The Consumer Credit and Sales Legal Practice Series

THE COST OF CREDIT

Regulation, Preemption, and Industry Abuses

Third Edition  With CD-Rom

Elizabeth Renuart

Kathleen E. Keest

Contributing Authors: Carolyn L. Carter, Alys I. Cohen, Chi Chi Wu

National Consumer Law Center
77 Summer Street, 10th Floor   Boston, MA 02110

www.consumerlaw.org

About NCLC

The National Consumer Law Center, a nonprofit corporation founded in 1969, assists consumers, advocates, and public policy makers nationwide who use the powerful and complex tools of consumer law to ensure justice and fair treatment for all, particularly those whose poverty renders them powerless to demand accountability from the economic marketplace. For more information, go to www.consumerlaw.org.

Ordering NCLC Publications

Order securely online at www.consumerlaw.org, or contact Publications Department, National Consumer Law Center, 77 Summer Street, Boston, MA 02110, (617) 542-9595 x1, FAX: (617) 542-8028, e-mail: publications@nclc.org.

Training and Conferences

NCLC participates in numerous national, regional, and local consumer law trainings. Its annual fall conference is a forum for consumer rights attorneys from legal services programs, private practice, government, and nonprofit organizations to share insights into common problems and explore novel and tested approaches that promote consumer justice in the marketplace. Contact NCLC for more information or see our web site.

Case Consulting

Case analysis, consulting and co-counseling for lawyers representing vulnerable consumers are among NCLC's important activities. Administration on Aging funds allow us to provide free consulting to legal services advocates representing elderly consumers on many types of cases. Massachusetts Legal Assistance Corporation funds permit case assistance to advocates representing low-income Massachusetts consumers. Other funding may allow NCLC to provide very brief consultations to other advocates without charge. More comprehensive case analysis and research is available for a reasonable fee. See our web site for more information at www.consumerlaw.org.

Charitable Donations and Cy Pres Awards

NCLC's work depends in part on the support of private donors. Tax-deductible donations should be made payable to National Consumer Law Center, Inc. For more information, contact Suzanne Cutler of NCLC's Development Office at (617) 542-8010 or scutler@nclc.org. NCLC has also received generous court-approved *cy pres* awards arising from consumer class actions to advance the interests of class members. For more information, contact Robert Hobbs (rhobbs@nclc.org) or Rich Dubois (rdubois@nclc.org) at (617) 542-8010.

Comments and Corrections

Write to the above address to the attention of the Editorial Department or e-mail consumerlaw@nclc.org.

About This Volume

This is the Third Edition of *The Cost of Credit* with a 2005 companion CD-Rom. The Third Edition and 2005 CD-Rom supersede all prior editions, supplements, and CDs, which should all be discarded. Continuing developments can be found in periodic updates to this volume and in NCLC REPORTS, *Consumer Credit & Usury Edition*.

Cite This Volume As

National Consumer Law Center, The Cost of Credit (3d ed. 2005).

Attention

> *This publication is designed to provide authoritative information concerning the subject matter covered. Always use the most current edition and supplement, and use other sources for more recent developments or for special rules for individual jurisdictions. This publication cannot substitute for the independent judgment and skills of an attorney or other professional. Non-attorneys are cautioned against using these materials to conduct a lawsuit without advice from an attorney and are cautioned against engaging in the unauthorized practice of law.*

About the Authors

Elizabeth Renuart is a staff attorney in NCLC's Boston office who focuses on consumer credit, Truth in Lending, and home ownership issues and heads NCLC's Home Defense Task Force. She is co-author of the Second Edition and prior supplements to this manual, co-author of *Truth in Lending* (5th ed. 2003), author of *Stop Predatory Lending*, editor of NCLC REPORTS, *Consumer Credit & Usury Edition*, and a former member of the Federal Reserve Board Consumer Advisory Council. Prior to joining NCLC, she was the managing attorney of a legal services office in Baltimore, Maryland, where she had a similar specialty and litigated cases involving RESPA, Truth in Lending, deceptive practices, and fraud. She has been a legal services attorney for over twenty-five years.

Kathleen Keest, presently with the Center for Responsible Lending, previously was with the Iowa Attorney General's Office, and also was an NCLC staff attorney from 1985 to 1996 specializing in Truth in Lending, usury, and other credit laws. Before that she was an attorney specializing in consumer law with the Legal Services Corporation of Iowa. She is the co-author of the prior two editions to this volume, co-author of *Truth in Lending* (1989, 1995, 1999, 2003) and *Usury and Consumer Credit Regulation* (1987). She is a past chair of the American Bar Association's Financial Services Committee and a former member of the Federal Reserve Board Consumer Advisory Council. She is the 1999 recipient of the Vern Countryman Consumer Award.

Carolyn Carter, contributing author, is of counsel with NCLC, and was formerly co-director of Legal Services, Inc., in Gettysburg, Pennsylvania, and director of the Law Reform Office of Cleveland Legal Aid Society. She is the editor of *Pennsylvania Consumer Law*, co-author of *Unfair and Deceptive Acts and Practices* (6th ed. 2004), *Fair Debt Collection* (5th ed. 2004), *Fair Credit Reporting* (5th ed. 2002), *Consumer Warranty Law* (2d ed. 2001), *Automobile Fraud* (2d ed. 2003), and contributing author to the prior edition of this volume, *Truth in Lending* (5th ed. 2003), and a number of other NCLC publications. She is a member of the Federal Reserve Board Consumer Advisory Council.

Chi Chi Wu is an NCLC staff attorney working on credit discrimination and consumer credit law issues. She is co-author of *Credit Discrimination* (4th ed. 2005) and a contributing author to *Fair Credit Reporting* (5th ed. 2002) and *Truth in Lending* (5th ed. 2003). She was formerly an Assistant Attorney General with the Consumer Protection Division of the Massachusetts Attorney General's Office, and an attorney with the Asian Outreach Unit of Greater Boston Legal Services.

Alys I. Cohen is a staff attorney at NCLC's Washington office, where she works on consumer credit issues. She is a contributing author to *Truth in Lending* (5th ed. 2003). Formerly, she was an attorney in the Federal Trade Commission's Bureau of Consumer Protection, Division of Financial Practices, where she was involved in credit discrimination and predatory lending matters.

Acknowledgments: The authors are indebted to the many people who helped with this manual. Foremost, this manual in large part builds upon *Usury and Consumer Credit Regulation* (1987), co-authored by Kevin Brown, with substantial contributions from Ernest Sarason and Robert Sable. Special note must be made of Mark Leymaster who wrote the Center's first usury volume, *Consumer Usury and Credit Overcharges* (1982), from which all subsequent work evolved, and who contributed the credit math program found on the CD-Rom. We also want to thank the many people who contributed to the prior two editions of this volume and, more recently, to Margot Saunders for her contributions to Chapter 4 and concerning E-Sign, Patricia McCoy for her contributions to Chapter 3, Jon Sheldon for the section on arbitration agreements, and Elizabeth De Armond, Kurt Terwilliger, and Mary Kingsley for legal research and writing.

Special thanks to Denise Lisio for editorial supervision; Nathan Day for editorial assistance; Shirlron Williams for cite checking; Shannon Halbrook for production assistance; Xylutions for typesetting services; Mary McLean for indexing, and Neil Fogarty of Law Disks for preparing the CD-Rom.

What Your Library Should Contain

The Consumer Credit and Sales Legal Practice Series contains 16 titles, updated annually, arranged into four libraries, and designed to be an attorney's primary practice guide and legal resource in all 50 states. Each manual includes a CD-Rom allowing pinpoint searches and the pasting of text into a word processor.

Debtor Rights Library

2004 Seventh Edition with CD-Rom, Including Law Disks' Bankruptcy Forms

Consumer Bankruptcy Law and Practice: the definitive personal bankruptcy manual, with step-by-step instructions from initial interview to final discharge, and including consumers' rights as creditors when a merchant or landlord files for bankruptcy. Appendices and CD-Rom contain over 130 annotated pleadings, bankruptcy statutes, rules and fee schedules, an interview questionnaire, a client handout, and software to complete the latest versions of petitions and schedules.

2004 Fifth Edition, 2005 Supplement, and 2005 CD-Rom

Fair Debt Collection: the basic reference in the field, covering the Fair Debt Collection Practices Act and common law, state statutory and other federal debt collection protections. Appendices and companion CD-Rom contain sample pleadings and discovery, the FTC's Official Staff Commentary, *all* FTC staff opinion letters, and summaries of reported and unreported cases.

2002 Fifth Edition, 2004 Supplement, and 2004 CD-Rom

Repossessions and Foreclosures: unique guide to VA, FHA and other types of home foreclosures, servicer obligations, motor vehicle and mobile home repossessions, threatened seizures of household goods, tax and other statutory liens, and automobile lease and rent-to-own default remedies. The CD-Rom reprints relevant UCC provisions and numerous key federal statutes, regulations, and agency letters, summarizes hundreds of state laws, and includes over 150 pleadings covering a wide variety of cases.

2002 Second Edition, 2004 Supplement, and 2004 CD-Rom

Student Loan Law: student loan debt collection and collection fees; discharges based on closed school, false certification, failure to refund, disability, and bankruptcy; tax intercepts, wage garnishment, and offset of social security benefits; repayment plans, consolidation loans, deferments, and non-payment of loan based on school fraud. CD-Rom and appendices contain numerous forms, pleadings, interpretation letters and regulations.

2004 Third Edition with CD-Rom

Access to Utility Service: the only examination of consumer rights when dealing with regulated, de-regulated, and unregulated utilities, including telecommunications, terminations, billing errors, low-income payment plans, utility allowances in subsidized housing, LIHEAP, and weatherization. Includes summaries of state utility regulations.

Credit and Banking Library

2003 Fifth Edition, 2004 Supplement, and 2004 CD-Rom

Truth in Lending: detailed analysis of *all* aspects of TILA, the Consumer Leasing Act, and the Home Ownership and Equity Protection Act (HOEPA). Appendices and the CD-Rom contain the Acts, Reg. Z, Reg. M, and their Official Staff Commentaries, numerous sample pleadings, rescission notices, and two programs to compute APRs.

National Consumer Law Center ■ **77 Summer Street** ■ **10th Floor** ■ **Boston MA** ■ **02110**
(617) 542-9595 ■ **FAX (617) 542-8028** ■ **publications@nclc.org**
Order securely online at www.consumerlaw.org

2002 Fifth Edition, 2005 Supplement, and 2005 CD-Rom	**Fair Credit Reporting:** the key resource for handling any type of credit reporting issue, from cleaning up blemished credit records to suing reporting agencies and creditors for inaccurate reports. Covers credit scoring, privacy issues, identity theft, the FCRA, the new FACT Act, the Credit Repair Organizations Act, state credit reporting and repair statutes, and common law claims.
2005 Third Edition with CD-Rom	**Consumer Banking and Payments Law:** unique analysis of consumer law (and NACHA rules) as to checks, money orders, credit, debit, and stored value cards, and banker's right of setoff. Also extensive treatment of electronic records and signatures, electronic transfer of food stamps, and direct deposits of federal payments. The CD-Rom and appendices reprint relevant agency interpretations and pleadings.
2005 Third Edition with CD-Rom	**The Cost of Credit: Regulation and Legal Challenges:** a one-of-a-kind resource detailing state and federal regulation of consumer credit in all fifty states, federal usury preemption, explaining credit math, and how to challenge excessive credit charges and credit insurance. The CD-Rom includes a credit math program and hard-to-find agency interpretations.
2005 Fourth Edition with CD-Rom	**Credit Discrimination:** analysis of the Equal Credit Opportunity Act, Fair Housing Act, Civil Rights Acts, and state credit discrimination statutes, including reprints of all relevant federal interpretations, government enforcement actions, and numerous sample pleadings.

Consumer Litigation Library

2004 Fourth Edition with CD-Rom	**Consumer Arbitration Agreements:** numerous successful approaches to challenge the enforceability of a binding arbitration agreement, the interrelation of the Federal Arbitration Act and state law, class actions in arbitration, collections via arbitration, the right to discovery, and other topics. Appendices and CD-Rom include sample discovery, numerous briefs, arbitration service provider rules and affidavits as to arbitrator costs.
2002 Fifth Edition, 2005 Supplement, and 2005 CD-Rom	**Consumer Class Actions: A Practical Litigation Guide:** makes class action litigation manageable even for small offices, including numerous sample pleadings, class certification memoranda, discovery, class notices, settlement materials, and much more. Includes a detailed analysis of the Class Action Fairness Act of 2005, recent changes to Rule 23, and other contributions from seven of the most experienced consumer class action litigators around the country.
2004 CD-Rom with Index Guide: ALL pleadings from ALL NCLC Manuals, including Consumer Law Pleadings Numbers One through Ten	**Consumer Law Pleadings on CD-Rom:** Over 1000 notable recent pleadings from all types of consumer cases, including predatory lending, foreclosures, automobile fraud, lemon laws, debt collection, fair credit reporting, home improvement fraud, rent to own, student loans, and lender liability. Finding aids pinpoint the desired pleading in seconds, ready to paste into a word processing program.

Deception and Warranties Library

2004 Sixth Edition with CD-Rom	**Unfair and Deceptive Acts and Practices:** the only practice manual covering all aspects of a deceptive practices case in every state. Special sections on automobile sales, the federal racketeering (RICO) statute, unfair insurance practices, and the FTC Holder Rule.
2003 Second Edition, 2005 Supplement, and 2005 CD-Rom	**Automobile Fraud:** examination of title law, odometer tampering, lemon laundering, sale of salvage and wrecked cars, undisclosed prior use, prior damage to new cars, numerous sample pleadings, and title search techniques.
2001 Second Edition, 2005 Supplement, and 2005 CD-Rom	**Consumer Warranty Law:** comprehensive treatment of new and used car lemon laws, the Magnuson-Moss Warranty Act, UCC Articles 2 and 2A, mobile home, new home, and assistive device warranty laws, FTC Used Car Rule, tort theories, car repair and home improvement statutes, service contract and lease laws, with numerous sample pleadings.

National Consumer Law Center ■ **77 Summer Street** ■ **10th Floor** ■ **Boston MA** ■ **02110**
(617) 542-9595 ■ **FAX (617) 542-8028** ■ **publications@nclc.org**
Order securely online at www.consumerlaw.org

NCLC's CD-Roms

Every NCLC manual comes with a companion CD-Rom featuring pop-up menus, PDF format, Internet-style navigation of appendices, indices, and bonus pleadings, hard-to-find agency interpretations and other practice aids. Documents can be copied into a word processing program. Of special note is *Consumer Law in a Box*:

July 2005 CD-Rom

Consumer Law in a Box: a CD-Rom combining *all* documents and software from 16 other NCLC CD-Roms. Quickly pinpoint a document from thousands found on the CD through keyword searches and Internet-style navigation, links, bookmarks, and other finding aids.

Other NCLC Publications for Lawyers

issued 24 times a year

NCLC REPORTS covers the latest developments and ideas in the practice of consumer law.

2003 First Edition with CD-Rom

The Practice of Consumer Law: Seeking Economic Justice: contains an essential overview to consumer law and explains how to get started in a private or legal services consumer practice. Packed with invaluable sample pleadings and practice pointers for even experienced consumer attorneys.

2002 First Edition with CD-Rom

STOP Predatory Lending: A Guide for Legal Advocates: provides a roadmap and practical legal strategy for litigating predatory lending abuses, from small loans to mortgage loans. The CD-Rom contains a credit math program, pleadings, legislative and administrative materials, and underwriting guidelines.

National Consumer Law Center Guide Series are books designed for consumers, counselors, and attorneys new to consumer law:

2005 Edition

NCLC Guide to Surviving Debt: a great overview of consumer law. Everything a paralegal, new attorney, or client needs to know about debt collectors, managing credit card debt, whether to refinance, credit card problems, home foreclosures, evictions, repossessions, credit reporting, utility terminations, student loans, budgeting, and bankruptcy.

2002 Edition

NCLC Guide to Mobile Homes: what consumers and their advocates need to know about mobile home dealer sales practices and an in-depth look at mobile home quality and defects, with 35 photographs and construction details.

2002 Edition

NCLC Guide to Consumer Rights for Immigrants: an introduction to many of the most critical consumer issues faced by immigrants, including international wires, check cashing and banking, *notario* and immigration consultant fraud, affidavits of support, telephones, utilities, credit history discrimination, high-cost credit, used car fraud, student loans and more.

2000 Edition

Return to Sender: Getting a Refund or Replacement for Your Lemon Car: Find how lemon laws work, what consumers and their lawyers should know to evaluate each other, investigative techniques and discovery tips, how to handle both informal dispute resolution and trials, and more.

Visit **www.consumerlaw.org** to order securely online or for more information on all NCLC manuals and CD-Roms, including the full tables of contents, indices, listings of CD-Rom contents, and **web-based searches of the manuals' full text.**

National Consumer Law Center ■ 77 Summer Street ■ 10th Floor ■ Boston MA ■ 02110
(617) 542-9595 ■ FAX (617) 542-8028 ■ publications@nclc.org
Order securely online at www.consumerlaw.org

Finding Aids and Search Tips

The Consumer Credit and Sales Legal Practice Series presently contains sixteen volumes, eight supplements, and sixteen companion CD-Roms—all constantly being updated. The Series includes over 10,000 pages, 100 chapters, 100 appendices, and over 1000 pleadings, as well as hundreds of documents found on the CD-Roms, but not found in the books. Here are a number of ways to pinpoint in seconds what you need from this array of materials.

Internet-Based Searches

www.consumerlaw.org

Electronically search every chapter and appendix of all sixteen manuals and their supplements: go to www.consumerlaw.org/keyword and enter a case name, regulation cite, or other search term. You are instantly given the book names and page numbers of any of the NCLC manuals containing that term, with those hits shown in context.

www.consumerlaw.org

Current indexes, tables of contents, and CD-Rom contents for all sixteen volumes are found at www.consumerlaw.org. Just click on *The Consumer Credit and Sales Legal Practice Series* and scroll down to the book you want. Then click on that volume's index, contents, or CD-Rom contents.

Finding Material on NCLC's CD-Roms

Consumer Law in a Box CD-Rom

Electronically search all sixteen NCLC CD-Roms, including thousands of agency interpretations, all NCLC appendices and almost 1000 pleadings: use Acrobat's search button* in NCLC's *Consumer Law in a Box CD-Rom* (this CD-Rom is free to set subscribers) to find every instance that a keyword appears on any of our sixteen CD-Roms. Then, with one click, go to that location to see the full text of the document.

CD-Rom accompanying this volume

Electronically search the CD-Rom accompanying this volume, including pleadings, agency interpretations, and regulations. Use Acrobat's search button* to find every instance that a keyword appears on the CD-Rom, and then, with one click, go to that location on the CD-Rom. Or just click on subject buttons until you navigate to the document you need.

Finding Pleadings

Consumer Law Pleadings on CD-Rom and Index Guide

Search five different ways for the right pleading from over 1000 choices: use the *Index Guide* accompanying *Consumer Law Pleadings on CD-Rom* to search for pleadings by type, subject, publication title, name of contributor, or contributor's jurisdiction. The guide also provides a summary of the pleading once the right pleading is located. *Consumer Law Pleadings on CD-Rom* and the *Consumer Law in a Box CD-Rom* also let you search for all pleadings electronically by subject, type of pleading, and by publication title, giving you instant access to the full pleading in Word and/or PDF format once you find the pleading you need.

Using This Volume to Find Material in All Sixteen Volumes

This volume

The Quick Reference at the back of this volume lets you pinpoint manual sections or appendices where over 1000 different subject areas are covered.

---

* Users of NCLC CD-Roms should become familiar with "search," a powerful Acrobat tool, distinguished from "find,"another Acrobat feature that is far slower and less powerful than "search." The Acrobat 5 "search" icon is a pair of binoculars with paper in the background, while the "find" icon is a pair of binoculars without the paper. Acrobat 6 and 7 use one icon, a pair of binoculars, that brings you to a menu with several search options.

Summary Contents

Contents xi

CD-Rom Contents xxxi

Chapter 1   Introduction 1

Chapter 2   Overview of Substantive Regulation of the Cost of Consumer Credit: State Laws 13

Chapter 3   Federal Preemption of State Laws Limiting Credit Charges and Regulating the Terms and Conditions of Lending 41

Chapter 4   Credit Math For Practitioners: Calculations of Interest Rate and Other Charges 125

Chapter 5   The Cost of Early Termination: Rebates of Unearned Charges and Prepayment Penalties 185

Chapter 6   The Cost of Refinancing: Calculation and Legal Issues 217

Chapter 7   Hidden Interest 237

Chapter 8   Credit Insurance 311

Chapter 9   The Statute: Determining the Applicable Statute and Principles of Statutory Construction 399

Chapter 10   The Trial: Jurisdiction; The Right to a Jury Trial; Elements of a Prima Facie Case; Creditor Defenses and Borrowers' Remedies 451

Chapter 11   The Credit Marketplace and a Sampling of Abuses *Du Jour* 557

Chapter 12   Beyond Usury: Statutory and Common Law Challenges to
              Overreaching Credit 605

Appendix A   State Lending Statutes 695

Appendix B   State Mortgage Broker Laws 707

Appendix C   National Bank Act 709

Appendix D   Home Owners' Loan Act 737

Appendix E   Federal Credit Union Act 773

Appendix F   Federal Deposit Insurance Act 789

Appendix G   Depository Institutions Deregulation and Monetary Control Act
              of 1980 805

Appendix H   Alternative Mortgage Transaction Parity Act of 1982 815

Appendix I   Gramm-Leach-Bliley Act 819

Appendix J   Other Federal Statutory Limits on Credit Terms 835

Appendix K   Real Estate Settlement Procedures Act 839

Appendix L   Sample Pleadings, Discovery, and Expert Witness Evidence 893

Appendix M   Websites Relating to Consumer Credit Issues 975

              Index 977

              Quick Reference to Consumer Credit and Sales Legal Practice Series . . 1017

              About the Companion CD-Rom 1029

Contents

CD-Rom Contents. xxxi

Chapter 1

Introduction

1.1 Purpose of This Manual 1
1.2 Scope of This Manual. 2
1.3 Purpose of Usury Laws and Their Progeny. 3
1.4 Organization of This Manual 4
1.5 References. 5
1.6 Getting Started. 6
    1.6.1 Introduction 6
    1.6.2 Analyzing the Contract: "Follow the Money" 7
    1.6.3 Analyzing the Legal Issues 9
        1.6.3.1 What Law Governs the Transaction? 9
            1.6.3.1.1 General 9
            1.6.3.1.2 Is it credit?. 9
            1.6.3.1.3 What state law applies? 9
            1.6.3.1.4 Is state law preempted?. 10
        1.6.3.2 Supplemental Checklist for Fixed-Term Consumer Credit Sales
        and Loans 11
            1.6.3.2.1 Check the arithmetic§§ 1.6.2, 4.11 11
            1.6.3.2.2 What are the interest charges? 11
            1.6.3.2.3 What is the principal amount? 11
            1.6.3.2.4 What are the maximum permissible charges? 12
            1.6.3.2.5 Are there non-rate violations in the contract? 12

Chapter 2

Overview of Substantive Regulation of the Cost of Consumer Credit:
State Laws

2.1 Introduction 13
2.2 Historical Development of Usury Laws 13
    2.2.1 Early Attitudes Toward Interest 13
    2.2.2 General Usury Statutes in the United States 14
    2.2.3 Special Usury Laws 15
        2.2.3.1 Laws Governing Loans. 15
        2.2.3.2 Laws Governing Sales 16
2.3 The Modern Consumer Credit Marketplace. 17
    2.3.1 Types of Creditors 17
        2.3.1.1 Introduction 17
        2.3.1.2 Depository Creditors 18
            2.3.1.2.1 Banks. 18
            2.3.1.2.2 Savings and loan associations 19

2.3.1.2.3 Credit unions. 20
2.3.1.3 Non-Depository Creditors 20
2.3.1.3.1 Finance companies and other licensed lenders 20
2.3.1.3.2 Retail sellers 20
2.3.1.3.3 Convenience creditors. 21
2.3.2 Types of Credit 21
2.3.2.1 Introduction 21
2.3.2.2 Loan vs. Credit Sales. 22
2.3.2.3 Open-End vs. Closed-End Credit 23
2.3.2.4 Security Taken in Credit Transactions. 25
2.3.3 Types of Special Usury Statutes 26
2.3.3.1 Introduction 26
2.3.3.2 Small Loan Laws and Their Progeny 26
2.3.3.3 Industrial Loan Laws 26
2.3.3.4 Installment Loan Laws 27
2.3.3.5 Retail Installment Sales Acts. 27
2.3.3.6 Insurance Premium Finance Regulations 28
2.3.3.7 Second Mortgage and Home Equity Loan Laws. 28
2.3.3.8 Open-End Loans and Credit Sales 29
2.3.3.9 Pawnbroker Statutes. 30
2.3.3.10 Comprehensive Consumer Credit Codes 30
2.3.3.11 Servicemembers Civil Relief Act 31
2.3.4 Relationship Between State Laws Regulating Credit Charges and the
Federal Truth in Lending Act. 31
2.4 Deregulation of Usury Law 33
2.4.1 Changing or Abolishing Interest Ceilings 33
2.4.2 Deregulation of the Residential Mortgage Market 37
2.5 Post-Deregulation: The Next Generation. 39

Chapter 3

Federal Preemption of State Laws Limiting Credit Charges and Regulating the Terms and Conditions of Lending

3.1 Introduction 41
3.1.1 Overview of the Relevant Statutes 41
3.1.2 Organization of This Chapter 43
3.2 Checking for Preemption: A Summary Guide 43
3.2.1 First Steps. 43
3.2.2 Preemption Analysis: A Step-by-Step Guide. 44
3.2.2.1 Overview 44
3.2.2.2 Step One: Is the Transaction Credit?. 44
3.2.2.3 Step Two: What Type of Loan Is It?. 44
3.2.2.4 Step Three: Identify the Type of Lender 44
3.2.2.5 Step Four: Which State's Law Would Ordinarily Apply? 45
3.2.2.6 Step Five: Which of the State's Usury Law Governs the Loan? . . . 45
3.2.2.7 Step Six: Who Is the Loan Holder? 45
3.2.3 Distinctions Based on the Type of Loan and the Location of its
"Making". 45
3.2.3.1 Non-Mortgage Loans/Intrastate 45
3.2.3.2 Non-Mortgage Loans/Interstate 46
3.2.4 Mortgage Loans. 47
3.2.4.1 Preemption of State Laws Regarding Interest Rates and Charges. . . 47
3.2.4.2 Preemption of Other Mortgage Contract Terms 47
3.2.5 Federal Consumer Lending Preemption Chart. 48
3.3 The Bureaucracy of Preemption 50

Contents

3.3.1 Who Regulates Which Lenders? 50
3.3.2 Deference to Agency Preemption Regulations and Opinions 51
3.4 The National Bank Act 52
3.4.1 History and Purpose of the National Bank Act 52
3.4.2 Calculating Alternative Interest Ceilings 53
3.4.3 Most Favored Lender Doctrine 53
    3.4.3.1 General 53
    3.4.3.2 "Competing Lender" Limitations on the Most Favored Lender
            Doctrine 54
    3.4.3.3 State Lender Limitation on Most Favored Lender Doctrine 55
    3.4.3.4 Most Favored Lender Must Comply with "Material" State
            Restrictions 56
3.4.4 Calculating the Rate Ceiling for National Banks: Some Practical
      Examples 57
3.4.5 Interstate Banking: National Banks and Rate Exportation 58
    3.4.5.1 Background: *Marquette* and Its Legacy 58
        3.4.5.1.1 Overview and constitutional concerns 58
        3.4.5.1.2 The role of a national bank's "location" 59
        3.4.5.1.3 National bank as an assignee 63
    3.4.5.2 Scope of the Term "Interest Rate" for Exportation Purposes 64
3.4.6 National Bank Act Preemption 68
    3.4.6.1 Conflict Preemption 68
    3.4.6.2 OCC's Broad 2004 Preemption Regulations 74
    3.4.6.3 Visitorial Powers of the OCC 76
    3.4.6.4 Preemption Rights of Operating Subsidiaries and Agents 78
3.5 The Home Owners' Loan Act and Federal Savings Associations 80
3.5.1 History and Purpose of the Home Owners' Loan Act 80
3.5.2 Most Favored Lender Doctrine and Exportation 80
3.5.3 HOLA and "Field" Preemption 81
3.5.4 Preemption Rights of Certain Subsidiaries and Agents 84
3.6 Federal Credit Union Act and Federal Credit Unions 85
3.6.1 Overview 85
3.6.2 Most Favored Lender Status 86
3.6.3 Beyond Usury Preemption 86
3.7 The Federal Deposit Insurance Act and State-Chartered Banks 87
3.7.1 The "Dual" Banking System and State-Chartered Bank Powers 87
3.7.2 Most Favored Lender Doctrine and Exportation 88
3.7.3 Other Preemption Rights Extended by Federal Law to State-Chartered
      Banks 89
3.7.4 Expansion of Bank Powers Through State Parity Acts 90
3.8 FHA- or VA-Insured Loans: Preemption of State Usury Law 90
3.8.1 General 90
3.8.2 State Opt-out of the FHA/VA Loan Preemption 91
3.9 The Depository Institutions Deregulation and Monetary Control Act of 1980
    (DIDA): Most Favored Lender Status for Federally-Insured Lenders; First Lien
    Mortgage Preemption 92
3.9.1 Introduction; Legislative History and Purpose 92
3.9.2 DIDA and Federally-Related Lenders 94
    3.9.2.1 Extension of Federal Alternate Interest Ceiling and Most Favored
            Lender Status to Federally-Related Lenders 94
    3.9.2.2 Interstate Banking Review: DIDA and Exportation 95
        3.9.2.2.1 General 95
        3.9.2.2.2 DIDA's exportation and choice of laws 97
3.9.3 DIDA's "First Mortgage" Preemption 98
    3.9.3.1 Overview 98

3.9.3.2 First Lien 100
   3.9.3.2.1 Definition of first lien 100
   3.9.3.2.2 Special Texas issue on first liens. 101
3.9.3.3 Qualifying Lenders 102
3.9.3.4 Mobile Home Loans and Credit Sales. 103
3.9.4 Opting Out of DIDA by State Legislation. 105
  3.9.4.1 General 105
  3.9.4.2 First Lien Preemption Opt-out: Interest Cap Versus Points and Fees Limitations 106
  3.9.4.3 DIDA'S Alternate Ceiling/Most Favored Lender Preemption Opt-Out 107
3.10 The Alternative Mortgage Transactions Parity Act (AMTPA): Preemption of State Non-Rate Mortgage Credit Regulation 108
  3.10.1 Scope of AMTPA's Preemption. 108
  3.10.2 AMTPA's Regulatory Scheme 110
3.11 Gramm-Leach-Bliley Act and Interstate Loan Pricing 113
3.12 Preemptive Effect of Federal Consumer Protection Statutes 114
3.13 Faux Bank Preemption: "Rent-a-Charter" Arrangements 114
  3.13.1 General 114
  3.13.2 Private Litigation and State Enforcement 115
  3.13.3 The OCC, OTS, and FDIC Enter the Fray 118
3.14 Usury Deregulation by State "Parity" Laws 120
  3.14.1 "Parity" Statutes Described 120
  3.14.2 Impact of State Parity Statutes 121
  3.14.3 Parity Statute Interaction with Federal "Most Favored Lender" 122
3.15 Federal Jurisdiction: Removal of Preemption Issues to Federal Court. 122

Chapter 4   Credit Math For Practitioners: Calculations of Interest Rate and Other Charges

4.1 Introduction 125
4.2 Interest Calculation: Single Payment Transactions 125
4.3 Interest Calculation: Installment Credit. 126
  4.3.1 Actuarial Interest 126
   4.3.1.1 Amortizing Credit Explained; Actuarial or Simple Interest Calculations 126
   4.3.1.2 Negative Amortization; Non-Amortizing Credit; Balloon Payments 130
  4.3.2 Add-on Interest 132
  4.3.3 Discount Interest 135
  4.3.4 Split Rate Interest—Graduated Rates 136
  4.3.5 Open-End Credit 138
   4.3.5.1 Calculation Distinctions Between Open- and Closed-End Credit . . 138
   4.3.5.2 Methods of Calculating Interest on Open-End Credit. 139
   4.3.5.3 Legal Treatment of Open-End Calculation Methods 140
  4.3.6 Variable Rates 140
   4.3.6.1 Variable Rate Transactions Described 140
   4.3.6.2 Calculating the Current Rate 141
   4.3.6.3 Amortizing Variable Rate Loans over Fixed Time Periods 143
   4.3.6.4 Caps and Floors in Variable Rate Transactions; Explanation and Requirements 143
   4.3.6.5 Legal Issues in Variable Rate Credit 145
4.4 Truth in Lending APR and Finance Charge Distinguished 146
  4.4.1 Purpose of the Truth in Lending APR; Finance Charge Explained, Distinguished From Interest 146

Contents

4.4.2 Calculation and Accuracy of the Annual Percentage Rate 148
4.5 Interest Bearing v. Precomputed 149
   4.5.1 Introduction. 149
   4.5.2 Interest Bearing 149
   4.5.3 Precomputed 150
4.6 Special Calculation Problems 151
   4.6.1 Compound Interest 151
      4.6.1.1 When Does Compounding Occur? 151
      4.6.1.2 Legal Restrictions on Compounding 153
   4.6.2 Odd Payment Periods and Odd Payment Amounts. 156
      4.6.2.1 General 156
      4.6.2.2 Weekly, Bi-Weekly Payment Periods; Legal Issues 157
   4.6.3 Daily Interest Rates and the 365/360 Method 158
      4.6.3.1 General 158
      4.6.3.2 365-Day Method 159
      4.6.3.3 360-Day Method 159
      4.6.3.4 365/360 Day Method: "The Bankers' Year" 159
      4.6.3.5 Effect of Late Posting of Payments. 161
   4.6.4 Rounding 162
   4.6.5 Spreading 163
      4.6.5.1 A Calculation Defense to Usury Claims in Fixed Term Loans. . . . 163
      4.6.5.2 Spreading in Open-End, Variable-Rate Transactions 165
      4.6.5.3 Spreading in Special Situations 165
      4.6.5.4 Contract Argument Against Spreading. 166
   4.6.6 Minimum Finance Charges or Service Charges 167
   4.6.7 Biweekly Mortgage Payment 167
   4.6.8 Daily Accrual Accounting 167
      4.6.8.1 Daily Accrual Without Compounding 167
      4.6.8.2 Daily Accrual with Compounding 169
      4.6.8.3 Daily Accrual and Application of Payments. 170
4.7 Points 170
   4.7.1 Calculation of Points. 170
   4.7.2 Legal Issues Arising in Calculation of Points 172
4.8 Calculation of Late Charges and Deferral Charges 173
   4.8.1 Late Charges 173
   4.8.2 Deferral Charges 174
   4.8.3 Payment Holidays for Interest-Bearing Loans 175
4.9 Transactions Involving Progress Payments 176
4.10 Proving Mathematical Issues in Court. 176
4.11 Practical Tips 178
   4.11.1 Developing a System for Analyzing Consumer Credit Issues 178
   4.11.2 Gathering Information from the Client 178
   4.11.3 Gathering Information from Creditor and Other Parties. 179
   4.11.4 Calculations and Analysis. 179

Chapter 5

The Cost of Early Termination: Rebates of Unearned Charges and Prepayment Penalties

5.1 Introduction 185
5.2 Overview of Statutes Regulating Rebates 186
   5.2.1 State Statutes. 186
   5.2.2 Federal Rebate Law 186
   5.2.3 Credit Secured by First Lien on Mobile Home 187
   5.2.4 Federal Law Regulating High-Cost Mortgages 187
   5.2.5 Bankruptcy Law. 188

5.3 Using This Chapter: Putting the Law into Practice 188
5.4 When Are Rebates Required? Precomputed Charges; Early Termination; Partial
    Prepayments. 189
    5.4.1 Precomputed Charges 189
    5.4.2 Early Termination. 189
    5.4.3 Partial Prepayments. 189
5.5 What Charges Are Subject to Rebate 190
    5.5.1 Contract Interest: Precomputed Transactions; Hidden Rule of 78
          Accounting in Interest-Bearing Transactions 190
    5.5.2 Other Charges and Fees. 192
          5.5.2.1 General 192
          5.5.2.2 Rebates and Points. 193
                  5.5.2.2.1 General. 193
                  5.5.2.2.2 Are points and other prepaid finance charges "earned at
                            consummation"? 193
                  5.5.2.2.3 Special issues under the federal rebate statute 194
          5.5.2.3 Other Theories to Attack Abusive Use of Points. 195
5.6 Calculating Rebates. 196
    5.6.1 Introduction. 196
    5.6.2 Payment Dates and Intervals. 196
          5.6.2.1 Fixing the Date for the Rebate Calculation 196
          5.6.2.2 Intervals: Rounding the Time Calculation 196
    5.6.3 Rebate Formulae 198
          5.6.3.1 Determining Which Formula to Use 198
          5.6.3.2 Pro Rata Rebates 199
          5.6.3.3 Rule of 78 199
                  5.6.3.3.1 Background and legal status. 199
                  5.6.3.3.2 Calculating a Rule of 78 rebate: a simplified step by
                            step guide for mathphobes. 201
                  5.6.3.3.3 The explanation of the Rule of 78 for those who care
                            (optional reading for the practitioner) 202
                  5.6.3.3.4 Sum of the balances method: a variant on the Rule
                            of 78 203
          5.6.3.4 Actuarial Rebates. 204
                  5.6.3.4.1 Legal status. 204
                  5.6.3.4.2 Calculation of actuarial rebates. 205
                  5.6.3.4.3 Actuarial rebates under actuarial split rate statutes. . . . 206
5.7 Proving Rebate Violations Are Illegal Charges. 207
    5.7.1 Usury Upon a Contingent Event 207
    5.7.2 Intent to Collect Unearned Charges; Verb-iage (What Constitutes
          "Charging," "Receiving," or "Contracting For" Unearned Charges) 208
          5.7.2.1 Whether Intent Is Required 208
          5.7.2.2 Does the Contract Show the Creditor's Intent to Charge Unearned
                  Interest? 208
          5.7.2.3 Has the Creditor Failed to Give the Rebate the Contract
                  Requires? 209
    5.7.3 Special Issues Regarding Remedies for Violation of the Federal Rebate
          Statute 210
5.8 Prepayment Penalties. 210
    5.8.1 General. 210
    5.8.2 High-Cost Mortgages 214
    5.8.3 Prepayment Penalties for Federal Lenders. 214
5.9 Preemptive Effect of the New Federal Consumer Protection Statutes. 215

Contents

Chapter 6

The Cost of Refinancing: Calculation and Legal Issues

6.1 Introduction 217
    6.1.1 Double Their Money: The "Flipping Penalty" 217
        6.1.1.1 Overview 217
        6.1.1.2 Small Loan Example 218
        6.1.1.3 Equity-Skimmers and the Flipping Penalty. 219
    6.1.2 Overview of Legal Issues in Refinancings 219
    6.1.3 Refinancing, Consolidation and Flipping Defined. 220
6.2 Usurious Taint in Refinanced Obligations 220
    6.2.1 Continuation of Taint in Renewal Transactions 220
    6.2.2 No Taint If First Debt Forms No Part of Consideration 221
    6.2.3 Novation vs. Waiver 222
6.3 The Cost of Refinancings 224
    6.3.1 The Elements of the Price Escalator 224
    6.3.2 Refinancing Calculations in Action: Another Walk-Through Case Study . . 225
6.4 Evaluating the Calculations. 227
    6.4.1 Rebates 227
        6.4.1.1 Calculating Proper Rebates 227
        6.4.1.2 Compounding 228
        6.4.1.3 Non-Rebatable Charges on Old Loan 228
    6.4.2 Imposition of Additional Charges on the New Loan 229
    6.4.3 Is the New Rate Proper? 230
6.5 Practice Tip: Evaluating Refinancing as a Way Out of Real Estate Mortgage
Foreclosure 231
6.6 Business or Consumer Loan? May Refinancing Change the Character of a
Loan? 235

Chapter 7

Hidden Interest

7.1 Introduction 237
    7.1.1 First Principles. 237
    7.1.2 Intersection with Preemption 238
7.2 Payments for Lender Services: What Is Interest? 238
    7.2.1 Fees Based on the Creditor's Expenses 238
    7.2.2 Points, Commitment Fees, and Other Percentage Fees 241
        7.2.2.1 General 241
        7.2.2.2 Legal Considerations 242
        7.2.2.3 Commitment Fees 244
    7.2.3 Non-Cash Compensation and Side Agreements 245
    7.2.4 Delinquency Charges. 247
        7.2.4.1 Introduction 247
        7.2.4.2 Late Fees As Interest 248
            7.2.4.2.1 "Common law" approach 248
            7.2.4.2.2 Late fee statutes. 250
        7.2.4.3 Pyramiding Late Charges 252
7.3 Payments for Third Party Services. 253
    7.3.1 General Principles. 253
    7.3.2 Broker Fees. 255
    7.3.3 Attorney Fees 258
        7.3.3.1 General 258
        7.3.3.2 Attorney Fees upon Default. 258
        7.3.3.3 Attorney Fees As a Closing Cost 259
7.4 Interest Hidden When Principal Amount Is Overstated 260
    7.4.1 Introduction. 260

7.4.2 Fees Added to Principal; General Methods of Overstating Principal 260
7.4.3 Wraparound Mortgages 262
7.4.4 Compensating Balances. 264
7.4.5 Indexing Loan Principal. 265
7.4.6 Hidden Interest in Credit Sales 265
    7.4.6.1 Inflating the Sale Price 265
    7.4.6.2 Seller's Points 268
7.5 Hidden Interest in "Non-Credit" Transactions 270
  7.5.1 Introduction. 270
  7.5.2 Sale and Repurchase or Leaseback Agreements: Secured Credit Disguised
      as an Outright Sale 270
    7.5.2.1 Equitable Mortgages. 270
    7.5.2.2 Personal Property. 272
    7.5.2.3 Auto Title Loans 272
      7.5.2.3.1 Overview 272
      7.5.2.3.2 Leaseback schemes. 273
      7.5.2.3.3 Auto title "pawns". 274
      7.5.2.3.4 Other schemes and disguises 275
      7.5.2.3.5 Auto title loan statutes 276
  7.5.3 Credit Sales Disguised As Leases: Rent-To-Own 277
    7.5.3.1 General 277
    7.5.3.2 Rent-to-Own contracts described 277
    7.5.3.3 Trends in the RTO industry. 279
    7.5.3.4 History of Legal Challenges to RTO contracts 280
    7.5.3.5 Industry-Friendly RTO Legislation 281
    7.5.3.6 Legal Challenges to RTO in Light of the Legislative Reality 283
      7.5.3.6.1 Overview 283
      7.5.3.6.2 Unconscionability and RTO pricing. 283
      7.5.3.6.3 Applicability of UDAP statutes to RTO transactions . . . 285
      7.5.3.6.4 "Optional" fees. 285
      7.5.3.6.5 Repossession tactics 286
      7.5.3.6.6 Discriminatory treatment claims 287
      7.5.3.6.7 Other high-cost credit disguised as RTOs. 287
  7.5.4 Tax Refund Schemes. 287
    7.5.4.1 Assignment of Tax Refunds As Disguised Credit 287
    7.5.4.2 Refund Anticipation Loans (RALs). 289
  7.5.5 Payday Loans/Check Advancement Loans 292
    7.5.5.1 Introduction 292
    7.5.5.2 Payday Lending: Big Business. 294
    7.5.5.3 The Lenders and the Loans Described. 295
    7.5.5.4 Types of Abuses 296
    7.5.5.5 State Regulation of Payday Lending 297
    7.5.5.6 Legal Claims. 298
    7.5.5.7 Bank Partnerships and "Rent-a-Finance" Company Arrangements. . . 303
    7.5.5.8 Special Defenses to Arbitration Clauses 303
    7.5.5.9 Checks and Electronic Fund Transfers in Payday Loans. 303
      7.5.5.9.1 Introduction. 303
      7.5.5.9.2 Conditioning payday loan on authorization for
           electronic fund transfer 303
      7.5.5.9.3 Repeated presentment of borrower's check. 304
      7.5.5.9.4 Amount that payday lender can obtain through check or
           electronic fund transfer 304
      7.5.5.9.5 Post-dated checks. 305
      7.5.5.9.6 Right to stop payment. 305
      7.5.5.9.7 Unauthorized payments 305

7.5.6 Bank Bounce Loans 306
7.5.7 Joint Venture Investments 307
7.5.8 Income Buyers 308
    7.5.8.1 General 308
    7.5.8.2 Assignment of Government Income 308
    7.5.8.3 Litigation Finance Companies 309

Chapter 8   Credit Insurance

8.1 Introduction 311
8.2 Economic Incentives; Market Failures 312
  8.2.1 Background 312
  8.2.2 Benefits to Creditor 312
  8.2.3 Excessive Cost of Credit Insurance 314
    8.2.3.1 Reverse Competition; Market Failures 314
    8.2.3.2 Low Loss-Ratios Demonstrate Excessive Cost 315
8.3 Credit and Credit-Related Insurance Products 318
  8.3.1 Types of Credit Insurance 318
    8.3.1.1 Overview 318
    8.3.1.2 Credit Life 318
    8.3.1.3 Credit Disability/Accident and Health 319
    8.3.1.4 Involuntary Unemployment Insurance 320
    8.3.1.5 Credit Property 320
        8.3.1.5.1 General 320
        8.3.1.5.2 Vendor's single interest insurance 321
        8.3.1.5.3 Dual interest 323
        8.3.1.5.4 Motor vehicle credit insurance: special issues 323
  8.3.2 Credit-Related Insurance 325
    8.3.2.1 Private Mortgage Insurance 325
    8.3.2.2 Title Insurance 327
    8.3.2.3 Debt Cancellation and Debt Suspension Agreements 329
  8.3.3 Non-Credit Insurance Distinguished 331
8.4 Types of Regulation 332
  8.4.1 Sources of Regulation 332
    8.4.1.1 Overview 332
    8.4.1.2 Insurance Statutes and Regulations 332
    8.4.1.3 Consumer Credit Laws Regulating Credit Insurance 333
    8.4.1.4 Unfair Trade Practices Laws 334
    8.4.1.5 Federal Laws 334
        8.4.1.5.1 Truth in Lending 334
        8.4.1.5.2 Bank Holding Company Act and the Gramm-Leach-
                Bliley Act 335
    8.4.1.6 Insurance Premium Financing Laws 337
  8.4.2 Substance of Credit Insurance Regulations 338
    8.4.2.1 Rates 338
        8.4.2.1.1 General 338
        8.4.2.1.2 Problems with prima facie rates 339
        8.4.2.1.3 Deviations 339
        8.4.2.1.4 Challenging prima facie rates 339
        8.4.2.1.5 Filed-Rate Doctrine 340
    8.4.2.2 Non-Rate Regulation 341
        8.4.2.2.1 NAIC model acts 341
        8.4.2.2.2 Substantive credit regulation and unfair trade practices
                statutes 343

8.5 Common Abuses and Possible Remedies 343
  8.5.1 Introduction. 343
  8.5.2 Voluntariness 344
    8.5.2.1 General: The Law and the Practice. 344
    8.5.2.2 Truth in Lending and Usury Distinguished. 345
    8.5.2.3 Compulsory Insurance and Usury. 346
      8.5.2.3.1 General. 346
      8.5.2.3.2 Choice of insurers 347
    8.5.2.4 Proving Coercion. 347
    8.5.2.5 Truth in Lending 351
    8.5.2.6 UDAP 352
    8.5.2.7 Antitrust; McCarran-Ferguson Act 353
      8.5.2.7.1 Unlawful tie-in arrangements 353
      8.5.2.7.2 Effect of the McCarran-Ferguson Act on antitrust
              challenges to credit insurance practices 355
  8.5.3 Excessive Cost of Credit Insurance 359
    8.5.3.1 Calculating Credit Insurance Charges 359
      8.5.3.1.1 Introduction. 359
      8.5.3.1.2 Credit life 360
      8.5.3.1.3 Credit accident & health 361
      8.5.3.1.4 Credit property insurance. 362
    8.5.3.2 Excess Premium Charges As Usury 363
      8.5.3.2.1 General. 363
      8.5.3.2.2 Creditor compensation as interest 365
    8.5.3.3 Excess Coverage As Illegal Overcharge. 367
      8.5.3.3.1 Level term credit life insurance 367
      8.5.3.3.2 Amount of coverage 367
    8.5.3.4 Special credit property issues. 368
      8.5.3.4.1 Scope of insurable interest. 368
      8.5.3.4.2 Force-placed insurance 369
      8.5.3.4.3 Phantom coverage 369
  8.5.4 Insurance Packing. 370
    8.5.4.1 Overview 370
    8.5.4.2 Packing As an Equity-Skimming Tool to Exceed Critical
         Statutory Thresholds. 370
    8.5.4.3 Packing with Sales of Non-Credit Insurance and Other Ancillary
         Products. 372
    8.5.4.4 Unnecessary Collateral, Duplicative Insurance 375
    8.5.4.5 Non-Filing Insurance 377
  8.5.5 Post-Claim Underwriting, Ineligibility 380
    8.5.5.1 Challenging the Sale of Insurance to Borrowers Unlikely to
         Benefit. 380
    8.5.5.2 Incomplete Coverage 381
    8.5.5.3 Collecting the Benefits of the Insurance Bargain. 382
      8.5.5.3.1 General. 382
      8.5.5.3.2 Theories of recovery against the insurer. 382
      8.5.5.3.3 Theories of recovery against the creditor 384
  8.5.6 Surpluses, Secondary Beneficiaries 386
8.6 Rebates 386
8.7 Remedies. 389
  8.7.1 Usury 389
  8.7.2 Breach of Fiduciary Duty. 390
  8.7.3 Breach of the Duty to Disclose; Fraud and Related Claims 391
    8.7.3.1 Duty to Disclose 391
    8.7.3.2 Fraud; Misrepresentation and Concealment 392

8.7.4 Unfair and Deceptive Acts and Practices 393
8.7.5 Unconscionability. 396
8.7.6 Arbitration in the Insurance Context 397

Chapter 9

The Statute: Determining the Applicable Statute and Principles of Statutory Construction

9.1 Introduction 399
9.2 Which Usury Statute Applies?. 399
   9.2.1 Nature of Distinctions Among Statutes; General Principles of Coverage . . 399
      9.2.1.1 Overview 399
      9.2.1.2 Methods of Distinguishing the Transaction. 399
      9.2.1.3 "Opting In" or Contracting for Coverage 400
      9.2.1.4 Deregulation; Criminal Usury 400
      9.2.1.5 Preemption. 400
      9.2.1.6 Substance Not Form Dictates Nature of Transaction 400
   9.2.2 Is the Loan for Consumer or Business Purposes?. 401
      9.2.2.1 Introduction 401
      9.2.2.2 Justification for Business Loan Exemption. 402
      9.2.2.3 Requiring Incorporation or an Affidavit of Business Purpose 403
      9.2.2.4 Criteria for Business vs. Personal Purpose 404
      9.2.2.5 Intermediaries; Refinancing 405
      9.2.2.6 Burden of Proof. 406
   9.2.3 Distinctions Based on the Type of Credit 406
      9.2.3.1 Introduction 406
      9.2.3.2 Open-End or Closed-End Credit. 406
      9.2.3.3 Loans v. Credit Sales; Body-Dragging. 409
      9.2.3.4 Land Installment Contracts 410
      9.2.3.5 The "Finance Charge" Requirement. 412
   9.2.4 Distinctions Based on the Type of Creditor. 412
      9.2.4.1 Introduction 412
      9.2.4.2 Frequency Standard, or "In the Business" of Extending Credit. . . 413
      9.2.4.3 State Depository Lenders 413
      9.2.4.4 Regulations Applicable to Federal Depository Lenders 414
      9.2.4.5 Non-Depository Creditors 414
      9.2.4.6 Challenging a Creditor's Efforts to Evade Licensing
            Requirements 416
   9.2.5 Distinctions Based on Loan Size; Loan-Splitting and Loan-Packing To
      Evade Regulation 418
      9.2.5.1 General 418
      9.2.5.2 Loan Splitting. 418
      9.2.5.3 Loan Packing 418
   9.2.6 Distinctions Based on Security Taken 420
   9.2.7 Criminal Usury Statutes; Unconscionability Standards to Regulate the
      Cost of Credit 421
   9.2.8 Usury in "Deregulated" States 422
      9.2.8.1 Exceeding an "Agreed Rate" Cap 422
      9.2.8.2 Hidden Interest in Agreed Rate Transactions 424
   9.2.9 Choice of Laws 428
      9.2.9.1 Overview 428
      9.2.9.2 Substantial Relationship Test 429
      9.2.9.3 Public Policy Concerns and the "Not Greatly In Excess"
            Requirement 430
      9.2.9.4 State Statutes Governing Choice of Laws 432

9.2.9.5 Contractual Choice of Law Clauses 433
9.2.10 Formal Requirements for Electronic Credit Transactions and the
Interplay Between State and Federal Law 434
9.2.10.1 Introduction 434
9.2.10.2 Overview of E-Sign and UETA 435
9.2.10.3 What Law Applies: E-Sign, UETA, or Other State Laws? 436
9.2.10.3.1 Introduction 436
9.2.10.3.2 States that have not passed a statute addressing
electronic commerce 437
9.2.10.3.3 States that passed non-uniform versions of UETA
before E-Sign was adopted 437
9.2.10.3.4 States that passed uniform versions of UETA before
E-Sign was adopted 437
9.2.10.3.5 States that passed UETA or other laws after E-Sign's
adoption 437
9.2.10.4 E-Sign and UETA Consumer Consent Requirements 438
9.2.10.4.1 E-Sign 438
9.2.10.4.2 UETA 438
9.2.10.5 Effect of E-Sign and UETA on Timing and Format
Requirements 439
9.2.10.6 Manner of Transmitting Electronic Credit Documents Under
E-Sign and UETA 439
9.2.10.7 Document Integrity 440
9.2.10.8 Validity and Enforceability of Electronic Contracts and
Signatures Under E-Sign and UETA 440
9.2.10.9 Subsequent Notices 441
9.2.10.10 Practice Tips When Dealing with Electronic Credit Contracts . . 442
9.3 Statutory Construction 442
9.3.1 Applying General Rules of Interpretation 442
9.3.1.1 Broad vs. Narrow Construction of Usury Statutes: Invoking the
History and Purpose of Usury Statutes 442
9.3.1.2 *Expressio Unius Est Exclusio Alterius*: Limiting the Creditor's
Ability to Add Extra Charges Not Specifically Authorized 446
9.3.1.3 Deference to Administrative Interpretations 447
9.3.2 Retroactive Amendment of Usury Statutes 447
9.3.2.1 General Standards 447
9.3.2.2 Variable or Floating Usury Ceilings Distinguished 450

Chapter 10

The Trial: Jurisdiction; The Right to a Jury Trial; Elements of a Prima Facie Case; Creditor Defenses and Borrowers' Remedies

10.1 Introduction 451
10.2 Long-Arm Jurisdiction over Out-of-State Lenders 451
10.2.1 Constitutional and Statutory Standards 451
10.2.2 Jurisdiction over Internet-Based Lenders 452
10.2.3 Personal Jurisdiction over Securitization Trusts 454
10.2.3.1 Overview 454
10.2.3.2 General Jurisdiction 455
10.2.3.3 Specific Jurisdiction When Claim Relates to Property in Forum
State 456
10.2.3.4 Specific Jurisdiction When Unsecured Debts Have Been
Assigned to a Trust 457
10.2.3.5 Jurisdiction in Bankruptcy Court and Over Counterclaims 458
10.3 The Enforceability of Arbitration Agreements 458

Contents

10.3.1 General 458

10.3.2 Where an Agreement Is Void: Usurious, Illegal and Unlicensed Loan
Agreements 459

10.3.3 Where a Contract Was Never Finalized: "Yo-Yo" and Other Condition
Precedent Contracts 460

10.3.4 Where Arbitration Agreement Is Superseded by Later Agreement 460

10.3.5 Where the Parties to a Dispute Are Not Parties to the Arbitration
Agreement 461

    10.3.5.1 Are Co-signers and Other Non-signatories Bound by Arbitration
Agreement? 461

    10.3.5.2 Can a Party Not Named in the Arbitration Agreement Force the
Consumer to Arbitrate Claims? 462

10.3.6 Special Rules for Insurance Transactions 463

    10.3.6.1 General 463

    10.3.6.2 Is a State Law One Enacted for the Purpose of Regulating
Insurance? 464

    10.3.6.3 Does State Insurance Law Restrict the Enforceability of
Arbitration Agreements? 464

10.3.7 Other Challenges to Agreement's Enforceability 464

10.4 Right to Jury Trial 465

10.5 Elements of a Prima Facie Case 466

10.5.1 General 466

    10.5.1.1 Overview of Elements 466

    10.5.1.2 Burden of Proof 467

    10.5.1.3 Contract Construction 468

10.5.2 Loan or Forbearance 470

    10.5.2.1 Introduction 470

    10.5.2.2 Credit Sales and the Time-Price Doctrine 471

        10.5.2.2.1 Time-price exception to usury laws 471

        10.5.2.2.2 The erosion of the time-price doctrine: direct
regulation of consumer credit sales and RISAs 473

    10.5.2.3 Forbearance and Detention 473

10.5.3 Absolute Obligation to Repay Principal 476

10.5.4 Interest Overcharge 476

    10.5.4.1 General 476

    10.5.4.2 Charging, Contracting For, or Receiving Excess Interest 477

    10.5.4.3 "Interest" or Regulated Charge 479

    10.5.4.4 Proving the Charge Is Excessive 481

10.5.5 Intent 481

    10.5.5.1 When Proof of Intent Is Required 481

    10.5.5.2 Usury Apparent on Face of Contract; Bona Fide Error 482

    10.5.5.3 Usury Not Apparent on Face of Contract 484

    10.5.5.4 Inference of Intent 486

10.6 Creditor Defenses 486

10.6.1 Defenses of Assignees and Holders in Due Course 486

    10.6.1.1 Overview of General UCC Rules and Consumer Exceptions . . . 486

    10.6.1.2 Consumer Exceptions to the Holder-in-Due-Course Doctrine:
State Limitations, the FTC Holder Rule, and High-Cost
Mortgages 487

        10.6.1.2.1 Rationale for consumer exceptions 487

        10.6.1.2.2 State laws and the FTC Rule 489

        10.6.1.2.3 Assignee liability for high-cost mortgages 491

    10.6.1.3 UCC Principles 492

        10.6.1.3.1 Basic prerequisites 492

10.6.1.3.2 Is the assignee a holder? 492
10.6.1.3.3 Is there a negotiable instrument? 493
10.6.1.3.4 Did the holder acquire the instrument in good faith, for value, and without notice? 494
10.6.1.3.5 What defenses can be asserted against a holder in due course? 494
10.6.1.3.6 Rights of subsequent transferees of negotiable instruments 494
10.6.1.3.7 Electronic negotiable instruments 494
10.6.1.3.8 Showing that a holder did not take usurious note in good faith and without notice of defenses 495
10.6.1.3.9 Whether usury can be asserted against a holder in due course 497
10.6.1.3.10 The UCC and waiver of defense clauses 497
10.6.2 Collection Agencies' Liability for Illegal Overcharges 498
10.6.3 Standing to Assert Usury 498
10.6.4 Estoppel and Waiver 501
10.6.4.1 Overview 501
10.6.4.2 Borrower's Knowledge 501
10.6.4.3 False Contractual Statements 503
10.6.4.4 Waiver 504
10.6.5 Voluntary Payment Defense 504
10.6.6 Res Judicata 508
10.6.7 Statutes of Limitations 509
10.6.8 De Minimis Violations 511
10.6.9 Industry Custom and Usage 512
10.6.10 Usury Saving Clauses 513
10.6.11 Correction of Error as a Defense 515
10.7 Special Defenses of Federal Receivers: *D'Oench* and Related Doctrines 515
10.7.1 Introduction 515
10.7.2 Does § 1823(e) Preempt *D'Oench* and the Federal Holder-in-Due-Course Doctrine? 516
10.7.3 *D'Oench* 517
10.7.3.1 Overview of the Doctrine 517
10.7.3.2 Treatment of Innocent Borrowers and Free-Standing Torts 518
10.7.4 12 U.S.C. § 1823(e) 519
10.7.4.1 Outline of § 1823(e) 519
10.7.4.2 Requirements for Enforceability of Agreements 520
10.7.4.3 What Is an "Agreement" Under § 1823(e)? 520
10.7.4.4 Requirement That the Agreement Tend to Diminish or Defeat FDIC's Interest in an Asset 521
10.7.4.5 Equitable Considerations 522
10.7.4.6 Differences Between § 1823(e) and *D'Oench* 522
10.7.5 Federal Holder-in-Due-Course Doctrine 523
10.7.6 Who Can Claim Protection Under *D'Oench* and Related Doctrines 526
10.7.6.1 Subsidiaries, Institutions That Are Not Federally Insured 526
10.7.6.2 Assignees 526
10.7.6.3 Whether Assignees Benefit from FIRREA's Limitations Period . . 527
10.7.7 Effect of the Consumer Limitations on the FTC Holder Rule 528
10.7.8 A Sampling of Claims and Defenses Making Inroads 529
10.7.9 FDIC/RTC Liability for Its Own Conduct 534
10.7.10 Claims Process 534
10.8 Remedies for Illegal Overcharges; Traditional Usury Remedies 535
10.8.1 Introduction 535

10.8.2 State Statutory Remedies 536
    10.8.2.1 Overview; Implying a Remedy When Statute Is Silent 536
    10.8.2.2 Forfeiture of Creditor's Right to Recover Principal, Interest, Other Illegal Overcharges, or to Collect Attorney Fees. 537
        10.8.2.2.1 Statutes that void the contract interest or other charges. . 537
        10.8.2.2.2 Statutes that void the entire obligation 538
    10.8.2.3 Borrower's Recovery of Payments Made 539
    10.8.2.4 Statutory Penalties 542
10.8.3 Equitable Remedies. 543
10.8.4 Consumer Remedies for Creditor's Failure to Obtain a License 545
    10.8.4.1 Unlicensed Lending 545
    10.8.4.2 Remedies Where Licensed Creditor Violates Conditions of Licensure Statute 547
10.8.5 Federal Remedies 547
    10.8.5.1 Remedies Under National Bank Act and DIDA 547
    10.8.5.2 Remedies for HOEPA Violations 548
    10.8.5.3 RICO. 548
        10.8.5.3.1 Overview of RICO 548
        10.8.5.3.2 Racketeering activity and the pattern requirement 549
        10.8.5.3.3 Alleging a RICO claim based on the collection of an unlawful debt. 551
        10.8.5.3.4 The "injury" element 552
        10.8.5.3.5 RICO and creditor overcharges. 553
        10.8.5.3.6 State RICO statutes. 555
10.8.6 Class Actions 556

Chapter 11

The Credit Marketplace and a Sampling of Abuses *Du Jour*

11.1 Market Forces—Market Rationales—Market Failures 557
11.2 Barriers: Information, Understanding, Choice, and Steering 557
11.3 High Rate and High Risk: Myth or Fact? 558
11.4 Fuel for the Subprime Market: Securitization. 563
11.5 Home-Secured Credit. 565
  11.5.1 Background: Equity-Skimming and Predatory Lending 565
  11.5.2 Home Improvement Credit 565
  11.5.3 Refinancing/Debt Consolidation. 567
  11.5.4 Loan Brokers/Mortgage Brokers 568
    11.5.4.1 The Role of the Loan Broker 568
    11.5.4.2 Legal Status of Brokers. 569
    11.5.4.3 Range of Legal Claims Arising from Broker Involvement. 569
  11.5.5 Post-consummation Profiteering. 571
  11.5.6 Property Flipping and Appraisal Fraud 574
11.6 Used Car Financing 577
  11.6.1 Introduction 577
  11.6.2 Lender-Imposed Financing Costs: Discounts and Acquisition Fees . . . 578
    11.6.2.1 Burying Credit Costs in Inflated Cash Prices 578
    11.6.2.2 Related Problems: Loan Packing or Shoddy Cars 581
  11.6.3 Negative Equity: Driving "Upside Down" 582
  11.6.4 Payment Packing. 585
  11.6.5 Yo-Yo Deals, a.k.a. Spot Delivery 586
  11.6.6 Yield Spread Premiums 588
  11.6.7 What's in a Name? Who's Who in a Vehicle Retail Installment Sale? . . 589
  11.6.8 Single Document and Disclosure Requirements 591
11.7 Credit Cards: Background, Abuses and State Law Claims 593

11.7.1 The Rise of the Credit Card 593
    11.7.1.1 The Massive Credit Card Debt Burden 593
    11.7.1.2 Escalating Debt Loads Caused by Industry Practices 594
11.7.2 Credit Card Abuses 595
    11.7.2.1 Historical Perspective . . . ., ... 595
    11.7.2.2 Junk Fees and Fee Income 596
        11.7.2.2.1 Introduction 596
        11.7.2.2.2 Late fees 597
        11.7.2.2.3 Over-limit fees 597
        11.7.2.2.4 Balance transfer fees 597
        11.7.2.2.5 Currency conversion fees 597
    11.7.2.3 Other Abuses 598
        11.7.2.3.1 Penalty rates and universal default 598
        11.7.2.3.2 Deceptive marketing 598
        11.7.2.3.3 Late payment practices and posting cut-off policies . . . 599
        11.7.2.3.4 Tiny minimum monthly payments 599
        11.7.2.3.5 Aggressive solicitation 600
        11.7.2.3.6 Shrinking grace periods 600
        11.7.2.3.7 Payment allocation order 600
        11.7.2.3.8 Debt collection abuses 600
        11.7.2.3.9 Use of mandatory arbitration clauses 601
    11.7.2.4 Unilateral Change in Terms Provisions 602
11.7.3 Challenging Credit Card Abuse 603
    11.7.3.1 Breach of Contract 603
    11.7.3.2 State UDAP Statutes 603
    11.7.3.3 Other Claims 603
    11.7.3.4 Intersection with Federal Truth in Lending Act 603
    11.7.3.5 Preemption and Credit Cards 604
        11.7.3.5.1 General 604
        11.7.3.5.2 TILA preemption 604
11.7.4 Assisting Consumers Overwhelmed by Credit Card Debt 604

Chapter 12

Beyond Usury: Statutory and Common Law Challenges to Overreaching Credit

12.1 Introduction 605
12.2 Federal and State Statutes Relating to Real Estate Secured Credit 606
  12.2.1 The Real Estate Settlement Procedures Act (RESPA) 606
    12.2.1.1 Scope 606
    12.2.1.2 Cost Disclosure Provisions 607
    12.2.1.3 Servicer Obligations 610
    12.2.1.4 Escrow Limitations 611
    12.2.1.5 Prohibition Against Kickbacks and Referral Fees 612
        12.2.1.5.1 Introduction 612
        12.2.1.5.2 Lender-paid broker fees and pre-HUD policy statement
                    court decisions 614
        12.2.1.5.3 1999 HUD policy statement on lender-paid broker fees . . 617
        12.2.1.5.4 Conflicting interpretations of the 1999 HUD policy
                    statement 619
        12.2.1.5.5 HUD's second policy statement and its domino effect
                    upon the courts 620
        12.2.1.5.6 Broker kickback practice issues 623
    12.2.1.6 Excessive, Unearned, and Duplicative Fees 625
    12.2.1.7 Steering by Seller to Title Insurance Company 631

Contents

12.2.1.8 Preemption.. 631
12.2.1.9 Electronic Provision of Information Required by RESPA 632
12.2.1.10 Practice Issues 633
12.2.2 Home Ownership and Equity Protection Act of 1994 635
12.2.2.1 Overview and Remedies 635
12.2.2.2 Covered Mortgages 636
12.2.2.3 Substantive Prohibitions 637
12.2.3 State High-Cost Mortgage Statutes 638
12.3 Fair Lending Statutes and Civil Rights 642
12.3.1 Scope and Substantive Prohibitions 642
12.3.2 ECOA Notice Requirements 643
12.4 Federal and State Credit Repair Statutes 643
12.4.1 Overview... 643
12.4.2 Federal Credit Repair Organizations Act.................... 644
12.4.2.1 Coverage 644
12.4.2.2 Substantive Prohibitions 644
12.4.2.3 Remedies 645
12.4.3 State Credit Repair Laws 646
12.4.3.1 Coverage 646
12.4.3.2 Substantive Prohibitions 647
12.4.3.3 Private Causes of Action.................................. 647
12.5 Unfair and Deceptive Acts and Practices (UDAP) Statutes........ 647
12.6 RICO As a Remedy for Overreaching and Fraud 653
12.7 Unconscionability 659
12.7.1 Overview... 659
12.7.2 Unconscionability as Outer Limit on Price of Credit........ 662
12.7.3 Improvident Lending as Unconscionable...................... 665
12.7.4 Challenging Terms Other Than Interest Rate as Unconscionable....... 666
12.7.5 Remedy for Unconscionability 669
12.8 Duty of Good Faith and Fair Dealing 669
12.9 Fiduciary or Quasi-Fiduciary Duty.............................. 673
12.9.1 Duties of a Fiduciary; Remedies for Breach of Fiduciary Duty........ 673
12.9.2 Mortgage/Loan Brokers 674
12.9.3 Creditors' Fiduciary or Quasi-Fiduciary Role 674
12.9.4 Intentional Interference with a Contractual Relationship 676
12.10 Fraud and Misrepresentation 677
12.10.1 Parties Liable 677
12.10.2 Substantive Conduct Subject to Fraud and Misrepresentation Claims... 682
12.10.2.1 General... 682
12.10.2.2 Home Improvement Fraud 682
12.10.2.3 Fraud in Home Sales and Refinancing 684
12.10.2.4 Hidden Fees and Other Credit Practices 685
12.10.2.5 Falsification and Forgery 687
12.10.2.6 Negligent Misrepresentation............................ 688
12.10.2.7 Effect of Credit Documents That Contradict Oral Misrepresentations......... 688
12.10.3 Constitutional and Statutory Restrictions on Punitive Damages....... 688
12.11 Other Lender Liability Theories............................... 689
12.11.1 Duty of Due Care 689
12.11.2 Estoppel... 689
12.12 Liability Chart: Lender and Assignee Liability 690

Appendix A   State Lending Statutes 695

Appendix B   State Mortgage Broker Laws 707

Appendix C   National Bank Act

                 C.1 Selected Statutory Provisions 709
                 C.2 Selected Regulations 719
                 C.3 OCC Interpretive and Advisory Letters 733
                 C.4 OCC Preemption Determinations 736

Appendix D   Home Owners' Loan Act

                 D.1 Selected Statutory Portions 737
                 D.2 Selected Regulations 755
                 D.3 OTS Interpretive Letters 767

Appendix E   Federal Credit Union Act

                 E.1 Selected Statutory Provisions 773
                 E.2 Selected Regulations 776
                 E.3 NCUA Interpretive Letters 785

Appendix F   Federal Deposit Insurance Act

                 F.1 Selected Statutory Provisions 789
                 F.2 Selected Regulations 801
                 F.3 FDIC Letters, Opinions, and Advisories 802

Appendix G   Depository Institutions Deregulation and Monetary Control Act of 1980

                 G.1 Statutory Provisions 805
                 G.2 Relevant Regulations 811

Appendix H   Alternative Mortgage Transaction Parity Act of 1982

                 H.1 Statutory Provisions 815
                 H.2 Relevant Regulations 817
                 H.3 OTS AMTPA Interpretive Letters 818

Appendix I   Gramm-Leach-Bliley Act

                 I.1 Selected Statutory Provisions Related to Insurance 819
                 I.2 Selected Banking Regulations Related to Credit Insurance 825
                      I.2.1 12 C.F.R. Part 14—Office of the Comptroller of the Currency Regulations
                             Regarding Consumer Protection in Sales of Insurance 825
                       I.2.2 82512 C.F.R. § 208—Membership of State Banking Institutions in the
                             Federal Reserve System (Regulation H) 827
                       I.2.3 82712 C.F.R. Part 343—Federal Deposit Insurance Corporation
                               Regulations Regarding Consumer Protection in Sales of Insurance 829
                       I.2.4 82912 C.F.R. Part 536—Office of Thrift Supervision Regulations
                               Regarding Consumer Protection in Sales of Insurance 831

Contents

Appendix J   Other Federal Statutory Limits on Credit Terms

J.1 Adjustable Rate Mortgages Caps 835
J.2 Federal Rebate Statute 835
J.3 Servicemembers Civil Relief Act 836

Appendix K   Real Estate Settlement Procedures Act

K.1 Selected Statutory Provisions 839
K.2 Selected Regulation X Provisions 847
K.3 HUD Policy Statements 870
    K.3.1 HUD Statement of Policy 1999-1: Regarding Lender Payments to
          Mortgage Brokers 870
    K.3.2 HUD Statement of Policy 2001-1: Clarification of Statement of Policy
          1999-1 Regarding Lender Payments to Mortgage Brokers, and Guidance
          Concerning Unearned Fees Under Section 8(b) 879
K.4 HUD Letters 888
    K.4.1 HUD Letter Regarding Statement of Policy 1999-1 888
    K.4.2 HUD Letter Regarding Disclosures on Good Faith Estimate and HUD-1
          Settlement Statement 888

Appendix L   Sample Pleadings, Discovery, and Expert Witness Evidence

L.1 RISA Violations in Car Sale 893
    L.1.1 Answer and Counterclaim 893
    L.1.2 First Set of Interrogatories 895
L.2 Insurance Packing, Loan Padding and Flipping 897
    L.2.1 Complaint 897
    L.2.2 Sample Request for Admissions 899
    L.2.3 Sample Expert Affidavit: Broker Fee as Hidden Finance Charge 901
    L.2.4 Expert Witness Testimony Regarding Loan Splitting (*Besta v. Beneficial
          Financial*) 906
    L.2.5 Sample Expert Report on the Economic Cost of Debt Consolidation 910
    L.2.6 Expert Report on the Spiraling Costs and Profits to Lenders Due to
          Multiple Refinancings 912
L.3 Disguised Credit 914
    L.3.1 Sample Complaint 914
    L.3.2 Sample Discovery 917
L.4 Rent-a-Bank 918
    L.4.1 Complaint Challenging Rent-a-Bank Arrangements Involving a
          State-Chartered Bank 918
    L.4.2 Complaint Challenging Rent-a-Bank Arrangements Involving a National
          Bank 928
L.5 Refund Anticipation Loan (RAL) Litigation 933
    L.5.1 Sample Amended Complaint 933
    L.5.2 Interrogatories to Bank 938
    L.5.3 Requests for Production of Documents Directed to Bank 943
    L.5.4 Interrogatories to Tax Preparer 946
    L.5.5 Requests for Production of Documents Directed to Tax Preparation Firm . . 950
L.6 RESPA Pleadings 953
    L.6.1 Answer and Affirmative Defenses 953
    L.6.2 Discovery 957
L.7 Bank Preemption Pleadings and Briefs 959
    L.7.1 Amicus Brief in Wachovia Bank v. Burke 959

L.7.2 Complaint in New York v. First Horizon Home Mortgage 966
L.7.3 Amended Complaint in Miller v. Bank of America 968

Appendix M   Websites Relating to Consumer Credit Issues 975

Index 977

Quick Reference to Consumer Credit and Sales Legal Practice Series . . 1017

About the Companion CD-Rom 1029

CD-Rom Contents

How to Use/Help

Text Search
Ten-Second Tutorial on Adobe Acrobat
Two-Minute Tutorial on Adobe Acrobat
Navigation: Bookmarks
Disappearing Bookmarks?
Navigation Links
Navigation Arrows
Navigation: "Back" Arrow
Acrobat Articles
View-Zoom-Magnification: Making Text Larger
Full Screen vs. Bookmark View
Copying Text in Acrobat
How to Copy Only One Column
Word Files
About This CD-Rom
How to Install Acrobat Reader, with Search
Finding Aids for NCLC Manuals: What Is Available in the Books

Map of CD-Rom Contents

Acrobat 6.0 Problem

Statutes

DIDMCA (Appendix G.1)
AMTPA (Appendix H.1)
National Bank Act (Appendix C.1)
Interstate Banking and Branching Efficiency Act (Appendix C.1)
Home Owners' Loan Act, Selected Portions (Appendix D.1)
Federal Credit Union Act, Selected Statutory Provisions (Appendix E.1)
Federal Insurance Deposit Act, Selected Provisions (Appendix F.1)
Gramm-Leach-Bliley Act (Appendix I.1)
Adjustable Rate Mortgage Caps (Appendix J.1)
Federal Rebate Statute (Appendix J.2)
Servicemembers Civil Relief Act (Appendix J.3)
RESPA, 12 U.S.C. §§ 2601–2617 (Appendix K.1)
State Lending Statutes Summarized (Appendix A)

Federal Regulations

Selected HUD RESPA Regulations (Appendix K.2)
Comptroller of the Currency National Bank Regulations (Appendix C.2)

Supplemental Info—Amendment to 12 C.F.R. § 5.34 (69 Fed. Reg. 64478 (Nov. 5, 2004))
Office of Thrift Supervision Regulations—Savings Associations (Appendix D.2)
Office of Thrift Supervision Regulations—Federally Related Mortgages (Appendix G.2)
National Credit Union Administration Regulations—Loans to Members (Appendix E.2)
Regulations Related to Federal Insurance Deposit Act (Appendix F.2)
Joint Regulations on Consumer Protections for Depository Institution Sales of Insurance
12 C.F.R. § 14: Consumer Protections in Sales of Insurance (Appendix I.2.1)
12 C.F.R. § 208: Membership of State Banking Institutions in the Federal Reserve System (Regulation H) (Appendix I.2.2)
12 C.F.R. § 343 (Appendix I.2.3)
12 C.F.R. § 536 (Appendix I.2.4)
OCC Regulations—Debt Cancellation Contracts and Debt Suspension Agreements, 12 C.F.R. § 37 (Appendix C.2)
Regulations Related to AMTPA (Appendix H.2)

Agency, Court Interpretations

HUD
HUD Statement of Policy 1999-1: Lender Payments to Mortgage Brokers (Appendix K.3.1)
HUD Statement of Policy 2001-1: Clarifying 1999-1 Statement of Policy (Appendix K.3.2)
HUD Letter: Statement of Policy 1999-1 (Appendix K.4.1)
HUD Letter: Disclosure on Good Faith Estimate and HUD-1 Settlement Statement (Appendix K.4.2)
NCUA
Interpretive Letters (Summarized) (Appendix E.3)
Interpretive Letters (Full)
March 12, 2004: NCUA Preemption of the Georgia Fair Lending Act
February 10, 2004: Preemption of the New Mexico Home Loan Protection Act
January 28, 2004: Debt Cancellation Agreements
January 28, 2004: Preemption of Fee Limitations on Debt Cancellation Products
January 28, 2004: New Jersey Homeownership Security Act of 2002
December 15, 2003: Texas Debt Collection Law
November 10, 2003: NCUA Preemption of the Georgia Fair Lending Act
May 23, 2003: Applicability of the District of Columbia (D.C.) Home Loan Protection Act of 2002 to Federal Credit Unions
December 23, 2002: Debt Cancellation Programs
October 4, 2002: North Carolina Mortgage Lending Act
October 3, 2002: Preemption of Connecticut Open-End Mortgage Law
July 29, 2002: Applicability of Georgia Fair Lending Act to Federal Credit Unions
June 26, 2002: Preemption of California Credit Card Disclosure Law
March 2, 2001: Applicability of State Lending Regulation to Federal Credit Unions
February 1, 1999: State Law Limiting Finance Charges on Retail Installment Sales of Cars
December 9, 1998: Federal Credit Unions Establishing ATMs in Wyoming
April 21, 1998: Preemption of State Law

September 4, 1997: Application of State Consumer Lending Laws to Federal Credit Unions

July 31, 1997: Preemption of State Law Concerning Late Fees

April 14, 1997: NCUA Preemption of State Law Affecting Finance Charge

December 30, 1996: Application of State of Arizona Transaction Privilege Tax

January 29, 1996: Preemption of State Law

April 26, 1995: Preemption of State Usury Laws

January 21, 1993: Preemption of Pennsylvania Laws Governing Mortgage Fees

July 7, 1992: Preemption of South Dakota Law on Disposition of Decedent Accounts

June 24, 1992: Preemption of Texas Law Governing Late Charges

June 11, 1992: Iowa Credit Card Registration Law

June 1, 1992: Preemption of State Laws Governing Grace Periods

May 18, 1992: Preemption of Late Charges

April 5, 1992: Iowa Credit Card Law

OCC

Interpretive and Advisory Letters (Summarized) (Appendix C.3)

Interpretive and Advisory Letters (Full)

January 2005, Preemption—*Wells Fargo v. Harris, Bank One v. Feinstein*

January 2005, Preemption—*Mass. v. Simon*

September 2004, Preemption of State Unclaimed Property Laws, No. 1006

September 2004, Preemption of State Laws by UCC, No. 1005

August 2004, Federal Bank Charging State-Parity Fees, No. 1004

August 2004, Preemption of Georgia Fair Lending Act, No. 1002

August 2004, Preemption, No. 1000

August 2004, Preemption of State Predatory Lending Laws, No. 999

August 2004, Preemption of State Anti-Discrimination Laws, No. 998

August 2004, Bank Not-Sufficient-Funds Charges, No. 997

July 2004, Bank Fiduciary Powers, No. 995

July 2004, Preemption Rule

April 2004, Secured Credit Cards

February 2004, Consumer Complaints Referred to National Banks From State Officials

December 2003, UPS Drop Boxes at Financial Centers, No. 980

September 2003, Interpretive Letter No. 974

September 2003, Interpretive Letter No. 971

July 2003, Interpretive Letter No. 968

March 2003, Interpretive Letter No. 959

March 2003, Interpretive Letter No. 958

March 2003, Interpretive Letter No. 957

February 21, 2003, Avoiding Predatory and Abusive Lending Practices in Brokered and Purchased Loans (AL2003-3)

February 21, 2003, Guidelines for National Banks to Guard Against Predatory and Abusive Lending Practices (AL2003-2)

February 2003, Interpretive Letter No. 956

February 2003, Interpretive Letter No. 954

February 2003, Interpretive Letter No. 952

November 25, 2002, Questions Concerning Applicability and Enforcement of State Laws: Contacts From State Officials (AL2002-9)

July 2002, Interpretive Letter No. 939 (ATMs Owned by Out-of-State Banks)

March 22, 2002, Guidance on Unfair or Deceptive Acts or Practices (AL2002-3)
May 22, 2001, Interpretive Letter No. 916, Order of Check Posting
January 19, 2001, Interpretive Letter No. 906, National Bank Authority to Charge ATM Fees
December 28, 2000, Interpretive Letter No. 903, Debt Suspension Products
October 28, 1999, Interpretive Letter No. 872
October 8, 1999, Interpretive Letter No. 866
June 29, 1998, Interpretive Letter No. 846
April 15, 1998, Interpretive Letter No. 838
February 17, 1998, Interpretive Letter No. 822
February 17, 1998, Interpretive Letter No. 821
January 7, 1998, Interpretive Letter No. 817
October 7, 1997, Interpretive Letter No. 803
July 7, 1997
June 27, 1997, Interpretive Letter No. 789
March 18, 1997, Interpretive Letter No. 776
March 6, 1997, Interpretive Letter No. 772
September 13, 1996, Interpretive Letter No. 749
August 21, 1996, Interpretive Letter No. 744
August 15, 1996, Interpretive Letter No. 739
August 9, 1996
January 18, 1996, Interpretive Letter No. 706
June 9, 1995, Interpretive Letter No. 674
May 15, 1995
May 3, 1995
February 9, 1995
March 24, 1994, Interpretive Letter No. 644
July 19, 1993, Interpretive Letter No. 628
July 13, 1993
June 3, 1993
May 10, 1993, Interpretive Letter No. 623
May 6, 1993
February 26, 1993, Interpretive Letter No. 616
February 1, 1993
January 15, 1993, Interpretive Letter No. 614
December 7, 1992
November 2, 1992
September 30, 1992
June 18, 1992, Interpretive Letter No. 590
June 10, 1992
February 4, 1992
January 15, 1992, Interpretive Letter No. 572
Preemption Interpretations (Summarized) (Appendix C.4)
Preemption Interpretations
August 5, 2003 (68 Fed. Reg. 46264)
October 9, 2001 (66 Fed. Reg. 51502)
May 23, 2001 (66 Fed. Reg. 28593)
May 10, 2001 (66 Fed. Reg. 23977)
March 20, 2000 (65 Fed. Reg. 15037)
OTS
Office of Thrift Supervision Opinion Letters (Summarized) (Appendix D.3)
Office of Thrift Supervision Opinion Letters (Full)
October 18, 1994, Wisconsin Law—Consumer Access to Credit Reports

December 14, 1994, Preemption of Virginia Law Regulating Money Order Services of Federal Savings Associations

May 10, 1995, Georgia Residential Mortgage Act

January 18, 1996, Colorado Law: Annual Reports to State

March 28, 1996, Interstate Trust Business

April 30, 1996, Effect of Parity Act on Wisconsin Prepayment Penalty Statute

June 21, 1996, Interstate Marketing of Trust Services

August 8, 1996, Interstate Trust Activities

November 27, 1996, Fixed-Rate Mortgage Loans with a Default Rate

December 24, 1996, Preemption of State Laws Applicable to Credit Card Transactions

February 10, 1997, State Law Restrictions of Adjustable Rate Mortgage Loans

August 19, 1997, New Jersey Licensed Lenders Act

August 25, 1997, Preemption of Ohio State Law Limiting Discount Points

September 2, 1997, Applicability of Virgin Islands Banking Board Order and Virgin Islands Licensing Statute

May 11, 1998, New York Special Mortgage Recording Tax

July 1, 1998, Preemption of State ATM Restrictions

July 1, 1998, Interstate Pre-Need Funeral Trust Services and Fiduciary Activities

December 22, 1998, Massachusetts Electronic Branch Restrictions

January 4, 1999, Preemption of State Branching Statute

March 10, 1999, California Unfair Competition Act

July 26, 1999, Preemption of State (MD, CT) Mortgage Lender Licensing Requirements

July 29, 1999, Preemption of State (MD) Lender Licensing Laws

November 22, 1999, Preemption of Local ATM Fee Restrictions

December 7, 1999, San Francisco ATM Fee Ordinance

April 21, 2000, State Law (NY) Limiting Payoff Statement Fees

June 2, 2000, Due-on-Sale Regulations—Reverse Mortgage Definition

January 3, 2001, Federal Savings Bank Authority to Exercise Trust Powers Through an Agency Office (VA)

May 16, 2001, State Credit Card Lending Requirements

June 26, 2001, Applicability of State Law to Federal Savings Associations (TX)

December 14, 2001, Preemption of Iowa Laws Regulating Loan Fees

January 10, 2002, Authority of an Operating Subsidiary of a Federal Savings Association to Conduct Fiduciary Activities

March 21, 2002, Arizona Credit Card Reporting Requirements

May 14, 2002, Applicability of the Wisconsin Motor Vehicle Consumer Lease Law

June 12, 2002, Oklahoma Restrictions on Cash Dispensing ATMs

October 1, 2002, Preemption of California Minimum Payment Statute

January 21, 2003, Preemption of Georgia Fair Lending Act

January 30, 2003, Preemption of New York Predatory Lending Law

July 22, 2003, Preemption of New Jersey Predatory Lending Act

September 2, 2003, Preemption of New Mexico Home Loan Protection Act

October 6, 2003, Preemption of New York Escrow Account Laws

December 2, 2003, Alternative Mortgage Transaction Parity Act

September 14, 2004, Underwriting Authority for Asset-Backed Securities by an Operating Subsidiary

September 17, 2004, Location and Exportation Authority

October 25, 2004, Authority of a Federal Savings Association to Perform Banking Activities Through Agents Without Regard to State Licensing Requirements

October 28, 2004, Illinois Corporate Fiduciary Act

Powers of Federal Savings Associations, March 1, 2002, OTS

OTS-OCC Q&A: Selling of Credit Insurance Products

OTS Interpretive Letters Relating to AMTPA (Appendix H.3)

OTS Brief—Changes to AMTPA Regulations

FDIC

Interpretive Letters and Advisories (Summarized) (Appendix F.3)

Interpretive Letters and Advisories (Full)

No. 10: Interest Charges Under Section 27 of the Federal Deposit Insurance Act, April 17, 1998

No. 11: Interest Charges by Interstate State Banks, May 18, 1998

Whether Certain Deposit Product Violates Prohibition Against Paying Interest on Demand Deposits (12 C.F.R. § 329.2): FDIC-92-27, April 25, 1992

Section 521 of the Depository Institutions Deregulation and Monetary Control Act of 1980 Authorizes Insured State-Chartered Banks to Export Same Fees and Charges on Interstate Loans That National Banks May Under 12 U.S.C. § 85: FDIC-92-47, July 8, 1992

Interest Rates for Loans Made to Out-of-State Bank Customer: FDIC-81-7, March 17, 1981

Interest Rate on Loans to Customers Residing in States That Have Rejected the Federal Preemption Provision: FDIC-83-16, October 20, 1983

Relationship of State Usury Preemption Laws: FDIC-88-45, June 29, 1988

12 U.S.C. § 1831d Preempts Contrary State Common Law Restrictions on Credit Card Loans: FDIC-93-27, July 12, 1993

Whether a Loan Production Office of an Insured Non-member Bank Qualifies as a "Domestic Branch" as Defined in § 3(o) of the FDI Act: FDIC-95-28, October 4, 1995

Does an Automated Loan Machine Constitute a "Remote Service Unit" Under Section 3(o) of the FDI Act: FDIC-97-5, July 8, 1997

Would Certain Courier/Messenger Services Constitute Branch Banking and, Therefore, Violate Branch Banking Laws: FDIC-97-6, September 26, 1997

Does Section 27 of the Federal Deposit Insurance Act Preempt the Michigan Motor Vehicle Sales Finance Act: FDIC-02-06, December 19, 2002

Financial Institution Letters

FIL-26-2004: Unfair or Deceptive Acts or Practices Under Section 5 of the Federal Trade Commission Act (March 11, 2004)

FIL-15-2003: Interagency Advisory on Mortgage Banking Activities (February 25, 2003)

FIL-2-2003: Federal Banking Regulatory Agencies Jointly Issue Account Management and Loss Allowance Guidance for Credit Card Lending (January 8, 2003)

FIL-131-2002: Interagency Advisory on the Accounting Treatment of Accrued Interest Receivable Related to Credit Card Securitizations (December 4, 2002)

FIL-57-2002: Unfair or Deceptive Acts or Practices: Applicability of the Federal Trade Commission Act (May 30, 2002)

FIL-18-2001: FFIEC Statement on Revision to Article 9 of the Uniform Commercial Code (February 28, 2001)

FIL-9-2001: Federal Banking Regulatory Agencies Jointly Issue Expanded Examination Guidance for Subprime Lending Programs (January 31, 2001)

FIL-94-99: Interagency Guidance on High Loan-to-Value Residential Real Estate Lending (October 12, 1999)

FIL-44-97: Risks Associated with Subprime Lending (May 2, 1997)

FRB Open End Credit Disclosures

Center for Responsible Lending, Comments to Advance Notice of Proposed Rulemaking—Regulation Z, Subpart B: Open-End Credit, Docket No. R-1217, March 28, 2004

State Agencies

Iowa Credit Administration, *Per Diem* Charge on Honored NSF Checks as Finance Charge (Aug. 12, 1999)

Court Orders, Opinions

Cummins v. H & R Block (W. Va. Cir. Ct, Kanawha Cty June 1, 2004) (order denying defendants' motion to compel arbitration in case challenging H&R Block's brokering of RALs)

Cummins v. H & R Block (W. Va. Cir. Ct. Kanawha Cty Dec. 30, 2004) (order granting class certification in case challenging H&R Block's brokering of RALs)

In re Josephine McCarthy (Bankr. E.D. Va. filed 2004) (credit card issuer failed to provide documentation of debt it was seeking to collect)

In re Blair (Bankr. W.D.N.C. Feb. 10, 2004) (relating to adequacy of card issuer's documentation for seeking debt of specified amount)

Pleadings/Practice Aids

Practice Pointers

Analyzing a Loan Flipping Case

Methods of Computing Interest on Revolving Credit

CFA Report on Payday Lending (Arkansas)

Complaints and Answers

Sample Answer and Counterclaim—Collection on Car Loan (Appendix L.1.1)

Sample Complaint—Insurance Packing, Loan Padding and Flipping (Appendix L.2.1)

Sample Complaint Against a Payday Lender (Appendix L.3.1)

Complaint Challenging Rent-a-Bank Arrangements Between State-Chartered Bank and Payday Lender (Appendix L.4.1)

Complaint Challenging Rent-a-Bank Arrangements Between National Bank and Payday Lender (Appendix L.4.2)

Refund Anticipation Loan Debt Collection Complaint (Appendix L.5.1)

Answer and Affirmative Defenses—RESPA (Appendix L.6.1)

Complaint Involving Bank Preemption—*New York v. First Horizon Home Mortg.* (Appendix L.7.2)

Amended Complaint Involving Bank Preemption—*Miller v. Bank of America* (Appendix L.7.3)

Class Action Complaint—Payday Lending

Class Action Complaint—Claims for High PMI Premiums Based on the FCRA's Adverse Action Provisions

Sample Complaint—RESPA

Complaint—Predatory Mortgage Lending

Complaint in Payday Loan Case
Amended Bill of Complaint in Auto Pawn Case
Class Action Amended Complaint in Auto Pawn Case
Complaint—Mortgage Refinancing
Amended Class Action Complaint—Mortgage Servicer Practices
Complaint—Failure to Pay Credit Life Insurance Claim
Answer, Counterclaim, and Third-Party Complaint, Foreclosure Defense
Complaint—Loan Flipping
Complaint—Use of Rule of 78

Discovery
Sample First Set of Interrogatories—Car Loan (Appendix L.1.2)
Sample Request for Admissions—Insurance Packing, Loan Padding and
    Flipping (Appendix L.2.2)
Sample Document Requests and Interrogatories to Payday Lender (Appendix
    L.3.2)
Interrogatories to Bank—Refund Anticipation Loan Debt Collection (Appendix
    L.5.2)
Interrogatories to Tax Preparer—Refund Anticipation Loan Debt Collection
    (Appendix L.5.4)
Document Request Directed to Bank—Refund Anticipation Loan Debt
    Collection (Appendix L.5.3)
Document Request Directed to Tax Preparation Firm—Refund Anticipation
    Loan Debt Collection (Appendix L.5.5)
Discovery—RESPA (Appendix L.6.2)
Interrogatories and Document Requests—Predatory Mortgage Lending Case
First Set of Interrogatories in Auto Pawn Case
Second Set of Interrogatories in Auto Pawn Case
Document Requests in Auto Pawn Case
Request for Admissions in Auto Pawn Case
First Set of Interrogatories—Mortgage Servicer Practices
Class-Related Interrogatories—Mortgage Servicer Practices
Document Request to First Defendant—Mortgage Servicer Practices
Document Request to Second Defendant—Mortgage Servicer Practices
Discovery—Failure to Pay Credit Life Insurance Claim
Interrogatories—Use of Rule of 78
Document Requests—Use of Rule of 78
Request for Admissions—Use of Rule of 78
Document Preservation Motion—Foreclosure Defense
Proposed Order—Foreclosure Defense

Affidavits and Expert Testimony
Sample Expert Affidavit—Broker Fee as Hidden Charge (Appendix L.2.3)
Expert Witness Testimony—Loan Splitting, from *Besta v. Beneficial Fin.*
    (Appendix L.2.4)
Expert Witness Testimony—Economic Cost of Debt Consolidation (Appendix
    L.2.5)
Expert Witness Testimony—Spiraling Costs, Profits from Multiple Refinancings
    (Appendix L.2.6)

Briefs, Motions, Orders
Sample Response to Motion to Dismiss in Payday Lending Case
Amicus Brief—Payday Lending
RESPA Motion for Summary Judgment
Amicus Brief—Payday Lending and Charter Renting
Amicus Brief—Bank Preemption, *Wachovia Bank v. Burke* (Appendix L.7.1)
Sample Memorandum in Support of Partial Summary Judgment—RESPA Case

Amicus Brief—National Bank Preemption of State Second Mortgage Laws
  Where Bank's Assignor Lacked Preemption Rights
Pre-Trial Brief in Payday Loan Case
Memorandum Supporting Temporary Injunction—Auto Title Pawn Case
Reply Memorandum Supporting Temporary Injunction—Auto Title Pawn Case
Brief in Opposition to Motion to Dismiss in Mortgage Refinancing Case
Brief in Opposition to First Defendant's Motion to Dismiss—Mortgage Servicer
  Practices
Brief in Opposition to Second Defendant's Motion to Dismiss—Mortgage
  Servicer Practices
Consumer's Opposition to Motion to Dismiss Consumer's Defenses and
  Counterclaims to Foreclosure Action
Consumer's Motion to Dismiss Foreclosure Action Because Plaintiff Not the
  Real Party in Interest
Class Certification and Notice
Memorandum in Support of Class Certification in Auto Title Pawn Case
Opening Memo in Support of Class Certification—Use of Rule of 78
Class Notice—Use of Rule of 78
Settlements, Injunctive Orders, and Judgments
Order—Rent-a-Bank Arrangements
Order—Payday Lending Case
NY AG Decision and Order—Payday Lending Case
Jury Instructions—Predatory Mortgage Lending Case
Verdict—Predatory Mortgage Lending Case
Jury Findings—Predatory Mortgage Lending Case
Jury Instructions in Case Alleging Fraud by Mortgage Lender and by
  Investment Banker Who Securitized the Paper
Verdict Form
Permanent Injunction and Order—Payday Loan Case
Letter Opinion of Trial Court in Payday Loan Case
Permanent Injunction and Judgment—Auto Title Pawn Case
Letter Opinion of Trial Court in Auto Title Pawn Case
Joint Motion for Preliminary Settlement Approval—Mortgage Servicer
  Practices
Settlement Agreement and Release—Mortgage Servicer Practices
Notice of Proposed Class Action Settlement—Mortgage Servicer Practices
Order Preliminarily Approving Settlement—Mortgage Servicer Practices
Stipulation—Proposed Settlement—Use of Rule of 78 (*Consumer Class
  Actions*, Appendix O.5)

Credit Math Software

Consumer Law Math
APR Program

Web Links (Appendix M)

The Cost of Credit Appendices on CD-Rom

Table of Contents
Appendix A, State Lending Statutes
Appendix B, State Mortgage Broker Laws
Appendix C, National Bank Act
Appendix D, Home Owners' Loan Act, Regulations and Interpretations
Appendix E, Federal Credit Union Act, Regulations and Interpretations

Appendix F, Federal Deposit Insurance Act
Appendix G, Depository Institutions Deregulation and Monetary Control Act of 1980
Appendix H, Alternative Mortgage Transaction Parity Act of 1982
Appendix I, Gramm-Leach-Bliley Act
Appendix J, Other Federal Statutory Limits on Credit Terms
Appendix K, Real Estate Settlement Procedures Act
Appendix L, Pleadings
Appendix M, Websites Relating to Consumer Credit Issues
Index
Word Pleadings, Practice Aids on CD-Rom
Quick Reference to *Consumer Credit and Sales Legal Practice Series*
What Your Library Should Contain

Word Pleadings, Practice Aids on CD-Rom

Practice Pointers
Complaints and Answers
Discovery
Affidavits and Expert Testimony
Briefs, Motions, Orders
Class Certification and Notice
Settlements, Injunctive Orders, and Judgments

Contents of NCLC Publications

Internet-Based Keyword Search of All NCLC Manuals
Detailed and Summary Tables of Contents for Each Manual
Short Description of Each Manual's Features with Link to Manual's Detailed Index
Short Index to Major Topics Covered in the 16-Volume Series
Descriptions of Other NCLC Books for Lawyers and Consumers
Features of *Consumer Law in a Box* (16 CD-Roms Combined into One Master CD-Rom)
Printer-Friendly 3-Page Description of All NCLC Publications, Latest Supplements
Printer-Friendly 25-Page Brochure Describing All NCLC Publications
Printer-Friendly Order Form for All NCLC Publications
Order Securely On-line

Consumer Education Brochures, Books

Legal and General Audience Books Available to Order from NCLC
The Practice of Consumer Law, Seeking Economic Justice
STOP Predatory Lending, A Guide for Legal Advocates, with CD-Rom
Return to Sender: Getting a Refund or Replacement for Your Lemon Car
The NCLC Guide to Surviving Debt (2005 ed.)
The NCLC Guide to Consumer Rights for Immigrants
The NCLC Guide to Mobile Homes
Printer-Friendly Order Form
Order Securely On-line
Brochures for Consumers on This CD-Rom
General Consumer Education Brochures
Consumer Concerns for Older Americans
Immigrant Justice in the Consumer Marketplace

Order NCLC Publications, CD-Roms

NCLC Manuals and CD-Roms
Order Publications On-line

CD-Rom Contents

    Printer-Friendly Order Form
    Consumer Law in a Box CD-Rom
    Credit Math, *Bankruptcy Forms* Software
    Printer-Friendly Publications Brochure
    NCLC Newsletters
    Case Assistance
    Conferences, Training
    Books for Lawyers, Consumers
    Consumer Education Pamphlets
    Consumer Web Links

About NCLC, About This CD-Rom

National Consumer Law Center
    Mission Statement
    Contact Information: Boston, Washington Offices
    Go to NCLC Website
    What Your Library Should Contain
    Order NCLC Publications On-line
    Learn More About NCLC Manuals, CD-Roms,
    Order Form: Order NCLC Publications via Mail, Phone, Fax
About This CD-Rom
    What Is Contained on This CD-Rom
    Finding Aids for NCLC Manuals: What Is Available in the Books?
    Disclaimers—Need to Adapt Pleadings; Unauthorized Practice of Law
License Agreement, Copyrights, Trademarks: Please Read
Law Disks: CD-Rom Producer, Publisher of *Bankruptcy Forms* Software

Acrobat Reader 5.0.5 and 7.0.1

Chapter 1   Introduction

1.1 Purpose of This Manual

It has been said that we have become a nation of debtors. In 2004, the outstanding consumer installment debt in this country was estimated at over $1.3 trillion, up from $162.2 billion in 1975.[1] During that same period, the nature of the consumer credit marketplace has changed dramatically. Legislative, judicial and administrative attitudes concerning the degree of regulation of that marketplace have undergone one of their periodic mood swings, with the rhetoric of deregulation dominating the public policy debates. To the extent the notion of consumer protection enters into the debate, disclosure, rather than substantive regulation, is urged as a "market-perfecting" mechanism. This general thrust has led many consumer law practitioners to assume that in a deregulated environment, there is no such thing as an "illegal" or usurious charge and that excessive charges for credit cannot be challenged directly. Some in the credit business have assumed the same thing, and attempted to take advantage of this perceived unconstrained liberty. Far too often, low-income consumers bear the consequences. Among the most troubling of those consequences is the rise in home equity lending, and a concurrent rise in foreclosure rates.[2] At the same time, the fringe credit market—payday lending, refund anticipation loans, rent-to-own transactions, title pawns, all of which often carry triple-digit interest rates—has expanded dramatically.[3]

But in fact the sky is not the limit for consumer credit charges. There remain significant limitations on the right of creditors to exact any yield they wish from borrowers in the most typical consumer credit transactions. Some are in the form of direct limitations on the charges, some in specific substantive limitations on contract terms which affect the yield, and some are in the form of broad theories which spring from fundamental notions of fairness and balance in the rules of the marketplace. The majority of states have not removed interest ceilings from their statutes governing small loans, nor from their Retail Installment Sales Acts, common sources of credit for low-income consumers. Even deregulated states may have a "ceiling"—it is simply one now set by individual contracts, rather than the legislature. Measured against that contractual ceiling, there still may be an illegal overcharge.[4] State statutes may limit the use of add-on or discount interest calculations, (which result in a higher dollar cost to the consumer than the numerical rate itself suggests[5]), even if there is no specific statutory interest rate cap set. Rebates are required in all consumer transactions, and, if not given at all or calculated improperly, an illegal overcharge has occurred.[6] The "non-interest" charges tacked onto credit transactions have grown tremendously, and they provide ample hiding places for illegal over-

---

1 *Compare* Federal Reserve Board, Federal Reserve Statistical Release, Consumer Credit, (Jan. 2005, G.19), *available at* www.federalreserve.gov/releases/g19/ *with* 62 Fed. Res. Bull. A46 (Dec. 1976). Mortgage debt grew from $491 billion in October 1975 to $7.5 trillion in 2004. Federal Reserve Board, Federal Reserve Statistical Release, Flow of Funds of the United States, Table B.100: Balance Sheet of Households and Organizations (Mar. 10, 2005), *available at* www.federalreserve.gov/releases/z1/Current/z1r-5.pdf; 62 Fed. Res. Bull. A42 (Dec. 1976). Credit card debt now stands at $827.5 billion, up from $9.5 billion in 1975. Federal Reserve Board, Federal Reserve Statistical Release, Consumer Credit, (Jan. 2005, G.19); 62 Fed. Res. Bull. A46 (Dec. 1976). Note that the credit card debt figure includes the 10% of cardholders who do not carry a balance and who use their cards for "convenience credit." For additional statistics, *see* Lynn Drysdale and Kathleen Keest, *The Two-Tiered Consumer Financial Services Marketplace: The Fringe Banking System and its Challenge to Current Thinking About The Socio-Economic Role of Usury Laws in Today's Society*, 51 S.C. L. Rev. __ (2000).

2 Between 1998 and 2001, the proportion of families with home-secured debt rose 1.5 percentage points, to 44.6 percent. The increase continues a trend that has been observed since 1992.

Ana M. Aizcorbe, Arthur B. Kennickell, and Kevin B. Moore, Recent Changes in U.S. Family Finances: Evidence from the 1998 and 2001 Survey of Consumer Finances, *in* Fed. Res. Bull. (Jan. 2003), *available at* www.federalreserve.gov/pubs/bulletin/2003/0103lead.pdf. *See* Lynn Drysdale and Kathleen Keest, *The Two-Tiered Consumer Financial Services Marketplace: The Fringe Banking System and its Challenge to Current Thinking About The Socio-Economic Role of Usury Laws in Today's Society*, 51 S.C. L. Rev. __ (2000). The foreclosure rate more than doubled from 1980 to 1998. U.S. Census Bureau, Statistical Abstract of the United States: 1999 at 526.

3 *See* Lynn Drysdale and Kathleen Keest, *The Two-tiered Consumer Financial Services Marketplace: The Fringe Banking System and its Challenge to Current Thinking About The Socio-Economic Role of Usury Laws in Today's Society*, 51 S.C. L. Rev. __ (2000); Ch. 7, *infra*.

4 *See* § 9.2.8, *infra*.

5 *See* §§ 4.3.2, 4.3.3, *infra*.

6 *See* Ch. 5, *infra*.

charges.[7] Both federal and many state laws limit some of the kinds of contract terms which can drive up the cost of credit, such as prepayment fees.[8] Simply the way the creditor structures a transaction, or a series of transactions, can so distort the cost in relation to the real consideration that the loan may be vulnerable to legal challenge even in the absence of violations of any technical requirements.[9] Finding effective ways to protect vulnerable consumers from those who would take advantage of them is more critical now than it ever was.[10]

It is with this problem in mind that this revised edition was written. The purpose of this manual is four-fold:

- To introduce the reader to the basics of "credit math," and to try to convey that it is neither as boring as it sounds to many nor as intimidating as many fear.[11] Understanding how the math works on any given transaction can open the door to some effective claims which would otherwise go undiscovered.[12]
- To provide a guide to the state and federal statutes and regulations which directly or indirectly limit the cost of consumer credit in both regulated and "deregulated" states, and to common credit practices which may violate these statutes.
- To sort out those areas where, as a result of federal law, such state laws may be preempted.[13]
- To provide an overview of the array of broader statutory and common law claims which may also be available to challenge overcharges and overreaching credit.

1.2 Scope of This Manual

The primary focus of this manual is the cost of credit. As such, the bulk of it is devoted to those state and federal statutes which restrict credit charges either directly or indirectly, through substantive limitations on credit contract terms. Since most of them are usury statutes and their descendants, the "common law"[14] of usury is considered throughout.

However, there are other statutes and common law legal theories which also may come into play as a viable means to challenge deception, excess or unfairness in the price of credit, and this manual provides an overview of these as well.[15]

The oldest of the statutes which limit the cost of credit are so-called "general" usury statutes which purport to set the maximum rate of interest that can be charged in any "loan" transaction in a jurisdiction. More recent and plentiful are the "special" usury laws, such as small loan laws, which are usually structured as exceptions to a general usury ceiling, and which govern interest charges only in connection with specified kinds of loans. Finally, there are numerous laws which regulate charges for credit, but which are not usually called "usury" laws. For example, retail installment sales acts technically limit charges assessed in connection with the sale of goods on credit rather than charges for "loans" covered by usury laws. Consumer Finance Acts or Consumer Loan Acts may or may not set a limit on the maximum allowable interest rate, but they usually have limitations on other terms which affect the cost of credit.

Similarly, banking regulations may restrict the kinds of charges which a bank may impose, such as prepayment penalties or various service charges, without specifically restricting the rate of interest that may be charged, as usury statutes traditionally have done.

Some part of the consumer credit market is "deregulated" to some extent in every state, whether by action of the state legislature or by federal preemption.[16] Even those transactions, however, are subject to some standards, and throughout the manual, an effort is made to highlight areas where overcharges are vulnerable to challenge whether there is a usury ceiling or not.[17]

Despite the distinctions which can be drawn among the various statutes described above, all of these statutes are the subject of this book.[18] Because of the interrelationship between cost limitations and some other substantive limitations on credit terms, both are frequently discussed throughout the book. For the sake of simplicity, they may be referred to as "usury" statutes, since "statutes regulating the substantive cost-related terms of credit" is a bit verbose.

---

7 *See* Chs. 6, 7 and 8, *infra.*

8 *See, e.g.,* §§ 5.8, 11.3.2, *infra.*

9 *See* Chs. 6 and 11, *infra.*

10 *Cf.* § 1.3, *infra.* This is not to imply that all, or even most, credit providers fall into that category. It is only to suggest that vulnerable and economically disadvantaged consumers are disproportionately affected by those credit providers who do.

11 NCLC welcomes any comments as to how to better accomplish this goal.

12 *See, e.g.,* §§ 6.1.1, 12.7, *infra.*

13 *See* Ch. 3 and § 5.9, *infra.*

14 The term is somewhat misleading, as usury is a statutory concept. Nonetheless, since usury laws have been around a long time and are widespread, what can be termed a common law of usury has arisen.

---

15 Some of these are themselves the subject of separate volumes in NCLC's Consumer Credit and Sales Legal Practice Series, and so are dealt with here only briefly. *See, e.g.,* National Consumer Law Center, Unfair and Deceptive Acts and Practices (6th ed. 2004 and Supp.); National Consumer Law Center, Truth in Lending (5th ed. 2003 and Supp.); National Consumer Law Center, Credit Discrimination (4th ed. 2005).

16 *See* Ch. 3, *infra.*

17 *See, e.g.,* § 9.2.8, *infra.*

18 Chapter 2 discusses the different kinds of statutes governing the current consumer credit marketplace, and their evolution.

1.3 Purpose of Usury Laws and Their Progeny

The purpose of almost all limitations on credit charges is the protection of the borrower. It has been recognized for centuries that borrowers and lenders often do not enter credit contracts on an equal footing. The absence of equal bargaining power may manifest itself in different ways. Most obviously, a debtor who, for example, has lost her job and has defaulted on her mortgage may agree to almost any terms to obtain new credit and to avoid losing his home. Usury statutes have traditionally been justified as attempts to prevent the exploitation of such a needy borrower by limiting the price that she may be asked to pay for the loan.[19]

Yet, modern credit laws often address more subtle effects of unequal borrowing power as well as flagrant exploitation.

It is a fact of the modern consumer credit market that creditors, not borrowers, draft loan documents, and that the terms of credit contracts offered to consumers are basically non-negotiable. A potential borrower can "take it or leave it" and go elsewhere, though sometimes the "elsewhere" is not so easy to find. Moreover, the increased complexity of credit makes it difficult for consumers to do any meaningful comparison shopping to determine whether it is best to "leave it" or not.[20] The ubiquity of adhesive credit contracts, combined with the ignorance of almost all consumers about the fine print contained in these contracts, leads to opportunities for the exploitation of borrowers that are just as great as those presented by the classic desperate borrower.

Consumer credit statutes have adopted several tactics to combat the vulnerability of borrowers in everyday transactions. Many of these laws are unrelated to direct limitations on the interest rate or other charges which a creditor may assess. For example, state credit statutes frequently render unenforceable some particularly one-sided contract clauses such as waivers of a borrower's legal rights. Disclosure statutes, as another example, attempt to inform consumers about the charges contained in a contract without placing legal limits on what those charges may be.

These statutes also play a role in protecting borrowers in everyday credit transactions. Either expressly in special usury statutes or through the judicial interpretation of general usury statutes, there may be limitations on attorneys' fees, credit insurance premiums, "service charges," appraisal fees, commitment fees and other charges for services, real or imagined, that a creditor may impose. The most obvious purpose of these limitations on the particular kinds of charges that a creditor may assess is to define what the "interest" charges are that are subject to usury rate ceilings.[21] Yet because this question of defining interest can be, and has been handled though traditional judicial interpretation of general usury ceilings, one senses that other purposes lie behind statutory restrictions on particular credit charges.

One such underlying motive is, no doubt, a dissatisfaction, often on the part of creditors, with the charges allowed

---

19 Nelson v. Associates Fin. Servs. Co., 659 N.W.2d 635 (Mich. Ct. App. 2002) (purpose of restrictions on prepayment penalties is to protect loan customers from being locked in to high interest rates). *See, e.g.*, Ghirardo v. Antonioli, 883 P.2d 960 (Cal. 1994) (purpose of usury law is " 'to protect the necessitous, impecunious borrower who is unable to acquire credit from the usual sources and is forced by his economic circumstances to resort to excessively costly funds to meet his financial needs.' "); Jersey Palm-Gross, Inc. v. Paper, 658 So. 2d 531, 534 (Fla. 1995) (purpose of usury laws is to "protect borrowers from paying unfair and excessive interest to overreaching creditors"; and "to bind the power of creditors over necessitous debtors and prevent them from extorting harsh and undue terms in the making of loans"); Trapp v. Hancuh, 530 N.W.2d 879 (Minn. Ct. App. 1995) (purpose of usury laws is "to protect the weak and necessitous from being taken advantage of by lender who can unilaterally establish the terms of the loan transaction"; distinguishing position of corporations, presumed to be in an equal bargaining position); Watkins v. Mississippi Bar, 589 So. 2d 660 (Miss. 1991) (central purpose of usury law is to protect borrowers from overreaching creditors); Scarr v. Boyer, 818 P.2d 381, 383 (Mont. 1991) ("Usury statutes protect borrowers who lack real bargaining power against overreaching by creditors"); Schneider v. Phelps, 41 N.Y.2d 238, 359 N.E.2d 1361, 1365 (1977) ("The purpose of usury laws, from time immemorial, has been to protect desperately poor people from the consequences of their own desperation. Law-making authorities in almost all civilizations have recognized that the crush of financial burdens causes people to agree to almost any conditions of the lender and to consent to even the most improvident loans. Lenders, with the money, have all the leverage; borrowers, in dire need of money have none."); Seidel v. 18 East 17th St. Owners, 598 N.E.2d 7 (N.Y. 1992) (same); Smith v. Mitchell, 616 A.2d 17 (Pa. Super. Ct. 1992) (purpose of usury law, which applied to business loans under $10,000, "to protect the citizenry . . . from being exploited at the hands of unscrupulous individuals seeking to circumvent the law at the expense of *unsuspecting* borrowers who may have no other avenue to secure backing for a, for example, business venture."); Whitworth & Yancy v. Adams, 5 Rand 333, 335, 26 Va. 333 (1827) ("These statutes were made to protect needy and necessitous persons from the oppression of usurers and monied men, who are eager to take advantage of the distress of others; while they, on the other hand, from the pressure of their distress, are ready to come to any terms; and with their eyes open, not only break the law, but complete their ruin."); Paulman v. Filtercorp, 899 P.2d 1259 (Wash. 1995) (usury laws' aim is "to protect vulnerable bor-

rowers from oppression"; the evil at which they are directed "is oppression of the borrower 'who by adversity and necessity of economic life [is] driven to borrow money at any cost.' "); Demopolis v. Galvin, 57 Wash. App. 47, 786 P.2d 804, 807 (1990) (purpose is to protect desperate borrowers "driven to borrow money at any cost").

20 Throughout Chs. 4–8 of this book are discussions of the multitude of ways in which the price of credit can be understated, which distorts the impact genuinely lower cost competitors can have on the market. Additionally, there are information, education and access barriers on the consumer's part that interfere with competition as a solution to the problem of abusive, adhesive contract terms. *See generally* § 11.1, *infra*.

21 *See generally* Chs. 7 and 8, *infra*, for what charges, other than the contract rate, may be considered interest.

by previous judicial decisions or with the uncertainties of the whole judicial process.[22] Another motive, generally unemphasized, for regulating particular credit fees exists in at least some special usury laws;[23] these regulations may attempt to prevent consumers from being nickel-and-dimed to death by miscellaneous fees which, realistically, they are powerless to dispute. This goal is somewhat akin to the purposes of disclosure statutes which force creditors to include various "fees" in the calculation of a disclosed interest rate, except that it is a substantive limitation rather than mere disclosure.

A final purpose of at least some usury statutes is to make consumer debt more easily repayable. For example, a special usury law which granted licensed creditors the right to collect a high interest rate might require that the interest rate be fixed and that it be repayable in equal monthly installments. Such conditions are common in small loan acts, installment loan laws, and retail installment sales acts. State and federal mortgage regulations often required similar repayment terms until mortgage laws were "deregulated" in the early 1980s. Because that change played some role in the rise of notorious "equity-skimmers,"[24] to whom an untold number of consumers lost their homes, some re-regulation was necessary to guard against saddling vulnerable consumers with unaffordable home equity loans.[25]

1.4 Organization of This Manual

This manual is divided into twelve chapters and contains thirteen appendices and a companion CD-Rom.

Chapter One explains the scope and purpose of the manual. It also includes a checklist that suggests a method to break down the cost of a credit transaction into its component parts. Once that is done, the practitioner can do two analyses. He or she can evaluate each part for compliance with statutory and contract requirements to determine

whether there are overcharges violating specific laws, regulations or the agreement itself. It will also enable the practitioner to look overall at the value the consumer received, and the price paid for it, to determine whether there is overreaching involved, irrespective of whether there are technical contract or statutory violations.

Chapter Two begins with an overview of the history of usury and its evolution into the patchwork of current regulation of the consumer credit marketplace. Since this is still primarily a matter of state law, Chapter Two concentrates on state law. However, the past two decades have seen more federal incursion into substantive credit regulation.

Chapter Three discusses federal preemption of state usury laws by the type of lender and by the type of loan involved.

Chapter Four explains how installment credit works, the different methods of calculating interest, and some of the legal issues that arise in conjunction with these basic calculation questions. It also explains the distinction between Truth in Lending and usury law, and between an APR and the contract rate.

Chapter Five focuses on the cost to the borrower of early termination of credit, whether through default and acceleration, refinancing or debt consolidation, or pay-off. Methods of calculating rebates are explained, and the various regulatory requirements concerning rebates are explored. It also explores limitations on prepayment penalties.

Chapter Six concentrates on the calculation and legal issues which arise in the context of refinancing, as that can be an extraordinarily expensive act for consumers, and one which is often manipulated by creditors to maximize their profit for a minimum of benefit to the borrower.

Chapter Seven surveys a number of the "non-interest" charges which are common sources of overcharges, or hidden interest, and some "non-credit" credit transactions which were similarly designed to evade restrictions on credit charges.

Chapter Eight is an in-depth look at credit insurance, a major tool for extracting extra profit from credit.

Chapter Nine is a guide to determining which of the maze of laws is the one applicable to a given transaction, including sources of regulation in deregulated states, and choice of laws issues. Statutory construction of usury laws is also discussed.

Chapter Ten lays out the elements of a prima facie case which a borrower needs to prove to establish a traditional usury claim, the range of defenses typically offered by creditors, and the range of remedies available when a usury claim is established.

Chapter Eleven discusses common industry abuses. While deregulation has limited the most traditional approach to challenging excessively priced credit, the inventiveness of credit providers in devising hidden ways to hike the price of credit has continued apace. (Actually, its pace has probably been accelerated by the current regulatory environment.[26])

---

22 The influence of the credit industry on the drafting of consumer credit legislation is hard to understate. The industry exerts constant pressure on Congress and state legislatures to loosen or remove whatever restrictions have been placed upon it, either legislatively or judicially. Due to a lack of consumer opposition and the limited understanding that many legislators have of credit legislation, this pressure often bears fruit, and credit regulations are gradually weakened, until some particularly egregious abuse draws public attention and restrictions are reimposed. This cycle of loosening and tightening of consumer credit regulation has been evident through much of the twentieth century; the past twenty years have been only the latest example. *Cf.* §§ 11.5.1 and 12.2.2, *infra.*

23 A good example is small loan laws, which were traditionally more strict with the purported non-interest charges that a creditor may impose.

24 *See* § 11.5.1, *infra.*

25 *See* § 12.2.2, *infra* (discussing the federal Home Ownership and Equity Protection Act of 1994, primarily codified at 15 U.S.C. § 1639). *See also* § 2.2.3, *infra* (discussing state statutes adopting and expending on the federal protections).

---

26 *See* § 2.5, *infra.*

Chapter Twelve discusses some of the statutes and common law theories outside the family of usury descendants which can be used to challenge excessively priced credit. The approach of letting "the market" take care of itself ignores the fact that "the market" is an amoral institution. The usury statutes from which credit regulation evolved, in contrast, stem from a moral perspective: abuse of economic power, like abuse of physical or political power should not be socially sanctioned. That moral base has not disappeared with the disappearance of statutorily prescribed interest rate caps. Consequently, some courts have been willing to use statutes and common law claims stemming from standards of fundamental fairness to evaluate creditor overreaching, and legislators have been willing to note that some activities simply go too far to be officially sanctioned.

Appendix A is a summary of state statutes regulating consumer credit charges.

Appendix B is a summary of state statutes regulating mortgage brokers.

Appendix C contains selected statutory and regulatory provisions of the National Bank Act, as well as some related OCC letters and formal preemption determinations.

Appendix D contains selected statutory and regulatory provisions of the Home Owners' Loan Act, as well as some related OTS letters.

Appendix E contains selected statutory and regulatory provisions of the Federal Credit Union Act, as well as some related NCUA letters.

Appendix F contains selected statutory and regulatory provisions of the Federal Insurance Deposit Act, as well as some related FDIC letters and advisories.

Appendix G contains selected statutory and regulatory provisions of the Depository Institutions Deregulation and Monetary Control Act of 1980.

Appendix H contains selected statutory and regulatory provisions of the Alternative Mortgage Transactions Parity Act, as well as some related OTS interpretive letters.

Appendix I contains selected statutory and regulatory provisions of the Gramm-Leach-Bliley Act.

Appendix J contains selected provisions regarding federal limits on credit terms, including adjustable rate mortgage caps, the federal rebate statute and the Servicemembers Civil Relief Act.

Appendix K contains selected statutory and regulatory provisions of the Real Estate Settlement Procedures Act, as well as some HUD policy statements and letters.

Appendix L contains containing sample pleadings, discovery, and briefs on subjects including: retail installment sales agreements; insurance packing and loan inflation; disguised credit; rent-a-bank; refund anticipation loans; RESPA; and bank preemption.

Appendix M contains a sampling of helpful website addresses.

This volume also includes a CD-Rom containing: all of the statutes, regulations and administrative letters found in the appendices; an array of pleadings, discovery, briefs, affidavits, expert testimony, settlements and orders; a program to calculate annual percentage rates and prepare amortization tables; the appendices to this volume; and information about NCLC's *Consumer Credit and Sales Legal Practice Series* and other NCLC publications. See *About the Companion CD-Rom* at the back of this volume for more information.

1.5 References

There are not many treatises on usury law, which is one of the reasons that this manual has been written. Apart from this manual, the most comprehensive treatments of usury issues are probably contained in the *Corpus Juris Secundum* (C.J.S.)[27] and *American Jurisprudence, Second Series* (Am. Jur. 2d)[28] articles on interest and usury. Fonseca in *Handling Consumer Credit Cases* (West Group 1986 and Supp.), has one chapter on interest limitations and one on credit insurance. Greenfield, in *Consumer Law: A Guide for Those Who Represent Sellers, Lenders, and Consumers* (Little, Brown 1995), includes a chapter on credit insurance and some discussion of legal controls on the substance of consumer contracts. Some of the lender liability theories discussed in Chapter Twelve are also discussed, though more in the commercial context, in Budnitz, *The Law of Lender Liability* (A.S. Pratt 1994).

This manual assumes that the reader has a basic knowledge of contract law, including topics such as default, acceleration of debt, and security interests in credit contracts. For greater detail on these topics, see National Consumer Law Center, *Repossessions and Foreclosures* (5th ed. 2002 and Supp.). Sales and warranty issues are addressed in National Consumer Law Center, *Consumer Warranty Law* (2d ed. 2001 and Supp.). This book also touches on fair lending law and unfair and deceptive acts and practices statutes, both of which are the subject of separate volumes, National Consumer Law Center, *Unfair and Deceptive Acts and Practices* (6th ed. 2004 and Supp.), and National Consumer Law Center, *Credit Discrimination* (4th ed. 2005). Finally, interest calculation and disclosure issues under the Federal Truth in Lending Act are discussed in National Consumer Law Center, *Truth in Lending*.[29] A companion disk to that manual includes a software program that will calculate APRs.

A good source for summaries of state credit laws is the looseleaf service *Consumer Credit Guide* published by Commerce Clearinghouse, Inc. More concise summaries can be found in the looseleaf, *The Cost of Personal Borrowing in the United States* (Financial Publishing Co./

---

27 47 C.J.S., *Interest & Usury; Consumer Credit* (West Group).

28 17 Am. Jur. 2d, *Consumer & Borrower Protection* (West Group); 45 Am. Jur. 2d, *Interest & Usury* (West Group).

29 (5th ed. 2003 and Supp.). *See generally* § 4.4, *infra.*

Carleton, Inc.). The latter source contains numerous rate tables tailored to individual state usury and credit insurance statutes and can be very helpful with rate calculation issues, but unfortunately it lacks statutory citations. The *Consumer Credit Guide* is therefore a better reference when citations to individual state statutes and decisions are needed.

Many unreported cases cited in NCLC manuals are available through Sargent Shriver National Center on Poverty Law (NCPL) (formerly known as the National Clearinghouse for Legal Services). Those unreported cases and other documents are cited by a "Clearinghouse" number. NCPL retains copies of these documents, organized by Clearinghouse number. Current case pleadings are available on NCPL's website (www.povertylaw.org). Summaries are available to the general public. Subscribers can download full text. (Subscription fees are $25/monthly or $200/annually.) For older case pleadings, call NCPL at (312) 263-3830, extension 223. A minimum copying and delivery fee will be charged. Other unreported decisions may be reprinted on the CD-Rom accompanying this volume.

1.6 Getting Started

1.6.1 Introduction

In analyzing a credit transaction, it is helpful to do a two-track approach. First, just look at how the money breaks out. For this, it is *absolutely necessary* to have some document which itemizes the components of the note principal or amount financed. If a Truth in Lending itemization of the amount financed was given,[30] that will suffice. In mortgage transactions subject to RESPA,[31] a good faith estimate of settlement costs must be given, which breaks out all closing costs. However, practitioners should be aware that these are "good faith estimates," and the actual figures may differ. Some loans, particularly home equity loans, may also have a disbursal sheet.

What you are looking for is very simple: into whose pocket does each dollar comprising the total obligation go. Obviously interest goes into the creditor's pocket, but what about all the other charges? Generally speaking, the busier that itemization looks, the more closely the transaction needs to be scrutinized. Start by making three lists. The first is one for those components which are of value to the borrower—proceeds, purchase price of goods, legitimate pay-offs of debts to third parties, legitimate refinanced balances. In the second, list those to be paid (or purported to be paid) to third parties. In the last, list the charges clearly identified as going to the creditor. On some loans there is a fourth "what's this?" list.

Here is a sample loan with 180 payments of $379.40.

Note Principal	$29,600	TIL Amount Financed	$26,178
Contract rate	13.25%	APR	15.721%
Contract interest	$38,692	TIL finance charge	$42,114

The difference in the two columns reflects the fact that there are "non-interest" charges on this loan which the creditor has excluded from the interest calculations for purposes of the state credit laws, while TIL requires that they be considered finance charges. Typically, prepaid finance charges such as points and origination fees or service charges account for the difference, although some third party charges may be treated differently, as well.[32]

Distilling from the itemization of the amount financed, the loan closing statement, and the settlement statement (all of which this client happens to have) the break-out of the $29,600 note principal looks like this:[33]

Borrower

proceeds	$ 316
prior loan payoff to lender	$19,368
payoffs of third party debts	$ 5,117
Total	$24,801

Third party fees

appraisal fee	$ 300
tax service fee	$ 69[34]
hazard insurance	$ 524 1 yr. premium +
	$ 441 mo. escrow
title-related fees and insurance	$ 386[35]
documentary stamps	$ 104
recording fees	$ 20
Total third party closing fees	$ 1,447

Creditor's pocket

prepaid interim interest	$ 150
10% origination fee	$ 2,953
loan fee	$ 250
Total lender closing fees	$ 3,353

The closing fees and up-front charges on this loan make up $4,800, 16% of the note "principal." A chunk of principal that big which goes to fees and costs is a cue to scrutinize this loan very carefully for overcharges or over-

---

30 TIL does not require that one be given, only that the consumer be informed of the right to request one. Reg. Z, § 226.18(c)(2). Many creditors, though, give one automatically.

31 *See* § 12.2.1, *infra.*

32 *See generally* § 4.4, *infra.*

33 All figures, which are from an actual loan sent to NCLC by a Legal Services attorney for analysis, are rounded off to the nearest dollar, so they will not add up precisely.

34 It is unclear from the documents whether this is a third party fee or kept by the creditor.

35 Consists of two separate charges, though it is not clear what specifically they each are for. This should be clarified in discovery.

reaching.[36] Moreover, the biggest chunk of the benefits to the borrower consists of a refinanced loan payoff, and debt consolidation. These charges should not go unexamined, as they, too, can be the source of problems giving rise to claims or defenses.[37]

1.6.2 Analyzing the Contract: "Follow the Money"[38]

I. What did the borrower actually get?

A. If loan . . .

   1. Proceeds to borrower   _____

   2. If refinancing, pay-off amount[39]   _____

     a. Was a rebate of the finance charge/interest necessary?[40]

     b. Does the applicable statute prescribe how the rebate is to be calculated, e.g., Rule of 78 or actuarial? Does the contract have a provision? Is it consistent with the statute?[41]

     c. Were any other charges required to be rebated, e.g., insurance?[42]

     d. Were the rebates properly calculated?[43]

     e. Overall, did the creditor vastly improve its lot at the expense of the borrower by the refinance, e.g., is borrower's home now security on an "upsold" loan; are payments higher; are rates higher or overall costs much higher?[44]

   3. If consolidation, who was paid off, what was that debt for, and what were its terms? (e.g., unsecured debts now secured by the home? low rate debt now a high rate debt?)[45]   _____

B. If sale, price of goods or services purchased?   _____

C. Is the price reasonable, or does it smell like price gouging?[46]

II. What went into the creditor's pocket?[47]

A. Interest (that portion linked to the term of the loan).[48] _____

   1. Is it high rate credit—maybe unconscionably high? usuriously high?[49]

   2. Was there "upselling" or "loan padding" to make it a bigger loan, and thereby increase the amount of interest the creditor would earn? (Be particularly watchful if the principal was padded with costs that benefited the creditor more than the borrower.)[50]

B. Prepaid finance charges, e.g., points, loan discount, loan origination fee, service charge, etc.[51] _____

   1. Be especially watchful for a high portion of prepaid finance charges by creditors who put their borrowers on a "frequent flipper" program (i.e., encourage them to refinance frequently).[52]

   2. Were there expensive add-ons, e.g., service contracts?

C. What transaction costs or costs of doing business has the creditor passed along to the borrower, thus saving the creditor the expense? (e.g., is the creditor making the borrowers pay its cost of doing business on top of interest and prepaid finance charges?) _____

_____(total)

   1. The law may determine either what types of charges may be passed along, or may place some limit on the amount of cost that can be passed along. If a charge crosses that line, the excess may be considered interest.[53]

   2. Under TIL, some are finance charges in non-real-estate-secured loans. In real-estate-secured loans, they might be considered part of the amount financed, but only if they are "bona fide and reasonable."[54]

---

36 In enacting the Home Ownership and Equity Protection Act of 1994, Congress defined high-cost mortgages to be those with either APRs that were 10% above a market benchmark or which meet a "fees and points" trigger of 8% of the loan amount. Congress noted that the "8 percent level for points and fees is well above the industry average," and through this trigger, it sought "to prevent unscrupulous creditors from using grossly inflated fees and charges to take advantage of unwitting consumers." S. Rep. No. 169, 103d Cong., 1st Sess. 24 (1993), codified primarily at 15 U.S.C. § 1639. (This loan is double that threshold. *See* § 12.2.2, *infra*.)

37 *See* Chs. 6, 11, *infra*.

38 Deep Throat, circa 1973.

39 *See generally* Chs. 5 and 6, *infra*.

40 *See* § 5.4, *infra*.

41 *See* § 5.6.3.1, *infra*.

42 *See* § 5.5, *infra*.

43 *See* § 5.6, *infra*.

44 *See* §§ 6.3.2, 6.4.3, 8.5.3, Ch. 11, *infra. See also* National Consumer Law Center, Unfair and Deceptive Acts and Practices § 5.1.9 (6th ed. 2004 and Supp.).

45 *See* § 6.4.3, Ch. 11, *infra. See also* National Consumer Law Center, Truth in Lending § 3.10 (5th ed. 2003 and Supp.); National Consumer Law Center, Unfair and Deceptive Acts and Practices § 5.1.11.2 (6th ed. 2004 and Supp.).

46 *See* § 7.4.6, *infra. See also* National Consumer Law Center, Truth in Lending § 3.10 (5th ed. 2003 and Supp.); National Consumer Law Center, Unfair and Deceptive Acts and Practices § 4.4.4 (6th ed. 2004 and Supp.); National Consumer Law Center, Consumer Warranty Law §§ 11.2.4.4.4, 11.2.8.3 (2d ed. 2001 and Supp.).

47 Don't forget anything from the first section that might end up there, too, such as improper rebates or hidden finance charges in inflated sales prices.

48 *See* Ch. 4, *infra*.

49 *See* Ch. 11, *infra*.

50 *See* §§ 7.2–7.5, 8.5, *infra. See also* National Consumer Law Center, Unfair and Deceptive Acts and Practices § 5.3.12 (6th ed. 2004 and Supp.).

51 *See generally* §§ 4.7, 5.5.2.2, 6.4.1.3, 7.2.2, *infra; see also* National Consumer Law Center, Truth in Lending §§ 3.8, 4.3.3.4, 4.3.4.5 (5th ed. 2003 and Supp.) for more than anyone is really interested in about prepaid finance charges.

52 *See* §§ 6.3.2, 6.4.1.3, Ch. 11, *infra*.

53 *See* § 7.2.1, *infra*.

54 *E.g.*, National Consumer Law Center, Truth in Lending §§ 3.2, 3.5–3.9 (5th ed. 2003 and Supp.).

3. Watch for charges which the creditor may misname in order to make it look on its face like something which can be legitimately passed on to the consumer, but is not in fact such an animal.[55]

D. What "third-party" charges may wind up in whole or in part in the creditor's pocket?

1. Insurance costs are usually quite profitable through high commission rates,[56] and the insurance companies whose products are sold are sometimes "captives," so that commissions go directly into the lenders' coffers and other profit goes to an affiliated entity. The latter may be direct, or indirect through "reinsurance" arrangements.[57]
2. There may be hidden interrelationships through which the creditor and the purported third party share the same pocket. Loan brokerage companies have on occasion been found to have the same principals and directors as the lenders to whom they refer customers.[58]
3. Be aware of what the typical market rates in your area are for these third party costs. If the charges are higher than usual, check it out. They may be selecting very expensive options as a means of upselling, or they may actually be hiding extra profits. (e.g., in real-estate-secured loans, charging more than actual (or bona fide and reasonable) attorneys fees, appraisal fees, etc., and skimming the profit or simply using it as a padding device).[59]

E. Any other odd-looking charges? If they are not conferring any obvious benefit on the consumer, or are an atypical type of charge on a credit transaction, start looking for how the creditor might be skimming something extra off it.

III. What went into third parties' pockets?   _____
                                                      (total)

A. See II.C, II.D, *supra.*

B. Look for insurance—credit and otherwise. It is a ripe area for abuse.[60]

1. Are all the insurances sold of a kind which *this* creditor is authorized to sell in *this* kind of loan?[61]
2. Even if it is an authorized type, are they ones where abuses have shown up, e.g., non-filing, VSI (vendor's single interest) policies.[62]
3. Does the state regulate the insurance *rates* for any of the types of insurance sold?[63]
4. Does the state regulate the amount of insurance coverage?[64]
5. Would the consumers qualify for benefits under the insurance policies purchased?[65]
6. Was the consumer led to believe the insurance was required?[66]
7. Viewed as a whole, is this just way the heck out of line?[67]

C. Look very closely at loan/mortgage brokers—often an area of abuse.[68]

IV. So what do you do after you've figured all this out? Once you've identified all the components of the loan. . . .

A. Compare how the creditor allocated the components as between the finance charge/interest side of the ledger and the amount financed/principal side of the ledger. There may be violations of Truth in Lending[69] or state credit statutes or both. These violations would not have shown up if you just did a numbers check, taking their figures and allocations at face value, rather than making your own check of each component.

B. Even if there is not a specific TIL or usury violation, the numbers may suggest lender overreaching. Then it is critical to look for other, more broad remedies. Depending on the facts and the extent of the overreaching, other potential causes of action include:

1. common law fraud and related theories;[70]
2. breach of fiduciary duty;[71]
3. RICO;[72]

---

55 *E.g.,* §§ 8.3.1.4, 8.5.4.5, *infra. See also* National Consumer Law Center, Truth in Lending § 3.9.6.3 (5th ed. 2003 and Supp.) (non-filing insurance).

56 Service contracts on auto loans may also be foisted onto a credit contract as a means of upselling the loan and earning a commission. *See* National Consumer Law Center, Truth in Lending § 3.6.5 (5th ed. 2003 and Supp.); National Consumer Law Center, Consumer Warranty Law Ch. 18 (2d ed. 2001 and Supp.); National Consumer Law Center, Unfair and Deceptive Acts and Practices § 5.4.3.5 (6th ed. 2004 and Supp.).

57 *See* § 8.2, *infra; see also* §§ 8.5.3–8.5.6, *infra.*

58 *E.g.,* § 7.3, *infra. See also* National Consumer Law Center, Truth in Lending, § 3.7.4 (5th ed. 2003 and Supp.); National Consumer Law Center, Unfair and Deceptive Acts and Practices § 5.1.11 (6th ed. 2004 and Supp.).

59 *See* §§ 7.3, 8.5, *infra. See also* National Consumer Law Center, Truth in Lending, §§ 3.2, 3.6.3, 3.9.5, 3.9.6 (5th ed. 2003 and Supp.).

60 Generally Ch. 8, *infra.*

61 *See* §§ 8.5.3.3, 8.5.4.3, *infra.*

62 *See* II.C.3, *supra.*

63 *See* §§ 8.4.2.1, 8.5.2.3, *infra.*

64 *See* §§ 8.4.2.2, 8.5.3.3, *infra.*

65 *See* §§ 8.5.4, 8.5.5, *infra.*

66 *See* § 8.5.2, *infra. See also* National Consumer Law Center, Truth in Lending § 3.9.4.5.2 (5th ed. 2003 and Supp.).

67 *See* § 8.5.4, *infra. See also* National Consumer Law Center, Unfair and Deceptive Acts and Practices §§ 5.1.9, 5.3.1.1 (6th ed. 2004 and Supp.).

68 *See* §§ 7.3.2, 11.5.4, *infra.*

69 This is particularly critical if this is a transaction that might be subject to the Truth in Lending rescission right. National Consumer Law Center, Truth in Lending, Ch. 6 (5th ed. 2003 and Supp.).

70 *See* § 12.10, *infra. See also* National Consumer Law Center, Unfair and Deceptive Acts and Practices §§ 9.5, 9.6.3 (6th ed. 2004 and Supp.).

71 *See* §§ 8.7.2, 12.9, *infra.*

72 *See* §§ 10.8.5.3, 12.6, *infra. See also* National Consumer Law

4. breach of duty of good faith;[73]
5. breach of duty to disclose;[74]
6. unconscionability;[75]
7. general contract theories, e.g., failure of consideration.

V. Conclusion

In short, if it looks like it's a rip-off, there's more than likely some cause of action. But you need to know how the rip-off works. Further, if you are able to quantify the problem, you can make it that much more dramatic for the judge or jury.

1.6.3 Analyzing the Legal Issues

1.6.3.1 What Law Governs the Transaction?

1.6.3.1.1 General

- Collect and examine as many documents as can be obtained. Scrutinize the numbers, as suggested in the prior checklist. — §§ 1.6.1, 1.6.2

1.6.3.1.2 Is it credit?

Transactions may involve credit despite their appearance. Begin by interviewing the client and reviewing the contract documents.

- Transactions labeled "leases" may actually be credit sales disguised as leases to circumvent state credit laws. — § 7.5.3
    — Appliance "leases," often called "rent-to-own," may be disguised credit sales.[76]
- Professional bills (from doctors, hospitals, lawyers) subject to late charges may be treated as credit. — § 10.5.2
- An agreement to cash a postdated check may conceal a loan. — § 7.5.5
- A pawn transaction may be a loan. — § 7.5.2.3
- Assignments of tax refunds may be loans. — § 7.5.4.1
- Sale and repurchase agreements may be loans. — § 7.5.2

- "Investment" agreements may be loans. — § 7.5.6
- Sales of government benefit monies, actual or potential legal settlements, or lottery winnings may be loans. — § 7.5.7

1.6.3.1.3 What state law applies?

State statutory schemes vary and you must develop a checklist for your own state. Appendix A, *infra* contains a list of statutes, organized by state, which can help you get started. To spot the controlling statute, consider some of the following factors:

- If the creditor is from another state or the contract was signed in another state, check conflict of laws and pre-emption rules. — § 9.2.9, Ch. 3
- "General" usury statutes apply to all loans or forbearances not subject to special usury laws, but may not regulate credit sales. — §§ 2.3.2.2, 10.5.2.1
- The permissible contract interest ceiling may be the "legal rate" if the agreement is not written or the rate is not specified in the contract. — § 9.2.8
- Consumer transactions are subject to comprehensive consumer credit statutes in: Alabama, Colorado, Idaho, Iowa, Indiana, Kansas, Maine, Oklahoma, South Carolina, Texas, Utah, West Virginia, Wisconsin, and Wyoming. — § 2.3.3.10
- In other states, numerous "special usury laws," frequently structured as exceptions to a "general" usury ceiling, must be examined to find the controlling law. Transactions may be distinguished by the following considerations:
    — Credit sales are usually regulated by installment sales acts. Different installment sales acts may govern sales of different kinds of goods: motor vehicles, mobile homes, and "other goods." — §§ 2.2.3.2, 2.3.2.2
    — Different kinds of lenders may be subject to different statutes: banks, savings and loan associations, credit unions, finance companies, industrial banks, small loan licensees, licensed pawnbrokers, etc. Be sure to consider federal preemption if the creditor is a depository institution such as a bank or thrift. — §§ 2.3.1, 9.2.4

Center, Unfair and Deceptive Acts and Practices § 9.2 (6th ed. 2004 and Supp.).

73 *See* § 12.8, *infra*.
74 *See* §§ 8.7.3, 12.9, *infra*.
75 *See* §§ 8.7.5, 12.7, *infra*.
76 Most states have, however, now adopted consumer rental transaction laws that purport to remove rent-to-own transactions from the state credit sales laws and to legitimize effective triple-digit interest rates. *See* § 9.5.3.2.3, *infra*. See also Lynn Drysdale & Kathleen Keest, *The Two-tiered Consumer Financial Services Marketplace: The Fringe Banking System and its Challenge to Current Thinking About The Socio-Economic Role of Usury Laws in Today's Society*, 51 S.C. L. Rev. __ (2000).

— Different statutes may apply depending on the size of a loan. §§ 2.3.3.2, 9.2.5

— The purpose of credit can be important. Consumer transactions are often subject to usury regulations while business transactions may not be. § 9.2.2

— The financing of insurance premiums is often separately regulated. § 2.3.3.6

— Credit secured by real estate may be separately regulated. First mortgages and junior mortgages are often treated differently. High-cost mortgages may implicate additional federal and state statutes. Be sure to consider federal preemption in all transactions secured by real estate. §§ 2.3.3.5, 3.9.3, 3.10, 11.3.2, 11.3.3

— Open-end credit, often associated with credit cards, is probably regulated by a different statute than fixed-term credit, and may be affected by federal preemption. § 2.3.3.8, Ch. 3

— If a lender is not properly licensed, the special usury statute may not permit it to lend at high rates. § 9.2.4.5

1.6.3.1.4 Is state law preempted?

State usury laws may be preempted in three basic situations: loans made by depository lenders; federally-insured loans; and mortgage loans. Check the usury preemption chart in § 3.2.5 for easy reference.

• Loans by depositories:

— National banks are governed by the National Bank Act and the regulations of the Office of the Comptroller of the Currency, but state laws may be relevant under the most favored lender and exportation doctrines. § 3.4

— Federal savings associations are governed by the Home Owner's Loan Act regulations of the Office of Thrift Supervision. § 3.5, Appx. D

— Federal credit unions are governed by the National Credit Union Act and the regulations of the National Credit Union Administration. § 3.6, Appx. E

— State-chartered federally-insured banks are governed by state laws, the federal deposit insurance act, and are "most favored lenders" regarding interest preemption. § 3.7, Appx. F, Appx. G

— Any federally-insured depository lender, including state banks, state and federal credit unions, and state and federal savings and loan associations, may lend at the "alternative" interest ceiling made available to national banks unless the state has "opted out" of DIDA (also referred to as DIDMCA). This may include exportation rights. §§ 3.9.2, 3.9.4

• Federally-insured loans § 3.8

— State usury laws are preempted for loans insured by the Federal Housing Administration or the Veterans Administration unless the state has opted out of this preemption.

• Mortgage Loans

— Credit secured by first liens on residential real estate or mobile homes may be exempt from state interest rate caps if the state has not opted out of this DIDA provision. Opt-out states are: Colorado, Georgia, Hawaii, Idaho, Iowa, Kansas, Maine, Massachusetts, Minnesota, Nebraska, Nevada, Puerto Rico, South Carolina, South Dakota. §§ 3.9.3, 3.9.5, Appx. G

— Credit secured by first liens on residential real estate or mobile homes may be exempt from state limits on points and fees if the state has not opted out of this DIDA provision. Practitioners need to check their state law to see whether a cap on points or fees has been enacted since March 31, 1980, DIDA's effective date. §§ 3.9.3, 3.9.4.2

— DIDA preemption applies to mobile home sales only if the seller complies with OTS consumer protection regulations. § 3.9.3.4

— DIDA first mortgage preemption may not apply to loans by some small lenders and does not apply to transactions before April 1, 1980. § 3.9.3

— Most housing creditors issuing senior or junior mortgage loans can invoke OTS regulations governing variable rate loans, balloon notes, etc., except in opt-out states. § 3.10, Appx. H

1.6.3.2 Supplemental Checklist for Fixed-Term Consumer Credit Sales and Loans

1.6.3.2.1 Check the arithmetic §§ 1.6.2, 4.11

- There should be a Truth in Lending disclosure statement in consumer credit sales and loans.
- The TIL amount financed plus the TIL finance charge must equal the TIL total of payments.
- The sum of the payments called for must equal the TIL total of payments.
- If the buyer made a down payment, it must have been properly credited.
- If the amount financed is itemized or if there is a separate itemization of disbursements, the items listed must equal the amount financed.
- If there is a separate note, the numbers on the note should conform with those on the TIL statement, recognizing different allocation rules for TIL and state credit laws. § 4.4
- Contract numbers must agree with the numbers on a bill of sale and the advertised price.

1.6.3.2.2 What are the interest charges?

- Payments specifically denoted as "time-price differential" in a sales contract are usually interest under retail installment sales acts. §§ 9.2.3.2, 10.5.2.1
- Fees for lender services (service charges, document preparation fees, etc.) are interest unless otherwise defined by statute. § 7.2
- Late fees are excluded from interest in many states but must be reasonable in amount and below any statutory limit. (Note the effect of exportation rules on late charges from out-of-state credit card issuers.) §§ 4.8, 7.2.4
- Brokers fees may be interest if broker is agent of seller or is closely connected to seller. Broker's conduct and charges may trigger other causes of action. §§ 7.3.2, 11.5.4
- Charges for the creditor's attorney are sometimes interest. § 7.3.3
- Credit insurance premium may be treated as interest if it is excessive or illegal; consider the following:

  — Did the seller require the buyer to purchase insurance (depending on state law, entire premium cost or seller's commission may be interest if purchase was required)? § 8.5.2
  — If regulated, is the credit insurance rate above the state maximum? §§ 8.5.3.1, 8.5.3.2
  — Was excessive coverage sold to the debtor relative to the amount of credit? § 8.5.3.3
  — Was the coverage duplicative of policies already held by debtor? §§ 8.5.3.3.3, 8.5.4.3
  — Was the debtor sold insurance that he or she was not eligible for? § 8.5.5
  — Did force-placed insurance include excess coverage? §§ 8.3.1.4, 8.5.3.4
- Other third party expenses may be excludable from interest if bona fide and reasonable and not above any statutory limit. §§ 7.3.1, 9.3.1.2
- Inflated cash price of goods or services may be interest; § 7.4.6.1
- Unearned interest or credit insurance premiums which a creditor does not rebate upon prepayment or acceleration should be included as interest in a rate calculation. Ch. 5, § 8.6

1.6.3.2.3 What is the principal amount?

- In a credit sale, the cash price of the goods, minus any down payment, is principal unless cash price is inflated for credit sale. § 7.4.6
- The face amount stated on a loan note frequently exceeds the true loan principal; some creditor techniques for inflating the apparent principal amount are:
  — Including sham fees in the face amount of the note; § 7.4.2
  — Requiring the borrower to maintain an account with the creditor; § 7.4.4
  — Seller's points; § 7.4.6.2
  — Wraparound mortgage notes which allow the credit or to charge interest on sums it did not advance; § 7.4.3
  — If the loan was refinanced, the pay-off on the prior loan may have been improperly inflated. Ch. 6
- Valid third party fees, if paid by creditor, may be treated as principal. § 7.3
- Creditor fees expressly excluded from interest by statute may be treated as principal if financed by the seller. § 7.2

1.6.3.2.4 What are the maximum permissible charges?

Using the principal amount you just calculated, determine the maximum charges that the creditor could legally have assessed under the usury ceiling. If the actual interest charges exceed the legal amount, a usury violation exists. If the contract sets the cap, does it exceed the stated contract rate?

- What interest calculation method does the statute authorize for fixed-term credit sales and is the method used by the creditor valid under the statute?
  - Actuarial (simple) interest;   § 4.3.1
  - Add-on interest (common in installment sales acts);   § 4.3.2
  - Discount interest;   § 4.3.3
- Is the credit precomputed or interest-bearing?   § 4.5
- What is the actual term of the credit?
  - Is the term permissible under the statute? Installment sales acts often state a maximum term for sales credit, and small loan acts may limit the term.
  - If the loan has been terminated prematurely through prepayment or acceleration, has this increased the effective interest rate charged by the creditor?   Ch. 5
  - Were proper rebates of unearned interest given if the interest was precomputed?   Ch. 5
  - Were proper credit insurance rebates given?   Ch. 5, § 8.6
- Does the statute provide a split rate interest ceiling?   § 4.3.4
- Can the interest charges be spread over the whole loan term for purposes of interest rate calculation?   § 4.6.5
- Does the contract call for compound interest and, if so, is the compounding permissible?   § 4.6.1
  - Compounding may occur when a creditor finances fees that are actually hidden interest charges;   § 4.6.1
  - Refinancing agreements often involve *de facto* compounding;   §§ 4.6.1, 6.4.1.2
  - The common law of many states discourages compounding.   § 4.6.1.2
- If the loan was refinanced, were charges added which are improper in a refinancing? Was the interest rate improperly raised?   Ch. 6
- Even if the contract rate is legal on its face, has the creditor in fact charged a higher rate?
  - Failure to provide rebates when a precomputed debt is prepaid or accelerated increases the contract rate;   Ch. 5
  - Demand or dunning letters asking for excessive payments may be usurious;   §§ 5.7.2, 10.5.4.2
  - Whether or not the loan is precomputed, must the lender rebate precomputed charges such as points?   §§ 5.5.1, 5.5.2, 6.4.1.3
  - If the loan has been voluntarily prepaid, have any prepayment penalties been imposed, and are they permissible?   § 5.8
- If a transaction is subject to no interest ceiling, is the rate so high as to be unconscionable or so deceptively understated as to be unconscionable?   § 12.7
- If the controlling statute allows the parties to agree to any interest rate, have the parties really agreed to the rate that was charged? An inflated cash price or hidden finance charge may violate an "agreed rate" statute.   § 9.2.8

1.6.3.2.5 Are there non-rate violations in the contract?

- Have TIL disclosures been given and are they proper?[77]
- Have state disclosure requirements been met?
- Does the controlling state law require payments to be made in equal installments? If so, balloon notes or open-end transactions may be impermissible.   §§ 4.6.2, 12.2.2
- Does the controlling state law regulate the type of security the creditor may accept.   §§ 9.2.6, 12.7
  - Retail installment sales acts often prohibit real estate security, as do some loan acts.
- If the amount due was accelerated:[78]
  - The contract may not authorize acceleration;
  - An applicable state right-to-cure law may have been violated;
  - There may not have been a right to accelerate on the date the contract was accelerated;
  - The parties' conduct may have modified the creditor's right to accelerate;
- Does the statute provide the same remedies for non-rate violations as for interest overcharges?

---

77 *See* National Consumer Law Center, Truth in Lending (5th ed. 2003 and Supp.).

78 Acceleration is discussed in National Consumer Law Center, Repossessions and Foreclosures Ch. 4 (5th ed. 2002 and Supp.).

Chapter 2

Overview of Substantive Regulation of the Cost of Consumer Credit: State Laws

2.1 Introduction

Statutes regulating credit are frequently described as a patchwork. This is a fair description, but perhaps one that is overly kind. Upon first exposure to the subject of credit regulation, the impression of the average attorney might be that the field is a maze, if not a mess, and probably both.

In a typical state, there may be a dozen or more statutes, each intended to address a different kind of credit transaction. The most common distinction is the type of creditor that each regulates. For example, banks, savings and loan or thrift institutions, credit unions, finance companies, and individual lenders may each fall under a different statute when making otherwise identical loans. Not only are different creditors statutorily distinguished, but supposedly distinct kinds of credit transactions are also treated differently. Credit sales of goods are usually distinguished from loans of money, and each of these categories may be further subdivided by the particular kind of goods sold or by the size of the loan. Consumer credit may be regulated apart from credit extended to businesses; fixed-term credit is usually distinguished from open-end accounts associated with credit cards; and credit secured by real estate is most often segregated from everything else.

The point of this discussion is not to drive a novice in the field of credit regulation to despair of ever understanding the subject. Rather, it is to emphasize that credit transactions are regulated (or not) by a large, overlapping set of statutes, which are often duplicative, which are riddled with exceptions, and which tend to draw arbitrary lines in the regulation of fundamentally similar transactions. The purpose of this chapter is to attempt to describe how the law got into this state and, in so doing, to provide a brief overview of what credit statutes are designed to do, and how, in the end, the consumer fares under them. Case law interpreting the distinction will be discussed in a later chapter, "Which Statute Applies," § 9.2, *infra*. The discussion initially takes a historical approach to the regulation of the cost of credit, since the perspective of history is the only one from which the current structure of credit laws makes any sense.

2.2 Historical Development of Usury Laws

2.2.1 Early Attitudes Toward Interest

The history of usury regulation[1] is in large part a history of the tension between the conviction that the lending of

---

1 The historical discussion contained in this chapter is admittedly cursory. It is designed to be an overview of credit regulation rather than a detailed analysis. Those interested in more detail should consult the following sources: Bodfish, History of Building and Loan Associations in the U.S. (1931); Cobb, Federal Regulation of Depository Institutions: Enforcement Powers and Procedures (1984); The Consumer Finance Industry: Its Costs and Regulation (Chapman & Shea, Eds., 1967); Curran, Trends in Consumer Credit Legislation (1966); Homer, A History of Interest Rates (1963); Hubachek, Annotations on Small Loan Laws (1938); Kawaja, Regulation of the Consumer Finance Industry: A Case Study of Rate Ceilings and Loan Size Limits in New York State (1971); Murray, History of Usury (1866); Saulnier, Industrial Banking Companies and Their Banking Practices (1940); Sherman, Modern Story of Mutual Savings Banks (1934); Welfling, Mutual Savings Banks (1968); 1 Credit Union Law Service ch. 1 (Matthew Bender 1987); James J. White, *The Usury Trompe l'Oeil*, 51 S.C. L. Rev. 445 (Spring 2000); Note, *Interest Rates and the Law: A History of Usury*, 1981 Ariz. St. L.J. 61; Curran, *Legislative Controls As a Response to Consumer-Credit Problems*, 8 B.C. Ind. & Com. L. Rev. 409 (1966–67); Lynn Drysdale & Kathleen Keest, *The Two-Tiered Consumer Financial Services Marketplace: The Fringe Banking System and its Challenge to Current Thinking About The Socio-Economic role of Usury Laws in Today's Society*, 51 S.C. L. Rev. 589 (2000); David J. Gerber, *Prometheus Born: The High Middle Ages and the Relationship Between Law and Economic Conduct*, 38 St. Louis L. J. 673 (1994); Edward L. Glaeser & Jose Scheinkman, *Neither a Borrower Nor a Lender Be: An Ecnomic Analysis of Interest Restrictions and Usury Laws*, 41 J. Law & Econ. 1 (1998); Jordan & Warren, *A Proposed Uniform Code for Consumer Credit*, 8 B.C. Ind & Com. L. Rev. 441 (1966–67); Littlefield, *Parties and Transactions Covered By Consumer-Credit Legislation*, 8 B.C. Ind. & Com. L. Rev. 463 (1966–67); Redfield, *Savings Banks and Savings and Loan Associations: The Past and the Future*, 16 Bus. Law 170 (1960); *Combating the Shark*, 8 Law & Contemp. Prob. 1-205 (Winter 1941) (series of articles on usury, small loan laws, and loan sharking); Roster, *Modern Role of Thrifts*, 18 Loyola L.A. L. Rev. 1099 (1985); Vincent D. Rougeau, *Rediscovering Usury: An Argument for Legal Con-*

money at interest is predatory and immoral, and the fact that such money lending is necessary for the formation of capital and the flow of commerce. The tension between these views continues to the present day, albeit in a somewhat altered scope. The question today is not whether the charging of interest *per se* is moral or proper, but rather what limits, if any, should be placed on the interest charged.

The lending of money or commodities such as grain in return for interest has been documented as early as 3000 B.C.[2] and no doubt, predates that. From its inception, the practice seems to have caused controversy in many societies. In part, the charging of interest was condemned on moral and religious grounds; it was considered ungodly and uncharitable for one man to profit from the need of another. Yet there were also many concrete grounds for opposing money lending. In hard times, a borrower could lose all his property and be sold into slavery to pay his debts. The evils caused by usury were very real, and moneylending was at times banned outright. For example, under the laws of the Old Testament, one Jew was forbidden to lend at interest to another.[3]

The complete abolition of money lending at interest is not, however, a realistic solution to the problems that lending can cause or exacerbate. First, if one person has money or some commodity which another needs, it will be difficult to thwart the combined self-interest of the former and desire of the latter. Loan contracts are, after all, consensual agreements, even if not always even-handed ones. Second, loans at interest do not invariably spell doom for the borrower. They can and do benefit both parties in most cases, especially in commercial transactions where they assist capital formation and commerce. Not surprisingly, early commercial societies were tolerant of moneylending although they frequently imposed limits on the interest rates that would be permitted. Conversely, even in societies which prohibited loans at interest, means were found to overcome the prohibitions. Thus, even while the Old Testament condemned usurers and forbade one Jew from collecting interest from another, it allowed the collection of interest from foreigners.[4]

Medieval Europe, under the powerful influence of the Catholic church, followed a similar path. The church repeatedly condemned the assessment of "usury" (i.e., interest),[5]

but Jews were permitted to operate pawnshops. As trade gradually increased through the centuries, Christian merchants developed various schemes to avoid the prohibitions, such as assignments of rents, "investments," and the use of bills of exchange. In England, it was not until 1545 that Parliament legalized charging interest in the modern sense,[6] and even this statute was repealed during the reign of Queen Mary, only to be reenacted in 1570 under Queen Elizabeth. From this date, interest ceilings in England were set at various rates below ten percent until the ceilings were entirely removed in 1854.

2.2.2 General Usury Statutes in the United States

English usury statutes, particularly the Statute of Anne, were adopted by the American colonies prior to independence. Variations on these statutes remain in effect to this day in many states, and are commonly referred to as "general" usury laws because they purport to set a ceiling for all loans of money or forbearance of debt in a jurisdiction, not just for particular types of lenders or credit transactions. With very few exceptions, general usury laws were the only statutes regulating credit costs in the United States prior to the twentieth century.

The influence of the general usury laws on modern credit regulation is difficult to over-emphasize. Their importance stems not so much from the language of the statutes or even from the particular interest ceilings that they set, because these features are easily altered through legislation. Rather, the influence of general usury statutes lies in their heredity; when these statutes were borrowed from English law, they brought with them the interpretation placed upon them by the English courts. This gloss of case law was adopted by American courts and represents an important source of authority in the interpretation of modern usury statutes. It is, at least in effect, a common law of usury which, in the absence of express statutory treatment, governs issues such as the elements of proof of a usury case or the definition of interest.

Many of the inconsistencies and irrationalities which exist in current credit laws can be traced to English case law and, through it, to even earlier origins in common law or canon

---

trols on Credit Card Interest Rates, 67 U. Colo. L. Rev. 1 (1996).

2 The records are Sumerian. *See* Homer, A History of Interest Rates 25 (1963). The discussion of ancient commercial practices is taken primarily from this source.

3 *See* Exodus 22:25, Leviticus 25:35–37, Deuteronomy 23:19–20. *See also* Commonwealth v. Donoghue, 63 S.W.2d 3 (Ky. App. 1933) (quoting 4th century Christian theologian's views of usury and referring to Old Testament prohibitions).

4 *See* Deuteronomy 23:19–20.

5 In medieval terms the word "usury," derived from the Latin "usera," equated with what we would call "interest" today. The prohibition of usury was essentially a prohibition of charging for the use of money. However, common law distinguished reim-

bursement for a loss associated with a loan from charges for the use of money and permitted the former while forbidding the latter. This legal compensation for loss was known as "interesse" from the Latin "intereo" meaning "to be lost." Thus legal charges associated with a loan appear to have evolved to the modern notion of "interest," while illegal charges eventually came to be called "usury." *See* Homer, A History of Interest Rates 73–74 (1963).

6 37 Hen. 8, C. 9 (1545). The statute was entitled "An Act Against Usury," doublespeak apparently having preceded George Orwell by several centuries. *See also* Commonwealth v. Donoghue, 63 S.W.2d 3 (Ky. App. 1933) (discussing the development of English usury law).

law. For example, the English courts ruled that a sale of goods on credit did not constitute a loan or forbearance and was thus exempt from the interest limitations of usury statutes.[7] This rule, known as the time-price doctrine, was adopted by American courts[8] and, despite much criticism, is still recognized in some states today.[9] In general, the time-price doctrine is the source of the separate regulation of loans and credit sales in virtually all states.

Another example of the ancient roots of modern usury law principles is the distinction between interest on a loan and "penalties," such as late fees, which can be assessed on overdue accounts, usually without usury limitations. (In many modern consumer statutes, however, late fees are separately regulated.) This distinction, which has been codified in most states, appears to have come to American law, through English case law, from a canon law rule that one could not exact gain from a loan (i.e., charge any interest), but that one could be compensated for loss incurred through a loan, including the loss suffered when the loan was not promptly repaid.[10] This convenient doctrine appears to have been used in the Middle Ages to evade the church's prohibition against interest,[11] just as it is used today to evade laws which limit the amount of interest that a lender may charge.[12]

2.2.3 Special Usury Laws

Although some states have repealed the general usury laws, the structure of credit statutes in most states today is a general usury ceiling riddled with statutory exceptions for particular creditors or transactions. These statutory exceptions are known as "special" usury laws because of their individually limited scopes. However, special usury laws have proliferated to such an extent that to view them as exceptions to a general usury ceiling is misleading. Today, the average credit transaction is governed, if at all, by a special usury statute. In order to understand the evolution of special usury laws, it is necessary to consider the United States credit market of the nineteenth century when only general usury laws were on the books.

2.2.3.1 Laws Governing Loans

Consumer credit as we know it today did not exist, for practical purposes, prior to the twentieth century.[13] Pawn-broking, of course, had been around for millennia, and personal loans secured by real estate were not unknown. Yet the vast majority of credit transactions were commercial. The total amount of credit available in the nineteenth century United States was limited, and most of it was directed towards industrial development where the profits available were higher and the risks lower, than for individual loans. Furthermore, demand for individual credit was lower than it is today. Not only was individual borrowing socially frowned upon, but the economy was not oriented toward the production of consumer durable goods. In the days before automobiles, televisions, refrigerators, and other modern appliances, there was less for an individual to buy on credit.

This is not to say that individual Americans had no need to borrow for personal expenses prior to the twentieth century, or that there was no demand for goods, but rather that the official credit system simply did not extend to the average wage-earner. Given interest ceilings under general usury statutes in the neighborhood of six percent, and the proportionately higher administrative expense in small personal loans than in large commercial loans, banks could make more money lending to businesses. Thus individuals in need of personal loans had to resort to loan sharks or "salary lenders." The typical arrangement seems to have been a loan for $5 on a Monday, repayable on Friday (pay day) for $6. Ignoring compounding, this is an annual interest rate of 1040%.[14]

The problem of loansharking was pervasive in the nineteenth century,[15] leading to increased recognition of both the financial plight of wage earners and their need for a legitimate source of credit. Early attempts to reform were small-scale, informal and uncoordinated, but seemed to follow one of three basic strategies. First, cooperative societies were formed, generally following models pioneered in Europe, in which individuals pooled their money for their mutual benefit. The earliest of these societies took the form of mutual savings banks, organized under existing banking laws, but catering to and owned by small depositors. As the name implies, however, mutual savings banks were primarily concerned with encouraging thrift rather than providing credit. Building and loan associations, on the other hand, were cooperative organizations established primarily to provide mortgage money to members. Both of these institu-

---

Response to Consumer Credit Problems, 8 B.C. Ind. & Com. L. Rev. 409 (1966–67).

7 *See* Beete v. Bidgood, 7 B. & C. 453, 108 Eng. Rep. 792 (K.B. 1827).

8 *See* Hogg v. Ruffner, 66 U.S. (1 Black) 115 (1861).

9 *See* § 10.5.2.2, *infra*. *See also* §§ 2.2.3.2, 2.3.2.2, *infra*.

10 The common law rule in turn seems to derive from Roman Law. *See* Homer, A History of Interest Rates 73–74 (1963).

11 J.B.C. Murray, *History of Usury* (J.B. Lippincott & Co. 1866).

12 For a discussion of delinquency charges under modern usury law, see § 7.2.4, *infra*.

13 *See generally* Note, *Interest Rates and the Law: A History of Usury*, 1981 Ariz. St. L.J. 61; Curran, *Legislative Controls As a*

14 *See* Commonwealth v. Donoghue, 63 S.W.2d 3 (Ky. App. 1933) and § 2.5, *infra* for a discussion of modern incarnations of this type of credit. *See also* Lynn Drysdale & Kathleen Keest, *The Two-Tiered Consumer Financial Services Marketplace: The Fringe Banking System and its Challenge to Current Thinking About The Socio-Economic role of Usury Laws in Today's Society*, 51 S.C. L. Rev. 589 (2000), for a fuller discussion of the historical antecedents of today's fringe lenders.

15 *See generally Combating the Loan Shark*, 8 Law & Contemp. Prob. 1-205 (Winter 1941) (issue devoted to articles on usury, small loan laws, and loan sharking).

tions, which were the precursors of modern savings banks and savings and loan associations respectively, had become widespread by the turn of the century.[16] A later model of the cooperative society, which did not emerge in the United States until the first decade of the twentieth century, was the credit union. Like its predecessors, credit unions emphasized the pooling of resources, but further required the existence of some common bond among the members, typically a common employer.[17]

A second response to the loan shark problem was more strictly philanthropic.[18] Organizations supported by donated funds made small loans at no charge except administrative expenses. Some employers apparently followed the same route. However, the money available through such organizations does not appear to have been sufficient to have made much of a dent in the demand for small loans.

The third and, chronologically, last strategy aimed at combating loansharking was to attract credit, which had previously been extended only to businesses, to the consumer credit market by making consumer lending a profitable prospect. While the philanthropic organizations and, at least in their early stages, the cooperative credit organizations posed no challenge to the existing general usury laws, the essence of this third strategy created exceptions to the general usury law for small, unsecured loans, thereby making them attractive, profitable investments for legitimate creditors. The concept of making small loans available by increasing their yield is most clearly manifested in the small loan laws and the industrial bank laws, both of which were first adopted in the early twentieth century.[19]

The small loan laws, pioneered by the Russell Sage Foundation[20] and the research that it supported, took a direct approach to attracting capital to the consumer market. The Uniform Small Loan Law, the first draft of which was issued in 1916, created a licensed class of small loan lenders authorized to charge rates significantly in excess of the general usury ceilings. In return, these lenders accepted regulation, the risk involved in personal lending, and the

higher administrative expense of small loans. For example, the fourth draft of the uniform law[21] allowed the charging of 3-1/2% *monthly* on loans of $300 or less. This rate was much higher than the general usury ceiling, but was nevertheless vastly lower than the rates charged by loan sharks. *See* § 2.3.3.2, *infra*.

Industrial banks, first organized under regular state banking laws early in the twentieth century, took a less direct approach to increasing the yields on consumer credit.[22] These institutions accepted individual deposits and made loans secured by those deposits. Arthur Morris devised a plan which treated loans as repayable in a single lump sum at the end of the agreed term and computed interest accordingly. However, the Morris Plan required the borrower to make regular "deposits" in the bank which were calculated to equal the total amount of principal and interest due at the end of the term. Essentially, the Morris Plan allowed industrial banks to increase yields by charging interest on sums the borrower had already repaid (i.e., by ignoring the declining principal balance on the loan). Although this device was really an evasion of existing general usury laws, rather than a clear-cut legal exception to them, many states adopted statutory exceptions to general usury laws to validate the practice, and industrial banks came to serve a market of consumers seeking loans in excess of the $300 limits set for small loan licensees. *See* § 2.3.3.3, *infra*.

Carving out statutory exceptions to the general usury laws proved an effective means of expanding the amount of available consumer credit. Not surprisingly, it also proved to be a trend which, once started, was difficult to limit. Although credit laws developed differently in each state, statutory usury exceptions were soon made not only for small loan lenders but also for industrial banks, as discussed above, credit unions, mortgage lenders such as savings banks and building and loan associations, and eventually, banks[23] making "installment loans" to finance consumer purchases.

2.2.3.2 Laws Governing Sales

It should be emphasized that the statutes discussed in the previous subsection were adopted as exceptions to the general usury statutes which, as interpreted by the courts, regulated only loans or forbearances of debt and not sales of goods on credit. Since the effective interest rate (technically, the "time-price differential") which a seller could impose in

16 *See generally* Bodfish, History of Building and Loan Associations in the U.S. (1931); Cobb, Federal Regulation of Depository Institutions: Enforcement Powers and Procedures (1984); Sherman, Modern Story of Mutual Savings Banks (1934); Welfling, Mutual Savings Banks (1968); Redfield, *Savings Banks and Savings and Loan Associations: The Past and the Future*, 16 Bus. Law 170 (1960).

17 For a brief description of the evolution of credit unions see 1 Credit Union Law Service ch. 1 (Matthew Bender 1987).

18 *See* Kawaja, Regulation of the Consumer Finance Industry: A Case Study of Rate Ceilings and Loan Size Limits in New York State 23 (1971).

19 The idea of increasing yield was applied to other creditors as well. For example, the early credit union statutes, modeled after a 1909 Massachusetts law, permitted credit unions to charge interest at rates above most general usury law limits.

20 *See generally* Curran, Trends in Consumer Credit Legislation (1966); Hubachek, *The Development of Regulatory Small Loan Laws*, 8 Law & Contemp. Prob. 108 (1941).

21 *Reprinted in* Hubachek, Annotations on Small Loan Laws (1938).

22 *See generally* Curran, Trends in Consumer Credit Legislation 52 *et seq.* (1966); Saulnier, Industrial Banking Companies and Their Banking Practices (1940).

23 Although installment loan laws seem primarily to address banks making consumer loans, their precise scope varies significantly from state to state. *See* Curran, Trends in Consumer Credit Legislation 65 *et seq.* (1966).

a credit sale was not limited by the general usury laws, there was no need to loosen the regulatory reins through special legislation as there was with loans. Consequently, consumer credit sales were largely unregulated by state legislatures until after the Second World War, and were governed instead by regular contract law.

When the attention of state legislatures finally did turn to credit sales transactions, the motivation was reversed from that for previous special usury laws; the idea was to tighten controls rather than to loosen them.[24] The retail installment sales acts (RISAs) and motor vehicle retail installment sales acts (MVRISAs) adopted after the war frequently imposed limits on finance charges where none had previously existed, and they universally emphasized consumer protections such as disclosure of credit terms and limitations on creditor remedies.[25] There is, of course, a sense in which the special lending laws were also protective; they allowed regulated lenders to charge high rates, thus sparing small borrowers from the even greater ravages of the loan sharks. Moreover, RISAs and special lending statutes address many of the same subjects, which is not surprising, since a credit sale is merely a secured loan in different legal clothing. For these reasons, this manual treats RISAs and MVRISAs as a subclass of special usury law. Yet, remember that the law has historically treated credit sales and loans distinctly, and that these historical distinctions still occasionally crop up in modern consumer credit cases. *See* §§ 9.2.3.3, 10.5.2.2, *infra*.

2.3 The Modern Consumer Credit Marketplace

2.3.1 Types of Creditors

2.3.1.1 Introduction

The most basic division between types of creditors in the credit marketplace is the distinction between depository lenders, such as banks and savings and loan associations, which accept deposits,[26] and non-depository creditors, such as finance companies, which do not accept demand deposits from the public. Both depository and non-depository creditors act as intermediaries in the sense that they obtain funds from disparate investors and lend them at a profit to those who want money.

Yet the acceptance of funds from the general public has distinguished depository creditors in two important ways. First, depositories have traditionally been regulated by either the federal or state governments in order to insure the safety of the public's deposits. Regulation of non-depositories is generally both more recent and more limited. Second, individual deposits such as passbook savings accounts traditionally provided a relatively inexpensive source of funds. Consequently depositories have been able to issue loans at lower interest rates than non-depositories and have run afoul of usury statutes less frequently. Faced with this competition, non-depository creditors traditionally specialized in supposedly higher risk loans to lower-income borrowers. Most of the more egregious forms of price-gouging and deceptive credit practices discussed in this manual have historically been the province of non-depository creditors.

While the use of credit cards and checking account overdraft loans has filled some of the need for small unsecured loans, a large number of consumers have been left without credit cards or other access to small loans due to declining availability.[27] The remainder of this market is now filled by companies offering payday loans (akin to salary lenders), auto title loans, tax refund anticipation loans, and rent-to-own transactions.[28] Some of these lenders simply ignore the small loan laws where they exist while others attempt to disguise their loans as something else. At the same time, these industries are spending a great deal of time and money pushing sweetheart legislation to avoid the reach of the small loan laws.

The small loan fringe market justifies its cost in part by its higher transaction costs and in part by the higher level of risk assumed to be associated with lending to customers who may not be able to find credit elsewhere. However, the rates of return for these lenders are much higher than for conventional lenders, such as banks and finance companies. For example, payday lenders in Tennessee showed a lucrative rate of return on assets of 22.72% and on equity of 30.37% in 1999.[29] A title lender reported a rate of return of 12%,

---

24 A more cynical view may be taken, however. At the time that many RISAs were being adopted in the 1950s and 1960s there was a clear trend in the courts toward the abolition of the time-price usury exception. The ultimate result of such a trend would have been the application of the low general usury ceilings to credit sales. RISAs and their relatively high ceilings can be seen as an attempt to preclude this result.

25 *See, e.g.*, Zachman v. Whirlpool Acceptance Corp., 841 P.2d 27 (Wash. 1992) for a discussion of the purpose and origins of RISAs. *See generally* Curran, Trends in Consumer Credit Legislation *et seq.* (1966).

26 These deposits frequently but not invariably are interest-bearing.

27 The finance companies and industrial loan associations that met these needs for many years left the market over the past 20 years in favor of greater profitability in larger loans.

28 For the most comprehensive information about the growth and characteristics of this industry, see Lynn Drysdale & Kathleen Keest, *The Two-Tiered Consumer Financial Services Marketplace: The Fringe Banking System and its Challenge to Current Thinking About The Socio-Economic role of Usury Laws in Today's Society*, 51 S.C. L. Rev. 589 (2000).

29 Tennessee Dep't of Fin. Institutions, Report to the 101st General Assembly on the Deferred Presentment Services Act, 1999 at 9; Duren Cheek, *Many Payday Lenders Skirt Law*, The Tennessean, Jan. 24, 1999.

whereas banks are satisfied with a 1.5% return on assets.[30] The way these transactions are structured often generates negligible risk of loss. For example, the payday lender takes a live check and the title lender holds the title to the car.

Despite historical generalizations and some continuing differences between depository and non-depository institutions, it should be emphasized that the current consumer credit market is in a state of flux. Deregulation of the interest rates paid on passbook savings accounts and the growth of alternative financial institutions increased the cost of lending for depository creditors and decreased their competitive edge.[31] Meanwhile, many non-depository creditors made conscious and generally successful attempts to branch out into middle-income consumer markets, such as the market for home equity loans.[32] Thus it is no longer strictly true that poor people go to finance companies while wealthier borrowers do business with banks and other depository lenders. It will be interesting to see whether the proclivity of many non-depositories toward sharp dealing will decrease as their share of presumably lower risk consumer loans increases, but unfortunately no such general trend is yet apparent. Instead, the trend seems to be toward depository lenders charging comparatively higher interest rates and other charges than previously and becoming involved in more consumer litigation, and even associating themselves with payday lenders in order to export triple-digit interest rates from deregulated states to states that have retained rate caps.[33]

2.3.1.2 Depository Creditors

2.3.1.2.1 Banks

The major types of depository lenders are banks, savings and loan institutions or thrifts, and credit unions. By far the oldest of these institutions are commercial banks, which significantly predate the founding of the United States. The Bank of England, for example, was founded in 1694, and this was preceded by major Italian and Dutch international banking enterprises.

In the United States, banks were first chartered and regulated, to the extent that they were regulated at all, by state law.[34] The system was chaotic; the federal government held the power of coinage, but any state bank could issue paper notes, and numerous kinds of paper notes were simultaneously in circulation. After a few abortive attempts and much political ado, the National Bank Act established a permanent federal banking system in 1864. Upon application, qualifying institutions were granted federal banking charters and special lending rights. In return, they agreed to maintain specified reserves and to comply with other federal regulations. Thus a dual state and federal banking system was established, with state banks regulated by state law and national banks regulated by federal law.

The federal banking system has been significantly modified since its inception. In 1913 the Federal Reserve System was established under which a set of regional federal reserve banks, with a single board of governors, was authorized to serve as a lender of last resort to member banks. Thus, a true central banking system was created. Then, in 1933 the Federal Deposit Insurance Corporation was created, and all federal banks were required to participate in the FDIC's insurance program. Qualifying state banks had the option of joining the FDIC, and by the 1980s virtually all state and federal banks were insured by the FDIC. Because of their participation in the FDIC, even state banks are subject to some federal regulation on issues such as reserve requirements or the percentage of funds which may be issued to any one borrower. But consumer protection regulation of state banks, such as usury or other substantive consumer credit restrictions, remains primarily a matter of state law. There are, however, inroads on this principle. The extent of federal preemption, arising from the deregulation legislation of the early 1980s,[35] and interstate banking legislation passed by Congress has undermined the ability of states to regulate state banks.

The laws of some states authorize the charter of more than one kind of state bank. As mentioned previously, commercial banks were generally uninterested in consumer credit until well into the twentieth century. But mutual savings banks, on the other hand, were organized in many eastern states in the nineteenth century under existing banking laws to provide banking service to small depositors.[36] Although these organizations may technically be "banks," their modern business is more akin to that of a savings and loan institution than to that of a commercial bank, and the applicable state regulations may be distinct from those governing regular commercial banks. Similarly, "industrial

---

30 Joseph B. Cahill, *License to Owe: Title-Loan Firms Offer Car Owners a Solution That Often Backfires*, Wall St. J., Mar. 3, 1999, at A1.
31 *See* John P. Caskey, Fringe Banking (1994).
32 *See* Cathy Lesser Mansfield, *The Road to Subprime "HEL" Was Paved with Good Congressional Intentions: Usury Deregulation and the Subprime Home Equity Market*, 51 S.C. L. Rev. 473 (2000), for a detailed analysis of the growth of subprime home equity lending by non-depository institutions.
33 *See* Lynn Drysdale & Kathleen Keest, *The Two-Tiered Consumer Financial Services Marketplace: The Fringe Banking System and its Challenge to Current Thinking About The Socio-Economic role of Usury Laws in Today's Society*, 51 S.C. L. Rev. 589 (2000), for a description of this development.
34 *See generally* Cobb, Federal Regulation of Depository Institutions: Enforcement Powers and Procedures (1984); Homer, A History of Interest Rates (1963); Hutchinson, Money, Banking, and the United States Economy (1967).
35 This legislation is not discussed in this manual except to say that the preemptive effect on state consumer protection legislation was the object of specific concern. *See generally* Ch. 3, *infra*.
36 *See generally* Sherman, Modern Story of Mutual Savings Banks (1934); Welfling, Mutual Savings Banks (1968). FDIC insurance is available to mutual savings banks.

banks," which were first organized in the early twentieth century under state banking laws, soon obtained separate regulation in most states and may most accurately be viewed as variants of consumer finance companies.[37]

Apart from these anomalous types of state banks, banks as a whole were slow to enter the field of consumer credit, becoming significantly involved only after the depression. Modern banks frequently issue mortgage loans or other well-secured consumer installment credit such as automobile loans. In recent years, banks have been leaders in promoting high-priced, frequently unsecured consumer credit in the form of open-end credit card accounts. Credit cards have particularly been employed by national banks which can afford major marketing campaigns and which can often charge higher rates than state banks because of favorable interstate banking rules allowing them to locate in a loosely regulated state and "export" that state's law to customers nationwide. Following federal deregulation in 1980, federally-insured state banks have successfully claimed similar rights.[38] A few banks in deregulated states have even begun associating with payday lenders in regulated states in order to export high rates.[39] The profitability of credit card business has led to the formation of specialized banks concentrating in that business.[40]

2.3.1.2.2 Savings and loan associations

Savings and loan associations (S&Ls), also known as "thrifts" or "thrift institutions," are descendants of the building and loan associations of the nineteenth century.[41] These were private cooperative organizations in which each of the members contributed periodic payments on his "share" in the organization in return for receiving a mortgage loan as sufficient funds became available to the cooperative. Early building and loan associations generally dissolved once houses had been built for all members. Yet by the turn of the century, building and loan associations had evolved to permanent organizations, chartered and regulated by many states, in which the accounts of shareholders and borrowers were separately maintained.

A parallel system of state and federal S&Ls, somewhat comparable to the dual state and federal banking system, was established during the depression when many S&Ls faced severe financial problems. Specifically, in 1932 the Federal Home Loan Bank System was created, modeled after the Federal Reserve System. Twelve regional federal home loan banks were established, under one Board, the Federal Home Loan Bank Board (FHLBB), to extend short- and long-term credit to member S&Ls.[42] In 1933, the Home Owners Loan Act provided for the chartering of federal S&Ls whose participation in the Federal Home Loan Bank System was mandatory. In 1934, the Federal Savings and Loan Insurance Corporation (FSLIC) was created, and deposits in all federal S&Ls and many state S&Ls were federally insured.

The lending authority of federal S&Ls and many state S&Ls was expanded in the late 1970s due to the pressure of high interest rates on institutions whose primary assets were long-term, low-yield mortgages. Federal S&Ls, for example, were authorized to issue consumer loans, home improvement loans, commercial real estate loans, credit cards, student loans, and many other forms of credit, although the percentage of an S&Ls assets which may be invested in some of these forms of credit is limited.[43] The lending authority of state S&Ls is generally specified by state law, although state S&Ls may be authorized to follow federal thrift lending regulations under some circumstances, and state S&Ls which carry federal insurance, as almost all do, may have most favored lender status.[44]

However, this expanded lending authority did not prove to be the anticipated boon for the savings and loan industry. In fact, it resulted in failure for an unprecedented number of thrifts, placing financial strains on the thrift insurer, FSLIC.[45] As a result, Congress passed the Financial Institutions Reform, Recovery and Enforcement Act of 1989 (FIRREA),[46] a general overhaul of the federal regulatory structure for thrifts. The Federal Home Loan Bank Board was abolished, and many of its supervisory functions were transferred to the Office of Thrift Supervision (OTS).[47]

37 *See generally* Curran, Trends in Consumer Credit Legislation 52 *et seq.* (1966); Saulnier, Industrial Banking Companies and Their Banking Practices (1940). In many states industrial banks may not accept demand deposits.

38 *See* §§ 3.4.5, 3.9.2.2, *infra.*

39 *See* Lynn Drysdale & Kathleen Keest, *The Two-Tiered Consumer Financial Services Marketplace: The Fringe Banking System and its Challenge to Current Thinking About The Socio-Economic role of Usury Laws in Today's Society,* 51 S.C. L. Rev. 589 (2000). "Rent-a-bank" shams are discussed in § 3.13, *infra.*

40 *See* Lynn Drysdale & Kathleen Keest, *The Two-Tiered Consumer Financial Services Marketplace: The Fringe Banking System and its Challenge to Current Thinking About The Socio-Economic role of Usury Laws in Today's Society,* 51 S.C. L. Rev. 589 (2000).

41 *See generally* Bodfish, History of Building and Loan Associations in the U.S. (1931); Sherman, Modern Story of Mutual Savings Banks (1934).

42 Mutual savings banks and insurance companies were also permitted to join the federal home loan bank system, although there have been no insurance company members since 1959. *See* Welfling, Mutual Savings Banks 92–94 (1968).

43 *See* 12 U.S.C. § 1464; 12 C.F.R. § 545.

44 *See* §§ 3.5, 3.10, 3.14, *infra.*

45 Even a brief overview of the S&L crisis is beyond the scope of this book, but one interesting and readable treatment of it is Kathleen Day, S&L Hell: The People and the Politics Behind the $1 Trillion Savings and Loan Scandal (W.W. Norton & Co. 1993). The jacket art is worth the price of the book.

46 Pub. L. No. 101-73, 103 Stat. 183 (Aug. 9, 1989).

47 As a successor agency, OTS has republished former FHLBB rules as they relate to topics discussed in this manual, generally

2.3.1.2.3 Credit unions

The last major type of depository creditor is the credit union. Credit unions are generally nonprofit cooperatives with membership open to a limited group of people who have some common bond. For example, employees of a single employer, members of a union, or residents of a specific region might be eligible to join a credit union organized for one of these groups. Depositors in a credit union are technically shareholders, and the funds deposited in the credit union are used to provide credit to the credit union's members.

The first American credit unions were established in New England at the turn of the last century and were based on European and Canadian models.[48] Massachusetts passed the first state statute authorizing the charter of credit unions in 1909. By 1930, following a substantial private publicity campaign funded primarily by the Boston merchant Edward A. Filene, credit union statutes modeled on the Massachusetts statute had been adopted in thirty-two states.

In 1934, the Federal Credit Union Act,[49] also based in part on the original Massachusetts statute, authorized the federal charter of credit unions, and a dual state and federal credit union system, similar to the dual banking and S&L systems, was established. Federal insurance, through the National Credit Union Share Insurance Fund, was required for deposits in federal credit unions and was made available to qualifying state credit unions. Today, virtually all credit unions are federally insured.

By their very nature, credit unions are small, consumer-oriented institutions. Because of their nonprofit status and their selective membership standards, credit unions are often able to provide more favorable terms than other institutions on both member deposits and loans. Just as one example, federal credit unions are prohibited from assessing any penalty when a consumer chooses to pay off a loan prematurely, before its scheduled retirement date.[50]

2.3.1.3 Non-Depository Creditors

2.3.1.3.1 Finance companies and other licensed lenders

There are essentially three varieties of non-depository consumer creditors: licensed lenders, retailers, and convenience creditors. Licensed lenders are corporations or individuals who have received a state license to issue consumer credit, frequently at high interest rates, under one or more of the numerous state special usury statutes. For example, small loan laws, industrial bank laws, and pawnbroking statutes generally require that a creditor receive a state license and comply with state regulations in order to lend at the generous rates that these statutes usually authorize.

As previously unregulated mortgage companies became the source of some abusive lending practices in the 1980s, some states added these to the list of those lenders requiring licensing and regulation.[51] Creditors that purport to operate under a special usury statute but fail to obtain the proper license may face serious penalties for violations of the state's general usury law.[52]

Probably the most common example of a licensed lender is the consumer finance company. Finance companies as a group have a history of sharp dealing, and can be very costly to an unwary consumer. These companies, the descendants of small loan lenders, have, in many cases, recently expanded their operations to include a more middle-class consumer market.[53] For example, many finance companies have made substantial profits through the cross-selling of credit insurance and other services in conjunction with their loans, through the repeated refinancing of outstanding consumer debt, and through questionable extensions of credit to insolvent borrowers on over-secured loans. Other types of lenders include payday lenders, rent-to-own operations, and auto title pawns.[54] Many of these practices are discussed more thoroughly later in this manual.[55]

2.3.1.3.2 Retail sellers

The second major class of non-depository creditor consists of retailers of consumer durable goods. Many consumers cannot afford to purchase big-ticket goods such as automobiles, furniture, refrigerators, and other appliances in cash. Retailers therefore are compelled to offer credit plans as a sideline to their sales business. The terms of the installment credit sales contracts which a retailer may employ, often including the maximum interest rate[56] and other

---

with only technical changes. 54 Fed. Reg. 49411 (Nov. 30, 1989). *See* Appx. D.2, *infra.*

48 *See generally* 1 Credit Union Law Service ch. 1 (Matthew Bender 1987).

49 *See* 12 U.S.C. § 1751 *et seq.* For a discussion of federal usury preemption for credit unions, see §§ 3.6, 3.10, *infra.*

50 *See* 12 C.F.R. § 701.21(c)(6), reprinted in Appx. E.2, *infra.*

51 *E.g.,* Mass. Gen. L. § 255E, Licensing of Certain Mortgage Lenders and Brokers (enacted 1991). Some states had previously regulated second mortgage lenders. *See* § 2.3.3.7, *infra.*

52 *See* § 9.2.4.6, *infra.*

53 *See* Lynn Drysdale & Kathleen Keest, *The Two-Tiered Consumer Financial Services Marketplace: The Fringe Banking System and its Challenge to Current Thinking About The Socio-Economic role of Usury Laws in Today's Society,* 51 S.C. L. Rev. 589 (2000).

54 While some of these transactions are not formally considered "loans," the structures of the transactions make it clear that the institutions are indeed lenders making loans at very high interest rates.

55 *See* Chs. 6 (refinancings), 7 (hidden interest) and 8 (credit insurance) *infra. See also* Ch. 11, *infra.*

56 Because the transaction is a sale rather than a loan, the charge assessed may be described as "time-price differential" or "finance charge" instead of "interest," but the difference is purely semantic. § 2.2.3.2, *supra,* §§ 2.3.3.5, 10.5.2.2, *infra.*

charges on the contract, are regulated in many states by retail installment sales acts or motor vehicle retail installment sales acts. Major retailers, such as department stores, where customers shop frequently, often offer revolving credit plans represented by "charge cards" as well as, or instead of, installment credit. These revolving credit accounts are usually regulated separately from installment credit under state law.

Retailers that enter into installment sales contracts with buyers often do not retain these contracts for long after they have been signed. Instead, in order to obtain cash with which to conduct their business, retailers often sell or assign the contracts[57] to other creditors, typically finance companies, or "acceptance" companies, at a discount from the amount that the consumer is obligated to pay over the term of the contract. For example, if a consumer has contracted to pay a retailer $100 over a period of a year, the retailer might sell the contract to a finance company in return for an immediate payment of $85.[58] The retailer and the finance company will generally enter into a "master contract" under which the finance company agrees to purchase some or all of the retailer's contracts on stated terms.

The assignment of a retail installment contract may or may not significantly affect the credit buyer. At the least, the buyer may receive a notice that payments should be made to the assignee rather than the retailer. If the buyer falls behind in payments, the effect may be greater. Depending on the terms of the master contract,[59] either the assignee may sue the buyer on the contract or the contract will be reassigned to the retailer, which will have to enforce the contract itself.[60] Alternatively, finance companies use assigned consumer contracts as a source of new customers, and if a buyer is not seriously in default, the finance company might use the opportunity of delinquency to convince the consumer to refinance the debt. Such refinancings can be extremely profitable for creditors, and finance companies encourage debtors with acceptable payment records to take out additional loans so that their debt may be refinanced and extended.[61] The costs of refinancing are explored in Chapter 6, *infra*.

2.3.1.3.3 Convenience creditors

A final category of non-depository commercial creditors may be called convenience creditors. Convenience creditors are sellers who forbear the collection of existing debts in return for installment payments with interest. Such creditors include doctors, lawyers, hospitals, utilities, oil companies, farm supply companies, and other businesses which have no formal charge account plan but which are willing to finance debts either to increase their volume of business or in order to avoid the collection process as long as their customers are making payments. These credit agreements are often evidenced merely by a sales receipt which states that a monthly charge will be imposed if the debt is not paid within thirty days.

Determining which statute controls a transaction with a convenience creditor may require a careful analysis of state law. Some states have separate interest ceilings for goods sold on open accounts. Others may treat convenience creditors under Retail Installment Sales Act (RISAs),[62] although RISAs do not always reach sellers that extend credit only infrequently. Alternately, usury statutes may apply to sales on account on the theory that interest is being charged for the seller's forbearance of debt.[63] In any case, charges assessed by convenience creditors should be examined closely because such creditors frequently violate credit statutes, either out of ignorance of the controlling law or because they fail to take credit limitations seriously.

2.3.2 Types of Credit

2.3.2.1 Introduction

The consumer credit marketplace is divided by the kinds of credit being extended, as well as the types of creditors that are extending credit. To some extent these two views overlap. Retailers generally extend sales credit while depository and non-depository lenders generally do not. Nevertheless, laws often distinguish and separately regulate

---

57 The credit contracts or notes associated with the sales contracts are often referred to as "consumer paper."

58 The precise amount of the discount will vary with the creditworthiness of the buyer, the quality of the security, and overall market interest rates.

59 Contracts between sellers and the assignees which purchase consumer paper are divided into "recourse" contracts, in which the assignee may force the credit seller to buy back the paper if the consumer defaults, "non-recourse" contracts in which the assignee has no such right, and "limited recourse" contracts in which the repurchase of the consumer contract can be compelled only for debts above a stated amount, for specified types of default, or for specified categories of transactions. Under some state laws, creditors may be obligated to inform the consumer of the assignment or reassignment of the credit contract.

60 Assignments of consumer credit sales contracts used to provide serious problems for consumers because assignees could claim to be immune to contract defenses which the buyer might have asserted against the seller. The Federal Trade Commission, however, has significantly restricted the extent to which consumer defenses in sales contracts may be waived. *See* § 10.6.1.2.2, *infra*.

61 Refinancing can be very profitable for the lender, and the borrower's obligation generally grows larger with each refinance. In the industry, the process of turning an involuntary customer (one obtained through a merchant's assignment) into a repeat finance company customer is called "the food chain," with the final goal to turn him or her into a home-equity loan borrower.

62 *See* § 2.3.3.5, *infra*.

63 *See* § 10.5.2.3, *infra*.

different types of credit transactions even if they are offered by the same creditor. For example, a single creditor may offer customers both fixed-term or open-end credit, and these two types of transactions will probably be separately regulated. This section discusses briefly the three major divisions in the kinds of credit generally available: loan vs. sales credit; fixed-term vs. open-end credit; and secured vs. unsecured credit. Case law interpreting the distinctions is discussed in § 9.2, *infra.*

2.3.2.2 Loan vs. Credit Sales

The legal distinction between a loan of money and the sale of goods on credit has been mentioned previously in this chapter.[64] English courts, interpreting the English usury statutes upon which American general usury laws were modeled, determined that the limitations in those statutes on interest paid for loans of money or forbearances of debt[65] did not apply to the price that a merchant could charge for goods. A seller could charge one price for the goods if the buyer paid immediately, and another, higher price if the buyer chose to pay over some agreed time. The difference between the "time price" and the "cash price" would not be considered interest under the usury statute. This so-called "time-price doctrine" was adopted by American courts interpreting American general usury laws. Consequently, the charges associated with the credit sale of goods were generally unregulated until specific statutory controls were adopted in the middle of the twentieth century. Charges for any other kind of credit were considered "interest" for a loan or forbearance and were subject to usury limitations.[66]

A credit sale is not just any credit which is eventually used to buy goods; rather, it is credit extended specifically by the seller in conjunction with the sale of specific goods.[67] Thus, if a consumer gets a finance company loan for the express purpose of buying furniture, the transaction, in most circumstances, is still a loan subject to loan, not sale, regulations.[68] Similarly, if the buyer charges the purchase on a bank credit card, the credit is a loan.[69] Yet, if the furniture store directly offers the consumer separate cash and time prices for the same goods, the transaction is a credit sale

which general usury laws do not reach, but which today will be controlled by retail installment sales acts (RISAs) in most states.[70]

The time-price doctrine may not have been completely unreasonable at the time it was originally adopted. Prior to the twentieth century there were some practical, if not theoretical, differences between credit extended in loans and sales. First retailers really did extend credit; they were not merely intermediaries between buyers and the assignees of consumer sales paper. Second, in some sense individuals in a less industrialized society were less dependent on manufactured goods, and it was not entirely unreasonable for courts to conclude that the compulsion facing an individual in need of money and his consequent need for statutory protection were much greater than the comparable needs of an individual who merely wanted to buy goods. To some extent, this rationale for distinguishing loans and sales is still valid today; few consumers face an genuine economic compulsion to purchase a home entertainment center. Nevertheless, a greater dependence on goods does now exist. A commuter whose car breaks down and who has no alternate transportation faces a need to replace the car which may be just as great as the compulsion facing many borrowers.[71]

Regardless of the original merit of the time-price doctrine, it was clear by the middle of the twentieth century that the distinction between credit sales and loans had become untenable. Lenders were avoiding usury restrictions by buying consumer paper at a discount from retailers rather than issuing loans for the purchase of goods. Furthermore, retailers were introducing open-end charge accounts and, under the time-price rule, were assessing unregulated charges on these accounts even though the accounts were not repayable over any set period, and even though the debt outstanding on the accounts at any given time might not easily be traced to individual purchases.

Under these circumstances, some courts began to reject the time-price usury exception, or at least to exclude charge accounts from the exception, thus exposing sales credit to usury limits.[72] Simultaneously, state legislatures became increasingly concerned that the application of commercial sales laws to consumer transactions was enabling deceptive practices in such transactions to go unremedied. The confluence of credit sellers' concerns about their potential

---

64 *See* §§ 2.2.2, 2.2.3.2, *supra.*

65 A forbearance is an agreement between a creditor and debtor in which the creditor agrees to postpone collection of the pre-existing debt between the parties in return for interest payments from the debtor. *See* § 10.5.2, *infra.*

66 For a discussion of the definition of "interest," see Ch. 7, *infra.*

67 Other limitations on the time-price doctrine exist. For example, the seller usually must disclose the separate time and cash prices prior to the transactions. *See generally* § 10.5.2.2, *infra.*

68 *See generally* § 9.2.3.3, *infra.*

69 *But cf.* Acker v. Provident Nat'l Bank, 512 F.2d 729 (3d Cir. 1975) (bank credit card account governed by state installment sales act ceiling under "most favored lender" doctrine). *See* §§ 3.4.3, 3.9.2, *infra* for discussion of most favored lender doctrine.

70 *See* § 9.2.3.3, *infra.*

71 Even assuming that a borrower is compelled to borrow money, while a purchaser is not compelled to buy goods, the time-price doctrine breaks down rather quickly. Why should the purchase of goods, whether necessities or luxuries, be unregulated when a loan, the proceeds of which are used to buy the same goods, is subject to usury ceilings? The distinction just does not make sense.

72 The earliest cases were Hare v. Gen. Contract Purchase, 220 Ark. 601, 249 S.W.2d 973 (1952) *reh'g denied* 222 Ark. 291, 262 S.W.2d 287 (1953); Elder v. Doerr, 175 Neb. 483, 122 N.W.2d 528 (1963). For more modern cases, see § 10.5.2.2.1, *infra.*

exposure to usury statutes and the demand for greater consumer protections led, primarily in the 1950s, to most jurisdictions adopting retail installment sales acts. These statutes may be viewed as special usury laws which often, but not invariably, set limits on the charges assessed in credit sale transactions. Nevertheless, even in states which have adopted RISAs, the time-price usury exception may continue to apply to sales transactions which, for whatever reason, fall outside the scope of the RISA.[73]

2.3.2.3 Open-End vs. Closed-End Credit

The consumer credit laws of most states distinguish closed-end or installment credit from open-end or revolving credit.[74] Generally, closed-end credit statutes address a single extension of credit between a creditor and a debtor which the debtor agrees to pay off in a fixed number of periodic installments of a specified amount. The credit sale of an automobile is a good example of such a transaction because any one sale will almost invariably represent the entire debt outstanding between the two parties. Although the consumer might go to the same dealer over many years to purchase more automobiles, each credit sale would be viewed as an isolated transaction, to be paid for individually.

Open-end credit statutes, on the other hand, contemplate frequent transactions between the parties in which the debt from each individual transaction is merged into the larger outstanding debt. A typical example of this arrangement is a bank credit card or a charge account at a department store. The debt from each purchase by a consumer is added to an outstanding balance, and the consumer receives a monthly statement giving the total outstanding balance, the accrued finance charge from the preceding month, and the minimum payment due. There is no set number of payments that the consumer will make on the account, and there is no expectation that the size of each payment will be equal. The consumer is required to pay only a stated minimum amount which will vary with the outstanding balance and which will, in most cases, at least equal the accrued finance charge for the previous month.[75] Of course, the consumer is free to pay off the entire balance whenever he or she wishes. Under the terms of most card agreements, finance charges may be avoided altogether if the full account balance is paid on time every month,[76] although annual "membership" fees are

usually imposed on bank credit cards regardless of the consumer's payment record.

Charge cards were introduced in about 1914 by department stores, hotels, oil companies, and Western Union.[77] These cards could only be used to purchase the issuer's goods and services, and the balance had to be paid in full each month. In the 1950s, Diners' Club and American Express began issuing general purpose cards that could be used at a variety of vendors. Several years later, banks entered the market and introduced credit cards, which allowed balances to be carried over from one month to the next. In the 1960s, groups of banks created national credit card transaction processing systems under the names VISA and MasterCard.[78] The great explosion in credit card lending occurred, however, only after the Supreme Court ruled that national banks could export interest rates from their home states by issuing credit cards to residents of other states.[79] The intense marketing of credit cards is characterized by teaser rates, bait and switch offers, and false promises of fixed rates and other favorable terms.[80] Some credit card lenders increase their income through high late fees, manipulation of due dates and posting dates, over-limit fees, transaction fees, inactivity fees, penalty interest rates that are imposed if a payment is late, and low minimum payments that allow finance charges to build up over a longer period of time.[81] Most recently, credit card issuers have added the practice of universal default, where a penalty rate is imposed for late payments to any of the consumer's *other creditors.*[82]

---

provided that the customer had entered the month with an account balance of zero. Some cards, however, provide no grace period, and interest is assessed from the day a purchase is recorded (i.e., "posted") by the creditor.

77 This summary of the development of the credit card industry is based on Diane Ellis, *Bank Trends—The Effect of Consumer Interest Rate Deregulation on Credit Card Volumes, Charge-Offs, and the Personal Bankruptcy Rate* (1999) (available at www.fdic.gov/bank/analytical/bank/bt_9805.html).

78 At least one court has found that VISA and MasterCard are not themselves creditors or card issuers; the bank or store retains that status. *See* Schwartz v. Visa Int'l Corp., 2003 WL 1870370 (Cal. Super. Ct. Apr. 7, 2003) (discussing liability for improper disclosure of currency conversion fees).

79 *See* § 3.4.5, *infra.*

80 MassPIRG Education Fund, *A Road Map to Avoiding Credit Card Hazards* (Mar. 2001). *See* Rossman v. Fleet Bank, 280 F.3d 384 (3d Cir. 2002) for an example of false promises of no annual fee.

81 MassPIRG Education Fund, *A Road Map to Avoiding Credit Card Hazards* (Mar. 2001). For a discussion of these practices, see also Comments of the National Consumer Law Center et al., Federal Reserve Board Advance Notice of Proposed Rulemaking Review of the Open-End Credit Rules of Regulation Z (2005), *available at* www.consumerlaw.org/initiatives/test_and_comm/content/open_end_final.pdf.

82 *See* Patrick McGeehan, *Plastic Trap—Debt That Binds: Soaring Interest Compounds Credit Card Pain for Millions,* N.Y. Times, Nov. 21, 2004. A survey of credit card issuers found that 44% of banks surveyed had a universal default policy. Linda Sherry, *Annual Credit Card Survey 2004,* Consumer Action (Spring

---

73 *See* § 9.2.3.3, *infra.*

74 For a good comparison of open-end and closed-end credit arrangements, see Seibert v. Sears, Roebuck & Co., 120 Cal. Rptr. 233 (Cal. Ct. App. 1975).

75 If the minimum payment is less than the monthly finance charge, the result of making the minimum payment every month is negative amortization, and the debtor owes progressively more and more money, even if no additional charges (i.e., credit purchases) are made on the account. *See* § 4.3.1.2, *infra.*

76 Many cards have a "grace period" during which the amount billed in the previous month can be paid without finance charge

Card issuers also are adopting abusive debt collection tactics and mandatory arbitration clauses.[83]

In the 1990s, credit card debt grew substantially among all American families. By 2001, 76% of American families held credit cards and 55% of those carried on-going debt, with an average balance of over $4,000.[84] The debt burden is greatest on families with annual incomes under $10,000.[85] For families in this category carrying on-going debt, the debt load increased 184% during the decade, with an average debt load of over $1,800, almost 20% of total gross income.[86] Credit card debt among older Americans with incomes under $50,000 (70 percent of seniors) has also increased. About one in five older families with credit card debt is in debt hardship—spending over 40% of their income on debt payments, including mortgage debt.[87] The average credit card debt among young adults increased by 55% between 1992 and 2001 to $4,088 dollars, and these households now spend nearly 24% of their income on debt payments.[88] The substantially worsening of the credit card consumer's condition has been accompanied by credit card earnings that have been consistently higher than returns on all commercial bank activities.[89]

The interest rate on both fixed-term or open-end credit may be either a fixed rate or a variable rate. For example, many variable rate mortgages have a fixed term of fifteen or thirty years, and the monthly payment fluctuates in size as the interest rate changes.[90] Conversely, a convenience creditor may charge a fixed rate on the balance of an open-end account without having the contractual authority to raise that rate. Yet, it is much more common for fixed-term transactions to be at a fixed rate and open-end transactions to be at a variable rate because the charges on the former are often precomputed[91] while charges on the latter are computed monthly. Open-end accounts thus lend themselves to a frequently changing interest rate.

The separate regulation of installment credit and open-end credit makes some sense because the two arrangements raise different concerns. For example, calculation of the monthly finance charge or the minimum amount due does not cause much problem in installment credit where the principal is paid down on a regular basis, but does not otherwise fluctuate. Conversely, rebates of unearned interest are not an issue in open-end accounts because the interest on such accounts is not precomputed.

While the distinctions between closed-end and open-end credit are generally reasonable and are rarely litigated, consumer law practitioners should be aware that even this line is not as clear as it at first may seem. If open-end credit allows creditors a higher interest ceiling, fewer restrictions, or fewer disclosures, some creditors will try to structure single transactions as lines of credit which fall under the open-end statutes. Due to the scarcity of litigation, the extent to which this practice is valid is unclear.[92]

2004), *available at* www.consumer-action.org/English/CANews/ 2004_May_CreditCard/.

83 Comments of the National Consumer Law Center et al., Federal Reserve Board Advance Notice of Proposed Rulemaking Review of the Open-End Credit Rules of Regulation Z (2005), *available at* www.consumerlaw.org/initiatives/test_and_comm/ content/open_end_final.pdf.

84 Tamara Draut & Javier Silva, Borrowing to Make Ends Meet 10 (2003) (discussing data from the Survey of Consumer Finances), *available at* www.demos-usa.org/pub1.cfm.

85 Although only 35% of these families hold credit cards, 67% of those with credit cards reported carrying a debt. *Id.*

86 *Id.*

87 Heather G. McGee & Tamara Draut, *Retiring in the Red: The Growth of Debt Among Older Americans* (Jan. 19, 2004), *available at* www.demos-usa.org/pub101.cfm.

88 Tamara Draut & Javier Silva, *The Growth of Debt Among Young Americans* (Oct. 2004), *available at* www.demos-usa.org/ pub295.cfm.

89 Board of Governors of the Federal Reserve System, *The Profitability of Credit Card Operations of Depository Institutions* (June 2004), *available at* www.federalreserve.gov/boarddocs/ rptcongress/creditcard/2004/ccprofit.pdf. While the profitability of the credit card industry as a whole has fluctuated somewhat over these years, this is largely due to the changeability of the group of banks included in the sample. *Id.* at 2. According to a Board Report, profitability increases reached 13.7% in 2003 when the credit card banks included in the sample were held constant. *Id.* at 3. When the cost of funds declines for the banks, the profit margins stay high; when the cost of funds increases, these expenses are passed along to consumers. Even when all other economic indicators are problematic, credit card companies experience increased profits. Lavonne Kuykendall, *Review 2004: Card Lenders Earned More Despite Weak Portfolio Growth*, American Banker (Jan. 3, 2005).

90 This is the normal approach, but different contracts may provide different terms. Some variable rate mortgage contracts include a "cap" which prevents the monthly payment from exceeding a certain size. Different contracts take different tacks once this size is reached. True caps limit the contract interest rate as well as the monthly payment size, and both the interest rate and the payment will remain at their respective upper limits until market rates decline. If, however, the cap limits the payment size but the interest rate is allowed to continue to rise, in times of rising rates there will be a reduction in the amount of the monthly payment attributed to paying down principal. This will ultimately result in an extension in the term of the loan, or a final "balloon" payment. In the worst case, the monthly payment will not satisfy the monthly interest charge, and the borrower's debt will increase every month rather than decrease. Contracts which allow this situation, known as negative amortization, to occur can be dangerous for consumers and should be avoided. *See* § 4.3.1.2, *infra*. Since 1987, federal law has required that some maximum interest rate be set for variable rate credit secured by the consumer's principal dwelling, but since it allows the cap to be set at any level negative amortization can still occur if the payment is capped before the rate reaches its cap. *See* § 4.3.6.4, *infra*.

91 In a precomputed contract, all interest charges are determined at the time the contract is entered into, and a fixed monthly payment size is set at a level sufficient to pay off both the interest charges and the principal debt over the term stated in the contract. This is the traditional format for a small loan or credit sale. *See* § 4.5.3, *infra*.

92 See § 9.2.3.1, *infra* for a discussion of relevant case law.

A related gray area between closed-end and open-end credit is the typical finance company practice of repeatedly refinancing its customers' outstanding loans.[93] The process works approximately as follows. A finance company either loans a consumer money or, more often, acquires pre-existing debt through assignment or debt consolidation. This initial transaction looks like regular installment debt: a fixed number of usually equal payments is required to retire the debt and there is no obligation or even expectation that the creditor will give the borrower any more loans. Yet, before the initial obligation is paid off, the debt often is refinanced. The new loan also appears to be a closed-end transaction, but its principal includes not only the outstanding principal from the previous loan, but also unpaid interest, various non-interest fees such as credit insurance premiums, and often a small new cash advance to the borrower. In effect, new charges have been added to the consumer's account. With each subsequent refinancing, the process is repeated and the consumer's debt is extended. Repeated refinancing creates a highly remunerative form of an open-end account which is composed of a series of closed-end transactions. In most situations the transformation is not usurious,[94] but it demonstrates that even the most widely accepted distinctions among credit transactions may prove fleeting.

2.3.2.4 Security Taken in Credit Transactions

A final factor which distinguishes kinds of consumer credit is the security on the credit. The law commonly distinguishes secured and unsecured credit and, within the former class, credit secured by different types of collateral. Security is the debtor's real or personal property in which the creditor may claim a legal right, pursuant to the credit contract, if the debtor defaults. For example, credit sales contracts usually give the seller and its assignees a security interest in the goods purchased. If the buyer defaults on the payments and the security interest is valid,[95] the creditor may be able to repossess the goods and sell them to satisfy the outstanding debt.[96]

The existence of security on a credit contract is largely independent of other credit terms. Although a few special usury statutes require or prohibit collateral in specified transactions,[97] both fixed-term and open-end credit generally may be secured, as may both loans and credit sales. Moreover, any kind of creditor may require security. Yet the kind of security which may legally be required frequently depends on the type of transaction involved. For example, a small loan licensee or a retailer operating under a RISA may be prohibited from taking a security interest in real estate.[98]

Security interests are important because they alter the risks undertaken by the parties to the transaction. A creditor that obtains a valuable security interest, such as a first lien on real estate, faces a much lower risk of non-payment than does an unsecured creditor, and well-secured loans such as first mortgages frequently carry a lower interest rate than unsecured credit such as the average credit card account.[99] Conversely, the consequences for a debtor of defaulting on a loan are much greater if the loan is secured. A borrower who defaults on a home or automobile loan may lose his or her house or car in short order. Faced with such consequences, a borrower may be forced to make payments on a loan even if meeting the payments may lead to severe privation. Indeed, small loan lenders and retailers frequently took security interests in household goods simply because of the value of the threat of repossession in obtaining payment, rather than because of the negligible cash value of the household goods themselves, prior to legal restrictions on the practice.[100]

Due to the varying risks in transactions secured by different kinds of collateral and to the different potentials for abuse in these transactions, special usury statutes are often aimed at transactions involving a particular kind of collateral. Many states have special RISAs which address only the sale of motor vehicles. Other statutes apply only to mobile home sales. Almost invariably, state credit laws separately regulate home mortgage transactions, and they frequently

---

93 For a more thorough treatment of refinancing, see Ch. 6, *infra. See* Porter v. Ace Cash Express, Inc., 2000 U.S. Dist. LEXIS 15996 (E.D. La. Oct. 25, 2000) (payday lender did not fall within revolving credit statute; insufficient evidence that parties contemplated repeat transactions), *aff'd*, 277 F.3d 1372 (5th Cir. 2001). *See generally* § 9.2.3.1, *infra.*

94 Even in the absence of a specific statutory violation, it may be possible to challenge refinancing as an unfair or deceptive practice or under common law theories. *See* Chs. 6, 11, *infra.*

95 The validity of security interests is governed by Article 9 of the Uniform Commercial Code. *See generally* National Consumer Law Center, Repossessions and Foreclosures Ch. 3 (5th ed. 2002 and Supp.).

96 A creditor that has no security interest can ultimately collect on its debt by obtaining a judgment on the debt and attaching the debtor's property pursuant to the judgment. However, this process is generally more costly and time-consuming than self-help

repossession or even foreclosure. Moreover, much of a debtor's property, including the debtor's home, may be immune to attachment because of state homestead exemption statutes. Garnishment of the debtor's wages is subject to similar limitations. *See generally* National Consumer Law Center, Fair Debt Collection (5th ed. 2004 and Supp.).

97 *See, e.g.*, Cal. Fin. Code § 22000 *et seq.* (security required by Personal Property Brokers' Law). *Compare* Tex. Fin. Code Ann. § 342.001 (certain collateral prohibited on very small loans).

98 *See* § 9.2.6, *infra.*

99 Not all credit cards are unsecured. So-called "home equity loans," one of the latest and most threatening (to consumers) forms of consumer credit, are lines of credit which are secured by the borrower's home and are often associated with a credit card.

100 An FTC rule states that it is an unfair trade practice for a creditor to take a non-purchase-money security interest in most household goods of the debtor. *See* 16 C.F.R. § 444 (effective Mar. 1, 1985); National Consumer Law Center, Unfair and Deceptive Acts and Practices § 5.1.3.1 (6th ed. 2004 and Supp.).

distinguish credit secured by a senior lien from credit secured by second or third mortgages or other junior liens.[101]

2.3.3 Types of Special Usury Statutes

2.3.3.1 Introduction

As the previous discussion has indicated, special usury statutes evolved in the twentieth century in tandem with changes in the consumer credit market. Each statute, either when originally adopted or when later amended, was aimed at problems associated with a particular type of creditor, a particular type of transaction, or some combination of these. The cumulative effect of numerous narrowly focused statutes is highly fragmented regulation.

Periodically, when the number of special credit laws on the books in a given state has become particularly unwieldy, attempts have been made to consolidate the outstanding rules into one, presumably simplified statute. The most widely recognized attempt at such simplification is the Uniform Consumer Credit Code (UCCC), forms of which have been adopted in approximately ten states.[102] However, the pressures which led to the adoption and ongoing amendment of special usury laws remain even as credit codes are adopted. Consequently, while such codes are more clearly written and internally consistent than the statutes they replace, they nevertheless maintain pre-existing distinctions between creditors or loan types as often as they abolish them. Furthermore, state attempts at simplification are inherently limited because, short of repealing state law, they cannot untangle overlapping state and federal regulation.

The following subsections list and summarize several common varieties of special usury laws. Readers interested in greater detail about statutes affecting depository lenders should check the following chapter on federal usury preemption and also § 9.2.4, *infra.*

2.3.3.2 Small Loan Laws and Their Progeny

Small loan laws were first adopted in the early twentieth century in response to the widespread problem of loansharking. They were largely the product of the research and promotional efforts of the Russell Sage Foundation which, between 1916 and 1942, published seven drafts of a Uniform Small Loan Law. This uniform law was widely adopted by the states, and language from the uniform statute appears in numerous consumer finance statutes today even though these statutes may no longer be called small loan laws,[103] and they may govern relatively large consumer loans.

The concept behind the small loan law was to drive loan sharks out of business by making it profitable for regular business enterprises to make small loans to individuals.[104] The uniform law created a class of licensed lenders which, in return for compliance with the limitations of the statute on bookkeeping, security interests, and collection practices, were authorized to issue loans of less than $300 at interest rates in the neighborhood of 3% or 3-1/2% per month.[105] The uniform law strictly limited the charges or fees other than interest that a lender could assess, and provided harsh penalties, including loss of principal, for statutory violations. (*See* § 2.2.3.1, *supra.*)

The original small loan laws have been substantially modified in many states. Most significantly, the size of the loan to which small loan laws or their successors may apply has been greatly increased, in many states to $25,000 and in a few states even higher. Other states have authorized discount or add-on interest calculation methods[106] which were prohibited by the uniform law. Finally, small loan laws have sometimes been combined with industrial loan laws and other credit statutes, and have been renamed "consumer finance" laws.

2.3.3.3 Industrial Loan Laws

Industrial loan laws are special usury statutes which, like the small loan laws, were first enacted to attract credit to a consumer market dominated by loan sharks. However, instead of straightforwardly raising interest rates for licensed lenders as the small loan laws did, the industrial loan laws raised yields on consumer loans by authorizing mathematical subterfuge.[107] In particular, industrial loan laws adopted "Morris Plan" banking, under which a prospective borrower and a lender authorized to issue industrial loans

---

101 *See* § 2.4.2, *infra.*

102 Some other states adopted portions of the U.C.C.C. and another model act, the National Consumer Act. *See* § 2.3.3.10, *infra.*

103 An invaluable source of information about the interpretation of

small loan laws is Hubachek, Annotations on Small Loan Laws (Russell Sage Foundation 1938). *See also* Curran, Trends in Consumer Credit Legislation (1966); Hubachek, *The Development of Regulatory Small Loan Laws*, 8 Law & Contemp. Prob. 108 (1941). Because small loan laws were based on a uniform statute, the terminology employed in the modern small loan and consumer finance statutes of different states may be similar or identical, and attorneys interested in the interpretation of particular provisions of these statutes may be able to find precedent in the decisions of courts in other states.

104 For a discussion of the history and purpose of small loan laws, see Berger v. State Dep't of Revenue, 910 P.2d 581 (Alaska 1996).

105 Later drafts of the uniform law authorized split rates under which the interest rate applied to the first $100 of the outstanding balance may exceed the rate charged on the remainder of the principal balance. *See generally* § 4.3.4, *infra.*

106 These methods enable a creditor to understate, relative to an actuarial calculation such as the Truth in Lending Act's "APR," the interest rate it is charging. *See* §§ 4.3.1–4.3.3, 4.4, *infra.*

107 For more detail on the subjects addressed by industrial loan laws and the variations among the states' laws, see 1 Consumer Credit Guide (CCH) ¶ 560.

entered into supposedly separate loan and investment contracts. The loan would be repayable in one lump sum at the end of an agreed-upon term, and interest would be deducted in advance. Simultaneously, the borrower would make periodic deposits, pursuant to the investment agreement, which would total the amount of the lump sum when the loan came due. Industrial "banks" were thus authorized, in effect, to charge discount interest[108] at the general usury ceiling. Separate service charges, apart from the stated interest, were also permitted by most industrial loan laws.[109]

Industrial bank acts were adopted in only about half of the states. The development of industrial banks was limited by competition from small loan lenders and by commercial banks, especially in states which did not authorize industrial banks to accept demand deposits. Nevertheless, industrial banks became established in many states as consumer lenders able to offer loans above the small loan limits.

It is important to note that industrial loan act provisions differ among the states which recognize these transactions. Many states abolished the dual loan and investment contracts, which originally characterized industrial loans, and instead authorized licensed industrial loan lenders to issue installment loans at a stated discount interest rate. Other states opened industrial lending terms to commercial banks and, often, allowed industrial banks to issue commercial loans under the standard banking provisions. Finally, a few states combined industrial loan and small loan regulations into consumer finance acts which covered most, if not all, non-depository consumer lending.

2.3.3.4 Installment Loan Laws

Installment loan laws are a diverse collection of statutes which authorize banks, and frequently other lenders, to issue standard installment-payment loans at high interest rates.[110] Most of these statutes seem intended to put banks on an equal or comparable footing with small loan lenders, industrial banks, credit unions, or other lenders with statutory authority to lend at rates above the general usury ceiling. Thus installment loan laws have usually been constructed to apply to loans which these competing lenders might make. For example, some installment loan statutes apply only to credit below a stated principal amount or to loans with terms of less than five or ten years. Installment loan statutes also focus on interest calculation methods which might give competing lenders undue advantages. For example, they frequently authorize the use of add-on or discount interest, and address the rebate issues which arise when such precomputed loans are prepaid.

Although installment loan laws may be seen primarily as a special usury law for banks, in many states other lenders may invoke their terms as well. Typically, these other lenders are savings and loan associations or thrifts, mutual savings banks, or other state-regulated creditors which do not have their own special usury statute. Yet, in a few states, installment loan laws may be used by any lender to avoid the general usury ceiling, thus representing a significant usury exception. The general usury ceiling in these states would, however, still apply to otherwise unauthorized loans that did not satisfy installment loan act requirements for equal periodic payments, rebates upon prepayment, disclosure, etc.

2.3.3.5 Retail Installment Sales Acts

Retail installment sales acts (RISAs) were first adopted by most states in the 1940s and 1950s. These statutes regulate traditional fixed-term credit sales of consumer goods which, prior to the adoption of these statutes, had generally been free from interest ceilings due to the time-price usury exception.[111]

The scope of RISAs varies significantly from state to state.[112] Some RISAs cover the installment sale of all goods or services. Some cover only goods. Frequently a state will have special RISAs which apply exclusively to the credit sale of particular kinds of goods such as motor vehicles or, especially in recent years, mobile homes. A few states have special RISA-type statutes for home improvement transactions,[113] and AARP has published a model home improvement finance law.[114] States which have enacted special motor vehicle RISAs may or may not have parallel statutes which govern the credit sale of all other goods or services. In the 1980s, many courts ruled that rent-to-own transactions were governed by state RISAs, but these transactions

---

108 For a discussion of discount interest, see § 4.3.3, *infra*.

109 Distinctions between "interest" and other "charges" for purposes of usury law are considered in § 7.2, *infra*.

110 For more detail on the subjects addressed by installment loan laws and the variations among them, see 1 Consumer Credit Guide (CCH) ¶ 570.

111 For discussion of the time-price doctrine, see §§ 2.2.3.2, 2.3.2.1, 2.3.3.5, *supra*, and § 10.5.2.2, *infra*.

112 For a chart describing the states' Retail Installment Sales Acts, see 1 Consumer Credit Guide (CCH) ¶ 520. *See also* Westside Health and Racquet Club, Inc. v. Jefferson Fin. Servs., Inc., 19 S.W.3d 796 (Tenn. App. 1999) (Tennessee RISA covers health spa's assignment of member contracts to finance company and places no limits on terms of the assignment).

113 Fla. Stat. Ann. §§ 520.60 to 520.98; Mich. Comp. Laws §§ 445.1101 to 445.1431; N.J. Rev. Stat. §§ 17:16C-62 to 17:16C-94; Pa. Stat. Ann. tit. 73, §§ 501-101 to 501-602; Tenn. Code § 45-3-705. *See* Gonzalez v. Old Kent Mortgage Co., 2000 U.S. Dist. LEXIS 14530 (E.D. Pa. Sept. 19, 2000) (applying Pa. statute to home improvement loan); Williams v. Empire Funding Corp., 109 F. Supp. 2d 352 (E.D. Pa. 2000) (interpreting the conflicting cancellation rights of Truth in Lending and Pa. home improvement financing statute); In re Barber, 266 B.R. 309 (Bankr. E.D. Pa. 2001) (applying Pa. statute to home improvement loan).

114 Margot Saunders and Elizabeth Renuart, *Home Improvement Financing: A Model State Law* (AARP Public Policy Institute Publication # D1765 Oct. 2000), *available at* http://research.aarp.org.

are now generally covered by special industry-sponsored statutes that exempt them from the state RISA on the pretext that they are not credit sales.[115]

The substance of RISAs also varies among the states. Generally, all RISAs emphasize the disclosure of contract terms and the need to inform purchasers of their legal rights. They require all credit sale contracts to be written and, usually, to contain an itemization of charges. RISA single document and disclosure rules are discussed in § 11.6.8, *infra*. However, other RISA provisions are less consistent between jurisdictions. Most motor vehicle RISAs establish maximum rates for interest charges and frequently authorize add-on interest calculations. RISAs governing the credit sale of "other goods," however, often contain no rate ceiling. Most RISAs do address late charges, prepayment rights, insurance disclosures, and penalties for statutory violations. Some RISAs also limit co-signor liability and/or require special notice to those signing as a guarantor.[116] Other RISAs prohibit the taking of a security interest in property other than the goods sold or serviced.[117]

As mentioned earlier in this chapter, retail sellers rarely hold onto installment sale contracts for any length of time. Rather, they assign these contracts to third parties in order to obtain cash with which to run their businesses. RISAs often require potential purchasers of installment sale contracts to obtain a state license before entering the sales finance business. Otherwise, the assignment process is largely unregulated.[118]

2.3.3.6 Insurance Premium Finance Regulations

The credit sale of insurance is regulated by insurance premium financing statutes in many jurisdictions. Most premium financing is initiated by insurance agents, who assign the contracts to specialized finance companies. The financing of automobile insurance premiums is particularly common because many people cannot afford to pay their entire annual premium in one installment.

Not surprisingly, insurance premium financing is rife with consumer exploitation. The main problem is the lack of competition, which invites overreaching by creditors. Those states which regulate insurance premium finance have, however, exacerbated the situation by setting absurdly high[119] interest ceilings, given that the credit sale of an insurance

policy is virtually risk-free. If a borrower defaults in the payments, the insurance policy is cancelled[120] and the creditor receives the rebate for the unearned portion of the policy.[121] Because credit sellers require a down payment of, perhaps, thirty percent of the premium, the amount of the rebate invariably exceeds the balance of the debt, and the creditor loses nothing. Despite this "perfect security," creditors frequently charge rates for insurance premium financing that are at or near high usury ceilings.

2.3.3.7 Second Mortgage and Home Equity Loan Laws

The most explosive consumer credit market in recent years has been the market for second mortgages, or home equity loans, on residential real estate. The growth of these loans has a number of causes: an increase in real property values and, consequently, in the amount of equity held by homeowners; the desire of finance companies to lower the risks associated with their loans by obtaining real estate collateral; the deregulation of the mortgage market in the early 1980s; changes in the tax code regarding the deductibility of consumer interest payments; and the growth of the secondary market, permitting mortgage lenders to originate greater volumes of loans by selling them to investors. Regardless of the precise causes, second mortgages have become a minefield for unwary consumers.

The risks take many forms. Variable interest rates on many mortgages put homeowners at the mercy of future market rate fluctuations. Non-amortizing mortgages with final "balloon" payments can prove difficult to pay off and leave the borrower either in default or in perpetual debt. Open-end credit associated with "home equity" lines of credit can lead to improvident borrowing, and the presence of real estate security can lead to improvident lending to over-extended homeowners. Finally, the bottom line risk is always that defaulting borrowers may lose their homes.

A number of states reacted to the problem of second mortgages by adopting special usury laws which govern only second mortgages, home equity loans, or home improvement loans.[122] These statutes may set interest ceilings

---

115 *See* §§ 7.5.3.2–7.5.3.6, *infra*.

116 Lee v. Nationwide Cassell, L.P., 675 N.E.2d 599 (Ill. 1996) (co-signor is liable under Illinois law only if he or she has physically received the car or is a parent or spouse of the buyer).

117 *See, e.g.,* Ohio Rev. Code Ann. § 1317.071; Parker Financial v. Matthews, 1999 Ohio App. LEXIS 338 (Feb. 3, 1999) (no remedy provided in Ohio's RISA for a violation of this prohibition, however).

118 The ability of creditors to use assignments as a defense in consumer credit actions is discussed in § 10.6.1, *infra*.

119 Current charges in many jurisdictions are around 18% plus administrative fees.

120 *See* Barnett v. Funding Plus of America, Inc., 740 So. 2d 1069 (Ala. 1999) (upholding premium finance company's use of power of attorney from borrower to cancel her insurance without statutory advance notice after she missed a payment).

121 Technically, the creditor takes a security interest in the rebate. This procedure is expressly authorized by insurance premium financing statutes.

122 *See generally* Annot. 43 A.L.R.4th 675 (1986) (Construction and Application of Second Mortgage Statutes). Some second mortgage statutes were passed in the 1960s, during a prior cycle of questionable second mortgage lending practices. For a discussion of what constitutes a "second" mortgage, see § 3.9.3.2.1, *infra*, in the federal preemption context; *see also* Chevy Chase Bank, F.S.B. v. Chaires, 715 A.2d 199 (Md. 1998) (court held that a lien created by a state shore erosion control

and regulate the closing costs such as points[123] and appraisal fees that may be charged to the borrower at the outset of a transaction.[124] In 1982, however, federal law—with passage of the Alternative Mortgage Transaction Parity Act (AMTPA)—largely preempted the ability of states to regulate the structure of home equity loans, for example by prohibiting balloon rates, or non-amortizing loans.[125]

Some home equity lenders, though, abused the freedom that the deregulation of interest rates and structural terms brought. In consequence, Congress revisited the issue, and passed the Home Ownership and Equity Protection Act of 1994,[126] which placed substantive limitations on certain home equity lenders' ability to impose some of the terms condoned by AMTPA. Among the restricted terms are negative amortization, balloon payments, and prepayment penalties. Moreover, the new legislation also specifically addresses lending based on the value of the collateral, without adequate attention to ability to repay ("improvident lending"). This legislation applies only to closed-end loans secured by the borrower's primary home which exceed certain cost-triggers.[127] Consciously or not, Congress utilized the same policy principles underlying the trade-off used originally by the framers of the Small Loan Act, saying

to lenders in effect "you are permitted to charge very high rates, but if you do, you will be more strictly regulated and your ability to extract extra costs from the borrower will be limited."[128]

States also have responded to the explosion in abusive home equity lending. A number of states have passed substantial restrictions on predatory home equity lending that go beyond HOEPA's limits.[129]

2.3.3.8 Open-End Loans and Credit Sales

Open-end or "revolving" credit is regulated separately from fixed-term credit in most states. Within the open-end category, open-end *loan* accounts, typically offered by banks, may fall under a different statute from open-end credit *sales* accounts, such as the charge accounts available at many department stores.[130] Most open-end accounts, whether constituting loans or credit sales, are associated with plastic "credit cards."[131]

Statutes which govern open-end credit require monthly statements to be sent to the borrower showing the debits, credits, and finance charges assessed on the account during the previous billing cycle. They often set a ceiling on the monthly interest rate that can be assessed on the outstanding balance of the account, and specify how that outstanding balance may be calculated.[132] Interest on an open-end credit

---

fund on a residential property prior to a construction loan rendered the construction loan a "second" lien and, therefore, the state's secondary mortgage law applied).

123 For a discussion of the treatment of "points" as interest charges under state usury law, see § 7.2.2, *infra*.

124 *See, e.g., Williams v. Seeley (In re Williams),* 227 B.R. 83 (Bankr. E.D. Va. 1998) (lender violated state law second mortgage points and fees cap of 5% of the principal amount of the loan by charging a total of 23.5% triggering penalty provision of twice the total usurious interest paid plus costs and attorney's fees; in determining the amount of the award, court assumed, without stating it, that the loan discount fee was earned at the inception of the loan).

125 *See* discussion of the Alternative Mortgage Transaction Parity Act (AMTPA) at § 3.10, *infra*.

126 Subtitle B of Title I, Riegle Community Development and Regulatory Improvement Act of 1994 (H.R. 3474), Pub. L. No. 103-325, 108 Stat. 2160 (Sept. 23, 1994) primarily codified at 15 U.S.C. § 1639. For the legislative history of this "high cost mortgage" legislation, *see Hearings on Problems in Community Development Banking, Mortgage Lending Discrimination, Reverse Redlining, and Home Equity Lending, Before the Senate Comm. on Banking, Housing and Urban Affairs,* 103d Cong., 1st Sess. (Feb. 3, 17, 24, 1993) (S. Hrg. 103-137; ISBN:0-16-041270-6, for sale by GPO); *Hearing on S.924 Home Ownership and Equity Protection Act, Before the Senate Banking Committee,* 103d Cong., 1st Sess. (May 19, 1993); *The Home Equity Protection Act of 1993, Hearings on H.R. 3153 Before the Subcommittee on Consumer Credit and Insurance of the House Committee on Banking, Finance and Urban Affairs,* 103d Cong., 2d Sess. (Mar. 22, 1994); *Hearing on Community Development Institutions, 103-2, before the House Subcommittee on Financial Institutions Supervision, Regulation and Deposit Insurance,* 103d Cong., 1st Sess. (Feb 2–4, 1993).

127 See § 12.2.2, *infra*, for an overview of this legislation. It is discussed in depth in National Consumer Law Center, Truth in Lending Ch. 9 (5th ed. 2003 and Supp.).

---

128 *See generally* §§ 2.2.3.1, 2.3.1.3.1, 2.3.3.2, *supra*.

129 For a discussion of state high-cost mortgage laws, see § 12.2.3, *infra*.

130 Major credit cards such as Visa, MasterCard, or American Express, are loan accounts. The creditor is the card issuer, although the credit is used to pay off debts to retailers. On the other hand, the creditor on a department store charge account is the retailer itself, and the transactions are generally considered credit sales rather than loans. For a discussion of whether a nationwide mail-order company extended credit under a retail credit card arrangement, see State v. Allied Marketing Group, 949 S.W.2d 816 (Tex. App. 1997) (mail order company's use of gold card giving a customer a $10,000 line of credit created a retail credit card arrangement under Texas law and not a series of closed-end sale transactions as claimed by the company; at stake was legality of a $29.95 annual fee).

131 Not all plastic cards are credit cards; some are "debit cards." A credit card is a card associated with a true line of credit from a bank or other creditor. For such a line of credit to exist, the borrower should not have to have any money deposited with the creditor, although in practice some banks may only issue credit cards to their depositors. A debit card acts more like a bank check. The cardholder must have money on deposit with the bank that issues the card, and the cardholder can only "charge" purchases with the card if the money deposited with the bank equals or exceeds the amount of the "charge." As soon as a "charge" on a debit card is received by the bank, the cardholder's bank account is debited by the amount of the purchase. Because the cardholder always has enough money on deposit with the bank to cover his or her purchases, the bank never actually extends credit to the cardholder; it merely processes the cardholder's bills for him or her.

132 *See* § 4.3.5, *infra*.

sale may be allowed upon notice by the creditor.[133] Finally, open-end credit statutes may limit the imposition of periodic (usually annual) "membership" fees as well as other fees such as late fees and fees for exceeding the authorized credit limit.

The effect of state statutes on credit card accounts issued by depository lenders, as opposed to retail charge card accounts, has been significantly limited, by the preemption of many state usury laws on behalf of federal depository lenders. Specifically, a national bank or other "most favored lender" with a branch office in a state may offer credit card accounts on the most favorable terms available under the law of that state, but a national bank with no branch in that state may be able to do even better; it may offer accounts by mail at whatever terms the law of its home state allows.[134] Case law has extended this exportation right to state-chartered banks.[135] This rule has enabled major credit card issuers to do business by mail from states which have high or non-existent interest ceilings, with borrowers in low-rate states and, in effect, to ignore the low ceilings in the borrowers' home states. It has also led to a "race to the bottom" in terms of consumer protection laws as local banks convince legislatures that they must become more "creditor friendly"[136] or risk losing businesses to states which are.

2.3.3.9 Pawnbroker Statutes

Pawnbroking is a form of secured lending which usually involves a small principal, a short term, and a high interest rate.[137] It differs from small loan lending in that the pawnbroker takes physical possession of the security pledged by the borrower at the time the loan is made.[138] When the loan is repaid, usually in a lump sum but occasionally in installments, the collateral is returned to the borrower. If the borrower fails to repay the loan within a set time, the pawnbroker is permitted to sell the collateral to recover its debt.

Most states have a special usury statute which exempts licensed pawnbrokers from the general usury ceiling[139] and

permits them to charge rates comparable to small loan lenders. The regulations applicable to pawnbrokers and to small loan lenders may differ significantly, however, because of the differences in the structure of credit. Debt collection, for example, is not a big issue with pawnbrokers, because the value of the collateral they accept invariably exceeds the debt they are owed. However, pawnbrokers must keep records to demonstrate that they are not fencing stolen property, and state laws or regulations usually restrict the manner in which a pawnbroker can dispose of pledged property. For example, many states require public sales and insist that any surplus from such a sale be turned over to the borrower. State law may also restrict the charges apart from "interest" that a pawnbroker may impose. For example, storage charges for holding the borrower's pledged property may be forbidden.

2.3.3.10 Comprehensive Consumer Credit Codes

Several states have rewritten and consolidated all or parts of their various special usury statutes in the form of consumer credit codes. Among these jurisdictions are: Alabama, Colorado, Idaho, Iowa, Indiana, Kansas, Maine, Oklahoma, South Carolina, Texas, Utah, West Virginia, Wisconsin, and Wyoming. Some of these states have adopted statutes which are unique to the adopting state. However, most of these jurisdictions have enacted comprehensive consumer codes adopted from some form of the Uniform Consumer Credit Code (UCCC).

The UCCC is a model statute which has been approved by the National Conference of Commissioners on Uniform State Laws and the American Bar Association. Two basic versions of the UCCC exist. The original 1968 draft was funded and written predominantly by representatives of the consumer credit industry. It relied primarily on competition rather than rate ceilings to restrain excessive charges for credit, although the statute did contain ceilings which vary with the class of loan or credit involved.[140] The adoption of this draft was opposed by many consumer groups on the ground that it provided insufficient consumer protection. Seven states have adopted some form of the 1968 draft.[141]

---

133 Harrell Oil Co. v. Case, 543 S.E.2d 522 (N.C. App. 2001).

134 *See* §§ 3.4.3, 3.4.5, 3.9.2, *infra.*

135 *See* § 3.9.2 (extension of most favored lender rules to "federally-related" lenders), *infra.*

136 Good discussions of the history, policy and problems underlying this phenomenon can be found in Greenwood Trust Co. v. Massachusetts, 776 F. Supp. 21 (D. Mass. 1991), *rev'd* 971 F.2d 818 (1st Cir. 1992). *See also* Ch. 3, *infra.*

137 For a more thorough description of pawnbroking, see John P. Caskey, Fringe Banking (1994).

138 Auto-title pawn or auto pawn/lease-back scams, which conceal interest rates of as much as 800–900%, have recently surfaced in a number of states. *See* § 7.5.2.3, *infra. See* Lynn Drysdale & Kathleen Keest, *The Two-Tiered Consumer Financial Services Marketplace: The Fringe Banking System and its Challenge to Current Thinking About The Socio-Economic role of Usury Laws in Today's Society*, 51 S.C. L. Rev. 589 (2000).

139 Depending on the state, unlicensed pawnbrokers are either prohibited or must operate under the state's general usury law.

An exemption may apply only to statutory pawn transactions, rather than all activities by a pawnbroker. *See* Agapitov v. Lerner, 133 Cal. Rptr. 2d 837 (Ct. App. 2003). For cases discussing whether the sale of personal property with a repurchase option falls under a state's pawnbroking statute, see § 7.5.2.2, *infra.*

140 *See* Luttenegger v. Conseco Fin. Servicing Corp., 671 N.W.2d 425 (Iowa 2003) (distinguishing between fees with and without caps under the U.C.C.C. and finding that borrower's breach of contract claim was precluded because the fees in question were permissible).

141 These states are Colorado, Indiana, Oklahoma, South Carolina, Utah, Wisconsin, and Wyoming. The 1968 draft has also been adopted in Guam. The Wisconsin statute is actually a combination of the 1968 U.C.C.C. draft and the National Consumer

In response to the deficiencies of the UCCC, the National Consumer Law Center issued an alternative consumer credit code, the National Consumer Act (NCA), in 1970. This statute and a subsequent abbreviated draft of the NCA, known as the Model Consumer Credit Act (MCCA), included significantly more comprehensive consumer protections than the 1968 UCCC.[142] For example, among other changes, the NCA abolished the traditional distinction between loans and credit sales, restricted security interests and credit insurance commissions, and addressed credit bureau abuses and deceptive trade practices.[143]

The NCA was not adopted in its entirety by any state. Yet many states incorporated individual NCA provisions in their credit laws.[144] The NCA served as a counterpoint to the 1968 UCCC, and significantly influenced the second draft of the UCCC which was issued in 1974. The 1974 draft went farther than its predecessor towards abolishing unnecessary distinctions among types of credit. It also improved upon the consumer protection of the 1968 draft and, accordingly, received much less industry support. The 1974 UCCC draft has been adopted to varying degrees in only four states.[145]

As suggested by the fact that there are two outstanding drafts of the UCCC, the statute is somewhat less than uniform in practice. Differences between the 1968 and 1974 drafts have been exacerbated by state legislatures which have declined to adopt either version in whole cloth, have exempted specific transactions from UCCC coverage, or have simply amended the statute of their own accord. Nevertheless, significant similarities among UCCC jurisdictions remain, and practitioners in one UCCC state should consult decisions from other UCCC jurisdictions on unclear points of law.[146]

2.3.3.11 Servicemembers Civil Relief Act

The Servicemembers Civil Relief Act is a statute that regulates interest rates in some situations. The Act provides that the interest rate on any obligation that was incurred by a person before entering into military service must be reduced to 6% while the person is in the service.[147] The interest rate must be reduced on the entire obligation, so both the servicemember and any cosigners are benefited.[148] The creditor can avoid this result by applying to a court for a determination that the debtor's ability to pay a higher rate is not materially affected by military service. This provision does not merely create a defense for a servicemember who is sued on a debt, but requires the creditor to reduce the rate of interest during the debtor's active duty, and gives the debtor a private cause of action if the creditor does not.[149]

In 2003, Congress made substantial amendments to the Act.[150] Under the amendments, when a creditor lowers the interest rate on a loan the interest must be forgiven, not just deferred.[151] Additionally, the periodic payment due from the servicemember must be reduced by the amount of the forgiven interest; creditors cannot require the same payment but simply apply a greater portion toward principal.[152] Other aspects of the Servicemembers Civil Relief Act are discussed in a different volume and should be reviewed closely in cases to which the Act may apply.[153]

2.3.4 Relationship Between State Laws Regulating Credit Charges and the Federal Truth in Lending Act

By the 1960s, the "patchwork" of general and special usury laws was firmly in place. The problem with this system was not that it offended some abstract standard of orderliness. A set of statutes, each of which governs a particular credit transaction, is not inherently an unworkable legal scheme. Rather, the problem with the proliferation of special usury statutes was that in most states the credit terms employed by the different statutes were inconsistent, and this inconsistency extended not only to the setting of interest ceilings, but also to the most fundamental credit issues such as the definitions of principal, interest, and interest rate in a transaction. Consequently, consumers could easily have a

Act. Utah technically repealed the U.C.C.C. in 1985, but the statute was replaced by a consumer code containing many U.C.C.C. provisions.

142 Copies of the National Consumer Act and the Model Consumer Credit Code are available for $5 each from the National Consumer Law Center, 77 Summer Street, 10th floor, Boston, MA 02110.

143 For comparisons of the U.C.C.C. and NCA, *see generally* Rothschild & Carroll, Consumer Protection: Text and Materials, 2d Ed. § 19.06E (1977); Boyd, *The U3C and the NCA: a Comment and Comparison in Consumer Viewpoints: Critique of the Uniform Consumer Credit Code* 663 (R. Elbrecht Ed. 1971).

144 The NCA had the greatest influence in Wisconsin which adopted a combined version of the NCA and U.C.C.C.

145 These states are Idaho, Iowa, Kansas, and Maine.

146 The 1968 model U.C.C.C. is published in 7 Uniform Laws Annotated (West 1985). The 1974 model U.C.C.C. is published in 7A Uniform Laws Annotated (West 1985).

147 50 U.S.C. app. § 527. Cathey v. First Republic Bank, 2001 U.S. Dist. LEXIS 13150 (W.D. La. July 6, 2001) (magistrate's report), *adopted by* 2001 U.S. Dist. LEXIS 13195 (W.D. La. Aug. 13, 2001).

148 Cathey v. First Republic Bank, 2001 U.S. Dist. LEXIS 13150 (W.D. La. July 6, 2001) (magistrate's report), *adopted by* 2001 U.S. Dist. LEXIS 13195 (W.D. La. Aug. 13, 2001).

149 Cathey v. First Republic Bank, 2001 U.S. Dist. LEXIS 13150 (W.D. La. July 6, 2001) (magistrate's report), *adopted by* 2001 U.S. Dist. LEXIS 13195 (W.D. La. Aug. 13, 2001); Moll v. Ford Consumer Fin. Co., 1998 U.S. Dist. LEXIS 3638 (N.D. Ill. Mar. 16, 1998).

150 Pub. L. No. 108-189, 117 Stat. 2835 (2003). These amendments included a change of the statute's name, which originally was known as the Soldiers' and Sailors' Civil Relief Act.

151 50 U.S.C. app. § 527(a)(2).

152 50 U.S.C. app. § 527(a)(3).

153 National Consumer Law Center, Fair Debt Collection § 9.10 (5th ed. 2004 and Supp.).

"5% add-on" car loan which was, unbeknownst to them, significantly more expensive than their 7% simple interest mortgage.[154] Moreover, even for the same kind of transaction, different creditors might use different interest rate calculation methods. As a result, it was extremely difficult for consumers to compare the credit terms offered by different lenders or credit sellers. The situation encouraged deceptive and anti-competitive credit practices.

The Federal Truth in Lending Act (TILA)[155] was adopted in 1968 with twin goals of providing a set of standardized rules for determining accurately the genuine cost of credit and a mandatory, uniform set of consumer credit disclosures concerning cost and terms which a buyer or borrower could use to make an informed choice in the credit marketplace. The primary mechanism by which the Act sought to achieve this goal was (and still is) a standardized disclosure statement which creditors in consumer credit transactions are required to give a consumer before a transaction is consummated.[156] Among other disclosures, this statement must contain the "Amount Financed," which may be thought of as a rough equivalent of the principal amount of a loan or other credit, the "Finance Charge," which can be considered the total dollar cost of the loan or other credit, and the "Annual Percentage Rate" (APR), which is a simple interest calculation of the cost of the credit. All of these figures must be calculated according to detailed regulations promulgated by the Federal Reserve Board.[157]

The TILA also contains some substantive consumer protections in addition to its required disclosures. Most importantly, the TILA gives consumers a three-day period in which to rescind any transaction giving a creditor a security interest in their home, and this three-day period may be extended to as much as three *years* if disclosures are not properly made. In 1994, the Home Ownership and Equity Protection Act amended TILA to impose some substantive restrictions on certain high-cost home equity loans.[158] Yet, at its core the TILA is a disclosure statute, the purpose of which is not to supplant state law, but to provide a separate, standardized mechanism which a consumer can use to shop for credit. With some very limited exceptions involving the terminology which may be employed in credit contracts,[159] the TILA does not preempt state usury laws. It does not alter

state usury ceilings or other cost caps, nor does it affect the way that interest rates are calculated for the purposes of state usury law.[160] Indeed, many consumer credit contracts currently state two interest rates—one on the contract or note which is calculated as required or permitted by state law, and one on the TILA disclosure statement which contains the APR and other disclosures as calculated under federal law. Thus the TILA and state regulatory usury laws are best regarded as separate statutory schemes, and compliance with one in no way guarantees compliance with the other.

Having emphasized the distinctness of the TILA and usury law, one must acknowledge that the impact of the TILA on the entire consumer credit marketplace has been tremendous, and in some states it has affected state regulation. Specifically, it is not unusual for state legislatures to incorporate federal standards when rewriting their state laws. For example, a state law may set an interest ceiling at 18% as calculated by the Federal Reserve Board's APR regulations. More frequently, a state law may provide that compliance with TILA disclosure regulations is deemed to constitute compliance with state disclosure rules often associated with the state's regulatory scheme. In either instance, federal regulations, in effect, become part of the substantive law of the state, but this transformation can occur only pursuant to specific state legislative action.

A second, less concrete effect of the TILA is its impact on the interpretation of ambiguous state usury provisions. The widespread use and acceptance of the TILA disclosures and the APR in particular have led to an unspoken assumption that the APR for a consumer credit contract is the "correct" or "true" interest rate on that contract and that a creditor which computes its interest rates in accordance with the TILA has, in the absence of any clear conflict with state law, calculated a "correct" rate by which its compliance with a state usury ceiling may be measured. This view can have unfortunate consequences for consumers.

It is unquestionably true that the APR calculation prescribed by the Federal Reserve Board is a dramatic improvement, as a true picture of the cost of credit to a consumer, over many interest formulae traditionally permitted in fixed-term transactions[161] by state law, such as "add-on" or

154 For example, a 30-month loan at 5% add-on interest is equivalent to a 9.33% simple interest loan of the same duration. *See* §§ 4.3.2, 4.4.1, *infra.*
155 The TILA is codified at 15 U.S.C. § 1601 *et seq.*
156 The discussion here of TILA requirements is cursory at best and is intended only as an overview of the statute. For a thorough treatment of the TILA, see National Consumer Law Center, Truth in Lending (5th ed. 2003 and Supp.).
157 The FRB's Truth in Lending regulations are contained in "Regulation Z," 12 C.F.R. § 226.
158 See § 12.2.2, *infra*, for a brief overview and National Consumer Law Center, Truth in Lending Ch. 9 (5th ed. 2003 and Supp.) for a detailed discussion.
159 *See* § 3.12, *infra*. The 1994 HOEPA amendments preempt less

protective state laws, but not more protective ones. *See, e.g.,* § 5.9, *infra.*
160 *See* Tavares v. Sprunk (*In re* Tavares), 298 B.R. 195 (Bankr. D. Mass. 2003) (distinguishing between usury laws, which shield debtors from high interest rates, and TILA and similar state statutes, which provide credit disclosures and enable comparison shopping). The 1994 HOEPA amendments restrict some of the disadvantageous terms, such as negative amortization and the Rule of 78. *See generally* § 12.2.2, *infra.*
161 In contrast, the APR is of very little use to consumers in variable rate transactions because the initial rate, however calculated, is subject to change. Using the APR to shop for variable rate credit can be extremely misleading because the creditors advertising the lowest initial rates may not be providing the lowest price over the term of the transaction. In general, consumers who are

"discount" interest. Yet neither Congress nor the Federal Reserve Board is immune to the political pressures which first led states to adopt what were essentially misleading interest calculation rules in their special usury laws and, before that, in their interpretations of general usury laws. Indeed, the TILA has been completely rewritten since its initial incarnation and in recent years the FRB and its staff have often adopted interpretations which show more concern for the convenience or desires of creditors than for accurate cost disclosures.[162] Simultaneously, many states have rewritten their credit laws and, depending very much on the state, have become increasingly sophisticated. In such an atmosphere, it is a mistake to assume that state credit laws are the weak sisters of federal regulation, or that state interest calculation rules are less accurate than the APR to the extent that they differ from it. Instead, there is a danger that the adoption of pro-creditor rules at the federal level could subvert the independent consideration of controversial issues under state usury law by preemption[163] or simply by setting an authoritative bad example.

2.4 Deregulation of Usury Law

2.4.1 Changing or Abolishing Interest Ceilings

The late 1970s and early 1980s were watershed years for usury law. As a result of federal monetary policy to fight inflation, short-term commercial market interest rates rose above twenty percent, significantly exceeding general usury ceilings and many special usury law ceilings. Because lenders themselves borrow the money they lend, their profits were squeezed as their interest expenses rose. As state usury ceilings became constricting on creditors, they feared they would have to cut back their volume of lending, losing customers and market share. There was a fear that creditors would be understandably reluctant to lend money at rates below their cost of funds and that mortgage loans and other kinds of consumer credit would dry up. A consensus among legislators and the credit industry emerged that something

had to be done about usury laws, and action was taken at both the federal and state levels.

In 1980, the federal reaction to the conflict between usury ceilings and rising market interest rates was to preempt many, but not all, state usury limitations.[164] First, Congress allowed all federally-insured depository lenders to operate under a variable interest ceiling which had previously been reserved for national banks. Second, this alternative ceiling was *temporarily* extended to all creditors issuing business or agricultural credit in excess of $1,000.[165] Finally, Congress preempted all interest ceilings for most major lenders for credit secured by first mortgages on borrower's homes, including mobile homes. All of these preemptions were passed subject to the proviso that a state could "opt out" of the preemption by adopting legislation proclaiming that the state did not want the federal preemption to apply to its usury laws. The effect of this statutory structure was to shift the legislative burden to the proponents of usury laws; if a state failed to adopt new usury provisions or to reenact its old ones, most usury restrictions in the state were, by default, repealed.[166]

Because of the federal usury preemptions, state legislatures were forced to consider what role, if any, usury statutes should play in a modern economy. This was not exactly a new issue.[167] For example, in 1787, the English philosopher Jeremy Bentham had published an influential essay, *Letters in Defense of Usury*, in which he had argued that usury ceilings limited the credit available to those who could not offer security, violated the principle of freedom of contract, and should be abolished. According to Bentham's view, interest rates should be governed by free market rules of supply and demand. This utilitarian school of thought led to the repeal of English usury statutes in 1854.

Although the fundamental issues facing state legislatures in the 1980s were essentially the same as in Bentham's day, they were generally not painted as broadly. Rather, most

---

considering variable rate transactions should pay attention to the index to which the contract rate is pegged, the spread between that index and the contract rate, and the contractual cap on the interest rate, rather than the APR advertised by the creditor.

162 An example of this tendency is Regulation Z's highly questionable exclusion of "seller's points" from the "finance charge." *See* § 7.4.6.2, *infra*. Another example is the FRB's logically indefensible decision to define "finance charge" differently for mortgage and non-mortgage transactions and to include in the finance charge in non-mortgage transactions fees which are excluded in mortgage loans. *See* National Consumer Law Center, Truth in Lending §§ 3.7.5.2, 3.9.6 (5th ed. 2003 and Supp.). These are the sorts of arbitrary and confusing distinctions that the TILA was supposed to eliminate.

163 *See, e.g.,* § 3.9.2, *infra*.

164 The statute containing the preemptions was the Depository Institutions Deregulation and Monetary Control Act of 1980 (DIDA) Pub. L. No. 96-221. DIDA and other federal usury preemption are discussed in depth in Ch. 3, *infra*. For a detailed discussion of the legislative history of DIDA, *see* Cathy Lesser Mansfield, *The Road to Subprime "HEL" Was Paved With Good Congressional Intentions: Usury Deregulation and the Subprime Home Equity Market,* 51 S.C. L. Rev. 473 (2000). *See also* James J. White, *The Usury Trompe l'Oeil,* 51 S.C. L. Rev. 445 (Spring 2000).

165 This temporary business and agricultural preemption expired April 1, 1983.

166 More accurately, the old law would remain on the books but its enforcement would be preempted. The distinction can be important when, for example, preemption is conditioned upon a creditor's compliance with federal regulations. In the absence of compliance, the preemption will not apply to a transaction, and the state usury law can be enforced. *See, e.g.,* § 3.9.3.4, *infra*.

167 *Cf. In re* Coxson, 43 F.3d 189 (5th Cir. 1995) (noting that Texas had abolished usury laws during Reconstruction, but "credit abuses arose in the absence of usury laws," and they were reintroduced).

states had in place a fairly complex set of general and special usury statutes, some of which, such as the small loan acts and RISAs, were relatively uncontroversial, and some of which, such as fixed-rate general usury statutes, were clearly unworkable in the face of sizeable fluctuations in market interest rates. The main issue was thus what to do about general usury statutes, and two basic paths were followed. Many states repealed general usury ceilings completely, allowing parties who were not regulated by special usury statutes to contract for the payment of any agreed rate.[168] Other states modified their general usury laws so that the ceilings would fluctuate with some published market interest rate. For example, several states set their ceilings to five or six percentage points above the federal discount rate. Most states simply raised their interest ceilings to a point not constricting on traditional lenders.

It should be emphasized that the primary focus of new usury legislation at the state level has been general usury ceilings. Many states raised, but did not eliminate special usury ceilings in RISAs, small loan laws, second mortgage statutes, etc. Although it is difficult to generalize about the different legislative schemes in different states, the states' retention of special restrictions for some types of consumer credit seems to constitute a tacit recognition of the fact that the market for consumer credit is not without its flaws. Clearly, consumers and creditors do not possess equal bargaining power when negotiating consumer credit contracts; in fact, consumers are offered contracts on a take-it-or-leave-it basis. Credit transactions are often complicated beyond most consumers' ability or willingness to understand. Furthermore, a consumer's desperate need for money, e.g., to prevent foreclosure may seem to justify paying an extraordinary high price for the credit, although in a credit market that worked well, the consumer's desperate need for credit would not affect its price. Consumer credit is thus fertile ground for profiteering, and the maintenance of consumer protections in the form of interest ceilings and other cost limitations may be appropriate, regardless of the merit of a deregulated free, efficient market.

Some commentators have criticized the retention of any interest ceiling, no matter how high, on the grounds that ceilings inherently deprive some high-risk borrowers of credit and interfere with the smooth operation of credit markets.[169] This argument has been criticized as more theo-

retical than practical. First, contrary to the theoretical model, competition among lenders does not appear to drive down rates as more players enter the fringe lending business.[170] For example, in the area of payday loans, competition has resulted in excessive solicitation and overlending. In fact, loan pricing has slightly increased due to deregulation of small loan rates. In Colorado, where payday lenders operated for several years without an interest rate cap, the situation for consumers worsened substantially. The number of payday loan stores increased from 188 in 1997 to 218 in 1998, and the total number of loans increased by 55.9%. During that same period, however, the average APR did not fluctuate. Competition did not lead to lower rates for consumers.[171] Moreover, in thirteen states where payday lending is authorized, 15% of payday lenders surveyed quoted rates higher than allowed. An additional 38% of payday lenders quoted rates identical to the allowable APR. Competition is not driving down rates.[172] Even assuming that any interest ceiling inherently limits the credit available to some borrowers whose risk is too high to justify a loan at the rate ceiling, the number of borrowers actually deprived of credit by reasonable ceilings is probably very low.[173] One research project showed that credit was much more available to low-income borrowers in Little Rock, Arkansas with an effective 10% usury ceiling than in states allowing much higher interest charges.[174]

---

168 For a discussion of the interpretation of "agreed rate" statutes, see § 9.2.8, *infra*.

169 *See, e.g.,* 1981 Ariz. St. L.J. 1 *et seq.* (entire issue devoted to discussion of usury law and usury deregulation in Arizona; the authors of these articles go to great length to demonstrate that usury statutes do not set interest rates in Arizona, but they ignore that usury laws are not intended to set market rates); Note, *Usury Legislation—Its Effects on the Economy and a Proposal for Reform,* 33 Vand. L. Rev. 199 (1980); T. Durkin, *An Economic Perspective on Interest Rate Limitations,* 9 Ga. St. U. L. Rev. 821 (1993); H. Nathan, *Economic Analysis of Usury Laws,* 10 J. Bank Research 200 (1980); R. Shay, *The Impact of*

State Rate Ceilings upon the Availability and Price of Credit, 4 National Commission on Finance Technical Studies (1973). *Compare* John P. Caskey, Fringe Banking (1994) (discussing arguments in favor of rate regulation of fringe lenders).

170 Lynn Drysdale & Kathleen Keest, *The Two-Tiered Consumer Financial Services Marketplace: The Fringe Banking System and its Challenge to Current Thinking About The Socio-Economic role of Usury Laws in Today's Society,* 51 S.C. L. Rev. 589 (2000).

171 Pearl Chin, *Payday Loans: The Case for Federal Legislation,* 2004 U. Ill. L. Rev. 723 (2004).

172 *Id.*

173 Consumer credit legislation, when originally proposed, virtually always has evoked dire predictions that consumers will be shut out of the credit market. These predictions almost invariably lack credible empirical support and fail to materialize once the legislation is adopted. *See* G. Wallace, *The Logic of Consumer Credit Reform,* 82 Yale L.J. 461 (1971). For example, proposed changes in the U.C.C. holder-in-due-course rule, to give consumers legal recourse against the assignees of consumer sales contracts, elicited protests from the consumer finance industry on the ground that the new liability would reduce the credit available for the purchase of consumer paper. Yet, when the FTC effectively eliminated the holder-in-due-course doctrine from consumer credit sales, (*see* § 10.6.1.2.2, *infra*) the sky did not fall. Instead, the consumer credit market expanded rapidly. In general, so long as credit restrictions do not make consumer lending unprofitable as an over-all business, concerns that these restrictions will shut individuals out of the credit market seem greatly exaggerated.

174 R. Peterson & G. Falls, Impact of a Ten Percent Usury Ceiling: Empirical Evidence (Credit Research Center, Purdue Univ. 1981). A study in Maine is also instructive. When Maine

Second, whatever this number of borrowers is, it must be weighed against the number of performing consumers who would pay higher rates but for the presence of usury ceilings.[175] This latter category of consumers exists because the interest rates set in consumer credit contracts are determined very little by the risk[176] and not solely by the costs of the loan. Consumers and creditors possess unequal bargaining power, and creditors attempt to increase their returns whenever possible. Without usury restrictions (and sometimes even with them) consumers may pay more for a loan than their risk alone would indicate. Indeed, there is growing evidence of what could be called "sucker-pricing" for credit in some segments of the market,[177] which is counter to the

fundamental societal goal of fairness. For example, there is some indication that African-Americans or Native Americans may be charged by some lenders more than white borrowers for credit without risk-based justifications.[178] Following beefed-up efforts by federal regulatory agencies at fair lending enforcement,[179] some regulators noticed differential pricing even *within* the same risk-classification by some lenders purporting to use a system of tiered pricing based on risk.[180] Obviously, any risk-related rationale for high rates collapses in such circumstances. By restricting profiteering, reasonable usury statutes undoubtedly benefit more borrowers by limiting contract interest rates than they harm by restricting credit.[181] They also help limit the dam-

---

restricted interest rates on refinanced high-rate loans, this provision went to the heart of the source of profitability for finance companies, (*see* § 6.1.1.1, *supra*) which subsequently became a small presence in the state. On one occasion, a survey was done in conjunction with a study suggesting this be repealed. Among the quite interesting, but unheralded findings of the survey, over half of the former finance company customers found alternative sources of credit, and 53% of those found *cheaper* alternatives in banks and credit unions. (This cuts against the normal rationale that higher rate finance companies serve higher risk customers. *Cf.* § 11.1, *infra*.) Significantly, of those who did not find (or seek) funds elsewhere, over three times as many felt they were *better off* to be "rid of the burden of the finance company" (36.3%) as felt they were worse off because no other alternatives were available to them (11.4%). George J. Benston, *An Analysis of Maine's 36-Month Limitation on Finance Company Small Loans*, 33–41 (Dec. 1972), reprinted in the National Commission on Consumer Finance, Technical Studies, Vol. II.

175 *See* J. Campen & L. Lazonick, *Regulation of Small Loan Interest Rates: Public Policy and Consumer Welfare*, 1 New England J. Bus. & Econ. 30 (1980); Robin Morris, *Consumer Debt and Usury: A New Rationale for Usury*, 15 Pepperdine L. Rev. 151 (1988).

176 For example, conventional wisdom explains the difference in consumer credit rates at finance companies and banks as based on risk and, inferentially, on income. However, there is no statistically significant demographic difference between consumers who use banks and those who use finance companies. A.C. Sullivan, *Competition in the Market for Consumer Loans*, 36 J. Econ. & Bus. 141 (1984); G. Boczar, *Competition Between Banks and Finance Companies*, 33 J. Fin. 245 (1978). *But cf.* United States v. Household Fin. Corp., 602 F.2d 1255 (7th Cir. 1979) (finance company's argument that it shared in same market as banks rejected). A consumer survey sponsored by the Federal Reserve Board further supports the lack of risk segmentation, showing income ($24,200 median, $30,160 mean at banks and $23,080 median, $24,099 mean at finance companies) and debt load ($7869 mean, $4430 median at banks and $6927 mean, $4183 median at finance companies) to be virtually the same. Avery, Elliehausen, Canner & Gustafson, *Survey of Consumer Finances, 1983: A Second Report*, 70 Fed. Res. Bull. 857, 867 (Dec. 1984). Further, some high-rate credit transactions may create the very risk they cite to justify their existence, by overburdening borrowers who would not be credit risks if they had access to more reasonable rates.

177 The term is derived from a study showing race-and gender-based discrimination in price negotiations for new cars. Ian Ayres, *Fair Driving: Gender and Race Discrimination in Retail Car Negotiations*, 104 Harv. L. Rev. 817 (1991). The author

speculated that the cause of the difference was not necessarily racial or gender-based animus. Rather, where profits are not spread evenly across all transactions, sellers seek to maximize profits from those transactions where they can, leading them to look for "suckers" willing to pay full price. Stereotypes about who those "suckers" might be lead them to treat those people differently in negotiations, which, in turn, leads to a self-fulfilling cycle of higher prices for those people.

Education, age, sophistication, race or ethnicity, gender and a perceived or genuine absence of alternatives might each be such a marked category of customer. *See generally Hearings on Problems in Community Development Banking, Mortgage Lending Discrimination, Reverse Redlining, and Home Equity Lending, Before the Senate Comm. on Banking, Housing and Urban Affairs*, 103d Cong., 1st Sess. (Feb. 3, 17, 24, 1993) (S. Hrg. 103-137; ISBN:0-16-041270-6, for sale by GPO); Kathleen Keest, *Some of the Poor Pay Even More: Is There a "Discrimination Tax" in the Marketplace*, 27 Clearinghouse Rev. 365 (1993).

178 *See* § 11.1, *infra; see generally* National Consumer Law Center, Credit Discrimination § 8.2 (4th ed. 2005).

179 A watershed study by the Federal Reserve Bank of Boston showed why the previous examination methods used by regulators had generally failed to uncover any discrimination. It found that in fact most credit applicants (80%) had flaws which would warrant denial of credit, but that, in essence, marginal white applicants tended to be given the benefit of the doubt more often than equally-positioned minority applicants. Munnell, Browne, McEneaney, Tootell, *Mortgage Lending in Boston: Interpreting HMDA Data*, Working Paper Series No. 92-7 (Federal Reserve Bank of Boston, Oct. 1992), available from Federal Reserve Bank of Boston, Research Library-D, P.O. Box 2076, Boston, MA 02016-2076, (617) 973-3397, and also available as Clearinghouse No. 47,967. *See generally* National Consumer Law Center, Credit Discrimination § 10.11 (4th ed. 2005).

180 Presentation to ABA, Consumer Financial Services Committee, Business Law Section (Apr. 1994). Note that this related to institutions scrutinized on a routine basis by examiners. The experience of many consumer practitioners suggests that non-depository lenders, such as second mortgage companies and finance companies, would likely show similar disparities for minority or elderly, unsophisticated borrowers. They, however, are not routinely examined by regulators able to do comparative analysis. *See generally* National Consumer Law Center, Credit Discrimination § 8.4 (4th ed. 2005).

181 G. Wallace, *The Uses of Usury: Low Rate Ceilings Reexamined*, 56 B.U.L. Rev. 451 (1976).

age "sucker-pricing" can do to vulnerable borrowers or those frozen out of alternative markets for reasons unrelated to genuine risk.

Another rebuttal to the contention that usury statutes restrict credit and should, therefore, be abolished is the realization that some credit restriction may not be a bad thing.[182] Depriving genuinely high-risk borrowers, who in the consumer context are generally borrowers already heavily in debt, of the opportunity to borrow more money by setting a usury ceiling is not obviously wrong. Usury statutes have always been explained as attempts to save this class of debtor from acts of its own desperation. While such a policy may be paternalistic, it is not inherently unwise, so long as the ceiling is set above the average market rate.[183] In retaining usury regulations in the form of special usury ceilings and, frequently, variable general usury ceilings, state legislatures appear to have rejected the notion that high-risk borrowers, who are already up to their necks in debt, must be guaranteed the freedom to go in over their heads.[184]

Usury ceilings also screen out fraudulent and predatory lenders who cannot survive under reasonable usury ceilings because of their high cost of business and lack of repeat customers.[185] These lenders serve no socially useful purpose and often leave a trail of legal havoc and misery for both their borrowers and investors. Restricting high risk credit benefits not only the borrowers and their families who would be faced with the high costs of default, but also traditional lenders or investors who are harmed by the consumer bankruptcies caused by predatory lending. The critics of usury laws respond that the problems of unscrupulous, predatory and fraudulent lenders are best dealt with directly by fraud and consumer protection laws that do not impinge upon the rest of the credit marketplace.[186] However, a response to this contention is that usury ceilings are more effective in *preventing* fraud and the entrance of unscrupulous lenders into the market and do not impinge on the rest of the market when set at reasonable levels. They further create a "bright line" standard which benefits both the industry and consumers. Industry knows in advance what is permitted and what is not, relieving it of uncertainty. Consumers would be protected by an even-handed limit, while more subjective standards, (e.g., unfair and deceptive, unconscionable) are subject to uneven application by different judges with differing values and perspectives.

Finally, the enormous credit binge of the 1980s and 1990s,[187] with its attendant risks to both individuals and to the national economy as a whole, suggested to some that usury may well be an important macroeconomic tool. One commentator noted that while excess debt may or may not lead to recession,

> there is little doubt that *in* a recession all consumers suffer, overleveraged consumers suffer most, and the more overleveraged our population is, the more our society will suffer. . . .
>
> As a value moderating the supply of consumer credit in society, national usury laws can moderate the competing interests in indebtedness and offer consumers and society protection in a time of diminished employment or recession which is the major problem of post-industrial development.[188]

---

182 *See, e.g.*, Vincent D. Rougeau, *Rediscovering Usury: An Argument for Legal Controls on Credit Card Interest Rates*, 67 U. Colo. L. Rev. 1 (1996).

183 *See, e.g.*, Eric A. Posner, *Contract Law in the Welfare State: A Defense of the Unconscionability Doctrine, Usury Laws, and Related Limitations on the Freedom to Contract*, 24 J. Legal Stud. 283 (1995).

184 G. Wallace, *The Uses of Usury: Low Rate Ceilings Reexamined*, 56 B.U.L. Rev. 451 (1976). *See also* Diane Ellis, *Bank Trends—The Effect of Consumer Interest Rate Deregulation on Credit Card Volumes, Charge-Offs, and the Personal Bankruptcy Rate* (1999) (available at www.fdic.gov/bank/analytical/bank/bt_9805.html) (attributing rise in personal bankruptcies to deregulation of credit card interest rates).

185 During the tenure of a Massachusetts Bank Commissioner with a reputation for consumer concern as well as the health of the industry, an industry request of an increase in small loans rates in Massachusetts was denied. The evidence indicated that the needs of efficiently operating lenders were adequately met by existing ceilings, while others were losing business because of non-competitiveness and inefficiency. The Commission denied a general rate hike, as the goal of the small loan rate was to encourage efficiently managed capital to the business, not to assure profits to inefficient, uncompetitive businesses. Greenleaf Finance Co. v. Small Loans Regulatory Bd., SJC-1415 (Feb. 12, 1979).

186 *See, e.g.*, Steven W. Bender, *Rate Regulation at the Crossroads of Usury and Unconscionability: The Case for Regulating Abusive and Commercial Interest Rates Under the Unconscionability Standard*, 31 Houston L. Rev. 721 (1994).

187 Consumer installment debt:

1950	$21.5 billion
1972	$137.2 billion
1981	$333.4 billion
1986	$567.4 billion
1993	$795.5 billion
2004	$1.3 trillion

Robin Morris, *Consumer Debt and Usury: A New Rationale for Usury*, 15 Pepperdine L. Rev. 151, 166 n.54 (1988); 80 Fed. Res. Bull. A39, Table 1.55 (Sept. 1994); Federal Reserve Board, Federal Reserve Statistical Release, Consumer Credit, (Jan. 2005, G.19), *available at* www.federalreserve.gov/releases/g19/.

188 Robin Morris, *Consumer Debt and Usury: A New Rationale for Usury*, 15 Pepperdine L. Rev. 151, 177–78 (1988). *See also* Diane Ellis, *Bank Trends—The Effect of Consumer Interest Rate Deregulation on Credit Card Volumes, Charge-Offs, and the Personal Bankruptcy Rate* (1999) (available at www.fdic.gov/bank/analytical/bank/bt_9805.html) (attributing rise in personal bankruptcies to exportation of interest rates).

2.4.2 Deregulation of the Residential Mortgage Market

The greatest effect of usury deregulation in most states has been on consumer credit secured by a first lien on residential real estate or mobile homes. As mentioned in the previous subsection, interest ceilings on first mortgage credit were preempted in 1980 subject to state opt-out rights. Yet, only sixteen jurisdictions opted out of the mortgage interest preemption,[189] which means that no limits exist on first mortgage interest rates in a majority of states.

A further deregulation of mortgage credit occurred in 1982 when Congress, in the Alternative Mortgage Transactions Parity Act (AMTPA),[190] allowed almost all state creditors issuing either senior or junior residential mortgage loans to follow some, but not all, of the then-recently-liberalized mortgage lending regulations which previously had applied only to federal depository lenders. Although AMTPA also contained an opt-out provision, only a few states took advantage of it,[191] so federal rather than state regulations now apply to a large majority of mortgage transactions. Under these regulations, creditors can issue variable rate mortgages, mortgage loans with large "balloon" payments at the end of their terms, and non-amortizing loans under whose provisions a borrower may pay only the interest portion of the mortgage debt without paying off any principal. (However, abuse of these privileges led to limited re-regulation in 1994.[192])

The intent of mortgage deregulation under both DIDMCA and AMTPA was to increase the supply of mortgage credit available to borrowers, purportedly to enable consumers to buy homes. Thus DIDMCA eliminated interest ceilings on first mortgage loans so that creditors could issue mortgages at profitable rates, and AMTPA enabled borrowers who could not qualify for a traditional fixed term mortgage to try to obtain credit through what were euphemistically called "creative financing techniques."[193] Unfortunately, as laudable as the goal of enabling individuals to buy homes may be, and as superficially sensible as the approaches of DIDMCA and AMTPA may seem, in practice these statutes have

proved overbroad and have placed a substantial amount of economic risk on homeowners.

DIDMCA is overbroad for several reasons. Most obviously, the complete elimination of interest ceilings instead of the imposition of a variable ceiling was entirely unnecessary for well-secured and, hence, low-risk credit such as first mortgages. Less apparent, but just as important, was the failure of DIDMCA to limit its preemptions to purchase-money mortgages. Instead, DIDMCA can apply to almost any credit secured by a first lien on real estate.[194] This loophole, in part, led to a proliferation of "home equity" lending since non-purchase mortgage loans may be secured by a first lien on real estate and are therefore covered by DIDMCA. Similarly, the absence of a purchase money provision in DIDMCA has enabled de facto second mortgage lenders to escape state usury regulation simply by paying off senior mortgages with the proceeds of a de facto second mortgage loan and then claiming first mortgage status. Through this gambit, low interest mortgages are replaced with high interest mortgages. Moreover, those higher rates are then applied to higher balances, since the new principal includes the pay-off balance of the prior, low-rate loan. As a result, costs spiral upward dramatically.[195]

Although the economic prudence of many of the mortgage provisions authorized by AMTPA is questionable even when employed with first mortgages, the main example of over breadth in AMTPA is its application to junior mortgages. It is not at all clear how the average home buyer is aided by the availability under AMTPA of such high-risk complexities as non-amortizing, variable-rate, balloon second mortgages. Yet it is clear how such credit can be extremely dangerous for the average second mortgage borrower—it can be very hard to pay off.

Mortgage deregulation has generally made the credit marketplace a riskier place for both home buyers and for home owners who may take out loans secured by their homes.[196] Many of the new credit terms are not well under-

---

189 For a list of opt-out states, see § 3.2.5, *infra* (Preemption Chart). It is important to distinguish DIDA's preemption of ceilings on interest rates, from which sixteen jurisdictions have opted out, and its preemption of state limitations on points and other charges, which does not require an express state opt-out to be removed. Close analysis of the law of each state is necessary to determine whether the state has opted out of the preemption of state limitations on points and other charges. See § 3.9.5.2, *infra*.

190 12 U.S.C. § 3801 *et. seq. See* § 3.10, *infra*.

191 *See* §§ 3.2.4, 3.10, *infra*.

192 *See* § 2.3.3.7, *supra*.

193 "Creative financing techniques" are essentially techniques which had traditionally been forbidden by state law or federal regulations because they were considered economically imprudent. *See* § 3.10, *infra*.

194 There are some limits. *See* § 3.9.3, *infra*.

195 Such overreaching might be challenged under UDAP statutes or common law theories. *See* Ch. 12, *infra*.

196 Subprime mortgage loan originations increased more than ninefold from 1994 to 2003—from $35 billion to about $332 billion. Roberto G. Quercia, Michael A. Stegman & Walter R. Davis, *The Impact of Predatory Loan Terms on Subprime Foreclosures: The Special Case of Prepayment Penalties and Balloon Payments,* Center for Community Capitalism (Jan. 25, 2005), *available at* www.kenan-flagler.unc.edu/assets/documents/foreclosurepaper.pdf (citing Mortgage Market Statistical Annual 2004). Within metropolitan areas alone, between 1993 and 2001, the subprime share of refinance loans climbed from 2.1% to 10.1%. *Id. (citing* FDIC data from 2004). Home equity lending has, unfortunately, been encouraged by the 1986 tax law which preserves the deduction for interest on consumer loans only if they are secured by the borrower's property. Although the purpose of this loophole was to preserve the deduction for mortgage interest, it is as overbroad as the usury

stood by most borrowers who may face unpleasant surprises in the form of balloon notes and interest rate increases; deregulated lines of credit secured by a borrower's home may lead to improvident borrowing. Yet, most importantly, the combination of variable rates and unlimited interest charges shifts greater risks onto even those homeowners and home buyers who borrow intelligently and for good cause. Global or national economic changes which cause a significant rise in market interest rates,[197] and are clearly beyond the control of individual consumers, can nevertheless place unbearable economic burdens on mortgage debtors and can force them to default or to sell their homes. Because of the sheer volume of mortgage lending, the implications of this risk on a large scale are clearly serious. There is a danger that mortgage deregulation has created not only a minefield for individuals, but a potential time bomb for the national economy. Indeed, the late 1980s and early 1990s saw record foreclosure rates.[198] Moreover, the inevitable correction of over-inflated real-estate values in some areas left some borrowers with mortgages greater than the value of their homes, and thus unable to refinance to take advantage of the lower interest rates of the early 1990s. The goals of mortgage deregulation could have been achieved by far more modest legislative changes.

The problem of predatory home equity lending had grown so great for the primary victims—minority, elderly and low-income borrowers—that Congress revisited the issue in 1993 and 1994.[199] In consequence, the Home Ownership and Equity Protection Act of 1994[200] somewhat circumscribed the damage done by AMTPA. It created a special category of closed-end, high-rate home equity mortgage, and, in those transactions alone, re-regulated some of the kinds of creative financing practices most commonly used by these lenders. The Act is described in greater detail in Chapter 11, *infra*.[201]

A growing development, especially among subprime mortgage lenders, is the securitization of debt. Instead of selling loans on the secondary market, the subprime lender groups the loans into pools and issues securities backed by the pool of mortgages. The securities are then sold by investment bankers to investors. Part of the interest on the loans paid by the borrowers goes to the investors. The remainder of the interest covers the risk of loss for the pool of loans and then goes to the lender to the extent that losses are not suffered in the pool of loans. A trustee supervises the loan servicer, distributes income to the investors, and files periodic reports on the financial status of pool of loans.[202]

Securitization tends to increase the supply of loan capital, and thus the pressure on loan originators to make more and more loans, including loans that are unnecessary and even harmful to consumers. It also tends to dilute the market's oversight of lenders. When loans are sold on the secondary market the file for each loan is reviewed by the buyer, but when debts are securitized the only review is done by bond rating agencies like Moody's, which look only at a small sample of the loans in a pool. As a result, problem loans are more likely to slip through, and there is less incentive for the originating lender to comply with state and federal consumer protection requirements.

Mortgage-backed securities are governed by highly complex agreements among the parties involved. Since there are few or no reporting requirements for non-depository lenders, their SEC filings provide the only public source of information about their practices.[203]

preemptions in DIDA and AMTPA because it is not limited to purchase money mortgages. *See Hearings on Problems in Community Development Banking, Mortgage Lending Discrimination, Reverse Redlining, and Home Equity Lending, Before the Senate Comm. on Banking, Housing and Urban Affairs*, 103d Cong., 1st Sess. 314–15 (Feb. 3, 17, 24, 1993) (S. Hrg. 103-137; ISBN:0-16-041270-6, for sale by GPO) for discussion of additional encouraging factors.

197 Individual misfortunes such as illness or unemployment can obviously cause borrowers to lose their homes too. Such calamities were possible with traditional mortgages as well, but the current proliferation of non-mortgage credit secured by a borrower's home, such as home equity lines of credit, means that a consumer's home will more frequently be at risk than it traditionally had been.

198 From 1980 to 1991, the foreclosure rate more than doubled. Though it declined during some periods, it never reached the starting level. Projections from Mortgage Bankers Association of America data indicated that nearly half a million more foreclosures were started in 1989 than 1980. *See* R. Hobbs, *Foreclosure in America* (NCLC for Rockefeller Family Fund, 1991). More recently, disturbing rates of foreclosure in the subprime market have come to light. Twenty percent of subprime loans originated from 1998 to 2000 were the subject of at least one foreclosure filing in the six-year period 1998 to 2003. Of those loans, 60% resulted in a foreclosure sale or home loss within the study period and another 20% were still in foreclosure. Roberto G. Quercia, Michael A. Stegman & Walter R. Davis, *The Impact of Predatory Loan Terms on Subprime Foreclosures: The Special Case of Prepayment Penalties and Balloon Payments*, Center for Community Capitalism (Jan. 25, 2005), *available at* www.kenan-flagler.unc.edu/assets/documents/foreclosurepaper.pdf (citing Mortgage Market Statistical Annual 2004).

199 *See, e.g., Hearings on Problems in Community Development Banking, Mortgage Lending Discrimination, and Home Equity Lending, Before the Senate Comm. on Banking, Housing and Urban Affairs*, 103d Cong., 1st Sess. (Feb. 3, 17, 24, 1993) (S. Hrg. 103-137; ISBN:0-16-041270-6, for sale by GPO). To a large extent, it was considered a civil rights matter, and linked to greater emphasis on regulatory and private enforcement of fair lending requirements on market-rate lenders. *Id.*

200 *See* § 12.2.2, *infra*.

201 *See also* National Consumer Law Center, Truth in Lending Ch. 9 (5th ed. 2003 and Supp.).

202 For example, 6% may be paid to the investors, but if the interest rate on the loans is 14% the remaining 8% would go first to cover losses in the pool and then to the lender. See § 11.3, *infra*, for further discussion of securitization.

203 Cathy Lesser Mansfield, *The Road to Subprime "HEL" Was Paved with Good Congressional Intentions: Usury Deregulation and the Subprime Home Equity Market*, 51 S.C. L. Rev. 473

2.5 Post-Deregulation: The Next Generation

The consumer credit marketplace was, for the most part, born at the beginning of the twentieth century. As the twenty-first century begins, the nature of consumer credit has changed enormously in some respects—especially the growth of the use of the family home as a tool for access to credit. As noted in the preceding subsection, along with that growth came abuses in the home equity mortgage market which led to minimal re-regulation.[204]

But in other respects, the market has come full circle. Particularly in the area of very small, short-term credit, the situation facing the policy-makers who designed the Uniform Small Loan Laws at the beginning of the century is resurfacing at its end.

Many of the finance companies, which grew out of that effort,[205] have themselves moved out of the genuinely small loan business into larger-balance, home-secured lending. This may not be a problem for most consumers, who typically use credit cards or retail charge accounts for small-sum, short-term credit. But for other consumers, a variety of alternate sources with effective rates that would make a loan shark jealous have sprung up. "Post-dated check loans," which operate with remarkable similarity to the old salary lenders,[206] are being offered (legally or not) in many states. These loans, in small amounts, for terms of only a week or so at a time, may have effective interest rates of 700 to 2000%.[207] Pawnbrokers are with us still, but some have developed new variations, such as the "auto-pawn," in which the borrower "pawns the title, and keeps the car." This is essentially an auto-secured loan at pawnbrokers' rates of over 900%.[208] Rent-to-own companies provide a species of retail sales credit for household goods at effective rates which can reach triple digits.[209] It is not unknown for those small loan companies which still do specialize in genuinely small loans to lend at triple-digit APRs.[210]

Such devices can be a challenge for practitioners to effectively address in a deregulated environment, though there clearly are grounds to do so.[211] But as to whether the resurgence of such players in the consumer credit market will again lead to a movement for strong regulatory reform in the new millennium remains to be seen.[212]

(2000). The EDGAR database, containing SEC filings, is available on line at www.sec.gov.

204 *See* §§ 2.3.3.7, 2.4.2, *supra.*

205 §§ 2.2.3.1, 2.3.1.3.1, 2.3.3.2, *supra.*

206 *See* § 2.2.3.1, *supra.*

207 *See* § 7.5.5, *infra. See also* Creola Johnson, *Payday Loans: Shrewd Business or Predatory Lending?*, 87 Minn. L. Rev. 1 (Nov. 2002) (analyzing survey data that vividly portrays the payday lending industry's abuses).

208 § 7.5.2.3, *infra.*

209 §§ 7.5.3.2–7.5.3.6, *infra. See* Creola Johnson, *Welfare Reform and Asset Accumulation: First We Need a Bed and a Car*, 2000 Wis. L. Rev. 1221 (2000) (describing the reasons welfare recipients are forced into RTO transactions to acquire basic necessities).

210 NCLC has received copies of such loans from Legal Services attorneys in Utah (deregulated) and Micronesia (still regulated).

211 In addition to the sections referred to above, see also § 9.2.8, and Ch. 11, *infra.*

212 *Cf. In re* Coxson, 43 F.3d 189 (5th Cir. 1995) (noting that Texas had abandoned usury laws during Reconstruction, but reintroduced them when credit abuses arose in their absence).

Chapter 3	**Federal Preemption of State Laws Limiting Credit Charges and Regulating the Terms and Conditions of Lending**

3.1 Introduction

3.1.1 Overview of the Relevant Statutes

Determining the legal limitations on consumer credit costs is greatly complicated by the existence of numerous federal statutes and regulations that preempt state usury and other laws with respect to some, but not all lenders, transactions, and practices which might otherwise lead to illegal overcharges[1] and to other claims based on overreaching behavior.[2]

While some of the current credit preemption debates present fascinating issues for constitutional scholars, it is assumed that most people will only read this chapter if they think they have to. Given the ever-expanding scope and complex nature of credit preemption, this chapter is now a "must-read." So, as a public service, this section will begin with an overview of the relevant federal preemption statutes, and follow with an analysis checklist and a chart listing applicable federal statutes and regulations.

To generalize somewhat, preemption of state usury and lending laws, to the extent permitted, is authorized by eight different federal statutes.[3]

First, the National Bank Act (NBA)[4] sets the ceiling for interest rates that may be charged by federally-chartered banks. Under this Act, federal banks are treated as "most favored lenders" and may charge the higher of: (1) the interest rate allowed lenders in the state where the bank is located; or (2) one percent above the discount rate on ninety-day commercial paper in effect at the Federal Reserve Bank in the district where the bank is located. This "most favored lender" status may be transported across state lines under certain circumstances. The NBA and court decisions also permit banks to operate in derogation of other types of state laws if those laws impair, destroy, or significantly interfere with federally-authorized bank functions.[5]

The second statute preempting state usury laws is the Home Owners' Loan Act (HOLA) enacted in 1933.[6] This act authorizes the Office of Thrift Supervision to provide for the organization, incorporation, examination, and regulation of federal savings associations. Like the NBA, HOLA sets the ceiling for interest rates that may be charged by these federal associations. Federal savings associations are likewise treated as "most favored lenders" and may charge the greater of: (1) 1% above the discount rate on 90-day commercial paper in effect at the Federal Reserve bank in the district in which such savings association is located; or (2) the rate allowed by the laws of the state in which the savings association is located.[7] Like national banks, federal associa-

---

1   To further complicate matters, one of the hotly litigated questions has been what, exactly, is a usury law regulating "interest rates." *See* § 3.4.5.2, *infra*.

2   See Chapter 11, *infra*, for an overview of non-usury claims that may be available to defend against creditor misbehavior.

3   This chapter concentrates on preemption statutes which may apply in consumer cases. Commercial usury preemption statutes are not fully treated. *See, e.g.*, Fed. Deposit Ins. Corp. v. Wood, 758 F.2d 156 (6th Cir. 1985), *cert. denied*, 474 U.S. 944 (1985) (FDIC, as receiver of a failed bank, is not subject to usury defense on assumed note); Fourchon v. La. Nat'l Leasing Corp., 723 F.2d 376 (5th Cir. 1984), *rev'g* 548 F. Supp. 1258 (M.D. La. 1982) ("interest rate" and "rate of interest" in preemptive federal Ship Mortgage Act includes interest on interest, which Louisiana law forbids); Fed. Land Bank of St. Louis v. Wilson, 719 F.2d 1367 (8th Cir. 1983) (12 U.S.C. § 2015 (1971) preempts Arkansas farm credit usury laws); Fed. Deposit Ins. Corp. v. Lattimore Land Corp, 656 F.2d 139 (5th Cir. 1981) (preemption of Georgia usury law). Also not treated here is the functional preemption associated with federal government agencies

which are successors in interest to private (and usually bankrupt) lenders. *See generally* § 10.7, *infra* for a discussion of special defenses of federal receivers.

A few federal statutes have specifically been held not to preempt state usury laws. *See In re* Seolas, 140 B.R. 266 (E.D. Cal. 1992) (ERISA does not preempt Cal. general usury law, despite Cal. law exempting ERISA from state usury limits; court held latter statute was preempted by ERISA, and yes, court recognized this seems odd; *id.* at n.8); Visioneering Inc. Profit Sharing Trust v. Belle River Joint Venture, 149 Mich. App. 327, 386 N.W.2d 185 (1986) (ERISA).

4   12 U.S.C. §§ 85, 86. Selected provisions of the NBA appear in Appx. C.1, *infra*.

5   *See* § 3.4.6.1, *infra*.

6   12 U.S.C. § 1461 *et seq*. Selected portions of HOLA appear in Appx. D.1, *infra*.

7   12 U.S.C. § 1463(g).

tions may export this most favored lender status across state lines. Unlike the NBA, however, the OTS interprets HOLA as occupying the field of lending regulation. Consequently, state law is completely preempted, unless the OTS says otherwise.[8]

Third, the National Credit Union Administration (NCUA) allows federally-chartered credit unions to assess interest of up to 15% per annum or any higher temporary rate set by the National Credit Union Administration Board.[9] Using this discretion, the Board raised the federal credit union ceiling to 21% in 1980. Since May 14, 1987, the rate has been set at 18% and will revert to 15% after September 8, 2006 unless extended.[10] Beyond usury issues, the preemption rights of federal credit unions are narrower than those granted or claimed by national banks or federal savings association.[11]

Fourth, pursuant to the National Housing Act, housing loans insured by the Federal Housing Administration (FHA) or the Veteran's Administration (VA) are exempted from state interest ceilings.[12] As the authority of the FHA to set its own ceiling has been revoked,[13] new FHA-insured housing loans have no interest ceiling even, arguably, in situations where DIDA does not apply, such as junior mortgages. Similarly, the parties to a VA-insured loan may agree to any interest rate. However, states may opt out of the FHA/VA preemption, so this form of preemption consequently will not apply in all jurisdictions.

The fifth statute preempting state usury law is the Depository Institutions Deregulation and Monetary Control Act of 1980 (DIDA or DIDMCA).[14] This law appears to extend the "most favored lender" treatment regarding interest rates for federally-chartered banks to any federally-*insured* commercial bank (including state-chartered federally-insured banks), savings association, or credit union. In the special case of loans secured by first mortgages on residential real estate or first liens on mobile homes, DIDA has essentially eliminated interest rate ceilings and has preempted state limitations on a lender's ability to assess "points," finance charges, or "other charges." States may "opt out" of the federal DIDA preemption through appropriate legislation, and at least fifteen states exercised this option to some extent. Many of these states, however, have repealed their opt-outs. Those that retain their opt-out can deregulate their state usury caps as well.

Sixth, the 1982 Depository Institutions Act (DIA) has preempted many state consumer credit restrictions without affecting state *interest rate* ceilings. In particular, Title VIII of the Act, known as the Alternative Mortgage Transactions Parity Act (AMTPA),[15] was designed to eliminate state laws restricting "creative [home] finance," e.g., state laws that require equal monthly payments, limit variable interest rates, or prohibit final "balloon" payments or negative amortization.[16] However, AMTPA also contains a limited "opt out" provision and so may not apply in all states.

Seventh, the Interstate Banking and Branching Efficiency Act of 1994 (IBBEA) (commonly called the Riegle-Neal Act),[17] which allows banks to establish branch banks in other states, continues (but does not expand), the current preemption authorized by the NBA and DIDA. Congress took special pains to emphasize that state consumer protection and fair lending laws apply to the extent not preempted by federal law, which certainly is an unmistakable message that it has no intent to "occupy the field" of consumer protection, thus leaving states free to continue to do so except where the *other* traditional tests for preemption dictate.[18] Indeed, the conference report admonished the national bank regulator not to find federal preemption unless "the legal basis is compelling and the Federal policy is clear."[19] Further, the Act imposes publication requirements regarding the issuance of agency opinions addressing national bank preemption of certain types of state law.[20]

Eighth, most recently, Congress enacted the Gramm-Leach-Bliley Act (GLB Act) that largely focuses upon eliminating the barriers separating the banking, insurance, and securities industries.[21] One provision, though, should have an effect on the ability of a limited number of states (perhaps only Arkansas!) to regulate the interest rates of the banks chartered within their boundaries in certain circum-

---

8   *See* § 3.5.3, *infra.*

9   *See* 12 U.S.C. § 1757(5)(A)(vi).

10 *See* 12 C.F.R. § 701.21(c)(7)(ii)(C); 70 Fed. Reg. 3861 (Jan. 27, 2005).

11 *See* 12 C.F.R. § 701.21(b)(2) *discussed in* § 3.6, *infra.*

12 12 U.S.C. § 1709-1a; 38 U.S.C. § 3728.

13 *See* 12 U.S.C. § 1709(b)(5).

14 Pub. L. No. 96-221, 94 Stat. 161 (1980) (codified throughout Title 12 of the U.S. Code, including 12 U.S.C. § 1831d(a) (state commercial banks), 12 U.S.C. § 1463(g) (savings and loans), 12 U.S.C. § 1785(g) (federally-insured credit unions), and 12 U.S.C. § 1735f-7a (mortgages)). See Appx. G, *infra* for statutory text.

15 12 U.S.C. § 3801.

16 This deregulation led to abuse sufficient to persuade Congress to impose limited re-regulation of some creative financing terms in certain transactions. *See* §§ 11.5.1, 12.2.2, *infra.*

17 12 U.S.C. § 36.

18 H.R. Conf. Rep. No. 103-651, at 53–55 (1994), *reprinted in* 1994 U.S.C.C.A.N. 2068, 2074–2076.

    There are three traditional preemption tests: is the state law in direct conflict with federal law; is federal law so comprehensive as to evidence a congressional intent to "occupy the field," or does the state law stand as an obstacle to achieving the purpose of the federal law. Where possible, state statutes should be construed to avoid finding a conflict.

19 H.R. Conf. Rep. No. 103-651, at 54–55 (1994), *reprinted in* 1994 U.S.C.C.A.N. 2068, 2074–2076. *See generally* Pennsylvania v. Nelson, 350 U.S. 497 (1956); 16 Am. Jur. 2d *Constitutional Law* § 291.

20 12 U.S.C. § 43.

21 Pub. L. No. 106-102 (1999), *codified as* 15 U.S.C. § 6701 *et seq.,* § 6801 *et seq.,* § 6901 *et seq., and amending* 12 U.S.C. § 1831u.

stances.[22] In addition, the GLB Act eliminates some barriers to banks and their operating subsidiaries from engaging in credit insurance sales, solicitations, or cross-marketing activity. This aspect of the GLB Act is addressed in § 8.4.1.5.2, *infra*.

Finally, some federal consumer protection legislation may preempt inconsistent or less protective state law. The Truth in Lending Act (TILA)[23] created a very narrow preemption of the disclosure terminology that may be required by state usury laws. Generally, state consumer credit statutes may not define TILA credit terms differently than they are defined by federal regulation and may not require the use of a different term for an amount identically calculated under TILA. The preemption is limited, however, and normally will not, for example, prevent states from compelling more extensive or detailed disclosure than that required under TILA.

Likewise, the 1994 Home Ownership and Equity Protection Act, (HOEPA)[24] which amends TILA, imposes substantive restrictions on some contract terms with respect to certain transactions. Less protective state laws are preempted.[25] Similarly, the 1992 federal rebate law, which requires rebates in consumer credit transactions and limits the use of the cost-distorting Rule of 78, preempts contrary state law.[26]

The most significant consequences of federal intervention in usury law have been felt since 1980. At that time, there was a dramatic increase in interest rates and other fees that may be charged by most depository institutions, such as banks, savings and loans, and credit unions.[27] Moreover, in the mortgage context, an increase occurred in the cost of credit from non-depository lenders such as mortgage companies and finance companies. It is significant that with respect to some transactions (credit cards and some types of home equity lending), the increase has persisted even when market rates fell.[28]

As may be surmised from this outline, federal preemption has significantly undermined state consumer protections regarding credit charges and lending. State protections have been further eroded by state deregulation, directly and through so-called "parity" laws. While state parity statutes take many forms, they are essentially attempts, comparable to the federal most favored lender approach, to put state lenders on an equal footing with federal lenders by allowing them to lend on the same terms. The result of these parity laws, however, is that the liberal federal lending rates and regulations may be extended across the board to state, as well as federal lending institutions.

3.1.2 Organization of This Chapter

The chapter first provides a step-by-step guide and discussion in § 3.2, which will help determine whether preemption may be an issue on a particular transaction. Following that is a chart, which summarizes the federal statutes and regulations pertinent to preemption, and which states have opted out of those federal statutes.

Section 3.3 provides an overview of the alphabet soup of federal regulatory agencies; what agency has interpretive authority for which statutes, and what agency regulates which lenders. Each of the preemptive federal statutes is dealt with in turn in §§ 3.4–3.11, broken down according to the type of lender and nature of the state regulation that may be preempted.

The preemptive effect of various federal statutes that provide consumer protections is briefly noted in § 3.12. "Renting" the charter of a depository institution is described in § 3.13. Section 3.14 addresses state parity laws and their impact on usury laws. Finally, § 3.15 covers relevant jurisdictional issues that have arisen in conjunction with certain usury preemption claims.

Many of the pertinent federal statutes and regulations are reprinted in Appendices C–J.

3.2 Checking for Preemption: A Summary Guide

3.2.1 First Steps

Determining whether some form of federal preemption applies to a particular credit transaction can be a tricky task for both the novice and the experienced practitioner. This section contains a summary analysis and discussion that a practitioner may use to approach usury preemption. The accompanying preemption chart is a guide to the applicable statutes and regulations. Permissible state opt-outs are noted.

---

22 Section 731, *amending* 12 U.S.C. § 1831u(f). For a discussion of this provision, see § 3.11, *infra*.

23 15 U.S.C. §§ 1601 *et. seq.*, *implemented by* 12 C.F.R. § 226 (Regulation Z). *See generally* National Consumer Law Center, Truth in Lending §§ 2.6.3, 2.7 (5th ed. 2003 and Supp.).

24 Home Ownership and Equity Protection Act, Subtitle B of Title I, Riegle Community Development and Regulatory Improvement Act of 1994, Pub. L. No. 103-325, 108 Stat. 2160.

25 *See generally* §§ 5.9, 12.2.2, *infra*.

26 15 U.S.C. § 1615. This statute is *reprinted in* Appx. J.2, *infra*. *See generally* §§ 5.2.2, 5.9, *infra*.

27 *See* Cathy Lesser Mansfield, *The Road to Subprime "HEL" Was Paved with Good Congressional Intentions: Usury Deregulation and the Subprime Home Equity Market*, 51 S.C. L. Rev. 473 (2000).

28 *See, e.g.*, §§ 3.4.5, 3.6.2.2 (credit card exportation under both the NBA and DIDA), 11.5 (equity-skimming), *infra*. *See also* Tamara Draut & Javier Silva, *Borrowing to Make Ends Meet: The Growth of Credit Card Debt in the 90's*, 34 (DEMOS 2003).

3.2.2 Preemption Analysis: A Step-by-Step Guide

3.2.2.1 Overview

STEPS	ANALYSIS
1	Determine if the transaction is credit.
2	If credit, decide what type of loan it is, i.e., mortgage or non-mortgage.
3	Identify the type of lender.
4	Which state's law would apply but for preemption?
5	Which of that applicable state's lending/usury laws apply?
6	Who is the loan holder?

3.2.2.2 Step One: Is the Transaction Credit?

A lender may dress a loan in the clothing of some other type of transaction in order to avoid various consumer protection laws, not the least of which are state usury laws and the federal Truth in Lending Act.[29] In evaluating a transaction, it is important not take labels at face value. Substance usually prevails over form.[30] For a discussion of the more common types of disguised loans, see § 7.5, *infra*. The elements of a loan are described in § 10.5, *infra*.

3.2.2.3 Step Two: What Type of Loan Is It?

The next step to approaching federal preemption should be to distinguish residential real estate loans, including the credit sale of mobile homes or any loan secured by the consumer's residence, from non-mortgage loans. Check the Truth in Lending disclosure, the loan note, any mortgage, or security agreement to see if the loan is secured and by what type of property.

The federal laws and regulations permitting the preemption of state usury and non-usury lending laws are broader when it comes to mortgage loans. The preemption distinctions between mortgage and non-mortgage loans are described in § 3.2.3 and 3.2.4, *infra*.

3.2.2.4 Step Three: Identify the Type of Lender

At this stage, the practitioner must decide whether the original lender is a national bank, federal savings association, federal credit union, state-chartered depository, an operating subsidiary of these, or a state-chartered or licensed non-depository lender. If one of these depository institutions in involved, it is a good bet that preemption is an issue. Whether a claim of preemption is valid is another story, one that is addressed in §§ 3.4–3.13, *infra*.

Often the lender's name will make this identification process easy. Certain words or abbreviations that appear in the lender's name are good clues. The chart below decodes this information for you.[31]

WHAT DOES THE NAME HAVE TO DO WITH IT?

IF THE LENDER HAS THIS IN ITS NAME:	IT IS A:
National Bank	national bank
N.A.	national bank
Federal Savings Bank	federal savings bank
F.S.B.	federal savings bank
Federal Savings	federal savings association
F.A.	federal savings association
State Bank	state-chartered bank
Bank or Savings Bank (without the word "National" in front of "Bank")	state-chartered bank
S.S.B.	state savings bank
Savings (other than "savings bank" or "federal savings bank")	state-chartered savings association
S.A.	state-chartered savings association
Credit Union	credit union

To eliminate the guesswork, however, practitioners may check the Federal Deposit Insurance Corporation's website.[32]

The more difficult situation arises when the lender does not appear to be a depository institution. In this case, the lender is likely to be either affiliated in some way with a depository institution or a state-regulated finance company. For information on how to determine if a lender is an operating subsidiary of a national bank, see § 3.4.6.4, *infra,* or is an operating subsidiary of a federal savings association, see § 3.5.4, *infra*. Another place to check is the state's appropriate regulatory agency to see if the lender is a licensed lender. If so, then it is likely to be a finance company that is not a subsidiary of a depository institution.[33]

---

29 For a discussion about disguised credit for Truth in Lending purposes, see National Consumer Law Center, Truth in Lending §§ 2.1.2, 2.5 (5th ed. 2003 and Supp.). *See also* § 1.6.3, *supra*, regarding analyzing the legal issues in a credit transaction.

30 *See* cases cited in § 9.2.1.6, *infra*.

31 Thanks to Patricia McCoy, Professor of Law, the University of Connecticut School of Law, for this chart.

32 Visit www2.fdic.gov/structur/search/findoneinst.asp and then type in the name of the institution and click on "Find My Institution." The search will tell you if the bank has FDIC insurance and the name of the primary regulator.

33 The OCC did not grants preemption rights to national bank subsidiaries formally until 2001. *See* § 3.4.6.4. As a result, some operating subsidiaries may continue to renew their state licenses inadvertently or due to inertia. Companies purchased by national banks since 2001 that become operating subsidiaries may also show up on agency records as licensed for a period of time as well.

3.2.2.5 Step Four: Which State's Law Would Ordinarily Apply?

The issue to resolve at this step is whether the law of the state in which the consumer resided at the time the loan was made applies or whether the law of some other state applies. The result of this analysis depends on where the transaction occurred, whether the lender had an office or some presence in the consumer's state, if the lender is a depository or operating subsidiary, where the depository is chartered, and whether the loan note or related documents contained a valid choice of law provision.

If the loan was made in the consumer's home state and the lender did business in that state through a storefront, then that home state's law would ordinarily apply, absent a valid choice of law provision to the contrary. However, if the residence or place of business of both parties, the real estate securing the loan, and the place where the loan was negotiated or executed are not all located in the same state, then conflicts of law analysis comes into play. For a discussion of these issues, see § 9.2.9, *infra*.

If the lender is a depository or an operating subsidiary of a depository, the law of the state where the depository is chartered, at least for usury purposes, is implicated. If the depository is chartered in a state where the consumer does not reside, then it is likely that the bank is "exporting" its home state's rate.[34] This almost always means that the bank is chartered in a state with no or very high usury caps.

On the other hand, if the depository is chartered in the consumer's home state or if the loan is "made"[35] at a branch of the depository in the consumer's home state, then the consumer's home state usury cap ordinarily applies.

Regardless of where the depository is chartered, the non-usury law of a state will apply to some aspects of the transaction. However, federal statutes and regulations purport to preempt a large swath of non-usury state law.[36]

3.2.2.6 Step Five: Which of the State's Usury Law Governs the Loan?

Once the practitioner concludes that the transaction is governed by a particular state's law, the next step is to figure out whether that state has any usury or lending laws that would apply to the transaction at issue. Chapter 2 contains an overview of the generic types of lending laws that states have enacted over the years.

3.2.2.7 Step Six: Who Is the Loan Holder?

If the loan holder did not originate the loan, it may be entitled, nonetheless, to preemption under federal statutes and regulations discussed in this chapter in at least two circumstances: (1) the loan originator was entitled to preempt the specific state law at issue;[37] (2) the claims that the consumer wishes to raise against the holder are based on the holder's own behavior (as opposed to the behavior of the originator or parties acting in concert with the originator) and the holder is protected from state law by the preemption doctrine.[38]

In the first situation, if the originating lender[39] is protected from certain state laws by preemption, then the holder or assignee may cloak itself in preemption if the claims are based on the behavior of the originator. The second situation arises, for example, when the holder or assignee is a depository institution entitled to preemption and the holder itself violates a state law. In this case, the preemption regime applicable to that type of depository institution may trump the state law claims.

3.2.3 Distinctions Based on the Type of Loan and the Location of its "Making"

3.2.3.1 Non-Mortgage Loans/Intrastate

The preemption of non-mortgage usury law normally is restricted to the amount of interest or other charges a lender may assess and, potentially, to other terms "material" to the interest rate,[40] and applies only to federally-insured depository lenders. Hence, the character of the lender is the controlling factor. All national banks and, as of 1980, all other federally-insured lenders located in states which did not opt out of this section of DIDA,[41] may lend at rates up to the federal alternative ceiling.[42] Federal credit unions may also charge the current rate set by the National Credit Union Administration.[43] National banks and savings associations may invoke the most favored lender doctrine to issue loans at the highest rate which state law allows any lender making

---

34 See discussion in § 3.4.5, *infra*.
35 For a discussion of the OCC's definition of where a loan is "made," see § 3.5.1.2, *infra*. *See also* the OTS's more expansive definition in § 3.5.3.
36 *See* §§ 3.4–3.12, *infra*.

37 *See* § 3.4.5.1.3, *infra*.
38 See in particular the broad preemption regulations applicable to national banks and federal savings associations described in §§ 3.4, 3.5, *infra*.
39 In 2004, the OCC issued an Interpretive Letter in which it opines that a national bank table-funding a loan is not an assignee but should be treated as the original lender, even though its name is not listed as the lender on the loan documents, relying on the definition of "lender" in the Real Estate Settlement Procedures Act. *Compare* OCC Interpretive Letter No. 1000 (Apr. 2, 2004) *with* OCC Interpretive Letter No. 1002 (May 13, 2004), summarized in Appx. C.3, *infra*. These letters are *reprinted in* full on the accompanying CD-Rom.
40 *See* § 3.4.3.4, *infra*.
41 *See* § 3.9.4, *infra*.
42 *See* §§ 3.4.2, 3.9.2.1, *infra*.
43 *See* § 3.6, *infra*.

comparable loans.[44] Other federally-insured depository lenders also now claim most favored lender status under DIDA, and the cases to date have generally accepted that claim.[45]

Note that preemption of non-mortgage usury applies only to federally-insured depository lenders. It does not extend, for example, to finance companies or other non-depository lenders or even to state depository lenders who lack federal insurance.[46] The only exception is the case of the operating subsidiaries of national banks and federal savings associations.[47]

Preemption also does not cover non-mortgage loans made by any lender, except national banks, federal saving associations (and their operating subsidiaries), and credit unions, if the lender is located in a state that opted out of DIDA §§ 521–523 and the loan in question was made after the state opted out.[48]

Finally, the regulations promulgated by the Office of the Comptroller of the Currency (OCC) governing national banks, by the Office of Thrift Supervision (OTS) governing federal savings associations, and, to a lesser extent, by the National Credit Union Administration (NCUA) governing federal credit unions, create long lists of state laws governing the terms of the loan that *are* preempted.[49]

3.2.3.2 Non-Mortgage Loans/Interstate

The question of the scope of federal preemption in interstate transactions has been the subject of a substantial amount of litigation. Both national banks (under the National Bank Act) and federally-insured lenders (under DIDA) are marketing credit cards and other types of loans from their home state base and "exporting" the law of that state nationwide. They are generally located in states which have no limits on "interest" rates, and which may statutorily define that term very broadly, usually encompassing charges not considered to be interest under traditional usury analysis. Virtually any time a practitioner sees a credit card late charge, over the limit fee, or other charge that exceeds state law limits, federal preemption and exportation rights under the NBA or DIDA will be at the heart of the legal analysis.[50]

The Supreme Court first dealt with this issue in 1978.[51] It again revisited the exportation controversy in 1996 regarding late fees on credit card accounts.[52] The Court sanctioned the exportation of late fees by giving deference to a regulation promulgated by the Comptroller of the Currency.[53] The Fourth Circuit also upheld the practice in a case involving refund anticipation loans extended electronically by an out-of-state national bank through an agreement with tax preparers in the borrower's home state.[54]

Given current technology, these cases raise worrisome implications for the future. Major finance companies, traditionally lending subject to special usury laws such as small loan laws and consumer finance laws containing consumer protections, have begun to obtain national bank, saving association or operating subsidiary status in deregulated states and are "exporting" unregulated small loans from there.[55] Federal preemption has gone farther than anyone—

---

44 *See* §§ 3.4.3, 3.5.2, *infra*.

45 E.g., Greenwood Trust Co. v. Massachusetts, 971 F.2d 818 (1st Cir. 1992); Gavey Properties/762 v. First Fin. Sav. & Loan Ass'n, 845 F.2d 519 (5th Cir. 1988); *see* §§ 3.4.3, 3.5.2, *infra*.

46 Be careful making assumptions, though. Some very familiar names in finance companies have now set up affiliations with national bank charters in order to take advantage of federal preemption.

47 *See* §§ 3.4.6.4, 3.5.4, *infra*.

48 *See* §§ 3.2.3.2, 3.4.5, 3.9.2.2, 3.9.4, *infra*, for the complications in interstate transactions. What the term "located" means for purposes of interest rate preemption for both national banks and federally-insured lenders is discussed in § 3.4.5.1.2, *infra*.

49 *See* §§ 3.4.6, 3.5.3, 3.6, *infra*.

50 *See* §§ 3.4.5, 3.9.2.2, *infra*.

51 Marquette Nat'l Bank of Minneapolis v. First of Omaha Serv.

Corp., 439 U.S. 299 (1978) (§ 85 allows a national bank to charge out-of-state credit card customers an interest rate allowed by the bank's home state, even when the rate is higher than what is permitted by the states in which the cardholders reside). *See* § 3.4.5.1, *infra*.

52 Smiley v. Citibank (S.D.), N.A., 517 U.S. 735, 116 S. Ct. 1730, 135 L. Ed. 2d 25 (1996). For a more in-depth discussion of *Smiley*, see 3.4.5.2, *infra*.

53 12 C.F.R. 7.4001(a); 61 Fed. Reg. 4869 (Feb. 9, 1996).

54 Cades v. H & R Block, Inc., 43 F.3d 869 (4th Cir. 1994); *see also* Christiansen v. Beneficial Nat'l Bank, 972 F. Supp. 681 (S.D. Ga. 1997) (Beneficial did not create "branch" offices in Georgia by extending loans through H & R Block offices in Georgia; therefore, the law of the state which is the bank's home state, in this case Delaware, applied); Basile v. H & R Block, Inc., 897 F. Supp. 194 (E.D. Pa. 1995) (plaintiffs challenge to the APR through a Pennsylvania UDAP statute failed; court held that because the claim arose from the national bank's interest rate charges, it was preempted by the National Bank Act). Note that other claims against such lenders can succeed. *See* § 7.5.4.2, *infra*.

55 This is exactly what has happened in the payday loan context. State FDIC-insured banks operate their main bank offices in a state that exempts payday lending from small loan act restrictions (including usury caps) and then make these loans through a national network of check-cashers or payday lenders. National banks were in this business until 2003, at which time the Office of the Comptroller of the Currency ended all such activity by national banks. *See* § 3.13, *infra*. *See also* Jean Ann Fox, Consumer Federation of America, Unsafe and Unsound: Payday Lenders Hide Behind FDIC Bank Charters to Peddle Usury 18, 19 (Mar. 2004), *available at* www.consumerfed.org (click on "payday loans" under "Finance"). The capacity for mischief inherent in this expansion of exportation authority is also exemplified by a situation reported by a consumer advocate in Michigan. A Michigan auto dealer arranged financing for its Michigan customers through a New York bank, purportedly to circumvent Michigan's former restriction on finders' fees to retail sellers. Mich. Comp. Laws § 492.131(a), (c). The OCC upheld the application of preemption principles to both the national bank and the car dealer, as agent, in a Preemption Determination issued in 2001. 66 Fed. Reg. 28593 (May 23, 2001). *See* § 3.4.6.1, *infra*. This is an ominous sign for consumers: combine the effects of both exportation and yield spread premiums in auto financing, and one can expect used car loan rates to rise even higher soon, despite any limitations in local motor vehicle retail installment sales acts (see §§ 11.5.4.3, 12.6, *infra*, for a discussion of yield spread premiums).

Congress included—ever envisioned. As is noted elsewhere, in 1994 Congress expressed concern about how far some preemption interpretations have gone and reinforced its position that states have "a legitimate interest in protecting the rights of their consumers."[56]

3.2.4 Mortgage Loans

3.2.4.1 Preemption of State Laws Regarding Interest Rates and Charges

Preemption of residential mortgage regulation is complicated because not only interest rate ceilings, but also the structure and terms of mortgage loans may be affected. Regarding mortgage interest ceilings, the most important preemptive statute is DIDA § 501 which, as of 1980, eliminated interest ceilings on all first residential mortgage loans and all loans giving a first lien on a mobile home, with the following provisos:[57]

- First, states were allowed to opt out of DIDA, so the preemption is inapplicable in some states.[58]
- Second, although most lenders are covered by the statute, the preemption may not reach some small lenders or credit sellers.
- Third, if the mortgage is originated by a lender not covered by the statute (e.g., a small home improvement contractor or broker), even a covered lender who holds the debt as an assignee cannot assert preemption rights.[59]
- Fourth, in order for credit sales of mobile homes to have preemptive protection, the sellers or lenders must comply with a set of consumer protection regulations promulgated by the Office of Thrift Supervision (OTS).[60]

If DIDA does not apply to a mortgage loan, because, for example, the loan is a junior mortgage, the lender purchased the loan from a non-covered lender, or the lender fails to comply with the mobile home consumer protection regulations, state usury law will apply unless some other preemptive statute applies. Other preemptive statutes which one should consider include the National Bank Act if the lender is a national bank,[61] the Home Owners' Loan Act if the lender is a federal savings association,[62] DIDA §§ 521–523 if the lender is another depository lender,[63] the National Credit Union Act, if the lender is a federally-chartered credit union,[64] or the National Housing Act if the loan is FHA- or VA-insured.[65]

3.2.4.2 Preemption of Other Mortgage Contract Terms

Turning to the structure of the residential mortgage loans, federally-chartered banks, savings and loans, and credit unions are controlled by federal mortgage regulations that preempt state law. First, the enabling statutes for national banks, federal savings associations, and federal credit unions have been interpreted by regulation to permit these depositories to preempt state laws related to the terms and conditions of the loan, not just the interest rates and fees.[66]

Second, as of 1982, licensed state housing creditors, including non-depository lenders or credit sellers which "regularly make" mortgage loans, were given the option under the Alternative Mortgage Transactions Parity Act (AMTPA) of following the appropriate set of federal regulations instead of state law when making "alternative" (i.e., variable rate, non-amortizing or otherwise untraditional) senior or junior mortgage loans or credit sales of mobile homes.[67] AMTPA potentially applies to almost all mortgage transactions except in those states which opted out of its provisions before its October 15, 1985 deadline.[68]

Conversely, as a result of considerable abuse of the freedom granted mortgage creditors under AMTPA in 1982, some of these same structural terms are now re-regulated in certain high-cost mortgage transactions as a result of the federal Home Ownership and Equity Protection Act of 1994.[69] These amendments to the Truth in Lending Act preempt any less protective state law that would otherwise allow them in covered transactions. As a more specific and more recent federal law, it should also outrank AMTPA or other general federal preemption law where they conflict.[70]

---

56 H.R. Conf. Rep. No. 103-651, at 53 (1994), *reprinted in* 1994 U.S.C.C.A.N. 2068; *see also* § 3.1.1, *supra*, §§ 3.4.5, 3.9.2.2, 3.15, *infra*.

57 *See* § 3.9.3, *infra*.

58 *See* § 3.9.4, *infra*.

59 *See* § 3.9.3.3, *infra*; *cf.* §§ 3.3, 3.4.1, *infra*.

60 *See* § 3.9.3.4, *infra*.

61 *See* § 3.4, *infra*.

62 *See* § 3.5, *infra*.

63 *See* § 3.9.2, *infra*.

64 *See* § 3.6, *infra*.

65 *See* § 3.8, *infra*.

66 *See* §§ 3.4.6.2, 3.5.3, 3.6, *infra*.

67 *See* § 3.10, *infra*.

68 *See* §§ 3.10.1, 3.10.2, *infra*.

69 Home Ownership and Equity Protection Act, Subtitle B of Title I, Riegle Community Development and Regulatory Improvement Act of 1994 (H.R. 3474), Pub. L. No. 103-325, 108 Stat. 2160 (Sept. 23, 1994), codified in 15 U.S.C. § 1639. *See generally* §§ 5.9, 12.2.2, *infra*.

70 *See* Williams v. Gelt Fin. Corp. (*In re* Williams), 232 B.R. 629 (Bankr. E.D. Pa.), *aff'd*, 237 B.R. 590 (E.D. Pa. 1999); *see also* Singer, Sutherland Statutory Construction § 51.05 (5th ed.) (where a general statute conflicts with a later, more specific statute, the latter is considered an exception to the former). *But see* Illinois Ass'n of Mortgage Brokers v. Office of Banks and Real Estate, 308 F.3d 762 (7th Cir. 2002) (court disagrees with the proposition that a state law passed to expand upon HOEPA is not preempted by AMTPA; case dealt with the issue of AMTPA trumping a state law, not AMTPA trumping HOEPA).

3.2.5 *Federal Consumer Lending Preemption Chart*

The accompanying "Federal Consumer Lending Preemption Chart" is an aid for locating federal statutes and regulations preempting state regulation of consumer credit rates and other credit terms. To use the chart:

- First determine the type of loan and lender involved in the transaction. Any loan secured by residential real estate is treated as a mortgage loan.
- Second, determine the statute(s) indicated under the appropriate row (lender type) and column (loan type), and then review the summary of that statute directly following the chart. The absence of any statute under a particular row and column indicates a probable absence of any federal preemption.

As the chart demonstrates, more than one federal statute may apply to any given transaction. This overlap does not necessarily imply a conflict because the statutes typically stack one type of preemption onto another. Nevertheless, more than one interest rate provision may frequently apply to a transaction, and generally the higher rate will prevail in such situations.[71] Practitioners faced with a conflict between the two interest rate provisions should check the exact statutory language to be certain of priority.

Note: The chart does *not* cover business or agricultural preemption or TILA preemption of state credit terminology. Nor does it include *state* "parity" statutes where some or all state lenders are permitted by state law to claim parity with deregulated, federally-chartered lenders. State "parity" statutes are discussed in § 3.14, *infra*. Note also that all regulations may not be cited.

---

71 DIDA § 528, found in note following 12 U.S.C. § 1735f-7. One exception to this general rule involves the financing of mobile home purchases and the interplay between the general preemption under § 501(a) of the Depository Institutions Deregulation and Monetary Control Act of 1980 and the more limited preemption in § 501(c). *See* § 3.9.3.4, *infra.*

FEDERAL STATUTORY AND REGULATORY CONSUMER LENDING PREEMPTION CHART

	First Residential Mortgage (including first lien on mobile home)	Junior Residential Mortgage (including junior liens on mobile homes)	Other Loan or Credit Transactions
Federally chartered commercial banks (i.e., national banks)	• DIDA (1st mortgage)[b] • National Bank Act[a] • DIA (OCC regulations)[f] • FHA/VA preemption[d]	• National Bank Act[a] • DIA (OCC regulations)[f] • FHA/VA preemption[e]	• National Bank Act[a]
Federal savings associations and federal savings banks	• DIA (AMTPA)[f] • FHA/VA preemption[d] • DIDA (1st mortgage preemption if lender is federally related or making over $1 million in residential real estate loans)[b] • HOLA[g]	• HOLA[g] • DIA (OCC regulations)[f] • FHA/VA	• HOLA[g]
Federally chartered credit unions	• DIDA (1st mortgage)[b] • National Credit Union Act[e] • DIA (NCUA regulations)[f] • FHA/VA preemption[d]	• National Credit Union Act[e] • DIA (NCUA regulations)[f] • FHA/VA preemption[d]	• National Credit Union Act[e] • DIDA (alternate ceiling)[c]
Other depository lenders (including state depositories, e.g., commercial banks, mutual banks, savings banks, savings and loans, credit unions)	• DIA (AMTPA)[f] • FHA/VA preemption[d] • DIDA (1st mortgage preemption if lender is federally related or making over $1 million in residential real estate loans)[b]	• DIA (AMTPA)[f] • FHA/VA preemption[d] • DIDA (alternative ceiling applies if lender is federally insured)[c]	• DIDA (alternate ceiling applies if lender is federally insured)[c]
Finance Companies Mortgage Companies Industrial "Banks"	• DIA (AMTPA) (if lender regularly makes mortgage loans or mobile home credit sales)[f] • FHA/VA preemption[d] • DIDA (1st mortgage preemption if lender is federally related or making over $1 million in residential real estate loans)[b]	• DIA (AMTPA) (if lender regularly makes mortgage loans or mobile home credit sales)[f] • FHA/VA preemption[d]	

| Retailers (goods or services) | • DIA (AMTPA) (if lender regularly makes mortgage loans or mobile home credit sales)[f]
• DIDA (1st mortgage preemption applies to mobile home credit seller making over $1 million in sales or assigning all or part of sales to qualifying lender)[b] | • DIA (AMTPA) (If lender regularly makes mortgage loans or mobile home credit sales)[f] | |
| Private owner-financed sales | • DIDA (1st mortgage)[b] | | |

Abbreviations used in this chart:

AMTPA — Alternate Mortgage Transaction Parity Act
DIA — Depository Institutions Act
DIDA — Depository Institution Deregulation & Monetary Control Act
FHA — Federal Housing Administration
HOLA — Home Owners' Loan Act
NCUA — National Credit Union Administration
OCC — Office of the Comptroller of the Currency
OTS — Office of Thrift Supervision
VA — Veterans Administration

a. National Bank Act, 12 U.S.C. § 85 (interest rates), § 24 (general bank powers), § 24a (financial subsidiaries), § 371 (real estate-secured lending), § 484 (visitorial restrictions)(original act effective date: 1873); [reprinted at Appx. C.1, *infra*].

Comment: National bank may charge higher of state most favored lender rate or alternative federal ceiling. Preemption of state laws affecting the business of lending permitted by regulation. Operating subsidiaries are entitled to same preemption rights as their parent banks, according to regulation.

State Opt-out? No

Regulations: 12 C.F.R. § 7.4000 (visitorial restrictions), 7.4001 (definition of interest), 7.4002 (non-interest fees) (replacing § 7.7310), § 7.4006 (applicability of state law to operating subsidiaries), 7.4008, 7.4009, 34.3, 34.4 (terms and conditions of loan and other related bank activities), 7.500 et seq. (electronic activities) [with the exception of § 7.500 et seq., reprinted at Appx. C.2, *infra*].

Manual: § 3.4

b. DIDA § 501(a) (first mortgage preemption), 12 U.S.C. § 1735f-7a (effective date Apr. 1, 1980) [reprinted at Appx. G.1, *infra*].

Comment: Preempts state usury ceilings on credit secured by first lien on residential real estate or mobile home. Lender must be federally related or making over $1 million per year in residential mortgage and mobile home loans or credit sales. Preemption only applies to mobile homes if creditor complies with OTS consumer protection regulations.

State Opt-out? Yes. State opportunity to opt-out of interest preemption on first mortgage expired April 1, 1983. Opportunity to opt-out of provisions regulating points or pre-paid charges does not expire, and may be done implicitly. Whole or partial opt-out jurisdictions include: CO, GA, HI, ID, IA, KS, ME, MA, MN, NB, NV, NC, PR, SC, SD (Wisconsin repealed its § 501(a)(1) opt-out effective May 4, 1998).

Regulations: 12 C.F.R. § 590 (general OTS first mortgage preemption regulations); 12 C.F.R. § 590.4 (OTS consumer protection regulations for mobile home loans or credit sales) [reprinted at Appx. G.2, infra].

Manual: § 3.9.3, 3.9.5.2

c. DIDA § 521–523 (alternate ceiling), 12 U.S.C. § 1463(g) (savings and loans), 1785(g) (credit unions), 1831d(a) (commercial banks) (effective Apr. 1, 1980) [reprinted at Appx. G.1, *infra*].

Comment: Allows federally insured depositories to charge interest up to the federal alternative ceiling and, by judicial interpretation, extends most favored lender status to these institutions.

State Opt-out? Yes, no expiration date on opportunity to opt-out. Jurisdictions remaining opted-out: IA, PR, WI (Nebraska opted out between 1982 and 1988; Massachusetts opted-out between 1981 and 1986; Colorado dropped its opt-out in 1994; Maine dropped its opt-out in 1995; North Carolina dropped its opt-out in 1995 as to loans, mortgages, credit sales, and advances made in the state after effective date of July 1, 1995).

Regulations: 12 C.F.R. § 560.110 (replacing 12 C.F.R. § 571.22, 61 Fed. Reg. 50,951, 50,965 (Sept. 30, 1996)) [reprinted at Appx. D.2, *infra*].

Manual: § 3.9.2, 3.9.5.3

d. FHA/VA preemption, 12 U.S.C. § 1709-1a, 1735f-7, 1709(b)(5); 38 U.S.C. § 3728. State law preempted June 30, 1976 and December 21, 1979. FHA authority to set interest ceiling revoked effective Nov. 30, 1983.

Comment: Preempts state interest ceilings on FHA or VA insured home loans.

State Opt-out?   Yes. See 12 U.S.C. § 1709-1a(b) (effective June 30, 1985) and 12 U.S.C. § 1735f-7(b) (effective Dec. 21, 1979). Adoption or amendment of applicable state usury law after effective date of federal statute negates preemption associated under § 1735f-7(b). Preemption extends to VA loans through 38 U.S.C. § 3728. Mere amendment or reenactment of usury law after effective date of preemption may satisfy opt-out requirement.

Regulations: 24 C.F.R. § 200 *et seq.* (FHA); 38 C.F.R. § 36.4201 et seq. (VA).

Manual: § 3.8

e. Federal Credit Union Act, 12 U.S.C. § 1757 (effective date 1934) (1980 amendment substituted the 15% annual ceiling for a 1% per month rate) [reprinted at Appx. E.1, *infra*].

Comment: Regulates the types of loans which federally chartered credit unions may make. Sets maximum interest rate at 15% unless temporarily raised at the discretion of National Credit Union Administration Board. The maximum was raised to 21% effective May 12, 1980, and changed to 18%, effective May 14, 1987, 52 Fed. Reg. 8061 (Mar. 16, 1987). It has remained at 18% since that time. It is scheduled to revert to 15% on September 8, 2006, unless otherwise provided by the NCUA Board. 12 C.F.R. § 701.21(c)(7)(ii).

State Opt-out?   No.

Regulations: 12 C.F.R. § 701.21 [reprinted at Appx. E.2, *infra*].

Manual: § 3.6

f. Depository Institutions Act, Pub. L. No. 97-320 (Oct 15, 1982) (including Alternate Mortgage Transactions Parity Act, codified at 12 U.S.C. § 3801–3805) (effective Oct. 15, 1982) [reprinted at Appx. H.1, *infra*].

Comment: Expanded authority of federally chartered lenders to issue variable rate mortgages and other creative financing terms and to enforce due-on sale clauses. AMTPA (DIA Title VIII) grants state lenders, which have received any state license(s) necessary to engage in home mortgage lending, the option of following the appropriate federal lending regulations. This statute does not affect interest rate ceilings.

State Opt-out?   Yes. Option expired Oct. 18, 1985. Opt-out states: AZ, MA, ME, NY, SC, WI (New York's opt-out does not apply to manufactured housing).

Regulations: 12 C.F.R. § 560 (federal savings and loans) [reprinted at Appx. D.2, infra]; 12 C.F.R. § 560.220 (state savings and loans, non-depository "housing creditors") [reprinted at Appx. H.2, infra]; 12 C.F.R. § 34.21(a) (national banks) [reprinted at Appx. C.2, infra]; 12 C.F.R. § 34.24 (state commercial banks) [reprinted at Appx. C.2, infra]; 12 C.F.R. § 701.21 (credit unions) [reprinted at Appx. E.2, *infra*].

Manual: § 3.10

g. Home Owners' Loan Act, 12 U.S.C. § 1461, 1463, 1464 (enactment date 1933) [reprinted at Appx. D.1, *infra*].

Comment: Federal savings and loan associations and subsidiaries may charge higher of state most favored lender rate or alternative federal ceiling. Broad preemption via regulation of other loan terms, conditions, and related activities.

State Opt-out?   No.

Regulations: 12 C.F.R. § 560.1 et seq., 559.3(h), (n) (operating subsidiaries), 591.1–.6 [reprinted at Appx. D.2, *infra*].

Manual: § 3.5

3.3 The Bureaucracy of Preemption

3.3.1 Who Regulates Which Lenders?

To determine when a transaction might be subject to federal preemption, and state law displaced by federal regulation, one should look at the type of lender involved. A chart listing the type of lender and its primary regulators appears at the end of this section.

Insofar as usury and credit law is concerned, national banks, federal credit unions, and federal savings and loan associations (the term includes federal savings banks) are generally regulated by the Office of the Comptroller of the Currency (OCC),[72] the National Credit Union Administration (NCUA),[73] and the Office of Thrift Supervision (OTS)[74] (since 1989, replacing the Federal Home Loan Bank Board

---

72 *See* 12 C.F.R. §§ 1–34.

73 *See* 12 C.F.R. §§ 700 *et seq.*; *see also* Crissey v. Alaska USA Fed. Credit Union, 811 P.2d 1057 (Alaska 1991) (federally-chartered credit unions subject to NCUA regulations which specifically preempt state laws on interest rates and late charges, 12 C.F.R. § 701.21(b)(1)).

74 *See* 12 C.F.R. § 560 *et seq.* These regulations make clear that OTS occupies the entire field of lending regulation for federal savings associations. 12 C.F.R. § 560.2(a); *see* § 3.5.3, *infra*.

(FHLBB)[75]), respectively. The major exception to this rule of thumb for federal lenders is that all lenders, including federal banks and credit unions, which wish to take advantage of the removal of interest ceilings on first mortgage loans provided by DIDA must follow OTS regulations, including the OTS consumer protection regulations governing mobile home sales.[76] Federally-insured depository institutions, including state-chartered banks (including state savings banks), are subject to some additional regulation by the Federal Deposit Insurance Corporation.[77] Preemption may not apply where the federally-chartered or related institution is merely an assignee of a note, rather than the originator.[78]

State lenders, as well as federal lenders, are regulated under state law unless that law has been preempted, in which case, federal law and regulations may apply. On the whole, the most pervasive preemption of state regulatory authority affects mortgage and mobile home loans. First, as mentioned above, all lenders must follow OTS regulations to take advantage of DIDA's removal of interest ceilings on first priority mobile home loans.[79] Second, under AMTPA, many state lenders may follow liberal federal regulations controlling the structure of mortgage loans.[80] Specifically, state commercial banks may invoke OCC mortgage regulations,[81] state credit unions may rely on NCUA mortgage regulations,[82] and all other "housing creditors" including non-depository mortgage lenders may follow the mortgage regulations of the OTS.[83] Finally, state parity laws may enable state lenders, especially depository institutions, to follow the federal regulations governing either mortgage or non-mortgage transactions which are used by competing federal lenders.[84]

The National Bank Act and the Home Owners' Loan Act and especially the regulations enacted pursuant to these acts grant extensive preemption rights to national banks, federal savings associations, and their operating subsidiaries. These preemption regimes related to real estate lending, non-real estate lending, and deposit-taking are discussed in detail in §§ 3.4.6, 3.5, *infra*.

WHO IS IN CHARGE

TYPE OF LENDER	PRIMARY REGULATOR(S)
National bank (and its operating subsidiaries)	OCC
National savings association, federal savings bank (and their operating subsidiaries)	OTS
Federal credit union	NCUA
State bank or state savings bank	State Banking Commissioner, Federal Reserve Board (if a member of the Federal Reserve System), FDIC (if not a member of the Federal Reserve System)
State credit union	State credit union administrator, National Credit Union Share Insurance Fund
Finance companies, other lenders	State financial institutions agencies

3.3.2 Deference to Agency Preemption Regulations and Opinions

The federal agencies that administer the statutes preempting state usury law in the past occasionally published official interpretations of their regulations or authorizing statutes in the *Federal Register* and the Code of Federal Regulations. The degree of deference that should be given to past agency interpretations and informal staff opinions as to the preemptive scope of these statutes has been called into question. Prior to August 1994, it might have been (and was) argued that they should be persuasive.[85]

However, Congress, in enacting the 1994 Interstate Banking Act (IBBEA) (more commonly called the Riegle-Neal Act) expressed concern that the regulatory agencies have been unduly "inappropriately aggressive," finding preemption of state law "in situations where the federal interest did not warrant that result."[86] As a result, agencies must now

---

75 In the wake of the savings and loan crisis, the Federal Home Loan Bank Board (FHLBB) was abolished and its functions transferred to the newly created Office of Thrift Supervision (OTS) as of August 9, 1989. Financial Institutions Reform, Recovery and Enforcement Act of 1989, Pub. L. No. 101-73, 103 Stat. 183 (FIRREA). Many of the relevant FHLBB rules were republished by OTS with only technical changes. 54 Fed. Reg. 49411 (Nov. 30, 1989).

76 *See* 12 C.F.R. § 590. *But see* Nelson v. River Valley Bank & Trust, 971 S.W.2d 777 (Ark. 1998) (see discussion of this case in § 3.6.3.4, *infra*). *See generally* § 3.9.3, *infra*.

77 *See* § 3.7, *infra*.

78 *See* §§ 3.4.1, 3.4.5.1.3, *infra*.

79 *See* 12 C.F.R. § 590. *But see* Nelson v. River Valley Bank & Trust, 971 S.W.2d 777 (Ark. 1998) (discussed in § 3.9.3.4, *infra*).

80 *See* 12 U.S.C. § 3803. *See generally* § 3.10, *infra*.

81 *See* 12 C.F.R. § 34.21.

82 *See* 12 C.F.R. § 701.21.

83 *See* 12 C.F.R. §§ 560, 590, 591. Former Part 545 was substantially revamped and now appears in new Part 560. 61 Fed. Reg. 50951 (Sept. 30, 1996). To compare the old provisions with the new, see chart in the Federal Register. *Id.* at 50969.

84 *See* § 3.14, *infra*.

85 *See, e.g.*, Stoorman v. Greenwood Trust Co., 888 P.2d 289 (Colo. Ct. App. 1994), *aff'd on other grounds*, 908 P.2d 133 (Colo. 1995); *see also* Quiller v. Barclays American/Credit, Inc., 727 F.2d 1067, 1071 (11th Cir. 1984), *aff'd en banc*, 764 F.2d 1400 (11th Cir. 1985); Mitchell v. Trustees of United States Mut. Real Estate Inv. Trust, 375 N.W.2d 424 (Mich. Ct. App. 1985) (discussing authority of Fed. Home Loan Bank Bd. opinion letter); *cf.* Ford Motor Credit Co. v. Milhollin, 444 U.S. 555 (1980) (addressing the FRB's rulemaking authority under Truth in Lending).

86 H.R. Conf. Rep. No. 103-651, at 53 (1994), *reprinted in* 1994 U.S.C.C.A.N. 2068. Congress challenged positions taken both

publish any proposed opinion letter or interpretive rules that would invoke the National Bank Act to preempt state consumer protection, fair lending, community reinvestment law, or state law regarding the establishment of intrastate branches.[87] (Though the requirement was enacted in the Interstate Banking and Branching Act, these requirements are applicable beyond interstate branching questions.[88]) By this means, Congress hoped to assure that preemption principles were applied in a balanced fashion, and that state consumer protection laws, among others, would only be preempted where clearly warranted by federal policy interests.[89]

The process is not required when the issue has already been "resolved" by the agency or courts,[90] but because some important questions about the scope of preemption are still in flux, the matters may not be judicially "resolved" until the Supreme Court has spoken. In the meantime, when litigating these issues, practitioners might point to this expression of congressional concern to indicate both that Congress does not intend to "occupy the field" of consumer protection laws[91] and that previously issued agency opinions which would preempt such laws should be taken with a grain of salt.

The First Circuit, in fact, dismissed an agency interpretation on a preemption question as "unpersuasive and entitled to no deference" where the agency failed to offer any analytical support for its position, which in the court's view, flew in the face of the statutory language.[92]

In the 1995 round of exportation cases, agency interpretations were given contrary receptions. The California and Colorado Supreme Courts granted OCC interpretations deference,[93] while the New Jersey Supreme Court, citing the

inconsistency in the agency's position(s) on the issue, found them unpersuasive.[94] On the issue of credit card late fees, the Supreme Court agreed with the California and Colorado courts giving deference to and applying a published 1996 OCC Interpretive Ruling.[95] The Court articulated that agency interpretations of ambiguous provisions of the NBA will be followed if the interpretations are "formal," directed to national banks generally, and "reasonable." The interpretive ruling at issue had been published in the *Federal Register*. Presumably, "formal" means published. Earlier OCC letters that were merely in response to an inquiry from or regarding a particular bank were specifically rejected.[96]

Since the ruling in *Smiley*, the courts, as a general rule, uphold the banking agencies' expressions, whether found in an *amicus* brief,[97] or in a fully promulgated regulation.[98]

3.4 The National Bank Act

3.4.1 History and Purpose of the National Bank Act

The National Bank Act (NBA) was enacted in 1863–64, when "[i]n a field quite apart from the monetary, federal and state authority were met in bloody combat."[99] It was designed both to help finance the war in the near term and in the long-run to restore to the still young federal government control of the monetary system.[100] As such, Congress could not expose the fledgling banks to "the hazard of unfriendly legislation by the states, or to ruinous competition with state banks."[101] Hence

---

in formally adopted interpretive rules (12 C.F.R. § 7.8000) and informal interpretive opinion letters.

87 12 U.S.C. § 43. *See also* discussion of OCC opinions and letters in § 3.4.6.1, *infra*.

88 H.R. Conf. Rep. No. 103-651, at 54 (1994), *reprinted in* 1994 U.S.C.C.A.N. 2068. Its full reach is unclear, but it appears to apply when national bank act preemption would be invoked to displace state law in one of the enumerated areas, or when the OCC intends to opine that state law would have a discriminatory effect on a local branch of an out of state national bank. Consequently, the OTS, NCUA, and FDIC are not covered, unless they opine on NBA preemption.

89 H.R. Conf. Rep. No. 103-651, at 53, 54 (1994), *reprinted in* 1994 U.S.C.C.A.N. 2068.

90 *Id.* at 55.

91 For discussions of laws regulating the cost of consumer credit as "consumer protection" laws, see § 1.3, *supra* and § 9.3.1.1, *infra*.

92 See Grunbeck v. Dime Sav. Bank, 74 F.3d 331 (1st Cir. 1996) (preemptive effect of DIDA § 501 on a state simple interest statute prohibiting negative amortization at issue).

93 Smiley v. Citibank (S.D.), N.A., 11 Cal. 4th 138, 900 P.2d 690, 44 Cal. Rptr. 2d 441 (1995), *aff'd*, 517 U.S. 735, 116 S. Ct. 1730, 135 L. Ed. 2d 25 (1996); Copeland v. MBNA Am. Bank, N.A., 907 P.2d 87 (Colo. 1995). The OCC issued a formal interpretive ruling adopting the interpretation, 12 C.F.R. § 7.4001, 61 Fed. Reg. 4869 (Feb. 9, 1996). The exportation

debate is discussed in §§ 3.4.5, 3.6.2.2, *infra*.

94 Sherman v. Citibank (S.D.), N.A., 668 A.2d 1036 (N.J. 1995), *vacated and remanded*, 517 U.S. 1241, 116 S. Ct. 2493, 135 L. Ed. 2d 86 (1996) (in light of *Smiley*); Hunter v. Greenwood Trust Co., 668 A.2d 1067 (N.J. 1995), *vacated and remanded*, 517 U.S. 1241, 116 S. Ct. 2493, 135 L. Ed. 2d 86 (1996) (in light of *Smiley*).

95 Smiley v. Citibank (S.D.), N.A., 517 U.S. 735, 116 S. Ct. 1730, 135 L. Ed. 2d 25 (1996). The substantive holding of this case is discussed in § 3.4.5.2, *infra*.

96 *Smiley*, 116 S. Ct. at 1734.

97 *See* Bank of America v. City and Council of San Francisco, 309 F.3d 551, 563 (9th Cir. 2002); American Bankers Ass'n v. Lockyer, 239 F. Supp. 2d 1000, 1003 (E.D. Cal. 2002).

98 *See* Wachovia Bank, N.A. v. Burke, 319 F. Supp. 2d 275 (D. Conn. 2004), *appeal pending*; Wachovia Bank, N.A. v. Watters, 334 F. Supp. 2d 957 (W.D. Mich. 2004), *appeal pending*.

99 Bray Hammond, *Banks and Politics in America from the Revolution to the Civil War* 724 (Princeton Univ. Press 1957). For a short history of the development of banking law in the United States, see § 2.3.1.2.1, *supra*. For a longer version, see Patricia A. McCoy, Patricia A. McCoy, Banking Law Manual ch. 2 (Lexis Pub. 2d ed. 2003).

100 Earlier efforts at a central banking system had fallen to "the centrifugal passion of the Jacksonians for *laisser faire* and states' rights." *Id. See also* the discussion in First Union Nat'l Bank v. Burke, 48 F. Supp. 2d 132 (D. Conn. 1999).

101 The NBA's history and purposes are also discussed, through different prisms, in the California and New Jersey Supreme Court cases on interest rate exportation, which reached differing

section 85 of the NBA[102] allows a national bank, *when originating credit*,[103] to charge the higher of the maximum rate allowed lenders under state law (the most favored lender doctrine)[104] or an alternative federal rate based on the federal discount rate.[105] A national bank lending intrastate can take advantage of this alternative federal rate whenever it exceeds the state's interest ceiling. As will be seen, as the NBA is currently interpreted, a national bank operating interstate from its home state also may take advantage of higher (or no) rate ceilings in that state in extending credit (such as credit cards) to consumers in other states, a result which would probably confound Alexander Hamilton.[106]

There were approximately 2,001 national banks by the end of 2003.[107] In 2004, the Office of the Comptroller of the Currency regulated about 55% of the entire banking industry when measured by loans outstanding.[108]

3.4.2 Calculating Alternative Interest Ceilings

The alternative federal rate is 1% above the discount rate on 90-day commercial paper in effect at the federal reserve bank in the district where the national bank is located.[109] This discount rate on 90-day commercial paper is the "federal discount rate" frequently mentioned in the press, and is

the rate at which federal reserve banks will make short-term loans to member banks. Borrowers may be required to establish the controlling discount rate, and hence, the relevant alternative ceiling, in usury cases against national banks.[110]

Probably the best way to find the federal discount rate in effect at the time and place of a transaction is to examine the then current *Federal Reserve Bulletin*, published monthly by the Board of Governors of the Federal Reserve System.[111] On August 5, 1994 the discount rate was 3.5% for all of the district banks, thus the alternative ceiling under the National Bank Act would have been 4.5% (i.e., 1% above the discount rate).[112]

It is worth noting that the federal discount rate is not a true market rate but is a managed interest rate set by the Federal Reserve. Other benchmark rates do exist which may more accurately reflect money market rates and which may be referenced under other statutes, regulations, or contracts.[113] For example, Table 1.35, entries 3 through 5, in the *Federal Reserve Bulletin* shows average private market rates for commercial paper.

3.4.3 Most Favored Lender Doctrine

3.4.3.1 General

Once the discount rate formula has been used to calculate the alternative federal rate, this rate must be compared to the maximum interest rate allowed to state lenders under state law. A national bank will be able to charge the *higher* of the two rates. However, determining the maximum rate allowed under a state's law can be complex because state laws frequently set different rates for different classes of lenders and different classes of loans.

results. *Compare* Smiley v. Citibank (S.D.), N.A., 11 Cal. 4th 138, 900 P.2d 690, 44 Cal. Rptr. 2d 441 (1995), *aff'd*, 517 U.S. 735, 116 S. Ct. 1730, 135 L. Ed. 2d 25 (1996) *with* Tiffany v. National Bank of Mo., 85 U.S. 409, 413 (1873); Sherman v. Citibank (S.D.), N.A., 668 A.2d 1036 (N.J. 1995), *vacated and remanded*, 517 U.S. 1241, 116 S. Ct. 2493, 135 L. Ed. 2d 86 (1996) (in light of *Smiley*); *see also* Jones v. BankBoston, N.A., 115 F. Supp. 2d 1350 (S.D. Ala. 2000) (in the course of deciding that the NBA does not completely preempt state law and remanding the case to state court, the court reviewed some of the history and purpose of the NBA); Burgess & Ciolfi, *Exportation or Exploitation: A State Regulator's View of Interstate Credit Card Transactions*, 42 Bus. Law 929, 933 (May 1987).

102 12 U.S.C. § 85. Selected provisions of the NBA are *reprinted in* Appx. C.1, *infra*.

103 The National Bank Act does not apply to credit initiated by another lender, such as a finance company, which is later assigned to a national bank. *See* § 3.4.5.1.3, *infra*.

104 *See* § 3.4.3, *infra*.

105 For an explanation of the federal discount rate, see § 3.4.2, *infra*. Section 86 of the National Banking Act provides a remedy for a violation of the usury limits contained in § 85. Section 86, however, does not provide a cause of action unless the borrower has actually paid the interest sought to be recovered. McCarthy v. First Nat'l Bank, 223 U.S. 493 (1912). Where, however, the bank sues for usurious charges that the borrower has not paid, § 86 provides the borrower with a defense.

106 *See* § 3.4.5, *infra*.

107 OCC, Financial Performance of National Banks, 23 Quarterly J. 180, 191 (Mar. 2004), *available at* www.occ.treas.gov/qj/qj23-1/10-FinancialPerformance.pdf.

108 Jathon Sapsford, *Critics Cry Foul Over New Rules on Bank Review*, Wall St. J. Jan. 8, 2004, at C1.

109 *See* 12 U.S.C. § 85.

110 *See* Kerper v. NCMB Nat'l Bank of Fla., 496 So. 2d 199 (Fla. Dist. Ct. App. 1986) (borrower loses usury case when no evidence of discount rate at time of transaction introduced).

111 The Federal Reserve Bulletin is available in many public libraries. It is also available by subscription for from: Publications Services, Board of Governors of the Federal Reserve System, Washington, DC 20551. It is found in the tables reflecting domestic financial statistics. Table 1.14.

112 There is a complication in calculating the alternative ceiling for transactions executed between March 17, 1980 and November 17, 1981 as the Federal Reserve added a surcharge to the basic discount rate during this period, ranging between zero and four percent. For example, on May 8, 1981, a national bank's alternative ceiling was 19%: 14% discount rate + 4% FRB surcharge + 1% margin granted by § 85.

113 The Federal Reserve Board also provides the federal discount rate on-line, though it is not broken down by federal reserve bank regions: www.federalreserve.gov/releases/h15 (look under "Selected Interest Rates" and "commercial paper" and then select the three-month rate).

Problems can arise if variable rate loans and variable interest ceilings are pegged to different indexes. *See, e.g.*, Blessing v. Zeffero, 149 Mich. App. 558, 386 N.W.2d 590 (1986). *See generally* § 4.3.6, *infra*.

The original point of the alternative reference to state law was to assure that states did not discriminate against the newly created national banks;[114] or in today's parlance, to assure a "level playing field" between state and national commercial banks.[115] But the current interpretation is that national banks have *most* favored lender" status.[116] While in 1864, state banks typically would have been a state's most favored lender, the 20th century brought in new credit providers allowed to charge high rates because they were (it was assumed) engaged in riskier lending.[117] (It remains to be seen what will be unveiled in this, the twenty-first century.[118]) Therefore, *most* favored lender status gave national banks an edge over state banks[119] in transactions where the most favored lender doctrine applied.

As is discussed later, this balance shifted again after 1980. Federally-insured state banks, among others, have been successful in convincing courts that DIDA bestowed upon them the same "most favored lender" status afforded national banks.[120] Once again, national banks and state banks are on a fairly "level playing field," but one that is now often at an elevated level of cost to the consumer.

The most favored lender doctrine, however, is not blanket authority for those with its status to browse through state statutes and charge the highest interest rate in them.[121] There are three major limitations on the most favored lender doctrine, each of which is discussed in the following subsections.

3.4.3.2 "Competing Lender" Limitations on the Most Favored Lender Doctrine

National banks that invoke the most favored lender doctrine cannot automatically claim the right to charge the highest interest rate that any lender is permitted to charge. Rather, the national bank may only claim the rate which competing lenders may use *when issuing the same type of loan.*[122] Thus, the bank may not use finance company rates if it is making a type of loan that finance companies are not authorized to make, because the finance companies do not compete with the bank for that type of loan.[123]

It is the legal authority, rather than the actual practice of the potentially "competing" state lenders that will determine whether or not a state lender is a competitor for purposes of the most favored lender analysis.[124] For example, in order to invoke an interest ceiling normally applicable to finance companies, a national bank will not be forced to prove that finance companies actually make the type of loan which the bank has made, but will only be required to establish that finance companies in the relevant state could legally make such loans if they chose to. Similarly, an OCC staff letter has indicated that state-chartered credit unions are competitors of a national bank for most favored lender purposes, even if no credit unions are located in the county or geographic banking market of the national

---

114 The goal was to protect "nascent national banks from discriminatory or oppressive state rate laws." Burgess & Ciolfi, *Exportation or Exploitation: A State Regulator's View of Interstate Credit Card Transactions*, 42 Bus. Law 929, 933 (May 1987); *see also* Finkelstein, *Most Favored Lender Status for Insured Banks*, 42 Bus. Law. 915 (1987) (purpose in enacting § 85 and its corollary in DIDA (see § 3.9.2, *infra*) was to put lenders on equal footing, not to give most favored lenders competitive advantage). *See generally* § 3.4.1, *supra*.

115 *See, e.g.*, Rockland-Atlas Nat'l Bank of Boston v. Murphy, 110 N.E.2d 638 (Mass. 1953); Note, 58 Iowa L. Rev. 1250 (1973).

116 *See, e.g.*, Marquette Nat'l Bank of Minneapolis v. First of Omaha Serv. Corp., 439 U.S. 299 (1978); Tiffany v. National Bank of Mo., 85 U.S. 409 (1873); Kenty v. Bank One, Columbus, N.A., 92 F.3d 384 (6th Cir. 1996); Annotation, 38 A.L.R. Fed. 805 (1978).

117 For example, small loan lenders lending under Small Loan Acts. *See generally* Ch. 2, *supra*. For a discussion of the merits of the high rate/high risk assumption, see § 11.1, *infra*.

118 A myriad of issues are percolating related to cyberspace lending, among them, the question of which state's law will apply to bank and non-bank lending entities. For example, what constitutes "contacts" with a state for purposes of jurisdiction, venue, and choice of laws. Depending on how electronic v. physical "contacts" in states are weighed, even non-banks may be able to jump on the exportation bandwagon by including anti-consumer choice of law provisions in electronic contracts which operate to divest the consumer's home state of any ability to regulate such entities.

119 *See, e.g.*, Nelson v. Citibank (S.D.), N.A., 794 F. Supp. 312, 318 (D. Minn. 1992) (citing Fisher v. First Nat'l Bank, 548 F.2d 255 (8th Cir. 1977)).

120 *See* § 3.6.2, *infra*.

121 When state law puts no limit on the interest rate a state bank may charge, 12 U.S.C. § 85 imposes a seven percent per annum rate. However, some courts have essentially ignored this pro-

vision and have held that, in the absence of a state ceiling on state institutions, federal banks are similarly unlimited under the most favored lender doctrine. *See* Hiatt v. San Francisco Nat'l Bank, 361 F.2d 504 (9th Cir. 1966) (the explicit 12 U.S.C. § 85 limitation of seven percent discount method interest for national banks in states that have not set an interest ceiling may be ignored and such banks may charge the same unrestricted amount of interest as state banks); *see also* Moore v. United Nat'l Bank, 821 S.W.2d 409 (Tex. App. 1991) (because bank subject to no rate limitation on residential first mortgage as a result of DIDA, national banks are also free of rate limitations on such loans).

122 *See* United Mo. Bank v. Danforth, 394 F. Supp. 774 (W.D. Mo. 1975); Att'y Gen. v. Equitable Trust Co., 294 Md. 385, 450 A.2d 1273 (1982); *see also* Saul v. Midlantic Nat'l Bank S., 572 A.2d 650 (N.J. Super. Ct. App. Div. 1990).

123 OCC Interpretive Letter No. 178, Consumer Cred. Guide (CCH) ¶ 97,239 (1981). Relevant letters from 1992 forward are reproduced on the CD-Rom accompanying this volume and are summarized in Appx. C.3, *infra*.

124 *See* United Mo. Bank v. Danforth, 394 F. Supp. 774 (W.D. Mo. 1985); VanderWeyst v. First State Bank of Benson, 425 N.W.2d 803 (Minn. 1988) (interpreting the "most favored lender" status which the court holds is extended to federally insured, state chartered banks under DIDA; *see* § 3.9.2.1, *infra*); *see also* Fisher v. First Nat'l Bank of Omaha, 548 F.2d 255 (8th Cir. 1977); First Bank of Cadillac v. Miller, 347 N.W.2d 715 (Mich. Ct. App. 1984).

bank and do not, therefore, create actual competition, provided that the credit unions are authorized to do business in that market.[125]

The OCC recently may have stretched the most favored lender doctrine to its limits. In a 2004 Interpretive Letter, the agency opined that a national bank may charge prepayment penalties in its home state by bootstrapping an Office of Thrift Supervision regulation into its home state's law via the state's parity act.[126] The OCC reached this conclusion using the following analysis: OCC regulation defines "interest" to include prepayment penalties; although the bank's home state prohibits the charging of prepayment penalties under some of its usury laws, the state's parity act permits a bank, including a state bank, to collect interest and charges on loans as allowed by state or federal law; OTS regulations authorize federal savings associations to charge prepayment penalties. Consequently, if the home state's authorities interpret the state parity act as allowing state banks the right to charge prepayment penalties, then national banks can as well (even if the national bank could not charge prepayment penalties under OCC regulations).

The competing lender rule also clearly places great importance on the classification of loan types, and it raises the question of how a class of credit should be defined for purposes of the most favored lender rule. One element to be used in defining a class of loans is any limitation placed on the total amount of the loan by the "borrowed" statute.[127] The most frequently litigated example of this issue is the treatment of credit card accounts issued by national banks. The courts have split on the question of whether a national bank can invoke a state's small loan ceiling in connection with its credit card accounts. Some courts have allowed the use of the small loan ceiling, despite the structural differences between open-end accounts and traditional small loans, on the ground that both small loans and credit cards are used to finance similar consumer purchases and that both may be repaid in installments.[128] Other courts have reasoned that the use of small loan ceilings for credit cards would lead to an obliteration of state distinctions between classes of

credit and that Congress did not intend such a result when it granted most favored lender privileges.[129]

In recent years, there has not been much litigation on this issue, as national banks circumvented this restriction by moving their credit card operations to highly deregulated states and "exporting" those states' lack of regulation nationwide. Thus, at least as to credit cards, it is now more often a matter for analysis under the exportation doctrine.[130] As is noted elsewhere, there are frightening indications that this stratagem is being groomed to enable traditionally high-cost lenders, dressed up with national bank charters, to *de facto* deregulate consumer credit nationwide, irrespective of what policy judgments the elected representatives in the consumer's home state may have made.[131]

3.4.3.3 State Lender Limitation on Most Favored Lender Doctrine

The second limitation on the most favored lender doctrine is that national banks may only adopt the rates of competing *state* lenders and not those of other *federal* lenders with whom they compete in a state.[132] This seemingly obvious limitation needs to be stated because between 1980 and 1987 federal credit unions were allowed to charge 21% interest under the National Credit Union Act,[133] and other lenders, including national banks, eyed this rate longingly. However, it is clear that the intent of the NBA's most favored lender doctrine is to prevent discriminatory state regulation in favor of state institutions, not to provide equality among federal lenders.[134] Thus, for example, the OCC warned a national bank that it could not use the most favored lender doctrine to charge the Federal Credit Union Act rate when it was at its peak.[135]

---

125 OCC Letter, Apr. 16, 1985, *discussed in* 44 Wash. Fin. Rep. (BNA) 800, 801 (May 6, 1985).

126 OCC Interpretive Letter No. 1004 (Aug. 4, 2004), available on the CD-Rom accompanying this volume.

127 OCC Interpretive Letter No. 178, Consumer Cred. Guide (CCH) ¶ 97,239 (1981). Relevant letters from 1992 forward are reproduced on the CD-Rom accompanying this volume. *See also* VanderWeyst v. First State Bank of Benson, 425 N.W.2d 803, 809 (Minn. 1988) (interpreting "most favored lender status" which court holds is extended to federally-insured, state-chartered banks under DIDA).

128 *See* Fisher v. First Nat'l Bank of Omaha, 548 F.2d 255 (8th Cir. 1977); United Mo. Bank v. Danforth, 394 F. Supp. 774 (W.D. Mo. 1975); *see also* OCC Interpretive Letter No. 178, Consumer Cred. Guide (CCH) ¶ 97,239 (1981) (invocation of RISA ceiling for credit card account under most favored lender doctrine). Relevant letters from 1992 forward are reproduced on the CD-Rom accompanying this volume.

129 *Cf.* Att'y Gen. v. Equitable Trust Co., 450 A.2d 1273 (Md. 1982) (interpreting most-favored lender status under DIDA).

130 *See* § 3.4.5, *infra.*

131 *See* Cades v. H & R Block, Inc., 43 F.3d 869 (4th Cir. 1994); §§ 3.4.5, 3.9.2.2, *infra.*

132 OCC Letter, Consumer Cred. Guide (CCH) ¶ 96,744 (Jan. 19, 1983). *See generally* Comment, *Federal Credit Unions—Competing Lenders For Purposes of the "Most Favored Lender" Doctrine?*, 5 Ann. Rev. Banking L. 349 (1986) (criticizing OCC position).

133 12 U.S.C. § 1757. Maximum rate temporarily set at 21% by 12 C.F.R. § 701.21(c)(7)(ii), effective May 12, 1980, reduced to 18% as of May 14, 1987, which is the maximum rate presently in effect. 12 C.F.R. § 701.21(c)(7)(ii).

134 *See* § 3.4.3.1, *supra.*

135 OCC Letter, Consumer Cred. Guide (CCH) ¶ 96,744 (Jan. 19, 1983). The Pennsylvania bank appeared to be reasoning by analogy to Op. Tenn. Att'y Gen. No. 220, Consumer Cred. Guide (CCH) ¶ 96,822 (1982) (twenty-one percent allowed for banks, savings and loans, and credit unions under state parity legislation and federal most favored lender doctrine, but eighteen percent for other creditors); *see also* Op. Tenn. Att'y Gen. No. 620, Consumer Cred. Guide (CCH) ¶ 96,966 (1981); Op.

This is, however, not the end of the story, because state parity laws, in conjunction with most favored lender analysis, may provide national banks with an indirect path to the credit union rates. In essence, if a state parity law allows a state credit union to use the federal credit union rate, and a national bank can in turn invoke the same rate as the state credit union under the most favored lender rule, the national bank has achieved the federal credit union rate, at least for loans in that state.[136] State parity laws are discussed at § 3.14, *infra*.

3.4.3.4 Most Favored Lender Must Comply with "Material" State Restrictions

The final limitation on a national bank's adoption of a state interest rate under the most favored lender doctrine is that the national bank must comply with any state restrictions on the relevant loan type which are "material" to determination of the interest rate on that type of loan.[137] If state law permits finance companies to issue high interest loans, but restricts their associated loan fees, a national bank cannot adopt only the state interest rate without complying with the fee restrictions because these restrictions are "material" to the interest rate allowed on the loan.

The materiality requirement can force national banks to comply with numerous state loan regulations if they want to adopt the state interest rate. Courts have found regulations concerning compounding of interest,[138] maximum loan

charges,[139] attorney fees,[140] and requirements that credit terms be in writing[141] to be material to the interest rates allowable. In one of the most comprehensive discussions of the materiality issue, Maryland's highest court in *Attorney General v. Equitable Trust Co.*[142] specified that state regulations governing fees, wage assignments, service charges, loan-splitting, postdefault interest rate reductions, refinancing, compounding of interest, credit insurance, part payment bookkeeping, non-sufficient fund fee limitations, prepayment penalties, and the duration of a credit extension were all material to the interest rate allowed under the state small loan law. Most importantly, the Maryland Court held that state loan duration limitations were material, and that credit card lenders in the state must track each credit card transaction separately in order to comply with the small loan maturity regulations if they wish to use small loan rates.[143]

In contrast, the same opinion held that a small loan provision prohibiting holder-in-due-course status for a lender financing a sale was not material to the interest rate permitted by the statute. Similarly, regulations governing licensing, capital requirements, reporting requirements, or the supervision of state-regulated lenders may not be material to the interest rate allowed on a class of loans.[144] Some dispute exists over the materiality of state disclosure requirements.[145] However, if a state requires greater disclosure

---

Tenn. Att'y Gen. No. 221, Consumer Cred. Guide (CCH) ¶ 96,824 (1982).

136 *See* OCC Interpretive Letter No. 1004 (Aug. 4, 2004) (national bank located in Michigan may charge prepayment penalties via a state parity act that applies loan-related charges imposed by state banks and which § 85 incorporates and applies to national banks), available on the CD-Rom accompanying this volume. *See also* Begala v. PNC Bank, Ohio, N.A., 214 F.3d 776 (6th Cir. 2000), *cert. denied*, 531 U.S. 1145 (2001) (national bank located in Ohio is entitled to use the interest rate allowed to building and loan associations and savings banks under most favored lender doctrine; payment holiday was not a new credit transaction and, therefore, was covered by this state law which allowed unlimited interest on "loans made").

137 12 C.F.R. § 7.4001(b), (c); 61 Fed. Reg. 4869 (Feb. 9, 1996); *see* OCC Unpublished Letter (June 10, 1992) (provision in Arkansas constitution allowing state banks to charge a maximum interest rate of 5% above the federal discount rate "at the time of the contract" was a material term). The full text is reproduced on the CD-Rom accompanying this volume. *See also* Kent v. Bank of Am., N.A., 2003 WL 327465 (Cal. Ct. App. Feb. 11, 2003), *cert. denied*, 124 S. Ct. 348 (2003) (bank is subject to state laws material to the determination of late payment and overlimit fees, the fees at issue in the case). For an interesting discussion of the OCC's vacillation on how materiality plays out in practice, see Sherman v. Citibank (S.D.), N.A., 668 A.2d 1036 (N.J. 1995), *vacated and remanded on other grounds*, 517 U.S. 1241, 116 S. Ct. 2493, 135 L. Ed. 2d 86 (1996).

138 *See* Haas v. Pittsburgh Nat'l Bank, 526 F.2d 1083 (3d Cir. 1975), *aff'd*, 627 F.2d 677 (3d Cir. 1980); Partain v. First Nat'l Bank of Montgomery, 467 F.2d 167 (5th Cir. 1972).

139 *See* Northway Lanes v. Hackley Union Nat'l Bank & Trust Co., 464 F.2d 855 (6th Cir. 1972).

140 *See* Rockland-Atlas Nat'l Bank of Boston v. Murphy, 329 Mass. 755, 110 N.E.2d 638 (1953).

141 *See* Landau v. Chase Manhattan Bank, N.A., 367 F. Supp. 992 (S.D.N.Y. 1973).

142 450 A.2d 1273 (Md. 1982). The court defined "material to the determination of the interest rate" to mean material to a judicial determination of whether the interest rate charged in a given transaction is unlawful. *Id.* at 1292. A cautionary note is in order. While the broad reading of "materiality" in this context often protected consumers by requiring national banks to comply with some of the strictures placed on higher rate state lenders as a *quid pro quo* for their higher rate authority, it has boomeranged against consumers when national banks (and others asserting most favored lender status) "export" their home state's lack of any corollary restrictions interstate. In the exportation contest, it has undermined state consumer protections nationwide. *See* §§ 3.4.5, 3.9.2.2, *infra*.

143 There is potentially an interesting conflict between these holdings and the OCC's new interpretive ruling on non-interest fees. If a state statute borrowed for most favored lender purposes limits a material, non-interest fee, for example, attorney fees, how will the OCC reconcile the "material" limitation of 12 C.F.R. § 7.4001(b) with its menu of "considerations" for acceptable non-interest fees in 12 C.F.R. § 7.4002(b), (d), which does not mention it? *See* 61 Fed. Reg. 4869 (Feb. 9, 1996); 66 Fed. Reg. 34792 (July 2, 2001).

144 *See* Burke & Kaplinsky, *Unraveling the New Federal Usury Law*, 37 Bus. Law. 1079, 1102, 1103 (1981–1982); *see also* OCC Interpretive Letter No. 178 (Jan. 12, 1981) Consumer Cred. Guide (CCH) ¶ 97,239 (RISA disclosure requirements not material). Relevant letters from 1992 forward are reproduced on the CD-Rom accompanying this volume.

145 Burke & Kaplinsky, *Unraveling the New Federal Usury Law*,

on high-rate consumer loans than on other classes of loans, these disclosure requirements should logically be deemed material to the higher rate.

The Minnesota Supreme Court considered (and applied) the materiality rule in the context of extending the most favored lender status to federally-insured state-chartered banks under DIDA.[146] It defined materiality as (1) pertaining to the manner in which the numerical rate of interest is calculated or (2) defining the "class of loans in such a way (as by size, type of borrower, or maturity)" as to affect the borrowed rate.[147] Licensing requirements would not be material, for example. The court specifically declined to decide whether attorney fees or loan-splitting provisions were material, as neither of these were part of the state statute the court chose to borrow.[148]

3.4.4 Calculating the Rate Ceiling for National Banks: Some Practical Examples

A few examples may help to clarify the interaction between the federal alternate interest rate ceiling and the state rate as calculated under the most favored lender doctrine. First, state banks in some jurisdictions are permitted to charge any rate agreed to by the parties to the loan. Under such circumstances, there will be no ceiling for federal banks either.[149] Similarly, when states have no ceiling *on particular types* of loans, federal banks arguably may charge unlimited interest *on loans of that type.*[150] This result appears to contradict that language in 12 U.S.C. § 85 which

establishes a 7% rate in the absence of a state ceiling, but it is otherwise consistent with most favored lender analysis.[151]

In some states, the usury ceiling for a particular type of loan may be the same for all lenders. This can occur when state banks are allowed to use the small loan rate without being licensed as small loan lenders. For example, if state banks may legally invoke the small loan rate ceilings on fixed term consumer credit up to $6,000 in amount financed (the scope of the small loan law), the national bank clearly may also use the small loan rate for small loans under that amount.

In many states, finance companies are allowed to charge more than the state banks on comparable loans. If, for example, the highest state rate ceiling is the finance company rate for smaller loans, then this rate may be adopted for loans of a type the finance companies are authorized to make as the national bank ceiling under the most favored lender approach.[152]

If the loan the national bank wishes to make is larger than loans finance companies are allowed to make, the national bank may not use the state finance company rate ceilings; it must look elsewhere to determine what the highest applicable legal rate under state law would be for that loan. For example, assume a national bank in state A wishes to make a fixed term loan of $4,000 to a consumer borrower. If the state's small loan law covers loans up to $3,000, that rate ceiling does not apply.[153] If, instead, the highest rate cap allowable for a $4,000 loan is, pursuant to a floating rate cap allowed to state banks, set at 9% on that date,[154] that is the most favored lender rate. The national bank now compares

---

37 Bus. Law. 1079, 1102, 1103 (1981–1982); *see also* Finkelstein, *Most Favored Lender Status for Insured Banks*, 42 Bus. Lawyer 915 (1987) (discussing materiality in the context of a parallel provision to § 85's most favored lender status, § 521 of DIDA, (*see* § 3.9.2, *infra*), questions the unexplained decision in First Bank East v. Bobeldyk, 391 N.W.2d 17 (Minn. Ct. App. 1986) that disclosure requirements are not "material." Article notes that a failure to provide disclosures may put that lender at a competitive advantage over those who must do so, thus defeating the purpose of most favored lender doctrine to provide for parity between banks and other state lenders).

146 VanderWeyst v. First State Bank of Benson, 425 N.W.2d 803 (Minn. 1988). See § 3.9.2, *infra*, for a discussion of most favored lender doctrine under DIDA.

147 VanderWeyst, 425 N.W.2d at 810.

148 *Id.* at 810, 811.

149 *See* Hiatt v. San Francisco Nat'l Bank, 361 F.2d 504 (9th Cir. 1966) (the explicit 12 U.S.C. § 85 limitation of seven percent discount method interest for national banks in states that have not set an interest ceiling may be ignored and such banks may charge the same unrestricted amount of interest as state banks); Comptroller's Ruling, 12 C.F.R. 7.7310(a).

150 *See* Keresey v. Nevada Nat'l Bank, 98 Nev. 315, 646 P.2d 1224 (1982); Patten v. Md. Bank, N.A., 126 S.W.3d 532 (Tex. App. 2003); Moore v. United Nat'l Bank, 821 S.W.2d 409 (Tex. App. 1991) (because state banks were subject to no rate limitations on first lien residential real estate as a result of DIDA, national banks are also free of rate limitations on such loans).

151 *See, e.g.,* Moore v. United Nat'l Bank, 821 S.W.2d 409 (Tex. App. 1991) (court rejected borrower's argument that because DIDA preempted any rate ceilings on residential first mortgages, "no rate is fixed by state law" and the alternate federal rate should apply; though the argument is compelling, such a reading is inconsistent with policy of assuring that national banks are not at competitive disadvantage).

The result is based on a 1900 Supreme Court decision, Daggs v. Phoenix Nat'l Bank, 177 U.S. 549, 20 S. Ct. 732, 44 L. Ed. 882 (1900), in which the language "if no rate is fixed by [state] law" was interpreted to authorize national banks to charge that rate when state law would otherwise not allow interest at all.

152 OCC Interpretive Letter 178, Consumer Cred. Guide (CCH) ¶ 97,239 (Jan. 12, 1981). Relevant letters from 1992 forward are reproduced on the CD-Rom accompanying this volume.

153 *Id.* The maximum amount is a "material" limit on the rate ceiling granted under state law, which the federal law respects.

154 When market interest rates spiked in the late 1970s, outstripping some of the fixed usury rate ceilings, all states responded, taking one or more of three approaches. One was to deregulate, leaving the rate to be determined by agreement of the parties (§ 9.2.8, *infra*). A second was to raise the statutory rate. A third approach was to set a ceiling tied to a specified market rate (for example, the Federal Reserve bank discount rate). A ceiling like this, "floating" with market conditions, has two advantages. It is self-correcting, avoiding the mismatch between changing market conditions and static statutory caps, and it balances both creditors and consumer interests, placing an outside limit to prevent abusive terms.

this rate to the federal discount rate.[155] If the discount rate were 4%, by adding the 1% allowed under section 85, the alternative federal ceiling would be 5%. For this loan, the state most favored lender rate would thus be higher than the federal ceiling, and the national bank would be permitted to use the 9% state bank rate.

Express exceptions for state and national banks from otherwise applicable usury limits may appear in state law.[156] Applicable state laws may be spread over several provisions or statutes. Consequently, practitioners should review the entirety of a state's credit law carefully.

It is also important to observe that the interest calculation method used to determine the most favored lender rate is the method set by state law. The use of state law for interest calculation has not always been the rule. In *Evans v. National Bank of Savannah*,[157] the Supreme Court decided to look to a state's numerical interest ceiling, but not its method of calculation, in setting the most favored lender rate. Thus, a state 8% usury ceiling was read to permit an 8% discount rate for a national bank even though no state lender could charge an equivalent rate under state law.

The Eighth Circuit has limited *Evans* to its facts, holding that state calculation methods apply except on short-term single-installment notes.[158] The Eighth Circuit's approach is more consistent with both the most favored lender doctrine and the modern lending environment than the *Evans* decision. Reading an 18% state usury ceiling as a discount rate for national banks, for example, would permit 200% simple interest on a five-year, $5,000 transaction.[159]

3.4.5 Interstate Banking: National Banks and Rate Exportation

3.4.5.1 Background: *Marquette* and Its Legacy

3.4.5.1.1 Overview and constitutional concerns

A 1978 Supreme Court decision, *Marquette National Bank of Minneapolis v. First of Omaha Service Corp.*,[160] gave national banks the right to take the most favored lender status from their home state across state lines, and preempt the law of the borrower's home state.[161] Therein lies the tale

of why so many of those credit card solicitations sent by mail every week come from Delaware or South Dakota: credit card issuers located there to export those unregulated states' *lack* of consumer protections nationwide, irrespective of what policy decisions other state legislatures have made about the proper balance between creditor and debtor interests.[162]

The full extent of the exportation right has not been fully determined although the picture is clearer.[163] Two questions have been central to the hotly contested post-*Marquette* litigation: what charges and contract terms are encompassed in the term "interest rate," and thus may be exported; and whether DIDA grants entities other than national banks the right to export "it," however it is defined.

The Supreme Court confronted the first question in *Smiley v. Citibank (South Dakota), N.A.*[164] This case is addressed in § 3.4.5.2, *infra*. The second question, that is, the special issues raised by boot-strapping the national banks' exportation right to state-chartered banks through DIDA, is discussed in § 3.9.2.2, *infra*.

A third issue, less explored to date, is whether *Marquette* limits the exportation right to entities with no branches in its target state.[165] This section will first discuss *Marquette* and one possible limitation derived from that decision.

---

155 *See* § 3.4.2, *supra*.

156 *See* Jones v. Wells Fargo Bank, 5 Cal. Rptr. 3d 835 (Cal. Ct. App. 2003) (exception in California's constitutional usury provisions for state and national banks where the bank is authorized to engage in trust business and is acting in its fiduciary relationship).

157 251 U.S. 108, 40 S. Ct. 58, 64 L. Ed. 171 (1919); *see* Annotation, 81 A.L.R.2d 1280 (1962).

158 First Nat'l Bank v. Nowlin, 509 F.2d 872 (8th Cir. 1975).

159 An 18% discount on a sixty-month transaction takes $4500 in interest, leaving only $500 as the financed amount. *See* § 4.3.3, *infra*.

160 439 U.S. 299, 99 S. Ct. 540, 58 L. Ed. 2d 534 (1978).

161 It is worth noting that there was no interstate banking when the NBA was passed. *See generally* § 3.4.1, *supra*.

162 South Dakota and Delaware, at the beginning of the explosive growth of the financial services industry around 1980, sought to attract that industry as part of their economic development strategy. They wanted to "provide [their] citizens with the jobs and benefits a large national credit card operation can provide (attracted by the ability to export limitless credit card rates to other states)," while, it should be noted, protecting their local banks from competition with the exporting banks. Indep. Cmty. Bankers' Ass'n of S.D. v. Board of Governors, Federal Reserve Sys., 838 F.2d 969, 975 (8th Cir. 1988). *Cf.* Eckman, *The Delaware Consumer Credit Bank Act and Exporting Interest Under § 521 of the Depository Institutions Deregulation and Monetary Control Act of 1980*, 39 Bus. L. 1264 (1984).

It worked, too. South Dakota's tax revenue from banks went from $3.2 million in 1980 to almost $27.2 million in 1987, with the comparable figures for Delaware rising from $2.4 million to almost $40 million. The Economist, July 2, 1988, pg. 26. Nonetheless, the strategy has had the effect of weakening the resolve of states which wish to retain strong consumer protections, as the local banks argue that having to comply with such laws puts them at a competitive disadvantage to the exporting banks, which do not. This is one of the factors behind the continuing push for deregulation at the state level, even though the lowest interest rates in decades mean statutory limitations no longer squeeze lenders' margins, as they did in the late 1970s and early 1980s.

163 For review of exportation and preemption developments, see Elizabeth R. Schiltz, *The Amazing, Elastic, Ever-Expanding Exportation Doctrine and Its Effects on Predatory Lending Regulations*, 88 Minn. L. Rev. 518 (2004).

164 517 U.S. 735, 116 S. Ct. 1730, 135 L. Ed. 2d 25 (1996); *see also* Doe v. Norwest Bank Minn., N.A., 107 F.3d 1297 (8th Cir. 1997).

165 For a discussion of *Marquette* and interstate banking, see Elizabeth R. Schiltz, *The Amazing, Elastic, Ever-Expanding Exportation Doctrine and Its Effects on Predatory Lending Regulations*, 88 Minn. L. Rev. 518 (2004).

The fundamental issue presented by exportation is the transformation of federal preemption into "sister-state" preemption, a fundamentally undemocratic concept alien to our organic system which respects the sovereignty of all states on an equal plane.[166] The courts are being asked to balance this profound interest against what is merely part of the momentum toward an interstate banking system. Looking at it from that perspective, one state court held that, to the extent section 85 of the National Bank Act would transform South Dakota law into federal law, it is an unconstitutional delegation of authority.[167] The Supreme Court, however, framed the issue in such a way so as to avoid constitutional analysis. The question for the Court was whether a bank can utilize a federal definition of interest to charge its fees in any state in which it does business.[168]

An unintended but not surprising effect of the *Marquette* ruling has been the enormous increase in credit card lending,

and, consequently, consumer credit card debt. Since 1978, the year *Marquette* was decided, this type of debt rose from approximately $50 billion to over $300 billion by 1995.[169] By 2001, credit card debt jumped to $692 billion.[170] According to one author, a result of the deregulated credit market place which occurred following this Supreme Court case has been an enormous increase in personal bankruptcy filings.[171]

3.4.5.1.2 The role of a national bank's "location"

In *Marquette*, the Supreme Court allowed a Nebraska national bank which had no Minnesota branches to employ the higher Nebraska rate ceiling for its credit card customers in Minnesota, where a lower state usury limit otherwise applied to banks. The Court held that the controlling rate ceiling was that of the lender bank's home state; therefore, interstate banking by mail was unaffected by usury laws in the consumer's home state. A bank's location was determined by the "charter address" in the bank's organization certificate. Thus out-of-state national banks from states with high or nonexistent rate limitations are not restricted by more protective local usury laws, at least as long as they have no authorized branch in the consumer's state. The court reasoned that this was no different from an out-of-state customer coming across a state line to obtain a loan in the second state.[172]

It is unclear whether the fact that the Nebraska bank had no branches in Minnesota was essential to the court's holding.[173] Certainly its analogy to the out-of-state customer coming into the second state for a loan would no longer hold, for lenders that take their shops into another state then have to comply with that state's laws.[174] A loan office of a nationally operating finance company, for example, must comply with the laws of the states in which it operates.[175]

---

166 It is undemocratic because the legislators of the exporting states are not accountable to citizens in other states, though their rights are determined by that "foreign" body. In contrast, all citizens can hold their *federal* legislators accountable at the polls, if they disapprove of *federal* preemption of their rights under state law. It is upon this basic fact that the exportation doctrine stumbles on its own terms. Were Congress (in 1864 or 1978) asked if they intended to let the Delaware state legislature set the standards for consumer protection nationwide, it is extremely doubtful they would have said yes, and constitutional scholarship suggests they could not have. *Cf.* Irwin v. Citibank (S.D.), Clearinghouse No. 50,419 (Pa. C.P. filed Dec. 9, 1993) (citing Lawrence H. Tribe, American Constitutional Law § 5-17 (1988)).

167 Irwin v. Citibank (S.D.), Clearinghouse No. 50,419 (Pa. C.P., filed Dec. 9, 1993) (citing, among other things, Gibbons v. Ogden, 22 U.S. (9 Wheat.) 1, 208 (1824)); *see also* Smiley v. Citibank (S.D.), N.A., 32 Cal. Rptr. 2d 562 (Ct. App. 1994) (dissent), *aff'd*, 517 U.S. 735, 116 S. Ct. 1730, 135 L. Ed. 2d 25 (1996) (Supreme Court dismissed the constitutional argument because the OCC had promulgated a regulation during the course of the litigation that defined interest to include late fees; thus, there was no transformation of South Dakota law into federal law, but rather federal law now controlled); Mazaika v. Bank One, Columbus, N.A., 653 A.2d 640 (Pa. Super. Ct. 1994), *rev'd on other grounds*, 680 A.2d 845 (Pa. 1996) (applying the holding in *Smiley*). *But see* First Nat'l Bank v. Burke, 48 F. Supp. 2d 132 (D. Conn. 1999) (court rejected a 10th Amendment constitutional challenge to the OCC's expansive reading of its right to enforce the National Banking Act; case involved Connecticut law prohibiting the imposition of ATM surcharges on non-depositors).

168 *See* Mazaika v. Bank One, Columbus, N.A., 653 A.2d 640 (Pa. Super. Ct. 1994) (interpreting *Marquette*), *rev'd on other grounds*, 680 A.2d 845 (Pa. 1996); *cf.* Fed. Home Loan Bank Bd., General Counsel Opinion No. 588 (Raiden, Dec. 11, 1984) (interpreting rate exportation under § 522 of DIDA, "multi-location" savings and loan is "located" in any state where its main office or any branch office is located; thus the lender can export the most favored lender rate of the state where the office at which the transaction is booked is located). Opinion No. 588 does not view *Marquette*'s interpretation of "located" under § 85 as controlling, as no branch locations were involved. This issue was not raised in Smiley v. Citibank (S.D.), N.A., 517 U.S. 735, 116 S. Ct. 1730, 135 L. Ed. 2d 25 (1996).

169 Diane Ellis, *Bank Trends—The Effect of Consumer Interest Rate Deregulation on Credit Card Volumes, Charge-Offs, and in the Personal Bankruptcy Rate*, FDIC—Division of Insurance (2000), *available at* www.FDIC.gov.

170 Tamara Draut & Javier Silva, Borrowing to Make Ends Meet: The Growth of Credit Card Debt in the 90's, 3 (DEMOS 2003).

171 Diane Ellis, *Bank Trends—The Effect of Consumer Interest Rate Deregulation on Credit Card Volumes, Charge-Offs, and in the Personal Bankruptcy Rate*, FDIC—Division of Insurance (2000), *available at* www.FDIC.gov.

172 The separate but related issue of the citizenship of a national bank for purposes of diversity jurisdiction is discussed in § 3.15, *infra*.

173 Even banks which establish branches in other states must ordinarily comply with the host state's law, unless "non-ministerial" functions are performed at the main office in the home state. See the discussion in this subsection of two OCC Interpretive letters.

174 Compliance with state law where the branch is located depends upon where the loan actually is "made." This issue is discussed later in this section.

175 At least one court has held that "body-dragging" a borrower to a lender's office in a second state in order to deny the borrower the protections of his home state's law will not, under a choice of laws analysis, warrant application of the lender's home base

The Cost of Credit: Regulation and Legal Challenges

A recent decision interpreted the "organized or existing in" language in the first sentence of section 85 of the National Bank Act.[176] Homeowners sued a national bank chartered in North Carolina that does business nationwide but maintains no branches outside of its home state. Rather, its home equity lending is conducted through "loan processing offices." The homeowners, residents of Pennsylvania, were charged interest on the loan principal prior to disbursement of the funds to them and third parties, in violation of North Carolina law. The bank argued that it "existed" in Pennsylvania due to the presence of its loan processing and, therefore, should be able to apply the law of that state to the transaction. The court rejected this theory, finding that the "existing" language in section 85 was meant to "guarantee the same status under state law provided to national banks organized under the 1864 Act to those banks already 'existing' under the earlier act."[177] Therefore, the bank could not use the more permissive Pennsylvania climate to shield itself from the laws of its home state. Only if the bank established a branch in Pennsylvania would the laws of that state potentially apply.[178] The court denied the bank's motion for summary judgment and certified a nationwide class. Three years later, the court vacated its opinion without discussion, presumably as part of a settlement of the case.[179]

Historically, there have been limitations on the right of banks to establish branches interstate,[180] though the passage of the Interstate Banking and Branching Efficiency Act of 1994[181] is undoubtedly making interstate branch banking more common, and thus brings this question to the fore.[182]

The legislative history of IBBEA indicates that Congress did not intend, by its passage, to tip the balance of existing law on preemption one way or the other. It leaves the judicial process to continue to take its course—whatever that may be.[183] It further expresses concern that the federal banking

---

state's law. Mayo v. Key Fin. Servs., Inc., Clearinghouse No. 49,969 (Mass. Super. Ct. June 22, 1994) (arguably such body-dragging is an unfair and deceptive practice as well).

176 Flannick v. First Union Home Equity Bank, 134 F. Supp. 2d 389 (E.D. Pa. 2001) (the bank first argued that any interest restrictions in North Carolina law are trumped by DIDMCA because the loan was a first lien mortgage; the court rejected this argument because North Carolina had opted out of the interest rate and points restrictions).

177 *Id.* at 396.

178 See the discussion in this subsection of two OCC Interpretive Letters regarding the application of the law of the home state and that of the state where branches exist.

179 Flannick v. First Union Equity Bank, N.A., 2004 WL 1218600 (E.D. Pa. Mar. 8, 2004).

180 The McFadden Act, 12 U.S.C. § 36, limited the national banks' right to establish branches in other states.

181 Pub. L. No. 103-328, 108 Stat. 2338 (Sept. 29, 1994) (codified at 12 U.S.C. § 36).

182 That interstate branching has expanded greatly since the passage of IBBEA is evident from court decisions upholding OCC decisions permitting branching. See, e.g., TeamBank, N.A. v. McClure, 279 F.3d 614 (8th Cir. 2002) (court upheld OCC order permitting TeamBank, headquartered in Missouri, to merge with an affiliated national bank in Kansas; following the OCC order, TeamBank moved its headquarters to Kansas and retained branches in both Kansas and Missouri); Ghiglieri v. Sun World N.A., 117 F.3d 309 (5th Cir. 1997) (Comptroller's decision to allow bank to relocate its main office to another state, to maintain its pre-existing branches in its ex-home state, and to

create additional branches in its ex-home state upheld); Ghiglieri v. Ludwig, 125 F.3d 941 (5th Cir. 1997) (same). *But see* McQueen v. Williams, 177 F.3d 523 (6th Cir. 1999) (court reversed OCC permission to a bank holding company located in Ohio to create a major regional banking network and to engage in interstate banking by converting a affiliated bank in Michigan to a national bank, relocate its main office in Indiana, maintain its existing branches in Michigan and to switch some main offices of banks to branches).

In addition, the Fourth Circuit held that the H & R Block office in South Carolina (where Beneficial National Bank made tax refund anticipation loans) did not constitute a branch and the exportation was sanctioned. Cades v. H & R Block, Inc., 43 F.3d 869 (4th Cir. 1994); Christiansen v. Beneficial Nat'l Bank, 972 F. Supp. 681 (S.D. Ga. 1997) (same). Recently, the OCC issued an amendment to Interpretive Ruling § 7.1012 addressing "messenger services." 64 Fed. Reg. 60092 (Nov. 4, 1999). The Supplementary Information clearly shows that the OCC intended to incorporate the more lax standard enunciated in *Cades* and *Christiansen* in determining under what circumstances the H & R Block office does not constitute a branch of the bank itself. The OCC distinguished between the situation where the agent (called the "messenger service") is affiliated with the out-of-state bank and when the agent is not affiliated. A non-affiliated service need only show that it has the discretion to determine, in its own business judgment, which customers it will serve and when. "In contrast, an affiliated service, because it may be more likely to favor its affiliates as a result of its common ownership or control, must show that it actually serves the public generally, including non-affiliated depository institutions." *Id.* The OCC carefully points out that the national bank cannot conduct its "core" activities in the borrower's home state (or else the H & R Block office would be acting as a branch). The upshot is that an H & R Block office will not be considered a branch as long as the out-of-state bank uses the local office to merely collect and transmit information to the bank and the bank makes it credit decisions and lends the money from its own office (which, of course, the bank wants to do so that it can export the lack of consumer protections in its home state to the borrower's state).

183 Pub. L. No. 103-328, § 102(b)(1), 108 Stat. 2338 (codified at 12 U.S.C. § 36(f)(1)) (national bank branches are subject to laws of host state regarding consumer protection, CRA, fair lending, and establishment of intrastate branches except when federal law preempts such state laws with respect to national banks); *see also* Pub. L. No. 103-328, § 102(b)(3), 108 Stat. 2338 (codified at 12 U.S.C. § 1831a(j)) (out-of-state state bank branches are subject to laws of host state regarding consumer protection, CRA, fair lending, and establishment of intrastate branches [*Editor's Note*: That section does not have a reference to federal preemption. See generally § 3.9.2.2, *infra*.]).

The Conference Committee Report is about as unequivocal as the 103d Congress knew how to be.

> States have a strong interest in the activities and operations of depository institutions doing business within their jurisdictions, regardless of the type of charter an institution holds. In particular, States have a legitimate interest in protecting the

regulatory agencies have been "inappropriately aggressive" in preempting state law "in situations where the federal interest did not warrant that result."[184]

Two recent Interpretive Letters issued by the OCC, however, pull the rug out from under the even-handedness that Congress was trying to achieve. In the first letter, a bank sought an opinion as to whether it could use interest rates permitted in its home state in extending credit cards to customers in states where it intended to merge with affiliated banks.[185] The bank intended to continue to perform virtually all of its credit card operations in its main office state.[186] The OCC agreed that the bank could export the interest rates of its home state to other states despite the anticipated location of branches in those states.[187]

Once the train started chugging, the OCC gave it a huge push with the Interpretive Letter of February 17, 1998.[188] In it, the chief counsel decided that a national bank may be located in *both* its home state and its host (or branch) states for purposes of exportation. Relying heavily on statements made by Senator Roth,[189] a co-sponsor of IBBEA, the chief counsel concluded that:

> [A]n interstate national bank may charge interest permitted by the laws of its home state unless the loan is made—that is, the loan is approved, credit is extended, and funds are disbursed—in a branch or branches of the bank in a single host state. If one or two of these three functions occur in a host state, the bank may, alternatively, charge the interest permitted by that state if, based on an assessment of all the facts and circumstances, the loan has a clear nexus to that state.[190]

Under this interpretation, therefore, national banks will be allowed to apply home state rates *unless*, regarding a particular loan, these non-ministerial functions[191] are *all* performed at one or more branches.

These Interpretive Letters create a cookbook which shows national banks with branches in other states how to design their business so they can apply their home states' laws to loans made through their branches, thus avoiding the application of the host states' consumer protection, fair lending, and community reinvestment laws. Alternatively, the national bank can select the host state's law even if all three non-ministerial functions are not performed in the branch. In addition, it will be quite difficult for borrowers (and their attorneys) to make an independent determination as to which state's usury rates should be applied to their loans. Such a determination will involve discovering where the decision to extend credit and communicate the decision, the

---

rights of their consumers, businesses, and communities.... Congress does not intend that [this Act] alter this balance and thereby weaken States' authority to protect the interests of their consumers, businesses, or communities.

It goes on to reiterate the standard judicial principles of interpretation: state law applies unless there is a direct conflict, or federal law is so comprehensive as to evidence congressional intent to occupy the field, or state law stands as an obstacle to accomplished the federal law's purposes. Thus safe and soundness is one factor to consider, but, on the other hand, courts usually "use a rule of construction which avoids finding a conflict where possible. This title does not change these judicially established principles." H.R. Conf. Rep. No. 103-651, at 53 (1994), *reprinted in* 1994 U.S.C.C.A.N. 2068.

184 H.R. Conf. Rep. No. 103-651, at 53, 54 (1994), *reprinted in* 1994 U.S.C.C.A.N. 2068.
    Congress singled out the example of an agency opinion preempting a state law restricting bank deposit account service charges. As a result of this concern, proposed agency interpretations preempting state law with respect to CRA, consumer protection, fair lending, or intrastate branches now must be published in the Federal Register for comment. 12 U.S.C. § 43; *see* § 3.3, *supra*.
    It is unclear the precise range of the term "consumer protection." Certainly limitations on the cost of consumer credit protect consumers. Given the Supreme Court's acceptance of the OCC's expansive definition of interest, it is difficult to know what constitutes "consumer protection," except for protections that have nothing to do with interest rates and fees, such as disclosure. *See* § 3.4.5.2, *infra*.

185 OCC Interpretive Letter No. 776 (Mar. 18, 1997). Interpretive Letters issued since 1996 can be obtained on the Internet at www.occ.treas.gov (look under "regulatory activities"). Summaries of OCC letters dealing with the preemption of state law and related topics issued since 1992 can be found in Appx. C.3, *infra*. The full text of these letters is reproduced on the CD-Rom accompanying this volume.

186 The laundry list of functions is quite long but, relevant to the extension of credit include: receiving and processing application for credit; obtaining credit reports; gathering and verifying information necessary to make the credit decisions; making of all underwriting and credit decisions; maintaining all credit card accounts; and providing customer service and collection functions. *See* OCC Interpretive Letter, at 2, 3 (Feb. 17, 1998).

187 As for what constitutes a "branch," *see* 12 C.F.R. § 7.1003, *reprinted in* Appx. C.2, *infra. See also* OCC Interpretive Letter

No. 980 (Dec. 24, 2003) (UPS drop box at various non-bank offices of a national bank do not constitute branches given the particular facts).

188 OCC Interpretive Letter No. 822 (Feb. 17, 1998). *See also* OCC Interpretive Letter No. 995 (June 22, 2004) (national bank may export the state fiduciary law of any state in which it conducts fiduciary services to any other state; a state's law that restrict foreign national banks from providing fiduciary services in its state unless certain conditions are met is preempted).

189 140 Cong. Rec. S12,789 (Sept. 13, 1994).

190 OCC Interpretive Letter No. 822, at 14, 15 (Feb. 17, 1998). *See also* FDIC General Counsel Opinion No. 11 (May 18, 1998), 63 Fed. Reg. 27282, adopting the OCC analysis and applying it to insured state-chartered banks. *Cf.* OTS Letter (Sept. 17, 2004) in which the OTS confirms that savings associations may charge the interest rate allowed by its home state regardless of where the loan is "made" or "booked"; or the state in which a branch exists, if the loan is "booked" in the branch's state. The OTS distinguishes the more restrictive standards set forth in OCC and FDIC letters on this issue.

191 These non-ministerial functions are: the decision to extend credit (and the communication of that decision); the extension of credit itself; and the disbursal of loan proceeds.

extension itself, and the disbursal of funds each actually occurred.[192]

Finally, it is unclear whether these letters have any binding effect because they were not issued in accordance with 12 U.S.C. § 46.[193]

In the realm of electronic transactions, the OCC enacted two relevant regulations.[194] One regulation addresses where a bank is located when it maintains technology in a state. It states that a national bank is not located in a state solely because it physically maintains technology, such as a server or automated loan center, in that state; nor is it located in a state because the bank's products or services are accessed through electronic means by consumers located in the state.[195] The second regulation deals banks operating solely via the Internet. Where a national bank is operating exclusively through the Internet, its main office is the office relevant for section 85 purposes.[196] However, the "main" office may be little more than an office suite and a "call center." Is this type of "main" office a sufficient "location" for purposes of section 85? The answer may turn on whether the bank has significantly outsourced functions that require physical assets or person-power to third parties.[197]

One other interesting development involves the interplay between the National Banking Act and the Electronic Funds Transfer Act as they affect the related issue of a state's ability to regulate electronic transactions.[198] The EFTA provides:

> A basic framework establishing the right, liabilities, and responsibilities of participation in electronic fund transfer systems. The primary objective of this subchapter, however, is the provision of individual consumer rights.[199]

One court denied a national bank's motion to enjoin the enforcement of Iowa's Electronic Funds Act which regulates the establishment of ATM machines in its borders by banks which have no in-state offices.[200] Specifically, Iowa law mandates that a bank (national or otherwise) maintain an in-state office in order to operate an ATM in Iowa; requires banks operating an ATM in Iowa to file an information statement, including a schedule of charges and agreements to comply with Iowa law; regulates the amount of "interchange fee"; provides for "universal access"; and limits the type of advertising placed on ATM machines.

The court held that none of the challenged provisions of Iowa law were inconsistent with the NBA.[201] More significantly, the court approved the more narrowly drawn EFTA which, by its terms, does not preempt state law except to, and only to, the extent of any inconsistency. Under this analysis, none of the Iowa provisions were inconsistent with the more consumer friendly EFTA.[202]

On appeal, however, the Eighth Circuit reversed.[203] The court stated that the National Bank Act preempts Iowa law because it grants national banks the authority to exercise any incidental powers as are necessary to carry on the business of banking. In addition, the court found that the deferral to state consumer protection laws present in the Interstate Banking and Branching Efficiency Act of 1994 (IBBEA)[204] does not apply because ATMs are specifically excluded from the definition of a "branch."[205] In cursorily dismissing the EFTA argument, the court merely asserts that "this anti-preemption provision is specifically limited to the provisions of the federal EFTA, and nothing therein grants the states any additional authority to regulate national banks." This holding fails to consider the fact that the EFTA was passed after the NBA. Thus, Congress chose to defer to state law in electronic transactions where state law is not inconsistent with the EFTA. Relying upon the IBBEA's exclusion of ATMs from coverage to mean that no other more specific federal law applies to electronic transactions at ATMs is misplaced. Because IBBEA does not apply, the law that arguably applies is the EFTA, not general principles enunciated by courts under the NBA.[206]

This issue heated up in California when two cities passed ordinances prohibiting financial institutions from charging

---

192   A good example of this problem arose in MorEquity, Inc. v. Naeem, 118 F. Supp. 2d 885 (N.D. Ill. 2000). There, residents of Illinois argued that the bank which made them a mortgage loan, though chartered in California, had established a branch in Illinois where the loan application was submitted. The consumers argued that Illinois usury law applied to the transaction. The court, however, found that the consumers failed to allege where the non-ministerial acts occurred and dismissed their usury claim.

193   *See* § 3.4.6, *infra*. While these letters are ostensibly not about preemption, their effect is to preempt the host states' laws on consumer protection, fair lending, and community reinvestment.

194   12 C.F.R. §§ 7.5008, 7.5009.

195   12 C.F.R. § 7.5008.

196   12 C.F.R. § 7.5009.

197   *See* discussion of these issues in Elizabeth R. Schiltz, *The Amazing, Elastic, Ever-Expanding Exportation Doctrine and Its Effects on Predatory Lending Regulations*, 88 Minn. L. Rev. 518, 558–559 (2004) (suggesting that even the OCC thought it was pushing the envelope with this regulation).

198   15 U.S.C. § 1693 *et seq.*

199   15 U.S.C. § 1693(b).

200   Bank One, Utah v. Gattau, Clearinghouse No. 52,148 (S.D. Iowa July 24, 1998), *rev'd*, 190 F.3d 844 (8th Cir. 1999), *cert. denied*, 529 U.S. 1087 (2000).

201   In so holding, the court found that the OCC letter on Connecticut ATM restrictions which opined that the state law was pre-empted by the NBA was an unreasonable interpretation of preemption law. *See* OCC Interpretive Letter No. 821 (Feb. 17, 1998) (reproduced on the CD-Rom accompanying this volume).

202   The court also dismissed the bank's arguments that these provisions violated the Commerce Clause, the First Amendment, and the Equal Protection Clause.

203   Bank One v. Gattau, 190 F.3d 844 (8th Cir. 1999), *cert. denied*, 529 U.S. 1087 (2000).

204   12 U.S.C. § 36(f)(1)(A); *see* § 3.1.1, *supra*.

205   12 U.S.C. § 36(j).

206   *See* the OCC's position on this issue in Interpretive Letter No. 906 (Jan. 19, 2001), *reproduced on* the CD-Rom accompanying this volume.

non-accountholders an ATM fee for the use of their machines. Financial institutions immediately sued. A federal district court permanently enjoined the implementation of these ordinances on the grounds that the NBA and HOLA preempt the municipalities right to regulate national banks and federal savings associations on this core issue.[207] The Ninth Circuit affirmed, probably sealing the fate of similar local ordinances that might be contemplated in other jurisdictions.[208] On the EFTA issue, the court agreed with the Eighth Circuit and added a second reason why the EFTA does not trump the bank preemption asserted in the case. The court held that the regulation of ATM fees is not the type of consumer protection measure contemplated by the EFTA.[209]

3.4.5.1.3 National bank as an assignee

There is one limitation on rate exportation that does seem clear. Courts have held that federal preemption rights granted to depositories apply only to credit *initiated* by the depository, not to that assigned to it.[210] In other words, a

bank cannot purchase a pre-existing usurious note executed by parties in a low-rate state and then claim that the note is no longer usurious on the theory that the laws of the high rate state should control. Such an approach would render usury ceilings for lenders other than national banks completely unworkable and has no foundation in the purposes of

207 Bank of Am. v. City & County of San Francisco, 2000 U.S. Dist. LEXIS 12587 (N.D. Cal. June 30, 2000).

208 Bank of Am. v. City & County of San Francisco, 309 F.3d 551 (9th Cir. 2002) (HOLA regulations leave no room for states to regulate federal savings associations; OCC preemption letters regarding ATM fee restrictions imposed by states or local jurisdictions upheld).

209 *Id.*; *see also* Wells Fargo Bank Texas v. James, 321 F.3d 488 (5th Cir. 2003) (court upholds injunction issued against the enforcement of a state law prohibiting banks from charging fees to non-account holders for cashing checks drawn on that bank); Metrobank N.A. v. Foster, 193 F. Supp. 2d 1156 (S.D. Iowa 2002) (state's anti-discrimination law, which when applied to national banks prevented them from charging fees to non-account holders when accessing ATM machines, is preempted). For press on this issue and the role of the OCC, see Jess Bravin & Paul Beckett, *Dependent on Lender Fees, The OCC Takes Banks' Side Against Local Laws*, Wall St. J., Jan. 28, 2002.

210 *See* Fed. Deposit Ins. Corp. v. Lattimore Land Corp., 656 F.2d 139 (5th Cir. 1981); Miller v. Pacific Shore Funding, 224 F. Supp. 2d 977 (D. Md. 2002), *aff'd on other grounds*, 92 Fed. Appx. 933, 2004 WL 144138 (4th Cir. 2004) (assignees stand in the shoes of the assignors and are subject to the same claims and defenses unless the holder-in-due-course defense applies); Fed. Nat'l Mortgage Ass'n v. Lefkowitz, 390 F. Supp. 1364 (S.D.N.Y. 1975) (where state law applies at loan origination, it continues to apply to the loan purchaser); *In re* Harrington, 6 B.R. 655 (Bankr. D.R.I. 1980) (assignment does not revive void note); Spitz v. Goldome Realty Credit Corp., 569 N.E.2d 43 (Ill. App. Ct. 1991), *aff'd*, 600 N.E.2d 1185 (Ill. 1992) (mortgage originated by lender which is a servicing corporation second-tier subsidiary of a federal savings bank was subject to state mortgage escrow account act; the preemption applicable to its parent did not extend to it); Viereck v. Peoples Sav. & Loan Ass'n, 343 N.W.2d 30 (Minn. 1984) (due-on-sale clauses contained in mortgage were not valid under applicable state law; as the originating lenders were not entitled to preemption, the federal savings association assignee was not entitled to preemption either); St. Paul Bank for Cooperatives v. Ohman, 402 N.W.2d 235 (Minn. Ct. App. 1987) (interest preemption in 12 U.S.C. § 2205 relating to loans from institutions of the Farm Credit

System did not apply to an assigned contract); Garrison v. First Fed. Sav. & Loan Ass'n of S.C., 402 S.E.2d 25 (Va. 1991) (federal savings and loan as assignee of mortgage company originated loan not entitled to preemption even though loan was one of large pool sold to the savings and loan). *Cf.* Adkison v. First Plus Bank, 143 S.W.3d 29 (Mo. App. Ct. 2004) (the bank was the lender since it was listed on the documents; court implies disapproval of the claim that the table-funding "lender," technically the assignee, is the lender).

In the credit card context, a recent decision by the Eighth Circuit highlights a national bank's rights after it acquires credit card accounts and becomes the originator of credit. Krispin v. The May Dep't Stores Co., 218 F.3d 919 (8th Cir. 2000) (consumer opened a revolving credit card account with the store located in Missouri sometime before 1996; in 1996, the store sold all of its accounts to May National Bank, not chartered in Missouri; all new accounts were also opened directly in the bank's name; agreement between the store and the bank provided that the store purchase the bank's new accounts on a daily basis as the assignee; bank increased the late fees and the customers sued charging that Missouri law was violated by the store; court found that the bank, and not the store, issued credit to the customers and thus was entitled to preempt Missouri late fee limits; note that if customers still owed debt extended by the store before 1996, late fees imposed on that debt should be limited by Missouri law as the bank would not have originated that debt; central question was whether the case should be remanded to state court.

The court in *Marquette* emphasized that it was not considering a transaction in which it was alleged that a state lender was the actual extender of credit. Marquette Nat'l Bank of Minneapolis v. First of Omaha Serv. Corp., 439 U.S. 299, 307, 308, 311 n.24, 99 S. Ct. 540, 58 L. Ed. 2d 534 (1978); *cf.* Grunbeck v. Dime Sav. Bank, 848 F. Supp. 294 (D.N.H. 1994) (issue not discussed, but the originator in that case would have been able to independently assert federal preemption of state law regarding method of computing interest under either DIDA § 501 or AMTPA), *vacated and remanded on other grounds*, 74 F.3d 331 (1st Cir. 1996) (DIDA does *not* preempt state simple interest statute; issue as to AMTPA's preemption apparently to be resolved on remand (lender made negatively amortizing mortgage loans); *see* §§ 3.9.3.3, 3.10, *infra*); Cohen v. Eisenberg, 697 N.Y.S.2d 625 (App. Div. 1999) (mortgage loan holder's motion for summary judgment denied where consumer alleged that originating lender (a lender entitled to preemption) was substituted at closing for the lender (not entitled to preemption) who provided the commitment letter; facts support allegation of intent to evade state usury laws). *But see* Saul v. Midlantic Nat'l Bank/South, 572 A.2d 650 (N.J. Super. Ct. App. Div. 1990) (court applied most favored lender doctrine of NBA to transaction in which an installment sale contract with a car dealer was assigned to a national bank). However, *Saul* does not discuss the distinction between a national bank's status as assignee and as originator, and the point was apparently not raised. As a result of that deficiency in its analysis, the case's precedential value should be viewed as questionable as support for an argument that a national bank is entitled to the NBA's preemption rights when it is an assignee. *See also* § 3.3, *supra*.

the National Bank Act or its counterpart statutes affecting other types of depository institutions. Further, the parties to a contract have the right to expect that the contract terms and the laws governing them are fixed as of the time the contract is consummated. If a national bank can successfully argue that its preemption rights regarding the interpretation and legality of a loan contract attach even if it is only the assignee of the contract, the ability to contract with certainty is completely undermined.

The OCC has spoken to some extent on this issue. Where the bank originates or table-funds the loan,[211] the bank's preemption rights "attach" to the loan and conflicting state laws are preempted.[212] Where the loan is arranged by a broker and made by another type of entity not entitled to preemption, the state law is not preempted.[213] Where the bank is merely the trustee of a pool of loans and did not originate the loan and did not fund the loan at inception, state law applies.[214]

Challenges to "sham" bank loans or "rent-a-charter" loans seek to look beneath the façade of the bank's name appearing on the loan documents to determine who is the true lender and, hence, whether the actual lender is entitled to preemption. This hot topic is discussed in § 3.13, *infra*.

3.4.5.2 Scope of the Term "Interest Rate" for Exportation Purposes

The position of the exporting lenders is that virtually any contract term which affects their ultimate yield is "material," can be considered as interest, and is therefore exportable. To date, they have been fairly successful in convincing courts of this position.[215] Charges and contract terms which have been held to fall within the scope of "interest rate" for purposes of most favored lender status (and hence exportation rights) are: late charges,[216] credit card over the limit (OTL) fees,[217] cash advance fees,[218] methods of computing interest,[219] bonus or commissions paid to lenders,[220] and closing costs.[221]

Prior to the *Smiley* decision there were some stirrings, questioning whether these courts went too far with too little thought.[222] Given the legislative history of the Interstate Banking Act which makes clear Congress did not (and does not) intend to occupy the field of consumer protection, even for national banks, a thoughtful dissent in a California

---

211 A table-funded transaction is one where a nominal lender is actually originating the loan for an entity whose money is used to fund the loan. The loan is transferred immediately to the table-funding lender. *See* § 12.2.1, *infra*, for a description of the implications of table-funding under the Real Estate Settlement Procedures Act.

212 OCC Interpretive Letter No. 1000 (Apr. 2, 2004); OCC Interpretive Letter No. 1002 (May 13, 2004), *reprinted on* the CD-Rom accompanying this volume. *But cf.* Adkison v. First Plus Bank, 143 S.W.3d 29 (Mo. App. Ct. 2004) (the bank was the lender since it was listed on the documents; court implies disapproval of the claim that the table-funding "lender," technically the assignee, is the lender).

213 *Id.*

214 OCC Letter to Private Attorneys regarding Wells Fargo Bank, Minnesota, N.A. v. Alberta Harris (Jan. 14, 2005), *reprinted on* the CD-Rom accompanying this volume. Securitization is described in § 11.3, *infra*, in National Consumer Law Center, *Unfair and Deceptive Acts and Practices* § 6.7.4 (6th ed. 2004 and Supp.), and in Kathleen C. Engel & Patricia A. McCoy, *Predatory Lending: What Does Wall Street Have to Do with It?*, 15 Housing Pol. J. 715, 717–718 (2004). One caveat in this OCC Letter is worth noting. The result may be different if the national bank purchases a loan as permitted by 12 C.F.R. § 34.4(a)(10). In that case, the preemption ought to be limited to state laws affecting purchase of the loan, not state laws affecting the origination. *Cf.* Abel v. Keybank USA, N.A., 313 F. Supp. 2d 720 (N.D. Ohio 2004) (a provision embedded in a state usury law that creates assignee liability and trumps the holder-in-due-course doctrine in the U.C.C. is preempted).

215 *See* Elizabeth R. Schiltz, *The Amazing, Elastic, Ever-Expanding Exportation Doctrine and Its Effects on Predatory Lending Regulations*, 88 Minn. L. Rev. 518 (2004). But in a different context, one court noted that such an argument goes too far. "The flaw in [this] argument may be demonstrated by asking whether a state's truth-in-lending statute would be preempted because it potentially reduces the return a [lending plan] may get on its loans by restricting its ability to cheat." *In re* Seolas, 140 B.R. 266, 273 (E.D. Cal. 1992) (discussing whether ERISA preempts state usury laws, and concluding it does not).

216 *See, e.g.*, Spellman v. Meridian Bank, 1995 WL 764548 (3d Cir. Dec. 29, 1995); Goehl v. Mellon Bank (Del.), 825 F. Supp. 1239 (E.D. Pa. 1993); Nelson v. Citibank (S.D.), N.A., 794 F. Supp. 312 (D. Minn. 1992); Tikkanen v. Citibank (S.D.), N.A., 801 F. Supp. 270 (D. Minn. 1992); Smiley v. Citibank (S.D.), N.A., 11 Cal. 4th 138, 900 P.2d 690, 44 Cal. Rptr. 2d 441 (1995), *aff'd*, 517 U.S. 735, 116 S. Ct. 1730, 135 L. Ed. 2d 25 (1996); Copeland v. MBNA Am. Bank, N.A., 907 F.2d 87 (Colo. 1995); *see also* Greenwood Trust Co. v. Massachusetts, 971 F.2d 818 (1st Cir. 1992) (late charges are interest for purposes of most favored lender status expanded to state banks under DIDA); Hill v. Chem. Bank, 799 F. Supp. 948 (D. Minn. 1992) (same); Stoorman v. Greenwood Trust Co., 908 P.2d 133 (Colo. 1995) (same).

217 *See, e.g.*, Watson v. First Union Nat'l Bank, 837 F. Supp. 146 (D.S.C. 1993) (NBA); Tikkanen v. Citibank (S.D.), N.A., 801 F. Supp. 270 (D. Minn. 1992); Hill v. Chem. Bank, 799 F. Supp. 948 (D. Minn. 1992) (DIDA).

218 Fisher v. First Nat'l Bank, 548 F.2d 255 (8th Cir. 1977).

219 *See* First Nat'l Bank in Mena v. Nowlin, 509 F.2d 872 (8th Cir. 1975) (discount interest prohibited for national banks, as it was for all state lenders). *But cf.* Grunbeck v. Dime Sav. Bank, 74 F.3d 331 (1st Cir. 1996) (DIDA does *not* preempt state simple interest statute [lender made negatively amortizing mortgage loans]).

220 *E.g.*, Cronkleton v. Hall, 66 F.2d 384 (8th Cir. 1933) (NBA §§ 85, 86).

221 *E.g.*, Northway Lanes v. Hackley Union Nat'l Bank & Trust, 464 F.2d 855 (6th Cir. 1972) (§ 85).

222 Some courts have gone so far as to hold that state court jurisdiction is preempted. *See* § 3.15 *infra*.

appellate decision examined what it perceived as the slender reed upon which these cases are based.[223] Despite this eloquent dissent, the California Supreme Court upheld the broad definition of interest.[224]

Several other courts[225] weighed in on each side of the question of what constitutes "interest" for exportation purposes, creating quite a conflict. Surprisingly, during this litigation over the scope of the word "interest," only one court noted the logical conundrum created in accepting the industry's position: to maximize revenues, it wants a "heads-I-win-tails-you-lose" interpretation. For exportation purposes, it wants "interest" defined broadly to include as many fees as possible; for usury purposes, it wants the term defined narrowly, to exclude as many fees as possible. Traditional usury law, for example, excludes late fees and other contingent fees from the definition of interest.[226] In *Mazaika v. Bank One*, the court recognized the irony of the fact that the fees the bank wished to export under Ohio law as "interest" would have made its contracts usurious if they were considered interest under Ohio's 25% usury ceiling.[227]

The inconsistency does make for some interesting contortions in trying to articulate a rational position without simply admitting the economic imperative. That brings us to the OCC's 1996 interpretive ruling that, for the most part,

formalizes the latest position its staff took in the exportation debate.[228] While a Martian looking at the ruling would likely scratch its head(s), the rule makes sense if one views it as letting the banks have their cake and eat it, too. The OCC's new definition of "interest" is any payment compensating a creditor or prospective creditor for extending credit or any default or breach by a borrower of a condition upon which credit was extended. It *includes* such fees as "numerical periodic rates, late fees, not sufficient funds fees (NSF fees), overlimit fees, annual fees, cash advance fees, and membership fees." Ordinarily *excluded* are "appraisal fees, premiums and commissions attributable to insurance guaranteeing repayment of any extension of credit, finders' fees, fees for document preparation or notarization or fees incurred to obtain credit reports."[229] However, if state law would not consider OCC's included fees to be interest, for, oh, say, state usury purposes, this federal definition of interest would not disturb that, according to the OCC.[230]

---

223 Smiley v. Citibank (S.D.), N.A., 32 Cal. Rptr. 2d 562, 572 (Ct. App. 1994).

224 900 P.2d 690 (Cal. 1995), *aff'd*, 517 U.S. 735, 116 S. Ct. 1730, 135 L. Ed. 2d 25 (1996).

225 *Reading "interest" rate to include late fees*: Spellman v. Meridian Bank, 1995 WL 764548 (3d Cir. Dec. 29, 1995) (also over the limit fees); Smiley v. Citibank (S.D.), N.A., 11 Cal. 4th 138, 900 P.2d 690, 44 Cal. Rptr. 2d 441 (1995), *aff'd*, 517 U.S. 735, 116 S. Ct. 1730, 135 L. Ed. 2d 25 (1996); Copeland v. MBNA Am. Bank, N.A., 907 P.2d 87 (Colo. 1995); *see also* Stoorman v. Greenwood Trust Co., 908 P.2d 133 (Colo. 1995) (similar holding under DIDA).

Reading "interest" rate to exclude late fees: Sherman v. Citibank (S.D.), N.A., 668 A.2d 1036 (N.J. 1995), *vacated and remanded*, 517 U.S. 1241, 116 S. Ct. 2493, 135 L. Ed. 2d 86 (1996); Mazaika v. Bank One, Columbus, N.A., 653 A.2d 640 (Pa. Super. Ct. 1994) (also excluded from sweep of interest rate preemption: annual fees, return check charge, over-the-limit fee), *rev'd*, 680 A.2d 845 (Pa. 1996); *see also* Hunter v. Greenwood Trust Co., 668 A.2d 1067 (N.J. 1995) (same under DIDA), *vacated and remanded*, 517 U.S. 1241, 116 S. Ct. 2493, 135 L. Ed. 2d 86 (1996).

226 The exception to this rule has been when late fees were held to be a device designed to circumvent usury caps. *See* § 7.2.4.2, *infra*; *see also* § 5.7.1, *infra*.

227 653 A.2d 640 (Pa. Super. Ct. 1994), *rev'd*, 680 A.2d 845 (Pa. 1996) (applying the holding in *Smiley*). The Ohio legislature had thoughtfully provided that the fees in question were not interest, "except for one, unique purpose"—that of exportation. *Id.* at 646, 647; *see In re Beck*, 248 B.R. 229 (Bankr. W.D.N.Y. 2000) (national bank cannot have its cake and eat it too, says the court in *dictum*; bank chartered in Arizona may not claim applicability of its home state law regarding the creation of a security interest and that of the consumer's residence, New York, by inserting a clause in the contract indicating that New York law applies regarding the security interest).

228 Prior to the exportation explosion, the OCC had articulated the traditional position that late fees were not interest. OCC Letter (June 25, 1964). Then, when the industry had gotten a few states to define interest broadly in order to export those states' "interest" rates, see § 3.4.5.1.1, *supra*, the OCC staff's opinion was that a late fee could be interest if the relevant state law so defined it. OCC Letter No. 452 [1988–1989 Transfer Binder] Fed. Banking L. Rep. (CCH) ¶ 85,676 (Aug. 11, 1988). Then, when using state law of the bank's home state started running into theoretical problems, because "sister-state" preemption does not have the basis in law that federal preemption does, see §§ 3.4.5.1.1, *supra*, and 3.9.2.2.1, *infra*, the OCC staff position became that a federal definition controlled, and crafted a broad federal definition. J. Williams, Chief Counsel, OCC Letter No. 676 [1994–1995 Transfer Binder] Fed. Banking L. Rep. (CCH) ¶ 83,618 (Feb. 17, 1995). Then the OCC formally proposed this interpretive ruling. 60 Fed. Reg. 11924 (Mar. 3, 1995).

229 12 C.F.R. § 7.4001(a), 61 Fed. Reg. 4869 (Feb. 9, 1996). This interpretive ruling is *reprinted in* Appx. C.3, *infra*. In 2001, the OCC clarified the definition of an NSF fee. 66 Fed. Reg. 34784 (July 2, 2001). If the bank imposes a fee when a borrower tenders payment on a debt with a check drawn on insufficient funds, that fee constitutes "interest" for purposes of this rule. 12 C.F.R. § 7.4001(a). Fees that a bank charges for its deposit account services, including overdraft and returned check charges, are not "interest." 66 Fed. Reg. at 34786. The OCC also amended 12 C.F.R. § 7.4002 which permits national banks to impose non-interest charges upon its customers. This interpretive ruling is *reprinted in* Appx. C.1, *infra*. The agency made it clear that national banks have the authority to decide the amount and method by which such fees are computed. 12 C.F.R. § 7.4002(b)(2); 66 Fed. Reg. 34784, 34787 (July 2, 2001). This regulation arguably ratifies an earlier OCC Interpretive Letter in which the agency allowed banks to post checks for payment in any order. OCC Interpretive Letter No. 916 (May 22, 2001). This letter is controversial with consumer because it condones a practice called "high-to-low" posting. Banks using this method pay the largest check from an account first in any given twenty-four-hour cycle. If a customer writes several checks against insufficient funds, posting the biggest check first causes more checks to bounce, generating more fees for the bank.

230 12 C.F.R. § 7.4001(b), 61 Fed. Reg. 4869 (Feb. 9, 1996). The section-by-section analysis in the supplementary material

The most important chapter to this story is that the Supreme Court gave deference to the OCC ruling and upheld its broad federal definition of interest finding it to be a reasonable interpretation of section 85.[231] It was not bothered by the agency's changing position over the years,[232] nor by the fact that the ruling may have been issued in response to this very litigation.[233] The Court opined that the agency's interpretations of ambiguous provisions of the National Banking Act will be accorded deference only if the interpretations are "formal,"[234] directed to national banks generally, and "reasonable." Arguably, from henceforth, in order to ensure deference, the OCC and other federal agencies may be required to address interpretive letters generally to all institutions they regulate and come from the agency itself or its chief official.[235]

On the merits, because the Court accorded deference to the OCC definition of interest as including late fees, that issue is settled. The Court found that the OCC regulation represented a reasonable interpretation of section 85 by drawing a distinction between "payment compensating a creditor or prospective creditor for an extension of credit, making available of a line of credit, or any default or breach by a borrower" and all other payments. "All other payments" consist essentially of payments made to third parties who performed services which assisted in the making or guaranteeing of the loan. Neither the ruling nor the Court drew any distinction between when a fee is due—prior to or after the extension of credit, or otherwise—and whether that fee constitutes interest under section 85.[236]

Despite the Interpretive Ruling's laundry list of charges that constitute interest and those that do not, there is wiggle room. A subsequent decision from the Eighth Circuit Court of Appeals held that insurance premiums attributable to force-place insurance covering loss of the purchased automobile due to fire, theft, and collision were not interest.[237] This finding was premised upon the court's belief that the premiums were more akin to premiums and commissions attributable to insurance guaranteeing repayment of any extension of credit (therefore, not interest under the OCC ruling) than to charges compensating a creditor for a default or breach by a borrower (therefore, interest). In reaching this result, the court contrasted premiums for insurance which compensate the creditor for the cost of protecting its security to a late fee which supposedly compensates a creditor solely

---

makes it abundantly clear that banks wanted to be sure that late fees and so forth would not be considered interest for usury purposes. 61 Fed. Reg. at 4858, 4859.

231 Smiley v. Citibank (S.D.), N.A., 517 U.S. 735, 116 S. Ct. 1730, 135 L. Ed. 2d 25 (1996); *see also* Kent v. Bank of Am., 2003 WL 327465 (Cal. Ct. App. Feb. 11, 2003) (late fees and overlimit charges are interest). Ironically, in a later case, the Supreme Court practically pontificated on the issue of one state imposing its own policy choices on sister states. BMW of N. Am., Inc. v. Gore, 517 U.S. 559, 116 S. Ct. 1589, 134 L. Ed. 2d 809 (1996) (reversing an award of punitive damage as excessive). Through the vehicle of exportation, that is precisely what is occurring when banks take the absence of usury protections in their home states on the road to more protective states.

232 *Smiley*, 116 S. Ct. at 1734, 1735 (the Court proved the point that the OCC had no consistent position when it said: "Nor can it even be argued that the two statements *reflect* a prior agency policy, since in addition to contradicting the regulation before us here, they also contradict one another—the former asserting that 'interest' is a nationally uniform concept, and the latter that it is to be determined by reference to state law. What these statements show, if anything, is that there was good reason for the comptroller to promulgate the new regulation, in order to eliminate uncertainty and confusion."; what the Court failed to mention is that the OCC letter asserting that "interest" is a nationally uniform concept defined "interest" to *exclude* late fees).

233 *Smiley*, 116 S. Ct. at 1733. Because the agency's position was in the form of a "full-dress" regulation (in other words, adopted pursuant to the notice and comment procedures of the Administrative Procedures Act), the Court distinguished the ruling from agency litigating positions that would be wholly unsupported by regulations, rulings, or administrative practices.

234 The Court dismissed as nonbinding those earlier OCC opinions that were too "informal," for example, a 1964 Comptroller letter to the President's Committee on Consumer Interests; or letters that were merely in response to an inquiry concerning "particular banks." 116 S. Ct. at 1734.

235 Where an interpretation of the OCC concludes that federal law preempts the application to a national bank of any state law regarding, among other things, consumer protections, the OCC must do three things first: 1) publish it in the Federal Register; 2) give interested parties at least thirty days in which to submit written comments; and 3) consider any comments provided in developing the final rule. [Note that this provision creates two exceptions to this requirement.] Short of this and where the interpretation involves the preemption clause of the statute, the

OCC interpretations should not be accorded deference. 12 U.S.C. § 43 (added by the 1994 Interstate Banking Act, Pub. L. No. 103-328).

The OCC ruling at issue in *Smiley* was properly promulgated under the Administrative Procedures Act so § 43 was not implicated. The Court did, however, note that the ruling involved the "substantive" meaning of § 85 as distinct, in the Court's mind, from whether the agency's interpretation of § 85 was preemptive. [It can be argued, though, that this Court's decision to defer to the OCC ruling has the effect of significantly expanding the preemptive scope of § 85.] *Cf.* Bowler v. Hawke, 320 F.3d 59 (1st Cir. 2003) (OCC letter that admittedly was informal does not create a "conflict" for federal jurisdiction purposes).

236 The Court explicitly rejected the borrower's arguments that late fees cannot constitute interest because they do not vary based upon the payment owed or the time period of delay and that late fees are "penalties" and cannot constitute interest. *Smiley*, 116 S. Ct. at 1735, 1736.

237 Doe v. Norwest Bank Minn., N.A., 107 F.3d 1297 (8th Cir. 1997) (this was not a victory for the borrower because the borrower's argument was that the state usury statute was violated if the premiums were interest); *see also* Richardson v. National City Bank of Evansville, 141 F.3d 1228 (7th Cir. 1998) (court agreed with the holding in *Doe* and added that the list of non-interest charges in § 7.4001(a) is merely illustrative, as opposed to exhaustive); Gutter v. Bank One, La., N.A., 1997 WL 722952 (E.D. La. Nov. 17, 1997) (because force-placed insurance premiums were not interest under *Doe*, § 85 was not implicated and removal to federal court was improper).

for the effects of the consumer's default. Even the portion of the premium attributable to waiver of repossession and waiver of salvage was not considered interest because these endorsements existed in all standard automobile insurance policies in Minnesota and which the consumer was supposed to maintain in any event.[238]

In another case, a bank charged its customers a fee under a deposit account agreement for checks presented for payment on an account with insufficient funds once the customers exceeded the limits of any applicable overdraft protection plan.[239] The court held that the fee was not "interest" under 12 C.F.R. § 7.4001(a) because it was not charged as part of an extension of credit or any default by a borrower of a condition upon which credit was extended.[240]

A federal court in Missouri decided that loan origination and discount fees constitute interest because these fees generally are not collected unless a loan is actually made.[241] Further, these fees are designed to eliminate potential risks based on the creditworthiness of the borrower. As such, the court rejected the claim that these fees were, in reality, paid to a third party broker or finder.

Since the promulgation of the OCC ruling, the OCC's Chief Counsel has issued two interpretive letters which add specific charges into the "interest" side of the equation. First, in Interpretive Letter No. 744, the OCC opines that prepayment penalties constitute interest for purposes of section 85 (and are exportable if the national bank's home state permits them).[242] The rationale offered is that prepayment penalties compensate the lender for risks incurred in connection with the lending of its money because the bank relinquishes its right to receive the anticipated earnings on the loan over its projected life.[243]

The second letter determined that certain fees charged in connection with home equity open-end accounts were interest under the ruling.[244] These fees included an "account opening fee,"[245] "fixed rate option fee,"[246] fees for prepaying a fixed rate option and for early closure of the account,[247] and some "rejected item" fees.[248] In light of this letter, the OCC seems ready to consider most fees charged by national banks interest unless they fall into the exclusion pigeonholes.

A number of other credit card and loan fees do not neatly fit into either the interest or non-interest category and may be the subject of litigation, however. For example, attorney fees and collection costs are assessed because of a default by the borrower but they do not compensate the *creditor* (as opposed to the third party collector) for nonpayment. Other fees that may not be considered interest arguably include certain insurance charges, real estate mortgage insurance premiums, other fees paid to third parties who guarantee or insure repayment of loans in the event of default, credit card replacement fees, copy and delivery fees, security interest filing and release or termination fees, and other types of secured loan closing and post-closing costs and fees.[249]

---

238 Certain variations of vendor's single interest insurance (VSI) pay the loan balance only in the event of loan default or repossession. *See* § 8.3.5.2, *infra*. Based upon this fact, the premium for this insurance should be interest under this court's analysis.

239 Terrell v. Hancock Bank, 7 F. Supp. 2d 812 (S.D. Miss. 1998); *see also* Video Trax, Inc. v. NationsBank, N.A., 33 F. Supp. 2d 1041 (S.D. Fla. 1998), *aff'd*, 205 F.3d 1358 (11th Cir.) (table), *cert. denied*, 531 U.S. 822 (2000) (honoring checks on an overdrawn account is not an extension of credit and fees related to honoring such checks do not constitute interest); Nicolas v. Deposit Guarantee Nat'l Bank, 182 F.R.D. 226 (S.D. Miss. 1998) (at issue was a NSF fee imposed on deposit account which did not include an overdraft feature).

240 For similar reasons, the fee was not "interest" for purposes of state usury limits. Terrell v. Hancock Bank, 7 F. Supp. 2d 812, 817 (S.D. Miss. 1998); *see also* Video Trax, Inc. v. NationsBank, N.A., 33 F. Supp. 2d 1041 (S.D. Fla. 1998), *aff'd*, 205 F.3d 1358 (11th Cir.) (table), *cert. denied*, 531 U.S. 822 (2000).

241 Phipps v. Guar. Nat'l Bank of Tallahassee, 2003 WL 22149646 (W.D. Mo. Sept. 17, 2003).

242 OCC Interpretive Letter No. 744 (Aug. 21, 1996), *reproduced on* the CD-Rom accompanying this volume.

243 The products described in the Letter were home equity loans in which the customers could choose to pay a lower interest rate in a loan that included a prepayment penalty or pay a higher

interest rate and avoid a prepayment penalty provision. [*Editor's Note*: the national bank which requested the letter sought an alternative source of preemption because it could not have taken advantage of DIDMCA's preemption. Many of these home equity loans would be second mortgages and that preemption does not apply to prepayment penalties (see § 3.10.3, *infra*); in addition, the OCC's regulations permitting the inclusion of prepayment penalty provisions applies only to variable rate mortgages (see 12 C.F.R. § 34.23), which may not have applied to the home equity loans described in this letter.]

244 OCC Interpretive Letter No. 803 (Oct. 7, 1997), *reproduced on* the CD-ROM accompanying this volume.

245 This fee was imposed simply for making available a line of credit. The Chief Counsel considered it interest because it compensated a creditor for an extension of credit.

246 The home equity account permitted the borrower to obtain fixed rate advances that were payable in regular monthly installments over a fixed term. The bank seeking the OCC opinion charged a fee for exercising this option. The Chief Counsel determined the fee to be interest because it also compensated the creditor for an extension of credit (assuming, it seems, that every draw on a line of credit is an "extension of credit").

247 These fees were essentially prepayment penalties and constituted interest, the OCC decided, because they compensated the bank for the risk that it would not receive the income it anticipated in extending the line of credit.

248 The bank required a $10 fee when it rejected an attempted draw on the account if the account had been suspended, the draw created an overdraft, or the attempted draw was less than the allowable minimum draw. The fees imposed in these circumstances constituted interest because they compensated the lender for the borrower's actions in connection with the extension of credit that were contrary to the terms of the credit agreement. Fees imposed for an attempted draw *after* an account was terminated, however, were not interest because no debtor/creditor relationship existed at that time.

249 If these fees are not interest under the OCC ruling, they cannot be exported by a bank. Whether they are interest for purposes of state

A related issue, the threat of nationwide deregulation through extension of the exportation doctrine to electronic lending, is discussed in § 3.2.3.2, *supra.* Refund anticipation loans, a common form of electronic loans, are discussed in § 7.5.4.2, *infra.* As more and more lending occurs over the Internet, the ability of states willing to protect its citizens via usury caps and other consumer protections will be eroded even further.

It should also be noted that one apparent result of the exportation conflict seems to be a "race to the bottom," as far as consumers are concerned, as local credit providers convince their state legislatures that they need to be able to charge higher fees to compete with the preemptors.[250] "Saving jobs," rather than consumer protection, thereby becomes the issue as it is framed by the industry for the state legislatures.

A clear example of this is provided by the New Jersey legislature. In direct response to the decision in *Smiley*, it enacted provisions relating to bank revolving credit plans which allow any state- or federally-chartered bank, savings or savings and loan association to charge any periodic interest rate, late fee, annual fee, transaction charge, returned payment charge, stop payment fee, over limit fee or other fee agreed to by the parties.[251] The only interest cap applicable is that provided by New Jersey's criminal usury statute that makes it a crime to charge more than thirty percent.[252] The legislature specifically noted the decision in *Smiley* and declared that these provisions were intended to make "this state as equally attractive as other states for the location of bank credit card operations."[253]

3.4.6 National Bank Act Preemption

3.4.6.1 Conflict Preemption

It is clear that national banks, though federally created creatures, are also subject to state laws in certain circumstances. As the Supreme Court put it:

---

usury limits is still a matter of state law. *See* 12 C.F.R. § 7.4001(c). Note that the NBA grants preemption rights to national banks under provisions other than § 85. *See* § 3.4.6, *infra.*

250 *See* Jeffrey I. Langer & Kathleen E. Keest, *Interest Rate Regulation Developments in 1995: Continuing Liberalization of State Credit Card Laws and "Non-Filing" Insurance as "Interest" Under State Usury Laws*, 51 Bus. Law. 887 (May 1996) for a tally.

251 N.J. Stat. Ann §§ 17:3B-41 to 17:3B-46 (West).

252 N.J. Stat. Ann. § 2C:21-19(a) (West).

253 1996 N.J. Laws Ch. 137, § 1 (note the contrast with the New Jersey courts which refused to allow the exportation of interest rates and fees from other states and whose decisions were vacated in light of *Smiley*). *See* Sherman v. Citibank (S.D.), N.A., 668 A.2d 1036 (N.J. 1995), *vacated and remanded*, 517 U.S. 1241, 116 S. Ct. 2493, 135 L. Ed. 2d 86 (1996); Hunter v. Greenwood Trust Co., 668 A.2d 1067 (N.J. 1995), *vacated and remanded*, 517 U.S. 1241, 116 S. Ct. 2493, 135 L. Ed. 2d 86 (1996).

In defining the pre-emptive scope of statutes and regulations granting a power to national banks, these cases take the view that normally Congress would not want States to forbid, or to impair *significantly*, the exercise of a power that Congress explicitly granted. To say this is not to deprive States of the power to regulate national banks, where (unlike here) doing so does not prevent or *significantly* interfere with the national bank's exercise of its powers.[254]

---

254 Barnett Bank of Marion County, N.A. v. Nelson, 517 U.S. 25, 31, 116 S. Ct. 1103, 134 L. Ed. 2d 237 (1996) (emphasis added); *see also* Anderson Nat. Bank v. Luckett, 321 U.S. 233, 248, 64 S. Ct. 599, 607, 88 L. Ed. 692 (1944) ("This Court has often pointed out that national banks are subject to state laws, unless those laws infringe the national banking laws or impose an undue burden on the performance of banks' functions."); McClellan v. Chipman, 164 U.S. 347, 358, 17 S. Ct. 85, 87, 88, 41 L. Ed. 461 (1896) (application to national banks of state statute forbidding certain real estate transfers by insolvent transferees would not "destro[y] or hampe[r]" national banks' functions); National Bank v. Commonwealth, 76 U.S. (9 Wall.) 353, 362, 19 L. Ed. 701 (1869) ("[Federal banks] are subject to the laws of the State, and are governed in their daily course of business far more by the laws of the State than of the nation. All their contracts are governed and construed by State laws. Their acquisition and transfer of property, their right to collect their debts, and their liability to be sued for debts, are all based on State law. It is only when the State law incapacitates the banks from discharging their duties to the government that it becomes unconstitutional."); Wells Fargo Bank of Tex., N.A. v. James, 321 F.3d 488 (5th Cir. 2003) (court reaffirmed the "prevent or significantly interfere with" *Barnett* standard; it then upheld the validity of the OCC regulation permitting banks to charge fees and affirmed preemption of a Texas statute prohibiting banks from charging check cashing fees to non-account holders); Bankwest, Inc. v. Baker, 324 F. Supp. 2d 1333 (N.D. Ga. 2004), *appeal pending* (court interprets *Barnett* standard to require significant impairment, contrasting it to the standards under the Federal Deposit Insurance Act); Abel v. Keybank USA, N.A., 313 F. Supp. 2d 720 (N.D. Ohio 2004) (affirms the *Barnett* standard but holds that the assignee liability provision of the state's retail installment act significantly interferes with an ability to negotiate promissory notes and lend money); Wachovia Bank, N.A. v. Burke, 319 F. Supp. 2d 275 (D. Conn. 2004), *appeal pending* (court articulates the *Barnett* significantly interfere standard but holds that the state laws prevent or significantly impairs the ability of national bank operating subsidiaries to do business); Fidelity Nat'l Info. Solutions, Inc. v. Sinclair, 2004 WL 764834 (E.D. Pa. Mar. 31, 2004) (repeats the *Barnett* forbid or significantly impair standard in context of deciding that the OCC 2004 preemption regulations are not implicated because the state law regulates and certifies real estate appraisers, not national banks directly; authority for the state regulation comes from another federal statute, the Financial Institutions Reform, Recovery, and Enforcement Act of 1989; Miller v. Bank of America N.T. & S.A., 2004 WL 3153009 (Cal. Super. Dec. 30, 2004) (standard in *Barnett* is narrower than claimed by the defendant in this case; *Barnett* standard is whether a state is prohibited from forbidding or significantly impairing the exercise of a bank's power, not merely impairing, obstructing, or conditioning that power). *But see* First Nat'l Bank of San Jose v. California, 262 U.S. 366, 43 S. Ct. 602, 67 L. Ed. 1030 (1923) (court uses "frustrates, impairs, conflicts with" language to

According to the Supreme Court, state law generally carries a presumption of validity, unless it conflicts with federal law, where Congress has legislated in a field that the state has traditionally occupied.[255] This type of "conflict" preemption involves a case-by-case determination of whether particular state laws prevent or significantly interfere with exercise of the national bank's powers.

In 1994, Congress concurrently endorsed and expanded upon these standards enunciated by the Supreme Court. In the course of enacting the Riegle-Neal Act, Congress instructed the OCC and courts to avoid finding conflicts between federal and state law where possible.[256] Though the Act as a whole expanded bank powers by permitting both state and national banks to establish branches and sister banks across state lines, the conference report accompanying the Act stated that Congress did not intend to weaken a

state's authority to protect the interests of its consumers or to change the substantive theories of preemption that existed in law at that time.[257] The conference report directly instructed the Comptroller to refrain from concluding that a state law is preempted unless "the legal basis is compelling and the Federal policy interest is clear."[258] Moreover, Congress recently expressly approved of the *Barnett* standard when it enacted the Gramm-Leach-Bliley Act in 1999.[259]

The Supreme Court has never held that the National Bank Act preempts the field of law relating to the permitted activities of national banks, except in one limited area. In 2003, the court created a narrow exception: in actions against national banks for usury, section 85 of the NBA provides for the exclusive cause of action and remedy even where the complainant relies entirely on state law.[260] Con-

---

preempt state escheat law); Ass'n of Banks in Ins., Inc. v. Duryee, 270 F.3d 397 (6th Cir. 2001) (court uses "frustrates, impairs, conflicts with" language and *Barnett* language); Video Trax, Inc. v. NationsBank, N.A., 33 F. Supp. 2d 1041, 1048 (S.D. Fla. 1998), *aff'd*, 205 F.3d 1358 (11th Cir.) (table), *cert. denied*, 531 U.S. 822 (2000) (case dealt with whether fees charged when overdrafts occurred on an account were interest; in the course of deciding these fees were not interest, the court observed: "The absence of express statutory preemption, conflict preemption may be implied where it is impossible to comply with both state and federal requirements, or where state law stands as an obstacle to achieving the intent of Congress."); Mayor of New York v. Council of New York, 780 N.Y.S.2d 266 (N.Y. Sup. Ct. 2004) (city ordinance limiting the lenders with whom the city will do business to "non-predatory" lenders is preempted because the local law stands as an obstacle to the accomplishment and execution of the full purposes of Congress in enacting the NBA); *In re* Hibernia Nat'l Bank, 21 S.W.3d 908 (Tex. App. 2000) (state law preventing a foreign corporation from suing until it obtained a certificate of authority to transact business in Texas infringed upon the powers of the national bank and was preempted).

255 Medtronic, Inc. v. Lohr, 518 U.S. 470, 485, 116 S. Ct. 1146, 91 L. Ed. 2d 700 (1996) (case dealt with the preemption of state tort law by the federal Medical Device Amendments). *See also* Nat'l State Bank, Elizabeth, N.J. v. Long, 630 F.2d 981 (3d Cir. 1980) (state anti-redlining law does not frustrate federal banking system and is not preempted). The Second and Ninth Circuits dispute this proposition in the context of the NBA. Flagg v. Yonkers Sav. & Loan Ass'n, FA, 396 F.3d 178 (2d Cir. 2005); Bank of Am. v. City & Council of San Francisco, 309 F.3d 551, 559 (9th Cir. 2002). The OCC relied upon the *Bank of America* decision to opine that a presumption against preemption no longer exists. 69 Fed. Reg. 1895, 1896, 1897 (Jan. 13, 2004).

In another context, the Fourth Circuit held that the " 'presumption against preemption is even stronger against preemption of state remedies, like tort recoveries, where no federal remedy exists.' " College Loan Corp. v. SLM Corp., 2004 WL 196540, *8 (4th Cir. Jan. 31, 2005), *quoting* Abbot v. American Cyanamid Co., 844 F.2d 1108, 1112 (4th Cir. 1988) (case involved a dispute between two lenders of student loans; court also stated: "The existence of comprehensive federal regulations that fail to occupy the regulatory field do not, by their mere existence, preempt non-conflicting state law." *8).

256 H.R. Rep. Conf. Rep. No. 103-651 at 53 (1994), *reprinted in* 1994 U.S.C.C.A.N. 2074.

257 *Id.* at 53, 55, *reprinted in* 1994 U.S.C.C.A.N. 2074, 2076. The conference report went on: "This process is not intended to confer upon the agency any new authority to preempt or to determine preemptive congressional intent in the [the area of consumer protection], or to change the substantive theories of preemption as set forth in existing law."

258 *Id.* at 55, *reprinted in* 1994 U.S.C.C.A.N. 2076.

259 15 U.S.C. § 6701(d)(2)(A) ("In accordance with the legal standards for preemption set forth in the decision of the Supreme Court of the United States in Barnett Bank of Marion County, N.A. v. Nelson, 517 U.S. 25 (1996), no State may, by statute, order, regulation, or other action, prevent or significantly interfere with the ability of a depository institutions or an affiliate thereof, to engage directly or indirectly, either by itself or in conjunction with an affiliate or any other person, in any insurance sales, solicitation, or cross-marketing activity."). The conference report related to the passage of the Interstate Banking and Branching Efficiency Act of 1994 also confirms that a strict conflict preemption standard applies to national banks. *See* § 3.1.1, *supra*.

Through this Act, Congress expanded the authority of banks to operate in disregard of state law in an area long considered a sacred cow of state regulation, that is, the sale of insurance. This preemption, however, is subject to thirteen exceptions that preserve the states' rights to regulate a bank's insurance sales under certain conditions. The nature and extent of this preemption is discussed more fully in § 8.4.1.5.2, *infra*.

260 Beneficial Nat'l Bank v. Anderson, 539 U.S. 1, 123 S. Ct. 2058, 156 L. Ed. 2d 1 (2003). *See also* Flowers v. EZPawn Oklahoma, 307 F. Supp. 2d 1191 (N.D. Okla. 2004) (*Anderson* not applicable where the complaint alleges that the real lender is the non-bank entity and the bank itself was not sued); OCC Letter to Mass. AG (Jan. 5, 2005) (complete preemption doctrine applies to usury claims, not to all state law claims), *reprinted on* the CD-Rom accompanying this volume. Other Supreme Court and lower court cases finding state laws were not preempted include: Anderson Nat'l Bank v. Luckett, 321 U.S. 233, 64 S. Ct. 599, 88 L. Ed. 692 (1944) (state law requiring the transfer of abandoned bank deposits to the state); Lewis v. Fid. Deposit Co. of Md., 292 U.S. 559, 54 S. Ct. 848, 78 L. Ed. 1425 (1935) (state law permitting national bank to be appointed depository of state funds and requiring a bond that creates a lien on the bank's assets is not preempted); First Nat'l Bank in St. Louis v. Missouri, 263 U.S. 640, 44 S. Ct. 213, 68 L. Ed. 486 (1924) (state law prohibiting branch banking upheld); Waite v. Dowley, 94 U.S. 527, 24 L. Ed. 181 (1876) (state law requiring national bank to annually transmit a list of bank stockholders and the

sequently, removal of a case filed in state court seeking damages against a national bank for state law violations was proper.[261]

The general powers granted to a national bank are delineated in 12 U.S.C. § 24.[262] Congress also addressed certain specific powers in other provision of the National Bank Act. For example, section 371 discusses real estate lending. In addition, the NBA provides that banks have incidental powers as may be necessary to carry on the business of banking.[263] The Supreme Court has held "that the 'business of banking' is not limited to the enumerated powers in § 24 Seventh and that the Comptroller therefore has discretion to authorize activities beyond those specifically enumerated. The exercise of the Comptroller's discretion, however, must be kept within reasonable bounds."[264] The fact that a national bank has certain powers does not mean that it is entitled to preempt all state laws that affect the ability to exercise that power, given the preemption standard in *Barnett.*

Until 2004, the OCC had not issued broad regulations preempting state laws related to the business of lending or deposit-taking. Instead, in the area of mortgage lending, the agency had promulgated regulations that trumped state law only with regard to:

- The amount of a loan in relation to the appraised value of the real estate;
- The schedule for the repayment of principal and interest;
- The term to maturity of the loan;
- The aggregate amount that could be loaned upon the security of real estate; and
- The covenants that must be contained in a lease to qualify the leasehold as acceptable security for a real estate loan.[265]

Instead, the OCC addressed particular state laws and their impact on national banks on an "as-needed" basis, through opinion letters that, until recently, had not been formally published.[266]

Despite paying lip-service to state authority to co-regulate national banks, in fact, over the last twenty years the OCC has issued few letters in which it upheld the applicability of state law. In one of seven such letters, the OCC confirmed the validity of an Arkansas constitutional usury cap when applied to a national bank located in Arkansas that sought to use the state's "most favored lender" rate.[267]

In another opinion, the OCC upheld a Texas regulation that prohibited banks from using any form of advertising that implied that a branch facility is a separate bank.[268] Because Congress had deleted a statutory requirement that the OCC approve of bank names or name changes, the OCC opined that issues of names and the advertising of the names is primarily a matter of the bank's business, subject to applicable state law. The OCC further found no evidence that the Texas rule unduly burdened the ability of national banks to discharge their duties.

In 1997, the OCC upheld a specific state law involved a New York statute permitting the inspection of books and records of a national bank's insurance agency to determine compliance with applicable state law.[269] Previously, the OCC had acknowledged the role of state insurance regulators to administer and oversee compliance with certain state laws that apply to national banks.[270]

---

amount paid for each share is not preempted); First Nat'l Bank v. Commonwealth of Kentucky, 76 U.S. (9 Wall) 353, 362, 19 L. Ed. 701, 703 (1870) (affirmed validity of state law taxing the bank shares; court also holds that state law regarding the right to contract and collect debts applies to national banks); National State Bank, Elizabeth, N.J. v. Long, 630 F.2d 981 (3d Cir. 1980) (state anti-redlining law); *cf.* Fed. Nat'l Mortgage Ass'n v. Lefkowitz, 390 F. Supp. 1364 (S.D.N.Y. 1975) (state law requiring the payment of interest on escrow accounts did not impose such a burden on Fannie Mae as to invalidate it). However, Supreme Court cases upholding preemption outweigh, in number, those that do not. These cases are summarized in Arthur E. Wilmarth, Jr., *The OCC's Preemption Rules Exceed the Agency's Authority and Present a Serious Threat to the Dual Banking System*, 23 Ann. Rev. Banking & Fin. L. 225 (2004).

261 Court decisions addressing the issue of removal to federal court where a national bank is the defendant are discussed in § 3.15, *infra.*

262 This section is *reprinted in* Appx. C.1, *infra.*

263 12 U.S.C. § 24 Seventh.

264 NationsBank of N.C., N.A. v. Variable Annuity Life Ins. Co., 513 U.S. 251, 258 n.2, 115 S. Ct. 810, 130 L. Ed. 2d 740 (1995).

265 12 C.F.R. § 34.4 (former regulation); *see also* 12 C.F.R.

§§ 34.20–34.25 (OCC regulations regarding adjustable rate mortgages); 12 C.F.R. §§ 34.61–34.62 (OCC regulations regarding real estate lending standards), *reprinted in* Appx. C.2, *infra.*

266 *See* Richard J. Hillman & Lynn H. Gibson, *Role of the Office of Thrift Supervision and Office of the Comptroller of the Currency in the Preemption of State Law*, General Accounting Office, OGC-00-51R (Feb. 7, 2000). Summaries of these letters from 1992 until the present can be found in Appx. C.3. The letters are reproduced on the CD-Rom accompanying this volume.

267 OCC Unpublished Letter (June 10, 1992). Interpretive letters issued since May 1996 can be obtained on the Internet at www.occ.treas.gov./interp/monthly.htm. Summaries of OCC letters dealing with the preemption of state law and related topics can be found in Appx. C.3, *infra.* The full text of these letters dating back to January 1992 is reproduced on the CD-Rom accompanying this volume.

268 OCC Interpretive Letter No. 674 (June 9, 1995). This letter is summarized in Appx. C.3, *infra.* The full text is reproduced on the CD-Rom accompanying this volume.

269 OCC Unpublished Letter (July 7, 1997). This letter is summarized in Appx. C.3, *infra.* The full text is reproduced on the CD-Rom accompanying this volume.

270 In this letter, the OCC relied upon Advisory Letter 96-8 entitled "Guidance to National Banks on Insurance and Annuity Sales Activities." *See also* Barnett Bank of Marion County, N.A. v. Nelson, 517 U.S. 25, 116 S. Ct. 1103, 134 L. Ed. 2d 237 (1996) (where state law conflicts with congressional grant of authority allowing national banks to act as the agent for any fire, life, or other insurance company authorized by state law to do business by soliciting and selling insurance in small towns, state law is

In 2002, the OCC released an advisory letter describing its role in enforcing state and federal unfair and deceptive acts or practices, providing guidance on what acts or practices might be unfair or deceptive, and discussing related matters.[271] In this letter, the OCC confirmed that state UDAP acts may apply, citing to California's as an example. It is worthy to note here, however, that the Office of Thrift Supervision also opined that state unfair and deceptive acts and practices laws that do not directly regulate credit transactions apply to federal savings associations.[272] At least two courts have confirmed that consumers and state agencies can enforce state unfair and deceptive acts and practices laws against national banks concerning a variety of types of misleading or fraudulent behavior.[273]

In a subsequent advisory letter, the agency listed several types of other state laws that are not preempted: contract, debt collection, acquisition and transfer of property, taxation, zoning, criminal, and tort laws.[274]

Recently, the agency opined that a state's Uniform Commercial Code applies to national banks. However, the OCC did not address the non-uniform provisions that individual states may include in the body of their state commercial codes.[275]

Finally, the OCC's chief counsel announced that state anti-discrimination laws generally are not preempted. The agency hedged a bit when it reserved the right to assess specific state laws on a case-by-case basis.[276] However, the OCC opined that state fair lending and anti-redlining laws are only enforceable against national banks by the OCC itself.

On the other hand, the OCC has released scores of letters finding that a variety of state laws *are* preempted.[277] Specifically in regards to consumer credit statutes, the OCC has opined that provisions requiring national banks to obtain licenses,[278] to maintain and allow inspection of certain records,[279] to pay annual or other fees,[280] and to provide

---

preempted; where state insurance law does not conflict with federal law relating to national banks, national banks may have to comply).

271 OCC Advisory Letter No. AL 2002-3 (Mar. 22, 2002). This letter is summarized in Appx. C.3, *infra*. The full text is reproduced on the CD-Rom accompanying this volume. The letter suggests that the OCC has the authority to enforce state UDAP acts.

272 *See* § 3.5.3, *infra*, for a discussion of preemption rights of federal savings associations under the Home Owners' Loan Act.

273 Minnesota *ex rel.* Hatch v. Fleet Mortgage Corp., 158 F. Supp. 2d 962 (D. Minn. 2001) (claims under state consumer fraud, deceptive practices, and false statement in advertising act not preempted where claims arose from practice of disclosing customer information to other companies without customer's knowledge); Miller v. Bank of America N.T. & S.A., 2004 WL 3153009 (Cal. Super. Dec. 30, 2004) (state UDAP claims based on a misrepresentation that the bank's accounts would be "safe" and secure is not preempted by the bank's deposit-taking authority). *Cf.* Barnes v. Fleet Nat'l Bank, N.A., 370 F.3d 164 (1st Cir. 2004) (court approves of a cause of action against the bank based on the state UDAP act; violation of the federal Truth In Savings Act is a violation of the state UDAP act; complaint alleges that the bank did not properly disclose the effective date of changes to fees and minimum balance requirements for customer bank accounts; preemption not explicitly discussed); West Virginia *ex rel.* McGraw v. Parrish Auto. Training Co., 147 F. Supp. 2d 470 (N.D. W. Va. 2001) (court remanded matter to state court on grounds that there was no federal jurisdiction where state sued in state court to enforce state unfair and deceptive practices act because car dealers allegedly failed to disclose interest rate markups to the customers; banks set the initial rate and then purchased the dealer loans; banks raised no claim that state UDAP did not apply to them). *But see* Am. Bankers Ass'n v. Lockyer, 239 F. Supp. 2d 1000 (E.D. Cal. 2002) (California's minimum payment disclosure law for credit cards preempted; court stated that consumer protection statutes are not reflected in the case law as an area in which states have traditionally been permitted to regulate national banks, though court was not addressing state unfair or deceptive acts or practices acts specifically).

274 OCC Advisory Letter No. AL 2002-9 (Nov. 25, 2002). This letter is summarized in Appx. C.3, *infra*. The full text is

reproduced on the CD-Rom accompanying this volume. *See also* Bank of Am. v. City & Council of San Francisco, 309 F.3d 551, 559 (9th Cir. 2002) (court adopts this same list).

275 OCC Interpretive Letter No. 1005 (June 10, 2004). This letter is summarized in Appx. C.3, *infra*. The full text is reproduced on the CD-Rom accompanying this volume.

276 OCC Interpretive Letter No. 2004 (Mar. 9, 2004), *reprinted on* the CD-Rom accompanying this volume.

277 *See* summaries of OCC letters in Appx. C.3, *infra*. For an article criticizing the OCC and OTS for "dismantling" state regulatory powers, see Stacy Mitchell, *Rogue Agencies Gut State Banking Laws*, New Rules (Fall 2001), at 4; *see also* Jess Bravin & Paul Beckett, *Dependent on Lender Fees, The OCC Takes Banks' Side Against Local Laws*, Wall St. J., Jan. 28, 2002, at A1.

278 OCC Unpublished Letter (Feb. 9, 1995) ("[a]s instrumentalities of federal government, national banks are not required to obtain state approval for the exercise of the powers granted to them by Congress") (reviewing Idaho Credit Code); OCC Interpretive Letter No. 644 (Mar. 24, 1994) (same) (reviewing Georgia's Residential Mortgage Act which required licensing of banks which do not maintain an office in that state); OCC Interpretive Letter No. 614 (Jan. 15, 1993) (same) (reviewing Idaho Credit Code which requires credit card issuers to obtain a license); OCC Unpublished Letter (Feb. 4, 1992) (same) (reviewing Iowa Lender Credit Card Act). These letters are summarized in Appx. C.3, *infra*. Their full text is reproduced on the CD-Rom accompanying this volume.

279 OCC Unpublished Letter (Feb. 9, 1995) (states cannot exert "visitorial" powers over a national bank; "visitation" includes any act of a state official to inspect, regulate, or control the operation of a bank to enforce its law) (reviewing Idaho Credit Code); OCC Unpublished Letter (May 6, 1993) (same) (reviewing Idaho Consumer Credit Code); OCC Interpretive Letter No. 614 (Jan. 15, 1993) (same) (reviewing Wisconsin and Wyoming Credit Codes which require that lenders file notification with the state when a finance charge exceeding a certain percent and to file annual reports thereafter); OCC Unpublished Letter (Feb. 4, 1992) (same) (reviewing Iowa Lender Credit Card Act). These letters are summarized in Appx. C.3, *infra*. Their full text is reproduced on the CD-Rom accompanying this volume.

280 OCC Unpublished Letter (Feb. 9, 1995) (while states can tax national banks to the same extent that they tax state banks, annual fees and the like are generally not "taxes" as they do not constitute general revenue, but, rather, are used for the purpose

certain disclosures are preempted.[281] In 2002, the agency published a list of activities that national banks may perform including citations to authority for such activities.[282]

As discussed in § 3.3, *supra*, Congress took care to emphasize that state consumer protection and fair lending laws apply to the extent not preempted by federal law in the Interstate Banking and Branching Efficiency Act of 1994 (IBBEA).[283] Congress further expressed concern that the federal banking regulatory agencies have been "inappropriately aggressive" in opining that federal law preempted some state consumer protections, doing so in cases where Congress did not think the federal interest warranted it. Consequently, those agencies must now go through the process of publishing in the *Federal Register* for a thirty day comment period any proposed opinion letter or interpretation that the National Bank Act preempts any state law regarding consumer protection, community reinvestment, fair lending, or the establishment of intrastate branches.[284] The only exceptions to this rule can occur when the issues involved are "essentially identical" to those previously resolved by the courts or have been the subject of an opinion letter or interpretive rule released by the agency prior to the passage of IBBEA.[285]

Arguably, OCC Interpretive Letter No. 822[286] should have been published for comment before it was issued.[287] In that letter, OCC's chief counsel decided that a national bank with interstate branches may charge interest permitted by either its home state or its host (or branch) states. The answer depends upon where the loan is "made" (that is, where the loan is approved, credit is extended, and funds are disbursed).[288] This informal letter essentially instructs na-tional banks with branches in other states how to design their business so they can apply their home states' laws to loans made through their branches, thus avoiding the application of the host states' consumer protection, fair lending, and community reinvestment laws.[289] By failing to formally publish this letter, its validity may be subject to attack.

Another recent OCC letter may suffer from the same defect.[290] The agency opined that a national bank may charge prepayment penalties in its home state by bootstrapping an Office of Thrift Supervision regulation into its home state's law via the state's parity act. The OCC reached this conclusion using the following analysis: OCC regulation defines "interest" to include prepayment penalties; although the bank's home state prohibits the charging of prepayment penalties under some of its usury laws, the state's parity act permits a bank, including a state bank, to collect interest and charges on loans as allowed by state or federal law; OTS regulations authorize federal savings associations to charge prepayment penalties; consequently, if the home state's authorities interpret the state parity act as allowing state banks the right to charge prepayment penalties, then national banks can as well.

Despite its resounding deference to the OCC's published interpretation regarding the definition of "interest," judicial deference to unpublished letters was criticized by the Supreme Court in *Smiley v. Citibank (South Dakota), N.A.*[291] The Court held that letters construing ambiguous provisions of the National Banking Act will be given deference only if the interpretations are "formal," directed to national banks generally, and "reasonable." Since the decision in *Smiley*, at least two courts have refused to give deference to OCC letters in other contexts.[292]

---

of funding a licensing or regulatory scheme; only the OCC can assess fees against national banks; reviewing Idaho Credit Code); OCC Interpretive Letter No. 644 (Mar. 24, 1994) (same) (reviewing Georgia's Residential Mortgage Act); OCC Unpublished Letter (May 6, 1993) (same) (reviewing Idaho Consumer Credit Code); OCC Unpublished Letter (Feb. 4, 1992) (same) (reviewing Iowa Lender Credit Card Act). These letters are summarized in Appx. C.3, *infra*. Their full text is reproduced on the CD-Rom accompanying this volume.

281 Am. Bankers Ass'n v. Lockyer, 239 F. Supp. 2d 1000 (E.D. Cal. 2002) (California's minimum payment disclosure law for credit cards preempted). In this case, the OCC filed an *amicus* brief (rather than issuing a letter) arguing preemption and the court gave it deference.

282 Activities Permissible for a National Bank, Office of the Comptroller of the Currency (Feb. 2002), *available at* www.occ.treas.gov/corpapps/bankact.pdf.

283 12 U.S.C. § 36(f)(1).

284 12 U.S.C. § 43.

285 12 U.S.C. § 43(c).

286 (Feb. 17, 1998).

287 *See also* § 3.4.5.1.2, *supra*.

288 *See also* 12 C.F.R. §§ 7.1002 (regarding national banks acting as finder), 7.1003 (regarding money lent at banking offices or at other than banking offices), 7.1004 (regarding loans originating at other than banking offices), 7.1005 (regarding credit decisions at other than banking offices).

289 *Cf.* 12 C.F.R. § 7.1003 (regarding where money is deemed to be "lent" for purposes of what constitutes a bank branch).

290 OCC Interpretive Letter No. 1004 (Aug. 4, 2004), summarized in Appx. C.3, *infra*, and available on the CD-Rom accompanying this volume.

291 517 U.S. 735, 116 S. Ct. 1730, 135 L. Ed. 2d 25 (1996); *cf.* Bowler v. Hawke, 320 F.3d 59 (1st Cir. 2003) (OCC letter that was admittedly "informal" does not create a conflict for federal court jurisdiction purposes).

292 McQueen v. Williams, 177 F.3d 523 (6th Cir. 1999) (court gave no deference to an OCC letter in which the agency opined that the National Bank Act does not prevent the relocation and merger plan of a particular bank especially as the conflicted with state law); Blackfeet Nat'l Bank v. Nelson, 171 F.3d 1237 (11th Cir. 1999) (OCC letter allowing a national bank to issue retirement certificates of deposit that guaranteed a continuing stream of payments constituted an unreasonable expansion of the powers of a national bank); *cf.* Heaton v. Monogram Credit Card Bank of Ga., 231 F.3d 994 (5th Cir. 2000), *cert. denied*, 533 U.S. 915 (2001) (district court reversed itself and refused to grant deference to an FDIC letter indicating that Monogram was a state "bank" for preemption or exportation purposes, even though its only depositor was its parent company, because the plaintiff showed that Monogram participated in the preparation of the FDIC letter; the appellate court dismissed the appeal of the district court's remand order to state court), *remand follow-*

Since 2000, the OCC has issued several preemption determinations in the *Federal Register*. During 2000 and 2001 alone, it published several Notices of Request for Preemption Determinations for comments and issued three formal preemption letters.[293] For consumers, one of the most important requests for a preemption determination relates to the ability of national banks headquartered in one state that wish to conduct motor vehicle sales financing in another state, without regard to the foreign state's retail installment sales act.[294]

The OCC opined that Michigan's motor vehicle retail installment act (MVRISA) did not apply to out-of-state national banks when car dealers acted as their agents in soliciting loans to finance motor vehicles.[295]

In an interesting footnote that has bearing on the "rent-a-charter" controversy discussed in § 3.13, *infra*, the OCC

reigned itself in on the use of agents by national banks. It distinguished the Michigan situation from one "where a loan product has been developed by a non-bank vendor that seeks to use a national bank as a delivery vehicle, and where the vendor, rather than the bank, has the preponderant economic interest in the loan."[296]

In late 2003, the OCC published a preemption determination regarding the Georgia Fair Lending Act, an anti-predatory mortgage lending law patterned on the federal Home Ownership and Equity Protection Act.[297] Two banks and an operating subsidiary filed the request for a determination.[298] This preemption determination will have far-reaching consequences for the attempts by states to curb predatory lending practices within their borders.[299]

In the request for preemption, the national banks claimed that the National Bank Act authorizes the OCC to occupy the field of real estate lending. This is an astonishing argument and would expand the preemption powers of banks beyond that envisioned by the OCC in the past. While not directly taking the bait dangled by the bank, the OCC ruled that the entire statute was preempted, even provisions typically found in state law, such as rights to cure, restrictions on brokers and home improvement contractors, assignee liability, and attorney fees.[300]

The OCC accomplished this result by re-tooling the conflict preemption standard. Under this iteration of the standard, state law applies to national banks if the law does not alter or condition a national bank's ability to exercise a power granted to it by federal law, and the state law provides the "legal infrastructure that surrounds and supports the conduct of that business."[301] Further, the OCC argued that there is no presumption that state law applies to national banks.[302] Finally, the agency reviewed the history of the express power to engage in real estate lending in the NBA § 371, finding it does not envision that the exercise of this power "would be subject to compliance with any state requirements."[303]

ing appeal, 2001 U.S. Dist. LEXIS 325 (E.D. La. Jan. 8, 2001) (court remanded to state court despite new FDIC opinion letter and change in Georgia law, finding that, while the bank had a deposit, it was not in the "business" of receiving deposits and, therefore, not entitled to preemption), *subsequent proceedings at* 297 F.3d 416 (5th Cir. 2002) (district court's order denying intervention to the FDIC reversed; federal court jurisdiction created by FDIC as a party; further remand to state court denied). This case has attracted some interesting press. *See, e.g.*, Paul Beckett, *Clashing Interests: Why Patricia Heaton Could Cause Problems for a GE-Owned Bank*, Wall. St. J., Mar. 30, 2001, at A1; Roger Furman, *Friends in High Places*, U.S. Banker, Mar. 2000, at 30. In late 2001, the FDIC abandoned the letter approach and enacted a regulation defining what being in the business of receiving deposits means under the Federal Deposit Insurance Act. 66 Fed. Reg. 54645 (Oct. 30, 2001). Not surprisingly, the agency stuck to its previous position that a bank need only maintain one or more non-trust deposit accounts in the minimum aggregate amount of $500,000. Whether, and the extent to which, courts will accord deference to this regulation given its controversial history remains to be seen.

293 One notice involved the applicability of a state statute regulating auctioneers who sell certificate of deposits on-line using an auction format. 65 Fed. Reg. 2455 (Jan. 14, 2000). The OCC published its Preemption Determination on this issue, finding that Pennsylvania law is preempted because it would limit the ability of the bank to exercise its powers under federal law to receive deposits, market, and use electronic means to engage in permissible activities and it would violate the OCC's exclusive visitorial powers. 65 Fed. Reg. 15037 (Mar. 20, 2000). Another request, involved an Ohio law that prohibits the public sale of reclaimed leased vehicles. 65 Fed. Reg. 63916 (Oct. 25, 2000). The OCC held that the ability of banks to sell reclaimed lease vehicles is part of the business of engaging in the leasing of automobiles, clearly a permitted business. State law frustrates the banks' ability to operate their leasing businesses in an economically efficient manner consistent with safe and sound banking principles and is, therefore, preempted. 66 Fed. Reg. 23977 (May 10, 2001). The OCC issued a preemption determination regarding West Virginia's insurance laws. That letter is discussed in § 8.4.1.5.2, *infra*. A brief summary of these preemption determinations can be found in Appx. C.4, *infra*. Their full text is reproduced on the CD-Rom accompanying this volume.

294 65 Fed. Reg. 63917 (Oct. 25, 2000).

295 66 Fed. Reg. 28593 (May 23, 2001). This Preemption Determination is discussed more fully in § 3.4.6.4, *infra*.

296 66 Fed. Reg. at 28595 n.6.

297 *Compare* Ga. Code Ann. § 7-6A-1 *et seq.* with 15 U.S.C. §§ 1602(aa), 1639. *See also* Mayor of the City of New York v. The Am. Fin. Servs. Ass'n, 780 N.Y.S.2d 266 (N.Y. Sup. Ct. 2004) (ordinance limiting the city's ability to contract with "predatory" lenders is preempted by the NBA, HOLA, and DIDA).

298 68 Fed. Reg. 8959 (Feb. 26, 2003).

299 68 Fed. Reg. 46264 (Aug. 5, 2003).

300 In 2004, the OCC issued two letters addressing questions from the Georgia banking agency regarding the limits of the OCC's Determination. OCC Interpretive Letter No. 1000 (Apr. 2, 2004); OCC Interpretive Letter No. 1002 (May 13, 2004), *reprinted on* the CD-Rom accompanying this volume. Letter No. 1000 states that the only part of the GFLA not preempted is the requirement that a lender terminate a foreclosure proceeding once a default is cured.

301 68 Fed. Reg. 46264, 46274, 46275 (Aug. 5, 2003).

302 68 Fed. Reg. 46275 (Aug. 5, 2003).

303 *Id.* Arguments contrary to the OCC's interpretation of § 371 can

The OCC's positions articulated in the Georgia preemption determination foreshadowed the agency's next major step to mirror the broad preemption available to federal savings associations under the Home Owners' Loan Act.[304]

3.4.6.2 OCC's Broad 2004 Preemption Regulations

In 2004, the OCC adopted four broad regulations that purport to preempt state laws in the areas of deposit-taking, non-mortgage lending, mortgage lending and, generally, the business of banking.[305] These rules declare that state laws are preempted if they "obstruct, impair, or condition a national bank's ability to fully exercise" its powers, either directly or through operating subsidiaries.[306] The OCC further defined "obstruct, impair, or condition" in the regulations.[307] Essentially the agency stated that *no* state law applies to national banks, unless the particular state law has

---

be found in Arthur E. Wilmarth, Jr., *The OCC's Preemption Rules Exceed the Agency's Authority and Present a Serious Threat to the Dual Banking System*, 23 Ann. Rev. Banking & Fin. L. 225 (2004).

304 For a discussion of preemption under HOLA, see § 3.5, *infra*. In the Supplementary Information accompanying the OCC's new regulations, the agency expressly claimed that its authority to preempt state laws is comparable in scope to that of the OTS. 69 Fed. Reg. 1904, 1912 n.62 (Jan. 13, 2004); *see also* Letter to Private Attorney regarding New OCC Preemption Regulations (July 20, 2004), *reprinted on* the accompanying CD-Rom.

305 12 C.F.R. §§ 7.4007 (deposit-taking), 7.4008 (non-mortgage lending), 7.4009 (business of banking generally), 34.3 (mortgage lending), 34.4 (mortgage lending); *see* 69 Fed. Reg. 1904 (Jan. 13, 2004). These regulations became effective on February 12, 2004 and are *reprinted in* Appx. C.2, *infra*. The OCC will likely claim that these regulations are retroactive given the position it took in the Supplementary Information: "The OCC therefore is issuing this final rule in furtherance of its responsibility to enable national banks to operate under Federal law, without interference from inconsistent state law, and in furtherance of their safe and sound operations. The final rule does not entail any new powers for national banks or any expansion of their existing powers." *Id.* at 1908.

The OCC discusses state unclaimed property and escheat laws in relation to its new deposit-taking regulation in OCC Interpretive Letter No. 1006 (Aug. 19, 2004), *reprinted on* the CD-Rom accompanying this volume.

In 2002, the OCC adopted regulations governing the electronic activities of national banks. 12 C.F.R. § 7.5000 *et seq.* These regulations contain a provision purporting to preempt state laws affecting the electronic activities of national banks. 12 C.F.R. § 7.5002(c). Relevant portions of these regulations appear in Appx. C.2, *infra*.

306 12 C.F.R. §§ 7.4007(b), 7.4008(d), 7.4009(b), 34.4(a).

307 The OCC surveyed federal court cases regarding conflict analysis, including the *Barnett* language "prevent or significantly impair," but ultimately concluded that there is not any one clear standard, citing Hines v. Davidowitz, 312 U.S. 52, 67, 61 S. Ct. 399, 85 L. Ed. 581 (1941). 69 Fed. Reg. 1904, 1910 (Jan. 13, 2004).

only an "incidental" effect on the business of banking.[308] State laws that have only an "incidental" effect are those that are part of the legal infrastructure that makes it practicable for national banks to conduct their authorized activities and that do not regulate the manner or content of the business of banking.[309] This standard is a *de minimus* one and appears to conflict with Supreme Court precedent and the congressional adoption of that precedent into statute.[310]

Each of these rules is structured in a similar fashion. First, each one describes the specific authority of national banks to conduct the covered banking activity. Second, each rule lists

---

308 12 C.F.R. §§ 7.4007(c), 7.4008(e), 7.4009(c)(2), 34.4(b). *See* discussion in the Supplementary Information accompanying the regulations. 69 Fed. Reg. 1904, 1911–1913 (Jan. 13, 2004).

309 69 Fed. Reg. 1904, 1913 (Jan. 13, 2004). The criticism of this articulation of the standard has been swift. *See* Arthur E. Wilmarth, Jr., *The OCC's Preemption Rules Exceed the Agency's Authority and Present a Serious Threat to the Dual Banking System*, 23 Ann. Rev. Banking & Fin. L. 225 (2004); *Hearing Before the Subcomm. on Oversight and Investigations, House Comm. on Fin. Services*, 108th Cong. (Jan. 28, 2004) (testimony of Thomas J. Miller, Iowa Att'y Gen.), *available at* http://financialservices.house.gov/media/pdf/012804tm.pdf. Ten Democrats on the Senate Banking Committee and twenty-two Democrats and one Independent on the House Financial Services Committee urged the OCC to put the rules on hold. *Trade Groups Back Hawke on Preemption; Question Sarbanes Request to Delay Rules*, 81 Banking Rep. 918 (2003); Todd Davenport, *OCC: States Should Focus on Nonbanks*, The Am. Banker, Dec. 13, 2004, at 3; *see also* Spitzer, *New York Officials Call for OCC to Reverse Position on Preemption Rules*, 81 Banking Rep. 901 (2003).

310 *See* § 3.4.6.1, *supra*. The OCC also may rely upon the express interest rate preemption under section 85 of the NBA as a springboard to argue that a national bank can pick and choose which state laws support its *infra*structure. However, section 85 does not authorize a national bank to completely ignore state limits. To the contrary, section 85 requires that the bank actually look at the state law that governs the "most favored lender" in the state. This means that the national bank may adopt the rate that applies to the most favored lender making similar types of extensions of credit and must comply with all other parts of the law "material" to the determination of that rate. *See* § 3.4.3, *supra*. Such state restrictions could include compounding of interest, maximum loan charges, fees, loan splitting, refinancings, NSF fee limitations, prepayment penalties, and the loan term. *See* § 3.4.3.4, *supra*. Thus, the application of the most favored lender doctrine forbids cherry-picking among state laws. The Supreme Court rejected an OCC argument that would have enabled national banks to do just that: "The Comptroller argues that Utah's statute 'expressly authorizes' state banks to have branches in their home municipalities. He maintains that the restriction, in the subsequent paragraph of the statute limiting branching solely to the taking over of an existing bank, is not applicable to national banks. It is a strange argument that permits one to pick and choose what portion of the law binds him." First Nat'l Bank of Logan v. Walker Bank & Trust Co., 385 U.S. 252, 261, 87 S. Ct. 492, 17 L. Ed. 2d 343 (1966). *See also* Attorney General v. The Equitable Trust Co., 450 A.2d 1273, 1289 (Md. Ct. Spec. App. 1982) ("If the most favored lending doctrine obliterates state law nondiscriminatory classifications of transactions, then consequences result which could never have been intended by Congress.").

the types of state laws that are presumptively preempted. Third, each rule explains the preemption standard to be applied to those state laws not previously identified. Fourth, each rule enumerates state laws that may not be preempted as long as they only incidentally affect the particular banking activity covered by that rule. Finally, each rule includes a "catch-all" provision that reserves to the OCC the right to decide if any other state law, not previously identified, is preempted.

In addition, the two new lending regulations create an "ability to repay" standard that national banks must follow when originating loans.[311] Essentially, the rules prohibit national banks from making a loan based "predominately" on the bank's realization of the value of any collateral without regard to the borrower's ability to repay. However, a bank may use any reasonable method of determining a borrower's ability to repay. These rules list certain types of documentation as examples of verification of ability to repay but also permit national banks to use "other relevant factors." Although the OCC touts the repayment ability standard as an anti-predatory lending protection,[312] it is unlikely to stop national banks or their operating subsidiaries from making loans that a borrower cannot repay because there is no bright line debt-to-income or residual income standard.[313]

The lending regulations also prohibit national banks from engaging in unfair or deceptive acts or practices within the meaning of the Federal Trade Commission Act. Embodying this prohibition in a regulation was unnecessary as the FTC Act already applies to banks.[314] Some observers wonder whether the OCC is attempting to prevent state consumer protection laws from applying to banks, despite its earlier pronouncement that they do apply.[315]

The types of state laws that the two regulations pertaining to lending identify as automatically preempted include those that relate to:

- Licensing, registration, filings, or reports by creditors;
- The ability of a creditor to require or obtain insurance for collateral or other credit enhancement or risk mitigant;
- Loan-to-value ratios;
- The terms of credit, including the schedule for repayment of principal and interest, amortization of loans, balance, payments due, minimum payments, term to maturity of the loan, or the ability to call the loan due and payable upon the passage of time or a specified event external to the loan;
- Escrow or similar accounts;
- Security property;
- Access to and use of credit reports;
- Disclosure and advertising requirements in credit application forms, credit solicitations, billing statement, credit contracts, or other related documents;
- Disbursements and repayments; and
- Rates of interest.

For real-estate-secured loans, additional state laws relating to the following subjects are preempted:

- The aggregate amount of funds that can be loaned upon the security of real estate;
- Processing, origination,[316] servicing,[317] sale, or purchase of, investment in, or participation in mortgages;
- Due on sale clauses, with some exceptions; and
- Covenants and restrictions that must be contained in a

---

311 12 C.F.R. §§ 7.4008(b), 34.3(b).

312 69 Fed. Reg. 1904, 1911 (Jan. 13, 2004). However, this standard arguably prohibits payday lending by national banks because the ability to repay typically is not an underwriting criteria. *See* § 7.5.5.3, *infra.*

313 The OCC describes these "consumer protection" provisions in more detail in OCC Interpretive Letter No. 999 (Mar. 9, 2004); Letter to Private Attorney regarding New OCC Preemption Regulations (July 20, 2004). *See also* Remarks by Julie L. Williams, Chief Counsel and First Senior Deputy Comptroller (Mar. 9, 2004) (discusses mischaracterizations of the OCC's preemption rule and the consumer protection provisions), *available at* www.occ.treas.gov/04rellst.htm.

314 *See* OCC Advisory Letter No. 2002-3 (reproduced on the CD-Rom accompanying this volume). In addition to the broad unfair and deceptive practices standards applicable through the FTC Act, the Federal Reserve Board enacted a regulation that applies to banks mirroring some, but not all, of the specific credit practices rules issued by the Federal Trade Commission. 12 C.F.R. § 227.

315 *See* OCC Advisory Letter No. 2002-3, at 3 n.2 (reproduced on the CD-Rom accompanying this volume); *Hearing Before the Subcomm. on Oversight and Investigations, House Comm. on Fin. Services,* 108th Cong. (Jan. 28, 2004) (testimony of Thomas J. Miller, Iowa Att'y Gen.), *available at* http://financialservices.house.gov/media/pdf/012804tm.pdf. What is clear is that the OCC has wrenched any

public enforcement of state consumer protection laws away from state officials in its new "visitorial powers" rule unveiled at the same time as these regulations, and in pronouncements leading up to that regulation. *See* 12 C.F.R. § 7.4000; 69 Fed. Reg. 1895 (Jan. 13, 2003). For an earlier OCC visitorial letter, see OCC Interpretive Letter No. 958 (Jan. 27, 2003) (reproduced on the CD-Rom accompanying this volume). When the OCC decided to get "religion" regarding the unfair or deceptive practices of national banks is unclear. A former general counsel of Citigroup's U.S. credit card business noted that the OCC ignored the "poster child of abusive consumer practices" in the credit card industry for ten years, until a state official took action. This "fiasco" was the turning point, he argues. Letter to the Editor, *Comptroller Has Duty to Clean up Card Pricing Mess,* The Am. Banker, Nov. 21, 2003, at 17.

316 *But cf.* Fidelity Nat'l Info. Solutions, Inc. v. Sinclair, 2004 WL 764834 (E.D. Pa. Mar. 31, 2004) (state regulation and certification of real estate appraisers only incidentally affects the origination of mortgage loans because the federal Financial Institutions Reform, Recovery, and Enforcement Act of 1989 states that sound appraisals are important for safety and soundness reasons and the consumer bears the cost of the appraisal, not the bank).

317 Since at least 1996, the Comptroller has stated that banks complying with the federal Real Estate Settlement Procedures Act are presumptively in compliance with any state laws. Comptroller's Handbook on Real Estate Settlement Procedures, Clearinghouse No. 55,550, at 14 (Aug. 1996).

lease to make it qualify as acceptable security for a real estate loan.[318]

Both lending rules then list the types of state laws that are *not* preempted *as long as* they only incidentally affect the exercise of national banks' lending powers.[319] They are: contract,[320] tort, criminal, homestead, rights to collect debts,[321] acquisition and transfer of property, taxation, and zoning laws. The OCC reserves the right to declare state laws not contained in this list preempted if they have more than an incidental affect on the banks' business of lending.

Noticeably absent from these lists of laws are the Uniform Commercial Codes (UCCs), foreclosure and repossession laws, and unfair and deceptive trade practices acts (UDAPs). At a hearing before the Subcommittee on Oversight and Investigations of the House Committee on Financial Services on January 28, 2004, Julie Williams, First Senior Deputy Comptroller and Chief Counsel to the OCC, testified that state UDAP acts are *not* preempted, in response to a question from a subcommittee member.[322] Whether this statement will be reflected in future regulations or interpretive letters remains to be seen.[323]

Since the effective date of these regulations, the OCC has released two interpretive letters agreeing that the Uniform Commercial Code[324] and state anti-discrimination laws are *not* preempted.[325]

It is important to note that these new preemption regulations apply on their face to national banks[326] (and, according to the OCC, to their operating subsidiaries[327]). This fact should reinforce court decisions holding that the NBA applies only to credit *initiated* by a national bank, not to that assigned to it.[328]

Another development in early 2005 occurred when the OCC released guidelines to assist banks in avoiding involvement in abusive, predatory, and unfair or deceptive mortgage lending practices.[329] The purposes of the guidelines are twofold: first, to assist a bank to manage the credit, legal, compliance, reputation, and other risks associated with mortgage lending activities; and second, to prevent the bank from becoming implicated in "abusive, predatory, unfair or deceptive practices, directly, [or] indirectly through mortgage brokers or other intermediaries, or through purchased loans."[330] The agency identified certain practices or loan terms that banks should avoid, including: equity stripping; fee packing; loan flipping; refinancing special mortgages; encouraging default; negative amortization; balloon payments in short-term transactions; lengthy prepayment penalties; default interest rates that rise to a level not commensurate with risk mitigation; high-cost loans as defined in the Homeownership and Equity Protection Act; and mandatory arbitration.[331]

Finally, the OCC amended its visitorial power regulation concurrently with the release of its 2004 preemption regulations.[332]

3.4.6.3 Visitorial Powers of the OCC

"Visitation" refers to "the act of a superior or superintending officer, who visits a corporation to examine into its manner [of] conducting business, and enforces an observance of its laws and regulation."[333] The OCC claims to have

318 *Compare* 12 C.F.R. § 7.4008(d) *with* 12 C.F.R. § 34.4(a).
319 12 C.F.R. §§ 7.4008(e), 34.4(b).
320 *See* Delaney v. Bank of America Corp., 2004 WL 1553518 (N.D. Miss. June 16, 2004) (in the context of a removal motion, court held that a claim based on breach of contract duties due to the charging of excessive interest rates is not preempted; fraud claims not preempted as well); Perdue v. Crocker Nat'l Bank, 702 P.2d 503 (Cal. 1985) (claim based upon the unconscionability of the NSF fee is not preempted; predated Smiley v. Citibank (South Dakota), N.A.); Best v. United States Nat'l Bank of Oregon, 739 P.2d 554 (Or. 1987) (claim based on the contract duty of good faith and fair dealing is not preempted; dealing with NSF fee; predated Smiley v. Citibank (South Dakota), N.A.).
321 One court recently held that the bank's practice of off-setting bank fees against bank accounts is a collection practice and is not preempted by the new regulations. Miller v. Bank of America N.T. & S.A., 2004 WL 3153009 (Cal. Super. Dec. 30, 2004).
322 Testimony of Julie L. Williams before the Subcommittee on Oversight and Investigations of the House Committee on Financial Services (Jan. 28, 2004), *available at* http://financialservices.house.gov/hearings.asp?formmode=detail&hearing=273&comm=4 (click on "Hearing transcript"). Her written testimony made no such promise. *See* Hearing Before the Subcomm. on Oversight and Investigations, House Comm. on Fin. Services, 108th Cong. (Jan. 28, 2004) (testimony of Julie Williams, First Senior Deputy Comptroller & Chief Counsel, Office of the Comptroller of the Currency), *available at* http://financialservices.house.gov/hearings.asp?formmode=detail&hearing=273&comm=4.
323 One court reviewed Ms. Williams' written testimony and observed that she implied that state consumer protections laws are preempted. Abel v. Keybank USA, N.A., 313 F. Supp. 2d 720, 729 (N.D. Ohio 2004).

324 OCC Interpretive Letter No. 1005 (June 10, 2004). The full text is reproduced on the CD-Rom accompanying this volume.
325 OCC Interpretive Letter No. 2004 (Mar. 9, 2004), *reprinted on* the CD-Rom accompanying this volume.
326 The 2004 regulations repeatedly describe the powers of national banks themselves and make no mention of non-bank originators or non-bank assignees or purchasers of loans.
327 12 C.F.R. § 7.4006; *see also* 69 Fed. Reg. 1904, 1913 (Jan. 13, 2004); 69 Fed. Reg. 1895, 1900–1902 (Jan. 13, 2004).
328 *See* discussion of court decisions and OCC Interpretive Letters on this point in § 3.4.5.1.3, *supra.*
329 70 Fed. Reg. 6329 (Feb. 7, 2005). The effective date is April 8, 2005.
330 70 Fed. Reg. at 6333.
331 70 Fed. Reg. at 6333–6334.
332 69 Fed. Reg. 1895 (Jan. 13, 2004).
333 Guthrie v. Harkness, 199 U.S. 148, 158, 26 S. Ct. 4, 7, 50 L. Ed.

exclusive visitorial powers over national banks and their operating subsidiaries under section 484 of the NBA.[334]

The OCC asserts that state or local governmental bodies have no right to take administrative action against or to sue national banks and their operating subsidiaries to enforce state laws that *do* apply to national banks. The only action that state officials may take is to sue for a declaratory judgment on the issue of whether a particular state law applies to the business of a national bank or is preempted.[335] However, once the court decides that the state law does apply to the national bank, only the OCC can then enforce that law.[336]

The extension of visitorial rights by the OCC over national bank operating subsidiaries is likely to be the most controversial aspect of the OCC's latest pronouncement on visitation.[337]

The OCC agrees that private civil cases filed in pursuit of personal claims against a national bank are permitted. Such cases do not amount to "visitation."[338] However, one court added a wrinkle to this exception. It held that a consumer could not bring a civil "private attorney general" lawsuit against a national bank or its subsidiary where the consumer asserted rights of the general public as opposed to alleging any personal harm.[339] This holding could have significant repercussions, if followed elsewhere, for the private enforcement of federal consumer protection laws.[340] In these statutes, Congress included fee-shifting provisions to encourage private attorney general enforcement. Arguably, where the consumer seeks any type of damages for herself, such as actual or statutory relief, the *Wilens* decision should be distinguished because the consumer is "alleging personal harm."

It is important to distinguish the primary jurisdiction doctrine from the OCC's visitorial rights over national banks. The primary jurisdiction doctrine permits a court to refer a matter over which it has jurisdiction to an agency regarding an issue within its special competence.[341] The court stays further proceedings until the agency issues a ruling. Moreover, the referral to the agency does not deprive the court of jurisdiction.[342]

Nevertheless, national banks may request courts to refer consumer protection statutory or other claims to the OCC, arguing that the OCC has some special expertise or ability to enforce those laws against national banks or claiming that the OCC's visitorial authority mandates the referral. These arguments should be unsuccessful for several reasons: first,

---

130 (1905); *see also* Wachovia Bank, N.A. v. Watters, 334 F. Supp. 2d 957 (W.D. Mich. 2004), *appeal pending*; Wells Fargo Bank v. Boutris, 265 F. Supp. 2d 1162, 1165 (E.D. Cal. 2003), *appeal pending*; First Union Nat'l Bank v. Burke, 48 F. Supp. 2d 132, 144 (D. Conn. 1999) (visitation means inspection, superintendence, direction, regulation).

334 12 C.F.R. § 7.4000; *see also* OCC Advisory Letter AL 2004-2 (Feb. 26, 2004); OCC Interpretive Letter No. 958 (Jan. 27, 2003); OCC Interpretive Letter No. 957 (Jan. 27, 2003) (all reproduced on the CD-Rom accompanying this volume). Section 484(a) of the NBA states: "No national bank shall be subject to any visitorial powers except as authorized by federal law, vested in the courts of justice or such as shall be, or have been exercised or directed by Congress or by either House thereof or by any committee of Congress or of either House duly authorized." Section 484(b) permits state auditors or examiners to review a bank's records "solely to ensure compliance with applicable State unclaimed property or escheat laws upon reasonable cause to believe that the bank has failed to comply with such laws." Three courts agree with the OCC's position regarding the scope of its supervision over operating subsidiaries. Wachovia Bank, N.A. v. Burke, 319 F. Supp. 2d 275 (D. Conn. 2004), *appeal pending*; Wachovia Bank, N.A. v. Watters, 334 F. Supp. 2d 957 (W.D. Mich. 2004), *appeal pending*; Wells Fargo Bank v. Boutris, 265 F. Supp. 2d 1162 (E.D. Cal. 2003), *appeal pending*; National City Bank of Ind. v. Boutris, 2003 WL 21536818 (E.D. Cal. July 2, 2003), *appeal pending*.

335 The OCC discusses this limited right in the Supplementary Information accompanying the regulation. 69 Fed. Reg. 1895, 1900 (Jan. 13, 2004).

336 For an extensive article refuting a number of positions taken by the OCC, including its stance on the scope of its visitorial powers, especially as they pertain to operating subsidiaries, see Arthur E. Wilmarth, Jr., *The OCC's Preemption Rules Exceed the Agency's Authority and Present a Serious Threat to the Dual Banking System*, 23 Ann. Rev. Banking & Fin. L. 225 (2004).

337 *See* Arthur E. Wilmarth, Jr., *The OCC's Preemption Rules Exceed the Agency's Authority and Present a Serious Threat to the Dual Banking System*, 23 Ann. Rev. Banking & Fin. L. 225 (2004); Bill Lockyer, *Other view: Banks slip regulation of state laws*, Sacramento Bee, May 21, 2003 (letter to the editor from California's Attorney General arguing that state oversight is not completely preempted, and the harm to consumer protections caused by the OCC's position).

338 69 Fed. Reg. 1895, 1900 (Jan. 13, 2004).

339 Bank One Del. v. Wilens, 2003 WL 21703629 (C.D. Cal. July 7, 2003) (consumer filed suit against the operating subsidiary and the bank initiated its own action seeking a declaratory judgment and injunction preventing the consumer from proceeding in state court; summary judgment granted to the bank because the OCC's visitorial power trumps state officials or their "delegatee" from exercising any supervision), *subsequent proceedings*, 2003 WL 21703627 (C.D. Cal. June 12, 2003) (consumer's motion to dismiss denied).

   Two other courts have ruled that Rhode Island's UDAP act does not apply to national banks due to an express exemption in that act for "regulated entities, finding that only the OCC may enforce the FTC Act against national banks. Roberts v. Fleet Bank (R.I.), N.A., 342 F.3d 260 (3d Cir. 2003); Chavers v. Fleet Bank (RI), N.A., 844 A.2d 666 (R.I. 2004).

340 For example, the federal Truth in Lending Act, the Equal Credit Opportunity Act, the Fair Debt Collection Practices Act, the Home Ownership and Equity Protection Act, the Fair Credit Billing Act, among others.

341 Reiter v. Cooper, 507 U.S. 258, 268–69, 113 S. Ct. 1213, 122 L. Ed. 2d 604 (1993); Owner-Operator Independent Drivers Ass'n, Inc. v. New Prime, Inc., 192 F.3d 778, 785 (8th Cir. 1999), *cert. denied*, 529 U.S. 1066 (2000).

342 This doctrine is not equivalent to an exhaustion requirement. Exhaustion *requires* a plaintiff to pursue an administrative remedy, if one is available, before filing a case in court. Reiter v. Cooper, 507 U.S. 258, 268–69, 113 S. Ct. 1213, 122 L. Ed. 2d 604 (1993).

it is well within the conventional expertise of judges to apply federal or state consumer laws or common law to the facts of a situation and render a decision; second, many consumer protection laws provide for a private right of action in *court* (not in the OCC); third, the interpretation and enforcement of consumer protection laws is not peculiarly within the OCC's discretion and does not require its expertise;[343] and, fourth, the OCC does not have a mechanism for hearing claims under these statutes.[344] Weighing these criteria, one court denied a motion to dismiss consumer fraud act and federal Truth in Lending Act claims on the ground that the primary jurisdiction doctrine did not mandate referral to the OCC.[345]

3.4.6.4 Preemption Rights of Operating Subsidiaries and Agents

Since at least 1966, the OCC has permitted national banks to purchase and own stock in subsidiary companies.[346] Until 2001, neither Congress nor the OCC had conferred national bank preemption rights upon national bank subsidiaries. However, following the example of the OTS,[347] the OCC promulgated a very short and seemingly innocuous regulation in 2001: "Unless otherwise provided by Federal law or OCC regulation, State laws apply to national bank operating subsidiaries to the same extent that those laws apply to the parent national bank."[348]

Nowhere has Congress explicitly addressed the extension of national bank preemption to operating subsidiaries. The Comptroller does not argue this point in the Supplementary Information accompanying the regulation expanding preemption to these entities.[349] Instead, he relies upon the OCC's longstanding approval of banks owning operating subsidiaries, Congress' more recent recognition of the role of operating subsidiaries *vis-a-vis* banks in the Gramm-Leach-Bliley Act,[350] and the fact that the Office of Thrift Supervision extended preemption rights to operating subsidiaries of federal savings associations in 1996.[351]

However, allowing banks to own operating subsidiaries and granting those non-bank entities the expansive right of preemption and its sister right of exportation are two completely different matters. At the time, critics expressed concern that granting preemption rights to subsidiaries prevents states from regulating these companies as they traditionally have under licensing, corporate governance, and consumer protection laws.[352] This move was controversial, and its legality is being questioned in several courts and by at least one banking expert.[353]

---

343 For example, under the federal Truth in Lending Act, the OCC is not the sole agency responsible for enforcing TILA. 15 U.S.C. § 1607. Several other banking agencies and the Federal Trade Commission share this responsibility. Further, state attorneys general may bring actions to enforce certain high-cost mortgage loan provisions of the Act. 15 U.S.C. § 1640(e).

344 The OCC created a customer assistance division that accepts consumer complaints and *may* attempt to resolve them informally. *See* OCC's website at www.occ.treas.gov, click on "Customer Complaints and Assistance." The website contains a disclaimer: "Many complaints stem from factual or contract disputes between the bank and the customer. Only a court of law can resolve those disputes and award damages. If your case involves such a dispute, we will suggest that you consult an attorney for assistance." (visited Feb. 16, 2005).

345 Richardson v. Standard Guar. Ins. Co., 853 A.2d 955 (N.J. Super. Ct. App. Div. 2004).

346 31 Fed. Reg. 11459, 11459, 11460 (Aug. 31, 1966) (codifying 12 C.F.R. § 7.10, which now appears at 12 C.F.R. § 5.34).

347 *See* § 3.5.4, *infra*.

348 12 C.F.R. § 7.4006; 66 Fed. Reg. 34784, 34788–789 (July 2, 2001). In 2003, the OCC issued a short interpretive letter to the effect that operating subsidiaries are entitled to preempt state laws generally and are specifically accorded "most favored lender" status just like their parent company. OCC Interpretive Letter No. 954 (Feb. 2003). A summary of this letter can be found in Appx. C.3, *infra*. The full text is provided on the CD-Rom accompanying this volume.

349 66 Fed. Reg. at 34788.

350 Pub. L. No. 106-102, § 121, 113 Stat. 1338 (1999) (codified at 12 U.S.C. § 24a(g)(3)). This Act appears to acknowledge the ability of national banks to own operating subsidiaries when it defined what constitutes a financial subsidiary. *Id.* Financial subsidiaries and operating subsidiaries are different entities. For a discussion of the additional burdens national banks acquire when taking on or creating a financial subsidiary, see Patricia A. McCoy, Banking Law Manual § 4.06[1] (Lexis Pub. 2d ed. 2003).

351 66 Fed. Reg. at 34788. As noted, there is no explicit authority in the National Bank Act. However, in a recent case, the OCC relied upon 12 U.S.C. § 24 (seventh) as support for this regulation. That provision grants national banks "incidental" powers necessary to carry on the business of banking. *See* Wells Fargo Bank, N.A. v. Boutris, 252 F. Supp. 2d 1065 (E.D. Cal.) (preliminary injunction granted to the operating subsidiary), *further proceedings at* 265 F. Supp. 2d 1162 (E.D. Cal. 2003) (summary judgment granted), *appeal pending*.

352 66 Fed. Reg. at 34788.

353 *See* Wachovia Bank, N.A. v. Burke, 319 F. Supp. 2d 275 (D. Conn. 2004), *appeal pending*; Wachovia Bank, N.A. v. Watters, 334 F. Supp. 2d 957 (W.D. Mich. 2004), *appeal pending*; Wells Fargo Bank, N.A. v. Boutris, 252 F. Supp. 2d 1065 (E.D. Cal.) (preliminary injunction granted to the operating subsidiary), *further proceedings at* 265 F. Supp. 2d 1162 (E.D. Cal. 2003) (summary judgment granted to the operating subsidiary), *appeal pending*; Arthur E. Wilmarth, Jr., *The OCC's Preemption Rules Exceed the Agency's Authority and Present a Serious Threat to the Dual Banking System*, 23 Ann. Rev. Banking & Fin. L. 225 (2004) (an excellent dissection of the National Bank Act and the lack of authority therein to extend preemption rights to operating subsidiaries); *see also* Elizabeth R. Schiltz, *The Amazing, Elastic, Ever-Expanding Exportation Doctrine and Its Effects on Predatory Lending Regulations*, 88 Minn. L. Rev. 518, 581–583, 621, 622 (2004) (discussing the phenomena of renting charters and co-branded credit cards; concluding that applying the exportation doctrine to non-bank lenders is not justified under principles of banking law). The *amicus* brief filed by 38 state attorneys general and the Conference of State Bank Supervisors in the Second Circuit Court of Appeals in Wachovia Bank, N.A. v. Burke is *reprinted in* Appx. L.7.1, *infra*. Appx. L.7.2 contains the complaint filed by the New York Attorney

In the first case to directly address the power of the OCC to enact this regulation, a federal court in California issued a preliminary injunction against the enforcement of state law against a subsidiary and later granted summary judgment to the operating subsidiary, finding it likely that section 7.4006 is a valid exercise of power by the OCC.[354] Two other courts subsequently upheld the operating subsidiary rule.[355] All three of these decisions have been appealed.

In any event, even if the Comptroller possessed the authority to enact 12 C.F.R. § 7.4006, by its own terms, that preemption provision applies only to operating subsidiaries. Financial subsidiaries are not entitled to preempt state laws.[356] The distinction between a "financial" subsidiary and an "operating" subsidiary may be hard to discern in real life. Certainly, a mortgage lending operation spun off into a subsidiary by a national bank appears to be engaging in "financial" activities.

A careful investigation of the actual relationship between a non-depository and its related depository institution is important. If the non-depository is only an affiliate or an operating subsidiary of a holding company and not a direct subsidiary of the bank itself, preemption rights do not attach.[357]

How can a practitioner or the public determine whether a particular company is an operating subsidiary of a national bank? At this point in time, the information available to the public is far from adequate. In February 2004, the OCC added a searchable list of many of the national bank subsidiaries that engage in consumer lending to its website. The site appears at www.occ.treas.gov. Click on "Customer Complaints and Assistance" and then on "Searchable list" under "What is an operating subsidiary of a national bank?" This list does not indicate when a company became an operating subsidiary or when it lost this status, if it was sold or reorganized. This information is critical because loans originated before or after a company was bought up or reorganized into an operating subsidiary would not be entitled to preemption.

Unfortunately, the list is not complete.[358] However, the OCC added new reporting requirements for national banks to its regulations in late 2004.[359] As of the annual reporting deadline of January 31, 2005, national banks must report: their name and charter number; the name, d/b/a name, abbreviated name, or trade names used to identify their operating subsidiaries when doing business directly with consumers, mailing address (including street address), e-mail address, and telephone number; principal place of business of the operating subsidiary, if different from the mailing address; and, the lines of business in which the operating subsidiary is doing business directly with consumers, using a special code system found on the OCC's website. This list will improve over time with this additional information. Unfortunately, the new regulation does not require the banks to report when a non-depository becomes an operating subsidiary or when it loses its status.

Finally, do mere agents of national banks gain any preemption rights by virtue of this relationship? In 2001, the OCC published a preemption decision, opining that Michigan's motor vehicle retail installment act (MVRISA) did not apply to out-of-state national banks when car dealers acted as their agents in soliciting loans to finance motor vehicles.[360] The OCC addressed the situation where the effect

---

General against the operating subsidiary of a national bank based on state law violations.

354 Wells Fargo Bank, N.A. v. Boutris, 252 F. Supp. 2d 1065 (E.D. Cal.) (preliminary injunction granted to the operating subsidiary), *further proceedings at* 265 F. Supp. 2d 1162 (E.D. Cal. 2003) (summary judgment granted to the operating subsidiary), *appeal pending.* The court relied upon a letter from the OCC to find that the mortgage lending arm of the bank was an operating subsidiary. *See also* Nat'l City Bank of Ind. v. Boutris, 2003 WL 21536818 (E.D. Cal. July 2, 2003) (same), *appeal pending.*

355 Wachovia Bank, N.A. v. Burke, 319 F. Supp. 2d 275 (D. Conn. 2004), *appeal pending*; Wachovia Bank, N.A. v. Watters, 334 F. Supp. 2d 957 (W.D. Mich. 2004), *appeal pending.*

356 12 C.F.R. § 5.34 (defining what is an operating subsidiaries and stating that the regulation does not apply to financial subsidiaries, which are governed by 12 C.F.R. § 5.39). The preemption regulation, however, only applies to "operating subsidiaries." 12 C.F.R. § 7.4006.

357 *See* Erick Bergquist, *Two states investigating unit of Wells*, American Banker, June 11, 2004, at 1.

358 One can also use the National Information Center of the Federal Reserve Board's website at www.ffiec.gov/nic. Using this site is problematic for two reasons. First, it is not easy to navigate. The second reason is that ultimately you cannot be sure whether the entity is an operating subsidiary or a financial subsidiary. Here is a quick lesson: At www.ffiec.gov/nic, click on "Institution Search" at the top and then type in Wells Fargo Home Mortgage, as an example. Do not add anything else and click on submit. You will get a screen with two listings. Click on "Wells Fargo Home Mortgage Inc." (not Wells Fargo Home Mortgage of Hawaii). You get a screen reading "Re Wells Fargo Home Mortgage Inc." Look at "Top Holder" and the name there is "Wells Fargo & Company." Click on "Organization Hierarchy" at the top, and this time type in Wells Fargo & Company (exactly as listed) and click submit. Two institutions are listed but click on Wells Fargo & Company. Then at the next screen, click on submit. Then click on Complete Summary Hierarchy Report and you get a pdf file that is a long list of names. Use the find function of PDF (Click on the binoculars) and type in Wells Fargo Home Mortgage, Inc. and you will get to line 188.

There, you will find the company in question. But at this point, you still do not know if it is an operating subsidiary of a national bank. So, you scroll up until you see the entity that is not indented as far into the page as is Wells Fargo Home Mortgage, Inc. In this case, scrolling up takes you to line 138 which lists Wells Fargo Bank, National Association. This is supposed to mean that Wells Fargo Home Mortgage Inc. is an operating subsidiary of Wells Fargo Bank. However, when you scroll across line 188, Wells Fargo Home Mortgage is listed as an "other company" so this does not tell you for sure that it is an operating subsidiary. Not a satisfactory result for all of this searching.

359 12 C.F.R. § 5.34(e)(6), *added by*, 69 Fed. Reg. 64478 (Nov. 5, 2004).

360 66 Fed. Reg. 28593 (May 23, 2001). This Preemption Determination also is discussed in § 3.4.6.1, *supra.*

of the Michigan law was to require that the dealer be licensed under the MVRISA; where the bank could not originate loans, only purchase them from the dealer; where the bank also had to be licensed; and where the MVRISA regulated the loan terms, including the permitted fees and interest rate, and required certain disclosures.

While banks had the authority to contract with agents before this opinion, the OCC pushed the preemption boundary further by finding that the car dealers, as agents, need not observe state licensing laws where to do so effectively restricts the ability of a national bank to exercise its ability to use agents at all.[361] The outer parameters of this determination have not been tested to date, though the Office of Thrift Supervision's letter pushes beyond whatever limits exist in OCC opinion.[362]

3.5 The Home Owners' Loan Act and Federal Savings Associations

3.5.1 History and Purpose of the Home Owners' Loan Act

In 1933, Congress enacted the Home Owners' Loan Act (HOLA).[363] This statute authorizes the Office of Thrift Supervision (OTS)[364] to provide for the organization, incorporation, examination, and regulation of federal savings and loan associations and federal savings banks.[365]

A product of the Great Depression of the 1930s, the Act was intended:

> [T]o provide emergency relief with respect to home mortgage indebtedness at a time when as many as half of all home loans in the country were in default. . . . Local institutions that had previously supplied funds to finance homes had ceased doing business or had discontinued such long-term loans, so that more than half the counties in the country, containing almost one-fifth of the total population, were without home-financing institutions.[366]

3.5.2 Most Favored Lender Doctrine and Exportation

Like the National Bank Act, the HOLA bestows upon federal savings associations "most favored lender" status by allowing them the right to charge a federal interest rate or the interest rate allowed by the home state.[367] Accordingly, federal savings associations may charge the greater of: (1) one percent above the discount rate on ninety-day commercial paper in effect at the Federal Reserve bank in the district in which such savings association is located; or (2) the rate allowed by the laws of the state in which the savings association is located. Calculating the alternative federal interest rate and the scope of the most favored lender doctrine are discussed earlier regarding national banks. The analysis of these issues appearing in §§ 3.4.2 and 3.4.3, *supra*, applies with equal validity to federal savings and loans.

Significantly, federal savings associations may also export interest rates across state lines, just like national banks.[368] However, the OTS has defined where an association is "located" more broadly than has the OCC for purposes of which state's usury law applies under the most favored lender doctrine.[369] In a letter issued in 2004, the OTS reiterated its position: that an association may export the most favored lender interest rate of its home office state, even when making loans to borrowers residing in a branch state *and* even if the loans are booked out of offices located in that branch state.[370] In this latter situation, the association need not demonstrate any special nexus between the loans and the association's home state. The association also may elect to use the most favored lender interest rate of the branch state when a loan is made in that branch state, regardless of whether the borrower resides in the branch state or a state in which the association is not located.

The same rule that applies to national banks regarding *when* preemption arises should apply equally to federal sav-

---

361 The portions of the opinion related to the ways in which the state law directly curbed the bank's right to make loans were not new or surprising.

362 See § 3.5.4, *infra*.

363 For a short history of the development of banking law in the United States, see § 2.3.1.2.1, *supra*. For a longer version, see Patricia A. McCoy, Patricia A. McCoy, Banking Law Manual ch. 2 (Lexis Pub. 2d ed. 2003).

364 The predecessor agency to the OTS was called the Federal Home Loan Bank Board.

365 12 U.S.C. §§ 1461, 1463. These provisions appear in Appx. D.1, *infra*. The definition of a federal savings association includes a federal savings bank. 12 U.S.C. §§ 1813, 1864. This chapter will use the broader term "federal savings association" to refer to both types of institutions.

366 Fidelity Fed. Sav. & Loan Ass'n v. de la Cuesta, 458 U.S. 141,

---

159, 160, 102 S. Ct. 3014, 73 L. Ed. 2d 664 (1982).

367 12 U.S.C. § 1463(g). This provision first appeared at 12 U.S.C. § 1730g when it was enacted as part of the Depository and Institutions Deregulation and Monetary Control Act of 1980. It was added later to HOLA. See Gavey Properties/762 v. First Fin. Sav. & Loan Ass'n, 845 F.2d 519 (5th Cir. 1988); *see also* Appx. G.1, n.2, *infra*.

368 *See* Gavey Properties/762 v. First Fin. Sav. & Loan Ass'n, 845 F.2d 519 (5th Cir. 1988); Cappalli v. Nordstrom, F.S.B., 155 F. Supp. 2d 339 (E.D. Pa. 2001) (Arizona-chartered federal savings bank may use Arizona law regarding the charging of a late fee on a credit card when extending credit to a Pennsylvania resident as long as it complies with Arizona law; applying *Smiley* principles in the HOLA context), *aff'd*, 28 Fed. Appx. 160 (3d Cir. 2002) (unpublished).

369 *Compare* OTS Letter No. P-2004-8 (Sept. 17, 2004) *with* OCC Interpretive Letter No. 822 (Feb. 17, 1998). Both of these letters are *reprinted on* the CD-Rom accompanying this volume. See discussion of the OCC letter in § 3.4.5.1.2, *supra*.

370 OTS Letter No. P-2004-8 (Sept. 17, 2004).

ings associations. The National Bank Act applies only to credit initiated by a national bank, not to that assigned to it.[371]

3.5.3 HOLA and "Field" Preemption

Congress granted the Federal Home Loan Bank Board (and its successor, the Office of Thrift Supervision) broad authority to regulate the lending practices of federal savings associations. Until 1996, the analysis applied by the courts to determine if a state law was preempted by HOLA or an OTS regulation was the same as that used when national banks were involved, that is, "conflict" preemption analysis.[372] When the OTS had issued regulations governing the behavior at issue which conflicted with state law on the same issue, the state law was preempted.[373]

In 1996, the OTS issued new regulations that claimed the authority to occupy the entire field of lending regulations regarding federal savings associations.[374] This declaration has been upheld by several courts.[375] On the other hand, a few courts have found that these regulations "support the conclusion that Congress has not occupied the entire field."[376]

These regulations list the types of state laws that are expressly preempted with respect to federal savings associations and those which are not.[377] For example, state laws relating to credit transactions are explicitly preempted. Such laws include those governing: licensing, registration, filings and reports by creditors; loan-to-value ratios; the terms of the credit transaction; loan-related fees;[378] escrow accounts; access to and use of credit reports; disclosure and advertising rules; the processing, origination, servicing, sale or purchase of or investment or participation in, mortgages; disbursements and repayments; usury and interest rate ceilings to the extent provided in certain enumerated federal laws; and due-on-sale clauses in certain circumstances.[379]

---

371 Viereck v. Peoples Sav. & Loan Ass'n, 343 N.W.2d 30 (Minn. 1984) (due-on-sale clauses contained in mortgage were not valid under applicable state law; because the originating lenders were not entitled to preemption, the federal savings association assignee was not entitled to preemption); Garrison v. First Fed. Sav. & Loan Ass'n of S.C., 402 S.E.2d 25 (Va. 1991) (federal savings and loan, as assignee of mortgage company which originated loan, not entitled to preemption even though loan was one of large pool sold to the savings and loan). *See also* the discussion in § 3.4.5.1.3, *supra*.

372 *See* Fidelity Fed. Sav. & Loan Ass'n v. de la Cuesta, 458 U.S. 141, 159 n.14, 102 S. Ct. 3014, 73 L. Ed. 2d 664 (1982) ("Because we find an actual conflict between federal and state law, we need not decide whether the HOLA or the Board's regulations occupy the field of due-on-sale or the entire field of federal savings and loan regulation. . . ."; interestingly, only one of the justices in the 6-2 majority is currently on the bench, and she (O'Connor, J.) filed a concurrence in which she stated: "[I]t is clear that HOLA does not permit the Board to pre-empt the application of all state and local laws to such institutions"; on the other hand, the two dissenters are still on the Court (Rehnquist, C.J. & Stevens, J.)); *see also* Departmento de Asuntos del Consumidor (DACO) v. Oriental Fed. Sav. Bank, 648 F. Supp. 1194 (D. P.R. 1986) (Home Owner's Loan Act did not preclude state regulation of federal savings and loan's retail installment sales contracts; federal regulations governing federally-chartered depository institutions preempt state law to the extent of direct conflict but do not preempt the field); *cf.* § 3.4.6.1, *supra* (regarding national banks).

373 *See, e.g.,* Fidelity Fed. Sav. & Loan Ass'n v. de la Cuesta, 458 U.S. 141, 102 S. Ct. 3014, 73 L. Ed. 2d 664 (1982) (state court decision prohibiting lenders from exercising due-on-sale clauses in mortgages is preempted by explicit Board regulation); Siegel v. Am. Sav. & Loan Ass'n, 258 Cal. Rptr. 746 (Cal. Ct. App. 1989) (reconveyance fees not explicitly regulated by the Board under regulation in effect at time case was decided [now superseded by 12 C.F.R. § 560]; state law not preempted).

Cases decided prior to the promulgation of § 560.2 holding that Congress did not intend to occupy the field of lending regulation for federal savings associations are no longer viable except to the extent that they concern state laws that fall into the preemption exception in § 560.2(c). *See, e.g.,* Fenning v. Glenfed Inc., 47 Cal. Rptr. 2d 715 (Ct. App. 1995) (and case cited therein).

374 12 C.F.R. § 560.2 (effective Jan. 1, 1997), *reprinted in* Appx. D.2, *infra*; *see also* Richard J. Hillman & Lynn H. Gibson, Role of the Office of Thrift Supervision and Office of the Comptroller of the Currency in the Preemption of State Law, General Accounting Office, OGC-00-51R (Feb. 7, 2000) (OTS claims that HOLA "occupies the field," a broader form of preemption than "conflict" preemption).

375 *See, e.g.,* Flagg v. Yonkers Sav. & Loan Ass'n, FA, 396 F.3d 178 (2d Cir. 2005); Bank of Am. v. City & County of San Francisco, 309 F.3d 551 (9th Cir. 2002); Am. Bankers Ass'n v. Lockyer, 239 F. Supp. 2d 1000 (E.D. Cal. 2002); Miller v. Bank of America N.T. & S.A., 2004 WL 3153009 (Cal. Super. Dec. 30, 2004) (court observes that the preemption standards under HOLA are broader than those under the NBA; intent of HOLA is to occupy the field); Moskowitz v. Wash. Mut. Bank, F.A., 768 N.E.2d 262 (Ill. App. Ct. 2002); Mayor of New York v. Council of New York, 780 N.Y.S.2d 266 (N.Y. Sup. Ct. 2004).

376 Konynenbelt v. Flagstar Bank, 617 N.W.2d 706, 713 (Mich. Ct. App. 2000); *see also* Bright v. Wash. Mut. Bank, 2002 WL 453725 (Cal. Ct. App. Mar. 25, 2002) (recognizes that not all state laws are preempted); Wash. Mut. Bank, F.A. v. Super. Ct., 115 Cal. Rptr. 2d 765 (Cal. Ct. App. 2002) (same); Gibson v. World Sav. & Loan Ass'n, 128 Cal. Rptr. 2d 19 (Cal. Ct. App. 2002) (same); Homecomings Fin. Network v. Sprow, Clearinghouse No. 54,568 (D.C. Super. Ct. Apr. 19, 2001) (though the OTS regulations purport to occupy the field, they expressly state that certain state laws are not preempted if they only incidentally affect the lending operations of the federal savings association); Pinchot v. Charter One Bank, F.S.B., 792 N.E.2d 1105 (Ohio 2003) (not all state laws are preempted); *cf.* Turner v. First Union Nat'l Bank, 740 A.2d 1081 (N.J. 1999) (court states that regulations occupy the field but holds, narrowly, that express preemption applies; state law which limits when the lender's attorney fee can be passed on to the borrower is preempted where the state law conflicted with a specific OTS regulation permitting the charging of attorney fees).

377 *Compare* 12 C.F.R. § 560.2(b) *with* 12 C.F.R. § 560.2(c). *See also* 12 C.F.R. § 550.136 (fiduciary powers can be exercised without regard to state law); 68 Fed. Reg. 53024 (Sept. 9, 2003).

378 *See also* 12 C.F.R. § 560.34 (preempts prepayment penalty prohibitions in state laws as does § 560.2(b)(5)); Stoneking v. Bank of Am., N.A., 43 P.3d 1089 (N.M. Ct. App. 2002).

379 12 C.F.R. § 560.2(b).

By contrast, state laws that are specifically enumerated in the regulation and only "incidentally" affect the lending operations of federal savings associations are not preempted. The types of state laws that fall into this latter category are: contract and commercial law; real property law; certain homestead laws; tort law; and criminal law.[380] In addition, the OTS may find that other state laws are not preempted if two conditions are met: the state law furthers a vital state interest and it either incidentally affects lending operations or is not otherwise contrary to the purposes of HOLA.[381] In analyzing whether a state law is or is not preempted, the OTS suggests a two-step process in the Supplementary Information to these regulations:

> When analyzing the status of state laws under § 560.2, the first step will be to determine whether the type of law in question is listed in paragraph (b). If so, the analysis will end there; the law is preempted. If the law is not covered by paragraph (b), the next question is whether the law affects lending. If it does, then, in accordance with paragraph (a), the presumption arises that the law is preempted. This presumption can be reversed only if the law can clearly be shown to fit within the confines of paragraph (c). For these purposes, paragraph (c) is intended to be interpreted narrowly. Any doubt should be resolved in favor of preemption.[382]

Since the promulgation of this regulation, the OTS has determined that one type of state law not mentioned in the regulation is *not* preempted—state unfair and deceptive acts and practices laws that do not directly regulate credit transactions.[383] This opinion letter specifically addressed whether Indiana's UDAP act was preempted. While Indiana's UDAP act affects lending to the extent that it prohibits misleading statements and practices in loan transactions, the OTS found that there is no indication that the law is aimed at any state objective in conflict with the safe and sound regulation of federal savings associations. "In fact, because federal thrifts are presumed to interact with their borrowers in a truthful manner, Indiana's general prohibition on deception should have no measurable impact on their lending operations." Several courts have recognized this distinction when deciding whether state UDAP acts applied to the activities of savings associations.[384] Unlike

the OCC,[385] the OTS has not addressed whether other common types of state statutes are preempted, such as the UCC and anti-discrimination laws.[386]

Both before and after the enactment of 12 C.F.R. § 560, the OTS has determined that numerous other types of state laws are preempted, including state anti-predatory mortgage lending (HOEPA-like) laws,[387] loan disclosure laws, loan-related charges regulation (including pre-payment penalty prohibitions), certain state insurance laws, fiduciary laws, statutes governing the trust activities of thrifts, licensing laws, laws or ordinance restricting the ATM fees, and a host of others.[388] Additionally, in 2002, the OTS published a list of the powers of federal savings associations with support-

---

380   12 C.F.R. § 560.2(c).

381   12 C.F.R. § 560.2(c)(6).

382   61 Fed. Reg. 50951, 50966, 50967 (Sept. 30, 1996).

383   OTS Chief Counsel Letter (Feb. 24, 1996). All OTS preemption letters issued since 1994 are summarized in Appx. D.3, *infra*. With one exception, the full text of the letters is reproduced on the CD-Rom accompanying this volume.

384   Boursiquot v. Citibank F.S.B., 323 F. Supp. 2d 350 (D. Conn. 2004) (UDAP act preempted where the issue is the collection of a fax/statement fee); Lopez v. World Sav. & Loan Ass'n, 130 Cal. Rptr. 2d 42 (Cal. Ct. App. 2003) (state law prohibition against charging for a payoff statement is within the field of

lending regulation and is preempted; UDAP claims are not preempted to the extent that the behavior complained of is outside of the list of lending related activities; in this case, concurrent UDAP claim was preempted; breach of contract and fraud claims not preempted but failed due to court's reading of the contract provision); Wash. Mut. Bank, F.A. v. Super. Ct., 115 Cal. Rptr. 2d 765 (Ct. App. 2002) (charging one day's pre-closing interest affects the "terms of credit"; state law prohibiting the imposition of this charge is preempted; court noted that state UDAP act is within state's police power and is subject to heightened presumption against preemption); Laskey v. Downey Sav. & Loan Ass'n, 2002 WL 31721686 (Cal. Ct. App. Dec. 5, 2002) (same); Kunert v. Bank of Am. Nat'l Trust & Sav. Ass'n, 2001 WL 1715929 (Cal. Super. Ct. Aug. 3, 2001) (interest rate upcharge in car financing is akin to a "loan-related fee" and state law prohibiting the charging of a secret upcharge is preempted; fraud claim is also preempted as it is based on the same "loan-related fee" issue); Moskowitz v. Wash. Mut. Bank, 768 N.E.2d 262 (Ill. App. Ct. 2002) (breach of contract and UDAP claims based upon the bank's practice of charging a payoff statement fee, found to be a "loan-related fee" under the OTS regulations, preempted); Rosenberg v. Washington Mut. Bank, F.A., 849 A.2d 566 (N.J. Super. Ct. App. Div. 2004) (consumer fraud and breach of contract claims based on allegedly deceptive monthly billing statements preempted as the claims are based on disclosures and disclosure laws are expressly preempted in § 560.2).

385   *See* §§ 3.4.6.1, 3.4.6.2, *supra*.

386   The OTS adopted its own anti-discrimination regulations. 12 C.F.R. §§ 528.2–528.9, *reprinted in* Appx. D.2, *infra*.

387   The OTS decided that the anti-predatory lending laws of New York, New Mexico, New Jersey, and Georgia are preempted. *See* Appx. D.3, *infra. See also* Mayor of New York v. Council of New York, 780 N.Y.S.2d 266 (N.Y. Sup. Ct. 2004) (city ordinance prohibiting the city from doing business with predatory lenders is preempted by HOLA).

388   *See* summary of OTS letters in Appx. D.3, *infra*. OTS letters related to restrictions on ATM fees and requirements related to the disclosure of the estimated length of time necessary to pay off credit card balances have been upheld by the courts. *See* Bank of Am. v. City & County of San Francisco, 309 F.3d 551 (9th Cir. 2002); Am. Bankers Ass'n v. Lockyer, 239 F. Supp. 2d 1000 (E.D. Cal. 2002). For an article criticizing the OCC and OTS for "dismantling" state regulatory powers, see Stacy Mitchell, *Rogue Agencies Gut State Banking Laws*, New Rules (Fall 2001) at 4; *see also* Jess Bravin & Paul Beckett, *Dependent on Lender Fees, The OCC Takes Banks' Side Against Local Laws*, Wall St. J., Jan. 28, 2002.

ing citations.[389] Practitioners should consult this list to determine the OTS's view on the nature and extent of the powers of federal thrifts before suing or defending this type of institution.

Issues of preemption of state laws in cases involving federal savings associations occur with greater frequency since the OTS adopted its broad preemption regulation. More often than not the court finds the state law in question to be preempted.[390] However, a growing number of deci-

sions hold that certain state laws are not preempted.[391]

---

state law prohibiting the charging of a secret upcharge is preempted; fraud claim is also preempted as it is based on the same "loan-related fee" issue); Moskowitz v. Wash. Mut. Bank, F.A., 768 N.E.2d 262 (Ill. App. Ct. 2002) (breach of contract and UDAP claims based upon the bank's practice of charging a payoff statement fee found to be a "loan-related fee" under the OTS regulations and preempted); Chaires v. Chevy Chase Bank, F.S.B., 748 A.2d 34 (Md. Ct. Spec. App. 2000) (Maryland secondary mortgage loan law containing prohibitions against the charging of certain fees is preempted); Rosenberg v. Washington Mut. Bank, F.A., 849 A.2d 566 (N.J. Super. Ct. App. Div. 2004) (consumer fraud and breach of contract claims based on allegedly deceptive monthly billing statements preempted as the claims are based on disclosures and disclosure laws are expressly preempted in § 560.2); Stoneking v. Bank of Am., N.A., 43 P.3d 1089 (N.M. Ct. App. 2002) (state law prohibition against prepayment penalties preempted by 12 C.F.R. § 560.34); Mayor of New York v. Council of New York, 780 N.Y.S.2d 266 (N.Y. Sup. Ct. 2004) (city ordinance limiting the lenders with whom the city will do business to "non-predatory" lenders is preempted); Albank F.S.B. v. Foland, 676 N.Y.S.2d 461 (City Ct. 1998) (OTS regulation trumped a state evidentiary law which prohibited a maker of a contract involving a consumer transaction from introducing the contract into evidence when the print is not clear and legible or is less than a specified type; the type size requirement is inconsistent with § 560.2(a) because that requirement would thwart the goal that there be a uniform set of federal lending regulations).

391   *See* Alkan v. Citimortgage, Inc., 336 F. Supp. 2d 1061 (N.D. Cal. 2004) (state debt collection law is not preempted because the act is not a lending law; the act does not come into play until after the loan is made; no reason why a savings association should not be subject to a state act that expands upon its federal counterpart, the FDCPA, by covering the original lender); Hussey-Head v. World Sav. & Loan Ass'n, 4 Cal. Rptr. 3d 171 (Cal. Ct. App. 2003) (state credit reporting act applies to savings association because it only incidentally affects the business of lending; factors the court relied upon were: that the savings association voluntarily chose to report to the credit bureaus, and that there was no evidence that the statute is specifically directed to the savings association, that the law was designed to regulate savings associations more than any other type of business, or that in practice the law has a disproportionate impact on lending institutions); Gibson v. World Sav. & Loan Ass'n, 128 Cal. Rptr. 2d 19 (Ct. App. 2002) (strong presumption against preemption when the state's police powers are involved; UDAP acts involve police power; UDAP and breach of contract claims do not implicate saving association's ability to force place insurance but rather they rely upon allegations that the insurance charge included fees for non-insurance and that the lender lied about that; preemption of state law principles do not extend to those voluntarily assumed in a contract); Homecomings Fin. Network v. Sprow, Clearinghouse No. 54,568 (D.C. Super. Ct. Apr. 19, 2001) (unconscionability claim in not preempted); Pinchot v. Charter One Bank, F.S.B., 792 N.E.2d 1105 (Ohio 2003) (state real estate law requiring recordation of a release within ninety days of the pay-off is not preempted as it only incidentally affects lending activities; the law does not affect "lending" as the lending relationship is over before the satisfaction is recorded; note: the Ohio intermediate appellate court, in 2002 WL 568400 (Ohio Ct. App. Apr. 11, 2002), also found that the state law is not akin to "servicing," an activity expressly mentioned in § 560.2 and the savings association admitted that prompt

---

389   Office of Thrift Supervision, Powers of Federal Savings Associations (Mar. 1, 2002). This document is reproduced on the CD-Rom accompanying this volume.

390   *See* Flagg v. Yonkers Sav. & Loan Ass'n, FA, 396 F.3d 178 (2d Cir. 2005) (HOLA trumps the state interest on escrow law and a related UDAP claim; choice of law provision incorporating state law generally, as opposed to a reference to a specific state law, is not sufficient to trump HOLA under contract theory); Bank of Am. v. City & County of San Francisco, 309 F.3d 551 (9th Cir. 2002) (ordinance prohibiting financial institutions from charging ATM fees to non-depositors preempted; court also construes federal anti-assignment provision); Lopez v. Wash. Mut. Bank, F.A., 302 F.3d 900 (9th Cir. 2002) (HOLA preempts state laws restricting deposit-related activities under a sister regulation, namely 12 C.F.R. § 557.12; court also construed the federal anti-assignment protections); Boursiquot v. Citibank F.S.B., 323 F. Supp. 2d 350 (D. Conn. 2004) (UDAP act preempted where the issue is the collection of a fax statement fee); Haehl v. Wash. Mut. Bank, F.A., 277 F. Supp. 2d 933 (S.D. Ind. 2003) (reconveyance fee is a "loan related fee" under 12 C.F.R. § 560.2 and Indiana law prohibiting the charging of such a fee is preempted; the court made this finding even though the lender allegedly kept the fee and never paid it out); Am. Bankers Ass'n v. Lockyer, 239 F. Supp. 2d 1000 (E.D. Cal. 2002) (California minimum payment credit card disclosure law preempted); Lopez v. World Sav. & Loan Ass'n, 130 Cal. Rptr. 2d 42 (Cal. Ct. App. 2003) (state law prohibition against charging for a payoff statement is within the field of lending regulation and is preempted; UDAP claims are not preempted to the extent that the behavior complained of is outside of the list of lending related activities; in this case, concurrent UDAP claim was preempted; breach of contract and fraud claims not preempted but failed due to court's reading of the contract provision); Wash. Mut. Bank, F.A. v. Super. Ct., 115 Cal. Rptr. 2d 765 (Cal. Ct. App. 2002) (charging one day's pre-closing interest affects the "terms of credit"; state law prohibiting the imposition of this charge is preempted; court noted that state UDAP act is within state's police power and is subject to heightened presumption against preemption); Laskey v. Downey Sav. & Loan Ass'n, 2002 WL 31721686 (Cal. Ct. App. Dec. 5, 2002) (same); Bright v. Wash. Mut. Bank, 2002 WL 453725 (Cal. Ct. App. Mar. 25, 2002) (state law prohibiting force-placed insurance at a cost exceeding the replacement value of the improvements of the property is preempted as it falls within provision preempting laws related to the ability of an association to require hazard insurance); Thompson v. WFS Fin., Inc., 2003 WL 22924458 (Cal. Super. Ct. Nov. 6, 2003) (OTS regulations prohibiting discrimination, 12 C.F.R. §§ 528.2 and 528.9, preempt claims based on state ECOA-like law; OTS regulation enacted after the federal ECOA supersede the more general ECOA and its express permission to states to enact more protective anti-discrimination laws); Kunert v. Bank of Am. Nat'l Trust & Sav. Ass'n, 2001 WL 1715929 (Cal. Super. Ct. Aug. 3, 2001) (interest rate upcharge in car financing is akin to a "loan-related fee" and

The Cost of Credit: Regulation and Legal Challenges

An interesting issue arises when the federal savings association incorporates specific state law provisions into its loan contracts. Does that contract provision reverse any preemption to which the association may be entitled? When faced with this situation Maryland's highest court held that the incorporated state law was not preempted outright.[392] According to this court, the question is a matter of state contract law and interpretation. The court held that the express preemption in 12 C.F.R. § 560.2(b) does not apply. It distinguished between a claim of preemption (being a defense requiring an analysis of federal law and the determination of the impact the relationship of the parties has on the ability of that law to fulfill its intended goal) and parties contracting to comply with a specific law (this analysis involves contract interpretation, and requires discerning the parties' intent and is a matter of state law). The court remanded the case to the trial court to make the ultimate decision. Practitioners should check for further developments in this case.

3.5.4 Preemption Rights of Certain Subsidiaries and Agents

The ability to preempt certain state laws enjoyed by federal savings associations also applies, by regulation, to operating subsidiaries of these federal associations.[393] This regulation limits the subsidiary's preemption right to that of the parent savings association, and no more.[394] Operating

subsidiaries must be distinguished from "service corporations" which explicitly cannot claim any preemption rights.[395] Separate regulations govern the requirements that savings associations must meet in order to establish or obtain an interest in an operating subsidiary or service corporation.[396]

A careful review of the provisions of the HOLA and the Federal Deposit Insurance Act upon which the OTS relied to promulgate this regulation reveals that Congress did not expressly address this issue.[397] In the Supplementary Information accompanying the regulation, the OTS relied upon its long-standing policy to treat the subsidiary in the same way as the parent federal savings association for purposes of preemption. Its rationale was that the operating subsidiary may only be engaged in activities permissible for its parent and must be controlled by the parent.[398] Whether this rationale will defeat a claim that the agency exceeded its legislative authority by extending preemption to the subsidiary remains to be seen.

However, such an argument must confront broad language in the seminal case regarding OTS authority under HOLA in *Fidelity Federal Savings & Loan v. de la Cuesta*.[399] There, the Supreme Court upheld the validity of a regulation promulgated by the predecessor to the OTS regarding due-on-sale clauses and the regulation's preemptive effect on California law. In the course of discussing this regulation, the court stated that "[f]ederal *regulations* have no less pre-emptive effect than federal *statutes*. . . . A pre-emptive regulation's force does *not* depend on express congressional authorization to displace state law. . . ."[400] The Court explicitly rejected the California appellate court's focus on whether the federal statute had impliedly preempted state law. The Court's actual holding was narrow, despite this broad language. It found a conflict between the express language of the federal regulation and the state law. Consequently, state law had to yield. The Court did *not* decide "whether the HOLA or the Board's regulations occupy the field of due-on-sale law or the entire field of federal savings and loan regulation."[401] Whether the Court

recordation is part of best practices); Chevy Chase Bank v. McCamant, 512 S.E.2d 217 (W. Va. 1998) (no express or implied preemption prevents the applicability of state debt collection laws to a federal savings bank).

392 Wells v. Chevy Chase Bank, F.S.B., 832 A.2d 812 (Md. 2003) (in the section captioned "Governing Law," the credit card agreement stated: "This Agreement is made in Maryland. It is governed by Subtitle 9 [Credit Grantor Revolving Credit Provisions] of Title 12 [Credit Regulations] of the Commercial Law Article of the Maryland Annotated Code."; this provision refers to one of Maryland's credit regulation statutes, the most flexible for lenders); *see also* Fidelity Nat'l Info. Solutions, Inc., 2004 WL 764834 (E.D. Pa. Mar. 31, 2004) (state regulation and certification of real estate appraisers enacted pursuant to the federal Financial Institutions Reform, Recovery, and Enforcement Act of 1989 does not regulate the credit activities of savings associations even though it does incidentally affect their operations).

393 12 C.F.R. § 559.3(h), (n); OTS Powers of Federal Savings Associations (Mar. 1, 2002) (reproduced on the CD-Rom accompanying this volume) (in its overview of the powers of operating subsidiaries, the OTS only cites to its own regulations and opinion letters in support of its position, and not to any statutory authority); *see* 61 Fed. Reg. 66561, 66563 (Dec. 18, 1996); *see also* WFS Fin. Inc. v. Dean, 79 F. Supp. 2d 1024 (W.D. Wis. 1999); Chaires v. Chevy Chase Bank, F.S.B., 748 A.2d 34 (Md. Ct. Spec. App. 2000); Malhotra v. Pac. Thrift & Loan Corp., 1999 Wash. App. LEXIS 1775 (Wash. Ct. App. Oct. 11, 1999).

394 *See* OTS Letter No. P-2004-5 (Sept. 14, 2004) (an operating subsidiary may own, sell, underwrite, and deal in asset-backed

securities because a federal association may engage in these activities either as an express power under HOLA or an incidental power).

395 12 C.F.R. § 559.3; 61 Fed. Reg. 66561, 66563 (Dec. 18, 1996); *see* Fenning v. Glenfed, Inc., 47 Cal. Rptr. 2d 715 (1995); *see also* 67 Fed. Reg. 60542, 60550, 60551 (Sept. 26, 2002) (OTS affirms its view of the rights of operating subsidiaries in the Supplementary Information accompanying changes to its AMTPA regulations and states that operating subsidiaries need not resort to AMTPA to preempt state law).

396 12 C.F.R. § 559.3 (and accompanying chart).

397 12 U.S.C. §§ 1462, 1463, 1464, 1662a, 1828.

398 *See* 61 Fed. Reg. 66561, 66563 (Dec. 18, 1996).

399 458 U.S. 141, 102 S. Ct. 3014, 73 L. Ed. 2d 664 (1982).

400 *Id.* at 153, 154 (emphasis added).

401 *Id.* at 159 n.14. Elsewhere, the Court stated: "Although the Board's power to promulgate regulations exempting federal savings and loans from the requirements of state law may not be

would apply the same standards to a regulation that creates preemption rights not for a federal savings association, which the OTS has broad authority to nurture from "cradle to grave" under HOLA, but for a subsidiary is unclear.[402]

The OTS maintains a searchable database on its website that will permit practitioners to determine if a lender or company is an operating subsidiary of a federal savings association. Go the OTS website[403] and click on "Consumer Inquiries" under "Consumer & Community." Next, click on "Related Organizations Directory" and follow the instructions.

Another question relates to whether third parties not corporately related to the savings association are entitled to preempt state law due to their contract relationships with the association. In 2004, the OTS released a preemption letter addressing the applicability of state licensing or registration laws to "agents" who market, solicit, and perform certain customer service activities related to the savings associations deposit-taking and loan products.[404]

The OTS described the relationship between the third party and the savings association this way: A third party "agent"[405] marketed and solicited customers for the association's deposit and loan products and services. This company worked exclusively for the association. It directed potential customers and borrowers to the association and assisted individuals in completing application forms and documentation, answering questions, and, at the customer's request, transmitting the completed application to the association. The agent did not open accounts, accept deposits or payments, cash checks, handle any deposit transfers or withdrawals, evaluate or review applications (except for completeness), approve loans, or make any other substantive decisions.

The OTS opined that the agent need not comply with state licensing or registration laws where the agent and the association enter into a written agreement specifying certain

duties and responsibilities; where the agent must undergo training from the association on the products and applicable laws before commencing its activities on behalf of the association; and where the agent is subject to the association's and OTS's supervision and control. Although the company was the exclusive agent of the association, this factor does not appear to be a precondition to the agent's qualifications for preemption.

The OTS based its decision on the notion that federal savings associations can engage in these activities directly without regard to state law and this principal does not change "merely because an association contracts with a third party to perform marketing, solicitation, and customer services."[406] The OTS also argued that this outcome "may result in greater credit distribution channels, which in turn, has the potential to lower the cost of credit."[407] Finally, the OTS was concerned about the costs to the agents (presumably passed on to the association) of complying with state licensing laws.

The OTS letter, on its face, addresses the applicability of licensing and registration laws—not substantive laws, like UDAPs, telemarketing laws, credit repair acts, and the like—and should be limited to those laws. Further, the letter states clearly that agents who perform banking or lending activities for entities other than federal savings associations would have to comply with any state licensing and registration requirements for those activities.[408]

However, the OTS letter expands savings association preemption to agents beyond what the OCC accomplished in its 2001 opinion.[409] The OCC limited its discussion to the facts of the car dealer situation. On the other hand, the OTS created a roadmap in the letter's Appendix for the preemption of licensing and registration laws for "agents" generally. Finally, to the extent that independent contractors of savings associations can claim preemption rights as well far exceeds where the OCC has gone before.[410]

3.6 Federal Credit Union Act and Federal Credit Unions

3.6.1 Overview

The Federal Credit Union Act of 1934 (FCUA)[411] regulates the operation of federally-chartered credit unions and

---

boundless, in this case we need not explore the outer limits of the Board's discretion." *Id.* at 167.

402 It is interesting to note that the only justices presently on the Court who took part in the *de la Cuesta* decision are Justices O'Connor and Stevens and Chief Justice Rehnquist. Justice O'Connor wrote a short concurrence emphasizing that the authority of the OTS's predecessor is not limitless. *Id.* at 171. Chief Justice Rehnquist and Justice Stevens joined in a dissent. There they reviewed the congressional intent manifested in the statute and found that HOLA did not empower the agency to determine when federal law should govern the enforceability of provisions contained in mortgages. After all, they said, mortgages, contracts, and real property are traditionally the domain of state law. "Congress did not intend to create a federal common law of mortgages." *Id.* at 174.

403 www.ots.treas.gov.

404 OTS Letter P-2004-7 (Oct. 25, 2004), *reprinted on* the CD-Rom accompanying this volume.

405 The OTS uses the word "agent" throughout the letter rather loosely because the facts revealed that the "agent" in this case was actually an independent contractor.

406 OTS Letter P-2004-7 at 10.

407 *Id.*

408 *Id.* at 14, n.46.

409 *See* § 3.4.6.1, *supra.*

410 Note that the authority of the OCC and OTS to extend preemption rights to operating subsidiaries has been upheld by courts at the moment. *See* § 3.4.6.4, *supra.* However, granting these rights to mere agents or independent contractors stands on very weak grounds.

411 12 U.S.C. §§ 1751 *et seq.*

sets the maximum interest rate that these credit unions may charge in the absence of a more specific statutory authority.[412] Since 1970, the primary regulator of federal credit unions has been the National Credit Union Administration (NCUA).[413] At that time, Congress also created the National Credit Union Share Insurance Fund, administered by NCUA, which provides insurance for federal credit unions and qualified state-chartered credit unions, up to $100,000 per member account.[414]

The Act was amended in 1980 to replace the former ceiling of 1% per month on loans made to credit union members with a 15% annual rate. However, the statute also contains an escape clause allowing NCUA to substitute a higher temporary rate if economic conditions so require.[415] Acting under this authority, the Board adopted a 21% ceiling effective May 12, 1980, and maintained the 21% rate until May 14, 1987, when it was lowered to 18%. This rate will remain in effect until September 8, 2006 and then revert to 15% for loans and lines of credit originated after that date, unless extended by the NCUA.[416]

3.6.2 Most Favored Lender Status

Like national banks and federal savings associations, the FCUA confers upon federal credit unions "most favored lender" status in particular circumstances. Section 1785 allows federal credit unions to charge a federal interest rate or the interest rate allowed by the home state for the particular type of loan *if* either of those rates exceeds the rate permitted by the NCUA (presently 18%).[417] This means that the federal credit union may charge the greater of: (1) one percent above the discount rate on ninety-day commercial paper in effect at the Federal Reserve bank in the district in which such credit union is located; or (2) the rate allowed by the laws of the state in which the credit union is located, if either exceeds 18%. The NCUA extended the most favored lender status to state-chartered credit unions by issuing an "interpretation."[418] Calculating the alternative federal interest rate and the scope of the most favored lender doctrine are discussed earlier regarding national banks. The analysis of these issues appearing in §§ 3.4.2 and 3.4.3, *supra,* applies with equal validity to federal credit unions.[419]

3.6.3 Beyond Usury Preemption

The preemption regime for federal credit unions, until recently, has been fairly narrow. It is clear that the Federal Credit Union Act preempts state usury law to the extent that state law conflicts with the Act, and that state usury statutes setting low interest ceilings create such a conflict.[420] However, the Act is not so comprehensive as to preempt all state regulation of federal credit unions. States retain regulatory authority in areas the Act does not address.[421] Thus, one court held that a state law limiting the maximum attorney fees that a lender could recover from a defaulting debtor was not preempted, and applied to a federal credit union.[422]

The NCUA defined the limited scope of federal credit union preemption by regulation.[423] The NCUA states that the FCUA grants it exclusive authority to regulate the "rates, terms or repayment and other condition of Federal credit union loans and lines of credit (including credit cards) to members."[424] The agency then identifies the specific types of state law that are preempted as laws purporting to limit or affect:

—Rates of interest and amounts of finance charges, including, terms related to variable rate loans and late charges;

—Closing costs, application, origination, or other fees;

—Terms of repayment, including, maturity of loans and lines of credit; the amount, uniformity, and frequency of payments; balloon payments; and prepayment limits;

—Conditions related to the amount or purpose of the loan or line of credit and the type or amount of security;

—The imposition and enforcement of liens on the shares (deposits) of borrowers and accommodating parties.[425]

The NCUA intends that this list be exclusive.[426] State laws that do not affect rates, terms of repayment, and other conditions are *not* preempted. The NCUA identifies some state laws that are not preempted, including: insurance laws;

---

412 12 U.S.C. § 1757(5)(A)(vi).

413 *See* Patricia A. McCoy, Banking Law Manual § 2.08 (Lexis Pub. 2d ed. 2003).

414 12 U.S.C. §§ 1782, 1783, 1787.

415 12 U.S.C. § 1757(5)(A)(vi)(I).

416 12 C.F.R. § 701.21(c)(7), *amended* 70 Fed. Reg. 3863 (Jan. 27, 2005).

417 12 U.S.C. § 1785(g). This provision was enacted as part of the Depository and Institutions Deregulation and Monetary Control Act of 1980. *See* Appx. G.1.

418 NCUA Statement of Interpretation and Policy (IRPS 81-31), 46 Fed. Reg. 24153 (Apr. 30, 1981), *amending,* IRPS 80-11, 45 Fed. Reg. 78624 (Nov. 26, 1980).

419 *See also* 45 Fed. Reg. 78624, 78625 (Nov. 26, 1980), *as*

---

amended by IRPS 81-3, 46 Fed. Reg. 24153 (Apr. 30, 1981) (NCUA opinion as to federally-insured credit unions and the most favored lender doctrine).

420 *See, e.g., Ex parte* Davis, 401 So. 2d 52 (Ala. 1981); Neal v. Redstone Fed. Credit Union, 447 So. 2d 805 (Ala. Civ. App. 1984); Christian v. Atlanta Army Depot Fed. Credit Union, 140 Ga. App. 277, 231 S.E.2d 7 (1976); Brooklyn Jenapo Fed. Credit Union v. Schucher, 41 Misc. 2d 368, 245 N.Y.S.2d 637 (Sup. Ct. 1963); McAnally v. Ideal Fed. Credit Union, 428 P.2d 322 (Okla. 1967).

421 *See Ex parte* Davis, 401 So. 2d 52 (Ala. 1981); *see also* McAnally v. Ideal Fed. Credit Union, 428 P.2d 322 (Okla. 1967).

422 *Ex parte* Davis, 401 So. 2d 52 (Ala. 1981).

423 12 C.F.R. § 701.21(b).

424 12 C.F.R. 21 701.21(b)(1), *citing* 12 U.S.C. § 1757(5).

425 *Id.*

426 12 C.F.R. § 701.21(b)(2).

laws relating to the transfer of and security interests in real and personal property (except relating to due-on-sale clauses); laws relating to collection costs and attorney fees; requirements that documents be in plain English; law addressing the circumstances in which a borrower may be in default; and cure statutes.[427]

Finally, the regulation states that NCUA does not intend to preempt state laws affecting aspects of credit transactions that are primarily regulated by other federal laws, for example, those state laws concerning credit cost-disclosure requirements, credit discrimination, credit reporting practices, unfair credit practices, and debt collection practices.[428] When these types of state laws are at issue, the agency will determine the applicability of such laws according to the preemption standards of the relevant federal law and regulations.

Like the OCC and OTS,[429] the NCUA has issued numerous preemption letters over the years.[430] These letters are more evenly divided between those approving and those disapproving the applicability of state laws to federal credit unions than are the opinions released by the OCC and OTS. For example, parts of a state credit card law, registration requirements in certain situations, laws relating to the deposits of a decedent, laws regulating the advertising of loans, state debt collection requirements, and prohibitions on fees for use of ATMs by nonmembers are *not* preempted.[431]

On the other hand, state usury laws, restrictions on changing the terms in open-end credit, laws relating to grace periods, minimum payment disclosures requirements relating to credit card plans, restrictions on establishing ATM machines in a state, conditions to the refinancing of a balloon payment, and state anti-predatory lending laws *are* preempted.[432]

Two areas where the NCUA has flip-flopped regarding preemption relate to car dealer originated loans purchased by credit unions ("indirect" loans) and state anti-predatory lending laws. Regarding the car dealer loans, in 1992, the NCUA opined that state motor vehicle retail installment sales laws apply to loans originated by car dealers and purchased by a federal credit union.[433] It reasoned that the

FCUA preemption only applies to loans originated by the credit union regardless of the fact that all parties contemplate that the loan will be assigned immediately to the credit union. In 1999, the NCUA reversed itself, without discussing the 1992 letter.[434]

Regarding state anti-predatory lending laws patterned on the federal Home Ownership and Equity Protection Act (HOEPA), the NCUA reviewed laws or regulations in effect in New York, Georgia, and North Carolina, deciding that certain provisions were not preempted, particularly where they mirrored HOEPA.[435] However, in 2003, the NCUA defined the preemption rights of federal credit unions more expansively, by arguing that any state law that *affects* the rates, terms, and conditions of the loan is preempted regardless of whether another federal law permits the state to enact it.[436] The NCUA opined that: "Based on this, NCUA's lending regulation preempts any state law, including one affecting aspects of lending primarily regulated by TILA, that regulates rates, terms of repayment and other conditions of loans and lines of credit."[437] The agency has not amended the limitation in its preemption regulation regarding state laws affecting aspects of credit transactions primarily regulated by other federal laws, however.[438] Consequently, the letters preempting the HOEPA-like laws in the District of Columbia, Georgia, and New Jersey may be challenged.

3.7 The Federal Deposit Insurance Act and State-Chartered Banks

3.7.1 The "Dual" Banking System and State-Chartered Bank Powers

As is evident from previous sections in this chapter, a large part of the banking industry operates under federal banking charters. There were approximately 2,001 national banks and 928 federal savings associations by the end of 2003.[439] The FDIC reports a total of 7,769 insured com-

---

427 *Id.*

428 12 C.F.R. § 701.21(b)(3).

429 *See* §§ 3.4.6, 3.5, *supra.*

430 The letters issued by the NCUA since 1992 are summarized in Appx. E.3, *infra.* These letters are reproduced on the CD-Rom accompanying this volume.

431 *See* NCUA Letters (Nov. 26, 2003; Jan. 29, 1996; July 7, 1992; June 11, 1992; May 18, 1992; Apr. 25, 1992).

432 *See* NCUA Letters (Mar. 12, 2004; Jan. 28, 2004; Nov. 10, 2003; May 23, 2003; Oct. 4, 2002; Oct. 3, 2002; July 29, 2002; June 26, 2002; Mar. 2, 2001; Feb. 1, 1999; Sept. 4, 1997). A court upheld the NCUA's letter opining that California's minimum payment disclosure law was preempted. American Bankers Ass'n v. Lockyer, 239 F. Supp. 2d 1000 (E.D. Cal. 2002).

433 NCUA Letter (June 24, 1992).

434 NCUA Letter (Feb. 1, 1999).

435 NCUA Letters (Mar. 2, 2001; July 29, 2002; Oct. 4, 2002).

436 NCUA Letters (May 23, 2003; Nov. 10, 2003; Jan. 28, 2004; Feb. 10, 2004; Mar. 12, 2004). The NCUA relies upon American Bankers Ass'n v. California, 238 F. Supp. 1000 (E.D. Cal. 2002) where the court stated that "there is no indication the savings clause reaches beyond TILA to control the preemption analysis applicable under any other federal laws, including the federal banking laws." *Id.* at 1009.

437 NCUA Letter (May 23, 2003) (preempting the District of Columbia's law).

438 12 C.F.R. § 701.21(b)(3).

439 OCC, *Financial Performance of National Banks*, 23 Quarterly J. 180, 191 (Mar. 2004), *available at* www.occ.treas.gov/qj/qj23-1/10-FinancialPerformance.pdf; OTS, *Thrift Industry Highlights Fourth Quarter 2003*, *available at* www.ots.treas.gov/docs/1/14340.html.

mercial banks in 2003.[440] Of these, state banks represented 5,768 of this total, down from 5,943 in 2001.[441] Even though state banks outnumber national banks, national banks control 55% of outstanding loans made or held by the entire banking industry.[442]

The banking system consists of two parallel tracks for banks and thrifts—those that operate under federal charters and those that operate under state charters. Depository institutions can choose to be chartered and regulated primarily by a federal or a state agency.[443] The types of bank powers and the extent of preemption rights available to a depository institution and the legal infrastructure under which it will operate flow from this choice.[444]

State banks are created by and operate primarily under the laws of their home state, with some exceptions. These banking powers are enumerated in state law and most state banking codes also include some type of "incidental" power provision.[445] An incidental power provision expands upon the enumerated powers by permitting banks to engage in activities that are related to the express powers.[446] Further, some states grant their banks, and sometime foreign banks, the same powers given to national banks, through state "parity" acts.[447]

A federal regulatory overlay exists due to the federal insurance that state banks typically purchase. In response to the devastation caused by the Great Depression, Congress created the Federal Deposit Insurance Corporation in 1933 to provide deposit insurance.[448] The FDIC's authority has expanded since then. It currently administers two insurance funds, the Bank Insurance Fund, which is available to national and state banks, and the Savings Association Fund, which is available to federal and state savings associations.[449]

If a state-chartered bank is a member of the Federal Reserve System, it is subject to federal oversight by the Federal Reserve Board.[450] However, the FDIC retains primary federal authority over insured state-chartered nonmember banks and regularly examines these institutions.[451]

3.7.2 Most Favored Lender Doctrine and Exportation

In 1980, Congress created parity between federally-insured state-chartered banks (including state savings banks) and national banks in one area. Congress extended the most favored lender status granted to national banks under the National Bank Act to these state institutions.[452] The purposes and scope of this Act, the Depository Institutions Deregulation and Monetary Control Act of 1980 (DIDA) are discussed in detail in § 3.9, *infra*.

As a result of receiving the mantle of the most favored lender, a federally-insured state-chartered financial institution may charge the greater of: (1) one percent above the discount rate on ninety-day commercial paper in effect at the Federal Reserve bank in the district in which such state bank is located; or (2) the rate allowed by the laws of the state in which the state bank is located.[453]

The FDIC has issued several letters over the years in which it opines that section 521 of DIDA should be interpreted in the same manner as section 85 of the National Bank Act. For example, the agency defines "interest" in the same manner as does the Office of the Comptroller of the Currency for national banks.[454] The FDIC interprets the scope of section 521 of DIDA to include the preemption of common law usury rate restrictions in addition to the preemption of statutory and constitutional restrictions.[455] Fi-

---

440 FDIC, Number of Institutions, Branches, and Total Offices, Table CB01, *available at* www2.fdic.gov/hsob/hsobRpt.asp.

441 John J. Schroeder, *"Duel" Banking System? State Bank Parity Laws: An Examination of Regulatory Practice, Constitutional Issues, and Philosophical Questions*, 36 Ind. L. Rev. 197, 201 (2003).

442 Jathon Sapsford, *Critics Cry Foul Over New Rules on Bank Review*, Wall S. J. Jan. 8, 2004, at C1.

443 *See* the chart in § 3.3.1, *supra*, listing the type of depository institution and its primary regulator. For a short history of the development of banking law in the United States, see § 2.3.1.2.1, *supra*. For a longer version, see Patricia A. McCoy, Patricia A. McCoy, Banking Law Manual ch. 2 (Lexis Pub. 2d ed. 2003).

444 *See* Patricia A. McCoy, Banking Law Manual ch. 3 (Lexis Pub. 2d ed. 2003) (discusses the history of the dual banking system, the choices among charters, and suggests that the dual banking system should be scrapped).

445 John J. Schroeder, *"Duel" Banking System? State Bank Parity Laws: An Examination of Regulatory Practice, Constitutional Issues, and Philosophical Questions*, 36 Ind. L. Rev. 197, 202 (2003).

446 Christian A. Johnson, *Wild Card Statutes, Parity, and National Banks—The Renascence of State Banking Powers*, 26 Loy. U. Chi. L.J. 351, 356 (1995).

447 *Id.* at 206. Under state parity acts, state-chartered banks may be allowed to operate as national bank "copycats." States cannot confer exportation rights beyond their borders.

448 Act of June 16, 1933, ch. 89, § 8, 48 Stat. 168, codified at 12 U.S.C. § 1811.

449 12 U.S.C. §§ 1821(a)(5)–(a)(6); *see also* Patricia A. McCoy, Banking Law Manual § 2.05 (Lexis Pub. 2d ed. 2003).

450 Patricia A. McCoy, Banking Law Manual § 2.05 (Lexis Pub. 2d ed. 2003).

451 12 U.S.C. § 1820(b)(2); Pub. L. No. 96-221, tit. v, § 521, 94 Stat. 164 (1980).

452 12 U.S.C. § 1831d(a) (state-chartered banks); 12 U.S.C. §§ 1463(g) (state savings banks); 1831(b) (definition of state savings association as including savings banks). At that time, Congress also granted federally insured or chartered savings associations and federally-insured credit unions most favored lender status. *See* § 3.9.2.1, *infra*.

453 12 U.S.C. § 1831d(a).

454 FDIC General Counsel Opinion No. 10, 63 Fed. Reg. 19258 (Apr. 17, 1998); FDIC Letter (July 8, 1992); FDIC Letter (Oct. 20, 1983). Relevant FDIC opinions and letters are *reprinted on* the CD-Rom accompanying this volume. *See also* Harris v. Chase Manhattan Bank, N.A., 35 Cal. Rptr. 2d 733 (Cal. Ct. App. 1994).

455 FDIC Letter (July 12, 1992), *reprinted on* the CD-Rom accom-

nally, the FDIC adopted OCC Letter No. 822, defining the "location" of the bank for exportation purposes.[456] Courts and other authorities agree with this analysis.[457] Calculating the alternative federal interest rate and the scope of the most favored lender doctrine are discussed earlier regarding national banks. The analysis of these issues appears in §§ 3.4.2 and 3.4.3, *supra.*

"Conflict" preemption analysis should be applied in the event that the most favored lender doctrine is arguably infringed upon by state law. The standard, as articulated by one court, is whether the state law stands as an obstacle to achieving the objectives of the federal law.[458]

The most favored lender status only applies to "banks" as defined by the Federal Deposit Insurance Act.[459] One court refused to grant deference to an FDIC letter claiming that the defendant was a state "bank" for preemption and exportation purposes because the consumer proved that the bank participated in the preparation of the agency letter and the bank was not engaged in the business of taking deposits as its only depositor was its parent company.[460] However, in late 2001, the FDIC enacted a regulation defining what "being in the business of receiving deposits" means.[461] Not surprisingly, the agency stuck to its position articulated in the letter discredited in *Heaton,* i.e., a bank need only maintain one or more non-trust deposit accounts in the minimum aggregate amount of $500,000. It remains to be seen how much deference the courts will give to this regulation given its controversial history.

Finally, the same rule that applies to national banks regarding *when* preemption arises should apply equally to state-chartered state banks. The National Bank Act applies only to credit initiated by a national bank, not to that assigned to it.[462]

3.7.3 Other Preemption Rights Extended by Federal Law to State-Chartered Banks

Beyond most favored lender interest rate preemption and the exportation rights that accompany it, the ability of federally-insured state-chartered banks to preempt other aspects of their home or host state's law is limited. As noted above, state-chartered banks are first and foremost creatures of state law.[463] The instances where federal law creates preemption rights related to consumer transactions are few in number and limited in scope. First, state-chartered banks may make adjustable rate mortgage loans in accordance with regulations issued by the OCC, regardless of any applicable state law restrictions. Congress extended this type of preemption to state banks in the Alternative Mortgage Transactions Parity Act (AMTPA).[464] Second, DIDA permits federally-insured depository lenders to charge any interest rate or any amount of points and fees that relates to the annual percentage rate in transactions involving residential first lien mortgage loans, unless the state opted out.[465] Third, Congress expanded the ability of state-chartered banks to preempt state laws when the bank branches into another state. The Interstate Banking and Branching Efficiency Act of 1994 (also known as the Riegle-Neal Act) provides that:

> The laws of the host state, including laws regarding community reinvestment, consumer protection, fair lending, and establishment of intrastate branches, shall apply to any branch in the host state of an out-of-State State bank to the same extent as such State laws apply to a branch in the host State of an out-of-State national bank.[466]

If the host state's law does not apply to the branch, then the bank's home state law applies.[467] The preemption of

---

panying this volume. *See* discussion of the scope of OCC Letter No. 822 in § 3.4.5.1.2, *supra.*

456 FDIC General Counsel Opinion No. 11, 63 Fed. Reg. 27282 (May 18, 1998), *reprinted on* the CD-Rom accompanying this volume.

457 *See* § 3.9.2.1, *infra. See also* Adkison v. First Plus Bank, 143 S.W.3d 29 (Mo. App. Ct. 2004).

458 BankWest Inc. v. Banker, 324 F. Supp. 2d 1333, 1345–1346 (N.D. Ga. 2004).

459 12 U.S.C. § 1813(a)(2) (state banks must engage in the business of receiving deposits).

460 Heaton v. Monogram Credit Card Bank of Ga., 1999 WL 1789422 (E.D. La. Nov. 22, 1999), *appeal dismissed,* 231 F.3d 994 (5th Cir. 2000), *cert. denied,* 533 U.S. 915 (2001), *remand following appeal,* 2001 WL 15635 (E.D. La. Jan. 5, 2001) (court remanded to state court despite new FDIC opinion letter and change in Georgia law, finding that, while the bank had a deposit, it was not in the business of receiving deposits and, therefore, not entitled to preemption), *subsequent proceedings,* 297 F.3d 416 (5th Cir. 2002) (district court's order denying intervention to the FDIC reversed; federal court jurisdiction created by FDIC as a party; further remand to state court denied). This case has attracted some interesting press. *See, e.g.,* Paul Beckett, *Clashing Interests: Why Patricia Heaton Could Cause Problems for a GE-Owned Bank,* Wall. St. J., Mar. 30, 2001, at A1; Roger Furman, *Friends in High Places,* U.S. Banker, Mar. 2000, at 30.

461 12 C.F.R. § 303.14(a); 66 Fed. Reg. 54645 (Oct. 30, 2001).

462 *See* § 3.4.5.1.3, *supra; see also* Adkison v. First Plus Bank, 143 S.W.3d 29 (Mo. App. Ct. 2004) (bank was the lender because it was listed on the loan documents). *But see* Terry v. Community Bank of N. Va., 255 F. Supp. 2d 817 (W.D. Tenn. 2003) (the court looked beyond the face of the loan documents to determine which entity actually funded the loan; court held that if the state-chartered bank did not fund the loan, the bank would not be entitled to preemption under § 521 of DIDA).

463 Christian A. Johnson, *Wild Card Statutes, Parity, and National Banks—The Renascence of State Banking Powers,* 26 Loy. U. Chi. L.J. 351, 358 (1995).

464 12 U.S.C. § 3803; 12 C.F.R. §§ 34.20–34.24. AMTPA is discussed at length in § 3.10, *infra.*

465 12 U.S.C. §§ 1735f-7a, 1735f-5(b). *See* § 3.9.3, *infra.*

466 12 U.S.C. § 1831a(j).

467 *Id.*

state law permitted under this act does not apply outside of the interstate branching context. Further, Congress did not intend to weaken the authority of states to protect the interests of consumers.[468] The scope of Congress' concern that consumer protections apply to in-state branches of out-of-state banks to the same extent as to branches of banks chartered by those states is evident in the Conference Report and is discussed in other sections of this chapter.[469]

Fourth, Congress created loan-pricing parity among state and local banks in the limited number of states (perhaps only Arkansas) with constitutional usury provisions limiting interest rates to under a certain percentage.[470] Fifth, the Gramm-Leach-Bliley Act opens the doors to financial institutions to engage in new activities previously restricted or prohibited, but relevant to consumer transactions. Banks can now sell, solicit, and cross-market credit insurance.[471] Sixth, certain federal consumer protections laws apply to "creditors" broadly defined.[472] As a general rule, these laws preempt inconsistent state laws.

Let us work through an example to flesh out when these preemption rights apply and when they do not. This example assumes that the bank is making a loan to a consumer for personal, family, or household purposes. It does not address the types of preemption created by Gramm-Leach-Bliley or the federal consumer protection statutes mentioned above. This example also assumes that neither of the states is Arkansas.

- If a state-chartered bank in State A makes a loan to a customer in State A, the bank must comply with all applicable state laws with two exceptions:[473] state interest-rate caps in the event that the DIDA first lien mortgage preemption applies[474] and restrictions to adjustable-rate mortgages if the loan falls within the scope of AMTPA.

- If a state bank chartered in State A does not branch into State B, it can charge customers in State B the interest permitted under the most favored lender doctrine in State A in non-mortgage transactions. In the mortgage context, if the bank enters into a first lien mortgage loan with a customer in State B, the bank may charge any interest rate and related fees that the parties agree to, unless the State B opted out of DIDA.[475] If the mortgage loan is secured by a subordinate lien or State B opted out of DIDA, the bank may charge the interest permitted under the most favored lender doctrine in State A and export that rate to State B. Without a branch, however, the bank cannot preempt other applicable laws of State B, unless State B expressly exempts foreign banks from its laws.

- Finally, if the bank establishes a branch in State B, then State B's law will apply to the same extent as it applies to a national bank with a branch in State B.[476]

3.7.4 Expansion of Bank Powers Through State Parity Acts

State parity acts may be the vehicle by which a state opens its doors to foreign banks by treating them the same as the state would treat its home banks. Parity acts are described in § 3.14, *infra*. Or a state may exempt home state and foreign depository institutions from selected laws, through express exclusionary provisions. When a federal law containing an express preemption does not apply to the transaction at issue, practitioners must look to the law of the state where the transaction occurred to determine if the state restricts the terms or conditions of the transaction and whether that law applies to the local or foreign bank.

3.8 FHA- or VA-Insured Loans: Preemption of State Usury Law

3.8.1 General

The Federal Housing Administration (FHA) and the Veterans Administration (VA) are authorized to insure loans for the purchase or improvement of houses and mobile homes,[477] and the state interest ceilings have been pre-

---

468 H.R. Conf. Rep. No. 103-651 at 53 (1994), *reprinted in* 1994 U.S.C.C.A.N. 2074.

469 H.R. Conf. Rep. No. 103-651 at 51 (1994), *reprinted in* 1994 U.S.C.C.A.N. 2072. *See also* 12 U.S.C. § 36(f)(1)(A). The concerns of Congress are discussed more fully in §§ 3.1.1, 3.3.2, 3.4.6.1, *supra*.

470 Section 731 of the Gramm-Leach-Bliley Act of 1999, *amending* 12 U.S.C. § 1831u(f). Pub. L. No. 106-102, 113 Stat. 1338 (1999). *See* § 3.11, *infra*.

471 15 U.S.C. § 6701(d). Banks and their affiliates may preempt state laws where they conflict with the new powers granted by Congress in the Gramm-Leach-Bliley Act, 15 U.S.C. § 6701(d). *See also* discussion in § 8.4.1.5.2, *infra*.

472 § 3.12, *infra*.

473 This scenario assumes that the most favored lender doctrine applies but that the federal interest rate is lower than the permissible state interest rate and the bank selected the state rate.

474 Note that the most favored lender doctrine *requires* bank to comply with the state usury cap for the type of loan it is offering, unless the bank chooses the federal rate. The federal rate is so low that banks are looking to state law to allow them to charge more.

475 *See* FDIC Letter (June 29, 1988), *reprinted on* the CD-Rom accompanying this volume. The FDIC adopted OCC Letter No. 822, defining the "location" of the bank for exportation purposes. FDIC General Counsel Opinion No. 11, 63 Fed. Reg. 27282 (May 18, 1998), *reprinted on* the CD-Rom accompanying this volume.

476 *See* the OCC and FDIC position on the "location" of the bank and where the loan is made that creates wrinkles in this otherwise straightforward analysis. §§ 3.4.5.1.2, 3.7.2.

477 *See* 12 U.S.C. § 1703; 38 U.S.C. § 3703.

empted for these loans.[478] Unfortunately, both the VA and the FHA permit borrowers and lenders to agree to any interest rate, though some restrictions on fees may apply.[479] As a result, in the absence of state opt-out legislation,[480] there is no interest ceiling on FHA-insured or VA-insured loans. However, regulations governing insurance, payment schedules, fees, and other charges associated with these FHA-insured and VA-insured loans exist.[481]

Practitioners should carefully scrutinize whether an out-of-state lender is authorized by the FHA to make insured loans in the client's state. If not, the loans are not entitled to exemption from state usury caps on this basis.[482] The FHA may approve a lender to make FHA-insured loans on a nationwide basis or in a restricted geographic area.[483] If the lender is limited to a geographical area, the FHA must specifically approve the making of loans from branch offices that must be located only in states contiguous to the state in which the approved main or branch offices are located. The Alabama Supreme Court held that one lender was not exempt from the state's cap on points charged in the making of mortgage loans because its Alabama branch was not contiguous to its main office in Louisiana and it had not obtained special approval from FHA to make insured loans in Alabama.[484]

The removal of state interest ceilings on mobile home loans insured by the FHA and VA has led to some conflict with the mobile home provisions of the Depository Institutions Deregulation and Monetary Control Act of 1980 (DIDMCA or DIDA).[485] DIDA preempts interest ceilings on first mobile home loans only on the condition that the mobile home lenders comply with OTS consumer protection regulations.[486] However, the Eleventh Circuit in *Doyle v. Southern Guaranty Corp.* held that lenders making FHA- or VA-insured first mobile home loans need not comply with the OTS (formerly FHLBB) regulations because the state interest ceilings on their loans are independently pre-

empted.[487] The *Doyle* court reasoned that both DIDA and the FHA/VA preemptions were written, almost simultaneously, by the same congressional committees, and that they were thus apparently intended to have independent effect. Furthermore, the court stated that the FHA and VA regulations appeared to protect borrowers adequately so that the additional imposition of the FHLBB regulations was unnecessary.

The elimination of the federal ceiling on interest which could be charged on loans insured by the FHA and the VA may create *indirect* rate deregulation in certain state consumer credit statutes which were pegged to this ceiling. The Pennsylvania Motor Vehicle Installment Sales Finance Act[488] is an example. This statute, which sets lender usury ceilings for automobile and mobile home financing, provides that its usury ceiling shall *not* apply to "any sale or credit or loan insured or guaranteed in whole or in part by the Federal Housing Administration, the Veterans Administration or any other department or agency of the United States Government: provided, that any such sale or credit or loan is subject to a maximum rate of interest established by law or by such department or agency."[489] The Pennsylvania legislature was sufficiently insightful to require that a "maximum rate of interest" be established, which probably does not include this statutory removal of any rate ceiling. But other statutes deferring to government regulation may not be so well written. If, for example, this statute had incorporated the FHA rate without conditions, FHA-insured mobile home loans could be exempt, as a matter of *state* law, from *state* usury ceilings.[490] Mobile home lenders making loans insured by the FHA would then have no need to invoke DIDA and comply with OTS mobile home regulations to escape the normal state usury ceiling.

3.8.2 State Opt-out of the FHA/VA Loan Preemption

States may opt-out of the FHA- and VA-insured loan preemptions, but, because several statutes are involved in the preemption, and because the opt-out language in these statutes is somewhat vague, the applicability of state law to any given insured loan can be a complicated question. The answer depends largely on the effective dates of the state opt-out statutes(s) and the transaction date. The first FHA/VA preemption law passed by Congress took effect on June 30, 1976[491] and the second on December 21, 1979.[492]

478 *See* 12 U.S.C. § 1709-1a; 38 U.S.C. § 3728.
479 *See* 38 U.S.C. § 3745; 38 C.F.R. §§ 36.4311, 36.4312; 60 Fed. Reg. 38256 (July 26, 1995) (VA). *See also* 12 U.S.C. § 1709(b)(5); 24 C.F.R. §§ 201, 203 (FHA).
480 *See* § 3.8.2, *infra.*
481 *See generally* 24 C.F.R. §§ 201, 203 (FHA) and 38 C.F.R. § 36.4312 (VA).
482 The lender may, however, be entitled to exemption under another provision of DIDA. *See* Jackson v. Mundaca Fin. Serv., Inc., 76 S.W.3d 819 (Ark. 2002) (assignee failed to prove that the contractor or lender were approved by the FHA to make Title 1 rehab loans; therefore, not entitled to preemption on this ground); § 3.9.3, *supra.*
483 24 C.F.R. §§ 202.3(a)(2)(iv), (v).
484 United Companies Lending Corp. v. McGehee, 686 So. 2d 1171 (Ala. 1996); *see also* Jackson v. Mundaca Fin. Servs., Inc., 76 S.W.2d 819 (Ark. 2002) (FHA preemption not available because the defendant did not prove that the lender was approved to make loans in Arkansas at the time the loan was made).
485 *See* § 3.9, *infra.*
486 *See* 12 U.S.C. § 1735f-7a; 12 C.F.R. § 590.4.

487 795 F.2d 907 (11th Cir. 1986). The Supreme Court denied *certiorari* in *Doyle*'s companion case Ft. Wayne Mtg. v. Wood, 484 U.S. 926 (1987).
488 Pa. Stat. Ann. tit. 69, § 619(F) (West).
489 *Id.*
490 *E.g.*, Ala. Code § 8-8-6.
491 *See* 12 U.S.C. § 1709-1a.
492 *See* 12 U.S.C. § 1735f-7. Note that this provision does not

State opt-out laws passed between those two dates would appear to cover only those loans issued[493] after the effective date of the state opt-out law and prior to the second preemption in 1979. FHA- and VA-insured loans issued after December 21, 1979, would not be subject to state-imposed[494] interest ceilings unless the relevant state passed its opt-out law after that date and prior to the loan transaction. That is, states which opted out of the 1976 preemption before or during most of 1979 would have to adopt a second opt-out law after December 21, 1979, to reimpose the state exemption.

Beyond the tangle of effective dates that must be examined to determine whether an FHA- or VA-insured loan is covered by state usury law, one must consider what language is required in state legislation for the legislation to constitute opt-out law. The Eleventh Circuit considered this issue in *Doyle v. Southern Guaranty Corporation*, and decided for two reasons that a state need only amend or reenact its usury law, and need not expressly reject the FHA/VA preemption to opt out of this preemption.[495] First, the court observed that the language in the statutes preempting state interest ceilings on FHA- or VA-insured loans is not as strict as that under the DIDA first mortgage interest rate preemption which requires a state opt-out law to express its intent "explicitly and by its terms."[496] Instead, the FHA/VA preemptions are effective until the effective date "of a provision of law of . . . [the] . . . state limiting the rate or amount of interest, discount points, or other charges" on any loan covered by the preemption.[497] Second, the *Doyle* court reasoned that the purpose of preemption was to assist states to raise their usury ceilings, and that once this purpose was accomplished, the congressional deference to state law indicated by the existence of an opt-out clause should prevail. Thus, the court determined that when a state reenacts or raises its usury limit on a particular class of loans, it overrides the FHA and VA preemptions for that type of loan in the absence of a contrary statement.

Practitioners should examine any amendments or reenactments of their state usury law which occurred after the effective dates(s) of the relevant preemption statutes(s) to determine whether their state may have wittingly or unwittingly opted-out of the FHA/VA preemption.[498] However, such a search of state law may instead reveal the express repeal of state usury and other state limitations on FHA- and VA-insured loans.[499] These repeals are fairly common because many states chose to rely on the federally administered interest ceilings, which existed for FHA-insured loans until November 30, 1983, and which existed for VA-insured loans until 1995, as a substitute for state usury regulation of these loans.[500]

3.9 The Depository Institutions Deregulation and Monetary Control Act of 1980 (DIDA): Most Favored Lender Status for Federally-Insured Lenders; First Lien Mortgage Preemption

3.9.1 Introduction; Legislative History and Purpose

Driven primarily by congressional concerns about the solvency of the savings and loan industry[501] caused, in part, by the spike in interest rates that occurred in 1979 to

---

expressly cover VA-insured loans but that it is apparently extended to VA-insured loans by 38 U.S.C. § 3728.

493 More precisely, the date of issue of a certificate of commitment by the government appears to be the effective date of the transaction for preemption purposes. *See* Maine Bureau of Consumer Credit Protection, Advisory Ruling No. 161, *reprinted at* Consumer Cred. Guide (CCH) ¶ 97,019 (Oct. 29, 1981).

494 Remember, however, that federally set interest ceilings were in effect on FHA loans until November 30, 1983.

495 795 F.2d 907 (11th Cir. 1986). The Supreme Court denied *certiorari* in *Doyle*'s companion case Ft. Wayne Mtg. v. Wood, 484 U.S. 926 (1987).

496 *See* DIDA § 501(b)(2), 12 U.S.C. § 1735f-7a(b)(2); DIDA § 525, *reprinted in* note to 12 U.S.C. § 1703g (main volume). Note, however, that the DIDA provision allowing states to opt out of the preemption on discount points and other charges does not contain the "explicitly and by its terms" language. *See* DIDA § 501(b)(4), 12 U.S.C. § 1735f-7a(b)(4).

497 *See* 12 U.S.C. § 1735f-7(b).

498 *See* Doyle v. S. Guar. Corp., 795 F.2d 907 (11th Cir. 1986) (amendment to Georgia statute constituted opt-out of FHA/VA preemption). The Supreme Court denied *certiorari* in *Doyle*'s companion case Ft. Wayne Mtg. v. Wood, 484 U.S. 926 (1987). *But cf.* Green v. Decatur Fed. Sav. & Loan Ass'n, 143 Ga. App. 368, 238 S.E.2d 740 (1977) (mere recodification insufficient).

499 Burris v. First Fin. Corp., 928 F.2d 797 (8th Cir. 1991) (court found such an express statement in amendment to Arkansas state constitution limiting interest rates but explicitly excluding interest rates governed by federal law); Williams v. Norwest Fin. Ala., Inc., 723 So. 2d 97 (Ala. Civ. App. 1998) (state law expressly exempted FHA lenders from most of the provisions regulating consumer finance transactions, including a prohibition on prepayment penalties).

500 *See, e.g.,* Ariz. Rev. Stat. § 44-1206; N.J. Stat. Ann. § 17:2-7 (West).

501 Interest rates were high and depositors were moving their funds into money market funds which paid higher interest than deposit accounts. This climate depressed the amount of funds deposited into savings and loans associations which, thereby, reduced the amount of available money to lend. *See* S. Rep. No. 96-368, at 3, 4 (1979), *reprinted in* 1980 U.S.C.C.A.N. 236, 238–240. For a detailed description of the events leading up to the passage of DIDA and its ramifications, see Cathy Lesser Mansfield, *The Road to Subprime "HEL" Was Paved with Good Congressional Intentions: Usury Deregulation and the Subprime Home Equity Market*, 51 S.C. L. Rev. 473 (2000).

1982,[502] as well as some sentiment toward deregulation, Congress extended federal preemption of state interest rates beyond that historically available under the National Bank Act.[503] Specifically, the Depository Institutions Deregulation and Monetary Control Act of 1980 (DIDA)[504] (1) provided alternate federal rate ceilings for various federally-chartered or federally-insured depository lenders, apparently extending most favored lender status to these lenders;[505] (2) completely removed interest ceilings for most first mort-

gages on residences and mobile homes;[506] and (3) temporarily permitted an alternate federal ceiling on most business and agricultural credit.[507]

In doing so, however, Congress recognized that it was venturing onto territory traditionally within the purview of states.[508] The century old National Bank Act had been a limited preemption, enacted to achieve a purpose when the national interest was clearly paramount.[509] In contrast, DIDA was enacted to address a temporary interest rate crunch,[510] and to respond to the state banks' arguments that they should be on an equal footing with national banks.[511]

Presumably recognizing that the national interest in this instance was less compelling, it made a compromise, deferring somewhat to principles of federalism. It built into the statute an opportunity for states to "opt-out." In this, DIDA differs considerably from the National Bank Act, where, after all, a state opt-out right would have completely defeated the purpose. DIDA, in contrast, reflects a "policy of permitting a state the *primary* opportunity to determine its usury statutes by permitting the state to reassert" or reinstate any usury ceilings which may have been preempted.[512]

---

502 The lowest of the domestic interest rates, the rate charged by federal reserve banks in making short-term loans to member banks, was 6% at the end of 1977. In May, 1981, it was 14%, with a 4% surcharge on some of those transactions. By way of comparison, in August 1994, that rate was 3.5% and in January 2001, the rate was 5.5%. 80 Fed. Res. Bull. A8, table 1.14 (Sept. 1994); 87 Fed. Res. Bull. A7, table 1.14 (Feb. 2001).

503 *See* § 3.4, *supra.*

504 Pub. L. No. 96-221, tit. v, 94 Stat. 164 (1980), *reprinted in* Appx. G.1, *infra.*

505 *See* 12 U.S.C. §§ 1831d(a) (state commercial banks), 1463(g) (federal savings and loans), 1785(g) (federal credit unions); § 3.9.2, *infra. See also* §§ 3.4.3, 3.4.5, *supra* for a discussion of most favored lender status as it has developed in the national bank context. To date, the courts have interpreted most favored lender issues under DIDA and the NBA consistently. *See, e.g.*, Gavey Properties 1762 v. First Fin. Sav. & Loan Ass'n, 845 F.2d 519 (5th Cir. 1988) ("consistent interpretations of § 85 and [DIDA § 522, currently codified at § 1463(g)(1)] appear warranted," so federally-insured savings and loan could export most favored lender rate from home state; court says savings and loan could "import" the rate of the borrower's home state if that were more favorable than the saving and loan's home state); *see also* Greenwood Trust Co. v. Massachusetts, 971 F.2d 818 (1st Cir. 1992). *But see* Heaton v. Monogram Credit Card Bank of Ga., 231 F.3d 994 (5th Cir. 2000), *cert. denied*, 533 U.S. 915 (2001) (district court reversed itself and refused to grant deference to FDIC letter indicating that Monogram was a state "bank" for preemption and exportation purposes, even though its only depositor was its parent company, because the plaintiff showed that Monogram participated in the preparation of the FDIC letter; thus, Monogram was not a state "bank" entitled to export; the appellate court dismissed the appeal of the district court's remand order to state court), *remand following appeal*, 2001 U.S. Dist. LEXIS 325 (E.D. La. Jan. 8, 2001) (court remanded to state court despite new FDIC opinion letter and change in Georgia law, finding that, while the bank had a deposit, it was not in the business of receiving deposits and, therefore, not entitled to preemption; *subsequent proceedings*, 297 F.3d 416 (5th Cir. 2002) (district court's order denying intervention to the FDIC reversed; federal court jurisdiction created by FDIC as a party; further remand to state court denied). This case has attracted some interesting press. *See, e.g.*, Paul Beckett, *Clashing Interests: Why Patricia Heaton Could Cause Problems for a GE-Owned Bank*, Wall. St. J., Mar. 30, 2001, at A1; Roger Furman, *Friends in High Places*, U.S. Banker, Mar. 2000, at 30. In late 2001, the FDIC abandoned the letter approach and enacted a regulation defining what "being in the business of receiving deposits" means. 12 C.F.R. § 303.14; 66 Fed. Reg. 54645 (Oct. 30, 2001). Not surprisingly, the agency stuck to its previous position that a bank need only maintain one or more non-trust deposit accounts in the minimum aggregate amount of $500,000. It remains to be seen how much deference the courts will give to this regulation given its controversial history.

506 *See* 12 U.S.C. § 1735f-7a (mobile home rate preemption is conditioned on compliance with consumer protections). The DIDA exemption can apply to a mobile home sale even if the sale includes other items. Draper v. Castle Home Sales, Inc., 711 F. Supp. 1499 (E.D. Ark. 1989) (refrigerator and range included in contract but not separately priced), *aff'd*, 894 F.2d 1341 (8th Cir. 1988) (table); *see* § 3.9.3, *infra.*

507 *See* 12 U.S.C. §§ 86a, 1831a (expired) (allowed five percent over discount rate for non-consumer loans of $1000 or more).

508 *See* S. Rep. No. 96-368, at 37, 41 (1979), *reprinted in* 1980 U.S.C.C.A.N. 236, 272, 277 (views of Sen. Morgan, an opponent of the bill).

509 *See* § 3.4.1, *supra.*

510 Ironically, however, the states had been moving to raise usury ceilings to deal with the problem. From December 1975 to June 1979, approximately twenty-eight states liberalized their usury ceilings to deal with the rising interest rates. About fifteen states also exempted FHA and VA loans from their usury caps. *See* S. Rep. No. 96-368, at 37, 41 (1979), *reprinted in* 1980 U.S.C.C.A.N. 236, 272, 277 (statement of Sen. Morgan); *see also* Cathy Lesser Mansfield, *The Road to Subprime "HEL" Was Paved with Good Congressional Intentions: Usury Deregulation and the Subprime Home Equity Market*, 51 S.C. L. Rev. 473 (2000); Burgess & Ciolfi, *Exportation or Exploitation: A State Regulator's View of Interstate Credit Card Transactions*, 42 Bus. Law 929, 931–933 (1987); Kreissman, *Administrative Preemption in Consumer Banking Law*, 73 Va. L. Rev. 911, 922–925 (1987).

511 *See* § 3.4.3.1, *supra*; *cf.* VanderWeyst v. First State Bank of Benson, 425 N.W.2d 803, 809 (Minn. 1988) (purpose of extending most favored lender status to federally-insured, state-chartered lenders under DIDA was to put state banks on parity with national banks, not give them "a leg up"); Finkelstein, *Most Favored Lender Status for Insured Banks*, 42 Bus. Lawyer 915, 918 (1987) (purpose in enacting NBA § 85 and DIDA § 521 to put lenders on equal footing, not to give most favored lenders competitive advantages).

512 S. Rep. No. 96-368, at 18, *reprinted in* 1980 U.S.C.C.A.N. 236, 254 (emphasis added); *see also* Fed. Deposit Ins. Corp., Opinion

However, the financial services industry, and, to date, the courts specifically addressing the issue, have not viewed DIDA as so circumscribed. In particular, sections 521–523 are now interpreted to give additional lenders the full measure of most favored lender status formerly reserved to national banks. While equality between national and state banks competing in local markets was undoubtedly intended, it is entirely possible that any interstate banking ramifications were unforeseen and unintended.[513] Nonetheless, as the courts have interpreted these sections to give other lenders "exportation" rights, DIDA joins with the NBA to threaten national deregulation by "sister-state preemption."[514] As noted earlier, Congress has since expressed a clear view that interstate banking concerns do not completely preempt state concerns about consumer protection and fair lending.[515] Its message is that there is a balance of state and federal concerns, which may have been inappropriately weighed in federal favor in the past.

The most favored lender and exportation issues under sections 521–523 are discussed in § 3.9.2, *infra*. The second category of transactions subject to DIDA's preemption, of particular import to consumers, are "first lien" mortgages, discussed in § 3.9.3, *infra*. Finally, DIDA's opt-out provisions will be addressed in § 3.9.4, *infra*. The question of federal jurisdiction over DIDA preemption questions is described in § 3.15, *infra*.

3.9.2 DIDA and Federally-Related Lenders

3.9.2.1 Extension of Federal Alternate Interest Ceiling and Most Favored Lender Status to Federally-Related Lenders

One significant, and controversial, effect of DIDA was the extension of the alternate federal interest ceiling,[516] formerly available only to national banks, to other federally-related depository institutions. The following lenders can take advantage of the federal alternative rate ceilings:

- State-chartered commercial banks using federal deposit insurance;[517]
- Federally-insured or federally-chartered savings and loan associations, including federal savings banks;[518]
- State mutual savings banks and savings and loan associations, if they are federally insured;[519] and
- Federally-insured credit unions.[520]

Because the language in DIDA extending the alternate interest ceiling to these federally-related lenders matches the most favored lender provision of the National Bank Act,[521] these lenders have argued that they have similarly been granted most favored lender status. The result of such an interpretation is that federally-insured state banks, savings and loans, and credit unions may charge the higher of the rate established for such institutions under state law, the federal alternate rate, or the highest rate allowed to any lender (particularly finance companies or deregulated lenders) making similar loans in the state.

Whether DIDA was intended to extend most favored lender status is unclear. The legislative history shows only that DIDA's most favored lender language was adopted as a last-minute compromise. However, most authorities, both regulatory agencies[522] and courts,[523] support the extension,

---

Letter, FDIC No. 88-45, *reprinted in* [1988-1989 Transfer Binder] Fed. Banking L. Rep. (CCH) ¶ 88,110 (Jones, Jan. 29, 1988) ("in an effort to preserve principles of federalism, . . . Congress enacted [a provision permitting states to "opt out" of these DIDA provisions] in order to enable States to recover authority [the preemption] had taken away."). Admittedly, it did make opting out a bit messy, placing different time limits on the opt out right with respect to different DIDA provisions, and varying the degree to which states could do so implicitly. *See* § 3.9.4, *infra*. It further attempted to circumscribe the impact of "interest" rate preemption, at least as to the first mortgage preemption, by clarifying that state consumer protections such as limitations on late charges, prepayment penalties and attorney fees are not preempted. *Cf.* S. Rep. No. 96-368, at 19, *reprinted in* 1980 U.S.C.C.A.N. 236, 255 (first lien preemption of Title V, Part A does *not* preempt state consumer protections on residential mortgage loans such as "limitations on prepayment charges, attorney fees, late charges or similar limitations designed to protect borrowers"). Courts have differed on the relevance of that to interpreting Title V, Part C (most-favored-lender extension, §§ 521–523). *Compare* Hill v. Chem. Bank, 799 F. Supp. 948, 954 (D. Minn. 1992) (not relevant) *with* Sherman v. Citibank (S.D.), N.A., 668 A.2d 1036 (N.J. 1995) (finding it instructive), *vacated and remanded*, 517 U.S. 1241, 116 S. Ct. 2493, 135 L. Ed. 2d 86 (1996).

513 *See* § 3.9.2.1, *infra*.
514 *See* § 3.4.5, *supra*, § 3.9.2.2, *infra*.
515 *See* §§ 3.1.1, 3.3, *supra* (discussing the Interstate Banking and Branching Efficiency Act of 1994).

516 *See* § 3.4.2, *supra*.
517 12 U.S.C. § 1831d(a).
518 12 U.S.C. § 1463(g) (formerly codified at 12 U.S.C. § 1730g).
519 12 U.S.C. § 1463(g).
520 12 U.S.C. § 1785(g).
521 *Compare* 12 U.S.C. §§ 1436(g), 1785(g), 1831d(a) *with* 12 U.S.C. § 85. The remedies also match. *Compare* 12 U.S.C. § 86 *with* 12 U.S.C. § 1463(g)(2).
522 *E.g.*, Fed. Home Loan Bank Bd., General Counsel Opinion No. 4 (Sept. 19, 1980) (FHLBB interpretation giving most favored lender status to an FSLIC-insured "thrift"); Fed. Banking L. Rep. (CCH) ¶ 81,635 and Consumer Cred. Guide (CCH) ¶ 95,511 (FDIC opinion letter applying it to an FDIC-insured state-chartered bank); Letter from Douglas H. Jones, Deputy Gen. Counsel, FDIC-93-27 (July 12, 1993), *reprinted on* the CD-Rom accompanying this volume; Letter of Oct. 20, 1983, *reprinted on* the CD-Rom accompanying this volume; FDIC General Counsel's Op., 63 Fed. Reg. 27282 (May 18, 1998), *reprinted on* the CD-Rom accompanying this volume; 45 Fed. Reg. 78624, 78625 (1980), *as amended by* IRPS 81-3, 46 Fed. Reg. 24153 (NCUA opinion as to federally-insured credit unions).
523 *See, e.g.*, VanderWeyst v. First State Bank of Benson, 425

though no legislative history supports that construction. The result presents the danger of obliterating traditional state regulatory schemes for institutions not otherwise regulated.[524]

Since courts are currently interpreting most favored lender status under DIDA and the NBA almost interchangeably, readers should refer to §§ 3.4.3.4 and 3.4.5.2, *supra* for discussions of the definition of the term "interest rate." Similarly the NBA limitations on the most-favored lender doctrine should be equally applicable to DIDA's most favored lenders. *See* § 3.4.3, *supra*.

It is important to note that the broader types of federal preemption available to national banks and federal savings associations do not apply to state-chartered depositories. The preemption available to state-chartered, FDIC-insured banks is the "narrowest preemption available to depositories."[525] The interest rate and "interest-like" fee preemption available under section 1831d(a) does not include licensing laws, loan terms unrelated to the interest rate, or the remainder of state law, including state consumer laws.[526]

3.9.2.2 Interstate Banking Review: DIDA and Exportation

3.9.2.2.1 General

The origin of the right granted to national banks to export interest rates across state lines is discussed in § 3.4.5, *supra*. The industry has assumed, and, since the First Circuit's decision in *Greenwood Trust v. Massachusetts*,[527] the courts have as well, that DIDA gives federally-related lenders exportation rights coextensive with the national banks. Granting these lenders competitive equality with national banks adds additional players to one team in the contest between what might be termed "bank-friendly" states[528] and consumer-friendly states.

Dressed in the armor of section 521 of DIDA, state-chartered banks ventured out into the credit card exporting business. Two of the issues raised by DIDA exportation are the same as those raised by national bank exportation, and the reader should refer to those earlier discussions: the scope of loan terms encompassed by the term "interest rate" which can be exported,[529] and the constitutionality of delegating federal preemptive authority to unaccountable state legislatures.[530]

There is, however, an additional issue presented by exportation under DIDA which, like the constitutional question, raises fundamental questions of comity and federalism. It is also one which the courts have yet to seriously address. That is how to reconcile the notion that Congress might have assumed federally-related lenders could export a deregulated transaction nationwide—to any state—while at the same time granting states the primary right to "just say no," and "reassert" or reinstate any usury ceilings which may have been preempted.[531]

Arguably the very existence of the opt-out right in DIDA should, as a matter of statutory construction, weigh against grafting the full exportation right under the National Bank Act onto DIDA, for otherwise the opt-out right is superfluous.[532] Nonetheless, two circuit courts have held that DIDA

N.W.2d 803 (Minn. 1988) (federally-insured state bank may invoke most favored lender doctrine; purpose of DIDA was to give state banks parity with national banks); *see also* Malhotra v. Pac. Thrift & Loan Corp., 1999 Wash. App. LEXIS 1775 (Wash. Ct. App. Oct. 11, 1999) (state-chartered insured depository institution located in California entitled to preempt Washington's usury cap even though a second lien mortgage). *See also* the exportation cases cited in § 3.9.2.2, *infra*. One senses some circular logic here, remembering that the original purpose of the National Bank Act was to give national banks parity with state banks. *See* § 3.4.3.1, *supra*.

524 One must wonder how many lenders can be treated as "most favored" before all distinctions between classes of lenders are eliminated. At that point, all lenders will be allowed to charge the highest permissible rates on any class of loan, consumers will be paying extremely high charges, and perversely, no lender will any longer be "most favored." In a special concurrence in Bandas v. Citizens State Bank of Silver Lake, 412 N.W.2d 818 (Minn. Ct. App. 1987), *rev'd and remanded on other grounds sub nom.* Vander Weyst v. First State Bank of Benson, 425 N.W.2d 803 (Minn. 1988) recognizes that the seminal case (First Bank E. v. Bobeldyk, 391 N.W.2d 17 (Minn. Ct. App. 1986)) arguably is based on a misreading of the statutes, but views a re-examination of the question as inappropriate, given the number of cases premised on it.

525 Darrell L. Dreher & Elizabeth L. Anstaett, *Common Misconceptions in Bank Interstate Credit Transactions*, 56 Consumer Fin. L.Q. Rep. 281, 282 (2002).

526 *Id. See also* the discussion regarding the effect of DIDA on the applicability of state laws to a branch of a state-chartered bank in the borrower's state in § 3.9.2.2.2, *infra*. The Federal Deposit Insurance Act and state-chartered banks are discussed more fully in § 3.7, *supra*.

527 971 F.2d 818 (1st Cir. 1992); *see also* Venture Properties, Inc. v. First S. Bank, 79 F.3d 90 (8th Cir. 1996); Hill v. Chem. Bank, 799 F. Supp. 948 (D. Minn. 1992); Stoorman v. Greenwood Trust Co., No. 93CA0224 (Colo. Ct. App. Apr. 17, 1994), *aff'd*, 908 P.2d 133 (Colo. 1995).

528 Irwin v. Citibank (S.D.), Clearinghouse No. 50,419 (Pa. C.P. Dec. 9, 1993).

529 *See* § 3.4.5.2, *supra*.

530 Smiley v. Citibank (S.D.), N.A., 517 U.S. 735, 116 S. Ct. 1730, 135 L. Ed. 2d 25 (1996).

531 *See* § 3.9.1, *supra*, § 3.9.4, *infra*.

532 *Cf.* Singer, Sutherland Statutory Construction ¶ 46.06 (5th ed.). *But see* Stoorman v. Greenwood Trust Co., 888 P.2d 289 (Colo. Ct. App. 1994), *aff'd on other grounds*, 908 P.2d 133 (Colo. 1995) (Colorado's opt-out only applies to loans "made" in state).

carries with it the exportation right.[533] However, both were to states which had not opted-out of the relevant portion of DIDA. The first simply opined that consistency in interpreting section 85 and DIDA § 522 "seems warranted,"[534] and failed entirely to discuss the significant statutory and policy differences between the two.[535] In the more prominent decision, *Greenwood Trust v. Massachusetts*,[536] the First Circuit allowed a Delaware state-chartered bank to export the high late charges on its Discover card to Massachusetts, where they were not allowed. The First Circuit, without analysis, avoided the issue by simply noting that Massachusetts had not opted out of section 521.[537]

To date, only one decision appears to have involved a state that did opt out. A Colorado intermediate appellate court held that the opt-out right applied only to loans "made" in the opting-out state. It made reference to a

Colorado law[538] that considered the contract made in Colorado if the lender received the agreement there. Hence the court found the opt-out would apply only to intrastate loans.[539] Note that the reference to state law was key. In contrast, were the question to arise in Iowa, another opt-out state, reference to state law would dictate that the debtor's residence determines where the contract is "made."[540] Thus seemingly *Stoorman* would, ironically, support Iowa's assertion of its opt-out status to enforce its laws over DIDA exporters. The question of where a loan is "made" is ordinarily analyzed in the choice of law context. Agency preemption interpretations on this point are not consistent.[541] Traditional conflicts principles may provide additional support to an argument that a state's opt out should stand as a shield against exporting DIDA lenders.

It should be noted, however, that one result of this whole controversy has been to erode the will of legislatures in "consumer-friendly" states as local financial services industry has worked hard (and generally successfully) for the freedom to charge more and higher fees, claiming that freedom is necessary to compete with those lenders who have the cloak of preemption.[542] In this race to the bottom, consumers have been the losers, as fee caps have risen.[543]

One of the other ironies that arises in this exportation context occurs when courts in far-flung states where credit card customers reside are called upon to resolve conflicts in the laws of the state where the bank was chartered. For example, an Illinois federal court found itself embroiled in a controversy over which provisions of Virginia usury law applied to regulate the allowable amount of late fees and the duration of the grace period.[544] The court initially construed

533 Greenwood Trust Co. v. Massachusetts, 971 F.2d 818 (1st Cir. 1992) (Delaware-chartered bank may override Massachusetts' late charge limitation under § 521); Gavey Properties 1762 v. First Fin. Sav. & Loan Ass'n, 845 F.2d 519 (5th Cir. 1988). *Accord* Hill v. Chem. Bank, 799 F. Supp. 948 (D. Minn. 1992). *Cf.* Malhotra v. Pac. Thrift & Loan Corp., 1999 Wash. App. LEXIS 1775 (Wash. Ct. App. Oct. 11, 1999) (state-chartered insured depository institution chartered in California entitled to preempt Washington's usury cap even though a second lien mortgage) (no explicit discussion of exportation).

534 Gavey Properties 1762 v. First Fin. Sav. & Loan Ass'n, 845 F.2d 519 (5th Cir. 1988).

535 *See* §§ 3.4.1, 3.9.1, *supra.*

536 971 F.2d 818 (1st Cir. 1992); *accord* Hill v. Chem. Bank, 799 F. Supp. 948 (D. Minn. 1992) (also involving a non-opt-out state). Several states filed an excellent brief as *amici*, which is available from National Clearinghouse for Legal Servs., Clearinghouse No. 47,943 (*see* § 1.5, *supra*).

537 It had originally opted out of DIDA entirely, but apparently implicitly rescinded its opt out of § 521 in 1986. *See also* Smiley v. Citibank (S.D.), N.A., 32 Cal. Rptr. 2d 562 (Ct. App. 1994) (dissent) for a thoughtful criticism of *Greenwood Trust*. The history of this case, however, highlights that the dissent was spitting into the gale-force wind of exportation as the Supreme Court upheld the majority. *See* § 3.4.5.2, *supra*. Industry in several states which originally opted out of DIDA's alternate ceilings have been successful in convincing state legislatures to reverse their opt-out decisions. Of the eight jurisdictions which originally opted-out under § 525, five have repealed their opt-out. *See* § 3.9.4.1, *infra*; *see also* Jeffrey I. Langer & Kathleen E. Keest, *Interest Rate Regulation Developments in 1995: Continuing Liberalization of State Credit Card Laws and "Non-Filing" Insurance as "Interest" Under State Usury Laws*, 51 Bus. Law. 887 (1996); *cf.* Flannick v. First Union Home Equity Bank, 134 F. Supp. 2d 389 (E.D. Pa. 2001) (national bank was chartered in North Carolina and made loan to Pennsylvania resident; issue was whether North Carolina or Pennsylvania law applied to issue of when interest charges on the loan could commence; the bank first argued that any interest restrictions in North Carolina law were trumped by DIDMCA because the loan was a first lien mortgage; the court rejected this argument because North Carolina had opted out of the interest rate and points restrictions) (*Editor's note*: Three years later, the court vacated its opinion without discussion, presumably as part of a settlement of the case. 2004 WL 121860 (E.D. Pa. Mar. 8, 2004)).

538 Colo. Rev. Stat. § 5-1-201(1).

539 Stoorman v. Greenwood Trust Co., 908 P.2d 133 (Colo. 1995) (the court mentioned in passing that § 525 had been repealed, which is incorrect; *see* § 3.9.4.3, *infra.*).

540 *See* Iowa Code § 537.1201.

541 *Compare* Fed. Home Loan Bank Bd. Opinion Letter No. 581 (Doyle, June 14, 1983) (where a contract is made depends on choice of law principles) *with* OCC Interpretive Letter No. 822 (Feb. 17, 1998) (which state law applies depends on where the loan is approved, credit is extended, and funds are disbursed) *and* FDIC General Counsel's Op., 63 Fed. Reg. 27282 (May 18, 1998) (adopts the OCC's definition). The full text of the OCC and FDIC letters is reproduced on the CD-Rom accompanying this volume.

542 See, for example, Jeffrey I. Langer & Kathleen E. Keest, *Interest Rate Regulation Developments in 1995: Continuing Liberalization of State Credit Card Laws and "Non-Filing" Insurance as "Interest" Under State Usury Laws*, 51 Bus. Law. 887 (1996), for a survey of state laws "liberalizing" credit card laws (read "raising fees").

543 *Id.* (noting that in 1995 alone, eleven states authorized or increased credit card late fees). Since penalty fee revenue for credit card banks has increased from $1.7 billion in 1996 to almost $15 billion in 2004. Cardweb.com, *Fee Party* (Jan. 13, 2005), *available at* www.cardweb.com/cardtrak/news/2005/january/13a.html (visited Mar. 2005).

544 Amaro v. Capital One Bank, 1998 U.S. Dist. LEXIS 8373 (N.D.

an alleged conflict in another state's law before that state's own court ever had the opportunity to do so, though it later reconsidered and appropriately certified the question to the Virginia Supreme Court.[545]

3.9.2.2.2 DIDA's exportation and choice of laws

Traditional conflict of law principles are discussed in § 9.2.9, *infra*, but some discussion of the considerations in the exportation context is warranted. At the outset, it should be noted that some factors weigh in both directions, so applying a choice of law analysis to these cases may be affected by "eye of the beholder" judgment. As these transactions are handled by mail, a substantial relationship exists in both states: all the lender's activity takes place in one state (mailing the solicitations and statements, receiving signed application agreements and payments);[546] all the borrower's activity takes place in another (in a sense, the "negotiation" takes place in the borrower's home, as he or she reads the solicitation, and signs the application/agreement).[547]

While there is a preference for adopting the law of the state that would uphold the contract, there are two limitations on that, both of which argue against adopting the law of the exporting state. The first is that invoking the preference should not undermine the public policy of the state whose laws are not followed. Here, the contest is between states that have elected to maintain consumer protections for their own citizens, on the one hand, and states that have invited lenders to locate there specifically in order to enable those lenders to ignore the public policy of other states.[548] It is hard to imagine a more clear instance of a case in which invoking the preference would significantly undermine the public policy of the other state.[549] Public policy should be a critical component of a conflicts analysis in these cases: because Congress specifically gave states the right to "just say no," statutory construction principles dictate that it be assumed they meant that others must respect that decision.[550]

As noted earlier, it is unlikely Congress meant to delegate to the Delaware or South Dakota legislatures powers it refused to exercise itself, and such delegation is arguably unconstitutional if it did.[551] As to the relative importance of the public policies of protecting consumers and facilitating interstate banking, Congress has specifically refused to say the latter outweighs the former. In the context of the 1994 interstate banking law, Congress makes that clear, both in the statutory text and legislative history. The new law's text specifically provides that branches of out-of-state banks are subject to the host states' laws on consumer protection and fair lending, unless the state law discriminates against the bank or is otherwise preempted by federal law. It makes that caveat with respect to out-of-state branching by both national and state-chartered banks.

Finally, another choice of law principle relating to usury cases recognizes the distinction between general and special usury laws.[552] Courts have recognized that commercial and consumer cases involve different public policy considerations,[553] another factor which should, in a conflicts analysis, tilt the balance in favor of the home state of the borrower whose only contact with the other state is to mail the application and payments there in a preaddressed envelope.

Even though the national bank's right to export has been upheld, as discussed in § 3.4.5, *supra*, the statutory and policy differences between DIDA and the NBA have yet to

---

Ill. May 19, 1998) (court opted for the position argued by the bank, that the Virginia provision applying to revolving accounts which permitted banks to charge any "charges and fees" as agreed to by the parties to the contract controlled). In some instances, if the case is filed in the federal courts sitting in the home state of the defendant bank, the federal court may dismiss the case on the grounds of lack of jurisdiction or certify the question of state law to the state's highest court. *See, e.g.*, Fleet Bank v. Burke, 160 F.3d 883 (2d Cir. 1998).

545 1999 WL 59968 (N.D. Ill. Feb. 2, 1999). The district court's initial inclination about how to resolve the conflict was later vindicated by Virginia's highest court. *See* Perez v. Capital One Bank, 522 S.E.2d 874 (Va. 1999). Practitioners filing a case in one state may end up litigating certain issues in the home state of the defendant. Consumers' counsel must have sufficient resources to carry the legal fight to a foreign forum, yet another burden placed upon consumers due to the effects of exportation.

546 *E.g.*, Stoorman v. Greenwood Trust Co., 888 P.2d 289 (Colo. Ct. App. 1994), *aff'd on other grounds*, 908 P.2d 133 (Colo. 1995).

547 *Cf.* Aldens, Ins. v. Miller, 610 F.2d 538 (8th Cir. 1979) (Iowa's mandatory choice of law provision upheld against Illinois-based mail-order open-end credit retailer). On the separate issue of whether a lender can be sued in the home state of the borrower, the Fifth Circuit recently determined that, in the electronic commerce context, a posted website with a toll-free number, a mailing address, an e-mail address, and a printable order form were insufficient "contacts" with a state to subject the company to personal jurisdiction. Minke v. AAAA Dev. Ltd. Liab. Co., 190 F.3d 333, 337 (5th Cir. 1999) ("This [patent infringement] case does not fall into the spectrum of cases where a defendant clearly conducted business over the Internet nor does it fall into the middle spectrum of interactivity where the defendant and users exchange information through the Internet.").

548 *See* § 3.4.5.1.1, *supra*.

549 At least one court gave the public policy analysis dominance when the laws of the foreign jurisdiction imposed no usury ceiling whatsoever. N. Am. Bank, Ltd. v. Schulman, 474 N.Y.S.2d 383 (County Ct. 1984). *But see* Amaro v. Capital One Bank, 1998 U.S. Dist. LEXIS 8373 (N.D. Ill. May 19, 1998) (court refused to apply the Illinois UDAP statute in a suit filed by Illinois credit card customers against a Virginia bank and dismissed public policy arguments simply because the credit card agreement stated that Virginia and federal law applied; the Virginia UDAP Act conveniently does not apply to credit transactions).

550 Singer, Sutherland Statutory Construction ¶ 46.06 (5th ed.).

551 *See* § 3.4.5.1.1, *supra*.

552 *See* §§ 2.2.2, 2.2.3, *supra*.

553 *See, e.g.*, State *ex rel.* Meierhenry v. Spiegel, Inc., 277 N.W.2d 298 (S.D. 1979). *See generally* § 9.2.9, *infra*.

be thoughtfully analyzed in an opinion. It is conceivable the Supreme Court will revisit *Marquette* and what it wrought.[554]

3.9.3 DIDA's "First Mortgage" Preemption

3.9.3.1 Overview

The one federal usury preemption with perhaps the greatest effect to date on low and moderate income consumers is DIDA's preemption of state laws limiting interest rates and charges on first mortgage loans. Specifically, DIDA § 501(a)(1) overrides state laws and state constitutional provisions which limit "the rate or amount of interest, discount points, finance charges, or other charges" on loans secured by first liens on either residential real estate or residential mobile homes.[555]

Unlike the most favored lender preemption, which, through controversial agency and judicial interpretations, currently encompasses a wide variety of charges within the definition of "interest,"[556] DIDA's first lien preemption covers only those limitations on costs that are included in the annual percentage rate.[557] It does not preempt state limitations designed to protect borrowers, such as prepayment charges, late charges, attorney fees, or similar limitations.[558] Nor does it preempt a state statute which prohibits

negative amortization[559] or a state statute which prohibits the charging of an escrow waiver fee.[560]

The extent of the first lien preemption is limited to state laws "expressly limiting the rate or amount of interest, discount points, finance charges, or other charges."[561] Arguably, laws that prohibit the financing of discount points or other charges are not preempted because such laws do not expressly limit the rate or amount of such fees, only when and how the consumer pays for them. Under principles of federalism, preemption is narrowly construed in light of the congressional purpose of the provision.[562]

---

554 *See In re* Beck, 248 B.R. 229 (Bankr. W.D.N.Y. 2000) (national bank cannot have its cake and eat it too, says the court in *dictum*; bank chartered in Arizona may not claim applicability of its home state law regarding the creation of a security interest and that of the consumer's residence, New York, by inserting a clause in the contract indicating that New York law applies regarding the security interest).

555 DIDA § 501(a)(1), 12 U.S.C. § 1735f-7a. For a discussion of the "residential" nature of a mortgage, see *In re* Lawson Square, Inc., 816 F.2d 1236 (8th Cir. 1987); Bank of New York v. Hoyt, 617 F. Supp. 1304 (D.R.I. 1985).

556 *See* §§ 3.4.3, 3.4.5.2, 3.9.2, *supra*.

557 S. Rep. No. 96-368, at 19, *reprinted in* 1980 U.S.C.C.A.N. 236; *see* Baughman v. Mellon Mortgage Co., 621 N.W.2d 776 (Minn. Ct. App. 2001) (tax service fee is included in the APR); *see also* Wells Fargo Bank, N.A., v. Boutris, 265 F. Supp. 2d 1162 (E.D. Cal. 2003) (state law restricting how many days of *per diem* interest can be charged is preempted because it expressly limits the amount of interest that can be charged). *See* § 4.4, *infra*, for a discussion of the APR.

558 12 C.F.R. § 590.3(c); *see* Larsen v. Countrywide Home Loans, Inc., 2001 WL 803689 (N.D. Ill. July 17, 2001) (court refused to dismiss the claim based on the charging of interest after the loan was prepaid in full because the charge is sufficiently like a prepayment penalty and does not appear to be related to the calculation of the APR); Gonzalez v. Old Kent Mortgage Company, 2000 U.S. Dist. LEXIS 14530 (E.D. Pa. Sept. 19, 2000) (non-interest rate charges are not subject to DIDMCA preemption); Barber v. Fairbanks Capital Corp. (*In re* Barber), 266 B.R. 309 (Bankr. E.D. Pa. 2001) (non-interest charges not preempted by DIDMCA); Nelson v. Associates Fin. Serv. Co. of Ind., Inc., 659 N.W.2d 635 (Mich. Ct. App. 2002) (state restriction on prepayment penalties is not related to the "rate or amount of interest" and is not preempted); Konynenbelt v. Flagstar Bank,

617 N.W.2d 706, 713 (Mich. Ct. App. 2000) (mortgage release fees not a component of the annual percentage rate and, therefore, not subject to DIDMCA preemption); Veytia v. Seiter, 740 S.W.2d 64, 66 (Tex. App. 1987) (quoting legislative history, § 501 would not protect usurious late charges), *aff'd*, 756 S.W.2d 303 (Tex. 1988). *Compare* Shelton v. Mut. Saving & Loan Ass'n, 738 F. Supp. 1050 (E.D. Mich. 1990) (court holds that a state law prohibiting precomputed interest, and prescribing simple interest method on mortgage loan would be preempted by DIDA and was not within the purview of the exception of § 590.3 [Practice at issue involved charging interest on funds prior to disbursement.]) *with* Currie v. Diamond Mtg. Corp., 83 B.R. 536 (N.D. Ill. 1987), *aff'd*, 859 F.2d 1538 (7th Cir. 1988) (effort to take advantage of § 590.3 exception by arguing points were essentially the same as prepayment penalties failed).

[*Editor's Note*: But note that some non-APR-related protections for consumers, such as late fees, may be otherwise preempted under the Alternative Mortgage Transactions Parity Act in some circumstances. *See, e.g.*, 12 C.F.R. § 34.23 (1996); § 3.10, *infra*. Some state retail installment sales acts (RISA) that apply to the purchase and financing of mobile homes may explicitly or in effect prohibit the financing of certain fees that would be allowed under DIDA, assuming the seller/lender is otherwise entitled to DIDA preemption. *See* § 3.9.3.4, *infra*. However, there is a strong argument that a prohibition against the *financing* of such points and fees does not fall within the scope of DIDA because this does not limit the amount of the fee that can be charged, only the method by which they are paid.]

559 *See* Grunbeck v. Dime Sav. Bank, 74 F.3d 331 (1st Cir. 1996) (court notes § 501 preempts only state law "*expressly* limiting the rate or amount of interest"; the simple interest statute did not limit lender's right to charge whatever rate would equal the amount recoverable through compounding; focus of preemption question is not whether such a statute might make it more difficult to command such a return in a better-informed marketplace; court rejects as unpersuasive contrary FHLBB and OTS agency opinions [*Editor's Note*: In case you're wondering why AMTPA's preemption of state laws forbidding negative amortization was not determinative, a close observer reports that there are apparently unresolved factual issues as to whether there was adequate compliance with federal regulations necessary to invoke AMTPA's preemptive protection, which may be dealt with on remand. *See generally* § 3.10.2, *infra*.]).

560 Stern v. Norwest Mortgage, Inc., 672 N.E.2d 296 (Ill. App. Ct. 1996), *aff'd*, 688 N.E.2d 99 (Ill. 1997). *But see* Baughman v. Mellon Mortgage Co., 621 N.W.2d 776 (Minn. Ct. App. 2001) (tax service fee is included in the APR).

561 DIDA § 501(a)(1), 12 U.S.C. § 1735f-7a.

562 Nelson v. Associates Fin. Servs. Co. of Ind., 659 N.W.2d 635 (Mich. Ct. App. 2002).

The legislative intent behind this provision was to stimulate the housing market during a period of high market interest rates, when there was a serious mismatch between generally low, fixed state usury ceilings for first mortgages and historically high market rates.[563] In this goal DIDA, no doubt, succeeded. Unfortunately, the broadly worded first mortgage preemption not only enabled home buyers to obtain mortgage loans, albeit at high interest rates, but also made consumers' homes the targets of many lenders who, in securing their loans with residential real estate, gained both access to the security in the case of default and an automatic removal of usury ceilings.

The fundamental flaw in DIDA's first mortgage preemption is that, despite the "first lien" restriction in the statute,[564] the law contains no express purchase money limitation. The preemption extends to any loan provided that the lender obtains a first lien on the borrower's home as security. This loophole was one of the factors leading to the proliferation of home equity loans, typically much higher balance loans than other consumer credit. These loans, which often were used for debt consolidation, placed the consumer's home at risk of foreclosure in the event of default.[565] Moreover, they often featured terms making them more costly, or difficult to repay, thus increasing the likelihood of default.[566]

The combination of the "first lien" language in DIDA § 501(a)(1) and the absence of a purchase money requirement has enabled *de facto* second mortgage lenders to claim usury preemption by paying off cheaper senior liens with part of the proceeds of the second mortgage loan, thus obtaining first lien status. Home equity lending exploded, rising from about $40 billion in 1986 to $420 billion in 1997 to over $736 billion by the first quarter of 2004.[567] The value of the mortgage-backed securities (MBS) issued by the subprime market grew from $11.05 billion in 1994 to $133 billion in 2002.[568]

In one of the most notorious instances of abuse of this preemption, a finance company specializing in financing used cars generally required first mortgages, as well as the car, to secure the loans at very high rates. Low-rate first mortgages were required to be paid off with the high rate car loan.[569] If the borrower did not have a home, a cosigner who did (not infrequently parents or grandparents) would be required. In this situation, the result of the defendant's invocation of federal preemption was to frustrate, rather than to facilitate the intended housing policy by placing homes at risk of foreclosure for high-rate used-car loans.[570] It was in respect to this lender that the Third Circuit originally, in an opinion later vacated, thought it would be "absurd to find that Congress intended lenders to be able to short circuit state usury limitations and increase the risk of foreclosure in order to enable the borrower to purchase a used car."[571] Nonetheless, it did just that, as it could not read a purchase money limitation into the statute.[572]

---

563 *See* S. Rep. No. 96-368, at 18, *reprinted in* 1980 U.S.C.C.A.N. 236, 254; H.R. Conf. Rep. No. 96-842, at 78, *reprinted in* 1980 U.S.C.C.A.N. 298, 308.

564 *See* DIDA § 501(a)(1), 12 U.S.C. § 1735f-7a.

565 For an excellent discussion of the effect of this first lien preemption and the rise of the subprime market, see Cathy Lesser Mansfield, *The Road to Subprime "HEL" Was Paved with Good Congressional Intentions: Usury Deregulation and the Subprime Home Equity Market*, 51 S.C. L. Rev. 473 (2000).

566 In that, they were aided by the 1982 mortgage preemption in AMTPA. *See* §§ 3.10, 11.1, *infra.*

567 David F. Seiders & Charles A. Luckett, Household Borrowing the Recovery, 64 Fed. Res. Bull. 153, 156 (Mar. 1978); Glenn B. Canner, Thomas A. Durkin & Charles A. Luckett, Recent Developments in Home Equity Lending, 84 Fed. Res. Bull. 241, 242–248 (Apr. 1998); Howard Lax, Michael Manti, Paul Raca, Peter Zorn, *Subprime Lending: An Investigation of Economic Efficiency*, 15 Hous. Pol'y Debate 533, 533 (2004). *See also* Cathy Lesser Mansfield, *The Road to Subprime "HEL" Was Paved with Good Congressional Intentions: Usury Deregulation and the Subprime Home Equity Market*, 51 S.C. L. Rev. 473 (2000).

568 Inside Mortgage Finance Publications, Inc., The 2003 Mortgage Market Statistical Annual, Vol. II, at 5–7.

569 As a consumer discount company, the lender would have been limited to a 9 1/2% discount ceiling on loans up to four years, equivalent to a 25.9% APR. With the first lien preemption, the result was frequently default on mortgage loans with rates up to 41%.

570 Some lender's practices are described in Smith v. Fidelity Consumer Discount Co., Nos. 88-1406, 88-1444, slip op. at 35 (3d Cir. June 27, 1989) (opinion vacated as to DIDA's rulings), *as modified*, 898 F.2d 907 (3d Cir. 1990), and the district court opinion, Laubach v. Fidelity Consumer Discount Co., 686 F. Supp. 504, 507 (E.D. Pa. 1988) (plaintiff Smith could not receive a loan unless his eighty-one-year-old mother cosigned so the loan would be secured by a mortgage); *see also* Curry v. Fidelity Consumer Discount Co., 656 F. Supp. 1129 (E.D. Pa. 1987); Solis v. Fidelity Consumer Discount Co. (*In re* Solis), 38 B.R. 293 (Bankr. E.D. Pa. 1984), *rev'd in part*, 58 B.R. 983 (Bankr. E.D. Pa. 1986) (in this case two homes—the buyer's and the cosigner's—secured the purchase of a $3500 Buick); Keller v. Fidelity Consumer Discount Co. (*In re* Keller), 34 B.R. 562 (Bankr. E.D. Pa. 1983). For other examples of Fidelity's lending practices, see *In re* Celona, 90 B.R. 104 (Bankr. E.D. Pa. 1988), *aff'd*, 98 B.R. 705 (E.D. Pa. 1989) (defendant reconstituted as Equitable National Bank); *In re* Russell, 72 B.R. 855 (Bankr. E.D. Pa. 1987).

571 Smith v. Fidelity Consumer Discount Co., Nos. 88-1406, 88-1444, slip op. at 36 (3d Cir. June 27, 1989) (opinion vacated as to DIDA's rulings), *as modified*, 898 F.2d 907 (3d Cir. 1990).

572 Smith v. Fidelity Consumer Discount Co., 898 F.2d 907, 909 (3d Cir. 1990) ("This is the kind of case in which we need to remain mindful of Lord Campbell's admonition that 'it is the duty of all courts of justice to take care, for the general good of the community, that hard cases do not make bad law.' However we may feel about the defendants' interest rates and business practices, it is our duty to give effect to that construction of § 501(a)(1) of DIDA that is most consonant with its text, its legislative history and the interpretations of the agency entrusted to administer DIDMCA." (citations omitted)); *see also* Brown v. Investors Mortgage Co., 121 F.3d 472 (9th Cir. 1997) (follows *Smith*); Gora v. Banc One Serv., Inc., 1995 WL 613131 (N.D. Ill. Oct. 17, 1995) (same, rejecting *Hicks*); *In re* L.G.H. Enterprises, Inc., 146 B.R. 612 (Bankr. E.D.N.Y. 1992) (not relevant whether loans were non-purchase money or for refinancing; statute requires only that they be first liens). *But cf.*

Because the application of the DIDA first mortgage preemption to a home loan can devastate a consumer's usury claim even if the interest charged is absurdly high, counsel representing defaulting homeowners should examine each loan transaction carefully to determine whether it falls within the scope of the preemption.[573] Several questions should be considered.

- Did the lender really obtain a first lien on residential property at the requisite time?
- Does the lender itself qualify under DIDA?
- In the case of mobile home loans, has the lender complied with the OTS consumer protection regulations?
- Finally, has the state exercised its right to opt out of either the interest rate or points provisions of DIDA?[574]

Significantly, lenders claiming DIDA preemption carry the burden of proving that DIDA applies to a particular transaction.[575]

3.9.3.2 First Lien

3.9.3.2.1 Definition of first lien

The usury preemption under DIDA § 501(a)(1) exempts "any loan, mortgage, credit sale, or advance which is—(A) secured by a first lien on residential real property" from state usury ceilings.[576] The OTS (formerly the FHLBB), which is charged with interpreting DIDA,[577] has defined "loans which are secured by a first lien on real estate" as loans secured by any instrument "of such a nature that, in the event of default, the real estate described in the instrument could be subjected to the satisfaction of the obligation with the same priority as a first mortgage of a first deed of trust in the jurisdiction where the real estate is located."[578] This definition clearly leaves some questions about the precise definition of "first lien" under DIDA, and state law determines the issue.[579]

As noted in the preceding section, it is now clear that there is no purchase money limitation inherent in the definition.[580] However, a wraparound mortgage[581] does not qualify as a first lien. In *Mitchell v. Trustees of United States Mutual Real Estate Investment Trust*,[582] a Michigan court of appeals determined that the lien held by a wraparound lender was clearly subordinate to the original, extant mortgage, even though the wraparound lender had the contractual and financial capacity to pay off the original mortgage at any time.

State recording statutes and second mortgage laws should be carefully checked to see when pre-existing liens are extinguished and what priority the refinancing lender has obtained. The first lien status of *de facto* second mortgage loans could be challenged if the lender neglected to pay off tax liens or other liens which may have previously arisen under state law.[583] In addition, liens created by state or federal government programs, such as deferred loans made for the purpose of rehabilitating residences, should destroy the "first lien" claim of a subsequent home equity loan and could subject that second loan to the state's second mortgage loan law.[584]

On the other hand, when the loan pays off a prior first, a short delay in retiring that debt will probably not defeat first lien status.[585] When the lender states its intention in the loan documents that it is relying upon the section 501 preemp-

---

Fidelity Fin. Servs. v. Hicks, 574 N.E.2d 15 (Ill. App. Ct. 1991) (indicates that DIDA preemption would apply only to purchase-money mortgages; the court may have been unaware of *Smith*, which was not cited).

573 For alternative theories to attack overreaching loans, see Ch. 11, *infra*.

574 *See* § 3.9.4, *infra*.

575 *See In re* Russell, 72 B.R. 855 (Bankr. E.D. Pa. 1987) (excellent discussion); Pac. Mortgage & Inv. Group, Ltd. v. Horn, 641 A.2d 913 (Md. Ct. Spec. App. 1994); Fidelity Fin. Servs. v. Hicks, 574 N.E.2d 15 (Ill. App. Ct. 1991).

576 *See* DIDA § 501(a)(1), 12 U.S.C. § 1735f-7a.

577 *See* § 3.3, *supra*.

578 *See* 12 C.F.R. § 590.2(c).

579 *See* Brown v. Investors Mortgage Co., 121 F.3d 472 (9th Cir. 1997) (lienholder of fixture lien arising from purchase of a furnace and water heater does not have same priority as a first

mortgage holder under state law); Mitchell v. Trustees of U.S. Mut. Real Estate Inv. Trust, 375 N.W.2d 424 (Mich. Ct. App. 1985); Fed. Home Loan Bank Bd., General Counsel Opinion Letter No. S86 (May 11, 1984); *see also In re* Russell, 72 B.R. 855 (Bankr. E.D. Pa. 1987) (first lien issue discussed, but case decided on other grounds); Cohen v. Eisenberg, 697 N.Y.S.2d 625 (App. Div. 1999) (burden on lender when lender files for summary judgment).

580 *See* § 3.9.3.1, *supra*.

581 *See* § 7.4.3, *infra*.

582 375 N.W.2d 424 (Mich. Ct. App. 1985).

583 *See, e.g., In re* Grigsby, 119 B.R. 479 (Bankr. E.D. Pa. 1990) (creditor's argument that parties intended that loan be secured by a first lien, where there already existed a small remaining first mortgage, ruled not sufficient to invoke DIDA), *rev'd on other grounds*, 127 B.R. 759 (E.D. Pa. 1991); Fidelity Fin. Servs. v. Hicks, 574 N.E.2d 15 (Ill. App. Ct. 1991).

584 *Cf.* Chevy Chase Bank, F.S.B. v. Chaires, 715 A.2d 199 (Md. 1998) (court held that a lien created by a state shore erosion control fund on a residential property prior to a later construction loan rendered the construction loan a "second lien" and therefore the state's secondary mortgage loan law applied; not a federal preemption case but instructive on what constitutes a "first lien" under state law); *see* § 2.3.3.7, *supra*. *But see* Pence v. Norwest Bank Minn., N.A., 768 A.2d 639 (Md. 2001) (city deferred loan and accompanying security agreement did not create a legal mortgage due to defective wording; there being no prior mortgage on the property, the home equity lender's lien was in first position).

585 *See* Laubach v. Fidelity Consumer Discount Co., 686 F. Supp. 504 (E.D. Pa. 1988), *aff'd sub nom.* Smith v. Fidelity Consumer Discount Co., 898 F.2d 907 (3d Cir. 1990); M & P Enterprises v. TransAmerica Fin. Servs., 944 S.W.2d 154 (Mo. 1997).

tion, it is not bound by that election if it may avoid a state usury cap under a different preemption provision.[586]

3.9.3.2.2 Special Texas issue on first liens

Until January 1, 1998, the Texas constitution and statutes limited the right to take a first lien—or indeed any lien—on the home.[587] The Texas electorate voted to amend its constitution and change the long-standing (since 1839) homestead protections.[588] Lenders can now make home equity loans for any purpose, although they are subject to a number of restrictions designed to prevent the abuses experienced by many homeowners in other states.[589] Of relevance to DIDA's first lien preemption, and AMTPA's alternative mortgage loan term preemption, is the revised Texas Constitution, art. 16, § 50(j), which states that if any of the provisions relating to home equity loans, liens for refinances of debt, written notice requirements, and other provisions are held to be preempted, all of those provisions are invalid. This has been called the "poison pill provision."[590]

Arguably, the effect of the poison pill provision will be to render the entire law invalid if the preemption clause is triggered. This provision creates a strong disincentive for lenders to raise *any* preemption argument. How the effect of the "poison pill" plays out remains to be seen.

Lawsuits have begun to percolate through the courts challenging various provisions of this Texas law. In one case, a home improvement contractor sued a lender after the lender refused to close on a loan at the offices of a "title abstract company" on the grounds that this was not a proper location under the special provisions in the amendment related to home improvement financing.[591] The court held that a title abstract company is not a "title company" under section 50(a) and the lender was correct to refuse to fund the loan. The court also rejected a variety of other challenges to this provision, including the claim that "title company" was unconstitutionally vague.

In another case, the Texas Supreme Court reviewed two apparently conflicting provisions regarding whether the homeowner could be required to pay off debts that were not secured by the homestead.[592] It held that the provisions creating the substantive protection (which allowed "debt to another lender" to be paid) trumped a provision requiring a special notice to the homeowner (which limited the debt to that owed the same lender).

More recently, the provision of the constitutional amendment that allows the lender to cure any defect in its obligations under the loan within a reasonable time after notice from the borrower came under scrutiny. At issue was whether a lender who charged closing fees in excess of the 3% cap could cure and avoid forfeiture of the principal and interest and maintain the lien on the property.[593] The bor-

---

586 *Paramjeet v. Pac. Thrift and Loan Co.*, 1999 Wash. App. LEXIS 1775 (Wash. Ct. App. 1999) (the lender did not acquire first lien status because the first lien holder refused to subrogate; lender can, nevertheless, avoid state usury cap under the § 521 preemption for state-chartered depository institutions).

587 The Texas Constitution art. 16, § 50 and Tex. Prop. Code Ann. § 41.001 (Vernon) precluded any waiver of the homestead exemption except for purchase money debts, property taxes, and home improvements contracted for in a specified manner. Hence any other type of home equity mortgage was invalid. Further, under the Texas Consumer Credit Code, Tex. Rev. Code Ann. § 5069-6.05 (Vernon), no retail installment contract could take a first lien on property, except for the acquisition of the structure. Thus while a home improvement sales contract could include a valid lien under the homestead law, it could not include a valid *first* lien under the Consumer Credit Code.

588 Tex. Const. art. 16, § 50(a)(6).

589 For example, only one equity loan at a time (in addition to a purchase money loan and any home improvement loans) may be secured by the homestead; lender cannot require a borrower to pay off existing debt to that lender with an equity loan (that is, no "required" flipping); balloon payments are prohibited; no open lines of credit allowed; prepayment penalties are prohibited; loan and all other indebtedness secured by the home cannot exceed 80% of the fair market value; points and fees are capped at 3%; loan cannot close until at least twelve days after application in writing; loan cannot close until one business day after the homeowner receives a final itemization of closing costs; borrower must receive at the closing copies of all documents signed; loan cannot close until at least one year from closing date of any other loan secured by the same property, except refinances in certain circumstances; the loan may be closed only at the office of an attorney, lender, or title company; only judicial proceeding can be used to foreclose; loan cannot impose personal liability on the borrower (that is, no deficiencies after foreclosure); wage assignments are prohibited; loan may be rescinded within three days after closing. For home improvement loans, there is a twelve-day waiting period between application for the loan and the performance of any work or purchase of materials; homeowner has a three-day rescission period; and the contract for the work and material must be executed only at the office of a third-party lender, attorney, or title company. Reverse mortgages and home equity lines of credit are permitted under certain circumstances. The penalty for noncompliance is forfeiture of all principal and interest if the lender fails to comply with its obligations within a reasonable time of notification of its failure to comply. Tex. Const. art. 16, § 50(a).

590 Tex. Const. art. 16, § 50(j) states: "Subsection (a)(6) and subsections (e)–(i) of this section are not severable, and none of these provisions would have been enacted without the others. If any of those provisions are held to be preempted by the laws of the United States, all of those provisions are invalid. This subsection shall not apply to any lien or extension of credit made after January 1, 1998 and before the date any provision under Subsection (a)(6) or Subsections (e)–(i) is held to be preempted."

591 *Rooms With a View, Inc. v. Private Nat'l Mortgage Ass'n*, 7 S.W.3d 840 (Tex. App. 1999).

592 *Stringer v. Cendant Mortgage Corp.*, 23 S.W.3d 353 (Tex. 2000).

593 *Doody v. Ameriquest Mortgage Co.*, 49 S.W.3d 342 (Tex. 2001); *see also Pelt v. U.S. Bank Trust, N.A.*, 359 F.3d 764 (5th Cir. 2004) (forfeiture penalty not triggered where homeowners received copies of all documents, though unsigned, at the closing and received copies of the signed ones shortly thereafter); *Vincent v. Bank of Am., N.A.*, 109 S.W.3d 856 (Tex. App.

rower argued that the cure provision only applied to the 3% restriction and not to the subsection voiding the lien. The court held that the lender was entitled both to cure and maintain its lien. In another decision, the Texas Court of Appeals held that the 3% cap on "fees" does not apply to discount points because discount points constitute "interest" when they are paid in exchange for a lower rate.[594] However, a federal court decided that a loan origination fee was a "fee" under the Texas Constitution for purposes of the 3% cap.[595] Both origination and discount fees are normally calculated as a percentage of the loan amount. There seems to be little reason to treat them differently for purposes of the statutory cap. The federal court noted this irony but insisted on applying the plain language of the constitutional provision.[596] The result: the lender had to forfeit all principal and interest.[597]

The Texas Finance Commission issued regulations ostensibly interpreting the Texas Constitution in 2003.[598] Almost immediately thereafter, a lawsuit was filed challenging the validity of the regulations on the grounds that they conflict with the constitutional provisions and go beyond the scope of the Constitution.[599]

3.9.3.3 Qualifying Lenders

A second question to be considered in determining whether state usury law has been preempted by DIDA's first mortgage provisions is whether the lender itself qualifies under DIDA. Generally, DIDA § 501(a)(1) applies to a loan or mobile home credit sale if:

- The loan or sale is made by a federally-insured depository lender;[600]

- The loan or sale is made, insured, or "assisted in any way" by HUD;[601]
- The lender is approved by the Secretary of HUD for participation in any National Housing Act mortgage insurance program;[602]
- The loan or sale is made by a "creditor"[603] who "makes or invests in" residential real estate loans or mobile home credit sales in excess of $1 million per year;[604]
- The loan is eligible for resale on the federal secondary mortgage market;[605]
- The mobile home seller is a "creditor" who assigns all or part of its credit contracts to one of the above qualifying lenders;[606] or
- The seller is the previous occupant of the property or mobile home who is taking back a mortgage.[607]

While these categories capture a great portion of the mortgage lending industry, there are occasions when the qualifying lender criterion is not met. Loans or mobile home credit sales made by small creditors or those who extend credit infrequently, perhaps as a sideline to a real estate or loan

---

Note that the complete removal of ceilings under DIDA § 501(a)(1) takes priority over DIDA's alternative ceiling provisions, discussed in § 3.9.2, *supra*, when federally-related lenders issue first mortgage credit. *See In re* Lawson Square, 816 F.2d 1236 (8th Cir. 1987).

601 12 U.S.C. § 1735f-5(b) (incorporated by DIDA § 501(a)(1)(C)).
602 *See* 12 U.S.C. § 1735f-7a (DIDA § 501(a)(1)(C)(6)).
603 The definition of creditor is taken from 15 U.S.C. § 1602(f), and includes persons who "regularly" extend consumer credit payable in four or more installments or involving a finance charge. *See* Mitchell v. Trustees of U.S. Mut. Real Estate Inv. Trust, 375 N.W.2d 424 (Mich. Ct. App. 1985). But qualifying lenders are not limited to those extending "consumer" credit. *See* OTS Gen. Counsel Opin., Fed. Banking L. Rep. (CCH) ¶ 82,504 (Sept. 18, 1989).
604 12 U.S.C. § 1735f-5(b) (incorporated by DIDA § 501(a)(1)(C)). *See generally* Brown v. Investors Mortgage Co., 121 F.3d 472 (9th Cir. 1997) (summary judgment on $1,000,000 threshold issue could be granted on basis of lender's affidavit based upon personal knowledge; borrower apparently produced no evidence to contradict lender's claims); *In re* Russell, 72 B.R. 855 (Bankr. E.D. Pa. 1987) (lender failed to carry burden of proof on $1,000,000 DIDA threshold). Practitioners should be cautious in reviewing a lender's evidence that it qualifies. One attorney, upon investigation, found that some of the purported "qualifying" loans were secured primarily by commercial property. A brief on the issue is available from Clearinghouse. Farran v. Penn Mortgage Co., Clearinghouse No. 51,259 (Bankr. D. Md. 1995) (reply to response to motion for summary judgment; reply memorandum in support of plaintiff's motion for summary judgment).
605 12 U.S.C. § 1735f-5(b). Generally, this means that the loan originator must have been approved by the Federal National Mortgage Association (Fannie Mae) or some other federal purchaser, and that the loan terms and structure must meet the federal purchaser's requirements.
606 DIDA § 501(a)(1)(C)(v), 12 U.S.C. § 1735f-7a.
607 DIDA § 501(a)(1)(C)(vi), 12 U.S.C. § 1735f-7a. This provision applies to sales on or after October 8, 1980.

2003) (forfeiture as a penalty only applies to constitutionally mandated provisions in the loan documents; breach of a non-mandated contract provision does not trigger forfeiture). *Cf.* Adams v. Ameriquest Mortgage Co. (*In re* Adams), 307 B.R. 549 (Bankr. N.D. Tex. 2004) (lender may use cure provisions to offer to enter into a new loan to cure the violations; cure provisions permit the lender to cure unilaterally).
594 Tarver v. Sebring Capital Credit Corp., 69 S.W.3d 708 (Tex. App. 2002); *see also* Pelt v. U.S. Bank Trust Nat'l Ass'n, 2002 WL 31006139 (N.D. Tex. Sept. 5, 2002) (same, applying *Tarver*), *later proceedings at* 2003 WL 193468 (N.D. Tex. Jan. 23, 2003) (motion for new trial on a different issue denied), *aff'd*, 359 F.3d 764 (5th Cir. 2004).
595 Thomison v. Long Beach Mortgage Co., 176 F. Supp. 2d 714 (W.D. Tex. 2001).
596 *Id.* at 716–718.
597 However, the parties subsequently asked the court to vacate its holding and it did so. Thomison v. Long Beach Mortgage Co., 2002 WL 32138252 (W.D. Tex. Aug. 9, 2002).
598 7 Tex. Admin. Code § 153.1 *et seq.* The Texas voters amended the constitution to give the department this authority in 2003. Tex. Const. art. 16, § 50(t).
599 ACORN v. Fin. Comm'n of Texas, Clearinghouse No. 55,456B (Tex. Dist. Ct. Jan. 29, 2004).
600 12 U.S.C. § 1735f-5(b) (incorporated by DIDA § 501(a)(1)(C)).

brokerage business may not qualify. Such lenders are the most likely to fail to meet the broadly written requirements for qualifying lenders under DIDA § 501(a)(1).[608] Second, when a contract was originated by one seller or creditor, and then assigned to a second, the question may arise as to which must be the "qualifying lender" in order to assert preemption. It is most likely to arise when a home improvement contractor or small mortgage lender who is not a qualifying lender assigns the contract to a larger entity which would qualify and which then tries to assert preemption based on its own status. While there appear to be no cases on point to date addressing DIDA's section 501 preemption, the issue has been litigated in the context of other federal preemption provisions, and the rule is that the *originator* must qualify for the preemption.[609] There is no reason for DIDA first lien preemption to be treated any differently.[610]

3.9.3.4 Mobile Home Loans and Credit Sales

An extremely important qualification to the mobile home preemption in DIDA § 501(a)(1) is that this section only applies if the mobile home loan or credit sale complies with the OTS's consumer protection regulations.[611] These regulations govern the refund of precomputed finance charges; prepayment penalties; late charges; deferral fees; and the consumer's right to notice before repossession, foreclosure, or acceleration.[612]

---

608 *Cf.* Mitchell v. Trustees of United States Mut. Real Estate Inv. Trust, 375 N.W.2d 424 (Mich. Ct. App. 1985) (insufficient evidence that trust was "creditor").

609 Fed. Deposit Ins. Corp. v. Lattimore Land Corp., 656 F.2d 139 (5th Cir. 1981); Miller v. Pacific Shore Funding, 224 F. Supp. 2d 977 (D. Md. 2002), *aff'd on other grounds*, 92 Fed. Appx. 933, 2004 WL 144138 (4th Cir. 2004) (assignees stand in the shoes of the assignors and are subject to the same claims and defenses unless the holder-in-due-course defense applies); Fed. Nat'l Mortgage Ass'n v. Lefkowitz, 390 F. Supp. 1364 (S.D.N.Y. 1975) (where state law applies at loan origination, it continues to apply to the loan purchaser); *In re* Harrington, 6 B.R. 655 (Bankr. D.R.I. 1980) (assignment does not revive void note); Spitz v. Goldome Realty Credit Corp., 569 N.E.2d 43 (Ill. App. Ct. 1991), *aff'd*, 600 N.E.2d 1185 (Ill. 1992) (mortgage originated by lender which is a servicing corporation second-tier subsidiary of a federal savings bank was subject to state mortgage escrow account act; the preemption applicable to its parent did not extend to it); Viereck v. Peoples Sav. & Loan Ass'n, 343 N.W.2d 30 (Minn. 1984) (due-on-sale clauses contained in mortgage were not valid under applicable state law; as the originating lenders were not entitled to preemption, the federal savings association assignee was not entitled to preemption either); St. Paul Bank for Cooperatives v. Ohman, 402 N.W.2d 235 (Minn. Ct. App. 1987) (interest preemption in 12 U.S.C. § 2205 relating to loans from institutions of the Farm Credit System did not apply to an assigned contract); Garrison v. First Fed. Sav. & Loan Ass'n of S.C., 402 S.E.2d 25 (Va. 1991) (federal savings and loan as assignee of mortgage company originated loan not entitled to preemption even though loan was one of large pool sold to the savings and loan). *Cf.* Adkison v. First Plus Bank, 143 S.W.3d 29 (Mo. App. Ct. 2004) (the bank was the lender since it was listed on the documents; court implies disapproval of the claim that the table-funding "lender," technically the assignee, is the lender).

In the credit card context, a recent decision by the Eighth Circuit highlights a national bank's rights after it acquires credit card accounts and becomes the originator of credit. Krispin v. The May Dep't Stores Co., 218 F.3d 919 (8th Cir. 2000) (consumer opened a revolving credit card account with the store located in Missouri sometime before 1996; in 1996, the store sold all of its accounts to May National Bank, not chartered in Missouri; all new accounts were also opened directly in the bank's name; agreement between the store and the bank provided that the store purchase the bank's new accounts on a daily basis as the assignee; bank increased the late fees and the customers sued charging that Missouri law was violated by the store; court found that the bank, and not the store, issued credit to the customers and thus was entitled to preempt Missouri late fee limits; note that if customers still owed debt extended by the store before 1996, late fees imposed on that debt should be limited by Missouri law as the bank would not have originated that debt; central question was whether the case should be remanded to state court.

The court in *Marquette* emphasized that it was not considering a transaction in which it was alleged that a state lender was the actual extender of credit. Marquette Nat'l Bank of Minneapolis v. First of Omaha Serv. Corp., 439 U.S. 299, 307, 308, 311 n.24, 99 S. Ct. 540, 58 L. Ed. 2d 534 (1978). *Cf.* Grunbeck v. Dime Sav. Bank, 848 F. Supp. 294 (D.N.H. 1994) (issue not discussed, but the originator in that case would have been able to independently assert federal preemption of state law regarding method of computing interest under either DIDA § 501 or AMTPA), vacated and remanded on other grounds, 74 F.3d 331 (1st Cir. 1996) (DIDA does not preempt state simple interest statute; issue as to AMTPA's preemption apparently to be resolved on remand (lender made negatively amortizing mortgage loans); *see* §§ 3.9.3.3, 3.10, *infra*); Cohen v. Eisenberg, 697 N.Y.S.2d 625 (App. Div. 1999) (mortgage loan holder's motion for summary judgment denied where consumer alleged that originating lender (a lender entitled to preemption) was substituted at closing for the lender (not entitled to preemption) who provided the commitment letter; facts support allegation of intent to evade state usury laws). *But see* Saul v. Midlantic Nat'l Bank/South, 572 A.2d 650 (N.J. Super. Ct. App. Div. 1990) (court applied most favored lender doctrine of NBA to transaction in which an installment sale contract with a car dealer was assigned to a national bank). However, Saul does not discuss the distinction between a national bank's status as assignee and as originator, and the point was apparently not raised. As a result of that deficiency in its analysis, the case's precedential value should be viewed as questionable as support for an argument that a national bank is entitled to the NBA's preemption rights when it is an assignee. *See also* § 3.3, *supra*.

610 But note that, for mobile home sellers who "regularly" extend credit, the act of assigning its contracts to a qualifying creditor makes the mobile home seller a qualifying lender. 12 U.S.C. § 1735f-7a(a)(1)(c)(v).

611 DIDA § 501(c), 12 U.S.C. § 1735f-7a; *cf.* Livingston v. Vanguard Fed. Sav. Bank, 563 A.2d 175, 180 (Pa. Super. Ct. 1989) (court notes that mobile home lender's contract did not contain Federal Home Loan Bank Board's consumer safeguards, so regulations under DIDA were irrelevant to issue of whether Home Owner's Loan Act and regulations issued thereunder preempted state law prohibiting prepayment penalties on mobile home installment contracts).

612 DIDA §§ 501(c)(1)–(4); 12 C.F.R. § 590.4; *cf.* Burris v. First Fin. Corp., 928 F.2d 797 (8th Cir. 1991) (holding an "acquisi-

Unfortunately, one court has created a loophole to the consumer protection qualification through which a Mack truck could maneuver. In *Nelson v. River Valley Bank & Trust*, the bank financed the consumer's purchase of a mobile home, taking a security interest in the home *and* obtaining a first lien on the ground owned by the consumer.[613] Relying upon the regulation implementing DIDA,[614] the court determined that the bank was entitled to the "first lien" preemption without a showing of compliance with the consumer protection conditions. In its haste, the court failed to notice that the statute itself exhibits no ambiguity, even if the implementing regulation arguably does.[615] Congress unequivocally intended that section 501(a) does not apply at all if the conditions set forth in section 501(c) have not been met when a first lien on a residential manufactured home arises as a result of the transaction.[616]

Exactly what happens in the absence of creditor's compliance with the OTS regulations will depend on what law applies to that creditor in the absence of the section 501(a)(1) preemption. There are two possibilities: either the creditor will be saved by some other provision which preempts state usury law, or state usury law will apply.

The only mobile home creditors which are likely to escape state usury law after violating the OTS consumer protection regulations are federally-insured depository lenders, who apparently could claim the right to charge the federal alternate interest rate even if section 501(a)(1) of DIDA did not apply.[617] Depository lenders who had exceeded the alternate federal ceiling would be subject to federal usury penalties. However, the federal alternate ceiling will not shelter other lenders or credit sellers, such as finance companies or mobile home dealers.

Another possible escape route for mobile home creditors who have violated OTS regulations is the National Housing Act which preempts state regulations of interest rates charged on loans insured by either the Federal Housing Administration or the Veterans Administration.[618] The statutes authorizing FHA- or VA-insured loans constitute a separate source of usury preemption, independent of DIDA.[619] Yet the effect of this preemption is often limited. First, it obviously applies only to those loans that are insured by the FHA or VA. Second, states can easily opt out of the FHA and VA preemptions merely by amending, reenacting, or recodifying their usury statutes,[620] and creditors who disregard the OTS consumer protection regulations in reliance on the FHA/VA preemptions are consequently treading on thin ice.[621] Finally, the regulations addressing FHA- and

---

613   971 S.W.2d 777 (Ark. 1998).
614   12 C.F.R. § 590.3(a). The court pounced upon how the regulation is structured to find: "This regulation defeats the Nelsons' argument because it clearly provides that compliance with consumer safeguards is not required when the loan is secured by a first lien on residential real property. We also find persuasive the fact that section 501 of the Monetary Control Act and regulation 590.3 are written in the disjunctive, thereby indicating that Congress intended our state usury law to be preempted if any one of three situations exists." 971 S.W.2d at 780.
615   The court applied § 528 of DIDA (*see* Appx. G.1, *infra*) which allows the highest applicable interest rate to apply if one or more provisions of the statute apply to the same transaction. However, § 528 is not triggered where only one preemption section applies. In this case, only § 501 applies and subsection (c) trumps subsection (a). The court was wrong to throw § 528 into the mix.
616   Though the legislative history is scant, it shows that Congress created special treatment for loans involving manufactured homes.

> Manufactured home financing is covered by the mortgage usury preemption as long as such financing complies with consumer protection provisions specified in regulations of the FHLBB. The conferees intend that in developing these regulations the Bank Board should look for guidance to regulations, handbooks and circulars of the FHA and VA regarding mobile home lending, the provisions of the standard conventional mortgage forms of FHLMC and FNMA, and the provisions of the Uniform Consumer Credit Code. The conferees wish to emphasize that consumer protection provisions regarding manufactured home financing adopted in regulations of the Bank Board shall not preempt any state law which provides stronger protection to the consumer.

H. Conf. Rep. No. 96-842, *reprinted in* 1980 U.S.C.C.A.N. 236, 309. Indeed, the consumer protection condition to the manufactured housing preemption was intended as a floor. States could enact greater protections. *But see* Fed. Home Loan Bank Bd., General Counsel Letter No. 555, Clearinghouse No. 52,149

---

tion charge" not refunded upon prepayment is not a prepayment penalty within 12 C.F.R. § 590.4).

(July 28, 1981) (FHLBB opines that in certain limited circumstances, a loan secured by a combination lot and mobile home may be treated as a loan secured by residential real property for purposes of § 501(a); applicability of this letter should be limited to the particular question at issue, that is, Fannie Mae's plans to finance subdivisions in several states consisting of lots in which mobile homes are affixed; the letter includes four factors that must be met, none of which applied to the facts contained in the *Nelson* case).
617   *See* 12 U.S.C. §§ 85, 1463(g), 1785(g), 1831d; *cf. In re* Lawson Square, 816 F.2d 1236 (8th Cir. 1987) (discussing relationship between DIDA first mortgage and alternative ceiling provisions).
618   *See* 12 U.S.C. § 1703 (FHA loans); 38 U.S.C. § 3703 (VA loans).
619   *See* Burris v. First Fin. Corp., 928 F.2d 797 (8th Cir. 1991); Doyle v. S. Guar. Corp., 795 F.2d 907 (11th Cir. 1986).
620   *See* § 3.8.2, *infra*.
621   *See, e.g.*, Doyle v. S. Guar. Corp., 795 F.2d 907 (11th Cir. 1986) (Georgia opted out of the FHA/VA preemption by amending its statutes; DIDA did not apply because creditors had ignored consumer protection regulations; consequently state law controlled); S. Guar. Corp. v. Doyle, 353 S.E.2d 510 (Ga. 1987) (same case as above; question certified to state Supreme Court) (amendment of Georgia usury law was not retroactive and did not exempt creditors from state rate ceilings that they violated in reliance on federal preemption).

VA-insured loans contain no interest rate caps, though they do limit the amount of certain fees that can be charged.

If, as in most cases, no federal preemption other than section 501(a)(1) of DIDA applies to a mobile home transaction, and the creditor loses the protection of section 501(a)(1) by violating the OTS regulations, state usury law will apply to the transaction. The results will depend on what the relevant state's usury law says. If the state has a high interest ceiling, or none at all on mobile home loans, the creditor may be in compliance with the state usury law and may not be harmed by the loss of the section 501(a)(1) preemption. However, if the state has a low or moderate usury ceiling applicable to these transactions, the creditor who has relied on the DIDA preemption to charge a higher rate will have violated the state usury law and will be subject to applicable penalties.

Practitioners should scrutinize mobile home loans carefully for compliance with those regulations. For example, with limited exceptions, a creditor cannot attempt to repossess, foreclose, or accelerate the debt without a thirty-day notice of default and right to cure.[622] Courts have scrutinized four major mobile home financiers' form contracts for compliance, and minor differences in contract language have made major differences in consequences for the lender.

In *Quiller v. Barclay's American/Credit, Inc.*,[623] the Eleventh Circuit held that mobile home creditors violated that regulation by including in their standard financing contract a clause allowing acceleration of the debt and repossession, both without notice, upon the buyer's default, "subject to any notice to cure." As a result, the DIDA preemption of state usury law did not apply and the plaintiffs therefore stated a claim under state usury law, which the creditors had clearly violated in reliance on the DIDA preemptions.

By contrast, the same court in *Grant v. General Electric Credit Corp.*,[624] decided that slightly different language in a different standard financing contract did not so infringe the debtor's right to cure as to violate the FHLBB consumer protection regulations. The agreement in this case allowed the creditor to "declare immediately due and payable any and all installments . . . [minus the unearned finance charge] . . . provided that the buyer shall be given notice of right to cure default before seller is permitted to exercise that right." Because this language did not grant the creditor the right to accelerate, repossess, and demand payment *without notice*, the court found compliance with the FHLBB regulations and held that DIDA preemption applied to the disputed mobile home loans.

In two other mobile home cases, the Eleventh Circuit stretched to read vague or ambiguous contract terms in a manner which complied with FHLBB rules, thereby finding DIDA applicable. In *Moyer v. Citicorp Homeowners,*

Inc.,[625] the court found that a contractual provision that the creditor's rights were "Subject to Buyer's Right to Notice of Default and Right to Cure such default, if any" was sufficient. Similarly, the same court upheld another boilerplate contract against a usury challenge, despite the need to resort to some convoluted logic to do so. At issue in *Atkinson v. General Electric Credit Corp.*[626] was a provision requiring that notice of right to cure would be given "if required by applicable law." There was also a contract provision setting forth Georgia law, which does not require notice of right to cure, as the governing law. The court held that, because the "seller of the mobile home intended to charge an interest rate that would be permissible under DIDA," the intent of the governing law provision must have been to apply to contract matters not covered by DIDA.[627] Furthermore, because FHLBB regulations did not require that the contract specify the notice of right to cure precisely[628] and because federal law is a part of state law, no conflict with FHLBB rules existed and DIDA operated to validate the contracts.

However, if a practitioner sees a contract with language like that in *Moyer* or *Atkinson*, and the creditor has accelerated, repossessed, or taken collection action without having given the OTS-required notice,[629] those cases should not protect the creditor from a usury challenge. In those cases, the court was looking prospectively, giving the creditor the benefit of the doubt by presuming its intention was to comply with federal rules. If, however, a creditor in fact does not comply when the time for collection action comes, the creditor clearly was defining its rights under state law, and thus, like *Quiller* should not be entitled to DIDA preemption.

3.9.4 Opting Out of DIDA by State Legislation

3.9.4.1 General

As is discussed in § 3.9.1, *supra*, Congress, in enacting DIDA intruded cautiously into this area of traditional state concern. It tempered DIDA's interest cap preemption by giving states the right to "opt-out," and reassert primary

---

622 12 C.F.R. § 590.4.
623 764 F.2d 1400 (11th Cir. 1985), *reinstating* 727 F.2d 1067 (11th Cir. 1984).
624 764 F.2d 1404 (11th Cir. 1985).

625 799 F.2d 1445 (11th Cir. 1986). *See also* Chambliss v. Oakwood Acceptance Corp. (*In re* Chambliss), 315 B.R. 166 (Bankr. S.D. Ga. 2004).
626 866 F.2d 396 (11th Cir.).
627 *Id.* at 398. It is interesting that the court neither mentioned the principle of construing contract ambiguities against the drafter, nor, apparently, found the buyer's intent to be at all relevant, only the seller's.
628 *See* Burris v. First Fin. Corp., 928 F.2d 797 (8th Cir. 1991) (the contract is not required to recite the borrower's thirty-day notice of right to cure under DIDA or 12 C.F.R. § 590.4(h)).
629 Assuming that one of the exceptions under FHLBB/OTS regulations is not applicable, in other words, abandonment or "other extreme circumstances," 12 C.F.R. § 590.4(h).

control over credit charges.[630] As a result, not all the DIDA preemptions apply in all states. Specifically, Colorado, Georgia, Hawaii, Idaho, Iowa, Kansas, Maine, Massachusetts, Minnesota, Nebraska, Nevada, North Carolina, Puerto Rico, South Carolina, and South Dakota have expressly reimposed all or part of their state usury laws.[631] Even in these states, however, the DIDA preemptions apply to transactions which occurred after March 31, 1980, and prior to the effective date of the relevant state opt-out statute.[632]

The requirements for opting out of the DIDA preemptions vary with the individual preemptions, and some states have been selective in opting out, so it is important to be precise about which of DIDA's preemptions is at issue. The chart in § 3.2.5, *supra*, attempts to provide a guide to state opt-outs.

3.9.4.2 First Lien Preemption Opt-out: Interest Cap Versus Points and Fees Limitations

As if DIDA were not confusing enough, there are two separate components to the first lien opt-out right, one of which expired in 1983, the other of which is continuing. In order to opt out of the section 501 first mortgage *interest rate* preemption, a state must have passed legislation or held a referendum prior to April 1, 1983, which "explicitly and by its terms" rejected the preemption.[633] However, this three-year cut-off does *not* limit the states' abilities to reregulate the assessment of *points or "such other charges"* on first mortgage loans.[634] DIDA imposes no deadline for such action and, unlike the interest rate opt-out does not require an express rejection of this preemption. Arguably, *any* legislation enacted after March 31, 1980, which amends or institutes limitations on points or charges other than the stated interest rate, constitutes opt-out legislation. The debate in the courts, primarily raging in federal and state courts in Illinois, is whether a reenactment of a law containing a points-and-fees cap with little or no changes is sufficient to constitute an opt out or whether something more is necessary.[635]

630   *See* Depository Institutions Deregulation and Monetary Control Act of 1980, Pub. L. No. 96-221, tit. v, §§ 501(b)(2), 501(b)(4), 525, 94 Stat. 132.

631   Colo. Rev. Stat. §§ 5-13-101 to-103 (general override originally passed as regards DIDA §§ 501(a)(1), 511, 521, 522, 523, 524; override dropped as to 521, 522 and 523 effective July 1, 1994); Ga. Code Ann. § 7-4-20 (overriding DIDA §§ 501(a)(1), 511) (effective Mar. 31, 1983); Haw. Rev. Stat. § 478-9 (effective Sept. 2, 1981) (overriding DIDA §§ 501(a)(1), 511) (despite this preemption, Hawaii exempts first lien mortgages from state usury caps under another state law; *see* Haw. Rev. Stat. § 478-8); Idaho Code § 28-49-105 (1983) (Michie) (overriding DIDA § 501(a)(1)); Iowa Code § 537 preamble (1980 Iowa Acts 1156, § 32) (general override: overriding DIDA §§ 501(a)(1), 511, 521, 522, 523, 524); Kan. Stat. Ann. § 16-207a (overriding DIDA § 501(a)(1)); Me. Rev. Stat. Ann. tit. 9A, § 1-110 (West) (overriding DIDA §§ 501, 521, 523); 1995 Me. Laws 137, §§ 1, 3; 1995 Me. Legis. Serv. 221 (West) (amendment to repeal opt-out of § 521–523); Mass. Gen Laws ch. 183, § 63 note (1980 Mass. Acts 385, originally overriding DIDA §§ 501(a)(1), 511(a), 521, 522, 523; 1986 Mass. Acts 177, amendment repealed the override of §§ 521–523); Minn. Stat. § 47.203 (effective June 2, 1981) (overriding DIDA § 501(a)(1)); Neb. Rev. Stat. § 45-1.104 (effective Apr. 7, 1989) (overriding §§ 501(a)(1), 511 and 524, curtailed its § 525 override to allow the alternate rate ceiling to federally-related lenders); 1981 Nev. Stat. 668, § 11 (effective June 14, 1981) (overriding DIDA § 501(a)(1), and § 511 with respect to business or agricultural loans in amounts of $1000 or more); N.C. Gen. Stat. § 24-2.3 (overriding DIDA § 501, 521, 522, 523, 524); 1983 N.C. Sess. Laws 126, § 1; 1995 N.C. Sess. Laws 387 (amended to repeal opt-out of § 521-524 as to loans, mortgages, credit sales and advances made on or after July 1, 1995); 10 P.R. Laws Ann. § 988l (general override: overriding DIDA §§ 501(a)(1), 511, 521, 522, 523, 524); 1982 S.C. Acts 385, § 1 (overriding DIDA §§ 501(a)(1), 511, 512); S.D. Codified Laws § 54-3-15 (Michie) (overriding DIDA §§ 501(a)(1), 511, 524). Wisconsin originally opted out. *See* 1981 Wis. Laws 45, § 50 (overriding DIDA §§ 501(a)(1), 511, 521, 522, 523). However, in 1998, Wisconsin repealed its opt-out. 1997 Wis. Laws 142.

    See also Greenwood Trust Co. v. Massachusetts, 971 F.2d 818 (1st Cir. 1992) (discussing Massachusetts' change of mind on its opting back in to § 525); Flannick v. First Union Home Equity Bank, 134 F. Supp. 2d 389 (E.D. Pa. 2001) (court rejected argument that any interest restrictions in North Carolina law are trumped by DIDMCA as the loan was a first lien mortgage and North Carolina opted out of the interest rate and points restrictions).

632   *See* DIDA §§ 501(b)(2), 525.

633   *See* DIDA § 501(b)(2), 12 U.S.C. § 1735f-7a(b)(2); *see also* Brown v. Investors Mortgage Co., 121 F.3d 472 (9th Cir. 1997) (Washington's 1981 enactment of its general usury statute setting an annual interest rate ceiling at the higher of 12% or 4% above the yield on twenty-six-week T-bills did not constitute an interest rate opt-out because it did not so state explicitly); Veytia v. Seiter, 756 S.W.2d 303 (Tex. 1988).

634   *See* DIDA § 501(b)(4), 12 U.S.C. § 1735f-7a(b)(4).

635   To follow the debate in the Illinois courts, compare Reiser v. Residential Funding Corp., 380 F.3d 1027 (7th Cir. 2004) (affirming Currie v. Diamond Mortgage Corp., 859 F.2d 1538 (7th Cir. 1988) which held that § 4.1a of the Illinois Interest Act was preempted by DIDA) (*Editor's note*: The Illinois legislature reenacted § 4.1a in 1991, three years after *Currie* was decided); Reed v. Worldwide Fin. Servs., Inc., 1998 WL 852854 (N.D. Ill. Nov. 27, 1998) (1991 re-enactment of § 4.1 of Illinois Interest Act which repealed the entire statutory section with amended portions did not evidence an intent by Illinois to re-assert its usury limitations in points; DIDMCA does not wholly preempt § 4.1 as the points limitation continues in effect for other loans and this re-enactment is not superfluous); Currie v. Diamond Mortgage Co., 83 B.R. 536 (N.D. Ill. 1987) (apparently no requirement that re-regulation of points explicitly refer to DIDA; however no implicit opt-out of federal preemption on points found in Illinois), aff'd, 859 F.2d 1538 (7th Cir. 1988); Smith v. Elzey (*In re* Smith), 280 B.R. 436, 443 n.5 (Bankr. N.D. Ill. 2002) (Illinois has not exercised its right to invoke its own usury statute, even though it effectively amended portions of Section 4.1a in 1992) *with* U.S. Bank N.A. v. Clark, 807 N.E.2d 1109 (Ill. App. Ct. 2004) (even if § 4.1a was preempted when Congress passed DIDA, the Illinois legislature reenacted § 4.1a in 1991, effective in 1992, and the legislature is presumed to have been aware of the *Currie* decision and of DIDA; rejects

To determine whether a particular state has opted out from the points and fees preemption, the state's credit laws

---

contention that for legislation to constitute an opt out, it must be "new," either in the sense of being different from the state's prior law or in the sense of occupying a different or new section of a state constitution or statutory code). *Cf.* Fidelity Fin. Servs., Inc. v. Hicks, 574 N.E.2d 15 (Ill. App. Ct. 1991) (reviewing history of § 4.1a but ultimately deciding that the lender did not show that the loan fell within the scope of DIDA because the loan was not a purchase-money mortgage loan).

For cases outside of Illinois, see Autrey v. United Companies Lending Corp., 872 F. Supp. 925 (S.D. Ala. 1995) (Alabama passed a cap on points after March 31, 1980 which qualifies as an override of DIDA); Baughman v. Mellon Mortgage Co., 621 N.W.2d 776 (Minn. Ct. App. 2001) (re-enactment of a restriction on the charging of a fee for the administration of an escrow account and the addition of a clause prohibiting the charging of a fee for allowing the mortgagor to discontinue the escrow account in 1998 was not a "significant" change for purposes of qualifying for an opt-out of a state law DIDA-like preemption [*Editor's Note*: Minnesota opted out of DIDA but then enacted a state version of the DIDA rate, points, and fees preemption.]); Hibbitt v. First United Equities, Inc., 2002 WL 745570 (Ohio Ct. App. Apr. 25, 2002) (1988 amendment to state statute limiting discount points to two percent was not an opt-out because no changes were made to the discount provision, only minor changes were made to other provisions and, in 1999, the legislature explicitly stated that the discount cap was preempted by DIDA).

For federal and state agency opinions on this issue, see OTS General Counsel Letter, Clearinghouse No. 52,146 (Aug. 25, 1997) (re-enactment of certain provisions of Ohio law including a cap on discount points does not constitute an opt-out where amendments were only technical and there was no evidence of an intent to limit discount points); Fed. Home Loan Bank Bd., General Counsel Opinion Letter No. S51 (Oct. 27, 1981) (amendment to North Carolina statute did not constitute opt out of discount points preemption); Vermont Dep't of Banking, Ins., Securities, & Health Care Admin., Banking Bulletin No. 19, Clearinghouse No. 52,158 (July 23, 1997) (re-enactment of a section of Vermont law which referenced another section capping and limiting certain fees merely a "consolidation," not a re-enactment for DIDMCA purpose (despite the fact that the legislature made new significant changes to the "consolidated" law, for example, increasing the allowable term of first and second lien mortgage loans, allowing lenders to make variable rate or variable payment loans)); New Mexico Att'y Gen., DIDMCA Letter, Clearinghouse No. 52,510 (Aug. 13, 1999) (New Mexico Mortgage Loan Company and Loan Broker Act (MLC Act) limiting broker's fees passed in 1983 is not preempted by DIDA; another state law governing commissions on loans paid to non-registrants under MLC Act though enacted in 1980 was not preempted by DIDA because New Mexico adopted/readopted the limitations on commissions in 1984 when it amended the provision to exclude certain business, commercial, and agricultural loans and loans secured by registrants under the MLC Act); Wisconsin Dep't of Fin. Institutions, Opinion Letter, Clearinghouse No. 52,147 (Jan. 26, 1999) (Wisconsin enacted a law at the same time as its express interest cap override in 1981 that implicitly trumped DIDA's preemption relating to points; opting back in to DIDA in 1998 did not affect this implicit points cap; thus, the points cap of two percent remains in effect).

For cases and agency opinions interpreting opt outs in other federal statutes, compare Doyle v. S. Guar. Corp., 795 F.2d 907

---

must be reviewed to determine if there was a points-and-fees cap on the effective date of DIDA. If so, it is preempted unless the state re-enacted it[636] (or passed any other statute which includes a points-and-fees cap) at any time following the enactment of DIDA. If so, then the points and fees can be effectively limited in that state (barring the invocation of other types of federal preemption discussed in earlier sections of this Chapter).

3.9.4.3 DIDA'S Alternate Ceiling/Most Favored Lender Preemption Opt-Out

As with the first lien interest rate preemption, explicit legislative action is required for states to reject DIDA's alternate interest ceiling (and most favored lender) provisions for federally-insured depository lenders.[637] No deadline exists before which a state must exercise its right, under section 525, to opt-out of this portion of DIDA.[638] For states concerned about protecting their consumer protection policies against erosion by exportation from out-of-state state-chartered banks,[639] this may be one solution. (Well, eventually it may be a solution. But, for the nonce, it is working in the opposite direction, as industry in three states which had opted out succeeded in getting the opt-outs repealed since 1994.[640])

Some explanation is warranted of a brief reference in a recent intermediate appellate court decision to the "repeal" of the section 525 opt-out right.[641] Though a look at the current volumes of the U.S. Code is confusing, DIDA § 525 has not been repealed. As is discussed with reference to the federal rebate statute,[642] fitting free-standing congressional enactments into the structure of the U.S. Code is an administrative decision, with no legal significance. Section 525 of DIDA, containing the opt-out, was labeled the "effective date" section for DIDA §§ 521-523, which amended three different statutes. The Office of Law Revision Counsel determines placement for an effective date of an amendment affecting multiple statutes by setting it out as a subsidiary note to the first one affected. It then just places cross-references to that one in the notes to subsequently-numbered affected statutes. The first code section affected by DIDA

(11th Cir. 1986) (analogous language under FHA/VA preemption statutes) with Fed. Home Loan Bank Bd., General Counsel Opinion Letter No. S50 (June 18, 1981) (citing Green v. Decatur Fed. Sav. & Loan Ass'n, 143 Ga. App. 368, 238 S.E.2d 740 (1977) (mere recodification insufficient)).

636 *But see* discussion above on the issue of whether a mere "re-codification" constitutes an "enactment."

637 *See* DIDA § 525, *reprinted in* Appx. G.1, *infra.*

638 *Id.*

639 *See* § 3.9.2.2, *supra.*

640 Colorado (1994), Maine (1995), North Carolina (1995). *See* § 3.9.5.1, *supra.*

641 Stoorman v. Greenwood Trust Co., 888 P.2d 289 (Colo. Ct. App. 1994), *aff'd on other grounds*, 908 P.2d 133 (Colo. 1995).

642 *See* § 5.7.3, *infra.*

§ 525 was 12 U.S.C. § 1730g, amended by DIDA § 522.[643] As it happened, that was the section extending the alternate rate privileges to federally-insured savings and loans.

And then it came to pass that the savings and loan industry collapsed, jeopardizing the federal insurance fund for thrifts, FSLIC. As part of the savings and loan bail-out, there was a wholesale revamping of the federal insurance fund by the Financial Institutions Reform, Recovery and Enforcement Act of 1989 (FIRREA). The old code subchapter creating FSLIC, of which section 1730g was a part, was repealed.[644] The new thrift laws now appear elsewhere.[645]

FIRREA, however, *only* repealed "Title 4 of the National Housing Act (1724 *et seq.*)"; it did not repeal DIDA, or any part thereof.[646] That codifiers had set DIDA § 525 out in full text as a subsidiary note there, instead of to one of the other affected sections, has no legal significance. The full text of DIDA § 525 is now a subsidiary note to 12 U.S.C. § 1785 and is cross-referenced in 12 U.S.C. § 1831d.

There may be a question about whether the opt-out *as to savings and loans only* was lost, as the relevant preemption applied, by definition, to FSLIC-insured thrifts, which no longer exist. However, there is no such question about FDIC-insured state commercial banks or credit unions. The right to opt-out of preemption for those institutions remains open-ended.

3.10 The Alternative Mortgage Transactions Parity Act (AMTPA): Preemption of State Non-Rate Mortgage Credit Regulation

3.10.1 Scope of AMTPA's Preemption

A second wave of mortgage deregulation by federal preemption occurred in 1982. In addition to usury ceilings, states frequently had limited various structural contract terms that might deceptively escalate the cost of credit, or make it more difficult to repay. Perhaps most importantly, fixed rates were often required, so mortgage lenders were, for example, holding thirty year mortgages written at 7% when the prime was at 17%, squeezing their margin.[647] To avoid that, lenders

wanted variable rate contracts that would permit their long-term credit to rise (or fall) with the market, and thus shift the risk of market fluctuations to the borrower.[648] As it is common for homes to be sold during the term of the mortgage, lenders also wanted to limit the right of new buyers to assume the old, low-rate mortgage, and enforce "due on sale" clauses, which would enable the lender to write new loans at current rates. Other types of "creative financing" were envisioned to revitalize the mortgage market: balloon payments, graduated payments, and the like.

To that end, one of the most sweeping federal preemptions of state consumer credit laws became effective on October 15, 1982. This Act, the Depository Institutions Act (DIA) was also known as the "Garn/St. Germain Act," after its architects, the Senate and House Banking Committee Chairmen. DIA revised federal lending authority extensively, granting many new powers to federal lenders, especially the savings and loan associations. It provided special aid to ailing lenders, preempted state law concerning due on sale clauses,[649] and altered Truth in Lending as well as other matters not treated here.

The primary DIA consumer usury preemption is contained in the Alternative Mortgage Transactions Parity Act (AMTPA).[650] AMTPA was designed to extend certain federal mortgage regulations, which previously had covered only federally-chartered lenders, to state lenders, and, thereby, to eliminate the "discriminatory" advantage which these liberal regulations may have given the federal institutions.[651] Practitioners should note both the substance and scope of this statute.

---

643 DIDA § 523 amended 12 U.S.C. § 1785, and DIDA § 521 amended 12 U.S.C. § 1831d.

644 Subch. 4, 12 U.S.C. §§ 1724–1730i, repealed by FIRREA, Pub. L. No. 101-73, tit. IV, § 407, 103 Stat. 183 (1989).

645 12 U.S.C. § 1461 *et seq.*

646 Pub. L. No. 101-73, tit. IV, § 407, 103 Stat. 183 (1989).

647 Essentially, lenders want to avoid interest-rate risk defined as: "the danger that rates on short-term funds, which are what a bank normally buys, will rise to such a level that the bank's longer-term loans, written at the lower interest rates of an earlier time, will become unprofitable." Martin Mayer, *The Money*

Bazaars: Understanding the Banking Revolution Around Us, at 179 (Mentor Books 1985).

648 In 1982, the thought that mortgage rates would fall back down to seven percent seemed remote indeed. For those borrowers whose variable rate loans did not have a floor in the way, the risk paid off. One court described the conditions prevailing in the marketplace at the time AMTPA was enacted as: "Interest rate volatility had impaired the ability of housing creditors to provide consumers with fixed-term, fixed-rate credit secured by residential property." McCarthy v. Option One Mortgage Corp., 362 F.3d 1008, 1010 (7th Cir. 2004).

649 The preemption of state "due on sale" clause laws may have been redundant, at least insofar as the regulation of federal savings and loans is concerned. *See* Fidelity Fed. Sav. & Loan Ass'n v. de la Cuesta, 458 U.S. 141, 102 S. Ct. 3014, 73 L. Ed. 2d 664 (1982). For OTS regulations restricting the rights of lenders to impose prepayment penalties when due on sale clauses are enforced, see 12 C.F.R. § 591.5(b)(2). *See also* W. Life Ins. Co. v. McPherson K.M.P., 702 F. Supp. 836 (D. Kan. 1988) (Garn/St. Germain preempted due-on-sale restriction on private lenders); McCausland v. Bankers Life Ins. Co., 110 Wash. 2d 716, 757 P.2d 941 (1988) (Washington common law restriction on due-on-sale clauses preempted by Garn/St. Germain Act).

650 12 U.S.C. § 3800.

651 *See* 12 U.S.C. § 3801; *see also* OCC Unpublished Letter (Sept. 30, 1992) (Pennsylvania state banks are not subject to state restrictions regarding the maximum amounts and term, amortization formula, and contract provisions such as balloon and

First, AMTPA does not affect interest ceilings on mortgage loans. Instead, it addresses the *structure* of mortgage loans by overriding certain state laws which restrict "creative finance," e.g., laws limiting variable interest rates, final "balloon" payments, or negative amortization.[652] These state statutes are replaced, at the option of the state lender,[653] by federal regulations. Specifically, OCC regulations may be invoked by state commercial banks, NCUA regulations by state credit unions, and OTS (formerly FHLBB) regulations by all other "housing creditors," including state savings and loans and finance companies. However, the state lender must follow either the applicable state laws or federal regulations, and cannot select and combine the most advantageous terms of each.[654]

Second, AMTPA only applies to "alternative mortgage transactions" as defined in the statute:

—loans in which the finance charge or interest rate may be adjusted or renegotiated[655] (for example, adjustable rate mortgages or mortgages in which the rate decreases if the borrower pays on time);[656]
—loans with fixed rates but which implicitly permit rate adjustments by having the debt mature at the end of an interval shorter than the term of the amortization schedule[657] (for example, loans with balloon payments);[658]
—loans involving any similar type of rate, method of determining return, term, repayment, or other variation not common to traditional fixed-rate, fixed-term transactions[659] (for example, loans that negatively amortize or those involving shared equity or appreciation).[660]

Once the loan meets one of these definitions, then certain state laws may be preempted.[661]

Third, AMTPA applies not only to state depository institutions, but to all "housing creditors" making "alternative mortgage transactions."[662] Housing creditors are broadly defined to include any depository lender, HUD-approved lender, or any lender who "regularly makes" loans or credit sales secured by residential realty or mobile homes, and any transferee of these lenders. Alternative mortgages include senior or junior residential mortgages or credit sales which have variable interest rates or maturity or other non-traditional terms such as shared equity. The broad scope of AMTPA is significant because non-depository lenders such as finance companies or mobile home dealers have a history of abuse of credit terms and have, consequently, been closely regulated in many states. AMTPA gives these creditors much greater freedom. However, state housing creditors must comply with any applicable state licensing laws and "regulatory requirements and enforcement mechanisms provided by State law."[663]

---

demand features due to AMTPA). This letter is summarized in Appx. C.3, *infra*. The full text is reproduced on the CD-Rom accompanying this volume. However, as the OTS notes, the regulations adopted by federal agencies supervising national banks, credit unions, and savings associations are not consistent in the area of real estate lending. *See* 67 Fed. Reg. 60542, 60446 (Sept. 26, 2002); National Home Equity Mortgage Ass'n v. Office of Thrift Supervision, Civil Action No. 1:02cv02506 GK (D.D.C. filed Mar. 7, 2003) (OTS brief in support of its motion for summary judgment, reproduced on the CD-Rom accompanying this volume).

652 Though not explicitly listed in the statute, prepayment penalties were permitted under AMTPA by OTS regulation from 1996 until July 1, 2003. *See* § 3.10.2, *infra*.

Reverse mortgages probably fall within the scope of AMTPA's preemptive sweep. *See* First Gibraltar Bank, F.S.B. v. Morales, 19 F.3d 1032 (5th Cir. 1994); Black v. Fin. Freedom Senior Funding Corp., 112 Cal. Rptr. 2d 445 (Ct. App. 2001) (reverse mortgages meet the definition of an "alternative mortgage transaction"). The state law in question in *First Gibraltar* was Texas homestead law, which limits the right to take enforceable security interests to three circumstances. A housing creditor (Beneficial) and a federal savings bank urged that AMTPA and the Home Owners Loan Act (*see* § 3.3, *supra*), respectively, enabled them to write reverse mortgages despite Texas law, a position which the Fifth Circuit adopted. However, Congress quickly amended HOLA (and, by extension AMTPA) to provide that a homestead law like Texas' (which no other state has) is not preempted. Pub. L. No. 103-328, § 102(b)(5), 108 Stat. 2338 (1994); H.R. Conf. Rep. No. 103-651, at 57 (1994), *reprinted in* 1994 U.S.C.C.A.N. 2068. *See generally* § 3.9.3.2.2, *supra*. *First Gibraltar* is probably still good law, though, as far as classifying reverse mortgages as a creative financing technique within the reach of AMTPA. If a state law *other* than a homestead exemption law is what stands in the way, it may still be preempted.

653 *See* 12 U.S.C. § 3803.

654 *E.g.*, Cooluris, *Variable Rates in Closed End Credit*, *reprinted in* Practicing Law Inst., Consumer Credit 1983, at 764 (1983) ("an alternative mortgage transaction is deemed to be in accordance with the applicable federal regulations to the extent it complies totally with the applicable regulation"). The DIA § 804(b) right to correct nonconforming contracts in order to preserve preemption reinforces the notion that when the federal option is chosen it must be followed completely. *See also* Rudolph, Schmeltzer & Weiner, *Federal Legislation Affecting Mortgage Credit*, 38 Bus. Law. 1311, 1320 (1983). The suggestion that "[n]onfederally chartered housing creditors may be expected to use title VIII only

to the extent that the provisions in the federal regulations applicable to them would be more attractive than lending under state law," should not be misread: No authority is there cited for either combining state law and federal law in the same contract *or* as among different borrowers using the same form.

655 12 U.S.C. § 3802(1)(A).

656 See examples of what constitute "alternative mortgage transactions" in the Supplementary Information accompanying the revised OTS AMTPA rule. 67 Fed. Reg. 60542, 60549 (Sept. 26, 2002).

657 12 U.S.C. § 3802(1)(B).

658 67 Fed. Reg. 60542, 60549 (Sept. 26, 2002).

659 12 U.S.C. § 3802(1)(C).

660 67 Fed. Reg. 60542, 60549 (Sept. 26, 2002).

661 *See* § 3.10.2, *infra*.

662 *See* 12 U.S.C. § 3802.

663 *See* 12 U.S.C. § 3802(2). *See also* McCarthy v. Option One Mortgage Corp., 362 F.3d 1008 (7th Cir. 2004) (preemption is an affirmative defense and the proponent of preemption must show "substantial" compliance with the relevant OTS regulations).

Fourth, six states used their now-expired ability to "opt out" of AMTPA provisions. October 15, 1985 was the deadline.[664] Those states are free to impose restrictions on state housing creditors regardless of whether the mortgage loan is an "alternative mortgage transaction."

Fifth, there was sufficient abuse of the freedom granted by AMTPA[665] to impose sometimes devastatingly expensive creative financing terms that Congress revisited the matter a decade later, and itself imposed a limited degree of reregulation. Trying to narrowly target the reregulation to the segment of the market where the abuses occurred, some of these terms are prohibited or restricted in specified high-cost, closed-end home equity loans. The reregulation of creative financing terms by the Home Ownership and Equity Protection Act of 1994 (HOEPA) is briefly described in § 12.2.2, *infra*, and in detail in NCLC's *Truth in Lending* Chapter 9.[666] The Act applies to certain real-estate-secured loans consummated on or after October 1, 1995. If a loan is covered by HOEPA, it, not AMTPA, will be the controlling statute to the extent they conflict.[667]

States that wish to regulate abusive mortgages in a fashion similar to HOEPA may run into claims that AMTPA trumps state law prohibitions related to balloon payments, variable rate loans, negative amortization, or prepayment penalties. The lending industry has challenged these laws on a variety of theories, this being but one. A federal court in Illinois granted summary judgment to the state and dismissed such a challenge on the grounds that HOEPA is the statute against which preemption ought to be measured, not AMTPA.[668] However, the Seventh Circuit vacated and remanded this decision.[669] The appellate court held that HOEPA does not affect AMTPA's ability to preempt state law as a general matter. AMTPA's preemptive effect on state law is separate and distinct.[670]

Sixth, the abuse by predatory lenders, some of which are non-depository "housing creditors," led the Office of Thrift Supervision to *remove* prepayment penalties and late fees from the designated loan terms that state housing creditors may place in their loans notwithstanding state law.[671] The effective date of this change was July 1, 2003.[672] This surprising change is discussed in more detail in § 3.10.2, *infra*.

3.10.2 AMTPA's Regulatory Scheme

As noted in the preceding section, state lenders may comply with state law with respect to creative financing terms, but if they wish instead to avail themselves of AMTPA, they must comply with federal regulations. Hence it is necessary to discuss the federal regulatory scheme briefly.

Probably the most important to those representing low-income homeowners are the regulations issued by the Office of Thrift Supervision (OTS).[673] The broad category of "state housing creditors,"[674] other than state banks and credit unions, must comply with OTS regulations.[675] State banks

664 *See* 12 U.S.C. § 3804. Arizona, Maine, Massachusetts, New York, South Carolina, and Wisconsin have opted out of all or part of AMTPA: Ariz. Rev. Stat. § 33-1571 (opt out until October 14, 1987 with respect to preemption of due-on-sale prohibitions for real property loans made between July 8, 1971 and October 15, 1982, and which are secured by one to four family units on two and one-half acres or less); Me. Rev. Stat. Ann. tit. 9A, § 1-110 (West); 1985 Mass. Acts 224; N.Y. Banking Law § 6-g (McKinney) (did not opt out with respect to residential manufactured homes); 1984 S.C. Acts 355, § 1 (not codified); 1983 Wis. Laws 389, § 11(1) (nonstatutory). *See generally* 1 Consumer Cred. Guide (CCH) ¶ 510. A state's statutory attempt to prohibit prepayment loan terms which occurred after the opt-out deadline will be not survive a legal attack. *See* Nat'l Home Equity Mortgage Ass'n v. Face, 64 F. Supp. 2d 584 (E.D. Va. 1999), *aff'd*, 239 F.3d 633 (4th Cir.), *cert. denied* 534 U.S. 823 (2001).

     The potential to control terms which fall within the scope of the statute, such as interest rates on variable rate home equity loans, is very limited in those states which failed to exercise their right to opt-out, however. *See* Op. Tenn. Att'y Gen. No. 87-147, 5 Consumer Cred. Guide (CCH) ¶ 95,916 (Sept. 15, 1987) (as Tennessee did not opt out of AMTPA, state law attempting to regulate rates charges on mortgages subject to AMTPA would be preempted).

665 *See* Cathy Lesser Mansfield, *The Road to Subprime "HEL" Was Paved with Good Congressional Intentions: Usury Deregulation and the Subprime Home Equity Market*, 51 S.C. L. Rev. 473 (2000) (article discusses the rise of the predatory subprime mortgage market resulting from the freedom allowed by both AMTPA and DIDA's first lien preemption).

666 National Consumer Law Center, Truth in Lending Ch. 9 (5th ed. 2003 and Supp.).

667 *See* Williams v. Gelt Fin. Corp. (*In re Williams*), 232 B.R. 629 (Bankr. E.D. Pa.), *aff'd*, 237 B.R. 590 (E.D. Pa. 1999); Singer, Sutherland Statutory Construction § 51.05 (5th ed.) (where a general statute conflicts with a later, more specific statute, the latter is considered an exception to the former).

668 Ill. Ass'n of Mortgage Brokers v. Office of Banks & Real Estate, 174 F. Supp. 2d 815 (N.D. Ill. 2001).

669 Ill. Ass'n of Mortgage Brokers v. Office of Banks & Real Estate, 308 F.3d 762 (7th Cir. 2002).

670 *See also* Thompson v. WFS Fin., Inc., 2003 WL 22924458 (Cal. Super. Ct. Nov. 6, 2003) (Home Owners' Loan Act preemption trumps the ECOA's permission to states to enact more protective laws).

671 67 Fed. Reg. 60542 (Sept. 26, 2002).

672 67 Fed. Reg. 76304 (Dec. 12, 2002).

673 Prior to Aug. 1989, the Federal Home Loan Bank Board (FHLBB) was the regulating agency.

674 *See* § 3.9.1, *supra*.

675 *See* 12 C.F.R. § 560.220. [*Editor's Note*: From 1988 to 1996, that provision was found in 12 C.F.R. § 545.33(f). *See* 61 Fed. Reg. 50969 (Sept. 30, 1996). Prior to 1988, that provision was contained in an Appendix to § 545. *See* 53 Fed. Reg. 18265 (May 23, 1988).] Note that only the regulations specified in 12 C.F.R. § 560.220 preempt state law on behalf of state "housing creditors." The remainder of the regulations preempts state law for federally-chartered savings associations only. *See* § 3.5.3, *supra. See also* McCarthy v. Option One Mortgage Corp., 362 F.3d 1008 (7th Cir. 2004) (preemption is an affirmative defense and the proponent of preemption must show "substantial"

may comply with regulations promulgated by the Office of the Comptroller of the Currency (OCC).[676] State credit unions look to NCUA rules.[677]

Until July 1, 2003, the OTS regulations overrode state restrictions for AMTPA lenders in the areas of: amortization, including deferral and capitalization of interest;[678] late fees and prepayment penalties;[679] interest rate, payment,

balance, and term adjustments during the course of the loans;[680] and disclosures.[681] The OTS also issued an opinion letter finding that housing creditors may include a provision that raises the interest rate in the event of a default, finding that this type of loan constitutes an "alternative mortgage transaction."[682] Disclosure requirements for fixed rate mort-

---

compliance with the relevant OTS regulations; evidence of office procedures to ensure compliance with OTS regulations, a cover letter indicating that certain variable-rate disclosures were sent to the borrower, signed acknowledgment of receipt, and no evidence to the contrary was sufficient).

676 *See* 12 C.F.R. § 34, Subpart B (specifically § 34.24 concerning applicability to state banks); 61 Fed. Reg. 11300 (Mar. 20, 1996). Prior to October 1, 1988, this provision was found in 12 C.F.R. § 29. *See* 53 Fed. Reg. 7891 (Mar. 11, 1988).

677 *See* 12 C.F.R. § 701.21(a) (statement of scope and purpose).

678 67 Fed. Reg. 60542, 60549 (Sept. 26, 2002). This provision would include negatively amortizing loans and possibly reverse mortgages. *See* First Gibraltar Bank, F.S.B. v. Morales, 19 F.3d 1032 (5th Cir. 1994) (regarding reverse mortgages); Black v. Fin. Freedom Senior Funding Corp., 112 Cal. Rptr. 2d 445 (Ct. App. 2001) (reverse mortgages meet the definition of an "alternative mortgage transaction"). The state law in question in *First Gibraltar* was Texas homestead law, which limits the right to take enforceable security interests to three circumstances. A housing creditor (Beneficial) and a federal savings bank urged that AMTPA and the Home Owners Loan Act (*see* § 3.3, *supra*), respectively, enabled them to write reverse mortgages despite Texas law, a position which the Fifth Circuit adopted. However, Congress quickly amended HOLA (and, by extension AMTPA) to provide that a homestead law like Texas' (which no other state has) is not preempted. Pub. L. No. 103-328, § 102(b)(5), 108 Stat. 2338 (1994); H.R. Conf. Rep. No. 103-651, at 57 (1994), *reprinted in* 1994 U.S.C.C.A.N. 2068. *See generally* § 3.9.3.2.2, *supra*. *First Gibraltar* is probably still good law, though, as far as classifying reverse mortgages as a creative financing technique within the reach of AMTPA. If a state law *other* than a homestead exemption law is what stands in the way, it may still be preempted.

679 Though not explicitly listed in the statute, prepayment penalties were permitted under AMTPA by OTS regulation from 1996 until July 1, 2003. *See* Nat'l Home Equity Mortgage Ass'n v. Face, 239 F.3d 633 (4th Cir.), *cert. denied*, 534 U.S. 823 (2001); Davis v. GN Mortgage Corp., 244 F. Supp. 2d 950 (N.D. Ill. 2003); Shinn v. Encore Mortgage Servs., Inc., 96 F. Supp. 2d 419, 425, 426 (D.N.J. 2000); Glukowsky v. Equity One, Inc., 848 A.2d 747 (N.J. 2004) (OTS's 1996 regulation was a reasonable interpretation of AMTPA at the time), *cert. denied*, 125 S. Ct. 864 (2005). For loans made during that period, housing creditors, who are not federal banks or credit unions (which must comply with OCC or NCUA rules, respectively), could include prepayment penalty provisions only in transactions that first meet the definition of an "alternative" transaction as defined in the statute, that is, one in which the interest rate or finance charge may be adjusted; one involving a fixed-rate, but which contains a balloon payment; or one involving "any similar type of rate, method of determining return, term, repayment, or other variation not common to traditional fixed-rate, fixed-term transactions. . . ." 12 U.S.C. § 3802(1). If the transaction met this definition and contained a prepayment penalty, that provision applied regardless of conflicting state law. 12 C.F.R. §§ 560.34, 560.220. Whether the transaction is an "al-

ternative" mortgage in the first instance should be the first question. In other words, if the loan is a conventional, fixed-rate mortgage with a prepayment penalty, that transaction arguably is not an alternative mortgage transaction because the presence of a prepayment penalty alone should not confer this status. Prepayment penalties are "common to traditional fixed-rate, fixed-term" loans and do not meet the definition in § 3802(1). The OTS used this same analysis in the Supplementary Information accompanying the recent change to its AMTPA regulations effective July 1, 2003. 67 Fed. Reg. 60542, 60549 (Sept. 26, 2002). *See also* McCarthy v. Option One Mortgage Corp., 362 F.3d 1008 (7th Cir. 2004) (preemption is an affirmative defense and the proponent of preemption must show "substantial" compliance with the relevant OTS regulations; evidence of office procedures to ensure compliance with OTS regulations, a cover letter indicating that certain variable-rate disclosures were sent to the borrower, signed acknowledgment of receipt, and no evidence to the contrary was sufficient); Shinn v. Encore Mortgage Servs., Inc., 96 F. Supp. 2d 419, 425, 426 (D.N.J. 2000) (court found that the lender met the threshold for AMTPA preemption of state law, that is, it qualified as a "housing creditor" and the loan met the definition of an alternative mortgage transaction (it contained a variable rate)). *But see* Nat'l Home Equity Mortgage Ass'n v. Face, 239 F.3d 633 (4th Cir.), *cert. denied*, 534 U.S. 823 (2001) (court's decision is not clear on the point of whether a prepayment penalty transforms an otherwise traditional loan into an alternative mortgage transaction; court relied on a 1982 regulation in support of its ultimate decision to uphold the OTS's 1996 regulation; however, that regulation permitted prepayment penalties in loans that otherwise met the definition of an "alternative mortgage transaction," in other words, the interest rate must remain fixed for at least five years after any initial rate adjustment); Op. Md. Att'y Gen No. 97-018, 1997 Md. AG LEXIS 22 (Aug. 19, 1997) (AMTPA preempts Maryland's restrictions on prepayment penalties; no indication that the opinion is limited to those transactions that qualify as alternative mortgage transactions).

There is an argument, not addressed by any of the courts upholding the 1996 OTS regulation, that DIDA expressly authorizes states to adopt laws limiting or prohibiting such charges as prepayment penalties and AMTPA did not override DIDA in this respect. It goes like this: DIDA authorized states to adopt laws limiting discount points and other charges on federally-related mortgage loans. 12 U.S.C. § 1735f-7a(b)(4). Congress made it clear that this section was designed to allow states to enforce limitations on prepayment charges, attorney fees, late charges, and the like. S. Rep. No. 96-368, *reprinted in* 1980 U.S.C.C.A.N. 236, 255. This expression of congressional intent is embodied in an OTS regulation, 12 C.F.R. § 590.3(c). AMTPA itself is silent on the issue of prepayment penalties and, consequently, could not have repealed the section of DIDA that gave states the green light to regulate.

680 12 C.F.R. § 560.35.

681 12 C.F.R. § 560.210, *as amended by* 63 Fed. Reg. 38463 (July 17, 1998).

682 OTS Chief Counsel Letter (Nov. 11, 1996). *See* summary of OTS letters in Appx. H.3, *infra*. The full text is reproduced on

gages were removed during a massive revision of OTS regulations in 1996.[683] Disclosure requirements for adjustable rate mortgages now track the Truth in Lending requirements.[684]

Significantly, for mortgage loans made on or after July 1, 2003, the OTS removed the prepayment penalty and late fee regulations from those that state housing creditors may use to trump state laws.[685] In other words, as of that date, any state law limiting prepayment penalties or late fees[686] will apply to new loans made by state housing creditors.[687] After July 1, 2003, state housing creditors may elect to preempt only state laws that cover adjustable rate mortgages.[688] Many states regulate late fees and a significant number prohibit or restrict prepayment penalties.[689] These laws will have a new life as of July 1, 2003.[690] This change is important because it revives state power to address the abusive nature of prepayment penalties in predatory mortgage loans.[691] One trade association sued the OTS, arguing that the agency exceeded its authority by limiting the scope of the statute through the rule-making process.[692] The federal district court rejected this claim and upheld the regulation.[693] Subsequently, the court of appeals affirmed this decision.[694]

The issue of whether the OTS regulation in effect from 1996 to 2003 was valid has been the subject of litigation. At this point in time, however, all of the courts to address this issue have upheld the regulation.[695]

Given the specificity in the OTS regulations as to the limited nature of state housing creditor preemption rights, a claim that AMTPA preempts all state laws applicable to a home transaction if the loan qualifies as an "alternative mortgage transaction" should fail. For example, state restrictions on the amount of attorney fees that the holder can collect in the event of default should not be preempted.[696] Claims of misleading or deceptive advertising and practices in the sale of reverse mortgages are not preempted.[697]

---

the CD-Rom accompanying this volume. However, the OTS did not list default interest rates in its definitions of alternative mortgage transactions in the Supplementary Information accompanying its recent AMTPA rule changes. 67 Fed. Reg. 60542, 60549 (Sept. 26, 2002). The validity of this older OTS letter is unclear.

683 *Compare* 12 C.F.R. § 560.210 *with* former 12 C.F.R. § 563.99(a)(2). *See also* 61 Fed. Reg. 50970 (Sept. 30, 1996).

684 12 C.F.R. § 560.210 (1996), *as amended by* 63 Fed. Reg. 38463 (July 17, 1998); *see also* 82 Op. Md. Att'y Gen. No. 97-018, 1997 Md. AG LEXIS 22 (Aug. 19, 1997) (various provisions of Maryland's usury laws regarding prepayment penalties were pre-empted for "housing creditors" as long as the extension of credit was made in accordance with AMTPA and the applicable federal regulations).

685 For the regulatory history of this revision, *see* 65 Fed. Reg. 17811 (Apr. 5, 2000) (request for input); 67 Fed. Reg. 20468 (Apr. 25, 2002) (proposed regulation); 67 Fed. Reg. 60542 (Sept. 26, 2002) (final regulation); and 67 Fed. Reg. 76304 (Dec. 12, 2002) (extension of effective date). Extensive discussion accompanied the proposals and final rule.

686 For manufactured housing loans, the federal regulation sets a floor. The grace period must be at least fifteen days and the fee cannot exceed five percent of the unpaid amount of the installment. 12 C.F.R. § 590.4.

687 12 C.F.R. § 560.220; 67 Fed. Reg. 60542 (Sept. 26, 2002).

688 12 C.F.R. §§ 560.35, 560.210, 560.220.

689 Regarding state laws that restrict or prohibit prepayment penalties in mortgage transactions, see, e.g., Ala. Code § 5-19-4; Alaska Stat. § 45.45.010 (Michie); Conn. Gen. Stat. §§ 36a-265(c), 519; D.C. Code Ann. § 28-3301; 815 Ill. Comp. Stat. § 205/4; Ind. Code § 28-1-13-7.1; Miss. Code Ann. §§ 75-17-31, 89-1-317; Mo. Rev. Stat. § 408.036; Neb. Rev. Stat. § 8-330; N.J. Stat. Ann. § 46:10B-2 (West); N.M. Stat. Ann. § 56-8-30 (Michie); N.C. Gen. Stat. § 24-1.1A(b); 41 Pa. Cons. Stat. § 405; R.I. Gen Laws § 34-23-5; Tex. Fin. Code Ann. § 302.102 (Vernon); Va. Code Ann. § 6.1-330.83 (Michie); W. Va. Code § 47-6-5b. This is not an exhaustive list so state law should be consulted.

690 67 Fed. Reg. 60542, 60548 (Sept. 26, 2002).

691 According to a report issued by the North Carolina Coalition for Responsible Lending, prepayment penalties are included in two percent of prime loans, yet they appear in about seventy percent of subprime loans. *See* North Carolina Coalition for Responsible Lending, Prevalence of Prepayment Penalties, *available at* www.responsiblelending.org/PL%20-%20Coalition%20Studies.htm. For a critique of prepayment penalties in the subprime market, see Eric Stein, *Quantifying the Economic Cost of Predatory Lending*, Center for Responsible Lending (July 25, 2001), *available at* http://responsiblelending.org/pdfs/Quant10-01.PDF. Finally, research shows that subprime refinance mortgage loans with prepayment penalties are more likely to experience a foreclosure than loans without these penalty clauses—by about 20 percent. Roberto G. Quercia, Michael A. Stegman, Walter R. Davis, *The Impact of Predatory Loan Terms on Subprime Foreclosures: The Special Case of Prepayment Penalties and Balloon Payments* (Kenan-Flagler Business School, UNC Jan. 2005), *available at* www.kenan-flagler.unc.edu/assets/documents/foreclosurepaper.pdf.

692 Nat'l Home Equity Mortgage Ass'n v. OTS, Clearinghouse No. 54,585 (D.D.C. filed Dec. 20, 2002) (complaint).

693 Nat'l Home Equity Mortgage Ass'n v. OTS, 271 F. Supp. 2d 264 (D.D.C. 2003). The OTS brief in support of its motion for summary judgment articulates the basis for its 1996 rule and the reasons for the shift in its position regarding prepayment penalties and late fees. The brief is reproduced on the CD-Rom accompanying this volume. In its brief, the OTS discredits a 1996 opinion letter that dealt with prepayment penalties under Wisconsin law. *See* Office of Thrift Supervision, Opinion Letter (Apr. 30, 1996) (reproduced on the CD-Rom accompanying this volume).

694 Nat'l Home Equity Mortgage Ass'n v. OTS, 373 F.3d 1355 (D.C. Cir. 2004).

695 Nat'l Home Equity Mortgage Ass'n v. Face, 239 F.3d 633 (4th Cir.), *cert. denied*, 534 U.S. 823 (2001); Davis v. GN Mortgage Corp., 244 F. Supp. 2d 950 (N.D. Ill. 2003); Shinn v. Encore Mortgage Servs., Inc., 96 F. Supp. 2d 419 (D.N.J. 2000); Glukowsky v. Equity One, Inc., 848 A.2d 747 (N.J. 2004) (OTS's 1996 regulation was a reasonable interpretation of AMTPA at the time), *cert. denied*, 125 S. Ct. 864 (2005).

696 *In re* Jones, 2000 Bankr. LEXIS 1741 (Bankr. E.D.N.C. Dec. 22, 2000). *Cf.* Arnold v. First Greenboro Home Equity, Inc., 327 F. Supp. 2d 1022 (E.D. Mo. 2004) (removal case). The issue of complete preemption for removal purposes is addressed in § 3.15, *infra*.

697 Black v. Fin. Freedom Senior Funding Corp., 112 Cal. Rptr. 2d 445 (Ct. App. 2001). *Cf.* Ansley v. Ameriquest Mortgage Co.,

Further, the OTS crafted its regulation to allow housing creditors who are not commercial banks, credit unions, or federal savings associations to follow certain of its regulations to preempt state law and no others.[698] The OTS regulations that provide much broader preemption apply only to federal savings associations.[699]

The OCC regulations that apply to AMTPA lenders[700] cover "adjustable-rate mortgages"[701] and address indexing,[702] and the availability of prepayment fees.[703] Rate caps were removed during the 1996 revision process.[704] Finally, notices and explanations of rate changes are required for transactions subject to Truth in Lending in accordance with the provisions of Regulation Z.[705] Generally, a borrower must receive notice of a rate change at least twenty-five days before payment at the new rate is due.[706]

The NCUA regulations specifically preempt state regulation of variable interest rates, late fees, closing and other charges, the manner of repayment (including balloon payments), the purpose of the loan, loan-to-value ratios, and due-on-demand clauses.[707] Significantly, state requirements for notice to the borrower of a change in interest rates have also been preempted.[708] However, the NCUA regulations expressly refrain from preempting other state laws including insurance laws, collection costs and attorney fees, state contractual "plain language" requirements, and state laws regarding security interests, default, and cure of default.[709]

With the exception of a provision guaranteeing borrowers the right to make early payments on a loan without penalty,[710] the NCUA regulations contain few substantive consumer protections. Disclosure requirements are absent, though the reason for this omission is probably the regulations' stated intention not to preempt state law "affecting aspects of credit transactions that are primarily regulated by federal law other than the Federal Credit Union Act."[711] Thus, both federal credit unions and state credit unions making alternative mortgages are subject to state law concerning credit cost disclosures, unfair credit practices, etc., if they are not otherwise preempted by federal law.[712]

3.11 Gramm-Leach-Bliley Act and Interstate Loan Pricing

In 1999, Congress enacted the Gramm-Leach-Bliley Act which largely focuses upon eliminating the barriers separating the banking, insurance, and securities industries.[713] The Act set off a wave of mergers in the financial services industry, reshaping the marketplace in ways that cannot yet be foreseen.

One provision, though, should have a profound effect on the ability of a limited number of states (perhaps only one)

---

340 F.3d 858 (9th Cir. 2003) (issue was whether removal to federal court was proper; court said no because AMTPA does not preempt all state laws, citing *Black*); Arnold v. First Greensboro Home Equity, Inc., 327 F. Supp. 2d 1022 (E.D. Mo. 2004) (removal case). The issue of complete preemption for removal purposes is addressed in § 3.15, *infra.*

698 12 C.F.R. § 560.220 specifically lists the applicable OTS regulations which deal with late charges (12 C.F.R. § 560.33), prepayments until July 1, 2003 (12 C.F.R.§ 560.34), adjustments to home loans (12 C.F.R. § 560.35), and disclosures for variable rate mortgages (12 C.F.R. § 560.210). *See* Black v. Fin. Freedom Senior Funding Corp., 112 Cal. Rptr. 2d 445 (Ct. App. 2001) (court discusses the fact that 12 C.F.R. § 560.220 lists just four regulatory provisions that apply to housing creditors; however, court decided the issue on broader grounds, namely, that the preemption language in AMTPA does not contain a clear manifestation of congressional intent to preempt all state laws concerning the terms and marketing of alternative mortgage transactions).

699 *See, e.g.,* 12 C.F.R. § 560.2. The OTS recently confirmed that the broad preemption available to federal thrifts under its supervision does not apply to state housing creditors who invoke AMTPA. 67 Fed. Reg. 60542, 60544, 60548 (Sept. 26, 2002); *see also* U.S. Bank N.A. v. Clark, 807 N.E.2d 1109 (Ill. App. Ct. 2004); § 3.5, *supra.*

700 *See* 12 C.F.R. § 34.1 *et seq.*

701 *See* 12 C.F.R. § 34.20.

702 12 C.F.R. § 34.22. Note that the index must be beyond the control of the lender.

703 12 C.F.R. § 34.23 (prepayment penalties permitted only in variable rate mortgages under certain circumstances). *See* OCC Interpretive Letter No. 744, discussed in § 3.4.5.2, *supra,* which finds that national banks chartered in a state permitting prepayment penalties can export prepayment penalty provisions to other states as "interest," thus avoiding the limitations in 12 C.F.R. § 34.23.

704 Prior to 1996, rate caps existed in former 12 C.F.R. § 34.8.

705 A specific reference to the applicability of the Truth in Lending Act to disclosures of ARM loan terms was deleted, however, during the 1996 revisions. *Compare* former 12 C.F.R. § 34.10 *with* 12 C.F.R. §§ 34.20–34.25. Despite this deletion, the TILA disclosure rules apply and are spelled out at Regulation Z, 12 C.F.R. § 226.20(c). *See generally* National Consumer Law Center, Truth in Lending § 4.8.2.2.5 (5th ed. 2003 and Supp.).

706 *See* 12 C.F.R. § 226.20(c).

707 12 C.F.R. §§ 701.21(b), 701.21(c)(7), 701.21(g)(6).

708 12 C.F.R. § 701.21(b)(1)(i)(A)(3).

709 12 C.F.R. § 701.21(b)(2).

710 *See* 12 C.F.R. § 701.21(c)(6).

711 *See* 12 C.F.R. § 701.21(b)(3).

712 *See* 12 C.F.R. § 701.21(b)(3). The absence of special NCUA disclosure regulations for variable rate transactions suggests that credit unions must follow normal TILA variable rate disclosures. The failure of banks or savings and loans to comply with relevant OCC or OTS ARM disclosures also invokes TILA coverage. *Cf.* 12 C.F.R. § 226.19 n.45a. As a result of the efforts of the interagency Federal Financial Institutions Examination Council (FFIEC), there is now, to a great degree, uniformity in the ARM disclosure requirements. *See* 53 Fed. Reg. 7885 (Mar. 11, 1988) (OCC implements FFIEC recommendations by deferring to TIL disclosure requirements where applicable); 53 Fed. Reg. 18265 (May 23, 1988) (FHLBB adopts FFIEC recommendations, enacting ARM disclosures similar to the Federal Reserve Board's Regulation Z requirements).

713 Pub. L. No. 106-102, 113 Stat. 1338 (1999) (codified at 15 U.S.C. §§ 6701 *et seq.,* 6801 *et seq.,* 6901 *et seq.,* and amending 12 U.S.C. § 1831u).

to regulate the interest rates of the banks chartered within their boundaries in certain circumstances.[714] This subsection contains two important limitations. First, the provision, by its terms, applies only to states with a constitutional provision limiting the maximum lawful annual percentage rate of interest on a contract at not more than 5% above the discount rate for 90-day commercial paper in effect at the federal reserve bank for the federal reserve district in which such state is located.[715] This may limit the effect of this provision to only one state, Arkansas.[716] Second, the subsection does not affect the interest that any insured depository institution may charge or receive under the Depository Institutions Deregulation and Monetary Control Act,[717] the National Bank Act,[718] or the Federal Deposit Insurance Act.[719]

If this part of the Act applies, a bank with FDIC insurance chartered in such a state may charge and collect interest, discount points, finance charges, or other similar charges as permitted by the home state of an out-of-state bank with a branch in that state or the maximum rate or amount of interest, discount points, finance charges, or other similar charges allowed in a similar transaction allowed a state insured depository institution chartered in that state (the state with the constitutional limitation) or a national bank or federal savings association whose main office is located in such state. The provision was designed to provide for loan pricing parity among interstate and local banks. Essentially, if an interstate bank can charge a particular interest rate, then a local bank in the state into which the interstate bank has branched, may charge a rate comparable to that which the home state of the interstate bank allows.[720]

A court applied this provision of the Gramm-Leach-Bliley Act to hold that a Texas consumer who received a credit card from an Arkansas-chartered bank could not complain of usury under Arkansas law.[721] Because a branch of an Alabama-chartered bank existed in Arkansas, the Arkansas bank need not comply with the Arkansas usury cap because Alabama law permitted the parties to contract for any interest rate.

3.12 Preemptive Effect of Federal Consumer Protection Statutes

Though this chapter has concentrated on those federal preemption statutes that override state limitations of credit cost terms, there are some federal consumer protection statutes that may preempt inconsistent or less protective state laws. Two of those, the federal rebate statute and the Home Ownership and Equity Protection Act (HOEPA), are discussed elsewhere in this book.[722]

Truth in Lending, a federal disclosure statute, preempts inconsistent state laws. Except to the extent it is amended by HOEPA, Truth in Lending neither regulates credit charges nor preempts state laws which do.[723] Its preemption is narrow, and relates largely to the definition of consumer credit terms. TILA requires extensive disclosures in consumer credit transactions, and its goal of standardized terms to use for comparison shopping requires uniform definitions. Thus TILA regulations[724] promulgated by the Federal Reserve Board define numerous credit terms, such as "finance charge" or "annual percentage rate," which must be disclosed to consumers. In the event that a state usury law defines these terms differently or requires the use of a different term, that state law may be preempted.[725] TIL preemption is discussed in more detail in NCLC's *Truth in Lending*.[726]

3.13 Faux Bank Preemption: "Rent-a-Charter" Arrangements

3.13.1 General

A recent and disturbing trend in the payday loan industry has drawn the ire of state and federal regulators and consumers. Payday lenders have courted both national and state-chartered banks to act as conduits for loans in a blatant attempt to avoid the application of state usury caps through the exportation doctrine.[727] As discussed in § 3.4.5, *supra*, this doctrine permits a bank chartered in a deregulated state

---

714 Section 731 (amending 12 U.S.C. § 1831u(f)).
715 Section 731 (amending 12 U.S.C. § 1831u(f)).
716 *See* Johnson v. Bank of Bentonville, 122 F. Supp. 2d 994 (W.D. Ark. 2000), *aff'd*, 269 F.3d 894 (8th Cir. 2001) (court indicates that Arkansas is the only state which has such a constitutional provision). [*Editor's Note*: The editors have not conducted independent research to verify this claim; practitioners should check their state law to determine the existence of such a provision.]
717 12 U.S.C. § 1831u(f)(2). No effect on 12 U.S.C. § 1735f-7a.
718 12 U.S.C. § 1831u(f)(2). No effect on 12 U.S.C. § 85.
719 12 U.S.C. § 1831u(f)(2). No effect on 12 U.S.C. § 1831d.
720 H.R. Rep. No. 106-434, at 184 (1999), *reprinted in* 1999 U.S.C.C.A.N. 245, 277; Johnson v. Bank of Bentonville, 122 F. Supp. 2d 994, 999 (W.D. Ark. 2000), *aff'd*, 269 F.3d 894 (8th Cir. 2001) (Congress has the power under the Commerce Clause to enact this preemption provision; bank chartered in Arkansas permitted to charge interest in excess of the constitutional cap).
721 Jessup v. Pulaski Bank, 327 F.3d 682 (8th Cir. 2003).

722 *See* §§ 5.9, 12.2.2, *infra*.
723 15 U.S.C. § 1601 *et seq. See generally* National Consumer Law Center, Truth in Lending (5th ed. 2003 and Supp.).
724 *See* 12 C.F.R. § 226.
725 *See* 12 C.F.R. § 226.28.
726 National Consumer Law Center, Truth in Lending § 2.6.3 (5th ed. 2003 and Supp.).
727 Indeed, this partnership scheme is the industry's action plan to avoid regulatory restrictions. *See* Stephens, Inc., Payday Advance—The Final Innings: Standardizing the Approach (2000); *see also* Elizabeth R. Schiltz, The Amazing, Elastic, Ever-Expanding Exportation Doctrine and Its Effects on Predatory Lending Regulations, 88 Minn. L. Rev. 518, 581–583, 621, 622 (2004) (discussing renting charters and concluding that applying the exportation doctrine to non-bank lenders is not justified under principles of banking law).

to ignore the usury laws in the borrower's home state, undermining that state's ability to enforce its usury laws. In the payday lending context, this means that payday lenders can partner with banks, make loans for the bank at its local storefront, buy back the loan, and claim that the borrower's home state usury laws do not apply.

The relationships between banks and check cashers, payday offices, and other storefronts can take several forms. For example, the bank originates or underwrites the loan and may or may not directly approve the extension of credit to the customer. The storefront often processes the loan by gathering relevant consumer information, transmitting the information to the bank, approving credit in some instances, servicing the loan, and collecting payments for the bank. Typically, the bank immediately sells the loans back to the payday lender and retains a small "participation" share. The payday lender may fully indemnify the bank from any legal liability.[728]

These types of arrangements can be very lucrative for the payday lenders because they allow these lenders (unless challenged) to enter markets that are otherwise forbidden to them. For example, one payday lender partners with four different banks to do business in five states.[729] This lender also maintains payday storefronts in twenty-eight other states. The revenues from just these five states accounted for about 30% of all revenues in 2003 and account for 27.5% of all revenues generated in 2004 as of June 30. Of a total of 2,208 stores nationwide, the payday company's bank model occurred in 521 of these stores, approximately 23% of the total. A disproportionate share of this payday lender's revenue stream comes from the bank model.

3.13.2 Private Litigation and State Enforcement

Consumers are challenging these partnerships, arguing that the payday lender is renting the bank charter. The first such lawsuit was filed against Dollar Financial Group, Inc., one of the largest check cashing companies, and Eagle National Bank of Pennsylvania in federal court in Los Angeles.[730] The case, in essence, alleged that the bank had "rented" its charter to allow the check casher to circumvent otherwise applicable state law restrictions. The parties settled this matter, leaving no precedent to guide other practitioners.

A second case filed in Florida state court alleged that Ace and Goleta National Bank of California entered into a master agreement in which Ace Cash Express offered Goleta loans through its retail site.[731] Ace purchased from Goleta all of the bank loans made on the previous day. Ace admitted that the loan purchases entitled it to substantially all of the interest and all of the risk of nonpayment. Consumers accessed the loan proceeds through the use of debit cards that bore the Ace or "Advance Cash Express" name. Ace indemnified Goleta for any risk it incurred, except in limited circumstances. The pleading concluded that the real purpose of the agreement between Goleta and Ace was to allow Ace to evade Florida usury laws by allowing Ace to utilize Goleta's name and national banking standing. The complaint sought damages for usury violations and under the state's unfair and deceptive trade practices act. The case was removed to federal court. But that court remanded the matter back to state court on the grounds that the National Bank Act does not apply to non-banks such as Ace and that the borrower's claims were not preempted by that Act.[732] This case later settled.

Meanwhile, consumers in Maryland, Texas, and Indiana filed class action suits in both federal and state courts attacking this particular brand of partnership between Goleta National Bank and Ace Cash Express.[733] The two cases filed in federal court, both of which named the national bank, were dismissed.[734] The *Purdie* suit was subsequently rein-

---

728 *See* descriptions of these arrangements and their variations in the following court decisions: BankWest Inc. v. Banker, 324 F. Supp. 2d 1333 (N.D. Ga. 2004); Flowers v. EZPawn Oklahoma, Inc., 307 F. Supp. 2d 1191 (N.D. Okla. 2004); BankWest Inc. v. Oxendine, 598 S.E.2d 343 (Ga. Ct. App. 2004).

729 The information in this paragraph is derived from Advance America, Cash Advance Centers, Inc.: Form S-1 SEC Registration Statement of 8/13/04, *available at* www.sec.gov/Archives/edgar/data/1299704/000104746904026511/a2141558zs-1.htm.

730 Phanco v. Dollar Fin. Group, Clearinghouse No. 53,034 (C.D. Cal. filed Feb. 8, 1999) (complaint).

731 Long v. Ace Cash Express, Clearinghouse No. 53,504A (Fla. Cir. Ct. undated) (complaint).

732 Long v. Ace Cash Express, Inc., Clearinghouse No. 53,504B (M.D. Fla. June 18, 2001) (order).

733 *See* Johnson v. Ace Cash Express, Inc., Clearinghouse No. 53,544 (D. Md. undated) (nationwide class) (case voluntarily dismissed); Purdie v. Ace Cash Express, Inc., Clearinghouse No. 53,545 (N.D. Tex. undated) (nationwide class); Brown v. Ace Cash Express, Inc., Clearinghouse No. 53,546 (Md. Cir. Ct. undated) (statewide class). The case filed in Indiana has been dismissed. *See also* Hudson v. Ace Cash Express, Inc., 2002 WL 1205060 (S.D. Ind. May 30, 2002), *amended complaint dismissed by* 2002 WL 31255461 (S.D. Ind. Sept. 27, 2002).

The complaint in Brown v. Ace Cash Express, Inc. appears in Appx. L.4.2, *infra*. Ace removed the case to federal court but the court remanded. Brown v. Ace Cash Express, Inc., Clearinghouse No. 53,546A (D. Md. Dec. 14, 2001) (mem.) (court held that Ace is not a national bank and none was named in the lawsuit; involvement by a national bank in these transactions is alleged to be nominal and pretextual; possibility that a claim could someday be asserted against Goleta does not provide original or removal jurisdiction).

734 Purdie v. Ace Cash Express, Inc., 2002 WL 31730967 (N.D. Tex. Oct. 29, 2002) (case was filed under the federal RICO statute; court held that the plaintiff failed to adequately plead an association in fact under strict Fifth Circuit RICO standards), *vacated*, 2003 WL 21447854 (N.D. Tex. June 13, 2003) (vacated upon plaintiff's motion in light of class action settlement); Hudson v. Ace Cash Express, Inc., 2002 WL 1205060 (S.D. Ind.

stated and then settled.[735] Of the two cases, the one relevant to this discussion is *Hudson v. Ace Cash Express, Inc.* There, the court refused to look behind the loan documents listing the bank as the lender at the motion to dismiss stage. Further, the complaint failed to allege that the lender was Ace, not the bank, a fact of importance to the court.[736]

Three states, Colorado, Ohio, and North Carolina, filed enforcement actions in state courts against Ace Cash Express, arguing that Ace, not Goleta, was the true lender. In the Colorado case, the complaint alleged that Ace violated Colorado's usury laws and committed unfair and deceptive acts.[737] Ace removed the case to federal court, arguing that Colorado's claims are completely preempted by the National Bank Act. The attorney general filed a motion to remand.[738] The federal court subsequently remanded the case to state court, following the example of the court in *Long v. Ace Cash Express*.[739] Subsequently, the Colorado Attorney General announced a settlement.[740]

In Ohio, Goleta, not a party to the state's case, filed an affirmative suit in federal court in an apparent preemptive strike, arguing that the state threatens to impair the bank's federal right to make loans to Ohio residents.[741] The Superintendent of Financial Institutions sought dismissal and the court agreed, holding that Goleta lacked standing as it will incur no direct injury due to the enforcement action filed against its non-bank partner.[742] Interestingly, attorney generals from seventeen other states filed an *amicus curiae* brief in support of the motion to dismiss.[743]

Following the lead of Colorado and Ohio, North Carolina's Attorney General filed a complaint against Ace contesting the rent-a-charter arrangement, seeking to stop its practice of making loans above the state's 36% interest rate.[744] Consistent with its actions in Ohio, Goleta Bank, though not named in the state enforcement action, filed an action in federal court seeking to enjoin the state action. The court abstained and held that the National Bank Act does not apply to non-bank entities.[745] Further, the court found that state laws regarding brokering apply to Ace even if Goleta was making the loans. In addition, Goleta had no standing to challenge the state action against Ace. The case subsequently settled.[746]

Finally, the Attorney General of Florida moved to intervene in two private cases filed after the *Long* case. After a court dismissed one of the cases and the private plaintiff's claims were dismissed in the other, the Attorney General settled with Ace. Ace agreed to apply for and the state agreed to grant it a license to make payday loans (called deferred presentment transactions in Florida) and agreed to

---

May 30, 2002), *amended complaint dismissed*, 2002 WL 31255461 (S.D. Ind. Sept. 27, 2002).

735 Purdie v. Ace Cash Express, Inc., 2003 WL 21447854 (N.D. Tex. June 13, 2003) (dismissal vacated), 2003 WL 22976611 (N.D. Tex. Dec. 11, 2003) (settlement approved).

736 Furthermore, the *Hudson* court relied upon the Eighth Circuit decision in Krispin v. May Dep't Stores Co., 218 F.3d 919 (8th Cir. 2000) for the proposition that one should look to the originating entity to decide whether the National Bank Act applies). The Eighth Circuit decided *Krispin* in the context of removal to federal court and held cursorily that the NBA completely preempts state law usury claims, a position that has been criticized. *See* § 3.15, *infra*. The *Krispin* court did not address a rent-a-charter situation. Finally, in that case the bank was a wholly-owned subsidiary of the named defendant, unlike the relationship between Ace and Goleta. *But see* Terry v. Cmty. Bank of N. Va., 255 F. Supp. 2d 817 (W.D. Tenn. 2003) (plaintiff sufficiently alleged that the state-chartered bank did not fund the loan to survive dismissal; if the plaintiff succeeds at trial, then the bank will not be protected by preemption under DIDA).

737 State *ex rel.* Salazar v. Ace Cash Express, Inc., Clearinghouse No. 53,537A (Colo. Dist. Ct. filed July 16, 2001).

738 State *ex rel.* Salazar v. Ace Cash Express, Inc., Clearinghouse No. 53,537A (Colo. Dist. Ct. filed July 16, 2001) (plaintiff's motion to remand).

739 State *ex rel.* Salazar v. Ace Cash Express, Inc., 188 F. Supp. 2d 1282 (D. Colo. 2002); *see also* Carson v. H & R Block, Inc., 250 F. Supp. 2d 669 (S.D. Miss. 2003) (plaintiffs were charged substantially more interest for tax refund loans than represented and disclosed; removal not proper when case was filed against only the tax preparation service).

740 The press release describing the settlement was located at www.ago.state.co.us/PRESREL/presrl2002/prsrl40.stm as of March 2004. Under the terms of the settlement: Ace Cash Express will pay $1.3 million in refunds of excess finance charges to consumers who renewed their loans more than once since July 1, 2000 or obtained loans from Ace regardless of whether or not renewed between January 1, 2001 and November 20, 2001, the dates Ace was not licensed in Colorado to make loans. Several thousand consumers are expected to receive refund checks; Ace was to become licensed as a supervised lender effective November 20, 2001 (Ace had filed applications for license during the pendency of the lawsuit and those appli-

cations were complete on Nov. 20, 2001); Ace terminated its relationship with Goleta National Bank effective July 1, 2002, and will immediately comply fully with Colorado's consumer credit and payday lending laws.

741 Goleta Nat'l Bank v. O'Donnell, Clearinghouse No. 53,550A (S.D. Ohio undated) (complaint), Clearinghouse No. 53,550B (S.D. Ohio Oct. 2001) (memorandum in support of motion for preliminary injunction), Clearinghouse No. 53,550C (S.D. Ohio Nov. 23, 2001) (defendant's answer to motion for preliminary injunction), Clearinghouse No. 53,550D (S.D. Ohio Nov. 23, 2001) (defendant's motion to dismiss).

742 Goleta Nat'l Bank v. O'Donnell, 239 F. Supp. 2d 745 (S.D. Ohio 2002).

743 This brief appears on the CD-Rom accompanying this volume.

744 State *ex rel.* Cooper v. Ace Cash Express, Inc., Clearinghouse No. 53,559 (N.C. Super. Ct. Jan. 2002) (complaint).

745 Goleta Nat'l Bank v. Lingerfelt, 211 F. Supp. 2d 711 (E.D.N.C. 2002). Ace also removed the state action to federal court but the judge remanded on the grounds that the state's claims against Ace are not completely preempted by the National Bank Act. State *ex rel.* Cooper v. Ace Cash Express, Inc., Clearinghouse No. 53,559B (E.D.N.C. May 14, 2002).

746 Ace agreed to refrain from conducting any payday loan business in North Carolina for one year either as the lender or as an agent for others unless the terms of the loans complied with North Carolina law. Ace agreed to drop its appeal in the Lingerfelt case. North Carolina *ex rel.* Cooper v. Ace Cash Express, Inc., Clearinghouse No. 53,559 (N.C. Super. Ct. Dec. 13, 2002) (consent judgment).

cancel all payday loans delinquent as of October 1, 2002 which remained unpaid as of December 30, 2002 and to notify credit bureaus that the debt were cancelled.[747]

In other developments, Advance America/Cash Advance Centers, Inc.'s[748] arrangement with BankWest, a state-chartered bank, is the focus of scrutiny by at least two state agencies. In Georgia, the Industrial Loan Commissioner served subpoenas upon Advance America on the grounds that payday loans were being made out of their offices under the name of BankWest, Inc. BankWest and its non-bank partners filed an action in state court attempting to stop the investigation. Recently, the Georgia court dismissed on the ground the commissioner has the authority to investigate the true nature of the relationship between the bank and non-bank entities to determine if state law as it may apply to the non-bank companies is being violated.[749] The Georgia Court of Appeals affirmed.[750]

To curb the sham rent-a-charter arrangements from circumventing its state law, the Georgia Legislature enacted a new chapter that presumes that an agent for an exempt entity, including a depository institution, is the actual lender and is subject to the Act if, under the totality of the circumstances, the agent holds, acquires, or maintains a predominant economic interest in the revenue generated by the loan.[751]

Before the effective date of the Georgia statute, Advance America and several other payday lenders and their state-chartered bank partners sued to enjoin the statute on a variety of grounds, one being federal bank preemption.[752] The district court refused to issue a preliminary injunction. Regarding preemption, the court held that the state law does not conflict with the Federal Deposit Insurance Act and is not preempted. The court found that the state law does not prohibit out-of-state banks from using agents, there was no evidence to show that banks could not operate profitably under the state law restraints on agents, and that federal banking regulators have recognized "that non-bank entities which partner with banks in an effort to avoid state usury laws are not entitled to the protection of the federal banking laws."[753]

In 2004, North Carolina's Department of Commerce and the Attorney General of North Carolina announced investigations into the agreements between Advance America, Cash Advance Centers, Inc. and its bank partners.[754] In addition, at least three private class action lawsuits were filed in 2004 against several payday lenders doing business in North Carolina through state-chartered banks.[755] In a case filed against EZPawn Oklahoma Inc. alleging usury violations, the federal district court remanded the case to state court because the defendant presented no proof to contradict the plaintiff's allegations that EZPawn was the true lender, not County Bank of Rehobeth Beach.[756]

Finally, the Attorney General of New York is challenging the rent-a-bank relationship between County Bank of Rehobeth Beach, DE and CRA Services, doing business as Cashnet and TC Services, doing business as Telecash.[757] Private attorneys filed a class action in state court in New Jersey alleging a variety of state law claims based on this same arrangement.[758]

---

747 *In re* Ace Cash Express, Inc., Clearinghouse No. 54,583 (Fla. Dep't of Banking & Fin. Dec. 30, 2002) (final administrative order). This settlement document provides the history of two private cases in which the attorney general moved to intervene.

748 Advance America and Cash Advance Centers, Inc. are one company. *See* http://www.sec.gov/Archives/edgar/data/1299704/000104746904026511/a2141558zs-1.htm.

749 BankWest, Inc. v. Oxendine, Clearinghouse No. 54,584 (Ga. Super. Ct. Feb. 19, 2003) (final order and judgment), aff'd, 598 S.E.2d 343 (Ga. Ct. App. 2004). In the course of reaching its decision, the trial court said that the record showed genuine issues of material fact as to whether Advance America is the de facto lender given that it holds the preponderant economic interest in those loans, pays the majority of the operating costs, uses "Tele-Track" to make underwriting decisions whether or not banks are involved, and makes loans directly in states that permit payday lending.

750 BankWest, Inc. v. Oxendine, 598 S.E.2d 343 (Ga. Ct. App. 2004) (the court upheld the authority of the commissioner to continue his investigation to determine if Advance America's activities fall within his regulatory authority, affirming a substance over form approach to analyzing these relationships). *Cf.* USA Payday Cash Advance Centers v. Oxendine, 585 S.E.2d 924 (Ga. App. Ct. 2003) (at issue was the commissioner's efforts to investigate the relationship between certain payday lenders and County Bank but the court held that the payday lenders failed to exhaust their administrative remedies).

751 Ga. Code Ann. §§ 16-17-2(b)(4), 16-17-6.

752 BankWest, Inc. v. Baker, 324 F. Supp. 2d 1333 (N.D. Ga. 2004), *appeal pending.*

753 *Id.* at 1348.

754 *AG Cooper launches investigation of state's largest payday lender* (Aug. 26, 2004), *available at* www.ncdoj.com/DocumentStreamerClient?directory=PressReleases/&file=Advance%20America.pdf.

755 For a copy of the complaint in one of these cases, Kucan v. Advance America, Cash Advance Centers of N.C., Inc., see Appx. L.4.2, *infra.*

756 Flowers v. EZPawn Okla., Inc., Clearinghouse No. 55,462 (N.D. Okla. Nov. 25, 2003) (mag.), *aff'd*, 307 F. Supp. 2d 1191 (N.D. Okla. 2004).

757 New York *ex rel.* Spitzer v. County Bank of Rehobeth Beach DE, Case No. 1:03-CV-1320 (N.D.N.Y. May 25, 2004) (remand decision), available on the CD-Rom accompanying this volume. For a press release about this decision, go to www.oag.state.ny.us/press/2004/may/may28a_04.html. For a copy of the complaint, go to www.oag.state.ny.us/press/2003/sep/payday_verified_complaint.pdf.

758 Muhammad v. County Bank of Rehobeth Beach, No. __ (N.J.

3.13.3 The OCC, OTS, and FDIC Enter the Fray

In 2000, both the Office of the Comptroller of the Currency and the Office of Thrift Supervision issued letters warning national banks and thrifts of the potential credit, transaction, reputation, compliance, and legal risks involved with payday lending.[759] While the OCC did not prohibit or limit national banks from entering into these partnerships, it created a set of guidelines that discourage rollovers and list certain disclosures that banks "should" make.

One of the most important statements of the OCC in its advisory letter is the following:

> Multiple renewals—particularly renewals without reduction in the principal balance, and renewals in which interest and fees are added to the principal balance, are an indication that a loan has been made without a reasonable expectation of repayment at maturity.[760]

This statement can be used to support an unfair and deceptive practices or unconscionability claim by arguing that the lender knew the consumer did not have the ability to repay at the time of each rollover.

Failure to follow these guidelines will be the subject of "careful" examination and follow-up by the agency. Whether these letters would have any long-term affect on the use of these partnerships was unclear until the OCC announced a consent order signed by Eagle National Bank on December 18, 2001.[761] In a press release, the OCC indicated that Eagle was in material noncompliance with an earlier memorandum of understanding and engaged in a number of unsafe and unsound activities in its payday lending arrangements with Dollar Financial Group. Eagle had "rented out its national bank charter to a payday lender in order to facilitate that non-bank entity's evasion of the requirements of state law that would otherwise be applicable to it."[762] Eagle agreed to cease its payday lending business by June 2002.

The OCC continued its tough stance on banks and their partners regarding payday lending during 2002. The OCC terminated the partnership between Goleta National Bank and Ace Cash Express, Inc., the subject of the numerous lawsuits and state enforcement actions discussed above. These entities agreed to cease all payday lending by December 31, 2002, though servicing and collecting on outstanding loans can continue. Ace agreed to be 100% responsible for outstanding loans and to pay a $250,000 civil penalty. Ace cannot partner with any other national banks without the permission of the OCC. Goleta consented to a $75,000 civil penalty.[763]

The OCC also shut down the smaller scale payday lending arrangements between Advance America and Cash Advance Centers and Peoples National Bank of Paris, Texas as well as the partnership between Cash America and First National Bank in Brookings, South Dakota.[764] As a result, no national bank is renting its charter as of late spring 2005 when this volume went to press.

Arguably, the OCC's preemption regulation issued in 2004 prevents national banks from engaging in payday lending directly. There, the OCC stated: "A national bank shall not make a consumer loan . . . based predominantly on the bank's realization of the foreclosure or liquidation value of the borrower's collateral, without regard to the borrower's ability to repay the loan according to its terms."[765] Assuming the holding of the check rises to the level of "collateral"

Super. Ct. filed 2004), available on the CD-Rom accompanying this volume.

759 *See* OCC Advisory Letter No. AL 2000-10 (Nov. 27, 2000), *available at* www.occ.treas.gov/advlst00.htm; OTS Letter (Nov. 27, 2000), *available at* www.ots.treas.gov/docs/2/25132.pdf. *See also* Office of Thrift Supervision, Letter P-2000-4 (Feb. 3, 2000) (OTS will conduct examinations of the thrift's partner in payday lending to the same extent as it will of the thrift). In addition, the Chair of the Federal Deposit Insurance Corporation (FDIC), the federal bank insurance agency, indicated in a speech that Congress did not contemplate that banks would use the exportation principle to take advantage of consumers and described the practice as, at the very least, inappropriate and "unbecoming." Remarks of Donna Tanoue, Chair, Fed. Deposit Ins. Corp. (June 13, 2000), *available at* www.fdic.gov/news/news/speeches/archives/2000/sp13june00.html.

The OCC reiterated many of its concerns in a bulletin issued in 2001. *See* OCC Bulletin No. 2001-47, *available at* www.occ.treas.gov (click on "issuances" and then "bulletins").

760 OCC Advisory Letter No. AL 2000-10 (Nov. 27, 2000), *available at* www.occ.treas.gov/advlst00.htm.

761 *See In re* Eagle Nat'l Bank, OCC No. 2001-104 (Dec. 18, 2001), *available at* www.occ.treas.gov/ftp/eas/ea2001-104.pdf. For an article discussing the Eagle Bank partnership written before the action taken by the OCC, see John Hackett, *Ethically Tainted*, The Am. Banker, Nov. 1, 2001, at 48.

762 OCC News Release 2002-01 (Jan. 3, 2002), *available at* www.occ.treas.gov (click on "issuances" and then on "new releases").

763 *In re* Goleta Nat'l Bank, EA No. 2002-93 (Oct. 25, 2002) (consent order), *available at* www.occ.treas.gov/ftp/eas/ea2002-93.pdf; *In re* Ace Cash Express, Inc., EA No. 2002-92 (Oct. 25, 2002), *available at* www.occ.treas.gov/ftp/eas/ea2002-92.pdf.

764 *In re* Advance Am., EA No. 2003-3 (Jan. 29, 2003) (consent order), *available at* www.occ.treas.gov/ftp/eas/ea2003-3.pdf; *In re* Peoples Nat'l Bank, EA No. 2003-2 (Jan. 29, 2003), *available at* www.occ.treas.gov/ftp/eas/ea2003-2.pdf; *In re* First Nat'l Bank in Brookings, EA No. 2003-1 (Jan. 17, 2003), *available at* www.occ.treas.gov/ftp/eas/ea2003-1.pdf. Peoples National Bank challenged the OCC's unsatisfactory examination rating based upon the bank's payday lending activities, seeking injunctive and declaratory relief. Peoples Nat'l Bank v. Office of the Comptroller of the Currency, 227 F. Supp. 2d 645 (E.D. Tex. 2002) (suit dismissed for lack of jurisdiction), *aff'd*, 362 F.3d 333 (5th Cir. 2004). Following the trial court's decision, Peoples Bank agreed to stop this type of lending.

765 12 C.F.R. § 7.4008(b). *See* § 3.4.6.2, *supra*.

under state law,[766] payday lending does not involve a real assessment of ability to repay or debt-to-income ratios.

The OTS was not nearly as busy as the OCC because federal saving associations have not partnered with payday lenders to date, except in two instances. Both of those arrangements have ended.[767]

In another significant move, the Office of the Comptroller of the Currency (OCC) filed an *amicus* brief in the Colorado case, *State ex rel. Salazar v. Ace Cash Express, Inc.*, in support of Colorado's motion to remand, discussed in § 3.13.1.2, *supra*. The OCC wrote:

> The standard for finding complete preemption is not met in this case. While the Defendant's Notice of Removal repeatedly refers to Goleta National Bank using Ace Cash Express, Inc. ("ACE") as its agent to solicit loans (see para. 7, 8, 16, and 17), ACE is the only defendant in this action, and ACE is not a national bank. Nor do the Plaintiffs' claims against ACE arise under the National Bank Act, or other federal law. Although Defendant apparently attempts to appropriate attributes of the legal status of a national bank for its own operations as a defense to certain of Plaintiffs' claims, such a hypothetical conflict between federal and state law does not give this court federal question jurisdiction under the doctrine of complete preemption.[768]

Finally (for now), certain state-chartered depositories come under the jurisdiction of the Federal Deposit Insurance Corp. (FDIC), if they are FDIC-insured banks. The FDIC issued Guidelines for Payday Lending in July 2003.[769] The guidelines emphasize safety and soundness concerns, limit the volume of payday loans to less than 25% of the bank's Tier 1 capital, and call for up to 100% capitalization of loans outstanding.[770] Examiners are to look at certain characteristics of their third-party lender programs but the FDIC did not create any firm prohibitions.[771] While the guidelines indicate that borrowers who request an extension, deferral, renewal, or rewrite should exhibit a renewed "willingness and ability to repay," they do not require banks to check credit history or debt-to-income ratios. Further, the guidelines only state that banks "should" limit the number and frequency of extensions, deferrals, renewals, or rewrites.[772]

Unfortunately, the FDIC guidelines have not prevented state-chartered insured banks from partnering with payday lenders. As of 2004, ten such banks partner with several national payday lending companies to make loans in states with firm usury caps.[773]

In February 2005, the FDIC released "Guidelines for Payday Lending" to supplement and clarify the 2003 guide-

---

767 Jean Ann Fox, Consumer Federation of America, *Unsafe and Unsound: Payday Lenders Hide Behind FDIC Bank Charters to Peddle Usury* 18, 19 (Mar. 2004), *available at* www.consumerfed.org (click on "payday loans" under "Finance").

768 State *ex rel.* Salazar v. Ace Cash Express, Clearinghouse No. 53,556 (D. Colo. Jan. 25, 2002) (order). In a speech given on February 12, 2002, Comptroller Hawke had the following to say about rent-a-bank concerns:

> Let me raise one other caution about preemption. The benefit that national banks enjoy by reason of this important constitutional doctrine cannot be treated as a piece of disposable property that a bank may rent out to a third party that is not a national bank. Preemption is not like excess space in a bank-owned office building. It is an inalienable right of the bank itself.
>
> We have recently seen several instances in which non-bank lenders who would otherwise have been fully subject to various state regulatory laws have sought to rent out the preemption privileges of a national bank to evade such laws. Indeed, the payday lending industry has expressly promoted such a "national bank strategy" as a way of evading state and local laws. Typically, these arrangements are originated by the payday lender, which attempts to clothe itself with the status of an "agent" of the national bank. Yet the

> predominant economic interest in the typical arrangement belongs to the payday lender, not the bank.
>
> Not only do these arrangements constitute an abuse of the national charter, they are highly conducive to the creation of safety and soundness problems at the bank, which may not have the capacity to manage effectively a multi-state loan origination operation that is in reality the business of the payday lender. As you probably saw, we recently took supervisory action against a small national bank that dramatically demonstrated its inability to manage such a relationship in a safe and sound manner.

This speech is *available at* www.occ.treas.gov/ftp/release/2002-10a.doc. *See also* Pearl Chin, *Payday Loans: The Case for Federal Legislation*, 2004 U. Ill. L. Rev. 723 (2004) (discussing why economic theory supports credit rationing and arguing in favor of closing the rent-a-charter loophole through federal legislation).

769 This document is *available at* www.fdic.gov/regulations/safety/payday/index.html.

770 However, banks that sell 85% to 95% of their loans or participation interests to their local storefront partners have little to capitalize.

771 *See* Jean Ann Fox, Consumer Federation of America, *Unsafe and Unsound: Payday Lenders Hide Behind FDIC Bank Charters to Peddle Usury* 18–19 (Mar. 2004), *available at* www.consumerfed.org (click on "payday loans" under "Finance").

772 FDIC Guidelines for Payday Lending 5 (2003), *available at* www.fdic.gov/regulations/safety/payday/index.html.

773 Jean Ann Fox, Consumer Federation of America, *Unsafe and Unsound: Payday Lenders Hide Behind FDIC Bank Charters to Peddle Usury* 13–15 (Mar. 2004), *available at* www.consumerfed.org (click on "payday loans" under "Finance").

lines.[774] The major differences between the two documents relate to when the guidelines apply and to concerns about ability to repay. First, the FDIC states that the 2005 guidelines apply regardless of whether a bank's payday lending program meets the credit exposure threshold (set at equal to or greater than 25% or more of tier 1 capital in the 2003 document).

Second, the banks should ensure that borrowers who request an extension, deferral, renewal, or rewrite exhibit an ability to repay. For the FDIC, this exhortation translates into a bright-line rule that the bank offer the customer or refer the customer to an alternative longer-term credit product when the customer has used payday loans for more than three months in the past twelve months. This means that the customer can have six two-week loans in the past year before the bank has to refuse to renew or provide another payday loan. For example, if the loan costs $17 per $100, a customer will have paid more than she borrowed and still owe the principal ($17 × 6 = $102). Whether this rule will cut into bank and partner profits enough to force the banks out of the business is unclear. Of course, banks could raise the loan fees and demand a greater share of the profits from their payday partner to cover any shortfall.

Unfortunately, the FDIC did not require its banks to determine ability to repay before making loans to consumers. Nor did it address the concern that renting a charter is an abuse of bank privileges which helps non-bank payday lenders evade state usury laws and consumer protections. Arguably, however, FDIC-insured state-chartered banks are prohibited from engaging in payday lending since national banks may not make loans based on the value of the collateral without to the borrower's ability to repay.[775]

But, interestingly, the FDIC did recognize that the non-bank firms associated with state banks *are* subject to state regulation.[776] And the FDIC instructed its examiners to look at the "economic substance" of a transaction to determine the number of rollovers that have occurred.[777]

Prior to the release of the 2004 amended FDIC Guidelines and smarting from the aggressive stance of the OCC and OTS, payday lenders simply switched their affiliations to state-chartered FDIC-insured banks. The federal usury preemption arises for these banks under the Depository Insti-

tutions Deregulation and Monetary Control Act.[778] Suits challenging these arrangements have begun.[779]

3.14 Usury Deregulation by State "Parity" Laws

3.14.1 "Parity" Statutes Described

In the early 1980s, many states enacted "parity" statutes as amendments to their special usury statutes. Presently, nearly every state has enacted some form of parity provision.[780] Such laws may effectively operate to put a state bank on parity with its federal counterpart in its home state.[781]

On their face, parity statutes provide in simple terms that one type of state creditor, such as a state savings and loan, may extend consumer credit under the same rate ceiling or under the same terms and conditions as another type of creditor, such as a federal savings association or national bank. However, the effects of such laws may be extremely complex, leading to legal arguments that the "parity" deregulation extends to transactions and creditors in ways that were unlikely to have been foreseen by the legislature enacting the parity laws.

The legislative goal of state parity laws is often considered to be the creation of competitive equality among different types of lenders. Further, interstate banks much prefer "seamless" regulation, meaning that they want to operate under one set of rules even when they do business in multiple states. Because of this, state parity laws have been analogized to the "most favored lender" doctrine of the National Bank Act.[782] State parity laws may not create competitive equality in interstate banking due to inconsistencies among the laws and because some laws may change only one aspect of the differences between two types of institutions—the rate ceiling—without changing the numerous other regulatory restrictions and powers which might be

---

774 FDIC Guidelines for Payday Lending (2005), *available at* www.fdic.gov/news/news/financial/2005/fil1405a.html.

775 *Compare* 12 U.S.C. § 1831a(a)(1) (state bank may not engage as principal in any type of activity that is not permissible for a national bank except in two circumstances) *with* 12 C.F.R. § 7.4008(b) (national bank regulation regarding ability to repay).

776 FDIC Guidelines for Payday Lending 2 (2005), *available at* www.fdic.gov/news/news/financial/2005/fil1405a.html.

777 *Id.* at 5. "Where the economic substance of consecutive advances is substantially similar to 'rollovers'—without appropriate intervening 'cooling off' or waiting periods—examiners should treat these loans as continuous advances and classify accordingly."

778 12 U.S.C. § 1831d(a); *see* § 3.9.2, *infra*.

779 *See* § 3.13.2, *supra*.

780 John J. Schroeder, *"Duel" Banking System? State Bank Parity Laws: An Examination of Regulatory Practice, Constitutional Issues, and Philosophical Questions*, 36 Ind. L. Rev. 197, 202 (2003). This article contains a chart of the state parity laws. *Id.* at 223–227. Only two states, Iowa and North Carolina, have not. However, another banking provision in Iowa permits state banks to exercise all powers necessary to effect any and all of the purposes for which the bank is organized. Iowa Code §§ 524.801(10). North Carolina law grants to state banks "powers conferred by law upon private corporations." N.C. Gen. Stat. § 53-43.

781 John J. Schroeder, *"Duel" Banking System? State Bank Parity Laws: An Examination of Regulatory Practice, Constitutional Issues, and Philosophical Questions*, 36 Ind. L. Rev. 197, 203, 204 (2003).

782 Culhane & Kaplinsky, *Trends Pertaining to the Usury Laws*, 38 Bus. Law. 1329, n.43 (1983).

very different for the different types of credit institutions subject to the parity statute. However, after reviewing the state parity acts, one author concludes that they are quite broad.[783]

A 1983 federal district court decision holding a Utah parity statute unconstitutional under the Utah Constitution may cast doubts on the constitutionality of the parity statutes in other states.[784] The court held that the state statute giving state savings and loans parity with federal savings and loans embodied an unconstitutional delegation of the state's legislative authority to Congress and federal agencies.[785] The court distinguished the situation in which the state legislature adopts existing federal law from the unconstitutional adoption of prospective federal law as state law. (Note that one court, and a dissent in a second case, have raised similar concerns about the reverse situation.[786]) In recent years, surprisingly, the constitutional issue has lapsed into dormancy. However, there appear to be strong arguments in favor of it due to the fact that parity acts provide for a prospective delegation and do not limit the provisions to existing federal legislation or regulation.[787] Furthermore, permitting state banks to engage in all of the activities granted by Congress to federal depositories is one thing but pegging state banks powers to federal *agency* opinions is quite another.

3.14.2 Impact of State Parity Statutes

A good example of the potential effect of a state parity law is given by a New Jersey attorney general ruling on revolving equity loans—credit cards secured by residential second mortgages. The state law did not directly authorize most lenders to engage in this hazardous form of second mortgage lending. However, a New Jersey attorney general's letter[788] based on the interplay of state parity legislation and federal credit deregulation, advised the state's banking commissioner that various state-chartered lenders may cre-

ate revolving consumer credit lines, accessible by credit card or check and secured by a junior residential mortgage.

The first step of the Attorney General's analysis was to note that while the revolving check loan law[789] did *not* authorize the use of real estate collateral, it did provide that lending "otherwise authorized by law or enforceable at law" is not prohibited. The Attorney General then relied on two different theories to argue that banks can secure revolving credit with real estate second mortgages. The first theory was that a state parity law authorized banks (savings and loans, commercial banks, and savings banks) to make junior residential mortgage loans "under the same terms and conditions" as allowed to second mortgage loan licensees.[790] The Attorney General interpreted the "same terms and conditions" to mean that state banks should have parity with second mortgage loan licensees to use real estate collateral. Even though second mortgage loan licensees historically extend only closed-end credit, the banks could use the real estate collateral to secure revolving credit—a type of credit the banks *are* authorized by state law to extend.

The second theory was that state law provided the banking commissioner with authority to create "competitive parity" between state-chartered and federally-chartered financial institutions. For example, state-chartered savings and loans should have powers, rights, benefits and privileges enjoyed by federal savings and loans regulated by the Federal Home Loan Bank Board (FHLBB).[791] As the FHLBB allowed the federal savings and loans revolving equity loans (including those with variable rates), parity requires that state-chartered savings and loans be allowed to make revolving equity loans. The New Jersey parity statutes for commercial and savings banks similarly gave the regulator of these banks the authority to extend to them the same lending authority as the Comptroller of the Currency gave to federally-chartered commercial banks and savings banks to extend revolving equity loans.[792]

This New Jersey example shows how state parity legislation can radically expand the impact of either federal or state credit deregulation legislation. Practitioners cannot judge the scope of credit deregulation statutes until they carefully consider the interaction of state parity legislation. Practitioners can usually find these state parity statutes in the state banking provisions that set out the state's charter-granting and regulatory authority.[793]

783 John J. Schroeder, *"Duel" Banking System? State Bank Parity Laws: An Examination of Regulatory Practice, Constitutional Issues, and Philosophical Questions*, 36 Ind. L. Rev. 197, 207 (2003). *See also* Christian A. Johnson, *Wild Card Statutes, Parity, and National Banks—The Renascence of State Banking Powers*, 26 Loy. U. Chi. L.J. 351, 368–379 (1995).

784 Utah League of Insured Sav. Ass'n v. State, 555 F. Supp. 664 (D. Utah 1983). *See also* cases discussed in John J. Schroeder, *"Duel" Banking System? State Bank Parity Laws: An Examination of Regulatory Practice, Constitutional Issues, and Philosophical Questions*, 36 Ind. L. Rev. 197, 209-214 (2003).

785 Utah League of Insured Sav. Ass'n v. State, 555 F. Supp. 664, 673–675 (D. Utah 1983).

786 § 3.4.5.1.1, *supra*.

787 John J. Schroeder, *"Duel" Banking System? State Bank Parity Laws: An Examination of Regulatory Practice, Constitutional Issues, and Philosophical Questions*, 36 Ind. L. Rev. 197, 211–218 (2003).

788 N.J. Att'y Gen. Letter, Revolving Credit Equity Loans (Apr. 13, 1983).

789 N.J. Stat. Ann. § 17:9A-59.1 (West).

790 *See* N.J. Stat. Ann. §§ 17:11A-34, 17:9A-24(14) (West).

791 N.J. Stat. Ann. § 17:B-4A (2) (West).

792 *See* N.J. Stat. Ann. §§ 17:9A-24a, 17:9-24b (West).

793 *See* the chart listing the citations to all state parity acts at the end of John J. Schroeder, *"Duel" Banking System? State Bank Parity Laws: An Examination of Regulatory Practice, Constitutional Issues, and Philosophical Questions*, 36 Ind. L. Rev. 197 (2003). For an example of a case applying a state parity law, see S. Pointe Dev. Co. v. Capital Bank, 573 So. 2d 939 (Fla. Dist. Ct. App. 1991).

3.14.3 Parity Statute Interaction with Federal "Most Favored Lender"

Usury analysis becomes more complicated when a state "parity" statute is invoked by a federal lender under the "most favored lender doctrine." For example, a national bank cannot directly use a federal credit union rate ceiling of 15% under the most favored lender doctrine because the doctrine only gives the bank equality with the most favored state lender,[794] and a federal credit union is not a state lender. Yet the national bank may be able to achieve the 15% rate indirectly in some states with parity statutes. For example, a state-chartered credit union in Tennessee is entitled by virtue of a state "parity" statute to charge the same rate as federal credit unions.[795] The federal most favored lender doctrine allows the national bank to do business under the state credit union rate ceiling because the state credit union may prove to be the most favored lender under state law. Because the state credit union can invoke the federal credit union rate under the parity statute, so can the national bank under the most favored lender rule. Essentially, the logic is that even if no statute authorizes creditor A to charge the same rates allowed to creditor C, still creditor A can achieve the same result if it is permitted to charge the same rates as creditor B, and creditor B can, in turn, charge the same rates as C.

The fundamental problem with this approach is that neither Congress nor the state legislature intended it. Congress intended that national banks and federal credit unions have different credit rate ceilings. And yet the national bank claims the benefit of the federal credit union rate ceiling by virtue of a state law intended to create parity only between state and federal credit unions.

The combination of state parity laws and the most favored lender doctrine may provide state as well as federal lending institutions with bootstrapping opportunities to raise their rates. For example, the legal rates nominally applicable in a 1984 Michigan case[796] limited state-chartered banks to a 7% interest charge and state credit unions to a 15% rate. However, a state parity law additionally authorized the state-chartered banks to impose rates as high as those received on comparable loans by national banking associations authorized to do business in the state. The court ruled that state credit unions were competing lenders of national banks in the areas of consumer and small business credit, that a

national bank could therefore charge the 15% state credit union rate under the most favored lender doctrine, and that the state-chartered banks were, consequently, also entitled to a 15% rate.

3.15 Federal Jurisdiction: Removal of Preemption Issues to Federal Court

The credit export industry which has been so aggressive in pushing the limits of "most favored lender doctrine" under both the NBA and DIDA,[797] has tried to keep state courts from ruling on questions concerning the scope of that doctrine. When the industry's right to export Delaware and South Dakota deregulation into other states has been challenged directly in state courts, it has sought removal to federal courts. The strategy of removing cases to federal court now appears to include litigation brought in state court raising claims based solely on state law whenever the defendant is a federally-regulated institution or related to one. The law, however, generally supports remand to state court in these situations.

Ordinarily, a federal question[798] must appear on the face of a complaint before a state court action can be removed to federal court. That there may be a defense rooted in federal law is not grounds for removal.[799] One way to avoid or defeat removal to federal court in litigation involving a national bank is to plead claims under state law principles only. This tactic has been successful in cases attacking forced-placed insurance practices.[800] As collateral protection premiums are not "interest" under the National Bank-

---

794 *See* § 3.4.3.3, *supra.*

795 Tenn. Code Ann. § 45-4-602(a)(2); *see also* Op. Tenn. Att'y Gen., Consumer Cred. Guide (CCH) ¶ 96,966 (Dec. 7, 1981).

796 First Bank of Cadillac v. Miller, 131 Mich. App. 764, 347 N.W.2d 715 (1984); *see also* Begala v. PNC Bank, Ohio, N.A., 214 F.3d 776 (6th Cir. 2000) (national bank located in Ohio is entitled to use the interest rate allowed to building and loan associations and savings banks under most favored lender doctrine; payment holiday was not a new credit transaction and, therefore, was covered by this state law which allowed unlimited interest on "loans made").

797 *See* §§ 3.4.5, 3.9.2.2, *supra.*

798 Federal jurisdiction is proper where a claim arises under the Constitution, laws or treaties of the United States. 28 U.S.C. § 1331.

799 *See, e.g.,* Beneficial Nat'l Bank v. Anderson, 539 U.S. 1, 123 S. Ct. 2058, 156 L. Ed. 2d 1 (2003); Rivet v. Regions Bank of La., 522 U.S. 470, 118 S. Ct. 921, 139 L. Ed. 2d 912 (1998) (case involved commercial mortgages and the preclusive effect of a bankruptcy court ruling); Hill v. Chem. Bank, 799 F. Supp. 948 (D. Minn. 1992).

800 *See, e.g.,* Green v. H & R Block, Inc., 981 F. Supp. 951 (D. Md. 1997); Gutter v. Bank One, La., N.A., 1997 WL 722952 (E.D. La. Nov. 17, 1997); Pippin v. Regions Bank, 1997 WL 627560 (E.D. La. Oct. 9, 1997); *see also* Smith v. Beneficial Nat'l Bank USA, 971 F. Supp. 513 (M.D. Ala. 1997) (same as *Hunter, infra*); Kenney v. Farmers Nat'l Bank, 938 F. Supp. 789 (M.D. Ala. 1996) (removal not allowed as NBA did not completely preempt consumer's state law claims of fraud, breach of contract, unconscionability, breach of fiduciary duty, and civil conspiracy in connection with the collection of premiums on vendor single-interest insurance on a mortgage); Giddens v. Hometown Fin. Servs., 938 F. Supp. 801 (M.D. Ala. 1996) (same with respect to the issuing and collecting of vehicle VSI premiums); Hunter v. Beneficial Nat'l Bank USA, 947 F. Supp. 446 (M.D. Ala. 1996) (same with respect to the purchasing and financing of satellite dishes and hearing aids).

ing Act,[801] plaintiff's well-pleaded complaint alleging only claims sounding in tort and contract law was not pre-empted by the NBA.

An exception to this "well-pleaded complaint rule" exists when the plaintiff fails to plead necessary federal questions.[802] In this situation, removal should be allowed only if federal law completely preempts an asserted state law claim.[803]

The Supreme Court recently carved out one portion of the National Bank Act as completely preempting state law: usury claims raised against national banks.[804] Resolving a split between two circuits,[805] the Court held that section 85 and section 86 of the National Bank Act provide the exclusive cause of action for *usury* claims against national banks. However, *Anderson* should not be the basis of removal of non-usury claims against national banks.[806] Cases decided

since the *Anderson* decision have made this distinction in cases involving not only national banks but also in cases involving federal savings associations, and state banks.[807]

---

801 *See* Doe v. Norwest Bank Minn., N.A., 107 F.3d 1297 (8th Cir. 1997).

802 Rivet v. Regions Bank of La., 522 U.S. 470, 118 S. Ct. 921, 139 L. Ed. 2d 912 (1998) (case involved commercial mortgages and the preclusive effect of a bankruptcy court ruling); Hill v. Chem. Bank, 799 F. Supp. 948 (D. Minn. 1992).

803 Beneficial Nat'l Bank v. Anderson, 539 U.S. 1, 123 S. Ct. 2058, 156 L. Ed. 2d 1 (2003); Cavette v. Mastercard Int'l, Inc., 282 F. Supp. 2d W.D. Tenn. 2003) (state law claims based on unfair and deceptive practices relating to failure to disclose and based on negligent misrepresentation a currency conversion fee are not a proper basis of removal; duties did not arise under federal law); Nelson v. Associates Fin. Servs. Co. of Ind., Inc., 79 F. Supp. 2d 813 (W.D. Mich. 2000) (" 'Complete preemption' applies only in the extraordinary circumstance when Congress intends, not merely to preempt a certain amount of state law, but also transfer jurisdiction to decide the preemption question from state to federal courts," *quoting* Musson Theatrical, Inc. v. Fed. Express Corp., 89 F.3d 1244, 1253 (6th Cir. 1996) where court held Congress did not intend to create an exclusively federal court question; DIDMCA does not completely preempt consumer's claims under state usury, licensing, and UDAP laws); Hill v. Chem. Bank, 799 F. Supp. 948 (D. Minn. 1992).

804 Beneficial Nat'l Bank v. Anderson, 539 U.S. 1, 123 S. Ct. 2058, 156 L. Ed. 2d 1 (2003).

805 *Compare* Anderson v. H & R Block, Inc., 287 F.3d 1038 (11th Cir. 2002) (finding of complete preemption is not warranted) *with* M. Nahas & Co. v. First Nat'l Bank of Hot Springs, 930 F.2d 608 (8th Cir. 1991) *and* Krispin v. May Dep't Stores Co., 218 F.3d 919 (8th Cir. 2000). For earlier cases, see Copeland v. MBNA Am., N.A., 820 F. Supp. 537 (D. Colo. 1993) (NBA: removal not warranted); Donald v. Golden Credit Union, 839 F. Supp. 1394 (E.D. Cal. 1993) (DIDA: same); Goehl v. Mellon Bank (DE), 825 F. Supp. 1239 (E.D. Pa. 1993) (NBA: removal granted); Watson v. First Union Nat'l Bank, 837 F. Supp. 146 (D.S.C. 1993) (same); Nelson v. Citibank (S.D.), N.A., 794 F. Supp. 312 (D. Minn. 1992) (NBA: removal granted); Tikkanen v. Citibank (S.D.), N.A., 801 F. Supp. 270 (D. Minn. 1992) (same); Hill v. Chem. Bank, 799 F. Supp. 948 (D. Minn. 1992) (DIDA § 521).

806 *See* Ansley v. Ameriquest Mortgage Co., 340 F.3d 858 (9th Cir. 2003) (AMTPA: issue was whether removal to federal court was proper; court said no because AMTPA does not preempt all state laws); Carson v. H & R Block, Inc., 250 F. Supp. 2d 669 (S.D. Miss. 2003) (claims relating to misrepresentation and suppres-

sion of facts by the tax preparation service that the interest was substantially less interest than it actually turned out to be are not grounds for removal); West Virginia *ex rel.* McGraw v. Parrish Auto. Training Co., 147 F. Supp. 2d 470 (N.D. W. Va. 2001) (NBA: remand granted where the state sued car dealers and banks, as assignees, over a UDAP claim for failure to disclose the dealer interest rate hikes and the receipt of the yield spread premium from the banks); Heaton v. Monogram Credit Card Bank of Ga., 2001 U.S. Dist. LEXIS 325 (E.D. La. Jan. 5, 2001) (FDIA: no complete preemption, relying on Jones v. BankBoston), *subsequent proceeding,* 297 F.3d 416 (5th Cir. 2002) (FDIC permitted to intervene, thus creating federal court jurisdiction; remand reversed on these grounds); Jones v. BankBoston, N.A., 115 F. Supp. 2d 1350 (S.D. Ala. 2000) (NBA: removal not warranted).

807 *See* Freunscht v. Banknorth, N.A., 2004 WL 540693 (D.N.H. Mar. 17, 2004) (NBA: case challenged practice of the assignee bank that failed to notify the credit insurer that the car loans were prepaid, as required by state law, which resulted in the consumers not receiving refunds of unearned premiums; no express federal preemption of this state law claim and the NBA does not wholly displace this cause of action; removal to federal court not appropriate); Wilson v. Bank of America Corp., 2004 WL 443881 (S.D. Miss. Feb. 20, 2004) (NBA: causes of action were based on the deceptive inducement of the consumer to enter into loans that were more expensive than loans for which they could have qualified; no allegation that the rates or fees were illegal; removal to federal court not appropriate); Cortazar v. Wells Fargo & Co, 2004 WL 1774219 (N.D. Cal. Aug. 9, 2004) (NBA: removal not appropriate where the consumer pled UDAP violations based in part on violations of federal laws, TILA, RESPA, HOEPA; state claims are not transformed into federal claims especially where the plaintiff is not seeking any of the federal remedies and where the state claims did not depend solely on the federal claims for survival; although preemption may ultimately be a defense to the claims, preemption does not present federal question supporting removal jurisdiction *per se*); Jacobs v. ABN AMRO Bank N.V., 2004 WL 869557 (E.D.N.Y. Apr. 21, 2004) (NBA: causes of action under the state property code, UDAP act, and common law based on the charging of a payoff statement fax fee and recording release fee do not support removal to federal court; just because the OCC may have visitorial powers does not translate to complete preemption); Delaney v. Bank of America Corp. 2004 WL 1553518 (N.D. Miss. June 16, 2004) (NBA: removal not appropriate where the claims raised due to the charging of allegedly excessive interest rates are fraud and breach of common law duties; these types of claims are not preempted by the NBA); McKenzie v. Ocwen Fed. Bank, F.S.B., 306 F. Supp. 2d 543 (D. Md. 2004) (HOLA: removal was not appropriate because HOLA does not create exclusive federal causes of action where claims were raised under state credit and fair debt laws, as well as for breach of contract, due to the thrift charging certain fess when servicing the loan; defendant's suggestion that the OTS has a consumer remedy division did not impress the court; the court did not directly address the issue that the thrift was only the servicer and not the originator); Dowd v. Alliance Mortgage Co., 339 F. Supp. 2d 452 (E.D.N.Y. 2004) (HOLA: the defendant's act of becoming an operating subsidiary of a thrift after the lawsuit was filed does not trigger federal question jurisdiction); Flowers v. EZPawn Oklahoma, Inc., 307 F. Supp.

Another hot issue that may make its way to the Supreme Court involves diversity jurisdiction and the citizenship of the bank. The Fourth, Fifth, and Seventh Circuit Courts of Appeal are split on the question. The Fourth Circuit held that the national bank is a citizen of the state where it maintains its principal place of business, the state listed in its organizational certificate, *and* the states in which it has branches, a very broad view.[808] The Fifth and Seventh Circuits defined citizenship more restrictively.[809] These courts decided that the national bank is only a citizen of the state where it maintains its principal place of business and the state listed in its organizational certificate.

On a related topic, the Second Circuit Court of Appeals dismissed an action filed by a national bank against a state banking commissioner challenging his interpretation of state law limits on ATM fees.[810] The court rejected the bank's assertion of federal court jurisdiction because the bank's federal preemption claim would arise only if the federal court first construed the disputed meaning of state law in favor of the banking commissioner.[811]

Removal is one more facet of the preemption debate. In addition to the discussion occurring in the courts, Congress has spoken on the proper balance of state and federal interests. As noted elsewhere in this chapter, Congress in 1994 enacted comprehensive interstate banking legislation. It took that opportunity to reiterate and reinforce its intent that state consumer protection and fair lending laws are not to be preempted wholesale. Standard preemption principles, not extraordinary ones, apply. Among those principles it specifically enumerates the "rule of construction that avoids finding a conflict between Federal and State law where possible."[812] These pronouncements address the substance of preemption, not jurisdictional issues. However, that Congress thinks the agencies have inappropriately interpreted the NBA to preempt state consumer protection law in the absence of a compelling federal interest suggests Congress does not count the NBA among that rare category of completely preemptive federal laws.[813]

2d 1191 (N.D. Okla. 2004) (FDIA: no complete preemption under the FDIA and remand is appropriate); New York *ex rel.* Spitzer v. County Bank of Rehobeth Beach DE, Case No. 1:03-CV-(LEK/DRH) (N.D.N.Y. May 25, 2004), *reprinted on* the accompanying CD-Rom (FDIA: same as *Flowers*); Hancock v. Bank of Am., 272 F. Supp. 2d 608 (W.D. Ky. 2003) (NBA: no complete preemption, and therefore removal not appropriate, where the lawsuit challenged the charging of a fee for faxing a loan payoff statement; the fee at issue is not "interest"); Phipps v. Guar. Nat'l Bank of Tallahassee, 2003 WL 22149646 (W.D. Mo. Sept. 17, 2003) (NBA: where lawsuit alleges violations of state law limiting the amount or type of certain closing fees, that is, origination and loan discount fees, state law is completely preempted; removal and dismissal are proper). *Cf.* Arnold v. First Greensboro Home Equity, Inc., 327 F. Supp. 2d 1022 (E.D. Mo. 2004) (AMTPA: borrower's suit to collect allegedly unlawful prepayment penalty under state law should be remanded because AMTPA does not completely preempt state law). *But see* Taylor v. Wells Fargo Home Mortgage, Inc:, 2004 WL 856673 (E.D. La. Apr. 20, 2004) (NBA: homeowner alleged state law contract and tort claims due to the bank operating subsidiary's demand for clerk costs and sheriff costs and commission arising due to attempted foreclosure sale; operating subsidiary argued that claims really arose under the FCRA, FDCPA, and RESPA; court held case was properly removed because the complaint sought punitive damages which are only available under the FCRA and where the allegation of excessive fees creates a federal cause of action under Beneficial Nat'l Bank v. Anderson).

808 Wachovia Bank, N.A. v. Schmidt, 388 F.3d 414 (4th Cir. 2004).

809 Horton v. Banc One, N.A., 387 F.3d 426 (5th Cir. 2004); Firstar Bank v. Paul, 253 F.3d 982 (7th Cir. 2001); *see also* RDC Funding Corp. v. Wachovia Bank, N.A., 2004 WL 717111 (D. Conn. Mar. 31, 2004) (same).

---

810 Fleet Bank v. Burke, 160 F.3d 883 (2d Cir. 1998).

811 The court's major concern was "that opening the federal courts to preemption claims by plaintiffs raising disputes about the meaning and application of state law risks a major and unwarranted incursion on the authority of state courts to construe state statutes." *Id.* at 892. *But see* Bank One, Utah v. Guttau, Clearinghouse No. 52,148 (S.D. Iowa July 24, 1998), *rev'd on other grounds*, 190 F.3d 844 (8th Cir. 1999) (court refused to abstain under the *Younger* doctrine because the federal plaintiff/ bank did not have an adequate opportunity for judicial review of its constitutional claims in a pending state proceeding involving an unrelated merchandise company with which the bank contracted to place its ATM machines; no issue or interpretation of state law raised), *cert. denied*, 529 U.S. 1087 (2000).

812 H.R. Conf. Rep. No. 103-651, at 53 (1994), *reprinted in* 1994 U.S.C.C.A.N. 2068.

813 The *Hill* court noted that the Supreme Court found complete preemption in only three areas; § 301 of the Labor Management Relations Act, ERISA and Indian Rights. 799 F. Supp. at 950; *see also* Rivet v. Regions Bank of La., 522 U.S. 470, 118 S. Ct. 921, 139 L. Ed. 2d 912 (1998) (Court cites to two other instances of complete preemption, namely, ERISA and the Labor Management Relations Act).

Chapter 4 — Credit Math For Practitioners: Calculations of Interest Rate and Other Charges

4.1 Introduction

The preceding chapters in this manual, as well as many of the remaining chapters, analyze the substance and interpretation of usury statutes. By contrast, this chapter focuses on mechanics: on how to make sense of the numbers and interest rates in individual consumer credit transactions.

In order to simplify the discussion, the authors have made several assumptions about the reader's knowledge. First, having read Chapter Two and having done some preliminary research, the reader is assumed to know which statute, such as a state RISA, applies to the transaction in question. Second, having looked at the statute, the reader is assumed to know the relevant maximum interest rate, for example 8% "add-on" interest or a rate "agreed to by the parties," if a deregulated transaction.[1] Finally, the reader is assumed to know how the statute defines "principal" and "interest" payments. In other words, this chapter generally assumes that the "principal" in a loan is the amount of cash received by the borrower and that all payments except those attributable to repayment of principal are "interest." A more detailed and realistic assessment of "interest" and "principal" follows in Chapters 7 and 8, *infra*.

What is not assumed is that the reader knows how to calculate the 8% "add-on interest" allowed by the RISA or the differences between, for example, add-on interest and actuarial interest. By carefully reading this chapter, and § 4.3.2 in particular, the reader should fairly quickly understand how to make "add-on" interest rate calculations.

Readers are urged to keep a pencil and paper (or a calculator) handy as they go through this chapter. The best way to understand the calculations presented is to try to duplicate the examples given. Before the mathematically faint-of-heart give up, let it be said that the mathematics of this chapter would not challenge a reasonably bright, well-educated sixth grade student. That is, the only skills required are addition, subtraction, multiplication, and division; almost any calculator, if it is easy to use and easy to read, can do the job.

But let there be no mistake: the emphasis here is on the numbers, the dollars and cents, of consumer usury, and there is no way to avoid these simple arithmetic calculations. The authors have tried diligently to make the text and the examples simple and elegant and not unduly complicated. A careful reading of this chapter should intellectually enrich the reader and, more importantly, financially benefit the client.

4.2 Interest Calculation: Single Payment Transactions

Nearly every schoolchild (even those who grow up to be lawyers) learns that the formula for savings account interest is $I = P \times R \times T$, where I = Interest ($), P = Principal ($), R = Rate of interest (%), and T = Time. The following example will illustrate the application of this formula.[2]

Suppose a depositor places $1,000 in a savings account which pays 8% simple interest on an annual basis. If the depositor does not withdraw any of the $1,000 for a year, how much interest will have been earned by the end of the year?[3] In this example, the principal, P = $1,000; the rate of interest, R = 8% per year; and the time, T = one year. Therefore $I = \$1,000 \times 8\% \; 1 = \$80$. At the end of the year, this prudent depositor will have $80 interest plus the original principal of $1,000, for a total of $1,080 in her account.

Another depositor puts her $1,000 in a savings account in the same bank at the same 8%, annual interest rate. This depositor, however, leaves the $1,000 in her account for three years. How much interest will have been earned by the end of three years?[4]

Again, P = $1,000 and R = 8%. This time, however, T = three years. Therefore, $I = \$1,000 \times 8\% \times 3 = \$240$. At the end of the three years, the depositor will have $240 in interest, plus the original $1,000 principal, for a total of $1,240.

At this point, impatient readers will point out that this discussion may be nostalgic and possibly even interesting,

---

1 Practitioners should not assume that issues of credit overcharges cannot arise in deregulated states: they can and do. *See* §§ 9.2.7, 9.2.8 and Ch. 11, *infra*.

2 The numbers used, however, may reflect only the experience of a very affluent schoolchild growing up in an inflationary, deregulated economy.

3 This discussion will assume that interest is not compounded, or added to principal, at any point except at the end of the particular time period in question.

4 *See* note 3, *supra*.

but of little relevance, since this manual is concerned with the problems of consumer borrowers, not consumer depositors. But turn the tables and think of a situation where a consumer, instead of enjoying the luxury of a $1,000 savings account, needs to *borrow* $1,000 for one year from the same bank which is lending money at the same annual interest rate of 8%. Instead of the bank "borrowing" the consumer's money and paying her interest, as in the first examples, now the consumer is borrowing the bank's money and paying the bank interest.

The bank uses the same formula for calculating interest, I = P × R × T. If the consumer needs to borrow $1,000 for one year at 8% annual interest, then P = $1,000; R = 8%; and T = 1. Then, I = $1,000 × 8% × 1 = $80. At the end of one year, the consumer will owe the bank $80 interest plus $1,000 principal for a total of $1,080.

If another consumer needs to borrow $1,000 at the same 8% rate from the same bank, but for three years, instead of one year, then P = $1,000; R = 8%; and T = 3. Therefore, I = $1,000 × 8% × 3 = $240. The consumer will owe the bank a total of $240 in interest. The bank may allow the consumer to pay all the interest at the end of the three-year term, at which point the consumer will owe $240 in interest plus $1,000 in principal, for a total of $1,240.[5]

This is the essence of simple-interest, one-payment transactions. As can be seen above, the maximum interest is relatively easy to calculate[6] and the method is relatively unambiguous.

4.3 Interest Calculation: Installment Credit

The explosive growth of consumer credit after World War II was marked by an almost exclusive reliance on *installment* credit[7] and by a bewildering array of methods to calculate consumer installment interest. Installment interest is premised on the assumption that the consumer will make payments on a periodic basis[8] and that if every payment is made on time, all of the principal, as well as all of the interest that has been earned over the life of the transaction,

will have been paid to the lender by the end of the loan term. This section will try to demystify the various interest methods: actuarial (simple), add-on, and discount.[9]

As a preview, consider whether an auto loan from a dealership at 6% is cheaper than the same loan from a credit union at 10%. The answer might seem obvious, but compare the following results on a three-year, $2,000 car loan. (It is a very old car.)

- 10% actuarial = $323.24 interest
- 6% add-on = $360 interest
- 6% discount = $439.02 interest

That anomalous result—the 10% loan is cheaper than two 6% loans, which themselves are not equal in cost—is, in short, why the Truth in Lending annual percentage rate (APR) was developed as a standard basis for comparison shopping for installment credit.[10]

4.3.1 Actuarial Interest

N.B.: The following discussion of actuarial interest must be mastered in order to understand the rest of the chapter. While this section should not be difficult to comprehend, it should not be skipped by the tyro.

4.3.1.1 Amortizing Credit Explained; Actuarial or Simple Interest Calculations

The reader will recall one of the examples from the discussion of simple interest[11] in which the consumer wanted to borrow $1,000 at 8% annual simple interest, repayable in one payment at the end of the year. Using the formula I = P × R × T, it became painfully clear that interest was $80 and at the end of the year the consumer would owe $80 interest and $1,000 principal, for a total of $1,080.

Now imagine that same consumer returned to the same bank that was still advertising the same "8% interest rate." Having once again been asked to lend another $1,000 for a year, the bank readily agreed, with one small, but very critical, change in terms. It would indeed give the consumer $1,000 for one year and would only charge the same $80 interest. This time, however, the bank would like the consumer to pay back the total amount owed ($1,080, of which $1,000 is principal and $80 is interest) in 12 monthly installments of $90 each.[12]

A smart consumer would not accept the bank's offer without first thinking about the difference between the two

---

5 Or the banks may require the consumer to pay interest as it is earned every year. Therefore the consumer will pay $80 interest at the end of the first year; $80 interest at the end of the second year; and $80 interest plus the $1,000 principal at the end of the third year.

6 Usury issues, such as compounding or rounding, may still arise, however, in simple interest, one-payment transactions. *See* §§ 4.6.1, 4.6.4, *infra. See also* Fried v. Bolanos, 629 N.Y.S.2d 538 (App. Div. 1995) (a determination of the loan term was necessary to establish whether the interest charge in a single payment loan was usurious; repayment date tied to an uncertain, contingent event was not sufficiently definite to permit a determination of the interest rate).

7 As opposed to the one-payment transactions discussed in § 4.2, *supra.*

8 The typical period is monthly, but weekly, semi-monthly, bi-monthly, etc. transactions are not unknown in the world of consumer credit.

9 A cause of action based on interest payment issues accrues when the interest is charged during the mortgage servicing process; it does not accrue at closing. Miller v. Pacific Shore Funding, 2004 WL 144138 (4th Cir. Jan. 28, 2004); Faircloth v. Fin. Asset Secs. Corp., 2004 WL 119364 (4th Cir. Jan. 23, 2004).

10 The APR is explained more fully in § 4.4, *infra. See also* National Consumer Law Center, Truth in Lending § 1.1.1 (5th ed. 2003 and Supp.).

11 *See* § 4.2, *supra.*

12 Since $1,080 ÷ 12 = $90.

loans. The loans are remarkably similar: they are both "8%" loans of $1,000 for one year. However, in the first loan, the consumer had the full use of the $1,000 for a full year. She could use the loan proceeds any way she wanted: she could invest the $1,000; spend it; or put it under her mattress. As long as she paid the bank the $1,080 at the end of the year, she had the full use of the $1,000 for a year.

In the second loan, there are more restrictions. First and foremost, the consumer will not be able to use the $1,000 for the full year. Instead, she will have to give the bank $90 one month after receiving the $1,000 loan, and then $90 every month thereafter, until all twelve $90 payments have been made. Each payment will be applied in some fashion partly to interest and partly to principal. Therefore, beginning with the very first payment of $90, each payment reduces the amount of principal the consumer has at her disposal. Intuitively, the consumer will realize that the first loan is much more economically attractive than the second loan. Each loan charges the same amount of interest, but the first loan gives her full use of the $1,000 for the full year. In order to make the two loans economically equivalent, the bank would have to charge less interest for the second loan.

The consumer's insights are correct. Indeed, applying the $80 simple interest for a one-year, one-payment $1,000 loan to a one-year, twelve-monthly payment, $1,000 loan almost doubles the *effective* annual interest rate. The effective annual interest rate for the first loan is obviously 8%, while the effective annual interest rate of the second is, not so obviously, 14.45%. Conversely, in order for the second loan's effective annual interest rate to be 8%, the same as that of the first loan, the monthly payments would have to be reduced from $90 to $86.99.[13] The interest charge for this transaction would only be $43.86, slightly more than half of the $80 charge in the other transaction.

All of the above is just a long way of saying that while there is more than one way of skinning the "8% interest" cat, there is essentially only one way to calculate simple or "actuarial" interest. *Actuarial interest is calculated by applying a periodic interest rate to the outstanding balance of the unpaid principal every repayment period for the term of the loan. The reduction over time of the outstanding balance, to produce "declining balances," is known as "amortization."* If we return once again to the two previous examples, the application of the actuarial method will become clearer.

The first example is the $1,000 loan for one year at 8% simple annual interest, with one payment at the end of the year. In this example, the repayment period is one year, so the periodic rate is 8%. Therefore, at the end of the one-year period, the 8% periodic rate is applied to the $1,000 outstanding balance of the unpaid principal which produces $80 in interest. The consumer now owes the original principal of $1,000, plus $80, for a total of $1,080. If the consumer

makes an $1,080 payment at that point, she will have completely satisfied her debt to the bank.

CHART 1
Amortization of $1,000 Loan at 8% Simple (Actuarial) Interest

Principal = $1,000

12 monthly payments

    Regular payment (#1 − #11) = $86.99

    Final payment (#12)   = $89.98

Total interest = $43.86

Simple Interest rate = 8%

Annual Percentage Rate = 8%

Payment #	Unpaid Balance	+	Monthly Interest	−	Payment	=	New Balance	Total Interest To Date
1	$1000.00		$6.67		$86.99		$919.68	$ 6.67
2	$ 919.68		$6.13		$86.99		$838.82	$12.80
3	$ 838.82		$5.59		$86.99		$757.42	$18.39
4	$ 757.42		$5.05		$86.99		$675.48	$23.44
5	$ 675.48		$4.50		$86.99		$592.99	$27.94
6	$ 592.99		$3.95		$86.99		$509.95	$31.89
7	$ 509.95		$3.40		$86.99		$426.36	$35.29
8	$ 426.36		$2.84		$86.99		$342.21	$38.13
9	$ 342.21		$2.28		$86.99		$257.50	$40.41
10	$ 257.50		$1.72		$86.99		$172.23	$42.13
11	$ 172.23		$1.15		$86.99		$ 86.39	$43.28
12	$ 86.39		$0.58		$86.97		$ 0.00	$43.86

Contrast this example with the example of borrowing $1,000 at 8% simple (or actuarial) annual interest for one year, repayable in twelve monthly installments, which is the basis for Chart 1. In this example, the monthly payment is $86.99. Since the repayment period is one *month*, the periodic rate is 8% ÷ 12 (as there are 12 months in a year) or .6667% or .006667. Therefore, at the end of the first one month period, the .6667% periodic rate is applied to the $1,000 outstanding balance of the unpaid principal, which produces $6.67 in interest.[14] If the consumer wanted to pay off her loan on this date, she would then owe the $1,000 principal plus the $6.67 interest, for a total of $1,006.67. However, the consumer is only contractually obligated to make a payment of $86.99. This payment is first applied to the $6.67 interest that has been earned. The remaining $80.32[15] is subtracted from the $1,000 principal to produce a new balance of $919.68. This process (called "amortization") is repeated every month, so that each month the outstanding balance "declines" until the unpaid balance has been reduced to zero.

The next month the process is repeated, except that interest will only be earned on a principal of $919.68. This month the loan will earn $6.13 in interest. This is calculated

---

13 The 12th final payment would be $86.97, $.02 less than the first 11 payments.

14 *See* Chart 1, Amortization of $1,000 Loan at 8% Simple Interest, third column.

15 $86.996 − 6.67 = $80.32.

by multiplying the $919.68 unpaid principal times 8% annual rate and dividing that by 12, since only 1 of 12 months has passed. $919.68 × .08 ÷ 12 = $6.13. The $86.99 payment is applied first to the $6.13 accrued interest. The remainder of the payment, $80.86 ($86.99 − $6.13 = $80.86), is applied to the principal. The unpaid balance is now $838.82 since $919.68 − $80.86 = $838.82.

Whenever an installment payment is made, the payment is applied first to interest; this includes both interest that has accrued since the last payment was made and any interest that remained unpaid when the last payment was credited. The remaining portion of any payment that is not applied to interest is then applied to the unpaid principal.

Chart 1 (Amortization of $1,000 Loan at 8% Simple Interest) illustrates this process. It also demonstrates that because the unpaid balance declines after every monthly payment, then the amount of interest earned on the unpaid balance declines every month as well.[16] If the payments are calculated correctly, then the final payment will equal the unpaid principal balance plus the interest earned over the last period, thereby reducing the unpaid balance to zero.

At this point, the impatient, pragmatic reader will protest "all of this theory is very interesting, but how do we calculate actuarial interest for installment transactions? We have the formula for simple or actuarial interest for one payment transactions (I = P × R × T). Now give us the formula for actuarial interest for installment transactions."

The unhappy answer is that there is no simple formula for calculating actuarial interest for installment transactions. As will be discussed in the subsection on annual percentage rate,[17] there are both complicated formulas[18] and tables[19] that can be used to calculate actuarial interest for installment transactions. There are also hand-held calculators[20] and computer programs, including one on the companion CD-Rom to this volume, which can precisely calculate actuarial interest rates, particularly when all the payment periods and payment amounts are identical.[21] Nonetheless, there is no relatively unsophisticated formula which creditors or consumer lawyers

can use to obtain quickly the actuarial interest rate or the maximum actuarial interest allowable in any transaction.[22]

However, it is helpful to have an understanding of the basic procedure employed in calculator and computer programs which determine the rate being charged in a transaction. Basically, they use the same trial and error technique anyone would use.[23] They take an educated guess at the actuarial interest rate needed to amortize a given loan amount at a given term with a given payment schedule. The final unpaid balance should be $0.00 after the final payment. If the final balance is higher than $0.00 (a positive number), then the interest rate should be reduced (so that the loan is amortized more quickly). On the other hand, if the final balance is less than $0.00 (a negative number), then the interest rate should be increased (so that the loan is not amortized so quickly). By trial and error, eventually an interest rate is found which creates a final unpaid balance of $0.00 and that is the true, actuarial rate for that transaction.

By way of illustration, let us return to Chart 1, where the $1,000, one-year loan, with 11 monthly payments of $86.99 and a 12th, final payment of $86.97 is amortized exactly at 8%. Let us assume for a moment, however, that we do not know what the true, actuarial interest rate is, but that we would like to find out.

CHART 2
Trial Amortization of $1,000 Loan at 10% Simple Interest

Principal = $1,000

12 monthly payments

    Regular payment (#1 − #11) = $86.99

    Final payment (#12)   = $86.97

Total interest = $55.52

Simple Interest rate = 10%

Payment #	Unpaid Balance +	Monthly Interest −	Payment =	New Balance	Total Interest To Date
1	$1000.00	$8.33	$86.99	$921.34	$ 8.33
2	$ 921.34	$7.68	$86.99	$842.03	$16.01
3	$ 842.03	$7.02	$86.99	$762.06	$23.03
4	$ 762.06	$6.35	$86.99	$681.42	$29.38
5	$ 681.42	$5.68	$86.99	$600.11	$35.06
6	$ 600.11	$5.00	$86.99	$518.12	$40.06
7	$ 518.12	$4.32	$86.99	$435.45	$44.38
8	$ 435.45	$3.63	$86.99	$352.09	$48.01
9	$ 352.09	$2.93	$86.99	$268.03	$50.94
10	$ 268.03	$2.23	$86.99	$183.27	$53.17
11	$ 183.27	$1.53	$86.99	$ 97.81	$54.70
12	$ 97.81	$0.82	$86.97	$ 11.66	$55.52

---

16 If this were not true, then $6.67, that is the monthly interest earned on the full $1,000 principal, would be earned every month; over twelve months, $80.00 in interest would be earned (12 × $6.67 = $80.00). This would create the obvious anomaly of the two loans generating the same amount of interest, despite the borrower getting less use of the principal in the second loan example.

17 *See* § 4.4, *infra.*

18 *See, e.g.,* 12 C.F.R. 226, Reg. Z, App. J. (1993).

19 *See, e.g.,* Fed. Reserve Board Annual Percentage Rate Tables. There are two volumes. Volume I is suitable for the overwhelming majority of consumer credit transactions, and Volume II is used when less common, irregular transactions are involved. Consumer law practitioners would rarely need Volume II. The tables may be ordered for $5.00 each from the FRB. Prepaid orders should be sent to: Publications Services, Mail Stop 127, Board of Governors of the Federal Reserve System, Washington, D.C. 20551, (202) 452-3000.

20 *E.g.,* Texas Instruments and Hewlett Packard business calculators.

21 *E.g.,* Financial Publishing Co. in Boston will also calculate actuarial interest rates. For more information, see note 153, *infra.*

22 Indeed, as is explained in § 4.3.2, *infra*, these computational difficulties explain the growth of single interest methods, such as add-on interest.

23 The critical difference is that the computer is much faster and unlikely to make the arithmetical mistakes that pass unnoticed by mere mortals.

Then let us assume that we make an educated guess that the actuarial interest rate for this transaction is 10%. We, therefore, carefully prepare an amortization of the above loan at 10% (reproduced at Chart 2, Trial Amortization of $1,000 Loan at 10% Simple Interest). That is, the first month we multiply the unpaid balance of $1,000 times the periodic rate of 10% ÷ 12 or .8333% and we get $8.33 interest. The $86.99 payment is applied first to the $8.33 interest, with the remaining $78.66 subtracted from the $1,000 unpaid balance, to create a new unpaid balance of $921.34. This process is repeated until all 12 payments have been made. As can be seen, in Chart 2, the final unpaid balance is $11.66. Since this is *higher* than zero, it means the actuarial interest rate must be *lower* than 10%.

CHART 3
Trial Amortization of $1,000 Loan at 6% Simple Interest

Principal = $1,000
12 monthly payments
    Regular payment (#1 − #11) = $86.99
    Final payment (#12)   = $86.97
Total interest = $32.50
Simple Interest rate = 6%

Payment #	Unpaid Balance	+ Monthly Interest	− Payment	= New Balance	Total Interest To Date
1	$1000.00	$5.00	$86.99	$918.01	$ 5.00
2	$ 918.01	$4.59	$86.99	$835.61	$ 9.59
3	$ 835.61	$4.18	$86.99	$752.80	$13.77
4	$ 752.80	$3.76	$86.99	$669.57	$17.53
5	$ 669.57	$3.35	$86.99	$585.93	$20.88
6	$ 585.93	$2.93	$86.99	$501.87	$23.81
7	$ 501.87	$2.51	$86.99	$417.39	$26.32
8	$ 417.39	$2.09	$86.99	$332.49	$28.41
9	$ 332.49	$1.66	$86.99	$247.16	$30.07
10	$ 247.16	$1.24	$86.99	$161.41	$31.31
11	$ 161.41	$0.81	$86.99	$ 75.23	$32.12
12	$ 75.23	$0.38	$86.97	−$ 11.36	$32.50

Therefore we try the lower actuarial interest rate of, for example, 6% and carefully prepare an amortization of the above loan at the 6% rate. As can be seen in Chart 3 (Trial Amortization of $1,000 Loan at 6% Simple Interest), the final unpaid balance is -$11.36. Since this is *less* than zero, it means that the actuarial interest rate for this transaction is *higher* than 6%.

At this point, then, we know that the true actuarial interest rate lies somewhere between 6% and 10%. Therefore we would try other interest rates within that range until we found one that worked exactly; that is, the amortization would produce a final unpaid balance of $0.00. As can be seen in Chart 1, the precise actuarial interest rate for this transaction is 8%. The computer would have arrived at this answer in a matter of seconds, while a paper and pencil calculation takes considerably longer. Nonetheless, the trial and error process would be the same.

The same process can be used to determine the proper monthly payment in an actuarial transaction. Someone or something takes an educated guess at the size of the payment needed to amortize a given loan amount at a given actuarial interest rate with a given number of periodic payments. The final unpaid balance should be $0.00 after the final payment. If the final balance is *higher* than $0.00, then the payment size should be increased (so that the loan is amortized more quickly). On the other hand, if the final balance is less than $0.00, then the payment size should be decreased (so that the loan is not amortized so quickly). By trial and error, eventually a payment size (or sizes) will be found that creates a final unpaid balance of $0.00.

By way of illustration, let us return to Chart 1, where the $1,000, one-year loan is amortized at 8% with 11 monthly payments of $86.99 and a 12th, final payment of $86.97. Let us assume for a moment, however, that we do not know (but would like to) what size monthly payments are needed to amortize this loan at 8% over 12 months.

CHART 4
Trial Amortization of $1,000 Loan at 8% Simple Interest with $85 Payments

Principal = $1,000
12 monthly payments
    Regular payment (#1 − #12) = $85.00
Simple Interest rate = 8%

Payment #	Unpaid Balance	+ Monthly Interest	− Payment	= New Balance	Total Interest To Date
1	$1000.00	$6.67	$85.00	$921.67	$ 6.67
2	$ 921.67	$6.14	$85.00	$842.81	$12.81
3	$ 842.81	$5.62	$85.00	$763.43	$18.43
4	$ 763.43	$5.09	$85.00	$683.52	$23.52
5	$ 683.52	$4.56	$85.00	$603.52	$28.08
6	$ 603.08	$4.02	$85.00	$522.10	$32.10
7	$ 522.10	$3.48	$85.00	$440.58	$35.58
8	$ 440.58	$2.94	$85.00	$358.52	$38.52
9	$ 358.52	$2.39	$85.00	$275.91	$40.91
10	$ 275.91	$1.84	$85.00	$192.75	$42.75
11	$ 192.75	$1.29	$85.00	$109.04	$44.04
12	$ 109.04	$0.73	$85.00	$ 24.77	$44.77

Then let us assume that we make an educated guess that $85 monthly payments will amortize this transaction at 8%. We, therefore, carefully prepare an amortization of the above loan with monthly payments of $85 (reproduced at Chart 4, Trial Amortization of $1,000 Loan at 8% Simple Interest with $85 Payments). As can be seen, the final unpaid balance is $24.77. Since this is *higher* than zero, it means the payment size must be higher than $85.00.

Therefore we try the higher payment size of $90 and carefully prepare an amortization of the above loan at the 8% rate. As can be seen in Chart 5, (Trial Amortization of $1,000 Loan at 8% Simple Interest with $90 Payments) the final unpaid balance is -$37.49. Since this is *less* than zero, it means that the payment size must be *lower* than $90.

CHART 5
Trial Amortization of $1,000 Loan at 8% Simple Interest
with $90 Payments

Principal = $1,000
12 monthly payments
    Regular payment (#1 − #12) = $90.00
Simple Interest rate = 8%

Payment #	Unpaid Balance	+	Monthly Interest	−	Payment	=	New Balance	Total Interest To Date
1	$1000.00		$6.67		$90.00		$916.67	$ 6.67
2	$ 916.67		$6.11		$90.00		$832.78	$12.78
3	$ 832.78		$5.55		$90.00		$748.33	$18.33
4	$ 748.33		$4.99		$90.00		$663.32	$23.32
5	$ 663.32		$4.42		$90.00		$577.74	$27.74
6	$ 577.74		$3.85		$90.00		$491.59	$31.59
7	$ 491.59		$3.28		$90.00		$404.87	$34.87
8	$ 404.87		$2.70		$90.00		$317.57	$37.57
9	$ 317.57		$2.12		$90.00		$229.69	$39.69
10	$ 229.69		$1.53		$90.00		$141.22	$41.22
11	$ 141.22		$0.94		$90.00		$ 52.16	$42.16
12	$ 52.16		$0.35		$90.00		−$ 37.49	$42.51

At this point, then, we know that the actual payment size lies somewhere between $85 and $90. Therefore we would try other payment sizes within that range until we found one that worked exactly; that is, the amortization would produce a final unpaid balance of $0.00. As can be seen in Chart 1, the payments required to amortize this loan at 8% are 11 payments of $86.99 and a final payment of $86.97. Therefore, the total interest earned in this transaction (assuming there are 12 regular payments), is $43.86.[24]

The companion CD-Rom to this volume includes a software program that calculates APRs and prepares amortization tables.

4.3.1.2 Negative Amortization; Non-Amortizing Credit; Balloon Payments

As discussed above, one of the principal features of amortization of actuarial interest transactions is "declining balances," in which the unpaid principal balance declines or decreases as payments are made. The more time that has passed, and the more payments that have been made, the faster the rate of decline; with successive payments, less interest is earned every period, so that a larger portion of each payment is applied to principal.

Not every actuarial transaction runs true to this form. In some transactions, either by design or by accident, there is a "negative amortization" in which the outstanding obligation (including the unpaid principal) increases over time, rather than declines over time. This process is called "negative amortization" because it is the opposite of regular amortization: instead of the outstanding obligation moving towards zero over time, it actually increases over time. The

---

24 (11 × $86.99) + (1 × $86.97) = $1,043.86. $1,043.86 − $1,000
    = $43.86.

practical results for the consumer may be, at best, quite astounding and, at worst, financially disastrous. (For this reason, Congress has recently limited the right of creditors to use negatively amortizing loans in certain high-cost home equity credit.[25])

A few examples may help to illustrate "negative amortization." Suppose a bank agrees to lend a consumer $1,000 at an 8% annual interest rate and the consumer agrees to repay the loan in eleven monthly payments of $5.00 each and a twelfth payment of the outstanding unpaid principal and interest.

CHART 6
Negative Amortization of $1,000 Loan
at 8% Actuarial Interest—Actuarial Rule

Principal = $1,000 12 monthly payments
    Regular payment (#1 − #11) = $5.00
    Final payment (#12)   = $1,025.75
Actuarial interest Rate = 8%

Payment #	Unpaid Balance	+	Monthly Interest	−	Payment	=	New Balance	Total Interest To Date
1	$1000.00		$6.67		$5.00		$1001.67	$ 6.67
2	$1001.67		$6.68		$5.00		$1003.35	$13.35
3	$1003.35		$6.69		$5.00		$1005.04	$20.04
4	$1005.04		$6.70		$5.00		$1006.74	$26.74
5	$1006.74		$6.71		$5.00		$1008.45	$33.45
6	$1008.45		$6.72		$5.00		$1010.17	$40.17
7	$1010.17		$6.73		$5.00		$1011.90	$46.90
8	$1011.90		$6.75		$5.00		$1013.65	$53.65
9	$1013.65		$6.76		$5.00		$1015.41	$60.41
10	$1015.41		$6.77		$5.00		$1017.18	$67.18
11	$1017.18		$6.78		$5.00		$1018.96	$73.96
12	$1018.96		$6.79		$1025.75		$ 0.00	$80.75

That consumer may well be shocked to find out how much she will owe for that final payment.[26] She would be less shocked if she made a few simple calculations before agreeing to the terms of the loan. If the annual interest rate is 8%, then during the first month, the $1,000 will earn $6.67 in interest.[27] Her $5.00 monthly payment will not even cover the $6.67 interest that has been earned over the first month. Therefore nothing remains of her payment to be applied to principal. With nothing to be applied to principal, the $1,000 unpaid principal balance is not going to decline. In fact,

---

25 Home Ownership and Equity Protection Act, Subt. B of Title I, Riegle Community Development and Regulatory Improvement Act of 1994, (H.R. 3474) Pub. L. No. 103-325, 108 Stat. 2160 (Sept. 23, 1994), primarily codified at 15 U.S.C. §§ 1605(aa), 1639. *See generally* § 12.2.2, *infra*; National Consumer Law Center, Truth in Lending Ch. 9 (5th ed. 2003 and Supp.). North Carolina recently passed a similar law. *See* § 2.3.3.7, *supra*.

26 Assuming that she either did not receive or did not read her Truth in Lending disclosure statement. Neither assumption, unfortunately, is very unusual.

27 $1,000 × 8% ÷ 12 (since there are 12 months per year) = $6.67.

depending on how the bank treats the unpaid interest every month, the unpaid principal balance may actually *increase*.

The bank may use the "actuarial rule,"[28] adding the unpaid interest every month to the unpaid principal balance, so that the unpaid principal balance increases every month. The results can be seen in Chart 6 (Negative Amortization of $1,000 Loan at 8% Actuarial Interest—Actuarial Rule). Every month, as the unpaid principal balance increases, the amount of interest earned on that balance will also increase.

For example, since $6.67 in interest was earned the first month, there was $1.67 in unpaid interest after the $5.00 payment was made.[29] $1.67 unpaid interest is added to the $1,000 unpaid principal balance to create a new unpaid balance of $1,001.67.

The next month, since the unpaid balance is slightly higher, the amount of interest earned is also slightly higher. Now $6.68 interest is earned, and after subtracting the $5.00 payment, $1.68 interest is unpaid. The $1.68 is added to the previous unpaid balance to create a new unpaid balance of $1,003.35. This process is repeated every month.

At the end of the 11th month, the unpaid balance has increased to $1,018.96. Since that balance will generate $6.79 in interest over the 12th month, the consumer will then owe a "balloon payment"[30] of $1,025.75,[31] which is more than the sum of the amount originally borrowed plus the $55 already paid over the first 11 months.

If the bank takes a more consumer-oriented view and follows the "U.S. Rule"[32] and does not add unpaid interest to the unpaid principal balance each month, there will still be a negative amortization; at the end of the 12th month, the consumer will still owe more than the $1,000 she borrowed. The results of this negative amortization can be seen in Chart 7 (Negative Amortization of $1,000 Loan at 8% Simple Interest—U.S. Rule).

For example, since $6.67 in interest was earned the first month, there was $1.67 in unpaid interest after the $5.00 payment was made. The $1.67 in unpaid interest is *not* added to the $1,000 unpaid principal balance (as in the actuarial method), but instead is kept separate in an unpaid interest column. No interest, under the U.S. Rule method, is earned on unpaid interest. The $1,000 unpaid principal balance remains the same.

The next month, and indeed every month (except for the last month), the same process is repeated. The $1,000 balance always remains the same; it always generates $6.67 in interest, of which only $5.00 is paid; and the $1.67 in unpaid interest is added to the unpaid interest column.

After 11 months, there is $18.37 in the unpaid interest column. In the 12th month, another $6.67 in interest is earned on the $1,000 unpaid principal balance. Therefore, to

CHART 7

Negative Amortization of $1,000 Loan

at 8% Simple Interest—U.S. Rule

Principal = $1,000 12 monthly payments

   Regular payment (#1 − #11) = $5.00

   Final payment (#12)   = $1,025.04

Simple interest Rate = 8%

Payment #	Unpaid Balance +	Monthly Interest −	Payment =	New Balance	Total Interest To Date	Total Unpaid Interest To Date
1	$1000.00	$6.67	$5.00	$1000.00	$ 6.67	$ 1.67
2	$1000.00	$6.67	$5.00	$1000.00	$13.34	$ 3.34
3	$1000.00	$6.67	$5.00	$1000.00	$20.01	$ 5.01
4	$1000.00	$6.67	$5.00	$1000.00	$26.68	$ 6.68
5	$1000.00	$6.67	$5.00	$1000.00	$33.35	$ 8.35
6	$1000.00	$6.67	$5.00	$1000.00	$40.02	$10.02
7	$1000.00	$6.67	$5.00	$1000.00	$46.69	$11.69
8	$1000.00	$6.67	$5.00	$1000.00	$53.36	$13.36
9	$1000.00	$6.67	$5.00	$1000.00	$60.03	$15.03
10	$1000.00	$6.67	$5.00	$1000.00	$66.70	$16.70
11	$1000.00	$6.67	$5.00	$1000.00	$73.37	$18.37
12	$1000.00	$6.67	$1025.04	$ 0.00	$80.04	$ 0.00

pay off the loan, the consumer must pay $1,000 + $6.67 interest + $18.37 unpaid interest for a total of $1,025.04. Again, there has been a negative amortization, in that the balance owed at the end of the loan is higher than that owed at the beginning.

A common example of negative amortization can be seen in "ARMs" or Adjustable Rate Mortgages.[33] In some ARMs, there may be a payment "cap" which limits the monthly payment increase, usually to a percentage of the previous payment. Because payment caps limit only the amount of payment increases but not interest rate increases, payments may not be large enough to cover all of the interest earned on a loan.

For example, if a consumer were to borrow $65,000 for 30 years (360 payments) at an initial annual rate of 12%, the payments would be $668.60 per month. After the first year, the unpaid balance would be $64,764.11. If the annual rate were then adjusted to 14% and there was a payment cap set at 7 1/2% above the initial payment size, the next month's interest would be $755.58,[34] but the next month's payment would only be $718.75,[35] so that $36.38 in interest would be unpaid.[36] If the lender followed the actuarial rule and "capitalized" the unpaid interest (that is, added it to the unpaid principal), at the end of the second year, the consumer would then owe $65,235.58, or almost $236 more than she had originally borrowed.

---

28 *See* § 4.6.1, *infra*.

29 $6.67 − $5.00 = $1.67.

30 *See* § 4.6.2, *infra*.

31 $1,018.96 + 6.79 = $1,025.75.

32 *See* § 4.6.1, *infra*.

33 *See* § 4.3.6, *infra* for a discussion of variable rate loans.

34 $64,764.11 × .14 ÷ 12 = $755.58.

35 $668.60 × 1.075 = $718.75.

36 $755.58 − $718.75 = $36.38.

Some ARMs contain a cap on negative amortization, often limiting the total amount owed to 125% of the original loan amount. When that point is reached, monthly payments may be increased, despite the payment cap, so that the loan is fully repaid over the remaining term. Of course, ordinarily nothing prohibits a consumer from voluntarily increasing her payment to avoid negative amortization. The main problems are whether the consumer realizes that negative amortization is occurring and whether the consumer can afford to increase her monthly payment.

A loan also may be designed to be an "interest-only" or non-amortizing loan, with the payment amount set at exactly the amount of interest earned for each payment period. The loan balance will not decline over time, as there is no portion of the installment payment left to apply toward reduction of principal. As with a negatively amortizing loan, the consumer then will be faced with the need to pay off the *entire* principal, plus the interest accrued since the penultimate payment, in one large balloon payment.

If, for example, our $1,000, 8% loan called for interest-only payments, with a final balloon payment of the outstanding principal balance plus earned interest, the repayment schedule would be eleven monthly payments of $6.67, and a twelfth balloon payment of $1,006.67.[37]

Balloon payments can create major problems for average wage-earners who do not have a lot of flexibility in their budget. For this reason, consumer credit statutes, for example RISAs, often limit or prohibit balloon payments, or require that the consumers be given the opportunity to refinance the loan on the same terms, absent changed circumstances.[38]

Balloon payments are a common feature in home equity credit, which began an explosive growth in the 1980s. As those tend to be higher balance loans, a balloon payment can be a hopeless obstacle to repayment for the average borrower. They are a particularly favorite tool of the "predatory" home equity lenders, who charge exceptionally (and unnecessarily) high rates on these loans. More typical of these loans than the $1,000, 8% loan used here for illustration, is a two-year balloon note, $20,000 at 18% interest.

The monthly interest-only payments on that loan are $300,[39] and the final balloon payment is $20,300 ($20,000 principal and final month's interest). Unless the consumer anticipated selling the house, receiving an inheritance, or winning the lottery, coming up with the funds to pay a balloon payment of that size will be difficult. The unfortunate borrower thus is likely to be placed between a rock and a hard place: facing foreclosure or seeking to refinance. As is discussed in Chapter 6, *infra*, the latter course too often is expensive, creating a downward spiral deeper into unmanageable debt. For this reason, Congress has limited balloon payments in some high-cost home equity loans,[40] and some states, such as North Carolina and Texas, flatly prohibit balloon payments in certain mortgage loans.[41]

Defending foreclosures arising out of home-secured credit with these and other abusive terms has become an increasingly important part of low-income consumer advocacy. In addition to possible specific statutory restrictions on negative amortization or balloon payments, a variety of other claims and defenses may be available in these cases.[42]

4.3.2 Add-on Interest

Creditors, particularly before the widespread use of computers, were troubled by the complexities of calculating simple or actuarial interest for installment transactions, as demonstrated by the discussion in the previous section.[43] If a consumer, for example, wanted to borrow $960.11 and to repay it in 18 monthly installments and the maximum legal interest rate was 8.5%, without a computer or a chart from a consumer finance publishing firm, there was no easy way to compute the maximum interest charge or the monthly payments.[44] What creditors needed was an easy way of calculating maximum interest charges, preferably one that drew upon their experience with the $I = P \times R \times T$ formula.[45] One method which became very popular was the add-on interest method. Add-on interest is used only for installment transactions, yet add-on interest is calculated as if there were no installments. It takes the $I = P \times R \times T$

---

37 $1,000 (principal) + $6.67 (final month's interest) = $1,006.67. *See also* § 4.6.2, *infra* on calculating balloon payments.

38 *See, e.g.*, W. Va. Dept. of Banking Reg., Ch. 31A-2-4(c)(11) § 2.01 (balloon payments prohibited in supervised loans); Utah Code § 70C-3-102 (right to refinance closed-end consumer debt on same terms if consumer creditworthy).

39 $20,000 × .18 ÷ 12 = $300.

40 Home Ownership and Equity Protection Act, Subt. B of Title I, Riegle Community Development and Regulatory Improvement Act of 1994, (H.R. 3474) Pub. L. No. 103-325, 108 Stat. 2160 (Sept. 23, 1994), primarily codified at 15 U.S.C. §§ 1605(aa), 1639. *See generally* § 11.3.2, *infra*; National Consumer Law Center, Truth in Lending Ch. 9 (5th ed. 2003 and Supp.).

41 *See* §§ 2.3.3.7 and 3.9.3.2.2, *supra*.

42 Calculation issues in prepayment and refinancing may arise. *See* Chs. 5 and 6, *infra*. Overcharges in closing costs, broker's fees or credit insurance, or excessive points are commonly found in these loans. *See* Chs. 7–8, *infra*. Deceptive practices or the fundamental unfairness of these loans may give rise to other claims. *See* Ch. 11, *infra*; National Consumer Law Center, Unfair and Deceptive Acts and Practices (6th ed. 2004 and Supp.). Often, Truth in Lending rescission is a possible remedy. *See* National Consumer Law Center, Truth in Lending, Ch. 6 (5th ed. 2003 and Supp.). Bankruptcy, too, may be a useful strategy to stave off foreclosure and raise these kinds of claims. *See* National Consumer Law Center, Consumer Bankruptcy Law and Practice (7th ed. 2004 and Supp.). For an overview of foreclosure defense strategies, see National Consumer Law Center, Repossessions and Foreclosures (5th ed. 2002 and Supp.).

43 *See* § 4.3.1, *supra*.

44 The maximum interest would be $65.89 and the monthly payments would be $57.00 each. (We have a computer.)

45 *See* § 4.2, *supra*.

formula (which is traditionally used only for one-payment, simple-interest transactions) and uses it to calculate installment interest.

Add-on interest is a method for calculating "precomputed" interest[46] in which the consumer agrees to pay the total of payments, which includes both interest and principal, as opposed to agreeing to pay the principal plus interest as it accrues at a certain rate. Because add-on interest is precomputed, the note or contract should contain an agreement as to how unearned interest will be rebated in the event of prepayment.[47]

CHART 8
Amortization of $1,000 Loan at 8% Add-On Interest
(14.45% Actuarial Interest)

Principal = $1,000
12 monthly payments
    Regular payment (#1 − #11) = $90.00
    Final payment (#12)   = $89.98
Total interest = $79.98
Add-on Interest rate = 8%
Annual Percentage Rate = 14.45%

Payment #	Unpaid Balance	+	Monthly Interest	−	Payment	=	New Balance	Total Interest To Date
1	$1000.00		$12.04		$90.00		$922.04	$12.04
2	$ 922.04		$11.10		$90.00		$843.14	$23.14
3	$ 843.14		$10.15		$90.00		$763.29	$33.29
4	$ 763.29		$ 9.19		$90.00		$682.48	$42.48
5	$ 682.48		$ 8.22		$90.00		$600.70	$50.70
6	$ 600.70		$ 7.23		$90.00		$517.93	$57.93
7	$ 517.93		$ 6.24		$90.00		$434.17	$64.17
8	$ 434.17		$ 5.23		$90.00		$349.40	$69.40
9	$ 349.40		$ 4.21		$90.00		$263.61	$73.61
10	$ 263.61		$ 3.17		$90.00		$176.78	$76.78
11	$ 176.78		$ 2.13		$90.00		$ 88.91	$78.91
12	$ 88.91		$ 1.07		$89.98		$ 0.00	$79.98

CHART 9
Simple Interest Rates Equivalent to Add-On Rates
on Loans with Equal Monthly Payments

Loan Duration (Months)	6% Add-on	8% Add-on	12% Add-on
12	10.90%	14.45%	21.46%
18	11.08%	14.65%	21.64%
24	11.13%	14.68%	21.57%
30	11.12%	14.63%	21.41%
36	11.08%	14.55%	21.20%
48	11.97%	14.35%	20.75%
60	10.85%	14.13%	20.31%

With installment payments, the average unpaid balance is only slightly more than one-half of the original principal.[48] With simple (actuarial) interest, the interest calculated when each payment is credited will decline, because the principal is declining.[49] In contrast, add-on interest is calculated at the outset of the loan on the full amount for the full term, as if the principal did not decline over the course of the loan. Compare the total interest earned on a one-year, $1,000 loan at 8% actuarial, $43.86 (Chart 1) with that earned at 8% add-on, $79.98 (Chart 8). Thus, the 8% add-on means more than $36 extra in earnings for this creditor[50] than for 8% actuarial. To earn an equivalent dollar amount, the creditor would obviously have to charge a higher *actuarial interest* rate. See Chart 9 (Simple Interest Rates Equivalent to Add-On Rates on Loans with Equal Payments) which illustrates the contrast between the nominal add-on rate and the effective simple interest rate. As the chart shows, add-on rates always dramatically understate the effective simple or actuarial interest rate.

Thus, an added benefit of add-on rates for creditors is that add-on rates can be used in a deceptive fashion to understate the true simple rate of interest. Not only may consumers be misled as to the true interest rates for their loans and sales transactions, but legislators may also be mislead. For example, if legislators are asked to raise rates for a particular class of transactions from 6% add-on to 8% add-on, they may not realize that (1) the former rates are the equivalent of nearly 12% simple interest for some transactions and (2) the new rates would be the equivalent of nearly 15% for some transactions.

The calculation of add-on rates is relatively simple. The *principal* is multiplied by the (annual) add-on *rate* times the number of *years* in the transaction. This produces the maximum amount of interest allowable under the add-on rate statute. $P \times R \times T = I$ where P = Principal, R = Rate (annual add-on rate), T = Time (number of years), and I = Interest. For example, if a consumer borrows $1,000 and agrees to pay the loan in 12 monthly installments, what is the maximum amount of interest that can be charged under an 8% add-on rate? In this example

P = $1,000
R = .08 (or 8%)
T = 1 year

$P \times R \times T = \$1,000 \times .08 \times 1 = \$80$. Therefore, $I = \$80$.

The consumer will have to pay a total of $1,000 principal + $80 interest, or $1,080. Each month, the consumer will have

---

46 *See* § 4.5, *infra*.

47 *See* Ch. 5, *infra*. *See also* Restaurant Dev., Inc. v. Cananwill, Inc., 80 P.3d 598 (Wash. 2003) (citing statutory provision for rebate of unearned charges as evidence that legislature intended interest rate to be an add-on rate).

48 *See, e.g.*, Chart 8 (Amortization of $1,000 Loan at 8% Add-On Interest). Note that after six payments, the unpaid balance is only $517.93, slightly more than half of the original unpaid balance of $1,000. The average unpaid balance for this transaction is $554.74, again slightly more than half of the original unpaid balance of $1,000.

49 *See* § 4.3.1, *supra*.

50 $79.98 − $43.86 = $36.12.

to pay $90.00 ($1,080 ÷ 12 = $90). Chart 8 (Amortization of $1,000 Loan at 8% Add-On Interest) shows the actuarial amortization of this loan.[51]

This was a comparatively easy example, although no add-on interest rate example is very difficult since add-on interest was designed to be easy to use. A more complicated example: if a consumer borrows $3,890.99 and agrees to repay the loan in 30 monthly installments, what is the maximum amount of interest that can be charged under an 8.25% add-on rate? In this example

$P = \$3,890.98$
$R = .0825$ (or 8.25%)
$T = 2.5$ years (or 30 ÷ 12 years)

$P \times R \times T = \$3,890.98 \times .0825 \times 2.5 = \$802.51$. Therefore, $I = \$802.51$.

The consumer will have to pay a total of $3,890.98 principal plus $802.51 interest, or $4,693.49. Each month, the consumer will have to pay $156.45.[52] Again, it is important to remember that the true simple interest rate, or annual percentage rate, for this transaction is 15.06%, or almost twice the nominal add-on rate of 8.25%.

A still more complicated example would involve "split rates" in which two or more add-on rates would apply to the transaction. For example, a usury statute might allow a creditor to apply an add-on rate of 10% to the first $500 of principal and an add-on rate of 8% to any original principal balance above $500. If a consumer borrows $748.28 and agrees to repay the loan in 24 monthly installments, what is the maximum amount of interest that can be charged under these add-on rates?

In this example, it makes the calculations easier if the loan principal is divided into two parts, P(1) or $500, to which the 10% add-on rate applies, and P(2) or $248.28, to which the 8% add-on rate applies. Therefore, $P = \$748.28 = P(1)$ $500.00 + P(2) \$248.28$.

The next step is to calculate the maximum interest that can be charged on each part of the principal.

$P(1) = \$500$
$R(1) = .10$ (or 10%)
$T(1) = 2$ years (or 24 months)

$P(1) \times R(1) \times T(1) = \$500.00 \times .10 \times 2 = \$100.00$. Therefore, $I(1) = \$100.00$.

$P(2) = \$248.28$
$R(2) = .08$ (or 8%)
$T(2) = 2$ years (or 24 months)

$P(2) \times R(2) \times T(2) = \$248.28 \times .08 \times 2 = \$39.72$
Therefore $I(2) = \$39.72$

The total interest $(I) = \$100 + \$39.72 = \$139.72$. The consumer will have to pay a total of $748.28 principal plus $139.72 interest, or $888. Each month, the consumer will have to pay $37 ($888 ÷ 12 = $37). Remember, again, that the true simple interest rate, or annual percentage rate, for this transaction is 17.01%, much higher than the "split" add-on rates of 8% and 10%.

Other computational problems, such as odd payment periods, rounding, and counting days,[53] may need to be considered, as with all interest methods. A careful look at the relevant add-on interest usury statute should be the very first step, as the statute itself may directly address these issues.[54] Even where the statute allows for a certain rate of add-on interest, a debtor in bankruptcy may be protected from such provisions.[55]

Generally, however, add-on interest statutes require all payments to be equal in size, with slight variations allowed in the first payment (particularly if the first payment period is longer than one month). If the payment sizes are not similar, particularly if the initial payments are considerably larger than the later payments, the effective annual interest rate is significantly increased.[56]

A final note of caution is that many add-on interest rate statutes do not use the words "add-on" to describe the rates therein. They may, for example, use such terms as "$8.00 per $100 per annum" to describe an 8% add-on rate.[57]

---

51 This is the same formula as the single-payment transaction described in § 4.2, in both cases yielding $80 in interest earned over one year. A 3-year, 8% add-on installment loan likewise would yield the same amount as a comparable-term, single-payment loan: $1,000(P) × .08(8%) × 3 (years) = $240 (I), for a total indebtedness of $1,240. *See* Corcoran v. TranSouth Fin. Corp. (*In re* Corcoran), 268 B.R. 882 (Bankr. M.D. Fla. 2001) (giving examples of calculation of add-on rates).

52 More precisely, the final payment will be $156.44, since 29 × $156.45 = $4537.05; 1 × $156.44 = $156.44; and $4537.05 + $156.44 = $4693.49.

53 *See* §§ 4.6.2, 4.6.4, and 4.6.3, respectively, *infra*.

54 For example, many add-on interest usury statutes allow a creditor to charge a full month's interest if an odd payment period is longer than 15 days. Under such a statute, if a loan is consummated on March 1 and the first payment is due on April 22, or one month and 22 days later, then the creditor may charge two full months, interest. *See* § 4.6.2, *infra*. *See also* Parten v. General Motors Acceptance Corp., 187 Ga. App. 516, 370 S.E.2d 778 (1988), where the court ruled against the borrower's usury claim based on an add-on transaction because the borrower failed to consider the special statutory section on irregular payments. The decision does not, however, give enough detail to determine whether the court's analysis is correct.

55 *In re* Pokrzywinski, 2004 WL 1663818 (E.D. Wis. July 21, 2004) (add-on interest not permitted in cramdown loan).

56 Indeed, some add-on statutes allow creditors to require irregular payments, as long as the effective interest rate is not higher than it would be if all payments were the same size.

57 Restaurant Dev., Inc. v. Cananwill, Inc., 80 P.3d 598 (Wash. 2003) ("$10 per $100 per year" states add-on rate). *See, e.g.,* Corcoran v. TranSouth Fin. Corp. (*In re* Corcoran, 268 B.R. 882) (Bankr. M.D. Fla. 2001) (interpreting "$17 per $100 per year" as add-on rate).

4.3.3 Discount Interest

The method for calculating discount interest is similar to that for calculating add-on interest. Discount interest, like add-on interest, is a method for calculating "precomputed" interest[58] in which the consumer agrees to pay the total of payments, which includes both interest and principal, as opposed to agreeing to pay the principal plus interest as it accrues at a certain rate. Because discount interest, like add-on interest, is precomputed, the note or contract should contain an agreement as to how unearned interest will be rebated in the event of prepayment.[59]

As with add-on interest, discount interest is calculated as if there were no installment payments. Instead, interest is calculated as if only one simple interest payment were going to be made at the end of the loan term. With discount interest, however, the interest is subtracted, or discounted, from the "face amount."[60] The remainder, or principal, is given to the consumer, who is obligated to repay the "face amount" (which consists of principal and interest). The net result of discount interest is to create an effective interest rate that is not only higher than the nominal simple interest rate but also higher than the effective add-on interest rate.[61]

A few examples will help clarify the discount interest method. Suppose a consumer takes out a one-year loan with a $1,000 "face amount" at 8% discount interest. The simple interest charge on a one-year loan with a $1,000 "face amount," if only one payment is made at the end of the term, is $80.00 ($80 = $1,000 × 8% × 1). However, the $80.00 interest charge is "discounted" or deducted from the $1,000 "face amount," leaving only $920.00 in principal which is given to the consumer. At the end of the year, the consumer is obliged to pay $1,000 to the lender. The effective annual interest rate (APR) is 8.7% and higher than the nominal interest rate of 8%, because $80 interest is being charged on a principal of only $920, and not $1,000.[62]

The next example is identical to the first example, except that the loan is repayable in 12 monthly installments. (Installment, discount interest is sometimes referred to as "discount per annum.") The amount of interest is again calculated the same way, as if there were a $1,000 simple interest 8% loan repayable in one payment at the end of one year. The interest charge, therefore, is again $80 ($1,000 ×

8% × 1 = $80). The $80 interest charge is deducted or "discounted" from the "face amount" of $1,000, leaving the consumer with $920 principal. This time, however, the consumer must make twelve monthly payments of $83.33 each.[63] The effective annual interest rate (APR) for this discount installment loan is 15.68%. This rate is not only almost twice the nominal interest rate of 8%, but it is also even higher than the effective interest rate (APR) of 14.45% for a one-year 8% add-on transaction. (Both the 8% add-on and 8% discount borrower pay $80 for their one-year loans, but the discount borrower is paying the same interest for less money. The effective rate is higher because $80 interest on $920 is more expensive credit than $80 interest on $1,000.)

The longer the term of a discount interest, installment transaction, the higher the effective annual interest rate (APR). For example, a $1,000 "face amount" loan at 8% discount interest repayable in 36 monthly installments (three years) of $27.78 each[64] would produce $240 of interest ($1,000 × 8% × 3 = $240). Therefore, the consumer would receive only $760 in principal ($1,000 − 240 = $760). The effective annual interest rate (APR) for this transaction would be 18.79%.

For this reason, discount interest rates, unlike most other interest rate methods, can only be used in relatively short-term loans. Otherwise, the effective annual interest rates for longer term, discount interest loans become extremely high; for example, the APR for a 120-month (10-year) 8% discount loan is almost 50%.

In addition, at some point for each discount interest rate, the amount of interest will exceed the amount of the loan. Since interest is deducted or "discounted" from the "face amount," in such a situation the consumer would receive nothing as principal but would be compelled to pay interest, at an infinite rate of interest, over the life of the loan. This would clearly be an absurd result. For example, if a consumer took out a 10-year loan with a face amount of $1,000, at 10% discount interest, he would owe $1,000 interest, which would immediately be "discounted" from the "face amount" of $1,000, leaving him with a principal of $0, but an obligation to repay the $1,000 over the next ten years.

Readers who want to calculate maximum discount interest charges in real-life consumer finance situations may object to the above formulas, which start with the total amount of the obligation rather than the amount the consumer wants to borrow. If a consumer wants to receive $1,000 in cash as a loan, the discount loan company (and the consumer law practitioner) must be able to calculate quickly discount interest on the principal and not the "face amount" which includes both principal and interest.

---

58 *See* § 4.5, *infra.*

59 *See* Ch. 5, *infra.*

60 Sometimes referred to as "statutory principal."

61 At this point, it should be noted that many usury statutes explicitly prohibit discount interest. Many other statutes have been interpreted to prohibit discount or "capitalized" interest. *See, e.g.,* Durant v. Olympic Sav. & Loan Ass'n, 582 F.2d 1090 (7th Cir. 1978). Other statutes allow it in limited form. *See, e.g.,* Grigg v. Robinson Furniture, 260 N.W.2d 898 (Mich. Ct. App. 1977).

62 *See also* Corcoran v. TranSouth Fin. Corp. (*In re* Corcoran), 268 B.R. 882 (Bankr. M.D. Fla. 2001) (giving example of discount interest calculations).

---

63 More precisely, the consumer must make 11 monthly payments of $83.33 each and a 12th, final payment of $83.37.

64 More precisely, the consumer must make 35 payments of $27.78 each and a 36th final payment of $27.70.

As the footnote below explains,[65] the formula for finding discount installment interest (I) on a principal (P) at a given discount interest rate (R) over a given time (T) is

$$I = \frac{P \times R \times T}{1 - (R \times T)}$$

For example, if a consumer borrows $1,000 principal at 8% discount interest repayable in 12 monthly installments (one year), then

$$P = \$1,000$$
$$R = 8\% = .08$$
$$T = 1$$
$$I = \frac{\$1,000 \times .08 \times 1}{1 - (0.8 \times 1)}$$
$$= \frac{\$80}{.92}$$
$$= \$86.96.$$

Therefore, the maximum interest that can be charged is $86.96, and the face amount of the loan note will be $1,086.96. The consumer would repay the loan in 12 installments of $90.58 each and the effective interest rate (APR) for this loan, as it is for all one-year 8% discount installment loans, is 14.45%. In this loan, it is important to remember that the consumer will receive the full $1,000 principal. He will generally be unaware that the $86.96 interest has been "discounted" from the "face amount" of $1,086.96.

In a similar example, if a consumer borrows $1,000 principal at 8% discount interest repayable in 36 monthly installments (three years), then

$$P = \$1,000$$
$$R = 8\% = .08$$
$$T = 3$$
$$I = \frac{\$1,000 \times .08 \times 3}{1 - (0.8 \times 3)}$$
$$= \frac{\$240}{.76}$$
$$= \$315.79.$$

Therefore, the maximum interest that can be charged is $315.79, and the face amount of the note will be $1,315.79. The consumer would repay the loan in 36 installments of $36.55 each[66] and the effective interest rate (APR) for this loan, as it is for all three-year, 8% discount installment loans, is 18.79%. Note that the maximum interest for a three-year loan ($315.79) is more than three times (indeed, it is nearly four times) the maximum interest for a one-year loan ($86.95).

4.3.4 Split Rate Interest—Graduated Rates

Consumer credit laws sometimes authorize lenders to charge "split" or graduated interest rates on some loans. In a split rate loan, one actuarial interest rate is applied to one part of the loan and a different actuarial interest rate is applied to the remaining part of the loan.[67] The overall interest charge for each payment on a split rate loan is the aggregate of the interest charges for each step. Usually, the highest interest rate is applied to the lowest part of the loan amount. The second highest interest rate is applied to the second lowest part of the loan amount, and so on.

For example, a small loan law may authorize a lender to charge an annual interest rate of 24% (or a monthly interest rate of 2%) on the first $500 of the loan and an annual interest rate of 18% (or a monthly interest rate of 1.5%) on the portion of the loan exceeding $500, up to $2,000.

Each month, the different interest rates are applied to the relevant parts of the loan principal. The amortization of a $1,000 loan, repayable over 24 months, under the above terms is set forth in Chart 10 (Amortization of $1,000 Split Rate Loan). As can be seen, the amortization of a split rate loan is similar to the amortization of a simple, single interest rate loan. The basic difference is that each month the different interest rates are applied to different parts of the unpaid balance.

For example, look at the first month. The $1,000 principal is divided into two parts, $500 (to which the 2% monthly rate is applied) and the remaining $500 (to which the 1.5% monthly rate is applied). On the first $500, the interest for that month is $10 ($500 × 2% = $10). On the second $500, the interest for that month is $7.50 ($500 × 1.5% = $7.50). Therefore the total interest for the first month is $17.50 ($10.00 + 7.50 = $17.50). After the $17.50 interest is subtracted from the $52.00 payment, the remaining $34.50 is applied to principal, thereby reducing the unpaid principal to $965.50 ($1,000 − 34.50 = $965.50).

This process is repeated the next month. The $965.50 unpaid balance is divided into two parts, $500 (to which the 2% monthly interest rate is applied to produce $10.00 interest) and $465.50 (to which the 1.5% monthly interest rate is applied to produce $6.98 interest). The total interest for that month is $16.98 ($10.00 + 6.98 = $16.98).

This process is repeated each month until the unpaid balance is reduced to less than $500. At this point, only the higher monthly interest rate of 2% is applied to the unpaid balance. The lower monthly interest rate of 1.5% is *not* applied to any portion of the unpaid balance because there is no balance above $500.

---

65 Discount interest is calculated on the "face amount" which includes both interest (I) + principal (P). Therefore:

$$I = (P + I) \times R \times T$$
$$I = PRT + IRT$$
$$I - IRT = PRT$$
$$I(1 - RT) = PRT$$
$$I = \frac{PRT}{1 - RT}$$

66 More precisely, the consumer must make 35 payments of $36.55 each and a 36th, final payment of $36.54.

67 *See* § 4.3.1, *supra.*

CHART 10
Amortization of $1,000 Split Rate Loan

Principal = $1,000.00
24 monthly payments
 Regular payment (#1 − #23) = $52.00
 Final payment (#24)   = $51.85
Split rate structure:
 $0–$500: 2%/month or 24%/year
 $500–$2000: 1.5%/month or 18%/year
Annual Percentage Rate = 22.24%

Payment #	Unpaid Balance	+	2% Monthly Interest	+	1.5% Monthly Interest	−	Payment	(Paid to Principal)	=	New Monthly Balance	Total Monthly Interest	Interest To Date
1	1000.00		10.00		7.50		$52.00	(34.50)		965.50	(17.50	17.50)
2	965.50		10.00		6.98		$52.00	(35.02)		930.48	(16.98	34.48)
3	930.48		10.00		6.46		$52.00	(35.54)		894.94	(16.46	50.94)
4	894.94		10.00		5.92		$52.00	(36.08)		858.86	(15.92	66.86)
5	858.86		10.00		5.38		$52.00	(36.62)		822.24	(15.38	82.24)
6	822.24		10.00		4.83		$52.00	(37.17)		785.07	(14.83	97.07)
7	785.07		10.00		4.28		$52.00	(37.72)		747.35	(14.28	111.35)
8	747.35		10.00		3.71		$52.00	(38.29)		709.06	(13.71	125.06)
9	709.06		10.00		3.14		$52.00	(38.86)		670.20	(13.14	138.20)
10	670.20		10.00		2.55		$52.00	(39.45)		630.75	(12.55	150.75)
11	630.75		10.00		1.96		$52.00	(40.04)		590.71	(11.96	162.71)
12	590.71		10.00		1.36		$52.00	(40.64)		550.07	(11.36	174.07)
13	550.07		10.00		0.75		$52.00	(41.25)		508.82	(10.75	184.82)
14	508.82		10.00		0.13		$52.00	(41.87)		466.85	(10.13	194.95)
15	466.95		9.34		0.00		$52.00	(42.66)		424.29	(9.34	204.29)
16	424.29		8.49		0.00		$52.00	(43.51)		380.78	(8.49	212.78)
17	380.78		7.62		0.00		$52.00	(44.38)		336.40	(7.62	220.40)
18	336.40		6.73		0.00		$52.00	(45.27)		291.13	(6.73	227.13)
19	291.13		5.82		0.00		$52.00	(46.18)		244.95	(5.82	232.95)
20	244.95		4.90		0.00		$52.00	(47.10)		197.85	(4.90	237.85)
21	197.85		3.96		0.00		$52.00	(48.04)		149.81	(3.96	241.81)
22	149.81		3.00		0.00		$52.00	(49.00)		100.81	(3.00	244.81)
23	100.81		2.02		0.00		$52.00	(49.98)		50.83	(2.02	246.83)
24	50.83		1.02		0.00		$51.85	(50.83)		0.00	(1.02	247.85)

For example, look at payment number 15 on Chart 10. At that point, the unpaid balance is $466.95 to which the 2% monthly interest rate is applied, producing $9.34 in interest. The 1.5% monthly interest rate is not applied because the unpaid balance is less than $500. This process is repeated every month, until the 24th payment which reduces the unpaid balance to $0.00.[68]

It is important to remember that the amortization of a split rate loan, as discussed above and in Chart 10, is, like all other amortizations, the amortization of a single loan of $1,000. It is not the amortization of two loans, one of $500 at 2% per month, and a separate loan of $500 at 1.5% per month.[69] To amortize those two loans concurrently over 24 months would require monthly payments of, respectively, $26.43 and $24.96, for a total of $51.39; contrast this with the fact, as illustrated in Chart 10, that monthly payments of $52.00 would be required to amortize the single split rate loan of $1,000.

This is not to suggest that the separate amortization of two loans always produces lower maximum payments than those produced by the correct, integrated amortization of a single loan. Sometimes the dual amortizations produce higher maximum payments.

For example, consider a small loan, split rate statute which allows lenders to charge 2.5% monthly interest on the first $500 and 2% interest on the balance above $500. The maximum monthly payment on a $1,200 loan repayable over 24 months at the split rates is $57.84. However, to amortize loans of $500 and $700 concurrently over 24 months at the respective monthly interest rates of 2.5% and 2% would require monthly payments, respectively, of $27.96 and $37.01, for a total of $64.97 per month.

Another important point to remember is that split rate loans, as do all loans, bear an effective annual interest rate (called annual percentage rate or APR)[70] that must be

---

68 These actuarial split rate loans should be distinguished from "add-on" split rate loans. The latter are described in different statutory terms (usually as two or more add-on or $__ per $100 per annum) and are much easier to calculate. *See* § 4.3.2, *supra.*

69 *Watson v. Avco Fin. Servs. Int'l,* 224 Neb. 778, 401 N.W.2d 485 (1987).

70 *See* § 4.4, *infra.*

determined independently of the method used to calculate maximum interest under the state usury law.[71] For example, the APR for the transaction described at Chart 10 is 22.24%.

However, it is also important to recognize that the APR, intuitively, should fall between the two split rates if the maximum allowable interest has been charged. Every month, the effective interest rate in a split rate amortization will never exceed the highest interest rate nor will it fall below the lowest interest rate. Therefore, it makes sense that the true, effective rate, or annual percentage rate, will fall between the two split rates.

For example, in the transaction described at Chart 10, the two split rates are 24% per year and 18% per year. The fact that the APR is 22.24% is a rough indicator that the interest charged was near or at the maximum. An annual percentage rate of 25% would be a good indicator that the interest charged exceeded the maximum lawful interest (assuming that the "finance charge" used to compute the annual percentage rate is synonymous with the interest charged).[72]

The final point is that the amortization of a transaction at the split rates is different from the amortization of the identical transaction at the annual percentage rate. Generally, the unpaid balance is reduced more slowly in the latter amortization.

For example, compare the split rate amortization at Chart 10 with the annual percentage rate amortization of the identical loan at Chart 11 (Amortization of $1,000 Split Rate Loan at 22.24% Annual Percentage Rate). Applying the split interest rates to the original unpaid balance of $1,000 creates a new balance after the first payment of $965.50. However, applying the APR to the same original unpaid balance produces a new balance of $966.53. The unpaid balance after the 12th payment is $550.07 on the split rate amortization and $554.78 on the annual percentage rate amortization.

This difference becomes important in the event of prepayment, refinancing, or acceleration after default. In the absence of state law requiring the computation of the unpaid balance by one method or the other, the consumer's attorney should argue that the unpaid balance should be calculated by the use of the split rates.[73]

---

[71] *See, e.g.,* Wilson v. St. Charles Mortg. & Loan, Inc., 756 So. 2d 514 (La. App. 2000) (noting difference between split rates and effective annual percentage rate).

[72] "Finance charge" and "annual percentage rate" are both terms defined by the Federal Truth in Lending Act, 15 U.S.C. § 1605. TIL requires that certain types of credit-related charges in addition to "interest," as that term is commonly used (and as it is used in this chapter), be considered a "finance charge" and factored into the calculation of the APR. The TIL definition of "finance charge" encompasses charges which state law often does not consider "interest." *See* § 4.4.1, *infra. See also* National Consumer Law Center, Truth in Lending Ch. 3 (5th ed. 2003 and Supp.).

[73] *See* § 5.6.3.4.3, *infra.*

CHART 11
Amortization of Loan at 22.24% Annual Percentage Rate

Amount Financed = $1,000.00
24 monthly payments
　　Regular payment (#1 − #23) = $52.00
　　Final payment (#24)　　　= $51.83
Annual Percentage Rate = 22.24%

Payment #	Unpaid Balance	+ Monthly Interest	− Payment	= New Balance	Total Interest To Date
1	$1000.00	$18.53	$52.00	$966.53	$ 18.53
2	$966.53	$17.91	$52.00	$932.44	$ 36.44
3	$932.44	$17.28	$52.00	$897.72	$ 53.72
4	$897.72	$16.63	$52.00	$862.35	$ 70.35
5	$862.35	$15.98	$52.00	$826.33	$ 86.33
6	$826.33	$15.31	$52.00	$789.64	$101.64
7	$789.64	$14.63	$52.00	$752.27	$116.27
8	$752.27	$13.94	$52.00	$714.21	$130.21
9	$714.21	$13.23	$52.00	$675.44	$143.44
10	$675.44	$12.52	$52.00	$635.96	$155.96
11	$635.96	$11.78	$52.00	$595.74	$167.74
12	$595.74	$11.04	$52.00	$554.78	$178.78
13	$554.78	$10.28	$52.00	$513.06	$189.06
14	$513.06	$ 9.51	$52.00	$470.57	$198.57
15	$470.57	$ 8.72	$52.00	$427.29	$207.29
16	$427.29	$ 7.92	$52.00	$383.21	$215.21
17	$383.21	$ 7.10	$52.00	$338.31	$222.31
18	$338.21	$ 6.27	$52.00	$292.58	$228.58
19	$292.58	$ 5.42	$52.00	$246.00	$234.00
20	$246.00	$ 4.56	$52.00	$198.56	$238.56
21	$198.56	$ 3.68	$52.00	$150.24	$242.24
22	$150.24	$ 2.78	$52.00	$101.02	$245.02
23	$101.02	$ 1.87	$52.00	$ 50.89	$246.89
24	$ 50.89	$ 0.94	$51.83	$ 0.00	$247.83

The companion CD-Rom to this volume includes a software program that will calculate APRs and prepare amortization tables for split rate loans.

4.3.5 Open-End Credit

4.3.5.1 Calculation Distinctions Between Open- and Closed-End Credit

The preceding discussions of interest calculation methods focused on closed-end credit: a single advance of credit, repayable in fixed payments over a fixed term. Interest may be calculated at the outset because all three variables in our formula—principal (P), rate (R) and time (T)—are known then.[74]

---

[74] Once the interest (I) is determined, the amount of the installment payments, too, can be determined by dividing the sum of P+I by the number of periods in the term. For example, our $1,000, 8% add-on, one-year loan gives a total obligation to repay of $1,080. ($1,000(P) + $80(I) = $1,080.) If the payment period is monthly, the monthly payment amount is $1,080 ÷ 12 = $90.

　　The predicted interest, however, assumes payment is made as scheduled. As will be discussed, irregular payment amounts or

Open-end credit, however, presents a different situation because two of the variables—principal (P) and time (T)—are not known at the outset. Open-end credit anticipates repeated use of the credit, so the principal balance will fluctuate, depending on the borrower's use of the account.[75] There also is not a fixed term for repayment of an open-end credit account,[76] and installment payments vary. (Typically, the contract requires minimum payments set at a specified percentage of the account balance.[77])

The response is to calculate the interest due at the time each installment payment is due. That may be simple, if a borrower only uses the credit card once each month, preferably on the first day of the billing cycle (to give the creditor a full 30 days of interest). That is not, however, a typical usage pattern for open-end credit, and consequently a variety of methods have been devised for calculating the "P" from which "I" is determined on open-end accounts.

4.3.5.2 Methods of Calculating Interest on Open-End Credit

The two most prevalent methods of computing interest on revolving credit are the Straight Average Daily Balance and the Two-Cycle Average Daily Balance.[78]

Following is an example to highlight how these methods work. Assume that a consumer, who has a revolving credit/credit card account which authorizes the creditor to charge interest at 18% APR (which is a monthly rate of 1.5% and a daily rate of .05%), enters into the following transactions:

Dates	Transaction	Amount
May 1	Previous balance	0
May 12	Purchase	$1,000
May 31	Ending balance	$1,000
June 1	Previous balance	$1,000
June 10	Purchase	$1,000
June 25	Payment	$ 500
June 30	Ending balance	$1,500

Under the straight Average Daily Balance method, no interest is assessed if the previous balance is zero, or if payments and credits equal the previous balance. However, if there is a previous balance and it is not paid in full, then an interest charge is made on the previous balance, plus purchases minus payments and credits, all weighted as of the date they occurred.

The formula for this method is: Sum of (interest rate ÷ 360 × daily balance) for each day in the billing cycle.[79] Interest would accumulate as follows.

Date	Balance	Daily Periodic Rate	Daily Interest Accrued	Month-to-Date Interest (sum)
1-May	0	0.050%	$——	$——
2-May	0	0.050%	$——	$——
3-May	0	0.050%	$——	$——
4-May	0	0.050%	$——	$——
5-May	0	0.050%	$——	$——
6-May	0	0.050%	$——	$——
7-May	0	0.050%	$——	$——
8-May	0	0.050%	$——	$——
9-May	0	0.050%	$——	$——
10-May	0	0.050%	$——	$——
11-May	0	0.050%	$——	$——
12-May	1,000	0.050%	$0.500	$0.50
13-May	1,000	0.050%	$0.500	$1.00
14-May	1,000	0.050%	$0.500	$1.50
15-May	1,000	0.050%	$0.500	$2.00
16-May	1,000	0.050%	$0.500	$2.50
17-May	1,000	0.050%	$0.500	$3.00
18-May	1,000	0.050%	$0.500	$3.50
19-May	1,000	0.050%	$0.500	$4.00
20-May	1,000	0.050%	$0.500	$4.50
21-May	1,000	0.050%	$0.500	$5.00
22-May	1,000	0.050%	$0.500	$5.50
23-May	1,000	0.050%	$0.500	$6.00
24-May	1,000	0.050%	$0.500	$6.50
25-May	1,000	0.050%	$0.500	$7.00
26-May	1,000	0.050%	$0.500	$7.50

---

irregular timing of payments can either decrease or increase the interest earned on an actuarial loan. *See* §§ 4.5, 4.6.2, 4.6.3 and 4.6.4, *infra*.

75 *See* § 2.3.2.3, *supra*.

76 Some open-end credit contracts, home-equity lines of credit (HELCs), for example, do not have an indefinite life. The contract may have a "call provision," where the piper must be fully paid when the creditor exercises it. Some may provide that it can be exercised in as little as three years, others in 15 years. Other HELCs may divide the account into, for example, a 10-year "draw" period, and then a 15-year "repayment" period, during which payment amounts will be set high enough to repay the entire debt.

77 Particularly in credit cards, that is a small percent, e.g., 4%, which does not reduce the principal very fast, which, in turn, increases interest earnings for the card issuer.

78 *See generally* Mark Furletti, *Credit Card Pricing Developments and Their Disclosure* (Payment Cards Center, The Federal Reserve Bank of Philadelphia, Jan. 2003); David S. Evans and Richard Schmalensee, *Paying with Plastic: The Digital Revolution in Buying and Borrowing*, 141–144 (MIT Press 2000). For a review of the varied types of interest calculation methods formerly used by credit card issuers, see *Historic Methods of Computing Interest on Revolving Credit* on the CD-Rom included with this volume.

79 This calculation could be done by dividing the rate by 360 or 365. See § 4.6.3, *infra*, for further discussion on these two approaches.

Date	Balance	Daily Periodic Rate	Daily Interest Accrued	Month-to-Date Interest (sum)
27-May	1,000	0.050%	$0.500	$8.00
28-May	1,000	0.050%	$0.500	$8.50
29-May	1,000	0.050%	$0.500	$9.00
30-May	1,000	0.050%	$0.500	$9.50
31-May	1,000	0.050%	$0.500	$10.00
1-Jun	1,000	0.050%	$0.500	$0.50
2-Jun	1,000	0.050%	$0.500	$1.00
3-Jun	1,000	0.050%	$0.500	$1.50
4-Jun	1,000	0.050%	$0.500	$2.00
5-Jun	1,000	0.050%	$0.500	$2.50
6-Jun	1,000	0.050%	$0.500	$3.00
7-Jun	1,000	0.050%	$0.500	$3.50
8-Jun	1,000	0.050%	$0.500	$4.00
9-Jun	1,000	0.050%	$0.500	$4.50
10-Jun	2,000	0.050%	$1.000	$5.50
11-Jun	2,000	0.050%	$1.000	$6.50
12-Jun	2,000	0.050%	$1.000	$7.50
13-Jun	2,000	0.050%	$1.000	$8.50
14-Jun	2,000	0.050%	$1.000	$9.50
15-Jun	2,000	0.050%	$1.000	$10.50
16-Jun	2,000	0.050%	$1.000	$11.50
17-Jun	2,000	0.050%	$1.000	$12.50
18-Jun	2,000	0.050%	$1.000	$13.50
19-Jun	2,000	0.050%	$1.000	$14.50
20-Jun	2,000	0.050%	$1.000	$15.50
21-Jun	2,000	0.050%	$1.000	$16.50
22-Jun	2,000	0.050%	$1.000	$17.50
23-Jun	2,000	0.050%	$1.000	$18.50
24-Jun	2,000	0.050%	$1.000	$19.50
25-Jun	1,500	0.050%	$0.750	$20.25
26-Jun	1,500	0.050%	$0.750	$21.00
27-Jun	1,500	0.050%	$0.750	$21.75
28-Jun	1,500	0.050%	$0.750	$22.50
29-Jun	1,500	0.050%	$0.750	$23.25
30-Jun	1,500	0.050%	$0.750	$24.00

Accordingly, this method produces $24 interest for the month of June.[80]

Under the Two-Cycle Average Daily Balance Method, the grace period is effectively eliminated when the consumer moves from paying the account on a non-revolving basis to a revolving basis. This occurs when a consumer who has paid in full during the previous month(s) carries a balance forward to the next month. Because that balance is not owed until the month after it was charged, this method captures interest earned for two months: the month in which the payment is due and the previous month when the balance

---

80 Many thanks to Mark Furletti at the Federal Reserve Bank of Philadelphia for helping us with this analysis and chart.

was initially carried over. Accordingly, the interest charged at the end of the month of June would be $34: the $24 accrued for June under the Average Daily Method Balance *plus* the $10 accrued during May.

4.3.5.3 Legal Treatment of Open-End Calculation Methods

The Uniform Consumer Credit Code (UCCC) illustrates that a statute may give creditors great leeway in selecting an interest calculation for open-end credit.[81] The 1974 UCCC § 202.2 gives creditors in open-end accounts several alternatives. Section 2.202.2(a) is an average daily balance method. Section 2.202.2(b) offers two alternatives depending on whether the bracketed language is adopted. Without the bracketed language, section 2.202.2(b) is the previous balance method. The brackets are offered as a pro-consumer alternative converting section 2.202.2(b) to the adjusted balance method.[82] However, the impact of this alternative is vitiated by the overall section language which permits the highest yielding method of sections 2.202.2(a), 2.202.2(b), or 2.202.2(c). Thus, a state which thought it adopted the adjusted balance method could still find itself authorizing the more expensive straight average daily balance method or even the most expensive true actuarial average daily balance method. The prefatory note to the UCCC[83] makes it clear that the drafters contemplated the use of all three methods, including the most expensive, "true actuarial average daily balance" method.

The Truth in Lending Act requires disclosure of only the general method of computing the balance on which the finance charge will be assessed.[84] The contract, and sometimes the creditor's actual practice, must be consulted to determine exactly how it is computing the balance.

4.3.6 Variable Rates

4.3.6.1 Variable Rate Transactions Described

In a traditional consumer loan, a borrower contracts to pay a fixed interest rate and/or a specified amount of interest. Assuming that the credit calculations are correctly made,

---

81 Because most lenders use one of the two mainstream methods, these provisions likely apply primarily to creditors operating closer to the margins.

82 For a discussion of these calculation methods, which are not so common in recent times, see *Historic Methods of Computing Interest on Revolving Credit* on the CD-Rom included with this volume.

83 U.C.C.C. Uniform Draft p.XXV. *See, e.g.,* Iowa Code § 537.2202 (authorizing charge which is "the greatest of" alternative methods described).

84 12 C.F.R. § 226.5a(g). *See* Hale v. MBNA America Bank, 2000 U.S. Dist. LEXIS 13403 (S.D.N.Y. Sept. 18, 2000) (creditor need not disclose details of method of computing balance).

and that all installments are paid on time,[85] then the size of the borrower's payments can be predicted with absolute certainty before credit is extended.

In contrast, the last couple of decades has witnessed the dramatic growth of variable rate contracts. While the early growth of these contracts is connected to higher interest rates,[86] more recently there has been an explosion of such loans in the subprime market. In 2004, two-thirds of all securitized subprime mortgages were adjustable rate mortgages.[87] In a variable rate loan, no rate of interest is guaranteed over the term of the loan. Instead, the rate may increase or decrease periodically and, absent special contract terms, the size of the borrower's payments will fluctuate with the rate. Because the contract rate and payments may change, variable rate loans cannot be precomputed; they are inherently interest-bearing transactions.[88] They may or may not be structured as open-end credit.[89]

A variable rate transaction is perhaps most easily viewed as a series of short-term fixed-rate transactions, the lengths of which depend upon the frequency with which the interest

rate on the variable loan can change.[90] For example, consider an open-end account on which the rate may change monthly. This is essentially a series of renewable one-month fixed-rate loans. The rate assessed during any one month does not change, although the rates charged during different months may be different. Similarly, a fifteen-year variable rate mortgage on which the rate may change annually is comparable to a series of fifteen one-year balloon notes,[91] the first fourteen of which the creditor is obliged to refinance upon maturity at the current market interest rate. Indeed, the similarity between a long-term variable rate loan and a series of short-term fixed-rate loans is so great that some creditors which would normally extend long-term credit have evaded statutes that prohibit interest variations during the term of a loan by employing short-term loans that are renewable at a renegotiated interest rate.[92]

4.3.6.2 Calculating the Current Rate

The interest rates charged under variable rate contracts normally do not fluctuate arbitrarily.[93] Rather, they vary

---

85 Late payments on interest-bearing debt will increase the interest earned by the creditor. The extra interest will throw off the anticipated repayment schedule and may cause the compounding of interest. *See* § 4.6.1, *infra*. With precomputed debt, late charges are often imposed for tardy payments, and these fees obviously increase the borrower's total payments. *See* §§ 4.8, 7.2.4, *infra*.

86 The popularity, at least among creditors, of variable rate contracts is traceable to the dramatic increase in interest rates in the late 1970s. Lenders which had entered into long-term, fixed-rate transactions, such as traditional 30-year mortgages, incurred serious losses, and some went bankrupt. The dramatic increase in the volume of variable rate lending reflects an attempt by creditors, generally with the blessing of their government regulators, to avert future losses by shifting the risk of interest fluctuations onto borrowers. Thus, if interest rates rise significantly in the future, it is the borrowers who will be hurt first, not the banks. Of course, borrowers can benefit from a decline in rates, but the risks associated with interest increases are greater than those associated with interest declines. Rates physically cannot drop below zero percent, whereas increases, unless limited by contract, are potentially infinite. (However, federal law has required, since 1987, that adjustable rate mortgage loans in fact include a cap. 12 U.S.C. § 3806. But the cap can be set very high, and other types of variable rate loans are not subject to this requirement.)

87 Roberto G. Quercia et al., *The Impact of Predatory Loan Terms on Subprime Foreclosures: The Special Case of Prepayment Penalties and Balloon Payments,* Center for Community Capitalism, Kenan Institute for Private Enterprise, (University of North Carolina at Chapel Hill Jan. 25, 2005), *available at* www.kenan-flagler.unc.edu/assets/documents/foreclosurepaper.pdf. This figure is particularly troubling because these loans are 50% more likely to end up in foreclosure than fixed rate loans, even after controlling for other risk factors. *Id.*

88 *See* § 4.5, *infra*, for a discussion of interest-bearing and precomputed transactions.

89 Typical examples of variable-rate open-end credit are credit card accounts and home equity lines of credit. Purchase money mortgages, on the other hand, usually have a fixed term of 10, 15, or 30 years even if they employ variable interest rates.

---

90 This view implies that the legality of a variable rate loan for usury purposes is determined by the rate charged in any one or more of the payment periods in the loan term. Thus, a variable loan under a fixed ten percent simple interest ceiling would be usurious if the rate assessed in any one month exceeded an annualized ten percent return, even if the rate charged during all the other months was well below the ceiling. Other views of variable transactions exist, however. Most importantly, it is possible to look only at the effective rate charged over the whole term of a variable rate loan, rather than at the rates assessed in individual payment periods. This approach presumes that interest payments can be "spread" across different payment periods. *See* § 4.6.5, *infra*.

91 Each of the fifteen loans would have to partially amortize the loan principal in order for the analogy to be precise.

92 *See* Barck v. Grant State Bank, 137 Mich. App. 440, 357 N.W.2d 872 (1984); Shebuski v. Lakeland State Bank, 345 N.W.2d 898 (Wis. Ct. App. 1984). A series of fixed-term balloon notes may have to be disclosed as a variable rate transaction under the TILA, however. *See* Official Staff Commentary to Reg. Z, 12 C.F.R. § 226.17(c)(1)-11 (1993). Another way that a creditor may obtain the advantages of a variable rate loan in a purportedly fixed rate transaction is to add a "demand clause" to a traditional fixed term transaction. Demand clauses authorize the creditor to require the borrower to pay the full balance on the loan. They often can be invoked by the creditor at any point in the loan term. Their purpose is not so much to give a creditor the power to compel the repayment of a loan, as it is to enable the creditor to compel the refinancing of the debt if interest rates increase significantly. As such, demand clauses are a hidden variable rate feature which can be more disadvantageous to borrowers than normal variable rate terms, because they will never be invoked if interest rates decline. Special (and ineffectual) TILA disclosure rules apply to demand obligations. *See* 12 C.F.R. §§ 226.17(c)(5), 226.18(i).

93 Some variable rate loans, especially open-end accounts, allow creditors to change the interest rate at will, although there may be limitations on the extent to which a new, higher rate can be applied to a prior balance. *See* Garber v. Harris Trust & Sav. Bank, 432 N.E.2d 1309 (Ill. Ct. App. 1982) (rate change on open-end account does not breach contract; each use of card is new contract, at least when no annual fee imposed); Op. Tenn.

according to a formula which is specified in each credit contract. Typically, such formulae tie the contract rate to an external interest rate or "index"[94] such as the prime lending rate at a specified bank, the federal discount rate,[95] a treasury bill rate, or sometimes a rate which represents the creditor's cost of funds. The contract also specifies a "margin" which is added to the index rate to arrive at the contract rate.[96]

Regardless of the precise formula used to set a variable rate, the method must be disclosed to the consumer in accordance with Truth in Lending rules, which vary, depending on the type of credit, the nature of the security, and the length of the term.[97] These disclosures, together with the contract itself, and a publication source for the index,[98] should enable the consumer or the practitioner to determine the appropriate rate.

In addition to the basics, (identifying the index and establishing the margin), the contract should also specify the frequency with which the rate may change, the reference date to use in identifying the index rate,[99] and any rounding rules.[100]

For example, a variable rate mortgage may specify that the rate will change semi-annually on the anniversary date of the first payment (the "change" date), the index will be that of the most recent yield at auction on six-month treasury bills, measured as of thirty days prior to the "change" date, and the index is three percent. If that yield, as of the reference date, was 8.5%, the contract rate would be 11.5% for at least the next six months.

More sophisticated interest rate formulae may attempt to limit the extent to which interest rates may vary in order to limit the risk of variable loans. For example, some variable rate contracts set "caps" and "floors" on the interest rate that may be charged, so that the rate may fluctuate only within a specified range. Other provisions limit the speed with which the contract rate may change. For example, a contract interest rate might be permitted to increase or decrease no more than one percent annually. Such limitations on the variation of rates are discussed in § 4.3.6.4, *infra*.

Calculation errors on ARMs are not uncommon. One lender found 178 types of mistakes in a review of its portfolio.[101] A bank which originates loans using Index A, measured 30 days before the change date, may purchase on the secondary market other loans, which may use Index B, or use Index A, but measured as of 45 days before the change date. The bank may nonetheless use the same computer program, geared to its own product, for all loans, irrespective of what the contract says. Such errors, of course, do not always work to the consumer's disadvantage. Unless the error is one which is systematically biased against borrowers, they may have been undercharged instead of overcharged. (Examples of errors which would systematically result in overcharges are where a creditor consistently rounds the rate up to the nearest one-eighth, instead of to the nearest one-eighth as the contract may provide; where an unethical lender is conscientious about following upward index rate adjustments, but not downward ones; or where the identification used is somewhat fluid (e.g., "most recent"), and the creditor looks for the index's highest point among several of the "most recent" announcements.)

As a result of fairly widespread publicity about ARM errors, actual calculation practice of ARM lenders has received increased focus from the lenders themselves, regulators, and consumers. *See* § 4.3.6.5, *infra*.

A.G. No. 296, Consumer Cred. Guide (CCH) ¶ 96,563 (1983) (statute says credit card rate increases cannot be applied to prior balances, nor can late charges be changed).

94   Variable-rate home-equity lines of credit (HELCs) are required by federal law to use an external index. 15 U.S.C. § 1647(a); Reg. Z, 12 C.F.R. § 226.5b(f)(1). *See* National Consumer Law Center, Truth in Lending § 5.11.3.2 (5th ed. 2003 and Supp.).

   Litigation has arisen over the use of "internal" indices, which are in the control of the lender, as that figure, not independently verifiable by the consumer, may be fudged. § 4.3.6.5, *infra*.

95   For discussion of the federal discount rate, see § 3.4.2, *supra*.

96   The average margin at the end of 1993 for home equity lines of credit was approximately 1.5%, and the index used on most HELCs was the prime rate. 62 BNA Banking Rpt. 873 (May 16, 1994). The average margin was 1.41% over the prime rate at the end of 1997, and 1.27% at the end of 1998. 70 BNA Banking Rpt. 982 (June 15, 1998).

97   15 U.S.C. § 1637a (HELCs); Reg. Z, 12 C.F.R. §§ 226.5a(b) (credit and charge card solicitations); 226.5b(d)(12) (HELCs); 226.18(f) (closed-end, not secured by a residence, or with a term of one year or less); 226.19(b) (closed-end, residence-secured with term longer than one year). *See generally* National Consumer Law Center, Truth in Lending §§ 4.8, 5.4.3.2.2, 5.5.5.10, 5.11.4.5.13 (5th ed. 2003 and Supp.).

98   The Wall Street Journal generally publishes rates on indices commonly used, or they may be found in the Federal Reserve Bulletin. In some states, where there is a usury cap which floats with an index, the regulatory agency may publish the index rates in a state administrative bulletin. CCH Consumer Credit Guide usually publishes such releases, too. (The TIL disclosure statement must disclose a source of information about the index for home-secured ARMs. Reg. Z § 226.5b(d)(12)(iii), § 226.19(b) (2)(ii).) LIBOR rates, often used as the index for subprime mortgages, can be found at www.bankfacts.org.uk.

99   Since those rates change, it is necessary to fix a point in time which will be the one used. *See, e.g.*, Hubbard v. Fidelity Fed. Bank, 824 F. Supp. 909 (C.D. Cal. 1993), *aff'd in part, rev'd in part*, 91 F.3d 75 (9th Cir. 1996), in which a lender changed its method of determining what date to use, with the result that the rate stayed higher in a time of falling rates.

100   A contract may provide that the rate will be rounded to the

nearest one-eighth percent, for example. If the index was 4.73%, and the margin was 3%, the contract rate would be 7.75%.

101   *See* Whitford v. First Nationwide Bank, 1992 WL 442864 (W.D. Ky. settled Nov. 1992). *See also* § 4.6.5, *infra* on the rule that the doctrine of spreading may be unavailable as a defense in open-end, variable-rate transactions. *See generally* Ch. 9, *infra*.

4.3.6.3 Amortizing Variable Rate Loans over Fixed Time Periods

In many ways, amortizing a variable rate loan is similar to the amortization calculation in a regular interest-bearing loan.[102] Each month (or other payment period) the current interest rate must be applied to the currently outstanding loan balance to determine the interest which has accrued. This accrued interest is deducted from the borrower's payment, and the remainder of the payment, if any, is used to pay down the loan balance.

The problem with a variable rate loan is that, because of the possibility of interest rate fluctuation, the amount of interest that will be accruing at any point in the loan cannot be predicted ahead of time. Consequently, the size of the monthly payment which will be needed to pay this interest and to retire the loan principal over a stated term cannot be known ahead of time either.[103] In short, in order to amortize a variable rate loan over a fixed period of time, the borrower's payments must be allowed to fluctuate to match the periodic interest rate changes.

Changing the size of a borrower's payment whenever the interest rate changes involves the reamortization of the loan at each change. For example, assume a 30-year variable rate mortgage of $100,000 with an initial interest rate of 12%. The borrower's initial payments would be set at $1,028.61 just as if this were a fixed rate loan.[104] If, however, the interest rate increased to 13% after one year, the debt would then be reamortized at the new rate. After one year of regular payments, the balance on the loan would be $99,637.14 and twenty-nine years would be left on the loan term. Thus, the loan would be reamortized as a $99,637.14 loan for twenty-nine years at 13% annual interest. The new monthly payments would increase to $1,105.41. Whenever the interest rate changed thereafter, the loan would be reamortized in the same manner, given the then-existing loan balance, interest rate, and remaining loan term.

4.3.6.4 Caps and Floors in Variable Rate Transactions; Explanation and Requirements

A loan with an unlimited variable rate can be quite risky for a borrower, especially if it is a large mortgage loan which consumes a high percentage of the borrower's income. Relatively small increases in the interest rate can significantly raise the monthly payment,[105] and larger rate increases can force many borrowers to default or to sell their homes.[106] In order to allay these risks, which many potential mortgage borrowers are unwilling to accept, creditors frequently offered variable rate loans with "caps" of different kinds. Since 1987, federal law has required all new variable rate home mortgages to include interest rate caps, though the creditor may set the cap as high as it chooses,[107] unless there is an applicable state ceiling.

As noted above, the concept of a variable rate loan shifts the risk of rising rates to the consumers, and in the 1980s borrowers indeed bore it. But a variable rate also gives the consumer the benefit of falling rates. Thus, when mortgage rates fell in the early 1990s to the lowest rates in twenty years, many consumers recognized significant benefits.

However, as unlikely as 7% mortgage rates may have seemed in 1988, some creditors also wanted to limit their risk in a climate of falling rates, and so set contract floors. A predatory home equity lender might, for example, have an initial contract rate of 19%, a very high cap of 33% and a floor fixed at the initial rate, no matter how low the index rate falls.[108] A borrower under that contract will thus be stuck at 19% even when rates are falling.[109]

Caps are essentially contractual limitations on the extent that the interest rate or the interest payments may vary during the loan term. They can provide borrowers with valuable safeguards against major fluctuations in market interest rates. However, all caps are not alike, and some may provide borrowers with little or no real protection. It is critical for attorneys who are reviewing proposed variable rate contracts to examine carefully the contractual language which defines the cap.

---

102 *See* § 4.3.1, *supra*.

103 Of course, not all variable rate transactions have a stated term. In open-end transactions, the monthly minimum payment is usually a percentage of the outstanding balance. So long as this percentage exceeds the monthly interest rate, borrowers who pay the minimum amount each month will eventually pay off any outstanding balance, even if the precise interest rate varies. Open-end contracts in which the minimum payments merely meet the currently accrued interest (i.e., which allow interest-only payments) or which do not meet the currently accrued interest (i.e., which allow negative amortization) should be approached cautiously since they can leave a borrower in a state of perpetual and, in the latter case, increasing debt.

104 In other words, equal monthly payments of $1,028.61 over thirty years would precisely amortize a $100,000 loan at 12% annual interest.

105 Rate increases will hike the borrower's payments the most when they occur early in the loan term when little principal has yet been paid off.

106 On a large scale, such sales or defaults would clearly depress real estate prices, hurting not only borrowers, but also creditors whose collateral might no longer fully secure their loans.

107 12 U.S.C. § 3806. Truth in Lending Reg. Z, 12 C.F.R. § 226.30 requires all "creditors," who regularly extend credit for personal, family, or household purposes, to include a limitation on the maximum interest rate that can be charged on an adjustable rate mortgage loan.

108 This description is based upon an actual case from NCLC service request files.

109 See also discussion of recapture, later in the subsection, where creditors recoup interest lost due to a cap when rates later decline.

The most important distinction among contractual caps is whether a cap restricts the interest *rate* that may be charged or only the monthly *payment*. A cap which limits the contract interest rate to a maximum of, say, 15% annual interest prevents the creditor from earning any more than fifteen percent interest, regardless of how high the loan's index rate may go. Thus, if the contract rate is normally the six-month treasury bill rate plus three percent, but the rate is capped at 15%, the interest earned on the loan would remain at 15% whenever the T-bill rate reached or exceeded 12%. This is the kind of "cap" that is now required for all new variable rate home mortgage transactions.[110]

Some capped mortgages, however, do not limit the contract interest rate, but merely restrict the size of the borrower's monthly payment. This arrangement can spell trouble for the borrower because the amount of interest that the creditor may earn is not limited; instead, only the amount of interest that the borrower can currently be required to pay is capped. If interest rates rise to the point where the payments needed to amortize the debt exceed the maximum monthly payment, then the amount of the monthly payment being used to pay down principal will be too small to retire the debt over the stated loan term, and the borrower will probably be left with a balloon payment at the end of the term.[111]

If interest rates go higher, the situation can get worse. At some point,[112] the interest that the creditor is earning on the debt will reach or exceed the payment that the borrower is making. When the accruing interest and the payments are equal, the borrower is not paying down the debt at all and, in the case of a mortgage, is building no equity in the home. When the accruing interest exceeds the borrower's maximum payment, the debt balance actually will increase.[113] Thus, if interest rates rise sufficiently, a mortgage borrower with a capped monthly payment, but without a capped interest rate,[114] can wind up losing equity in his home, despite making all of the maximum monthly payments as they come due. In the worst case, at the end of the loan term, the borrower may face a balloon payment which exceeds the amount of money originally borrowed.

A second issue regarding the interpretation of caps is what happens when interest rates decline after the rate cap or the monthly maximum payment has been reached. Some credit contracts authorize the creditor to recapture or "carry over" any interest which it would have earned or collected but for the cap, by refusing to lower the borrower's payments when market interest rates decline. The precise recapture mechanism will depend on the type of cap in the contract. Generally a contract with an interest rate cap might permit a recapture by authorizing the creditor to refuse to lower its rates, while a contract with a maximum payment provision might require the borrower to continue making the maximum payment until the loan could be amortized by reduced payments.[115]

A variation of a recapture clause appears in a California case involving a disputed mortgage.[116] The contract in question capped the interest rate at 2.5% above the initial rate and limited any change in the contract rate to 0.25% during any six-month period. Rate increases were optional with the creditor while decreases were described as mandatory. However, the contract also provided that the contract rate should maintain the same margin above its index rate as existed when the contract was consummated. On the basis of this last provision, and on the basis of a clause which stated that the failure of the creditor to invoke an increase did not constitute a waiver of its right to do so later, the creditor claimed the right to carry over rate increases, including apparently both increases which it voluntarily waived and those which it was precluded from invoking by either the 2.5% cap or the 0.25% maximum six-month increase.[117] Thus, when the market index, to which the contract rate was pegged, rapidly increased, the creditor built up a large reserve of "unapplied interest increases." When the index subsequently declined, the creditor refused to lower the contract rate, despite the mandatory decrease provision, but instead offset the decrease against its previously unused increases.

After a careful analysis of the mortgage contract, the California Court of Appeals determined that the creditor's actions were contractually permissible, and, purely as a matter of contract construction, this conclusion may be correct.[118] Yet it is clear that this interpretation was not

---

110   12 U.S.C. § 3806 specifies an interest *rate* limitation.

111   While balloon payments are probably the most common way for a creditor to recover payments which it could not previously assess, other mechanisms are possible. As discussed later in this subsection, some contracts may allow the creditor to refuse to lower the borrower's payment when the index rate later declines.

112   Early in the loan term, relatively modest interest rate increases can significantly raise the amount of interest accruing so that interest-only payments or negative amortization are most likely to occur at this stage in the transaction. Late in the loan term, the principal balance has been reduced, and a much greater interest rate increase would be necessary before all of the capped monthly payment would be eaten up by accruing interest.

113   In other words, negative amortization would occur. *See* § 4.3.1.2, *supra*.

114   Or with a cap too high to prevent negative amortization.

115   Either of these mechanisms would prevent the borrower's payments from declining, but the interest due to the carry-over in the former system would be charged as it was earned, thus avoiding compounding.

116   Gabbard v. American Savings, 188 Cal. App. 3d 230, 233 Cal. Rptr. 610 (1986).

117   *Id.* At one point in the loan term, the creditor's carry-over exceeds 2.5% even when the contract rate has already been increased by 0.5%. Thus, through the carry-over mechanism, the creditor is claiming the advantage of rate increases which the 2.5% cap would otherwise seem to preclude. The court did not discuss this issue directly.

118   One problem with the court's conclusion is that the clause allowing the creditor to invoke increases which it had previ-

anticipated by the borrower, and given the vagueness of the contract and the "mandatory decrease" language which it contained, it is not obvious that even a careful, intelligent borrower could have deciphered the terms of the caps in the contract.[119] The lesson for attorneys who have the opportunity to review variable rate contracts before they are signed is to insist on precision in the definition of any contractual cap and, in particular, to require a written example of the effects of a market interest rate decline after a contract cap has been reached. In a home-secured transaction, the practitioner should be aided by additional TIL disclosure requirements effective in 1987.[120]

4.3.6.5 Legal Issues in Variable Rate Credit

Variable rate consumer credit has become quite common in the last two decades. In many types of consumer transactions, creditors are statutorily authorized to set variable rates. For example, statutes regulating open-end credit generally allow variable rates, and because of federal preemption of mortgage regulations, creditors may contract for variable rates in almost any mortgage transaction.[121] However, as noted in § 4.3.6.2, *supra*, calculation errors in ARMs have been relatively common, engendering litigation, enhanced regulatory attention, and more self-audits by industry. Moreover, it is important for attorneys who are examining consumer transactions to remember that variable rates are a fairly recent phenomenon in consumer credit, and older statutes may explicitly or implicitly prohibit variable transactions.

A few states have adopted explicit variable rate controls. Yet, even ignoring the effects of federal preemption, creditors may find it easy to circumvent such statutes if they are not well written. For example, if a statute prohibits variable rates, but not balloon notes, a creditor can simulate variable rates by issuing a series of short-term fixed-rate balloon notes to a borrower.[122] The rate on each individual note may be fixed, but if different notes have different rates, the over-all transaction is effectively variable.

The most widespread prohibition of variable rates is in those statutes which require debts to be paid off in substantially equal monthly installments over a fixed term. Variable rate contracts cannot meet these requirements because a change in interest rate will require either a change in the monthly payments, a final balloon payment, or a change in the loan term to compensate for the altered interest charges. The statutes which most commonly require a fixed loan term and equal monthly installments are installment sales acts (RISAs) and small loan laws. Consumer law practitioners should be particularly suspicious of variable rate contracts which otherwise seem to fall within the scope of these statutes.

Most importantly, a variable rate transaction should also be assessed for compliance with the contract itself, as well as with applicable statutes, for adjustment errors have been quite common. For example, some variable rate contracts tie the interest rate charged to an internal, rather than external index.[123] An internal index could be the bank's own "prime rate," often defined as the lowest rate regularly charged by the bank to its commercial customers with the highest credit rating, rather than the prime rate charged by a nonparty bank or a federal index. Sometimes a borrower may find that a "prime rate" within the creditor's control is a rather fluid concept, and that the bank may be charging the borrower a higher rate than other commercial borrowers.[124] (Readers should be aware that some real-estate-secured adjustable-rate mortgages must be tied to an index that is beyond the lender's control.[125])

---

ously omitted spoke only of "permissible" increases. Yet, as discussed in the preceding footnote, the carry-over at times exceeded the 2.5% cap, which does not appear to be "permissible" under the contract.

119 The obvious question is whether the nature of this "cap" was properly disclosed. The Truth in Lending Act then required creditors to disclose any limitations on the increase of a contract's APR. 12 C.F.R. § 226.18(f)(2) (1993). However, the section of the *Gabbard* opinion dealing with disclosure is unpublished, and it is not clear whether the TILA applied to the case. *See also* Mayne v. Bank of America, 242 Cal. Rptr. 357 (Ct. App. 1987) (even though lender's personnel informed borrower that rate would generally rise and fall with the index, and the documents explaining the recapture mechanism were difficult to understand, the documents contained an accurate explanation of the formula and therefore there was no violation of statutes prohibiting false, deceitful or misleading representations. [*Ed. note*: The court specifically notes the education and business experience of this borrower. While it does not say it would rule differently for a less educated and sophisticated borrower, this may serve as a relevant distinction in other cases.]).

120 *See* 12 U.S.C. § 3806(a) and 12 C.F.R. § 226.30, which require a rate cap to be set for ARMs. On open-end home equity plans, the creditor must disclose a cap and its rules on rate and payment limitations and rate carryover. Reg. Z, 12 C.F.R. § 226.5b(d)(12)(viii), ix. *See* Reg. Z, 12 C.F.R. § 226.19(b) for the disclosure rules for closed end ARMs.

121 *See* § 3.10, *supra* (AMTPA).

122 *See, e.g.,* Barck v. Grant State Bank, 137 Mich. App. 440, 357 N.W.2d 872 (1984); Shebuski v. Lakeland State Bank, 345 N.W.2d 898 (Wis. Ct. App. 1984); *see also* Lage v. Pan Am. Bank, 529 So. 2d 1242 (Fla. Dist. Ct. App. 1988) (where statute required special disclosure of balloon payments in transaction with "regular payment," payments under variable-rate contract at fixed intervals were "regular"); Manufacturers Nat'l Bank v. Pink, 341 N.W.2d 181 (Mich. Ct. App. 1983) (contract with integral variable rate does not violate statute forbidding changes in credit contract rates where index is beyond control of lender).

123 *See* § 4.3.6.2, *supra* for identification of common external indices used to calculate the applicable rate.

124 *See, e.g.,* Briggs Transportation Co. v. Second Northwestern Nat'l Bank, 406 N.W.2d 7 (Minn. Ct. App. 1987) (issue of fact precluding summary judgment where borrower alleged banks made loans to their commercial customers at lower rate than the announced prime upon which his rate was based). Similar complaints have formed the basis for several RICO cases.

125 *See, e.g.,* 15 U.S.C. § 1647, 12 C.F.R. § 226.30 (variable-rate consumer credit transactions subject to the Truth in Lending Act

More basically, errors occur when the wrong index is used, or the wrong reference date for valuing the index, and so forth.[126] A fair amount of litigation has arisen from ARM adjustment errors, mostly unreported, settled cases. The typical claims raised are Truth in Lending,[127] breach of contract, negligence and fraud.[128] Additionally, regulators have issued guidelines to lenders and services for ARM audits and adjustments. For example, a Fannie Mae servicing guideline provides that borrowers should receive refunds or, in certain circumstances, credits for overcharges, though no repayment of undercharges is required. Lenders and servicers may net overcharges against undercharges made on that account to determine whether the borrower or the lender is ultimately the one short-changed by the error.[129]

If the contract specifies as the index the prime rate of a bank which fails, the question may arise as to what index should then be used. The Fifth Circuit has allowed the substitution of an analogous rate.[130]

Variable rate contracts may be subject to an absolute statutory ceiling. Most courts have held that the interest rate may never exceed the cap even if on average it is below the ceiling.[131] To hold otherwise would require the borrower to pay excess interest during the term of the transaction, not knowing whether the payments were legal until the end of the payment period.

Where the contract contains an escalator clause which has no limits or reference to an index by which an interest charge may be determined, the contract may be subject to challenge. In *Preston v. First Bank of Marietta*,[132] borrowers

signed a note which simply allowed the bank to raise the interest on 30-days' notice. The court held that the clause, with neither limit nor definition, was too uncertain to be enforceable. Moreover, while the contract allowed for a decrease in rates, the borrower had no right to force a decrease when the bank's cost of money declined. To enforce such contracts, which lacked mutuality and definition, would have been unconscionable. The court ordered that the notes be calculated at their original rates.[133] (But similar provisions, when agreed to by an astute business person for whom refinancing is a viable escape from such an agreement, may be held to be enforceable.[134]) Finally, if the lender misrepresents the nature of a variable rate provision, the court may refuse to enforce it.[135]

4.4 Truth in Lending APR and Finance Charge Distinguished

4.4.1 Purpose of the Truth in Lending APR; Finance Charge Explained, Distinguished From Interest

As was noted in the discussion in § 4.2.2, when one creditor advertises that it lends money at "8% interest," and another creditor advertises "12% interest," the consumer would ordinarily have no way of knowing which creditor was offering a better deal. For example, an 8% "add-on" rate[136] is considerably more expensive than a 12% "actuarial" or "simple interest" rate.[137]

Theoretically, a consumer could ask each creditor how large the payments would be as a basis of comparison.

and secured by a dwelling); 12 C.F.R. § 34.22 (OCC regulations governing national banks and corresponding AMTPA lenders, applicable only to certain consumer credit transactions); 12 C.F.R. § 560.220 (FHLBB/[OTS after August, 1990] regulations governing federal S & Ls and AMTPA state housing creditors). *See* § 3.10, *supra* for a fuller discussion of AMTPA.

126 *See* § 4.3.6.2, *supra*.

127 For TIL variable-rate disclosure requirements, see National Consumer Law Center, Truth in Lending §§ 4.6.4 (closed-end), 5.5.5.10 (open-end, general), 5.11 (HELCs) (5th ed. 2003 and Supp.).

128 *See, e.g.*, Hubbard v. Fidelity Fed. Bank, 824 F. Supp. 909 (C.D. Cal. 1993) (TIL violated, but claim time-barred), *aff'd in part and rev'd in part*, 91 F.3d 75, 78 (9th Cir. 1996) (a consumer can state a claim for breach of contract if the loan documents require notice of periodic rate changes and the lender does not provide proper notice; if such a breach occurred, the court held that Truth in Lending could be violated as well); Whitford v. First Nationwide Bank, 1992 WL 442864 (W.D. Ky. settled Nov. 1992).

129 Fannie Mae Servicing, Sec. 4, Ch. 5, "Correction of Adjustment Errors" (Sept. 30, 1996) (Clearinghouse No. 52,527).

130 Ginsberg 1985 Real Estate P'ship v. Cadle Co., 39 F.3d 528 (5th Cir. 1994). Note that many variable rate contracts provide for such a contingency.

131 *See* the discussion of spreading at § 4.6.5, *infra*, for a more detailed analysis and case citations.

132 16 Ohio App. 3d 4, 473 N.E.2d 1210 (1983). *See also In re Computer Optics*, 126 B.R. 664, 669 n.9 (Bankr. D.N.H. 1991) (in *dictum*, court notes that bank's unfettered discretion to raise

or lower the interest rate without reference to a contractual formula would not be enforceable).

133 *Preston*, 473 N.E.2d at 1214–15. Note that the lender had also failed to comply with the Truth in Lending disclosure requirements. The appellate court held the trial court's remedy authorized both as actual damages under TIL, and under the common law contract rule that a court may enforce part of a contract and refuse to enforce other parts. *See also* Baxter v. First Bank of Marietta, 1992 WL 330252 (Ohio Ct. App. 1992).

134 Bank of New Hampshire v. Scanlon, 743 A.2d 842 (N.H. 1999) (bank allowed to recover deficiency on commercial loan even though variable rate was discretionary rather than tied to some external index; court holds this did not violate statute requiring disclosure of rate); Murello Constr. Co. v. Citizens Home Savings Co., 29 Ohio App. 3d 333, 505 N.E.2d 637 (1985) (distinguishing *Preston*).

135 *See* Baxter v. First Bank of Marietta, 1992 WL 330252 (Ohio Ct. App. 1992) (loan officer told homeowners it was a fixed-rate loan and to ignore variable rate provision; court found this to be "inconsistent additional information" which violated Truth in Lending, and held proper actual damages was refusal to enforce variable rate provision. *NB*: These facts also state a UDAP claim in states where the creditor is covered under the UDAP statute).

136 *See* § 4.3.2, *supra*.

137 *See* § 4.3.1, *supra*.

However, assuming that both creditors disclosed accurate information, the 8% add-on creditor might disclose that the consumer would have to pay $48.33 a month for 24 months, while the 12% actuarial creditor might disclose that the consumer would have to pay $88.84 a month for 12 months. Would arming the consumer with that information make his decision as to which offer was more financially attractive any more rational? At best, the theoretical consumer would still feel like he was comparing apples and oranges, with no common standard for evaluating the two loans.

With the explosive growth of consumer credit after World War II, Congress was concerned about the need for a standard basis of comparison for the costs of credit. Better-informed consumers presumably would choose creditors who offered the lowest costs, thus encouraging competition among creditors and theoretically lowering costs for consumer credit. Thus, Congress passed the Truth in Lending Act (TILA) in 1968[138] which requires creditors to disclose the costs of consumer credit using a standardized format and terminology.

Creditors must make numerous disclosures under the TILA, most of which are not discussed in this manual.[139] However, the two most important TILA disclosures will be briefly discussed here. They are the "finance charge" and the "annual percentage rate" or APR. Basically, the finance charge is the cost of credit on a dollar basis. It is conceptually comparable to the total interest charge on a credit contract, except that the finance charge is broadly defined[140] and generally includes charges that are often excluded from the definition of interest under state usury laws. The APR, on the other hand, is essentially an actuarial rate. Because it accurately reflects the effective cost of credit when declining balances are taken into account, unlike add-on or discount notes, the APR "truthfully" discloses the cost of credit. In most fixed term transactions, it is the rate which amortizes the finance charge and the "amount financed" (in TILA terminology)[141] at the scheduled repayment terms. (The amount financed is conceptually comparable to the loan principal. However, as TIL defines the finance charge more broadly than state usury law defines interest, the amount financed conversely is more narrowly defined than principal is defined for state usury law purposes.)

These distinctions between TIL finance charge and state law interest, and TIL amount financed and state law-defined principal are critical to remember.

The TIL finance charge includes not only that which is classified as "interest" under state usury law, but many of the numerous fees imposed by the lender which state laws often exclude from "interest," and which are instead frequently included in the face amount of the note, or principal.[142] For example, many usury statutes allow creditors to exclude points[143] or a "service charge" or "processing charge," which is often one or two percent of loan proceeds, from "interest" on a loan. Such provisions enable creditors to increase their return without exceeding the express "interest" ceilings of usury laws. These loopholes also permit creditors to understate the actual cost of credit to the borrower, a problem that TIL was specifically designed to cure. Thus, even though state law excludes a service charge from the law's definition of interest, under TIL's general definition, the service charge is a charge payable by the consumer and imposed by the creditor as a condition of the extension of credit and therefore must be included in the finance charge.[144]

By using an actuarial calculation method and a more realistic, inclusive definition of the cost of credit (the finance charge), the APR is the more accurate measure of the cost of credit.

Because the TIL finance charge in a credit contract thus often exceeds the "interest" as defined by state law, the APR, which uses the finance charge as one component of its calculation, in turn, will often exceed the "interest rate" shown on the contract, even if the contract interest rate is computed actuarially.[145] Indeed, given the nature of most usury laws and creditor practices, any disclosed finance charge and APR which do not exceed the corresponding "interest" and "interest rate" on the note should be viewed with some suspicion.[146] For purposes of examining a trans-

---

138 15 U.S.C. § 1601. *See also* 12 C.F.R. § 226 (Regulation Z); National Consumer Law Center, Truth in Lending (5th ed. 2003 and Supp.).

139 The TILA discussion in this manual is greatly simplified. It is designed to give practitioners the basic concepts behind the TILA and, in particular, its APR disclosure. Attorneys who need to know about the TILA in any detail, or who want to calculate an APR, should consult National Consumer Law Center, Truth in Lending (5th ed. 2003 and Supp.).

140 The finance charge includes any charge payable directly or indirectly by the consumer, imposed directly or indirectly by the creditor, as an incident to or a condition of the extension of credit. 15 U.S.C. § 1605(a); 12 C.F.R. § 226.4(a). *See generally* National Consumer Law Center, Truth in Lending Ch. 3 (5th ed. 2003 and Supp.). For a discussion of the rationale behind the U.C.C.C.'s expansive definition of finance charge, see Luttenegger v. Conseco Fin. Serv., 671 N.W.2d 425 (Iowa 2003).

141 This is a simplification, especially when irregular payments are involved. The APR in open-end credit transactions is generally a periodic rate, rather than a rate used to amortize the debt. See

National Consumer Law Center, Truth in Lending (5th ed. 2003 and Supp.) for more detail.

142 *See, e.g.,* Am. Gen. Fin. v. Bauer, 2001 Ohio App. LEXIS 2228 (May 4, 2001) (explaining difference between "interest" as defined by state mortgage loan act and "finance charge" as defined by TILA). The definition of "interest" under state usury law, including the treatment of various fees as interest, is discussed in Ch. 7, *infra.*

143 *See* § 7.2.2, *infra.*

144 *See* 12 C.F.R. § 226.4(b)(2), (3).

145 *See, e.g.,* Am. Gen. Fin., Inc. v. Bauer, 2001 Ohio App. LEXIS 2228 (May 4, 2001) (noting differences between TIL APR and rate under state mortgage loan act).

146 However, in some consumer credit transactions, the finance charge will include only "interest." In those situations, the APR

action for usury violations, however, it is the state law definitions of interest and interest rate that are dispositive, not the TIL-defined APR and finance charge.[147]

Let us return to the example given at the beginning of this section. Which loan is more advantageous to the consumer, an 8% add-on loan for two years or a 12% actuarial loan for one year? Assuming that there are no costs of credit other than interest, the former loan has an APR of 14.68% while the latter loan has an APR of 12%. Assuming the total cost of the credit is the most important consideration for the consumer, the 12% actuarial loan for one year is better for the consumer, who would save $93.84. (However, if monthly cash flow is the most critical factor for the borrower, he or she may consider saving $40.51 in payments for each of 12 months worth paying an extra $93.84 over the life of the loan.[148])

Since the state law definitions of interest and interest rate are the relevant ones for a usury analysis, is the APR of any relevance to an analysis of a contract for state law claims? Assuming the creditor has properly calculated the APR, a great disparity between the note interest rate and the APR may indicate excessive points were charged, or the loan was otherwise padded. Some difference is to be expected, but, for example, an 18% note rate and 28% APR suggests excessive prepaid finance charges which should be closely scrutinized.[149]

4.4.2 Calculation and Accuracy of the Annual Percentage Rate

As suggested in the preceding subsection, the APR is basically an actuarial rate which states the cost of credit as a yearly percentage rate. However, the Federal Reserve Board (FRB), which is charged with promulgating regulations to implement the TILA,[150] allows the APR to be calculated either on a strict actuarial basis, or through the use of the "United States Rule" (U.S. Rule).[151] The two methods are similar in that each requires the application of an interest rate to an unpaid balance to produce the interest accrued during each payment period. In most fixed term transactions the two methods will produce identical results. The use of the U.S. Rule, however, prevents the compounding of interest charges when interest accrues faster than it is paid off.

Unfortunately for both creditors and consumers, just as there is no formula for calculating actuarial rates in general, there is no simple formula to calculate the annual percentage rate using either the strict actuarial method or the U.S. Rule. Appendix J of the FRB's Regulation Z sets out in great detail "instructions and equations for the actuarial method."[152] These instructions and equations will probably intimidate, rather than enlighten most creditors and consumers. One alternative is to turn to experts who have produced computer programs, programmable and programmed calculators, and charts which can calculate annual percentage rates.[153]

Another alternative is to use the Federal Reserve Board's Annual Percentage Rate Tables. Volume I of these Tables can be used to compute annual percentage rates for "regular" transactions and for transactions with irregular first payments, irregular first periods, and irregular final payments.[154]

Volume II of the FRB's Annual Percentage Rate Tables can be used to calculate annual percentage rates for "irregular" transactions. An "irregular" transaction is one that includes one or more of the following features: multiple advances, irregular payment periods, or irregular payment amounts (other than an irregular first period or an irregular first or final payment).[155] Very few transactions subject to TIL will require the use of Volume II.

Creditors are allowed to use the Tables in calculating annual percentage rates but are not required to do so. They may use any other computation tool to calculate the annual percentage rate as long as the tool determines an annual

---

can be viewed as the actuarial interest rate for the transaction. (This assumes that the APR has been accurately disclosed.)

147 Some state statutes utilize the TIL rules in their definitions, in which case the properly calculated APR would be the relevant figure. *See also* Olympic Coast Investment v. Wright (*In re* Wright), 256 B.R. 626 (Bankr. D. Mont. 2000) (accepting APR as persuasive indication of compliance with Montana usury law).

148 Of course, an appraisal of relative values can be even further complicated. If the amount financed is concealing hidden finance charges, or if there are high closing costs legitimately excluded from the APR, the disclosed APR may not be a meaningful tool for comparison to other loans with higher APRs but fewer closing costs or no hidden finance charges. Similarly, refinancings involving points and closing costs can lessen the effectiveness of the APR as a meaningful tool. *See generally* Ch. 7 (hidden interest); §§ 6.3 and 6.5 (refinancing), *infra*.

149 *See* Ch. 7, *infra* (points), and Ch. 11, *infra* on other state law claims which also may be available.

150 The TILA regulations, known as Regulation Z, and the Official FRB Staff Commentary to Regulation Z are found at 12 C.F.R. § 226.

151 *See* 12 C.F.R. § 226.22(a) (Regulation Z). The U.S. Rule is discussed in greater detail in § 4.6.2, *infra*.

152 12 C.F.R. 226, Appx. J.

153 For example, Financial Publishing Co., 6 Beacon St., Boston, MA 02108 (617-262-4040) publishes many such charts and will calculate APR's for a nominal fee; the National Consumer Law Center will also calculate APR's free for Legal Services lawyers and at a nominal fee for others; the Texas Instrument business calculators and certain other hand-held calculators will compute APR's for many transactions. An APR program is also included on the companion CD to this volume.

154 There are two volumes. Volume I is suitable for the overwhelming majority of consumer credit transactions, and Volume II is used when less common, irregular transactions are involved. Consumer law practitioners would rarely need Volume II. The tables may be ordered for $5.00 each from the FRB. Prepaid orders should be sent to: Publications Services, Mail Stop 127, Board of Governors of the Federal Reserve System, Washington, D.C. 20551, (202) 452-3000.

155 12 C.F.R. § 226.22(a)(3), note 46.

percentage rate equal to the precise actuarial or U.S. Rule annual percentage rate, within the required degree of accuracy.[156] Other computation tools may produce annual percentage rates within the required degree of accuracy but different from the annual percentage rates computed using the Tables. Therefore, the fact that an annual percentage rate computed with the Tables is different from the disclosed annual percentage rate is only an indication that the annual percentage rate has not been disclosed accurately, not conclusive proof.

Another caveat is that creditors have the option of disregarding some payment schedule irregularities that arise from an irregular first payment period.[157] Since a creditor need not disclose whether it has disregarded the irregularity, the annual percentage rate in those situations should be calculated both ways, once disregarding the irregularity and once taking it into account.

Finally, TIL defines an "accurately" disclosed APR to allow some leeway. For most consumer credit transactions, there is an allowable tolerance of 1/8 of 1% (.125%).[158] For those who wish a more detailed explanation of TIL standards for calculating the APR, see NCLC's *Truth in Lending*.[159]

4.5 Interest Bearing v. Precomputed

4.5.1 Introduction

Section 4.3, *supra* referred to two basic ways of structuring consumer credit transactions: "interest bearing" and "precomputed." Both will be explained below, with the following hypothetical used to illustrate the differences. Consumer A and Consumer B each borrow $1,000 at an actuarial interest rate of 14.45% and are obligated to make 11 monthly payments of $90.00 each and a final, 12th monthly payment of $89.98. Both consumers make five monthly payments of $90 exactly as scheduled and then, having shared a lottery win, both prepay their loans. The only difference between the two loans is that A's loan is "interest bearing" and B's loan is "precomputed." The important thing to remember is that if A and B had each made all 12 payments exactly on time, there would have been no discernible difference between the two loans.

4.5.2 Interest Bearing

The traditional way to compute interest is on an "interest-bearing" basis. In an interest-bearing transaction, the consumer agrees to pay the principal (or amount financed, etc.)

plus interest as it accrues at a certain periodic rate. Usually, the consumer signs a note agreeing to pay the principal "together with interest thereon at an annual rate of ___ %."

With an "interest-bearing" note, the lender sets up the loan on a "declining balances" basis.[160] Every time a periodic payment is made, a periodic interest rate (the annual rate divided by the number of periods) is applied to the outstanding balance. The interest that is produced (plus late charges, if any) is subtracted from the payment; the remainder of the payment is applied to the outstanding balance, thereby reducing it. Each time a payment is made, the same process is repeated, until the outstanding balance is reduced to zero.

If at any time the amortization is interrupted (because of prepayment, acceleration, refinancing, etc.), the outstanding balance can be quickly determined by adding any interest (and other charges) that has accrued since the last payment to the previous outstanding balance. Ordinarily, no "rebates" of unearned interest charges have to be calculated, since the consumer is only being charged for interest that has been earned.[161]

Additional payments toward principal only will be applied as such where the consumer specifies the purpose of the additional funds. Where a consumer makes an unidentified partial payment mid-month, or adds additional money to a monthly payment, the payment will not be applied but instead will be held until enough money comes in to make a full payment.[162]

In our hypothetical, Consumer A has signed an "interest-bearing" note because she has agreed to pay "$1,000 together with interest thereon at the annual rate of 14.45%." She has also agreed to the payment schedule described above. Once the loan has been consummated, the lender sets up its books or computer on a declining balances method at an annual actuarial interest rate of 14.45%, a monthly periodic rate of 1.204% (14.45% divided by 12), or on a daily rate, using a 365-day year, of .0396% (14.45% divided by 365).[163] Assuming that Consumer A makes monthly payments exactly as scheduled, every time Consumer A makes a payment, the outstanding balance is multiplied by the monthly periodic rate of 1.204% to produce the interest earned during the previous month. The interest is subtracted from the payment, the remainder of which reduces the outstanding balance.

156 12 C.F.R. § 226.22(b)(2).

157 *See* 12 C.F.R. § 226.17(c)(4).

158 15 U.S.C. § 1606(c); 12 C.F.R. § 226.22(a)(2).

159 National Consumer Law Center, Truth in Lending §§ 4.6.4.3, 4.6.4.6 (5th ed. 2003 and Supp.).

160 *See* § 4.3.1, *supra*.

161 *See, however,* § 5.5.2.2, *infra*.

162 *See* § 5.4.3, *infra*, for a discussion of partial prepayments.

163 For a case dealing with the details of converting a daily rate to an annual rate under a state statute that incorporated TIL's calculation methods, see Hooks v. Cobb Center Pawn & Jewelry Brokers, Inc., 527 S.E.2d 566, 241 Ga. App. 305 (1999) (where statute allowed 25% interest "per 30 day period," annual rate was to be computed by dividing 25% by 30 to get a daily rate, and then multiplying the daily rate by 365, rather than by multiplying the 30-day rate by 12).

Chart 8 (Amortization of $1,000 Loan At 8% Add-on Interest) illustrates the process. For example, with the first monthly payment, the 1.204% periodic monthly rate is multiplied times the $1,000 unpaid balance to produce $12.04 interest. This interest is subtracted from the $90 payment and the $77.96 remainder is applied to the $1,000 unpaid balance, thereby reducing it to $922.04.[164] Every month the same process is repeated. If Consumer A made every $90 payment (and the final $89.98 payment) exactly on time, at the end of the twelve months, the balance would be zero.

However, under the hypothetical, Consumer A decides to pay off her loan immediately after making the fifth $90 payment. As can be seen, the new unpaid balance *after* the fifth payment is credited is $600.70. Assuming that there are no prepayment penalties, other additional charges, or any unearned charges which would have to be rebated (for example, unearned credit insurance premiums),[165] Consumer A need only pay the lender $600.70 to pay off the loan completely. Consumer A has been charged only for interest that has been earned. As noted on Chart 8, after five months $50.70 in interest has been earned.[166]

4.5.3 Precomputed

The other principal way of structuring consumer credit transactions is on a "precomputed" basis. Until fairly recently, almost all consumer credit installment transactions, with the notable exception of mortgages, were structured on a "precomputed" basis.

"Precomputed" is clearly a term of art, because in both "interest-bearing" and "precomputed" transactions, the interest which would be earned if every payment were made on time is precomputed in the sense that it is calculated in advance. However, "precomputed" transactions are called such because the interest for the transaction has been included in the amount the consumer *contractually* agrees to pay.

In a "precomputed" transaction, the consumer agrees to pay the *total of payments*, which includes both principal and all anticipated interest.[167] At the beginning of a precomputed transaction, the creditor calculates the interest that will be earned over the course of the transaction. However, during the life of the transaction, the creditor will not calculate the interest earned during each periodic payment interval. The creditor will not set up the loan on a "declining balances" basis and indeed, unless the loan is prepaid in some fashion, the creditor need not ever make any "interest" calculations.

Instead, every time a periodic payment is made, the creditor will subtract the payment from the original total of payments. If the consumer makes every payment on time, the total of payments will be reduced to zero and the loan will be fully paid.

If the consumer makes a late payment, clearly the creditor cannot charge extra interest, since interest calculations are not made during the life of the precomputed transaction. That is not to say, however, that a lender will not be compensated for the late payment. First, the relevant law and contract will usually authorize the lender to impose a late charge.[168] This late charge often exceeds the amount of interest that would be earned in an interest-bearing transaction.

Second, the lender may also be allowed to impose a "deferral" fee, the payment of which allows the consumer to make one or more payments later than originally scheduled. Again, the deferral fee often exceeds the amount of interest that would be earned in an interest-bearing transaction. Finally, the lender has various debt collection techniques, ranging from simple moral suasion to threats of acceleration or repossession, that may discourage the consumer from making late payments.

Precomputed transactions clearly offer creditors a simple bookkeeping method. Instead of being concerned about declining balances, periods between payments, interest earned during each period, etc., the creditor need only keep a simple record or ledger of the account. It starts with the total of payments. Then, each payment is subtracted from the total of payments (and late charges are added to the total of payments). Assuming that the creditor's records and addition/subtraction are accurate, the loan will be fully paid when the total of payments has been reduced to zero.

Prepayment, poses some difficulty, however. It would be unfair to require the consumer to simply pay the unpaid total of payments, since that includes interest that would have been earned over the full loan term, but has not yet been earned at the time of prepayment. Hence most state laws governing consumer credit transactions have long required that unearned interest and other unearned charges be rebated when a precomputed contract is terminated early, and in 1992 Congress mandated rebates of unearned interest in all consumer credit transactions.[169]

The simplicity inherent in bookkeeping for precomputed transactions is directly related to the inherent simplicity of the add-on and discount methods of calculating interest.[170] Just as the difficulty of calculating actuarial interest for installment transactions led to the widespread use of add-on and discount interest, so the relative complexity of keeping books on an interest-bearing basis has led to the widespread use of precomputed transactions.

---

164 $1,000.00 − $77.96 = $922.04.

165 *See* § 8.6, *infra*.

166 This is the sum of $12.04, $11.10, $10.15, $9.19, and $8.22, the interest earned each month during the first five months.

167 Contrast this with an "interest-bearing" transaction in which the consumer agrees to pay the *principal* plus interest as it accrues. *See* Foster v. Centrex Capital Corp., 80 S.W.3d 140 (Tex. App. 2002) (construing contract as a precomputed transaction).

168 *See* §§ 4.8, 7.2.4, *infra*.

169 15 U.S.C. § 1615(a)(1). How rebates of unearned charges are calculated is discussed in Ch. 5, *infra*.

170 *See* §§ 4.3.2, 4.3.3, *supra*. Indeed those two methods are generally used only in precomputed transactions.

In the hypothetical, we know that Consumer B signed a "precomputed" note because she has agreed to pay $1,079.98 (total of payments) in eleven monthly installments of $90 each and a twelfth monthly installment of $89.98. This total of payments includes $1,000 principal and $79.98 precomputed interest. The promise-to-pay portion of the Note need not refer to any interest rate, because the interest has been "precomputed" and already included in the total of payments.

Once the loan has been consummated, the lender sets up its books or computer on a declining total of payments method, beginning with a total of payments of $1,079.98. Every time Consumer B makes a $90 payment, the payment is subtracted from the unpaid total of payments. The lender will also *add* to the unpaid total of payments any late charge or other charges that have been earned since the last payment. For example, after Consumer B has made her first $90 payment, the lender subtracts $90 from the $1,079.98 unpaid total of payments for a new balance of $989.98.[171]

Every month the same process is repeated. If Consumer B makes every $90 payment (and the final $89.98 payment) exactly on time (or at least does not make any late payments and thereby avoids late charges), at the end of the twelve months, the balance will be zero.[172] As mentioned previously, there are no practical differences between interest-bearing and precomputed transactions when every payment is made on time and all payments are made.

However, under the hypothetical, Consumer B decides to pay off her loan immediately after making her fifth $90 payment. The unpaid balance after five payments of $90 is $629.98,[173] assuming that no late charges or other charges have been added on. If the lender asked Consumer B to pay $629.98, Consumer B would point out that this would be unfair. The $629.98 unpaid total of payments includes interest that would have been earned if the loan went the full twelve months, but only five months' interest has been earned. In other words, not all of the $979.98 precomputed interest has been earned after five months, and some of it should be rebated.

At this point, the lender suddenly remembers his legal, contractual, and moral obligation to rebate unearned interest in the event of prepayment.[174] The lender calculates the rebate by using the Rule of 78, which, as is explained in § 5.6.3.3, *infra*, gives it a rebate percentage of 35.90% or .3590.[175] Multiplying 35.90% times the precomputed interest of $79.98 produces a rebate of unearned interest of $28.71.[176] (This means that *earned* interest = $79.98 − $28.71 = $51.27.) The *unearned* interest of $28.71 is

subtracted from the unpaid total of payments of $629.98 to produce a "payoff" balance of $601.27.[177]

Note that this figure is slightly higher than the $600.70 "payoff" balance for the interest-bearing loan. The difference resulted because in the interest-bearing transaction, only $50.70 in interest was earned after the fifth payment, while in the precomputed transaction, $51.27 was considered "earned" after the fifth payment.[178]

4.6 Special Calculation Problems

4.6.1 Compound Interest

4.6.1.1 When Does Compounding Occur?

Most attorneys are probably familiar with the concept of compound interest. In essence, compounding is the practice of charging interest on interest, or in other words, of adding accrued interest to the principal amount of a debt and making subsequent interest calculations on the basis of this new, increased principal amount. The effect of compounding is to increase the effective interest rate paid on the debt.

A common example of the compounding of interest can be found in the typical bank savings account. Interest on such accounts is computed at some stated interval: daily, monthly, or quarterly. At the end of each interval, the amount of interest earned during that interval is calculated and credited to the account. In subsequent intervals, the interest payments which have previously been credited to the account themselves bear interest, just like cash deposited in the account. For example, if a depositor opens a savings account with a $1,000 deposit, and the account pays 5% interest, compounded monthly, then the following calculations would apply. First, the *monthly* interest rate is 5/12% or .0041666. Thus, after the first month, if there have been no new deposits or withdrawals, the account will have earned $1,000 × 0.0041666 = $4.17 (rounded) in interest. This $4.17 is credited to the account and bears interest in subsequent months. Therefore, the interest earned in the second month will be slightly higher: $1,004.17 × 0.0041666 = $4.18 (rounded). The balance after two months is $1,008.35. As a result of the monthly compounding, the effective annual interest rate paid will be 5.116% rather than 5.0%.[179] In general, the more frequently interest

---

171 $1,079.98 − $90.00 = $989.98.

172 $1,079.98 − (11 × $90 + 1 × $89.98) = 0.

173 5 × $90 = $450.00. $1,079.98 − $450.00 = $629.98.

174 Rebates of unearned interest are discussed in much greater detail in Ch. 5, *infra*.

175 (7 × 8) ÷ (12 × 13) = .3590.

176 $79.98 × .3590 = $28.71.

177 $629.98 − $28.71 = $601.27.

178 The Rule of 78, used in this hypothetical, is a short-cut formula for calculating interest which has a consistent bias in favor of the creditor. For this reason, there are legal restrictions on its use. *See* § 5.6.3.3, *infra*.

179 This difference may not seem large at first glance. Yet, apparently small differences in interest rates have significant consequences in large, long-term transactions. For example, consider a mobile home purchase, purportedly at 24% annual interest, which is actually computed with daily compounding. The ef-

on an account is compounded, the more the compounding increases the effective interest rate.

Interest can compound on an interest-bearing loan[180] in essentially the same manner that it compounds in a savings account. Indeed, a bank account can be regarded as a variety of interest-bearing loan, repayable on demand, in which the depositor is the creditor and the bank is the debtor. Compounding in interest-bearing consumer loans is, however, not a certainty. Rather, it depends first on whether interest on the loan is charged faster than it is paid off and, second, on how any excess interest is treated after it accrues.

In order for compounding to occur, interest must in some fashion be charged on a loan more rapidly than it is paid off.[181] This can happen in several ways. For example, if interest on a loan is calculated and charged daily while payments are due only monthly, then the interest cannot be paid as rapidly as it accrues and compounding may occur, even if all payments are made as scheduled.[182] Alternatively, if the amount of interest which accrues during a payment interval is larger than the payment due in that interval,[183]

_____

fective yield thus will be 24.234% per annum. Over a 30-year loan of $40,000, the borrower would pay $248,231 for the 24% simple interest loan, but $251,021 for the same loan with daily compounding. The compounding costs the borrower $2,790.

180 The discussion in this subsection is limited to interest-bearing transactions except where otherwise indicated. For a discussion of the distinction between interest-bearing and precomputed transactions, see § 4.5, *supra*.

181 The assumption made here is that payments on a loan are attributed first to the interest which accrued in the previous interval and subsequently to the principal debt. This is the standard procedure in actuarial calculation. *See, e.g.,* 12 C.F.R. § 226 Appendix J(a) (actuarial calculations under Regulation Z). Compare, however, the methods used to calculate damages in usury cases (§ 10.8.2.2, *infra*).

182 Compounding will occur whenever interest is calculated more frequently than it is paid, provided that the interest is added to the outstanding principal balance as soon as it is computed.

183 The periodically accruing interest can exceed the scheduled periodic payment in several situations. In some variable rate mortgages, the size of the monthly payment is capped, but the interest rate that may be charged did not have to be capped until 1987, and even after 1987 the cap can be set at any level. Under such contracts, the interest charged will exceed the monthly payment if the contract rate goes high enough, and negative amortization will occur. Similarly, accruing interest can exceed the required monthly payment on an open-end account if the minimum payment is not set high enough. *Cf.* Grunbeck v. Dime Savings Bank, 74 F.3d 331 (1st Cir. 1996) (allegation that negative amortization resulting from similar circumstances in variable rate loans violated state simple interest statute; issue on appeal was preemption [*see* § 3.9.3.1, *supra*]).

A different situation in which accruing interest can exceed scheduled payments involves scheduled balloon interest payments. Such terms are not uncommon. For example, when "points" are charged in conjunction with a loan and are "financed" by the lender, the dollar amount of the points will probably exceed any concurrently scheduled payments, causing compounding even if the borrower makes all payments as scheduled. *See* § 7.2.2, *infra* for a discussion of "points" as interest charges.

then the excess accrued interest will probably be added to the outstanding loan balance, causing compounding in subsequent interest calculations. Finally, and perhaps most commonly, excess interest will accrue when a borrower makes late payments or misses payments on an interest-bearing debt.[184]

The second prerequisite for compounding interest on an interest-bearing debt is that any accrued, unpaid interest be added to the outstanding principal balance of the debt and treated as principal in subsequent interest calculations.[185] The addition of accrued interest to the principal debt in this manner is known as the "actuarial rule" and is widely employed, especially in open-end credit accounts.[186] However, the actuarial rule is not the only way to handle excess interest. In fact, the U.S. Supreme Court has ruled that overdue interest generally should *not* be added to principal to allow compounding.

> The correct rule in general is, that the creditor shall calculate interest whenever a payment is made. To this interest the payment is first to be applied; and if it exceed the interest due, the balance is to be applied to diminish the principal. If the payment fall short of the interest, the balance of interest is not to be added to the principal so as to produce interest. This rule is equally applicable whether the debt be one which expressly draws interest, or on which interest is given in the name of damages.[187]

This latter approach to accounting for accrued interest, which has become known as the "U.S. Rule," essentially requires creditors to maintain separate accounts for principal

_____

184 Compounding is most readily justified in this latter situation because the creditor suffers a loss due to the late payment and the compounding may compensate for this loss if it is not otherwise compensated by special late fees. *See* § 7.2.4, *infra*. *Cf.* Norman v. Norman, 506 N.W.2d 254 (Mich. Ct. App. 1993) (simple interest mandated in absence of statute, explicit agreement or "special circumstances dictating otherwise;" *in dicta*, court speculates that equitable compound interest may be appropriate if a debt arising out of a divorce judgment was significantly delinquent, requiring the creditor-spouse to seek court aid in enforcing judgment). However, at least one court has held that an erratic and incomplete payment history is no defense to a usury challenge to compounding. A.J. Reynolds v. Succession of Williams, 628 So. 2d 1 (La. Ct. App. 1993).

In contrast, compounding which cannot be avoided by the borrower's timely payment of installments is merely a ruse for charging more than the stated contact rate.

185 *See, e.g.,* Niggeling v. Michigan Dep't of Transp., 488 N.W.2d 791, 792 (Mich. Ct. App. 1992). *But see* Pentico v. Mad-Wayler, Inc., 964 S.W.2d 708 (Tex. App. 1998) (adding late fees to outstanding balance resulting in an increase of the principal balance upon which interest is charged does not constitute compounding).

186 Estate of Baxter v. Shaw Assocs., Inc., 797 So. 2d 396 (Miss. App. 2001) (construing statute allowing "actuarial" interest as allowing compounding).

187 Story v. Livingston, 38 U.S. (13 Pet.) 359, 371 (1839).

and unpaid interest and allows the assessment of interest only on the principal account.[188]

An example may help to illustrate the differences between the actuarial rule and the U.S. Rule. Assume that the outstanding principal balance of a mortgage loan is $50,000, that all payments are up to date, that the interest rate is 1% monthly, and that the interest which consequently accrues on the debt in the current month is $500. Assume further that the normal monthly mortgage payment is $800. If the borrower makes this regular $800 payment, or indeed if the borrower makes any payment which meets or exceeds the accrued interest of $500, the results under the actuarial rule and U.S. Rule will be the same; the first $500 of the payment will be attributed to the accrued interest and any remainder will be used to pay down the $50,000 principal balance. If, however, the borrower for some reason makes a lower payment, say $400, there will be accrued but unpaid interest of, in this example, $100, and the difference between the actuarial rule and U.S. Rule comes into play.

Under the actuarial rule, the $100 in unpaid interest will be added to the $50,000 balance, and the sum of $50,100 will be used to compute the following month's interest which, at the 1% monthly rate, will be $501. If the normal $800 payment is made the next month, the first $501 of that payment is attributed to interest and the remaining $299 is used to pay down the principal debt, leaving a balance of $49,801.

Under the U.S. Rule, the $100 of accrued but unpaid interest is not added to the $50,000 balance but is kept separately and does not bear interest. Thus, the $50,000 balance is unchanged and the following month's interest remains $500. If the normal $800 payment is then made the next month, $100 of the payment will first be used to pay off the existing accrued interest, $500 of the payment will be attributed to the interest that has just accrued, and the remaining $200 will be used to pay down principal, leaving a balance of $49,800. The use of the U.S. Rule has left the borrower with a balance which is one dollar lower than the balance computed with the actuarial rule. The borrower's savings are not just one dollar, however. Rather, the borrower will continue to save money, initially at the rate of one cent per month,[189] throughout the loan term because his balance will always be slightly lower than it would have been under the actuarial rule. Thus, slightly less interest will

accrue every month and the principal will be paid down slightly faster. Depending on the time the loan remains outstanding, the savings from the U.S. Rule to the borrower in this example could be several dollars. The difference would be much greater if there were multiple missed, partial, or late payments.[190]

Although compound interest is most often thought of in conjunction with interest-bearing accounts, the two components of compounding—a charge of interest in excess of any concurrent payment, and the addition of this excess to the principal balance—are by no means so limited. Indeed, compounding is an element in many credit practices which are commonly used to increase yield on all kinds of consumer loans. For example, discount interest,[191] which is invariably associated with precomputed debt, employs compounding because the borrower is assessed interest on a greater sum than is actually received and because, under most usury statutes, the difference between the amount the borrower receives and the amount on which the interest is calculated is, itself, interest. Similarly, when creditors charge "points" or other fees at the consummation of a loan,[192] and then "finance" those charges by including them in the face amount of a loan note instead of demanding immediate cash payment, compound interest is being assessed. The fees themselves are usually interest payments unless a statute says otherwise,[193] and once these fees are added to loan principal, they themselves bear interest. In general, any time a creditor includes interest charges in the face amount of a loan note, it is assessing compound interest.[194]

4.6.1.2 Legal Restrictions on Compounding

The law traditionally has taken a dim view of the compounding of interest. The courts have recognized that compounding increases the yield which a creditor receives, and have questioned the use of compounding even when the ultimate yield that it provides is below the usury ceiling.[195] The basic concern seems to be that compounding is deceptive, so that "an improvident debtor is not likely to realize the

---

188   All payments are attributed first to paying off any accrued interest. Only after all accrued interest in the interest "account" is paid off are payments attributed to principal. *See* 12 C.F.R. § 226, Appendix J(a) (Federal Reserve Board explanation of U.S. Rule).

189   At a 1% monthly interest rate, the mortgage balance under the actuarial rule, which is $49,801, will earn one cent more in one month than the U.S. Rule balance of $49,800. Thus, after an additional month, the difference between the balances will increase from $1.00 to $1.01. Due to the effects of continued compounding, the difference between the balances will increase for as long as the debt is outstanding.

190   *See, e.g.*, American Bank v. Wegener, 776 S.W.2d 922, 923 (Mo. Ct. App. 1989) (compounding would have added $40,804.17 in interest).

191   *See* § 4.3.3, *supra*. Of course, if discount interest is authorized by statute, then the compounding is probably legal.

192   *See* §§ 4.7, 7.2.2, *infra*.

193   In general, the statutory definition of "interest" must be addressed before the presence of compounding, at least from a legal standpoint, can be determined. If "points" or other fees are interest under the controlling statute, but are treated as loan principal in a credit contract, then compounding is inevitable. If the creditor may legally exclude points or other up-front fees from "interest," then compounding may not technically be present, although the economic consequences are the same.

194   Hidden interest is discussed in Ch. 7, *infra*.

195   *See* Citizens Nat'l Bank v. Donnell, 195 U.S. 369 (1904); Acker v. Provident Nat'l Bank, 512 F.2d 729 (3d Cir. 1975).

extent to which the interest will accumulate."[196] Of course, this concern could just as well be voiced (and sometimes is) about myriad other practices which creditors use to increase yield. Nevertheless, perhaps because the effects of compounding are easy to perceive, the courts have been especially vigorous in its condemnation. Sufficient case law exists to make compounding open to challenge in many jurisdictions if it is not expressly authorized by statute.[197]

Many cases which discuss the validity of compound interest are not usury cases. Rather they are cases argued under common law contract principles which have challenged compounding on public policy grounds.[198] In many jurisdictions, although not all, agreements requiring the payment of compound interest have been held to violate public policy.[199] However the courts which take this position against compounding have distinguished agreements to compound interest in connection with debts not yet owed, from agreements to pay interest on interest obligations which have already come due, and have declared that the latter do not involve "compounding."[200] For example, a

provision in a loan agreement to charge interest on any future interest installments which the borrower does not pay on time might be void, while an agreement made after an installment was overdue to pay interest on the overdue installment might be valid. The reason for this somewhat unlikely distinction appears to be a belief that the former transaction allows debts to mount without the borrower's knowledge while the latter merely compensates the creditor for its loss.[201]

Although contract law arguments against the imposition of compound interest are worth considering in many consumer transactions, they have one major drawback. Specifically, the remedy for an impermissible agreement to compound interest may be limited to the voiding of the improper contract clause. Thus, whenever possible, it is to a consumer's advantage to argue that compounding is prohibited not only by contract law, but also by a usury statute which contains more expansive remedies.

There are two ways in which compounding can lead to a usury violation. First, compounding can violate a usury statute if the effect of the compounding is to raise the creditor's yield above the statutory ceiling. Thus, a 7.5% simple interest ceiling is violated when a lender charges interest at 7.5%, compounded quarterly, because the actual return is 7.72%.[202]

---

196 Household Fin. Corp. v. Goldring, 33 N.Y.S.2d 514 (App. Div.), *aff'd*, 43 N.E.2d 715 (N.Y. 1942).

197 *See, e.g.*, Iowa Sup. Ct Bd. of Prof. Ethics & Conduct v. McKittrick, 683 N.W.2d 554 (Iowa 2004) (compound interest generally not permitted without agreement between parties and specifically not permitted on finance charge for accounts receivable); A.J. Reynolds v. Succession of Williams, 628 So. 2d 1 (La. Ct. App. 1993) (creditor compounded in a transaction not subject to one of Louisiana's statutory exceptions to general rule against compounding). *See generally* Annot., 10 A.L.R.3d 421 (1966) (definition of compound interest in statutes prohibiting compounding); Annot. 57 A.L.R.2d 630 (1958) (interest taken in advance as usury); Annot. 37 A.L.R. 325 (1925) (validity of agreement to pay interest on interest) *supplemented at* 76 A.L.R. 1484 (1932).

198 A few statutes apart from regular usury laws have also prohibited compounding. *See, e.g.*, Re Chinese Am. Bank, 36 Hawaii 571 (1943) (no compounding found in transaction); Lee v. Melby, 93 Minn. 4, 100 N.W. 379 (1904).

199 Many of the cases are quite old. They are collected in Annot., 37 A.L.R. 325 (1925) *supplemented at* 76 A.L.R. 1484 (1932). Numerous New York opinions have stated that compounding contravenes public policy. *See, e.g.*, Debentureholders Protective Committee v. Continental Inv. Corp., 679 F.2d 264 (1st Cir. 1982), *cert. denied*, 459 U.S. 894 (1982) (interpreting New York law); *In re* Rosner, 48 B.R. 538 (Bankr. E.D.N.Y. 1985); *In re* Webb, 29 B.R. 280 (Bank. E.D.N.Y. 1983); Giventer v. Arnow, 333 N.E.2d 366 (N.Y. 1975). *But see* Elliott Assocs. v. Banco De La Nacion, 194 F.R.D. 116 (S.D.N.Y. 2000) (applying statutory amendment allowing compound interest); Spodek v. Park Property Development Assocs., 759 N.E.2d 760 (N.Y. 2001) (allowing post-judgment interest on judgment that represented both principal and interest); Steinberg v. Williams, 558 N.Y.S.2d 188 (App. 1990) (negative amortization in mortgage was not compounding; also, loan was a purchase money mortgage to which usury law did not apply); Harris v. Coles, 60 S.W.3d 848 (Tenn. App. 2001) (compound interest allowed, but only if parties have agreed to it).

200 *See* Smith v. MRCC P'ship, 792 S.W.2d 301 (Ark. 1990) (not usury to add accrued, unpaid interest on antecedent debt to principal on new debt and write new contract with maximum

rate of interest on whole amount); Coupounas v. Madden, 514 N.E.2d 1316 (Mass. 1987); Beneficial Fin. Co. v. Fusco, 203 A.2d 457 (Me. 1964); Giventer v. Arnow, 333 N.E.2d 366 (N.Y. 1975); Household Fin. Co. v. Goldring, 33 N.Y.S.2d 514 (App. Div.) *aff'd*, 43 N.E.2d 715 (N.Y. 1942). *See also In re* Rosner, 48 B.R. 538 (Bankr. E.D.N.Y. 1985) (compounding by prior agreement void); Matter of Estate of Jackson, 508 N.Y.S.2d 671 (App. Div. 1986).

201 Giventer v. Arnow, 333 N.E.2d 366 (N.Y. 1975). *See, e.g.*, Boatmen's First Nat'l Bank of Kansas City v. Bogina Petroleum Engineers, 794 S.W.2d 703 (Mo. Ct. App. 1990). *See also* Strawn Furniture Co. v. Austin, 655 S.W.2d 397 (Ark. 1983) (10/12% per month compounds to 10.76% annually, exceeding 10% usury ceiling). *But see* North Dade Church of God v. JM Statewide, 851 So. 2d 194 (Fla. Dist. Ct. App. 2003) (allowing the payment of interest on past-due interest because such payment "supplies the place of prompt payment and indemnifies the creditor for his or her forbearance").

202 In Giventer v. Arnow, 333 N.E.2d 366, 368 (N.Y. 1975) the court states: "it is considered against public policy to encourage creditors to silently permit debts to progressively mount at the expense of debtors who, often unaware of the consequences of the prior agreement, tend to confuse forbearance with indulgence." *Cf.* Haider v. Montgomery, 423 N.W.2d 494 (N.D. 1988) (though compounding prohibited, forfeiture penalty inapplicable; forfeiture penalty only applies where interest exceeds maximum allowable rate (in this case 13.854%) and effective rate resulting from compounding herein was 13.497%); Ervin v. Muller, 2003 WL 21744332 (Wash. Ct. App. July 29, 2003) (contract, which allowed for compound interest, was permissible; effective rate did not exceed statutory usury ceiling). Note that this argument can be made in deregulated states, too, where the statute provides that the permissible rate is that "agreed to" by the parties. *See* § 9.2.8, *infra*. Unless the contract itself specifically provides for compounding, it can be

The second situation in which compounding of interest may violate usury laws occurs when a usury statute prohibits compounding, either explicitly or implicitly, regardless of the resulting yield.[203] The most significant examples of such statutes were the earlier drafts of the Uniform Small Loan Law which provided that: "Interest shall not be paid, deducted, or received in advance. Interest shall be computed and paid only on unpaid principal balances and shall not be compounded."[204]

This clause clearly prohibits compounding through the use of open-end credit accounts.[205] It has also been read by many courts to prohibit a creditor from refinancing an existing debt and adding the unpaid interest which had accrued under the existing loan to the principal of the new obligation.[206] A minority of courts, however, has permitted such *de facto* compounding through refinancing, despite the small loan law provisions, by reading into the act the

common law distinction between agreements which automatically compound interest and those which provide only for the payment of interest on interest which has already accrued.[207]

In addition to small loan laws, other usury statutes may limit or prohibit compounding.[208] In some jurisdictions, usury statutes allow compounding only if the parties expressly agree to the practice.[209] Case decisions suggest that courts will require any such agreement to be explicit, so the practitioner should carefully review the contract language where the creditor has compounded interest.[210]

---

argued that the effect of compounding is to charge more than the "agreed-to" cap.

203 *Cf.* Grunbeck v. Dime Savings Bank, 74 F.3d 331 (1st Cir. 1996) (involving allegation that negative amortization resulting from minimum payments too low to pay accrued interest on variable rate mortgage increases violated New Hampshire's simple interest statute; issue on appeal was preemption [*see* § 3.9.3.1, *supra*]); A.J. Reynolds v. Succession of Williams, 628 So. 2d 1 (La. Ct. App. 1993) (court found implied contract for usury where creditor's accounting method on erratically paid loan compounded interest annually, in violation of general rule against compounding, over twenty-three year life of transaction; fact that amount paid was less than would have been paid had loan been fully paid according to terms did not negate the usury inherent in the compounding, nor did the fact that debtor still may have owed something in true principal when usury was asserted).

204 Uniform Small Loan Law, 6th Draft, § 13 (1935) *reprinted in* Hubachek, Annotations On Small Loan Laws (Russell Sage Foundation 1938). Earlier drafts contained similar prohibitions against compounding. The seventh draft, however, gives creditors a limited right to compound when refinancing small loans:

> [c]harges shall not be compounded; provided that, if part or all of the consideration for a loan contract is the unpaid principal balance of a prior loan, then the principal amount payable under such loan contract may include any unpaid charges on the prior loan which have accrued within sixty days before the making of such loan contract.

Uniform Small Loan Law, 7th Draft, § 13 (1942) *reprinted in* Curran, Trends In Consumer Credit Legislation (University of Chicago Press, 1966).

205 *See* Partain v. First Nat'l Bank of Montgomery, 467 F.2d 167 (5th Cir. 1972).

206 *See* Madison Personal Loan, Inc. v. Parker, 124 F.2d 143 (2d Cir. 1941) (applying New York law) (excellent discussion, but its authority in New York is questionable due to later state court decisions); Vann v. Accounts Supervision Co., 88 So. 2d 548 (Fla. 1956); Lanier v. Consolidated Loan & Fin. Co., 170 S.E. 99 (Ga. App. 1933); Securities Fin. Co. v. Maranto, 119 So. 2d 120 (La. Ct. App. 1966); Vaughn v. Graham, 121 S.W.2d 222 (Mo. App. 1938); Commonwealth v. State Loan Corp., 176 A. 516 (Pa. Super. 1935).

207 *See* Beneficial Fin. Co. v. Fusco, 203 A.2d 457 (Me. 1964); Rouse v. Jennings, 249 N.W. 10 (Mich. 1933); Household Fin. Corp. v. Goldring, 33 N.Y.S. 514 (App. Div.), *aff'd*, 43 N.E.2d 715 (N.Y. 1942).

208 *See, e.g.,* American Bank v. Wegener, 776 S.W.2d 922 (Mo. Ct. App. 1989) (statute limits compounding to once annually); N.D. Cent. Code § 47-14-09 a violation of which was found in Haider v. Montgomery, 423 N.W.2d 494 (N.D. 1988) (compounded interest forfeited but not all interest because compounding did not raise interest rate above usury limit); Northwestern Equipment, Inc. v. Badinger, 403 N.W.2d 8 (N.D. 1987) (seller compounded interest on account receivable; because it failed to prove that it fell within an exception to the prohibition against compounding, summary judgment in its favor reversed).

209 Fielder v. Credit Acceptance Corp., 19 F. Supp. 2d 966 (W.D. Mo. 1998) (interpreting Mo. Rev. Stat. § 408.080) (parties did not contract to collect compound interest; creditor practice of compounding interest in connection with its repossession and deficiency actions subjects it to the penalty provisions of the state Motor Vehicle Time Sales Act), *vacated on jurisdictional grounds*, 188 F.3d 1031 (8th Cir. 1999) (ordering interest overcharge portion of case severed and remanded to state court).

210 *See, e.g.,* Pennsylvania Truck Lines, Inc. v. Solar Equity Corp., 127 F.R.D. 127 (N.D. Ill. 1988) (compounding would render inconsistent parties' agreement to "1 1/2% per month (18% per annum)"), *aff'd on other grounds*, 882 F.2d 221 (7th Cir. 1989); *In re* Brummer, 147 B.R. 552 (Bankr. D. Mont. 1992) (under Montana statute, contract must unequivocally provide for compounding; parties' intent or market practice will not suffice); *In re* Charleston Medical Center, Ltd., 100 B.R. 962 (Bankr. S.D. Ohio 1989) (contract provision that interest is to be computed and payable "on a monthly basis" does not expressly allow compounding of interest, since it speaks merely to periodicity rather than to method of computation); Ninety Five Ten v. Crain, 282 Cal. Rptr. 141 (Ct. App. 1991) (note calling for interest "per annum-monthly" calls for simple, not compound interest; creditor could not circumvent requirement for agreement to compound by seeking pre-judgment interest); Haughton v. Namano, Inc., 222 Ga. App. 644, 476 S.E.2d 31 (1996) (may be usurious to charge interest on interest on an open account, in absence of agreement); Weigel Broadcasting Co. v. Smith, 289 Ill. App. 3d 602, 682 N.E.2d 745 (1996) (compound interest disfavored; available only when no statutory bar and the parties specifically agree); Helland v. Helland, 573 N.E.2d 357 (Ill. App. Ct. 1991) ("8% per annum" specified in contract did not permit compounding); Norman v. Norman, 506 N.W.2d 254 (Mich. Ct. App. 1993) (in absence of statute, explicit agreement of parties or special circumstances dictating otherwise, rule is to calculate interest on simple, not compound basis); Lincoln Lumber Co. v. Fowler, 533 N.W.2d 898 (Neb. 1995) (in absence of statute or contract, compound interest not allowed; documents signed by

155

Usury violations have been found where no specific agreement existed.[211]

Finally, consumer law practitioners should consider whether any provisions of a usury statute may impliedly prohibit compounding of interest. For example, the Third Circuit held that a Pennsylvania installment sales act which authorized the assessment of "simple" interest was violated by compounding even though the effective yield received by the creditor did not exceed the simple interest ceiling.[212] In general, the distaste which courts have shown for compounding suggests that statutes must clearly authorize the practice before it will be permitted.[213] For example, the

Vermont Supreme Court has held that, without further expression of legislative intent, the use of the phrase "computed by the actuarial method" in the statute on judgment interest was not sufficient to change the common law rule which required computing by simple interest and prohibited compounding.[214]

4.6.2 Odd Payment Periods and Odd Payment Amounts

4.6.2.1 General

Most of the discussion thus far of installment interest methods and calculations has rested on the assumption that in any particular transaction all of the payment periods are equal[215] and that all of the payment amounts are also equal.[216] This assumption holds true for most consumer credit installment transactions. Indeed, many consumer credit laws, particularly add-on interest usury laws,[217] require creditors to impose payment schedules with equal payment periods and/or equal payment amounts.

The reason for these requirements is that unequal periods or amounts can affect the effective interest rate (and, of course, the annual percentage rate).[218] Generally, *higher* effective interest rates will be created by relatively shorter initial payment periods and higher initial payments because the consumer must repay the loan more quickly. (For this reason, it is not uncommon for used car dealers to run afoul of both usury laws and TIL when they require repayment periods shorter than one month, as will be discussed in more detail below, § 4.6.2.2.)

Conversely, *lower* effective interest rates will be created by relatively longer initial payment periods, lower initial payments, and larger final payments, because the consumer repays the loan more slowly.

---

guarantor did not specify compound interest, so creditor limited to simple interest); Campbell v. Lake Terrace, Inc., 905 P.2d 163 (Nev. 1995) (compound interest disfavored; allowed only if statute or agreement specifically provides); Christensen v. Munns, 812 P.2d 69 (Utah App. Ct. 1991) (compound interest not authorized where contract specified the variable rate to be applied to the principal until maturity, and specified no post-maturity rate); Mountain States Broadcasting v. Neale, 776 P.2d 643 (Utah App. 1989) (note providing that unpaid interest would "bear like interest as the principal" did not explicitly allow monthly compounding). *Cf.* Southfield Western, Inc. v. City of Southfield, 520 N.W.2d 721 (Mich. 1994) (construing statute to allow pre-judgment interest to be included in amount on which post-judgment interest is charged, since statute made a distinction between pre- and post-judgment); American Bank v. Wegener, 776 S.W.2d 922 (Mo. Ct. App. 1989) (agreement to compound interest found in provision that note and all installments were to bear interest after maturity, since installments included interest; compounding limited by statute to once annually); Ervin v. Muller, 2003 WL 21744332 (Wash. Ct. App. July 29, 2003) (upholding mortgage contract provision providing that unpaid interest will be added to the principal).

211 *See* McConnell v. Merrill Lynch, Pierce, Fenner, & Smith, 578 P.2d 1375 (Cal. 1978) *later opinion at* 662 P.2d 916 (Cal. 1983) (form contract which authorized interest charges in accordance with broker's "usual custom" did not constitute agreement to compound); Crest Savings & Loan Ass'n v. Mason, 581 A.2d 120 (N.J. Super. Ct. 1990). *See also* Acker v. Provident Nat'l Bank, 512 F.2d 729 (3d Cir. 1975); Helland v. Helland, 573 N.E.2d 357 (Ill. App. Ct. 1991) (compounding authorized only when parties specifically agree to it and no statute bars it); Coupounas v. Madden, 514 N.E.2d 1316 (Mass. 1987) (in absence of express agreement to pay compound interest on interest-bearing account invoices due, creditor cannot compound interest); William C. Dear & Assocs., Inc. v. Plastronics, Inc., 913 S.W.2d 251 (Tex. App. 1996) (commercial case where parties did not agree to any interest rate; in absence of written agreement Tex. Rev. Civ. Stat. Ann. art. 5069-1:03 applied; statute does not expressly allow compounding so court held it is prohibited).

212 Acker v. Provident Nat'l Bank, 512 F.2d 729 (3d Cir. 1975). *See also* Stovall v. Illinois Central Gulf R.R., 722 F.2d 190 (5th Cir. 1984) ("actuarial method" allows compounding only annually).

213 *Compare* Stovall v. Illinois Central Gulf R.R., 722 F.2d 190 (5th Cir. 1984) (no compounding in absence of express statutory authorization); Acker v. Provident Nat'l Bank, 512 F.2d 729 (3d Cir. 1975) (same); *and* Westbrook v. Fairchild, 9 Cal. Rptr. 2d 277 (Cal. Ct. App. 1992) (statute permitting post-judgment interest of 10% per annum on the principal construed to prohibit compounding; similar provision in state constitution construed

in same way); Simon v. CNA Ins. Co., 543 A.2d 110 (N.J. Super. App. Div. 1988) (omission of word "simple" from amended statute on rate of judgment interest did not permit compounding); William C. Dear & Assocs., Inc. v. Plastronics, Inc., 913 S.W.2d 251 (Tex. App. 1996) (no compounding in absence of express statutory authorization) *with* Grigg v. Robinson Furniture Co., 260 N.W.2d 898 (Mich. App. 1978) (general state prohibition of compound interest does not prevent compounding of time-price differentials).

214 Greenmoss Builders v. Dun & Bradstreet, 543 A.2d 1320 (Vt. 1988). *But cf.* Boatmen's First Nat'l Bank v. Bogina Petroleum Engineers, 794 S.W.2d 703 (Mo. Ct. App. 1990) (statute prohibiting compounding of interest applies only to contract interest, not judgment interest; court held awarding judgment interest on judgment amount including interest was permissible).

215 Indeed, every example so far has used equal monthly payment periods.

216 Sometimes, the last payment had to be adjusted by a few cents due to rounding, and the discussion of balloon payments obviously, does not rest on that assumption.

217 *See* § 4.3.2, *supra.*

218 *See* § 4.4, *supra.*

For example, suppose a creditor agrees to lend a consumer $1,000 repayable in 12 monthly installments and charges $80 interest. This loan is identical to the $1,000 8% add-on loan illustrated in Chart 8, except that the first payment is due only ten days after the loan is consummated and all other payments are due monthly. This change in terms, without affecting the amount of principal, the amount of interest, or the number or size of the payments, raises the effective annual interest rate (APR) from 14.45% to 16.16%.

Similarly, another creditor might extend the same loan with equal payment periods but requiring a first payment of $145 and 11 more payments of $85. Again, it is the same total of payments as the original loan, but this payment schedule would also raise the effective interest rate, this time from 14.45% to 15.20%.

While both of these examples might violate a state's add-on interest usury law, it is not unusual for consumers to enter credit agreements with unequal ("odd") payment periods or payment amounts. Sometimes, transactions are structured this way for the convenience of the consumer. For example, a consumer who obtains a loan on August 16 may not receive her first paycheck until October 1. Changing the first monthly payment due date from September 16 to October 1 will certainly help the consumer get off to a good start.

This change will also benefit the creditor. First, the creditor will usually be able to charge more interest for the first payment period since it is longer than a month. Second, many consumer credit usury statutes (particularly add-on interest statutes) allow a creditor to charge two full months' interest for the first payment period if that period is at least one month and 15 days (or 1.5 months) long. The same $1,000, one-year, 8% add-on loan, but with an August 16 to October 1 first payment period, would allow the lender to charge interest as if the loan had 13 payments rather than 12. Because of the "odd" first period of one month and 15 days, it could charge an extra $6.67 in interest[219] without exceeding the maximum interest charge allowable under the statute. At the same time, however, the effective annual interest rate (APR) would be raised slightly from 14.45% to 14.47%.

The same creditor could, of course, ignore the odd first period and merely charge the same interest as if all the payment periods were equal. Since the odd first period is longer than the others, the effective annual interest rate (APR) would be lowered from 14.45% to 13.39%.

Other credit statutes may also give creditors the option of ignoring odd payment periods or odd payment amounts. For example, in calculating and disclosing annual percentage rates, for Truth in Lending purposes, creditors may ignore first periods up to 11 days shorter or 21 days longer than a regular period in transactions with terms between one and ten years.[220]

Reducing the size of the initial payments can have a significant financial impact on the consumer; the reduction in initial payments may require the consumer to make a "balloon" payment, or a final payment that is significantly larger than the other payments. At a constant interest rate, the lower the initial payments, the higher the "balloon" payment. If the balloon payment is very high and the creditor does not guarantee refinancing on reasonable terms, the consumer may be unable to make the payment and may be compelled to default or to refinance the debt on very expensive terms.

For an illustration of a balloon payment, see Chart 6.[221] The first 11 payments are very low and do not even cover interest. As a consequence, the 12th payment of $1,025.75 is a "balloon" payment and is even higher than the original principal. If the consumer originally needed to borrow $1,000, it is unlikely that he will be able to make a $1,025.75 payment only one year later.

The consumer lawyer should ask the following questions if there are any irregular payment periods or payment amounts in a particular consumer credit transaction:

- Does any relevant law prohibit that irregularity (or require all payment periods or payment amounts to be equal)?
- If the irregularity is allowed or not prohibited, does the law establish special rules for the adjustment of interest charges to reflect the effect of the irregularity?
- Has the creditor accurately adjusted the interest charges to reflect the effect of the irregularity?
- Has the creditor correctly disclosed the APR, keeping in mind the tolerance allowed by Regulation Z?[222]

APRs for transactions with irregular payment amounts can be calculated with the APR program on the companion CD-Rom to this volume.

4.6.2.2 Weekly, Bi-Weekly Payment Periods; Legal Issues

The most common regular repayment period in consumer transactions is monthly. However, other periods are sometimes used. Used car financing contracts, for example, may call for weekly, bi-weekly, or semi-monthly repayment periods. Absent some specific prohibition, such shorter periods are legitimate. However, practitioners have found that it is relatively common for the dealers to run afoul of usury laws or TIL (or both) in doing so.

The common mistake is a simple one. As noted in the preceding section, a shorter repayment term results in a

---

219   $1,000 × 8% × 13 ÷ 12 = $86.67. $1,000 × 8% × 12 ÷ 12 = $80.00. $86.67 − 80.00 = $6.67.

220   12 C.F.R. § 226.17(c)(4)(ii). Section 226.17(c)(4) also lists the rules for shorter and longer transactions.

221   Negative Amortization of $1,000 Loan At 8% Actuarial Interest—Actuarial Rule. *See generally* § 4.3.1.2, *supra*.

222   *See* 12 C.F.R. §§ 226.17(c)(4), 226.22(a).

higher APR. Take, as an example, a $2,000 loan, repayable in 24 installments of $105.75, for a total repayment obligation of $2,538.

- monthly installments—24% APR[223]
- semi-monthly installments—48% APR[224]
- bi-weekly installments—52% APR[225]
- weekly installments—104% APR[226]

If the dealer, (not having read this chapter), uses the computer program or charts for 24 *monthly* repayment periods, while the contract calls for shorter repayment periods, the APR, as is evident above, will be seriously understated, and hence a TIL violation.[227]

It may also be a usury violation. If the statutory limit on a car of that age is 28% actuarial interest,[228] any repayment period other than monthly will result in an overcharge. Even in deregulated states, where there is no rate cap other than the one "agreed-to" by the parties, the *agreed rate* on this loan is probably disclosed as 24%, so that cap, too, is violated.[229] Some statutes may specifically allow repayment on other than a regular monthly basis, but nonetheless provide that the yield cannot exceed the yield in a monthly payment contract. Thus, in the above example, a payment schedule more frequent than monthly would make this a usurious transaction.[230]

4.6.3 Daily Interest Rates and the 365/360 Method

4.6.3.1 General

Lenders with interest-bearing accounts may choose to ignore (within certain limits) the exact date a payment is made. If a consumer makes a payment a few days before the payment due date or a few days after the payment due date, the lender may nonetheless charge interest as if the payment were made exactly when due.[231] Many mortgage lenders, for example, follow this practice, much to the benefit of consumer mortgagors who consistently make their payments a few days late.[232]

Other lenders, particularly those with more sophisticated computer programs, may charge their borrowers a daily rate of interest. The general effect of applying daily rates undoubtedly increases the yield of their loans, since payments are more likely to be made after their due dates than before their due dates. While an argument should be made that lenders should clearly disclose that the application of daily interest rates could cost borrowers more money in interest charges and could lengthen their repayment schedules, or result in a higher final payment generally, the application of daily interest rates, in itself, does not pose special usury problems.[233]

However, the use of daily interest rates can pose computational problems. There are two basic, intertwined issues: one is how to compute the daily rate and the other is how to count the number of days in a particular payment period.

---

223 Thirty-day period, 12 periods per year.
224 Fifteen-day period, 24 periods per year. (Calculated on the basis of a 30-day month, *see generally* § 4.2.3.4, *supra*.)
        A second arguable TIL violation is also common on these in-between payment periods. Sometimes the creditor will call for a "bi-monthly" repayment period. According to the dictionary, the first definition of bi-monthly is every two months, and the second definition is twice a month, or semi-monthly. Hence, with a disclosed schedule of 24 payments, "bi-monthly," the consumer has to guess whether payments are due every 2 weeks, or every 8 weeks. That, it can certainly be argued, is not a "clear" disclosure of the payment schedule as TIL requires. 15 U.S.C. §§ 1632(a), 1638(a)(6); Reg. Z, §§ 226.17(a), 226.18(g); National Consumer Law Center, Truth in Lending §§ 4.2.4, 4.6.6 (5th ed. 2003 and Supp.).
225 Fourteen-day periods, 26 periods per year.
226 Seven-day periods, 52 periods per year.
227 15 U.S.C. § 1638(a)(4); Reg. Z §§ 226.18(e), 226.22; National Consumer Law Center, Truth in Lending § 4.6.4 (5th ed. 2003 and Supp.).
228 It is fairly common for a state to have tiered rate caps, with older cars subject to significantly higher rates than new cars. *See, e.g.,* Fla. Stat. Ann. § 520.08.
229 *See* § 9.2.8, *infra*. If the statute provides that the parties agree to a *rate*, the disclosure of the $538 finance charge is not an effective defense. *See* Chroniak v. Golden Inv. Corp., 983 F.2d 1140 (1st Cir. 1993) (note which specified interest in dollar amount, but no rate, violated an as-agreed statute, invoked statutory penalties; court also rules this is a UDAP violation, as full disclosure of interest rates takes on added significance with the elimination of usury ceilings).
230 *See, e.g.,* Fla. Stat. Ann. § 520.08, of the Motor Vehicle Retail Installment Sales Act. Subsection (1) states the maximum

add-on rates. (*See* § 4.2.2.2, *supra*.) Subsection (2) says that the maximum finance charge allowable "shall be computed . . . on contracts payable in successive monthly payments substantially equal in amount." Subsection (3) states that when the contract calls for unequal or irregular installment payments, "the finance charge may be at a rate which will provide the same yield as is permitted on monthly payment contracts under subsections (1) and (2), *having due regard for the schedule of payment*." (emphasis added).
        Thus, for example, on a 5-year-old car, the maximum rate is 17% add-on, which on a 24-installment monthly repayment basis has an actuarial equivalent of 29.85%. If the 24 installments in the same amount were repayable more frequently than monthly the finance charge would have a much higher yield than 29.85%, as shown in the text, and so, "having due regard" for the payment schedule, such a loan would be usurious.
231 Of course, the lender may impose a late charge or accelerate the loan if the payment is made too many days late.
232 *See, e.g.,* Fannie Mae Servicing Guide, Part III, Ch. 1, § 101 (requiring servicer to charge 30 days' interest each month for first mortgages but allowing payment-to-payment calculation of interest (taking into account the actual number of days between payments) for second mortgages if the mortgage instrument requires it).
233 With one exception. *See* § 4.6.3.5, *infra*.

Chart 12

DAY COUNTING METHODS

Principal = $1,000 (remains unchanged)

Annual interest rate = 18%

Date of transaction: March 1, 1999

Date of Interest-Only Payments	365 day Method Interest[1]	360 day Method Interest[2]	365/360 day Method Interest[3]
April 1, 1999	$15.28 (31 days)	$15.00 (30 days)	$15.50 (31 days)
May 1, 1999	$14.79 (30 days)	$15.00 (30 days)	$15.00 (30 days)
June 15, 1999	$22.18 (45 days)	$22.00 (44 days)	$22.50 (45 days)
Total Interest	$52.25	$52.00	$53.00

1 Daily interest rate: 18%/365 = .0493%

2 Daily interest rate: 18%/360 = .05%

3 Daily interest rate: 18%/360 = .05%

For the purposes of illustrating the different methods, assume that a consumer borrows $1,000 at 18% on March 1, 1999 and makes interest-only payments on April 1, 1999; May 1, 1999; and June 15, 1999. The results of the different methods are explained below and summarized at Chart 12, Day Counting Methods.

4.6.3.2 365-Day Method

The most obvious solution to these issues is to divide the relevant annual interest rate by 365 (the number of days in a year)[234] and then simply to count the exact number of days that have elapsed in each period. For example, consider the first payment on April 1, 1999. The daily interest rate is .0493% (18% ÷ 365 = .0493%). The number of days between March 1 and April 1 is 31. Therefore, the interest that is earned during that period is $15.28 ($1,000 × .0493% × 31 days = $15.28).

If the consumer made a second payment on May 1, the same process would be repeated. The daily interest rate is .0493%. The number of days between April 1 and May 1 is 30. Therefore, the interest that is earned during that period (assuming that the unpaid principal remains unchanged at $1,000), is $14.79 ($1,000 × .0493% × 30 days = $14.79).

If the consumer made a third payment on June 15, the same process would again be repeated. The number of days between May 1 and June 15 is 45. Therefore, the interest that is earned is $22.18 ($1,000 × .0493% × 45 days = $22.18). The total interest earned between March 1 and June 15 is $52.25.

---

234 Scientific purists may point out that a year actually has 365 1/4 days; however, more practical, but no less precise, observers may also point out that a *calendar* year, with the exception of a leap year, has exactly 365 days.

4.6.3.3 360-Day Method

Another method, which many creditors prefer because it is easier to apply, is to divide the annual interest rate by 360 and to assume that all monthly periods have 30 days. This assumption is maintained regardless of whether the actual number of days in a monthly period is 28, 29, 30 or 31.

In the first example, of a payment period between March 1 and April 1 at an annual rate and a principal of $1,000, the daily interest rate is .05% (18% ÷ 360 = .05%). While the exact number of days between March 1 and April 1 is 31, under the 360-day method, it is assumed that this monthly period is 30 days. Therefore, the interest that is earned during that period is $15.00.

If the consumer made another payment on May 1, the same process would be repeated. The daily interest rate is .05%. It is another monthly period so the number of days again is 30 (although this time, the 30 days coincides with the exact number of days). Therefore, the interest earned during that period is again $15.00 ($1,000 × .05% × 30 days = $15.00).

If the consumer made a third payment on June 15, the same process would again be repeated. The monthly period between May 1 and June 1 is considered 30 days (even though the exact number of days is 31). The period between June 1 and June 15 is considered 14 days, for a total of 44 days. Therefore, the interest earned during that period is $22.00 ($1,000 × .05% × 44 days = $22.00). The total interest earned between March 1 and June 15 is $52.00, or slightly less than the 365-day method.

This comparison between the 365-day method and the 360-day method is typical. If both methods are correctly applied, then they will generate approximately the same amount of interest, particularly over the long term. Indeed, if a consumer made every monthly payment exactly on time over a year, then each method would produce the exact same amount of interest.

4.6.3.4 365/360 Day Method: "The Bankers' Year"

A third method, the 365/360 method, however, not only combines aspects of the first two methods but consistently generates interest higher than that produced by the other methods. The 365/360 method uses a 360-day year to calculate the daily interest rate, so that each day earns more interest. However, it also uses a 365-day year to count the number of days in any given payment period; it does not assume that each monthly payment period has 30 days, regardless of the actual number of days in a particular payment period. As a result, a lender who uses the 365/360 method will collect an extra five (5) days of interest every year. This has the effect of increasing the interest rate by 1.39% (5 ÷ 360 = .0139). For example, in the 18% annual interest rate example discussed above, the effective interest rate under the 365/360 method would be 18.25% (18% × 1.0139 = 18.25%).

The application of the 365/360 method to the above example is summarized at Chart 12. In each instance, the daily interest rate is .05% (18% ÷ 360 = .05%). In the first payment period between March 1 and April 1, there are 31 days. Therefore, the interest generated is $15.50 ($1,000 × .05% × 31 = $15.50). This method produced $.50 more interest than that generated by 360-day method which assumed that there were only 30 days in a monthly payment period.

The second payment period produced $15.00 in interest, the same as that produced by the 360-day method, because the number of actual days in the period (30) is the same as the assumed number of days in the monthly period (30). Therefore, the interest generated during that period is $15.00 ($1,000 × .05% × 30 days = $15.00).

However, the third payment period again illustrates the discrepancies between the 365/360 method and the 360-day method. Counting the exact number of days between May 1, 1999 and June 15, 1999 produces 45 days. Therefore, the interest generated during this period is $22.50 ($1,000 × .05% × 45 days = $22.50). Again this method produced $.50 more interest than that generated by the 360-day method which assumed that there were only 30 days between May 1 and June 1 and counted 14 days between June 1 and June 15, for a total of 44 days. The total interest earned between March 1 and June 15 is $53.00, which is more than 1% higher than the 365-day method and nearly 2% higher than the 360-day method.

The 365/360 method of interest calculation has been widely used in the banking industry for the past two centuries. A 1971 Federal Reserve Board study indicated that 82% of all commercial banks used this method on at least some loans. In 1971 Congressman Wright Patman estimated that of the total amount of interest collected annually in the United States, $145 million is due to the difference between stated and actual rates that results from use of the 365/360 method.[235]

Borrowers charged interest computed by means of the 365/360 method at the maximum rate allowed by law have frequently brought usury actions against their lenders. In the first such reported case, *New York Firemen Insurance Co. v. Ely & Parsons*,[236] the court found the challenged loan usurious. Throughout the remainder of the nineteenth century and the first half of the twentieth century, however, the vast majority of courts rejected the *Ely & Parsons* view.[237]

The courts that rejected the *Ely & Parsons* rationale usually found that established banking custom and the need

for easy calculation justified the use of the 365/360 method. It was said that computation of interest under the 365/365 method was far more difficult than under the 365/360 method. In addition, some courts found that there was no legislative intent to interfere with this long-established custom. Other courts dismissed the problem as insignificant, because each borrower suffers only slight harm.[238]

In recent years, with the advent of computerized banking, the rationale of these earlier cases has been carefully reconsidered. As one commentator noted,

> [i]nterest is now calculated, not by uneducated bank clerks, but by computers that can easily be programmed to use any method of calculation. The advanced technology would seem to support an inference that the lender using the 365/360 method does so in order to collect the excess interest rather than to promote convenience.[239]

The United States Court of Appeals for the Ninth Circuit, applying Oregon law, agreed with this rationale in *American Timber & Trading Co. v. First National Bank of Oregon*.[240] The Ninth Circuit agreed with District Judge Goodwin's conclusion that the usury statute "should be construed with regard to its net effect upon the borrower rather than upon the bookkeeping burden, custom, or convenience of the lender."[241] The Ninth Circuit was especially skeptical of the defendant bank's convenience argument in view of the fact that the bank used the 365/365 method to compute interest it paid to its depositors.[242]

American Timber has been received enthusiastically.[243] More importantly, the decision has been expressly followed by most courts which subsequently considered the issue.[244]

---

235 *See* Comment, *Legal Aspects of the Use of "Ordinary Simple Interest*,*"* 40 U. Chi. L. Rev. 141, 142–43 (1972).

236 2 Cow. 678 (N.Y. 1824).

237 *See generally* Comment, *Legal Aspects of the Use of "Ordinary Simple Interest*,*"* 40 U. Chi. L. Rev. 141, 145–52 (1972); Annot., 35 A.L.R.2d 842, 843–50 (1954).

238 *See* cases cited in Comment, *Legal Aspects of the Use of "Ordinary Simple Interest*,*"* 40 U. Chi. L. Rev. 141, 145–50 (1972); Annot., 35 A.L.R.2d 842, 843–48 (1954).

239 Comment, *Legal Aspects of the Use of "Ordinary Simple Interest*,*"* 40 U. Chi. L. Rev. 141, 148 (1972).

240 511 F.2d 980, 983–84 (9th Cir. 1974), *cert. denied*, 421 U.S. 921 (1975).

241 *Id.* at 983.

242 *Id.* at 983–84.

243 *See, e.g.*, Comment, *Legal Aspects of the Use of "Ordinary Simple Interest*,*"* 40 U. Chi. L. Rev. 141, 148–49 (1972); Note, 6 U. Tol. L. Rev. 541, 559 (1975).

244 *See In re* Rosner, 48 B.R. 538 (Bankr. E.D.N.Y. 1985) (loan nominally at maximum legal interest rate made usurious by use of 365/360 method); Ellis Nat'l Bank of Tallahassee v. Davis, 359 So. 2d 466 (Fla. 1978); Perlman v. First Nat'l Bank, 305 N.E.2d 236 (Ill. App. Ct. 1978), *appeal dismissed*, 331 N.E.2d 65 (Ill. 1975) (defense of "customary practice" rejected); Nicoladze v. Lomas & Nettleton Mortgage Investors, 679 S.W.2d 671 (Tex. App. 1984) (usury found on one of several loans because of undisclosed 365/360 calculations), *aff'd in relevant part, rev'd in part on other grounds sub nom.* Lawler v. Lomas & Nettleton Mortgage Investors, 691 S.W.2d 593 (Tex. 1985); O'Brien v. Shearson Hayden Stone, Inc., 90 Wash. 2d 680, 586 P.2d 830, 836 (1978). *See also* Hamilton v. Ohio Savings Bank, 694 N.E.2d 442 (Ohio 1998) (ordering certification of class action challenging lender's use of 365/360 method).

Also, the California Supreme Court relied on *American Timber* in reaching its conclusion that use of the 365/360 method constitutes false and misleading advertising.[245]

Not all courts have followed *American Timber*, however. In *Beazley v. Georgia Railroad Bank & Trust Co.*,[246] a Georgia intermediate court followed a 1906 decision of the Georgia Supreme Court and found that a loan which yielded interest at the maximum legal rate was not usurious, even though the 365/360 method was used. And the Arkansas Supreme Court, with one justice dissenting, concluded with "no hesitancy" that "for practical, legal, and historical reasons, . . . the use of the 360-day year is lawful even when the interest is [the legal maximum]."[247] Finally, some courts have recognized the defense of mistake in 365/360 cases.[248]

To avoid the uncertainty which the above cases illustrate, some states prohibit using 1/360th for a daily rate[249] and punish violations as usury.[250] Other statutes seem to authorize the use of 365/360 method.[251]

On a more elementary level, a creditor who casually counts the days that a loan is outstanding may find that it has committed usury. For example, in *Ex Parte Underwood*,[252]

a contract was executed on August 26, 1982, with a final payment due on August 15, 1984. The exact time period was one year, 354 days, but the creditor charged interest on a two-year basis. This slight overcharge violated the Alabama Mini-Code. Additionally, a lender that calculates interest based on the 365/360 method will face a legal challenge if the loan contract contains an interest rate based on a less expensive calculation method.[253]

4.6.3.5 Effect of Late Posting of Payments

If the lender intentionally delays posting the payments, more interest may accrue over the term of the loan than contracted for or allowed by law. For example, assume a $1,000 simple interest loan made on April 1, with a monthly payment of $86.99 at 8%. See loan in Chart 6, *supra*. Assume that the lender calculates interest on a 365-day year, so the daily rate is .0219%. If the borrower pays the scheduled amount of $86.99 on time each month but the lender fails to post the payment for 15 additional days, the interest charges would look like this:

Chart 13
Simple Interest One-Year Loan With 8% Simple Interest Computed on Daily Basis, Showing Effect of Late Posting of Payments

Pay-ment	Due Date[254]	Unpaid Balance	# of Days of Interest[255]	Interest	Pay-ment	New Balance
1	5/1	$1,000.00	45	9.86	86.99	922.87
2	6/1	$ 922.87	31	6.27	86.99	842.15
3	7/1	$ 842.15	30	5.72	86.99	760.88
4	8/1	$ 760.88	31	5.17	86.99	679.06
5	9/1	$ 679.06	31	4.61	86.99	596.68
6	10/1	$ 596.68	30	3.92	86.99	513.61
7	11/1	$ 513.61	31	3.49	86.99	430.11
8	12/1	$ 430.11	30	2.82	86.99	345.95
9	1/1	$ 345.95	31	2.35	86.99	261.31
10	2/1	$ 261.31	31	1.77	86.99	176.09
11	3/1	$ 176.09	28	1.08	86.99	90.18
12	4/1	$ 90.18	31	0.61	86.99	3.80

---

245 Chern v. Bank of America, 15 Cal. 3d 866, 127 Cal. Rptr. 110, 544 P.2d 1310 (1976) (en banc). *Compare* South Bay Chevrolet v. GMAC, 85 Cal. Rptr. 2d 301 (App. 1999) (financially sophisticated automobile dealer that knew its floor plan financer used 365/360 method could not assert UDAP claim). *See generally* National Consumer Law Center, Unfair and Deceptive Acts and Practices § 5.1.8.2 (6th ed. 2004 and Supp.).

246 241 S.E.2d 39, 40 (Ga. App. 1977). *See also* Mom Corp. v. Chattahoochee Bank, 418 S.E.2d 74 (Ga. App. Ct. 1992) ("daily charge equal to annual percentage rate divided by 360 is not usurious *per se*"; method of counting days not at issue).

247 Martin v. Moore, 601 S.W.2d 838, 839 (Ark. 1980). *But see* Cagle v. Boyle Mortgage Co., 261 Ark. 437, 549 S.W.2d 474 (1977).

248 *See, e.g.*, First Am. Nat'l Bank v. Booth, 606 S.W.2d 70 (Ark. 1980); Libowsky v. Lake Shore Commercial Fin. Corp., 330 N.W.2d 248 (Wis. App. 1982) (charged 365/360 by error of programmer).

249 *See, e.g.*, Fla. Stat. § 687.03. For mortgages held by Fannie Mae, interest for a partial month must be calculated on the basis of a 365-day year. *See* Servicing Guide, Part II, Ch. 5, § 501, Part VI, Ch. 1, § 102.01.

250 Ellis Nat'l Bank v. Davis, 359 So. 2d 466 (Fla. Dist. Ct. App. 1978), *cert. denied*, 365 So. 2d 711 (Fla. 1978), *cert. denied*, 440 U.S. 976 (1979), *aff'd*, 379 So. 2d 1310 (Fla. Dist. Ct. App. 1980); S.C. Dept. of Consumer Affairs Admin. Interp. No. 3.508-7702, Consumer Cred. Guide (CCH) ¶ 98,214 (1977).

251 *See, e.g.*, Voitier v. First Nat'l Bank of Commerce, 514 F. Supp. 585 (E.D. La. 1981).

252 496 So. 2d 46 (Ala. 1986). *See also* Yates Ford, Inc. v. Ramirez, 692 S.W.2d 51 (Tex. 1985), *rev'g* 675 S.W.2d 232 (Tex. App. 1984) (creditor permitted to count odd days backwards from one month prior to first due date instead of forward from one month following date of consummation. The statute appears to mandate the latter, while Reg. Z, Appendix J mandates the latter. The Texas Supreme Court gave effect to an administrative ruling that permitted the use of either method as long as a creditor used it consistently. The ruling allowed the creditor to earn 15 days interest, rather than 14).

253 Hamilton v. Ohio Sav. Bank, 694 N.E.2d 442 (Ohio 1998) (certifying class action where lender calculated interest with the 365/360 method and consumers' interest payments exceeded the agreed rate; one subclass of plaintiffs also had loans that would not fully amortize within agreed loan terms and thus would face a balloon payment).

254 In this example it is assumed that the borrower makes every payment on time, so the due date is the same as the date of receipt of the payment.

255 In this example, the lender charged interest for 45 days (the 30 days from April 1 to May 1, plus the 15 days during which posting was delayed) for the first payment period. For the second payment period, the lender charged interest for the 31 days from May 15 to June 15. The number of days in succeeding periods varies depending on the number of days in the month.

The total interest earned is $47.67, as compared to $43.86 if the payments had been credited on time, plus the borrower still owes $3.80 after 12 months of payments. While the additional interest is certainly a small amount, in a 30-year $40,000 second mortgage loan at 8.23% simple interest per year, a pattern of posting payments 15 days late will cost the borrower $370.80 in interest.

Creditors may also post payments late as a means of generating revenue in the form of late charges.[256] This practice is prohibited by the Truth in Lending Act for certain types of transactions (e.g., credit cards)[257] but creditors may still attempt to manipulate grace periods and due dates to evade this prohibition. A major credit card bank entered into a $300 million settlement in 2000 with the Office of the Comptroller of the Currency and the San Francisco District Attorney's Office that required it, *inter alia*, to refund late fees it had charged due to delayed posting of payments.[258] Some states also have laws requiring prompt crediting of payments.[259]

4.6.4 Rounding

Attorneys calculating interest rates and payments will inevitably encounter the issue of rounding. Specifically, rounding is necessary whenever the product of a multiplication operation or the quotient (i.e., the result) of a division operation cannot be expressed precisely within some specified number of decimal places.

Perhaps the two most common examples of rounding problems in interest calculations are the determination of a periodic interest rate, and the multiplication of the balance of a debt by this periodic rate to obtain a borrower's monthly payments. For example, assume that an interest-bearing loan states a 10% annual interest rate. The first step in determining the borrower's monthly payment is to find the monthly interest rate, which will be the annual rate divided by twelve.[260] But $10 \div 12\%$ cannot be expressed precisely in decimal form; on an eight-digit calculator it is rounded (down) to 0.0083333.

The next step in determining the monthly payment is to multiply the outstanding balance, which for simplicity we will say is $1,000, by the monthly rate, here 0.0083333, to obtain the interest earned in the month, which will be $8.3333. The problem is that the borrower cannot pay $8.3333; he must pay either $8.33 or $8.34. But in the former case, the creditor is losing a third of a cent which it has earned, while in the latter case, the creditor will be receiving two-thirds of a cent which it did not earn. This may not seem significant, but over a long-term transaction, the difference can amount to a few dollars.[261]

There are basically three ways in which rounding can be handled: numbers can be rounded up, down, or to the nearest digit. The fairest technique is probably rounding to the nearest digit.[262] Using this method over a series of calculations, charges which are slightly too high because of rounding error tend to be offset by charges which have been rounded down, and rounding error is thus minimized. Some creditors, however, consistently round payments up one penny to maximize their profits.

Usury statutes are generally silent as to permissible rounding practices, as they are with many calculation techniques. However, rounding can be a usury issue because a creditor which consistently rounds earned interest up a penny is slightly increasing the effective interest rate it is charging. If a credit contract is already set at the maximum rate permitted by statute, then any increase in effective rate, no matter how small, exceeds the usury ceiling. Of course, such small overcharges may be subject to a *de minimis* defense in some jurisdictions.[263] Yet, overcharges due to a systematic practice of rounding up a penny should not be lightly dismissed. There is really no justification for this practice other than maximizing profits, and if creditors are permitted to maximize profits despite statutory prohibitions, the law will rapidly lose meaning.

With variable rate notes, the interest rate itself may involve rounding issues, as the index rates commonly used may be odd numbers, e.g., 7.56%. Often, the variable rate contracts will provide for rounding the rate to the nearest one-eighth percent. As noted in § 4.3.6.2, *supra*, a creditor may sometimes use a rate obtained by rounding up, instead of rounding

---

256 *See* MassPIRG Education Fund, *A Road Map to Avoiding Credit Card Hazards* (Mar. 2001).

257 15 U.S.C. § 1666c. *See* National Consumer Law Center, Truth in Lending § 5.8.9.1 (5th ed. 2003 and Supp.).

258 *In the Matter of* Providian Nat'l Bank, #2000-53 (U.S. Dept. of Treas., Office of the Comptroller of the Currency), available at www.occ.treas.gov/ftp/release/2000-49.txt. *See also In re* Providian Fin. Corp. Securities Litigation, 152 F. Supp. 2d 814 (E.D. Pa. 2001) (denying motion to dismiss claims by investors who alleged that credit card bank concealed fact that its high returns were based on misrepresentations to consumers); Mangone v. First USA Bank, 206 F.R.D. 222 (S.D. Ill. 2001) (approving settlement of class action involving late posting of payments); Capital One Bank v. Rollins, 106 S.W.3d 286 (Tex. App. 2003) (reversing certification of class challenging manipulation of payment crediting dates in order to impose late charges; remanding for further analysis of existence of individual issues).

259 *See, e.g.,* Iowa Code § 535.14.

260 This assumes all months are of equal length. Some creditors

recognize the different lengths of months, in which case the answer is slightly different. *See* § 4.6.3, *supra*.

261 If a creditor rounded up on all payments in a 360 payment loan and gained, on average, an extra half cent from each payment, it would earn an extra $1.80 directly. The actual extra earnings would be higher due to compounding.

262 Specifically, earnings of 0.5¢ and above are rounded to 1.0¢ while earnings below 0.5¢ are rounded to 0.0¢. This is the technique used in the charts in this manual. Whatever method is employed should be used consistently. When checking the interest calculations in the credit contract, it may be advisable for a consumer's attorney to round up on all calculations. This method gives the creditor its highest possible earnings. If the creditor is claiming an even higher amount, the attorney can be certain that the difference is not due to rounding error.

263 *See* § 10.6.8, *infra*.

down to a nearer mark. Section 4.3.6.2 discusses some claims which may arise from such a contract violation.

4.6.5 Spreading

4.6.5.1 A Calculation Defense to Usury Claims in Fixed Term Loans

The rate of interest charged on many loans fluctuates during the term of the credit. This fluctuation may be obvious, as in the case of loans in which the interest rates are pegged to some market rate such as the federal discount rate, or it may be concealed, as in the case of apparent fixed-rate loans in which the borrower must pay various one-time fees at the outset of the transaction as well as the constant monthly payments.[264] In either situation, a tricky usury issue may arise. Specifically, it is possible that the interest rate will exceed the usury ceiling for one or more payment periods during the loan without exceeding the ceiling for the loan term as a whole. For example, consider a variable rate account, over a six-month period, with a constant outstanding balance, in a state with a ten percent simple interest ceiling. If interest is charged on the account at an annual rate of 9% for the first five months, but the rate then jumps to 11% for the last month before the debt is paid off, is the transaction usurious? The answer obviously depends on whether each monthly payment period is viewed individually, in which case a usury violation occurs in the last month of the loan, or whether the loan is viewed as a whole and the interest charges are averaged, in which case the overall contract rate is 9.33%, significantly below the usury ceiling.[265]

Or consider an 18% second mortgage loan, with 20 points charged, in theory earned at consummation. During the first month of the loan, those 20 points[266] added to the regular 18% interest for one month, will result in a significantly higher yield than 1.5% (.18% ÷ 12 = 1.5%). As in the previous example, whether the loan is usurious or not depends upon whether the court looks at the return for one month, or the life of the loan.

Courts reviewing traditional fixed-term loans have generally applied usury ceilings to the overall rate of return for credit transactions and have done so through a doctrine which is often called "spreading."[267] Although it may be stated differently in different jurisdictions, the spreading doctrine essentially instructs a court to calculate the maxi-

---

264 Because of the one-time fees, the *effective* interest rate will usually be higher at the beginning of the transaction than later in the loan term even though the contract describes the interest rate as fixed.

265 This example assumes that the accrued interest is paid off monthly with no monthly payments to principal. The assumption of a constant principal balance is a bit unrealistic since the balances of most accounts fluctuate; however, it is made here to simplify the example. If the monthly balances in the example varied, it would not be sufficient merely to average the monthly rates, as this example does. Instead, the maximum charge for each month, given its particular outstanding balance, would have to be computed. Under the "spreading" rule, the sum of these monthly maximum charges would thus be compared to the actual charge. If the outstanding balance for the last month, when 11% annual interest was charged, sufficiently exceeded the balances for the previous months, the loan would be usurious even after spreading was done. *See* text accompanying notes 284–285, *infra* for discussion of spreading in open-end, variable-rate transactions. For a discussion of Texas law and calculation issues in the spreading context, see Frank A. St. Claire, *The "Spreading of Interest" Under the Actuarial Method*, 10 St. Mary's L.J. 753 (1979), cited in Groseclose v. Rum, 860 S.W.2d 554 (Tex. App. 1993), a rather odd case involving graduated interest rates and a court which seemingly forced a usury theory into the case in order to invoke the spreading doctrine.

266 Points are discussed in §§ 4.7, 7.2.2, *infra*.

267 For cases applying spreading in fixed-term transactions, *see, e.g.,* Perry v. Stewart Title Co., 756 F.2d 1197 (5th Cir. 1985) (applying Texas law); Kissell Co. v. Gressley, 591 F.2d 47 (9th Cir. 1979) (applying Arizona law) (transaction usurious despite spreading); C.I.O.S. Fdn. v. Berkston Ins. A.V.V., 2000 U.S. Dist. LEXIS 2337 (N.D. Miss. Jan. 28, 2000) (applying Texas spreading law to find loan not usurious); *In re* Auto Int'l Refrigeration, 275 B.R. 789, 809–16 (Bankr. N.D. Tex. 2002), *aff'd,* 307 B.R. 849 (N.D. Tex. 2002); Olympic Coast Investment v. Wright (*In re* Wright), 256 B.R. 626 (Bankr. D. Mont. 2000) (origination fees and similar charges must be spread over full term of loan); Wooten v. Davis, 293 Ark. 496, 739 S.W.2d 669 (1987) (concept, though not word, utilized to determine no usurious overcharge); White v. Sweeney, 291 P.2d 77 (Cal. 1955); St. Petersburg Bank & Trust Co. v. Hamm, 414 So. 2d 1071 (Fla. 1982); Ransom v. Fleet Fin., Inc., 466 S.E.2d 686 (Ga. App. 1996) (doctrine invoked, though not by name); Fleet Fin., Inc. v. Jones, 430 S.E.2d 352 (Ga. 1993) (doctrine invoked, though not by name); Mayfield v. Oklahoma State Bank, 460 P.2d 414 (Okla. 1969) (word "spreading" not used, but doctrine otherwise followed); Danziger v. San Jacinto Sav. Ass'n, 732 S.W.2d 300, 303 (Tex. 1987); Tanner Dev. Co. v. Ferguson, 561 S.W.2d 777 (Tex. 1977) (lengthy discussion); Torres v. Overby, 2000 Tex. App. LEXIS 2493 (Apr. 17, 2000) (unpublished, citation limited); Pentico v. Mad-Wayler, Inc., 964 S.W.2d 708 (Tex. App. 1998); R.V. Indus. v. Urdiales, 851 S.W.2d 306 (Tex. App. 1992) (interpreting Tex. Rev. Civ. Stat. Ann. § 5069-1.07 which mandates use of spreading doctrine to determine whether real-estate-secured loan is usurious), *rev'd in part on other grounds,* 851 S.W.2d 216 (Tex. 1993); Nicoladze v. Lomas & Nettleton Mortgage Inv., 679 S.W.2d 671 (Tex. App. 1984). *But cf. In re* Brummer, 147 B.R. 552 (Bankr. D. Mont. 1992) (under Montana law, spreading doctrine does not apply where transaction facially usurious, but does where usurious interest due to borrower's action; i.e., prepayment or default); Hoffman v. Key Federal Sav. & Loan Ass'n, 416 A.2d 1265 (Md. 1979) (statutory allowance of "yield to maturity" allowed spreading only of points or other charges made at loan inception; not applicable where creditor allegedly improperly charged interest on progress payments in advance of disbursement; court "unable to effectively counter" the argument that spreading is much like "reasoning that if one who must travel 600 miles drives 375 m.p.h. in the first hour and 25 m.p.h. for each of the next nine hours, a permissible rate of 60 m.p.h. has been achieved." *Id.* at 1271); Benchmark Land Development, Inc. v. Wooley, 2001 Tex. App. LEXIS 8390 (Dec. 20, 2001) (usurious interest cannot be saved by spreading it out over three subsequent signed notes).

mum charges which a creditor could assess on a credit transaction and to compare this figure with the charges actually assessed. If the actual charges do not exceed the permitted charges for the over-all transaction, then fluctuations in the effective rate of return during the loan term are ignored. Conceptually, the interest overcharges during some payment periods are "spread" over other payment periods and are offset by the amounts of extra interest which the creditor might legally have charged,[268] but did not actually charge, during those other payment periods.

The notion of spreading interest seems fairly reasonable at first glance, and it clearly makes calculations easier for courts reviewing usury cases. Nevertheless, the doctrine may allow creditors to obtain an effective yield in excess of the usury ceiling because it ignores the timing of payments that the creditor receives. Essentially, payments made early in a loan term are more valuable to a creditor than later payments because the creditor has use of the money for a longer time. This is one reason that creditors often require one-time interest payments in the form of points, commitment fees, service charges, and other charges, at the outset of a credit transaction.[269] To the extent that the spreading doctrine ignores the time value of payments in a credit transaction, it can be a loophole in the usury ceiling.

An example may help to show the potential effect of spreading. Assume a twelve-month $1,000 loan, repayable in equal monthly installments, under a 10% simple interest ceiling. The permissible interest charge over the term of this loan is $55.[270] Under the spreading doctrine, it theoretically does not matter when the creditor imposes this $55 charge. In the extreme case, the creditor could require that the borrower pay the $55 at the outset of the transaction, in which case the borrower is effectively receiving not $1,000 in loan proceeds, but only $945.[271] However, the simple interest yield on a twelve-month loan of $945 with equal monthly payments and total interest charges of $55 is approximately 10.57%. Thus, in this example, spreading could increase the yield of the loan by 0.57%.

It should be emphasized that this example is a bit extreme in that all the interest charges were imposed at the outset of the transaction. Many courts which recognize the spreading doctrine would treat this transaction as a $945 loan. For example, under Texas law, it is clear that the "true principal" of a transaction must be determined before spreading is applied,[272] and that the $55 deducted at the outset of the loan would not be treated as principal. However, an interpretation of a Florida spreading statute by that state's Supreme Court suggests that one Florida usury statute would permit a creditor to increase its yield, under the guise of spreading, in precisely the manner that the example indicates.[273] Furthermore, the increase in yield illustrated by the example would occur, albeit to a lesser extent, in any transaction where apparent overcharges early in the term of the loan are spread over later payment periods.[274]

A good illustration of the spreading doctrine, the distortions caused by it, and the vagaries of usury litigation is the interpretation of a statute limiting the yield "per month" in Georgia. The most recent word is that of the Georgia Supreme Court, which invoked the doctrine (though not by name), to salvage contracts with more than 20 points from a usury challenge.[275] Though the civil usury ceiling in Georgia has been removed, a criminal usury cap of "5% per month"[276] was retained. In the wake of deregulation, extremely expensive loans with an extraordinary number of points flooded the state. Those points meant that the yield in the first month, when the creditors claimed the points were earned (as all creditors do),[277] was well in excess of 5%.[278] These loans, primarily home equity loans, were the subject of a great deal of litigation,[279] and, prior to the resolution of the question in

---

268 This reference is to the amount that the creditor might legally have charged under the usury ceiling, not the amount it might permissibly charge under the terms of the contract. *See, e.g.,* Rent America, Inc. v. Amarillo Nat'l Bank, 785 S.W.2d 190 (Tex. App. 1990) (spreading doctrine used to find that interest calculation sought in court pleading did not exceed statutory usury ceiling, though it did include unearned interest in excess of rate agreed upon in contract).

269 *See* § 7.2.2.1, *infra* for further discussion of the attraction of points for creditors.

270 Actually it's $55.04, but the amounts are rounded in this example.

271 The process amounts to charging a form of discount interest. *See* § 4.3.3, *supra.*

272 *See, e.g.,* Perry v. Stewart Title Co., 756 F.2d 1197 (5th Cir. 1985) (applying Texas law); Tanner Dev. Co. v. Ferguson, 561 S.W.2d 777 (Tex. 1977).

273 St. Peterburg Bank & Trust Co. v. Hamm, 414 So. 2d 1071 (Fla. 1982) (face amount of note, including "interest" charges, used to calculate contract rate under state spreading statute).

274 In most cases where spreading is an issue, the creditor has collected interest payments throughout the loan term, but has exacted more interest at the beginning of the loan than later in the term. To some extent, of course, this practice of collecting more interest early in the loan term is actuarially justified because the outstanding principal balance is greater than it is later in the term. Yet the size of the interest payments which lenders collect in the form of points and other "up-front" fees more than compensates for this actuarial effect and raises the effective interest rate at the beginning of the loan term. The increase in effective yield occurs even when the one-time fees are quite small, although the smaller the fee, the smaller the increase.

275 Fleet Fin., Inc. of Georgia v. Jones, 430 S.E.2d 352 (Ga. 1993).

276 Ga. Code Ann. § 7-4-18. *See generally* § 9.2.7, *infra.*

277 *See* § 7.2.2.1, *infra.*

278 The first month's yield in the named plaintiff's contract would have been 23%.

279 *Cf.* Norris v. Sigler Daisy Corp., 392 S.E.2d 242 (Ga. 1990) (points are interest for the purposes of interpreting the criminal usury statute); Moore v. Comfed Sav. Bank, 908 F.2d 834 (11th Cir. 1990) (same; notes "outrageous" charges); Alexander v. Kaye-Co, Clearinghouse No. 46,763 (Ga. Super. Ct. Oct. 2, 1992) (reverse redlining case alleging that African-Americans targeted for these loans in violation of Georgia Fair Housing Act). The Georgia loans were also a major reason that Congress considered regulating high-cost mortgages; Home Ownership & Equity Pro-

Jones, there was a split in Georgia's federal courts as to whether they violated the state's criminal usury ceiling.[280]

However, it may be that even the *Jones* decision should not be the final word as to whether spreading is available where the statute clearly sets a "*per month*" cap. An earlier decision interpreted similar language in Georgia's small loan act exactly as the *Jones* borrowers argued.[281] It is possible that the fact it was a criminal statute may have been the critical factor which led the *Jones* court to use the spreading doctrine in the face of the statutory language and long-standing precedent.[282] It may be that a civil statute, particularly a special usury statute such as a small loan act or its successor, would still be interpreted as in the earlier decision.[283]

4.6.5.2 Spreading in Open-End, Variable-Rate Transactions

Although numerous courts have applied the spreading doctrine in fixed-term transactions, several courts have refused to extend spreading to open-end, variable-rate transactions.[284] The reason seems to be the tenet of usury law that a transaction is usurious at its inception if it is usurious at all. Courts considering the application of spreading to open-end

accounts have recognized that usury in such accounts could never be determined until the account was terminated if spreading were allowed, because any monthly overcharges could theoretically be spread to later payment periods in which the maximum rate was not charged.

Conversely, any apparently non-usurious account could be made usurious by later overcharges. Faced with the possibility that the presence of usury in an open-end account might depend entirely on the date that the account terminated, some courts seem to have concluded that spreading is unworkable in open-end transactions, and that these transactions are better viewed as a series of (monthly) loans or forbearances which must be individually examined for usury. Other courts, however, have had no problem with the idea of testing for usury at the time an open-end account is terminated and have applied the spreading doctrine to open-end transactions.[285]

4.6.5.3 Spreading in Special Situations

A final issue raised by the concept of spreading is the term over which interest payments may be spread. This issue can arise in two basic situations: when the term of the credit is shortened, usually by default or prepayment; and when there is more than one credit transaction between the same debtor and creditor.

As suggested earlier in this discussion, a creditor which assesses one-time fees at the beginning of the term of a loan is charging a higher effective interest rate at the beginning of the term than later in the loan. Under the spreading doctrine, this practice is permissible if the over-all contract rate is below the usury ceiling. Yet what happens when the term of the loan is cut short, perhaps by prepayment? Logically, even under the spreading doctrine, the lender will have charged a higher rate of interest than it would have if the loan had remained in effect for the originally anticipated term, because there will now be fewer payment periods over which the one-time fees can be spread.[286] If the contract interest rate exceeds the statutory limit when the fees are spread over the shortened loan term, usury should result.[287]

There is, however, a major limitation on the argument that the premature termination of credit can cause usury: courts are reluctant to find usury violations based on contingencies

tection, S. 1275 Subtitle B, Cong. Rec. S 3334 (Mar. 21, 1994) (*Problems in Community Development Banking, Mortgage Lending Discrimination, Reverse Redlining, and Home Equity Lending, Hearings Before the Committee on Banking, Housing & Urban Affairs*), (103d Cong., 1st Sess., Feb. 3, 17, 24, 1993).

280 *Compare In re* Dent, 130 B.R. 623 (Bankr. S.D. Ga. 1991) and *In re* Evans, 130 B.R. 357 (Bankr. S.D. Ga. 1991) with Johnson v. Fleet Fin., 785 F. Supp. 1003 (S.D. Ga. 1992), *aff'd*, 4 F.3d 946 (11th Cir. 1993).

281 Hartsfield Co. v. Fulwiler, 200 S.E. 309 (Ga. 1938).
    For excellent briefs on this issue, see briefs in two of the pre-*Jones* cases: Johnson v. Fleet Fin., 4 F.3d 946 (11th Cir. 1993) (appellants' brief available as Clearinghouse No. 47,940) and *In re* Wright, 144 B.R. 943 (Bankr. S.D. Ga. 1992) (appellants' brief on appeal to district court available as Clearinghouse No. 47,941).

282 The court noted that the statute was susceptible of multiple interpretations, and as a criminal statute, it must be construed most favorably to the potentially liable party.

283 *See* § 9.3.1.1, *infra* on statutory construction.

284 *See* Connell v. Merrill, Lynch, Pierce, Fenner, & Smith, 578 P.2d 1375 (Cal. 1978), *later opinion at* 662 P.2d 916 (Cal. 1983); Arneill Ranch v. Petit, 134 Cal. Rptr. 456 (App. 1976); *see also* Voitier v. First Nat'l Bank of Commerce, 514 F. Supp. 585 (E.D. La. 1981) (spreading argument rejected although "spreading" terminology not used); Superior Improvement v. Mastic Corp., 604 S.W.2d 950 (Ark. 1980) (same); Sailboat Apartment Corp. v. Chase Manhattan Mortgage & Realty Trust, 363 So. 2d 564 (Fla. Dist. Ct. App. 1978); Norstar Bank v. Pickard & Anderson, 529 N.Y.S.2d 667 (App. Div. 1988) (cannot "average" the return on a variable-rate loan over life of loan for purposes of determining usury; to rule otherwise would compel borrowers to pay excessive interest and not seek relief until end of term; creditor, on other hand, could have avoided problem by use of caps or use of an index which would have avoided usury). *See generally* Annotation, *Usury in Connection with Loan Calling for Variable Interest Rate*, 18 A.L.R.4th 1068.

285 *See* American Timber & Trading Co. v. First Nat'l Bank of Oregon, 690 F.2d 781 (9th Cir. 1982); S & A Indus., Inc. v. Bank Atlanta, 543 S.E.2d 743 (Ga. App. 2000) (spreading applied to line of credit even though term of repayment period not defined); O'Brien v. Shearson, Hayden, Stone, Inc., 90 Wash. 2d 680, 586 P.2d 830 (1978), *on reconsideration* 605 P.2d 779 (Wash. 1980). *See also In re* Auto Int'l Refrigeration, 275 B.R. 789, 817–18 (Bankr. N.D. Tex. 2002) (using total amount borrower could have borrowed under line of credit, rather than smaller amount actually borrowed), *aff'd*, 307 B.R. 849 (N.D. Tex. 2002).

286 This is illustrated in § 7.2.2.1, *infra*.

287 *See* Kissell v. Gressley, 591 F.2d 47 (9th Cir. 1979) (applying Arizona law).

within the control of the borrower.[288] Most courts view prepayment and default as contingencies within the borrower's control. Thus, it is probable that the premature termination of a loan through acceleration or prepayment will not in itself cause usury even if the effective interest rate charged on the shortened loan exceeds the usury ceiling.[289] (Yet acceleration caused by the lender's wrongdoing can trigger a usury violation if the effective contract rate caused by the shortened loan term is too high.[290]) Moreover, many modern credit statutes require the creditor to rebate enough interest to the borrower upon early loan termination to insure that the effective interest rate over the shortened contract term does not exceed the usury ceiling.[291] Failure to provide these rebates may be usurious even if the early termination is caused by the borrower.[292]

The second situation in which the term of a loan can be an issue under the spreading doctrine arises when there is more than one transaction between the debtor and creditor. If some, but not all of the obligations between the parties are usurious when viewed individually, creditors may attempt to spread the excess interest in the apparently usurious notes across the non-usurious obligations to defeat a usury claim. This tactic presumes, of course, that the over-all interest charge when the notes are aggregated is below the maximum permissible for a loan of the size of the aggregated debts.

The validity of spreading interest across two or more notes appears to depend on the relationship, if any, between the notes. Clearly, interest cannot be spread across unrelated debts.[293] However, if a series of notes is created pursuant to a single financing agreement, the notes apparently may be aggregated and the interest spread among them.[294] Similarly, if two notes represent the same debt spreading may be permissible, although determining when a renewal note represents the same debt as its predecessor can be a tricky problem.[295] For example, one Texas court allowed the spreading of interest across a refinancing transaction on the grounds that the old debt was never extinguished,[296] while a bankruptcy court in California refused to spread interest across a transaction in which a credit sale contract (in the guise of a lease) was rewritten as a forbearance at usurious rates.[297]

4.6.5.4 Contract Argument Against Spreading

Consumer law practitioners should observe that spreading usually appears as a defense in a usury action. It is rarely mentioned in the contract itself and may not be closely considered when the contract is drafted. Therefore, creditors may unwittingly insert clauses in the credit contract that are inconsistent with a spreading defense. For example, one of the justifications for the spreading of loan fees over the term of a loan is that these charges are related to the entire term of the loan and should not be attributed entirely to any one payment period.[298]

Yet, to avoid rebates of unearned charges, creditors usually claim that various loan fees are earned at the outset of the loan transaction. Such claims are clearly incompatible with a spreading defense, although whether they would defeat the defense in a jurisdiction which recognizes spreading is unclear.[299] While the argument was unsuccessful in

---

288 *See* discussion in § 5.5, *infra*.

289 *See, e.g., In re* Brummer, 147 B.R. 552 (Bankr. D. Mont. 1992) (under Montana law, spreading doctrine applies where usurious interest results from borrower's action, i.e., prepayment or default, though does not apply where transaction facially usurious); French v. Mortgage Guarantee Co., 104 P.2d 655 (Cal. 1940). *But see In re* Auto Int'l Refrigeration, 275 B.R. 789, 809–16 (Bankr. N.D. Tex. 2002) (acceleration of note would have meant that interest was to be spread over shortened term, but not shown here), *aff'd*, 307 B.R. 849 (N.D. Tex. 2002); *In re* Abramoff, 92 B.R. 698 (Bankr. W.D. Tex. 1988) (lender's acceleration itself precludes spreading over the original contract term; court permits spreading over actual period borrower had use of funds); Armstrong v. Steppes Apts., Ltd., 57 S.W.3d 37 (Tex. App. 2001) (finding loan usurious after spreading charges only over the shortened term after lender accelerated); Financial Security Servs. v. Phase I Electronics, 998 S.W.2d 674 (Tex. App. 1999) (an advance payment of interest can be spread only over actual period borrower had use of funds where lender accelerated debt and borrower paid accelerated amount after one year of five-year loan).

290 *See* Kissell v. Gressley, 591 F.2d 47 (9th Cir. 1979); Foster v. Universal CIT Credit Corp., 231 Ark. 230, 330 S.W.2d 288 (1959) (involuntary prepayment). *Cf. In re* Abramoff, 92 B.R. 698 (Bankr. W.D. Tex. 1988) (lender's acceleration itself precludes spreading over the original contract term; court permits spreading over actual period borrower had use of funds).

291 The Texas spreading statute requires rebates, for example. *See* Danziger v. San Jacinto Sav. Ass'n, 732 S.W.2d 300 (Tex. 1987); Coppedge v. Colonial S & L Ass'n, 721 S.W.2d 933 (Tex. App. 1986).

292 *Id.* For a discussion of rebates of unearned interest apart from the context of spreading, see Ch. 5, *infra*.

293 *See* American Timber & Trading Co. v. First Nat'l Bank of Oregon, 690 F.2d 781, 790 (9th Cir. 1982).

294 *See* American Timber & Trading Co. v. First Nat'l Bank of Oregon, 690 F.2d 781, 789 (9th Cir. 1982); Mayfield v. Oklahoma State Bank, 460 P.2d 414 (Okla. 1969). For a discussion of a closely related issue, the aggregation of debt for purposes of determining loan size, *see* § 9.2.5, *infra*.

295 The issue is similar to the question of whether a renewal note represents the same debt as a preceding usurious note and is therefore tainted with the pre-existing usury. *See* § 6.2, *infra*.

296 Nicoladze v. Lomas & Nettleton Mortgage Investors, 679 S.W.2d 671 (Tex. App. 1984).

297 Fox v. Peck Iron & Metal, 25 B.R. 674 (Bankr. S.D. Cal. 1982).

298 *See* Arneill Ranch v. Petit, 134 Cal. Rptr. 456 (App. 1976).

299 Although it may not be immediately obvious, the issues of spreading and rebates are closely related. (For a discussion of rebates, *see* Ch. 5, *infra*.) If a loan fee is "earned" at the outset of a transaction and is therefore exempt from rebate calculations, it would be inconsistent to spread the fee over the term of the loan for rate calculation purposes because the former theory presumes that the whole fee is earned at once, while the latter presumes that part of the fee is earned in each payment period. A creditor which

the Georgia Supreme Court, that case involved a criminal usury statute, "susceptible of multiple interpretations," which the court said must be construed strictly in favor of the creditor.[300] In the civil context, a court might be more willing to hold the creditor—who drafted the contract—to its own words.[301]

4.6.6 Minimum Finance Charges or Service Charges

Some credit statutes, like the Indiana version of the UCCC, authorize a minimum finance charge. The interrelationship between this charge and a statutory interest rate cap can be confusing. In Indiana, payday lenders argued that the $30 minimum finance charge provision meant that they could charge $30 for any transaction, no matter how short, even if it pushed the APR far above the statutory cap of 36%. The Indiana Supreme Court disagreed, holding that the minimum finance charge merely represented the amount that the lender was entitled to retain out of the finance charge if the borrower prepaid the loan.[302] The finance charge for the full term of the loan as written still had to be within the 36% cap.

4.6.7 Biweekly Mortgage Payment

Some mortgage lenders offer biweekly payment plans as a way for people to pay off their mortgages more quickly. The consumer pays half of the mortgage payment every two weeks, rather than a full payment every month. Since there are 52 weeks in a year, the consumer ends up making 26 half-payments instead of 12 whole payments, resulting in one extra payment per year. Applying an extra payment to reduce the principal can dramatically reduce the term and amount of interest that the consumer pays. For example, paying a $100,000 loan at 11.627% at $1,000 a month requires 30 years of payments and results in a finance charge of $260,000. Paying the same loan at the same interest rate at $500 every two weeks requires only 19-1/2 years of payments and results in a finance charge of only $152,000.

In some areas, independent companies offer to set up biweekly payment plans for mortgage debtors, typically charging a flat fee plus a percentage of each payment for this service. Some mortgage lenders also charge a monthly fee for setting up such a payment plan. These fees eat into the benefit that the consumer realizes from the biweekly payment. Some of these independent companies have also been accused of failing to forward payments promptly to the mortgage holder and making misleading representations about the nature of the plan and the extent of the benefits.[303]

4.6.8 Daily Accrual Accounting

4.6.8.1 Daily Accrual Without Compounding

Even as consumers have become more aware of the cost saving benefits of having lower interest rates on loans—especially those for large amounts and for long terms, like home mortgages—many in the financial services industry have found creative ways to extract more money from consumers. One particularly pernicious way is the *daily accrual* method of charging interest on home mortgages. Although the accounting rules used in this method are the consumer friendly "simple interest" method, the effect of using the daily accrual method on home mortgages can cost home owners tens of thousands of dollars over the course of a mortgage.

It should be noted that in years past, the simple interest method of accounting has always been the preferred method for charging interest on long-term loans. The simple interest method is still the preferred way to *calculate* the amount of interest that will be due on the loan when the loan is first established and when the loan is prepaid.[304]

Conventional mortgage loans, which are sold on the secondary market to Fannie Mae or Freddie Mac, generally use what is called the scheduled method of accounting. On a scheduled loan, for purposes of determining how much interest is due on the loan, each payment is counted as made on the date it is *scheduled* to be paid, rather than the date it is *actually* paid.[305] This means that whether the payment is

---

invokes the spreading doctrine, while denying that the fees which it wants to spread are rebateable, is trying to have its cake and eat it too. However, if statutes authorize both spreading and the treatment of points or other fees as earned upon the consummation of a transaction, challenging the inconsistency may be difficult. If the statutes are worded permissively (i.e., points *may* be treated as earned at consummation), then it might be argued that the contractual choice to treat the points as earned should constitute a waiver of a subsequent spreading defense.

300 Fleet Fin., Inc. v. Jones, 430 S.E.2d 352 (Ga. 1993); *see* § 4.6.5.1, *supra*. For statutory construction rules in civil usury statutes, see § 9.3.2.1, *infra*. Cf. Fisher v. Westinghouse Credit Corp., 760 S.W.2d 802 (Tex. App. 1988) (lender cannot spread illegal late charge interest over term of underlying note).

301 At the very least, it might consider the contract to be ambiguous, and as such, should be construed against the drafter.

302 Livingston v. Fast Cash USA, Inc., 753 N.E.2d 572 (Ind. 2001).

303 Eva v. Midwest Nat'l Mortgage Banc, Inc., 143 F. Supp. 2d 862 (N.D. Ohio 2001) (denying motion to dismiss state and federal RICO, Fair Housing Act, fraud, unconscionability, conversion, and civil conspiracy claims against independent biweekly payment plan company; dismissing certain other claims); *Washington State Department of Financial Institutions, Expanded Report of Examination of Household Finance Corporation III as of April 30, 2002,* Clearinghouse No. 54,580 (documenting one lender's deceptive disclosure of effective rate that borrower would theoretically achieve by enrolling in biweekly payment plan).

304 See discussion in § 4.3.3, *supra*, on discount interest and discussion in § 5.6.3.3, *infra*, on Rule of 78 and other prepayment penalties.

305 *See, e.g.*, Multistate Fixed Rate Note—Single Family—Fannie Mae/Freddie Mac Uniform Instrument Paragraph 3(A): "Each monthly payment will be applied as of its scheduled due date and will be applied to interest before principal. . . ."

received on the first day, the third day or the seventeenth day of the month (or even not until the following month), the same amount of interest is charged for that month, and it is based on the particular day that the payment was *scheduled* to be paid. For scheduled loans, the only events which will alter the actual amortization of the mortgage from the way it was predicted to amortize when the loan was made will be prepayments of principal. This rule of accounting applies until and unless the loan goes into default, or is prepaid.

In contrast, the daily accrual method of accounting calculates the amount of interest to be due during the term of the loan, rather than at the time the loan is established, or at the time the loan is prepaid. The subprime mortgage lenders who use this method count the actual number of days between payments (generally using an interest rate based on a 360-day year,[306] and counting the days between payments by counting like days to like days of each month). In other words, the actual yearly note rate of the loan will be divided by 360 to determine the daily rate and this daily rate will be multiplied by the number of days that have lapsed between payments. The like day rule will count thirty days between January 10 and February 10, even though there are actually thirty-one, and thirty days between February 10 and March 10, although there are actually only twenty-eight, unless it is a leap year.

The actual arithmetic in a daily accrual loan works as follows. For each payment received, the following math must be done:

1) *Determining the daily interest rate.* The note rate, which is based on the full year, is divided by 360 to determine the daily interest rate.

2) *Finding the number of days to apply the daily interest rate.* The date the payment is made is compared to the date payment was made in the previous month. Counting like days to like days as thirty, the difference in days will be determined. So from February 12 to March 14 will be considered thirty-two days, despite the fact that anyone looking at a real calendar would count thirty days (or thirty-one if it is leap year).[307]

3) *Determining the periodic interest rate.* The daily interest rate found in step 1 is multiplied by the number of days found in step 2 to yield a "periodic interest rate."[308]

4) *Determining the amount of interest to be collected from this payment.* The periodic interest rate is multiplied by the previous month's remaining balance to determine the amount of interest due this month.

5) *Determining the amount of the payment to be applied to principal, if any.* The amount of interest due is deducted from the monthly payment, and any remaining funds are applied to reduce the principal balance of the loan.

6) *Determining earned but unpaid interest.* If the amount of interest calculated to be due this month exceeds the amount of the payment, this is called "earned but unpaid interest." Unless interest is compounded (*see* § 4.6.8.2, *infra*) this earned but unpaid interest is isolated as a separate line and accumulated until paid off from subsequent payments, so that one month's earned but unpaid interest is added to the subsequent month's amount. However, the cumulative amounts of earned but unpaid interest do not affect the balance of the loan, and no interest is earned on this unpaid interest.

7) *Paying off earned but unpaid interest.* The following month steps one through four are repeated, except that before any amount of the payment is applied to reduce the principal of the loan, the payment is first applied to reduce the previous month's earned but unpaid interest. This step is repeated until all earned by unpaid interest amounts have been paid off. Only when the cumulative total of all previous months' earned but unpaid interest has been paid off is any portion of the monthly payment applied to reduce the principal balance of the loan.

Consider the following example, covering the first two years of otherwise identical loans of $75,000 at a 12% interest rate for thirty years. Assume the loan was made on December 1, 2001, and that the payments are due the first of each month, with a late charge owing only if the payment is made fifteen days late. In the example below, not a single payment is made after the fifteen-day grace period, every payment is made in full, and the additional interest charges assessed each month are *not compounded*. Yet after one year's payments, each payment of which is on time and made in full, the home owner owes an additional $179.

After thirty years of timely, full payments, using the daily accrual method the amount of additional interest owed will exceed $8,900. In real life, however, mortgage payments on subprime mortgages are rarely always made on time, and in the exact amount required. This is largely because, even

---

306 Most of the subprime lenders who use daily accrual accounting appear to use the 360-day rule to arrive a the daily interest rate, but some may use 365 days. Use of the 360-day rule to calculate the daily interest rate seems to require, but does not necessarily require, use of the like day rule to determine the number of days between payments. See § 6.3, *infra*, regarding the use of the 360- or 365-day method.

307 Whether lenders count leap year when they use the 360-day rule to calculate interest is a whole bag of worms in itself, and seems to be left up to the vagaries of the person doing the counting. Although the Microsoft Excel spreadsheet does offer some explanation of the different uses of these methods, the authors have not been able to determine that any rules of law govern this specific question.

308 It is conceivable that the daily interest rate may be determined

by dividing the annual note rate by 365, however, that would probably only be done if required by law or contract. If the daily rate were determined by dividing 365 days, that does not necessarily mean that the number of days between payments would be determined by counting actual days. This would also generally be determined by the individual creditor, unless required by law or contract.

Chart 14

First Two Years of Thirty Year $75,000 Loan at 12% Per Annum,
Showing Difference Between Daily Accrual and
Scheduled Payment Methods

Payment Number	Date of Payment	Days From Last Payment	Payment Amount	Periodic Interest Rate	Interest Earned	Daily Accrual New Balance	Scheduled Payment New Balance	Difference in *Balance* between Daily Accrual and Scheduled
						$75,000.00		
1	1/15/2002	44	$771.45	1.47%	$1,100.00	$75,000.00	$74,978.55	−$ 21.45
2	2/13/2002	28	$771.45	0.93%	$ 700.00	$75,000.00	$74,956.88	−$ 43.12
3	3/15/2002	32	$771.45	1.07%	$ 800.00	$75,000.00	$74,934.99	−$ 65.01
4	4/15/2002	30	$771.45	1.00%	$ 750.00	$75,000.00	$74,912.88	−$ 87.12
5	5/9/2002	24	$771.45	0.80%	$ 600.00	$75,000.00	$74,890.55	−$109.45
6	6/15/2002	36	$771.45	1.20%	$ 900.00	$75,000.00	$74,868.00	−$132.00
7	7/15/2002	30	$771.45	1.00%	$ 750.00	$75,000.00	$74,845.23	−$154.77
8	8/15/2002	30	$771.45	1.00%	$ 750.00	$75,000.00	$74,822.23	−$177.77
9	9/5/2002	20	$771.45	0.67%	$ 500.00	$74,906.95	$74,799.00	−$107.95
10	10/15/2002	40	$771.45	1.33%	$ 998.75	$74,906.95	$74,775.54	−$131.41
11	11/14/2002	29	$771.45	0.97%	$ 724.10	$74,906.95	$74,751.84	−$155.11
12	12/15/2002	31	$771.45	1.03%	$ 774.03	$74,906.95	$74,727.90	-$179.05

when the home owner is in the habit of paying in a timely manner, these subprime mortgagors *encourage untimely payments*. "Skip a payment!" "Take a holiday from payments!" are standard offers from some subprime mortgage companies. And missed payments can have devastatingly expensive consequences on a mortgage which uses a daily accrual method of calculating interest.

Considering the sample mortgage described above, now assume that the daily accrual method is combined with just *one* missed payment (assume it is the sixth payment). The borrower's otherwise timely and full payments will not reduce principal for forty-six months. The extra amount owed at the end of the thirty-year mortgage will exceed $29,000.

Actually this additional interest cost is less a matter of interesting mathematics than of the differing practices—and dramatically different incentives—of the mortgagees that employ the two different methods. In a scheduled mortgage, because the payment is always applied as if it were made on time, the home owner would never be encouraged to skip a payment because the servicer does not receive any added interest, or other benefit, from the fact that the home owner has paid late. However, if one does the math on the effect of a missed sixth payment on a scheduled mortgage, the mortgage balance would not be paid down until the fortieth timely payment, and the extra interest owed at the end of the mortgage would be over $22,000. While this additional interest would be $6,000 less than what would be due under the daily accrual mortgage, the chief distinction between the

two is that the daily accrual accounting method provides an incentive to encourage missed payments. In contrast, in a scheduled mortgage the servicer has every incentive to ensure the borrower pays on time, because the servicer has to advance these amounts to the investor and the servicer earns only the late charge for that late payment.

4.6.8.2 Daily Accrual with Compounding

Lenders and servicers can exacerbate the effect of the daily accrual method by both charging interest on a daily basis, and compounding earned but unpaid interest. This practice can more than double the added cost of daily accrual accounting.

The arithmetic involved in a daily accrual loan with compounding is identical to that used in the daily accrual method without compounding (*see* § 4.6.8.1, *supra*) until one reaches step six. Step six involves the compounding of unearned interest:

6) *Dealing with earned but unpaid interest.* If the amount of interest calculated to be due in the current month exceeds the amount of the payment, the excess is *added* to the balance of the loan, increasing the previous month's balance by the amount of the interest earned in this month which exceeds the payment.

7) *Repeat steps.* The following month these steps are repeated.

Chart 15

First Two Years of Thirty Year $75,000 Loan at 12% Per Annum,
Showing Difference Between Daily Accrual and
Scheduled Payment Methods *with Compounding*

Payment Number	Date of Payment	Days From Last Payment	Payment Amount	Periodic Interest Rate	Interest Earned	Daily Accrual New Balance	Scheduled Payment New Balance WITH COM-POUND-ING	Difference in *Balance* between Daily Accrual and Scheduled WITH COM-POUND-ING
1	1/15/2002	44	$771.45	1.47%	$1,100.00	$75,328.55	$74,978.55	-$350.00
2	2/13/2002	28	$771.45	0.93%	$ 703.06	$75,260.16	$74,956.88	-$303.28
3	3/15/2002	32	$771.45	1.07%	$ 802.77	$75,291.48	$74,934.99	-$356.49
4	4/15/2002	30	$771.45	1.00%	$ 751.91	$75,272.94	$74,912.88	-$360.06
5	5/9/2002	24	$771.45	0.80%	$ 602.18	$75,103.67	$74,890.55	-$213.12
6	6/15/2002	36	$771.45	1.20%	$ 901.24	$75,233.46	$74,868.00	-$365.46
7	7/15/2002	30	$771.45	1.00%	$ 752.33	$75,214.34	$74,845.23	-$369.11
8	8/15/2002	30	$771.45	1.00%	$ 752.14	$75,195.03	$74,822.23	-$372.80
9	9/5/2002	20	$771.45	0.67%	$ 501.30	$74,924.88	$74,799.00	-$125.88
10	10/15/2002	40	$771.45	1.33%	$ 998.99	$75,152.42	$74,775.54	-$376.88
11	11/14/2002	29	$771.45	0.97%	$ 726.47	$75,107.44	$74,751.84	-$355.60
12	12/15/2002	31	$771.45	1.03%	$ 776.11	$75,112.10	$74,727.90	-$384.20

Using our sample thirty-year mortgage for $75,000 at 12%, the effect of compounding doubles the amount of additional interest owing after one year of timely payments.

Again, while the math works its magic to yield more profits for the lender, the true benefit to the lender is the way that both the daily accrual method and the compounding of interest reward the lender for encouraging borrowers to skip payments. On the other hand the scheduled payments method of accounting yields no benefit for the servicer if the borrower is late—indeed the servicer generally has to advance the payment to the investor—so the servicer has every incentive to encourage timely and full payments.

A loan which compounds interest creates negative amortization. If the loan is a covered loan under HOEPA (Home Ownership and Equity Protection Act)[309] such a loan would violate the statutory provisions which prohibit negative amortization at any time during the course of the loan.[310] A loan whose amortization chart at the outset does not appear to use negative amortization will still violate HOEPA if, in practice, the lender uses the daily accrual method of accounting and compounds interest.[311]

4.6.8.3 Daily Accrual and Application of Payments

Daily accrual accounting also rewards lenders and servicers for changing the standard method of applying payments. In conventional mortgages, servicers apply the payments first to interest, then to principal, then to escrow payments due, and finally to late charges.[312] In contrast, some subprime servicers will apply payments first to advances made (such as for forced place insurance), then to interest, then to late charges, and last to principal. This change in the order of the application of the money received in each payment can also have very expensive long-term consequences for borrowers.

4.7 Points

4.7.1 Calculation of Points

Often, the charges which a borrower must pay to obtain credit are not limited to monthly interest payments. Points,

---

309 15 U.S.C. § 1602(aa); *see* National Consumer Law Center, Truth in Lending Ch. 9 (5th ed. 2003 and Supp.).

310 15 U.S.C. § 1639(f).

311 *See* National Consumer Law Center, Truth in Lending § 9.4.5 (5th ed. 2003 and Supp.).

312 *See* Fannie Mae Single Family Servicer Guidelines III, § 101.03: Payment Shortages (2002 and Supp.); General Freddie Mac Policies, Single Family Seller/Servicer Guide § 51.15(a) Accounting Methods (1989 and Supp.).

which have been mentioned previously in this chapter, are a prime example. Especially in real estate transactions, borrowers normally are assessed one-time fees at the consummation of a transaction, in addition to their regular monthly installments. Some of these fees directly compensate the creditor for specific third-party expenses, such as filing fees or appraisal fees, and generally do not present problems in calculation. Other fees, however, are not directly connected to expenses that the creditor has incurred and are expressed in terms of a percentage of the loan that the borrower is receiving. Such fees are called points, discount points, origination fees, commitment fees, service charges, or just loan fees.[313] Throughout most of this manual, they are referred to simply as "points." In normal industry usage, one point is equal to one percent of the face amount of the loan note that the borrower signs.[314]

Although points are often described by creditors as a fee which a borrower must pay, this is not precisely the way they normally work. Instead, points are usually treated as a discount[315] withheld from the loan, thus reducing the amount that the borrower receives. For example, assume that a borrower goes to a bank seeking a $100,000 mortgage. The bank offers to make the loan at ten percent simple interest, plus three points. Since one point is one percent of the nominal loan amount, in this case one point will equal $1,000. Therefore the bank is demanding $3,000 (three points) in addition to the ten percent stated interest. If the borrower agrees to these terms, he will sign a note for $100,000 and will pay ten percent on this amount, but he will receive only $97,000 in loan proceeds because of the points.[316]

It does not take great insight to see that the use of points increases a creditor's yield on a loan, and that the stated ten percent contract rate in the example is misleading.[317] The

precise increase in yield depends on the term of the loan; the shorter the term, the greater the increase.[318] If the loan in the example is a 30-year fixed-rate mortgage which is not paid off early, the lender's yield will be 10.3657% simple interest, or more than a third of a percentage point higher than the stated rate.[319] Most mortgage loans are retired early, however, so in practice the increase in the loan yield may be significantly higher.[320]

An alternate method of calculating points exists, although it is less often used than the practice just described. This alternative is to calculate points as a percentage of the loan proceeds which the borrower actually receives, rather than as a percentage of the face amount of the loan note. The points are then added on to the proceeds to calculate the amount of the note. Thus, if the borrower wants a $100,000 loan and must pay three points, he would sign a note for $103,000. The yield to the lender under this system, although still above the ten percent rate stated on the note, is lower than when the same number of points are treated as a discount,[321] and the disparity may explain why the discount system is more frequently used.

---

313 Though these are clearly compensation to the creditor, whether they are legally characterized as interest varies, dependent upon state law. *See* §§ 7.2–7.3, *infra*. Points are always treated as "finance charge" under the federal Truth in Lending Act, even when they are not "interest" under state usury law. *See* 12 C.F.R. § 226.4(b)(3) (Regulation Z).

314 As discussed later in this section, points may also be calculated as a percentage of the sum that the borrower actually receives.

315 This discount is technically not "discount interest," discussed in § 4.3.3, *supra*, because there is no time factor in the calculation. Three points on a short-term loan is the same dollar amount as three points on a long-term loan of the same principal, although the charging of points on a short-term loan will increase a lender's yield more than the charging of the same number of points on a long-term loan.

316 If the borrower needs the full $100,000 in cash, the creditor will probably just increase the amount of the loan note so that $100,000 will remain after three points have been subtracted. Specifically, if the borrower signed a note for $103,092.78, three percent of this amount (i.e., three points) would be $3,092.78, and the borrower would be left with exactly $100,000 after the points were subtracted.

317 The Truth in Lending Act disclosures should accurately reflect the interest rate being charged because the points must be

included in the TILA finance charge and APR. However, the TILA calculations assume that the contract will run its full term. If it does not, and most consumer loans do not, the APR will also be understated unless the points are subject to rebate. For discussion of the need to rebate points, *see* § 5.5.2.2, *infra*.

318 *See, e.g.*, Bandas v. Citizens State Bank, 412 N.W.2d 818 (Minn. Ct. App. 1987) (stated APR was 14.25%, not including a 1 1/2% loan origination fee; since note due in 14 days, including loan origination fee as interest raised effective interest rate to a usurious rate of 51.52%), *rev'd and remanded on other grounds sub nom.* VanderWeyst v. First State Bank of Benson, 425 N.W.2d 803 (Minn. 1988), *cert. denied*, 488 U.S. 943 (1988).

319 The yield can be calculated in the following manner. First, the monthly payment required to amortize a 10% simple interest loan of $100,000 in equal monthly installments is $877.57, so this is the payment the borrower will be making. However, the borrower is receiving only $97,000, not $100,000, because of the points. The APR on a 30-year loan of $97,000 with equal monthly payments of $877.57 is 10.3657%, and this is the correct yield. Note, however, that state "spreading" statutes may dictate different methods for calculating the increase in yield due to points. These methods generally understate the increase. Spreading is discussed in § 4.6.5, *supra*.

320 This assumes that the points are not subject to statutory rebate requirements. If points must be rebated upon prepayment, and there is a serious argument that they should be (*see* § 5.5.2.2, *infra*), then prepayment would not increase the loan yield.

321 Specifically, the actuarial yield from this method of calculating points is 10.3548%, which is 0.0109% lower than the yield when points are discounted. The calculation works as follows. The borrower signs a note for $103,000 bearing ten percent simple interest. Amortization of this note over thirty years will require equal monthly payments of $903.90. However, the borrower is only getting $100,000, not $103,000. The APR for a $100,000 loan with equal monthly payments of $903.90 over thirty years (which, again, is the payment that the borrower will actually be making) is 10.3548%.

4.7.2 Legal Issues Arising in Calculation of Points

The legal characterization of points and similar charges as interest generally is discussed in § 7.2.2, *infra*. This discussion focuses on legal issues that may arise regarding the *calculation* of points.

Usury statutes frequently limit themselves to restricting the effective interest rate that a creditor may charge and may not dictate the manner in which a creditor can calculate its fees. Thus, creditors often may calculate points however they please, so long as the resulting interest rate, including the charges for points, does not surpass the usury ceiling. On the other hand, some states have specific limitations on points. These limits should be investigated carefully, since they may continue to apply even if the state eliminates the interest rate ceiling applicable to a transaction.[322]

First, some statutes prohibit "paying, adding, or deducting interest in advance," which arguably is violated when points are charged.[323]

Second, if a usury statute either restricts the absolute number of points that a creditor may assess or excludes a stated number of points from the statute's definition of "interest," then the manner in which these points are calculated is clearly significant, and the consumer's attorney must read the statutory language very carefully. One critical question is of which amount the points are a percentage. For example, if a statute allows a creditor to charge only three points, and if points are described as a percentage of loan "principal,"[324] the definition of principal must be checked. Generally, "principal" does not include interest charges such as points, so under these circumstances the points would have to be calculated on the basis of the money actually received by the borrower or paid on his behalf for non-interest expenses. The calculation of points as a discount in this example could be usurious.[325]

Unfortunately, when usury statutes do restrict points, they are often imprecise. Consider, for example, a Missouri statute which permits a lender to charge "a fee not to exceed one percent of the loan amount. . . ."[326] What is the loan amount? Is it the amount of the note? Is it the amount the borrower receives? The answer is not immediately obvious, although a dissection of Missouri case law, or perhaps a closer reading of the statute, might provide some clues. For an example of the differing approaches taken to bring some clarity to these statutes, compare *In re Bogan*,[327] in which "principal amount loaned" was interpreted to exclude the percentage-based loan fee in question, with *Lee v. Beneficial Finance Co.*,[328] in which "face amount of contract" was interpreted to include the loan fee.

Another issue which can arise when a statute restricts the number of points which can be charged is whether excess points are buried among other costs. This issue has been raised in connection with "yield spread premiums," a device whereby the creditor charges a higher rate than it would otherwise impose on a loan, and gives the difference, or some portion of it, to a referring broker. Among other challenges to the practice, plaintiffs in *Smith v. First Family Financial Services, Inc.*[329] alleged that the table-funding[330] arrangement between a broker and lender was a device to circumvent Alabama's five-point cap. The Alabama Supreme Court held that "[i]t is a part of the origination fee paid to the mortgage broker on the front end of the loan," and that it was a question of fact whether the arrangement

---

322 *See* Watley v. Transamerica Fin. Servs. (*In re* Watley), 708 So. 2d 890 (Ala. 1997) (statutory cap on points continues to apply even though interest rate is deregulated).

323 *E.g., In re* Peterson, 93 B.R. 323 (Bankr. D. Vt. 1988) (allegation that prepaid interest was charged states a viable cause of action, interpreting 9 Vt. Stat. Ann. 41a(d)(1)).

324 *E.g.*, 815 Ill. Comp. Stat. § 205/4.1a, which, unfortunately, nowhere defines principal amount.

325 The improper calculation of points could violate the statute even if the resulting rate were otherwise permissible, because an express statutory limitation on the number of points which may be charged would have been infringed. *See, e.g.*, Cheshire Mortgage v. Montes, 223 Conn. 80, 612 A.2d 1130 (1992) (calculating 10% prepaid finance charge on principal amount including the prepaid finance charge impermissible; effective prepaid finance charge was thus 11%, which exceeded statutory maximum). *See also In re* Bogan, 281 F. Supp. 242 (W.D. Tenn. 1968) (statute allowing loan fee of 4% of "principal amount loaned" interpreted to mean principal *before* loan fee added; fee could not be based on fee itself; since creditor did so, it constituted usury). *But see* Watley v. Transamerica Fin. Servs.,

708 So. 2d 890 (Ala. 1997) (points can be included in the "original principal balance" on which points are calculated, where statute also provided that points could be "deducted from the proceeds and included in the original principal"; change in law to add a reference to "original amount financed" may, however, require different interpretation in future).

326 Mo. Rev. Stat. § 408.052 (1990). The quoted language, which addresses construction loans, is actually more precise than other sections of the statute which refer simply to a one percent origination fee without saying what this fee is a percentage of. Of course, a reasonable interpretation would be to construe this fee also as a percentage of the "loan amount," but that does not help much.

327 281 F. Supp. 242 (W.D. Tenn. 1968). *See also* Cheshire Mortgage v. Montes, 612 A.2d 1130 (Conn. 1992) (calculating prepaid finance charge on amount including prepaid finance charge is impermissible).

328 282 S.E.2d 770 (Ga. Ct. App. 1981). It is worth noting that it took 24 years and five appellate decisions to pin down the meaning of that phrase in Georgia. *See, e.g.*, Financeamerica Corp. v. Drake, 270 S.E.2d 449 (Ga. App. Ct. 1980); Consolidated Credit Corp. v. Peppers, 240 S.E.2d 922 (Ga. App. Ct. 1977).

329 626 So. 2d 1266 (Ala. 1993).

330 A table-funded loan is one in which a broker, or "correspondent lender," with no money, closes the loan *in his or her name* with funds supplied by a genuine lender, and immediately assigns the loan to the lender. (Note that for purposes of the Real Estate Settlement Procedures Act, (RESPA), the "assignee" is considered the creditor, and the correspondent lender is considered a broker. *See* § 12.2.1, *infra*.)

was designed to evade the statutory point cap.[331] (Yield spread premiums raise a number of other issues as well, and are discussed further in Chapters 7 and 11, *infra*.) In addition to yield spread premiums, points may be higher than stated if the points are financed and the lender then charges points on the new loan amount that includes the financed points. Compounding points on financed points will result in a dollar figure for points that is higher than the original points figure, and thus may exceed a state cap. Moreover, some states prohibit compounding points altogether.

Determining the principal amount on which points can be based raises even more questions when the new loan refinances an old loan from the same lender. Some states allow points to be assessed only on the new funds advanced, i.e., the difference between the principal of the new loan and the unpaid balance of the old loan.[332] A Tennessee Supreme Court decision holds that the net payoff amount of the old loan, not the full balance including unearned interest, should be used in making this calculation.[333] In *Gonzales v. Associates Fin. Servs.*,[334] however, the Kansas Supreme Court interpreted its statute to allow a 2% origination fee to be imposed upon the whole principal of the new loan, not just the new money.

4.8 Calculation of Late Charges and Deferral Charges

4.8.1 *Late Charges*

Usury statutes often allow creditors to contract for the payment of late charges on delinquent credit accounts. Generally these charges may be imposed only after the expiration of a grace period, frequently ten days, which runs from the date on which an installment payment is contractually due.[335] The legal status of late charges as interest or non-interest charges is discussed in section 7.2.4.2, *infra*.

In most transactions, the calculation of late charges is straightforward. They are typically expressed as a percentage of the overdue installment, provided that they do not exceed some amount specified by statute. For example, a usury statute might allow a creditor to assess a late fee of 5% of an overdue installment, not to exceed $5.00.[336] Under this

formula, the charge on an overdue installment of $50 would be $2.50 (i.e., 5% of $50), but the fee for an overdue $150 installment would be only $5.00, not $7.50, because of the fixed $5.00 limit in the statute.

Both usury statutes and credit contracts should be carefully read to determine the size of the late fee which may be imposed when a debtor pays only part of the monthly installment on time. The issue in this situation is whether the late fee is calculated as a percentage of the full installment, even though the debtor has actually paid some of this amount on time, or as a percentage of only that part of the installment which is actually late. For example, if a debtor pays only $30 of a regular $50 installment, is the late fee $2.50 (i.e., 5% of $50) or only $1.00 (i.e., 5% of the unpaid portion, $20)? Most usury statutes seem to take the latter approach and limit the late charge to a percentage of the amount actually overdue.[337] This approach makes sense because it provides the debtor with an incentive to make a timely partial payment, rather than no payment at all, and because it reflects the lesser damages incurred by a creditor when a partial payment is made.[338]

If a usury statute does permit a creditor to follow the more lucrative technique of ignoring partial payments in the calculation of late fees, a consumer's attorney should pay close attention to the contractual description of late charges. Late fees may be imposed only as authorized by contract.[339] Furthermore, a Truth in Lending violation may exist if a consumer credit contract does not unambiguously describe the method to be used to calculate a late fee in the event of a partial payment.[340]

A second calculation issue related to late fees is the manner in which a borrower's regular payments are treated once a late charge has been imposed. Most usury statutes limit a creditor to one late charge per installment. However, a single late payment can be transformed into multiple late charges if a borrower's regular installment payments are attributed first to any outstanding late fees and only second to the installment(s) which have come due. This practice, which is known as the "pyramiding" of late charges, is discussed in detail in § 7.2.4.2, *infra*.

---

allowing late fees as percentage of overdue installment and upholding a similar late fee clause in a contract between two sophisticated commercial parties).

337 *E.g.*, U.C.C.C. § 2.502(1) (1974 Model Act).

338 Late charges are generally justified either as an incentive for prompt payment or as compensation to the creditor for the income it loses through the late receipt of payments. *See* § 7.2.4.2, *infra*.

339 *See* Metro Hauling, Inc. v. Daffern, 723 P.2d 32 (Wash. Ct. App. 1986). *See also* § 7.2.4.2, *infra* for case law on improperly calculated late charges as interest or overcharge.

340 *See* In re Whitley, 772 F.2d 815 (11th Cir. 1985); Watts v. Key Dodge Sales, Inc., 707 F.2d 847 (5th Cir. 1983). *See generally* National Consumer Law Center, Truth in Lending § 4.7.7 (5th ed. 2003 and Supp.). While statutory damages are not available for failure to disclose late charges, this violation is very suitable for actual damages. *Id.* §§ 8.5, 8.6.5.2.

---

331 Smith v. First Family Fin. Servs., Inc., 626 So. 2d 1266, 1271 (Ala. 1993).

332 See Ch. 6, *infra*, for a detailed discussion of the calculations involved in refinancing.

333 Hathaway v. First Family Fin. Servs., 1 S.W.3d 634 (Tenn. 1999).

334 266 Kan. 141, 967 P.2d 312 (1998).

335 Note that, if the transaction is interest-bearing, the grace period does not affect the accumulation of interest, which accrues during the grace period.

336 *See, e.g.*, Metlife Capital Fin. Corp. v. Washington Avenue Assocs., 732 A.2d 493 (N.J. 1999) (reciting New Jersey statutes

Another issue is whether a creditor who is charging interest on a daily basis can also charge a late charge for a payment that is paid late. The answer will probably depend on the exact language of the statute. A Pennsylvania court found both authorized by its Motor Vehicle Sales Finance Act.[341] Even though the daily interest should be full compensation to the lender for the delay in payment, lenders will seek to justify the late charge in the name of deterrence.

In addition to calculation issues, questions often arise as to whether the creditor had the right to impose the late charge. The statute may require a written agreement[342] or at least a disclosure,[343] and may mandate a grace period. Some creditors have been charged with deliberately posting payments late in order to maximize their revenue from late charges.[344]

4.8.2 Deferral Charges

In addition to allowing late charges, many consumer credit statutes permit creditors to collect a deferment charge (sometimes called an extension or forbearance charge) when monthly payments are deferred for a period of time, extending the maturity date of the loan. Where deferral charges are not specifically addressed by statute, a court may treat such charges as separate forbearance agreements, subject to the relevant usury ceiling.[345]

Deferral charge provisions generally apply only to *precomputed* consumer loans repayable in substantially equal monthly installments.[346] (On interest-bearing accounts, the interest continues to accrue during the deferred period, so there is automatically an adjustment to compensate the creditor for the delay. Precomputed interest, by contrast, is fixed at consummation, on the assumption that the loan will be paid as originally scheduled. Any delay, therefore, requires some adjustment if the creditor is to be compensated for it.[347])

Typical consumer credit statutes provide that a deferral agreement must be in writing[348] or the original loan contract must specifically allow the imposition of a deferral

charge.[349] Some state laws specify that the creditor cannot impose or retain a late charge if a deferral charge is applied to the delinquency period.[350] Other aspects of statutory deferral provisions a consumer's attorney should check include: whether deferral of partial monthly installments is allowed and, if so, how it is to be calculated;[351] whether appropriate additional charges (e.g., official fees and taxes, insurance charges, annual credit card fees) may be added to the amount deferred for purposes of computing the deferral charge;[352] whether the original loan contract may allow the creditor to unilaterally grant a deferral and impose related charges where a monthly payment is not made within a set period of time from its due date;[353] and whether the deferment charge is partially refundable if the loan is prepaid during that period.[354]

A sampling of statutes addressing deferral fees shows three methods articulated, which are harder to read than to calculate. Assume that Carl's job got downsized soon after he took out a precomputed $1,000 loan at 10% for one year on February 1. After making only the first payment of $87.92 on March 1,[355] he finds he needs to ask for a deferral. A partial amortization chart for his loan would show that the interest earned during his second payment interval, due April 1, is $7.67.

Balance	Interest	− Payment	= New Bal	Due Date
$1,000.00	$8.33	$87.92	$920.41	Mar. 1
$920.41	$7.67	$87.92	$840.16	Apr. 1

We can use Carl's request to see how much a deferral would cost him under each of the three sample statutory methods.

1. *"The deferment charge for a one month period may not exceed the applicable interest for the installment period immediately following the due date of the last undeferred payment."*[356]

---

341 Harrell v. Chrysler Fin. Co., 811 A.2d 597 (Pa. Super. 2002).

342 Aldrich & Co. v. Ellis, 52 P.3d 388 (Mont. 2002) (merchant must have written agreement to collect late payment charges on retail installment sales and retail charge accounts but it is unnecessary for accounts receivable).

343 *See* § 11.6.8, *infra*.

344 *See* §§ 4.6.3.5, *supra*, 11.5.5, *infra*.

345 *Cf.* Sunburst Bank v. Keith, 648 So. 2d 1147 (Miss. 1995) (oral deferral agreements entered into on business loans were separate forbearance agreements subject to maximum annual interest allowed by statute, to be calculated by statutorily required actuarial method; lender exceeded ceiling by using a pro rata calculation in arriving at deferral charge, which failed to take into account declines in the principal balance at the time of deferrals). *See generally* § 10.5.2, *infra* on forbearance.

346 *See, e.g.*, Cal. Fin. Code § 22400(a)(4); Tex. Fin. Code § 342.001; 205 Ill. Comp. Stat. § 670/15(f)(5).

347 *See generally* § 4.5, *supra*.

348 *See, e.g.*, Iowa Code Ann. § 537.2503(1); Colo. Rev. Stat. § 5-3-204(1); Mass. Gen. Laws ch. 140, § 100, Mass. Regs. Code tit. 209, § 26.06(4)(d) (small loans).

349 *See, e.g.*, N.Y. Banking Law § 351(5)(c) (McKinney); Cal. Fin. Code § 22400(a)(4).

350 *See, e.g.*, Colo. Rev. Stat. § 5-3-204(4); Iowa Code Ann. § 537.2503(4); 209 Mass. Regs. Code § 26.06(d). Since the borrower is essentially buying the right to not make the payment, it is not a late payment.

351 *Compare, e.g.*, Colo. Rev. Stat. § 5-3-204(1) (deferral of part of unpaid installments allowed) *with* 205 Ill. Comp. Stat. § 670/15(f)(5) (allowing only deferment of wholly unpaid installments, though allowed proportionally for partial months).

352 *See, e.g.*, Colo. Rev. Stat. § 5-3-204(2); Iowa Code Ann. § 537.2504(2).

353 *See, e.g.*, Colo. Rev. Stat. § 5-3-204(3); Iowa Code Ann. § 537.2504.

354 *See, e.g.*, Tex. Fin. Code §§ 342.202 to 342.204; 205 Ill. Comp. Stat. § 670/15(f)(5).

355 The lender used the actuarial method, assuming all payments would be made as scheduled, to precompute the interest. *See, e.g.*, 205 Ill. Comp. Stat. § 670/15(b). His monthly payments are $87.92, and the total finance charge for the twelve month period would be $55.04. *See generally* § 4.3.1, *supra*.

356 205 Ill. Comp. Stat. § 670/15(f)(5). *See also* Cal. Fin. Code § 22400(a)(4).

Under this method, Carl's charge to defer the April payment one month, until May 1, is $7.67. The "due date of the last undeferred payment" is March 1, and the interest due for the period between March 1 and April 1 is $7.67, according to the amortization chart.[357] He is in effect buying the right to keep his outstanding principal at $920.41 for two months, instead of one, and is paying an extra month's interest at the contract rate to do so.

2. The lender may collect *a charge not exceeding the rate previously stated to the debtor pursuant to the provisions on disclosure . . . applied to the amount or amounts deferred for the period of deferral. . . .*"[358]

If the disclosed APR in Carl's loan was 10%, one month's deferral would be $7.67 by this method, as well:

$920.41 × 10% ÷ 12 (monthly rate) × 1 (month) = $7.67.[359]

3. *"The interest for such deferment may be equal to the difference between the refund which would be required for prepayment in full, as of the date of deferment and the refund which would be required for prepayment in full as one month prior to such date multiplied by the number of months in the deferment period. . . ."*[360]

Carl is a little confused here, because he has not read Chapter Five, about rebates upon prepayment yet, and does not understand why rules for paying a loan off early should have anything to do with paying to make a loan last longer. But he forges ahead. Taking a detour to that chapter, he sees that there are two customary ways to calculate a rebate upon prepayment: the actuarial method[361] and the Rule of 78.[362] The second method, the Rule of 78, has an inherent bias which overcompensates the creditor upon prepayment, and that bias can carry over into deferral fee calculations if the Rule of 78 is the refund rule which serves as the point of reference for the deferral charge calculation.

If the statute governing Carl's loan calls for actuarial rebates, those are, as he sees in Chapter Five, calculated by subtracting the interest as computed by the actuarial method at time of prepayment from the total precomputed interest, and refunding the difference. The refund which would be due on Carl's loan if there were a prepayment one month prior to deferral (March 1) would be: $55.04[363] − $8.33 = $46.71. The refund which would be due if there were a prepayment on the date of deferral (April 1) would be: $55.04 − ($8.33 + $7.67) = $39.04. The difference between those two refunds is—voilà—$7.67.[364] The deferral charge by this method is the same as the previous two.

However, if the relevant statute would permit a prepayment rebate calculated by the Rule of 78 (not all do), it is a different story. Using the formula he learns from peeking at the next chapter,[365] he calculates the rebate as of March 1 to be $46.57.[366] As of April 1, it would be $38.81.[367] The difference, and hence the deferral fee, would be $7.76—a bit more than a deferral fee calculated without using rebates as a reference. Not by much, but pennies can add up across a lot of customers and a lot of deferrals.

4.8.3 Payment Holidays for Interest-Bearing Loans

In an interest-bearing loan, as noted above, the interest continues to accrue during any deferral period, so the lender is compensated for the delay. The borrower is nonetheless required to adhere to the payment schedule set forth in the contract. Some lenders occasionally offer "payment holidays," by which the debtor can skip a payment, sometimes in return for a deferral fee. If the deferral fee is not high enough to cover the extra interest that accrues due to the deferral, the borrower will be surprised by a balloon payment due at the end of the contract.[368] A lender who misrepresents the effect of deferral may face UDAP liability.[369]

---

357 $920.41 (principal) × 10%/12 (monthly rate) × 1 (month) = $7.67. *See* § 4.3.1.1, *supra*.

For the aficionado of mathematical minutiae, there is arguably an ambiguity in the Illinois statute used in this example. On the one hand, it says that the precomputed loan includes interest "computed actuarially in advance, assuming all payments will be made when scheduled." 205 Ill. Comp. Stat. 670/15(b). Yet in the same section, it defines "applicable interest" in language that seems to describe the sum of the balances method, a variant on the Rule of 78. (*See* § 5.6.3.3.4, *infra*.) As is discussed below in connection with the third type of sample deferral formula, that can be a bit more expensive for the borrower.

358 Colo. Rev. Stat. § 5-3-204(1). *Compare* Iowa Code Ann. § 537.2503(1) (1 1/2% per month, not to exceed the disclosed APR applied to the amount deferred for the time deferred).

359 *See* § 4.3.1.1, *supra*.

360 Tex. Fin. Code § 342.204; *See also* N.Y. Banking Law § 351(5)(c) (McKinney).

361 *See* § 5.6.3.4, *infra*.

362 *See* § 5.6.3.3, *infra*.

363 Remember that the interest on $1000 at 10% actuarial for 12 months is $55.04. *See* note 355, *supra*.

364 $46.71 − $39.04 = $7.67

365 *See* § 5.6.3.3.2, *infra* for the formula, and § 5.6.3.3.1 for a discussion of legal limitations on the use of the Rule of 78.

366 ($55.04) × (.8462) = $46.57.

367 ($55.04) × (.7051) = $38.81.

368 Or, in the case of open-end credit, the borrower may find that the debt is not paid off even after adjusting the originally projected term to take the deferral period into account.

369 Begala v. PNC Bank, 1999 Ohio App. LEXIS 6331 (Dec. 30, 1999) (ordering class certification). For further information about the nature of the loan, see Begala v. PNC Bank, 163 F.3d 948 (6th Cir. 1998) (upholding denial of TIL claims). *See also* Begala v. PNC Bank, 214 F.3d 776 (6th Cir. 2000) (upholding denial of RICO and National Bank Act claims), *cert. denied*, 531 U.S. 1145 (2001).

4.9 Transactions Involving Progress Payments

It is not unusual for home improvement contracts to provide for progress payments, whereby the loan proceeds are disbursed in installments to the contractor as the work proceeds. If such a contract provides for interest on the full amount of the loan from consummation, the creditor may be in trouble.

In *Danziger v. San Jacinto Savings Ass'n*,[370] the borrowers entered into a precomputed contract which provided that the loan principal would be placed in escrow, to be disbursed in installments to the contractor. The interest was calculated at 8% add-on on the full amount of the principal from the loan date. After disbursement, the lender calculated how much of the principal was in the escrow during each payment period, and then credited the account "to return interest charged on the money prior to its being disbursed."[371] The Texas Supreme Court held the practice of contracting for interest on the entire principal, where the contract provides for multiple disbursements, to constitute the charging of usurious interest within the meaning of the applicable statute.[372] The practice of crediting back the overpaid interest did not purge the usury.

4.10 Proving Mathematical Issues in Court

Once computations have been made which suggest usury claims, the next question is how to prove the mathematical issues to the court.[373] The first step is to translate the words of the relevant statute into the proper formula. If the statute uses a phrase commonly understood, such as Rule of 78 rebate, or "add-on" interest, that translation is not difficult. However, sometimes no clarifying words are used,[374] and it is a question of law as to what formulation is authorized, which may be determined by ordinary rules of statutory construction. Sometimes a statute describes a computational method, and it becomes an issue as to precisely what formula those words describe.[375] Banking department regulations should always be checked, as they may clarify the statute.

The question of what the statute requires or permits is a question of law. However, as a practical matter, the statutory language may be technical, readily understandable by those experienced in the area but less accessible to those who are not—including judges who may not frequently hear such cases. Therefore, there may be confusion as to what computational system is authorized, and it may be useful to make that clear for the court. In most cases, the parties (both presumably familiar with the state's scheme) will not disagree.[376] A request for admission or stipulation would be the simplest way to avoid the problem. If it becomes an issue, affidavits from the Banking Department or other relevant regulatory authority may be useful,[377] and could be the basis for a motion for partial summary judgment.

Once the statutorily prescribed method is established—actuarial rebate or Rule of 78 rebate; simple interest or add-on interest, etc.—the next step is to determine the proper formula which expresses that system. A number of sources which discuss financial mathematics may be used to

---

370 732 S.W.2d 300 (Tex. 1987).

371 *Id.* at 302.

372 *Id.* at 302–03. The Texas statute at issue in *Danziger* does not require that usurious interest actually be paid by the borrower, but that it be contracted for, charged or received. *Id.* at 304. *See generally* § 10.5.4.2, *infra*. *See also* Hoffman v. Key Federal Sav. & Loan Ass'n, 286 Md. 28, 416 A.2d 1265 (1979) (if funds delivered by borrowers to a *bona fide* escrow agent, lenders can charge interest on that sum; if lender in effect only disbursed part of proceeds, lender cannot charge interest on portion not disbursed).

373 Other elements of proof necessary to establish a usury claim are discussed in Ch. 10, *infra*.

374 *See, e.g.*, Skolnick v. Ford Motor Credit Co., 465 A.2d 1064 (Pa. Super. Ct. 1983), *appeal dismissed*, 482 A.2d 275; Dear v. Holly Jon Equip. Co., 423 A.2d 721 (Pa. Super. Ct. 1980) (whether MVRISA statute authorizing 7 1/2% per year permitted use of add-on calculation).

375 *See, e.g.*, Kenney v. Landis Fin. Group, Inc., 349 F. Supp. 939 (N.D. Iowa 1972) (on motion for summary judgment, court held state small loan rebate provision mandates use of actuarial method), *rev'd*, 376 F. Supp. 852 (N.D. Iowa 1974) (after trial, upon defendant's presentation of expert testimony and exhibits regarding state department of banking interpretation, court held the relevant provision states the Rule of 78); Watson v. Avco Fin. Servs., Int'l, 401 N.W.2d 485 (Neb. 1987) (manner of computing split-rate interest at issue). *See also* Dechow v. Sko-Fed Credit, 536 N.E.2d 1382 (Ill. App. 1989) (statute precluding interest for any time period after payment in full precluded use of Rule of 78 rebate); Denley v. Peoples Bank, 553 So. 2d 494 (Miss. 1989) (use of Rule of 78 rebate improper under applicable statute which provided that parties could agree to "pay a finance charge which will result in a yield not to exceed [specified percentages] each calculated according to the actuarial method"; though contract rate was legal on its face if loan paid according to original terms, where there is prepayment, the "yield" must be recalculated to account for the altered term so that the yield does not exceed the specified rate according to the actuarial method).

376 However, creditors generally favor the interpretation which permits them the greatest return, so while the "conventional wisdom" may dictate one interpretation, that does not mean it is unassailable. Practitioners should always review the statute, regulations, and case law carefully, and make their own informed judgments. A good example of a successful challenge to conventional assumptions is Steele v. Ford Motor Credit, 783 F.2d 1016 (11th Cir. 1986) in which the practitioners urged that interest retained for a period after a loan was refinanced because of the creditor's rounding up when calculating a Rule of 78 rebate constituted a finance charge for Truth in Lending purposes. The court agreed, allowing the borrower to rescind based on that material violation.

377 *See* cases cite in notes 374 and 375, *supra*.

provide the proper formula.[378] Reference to such treatises as authority for a formulaic expression of the method of calculation should be adequate. Arguably, this, too, is a question of law, although even if it is viewed as a factual question, it may be viewed as a type of "verifiable fact" of which courts may take judicial notice.[379] Requests for admission, interrogatories or stipulations are also simple means of presenting the proper formula to the court. Of course, disputes are likely to arise as to how to treat irregularities in the transaction, such as whether odd days may be rounded in calculating a prepayment rebate, and if so, should they be rounded up or down. Such issues, of course, are ones of law. Again, banking department regulations should be checked, since the department may have promulgated rules to deal with accounting details such as rounding, 360/365 day years and other similar issues.

The final step is to carry out the computations in accordance with the relevant formula. Since this is no more than multiplication, division, subtraction, and addition, the calculations themselves are facts of which courts certainly may take notice.[380]

In order to establish whether there is a usurious overcharge, a number of courts simply calculate the maximum allowable charge under the statute, and compare that to the charge actually imposed.[381] That is a simple, straightforward method of establishing an overcharge, and one which avoids the necessity of "proving" the rate actually charged. While some parties have used experts, CPAs, for example, to testify as to the effective rate of return on the transaction,[382] that does not appear to be necessary. The same information can be developed by use of financial calculators,[383] which are relatively cheap, and widely used and accepted. The companion CD-Rom to this volume includes a program that will also calculate APRs and prepare an amortization table. Calculations so derived may simply constitute judicially noticed mathematics which may be spelled out in the memorandum of law.[384] Requests for admissions as to specific computations are another useful method of establishing numbers, particularly if the jurisdiction has a sanctions rule similar to Fed. R. Civ. P. 37(c), which provides that a party failing to admit the truth of any matter as requested may be required, in certain circumstances, to pay the opposing party the expenses incurred in establishing the proof of such matter. (See Appx. L.2.2, *infra*, for a sample request for admission.) The practitioner who does wish to present expert evidence, either as a convenient method to prove the calculations or to establish more complex mathematical analysis, may do so either through the use of affidavits or testimony. Appendices L.2.3–L.2.6, *infra*, contain a sample affidavit and portions of sample expert testimony.

---

378 This source, for example. Some formulae are also described in Comment, *Usury: Issues in Calculation*, 34 Ark. L. Rev. 442 (1980); Financial Publishing Co., The Cost of Personal Borrowing. A general reference is David Thorndike, Encyclopedia of Banking & Financial Tables, Warren, Gorham & Lamont (3d ed. 1987).

379 *See, e.g.*, Fed. R. Evid. 201(b)(2), which provides that courts may take judicial notice of facts not subject to reasonable dispute, such as ones verifiable "by resort to sources whose accuracy cannot reasonably be questioned." *See also In re Jungkurth*, 74 B.R. 323, 328 n.1 (Bankr. E.D. Pa. 1987) (taking judicial notice of rebate calculations pursuant to Fed. R. Evid. 201(b)); *In re Russell*, 72 B.R. 855, 860, 865–66 n.1 (Bankr. E.D. Pa. 1987).

380 *Miller v. Federal Land Bank*, 587 F.2d 415, 422 (9th Cir. 1978), *cert. denied*, 441 U.S. 962 (1979) (the amount of interest saved by a reduction of principal and shortening of the amortization period is a question of mathematics, of which the court can and should take judicial notice). *See also In re Jungkurth*, 74 B.R. 323, 328 n.1 (Bankr. E.D. Pa. 1987) (taking judicial notice of rebate calculations pursuant to Fed. R. Evid. 201 (b)); *In re Russell*, 72 B.R. 855, 860, 865–66 n.1 (Bankr. E.D. Pa. 1987); *Dillon v. RTC*, 811 S.W.2d 765, 766–767 (Ark. 1991) ("It requires no expert testimony to compute the interest which would be owed at 13% per annum."); *Parks v. E.N. Beard Hardwood Lumber, Inc.*, 565 S.W.2d 615 (Ark. 1978); *Vela v. Yates Ford*, 675 S.W.2d 232 (Tex. App. 1984), *rev'd on other grounds sub nom. Yates Ford, Inc. v. Ramirez*, 692 S.W.2d 51 (Tex. 1985) (court simply goes through equations, apparently taking judicial notice of arithmetic principles). *But cf.* dissent, in which one judge opines that complex calculations from F.R.B. Appendix J should "be supported by expert testimony and explanations of the mathematical intricacies involved." *Id.* at 57); *Cuevas v. Montoya*, 740 P.2d 858, 861 n.1 (Wash. Ct. App. 1987) (court apparently prepared its own calculations).

381 *E.g.*, *Williams v. Seeley (In re Williams)*, 241 B.R. 387 (Bankr. E.D. Va. 1999) (court did its own calculations, using business calculator), *rev'd in part on other grounds*, 11 Fed. Appx. 344 (4th Cir. 2001); *In re Russell*, 72 B.R. 855, 860, 865–66 (Bankr. E.D. Pa. 1987); *Parks v. E.N. Beard Hardwood Lbr., Inc.*, 565 S.W.2d 615 (Ark. 1978); *Cappaert v. Bierman*, 339 So. 2d 1355 (Miss. 1976); *Butler v. Holt Machinery Co.*, 741 S.W.2d 169 (Tex. App. 1987), *corrected on denial of rehearing*, 739 S.W.2d 958 (1987). *See also A.J. Reynolds v. Succession of Williams*, 628 So. 2d 1 (La. Ct. App. 1993) (where creditor calculated charge annually and added it to the balance, court calculated maximum annual interest charge to establish compounding, which rendered transaction usurious).

382 *E.g.*, *Olympic Coast Investment, Inc. v. Wright (In re Wright)*, 256 B.R. 626 (Bankr. D. Mont. 2000) (finding mortgage banker's and accountant's expertise more persuasive re interest rate calculation than that of economist who did not have experience in financial industry); *Smith v. MRCC P'ship*, 792 S.W.2d 301 (Ark. 1990); *Wooten v. Davis*, 739 S.W.2d 669 (Ark. 1987); *Cappaert v. Bierman*, 339 So. 2d 1355 (Miss. 1976); *Equilease Corp. v. Belk Hotel Corp.*, 256 S.E.2d 836 (N.C. Ct. App. 1979).

383 *E.g.*, Texas Instruments or Hewlett Packard business calculators. The practitioner should make sure that the calculator performs amortizations.

384 *See* note 380, *supra*. Also, *cf. Besse v. Burlington-Northern, Inc.*, 79 F.R.D. 623 (D. Minn. 1978) (in valuing damages in a personal injury case, court may take judicial notice of a present value table). Submitting amortization schedules from recognized publishers may also be adequate. *See Hoffman v. Key Fed. Sav. & Loan Ass'n*, 286 Md. 28, 416 A.2d 1265 (1979) (utilized schedule published by Financial Publishing Co., "relied upon by many lenders").

4.11 Practical Tips

4.11.1 Developing a System for Analyzing Consumer Credit Issues

Generally, clients do not complain to their attorneys about specific usury issues. For example, it would be fairly unusual for a client to waltz into the office saying, "I think the bank overcharged me $.39 for credit insurance which is arguably interest and possibly a usury violation." More likely a client will appear after the transaction has gone sour for one reason or another. It then becomes the attorney's job to analyze the facts and issues relevant to the transaction.

The beginning of this chapter, as well as the other chapters of this manual, should give the reader insight into some of the more common legal and computational usury issues which arise in consumer credit transactions. The consumer lawyer, however, needs more than this raw knowledge. He or she also needs to take a methodical approach to every consumer credit case, in order to uncover potential overcharge issues. The following discussion represents the author's approach to gathering and analyzing the numbers in a consumer credit transaction, as illustrated by a hypothetical used car credit transaction. This approach works for the author, but it may not work for other lawyers. The important thing is not which method the lawyer adopts but the fact that the lawyer has a method. Every consumer lawyer who wants to represent the client vigorously must develop his or her own approach. Chapter 1, *supra* contains a checklist which may be useful in this process.

The hypothetical situation is far less complicated than most consumer credit transactions. However, it will help to illustrate a methodical approach to documentary analysis. On January 1, 2000, the client, Connie Consumer ("Consumer"), bought a used car from C.R. Pyle Clean Used Cars ("Pyle") which provided financing. After Consumer made only three payments, Pyle repossessed the car, sold it at auction, and sent Consumer a letter demanding payment of a $3,800 deficiency balance. This transaction will suggest many consumer law issues[385] but the primary focus of this discussion will be the overcharge issues.

4.11.2 Gathering Information from the Client

The first step is to gather as much information as possible directly from the client. Obviously the client must be carefully and methodically interviewed, to get the entire story, from the beginning to the end of the transaction. As explained below, the client must also be asked to give the lawyer all of the relevant documents from the transaction.

In the hypothetical, the following questions suggest possible lines of inquiry for the client interview:

- Why did Consumer go to Pyle (previous transactions; advertising; recommendation of a friend)?
- What representations were made by Pyle about the cost of the car and the cost of the financing?
- What representations were made about non-interest charges in connection with the transaction (e.g., official fees, insurance premiums, service contracts, etc.)?
- What charges did Consumer think were compulsory, what charges did she think were optional, and of what charges did she only later become aware?
- What oral representations, if any, induced client to enter into the transaction with Pyle?
- What, if any, down payment did Consumer make, in cash and/or a trade-in?
- What documents did Consumer receive from Pyle or third parties, and when did she receive them?[386]
- What payments did Consumer make and when did she make them?
- What communications, oral or written, did she receive from Pyle after default, repossession, or the sale of her car at auction?

In addition to a methodical interview, the consumer lawyer should also ask the client to produce all of the relevant documents in her possession, since the simplest and cheapest way to obtain the relevant documents is through the client. As all lawyers know, there is no way to predict which documents the client will show up with at the initial interview: possibilities range from shopping bags filled with every scrap of paper to nothing at all, not even the notice of the foreclosure sale scheduled for that afternoon. Regardless of that range, the lawyer must stress to the client how important it is to bring in the documents, as well as giving the client direction as to what documents to look for.

In the hypothetical, the following documents should be obtained, if possible, from the client:[387]

- Newspaper advertisement by Pyle;
- Purchase order;
- Bill of sale;
- Contract;
- Truth in Lending disclosure statement, including, if given, itemization of Amount Financed;
- Odometer disclosures;
- Insurance documents (credit insurance, physical damage insurance, liability insurance, etc.);
- Warranty documents;

---

385 *E.g.*, Truth in Lending, repossessions, deceptive practices, etc.

386 *See* discussion at § 4.11.3, *infra*.

387 If the documents cannot be obtained from the client, then the lawyer or client should try to obtain them from the creditor and third parties. *See* § 4.11.3, *infra*.

- FTC Used Car Notice;
- Service contract;
- Title and registration;
- Receipts (down payment; regular payments);
- Payment book;
- Correspondence from Pyle or third parties (dunning notices, repo notices, deficiency claim notices, etc.);
- Legal documents (e.g., complaint, notice of judgment, etc.).

After the documents have been obtained (both from the client and from third parties), the lawyer must compare the information in the documents with that obtained from the client interview; the client should then be asked to explain, if possible, any disparities.

4.11.3 Gathering Information from Creditor and Other Parties

Not only is there a wide range of documents that clients will bring to the initial interview, but everyone has different record-keeping habits. Therefore, few clients will have all of the documents listed above. Since these documents can be very important in a consumer credit case, other sources must be explored, particularly the creditor.

In addition to the documents described above, there are also important documents that can only be obtained from the creditor or other parties. These documents are records of the creditor's financial transactions with the client, as well as with third parties, such as insurance companies, state title agencies, repossession companies, etc.

There are a variety of ways these documents can be obtained. Obviously, one way is to file suit and obtain the documents through formal discovery. However, since these documents generally are necessary to evaluate the case at the outset, formal discovery is not an efficient method. Moreover, if one does not have other facts suggesting the existence of colorable claims, it is of dubious ethics. Nor may it be strategically advisable (if there are documents which might be destroyed after a claim has been filed), or financially feasible (considering the costs of litigating unsuccessful claims).[388]

But there are other, informal approaches to obtaining the desired documents from the creditor. For example, depending on the client's or lawyer's relationship with the creditor, the lawyer could be very straightforward with the creditor. He or she could say, "I am trying to advise my client what to do about your claim against him. I cannot properly advise her as to either her rights or her responsibility to you without having this information. It would be helpful to get your side

of the story, including copies of your records." Another more aggressive approach would be to tell the creditor that litigation is being considered but that it would not be filed until the lawyer has had a chance to study the creditor's records.

Third parties may be another source of records. It can be helpful to get records from the attorney general or consumer protection agency, if the client has already filed a complaint; from other state agencies, such as the title bureau; and from insurance companies.

In the hypothetical, the following documents, possibly available from Pyle and other parties, would be helpful:

- Pyle's "ledger card" and other records of payments, late charges, and other charges;
- Master group credit insurance and automobile insurance policies;
- Title or other documents with information on liens and other security interests on the client's car.

4.11.4 Calculations and Analysis

Once all the available documents have been gathered together, the consumer law practitioner can begin the calculations and analysis necessary to uncover the client's potential usury claims. For the purposes of the hypothetical, we have gathered only (because this is an imperfect world) four documents: the Truth in Lending disclosure statement;[389] portions of the sales contract and itemization of the Amount Financed;[390] Pyle's ledger card;[391] and a letter from Pyle to Consumer following the repossession sale of her car.[392]

---

388 *See also* Fed. R. Civ. P. 11 (sanctions for filing unwarranted claims).

389 *See* Chart 16, Truth in Lending Disclosure Statement.
390 *See* Chart 17, Sales Contract.
391 *See* Chart 18, Ledger Card.
392 *See* Chart 19, Deficiency Collection Letter.

CHART 16
Truth in Lending Disclosure Statement
C.R. Pyle Clean Used Cars

ANNUAL PERCENTAGE RATE The cost of your credit as a yearly rate	FINANCE CHARGE The dollar amount the credit will cost you.	Amount Financed The amount of credit provided to you or on your behalf.	Total of Payments The amount you will have paid after you have made all payments as scheduled.	Total Sale Price The total cost of your purchase on your downpayment of $653.88.
21.48%	$1535.51	$4196.05	$5731.56	$5385.44

You have the right to receive at this time an itemization of the Amount Financed.

☒ I want an itemization.   ☐ I do not want an itemization.

Your Payment schedule will be:

Number of Payments	Amount of Payments	When Payments Are Due
36	$159.31	Monthly beginning 2/1/99

Insurance
Credit life insurance and credit disability insurance are not required to obtain credit, and will not be provided unless you sign and agree to pay the additional cost.

Type	Premium	Signature	
Credit life	$103.17	I want credit life insurance	_____ Signature
Credit Disability	$186.58	I want credit disability insurance	_____ Signature
Credit Life and Disability		I want credit life and disability insurance	_____ Signature

You may obtain property insurance from anyone you want that is acceptable to (Creditor). If you get the insurance from (Creditor). You will pay $ *N.A.*

Security: You are giving a security interest in:

☒ the goods or property being purchased.
☐ (brief description of other property).

Filing fees: $ 46.30   Non-filing insurance $_____—_____

Late Charge: If a payment is more than ten days late, you will be charged $ 5.00 / 5 % of the payment, whichever is less.

Prepayment: If you pay off early, you

☐ may   ☐ will not   have to pay a penalty
☒ may   ☐ will not   be entitled to a refund of part of the finance charge.

See your contract documents for any additional information about nonpayment, default, any required repayment in full before the scheduled date, and prepayment refunds and penalties.

_____

@ means an estimate

CHART 17
Sales Contract

BUYER	*SELLER*
CONNIE CONSUMER	C.R. PYLE CLEAN USED CARS

You, the Buyer, may buy the vehicle described below for cash or on credit. The cash price is shown below as "Cash Price." The credit price is shown below as "Total Sale Price". By signing this contract, you choose to buy the vehicle on credit under the agreements on the front and back of this contract.

New or Used	Year and Make	Series (Model)	Body Style	No. Cyl.	M Truck Ton Capacity	Vehicle Identification Number	Use For Which Purchased
USED	1995 FORD	ESCORT	4/DR	6		123456789	☐ Personal ☐ Agricultural ☐ Commercial ☐

INCLUDING:

☐ Radio ☐ Air Conditioner ☐ Automatic Transmission ☐ Power Steering ☐ _____ ☐ _____

TRADE-IN	1992 Toyota	$ 2,000	$ 1,546.12
	Year and Make	Gross Allowance	Amount Owing

ITEMIZATION OF AMOUNT FINANCED

Cash Price .... $ 3727.50 (1)
Down Payment
    (a) Cash Paid .... $ 200.00
    (b) Pickup Payment due _____ 19_____ .... $ N.A.
    (c) Cash Down Payment (a plus b)........................... $ 200.00
    (d) Trade-in (Description Above) .... $ 453.88
           Total Down Payment (c plus d)................. $ 653.88 (2)
Unpaid Balance of Cash Price (1 minus 2)...................... $ 3073.62 (3)
Amounts Paid on Your Behalf
To Public Officials (i) for license, title & registration fees $40.00
    (ii) for official fees $ N.A. .
    (iii) for documentary stamps $ 6.30 .
    (iv) for taxes (not in Cash Price) $ 186.38......................... $ 232.68
To Insurance Companies for
    Vehicle Insurance .... $ N.A.
    Credit Life Insurance.. $ 103.17
    Credit Disability Insurance.................................. $ 286.58
    _____ _____ .... $ N.A.
To _____ for _____ ... $ N.A.
To _____ for _____ ... $ 500.00
To TOW MOTOR CO. for EXTENDED SERVICE PLAN ... $ N.A.
      TOTAL.. $ 1122.43 (4)
Amount Financed (3 plus 4)................................... $ 4196.05 (5)

CHART 18
Ledger Card
C.R. Pyle Clean Used Cars

Total of Payments: $5731.56
Payment Schedule: 36 × $159.31 Due Date: 1st
First Payment: 2/1/00
LC: $7.97

Date	Payment	LC	New Balance
2/1/00	$159.31	—	$5573.25
3/9/00	$159.31	$7.97	$5421.91
4/11/00	$ 79.88	$7.97	$5350.00
5/12/00	Call — will send check		
6/12/00	Repo.		
6/28/00	Sale — $3000.00		

CHART 19
Deficiency Collection Letter

July 18, 2000

Connie Consumer
11 Beacon Street
Boston, MA 02108

Dear Ms. Consumer:

As you can see from the attached report, your car has been sold and you now are obligated for a deficiency of $3,800.

Amount Owed	$5350
Repossession Expenses	300
Storage Charges	150
Sales Expenses	200
Reconditioning Expenses	300
Attorney's Fees	500
	$6800
Less Sale Price of	3000
	$3800

Please forward this amount to us immediately.

Yours truly,

C.R. PYLE CLEAN USED CARS

The first step is to examine the documents generally to get an overall sense of the transaction and to look for numbers or other data that are not consistent with the client's story or with the lawyer's knowledge of the facts. The relevant numbers should also match on all documents. Not all discrepancies will necessarily be important, relevant, or actionable, especially after further investigation, but some may prove helpful to the client. The basic question to ask is: "Do these numbers make sense?"

For example, in the hypothetical, the lawyer makes note of the following observations:

1. *Trade-in*: Consumer traded in her 1992 Toyota and only received a gross $2,000 credit for it.[393] The lawyer might investigate the approximate value of a 1992 Toyota on January 1, 2000, the date of the trade-in. The lawyer might discover that the Toyota had just been "totaled" in an accident or perhaps that Pyle unconscionably took advantage of Consumer's ignorance of the Toyota's value. Perhaps Pyle would also be liable to a claim for "hidden interest" in the amount of the undervaluation.[394]

2. *Service contract*: The lawyer notices a $500 charge to Tow Motor Co. for an "Extended Service Plan." Consumer did not mention this plan, which may well be a form of service contract; indeed, Consumer provided quite a long narrative about all the car repairs she had to pay for on the 1995 Ford Escort she purchased from Pyle. In addition to obvious contract and warranty claims, Consumer may well have paid $500 for a non-existent contract or for illusory warranty coverage, either of which may also be "hidden interest."[395]

3. *Credit disability insurance*: The itemization of the Amount Financed shows that the premium for credit disability ("A&H") insurance is $286.58, while the Truth in Lending disclosure statement, in the credit insurance authorization section, shows a premium of only $186.58, a $100 difference. If Consumer were truly charged the higher figure, this would probably be a Truth in Lending violation. In addition, she may have a claim that the $100 "overcharge" was actually interest for usury purposes, since she only "contracted" (via the authorization) to pay the lower premium.

4. *Missing payment*: Consumer told the lawyer that she paid Pyle $80 in cash at the end of April (to make up a partial payment earlier in the month) but did not get a receipt. This payment does not appear on the ledger card. If this issue of fact can be resolved in Consumer's favor, not only would Consumer save at least $80, but she might also have a usury claim.[396]

---

393   After subtracting the $1,546.12 pay off on the debt secured by the Toyota, Consumer only received a $453.88 net credit for her trade-in. Another question is whether the payoff figure was accurately calculated. *See* §§ 6.4, 8.6, *infra*.

394   The hidden interest claim would depend on whether Pyle would have given Consumer a better deal on the trade-in or the Escort's sales price if Consumer had paid cash. The client should be asked how the price of the trade-in and new purchase was set. *See* § 7.4.6, *infra*. There is evidence that prices may be routinely hiked for certain categories of consumers, such as the elderly, Native Americans, African-Americans, and women. In addition to hidden interest claims, such differential pricing based on race, age, gender, ethnicity, etc. may violate UDAP laws, civil rights laws, and may arguably implicate fair lending laws, where the purchase is financed. *See* National Consumer Law Center, Credit Discrimination §§ 8.2, 8.5.4 (4th ed. 2005).

395   *Id.*

396   Failure to credit payments properly will lead to an excessive balance on the consumer's account. When the overcharge is

The next step is to see whether the numbers are internally and mathematically consistent: do the numbers bear a mathematical relationship to each other, is the arithmetic correct? In the hypothetical, for example, the lawyer would look at the itemization of the Amount Financed[397] to make sure the numbers add and subtract properly; the payment schedule on the Truth in Lending disclosure statement[398] to make sure that the payments equal the "Total of Payments"; the ledger card[399] to make sure that payments are subtracted properly from the running balance and the late charges are properly added thereto; and at the July 18 collection letter[400] to make sure that the numbers are added and subtracted correctly.

After examining these documents, the lawyer might make note of the following problems:

- *Payment schedule*: According to the Truth in Lending disclosure statement, Consumer was supposed to pay 36 monthly payments of $159.31 each. However, the product of 36 × $159.31 is $5,735.16, or $3.60 higher than the disclosed Total of Payments. Not only is this a possible Truth in Lending violation, it may also provide a usury claim for the client.[401]
- *Late charges*: The lawyer uncovers several problems with the late charges. First, according to the Truth in Lending disclosure statement, the maximum late charge is supposed to be $5.00 or 5% of the payment, whichever is *less*. Consumer was twice charged $7.97, which may not only be a violation of the contract, but may also violate state usury laws; the overcharge may be considered "interest."[402] Another problem with the late charges is that, again according to the Truth in Lending disclosure statement, late charges should only be imposed "if a payment is more than ten days late." Yet Pyle imposed a late charge on Consumer when she made her March 1, 1994 payment on March 9, 1994, only eight days after it was due. Similar contractual and usury claims may also arise from this problem.

---

treated as interest, it will increase the effective rate charged by the creditor, possibly causing usury. The consumer should be aware of the possibility of a good faith error defense, however. *See* § 12.8, *infra*.

397 *See* Chart 17.

398 *See* Chart 16.

399 *See* Chart 18.

400 *See* Chart 19.

401 If the creditor were already charging the highest permissible interest rate, a $3.60 overcharge would be usurious. a misstatement of the number or amount of payments is a TIL violation for which statutory damages are available, and TILA does not provide any tolerance for minor inaccuracies in the payment schedule. However, the creditor might try to recharacterize this misstatement as an inaccuracy in the total of payments, for which statutory damages are not available. 15 U.S.C. §§ 1638(a)(6), 1640(a). *See* National Consumer Law Center, Truth in Lending §§ 4.6.5, 8.6.5.2 (5th ed. 2003 and Supp.).

402 *See* § 7.2.4, *infra*; *see also* discussion *infra*.

The third step in the analysis is to determine which state and federal laws apply to this transaction and to decide whether any of these laws have been violated. While many states have recently "deregulated" consumer credit transactions, one of the basic tenets of consumer law still holds true: nearly every charge and every term of a consumer credit contract is specifically regulated, controlled, or limited by a statute or regulation, *even if the statute or regulation merely says that a charge may be set by agreement between the parties.*[403]

Therefore it is important for the consumer lawyer to become familiar with the relevant laws and regulations. In addition, the lawyer must carefully check the charges and terms of each transaction. In the hypothetical, the following charges should be carefully scrutinized:

- Interest and finance charge;
- Annual percentage rate;
- Credit insurance charges;
- Documentary fees (license, title, registration);
- Taxes;
- Late charges;
- Rebates (in the event of prepayment, acceleration, repossession, etc.);
- Attorney fees.

Having looked at these charges and the relevant laws, the lawyer might make note of the following:

1. *Interest*: Interest rates for financing used cars is governed by the state's Motor Vehicle Retail Installment Sales Act (MVRISA). MVRISA states that the maximum rate of charge for financing a used car between three and five model years old[404] is "$12 per $100 per annum" or 12% add-on.[405] Multiplying $4,196.05 (principal or Amount Financed) × 12% (maximum add-on rate) × 3 (years) produces a maximum charge of $1,510.58. However, Pyle charged Consumer $1,535.51, for an overcharge of $24.93,[406] which could implicate the statutory usury penalties.

2. *Credit life insurance*: By state regulation, the maximum charge for credit life insurance on the borrower is $.50/$100/year. Multiplying $.50 × $5,731.56 ÷ 100 (Total of Payments divided by 100) × 3 (years) produces a maximum premium charge of $85.97.[407] However, Pyle charged Consumer $103.17, for an overcharge of $17.20.[408] Depending on the various statutes and regulations, this overcharge may

---

403 *See* § 9.2.8, *infra* on interpreting deregulated statutes.

404 This provision applies because Consumer purchased in 2000 a 1995 Ford, a car which was five model years old.

405 *See* § 4.3.2, *supra*.

406 $1,535.51 − 1,510.58 = $24.93.

407 *See* § 8.5.3.1, *infra* for discussion on calculating credit insurance premiums.

408 $103.17 − $85.97 = $17.20. Apparently, Pyle charged Consumer $.60/$100/year, instead of $.50/$100/year. $.60 × $5,731.56 ÷ 100 × 3 = $103.17.

also invoke usury penalties.[409] At the very least, Consumer will save $17.20 plus interest less the rebate.[410]

3. *Fees*: Consumer paid $40 for license, title, and registration fees, yet the maximum fees under state law are only $37.50. The $2.50 overcharge may be a form of "hidden interest."[411]

4. *Late charges*: Under the MVRISA, as well as under the contract, the maximum late charge is $5.00 or 5% of the payment, whichever is *less*. As noted above, Pyle has overcharged on two late charges (by exceeding the $5.00 ceiling) and has also imposed a late charge when a payment was less than 10 days late. In addition, Pyle also imposed a full late charge on April 11, even though a partial payment of $79.88 was made. The question of whether Pyle could charge a full late charge (that is, up to the $5.00 legal maximum), a partial late charge, or no late charge at all, should be investigated further.[412]

5. *Rebates*: Under the applicable MVRISA, the creditor must rebate unearned interest when a precomputed transaction is prepaid or otherwise "terminated" before the final payment. The statute authorizes the use of the Rule of 78 to calculate the rebate of unearned precomputed interest.[413] Obviously, one must first determine whether this is a "precomputed" transaction, as opposed to an interest-bearing transaction.[414] Since the Truth in Lending statement refers to prepayment rebates, rather than penalties, and the ledger card was not kept on an interest-bearing basis, this appears to be a precomputed transaction. Another sign is that add-on interest was charged, which is generally precomputed.[415] The use of add-on interest generally binds the consumer to pay the total of payments. To be completely sure, the rest of the contract, not yet available, must be examined. If it says that Connie Consumer agrees to pay the "total of payments listed above, $5,731.56" or some variant, it is precomputed. If, under the contract, Connie Consumer promises to pay "the amount financed together with interest thereon . . ." or "$4,196.05 together with interest thereon. . . ." or similar language, it is interest-bearing, and no interest rebate is required.[416]

The lawyer notes that the "Amount Owed" on the July 18 letter ($5,350) is the same as the April 11 "New Balance"

on the Ledger Card ($5,350). Therefore, the lawyer is fairly certain that the unearned interest has not been rebated or otherwise credited to Consumer's account, but is less certain about the amount of the rebate to which Consumer is entitled. (That's because he hasn't yet read § 5.6.3.3, *infra*, which unveils the mysteries of the Rule of 78. But, if he makes a quick detour there now, he can confidently go forward with his analysis of Consumer's case.) There are at least two issues which have to be resolved before the exact amount of the rebate can be determined:

- Which event triggers the rebate: the last payment (April 11), the date of acceleration (date unknown), the repossession (June 12), the repossession sale (June 28), the date of the demand letter (July 18)?[417]
- Since none of the above events took place on a payment due date (the 1st of every month), should the rebate be calculated as of the nearest payment date, the previous payment date, or the next payment date?[418]

Without yet knowing the answers to those questions, the lawyer can still calculate the rebate on the terms most favorable to the creditor. It is to the creditor's advantage to calculate the rebate on the latest possible date, since that produces the smallest rebate. Therefore, the lawyer uses the July 18 letter as the triggering event and uses the next payment date, August 1, as the rebate date.

As of August 1, seven payment dates have passed[419] so 29 payments remain.[420] The rebate fraction would then equal $(29 \times 30) \div (36 \times 37) = 65.32\%$ or .6532. Multiplying $65.32\% \times \$1,535.51$ (interest charge) $= \$1,003$. The lawyer knows that the client, Consumer, is entitled to a rebate of $1,003 at the very least.

In addition, the lawyer knows that Consumer is entitled to a Rule of 78 rebate of the unearned portion of the $389.75 credit insurance premiums.[421] Again using the most conservative assumptions, the lawyer multiplies $65.32\% \times \$389.75$ to get a $254.58 credit insurance rebate.

Therefore, even without raising usury issues relating to initial charges,[422] and using conservative assumptions, the lawyer has reduced Pyle's claim by $1,257.58.[423]

---

409 *See* § 8.5.3.2, *infra*.
410 *See* § 8.6, *infra* for further discussion of rebates of credit insurance premiums.
411 *See* § 7.3.1, *infra*.
412 *See* § 4.8, *supra*.
413 *See* § 5.6.3.3, *infra*.
414 *See* § 4.5, *supra*.
415 *Id.*
416 *Id.* Rebates of credit insurance, however, may still be required. *See* § 8.6, *infra*.

417 Pyle might argue that no rebate is due until judgment or payment of judgment. *See* § 5.6.2, *infra*.
418 *See* § 5.6.2, *infra*.
419 February, March, April, May, June, July, August.
420 $36 - 7 = 29$.
421 $103.17 (credit life) + $286.58 (credit disability) = $389.75. *See* § 8.6, *infra*, as to when insurance rebates are required.
422 Indeed, the failure to rebate interest and/or credit insurance premiums itself gives rise to usury claims. *See* §§ 5.7, 8.6, *infra*.
423 $1,003.00 + 254.58 = $1,257.58.

Chapter 5	The Cost of Early Termination: Rebates of Unearned Charges and Prepayment Penalties

5.1 Introduction

A distinct form of overcharge often appears when credit is retired early by prepayment of the debt (including by refinancing) or when a debt matures early because of default and acceleration. Since the amount of interest due is in part a function of the time the credit is outstanding,[1] shortening the time should, as a matter of logic and fairness, reduce the amount of interest the borrower pays. But that may not always happen. The creditor may impose hidden charges, consisting of any unearned amount of insurance premiums and precomputed interest that it retains upon the early termination of credit.

An example may help to explain how unearned interest is extracted when precomputed credit is paid off early. If a consumer receives a $1,000 loan which is to be paid off over two years with precomputed add-on interest of 24% per year, the total amount repayable will be $1,000 principal + $480 interest = $1,480. In a precomputed transaction, the note would obligate this consumer to pay the full $1,480, typically in equal monthly installments.

After one year of regular payments, the consumer will have paid off half the debt, leaving a balance of $740. At this point, assume that the consumer wins the lottery and wants to pay off the debt. Or assume, more realistically, that the lender accelerates the debt and demands full payment because the consumer has been laid off and defaulted on the payments. Or assume, most realistically, that the lender hears of the consumer's unemployment and sympathetically agrees to refinance the debt with a new loan, most of the proceeds of which will be used to pay off the old debt. In any of these situations, the remaining obligation to be paid off is apparently $740. Yet, if the consumer pays this amount, two years' interest ($480) will have been paid for a loan which actually lasted only one year. This would be an effective add-on interest rate of 48%, caused by the lender's retaining the second year's unearned interest charges.

Similarly, if the borrower purchases a two-year credit life insurance policy, it is common for the lender to deduct the entire two-year premium from the proceeds of the loan.[2] If

the loan is then paid off after only one year, the consumer will have received only part of the coverage paid for. The premium for the second year is unearned and, if not rebated, will constitute a hidden overcharge.[3] Note that insurance premium rebates will be necessary even if the loan is interest-bearing and not precomputed, because, regardless of the method of interest calculation, the insurance premium often is calculated and prepaid on the assumption of a two-year credit repayment period. In other words, the insurance premium may be precomputed even if the loan is not.[4]

This chapter discusses the legal mandates regarding rebates, and explains the necessary formulae to make the calculations to assess a consumer credit transaction for this kind of an overcharge. It also discusses prepayment penalties, conceptually distinct, but treated here because, like unrebated charges, they economically penalize consumers who want to retire their debt early. Moreover, for consumers who refinance their debt, this inflated (legally or not) payoff, which becomes part of the principal of the new loan, in turn inflates the cost of the new loan. The interaction of prepayment costs (the subject of this chapter) with refinancing costs (the subject of the next chapter) can make the cost of the credit spiral upward all out of proportion to its

---

1 See §§ 4.2, 4.3, supra.
2 In open-end credit, by contrast, the credit insurance premium is

usually paid month-by-month, for one month of coverage at a time. Because of pressure from consumers and regulators, some closed-end lenders are also now charging for credit insurance on a month-by-month basis, rather than deducting the entire premium for the full term of the loan from the loan proceeds.

3 See, e.g., Varner v. Century Fin. Co., 738 F.2d 1143 (11th Cir. 1984) (interest and charges forfeited under Georgia Industrial Loan Act when loan agreement failed to provide for rebate of unearned insurance premium); Clyde v. Liberty Loan Co., 287 S.E.2d 551 (Ga. 1982) (usury for failure to rebate insurance premiums); Brown v. Associates Fin. Servs. Corp., 346 S.E.2d 873 (Ga. Ct. App. 1986); compare Greeley Nat'l Bank v. Sloan, 677 P.2d 409 (Colo. Ct. App. 1983) (usury avoided when complaint failed to credit borrower with insurance rebate but proper adjustment then made). See § 8.6, infra.

4 See generally §§ 5.4, 5.5, 8.4.2, infra. In some cases, lenders have failed to cancel credit insurance upon acceleration and, consequently, have not given an insurance premium rebate. See, e.g., Williams v. Charter Credit Co., 347 S.E.2d 635 (Ga. App. 1986). For a discussion of when creditors are obligated to cancel credit insurance, see § 8.5, infra.

nominal cost. Chapter Six will provide some examples of this. Practitioners should note that even if a creditor does not impose any illegal overcharges—that is, it calculates each individual charge correctly, and calculates all rebates correctly—the overall transaction may nonetheless be so overreaching that other legal claims may be available. See Chapter 11, *infra*.

5.2 Overview of Statutes Regulating Rebates

5.2.1 State Statutes

The windfall that a creditor would receive if it could retain unearned charges upon prepayment or acceleration of precomputed debt has been widely recognized, and almost all state consumer credit statutes have long required the rebate of unearned interest and insurance charges.[5] Failure to give those rebates, or to calculate them correctly, gives rise to usury or overcharge claims.[6]

Nevertheless, there are exceptions and limitations, many of which were adopted through credit industry lobbying and make no sense except when viewed as efforts to limit the size of the rebates which creditors must provide. The widespread, too-often legally sanctioned use of the Rule of 78 rebate calculation formula, with its creditor bias,[7] for example, can only be explained in this light, as can statutes exempting some charges from rebate requirements.[8] And, the rise of loans laden with an exorbitant amount of points and other prepaid charges may mean that statutory rebate mandates do not fully protect consumers.[9]

5.2.2 Federal Rebate Law

Congress somewhat narrowed the loopholes in 1992, when it required that rebates of unearned interest be made on *all* consumer credit transactions.[10] To the extent that such rebates were not already mandated by state law, they are now by federal law. Moreover, Congress prohibited the use of the controversial Rule of 78 to calculate rebates in

---

5 *See, e.g.*, Ala Code § 5-18-15 (Rule of 78 for small loan prepayment), § 5-19-4 (prepayment rebates by Rule 78 except pro rata for refinancing within 90 days), § 8-8-14 (pro rata refund of interest surcharge); Alaska Code § 45.10.070 (Rule of 78 under state RISA), § 06.40.120 (insurance premium finance), § 06.40.150 (unearned insurance premiums); Ariz. Rev. Stat. Ann. § 44-6002 (actuarial rebate required for RISA transactions as of Oct. 1, 1980), § 44-1205 (actuarial rebate on loan transactions as of Oct. 1, 1980), § 6-626 (actuarial rebate); Cal. Civ. Code § 1806.3 (Rule of 78 upon prepayment under Unruh Act); Cal. Fin. Code § 22400 (Consumer Finance Lenders); Mich. Comp. Laws § 445.858 (RISA); N.J. Stat. Ann. § 17:3B-22 (simple interest rebate), § 17:3B-23 (limiting acceleration clauses), §§ 17:16C-35, 17:16C-43 (RISA), § 17:16D-14 (insurance premiums); Pa. Stat. Ann. tit. 69, § 623(G)(5) (mobile homes), § 1603 (actuarial).

   Even in the absence of a specific statute or contract provision requiring a rebate, a court may impose such a requirement upon an equitable principle that unearned interest must be deducted upon acceleration and payment of a debt prior to maturity. *See, e.g.*, *In re* Coxson, 43 F.3d 189 (5th Cir. 1995) (Texas follows equitable rule requiring surrender of unearned interest to obtain a foreclosure; rule invoked to avoid usurious construction of contract silent about rebate upon acceleration); Aardwoolf Corp. v. Nelson Capital Corp., 861 F.2d 46 (2d Cir. 1988).

6 *See, e.g.*, Circle v. Jim Walter Homes, Inc., 470 F. Supp. 39 (W.D. Okla. 1979), *aff'd*, 654 F.2d 688 (10th Cir. 1981); Clyde v. Liberty Loan Co., 287 S.E.2d 551 (Ga. 1982) (contract was usurious where it allowed acceleration without a rebate); Palace Indus., Inc. v. Craig, 339 S.E.2d 313 (Ga. App. 1985) (acceleration without rebate is usurious); Jim Walter Homes v. Schuenemann, 668 S.W.2d 324 (Tex. 1984) (acceleration clause that would call for payment of unearned time-price differential was usurious); Moore v. White Motor Credit Corp., 708 S.W.2d 465 (Tex. App. 1985) (suit for accelerated amount without rebating unearned interest was usurious; note that the Texas Supreme Court has since held in George A. Fuller Co. v. Carpet Servs., Inc., 823 S.W.2d 603 (1992) that merely seeking unearned interest in a pleading is not a "charge" so does not

trigger usury penalties]); Dryden v. City Nat'l Bank of Laredo, 666 S.W.2d 213 (Tex. App. 1984) (demand for full amount, without rebate of unearned interest, is usurious); Commercial Credit Corp. v. Chasteen, 565 S.W.2d 342 (Tex. Ct. App. 1978) (accelerating debt and demanding unearned interest is usurious); *see also* Denley v. Peoples Bank, 553 So. 2d 494 (Miss. 1989) (even though statute was silent as to prepayment rebate method, use of Rule of 78 was usurious when it caused lender's yield to exceed statutory ceiling stated as actuarial rate; that implies a requirement of an actuarial rebate on precomputed loans); Brookshire v. Longhorn Chevrolet, Inc., 788 S.W.2d 209 (Tex. App. 1990) (acceleration clause in contract rendered it usurious on its face where it expressly entitled creditor, upon happening of the contingency of default and acceleration, to exact greater than lawful interest by demanding the unpaid balance of the "Total of Payments," which includes the finance charges. [Texas law provides that usury penalties are triggered where excess interest is contracted for.]). *Cf.* Greeley Nat'l Bank v. Sloan, 677 P.2d 409 (Colo. Ct. App. 1983) (rebate required, but adjustment voluntarily made within reasonable time and penalty avoided); Union Trust Co. of Md. v. Tyndall, 428 A.2d 428 (Md. 1981) (rebate required; no damages considered); Naumburg v. Pattison, 711 P.2d 1387 (N.M. 1985) (prepayment prohibition was penalty in violation of statute, but tender of debt insufficient; damages issue not reached). *But see* Horton v. Middle Georgia Bank, 191 Ga. App. 51, 380 S.E.2d 749 (1989) (method of acceleration rebate could not give rise to usury claim because there was no interest rate ceiling for this type of loan; perhaps borrower had breach of contract claim).

7 *See* § 5.6.3.3.1, *infra*.

8 *See* § 5.5.2, *infra*. Statutes which permit an acquisition charge to be deducted from the interest prior to calculating the rebate also fall into this category. *See, e.g.*, Ga. Code § 10-1-3(i) (RISA authorizes Rule of 78 rebate after deducting a $20 acquisition charge from the interest). *See generally* James H. Hunt, *The Rule of 78: Hidden Penalty for Prepayment in Consumer Credit Transactions*, 55 B.U. L. Rev. 331, 358 (1975).

9 *See* § 5.5.2, *infra*. For examples of how this is compounded in refinancings, see Chapter 6, *infra*.

10 15 U.S.C. § 1615(a).

long-term transactions, where it is most costly to consumers.[11] Any precomputed consumer credit transaction with a scheduled term longer than sixty-one months, consummated after September 30, 1993, is required to use the actuarial method of calculating rebates.[12] The federal rebate law incorporates the Truth in Lending Act's definition of consumer credit transaction, except that "creditor" includes any assignee.[13] Since, however, the federal rebate law is not part of the Truth in Lending Act (even though it is codified there[14]), TILA's exemption of various types of transactions does not affect the scope of the rebate law.[15] The scope of the rebate law is also unaffected by the exemptions from portions of TILA that the Federal Reserve Board has given to five states.[16]

5.2.3 Credit Secured by First Lien on Mobile Home

The Depository Institutions Deregulation and Monetary Control Act of 1980 (DIDA)[17] preempts state interest rate ceilings for credit secured by a first lien on a mobile home. To take advantage of this preemption, however, the creditor must comply with certain consumer protections set forth in an Office of Thrift Supervision (OTS) rule.[18] Two key requirements of the rule are that there can be no prepayment penalties in such credit,[19] and all rebates must be computed by the actuarial method.[20] This rule, which is discussed in detail in § 3.9.3.4, *supra*, does not mean that prepayment penalties and non-actuarial rebates are prohibited, but a creditor that does not comply with the rule cannot take advantage of federal preemption so is subject to state usury law and its penalties. Since most extensions of credit that are secured by first liens on mobile homes will be for terms longer than sixty-one months, the federal rebate law discussed in the previous subsection will prohibit non-actuarial rebates in most transactions to which the OTS rule would apply.

5.2.4 Federal Law Regulating High-Cost Mortgages

Consumers received some additional protection when congressional concern about predatory home equity lending and "equity skimming" led to the Home Ownership and Equity Protection Act of 1994 (HOEPA).[21] This Act applies solely to certain high-cost closed-end home equity loans considered to be "potentially dangerous when misused."[22] Rather than simply imposing a usury ceiling, it limits or prohibits some of the more common abusive practices in those loans.

The protections of the legislation are triggered when a closed-end home equity loan[23] meets one of two alternative cost thresholds. If the APR for a first lien mortgage loan is eight percentage points higher than the yield on Treasury securities for comparable maturities, the loan is covered.[24] (Prior to October 1, 2002, the trigger was ten percentage points.[25]) For junior mortgage loans the loan is covered if

---

11 *See* §§ 5.6.3.3.1, 5.7.3, *infra.*

12 15 U.S.C. § 1615(d).

13 15 U.S.C. § 1615(d)(3).

14 *See* § 5.7.3, *infra.*

15 15 U.S.C. § 1603 (stating that "this subchapter does not apply" to certain specified transactions; the federal rebate law is not part of the subchapter that includes TILA).

16 15 U.S.C. § 1633; FRB Official Staff Commentary § 226.29(a)-4 (granting exemptions to Connecticut, Maine, Massachusetts, Oklahoma, and Wyoming).

17 Pub. L. No. 96-221, tit. v, 94 Stat. 164, § 501(c) (1980), 12 U.S.C. § 1735f-7a.

18 12 U.S.C. § 1735f-7a(c).

19 12 C.F.R. § 590.4.(d).

20 12 C.F.R. § 590.4(c).

21 Home Ownership and Equity Protection Act, Subt. B of Title I, Riegle Community Development and Regulatory Improvement Act of 1994, (H.R. 3474) Pub. L. No. 103-325, 108 Stat. 2160 (Sept. 23, 1994), primarily codified at 15 U.S.C. §§ 1605(aa), 1639. *See Hearings on Problems in Community Development Banking, Mortgage Lending Discrimination, Reverse Redlining, and Home Equity Lending, Before the Senate Comm. on Banking, Housing and Urban Affairs*, 103d Cong., 1st Sess. (Feb. 3, 17, 24, 1993) (S. Hrg. 103-137; ISBN:0-16-041270-6, for sale by GPO) [hereinafter 1993 Senate Hearings]; *Hearing on S.924 Home Ownership and Equity Protection Act, before the Senate Banking Committee*, 103d Cong., 1st Sess. (May 19, 1993); *The Home Equity Protection Act of 1993, Hearings on H.R. 3153 Before the Subcommittee on Consumer Credit and Insurance of the House Committee on Banking, Finance and Urban Affairs*, 103d Cong., 2d Sess. (Mar. 22, 1994); *Hearing on Community Development Institutions, 103-2, before the House Subcommittee on Financial Institutions Supervision, Regulation and Deposit Insurance*, 103d Cong., 1st Sess. (Feb. 2–4, 1993).

22 H.R. Conf. Rep. No. 652, 103d Cong., 2d Sess. 1 (1994). The bill initially denominated covered mortgages "high cost mortgages," but the term, considered pejorative by some, was deleted from the bill at the industry's behest as the legislation made its way to enactment. As there was no easily referenced alternative name given loans subject to this statute, and since in fact the only covered loans are the expensive ones, this manual will refer to them as high-cost mortgages for simplicity's sake. (Apologies to any reader who may be offended by the terminology.)

23 There are certain other requirements for coverage: the mortgage must be on the consumer's principal dwelling; open-end credit, acquisition money mortgages, and reverse mortgages are exempt. 15 U.S.C. § 1602(aa)(1). See National Consumer Law Center, Truth in Lending Ch. 9 (5th ed. 2003 and Supp.) for a more detailed discussion of this legislation and the issues arising under it. *See also* Ch. 11, *infra.*

24 15 U.S.C. § 1602(aa)(1)(A); 12 C.F.R. § 226.32(a)(1)(ii).

25 The statute specifies a trigger of ten percentage points, but allows the Federal Reserve Board to adjust it up to two percentage points in either direction in certain circumstances. 15 U.S.C. § 1602(aa)(2). The FRB used this discretionary authority

the APR exceeds the federal benchmarks by ten percentage points. There is an alternative trigger, included because many predatory lenders keep the disclosed APR artificially low by padding the amount financed. If total points and up-front fees exceed the greater of 8% of the total loan amount or $400 (adjusted annually for inflation), the loan is covered.[26]

This legislation is discussed in more detail in Chapter 11, *infra*, and National Consumer Law Center, *Truth in Lending* Chapter 9 (5th ed. 2003 and Supp.). For covered loans, HOEPA prohibits prepayment penalties irrespective of the loan term.[27] Further, it defines the use of the Rule of 78 as a prepayment penalty, forbidding its use, with one complex, narrow exception that is discussed in § 5.8.2, *infra*.[28] The use of the Rule of 78 is completely prohibited where the creditor has accelerated a covered loan due to default.[29]

5.2.5 Bankruptcy Law

Bankruptcy law is an overlay upon federal and state rebate law. Section 502(b) of the Bankruptcy Code requires the bankruptcy court to determine the amount of each claim filed by a creditor that will be allowed. This determination is to be made as of the date the bankruptcy petition was filed, and claims cannot include "unmatured interest."[30] This means that interest on a debt is collectible from the bankruptcy estate only to the extent it is earned before the filing of the bankruptcy petition.[31]

Some courts have construed this language to prohibit use of the Rule of 78 to compute the rebate of interest on a debt in bankruptcy, even if the contract and state or federal rebate law would allow use of the Rule.[32] These courts have

reasoned that application of the Rule of 78 formula provides only an approximation of the amount of unearned interest and always favors the lender.[33] This error in favor of the lender can be viewed as a penalty charge,[34] which is detrimental to the debtor, the estate, and the other creditors because it causes less money to be distributed to other creditors.[35] In addition, the Rule of 78, which computes rebates on a monthly basis, is inconsistent with the Bankruptcy Code's mandate that the court determine the amount of the claim as of the date the bankruptcy petition is filed.[36] Further, some state statutes only authorize Rule of 78 rebates in the event of prepayment.[37] The bankruptcy court may be willing to make a distinction between prepayment and the acceleration that occurs when a bankruptcy petition is filed.[38]

5.3 Using This Chapter: Putting the Law into Practice

Since there is no longer any question as to whether rebates are required in consumer credit transactions—if state law did not already require it, federal law now does—the practitioner can concentrate on the calculations and on the finer points of the statute when assessing a transaction for overcharges arising out of early termination. The remaining sections of this chapter address these questions:

- The time when rebates must be given;
- The particular charges that are subject to rebate;
- Which rebate calculation formula is required;
- How to calculate a rebate by each of the standard rebate methods;
- The point at which a creditor has charged illegal unearned interest.

Finally prepayment penalties, which, like unrebated charges, penalize consumers who want to retire their debts early, are discussed. The chapter concludes with an exploration of the relationship between state and federal rebate law.

---

to reduce the trigger to eight percentage points above comparable securities for first position loans, effective Oct. 1, 2002. 66 Fed. Reg. 65604 (Dec. 20, 2001).

26 15 U.S.C. § 1602(aa)(1)(b), (3). The $400 amount has been adjusted to $510 for transactions consummated in 2005. FRB Official Staff Commentary § 226.32(a)-2(x).

27 15 U.S.C. § 1639(c).

28 *See* § 5.8.2, *infra*.

29 15 U.S.C. § 1639(d).

30 11 U.S.C. § 502(b)(2); *see also* National Consumer Law Center, Consumer Bankruptcy Law and Practice § 12.6.2 (7th ed. 2004).

31 *See, e.g.*, Gass v. Mid-State Homes, Inc. (*In re* Gass), 57 B.R. 109 (Bankr. E.D. Tenn. 1985); for legislative history supporting this general rule, see S. Rep. No. 989, 95th Cong., 2d Sess. at 62–63 (1978), *reprinted in* 1978 U.S.C.C.A.N. 5787, 5848–49. Note that in certain circumstances, post-petition interest may be charged and collected by creditors. *See* National Consumer Law Center, Consumer Bankruptcy Law and Practice §§ 11.6.1.3.3.4, 12.6.2 (7th ed. 2004).

32 *In re* McMurray, 218 B.R. 867 (Bankr. E.D. Tenn. 1998); Gass v. Mid-State Homes, Inc. (*In re* Gass), 57 B.R. 109 (Bankr. E.D. Tenn. 1985); General Motors Acceptance Corp. v. Willis (*In re* Willis), 6 B.R. 555 (Bankr. N.D. Ill. 1980). *But see* Meeker v. Bloomington Fed. Sav. & Loan Ass'n (*In re* Hughes), 61 B.R. 400 (Bankr. C.D. Ill. 1986); *In re* Watson, 32 B.R. 491 (Bankr.

W.D. Wis. 1983); *In re* Clausel, 32 B.R. 805 (Bankr. W.D. Tenn. 1983). *See* National Consumer Law Center, Consumer Bankruptcy Law and Practice § 13.4.3.4.3 (7th ed. 2004).

33 *See* § 5.6.3.3.1, *infra*.

34 James H. Hunt, *The Rule of 78: Hidden Penalty for Prepayment in Consumer Credit Transactions*, 55 B.U. L. Rev. 331, 339 (1975).

35 *In re* McMurray, 218 B.R. 867 (Bankr. E.D. Tenn. 1998).

36 *In re* McMurray, 218 B.R. 867 (Bankr. E.D. Tenn. 1998).

37 *See, e.g.*, Tenn. Code Ann. § 45-5-402(b).

38 *See In re* McMurray, 218 B.R. 867 (Bankr. E.D. Tenn. 1998). The legislative history of section 502(b) indicates that: "bankruptcy operates as the 'acceleration' of the principal amount of the claims against the debtor." S. Rep. No. 989, 95th Cong., 2d Sess. at 62–63 (1978), *reprinted in* 1978 U.S.C.C.A.N. 5787, 5848–49.

5.4 When Are Rebates Required? Precomputed Charges; Early Termination; Partial Prepayments

5.4.1 Precomputed Charges

One of the two key words in determining when rebates are necessary is "unearned." Issues about the proper rebate of *interest* should arise only with respect to *precomputed* credit, because, by definition, interest is added to the debt only as it is earned in an interest-bearing contract.[39] Thus as a general rule, there is no unearned interest involved in interest-bearing credit, though, as is discussed below, that is not an absolute. A precomputed transaction, in contrast, folds into the borrower's legal obligation at the outset all the interest to be earned over the originally scheduled life of the loan. As payments are made, they are subtracted from the "total of payments" and not allocated between interest and principal,[40] so at any point prior to the scheduled maturity, the remaining debt (the sum of the remaining payments due) will include some interest not yet earned. It is primarily this context in which rebate issues arise.

However, rebate issues can also arise in interest-bearing transactions, as contract interest may not be the only type of charge imposed. Most commonly, both precomputed and interest-bearing loans may contain other charges which are priced in relation to time, such as credit insurance premiums. These will need to be rebated upon early termination.[41] Arguments may arise about other charges, such as points, origination fees, or service charges, which may be imposed in both precomputed and interest-bearing transactions. Creditors argue that these kinds of charges are "earned at consummation" and therefore are not subject to rebate.[42] Finally, an examination of some lenders' amortization schedules for interest-bearing loans may show that the "interest earned" figures have been calculated upon the infamous Rule of 78, rather than the true, actuarial method of calculation. Trying to use the Rule, with its inherent bias

in the creditor's favor, as a method of accruing interest during the life of the loan also raises the possibility of effectively charging unearned interest, even if the loan appears to be interest bearing.[43]

5.4.2 Early Termination

The second key word is "early." If a borrower defaulted on the last two payments of a loan, which was scheduled to mature on April 1, 1994, but the creditor did not file a collection action until June 1, 1994, there will be no rebate issues. Since the loan went to (and past) maturity, all the precomputed interest would have been fully earned, as would any credit insurance premiums.[44]

Also related to the "early termination" prerequisite is how rebates are to be handled when the transaction is involuntarily terminated prior to scheduled maturity. In the event of default, the loan may mature early through acceleration. Involuntary early termination of a consumer credit transaction triggers rebate requirements, under both the 1992 federal rebate law[45] and the Home Ownership and Equity Protection Act's absolute prohibition against the Rule of 78 in high-cost mortgages.[46] Much state law mandates rebates upon involuntary early termination, as well.[47] (However, as will be seen in § 5.6.2, *infra*, fixing the precise date to use in making the calculations is not as obvious as it is when a voluntary pay-off has occurred.)

5.4.3 Partial Prepayments

The federal law and most state laws typically do not require rebates for "partial prepayments."[48] These are early payments which are too small to retire the consumer's total

---

39 At any given time, the amount due on an interest-bearing contract is the unpaid principal balance plus accrued interest. *See* § 4.5.1, *supra*. *See, e.g., In re* Curtis, 83 B.R. 853 (Bankr. S.D. Ga. 1988); Wombold v. Associates Fin. Servs. Co., 104 P.3d 1080, 1089 (Mont. 2004) (rebate formula only applies to add-on loans, not interest-bearing loans); Foster v. Centrex Capital Corp., 80 S.W.3d 140 (Tex. App. 2002) (finding that finance charge was precomputed, so statutory rebate formula applied); Myles v. Resolution Trust Corp., 787 S.W.2d 616 (Tex. App. 1990) (no usury contracted for in acceleration clause of interest-bearing contract).

40 *See* § 4.5.3, *supra*; James H. Hunt, *The Rule of 78: Hidden Penalty for Prepayment in Consumer Credit Transactions*, 55 B.U. L. Rev. 331 (1975), p.331, n.2.

41 *See* §§ 5.5.2, 8.5, *infra*.

42 *See* § 5.5.2.2, *infra*.

43 *See* § 5.5.1, *supra*.

44 There may be another issue, however, as to how the creditor calculated any interest due after maturity and before the legal action. Some contracts provide for lower post-maturity rates (though rarely these days), others provide for continuing at the original rate, and yet others provide for a higher "default" rate. Some predatory home equity lenders have contracted for default rates of 36 to 42% on fully secured loans. As a consequence Congress limited default rates on high-cost mortgages. Home Ownership and Equity Protection Act, 15 U.S.C. § 1639(d). Some state statutes may regulate default rates, as well. *See, e.g.,* Ala. Code § 5-18-15(j) (small loan maximum interest reduced to 8% six months after maturity).

45 15 U.S.C. § 1615(a)(3).

46 15 U.S.C. § 1639(d).

47 *See, e.g.,* Iowa Code § 537.2510(6). *See also* Union Trust Co. v. Tyndall, 428 A.2d 428 (Md. 1981); First Va. Bank v. Settles, 588 A.2d 803 (Md. Ct. App. 1991) (repossession sale equated with prepayment).

48 *See, e.g.,* 15 U.S.C. § 1615(a); Neb. Rev. Stat. § 45-1024(2)(b), (c) (requiring rebates for "prepayment in full"). *But see* Cal. Fin. Code § 22400(a)(3) (recomputation required for partial prepayment of three or more installments).

debt. If, for example, a borrower took out a loan repayable in twenty-four equal monthly installments and then paid both the fifth and sixth installments when only the fifth had come due, the borrower would have made a partial prepayment on the loan. If the lender in this example were using interest-bearing bookkeeping,[49] the partial prepayment would work to the borrower's advantage because the extra payment would be used to pay down the outstanding principal balance of the loan. Subsequent monthly interest payments would be calculated using this reduced principal amount, and the borrower would save on interest charges.[50]

In a precomputed transaction, on the other hand, the borrower will frequently receive no economic benefit from a partial prepayment unless the contract provides for some interest adjustment.[51] The reason is that the total amount of interest due on the contract has been predetermined, and despite the fact that the partial prepayment will render some of this interest unearned, most usury laws require no rebates of unearned interest in the case of partial prepayments. To the extent that any justification exists for this legal omission, it is that creditors do not want to have to recalculate precomputed debts whenever a partial prepayment is made, and partial prepayments can conceivably occur many times in the term of a single loan.

Practitioners representing borrowers who have made partial payments in precomputed transactions should check the language of both the state usury statutes and the credit contract to see how partial payments are treated. A few state statutes do require that the consumer receive credit for partial prepayment by some mechanism.[52] Typically, how-

ever, usury statutes will neither require nor prohibit rebates for partial prepayment, and the contract language will therefore control.[53] If the contract does not specifically distinguish full and partial prepayments, contract provisions providing rebates of unearned interest may arguably apply to both types of prepayment. However, most precomputed credit contracts expressly deny any creditor obligation to give rebates for partial prepayments, and absent the mandate of a state statute, consumers who have voluntarily made partial prepayments are not entitled to any rebates.

5.5 What Charges Are Subject to Rebate

5.5.1 *Contract Interest: Precomputed Transactions; Hidden Rule of 78 Accounting in Interest-Bearing Transactions*

In all consumer credit transactions, the creditor must "promp[tly] refund the unearned interest."[54] In precomputed transactions, by definition there will be unearned interest when the loan is prepaid,[55] and so a refund is necessary.

In contrast, as discussed in § 5.4.1, *generally* there is no unearned interest to rebate in an interest-bearing transaction, when it is properly amortized. Unfortunately for the number-numbed practitioner, however, it is nonetheless necessary to check the creditor's accounting on interest-bearing loans, too. Computers have made it easy for lenders, borrowers, and attorneys alike to blithely run off amortization schedules without knowing how the machine arrived at those numbers. Careful examination of some lenders' amortization schedules—even for interest-bearing loans—may show that the "interest earned" for each period does not jive with an actuarial accounting.[56] The computer instead used the Rule of 78 to allocate the interest from each payment.

The Rule of 78 is discussed in detail in § 5.6.3.3, *infra*, but for now, suffice it to say that it is neither an accurate nor a fair method of determining earned interest. Rather, it is a

---

49 *See* § 4.5.1, *supra.*

50 On the other hand, the borrower receives no benefit from prepayment under a purportedly interest-bearing system used by a few lenders which treats prepayments as pre-paid interest instead of crediting them against the principal balance. Such manipulative bookkeeping could be usurious if it raised a lender's yield above the usury ceiling. Otherwise it might be challenged as a breach of contract or as a violation of state statutes prohibiting unfair or deceptive acts and practices. Another technique some lenders use is to hold a prepayment in a suspense account until the next regularly scheduled payment date arrives. These lenders may, however, apply the prepayment to reduce the principal if the borrower so specifies when making the payment.

51 Of course, the borrower would gain some benefit if he or she made a partial prepayment of at least the amount of one installment and then continued to make regular payments. Under this scenario, the debtor would ultimately make a full prepayment one or more installment periods before the loan had been scheduled to be retired, and the debtor would receive some rebate at that point.

52 *See, e.g.,* Cal. Fin. Code § 22400(a)(3) (contract must be recomputed when a prepayment of three installments or more is made); Md. Com. Code § 12-308(c)(2) (partial prepayments must be applied first to accrued interest, then to reduce the principal balance).

    The federal act requires rebates only in the event of complete prepayment, 15 U.S.C. § 1615(a), but that is a minimum standard. It should not preempt more protective state laws, § 5.9,

---

infra, and certainly parties can contract for it. *Cf.* Sanders v. Lincoln Serv. Corp., 1993 WL 112543 (N.D. Ill. 1993) (2-month cap for mortgage escrow funds under RESPA is a cap, not a floor; parties can contract for smaller cushion).

53 *See, e.g.,* Saul v. Midlantic Nat'l Bank/South, 572 A.2d 650 (N.J. Super. App. Div. 1990).

54 15 U.S.C. § 1615(a). Rebates of unearned interest in precomputed consumer credit transactions were required under most, if not all, state laws prior to the federal law. *See* § 5.2.1, *supra.*

55 See §§ 4.5.3, 4.11, *supra* for tips on how to identify a precomputed transaction.

56 *See* § 4.3.1, *supra.*

shorthand formula devised in "the pre-electronic world"[57] to *approximate* earned interest in short term loans with low rates,[58] and one which is always biased in the creditor's favor.[59] In longer term or higher rate transactions, the distortion is "absurd"[60] and should not be used.

If the Rule of 78 would not otherwise be permitted in connection with the transaction, a creditor's effort to nonetheless extract its extra profit from the consumer upon early payment by the artifice of "earning" it each period prior to pay-off on an interest-bearing contract should be viewed as an impermissible device to evade the law.[61] It is difficult for a creditor to offer a legitimate reason to use it when "address[ing] the issue from first principles" and "as a matter of logic and statutory construction."[62] Generally accepted

accounting principles do not permit interest to be imputed by the Rule except where the result is "not materially different" from the interest method.[63] The IRS takes the position that, even when a loan agreement provides that interest shall be earned by the Rule of 78, "no deduction for interest will be allowed for any year in excess of the economic accrual of interest,"[64] because of the high degree of distortion it creates.[65] And courts have generally disfavored the Rule except when it was *explicitly* sanctioned by statute or administrative rule.[66] Consequently, absent ex-

---

57 Kedziora v. Citicorp Nat'l Servs., 780 F. Supp. 516, 525 (N.D. Ill. 1991), *quoting* Peter Canellos & Edward Kleinbard, *The Miracle of Compound Interest: Interest Deferral and Discount after 1982*, 38 Tax. L. Rev. 565, 566 (1983).

58 Canellos & Kleinbard, *supra* note 57 at 581; James H. Hunt, *The Rule of 78: Hidden Penalty for Prepayment in Consumer Credit Transactions*, 55 B.U. L. Rev. 331–332, 338, 344 (1975).

59 A comparative schedule shows that the remaining balance under the 78's method is "always higher" than the simple interest method, except at the final installment where the balance is $0. "This is always true; the 78's method favors the lender." Financial Publishing Co., Financial 78's Method Handbook, p.6 (Pub. No. 841 Rev. Apr. 1982). *See also* James H. Hunt, *The Rule of 78: Hidden Penalty for Prepayment in Consumer Credit Transactions*, 55 B.U. L. Rev. 331, 338, 345–346 (1975).

60 Financial Publishing Co., Yields If Prepaid, vi (1970), quoted in James H. Hunt, *The Rule of 78: Hidden Penalty for Prepayment in Consumer Credit Transactions*, 55 B.U. L. Rev. 331, 338 (1975). In longer-term, higher rate loans, allocating interest from each payment by the Rule of 78 can actually make the loan appear to be negatively amortizing, (*See* § 4.3.1.2, *supra*) thus *increasing* the loan balance in the early months. Canellos & Kleinbard, *supra* note 57 at 585.

For examples of the unfairness of the use of the Rule in long-term loans, see Livingston v. Vanguard Fed. Sav. Bank, 563 A.2d 175 (Pa. Super. Ct. 1989) in which mobile home buyers, despite making payments for 4 1/2 years on a 15-year contract, would have had a pay-off of about $700 more than they borrowed (borrowers were challenging the use of the Rule as a prepayment penalty, which was prohibited by state law, but case decided on other grounds). *See also* Draper v. American Funding, Ltd., 285 Cal. Rptr. 640 (Ct. App. 1991) (use of Rule of 78 instead of actuarial method cost borrower $17,410); Pysh v. Security Pacific Housing Serv., 610 A.2d 973 (Pa. Super. Ct. 1992) (use of Rule of 78 would result in early pay-off balance approximately $3,000 greater than actuarial method; borrowers had alleged use of Rule violated MVSFA's prohibition against prepayment penalty. But since MVSFA and banking regulations also specifically authorized use of Rule to calculate rebate, court reconciled two provisions by holding use of Rule to calculate unearned interest and prepayment penalty provision prohibits imposition of separate charge or penalty for prepayment).

61 *See* § 9.2.1.6, *infra*, on courts looking to substance, not form of transaction.

62 Kedziora v. Citicorp Nat'l Servs., 780 F. Supp. 516, 524 (N.D. Ill. 1991) (claim that the use of the Rule upon early termination of a lease was an unenforceable penalty survived a motion to dismiss). After suit was filed, the creditor in that case abandoned

its use of the Rule of 78 for the plaintiff and certain other lessors, so on summary judgment the court did not reach the question of whether use of the Rule of 78 resulted in a penalty. Kedziora v. Citicorp Nat'l Servs., 883 F. Supp. 1155 (N.D. Ill. 1995). The case reached the Seventh Circuit on other issues, Channell v. Citicorp Nat'l Servs., 89 F.3d 379 (7th Cir. 1996).

63 Financial Accounting Standards Board, FASB Accounting Standards, § I.69.108 (2004–05 ed.). The FASB is a trade association council which sets generally accepted accounting standards.

64 Rev. Rul. 83-84, 1983-1 CB97, 1983 IRB LEXIS 390. The Ruling has a chart comparing economic accrual to Rule of 78 accrual on a $100,000, 12% loan payable in 30 annual installments. The difference in the first year is over $5,500.

65 *See* Prabel v. Commissioner, 882 F.2d 820 (3d Cir. 1989); Mulholland v. United States, 22 F.3d 1105 (table), 1994 U.S. App. LEXIS 5109 (Fed. Cir. 1994); LaVerne v. Commissioner, 94 F.T.C. 637 (1990), *aff'd on other grounds*, 956 F.2d 274 (9th Cir. 1992) (table); Levy v. Commissioner, 92 F.T.C. 1360 (1989). *See also* German v. Commissioner, 1993 WL 42850 (U.S. Tax. Ct. Feb. 22, 1993), *aff'd*, 46 F.3d 1141 (9th Cir. 1995).

There was formerly an exception for short-term consumer loans, Rev. Proc. 83-40, 1983-1 CB 774, 1983 IRB LEXIS 481. This exception has been eliminated, however, and "the Rule of 78s is no longer an acceptable method of accounting for federal income tax purposes." § 5.04 of Rev. Proc. 99-49, 1999 IRB LEXIS 456 (Dec. 27, 1999). *See also* Rev. Proc. 97-37, 1997 IRB LEXIS 241 (Aug. 18, 1997). A borrower who actually pays a "78 penalty" (*see* § 5.6.3.3.1, *infra*) upon prepayment may deduct it. Rev. Rul. 86-42, 1986-1 CB82; 6-1b. The Third Circuit, in *Prabel*, though, stated that in the event of prepayment, the difference between the economic accrual interest owed and that determined to be owed under the Rule of 78 "should be considered a prepayment penalty." 882 F.2d at 827. *See also* Canellos & Kleinbard, *supra* note 47 at 585 (78 "should be viewed as a hidden prepayment penalty, not an accurate measure of the interest cost per period.").

66 *See In re* Jungkurth, 74 B.R. 323 (Bankr. E.D. Pa. 1987) (where statute prohibits prepayment penalties but does not specify a method of calculating rebates, the actuarial method must be used. Unless expressly authorized by statute, use of the Rule of 78 would constitute a prepayment penalty); Dechow v. Sko-Fed Credit Union, 181 Ill. App. 3d 367, 536 N.E.2d 1382 (1989) ("it is untenable to suggest that interest 'accrues' according to the Rule of 78s"); Denley v. Peoples Bank, 553 So. 2d 494 (Miss. 1989) (even though statute was silent as to prepayment rebate method, use of Rule of 78 was usurious when it caused lender's yield to exceed statutory ceiling stated as actuarial rate; that implies a requirement of an actuarial rebate on precomputed loans); see also Kedziora v. Citicorp Nat'l Servs., 780 F. Supp. 516 (N.D. Ill. 1991) for an excellent discussion. *But see* Ortegel v. ITT Thorp Corp., 569 N.E.2d 586 (Ill. App. Ct. 1991) (use of Rule of 78 is not a prepayment penalty and was not prohibited

press authorization, any use of it—whether to calculate rebates in precomputed transactions, or to accrue interest in interest-bearing transactions—should be challenged.

5.5.2 Other Charges and Fees

5.5.2.1 General

As is discussed elsewhere in this manual, creditors usually charge debtors numerous fees in addition to the stated contract interest.[67] One advantage is that this enables a creditor to understate the actual interest rate it is charging,[68] but it is also attractive to creditors because it may allow them to limit the size of the rebates they must give upon acceleration or prepayment. (A graphic example of how this can increase the creditor's actual yield upon prepayment is described in § 7.2.2.1, *infra*.)[69] The trick stems from the theory that rebates apply only to charges that are unearned as a result of the early termination of credit. Creditors typically claim that fees are earned at the consummation of the credit contract and need not be rebated because they are unrelated to the term of the credit. The validity of this argument depends on the particular type of fee which has been assessed and the language of the controlling statute.

The argument that a fee is earned at the outset of a credit transaction makes no sense in the case of fees that are clearly related to the term of credit. Credit insurance premiums, for example, usually vary with the term of credit, and the difference between a two-year premium and a one-year premium is unearned if prepayment occurs after one year.[70] The same principle may apply to other types of fees. One court has held that a broker's fee had to be reduced upon the involuntary prepayment of a note when the broker's services were supposed to extend over the full term of the loan.[71] Separate charges associated with credit sales for repair contracts on appliances might similarly be rebatable, particularly if one assumes that more repairs would be likely at the end of the contract term, after the appliance has been subjected to normal wear and tear, than at the beginning of the contract when the appliance is new.

Service contracts on cars, which are both expensive and sold for a particular time period, may present rebate issues. If a consumer wanted to pay off the car loan early, but wanted both to keep the vehicle and to continue the service contract on it in force, there is no reason for a rebate on the service contract. However, if during the period it is in force, the car is repossessed or traded in, the service contract should be cancelled, and the unearned portion of the cost rebated; the borrower should not have to subsidize coverage for a subsequent owner.[72]

The logical relationship between a fee and the term of credit is, however, only part of the rebate story. As with other usury issues, whatever fee the controlling statute says is rebatable is rebatable, and whatever fee the statute excuses from rebates need not be rebated, common sense notwithstanding. Thus, a one-time appraisal fee which a statute treats as part of the finance charge must be rebated if the statute requires the rebate of "finance charges,"[73] and a service charge need not be if the statute so specifies.[74]

Statutes can and frequently do exclude all or part of various fees, including basic interest charges, from rebate requirements with no apparent reason. For example, many statutes provide for the subtraction of an acquisition fee from the total finance charge before a rebate is calculated.[75] Similarly, statutes frequently allow creditors to ignore rebates which would be less than one dollar.[76]

---

in a 1983 mortgage in excess of $25,000. *Note*: It is clear from the court's discussion that it was confused about the nature of the Rule (e.g., "the borrower must pay the interest even if the loan is not prepaid," *id*. at 590], so this case should be viewed as an anomaly).

67   *See* §§ 7.1–7.3, Ch. 8, *infra*.

68   For purposes of the disclosure required by the Truth in Lending Act, some, but not all, of these charges must be included in the calculation of the APR. *See generally* National Consumer Law Center, Truth in Lending Ch. 3 (5th ed. 2003 and Supp.).

69   *See also* Ch. 6, *infra*.

70   *See* Varner v. Century Fin. Co., 738 F.2d 1143 (11th Cir. 1984); Clyde v. Liberty Loan Co., 287 S.E.2d 551 (Ga. 1982) (maintenance charges and credit insurance premiums must be rebated if unearned); Brown v. Associates Fin. Servs. Corp., 346 S.E.2d 873 (Ga. Ct. App. 1986). But note that some types of credit may charge for credit insurance on a monthly installment basis, as is typically the case with credit cards, rather than on a precomputed basis.

71   Jackson Inv. Co. v. Bates, 366 So. 2d 225 (Miss. 1978).

72   *Cf.* Jackson Inv. Co. v. Bates, 366 So. 2d 225 (Miss. 1978). *See generally* National Consumer Law Center, Consumer Warranty Law Ch. 17 (2d ed. 2001 and Supp.). Advocates should also be alert for price-gouging in the initial cost of service contracts, which may be attacked as a hidden finance charge. *See* § 7.4.6.1, *infra*; National Consumer Law Center, Unfair and Deceptive Acts and Practices § 5.4.3.6 (6th ed. 2004 and Supp.).

73   *See* S.C. Dep't of Consumer Affairs Interp. 3.210-8109, Consumer Cred. Guide (CCH) ¶ 97,043 (Sept. 8, 1981).

74   *In re* Tucker, 74 B.R. 923 (Bankr. E.D. Pa. 1987) (though persuasive authority and public policy suggest a "service charge" *should* be rebated, the controlling statute is clear that no such rebate is required).

75   Alaska Stat. § 45.10.070 ($10 except for $25 for automobile credit sale under state RISA); Ga. Code Ann. § 10-1-3 ($20); Mich. Comp. Laws § 445.857 ($10); Ohio Rev. Code Ann. § 1317.09 ($10); Foster v. Centrex Capital Corp., 80 S.W.3d 140 (Tex. App. 2002) (creditor need not rebate acquisition charge even though contract does not specifically allow this, since statute allows it); Restaurant Dev., Inc. v. Cananwill, Inc., 80 P.3d 598 (Wash. 2003) (construing provision of insurance premium finance law to require rebate of unearned finance charges but not acquisition fee). *See generally* James H. Hunt, *The Rule of 78: Hidden Penalty for Prepayment in Consumer Credit Transactions*, 55 B.U. L. Rev. 331, 339 (1975).

76   Ala. Code §§ 5-19-4 ($1), 8-8-14 ($25); Alaska Stat. §§ 06.40.150, 45.10.070; Mich. Comp. Laws § 445.858(b); Pa. Stat. Ann. tit. 69 § 1603.

5.5.2.2 Rebates and Points

5.5.2.2.1 General

One potential area of dispute is whether the federal or a relevant state law governing the transaction requires the rebate of points, service charges, origination charges or other one-time fees charged at the time the loan is consummated.[77] The question is significant if only because of the size of these fees, especially in mortgage transactions. Borrowers charged ten non-rebatable points on a $10,000 mortgage loan, which was then immediately accelerated, would forfeit $1,000. Or consider a five-year loan at 15% contract interest with a note principal of $6,169, which includes $1,169 in points. The APR for Truth in Lending purposes would be 25%,[78] yet if the loan is prepaid after two years, the impact of the "nonrefundable" points is that the borrower pays an effective interest rate of 29 1/2% for those two years—almost double the 15% contract rate. (The borrower would actually pay $540 more for a prepaid loan structured this way than if the loan had been initially written at a straight 25% contract rate with no points.[79])

5.5.2.2.2 Are points and other prepaid finance charges "earned at consummation"?

Some state statutes, particularly ones regulating real-estate-secured loans, explicitly permit the exclusion of points and other prepaid finance charges from the rebate by denominating them as "nonrefundable" or stating that they are to be considered earned at consummation.[80] Other states may specifically curtail the practice.[81]

On other occasions, statutes are silent on the matter. Even within a state, the statutory treatment may not be consistent. There may be an express provision denominating points as nonrefundable in real estate transactions, with no similar provision regarding points or origination fees in other types of credit.[82] Where not expressly addressed, a mandate to rebate points may nevertheless follow directly from standard statutory rebate language. Statutes may simply require the rebate of "unearned interest" or "unearned finance charge" according to a particular rebate formula, such as the Rule of 78 or the actuarial method.[83] Where points or similar fees fall within the definition of "interest" or "finance charge," whichever the statute uses, one element of that test is met.[84]

The next question, then, is whether those charges are "earned" at the outset of the transaction. In the absence of any controlling statute or case law, the need to rebate points may depend on the underlying economic validity of the creditor's argument that they are.[85] This argument depends on the existence of some separate service which the creditor provides at the beginning of a credit transaction and for

---

77 For a discussion of points as interest, see § 7.2.2, *infra*. The calculation of points is treated in § 4.7, *supra*.

78 *See* § 4.4, *supra* on the difference between APR and interest. Points are considered part of the finance charge by TIL.

79 This example is described in more detail in § 7.2.2, *infra*. *See also* § 6.4.1.3, *infra*.

80 *See, e.g.*, Ga. Code Ann. § 7-4-2(a)(3) (points and origination fees on mortgage loans excluded from both definition of "interest" and rebate calculations); *see also In re* Tucker, 74 B.R. 923 (Bankr. E.D. Pa. 1987) (though persuasive authority and public policy suggest a "service charge" *should* be rebated, the controlling statute is clear that no such rebate is required). However, even where authorized, if it is a part of a pattern of overreaching, other theories may be used to attack the creditor's overall conduct. *See generally* Chs. 6, 11, *infra*.

81 Ala. Code § 8-8-14 (pro rata refund of 2% interest surcharge for prepayment within 90 days); La. Rev. Stat. Ann. § 9-3532(B) (rebate of prepaid finance charge in simple interest transaction unless amount financed exceeds $10,000; scheduled term of credit is 36 months or more; and prepaid finance charge is less than 5% of amount financed).

82 *See* Ala. Code § 5-19-4(g) (5 point limit in real-estate-secured loans, earned at consummation and may be excluded from finance charge for purposes of calculating the refund).

83 For a discussion of rebate formulae, see § 5.6.3, *infra*.

84 *See, e.g.*, S.C. Dep't of Consumer Affairs, Admin. Interp. No. 3.109-8010 (Sept. 3, 1980) (rebate of "unearned portion of the loan finance charge," which includes points within its definition under Consumer Protection Code). *Compare* 1989 S.C. Op. Atty. Gen., No. 89-25 p.7, 1989 S.C. AG LEXIS 61 (Feb. 28, 1989) (no refund of points required upon payment of first mortgage not subject to Consumer Protection Code).

Where a statute requires actuarial computation, it also can be argued that points are inconsistent with that requirement. State of Kansas, Consumer Credit Commissioner, Admin. Interp. No. 107 (Jan. 2, 1985) (limit of 3 points on mortgage loans; points prohibited for other consumer transactions by Kan. Stat. Ann. § 16a-2-401 because inconsistent with actuarial computation requirement [Kansas law has since been amended to allow two points on non-real estate loans, so this interpretation is no longer effective, but the analysis might apply in other states]).

85 *Cf. In re* Tucker, 74 B.R. 923 (Bankr. E.D. Pa. 1987) (though persuasive authority and public policy suggest a "service charge" *should* be rebated, the controlling statute is clear that no such rebate is required).

It is interesting to note the inconsistency between the creditor argument in rebate cases that interest fees such as points are earned at the outset of a transaction and the doctrine of "spreading" frequently advocated by creditors in rate calculation disputes. (*See* § 4.6.5, *supra* for a discussion of spreading.) It is not at all clear why a creditor should be able to claim that points are earned at the consummation of a transaction, but that the effective interest rate should be calculated by treating the points as being earned throughout the term of the loan. *Cf.* Williams v. Seeley (*In re* Williams), 2001 U.S. App. LEXIS 13246 (4th Cir. June 13, 2001) (points are not considered "paid" at outset of the transaction when the lender merely reserves them from the proceeds of the loan); Fleet Fin. Inc. v. Jones, 430 S.E.2d 352 (Ga. 1993) (adopting spreading doctrine when points would have exceeded usury cap if attributed to first month; court notes it was not called upon to decide whether usury might result if loan period shortened by acceleration); Danziger v. San Jacinto Savings Ass'n, 708 S.W.2d 1 (Tex. App. 1986), *rev'd in part*, 732 S.W.2d 300 (Tex. 1987) (discussing Texas rebate rules when spreading doctrine applied).

which it may claim immediate compensation. Some courts considering the nature of points and similar fees have found no such separate service and have held instead that these fees merely constitute profit or compensation for overhead expense.[86] Such decisions suggest that points should be subject to rebate because there is no reason to consider income designated as profit or compensation for overhead expense to be earned at the outset of a transaction.[87]

Additional authority for this proposition is found in generally accepted accounting principles. The Financial Accounting Standards Board (FASB)[88] issued an accounting standard in 1987 in which it recognized that originating a loan is not a separate income-producing activity and therefore requires that origination fees, commitment fees, and other loan fees be recognized as income to the lender over the life of the loan.[89] Thus, if the lender's books are prepared in accord with generally accepted accounting standards, their own records may belie the notion that points are earned at the outset of a loan.

One final problem concerning the rebate of points should be mentioned. Many rebate statutes require rebates of unearned charges solely in "precomputed *transactions*," because as discussed above, theoretically there is no unearned interest in an interest-bearing loan.[90] Points and similar charges are in fact "precomputed *charges*," but they are often imposed on interest bearing transactions, particularly mortgage loans.[91] Even assuming that these prepaid charges are really earned over the term of the credit and not at consummation of the transaction, these mixed transactions might nevertheless escape rebate if the rebate statute addresses only "precomputed transactions" and does not define a precomputed transaction broadly enough to cover points on interest-bearing debt.[92] For example, Colorado follows the rule that a transaction is precomputed only if at least 50% of the finance charge is precomputed,[93] and under such an approach, points on nominally interest-bearing debt will rarely be rebatable. Recognizing this problem, other states have either limited the number of points that may be assessed or have expanded their rebate requirements so that they are no longer limited to "precomputed" credit.[94]

5.5.2.2.3 Special issues under the federal rebate statute

As discussed above, in the absence of specific language excluding points and similar charges from rebate requirements, the need to rebate them may be inferred from the rebate statute—if it requires that "unearned interest" be rebated, then the argument depends on whether points are interest, and whether they are earned at consummation.

The federal rebate statute requires that "[i]f a consumer prepays in full the financed amount under any consumer credit transaction, the creditor shall promptly refund any unearned portion of the interest charge to the consumer."[95] Whether points are "interest" for purposes of this statute is a particularly interesting issue.

One might think (wrongly) that the answer would be easy: since it is codified amidst the Truth in Lending Act, Truth in Lending definitions apply, and interest, for Truth in Lending purposes, has a separate identity from points.[96] (Both, though, are part of the broader category "finance charge."[97]) However, it is by no means clear that TIL definitions do—or should—apply, for the rebate statute is not part of TILA despite its location in the code books. Rather, it was a free-standing part of the Housing and Urban Development Act of 1992, and is specifically denominated as *not* being part of Truth in Lending.[98] The decision as to where it would be codified was made subsequently by a House body called the Office of the Law Revision Counsel.[99]

Outside of the TIL context, there has grown up what one court has termed the "federal common law" definition of interest.[100] An appealing argument can be made that, since

---

86 *See* § 7.2.2, *supra*.

87 *Cf.* Smith v. Anderson, 801 F.2d 661 (4th Cir. 1986) (Va. law) (court distinguishes "service charge," compensation for investigating and processing a loan, from points).

88 The FASB is a trade association council which sets generally accepted accounting standards.

89 *See* FASB Statement No. 91, Accounting for Nonrefundable Fees and Costs Associated With Originating or Acquiring Loans and Initial Direct Costs of Leases (effective for fiscal years beginning after Dec. 15, 1987). *See generally* FASB Statement of Accounting Concepts No. 7, App. B at 51 (Feb. 2000); FASB Accounting Standards, § L20 (2004-05 Ed.).

90 § 5.4.1, *supra*. *See* Wombold v. Associates Fin. Servs. Co., 104 P.3d 1080, 1089 (Mont. 2004) (rebate formula only applies to add-on loans, not interest-bearing loans, but charging points violated another portion of the statute). Some statutes and regulations avoid the problem of unearned interest and rebates by forbidding precomputation, at least for long-term debt. *See, e.g.*, 38 C.F.R. § 36.4309 (FHA-insured mobile home loans with term over 5 years); Cal. Civ. Code § 2981.7 (motor vehicle credit sales with term over 62 months).

91 *Compare* Colorado Dep't Law, Admin. Interp. Nos. 2.201, 3.201, 3.508-8301 (Oct. 14, 1983) (no rebate of prepaid finance charges required in non-precomputed transactions; note that Colorado regulations, 4 Colo. Code Regs. 902-1 Rule 13, now require such a rebate if refinancing occurs within the first year) *with* Mass. Gen. Laws Ann. ch. 255, § 13L (requiring rebate of all "precomputed charges").

92 *See* Colorado Dep't Law, Admin. Interp. Nos. 2.201, 3.201, 3.508-8301 (Oct. 14, 1983). This might be argued as a prepayment penalty. *See* § 5.8, *infra*.

93 *See, e.g.*, Colo. Rev. Stat. § 5-1-301(35).

94 La. Rev. Stat. Ann. § 9:3532(B) (limiting nonrebatable prepaid finance charge on simple interest transactions).

95 15 U.S.C. § 1615(a)(1).

96 Reg. Z, 12 C.F.R. § 226.4(b)(1) and (3).

97 15 U.S.C. § 1605(a)(1); Reg. Z, § 226.4(b).

98 15 U.S.C. § 1615, Historical Note on Codification.

99 Roland E. Brandel, Joseph E. Terraciano, & Barry A. Abbott, *Truth in Lending* (2d ed.) ¶ 33.02[1] (1994 Supp.).

100 Greenwood Trust Co. v. Massachusetts, 971 F.2d 818, 829 (1st Cir. 1992).

the federal rebate statute is not part of TIL, the federal common law definition of "interest" should be the relevant one. Much litigation over the definition of interest has arisen in the context of federal preemption and exportation, and most favored lender status, where the majority of courts have interpreted the term broadly.[101] Among the charges courts have held to be interest are late charges,[102] over-the-limit fees on credit cards,[103] a compensating balance requirement,[104] cash advance fees,[105] bonus or commissions paid to lenders,[106] and closing costs.[107] One of the federal banking agencies has issued a regulation defining interest to include many of these charges.[108] It has also been held to encompass the method of calculating interest, as that affects the effective yield.[109] Using this body of law as the relevant definition, then, would mean that a great many kinds of charges, such as points, would be "interest charges" subject to the federal rebate mandate. It certainly has the appeal of fairness that a federal common law definition of "interest" should be interpreted with consistency irrespective of whether it benefits the creditor or the borrower.

As with state laws, there remains the question of whether a given item in that broad category of charges is "unearned." For some charges under the federal definition, it should not be a difficult determination: late fees, for instance, are not imposed except where a payment is late, and so those charges would be earned. For points and similar prepaid finance charges, the analysis should be the same as was mentioned in the preceding section.[110]

Though no agency has official interpretive authority for this statute,[111] it is possible that regulatory agencies may issue compliance guidelines. Like the courts, these agencies have generally utilized a broad definition of interest when it served the creditors' interest.[112] It is to be hoped that they would be consistent in interpreting the term broadly when determining what charges are subject to rebate.[113] However, the statute has been in effect since 1993 without any regulatory agency having issued guidelines and action at this point seems unlikely.

5.5.2.3 Other Theories to Attack Abusive Use of Points

Non-rebatable fees can be both costly and deceptive. As such, they are a favored tool of some of the overreaching lenders, particularly where early termination is likely, as in the case of refinancing or predictable default.[114] Consumers should consider other theories to challenge the practice. Where not explicitly sanctioned, a failure to rebate points might be argued as a prepayment penalty.[115] If the points are excessive, as some high-rolling mortgage lenders imposed in the mid-1980s (25 to 40 points),[116] borrowers might also challenge such nonrefundable fees as unconscionable,[117]

---

101   *See* Ch. 3, *supra.*

102   *See, e.g.,* Smiley v. Citibank (South Dakota), N.A., 517 U.S. 735, 116 S. Ct. 1730, 135 L. Ed. 2d 25 (1996) (approving of and giving deference to the definition of interest contained in the 1996 OCC Interpretative Ruling, see Appx. C.3, *infra*); Greenwood Trust Co. v. Massachusetts, 971 F.2d 818 (1st Cir. 1992) (§ 521 of DIDA).

103   *See, e.g.,* Watson v. First Union Nat'l Bank, 837 F. Supp. 146 (D.S.C. 1993) (§ 85 of NBA).

104   *See, e.g.,* McAdoo v. Union Nat'l Bank, 535 F.2d 1050 (8th Cir. 1976) (§ 85 of NBA based on Arkansas law).

105   *See, e.g.,* Fisher v. First Nat'l Bank, 548 F.2d 255 (8th Cir. 1977) (NBA § 85).

106   *See, e.g.,* Cronkleton v. Hall, 66 F.2d 384 (8th Cir.), *cert. denied,* 290 U.S. 685 (1933) (NBA § 85, 86).

107   *See, e.g.,* Northway Lanes v. Hackley Union Nat'l Bank & Trust, 464 F.2d 855 (6th Cir. 1972) (§ 85).

108   12 C.F.R. § 7.4001(a).

109   First Nat'l Bank in Mena v. Nowlin, 509 F.2d 872 (8th Cir. 1975) (discount interest prohibited for national banks, as it was for all state lenders). *But cf.* Grunbeck v. Dime Savings Bank, 74 F.3d 331 (1st Cir. 1996) (DIDA does not preempt state simple interest statute).

110   *See* § 5.5.2.2.2, *supra.*

111   In fact, the FRB, with interpretive authority over TIL, has indicated it has no interpretive authority over the federal rebate statute, and as such, cannot issue any clarifying rules.

112   *See* 12 C.F.R. § 7.4001(a). *See also* Grunbeck v. Dime Savings Bank, 848 F. Supp. 294, 298 (D.N.H. 1994).

113   Readers should be aware that an industry representative obtained a post-enactment letter from the bill's sponsor, Congressman Torres, indicating that it was not intended to require a rebate of points. *See* Roland E. Brandel, Joseph E. Terraciano, & Barry A. Abbott, *Truth in Lending* ¶33.03[2] n.3 (2d ed. Supp. 1994). However, general rules of statutory construction do not give much weight to the post-enactment statements of a single legislator, and they are not part of the legislative history. Singer, *Sutherland Statutory Construction* ¶ 48.16 (6th ed. 2000).

114   *See* Chs. 6, 11, *infra.*

115   *See* § 5.8, *infra. Cf. In re* Jungkurth, 74 B.R. 323 (Bankr. E.D. Pa. 1987) (absent statutory authorization, Rule of 78 is a prepayment penalty).

116   *See, e.g.,* First Am. Mortgage Co. and Landbank Equity, two major multi-state lenders, both of which eventually went into bankruptcy, leaving their loans in the hands of other lenders which had purchased them on the secondary mortgage market.

117   *See, e.g.,* Johnson v. Tele-Cash, 1999 U.S. Dist. LEXIS 20632 (D. Del. Dec. 29, 1999) (interest rate may be unconscionable even in a deregulated state) (denial of motion to dismiss), *rev'd on other grounds,* 225 F.3d 366 (3d Cir. 2001) (enforcing arbitration clause); United Companies Lending Corp. v. Sargeant, 20 F. Supp. 2d 192 (D. Mass. 1998) (charging 10 discount points violated Massachusetts UDAP regulation prohibiting points that deviate significantly from industry-wide standards; court declines to rule on unconscionability but exercises its equitable powers to award borrower opportunity to rescind); Williams v. E.F. Hutton Mortg. Corp., 555 So. 2d 158 (Ala. 1989) (40 nonrefundable points challenged as unconscionable; this claim dismissed because was on behalf of class of prepaid borrowers, and unconscionability is available defensively, not as basis for affirmative relief; further, noteholder in fact may have given rebates upon prepayment. Discussion indicates a companion case on behalf of existing, non-prepaid borrowers settled); Commonwealth v. First Alliance Mortgage Co., Clearinghouse No. 52,511 (Mass. Super. Ct. Nov. 27, 1998)

particularly in the context of refinancings.[118] These theories are discussed in more detail in Ch. 12, *infra*.

5.6 Calculating Rebates

5.6.1 Introduction

Once the particular credit charges that are subject to rebate have been identified, the next step is to determine exactly how much of those charges must be refunded to the debtor. This determination will depend on two factors: the time that the credit has been outstanding, and the particular rebate formula that is used.

5.6.2 Payment Dates and Intervals

5.6.2.1 Fixing the Date for the Rebate Calculation

That the size of a rebate depends on the time when the debt is prepaid or otherwise matured makes intuitive sense. If a borrower pays off a two-year loan after only one month, the creditor has earned less interest and should have to refund more money than if the consumer paid off the same loan after twenty-two months. The reason is that the borrower who prepays early in the term of the loan has had the use of the borrowed principal for less time than the borrower who prepays near the end of the term of the loan.

The first step in any rebate calculation is to determine the precise date as of which the rebate must be calculated. If a loan is prepaid, either directly by the borrower or through refinancing, the controlling date will be the date of prepayment, although as discussed subsequently, that date may be rounded to the nearest regular payment date preceding or following the actual date of prepayment. If a debt is matured through acceleration rather than voluntary prepayment, however, determining the date when a rebate must be credited is more complicated.[119]

In some states acceleration is simply treated as a form of prepayment and the controlling date for rebate calculations is the date on which the creditor accelerates the debt.[120] Some courts have held that rebates are required when a post-repossession sale is held.[121] In other states, however, acceleration is not viewed as terminating the credit, and the creditor continues to earn interest until some later date, such as the date the creditor files an action on the debt, or the date of final judgment on the debt.[122] If the date of filing or the judgment date, as the case may be, is later than the date on which the debt was originally scheduled to terminate, the creditor will have earned all the interest due under the contract, and no rebate will be required.

5.6.2.2 Intervals: Rounding the Time Calculation

The next complication in calculating the time that a precomputed loan has been outstanding is that contractually interest is "earned" and payments are due at specific intervals, usually monthly, during the term of the loan, but prepayments and accelerations generally do not occur exactly on a payment date. Rather than giving the borrower a partial rebate for the days remaining in the payment interval,[123] lenders have traditionally rounded up to the next payment date (rarely back to the previous payment date). Thus a borrower who prepaid a twelve month loan after only

---

(granting preliminary injunction on claim that charging 23 discount points violates Massachusetts regulation prohibiting points that deviate significantly from industry-wide standards); S.C. Dep't of Cons. Affairs, Admin. Interp. No. 10.103-9302 (Sept. 7, 1993) (discussing such practices as precipitating legislative action, granting Administrator right to address excessive prepaid fees as unconscionable). *But see* Gonzales v. Associates Fin. Serv., 967 P.2d 312 (Kan. 1998) (charging of maximum allowable origination fee in each of a series of refinances may be unconscionable in the right case; no finding of unconscionability in this case since the doctrine can only be raised defensively). *See generally* § 11.7, *infra* for a discussion of unconscionability.

118 *See* Ch. 6, *infra*.

119 Of course, accelerating an interest-bearing debt, instead of a precomputed debt, will not require any rebates, as there is no

unearned interest to rebate. *See In re* Curtis, 83 B.R. 853 (Bankr. S.D. Ga. 1988); Myles v. Resolution Trust Corp., 787 S.W.2d 616 (Tex. App. 1990) (no usury contracted for in acceleration clause of interest-bearing contract). *See generally* §§ 5.4.1, 5.5.1, *supra*.

120 *See, e.g.*, Iowa Code Ann. § 537.2510(6) (if judgment is obtained, rebate is calculated as of date of acceleration); N.Y. Pers. Prop. Law § 408(6); N.C. Gen. Stat. § 25A-32 (the earlier of date judgment obtained or 15 days after repossession); Pa. Stat. Ann. tit. 69, § 622(B); Va. Code § 6.1-330.89. *See also* Palace Indus., Inc. v. Craig, 177 Ga. App. 338, 339 S.E.2d 313 (1985); Berman v. Schwartz, 59 Misc. 2d 184, 298 N.Y.S.2d 185 (Sup. Ct. 1968), *aff'd*, 33 A.D.2d 673, 305 N.Y.S.2d 1019 (1969); G.M.A.C. v. Uresti, 553 S.W.2d 660 (Tex. Civ. App. 1977).

121 Union Trust Co. v. Tyndall, 428 A.2d 428 (Md. 1981); First Va. Bank v. Settles, 588 A.2d 803 (Md. Ct. App. 1991).

122 For example, both the 1968 and 1974 versions of the U.C.C.C. provide that "if the maturity is accelerated for any reason and judgment is entered, the consumer is entitled to the same rebate as if payment had been made on the date judgment is entered." U.C.C.C. §§ 2.210(8) 3.210(8); U.C.C.C. § 2.510(7). *See also* Neb. Rev. Stat. § 45-1024(2)(c); W. Va. Code § 46A-3-111.

123 Such partial rebates may be required only for prepayments in the first 30 or 60 days of a loan. *See, e.g.*, Ohio Rev. Code Ann. §§ 1321.13 (small loans); 1321.57 (second mortgages) (if payment is made before first installment is due, lender may keep 1/30 of monthly finance charge per day loan was outstanding). They are unpopular with creditors because they do not mesh with the Rule of 78 rebate formula which does not recognize the existence of fractional intervals. Not surprisingly, the industry has preferred to use the lucrative technique of rounding payment intervals so that it may then employ the lucrative Rule of 78 formula.

four months and two days would receive a rebate for only the last seven months of interest, not for seven months and twenty-eight days.[124] Such self-serving calculations are profitable for lenders because consumer credit is frequently refinanced, and with each refinancing a lender that follows this practice may retain nearly one full month's worth of unearned interest and insurance premiums while charging interest on it under the new contract—in effect "double-dipping."[125] Moreover, prepayment shortly after a regular payment date, when the rebate calculation most favors the lender, is often guaranteed by lenders who stall for a few days before processing prepayments received late in the monthly payment period. By such simple expedients, creditors can minimize rebates and maximize profits.

The practice of rounding payment intervals in a lender's favor has traditionally been sanctioned by state law. Many small loan acts, for example, required rebates of unearned charges based on the installment date scheduled to follow prepayment, although some state versions of the small loan law based rebates on the installment date nearest the date of prepayment.[126] As consumers and regulators have become more sophisticated, however, more and more statutes have prohibited the rounding of intervals in the creditor's favor during the first fifteen days of the payment period,[127] and improper rounding has been challenged in court.[128] Specific

statutory rounding rules, even if they still favor creditors,[129] provide clear standards against which a creditor's calculations may be measured. Creditors who claim excess interest through improper rounding will be charging illegal hidden interest.[130]

The difficulty with statutes controlling the rounding of payment intervals is two-fold. First, the statutes are frequently unenforced because they are still poorly understood by many practitioners. Second, creditors can still avoid the effect of the statutes by refusing to accept prepayments during the first half of the month. Such a manipulation of the rebate provisions could, however, be revealed by an examination of a creditor's ledger cards. A pattern of prepayment in the second half of the month, if sufficiently dramatic, might support a claim alleging a systematic effort to evade the statute, and thus state a usury claim.[131] (Moreover, if there is also a statute prohibiting prepayment penalties, one could argue that refusal to accept prepayment when tendered violates that statute.[132])

A second form of miscounting of payment intervals frequently occurs when the first payment period in the transaction is longer than the later periods. For example, the first payment on a loan might not be due until forty-five days after the loan proceeds are disbursed, while subsequent payments would be due at regular monthly intervals thereafter. Lenders may attempt to count the initial forty-five days as 1 1/2 or even two intervals for rebate purposes, thus exaggerating the number of intervals for which interest has been earned and need not be rebated.

The technique works approximately as follows. Assume that an initial forty-five-day payment period is counted as 1 1/2 intervals, and that a statute requires rounding to the closest payment date. If prepayment occurs after sixty-one days, then the first forty-five days are treated as 1 1/2 intervals, and the next sixteen days are treated as another full interval through rounding. This yields 2 1/2 intervals of earned interest, and because fractional intervals cannot be used in the Rule of 78, a second rounding is used which boosts the 2 1/2 intervals to three full intervals. Thus, upon prepayment after sixty-one days, which by almost any other counting method would be treated as two intervals, the lender obtains three full intervals of "earned" interest. Such

---

124 *See* Steele v. Ford Motor Credit Co., 783 F.2d 1016 (11th Cir. 1986) (Truth in Lending case; unrebated interest due to improper rounding is finance charge in refinanced loan); Fitch v. General Motors Acceptance Corp., 351 S.E.2d 215 (Ga. App. 1986) (pro rata rebate need not be calculated on a daily basis) (is it just coincidence that the creditor chose to accelerate this note two days into a payment period?); Beaty v. Land of Lincoln Savings & Loan, 468 N.E.2d 1259 (Ill. App. 1984) (entire month's interest earned on first day of month under mortgage contract).

125 For a case study of how this, among other cost-enhancing practices used in "the frequent flipper" program in which many finance companies indulge, costs consumers considerable amounts of money, *see* § 6.1.1, *infra*.

126 *See, e.g.*, Ariz. Rev. Stat. Ann. § 6-634 (rebate applicable to all fully unexpired months . . . which follow the installment date nearest the date of prepayment; rounding in creditor's favor thereby guaranteed). For a chart detailing states' methods for determining prepayment rebates, see 1 Consumer Credit Guide (CCH) ¶ 540.

127 *See, e.g.*, Ala. Code § 5-19-4; Neb. Rev. Stat. § 45-1124(2)(c); Ohio Rev. Code Ann. §§ 1321.13, 1321.57; S.C. Dep't of Consumer Affairs 3.210-7609 Consumer Cred. Guide (CCH) ¶ 98,318 (Oct. 21, 1976) (one day cannot be treated as one month for rebate purposes); *see also* Tex. Fin. Code § 342.352 (pro rata earnings for odd days when prepayment is not on installment date).

128 *Compare* Steele v. Ford Motor Credit Co., 783 F.2d 1016 (11th Cir. 1986) (Truth in Lending case) *with In re* Jones, 79 B.R. 233 (Bankr. E.D. Pa. 1987) (state law permits use of Rule of 78 and rounding forward to allow a fraction of a month to be considered a full month). *See also* Webster v. International Harvester Credit Corp., 367 N.E.2d 924 (Ohio App. 1977).

129 For example, the Ohio RISA, Ohio Rev. Code Ann. § 1317.06(A)(2), arbitrarily requires rounding in the borrower's favor only in the first ten days of the payment interval. *See* Webster v. International Harvester Credit Corp., 367 N.E.2d 924 (Ohio App. 1977).

130 *Cf.* Steele v. Ford Motor Credit Co., 783 F.2d 1016 (11th Cir. 1986) (hidden finance charge under Truth in Lending Act).

131 *See* § 9.2.1.6, *infra*. See also Ch. 11, *infra*.

132 *Cf.* Groselose v. Rum, 860 S.W.2d 554 (Tex. App. 1993) (contract clause prohibiting prepayment is a penalty or charge, violative of statute prohibiting prepayment penalties).

counting machinations have been expressly forbidden in several jurisdictions[133] and are probably invalid in most states.

5.6.3 Rebate Formulae

5.6.3.1 Determining Which Formula to Use

Once the particular charges that are subject to rebate are identified and the duration of the credit has been determined, the final step in computing the amount of the rebate is to apply to these figures one of the three rebate formulae which are generally used: the pro rata formula, the actuarial formula, or the Rule of 78. For transactions consummated prior to September 30, 1993, the appropriate formula will be a question of state law. However, for consumer credit transactions with terms longer than 61 months consummated after that date, federal law now prohibits the use of the Rule of 78. It requires instead the use of a formula at least as favorable to the borrower as the actuarial method.[134] This federal law will preempt any contrary state law.[135] Further, certain closed-end, high-cost home equity loans consummated on or after October 1, 1995, are subject to the requirements of the Home Ownership and Equity Protection Act of 1994.[136]

But for transactions consummated prior to the effective date of these federal statutes, and for transactions not subject to it, the appropriate rebate formula remains a matter of state law[137] or a matter of contract law, in the absence of applicable state law.[138] State credit statutes often authorize the use of the Rule of 78, also known as the "sum of the digits" formula, because it maximizes the amount of interest and other charges which the creditor can claim to be earned, and can therefore exclude from the rebate, when prepayment occurs. (However, the applicable statute should be checked carefully to ensure that the statute in fact allows it. Where the statute describes a system, rather than naming it, creditors may improperly interpret it to their benefit.[139]) In many states, the rebate formula which should be used will vary from statute to statute and may depend on how the debt matures, or on the originally anticipated duration of the credit. Thus, even prior to the federal limitation, actuarial rebates might have been mandated for mortgage loans, while Rule of 78 rebates were authorized for small loans or credit sales.[140] Similarly, some states require pro rata rebates

---

133 *See, e.g.,* Iowa Code § 537.2510(2); S.C. Dep't of Consumer Affairs Interp. No. 3.210-8205, Consumer Cred. Guide (CCH) ¶ 96,746 (Dec. 30, 1982). In contrast, if a lender does not attempt to manipulate the Rule in this way where there is a long first period, a court may view the creditor's rounding forward at the end of the contract as less inequitable, *In re* Jones, 79 B.R. 233 (Bankr. E.D. Pa. 1987). Thus, if the advocate is considering a challenge to a creditor's rounding up to the next due date, the attorney should be careful to see if any resulting excess interest could be offset by "earned" interest from the long first period for which the Rule of 78 formula may not account. For example, consider a loan made on January 1, with the first payment due February 10, and the 10th of each month thereafter, with all payments being equal in amount. A refinancing occurs on October 1st, with the creditor rounding forward to October 10 in counting intervals to make the Rule of 78 calculation. If the lender did not also count the 10 extra days in the first period as a full interval, the court may consider that the extra 10 days of unearned interest claimed by the creditor for the last month could simply be offset against the extra days of interest in the first interval which was earned, but not accounted for in making the Rule of 78 calculation.

134 15 U.S.C. § 1615. *See* §§ 5.2.2, *supra*, 5.7.3, *infra.*

135 § 5.9, *infra*

136 15 U.S.C. § 1639. *See* § 5.8.2, *infra*; National Consumer Law Center, Truth in Lending § 9.1.1 (5th ed. 2003 and Supp.).

137 Certain transactions may be subject to other federal law which may also prohibit the use of the Rule of 78, such as federally

related loans secured by first liens on mobile homes. *See* 12 C.F.R. § 590.4.

138 Zwayer v. Ford Motor Credit Co., 665 N.E.2d 843 (Ill. App. 1996) (rebates computed by the Rule of 78 are not allowed where contract terms are ambiguous).

139 Because creditors may try to construe ambiguous statutes in their favor, they may well be routinely using a more generous formula than the law allows. *See, e.g.,* Dechow v. Sko-Fed Credit Union, 536 N.E.2d 1382 (Ill. App. 1989) (statute governing transactions secured by residential real estate provided that interest could not be "computed, calculated, charged or collected for any period of time occurring after the date on which the total indebtedness [except late charges] is paid in full" precludes use of Rule of 78; statute requires actuarial calculation; court rejects creditor argument that Rule of 78 is method of calculating interest accruing prior to prepayment); Denley v. Peoples Bank, 553 So. 2d 494 (Miss. 1989) (use of Rule of 78 rebate improper and usurious under applicable statute which was silent as to rebate method but provided that parties could agree to "pay a finance charge which will result in a yield not to exceed [specified percentages] each calculated according to the actuarial method"; though contract rate was legal on its face if loan paid according to original terms, where there is prepayment, the "yield" must be recalculated to account for the altered term so that the yield does not exceed specified rate according to the actuarial method). *See also In re* Jungkurth, 74 B.R. 323 (Bankr. E.D. Pa. 1987) (where statute prohibits prepayment penalties but does not specify a method of calculating rebates, the actuarial method must be used. Unless expressly authorized by statute, use of the Rule of 78 would constitute a prepayment penalty). *But see* Dennis v. Old Republic Ins. Co., 578 N.E.2d 1010 (Ill. App. Ct. 1991) (appears to question *Dechow's* interpretation in dicta).

140 *See, e.g.,* Dechow v. Sko-Fed Credit Union, 536 N.E.2d 1382 (Ill. App. 1989) (statute governing transactions secured by residential real estate provided that interest could not be "computed, calculated, charged or collected for any period of time occurring after the date on which the total indebtedness [except late charges] is paid in full" precludes use of Rule of 78; statute requires actuarial calculation; court rejects creditor argument that Rule of 78 is method of calculating interest accruing prior to prepayment); Denley v. Peoples Bank, 553 So. 2d 494, 501 n.6 (Miss. 1989). *Cf.* Draper v. American Funding, Ltd., 285 Cal. Rptr. 640 (Ct. App. 1991) (applicable statute was personal property brokers law, which at the time authorized Rule of 78,

when a debt is accelerated, but allow the Rule of 78 if the debt is voluntarily prepaid.[141] Finally, separate regulations often cover insurance premium rebates, so an insurance premium may be rebated under the Rule of 78, while the other charges are rebated actuarially.

5.6.3.2 Pro Rata Rebates

The simplest but least used rebate formula is the pro rata method. This formula assumes that interest is earned in direct proportion to the time that a loan or credit has been outstanding. If a prepayment occurs four months into the term of a precomputed loan that had been scheduled to be repaid in twelve months, the pro rata method provides that 4/12 of the interest has been earned. Consequently, the remaining 8/12 of the interest is unearned and must be rebated. If the total finance charge subject to rebate had been $1,000, then $8/12 \times \$1,000 = \$666.67$ should be rebated to the consumer.

The pro rata rebate method is simple to apply, but it is mathematically very crude because it fails to consider the effect of a declining principal balance on the earning of interest. Because a borrower has the use of all or most of the loan principal at the beginning of the term of a loan, the interest earned in the earlier payment intervals is greater than that earned in later intervals when much of the principal has already been paid back; about two thirds of the total interest on an amortization schedule is earned before the midpoint of the term of an installment loan. By ignoring the effect of the declining principal balance, the pro rata method recognizes less interest as "earned" at any given point in the

loan term than would otherwise be the case. When a prepayment occurs, the lender is deemed to have earned less interest and must pay a larger rebate under the pro rata method than if a formula recognizing the effect of declining balances had been used.

Not because of its mathematical inaccuracy, but because the pro rata method yields larger rebates for borrowers than other methods, it is rarely used. The fundamental statistical flaw in the pro rata calculation method is its failure to recognize declining principal balances. Yet, add-on and discount interest calculations have exactly the same flaw,[142] and these methods are widely authorized and used, supposedly for their simplicity, but actually for their profitability.

Statutes requiring pro rata rebates do, nevertheless, crop up at times, particularly for those rebates required when a creditor accelerates a debt because of default or some other contingency,[143] or in the event of a quick-flip on a loan.[144] Practitioners should be sure that these rebates are properly calculated and credited to the consumer's account. Furthermore, in any add-on or discount interest transaction for which a rebate formula is not statutorily or administratively specified, practitioners should argue that pro rata rebates are appropriate. If interest is earned in precomputed transactions without regard to declining balances, fairness and consistency demand it should be rebated in the same fashion.[145]

5.6.3.3 Rule of 78

5.6.3.3.1 Background and legal status

As the reader who has been introduced to the Rule of 78 in other parts of this book may have gathered,[146] this method of calculating rebates is a bane to consumers and a boon to creditors. It is also an anachronism; since the advent of widely available computers, there is no reason for it other than to maximize income for creditors.[147]

In the pre-computer era, it was a tedious task to calculate how much interest was earned at a given point prior to maturity on a precomputed loan. If a borrower wanted to

---

not statute governing residential property loans). *But see* Dennis v. Old Republic Ins. Co., 578 N.E.2d 1010 (Ill. App. Ct. 1991) (appears to question *Dechow's* interpretation in dicta; avoids direct conflict by holding different statute applicable. [*Ed. Note*: the case appears to be rather result-oriented, as it invokes the statutory construction principle that the more specific statute governs over the more general in the case of a conflict. It proceeds to find that a statute governing all secured or unsecured installment loans except certain purchase money mortgages is *more* specific than the statute applying to loans secured by residential real estate. That is a judgment call about which reasonable minds may differ.]); Jacobson v. General Fin. Corp., 592 N.E.2d 1121 (Ill. App. Ct. 1992) (decision sorting out morass remaining after amendments to interest statutes which followed *Dechow* decision, finds use of Rule acceptable. *Ed. Note*: Illinois borrowers—and bewildered attorneys—can be grateful that the new federal legislation prohibiting the use of the Rule of 78 on long-term consumer loans make it unnecessary to sort out the Illinois scheme for loans consummated after Sept. 30, 1993. *See* 15 U.S.C. § 1615.

141 *See* Varner v. Century Fin. Corp., Inc., 317 S.E.2d 178 (Ga. 1984) (Rule of 78 may be used for rebates pursuant to refinancing or voluntary prepayment, but pro rata rebate must be given if debt is accelerated pursuant to a default); Carter v. First Fed. Sav. & Ass'n of Atlanta, 347 S.E.2d 264 (Ga. App. 1986) (MVRISA).

142 *See* §§ 4.3.2–4.3.3, *supra*.

143 *See, e.g.,* Walter E. Heller & Co. v. Mall, Inc., 267 F. Supp. 343 (E.D. La. 1967) (pro rata refund of discount interest upon acceleration under Louisiana law); Varner v. Century Fin. Corp., Inc., 317 S.E.2d 178 (Ga. 1984) (interpreting Ga. Code Ann. § 7-4-2(b)(1) (effective Mar. 1, 1983)); Fitch v. G.M.A.C., 351 S.E.2d 215 (Ga. App. 1986) (pro rata rebate required, but calculation need not be on a daily basis, only a monthly basis); Bozeman v. Tifton Fed. S&L Ass'n, 297 S.E.2d 49 (Ga. Ct. App. 1982) (pro rata rebate required upon acceleration by motor vehicle special usury law).

144 *Eg.,* Ala. Code § 5-19-4(d) (pro rata rebate if refinanced by same creditor or affiliate with 120 days).

145 *See In re* Lowell, Clearinghouse No. 30,955 (S.D. Me. 1972).

146 *See, e.g.,* §§ 4.11, 5.5.1, *supra*, § 6.1, *infra*.

147 *See* § 5.5.1, *supra*.

terminate a loan 36 months into a 48-month term, determining the actual interest earned to that point would require that an amortization be prepared for the loan, calculating the interest due at each payment interval on the declining principal balance.[148] While not a difficult task, it was time-consuming and labor-intensive, requiring in the above example 36 separate three-step calculations.[149] The Rule of 78 is nothing more than a shorthand formula designed to *approximate* the results of an actual amortization with a single, simple five-step formula, which is all the more efficient because it can be applied to all transactions irrespective of term or interest rate. There is, however, a hitch in this shorthand approximation: it has an inherent bias in the creditor's favor. There will always be a smaller rebate to the consumer when the Rule of 78 is used than when the actuarial method is used, so the borrower always loses.[150] The difference between the two amounts can be termed a "78s' penalty."[151] In short-term, small balance loans, the degree of error is relatively small. For example, in a $1,000, one-year, 10% loan prepaid at 6 months, the 78s' penalty the borrower pays would be only 25 cents. At that scale, the lender bias might have been economically rationalized in the 1930s, when it was first legally sanctioned,[152] by arguing that the bias cost the consumer less than the increased operational expenses which would have been passed onto borrowers if the labor-intensive actuarial calculations were required.

However, the longer the term, the higher the rate, and, of course, the higher the balance, the greater the distortion. The use of the Rule on a 15-year, $30,000, 16% mobile home contract, prepaid at the 60th month penalizes the consumer to the tune of almost $4,600.[153] Unfortunately, during the 1980s, the trend in the consumer credit market was toward longer loan terms, larger loan sizes, and, for much consumer

debt, higher interest rates—the very characteristics which result in the greatest distortion when the Rule of 78 is used. When Congress first examined the Rule in 1979, it was estimated that its use cost consumers as much as half a billion dollars.[154] By 1992, when Congress next examined it, several states had limited its use at least in consumer credit transactions,[155] but any savings consumers realized from that was probably counteracted by the greater cost to borrowers which resulted from the changing nature of the market in the remaining states.

While the Rule's burden on consumers burgeoned, changing technology rendered the Rule obsolete. The widespread availability of computers and programmed calculators which can do amortizations in a matter of seconds completely undid the rationale for the Rule. There is now no legitimate reason for it.[156]

Because of its inherent unfairness, the Rule had come under legal attack long before the 1992 congressional action. Because it was specifically authorized in many jurisdictions, much litigation in the 1970s focused on the disclosure of the Rule under the Truth in Lending Act.[157] The

---

148 Preparing an amortization was a task the simplified methods of precomputing loans—the add-on and discount methods—were intended to avoid. §§ 4.3.2, 4.3.3, *supra*.

149 (1) Calculate the interest due for the payment period; (2) allocate a portion of the payment to the accrued interest; and (3) apply the remaining payment to the principal balance to obtain the new principal balance. The process is repeated for each payment period. *See* § 4.3.1, *supra*.

150 Bonker, *The Rule of 78*, XXXI Journal of Finance 877, 885 (No. 3, June 1976); Hunt, *The Rule of 78: Hidden Penalty for Prepayment in Consumer Credit Transactions*, 55 B.U. L. Rev. 331 (1975). *See* § 5.5.1, *supra*.

151 *In re* McMurray, 218 B.R. 867 (Bankr. E.D. Tenn. 1998).

152 Financial Publishing Co., 78's Method Handbook 5 (Pub. No. 841 Rev. Apr. 1982).

153 Even at a more modest 10% rate on a 20-year, $37,000 mobile home contract, prepaid in year 8, the interest earned by the actuarial method is $27,157.84; by the Rule of 78 $31,106.52—nearly a $3,950 Rule of 78 penalty.

One financial publication charts the augmented returns resulting from the use of the Rule of 78. Financial Publishing Co., 78's Method Handbook (Pub. No. 841 Rev. Apr. 1982). For example, a 24%, 120-month loan prepaid after 24 months means the true interest paid is 28 3/4%.

154 *Restrict the Use of the Rule of 78*: *Hearings Before the Subcommittee on Consumer Affairs of the Senate Comm. on Banking, Housing, and Urban Affairs on S. 2002*, 96th Cong., 1st Sess. (1979) (statement of Willard Ogburn and Bonnie Freeman, 118–19).

155 *See, e.g.*, Kan. Stat. Ann. § 16a-2-201(5)(b) (prohibited in long-term loans as of 1982; note that Kan. Stat. Ann. § 16a-2-201 now requires the actuarial method for rebates in closed-end credit sales); Md. Comm. Law Code Ann. §§ 12-612(c) (actuarial rebates for consumer installment sales executed on or after Jan. 1, 1981) (effective July 1, 1984) 12-505(e) (effective July 1, 1986); Va. Code § 6.1-330.86:1 (prohibited in long-term loans made after Jan. 1, 1991). *See also* Draper v. American Funding, Ltd., 285 Cal. Rptr. 640 (Ct. App. 1991) (interpreting former Cal. Fin. Code § 22482, governing personal property brokers; that provision, requiring actuarial rebates, was passed too late to save the plaintiff the $17,410 excess cost caused by the use of the Rule of 78). *But see* Jacobson v. General Fin. Corp., 592 N.E.2d 1121 (Ill. Ct. App. 1992) (upholding legislative amendment that, bowing to industry pressure, allowed continued use of Rule of 78 on certain loans).

Some courts, recognizing that the Rule of 78 is a hidden charge "burdensome to the consumer and unjustified by the economic needs of the lender," encouraged legislative correction of the inequities created by the use of the Rule. Drennan v. Security Pac. Nat'l Bank, 621 P.2d 1318, 1327 (Cal. 1981); Lanier v. Associates Fin., Inc., 499 N.E.2d 440, 447 (Ill. 1986); Dennis v. Old Republic Ins. Co., 578 N.E.2d 1010 (Ill. App. Ct. 1991).

156 Kedziora v. Citicorp Nat'l Servs., 780 F. Supp. 516, 525 (N.D. Ill. 1991) (programmed calculators and computers reduce ease-of-use factor to *de minimis* proportions, and weight of independent thinking tips toward view of it as penalty "unrelated to real economic interest." Court notes FRB view otherwise "looks more and more like the result of lender lobbying rather than thoughtful analysis." Consumer Leasing Act case).

157 *See, e.g.*, Gallois v. Commercial Securities Co., 661 F.2d 901 (5th Cir. 1981); Gantt v. Commonwealth Loan Co., 573 F.2d 520 (8th Cir. 1978); Grant v. Imperial Motors, 539 F.2d 506 (5th Cir. 1976); Bone v. Hibernia Bank, 493 F.2d 135 (9th Cir. 1974).

TIL challenges were ultimately unsuccessful, but they were critical to raising public awareness of the Rule's inequities.

Other theories have also been used to challenge the Rule in litigation, such as alleging it violates statutes limiting prepayment penalties, or UDAP statutes. These have met with mixed success.[158]

Congress, however, finally acted in 1992. Compromising by eliminating it where its impact is most pronounced, the use of the Rule now is prohibited in all precomputed consumer credit transactions with terms longer than 61 months consummated after September 30, 1993.[159] Under the new federal law, rebates in these transactions must be calculated by "a method at least as favorable to the consumer as the actuarial method,"[160] which is explained in § 5.6.3.4, *infra*. Remedies for violation of this statute are discussed in § 5.7.3, *infra*.

In 1994, Congress took another step toward curbing it in an area where both the distortion and harm to consumers is great. The Home Owners and Equity Protection Act, regulating certain high-cost home equity loans, defines the use of the Rule as a prepayment penalty, which is forbidden irrespective of the term of the transaction.[161] In addition, in the bankruptcy context, some courts have refused to apply the Rule of 78 when determining the amount of a creditor's allowed claim.[162]

5.6.3.3.2 Calculating a Rule of 78 rebate: a simplified step by step guide for mathphobes

The congressional action still leaves open the possibility for the Rule to be applied in precomputed transactions of 60 months and under. Since it is also the overwhelming choice of rebate calculation for unearned credit insurance premiums,[163] and some creditors use computer programs which amortize loans by the Rule of 78,[164] it is still necessary for the thorough practitioner to know how to calculate a Rule of 78 rebate.

Fortunately, as you may recall from high school, if you know the formula, you can get the right answer even if you do not know how the formula was derived.[165] So, herewith, the formula:

$$rebate = \frac{R(R+1)}{N(N+1)} \times FC$$

where

N = originally scheduled number of installments;

R = number of scheduled installments remaining after date of prepayment (use rounding formula specified in statute);

FC = total finance charge (i.e., total interest subject to rebate).

Applying that formula is a simple matter (honestly), as can be seen from working through an example. Bob Borrower signed a loan on December 1, 1992, with the following terms: $5,000 principal, 18% interest, 48 monthly payments of $146.87.[166] The $5,000 principal does not include any points, service charge or other prepaid finance charge. It does include credit insurance premiums in the amount of $215. A late charge of five dollars may be imposed if a payment is more than ten days late. On March 17, 1994, Bob refinanced. To determine the proper amount to be rebated under the Rule, follow this step by step guide.

1. Determine which charges are subject to rebate requirements. (§ 5.5, supra)

Examining the documents, we determine that this is a precomputed contract,[167] so there is unearned interest to be rebated. As there are no prepaid finance charges,[168] the $215 credit insurance premiums are the only other charges which should be rebated.[169]

Other challenges were unsuccessfully made based on contract, UDAP, or public policy grounds. *See, e.g.*, Drennan v. Security Pac. Nat'l Bank, 621 P.2d 1318 (Cal. 1981); Lanier v. Associates Fin., Inc., 499 N.E.2d 440 (Ill. 1986) (note concurrence, suggesting claim stated under disclosure provisions of Illinois Interest Act may have met with more success. *Id.* at 448–49 [*cf.* Dechow v. Sko-Fed Credit, 536 N.E.2d 1382 (Ill. App. 1989)]). *See* Kedziora v. Citicorp Nat'l Servs., 780 F. Supp. 516 (N.D. Ill. 1991), for a historical perspective on the case law.

158 *Prepayment penalties*: *Compare In re* Jungkurth, 74 B.R. 323 (Bankr. E.D. Pa. 1987) (unless specifically authorized by statute, use of Rule would constitute a prepayment penalty) *with* Jacobson v. General Fin. Corp., 592 N.E.2d 1121 (Ill. Ct. App. 1992) (court declines to rule, but appears to disfavor argument); Pysh v. Security Pacific Housing Serv., 610 A.2d 973 (Pa. Super. Ct. 1992) (use of Rule of 78 would result in early pay-off balance approximately $3,000 greater than actuarial method; borrowers alleged use of Rule violated MVSFA's prohibition against prepayment penalty, but since MVSFA and banking regulations also specifically authorized use of Rule to calculate rebate, court reconciled two provisions by allowing use of Rule to calculate unearned interest, but prohibiting imposition of separate charge or penalty for prepayment); *see generally* Kedziora v. Citicorp Nat'l Servs., 780 F. Supp. 516 (N.D. Ill. 1991) for a historical perspective.

UDAP: *See In re* Milbourne, 108 B.R. 522 (Bankr. E.D. Pa. 1989); *In re* Tucker, 74 B.R. 923 (Bankr. E.D. Pa. 1987) (dicta).

159 15 U.S.C. § 1615(d). Contrary state law is preempted. § 5.9, *infra*.

160 15 U.S.C. § 1615(b).

161 There is a limited exception to this prohibition. *See* § 5.8.2, *infra*. *See also* § 5.2.4, *supra*, and § 12.2.2, *infra* for a discussion of what loans fall within the scope of the legislation.

162 *See* discussion in § 5.2.5, *supra*.

---

163 This is the case even in states which do not permit the use of the Rule to calculate interest rebates.

164 *See* § 5.5.1, *supra*.

165 For those who enjoy that sort of thing, the derivation is explained in the next subsection. For those who do not enjoy that sort of thing, the next subsection can be safely ignored.

166 The last payment should be adjusted to account for rounding.

167 *See* §§ 4.5.3, 4.11.4, *supra*.

168 *See* § 5.5.2.2, *supra*.

169 *See* § 5.5.2.1, *supra*; § 8.6, *infra*.

We can obtain the precomputed interest figure in a number of ways: if the documents list a loan principal and an interest charge, it's handed to us. If it lists a loan principal only, we can subtract that amount from the total of payments to come up with the interest. Or if there are no prepaid finance charges or other non-interest finance charges, as in this case, we can just use the "finance charge" as disclosed on the TIL disclosure statement. In Bob's loan, we find that the disclosed finance charge is $2,049.76.[170]

2. Determine how the statute authorizing the Rule of 78 rebate defines which payment dates and intervals to use.[171] (§ 5.6.2, supra)

Assume the applicable statute requires rounding to the regular payment due date nearest to the date of prepayment. Following that rounding rule, the April 1, 1994 payment due date is the closest to the March 17 refinancing.

Having determined that April 1 is the appropriate date, we calculate that 16 payment intervals have "fully elapsed" on that date.[172] (January 1, 1993 to April 1, 1994 = 16 fully elapsed payment periods.)

3. Determine how many months are remaining in the scheduled loan term: number of months originally scheduled (n) minus number of elapsed months = number of months remaining (r):

48 months (originally scheduled term) minus 16 elapsed months = 32. (Or, you can just count them up.) This number is called "r" in the formula (for "remaining"—clever, eh?).

4. Determine the rebate fraction (or rebate factor), by use of the formula set out at the beginning of this subsection.

$$\frac{r(r+1)}{n(n+1)}$$

$$r = 32, \ n = 48$$

$$\frac{32(32+1)}{48(48+1)} = \frac{32(33)}{48(49)} = .4490$$

5. Multiply the charges subject to the Rule's rebate by the rebate factor.

As we determined in step 1, in Bob's loan FC = $2,049.76 interest subject to rebate + $215 credit insurance premiums subject to rebate = $2,264.76.

($2,049.76) × (.4490)   = $920.34 unearned interest to be rebated.[173]

($215) × (.4490)   = $96.54 unearned insurance to be rebated.

$1,016.88 total unearned charges to be rebated.

To determine the actual payoff amount on Bob's loan, we must also credit all payments made, and add all late charges which he may have incurred. In Bob's case, if he made all payments timely through February 1, he would have paid 14 payments, for a total of $2,056.18. As the March 1 payment would have been late on the date of refinancing, Bob incurred one $5 late charge.

Total of payments	$7,049.76 (48 @ $146.87)
Minus Payments made	−2,056.18 (14 @ $146.87)
Minus Rebates	−1,016.88
Plus Late charge	+ 5.00 (1 @ $5.00)
Pay off balance	$3,981.70

If the creditor is asking for a larger payoff than this, there is an overcharge.

For mathphobes, this is all that is necessary; you may safely ignore the next section. For those who are curious, the theory behind it is explained there.

5.6.3.3.3 The explanation of the Rule of 78 for those who care (optional reading for the practitioner)

So how does the Rule of 78 work? Like the pro rata method, the Rule of 78 calculates the fraction or percentage of the finance charge which has been earned at any point in the loan. Unlike the pro rata method, however, the Rule of 78 does not assume that the interest earned in each month (or other interval) of the loan is equal. Instead, it weights the earliest months in the loan term most heavily and attributes progressively less interest to later months. As a general approach, this concept of attributing more interest to months early in the loan term than to months later in the term is correct because of the declining principal balance owed on

---

170 Remember that the TIL finance charges may include some charges which under state law may not need to be rebated, such as points. *See* § 4.4.1, *supra*. So if we are using only the disclosure statement on a loan with prepaid finance charges, we may need to make an adjustment.

    For example, if there had been a 2% origination fee on Bob's loan (2% of $5,000 principal = $100), the TIL disclosure statement would have listed the finance charge as $2,149.76. (The interest on $5,000 at 18% for 4 years, plus the $100 origination fee.)

    If, under applicable state law, origination fees are considered "earned at consummation," and do not need to be rebated, (*see* § 5.5.2.2, *supra*) then we must subtract that fee from the TIL finance charge in order to obtain the interest charge subject to rebate. $2,149.76 (TIL finance charge) minus $100 (origination fee) = $2,049.76 interest subject to rebate.

171 If the statute does not specify rounding rules, the banking department or other regulatory agency may have rules which do so. Administrative regulations should be reviewed, or simply call the regulator and ask.

172 That language commonly appears in statutes or regulations governing rules for rounding intervals.

173 Compare this to the actuarial rebate of $1,020.57, over $100 more to consumer. *See* § 5.6.3.4, *infra*.

the loan. However, the method used by the Rule of 78 weights the early months too heavily and the later months too lightly and thus, when a loan is prepaid, credits the lender with more earned interest than it is actuarially due.[174]

The method by which the Rule of 78 weights the income earned in each payment interval of a loan is as follows. First, the total number of payment intervals (usually months) in the originally anticipated loan term is counted. In a one-year loan with payments due monthly, there will be twelve payment intervals. In a similar two-year loan, there will be twenty-four intervals.

Second, the denominator of the rebate fraction is determined by adding up all of the integers from one to the number of payment intervals originally anticipated for the loan. For the one year loan mentioned above, this sum is: $1+2+3+4+5+6+7+8+9+10+11+12 = 78$. This sum of 78 is the origin of the name of the Rule of 78, but the sum is 78 only for a loan with twelve equal repayment intervals. For the two-year loan, for example, the denominator of the rebate fraction will be $1+2+3+4+ \ldots +21+22+23+24 = 300$. In general, the formula for determining the sum of the digits from one to the number of payment intervals is: sum = $[N \times (N + 1)] \div 2$ where N represents the number of payments originally anticipated for the loan.

Third, each month is given a weight that is the opposite of its order of repayment. Thus, the first month of a one-year loan with equal monthly installments is given a weight of twelve, the second month is given a weight of eleven, the third ten, etc. The final month of any loan, regardless of the length of the term, will always be given a weight of one. Each month's weight represents the amount of interest that is earned in that month according to the Rule. Remembering that the denominator of the rebate fraction for a one-year loan is 78, the amount of interest earned in the first month of the loan is 12/78ths or about 15.38% of the total interest.[175] Similarly, the amount of interest earned during the second month of the loan is 11/78ths of the total or about 14.1%. The interest credited to the third month will be 10/78ths of the total, and so on. As a result, the amount of interest earned during the first three months of this one-year loan would be $12/78 + 11/78 + 10/78 = 33/78$ths of the total contract interest, or about 42.3%. At the same time, the amount of unearned interest which must be rebated is the fraction attributed to the last nine scheduled months which is, starting with the interest earned in the twelfth month:

$1/78 + 2/78 + \ldots + 8/78 + 9/78 = 45/78$ or about 57.7% of the total interest charge.[176]

From this is derived the rebate formula used in the preceding section.

5.6.3.3.4 Sum of the balances method: a variant on the Rule of 78

An important variant of the Rule of 78, or sum of the digits method, is the ''sum of the balances'' method. Its impact lies in loans where the scheduled payments are unequal, particularly where a final balloon payment is called for. It provides that the fraction of the total contract interest that must be rebated at any given time in the loan term is the sum of the monthly loan balances for the months remaining in the originally scheduled loan term divided by the sum of the monthly balances for all the months in the scheduled loan term.[177] Thus, for a six-month loan of $600 which is scheduled to be repaid in $100 monthly installments, the rebate fraction after two months would be:

$$\frac{400+300+200+100}{600+500+400+300+200+100} = \frac{1000}{2100} = \frac{10}{21} = 0.476 \ (rounded).$$

This fraction would be multiplied by the finance charge (i.e., the total contract interest subject to rebate) to obtain the actual dollar amount of unearned interest. If $40 of that $600 total of payments was the interest, the amount rebated would be $19.04.[178]

The rebate fraction obtained with the sum of the balances formula in the example above is identical to the fraction which would be produced by the Rule of 78.[179] For any loan which is paid off in equal monthly installments, the sum of the balances method and the Rule of 78 will provide identical rebates. However, if a loan schedule contains unequal payments, and especially if the loan is scheduled to be retired by a final balloon installment, the rebates under the sum of the balances method and the Rule of 78 are *not* the

---

174 *See generally* Hunt, *The Rule of 78: Hidden Penalty For Prepayment in Consumer Credit Transactions*, 55 B.U. L. Rev. 331 (1975). *See also* Kedziora v. Citicorp Nat'l Servs., 780 F. Supp. 516 (N.D. Ill. 1991); Denley v. Peoples Bank, 553 So. 2d 494, 498–99 (Miss. 1989) (discussion of how Rule of 78 ''skews the accrual'' of finance charges); IRS Rev. Ruling 83-84, 1983-1 CB97.

175 The interest earned in the first month of a two-year, 24-installment loan would, in contrast, be 24/300ths of the total interest or 8 percent.

176 Note that you can use the formula previously given, sum = $[N \times (N + 1)] \div 2$, to figure out that the sum of the integers from one to nine is forty-five, i.e., $[9 \times (9 + 1)] \div 2 = 90 \div 2 = 45$. Thus the numerator of the rebate fraction can be calculated as easily as the denominator. All you have to do is to decide how many intervals (usually months) remain after the date of prepayment, and then apply the formula.

177 Statutes which call for a sum of the balances rebate are often difficult to decipher. The typical language might provide for a rebate of ''at least as great a proportion of the finance charge as the sum of the monthly balances after the date of prepayment bears to the sum of all the monthly balances under the schedule in the contract.'' The average statute also has language describing the rounding method for determining the number of remaining installments.

178 $(.476) \times (\$40) = \$19.04$.

179 The rebate fraction calculated by the Rule of 78 would be:

$$\frac{4+3+2+1}{6+5+4+3+2+1} \times \frac{10}{21}$$

same. Instead, the more the repayment schedule is loaded with large payments near the end of the loan term, the more the sum of the balances method will favor the borrower in comparison with the Rule of 78. Creditors which give standard Rule of 78 rebates on balloon note transactions when the statute prescribes the sum of the balances method are probably violating the state law. Practitioners should be particularly alert to this, because it can reasonably be anticipated that balloon notes, particularly five-year balloon notes, will be on the rise among creditors trying to minimize the impact of two recent federal consumer protection enactments.[180] Since a number of state statutes do specify the sum of the balances method, instead of the sum of the digits or the Rule of 78, this issue may become more important now.

The only way to calculate a sum of the balances rebate on a transaction with several unequal monthly payments is to laboriously add up all the monthly balances. However, if all the payments are the same size except for a final balloon payment, the sum of the balances rebate can be calculated by the following formula:

$$rebate = \left[(R \times B) + \left(\frac{R(R-1)}{2} \times P\right)\right] \times FC \div \left[(N \times B) + \left(\frac{N(N-1)}{n} \times P\right)\right]$$

where

N = originally scheduled number of installments;

R = number of scheduled installments remaining after date of prepayment (use rounding formula specified in statute);

FC = total finance charge (i.e., total interest subject to rebate);

B = balloon payment due as last installment;

P = regular payment amount.

---

180 For certain high-cost loans, the Home Ownership and Equity Protection Act of 1994 prohibits balloon payments on any note with a term less than five years. Lenders may structure high-cost loans to be exactly five years in order to avoid this prohibition, so that they can include a balloon payment. At the same time, the 1992 federal rebate law prohibits the use of the Rule of 78, or any rebate calculation method less favorable to the consumer than the actuarial method, in consumer credit transactions with terms longer than sixty-one months. 15 U.S.C. § 1615(b). *See* §§ 5.2.2, 5.5.2.2.3, *supra.* Thus a high-cost loan with a term of exactly five years could have a balloon payment and would not be subject to the rebate law's prohibition of a non-actuarial rebate. HOEPA also restricts use of rebate formulae such as the Rule of 78 that are less favorable to the consumer than the actuarial method, but it allows non-actuarial methods to be used in some circumstances for prepayments in the first five years of the loan. 15 U.S.C. § 1639(c).

Even if a lender structures a sixty-month balloon loan that avoids these federal restrictions, it must still comply with state law, §§ 5.8.2, 5.9, *infra.* If the state law rebate statute uses the sum of the balances method, instead of the sum of the digits method, the use of the standard Rule of 78 likely will result in an overcharge.

Keep in mind, though, that this will ordinarily not be an issue on interest-bearing loans. *See* §§ 5.4.1, 5.5.1, *supra.*

As an example of the use of this formula, consider the same six-month loan for $600 that was mentioned earlier in this section, but assume that instead of equal monthly payments of $100, the loan is repayable in five installments of $60 and a final $300 balloon installment. Following the formula, the rebate upon prepayment after two months is:

$$\left[(4 \times 300) + \left(\frac{4 \times 3}{2} \times 60\right)\right] \times FC \div \left[(6 \times 300) + \left(\frac{6 \times 5}{2} \times 60\right)\right]$$

$$= \frac{1200 + 360}{1800 + 900} \times FC$$

$$= \frac{1560}{2700} \times FC$$

$$= 0.578 \ (rounded) \times FC$$

Thus the difference between the sum of the balances rebate and the Rule of 78 rebate on this loan is more than one tenth of the total finance charge.[181] Again assuming that $40 of the $600 total of payments was the interest subject to rebate, the amount of the rebate is $23.12,[182] compared to the $19.04 rebated yielded by a straight Rule of 78 method.[183] On large loans with high finance charges this difference can be thousands of dollars.

5.6.3.4 Actuarial Rebates

5.6.3.4.1 *Legal status*

The most accurate and the fairest way to balance creditor and debtor interests in a rebate calculation is to determine the actuarial interest that the creditor has earned at the time of prepayment and to refund to the borrower the difference between the total contract interest and this actuarially earned amount. Generally accepted accounting principles consider this the economic reality.[184] The extreme distortion caused by the Rule of 78, particularly for contracts with longer terms and high principal amounts, led many states to require the actuarial method, at least in long-term loans, prior to the 1992 federal law which now mandates it for all consumer credit transactions with terms longer than 61 months.[185] Even prior to the 1992 federal rebate statute, actuarial rebates were frequently required by state statutes and federal regulations, especially for contracts with longer terms and high principal amounts, because of the Rule of 78 inaccuracy for such

---

181 The difference is 0.578 − 0.476 = 0.102.

182 (.578) × ($40) = $23.12.

183 *See* note 178, *supra.*

184 James H. Hunt, *The Rule of 78: Hidden Penalty for Prepayment in Consumer Credit Transactions*, 55 B.U. L. Rev. 331 (1975). *See* § 5.5.1, *supra.*

185 15 U.S.C. § 1615(b) (Rule of 78 prohibited on precomputed consumer credit transactions consummated after September 30, 1993 with term longer than 61 months; method at least as favorable to consumer as actuarial method must be used). *See* §§ 5.2.2, *supra*, 5.7.3, *infra.*

transactions.[186] Moreover, any home equity loans which fall within the scope of the 1994 Home Ownership and Equity Protection Act are prohibited from using the Rule irrespective of length of term, with one narrow exception.[187]

5.6.3.4.2 Calculation of actuarial rebates

The computation of an actuarial rebate requires the construction of an amortization schedule. There is no easy formula to calculate the rebate. At the time each payment is made from the beginning of the loan to the point of prepayment, the interest earned during the preceding period or fractional period must be computed by multiplying the outstanding principal balance by the periodic interest rate, and the payments received must be used, first to pay off the accrued interest and, second, to reduce the outstanding principal balance. The process may be tedious, especially in precomputed transactions where no amortization schedule is otherwise needed, but it is the most economically accurate and fairest of the three rebate methods: the lender receives income for the actual use of its funds and the borrower does not overpay interest.

The companion CD-Rom to this volume includes two programs that will prepare and print amortization schedules so that actuarial rebates can be determined. Practitioners using the program should also be familiar with the manual calculations necessary to check the amortization schedule that are discussed in this subsection and § 4.3.1, *supra*. When presenting the amortization schedule to a court, it is important to be able to demonstrate its accuracy by doing the simple arithmetic necessary to check it.[188]

The calculation of actuarial interest has previously been discussed in this manual,[189] but a brief example of the use of an actuarial calculation to compute the size of a rebate will nevertheless be given here. Assume that a consumer takes out a precomputed one-year loan of $1,000 repayable in equal monthly installments with 14% add-on interest and an APR of 24.91%. The total amount repayable will be $1,000 principal + ($1,000 × 0.14) interest = $1,140. The monthly installment will be $1,140 ÷ 12 = $95. If the consumer prepays the loan after exactly three months and the relevant statute calls for an actuarial rebate of the unearned interest, then the amount of interest that the lender has earned in the three months that the loan was outstanding must be calculated. The difference between the total interest of $140 and the amount that the lender has earned will be the amount of the rebate.

The following partial amortization table shows the appropriate actuarial earnings.[190] Note that the periodic (here, monthly) rate is 24.91 ÷ 12 = 2.07583%.[191]

The interest earned each month is calculated by multiplying the current principal balance by the periodic interest rate. This earned interest is deducted from the monthly payment and the remainder of the payment is used to reduce the balance of the loan. The following month's interest is calculated using this new, reduced balance.

In this example, the lender has earned $57.62 in interest over the three months of the loan, and the borrower is entitled to a rebate of: $140 total precomputed interest − $57.62 earned interest = $82.38. The total amount repayable of $1,140 minus the amount that the borrower has already paid (3 × $95 = $285) equals $855, the amount the lender shows as due after three months. When the rebate of $82.38 is subtracted, the balance is $772.62, which is the amount that the borrower will have to pay to retire the loan at this point.

	Old Periodic Balance	+	2.07583% Monthly Interest	−	Monthly Installment Payment	=	New Periodic Balance	Monthly Paid To Principal	Cumulative Interest Earned
Jan.	$1,000.00		$20.76		$95.00		$925.76	$74.24	$20.76
Feb.	$925.76		$19.22		$95.00		$849.98	$75.78	$39.98
Mar.	$849.98		$17.64		$95.00		$772.62	$77.36	$57.62
Apr.	$772.62								

The example given here assumes that the first three installments of the loan were paid on time. If a payment had been missed or paid late, additional portions of the borrower's payments would be attributed to interest or late fees, and the rebate would be reduced. On the other hand, if some of the payments had been made early, the lender would have earned less interest and the rebate would increase. However, many statutes allow actuarial rebates to be calculated using the assumption that all installments were paid on time.[192]

---

186 *See, e.g.,* 12 C.F.R. § 590.4(c) (1994) (OTS mobile home regulations applicable to creditors claiming usury preemption under DIDA); 12 U.S.C. § 1735f-7a(c)(3); Mo. Rev. Stat. §§ 364.120, 365.140, 408.170 (as amended June 19, 1986 effective Aug. 13, 1986) (term over 61 months); Okla. Stat. Ann. tit. 14A, § 2-210(3) (as amended June 24, 1986, effective Nov. 1, 1986) (term over 61 months). *See also In re* Jungkurth, 74 B.R. 323 (Bankr. E.D. Pa. 1987) (where statute prohibits prepayment penalties but does not specify a method of calculating rebates, the actuarial method must be used; unless expressly authorized by statute, use of the Rule of 78 would constitute a prepayment penalty).

187 *See* § 5.8.2, *infra*.

188 *See also* § 4.10, *supra*.

189 § 4.3.1, *supra*.

190 This table rounds fractions of cents to the nearest penny.

191 24.91% is the actuarial equivalent of 14% add-on rate for 12 months.

192 *See, e.g.,* Ariz. Rev. Stat. Ann. § 6-634.

Whenever a debt is accelerated or prepaid on any day other than the scheduled monthly payment date, the effect of the fractional payment interval must be taken into account. For example, if the borrower had prepaid the loan after three months and one day instead of after exactly three months, the lender would have earned an extra day's interest. That one day's interest would be: $772.62 (the loan balance after three months) × 0.0207583 (the monthly rate) × 1/30 (assuming one day to be one thirtieth of a month) = $0.53. Therefore, after three months and one day, the lender would have earned $57.62 + $0.53 = $58.15, and the borrower would be entitled to a rebate of $140 − $58.15 = $81.85.

Lenders may attempt to round fractional intervals in their favor. Thus, when prepayment occurs after three months and a day, a lender might claim four months of interest. Although this practice may be permitted by some rebate statutes,[193] it is important to recognize that such rounding is not actuarial. Actuarially, a lender can earn only one day's interest in one day, not a whole month's interest.[194] Therefore, the very fact that a statute requires an "actuarial" rebate should preclude such rounding unless the statute specifically permits it.

5.6.3.4.3 Actuarial rebates under actuarial split rate statutes

A special rebate calculation issue arises under actuarial "split rate" usury statutes, which apply one interest rate to part of the outstanding balance and another, usually a lower rate, to the rest.[195] Such statutes do not produce a simple interest amortization pattern. Yet, when calculating rebates for precomputed transactions under actuarial split rate statutes,[196] creditors frequently assume simple interest amortization, using one twelfth of the APR as the monthly interest

rate. Such an assumption changes the earnings pattern mandated by the split rate statute, and, assuming that the rate permitted for the first part of the outstanding balance is higher than the rate permitted for the rest, causes lower rebates.[197] An example may help to illustrate this point.

Assume a split rate debt of $1,000 where the actuarial interest rate is 2% per month on the first $500 of credit and 1.5% per month on the remaining $500, creating a total precomputed interest charge of $247.99 over 24 months. The regular monthly payment is $52. The first three months' amortization of the loan is shown in the following chart, where "Interest 1" is the interest generated by the first incremental rate (2% on the first $500) and "Interest 2" is generated by the second incremental rate (1.5% on the balance over $500):

Old Balance	+ Interest 1	+ Interest 2	− Payment	= New Balance
$1,000.00	$10.00	$7.50	$52.00	$965.50
$965.50	$10.00	$6.98	$52.00	$930.48
$930.49	$10.00	$6.46	$52.00	$894.94

The total interest earned (adding the Interest 1 and Interest 2 columns) in three months is $50.94. The rebate at this point would be $197.05 ($247.99 − 50.94 = $197.05).

The APR for this transaction is 22.2267%. But if the APR is used to work out the amortization at 1.852% per month (22.226% ÷ 12 = 1.852%), the same total interest is earned overall but the pattern in which interest is earned is different:

---

193 See § 5.6.2.2, *supra*. Cf. Beaty v. Land of Lincoln Sav. & Loan, 468 N.E.2d 1259 (Ill. App. 1984) (full month's interest earned on mortgage contract when prepaid on second day of month; court finds no "prepayment penalty" but does not consider whether such earnings are actuarial).

194 See Financial Publishing Co., The Cost of Personal Borrowing in the United States p.32 (2004); *see also* 12 C.F.R. § 226, Appendix J(b)(6) (1986) (Regulation Z; definition of percentage rate for fraction of a unit period).

195 The issue arises only under actuarial split rate statutes as opposed to split rate statutes that allow add-on or discount interest calculations. The reason is that only actuarial computation takes the declining principal balance of the credit into account and, thus, causes the effective interest rate to rise during the term of the transaction as the part of the principal balance to which the lower rate applies is paid off. Split rate calculations are discussed in § 4.3.4, *supra*.

196 The concept of precomputed actuarial interest may seem contradictory, but actually it need not be. If permitted by the applicable statute, a creditor may simply calculate actuarial interest with an amortization table by assuming that payments are made on the scheduled installment dates. It then adds this precomputed actuarial interest to the principal amount and requires the borrower to sign a note for the total amount.

197 The difference between the earnings pattern under a simple interest rate, such as the APR, and the pattern created by a split rate statute can be viewed in the following manner. A simple interest amortization assumes that a single unchanging rate is applied, usually monthly, to the total outstanding balance at the time of each installment payment. Under a split rate statute, however, two or more different rates may apply simultaneously to different portions of the outstanding balance. Usually a higher rate applies to the first $500 or $1,000 of the outstanding balance, and one or more progressively lower rates apply to any additional portions of the outstanding balance. The critical point to recognize is that the "upper" portion(s) of the principal balance, to which the lower rate(s) apply, are paid off first. Thus, the lower rate(s) apply only during the beginning of the loan term while the higher incremental rate which applies to the first $500 or $1,000 will apply throughout the entire loan term. Consequently, under a split rate statute, the effective interest rate on the outstanding balance increases as the term of the loan progresses.

If a single flat interest rate, specifically the APR, is substituted for the split interest rate, the total amount of interest earned over the entire loan term will be the same, but the effective interest rate and the interest earned at the beginning of the loan term will be exaggerated, while the effective rate and the interest earned at the end of the term will be understated. Therefore, a creditor which uses the APR in a rebate calculation will be claiming more earnings early in the credit term than it is due under a split rate amortization, and will provide a lower rebate than that to which the borrower may be entitled.

Old Balance	+ Interest	− Payment	= New Balance
$1,000.00	$18.52	$52.00	$966.52
$966.52	$17.90	$52.00	$932.42
$932.42	$17.27	$52.00	$897.69

The total interest earned by the creditor after three months using this amortization is $53.69, or $2.75 more than would be generated using the split rate. Using the APR for amortization, the rebate would only be $194.30 ($247.99 − $53.69 = $194.30).

State laws and regulations must be consulted to determine which of these two actuarial rebates is correct. In a few states the problem has been directly addressed by statute.[198] However, if the applicable statute simply requires an "actuarial" rebate and does not specify that a simple interest amortization may be used for the rebate calculation, consumer Practitioners should argue that the very existence of the split rate statute constitutes a statutory specification that interest may only be earned in accordance with a split rate amortization pattern. The use of a simple interest amortization under such circumstances should be recognized as no more than a self-serving method of retaining illegal unearned interest.

5.7 Proving Rebate Violations Are Illegal Charges

5.7.1 Usury Upon a Contingent Event

Until the 1960s, it was common for usury statutes to neglect the issue of rebates upon the early termination of precomputed debt. With the exception of small loan laws or other special usury statutes, most usury laws simply provided interest ceilings, and many courts, adopting a strict construction of usury provisions, held that these ceilings applied only to the terms of a contract at the time of its execution.[199] Thus, a contract which would not have been usurious if its anticipated payment schedule had been met could not be made usurious by some "contingency," such as the "voluntary" action of the debtor in prepaying or defaulting on the debt.[200]

The rule against the creation of usury through contingencies can be criticized on its own terms. The notion that contractual default and acceleration is caused by the voluntary action of the debtor is, to say the least, strained.[201] Similarly, the position that voluntary prepayment is unanticipated at the time a credit contract is executed lacks credibility, given the high percentage of consumer loans that are prepaid or refinanced.[202] Such common sense arguments aside, it is critical for practitioners to recognize that the rule against the existence of usury in contingencies is simply a rule of construction developed by courts interpreting statutes that were silent on the need for rebates.[203] If a statute specifically requires the rebate of unearned interest or premiums, as do almost all modern statutes regulating precomputed consumer credit, then the failure of the creditor to provide such rebates triggers whatever remedies that statute provides for in the event its terms regarding allowable charges are violated. These remedy provisions often apply even absent intent,[204] but in any case, the intentional failure of the creditor to provide required rebates is usurious.[205] The question then is: when does a creditor manifest an intent to deny the rebate to which the consumer is entitled?

---

198 *See* Cal. Fin. Code § 24308.

199 This result may still hold if a statute regulates only the interest "contracted for," as opposed to the interest "contracted for or received," especially if the legislature used the latter language in another statute. Concord Realty Co. v. Continental Funding Corp., 776 P.2d 1114, 1120 (Colo. 1989) (*en banc*). *See also* § 5.7.2, *infra*.

200 *See, e.g.*, Lederman Enters., Inc. v. Westinghouse Credit Corp., 347 F. Supp. 1291 (D. Colo. 1972) (prepayment penalty); Winkle v. Grand Nat'l Bank, 601 S.W.2d 559 (Ark. 1980), *cert. denied*, 449 U.S. 880 (1980); B.F. Saul Co. v. West End Park North, Inc., 246 A.2d 591 (Md. 1968) (prepayment); Industrial Nat'l Bank v. Stuard, 318 A.2d 452 (R.I. 1974) (default and

acceleration). *But see* C.I.O.S. Foundation v. Berkston Ins. A.V.V., 2000 U.S. Dist. LEXIS 2337 (N.D. Miss. 2000) (Texas law) (usury penalties apply if any contingency would make loan usurious, but court applies spreading doctrine to avoid usury); Dixon v. Brooks, 604 S.W.2d 330 (Tex. Ct. App. 1980) (usury exists as a matter of law when any contingency exists under which the creditor can receive more than the maximum rate).

201 *See* Begelfer v. Najarian, 409 N.E.2d 167 (Mass. 1980) (late fees). *Cf.* Texas Airfinance Corp. v. Lesikar, 777 S.W.2d 559 (Tex. App. 1989) (upon acceleration borrower has not sought privilege of early payment and therefore prepayment penalty is impermissible).

202 Small loan data have shown that approximately 80% of small loan transactions involve refinancing or consolidation of debt and 50% involve four or more consolidations. *See In re* Lowell, Clearinghouse No. 30,955 (S.D. Me. 1972) *cited in* Hunt, *The Rule of 78: Hidden Penalty For Prepayment in Consumer Credit Transactions*, 55 B.U. L. Rev. 331 (1975). *See also* Mark C. Kramer & Raymond N. Neihengen, Jr., *Analysis of Finance Company Ratios in 1992*, J. of Commercial Lending (Sept. 1993) (63.1% "loans to present borrowers" 1992 survey) Table 2.

203 *See* B.F. Saul Co. v. West End Park North, Inc., 246 A.2d 591 (Md. 1968) (distinguishing loans to which rebate statute applies).

204 *See* § 5.7.2, *infra*.

205 *See, e.g.*, Matter of Sprouse, 577 F.2d 989 (5th Cir. 1978); Aetna Fin. Co. v. Brown, 323 S.E.2d 720 (Ga. App. 1984); Union Trust Co. of Md. v. Tyndall, 428 A.2d 428 (Md. 1981); Jim Walter Homes, Inc. v. Schuenemann, 668 S.W.2d 324 (Tex. 1984); Nationwide Fin. Corp. v. English, 604 S.W.2d 458 (Tex. Ct. App. 1980), *writ granted*, 24 Tex. Sup. Ct. J. 464 (Tex. 1981), *set aside, cause dismissed* (Oct. 14, 1981). Even if a statute is silent as to rebates, it can be interpreted as requiring whatever rebates are necessary to prevent an illegal amount of interest from being contracted for "or received." Denley v. Peoples Bank, 553 So. 2d 494, 500 (Miss. 1989). Or equitable principles may be held to require rebate upon acceleration. Aardwoolf Corp. v. Nelson Capital Corp., 861 F.2d 46 (2d Cir. 1988).

The rule against usury through contingencies nevertheless continues to affect some consumer transactions. First, the rule may preclude the need for rebates in some credit transactions which are nominally interest-bearing but which include significant prepaid finance charges, such as points. If a rebate statute applies only to precomputed transactions and the definition of "precomputed" does not encompass such mixed transactions, the traditional rule against usury in contingency situations could be invoked to preclude the need to rebate the prepaid charges.[206]

Second, the contingency rule occasionally rears its head even in situations where rebates are clearly required. In a few cases where the evidence strongly suggested a lender's intent to retain unearned charges, courts have nevertheless inferred the intent to make the proper rebate, citing the contingency rule as justification.[207]

5.7.2 Intent to Collect Unearned Charges; Verb-iage (What Constitutes "Charging," "Receiving," or "Contracting For" Unearned Charges)

5.7.2.1 Whether Intent Is Required

Under some consumer credit statutes, specific remedies are authorized wherever finance charges (or simply charges) in excess of that allowed are charged,[208] or more generally where provisions of the act are violated.[209] Any time the statute provides for a specific remedy for imposing charges in excess of that allowed, a provision requiring rebates should be considered to be encompassed by that language.[210] Some statutes make it quite clear there is no intent requirement, either by specifying the available defenses, such as "bona fide error,"[211] or by narrowing defenses or

enhancing remedies when the violations are intentional or in reckless disregard.[212]

In other cases, given a statute that requires the rebate of unearned charges upon prepayment or acceleration, proof of usury may depend primarily on a demonstration of the creditor's intent to collect unearned charges in violation of the statute. Interpretations of usurious intent vary significantly from jurisdiction to jurisdiction, and the subject as a whole is treated elsewhere in this manual.[213] Nevertheless, the intent to collect unearned charges presents some special issues which will be mentioned here.

5.7.2.2 Does the Contract Show the Creditor's Intent to Charge Unearned Interest?

There are two ways in which a creditor may violate usury law rebate requirements: either the creditor can provide a contract which on its face fails to provide for the appropriate rebate, or it can neglect in actual practice to give a rebate which it is both contractually and statutorily required to give. Where intent is required, demonstrating a usury violation in the first situation may be considerably easier than in the second because the contract itself can show the creditor's intent. In many jurisdictions, it is usurious merely to "contract for" usurious payments. Any contract calling for the collection of unearned charges upon acceleration or prepayment is therefore facially usurious and justifies statutory sanctions even if the contingency of acceleration or prepayment never occurs.[214]

This rule has led to a significant amount of litigation in some states, especially Georgia and Texas, over the construction of acceleration clauses, and the courts involved have drawn some very fine lines between the precise contract language that must be construed as requiring payment

---

206 *See* Colorado Dep't of Law, Admin. Interp. Nos. 2.201, 3.201 and 3.508-8301 (Oct. 14, 1983) (interpretation of Colorado U.C.C.C. finding no statutory rebate requirement for prepaid finance charges in nonprecomputed transactions unless prepayment was originally anticipated; note that Colorado regulations, 4 Code Colo. Regs 902-1 Rule 13, now require such a rebate if refinancing occurs within the first year).

207 *See* Jackson Inv. Co. v. Bates, 366 So. 2d 225 (Miss. 1978).

208 *See, e.g.*, Ala. Code § 5-19-19 (consumer credit code); Iowa Code § 537.5201(2),(3) (consumer credit code). *See generally* § 10.8, *infra*.

209 *See, e.g.*, Mich. Comp. Laws § 445.868 (RISA).

210 Since failure to rebate unearned interest results in excess charges, that should trigger any remedy authorized for excess charges. For such statutes, the question may be whether the excess was "charged," or whatever the operative verb in the statute is, as is discussed *infra*.

211 *See, e.g.*, Ky. Rev. Stat. § 371.990(3). An unintentional error does not generally equate to a "bona fide error," in the context of consumer credit legislation. For example, the Truth in Lending Act, which provides for statutory remedies is a strict liability

statute; absent the creditor's proof of one of the specified defenses, consumers must be awarded the full remedy. National Consumer Law Center, Truth in Lending § 1.4.2.3 (5th ed. 2003 and Supp.).

212 *See, e.g.*, Ala. Code § 5-19-19 (greater penalty for deliberate or reckless violations); Ky. Rev. Stat. § 371.990(4) (no correction of error permitted for willful and intentional failure to comply). *See also* W. Va. Code § 46A-5-101 (in no event does consumer have to pay excess charges, and has right to recover them; creditor contracting for or receiving excess charge additionally liable for statutory penalty, absent correction or error or successful defense of bona fide error notwithstanding maintenance of procedures reasonably adopted to avoid error). Both of those defenses are adopted from the Truth in Lending Act, and cases decided under that act should be relevant analogies to any similar state law. National Consumer Law Center, Truth in Lending §§ 7.4.3, 7.4.5 (5th ed. 2003 and Supp.).

213 *See* § 10.5.5, *infra*.

214 *See, e.g.*, G.A.C. Fin. Corp. v. Hardy, 208 S.E.2d 453 (Ga. 1974); Coastal Cement Sand Inc. v. First Interstate Credit Alliance, Inc., 956 S.W.2d 562 (Tex. App. 1997) (commercial case applying *Schuenemann* holding); Jim Walter Homes, Inc. v. Schuenemann, 668 S.W.2d 324 (Tex. 1984); Commercial Credit Corp. v. Chasteen, 565 S.W.2d 342 (Tex. Ct. App. 1978).

of unearned charges, and the language that does not necessarily manifest an intent to collect unearned charges. For example, in Georgia, contract clauses permitting the acceleration of "all installments,"[215] "the entire balance,"[216] and "all remaining payments"[217] were usurious, while a contract allowing the acceleration of "all liabilities"[218] was not. Similarly, in Texas acceleration of an entire "note" has been held to be usurious when the note includes unearned interest, while the acceleration of "debt" has been held not to violate usury law because the "debt" can be construed not to include unearned interest.[219]

In jurisdictions where case law has not already determined the standard for interpreting acceleration and prepayment clauses, practitioners should argue that such clauses should be read as an average consumer would read them.[220] It is important to recognize that the reason that dozens of judicial interpretations of acceleration clauses have been necessary is not that the consumer credit industry is incapable of drafting an acceleration clause that clearly and unambiguously provides for the rebate of unearned interest. The only conclusion that can be drawn from the amount of litigation construing acceleration clauses is that the drafting of consumer contracts is often deliberately opaque and designed to convince lay debtors that a creditor has greater rights than the law actually allows. Moreover, overly broad acceleration clauses should not be excused as attempts by creditors to insure that they do not sacrifice any of their rights upon a borrower's default, because the debtor's entitlement to a rebate of unearned charges in precomputed consumer contracts is now beyond dispute.[221]

The muddying of consumers' clear statutory rights through the use of vague contract language should be combated by construing these clauses as debtors would interpret them rather than through the construction of fine legal distinctions which would never occur to the average consumer. Thus practitioners should argue that if a debtor reading an acceleration clause would believe that the creditor could retain or collect unearned charges, the clause should be so interpreted and the contract held to be illegal.[222]

5.7.2.3 Has the Creditor Failed to Give the Rebate the Contract Requires?

If a credit contract properly provides for a rebate upon the early termination of a precomputed debt, the next question is whether, when the prepayment or acceleration finally occurs, the creditor actually gives the rebate properly. Statutorily, the issue is typically whether the creditor "charged" or "collected" usurious interest, and a significant number of cases have focused on this point.[223]

Generally, the "charging" of unearned interest involves some demand by the creditor for the payment of a sum in excess of that to which it is entitled at the time of the demand. Illegal charging has been found in demand letters,[224] in statements of account,[225] and in court pleadings,[226] including affidavits.[227] However, courts have at times allowed creditors to amend apparently usurious court pleadings, and thereby to avoid usury, by removing unearned charges from the judgment originally sought.[228] This practice is extremely unwise, as some courts have recognized, because it enables unscrupulous creditors to circum-

---

215 Lewis v. Termplan, Inc., 184 S.E.2d 473 (Ga. App. 1971).
216 Hardy v. G.A.C. Fin., 205 S.E.2d 526 (Ga. App. 1974), *aff'd*, 208 S.E.2d 453 (Ga. 1974).
217 Frazier v. Courtesy Fin. Co., 208 S.E.2d 175 (Ga. App. 1974).
218 Goodwin v. Trust Co. of Columbus, 242 S.E.2d 302 (Ga. App. 1978).
219 Jim Walter Homes v. Schuenemann, 668 S.W.2d 324 (Tex. 1984) (citing Texas cases); *see also* Mack v. Newton, 737 F.2d 1345 (5th Cir. 1984) (discussing Texas law). Interestingly, the acceleration of a "note" may not call for the collection of unearned interest under Georgia law, at least when proper language exists elsewhere in the contract. *See* Plant v. Blazer Fin. Servs., 598 F.2d 1357 (5th Cir. 1979).
220 *See* Matter of Sprouse, 577 F.2d 989 (5th Cir. 1978) (discussing effect of overreaching contract language on consumers in transactions which are not litigated).
221 *See* § 5.2, *supra.*
222 *See* Matter of Sprouse, 577 F.2d 989 (5th Cir. 1978).

223 *See also* § 10.5.4.2, *infra,* for cases on this point.
224 *See* Palace Indus., Inc. v. Craig, 339 S.E.2d 313 (Ga. App. 1985) (demand letters and complaint); Dryden v. City Nat'l Bank of Laredo, 666 S.W.2d 213 (Tex. App. 1984) (demand letters were "charge" even though debtor's account properly credited with rebate). *Cf.* Woodcrest Assocs. Ltd. v. Commonwealth Mortgage Corp., 775 S.W.2d 434 (Tex. App. 1989) (demand letter constituted "charge" but savings clause avoided usury). *See also* § 10.5.4.2, *infra.*
225 *See* Danziger v. San Jacinto Sav. Ass'n, 732 S.W.2d 300 (Tex. 1987) (inclusion of excess interest in pay-off quote constituted "charging" illegal interest); Cigna Ins. Co. v. TPG Store, Inc., 894 S.W.2d 431 (Tex. App. 1995) (statement including unrebated interest constituted usurious "charging"; subsequent credit cannot purge the usury); Williams v. Bach, 624 S.W.2d 272 (Tex. Ct. App. 1981) (undelivered statement of account). *But cf.* Mack v. Newton, 737 F.2d 1345 (5th Cir. 1984) (telephone conversation). *See generally* § 10.5.4.2, *infra.*
226 *See* Bell v. Loosier of Albany, Inc., 229 S.E.2d 374 (Ga. 1976); Palace Indus., Inc. v. Craig, 339 S.E.2d 313 (Ga. App. 1985); Moore v. White Motor Credit Corp., 708 S.W.2d 465 (Tex. App. 1985); Rick Furniture Distrib. Co. v. Kirlin, 634 S.W.2d 738 (Tex. App. 1982); Nationwide Fin. Corp. v. English, 604 S.W.2d 458 (Tex. Ct. App. 1980). *See also* Missouri-Kansas-Texas Railroad Co. v. Fiberglass Insulators, 707 S.W.2d 943 (Tex. App. 1986) (testimony of one lender witness about interest sought did not constitute "charging" when pleadings did not state a usurious rate). *But cf.* George A. Fuller Co. v. Carpet Serv., Inc., 823 S.W.2d 603 (Tex. 1992). *See* § 10.5.4.2, *infra.*
227 *See* GMAC v. Uresti, 553 S.W.2d 660 (Tex. Ct. App. 1977).
228 *See* Greeley Nat'l Bank v. Sloan, 677 P.2d 409 (Colo. Ct. App. 1983); Northwestern Bank v. Barber, 339 S.E.2d 452 (N.C. Ct. App. 1986). *Compare* Carter v. First Fed. Sav. & Loan Ass'n of Atlanta, 347 S.E.2d 264 (Ga. App. 1986) (statute violated despite amendment of amount sought). *See also* Gergora v. Goldstein Professional Ass'n, 500 So. 2d 695 (Fla. Dist. Ct. App. 1987) (lender dismissed action claiming usurious interest; sent letter reducing note rate to legal rate, then refiled lawsuit; this complied with state's statutory "purge" provision).

vent the usury law.[229] Because defaults on consumer credit are rarely contested, such a rule allows a creditor to charge and collect unearned interest as a general policy, amending its complaint and providing proper rebates only in the rare instances when it is challenged.[230] It thus keeps the illegal gains and completely avoids any sanction in the majority of cases where it is not caught.

5.7.3 Special Issues Regarding Remedies for Violation of the Federal Rebate Statute

The federal rebate statute does not include any provisions for a specific remedy in the event a creditor violates it. Its codification in the midst of a statute of which it is not officially a part creates confusion as to applicable remedies, just as it creates confusion as to definitions.[231] Nonetheless, there are several viable theories which the consumer can assert in the event a creditor violates the statute.

Truth in Lending: Given its location, the immediate thought would be to look to Truth in Lending Act remedies. However, irrespective of whether it is considered part of TIL or not, a violation of the federal rebate statute probably does *not directly* lead to a viable claim for private TIL remedies.[232] But equally irrespective of whether it is part of TIL or not, a violation may lead *indirectly* to a TIL violation. In the event the creditor[233] refinances its own loan (or a holder or servicer refinances a loan it is holding or servicing),[234] and calculates the prior loan's payoff in violation of the statute—either by failing to give rebates or by using the Rule of 78 when the actuarial method is required—the new loan will include an "unearned portion of the old finance charge that is not credited to the obligation."[235] Under TIL

rules, that is to be considered part of the finance charge in the new loan.[236] Thus, the disclosed amount financed, finance charge, and APR on the new loan all will be inaccurately disclosed,[237] and those violations, in turn, lead to TIL statutory damages as well as actual damages.[238]

UDAP: Failure to comply with the rebate law should also state a UDAP claim, where the transaction and lender are subject to the statute: the amount of the improperly calculated rebate would be actual damages.[239] The mere presence of a contract clause which indicates no rebate would be made, or that the Rule of 78 would be used in violation of the statute, might be considered a UDAP violation even if never invoked.[240]

Contract law: Common law contract principles may also be invoked to seek a remedy, as applicable law is an implied term of every contract.[241]

5.8 Prepayment Penalties

5.8.1 General

In its simplest form, a prepayment penalty is a fee that a borrower is contractually obligated to pay if he or she chooses to pay off a debt prior to its scheduled retirement date. The justification for such a fee is that the creditor has lost the profit which it would have made from the contract after the prepayment.[242] In truth, such a loss exists only when interest rates have declined since the execution of the

---

229 *See* Thomas v. Universal Guardian Corp., 243 S.E.2d 101, 102 (Ga. Ct. App. 1978); Nationwide Fin. Corp. v. English, 604 S.W.2d 458 (Tex. Ct. App. 1980). *Cf.* Danziger v. San Jacinto Savings Ass'n, 732 S.W.2d 300 (Tex. 1987) (once usurious sum is charged, usury cannot be cured by rebate of excess charges to debtor's account).

230 *See* Matter of Sprouse, 577 F.2d 989 (5th Cir. 1978) (discussing effect of overreaching contract language on consumers in transactions which are not litigated).

231 § 5.5.2.2.3, *supra*.

232 Civil liability applies to violations of Parts B, D and E of TIL. 15 U.S.C. § 1640. The rebate statute was codified in Part A, 15 U.S.C. § 1615.

233 The rebate statute defines creditor by reference to TIL's definition, but specifically includes assignees as creditors, as well. 15 U.S.C. § 1615(d).

234 Federal Reserve Board, Official Staff Commentary on Regulation Z, § 226.20(a)-5.

235 Reg. Z, 12 C.F.R. § 226.20(a). *See, e.g.,* Steele v. Ford Motor Credit Co., 783 F.2d 1016 (11th Cir. 1986). *See generally* National Consumer Law Center, Truth in Lending § 3.7.2.2.3 (5th ed. 2003 and Supp.). Note that this would also be the case when a creditor used the rule in violation of any other applicable statute. *See* Steele, *supra*.

236 Reg. Z, 12 C.F.R. § 226.20(a).

237 That assumes, of course, that the creditor included the full payoff balance of the prior loan in the amount financed on the new loan. It is unlikely that a creditor would go to the trouble of separating out an illegal overcharge to properly account for it in its TIL calculations.

Even if it did so, arguably there is still a TIL violation. TIL requires that disclosures reflect the legal obligation, Reg. Z, 12 C.F.R. § 226.17(c). At least with respect to the finance charge, the legal obligation is to pay charges in accord with applicable law. Applicable law says that the consumer should not have to pay the excess charge at all, irrespective of whether denominated finance charge or amount financed, thus all the financial disclosures would be skewed, because the total loan should be less. *See In re* Brown, 134 B.R. 134 (Bankr. E.D. Pa. 1991); National Consumer Law Center, Truth in Lending § 4.4.1 (5th ed. 2003 and Supp.).

238 15 U.S.C. § 1640; National Consumer Law Center, Truth in Lending §§ 8.5, 8.6 (5th ed. 2003 and Supp.).

239 For a discussion of scope issues under UDAP statutes, see National Consumer Law Center, Unfair and Deceptive Acts and Practices § 2.2, 2.3 (5th ed. 2001 and Supp.). For a discussion of UDAP damages, see *id.* Ch. 8.

240 *Id.* § 7.5.2; Leardi v. Brown, 474 N.E.2d 1094 (Mass. 1985). *Cf.* § 5.7.2, *supra*, on contract provisions calling for payment of illegal charges upon prepayment triggering usury remedies.

241 17A Am. Jur. 2d, Contracts § 371 (2004).

242 *See, e.g.,* Norwest Bank v. Blair Road Assocs., 252 F. Supp. 2d 86, 97 (D.N.J. 2003); Affiliated Capital v. Commercial Fed. Bank, 834 S.W.2d 521 (Tex. App. 1992).

credit contract, so that the creditor cannot re-lend its funds to a new borrower at the same rate that it was previously receiving. In times of rising rates, the lender can actually re-lend the funds more profitably.

Subprime lenders frequently include prepayment penalties in their loan contracts. While less than 2% of prime mortgages contain prepayment penalties, up to 80% of subprime mortgages do, leading to increased foreclosure risk.[243] Some home equity lenders have imposed prepayment penalties of as high as six months' interest, which can be thousands of dollars. Borrowers who wished to refinance their high rate debt at market rates would be held captive by these stiff prepayment penalties. In the most extreme forms, some fringe lenders' contracts have authorized such penalties even when the lender accelerates the loan and forecloses, or when the lender refinances, to inflate that portion of the new loan that consists of the prior loan's pay off. Thus such penalties are one of the favored tools of the equity-skimmers,[244] and were ultimately limited by Congress in certain high-cost loans.[245]

In the absence of statute or contract authorization, common law may prohibit prepayment of a debt.[246] However, in the consumer credit context, most state laws require that borrowers be allowed to prepay their debts and often limit or prohibit prepayment penalties.[247] (And prohibiting prepay-

ment is itself a prepayment penalty, so lenders cannot circumvent such limitations by that artifice.[248]) Such statutory provisions are usually closely associated with the state's rebate requirements because the failure to provide a proper rebate upon the prepayment of a precomputed debt is essentially a form of prepayment penalty.[249] In general, rebate issues, whenever they arise in connection with the prepayment of a debt, can be framed as questions of prepayment penalties. For example, where not specifically authorized, creditors' use of the Rule of 78 to calculate rebates upon prepayment may be challenged as an illegal prepayment penalty.[250]

---

243 John Farris and Christopher Richardson, *Geography of Subprime Mortgage Prepayment Penalty Patterns*, Housing Policy Debate vol. 15 no. 3 (2004) at 688; Roberto G. Quercia, Michael A. Stegman, and Walter R. Davis, *The Impact of Predatory Loan Terms on Subprime Foreclosures: The Special Case of Prepayment Penalties and Balloon Payments* (Jan. 25, 2005) at 7 (*available at* www.kenan-flagler.unc.edu/assets/documents/foreclosurepaper.pdf).

244 *See* Office of Thrift Supervision, Final Rule, 67 Fed. Reg. 60542, 60548 (Sept. 26, 2002) ("High penalties that are repeatedly financed into the cost of successive loans may be used by lenders to strip borrowers' equity in the home"); John Farris and Christopher Richardson, *Geography of Subprime Mortgage Prepayment Penalty Patterns*, Housing Policy Debate vol. 15 no. 3 (2004) at 688 ("these penalties may be used in the subprime market to extract rents from homeowners by stripping the equity from their homes").

245 §§ 5.2.5, *supra*, 5.8.2, *infra*.

246 *See, e.g.*, Norwest Bank v. Blair Road Assocs., 252 F. Supp. 2d 86, 97 (D.N.J. 2003); MONY Life Ins. Co. v. Paramus Parkway Bldg., Ltd., 834 A.2d 475 (N.J. Super. Ct. App. Div. 2003) (commercial loan); Westmark Commercial Mortgage Fund IV v. Teenform Assocs., 827 A.2d 1154 (N.J. Super. Ct. App. Div. 2003) (commercial loan); C.C. Port, Ltd. v. Davis-Penn Mortgage Co., 61 F.3d 288 (5th Cir. 1995) (Texas law); Metropolitan Life Ins. Co. v. Strnad, 876 P.2d 1362 (Kan. 1994).

247 *See, e.g.*, Del. Code tit. 6, § 4322 (RISA: right to prepay and receive rebate of unearned interest); Md. Code Ann. Com. Law § 12-308 (Consumer Loan Law: same); Miss. Code § 63-19-47 (MVRISA: same); Garver v. Brace, 55 Cal. Rptr. 2d 220 (App. 1996) (prohibitions and limitations in Cal. Civil Code § 2954.9(b) against prepayment penalty in mortgages on owner-occupied residential real property include the situation where the borrower builds a home on the property after the loan is executed but before the prepayment fee is paid). *See also* Nelson

v. Associates Fin. Servs. Co., 659 N.W.2d 635 (Mich. Ct. App. 2002) (construing Mich. Comp. Laws §§ 438.31 and 438.31c to place cap on prepayment penalties for certain deregulated first mortgage loans). *But cf. In re* Curtis, 83 B.R. 853 (Bankr. S.D. Ga. 1988) (Ga. Code Ann. § 7-4-2 prohibits prepayment penalties only in absence of contractual agreement for one; court validated express provision for prepayment penalty of 3 years' interest); Glukowsky v. Equity One, Inc., 848 A.2d 747 (N.J. 2004) (former OTS regulation preempting state prepayment penalty laws was within OTS's authority and allowed credit to charge prepayment penalty despite state law prohibition); George v. Fowler, 978 P.2d 565 (Wash. Ct. App. 1999) (clause prohibiting prepayment is valid in absence of legislative ban on such clauses).

248 *See, e.g.*, Naumburg v. Pattison, 711 P.2d 1387 (N.M. 1985) (prohibition of prepayment is, in itself, a prepayment penalty); Grosedlose v. Rum, 860 S.W.2d 554 (Tex. App. 1993); *cf.* McCausland v. Bankers Life Ins. Co., 757 P.2d 941 (Wash. 1988) (upholding prohibition of prepayment clause in commercial case but suggesting it might be unenforceable in consumer case). *But see* Prudential Ins. Co. v. Rand & Reed Powers P'ship, 972 F. Supp. 1194 (N.D. Iowa 1997) ("no prepayment" clause is not a prepayment penalty, so not prohibited; case involved commercial transaction), *aff'd*, 141 F.3d 834 (8th Cir. 1998). *But cf.* Carey v. Lincoln Loan Co., 998 P.2d 724 (Or. App. 2000) (statute prohibiting restrictions on prepayment of loans did not apply to installment land sale contract).

249 Even if the statute does not spell out the right to prepay, that right is implicit in any statute which requires a rebate upon prepayment.

250 *See In re* Jungkurth, 74 B.R. 323 (Bankr. E.D. Pa. 1987) (failure to provide a fair rebate constitutes prepayment penalty; court orders actuarial rebate; *In re* Tucker, 74 B.R. 923 (Bankr. E.D. Pa. 1987) (absent specific statutory authorization for Rule of 78, use of any rebate formula other than the Rule of 78 would be a prepayment penalty, and thus usurious; controlling statute at issue did authorize the Rule); *In re* Jones, 79 B.R. 233 (Bankr. E.D. Pa. 1987). *See also* Livingston v. Vanguard Fed. Sav. Bank, 563 A.2d 175 (Pa. Super. Ct. 1989) (challenging use of Rule of 78 as contravening state statute prohibiting prepayment penalties in mobile home contracts; case decided on other grounds). *Cf.* Prabel v. Commissioner, 882 F.2d 820, 827 (3d Cir. 1989) (court notes that in event of prepayment, the difference between the economic accrual of interest owed and that owed under the Rule of 78 "should be considered a prepayment penalty." IRS case); Kedziora v. Citicorp Nat'l Servs., 780 F. Supp. 516 (N.D. Ill. 1991) (discussing Rule of 78 as method of determining early termination penalty in auto lease under Consumer Leasing Act). *But see* Ortegel v. ITT Thorp Corp., 569 N.E.2d 586 (Ill. App. Ct. 1991) (use of Rule of 78 was not a prepayment penalty.

Similarly, the failure to rebate points upon prepayment may be viewed as a prepayment penalty.[251] Finally, as with the collection of unearned finance charges, the assessment of a prepayment penalty will only be viewed as the collection of usurious interest if the practice is specifically prohibited by state or federal law, because the payment will otherwise be seen as contingent upon the voluntary choice of the borrower to prepay the debt, and courts generally refuse to find usury in contingencies.[252]

Despite these similarities, it would be a mistake to regard rebate requirements and prepayment penalty prohibitions as interchangeable. The most obvious difference is that statutes prohibiting prepayment penalties typically are invoked when debt is retired through voluntary prepayment,[253] while rebate requirements apply to precomputed debt regardless of whether it is prepaid, accelerated, or otherwise matured.[254] As one court viewed it, a statutory Rule of 78 rebate authorization deals with the calculation of unearned interest, while a prepayment penalty prohibition forbids imposing a separate charge or penalty "simply for the privilege of prepaying."[255] Another court distinguished between voluntary prepayment and acceleration to decide whether the Rule of 78 could be used by a creditor upon acceleration when the contract clause in the loan regarding acceleration was silent as to the method of rebate but the clause regarding prepayment allowed the rebate to be computed using the Rule of 78.[256] The court held that the contract was ambiguous, would be construed against the maker, and therefore, the use of the Rule of 78 was prohibited.[257]

Note: the precedential value of this case should be limited, as the court's analysis suggests it was confused as to the nature of the problem, e.g., " . . . the borrower must pay the interest even if the loan is not prepaid," and "plaintiffs would have paid [interest charges] regardless of early payment." *Id.* at 590, 588 respectively. That begs the question, which is the 78 penalty upon prepayment. *See* §§ 5.5.1, 5.6.3.3, *supra*).

Early Truth in Lending cases discussed the issue of whether the Rule was a prepayment penalty which should have been disclosed as such under TILA. *Compare* Bone v. Hibernia Bank, 493 F.2d 135 (9th Cir. 1974) *and* Drennan v. Security Pacific Nat'l Bank, 28 Cal. 3d 764, 621 P.2d 1318, 170 Cal. Rptr. 904 (1981), *cert. denied*, 454 U.S. 833 (1981) (no TILA violation) *with* Ballew v. Associates Fin. Servs. Co. of Neb., 450 F. Supp. 253 (D. Neb. 1976) (TILA violation). *See* Kedziora v. Citicorp Nat'l Servs., 780 F. Supp. 516 (N.D. Ill. 1991) for a discussion and criticism of the TIL treatment of the Rule as a prepayment penalty.]

The new federal legislation regulating certain high-cost home equity loans specifically labels any rebate method less favorable than the actuarial method a prepayment penalty. *See* § 5.8.2, *infra*.

Where challenging the Rule as a prepayment penalty or as a UDAP violation, advocates may wish to obtain "78's Method Handbook," Financial Publishing Co., 82 Brookline Ave., Boston, MA 02215 (1984). While it is currently out of print, it may still be available in libraries. This volume enables the advocate to pinpoint the effective interest rate obtained by the lender when a 78 rebate is calculated. Additionally, the advocate may compare for the court the dollar amount difference between a Rule of 78 rebate and an actuarial rebate. §§ 5.6.3.3, 5.6.3.4, *supra*. Concretely identifying the amount of the overcharge may bolster the argument. *See, e.g., In re* Milbourne, 108 B.R. 522 (Bankr. E.D. Pa. 1989). These calculations can also be performed using the programs on the companion CD-Rom to this volume.

251 *Cf.* § 5.5.2.2, *supra*. An alternative to challenging excessive, nonrefundable points is unconscionability. *See generally* § 12.7, *infra* for a discussion of unconscionability.

252 *See* Lederman Enters., Inc. v. Westinghouse Credit Corp., 347 F. Supp. 1291 (D. Colo. 1972); Winkle v. Grand Nat'l Bank, 601 S.W.2d 559 (Ark. 1980), *cert. denied*, 449 U.S. 880 (1980); B.F. Saul Co. v. West End Park North, Inc., 250 Md. 707, 246 A.2d 591 (1968); Affiliated Capital v. Commercial Fed. Bank, 834 S.W.2d 521 (Tex. App. 1992) (prepayment penalty could be applied upon acceleration where note so provided; subject to application of spreading doctrine and savings clause, so not usurious [commercial loan]); Boyd v. Life Ins. Co. of the Southwest, 546 S.W.2d 132 (Tex. Civ. App. 1977). *Cf.* C.C. Port, Ltd. v. Davis-Penn Mortgage Co., 61 F.3d 288 (5th Cir. 1995) (Texas law) (prepayment premium is charge for option of prepayment, not interest; commercial case). *Compare* Texas Airfinance Corp. v. Lesikar, 777 S.W.2d 559 (Tex. App. 1989) (prepayment penalty is not interest and therefore cannot be usurious, but is unenforceable with acceleration because borrower is not seeking privilege of early payment). *See* § 5.7.1, *supra*.

253 *See In re* LHD Realty Corp., 726 F.2d 327 (7th Cir. 1984) ; *In re* Planvest Equity Income Partners IV, 94 B.R. 644 (Bankr. D. Ariz. 1988) (prepayment penalty not allowed upon liquidation or acceleration); Broadway Bank v. Star Hospitality, Inc., 2004 WL 2677658 (Iowa App. Nov. 24, 2004) (prepayment penalty not available when lender accelerates debt). *Cf. In re* Imperial Coronado Partners, Ltd., 96 B.R. 997 (B.A.P. 9th Cir. 1989) (prepayment penalty not available where creditor accelerates, but if borrower opted to sell the property and pay off the loan after acceleration instead of exercising right of reinstatement under state law or deacceleration under bankruptcy, prepayment was voluntary and penalty could be collected [due-on-sale clause not an issue]); LaSalle Bank v. Mobile Hotel Props., LLC, 2004 WL 2020084 (E.D. La. Sept. 7, 2004) (lender not entitled to collect prepayment fee upon acceleration unless contract explicitly provides). *But see* Financial Center Assocs. v. TNE Funding Corp. (*In re* Financial Center Assocs.), 140 B.R. 829 (Bankr. E.D.N.Y. 1992) (prepayment penalty may be charged upon acceleration if note so provides); Westmark Commercial Mortgage Fund IV v. Teenform Assocs., 827 A.2d 1154 (N.J. Super. Ct. App. Div. 2003) (prepayment penalty is available upon acceleration of commercial loan unless it is unreasonable).

254 The existence of a statute requiring rebates upon prepayment, in the absence of a statute compelling rebates upon default and acceleration, need not, however, be read as allowing the retention of unearned interest upon acceleration. *See* Glacier Lincoln-Mercury, Inc. v. Freeman, Consumer Cred. Guide (CCH) ¶ 99,567 (Alaska Dist. Ct. 1970).

255 Pysh v. Security Pacific Housing Serv., 610 A.2d 973 (Pa. Super. Ct. 1992) (court recognizes that use of Rule of 78 results in an early pay-off balance some $3,000 greater than actuarial method, but applicable statute specifically authorized Rule while prohibiting prepayment penalties, so court reconciled the two provisions).

256 Zwayer v. Ford Motor Credit Co., 665 N.E.2d 843 (Ill. App. 1996).

257 *Id.* at 846 (the court also noted that Illinois Motor Vehicle Resale Installment Sales Act permits the use of the Rule of 78 but does not require its use).

A second significant difference between the prohibition of prepayment penalties and rebate requirements is that rebates apply only to precomputed debt whereas statutes forbidding prepayment penalties usually encompass interest-bearing transactions, such as the typical mortgage. As a result, a lender's failure to rebate points or other prepaid finance charges on nominally interest-bearing debt may be better attacked as a prepayment penalty, (assuming that the debt is retired through prepayment) than as a rebate violation.

Prepayment penalties may be challenged on contract, fraud, or UDAP grounds.[258] Courts may find an unreasonable prepayment charge to be a liquidated damages clause that is unenforceable as a penalty.[259] In the bankruptcy context, where a claim is oversecured, the bankruptcy court may disallow a prepayment penalty if it is unreasonable.[260]

Another issue that may arise at the time of prepayment is the lender's exaction of "junk fees" as a condition of disclosing or accepting the prepayment. The lender is in a position to impose such fees because the debtor, especially when selling a home, may be under time pressure that prevents negotiation about questionable fees. State law[261] or the parties' contract[262] may restrict such fees. Even if no specific state statute outlaws a fee, it may be a UDAP violation to require the debtor to pay a fee for a service that the lender does not actually perform.[263] Courts have, however, declined to characterize fees for providing payoff statements as prepayment penalties, since satisfaction of the mortgage is not conditioned upon obtaining a payoff statement.[264]

258 *Cf.* Davis v. G.N. Mortg. Corp., 2005 WL 196673 (7th Cir. 2004) (rejecting fraud, contract, and UDAP challenges on factual grounds).

259 *In re* A.J. Lane & Co. , 113 B.R. 821 (Bankr. D. Mass. 1990). *But see* Financial Center Assocs. v. TNE Funding Corp. (*In re* Financial Center Assocs.), 140 B.R. 829 (Bankr. E.D.N.Y. 1992) (prepayment penalty clause not unenforceable as a penalty because actual damages uncertain at time of contracting); *In re* A.J. Lane & Co. , 113 B.R. 821 (Bankr. D. Mass. 1990) (prepayment penalty unreasonable where it would compensate lender even if market rates rose); *In re* Kroh Bros. Development Co., 88 B.R. 997 (Bankr. W.D. Mo. 1988) (prepayment charge unenforceable as penalty where it was disproportionate to actual damages).

260 11 U.S.C. § 506(b). *See* Imperial Coronado Partners, Ltd. v. Home Fed. Sav. & Loan Ass'n, 96 B.R. 997 (B.A.P. 9th Cir. 1989) (prepayment penalty must be limited to actual damages, i.e., difference between contract rate and market rate if market rate has dropped); *In re* Bess Eaton Donut Flour Co., 2004 WL 2609266 (Bankr. D.R.I. Oct. 8, 2004) (requiring evidentiary hearing on reasonableness); Sachs Elec. Co. v. Bridge Information Sys., Inc. (*In re* Bridge Information Sys., Inc.), 288 B.R. 556 (Bankr. E.D. Mo. 2002) (claimant has burden of demonstrating reasonableness of prepayment penalty; not met here without evidence of market rates for this type of loan); *In re* Schwegmann Giant Supermarkets P'ship, 264 B.R. 823 (Bankr. E.D. La. 2001) (disallowing prepayment penalty as unreasonable where lender introduced no evidence of actual damages); *In re* Duralite Truck Body & Container Corp., 153 B.R. 708 (Bankr. D. Md. 1993) (prepayment penalty unreasonable where it presumed a loss, regardless of whether market rates had risen or fallen); *In re* A.J. Lane & Co., 113 B.R. 821 (Bankr. D. Mass. 1990) (prepayment penalty unreasonable where it would compensate lender even if market rates rose); *In re* Kroh Bros. Development Co., 88 B.R. 997 (Bankr. W.D. Mo. 1988) (prepayment penalty unreasonable where it charged debtor same amount if interest rates rose). *But cf.* Anchor Resolution Corp. v. State Street Bank & Trust Co., 221 B.R. 330 (Bankr. D. Del. 1998) (prepayment penalty was reasonable where it was measured against actual market rates); *In re* Outdoor Sports Headquarters, Inc., 161 B.R. 414 (Bankr. S.D. Ohio 1993) (allowing prepayment penalty where it was set by reference to market rates for comparable investments, so was equivalent to actual damages); Financial Center Assocs. v. TNE Funding Corp. (*In re* Financial Center Assocs.), 140 B.R. 829 (Bankr. E.D.N.Y. 1992) (prepayment penalty valid under New York law and § 506(b); actual damages include cost of finding substitute borrower, additional risk, and other factors besides interest rate difference).

261 Negrin v. Norwest Mortgage, Inc., 700 N.Y.S.2d 184 (App. Div. 1999) (state real estate law required lender to provide payoff statement at no charge; violation may be UDAP violation). *But see* Boursiquot v. Citibank F.S.B., 323 F. Supp. 2d 350 (D. Conn. 2004) (OTS regulations preempt claim that fax fee violated state law); Lopez v. World Sav. & Loan Ass'n, 105 Cal. App. 4th 729, 130 Cal. Rptr. 2d 42 (2003) (OTS regulations preempt claim that federally-chartered savings and loan association's fax fee violated state law); Moskowitz v. Washington Mut. Bank, 768 N.E.2d 262 (Ill. App. 2002) (same as *Lopez*).

262 *See* Sandlin v. Shapiro & Fishman, 919 F. Supp. 1564 (M.D. Fla. 1996) ($60 payoff fee may violate loan contract; collector's motion for summary judgment denied). *But see* Stone v. Mellon Mortg. Co., 771 So. 2d 451 (Ala. 2000) (charging fax fee did not breach contract; contract need not specify every possible charge); Colangelo v. Norwest Mortgage, Inc., 598 N.W.2d 14 (Minn. App. 1999); Stutman v. Chemical Bank, 731 N.E.2d 608 (N.Y. 2000) ($275 attorney fee for special service of attending closing and releasing mortgage simultaneously with acceptance of payoff amount was not prepayment penalty so did not violate contract); Cain v. Source One Mortg. Serv. Corp., 1999 WL 674776 (Wash. Ct. App. Aug. 30, 1999) (unpublished, citation limited) (charging fax fee did not breach lender's promise to reconvey property without charge upon payoff).

263 Negrin v. Norwest Mortgage, Inc., 700 N.Y.S.2d 184 (App. Div. 1999) (charging fee to record the satisfaction of the mortgage may be a UDAP violation where lender did not actually handle the recordation). *But see* Stutman v. Chemical Bank, 731 N.E.2d 608 (N.Y. 2000) ($275 attorney fee for special service of attending closing and releasing mortgage simultaneously with acceptance of payoff amount was not prepayment penalty so bank's promise that there would be no prepayment penalty was not deceptive). *But compare* Westfall v. Chase Lincoln Bank, 685 N.Y.S.2d 181 (App. Div. 1999) (plaintiffs' voluntary payment of inflated recording fee bars UDAP and common law claims).

264 Jerik v. Columbia Nat'l, Inc., 1999 WL 1267702 (N.D. Ill. Sept. 30, 1999) (neither $10 quote fee nor $5 fax fee is prepayment penalty); Krause v. GE Capital Mortg. Servs., Inc., 731 N.E.2d 302 (Ill. App. 2000) (fax and quote charges not prepayment penalties); Colangelo v. Norwest Mortgage, Inc., 598 N.W.2d 14 (Minn. App. 1999) (fee for faxing payoff statement not a prepayment penalty). *But cf.* Dwyer v. J. I. Kislak Mortg. Corp., 13 P.3d 240 (Wash. Ct. App. 2000) (reversal of summary judgment for lender) (inclusion of fax fees in payoff statement, which misled borrowers to believe they were required by contract before mortgage would be released, would be violation of state deceptive practices statute).

5.8.2 High-Cost Mortgages

The 1994 federal legislation enacted to curb the abuses of equity-skimming and reverse redlining in high-cost home equity lending addresses the Rule of 78 penalty and prepayment penalties as a package.[265] For most covered loans,[266] no prepayment penalties are permitted at all, and use of any method of rebate less favorable than the actuarial rule is specifically defined to constitute a prepayment penalty.[267] There is one very narrow, complex exception. A prepayment penalty, including use of the Rule of 78 to calculate rebates, may be imposed where *all* elements of a five-prong exception are met:

- As of the time of consummation, the consumer will be paying less than 50% of monthly gross income to "monthly indebtedness payments," including the payments due under the loan being consummated.[268]
- The borrower's income and expenses are verified by a financial statement signed by the consumer, by a credit report, and, in the case of employment income, by payment records or employer records.[269]
- The penalty can only be imposed where the consumer is paying off the debt with funds from sources other than the creditor or its affiliate. (In other words, a creditor cannot profit from prepayment penalties when it is refinancing its own loans.[270])
- The penalty can only be imposed during the first five years, counting from the date of consummation.[271]
- A prepayment penalty can be imposed in these circumstances only if other applicable law permits it. It is thus clear that this exemption from the federal prohibition on prepayment penalties does not preempt any state or other federal law which would prohibit such penalties in the transaction.[272] For example, the federal rebate law continues to prohibit use of the Rule of 78 in transactions with terms exceeding sixty-one months.[273]

The background of this legislation, and the issues arising under it, are discussed more fully in National Consumer Law Center, *Truth in Lending* Chapter 9,[274] and anyone evaluating a transaction subject to it should refer to that chapter.[275]

---

265 15 U.S.C. § 1639(c).
266 *See* § 12.2.2, *infra* for an explanation of the Act's scope.
267 15 U.S.C. § 1639(c)(1).
268 15 U.S.C. § 1639(c)(2)(A)(i).
269 15 U.S.C. § 1639(c)(2)(A)(ii).
270 15 U.S.C. § 1639(c)(2)(B).
271 15 U.S.C. § 1639(c)(2)(C).
272 15 U.S.C. § 1639(c)(2)(D).
273 *See* § 5.6.3.3.1, *supra*. This legislation does not alter that. *See generally* National Consumer Law Center, Truth in Lending Ch. 9 (5th ed. 2003 and Supp.).
274 (5th ed. 2003 and Supp.).
275 Chapter 11, *infra*, contains a brief overview of the legislation.

5.8.3 Prepayment Penalties for Federal Lenders

The laws of most states forbid or restrict prepayment penalties in consumer credit transactions, but borrowers' attorneys should be aware that these prohibitions have been overridden in the case of some mortgage loans.[276] Specifically, if permitted by a loan contract, state and national banks may impose prepayment penalties on adjustable-rate mortgage loans,[277] and federally-chartered savings and loan institutions (thrifts) may impose prepayment penalties on both fixed and variable rate mortgage loans.[278] It is important to note one limitation on the Office of Thrift Supervision (OTS) regulations which allow federal thrifts to assess penalties upon prepayment. The OTS forbids collection of prepayment penalties by federal thrifts when they accelerate mortgage notes pursuant to due-on-sale clauses.[279]

Up until July 1, 2003, OTS allowed "housing creditors," defined as non-depository lenders who regularly make loans or credit sales secured by residential realty or mobile homes, to impose prepayment penalties in loans that fell under the Alternative Mortgage Transactions Parity Act.[280] Effective July 1, 2003, however, OTS amended its rules to delete the

---

276 For a general discussion of federal preemption of mortgage loan limitations, see §§ 3.4–3.12, *supra*. Note, however, that federal preemption of usury ceilings on first mortgage loans under § 501 of DIDA does not preempt state limitations on prepayment charges. 12 C.F.R. § 590.3(c). *See also* S. Rep. No. 368, 96th Cong. 2d Sess. 19 *reprinted in* 1980 U.S.C.C.A.N. 236, 255.
277 *See* 12 C.F.R. §§ 34.23, 34.24 (regulations of the Comptroller of the Currency) [*reprinted in* Appx. C.2, *infra*].
278 12 C.F.R. § 560.34. Prepayment penalties must be disclosed under 12 C.F.R. § 560.210 [reprinted at Appx. H.2, *infra*].
279 12 C.F.R. § 591.5 (1994) [*reprinted in* Appx. D.2, *infra*]. *See also* § 3.12, *supra*.
280 See description of former 12 C.F.R. § 560.220 in 67 Fed. Reg. 60542 (Sept. 26, 2002). It allowed "housing creditors" to make alternative mortgage transactions, which under former 12 C.F.R. § 560.34 could include prepayment penalties. *See* McCarthy v. Option One Mortg. Corp., 362 F.3d 1008 (7th Cir. 2004) (finding lender was a state housing creditor and complied with OTS regulations, so former version of OTS regulation preempted state restrictions on prepayment penalties); National Home Equity Mortg. Assn. v. Face, 239 F.3d 633 (4th Cir. 2001); McCarthy v. Option One Mortg. Corp., 2001 U.S. Dist. LEXIS 22711 (N.D. Ill. Feb. 11, 2001) (non-federally-chartered housing creditor can charge prepayment penalty, but only if it complies with OTS regulations); Shinn v. Encore Mortg. Servs., 96 F. Supp. 2d 419 (D.N.J. 2000) (housing creditor that complied with OTS regulations could charge prepayment penalty notwithstanding state law restrictions); Glukowsky v. Equity One, Inc., 848 A.2d 747 (N.J. 2004) (former OTS regulation preempting state prepayment penalty laws was within OTS's authority and allowed credit to charge prepayment penalty despite state law prohibition). *See also* § 3.10.2, *supra*, regarding changes to the AMPTA regulations that revive state law restrictions on prepayment penalties in the mortgage loan context.

authorization for these lenders to impose fees for prepayment.[281] As a result, these creditors are subject to any state restrictions on prepayment penalties.

Federal credit unions are specifically prohibited from receiving prepayment penalties,[282] as are any lenders making FHA-insured mortgage loans.[283] Further, the 1994 federal law regulating high-cost mortgages[284] is the controlling law on mortgages within its scope, irrespective of whether these preemption laws would otherwise permit it. Under rules of statutory construction, the high-cost mortgage legislation is the more specific, and more recent, and therefore would control.[285]

Generally, due-on-sale clauses permit lenders, upon the sale of a mortgaged property, to refuse to permit the purchasers to assume the outstanding mortgage, and instead allow the lender to accelerate the debt, requiring full payment of the mortgage at the time of sale. State laws prohibiting the enforcement of due-on-sale clauses were preempted by federal law in order to assist lenders, especially S&Ls, which were being placed in serious financial difficulty by the combination of rising interest rates and existing portfolios of long-term, low-interest mortgage loans during the late 1970s and early 1980s.[286] Unfortunately, many lenders were not content merely to improve their loan portfolios by forcing borrowers to prepay their mortgages at the time of resale, and many of these lenders simultaneously invoked the prepayment penalty clauses of the old mortgages, thereby not only forcing borrowers to prepay the mortgages upon the sale of the mortgaged property, but also compelling them to pay for the privilege.[287]

The OTS's predecessor, the FHLBB,[288] issued regulations prohibiting the imposition of prepayment penalties whenever the lender actually accelerated a mortgage pursuant to a due-on-sale clause.[289] However, many lenders evaded this regulation by dragging their feet when borrowers were attempting to close on the sale of the mortgaged property. By refusing to act on the borrower's application to allow the purchaser to assume the existing mortgage, lenders were able to force purchasers to seek a new mortgage, and thus, were able to compel prepayment without actually accelerating the old note.

To address this problem, the FHLBB amended its regulations, effective December 13, 1985,[290] so that a lender is deemed to have exercised a due-on-sale clause if it fails to act on the borrower's application within 30 days.[291] If the borrower voluntarily prepays the loan, however, even in anticipation of the sale of the mortgaged property, prepayment penalties may still be imposed.[292] Borrowers' attorneys should make sure that applications requesting permission for the purchasers' assumption of the mortgage are filed with the bank more than thirty days prior to closing, thus forcing lenders to permit the assumption or to call in the old mortgage.

5.9 Preemptive Effect of the New Federal Consumer Protection Statutes

The early 1980s saw federal law, directed at protecting financial institutions, preempting consumer protections under many state laws.[293] But, as often happens, the pendulum swings, and the early 1990s saw new federal consumer protection laws, aimed at curbing some of the abuses of deregulation. In some cases, the federal rebate statute[294] and the high-cost mortgage statute[295] will provide greater protections to borrowers than they would otherwise have under

281 12 C.F.R. § 560.220 [*reprinted in* Appx. H.2, *infra*] (as amended by 67 Fed. Reg. 60542 (Sept. 26, 2002)); *see* National Home Equity Mortgage Ass'n v. Office of Thrift Supervision, 373 F.3d 1355 (D.C. Cir. 2004) (upholding amended regulation as within discretion of OTS); § 3.12, *supra*.
282 *See* 12 C.F.R. § 701.21(c)(6) [*reprinted in* Appx. E.2, *infra*].
283 *See* 24 C.F.R. §§ 201.17, 203.22(b).
284 § 5.8.2, *supra*.
285 Williams v. Gelt Fin. Corp., (*In re* Williams), 232 B.R. 629 (Bankr. E.D. Pa. 1999), *aff'd* 237 B.R. 590 (E.D. Pa. 1999); Singer, Sutherland Statutory Construction ¶ 51.02 (6th ed. 2000). The HOEPA restriction is clearly intended to prohibit prepayment penalties that are not prohibited by other law. Otherwise, when listing the circumstances in which a prepayment penalty is allowed, the statute would not have had to list four other criteria besides not being prohibited by other law. 15 U.S.C. § 1639(c)(2)(A)–(E).
286 *See* Fidelity Fed. Savings & Loan Ass'n v. de la Cuesta, 458 U.S. 141, 102 S. Ct. 3014, 73 L. Ed. 2d 664 (1982). This ruling was reinforced and extended by Congress with the passage of the Depository Institutions Act, Pub. L. No. 97-320. *See* the discussion in § 3.10, *supra*. In the absence of federal preemption, many state courts had narrowly interpreted due on sale clauses. *See, e.g.,* Snow v. Western Savings & Loan Ass'n, 730 P.2d 204 (Ariz. 1986).
287 *Cf. In re* Abramoff, 92 B.R. 698 (Bankr. W.D. Tex. 1988) (a prepayment charge and a due-on-sale clause combined to create an unreasonable restraint on alienation). *See also* Tan v. California Fed. Sav. & Loan Ass'n, 189 Cal. Rptr. 775 (App. 1983)

(upholding due-on-sale clause in light of federal preemption of state restrictions, but construing ambiguous contract against lender and disallowing prepayment penalty).
288 Federal Home Loan Bank Board, which was abolished as of August 9, 1989, and its functions transferred to the OTS.
289 *See* 12 C.F.R. § 591.5.
290 If prepayment penalties imposed prior to that date are at issue, counsel for borrowers should closely examine the language of the prepayment penalty clause to see if the contract permits the imposition of these penalties when the lender accelerates the debt, forcing prepayment.
291 12 C.F.R. § 591.5(b)(3) [*reprinted in* Appx. D.2, *infra*].
292 *See* commentary at 50 Fed. Reg. 46744 (Nov. 13, 1985), *amending* 12 C.F.R. § 591.5.
293 *See* Ch. 3, *supra*.
294 15 U.S.C. § 1615 [*reprinted in* Appx. J.2, *infra*].
295 U.S.C. § 1639(c). *See* § 5.2.4, *supra*, § 12.2.2, *infra*; National Consumer Law Center, Truth in Lending Ch. 9 (5th ed. 2003 and Supp.).

state or other federal law. In other states, though, state law may still provide greater protection.

The high-cost mortgage statute is explicit about preemption. Even in the limited circumstances where a creditor is permitted to impose a prepayment penalty in a covered loan under that statute, it can only do so if otherwise applicable law also permits it.[296] Further, the new disclosure and substantive prohibitions do not affect state law "except to the extent that those State laws are inconsistent, and then only to the extent of the inconsistency,"[297] by which Congress intended "to allow states to enact more protective provisions than those in this legislation."[298]

The federal rebate statute included no specific preemption language. So, for example, if the federal rebate statute is ultimately interpreted to permit a creditor to exclude points from rebatable charges, would that preempt a state law that did not? It, too, should not preempt state laws more protective of the consumer. Consumer protection statutes are to be liberally construed to effectuate their purposes.[299] The purpose of this legislation was to assure that consumers were given rebates, and were not financially harmed by the gross distortions of the Rule of 78 in long-term loans.[300] While the odd history of the placement of the rebate statute in the code books again muddies the waters,[301] in this case the end should be the same whether TIL preemption language or general preemption principles apply.

If considered part of TILA, the federal rebate statute does not affect state laws relating to "types, amounts or rates of charges, or any element or elements of charges,"[302] except to the extent of the inconsistency. Thus state statutes which would permit a creditor to keep unearned interest are preempted, as are state statutes which would allow use of the Rule of 78 in long-term transactions, as a creditor could not do either without violating the federal act. In contrast, it is not inconsistent to protect consumers from overcharges created by skewed methods of calculating rebates.

Even absent the TIL preemption language, the more protective statutes are not preempted. Preemption may be found where language in the federal statute reveals an explicit intent to preempt state law. It may also be found where the federal statute's structure and purpose, or nonspecific statutory language, reveal an implicit preemptive intent, either because the federal regulatory scheme is so pervasive as to make it reasonable to infer Congress intended to occupy the field, or because the federal law is in irreconcilable conflict with the state law.[303] An irreconcilable conflict may be found if compliance with both the federal and the state law is physically impossible, or the state law stands as an obstacle to the accomplishment of Congress's purpose.[304]

These limited congressional forays into providing minimum standards of consumer protection cannot be reasonably assumed to occupy the field of the substantive regulation of consumer credit, particularly since credit regulation has historically been an area of state concern.[305] Finally, more protective state laws supplement, rather than conflict with, the rights given under the federal law. A creditor can comply with state statutes giving greater protection to consumers without running afoul of the federal law.[306] The federal statute thus sets the minimum consumer protection, not the maximum.

---

296   15 U.S.C. § 1639(c)(2)(D). *See* H.R. Conf. Rep. No. 652, 103d Cong., 2d Sess. 1 (1994) at 162.

297   15 U.S.C. § 1610(b).

298   H.R. Conf. Rep. No. 652, 103d Cong., 2d Sess. 1 (1994), at 162.

299   Singer, Sutherland Statutory Construction ¶ 73.1 (6th ed. 2003); *see* § 9.3.1.1, *infra*; National Consumer Law Center, Truth in Lending § 1.4.2.3 (5th ed. 2003 and Supp.).

300   *Mortgage Refinancing Reform Act of 1992: Hearings On H.R. 5170 before the House Subcommittee on Consumer, Affairs and Coinage of the Committee on Banking, Finance and Urban Affairs*, 102d Cong. 2d Sess. (May 27, 1992). The rebate provision of H.R. 5170 resurfaced as § 933 of the Housing and Community Development Act of 1992, Pub. L. No. 102-550.

301   *See* §§ 5.5.2.2.3, 5.7.3, *supra*.

302   15 U.S.C. § 1610(b). The preemption language of § 1610(a) speaks only to disclosures.

303   Barnett Bank v. Nelson, 517 U.S. 25, 31, 116 S. Ct. 1103, 134 L. Ed. 2d 237 (1996). *See* § 3.4.6.1, *supra*.

304   *Id.*

305   In contrast, for example, to foreign policy, which is the classic example of a dominant federal concern.

306   Hillsborough County v. Automated Medical Labs, 471 U.S. 707, 105 S. Ct. 2371, 85 L. Ed. 2d 714 (1985) (FDA and state health ordinances imposing more requirements can co-exist).

Chapter 6 — The Cost of Refinancing: Calculation and Legal Issues

6.1 Introduction

6.1.1 Double Their Money: The "Flipping Penalty"

6.1.1.1 Overview

Refinancing, in the right circumstances, and with the right lender, is a good deal for both parties, as demonstrated by the tremendous number of consumers who replaced the 10% to 11% purchase money mortgages written in the 1980s with 7% to 8% mortgages available when interest rates dipped to surprising lows in the early 1990s.

But refinancing is not always so mutually beneficial. It can be a trap for unwary consumers, and it is on the hidden costs which can attend refinancing from some lenders that this chapter focuses.[1] Being a repeat customer at the neighborhood finance company, for example, frequently is not quite the same thing as being a repeat customer at the neighborhood grocery store (or bank, for that matter). At the grocery store, the price of a loaf of bread marked $1.29 really is $1.29 for everybody, every time. A $1,000 loan at 30% for two years should be marked to sell for $342 in interest.[2] But a customer refinancing to borrow an extra $1,000 at 30% can pay a lot more than $342 for that extra $1,000.

That is why some segments of the industry encourage refinancing. They urge borrowers to combine medical, dental, credit card, and utility bills into a single debt for the "ease of a single monthly payment." Solicitous letters arrive regularly to existing customers asking if they would like more money.[3] But the aggressive marketing of refinancing and consolidation loans is almost inherently deceptive: they never advertise that the transaction may double the total cost of the existing debt, or that it may put the borrower's home on the line if it becomes collateral on the new loan.

These omissions might not be so serious if they were readily understood by consumers, but frequently they are not.

The effort pays off. Statistics show that over 60% of the outstanding loans issued by consumer finance lenders are refinancings of existing debt.[4] The "flipping penalty"—the added cost of borrowing which can result from refinancing—paid by consumers thus contributes to the record profits finance companies booked even during the recession of the early 1990s.[5] Borrowers, in the meantime, remain indebted for a much longer period of time than originally envisioned. Repeated refinancing of mortgage loans is a way for the lender to strip the equity out of a home.[6] Loan flipping is similar to "twisting" in the insurance industry or "churning" in the securities field.[7]

---

1 § 6.5, *infra*, discusses how to assess the benefits of a refinancing.

2 /$341.91, to be more precise. *See generally* § 4.3.1.1, *supra*.

3 *See* Emery v. American General Fin., Inc., 71 F.3d 1343 (7th Cir. 1995) for one such letter.

4 Small loan data have shown that approximately 80% percent of small loan transactions involve refinancing or consolidation of debt and 50% involve four or more consolidations. *See In re* Lowell, Clearinghouse No. 30,955 (S.D. Me. 1972) *cited in* Hunt, *The Rule of 78: Hidden Penalty For Prepayment in Consumer Credit Transactions*, 55 B.U. L. Rev. 331 (1975). *See also* Kramer & Neihengen, Jr., *Analysis of Finance Company Ratios in 1992*, 76 J. of Comm. Lending No. 1, 37 (Sept. 1993) (63% loans to present borrowers). Refinancing to existing customers has advantages beyond the profitability of the individual loan; the lender knows the borrower's habits and capabilities, so investigations are streamlined. Larger loan sizes also marginally reduce administrative costs.

5 During the 1990–1991 recession, finance companies' return on equity was 18%. In 1992, it was 19%. Kramer & Neihengen, Jr., *Analysis of Finance Company Ratios in 1992*, 76 J. of Comm. Lending No. 1, 37 (Sept. 1993), Table 1. By 1994 it had risen to 21.6%. Artz & Neihengen, Jr., *An Analysis of Finance Company Ratios in 1994*, 78 J. of Comm. Lending No. 1, 33 (Sept. 1995).

6 Office of Thrift Supervision, Final Rule, 67 Fed. Reg. 60542, 60548 (Sept. 26, 2002).

7 *Cf.* Emery v. American General Fin., Inc., 71 F.3d 1343 (7th Cir. 1995) (noting similarity to twisting); Jerry Ackerman, *Hancock Pays $1m Fine to Insurance Regulators in N.Y.: Charged with Misleading Customers to Sell Policies, Generate More Fees*, Boston Globe, Jan. 4, 1996, at 50. The parallels to insurance twisting are particularly apt, since loans which are frequently flipped often involve insurance packing as well. *See generally* Ch. 8, especially § 8.5.4, *infra*.

6.1.1.2 Small Loan Example

Here is a sample of how it works.[8] The consumer made a retail purchase for $747 on a "90-day same as cash" basis. The seller assigned the paper to a finance company, a common introduction to finance company borrowing. Over the course of the next six years, the consumer received approximately $6,000 from eleven separate loans. Each of the advances was a small sum, less than $1,000. Had these advances been written as eleven separate loans, giving equal value to the consumer, while allowing the lender maximum legal interest rates and prepaid finance charges, and the same credit insurance protection, the cumulative total of payments the consumer would have been obligated to pay was $6,926. In contrast, his total obligation for the series of refinanced loans was $16,000. Same benefit to the customer; comparable return and insurance protection for the lender in both cases, but over $9,000 difference in cost!

How does that happen? A variety of factors converge to create a flipping penalty, not all present in every case, but this example illustrates most of them.

The Rule of 78 Penalty: As was discussed in the preceding chapter, the pay-off balance on a loan being refinanced is artificially inflated when the Rule of 78 is used to calculate the rebate of unearned interest.[9] Both the unearned insurance premiums and unearned interest were calculated by the Rule on each of these refinancings.

To add insult to injury, this series of loans illustrates one of the glosses on the Rule, double-dipping. Recall that the Rule does not use fractional time intervals.[10] So, for example, when one loan with a due date on the first of the month was refinanced on April 6, the lender rounded forward to the May 1 due date. By virtue of the Rule, the lender "earned" interest and calculated it into the old loan's pay-off balance (at 25.8%) for 24 days *after* it was paid off. At the same time, it also charged interest on the old-loan portion of the new loan principal (at 25.8%) for the same 24 days.[11]

Service Charges: Pennsylvania's consumer discount law permits a service charge of $1 per $50 of the loan.[12] Obviously, as the total obligation grows, the amount of that fee grows. With the unflipped loan series, the service charge never gets above $20 per loan, since no individual loan exceeds $1,000. With the series of flipped loans, the service charge reaches a $100 statutory cap half-way through the flipping sequence and stays there. As written, the consumer was charged $944.79 in service charges. Without flipping, the total of eleven maximum allowable service charges would have been $138.50. These prepaid finance charges are useful to the creditor in two ways other than their face value: the interest clock gets to tick on them;[13] and they are considered "earned" at consummation, so they generally are not subject to any rebate requirement when the next refinancing occurs.[14]

Credit Insurance: Like the service charges, credit insurance is calculated on the total of payments, so burgeoning loans make for bigger premiums, which in turn, further bloat the loans.[15] Credit life insurance protection for the parties cost $374.26 in the refinanced series, ten times more than equally full protection in an unflipped series ($34.62).[16]

Stretching the Loan Term: Since interest and credit insurance premiums are time-sensitive components of the cost of credit, the longer the loan term, the higher both those figures are. In Pennsylvania, which authorizes a 9.5% discount rate ceiling for these loans, the problem is exacerbated by the nature of discount interest. Recall from Chapter 4, *supra*[17] that discount interest is deducted in advance, so the longer the term, the greater the amount deducted, and the higher the effective yield to the creditor.[18]

The initial $817 loan started at 36 months, for which the equivalent yield is 23.27%. The first seven loans were for 36 months, and the last four were for 48 months, a period which has an equivalent yield of 25.8%. Since these advances were all for less than $1,000, there was no reason to write

---

8   This example is taken from a Pennsylvania legal services' client's experience with a nationally known finance company. The case was settled (NCLC files).

9   *See* §§ 5.5.1, 5.6.3.3, *supra*.

10 *See* §§ 5.6.2, 5.6.3.3.2, *supra*.

11 When a refinancing occurs late in the monthly cycle, this "double dipping" effect is minimized, but several of these loans seemed to happen early in the cycle. Pennsylvania state law requires that credit insurance premium rebates be rounded to the nearest due date, but has no such requirement for interest rebates.

12 The allowable service charge under Pennsylvania law was increased in 1998 to $1.50 for every $50, with a maximum of $150, so this analysis understates the costs if refinancing occurred after 1998.

13 For Truth in Lending purposes, they are considered a finance charge and are considered in calculating the TIL-APR. But authorized points, service charges and the like are generally permitted to be included in the loan principal for usury purposes under state law, so the note interest rate is applied to that amount. *See generally* § 7.2.1–7.2.2, *infra*.

14 *See* §§ 5.4.1, 5.5.2, *supra*. *See also* § 6.4.1.3, *infra*.

15 *See* Ch. 8, *infra*. As is the case with many of the national finance companies, this one sells the insurance products of its own insurance affiliates, thus further bolstering corporate profits on each loan.

16 The problem is even worse when disability, unemployment and property insurance are also packed into a loan. *See* § 8.5.4, *infra*.

17 *See* § 4.3.3, *supra*.

18 "In general, the longer the term, the higher the annual percentage rate," an effect which becomes more pronounced as the term increases. A 10% discount loan for 10 years means the borrower receives nothing and pays it off for 10 years. The Cost of Personal Borrowing, 6–7 (Financial Publishing Co.). This publication charts the APR equivalents of discount rates for various terms. A 9.5% discount rate equals:
>   18.84% APR at 12 months
>   21.11% APR at 24 months
>   23.27% APR at 36 months
>   25.80% APR at 48 months
>   *Id.* at T132–133.

36-month loans.[19] A 12-month loan term would be more appropriate. The yield on a 12-month 9.5% discount loan is "only" 18.84%—a full 4 1/2% lower than writing the same loan for 36 months, and 7% lower than writing it for 48 months.

Along with lower effective interest rates, the principal to which those rates are applied is also lower when not inflated by the repeated flippings. Hence the dramatic savings between writing eleven separate 9.5% discount loans and writing eleven flipped 9.5% discount loans.

The following chart summarizes the way the cost of the $1.29 loaf of credit rises beyond its price tag.[20]

	11 no-flip, no-stretch loans	11 flipped & stretched loans (as written)
Proceeds to Borrower (including debt consolidation)	$6,094.88	$ 5,977.61
Credit Life Premium ($ .50/$100)	$ 34.62	$ 1,117.30 Charged – 743.04 Rebates Made* ———— $ 374.26
Service Charge/Prepaid Finance Charge ($1/$50)	$ 138.50	$ 944.79
Interest (Max. 9.5% discount)	$ 657.56	$18,533.69 Charged –12,464.79 Rebates Made* ———— $ 6,068.90
Cumulative Total of Payments	$6,925.56	$ 7,440 ** + 8,561*** ———— $16,001

Total Besta/Milbourne[21] Penalty = $9,075.44
($16,001.00 − $6,925.56)

*According to creditors accounting records
**The total obligation on the final loan to maturity
***The sum of all payments made on loans 1 to 10, prior to the time each was refinanced, according to creditor's accounting

6.1.1.3 Equity-Skimmers and the Flipping Penalty

The hidden surcharge on refinancings is often accompanied by increased risk for the borrower, as there may be a simultaneous attempt by the lender to obtain real estate security. Thus a borrower who refinances an unsecured small loan or who obtains a consolidation loan to pay off outstanding unsecured bills may well end up giving his or her home as security for the new debt. Some of the risks in this change are obvious: if the borrower now defaults, his or her home may be lost. The addition of real estate security to a debt also changes the risks in a less conspicuous way, by permitting the lender to engage in "asset-based" lending. It may look more to the equity in the home than to the borrower's income when deciding whether to extend additional credit. If the borrower cannot meet the monthly payments on the refinanced debt from his or her current income, a cycle of default and refinancing begins which leads inexorably to a higher and higher debt and, ultimately, to the loss of the consumer's home.[22]

The smoke and mirrors growth of the debt explains why some of the equity-skimming home equity lenders are fond of refinancing.[23] Using the same kind of analysis as above for small loans, a series of just three home equity loans written over an eleven-month period imposed a $32,800 flipping penalty on one homeowner.[24]

6.1.2 Overview of Legal Issues in Refinancings

The prevalence of refinancings suggests that attorneys should make it a habit to ask consumer clients whether their current loan has replaced an earlier credit transaction. If so, it is a good idea to analyze the transaction from both a "micro and macro" perspective. The small loan example shows that there are a number of steps in making calculations and imposing charges where the creditor may have run afoul of statutory or regulatory strictures. It is on these issues that this chapter will focus, and the next section walks the reader through the calculations. But it is also important to keep the big picture in mind. Even if each separate calculation and charge is within the letter of the law, the overall picture of the transaction may violate broader fairness standards. Unconscionability, unfair and deceptive practices and fraud stan-

---

19 *Cf.* Besta v. Beneficial Loan Co., 855 F.2d 532 (8th Cir. 1988).

20 To calculate the total cost for the flipped series, the total of payments made on all the prior loans was added to the total obligation on the final loan in the series.
    Compare that with the cumulative total of payments due on the series of unflipped loans. The difference is the hidden penalty.

21 Besta v. Beneficial Loan Co., 855 F.2d 532 (8th Cir. 1988); *In re* Milbourne, 108 B.R. 522 (Bankr. E.D. Pa. 1989). *See* § 6.1.2, *infra.* For another example of the cost of repeated refinancings, see the affidavit in Appxs. L.2.4–L.2.6, *infra,* which was prepared for the consumer's counsel in Hager v. American General Fin., Inc., 37 F. Supp. 2d 778 (S.D. W. Va. 1999).

22 *See* Mansfield, *The Road to Subprime "HEL" Was Paved with Good Congressional Intentions: Usury Deregulation and the Subprime Home Equity Market,* 51 S.C. L. Rev. 473 (2000), for a discussion of equity skimming.

23 *See* § 11.5, *infra.*

24 Her total indebtedness under the three loans as actually written was over $112,000. Writing separate loans, again with comparable insurance charges and maximum allowable charges to the creditor, would have cost her $79,300 (NCLC case file).

dards have been successfully used to attack overreaching credit practices,[25] and refinancings should be assessed for the possible claims and defenses discussed in Chapter 11, *infra*, in addition to specific illegal overcharges.

This chapter first deals with the question of whether a subsequent loan cures an earlier loan of usury, or stated differently, whether an earlier usurious loan taints the subsequent loan. Following that discussion, it identifies some of the potential problems which may give rise to overcharge-related claims in the refinancing itself. Next it attempts to elucidate how to evaluate when a refinancing may be helpful, particularly as a strategy to fend off a foreclosure. Finally it examines whether a business purpose loan can become a consumer loan upon refinancing.

6.1.3 Refinancing, Consolidation and Flipping Defined

This chapter applies to credit transactions, primarily between parties with an existing debtor-creditor relationship, in which one or more pre-existing credit obligations are replaced by new debt. (The calculation issues, however, are the same irrespective of whether the same creditor refinances the earlier debt.) At the outset, it may be helpful to define some of the terms which are used to describe different kinds of credit renewals. While "refinancing" is seldom statutorily defined, it means to "finance something new," usually after a renegotiation of credit terms.[26] On paper, a "refinancing" is a new loan, generally between an existing creditor and debtor, the proceeds of which are used to pay off the pre-existing debt.

"Consolidation" converts several debts into one new debt. The greatest abuse of consolidation occurs when several short-term, low-interest loans are consolidated into one very expensive loan, secured by the equity in the borrower's home. Consolidation may also occur when a pre-existing debt with the same lender is refinanced and a new advance is made. Whether the amount of a new advance is sufficient to change its character as refinanced debt may be important, for there are instances in which there are limits on the charges which can be imposed on a refinanced loan.[27]

The term "flipping" may be used to describe refinancing in general, though it is sometimes used more restrictively to describe situations in which new credit is extended at a higher rate than the refinanced credit. This chapter generally uses the former, broader meaning.

In examining a refinanced or consolidation loan, a practitioner must look for overcharges in the same manner as examining an original loan. However, unlike an original loan, the analysis cannot stop there; the credit agreements being refinanced or consolidated must also be examined, for the earlier loans themselves may give rise to a usury claim, tainting any subsequent loan. Additionally, the subsequent loan also may exceed applicable cost limitations if the outstanding balance from the earlier loan was improperly calculated, or if improper finance charges are imposed on the pre-existing balance.[28]

6.2 Usurious Taint in Refinanced Obligations

6.2.1 Continuation of Taint in Renewal Transactions

Because consumer debt is frequently refinanced, it is important to consider the extent to which the presence of usury in one obligation affects the validity of a subsequent agreement between the same parties when they renew or extend the outstanding debt. The question is particularly significant when the new agreement calls for interest at a legal rate and would be valid but for the previous usury. For

---

25 *See, e.g.*, Besta v. Beneficial Loan Co., 855 F.2d 532 (8th Cir. 1988) (*see* § 12.7, *infra*); *In re* Milbourne, 108 B.R. 522 (Bankr. E.D. Pa. 1989) (*see* § 12.5, *infra*); Villegas v. Transamerica Fin. Servs., 708 P.2d 781 (Ariz. Ct. App. 1985) (*see* § 12.5, *infra*). *See also* Emery v. American General Fin., Inc., 71 F.3d 1343 (7th Cir. 1995); Hager v. American General Fin., Inc., 37 F. Supp. 2d 778 (S.D. W. Va. 1999) (unconscionability and fraud claims withstand motion for summary judgment where consumers were in immediate financial need due to fire; lender allegedly misrepresented that credit insurance was required, and lender began flipping the loan just 9 days after the original transaction); Maxwell v. Fidelity Fin. Servs., Inc., 907 P.2d 51 (Ariz. 1995) (reversing grant of summary judgment for lender on unconscionability claim where inoperable water heater costing over $6,500 was financed at 19.5%, then refinanced along with a $800 cash advance to create a total deferred price of over $17,000). *See* §§ 12.6, 12.10, *infra*. *But see* Gonzales v. Associates Fin. Serv., 967 P.2d 312 (Kan. 1998).

26 Bar Harbor Bank & Trust v. Supt. of Bureau of Cons. Protection, 471 A.2d 292 (Me. 1984); Moore v. Canal Nat'l Bank, 409 A.2d 679, 684 (Me. 1979); Springhill Lake Investors Ltd. v. Prince George's County, 690 A.2d 535 (Md. App. 1997) (definition of refinancing was in context of imposition of transfer taxes by county recordation offices). The terms renewal and refinancing are generally used interchangeably. *See* Bar Harbor Bank & Trust, *supra*, 471 A.2d at 295.

27 *See* § 6.4.3, *infra*.

28 If renewals are done improperly there may be usury. Henson v. Dixie Fin. Co., 296 S.E.2d 593 (Ga. 1982) (limiting usury penalty to tainted principal); McNair v. Gold Kist, Inc., 305 S.E.2d 478 (Ga. App. 1983) (taint of usury continues through refinancing); Gold Kist v. McNair [different party], 303 S.E.2d 290 (Ga. App. 1983), *cert. denied*, 464 U.S. 937 (1983); Bar Harbor Bank & Trust Co. v. Supt. of Bureau of Consumer Protection, 471 A.2d 292 (Me. 1984)(loans renegotiated at end of term are refinancings under U.C.C.C., so increasing interest rate violates Maine statute); Manufacturer Hanover Trust v. Meadowdale Dev. Co., 458 N.Y.S.2d 700 (App. Div. 1983) (no summary judgment, since usury defense is good even with release in refinancing contract when alleged duress includes hidden interest claim).

example, assume that a borrower takes out a loan at the maximum legal interest rate, but that the transaction is usurious because the lender exacts a hidden interest fee in addition to the stated interest. If this loan is later renewed at the same rate, but no new fees are assessed, is the renewal note valid?[29]

The short answer to this question is no. The rule followed by almost all courts is that once a debt is tainted by usury, the usury will follow the debt through any number of renewal transactions.[30] Depending on the state, the taint may invalidate the new obligation to the same extent that it invalidated the original transaction.[31]

Courts have recognized that usury laws would be seriously undermined if the mere renewal of a usurious obligation could purge the debt of usury.[32] To regard renewal notes as valid as long as they state a legal interest rate would be

to ignore the inflation of the principal of the renewal note at least by the amount of the usurious charges in the previous transaction, and additionally by the amount of any void principal or interest carried over from the previous loan.[33] Furthermore, allowing renewals to purge usury would give borrowers significant problems with usury statutes of limitations. For example, a lender could conceivably charge a 50% commitment fee on a ten-year second mortgage loan, arrange a renewal of the debt a year or so later, and be beyond the usury statute of limitations a year or two beyond that.[34] A borrower who brought a usury action after five years of what appeared to be a ten-year term would arguably be time barred because of the renewal transaction.

6.2.2 No Taint If First Debt Forms No Part of Consideration

Despite the general rule against the purging of usury through renewal or replacement contracts, the courts do recognize circumstances under which the usury in one obligation will not taint a subsequent transaction between the parties. If the debt created by the first transaction forms no part of the consideration for the second obligation, then the two notes will be viewed as distinct, and usury in one note will not affect the legality of the other, unless the two are actually parts of a single usurious scheme.[35] This exception to the general rule of taint, however, is merely a statement that a second note between two parties will not be affected by usury in the prior note if in fact it is not a renewal of the previous note. Since refinancing transactions by definition involve the renewal of outstanding debt, this exception should seldom be of concern to practitioners considering taint in refinanced obligations.

---

29 Such facts are fairly common. *See, e.g., In re* Feldman, 259 F. Supp. 218 (D. Conn. 1966) (commitment fee); Cherry v. Berg, 508 S.W.2d 869 (Tex. Civ. App. 1974) (usurious discount in original notes).

30 Aaron v. Mattikow, 146 F. Supp. 2d 263 (E.D.N.Y. 2001). *See, e.g.,* Bowen v. Mt. Vernon Savings Bank, 105 F.2d 796 (D.C. Cir. 1939); *In re* Feldman, 259 F. Supp. 218 (D. Conn. 1966); Family Fed. Sav. & Loan v. Davis, 172 B.R. 437 (Bankr. D.D.C. 1994); Sanders v. Barron, 282 So. 2d 237 (Ala. 1973); American Savings Life Ins. Co. v. Financial Affairs Management Co., 474 P.2d 51 (Ariz. App. 1970); Westman v. Dye, 4 P.2d 134 (Cal. 1931); Coral Gables First Nat'l Bank v. Constr. of Fla., 119 So. 2d 741 (Fla. Dist. Ct. App. 1960); Henson v. Dixie Fin. Corp., 296 S.E.2d 593 (Ga. 1982); Harrison v. Arrendale, 147 S.E.2d 356 (Ga. App. 1966) (stating rule); Dickey v. Bank of Clarksdale, 184 So. 314 (Miss. 1938); Nelson v. Gen. Credit Corp., 90 N.W.2d 799 (Neb. 1958); State *ex rel.* Beck v. Associates Discount Corp., 77 N.W.2d 215 (Neb. 1956); Henderson v. Security Mortgage & Fin. Co., 160 S.E.2d 39 (N.C. 1968); Crabb v. Cole, 84 S.W.2d 597 (Tenn. App. 1935); Wallace v. D.H. Scott & Son, 127 S.W.2d 447 (Tex. 1939); Lentino v. Cullen Center Bank & Trust, 919 S.W.2d 743 (Tex. App. 1996). *See also* Federal Home Loan Mortgage Corp. v. 333 Neptune Ave. Ltd. P'ship, 1999 U.S. App. LEXIS 32056 (2d Cir. Dec. 2, 1999) (unpublished) (remanding case for determination of relationship between earlier and later transaction and for reevaluation of whether to exercise supplemental jurisdiction). *See generally* 47 C.J.S. *Interest & Usury* §§ 183-188.

31 *See, e.g., In re* Feldman, 259 F. Supp. 218 (D. Conn. 1966) (both principal and interest uncollectible); Henson v. Dixie Fin. Corp., 296 S.E.2d 593 (Ga. 1982) (interest and charges on original usurious loan forfeited, but lender may recover legal interest on new cash advanced upon refinancing); Dickey v. Bank of Clarksdale, 184 So. 314 (Miss. 1938) (interest on renewal notes void); Highway Equip. & Supply Co. v. Jones, 153 N.W.2d 859 (Neb. 1967) (interest forfeiture); Nelson v. Gen. Credit Corp., 90 N.W.2d 799 (Neb. 1958) (renewal note void); Lentino v. Cullen Center Bank & Trust, 919 S.W.2d 743 (Tex. App. 1996); Wallace v. D.H. Scott & Son, 127 S.W.2d 447 (Tex. 1939) (creditor can charge interest on new money advanced in refinancing but not on tainted principal); Cherry v. Berg, 508 S.W.2d 869 (Tex. Civ. App. 1974) (interest forfeiture).

32 *See* Bowen v. Mt. Vernon Savings Bank, 105 F.2d 796 (D.C. Cir. 1939); Family Fed. Sav. & Loan v. Davis, 172 B.R. 437 (Bankr. D.D.C. 1994).

33 *See In re* Feldman, 259 F. Supp. 218 (D. Conn. 1966) (borrower owed nothing when refinanced debt was void).

34 This is not an imagined problem. *See* Valley View State Bank v. Caulfield, 731 P.2d 316 (Kan. Ct. App. 1987)(series of refinancing agreements evidenced by as many as 47 notes over seven years; court's extremely narrow reading of U.C.C.C. cuts off consumer defenses from earlier notes in creditor's mortgage foreclosure action). Observe that the purging of usury from a debt validates only the new note. It does not eliminate the usury from the pre-existing note. Yet, the refinancing transaction does start the clock for the statute of limitations on the borrower's usury claim. *See* Crabb v. Cole, 84 S.W.2d 597 (Tenn. App. 1935).

35 *See* Dichter v. Viking Office Products, Inc., 501 N.Y.S.2d 420 (App. Div. 1986). *Compare* Brookshire v. Coffman, 696 S.W.2d 748 (Ark. 1985) (single usurious scheme) *and* Johnson v. Ronamy Consumer Credit Corp., 515 A.2d 682 (Del. 1986)(second mortgage and collateral guarantees were parts of single unenforceable transaction) *with* Thomas v. Estes, 229 S.E.2d 538 (Ga. App. 1976) (separate transactions). Similarly, a valid obligation will not be tainted by subsequent usurious agreements between the parties.

6.2.3 Novation vs. Waiver

There is a more serious limitation to the rule that the taint of usury will follow a debt through a renewal transaction. It is widely recognized that a usurious obligation may be purged of its usury by a subsequent agreement between the parties through which the usurious contract is completely abandoned with the "full knowledge and consent" of the borrower, and "new or independent" consideration is provided for the new contract.[36] In other words, courts allow usury to be purged through a "novation," which they regard as distinct from a mere "renewal." Yet because the continuation of at least some portion of the old debt as part of the consideration in a new credit contract apparently does not preclude the existence of a novation, figuring out the real difference between a renewal and a novation for usury purposes can be a problem. Despite the plethora of opinions which state that usury may be purged by a novation but not by a renewal, only a few courts have attempted to provide any general guidelines for distinguishing the two transactions.

The most logical rule for distinguishing between renewals and novations is that a refinancing may not be seen as a novation which purges a debt of usury unless the transaction in some manner credits the borrower with the amount of the usurious charges assessed in the previous transaction. Thus, any transaction which rolls over the full amount of an outstanding usurious obligation into a new note would be a renewal, not a novation, because the debt quite literally has not been purged of usurious charges.

A few courts have expressly stated the requirement that an agreement must at least credit the borrower with all usurious charges assessed on the pre-existing debt in order to purge the debt of usury.[37] Moreover, this proviso is consistent with many less explicit opinions which have found transactions that provided no such credit to be mere renewals.[38] It should nevertheless be observed that courts take a more metaphysical approach to the question of novation, and seem to worry a great deal about whether the usurious agreement has been "abandoned" or whether the new agreement is truly distinct from the old.[39] Clauses in refinancing agreements which reaffirm the former debt or which adopt the provisions of the original agreement have frequently been brandished as evidence of the entirely obvious fact that the new credit contracts are mere continuations of the old.[40]

In a slightly different vein, some courts emphasize the intent of the parties in entering the new transaction to see whether usury was purged,[41] although it may not be entirely clear what type of intent the court is examining. It has been stated that a specific intent to purge usury is unnecessary,[42] which suggests that the courts are looking exclusively at the intent of the parties to retire old debt and form an entirely new contract. But looking for such intent is a bit unrealistic. In the real world, if they think about the subject at all, debtors and creditors almost invariably view refinancing agreements as modifications of existing agreements and extensions of existing debt. Furthermore, one can question whether the intent of the parties to form a completely new contract, even if demonstrated, should be allowed to purge usury from the new note unless the refinancing agreement has been negotiated at arm's length. Otherwise, borrowers

---

36 *See* American Savings Life Ins. Co. v. Fin. Affairs Management Co., 474 P.2d 51 (Ariz. App. 1970) (stating rule). For cases holding that a new agreement purged an outstanding debt of usury, see Kogan v. Bergman, 53 Cal. Rptr. 371 (App. 1966); Ronen v. Teer, 498 P.2d 1284 (Idaho 1972); Matter of Estate of Jackson, 508 N.Y.S.2d 671 (App. Div. 1986)(borrower failed to meet his burden of proof).

37 *See* Bowen v. Mt. Vernon Savings Bank, 105 F.2d 796 (D.C. Cir. 1939); Family Fed. Sav. & Loan v. Davis, 172 B.R. 437 (Bankr. D.D.C. 1994) (lender not only did not purge original loan of usury, but condoned further unscrupulous activity by third parties in the process of settling litigation over the original loan); *In re* Bishop, 79 B.R. 94 (Bankr. D.D.C. 1987); Whittemore Homes, Inc. v. Fleishman, 12 Cal. Rptr. 235 (App. 1961); Henson v. Dixie Fin. Corp., 296 S.E.2d 593 (Ga. 1982). *See also* Kogan v. Bergman, 53 Cal. Rptr. 371 (App. 1966) (quoting *Whittemore, supra*).

38 *See, e.g.*, Rollins v. Odom, 519 So. 2d 652 (Fla. Dist. Ct. App. 1988) (usury becomes part of subsequent agreement unless all usurious elements of original loan abandoned and borrower

---

voluntarily agrees to new obligation); Coral Gables First Nat'l Bank v. Constructors of Fla., 119 So. 2d 741 (Fla. App. 1960) (new contract must be free from the vice of the old); Gemperle v. Crouch, 724 P.2d 375 (Wash. Ct. App. 1986) ("new, clean, and different transaction" required). Along the same line, cases in which a new note is held free of usury often involve some credit to the debtor. *See* Kogan v. Bergman, 53 Cal. Rptr. 371 (App. 1966); Ronen v. Teer, 498 P.2d 1284 (Idaho 1972) (total interest collected was at legal rate). *But see* Negaard v. Miller Constr. Co., 396 N.W.2d 833 (Minn. Ct. App. 1986)(court rules that payments on note applied first to interest, including usurious interest, so renewal note consists entirely of principal and is free of usury).

39 *See, e.g.*, Highway Equip. & Supply Co. v. Jones, 153 N.W.2d 859 (Neb. 1967).

40 *In re* Feldman, 259 F. Supp. 218 (D. Conn. 1966); Maze v. Sycamore Homes, Inc., 41 Cal. Rptr. 338 (App. 1964); Henderson v. Security Mortgage & Fin. Co., 160 S.W.2d 39 (N.C. 1968); Lawler v. Lomas & Nettleton Mortgage Invs., 691 S.W.2d 593 (Tex. 1985); Cherry v. Berg, 508 S.W.2d 869 (Tex. Ct. App. 1974).

41 This seems to be the approach taken in Texas. *See* Wallace v. D.H. Scott & Son, 127 S.W.2d 447 (Tex. 1939) (no intent to purge contract of usury). *See also* Matter of Estate of Jackson, 508 N.Y.S.2d 671 (App. Div. 1986) (borrower failed to prove usurious intent behind consolidated note). *Cf.* Lawler v. Lomas & Nettleton Mortgage Inv., 691 S.W.2d 593 (Tex. 1985) (question of intent does not entirely resolve issue; court also cites differences in terms of the two notes and fact that new note paid off old note); Cherry v. Berg, 508 S.W.2d 869 (Tex. Ct. App. 1974).

42 *See* Ronen v. Teer, 498 P.2d 1284 (Idaho 1972). *But cf.* Henderson v. Security Mortgage & Fin. Co., 160 S.E.2d 39 (N.C. 1968) (renewal of note was not settlement of usury claim when issue of usury had not arisen at time of renewal).

could be compelled upon refinancing to waive rights that could not be waived at the consummation of the original transaction.[43]

The issue of arm's length bargaining in refinancing agreements brings up an interesting point. Although a large majority of courts appear to view the question of taint in refinancing agreements as a matter of distinguishing novation from mere renewal, the issue of usury in refinancing agreements can be and, in a few cases, has been approached through an entirely different line of reasoning. Rather than considering whether a refinancing agreement constitutes a novation which may purge usury, it is just as plausible to consider whether the refinancing agreement constitutes a settlement and release of the parties' outstanding claims against each other, including usury.[44] It is generally recognized that the parties to a usurious agreement may enter into a settlement of a usury claim provided that the agreement is negotiated at arm's length.[45] Thus, it is possible to view the

issue of the purging of usury through refinancing as a question of whether the borrower released his or her usury claim pursuant to an arm's length settlement in the form of a refinancing agreement. The cases suggest that such a release may occur provided that the agreement actually contained a release clause, and provided that the borrower was represented by counsel during the negotiations.[46] It seems that neither a specific waiver of usury claims nor a credit for usurious payments is a prerequisite for a valid release, apparently because the representation of the borrower by counsel is presumed (rightly or wrongly) to ensure that the borrower's interests have been protected.[47]

Predicting whether a court will follow a "purging" or a "release" line of reasoning in any refinancing case can be difficult, especially since some jurisdictions profess to recognize both doctrines. Generally, the concept of release seems aimed at the settlement of ongoing disputes where both parties are adequately represented, while the concept of purging seems better suited to modifications prior to any litigation, although the line between these two situations can be difficult to draw.[48]

It is important to recognize that under either line of reasoning, the average consumer refinancing will not terminate pre-existing usury. If the court applies the "purging" doctrine, there is a strong argument that the usurious taint will infect the refinanced note unless the lender has taken the

---

43 *See* Bowen v. Mt. Vernon Savings Bank, 105 F.2d 796 (D.C. Cir. 1939). *See also* Krehling v. Barron, 1997 U.S. Dist. LEXIS 9956 (M.D. Fla. July 10, 1997) (distinguishing *Gunn* and holding that intent of parties in executing restructured notes could not be decided on summary judgment). *See generally* § 10.6.4, *infra*. *Cf.* Metro Hauling, Inc. v. Daffern, 723 P.2d 32 (Wash. Ct. App. 1986)(policy behind usury statutes would not be served if parties could modify agreements after default and provide for excessive interest on late payments). Several courts have refused to give effect to usury waiver or release clauses in renewal notes, although the result may depend on whether the borrower was represented by counsel when the renewal agreement was reached. *Compare* Aspeitia v. Calif. Trust Co., 322 P.2d 265 (Cal. App. 1958) *and* Coral Gables First Nat'l Bank v. Constructors of Fla., 119 So. 2d 741 (Fla. App. 1960) *with* Gunn Plumbing, Inc. v. Dania Bank, 252 So. 2d 1 (Fla. 1971) *and* Munilla v. Perez-Cobo, 335 So. 2d 584 (Fla. App. 1976).

44 This approach was taken in Gunn Plumbing, Inc. v. Dania Bank, 252 So. 2d 1 (Fla. 1971), although the court attempted to distinguish the concepts of release and purging. *See also* Duderwicz v. Sweetwater Savings Ass'n, 595 F.2d 1008 (5th Cir. 1979) (view of purging as settlement with new contract); LaBarr v. Tombstone Territorial Mint, 580 P.2d 744 (Ariz. Ct. App. 1978), *adopted* 582 P.2d 639 (Ariz. 1978) (settlement did not cover usury claim); Munilla v. Perez-Cobo, 335 So. 2d 584 (Fla. Dist. Ct. App. 1976) (following *Gunn Plumbing, supra*); McNair v. Gold Kist, Inc., 305 S.E.2d 478 (Ga. App. 1983) (note in payment of an open-end account did not cut off usury defense despite rules applicable to other contract defenses such as failure of consideration); Ronen v. Teer, 498 P.2d 1284 (Idaho 1972) (settlement purges usury); Henderson v. Security Mortgage & Fin. Co., 160 S.E.2d 39 (N.C. 1968) (renewal note was not a settlement).

45 *See, e.g.,* Gunn Plumbing, Inc. v. Dania Bank, 252 So. 2d 1 (Fla. 1971); Munilla v. Perez-Cobo, 335 So. 2d 584 (Fla. Dist. Ct. App. 1976); Thompson v. First Nat'l Bank of Tucker, 300 S.E.2d 529 (Ga. App. 1983); Carter v. Warde Capital Corp., 838 P.2d 327 (Idaho Ct. App. 1992) (prejudgment stipulation made after action brought to apply non-usurious interest rate purged usury from loans; dissent argues post-commencement agreement cannot purge usury); Bokum v. First Nat'l Bank in Albuquerque, 740 P.2d 693 (N.M. 1987) (accord and satisfaction agreement between bank and sophisticated, experienced busi-

nessman-borrower who was represented by counsel purged previous series of refinanced loans of usury); Vordenbaum v. Rubin, 611 S.W.2d 463 (Tex. Ct. App. 1980); Dunbabin v. Brandenfels, 566 P.2d 941 (Wash. Ct. App. 1977). *But cf. In re* Vehm Eng'g Corp., 521 F.2d 186 (9th Cir. 1975)(narrow construction of release clause; usury not waived); *In re* Giorgio, 62 B.R. 853 (Bankr. D.R.I. 1986) (settlement binds debtor but does not later bind debtor's trustee in bankruptcy); Victoria Bank & Trust Co. v. Brady, 779 S.W.2d 893 (Tex. Ct. App. 1989) (jury's finding that release was invalid upheld on various grounds, including borrower's ignorance of usury claim and failure of consideration), *rev'd on other grounds*, 811 S.W.2d 931 (Tex. 1991) (finding no usury).

46 *See* Gunn Plumbing, Inc. v. Dania Bank, 252 So. 2d 1 (Fla. 1971); Munilla v. Perez-Cobo, 335 So. 2d 584 (Fla. App. 1976); Victoria Bank & Trust Co. v. Brady, 779 S.W.2d 893 (Tex. Ct. App. 1989) (jury's finding that release was invalid upheld on various grounds, including borrower's ignorance of usury claim and failure of consideration). *Cf.* Henderson v. Security Mortgage & Fin. Co., 160 S.E.2d 39 (N.C. 1968) (no attorney representation).

47 *But see* Family Fed. Sav. & Loan v. Davis, 172 B.R. 437 (Bankr. D.D.C. 1994) (though represented by counsel, debtor did not believe he had claims, so thought waiver a moot point; court held waiver was not knowing or deliberate relinquishment of usury defense); *In re* Bishop, 79 B.R. 94 (Bankr. D.D.C. 1987) (parties, through counsel, had settled earlier action based on claims of usury and fraud and included a release clause; creditor's motion for summary judgment based on previous settlement denied; claim presents complex questions of law and fact not susceptible to determination on summary judgment).

48 *See* Gunn Plumbing, Inc. v. Dania Bank, 252 So. 2d 1 (Fla. 1971) (compare majority and dissenting opinions).

unusual step of crediting the borrower with the usurious charges. If, on the other hand, the court looks for a valid release in a consumer refinancing, it will not usually find one because consumers are rarely represented by counsel in such transactions, and thus the purported settlement will probably not have been reached through arm's length negotiations.

It is critical to note that some agreement is required before any purging of usury is possible. Unless expressly authorized by statute, a creditor cannot purge a debt of usury through its own unilateral action.[49] Florida and some other states have statutes which specifically allow a creditor to purge a contract of usury unilaterally, prior to the raising of a usury claim or defense, by notifying the debtor of the usury and crediting him with the overcharge.[50] Under such statutes, a borrower should be extremely careful about revealing the presence of a usury claim to the creditor prior to the filing of some formal notice such as the debtor's answer. For example, in a Florida case, counsel for a debtor made the mistake of informing the creditor's counsel of the debtor's usury claim before the debtor's answer had been filed in the creditor's action on a debt. The creditor immediately withdrew its complaint, sent the debtor a "purge" letter, and then refiled the action on the debt. The court subsequently found that the creditor lacked the "corrupt intent" which, under Florida law, the debtor must prove to establish usury.[51]

6.3 The Cost of Refinancings

6.3.1 The Elements of the Price Escalator

In assessing a series of refinancings, as suggested earlier it is useful to keep both a micro and macro viewpoint. Illegal overcharges can occur even if the transaction as a whole does not breach standards of ethical dealing. Conversely, the creditor's dealings may well violate community standards even if no specific illegal overcharge was imposed. Following are charges to evaluate for proper treatment in a series

of refinancing. But do so keeping in mind the true value the consumer received out of the transactions. What is the cumulative amount from the whole series which actually formed the consideration to the borrower: proceeds; payoffs of legitimate debts; purchase price of goods and services?[52] Then consider how the other costs imposed grow in relation to that sum over the course of the clients' history with the company.

- *Unearned interest in prior loans*: Precomputed loans will raise questions of proper rebates.[53] In some states, even interest-bearing transactions may raise questions, as there may be a limit on how much accrued, but unpaid interest can be included in a refinancing.[54]
- *Insurance premiums*: Rebates are required for unearned premiums and they most commonly use the more expensive Rule of 78. (A favored tool for padding loans, these create such a wide array of potential issues that an entire chapter (8) is devoted to credit insurance.)
- *Non-rebatable charges*: Points, origination fees, and service charges, if unusually high, are a good sign of trouble in a series of refinancings, because of the way they skew the yield.[55] Closing costs work the same way.
- *Invoking prepayment penalty clauses in refinancing*: This is another warning sign. Since the ostensible purpose of such clauses is to compensate the creditor for the loss of its intended bargain,[56] it has no place in a same-creditor refinancing, which is essentially an extension of the bargain.
- *Delinquency costs*: If a borrower is delinquent in paying the refinanced loan, earned, unpaid interest will also be added to the principal of the new loan, along with the cost of any deferral charges or late fees which may have been imposed. These charges, considered "interest" on the old loan, will become principal on the new loan, again increasing the interest cost on the new loan.

Having calculated the pay-off on the existing loan to its maximum profit, the lender is likely to add more charges to the new loan. In addition to more interest on a higher principal (usually for a longer term), and more insurance premiums (on a larger loan, for a longer term),[57] other charges may be repeated: service charges, filing fees, title opinions or title searches (if the credit is secured by real estate), document preparation fees and other such charges.

Repeated refinancings compound these hidden costs. Borrowers are encouraged to refinance when they show signs of having trouble making their scheduled payments on time. They may be encouraged to rewrite a loan to lower their

---

49 *See, e.g.*, Duderwicz v. Sweetwater Savings Ass'n, 595 F.2d 1008 (5th Cir. 1979); Davidson v. Commercial Credit Equip. Corp., 499 S.W.2d 68 (Ark. 1973) (subsequent disclaimer); United-Bilt Homes, Inc. v. Teague, 432 S.W.2d 1 (Ark. 1968) (suit for legal interest only does not purge usury); State *ex rel.* Beck v. Associates Discount Corp., 77 N.W.2d 215 (Neb. 1956); Yakutsk v. Alfino, 349 N.Y.S.2d 718 (App. Div. 1973); Danziger v. San Jacinto Savings Ass'n, 732 S.W.2d 300 (Tex. 1987); Financial Commerce, Inc. v. McLean, 435 P.2d 932 (Wash. 1968).

50 *See, e.g.*, Fla. Stat. Ann. § 687.04(2).

51 Gergora v. Goldstein Professional Ass'n Defined Benefits Pension Plan Trust, 500 So. 2d 695 (Fla. Dist. Ct. App. 1987). *Cf.* Beausejour Corp., N.V. v. Offshore Dev. Co., 802 F.2d 1319 (11th Cir. 1986) (statutory cure provisions not satisfied where creditor's letter did not state that transaction was usurious, did not refund any portion of sum paid under contract, and did not make formal adjustments to the contract).

52 But note that cash prices, too, can be inflated. *See* § 7.4.6, *infra*.

53 *See* Ch. 5, *supra*.

54 *See, e.g.*, Fla. Stat. § 516.031(5).

55 *See* § 5.5.2.2, *supra*, § 7.2.2, *infra*.

56 *See* § 5.8, *supra*.

57 For an explanation of the relation of the cost of insurance to the loan size and term, see § 8.5.3.1, *infra*.

payments, but the payments may be reduced only minimally (or not at all), while the total cost to the borrower is greatly increased.[58] As the loan size rises, the APR may even decline, though the real cost to the borrower rises. This works simply because so much of the cost is now buried in the loan principal.

In addition to directly increasing the total amount due, the lender may have other incentives to increase the principal on a new loan. Where statutes prohibit using real estate as security on loans under certain dollar amounts, refinancing can be an effective way of padding the principal past the magic threshold, so that the lender can take the borrower's home as collateral.[59] In states where interest rates are deregulated except for small loans,[60] inflating the principal through refinancing also may enable the lender to enter a deregulated lending arena.

6.3.2 Refinancing Calculations in Action: Another Walk-Through Case Study[61]

This section examines a finance company loan, secured by a second mortgage, and the calculations which the lender would make to prepare the refinanced loan. By highlighting the numerous calculations which must be made in deriving the figures for the new loan, this example demonstrates the myriad opportunities for improperly calculating rebates, or ignoring rebates, which may give rise to a usury claim. The example thus suggests information which should be sought through discovery in cases involving refinanced loans. While the complexity of the information needed may seem intimidating, pattern interrogatories are easily designed to elicit the necessary facts.

Assume a loan statement[62] shows the following components:

Principal $3,250
Includes:

$2,685	proceeds to borrower
156	credit life insurance
150	real property fees
9	filing fees
40	service charge
210	loan origination fees

Scheduled Interest	$1,550[63]
Total of Payments	$4,800
Rate of Charge	16.56%[64]

This precomputed loan is to be repaid over five years, in 60 monthly installments of $80 each. The contract authorizes a late charge of $4 per late installment. The applicable usury statute authorizes a 12% add-on rate.[65]

Assume that, after 17 months of prompt payment, this borrower had trouble making payments. The 18th and 19th payments were a week late, and then he was unable to make the 20th payment at all. Thirteen days after the due date for the 20th payment, the lender calls to ask about it. The lender suggests refinancing to bring the account current. The borrower inquires about getting an additional $200 cash advance, as he needs to pay a medical bill.

Because this was a precomputed loan, the current balance showing on the ledger card is simply the Total of Payments ($4,800) less the sum of the payments actually paid, $1,520 ($80 × 19), for a current balance of $3,280 ($4,800 − 1,520 = $3,280). To determine the pay-off balance, the lender will

---

58 *Cf.* Villegas v. Transamerica Fin. Servs., 708 P.2d 781 (Ariz. Ct. App. 1985).

59 For an example of padding for such a purpose, *cf.* Besta v. Beneficial Loan Co., 855 F.2d 532 (8th Cir. 1988).

60 *Compare* Ariz. Rev. Stat. § 6-632 *with* Ariz. Rev. Stat. § 44-1201.

61 *See* §§ 4.11, 5.6.3.3.2, *supra* for others.

62 The Truth in Lending Act does not require an itemization of the finance charge, even though it might have several components, *see, e.g.*, 12 C.F.R. § 226.4(b). However, many creditors do itemize such charges. Creditors are required to disclose the components of the amount financed on a closed-end transaction, or to notify the borrower of the right to obtain such an itemization, 12 C.F.R. § 226.18(c). If the client does not have an itemization, that should be obtained through formal or informal discovery as quickly as possible. (RESPA settlement statements or disbursal statements also may contain the necessary itemization.) Though the characterization of interest and finance charges are not always the same for TIL and usury laws, *see* § 4.4.1, *supra*, the disclosure statement is nonetheless an invaluable starting point for any usury analysis to reveal what charges the creditor has imposed.

63 The TIL disclosure statement would break down the charges differently:

Amount Financed	$3000
Finance Charge	$1800
Total of Payments	$4800
APR	20.31%

TIL requires the service charges and loan origination fee to be considered part of the finance charge, while the lender included these fees in the "principal" to which it applied a 16.56% (rounded) rate to derive the "scheduled interest."
   See § 4.4.1, *supra*.

64 Rate of charge rounded; actual charge 16.5577% (actuarial). Note the distinction between the APR and the "rate of charge" as this creditor uses that term. The "rate of charge" as used here is applied to a "principal" which includes both the elements of the amount financed and the prepaid finance charges (service charge and loan origination fee). The creditor then applied a "rate of charge" to the "principal," so defined, to derive the interest earned over time. In practice, the creditor probably selected a "rate of charge" which yields a "scheduled interest amount," which, when added to the prepaid finance charges (generally considered interest) will result in a total interest yield equivalent to 12% add-on for $3,000. The creditor's use of the term "principal" to refer to the $3,250 is somewhat misleading, because $250 of that sum is a prepaid finance charge, generally considered interest, but the creditor is financing it. *See* § 7.2.2, *infra*.

65 Note that even if no externally defined rate cap exists, the contract itself may set the applicable cap. *See* § 9.2.8, *infra*.

add any accrued charges not already reflected, such as late charges. It must also credit any required rebates to the consumers balance.

Unless applicable law clearly prohibits it, both interest rebates and credit insurance will likely be calculated according to the Rule of 78. Because the refinancing takes place 13 days into the 21st month of the loan, the lender decides to count the 21st month as a full month for purposes of computing the earned interest and insurance premiums. Thus, when using the Rule of 78 formula[66] the lender considers the number of remaining months in the loan term to be 39 (60 − 21 = 39). Next, it derives a rebate factor of 42.62% ((39 × 40) ÷ (60 × 61)). Because the lender characterized $250 ($40 service charge + $210 loan origination fee) as charges earned at the time this loan was consummated, it does not consider that amount to be subject to the rebate requirements. Therefore, it only applies the rebate factor to the "scheduled interest" of $1,550. So the borrower is credited with an unearned interest rebate of $660.61 ($1,550.00 × 42.62% = $660.61).[67]

The credit life insurance rebate is determined by the same formula,[68] so the rebate credited to the account balance would be as follows: $156.00 × 42.62% = $66.49

Having determined the rebates which must be credited to the current balance, the lender then determines whether there are additional charges to be added to the current balance. Assume two $4 late charges are added. (Although three payments were late, the first two may have been made within a contractual grace period, in which case it may be improper to impose a late charge on one of those payments.)

Thus, the current pay-off is:
$3,280.00 (current balance)
+   8.00 (late charges)
− 660.61 (interest rebate)
− 66.49 (insurance rebate)
────
$2,560.90 NET PAY-OFF

To this pay-off of the current loan, the lender will add the $200 which the consumer wants to borrow to pay a medical bill. Then the lender determines what other charges to add onto this loan. Theoretically, the insurance charges will only

be added if the debtor chooses to purchase the insurance. As a practical matter, however, many lenders automatically include such charges in the documents before the borrower arrives.[69]

If the lender continues to insure the loan,[70] and again writes it for a five-year term at the same interest rate used in the prior loan,[71] the critical loan components are as follows:

Amount Financed	$3,080.06
Includes:	
Net pay-off prior loan	$2,560.90
Amount given to borrower	200.00
Real Estate Fees	150.00
Filing Fees	9.00
Credit Life Insurance	160.16
Finance Charge	1,848.04
Total of Payments	4,928.10

The refinancing does not lower the monthly payment for this borrower, but raises it slightly to $82.14.[72] In fact, refinancing from this lender and borrowing $200 extra turns out to be very expensive for the borrower. A simple comparison of the first loan to the second is ample demonstration of how adversely refinancing can affect borrowers.

The borrower is again charged fees totalling $159 in connection with the security, along with interest on those repeat fees. This artificially inflated pay-off in turn inflates the interest yield on the new loan. The use of the Rule of 78, instead of the actuarial method, to calculate the interest rebate due on the first loan cost the borrower an extra $77.88.[73] Failure to rebate any of the loan origination fee cost the borrower another $89.50.[74] Together, these rebate bonuses, now part of the new principal, increase the interest yield on the new loan by $100.43 ($167.38 at 12% add-on for 5 years), thus costing the borrower an extra $267.81. However, it is even more dramatic to compare this to the cost of a $200 loan as the borrower probably imagined it. Since a $200 loan would probably be unsecured, there

---

66 *See* § 5.6.3.3.2, *supra.*

67 *See* § 5.6.2.2, *supra* on rounding intervals. Notice the impact of a Rule of 78 calculation. Though the loan is only one-third into its scheduled term, over 57% of the scheduled interest ($889.39) is considered earned ($1,550 − 660.61 = $889.39). Compare this to an actuarial rebate, which would have resulted in a rebate of $738.49 of scheduled interest; only 52.35% ($811.51) of the interest would have been earned. (The actuarial calculation includes 43 days of daily interest on a 360 day year earned after the last payment was made in the 19th month.) Thus the borrower paid a Rule of 78 penalty of $77.88.

68 It is likely that the insurance company issuing the policy considers premiums earned on an actuarial basis. If that is the case, then figuring the borrower's premium rebate by the Rule of 78 allows the lender to retain an insurance bonus, as well.

69 *See* § 8.5.2, *infra.*

70 In this hypothetical case, the legal credit life insurance rate is 65¢/$100/year. For further details on credit insurance calculations, see § 8.5.3.1, *infra.*

71 The add-on rate on the prior loan was 12%, with an actuarial equivalent of 20.31%. For the sake of simplicity, the finance charge is not further broken down into a service charge, loan origination fee, and scheduled interest, as was done on the original loan. *See* notes 63–64, *supra* for explanation of the difference in the way the first loan was structured.

72 $4,928.10 ÷ 60 = 59 at $82.14 and 1 at $81.84. To lower the payments, the lender may stretch the term yet longer, further increasing the total cost. A lender also may structure the loan with a balloon payment at the end in order to "lower" the monthly payments on a refinanced loan.

73 *See* note 67, *supra.*

74 *See* § 6.4.1.3, *infra.* This actually understates the rebate bonus, because the $89.50 rebate of the loan origination fee was calculated by the Rule of 78, not the actuarial method.

would be no filing fees, real estate fees or property insurance, as there likely would be on a real estate secured loan.[75] Even borrowing that amount separately at high Small Loan Act rates,[76] and spreading payment out over two years, the loan would consist of:

Proceeds to borrower	$199.49[77]
Credit Life	3.74
Amount Financed	203.23
Finance Charge	84.77
Total of Payments	288.00
Monthly Payment	12.00

The combined monthly payments on the two loans would be $92, just $12 more over two years. The gross cost, however, would be $1,360.10 less. This can be seen by comparing the total of payments due on the two separate loans ($4,800 + $288 = $5,088) to the total of payments due on the new loan plus payments already made on the earlier loan ($4,928.10 + $1,520.00 = $6,448.10).[78]

The cost of a non-refinanced loan for $200 could further be reduced by repaying it over a shorter period, or by borrowing from a lower rate lender. Merely paying off the medical bill at the 1 1/2% per month on outstanding balances often charged by service providers would be cheaper in the long run, and would be an unsecured debt. In short, a borrower who chooses refinancing in order to obtain additional credit, such as the $200 in this example, is paying far too much for the credit and may be putting his or her home at risk to boot.

Making the effort to work through the calculations in a refinancing can be very valuable for the client. It was the mathematical consequences to the borrower ($3,000 more than obtaining new, separate loans for new advance) which led one court to hold that it was opportunistic conduct rising to the level of an unfair practice to fail to disclose the lender's advantage and the borrower's disadvantage in choosing a refinancing option.[79] This followed a similar

analysis also showing a hidden penalty of about $3,000, which led another court to declare the transaction unconscionable.[80]

6.4 Evaluating the Calculations

6.4.1 Rebates

6.4.1.1 Calculating Proper Rebates

The example in the previous section illustrates the numerous computational steps in which a lender can err in determining the cost of a new loan to the borrower. The first step for the practitioner is to check the regulatory statute applicable to the transaction to determine two things: the charges which must be rebated from the prior loan;[81] and the formula to be used in computing those rebates.[82] All states require that credit insurance be cancelled and rebates given upon refinancing.[83] Precomputed interest also must be rebated.[84] If refunds are not made or if the wrong formula is used—one which would result in a higher "earned" premium or interest figure than the prescribed formula—the transaction is subject to challenge for illegal overcharge.[85]

Even a lender who uses the proper rebate formula may apply it improperly. In the example in the preceding section, the loan was refinanced on the 13th day of the loan's 21st month. Even if the applicable statute authorizes use of the Rule of 78 to compute the insurance rebates, the statute may not permit the lender to consider the insurance earned for the 21st period. A number of states provide that no insurance premium charge may be made if 15 days or less in a month have elapsed, though a full month's charge may be imposed if 16 or more days have elapsed. Under such a statute, the insurance premium in the example would have been improperly calculated, giving the lender an excessive charge.

---

75 Property insurance should be written only on collateral.

76 Assume the state has a split rate small loan ceiling authorizing 36% per year on an amount financed up to $250 of amount financed, and 24% per year on the excess to $400. The actuarial equivalent APR on this loan would be 36%.

77 As is often the case with real loans, the components of this loan are in odd amounts to reflect the way the creditors' computational charts are constructed.

78 The comparison, of course, is not a direct one because the separate $200 advanced with the refinancing of the previous balance was financed over five years. However, it is a legitimate cost comparison, because it illustrates one of the pitfalls borrowers face in refinancing: the repayment period is lengthened, thus making the loan more expensive, often providing little or no advantage to the borrower. Further, a lengthened term renders this borrower vulnerable to external events which may interrupt income and make him subject to foreclosure for a total of 80 1/2 months, instead of 60 months.

79 *In re* Milbourne, 108 B.R. 522 (Bankr. E.D. Pa. 1989). *See also*

Hager v. American General Fin., Inc., 37 F. Supp. 2d 778 (S.D. W. Va. 1999) (denying lender's motion for summary judgment on unconscionability claim); *In re* Tucker, 74 B.R. 923, 927 (Bankr. E.D. Pa. 1987) (court in dicta noted the lopsided math and suggested that failure of a usury claim would not forestall a UDAP claim).

80 Besta v. Beneficial Loan Co., 855 F.2d 532 (8th Cir. 1988). *See also* Hager v. American General Fin., Inc., 37 F. Supp. 2d 778 (S.D. W. Va. 1999) (denying lender's motion for summary judgment on unconscionability claim).

81 *See* § 5.5, *supra.*

82 *See* § 5.6.3, *supra.*

83 *See* § 8.6, *infra.* Usually, rebates of less than $1.00 need not be made.

84 *See generally* Ch. 5, *supra.*

85 *See generally* Ch. 5, *supra. See also In re* Jungkurth, 74 B.R. 323 (Bankr. E.D. Pa. 1987); *In re* Tucker, 74 B.R. 923, 927 (Bankr. E.D. Pa. 1987) ("any formula other than the 'actuarial method' of calculating rebates, unless such a formula is specifically authorized by state law, would constitute the imposition of a prepayment penalty and hence be usurious").

The number of months remaining in the loan term should have been 40, instead of 39. Thus the Rule of 78 rebate factor to be applied to the insurance should have been 44.81% (($40 \times 41) \div (60 \times 61)$) instead of 42.62%. The insurance rebate should have been $69.90 ($156 × 44.81), instead of $66.49 ($156 × 42.62%), for an insurance overcharge of $3.41. When a loan being refinanced is packed with very high insurance premiums,[86] substantial overcharges can result from improper calculations of insurance rebates.

Similarly, the statute applicable to interest rebates may only allow the lender to claim 13 days of interest for the last 13 days of the loan, and prohibit the rounding of the 13 days to a full month for rebate purposes. If the lender rounds up to a full month anyway, an overcharge occurs.[87] Note that some statutes prescribe different rules for calculating rebates where the transaction is refinanced after a short term.[88]

6.4.1.2 Compounding

The calculations in a refinancing transaction should be checked to see whether, in determining the pay-off on the prior loan, the lender improperly compounded interest. One of the reasons that refinancing to bring delinquent accounts current is expensive for borrowers is that earned, but unpaid interest from the delinquent account is added to the principal in the new account, thus swelling the basis upon which interest on the new account is calculated. Absent the refinancing, ordinarily no interest can be imposed on earned but unpaid interest.[89]

The general rule about compounding is that interest may be charged on accrued unpaid interest by an agreement made after the interest becomes due.[90] However, the applicable statute should be carefully reviewed. Though the courts are divided, a line of cases holds that including earned, unpaid interest in the principal of a refinanced loan constitutes illegal compounding under a state's small loan act. The rationale of these cases is that small loan acts prohibit compounding interest, and further prohibit taking excess

charges "directly or indirectly." A Louisiana appellate court held the practice to be illegal under that state's Small Loan Act, despite a specific statutory provision in Louisiana's general civil code adopting the general compounding rule that interest may be charged on accrued unpaid interest by an agreement made after the interest becomes due. The court considered the special purposes of the Small Loan Act to be critical in distinguishing the Act's treatment of compounding from the general compounding rule.[91] Other states' small loan acts specifically provide that only unpaid interest which accrued within the 60 days prior to refinancing may be included in the new loan principal.[92] Consequently, the inclusion of any unpaid interest beyond 60 days in the new principal would result in illegal interest.

6.4.1.3 Non-Rebatable Charges on Old Loan

The sample refinanced loan exhibits another characteristic which should act as a red flag for practitioners: the characterization of portions of the finance charge as nonrebatable fees, such as service charges, points or loan origination fees. Many statutes specifically authorize the imposition of service charges or points either in a prescribed amount or in a "reasonable" amount. To the extent the service charge imposed falls within the statutorily prescribed limit, the failure to rebate is probably legitimate.[93] (If it exceeds the statutory limit, of course, it is subject to attack.[94]) However, the use of points or loan origination fees outside the purchase money mortgage lending context is relatively new. Consequently, some special credit statutes, such as industrial loan acts or small loan acts, may not list them as specifically authorized charges.[95] If the applicable statute retains model small loan language prohibiting

---

86 Insurance packing is discussed at § 8.5.4, *infra*.
87 *See* § 5.6.2, *supra*. Irrespective of the impact of rounding on usury laws, such rounding up may constitute a finance charge for TIL purposes. Steele v. Ford Motor Credit, 783 F.2d 1016 (11th Cir. 1986). *See* National Consumer Law Center, Truth in Lending § 3.7.2.2 (5th ed. 2003 and Supp.).
88 *See, e.g.*, Ala. Code 5-19-4(d) (pro rata refund if renewed or refinanced by same creditor or affiliate within 120 days of original loan); Colo. Rev. Stat. § 5-2-207(2) (where prepaid finance charge was imposed on loan being refinanced or consolidated within one year, creditor must either limit new prepaid finance charge to new advance, or must rebate prepaid finance charge on old loan according to actuarial method).
89 *See* § 4.6.1, *supra*.
90 *Id. See, e.g.*, Smith v. MRCC P'ship, 792 S.W.2d 301 (Ark. 1990) (not usury to add accrued, unpaid interest on antecedent debt to principal on new debt and write new contract with maximum legal rate of interest on whole amount).
91 Securities Fin. Co. v. Maranto, 119 So. 2d 120 (La. Ct. App. 1960).
92 *See, e.g.*, Fla. Stat. § 516.031(5); N. H. Rev. Stat. § 399-A:11(IV). This is the provision in the seventh draft of the Uniform Small Loan Act, *reprinted in* Curran, Trends in Consumer Credit Legislation 30 (1965).
93 *In re* Tucker, 74 B.R. 923 (Bankr. E.D. Pa. 1987) (though persuasive authority and public policy suggest a service charge *should* be rebated, the controlling statute makes it clear that no such rebate is required).
94 *See, e.g.*, Williams v. Seeley (*In re* Williams), 241 B.R. 387 (Bankr. E.D. Va. 1999), *rev'd in part*, 2001 U.S. App. LEXIS 13246 (4th Cir. June 13, 2001) (points are not considered "paid" at outset of transaction when lender merely reserves them from the proceeds of the loan, so they could not be part of penalty under statutory formula); Mayo v. Key Fin. Servs., Inc., 1994 Mass. Super. LEXIS 549 (Mass. Super. Ct., June 22, 1994) (implied private right of action for violation of statute limiting points; assertable by a suitable common law remedy; borrowers choose to assert common law restitution), *aff'd on other issues*, 678 N.E.2d 1311 (Mass. 1997). If refinanced, the excess would taint the new loan, as well. *See* § 6.2, *supra*.
95 *See, e.g.*, Ariz. Rev. Stat. § 6-632 (points prohibited except in home equity loans).

charges which are "paid, deducted or received in advance," points should be impermissible.

Even absent a clear statutory prohibition, issues concerning the legality of such charges may arise where there is no affirmative authorization for them. The imposition of the charge itself may violate the statute.[96] Alternatively, if the points are "financed," their inclusion in the principal of the loan may give rise to illegal compounding. Even if points are allowed and the *de facto* compounding that they involve is disregarded, it still is arguable that their effect in limiting rebates creates an illegal overcharge. Most statutes regulating consumer credit require a rebate of unearned interest. If there is not a specific authorization for a charge which is non-rebatable, such as points or loan origination fees, the division of interest into rebatable and non-rebatable categories should be viewed as a "device or subterfuge" to exact usury, and an effort to circumvent or evade the law's requirement that interest be rebated.[97] This argument should be especially persuasive in the context of statutes which prohibit directly or indirectly taking charges not specifically authorized.[98]

Again, the example reviewed in § 6.3, *supra*, is telling. Assume that the statute authorizes a maximum $40 service charge, and makes no reference to points. In such a case, only the $40 should be considered non-rebatable, not the $210 loan origination fee. Thus, applying the 42.62% rebate factor[99] to the loan origination fee of $210, the interest rebate would be $89.50 in addition to the rebate applied to the scheduled interest.[100] The lender thus retained an extra $89.50 to which it was not entitled under the statute. Furthermore, because the $89.50 was not credited to the pay-off

balance, the principal of the new loan was improperly increased by that amount, and it is now generating additional interest at the new loan rate ($89.50 at 12% add-on for 60 months = $53.70) which should also be considered illegal interest. Thus the total overcharge to the borrower arising simply from the lender's failure to rebate the "origination fee" is $143.20.

6.4.2 Imposition of Additional Charges on the New Loan

The practitioner should examine the new, refinancing transaction and check the legitimacy of any new charges imposed. For example, some regulatory statutes explicitly prohibit imposing any points, service charges or administrative fees on loans which are refinanced within a specified amount of time, commonly six months to one year.[101] Other statutes, while allowing non-rebatable acquisition charges at the time of the initial transaction, may disallow them altogether at refinancing.[102] Statutes may also prohibit assessing service charges, and other such changes, on that portion of a loan used to pay off a prior loan, irrespective of time limits.[103] If the lender ignores this prohibition, the excess service charge is interest, and if, when added to the other interest charged, the total exceeds the allowable amount, the loan is usurious.[104]

Even where there are no specific limitations on the use of such charges on refinanced loans, these charges still may be subject to challenge. The Tennessee Supreme Court, interpreting a state statute in light of a former provision of the state constitution, articulated a series of standards against which statutorily authorized service charges should be measured. Such charges must bear a reasonable relation to the expenses and services of the lender, and may not include compensation for overhead expenses, such as rents, salaries,

---

96 *Id*. Also some statutes such as small loan laws, for example, list the charges that a creditor is permitted to assess and prohibit the imposition of all "other charges." The imposition of an unauthorized charge violates the statute even if the effective interest rate charged is below the small loan ceiling. *See, e.g.*, Ex parte New Fin. Ltd., 225 So. 2d 782, 784 (Ala. 1969). *See also* Attorney General of Md. v. Equitable Trust Co., 450 A.2d 1273, 1292 (Md. Ct. App. 1982). *See generally* § 9.3.1.2, *infra*.

97 A creditor argument that these charges are "earned" at consummation should not withstand scrutiny, in view of the fact that the types of costs points were originally designed to cover are generally separately charged to the borrower. Further, even if that legal fiction had merit, attributing an unreasonably large amount of compensation to non-rebatable charges, e.g., 15 points, could not withstand scrutiny. *See* § 5.5.2.2, *supra* for further discussion of points as rebatable charges. *See also* Cumberland Capital Corp. v. Patty, 556 S.W.2d 516 (Tenn. 1977)(similar analysis regarding the imposition of service charges). *Cf*. Moore v. Comfed Sav. Bank, 908 F.2d 834 (11th Cir. 1990), *rehearing denied* (11th Cir. 1990) (a matter for the trial court to determine whether 20 to 40 points were a device to take excess charges). [*Note*: The Georgia Supreme Court ultimately salvaged these loans from usury charges by invoking the spreading doctrine, but seemed to invite a UDAP challenge. Fleet Fin., Inc. v. Jones, 430 S.E.2d 352 (Ga. 1993).]

98 *See* § 9.3.1.2, *infra* (statutory construction).

99 Assuming that is the correct factor, see § 6.4.1.1, *supra*.

100 *See* § 6.3.2, *supra*.

101 *See, e.g.*, Cal. Fin. Code § 18212.2 (West 1989) (Industrial Loan Act). *See also* Colo. Rev. Stat. § 5-2-207(2) (where prepaid finance charge was imposed on loan being refinanced or consolidated within one year, creditor must either limit new prepaid finance charge to new advance or must rebate prepaid finance charge on old loan according to actuarial method); Ohio Rev. Code Ann. § 1321.57(G) (cannot either charge new points on refinancing real-estate secured loan within one year where prior loan had points charged, or impose a prepayment penalty).

102 *See* Independent Fin. Institute v. Clark, 990 P.2d 845 (Okla. 1999), which interprets a pre-1997 version of Oklahoma's Consumer Credit Code to prohibit non-rebatable acquisition fees upon refinancing, even for loans that qualified for these fees when initially made. The Oklahoma legislature amended the statute in 1997 to allow acquisition fees upon refinancing of some very small loans, but to make these fees subject to rebate. Okla. Stat. tit. 14A, §§ 3-205, 3-508B.

103 *See, e.g.*, Tenn. Code Ann. § 45-5-403 (Industrial Loan).

104 Coleman v. Allstate Loan & Inv. Co., Consumer Cred. Guide (CCH) ¶ 97,322 (E.D. Tenn. June 23, 1980).

and loan losses.[105] The legislative definition of a maximum permissible charge should not be construed as granting creditors permission to automatically charge that maximum amount to all borrowers. Rather, when the fee is within the statutory limits, it is considered to be prima facie valid, and the burden shifts to the borrower to show that the charge does not bear a reasonable relation to expenses and services rendered.[106] When a lender repeatedly refinances loans over a relatively short interval, imposing new charges each time, no legitimate justification for such charges exists. Repeated, unnecessary charges should properly be considered to be a device to obtain excessive interest.[107] Creditors should not, for example, be permitted to impose non-interest fees for title searches or real estate appraisals every time a second mortgage is refinanced; such repeated costs are not "reasonable."

6.4.3 Is the New Rate Proper?

The economic injury caused by refinancing or consolidation is compounded when the new loan is written at a higher rate than the loan being refinanced. In some cases, the rate increase can be challenged.

A few states explicitly restrict the right of a lender to raise the interest rate on a refinanced loan. For example, in Iowa, if the rate on the original loan exceeded 18%, the rate cannot be increased on the refinancing of the unpaid balance.[108]

More common than such general rate restrictions on refinancing are provisions in Retail Installment Sales Acts (RISAs) which provide that refinanced sales contracts retain their character as sales contracts, subject to the terms of the RISA.[109] Many of these statutes apply this restriction to all *holders* of retail sales contracts, not just to the original seller.

Historically, one of the notable abuses in refinancing occurred when retail sales contracts were assigned to finance companies. Because the rate limitations applicable to loans made by finance companies were often considerably higher than those applicable to credit sales, the assignee-finance companies would flip the assigned credit sale into one of its own loans, using the higher small loan or industrial loan rate. Requiring that refinanced contracts continue to be treated under the terms of the RISA when refinanced by a "holder" prevents the finance company from treating it as a loan regulated by the small loan law. (The same incentive to flip applies when the RISA is rate regulated, but a consumer loan is not.)

Nevertheless, it is not uncommon for finance companies to violate these RISA provisions. In *Vasquez v. Schwoeble*,[110] the trial court found that AVCO Financial Services of Southern California had engaged in a widespread flipping scheme whereby borrowers were deceptively and unfairly persuaded to flip lower cost credit sales into high cost loans. AVCO was prohibited from engaging in a number of abuses, including imposing finance charges greater than those permitted under the lower rate RISA and selling new credit insurance plans prior to cancellation of old ones.[111] AVCO was also ordered to disclose the true cost of the refinancing and any new costs imposed, to avoid misrepresenting the availability of new money if existing contracts were not flipped or consolidated, and to stop asserting that refinancing required further household goods as collateral.[112]

Vasquez also provides guidance as to how to treat the common situation in which a credit sale refinancing is accompanied by a new cash advance from an assignee-lender. In calculating restitution due to the consumers, the court ordered that where AVCO's refinancing was accompanied by a new cash advance, the RISA rate be applied to the credit sales balance, and the loan rate be applied only to new advances made in the debt consolidation. Some states explicitly specify by statute or regulation how to treat such "mixed" consolidations.[113]

---

105 Cumberland Capital Corp. v. Patty, 556 S.W.2d 516, 535–6 (Tenn. 1977). The state constitution was amended soon after *Cumberland Capital* to give more discretion to the state legislature. *See In re* Henley, 228 B.R. 425 (Bankr. E.D. Ark. 1998) (interpreting current version of Tenn. constitution not to limit legislature's authority to set interest rates).

106 *Id.*

107 *In re* Bogan, 281 F. Supp. 242, 250 (W.D. Tenn. 1968); *In re* Branch (Bankr. E.D. Tenn. 1966), *reprinted in* Greenfield, Consumer Transactions 424 (3d ed. 1999).

108 Iowa Code Ann. § 537.2504. It should be noted that the "unpaid balance" is defined to include new charges such as insurance premiums, filing fees, and closing costs on real estate secured loans. § 537.2504(2). In other words, such charges on the new loan cannot be considered new advances which could escape the rate limitation.

109 *See, e.g.*, Cal. Civ. Code §§ 1807.2 (explicitly regulating refinancing), 1807.3; Mass. Gen. Laws Ann. 255D, § 17; 69 Pa. Stat. § 1702. *But cf.* Mich. Comp. Laws Ann. § 445.861(d)(2) (holder who refinances retail installment contract may charge rate of interest or finance charge under Credit Reform Act, Mich. Comp. Laws Ann. § 445.1854). Also a number of RISA statutes provide protections regarding the right to refinance a balloon payment on a RISA contract.

110 Clearinghouse No. 30,321 (Cal. Super. Ct., Los Angeles, Cty., Sept. 20, 1982). *Cf.* Brewer v. Home Owners Auto Fin. Co., 10 Cal. App. 3d 337 (1970) (motor vehicle contract assigned immediately to finance company, which modified shortly thereafter to increase balance and take deed of trust; court held dealer and financer actually acting jointly, and conditional sales limitation on land as security applied despite this effort to evade that restriction).

111 This is forbidden under credit insurance laws, as well. *See* § 8.6, *infra*.

112 Many RISA statutes restrict the creditor's right to take a security interest in goods other than those sold. The FTC limits the right to take non-purchase money security interests in household goods, 16 C.F.R. 444, but finance companies still often use those household goods that fall through the definitional cracks in order to sell property insurance. *See* § 8.5.4.4, *infra*.

113 *See, e.g.*, Iowa Code Ann. § 537.2505(3) (West 1987) (where debts consolidated include a debt from a credit sale, the finance

6.5 Practice Tip: Evaluating Refinancing as a Way Out of Real Estate Mortgage Foreclosure

One situation where refinancing should be carefully considered as a useful option for a borrower is when a mortgage foreclosure threatens. Refinancing may prevent the loss of the home, or it may get the borrower deeper in debt. Where attorneys are involved early enough, they are in a position to help direct their clients to the positive use of a refinance. (Selling a house that is simply beyond the borrowers' means may be the only solution in some cases, but many borrowers would prefer to remain in their home—to keep the ties to their neighbors, their schools, and their community.)

Defending a foreclosure can be a complicated endeavor, involving consumer protection,[114] housing[115] and bankruptcy law, as well as traditional foreclosure law.[116] The dramatic rise in foreclosures which followed the explosion in home-secured lending[117] makes home defense a critical area. The foreclosure section of NCLC's *Repossessions and Foreclosures* has several chapters devoted to foreclosure defense. The following discussion touches only briefly on legal issues, instead focusing on how to determine when refinancing can help, instead of hurt, the client.

Though it may seem that borrowers in foreclosure are not good candidates for new credit,[118] even homeowners who are seriously delinquent on a mortgage may qualify for refinancing. If the refinancing lowers the monthly payment, the homeowners' income may be adequate to meet that lowered monthly obligation, making the borrowers more creditworthy to lower rate lenders.[119] In addition, many banks and savings banks are concerned about (or can be reminded of) their Community Reinvestment Act obligations if they are reluctant to lend to clients.[120] Many states and communities also have government sponsored or community development agency sponsored lending programs for low and moderate income homeowners.

First, it is important to make a realistic assessment of a client's financial capabilities. The amount of the monthly payment is the most important single factor. For example, clients with a high rate 25%, ten-year loan on a $15,000 second mortgage could reduce the monthly payments from $341.24 to $161.19 by refinancing the $15,000 at 10% for 15 years. This difference may make the debt load affordable, and make it more likely that the clients will be accepted for new financing. (Lenders commonly use a rule of thumb of 40% or so of income which should be devoted to housing. Of course, a budget based on actual monthly expenses should be used for determining clients' monthly mortgage payment capability.)

The next step is to examine the existing loan to determine what claims and defenses exist. The cost of any loan is a function of three main interrelated variables: the amount of the principal, the interest rate, and the payment term of the loan. Anything that can be done to reduce the principal on the new loan will reduce the cost of that loan, and reducing the pay-off balance on the existing loan is a critical way to accomplish that. In negotiating with the old lender, legitimate claims and defenses concerning the existing loan can be used as leverage to reduce the pay-off of the existing obligation, sometimes by a significant amount, and thus lower the cost of refinancing that loan.

It is necessary to look at the possibility of claims and defenses concerning the existing loan before looking at refinancing for three reasons. First, for some loans, the defenses available may be so powerful as to make the debt unenforceable and refinancing unnecessary. In that case it would be inappropriate (malpractice?) to unthinkingly advise the clients to refinance what in fact may be an unenforceable debt. The most dramatic examples are certain small loan and second mortgage laws, which void the obligation or at least any interest obligation, if the transaction violates the statute.[121] Second, the foreclosure process or refinancing may cut off some of the homeowners' claims or remedies, such as Truth in Lending (TIL) rescission.[122] It

---

114 *See, e.g.*, Ch. 11, *infra. See also* National Consumer Law Center, Repossessions and Foreclosures §§ 16.7, 16.10 (5th ed. 2002 and Supp.).

115 *See, e.g.*, National Consumer Law Center, Repossessions and Foreclosures Ch. 16 (5th ed. 2002 and Supp.).

116 *Id.* Chs. 14, 16, 17. Workout agreements are discussed at *id.* Ch. 15. For special issues on tax liens and tax foreclosures, see *id.* at Ch. 18.

117 *See* § 11.5.1, *infra*.

118 Lenders whose ads play to those with credit problems should be avoided, generally, as they most often make exorbitantly expensive loans, which will likely compound the client's problem, rather than solving it.

119 An attorney advising clients should be careful not to assume that credit would be unavailable from lower rate lenders. Data available from a Federal Reserve Board 1983 Survey of Consumer Finances, among other sources, indicates that the financial profile of commercial bank borrowers is not significantly different from that of finance company borrowers. This data does not support the commonly held notion that high rate lenders are entitled to those high rates because they serve high

---

charge is subject to the credit sale finance charge limitations); W. Va. Code § 46A-3-108 (1992) (where consolidation loan is mixed, credit sale rate limitations apply to the portion of the amount financed representing the sale balance, and loan limitations apply to the loan portion of the amount financed).

risk customers. *See generally* § 11.3, *infra*.

120 12 U.S.C. §§ 2901–2908. The Center for Community Change, 1000 Wisconsin Ave., N.W., Washington, D.C. 20007, (202) 342-0519, maintains a website, www.communitychange.org, with information about the CRA and links to government organizations' CRA data.

121 *See, e.g.*, Gottesfeld v. Kaminski, 524 A.2d 872 (N.J. Super. App. Div. 1987). *See generally* § 10.8, *infra*.

122 Some cases, however, have permitted rescission of refinanced loans under TIL if there are valid grounds and it is within three years of consummation. *See* National Consumer Law Center, Truth in Lending § 6.3.2.3 (5th ed. 2003 and Supp.). The right

therefore is important that these claims be determined and asserted before the foreclosure process finishes. Third, as noted earlier, the attorney can use any legitimate claims and defenses to reduce the pay-off on the existing loan through negotiation. For example, some usury statutes provide for forfeiture of interest.[123] In such a case, all payments previously made generally should be applied to reduce the principal (rather than both principal and interest).[124] This can significantly lower the pay-off on the existing loan. Alternatively, the attorney may be able to negotiate a new payment schedule, and thus alleviate the need for refinancing.

While the facts of each case must be examined to determine the available defenses, certain common inquiries are suggested for certain types of transactions. Non-purchase money mortgage loans should be routinely examined for material Truth in Lending violations which may make the transaction rescindable,[125] for usury claims that may eliminate finance charges or additional amounts due,[126] or overreaching in general.[127] Routinely, home improvement transactions should be examined as well for deceptive sales practices.[128] A mobile home purchase may often involve warranty[129] or usury[130] claims.

Once the client's financial situation and legal claims have been assessed, the next step is to assess the cost of refinancing. Unfortunately, it is not as easy as it might seem to determine the real cost of refinancing, and how it compares to the current obligation. While most mortgages are interest-bearing, and so interest rebates are a less important consideration, they often have non-rebatable points and high closing costs which complicate an evaluation of this option.[131] Simply looking for a lower interest rate or a longer repayment period will not necessarily lead to a cheaper loan. Other factors must be assessed as well, such as prepayment penalties or unfavorable rebate terms on the existing loan

(which would increase the principal balance being refinanced) and closing costs for the new loan which could further increase the principal balance on a new loan. However, *where appropriate*, refinancing at a lower rate can make a big difference to a client facing foreclosure. Chart 1 shows that, for example, refinancing a $10,000, ten-year, 25% loan at 15% for fifteen years would reduce monthly payments from $227.49 to $139.96.

CHART 1
PAYMENT ON VARIOUS LOANS

Amount Financed	APR	10 Years	15 Years	30 Years
$10,000	10%	$132.15	$107.46	$87.76
	15%	161.33	139.96	126.44
	20%	193.26	175.63	167.10
	25%	227.49	213.55	208.46
$15,000	10%	198.23	161.19	131.64
	15%	242.00	209.94	189.67
	20%	289.88	263.44	250.65
	25%	341.24	320.33	312.69
$20,000	10%	264.30	214.92	175.51
	15%	322.67	279.92	252.89
	20%	386.51	351.26	334.20
	25%	454.99	427.11	416.92

Any evaluation of the advantages of refinancing is complicated by the number of interdependent variables involved in the credit transactions being examined, as mentioned earlier.[132] These variables include the *principal*, which varies with claims and defenses, closing costs, broker's fees, origination fees or points, and other charges permitted in many states.

Another variable, the *interest rate*, varies greatly with the general economy, and from lender to lender. It may be fixed or adjusted during the term of the mortgage. The rate also may involve elements considered "earned" by the creditor on the day of loan (e.g., points or other precomputed finance charges) and elements that are earned over time during each payment period (e.g., interest, monthly service charges).

A third variable is the *term*, or duration of the loan, which may vary from three to thirty years, depending on the type of mortgage and lender. Other factors are the amount and timing of the *payments*, which can be equal amounts, involve a large balloon payment, complex graduated payments, bi-monthly rather than monthly payments, or other complexities. *Other terms*, such as prepayment penalties and the Rule of 78 affect the refinancing.

Finally, each of these variables must be examined for both the existing and new mortgage extensions, which could involve any number of mortgages; e.g., an existing first and second mortgage refinanced by a new first mortgage only or a new first and second mortgage.

to cure a default in a chapter 13 bankruptcy may also be lost. National Consumer Law Center, Consumer Bankruptcy Law and Practice § 11.6.2 (6th ed. 2000 and Supp.). *See also* § 6.2, *supra*, for a discussion of whether usury claims survive a refinancing.

123 *See* § 10.8, *infra*.

124 *Id.*

125 *See* National Consumer Law Center, Truth in Lending Ch. 6 (5th ed. 2003 and Supp.).

126 *See, e.g.*, Chs. 4 through 8.

127 *See* Ch. 11, *infra*.

128 *See* § 11.5.3, *infra*. National Consumer Law Center, Unfair and Deceptive Acts and Practices § 5.6.1 (5th ed. 2001 and Supp.).

129 *See* National Consumer Law Center, Truth in Lending § 6.3.2.3 (5th ed. 2003 and Supp.).

130 Federal preemption laws have created special rules for mobile home financing, which creditors must comply with to take advantage of preemption. Failure to comply with the federal rules may result in the violation of the state usury law. *See* Quiller v. Barclay's Am. Credit Ins., 764 F.2d 1400 (11th Cir. 1985), *affirming and reinstating* 727 F.2d 1067 (11th Cir. 1984), *cert. denied*, 476 U.S. 1124 (1986); § 3.9.3.4, *supra*.

131 *See* §§ 5.5.2.2, 6.4.1.3, *supra*.

132 *See generally* Chs. 4 and 5, *supra*.

CHART 2
EFFECTIVE ANNUAL COST OF CLOSING COSTS

Amount Financed (AF) & Closing Costs (CC)	APR	1 Yr.	2 Yr.	5 Yr.	10 Yr.	20 Yr.
1,000(AF)	10% APR	167%	92%	46%	30%	23%
500(CC)	12% APR	170%	95%	48%	33%	26%
10,000(AF)	10% APR	19.81%	15.18%	12.24%	11.24%	10.76%
500(CC)	12% APR	21.86%	17.23%	14.28%	13.29%	12.82%
10,000(AF)	10% APR	30%	21%	14.65%	12.58%	11.58%
1,000(CC)	12% APR	32%	23%	16.57%	14.69%	13.72%
15,000(AF)	10% APR	16.4%	13.41%	11.47%	10.82%	10.50%
500(CC)	12% APR	18.49%	15.44%	13.50%	12.85%	12.54%

Thus, a simple comparison of the Annual Percentage Rates (APR) of the old and new mortgage will not determine whether it is financially advantageous to refinance an existing mortgage, even if the new mortgage's APR is several percentage points lower than the old. A simple APR comparison is uninformative, because it does not adequately take into account other variables, such as closing costs, points, origination and application fees and other front-end charges on the new mortgages,[133] or prepayment penalties and incomplete rebates of unearned interest or insurance premiums on the old mortgage.[134]

The impact of points and closing costs makes refinancing decisions difficult, because they may make any savings in the finance charge illusory. These front-end and prepayment penalty costs are one-time expenses, and their impact on the real cost of borrowing *per year* will depend on how many years their cost will be spread over before the next refinancing or the sale of the house. A good rule of thumb to apply when points were charged on the existing loan is not to refinance unless the *contractual interest rate* on the existing note is at least two to four percentage points higher than the TIL-disclosed Annual Percentage Rate on the new note.[135]

Where the loan in question is a first lien, there are some special advantages to refinancing with a first mortgage instead of taking out a second mortgage or an unsecured loan. Rates on first mortgages from reputable lenders are usually lower than for other types of loans, the repayment period is likely to be the longest available, and there may be a better choice of fixed (as opposed to variable) rate mort-

gages available. The main disadvantage of a first mortgage refinancing is that there may be a lengthy application period, during which interest rates may rise. While some first mortgage loans may include higher closing costs and points, in recent years second mortgage lenders have become more expensive in this regard. The unsecured loan option may be preferable if the consumer later needs to file a chapter 13 bankruptcy.

The closing costs and points on the consolidation of an existing first and second mortgage into a single new first mortgage usually will be higher than if only the second mortgage were refinanced, since some of these are percentage-based fees. In addition, homeowners often finance these higher closing costs and points, driving up the loan balance, and consequently, the finance charges over the life of the loan even more. Chart 2 shows the effective annual cost of closing costs on a mortgage.[136] The cost is particularly high in the short run. For example, the effective annual cost is 167% for a $500.00 closing cost if only $1,000 is borrowed for one year at a 10% APR.

Because of points on either the existing or new loan and closing costs for the new loan, refinancing at a *lower* APR *may cost more in the short run* than staying with the existing, higher-rate APR mortgage. So, when considering refinancing, the rate on the new mortgage must be significantly lower if your clients do not expect to have the new mortgage for ten years or more. If your clients expect, for example, to retire after five years and sell their home, they could be worse off in terms of their *total cost* by refinancing at a lower APR with somewhat lower payments. This is in part because the closing costs and points on the new mortgage increase the new loan's principal balance compared to the existing loan's principal balance. It may also be explained by the effect of any front-end charges (e.g., points or closing costs) incurred on the existing mortgage, to the extent these were included in the APR, as Chart 2 demonstrates.

---

133 Some closing costs may not be reflected in the APR at all. Rather, they are considered part of the amount financed in most circumstances. *See, e.g.*, Reg. Z, 12 C.F.R. § 226.4(c)(7) (closing costs) and Official Staff Commentary to Reg. Z § 226.4(a)-3 (broker's fees). *See generally* § 4.1.1, *supra*; National Consumer Law Center, Truth in Lending Ch. 3 (5th ed. 2003 and Supp.).

134 *See* § 6.3, Ch. 5, *supra*.

135 This is because contractual interest rates usually are charged on top of points, while Truth in Lending requires the APR to include points in its calculation. *See* National Consumer Law Center, Truth in Lending §§ 3.2.3, 3.7.5 (5th ed. 2003 and Supp.).

---

136 In some parts of the country where home equity loans are being heavily marketed, some lenders may sporadically waive closing costs.

CHART 3

Terms of Refinance[137]	Current Balance	Monthly Payment	Nominal Rate	Balance After 5 More Years	5 Year Balance Increase	5 Year Savings on Payments (Loss)	20 Years Savings Loss
No Refinance[138] (12% APR) (4 points)	$47,631.78	$505.55	11.43%	$43,449.92	—	—	—
11% APR $1,500 closing fee; 0 points	49,131.78	507.13	11%	44,618.50	1,168.58	(94.80)	(379.20)
10.5% APR $1,500 closing fee; 0 points	49,131.78	490.52	10.5%	44,375.09	925.17	901.80	3,607.20
10.5% APR $1,500 closing fee; 2 points	50,114.42	490.61	10.21%	45,113.73	1,663.81	896.40	3,585.60
10% APR $1,500 closing fee; 2 points	50,114.42	474.03	9.71%	44,848.84	1,398.92	1,891.20	7,564.80

Chart 3 illustrates the short-term effect that closing costs and points have on refinancing a mortgage. The new mortgage's closing costs and points increase the mortgage payout at first. For example, a homeowner with a 12% APR mortgage is interested in refinancing at a lower rate. Even with low closing costs of $1,500, an 11% APR mortgage puts the homeowners in a worse position for the first five years. The balance at the end of five years is $1,168.58 higher than without a refinancing, and $94.80 has been lost over five years in higher monthly payments. Over the full 20-year term the homeowner would be $379.20 behind. Even if closing costs were only $1,500, the homeowner would have to get a 10.5% APR mortgage with no points to be roughly even in five years, and just $3,607.20 ahead after twenty years. If the new mortgage also included 2 points, the homeowner would have to get a mortgage below 10.5% APR with low closing costs to be ahead in five years. This is important because most Americans hold onto their mortgages for less than ten years.

The difference between the contractual interest rate on the existing mortgage and the Annual Percentage Rate, as disclosed on the TIL disclosure statement on the new mortgage, probably has to be two percentage points or more to make a refinancing worthwhile in the five to ten-year horizon, depending upon the amount of the new closing costs and the old and new points. If your clients are considering refinancing a mortgage and keeping it for less than ten years, an accountant or other credit expert should calculate the payout at five- or ten-year intervals to see if the refinancing will cost more than it saves.

If the client facing foreclosure is elderly, there is one additional refinancing avenue to consider: the reverse mortgage. Reverse mortgages are not universally available, nor are they universally suitable for seniors. However, where appropriate, they may offer the elder homeowner a chance to avoid foreclosure without incurring a further burdensome repayment obligation.[139]

These examples show just some of the complexities involved in evaluating the effectiveness of refinancing as a tool to prevent foreclosure. When "creative financing" options are considered for the new loan—variable-rate/variable-payment mortgages, negatively amortizing mortgages with large balloons—a realistic assessment requires educated guesses about both the direction of interest rate movement in the future, and the stability of the clients' future earnings.[140] It is difficult for economists and financial advisors to do this with much accuracy, much less poor mortal lawyers. Nonetheless, all of these factors must at least be assessed. If it can be done, lowering payments by a meaningful amount through refinancing can be the best solution for the clients. An ill-considered refinance, however, may mean the clients pay more just to end up with the same dilemma a little later.

---

137 Balance of existing loan plus points and closing costs refinanced for 20 years.

138 Five-year-old, 25-year mortgage at 12% APR, 4 discount points, original amount financed was $48,000.

139 *See generally Spending the Home*, 13 NCLC REPORTS *Consumer Credit and Usury Ed.* 5 (Sept./Oct. 1994) for a brief explanation of reverse mortgages and some of the pros and cons.

140 Variable-rate transactions are discussed in § 4.3.6, *supra*. Negatively amortizing loans are described in § 4.3.1.2, *supra*.

6.6 Business or Consumer Loan? May Refinancing Change the Character of a Loan?

As is discussed elsewhere,[141] whether a loan has a consumer purpose or a business purpose is sometimes critical in determining which regulatory statute applies. However, renewals may complicate the question. A consolidation may combine both consumer and business purpose loans. What then is the character of the consolidation loan? Usually the same standards will be used as to evaluate an original loan with mixed purposes. The court likely will look at the "primary" purpose of the loan, and if the bulk of the proceeds is business-related, it will be considered a business loan.[142]

A business loan secured by residential real estate may be refinanced in order to stave off foreclosure on the family home. Does that make the refinancing a consumer loan? In *Toy National Bank v. McGarr*,[143] one court articulated a *per se* rule. The court rejected the notion of shifting purposes, stating that the "only workable approach is to characterize a loan transaction by the use to which the proceeds are originally placed and maintain the same characterization throughout the life of the loan."[144] In *Toy* the consolidation loan at issue had a ratio of personal purpose to business purpose of 1 to 12, hence the court held it was not primarily for personal purposes even though the purpose of the consolidation may have been to forestall foreclosure.

Other courts do not adopt a *per se* approach, but make a determination after evaluating all the circumstances. *Anderson v. Lester*[145] held a renewal to be a personal loan where the borrowers' primary motivation was to protect their home from seizure. The proceeds were used to pay off those debts most immediately threatening the home, and the creditor knew of this motivation. A third court found the *Toy National Bank per se* rule unduly broad, but nonetheless held the renewal to be a business purpose loan where the borrowers had emphasized the business purpose to the lender, intentionally obfuscating matters, and the lender was unaware of any non-business purpose to the loan.[146]

There seems to be less ambiguity in the converse situation, where a personal loan is refinanced as part of a business purpose transaction. Paying off a second mortgage personal loan with proceeds of a loan specifically obtained to start a business has been held to be a business loan.[147]

---

141 *See* § 9.2.2, *infra*.

142 Toy Nat'l Bank v. McCarr, 286 N.W.2d 376 (Iowa 1979). *See also* § 9.2.2.2, *infra*. Standards for use in determining business purpose loans under Truth in Lending may also be helpful. *See* National Consumer Law Center, Truth in Lending § 2.4.2.2 (5th ed. 2003 and Supp.).

143 286 N.W.2d 376 (Iowa 1979). *Accord In re* Stipetich, 294 B.R. 635 (Bankr. W.D. Pa. 2003) (Md. law) (loan that refinanced business loan not consumer loan even though borrower obtained it to prevent foreclosure).

144 286 N.W.2d 376, 378 (Iowa 1979). This court also articulates the rule that a business purpose loan is not changed by the character of the security. But that is a different question than whether, when the primary purpose and motivation of a subse-

quent credit transaction is to save the family home, the new primary purpose overrides the old primary purpose.

145 382 So. 2d 1019 (La. Ct. App. 1980), *cert. denied*, 450 U.S. 1045 (1980).

146 Conrad v. Smith, 712 P.2d 866 (Wash. Ct. App. 1986). Another court discusses the lack of compelling authority for the question of whether refinancing a business loan to save a home converts it to a personal loan, but decides it is easier to find a different issue on which to determine the outcome of the case before it. *In re* Jackson, 42 B.R. 76, 79–81 (Bankr. D.D.C. 1984). *See also* Gregory v. Federal Land Bank, 515 So. 2d 1200 (Miss. 1987) (where loan refinanced agricultural debt, loan application stated purpose was agricultural in several places, and a purchase of a home with the proceeds would have violated the lending agreement, borrower's contention that TIL applied to transaction because its purpose was to prevent foreclosure on his farm and to finance purchase of a house failed).

147 Anderson v. Foothill Indus. Bank, 674 P.2d 232 (Wyo. 1984).

Chapter 7   Hidden Interest

7.1 Introduction

7.1.1 First Principles

For as long as usury restrictions have existed, creditors have attempted to circumvent their limitations. In medieval Europe, when it was completely forbidden to charge interest on loans, lenders constructed transactions, such as joint venture investments and sales of bills of exchange, which they claimed were not loans, and the profit from which they claimed was not interest. Along the same lines, they promoted legal fictions such as the notion that charges assessed on a loan once its repayment was overdue were not interest, but were merely permissible penalties.

With the legalization of interest by the first usury statutes in sixteenth century England, these credit machinations did not disappear, but rather changed their focus. The techniques which had formerly been used to conceal the assessment of any interest were adapted to conceal the extent of interest being charged. Most of these tactics, in modified form, are still with us today, and they are addressed in this chapter under the title of "hidden interest."

For the purposes of this chapter, "hidden interest" refers to charges (or other consideration) paid in conjunction with a credit contract which are classified as interest under state law regulating the transaction but which are not described as such, or are not described at all, in the contract, and which are consequently not included in the stated interest rate. To use a simple example, if a lender charges the maximum interest rate on the face of a loan contract and, in addition, imposes a $100 "loan fee," that fee may constitute usurious hidden interest unless it is specifically allowed as a non-interest charge under state law. Hidden interest may also exist if the creditor attributes excess payments to supposedly independent third parties, if the creditor misstates the amount of principal on which interest is being charged,[1] or if a credit transaction is restructured so that both the extension of credit and the payment of any "interest" are concealed. All of these hidden interest transactions are discussed below.[2]

This chapter examines some of the favorite hiding places for interest. Yet, because of the ingenuity of lenders who are constantly searching for new paths around usury statutes, it is unlikely that every possible subterfuge will be mentioned. Consequently, it is critical for practitioners to keep one fundamental principle in mind: "credit" and "interest" are what state law, not the credit contract, defines them to be.[3] Do not accept the contract's characterization of any payment as non-interest, or even its description of the over-all transaction if an extension of credit may be concealed.[4] Instead, read and rely on the state statutes and case law.

Although a number of states have deregulated their interest rates, it is important for practitioners to keep an eye open for hidden interest even in these deregulated states. Despite the absence of fixed usury caps, some lenders try to understate the interest rate as a deceptive sales device, and that may constitute a violation of the deregulated usury statutes. *See* §§ 9.2.7, 9.2.8, *infra*.

A good tip-off to the presence of hidden interest is the Truth in Lending disclosure which must accompany a consumer credit contract.[5] The definition of interest under state usury laws frequently differs from the costs of credit which must be included in the Truth in Lending Annual Percentage Rate (APR) disclosure, so it often happens that the APR will be slightly higher than the contract rate. Nevertheless, any *significant* difference between the interest rate stated in the contract and the APR, or between the TIL "amount financed" and the face amount of the note signed by the consumer strongly suggests that the contract contains hidden

---

1   *See generally* § 7.4, *infra*.

2   Hidden interest, in the form of unearned charges, may also exist when a precomputed debt is accelerated or prepaid and the

creditor fails to rebate unearned credit insurance premiums or interest. *See* Ch. 5, *supra*. It may also be present in refinancing in a variety of forms. *See* Ch. 6, *supra*. Chapter 8, *infra* discusses credit insurance as a device to hide additional profit.

3   This principle can cut both ways. Although amounts described as "interest" in the contract are almost always treated as such, the contract will not control if the law says otherwise. *See* Lowell & Austin, Inc. v. Traux, 507 A.2d 949 (Vt. 1985).

4   *See, e.g.,* Skinner v. Cen-Pen Corp., 414 S.E.2d 824 (Va. 1992) (courts not bound by contractual recitations in usury case; will look behind formal documents to true nature of transaction). *See generally* § 9.2.1.5, *infra*.

5   *See* § 4.4.1, *supra*; National Consumer Law Center, Truth in Lending (5th ed. 2003 and Supp.). A few statutes incorporate the TILA "finance charge" within the statutory definition of "interest." *See* Thelen v. Ducharme, 151 Mich. App. 441, 390 N.W.2d 264 (1986).

interest of some kind and should be closely examined. Furthermore, the itemization of the amount financed[6] may reveal a kind of charge often mislabeled for both usury and Truth in Lending purposes,[7] which also should trigger further investigation.

7.1.2 Intersection with Preemption

Much of the discussion in this chapter must be tempered by considerations of rate exportation and federal preemption, a topic discussed in Chapter 3, *supra*. The lenders who can take advantage of rate exportation, mainly banks and thrifts, are often chartered in states with few if any restrictions on their charges. Thus they are permitted to charge anything they want in terms of "interest," irrespective of the law in the borrower's home state.

Because of rate exportation, these lenders sought—and have obtained—a very broad definition of "interest" charges to include charges such as late fees and overlimit fees.[8] This broad definition allows the lender to charge whatever it wants—it is the consumers who have lost by classifying fees as interest in these cases. Making the situation even worse, some courts have held that certain fees are considered "interest" for the purposes of rate exportation, but are not "interest" for purposes of determining whether they violate state usury laws.[9]

7.2 Payments for Lender Services: What Is Interest?

7.2.1 Fees Based on the Creditor's Expenses

"Interest" can be defined as compensation paid to a lender for the use of money or the forbearance of a debt.[10] Broadly applied, such a definition would include any payment to a lender, regardless of whether the lender used the payment to cover expenses or instead attributed it to profit. However, in an attempt to circumvent the interest ceilings set by statute or agreement and to disguise the actual costs of a loan to the borrower, creditors have traditionally argued that certain specific expenses associated with a loan, such as closing costs or credit insurance, especially those costs attributable to third party services,[11] are not compensation for the loan. Instead, creditors argue, the expenses are separate payment for the specific services provided. Because the separate fees are not compensation for the loan, the argument concludes, they are not "interest." This analysis allows creditors to pass many of their costs on to borrowers, increasing their profit with no ostensible increase in interest rate.

The separation of "interest" from other costs of credit is a fundamentally flawed view of a credit transaction since it regards what is actually one transaction as a set of smaller transactions each of which may be separately compensated. The problem is that many of the separate services are tied to the loan transaction and are only "purchased" by the borrower so that the credit may be obtained. Furthermore, some of the "services" would not be purchased separately from the loan under any circumstances. Consider the absurdity of a consumer paying for "document preparation" or "processing" if he or she were not trying to get a loan.[12]

Despite the illogic of allowing lenders to assess non-interest fees for loan-related expenses, this approach is widely accepted under state law even when the separate services primarily benefit the lender.[13] As a general rule, recognized lender fees may be excluded from interest if they compensate the lender for reasonable expenses actually incurred in connection with a particular loan.[14] Following

---

6   The TIL itemization of the amount financed may not have been automatically given to the borrower, as the creditor is not required to do so. Reg. Z, 12 C.F.R. § 226.18(c)(2). However, in most transactions, the components of the amount financed and loan principal can be determined from either the TIL itemization, or in mortgage transactions, a settlement sheet or dispersal sheet. If none of these are immediately available, the advocate should obtain this information, if necessary through discovery. It is impossible to adequately evaluate a consumer credit transaction for a possible usury defense or claim without it. As a matter of fact, it is impossible to adequately evaluate a consumer credit transaction for TIL, UDAP, fraud or any other of a wide variety of potential claims and defenses without the mathematical break-down of the loan this information provides.

7   Regulation Z, which implements TILA, also excludes a number of fees from treatment as a "finance charge." *See* National Consumer Law Center, Truth in Lending Ch. 3 (5th ed. 2003 and Supp.).

8   Smiley v. Citibank (South Dakota), 517 U.S. 735, 116 S. Ct. 1730, 135 L. Ed. 2d 25 (1996).

9   Video Trax, Inc. v. NationsBank, N.A., 33 F. Supp. 2d 1041 (S.D. Fla. 1998) (overdraft fees are interest for purposes of the National Bank Act, but are not interest for usury analysis), *aff'd without op.*, 205 F.3d 1358 (11th Cir. 2000), *cert. denied*, 531 U.S. 822 (2000); Nicolas v. Deposit Guar. Nat. Bank, 182 F.R.D. 226 (S.D. Miss. 1998) (same).

10   *See, e.g.*, Black's Law Dictionary (7th ed. 1999).

11   *See* § 7.3, *infra*.

12   Though, as is discussed below, sometimes such fees may be considered interest.

13   *See* Eskridge, *One Hundred Years of Ineptitude: The Need For Mortgage Rules Consonant With the Economic and Psychological Dynamics of the Home Sale and Loan Transaction*, 70 Va. L. Rev. 1083, 1092 (1984).

14   *See, e.g.*, Matter of Ferris, 764 F.2d 1475 (11th Cir. 1985) (document preparation fee not interest in Georgia); Fikes v. First Fed. S&L of Anchorage, 533 P.2d 251 (Alaska 1975); Harris v. Guaranty Fin. Corp., 244 Ark. 218, 424 S.W.2d 355 (1968); Klett v. Security Acceptance Corp., 38 Cal. 2d 770, 242 P.2d 873 (1952); Collins v. Union Federal S&L Ass'n, 662 P.2d 610

the same approach, any charge which cannot be attributed to a specific loan-related expense is designed merely to cover the lender's overhead expenses or to contribute to its profit, and is interest on the loan unless a statute specifically says otherwise.[15]

Because the types and amounts of fees which may be excluded from interest vary widely from state to state and may, within any state, vary with the class of lender and loan, the first step to determining whether a lender has properly excluded specific fees from interest on a contract must be to check the relevant state code. In many states, the statute will provide a clear distinction between interest and non-interest charges by itemizing all the allowable non-interest charges or by setting a non-interest percentage fee to cover all expenses.[16] Some states may prohibit the charging of or limit the amount of fees in certain types of transactions in non-usury statutes, e.g., in statutes relating to real estate mortgages, some states limit the fees chargeable by lenders or their attorneys that can be passed onto borrowers.[17]

Other statutes may simply allow "reasonable" expenses to be excluded from interest,[18] while still other state codes

---

(Nev. 1983). *See also* Eskridge, *One Hundred Years of Ineptitude: The Need For Mortgage Rules Consonant With the Economic and Psychological Dynamics of the Home Sale and Loan Transaction,* 70 Va. L. Rev. 1083, 1096 (1984).

15 *Id. See also* Johnston v. Citizen's Bank & Trust Co., 659 F.2d 865 (8th Cir. 1981) (applying Arkansas law); Anderson v. Chainani (*In re* Kemper), 263 B.R. 773 (Bankr. E.D. Tex. 2001) (summary judgment inappropriate on issue of whether a "consulting fee" is interest as parties dispute whether any services were actually performed); Modern Pioneers v. Nancleen, 437 P.2d 658, 664–65 (Ariz. 1968) (tax service fee, which was a payment for a service that checks property tax payments twice a year, is overhead and constitutes interest); First Nat'l Mortgage Co. v. Arkmo Lumber & Supply Co., 277 Ark. 298, 641 S.W.2d 31 (1982) (commitment fee covers cost of doing business); Winston v. Personal Fin. Co., 220 Ark. 580, 249 S.W.2d 315 (1952) (fees for services performed by lender's employees were interest); Whittemore Homes, Inc. v. Fleishman, 190 Cal. App. 2d 554, 12 Cal. Rptr. 235 (1961) (fee for "other services and things of value" was interest); First Fed. Savings v. Norwood Realty Co., 212 Ga. 524, 92 S.E.2d 763 (1956) (service charge was interest); Vikowsky v. Savannah Appliance Serv. Corp., 179 Ga. App. 135, 345 S.E.2d 621 (1986) ($50 "administrative fee" was not an "official fee" that could be excluded from interest under state RISA); Real Estate Trust v. Lentz, 153 Md. 624, 139 A. 351 (1927); Vee Bee Serv. Co. v. Household Fin. Corp., 51 N.Y.S.2d 590 (Sup. Ct. 1944), *aff'd,* 55 N.Y.S.2d 570 (1945); O'Connor v. Lamb, 593 S.W.2d 385 (Tex. Ct. App. 1979); Cuevas v. Montoya, 48 Wash. App. 871, 740 P.2d 858 (1987) (attorney fees and "set-up" fee were charges for services normally incidental to making a loan, thus were interest); Aetna Fin. Co. v. Darwin, 691 P.2d 581 (Wash. Ct. App. 1984) ($1000 "loan funding fee" to prepare documents, arrange payoffs, etc. was interest; "[c]harges for making a loan and for the use of money are interest; charges are not interest if they are for services actually provided by the lender, reasonably worth the price charged, and for which the borrower agreed to pay."). *But cf.* Barnett Bank of West Orlando v. Abromowitz, 419 So. 2d 627 (Fla. 1982) (court appears to include "service fee" in interest calculation while stating that it is not interest).

Some state statutes do permit lenders additional fees to cover their overhead expenses. *See, e.g.,* Henley v. Cameron Auto Pawn (*In re* Henley), 228 B.R. 425 (Bankr. E.D. Ark. 1998) (Tennessee auto title pawn law permits lender to charge 2% interest plus "customary fee to defray the ordinary costs of operating a title-pledge office"; in this case, lender permitted to charge "customary fee" of $432 per month on loan of $2,400; court noted that generally Tennessee law indicated that lender charges should not include overhead, but the auto title pawn statute was legislatively created exception).

16 *See, e.g.,* Md. Com. Law Code Ann. §§ 12-105 (specifying charges excludable from interest on most loans), 12-307 (fees on consumer loans); Va. Code Ann. § 6.1-330.71–.72 (1988 Replacement Volume) (certain second mortgage lenders allowed 2% "loan fee" and specified fees); Wash. Rev. Code § 19.52.020 (for loans under $500, 4% or $15 "set-up" fee may be charged and shall not be considered interest). Such statutes should be read closely. By statutorily enumerating allowable charges, non-enumerated charges thus may be considered interest. *See, e.g.,* Garrison v. First Fed. Saving & Loan Ass'n, 402 S.E.2d 24 (Va. 1991) ("risk management fee" was interest where it was not specifically authorized by statute; appraisal charge in excess of actual cost was interest); Cuevas v. Montoya, 48 Wash. App. 871, 740 P.2d 858 (1987) (set-up fees in connection with loans larger than $500 are interest [*cf.* Wash. Rev. Code § 19.52.020]). *Compare* Opinion of the Mich. Att'y Gen., No. 6594, 5 Consumer Cred. Guide (CCH) § 95,775 (July 17, 1989) (documentary fees, services fees or inspection fees imposed on installment buyer as part of cash price or amount financed were not specifically provided for in MVRISA and therefore violated the statute's limitation on charges) *with* Opinion of the Tenn. Att'y Gen., No. 87-192, 5 Consumer Cred. Guide § 95,918 (CCH) (Dec. 16, 1987) (in response to question about whether document preparation fees could be assessed, opinion says "yes, but . . .," federal law prohibits charging for preparation of RESPA or TIL statements, and other document preparation fees would generally fall within guidelines for loan charges or similar provisions applicable under relevant state or federal general or special usury statute). *See generally* § 9.3.1.2, *infra.* *But see* Grantham v. First Union Home Equity Bank, 685 So. 2d 748 (Ala. Civ. App. 1996) (the cost of an appraisal performed by creditor's employee was properly included in the finance charge under Ala. Code § 5-19-1; § 5-19-1 merely defines the charges to be included in the finance and does not prohibit the charging of any particular fee); Colangelo v. Norwest Mortgage, Inc., 598 N.W.2d 14 (Minn. App. 1999) (maxim of contract construction *expressio unius est exclusio alterius* (the mention of one thing excludes the other) may not be helpful to argue that a list of allowable fees means that fees not listed are prohibited when the mortgage also lists charges that are prohibited).

17 *See, e.g.,* Turner v. First Union Nat'l Bank, 740 A.2d 1081 (N.J. Sup. Ct. 1999) (interpreting an act guaranteeing borrowers the right to independent legal representation and limiting attorney fees that can be charged by lender attorneys); Negrin v. Norwest Mortgage, Inc., 700 N.Y.S.2d 184 (N.Y. App. 1999) (interpreting N.Y. law requiring that mortgage liens be promptly released upon payment in full and limiting fees for the provision of a payoff amount). *But see* Baughman v. Mellon Mortgage Co., 621 N.W.2d 776 (Minn. App. 2001) (tax service fee, a one-time fee imposed even if an escrow account is not established, is allowed under Minnesota law).

18 *See* Fikes v. First Fed. S&L Ass'n, 533 P.2d 251, 265 (Alaska 1975) (interpreting Alaska Stat. § 06.30.590); Luttenberger v.

may not treat the matter at all. In either of the latter two circumstances, the attorney for a borrower who has been assessed supposedly non-interest charges should consider several questions. First, does the fee cover specific expenses related to his or her client's specific loan? Fees covering only overhead or profit might be challenged as hidden interest.[19] Second, were the fees actually incurred? Appraisal fees for appraisals which never were made or filing fees for documents which were never filed are good examples of concealed interest.[20] Finally, was the size of the fee reasonably related to the costs of the services involved? Excessive charges for otherwise valid services are not actually attributable to those services to the extent they are excessive, and should be considered interest to that extent.[21]

Loan document preparation fees present an interesting issue that other fees do not. In addition to the potential claim that these fees may not be authorized by state law and that they may be interest, practitioners should explore whether the entity preparing the documents was engaged in the unauthorized practice of law.[22] If the lender or other entity charged a fee for preparing or filling in the blanks on legal documents and this activity was incidental to the entity's business, the lender or entity may be engaged in the unauthorized practice of law.[23] Note that the charging of a fee that is otherwise illegal may have Truth in Lending implications depending upon whether that fee is treated as a finance charge.[24]

In the automobile financing context, dealers often separately impose charges for specific "services." Traditionally dealers treated many of these "services" as part of their overhead. Fees that dealers commonly tack onto the cost of the car include delivery and handling fees and conveyance

---

Conseco Fin. Servs. Corp., 671 N.W.2d 425 (Iowa 2003) (Iowa law permits lender to charge any closing cost agreed to in writing by borrower for a home-secured loan.).

But note that authorization of "reasonable" charges does not necessarily grant the creditor authority to charge them automatically on every loan. Thus, if a fee is unreasonable under the facts of an individual case, it may be usurious even if it is below a statutory maximum. *See In re* Bogan, 281 F. Supp. 242 (W.D. Tenn. 1968) (repeated assessment of investigation fee in a series of refinancing transactions was unreasonable and usurious).

19 *See* Eskridge, *One Hundred Years of Ineptitude: The Need For Mortgage Rules Consonant With the Economic and Psychological Dynamics of the Home Sale and Loan Transaction*, 70 Va. L. Rev. 1083, 1092 (1984).

20 *E.g.*, Matter of Mickler, 50 B.R. 818 (Bankr. M.D. Fla. 1985) (sham referral and consulting fees); *In re* Rosner, 48 B.R. 538 (Bankr. E.D.N.Y. 1985) (sham consulting fee); United-Bilt Homes v. Knapp, 239 Ark. 940, 396 S.W.2d 40 (1965) (usury when credit life insurance premium and appraisal fees not expended); Garrison v. First Fed. Saving & Loan Ass'n, 402 S.E.2d 24 (Va. 1991) (appraisal fee in excess of actual cost was interest).

21 *In re* Bogan, 281 F. Supp. 242 (W.D. Tenn. 1968); Fikes v. First Fed. S&L of Anchorage, 533 P.2d 251 (Alaska 1975); Altherr v. Wilshire Mortgage Corp., 104 Ariz. 59, 448 P.2d 859 (1969); U.S. Home & Realty Corp. v. Lehnartz, Clearinghouse No. 43,259, Case No. 87-SP-930 (Mich. Dist. Ct. Sept. 30, 1987) (creditor "purchased" borrower's property from her for $20,000 (less $5200 in fees), and immediately resold it to her for $32,000 at 9%–11% interest; the creditor apparently retained $4200 as a realtor fee; court held standard realty fee sales commission is 7%; fee in excess of 20% was "unwarranted, unconscionable and has no reasonable basis in standard realty fee"; also, creditor rendered no services to warrant commission). Kickbacks to the lender from third party service fees may also be interest. *See* Aclin Ford Co. v. Cordell, 274 Ark. 341, 625 S.W.2d 459 (1981) (insurance sales commission); B.F. Saul Co. v. West End Park N., Inc., 250 Md. 707, 246 A.2d 591 (1968); Stubbs v. Security Consumer Discount, 426 A.2d 1014 (N.J. 1980). *But see* Durante Bros. & Sons Inc. v. Flushing Nat'l Bank, 652 F. Supp. 101, 105 (E.D.N.Y. 1986) (exaggeration or misrepresentation of lender's own costs in connection with loan support claim of fraud rather than usury). *But cf.* Pechinski v. Astoria Fed. Sav. & Loan Ass'n, 238 F. Supp. 2d 640 (S.D.N.Y.), *aff'd*, 345 F.3d 78 (2d Cir. 2003) ("assignment fee" constituting 0.875% of outstanding mortgage balance was not finance charge under TILA, despite fact that bank conceded fee bore little relationship to cost of assignment.).

22 *See, e.g.*, Lawson v. First Union Mortgage Co., 786 N.E.2d 279 (Ind. Ct. App. 2003) (reversing trial court's dismissal of a consumer's equitable claim for return of a document preparation fee; court held that while a lender's lay employees did not commit the unauthorized practice of law by preparing mortgage loan documents, the lender could not charge a separate fee for such documents). *See also In re* Van Dyke, 296 B.R. 591 (Bankr. D. Mass. 2003) (real estate settlement services provided by non-attorney would be unauthorized practice of law, citing Mass. Conveyancers Ass'n v. Colonial Title & Escrow, 2001 WL 669280 (Mass. Super. Ct. June 5, 2001)); Doe v. McMaster, 585 S.E.2d 773 (S.C. 2003) (preparation of mortgage documents, as well as title search and documentation, constitutes practice of law). *But see* King v. First Capital Fin. Servs. Corp., 798 N.E.2d 118 (Ill. App. Ct. 2003) (lender did not commit unauthorized practice of law by preparing mortgage documents for its own use, because it was acting *pro se*), *appeal granted*, 807 N.E.2d 976 (Ill. 2003); Dressel v. Ameribank, 664 N.W.2d 151 (Mich. 2003) (bank did not engage in unauthorized practice of law by preparing mortgage documents using standard form documents, because it did not require the use of legal discretion or "profound legal knowledge").

23 The issue of non-attorneys preparing mortgage documents is a hotly contested one between the legal profession and non-legal entities. *See* Michael C. Ksiazek, Note, *The Model Rules Of Professional Conduct And The Unauthorized Practice Of Law: Justification For Restricting Conveyancing To Attorneys*, 37 Suffolk U. L. Rev. 169 (2004); Joyce Palomar, *The War Between Attorneys and Lay Conveyancers—Empirical Evidence Says "Cease Fire!,"* 31 Conn. L. Rev. 423 (1999). Ironically, the Federal Trade Commission and U.S. Department of Justice have weighed in on the side of the lending industry, believing that permitting non-lawyers to prepare mortgage loan documents is consumer-friendly because it supposedly increases competition and reduces the cost of document preparation. Fed. Trade Comm'n & United States Dep't of Justice, Comments on the American Bar Association's Proposed Model Definition of the Practice of Law (Dec. 20, 2002).

24 *See* National Consumer Law Center, Truth in Lending § 3.9.6.2.3 (5th ed. 2003 and Supp.) (document preparation fees charged in a real-estate-secured loan must be bona fide and reasonable to be disclosed as part of the amount financed; if fee is illegal, it cannot be either bona fide or reasonable).

charges. To justify the delivery and handling charge, dealers claim that they inspect and inventory the car and then clean the interior and exterior. Dealers impose a conveyance fee to register title to the vehicle with the state motor vehicle department.

These fees may constitute interest when the dealer is the lender for a variety of reasons. The dealer may not perform the service, may inflate the actual cost, or may be reimbursed by a third party, such as the manufacturer for the cost.[25] For example, manufacturers may reimburse the dealers for some or all of services performed for a "delivery and handling" fee. Many dealers register title to a vehicle on-line through a computer onsite. In this instance, there is no justification for a $400 conveyance fee.

Further, the state retail installment act may limit the types of fees which the lender may impose. Fees not specifically allowed should constitute interest and support a usury claim.[26] In addition to usury claims, such fees may be challenged under state UDAP acts[27] and the Truth in Lending Act.[28]

Another practice that may create hidden interest is failing to post payments on the date they are received. In loans where interest is calculated using the simple or actuarial method,[29] less interest may be owed over the life of the loan if a consumer makes the periodic payments early. This is so because the amount of each payment which is attributed to interest depends, in part, upon the length of time between payments. If the actual amount of interest charged due to late posting exceeds either the usury cap in that state or the contract rate, the consumer may have a claim for usury.[30]

---

25 *See, e.g.*, Motzer Dodge Jeep Eagle, Inc. v. Ohio Atty. Gen., 642 N.E.2d 20 (Ohio Ct. App. 1994) (some of services covered by a non-optional $95 "delivery and handling" fee were paid for by the manufacturer).

26 *See* § 2.3.3.5, *supra* and § 9.3.1.2, *infra*.

27 Negrin v. Norwest Mortgage, Inc., 700 N.Y.S.2d 184 (N.Y. App. Div. 1999) (allegation that the mortgage lender imposed an unlawful fax fee and a fabricated recording fee during the payoff or refinancing of a loan stated a UDAP claim); Motzer Dodge Jeep Eagle, Inc. v. Ohio Atty. Gen., 642 N.E.2d 20 (Ohio Ct. App. 1994) (fee violated Ohio UDAP Act where delivery and handling fee, supposedly optional, was actually mandatory, where dealer fails to itemize the activities performed for the fee, and where manufacturer actually reimburses for some of the services).

28 If the fee is imposed on credit customers and not loan customers, it should be included in the finance charge. *See* National Consumer Law Center, Truth in Lending § 3.6.5 (5th ed. 2003 and Supp.).

29 *See* discussion in § 4.5, *supra*.

30 In the credit card context, the Truth in Lending Act requires that payments must be credited as of the date of receipt. *See* Reg. Z § 226.10 (same day posting as long as the creditor credits it as the date of receipt, Official Staff Commentary (226.10(a)-1); National Consumer Law Center, Truth in Lending § 5.8.9.1 (5th ed. 2003 and Supp.). There is no corresponding TIL mandate on the closed end transaction side. Practitioners should look to state law or the contract to see if prompt crediting is required. Regardless, a UDAP claim should be considered because the

7.2.2 Points, Commitment Fees, and Other Percentage Fees

7.2.2.1 General

One type of ostensibly non-interest charge that is often used and misused by lenders is a fee calculated as a percentage of loan principal. Depending on the type of lender and loan involved, this fee may be variously described as an "origination fee," "commitment fee," "service charge," or "loan fee," but is perhaps best known as "points" or "discount points," with one point being a sum equal to one percent of the loan principal.[31] The use and misuse of points create a number of potential issues apart from their characterization as interest or not. Because of the significant added cost to borrowers, and their inherent capacity for deception, they are discussed in some detail elsewhere in this volume in relation to other trouble spots. General calculation issues are discussed in § 4.7, *supra*, the special rebate questions they present are discussed in § 5.5.2.2, *supra* and the distortions they cause in refinancing are discussed in §§ 6.3.2 and 6.4.1.3, *supra*.

Regardless of the precise name used or the precise manner of calculation, points are essentially a "bonus": an additional incentive or inducement supposedly offered to the lender to convince it to issue a loan. As such, it is logically very difficult to characterize points as anything but interest, both because they are clearly compensation to the lender for the use of money, and because it is extremely hard for a lender to discover any separate service, apart from general overhead expense or risk assumed, which varies with the size of the loan and can thus justify a non-interest percentage fee.[32]

For example, points on home mortgages have been alternately described as compensation to the lender for the costs of packaging a loan for resale on the secondary mortgage

---

creditor is engaging in an unfair or deceptive practice to make additional profit.

31 *See generally*, Eskridge, *One Hundred Years of Ineptitude: The Need For Mortgage Rules Consonant With the Economic and Psychological Dynamics of the Home Sale and Loan Transaction*, 70 Va. L. Rev. 1083, 1093 (1984).

32 *See* Fikes v. First Fed. S&L of Anchorage, 533 P.2d 251 (Alaska 1975) (among other considerations listed, the variation of a "loan fee" with the amount or risk of a loan suggests interest).

Under a Financial Accounting Standards Board standard, lenders must recognize income received from origination or similar fees over the entire loan term rather than at the consummation of the loan because, as a matter of generally accepted accounting practice, originating a loan is not a separate income-producing activity apart from the lending of money itself. If originating a loan is an integral part of the over-all lending process, then expenses incurred through loan origination are part of a lender's overhead expense which cannot be compensated by non-interest fees. FASB Statement No. 91, *Accounting for Nonrefundable Fees and Costs Associated with Originating or Acquiring Loans and Initial Direct Costs of Leases*.

market ("origination fees"), or as compensation for the discounted price at which the mortgage must be resold ("discount points"). However, the first justification fails when one realizes that the costs of "originating" a mortgage either have already been passed on to the borrower in the form of appraisal fees, attorney fees, etc., or are just overhead costs. The second justification similarly fails because compensating the lender for the discount on resale is no different from guaranteeing its profit margin.[33]

Whatever the theoretical justification, points are particularly subject to abuse by high rate lenders for two reasons. The first reason is that they offer an effective way for creditors to understate the real cost of credit (and thereby undercut legitimate competitors) when trying to sell the credit to prospective borrowers.[34]

Consider this scenario: A borrower needs $5,000; she and the loan officer discuss the monthly payments for a five-year term.[35] The loan officer explains that her monthly payments at 15% will be $146.76. And indeed, 15% is the interest rate specified in the promissory note, but the stated principal is $6,169, not $5,000. The lender has capitalized (treated as principal, not interest) 19 points in drafting the note and making the calculations.[36] The lender's compensation for that $5,000 loan is $3,805.60: $2,636.60 "interest" (15% for 5 years on the proceeds plus points), plus $1,169 (19 points). Somewhere in the mound of loan papers there should be a Truth in Lending disclosure statement which, if properly done, discloses the cost of credit more accurately as an APR of 25%.[37] But the borrower may not notice this buried document, or understand its significance if she does, and the lender encourages (or at least does not discourage) the impression that this is a 15% loan.[38]

The second reason that points are subject to abuse is the advantage to a lender of taking a sizeable portion of the compensation for a loan in points is in the event of prepayment, by refinancing, outright pay-off or acceleration in the event of default. Because lenders treat points as "earned" at consummation, they generally do not treat points as subject to rebate.[39] To see how that affects the borrower, assume the above loan is paid off after twenty-four months. If treated simply as a $5,000, 25% loan, the lender would have earned $2,213.22 in interest; but when treated as a $6,169, 15% loan the lender will have earned $1,586.86 in regular interest, plus the $1,169 in points, for a total of $2,755.86. The borrower paid over $540 more for the "15%" loan. The effective interest rate the borrower paid on her $5,000 for those two years was thus 29 1/2% when the impact of the points is considered. Given the frequency of refinancing, particularly in some segments of the consumer credit industry, such an example makes clear the impetus to abuse the concept of points.[40]

7.2.2.2 Legal Considerations

When statutes do not address the issue, lenders carry the burden of demonstrating that points and other fees are justified by actual recognized costs associated with a loan

---

33 *See* Bernhardt v. Atlantic Fin. Corp., 40 A.2d 713 (Mass. 1942) (discount was interest). Also, in some cases, there is no "discounting" of the interest rate that the discount points allegedly pay for. The practice of a lender in charging "discount points" but not providing lower interest rates in exchange for these fees may be challengeable under state UDAP laws. Vandenbroeck v. CommonPoint Mortg. Co., 2004 WL 1778933 (Mich. Ct. App. Aug. 10, 2004).

34 *See, e.g., In re* First Alliance Mortgage Co., 298 B.R. 652 (C.D. Cal. 2003) (describing how FAMCO loan officers were trained to give sales presentations designed to obfuscate loan origination fees (points) and other fees.).

35 The conventional wisdom is that most consumer borrowers focus foremost on the amount of the monthly payment. That is one reason that lenders can manipulate the other loan terms without the borrower's being aware of it in many cases.

36 *See* § 4.7.1, *supra* on calculating points.

37 Points, service charges etc. are considered a finance charge, and hence calculated in the APR, for purposes of the Truth in Lending Act. Thus the amount financed would be disclosed as $5000 and the finance charge as $3805.60, which includes the points as a $1169 prepaid finance charge. 15 U.S.C. § 1605(a)(1), (3); Reg. Z § 226.4(b)(3). *See* National Consumer Law Center, Truth in Lending §§ 3.7.5, 3.8 (5th ed. 2003 and Supp.).

38 Experience with some of the high rate lenders has shown various ways lenders encourage the misunderstanding. An in-

ternal memo from a loan officer to his colleagues in one infamous second mortgage company which routinely charged 20 to 40 points noted that he had success by concentrating on the note rate, never specifying the number of points (e.g., "19 points"), and, if asked about the charge simply explaining it as needed to cover their expenses. Moreover, that company characterized points as "discount" points, and some borrowers later reported that they had understood that to be a *discount*, not an additional charge. *See* § 11.2, *infra* for a discussion of general consumer understanding of credit costs. Practitioners should note that deceptive sales techniques such as these may be actionable under state UDAP statutes. *See generally* National Consumer Law Center, Unfair and Deceptive Acts and Practices § 5.1.7 (6th ed. 2004 and Supp.).

39 *See generally* § 5.5.2.2, *supra. See also* Hathaway v. First Family Fin. Servs., 1 S.W.3d 634 (Tenn. 1999) (points are not rebated upon refinancing under court's interpretation of state law). However, while lender's may treat them as earned at the time of settlement, points are often not considered "paid" by consumers at the same time. *See, e.g.,* Williams v. Seeley (*In re* Williams), 11 Fed. Appx. 344 (4th Cir. 2001) (discount fees are not considered paid at settlement, at least for purposes of interpreting the damage provision of Virginia's usury law; court relied upon a Supreme Court case in McCarthy v. First Nat'l Bank of Rapid City, 223 U.S. 493 (1912) for this proposition; however, the Supreme Court seems to be discussing loans where the interest was not collected until the maturity date of the loan and the interest was deducted in advance (from the total of payments, presumably); the court does not address points as charged in the mortgage marketplace in more recent times, as was the case in *Seeley*).

40 *See* §§ 5.5.2.2, 6.3, 6.4.1.3, *supra* for further discussion of both the mathematics and legal considerations surrounding points and early termination.

and are not merely extra profit or compensation for overhead expense.[41] In the case of points, it is a burden that lenders can seldom carry, and numerous courts have found points and similar fees to constitute hidden interest.[42] Practitioners

reviewing credit contracts which contain a higher than usual amount of points should view them with particular suspicion.[43]

More commonly, the relevant state statute specifically permits the exclusion of points, often allowing one or two points to be excluded from interest.[44] Sometimes this exclusion is granted in lieu of permitting other charges to be passed on to borrowers.[45] In any event, the existence of such statutes is helpful to consumers in at least one way: by specifying how many points and other fees may be excluded from interest, these statutes clearly imply that any additional fees are to be treated as interest.[46]

---

41 *See, e.g.,* United-Bilt Homes, Inc. v. Teague, 245 Ark. 132, 432 S.W.2d 1 (1968); VanderWeyst v. First State Bank of Benson, 425 N.W.2d 803 (Minn. 1988) (origination fee is interest if not related to expenses; affidavit of bank officer simply making that assertion not adequate to establish that; case remanded for factual determination), *cert. denied,* 488 U.S. 943 (1988); Freeman v. Gonzales Cty. Sav. & Loan Ass'n, 526 S.W.2d 774 (Tex. Ct. App. 1975), *aff'd,* 534 S.W.2d 903 (Tex. 1976) (2% "loan fee" not proven reasonable and thus constituted usury under statute). *See also* Moore v. Comfed Sav. Bank, 908 F.2d 834 (11th Cir. 1990); Norris v. Sigler Daisy Corp., 392 S.E.2d 242 (Ga. 1990) (both cases interpreting Georgia's criminal usury statute, O.C.G.A. 7-4-18; it does not exclude points from the definition of interest, so the effect of points would be considered in determining whether the criminal usury ceiling was violated even though the civil usury code excludes points from definition of usury).

42 *See, e.g.,* Smith v. Anderson, 801 F.2d 661 (4th Cir. 1986) (applying Virginia law); Perry v. Stewart Title Co., 756 F.2d 1197 (5th Cir. 1985) (front end charges were interest, but "spreading" of interest avoids usury violation); Johnston v. Citizen's Bank & Trust, 659 F.2d 865 (8th Cir. 1981) (applying Arkansas law); Imperial Corp. of Am. v. Frenchman's Creek Corp., 453 F.2d 1338 (5th Cir. 1972) (applying Texas law); Bowen v. Mt. Vernon Savings Bank, 105 F.2d 796 (D.C. Cir. 1939); First Nat'l Mortgage Co. v. Arkmo Lumber & Supply Co., 277 Ark. 298, 641 S.W.2d 31 (1982); Pazianos v. Schenker, 366 A.2d 440 (D.C. Ct. App. 1976); Montgomery Fed. Sav. & Loan Ass'n v. Baer, 308 A.2d 768 (D.C. Ct. App. 1973); Eisenstein v. Diprimo, 2000 Ga. App. LEXIS 1140 (Ga. App. Sept. 15, 2000); First Fed. Sav. v. Norwood Realty Co., 212 Ga. 524, 92 S.E.2d 763 (1956); Saskill v. 4-B Acceptance, 117 Ill. App. 3d 336, 453 N.E.2d 761 (1983); Luttenberger v. Conseco Fin. Servs. Corp., 671 N.W.2d 425 (Iowa 2003) (loan origination and processing fees are included in Iowa U.C.C.C. definition of "finance charge" for consumer loans; such fees permissible so long as resulting finance charge does not exceed 21% cap); B.F. Saul Co. v. West End Park N., Inc., 250 Md. 707, 246 A.2d 591 (1968) (excellent discussion); Bernhardt v. Atlantic Fin. Corp., 40 A.2d 713 (Mass. 1942) (discount was interest); Hope v. Contemporary Funding Group, 513 N.Y.S.2d 171 (1987) (discount retained by lender is additional interest); Vee Bee Serv. Co. v. Household Fin. Corp., 51 N.Y.S.2d 590 (N.Y. Sup. Ct. 1944), *aff'd,* 55 N.Y.S.2d 590 (1945); Hilal v. Lipton, 642 N.Y.S.2d 78 (App. Div. 1996); Tarver v. Sebring Capital Credit Corp., 69 S.W.3d 708 (Tex. App. 2002) (Texas constitutional 3% cap on fees does not apply to discount points paid in exchange for a lower rate; such points are considered interest); Gonzales County Sav. & Loan Ass'n v. Freeman, 534 S.W.2d 903 (Tex. 1976); Riverdale Mall Inc. v. Larwin Mortgage Invs., 515 S.W.2d 5 (Tex. Ct. App. 1975); Garrison v. First Fed. Savings & Loan Ass'n, 402 S.E.2d 24 (Va. 1991) (points, or loan discount fee, are interest); Aetna Fin. Co. v. Darwin, 691 P.2d 581 (Wash. Ct. App. 1984). *But see* Thomison v. Long Beach Mortgage Co., 176 F. Supp. 2d 714 (W.D. Tex. 2002) (loan origination fee held not interest and therefore subject to the 3% cap; court noted irony of treating discount fee and origination points differently); Olympic Coast, Inc. v. Wright (*In re* Wright), 256 B.R. 626 (Bankr. D. Mont. 2000) (in a commercial case, court held origination fee is not interest or, at least,

not usurious, using the spreading doctrine); Wombold v. Associates Fin. Serv. Co., 104 P.3d 1080 (Mont. 2004) (points were not interest; however, lender's charging of points violated Montana Consumer Loan Act's restriction on fees not authorized by statute).

43 The Home Ownership and Equity Protection Act provisions of the Truth in Lending Act are triggered if fees and points comprise 8% of a home-secured loan. *See generally* § 12.2.2, *infra;* National Consumer Law Center, Truth in Lending Ch. 9 (5th ed. 2003 and Supp.).

44 *See, e.g.,* Kan. Code § 16a-2-401(9) (3 points authorized in real estate loans; 2 points on other closed-end loans); Md. Com. Law Code Ann. § 12-401. Practitioners should check statutes which permit the exclusion of a percentage fee from interest to see how this fee may be calculated. Equitably, fees should be calculated as a percentage of the sum received by the borrower. Yet, lenders often collect a percentage of every sum that they finance, including previously assessed fees and the points themselves. Depending on the precise statutory language, this practice of assessing fees on fees may well be usurious. *See also In re* Bogan, 281 F. Supp. 242 (W.D. Tenn. 1968); Md. Com. L. § 12-107. *Cf.* Miller v. Pac. Shore Funding, 224 F. Supp. 2d 977 (D. Md. 2002) (Maryland's 10% cap on loan origination fees for secondary mortgages is calculated based upon "net proceeds" of loan; statute provides formula for calculating net proceeds), *aff'd on other grounds,* 92 Fed. Appx. 933 (4th Cir. 2004) (affirming dismissal of claims based on statute of limitations and standing grounds). *See generally* § 4.7.1, *supra.*

45 *See* Va. Code Ann. § 6.1-330.72 (broker fee by lender payable as part of "loan fee" or interest); Tavares v. Sprunk (*In re* Tavares), 298 B.R. 195 (Bankr. D. Mass. 2003) (broker fees and attorney fees included in calculation of interest rate for purposes of determining whether loan violates Massachusetts criminal usury statute).

46 *See* Williams v. Seeley (*In re* Williams), 11 Fed Appx. 344 (4th Cir. 2001) (discount fees are not considered paid at settlement, at least for purposes of interpreting the damages provision of Virginia's usury law); Smith v. Anderson, 801 F.2d 661 (4th Cir. 1986) (applying Virginia law); Miller v. Pac. Shore Funding, 224 F. Supp. 2d 977 (D. Md. 2002) (lender exceeded Maryland's 10% cap on loan origination fees for secondary mortgages by charging both origination fee and "non-interest, non-recording" fees that, when combined, were greater than 10% of "net proceeds"), *aff'd on other grounds,* 92 Fed. Appx. 933 (4th Cir. 2004) (affirming dismissal of claims based on statute of limitations and standing grounds); United Companies Lending Corp. v. Autrey, 723 So. 2d 617 (Ala. 1998) (points equal finance charge and excess over 5% cap violates Alabama's Mini-Code; issue arose in context of resolving which of two possible remedy provisions apply); Bandas v. Citizens State

It is arguable that even when the points imposed are within a statutorily authorized amount, the implicit reasonableness standard described above must be met. In assessing a series of refinancings in which service charges (which, like points, were designed to compensate for the lender's expenses and services), were repeatedly assessed, the Tennessee Supreme Court said that such a charge within the authorized maximum was merely prima facie valid, but the borrower might show it did not bear a reasonable relation to those costs.[47] The logic is equally persuasive whether the fee is denominated points or service charges.

Where the statute specifically excludes points from interest without any numerical limitation, there still are grounds to challenge an excessive number of points. In Georgia, though the civil usury statute excludes points from interest without limit,[48] the criminal statute does not exclude points from its definition of interest at all.[49] Points were also what

took a nominal 15% loan over New York's 25% criminal usury cap.[50]

Similarly, in a deregulated state, where the contract itself defines the maximum allowable rate, a failure to properly treat points creates an illegal overcharge, triggering the prescribed penalties.[51] In states that have removed any cap on interest rates, points may violate laws that limit non-interest fees, if they are *not* considered interest.[52]

Finally, an excessive number of points is a clue that the transaction may be vulnerable to one of the more broad fairness-based theories discussed elsewhere in this manual.[53]

7.2.2.3 Commitment Fees

When statutes do not control this issue, a few courts have recognized the exclusion of a percentage fee from interest in one other situation: the commitment fee. Commitment fees are assessed when a lender agrees to hold open a line of credit for a certain time, at a given interest rate. Some courts have viewed commitment fees as proper non-interest compensation due to the lender for granting the borrower an ongoing option to borrow money,[54] although there is authority for the

---

Bank, 412 N.W.2d 818 n.1 (Minn. Ct. App. 1987) (controlling statute designates permitted charges which are not interest; loan origination fee is not listed, therefore is interest), *rev'd and remanded on other grounds sub nom.* VanderWeyst v. First State Bank, 425 N.W.2d 803 (Minn. 1988) (different statute controlled transaction), *cert. denied,* 488 U.S. 943 (1988); Aetna Fin. Co. v. Darwin, 691 P.2d 581 (Wash. Ct. App. 1984). *See also* Mayo v. Key Fin. Servs., Inc., Clearinghouse No. 49,969 (Mass. Super. Ct. June 22, 1994) (implied private right of action for violation of statute limiting points; assertable by a suitable common law remedy; borrowers choose to assert common law restitution). *Cf.* Fidelity Fin. Servs. v. Hicks, 574 N.E.2d 15 (Ill. App. Ct. 1991) (allegation that creditor which charged 13 points violated statute limiting loan to 3 points survived motion to dismiss; court rejected creditor's argument that statute deregulating interest rates had impliedly repealed limitation on points).

47 Cumberland Capitol Corp. v. Patty, 556 S.W.2d 516 (Tenn. 1977). *See also In re* Bogan, 281 F. Supp. 242 (W.D. Tenn. 1968). *But see* Hathaway v. First Family Fin. Servs., Inc., 1 S.W.3d 634 (Tenn. 1999) (wherein court describes a change in Tennessee's constitution in response to the *Cumberland* decision and the enactment of a statute allowing a 4% service charge; unclear whether the Cumberland "reasonable" standard survived). *But cf. In re* Curtis, 83 B.R. 853 (Bankr. S.D. Ga. 1988) (unlimited number of points excluded from state's civil usury definition of interest); Gonzales v. Associates Fin. Serv., 967 P.2d 312 (Kan. 1998) (issue not raised in this flipping case where consumer argued that origination fee of the lesser 2% or $100 was improperly calculated on both the refinanced principal plus the new extension of credit. If raised, this may have been a more successful way to attack the lender's practice of charging maximum fee available to originate a new loan when the new monies to the borrower were very small sums.).

48 *See In re* Curtis, 83 B.R. 853 (Bankr. S.D. Ga. 1988); *In re* Cleveland, 67 B.R. 144 (Bankr. M.D. Ga. 1986).

49 *See* Moore v. Comfed Sav. Bank, 908 F.2d 834 (11th Cir. 1990); Eisenstein v. Diprimo, 2000 Ga. App. LEXIS 1140 (Ga. App. Sept. 15, 2000); Norris v. Sigler Daisy Corp., 392 S.E.2d 242 (Ga. 1990). The *Moore* court characterized taking 20–40 points as "outrageous" simply by taking judicial notice of the deviation from the average number of points (approximately 2 1/2) being charged as shown by data from Bureau of Census' Statistical abstract. Similarly, the same data showed average residential mortgage APRs to be 11% to 12%, while these APRs

ranged from 25 1/2% to 30%. The Georgia Supreme Court ultimately applied the spreading doctrine to salvage these loans from a finding of criminal usury. Fleet Fin. Inc. v. Jones, 430 S.E.2d 352 (Ga. 1993).

50 Kidd v. Delta Funding Corp., 2000 N.Y. Misc. LEXIS 29 (N.Y. Sup. Ct. Feb. 22, 2000) (processing fee which was not identified as a permitted "application" fee violates N.Y. Banking regulation for motion to dismiss purposes); Fareri v. Rain's Int'l Ltd., 589 N.Y.S.2d 579 (App. Div. 1992) (15% loan with $30,000 origination fee resulted in an effective rate of 26.14%, which violated criminal usury ceiling, thus loan was void *ab initio*).

51 *See* Garrison v. First Fed. Savings & Loan Ass'n, 402 S.E.2d 24 (Va. 1991), discussed in detail in § 9.2.8, *infra.*

52 Wombold v. Associates Fin. Serv. Co., 104 P.3d 1080 (Mont. 2004) (points were not interest; however, lender's charging of points violated Montana Consumer Loan Act's restriction on fees not authorized by statute). Note that Montana's restrictions on non-interest fees no longer applies to first lien mortgages.

53 *See* §§ 5.5.2.2.3, 6.1, *supra*; Ch. 11, *infra.* Note that when the Georgia Supreme Court finally invoked the spreading doctrine to save the loans at issue in Moore v. Comfed Sav. Bank, 908 F.2d 834 (11th Cir. 1990), it seemed to almost invite a UDAP challenge. Fleet Fin. Inc. v. Jones, 430 S.E.2d 352 (Ga. 1993). For certain home-secured loans, points and fees in excess of 8% of the loan amount will trigger application of the Home Ownership and Equity Protection Act provisions of the Truth in Lending Act. § 12.2.2, *infra;* National Consumer Law Center, Truth in Lending, Ch. 9 (5th ed. 2003 and Supp.).

54 *E.g.*, Mims v. Fidelity Funding, Inc. (*In re* Auto Int'l Refrigeration), 275 B.R. 789 (Bankr. N.D. Tex. 2002) (bona fide commitment fee not interest if reasonable and supported by "separate and additional consideration"); St. Petersburg Bank & Trust Co. v. Hamm, 414 So. 2d 1071 (Fla. 1982); People v. Central Fed. S&L Ass'n, 46 N.Y.2d 41, 385 N.E.2d 555, 412 N.Y.S.2d 815 (1978); Stedman v. Georgetown S&L Ass'n, 595 S.W.2d 486 (Tex. 1979) (bona fide commitment fee not interest); Rollingbrook Investment Co. v. Texas Nat'l Bank of

position that the fee must be reasonable to be excluded from "interest."[55] Other courts have held that commitment fees merely compensate the lender for normal overhead risk involved in lending, and are therefore interest.[56]

The latter view should prevail in consumer cases because, in the average consumer credit transaction, only one loan is sought and the borrower will almost certainly exercise his or her "option" to borrow as soon as the lender allows it. Under such circumstances, the notion of payment for an option loses all credibility.[57] An exception may be the annual fee imposed on many credit card users. Such fees closely resemble commitment fees since the cardholder obtains a true line of credit which may or may not be used. The validity of such annual fees, however, is almost invariably controlled by statute.

A variation on commitment fees is the "rate lock fee," which consumers pay to obtain a certain interest rate for a mortgage.[58] However, this fee is different in that it does not

guarantee the option to borrow, but instead guarantees the price of borrowing if the loan is approved.

7.2.3 Non-Cash Compensation and Side Agreements

Payments to a creditor under a contract may take forms other than the stated interest or the various cash fees such as points and service charges. Non-cash bonuses may also be exacted by lenders in consideration for the extension of credit, and may constitute hidden interest in the same manner as cash payments.[59] For example, the borrower's agreement to guarantee or cosign a third party debt owed to the lender may be interest on the contract,[60] as may a sharing of rents from mortgaged property.[61] Similarly, borrowers who are forced to enter side contracts, favorable to the lender and supposedly independent of the extension of credit, may in fact be paying hidden interest.[62] For example, courts have

---

Baytown, 790 S.W.2d 375 (Tex. App. 1990) (bona fide commitment fee may be charged for renewal option where commercial borrower had no right to renew and fee in fact was consideration for an option to borrow in the future; under circumstances, fact that no new money was advanced in the renewal was immaterial); Gibson v. Drew Mortgage Co., 696 S.W.2d 211 (Tex. App. 1985). *But cf.* Brazosport Bank v. Oak Park Townhouses, 837 S.W.2d 652 (Tex. App. 1992) (evidence inconclusive that up-front fee was a bona fide commitment fee or authorized interest, so court upheld trial finding that it was an unauthorized fee for making loan; appellate court held appropriate penalty under relevant statute was disallowance of fee rather than a usury violation), *rev'd on other grounds*, 851 S.W.2d 189 (Tex. 1993). *See generally* Annot. 93 A.L.R.3d 1156 (1979).

55 *See* Mims v. Fidelity Funding, Inc. (*In re* Auto Int'l Refrigeration), 275 B.R. 789 (Bankr. N.D. Tex. 2002) (commitment fee must be reasonable to be excluded from interest); Altherr v. Wilshire Mortgage Corp., 104 Ariz. 59, 448 P.2d 859 (1968) (*reasonable* commitment fee); First Am. Bank & Trust v. Windjammer Time Sharing Resort, Inc., 483 So. 2d 732 (Fla. Dist. Ct. App. 1986) (reasonableness depends on market conditions and industry practice; 20% commitment fee was clearly unreasonable when industry norm was between 1.5% and 5%).

56 *See* Henslee v. Madison Guaranty Sav. & Loan, 297 Ark. 183, 760 S.W.2d 842 (1988); First Nat'l Mortgage Co. v. Arkmo Lumber & Supply Co., 277 Ark. 298, 641 S.W.2d 31 (1982). *See also* Johnston v. Citizens Bank & Trust, 659 F.2d 865 (8th Cir. 1981) (applying Arkansas law); *In re* Feldman, 259 F. Supp. 218 (D. Conn. 1966) ("commitment fee" was interest).

57 *See* Mims v. Fidelity Funding, Inc. (*In re* Auto Int'l Refrigeration), 275 B.R. 789 (Bankr. N.D. Tex. 2002) (commitment fee was not bona fide and thus was interest when it was paid, not to hold option open, but at closing after loan was entered into and as a condition of receiving the funds); Gonzales Cty. Sav. & Loan Ass'n v. Freeman, 534 S.W.2d 903 (Tex. 1976) (distinguishing bona fide commitment fee for option permitting borrower to enter into loan in future from fee arising after parties had entered into loan agreement).

58 *See, e.g.,* Jones v. E*Trade Mortgage, 397 F.3d 810 (9th Cir. 2005) (rate-lock fee required to be refunded when a consumer exercises right of rescission under Truth in Lending Act).

59 *See, e.g.,* Pacific Eastern Corp. v. Gulf Life Holding Co., 902 S.W.2d 946 (Tenn. Ct. App. 1995) (where insurance company was a lender, question of fact whether life insurance policy required as collateral on life of a principal in a commercial loan was pretext for usury).

60 *See, e.g.,* Darden v. Schussler, 154 Ala. 372, 45 So. 130 (1907); Curtiss Nat'l Bank of Miami Springs v. Solomon, 243 So. 2d 475 (Fla. Dist. Ct. App. 1971); Simpson v. Charters, 188 Ga. 842, 5 S.E.2d 27 (1939); Winder Nat'l Bank v. Graham, 38 Ga. App. 552, 144 S.E. 357 (1928); Canal-Commercial Trust & Sav. Bank v. Brewer, 143 Miss. 146, 108 So. 424 (1926); Ferdon v. Zarriello Bros. Inc., 87 N.J. Super. 124, 208 A.2d 186 (1965); Vee Bee Serv. Co. v. Household Fin. Corp., 51 N.Y.S.2d 590 (Sup. Ct. 1944), *aff'd*, 55 N.Y.S.2d 570 (1945); Alamo Lumber Co. v. Gold, 661 S.W.2d 926 (Tex. 1983); Laid Rite, Inc. v. Texas Indus., Inc., 512 S.W.2d 384 (Tex. Ct. App. 1974); Janes v. Felton, 99 W. Va. 407, 129 S.E. 482 (1925). *Cf.* Durante Bros. & Sons, Inc. v. Flushing Nat'l Bank, 652 F. Supp. 101, 104 (E.D.N.Y. 1986) (assumption or repayment of third-party debt usurious only if lender acted with usurious intent, for example with knowledge that the third-party could not or would not pay); Standard Sav. Ass'n v. Greater New Canaan Missionary Baptist Church, 786 S.W.2d 774 (Tex. App. 1990) (payment of third party debt interest only when required as condition of making loan; it is a question of fact, though borrower's affidavit alone insufficient to warrant finding of usury on motion for summary judgment; stricter standard of proof required); Dodson v. Citizens State Bank of Dalhart, 701 S.W.2d 89 (Tex. App. 1986) (assumption of third party debt is interest only when it is a condition for the extension of credit). *But cf.* Victoria Bank & Trust Co. v. Brady, 811 S.W.2d 931 (Tex. 1991) (amount of third party debt owed to a *different* lender that borrower was required to assume is not interest; it was third party expense to protect priority as to creditor's security, which is not necessarily interest. [Note dissent]). *See generally* Annot. 31 A.L.R.3d 763 (1970).

61 *See* Annot. 16 A.L.R.3d 475 (1967) (sharing earnings from property as usurious). *See also* Bagri v. Desai, 349 S.E.2d 309 (N.C. Ct. App. 1986) (loan for purchase of motel; profits from motel shared with lender).

62 *See* Boyles v. Smith, 759 P.2d 518 (Alaska 1988) (side-sale agreement held to be hidden interest); Brabson v. Valentine, 804

held payments to lenders under sham consulting contracts to be interest.[63] On the other hand, some courts have found no additional interest present when the obligations undertaken by the borrower are supported by independent consideration and are therefore not given as payment for the loan.[64]

A major impediment to the claim that non-cash bonuses are hidden interest may be encountered if the benefit to the lender is contingent[65] or if the value of the bonus for some other reason cannot be quantified.[66] This problem arises most frequently when a loan contract grants the lender a share of the profits from the borrower's business or investment in consideration for making the loan.[67] Contracts of this nature were traditionally been structured as partnerships or joint ventures, but they have branched into the home mortgage market in the form of "lender participation" mortgages in which lenders and borrowers share any appreciation in the value of the mortgaged property.[68] In either case, the relevant usury question is whether the lender's

---

S.W.2d 451 (Tenn. Ct. App. 1990) (where lending bank required borrower to purchase an investment certificate from it, the transaction was usurious; court applied the common sense perspective that where the loan proceeds were $126,340, and the bank required the borrower purchase a $100,000 investment certificate, the bank only loaned $26,340 of its money); Glover v. Buchman, 104 S.W.2d 66 (Tex. Civ. Ct. App. 1937) (borrower forced to buy cash discount coupons from lender). *See also* Ransom v. S&S Food Center, Inc., 700 F.2d 670 (11th Cir. 1983) (mandatory service contract is TIL finance charge); Carney v. Worthmore Furniture, Inc., 561 F.2d 1100 (4th Cir. 1977) (mandatory service policy tied with credit sale was Truth in Lending "finance charge"). *Cf.* West Virginia v. Scott Runyan Pontiac-Buick, 461 S.E.2d 516 (W. Va. 1995) (auto dealer collected purchase price of extended service contracts but failed to purchase them from warranty company; assignees of financing contracts held liable for refunds). *See generally* Annot. 81 A.L.R.2d 1280 (1962).

63 *See, e.g., In re* Marill Alarm Sys., Inc., 68 B.R. 399 (Bankr. S.D. Fla. 1986); Matter of Mickler, 50 B.R. 818 (Bankr. M.D. Fla. 1985); *In re* Rosner, 48 B.R. 538 (Bankr. E.D.N.Y. 1985); Antonelli v. Neumann, 537 So. 2d 1027 (Fla. Dist. Ct. App. 1988) (a landscape consulting contract with lender held to be subterfuge to conceal usurious transaction: lender had letter indicating desire to extract 2% excess interest; the "landscape consulting fees" were coincidentally 2% payments made contemporaneously with each loan payment, rather than for work as performed; lender never testified the 2% payments were credited to the consulting fee).

64 *E.g.,* Zer-Ilan v. Frankford (*In re* CPDC, Inc.), 337 F.3d 436 (5th Cir. 2003) (consulting agreement payments did not constitute usurious interest because agreement was with third party company, not lender, and services were actually provided—despite the fact that lender owned the third party company and the agreed price was over eighteen times the real worth of the services); Durante Bros. & Sons, Inc. v. Flushing Nat'l Bank, 652 F. Supp. 101, 105 (E.D.N.Y. 1986); Feinberg v. Old Vestal Road Assocs., 550 N.Y.S.2d 482 (App. Div. 1990) (though courts may look beyond form of transaction to ascertain its real nature, in this commercial loan, court found that a separate agreement with an individual lender for a finder's fee to the lender was not a front for a usurious loan where the lender's own collateral was tied up by the loan, the borrower sought advice and assistance, and the borrower's attorneys drafted the agreements); Goldring v. Texas Commercial Bank, 665 S.W.2d 103 (Tex. 1984) (attorney fee based on consideration apart from loan); Sunwest Bank of El Paso v. Gutierrez, 819 S.W.2d 673 (Tex. App. 1991) (creditor's purchase of VSI insurance on collateral was not "unauthorized," usurious charge; it was rather a charge for separate and additional consideration, which allows creditors to pass on expenses for protection of collateral); Moody v. Main Bank of Houston, 667 S.W.2d 613 (Tex. App. 1984) (separate consideration for guarantee of third party debt). *See also* S.C. Dept. of Consumer Affairs Adm. Interp., No. 2 110-8701, Consumer Cred. Guide (CCH) 95,911 (Dec. 30, 1987) (bona fide and optional sale of service contract in conjunction with auto sale is properly considered part of cash price of transaction, and hence amount financed; notes that if such collateral sales not offered to cash customers or arranged so that

cash sales are rarely or never made, may be interest "incident to extension of credit"; Department will make determination on case by case basis, looking at substance, not form of transaction). *Cf.* Heine v. Schendel, 797 S.W.2d 278 (Tex. App. 1990) (borrower who agreed to perform work for the creditor at one-half borrower's usual price failed to establish that was device to give creditor additional interest).

65 *See also* D-Beam Ltd. P'ship v. Roller Derby Skates, 366 F.3d 972 (9th Cir. 2004) (when promissory notes limited repayment to borrower's interest in royalty payments, loans were not usurious because of contingency); Dopp v. Yari, 927 F. Supp. 814 (D.N.J. 1996) (following Kraft v. Mason.); Kraft v. Mason, 668 So. 2d 679 (Fla. Dist. Ct. App. 1996) (fact that payment of interest depended on contingency of successful lawsuit showed lack of corrupt intent to render loan usurious). *Compare* Beavers v. Taylor, 434 S.W.2d 230 (Tex. Ct. App. 1968) ("no interest" contract that gave lender a percentage of business' gross receipts was not usurious because payments were contingent on existence and quantity of any gross receipts) *with* Najarro v. SASI Int'l, Ltd., 904 F.2d 1002 (5th Cir. 1990), *cert. denied,* 498 U.S. 1048 (1991) (a contract is usurious if there is any contingency by which the lender can receive usurious interest). In First USA Mgmt., Inc. v. Esmond, 911 S.W.2d 100 (Tex. App. 1995), *rev'd on other grounds,* 960 S.W.2d 625 (Tex. 1997) the court reconciled the apparent conflict by noting that in *Beavers,* the sum which would be payable under the contract in the event of the contingency was uncertain, and would not necessarily have been usurious. By contrast, in *Najarro,* the amount of contingent interest written into the contract was usurious: if the contingency occurred, the amount payable would definitely be usurious. *See generally* § 10.5.3 *infra.*

66 For example, in Swank v. Sverdlin, 121 S.W.3d 785 (Tex. App. 2003), a jury had found usury when the compensation for a loan included interest, stock options, and a patent assignment. However, the appellate court reversed, holding there was no usury because the value of the patent assignment to the lender was much less than its estimated $25 million worth, due to fact that the lender was prohibited from licensing the patent to anyone but the borrower.

67 *See* § 7.5.7, *infra.*

68 *E.g.,* Jones v. Wells Fargo Bank, 5 Cal. Rptr. 3d 835 (Ct. App. 2003) (example of a "classic shared appreciation loan arrangement" in real estate investment context; no usury because California law exempted from usury cap national banks acting as a fiduciary for a trust). *See generally,* Kiefer, *Participating Mortgages: The Risk for Lenders,* 14 Real Estate L.J. 218 (Winter 1986); Burnes, *The Shared Appreciation Mortgage—A Joint Venture, A Relationship Between Debtor and Creditor, or Both?* 12 J. Real Estate Tax'n 195 (1985) (tax analysis conclud-

return is truly contingent on the success of the borrower's enterprise, and is consequently an investment, or whether instead the lender's return is guaranteed and is thus potentially usurious interest. Even if there is a genuine contingency involved, though, a contract which would obligate the borrower to pay illegal interest upon its occurrence may be viewed as usurious.[69]

Transactions which grant a lender equity participation in the borrower's enterprise vary widely in their structure, and usury issues are easily answered only in the more extreme cases. When an investor risks its capital and is rewarded only upon the success of the enterprise in which it has invested, its ultimate return is not interest subject to usury limits.[70] On the other hand, a lender whose loan is absolutely repayable and who receives interest payments at the statutory limit should not additionally receive equity participation under the guise of a purported investment even if the value of its equity is uncertain.[71]

Equity participation is most likely to be held to be interest when the evidence indicates that the parties intended the transaction to be a loan, when a large difference exists between the proceeds advanced by the lender and the fair market value of the equity, when little or no additional consideration is given to the borrower for the equity, and when unequal bargaining power was evident.[72] Statutes in a few states control whether equity participation may be interest.[73]

7.2.4 Delinquency Charges

7.2.4.1 Introduction

In a typical credit contract, borrowers are obliged to pay off their debt in installments, with each installment being due on a particular date, such as the first day of each month. Credit contracts usually provide a grace period, e.g., ten days, beyond the due date of an installment, and borrowers may pay an installment without penalty[74] during this grace period even though the payment is technically late. (Note that charging interest during a grace period when none is due constitutes usury.[75]) However, if an installment is paid after the expiration of the grace period, credit contracts generally authorize the creditor to impose a "late fee" or "delinquency fee" on the borrower.

Late charges may be imposed only if the contract authorizes it.[76] However, many credit contracts are now written broadly to allow creditors to impose both late fees, as well as other fees after a delinquency, such as attorney fees[77] or "property inspection fees" for home-secured loans.[78]

It is important to recognize that the imposition of a late fee does not mean that a borrower is in default, although the contract may technically grant the lender the right to declare default on the basis of a single missed payment, and, subject to notice requirements,[79] to pursue remedies such as accel-

---

ing that debtor-creditor relation prevails in shared appreciation mortgages).

69 *See* First USA Mgmt., Inc. v. Esmond, 911 S.W.2d 100 (Tex. App. 1995) (interpreting Najarro v. SASI Int'l, Ltd., 904 F.2d 1002 (5th Cir. 1990), *cert. denied*, 498 U.S. 1048 (1991), and distinguishing cases where the amount to be paid upon the occurrence of the contingency was uncertain, and not necessarily usurious), *rev'd on other grounds*, 960 S.W.2d 625 (Tex. 1997). *See also* Jersey Palm-Gross, Inc. v. Paper, 658 So. 2d 531 (Fla. 1995) (15% equity interest in business partnership was valued as of date of transaction which rendered transaction usurious).

70 *E.g.*, Securities & Exchange Comm'n v. First Securities Co., 507 F.2d 417 (7th Cir. 1974).

71 *E.g.*, Thomas v. Estes, 139 Ga. App. 738, 229 S.E.2d 538 (1976); Kessing v. National Mortgage Corp., 180 S.E.2d 823 (N.C. 1971); Bagri v. Desai, 349 S.E.2d 309 (N.C. Ct. App. 1986) (loan for purchase of motel; 15% interest and one-sixth of motel's profits plus one-sixth of any gain on resale was usurious); Johns v. Jaeb, 518 S.W.2d 857 (Tex. Ct. App. 1974).

72 *See* Comment, *Equity Participation in Texas: A Lender's Dream or a Usurious Nightmare?* 34 S.W.L.J. 877 (1980).

73 *E.g.*, Fla. Stat. Ann. § 687.03(4) (loans exceeding $500,000).

74 However, the economic reality is that a penalty does, in fact, exist if the lender uses interest-bearing bookkeeping. Because interest may continue to accrue through the grace period more of the next payment will be allocated to interest and less to principal. *See generally* §§ 4.5, 4.8, *supra*.

75 Steves Sash & Door Co. v. Ceco Corp., 751 S.W.2d 473 (Tex. 1988) (invoice specified finance charges to be imposed after 30 days on amounts unpaid).

76 *See* Bank of Crockett v. Culliper, 752 S.W.2d 84 (Tenn. Ct. App. 1988) (imposing substantial late charges in absence of contractual authorization to pressure repayment was unconscionable conduct under state statute); Bowman Plumbing, Heating & Elec. v. Logan, 59 Va. Cir. 446 (2002) (Virginia late payment statute requires late payment fee to be specified in the contract); Metro Hauling, Inc. v. Daffern, 44 Wash. App. 719, 723 P.2d 32 (1986).

   Late fees should be distinguished from "deferral fees" which are payments that a debtor may be permitted to make to delay the date when a payment is due and, thereby, to avoid default. *See generally* Hayes v. First Nat'l Bank, 507 S.W.2d 701 (Ark. 1974); Watson v. Avco Fin. Servs. Int'l, Inc., 224 Neb. 778, 401 N.W.2d 485 (1987). Deferral fees are less common because creditors usually prefer refinancing, but in any case it is clear that the borrower must agree to the deferral arrangement and the deferral fee before deferral charges may be imposed. Some states regulate the manner in which deferral fees may be assessed. *See* Reliable Credit Corp. v. Smith, 406 So. 2d 231 (La. Ct. App. 1981), *amended* 418 So. 2d 1311 (La. 1982). *See generally* § 4.8.1, *supra*.

77 *See* § 7.3.3.2, *infra*.

78 *See, e.g.*, Walker v. Countrywide Home Loans, 121 Cal. Rptr. 2d 79 (Ct. App. 2002) (property inspection fees are not late fees, and may be charged in addition to late fees, which are capped by California law).

79 State law may require a creditor to give written notice of default and to provide an opportunity for the debtor to cure the default before other remedies such as acceleration or repossession may be pursued. *See, e.g.*, Iowa Code § 537.5110. *See generally* National Consumer Law Center, Repossessions and Foreclosures § 4.7 (5th ed. 2002 and Supp.).

eration of the debt,[80] repossession of collateral, and collection. In fact, the law may treat post-default charges differently than late charges.[81] In practice, however, consumer credit payments are frequently late, and creditors are content to collect generous late charges unless and until accounts become seriously overdue.

Late fees, like any other payments made to a lender, are a potential source of hidden interest and should be closely scrutinized.[82] A lender's ability to exclude late charges from interest on a contract varies widely from state to state, and reference to the relevant state's statutes and case law is essential to the analysis of any particular case. This section will examine the various general approaches taken by courts considering whether late fees should be classified as interest.[83]

7.2.4.2 Late Fees As Interest

7.2.4.2.1 "Common law" approach

To the extent that a common law[84] treatment of late fees exists, the general rule is that late fees are excluded from interest because the fees are avoidable or, more precisely,

are contingent on the performance of the borrower.[85] Courts have frequently viewed late payment as a voluntary act of the borrower and the delinquency fee as a consequence of the borrower's voluntary act. These courts have been reluctant to allow the borrower to transform an otherwise valid contract into a usurious one through voluntary late payment, and have therefore either excluded the late fee from interest[86] or ruled that creditors may validly receive more than

---

80 In some cases, mostly involving commercial loans, lenders have even been permitted to charge "prepayment fees" for a default, under the theory that an acceleration of the loan after default constitutes a "prepayment." *See, e.g.,* Norwest Bank v. Blair Road Assocs., 252 F. Supp. 2d 86 (D.N.J. 2003) (permitting lender to charge both late fee and "prepayment premium," as well as permitting a default interest rate increase); MONY Life Ins. Co. v. Paramus Parkway Bldg., Ltd., 834 A.2d 475 (N.J. Super. Ct. App. Div. 2003) (same); Westmark Commercial Mortgage Fund IV v. Teenform Assocs., Ltd. P'ship, 827 A.2d 1154 (N.J. Super. Ct. App. Div. 2003) (same).

81 *See* First Nat'l Bank of Lakewood v. Union Tavern Corp., 794 P.2d 261 (Colo. Ct. App. 1990) (court distinguishes between delinquency charges and default interest; statute permitted the former but prohibited the latter, thus contract provision calling for default interest was unenforceable); Crest Savings & Loan Ass'n v. Mason, 581 A.2d 120 (N.J. Super. Ct. 1990) (late charges on installment payments cannot be imposed after acceleration; creditor has no right to be compensated for expenses connected to late payment when borrower no longer has a right to make installment payments).

82 Even if late fees are considered to be interest, courts may apply the spreading doctrine to hold that the late fees do not make the loan usurious. Torres v. Overby, 2000 Tex. App. LEXIS 2493 (Tex. App. Apr. 17, 2000). For a discussion of the spreading doctrine, see § 4.6.5, *supra.*

83 *See* § 9.3.1.1, *infra* on statutory construction.

84 The use of the term "common law" here may be somewhat misleading because usury is a statutory offense. Nevertheless, a broadly accepted gloss of usury law has grown from decisions interpreting individual usury statutes. For example, the general principle that usury statutes do not apply when payments to the lender are contingent is not expressly stated in many usury statutes, but is still a widely accepted view. The "common law rules" mentioned in this section refer to such generally accepted case law interpretations.

85 *See, e.g.,* Alston v. Crown Auto, Inc., 224 F.3d 332 (4th Cir. 2000); Camilla Cotton Oil Co. v. Spencer Kellogg & Sons, Inc., 257 F.2d 162 (5th Cir. 1958); Bunn v. Weyerhauser Co., 268 Ark. 445, 598 S.W.2d 54 (1980) (stating rule); Hayes v. First Nat'l Bank, 507 S.W.2d 701 (Ark. 1974) (distinguishing late fees from extension fees); Harris v. Guaranty Fin. Corp., 244 Ark. 218, 424 S.W.2d 355 (1968); O'Connor v. Televideo Sys., Inc., 218 Cal. App. 3d 709, 267 Cal. Rptr. 237 (1990); First Am. Title Ins. v. Cook, 12 Cal. App. 3d 592, 90 Cal. Rptr. 645 (1970); Gaddis v. Stardust Hills Owners Assoc., 804 N.E.2d 231 (Ind. Ct. App. 2004); Barbour v. Handlos Real Estate & Bldg. Corp., 393 N.W.2d 581 (Mich. Ct. App. 1986); Lew v. Goodfellow Chrysler Plymouth, Inc., 6 Wash. App. 226, 492 P.2d 258 (1971); Union Bank v. Kruger, 1 Wash. App. 622, 463 P.2d 273 (1969); Randall v. Home Loan & Inv. Co., 244 Wis. 623, 12 N.W.2d 915 (1944). *But see* Dikeou v. Dikeou, 928 P.2d 1286 (Colo. 1997) (in commercial loan context, late fee held to be interest which, when added to contract interest rate, did not exceed the usury cap); Torres v. Overby, 2000 Tex. App. LEXIS 2493 (Tex. App. Apr. 17, 2000) (late fees are interest under statutory definition).

86 *See, e.g.,* Nolen v. Nucentrix Broadband Networks, 293 F.3d 926 (5th Cir.), *cert. denied*, 537 U.S. 1047 (2002) (cable TV provider's late fee of up to 30% per month was not interest and thus not usurious); Alston v. Crown Auto, Inc., 224 F.3d 332 (4th Cir. 2000); Camilla Cotton Oil Co. v. Spencer Kellogg & Sons, Inc., 257 F.2d 162 (5th Cir. 1958); *In re* Borum, 60 B.R. 516 (Bankr. E.D. Ark. 1986); Tackett v. First Savings of Arkansas, 810 S.W.2d 927 (Ark. 1991); Hayes v. First Nat'l Bank, 507 S.W.2d 701 (Ark. 1974); Southwest Concrete Co. v. Gosh Constr., 51 Cal. 3d 701, 798 P.2d 1247, 274 Cal. Rptr. 404 (1990); Mallard v. Forest Heights Water Works, 580 S.E.2d 602 (Ga. Ct. App. 2003) (late payment penalty of 10% of monthly water bill did not constitute interest; Georgia law required a "loan or forbearance of money" as element of usury); Widmark v. Northrup King Co., 530 N.W.2d 588 (Minn. Ct. App. 1995) (commercial transaction); Seaton v. City of Lexington, 97 S.W.3d 72 (Mo. Ct. App. 2002) (late payment fee designed to ensure prompt payment of municipal sewer bill is not the equivalent of interest charged for the use of money, despite fact that statute authorizing late payments referred to the bearing of "interest"); Garcia v. Tex. Cable Partners, Ltd. P'ship, 114 S.W.3d 561 (Tex. App. 2003) (cable TV late fee not interest because no use, forbearance, or detention of money involved); Domizio v. Progressive County Mut. Ins. Co., 54 S.W.3d 867 (Tex. App. 2001) (payment of insurance premiums in installments does not equal credit; therefore, late fees are not subject to usury claim; no evidence presented regarding the liquidated damages claim); Alaskan Fireplace, Inc. v. Everett, 667 N.W.2d 378 (Wis. Ct. App. 2003) (table) (text available at 2003 WL 21397747) (1.5% per month late charge not a finance charge when it was imposed for actual, unanticipated late payment and seller viewed buyers as in default). This approach has ancient roots. *See* § 2.2.2, *supra.*

the legal interest rate on delinquent payments.[87] Those courts which exclude the fee from interest typically describe it instead as a "penalty" designed to encourage prompt payment.

The logic of this common law approach is questionable in many consumer credit cases because the late payment is often not so much a matter of the borrower's voluntary decision as one of economic necessity.[88] Furthermore, although a late fee provides an incentive for prompt payment when the borrower actually has the ability to make a payment, the notion of incentive loses its value when the borrower has no money.

Despite such objections, the common law approach of regarding late fees as contingent and labeling them as penalties rather than interest is widely applied.[89] Challenges to late fees in jurisdictions which take this approach are likely to succeed only when the late fees are so large as to obviate the notion that the fee is merely an incentive for prompt payment,[90] when the common law rule that the

damages collectible for failure to pay a sum of money are limited to interest at the legal rate, if one exists, or at market rates has not been statutorily repealed,[91] or when it can be shown that the parties expected late fees to be imposed at the time the contract was created and that the fees are therefore not contingent.[92] Such expectations may be difficult to prove, but numerous courts applying the common law approach have at least paid lip service to the idea that the rule should not control if evidence exists that the late fees have been imposed with an intent to avoid usury law.[93]

---

87 *See, e.g.,* Ruminant Nitrogen Products v. Zittle, 433 N.Y.S.2d 644 (1980); Union Bank v. Kruger, 1 Wash. App. 622, 463 P.2d 273 (1969). *Cf.* Stuchin v. Kasirer, 237 N.J. Super. 604, 568 A.2d 907 (App. Div. 1990) (contract providing for post-maturity interest rate higher than legal rate does not render contract usurious, at least provided parties did not contemplate at consummation that loan would not be paid at maturity; court said the clause should be examined to determine whether it was an unenforceable penalty); Klapper v. Integrated Agricultural Mgmt. Co., 539 N.Y.S.2d 812 (App. Div. 1989) (usury defense inapplicable where terms of note impose higher rate than statutory maximum only after maturity of note).

88 This point was recognized in Begelfer v. Najarian, 409 N.E.2d 167 (Mass. 1980). *See also* Scarr v. Boyer, 818 P.2d 381, 383 (Mont. 1991) ("Usury statutes protect borrowers who lack real bargaining power against overreaching by creditors." Default does not alter this public policy, and in fact increases the need; "a debtor who cannot retire a debt compounded by legal interest certainly lacks the resources to pay usurious interest").

89 However, late fees are considered interest for purposes of federal preemption and the rate exportation rights of depository institutions. *See* § 7.1.2, and Ch. 3, *supra*. In this case, treating late fees as interest results in fewer protections for consumers, because it permits depository institutions to ignore the laws of the consumer's home state regulating late fees.

90 *Cf. In re* Jordan, 91 B.R. 673 (Bankr. E.D. Pa. 1988) (late charge calculated at 1 1/2% of entire delinquency each month impermissible for several reasons: though creditor's evidence unclear, appears it may have compounded (pyramided) late charges; excessive late charges constitute additional interest; excessive late charge in relation to creditor's damage is an unenforceable penalty clause; and courts have inherent equitable authority to disallow even nonusurious, contractual interest when amount sought is so disproportionate to damages as to constitute penalty for late payment, especially in light of unequal bargaining power); Garrett v. Coast & So. Fed. Sav. & Loan Ass'n, 9 Cal. 3d 731, 511 P.2d 1197, 108 Cal. Rptr. 845 (1973) (liquidated damages analysis; late fee was unrelated to actual damages incurred); Beasley v. Wells Fargo Bank, N.A., 1 Cal. Rptr. 2d 446 (Cal. Ct. App. 1991) (three dollar minimum late charge on installments due under bank credit card plan held to be a penalty); Dikeou v. Dikeou, 928 P.2d 1286 (Colo. 1997) (see the

dissent's analysis in this commercial loan case; majority held late fee constituted interest). *But see* Smith v. Figure World Plus, Inc., 705 S.W.2d 432 (Ark. 1986) (100% late fee was not usurious interest, but rather was penalty, because charge was a fixed amount and was a one-time fee); Gaddis v. Stardust Hills Owners Assoc., 804 N.E.2d 231 (Ind. Ct. App. 2004) (late fee of 1% per day or 365% annually not usurious interest); Seaton v. City of Lexington, 97 S.W.3d 72 (Mo. Ct. App. 2002) (late payment penalty of 10% of monthly bill, or minimum of $10, did not constitute interest); Metlife Capital Fin. Corp. v. Washington Avenue Assoc. L.P., 732 A.2d 493 (N.J. 1999) (in commercial context, 5% late fee is judged under the following standard: whether the amount is reasonable in light of the totality of the circumstances; though 5% is a large amount on a large contract, but not unreasonable where the loan involved an arms-length, fully negotiated transaction between two sophisticated commercial parties, each represented by counsel and the per cent fee was within the normal industry standard).

91 *See* United Cable TV of Baltimore L.P. v. Burch, 732 A.2d 887 (Md. 1999) (5% late fee assessed by cable TV company for bill for service is an unlawful penalty and not a valid liquidated damages provision; common law not abrogated by statute; applicable legal interest rate is 6%). *But see* Perez v. Capital One Bank, 522 S.E.2d 874 (Va. 1999) (common law rule abrogated by specific statute allowing any fee agreed to by the parties). *The decision in United Cable TV v. Burch was legislatively overruled by 2000 Md. Laws ch. 59, §§ 1 and 2. See* Dua v. Comcast Cable, 805 A.2d 1061 (Md. Ct. App. 2002).

92 *See also* Bunn v. Weyerhauser Co., 268 Ark. 445, 598 S.W.2d 54 (1980); Metro Hauling, Inc. v. Daffern, 44 Wash. App. 719, 723 P.2d 32 (1986) (no contingency when contract modified after default to allow previously unauthorized late charges). *Cf.* Eriksen v. Fisher, 421 N.W.2d 193 (Mich. Ct. App. 1988) (charges for actual, unanticipated late payments are not interest).

93 *E.g.,* Camilla Cotton Oil Co. v. Spencer Kellogg & Sons, Inc. 257 F.2d 162 (5th Cir. 1958); Smith v. Figure World Plus, Inc., 705 S.W.2d 432 (Ark. 1986); Hayes v. First Nat'l Bank, 507 S.W.2d 701 (Ark. 1974); Loigman v. Keim, 594 A.2d 1364 (N.J. Super. Ct. 1991) (usury statute does not apply to interest on defaulted obligations, but that narrow exception does not apply where default is expected [dicta]); Lew v. Goodfellow Chrysler Plymouth, Inc., 6 Wash. App. 226, 492 P.2d 258 (1971); Randall v. Home Loan & Inv. Co., 244 Wis. 623, 12 N.W.2d 915 (1944). *See also* Administrative Interpretation #10, Maine Department of Business Regulation, Bureau of Consumer Protection Consumer Cred. Guide (CCH) § 98,617 (Jan. 29, 1975) (late charges on open account may be finance charge subject to Maine Consumer Credit Code if creditor continues to extend credit to debtor and fee is actually a periodic charge for delaying payment).

A second justification for the imposition of late fees is that such fees compensate creditors for expenses incurred when payments are made late, such as dunning costs[94] and loss of use of the principal which was due. Legislation which validates the assessment of non-interest late fees under specified circumstances reflects this justification by capping fees at certain amounts.

The concept of late fees as compensation to a lender is also subject to some criticism. At least in the case of lenders using interest-bearing bookkeeping, interest continues to accrue on a payment until it is received, and a lender which additionally imposes a fee on late payments is receiving double compensation.[95] Such lenders should not be allowed to claim that some other expenses, such as dunning costs, justify the imposition of late fees unless they can demonstrate that these costs are actually incurred when payments are made late.[96]

7.2.4.2.2 Late fee statutes

Statutes which govern late fees are generally more advantageous for consumers than the common law rule. A common statutory formula allows the lender to collect the lesser of $5 or 5% of the regular installment as a late fee, and restricts the lender to one late fee per installment no matter how late the installment is paid.[97] Some statutes also specify a minimum grace period which must be allowed before a late fee may be imposed.[98]

First, late fee statutes often specify the limits of the permissible fees, and late fees will clearly be interest to the extent that they exceed the statutory limit.[99] Second, fees assessed prior to the expiration of statutory grace periods constitute interest.[100] Third, statutes governing late payment fees may contain other requirements in addition to capping the amount of the fee. Failure to meet those requirements may also give rise to a usury claim.[101] Finally, a late fee may be challengeable under contract or other theories.[102]

---

94 *See, e.g.,* Gaddis v. Stardust Hills Owners Assoc., 804 N.E.2d 231 (Ind. Ct. App. 2004) (late fee of 1% per day or 365% annually was justified because association was required to incur expenses due to homeowner's delinquency). *Cf.* Opinion of the Kansas Att'y General No. 88-30, Consumer Cred. Guide (CCH) § 95,908 (Mar. 3, 1988) (reasonable late charge assessed by cable television company is not interest, so long as actual efforts to collect are made and delinquent users are not offered alternative options for payment).

95 *E.g.,* Iowa Code § 537.2502 (except on third-party credit card transactions); Opinion of the Attorney General of Michigan, No. 5486 (Apr. 30, 1979), *summarized at* Consumer Cred. Guide (CCH) ¶ 97,758; Harrell v. Chrysler Fin. Co., 811 A.2d 597 (Pa. Super. 2002) (statutory 2% limit on late payment fees did not prohibit lender from collecting both late fee and additional interest under simple interest method for late payment).

96 Collection costs are usually limited to actual out-of-pocket expenses. *See, e.g.,* La. Rev. Stat. Ann. § 6:956(G)(2) (note, though, that 6:956(G)(1) allows the imposition of a percentage late fee in addition to actual out of pocket expenses). In general, borrowers bear the burden of demonstrating that late fees bear no relationship to creditors' collection expenses. *See* Metlife Capital Fin. Corp. v. Washington Avenue Assoc. L.P., 732 A.2d 493 (N.J. 1999) (commercial transaction); Smith v. Figure World Plus, Inc., 705 S.W.2d 432 (Ark. 1986). An example of a case successfully meeting that burden is Beasley v. Wells Fargo Bank, N.A., 1 Cal. Rptr. 2d 446 (Ct. App. 1991).

97 *See, e.g.,* Cal. Civ. Code § 1803.6 (Retail Installment Act); U.C.C.C. § 2.502 (1974 Model Code). *See also* Bowman Plumbing, Heating & Elec. v. Logan, 59 Va. Cir. 446 (Va. Cir. Ct. 2002) (Virginia late payment statute caps fees at 5%).

98 *See, e.g.,* 24 C.F.R. § 203.25 (FHA-insured loans; 4% late fee

allowed on installments more than 15 days late); 38 C.F.R. § 36.4212 (VA-insured loans, 4% late fee allowed on installments more than 15 days late); Cal. Civ. Code § 1803.6 ($10 if less than 10 days late; $15 if less than 15 days late); U.C.C. § 2.502(1) (1974 Model Code) (10 days).

99 *See, e.g.,* Fisher v. Westinghouse Credit Corp., 760 S.W.2d 802 (Tex. App. 1988) (late fee computed as interest on past due payments, rather than one-time charge; late fee is a separate agreement tested separately for usury from underlying contract). *See also In re* Crotzer, 147 B.R. 252 (Bankr. N.D. Ala. 1992) (imposing late fees in excess of statutory maximum resulted in creditor's forfeiture of *all* late fees; to rule otherwise by permitting creditor to retain the legal amount would give creditors an incentive to break the law). One court, however, refused to apply the usual usury penalty of forfeiture of all interest as a remedy for excessive late charges, instead holding the lender forfeited all late charges to which it would otherwise be entitled. Swindell v. FNMA, 409 S.E.2d 892 (N.C. 1991) *modifying and aff'g* 387 S.E.2d 220 (N.C. App. 1990).

100 *See* Reliable Credit Corp. v. Smith, 406 So. 2d 231 (La. Ct. App. 1981), *amended* 418 So. 2d 1311 (La. 1982) (improperly imposed extension fee); Bumpus v. Vandeford, Clearinghouse No. 54,570 (N.D. Miss. Mar. 27, 2002) (late fee imposed prior to expiration of 15-day statutory period is finance charge); Steves Sash & Door Co. v. Ceco Corp., 751 S.W.2d 473 (Tex. 1988) (charging interest during a grace period when none is due is interest).

101 *See, e.g.,* Aldrich v. Ellis, 52 P.3d 388 (Mont. 2002) (seller failed to meet requirements of Montana statute governing imposition of late payment charges for accounts receivables; buyer permitted to amend complaint to add usury claim); Bowman Plumbing, Heating & Elec. v. Logan, 59 Va. Cir. 446 (2002) (Virginia late payment statute requires late payment fee to be specified in the contract between seller and consumer; failure to include fee in contract bars seller from collecting late fee).

102 For example, in a case involving a UDAP claim, rather than a usury claim, a careful parsing of contract language setting the amount of a permissible charge showed the creditor overcharged on late fees. Depending on the language of the statute involved, a similar analysis may prove fruitful. *See In re* Andrews, 78 B.R. 78 (Bankr. E.D. Pa. 1987) (mortgage contract called for late charge of 4% on installment—interpreted to be the principal and interest amount, but creditor calculated charges on basis of aggregate monthly payment amount which also included insurance and tax escrow). *Contra* Moore v. Lomas Mtg. USA, 796 F. Supp. 300 (N.D. Ill. 1992).

Late fees imposed pursuant to state statutes that permit any late fee agreed to by the borrower might be subject to attack as an unenforceable penalty. *See, e.g.,* Rea v. Breakers Ass'n, 674 So. 2d 496 (Miss. 1996) (applying Mississippi usury and late fee limitations to condominium associations).

Not all statutes which regulate lender fees permit any exclusion of late fees from interest.[103] Courts in several states have determined that late fees fall within statutory definitions of interest in the absence of an express statutory exception.[104] One theoretical basis for this is that failure to make a payment when due is a "detention" of money, the compensation for which constitutes interest in some states.[105]

A few states, including California, view late fees as liquidated damages.[106] However, the California late fee cap has been interpreted to apply only to fees formally denominated as late fees by the creditor.[107]

Contract provisions calling for liquidated damages may be valid if they represent a good faith effort of the parties at the time of the creation of the contract to assess and compensate for the damage which will be caused by a specified breach of contract.[108] However, liquidated dam-

---

103 Cantrell v. Walker Builders, Inc., 678 So. 2d 169 (Ala. Civ. App. 1996) (approves of an Alabama attorney general's opinion which opined that "interest" as defined in Ala. Code § 8-8-5 includes a late fee; only limit on the size of the late fee under § 8-8-5 is whether the fee is unconscionable).

104 *E.g.*, Reliable Credit Corp. v. Smith, 418 So. 2d 1311 (La. 1982); Wright Ins. Agency v. Scott, 371 So. 2d 1207 (La. Ct. App. 1979); Begelfer v. Najarian, 409 N.E.2d 167 (Mass. 1980); Hardwick v. Austin Gallery of Oriental Rugs, Inc., 779 S.W.2d 438, 443 (Tex. App. 1989); Veytia v. Seiter, 740 S.W.2d 64 (Tex. App. 1987); Dixon v. Brooks, 604 S.W.2d 330 (Tex. Ct. App. 1980). *Cf.* United Cable TV of Baltimore L.P. v. Burch, 732 A.2d 887 (Md. 1999) (though court found the 5% late fee to be an unenforceable penalty, it stopped short of finding the excess to be usurious).

105 *See, e.g.*, Scarr v. Boyer, 818 P.2d 381 (Mont. 1991) (Montana's usury statute applies to compensation for detention of money, thus it includes post-default interest within definition of interest, joining Texas and South Dakota courts' interpretation of detention); *In re* Brummer, 147 B.R. 552 (Bankr. D. Mont. 1992) (applying *Scarr*, holds a "reinvestment premium" due to satisfy the accelerated amount due after a default is a charge for the detention of money, and therefore interest); Swindell v. FNMA, 409 S.E.2d 892 (N.C. 1991), *modifying and aff'g* 387 S.E.2d 220 (N.C. App. 1990) (late fee has two purposes: one to encourage prompt payment, second to compensate lender for delay; in latter use it is interest on the detention of money or for forbearance in collection); Butler v. Holt Machinery Co., 741 S.W.2d 169, 174 (Tex. App. 1987) *corrected on denial of rehearing*, 739 S.W.2d 958 (1987) (contract had neither provided for nor disclosed late fees. Though they constituted interest, there was no usury because the resultant increase did not exceed the legal maximum). *But see* Domizio v. Progressive County Mut. Ins. Co., 54 S.W.3d 867 (Tex. App. 2001) (payment of insurance premiums in installments does not equal credit; therefore, late fees are not subject to usury claim).

Not all states include compensation for the detention of money as interest: some include only "loans or forbearance" within their scope. For example, a New York court held there was no "loan or forbearance" involved in a statutorily authorized late fee on overdue sewer and water assessments, thus a usury claim failed. Matter of City of Binghamton, 521 N.Y.S.2d 141 (1987). *See also* O'Connor v. Televideo Sys., Inc., 218 Cal. App. 3d 709, 267 Cal. Rptr. 237 (1990) (no forbearance involved where past due accounts subject to 18% annual late charge; court noted that this was commercial transaction between parties of equal bargaining power and no evidence it was a device to evade usury laws); Southwest Concrete Co. v. Gosh Constr., 51 Cal. 3d 701, 798 P.2d 1247, 274 Cal. Rptr. 404 (1990); Irwin Rogers Ins. Agency v. Murphy, 833 P.2d 128 (Idaho Ct. App. 1992) (late charges were not interest; usury required excessive compensation for loan, forbearance or extension of payment on existing debt, and there was no evidence of agreement for extended time for payment in consideration of late charges). For a discussion of loan or forbearance, see § 10.5.2, *infra*, and forbearance and detention, see § 10.5.2.3, *infra*.

106 *See* Beasley v. Wells Fargo Bank, N.A., 1 Cal. Rptr. 2d 446 (Ct. App. 1991); O'Connor v. Televideo Sys., Inc., 218 Cal. App. 3d 709, 267 Cal. Rptr. 237 (1990); Garrett v. Coast & So. Fed. Sav. & Loan Ass'n, 9 Cal. 3d 731, 511 P.2d 1197, 108 Cal. Rptr. 845 (1973).

See also In re Union Square Dev., 140 B.R. 544 (D. Colo. 1992) (Colorado law); St. Hilaire & Assoc. v. Harbor Corp., 607 A.2d 905 (Me. 1992) (suggests Maine adopts a liquidated damage analysis; contractual collection charges are enforceable if they are reasonable, reflect actual or anticipated loss and are not usurious or excessive as to constitute a penalty; interest and attorney fees at issue). *Cf.* Southwest Concrete Co. v. Gosh Constr., 51 Cal. 3d 701, 798 P.2d 1247, 274 Cal. Rptr. 404 (1990) (California Supreme Court analyzes late fee on other grounds than liquidated damages); Grausz v. Farber, 2002 WL 1399123 (Cal. Ct. App. June 28, 2002) (follows analysis of Southwestern Concrete v. Gosh; even if late payment fees were interest, usury law does not apply to commercial accounts); Domizio v. Progressive County Mut. Ins. Co., 54 S.W.3d 867 (Tex. App. 2001) (payment of insurance premiums in installments does not equal credit; therefore, late fees are not subject to usury claim; no evidence presented regarding the liquidated damages claim). *See generally* Annot., 63 A.L.R.3d 50 (1975).

107 Walker v. Countrywide Home Loans, 121 Cal. Rptr. 2d 79 (Ct. App. 2002) (property inspection fees are not late fees, and may be charged in addition to late fee capped by California law). This analysis would appear to undermine the concept of late fees as a form of liquidated damages. The reason for treating late fees as liquidated damages is to compensate the creditor for expenses from a delinquency that are impractical to quantify; thus, the creditor is permitted a single flat charge to compensate for the expenses. Once the creditor is permitted pile on additional fees for discrete expenses, it becomes apparent that the late fee is simply a penalty.

108 *In re* Union Square Dev., 140 B.R. 544 (D. Colo. 1992) (Colorado test is whether parties intend to liquidate damages; damages must be uncertain or difficult to prove; and must be a reasonable amount not grossly disproportionate to presumed loss; late fee of 4% of unpaid balloon payment at issue); Beasley v. Wells Fargo Bank, N.A., 1 Cal. Rptr. 2d 446 (Ct. App. 1991) (late charge calculated to include indirect costs and collection agency expenses did not constitute good faith effort to compensate for damage caused by a specific default. *Note*: case is informative on methodology in setting fees; that bank seemed to have viewed late and over-the-limit fees as a revenue source probably was a factor in result); Stuchin v. Kasirer, 237 N.J. Super. 604, 568 A.2d 907 (App. Div. 1990) (appellate court remanded case to trial court to determine whether 15% increase in post-maturity rate was unenforceable penalty; court gave illustrative guidance as to test for whether it was penalty or acceptable recompense, e.g., if lender resorted to commercial borrowing to replace lost income, difference between rate of his borrowing and rate he charged as lender might be a measure of damages). *Cf.* Metlife Capital Fin. Corp. v. Washington Avenue

ages provisions which go beyond the mere compensation of the injured party, and which act as punishment[109] for the breach are void. Applying this approach, a late fee calculated as a percentage of outstanding loan balance, rather than as a percentage of the delinquent amount, may be void as a penalty.[110] Furthermore, the creditor must be able to genuinely justify the charge—attributing indirect costs, unrelated overhead costs, and collection agency percentage-based fees do not meet the test for a valid liquidated damages clause.[111]

Note, however, that if a court finds that a liquidated damages clause is actually a penalty clause, the court may simply refuse to enforce the penalty clause, and may thus not find a usury violation. An affirmative action for damages may lie, however.[112]

7.2.4.3 Pyramiding Late Charges

The "pyramiding" of late charges is one method that creditors use to assess multiple late charges on an account after as little as one late payment. Pyramiding is accomplished by attributing a borrower's current payments first to outstanding late charges or overdue amounts and only second to the installment which is currently due. For example, if a borrower must make $100 monthly payments on a loan, due on the first of each month, and the borrower makes her January payment of $100 after the grace period has expired, on January 20th, a $5 late fee will be assessed for the late January payment. When the borrower makes a $100 February payment, even if that payment is properly made on February 1st, the first $5 of the payment will be attributed to the January late charge rather than to the February installment. As a result, the borrower will be $5 short in her February payment, unless she has thought to include an extra $5 with the February payment to cover the outstanding late fee. If the February payment is short by $5, the lender will add another late fee for the February payment, and the account will now have a $10 outstanding balance before the March payment comes due. The process will repeat with a late fee being added in March and every subsequent month even if all these payments are made on time.

The pyramiding of late charges presents a hidden interest problem in that the monthly addition of late charges to a debtor's account, when only one or two payments may actually have been late, constitutes a *de facto* increase in the interest rate. However, proving hidden interest through pyramiding may not be an easy case in many states, at least in the absence of a statute prohibiting the practice.[113]

Assoc. L.P., 732 A.2d 493 (N.J. 1999) (court adopted a more relaxed standard, at least in commercial cases, where the parties are have equal bargaining power; issue is whether the damage clause is reasonable under the totality of the circumstances).

109 Note that the use of the term "penalty" under a liquidated damages analysis has a very different meaning than under the common law usury approach. In many states, late fees are upheld as a "penalty" designed to discourage late payment. However, under a liquidated damages analysis, late fees could be upheld if they constituted a reasonable attempt to compensate a lender for the actual damages that it might incur upon late payment, but would be void if they were found to be a "penalty." N. Bloom & Son (Antiques), Ltd. v. Skelly, 673 F. Supp. 1260 (S.D.N.Y. 1987) (sales invoices called for interest at 2% per month on balances unpaid for more than 30 days; given amounts involved this was an impermissible penalty and thus void). *See also* St. Hilaire & Assoc. v. Harbor Corp., 607 A.2d 905 (Me. 1992) (contractual collection charges enforceable if reasonable, and not usurious or so excessive as to constitute a penalty; interest and attorney fees at issue). *Cf. In re* Kalian, 178 B.R. 308 (Bankr. D.R.I. 1995) (a 36% default rate considered under bankruptcy law; dicta notes default interest rates also may be unenforceable penalty under state law).

110 *See* Garrett v. Coast & So. Fed. Sav. & Loan Ass'n, 9 Cal. 3d 731, 511 P.2d 1197, 108 Cal. Rptr. 845 (1973). *See also In re* Jordan, 91 B.R. 673 (Bankr. E.D. Pa. 1988) (1 1/2% monthly late fee calculated on full amount of delinquency impermissible for a variety of reasons, *inter alia* late charges excessive in relation to creditor's damage an unenforceable penalty; particularly so here, where APR was already over 24%); *In re* Hein, 60 B.R. 769 (Bankr. S.D. Cal. 1986) ($500/day late fee was unenforceable penalty).

111 United Cable TV of Baltimore Ltd. v. Burch, 732 A.2d 887 (Md. 1999) (subscription contract for cable TV is a contract for the payment of money; damages for failure to pay or late payment of monthly fee is interest at lawful rate [6% per annum under Maryland law]; $5 late, therefore, is an unenforceable penalty). *But see* Gaddis v. Stardust Hills Owners Assoc., 804 N.E.2d 231 (Ind. Ct. App. 2004) (late fee of 1% per day or 365% annually was a valid liquidated damages provision and not a penalty); MetLife Capital Fin. Corp. v. Washington Avenue Ass'n, L.P., 732 A.2d 493 (N.J. 1999) (commercial loan case; 5% late fee is not an unenforceable penalty; reasonable under circumstances); Norwest Bank v. Blair Road Assocs., 252 F. Supp. 2d 86 (D.N.J. 2003) (following *MetLife*, court holds that late fee, plus default interest rate increase of 3%, plus a "prepayment premium" of at least 3% of the principal remaining, were enforceable as reasonable; burden was on commercial borrower to establish that these fees were unreasonable, which the borrower did not do); MONY Life Ins. Co. v. Paramus Parkway Bldg., Ltd., 834 A.2d 475 (N.J. Super. Ct. App. Div. 2003) (same); Westmark Commercial Mortgage Fund IV v. Teenform Assocs., Ltd. P'ship, 827 A.2d 1154 (N.J. Super. Ct. App. Div. 2003) (same); Waterbury v. City of Oswego, 674 N.Y.S.2d 530 (App. Div.

1998) (late fees not unenforceable penalty imposed by a municipality operating its own water supply).

112 United Cable TV of Baltimore Ltd. v. Burch, 732 A.2d 887 (Md. 1999). *The decision in United Cable TV v. Burch was legislatively overruled by 2000 Md. Laws ch. 59, §§ 1 and 2. See* Dua v. Comcast Cable, 805 A.2d 1061 (Md. Ct. App. 2002).

113 Such prohibitions do exist. *E.g.*, 24 C.F.R. § 203.25 (FHA loans) 38 C.F.R. § 36.4212 (VA loans); U.C.C.C. § 2.502(3) (1974 Model Code). However, one court held that pyramiding or "compounding" late fees was unlawful under a statute that did not directly address this issue. Waterman Convalescent Hospital, Inc. v. Jurupa Community Servs. District, 62 Cal. Rptr. 2d 264 (Cal. Dist. Ct. App. 1996) (statute at issue allowed for a 10% penalty for late payments and an additional penalty not exceeding 1/2 of 1% per month for nonpayment of the charges and the basic penalty; charging 10% on the 10% penalty violated the clear language).

A Federal Trade Commission (FTC) rule prohibits certain types of late charge pyramiding. The FTC Credit Practices Rule[114] declares that various credit contract practices, including late fee pyramiding, are "unfair" under section 5 of the Federal Trade Commission Act.[115] Under the FTC Rule, it is an "unfair act or practice" for a creditor to impose a late charge "when the only delinquency is attributable to late fee(s) or delinquency charge(s) assessed on earlier installments."[116]

Thus, the FTC Rule would prohibit the type of pyramiding described in the example at the beginning of this section. However, it does not reach pyramiding which results from a skipped payment rather than a late payment.[117] For example, if a borrower makes no January payment on a loan, the creditor may validly attribute the February 1st payment to the outstanding January debt, and may later attribute the March 1st payment to the February debt, etc. Under this accounting method, every payment is viewed as one month late and late charges are validly assessed every month.[118] This practice is prohibited if the loan is precomputed in those states which have adopted the 1974 draft of the U.C.C.C.[119]

7.3 Payments for Third Party Services

7.3.1 General Principles

Credit contracts frequently contain not only fees which are assessed for various services provided by the lender, but also fees collected by the lender on behalf of third parties who have, in fact or theory, provided some service to the borrower in connection with the contract. Third party payments may cover a myriad of services: broker fees, appraisal fees, recording fees, credit insurance, inspection fees, and attorney fees, to name but a few. In fact, the type of services provided by third parties can overlap with the type of services which lenders themselves at times provide and charge for, the only difference being the identity of the party which does the work and ultimately receives the fee.

Some state statutes expressly limit the amount or types of fees that can be charged in a particular transaction.[120] A few

states include fees of third parties in the calculation of the finance charge.[121] Generally, however, case law and statutes exclude reasonable, bona fide third party payments from interest on credit contracts.[122] The rationale is essentially the same as that which allows lenders to assess some non-interest fees directly; the services provided are regarded as separate from the extension of credit and, therefore, as separately compensable.[123] The argument for excluding fees from interest is stronger, however, in the case of third party payments than in the case of direct lender fees. First, the lender presumably does not retain the fee, so it is not compensation to the lender for an extension of credit, although the creditor may in fact attempt to reduce its overhead expense by contracting out work that would otherwise be done by its employees. Second, third party services are typically more concrete and easily distinguished

---

114 16 C.F.R. § 444.4. *See also* 49 Fed. Reg. 7740 (Mar. 1, 1984) (Statement of Basis and Purpose). Other regulatory agencies have adopted parallel rules. *See* 12 C.F.R. § 560.33 (OTS).

115 15 U.S.C. § 45(a).

116 16 C.F.R. § 444.4.

117 *See* FTC Staff Advisory Letter (June 21, 1985) *reprinted in* Consumer Cred. Guide (CCH) ¶ 96,257; FTC Staff Advisory Letter (May 31, 1985), *reprinted in* Consumer Cred. Guide (CCH) ¶ 96,309.

118 For a thorough treatment of this subject, see National Consumer Law Center, Unfair and Deceptive Acts and Practices §§ 3.4.5, 5.1.1.2, 5.1.1.3 (6th ed. 2004 and Supp.).

119 U.C.C.C. § 2.502 (1974); for a discussion of the U.C.C.C., see § 2.3.3.10, *supra*.

120 *See, e.g.*, Turner v. First Union Nat'l Bank, 740 A.2d 1081 (N.J.

1999) (imposition of document preparation fee by lender's attorney limited to certain circumstances, though, a careful read of the decision reveals that the court's interpretation of the statute eliminates any prohibition).

121 *See, e.g.*, Tavares v. Sprunk (*In re* Tavares), 298 B.R. 195 (Bankr. D. Mass. 2003) (fees to third parties included in calculation of interest rate for purposes of determining whether loan violates Massachusetts criminal usury statute); Luttenberger v. Conseco Fin. Servs. Corp., 671 N.W.2d 425 (Iowa 2003) (courier fee was included in Iowa U.C.C.C. definition of "finance charge" for consumer loans; such fees permissible so long as resulting finance charge does not exceed 21% cap); Gardin v. Long Beach Mortgage Co., 661 N.W.2d 193 (Iowa 2003) (Iowa's 2% cap on loan processing fees for home-secured loans applies to fees paid to third parties for credit reports, appraisal, and broker fees, if they are collected by lender; however, cap does not apply to fees directly charged by third party).

122 *See, e.g.*, *In re* Richards, 272 F. Supp. 480 (D. Me. 1967) (credit insurance); Grantham v. First Union Home Equity Bank, 685 So. 2d 748 (Ala. Civ. App. 1996) (interpreting Ala. Code §§ 5-19-1 and 5-19-4(b)); Cooprider v. Security Bank, 890 S.W.2d 240 (Ark. 1994) (reasonable fees, "made in good faith," to third parties "for something appropriate to establishing or protecting the lender's security"; title insurance at issue); Concord Realty Co. v. Continental Funding Corp., 776 P.2d 1114 (Colo. 1989) (*en banc*) (appraisal fee, inspection fee, credit reports, federal express charges, legal fees at closing); Swanson v. Gulf W. Int'l Corp., 429 So. 2d 817 (Fla. Dist. Ct. App. 1983) (broker fee); Palmer v. Bank of Louisville & Trust Co., 682 S.W.2d 789 (Ky. Ct. App. 1985) (appraisal fees, title insurance fees, title search fees actually paid to third parties were not interest); Goldring v. Texas Commercial Bank, 665 S.W.2d 103 (Tex. 1984) (attorney fee); Durias v. Boswell, 791 P.2d 282 (Wash. Ct. App. 1990) (a reasonable fee for actual services performed is not interest; whether it is so is a question of fact [broker fee at issue]). *See also* 12 C.F.R. § 7.4001 (interest for purposes of National Bank Act § 85 does not include several enumerated charges typically payable to third parties, though not couched in terms of third party payments).

123 *See generally In re* Richards, 272 F. Supp. 480 (D. Me. 1967); Sunwest Bank of El Paso v. Gutierrez, 819 S.W.2d 673 (Tex. App. 1991) (creditor's purchase of VSI insurance on collateral was not "unauthorized," usurious charge; it was rather a charge for separate and additional consideration, which allows creditors to pass on expenses for protection of collateral. Note: *But see* Ch. 8, *infra*.).

from the extension of credit than many lender "services," even if the third party services are still closely tied to the credit transaction. Thus, a borrower who purchases credit insurance through the lender theoretically receives some service apart from the loan itself, although the distinction between compensation for the loan and compensation for the "separate" service blurs when one realizes that the insurance benefits the lender as much as or more than the borrower.[124] In some cases, though, this rationale fails almost entirely. For example, appraisal fees and title-related costs are commonly excluded from characterization as interest in real-estate-secured transactions. In purchase-money mortgages, such services do provide some benefit to both parties—assuring the borrowers they will obtain clear title to property worth the sales price, and the lenders that they are adequately protected by the collateral. In non-purchase money mortgages, however, they have little relevance to the homeowners, and almost exclusively serve the lenders' interest in adequate protection.[125]

Despite the general rule that bona fide third party payments are not interest payments, hidden interest issues arise in several important situations. The first question is: what is a bona fide third party? Usury laws could easily be circumvented if a subsidiary or agent of the lender could collect non-interest payments on the lender's behalf, and courts have held that payments to a creditor's agents or employees are not bona fide third party payments.[126] Similarly, fees attributed to third parties, but not actually expended in whole or in part are held to be interest.[127]

Third party payments may involve hidden interest when the bona fide third party kicks back a percentage of its fee to the lender.[128] Consider the commission which lenders or their employees receive from insurance companies for selling credit insurance to borrowers. These payments often exceed half the insurance premium.[129] Logically, commissions should be interest because they are either direct income to the lender from the loan transaction or a significant supplement to its employees' incomes and, therefore, to its overhead,[130] and sometimes are so held.[131] However, courts have usually found insurance commissions to be hidden interest only when the borrower was required to purchase insurance from the creditor, or when evidence suggested either overpricing or the sale of unnecessary insurance.[132] Kickbacks other than insurance commissions have been held to be hidden interest.[133]

---

124 *See generally In re* Richards, 272 F. Supp. 480 (D. Me. 1967); Lockhart v. G.M.A.C., 252 Ark. 878, 481 S.W.2d 350 (1972) (borrower charged for vendor single interest insurance); Ch. 8, *infra.*

125 This point has been made in regard to Truth in Lending's exclusion of "bona fide and reasonable" closing costs from the finance charge. Ralph Rohner, The Law of Truth in Lending, ¶ 3.03[1], discussing 15 U.S.C. § 1605(e) and Reg. Z, 12 C.F.R. § 226.4(c)(7).

   Of course, even more irrationally, such fees may not be treated as interest even if the services admittedly serve the lender, as is discussed in this section.

126 *See, e.g., In re* Vehm Eng'g Corp., 521 F.2d 186 (9th Cir. 1975) (fee paid to lender's sister corporation was usurious interest); Matter of Dukes, 24 B.R. 404 (Bankr. E.D. Mich. 1982) (broker was not bona fide third party); Winston v. Personal Fin. Co. of Pine Bluff, 220 Ark. 580, 249 S.W.2d 315 (1952) (fees for services performed by lender's employees); Howes v. Curtis, 104 Idaho 563, 661 P.2d 729 (1983) (no independent broker). *See also* Hicki v. Choice Capital Corp., 694 N.Y.S.2d 750 (N.Y. App. Div. 1999) (question of whether broker commission constituted interest is a question of fact).

127 *See* United-Bilt Homes v. Knapp, 239 Ark. 940, 396 S.W.2d 40 (1965) (usury when charges for credit life insurance and appraisals not expended); Westervelt v. Gateway Fin. Serv., 190 N.J. Super. 615, 464 A.2d 1203 (1983) ($3000 for credit life insurance which was not procured); Garrison v. First Fed. Saving & Loan Ass'n, 402 S.E.2d 24 (Va. 1991) (appraisal fee in excess of actual charge was interest). *Cf.* National Consumer Law Center, Truth in Lending § 3.9.6.3 (5th ed. 2003 and Supp.) (real estate closing

costs that are not "bona fide" are finance charges under Truth in Lending). *But see* Durante Bros. & Sons Inc. v. Flushing Nat'l Bank, 652 F. Supp. 101, 105 (E.D.N.Y. 1986) (exaggeration or misrepresentation of lender's own costs in connection with loan support claim of fraud rather than usury).

128 *E.g.*, Kenty v. Bank One, Columbus, N.A., 1992 WL 170605 (S.D. Ohio Apr. 23, 1992) (where a bank charges a higher premium on force-placed property insurance than it actually pays, the excess is interest; thus if bank received "kick-backs" or rebates from premium charged to consumer's account without crediting that account, that constitutes interest), *aff'd in part and rev'd in part*, 92 F.3d 384 (6th Cir. 1995) (though excessive premium may be interest, usury cap not applicable by virtue of state law and the most favored lender doctrine).

129 *See* FDIC v. Gulf Life Ins. Co., 737 F.2d 1513 (11th Cir. 1984) (65% commission revealed); United Fin. & Thrift Corp. v. Smith, 387 S.W.2d 752 (Tex. Civ. App. 1965) (85% commission). *See generally* §§ 8.2.2, 8.5.3.2.2, *infra.*

130 For example, the commissions received by a bank officer in FDIC v. Gulf Life Ins. Co., 737 F.2d 1513 (11th Cir. 1984) work out to a minimum of approximately $120 per loan.

131 *See, e.g.*, Kenty v. Bank One, Columbus, N.A., 1992 WL 170605 (S.D. Ohio Apr. 23, 1992) (rebates or kickbacks to creditor from force-placed property insurance premium is interest), *aff'd in part and rev'd in part*, 92 F.3d 384 (6th Cir. 1995) (though excessive premium may be interest, usury cap not applicable by virtue of state law and the most favored lender doctrine). *See also* § 8.5.3.2.2, *infra.*

132 *See* Bailey v. Defenbaugh & Co., 513 F. Supp. 232 (N.D. Miss. 1981); Aclin Ford Co. v. Cordell, 274 Ark. 341, 625 S.W.2d 459 (1981) (citing Arkansas cases); B.F. Saul v. West End Park N. Inc., 250 Md. 707, 246 A.2d 591 (1968); Equitable Life Assurance Soc'y v. Ins. Commissioner, 251 Md. 143, 246 A.2d 604 (1968); North Am. Acceptance Corp. v. Warren, 451 S.W.2d 921 (Tex. Ct. App. 1970) error ref. nre (citing Texas cases). *But see* Equitable Life Assurance Soc'y of U.S. v. Scali, 38 Ill. 2d 544, 232 N.E.2d 712 (1967) (required life insurance generally not interest). *See generally* Annot. 91 A.L.R.2d 1344. Credit insurance is discussed in (much) greater depth in Ch. 8, *infra*; *see especially* § 8.5.2.3, *infra* (compulsory insurance); § 8.5.3, *infra* (excessive cost and coverage).

133 *See* Stubbs v. Security Consumer Discount Co., 426 A.2d 1014 (N.J. 1980). *Cf.* Kovian v. Fulton Nat'l Bank & Trust Co., 647 F. Supp. 830 (N.D.N.Y. 1986) (kickback of finder's fees; insufficient allegations to state usury claim).

Another issue is whether the fees purchase the product or service which was intended. For example, discovery in litigation[134] unearthed a purported "non-filing insurance," which bears no discernable resemblance to non-filing coverage, routinely being added to personal-property secured retail installment sales. Creditors taking personal property as collateral may elect to purchase "non-filing insurance" to protect their secured party status as against other secured parties who may later acquire an interest in the same collateral. Truth in Lending permits the cost of non-filing insurance to be excluded from the finance charge provided it meets certain conditions,[135] and state usury law may similarly permit such a charge.[136] However, though the creditor indeed purchased what is labeled a non-filing insurance policy, the arrangement actually resembled a default reserve, whereby most of the "premium" fees were returned to the creditor to compensate for bad debt losses—bankruptcies, skips, and so forth.[137] Since this clearly is not non-filing insurance, it should be subject to challenge as hidden interest. Similarly, premiums for property insurance, which creditors may require to protect collateral, may purchase coverage beyond that authorized by the contract or by law. A number of lawsuits have alleged that some "force-placed" insurance policies (purchased by creditors when borrowers failed to provide insurance or allowed theirs to lapse) included additional coverage such as conversion, embezzlement and secretion, mechanics liens, premium deficiency, repossession expense, repossession storage expense, and repossessed vehicle coverage. The premium cost attributable to such charges "that are unauthorized and unnecessary to protect the collateral" are interest.[138]

A final hidden interest issue in third party payments is whom the services really benefit. Some services provided by third parties benefit both the creditor and the borrower.

Credit insurance, for example, guarantees payment of outstanding debt if the debtor becomes ill or if the collateral is damaged. If both creditor and debtor benefit from the guarantee, the existence of some lender benefit will not alone demonstrate hidden interest.[139]

However, as the services become less beneficial to the borrower, the services begin to resemble non-cash compensation to the lender. For example, if a borrower pays for a credit report to be given to the lender, this payment should be treated as interest, even if the credit reporting company is a bona fide third party which retains all of the fee, because the report solely benefits the lender.[140] Similarly, a fee for recording the creditor's assignment of the mortgage has been held to be a part of the finance charge for both usury and Truth in Lending purposes.[141] Courts and statutes often deal with this problem by requiring third party expenses to be "reasonable" or "necessary and incidental" to the loan.[142] Furthermore, other courts have recognized that the benefit received from third party services is at least one factor to be considered in determining whether payments are interest.[143]

7.3.2 Broker Fees

One example of a third party payment which has frequently been revealed to be usurious hidden interest is the commission charged by a loan broker. In theory, loan brokers provide a service to borrowers by finding lenders who

---

134 *See* Edwards v. Your Credit, Inc., 148 F.3d 427 (5th Cir. 1998); Dixon v. S&S Loan Serv. of Waycross, 754 F. Supp. 1567, 1572–1574 (S.D. Ga. 1990); Walmsley v. Mercury Fin. Co., Clearinghouse No. 49,164 (S.D. Fla. order on motions to dismiss Sept. 10, 1993).

135 15 U.S.C. § 1605(d)(2); Reg. Z, 12 C.F.R. § 226.4(e); Official Staff Commentary to Reg. Z, § 226.4(e)-4. *See* National Consumer Law Center, Truth in Lending § 3.9.7.3 (5th ed. 2003 and Supp.).

136 *See, e.g.,* Fla. Stat. § 516.031(3)(a)-6.

137 Edwards v. Your Credit, Inc., 148 F.3d 427 (5th Cir. 1998) (court reversed grant of summary judgment to creditor, finding that the sheer magnitude of the evidence showed a dispute of material fact over whether the policy was really a general default policy cloaked in nonfiling garb). *See also* Adams v. Plaza Fin. Co., 168 F.3d 932 (7th Cir. 1999) (same). For a lengthy discussion in the context of insurance "packing," see § 8.5.4.5, *infra.*

138 Kenty v. Bank One, Columbus, N.A., 1992 WL 170605 (S.D. Ohio Apr. 23, 1992), *aff'd in part and rev'd in part*, 92 F.3d 384 (6th Cir. 1995) (though excessive premium may be interest, usury cap not applicable by virtue of state law and the most favored lender doctrine). *See generally* National Consumer Law Center, Unfair and Deceptive Acts and Practices § 5.3.11 (6th ed. 2004 and Supp.) for further discussion of these cases.

139 *See* Lockhart v. G.M.A.C., 252 Ark. 878, 481 S.W.2d 350 (1972).

140 Winston v. Personal Fin. Co. of Pine Bluff, 220 Ark. 580, 249 S.W.2d 315 (1952). Such fees also may be statutorily excluded from interest in some states. *E.g.,* W. Va. Code § 46A-3-109(a)(4).

141 *See* Cheshire Mortgage v. Montes, 223 Conn. 80, 612 A.2d 1130 (1992) (charge is a TIL finance charge; court also calculated the mortgage assignment fee as part of a prepaid finance charge in deciding that the charge exceeded state law limitations on points or prepaid finance charges). *See also* Brown v. Credithrift of Am. Consumer Discount Co. (*In re* Brown), 106 B.R. 852 (Bankr. E.D. Pa. 1989) (charge is includable in finance charge for TIL purposes).

142 *E.g.,* Alaska Stat. § 06.30.590 *interpreted in* Fikes v. First Fed. S&L Ass'n Anchorage, 533 P.2d 251 (Alaska 1975); Va. Code Ann. § 6.1-330.70 (fees charged in connection with residential mortgage loans must be reasonable and necessary); U.C.C.C. § 2.501 (1974 Model Act) (charges "reasonable" in relation to benefits received).

143 *See* United-Bilt Homes, Inc. v. Teague, 245 Ark. 132, 432 S.W.2d 1 (1968) (appraisal fee); Winston v. Personal Fin. Co., 220 Ark. 580, 249 S.W.2d 315 (1952); Sparkman & McLean Income Fund v. Wald, 10 Wash. App. 765, 520 P.2d (1974). *See also In re* Marill Alarm Sys., Inc., 68 B.R. 399 (Bankr. S.D. Fla. 1986), *aff'd*, 81 B.R. 119 (S.D. Fla. 1987) ("consulting fees" paid third party in conjunction with loan were interest where no documentation reflecting basis for consulting arrangement and no satisfactory explanation of services provided to earn the fee); S.C. Code Ann. § 37-2-202(e); U.C.C.C. § 2.501 (1974 Model Act).

are willing to issue borrowers loans. This dubious service may amount to as little as arranging a loan from a finance company, but it invariably leads to a large fee.

Fees to bona fide third party brokers are valid third party expenses in most jurisdictions[144] and are expressly regulated in some states.[145] Yet precisely because they are nominally valid, broker fees have provided a convenient artifice for lenders attempting to collect excessive interest.[146] Less sophisticated lenders may impose the fee directly, paying themselves a broker fee assuming that it will go unchallenged. More frequently, the fee will be paid to a supposedly independent party which is in fact associated with the lender in some way. In either situation, the fees are hidden interest and should be challenged as such.[147]

Numerous courts have held that broker fees are interest on a loan when the broker is an agent of the lender and hence

is not a bona fide third party.[148] However, no universal test exists for determining when a broker is actually the lender's agent, and courts typically view the issue as a question of fact which must be examined on a case-by-case basis.[149] A

---

144 *See* Family Fed. Sav. & Loan v. Davis, 172 B.R. 437 (Bankr. D.D.C. 1994); *In re* Bryant, 39 B.R. 313 (Bankr. D. Nev. 1984); Walker v. Pliss, 34 B.R. 432 (Bankr. D. Or. 1983); *In re* Verdini Enters., 13 B.R. 739 (Bankr. S.D. Fla. 1981); Swanson v. Gulf W. Int'l Corp., 429 So. 2d 817 (Fla. Dist. Ct. App. 1983); Gardin v. Long Beach Mortgage Co., 661 N.W.2d 193 (Iowa 2003) (Iowa's 2% cap on loan processing fees for home-secured loans does not apply to broker fees, because broker fees are not "collected" by lender); Ashland Nat'l Bank v. Conley, 231 Ky. 844, 22 S.W.2d 270 (1929). *See also* Wood v. Froerer Corp., 611 P.2d 193 (Nev. 1980) (broker was bona fide third party to loan transaction where lenders had no knowledge of and did not share in commission; promissory note was made payable to broker only as convenience to multiple lenders); Annot. 52 A.L.R.2d 703 (1957).

145 *See* Diane Inc. v. Kapnison, 667 P.2d 450 (N.M. 1983) (interpreting N.M. Stat. Ann. § 56-8-7 (1978)). However, such statutes frequently contain broad loopholes. The Nebraska statute governing loan brokers, for example, excludes attorneys, real estate brokers, real estate salespeople, and most lenders. Neb. Rev. Stat. § 45-190 (1983). *See generally* § 11.5.4, *infra*.

A number of states regulate loan brokers through their state credit services organization act. *See* National Consumer Law Center, Fair Credit Reporting, § 15.3 (5th ed. 2002 and Supp.). While these statutes do provide for some consumer protections, such as a cooling-off period, they do not cap broker fees. At least one court has held that the lack of a fee cap in a state credit services organization act permits a broker to charge whatever fee it wants, and that the act insulates broker fees from challenge under state usury laws. Lovick v. Ritemoney, Ltd., 378 F.3d 433 (5th Cir. 2004).

146 An example of a high-cost lender disguising its loan fee as a broker fee can be seen in Lovick v. Ritemoney, Ltd., 378 F.3d 433 (5th Cir. 2004). In *Lovick*, the broker charged a $1,500 fee for "brokering" a $2,000 auto title loan. The broker also undertook many of the tasks usually handled by the lender, such as performing credit checks, arranging for the agreement and note to be signed, issuing the loan principal check, and collecting payments. Despite raising its eyebrows at the amount of the broker fee, the Fifth Circuit held that the arrangement was permissible under the Texas Credit Services Organization Act.

147 *Cf.* Blon v. Bank One, Akron N.A., 35 Ohio St. 3d 98, 519 N.E.2d 363 (1988) (no duty to disclose a finder's fee hidden in the finance charge. [Note that the fee in question was an undisclosed part of the finance charge, not hidden in the amount financed.]).

148 *See, e.g.*, Tavares v. Sprunk (*In re* Tavares), 298 B.R. 195 (Bankr. D. Mass. 2003) (broker fees explicitly included in calculation of interest rate for purposes of determining whether loan violates Massachusetts criminal usury statute); Matter of Dukes, 24 B.R. 404 (Bankr. E.D. Mich. 1982); Browne v. Nowlin, 570 P.2d 1246 (Ariz. 1977); Bayne v. Jolley, 227 Cal. App. 2d 630, 38 Cal. Rptr. 873 (1964); North Am. Investors v. Cape San Blas Joint Venture, 378 So. 2d 287 (Fla. 1978); Feemster v. Schurkman, 291 So. 2d 622 (Fla. Dist. Ct. App. 1974); Applebaum v. Laham, 161 So. 2d 690 (Fla. Dist. Ct. App. 1964); Williamson v. Clark, 120 So. 2d 637 (Fla. Dist. Ct. App. 1960); Howes v. Curtis, 104 Idaho 563, 661 P.2d 729 (1983); Duckworth v. Bernstein, 55 Md. App. 710, 466 A.2d 517 (1983); Coner v. Morris S. Berman, Unlimited, 501 A.2d 458 (Md. Ct. Special App. 1985) (violation of state secondary mortgage and finders fees laws); Julian v. Burrus, 600 S.W.2d 133 (Mo. App. 1980); De Lee v. Hicks. 96 Nev. 462, 611 P.2d 211 (1980); United Mortgage Co. v. Hildreth, 559 P.2d 1186 (Nev. 1977); O'Connor v. Lamb, 593 S.W.2d 385 (Tex. Ct. App. 1979) (purported broker was the actual lender); Terry v. Teachworth, 431 S.W.2d 918 (Tex. Ct. App. 1968); Durias v. Boswell, 791 P.2d 282 (Wash. Ct. App. 1990) (broker fee is interest where broker is agent of lender); Sparkman & McLean Income Fund v. Wald, 10 Wash. App. 765, 520 P.2d 173 (1974); Busk v. Hoard, 396 P.2d 171 (Wash. 1964). *See also* U.S. Home & Realty Corp. v. Lehnartz, Clearinghouse No. 43,259, Case No. 87-SP-930 (Mich. Dist. Ct. Sept. 30, 1987) (arranger's fee was a finder's fee which should have been paid by creditor, not borrower, amount was considered interest; context suggested that broker and creditor were guilty of taking advantage of uneducated, financially desperate borrower.); Hicki v. Choice Capital Corp., 694 N.Y.S.2d 750 (N.Y. App. Div. 1999) (whether broker fee constituted interest is a question of fact). *Cf.* Mills v. State Nat'l Bank, 329 N.E.2d 255 (Ill. App. 1975) (bank's inclusion of brokers' commission as "service charge" on finance charge disclosure form did not, absent other indicia of bank's authority or control over brokers, create agency relationship); Farrell v. Lincoln Nat'l Bank, 320 N.E.2d 208 (Ill. App. 1974) (listing of broker fee as "service charge" on truth-in-lending disclosure form did not give rise to inference of principal-agent relationship between bank and brokers where there was no other evidence of agency). *See generally* Annot. 52 A.L.R.2d 703 (1957).

149 *See, e.g.*, Hicki v. Choice Capital Corp., 694 N.Y.S.2d 750 (N.Y. App. Div. 1999) (whether broker fee constituted interest is a question of fact); Argo Air, Inc. v. Scott, 197 S.E.2d 256 (N.C. App. 1973) (new trial ordered for failure of court to make factual determination on issue of whether broker was agent for borrower or lender). Note that courts in some jurisdictions may apply the more stringent clear and convincing evidence standard of proof, at least where criminal usury is alleged. *See, e.g.*, Rumbaut v. Reinhart, 628 N.Y.S.2d 75 (App. Div. 1995); Feinberg v. Old Vestal Road Assocs., Inc., 550 N.Y.S.2d 482 (1990) (presumption against finding of usury by defendant who claimed entitlement to finder's fee was not rebutted by clear and convincing evidence; criminal usury alleged). Some common indicia of a broker's agency are also discussed in § 11.5.4.2, *infra*.

few state statutes do specify that when a broker acts as agent for both the lender and borrower, it will be deemed to be the agent of the lender.[150]

Practitioners whose clients have been assessed broker fees should closely examine the transaction. As with other third party payments, fees which are collected when no third party exists,[151] which are never forwarded to a third party,[152] or which are kicked back to the lender,[153] are interest. Furthermore, illegal broker fees exacted with the knowledge of the lender have been treated as interest.[154]

In some cases, the lender and broker will split an interest rate upcharge called a "yield-spread premium."[155] An Alabama case that alleged this arrangement to be a concealed device to evade state's 5% cap on points was permitted to go to the jury.[156]

When broker fees have been paid to apparently independent brokers, practitioners should examine the relationship between the broker and lender. If the lender or its officers hold a financial interest in the broker, there may be an

agency relationship indicated.[157] Agency is also suggested if the broker arranges loans largely or exclusively for one lender,[158] or if the broker uses the lender's forms or offices to conduct its business.[159] Where the broker and lender are related by family ties, the possibility of the creditor sharing the benefits of the broker fees should be explored.[160] Finally, some courts have looked to the relative benefits which the broker provides to the borrower and lender. If the broker takes care of the loan application paper work for the lender

---

150 *See, e.g.*, Neb. Rev. Stat. § 45-105; N.M. Stat. Ann. § 56-8-12; Wash. Rev. Code Ann. § 19.52.030(2), interpreted in Durias v. Boswell, 791 P.2d 282 (Wash. Ct. App. 1990) (broker fee is interest where broker is agent of lender; factors relevant to determining agency include lender's reliance on broker for information concerning creditworthiness of borrower, preparation of documents necessary to close and adequately secure the loan, and performing record keeping functions; not relevant whether lender knew of broker fee, as Washington law provides that where broker acts as agent for both borrower and lender, it is deemed lender's agent for purposes of usury statute).

151 *See* Matter of Mickler, 50 B.R. 818 (Bankr. M.D. Fla. 1985) (sham referral fee); Howes v. Curtis, 104 Idaho 563, 661 P.2d 729 (1983); Henderson v. Security Mortgage & Fin. Co., 273 N.C. 253, 160 S.E.2d 39 (1968); Terry v. Teachworth, 431 S.W.2d 918 (Tex. Ct. App. 1968)

152 *Cf.* United-Bilt Homes v. Knapp, 239 Ark. 940, 396 S.W.2d 40 (1965) (credit life insurance and appraisal fees not actually expended).

153 *See* Stubbs v. Security Consumer Discount Co., 426 A.2d 1014 (N.J. 1980); National Am. Life Ins. Co. v. Bayou Country Club, Inc., 403 P.2d 26 (Utah 1965). *See also* Kenty v. Bank One, Columbus, N.A., 1992 WL 170605 (S.D. Ohio Apr. 23, 1992) (insurance kickbacks), *aff'd in part and rev'd in part*, 92 F.3d 384 (6th Cir. 1995). *Cf.* Kovian v. Fulton Nat'l Bank & Trust Co., 647 F. Supp. 830 (N.D.N.Y. 1986) (insufficient factual allegations to state claim); In re Salzman, 83 B.R. 233 (Bankr. S.D.N.Y. 1988) (in absence of evidence that brokerage fee inured to benefit of creditor in any way, brokerage fee paid to brother of one of the creditors was not interest).

154 *See* Pease v. Taylor, 496 P.2d 757 (Nev. 1972) (where lender either charged purported broker fee himself or ratified charge, agency established and fee treated as interest under usury law); Hubschman v. Broda, 103 N.J. Super. 494, 247 A.2d 698 (1968); National Am. Life Ins. Co. v. Bayou Country Club, Inc., 403 P.2d 26 (Utah 1965) (lender and broker shared an illegal additional charge; broker's share also attributed to lender as interest).

155 This arrangement is discussed in detail in § 11.5.4.3, *infra*.

156 Smith v. First Family Fin. Servs., Inc., 626 So. 2d 1266 (Ala. 1993).

157 *Compare* United Fin. & Thrift Corp. v. Smith, 387 S.W.2d 752 (Tex. Civ. App. 1965) *with* Huski-Bilt Inc. v. First Citizens Bank & Trust Co., 271 N.C. 662, 157 S.E.2d 352 (1967) (both cases considering effect of lender or its officers holding financial interests in companies selling credit insurance). *See also* Bourgeois v. Mortgage Funding Corp., Clearinghouse No. 52,162, No. 95-1541 (Bankr. D. Mass. Mar. 6, 1998) (TIL case; lender made about 90% of its loans through the broker; payment of the broker fee was a condition of settlement; broker and lender were owned, in whole or in part, by the same person); In re Whitley, 177 B.R. 142 (Bankr. D. Mass. 1995) (TIL case; broker and lender shared business address and parent company); Modern Pioneers Ins. Co. v. Nandin, 437 P.2d 658 (Ariz. 1968); Kamrath v. Great Southwestern Trust Corp., 551 P.2d 92 (Ariz. App. 1976); Coner v. Morris S. Berman, Unlimited, 501 A.2d 458 (Md. Ct. Spec. App. 1985) (secondary mortgage law violated where brokerage actually run by lender although nominally owned by lender's wife). *Cf.* Vezzani v. Tallant, 172 S.E.2d 858 (Ga. App. 1970) (allegation that lender controlled corporation to which borrower paid brokerage fee insufficient to uphold defense of usury on motion to dismiss).

158 Matter of Dukes, 24 B.R. 404 (Bankr. E.D. Mich. 1982); In re Mandell, 6 B.R. 961 (Bankr. D.R.I. 1980). *But cf.* Lovick v. Ritemoney, Ltd., 378 F.3d 433 (5th Cir. 2004) (special agency relationship between lender and broker, in which lender made all its loans through broker, did not transform broker fees into interest; court cites state credit services organization act as allowing unlimited broker fee arrangements); Thunderbird Inv. Corp. v. Rothschild, 19 Cal. App. 3d 820, 97 Cal. Rptr. 112 (1971) (fact that loan broker split commission with attorney employed by lender to investigate and advise lender of real estate investments did not render transaction usurious where lender did not know of or share in payment).

159 Modern Pioneers Ins. Co. v. Nandin, 437 P.2d 658 (Ariz. 1968) (corporate lenders and broker shared same suite in office building, same receptionist and same telephone number); Kamrath v. Great Southwestern Trust Corp., 551 P.2d 92 (Ariz. App. 1976) (corporate lender and brokers had interlocking directors and officers and offices were linked by an intercom system); Wheeler v. Superior Mortgage Co., 196 Cal. App. 2d 822, 17 Cal. Rptr. 291 (1961) (corporate lender and broker did business in same building, at same location and shared telephone number; broker's offices had no identification to distinguish them from lender's). *Cf.* Matter of Dukes, 24 B.R. 404 (Bankr. E.D. Mich. 1982) (broker completed all paper work).

160 *Compare* Rollins v. Odom, 519 So. 2d 652 (Fla. Dist. Ct. App. 1988) (brokerage fee went to lender's wife, who kept books for herself and her husband); Bayne v. Jolley, 227 Cal. App. 2d 630, 38 Cal. Rptr. 873 (1964) (commission to lender's broker daughter was usurious; she was lender's agent); Miller v. York, 548 P.2d 941 (Nev. 1976) (brokerage commission paid to lender's son-in-law was interest, rendering loan usurious) *with* In re Salzman, 83 B.R. 233 (Bankr. S.D.N.Y. 1988) (no evidence lender benefited from broker fee paid to his brother).

or otherwise performs as the lender's employee, the broker fee may actually be a device to shift the lender's overhead expenses to the borrower and would therefore constitute hidden interest.[161] Broker agreements between the broker and borrower may claim that the broker is not the agent of any lender. Where such an agreement exists, close scrutiny of the actual relationship between the lender and broker as discussed is essential to overcome the written disclaimer.[162]

Practitioners should also note that the Real Estate Settlement Procedure Act (RESPA) has an anti-kickback provision which may be implicated in some broker-lender arrangements. RESPA is discussed in § 12.2.1, *infra*. Other theories which may be available where excessive broker fees have been charged are also discussed in Chapters 11, 12, *infra*.

---

161 *See* Matter of Dukes, 24 B.R. 404 (Bankr. E.D. Mich. 1982); Busk v. Hoard, 396 P.2d 171 (Wash. 1964) (mortgage broker held individual lender's agent where broker, without charge to lender, checked title, prepared legal instruments for loan and mortgage on borrower's home, collected loan payments, maintained records regarding payments and made remittances to lender; brokers' knowledge of usury imputed to lender based on agency principles); Sparkman & McLean Income Fund v. Wald, 10 Wash. App. 765, 520 P.2d 173 (1974); Durias v. Boswell, 791 P.2d 282 (Wash. Ct. App. 1990) (broker fee is interest where broker is agent of lender; factors relevant to determining agency include lender's reliance on broker for information concerning creditworthiness of borrower, preparation of documents necessary to close and adequately secure the loan, and performing record keeping functions; not relevant whether lender knew of broker fee, as Washington law provides that where broker acts as agent for both borrower and lender, it is deemed lender's agent for purposes of usury statute). *But see* Lovick v. Ritemoney, Ltd., 378 F.3d 433 (5th Cir. 2004) (fact that broker performed many services of behalf of lender—such as performing credit checks, arranging for the agreement and note to be signed, issuing the loan principal check, and collecting payments—was insufficient to make broker fee "interest."); Farrell v. Lincoln Nat'l Bank, 320 N.E.2d 208 (Ill. App. 1974) (brokers who handled loan application paperwork on behalf of lender bank were not bank's agents where bank had no role in brokers' decision to submit applications, brokers submitted loan applications on behalf of customers to other banks, bank accepted applications through other brokers, brokers had no authority over bank's decision to grant loans, brokers did not service loans after they were made and bank did not control or receive any portion of broker fees; under these circumstances, inclusion of broker fee as "service charge" on Truth in Lending finance charge disclosure form did not make broker fee interest for purpose of usury law); Mills v. State Nat'l Bank, 329 N.E.2d 255 (Ill. App. 1975) (borrowers' claim that brokers who prepared loan application were agents of lender bank rejected based on reasoning in *Farrell, supra*). *See generally* § 11.5.4.2, *infra*, and National Consumer Law Center, Truth in Lending § 3.7.4.3.2 (5th ed. 2003 and Supp.) for other discussions of brokers as lender's agents.

162 Middleton v. Southern Atlantic Fin. Servs., Inc., 512 S.E.2d 525 (S.C. App. 1999) (evidence to contradict the written broker agreement disclaiming agency not presented in this case; parol evidence rule may prevent the introduction of oral representations of broker absent claims of fraud).

7.3.3 Attorney Fees

7.3.3.1 General

A different third party expense for which creditors often bill debtors is the fee of the creditor's attorney. There are two situations in which a borrower may face such a bill. First, many credit contracts provide that the creditor may obtain a judgment for its attorney fees if the borrower defaults and the debt must be referred to an attorney for collection. Second, creditors sometimes charge borrowers for attorney fees incurred during loan application or closing. These two types of legal fees should be distinguished because their validity under usury law as non-interest creditor expenses may be different.

7.3.3.2 Attorney Fees upon Default

If the recovery is authorized by contract, most states allow creditors to obtain a judgment for the attorney fees that they incurred in collecting a debt from a defaulting debtor.[163] There are limits on the recovery; generally, the fee must be reasonable,[164] a fee may not be recoverable if the creditor is

---

163 *See* National Consumer Law Center, Fair Debt Collection, § 15.2 (5th ed. 2004 and Supp.). A few older cases had found charges for attorney fees incurred during collection to be usurious, 17 A.L.R.2d 288 § 16, and some courts have ruled that these charges violate small loan laws. *Compare* Consolidated Plan of N.J. v. Shanholtz, 7 N.J. Misc. 876, 147 A. 401 (Sup. Ct. 1929), *aff'd*, Consolidated Plan of N.J. v. Palkowitz, 107 N.J.L. 517, 153 A. 906 (1931) *and* Ulin v. Walowitz, 147 Misc. 724, 265 N.Y.S. 745 (Mun. Ct. 1933) *with* Unity Plan Fin. Co. v. Green, 179 La. 1070, 155 So. 900 (1934). *See generally* Hubachek, Annotations on Small Loan Laws (Russell Sage Foundation 1938). However, most courts which have struck down contract clauses providing for payment of attorney fees upon default have done so on public policy grounds and have not found the offending contracts usurious. *See, e.g.*, Bank of Commerce v. Markakos, 22 N.J. 428, 126 A.2d 346 (1956); State Wholesale Supply, Inc. v. Allen, 30 N.C. App. 272, 227 S.E.2d 120 (1976) (finding usury on grounds apart from attorney fee clauses).

164 *E.g.*, Albanese v. Portnoff Law Assoc., 301 F. Supp. 2d 389 (E.D. Pa. 2004) (state municipal lien statute does not permit unreasonable attorney fees); Fleet Bank of Maine v. Steeves, 793 F. Supp. 18 (D. Me. 1992) (creditor's attorney fee request of over $25,000 for foreclosure action unreasonable and therefore reduced by court); Korea First Bank v. K.Y. Lee, 14 F. Supp. 2d 530 (S.D.N.Y. 1998) (commercial case; fee must be reasonable, i.e., related to the amount of time and effort expended regardless of percentage allowed in contract); Equitable Lumber Corp. v. IPA Land Dev. Corp., 381 N.Y.S.2d 459 (App. Ct. 1976) (same; suggesting in proper case that attorney fee provision may be unconscionable). Note that the justification for attorney fees upon default is compensation for creditor expense, not the imposition of a penalty for nonpayment. *See* Owens v. Connelly, 77 Ariz. 349, 272 P.2d 345 (1954); Community Credit Union v. Connors, 141 Conn. 301, 105 A.2d 772 (1954); St. Hilaire & Assoc. v. Harbor Corp., 607 A.2d 905 (Me. 1992).

guilty of some form of wrong-doing,[165] and, in many states, it may not exceed a statutorily specified percentage of the debt.[166] Moreover, in some states attorney fee clauses are unenforceable[167] or are enforceable only in specified kinds of contracts.[168] However, there seems to be general agreement that contractual provisions for the payment of attorney fees in the event of default are exempt from usury restrictions unless they are somehow used as a "cloak" for usury.[169] The most frequently mentioned reason for this rule is that a charge for attorney fees upon default is not a charge for the use of the creditor's money and hence is not "interest."[170] In addition, the charge is contingent on the borrower's performance and thus should not be included in the interest calculation for usury purposes.[171]

The charge must therefore be reasonable in amount, and the expense must actually have been incurred. *See generally* National Consumer Law Center, Fair Debt Collection § 15.2 (5th ed. 2004 and Supp.).

165 *See, e.g.,* Dent v. Associates Fin. Servs. of Am., Inc., 137 B.R. 78 (Bankr. S.D. Ga. 1992) (attorney fees for creditor found to violate criminal usury law are not "reasonable"); Szenay v. Schaub, 496 So. 2d 883 (Fla. Dist. Ct. App. 1986) (creditor's recovery of attorney fees would be inequitable where creditor, despite absence of usurious intent, had sought an excessive recovery). *See also* § 10.8.2.2.2, *infra*.

166 A common maximum seems to be 15% of the unpaid balance of the debt. Some states have special limits for particular kinds of actions. For example, New Jersey has special limits on the creditor's recovery of attorney fees in foreclosures. *See* Bank of Commerce v. Markakos, 22 N.J. 428, 126 A.2d 346 (1956); First Peoples Nat'l Bank of N.J. v. Brown, 178 N.J. Super. 549, 429 A.2d 623 (1981).

167 Some courts have ruled that small loan laws prohibit the collection of attorney fees upon default. *See* New Fin., Ltd. v. Ellis, 284 Ala. 374, 225 So. 2d 784 (1969). RISAs may also prohibit attorney fees. *Cf.* Watson v. Avco Fin. Servs. Int'l, Inc., 224 Neb. 778, 401 N.W.2d 485 (1987) (open question whether Nebraska RISA permits contracting for attorney fees). *See generally* National Consumer Law Center, Fair Debt Collection § 15.2.5.4 (5th ed. 2004 and Supp.).

168 *See* State Wholesale Supply, Inc. v. Allen, 30 N.C. App. 272, 227 S.E.2d 120 (1976) (statute permits attorney fee clause only in notes or other evidence of indebtedness which was held not to include a creditor's sales receipts or invoices). *Cf.* Quinn v. McCoy, 2002 WL 1303407 (Cal. Super. Ct. June 14, 2002) (while deed of trust authorized lender to impose attorney fees to enforce loan contract, lender not entitled to attorney fees for successful defense against borrowers' lawsuit for wrongful foreclosure, since such claims sounded in tort.).

169 In a few cases, creditors which have assessed usurious charges have retroactively attempted to justify them as valid charges for attorney fees. This gambit has not held up in court. *See* Ganus v. Jopes, 470 So. 2d 237 (La. Ct. App. 1985); Coppedge v. Colonial Sav. & Loan Ass'n, 721 S.W.2d 933 (Tex. App. 1986).

170 *See* Community Credit Union v. Connors, 141 Conn. 301, 105 A.2d 772 (1954); Armin Corp. v. Kullman, 127 N.J. Super. 600, 318 A.2d 448 (1974). *Cf.* Oyster Creek Fin. Corp. v. Richwood Investments II, Inc., __ S.W.3d __, 2004 WL 1794706 (Tex. App. Aug. 12, 2004) (upholding jury's finding that lender did not charge usurious interest in demanding amount that included principal, interest, and attorney fees.).

171 *See* Powell v. Sowell 145 So. 2d 168, *suggestion of error*

7.3.3.3 Attorney Fees As a Closing Cost

Charges for the services of an attorney in preparing loan papers or searching real estate title are quite different from charges associated with debt collection. Most noticeably, fees for an attorney's services in the loan preparation process are in no way contingent on the borrower's actions. Moreover, it is much more difficult to distinguish fees for the loan preparation activities of an attorney from the normal overhead expenses of the creditor than it is to distinguish fees for debt collection from normal overhead expense. Indeed, some courts have ruled that a creditor's charge for legal fees incurred in loan preparation are merely overhead expense and, as such, are interest subject to usury law.[172] Other courts have been more lenient with creditors and have ruled that such attorney fees, if paid to a bona fide third party attorney,[173] are valid third party expenses which may be charged to the borrower without being treated as interest.[174] As with other types of closing costs, applicable statutes may dictate the appropriate treatment of attorney fees for this type of service.[175]

---

overruled 146 So. 2d 576 (Miss. 1962); Annot. 17 A.L.R.2d 228 (1951).

172 *See* Brown v. Nowlin, 117 Ariz. 73, 570 P.2d 1246 (1977). *See also* Ganus v. Jopes, 470 So. 2d 237 (La. Ct. App. 1985) (dictum). *Cf.* Cuevas v. Montoya, 48 Wash. App. 871, 740 P.2d 858 (1987) (lender/attorney's own fees to set up a loan were interest).

173 *E.g.,* In re Salzman, 83 B.R. 233 (Bankr. S.D.N.Y. 1988) (no evidence that attorney was not independent of creditors or that legal fee incurred to benefit of creditors, therefore legal fees were not interest). An attorney who was an employee of the creditor would probably not be a bona fide third party because the creditor would have to pay no separate fee on account of any particular transaction. Rather, the attorney's salary would be overhead expense. The same logic applies to fees for collection of debt. Some statutes which authorize the award of fees for collection of debts specifically exclude fees charged on behalf of an attorney who is a creditor employee. *See* Md. Com. Law. Code Ann. § 12-623. On the general question of charging fees for services performed by creditor employees, see Winston v. Personal Fin. Co. of Pine Bluff, 220 Ark. 580, 249 S.W.2d 315 (1952) (fees were interest).

174 This is the rule in Texas. *See* Imperial Corp. of Am. v. Frenchman's Creek Corp., 453 F.2d 1338 (5th Cir. 1972) (applying Texas law); Goldring v. Texas Commercial Bank, 665 S.W.2d 103 (Tex. 1984); Nevels v. Harris, 129 Tex. 190, 102 S.W.2d 1046 (1937).

175 *See, e.g.,* Tavares v. Sprunk (In re Tavares), 298 B.R. 195 (Bankr. D. Mass. 2003) (attorney fees included in calculation of interest rate for purposes of determining whether loan violates Massachusetts criminal usury statute); Turner v. First Union Nat'l Bank, 740 A.2d 1081 (N.J. 1999) (imposition of document preparation fee by lender's attorney limited by statute to certain circumstances, though, a careful read of the decision reveals that the court's interpretation of the statute eliminates all of the protections in the law).

The closing attorneys used by some of the equity-skimming lender, § 11.5, *infra* may be linked by very close ties. In some circumstances, it may be appropriate to apply the same analysis

7.4 Interest Hidden When Principal Amount Is Overstated

7.4.1 Introduction

Another way of hiding interest is to exaggerate the amount of principal which a borrower has received. The idea behind inflating the principal amount is essentially a variation on the use of discount interest.[176] To use a simplistic example, a borrower might receive $100 from a lender while signing a note obliging him or her to pay back $120 in "principal" a year later. The $20 difference is clearly interest, although such arrangements are occasionally touted as no-interest loans.[177] Similarly, a check casher may "defer presentment" of a check with a face amount of $120, give the consumer $100, and either deposit the check or require the consumer to cover the check in two weeks hence. The $20 difference is a finance charge which translates into a 520% annual percentage rate.[178]

Of course, the "hiding" of the interest in these examples is quite transparent and would likely be questioned even by unsophisticated consumers. However, if some justification is given for the $20 increase in principal, the transaction begins to look reasonable. Even though it is more expensive than the loan described above, a borrower might be less likely to question a transaction in which the lender gave him or her $100, added a $20 "processing fee," and then charged 10% interest on the $120. Similarly, the borrower might not question a transaction in which a retail seller took what would normally be a $100 radio, marked the price up to $120, and then offered it on "easy credit" terms. Yet, in essence, all of these transactions are the same; the creditor in some manner inflates the principal amount of the loan or the price of the goods sold, and then charges interest on the inflated total.

7.4.2 Fees Added to Principal; General Methods of Overstating Principal

Undoubtedly the most common technique used to inflate loan principal is the inclusion of various fees in the face amount of the note signed by the borrower. The practice works approximately as follows. Assume that a borrower applies for a $1,000 loan from a finance company. The finance company approves the loan, but tells the borrower that he will have to pay a $10 credit investigation fee, a $20 service charge, and $70 for credit property insurance on his car which, by the way, he will have to provide as security. The borrower is unlikely to have $100 in cash for the fees, and the finance company lends the borrower the $100 for the fees as well as the $1,000 that he wanted originally. The borrower signs a $1,100 note which provides for interest at the statutory maximum, the lender deducts $100 for the fees, and the borrower keeps $1,000.[179]

Some of these devices can be extraordinarily expensive. One device, seen in several variations utilized by some of the more deviously ingenious high rate lenders, might be called "the prepaid payment pyramid." In its most extreme form, a lender wrote a one-payment, one-year balloon note, but deducted up-front the equivalent of twelve monthly interest-only payments from the face amount of the note. As this is, in effect, discount interest,[180] the real interest rate on this purported 24% loan was really 66.67%.[181]

---

to these closing attorneys as is used for the brokers linked to these lenders. *See* § 7.3.2, *supra*, Ch. 11, *infra*. Moreover, such attorneys may be held to account for participation in equity-skimming schemes before bar ethics commissions. *See, e.g., In re* Vaccaro, 539 A.2d 1094 (D.C. Ct. App. 1988) (following conviction for conspiracy to violate Truth in Lending and interstate transportation in furtherance of fraud, an equity-skimming lawyer was disbarred); *Lawyer Suspended for Actions in Abetting Second Mortgage Scam*, 10 NCLC REPORTS Consumer Credit & Usury Ed. 29 (Sept./Oct. 1991) (Massachusetts lawyer involved with "foreclosure prevention" lender was suspended by Bar Overseers).

176 *See also* the discussion of selling car loans at discounts in § 11.6.1, *infra*. *See generally* § 4.3.3, *supra*.

177 *E.g.*, National Travis Inc. v. Gialousakis, 120 Misc. 2d 676, 466 N.Y.S.2d 624 (Sup. 1983). *See also* Wilner v. O'Donnell, 637 S.W.2d 757 (Mo. Ct. App. 1982) ($25,000 is true loan principal when lender receives immediate $5000 kickback from $30,000 loan); Clausing v. Virginia Lee Homes, 384 P.2d 644 (Wash. 1963) (loan was usurious where promissory note stated loan amount was $67,500, but borrowers only received $56,000 in cash.).

178 "Payday" loans are discussed in § 7.5.5, *infra*.

179 Observe how profitable the financing of fees can be for the lender. Assuming that all the fees assessed by the lender are statutorily excluded from "interest," most of the fees such as "service charges" will nevertheless not represent out-of-pocket creditor expenses. Even the credit insurance premium, which must be paid to an insurance company, contains a significant commission that will be returned to the lender. Thus, the creditor cannot only charge a borrower for sums which largely represent overhead expense or profit, but it can simultaneously charge interest on those sums. A few statutes, however, do prohibit lenders from charging interest on certain financed costs because of the expense and deception involved. *See* Brown v. Nowlin, 117 Ariz. 73, 570 P.2d 1246 (1977). *Cf. In re* Bogan, 281 F. Supp. 242 (W.D. Tenn. 1968) (no assessment of fees on fees permitted). *But cf.* Dietrich v. Camargo Cadillac Co., 29 Ohio App. 3d 277 (1986) (sales tax could be included in "cash price" and could be financed by seller); Fanning v. Fritz's Pontiac-Cadillac-Buick, Inc., 472 S.E.2d 242 (S.C. 1996) (court held that a procurement fee was legitimately part of the sales price of a car because the consumer was aware of the fee prior to signing the credit agreement even though S.C. Code Ann. §§ 37-1-102 and 37-2-202 defined cash price to exclude hidden charges and only permits certain fees to be charged).

180 *See* § 4.3.3, *supra*.

181 The proceeds to the borrower was $24,000. The note was for $40,000, and $9600 in prepaid payments was deducted along

At least two usury issues are raised by such transactions. First, as discussed in §§ 7.2 and 7.3, *supra* a consumer's attorney must question whether the fees assessed by the creditor fall within the definition of interest under state law. If the controlling statute allows the exclusion of credit insurance premiums from interest, but makes no such provision for credit investigation or service charges, then the contract contains $30 of hidden interest, even if the borrower pays the fees out of his or her pocket. Because the contract rate is already at the statutory maximum without this $30, then the addition of the $30 renders the contract usurious.

The usury in this contract, however, does not stop at the $30.[182] The fact that the lender financed the hidden interest fees means that the face amount of the note signed by the borrower includes interest charges. Since the lender has been charging interest on the full face amount of the note including the $30 of hidden interest, it obviously has been assessing interest on interest, i.e., compounding. This compounding leads to a second overcharge in addition to the $30.[183] Specifically, if the contract rate were 10% add-on interest, the compounding would create a $3 annual overcharge. Given a two-year loan term, the total overcharge would be $36.

If the compounding raises the effective rate above the usury ceiling, usury will result.[184] But the presence of compounding also raises issues beyond the legality of the effective interest rate charged by the lender. Courts traditionally frown upon the use of compound interest, and merely the presence of compounding may be treated as a contract overcharge in some jurisdictions, even when the usury ceiling has not been breached.[185] Similarly, the inclusion of interest charges in the face amount of a note amounts to the assessment of discount interest, at least in part, on the credit contract.[186] While a majority of usury statutes limit only the effective interest rate charged by a creditor and do not regulate the precise method by which a creditor may calculate contract interest, a few statutes do prohibit the assessment of discount interest.[187] The inclusion of hidden interest fees in the face amount of a note could thus violate a statutory prohibition of discounting and could, depending on the statute, lead to usury penalties even if the effective interest ceiling had not been exceeded.

Another fee that has been the subject of litigation in the Truth in Lending context is an "upcharge." A common example of this occurs when an auto dealer sells an extended warranty to the customer.[188] Frequently, the dealer (who also finances the sale) keeps a portion of this fee and passes on the remainder to the warranty provider. In this situation, the dealer may add the whole fee into the principal amount of the loan even though the portion it keeps is analogous to points. For example, if the principal amount of the loan is $10,000, the total extended warranty fee is $1,000, and the dealer's portion is $100, the dealer keeps 1% of the loan amount. This could violate the applicable state statute on points and fees limitations.[189] In addition, if the upcharge,

---

with other interesting closing costs. The effective rate is 66.67%. Such machinations are the reason the Home Ownership and Equity Protection Act provisions of the Truth in Lending Act limits prepaid payments. *See* § 12.2.2, *infra*.

182 When the added fees are, in fact, hidden interest fees, the interest rate should be calculated on the basis of the principal actually received by the borrower, not on the face amount of the note. *See, e.g.,* Rollins v. Odom, 519 So. 2d 652, 656 (Fla. Dist. Ct. App. 1988) (for purpose of statute on computing effective rate of interest, the principal is the "actual amount of money which the lender turns over to the borrower."); Gibson v. Drew Mortgage, 696 S.W.2d 211 (Tex. Ct. App. 1985); Sparkman & McLean Income Fund v. Wald, 10 Wash. App. 765, 520 P.2d 173 (1974). *See also* Kenty v. Bank One, Columbus, N.A., 1992 WL 170605 (S.D. Ohio Apr. 23, 1992) (if force-placed insurance includes unnecessary and unauthorized coverage, excess premium is interest), *aff'd in part and rev'd in part,* 92 F.3d 384 (6th Cir. 1995) (though excessive premium may be interest, usury cap not applicable by virtue of state law and the most favored lender doctrine). *But cf.* Barnett Bank of West Orlando v. Abromowitz, 419 So. 2d 627 (Fla. 1982).

183 *See* United-Bilt Homes, Inc. v. Teague, 245 Ark. 132, 432 S.W.2d 1 (1968); Westervelt v. Gateway Fin. Serv., 190 N.J. Super. 615, 464 A.2d 1203 (1983). *See also* Kenty v. Bank One, Columbus, N.A., 1992 WL 170605 (S.D. Ohio Apr. 23, 1992) (if force-placed insurance includes unnecessary and unauthorized coverage, excess premium is interest, as is interest charged on excess premium), *aff'd in part and rev'd in part,* 92 F.3d 384 (6th Cir. 1995) (though excessive premium may be interest, usury cap not applicable by virtue of state law and the most favored lender doctrine). *Cf.* Clark v. Aetna Fin. Corp., 340 N.W.2d 747 (Wis. Ct. App. 1983) (interest charged on funds never received by borrower).

184 *See* Giventer v. Arnow, 37 N.Y.2d 305, 372 N.Y.S.2d 63 (1975).
185 *See* § 4.6.1.2, *supra.*
186 *See* § 4.3.3, *supra.* This form of discount is a one-time charge, however, and includes no time factor in its calculation as does traditional "discount interest."
187 *See* Ark. S&L Ass'n v. Mack Trucks of Arkansas, 263 Ark. 264, 566 S.W.2d 128 (1978) (discounting only up to 36 months permitted). Discounting was prohibited under the Uniform Small Loan Law, upon which many existing small loan and consumer loan statutes are based. *See* Uniform Small Loan Law, Seventh Draft § 13(b) (1942), *reprinted in* Curran, Trends in Consumer Credit Legislation (1966) (charges "shall not be paid, deducted, or received in advance").
188 Gibson v. Bob Watson Chevrolet-Geo, Inc., 112 F.3d 283 (7th Cir. 1997); Cirone-Shadow v. Union Nissan of Waukegan, 955 F. Supp. 938 (N.D. Ill. 1997); Alexander v. Continental Motor Werks, Inc., 933 F. Supp. 715 (N.D. Ill. 1996); Ritter v. Durand Chevrolet, Inc., 932 F. Supp. 32 (D. Mass. 1996); Taylor v. Quality Hyundai, Inc., 932 F. Supp. 218 (N.D. Ill. 1996), *aff'd in part, rev'd in part,* 150 F.3d 689 (7th Cir. 1998); Bernhauser v. Glen Ellyn Dodge, Inc., 683 N.E.2d 1194 (Ill. App. 1997). These cases primarily raise Truth in Lending and UDAP claims based upon the failure of the dealer to disclose that it retained a significant portion of the fee. *See* National Consumer Law Center, Truth in Lending § 4.7.4.3.2 (5th ed. 2003 and Supp.).
189 *See* discussions in § 4.7, *supra* and in § 10.5.4.3, *infra.*

arguably interest, is added to the principal and financed over the term of the loan, compounding occurs and the usury limits may be exceeded.

Similarly, the difference between a "GAP" insurance premium and the total fee charged by the dealer may be a finance charge if pocketed by the dealer. GAP insurance (a.k.a. debt cancellation agreement, a.k.a. balance protection plan) is a product that is mostly added on to car loans. It covers the risk of a "gap" between the outstanding loan balance and the amount paid out by the property insurer after a covered loss occurs on the collateral. It differs from property insurance on the collateral, as it covers the debt remaining after the property insurance was paid out.[190] If the dealer fails to pass on all of the amount paid by the borrower (for example, fee charged is $475, but the insurance is only $175) the dealer keeps the difference.[191] State usury laws should be checked because some states have not sanctioned it as an authorized charge which can be excluded from the interest rate calculation for usury purposes.[192] Further, the amount pocketed by the dealer is arguably interest and could, like dealer upcharges discussed above, violate the applicable state statute on points and fees limitations or cause the interest charges to exceed state usury limits.[193] Finally, if the insurance is required as part of the credit transaction, the fee may be illegal under state law for this reason.[194]

Discounts[195] and acquisition fees in the car financing context can also cause the sale price of a car to be significantly inflated. An example of this phenomenon is described in § 11.6.1, *infra*.

A creditor may inflate the loan principal in ways other than padding it with fees. For example, where a creditor erroneously required the borrower to make the first payment on the date of consummation, rather than thirty days later, the payment should have been treated as a down payment, rather than a part of the principal upon which interest was charged.[196] Or, charging interest on the full amount of the loan from the date of consummation when some of it was withheld by the creditor in escrow for later disbursal may improperly inflate the principal.[197]

Another scheme from Illinois involves a creditor that required its customers to deposit $250 in order to obtain a loan for $750. The lender placed the cash money in its general operating account to return to the consumers after they made all of the payments on the $750 loan.[198] However, the lender disclosed the amount financed as $750, not $500, even though the net effect of the transaction was that the consumers received a $500 loan. The Seventh Circuit confirmed the consumers' TILA claims and reversed the lower court's denial of class certification which included an unfair and deceptive practices claim.

7.4.3 *Wraparound Mortgages*

A fairly novel transaction in which interest may be hidden by the exaggeration of the loan principal is the "wraparound" mortgage. A wraparound mortgage is defined as a junior mortgage which secures a promissory note, the face amount of which is equal to the sum of: (1) the principal balance remaining on the existing senior mortgage; and (2) any additional money advanced by the wraparound lender.[199]

Wraparound mortgages may be structured either as purchase money mortgages or as mortgages executed for refinancing purposes.[200] In either instance, the purpose of wraparounds is to take advantage of an existing low-interest,

---

190 As to the Truth in Lending implications, see National Consumer Law Center, Truth in Lending § 3.9.4.7 (5th ed. 2003 and Supp.).

191 These were the facts in Lopez v. Orlor, Inc., 176 F.R.D. 35 (D. Conn. 1997) which involved Truth in Lending claims only.

192 *Cf.* Hawkins v. Thorp Credit & Thrift Co., 441 N.W.2d 470 (Minn. 1989) (sale of insurance not specifically authorized by statute is prohibited).

193 The definition of interest promulgated by the OCC and upheld in Smiley v. Citibank (*see* § 3.4.5.2, *supra*, and 12 C.F.R. § 7.4001, App. D.1.1, *infra*) arguably includes dealer upcharges because the amount pocketed does not constitute the premium "attributable to insurance guaranteeing repayment of any extension of credit." It is not arguably a commission paid for securing such insurance since the sum never left the dealer's pocket and was not paid back to the dealer in the form of a commission. More importantly, where the amount of the upcharge is two or more times the amount of the premium, it should not be considered a true commission, but rate gouging instead.

194 *See* Compton v. Altavista Motors, Inc., 121 F. Supp. 2d 932 (W.D. Va. 2000) (summary judgment denied on whether GAP insurance was voluntary; if required, the premium was an unlawful finance charge under state law).

195 Here, the term "discount" refers to the practice whereby the dealer sells the loan to the lender for less than the face value of the note. The dealer makes up for the anticipated "loss" by inflating the cash price or tacking on additional inflated charges.

196 Edwards v. Alabama Farm Bureau Mut. Casualty Ins. Co., 509 So. 2d 232 (Ala. Civ. App. 1986), *cert. quashed*, 509 So. 2d 241 (1987) (creditor failed to carry burden that this was a bona fide computation error).

197 *See* Danziger v. San Jacinto Savings Ass'n, 732 S.W.2d 300 (Tex. 1987). *But see* McPherson Ent. v. Producers Co-op., 827 S.W.2d 94 (Tex. App. 1992) (interest rate applied to improper principal held not usury. *Ed. Note*: The court for inscrutable reasons did not deal with this as a bona fide error case (*see* § 10.5.5, *infra*), which would have made sense in the circumstances. As it is, this intermediate court case looks to be at odds with *Danziger*).

198 Williams v. Chartwell Fin. Servs., Ltd., 204 F.3d 748 (7th Cir. 2000); Sharp v. Chartwell Fin. Servs. Ltd., 2000 U.S. Dist. LEXIS 3143 (N.D. Ill. Feb. 28, 2000).

199 Mitchell v. Trustees of U.S. Real Estate Inv. Trust, 375 N.W.2d 424 (Mich. App. 1985).

200 For a description of different types of wraparound transactions, see Arditto, *The Wraparound Deed of Trust: An Answer to the Allegation of Usury*, 10 Pac. L.J. 923 (1979).

non-assumable mortgage, by combining it with a higher interest, junior mortgage loan and offering the borrower a blended rate.

An example may clarify the arrangement. The average purchase money wraparound mortgage involves four parties: the seller of the property (the original mortgagor); the original lender (the original mortgagee) with whom the seller has an outstanding low-interest mortgage; the buyer (wraparound mortgagor); and the wraparound lender (wraparound mortgagee) which is issuing the wraparound mortgage. Assume that the purchase price of the property is $100,000, that the buyer puts down a $10,000 deposit, and that a mortgage of $40,000, issued by the original lender, is still outstanding on the property. Clearly the buyer needs a $90,000 mortgage loan. In a normal non-wraparound transaction, the buyer would obtain a full $90,000 from some bank or other lender, $40,000 of this loan would pay off the old mortgage, the seller would be left with $50,000 plus the $10,000 deposit, and the buyer would own the property subject to one $90,000 mortgage.

In a wraparound transaction, the original mortgage is never retired or assumed. Instead, the wraparound lender advances the buyer only $50,000 which is, in turn, paid over to the seller. The buyer then signs a mortgage note for a full $90,000 even though the wraparound lender only advanced $50,000. The buyer pays interest on the full $90,000 face amount of the note, and the wraparound lender is contractually obliged to pay the installments on the original mortgage as they come due. The wraparound lender pockets the difference between the payments it receives from the buyer and the installments due on the original low-rate mortgage.

The advantage to the buyer in a wraparound mortgage is that he or she receives a lower stated interest rate on the wraparound mortgage than if he or she had received a conventional mortgage for the full $90,000.[201] The major risk is that the wraparound lender will fail to remit the appropriate portion of the buyer's payments to the original mortgage lender. If the original mortgage lender does not receive its payments, it can foreclose on the property even if the buyer has made all payments to the wraparound lender. The arrangement also holds risks for the seller, who remains primarily liable on the original mortgage, although the value of the property upon foreclosure would normally cover his or her liability.

The usury issue in wraparound mortgages exists because the wraparound lender is charging interest on a supposed $90,000 principal when in fact it only advanced $50,000. The initial question is whether state law recognizes the fiction that the buyer has received $90,000, or instead looks to the true principal advanced when the interest is calculated. If the total finance charge on the wraparound note was $52,723 over a ten-year term, the APR would be 10% if the principal is $90,000, but 16.58% if the actual principal of $50,000 is used.[202] Even if the payments which the wraparound lender remits to the original mortgage lender are excluded from interest on the wraparound mortgage, the annual rate will rise above 10% because the wraparound lender is retaining not only the interest and principal payments on the $50,000 which it actually advanced, but also the spread between the interest rate in the wraparound note and the lower rate on the original mortgage.[203]

Litigation testing the validity of wraparound mortgages under state usury laws is quite sparse.[204] A 1985 Michigan case recognized that wraparound mortgages executed for refinancing purposes are not subject to federal usury preemption under the Depository Institutions Deregulation and Monetary Control Act of 1980 because they are not secured by first liens as required by the Act.[205] Thus, wraparound mortgages should be subject to state usury laws.

The Virginia Supreme Court refused to buy the fiction behind wraparounds and held that the lender's taking responsibility to forward the monthly payments on a first mortgage did not convert a $4,300 loan into a $50,000 loan. Thus in *Skinner v. Cen-Pen Corp.*, the purported 13 1/4%, $50,000 "wrap" loan was really a usurious 31.2%, $4,298 loan.[206] Furthermore, the Florida Supreme Court has ruled that a lender commits usury when it fails to pay off a first mortgage with part of the proceeds of a second mortgage loan, but instead retains those proceeds, paying only the installments on the first mortgage as they come due.[207] However, other opinions have reached the opposite result.[208]

---

201 There may also be tax advantages when higher interest payments are generated. *See* Bronner, *The Wraparound Mortgage: Its Structure, Uses and Limitations*, 12 J. Real Estate Tax'n 315 (Summer 1985).

202 The Truth in Lending Act disclosures are quite misleading in the case of wraparound notes because they are based on the fiction that the first mortgage is refinanced which, in fact, it is not.

203 Here is how one court calculated it: The wraparound lender wrote a $50,000, 13 1/4% loan, with 122 monthly payments of $589.24. However, it advanced only $4,98.18. The monthly payments forwarded to the senior creditor were $472.31. Thus the borrower paid $116.93 a month for 122 months to the wraparound lender to pay-off the $4300 debt. That works out to an effective rate of 31.22%. *See* Skinner v. Cen-Pen Corp., 414 S.E.2d 824 (Va. 1992).

204 *See, e.g.*, Summers v. Consolidated Capital Special Trust, 783 S.W.2d 580 (Tex. 1989) (payoff bid at foreclosure sale of wraparound mortgage should include the wrapped debt even if borrower was exempted from liability on the debt by the mortgage); Greenland Vista v. Plantation Place, 746 S.W.2d 923 (Tex. App. 1988) (upon acceleration of wraparound note, permissible to include demand for underlying lien balance and accrued interest along with balance of wrap loan). *See generally* Annot. 36 A.L.R.4th 144 (1985) (validity and effect of wraparound mortgages).

205 Mitchell v. Trustees of U.S. Real Estate Inv. Trust, 375 N.W.2d 424 (Mich. Ct. App. 1985). *See generally* § 3.9.3.2, *supra*.

206 414 S.E.2d 824 (Va. 1992).

207 Mindlin v. Davis, 74 So. 2d 789 (Fla. 1954). *See also In re* Hamlett, 63 B.R. 492 (Bankr. M.D. Fla. 1986) (finance company wraparound was usurious).

208 Hibbs v. Perry, 581 So. 2d 235 (Fla. Dist. Ct. App. 1991) (seller's wraparound at issue); Hool v. Rydholm, 467 So. 2d

Despite these rulings, the validity of wraparound mortgages will probably be determined by the definitions of principal and interest in individual usury statutes.[209] Wraparounds have been expressly validated in some state codes,[210] but may be prohibited by the provisions of some second mortgage statutes. The terms of the individual statutes should be carefully examined to determine whether the lender may include any sum not actually advanced to the borrower in the principal of the note.

7.4.4 Compensating Balances

Another method through which a creditor may overstate the principal amount of a loan and, thereby, understate the true interest rate on the loan is to require that the borrower maintain an account with the lender with a minimum deposit of, perhaps, ten percent of the stated amount of the loan. This "compensating balance" which remains in the lender's control is frequently described as "security" which is supposed to guarantee payments on the loan. In fact, it is just another form of discount because the borrower is paying interest on a larger sum than he or she is actually receiving. Frequently, no formal account will be maintained, but the lender's books will simply be adjusted to show a higher principal amount than the amount actually disbursed.

Compensating balance requirements have a long history in usury law, and it is generally recognized by the courts that a credit contract is usurious if a borrower is required to maintain a compensating balance as a condition of receiving the loan, and if the resulting interest rate, based on the principal actually received by the borrower, exceeds the state's interest ceiling.[211] The critical question is whether the lender requires the deposit and maintains control over it.[212] Such control is strongly suggested when a lender commingles the deposit with its own funds.[213]

The Tennessee Supreme Court, considering a variant in which the lender required the borrower to purchase an investment certificate as a condition of receiving the loan, sensibly observed that the borrower is, in effect, funding his own loan to the extent of the required investment. Since interest is, in theory, payment for the use of the lender's money, this creates a conceptual problem. In a case in which the lender required the purchase of a $50,000 investment certificate to secure a $100,000 loan, the court explained it this way: The borrower was paying 9 1/2% on $50,000 of the bank's money and $50,000 of his own money, while receiving only a 5 1/2% return on his investment certificate. The bank thus netted 4% on the borrower's $50,000, effectively receiving 13 1/2% interest on its money, a usurious return under applicable law.[214]

However, courts have refused to find usury when the evidence failed to establish that the lender *required* the borrower to maintain the compensating balance.[215] Similarly, deposits in escrow accounts which are not controlled by the lender may not be usurious.[216] Finally, a few courts have declined to find usury when a loan commitment required the lender to release loan proceeds on a certain date, but the lender instead placed the proceeds in an account pending the borrower's completion of some contract requirement.[217] Such lender delays in the disbursal of loan

1038 (Fla. Dist. Ct. App. 1985) (addressing only a seller's wraparound transaction).

209 For a discussion of wraparound notes under California law, see Arditto, *The Wraparound Deed of Trust: An Answer to the Allegation of Usury*, 10 Pac. L.J. 923 (1979).

210 *See, e.g.,* Minn. Stat. § 47.20.

211 *See, e.g.,* American Timber & Trading Co. v. First Nat'l Bank, 690 F.2d 781 (9th Cir. 1982); Harris v. McCann, 229 Ark. 972, 319 S.W.2d 832 (1959); Tri-County Fed. Sav. & Loan Ass'n v. Lyle, 371 A.2d 424 (Md. 1977); Grundel v. Bank of Craig, 515 S.W.2d 177 (Mo. Ct. App. 1974). *See generally* Annot. 92 A.L.R.3d 769 (1970).

212 American Timber & Trading Co. v. First Nat'l Bank, 690 F.2d 781 (9th Cir. 1982). *See generally* Annot. 92 A.L.R.3d 769 (1979).

213 *See* American Acceptance Corp. v. Schoenthaler, 391 F.2d 64 (5th Cir. 1968), *cert. denied,* 392 U.S. 928 (1968); Bank of Lumpkin v. Farmers' State Bank, 161 Ga. 801, 132 S.E. 221 (1926); Lyle v. Tri-County Fed. Sav. & Loan Ass'n, 363 A.2d 642 (Md. App. 1976), *aff'd,* 371 A.2d 424 (Md. 1977); Miller v. First State Bank, 551 S.W.2d 89 (Tex. Ct. App. 1977), *modified on other grounds,* 563 S.W.2d 572 (Tex. 1978). *But cf.* Starness

v. Guaranty Bank, 634 S.W.2d 325 (Tex. App. 1982) (commingling of funds ignored when interest-bearing certificate of deposit required by lender was not purchased with loan proceeds).

214 Continental Bankers Life Ins. Co. v. Bank of Alamo, 578 S.W.2d 625, 636 (Tenn. 1979), *quoted* in Brabson v. Valentine, 804 S.W.2d 451 (Tenn. Ct. App. 1990).

215 *See, e.g.,* Rebman v. Flagship First Nat'l Bank of Highlands County, 472 So. 2d 1360 (Fla. Dist. Ct. App. 1985) (no-interest escrow account was not compensating balance because not required by contract); Swanson v. Gulf W. Int'l Corp., 429 So. 2d 817 (Fla. Dist. Ct. App. 1983); Reid v. National Bank of Georgia, 256 S.E.2d 82 (Ga. App. 1979).

216 *Compare In re* Bryant, 39 B.R. 313 (Bankr. D. Nev. 1984) ("undisbursed principal" was not usurious when held by broker and available to lenders only with restrictions); Knight v. First Fed. Sav. & Loan Ass'n, 260 S.E.2d 511 (Ga. App. 1979) *with* Hoffman v. Key Fed. Sav. & Loan Ass'n, 416 A.2d 1265 (Md. 1979) (borrower stated usury claim when interest assessed on escrow account if all or part of it was under sole control of lender) *and* Danziger v. San Jacinto Savings Ass'n, 732 S.W.2d 300 (Tex. 1987) (when borrower did not receive all of loan proceeds, practice of charging interest on all of proceeds and periodically rebating excess charges to escrow account was usurious). *See also In re* Curtis, 83 B.R. 853 (Bankr. S.D. Ga. 1988) (where required escrow bears realistic relationship to charges it is designed to cover, it is a permissible charge, distinguishing Knight v. First Fed. Sav. & Loan, 260 S.E.2d 511 (Ga. App. 1979)); Concord Realty Co. v. Continental Funding Corp., 776 P.2d 1114, 1122 (Colo. 1989) (en banc) (reserve accounts for payment of prior encumbrances and interest during one-year term of note constituted principal; commercial transaction, but U.C.C.C. used as guide in determining principal and interest).

217 *E.g.,* Bettum v. Montgomery Federal Savings & Loan Ass'n, 277 A.2d 600 (Md. 1971).

proceeds are only justified, however, when the delay is caused by the borrower.[218]

7.4.5 Indexing Loan Principal

A less common method of inflating loan principal is to adjust the principal periodically in order, for example, to compensate for currency inflation.[219] The simplest way to do this is to peg the principal to an inflation index, such as the consumer price index. Thus, if the consumer price index showed a 5% annual inflation rate over several years, and the contract provided for annual adjustments, the outstanding loan principal would be multiplied by a factor of 1.05 at the end of each year. Payments for the subsequent year would be calculated using this adjusted principal amount.

The few courts which have directly considered the indexing of loan principal have agreed that the amount of an upward adjustment in principal is, in fact, hidden interest which may render the loan usurious.[220] Their reasoning is essentially that the risk of inflation is inherent in the act of lending money. The lender is compensated for this risk through the payment of interest, and interest rates at the time a contract is consummated reflect the level of inflation anticipated over the term of the loan.[221] Thus, additional loan payments, made possible by an indexed principal, are additional payments for a risk the lender has already incurred and, as such, are interest.

7.4.6 Hidden Interest in Credit Sales

7.4.6.1 Inflating the Sale Price

Interest can be hidden in the price of goods purchased on credit in the same manner that it is concealed in the principal amount of a loan. The practice works approximately as follows. Buyer A goes to a car dealer and expresses interest in a certain car. The dealer learns that Buyer A intends to pay cash and quotes a price of $500. Subsequently, Buyer B inquires about the same car. The dealer learns that Buyer B plans to buy on credit and offers him the identical car for $600 at the "low rate" of, say, 5% add-on interest over thirty months, with no down payment, total interest charges of $75, and an apparent APR of 9.33%. While the interest rate seems reasonable if the true cash price of $500 is used as the amount financed, the total interest payments jump from $75 to $175 with an APR of almost 25%. Practitioners seeing figures like those should consider the possibility of both TILA and usury violations, though at least one jury has treated hiding interest in this manner as outright fraud, warranting a hefty punitive damage award of over $50 million.[222]

Car dealers often sell car loans to pre-arranged lenders at a discount. In this situation, the dealer sells the loan to the lender for 60–80% below the amount financed listed on the note. An example of this common phenomenon is described in § 11.6.2.1, *infra*. To make up for the "loss," the dealer often inflates the sales price, sells the consumer "extras" (service or warranty contracts at marked-up prices), or charges additional fees.

What is surprising about this form of hidden interest is not that it exists, nor even that it is common, but rather that burying finance charge in the cash price is so openly practiced. For example, all the major American automobile manufacturers at times have offered supposedly below-market-rate financing for credit sales with advertised interest rates as low as 0.0%, while simultaneously offering rebates of as much as $1,000 to buyers who paid cash. Such sales gimmicks may well violate the Truth in Lending Act because of the misstatement of the amount financed (i.e., the sale price) in the credit purchases.[223] Indeed, the practice of burying finance charges (i.e., interest) in the amount financed (i.e., sale price) has been noted by the U.S. Supreme Court,[224] and has been held to violate the TILA in several cases.[225]

Deceptive price inflation may be subject to a variety of claims of the sort discussed in Chapter 11, *infra*. But, at least in theory, the concealment of interest in an inflated cash price should cause a usury violation as well, if the true interest rate exceeds the statutory limit.[226] The principles

---

218 *See* Williamson v. Clark, 120 So. 2d 637 (Fla. Dist. Ct. App. 1960). *See also* Danziger v. San Jacinto Savings Ass'n, 732 S.W.2d 300 (Tex. 1987) (when borrower did not receive all of loan proceeds, practice of charging interest on all of proceeds and periodically rebating excess charges to escrow account was usurious).

219 *See generally* Note, *Indexed Principal: A Way Around Usury Laws?* 31 Ark. L. Rev. 141 (1977); Note, *Purchasing-Power Adjusted Loans*, 45 U. Mo. K.C.L. Rev. 140 (1976–77); Note, *Indexing The Principal: The Usury Laws Hang Tough*, 37 U. Pitt. L. Rev. 755 (1976).

220 Olwine v. Torrens, 344 A.2d 655 (Pa. Super. Ct. 1975); Aztec Properties v. Union Planters Nat'l Bank of Memphis, 530 S.W.2d 756 (Tenn. 1975).

221 This approach, of course, puts the lender in a serious bind when the anticipated inflation rate approaches or exceeds a fixed usury ceiling, but no such problem exists under a variable usury ceiling which already incorporates market expectations of inflation.

222 *See* Johnson v. Mercury Fin., Clearinghouse No. 50,407, Case No. CV 93-952 (Ala. Cir. Ct. jury verdict Aug. 1994).

223 The only argument that might protect these financing arrangements from the TILA is the possibility that they are seller's points which, under the current TILA, may be excluded from the finance charge. *See* § 7.4.6.2, *infra*.

224 *See* Mourning v. Family Publications Serv., 411 U.S. 356, 93 S. Ct. 1652, 36 L. Ed. 2d 318 (1973).

225 *See generally* National Consumer Law Center, Truth in Lending §§ 3.6.3.4, 3.10 (5th ed. 2003 and Supp.).

226 *See In re* Stewart, 93 B.R. 878 (Bankr. E.D. Pa. 1988) (goods priced at $2000 which were readily available at a retail price of $900 concealed a finance charge of over 80% instead of the disclosed 18%, thus violating state RISA); Riley v. Red River

involved are the same as those under the TILA, and cases decided under the TILA should constitute persuasive authority for the proposition that a cash price may actually include interest charges. Nevertheless, several obstacles to an assertion of usury exist.

The first problem is the traditional "time-price exception" to state usury laws.[227] A state which recognizes the time-price fiction has no usury ceiling for bona fide sales of goods, and a seller can charge whatever time-price it can extract, short of unconscionability. Sellers in such jurisdictions may still inflate their sales price so that the interest they are charging will appear to be low, and buyers may therefore have valid TILA claims. However, the time-price doctrine will preclude usury unless the purchaser can convince a court that the seller's failure to state an accurate cash price removes the transaction from the time-price usury exception.[228]

However, the time-price doctrine has been abolished in many states, to be replaced by Retail Installment Sales Acts or other statutes which limit the finance charge that a seller can collect in a credit sale.[229] In such situations, the difference between the stated sale price and the actual value of the goods purchased is a clear example of hidden interest which, when included in the rate calculations, may cause usury. The difficulty here is proving the actual value of the goods.

Probably the best way to establish the true cash price of goods is to obtain an admission from the seller. Although unwary sellers may openly admit that they charge different cash and credit prices, or may stipulate to a maximum fair market value of the goods,[230] it may be both more realistic and more advantageous for a consumer to gain admission by sending a credible third party to the seller's place of business to price the goods after letting the seller know that he or she will pay in cash.[231] Such a strategy should work if the goods that the buyer purchased are not unique and if the time of the third party's visit is not too distant from the time that the seller offered the higher credit price.[232] A variety of other types of evidence have been viewed by courts as convincing in establishing the true cash price.[233]

Marine, Inc., 664 S.W.2d 200 (Ark. 1984) (where car price raised by $200 from price on original bill of sale to price on subsequent retail installment sale agreement, the $200 inflated price constituted interest and rendered the transaction usurious); United-Bilt Homes, Inc. v. Elder, 272 Ark. 496, 615 S.W.2d 367 (1981) (usury in inflated price of insulation and cabinets in prefabricated home revealed when buyers were required to obtain their own installation); Rowe Auto & Trailer Sales, Inc. v. King, 257 Ark. 484, 517 S.W.2d 946 (1975) (allegations of TILA and usury violations in inflated price of used car). *See also* American Sav. Life Ins. Co. v. Fin. Affairs Mgmt. Co., 474 P.2d 51 (Ariz. App. 1970) (loan principal included deliberately over-valued stock); Mutual Home Dealers Corp. v. Alves, 258 N.Y.S.2d 786 (App. Div. 1965) (allegation of inflated cash price as cloak for usury in credit sale was meritorious defense sufficient to vacate default judgment). *But see* King v. Western United Assurance Co., 997 P.2d 1007 (Wash. Ct. App. 2000) (discount that consumer could have gotten in the sale price of real estate if she paid in cash is not interest where the financed price was no higher than the appraised price).

227 For a more complete discussion of the time-price doctrine, see §§ 2.3.2.2, *supra*, 10.5.2, *infra*.

228 Generally speaking, a transaction will not fall within the time-price doctrine if it looks too much like a loan. This may happen if the niceties of quoting separate cash and time prices are not observed, Daniel v. First Nat'l Bank of Birmingham, 227 F.2d 353 (5th Cir. 1955), *reh'g denied*, 228 F.2d 803 (5th Cir. 1956); if the seller appears to be a mere front for a lender to whom the credit sale contract is immediately sold, Hare v. General Contract Purchase Corp., 220 Ark. 601, 249 S.W.2d 973 (1952); Midland Guardian Co. v. Thacker, 280 S.C. Rep. 563, 314 S.E.2d 26 (Ct. App. 1984); or if the goods being sold are a sham, W.T. Grant Co. v. Walsh, 100 N.J. Super. 60, 241 A.2d 46 (Middlesex Co. Ct. 1968) (coupons/script), Tuition Plan, Inc. v. Zicari, 70 Misc. 2d 918, 335 N.Y.S.2d 95 (Dist. Ct. 1972) (retail installment contract for tuition money was loan). Also where a seller raises its sale price based on the reasonable assurance of discounting its credit contracts to a finance company, the transaction may be in substance a loan subject to usury laws rather than a bona fide credit sale. *See* Hare v. Gen. Contract Purchase Corp., 220 Ark. 601, 249 S.E.2d 973 (1952). *See also* Butler v. Holt Machinery Co., 741 S.W.2d 169 (Tex. App. 1987), *corrected on denial of rehearing*, 739 S.W.2d 958 (1987) (where creditor added interest charges which were neither agreed to nor disclosed to the time-sale price in what was really a lending

transaction rather than a credit sale, such charges should be deducted from the price). It may also be fraud. *See* Johnson v. Mercury Fin., Clearinghouse No. 50,407, Case No. CV 93-952 (Ala. Cir. Ct. jury verdict Aug. 1994); § 12.10, *infra*.

229 *See* § 2.3.3.5, *supra*, § 10.5.2.2, *infra*. *But see* Perez v. Rent-A-Center, 866 A.2d 1000 (N.J. Super. 2005) (criminal usury statute does not apply in the context of time-price differentials for sales transactions governed by New Jersey RISA).

230 *See, e.g.*, Killings v. Jeff's Motors, Inc., 490 F.2d 865 (5th Cir. 1974).

231 This strategy was used by the buyer in Rowe Auto & Trailer Sales, Inc. v. King, 257 Ark. 484, 517 S.W.2d 946 (1975), to demonstrate that the seller followed the general practice of hiding interest in the sale price.

232 *But cf.* Johns v. Ford Motor Credit Co., 551 N.E.2d 179 (Ohio 1990), in which the Ohio Supreme Court defined "cash price" as the "bottom line" negotiated price, not the generally available starting price, such as the manufacturer's suggested retail price on a car. The court was interpreting the Ohio RISA provision prohibiting inclusion in a RISA contract indebtedness exceeding a specified amount tied to the "cash price." The court did limit its holding to the extent that the negotiated price must be agreed upon *in good faith*. (Case involved dealer's practice of raising the sale price to compensate for negative equity on trade-in, where buyer and seller both aware of practice and acting "in good faith.") *Cf.* Orosco v. Partyka Chevrolet, Inc., Clearinghouse No. 45,908, Civ. No. N-89-606 (D. Conn. order on motions for summary judgment, July 18, 1990) (TILA case holding it was a question of fact whether dealer's practice of adding $800 to the sticker price occurred in both cash and credit transactions. *NB*: the TIL definition of cash price must be interpreted to require reference to the starting price, not the negotiated "bottom line" price. *See* Reg. Z, 12 C.F.R. 226.2(a)(9): " . . . price at which a creditor, *in the ordinary course of business, offers to sell.* . . ." Emphasis added. The Ohio RISA definition of cash price, by contrast, referred to the price agreed upon in good faith by the parties.).

233 *See, e.g.*, In re Stewart, 93 B.R. 878 (Bankr. E.D. Pa. 1988)

The value of goods, such as used cars, which cannot be directly priced once they have been sold, may be established by comparison with the market price of comparable goods. This proof will probably require expert testimony. In the case of used cars, the National Automobile Dealers Association's *Official Used Car Guide* may establish an approximate market value, but the *Guide* may be inadmissible unless introduced into evidence through an expert who is familiar with the local car market, the accuracy of the *Guide*, and the effect of the car's condition on its precise price.[234] Such an expert might be a used car lot manager at another dealer, an insurance adjuster, a loan officer at a bank or finance company, or the dealer may in fact admit that it relies upon the guide.

A final approach to proving the actual price of goods is to determine during discovery if the note that the credit purchaser signed was sold to a third party and, if so, the discount at which it was sold. Selling at a discount means that the assignee buys the paper from the original creditor

for less than the face value of the debt, in effect imposing a cost on the original creditor. For example, if a credit contract for $2,500 with a stated interest rate of 0.0% is resold, immediately after signing, for $2,100, it is arguable that the true value of the goods is not $2,500, but only $2,100.[235] This theory was used to establish TILA violations in several cases[236] prior to a revision of Regulation Z which arbitrarily excluded discounts upon the resale of consumer credit contracts from the definition of "finance charge" unless the cost was separately imposed upon the borrower.[237] Despite the amendment of Regulation Z, these cases remain as authority for the proposition that discounts may constitute hidden finance charge in the absence of express statutory or regulatory statements to the contrary.

The discount paid by the assignee was at the crux of the fraud verdict awarded against the assignee-lender in *Johnson v. Mercury Finance*.[238] The car buyer in that case used evidence of the price for which the dealer bought the car ($1,900) and at which the dealer offered it for cash sale ($3,000). The credit price, hiked by a "dealer reserve," was almost $3,700. With insurance add-ons, the loan principal was over $4,000, written at 26.3%. The assignee paid the dealer only $2,700 for this note. The jury, as demonstrated by its sizeable punitive damage award, believed this arrangement fraudulently concealed an effective 50% return to the lender on the car loan.

Practitioners who are considering demonstrating usury through the existence of discounts should be aware that this is not an easy proposition. Courts generally hold that a seller or lender who has given value for a note may subsequently sell that note just like any other commodity for whatever price it can get, and that, for a discount to be usurious, the borrower must show that value was received before the note was discounted.[239] Unfortunately, the average purchaser has

(creditor/seller sold goods on credit from the showroom of another retailer, who would have charged a cash price to its own customers for less than 1/2 of seller's "cash price," concealed a hidden finance charge of 80% instead of 18%; the actual value was established at the price available from the other retailer); Riley v. Red River Marine, Inc., 664 S.W.2d 200 (Ark. 1984) (car price raised by $200 from original price on bill of sale to price listed on subsequent retail installment sales agreement; court also noted the sales tax was still calculated on the original, lower figure). *See also* El Paso Dev. Co. v. Berryman, 729 S.W.2d 883 (Tex. App. 1987) (borrower's claim that inflated sales price of real estate constituted interest, instead of valid time-price differential, sufficiently established to warrant temporary injunction preventing foreclosure pending final resolution of usury claim; sale price in a cash contract for sale of property executed five months earlier than a renegotiated credit sales contract for purchase of same property should be considered in determining if a cash price existed, raised substantial questions of law and facts), *later proceeding*, 769 S.W.2d 584 (Tex. App. 1989) (found to be interest).

One Legal Services advocate, in challenging "0%" used car loans as containing a hidden finance charge for TIL purposes, establishes the actual value by showing what the dealer paid for it before selling it to the consumer, and what it got for it at a repossession sale.

Another possibility is to check newspaper ads for the advertised price for the vehicle. In addition to providing evidence that the vehicle was inflated to bury financing costs, it is also evidence of a UDAP violation in states where selling a vehicle above the advertised price violates UDAP. *See, e.g.,* N.M. Admin. Code tit. 1, § 2.4.1 *et seq.* (1998) [At a minimum, that practice may be attacked as "low-balling" under standard UDAP theory. *See* National Consumer Law Center, Unfair and Deceptive Acts and Practices § 4.6.5 (6th ed. 2004 and Supp.).]; Motzer Dodge Jeep-Eagle v. Ohio Atty. Gen, 642 N.E.2d 20 (Ohio App. 1994); Sanders v. Francis, 561 P.2d 1003 (Or. 1977).

234 *See* Vines v. Hodges, 422 F. Supp. 1292, 1300 (D.D.C. 1976); Rowe Auto & Trailer Sales, Inc. v. King, 257 Ark. 484, 517 S.W.2d 946 (1975). See generally National Consumer Law Center, Automobile Fraud § 9.10.1.5 (2d ed. 2003 and Supp.) for a discussion of using guides as evidence of the true value of an automobile.

235 Assuming a one year contract, repayable in equal monthly installments of $208.33, with adjustment for odd cents in the final installment, the effective APR would be 33.48%.

236 *See* Joseph v. Norman's Health Club, Inc., 532 F.2d 86 (8th Cir. 1976); Schleimer v. McPherson, 400 N.Y.S.2d 566 (1978), *appeal dismissed*, 44 N.Y.2d 730, 405 N.Y.S.2d 460, 376 N.E.2d 933 (1978). *But see* Jennings v. Edwards, 454 F. Supp. 770 (M.D.N.C. 1978), *aff'd*, 598 F.2d 614 (4th Cir. 1979) (table) (discount at which credit contract was purchased by bank did not have to be disclosed as a finance charge under TILA).

237 *See* Reg. Z, 12 C.F.R. § 226.4(b)(6), *as interpreted*, in Official Staff Commentary § 226.4(a)-2. As subprime automobile financing has increased the size of these discounts, with increasingly distorted prices of both the vehicles and the credit pricing, this Truth in Lending provision is again the focus of litigation. *See generally* § 11.6.2, *infra*; National Consumer Law Center, Truth in Lending §§ 3.7.8, 3.10 (5th ed. 2003 and Supp.).

238 Clearinghouse No. 50,407, Case No. CV 93-952 (Ala. Cir. Ct. jury verdict Aug. 1994).

239 *Compare* Baske v. Russell, 67 Wash. 2d 268, 407 P.2d 434 (1965) (note discounted through sham third party lender was usurious) *with* Maynard v. England, 13 Wash. App. 961, 967–68, 538 P.2d 551, 555 (1975) (discount was not interest where credit purchasers receive value for their note) *and* Chancellor v.

received some value for the note (i.e., the goods purchased), just not full value, and to prove that the purchaser did not get full value, the purchaser must arguably show that the price of the goods was inflated, which is what he or she had to prove in the first place.[240]

The existence of this legal Catch-22 suggests that the discounted resale of a consumer's note may be more useful in demonstrating the amount by which a sale price was inflated than in showing the initial fact that it was inflated. For example, the following strategy might be used. Two or more credible witnesses could be sent to a seller's place of business to obtain cash and credit prices for the goods being sold. If these prices were different, the fact that the seller generally inflated the sale price of goods sold on credit could be established.[241] At this point, the discount at which the consumer's particular contract was sold might be used to establish the amount of interest hidden in the price of the particular goods that a consumer had purchased. In the automobile financing context, if the lender pays a discount as a percentage of the amount financed, it may also cap the amount by which the dealer can recoup the discount in an inflated sale price. For example, the lender-dealer contract may cap the amount the financier will pay at 120% of NADA trade-in value. In that case, the dealer is likely to make up for the lender discount by packing add-ons, such as insurance and service contract charges, into the amount financed. Such practices raise issues of loan packing,[242] UDAP,[243] and fraud.[244] Discounting and related lender-imposed finance costs in the automobile financing context are discussed in greater detail at § 11.6.2, *infra*.

Gateway Lincoln-Mercury, 502 S.E.2d 799 (Ga. App. 1998) (discount not interest where consumers were obligated to repay same amount with or without the discount).

240 *See* Maynard v. England, 13 Wash. App. 961, 538 P.2d 551 (1975) (purchaser fails to prove inflated price). *Cf.* April v. Union Mortgage, 709 F. Supp. 809 (N.D. Ill. 1989) (home improvement contract listed cash price as $20,000; that included a $3300 discount, reflecting practice of selling commercial paper for less than face value, which did not constitute interest or TIL finance charge. *NB*: Some indication in opinion that ruling may have been otherwise had borrowers been able to establish that $20,000 was not the price charged in comparable cash transactions). *But cf.* Hare v. General Contract Purchase Corp., 220 Ark. 601, 249 S.W.2d 973 (1952) (court looks to seller's reasonable assurance that credit sale contract can be discounted).

241 *See* Rowe Auto & Trailer Sales, Inc. v. King, 257 Ark. 484, 517 S.W.2d 946 (1975). *But see* Thrifty Oil Co. v. Superior Ct. of Los Angeles County, 111 Cal. Rptr. 2d 253 (Cal. Ct. App. 2001) (two-tier pricing at a gas station does not meet the definition of an illegal surcharge because the difference in the price for gas purchased with cash and gas purchased with a credit card was based on the additional cost to the merchant for credit card sales).

242 *See* discussion in § 9.2.5, *infra*.

243 *See* discussion in § 12.5, *infra*. *See generally* National Consumer Law Center, Unfair and Deceptive Acts and Practices (6th ed. 2004 and Supp.).

244 Johnson v. Mercury Fin., Clearinghouse No. 50,407, Case No. 93-952 (Ala. Cir. Ct. Jan. 1995), also discussed in § 12.10, *infra*.

7.4.6.2 Seller's Points

A special method by which interest costs may be hidden in the sale price of goods or real estate is the use of "seller's points." Seller's points occur most frequently in real estate transactions when the real estate seller, typically a builder, pays points to a bank or other lender in return for the lender's commitment to issue "low-interest" loans to qualified buyers. Such an arrangement might appear to be a boon to buyers and, indeed, seller's points would not be deceptive or usurious, if the seller did not recover its expense by raising the selling price of the real estate. In real life, however, seller's points are frequently, if not invariably, just a sales gimmick whose cost is passed on to the buyer in the form of an inflated sale price.[245] Thus, the only real difference between a transaction involving seller's points and one in which the seller raises its sale price to hide interest charges is the identity of the creditor.[246]

Even the distinction between the seller and the financier may become fuzzy, if indeed it exists at all, in some supposed seller's points transactions. Consider the interconnected network of an automobile manufacturer, its financing subsidiary, and its nominally independent dealers. To boost sales, the manufacturer offers rebates to cash buyers and, instead, offers "2% financing," through its finance company, to credit buyers. The finance company either receives a sum approximating the rebate from the manufacturer to compensate it for the below-market rate, or it takes a loss which, because the finance company is a subsidiary, is eventually passed on to the manufacturer. If the dealer, the manufacturer, and the finance company are viewed as one entity, this arrangement clearly involves an inflated credit sale price. Yet, if the seller (the dealer and/or manufacturer) and the finance company are seen as distinct entities, then the transaction seems to involve seller's points, with the seller paying the third party lender, either directly or indirectly, to reduce its rate.

Whether a transaction is viewed as one with a directly inflated credit sale price or one with a credit price indirectly inflated through seller's points really makes no economic difference to the buyer. In either case, the interest rate that the buyer is supposedly getting is illusory. However, it can make a difference in the legality of the transaction.

---

245 *See* William N. Eskridge, Jr., *One Hundred Years of Ineptitude: The Need For Mortgage Rules Consonant With the Economic and Psychological Dynamics of the Home Sale and Loan Transaction*, 70 Va. L. Rev. 1083, 1136, n.167 (1984).

246 In both situations, a seller may raise its sale price by, say, 5%. This cushion will then be used either directly by the seller to offset the costs of giving the buyer a low nominal interest rate (regular inflated sale price transaction) or will be paid to a third party lender in consideration for the lender's agreement to finance the sale, perhaps at below-market rates (seller's points transaction). In both cases, the inflated price effectively "buys down" the interest rate.

The main problem is that under the current version of Regulation Z, discounts for payments by cash instead of credit must be disclosed as finance charges for TILA purposes,[247] while seller's points need not be, even if the points are passed on to the buyer.[248] Broadly interpreted, this seller's points exception would amount to a TILA loophole that auto manufacturers could drive a truck through, or at least a lot of cars, and for that very reason it should be read narrowly. However, the open conflict between the seller's points loophole and the requirement that discounts for cash payment be disclosed as finance charge has yet to be litigated. In light of this uncertainty, the validity of seller's points under state usury laws becomes a particularly important issue.[249]

The technical distinction between a seller's points transaction, which involves a third party lender, and a credit sale in which the seller inflates its price to subsidize its "own" financing can be important for usury as well as TILA purposes, because the time-price exception to usury laws does not apply when a third party makes a direct loan to the buyer.[250] Thus, creditors who attempt to circumvent the TILA by using seller's points in loans have taken the first step toward usury violations. The question, as always, will be whether the seller's points are interest under the usury laws of any given state, and whether the interest rate resulting when seller's points are considered exceeds the statutory limit.

The few usury statutes that specifically consider payments by sellers to lenders usually treat the payments just as points paid directly by buyers,[251] although at least one statute begs the question by legitimizing seller's points provided that they are not passed on to buyers.[252] In the absence of express statutory treatment, practitioners should examine the underlying structure of the usury statute. If the statute defines interest as payments received by the lender without discussing who makes the payments, then a strong argument can be made that any payment to the lender, including seller's points, are interest.[253]

If the relevant statutory language is inconclusive, it is possible to argue that seller's points should always be seen as interest because they inherently involve the inflation of the sale price beyond what it would be in their absence. The most important point is recognizing that the seller's points are part of the consideration buyers receive for their purchase money. Buyers of a house in a seller's points transaction do not just purchase a house; they receive a house plus financing. This financing costs the seller a specific sum, the amount of points paid to the lender. Thus, the value of the house alone is the stated sale price minus the seller's points. The seller's points are simply buyer's points which use the seller as a conduit to the lender, and generally speaking, buyer's points are interest.

Despite the appeal of this argument, for which at least some support exists,[254] practitioners should recognize that there is a strong predisposition among the courts to rule that a seller can name whatever price it wants for its property without usury becoming an issue. To overcome this predisposition, it may be necessary to prove that the seller literally raised its price to compensate for points.[255] Such a proof

---

247 Reg. Z, 12 C.F.R. § 226.4(b)(9).

248 Reg. Z, 12 C.F.R. § 226.4(c)(5) *as interpreted in* Official Staff Commentary § 226.4(c)(5). Prior to the "simplification" of Regulation Z, seller points were treated as finance charge only if they were passed on to the buyer in the sale price. *See* Official F.R.B. Interpretation 226.406 (Oct. 23, 1970).

249 For a discussion of agreed rate statutes and their potential effect on seller's points transactions, see § 9.2.8, *infra.*

250 *See, e.g.,* Daniel v. First Nat'l Bank of Birmingham, 227 F.2d 353 (5th Cir. 1955), *reh'g denied,* 228 F.2d 803 (5th Cir. 1956); Dehart v. R/S Fin. Corp., 337 S.E.2d 94 (N.C. Ct. App. 1985).

251 Mich. Comp. Laws § 438.31c(1c)-2-b (lender prohibited from imposing discount or points on purchaser or seller except as specified); Ohio Rev. Code Ann. § 1343.011 (discount points are any charge paid by seller or buyer to lender); 41 Pa. Cons. Stat. Ann. §§ 101, 402 *interpreted in* 10 Pa. Admin. Code § 7.2 (points are paid for by seller); W. Va. Code § 47-6-5b(g) (defining points). *See also* B.F. Saul Co. v. West End Park N., Inc., 246 A.2d 591 (Md. 1968) (statutory language—"extracted by a lender from either the borrower or any other person"—covers sellers points).

252 *See* Md. Com. Law Code Ann. § 12-105(d). *See also* Maine Bureau of Consumer Credit Protection Advisory Ruling No. 56, Consumer Cred. Guide (CCH) ¶ 97,083 (Aug. 11, 1981); Opinion of the Wisconsin Attorney General, No. OAG 116-79 Consumer Cred. Guide (CCH) ¶ 97,537 (Nov. 30, 1979). Such

a position begs the question of whether sellers points are interest because it is possible to argue that sellers points are inherently passed on to buyers. By implying that not all sellers points are really paid by buyers, these statutes and interpretations apparently reject this argument, but they fail to clarify when the points are being passed on and when they are not, which is the crux of the issue.

253 *See* Yasner v. Commercial Mortgage Co., 295 A.2d 209 (N.J., Essex Cty. Ct. 1972). *See also* B.F. Saul Co. v. West End Park N., Inc., 246 A.2d 591 (Md. 1968). *But see* McArthur v. Schenck, 31 Wis. 673 (1873).

254 *See* Johnson v. Federal Nat'l Mortgage Ass'n, 609 S.W.2d 60 (Ark. 1980) (Smith, J. concurring). In his concurring opinion, Judge Smith succinctly describes the essence of a seller's points transaction. The buyer, seller, and lender sit down at a table. The lender gives the buyer, say, $100,000 in return for a promissory note. The buyer hands over the $100,000 to the seller for the purchase price, and the seller then gives perhaps $2000 back to the lender (2 points). Seen in this light, it is difficult to consider the two seller's points to be anything but discount interest, paid by the buyer. This approach to seller's points is effectively ratified by the numerous statutes which treat all seller's points as interest.

255 *See* Johnson v. Federal Nat'l Mortgage Ass'n, 609 S.W.2d 60 (Ark. 1980); Maynard v. England, 538 P.2d 551 (Wash. Ct. App. 1975). The idea that a buyer must prove that the seller literally raised an earlier price to recover the cost of seller's points does not make much sense because there is no real difference between that situation and one in which the seller sets the original price in contemplation of recovering its seller's points, or one in which the seller agrees to pay points instead of lowering the sale price. *Compare* Johnson v. Federal Nat'l Mortgage Ass'n, 609

might be established by evidence that preliminary sale negotiations, before seller's points were involved, contemplated a lower price than the final agreement; by evidence that the buyers were offered a better sale price on the condition that they obtained their own financing; or by evidence that cash buyers of the seller's property in general received better prices than credit buyers who used seller's points financing.

7.5 Hidden Interest in "Non-Credit" Transactions

7.5.1 Introduction

Perhaps the ultimate way to hide interest in a credit contract is to conceal the very fact that credit is being extended. This obfuscation is typically accomplished by structuring a loan as a sale or assignment of the collateral, or by transforming a credit sale into a long-term lease, concealing the interest charge in the sale price or lease payments. Among the examples in this section are varieties of hidden credit offered by the "fringe-banking" industry, which operates primarily in areas underserved by traditional banks.[256] Because the human imagination is a wondrous thing, one should not assume that this is an exhaustive listing. Rather these are merely common illustrations of the fundamental principle that courts will look behind the face of a transaction to ascertain its real nature.[257]

7.5.2 Sale and Repurchase or Leaseback Agreements: Secured Credit Disguised as an Outright Sale

7.5.2.1 Equitable Mortgages

One of the egregious forms of hidden interest occurs when a debtor, seeking to obtain or refinance a mortgage, ends up selling his or her home instead. A typical example is a homeowner—falling behind in his or her mortgage payments and facing foreclosure—who enters into a "sale"

agreement with a second mortgage lender.[258] The homeowner transfers title to the property in return for both the lender's agreement to pay off the first mortgage and an option to repurchase the property, usually within a year of the "sale," for a sum which greatly exceeds the amount actually expended by the second mortgage lender. The homeowner may also be asked to make "rent" or "lease" payments on the property until the option to repurchase expires. Invariably the homeowner cannot make the balloon payment required to repurchase the home, and when the option expires, the second mortgage lender claims clear title to the property.[259]

The courts have recognized that such "sales" with repurchase options may, in fact, be usurious loans and that the deeds at issue should be construed to be equitable mortgages.[260] The interest on the mortgage is the difference

---

258 For a discussion of these schemes and claims that might be brought to challenge them, see *Challenges to Fraudulent Homesavers*, 22 NCLC REPORTS *Deceptive Practices & Warranties Ed.* 22 (May/June 2004). *See also* National Consumer Law Center, Unfair and Deceptive Acts and Practices § 5.1.2.1 (6th ed. 2004 and Supp.). A variation of this scheme involves companies that offer land installment contracts or "bond for deed" leases to aspiring homeowners, sometimes on foreclosed or otherwise distressed properties. *See* § 9.2.3.4, *infra*.

259 Another reported scheme involved two partners, one of whom persuaded borrowers with substantial equity to sell the house to him and finance part of the sale by taking a second deed of trust. The other partner would finance the balance at 25% interest, but would loan the first partner substantially more than the balance with a balloon payment after one year. Needless to say, the first partner would walk away with the extra funds and default after a year, and the second partner would foreclose. This was the scheme discussed in Bowcutt v. Delta North Star Corp., 976 P.2d 643 (Wash. Ct. App. 1999), *later proceedings at* 110 Wash. App. 1041 (2002) (upholding, *inter alia*, trial court finding of no clear and convincing evidence of conspiracy).

260 *See* Metcalf v. Bartrard, 491 P.2d 747 (Alaska 1971); Merryweather v. Pendleton, 372 P.2d 335 (Ariz. 1962) (financially distressed businessman's sale of his stock in ranch with option to repurchase would be treated as equitable mortgage; court establishes six criteria for application of doctrine); Oregrund Ltd. P'ship v. Shieve, 873 So. 2d 451 (Fla. Dist. Ct. App. 2004) (sale-option transaction held to be a disguised loan given the disparity in the "sale" amount and the true value of property); Kawauchi v. Tabata, 413 P.2d 221 (Haw. 1966) (equitable mortgage); Thomas v. Klemm, 43 A.2d 193 (Md. 1945) (equitable mortgage; usury not an issue); Fales v. Glass, 402 N.E.2d 1101 (Md. Ct. App. 1980) (equitable mortgage, usury not at issue); Wilcox v. Moore, 93 N.W.2d 288 (Mich. 1958) (found to be usurious loan with mortgage taken); Boyd v. Layher, 427 N.W.2d 593 (Mich. App. 1988) (purported sale of interest land contract was usurious loan); Redmond v. McClelland, 2000 WL 1015774 (Minn. Ct. App. July 25, 2000) (unpublished, citation limited) (deeds created equitable mortgage even without explicit option to repurchase, in light of parties' intent and their relative sophistication), subsequent proceeding at 2001 WL 766779 (Minn. Ct. App. July 10, 2001) (upholding trial court's decision to give borrower an opportunity to redeem); Henderson v. Security Mortgage & Fin. Co., 160 S.E.2d 39 (N.C. 1968); McConnell v. Sutherland, 898 P.2d 254 (Or. Ct. App. 1995)

S.W.2d 60 (Ark. 1980) *with* Hare v. General Contract Purchase Corp., 220 Ark. 601, 249 S.W.2d 973 (Ark. 1952) (price inflated in anticipation of discount).

256 *Cf.* § 2.5, *supra*. A good overview of "fringe" or "alternative" financial services market and high-rate loan products, *see* Lynn Drysdale and Kathleen E. Keest, *The Two-Tiered Consumer Financial Services Marketplace: The Fringe Banking System and its Challenge to Current Thinking About the Socio-Economic Role of Usury Law in Today's Society*, 51 S.C. L. Rev. 589 (2000). *See also* Merchants of Misery (Michael Hudson, ed.) (Common Courage Press 1996); Southern Exposure magazine on *Banking on Misery* (June 2003).

257 *See generally* § 9.2.1.6, *infra*.

between the sale price and the option price plus any additional payments made by the homeowners and, given the short period before the repurchase option typically expires, the resulting interest rate can be astronomical.[261] Thus, the more difficult usury question is not whether the effective interest rate exceeds legal limits, but rather whether the transaction is covered by the usury statute. Often the key consideration is whether the borrower is under an absolute obligation to repay the loan. Many courts have looked to the underlying intent of the parties to find such an obligation to repay, and have held the transactions to be usurious.[262]

Other factors which indicate a loan are the "seller's" financial distress[263] and an unreasonably low "sale" price[264] and the relative sophistication of the parties.[265]

(deed with option to repurchase was an equitable mortgage; issue remained whether loan was subject to a statutory usury exemption); Johnson v. Cherry, 726 S.W.2d 4 (Tex. 1987) (equitable mortgage found, usury not at issue); Bantuelle v. Williams, 667 S.W.2d 810 (Tex. App. 1983) (sale of home with repurchase option construed as usurious mortgage); Sudderth v. Howard, 560 S.W.2d 511 (Tex. Ct. App. 1977) (equitable mortgage theory; party waived usury claim); Bown v. Loveland, 678 P.2d 292 (Utah 1984) (sale with oral repurchase option construed as equitable mortgage). *Cf.* Rabutaso v. Canga, 2002 WL 1064738 (Cal. Ct. App. May 29, 2002) (requiring rescission of fraudulent transaction where home worth $415,000 was sold for $351,000 and a prepaid lease of 10 months; buyer and brokers had forged homeowners' signatures on sales agreement and other documents); Howard v. Diolosa, 574 A.2d 995 (N.J. Super. Ct. App. Div. 1990) (equity would void sale-leaseback transaction when house worth over $100,000 was "sold" for $25,000 and a five-year lease; court rejects argument that the transaction was a mortgage loan, instead finding it unconscionable because of "such patent unfairness in the contract that no reasonable person not acting under compulsion or out of necessity would accept its terms"). *But see* Franchi v. Farmholme Inc., 191 Conn. 201, 464 A.2d 35 (Conn. 1983) (sale and leaseback is not an equitable mortgage); Hess v. Ellwanger, 2000 Minn. App. LEXIS 922 (Minn. Aug. 29, 2000) (no equitable mortgage in a commercial case).

261 In Bantuelle v. Williams, 667 S.W.2d 810 (Tex. App. 1983), the borrowers "sold" their home for $1342.52, the amount overdue on their first mortgage, and received an option to repurchase within two months for $2342.52. This is approximately 74% interest over two months or 444% annually. *See also* U.S. Home & Realty Corp. v. Lehnartz, Clearinghouse No. 43,259, Case No. 87-SP-930 (Mich. Dist. Ct. Sept. 30, 1987) (lender bought borrower's house for $20,000, withholding $5200 in broker's commissions, and immediately resold home to borrower for $32,000 at 9–11% interest; court held true principal was $14,800 [the $20,000 less the "unwarranted and unconscionable" fees]; court voided transaction and ordered repayment of $14,800 at 7%, with all previous payments credited against principal balance).

262 *E.g.,* Redic v. Gary H. Watts Realty Co., 762 F.2d 1181 (4th Cir. 1985); Woods-Tucker Leasing Corp. of Ga. v. Hutcheson-Ingram Dev. Co., 642 F.2d 744 (5th Cir. 1981); Sachs v. Ginsberg, 87 F.2d 28 (5th Cir. 1936); James v. Ragin, 432 F. Supp. 887 (W.D.N.C. 1977); Matter of Offshore Dev. Corp., 37 B.R. 96 (Bankr. M.D. Fla. 1984); Fox v. Peck Iron & Metal Co., 25 B.R. 674 (Bankr. S.D. Cal. 1982); Metcalf v. Bartrand, 491 P.2d 747 (Alaska 1971); McElroy v. Grisham, 810 S.W.2d 933 (Ark. 1991); Redmond v. McClelland, 2000 WL 1015774 (Minn. Ct. App. July 25, 2000) (unpublished, citation limited) (intent of parties at time of conveyance is key; court also looks

to their relative sophistication), *subsequent proceeding at* 2001 WL 766779 (Minn. Ct. App. July 10, 2001); Long v. Storm, 622 P.2d 731 (Or. App. 1980); Johnson v. Cherry, 726 S.W.2d 4 (Tex. Sup. Ct. 1987); Bantuelle v. Williams, 667 S.W.2d 810 (Tex. App. 1983); Brown v. Loveland, 678 P.2d 292 (Utah 1984). *But cf.* Bray v. McNeely, 682 S.W.2d 615 (Tex. App. 1984) (contract for purchase of land with option to compel seller to repurchase at higher price was contingent, not usurious).

263 *E.g.,* James v. Ragin, 432 F. Supp. 887 (W.D.N.C. 1977); Metcalf v. Bartrand, 491 P.2d 747 (Alaska 1971); Redmond v. McClelland, 2000 WL 1015774 (Minn. Ct. App. July 25, 2000) (unpublished, citation limited) (borrower's financial position and relative lack of expertise are factors), *subsequent proceeding at* 2001 WL 766779 (Minn. Ct. App. July 10, 2001); Long v. Storm, 622 P.2d 731 (Or. App. 1981); Johnson v. Cherry, 726 S.W.2d 4 (Tex. Sup. Ct. 1987); Brown v. Loveland, 678 P.2d 292 (Utah 1984). *Compare* Merryweather v. Pendleton, 91 Ariz. 334, 372 P.2d 335 (1962) *with* Weston v. Denny, 14 Ariz. App. 1, 480 P.2d 24 (1971); Browner v. District of Columbia, 549 A.2d 1107 (D.C. App. 1988) ("foreclosure specialists" soliciting sale/leaseback business from persons facing foreclosure were successfully prosecuted for making unlicensed loans in violation of Loan Sharking Act). *See also* McElroy v. Grisham, 810 S.W.2d 933 (Ark. 1991) ("seller"/borrower in dire financial straights, which creditors knew).

264 *E.g.,* James v. Ragin, 432 F. Supp. 887 (W.D.N.C. 1977); Metcalf v. Bartrand, 491 P.2d 747 (Alaska 1971); Oregrund Ltd. P'ship v. Shieve, 873 So. 2d 451 (Fla. Dist. Ct. App. 2004) (sale-option transaction held to be a disguised loan given the disparity in the "sale" amount and the true value of property); Howard v. Diolosa, 574 A.2d 995 (N.J. Super. Ct. App. Div. 1990) (equity would void sale-leaseback transaction when house worth over $100,000 was "sold" for $25,000 and a five-year lease; court rejects argument that the transaction was a mortgage loan, instead finding it unconscionable because of "such patent unfairness in the contract that no reasonable person not acting under compulsion or out of necessity would accept its terms"); Long v. Storm, 622 P.2d 731 (Or. App. 1981); Johnson v. Cherry, 726 S.W.2d 4 (Tex. Sup. Ct. 1987); Brown v. Loveland, 678 P.2d 292 (Utah 1984). *But see* Pacific Eastern Corp. v. Gulf Life Housing Co. (*In re* Pacific Eastern Corp.), 223 B.R. 523 (Bankr. M.D. Tenn. 1998) (commercial lease with repurchase option not a loan where the property was sold for fair market value). *Compare* Merryweather v. Pendleton, 91 Ariz. 334, 372 P.2d 335 (1962); Bermil Corp. v. Sawyer, 353 So. 2d 579 (Fla. Dist. Ct. App. 1977) *and* Kawauchi v. Tabata, 413 P.2d 221 (Haw. 1966) *with* Weston v. Denny, 14 Ariz. App. 1, 480 P.2d 24 (1971) *and* Rinya v. Teal, 593 S.W.2d 759 (Tex. Ct. App. 1979). *See also* McElroy v. Grisham, 810 S.W.2d 933 (Ark. 1991) (land valued at $235,000 "sold" for $80,000); Browner v. District of Columbia, 549 A.2d 1107 (D.C. App. 1988) (one customer "sold" home with equity worth $38,185 for $6988, and her monthly "rental" payments were more than twice her old mortgage payments).

265 Shelton v. Cunningham, 508 P.2d 55 (Ariz. 1973) (no equitable mortgage when lender and borrower were both older men with little education; court notes it might have ruled differently if one of the parties had been a mortgage banker or other person engaged in the business of loaning money); Redmond v. McClelland, 2000 WL 1015774 (Minn. Ct. App. July 25, 2000) (unpublished, citation limited) (borrower's financial position

Of course, aside from the usury issues involved, such sham sales may raise claims under the Truth in Lending Act (especially giving rise to rescission rights),[266] state deceptive practices statutes[267] or common law fraud, because the borrowers are seldom told the true nature of the transaction. At least two states have enacted a law governing purported sales/leasebacks of homes.[268] Additionally, practitioners should determine whether, if the sale/leaseback or repurchase is in reality a loan, the buyer/lender should be licensed under a special licensing law.[269] If the lender does not have the required lending license, one can argue the transaction should be void and unenforceable.[270] Practitioners should also investigate whether state and federal credit services organization laws, state home solicitation sales laws, state loan broker laws, or state and federal telemarketing laws might apply.[271]

7.5.2.2 Personal Property

A sale/repurchase or sale/leaseback transaction involving personal property instead of real estate also may be a loan structured to evade usury laws.[272] As with real estate based transactions, intent is a relevant factor, as is financial distress and a grossly inadequate price.[273] Licensing can be an issue with personal property sale/repurchase transactions, too. It may be viewed as a pawnbroking arrangement, which may violate usury laws if the lender is not properly licensed.[274] Further, licensed pawnbrokers cannot evade the restrictions on their business by trying to disguise what is in reality a pawn loan as a sale/repurchase agreement.[275] If the sale/leaseback transaction contains a terminable at will clause, the deal may be covered by the state rent-to-own law which could raise claims and defenses if the lender did not comply with it.[276]

7.5.2.3 Auto Title Loans

7.5.2.3.1 Overview

A form of high-cost lending that has grown tremendously in the last two decades is the "auto title loan."[277] These transactions are small loans for which the borrower in some manner pledges the title to his or her vehicle. The borrower generally keeps possession of the vehicle during the term of

---

and relative lack of expertise are factors), *subsequent proceeding at* 2001 WL 766779 (Minn. Ct. App. July 10, 2001).

266 James v. Ragin, 432 F. Supp. 887 (W.D.N.C. 1977); Long v. Storm, 622 P.2d 731 (Or. App. 1980). *See also* National Consumer Law Center, Truth in Lending § 2.5.3 (5th ed. 2003 and Supp.).

267 Bryant v. Woodland (*In re* Bryant), 111 B.R. 474 (Bankr. E.D. Pa. 1990). *See* National Consumer Law Center, Unfair and Deceptive Acts and Practices § 5.1.2.1 (6th ed. 2004 and Supp.).

268 *E.g.*, Ga. Code Ann. § 10-1-393(b)(20)(c) (regulating "foreclosure recovery sales," in which a lender purchases a dwelling from a borrower in default, and the borrower remains in possession of the dwelling after the purchase); Minn. Stat. §§ 325N.01 to 325N.09 (regulating "foreclosure recovery consultants," and "foreclosure reconveyances"). *Cf.* Greene v. Team Properties, 544 S.E.2d 726 (Ga. Ct. App. 2001) (discussing Georgia statute but holding that borrower's claim past statute of limitations).

269 *Cf.* Browner v. District of Columbia, 549 A.2d 1107 (D.C. App. 1988) (sale/leaseback perpetrators successfully prosecuted under statute prohibiting loaning money at greater than 6% without a license).

270 *See* § 9.2.4.6, *infra*.

271 National Consumer Law Center, Unfair and Deceptive Acts and Practices §§ 5.1.2.1, 5.1.2.2, 5.8, 5.9 (6th ed. 2004 and Supp.).

272 Sal Leasing, Inc. v. State *ex rel.* Napolitano, 10 P.3d 1221 (Ariz. 2000); B & S Mktg. v. Consumer Prot. Div., 835 A.2d 215 (Md. Ct. Spec. App. 2003) (sales/leasebacks of personal property found to be usurious loans under "pretend purchase" provisions of Maryland Consumer Loan Law; court found subterfuge when lender never sought to repossess property and did not inform consumers of option of returning property instead of "repurchasing" it; lender charged rates of up to 730%); Halco Fin. Servs., Inc. v. Foster, 770 S.W.2d 554 (Tenn. Ct. App. 1989). *Cf.* Burnett v. Ala Moana Pawn Shop, 3 F.3d 1261 (9th Cir. 1993) (pawn was really loan subject to Truth in Lending); Mertens v. Division of Consumer Servs., 596 So. 2d 89 (Fla. Dist. Ct. App. 1992) (state challenging auto sale/leaseback/repurchase ar-

rangement as usurious loans with interest rates of 200% to 1000%; decision addresses creditor's Fifth Amendment right to decline to produce documents to state agency). *But see* People v. Lee, 526 N.W.2d 882 (Mich. 1994) (sale with repurchase option not a loan because no obligation to repay; *NB*: This was a 4-3 decision in a criminal usury prosecution).

273 *See* Sal Leasing, Inc. v. State *ex rel.* Napolitano, 10 P.3d 1221 (Ariz. 2000); B & S Mktg. v. Consumer Prot. Div., 835 A.2d 215 (Md. Ct. Spec. App. 2003) (in finding sales/leasebacks of personal property to be usurious loans, court noted that lender would "purchase" personal property for flat $100 whether the items were worth more or less; appraiser found that average item "purchased" was worth $90; Dillree v. Devoe, 724 P.2d 171 (Mont. 1986) (sale/repurchase of personal property may be upheld if the court finds necessary factors not present). *See also* § 7.5.2.1, *supra*.

274 *See* Kuykendall v. Malernee, 516 P.2d 558 (Okla. Ct. App. 1973) (application of U.C.C.C.).

275 Rhodes v. Hartford, 201 Conn. 89, 513 A.2d 124 (1986); Lane v. Fabert, 178 Ill. App. 3d 698, 533 N.E.2d 546 (1989). *See also* discussion in § 7.5.2.3, *infra*.

276 *See* § 7.5.3.2, *infra*. *Cf.* Aple Auto Cash Express, Inc. of Okla. v. State *ex rel.* Oklahoma Dep't of Consumer Credit, 78 P.3d 1231 (Okla. 2003) (Department of Consumer Credit revokes rent-to-own license of RTO company engaged in auto title pawns).

277 For an overview of this industry, see Amanda Quester & Jean Ann Fox, Center for Responsible Lending and Consumer Federation of America, *Car Title Lending: Driving Borrowers to Financial Ruin*, Apr. 14, 2005. *See also* Lynn Drysdale and Kathleen E. Keest, *The Two-Tiered Consumer Financial Services Marketplace: The Fringe Banking System and its Challenge to Current Thinking About the Socio-Economic Role of Usury Law in Today's Society*, 51 S.C. L. Rev. 589 (June 2000). For sample pleadings in auto pawn cases, see National Consumer Law Center, Consumer Law Pleadings No. 3, §§ 4.2, 4.3 (Cumulative CD-Rom and Index Guide).

the loan, but may be required to leave the title, and sometimes a set of keys, with the lender. These loans have been seen with effective (and sometimes undisclosed) APRs of as much as 900%.

Most title loans are made for amounts far less than the value of the vehicle that secures the loan. Oversecuring the loan allows the lender to make these high-cost loans without regard to the borrower's ability to repay.

The auto title loan industry has grown rapidly.[278] For example, one state alone (Mississippi) had 272 licensed auto title lenders by the end of 2003, with nearly $25 million in loans outstanding.[279]

7.5.2.3.2 Leaseback schemes

The first wave of auto title loan schemes attempted to disguise their nature as a loan and their high interest rates using a leaseback pretense. A good example of these schemes is described in *Pendleton v. American Title Brokers, Inc.*,[280] one of the first reported cases about these loans. American Title Brokers advertised "Pawn your title, keep your car." The borrower pledged the car in exchange for $100, with an interest charge of $3.50, repayable in ten weekly installments. (So far that is only about a 33% APR—not cheap, but within with many states' small loan rate ceilings.) But simultaneously, the customer executed a separate leaseback for the car she had just pledged (with a right of repossession in the event of a default). The lease payments for the ten-week period were $10. (The weekly rental was always set at 10% of the loan size.) Credit insurance and an undisclosed processing fee were also added. Her total weekly payments would have been $22.88, with a total pay-back of $228.80—an effective APR of 977%. A second, $400 advance, would have yielded a 903% APR. The court had little problem deciding that Alabama's consumer credit code applied to the transaction.

American Title Brokers, like many other auto title lenders, attempted to avoid small loan requirements by claiming it was exempt as a pawnbroker. The court found it was not a bona fide pawnbroker, as its practice of renting back the car was contrary to a traditional hallmark of the pawnbroking business—that of retaining possession of the collateral.[281] It was, in essence, simply an effort to evade the state

small loan law, and the company was operating as an unlicensed small loan lender.[282]

The court also found that the rental transaction was subject to Truth in Lending, and that the full amount of the "rental" payments on the leaseback were a TIL finance charge, as they were a cost imposed by the creditor *incident* to the extension of credit, even though the leaseback was not a mandatory condition of obtaining the pawn loan.[283] The same analysis should establish the cost as interest under state usury laws.[284]

Another sale and leaseback auto title loan scheme was analyzed by the Arizona Court of Appeals, which developed a six factor–test to determine that the transaction was really a loan and subject to the state's small loan law.[285] The court reviewed the prior negotiations of the parties, the distress of the customer, whether the amount advanced was the amount the grantor needed, the disparity between the amount of cash received and the actual value of the property "leased" back, a contemporaneous agreement to repurchases, and whether the parties' subsequent acts shed light on the true nature of the transaction. The scheme involved advertisements to those needing "quick cash 4 your car/keep to drive." When consumers arrived at the storefront, they are told that the

278 *See* Amanda Quester & Jean Ann Fox, Center for Responsible Lending and Consumer Federation of America, *Car Title Lending: Driving Borrowers to Financial Ruin*, Apr. 14, 2005, at 9.
279 *Id.*
280 754 F. Supp. 860 (S.D. Ala. 1991). *See also* Quick Cash of Clearwater, Inc. v. State, Dep't of Agric., 605 So. 2d 898 (Fla. Dist. Ct. App. 1992) (case determining extent of regulatory authority, but contains a good description of the scheme), *additional proceedings*, 609 So. 2d 735 (Fla. Dist. Ct. App. 1992).
281 Pendleton v. American Title Brokers, Inc., 754 F. Supp. 860 (S.D. Ala. 1991). For other cases in which courts have found that auto title loans are not true pawns, see § 7.5.2.3.3 *infra*.
282 *See also* Virginia v. Car Pawn of Virginia, Inc., Clearinghouse No. 51,261, No. HG-402-3 (Cir. Ct. Richmond, VA, letter opinion Dec. 5, 1995) (title pawn is unlicensed small loan). The relevant statute will usually prescribe the penalty for operating without a required license, but it may also be possible to argue that failure to have such a license voids the transaction. *See* § 9.2.4.6, *infra*.
283 *See also* Wiley v. Earl's Pawn & Jewelry, Inc., 950 F. Supp. 1108 (S.D. Ala. 1997) (court held that auto title pawnbroker (no leaseback) was a creditor under TILA); Barlow v. Evans, 992 F. Supp. 1299 (M.D. Ala. 1997) (same); Bumpus v. Vandeford, Clearinghouse No. 54,570 (N.D. Miss. Mar. 27, 2002) (following Wiley v. Earl's Pawn and Barlow v. Evans). *See generally* National Consumer Law Center, Truth in Lending § 3.6.4 (5th ed. 2003 and Supp.).
284 *See* State v. R & A Investment Co., 985 S.W.2d 299 (Ark. 1999) (auto title lender violated state usury cap of 17% contained in the state's constitution rendering the transaction unconscionable and subject to usury remedies and UDAP enforcement by the attorney general) [Note that the court indicated that true annual interest rate on these transactions was 65% but that analysis was wrong; fees of 25% on amount of cash back yield an APR of 650%]; Quick Cash of Clearwater, Inc. v. State, Dep't of Agric., 605 So. 2d 898 (Fla. Dist. Ct. App. 1992) (court notes it does not decide whether consumers could bring action to void as unconscionable lease or for damages under other theories, or whether transactions are usurious, as question at issue is extent of department's regulatory authority; court does find the pawn/loan agreement subject to usury law and UDAP statute so case remanded to allow state to proceed to present its case), *additional proceedings*, 609 So. 2d 898 (Fla. Dist. Ct. App. 1992). *See also* Colorado Uniform Consumer Credit Administrator Letter (Mar. 20, 1999), Clearinghouse No. 52,498 (proposed sale/leaseback scheme involving cars likely constitutes consumer loans subject to 12% usury cap).
285 Sal Leasing, Inc. v. State *ex rel.* Napolitano, 10 P.3d 1221 (Ariz. Ct. App. 2000).

only way to get cash is to sign a sale/lease-back arrangement. The amount of cash the consumers received was close to the amount of their need and had no relationship to the value of the car. The proceeds typically equal only 18% of the car's retail value and no more than 30% of the low wholesale value. Further, the "lease fees" translated to interest rates of 218% per year, with payments set at $5 to $12 per day. In addition, if a payment was late, the company added $5 per day to the remaining lease payments together with a one-time charge of $25. The lender required its customers to maintain their own car insurance during the lease term. Finally, the company repossessed about 18% of all vehicles "sold" and leased-back.

7.5.2.3.3 Auto title "pawns"

As in *Pendleton v. American Title Brokers, Inc.*, many auto title lenders will characterize their loans as pawns. A number of cases have found that auto title loans are not true pawns and thus do not qualify for the special treatment allowed by state pawnbroker statutes.[286] However, a few states do allow auto title lenders to take advantage of pawn statutes.[287]

Some auto title lenders omit the pretense of the leaseback, opting to assert that the transaction is a straight pawn.[288]

Lenders will use contractual language that gives the "pawn-broker" a security interest in the property or title and the borrower the option of keeping possession of the collateral or turning it over.[289] (The preprinted language in one contract may go on to say " . . . you have made a knowing choice to maintain possession.") As with American Title Brokers, the "interest" charge is comparable to small loan rates—2% per month (24% per year). However, an additional "service charge" is added to that, set at 40% of the principal, plus a fixed processing fee. So a ten-week repayment plan for a $500 auto pawn loan requires a total payback of $1,033, with $103.30 weekly payments. The APR on that transaction is 830%.

This seems plainly to be a loan secured by an Article 9 security interest, and thus an even easier case to make than in *Pendleton*, though that court's analysis will be helpful both in establishing the "service charge" charge as interest and in distinguishing the transaction from a true pawn.[290] Indeed, in a later Alabama case, one court found that the pawn documents created an Article 9 security interest in both the title and the car, although only the security interest in the title documents in possession of the pawnbroker was perfected as of the date of the pawn transaction.[291]

---

286   Lynn v. Financial Solutions Corp. (*In re* Lynn), 173 B.R. 894 (Bankr. M.D. Tenn. 1994) (title pawn not true pawn and was subject to Article 9 of U.C.C.; even if it were, violated pawnbroker statute's reasonableness limitation on supplemental fees; transaction ruled void *ab initio* and court referred matter to attorney general); Commonwealth *ex rel.* Chandler v. Kentucky Title Loans, Inc., 16 S.W.3d 312 (Ky. App. 1999) (pawnbrokers who held certificate of title and set of car keys not pawnbroker under state statute which required that loans be made on deposit of personal property); State *ex rel.* McGraw v. Pawn America, 1998 WL 407101 (W. Va. 1998) (pawnbroker who retains only title but not the car itself is not entitled to pawnbroker exception to consumer credit laws); Commonwealth v. Car Pawn of Virginia, Inc., 37 Va. Cir. 412 (1995) (same). *Note: The decision in Lynn v. Financial Solutions Corp. was legislatively overruled. See* Henley v. Cameron Auto Pawn (*In re* Henley), 228 B.R. 425 (Bankr. E.D. Ark. 1998) (Tennessee auto title pawn law enacted in response to Lynn v. Financial Solutions Corp. permitted lender to charge 2% interest plus "customary fee"; in this case, lender permitted to charge "customary fee" of $432 per month on loan of $2,400).

287   *See, e.g.*, Floyd v. Title Exchange & Pawn of Anniston, Inc., 620 So. 2d 576 (Ala. 1993); Opinion of the Nevada Attorney General, No. 95-20 (Nov. 17, 1995), *available at* 1995 WL 737002 (Nevada attorney general opining that auto title pawn constitutes a "pawn" and the creditor is, therefore, not subject to licensing as an installment lender). Some states have permitted auto title "pawns" legislatively. *E.g.*, Ga. Code Ann. § 44-12-130(5); Minn. Stat. § 325J.06(c).

288   *See, e.g.*, State v. R & A Investment Co., 985 S.W.2d 299 (Ark. 1999); Churchwell v. National Title Loan, Inc., Case No. 96-5098-CA (Cir. Ct. Duval County Fla. Dec. 2, 1997) (order certifying class), Clearinghouse No. 52,155, (Cir. Ct. Duval County Oct. 23, 1998) (summary judgment granted to consumer

on TILA claim), Clearinghouse No. 52,155A; Commonwealth *ex rel.* Chandler v. Kentucky Title Loans, Inc., 16 S.W.3d 312 (Ky. App. 1999).

289   The contract gives the "pawn-broker" the right to repossess, with a minimum repossession fee of $125, and includes boilerplate language purporting to waive the right to object to repossession.

290   *See* Lynn v. Financial Solutions Corp. (*In re* Lynn), 173 B.R. 894 (Bankr. M.D. Tenn. 1994) (title pawn not true pawn; contract called for security interest, so lender was subject to Article 9, which lender violated). *Note: The decision in Lynn v. Financial Solutions Corp. was legislatively overruled. See* Henley v. Cameron Auto Pawn (*In re* Henley), 228 B.R. 425 (Bankr. E.D. Ark. 1998) (Tennessee auto title pawn law enacted in response to Lynn v. Financial Solutions Corp. permitted lender to charge 2% interest plus "customary fee"; in this case, lender permitted to charge "customary fee" of $432 per month on loan of $2,400).

291   Mattheiss v. Title Loan Express (*In re* Mattheiss), 214 B.R. 20 (Bankr. N.D. Ala. 1997) (the opinion addresses the implications of this holding in the bankruptcy context). *See also In re* Burnsed, 224 B.R. 496 (Bankr. M.D. Fla. 1998) (written auto title pawn agreement created a security interest under state law, making the lender a secured creditor); *In re* Lopez, 163 B.R. 189 (Bankr. D. Colo. 1994) (same holding in true pawn transaction). *But see* Jones v. Mayhall Enterprises (*In re* Jones), 304 B.R. 462 (Bankr. N.D. Ala. 2003) (vehicle not part of bankruptcy estate after debtor's right of redemption had expired; while trustee could avoid transfer because the debtor did not receive a reasonably equivalent value, title lender entitled to sell car to recover payment of its claim); Bell v. Instant Car Title Loans (*In re* Bell), 279 B.R. 890 (Bankr. N.D. Ga. 2002) (vehicle not part of estate when auto title lender repossessed it under Georgia law and redemption period had expired; however, debtor might be able to challenge repossession as a fraudulent transfer.); Oglesby v. Max (*In re* Oglesby), 2001 WL 34047880 (Bankr. S.D. Ga. Oct. 23, 2001) (when auto title lender repossessed

Of course, causes of action for fraud, misrepresentation, and unfair and/or deceptive acts should be pled to remedy overreaching or fraudulent conduct by such pawnbrokers.[292] If the interest charged exceeds twice that allowed under state law, the pawnbroker can also face RICO claims on the grounds that it is collecting an unlawful debt as long as the pawnbroker is operating as an "enterprise."[293] These claims are strengthened when, as often is the case, the title lender is also a used car dealer.

7.5.2.3.4 Other schemes and disguises

A case from Oklahoma involved a lender that claimed that its auto title loans were rent-to-own (RTO) transactions.[294] The Oklahoma Supreme Court disagreed, and using the six-factor analysis from the Arizona Supreme Court in *Sal Leasing, Inc.*,[295] determined that the transactions were loans. The court noted that a typical RTO business does not require the consumer to sell her property to the store at a significantly reduced price and then rent it back. The court also found significant the fact that the lender had no inventory and did not offer goods generally available to RTO customers. In this case, the auto title loans carried interest rates of 285%, 290%, and 484%.

In another case,[296] a $1,500 loan fee on a $2,000 title loan was disguised as a broker fee. The scheme involved two entities, one which allegedly was the broker, and the other which was the nominal lender. Unfortunately, the Fifth Circuit permitted the lender to get away with this ruse, holding that the Texas Credit Services Organization Act permitted such a brokerage arrangement.[297]

Some auto title lenders have been characterizing auto title loans as open-end lines of credit.[298] This variation seeks to take advantage of state laws that permit lenders to contract for any rate of interest for open-end credit.[299] In addition, Truth in Lending disclosures for open-end credit are much less informative than disclosures for closed-end credit.[300] These auto title "lines of credit" may be challenged as spurious open-end credit under Truth in Lending[301] and state loan laws.

Auto title lenders often increase these fees by using questionable add-on. Typical fees include late fees, repossession fees, and even fees to "call off" a repossession.[302] Other hidden loan fees are disguised in the form of charges for credit insurance, "auto club memberships," or other services.[303]

---

vehicle under Georgia law, property not part of estate even though debtor retained right to redeem under Georgia law); *In re* Walker, 204 B.R. 812 (Bankr. M.D. Fla. 1997) (auto repossessed prior to bankruptcy filing in title pawn transaction and debtor's failure to redeem within 60 days of filing extinguished any property right to car). For the bankruptcy implications of dealing with secured creditors in chapter 13 cases and the opportunity this presents to modify the creditor's rights, see National Consumer Law Center, Consumer Bankruptcy Law and Practice §§ 11.6 and 11.9 (7th ed. 2004 and Supp.). *See also In re* Davis, 269 B.R. 914 (Bankr. M.D. Ala. 2001) (auto title lender failed to perfect security interest by recording lien on certificate of title; security interest avoided in bankruptcy); State *ex rel.* Morgan v. Thompson, 791 So. 2d 977 (Ala. Ct. App. Jan. 12, 2001) (under state drug asset forfeiture law, auto title lender is not a bona fide owner of the vehicle but is only a bona fide lienholder; lender is only entitled to value of the lien, not possession of the vehicle); Cobb Center Pawn and Jewelry Brokers, Inc. v. Gordon, 529 S.E.2d 138 (Ga. App. 2000) (security interest is not perfected as against third party purchaser). Note, however, that in some states pawnbrokers do not have to perfect their security interest. This ironically may give pawnbrokers a superior interest to that of even a legitimate purchase money lender, if the latter failed to record his lien. *E.g.*, Kubota Credit Corp. v. Tillman, 2002 WL 31845225 (Tenn. Ct. App. Dec. 16, 2002).

292 *See* discussion in §§ 12.5, 12.7, 12.10, *infra. See also* Barlow v. Evans, 992 F. Supp. 1299 (M.D. Ala. 1997) (failure to disclose TILA-required costs of transaction states a claim of fraud by suppression under Alabama law); *Ex parte* Coleman (*In re* Coleman v. Higginbotham*), 861 So. 2d 1080 (Ala. 2003) (consumer alleged that pawnbroker repossessed vehicle in violation of oral agreement; court permitted consumer to bring claims for breach of contract and conversion, but not fraud or outrage.); Sal Leasing, Inc. v. State *ex rel.* Napolitano, 10 P.3d 1221 (Ariz. 2000) (reversed dismissal of UDAP claims in light of holding that sale/leaseback auto scheme created loans which violated state usury law). *But see* Miller v. Pawn World, Inc., 705 So. 2d 467 (Ala. Civ. App. 1997) (court dismissed fraud claims on ground that representations about selling the pawned property were part of the contract; borrower failed to read the contract and failed to meet his burden that the pawnbroker misrepresented that the loan would "roll over" more than once).

293 *See* Markham v. Gibson, Clearinghouse No. 52,067, No. 97-01651 SPK (D. Haw. July 7, 1998) and discussion in § 10.8.5.3, *infra.*

294 Aple Auto Cash Express, Inc. of Okla. v. State *ex rel.* Oklahoma Dep't of Consumer Credit, 78 P.3d 1231 (Okla. 2003) (following Sal Leasing, Inc. v. State *ex rel.* Napolitano).

295 Sal Leasing, Inc. v. State *ex rel.* Napolitano, 10 P.3d 1221 (Ariz. Ct. App. 2000). *See* § 7.5.2.3.2, *infra.*

296 Lovick v. Ritemoney Ltd., 378 F.3d 433 (5th Cir. 2004).

297 *Id. See* § 7.3.2, *supra*, for a discussion regarding challenging broker fees as disguised interest.

298 Amanda Quester & Jean Ann Fox, Center for Responsible Lending and Consumer Federation of America, *Car Title Lending: Driving Borrowers to Financial Ruin*, Apr. 14, 2005.

299 Iowa Code Ann. § 537.2402; Va. Code Ann, § 6.1-330.78.

300 *See generally* National Consumer Law Center, Truth in Lending Ch. 5 (5th ed. 2003 and Supp.).

301 *Id.* § 5.2.3.

302 *See* Marc Perrusquia, *Last-Resort Loans*, Memphis Commercial Appeal, July 11, 2004, at A1 (documenting illegal late fees, $175 repossession fee, and $75 "call off" fee charged by one auto title lender). See § 7.2.4.2, *supra*, for a discussion of challenging late fees as hidden interest.

303 *See, e.g.*, Low Cost Auto Pawn, Inc. v. Greco, 851 So. 2d 768 (Fla. Dist. Ct. App. 2003) (affirming summary judgment awarding borrower $32,656 against auto title lender who disguised loans as a "marketing agreement"); Tom Kertscher, *Car-title Loan Company Takes Borrower for a Ride, Suit Says,* Milwaukee Journal Sentinel, July 13, 2002, at 1B.

7.5.2.3.5 *Auto title loan statutes*

In the wake of adverse judicial rulings, the industry in some states sought a legislative stamp of approval for auto title loans.[304] Such statutes often operate to trump otherwise applicable usury caps, even those found in criminal statutes.[305]

Even so, such transactions may well run afoul of the law. Where the applicable law allows only certain fees up to certain amounts or percentages of the loan, no other charges can be imposed.[306] In addition, repossessing and selling the car and keeping the excess above the amount owed in violation of state law can also violate the fee or rate cap.[307]

Failure to comply with other requirements of a state pawn-broker law may also render the transaction voidable[308] or subject to a usury claim.[309]

If the auto title pawn is not specifically authorized by the state's pawnbroking statute, mere possession of a title certificate does not create a valid security interest under the UCC.[310] Wrongful repossession of the car in this instance creates a wide range of claims.[311]

A few states have sought to limit auto title "pawns" by explicitly requiring that the "pawnbroker" take possession of the vehicle or by excluding pawns made solely against the title of a vehicle.[312] Some municipalities have responded to the growth of the auto title lending industry by enacting their own more protective regulation or through zoning actions.[313]

---

304 *E.g.*, Fla. Stat. Ann §§ 537.001 to 537.018 (in 2000, Florida slashed the permissible interest rate from 20% per month to 30% per year on the first $2,000, 24% per year on the amount between $2,000 and $3,000, and 18% on amounts above $3,000, forcing the industry to abandon the state); Ga. Code Ann. § 44-12-130 to 44-12-138; Ky. Rev. Stat. Ann. §§ 368.200–.285, 368.991 (Kentucky caps title loan charges to 36% per year); Minn. Stat. §§ 325J.01 to 325J.13.; Miss. Code Ann. §§ 75-67-401 to 75-67-449; Mo. Rev. Stat. §§ 367.500 to 367.533; Mont. Code Ann. §§ 31-1-801 to 31-1-827; N.H. Rev. Stat. Ann. §§ 398:1 to 398:14 and §§ 399-A:1 to 399-A:19; Or. Rev. Stat. §§ 725.600 to 725.625; S.C. § 37-3-413; Tenn. Code Ann. §§ 45-15-101 to 45-15-120; Utah Code Ann. §§ 7-24-101 to 7-24-305. In Illinois, the Department of Financial Institutions has promulgated regulations, Ill. Admin. Code tit. 38, §§ 110.300 to 110.410, governing auto title loans as well as payday loans. These regulations were upheld in South 51 Development Corp. v. Vega, 781 N.E.2d 528 (Ill. Ct. App. 2002). Oregon similarly promulgated regulations, Or. Admin. R. § 441-730-0005 to 441-730-0320, that withstood an initial challenge. Northwestern Title Loans v. Division of Fin., 42 P.3d 313 (Or. Ct. App. 2002). *See also* N.M. Admin. Code tit. 12, §§ 18.4 to 18.6. In Alabama, a court decision permits auto title lending given the broad interpretation it gave to the definition of a pawn transaction. Floyd v. Title Exchange and Pawn of Anniston, Inc., 620 So. 2d 576 (Ala. 1993) (interpreting Ala. Code §§ 5-19A-1 to 5-19A-20 to permit auto title lending). In Nevada, the attorney general has opined that auto title loan constitutes a "pawn" and the creditor is, therefore, not subject to licensing as an installment lender. Opinion of the Nevada Attorney General, No. 95-20 (Nov. 17, 1995), *available at* 1995 WL 737002.

305 *See* Glinton v. And R, Inc., 524 S.E.2d 481 (Ga. 1999) (state pawnbroker law and criminal usury statute cannot be harmonized; the pawnbroker law prevails). *But see* Fryer v. Easy Money Title Pawn, Inc., 183 B.R. 322, *rehearing denied*, 183 B.R. 654 (Bankr. S.D. Ga. 1995) (harmonizing these two statutes).

306 *See* Advisory Legal Opinion, Office of the Florida Attorney General, Clearinghouse No. 52,497, AGO 99-38 (June 14, 1999) (repossession fee or other fee in excess of 22% per month allowable rate violates title loan cap).

307 *Id. See also* Yazzie v. Ray Vicker's Special Cars, Inc., 12 F. Supp. 2d 1230 (D.N.M. 1998) (in this true pawn case [car was held, not merely the title], pawnbroker violated the state pawnbroker law by charging "pawn service" fees above the legal limit and by failing to provide a physical description of the consumer on the pawn tickets); Lynn v. Financial Solutions Corp. (*In re Lynn*), 173 B.R. 894 (Bankr. M.D. Tenn. 1994) (title pawn not true pawn, but in any event lender also violated

pawnbroker statute's reasonableness limitation on supplemental fees; transaction held void *ab initio*); Advisory Legal Opinion, Office of the Florida Attorney General, Clearinghouse No. 52,497, AGO 99-38 (June 14, 1999) (difference between sale price of car and debt upon repossession is also an unauthorized fee if it and all other fees charged exceed the statutory rate cap). *But see* Henley v. Cameron Auto Pawn (*In re Henley*), 228 B.R. 425 (Bankr. E.D. Ark. 1998) ("reasonable" limitation on fees was apparently removed after the decision in *In re Lynn*; court, construing Arkansas law, found that a fee of 18% of the amount borrowed for 30 days did not violate the auto title act since the act only capped the interest rate [no discussion of when the size of a fee will cross an unconscionable line]).

308 Johnson v. Speedee Cash (*In re* Johnson), 289 B.R. 251 (Bankr. M.D. Ga. 2002) (auto title lender failed to include statutorily required terms in contract, such as 30-day redemption period; loan voidable in bankruptcy). *See also* Brown v. Speedee Cash (*In re* Brown), 304 B.R. 544 (Bankr. M.D. Ga. 2004) (following Johnson v. Speedee Cash.). *See also* Opinion of the Nevada Attorney General, No. 97-13 (Apr. 1, 1977), *available at* 1997 WL 169235 (if an auto title loan contains terms prohibited by state pawn statute, lender must comply with installment loan act.).

309 Bumpus v. Vandeford, Clearinghouse No. 54,570 (N.D. Miss. Mar. 27, 2002) (auto title lender failed to obtain license as a title-pledge creditor; loan subject to Mississippi usury cap of 10%.).

310 U.C.C. § 9-203.

311 National Consumer Law Center, Repossessions and Foreclosures § 3.10 (5th ed. 2002 and Supp.).

312 La. Rev. Stat. Ann. §§ 37:1801.D; Me. Rev. Stat. § 30-A:3960; Ohio Rev. Stat. §§ 4505.102, 4727.01(A) and 4727.08(E); S.C. Code Ann. § 40-39-10(3). However, South Carolina permits auto title lending not structured as a pawn transaction. *See* S.C. Code Ann. § 37-3-413.

313 *See* Malish v. City of San Diego, 101 Cal. Rptr. 2d 18 (Cal. Ct. App. 2000) (upholding city's right to require pawnbroker to obtain local permit, but striking down parts of ordinance that were inconsistent with state pawnbroker licensing law); Missouri Title Loans v. City of St. Louis Board of Adjustment, 62 S.W.3d 408 (Mo. Ct. App. 2001) (zoning action); Circle D Pawn #2, Inc. v. Norman, 956 P.2d 931 (Okla. Ct. App. 1998) (local law did not conflict with the state act). *See also* Meredith Fischer and Paige Akin, Board Rules Against Lender: Chesterfield Calls Store Site Wrong, Richmond Times-Dispatch, Jan. 3, 2003, at A12; Dan Kulin, City Considers Restrictions For Payday, Car Loan Firms, Las Vegas Sun, Nov. 5, 2002, at 3.

The Office of the Comptroller of the Currency issued a warning to national banks about safety and soundness and other risks associated with this type of lending as banks decide whether to partner with local entities to fund these loans.[314] The letter advises banks to tread carefully given the potential for claims based the fact that such loans may be based upon the value of the collateral and not on the consumer's ability to repay; lenders fail to rebate the net proceeds to the borrower upon the sale of the car; and some lenders fail to treat these transactions as loans, thus running afoul of the Truth in Lending Act.

7.5.3 Credit Sales Disguised As Leases: Rent-To-Own

7.5.3.1 General

A more common method of restructuring a credit transaction is to transform it into a lease. This is a common commercial practice, and a vast body of case law considers whether business transactions are secured credit sales or true leases.[315] Numerous decisions have recognized that supposed leases may in fact be credit sales especially when the lessee holds an option to purchase the property at the end of the lease term for nominal consideration, and when the lessee is responsible for insuring and maintaining the leased property during the term of the lease.[316] For example

"leases" of mobile homes have been held to be credit sales in several cases.[317]

In a consumer context, retailers have few reasons to structure credit sales as leases except to attempt to avoid the disclosures, interest ceilings, and repossession limitations imposed by the Truth in Lending Act, state retail installment sales acts, and the Uniform Commercial Code, respectively.[318] Therefore, practitioners who are examining purported leases under which ownership may ultimately be transferred to the consumer, should be particularly suspicious of the possibility that violations of these statutes may exist.

7.5.3.2 Rent-to-Own contracts described

By far, the most prevalent use of leases to conceal consumer credit sales is the "Rent-to-Own" (RTO) industry. RTO businesses are essentially appliance, electronics, and furniture retailers which arrange lease agreements rather than typical installment sales contracts for those customers who cannot purchase goods with cash or who are unsophisticated about money management. These lease agreements contain several special features. First, the lease agreements contain purchase options which typically enable the lessees to obtain title to the goods in question by making a nominal payment at the end of a stated period, such as eighteen months. Second, the leases are short term, so that "rental payments" are due weekly or monthly. Third, the leases are "at will." In other words, the leases theoretically need not be renewed at the end of each weekly or monthly term.[319]

---

314 OCC Advisory Letter, No. AL 2000-11 (Nov. 27, 2000), *available at* www.occ.treas.gov/advlst00.htm.

315 For a discussion of leases as secured sales under the U.C.C. see National Consumer Law Center, Repossessions and Foreclosures §§ 2.1.5, 14.1.2 (5th ed. 2002 and Supp.). *See also* Annot. 4 A.L.R.4th 85 (1981) ("sale" within scope of U.C.C. Article 2).

316 *See, e.g.*, Davis v. Colonial Securities Corp, 541 F. Supp. 302 (E.D. Pa. 1982), *appeal dismissed*, 720 F.2d 661 (3d Cir. 1983) (house lease actually a TILA credit sale); Hill v. Bentco Leasing Inc., 708 S.W.2d 608 (Ark. 1986) (purported lease was usurious despite absence of purchase option; no residual value in property at end of "lease"); Garrison Motor Freight v. Hammons, 628 S.W.2d 567 (Ark. 1982) (lease disguised as credit sale; free services to credit buyers held element of principal); Bell v. Itek Leasing Corp., 262 Ark. 22, 555 S.W.2d 1 (1977) (purported lease was usurious loan); Barco Auto Leasing Corp. v. House, 202 Conn. 106, 520 A.2d 162 (1987) (lease actually a credit sale subject to RISFA; little discussion of factors, but rider to lease had required lessee to purchase car at end of lease term); Halco Fin. Servs., Inc. v. Foster, 770 S.W.2d 554 (Tenn. Ct. App. 1989) (sale/leaseback of personal property with purchase option was disguised loan subject to usury laws); Vela v. Elberts Mobile Homes Inc., 630 S.W.2d 434 (Tex. App. 1982) (mobile home credit sale disguised as lease); Rouse v. Peoples Leasing Co., 96 Wash. 722, 638 P.2d 1245 (1982) (motor vehicle leases actually loans; lessor received fixed profit and lessee assumed risks). *See also* § 7.5.2, *supra*. *Cf.* Wight v. Agristor Leasing, 652 F. Supp. 1000 (D. Kan. 1987) (true lease); *In re* Pellegrino, 205 B.R. 479 (Bankr. E.D. Pa. 1997) (true lease; no evidence presented to show "body-dragging" or gross overcharging and parties

treated contract as a lease not a sale); Goodtimes v. IFG Leasing Co., 117 Idaho 452, 788 P.2d 853 (1990) (true lease); State *ex rel.* Celebrezze v. Telecommunications, Inc. 601 N.E.2d 234 (Ohio Ct. Cl. 1990), *reconsideration denied*, 601 N.E.2d 257 (1991) (true lease); Baldwin v. Liberty Leasing Co., 2000 Tex. App. LEXIS 4097 (Tex. App. June 20, 2000) (true lease in a commercial case); Potomac Leasing v. El Paso Housing Auth., 743 S.W.2d 712 (Tex. App. 1988) (no usury where pure lease with no claim made of a lease-purchase agreement). *See generally* Annot. 94 A.L.R.3d 640 (1979) (application of usury law to "leases"); *Equipment Lease as Usurious Loan*, 25 Proof of Facts 2d 521 (1981).

317 Gulf Homes, Inc. v. Gonzales, 139 Ariz. 1, 676 P.2d 635 (Ct. App. 1983), *aff'd in part, rev'd in part on other grounds*, 138 Ariz. 596, 676 P.2d 628 (1984); Vela v. Elberts Mobile Homes Inc., 630 S.W.2d 434 (Tex. App. 1982).

318 *See* National Consumer Law Center, Truth in Lending (5th ed. 2003 and Supp.); National Consumer Law Center, Repossessions and Foreclosures Ch. 14 (5th ed. 2002 and Supp.).

319 For detailed descriptions of a rent-to-own contracts, see Sight & Sound of Ohio, Inc. v. Wright, 36 B.R. 885 (S.D. Ohio 1983); *In re* Puckett, 60 B.R. 223 (Bankr. M.D. Tenn. 1986), *aff'd*, 838 F.2d 470 (6th Cir. 1988); Miller v. Colortyme, Inc., 518 N.W.2d 544 (Minn. 1994). A variation of an RTO contract can have an initial non-terminable term of five months which becomes terminable month-to-month thereafter. Others may be a fixed term, non-terminable lease with an option to purchase.

The RTO industry aims its marketing efforts at low-income consumers by advertising in minority media, buses, and in public housing projects, and by suggesting it has many features attractive to low-income consumers: quick delivery, weekly payments, no or small down payments, quick repair service, no credit checks, and no harm to one's credit rating if the transaction is canceled.[320] Most RTO customers enter into these transactions with the expectation of buying an appliance and are seldom interested by the rental aspect of the contract.[321] This attitude is encouraged by RTO dealers who emphasize the purchase option in their marketing even while they are minimizing its importance in the written contract. Of course, if and when a transaction is challenged in court, a RTO dealer will point to the rental provisions of the contract and claim that statutes which control traditional retail installment sales are irrelevant to RTO agreements.

The chief problem with RTO contracts is not only that these supposed leases are used to mask installment sales, but also that these sales are made at astronomic and undisclosed effective interest rates. Under most RTO contracts, the customer will pay between $1,000 and $2,400 for a TV, stereo, or other major appliance worth as little as $200 retail, if used, and seldom more than $600 retail, if new. This means that a low-income RTO customer may pay 1 1/2 to 12 times what a cash customer would pay in a traditional retail store for the same appliance.[322]

The finance charge and interest rate or annual percentage rate (APR) of an RTO contract depends on the retail cash value of the appliance (especially whether new or used) and the timing, amount, and number of payments. The following chart illustrates the APR computations, assuming no payments in arrears.[323]

---

320   The Association of Progressive Rental Organizations (APRO), the RTO trade association, publishes information on RTO at its website. *See* www.aprovision.org. It reports that about half of RTO customers (48%) have annual incomes under $36,000 and most (75%) have incomes under $50,000; over 57% are under the age of 45; over 65% have a high school education or less; and about 70% are Caucasian. The Federal Trade Commission conducted a survey of 532 RTC customers and found that 79% of those customers who used RTO in the last year had incomes under $40,000 (over the last five years, about 70% of these customers had incomes under $40,000). James M. Lacko, Signe-Mary McKernan & Manoj Hastak, *Survey of Rent-to-Own Customers*, Federal Trade Commission (Apr. 2000), *available at* www.ftc.gov/reports/index.htm (the survey also reports on other customer characteristics, such as, age, sex, race/ethnicity, education, employment, marital status, homeownership, geographical distribution, among other things). *See also* Creola Johnson, *Welfare Reform and Asset Accumulation: First We Need a Bed and a Car*, 2000 Wis. L. Rev. 1221, 1254 (2000) (citing an industry survey done in 1994 that revealed that 31% of RTO customers were on some form of public assistance); Warren B. Rudman, *Market Survey Results and Economic Analysis* (Feb. 1994) at 14 (report to the Board of Directors of Thorn EMI PLC concerning the operations of the Rent-A-Center Division of Thorn Americas Inc; report found that 61% of the respondents surveyed in 1994 had personal earnings less than $20,000 and 29% earned less than $10,000.).

321   A telephone survey of RTO customers that was commissioned by APRO found that 90% of customers intended to own the product they were renting, but only 40% managed to keep the product. Ed Winn, *The RTO Customer Survey See-Saw*, Progressive Rentals, May–June 2004. APRO claims on its website that less than one-quarter of its customers purchase the "rented" goods. *See* www.aprovision.org/industrystats.html. However, its method of deriving that statistic is suspect. According to testimony by Rent-A-Center's experts in one case, 64% of that company's inventory was sold to its customers. Perez v. Rent-A-Center, 866 A.2d 1000 (N.J. Super. 2005). The Federal Trade Commission conducted a survey of 532 RTC customers and found that 70% of RTO merchandise was purchased by the customer. Furthermore, 90% of the merchandise on which customers had made substantial payments (of six months or more) was purchased. James M. Lacko, Signe-Mary McKernan & Manoj Hastak, Survey of Rent-to-Own Customers, Federal Trade Commission (Apr. 2000), *available at* www.ftc.gov/reports/index.htm. One conclusion to draw from this latter statistic is that if the RTO contract fails, this most often occurs within the first six months. *See also* Creola Johnson, *Welfare Reform and Asset Accumulation: First We Need a Bed and a Car*, 2000 Wis. L. Rev. 1221, 1259–70 (2000) (arguing that most customers intend to purchase the items leased but fail to do so, citing an industry source; the author posits several reasons

why low-income consumers had difficulty saving, or in utilizing alternatives to RTO.).

Data obtained from RTO dealer's databases from different chains in several states show that 75% or more of RTO gross revenue is derived from customers who purchase goods. For example, RTO Enterprises Inc., Canada's largest rent-to-own company, reports that approximately 85% of RTO's revenues are generated through the rent-to-own program and approximately 87% of all rent-to-own customers purchase the merchandise at the end of the rental term. *See* www.stockdepot.com/buylowsellhigh/rto.html (as of 1998) for RTO Enterprises Inc. (This website is now available to subscribers only.) Discovery obtained in one class action against a major RTO company showed that 66% of one year's inventory was sold, and between 73% and 77% of the company's revenues came from sales, not rentals. *See* Ramp, *Renting-To-Own in the United States*, 24 Clearinghouse Rev. 797 (Dec. 1990).

322   Another issue is the public health risk inherent in certain goods if they are previously used, such as mattresses. A former Rent-A-Center manager filed a complaint with the Illinois Attorney General's Office detailing how stores in that chain would rent used mattresses, including ones that had been contaminated with human urine, blood, animal excrement, pet hairs, fleas, and dirt. Letter of Lawrence Martin to Illinois Attorney General Lisa Madigan re: Public Health Violations, June 3, 2004.

323   Payments in advance are called "annuity due" transactions, as contrasted with "ordinary annuities" as used in Truth in Lending's Regulation Z, Appendix J. For example, the top line of the chart shows different APRs if RTO payments are made at the beginning of each week: 52 weeks at $16 bears an APR of 445%, seventy-eight weeks at $16 amounts to 451% APR, and 104 weeks yields 452%, because the time value is different. The entire chart would show greater APRs for payments in advance. Because RTO dealers usually demand payments at the beginning of each week, the astronomic APR's in this chart are probably understated.

Amount Financed	Weekly Payment	52 Weeks		78 Weeks		104 Weeks	
		Finance Charge	APR	Finance Charge	APR	Finance Charge	APR
200	$16	$632	408%	$1,048	415%	$1,464	416%
	$18	$736	462%	$1,204	467%	$1,672	468%
300	$16	$532	254%	$ 948	272%	$1,364	276%
	$18	$636	294%	$1,104	309%	$1,572	311%
400	$16	$432	68%	$ 848	197%	$1,264	204%
	$18	$536	201%	$1,004	226%	$1,472	231%
500	$16	$332	111%	$ 748	148%	$1,164	159%
	$18	$436	140%	$ 904	173%	$1,372	182%
	$20	$540	168%	$1,060	197%	$1,580	204%
600	$16	$232	68%	$ 648	113%	$1,064	128%
	$18	$336	95%	$ 804	135%	$1,272	147%
	$20	$440	121%	$ 960	156%	$1,480	167%
700	$18	$236	60%	$ 704	106%	$1,172	122%
	$20	$340	84%	$ 860	125%	$1,380	139%
	$22	$444	107%	$1,016	144%	$1,588	156%

For example, a brand new big-screen conventional television sells for about $1,000 from a leading electronics retailer. Therefore, if an RTO customer leases that big screen television (worth $1,000) for $37 per week for 52 weeks,[324] the APR would be about 192%. However, if the customer leased a *used* big screen television (worth about $700 or less) for the same payment terms, the APR could be 275% or more.

7.5.3.3 Trends in the RTO industry

The Association of Progressive Rental Organizations (APRO), the RTO trade association, maintains a website.[325] As of 2004, APRO reports that RTO is a $6.2 billion a year industry serving about 2.7 million customers per year. Thus, the average RTO customer is spending over $2,296 a year or $191 per month on RTO merchandise.

Year	Total RTO revenues (in billions)	Total RTO customers (in millions)	Average RTO customer payment
2004	$6.2	2.7	$2,296
2003	$6	2.9	$2,069
2002	$5.6	2.9	$1,931
2001	$5.30	3.1	$1,710
2000	$5	3.1	$1,613
1999	$4.70	3.30	$1,424
1996	$3.98	2.85	$1,396
1994	$3.85	2.73	$1,410
1993	$4.49	3.43	$1,282
1991	$3.57	2.91	$1,226

324 This was the weekly rental fee reported for a big screen TV in Rent-A-Center v. Duron, 2004 WL 2403571 (Tex. App. Oct. 28, 2004).

325 www.aprovision.org.

Source: APRO

With the enactment of protective state laws[326] and the resolution of IRS disputes,[327] banks and Wall Street have recog-

326 *See* § 7.5.3.5, *infra*.

327 One of the most significant financial advantages enjoyed by RTO dealers that is not available to retail firms is the ability to depreciate household goods as rental merchandise. Retail merchants offering identical households goods cannot depreciate their inventory. For a discussion of the importance of the depreciation issue for RTO dealers, see Susan Lorde Martin & Nancy White Huckins, *Consumer Advocates v. The Rent-to-Own Industry: Reaching a Reasonable Accommodation*, 34 American Bus. L.J. 385, 416 (1997); Laura Saunders, "Taxing Matters," Forbes, Mar. 10, 1997, at 84. The RTO industry and the IRS have disputed the speed with which dealers can depreciate their merchandise. Dealers have argued that they should be able to depreciate very quickly since, on average, nearly all merchandise is disposed of in two to three years. In 1996, the industry prevailed on this issue in ABC Rentals & San Antonio Inc. v. Commissioner, 86 F.3d 392 (10th Cir. 1996). The court permitted RTO dealers to use a much faster depreciation methodology than the IRS argued was allowable. However, this decision was undermined by a change in the Code added by Section 1086 of the Taxpayer Relief Act of 1997 which allows RTO dealers the ability to depreciate their goods over three years if they have "qualified rent-to-own property." Pub. L. No. 105-34, codified at 26 U.S.C. § 168(g)(14). The impact of this tax provision on rent-to-own operations and customers may be profound since under the Act dealers are only entitled to use the three year depreciation schedule "if a substantial portion of the rent-to-own contracts terminate and the property is returned." I.R.C. § 168(i)(14)(B). This provision provides an even greater financial motivation for RTO dealers to immediately repossess goods rather than refinance the contract, permit the customer to reinstate the contract with payment of a late fee or otherwise negotiate an extension for late payment. Previously, many RTO dealers permitted the customer to retain the goods in their home while a new contract was substituted for the prior one.

nized the tremendous profit potential of RTO. The industry has consolidated into a few dominant national companies.[328]

The industry will need to expand its customer base if it wants to maintain its earnings record. Some companies have expanded their product offerings from basic consumer commodities to high-end items, such as big-screen televisions and flashy oversize chrome auto wheels aimed at young urban drivers.[329]

Despite RTO successes, there have been problems for the industry. Industry giant Rentway was one of the companies caught in the accounting fraud scandals at the beginning of the decade.[330] Customer satisfaction is low, and the image of the industry is mostly negative, although the industry's public relations efforts are having some effect.[331] Press on RTO remains overwhelming negative.[332]

7.5.3.4 History of Legal Challenges to RTO contracts

RTO transactions attempt to circumvent numerous consumer protection statutes and therefore have been attacked on many different levels.[333] Leases under which the lessee agrees to pay a sum equal to or exceeding the value of

goods, and under which the lessee acquires an option to purchase for nominal consideration, had been challenged as credit sales requiring Truth in Lending disclosures.[334] However, in 1981, Regulation Z, which implements the TILA, was amended to exclude from its coverage leases "terminable without penalty or at any time by the customer."[335] Many RTO contracts are drafted to fall into that loophole.[336]

RTO leases were also challenged as security interests under the UCC and may subject to UCC repossession limitations.[337] Similarly, RTO transactions were alleged to be security agreements rather than true leases under the Bankruptcy Code, thereby giving bankrupt consumers greater rights than normal lessees.[338] Last, but not least,

---

This can no longer be done because the Code requires that the property must be returned to the dealer. The net effect of this provision may well be an increase in repossessions for RTO customers, an event that has repeatedly led to litigation in the past. *See, e.g.*, Mercer v. DEF Inc., 48 B.R. 563 (Bankr. D. Minn. 1985); Murphy v. McNamara, 416 A.2d 170 (Conn. Super. Ct. 1979); Fassitt v. United TV Rental, Inc., 297 So. 2d 283 (La. Ct. App. 1974); State v. Action TV Rentals, Inc., 467 A.2d 1000 (Md. 1983); Kimble v. Universal TV Rental, Inc., 417 N.E.2d 597 (Ohio Mun. Ct. 1980).

328 Phillip M. Perry and Julie Sherrier, 2005 Economic Forecast, *Progressive Rentals*, Nov.–Dec. 2004 (describing RTO industry as consisting of national chains and single store "Mom & Pop" outlets.). For an account of consolidations within the RTO industry between 1994 and 1996, see Susan Lorde Martin & Nancy White Huckins, *Consumer Advocates v. The Rent-to-Own Industry: Reaching a Reasonable Accommodation*, 34 American Bus. L.J. 385, 405–06 (1997).

329 Chris Woodyard, *Spinning Wheels Got To Go Round for Hip Divers*, USA Today, Jan. 24, 2005 (noting one consumer who was paying $60 per week, or a total of more than $3,000, for a set of "bling-bling" rims retailing for $1,560).

330 Charles Duhigg, *3 Rent-Way Executives Plead Guilty*, Washington Post, July 23, 2003.

331 A survey commissioned by APRO revealed that 40% of RTO customers were unhappy with their experience, and 24% felt they had been treated with disrespect by the RTO employees. Among non-RTO customers, 55% had a negative image of the industry, down from 64% in 1997. Ed Winn, *The RTO Customer Survey See-Saw*, Progressive Rentals, May–June 2004.

332 *See, e.g.*, Anya Schiffrin, *Pay Now, Pay Later*, Mother Jones, May/June 2005; David Abel, *Yours, For A Price*, Boston Globe, Feb. 17, 2003, at B1; NBC Nightly News, "The Fleecing of America" Feb. 25, 1998.

333 See National Consumer Law Center, Consumer Law Pleadings No. 2, Ch. 8 (Cumulative CD-Rom and Index Guide) for pleadings in one RTO case.

334 *See* 15 U.S.C. § 1602(g); *compare* Clark v. Rent-It Corp., 685 F.2d 245 (8th Cir. 1982), *cert. denied*, 459 U.S. 1225 (1983); Green v. Continental Rentals, Clearinghouse No. 50,403 (N.J. Super. Ct. Law Div., Passaic County, Mar. 25, 1994) (RTO agreement a credit sale subject to TIL) *with* Smith v. ABC Rental Sys., 491 F. Supp. 127 (E.D. La. 1978), *aff'd*, 618 F.2d 397 (5th Cir. 1982). *See generally* Annot. 59 A.L.R. Fed. 929 (1982) (leases as TILA credit sales).

335 Reg. Z 12 C.F.R. § 226.2(a)(16).

336 However, at least one court has held that if the transactions are used as a means of purchase, rather than true short-term rentals, they may still be credit sales subject to TIL despite that language. *See In re* Hanley, 105 B.R. 458 (Bankr. C.D. Ill. 1989), *on motion to alter or amend*, 111 B.R. 709 (Bankr. C.D. Ill. 1990). Courts differ on whether the fact that a customer forfeits any built-up equity is properly considered as a penalty within the meaning of the Regulation. *Compare In re* Hanley, 105 B.R. 458 (Bankr. C.D. Ill. 1989), *on motion to alter or amend*, 111 B.R. 709 (Bankr. C.D. Ill. 1990); Starks v. Rent-A-Center, Clearinghouse No. 45,215 (Minn. Dist. Ct. 1990) *with* Green v. Continental Rentals, Clearinghouse No. 50,403 (N.J. Super. Ct. Law Div., Passaic County, Mar. 25, 1994) (customer had paid $3336 on $2785 worth of goods at time of repossession; court held penalty includes a forfeiture).

337 *See* Sight & Sound of Ohio, Inc. v. Wright, 36 B.R. 885 (S.D. Ohio 1983); Murphy v. McNamara, 416 A.2d 170 (Conn. Super. Ct. 1979) (RTO agreement was unconscionable sale); Broad v. Curtis Mathes Sales Co., Clearinghouse No. 36,376, CV-82-1254 (Me. Sup. Ct., Feb. 6, 1984). *See generally* National Consumer Law Center, Repossessions and Foreclosures § 14.3 (5th ed. 2002 and Supp.).

338 *See In re* Puckett, 60 B.R. 223 (Bankr. M.D. Tenn. 1986), *aff'd*, 838 F.2d 470 (6th Cir. 1988). *See also* Michaels v. Ford Motor Credit Co., 156 B.R. 584 (Bankr. E.D. Wis. 1993) (court found that the intent of the parties determined that the agreement was a disguised security agreement even though it was called a "Rental Agreement"). *But see In re* DWE Screw Products, Inc., 19 B.R. 313 (Bankr. N.D. Ohio 1993) (lease of nonresidential property was true lease even though the lessee had the option to purchase at any time without additional consideration, because the intent of the parties was to create a true lease and not a financing arrangement); *In re* Spears, 146 B.R. 772 (Bankr. S.D. Ill. 1992) (under U.C.C. § 1-201(37), RTO contract was true lease, not a security agreement, where consumer would become owner upon making all weekly rental payments or paying 60% of remaining payments in lump sum); *In re* Hardy, 146 B.R. 206 (Bankr. N.D. Ill. 1992) (RTO contract for beepers was lease, not security agreement where lessor relied on its provision of air time to lessees to make a profit); *In re* Frady, 141 B.R. 600

RTO agreements were challenged as usurious under state installment sales acts.[339]

For the past thirty years legal service attorneys, state attorneys general, and private practitioners have challenged RTO transactions with mixed success.[340] During this same period, the RTO industry has aggressively (and successfully in most cases) lobbied state legislatures and the Congress for a statutory exemption from consumer protection statutes, from annual percentage rate disclosure requirements, and from usury rate limitations.[341]

In nearly every state there are now RTO statutes which were carefully drafted by the industry to insulate dealers from claims of consumer abuse.[342] The RTO industry has contin-

---

(Bankr. W.D.N.C. 1991) (true lease because chapter 13 bankruptcy debtor did not have to finish paying; plan treating RTO as disguised security interest could not be confirmed).

Some courts have held that RTO leases are not security agreements as a result of industry-friendly legislation enacted in most states. *E.g.*, Ohio Rev. Code Ann. 135-01(F) (creating irrebuttable presumption that RTO transactions cannot be "intended for security," an element of the U.C.C. test). *See In re* Lepri, 2004 WL 1242556 (Bankr. D. Vt. May 5, 2004) (Vermont law prohibits RTO agreement from being considered a security interest under U.C.C. Article 9); *In re* Minton, 271 B.R. 335 (Bankr. W.D. Ark. 2001) (RTO agreements were true leases and not conditional sales because they fit the definition of "rental-purchase agreements" under Arkansas law); *In re* Mitchell, 108 B.R. 166 (Bankr. S.D. Ohio 1989) (agreement with regard to washer and dryer satisfied Ohio statutory definition of "lease purchase agreement" and therefore was not an installment sale with a disguised security agreement; as a consequence, debtor in bankruptcy could retain possession of property only by meeting requirements of § 365 of Bankruptcy Code, which include curing default. *See generally* National Consumer Law Center, Consumer Bankruptcy Law and Practice § 11.8 (7th ed. 2004 and Supp.) (rent-to-own transactions in bankruptcy).

339 *See* Burney v. Thorn America, Inc., 944 F. Supp. 762 (D. Minn. 1996) (measure of damages is the difference between the finance charge and a 5% interest rate; finance charge includes everything except the retail price); *In re* Rose, 94 B.R. 103 (Bankr. S.D. Ohio 1988); Murphy v. McNamara, 416 A.2d 170 (Conn. Super. Ct. 1979); Miller v. Colortyme, Inc., 518 N.W.2d 544 (Minn. 1994); Starks v. Rent-A-Center, Clearinghouse No. 45,215 (Minn. Dist. Ct. 1990); Robinson v. Thorn Americas, Inc., #L-003697-94, Clearinghouse No. 52,047 (N.J. Super. Ct. Dec. 19, 1997); Green v. Continental Rentals, Clearinghouse No. 50,403 (N.J. Super. Ct. Law Div., Passaic County, Mar. 25, 1994); Commonwealth of Pennsylvania v. Riverview Leasing, Inc., Clearinghouse No. 50,401, No. 325 M.D. 1993 (Pa. Commw. Ct. Aug. 5, 1994); Chandler v. Riverview Leasing, Inc., Clearinghouse No. 40,628 (Pa. C.P. Northampton Cty. May 15, 1986); State v. Rentavision Corp. of Am., Clearinghouse No. 35,731 (Tenn. Chanc. Ct. 1983); LeBakken Rent-to-Own v. Warnell, 589 N.W.2d 425 (Wis. Ct. App. 1998); Rent-A-Center, Inc. v. Hall, 510 N.W.2d 789 (Wis. Ct. App. 1993); Palacios v. ABC TV & Stereo Retail, 123 Wis. 2d 79, 365 N.W.2d 882 (Ct. App. 1985). *See also* Anoushian v. Rent-Rite, 2002 WL 1023438 (Pa. Commw. Ct. May 10, 2002) (Pennsylvania Retail Installment Sales Act, not RTO statute, governed lease agreement with option to purchase). *Anoushian* was legislatively overruled in 2003, see KFJ Enterprises, Ltd. Liab. Co. v. Rembert (*In re* Rembert), 293 B.R. 664 (Bankr. M.D. Pa. 2003), and abrogated by Griffin v. Rent-A-Center, 843 A.2d 393 (Pa. Super. Ct. 2004) (2003 amendments were a clarification, which the court applied retroactively). *Cf.* Fogie v. Rent-A-Center, Inc., 1995 WL 649575 (D. Minn. 1995) (RTO contracts are credit sales for all purposes, and are subject to general contract usury ceiling), *aff'd sub nom.*, Fogie v. Thorn Americas, Inc., 95 F.3d 645 (8th Cir. 1996), *subsequent appeal on different grounds*, 190 F.3d 889 (8th Cir. 1999) (RICO claim dismissed). *But see* Givens v. Rent-A-Center, Inc., 720 F. Supp. 160 (S.D. Ala. 1988), *aff'd mem.*, 885 F.2d 879 (11th Cir. 1989) (rental agreement not credit sale under Alabama Consumer Fin. Act); Hawkes Television Inc. v. Maine Bureau of Consumer Credit Protection, 462 A.2d 1167 (Me. 1983); State v. Action TV Rentals, Inc., 467 A.2d 1000 (Md. 1983). *See also* Remco Enters., Inc. v. Houston, 677

P.2d 567 (Kan. App. 1984) (RTO contract not unconscionable).

340 In addition to the cases cited in § 7.5.3.4, *supra*, the following law review articles discuss the case law regarding rent-to-own and the application of credit sales law. Adoption of the RTO industry's state laws make much of this material of historical interest only. Susan Lorde Martin & Nancy White Huckins, *Consumer Advocates v. The Rent-to-Own Industry: Reaching a Reasonable Accommodation*, 34 American Bus. L.J. 385, 389 (1997); James Nehf, *Effective Regulation of Rent-to-Own Contracts*, 42 Ohio St. L.J. 751, 758 (1991); Scott J. Burnham, *The Regulation of Rent-to-own Transactions*, 3 Loy. Consumer L. Rep. 40, 41 (1991); David L. Ramp, *Renting To Own in the U.S.*, 24 Clearinghouse Rev. 797 (1990); Karen F. Meenan, Note, *The Applicability of the Federal Truth in Lending Act to Rental Purchase Contracts*, Cornell L. Rev. 118, 132–133 (1980).

341 For a discussion of the RTO industry's legislative efforts between 1983–1991, see James Nehf, *Effective Regulation of Rent-to-Own Contracts*, 42 Ohio State L.J. 751, 821 (1991). (It should be noted that prior to becoming a law professor, James Nehf was a member of a law firm that represented Rent-A-Center and the Association of Progressive Rental Organizations (APRO), the RTO trade association. This law firm wrote most of the industry's model RTO bills. N.Y. Times, June 4, 1988, at 56. Prof. Nehf does not acknowledge his previous connection with the rent-to-own industry and the effect it had on his observations in his article.)

342 Ala. Code §§ 8.25.1 to 8.25.6; Alaska Stat. §§ 45.35.010 to 45.35.099; Ariz. Rev. Stat. Ann. §§ 44.6801 to 44.6814; Ark. Code Ann. §§ 4.92.101 to 4.92.107 (Michie); Cal. Civ. Code §§ 1812.620 to 1812.649; Colo. Rev. Stat. §§ 5.10.101 to 5.10.1001; Conn. Gen. Stat. §§ 42-240 to 42-253; 49 D.C. Reg. 1000; Del. Code Ann. tit. 6, §§ 7601 to 7616; Fla. Stat. §§ 559.9231 to 559.9241; Ga. Code Ann. §§ 10.1.680 to 10.1.689; Haw. Rev. Stat. §§ 481M-1 to 481M-18; Idaho Code, §§ 28.36.101 to 28-36-111; 815 Ill. Comp. Stat. §§ 655/.0.01 to 655/5; Ind. Code §§ 24-7-1-1 to 24-7-9-7; Iowa Code §§ 537.3601 to 537.3624; Kan. Stat. Ann. §§ 50.680 to 560.690; Ky. Rev. Stat. Ann. §§ 367.976 to 367.985; La. Rev. Stat. §§ 9:3351 to 9:3362; Me. Rev. Stat. Ann. tit. 9-A, § 11-1101 (West); Md. Code Ann., Com. Law II, §§ 12-1101 to 12-1112; Mass. Gen. Laws Ann. ch. 93 §§ 90 to 94; Mich. Comp. Law Ann. §§ 445.951 to 445.970 (West); Minn. Stat. Ann. §§ 325F.84 to 325F.97; Miss. Code §§ 75-24-1-51 to 75-24-175; Mo. Rev. Stat. §§ 407.660 to 407.665; Mont. Code §§ 30-10-101 to 30-10-116; Neb. Rev. Stat. §§ 69-2101 to 69.2119; Nev. Rev. Stat. §§ 597.010 to 597.110; N.H. Rev. Stat. Ann. §§ 358-P:1 to 358-P.12; N.M. Stat. Ann. §§ 57-26-1 to 57-26-12; N.Y. Pers. Prop. Law §§ 500–507; N.D. Cent. Code §§ 47-15.1-01 to 47-15.1-08; Ohio Rev. Code Ann. §§ 1351.01 to 1351.09; Okla. Stat. tit. 59, §§ 1950 to 1957; Or. Rev. Stat. §§ 646-245 to 646-259; 42

ued to seek a "federal fix" as well.[343] Thus, practitioners must acknowledge the current state of the law when looking for ways to seek redress for their clients' RTO problems.

The specific exemption of RTO transactions from other state and federal laws is the essential feature of these RTO statutes. All of the RTO laws provide that transactions that comply with their provisions are not "credit sales." Many statutes explicitly exempt RTOs from the state's home solicitation sales laws and from UCC Article 9 security interest definitions.[344]

Although there are variations, nearly all RTO statutes require certain disclosures in the contract including: the number and timing of the payments necessary to acquire ownership of the property; a statement declaring that the consumer will not own the property until the consumer has made the total payment necessary to acquire ownership; the cash price of the property (most commonly defined as whatever price the lessor sets); and a statement as to whether the property is new or used.[345] Although many state statutes provide that these disclosures must be made clearly and conspicuously, none require that the information be given on a separate document or separately segregated. The mandated disclosures, therefore, often appear scattered throughout the contract. State statutes generally do not mandate in-store price tag disclosures.

All RTO statutes contain "consumer remedy" provisions but these must be read carefully. For example, Florida provides for statutory damages with attorney fees and costs. Dealers, however, are only liable if they were notified of the violation in writing and failed to correct it within thirty days.[346] In Maryland, dealers escape liability if they can show that the error was unintentional, resulted from a bona fide error notwithstanding the maintenance of procedures reasonably adopted to avoid that type of error, and that the error was corrected within thirty days of discovering or receiving notice of the error.[347] Some states provide for a mandatory minimum recovery of, say, $100 which is not permitted if the case is filed as a class action.[348] Other states statutes do not include a minimum statutory award.[349]

It is evident that the RTO statutes were intended to provide dealers with complete insulation from consumer claims that the transactions are disguised credit sales.[350] Practitioners who are seeking effective remedies for clients will, therefore, need to look outside the RTO statutes in nearly all cases to challenge these so-called leases.[351]

Pa. Cons. Stat. Ann. §§ 6901 to 6911; R.I. Gen. Law §§ 6-44-1 to 6-44-10; S.C. Code Ann. §§ 37-2-701 to 37-2-714 (Law. Coop.); S.D. Codified Laws §§ 54-6A-1 to 54-6A-10; Tenn. Code Ann. §§ 47-18-601 to 47-18-614; Tex. Bus. & Com. §§ 35.71 to 35.74; Utah Code Ann. § 15-8.1; Vt. Stat. Ann. tit. 9, § 41b and Rule C.F. § 115.04; Va. Code Ann. §§ 59.1-207.17 to 59.1-207.27; Wash. Rev. Code §§ 63.19.010 to 63.19.901; W. Va. Code §§ 46B-1-1 to 46B-1-5; Wis. Stat. §§ 218.61 to 218.617; Wyo. Stat. Ann. §§ 40-19-101 to 40-19-120.

343 *See, e.g.*, H.R. 996, 108th Cong. (2003); S. 2947, 108th Cong. (2003); H.R. 2803, 103d Cong. 1st Sess. (1993); H.R. 2820, 104th Cong., 1st Sess. (1995); H.R. 2019, 105th Cong. 1st Sess. (1997). Many of these bills are virtually identical, and contain the type of provisions that have been criticized as those that "would make the whole law a sham." Lorde Martin & Nancy White Huckins, *Consumer Advocates v. The Rent-to-Own Industry: Reaching a Reasonable Accommodation*, 34 Am. Bus. L.J. 385, 396 (1997). For example, dealers would not be liable for disclosure violations if, within fifteen days of learning of the violation, they adjust the consumer's account so that the consumer would not have to pay more than was actually disclosed. This provision may well encourage dealers to ignore disclosure requirements because they suffer no penalty so long as they adjust once the consumer complains. The most recent RTO bills would also preempt those provisions in state laws that are more protective.

344 For instance, Ohio enacted legislation precluding lease-purchase agreements from being "intended" for security, Ohio Rev. Code § 135-01(F), which explains the differing results in *In re* Rose, 94 B.R. 103 (Bankr. S.D. Ohio 1988) and *In re* Mitchell, 108 B.R. 166 (Bankr. S.D. Ohio 1989).

345 The disclosure of an effective interest rate is never required, although consumers have tried to convince a court that it should be disclosed under New York law, despite its silence. Colon v. Rent-A-Center, Inc., 716 N.Y.S.2d 7 (N.Y. App. Div. 2000).

346 Fla. Stat. § 559.9239.

347 Md. Code Ann., Com. Law II § 12-1110.

348 *See, e.g.*, Ky. Rev. Stat. Ann. § 367.983(c).

349 *See, e.g.*, Iowa Code § 537.3621.

350 There are several ways in which state RTO legislation can be improved. Most state RTO laws do not require price tag disclosures, only contract disclosures. By the time the customer gets the contract the decision to proceed with the transaction has often been made. Price tag disclosures provide information before the commitment to rent to own has been made. Price tag disclosures should include information that will simply convey information about the high relative cost of renting to own to the prospective purchaser.

An important component of price is a comparison of the cash price to the total rent-to-own price. Virtually every state RTO law that requires a cash price disclosure permits RTO dealers to set the price wherever they choose. Some states such as Hawaii and California enacted statutory cash price-fixing formulas which produce greatly inflated cash prices. States should not be setting the cash price. In order to convey more accurate information about the cost of using rent-to-own, the cash price should reflect the fair market value and should be defined as such in law.

Another major improvement to existing state RTO laws would be the itemization of cost-of-lease services. The RTO industry in its model statutes has resisted itemization of lease services, choosing instead to disclose one unitary price. Litigation has revealed that the industry considers the value of terminability to be the most expensive lease service by far. Consumers with limited discretionary dollars should know that they will be charged hundreds of dollars for the right to terminate a contract.

351 Attempts to bring actions against RTO businesses have not been successful even with blatant violations of existing industry-friendly RTO laws. *See, e.g.*, Rent-A-Center v. Duron, 2004 WL 2403571 (Tex. App. Oct. 28, 2004) (reversing trial court's certification in class action for Rent-A-Center's imposition of late fee in excess of statutory limit.).

The exception to the above analysis has been four states: Minnesota,[352] Wisconsin,[353] New Jersey,[354] and Vermont.[355] However, a 2005 decision from a New Jersey appellate court has held that RTO contracts are not credit sales under that state's retail installment sales act, putting that state in the RTO-friendly column.[356]

7.5.3.6 Legal Challenges to RTO in Light of the Legislative Reality

7.5.3.6.1 Overview

Despite the wave of RTO legislation that has washed over the country, litigation challenges remain which differ in some significant ways from the earlier legal contests.

7.5.3.6.2 Unconscionability and RTO pricing

An evaluation of any unconscionability claim requires an understanding of RTO pricing. RTO pricing formulas are commonly applied to all goods thus making it possible to criticize the application of the formula to all customers. In actual practice, dealers typically set RTO prices in reference to weekly or monthly rates (e.g., $15.99 a week) and will determine the number of terms needed to acquire ownership. For example, a low-end stereo may be priced at $15.99 a week for seventy-eight weeks for a total of $1,247.22.

Many state statutes require dealers to disclose the cash price of the goods in addition to the total rent-to-own price. It has been accepted practice in the industry to set the cash price as a percentage of the total RTO price. This percentage varies from state to state but typically the cash price is an amount equal to 55–60% of the total rent-to-own price, although it may be as low as 30% of the total RTO price. The balance of the total rent-to-own price less cash price is disclosed where required as the "cost of leased services."[357] Using the example set forth above, the cash price for the stereo might be set as 60% of $1,247.22 or $748.33. The cost of leased services would be $498.88, 40% of $1,247.22.

An argument that the transaction is unconscionable must include an analysis of whether the cash price is excessive in relation to the actual cost to purchase the item in a retail store and whether the remainder of the total RTO price is justifiable.

Most early RTO litigation focused on the total rent-to-own price, the value of the rental goods, and the cash price as grossly excessive to support a claim or defense of unconscionability.[358] The argument centered around the idea that the padding in the total rent-to-own price above the value of the goods themselves constituted interest and, was thus, unconscionable. For example, if an RTO customer leases a new 27-inch color TV (worth $300) for $16 per week for fifty-two weeks, the customer would pay a total of $832. The APR would be about 254%, arguably unconscionable.

The industry, however, has claimed that the difference between the value of the goods and the total rent-to-own price consists of the "cost of leased services." When the industry raises this argument, however, it has been required to justify the cost of providing these services and, even more intangibly, the dollar value of these services to the customer.[359]

352 The Minnesota cases include Starks v. Rent-A-Center, Clearinghouse No. 45,215 (Minn. Dist. Ct. 1990), which involved a statute that included terminable leases within the definition of credit sale in certain circumstances. This statute was superseded by Minn. Stat. § 325F.82 to 95, which in turn was interpreted in Miller v. Colortyme, Inc., 518 N.W.2d 544 (Minn. 1994) and Fogie v. Rent-A-Center, Inc., 1995 WL 649575 (D. Minn. 1995) (RTO contracts are credit sales for all purposes; thus are subject to general contract usury ceiling, *aff'd sub nom.* Fogie v. Thorn Americas, Inc., 95 F.3d 645 (8th Cir. 1996), *subsequent appeal on different grounds*, 190 F.3d 889 (8th Cir. 1999) (RICO claim dismissed).

353 The Wisconsin cases include Rent-A-Center, Inc. v. Hall, 510 N.W.2d 789 (Wis. Ct. App. 1993), *review denied*, 115 N.W.2d 715 (Wis. 1994). In addition, the Wisconsin Attorney General has reached several settlements with RTO companies over their failure to make finance charge and rate disclosures. Press Release, State Reaches Major Settlement with Rent-to-Own Company, Wisconsin Attorney General's Office, Nov. 12, 2002 (noting this was the Wisconsin Attorney General's fifth settlement with an RTO company over violations of the Wisconsin Consumer Act.)

354 The New Jersey cases successfully challenging RTO practices include Robinson v. Thorn Americas, Inc., Clearinghouse No. 52,047, #L-003697-94 (N.J. Super. Dec. 19, 1997) (after plaintiffs won summary judgment on the merits, the damage portion of the case (and two other related suits) was settled for almost $60 million); Green v. Continental Rentals, 678 A.2d 759 (N.J. Super. 1994).

355 A Vermont court upheld a state attorney general rule requiring RTO companies to disclose the effective annual percentage rate of their RTO transactions. Thorn, Americas, Inc. v. Vermont Attorney General, Clearinghouse No. 51,957 (Vt. Super. Ct. Mar. 7, 1997).

356 Perez v. Rent-A-Center, 866 A.2d 1000 (N.J. Super. 2005). The court in *Perez* explicitly disagreed with the prior decision in Green v. Continental Rentals, 678 A.2d 759 (N.J. Super. 1994) as well as Robinson v. Thorn Americas, Inc., Clearinghouse No. 52,047, #L-003697-94 (N.J. Super. Ct. Dec. 19, 1997). The court held that RTO transactions were not credit sales despite the fact that the New Jersey retail installment sales act explicitly includes leases with the options to purchase the goods. The court stated its concern that permitting a challenge to RTO practices would "eliminate the availability of that option to persons ineligible for loans or who cannot afford to purchase a product outright or qualify under a retail sales installment contract."

357 Disclosure of the cost of leased services is required in Arizona, California, Connecticut, Georgia, Minnesota, Pennsylvania, Vermont, and West Virginia.

358 *See, e.g., In re* Unger, 95 B.R. 761 (Bankr. D. Or. 1989); Murphy v. McNamara, 416 A.2d 170 (Conn. Super. Ct. 1979).

359 Fogie v. Rent-A-Center, Inc., 1995 WL 649575 (D. Minn. 1995), *aff'd sub nom.*, Fogie v. Thorn Americas, Inc., 95 F.3d 645 (8th Cir. 1996) (in the district court opinion in this case, the court noted that the cost of lease services was disclosed as one

At present, every RTO contract in the United States discloses the cost of leased services as a single, undifferentiated number, if it is disclosed at all. Dealers argue that there are many components to the cost of leased services, most notably the right to return the goods and the servicing of merchandise. Because the RTO contract does not itemize these charges, dealers are compelled to justify these charges after the fact. Dealers and the experts they hire have used many approaches to try and justify these charges. In several cases, these arguments have not been accepted by the courts.[360]

RTO dealers have argued that the interest rate implicit in rent-to-own transactions is very low or non-existent. This assertion depends upon attaching high values for services and costs.[361] RTO dealers also claim an extraordinary cost

for providing terminability. This assertion is unjustified because RTO dealers frequently receive more money for the same goods after repossession than they would have received had the first customer been able to pay in full.[362] RTO dealer experts have also asserted that terminability is extraordinarily valuable to the customer. The industry has funded a number of market surveys in an attempt to justify this claim.[363] These surveys are highly questionable.[364]

charge; the lack of itemization of the services allegedly provided to customers made it impossible for the court to find that the services were bona fide and/or reasonable), *subsequent appeal on different grounds*, 190 F.3d 889 (8th Cir. 1999) (RICO claim dismissed); Miller v. Colortyme, Inc., 518 N.W.2d 544 (Minn. 1994); Rent-A-Center, Inc. v. Hall, 510 N.W.2d 789 (Wis. Ct. App. 1993), *review denied*, 115 N.W.2d 715 (Wis. 1994); Robinson v. Thorn Americas, Inc. Clearinghouse No. 52,047, #L-003697-94 (N.J. Super. Ct. Dec. 19, 1997).

360 Fogie v. Rent-A-Center, Inc., 1995 WL 649575 (D. Minn. 1995), *aff'd sub nom.*, Fogie v. Thorn Americas, Inc., 95 F.3d 645 (8th Cir. 1996) (in the district court opinion in this case, the court noted that the cost of lease services was disclosed as one charge; the lack of itemization of the services allegedly provided to customers made it impossible for the court to find that the services were bona fide and/or reasonable), *subsequent appeal on different grounds*, 190 F.3d 889 (8th Cir. 1999) (RICO claim dismissed); Miller v. Colortyme, Inc., 518 N.W.2d 544 (Minn. 1994); Rent-A-Center, Inc. v. Hall, 510 N.W.2d 789 (Wis. Ct. App. 1993), *review denied*, 115 N.W.2d 715 (Wis. 1994); Robinson v. Thorn Americas, Inc. Clearinghouse No. 52,047, #L-003697-94 (N.J. Super. Ct. Dec. 19, 1997).

361 For a lengthy discussion of the impact of the cost of leased services on the interest rate, see Michael Walden, *The Economics of Rent-to-Own Contracts*, 24 J. of Consumer of Affairs No. 2, 326 (1990). Professor Walden developed an economical model to determine implicit interest rates in RTO transactions. According to Walden, previous attempts treated RTO transactions as purchases, a shortcoming which created uncertainty in results and left allegations of high interest rates open to attack. Using industry estimates, Walden builds four cost factors into his calculations in order to address the specificity of the RTO transactions: the cost of depreciation; the cost of maintenance and repair; the cost of servicing the RTO contract (which includes collecting and processing payments); and opportunity cost. *Id.* at 327.

In most cases, Professor Walden's calculations yield lower implied interest rates than those that treated RTO transactions as sales. Implied interest on a 20-inch TV, for example, was 71.5% calculated as a sale; calculated according to Walden's model, that rate drops to 60%. Overall, implicit interest rates in Walden's empirical study ranged from about 33% to 125%, with the lion's share above 60%. *Id.* at 330–31. Interestingly, Walden was able to account for some of that variation based on demographics, concluding that implied interest rates were inversely proportional to average income in the tract where the RTO dealer was located. *Id.* 334–35. This may support a claim of

discrimination under the Equal Credit Opportunity Act if the census tracts with the lowest incomes served by the dealer also include large numbers of minority customers. *See* National Consumer Law Center, Credit Discrimination (4th ed. 2005).

Although Walden's model improves previous calculations of interest for RTO transactions—and makes allegations of usurious rates more defensible—some aspects of his paper pose problems. First, Walden uses industry estimates for costs and keep rates that are disputed both inside and outside the industry. (The keep rate is the ratio of number of contracts that result in a purchase compared to the number of contracts that do not result in a sale.) As Walden notes, it is likely that industry estimates would bias interest rates downward by overestimating dealer costs. Second, although Walden finds significant variation in interest rates among different products, his study does not include all of the kinds of products rented by typical RTO dealers. Furniture, which may be the product class with the highest interest rates, is conspicuously absent in the study. Third, Walden does not consider the value of terminability, the customer's right to end the RTO agreement at any time. If terminability were included, his interest rates might have to be adjusted downward. But recent attempts at calculating this intangible have been inconclusive, and in many cases, amount to little more than an attempt on the part of the industry to disguise interest. Finally, Walden does not balance out RTO dealers' depreciation costs with the enormous tax shields, to which they are now entitled. *See* § 7.5.3.3, *supra*.

362 Michael Walden, *The Economics of Rent-to-Own Contracts*, 24 J. of Consumer of Affairs No. 2, 415 (1990).

363 *See, e.g.*, Warren B. Rudman, "Market Survey Results and Economic Analysis" (Feb. 1994) at 14 (report to the Board of Directors of Thorn EMI PLC concerning the operations of the Rent-A-Center Division of Thorn Americas Inc.).

364 For example, a large CPA firm compared the cost of short term and long-term rentals, asserting that the difference between the two prices represented the value of terminability. Among the items surveyed were sports cars and construction equipment. Short term and long-term rental prices were significantly different for these items, whereas short and long-term rates for rentals of household goods did not show a wide price spread. The CPA firm averaged the difference of the total price paid for both type of rentals (short and long) for all items, including sports cars and construction equipment to justify a very high price for terminability for RTO. *See* Coopers & Lybrand Study, Nov. 10, 1995 (performed in connection with litigation in Burney v. Thorn America, Inc.), Clearinghouse No. 52,051 (This study is problematic for a variety of reasons: First, the markets chosen for comparisons are not comparable. Some of the comparisons include high-end automobiles, and most of them include office equipment, which has a higher rate of obsolescence than the majority of the products (furniture, appliances) offered by an RTO dealer. Higher obsolescence means higher terminability values. No market this second account firm considered is parallel to the RTO furniture market, where both maintenance and obsolescence are low. Second, the analysis

There is no support in any of the industry surveys to suggest that people understand that nearly 40% of the RTO payment is being charged for the right to terminate the contract.

Finally, charges added into the cost of lease services for delivery and maintenance are problematic because many dealers advertise these charges as "free." Challenging the cost of leased services added to the already arbitrary method by which the RTO cash price is determined (i.e., a percentage of the total RTO cost) can significantly increase the likelihood of success of an unconscionability claim even in the current deregulated climate.

Traditionally, common law unconscionability claims could only be raised defensively.[365] Since all RTO leases are terminable and because RTO dealers repossess and re-sell the goods (and do not sue to collect any unpaid "rent"), consumers rarely find themselves in a defensive posture. However, a number of state UDAP statutes prohibit unconscionable practices.[366] In addition, in those states which have adopted Article 2A of the UCC governing leases,[367] practitioners can seek affirmative relief from an unconscionable RTO transaction under section 2A-108.[368]

7.5.3.6.3 Applicability of UDAP statutes to RTO transactions

RTO practices are almost always within the scope of a state UDAP statute. UDAP statutes can effectively address a wide range of abuses, including: false or deceptive advertising; switch and bait practices; misrepresentation of the terms of the RTO contract; failures to disclose material facts about the transaction; padding the retail value of the goods being leased with unjustifiable and sometimes phantom costs of leased services; renting used appliances as new; delivering defective goods; failing to repair as promised; utilizing misrepresentations, deceptions, or illegal tactics to repossess the goods; violating the rent-to-own statute or

other applicable laws.[369] A more detailed discussion of how UDAP statutes can provide an effective remedy against RTO abuses can be found in NCLC's *Unfair and Deceptive Acts and Practices*.[370]

Finally, it is important to note that many state UDAP statutes prohibit "unfair" practices, in addition to deceptive acts.[371] Arguably, the notion of unfairness is broader than that of unconscionability since unconscionability implies "shocking the conscience of the court." Given the unjustified overpricing in RTO transactions, as discussed above, raising claims based on unfairness under the state UDAP statute may succeed where unconscionability may not.

7.5.3.6.4 "Optional" fees

A widespread abuse involves the inclusion of so-called "optional fees," such as liability damage waivers (LDW). LDW programs purport to relieve customers of any further responsibility for the fair market value of the property if the property is stolen or destroyed by certain specified acts.

The value of LDW is highly questionable.[372] RTO dealers rarely if ever sue customers. They expect their customers to be judgment proof. Further, many RTO dealers report that 95% or more of contracts include so called "optional" fees. In fact, it appears that the fee in many cases is not truly optional but mandatory. RTO contracts are frequently prepared at the store and taken to the customer's home with the goods. The contract may have the liability damage waiver fee already added to the rental rate. If the customer objects to the fee, the delivery person states that the contract will have to be rewritten and threatens that the goods cannot delivered. Faced with this alternative the customer may elect to sign the contract with the optional fee included.

RTO companies argue that LDW is not insurance because the plan does not offer to replace the lost property. This fact may not be dispositive of whether this product is insurance. The analysis depends upon state insurance law. Generally, a contract for insurance is created where there is a risk of loss to which one party is subject based on contingent or future events and the contract shifts that risk to another.[373] To the

---

only considers value to the consumer, not cost to the service provider; yet the accountant did not survey any customers to find out how much they value a particular service. Since the services are advertised as "included," consumers have no opportunity to evaluate the costs of these services or the terminability provision in order to comparison shop. Finally, many of these values (services or terminability) vary from item to item, yet the only differentiation provided for in this instance was between small and large items in delivery. The analysis does not take into account customers who do not use the delivery service or customers whose merchandise has low obsolescence rates or low maintenance costs).

365 *See* § 12.7, *infra.*
366 *See* National Consumer Law Center, Unfair and Deceptive Acts and Practices, § 4.4 (6th ed. 2004 and Supp.).
367 At least 45 states and the District of Columbia have adopted some form of Article 2A. *See* National Consumer Law Center, Consumer Warranty Law, § 19.2.1 (2d ed. 2001 and Supp.).
368 *Id.* § 18.4. Further, virtually none of the RTO statutes contain a specific exemption from Article 2A coverage.

369 For example, one court denied summary judgment to the RTO company and sent the case to the jury on the issue of whether the state's UDAP act was violated due to an overly inflated cash price. Colon v. Rent-A-Center, Inc., 716 N.Y.S.2d 7 (N.Y. App. Div. 2000).
370 *See* National Consumer Law Center, Unfair and Deceptive Acts and Practices, § 5.7.4 (6th ed. 2004 and Supp.).
371 *Id.* § 4.3 (6th ed. 2004 and Supp.).
372 There is a detailed discussion of LDW and other miscellaneous charges such as processing fees and reinstatement fees in James Nehf, *Effective Regulation of Rent-to-Own Contract*, 42 Ohio St. L.J. 751, 824 (1991). Nehf recognizes that these miscellaneous charges can present some of the most offensive aspects of RTO contracts because even a capable customer who has read the contract will have difficulty understanding these fees.
373 *See, e.g.,* Hertz Corp. v. Home Ins. Co., 18 Cal. Rptr. 267 (App. 1993) (contains compilation of cases regarding LDW in the car

extent that the purchase of LDW shifts the risk of loss to another party in the event of theft or destruction of the property in certain circumstance, it certainly looks and smells like insurance. If so, claims of coercion in the sale of LDW can be attacked in the same ways that allegations of coercion in the sale of credit insurance are addressed. Causes of action could include usury, UDAP, fraud, and misrepresentation.[374] These issues are discussed in detail in § 8.5, *infra*. Further, if the product is insurance, practitioners should determine if the "insurer" complied with the state insurance code in all respects.[375]

7.5.3.6.5 Repossession tactics

Even if the state RTO statute exempts the transaction from UCC Article 9 applicability, some repossession tactics remain suspect. The term "repossession" is used generally here to include collection-related conduct by an RTO dealer. The more outrageous examples include:

- RTO employees struggling with the customer in the home over possession of the television set, picking up a nearby object and smashing the set;[376]
- An employee breaking and entering a customer's home only to be shot and killed as a result;[377]
- Employees breaking and entering into a customer's home, and not only repossessing the RTO merchandise but stealing the customer's other possessions;[378]
- Filing criminal charges when the customer does not return RTO merchandise.[379]

Each RTO statute will need to be reviewed in order to determine what legal remedy is available for wrongful repossession by an RTO dealer. Most states have adopted Article 2A of the UCC which specifically applies to consumer leases. Section 2A-525(3) prohibits seizures that breach the peace. Section 2A-108 provides a consumer remedy for unconscionable conduct in the collection of a claim under the contract. Consumers may recover "appropriate relief" and attorney fees in such cases.[380]

In a few states, e.g., Michigan and Illinois, the RTO statutes omit the specific exclusion of the transactions from Article 9 applicability. In those states, practitioners can raise Article 9 objections to wrongful repossessions. Even where the UCC does not apply, customers have successfully pursued tort claims such as assault, battery, and trespass against dealers.[381]

Many RTO dealers when faced with an incident of wrongful repossession will attempt to accuse the employee of unforeseen misconduct.[382] While most RTO companies are going to have written policies that prohibit the use of force during a repossession, it should be possible in most cases to prove that the employer knew or should have known that force and threats of force are commonly used and approved during repossessions. Many RTO contracts have clauses which attempt to sanction entry into the customer's residence even when the customer is not home.[383] The use of

---

rental context); Norwest Corp. v. State Dept. of Ins., 571 N.W.2d 628 (Neb. 1997) (title product found to be insurance); Lawyers Title Ins. Corp. v. Norwest Corp., 493 S.E.2d 114 (Va. 1997) (title product found not to be insurance).

374 RTO dealers recognize that they are vulnerable to claims of fraud or other misconduct in connection with LDW when employees automatically add the "optional" fee to the rental charges. Ed Winn, "Risk of Option Fees," Progressive Rentals, p.14 (Dec. 1996/Jan. 1997). *But see* South Carolina Dept. of Consumer Affairs v. Rent-A-Center, Inc., 547 S.E.2d 881 (S.C. Ct. App. 2001) (state RTO law does not expressly limit allowable fees to those included in the statute; therefore, LDW is a permissible charge; no allegation that the fee was unconscionable).

375 *See, e.g.*, Norwest Corp. v. State Dept. of Ins., 571 N.W.2d 628 (Neb. 1997) (the Nebraska Department of Insurance issued a cease and desist order, finding that Norwest had engaged in the unauthorized business of insurance; order was affirmed on appeal).

376 *See, e.g.*, State v. Action TV Rentals, 467 A.2d 1000 (Md. 1983).

377 *See, e.g.*, State v. Stewart, 288 N.W.2d 751 (Neb. 1980).

378 Partridge v. Harvey, 805 So. 2d 668 (Miss. Ct. App. 2002).

379 Bragg v. Rent to Own, 570 S.E.2d 671 (Ga. Ct. App. 2002); State v. Cox, 2002 WL 1083897 (Ohio App. Dist. Ct. May 14, 2002). The filing of a criminal charge may give rise to tort claims against the RTO business. *See, e.g.*, Bragg v. Rent to Own, 570 S.E.2d 671 (Ga. Ct. App. 2002) (customer sued RTO

company for malicious prosecution and intentional infliction of emotional distress in obtaining an arrest warrant against him; tort claims were permitted to go to trial but trial court then directed verdict for RTO company on the basis that the company was not responsible for actions of employee).

380 For a fuller discussion of limitations on the seizure of RTO goods, see National Consumer Law Center, Repossessions and Foreclosures § 14.3.4 (5th ed. 2002 and Supp.).

381 *See, e.g.*, Botello v. Remco, No. 300,458, Clearinghouse No. 52,036 (Tex. Dist. Ct. 1985). Jury returned a verdict for nearly $130,000 against a rental company for injuries to a customer which occurred during an attempted repossession.

382 *See, e.g.*, Partridge v. Harvey, 805 So. 2d 668 (Miss. Ct. App. 2002).

383 The contract used by one large company contained the following provision: "Lessor shall have the right forthwith and without prior notice to enter any premises where said property is located and take immediate possession of said property without the necessity of any legal or judicial process and the Lessee shall be obligated to reimburse Lessor for any and all expenses related to any reasonable effort to repossess its property including reasonable attorneys fees." Similar contract language was in the RTO contract in Kimble v. Universal TV Rental, Inc., 65 Ohio Misc. 17, 417 N.E.2d 597 (1980). Despite the contract language, the court rejected the argument that the repossession was in fact peaceful since the customer was not home at the time and concluded that the entry of locked premises constituted a trespass. Other courts have similarly found a dealer's attempt to use right of entry clauses in a contract as not a defense to wrongful repossession claims. In Fassitt v. United TV Rental, Inc., 297 So. 2d 283 (La. Ct. App. 1974), the RTO contract had similar reentry language. The dealer entered the house and repossessed a stereo when the only person in the house was the

such clauses should be construed as evidence that dealers know, anticipate and even sanction wrongful repossessions despite company manual language to the contrary.[384]

7.5.3.6.6 Discriminatory treatment claims

There is some evidence that RTO dealers treat delinquent customers differently based on their race.[385] African-American customers may experience more rapid repossession and are less likely to have late fees waived than white customers.[386] The Equal Credit Opportunity Act arguably applies to RTO transactions.[387] If so, RTO dealers cannot treat customers differently post-default based on prohibited reasons.[388] Actual and punitive damages are available under the Act as well as attorney fees and costs.[389]

7.5.3.6.7 Other high-cost credit disguised as RTOs

Because of lenient RTO statutes in almost all states, other high-cost creditors have attempted to disguise their loans as rent-to-own transactions. There is some indication that automobile dealers may structure car sales as rent-to-own deals. In this instance, the state RTO act and the motor vehicle retail installment sales act (MVRISA) should be carefully reviewed. States may not have specifically exempted RTO deals from their MVRISAs which often cover leases. In those instances, it is likely that the MVRISA applies and was violated.

Auto title pawn lenders have also attempted to structure their loans as rent-to-own transactions. One court has rejected such an attempt, noting that a typical RTO business does not require the consumer to sell her property to the store at a significantly reduced price and then rent it back.[390] The court also noted that the lender had no inventory and did not offer goods generally available to RTO customers.

7.5.4 Tax Refund Schemes

7.5.4.1 Assignment of Tax Refunds As Disguised Credit

Another form of "non-credit" transaction that may be a disguised loan containing hidden interest is the assignment of a taxpayer's expected tax refund in return for an immediate cash payment; though this scheme has evolved into the now more prevalent Refund Anticipation Loans.[391] These latter "RALs" do not disguise their character as credit, though they frequently involve hidden interest.[392]

The disguised credit version of the "tax refund assignment" is often characterized as the sale of a chose in action, in which the lenders claim that they are buying the borrower's right to receive the refund. As with other disguised credit transactions, these loans frequently conceal extremely high rates of interest. For example, the assignment of a $100 tax refund for a $60 cash payment produces a $40 profit in a relatively short period of time. Depending upon the precise length of time between the $60 payment and the lender's receipt of the refund, the effective annual interest rate may reach 1,700 percent.

Whether such a transaction is subject to usury law depends on whether a court is willing to accept the transaction as the sale of a chose in action. Generally, it is permissible to sell notes or other obligations at a discount without the interference of usury ceilings,[393] so long as the seller is not the maker of the note.[394] At least one court has held that the assignment of a tax refund falls within this exception to

---

customer's eleven-year-old daughter. The court in *Fassitt* held that the reentry language was void as against public policy.

384 The industry often incorporates each individual store as a separate entity which may have no assets to pay a judgment. The parent corporation will deny responsibility for the misconduct of its subsidiaries. Practitioners faced with this situation should review their state law regarding piercing the corporate veil.

385 *See* Testimony of David Ramp regarding S.R. 1566, 1956, United States Senate Banking Committee, May 13, 1994, Clearinghouse No. 49,965.

386 *Id.*

387 *See* National Consumer Law Center, Credit Discrimination § 2.2.2.2.5 (4th ed. 2005).

388 *Id.* § 9.2.4.

389 *Id.* at Ch. 11.

390 Aple Auto Cash Express, Inc. of Okla. v. State *ex rel.* Oklahoma Dep't of Consumer Credit, 78 P.3d 1231 (Okla. 2003).

391 *See* § 7.5.4.2, *infra.*

392 NCLC and the Consumer Federation of America have issued several annual reports focusing on the RAL industry, the cost to consumers, the effect upon the Earned Income Tax Credit, and RAL litigation. For the first and most comprehensive of these reports, see Chi Chi Wu, Jean Ann Fox & Elizabeth Renuart, National Consumer Law Center & Consumer Federation of America, *Tax Preparers Peddle High Cost Tax Refund Loans: Millions Skimmed from the Working Poor and the U.S. Treasury* (Jan. 31, 2002). All of the RAL reports are *available at* www.consumerlaw.org. *See also* Lynn Drysdale and Kathleen E. Keest, *The Two-Tiered Consumer Financial Services Marketplace: The Fringe Banking System and its Challenge to Current Thinking About the Socio-Economic Role of Usury Law in Today's Society,* 51 S.C. L. Rev. 589 (2000).

393 This rule comes from the longstanding usury distinction between sales and loans and is a good example of the illogic of the distinction.

394 The use of a sham intermediary will not prevent the application of usury laws. *See, e.g.,* Graham & Locke Inv. v. Madison, 295 S.W.2d 234 (Tex. 1956); Baske v. Russell, 67 Wash. 2d 268, 407 P.2d 434 (1965). The argument can be made in the tax refund context that the IRS is merely a sham intermediary for the borrower/assignor's payment to the lender/assignee since the refund is technically the borrower's money. *See* Opinion of the Attorney General of Kentucky, Clearinghouse No. 41,261 (May 3, 1982).

usury law, and that the assignment is not a loan because the taxpayer is never obligated to repay anything to the assignee.[395]

The problem with this analysis is that it ignores the basic obligation of a court in a usury case to look beyond the legal formalities of a transaction and to examine its substance.[396] The substance of the tax refund transaction is that the taxpayer, who needs money immediately, obtains that money from another party such as a tax return preparer, and that the other party receives in return a larger payment at a later date. If that larger payment were made directly by the taxpayer, the transaction would be a textbook loan. To say that the transaction is not a loan because the later payment does not literally come from the taxpayer's pocket is to ignore the reality of the transaction.

Some courts and authorities have been willing to look at the substance of tax refund assignments, and have concluded that the transactions are loans which may violate usury laws. A New York court held that an individual who paid $5,500 for an assignment of a $7,500 interest in an estate was guilty of usury.[397] An opinion of the Attorney General of Kentucky determined that tax refund assignments in that state were loans which could violate that state's usury law.[398] Similarly, a scheme whereby tax refunds were "purchased" at deep discounts from the taxpayer was found to constitute the lending of money; the regulator considered a provision in the contract that required repayment of the *full* refund amount after six weeks if the refund has not been paid by the government to be a significant factor.[399]

The most recent decision is from the highest court in Colorado, where the lender claimed that the transaction was not a loan because it did not require the borrower to repay the advance unless the amount of the refund received was less than anticipated.[400] The Colorado Supreme Court re-

jected this argument, holding that the borrower's obligation to repay if the expected tax refund did not come through was sufficient to make the transaction a loan under the UCCC.[401] While the court stressed the differences between the UCCC and other states' definitions of "loan," its reasoning should be persuasive in other states, as the court debunked the claim that the transaction was merely the sale of a chose in action.[402]

As this case demonstrates, terming the obligation to repay a tax refund assignment as contingent is unjustified in many cases, because the agreement will require the consumer to repay the lender if the government fails to pay the full refund. Either the lender will be paid the principal plus interest by IRS's payment of the refund or the borrower will pay that exact same amount. There is no uncertainty in the amount of the payment. Neither the repayment itself nor the amount of the repayment is contingent upon a future event. The lender has not accepted any risk or uncertainty beyond those present in a typical consumer loan. In fact, the risk of nonpayment is less since the IRS's ability to pay the refund is unquestioned, so the creditor is relying less on the changeable financial circumstances of an individual.

Since the money from the IRS is the taxpayer's money in the first place, which is being temporarily held by the government, the only uncertainty is how the borrower pays—directly, or through the IRS as an intermediary. Repayment is no more contingent than when a borrower gives a post-dated check for the principal plus interest and remains liable for repayment if the check does not clear. In both cases, there are two routes by which the borrower's money will reach the lender, but the borrower's obligation to repay the principal plus the interest is not subject to any contingency. Other courts have followed the maxim that substance prevails over form and have seen through alleged contingencies to recognize the underlying absolute obligation of the borrower to repay.[403]

---

395 *See* Cullen v. Bragg, 350 S.E.2d 798 (Ga. Ct. App. 1986).

396 *See* § 9.2.1.6, *infra*.

397 *See* Leavitt v. Enos, 140 N.Y.S. 862 (1913).

398 Opinion of the Attorney General of Kentucky, Clearinghouse No. 41,261 (May 3, 1982).

399 *In re* Income Tax Buyers, S.C. Dep't of Consumer Affairs, Docket No. 9004 (order Feb. 5, 1991), *on rehearing*, (June 19, 1991), Clearinghouse No. 46,756, *aff'd*, Income Tax Buyers, Inc. v. Hamm, 1992 WL 12092431 (S.C. Ct. Common. Pleas 1992) (company giving consumers advances on their tax refunds, discounted by 20%–40%, in exchange for their full refunds (equivalent to 200% APRs) were engaged in loaning money and required to be licensed; administrator rejected Cullen v. Bragg, 350 S.E.2d 798 (Ga. Ct. App. 1986), and the argument that these were sales of chose in action). The regulator also noted that the assignment of the right to a tax refund before it is processed and issued runs afoul of the Assignment Act, 31 U.S.C. § 3727, and that IRS rules make clear that advertisements for these anticipated refunds must be described as loans. *See* IRS Publication 1345, Revenue Procedures for Electronic Filing of Individual Income Tax Returns at 44 (2004).

400 State *ex rel.* Salazar v. The Cash Now Store, Inc., 31 P.3d 161 (Colo. 2001). An excellent brief filed by the attorney general and code administrator in this case can be obtained from

Clearinghouse Review. Clearinghouse No. 52,151. On remand, the attorney general obtained a final judgment in excess of $49 million in damages and penalties. State *ex rel.* Salazar v. The Cash Now Store, Inc., Clearinghouse No. 55,601 (Colo. Dist. Ct. Mar. 8, 2004) (order and final judgment).

401 State *ex rel.* Salazar v. Cash Now Store, Inc., 31 P.3d 161 (Colo. 2001).

402 *Id.* at 167 (noting that the lender demonstrates that it does not view the refund as a chose in action because the borrower owes it a sum of money whether the refund or "chose" is valuable to the lender or not). *See also* Lawsuit Fin., L.L.C. v. Curry, 683 N.W.2d 233 (Mich. App. 2004) (obligation to repay litigation funding company was not contingent where borrower signed agreement after tortfeasor had admitted liability and jury had returned $27 million verdict); Income Tax Buyers, Inc. v. Hamm, 1992 WL 12092431 (S.C. Com. Pleas Jan. 14, 1992) (discounted sale of right to receive income tax refund is loan because contract obliges borrower to pay the amount of the refund if IRS does not).

403 *See, e.g.,* Tiffany v. Boatman's Sav. Inst., 85 U.S. 375, 18 Wall. 375, 21 L. Ed. 868, 870 (1873); Britz v. Kinsvater, 351 P.2d 986

Some courts have found that, when a person transfers a note or account to another at a discount, and guarantees payment, the guarantee makes the transaction a loan.[404] The more generally accepted holding, however, is that there is no *per se* rule, but a guarantee is one factor in determining whether the transaction is a disguised loan.[405] Thus, the borrower's guarantee of payment in a refund anticipation transaction may be insufficient in and of itself to persuade the court that the transaction is a loan. But tax refund assignment cases are significantly more clear-cut, because the tax refund represents the consumer's own money and because the financial solidity of the IRS means that the creditor is less at risk than in the typical loan.

Thus, practitioners whose clients have been the victims of tax refund assignment schemes should closely examine the transaction for terms which reveal the true extension of credit. For example, if the taxpayer is in any way liable to the "assignee" if the refund is smaller than expected, the argument that the transaction is merely a sale of a chose in action would be rebutted. Practitioners should also consider potential liability under disclosure statutes[406] or under statutes forbidding deceptive trade practices if the purported assignee in any way conceals the nature or terms of the transaction.[407]

7.5.4.2 Refund Anticipation Loans (RALs)

Some major lenders now offer "Refund Anticipation Loans," thus dropping the pretense that no credit is involved.[408] The refund is deposited directly into a "dummy account" the borrower sets up as part of the transaction at a bank affiliated with the creditor. Commonly, the note is formally designated a demand note, and the creditor's compensation is a flat fee. Since these loans typically are made through tax preparers, the consumer will pay a tax preparation fee, a separate fee to the tax preparer for processing the loan application, and, often, a fee to cash the refund loan proceeds on top of the RAL fee to the lender. These fees can be substantial, sometimes over $250 per loan. One report estimates that taxpayers paid over $1 billion in RAL fees alone.[409] RAL growth has been significant, rising from 10.8 million loans in 2000[410] to 12.1 million in 2003.[411]

(Ariz. 1960); Seargeant v. Smith, 163 P.2d 680 (Ariz. 1945). *Cf.* Baxter v. Stevens, 773 P.2d 890 (Wash. Ct. App. 1989) ("sale" of promissory note with recourse guarantee was a loan). *See generally* § 7.2.3, *supra*, and §§ 7.5.6, 9.2.1.6, 10.5.3, *infra. But see* Berger v. State, 910 P.2d 581 (Alaska 1996) (assignments of anticipated distributions of oil "manna" [called "permanent fund dividends"] to Alaskans not a disguised loan; case distinguishable because the assignment did not involve one's own money, as tax refunds do; further, court erroneously found that the assignors did not have an unconditional obligation to repay).

404 Western Auto Supply Co. v. Vick, 277 S.E.2d 360 (N.C. 1981) (seller transferred rights under chattel paper to lender, with a guarantee of payment; seller then collected the money from the account debtors and transmitted it to lender); Baxter v. Stevens, 773 P.2d 890 (Wash. Ct. App. 1989). *See generally* 45 Am. Jur. 2d *Interest and Usury* § 127 (1999).

405 *See, e.g.,* Berger v. State, 910 P.2d 581 (Alaska 1996) (repayment guarantees do not necessarily turn sales into loans; sale of rights to Alaska permanent fund distributions was not a loan even though borrower guaranteed payment); Carter v. Four Seasons Funding Corp., 97 S.W.3d 387 (Ark. 2003) (warranty that accounts would be collectable within ninety days and agreement to repurchase uncollectible accounts did not make sale of accounts receivable a loan); Investors Thrift v. AMA Corp., 63 Cal. Rptr. 157 (Ct. App. 1967) (agreement to repurchase uncollectible or disputed accounts did not make transaction a loan, but court suggests that it might have ruled differently if more indicia of a loan had been present). *See also* Ravkind v. Mortgage Funding Corp., 881 S.W.2d 203 (Tex. App. 1994) (assignment of payments due on contract for deed not a loan even though assignee had recourse against assignor); § 10.5.3 *infra*.

406 *But see* Cullen v. Bragg, 350 S.E.2d 798 (Ga. Ct. App. 1986) (neither state usury law nor the TILA applied to refund assignment). For a discussion of Truth in Lending rules on tax refund anticipation loans, see National Consumer Law Center, Truth in Lending § 4.4.10.2 (5th ed. 2003 and Supp.).

407 *See* Consent Order, 94 F.T.C. 425 (Sept. 12, 1979) *modified* 51 Fed. Reg. 43587 (Dec. 3, 1986). (Beneficial Fin. precluded from using the terms "instant tax refund" or "immediate tax refund" except in immediate conjunction with the word "loan.") For a compilation of enforcement actions filed by state attorney generals based upon this mischaracterization, see JTH Tax v. H & R Block, 128 F. Supp. 2d 926, 938 (E.D. Va. 2001), *aff'd in part, vacated in part, and remanded in part*, 28 Fed. Appx. 207 (4th Cir. 2002). *See also* Chi Chi Wu, Jean Ann Fox & Elizabeth Renuart, National Consumer Law Center & Consumer Federation of America, *Tax Preparers Peddle High Cost Tax Refund Loans: Millions Skimmed from the Working Poor and the U.S. Treasury* 25 (Jan. 31, 2002), *available at* www.consumerlaw.org.

408 For a review of the bank lenders and their tax preparer partners, *see* Chi Chi Wu, Jean Ann Fox & Elizabeth Renuart, National Consumer Law Center & Consumer Federation of America, *Tax Preparers Peddle High Cost Tax Refund Loans: Millions Skimmed from the Working Poor and the U.S. Treasury* 11–15 (Jan. 31, 2002), *available at* www.consumerlaw.org.

409 Chi Chi Wu & Jean Ann Fox, National Consumer Law Center & Consumer Federation America, *Picking Taxpayers' Pockets, Draining Tax Relief Dollars: Refund Anticipation Loans Still Slicing Into Low-Income Americans' Hard-Earned Tax Refunds* (Jan. 2005), *available at* www.consumerlaw.org. *See also* Alan Berube, Anne Kim, Benjamin Foman, & Megan Burns, Brookings Institution and Progressive Policy Institute, *The Price of Paying Taxes: How Tax Preparation and Refund Loan Fees Erode the Benefits of the EITC* (May 2002), *available at* www.brookings.org (estimated $1.75 billion diverted from the Earned Income Tax Credit to pay for RALs plus tax preparation and electronic filing).

410 Chi Chi Wu, Jean Ann Fox & Elizabeth Renuart, National Consumer Law Center & Consumer Federation of America, *Tax Preparers Peddle High Priced Tax Refund Loans: Millions Skimmed from the Working Poor and the U.S. Treasury*, (Jan. 31, 2002), *available at* www.consumerlaw.org.

411 Chi Chi Wu & Jean Ann Fox, National Consumer Law Center & Consumer Federation America, *Picking Taxpayers' Pockets, Draining Tax Relief Dollars: Refund Anticipation Loans Still*

While there has been activity as to the Truth in Lending implications of this arrangement,[412] there has been little challenge under usury laws. While the effective interest rates on these short-term loans could be from 40% to over 700%,[413] usury claims will run into the federal preemption/exportation snag.[414] All of the major RAL lenders are federally-chartered banks. The claim of the largest RAL lender, Beneficial National Bank (now HSBC Bank) that it has the right to export Delaware law (which permits any rate of interest agreed to by a lender and borrower) to wherever the RALs are written has been upheld by the Fourth Circuit at least in states where Beneficial has no branch offices.[415]

A few states have addressed tax refund loans through legislation. North Carolina focused on regulating the facilitator of RALs, rather than on the lender. The law does allow the Commissioner of Banks to review RALs for "unconscionable fees," which could make lenders liable for three times the fee and possible revocation of the right to make such loans. Examples of APRs, using the estimated repayment date for the loans involving direct deposit accounts receiving the refund, must be given.[416]

Wisconsin imposes only disclosure requirements on the lender.[417] Connecticut and Illinois regulate the tax preparer not the lender, but they too only impose limited disclosure requirements.[418] Minnesota requires tax preparers facilitating RALs to make disclosures using mandatory language and 14-point type.[419] New York City and Seattle have also passed ordinances requiring similar disclosures for RALs, as well as disclosures in RAL advertising.[420] State and municipal regulators have on occasion taken actions against tax preparers over deceptive advertising of RALs.[421]

Slicing Into Low-Income Americans' Hard-Earned Tax Refunds (Jan. 2005). *See also* Chi Chi Wu & Jean Ann Fox, *All Drain, No Gain: Refund Anticipation Loans Continue to Sap the Hard-Earned Tax Dollars of Low-Income Americans*, National Consumer Law Center & Consumer Federation of America (Jan. 2004); Chi Chi Wu & Jean Ann Fox, *The High Cost of Quick Tax Money: Tax Preparation, "Instant Refund" Loans, and Check Cashing Fees Target the Working Poor*, National Consumer Law Center & Consumer Federation of America (Jan. 30, 2003). All of these reports are available at www.consumerlaw.org.

412 National Consumer Law Center, Truth in Lending § 4.4.10.2 (5th ed. 2003 and Supp.).

413 Chi Chi Wu & Jean Ann Fox, National Consumer Law Center & Consumer Federation America, *Picking Taxpayers' Pockets, Draining Tax Relief Dollars: Refund Anticipation Loans Still Slicing Into Low-Income Americans' Hard-Earned Tax Refunds* (Jan. 2005). In 2003, the average tax refund was slightly over $2,000. With a RAL, borrowers typically receive their loan in one or two days, while the average time to process an electronically filed return is 8 to 15 days. Since the refund automatically gets deposited directly into the dummy account with the lender, the loan term can be realistically expected to average 10 days. If the flat fee is $100, that fee translates to an effective yield of 187%. *See also* United States Gen. Accounting Office, Pub. No. GAO-04-70, *Tax Administration: Most Taxpayers Believe They Benefit from Paid Tax Preparers, but Oversight for IRS is a Challenge* 10 (Oct. 31, 2003) (findings include fact that GAO investigators were quoted loan fees ranging from $130 on a $1,200 refund—or 400% APR—to $174 on a $700 refund—or 900% APR), *available at* www.gao.gov/cgi-bin/getrpt?GAO-04-70.

414 *See* Chapter 3, *supra.*

415 Cades v. H & R Block, Inc., 43 F.3d 869 (4th Cir. 1994) (H & R Block office itself did not constitute a "branch" office). *See also* Christiansen v. Beneficial Nat'l Bank, 972 F. Supp. 681 (S.D. Ga. 1997) (same relying upon *Cades* decision). The OCC issued an amendment to Interpretive Ruling (7.1012 addressing "messenger services."). 64 Fed. Reg. 60092 (Nov. 4, 1999). The Supplementary Information clearly shows that the OCC intended to incorporate the more lax standard enunciated in *Cades* and *Christiansen* in determining under what circumstances the H & R Block office does not constitute a branch of the bank itself. *See* discussion in § 3.4.5.1.2, *supra. Editor's note*: At the time *Cades* was decided, H & R Block had no ownership interest in the loans. Since 1996, however, it buys back a 49.9% interest in each loan it processes with Beneficial Bank. *See* Chi Chi Wu, Jean Ann Fox & Elizabeth Renuart, National Consumer Law Center & Consumer Federation of America, *Tax Preparers Peddle High Cost Tax Refund Loans: Millions Skimmed from the Working Poor and the U.S. Treasury* 12 n.53 (Jan. 31, 2002), *available at* www.consumerlaw.org.

A preemption issue in a RAL case that reached the Supreme Court is the scope of the National Bank Act's preemption for state usury claims, that is, whether such claims are subject to conflict preemption or complete preemption. The Supreme Court held that the NBA did completely preempt any usury claims against H & R Block and Household concerning RALs. Beneficial Nat'l Bank v. Anderson, 539 U.S. 1, 123 S. Ct. 2058, 156 L. Ed. 2d 1 (2003). *See* § 3.15, *supra.*

416 N.C. Gen. Stat. § 53-245 *et seq.* This statute has withstood a federal preemption challenge. North Carolina Ass'n of Electronic Tax Filers, Inc. v. Graham, 429 S.E.2d 544 (N.C. 1993).

417 Wis. Stat. §§ 421.301 *et seq.*

418 Conn. Gen. Stat. § 42-480; Ill. Comp. Stat. Ann. ch. 815, § 177/1 *et seq.*

419 Minn. Stat. § 270.30.

420 N.Y. City Admin. Code § 20-739; ACORN Press Release, *Seattle Passes Anti-RAL Legislation*, Sept. 24, 2004.

421 *See, e.g.,* Beneficial Corp. v. Federal Trade Commission, 542 F.2d 611 (3d Cir. 1976). Several state enforcement actions are discussed in JTH Tax v. H & R Block, 128 F. Supp. 2d 926 (E.D. Va. 2001) (citing *In re* H & R Block Eastern Tax Services, No. 93-410039 (Fla. Office Attorney Gen. Jan. 6, 1994) (assurance of voluntary compliance); Cerullo v. H & R Block, No. 95-409497 (N.Y. Gen. Term) (consent order); *In re* H & R Block, No. 93-198 (Conn. Comm'r Consumer Prot. July 27, 1993)), *aff'd in part, vacated in part, and remanded in part*, 28 Fed. Appx. 207 (4th Cir. 2002).

The New York City Department of Consumer Affairs (DCA) filed a lawsuit against H & R Block over the company's allegedly deceptive advertising. As a result of its investigation, DCA found that 86% of the company's branches in the city failed to differentiate between true refunds and RALs. Dykstra v. H & R Block, Clearinghouse No. 54587A (N.Y. Sup. Ct. Mar. 12, 2002) (complaint). In addition, DCA reached an agreement with Jackson Hewitt over charges of deceptive promotion of RALs. Press Release, *New York City Department of Consumer Affairs, Consumer Affairs Releases Preliminary Results of Tax Preparer Enforcement and Monitoring for 2004 Season*, Apr. 5, 2004, *available at* www.ci.nyc.ny.us/html/dca/pdf/pr40504.pdf.

RALs sometimes become the issue of regulatory action because they are involved in tax fraud cases. *See, e.g.,* United States v. Kissi, 2004 WL 2903720 (S.D.N.Y. Dec. 15, 2004) (tax

Aside from usury issues, borrowers can raise a myriad of other state law claims, particularly against the tax preparer, for example, breach of fiduciary duty, fraud, negligent misrepresentation, UDAP, breach of duty of good faith and fair dealing, civil conspiracy, and RICO.[422] These claims often arise if the tax preparer receives a undisclosed kickback from the lender to make the loan and when the tax preparer advertises the loans as "advances."[423] One court held that a tax preparation company that continued to advertise RALs as "advances" and not as "loans" in the face of numerous consent orders and enforcement actions operated in bad faith and issued a nationwide injunction.[424] In other decisions, courts have split on whether to dismiss or grant summary judgment on claims alleging breach of fiduciary duty and breach of duty of good faith and fair dealing.[425] One barrier

to RAL litigation is the prevalence of mandatory arbitration clauses in RAL contracts.[426]

Many of the class actions against the largest tax preparation chain, H & R Block, and its lending partner, Beneficial Bank (now HSBC Bank) were at risk of being snuffed out by a controversial $25 million global settlement.[427] The

---

fraud involving RALs); United States v. Ankamah, 2004 WL 744487 (S.D.N.Y. Apr. 6, 2004) (same). The Director of the IRS Criminal Investigation Division's Refund Crimes Unit noted that 80% of fraudulent e-filed returns are tied to either a RAL or other refund financial product. Allen Kenney, *IRS Official Shines Spotlight on E-Filing Fraud*, Tax Notes Today, 2004 TNT 130-4, July 6, 2004.

422 *See, e.g.,* Peterson v. H & R Block Tax Servs., 22 F. Supp. 2d 795 (N.D. Ill. 1998); Affafato v. Beneficial, 1998 U.S. Dist. LEXIS 12447 (E.D.N.Y. Aug. 7, 1998); Green v. H & R Block, 735 A.2d 1039 (Md. 1999); Basile v. H & R Block, Inc., 761 A.2d 1115 (Pa. 2000) (holding no fiduciary relationship on the basis of an agency relationship, but remanding for findings on the basis of a confidential relationship), *subsequent proceeding at* 777 A.2d 95 (Pa. Super. Ct. 2001) (finding confidential relationship); H & R Block v. Haese, 976 S.W.2d 237 (Tex. App. 1998). See Ch. 11, *infra*, for a broader discussion of these claims.

423 See discussion of fees and advertising practices in Chi Chi Wu, Jean Ann Fox & Elizabeth Renuart, National Consumer Law Center & Consumer Federation of America, *Tax Preparers Peddle High Cost Tax Refund Loans: Millions Skimmed from the Working Poor and the U.S. Treasury* (Jan. 31, 2002), *available at* www.consumerlaw.org.

424 JTH Tax v. H & R Block, 128 F. Supp. 2d 926, 938 (E.D. Va. 2001), *aff'd in part, vacated in part, and remanded in part*, 28 Fed. Appx. 207 (4th Cir. 2002) (appellate court upheld the finding of bad faith, though it modified the scope of the injunction) (in determining whether the various advertisements were misleading, the district court relied upon survey evidence showing that 22% of the surveyed consumers believed the poster advertisement was deceptive; the court found this degree of deception to be substantial; interestingly, H & R Block's own research indicated that most consumers would not associate an "advance" with a loan).

425 *See also* Basile v. H & R Block, Inc., 761 A.2d 1115 (Pa. 2000) (holding no fiduciary relationship on the basis of an agency relationship, but remanding for findings on the basis of a confidential relationship), *subsequent proceeding at* 777 A.2d 95 (Pa. Super. Ct. 2001) (finding confidential relationship). *Cf.* Kleven v. Household Bank, 334 F.3d 638 (7th Cir.) (trustee could not set aside repayment of RALs by taxpayers who filed for bankruptcy shortly after receiving a RAL; however, court remarks on the predatory nature of RALs, noting: "an attack on RALs based on fairness and equity would certainly have some appeal"), *cert. denied*, 124 S. Ct. 924 (2003). *Compare* Peterson v. H & R Block Tax Servs., Inc., 971 F. Supp. 1204 (N.D. Ill.

1997) (motion to dismiss on breach of duty of good faith and fair dealing denied; granted as to breach of fiduciary duty, 174 F.R.D. 78 (N.D. Ill. 1997) (class certification granted on RICO and UDAP claim), 22 F. Supp. 2d 795 (N.D. Ill. 1998) (RICO claim dismissed due to inability to show H & R Block's deliberate fraud in failing to advise customers that tax refunds where the earned income tax credit is sought may be delayed beyond three weeks; state law claim remanded to state court)); Green v. H & R Block, Inc., 735 A.2d 1039 (Md. 1999) (tax preparer found to be agent of consumer thus creating fiduciary duty to advise the consumer that it receives payments and other benefits from the lender for facilitating the making of the loan) Haese v. H & R Block, Clearinghouse No. 54586 (105th Jud. Tex. Dist. Ct. Nov. 6, 2002) (one page letter ruling in which court held that tax preparer owed fiduciary duty to consumers; court found that Block had violated that duty and assessed a forfeiture of all of the company's tax preparation fees in Texas for a 5-year period) *with* Beckett v. H & R Block, Inc., 714 N.E.2d 1033 (Ill. App. 1999) (tax preparer not an agent; no duty to disclose secret profit to consumer). *But cf.* Sorenson v. H & R Block, 2002 WL 31194868 (D. Mass. Aug. 27, 2002) (court held in this non-RAL case that, under Massachusetts law, a tax preparer does not owe *per se* fiduciary duty to client), *aff'd*, 2004 WL 1858182 (1st Cir. Aug. 20, 2004).

426 *See* Carbajal v. Household Bank, Fed. Sav. Bank, 372 F.3d 903 (7th Cir. 2004) (affirming order compelling arbitration of claims against Household, H & R Block, and other RAL lenders.). In *Carbajal*, the Seventh Circuit made some astounding assumptions about the RAL business. The court stated its belief that one-sided form contracts are beneficial because "[f]orms reduce transaction costs and benefit consumers because, in competition, reductions in the cost of doing business show up as lower prices (here, a slightly lower rate of interest on the loan)." The court apparently had not seen the astronomical prices of RALs, nor read its own prior opinions discussing the predatory nature of RALs in Kleven v. Household Bank, 334 F.3d 638,640 (7th Cir.), *cert. denied*, 540 U.S. 1073 (2003), which noted that "[t]he bargain struck [for a RAL] is a good one for only one of the two parties. Guess which one?"). The court also apparently had not noticed there is little competition or "shopping around" for RAL prices, which differ between the handful of RAL lenders by only a few dollars.

In contrast, the Pennsylvania Supreme Court denied a motion to compel arbitration in part on the basis that the arbitration clause in the RAL agreement was unconscionable towards consumers. McNulty v. H & R Block, 843 A.2d 1267 (Pa. Super. 2004), *cert. denied*, 125 S. Ct. 667 (2004). The Pennsylvania court noted that the RAL Agreement is a contract of "adhesion," and that the arbitration provision unreasonably favors Block, in that it required the consumer to pay a $50 fee that exceeded the $37 e-filing fee at issue in the case. *See also* Cummins v. H & R Block, Civil Action No. 03-C-134 (Circuit Court of Kanawha County June 1, 2004) (order denying defendants' motion to compel arbitration in case challenging H & R Block's brokering of RALs under West Virginia Credit Services Organization Act), available on the companion CD-Rom.

427 Zawikowski v. Beneficial Nat'l Bank, 2000 WL 1051879 (N.D.

Seventh Circuit, however, overturned the approval of the settlement. The court held that the district court judge abused his discretion in approving the settlement and sent the case back to the district court with the requirement that the case be assigned to a different judge.[428] On remand, the district court rejected the settlement on the basis that the class counsel who negotiated the settlement were inadequate representatives for the plaintiff class.[429] Subsequently, the district court permitted a nationwide class action to go forward on a RICO claim, plus a breach of contract claim against Household alone.[430]

Tax preparers who facilitate RALs may also run afoul of state laws governing loan brokers or credit services organizations.[431] For example, the Massachusetts Commissioner of Banks issued a warning letter to tax preparers that they would be required to obtain a small loan company license under Massachusetts law if they were offering RALs, regardless of whether the preparer originated the loan. The warning letter also noted that any person brokering small loans in Massachusetts must abide by Massachusetts regulations limiting the interest rates on small loans to 23% APR.[432] The Mississippi Commissioner of Banking and Consumer Finance has issued a similar letter.[433]

A significant risk to RAL consumers is the practice of cross-lender debt collection, by which all of the RAL lenders have included a provision in their RAL agreements allowing them to take a consumer's tax refund and use it to pay back any prior RAL debts for any other RAL lender.[434] There have been several lawsuits filed against RAL lenders and tax preparers over these cross-lender debt collection provisions.[435]

The Office of the Comptroller of the Currency requires RALs to be subject to a 100% risk weight, instead of the lower 20% risk weight for loans guaranteed by the federal government. A RAL lender had requested to carry the loans at the 20% risk weight, arguing that RALs should be considered low-risk loans because they are effectively collateralized by a direct obligation of the U.S. government. The OCC disagreed, noting that the bank's actual loss experience (1.5% of RAL borrowers) suggests that RALs do not perform as if the federal government guarantees them.[436]

7.5.5 Payday Loans/Check Advancement Loans

7.5.5.1 Introduction

As was discussed in Chapter Two, the market has come almost full circle in the last one hundred years for some wage-earners who want to borrow small sums for a short time.[437] The old "salary-lenders"[438] of the turn of the last century are cropping up now in the form of check lenders, or payday lenders.

Some traditional small loan providers have left the market, leaving a vacuum which is now being filled by companies offering payday loans, extremely high interest loans that

---

Ill. July 28, 2000) (objections to the settlement included allegations that it would only pay pennies on the dollar and that it was a product of collusion between Block, Beneficial, and some "friendly" plaintiffs' attorneys). Following the settlement, Household and H & R Block filed actions seeking to enforce arbitration clauses against any class members who opted out of the *Zawikowski* settlement (and there were about 2,100 such consumers). Household Bank, F.S.B. v. JFS Group, 320 F.3d 1249 (11th Cir. 2003); Household Bank, F.S.B. v. Allen, 2001 WL 737532 (S.D. Miss. May 25, 2001).

428 Reynolds v. Beneficial Nat'l Bank, 288 F.3d 277 (7th Cir. 2002).

429 Reynolds v. Beneficial Nat'l Bank, 260 F. Supp. 2d 680 (N.D. Ill. 2003).

430 Carnegie v. Household Int'l, Inc., 220 F.R.D. 542 (N.D. Ill. 2004) (in addition, court dismissed the breach of contract claim as to H & R Block, and withdrew class certification for several state claims on the basis that a fifty state legal analysis would be required to resolve them, presenting an intractable class manageability problem; court also reaffirmed a ruling by prior judge enforcing mandatory arbitration clauses against those RAL customers whose contracts included them), *aff'd*, 376 F.3d 656 (7th Cir. 2004).

431 *E.g.,* Cummins v. H & R Block, Civil Action No. 03-C-134 (Circuit Court of Kanawha County Dec. 30, 2004) (order granting plaintiffs' motion for class certification in case challenging H & R Block's brokering of RALs under West Virginia Credit Services Organization Act), available on companion the CD-Rom. For a discussion of how state credit services organization laws may apply to credit arrangers, see National Consumer Law Center, Fair Credit Reporting § 15.3.4 (5th ed. 2002 and Supp.).

432 Letter from Thomas J. Curry, Mass. Commissioner of Banks, Division of Banks Warns Tax Preparers That They Must Be Licensed to Provide Refund Anticipation Loan (Mar. 5, 2003), *available at* www.state.ma.us/dob/taxprep.htm.

433 Memorandum from Commissioner John Allison re: Department Warns Mississippi Tax Preparers They May Have to Obtain a

License to Provide Refund Anticipation Loans, Aug. 19, 2003, *available at* www.dbcf.state.ms.us/documents/cons_finance/tax-preparers-1st-memo.pdf.

434 Thus, if a taxpayer owes money to one RAL lender from a prior year and applies for a RAL from a different lender, her RAL will be denied and her refund will be gone. The second lender will take her refund and use it to repay the prior RAL debt to the first lender.

435 Carbajal v. Household Bank, Fed. Sav. Bank, 372 F.3d 903 (7th Cir. 2004) (affirming order compelling arbitration of claims against Household, H & R Block, and other RAL lenders for violation of Fair Debt Collection Practices Act, the Equal Credit Opportunity Act, and Illinois consumer protection laws); Hood v. Santa Barbara Bank & Trust, Civ. Action No. 1156354 (Santa Barbara Super. Ct. filed Mar. 18, 2003) (class action and representative action under California's debt collection and unfair trade practices laws), *reprinted in* Appx. L, *infra*.

436 Tommy Snow, Director of Capital Policy, Office of the Comptroller of the Currency, Interpretive Letter No. 959 (Feb. 13, 2003), *available at* www.occ.treas.gov/interp/mar03/int959.pdf.

437 See § 2.5, *supra*.

438 See § 2.2.3.1, *supra*.

extend until the borrower's next pay check.[439] Many main-stream institutions prefer not to write small loans because, while the return on a $5,000 loan is greater than if only $500 is borrowed, the originating and servicing costs are not significantly different. Many of the national finance companies, which were initially founded to meet precisely this credit need, have moved up and out of this type of small lending. As a result, the availability of small-sum, short-term credit has been curtailed.[440]

Much of the market for small, unsecured loans today has been replaced by the use of checking account overdraft loans and credit cards, even for relatively lower income households. This still leaves a large number of consumers without sufficient credit card limits or bank overdraft protection to meet their needs for relatively small unsecured loans.[441]

Payday lenders particularly target military personnel for a variety of reasons.[442] Military bases provide a large potential customer base in one location. Consequently, payday lenders cluster near base gates. Many personnel are low-income consumers. Periods of deployment are vulnerable times. Military codes of conduct stress the need for orderly finances. Some lenders advertise on the base through "military" newspapers perceived to be "official" by service members. Two researchers recently mapped the locations of payday lenders in relation to military bases in twenty states that "regulate" payday lending in a variety of ways.[443] Despite claims to the contrary, these authors found conclusively that payday lenders target the military, even when controlling for commercial development patterns and zoning ordinances with bank locations.

African Americans are another target of payday lenders, according to a study released in 2005.[444] The authors discovered that African-American neighborhoods have three times as many stores per capita as white neighborhoods. Further, the disparity grows when the proportion of African Americans in a neighborhood increases. The disparity is not affected when the authors controlled for income, homeownership, poverty, unemployment rate, urban location, age, education, share of households with children, and gender characteristics of the neighborhoods. The findings raise serious red flags and could support a race discrimination claim under the Equal Credit Opportunity Act.[445]

439 For the most comprehensive information about the growth and characteristics of this industry, see Lynn Drysdale & Kathleen E. Keest, *The Two-Tiered Consumer Financial Services Marketplace: The Fringe Banking System and its Challenge to Current Thinking About the Socio-Economic Role of Usury Law in Today's Society*, 51 S.C. L. Rev. 589 (2000); Creola Johnson, *Payday Loans: Shrewd Business or Predatory Lending?*, 87 Minn. L. Rev. 1, 33, 34 (Nov. 2002); *see also* Uriah King, Wei Li, Delvin Davis & Keith Ernst, *Race Matters: The Concentration of Payday Lenders in African-American Neighborhoods in North Carolina* (Center for Responsible Lending Mar. 22, 2005), *available at* www.responsiblelending.org/research/index.cfm?tid=2&tyid=2; Steven M. Graves & Christopher L. Peterson, *Predatory Lending and the Military: The Law and Geography of "Payday" Loans in Military Towns* (Mar. 29, 2005), *available at* www.responsiblelending.org/research/index.cfm?tid=2&tyid=2; Pearl Chin, *Payday Loans: The Case for Federal Legislation*, 2004 U. Ill. L. Rev. 723 (2004) (discussing why economic theory supports credit rationing and arguing in favor of a federal usury cap); Jean Ann Fox & Anna Petrini, *Internet Payday Lending: How High-Priced Lenders Use the Internet to Mire Borrowers in Debt and Evade State Consumer Protections* (Consumer Federation of America Nov. 30, 2004); Uriah King & Keith Ernst, *Quantifying the Cost of Predatory Payday Lending*, (Center for Responsible Lending Dec. 2003), *available at* www.responsiblelending.org/research/index.cfm?tid=2&tyid=2; Lisa Blaylock Moss, *Modern Day Loan Sharking: Deferred Presentment Transactions and the Need for Regulation*, 51 Ala. L. Rev. 1725 (2000); Deborah A. Schmedemann, *Time and Money: One State's Regulation of Check-Based Loans*, 27 Wm. Mitchell L. Rev. 973 (2000); Jean Ann Fox, Consumer Federation of America, *Unsafe and Unsound: Payday Lenders Hide Behind FDIC Bank Charters to Peddle Usury* (Mar. 2004); Jean Ann Fox & Edmund Mierzwinski, *Consumer Federation of America & U.S. PIRG, Rent-a-Bank Payday Lending: How Banks Help Payday Lenders Evade State Consumer Protections* (Nov. 2001); Edmund Mierzwinski & Jean Ann Fox, U.S. PIRG & Consumer Federation of America, *Show Me the Money! A Survey of Payday Lenders and Review of Payday Lender Lobbying in State Legislatures* (Feb. 2000); Jean Ann Fox, Consumer Federation of America, *The Growth of Legal Loan Sharking: A Report on the Payday Loan Industry* (Nov. 1998). Note that all of Consumer Federation of America's reports on payday lending can be found on its website at www.consumerfed.org (click on "Finance").

440 A virulent exception to this general observation persists. Some finance companies market small loans to hook consumers into a refinancing mill. See Emery v. Am. Gen. Fin., 71 F.3d 1343 (7th Cir. 1995) and discussion of this case in § 12.6, *infra*.

441 Credit unions have begun to reach out to communities with small sum, short-term cash needs. *See* Marva Williams & Kathryn Smolik, *Affordable Alternatives to Payday Loans: Examples from Community Development Credit Unions*, Woodstock Institute Reinvestment Alert (Mar. 2001), *available at* www.woodstockinst.org/alert16.pdf; Edward J. Gallagly & Darla Dernovsek, Credit Union Ass'n, Inc., Fair Deal: Creating Credit Union Alternatives to Fringe Financial Services (2000); Credit Union Ass'n, Inc., Alternatives to Payday Loans: The Credit Union Option (Dec. 2000).

442 An in-depth look at high-cost debt targeted at the military can be found in Steve Tripoli & Amy Mix, National Consumer Law Center, In Harm's Way—At Home: Consumer Scams and the Direct Targeting of America's Military and Veterans (May 2003), *available at* www.nclc.org (look under "Special Reports"); *see also* Mark Muecke, Consumers Union, *Payday Lenders Burden Working Families and the U.S. Armed Forces* 2 (July 2003).

443 Steven M. Graves & Christopher L. Peterson, *Predatory Lending and the Military: The Law and Geography of "Payday" Loans in Military Towns* (Mar. 29, 2005), *available at* www.responsiblelending.org/research/index.cfm?tid=2&tyid=2.

444 Uriah King, Wei Li, Delvin Davis & Keith Ernst, *Race Matters: The Concentration of Payday Lenders in African-American Neighborhoods in North Carolina* (Center for Responsible Lending Mar. 22, 2005), *available at* www.responsiblelending.org/research/index.cfm?tid=2&tyid=2

445 *See* § 12.3, *infra*.

7.5.5.2 Payday Lending: Big Business

Payday lending is a booming business. Some states that have legalized payday lending collect data on industry size and volume of business. For example, Colorado consumers borrowed over $291 million in 2003 from 387 lenders, a significant increase from the $106 million loaned in 2000 by 186 lenders.[446] In Indiana, the number of registered lenders jumped from 15 in 1994 to 117 (with 580 outlets) in 2001. By 2003, the number of licensees declined to 44 operating out of 313 offices, due to the impact of an Indiana Supreme Court decision and subsequent revisions to Indiana law. Since Mississippi legalized payday lending in 1998, it has issued at least 625 payday loan licenses. There are approximately 450 such lenders in Ohio. Washington has licensed 124 lenders with 378 outlets that made over $1 billion in loans in 2003, up from 90 licensed lenders with 287 outlets making loans of $580 million in 1999. By the end of 1999, North Carolina had licensed 220 lenders who lent over $720 million.[447] Even though payday lending is now illegal in North Carolina, the number of storefronts that make these loans with bank partners or by using subterfuges are estimated to range from 385 to 612.[448] During 2004, Missouri issued 1,198 payday loan licenses. These licensees made almost 2.6 million loans.[449] As of November 2003, the industry in Florida had 1,035 locations owned by 208 lenders and earned about $129 million in fees on $1.1 billion

in loans.[450] By 2004, payday lenders in Florida made 3.9 million loans totaling $1.5 billion which generated $158.2 million in loan fees.[451] Oklahoma reports 404 licensees originating $95.2 million in loans and generating advance fees totaling $13.3 million.[452] During 2004, two researchers compiled information regarding the number of storefronts in twenty states and the results are listed in their report.[453]

Nationally, about 15,000 licensed storefronts are now open.[454] The "mature" market is estimated to be 25,000 offices generating $6.75 billion annually in fees alone.[455] One of the publicly-traded national payday lenders announced its loan volume for fiscal 2003 at about $485.8 million, including $63.8 million in loan volume "processed" for Republic Bank, compared to over $105 million in 1998. Net charge-offs were only 5.4% of loan volume.[456] This company's average loan amount for its non-Republic Bank loans was $268.00 and average fee was $42.71, resulting in an average annual percentage rate (APR) of 494.26%.[457]

The largest payday lender filed extensive information with the Securities and Exchange Commission at the time it decided to become a publicly traded company in 2004.[458] That document revealed that the company made over 10 million loans in 2003 for a loan volume of almost $3.3 billion.[459] The company maintained 1,949 stores in 34 states, California being the biggest revenue producing state. The company partnered with BankWest in Pennsylvania,

---

446 *Cf.* Colorado Department of Law 2003 Deferred Deposit Lenders Annual Report *with* Colorado Department of Law 2000 Deferred Deposit Lenders Annual Report *available at* www.ago.state.co.us/UCCC/UCCCHOME.htm.

447 Jean Ann Fox & Edmund Mierzwinski, Consumer Federation of America & U.S. PIRG, Rent-a-Bank Payday Lending: How Banks Help Payday Lenders Evade State Consumer Protections (Nov. 2001); Jean Ann Fox, Consumer Federation of America, Safe Harbor for Usury: Recent Developments in Payday Lending (Sept. 1999); North Carolina Office of the Commissioner of Banks in its Report to the General Assembly on Payday Lending (Feb. 22, 2001), *available at* www.nccob.org/NR/rdonlyres/2A95D7DA-75C0-49F3-B896-CAC45D947727/0/CheckCashersReporttoGenAssembly.pdf; Indiana Department of Financial Institutions, Annual Report for Year Ended Dec. 31, 2003, at 47–51, *available at* www.in.gov/dfi/publications, go to "Annual Reports"; Washington State Department of Financial Institutions Payday Lending Report: Statistics and Trends for 2003, *available at* www.dfi.wa.gov/news/DFI_PaydayReport.pdf.

448 *Compare* Uriah King, Wei Li, Delvin Davis & Keith Ernst, *Race Matters: The Concentration of Payday Lenders in African-American Neighborhoods in North Carolina* at 8 (Center for Responsible Lending Mar. 22, 2005), *available at* www.responsiblelending.org/research/index.cfm?tid=2&tyid=2 *with* Steven M. Graves & Christopher L. Peterson, *Predatory Lending and the Military: The Law and Geography of "Payday" Loans in Military Towns* at 132 (Mar. 29, 2005), *available at* www.responsiblelending.org/research/index.cfm?tid=2&tyid=2

449 Missouri Division of Finance Report (Jan. 18, 2005), *available at* www.missouri-finance.org/pdfs/survey.pdf (the 2002 figures were 912 licensees extending 2 million loans).

450 Florida Office of Financial Regulation Deferred Presentment Program, Annual Report to Legislature 6 (Jan. 1, 2004).

451 Veritec, *Florida Trends in Deferred Presentment: State of Florida Deferred Presentment Program* (Dec. 2004), *available at* www.veritecs.com/FL_Trends_Dec_2004.pdf.

452 Veritec, *Oklahoma Trends in Deferred Presentment: Oklahoma Deferred Presentment Program* (Dec. 2004), *available at* www.veritecs.com/OK_Trends_12_2004.pdf.

453 Steven M. Graves & Christopher L. Peterson, *Predatory Lending and the Military: The Law and Geography of "Payday" Loans in Military Towns* (Mar. 29, 2005), *available at* www.responsiblelending.org/research/index.cfm?tid=2&tyid=2.

454 Jerry L. Robinson, Stephens, Inc., Update on the Payday Loan Industry: Observations on Recent Industry Developments (Sept. 26, 2003). Stephens, Inc. is a Little Rock, Arkansas investment firm; its website is located at www.stephens.com.

455 Stephens, Inc., Non-Bank Financial Services Industry Notes (Mar. 23, 2000); Stephens, Inc., Developing "Payday Advance" Business (Sept. 28, 1999); Bob Van Voris, *Payday Loans Under Scrutiny*, The Nat'l L.J., May 17, 1999, B1 at 4.

456 Ace Cash Express, 2003 Form 10-K: Annual Report Pursuant to Section 13 or 15(d) of the Securities Exchange Act of 1934, at 23, 24, *available at* www.sec.gov/Archives/edgar/data/849116/000095013403013059/d09248e10vk.htm#007.

457 *Id.* The APR was calculated by assuming the amount financed was $225.29 ($268.00 minus $42.71), payment due was $268.00, and the loan was outstanding for 14 days.

458 Advance America, Cash Advance Centers, Inc.: Form S-1 SEC Registration Statement of Aug. 13, 2004, *available at* www.sec.gov/Archives/edgar/data/1299704/000104746904026511/a2141558zs-1.htm.

459 *Id.* at 2.

First Fidelity Bank in Michigan, Republic Bank & Trust in North Carolina and Texas, and Venture Bank in Arkansas.[460] The bank partnerships accounted for about 30% of all revenues in 2003.[461] The bank model was used in 521 of its stores (about 20% of all stores) in these five states.[462] Interestingly, in 2003, 69.4% of customers repaid their payday loans in full on or before the due date; 95.4% repaid in full on or before the due date or within 14 days thereafter; 0.2% repaid before the check was deposited in bank for collection. Only approximately 4.4% of all checks were deposited and of those 66.5% cleared or were ultimately collected. Roughly, only 1.7% of the total amount loaned was not recovered.[463] This does not take into account additional fees added, such as late fees, non-sufficient fund fees, and extra civil penalties in some states.

Given the high fees charged and low net charge-offs, it is not surprising that this business is lucrative. Though most of the payday lenders are private companies (which makes it difficult to obtain financial information about them), payday lenders in Tennessee showed a return on assets of 22.72% and a return on equity of 30.37%.[464] One of the state-chartered banks (County Bank, Rehobeth Delaware) partnering with payday lenders in 2003 experienced a 2.69% return on average assets (excellent for a bank since a good return is 1% or more) and a 32.10% return on average equity.[465]

7.5.5.3 The Lenders and the Loans Described

Payday loans go by a variety of names, including "deferred presentment," "cash advances," "deferred deposits," or "check loans." They all work like this: the consumer provides the lender a live or a post-dated check written on his or her bank account for the amount borrowed plus a fee.[466] The fee is stated as either a percentage of the check or loan amount or in a dollar amount. This fee translates into annual percentage rates typically not less than 390% and averaging close to 500%, though advocates and credit code enforcement agencies have noted rates of 1300% to 7300%.[467] The check is then held for one to four weeks (usually until the customer's payday), at which time the consumer redeems the check by paying the face amount, allows the check to be cashed, or pays another fee to extend the loan.

These loans are marketed as a quick and easy way to get cash until the next payday. To qualify, consumers need only be employed for a period of time with the current employer, maintain a personal checking account, and show a pay stub and bank statement. The lender may use Telecheck to determine if another payday loan to the same customer is outstanding or to discover if the customer has bounced checks in the past. Otherwise, credit checks or other inquiries about ability to repay are not routinely performed.

The largest segment of the industry consists of storefronts that provide only one product: payday loans. The leading examples as of mid-2003 include Advance America (1,750 stores in 32 states, up from 1,325 outlets in 23 states in 2000), CNG (Cash'n Go) Financial (750 stores in 25 states, up from 658 stores in 23 states in 2000), and Check Into Cash (705 stores in 21 states, up from 500 stores in 15 states in 2000). Other payday lenders offer other products as well, such as pawn loans and check cashing services. The largest of these "full-service" lenders include Ace Cash Express (862 offices in 31 states, down from 1,000 locations in 29 states in 2000), Dollar Financial (621 locations in 17 states and 409 MoneyMart Express document transmitter locations, up from 244 stores in 12 states in 2000), and Cash America (504 stores in 16 states).[468]

---

460 *Id.* at 13–14.

461 *Id.* at 14.

462 *Id.* at 63.

463 The math is as follows: 10.178 million loans times 4.4%. Result is 447,832. Of these, 33.5% was not recovered (100 minus 66.5% that were ultimately recovered). Result is 150,023. Multiply this by the average amount of each check in 2003 ($321 + $52) and the result is $55,958,847. Divide this by $3.271 billion in loans made in 2003 and the result is 1.7%. Results are based on the assumption that loans made and customers are the same number.

464 Tennessee Department of Financial Institutions, Report to the 101st General Assembly on the Deferred Presentment Services Act 1999 at 9; Jean Ann Fox, Consumer Federation of America, The Growth of Legal Loan Sharking: A Report on the Payday Loan Industry (Nov. 1998).

465 American Banker (Mar. 31, 2004) (list of the community banks with the highest rates of return).

466 Many such lenders offer check-cashing or pawnbroking services. There are also "stand alone" payday lenders.

467 Data collected by the Colorado and Indiana credit code enforcement agencies show an average APR of 486% and 498%, respectively. *See* State of Colorado, Department of Law 1998 Post-Dated Check Cashers Supervised Lenders' Annual Report; Indiana Department of Financial Institutions, Summary of Payday Lender Examinations Conducted from July through October 1999. The Indiana audit revealed at least one transaction with an APR of 7,300%. *See also* Jean Ann Fox, Consumer Federation of America, The Growth of Legal Loan Sharking: A Report on the Payday Loan Industry (Nov. 1998). Table One of this report shows that the payday lenders surveyed charged fees that produce annual percentage rates ranging from a minimum of 521% to 1250% for a 7-day loan and 261% to 625% for a 14-day loan. A report by the North Carolina Office of the Commissioner of Banks states that the APR on almost 63% of all loans made in 1999 ranged from 460% to 805% while 9.83% of the loans ranged from 920% to 6,441%! Office of the North Carolina Commissioner of Banks, Report to the General Assembly on Payday Lending (Feb. 22, 2001).

468 *Compare* Jerry L. Robinson, Stephens, Inc., Update on the Payday Loan Industry: Observations on Recent Industry Developments (Sept. 26, 2003) *with* Stephens, Inc., Non-Bank Financial Services Industry Notes (Mar. 23, 2000).

7.5.5.4 Types of Abuses

The abuses occur in the making and collection of payday loans in a variety of ways. Cash-strapped consumers rarely have the ability to repay the entire loan when their payday arrives because that leaves little or nothing on which to live until the next paycheck. Lenders then encourage consumers to rollover or refinance one payday loan with another. The result is that the consumer pays another round of charges and fees and obtains no additional cash in return. Lawsuits and news reports reveal scores of consumers who are unable to climb out of this debt treadmill.[469] State agency audits show that, on average over a twelve month period, consumers renewed their loans from ten to twelve times, though one consumer renewed sixty-six times.[470]

Further, payday lenders often threaten to use the criminal system to collect these debts or routinely file criminal charges when a check is returned for insufficient funds. These *in terrorem* tactics are only possible because the lenders are holding checks. This fact makes the collection process easier and more reliable than when consumers only sign a promissory note to repay. Whether or not the checks technically constitute collateral for the loans, the retention of the checks, in effect, gives these lenders a huge advantage in collecting on their loans.

Payday lenders may fail to give Truth in Lending disclosures, making it impossible to understand the true cost of these loans. Some consumers are likely to forego such a loan if the paperwork told them that the APR was 520%, rather than 20% of the check. Even when TILA disclosures are given, they may be inaccurate.

Finally, payday lenders in usury cap states disguise these transactions, claiming that they are not making loans. In Texas, for example, the two main subterfuges presently used are "sale-leaseback" transactions and "cash-back ad sales."[471] In the sale-leaseback scam, the lender "buys" an

---

469   *See, e.g.*, Smith v. Short Term Loans, Ltd. Liab. Co., 2001 U.S. Dist. LEXIS 1554 (N.D. Ill. Feb. 9, 2001) (one named plaintiff received 15 payday loans in a 9 month period, while the other plaintiff obtained 11 loans in an 8 month span); Turner v. E-Z Check Cashing, Inc., 35 F. Supp. 2d 1042 (M.D. Tenn. 1999) (renewing the loan eight times cost the consumer in this case $840 in fees alone to obtain $300 in cash); Goldx Fin. Services, Inc. v. Bank of Am., 2001 WL 1219238 (Cal. Ct. App. Oct. 11, 2001) (payday lender involved in this suit against its bank claimed that the average number of transactions per customers at two of its locations was about 21); Wirdzek v. Serv. Annex, Ltd. Liab. Co., Clearinghouse Nos. 53,555A (complaint), 53,555B (class action settlement agreement) (Cal. Super. Ct., Kern County, Mar. 22, 1999) (named plaintiff either rolled over or obtained new loans 14 times in six months from the same lender); Johnson v. The Cash Store, 68 P.3d 1099 (Wash. Ct. App. 2003) (15 rollovers in 7 months); Keith Ernst, John Farris, & Uriah King, Center for Responsible Lending, *Quantifying the Economic Cost of Predatory Payday Lending* 5 (Dec. 18, 2003) (borrowers who received five or more payday loans per year account for 91% of industry revenue; 56% of revenue is obtained from customers with thirteen or more loans); Steven Rothman, *Officials Call Payday Financing "Loan Sharking,"* Bank Rate Monitor Online, Feb. 18, 1998 (describes a Kentucky consumer who borrowed $150 but paid more than $1000 in fees over a six month period to renew); David Horst, *Hard Lesson Learned in Borrowing on Paycheck,* The Post-Crescent (Wisconsin), Jan. 4, 1998 (consumer borrowed $1200 from five payday lenders and paid $200 every two weeks just to cover the renewal fees); *see also* Editorial, *Advance to Quicksand,* The Orlando Sentinel, Mar. 31, 1999; Editorial, *Legalized Loan Sharking: State should stop gouging by payday lenders,* The San Diego Union Tribune, Mar. 25, 1999.

470   Indiana Department of Financial Institutions, Summary of Payday Lender Examinations Conducted from July through October 1999. Further, the Department reported that of the 54,508 loans reviewed, the average amount financed was $165.74 and average finance charge was $27.29. Because the average consumer renewed 10 times each year, she paid $272.90 ($27.29 × 10) in fees alone to borrow $165.74. *See also* Washington State Department of Financial Institutions Payday Lending Report: Statistics and Trends for 2003, *available at* www.dfi.wa.gov/news/DFI_PaydayReport.pdf (shows that 51.4% of borrowers took out 6 or more loans in a year); Florida Office of Financial Regulation Deferred Presentment Program, Annual Report to Legislature 14 (Jan. 1, 2004) (on average consumers took out

7.6 loans per year); Illinois Department of Financial Institutions, Short Term Lending Final Report 26 (2000) (Department found an average of 13 contracts per payday loan customer, during an average six-month period). The Iowa Division of Banking also surveyed its payday loan licensees and found that the average number of loans per year was 12.5 (Dec. 2000). The North Carolina Office of the Commissioner of Banks reported that over 38% of all customers made 10 to 19 such loans in 1999. N.C. Office of the Commissioner of Banks, Report to the General Assembly on Payday Lending (Feb. 22, 2001). Further, the average number of loans each payday borrower obtained in North Carolina in 2000 was seven. *See* Michael A. Stegman & Robert Faris, *Payday Lending: A Business Model that Encourages Chronic Borrowing,* 17 Econ. Dev. Q. 8 (Feb. 2003), *available at* www.kenaninstitute.unc.edu/Centers/CCC/CCC_Publications_Presentations/PaydayChronicEDQ.pdf. Professor Stegman notes that the North Carolina figures "understate the real magnitude of the problem because they do not account for a family's use of more than one payday lender at a time or the use of a loan from one payday lender to pay off another." *Id.* at 20. His study concludes that financial performance of payday lenders *hinges* on the successful conversion of borrowers into chronic payday loan users, in large measure. *Id.* at 25. Interestingly, the Comptroller of the Currency found that one payday loan company provided incentives to its employees to actively promote repeat borrowing. Office of the Comptroller of the Currency, Fact Sheet: Eagle National Bank Consent Order 2 (Jan. 3, 2002), *available at* www.occ.treas.gov/02rellst.htm.

471   *See* Ruth Cardella, Consumers Union, Wolf in Sheep's Clothing: Payday Loans Disguise Illegal Lending (Feb. 1999); Consumers Union, Sale-Leaseback Lenders Defy Regulation (Feb. 2001); *see also* Upshaw v. Ga. Catalog Sales, 206 F.R.D. 694 (M.D. Ga. 2002) (class certification granted in catalog sales case); Cashback Catalog Sales, Inc. v. Price, 102 F. Supp. 2d 1375 (S.D. Ga. 2000) (catalog sale sham); Fed. Trade Comm'n v. Consumer Money Markets, Clearinghouse No. 53,282 (D. Nev. Oct. 2000) (FTC enforcement action against credit card lender for marketing a cash back catalog scheme); Henry v. Cash Today, Inc., 199 F.R.D. 566 (S.D. Tex. 2000) (class certification

item of personal property from the consumer, for example, a television, and "leases" it back for a "rental payment" which is due in two weeks. The cash-back ads are even more transparent. The consumer must "buy" an advertisement of one line for every $100 borrowed and pay an "ad fee" of $33 per $100 (translating to an APR of 858%). In both scenarios, the lender requires a signed check just in case the consumer fails to make the payment in two weeks hence.

Other newly developed schemes include loans that are *de facto* secured by Social Security or SSI benefits as alleged in one case.[472] Payday loans also are disguised as Internet service.[473] These deals advertise cash back for signing up for Internet access through in-store computers.[474] Others offer cash back for joining a website at a cost of $6 per day or $180 per month.[475] Advertisements directed at check cashers and payday lenders tell them: "Kiss Regulators Goodbye: The Internet Advantage."[476] Internet initiated payday loans are described in detail in a 2004 report issued by Consumer Federation of America.[477] This is a "must read"

---

granted in cash back ad sale case on TILA, RICO, usury, UDAP, and civil conspiracy claims); SAL Leasing, Inc. v. Arizona *ex rel.* Napolitano, 10 P.3d 1221 (Ariz. Ct. App. 2000) (sale-leaseback in car context are loans); State *ex rel.* Salazar v. The Cash Now Store, Inc., 31 P.3d 161 (Colo. 2001) (tax refund assignments are loans); New York *ex rel.* Spitzer v. JAG NY, L.L.C., No. 5302 (N.Y. Sup. Ct. Jan. 20, 2005) (cash back catalog sale is a sham; court issues permanent injunction and sets up a restitution proceeding), available on the CD-Rom accompanying this volume.

472 *See* Favors v. Stewart, Clearinghouse No. 54,590 (Ga. Super. Ct. July 9, 2002) (complaint) (the lender obtains its "security" for the loan by requiring that the consumer directly deposit his or her stream of Social Security of SSI payments into bank accounts controlled by the lender).

473 Morton v. Cyber Services Technology, Clearinghouse No. 54,588 (Ala. Cir. Ct. May 16, 2002) (complaint); Short On Cash.Net of New Castle, Inc. v. Dept. of Fin. Inst., 811 N.E.2d 819 (Ind. Ct. App. 2004) (sale of Internet service with immediate cash back of $100, the sale of multiple accounts so that customers can receive multiples of $100, and the restricted use of the Internet at the storefront render these transactions loans); North Carolina, *ex rel.* Cooper v. NCCS Loans, Inc., No. 02 CVS 1844 (N.C. Just. Ct. June 10, 2004) (Order) (Internet rebate scheme is a disguised loan; loans voided; permanent injunction issues), available on the CD-Rom accompanying this volume. See also the discussion of checks and electronic fund transfers in § 7.5.5.8, *infra*.

474 Jean Ann Fox & Anna Petrini, *Internet Payday Lending: How High-Priced Lenders Use the Internet to Mire Borrowers in Debt and Evade State Consumer Protections* (Consumer Federation of America Nov. 30, 2004); Jean Ann Fox, *Unsafe and Unsound: Payday Lenders Hide Behind FDIC Bank Charters to Peddle Usury* 7–9 (Consumer Federation of America Mar. 2004); Mark Muecke, Consumers Union, *Payday Lenders Burden Working Families and the U.S. Armed Forces* 2 (July 2003).

475 Mark Muecke, Consumers Union, *Payday Lenders Burden Working Families and the U.S. Armed Forces* 4 (July 2003).

476 Jean Ann Fox, Consumer Federation of America, Unsafe and Unsound: Payday Lenders Hide Behind FDIC Bank Charters to Peddle Usury 7 (Mar. 2004).

477 Jean Ann Fox & Anna Petrini, *Internet Payday Lending: How*

---

for practitioners or consumers concerned about the special abuses that arise in this context.

7.5.5.5 State Regulation of Payday Lending

Whether payday loans and the accompanying abuses violate a panoply of state and federal laws often depends, in the first instance, on the state of the law in the state where the loan transaction took place.[478] The states fall into three categories.

Category one: Fourteen states, the Virgin Islands, and Puerto Rico require payday lenders to comply with the state's small loan or criminal usury laws which maintain interest rate caps, most commonly, of 36% per annum.[479]

High-Priced Lenders Use the Internet to Mire Borrowers in Debt and Evade State Consumer Protections (Consumer Federation of America Nov. 30, 2004).

478 A notable and increasingly problematic exception applies to national and state banks and similar entities, discussed in § 3.13, *supra*.

479 These states are: Arkansas; Connecticut; Georgia; Maine; Maryland; Massachusetts; Michigan; New Jersey; New York; North Carolina (payday loan law expired on Aug. 31, 2001); Pennsylvania; Puerto Rico; Rhode Island; Vermont; Virgin Islands; West Virginia. The citations to these statutes can be found in Appx. A, *infra*.

The Attorneys General in Florida, Indiana, Maryland, and New York have issued opinions letters finding that payday loans do, indeed, violate the laws of those states. The New York Banking Department has issued a letter warning against payday lending in excess of that state's usury cap.

The Indiana Attorney General opinion was expressly upheld by Indiana's highest court. Livingston v. Fast Cash USA, Inc., 753 N.E.2d 572 (Ind. 2001). Subsequently, a number of class action cases were filed against payday lenders in Indiana. *See, e.g.,* Smith v. Steinkamp, 318 F.3d 775 (7th Cir. 2003) (affirming partial denial of motion to compel arbitration); Jump v. ACP Enterprises, 224 F. Supp. 2d 1216 (N.D. Ind. 2002) (lender's motion to dismiss TILA claims denied); Bullock v. Credit Bureau of Greater Indianapolis, 272 F. Supp. 2d 780 (S.D. Ind. 2003) (FDCPA claim barred by Rooker-Feldman doctrine). However, the Indiana legislature responded by passing payday loan legislation in 2002.

Massachusetts shut down a payday loan store. *See In re* Jay Patel, Naranbhai Patel, & Mailboxes, Etc., Clearinghouse No. 53,033 (Mass. Comm'r of Banks, Apr. 20, 2000) (order to cease and desist).

Arkansas's usury cap is located in its constitution. Despite that provision, the state legislature enacted a payday loan law (called the "Check-Casher's Act") permitting "fees" (and avoiding the use of the word "interest") which exceeded the constitutional usury cap. The highest court held that the transactions were loans, paving the way for the lower court to find the payday loan law unconstitutional. Luebbers v. Money Store, Inc., 40 S.W.3d 745 (Ark. 2001). A number of class actions have been filed in the last few years against payday lenders in Arkansas, including one seeking to enjoin the relevant Arkansas agency from issuing any further licenses to payday lenders on the grounds that the fees charged by the lenders are illegal under the state constitution and the agency's use of public funds to finance its operation is illegal. McGhee v. Arkansas State Board

These laws typically contain extensive provisions specifying the maximum loan amount, the maximum and/or minimum term, the maximum interest rate and permitted charges, the penalties for the charging of excessive interest and other violations, the licensing requirements, the prepayment rebate formulas, the conditions under which lenders can require insurance, if annual reports must be filed, the required contract provisions, and the prohibited contract provisions.[480] Because the allowable interest rates and fees are substantially below that which the payday industry charges, the lenders in these states are usually operating illegally by ignoring the small loan law.[481] It is in these states where the industry has the greatest incentive to disguise the transaction or to partner with banks.

Category two: The small loan laws of two states permit payday lenders to operate and charge any interest rate or fee which the parties to the loan agree to pay. The lenders in these states usually must comply with other provisions of the state's small loan act, however.[482]

Category three: Thirty-four states and the District of Columbia have enacted industry-backed laws or regulations specifically authorizing payday lending, usually in derogation of a protective usury statute.[483] Generally, these laws require either licensing or registration. Some mandate that the lenders put up a bond and/or maintain a certain level of net assets or worth. They typically specify a maximum term and maximum amount of the loan and fix the interest rate or fees to be charged.[484] While these fees seem small in the abstract, $15–$33 per $100, they translate into enormous annual percentage rates.[485]

Where payday loans are authorized in category three states, many obligate the lender to provide a written agreement to the consumer. More than half of these states prohibit rollovers, that is, the refinancing or repaying of one such loan with another, at which time the consumer incurs another round of charges. Many payday lenders avoid this prohibition however by refinancing the loan rather than renewing it. Other states set a maximum number of such loans that a consumer may have outstanding at any one time. Additionally, most states create some type of criminal or administrative penalties. However, only a few states provide for some type of limited private right of action allowing the consumer to obtain relief against the lender. Several states prohibit the lender from threatening to file or filing criminal charges against a consumer as a mechanism to collect on the debt. Finally, in seven of these states, only check cashers are allowed to make payday loans.

7.5.5.6 Legal Claims

The first line of defense raised by payday lenders when sued in states where such loans are illegal is to claim that the transaction is not a loan at all. The industry likes to characterize these deals as the deferred presentment of a check

---

of Collection Agencies, 2005 WL 107125 (Ark. Jan. 20, 2005). *See also* USA Check Cashers v. Island, 76 S.W.3d 243 (Ark. 2002) (class action certification granted); The Money Place, Ltd. Liab. Co. v. Barnes, 78 S.W.3d 730 (Ark. 2002) (same); THE/FRE, Inc. v. Martin, 78 S.W.3d 723 (Ark. 2002) (same); F & G Fin. Serv., Inc. v. Barnes, 82 S.W.3d 162 (Ark. 2002) (same). One of these cases resulted in a settlement that was challenged because the award to the class consisted of savings bonds that would not mature for another 16 years. Ballard v. Martin, 79 S.W.3d 838 (Ark. 2002), *cert. denied*, 123 S. Ct. 871 (2003) (court upheld settlement).

480 For a description of the history surrounding the need for and the passage of small loan laws, see § 2.3.3.2, *supra*.

481 One *caveat* is that the state enforcement agency may attempt to exempt payday lenders from the reach of the small loan act by administrative fiat. For example, while the Florida Attorney General did issue an opinion that "deferred deposit" checks were actually loans, the opinion provided a *de facto* safe harbor for check cashers who charged fees within the statutory limit for check cashing. See Betts v. Advance Am., 213 F.R.D. 466 (M.D. Fla. 2003). More importantly, the Department of Banking and Finance issued an opinion that not only included the same safe harbor, but also characterized the "deferred deposit" transactions as check cashing, not loans. The Florida Legislature affirmed this characterization by enacting a law permitting "deferred presentments" in 2001. Florida courts are now split on the issue of whether payday loans made before the effective date of the 2001 law constitute loans. *Compare* Betts v. McKenzie Check Advance of Florida, L.L.C., 879 So. 2d 667 (Fla. Dist. Ct. App. 2004) (the transactions constitute loans) *with* Betts v. ACE Cash Express, 827 So. 2d 294 (Fla. Dist. Ct. App. 2002) (the transactions do not constitute loans).

482 These states are: New Mexico and Wisconsin. See citations in Appx. A, *infra*.

483 These states are: Alabama, Alaska, Arizona, California, Colorado, Delaware, the District of Columbia, Florida, Hawaii, Idaho, Illinois, Indiana, Iowa, Kansas, Kentucky, Louisiana, Minnesota, Mississippi, Missouri, Montana, Nebraska, Nevada, New Hampshire, North Dakota, Ohio, Oklahoma, Oregon, South Carolina, South Dakota, Tennessee, Texas, Utah, Virginia, Washington, Wyoming. See citations in Appx. A, *infra*. In 2000, the Texas Finance Commission adopted regulations to permit small loan lenders to hold a check; other provisions of the small loan act apply, though the allowable rates are higher than for other small loans. Regulations in Illinois and Oregon have both survived initial challenges by the payday loan industry. *See* S. 51 Dev. Corp. v. Vega, 781 N.E.2d 528 (Ill. App. Ct. 2002) (legislation contained a permissible delegation of authority to the state agency; subsequent regulations were not void or issued in violation of state administrative procedures act); Northwest Title Loans v. Div. of Fin., 42 P.3d 313 (Or. Ct. App. 2002). Delaware, which does not have a usury cap, passed a payday loan law in 2002 that provides very limited protections for payday loan borrowers. South Dakota, another state without a usury cap, passed a similarly limited payday loan law in 2002.

484 *See, e.g.*, Porter v. Ace Cash Express, Inc., 2000 WL 1610632 (E.D. La. Oct. 26, 2000), *aff'd*, 277 F.3d 1372 (5th Cir. 2001) (table) (interpreting Louisiana's various credit laws to find that a payday loan flipped 10 times was legal; Louisiana's payday loan law not applicable as loans were consummated before its effective date).

485 *See* Jean Ann Fox, Consumer Federation of America, The Growth of Legal Loan Sharking: A Report on the Payday Loan Industry (Nov. 1998).

(or create the sale-leaseback or ad sale disguise). In category one states, the courts have uniformly pierced this smoke-screen to hold that the transaction is, in substance, a loan.[486] Several consequences flow from this fundamental finding. The state usury law is violated not only because the usury cap is exceeded (often by more than 100 times) but also because, in small loan states, licensing and other require-ments are ignored. Payday companies routinely fail to give Truth in Lending disclosures because of the pretense that the arrangement is not a loan.[487]

In addition, several courts have addressed the viability of a RICO claim and ruled favorably.[488] In the payday loan context, the claim arises where the state usury law is vio-lated and the amount of interest charged or collected exceeds twice the cap.[489] Violating RICO is particularly significant

---

486 Cashback Catalog Sales, Inc., 102 F. Supp. 2d 1375 (S.D. Ga. 2000); Turner v. E-Z Check Cashing, Inc., 35 F. Supp. 2d 1042 (M.D. Tenn. 1999); Burden v. York, Clearinghouse No. 52,502 (E.D. Ky. Sept. 29, 1999); Hamilton v. HLT Check Exch., 987 F. Supp. 953 (E.D. Ky. 1997); USA Payday Cash Advance Centers v. Oxendine, 585 S.E.2d 924 (Ga. Ct. App. 2003) (payday lender failed to exhaust administrative remedies before challenging the authority of the state loan commissioner; in doing so, court confirms that payday transactions come within the definition of "loan" under the Industrial Loan Act); Indus. Loan Comm'r v. Edwards Fin. Services, Clearinghouse No. 54,589 (Ga. Super. Ct. Oct. 14, 2002) (Civ. Action No. 1998cv02055) (granting Commissioner summary judgment on small loan act and TILA claim); Short On Cash.Net of New Castle, Inc. v. Dept. of Fin. Inst., 811 N.E.2d 819 (Ind. Ct. App. 2004) (sale of Internet service with immediate cash back of $100, the sale of multiple accounts so that customers can receive multiples of $100, and the restricted use of the Internet at the storefront render these transactions loans); White v. Check Holders, Inc., 996 S.W.2d 496 (Ky. 1999); New York ex rel. Spitzer v. JAG NY, L.L.C., No. 5302 (N.Y. Sup. Ct. Jan. 20, 2005) (cash back catalog sale is a sham; court issues permanent injunction and sets up a restitution proceeding), available on the CD-Rom accompanying this volume; North Carolina, ex rel. Cooper v. NCCS Loans, Inc., No. 02 CVS 1844 (N.C. Just. Ct. June 10, 2004) (Order) (Internet rebate scheme is a disguised loan; loans voided; permanent injunction issues), available on the CD-ROM accompanying this volume; Commonwealth v. Allstate Express Check Cashing, No. HD-44-1 (Cir. Ct. Rich-mond, Va. Oct. 20, 1993); see also Upshaw v. Ga. Catalog Sales, 206 F.R.D. 694 (M.D. Ga. 2002) (class certification granted in catalog sale case); Henry v. Cash Today, Inc., 199 F.R.D. 566 (S.D. Tex. 2000) (class certification granted in cash back ad sale case); Arrington v. Colleen, Inc., 2000 U.S. Dist. LEXIS 20651 (D. Md. Aug. 7, 2000) (order and memorandum denying lend-er's motion for summary judgment); SAL Leasing, Inc. v. Arizona ex rel. Napolitano, 10 P.3d 1221 (Ariz. Ct. App. 2000) (sale-leaseback in car title loan context); USA Check Cashers v. Island 76 S.W.3d 243 (Ark. 2002) (class certification granted; court noted class action vehicle well-suited for usury claim); Money Place v. Barnes, 78 S.W.3d 730 (Ark. 2002) (same); cf. Advance Am., Cash Advance Centers of Arkansas, Inc. v. Garrett, 40 S.W.3d 239 (Ark. 2001) (class certification reversed on usury and other claims and remanded as trial court imper-missibly ruled on the merits of the underlying claims). But compare Betts v. McKenzie Check Advance of Florida, L.L.C., 879 So. 2d 667 (Fla. Dist. Ct. App. 2004) (the transactions constitute loans) with Betts v. ACE Cash Express, 827 So. 2d 294 (Fla. Dist. Ct. App. 2002) ("deferred deposit" transaction constituted check cashing, not loan, based on the statutory definition; court relied on opinion confirming this position from the state Dept. of Banking) and Betts v. Advance Am., 213 F.R.D. 466 (M.D. Fla. 2003) (same, relying upon Betts v. ACE Cash Express).

487 Arrington v. Colleen, Inc., 2000 U.S. Dist. LEXIS 20651 (D. Md. Aug. 7, 2000) (order and memorandum denying lender's motion for summary judgment); Turner v. E-Z Check Cashing, Inc., 35 F. Supp. 2d 1042 (M.D. Tenn. 1999); Hamilton v. HLT Check Exch., 987 F. Supp. 953 (E.D. Ky. 1997); Indus. Loan Comm'r v. Edwards Fin. Services, Clearinghouse No. 54,589 (Ga. Super. Ct. Oct. 14, 2002) (granting Commissioner sum-mary judgment on small loan act and TILA claim).

The Federal Reserve Board, which promulgates regulations and interpretations under the Truth in Lending Act, amended the definition of credit in the Official Staff Commentary to include payday loans. 65 Fed. Reg. 17129 (Mar. 31, 2000). Payday lenders have argued with partial success that disclosures need not be given in loans entered into before the effective date (Oct. 1, 2000) of this Commentary addition. Compare Clement v. Amscot Corp., 176 F. Supp. 2d 1292 (M.D. Fla. 2001); Ballard v. AA Check Cashers, Inc., Clearinghouse No. 53,502 (W.D. Ark. Nov. 21, 2000) (order of dismissal), aff'd, 19 Fed. Appx. 468 (Sept. 25, 2001); Cox v. AA Check Cashers, Clearinghouse No. 53,502 (W.D. Ark. Nov. 8, 2000) with Arrington v. Colleen, Inc., 2000 U.S. Dist. LEXIS 20651 (D. Md. Aug. 7, 2000) (order and memorandum denying lender's motion for summary judgment); see also Clay v. Johnson, 264 F.3d 744 (7th Cir. 2001) (court finds that a FRB statement to the effect that a regulation or commentary change is a "clarification," and not a change in the law, is entitled to deference; case involved the payment schedule disclosure on a home improvement financing contract). See generally National Consumer Law Center, Truth in Lending § 2.5.5 (5th ed. 2003 and Supp.).

488 Cashback Catalog Sales, Inc., 102 F. Supp. 2d 1375 (S.D. Ga. 2000); Arrington v. Colleen, Inc., 2000 U.S. Dist. LEXIS 20651 (D. Md. Aug. 7, 2000) (order and memorandum denying lend-er's motion for summary judgment); Burden v. York, Clearing-house No. 52,502 (E.D. Ky. Sept. 29, 1999); Hamilton v. HLT Check Exch., 987 F. Supp. 953 (E.D. Ky. 1997); see also Upshaw v. Ga. Catalog Sales, 206 F.R.D. 694 (M.D. Ga. 2002) (class certification granted in catalog sales case on RICO and usury claims); Henry v. Cash Today, Inc., 199 F.R.D. 566 (S.D. Tex. 2000) (class certification granted in cash back ad sale case). But see Betts v. Advance Am., 213 F.R.D. 466 (M.D. Fla. 2003) (as the Florida statute defines payday loans as check cashing and, as such, they are not illegal, RICO claim based on collection of an unlawful debt is dismissed); Purdie v. ACE Cash Express, 2002 WL 31730967 (N.D. Tex. Oct. 29, 2002) (dismissing RICO claim against lender and bank for failure to establish an association-in-fact enterprise), vacated upon par-ties' motion, 2003 WL 21447854 (N.D. Tex. June 13, 2003) (class settlement and motion for leave to amend the complaint); Bellizan v. Easy Money of La., Inc., 2002 WL 1611648 (E.D. La. July 19, 2002) (RICO claims dismissed).

489 For a discussion of the elements of a RICO claim in the credit transaction context, see §§ 10.8.5.3.2, 12.6, infra. Many states have enacted their own version of a RICO statute that may offer a remedy in state court. See 10.8.5.3.2, infra. But see State v. Roderick, 704 So. 2d 49 (Miss. 1997) (state RICO act is unconstitutionally vague as applied to the defendant; the payday

for recovery purposes because the act allows the consumer to hold the individuals liable as well as the company as an entity.[490] Further, a judicial finding that RICO has been violated is often predicated upon fraudulent conduct which may render the judgment non-dischargeable in bankruptcy.[491]

If the lender threatens or uses the criminal bad check law to collect the debt, such behavior may violate the state unfair or deceptive trade practices act.[492] The *Turner* court found that the transaction did not involve the passing of a "bad" check, that is, the lender knew the consumer did not have sufficient funds in the checking account at the time of the loan to cover the amount of the cash advanced.[493] It con-

stituted an unfair or deceptive act to threaten to do what the creditor had no legal right to do. Though not an issue raised in the *Turner* case, such conduct also violates state fair debt collection practices acts that apply to creditors as collectors (and the federal act where the collector is a third party).[494] Further, the lender's employee, an attorney, may be liable under the federal Fair Debt Collection Practices Act for the content of collection letters sent to the consumer while wearing her attorney hat.[495]

State federal credit repair laws may provide additional remedies in the payday lending context. Typically, these laws require registration, bonding, disclosures, and a right to cancel. Almost all offer a private cause of action, often with minimum damages, punitive damages, and attorney fees. Significantly, most of these state statutes cover organizations that assist or offer to assist consumers in obtaining extensions of credit.[496] Local storefronts who partner with banks

---

loan company had relied upon a green light it received from the attorney general's office to set up shop).

490 Short of succeeding on a RICO claim, disgorging the enormous profits made by lenders may be difficult, especially where the payday lender is a corporate entity and possesses little or no assets by the time litigation is concluded. An aggressive attorney general sued the individuals who owned the stock of and operated the payday loan business as a corporation seeking to pierce the corporate veil and claim the principals actively participated in the illegal operation. Greenberg v. Commonwealth *ex rel.* Virginia Att'y Gen., 499 S.E.2d 266 (Va. 1998). Though these claims failed against one of the principals (and the other settled) due to the particular facts of the case and peculiarities of Virginia law, the creative approach provides guidance to others seeking to get to the heart of the matter, punishing the individual as well as corporate wrongdoers.

491 *See* 11 U.S.C. § 523(a)(6); Kawaauhau v. Geiger, 523 U.S. 57, 118 S. Ct. 974, 140 L. Ed. 2d 90 (1998).

492 *See* Turner v. E-Z Check Cashing, 35 F. Supp. 2d 1042 (M.D. Tenn. 1999); Johnson v. The Cash Store, 68 P.3d 1099 (Wash. Ct. App. 2003) (court affirms trial court's refusal to re-open default judgment against the payday lender on this issue; $26,701 damage award affirmed).

493 Jones v. Kunin, 2000 U.S. Dist. LEXIS 6380 (S.D. Ill. May 1, 2000) (motion to dismiss denied in case where consumer sued under the Fair Debt Collections Practices Act based upon threats that the consumer engaged in unfair and deceptive acts by writing post-dated checks which were dishonored when presented for payment; court held that there was no intent to defraud when the parties agreed at the time a check is written that there are not sufficient funds to cover it); Hartke v. Ill. Payday Loans, Inc., 1999 U.S. Dist. LEXIS 14937 (C.D. Ill. Sept. 13, 1999) (in the course of denying the defendants' motion to dismiss, court observes that the Illinois bad check statute does not apply to agreements to hold post-dated checks because the payee knows the check is no good when written); Iowa Dep't of Justice, Informal Advisory No. 87, Clearinghouse No. 52,156 (Feb. 18, 1999) (in addition to interpreting the criminal code, the Attorney General's office reviewed Iowa's payday loan law, finding that the Legislature intended the non-sufficient fund fee contained therein to be the exclusive penalty available; collectors must resort to civil, not criminal court to collect). This opinion provides an excellent guide to advocates in examining their state bad check law to determine if payday loan hot checks constitute "bad" debts. *Cf.* Thompson v. Adcox, 63 S.W.3d 783 (Tenn. Ct. App. 2002) (post-dated check is not a "check" under the criminal worthless check statute at the time of its passing; however, borrower later committed fraud when he subsequently failed to pay check after notice of its nonpayment).

494 *See, e.g.,* Boyce v. Attorney's Dispatch Serv., 1999 WL 33495605 (S.D. Ohio Apr. 27, 1999) (court found "egregious conduct" on the part of a collector of a payday loan which violated the Fair Debt Collection Practices Act; the collector identified himself as a police officer and threatened criminal prosecution); King v. Cashland, Inc., 2000 Ohio App. LEXIS 3943 (Ohio Ct. App. Sept. 1, 2000) (court reversed grant of summary judgment on an invasion of privacy claim based upon payday lender's attempts to collect the debt). A jury awarded $310,000 in damages (including $290,000 in punitive damages) against a payday lender who wrongfully garnished $177 from a borrower's wages. Bill Braun, *Small Claims Case Grows to $310,000,* Tulsa World, Oct. 26, 2001. If the payday lender has already obtained a judgment against the borrower, however, a Fair Debt Collection Practices Act claim based on the illegality of the payday loan may be barred by the Rooker-Feldman doctrine. *See* Bullock v. Credit Bureau of Greater Indianapolis, 272 F. Supp. 2d 780 (S.D. Ind. 2003); Witt v. Westfield Acceptance Corp., 2002 WL 826372, (S.D. Ind. Mar. 25, 2002). *See generally* National Consumer Law Center, Fair Debt Collection § 7.6 (5th ed. 2004 and Supp.).

495 Smith v. Short Term Loans, Ltd. Liab. Co., 2001 U.S. Dist. LEXIS 1554 (N.D. Ill. Feb. 9, 2001); *see also* Nance v. Ulferts, 282 F. Supp. 2d 912 (N.D. Ind. 2003) (attorney violated FDCPA because he attempted to collect on an illegal payday loan and to collect treble damages not yet awarded by a court; court refused to apply the bona fide error defense as the court decision finding payday lending illegal only confirmed the state of the law and did not change the law); National Consumer Law Center, Fair Debt Collection § 4.2.4 (5th ed. 2004 and Supp.). *But see* Bullock v. Credit Bureau of Greater Indianapolis, Inc., 272 F. Supp. 2d 780 (S.D. Ind. 2003) (FDCPA claims based upon illegal interest charge and the collection of treble damages cannot be brought in federal court once a judgment in state court against the consumer has been obtained; Rooker-Feldman doctrine defeats federal court jurisdiction, citing Epps v. Creditnet, Inc., 320 F.3d 756 (7th Cir. 2003)).

496 For a detailed discussion of state credit repair laws, *see* National Consumer Law Center, Unfair and Deceptive Acts and Practices § 5.1.2.2.3 (6th ed. 2004 and Supp.). For a case where a state filed a proceeding (in collaboration with the Federal Trade Commission) to enforce its credit repair law against a payday lending scheme, *see* Fed. Trade Comm'n v. Consumer Money Markets, Inc., Civil Action No. CVS001071-PMP-RJJ (D. Nev.

to assist the customer in obtaining credit, for example, should be covered. Similarly, state statutes governing loan brokers may cover payday lenders using rent-a-charter arrangements.[497] The federal Credit Repair Organizations Act may have a more limited use in the payday lending context, unless the creditor expressly or impliedly claims that the payday loan will improve the customer's credit record.[498]

Some lenders may market payday loans as "credit lines" or even credit cards. The Federal Trade Commission brought an enforcement action against one such company for its conduct during the telemarketing and opening of "pre-approved" credit lines supposedly worth thousands of dollars, regardless of their credit.[499] According to the FTC, the solicitation implied that the company's credit card could be used like an ordinary credit card for general shopping. However, after paying a membership fee of almost $170, though an automatic debit of the consumer's checking or credit card account, consumers received a company catalog. Not until then were the consumers informed that they could only purchase goods from the catalog and had to pay a 30% down payment on the purchases. Cash advances on the "line of credit" were not available. In order to draw cash, consumers had to deal with a different company to obtain loans of $20, payable in 30 days, for which consumers had to post-date personal checks in the amount of $26. The FTC and the State of Nevada sued on various claims, including, the Truth in Lending Act (the cash loans were really closed-end credit), the FTC Act (misrepresentations), and the Nevada Credit Services Organization Act (for failure to register), and the state UDAP act. The settlement required the defendants to disgorge $350,000 received from consumers and to forgive $1.6 million in debts.

Viable defenses to payday lending exist even in states whose laws expressly permit these transactions. Truth in Lending disclosures may be inaccurate.[500] Even where such disclosures are correct, the lender may present additional information in such a way so as to violate the requirement that the disclosures be clear and conspicuous and separately segregated. In *Smith v. The Cash Store Management, Inc.*, the Seventh Circuit reinstated a TILA claim based upon the creditor's practice of stapling a receipt over part of the TILA disclosure.[501] The receipt listed the finance charge as a "deferred deposit check fee." In another case, the Seventh Circuit held that failure to disclose the annual percentage rate and finance charge more conspicuously violated the Act.[502] Lastly, the check itself may be security for the loan and must be properly disclosed as such.[503] For other Truth in Lending claims raised in the payday loan context, see NCLC's *Truth in Lending*.[504]

In addition, the doctrine of unconscionability can be used to challenge the amount of fees and interest that is charged in states with no caps. Courts have refused to dismiss substantive unconscionability claims in payday loan cases filed in states where usury caps had been eliminated by the state legislatures[505] or, in one case, in a state with a payday

Sept. 6, 2000) (complaint and stipulated final judgment and order), *available at* www.ftc.gov/os/2000/09/Index.htm.

497 *See, e.g.*, Goleta v. Lingerfelt, 211 F. Supp. 2d 711 (E.D.N.C. 2002) (noting in *dicta* that if fact-finder determined that national bank was true lender, state agency had a viable alternative claim under the North Carolina Loan Broker Act).

498 The federal act is discussed in National Consumer Law Center, Unfair and Deceptive Acts and Practices § 5.1.2.2 (6th ed. 2004 and Supp.).

499 Fed. Trade Comm'n v. Consumer Money Markets, Inc., Civil Action No. CVS001071-PMP-RJJ (D. Nev. Sept. 6, 2000) (complaint and stipulated final judgment and order), *available at* www.ftc.gov/os/2000/09/Index.htm.

500 Checking the TILA math to determine if the APR, finance charge, amount financed, total of payments, and payment schedule can prove fruitful. *See* Yarnall v. Four Aces Emporium, Inc. (*In re* Boganski), 2005 WL 705233 (B.A.P. 9th Cir. Jan. 14, 2005) (payday store grossly understated the APR; lender did not prove all elements of the bona fide error defense); Jump v. ACP Enterprises, 224 F. Supp. 2d 1216 (N.D. Ind. 2002); Gilkey v. Cent. Clearing Co., 202 F.R.D. 515 (E.D. Mich. 2001) (class certified on TILA claims that the finance charge and annual percentage rate did not include the check cashing fee and that

additional information detracted from the finance charge disclosure); *see also* Jean Ann Fox & Anna Petrini, *Internet Payday Lending: How High-Priced Lenders Use the Internet to Mire Borrowers in Debt and Evade State Consumer Protections* at 23 (Consumer Federation of America Nov. 30, 2004) (survey of Internet payday lending sites revealed an instance of an inaccurately calculated APR; violations of the TILA advertising rules documented).

501 200 F.3d 511 (7th Cir. 1999); *see also* Gilkey v. Cent. Clearing Co., 202 F.R.D. 515 (E.D. Mich. 2001) (class certified on TILA claims that the finance charge and annual percentage rate did not include the check cashing fee and that additional information detracted from the finance charge disclosure).

502 Brown v. Payday Check Advance, Inc., 202 F.3d 987 (7th Cir.), *cert. denied*, 531 U.S. 820 (2000) (also, including itemization of the amount financed in the federal box violates the segregation requirement but statutory damages not available for this violation). For a critique of the holding relating to statutory damages, see National Consumer Law Center, Truth in Lending § 8.6.5 (5th ed. 2003 and Supp.).

503 Smith v. Cash Store Mgmt., Inc., 195 F.3d 325 (7th Cir. 1999) (payday lender can obtain a security interest in a post-dated check because the check secures payment beyond the mere promise to repay and can be collateral for the loan; disclosing the post-dated check as security did not, therefore, violate the Act); Jump v. ACP Enterprises, 224 F. Supp. 2d 1216 (N.D. Ind. 2002) (failure to disclose post-dated check as security interest violates TILA); *see also* Hahn v. McKenzie Check Advance of Ill., 202 F.3d 998 (7th Cir. 2000) (relying upon *Smith* to hold that post-dated check is security for loan even though consumer agreed in loan note to pay a $25 fee if check is dishonored and attorney fees necessary to collect); Van Jackson v. Check 'N Go of Ill., Inc., 123 F. Supp. 2d 1079 (N.D. Ill. 2000).

504 National Consumer Law Center, Truth in Lending §§ 4.2.4, 4.2.6, 4.2.8, 4.6.7.2 (5th ed. 2003 and Supp.).

505 Donnelly v. Illini Cash Advance, Inc., 2000 U.S. Dist. LEXIS 11906 (N.D. Ill. Aug. 16, 2000) (motion to dismiss denied; court observes that Illinois recognizes the doctrine of substantive unconscionability); Davis v. Cash for Payday, Inc., 193 F.R.D. 518 (N.D. Ill. 2000) (same in the class certification context); Van Jackson v. Check 'N Go of Ill., Inc., 193 F.R.D.

loan law that prohibited rollovers.[506]

Finally, some state enforcement agencies and other researchers have uncovered numerous violations of their payday laws during annual audits and investigation.[507] Comparing the law to the transaction may reveal defenses even under these permissive acts.[508] Noncompliance with these laws can arguably void the loan if only criminal penalties are imposed.[509] Violation of the act may also trigger UDAP liability.[510]

Municipalities may retain certain powers to limit the business hours and density of payday lending storefronts.[511]

---

544 (N.D. Ill. 2000) (same); Sharp v. Chartwell Fin. Services Ltd., 2000 U.S. Dist. LEXIS 3143 (N.D. Ill. Feb. 28, 2000) (same); Hartke v. Ill. Payday Loans, Inc., 1999 U.S. Dist. LEXIS 14937 (C.D. Ill. Sept. 13, 1999) (same); Johnson v. Tele-Cash, Inc., 82 F. Supp. 2d 264 (D. Del. 1999), *rev'd on other grounds*, 225 F.3d 366 (3d Cir. 2000), *cert. denied*, 531 U.S. 1145 (2001) (unconscionability can be the outer limit to interest charges in a state where there is no usury cap); *see also* Smith v. Short Term Loans, Ltd. Liab. Co., 2001 U.S. Dist. LEXIS 1554 (N.D. Ill. Feb. 9, 2001) (class certification granted on unconscionability claim under Illinois law); Dienese v. National Cash Advance, 2000 U.S. Dist. LEXIS 20389 (E.D. Wis. Dec. 11, 2000) (class certification granted on unconscionability claim under Wisconsin law); *cf.* Smith v. Steinkamp, 318 F.3d 775 (7th Cir. 2003) (in upholding trial court's decision to deny in part defendant's motion to compel arbitration, the Seventh Circuit noted that "[a] cynic might argue that, given the desperation of people who take out payday loans, these plaintiffs would have signed anything. . . . The defendants do not make this argument, however, perhaps fearing that it would invite a conclusion that payday loans are unconscionable and therefore unenforceable even in states that do not deem them usurious.").

506 Johnson v. The Cash Store, 68 P.3d 1099 (Wash. Ct. App. 2003) (in affirming trial court's refusal to re-open a default judgment against a payday lender on an unconscionability claim, the court held that back-to-back transactions and the payment of a non-amortizing fee every two weeks constituted rollovers, prohibited by the state payday lending law; court rejects lender's argument that providing disclosures is a defense to unconscionability; damages of $26,701, including emotional distress affirmed).

507 Candace Heckman, *State Accuses Paycheck Lender of Collection Abuses*, Seattle Post-Intelligencer (Sept. 28, 2004) (consumer complaints and investigation allege abusive debt collection practices, overcharging on fees, and lying about the loan percentage rates); Steven M. Graves & Christopher L. Peterson, *Predatory Lending and the Military: The Law and Geography of "Payday" Loans in Military Towns* at 190 (Mar. 29, 2005), *available at* www.responsiblelending.org/research/index.cfm?tid=2&tyid=2 (observing a significant number of payday lenders openly doing business that were not registered or licensed under state laws); Creola Johnson, *Payday Loans: Shrewd Business or Predatory Lending?*, 87 Minn. L. Rev. 1, 33, 34 (2002) (a law professor and law students conducted a survey of payday lenders in Franklin County, Ohio; the following lender practices were uncovered: refusing to provide customers with basic written information about the payday loan transaction, giving consumers false or misleading information about the cost of credit, failing to advertise the cost of credit using APRs, refusing to supply customers with written disclosures prior to contract consummation, claiming no credit check would be conducted but doing so anyway without obtaining consumer consent, including clauses in their loan documents that appear to be illegal or unconscionable, representing that consumers have the right to rescind the contract at no cost, allowing consumers to roll over payday loans in violation of state law, representing to consumers that the lenders have the ability to collect treble damages from defaulting consumers, and intimidating consumers with the threat of physical violence and criminal prosecution); Mark Muecke, Consumers Union, *Payday Lenders Bur-*

den Working Families and the U.S. Armed Forces (July 2003) (Consumers Union surveyed 31 payday lenders in Austin, Dallas, Lubbock, Fort Worth, Houston, and San Antonio, Texas, finding that none of the companies came close to meeting the fee caps in Texas regulations and found other violations); North Carolina Office of the Commissioner of Banks, Report to the General Assembly on Payday Lending (Feb. 22, 2001) (indicates that in 2000, it found 4,383 violations of certain provisions of the state's payday loan law); *see also* Indiana Dep't of Financial Institutions, Summary of Payday Lender Examinations Conducted from July through October 1999; Check 'N Go of Florida, Inc., 790 So. 2d 454 (Fla. Dist. Ct. App. 2001) (enforcement action which went up on appeal on issue of scope of the state's subpoena for records evidencing rollovers); Advance Am. v. State, 801 So. 2d 310 (Fla. Dist. Ct. App. 2001) (same). Private litigation raising violations of state payday lending laws have been pursued as well. *See, e.g.*, Wirdzek v. Serv. Annex, Ltd. Liab. Co., Clearinghouse Nos. 53,555A (complaint), 53,555B (class action settlement agreement) (Cal. Super. Ct., Kern County, Mar. 22, 1999) (alleged violations of state payday loan law include rollovers beyond 30 days and failing to provide certain written notices). The Office of the Comptroller of the Currency obtained a consent order against ACE Cash Express and Goleta National Bank terminating that rent-a-bank arrangement and imposing $325,000 in civil penalties in part based upon ACE's disposal of 641 customer loan files in a trash dumpster in violation of TILA, the Equal Credit Opportunity Act and the Gramm-Leach-Bliley Act. Office of the Comptroller of the Currency, News Release No. 2002-85 (Oct. 29, 2002), *available at* www.occ.treas.gov/ftp/release/2002%2D85.doc.

508 *See, e.g.*, Bellizan v. Easy Money of La., Inc., 2002 WL 1611648 (E.D. La. July 19, 2002) (describes loan splitting scheme by lender in order to extract fees in excess of Louisiana payday loan rate cap; however, court dismissed or granted summary judgment for the defendant on all of the plaintiff's claims).

509 *See, e.g.*, Lynn v. Fin. Solutions Corp. (*In re* Lynn), 173 B.R. 894 (Bankr. M.D. Tenn. 1994) (case involved failure of a pawnbroker to comply with Tennessee's pawnbroker act; court voided auto title pawn transaction); *cf.* Bumpus v. Vandeford, Clearinghouse No. 54,570 (N.D. Miss. Mar. 27, 2002) (auto title pawn case; lender failed to obtain license and thus loan subject to Mississippi usury cap). See also discussion regarding the effect of the failure of a lender to obtain a required license in § 9.2.4.6, *infra*.

510 California's act specifically declares that it is an unfair and deceptive act to fail to post required information or to charge fees in violation of the act.

511 The Payday Loan Store of Wisconsin v. Madison, 339 F. Supp. 2d 1058 (W.D. Wis. 2004) (city ordinance that required payday loan stores to close by 6:00 p.m. and prohibited stores from being within 5000 feet of each other upheld).

7.5.5.7 Bank Partnerships and "Rent-a-Finance" Company Arrangements

Relationships between payday lenders and banks or thrifts are increasing, due to the doctrine of "exportation."[512] *See* § 3.2.3.2, *supra*. This principle allows a bank chartered in a deregulated state to ignore usury laws in the borrower's home state, undermining that state's ability to protect its citizens from out-of-state exploiters. Consumers claim that banks are "renting" their charters to payday companies, in an attempt to usurp state usury laws. This controversial issue is discussed in § 3.13, *supra*. Removal from state court to federal court based on the claim that federal usury laws apply, rather than state law, in cases involving banks is discussed in § 3.15, *supra*. To date, attempts by states to shut down this sham through enforcement actions and legislation have been successful.[513]

Yet another attempt to avoid state law involved a finance company licensed in South Dakota that is lending through Arkansas storefronts to make payday loans. The South Dakota company allegedly originates no loans in South Dakota and was formed by Arkansas payday lenders to facilitate their lending in Arkansas.[514] The loan contracts contain a choice of law provision selecting South Dakota law. The legality of choice of law provisions is discussed in § 9.2.9, *infra*.

7.5.5.8 Special Defenses to Arbitration Clauses

Payday lenders, like many finance companies, are placing arbitration clauses in their contracts. In those states where payday loans are illegal because they violate the usury cap, the courts may refuse to enforce arbitration on the theory that the underlying transaction, the loan, is unenforceable or unconscionable. This and other defenses to arbitration clauses are discussed in § 10.3, *infra*.

7.5.5.9 Checks and Electronic Fund Transfers in Payday Loans

7.5.5.9.1 Introduction

As payday lenders base their business on checks or on authorizations to debit the consumer's bank account, the law governing these payment mechanisms is important. If the consumer gives the lender a paper check, it is governed by Articles 3 and 4 of the Uniform Commercial Code (UCC). If the holder of the paper check re-presents it to the consumer's bank electronically, both the UCC and the rules of the National Automated Clearing House Association (NACHA) also apply. Attempts to electronically transfer the bounced check or other fee from the consumer's account are covered by the Electronic Fund Transfer Act (EFTA).[515]

If the payday lender has the consumer authorize an electronic fund transfer rather than sign a paper check,[516] the EFTA and NACHA Rules, rather than the UCC, govern. The distinction between a paper check and an electronic fund transfer will not always be clear to the consumer, because the consumer can authorize an electronic fund transfer by giving the payday lender a paper check to use as a "source document." The lender uses information on the check to initiate an electronic fund transfer.

Transactions consummated by telephone or over the Internet can involve either Article 3 checks or electronic fund transfers. If the payday lender obtains authorization to sign the consumer's name to a paper check (a "telecheck" or "demand draft"), UCC Article 3 applies. In the alternative, the payday lender can obtain the consumer's authorization for an electronic fund transfer. The consumer will probably be unable to tell the difference between these two mechanisms, but the consumer's monthly bank statement will list them differently. The law of checks, electronic fund transfers, and other payment mechanisms is discussed in detail in another NCLC manual.[517]

7.5.5.9.2 Conditioning payday loan on authorization for electronic fund transfer

Since they cannot conveniently accept paper checks, Internet-based payday lenders commonly have the borrower

---

512 In fact, the industry has touted this collaboration as the best way to avoid legislative or regulatory headaches. *See* Stephens, Inc., Payday Advance—The Final Innings: Standardizing the Approach (Sept. 22, 2000).

513 *See* § 3.14, *supra*; *see also* Bankwest Inc. v. Baker, 324 F. Supp. 2d 1333 (N.D. Ga. 2004) (upholding Georgia's new law which prohibits a storefront from partnering with a bank where it obtains or retains a predominate interest in the loan proceeds).

514 Letter from Arkansans Against Abusive Payday Lending to Arkansas Attorney General (Oct. 15, 2004), available on the CD-Rom accompanying this volume.

515 15 U.S.C. § 1693 *et seq.*

516 For a description of some payday lenders' use of electronic fund transfers, see Jean Ann Fox, *Unsafe and Unsound: Payday Lenders Hide Behind FDIC Bank Charters to Peddle Usury* (Mar. 30, 2004); Jean Ann Fox & Anna Petrini, *Internet Payday Lending: How High-Priced Lenders Use the Internet to Mire Borrowers in Debt and Evade State Consumer Protections* at 17 (Nov. 30, 2004). Both reports are available at www.consumerfed.org.

517 National Consumer Law Center, Consumer Banking and Payments Law (3d ed. 2005).

authorize an electronic fund transfer to repay the loan.[518] The EFTA prohibits any person from conditioning the extension of credit upon the consumer's repayment by means of a preauthorized electronic fund transfer.[519] Because a "preauthorized electronic fund transfer" is defined as one authorized in advance to recur at substantially regular intervals,[520] and payday lenders generally withdraw the entire debt all at once, this prohibition will not usually affect payday lenders. However, the repayment authorization should be examined carefully, as some payday lenders reportedly obtain authorization from the consumer for multiple withdrawals.[521] State law should also be checked for any restrictions. Virginia, for example, prohibits payday lenders from using any authorization of electronic fund transfer as security for repayment of a loan.[522]

7.5.5.9.3 Repeated presentment of borrower's check

One of the worst problems for payday loan borrowers is the bounced check fees incurred if the lender presents the check but there are insufficient funds to cover it. The problem is most severe when the lender repeatedly re-presents the dishonored check, incurring more bounced check fees each time.

UCC Article 3 does not explicitly limit the number of times a check can be presented. However, the UCC's general rules of good faith govern presentment of checks.[523] Good faith is defined as honesty in fact and the observance of reasonable commercial standards of fair dealing.[524] Repeated resubmission of an insufficient funds check may violate this standard.

If the payday lender presents the borrower's check electronically, rather than presenting the physical check, the rules of the National Automated Clearing House Association (NACHA) prohibit more than the original presentment of the check plus two re-presentments.[525] NACHA rules also prohibit *any* re-presentment of "demand drafts" or "tele-checks," which are paper checks that a lender or seller signs on behalf of the consumer, usually based on the consumer's telephone authorization.[526]

State law may impose additional restrictions. Virginia, for example, prohibits payday lenders from depositing or otherwise presenting a check more than two times, or recovering more than $25 in returned check fees for a single check.[527]

If a payday lender is prohibited from presenting a check additional times, it can still sue the borrower on the check.

7.5.5.9.4 Amount that payday lender can obtain through check or electronic fund transfer

A payday lender may claim that it is entitled to not only the face amount of the consumer's check, but also a dishonored check fee or some other charge. If the payday lender submits a paper check, no bank will negotiate that check for more than the amount of the check, and will not

---

NACHA Rule 2.8.2 (2005) regulates "RCK" checks (checks that are re-presented electronically through the Automated Clearing House). It provides:

> An RCK entry must relate to an item that (1) is an item within the meaning of Revised Article 4 of the Uniform Commercial Code (1990 Official Text); (2) is a negotiable demand draft drawn on or payable through or at a Participating DFI, other than a Federal Reserve Bank or Federal Home Loan Bank; (3) contains a pre-printed serial number; (4) is in an amount less than $2,500; (5) indicates on the face of the document that the item was returned due to "Not Sufficient Funds," "NSF," "Uncollected Funds," or comparable language; (6) is dated 180 days or less from the date the entry is being transmitted to the RDFI (i.e., the item to which the RCK entry relates is not stale dated); (7) is drawn on a Consumer Account; and (8) has been previously presented (a) no more than two times in its physical form, if the entry is an initial RCK entry; or (b) no more than one time in its physical form and no more than one time as an RCK entry, if the entry is a reinitiated RCK entry pursuant to subsection 2.1 1 (Reinitiation of Returned Entries by Originators).
>
> Ineligible items include, but are not limited to, noncash items (as defined in Section 229.2(u) of Regulation CC); drafts drawn on the Treasury of the United States, a Federal Reserve Bank, or a Federal Home Loan Bank; drafts drawn on a state or local government that are not payable through or at a Participating DFI; United States Postal Service money orders; items payable in a medium other than United States currency; items which are third-party items; and demand drafts and third-party drafts that do not contain the signature of the Receiver.

The NACHA rules are discussed in detail in National Consumer Law Center, Consumer Banking and Payments Law Ch. 8 (3d ed. 2005).

---

518 *See* Jean Ann Fox & Anna Petrini, *Internet Payday Lending: How High-Priced Lenders Use the Internet to Mire Borrowers in Debt and Evade State Consumer Protections* at 17, 32 (Nov. 30, 2004), *available at* www.consumerfed.org.

519 15 U.S.C. § 1693k.

520 15 U.S.C. § 1693a(9).

521 Jean Ann Fox & Anna Petrini, Internet Payday Lending: *How High-Priced Lenders Use the Internet to Mire Borrowers in Debt and Evade State Consumer Protections* at 17, 28, 34 (Nov. 30, 2004), *available at* www.consumerfed.org.

522 10 Va. Admin. Code § 5-200-70(C) (West).

523 U.C.C. § 1-203.

524 U.C.C. §§ 3-103(a)(4), 4-104(c).

525 NACHA Rules can be obtained for $55 plus shipping at http://pubs.nacha.org/, or by phone at 800-487-9180. The book purchase also provides access to the rules on a website. Whether there is a private right of action to enforce NACHA Rules is examined at National Consumer Law Center, Consumer Banking and Payments Law Ch. 1 (3d ed. 2005).

526 NACHA Rule 2.8.2 (2005).

527 10 Va. Admin. Code § 5-200-70(B) (West).

pay the lender additional fees from the consumer's account. In addition, if the lender re-presents a paper check electronically, NACHA rules prohibit asking for more than the face amount of the check.[528]

If the lender obtains a paper check but re-presents it electronically, the UCC applies to the presentment of the check, but the Electronic Fund Transfer Act (EFTA) applies to any attempt to obtain an amount greater than the face amount of the check.[529] Under the EFTA, the consumer is not liable for an unauthorized transfer,[530] so if the consumer did not authorize the payday lender to obtain an electronic transfer of the additional fee, the consumer's bank must re-credit the amount.

7.5.5.9.5 Post-dated checks

Most consumers do not realize that, under the UCC, a check is payable when it is presented to the bank, even if it is post-dated.[531] Consumers can require their bank to wait until the date on the check only by first giving the bank notice of the post-dating and describing the check with reasonable certainty.[532] Regardless of whether the consumer has given notice to the bank, if a payday lender presents a post-dated check before its date, the consumer should be able to press UDAP and breach of contract claims against the lender.

7.5.5.9.6 Right to stop payment

The consumer's stop payment order on a paper check or electronic transfer will prevent the immediate transfer of funds to the payday lender, but will not resolve the issue of the consumer's liability to the payday lender. The consumer has the right to stop payment on a paper check if the consumer describes the check to the consumer's bank with reasonable certainty and at a time and in a manner that affords the bank a reasonable opportunity to act on it.[533]

Similarly, with electronic transfers, the consumer must provide the stop payment order orally or in writing at such time and in such manner as to allow the consumer's bank a reasonable opportunity to act upon the stop payment or-der.[534] For "preauthorized" electronic fund transfers, i.e., those authorized in advance to recur at substantially regular intervals, the consumer has the right under the Electronic Fund Transfer Act (EFTA) to stop payment by notifying the financial institution where the account is located.[535] Either oral or written notice is effective, as long as it is given at least three business days before the scheduled date of the transfer.[536] One example of a preauthorized electronic transfer to a payday lender is where the lender obtains the consumer's agreement to automatic renewal of the loan every two weeks, resulting in a series of interest-only debits to the consumer's account.[537]

NACHA rules also allow the consumer to withdraw authorization for recurring debits to an account. The consumer must inform payday lender directly as well as the financial institution where the account is maintained, and must sign a form under pain of perjury.[538] But the consumer still is protected if the consumer complies with the EFTA, and not with NACHA rules.

7.5.5.9.7 Unauthorized payments

The UCC sets out rules for a forged or altered check, and in general the consumer is not liable for such a check the payday lender may present for payment.[539] For an unauthorized electronic fund transfer (either because no amount was authorized to be transferred or because the wrong amount was transferred), the EFTA specifies that the consumer has no liability. Because no debit card or other access device is involved, the only liability the consumer has is if the unauthorized transfer appears on a monthly bank statement, and the consumer does not report it for sixty days. Even then, the consumer's liability is limited just to any *new* unauthorized transfers occurring *after* that sixty-day period.[540]

In addition, under the EFTA, the consumer can require the bank to institute a procedure to resolve any error in the transfer. While the consumer is not entitled to an immediate re-credit, the bank must promptly re-credit the amount if its investigation discovers the transfer was unauthorized. If the bank does not complete its investigation within ten business days, it must provisionally re-credit the amount to the consumer.[541]

---

528 "Re-presented Check Entries may be originated only for the face amount of the check. No collection fees may be added to the amount of the item when it is transmitted as an ACH entry." NACHA Operating Guidelines 170 (2005).

529 Official Staff Interpretations of Reg. E, 12 C.F.R. § 205.3-3(c)(1).

530 Reg. E, 12 C.F.R. § 205.6(b)(3); Official Staff Interpretations of Reg. E, 12 C.F.R. § 205.6(b)(3)-2. Note that the consumer must notify the bank within sixty days after the bank sends a statement showing the unauthorized debit. If the consumer does not, then the consumer may be stuck with any additional debits that occur after the sixty-day period.

531 U.C.C. § 4-401(c).

532 U.C.C. § 4-401(c).

533 U.C.C. § 4-403(a).

534 2005 NACHA Rule 8.4.

535 12 C.F.R. § 205.10(c).

536 *Id.*

537 *See* Jean Ann Fox & Anna Petrini, *Internet Payday Lending: How High-Priced Lenders Use the Internet to Mire Borrowers in Debt and Evade State Consumer Protections* at 27–28 (Nov. 30, 2004), *available at* www.consumerfed.org.

538 NACHA 2005 Operating Guidelines, 21–22, "Revocation of Authorization."

539 *See* National Consumer Law Center, Consumer Banking and Payments Law Ch. 2 (3d ed. 2005).

540 Reg. E, 12 C.F.R. § 205.6.

541 Reg. E, 12 C.F.R. § 205.11.

NACHA Rules provide similar protections, but, if the consumer files an "Affidavit of Unauthorized ACH Withdrawal" form at their bank, the consumer's bank must promptly re-credit the disputed amount.[542] Under NACHA rules, consumers must report the error within fifteen days in writing and under penalty of perjury. But, even if the consumer does not comply with this NACHA requirement, the bank must still conduct the error resolution procedure required by the EFTA.

7.5.6 Bank Bounce Loans

Bounce loans[543] are a form of overdraft coverage that some banks are using to boost their revenue. Bounce loans plans are a systematic attempt to induce consumers into using overdrafts as a form of high-cost credit. These plans offer short-term credit at triple-digit rates.[544] Bounce loans can be accessed both by writing checks and, in many cases, by withdrawing cash from an automated teller machine or using a debit card at a point of sale. Consumer assent is not necessary; consumers often are held accountable for fees unilaterally imposed by banks. Bounce loan plans are often administered through computer software and are formal programs developed by third party vendors.[545]

When a consumer uses a bounce loan, the bank recovers the amount advanced under the plan, plus a fee, by setting off that amount from the consumer's next deposit, even when that deposit is protected income, such as a welfare or Social Security check. The fee is often the same amount charged as an insufficient funds fee on a returned check or as the fee for traditional, *ad hoc* discretionary overdrafts. In some cases the bank also charges an additional per-day fee.[546]

A fundamental question is whether this product is covered by the definition of "credit" or "loan" under state lending laws. Bounce loans are clearly credit under TILA's definition of credit as "the right granted by a creditor to a debtor to defer payment of a debt or to incur debt and defer its payment."[547] The fees for bounce loans should be considered finance charges under TILA, but banks have exploited loopholes in Regulation Z to claim they are not.[548]

Several courts have held that traditional, *ad hoc* discretionary overdrafts are not loans and that their fees do not constitute "interest" under state laws.[549] These cases are distinguishable in that there are key differences between bounce loans and traditional, *ad hoc* overdrafts. With traditional, *ad hoc* overdrafts, banks pay an insufficient funds check on a discretionary basis as a courtesy to favored customers, not as a profit generator, and thus it is not illogical to treat the payment of an overdraft as the equivalent of a returned check, and find the fee to be a similar service charge. In contrast, banks actively promote bounce loans as a source of funds from which the consumer can not only write checks, but can also withdraw as cash from an automated teller machine (ATM), or use to pay merchants with a debit card.[550]

In the cases which have held that fees for traditional, *ad hoc* overdrafts are not interest, the courts found it to be significant that these fees served as a deterrent to discourage

---

542 2005 NACHA Rule 8.6.1.

543 Bounce "protection" or "courtesy overdrafts" are euphemisms sometimes used by banks to describe this high-cost credit product.

544 For example, a $100 overdraft will usually incur a fee of at least $20. If the consumer pays the overdraft back in 30 days, the APR is 243%. If the consumer pays the overdraft bank in 14 days, which is probably more typical for a wage earner, the APR is 520%. This arrangement is much more expensive than other alternatives that most banks offer, such as overdraft lines of credit, linking the account to a credit card, and transfers from savings.

545 Consumer Federation of America & National Consumer Law Center, *Bounce Protection: How Banks Turn Rubber Into Gold By Enticing Consumers to Write Bad Checks* (Jan. 27, 2003), *available at* www.consumerlaw.org/initiatives/test_and_comm/appendix.shtml.

546 *Id.*

547 15 U.S.C. § 1602(e). The Office of the Comptroller of the Currency has recognized that bounce loans are credit as defined by TILA. Daniel P. Stipano, Deputy Chief Counsel, Office of the Comptroller of the Currency, Interpretive Letter No. 914 (Sept. 2001), *available at* www.occ.treas.gov/interp/sep01/intsep01.htm. Regulators in Indiana and Colorado have reached the same conclusion. Indiana Dep't of Financial Institutions, Newsletter—Winter 2002 Ed. (Nov. 2002), at 2; Letter from Ass't Att'y Gen. Paul Chessin, Colorado Dep't of Law, Consumer Credit Unit, to Administrator, Colorado Uniform Consumer Credit Code (Mar. 21, 2001). The Indiana and Colorado opinions are available on the CD-Rom accompanying NCLC's Truth in Lending volume (5th ed. 2003 and Supp.). *Cf.* 12 C.F.R. § 215.3(a)(2) (defining overdrafts as "credit" under Federal Reserve Board's Regulation O, which governs loans to bank insiders).

548 *See* National Consumer Law Center, Truth In Lending §§ 3.6.5.2, 3.9.3.3 (5th ed. 2003 and Supp.), for a discussion of why bounce loan fees fit within TILA's finance charge definition. *But see* Order re: Defendant's Motion to Dismiss, *In re* Washington Mutual Overdraft Protection, Case No. CV 03-2566 (C.D. Cal. Apr. 26, 2004) (dismissing TILA claim on basis that bounce loan fees were not finance charges under TILA). This case is available on the CD-Rom accompanying NCLC's Truth in Lending (5th ed. 2003 and Supp.).

549 Video Trax v. Nationsbank, N.A, 33 F. Supp. 2d 1051 (S.D. Fla. 1998), *aff'd*, 205 F.3d 1358 (11th Cir.), *cert. denied*, 531 U.S. 822 (2000); Terrell v. Hancock Bank, 7 F. Supp. 2d 812 (S.D. Miss. 1998); First Bank v. Tony's Tortilla Factory, Inc., 877 S.W.2d 285 (Tex. 1994).

550 In Video Trax v. Nationsbank, N.A, 33 F. Supp. 2d 1051 (S.D. Fla. 1998), the court considered it significant that with traditional, *ad hoc* overdrafts the banks do not have a "corrupt intent," one of the factors under Florida law in determining whether a transaction is usurious. Thus, the fact that banks do have a different intent with bounce loans, that is, to induce consumers to use overdrafts as a credit source in order to generate large profits as opposed to providing a service to favored customers, is significant in analyzing whether bounce loan fees are usurious interest.

overdrafts, or covered the processing costs for a transaction that the bank unexpectedly had to bear. With bounce loans, the fee can no longer be characterized as compensation for unexpected processing costs or as a deterrent, because the bank has deliberately sought to encourage these transactions in order to generate fees.[551]

Furthermore, the reasoning of these cases should not apply when it comes to the per-day fee that some bounce loan plans charge. A consumer pays a single insufficient funds fee for a returned check but does not pay per-day charges. State banking regulators have stated that these daily fees are finance charges under state law.[552]

Finally, the argument that bounce loan fees are not interest because they are the same as returned check fees does not make any sense when it comes to non-check methods of accessing the product, such as access through ATMs, debit cards, and on-line banking transactions. With these payment mechanisms, there is no comparison to a returned check. For example, when a consumer without bounce loan access attempts to withdraw more money from an ATM than the consumer has in the account, the machine simply declines to give the consumer the money, and the consumer is charged nothing for making the attempt.

Even if bounce loan fees are considered interest they may not violate state usury laws because bounce loans are generally made by federally-chartered financial institutions.[553]

The federal banking regulators have issued a *Joint Guidance* document concerning bounce loans.[554] The *Joint Guidance* requires financial institutions to charge off bounce loans 60 days after the overdraft occurs.[555] It reviews legal risks for institutions offering bounce loans under several of the statutes in the federal Consumer Credit Protection Act, but ultimately does not conclude that these loans violate any of the laws.[556] The *Joint Guidance* also sets forth "best practices" for institutions offering bounce loans, the most meaningful of which recommends alerting consumers, if feasible, that a transaction may trigger an overdraft.[557] However, the best practices are not mandatory.

In addition, the Federal Reserve Board has proposed regulating bounce loans under the Truth in Savings Act (TISA), not under Truth in Lending Act.[558] Neither the *Joint Guidance* nor the proposed TISA regulations contain restrictions that would reduce or eliminate the most serious abuses of bounce loans.

7.5.7 Joint Venture Investments

Another type of "non-credit" transaction which at times may conceal a usurious loan is a joint venture investment where the investor (lender) provides cash to a business enterprise, typically in return for a share of any profits made by the enterprise.[559] The investor's return may be very large, but it is contingent on the success of the enterprise and is thus, in a true joint venture, exempt from usury law.[560]

---

551 A hypothetical from a non-financial services context may be instructive. Compare two stores that imposed a $50 fine for shoplifting. In store A, shoplifting is discouraged. The store manager requires the shoplifter to return the goods and pay a $50 penalty. In some cases, if the manager is in a good mood, he will permit the shoplifter to keep the goods if he pays for them, plus the $50 fee. In store B, however, the store manager permits "shoplifting." The manager has posted signs stating "You can take goods and pay for them when you have the money. You will be charged $50 in addition to the sale price of the goods."

In Store A, the $50 fee is clearly a penalty for shoplifting, whether the goods are returned or the purchase price paid. Store B, however, has entered into the business of granting credit to shoppers who do not have the money at hand to buy the store's goods. The $50 fee now represents revenue from allowing shoppers to essentially "buy on credit" and the only feature it shares in common with Store A's fee is that it is the same amount.

552 The Alabama Banking Department advised banks that charging a $2 daily fee on overdrawn accounts is considered a finance charge under Alabama law. V. Lynne Windham, Associate Counsel, Alabama State Banking Department, letter to redacted company, August 14, 2001, *available on* the companion CD-Rom. *See also* Iowa Consumer Credit Code Administrator, Informal Advisory # 88, *Per Diem Charge on Honored NSF Checks as a Finance Charge Under the ICCC and Iowa Common Law*, Aug. 12, 1999, *available on* the companion CD-Rom. Even a consultant who promotes bounce protection has conceded that per day fees are finance charges and has warned against imposing them. Alex Sheshunoff, *A New Approach to Covering Overdrafts*, Bank Director, Apr. 1, 2002.

553 *See* Ch. 3, *supra. Cf.* Video Trax, Inc. v. NationsBank, N.A., 33

F. Supp. 2d 1041 (S.D. Fla. 1998) (overdraft fees are interest for purposes of National Bank Act preemption, but are not interest for usury analysis), *aff'd without op.*, 205 F.3d 1358 (11th Cir. 2000), *cert. denied*, 531 U.S. 822 (2000); Nicolas v. Deposit Guar. Nat. Bank, 182 F.R.D. 226 (S.D. Miss. 1998) (same).

554 Office of the Comptroller of the Currency, Federal Reserve Board, Federal Deposit Insurance Corporation, and National Credit Union Administration, *Joint Guidance on Overdraft Protection Programs*, 70 Fed. Reg. 9127 (Feb. 24, 2005). The Office of Thrift Supervision issued its own separate Guidance. Office of Thrift Supervision, *Guidance on Overdraft Protection Programs*, 70 Fed. Reg. 8428, (Feb. 18, 2005). The main difference with the OTS Guidance is that it avoids the use of the term "credit" to describe bounce loans.

555 *Joint Guidance*, 70 Fed. Reg. at 9129; OTS Guidance, 70 Fed. Reg. at 8430.

556 *Joint Guidance*, 70 Fed. Reg. at 9130–9131.

557 *Joint Guidance*, 70 Fed. Reg. at 9132; OTS Guidance, 70 Fed. Reg. at 8431.

558 69 Fed. Reg. 31,760 (June 7, 2004).

559 *See, e.g.*, Burge v. Pack, 785 S.W.2d 207 (Ark. 1990) for discussion of evidence necessary to establish a joint venture. *See generally* Existence of Joint Venture, 12 Proof of Facts 2d 295 (1977).

560 Securities & Exchange Comm'n v. First Securities Co., 507 F.2d 417 (7th Cir. 1974); *In re* York Furniture Co., 32 B.R. 211 (Bankr. S.D.N.Y. 1983) (transaction constituted joint venture, not loan); Donatelli v. Siskind, 565 N.Y.S.2d 224 (App. 1991) (arrangement found to be joint venture, not loan). *Cf.* D-Beam

The joint venture begins to look more like a high-interest loan, however, as the investor's risk of losing its investment decreases. An "investment" which is absolutely repayable is, in fact, a loan rather than an investment. Courts have found joint ventures to be usurious credit transactions when the investor's return on its funds is guaranteed by the contract,[561] or where the contingency under which the business may avoid repayment is a practical impossibility.[562] For example, in a Florida case, a contract supposedly for the construction and purchase of a condominium complex was found to be a usurious loan when the developer (i.e., borrower) received a $372,800 "preconstruction purchase price" minus a $36,200 "finders fee" and was obliged to complete the condominiums in twenty months or, alternatively, to repay $559,200. The court determined that the

complex could not have been constructed in the allotted twenty months and that usury law applied regardless of the outward appearance of the transaction.[563]

7.5.8 Income Buyers

7.5.8.1 General

Another form of high-cost lending occurs when companies buy the rights to certain future income sources in exchange for immediate cash payment. Most times, lenders will not characterize these transactions as loans, but will call them an assignment, sale of income, advance, or similar name.[564] The annualized interest rates on these loans have been reported to be as high as 280%.[565]

7.5.8.2 Assignment of Government Income

One popular target for income buyers are streams of government benefits. Loan schemes have involved assignment of Social Security benefits,[566] veteran's pensions,[567] and workers' compensation.[568] Another stream of govern-

---

Ltd. P'ship v. Roller Derby Skates, 366 F.3d 972 (9th Cir. 2004) (when promissory notes limited repayment to borrower's interest in royalty payments, loans were not usurious because of contingency); Concord Realty Co. v. Continental Funding Corp., 776 P.2d 1114 (Colo. 1989) (en banc) (usury law does not apply if return of principal is guaranteed but profit is uncertain). See generally § 7.2.3, *supra*, regarding whether a loan is usurious when part of the compensation is a contingent share of profits.

561 Beausejour Corp., N.V. v. Offshore Dev. Co., 802 F.2d 1319 (11th Cir. 1986); Hufnagel v. George, 121 F. Supp. 2d 305 (S.D.N.Y. 2000) (agreement creates a loan, not a joint venture, where advanced money was repayable on a date certain; no profits existed to pay the interest or return on the investment), *subsequent proceeding at* 135 F. Supp. 2d 406 (S.D.N.Y. 2001) (affirming that agreement creates a loan and voiding loan for violation of N.Y. criminal usury statute); Peterson v. Harville, 455 F. Supp. 16 (D. Or. 1977), *aff'd*, 623 F.2d 611 (9th Cir. 1980) (also emphasizing intent of parties); Dennis v. Bradbury, 236 F. Supp. 683 (D. Colo. 1964), *aff'd*, 368 F.2d 905 (10th Cir. 1966); Maze v. Sycamore Homes, Inc., 230 Cal. App. 2d 746, 41 Cal. Rptr. 338 (1964); Whittemore Homes, Inc. v. Fleishman, 190 Cal. App. 2d 554, 12 Cal. Rptr. 235 (1961); Oregrund Ltd. P'ship v. Shieve, 873 So. 2d 451 (Fla. Dist. Ct. App. 2004) (sale-option transaction held to be a disguised loan given the disparity in the "sale" amount and the true value of property); Dang v. F & S Land Dev. Corp., 618 P.2d 276 (Haw. 1980); Grotjohn Precise Connexiones Int'l, S.A. v. JEM Fin., Inc., 12 S.W.3d 859 (Tex. App. 2000); Johns v. Jaeb, 518 S.W.2d 857 (Tex. Ct. App. 1974). *See also In re* Venture Mortgage Fund, Ltd. P'ship, 245 B.R. 460 (Bankr. S.D.N.Y. 2000) (religious document creating a joint venture to avoid a religious ban on charging interest has no effect on whether the transaction is a usurious loan; court found business loan violated the New York criminal usury law), *aff'd*, 282 F.3d 185 (2d Cir. 2002). *Cf.* Jones v. Wells Fargo Bank, 5 Cal. Rptr. 3d 835 (Ct. App. 2003) (shared appreciation mortgage; parties did not dispute that arrangement was a loan, but court held no usury because California law exempted from usury cap national banks acting as a fiduciary for a trust). *But see* Florida Trading & Inv. Co. v. River Constr. Servs., 537 So. 2d 600 (Fla. Dist. Ct. App. 1988) (fact that agreement does not explicitly provide for sharing losses does not preclude its characterization as investment, where entity supplying capital was fully integrated into the operation).

562 Schwartz v. Lincoln Constr. & Dev. Corp., 455 So. 2d 612 (Fla. Dist. Ct. App. 1984).

563 *Id.*

564 *See, e.g.*, Structured Investments Co. v. Price (*In re* Price), 313 B.R. 805 (Bankr. E.D. Ark. 2004) (lender claimed that loan was a "sale of income stream"); Stone Street Capital v. Granati (*In re* Granati), 270 B.R. 575 (Bankr. E.D. Va. 2001) (lender characterized its purchase of an income stream as an assignment not a loan, court agreed with lender that it had a non-dischargeable property interest in the income stream), *aff'd*, 63 Fed. Appx. 741 (4th Cir. 2003); Rancman v. Interim Settlement Funding Corp., 2001 WL 1339487 (Ohio App. Ct. Oct. 31, 2001) (lender characterized payment collateralized by possible settlement a "contingent cash advance" not a loan; court disagreed), *aff'd on other grounds*, 789 N.E.2d 217 (Ohio 2003). *See generally*, §§ 7.5.4.1, *supra*, and 10.5.3, *infra*, concerning *choses* in action.

565 *See, e.g.*, Rancman v. Interim Settlement Funding Corp., 2001 WL 1339487 (Ohio App. Ct. Oct. 31, 2001), *aff'd on other grounds*, 789 N.E.2d 217 (Ohio 2003).

566 *See, e.g.*, Stewart v. Favors, 590 S.E.2d 186 (Ga. Ct. App. 2003) (lawsuit challenging loan arrangement that required borrowers to deposit their Social Security or SSI payments into bank accounts controlled by the lender; motion to compel arbitration denied.).

567 *See, e.g.*, Structured Investments Co. v. Price (*In re* Price), 313 B.R. 805 (Bankr. E.D. Ark. 2004) (assignment of veteran's pensions as security for loan); Amos v. Advanced Funding, Inc., Civ. Ac. 04-CV-0911 (N.D. Ga. Oct. 5, 2004) (complaint), *available at* www.consumerlaw.org (challenging loan scheme aimed at veterans claiming to "purchase" right to receive their benefits.). *See generally* Steve Tripoli, National Consumer Law Center, *In Harm's Way—At Home: Consumer Scams and the Direct Targeting of America's Military and Veterans* 25 (May 2003), *available at* www.consumerlaw.org.

568 *See, e.g.*, Florida Asset Financing v. Utah Labor Commission. 98 P.3d 436 (Utah Ct. App. 2004) (beneficiary pledged worker's compensation disability payments as security for loan; lender used sham trust to direct benefits payments to itself.).

ment income often "bought" in these schemes are lottery winnings that are paid out over many years.[569] In addition to usury claims, these loan schemes are often challengeable because the income source is statutorily protected from assignment.[570]

7.5.8.3 Litigation Finance Companies

An entire industry has developed around the concept of "litigation finance."[571] These are loans that are secured by the potential settlement of legal actions.[572] These loans have been justified as a way to provide injured plaintiffs, who may be in dire financial straits due to their injury or unemployment, with funds while they pursue a lawsuit. (Of course, the dire financial straits of consumers is often used as a justification for lending them money at astronomical prices.)

Challenging litigation finance as a disguised loan may be difficult because repayment is contingent upon the success-

ful settlement of a lawsuit.[573] An Ohio intermediate appellate court was willing to hold that a litigation finance arrangement was really a usurious loan, noting there was ample evidence to support the trial court's determination that no real risk of non-payment existed,[574] but the Ohio Supreme Court affirmed this decision on the basis that the arrangement was void as champerty, without considering the usury issue.[575] A settlement advance was held to be a loan where the borrower had already obtained a $27 million jury verdict in a case, but there was an issue as to whether the award would be reduced as excessive.[576] In that case, court reasoned there was no contingency and the lender has established an absolute right to repayment.

Litigation finance companies have attracted regulatory scrutiny. The New York Attorney General reached settlements with a number of litigation finance companies requiring them to make better disclosures of the cost of the advance and the total amount to be repaid.[577]

Not all litigation funding is contingent. Some agreements require a minimum specific repayment regardless of the outcome of the borrower's lawsuit.[578] However, the fact that principal must be repaid, but the amount of interest being charged is contingent upon success of the lawsuit, may insulate the lender from a usury claim.[579]

Also, some lenders will make loans secured by existing settlement that are paid over the course of several years instead of a lump sum.[580] These transactions should be more easily challenged as loans. These transactions may present usury claims,[581] as well as claims under state UDAP stat-

---

569 *See, e.g.*, Singer Asset Fin. v. Duboff Family Investments (*In re* Duboff), 290 B.R. 652 (Bankr. C.D. Ill. 2003) (assignment of Illinois lottery prize payments); Settlement Funding v. Jordan, 2003 WL 734531 (Mass. Super. Ct. Feb. 7, 2003) (loan secured by lottery winnings).

570 *See* 42 U.S.C. § 407(a) (prohibiting assignment of Social Security benefits); 37 U.S.C. § 701(c) (prohibiting assignment of military pay). *See also* Structured Investments Co. v. Price (*In re* Price), 313 B.R. 805 (Bankr. E.D. Ark. 2004) (assignment of benefits was prohibited by federal law; provision of agreement waiving borrower's right to raise issue of illegality was unconscionable under U.C.C.); Singer Asset Fin. v. Duboff Family Investments (*In re* Duboff), 290 B.R. 652 (Bankr. C.D. Ill. 2003) (assignment of Illinois lottery prize payments violated Illinois lottery law and thus was void); Florida Asset Financing v. Utah Labor Commission. 98 P.3d 436 (Utah Ct. App. 2004) (Utah law does not prohibit assignment of workers' compensation benefits, but state commission must comply with beneficiary's instruction to redirect payments from lender to beneficiary).

571 This industry grew quickly in the early 2000s. For example, the chair of the American Legal Fin. Association, which is the trade association for this industry, started making loans in 2000. By 2005, his company, LawCash, had made 3,000 loans with $25 million in loan volume. Joseph Fried, *Wanting to Settle a Lawsuit? Beware of Cash Advances*, New York Times, Apr. 4, 2005.

572 *See, e.g.*, Sparks v. Stone Street Capital, 2002 WL 1575404 (N.D. Tex. July 15, 2002) (class action on behalf of consumers who transferred their interests in structured settlement payments in exchange for money; motion to compel arbitration granted); Rancman v. Interim Settlement Funding Corp., 2001 WL 1339487 (Ohio App. Ct. Oct. 31, 2001) (payment collateralized by possible settlement in personal injury litigation), *aff'd on other grounds*, 789 N.E.2d 217 (Ohio 2003). Some commentators have suggested legalizing litigation funding, but setting up a regulatory structure to govern these transactions, and limiting fees to the state usury cap or 25% of the amount loaned. *See* Yifat Shaltiel, John Cofresi, *Litigation Lending for Personal Needs Act: A Regulatory Framework to Legitimize Third Party Litigation Fin.*, 58 Consumer Fin. L. Q. Rep. 347 (Winter 2004).

573 *See* § 7.2.3, *supra*, and § 10.5.3 *infra*.

574 Rancman v. Interim Settlement Funding Corp., 2001 WL 1339487 (Ohio App. Ct. Oct. 31, 2001).

575 Rancman v. Interim Settlement Funding Corp., 789 N.E.2d 217 (Ohio 2003).

576 Lawsuit Fin., L.L.C. v. Curry, 683 N.W.2d 233 (Mich. Ct. App. 2004).

577 John Caher, *State, Legal Settlement Advance Business Agree on Measures to Protect Consumers*, New York Law Journal, June 29, 2004, at 1.

578 *See, e.g.*, Houston v. Cohen (*In re* Cohen), 305 B.R. 886 (B.A.P. 9th Cir. 2004) (debtor's assignment of anticipated settlement proceeds was a loan because debtor obligated to pay off "promissory note" whether or not lawsuit was successful).

579 *See* Kraft v. Mason, 668 So. 2d 679 (Fla. Dist. Ct. App. 1996) (fact that payment of interest depended on contingency of successful lawsuit, and that the lender was an unsophisticated party, showed lack of corrupt intent to render loan usurious); Dopp v. Yari, 927 F. Supp. 814 (D.N.J. 1996) (following Kraft v. Mason; note this was a commercial case.). See generally § 7.2.3, *supra*, regarding whether a loan is usurious when part of the compensation is a contingent share of profits.

580 *See, e.g., In re* Wiggins, 273 B.R. 839 (Bankr. D. Idaho 2001) (loan in which young accident victim suffering from brain injuries sold his rights to a structured annuity).

581 Lawsuit Fin., L.L.C. v. Curry, 683 N.W.2d 233 (Mich. Ct. App. 2004) (settlement advances were loans when borrower had already obtained jury verdict; loans were usurious where agreement required borrower to pay $887,500 for principal advances totaling $177,500.).

utes.[582] Note that the terms of the settlement income source may prohibit assignment.[583] Assignments of legal settle- ments may require court approval in some states,[584] or may be subject to the filing requirements of Article 9 of the Uniform Commercial Code.[585]

---

582 *See, e.g., In re* Wiggins, 273 B.R. 839 (Bankr. D. Idaho 2001) (income buyer violated Idaho UDAP statute in convincing young accident victim suffering from brain injuries to sell his rights to a structured annuity).

583 Many settlements of tort claims result in annuities being paid to the plaintiff that often contain an anti-assignment clause. *See, e.g.,* Liberty Life Assurance Company v. Stone Street Capital, 93 F. Supp. 2d 630 (D. Md. 2000) (anti-assignment clause of structured settlement was enforceable by insurer that paid an- nuity); Grieve v. General Am. Life Ins., 58 F. Supp. 2d 319 (D. Vt. 1999) (same); First Providian, Ltd. Liab. Co. v. Evans, 852

So. 2d 908 (Fla. Dist. Ct. App. 2003). There may be an issue of whether these anti-assignment clauses are prohibited by Article 9 of the U.C.C. *See* National Consumer Law Center, Reposses- sions and Warranties § 2.1.8 (5th ed. 2002 and Supp.).

584 *See, e.g.,* First Providian, Ltd. Liab. Co. v. Evans, 852 So. 2d 908 (Fla. Dist. Ct. App. 2003).

585 Houston v. Cohen (*In re* Cohen), 305 B.R. 886 (B.A.P. 9th Cir. 2004) (debtor's assignment of anticipated settlement proceeds was security interest for a loan subject to filing requirements of U.C.C. Article 9.).

Chapter 8   Credit Insurance

8.1 Introduction

One of the most remunerative methods for imposing extra costs on a credit transaction (open- or closed-end) is through the sale of credit insurance. The most common basic types of credit insurance include:

- Credit life, which protects the account against the loss of the borrower's life;
- Credit disability or accident and health (A&H), which is an indemnity insurance to cover payments in the event the borrower's income is interrupted for health reasons;
- Credit property, which protects the collateral;
- Loss of income, an indemnity policy to provide limited payments in the event of involuntary loss of employment;
- Private mortgage insurance, an indemnity policy required by mortgage lenders to cover a percentage of the losses they could incur if the borrower defaults and the property is foreclosed; and
- Debt cancellation or suspension agreements, a new entrant into the market, works like the credit life, disability, and loss of income insurances described above from the consumer's perspective but is not considered "insurance" under many state laws.

Because it is so profitable for both the creditors and insurance industry, the pressures to sell credit life, disability, property, and loss of income products are enormous. As a consequence, consumers spend as much as $6 billion per year on credit insurance, often with little understanding of what they have bought.[1] This volume of business conceals annual overcharges of $2.5 billion[2] where "overcharge" is defined in an economic sense rather than a legal sense.[3] Consequently, for many years advisors outside the credit industry have recommended that most consumers do not purchase these products.[4]

Though credit insurance is regulated to varying degrees in every state, neither the state regulatory bodies nor competitive pressures successfully control the problems.[5] This lack

---

1 Jack Gillis, James Hunt, D.J. Powers, Birny Birnbaum, *Credit Insurance Overcharges Hit $2.5 Annually*, Consumer Federation of America and Center for Economic Justice (Nov. 2001), *available at* www.consumerfed.org/credins.pdf (in 2000, consumers paid about $6 billion for the traditional credit insurance products). *See also* Mary Griffin & Birny Birnbaum, *Credit Insurance: The $2 Billion a Year Rip-Off*, Consumers Union and the Center for Economic Justice (Mar. 1999) (from 1995 to 1997, more than $17 billion of credit insurance was sold in the U.S., excluding private mortgage insurance). This is up from $2.5 billion in 1979. *See Credit Life Insurance Hearing Before the Subcomm. on Antitrust, Monopoly and Business Rights of the Senate Comm. on the Judiciary*, 96th Cong, 1st Sess. 48 (1979) (statement of Robert Sable).

2 Jack Gillis, James Hunt, D.J. Powers, Birny Birnbaum, *Credit Insurance Overcharges Hit $2.5 Annually*, Consumer Federation of America and Center for Economic Justice (Nov. 2001), *available at* www.consumerfed.org/credins.pdf.

3 Overcharges in this report were calculated as the difference between the total cost of the premiums that were actually charged and the total of the premiums that would have been charged if the states had implemented 60% loss-ratios. *Id.* at 2–3.

4 *E.g.*, *Credit Insurance: The Quiet Overcharge*, Consumer Reports at 415 (July 1979); *Credit Life Insurance: Oversold and Overpriced*, Changing Times at 62 (Mar. 1980); *Credit Life Insurance: The Nation's Worst Insurance Rip Off*, Statement of Consumer Federation of America and National Insurance Consumer Organization (June 4, 1990), Clearinghouse No. 45,773 (updated May 20, 1992, Clearinghouse No. 45,773A) (and updated again July 25, 1995, Clearinghouse No. 45,773B); Jack Gillis, James Hunt, D.J. Powers, Birny Birnbaum, *Credit Insurance Overcharges Hit $2.5 Annually*, Consumer Federation of America and Center for Economic Justice (Nov. 2001), *available at* www.consumerfed.org/credins.pdf.

    One of the exceptions is where a credit union is the creditor. That credit insurance typically meets the recommended standards for price-to-value.

5 Jack Gillis, James Hunt, D.J. Powers, Birny Birnbaum, *Credit Insurance Overcharges Hit $2.5 Annually*, Consumer Federation of America and Center for Economic Justice (Nov. 2001), *available at* www.consumerfed.org/credins.pdf. (according to this report, the 2000 national loss-ratio for credit life was 40.7%, for credit disability was 46.1%, for credit unemployment was 5.8% and for credit property was 14.7%, generally *down* from previous years; there were only 11 states and the District of Columbia that scored above 50% in their loss-ratios for either credit life or disability or both; of these 11 states, the loss-ratios for credit life *or* disability in only 5 states exceeded 60%; in *no* state did the loss-ratios for both credit life *and* disability exceed 60%).

    Some states, however, have recently lowered prima facie rates for credit insurance. *See, e.g.*, Colorado, Department of Regulatory Agencies, Div. of Ins., Amended Regulation § 4-9-2 (setting forth an appendix of "reasonable" credit insurance rates based on a 40% loss ratio in lieu of prima facie rates and providing an alternative method in which maximum rates are listed by type of coverage and base of coverage) *available at*

of control, combined with the product's profitability, leads to great potential for abuse.[6] Nevertheless, practitioners rarely explore credit insurance issues. This chapter will seek to identify some of the potential overcharge claims that may arise in the credit insurance context, and to identify other theories which also may be used to challenge various common credit insurance practices. It is necessary first to have some understanding of the nature of the industry in order to identify the issues and critically evaluate a case.

8.2 Economic Incentives; Market Failures

8.2.1 Background

Credit life insurance initially was sold in connection with Morris Plan Bank loans in 1917, its purpose admittedly to protect the creditor in the event of the borrower's death, and the premium cost was paid by the creditor.[7] Today, most lenders sell insurance for which the borrower pays a separate premium charge.

Credit insurance may be written as an individual policy, sold directly to the borrower. More often, however, it is a group policy, issued by the insurer to the creditor. The actual terms of the policy are set forth in the master policy between the creditor and the insurer. The group eligible to be insured under this policy is the creditor's borrowers, who are "enrolled" as members of the group if they purchase the insurance. Instead of receiving an insurance policy, a borrower receives a certificate of insurance.

Group insurance has administrative economies which should make it cheaper than individual policies, as there is less administrative work for the insurer. However, because of other pressures,[8] group credit insurance provides no cost advantage for consumers. (In fact, the use of group policies, by which the creditor merely enrolls a borrower, may allow the creditor to avoid licensing or other regulatory requirements of a state insurance department.)

8.2.2 Benefits to Creditor

The impetus for selling credit insurance comes from the three important ways in which a creditor benefits from its sale.

1. *The creditor receives significant compensation from the sale of insurance from the insurer whose product they sell.* Because the lender receives commissions at a specified percentage of each premium dollar, sometimes as much as 40–50%, the lender has a strong financial incentive to sell the most expensive insurance to borrowers, rather than the cheapest.[9] In fact, cheaper providers may be driven out of

---

www.dora.state.co.us/insurance/regs/4-9-2.pdf; Ind. Admin. Code tit. 760, r. 1-5.1 (lowering prima facie rates and establishing new standards for the sale of credit life insurance and credit accident and health); Memorandum from Randall Ward Regarding Credit Insurance Rate Modification, Clearinghouse No. 54594 (Ohio Dep't of Ins. Oct. 28, 2002) (ordering a 7.5% reduction in prima facie rates); South Carolina Dept. of Ins. Bulletin, No. 1999-06, Dec. 3, 1999 (gradually lowering prima facie rates in 2001 and then again in 2003), *available at* www.doi.state.sc.us/Eng/Public/bulletins/Bulletin996.asp.

6   Indeed, a former chair of the California Senate Insurance Committee took bribes from the credit insurance industry to push (successfully) for legislation which helped hike the price of the product. A consumer's RICO action against the legislator was blocked by a finding of legislative immunity, Chappell v. Robbins, 73 F.3d 918 (9th Cir. 1996). (It is unclear why the bribers were not sued, instead of the bribee.)

7   College of Bus. Adm., Ohio Univ., Consumer Credit Life and Disability Insurance, 7–8 (C. Hubbard, ed. 1973); National Ass'n of Ins. Comm'rs, A Background Study of the Regulation of Credit Life and Disability Insurance, 3 (1970); Dobson, *Credit Insurance: The Hidden Insurance*, 65 Mich. Bar Journal 166, 167 (Feb. 1986). (Arthur Morris and the Morris Plan Banks may merely have brought about the rebirth of the concept. There is apparently reference to credit insurance in the Code of Hammurabi.)

8   *See* §§ 8.2.2, 8.2.3, *infra*.

9   One company's 1998 SEC 10-K filing revealed both its philosophy of reverse competition as well as the commissions paid for 1994–1998:

> The Company uses contracts which allow the Company's clients [i.e., creditors] to participate in the underwriting results of policies they market to their customers. The "Retro Plan" contract links a client's overall commission to the claims experience on policies marketed to its customers, so that low loss-ratios result in higher commissions for the client and the high loss-ratios result in lower commissions. Another form of participation is a profit sharing contract under which the client earns up to 50% of the profits generated from its insurance business. The Company also reinsures premiums generated by certain clients to the clients' own captive insurance companies or to reinsurance subsidiaries in which clients have an ownership interest.

See American Bankers Ins. Group, 1998 10-K Filing (Mar. 30, 1999), *available at* www.sec.gov. The same filing reported the following loss-ratios, commissions, and return on equity: In 1994, percent of net premiums earned of benefits/claims, losses/settlement expenses were 40%, commissions were 40% and return on equity was 14.1%. The same percentages in 1995 were 37.3% (benefits/claims, losses/settlement expenses), 42.4% (commissions), 15.7% (return on equity). The same percentages in 1996 were 37.9% (benefits/claims, losses/settlement expenses), 41.5% (commissions), 16.5% (return on equity). The same percentages in 1997 were 36.6% (benefits/claims, losses/settlement expenses), 42.2% (commissions), 16.6% (return on equity). The same percentages in 1998 were 35.5% (benefits/claims, losses/settlement expenses), 43.7% (commissions), 31.4% (return on equity). *Id.* at 37. *See also* Spears v. Colonial Bank of Alabama, 514 So. 2d 814 (Ala. 1987) (car dealer, who received a 50% commission from each premium, earned profits of nearly a quarter million dollars in one year from his insurance sales); Higgins v. Harold-Chevrolet-GEO, 2004 WL 2660923 (Minn. Ct.

the market.[10] This financial stake in the credit insurance sale, coupled with market deficiencies which prevent consumers from exerting countervailing pressures,[11] sets the stage for reverse competition. Instead of competing to offer the cheapest insurance, insurers compete "in reverse" to offer the most expensive insurance so they can offer the highest commissions.

In addition to commissions, creditors may receive compensation in other forms. The insurer may also pay dividends or retrospective rate credits to the lender if the insurer has a favorable claims experience.[12] Further, many of the larger finance companies market the policies of a "captive insurer"—one which is affiliated with or wholly-owned by the finance company. ITT Financial (formerly Thorp Finance and Aetna Finance), for example, sold the insurance products of its affiliates ITT Lyndon Life and ITT Lyndon Property, among other affiliates. Beneficial has sold insurance through its subsidiary, Central National Life of Omaha. The same funneling of the insurance profits to other relatives in the creditor's corporate family may occur through reinsurance agreements. In these arrangements, the creditor initially purchases policies from an independent insurer, which then shares the risk, by reinsuring with an insurer affiliated with the creditor.[13] It should be noted, too, that

individual employees may receive some form of incentive or bonuses based on their insurance sales,[14] thus giving an individual loan officer economic pressures to sell insurance which are personal, as well as institutional.

Creditors also profit from investment income. Even though the borrower theoretically pays a single premium in advance for the entire loan term, the lender frequently does not forward the premium to the insurer. Rather, it is placed in escrow, and the creditor computes a monthly group premium due (after subtracting any premium refunds and creditor compensation) and then remits the insurer's share to the insurer.[15] The result is that the creditor may get investment interest earnings on the borrower's premium in addition to the interest the borrower pays directly.

2. *The creditor is the primary beneficiary.* Quite simply, the insurance is added security on the account. Though the borrower or the family may be protected from the hardships of a delinquent debt in the event of death or other misfortune, the major function "is to protect the lender, not the borrower, by insuring that a loan will be repaid despite destruction of collateral or impairment of the borrower's earning ability."[16]

3. *Interest is charged on the premium.* If the purchase of the credit life or A&H is voluntary, or if the borrower has a choice of providers on required property insurance on collateral, the Truth in Lending Act and most state credit laws[17] permit the cost of the premium to be included in the principal or amount financed. Obviously, the larger the principal, the greater the dollar yield to the creditor in interest; while the larger the portion of a debt attributed to the principal, the lower the interest rate will appear. (The same impact occurs with the Truth in Lending calculations.) Given the trend toward longer terms and larger loans, the premiums can significantly inflate the cost of the loan, by several thousand dollars in a mobile home or second mortgage loan. Consider this example where the credit insurance premium was financed as part of the principal in a subprime mortgage loan. The credit life insurance premium added $10,000 to the loan principal.

App. Nov. 23, 2004) (unpublished opinion) (car dealer retained almost one-half of the cost of credit insurance premiums and the commission was not disclosed to the consumer); Credit Life Insurance Revisited II (second update of Consumer Federation of America/National Insurance Consumer Organization July 25, 1995, n.12, Clearinghouse No. 45,773B) (commission and other compensation to creditors from credit life averages 45% nationally; range is from 20% or less in NY to *70% or more in LA*; this excludes additional finance charge on premiums; return also varies with type of creditor, with auto dealers receiving the largest margin). *See generally* § 8.2.3.1, *infra*. The benefits to the lender increase when the loan is flipped or refinanced several times over, especially if the Rule of 78 is used to rebated unearned insurance premiums. For an example of flipping and the sale of insurance on each transaction, see Hager v. American Gen. Fin., Inc., 37 F. Supp. 2d 778 (S.D. W. Va. 1999).

10 Prudential Insurance explained in one proceeding that it lost "millions of dollars in credit insurance, millions of it" because it "indulge[d] in the sin of not charging enough for its coverage." Testimony of W.L. Skinner, Sept. 4, 1964 before the Committee to Investigate All Insurance Rates and Practices Concerning Credit Life, Credit Accident and Health, Credit Property Insurance Sold in South Carolina, cited in Hearings on the Consumer Credit Industry *(Credit Insurance) Before the Subcommittee on Antitrust and Monopoly of the Committee on the Judiciary of the U.S. Senate*, 90th Cong., 1st Sess. (1967) 96, n.19.

11 *See* § 8.2.3.1, *infra*. *See, e.g.*, Spears v. Colonial Bank of Alabama, 514 So. 2d 814, 817–18 (Ala. 1987) (special concurrence).

12 College of Bus. Adm., Ohio Univ., Consumer Credit Life and Disability Insurance 29–31 (C. Hubbard, ed. 1973); Fagg, Credit Life and Disability Insurance, 94–99 (1986). *See, e.g.*, Kenty v. Bank One, Columbus, N.A., 92 F.3d 384 (6th Cir. 1996).

13 College of Bus. Adm., Ohio Univ., Consumer Credit Life and Disability Insurance 30 (C. Hubbard, ed. 1973). For further description of reinsurance arrangements, see Alinco Life Ins.

Co. v. United States, 373 F.2d 336 (Ct. Cl. 1967).

14 *See Equity Predators: Stripping, Flipping and Packing Their Way to Profits: Hearing before the Special Committee on Aging United States Senate*, 105th Cong. 2d Sess. 33-34, Serial No. 105-18 (Mar. 16, 1998) (statement of Jim Dough, former employee of predatory lender); Fagg, Credit Life and Disability Insurance 50 (1986).

15 College of Bus. Adm., Ohio Univ., Consumer Credit Life and Disability Insurance 35 (C. Hubbard, ed. 1973). *See generally* Fagg, Credit Life and Disability Insurance 94–100, 106–108 (1986).

16 Bailey v. Defenbaugh & Co. of Cleveland, Inc., 513 F. Supp. 232, 243 (N.D. Miss. 1981).

17 *See* § 8.5.2, *infra*. *See also* Hearing on *Equity Predators: Stripping, Flipping and Packing Their Way to Profits: Hearing before the Special Committee on Aging United States Senate*, 105th Cong. 2d Sess. 33–34, Serial No. 105-18 (Mar. 16, 1998) (statement of Jim Dough, former employee of predatory lender).

	WITH CREDIT INSURANCE	WITHOUT CREDIT INSURANCE
Principal	$68,593	$58,366
Note Rate	14.79%	14.79%
Monthly Payment	239 @ $856 plus 1 @ $54,327	240 @ $759.52
Total of Payments	$258,866	$182,280

The total cost difference between these two loans, the first a real loan, and the second, the same loan without the credit insurance, is over $96 per month plus the final balloon payment of $76,586.[18] The loan would have amortized in full over 240 months but for the credit insurance premium! It accounts for the balloon payment.

This inflation is exacerbated by the fact that most states permit insurance premiums to be calculated on the total of payments, which, in turn, includes the cost of the premiums and the finance charge, thus spiraling the cost.[19]

The only exception to this discussion involves private mortgage insurance. This type of insurance is required by mortgage lenders but the premium is usually collected as part of the monthly payment and included in the escrow, like the premium for hazard insurance and property taxes. Creditors are not, therefore, collecting interest on the premiums.[20]

8.2.3 Excessive Cost of Credit Insurance

8.2.3.1 Reverse Competition; Market Failures

Credit insurance, for the most part, is an overpriced insurance product. As the previous section suggests, the price the consumer pays for this insurance goes as much for additional profits to the creditor and insurer as it does for the protection it provides the borrower. In the absence of more stringent regulation than has occurred in the past, credit insurance is likely to remain overpriced.

The phenomenon of reverse competition is the primary explanation for the excessive cost of credit insurance. Reverse competition is the result of two intertwined factors: the financial incentives to the creditor to sell the most expensive insurance to its customers on the one hand; and the inability of consumers, for a variety of reasons, to force the price down by their market behavior on the other.

The economic impetus for creditors to push hard the sale of credit insurance is largely explained by how much profit

they make from credit insurance sales. Evidence in a Virginia rate-setting hearing for small loan companies showed that those companies received *one-third* of their net income from credit insurance.[21] Other studies show credit insurance constituting 30%–50% of pre-tax income for some lenders.[22] Insurance profits can even exceed the profits creditors make from their credit business.[23] Another way to measure the excessive compensation earned by lenders is to review the compensation ratio, i.e., the relationship of the commissions paid to the lenders to the total premiums charged for the product. For one major credit insurance company, the ratio ranged from 40% in 1994 to 43.7% in 1998.[24]

One startling example of the degree of the inflation in the cost of credit insurance due to the reverse competition effect is discussed in an Eleventh Circuit decision in which an insurer sought to avoid paying the FDIC the cost of rebates on unearned insurance premiums for approximately 300 prematurely terminated mortgage loans.[25] The insurance company defended on the ground that it had received only 35% of the premiums, the other 65% having been paid to the creditors' officers and employees or distributed to the creditors' stockholders![26] Ten years later, the picture had little improved generally. A 1994 CFA/NICO study reports that creditor compensation, *exclusive* of extra finance charge income, averages nearly 45% of the insurance cost.[27]

This loading of hidden creditor-profit into the costs of the product helps explain why credit insurance is no bargain for consumers. A comparison with regular term life insurance is

---

18 *Hearing on Predatory Mortgage Lending: The Problem, Impact and Responses*, Hearing before the Senate Committee on Banking, Housing, and Urban Affairs, July 26, 2001, *available at* www.senate.gov/%7Ebanking/01_07hrg/072601/miller.htm (this example appeared in Appendix B of the written testimony of Attorney General Thomas J. Miller of Iowa).

19 *See* § 8.5.3.1, *infra*.

20 *See* discussion below in § 8.3.2.1, *infra*.

21 *Credit Life Insurance Hearing Before the Subcomm. on Antitrust, Monopoly and Business Rights of the Senate Comm. on the Judiciary*, 96th Cong, 1st Sess. 48 (1979) (statement of Robert Sable). *See also* Spears v. Colonial Bank of Alabama, 514 So. 2d 814 (Ala. 1987) (car dealer, who received a 50% commission from each premium, earned profits of nearly a quarter million dollars in one year from his insurance sales); *Equity Predators: Stripping, Flipping and Packing Their Way to Profits: Hearing Before the Special Committee on Aging United States Senate*, 105th Cong. 2d Sess., 33–34, Serial No. 105-18 (Mar. 16, 1998) (statement of Jime Dough, former employee of predatory lender).

22 *Credit Life Insurance Hearing Before the Subcomm. on Antitrust, Monopoly and Business Rights of the Senate Comm. on the Judiciary*, 96th Cong, 1st Sess. 48 (1979) (statement of Robert Sable).

23 Dobson, *Credit Insurance: The Hidden Insurance*, 65 Mich. Bar Journal 167 (Feb. 1986).

24 American Banker's Insurance Group, 1998 10-K Filing (Mar. 30, 1999) at 37, *available at* www.sec.gov.

25 Federal Deposit Ins. Corp. v. Gulf Life Ins., 737 F.2d 1513 (11th Cir. 1984).

26 The insurance company lost on this issue, but it did recover a $36,349 judgment for overpaid commissions from a former employee of the creditor.

27 Credit Life Insurance Revisited II (second update of Consumer Federation of America/National Insurance Consumer Organization July 25, 1995, Clearinghouse No. 45,773B) (ranging from a low of 20% to less in NY to high of 70% or more in LA). Auto dealers generally have the highest margins. The figures include both the upfront commissions and back-end compensation.

telling; the premium for a credit life policy on a $10,000 car loan at 13% for four years might cost $438.64 (including interest), while a term life policy for the same amount might cost $229.[28]

The financial benefits of expensive insurance explains creditors' failure to seek the lowest cost insurance, but consumers' failure to bring competitive pressures to bear must also be explained. Quite simply, the matter of insurance is of peripheral concern to most borrowers. The absolute dollar cost of the premium may seem small in comparison to their total obligation; the *idea* of credit insurance seems sound, and consumers have no way of knowing what a genuinely reasonable cost for the protection would be.[29] If the consumer does any comparison shopping, it is for the primary product—the credit—not an ancillary product such as insurance.[30] Further, all too often, borrowers are unaware that they purchased insurance, or felt coercion in purchasing the insurance.[31]

8.2.3.2 Low Loss-Ratios Demonstrate Excessive Cost

That credit insurance is overpriced can be demonstrated by reviewing what is called the "loss-ratio" of credit insurers.[32] A loss-ratio is the percentage of each premium dollar which is paid out to insureds in claims benefits. In other words, if an insurer has a 35% loss-ratio, then 35% of each premium dollar is paid out to insureds for claims. The other 65% is retained for the insurer's expenses and profit and the creditor's compensation. Insurance with a "high" loss-ratio means that most of the premium dollar is spent for the benefit of insureds, and that the insurance may be a good buy for consumers.

Credit insurance, however, historically has had low loss-ratios. The most recent of several Congressional examinations of credit insurance (in 1979) found that data indicated that typical loss-ratios were in the 35% to 40% range for credit life insurance.[33] The 1979 average compares unfavorably with the 80% loss-ratio then required in Canada[34] or sometimes found in group life insurance plans sold to employers.[35] By 1990, the loss-ratio had only progressed to a 41.5% average nationwide.[36] In the wake of negative publicity, some states responded by lowering rates resulting in another incremental advance to an estimated 44% average loss-ratio nationally,[37] though by 1997, the national average was only 41.6%.[38] By 2000, the national average declined to 40.7%.[39] These loss-ratios compare unfavorably with the 60% minimum loss-ratio recommended by the National Association of Insurance Commissioners.[40]

---

28 Dobson, *Credit Insurance: The Hidden Insurance*, 65 Mich. Bar Journal 167 (Feb. 1986). This regular term life premium assumed a 40-year-old male. *Id.* at 167, n.14. Regular life insurance takes age and sex into account in establishing cost, while credit insurance does not. *Id.* The industry sometimes touts this lack of underwriting factors in pricing as an advantage. However, the common practice of post-claim underwriting counterbalances that. *See* § 8.5.5, *infra*.

29 While the industry likes to point to studies showing a lack of buyer resentment as to credit insurance, e.g., Fagg, Credit Life and Disability Insurance 463–470 (1986), the survey questionnaires do not fully set the stage for the respondents. As yet, no survey has prefaced its questions with an explanation that the product is as much as 4 times more expensive than comparable non-credit insurance, that as much as 30-65 cents of each premium dollar is paid to the creditor on top of the interest the borrower is already paying, and that the premiums cause an inflation of the interest they pay. If the consumers balance that background information against the benefits of convenience in the event of an insured loss, evidence of buyer resentment may rise. (One of the problems about hidden charges to consumers is that they do not complain about that which they can not see.)

As an interesting side note, however, the most recent, admittedly unscientific, NCLC priority survey found the excessive cost of credit insurance to be listed as a high priority by 41% of the client respondents.

30 Alinco Life Ins. Co. v. United States, 373 F.2d 336, 338 n.3 (Ct. Cl. 1967); Spears v. Colonial Bank of Alabama, 514 So. 2d 814, 818 (Ala. 1987) (special concurrence).

31 *See* § 8.5.2, *infra*.

32 This is a term which also must be understood in order to appreciate the regulatory scheme for credit insurance. *See* § 8.4.2.1, *infra*.

33 *Credit Life Insurance Hearing Before the Subcomm. on Antitrust, Monopoly and Business Rights of the Senate Comm. on the Judiciary*, 96th Cong, 1st Sess. 3 (1979).

34 *Credit Life Insurance Revisited: A Continuing Consumer Ripoff*, Statement of Consumer Federation of America and National Insurance Consumer Organization, Clearinghouse No. 45,773A (May 20, 1992).

35 Fonseca, Handling Consumer Credit Cases § 12:10 at 497 (3d ed. 1986). Compare it, too, with the 75% loss-ratio target for Medicare Supplement group policies (65% individual). Credit Life Insurance Revisited II (second update of Consumer Federation of America/National Insurance Consumer Organization July 25, 1995, n.6, Clearinghouse No. 45,773B).

36 *Credit Life Insurance Revisited: A Continuing Consumer Ripoff*, Statement of Consumer Federation of America and National Insurance Consumer Organization, Clearinghouse No. 45,773A (May 20, 1992). (This updates a report issued June 4, 1990, available as Clearinghouse No. 45,773.) *See also In re* Universal Underwriters Life Ins. Co., 685 N.W.2d 44 (Minn. Ct. App. 2004) (upholding state's action disallowing as excessive an insurer's credit life and disability rates, where the insurer's average loss ratio was significantly below 50%, even though the rates were within the prima facie range).

37 *Credit Life Insurance Revisited II* (second update of Consumer Federation of America/National Insurance Consumer Organization July 25, 1995, Clearinghouse No. 45,773B).

38 Mary Griffin & Birny Birnbaum, *Credit Insurance: The $2 Billion a Year Rip-Off*, Consumers Union and the Center for Economic Justice (Mar. 1999).

39 Jack Gillis, James Hunt, D.J. Powers, Birny Birnbaum, *Credit Insurance Overcharges Hit $2.5 Annually*, Consumer Federation of America and Center for Economic Justice 3 (Nov. 2001). This report lists the loss-ratios per type of credit insurance by state.

40 In 1990, only New York, Maine and DC met that standard. Only nine others met even a 50% loss-ratio. *Credit Life Insurance Revisited: A Continuing Consumer Ripoff*, Statement of Con-

Credit disability insurance fares slightly better in loss-ratios. In 1997, the national loss-ratio was 48.6%.[41] Six states and Puerto Rico exceeded the 60% benchmark.[42] However, by 2000, the loss-ratio dropped to 46.1%, with only five states reaching or exceeding the 60% mark.[43]

Credit property insurance, which is generally not rate regulated, has even lower loss-ratios (though the NAIC passed a model credit property act containing a 60% loss-ratio requirement in 2001). An early credit property insurance study found loss-ratios ranging between 7% and 25%.[44] A 1997 investigation revealed that the average loss-ratio was 26.3%.[45] By 2000, however, that ratio declined to an abysmal 14.7%.[46]

Finally, in 1997, unemployment insurance posted a dismal 12.6% national loss-ratio.[47] By 2000, this ratio had dropped to 5.8%.[48]

In theory, rate regulation of credit life and A&H focuses on loss-ratios in an effort to assure that the cost of credit insurance is reasonable in relation to the benefits.[49] For a number of reasons, rate regulation has not made credit insurance a cost-effective purchase for consumers. First, where rates are set by reference to a targeted, or "benchmark" loss-ratio, the benchmark is most often 50% or 60%.[50] This probably is overly generous, given that the insurers' expenses average only 22¢ to 26¢ per premium dollar.[51]

Second, the insurance rates set for credit life and A&H are the result of an estimate as to what rate would result in achieving the benchmark loss-ratio.[52] However, it is an estimating process that is often wrong and rarely re-examined. The 1979 Senate hearings showed that the credit life rates in forty states would produce loss-ratios of less than 50%; sixteen states had rates that would produce loss-ratios of less than 40%.[53] A decade later only two states and the District of Columbia had loss-ratios over 60%; nine states had 50–60% loss-ratios; eight states had 40–50% loss-ratios. The remainder were below 40%.[54] By 1995, these figures had not improved significantly: three states and the District of Columbia had loss-ratios over 60%; seven states had loss-ratios between 50–60%; fifteen states had 40–50% loss-ratios; and twenty-five states were below 40%.[55] Most

sumer Federation of America and National Insurance Consumer Organization (May 20, 1992), updating *Credit Life Insurance: The Nation's Worst Insurance Ripoff* (June 4, 1990). The two reports are available as Clearinghouse No. 45,773 and 45,773A. As of 1994 only one more state—Vermont—met the NAIC 60% target. *Credit Life Insurance Revisited II* (second update of Consumer Federation of America/National Insurance Consumer Organization July 25, 1995, Clearinghouse No. 45,773B). By 1997, only New York exceeded that 60% mark by posting a loss-ratio of 67.6%. Mary Griffin & Birny Birnbaum, *Credit Insurance: The $2 Billion a Year Rip-Off*, Consumers Union and the Center for Economic Justice 7 (Mar. 1999). Discovery in a post-claim eligibility case filed in Hawaii produced some interesting figures. *See* Lopez v. Associates Fin. Servs. of Hawaii, Inc., Clearinghouse No. 52,509 (D. Haw. Motion for Summary Judgment filed Oct. 29, 1998) (Associates answers to interrogatories show that in 1995, it made 689 mortgage loans in Hawaii, 408 of which included credit life [59%]; in 1996, it made 628 mortgage loans, 341 of which included credit life [54%]; and in 1997, it made 530 mortgage loans, 197 of which included credit life [37%]. The number of claims filed in 1995 were only 46; in 1996, 63, in 1997, 66. The loss-ratios were not obtained in discovery. Employee bonus programs are also attached.).

41 Mary Griffin & Birny Birnbaum, *Credit Insurance: The $2 Billion a Year Rip-Off*, Consumers Union and the Center for Economic Justice 3 (Mar. 1999).

42 *Id.* at 7. These states were Maine, New Jersey, New York, Pennsylvania, Vermont, West Virginia.

43 Jack Gillis, James Hunt, D.J. Powers, Birny Birnbaum, *Credit Insurance Overcharges Hit $2.5 Annually*, Consumer Federation of America and Center for Economic Justice 3 (Nov. 2001). These states are West Virginia (80%), South Carolina (60%), Maine (78%), Pennsylvania (63%), and New Jersey (64%).

44 *Credit Life Insurance Hearing Before the Subcomm. on Antitrust, Monopoly and Business Rights of the Senate Comm. on the Judiciary*, 96th Cong, 1st Sess. 43 (1979) (statement of Robert Sable).

45 Mary Griffin & Birny Birnbaum, *Credit Insurance: The $2 Billion a Year Rip-Off*, Consumers Union and the Center for Economic Justice 3 (Mar. 1999) (this loss-ratio relates only to credit property insurance sold in conjunction with closed-end loans; on the other hand the loss-ratio drops to only 11.6% for credit property sold to credit card holders).

46 Jack Gillis, James Hunt, D.J. Powers, Birny Birnbaum, *Credit Insurance Overcharges Hit $2.5 Annually*, Consumer Federation of America and Center for Economic Justice 3 (Nov. 2001).

47 Mary Griffin & Birny Birnbaum, *Credit Insurance: The $2 Billion a Year Rip-Off*, Consumers Union and the Center for Economic Justice 3 (Mar. 1999).

48 Jack Gillis, James Hunt, D.J. Powers, Birny Birnbaum, *Credit Insurance Overcharges Hit $2.5 Annually*, Consumer Federation of America and Center for Economic Justice 3 (Nov. 2001).

49 *See* § 8.4.2.1, *infra*.

50 Consumer Credit Insurance Association Info. Bull., Vol. XXXV, No. 61 (July 16, 1986). *See also* Fagg, Credit Life and Disability Insurance Appx. D (1986).

51 Dobson, *Credit Insurance: The Hidden Insurance*, 65 Mich. Bar Journal 169 (Feb. 1986).

52 This is discussed in more detail in § 8.4.2.1, *infra*.

53 *Credit Life Insurance Hearing Before the Subcomm. on Antitrust, Monopoly and Business Rights of the Senate Comm. on the Judiciary*, 96th Cong, 1st Sess. 2 (1979).

54 *Credit Life Insurance: The Nation's Worst Insurance Ripoff*, Statement of Consumer Federation of America and National Insurance Consumer Organization, Clearinghouse No. 47,773 (June 4, 1990), updated by *Credit Life Insurance Revisited: A Continuing Consumer Ripoff*, Clearinghouse No. 47,773A (May 20, 1992). *See also* § 8.4.2.1.1, *infra*. CFA/NICO's 1994 review lists only 4 jurisdictions meeting the NAIC 60% target loss-ratio and seventeen states showing "minimally effective regulation" at 50% loss-ratio and/or rates of 40¢/$100/year. Of the thirty states that do not meet these minimal standards, six are under 30% (AL, HI, KS, LA, MS, MN). *Credit Life Insurance Revisited II* (second update of Consumer Federation of America/National Insurance Consumer Organization July 25, 1995, Clearinghouse No. 45,773B).

55 Most Credit Life Insurance Still a Rip-Off, Clearinghouse No. 45,773C (update to Consumer Federation of America/National

recently, a report issued in 2001 lists only five states with loss-ratios of 60% or more for one type of credit insurance and only seven additional states and the District of Columbia posted loss-ratios exceeding 50%.[56] Further rate regulation usually allows significant commissions to creditors, though the need to allow creditor compensation as a part of each premium dollar itself is open to question. Even without commissions, creditors would probably continue to sell credit insurance due to the added yield resulting from financing the premiums and the added loan security it provides them.[57] Finally, credit property and involuntary unemployment are generally not rate regulated at all and the loss-ratio therefore is likely to be very low.[58] As a result of recent attention focused on the high price of credit insurance, the past few years have seen more states reviewing their credit life and disability rates, most often resulting in a lowering of the rates.[59] A trend toward closer scrutiny and reasonable pricing would be welcome news for consumers.

Nevertheless, it is too soon to say the problem has been cured. The convergence of all the above factors makes the credit insurance area one ripe for abuse,[60] so much so that it has been called "The Tail That Wags the Dog."[61] Consequently, any responsible evaluation of a consumer credit transaction must include an in-depth assessment of the facts and circumstances surrounding the sale of credit insurance. The National Association of Insurance Commissioners (NAIC) compiles raw data which it translates into loss-ratios. This information is available for credit life and disability insurance.[62]

Insurance Consumer Organization July 25, 1995, Clearinghouse No. 45,773B).

56 Jack Gillis, James Hunt, D.J. Powers, Birny Birnbaum, *Credit Insurance Overcharges Hit $2.5 Annually*, Consumer Federation of America and Center for Economic Justice 6 (Nov. 2001).

57 *Credit Life Insurance Hearing Before the Subcomm. on Antitrust, Monopoly and Business Rights of the Senate Comm. on the Judiciary*, 96th Cong, 1st Sess. 11–12 (1979) (testimony of James H. Hunt, Director, State Rating Bureau, Div. of Ins., Commonwealth of Massachusetts).

58 *See* Mary Griffin & Birny Birnbaum, *Credit Insurance: The $2 Billion a Year Rip-Off*, Consumers Union and the Center for Economic Justice 3 (Mar. 1999) (26.3% loss-ratio for property insurance; 12.6% for unemployment insurance; study also shows loss-ratios for these products by state).

59 Eighteen states lowered their rates between 1990 and mid-1994. The bulk of the resulting estimated $200 million in savings to consumers came in Georgia, Texas, North Carolina and Florida. In some states, though, the improvement still leaves much to be desired. Even after reducing its rates, Alabama, for example, still has among the highest rates and lowest loss-ratios. *See Credit Life Insurance Revisited II* (second update of Consumer Federation of America/National Insurance Consumer Organization July 25, 1995, Clearinghouse No. 45,773B). (That fact may have played a role in a determination that a $2 million punitive damage award was an appropriate deterrent "to exorcise fraud and inequity from the marketing of credit life policies." Union Security Life Ins. Co. v. Crocker, 667 So. 2d 688 (Ala. 1995) (over four years, creditor sold nearly $40 million in premiums, loss-ratios ranged from 16.3% to 21.1% during the period), *vacated on other grounds*, 116 S. Ct. 1872 (1996) ($2 million punitive damage award was sent back to Alabama Supreme Court for further consideration in light of BMW of N. Am., Inc. v. Gore, 517 U.S. 559, 116 S. Ct. 1589 (1996), *upon remand from Supreme Court*, 709 So. 2d 1118 (Ala. 1997) (court reduced punitive damages award to $1 million by weighing reprehensible conduct of insurance company's agent (though an apparently isolated instance) coupled with the "catastrophic" economic injury to Ms. Crocker facing foreclosure of her mobile home in the wake of her husband's death against percentage of $2 million award to insurance companies' net worth).)

Finally, Montana lowered its rates in 1996 by 20% to correct its low 1995 loss-ratio of 31%. *See Most Credit Life Insurance*

Still a Rip-Off, Clearinghouse No. 45,773C (update to Consumer Federation of America/National Insurance Consumer Organization July 25, 1995, Clearinghouse No. 45,773B).

Despite some attempts to curb excessive premiums for these credit insurance products, many states fail to even enforce existing laws. *See* Jack Gillis, James Hunt, D.J. Powers, Birny Birnbaum, *Credit Insurance Overcharges Hit $2.5 Annually*, Consumer Federation of America and Center for Economic Justice 14–21 (Nov. 2001). Table 6 of this Report lists these 23 negligent states. The authors note that, in 2001, they contacted at least six states with particularly low loss-ratios urging them to take action. None of those states responded, with the exception of Indiana.

60 In a major enforcement action, the OCC accused Providian National Bank with unfair and deceptive behavior for, among other things, failing to tell its customers that a "credit protection plan" (CPP) (a package of credit insurances) sold in conjunction with credit cards accounts was limited to the number of months that the consumer paid in, rather than the 18 months claimed by telemarketers; that the involuntary unemployment insurance was unavailable if the consumer was self-employed and did not commence until the consumer had paid in three months of premiums; that the hospitalization, illness, or disability coverage was unavailable for pre-existing conditions unless the consumer had paid six months of premiums; that CPP could be denied if the consumer's account was not current or over-limit; that CPP could be denied if the consumer paid more than the minimum payment to any credit card account other than Providian's; that CPP could be denied if the consumer accessed credit from any credit card other than Providian's. The matter settled and Providian must compensate consumers nationwide under formulas described in the Consent Order in In the Matter of Providian National Bank. Department of Treasury, #2000-53 (June 28, 2000) *available at* www.occ.treas.gov/ftp/eas/ea2000-53.pdf. *See also* allegations raised by the Federal Trade Commission in an enforcement action recently filed against Associates Corporation and Associates First Capital Corporation and their new parent, Citigroup, Inc. FTC v. Citigroup, Inc., Civil No. 010CV-0606 (N.D. Ga. filed Mar. 6, 2001), *available at* www.ftc.gov/os/2001/03/citigroupcmp.pdf (the FTC alleges that the Associates trained its employees to add the cost of a "total payment protection" package of credit insurance products to the monthly payment which they quoted to borrowers without explaining that this payment included the premium charges; employees instructed to discuss only the "benefits" of the insurance and not the costs or limitations on coverage).

61 Fonseca, Handling Consumer Credit Cases, Ch. 12 (3d ed. 1986).

62 Practitioners can contact the publications department at NAIC at (816) 374-7259. NAIC's website is located at www.naic.org. For a helpful guide to understanding insurance data, see David Birnbaum, *A Consumer Advocate's Guide to Getting, Under-*

8.3 Credit and Credit-Related Insurance Products

8.3.1 Types of Credit Insurance

8.3.1.1 Overview

The two most commonly sold types of credit insurance are credit life and credit A&H, designed to make payments on the account in the event of the borrower's death or disability.[63] Credit property protects collateral for the account. Another type of credit insurance began to be aggressively marketed in the mid-1980s: a loss-of-income coverage which makes limited payments on an account in the event of the borrower's involuntary unemployment. The first two kinds of insurance are ordinarily subject to rate regulation of some degree, the latter two are not—at least yet.[64] A fifth type of required credit insurance reared its head in the 1990s—private mortgage insurance. This insurance also tends to be unregulated in the traditional sense, e.g., regarding rates.[65]

The National Association of Insurance Commissioners now makes information regarding consumer complaints about credit insurance available by state, by type of insurance, and by insurance company.[66]

8.3.1.2 Credit Life

Credit life pays off an outstanding obligation in the event of the borrower's death. There are two types of credit life:

- *Decreasing or declining term credit life insurance*: this is the most commonly sold type of credit life. "Decreasing term" means that the amount of coverage decreases as the balance on the loan declines because of the installment payments. Theoretically, the benefits payable in the event of death will cover only the outstanding balance on the loan at the time the death occurs.[67] In most states the amount of coverage is based

on the remaining monthly payments at the time of death.[68] This coverage, called "gross coverage," overinsures the loan because it includes unearned interest. A few states require "net coverage," which covers only the remaining principal excluding unearned interest.[69] If gross coverage is prohibited, the sale of such insurance would also raise the possibility of a claim based on the excess charge, as net coverage should be cheaper. The method of determining the benefits payable at a given time may vary according to the policy terms.[70] These terms should be carefully reviewed to determine whether the policy will pay off the indebtedness in full in the event of death. The allegations in one case describe how the named plaintiff was told that the policy would always pay off the mortgage, though this was not the case based upon a standardized form.[71]

- *Level term credit life insurance*: in this type of policy, the amount of coverage or benefits payable does not decrease despite the fact that the installment payments reduce the account balance. The benefits payable remain level over the entire term of the policy.

Because the coverage does not decline with the loan balance, level life overinsures the loan even more than gross coverage decreasing insurance; it provides excessive coverage for which the borrower pays. It is more expensive than declining term; premium rates may be over 50% higher. For these reasons, it is illegal to write level term credit life on amortized loans in most states. Creditors may wish to sell level term because financing the higher premium will result in a greater interest yield. If it is sold impermissibly, an overcharge claim may be raised.[72]

Level term insurance may be justified and legally permitted where it is written in conjunction with interest-only loans, with the coverage on the policy set at the principal amount of the loan. In this type of loan, the monthly payments pay only the interest accrued each month, the principal never declines. The principal is due in one lump-sum "balloon" payment at the end of the loan term.

There are also credit life variations depending on the debtors covered. Single life protects only one named debtor.

---

standing, and Using Insurance Data, Center for Economic Justice (Aug. 1999), *available at* www.cej-online.org/intro.php.

63 Insurance generally should cover balloon payments as well as regular monthly payments. *See* Wallace v. First Assurance Life of Am., 862 So. 2d 374 (La. Ct. App. 2003). Note that decreasing life policies and those that list a specific monthly payment will not cover balloon payments.

64 As discussed in §§ 8.3.1.5.1 and 8.4.2.1.1, *infra*, the National Association of Insurance Commissioners adopted a model act to regulate property insurance in 2001. Whether states will adopt this act remains to be seen.

65 A new federal law effective July 29, 1999 creates automatic termination dates on such insurance and mandates additional disclosures. *See* § 8.3.2.1, *infra*.

66 *See* www.naic.org/servlet/cis

67 *See* Pena v. Associates Fin. Life Ins. Co., 77 Fed. Appx. 259 (5th

Cir. 2003) (holding that amount payable upon insured's death was limited to mortgage balance, not the $100,000 listed as the maximum coverage offered by the policy).

68 *See, e.g.*, Printis v. Bankers Life Ins. Co., 583 S.E.2d 22 (Ga. 2003).

69 *See* § 8.5.3.1.2, *infra*. The NAIC consumer credit insurance model act would mandate net coverage. NAIC Consumer Credit Insurance Model Act § 4(A) (1994).

70 *See* § 8.5.5, *infra*. Fagg, Credit Life and Disability Insurance 14–15 (1986).

71 Siemer v. Associates First Capital Corp., 2000 U.S. Dist. LEXIS 21244 (D. Ariz. Dec. 14, 2000) (magistrate recommended class certification), *aff'd*, 2001 U.S. Dist. LEXIS 12810 (D. Ariz. Mar. 30, 2001).

72 *See* § 8.5.3.3.1, *infra*.

Joint life protects two debtors who are obligated on an account. Most often, joint life is sold where a husband and wife are both obligated on an account. Joint coverage, however, means only that the policy will pay if *either* borrower dies. If both borrowers die, there are no additional benefits. The premium rate for joint life is more expensive than single life—from 1.40 to 1.75 times more expensive than single life. While this higher premium is attractive to creditors, the extra benefit to consumers may be marginal if repayment of the loan depends on the earning capacity of only one spouse.[73]

State law may restrict the insurer from selling credit insurance products with terms longer than ten years or from selling insurance in conjunction with loans having a term in excess of ten years.[74] In the mortgage lending context, these restrictions result in lenders marketing "truncated" insurance policies, i.e., policies with terms that are shorter than the term of the loan. Even where no such restriction exists, lenders commonly sell 5- or 10-year policies in conjunction with mortgage loans of 15- or 30-year terms. In these situations, the consumers pay the premium over the full term of the loans, often at high interest rates on subprime loans, even though the coverage ends well before the loan term ends. Even if these loans are prepaid, much of the truncated policy premiums are "earned" by that point, so that much of the principal reduction during the life of the loan simply paid off the over-priced insurance premiums. While this practice may not be illegal *per se*, practitioners should scrutinize the written and oral representations made about the policy. Some lenders may lead consumers to believe that the insurance policy will pay off the loan . . . and fail to state that this is true for only a portion of the loan term.

8.3.1.3 Credit Disability/Accident and Health

Credit disability insurance developed later than credit life insurance, but in much the same manner and for the same purpose. Creditors were looking to borrowers' wages to repay debt; death and disability are two major unforeseen circumstances that could interrupt wages. The purpose of credit disability insurance is to insure that payments on a loan or credit sale will still be made should sickness or accident cause a significant unanticipated interruption in income. Credit disability is indemnity coverage, which makes the monthly payments while the insured borrower is unable to work due to a disability covered under the policy—a "covered loss."

Two critical terms determine what type of credit disability insurance is offered: "waiting period" and "elimination period." The waiting period is the number of continuous days a person is required to be "disabled" by sickness or accident before the disability comes within the coverage provisions of the policy. The elimination period is the initial number of days in the period of disability for which there are no benefits payable by the policy. The waiting period is an essential element indicating to the policyholder if there is a covered disability or not. The elimination period, if there is one, operates like a deductible.

The following waiting periods are generally used for credit disability insurance: seven days, fourteen days, and thirty days. The elimination periods will be stated by using one of two terms, "retroactive" or "non-retroactive." The elimination period will be either the same length of time as the waiting period (non-retroactive), or there will be no elimination period (retroactive).

To illustrate the difference between retroactive and non-retroactive policies, an insured debtor with a fourteen-day non-retroactive policy must be sick or injured continuously for more than fourteen days to have a covered disability; benefits begin to accrue on the fifteenth day. With a fourteen-day retroactive policy, the insured debtor still must be sick or injured continuously for more than fourteen days to have a covered disability, but benefits are payable effective back to the first day of the disability.

Retroactive insurance is more expensive than non-retroactive, and the shorter the waiting period the more expensive the insurance. Since creditor profits are greatest with the largest insurance premium, finance companies generally sold the most expensive type of credit disability insurance— seven day retroactive. However, seven day retroactive policies are no longer approved by state insurance departments in many states. The most popular policy now in the consumer finance industry is the second most expensive— fourteen day retroactive.

Other restrictions may apply and insurance policies and information provided the consumer should be carefully reviewed. For example, one bank offered a "credit protection plan" (CPP) (a package of credit insurances) sold in conjunction with credit card accounts. Restrictions related to the hospitalization, sickness, or disability coverage included: the consumer could only collect for the number of months that the consumer paid in; claims could be denied for pre-existing conditions unless the consumer had paid six months of premiums, if the consumer's account was not current or over-limit, if the consumer paid more than the minimum payment to any credit card account other than the bank's, and if the consumer accessed credit from any credit card other than the bank's.[75]

73 *Cf.* Tomaszewski v. McKeon Ford, Inc., 573 A.2d 501 (N.J. App. Div. 1990) (breach of fiduciary duty to fail to inform borrower of significance of failing to insure the principal wage earner).

74 *See, e.g.,* Ga. Code Ann. § 33-31-2(c).

75 *See* In the Matter of Providian Nat'l Bank, Department of Treasury, Consent Order #2000-53 (June 28, 2000) *available at* www.occ.treas.gov/ftp/eas/ea2000-53.pdf.

8.3.1.4 Involuntary Unemployment Insurance

A newer addition to the credit insurance zoo is loss-of-income or involuntary unemployment insurance. It is an extension of the desire to protect an account against an interruption of the borrower's income. This protection is aimed primarily at loss of income caused by lay-offs, though some policies will also make monthly payments on a credit account if, in certain circumstances, the borrower goes out on strike or is fired. Unemployment insurance may be sold separately, or in combination with credit disability coverage. This combination coverage may raise special cost and voluntariness questions which should be explored.[76]

As with other types of credit insurance, the actual premium cost of involuntary unemployment insurance will seem to be a small portion of most loans, and so will not be likely to raise questions from consumers. The premium amount, considered in a vacuum, may even seem small enough to be attractive protection. However, two factors suggest that its cost may be very expensive in relation to the benefits.

- *Low loss-ratio*: A recent study lists the 1997 national loss ratio for this type of insurance at a whopping low 12.6%.[77]
- *Limited benefits*: The second factor, which suggests that involuntary unemployment insurance may not be a bargain, is that most policies provide protection only against short-term unemployment. The insurer will pay only a limited number of monthly payments on an account during each period of unemployment.[78] California, among only a few states thus far to establish an standards on involuntary unemployment insurance requires a minimum benefit period of only four loan installments,[79] and Tennessee sets the minimum at one-third the number of months covered by the policy.[80]

In addition to the limited number of monthly payments, the policy is likely to have a maximum ceiling on the total benefits or a maximum duration.[81] The duration of a policy sold in connection with a closed-end loan may be shorter than the term of the loan, further reducing the statistical odds that a covered loss will occur within the policy term and that the policy will provide a benefit to the borrower.

Finally, when sold in conjunction with open-end credit, such as a credit card, the monthly benefit may be limited to the *minimum* monthly payment established by the creditor. This can be as little as ten dollars, depending on the outstanding balance of the account.[82] If a policy provides six months' maximum benefits, and is limited to a ten dollar minimum monthly payment, the maximum benefit of the policy could be sixty dollars, whether the borrower was continuously unemployed for six months or two years. In addition, recent products sold in conjunction with credit card accounts may limit coverage to the number of months that the consumer paid in or if the consumer is self-employed and may deny claims if the consumer's account was not current or over-limit, if the consumer paid more than the minimum payment to any credit card account other than the bank's, and if the consumer accessed credit from any credit card other than the bank's.[83] Others may fail to pay the minimum monthly payment due on the credit card.[84]

8.3.1.5 Credit Property

8.3.1.5.1 General

Credit property insurance insures the borrower's property, rather than health or life. The coverage is designed to protect the creditor against loss to the collateral taken as security on the insured loan. However, it is not unknown for credit property insurance to be written on property unrelated to the loan, or for coverage to be written in amounts greater than the loan despite the fact that this practice may be illegal in many states.[85] Further, the creditor may sell insurance that may not bear a reasonable relation to the risk of loss, for example, where the policy covers only loss or damage caused by fire and lightning and then only if certain conditions unrelated to these occurrences also exists (i.e., the insured had defaulted in payment, the property has been repossessed, and the interest of the insured creditor has become impaired as a result of a loss covered by the policy)

---

76 *See* § 8.5.2, *infra.*

77 Mary Griffin & Birny Birnbaum, *Credit Insurance: The $2 Billion a Year Rip-Off*, Consumers Union and the Center for Economic Justice 3, 8 (Mar. 1999). The highest loss ratio (35%) is attributed to Pennsylvania, while the lowest (3.6%) is awarded to South Dakota. More dramatically, all but two states (Pennsylvania and New York) can boast of loss ratios above 20%.

78 Some policies permit the insured to re-qualify for benefits after being re-employed for a specified period of time.

79 Cal. Fin. Code § 18292.5(d) (industrial loan companies); Cal. Fin. Code § 22321 (property-brokers loans).

80 Tenn. Stat. Ann. § 45-5-305(3)(D) (Industrial Loans).

81 The involuntary unemployment insurance in one 42-month loan provided maximum benefits of 9 monthly payments. The premium for the policy amounted to 20% of the maximum benefits!

82 The method for determining the minimum monthly payment will vary. It is usually set by the contract which may, for example, be set at 4% of the outstanding balance, or a minimum of $10, whichever is greater.

83 *See* In the Matter of Providian Nat'l Bank. Department of Treasury, Consent Order #2000-53 (June 28, 2000) *available at* www.occ.treas.gov/ftp/eas/ea2000-53.pdf.

84 *See, e.g.*, Hammett v. American Bankers Ins. Co. of Florida, 203 F.R.D. 690 (S.D. Fla. Nov. 19, 2001) (nationwide class action denied on RICO claim due to reliance issues and on state breach of contract claim due to the possibility of variances in the laws of 50 states).

85 *See* § 8.5.3.4, *infra.*

or "collision or overturn while being transported by land" but does *not* cover the more common occurrence of theft or vandalism.

Credit property insurance is less thoroughly regulated than credit life and A&H, and generally is not rate regulated at all. Such rate regulation as exists may be vague, such as that it must be sold "at standard rates."[86] Some credit property insurance may be subject to a state's general property insurance laws, but credit property is often classified as "inland marine," which is subject to little or no meaningful regulation.[87] In 2001, the National Association of Insurance Commissioners adopted a credit personal property insurance model act.[88] If enacted by the states, this act will curb some of the abuses in this market, most especially its excessive cost. Its key provisions include requirements that: gross debt not be used in calculating the premium; benefits provided by the credit insurance be reasonable in relation to the premium charged which is met if the loss-ratio is at least 60%; rebates be made by the pro rata method; for closed-end loans, the credit insurance cannot exceed the amount of the underlying debt, and the credit insurance cannot be sold unless the loan amount exceeds a minimum amount set by each state; the insurance cannot be bundled with other types of insurance; it must be an option and not a condition of obtaining credit approval; consumers receive a pre-purchase disclosure describing certain rights; consumers receive a certificate of insurance.

This historical lack of regulation makes credit property insurance even more lucrative for creditors and insurers than does credit life and disability. Though there is less data available on credit property, the lack of regulation seems to result in exorbitant pricing compared to the benefits. One study found credit property loss ratios of only 7% to 25%, with commissions to creditors as high as 60%.[89] A 1997 report reveals the national loss-ratio to be only 22.3% for credit property sold in conjunction with closed-end accounts and 11.6% for insurance sold to credit card holders.[90] The most recent review of loss-ratios shows that the national credit property loss-ratio logged in at an abysmal 14.7% in 2000.[91] Probably because of this profitability, credit property insurance has played a central role in the phenomenon of "insurance-packing," the loading of loans with unnecessary insurance which has been the subject of frequent litigation.[92]

8.3.1.5.2 Vendor's single interest insurance

Vendor's Single Interest Insurance (VSI) protects only the creditor's interest in the property. Generally it pays the lesser of the actual loss on the property or the outstanding balance on the loan. Any equity the borrower has in the property is not protected. Thus, if the borrower's insured car is worth $2,000 at the time of loss, and she owes only $500 on the car loan, the policy will pay only the $500 loan balance. The borrower simply loses the $1,500 equity. On the other hand, if the property is worth only $500 and a $2,000 balance remains on the loan, the insurance will pay only the value of the property, and the borrower will still owe $1,500.

In reviewing transactions in which VSI is sold, practitioners may wish to probe the precise nature of that insurance. It appears that the same term may be used to apply to two different kinds of single interest insurance, which might be subject to different treatment under state credit licensing laws or Truth in Lending. As described above, VSI insures the *collateral* against risks defined by the policy.[93] However, some policies termed VSI seem in fact to be *deficiency* insurance—a type of credit loss insurance which may not be an authorized charge under the applicable licensing law.

One industry writer describes "blanket single interest insurance" as follows:[94]

---

86 *E.g.*, Cal. Fin. Code § 18294 (Industrial Loans).

87 Insurance on motor vehicles, however, will not fall into the inland marine category.

88 *See* NAIC Credit Personal Property Insurance Model Act, Clearinghouse No. 53,564.

89 National Consumer Law Center, *Limitation and Regulation of Credit Property Insurance* 41 (U.S. Dept. of Housing & Urban Development, Office of Federal Insurance Administration 1978); *Credit Life Insurance Hearing Before the Subcomm. on Antitrust, Monopoly and Business Rights of the Senate Comm. on the Judiciary*, 96th Cong, 1st Sess. 42 (1979) (statement of Robert Sable). As a result of recent changes to standard reporting forms, practitioners may soon be better able to determine loss-ratios for a credit property insurance company. The information may be on file with the state insurance commission, in the Credit Insurance Supplement, Experience Exhibit, or it may be available through the NAIC's database.

90 Mary Griffin & Birny Birnbaum, *Credit Insurance: The $2 Billion a Year Rip-Off*, Consumers Union and the Center for Economic Justice 3 (Mar. 1999).

91 Jack Gillis, James Hunt, D.J. Powers, Birny Birnbaum, *Credit Insurance Overcharges Hit $2.5 Annually*, Consumer Federation of America and Center for Economic Justice 3 (Nov. 2001).

92 *See* § 8.5.4, *infra*.

93 The benefits payable in a property insurance policy normally are tied to the value of the insured property by some measure defined in the policy—replacement cost, cost of repair, depreciated cost at time of loss. (However, some credit property policies, both dual and single interest, may define the measure of loss as the outstanding loan balance, irrespective of how that relates to the value of the property. This loan value measure of future loss valuation, though having the same results as the second kind of VSI which is discussed in this section, is conceptually distinct.)

94 It is not the fact that it is a "blanket" policy (as opposed to a policy written on a specified transaction) that creates problems under TIL and state credit laws. It is what these policies *insure* that is the problem, as the following discussion will indicate. In fact, *blanket* single interest insurance and *specific* single interest insurance· are both treated the same for purposes of Truth in Lending rules. Official Staff Commentary to Reg. Z § 226.4(d)-5. Thus they are both excludable when they meet the requirements for exclusion from the finance charge and are finance charges when they do not. These blanket policies as described do not meet the TIL requirements for exclusion.

Under [this type of] policy, a lender purchases coverage for all loans secured by property as collateral. A premium is paid monthly by the lender to the insurer. Rates are a flat premium per loan or a monthly outstanding balance premium per $1,000 of loan balances. Premiums are usually absorbed by the lender, although a charge may be passed on to the borrower in some states.

Coverage protects only the lender. For benefits to be payable, the loan must be in default and the property repossessed.[95] *The insurance covers only the difference between the value of the property at repossession and the loan balance at the time of repossession.* A benefit is paid only if the loss is caused by damage to the property. Perils covered are similar to standard collision and comprehensive coverage. The lender must require the borrower to carry insurance. (Emphasis added.)[96]

Some case law, in referring to single interest insurance, seems to be referring to a similar type of blanket single interest insurance. *Cordova & Simonpietri Ins. Agency v. Chase Manhattan Bank*,[97] describes "single interest" policies as insuring auto dealers against loss of the unpaid amount on each car that he sells.

If, for example, a customer buys a $5,000 car, finances it with a $3,000 loan, *and then refuses to pay the loan*, the policy satisfies the dealer's obligation on the loan and would pay $3,000 directly to the bank that had financed the purchase of the car. (Emphasis added.)[98]

As described, neither of these insure the collateral, thus are not credit property insurance.[99] Rather they describe a type of default or "credit loss insurance," which under many state consumer financing laws may not be a permissible charge to separately pass on to borrowers.[100] The consumer may also have a Truth in Lending claim for credit loss insurance premiums which are a finance charge under TIL rules.[101]

VSI appears on many automobile retail installment contracts as an additional charge of $15 to $50. Sometimes the car dealer, i.e., the vendor, has no relationship with the insurance company. Instead, the assignee purchasing the loan from the dealer has a group policy with an insurance company for the purchase of a policy. The charge for that policy is passed through the dealer to the consumer.

Arguably, the charge is not for "vendor's" insurance because the vendor, i.e., the dealer, did not actually sell any insurance to the consumer. The "VSI" charge, in this instance, may be simply a charge by a third party to accept assignment of the contract. In addition, the consumer may have had no real "choice" about the charge because the business practice between the dealer and the assignee is that every retail installment contract must contain the charge in order to be assigned.

As a practical matter, the agreement between the dealer and the assignee should be reviewed. It may include provisions spelling out whether the VSI fee is a mandatory charge. The practice of the insurance company regarding premium pricing may be revealing. The charge may be higher on indirect loans, i.e. loans between the dealer and consumers, than on direct loans, i.e., loans between the

---

95 A creditor subsequently may report such an insurance-mandated repossession as an ordinary repossession on the borrower's credit record, which certainly should be disputable under the Fair Credit Reporting Act and is arguably a UDAP violation. *See generally* National Consumer Law Center, Fair Credit Reporting (5th ed. 2002 and Supp.); National Consumer Law Center, Unfair and Deceptive Acts and Practices (6th ed. 2004 and Supp.).

96 Fagg, Credit Life and Disability Insurance 523 (1986). Since the lender must require the borrower to carry insurance on the collateral itself, and the covered risk is the gap between the property's value and the outstanding debt it is clear this insurance does *not* insure the *tangible property*, as contemplated for example by the TIL definition of VSI in Official Staff Commentary § 226.4(d)-10.

97 649 F.2d 36 (1st Cir. 1981). The case itself does not deal with the issues raised in this section.

98 *Id.* at 37.

99 *See also* §§ 8.5.3.4, 8.5.4.4, *infra* on what can be the proper subject of credit property insurance; Iowa ICCC Informal Advisory #86 (Nov. 30, 1998), Clearinghouse No. 52,156 (Iowa's Consumer Credit Code Commissioner clarified the difference between VSI and default insurance). *Cf.* Official Staff Commentary to Reg. Z § 226.4(d)-10 VSI protects "tangible property. . . ."

100 Many consumer financing laws define exclusively permissible charges, and credit loss insurance premiums are unlikely to be among them. *Cf.* §§ 7.3.1, *supra*, 8.3.2.1, 8.5.3.2.1, *infra*. (Though in some states, a premium for mortgage guaranty insurance on real estate-secured loans, another type of credit loss insurance, may be an exception.) *Cf.* Kenty v. Bank One, Columbus, N.A., 1992 WL 170605 (S.D. Ohio Apr. 23, 1992), *aff'd in part, rev'd in part on other grounds*, 92 F.3d 384 (6th Cir. 1996) (excess premium charge for coverage unauthorized and unnecessary to protect the collateral is interest; alleged unauthorized coverage purchased with property insurance premium included: conversion, embezzlement, secretion, mechanics lien, premium deficiency, repossession expense, repossession storage expense, and repossessed vehicle coverage).

It is important to make the distinction for a court if the issue is raised in a case. In Dixon v. S&S Loan Serv. of Waycross, 754 F. Supp. 1567 (S.D. Ga. 1990), the borrower claimed that the VSI insurance did not comport with Ga. Code Ann. § 33-24-4(c), which defines an insurable property interest. The court did not address it, saying it had not been raised in the complaint. Since there was no discussion of exactly what the VSI policy in question did provide for, it is unclear whether it was insuring the collateral or the deficiency.

101 15 U.S.C. § 1605(a)(5); 12 C.F.R. § 226.4(b)(5). The creditor is likely to have included the premium as part of the amount financed, treating it under VSI credit property insurance rules, 15 U.S.C. § 1605(c); 12 C.F.R. § 226.4(d)(2). *See generally* National Consumer Law Center, Truth in Lending § 3.9.4.7 (5th ed. 2003 and Supp.).

lender and consumers. The difference suggests that insurance sold by the assignee is not "vendor's" coverage.

An issue about the legality of the charge for VSI arises in those states whose retail installment acts, other applicable usury statutes, or credit insurance laws mandate that a lender requirement that VSI be purchased be clearly and conspicuously disclosed to the borrower. If the lender fails to check a box indicating that such insurance is required or otherwise fails to clearly and conspicuously disclose this fact, the vendor may be vulnerable to a claim of usury or subject to a statutory penalty. Whether the insurance premium constitutes an "unauthorized charge" or usury will depend upon the language of the relevant acts.[102]

Finally, many automobile financing documents require the purchaser to maintain insurance on the car until the loan is repaid and permits the purchaser to fulfill this requirement by providing her own insurance or authorizing the lender to purchase physical damage insurance. A recent case illustrates that a RICO claim can survive a motion to dismiss (at least against the lender) where the lender purchased a more expensive type of VSI which covered the lender's interest only.[103]

8.3.1.5.3 Dual interest

Dual interest protects the value of the insured property including the borrower's equity, and is not limited by the outstanding balance on the loan. In the above example with the $2,000 property and $500 loan balance, dual insurance would pay the $500 outstanding balance on the loan to the creditor, and $1,500 to the borrower.

8.3.1.5.4 Motor vehicle credit insurance: special issues

The sale of credit property insurance on car loans has special potential for unpleasant surprises for the borrower. As with other types of credit property, credit property insurance on cars can be either VSI or dual interest. If VSI coverage is purchased, the example in § 8.3.1.5.2, *supra* demonstrates one such surprise where the coverage is limited by the amount of the debt and the debtor's equity exceeds the debt. Further, neither VSI nor dual interest property insurance provides personal injury or personal

liability protection,[104] nor do they protect against routine property damage, or cover the car's replacement value. It is very difficult for a consumer to accurately compare the cost of credit property insurance on a motor vehicle with ordinary auto insurance. However, the much-less-comprehensive coverage of credit property insurance usually does not result in much cheaper premiums.[105]

Auto loans have been a prime source of problems with force-placed insurance, or collateral protection insurance (CPI).[106] Creditors have a legitimate interest in requiring that their collateral is insured against collision, theft and fire. Most auto loan contracts provide that the creditor has the right to purchase property insurance and add the cost to the debt if borrowers let their coverage lapse or otherwise fail to provide it. While this might sound perfectly convenient and unobjectionable for the borrower, the force-placed insurance is generally VSI, leaving the borrower's equity unprotected. More to the point, it is very expensive. The same forces driving other credit insurance abuses drive this, too: the coverage is purchased from affiliated companies; large commissions and rebates are given to the creditors.

Some of the additional expense of force-placed insurance derives from purchasing default protection for the lender, in addition to insuring the collateral. The premium price for this add-on coverage has been held to constitute interest.[107] A wide range of other abuses have made force-placed insurance the subject of litigation resulting in $300 million settlements.[108] These cases are discussed in more detail in another volume in this series,[109] and the widespread nature of the abuses suggests that any force-placed insurance on a

---

102 *Compare* Sunwest Bank of El Paso v. Gutierrez, 819 S.W.2d 673 (Tex. App. 1991) (unauthorized VSI premium did not constitute interest; rather it was assessed for separate and additional consideration) *with* Partridge v. Investment Co. of the Southwest, BankTexas, N.A., 1996 WL 732469 (Tex. App. 1996) (court agrees with *Sunwest* as far as it went but indicates that the failure to check the box may not satisfy the clear and conspicuous disclosure required in Texas' MVRISA, thus subjecting the lender to the statutory penalty of twice the amount of the unauthorized charge; borrower, however, did not properly plead this violation).

103 LaBarre v. Credit Acceptance Corp., 175 F.3d 640 (8th Cir. 1999).

104 With the advent of strict state financial responsibility laws for motor vehicle owners, this deficiency in credit property insurance coverage raised the possibility for confusion. Consequently, some states now require a conspicuous disclaimer on credit property insurance disclosures that it does not provide liability coverage.

105 The less comprehensive coverage for typical property insurance risks may be supplemented by coverage for credit loss risks; e.g., repossession expenses, premium deficiency, etc. *See, e.g.,* Kenty v. Bank One, Columbus, N.A., 1992 WL 170605 (S.D. Ohio Apr. 23, 1992), *aff'd in part, rev'd in part,* N.A., 92 F.3d 384 (6th Cir. 1996); Kenty v. Transamerica Premium Ins. Co., 650 N.E.2d 863 (Ohio 1995). *See* § 8.5.3.4, *infra* for a discussion of issues raised by such extraneous coverage.

106 This type of insurance has recently crept into the mortgage lending context as well. *See, e.g.,* Kirkland v. Midland Mortgage Co., CV198-083 (S.D. Ga. Jan. 4, 2000) (defendant's motion for reconsideration of denial of summary judgment and grant of class certification denied; motion for certification of interlocutory appeal granted), Clearinghouse No. 52,504 and 52,504A.

107 *See* § 8.5.3.4, *infra.*

108 *See* Mark A. Chavez, *If You Can't Beat Them, Change the Rules: The Industry Response to Force-Placed Insurance Litigation,* The Consumer Advocate, Vol. 3, Issue 5 (Nov./Dec. 1997).

109 *See* National Consumer Law Center, Unfair and Deceptive Acts and Practices § 5.3.11 (6th ed. 2004 and Supp.); National Consumer Law Center, Consumer Law Pleadings No. 1, Ch. 2 (Cumulative CD-Rom and Index Guide).

credit contract warrants careful investigation.[110] Given the

extensive litigation and the associated costs, some major automobile lenders have either eliminated or scaled back the program.[111]

In those states that have adopted it, the UCCC requires that, within a reasonable time after advancing sums, a lender that obtains the insurance must send the borrower a written notice listing the amount advanced, any charges with respect to the advances, any revised payment schedules, and, in certain circumstances, a brief description of the insurance including the type and amount.[112] The failure to send this notice triggers a refund of the charge in excess of that allowed under the Code.[113] Consequently, the entire amount of the premium for the force-placed insurance was forfeited because the entire fee was illegal.[114]

Review of the state's motor vehicle retail installment act, licensing laws, and applicable insurance statutes and regulations may also uncover requirements that the consumer be notified within a specified time of the purchase of the insurance and terms of coverage as well as other substantive obligations and prohibitions.[115]

The National Association of Insurance Commissioners (NAIC) drafted a "Creditor-Placed Insurance Model Act" which states are urged to adopt. Unfortunately, this act

---

110 *See* American Bankers Ins. Co. of Florida v. Alexander, 818 So. 2d 1073 (Miss. 2001) (motion to dismiss misrepresentation claim denied; filed-rate doctrine does not prevent a consumer from bringing breach of good faith and fair dealing, breach of fiduciary duty, UDAP, and common law fraud claims based upon allegations that American Bankers consciously ignored its filed rates and that the manner in which the policies were force-placed was calculated to benefit the insurance company through a kickback scheme); Pitts v. American Security Ins. Co., 550 S.E.2d 179 (N.C. App. 2001) (class certification denial reversed on appeal), *aff'd*, 569 S.E.2d 647 (N.C. 2002). *See, e.g.,* Kenty v. Bank One, Columbus, N.A., 92 F.3d 384 (6th Cir. 1996) (RICO, usury, antitrust); Kirkland v. Midland Mortgage Co., CV198-083 (S.D. Ga. Jan. 4, 2000) (defendant's motion for reconsideration of denial of summary judgment on the claim of breach of fiduciary duty and grant of class certification denied; motion for certification of interlocutory appeal granted), Clearinghouse Nos. 52,504 and 52,504A; Ruiz v. Stewart Assocs., Inc., 171 F.R.D. 238 (N.D. Ill. 1997) (insurance company's motion for summary judgment on RICO claim denied; borrowers adequately pled misrepresentation and causation; class certified); Bermudez v. First of America Bank Champion, N.A., 860 F. Supp. 580 (N.D. Ill. 1994), *case subsequently withdrawn pursuant to settlement agreement*, 886 F. Supp. 643 (N.D. Ill. 1995) (RICO, TIL and state law challenges survived motion to dismiss); Moore v. Fidelity Fin. Servs., Inc., 884 F. Supp. 288 (N.D. Ill. 1995) (RICO, TIL and state law challenges survived motion to dismiss. [But later the court dismissed the RICO count in *Moore*, 897 F. Supp. 378 (N.D. Ill. 1995) (failure to adequately plead an "enterprise") and dismissed RICO from the second amended complaint in Moore v. Fidelity Fin. Servs., Inc., 949 F. Supp. 673 (N.D. Ill. 1997) but granted class certification on the TILA, breach of contract and duty of good faith and fair dealing, and UDAP claims, 1998 WL 210941 (N.D. Ill. 1998).]); Dixon v. TCF Bank, 1995 WL 622409 (N.D. Ill. 1995) (RICO challenge dismissed); Gordon v. Ford Motor Credit Co., 868 F. Supp. 1191 (N.D. Cal. 1992) (RICO claim dismissed based on McCarran-Ferguson Act; *NB*: in so ruling, this decision is in the minority, see § 8.5.2.7, *infra*); Logan v. Norwest Bank Minnesota, N.A., 603 N.W.2d 659 (Minn. App. 1999) (summary judgment for lender on breach of contract claim for charging consumer for excessive coverage reversed; discussion of damages available to consumer); Kenty v. Transamerica Premium Ins. Co., 650 N.E.2d 863 (Ohio 1995) (tortious interference with a contractual relationship, civil conspiracy). *But see* Weathersby v. The Assocs. Fin. Servs. Co., 1999 U.S. Dist. LEXIS 6392 (E.D. La. Apr. 28, 1999) (RICO claim dismissed due to failure to allege injury related to the defendants' investment of racketeering proceeds or to RICO person gaining an interest in or control of the enterprise through a pattern of racketeering activity); Weinberger v. Mellon Mortgage Co., 1998 WL 599192 (E.D. Pa. 1998) (RICO claim against insurance company in this mortgage loan case dismissed because mortgage servicer had warned homeowner in writing that the forced-placed hazard insurance would cost substantially more and provide less coverage; therefore, no scheme to defraud even though the homeowner was not informed about the commissions paid by and between the insurer and servicer); Washington Mutual Bank, FA v. The Superior Court of Orange County, 15 P.3d 1071 (Cal. 2001) (nationwide class certification in a mortgage loan case reversed due to trial court's failure to adjudicate effect of choice of law provisions in the mortgages); Norwest Mortgage, Inc. v. The Superior Court of San Diego

County, 85 Cal. Rptr. 2d 18 (Cal. Ct. App. 1999) (nationwide class certification denied where case was filed under the California unfair competition law which cannot apply to Norwest which, though incorporated in California, conducted all relevant business from other states in the making of mortgage loans to non-Californians; leave granted to amend class definition); General Motors Acceptance Corp. v. Baymon, 732 So. 2d 262 (Miss. 1999) (jury verdict for consumer for $35,000 in compensatory damages and $5 million in punitive damages reversed and remanded for new trial on issue of breach of contract claim; court finds that GMAC did not breach its duty of fair dealing and good faith, that no fraud occurred, and no fiduciary relationship existed between the creditor and debtor; court found that evidence of disproportionate impact on minorities from the purchase of force placed insurance irrelevant and prejudicial; evidence of excessive profits, that rates amounted to "gouging" and that GMAC has manipulated the rate approval process held not relevant to issue of overcharging); Brannon v. Boatman's Nat'l Bank of Oklahoma, 976 P.2d 1077 (Okla. Ct. App. 1998) (claims of breach of contract, violations of state U.C.C.C., and unfair and deceptive acts based upon the purchase of more than "casualty" insurance, of insurance for periods of time exceeding than the uninsured period, and the payment of undisclosed commissions dismissed over strong dissent which lays out the telling facts).

111 *See* Mark A. Chavez, *If You Can't Beat Them, Change the Rules: The Industry Response to Force-Placed Insurance Litigation*, The Consumer Advocate, Vol. 3, Issue 5 (Nov./Dec. 1997).

112 U.C.C.C. § 2-208(1).

113 U.C.C.C. § 5-202(3).

114 Bank of Oklahoma, N.A. v. Portis, 942 P.2d 249 (Okla. App. 1997).

115 Ortiz v. General Motors Acceptance Corp., 673 N.E.2d 424 (Ill. App. 1996) (while the court ultimately dismissed the consumer's claims for violation of Illinois' MVRISA and Sales Finance Agency Act, the scrutiny which the practitioners applied to these laws to find a cause of action is instructive).

legitimizes many of the consumer complaints raised in litigation. For example, while the model act prohibits tacking on certain types of excess coverages, it permits those not listed. Further, lenders are allowed to pass on certain incidental costs to borrowers as well as pay commissions and other compensation to an "insurance producer," i.e., lenders. Finally, the model act eliminates any private right of action consumers may have, and instead grants state insurance commissioners exclusive oversight and enforcement authority over claims against the insurers.[116] Versions of this model have been passed in some states.[117]

8.3.2 Credit-Related Insurance

8.3.2.1 Private Mortgage Insurance

Private mortgage insurance (PMI) covers the mortgage lender against loss caused by a mortgagor's default. It may cover all or part of the loss and it may or may not relieve any liability on the borrowers part if default on the mortgage occurs. Private mortgage insurance was developed so that borrowers could purchase a home without making a 20% downpayment, a requirement of many banks and mortgage lenders. The insurance essentially serves one major purpose—it helps protect the lender in the event of losses incurred as a result of the borrower's default. In addition, it makes it easier for first-time homebuyers who cannot afford a large downpayment to purchase a home. In most transactions where the lender requires private mortgage insurance, the borrower pays the premium.

For conventional loans, the premium may be paid on an annual, monthly or single premium plan.[118] Most loans provide for monthly payments which are escrowed along with the hazard insurance premium and property taxes. The premiums are based on the amount and term of the loan and may vary according to the loan-to-value, type of loan, term of loan, and the amount of coverage required by the lender. The less the borrower puts down the higher the premium.

Given abuses in the PMI market, particularly with the failure of lenders to terminate it once the loan-to-value reaches 80%,[119] Congress passed the Homeowner's Protection Act of 1998 which applies to loans made after July 1, 1999.[120] Under certain circumstances, the consumer may initiate cancellation at 80% loan-to-value.[121] In any event, automatic termination must occur when the loan-to-value ratio drops to 78% based upon the initial amortization schedule.[122] New disclosures of the homeowner's rights and exemptions must be made at the time of loan consummation and annually thereafter.[123] Finally, the Act creates a private right of action and the homeowner may recover actual and statutory damages, attorney fees, and costs.[124]

In recent years a few states have enacted legislation to regulate PMI. For example, in California, if PMI is required as a condition of securing a loan, the lender must notify the

---

116 For a longer discussion of this model act, see Mark A. Chavez, *If You Can't Beat Them, Change the Rules: The Industry Response to Forced-Place Insurance Litigation*, The Consumer Advocate, Vol. 3, Issue 5 (Nov./Dec. 1997).

117 *See, e.g.*, N.J. Stat. Ann. § 17:16V-1 through 12; Tenn. Code Ann. §§ 56-49-101 to 115, effective Oct. 2, 1999.

118 A VA or FHA insured loan works differently. A VA loan is guaranteed by the Veterans Administration (VA) and the lender is required to collect an up-front one-time fee at closing called the "funding fee." This amount is between .50% and 3.00% of the loan amount depending upon the status of the veteran and if the veteran has used his or her VA benefits previously to purchase a home. There is no monthly premium and there is no refund of the Funding Fee when the loan-to-value is reduced below 80% or if the loan is paid off early.

On the other hand, the Federal Housing Administration (FHA) requires a one time upfront fee of 2.25% of the loan amount which may be financed in with the loan. In addition to the upfront fee there is a yearly fee of .50% of the unpaid balance of the loan which is divided into 12 equal payments and paid monthly in the house payment. If the loan is paid in full within the first 7 years there may be a prorated refund of the upfront premium paid. The monthly mortgage insurance premium may not be waived regardless of the loan to value.

119 *See, e.g.*, Kochlin v. Norwest Mortgage, Inc., 2001 WL 856206 (Minn. App. July 31, 2001) (affirming the trial court's finding that, under the terms of the mortgage contract, the individual plaintiffs were entitled to a refund of PMI premiums paid after the LTV reached 80%, while upholding a denial of class certification). The failure to terminate the insurance where required by contract or state law can state a UDAP claim. *See* § 12.5, *infra* and cases cited therein.

120 12 U.S.C. § 4901 *et seq.* This act was amended by the American Homeownership and Economic Opportunity Act of 2000, Pub. L. No. 106-569, §§ 401–405. Unfortunately, certain high-risk loans and affordable housing program loans are exempted. § 4902(g). For these types of loans, cancellation must automatically occur when "based solely on the initial amortization schedule for that mortgage, and irrespective of the outstanding balance for that mortgage on that date, [the loan] is first scheduled to reach 77 percent of the original value of the property securing the loan." There are slightly different rules if the "high risk loan" is a variable rate loan. *See* 12 U.S.C. § 4902(g)(1)(B)(ii).

121 12 U.S.C. § 4902(a). The borrower must have a "good payment" history as defined in § 4901(4); show that the property has not declined below the original value; and certify that there are no subordinate liens on the property. The value of the house is based on the original value, so a new appraisal is not required. 12 U.S.C. § 4901(2).

122 12 U.S.C. §§ 4901(18), 4902(b). When the 78% is reached varies, however, for fixed rate and variable rate mortgages. *Compare* 12 U.S.C. § 4901(18)(A) *with* 12 U.S.C. § 4901(18)(B). Further, the changes to the Act in 2000, *see supra* note 120, define mortgages with balloon payments as an "adjustable rate mortgage." § 4901(1). How loan modifications affect the automatic termination date is now addressed in § 4902(d).

123 12 U.S.C. § 4903. Significantly, the Act prohibits lenders or servicers from imposing a fee upon the homeowner to provide these disclosures. § 4906. Different disclosure rules apply if the lender requires the insurance and pays for it. § 4905.

124 12 U.S.C. § 4907.

borrower whether he or she has a right to cancel the insurance and under what conditions the insurance can be canceled.[125] In Minnesota, borrowers have the right to cancel PMI when the unpaid principal balance of the loan falls below eighty percent of the current fair market value of the property.[126] These state statutes remain relevant to the extent that the new federal law does not preempt them.[127]

There are Truth in Lending implications regarding the disclosure of the payment schedule where a monthly private mortgage insurance payment is collected. The payment schedule must list a certain number of payments in a monthly amount that includes the premium followed by the remaining number of payments in an amount that does not include the premium.[128] Abuses in the area of private mortgage insurance most recently have taken the form of extraordinarily high PMI premiums attributable primarily to a borrower's credit score. Whereas premiums used to be priced based only on loan characteristics such as loan term, loan type and downpayment (i.e., loan-to-value ratio),[129] the addition of credit history has raised monthly premiums for some borrowers from an average of under $100 to amounts ranging from $200 to over $900.[130] Such a premium increase can raise a consumer's monthly mortgage payment by 50% or more. The creditor's determination of the consumer's repayment ability (that is, the calculation of the monthly payment based on principal, interest, taxes and insurance, that goes toward the debt in the debt-to-income ratio) is supposed to include the actual PMI payment that the consumer will be required to pay.[131]

The insurance companies that provide private mortgage insurance post prices incorporating credit scores on their websites,[132] but creditors who are dealing directly with consumers (and who themselves choose the PMI provider), generally do not inform borrowers of these prices prior to closing (and at least in some cases do not appear to include the high PMI payment caused by a low credit score in the analysis of a consumer's repayment ability). As a result, a borrower could arrive at a loan closing only to find that her monthly payment is several hundred dollars higher (or more) than she was expecting. The borrower may not be able to afford this, but may feel pressured to sign the loan papers because she needs the loan. Because no prior notice has been provided, the borrower is not in a position to shop around.[133]

A consumer facing such a situation prior to December 2004 was able to bring a private cause of action under the Fair Credit Reporting Act (FCRA) against the creditor and the insurer for failure to provide an adverse action notice (the adverse action being the charging of a higher premium due to credit score).[134] Recent amendments, however, make the availability of a private action less clear.[135] A consumer also may be able to raise claims against the broker, creditor and the insurer for fraud, unconscionability, breach of fidu-

---

125 Cal. Ins. Code §§ 117; Cal. Civ. Code §§ 2954.6, 2954.7 (West); *see also* Conn. Gen. Stat. §§ 36a-725 to 36a-726 (lender must notify borrower whether borrower has right to cancel).

126 Minn. Stat. § 47.207.

127 *See* 12 U.S.C. § 4908 (a description of protected state laws).

128 Official Staff Commentary § 226.18(g)-5. *See also* National Consumer Law Center, Truth in Lending § 4.6.5.3 (5th ed. 2003 and Supp.).

129 *See* www.bankrate.com/brm/news/mtg/20010601b.asp.

130 Preston v. Mortgage Guar. Ins. Corp. of Milwaukee, Clearinghouse No. 55618, Case No.5:03-cv-111 (M.D. Fla. Mar. 27, 2003) (complaint) (monthly PMI premium of $762.29); Glatt v. The PMI Group, Inc., Clearinghouse No. 55617, Case No. 2:03-cv-326 (M.D. Fla. Sept. 15, 2003) (amended complaint) (monthly PMI premium of $604.06); Price v. United Guar. Residential Ins. Co., Clearinghouse No. 55613, Case No. 3-03-cv-2643R (N.D. Tex. Oct. 29, 2003) (complaint) (monthly PMI premium of $292.85); Broessel v. Triad Guar. Ins. Corp., Clearinghouse No. 55615, Case No. 1:04-cv-4 (W.D. Ky. Jan. 7, 2004) (complaint) (monthly PMI premium of $342.60); Whitfield v. Radian Guar., Inc., Clearinghouse No. 55616, Case No. 04-cv-111 (E.D. Pa. Jan. 12, 2004) (complaint) (monthly PMI premium of $905); Portis v. G.E. Mortgage Ins. Corp., Clearinghouse No. 55612, Cause No. 040-0300 (N.D. Ill. Jan. 15, 2004) (complaint) (monthly PMI premium of $574.08); Brantley v. Republic Mortgage Ins. Co., Clearinghouse No. 55614, Case No. 2-04-0805-23 (D.S.C. Mar. 15, 2004) (complaint) (monthly PMI premium of $590.43).

131 *See* www.efanniemae.com/singlefamily/pdf/gtu.pdf (showing that in Chapter 4 of Fannie Mae's guide to the Desktop Under-

writer program, under the section on total expense qualifying ratio calculations, the guide clearly explains that "piti" includes the PMI payment, and that the creditor must manually insert the actual PMI amount).

132 *See, e.g.,* http://mgic.com/ratecards.html; www.pmigroup.com/lenders/pmirates.html; www.ugcorp.com/rates.html; www.tgic.com/body_whatsnew_rates.htm; www.radiangroupinc.com/mortgage/rates.aspx; www.rmic.com/rates/ratecards.cfm.

133 One might also raise the additional issue of whether a borrower whose credit score causes the PMI premium to be raised significantly is really in a position to repay such a mortgage loan.

134 15 U.S.C. §§ 1681(a) & (b). *See* Karwo v. Citimortgage, Inc., 2004 WL 2033445 (N.D. Ill. Sept. 2, 2004) (court denied creditor's motion to dismiss where consumer alleged that the creditor failed to provide him with the requisite "adverse action notice" when he was charged a PMI premium higher than the lowest available rate due to the consumer's credit report; court found that consumer's claim fell under the "catch-all" provision of the statute, 15 U.S.C. 1681a(k)(1)(B)(iv)); Glatt v. The PMI Group, Inc., Clearinghouse No. 55619, Case No. 2:03-cv-326 (M.D. Fla. Dec. 23, 2003) (order) (denying defendants' motion to dismiss plaintiff's FCRA claim and holding that the FCRA's definition of adverse action in the insurance context could be applicable; even if statutory section on credit transactions applies instead, the provision that eliminates the need for an adverse action notice in case of a counteroffer does not necessarily apply); Preston v. Mortgage Guaranty Ins. Corp. of Milwaukee, Clearinghouse No. 55620, Case No.5:03-cv-111 (M.D. Fla. Dec. 19, 2003) (order) (denying defendants' motion for judgment on the pleadings and holding that plaintiffs' FCRA claims are supported by facts alleged).

135 15 U.S.C. §§ 1681m(h)(8)(A), (B). Under the amended provisions, it is not clear whether a private cause of action is unavailable simply for risk-based pricing notice claims or for all claims regarding notice violations.

ciary duty, or deception.[136] Where the insurer has paid illegal kickbacks to the mortgage company for the referral of business (since creditors, and not borrowers, choose the PMI company), the consumer should explore bringing a RESPA claim against the insurer and creditor.[137] State regulation currently provides no specific protection from such predatory pricing.

8.3.2.2 Title Insurance

Title insurance generally is required on all real-estate-secured loans.[138] It protects against loss to the mortgage creditor or homeowner related to defects in the title of a specific parcel of real property. Title coverage can be provided through a lender's policy (also called a loan policy) or a homeowner's policy. Lenders generally require a lender's policy to protect their loans and the coverage, which decreases during the loan term, is usually based upon the initial loan amount. An owner's policy is issued for the amount of the purchase price and coverage remains in force as long as the consumer or her heirs own the home. This coverage protects against title deficiencies not discovered in the title search and pays for a legal defense of a claim against the consumer's title.[139] This section focuses on lender policies.

Title protection ensures that lenders can sell their mortgage paper on the secondary market. Unlike other types of insurance, title insurance only covers losses arising from events that occurred prior to the date of the policy.[140] Losses typically covered by title insurance include claims against the homeowner's title caused by forged deeds, recording errors in legal documents, undisclosed heirs to previous owners, unpaid taxes or liens, and unrecorded easements.[141]

In addition to this coverage, title insurance premiums in some regions also include: searching public land, tax assessor, and court records to determine that title is clear; disposing of any issues that might cloud title; and preparing the necessary title-related documents.[142]

Unlike other types of insurance, which are based on actuarial loss data to predict the likelihood of future claims, title insurance rates, because they primarily protect against past events, are set mainly based on the costs of acquiring and preparing the insurance policy. In some states, title search and exam fees also are included in the price. Where they are not included, separate fees also may be assessed for a title opinion, attorney fees, closing charges, and escrow fees. These fees generally are not regulated when they are charged separately and therefore are subject to negotiation.[143] Three states set uniform rates[144] and most of the other states regulate rates through some form of a filed-rate system.[145] Iowa does not authorize the sale of title insurance and instead has established the state-run title guaranty pro-

136 State claims, however, may face assertions of preemption under the FCRA. *See* Glatt v. The PMI Group, Inc., Clearinghouse No. 55619, Case No. 2:03-cv-326 (M.D. Fla. Dec. 23, 2003) (order) (dismissing state UDAP claim as preempted by the FCRA under 15 U.S.C. § 1681t(b)); Preston v. Mortgage Guaranty Ins. Corp. of Milwaukee, Clearinghouse No. 55620, Case No.5:03-cv-111 (M.D. Fla. Dec. 19, 2003) (order) (same).

137 *See* 12 U.S.C. § 2601(a); Patton v. Triad Guaranty Ins. Corp., 277 F.3d 1294 (11th Cir. 2002) (where consumer alleged that insurer had provided illegal kickbacks to creditor in exchange for referrals of mortgage insurance business, application of RESPA anti-kickback provisions not barred by McCarran-Ferguson).

138 For a history and overview of the role of title insurance in real-estate conveyances, see Charles Szypszak, *Public Registries and Private Solutions: An Evolving American Real Estate Conveyance Regime*, 24 Whittier L. Rev. 663 (Spring 2003).

139 For general information about title insurance, see www.alta.org/consumer/questions.cfm.

140 Coverage reaches only to events on the date the policy is issued and extends backwards indefinitely.

141 In some instances, the policy also may cover fraud or dishonesty by the title insurance agent. Practitioners report, however, that such coverage may be addressed in a general letter from the insurer to the agent that applies to all policies issued by the agent, rather than in the main insurance policy itself.

142 *See* Jack Guttentag, *Ask the Mortgage Professor, available at* www.mtgprofessor.com/A%20-%20Title%20Insurance/Questions%20About%20Title%20Insurance.htm. A lender will not be able to avail itself of the coverage, however, where there is no insurable interest. For example, in one case a lender sought payment from a title insurer due to forgery of a grantor's signature on a deed, but the court found that the lender did not have an insurable interest because it had charged usurious interest to the homeowners. Usury was an explicit exception to coverage under the policy. Lawyers Title Ins. Corp. v. Wells, 881 So. 2d 668 (Fla. Ct. App. 2004) (insured lender had no insurable interest where the interest rate charged—over 92%—was criminally usurious).

143 *See* Title Resources Guaranty Company, Learning Center, *available at* www.trgc.com/center/comp.htm; North Carolina Department of Insurance, A Consumer's Guide to Title Insurance, *available at* www.ncdoi.com.

144 Fla. Stat. §§ 627.7711–627.798; N.M. Stat. Ann. § 59A-30-6; Tex. Ins. Code Ann. § 2703.151. These states also set commission splits for agents and underwriters.

145 *See, e.g.,* Md. Code Ann. § 11-401 through 11-409. State-licensed rating bureaus, which establish and file rates for their members, fell out of favor after legal actions against some of the nations largest title insurers. *See* FTC v. TICOR Title Ins. Co., 504 U.S. 621 (1992) (where the FTC claimed price fixing of title search and exam fees, the Court held that defendants could not claim immunity from antitrust laws for title insurance price-setting under the states' regulatory schemes; the administrative law judge previously found that five of nation's largest title insurers, which together accounted for 57% of national industry revenue, had engaged in price-fixing in four states); Brown v. Ticor Title Ins. Co., 982 F.2d 386 (9th Cir. 1992) (where plaintiffs alleged antitrust violations in connection with insurers' participation in state-licensed rating bureaus, the court held that the filed-tariff doctrine did not bar the antitrust claim). Since then, several states including Delaware, New York, Pennsylvania, New Jersey and Ohio have allowed the establishment of such bodies. *See* Jack Guttentag, *Ask the Mortgage Professor, available at* www.mtgprofessor.com/A%20-%20Title%20Insurance/Questions%20About%20Title%20Insurance.htm. *See also* Title Insurance Rating Bureau of Pennsylvania Filing for Approval of Rate Increase and Revisions to Rating Manual, 31 Pa. Bull. 5338 (Sept. 14, 2001), *available at* www.pabulletin.com/secure/data/vol31/31-37/1707.html.

gram to protect homeowners from title-related loss.[146] The cost of title insurance varies widely from state to state due in part to the nature and degree of state regulation and local costs.

Reverse competition is a major reason why consumers pay more than they should for title insurance.[147] Title insurers (underwriters) market their products to the title companies and closing attorneys (agents), rather than to the consumers actually purchasing the policy. The agent generally splits the title insurance premium with the insurer. RESPA requires that the actual dollar amount of the commission earned by the settlement agent for issuing the title insurance policy be disclosed on the HUD-1 form.[148] While in some states this split is governed by state law, in many states the agent—unbeknownst to the consumer—retains a majority of the premium.[149] The underwriter expects a set amount for a certain policy and the agent then has flexibility to set a higher price. While sometimes the agent decreases this amount to give the buyer a lower premium, in many instances the higher amount simply serves as a kickback for referring business. There does not appear to be a relationship between these fees and services rendered. Because consumers purchase title insurance only a few times in a lifetime, and because this cost is associated with the much larger transaction of purchasing or refinancing a home, they are not likely to shop around for title insurance or realize they can.[150]

Kickbacks (which are paid by title insurance agents to "producers" such as realtors and homebuilders who refer business to the agent) and padded fees flourish in this reverse-competition environment.[151] Refinancings in the subprime market particularly are subject to title insurance abuse because, while lower rates generally apply to such transactions, some lenders charge the higher purchase-money rate to their clients.

Fee-padding implicates the Truth in Lending Act, because title insurance costs must be bona fide and reasonable.[152] Where a kickback inflates the premium price, a RESPA claim may be available.[153] For example, several federal bank regulatory agencies recently settled an action against a nationwide title insurer for such violations.[154] A consumer seeking to challenge abusive title insurance practices, such as failure to disclose the availability of a lower refinancing rate or failure to disclose kickbacks, also should consider bringing a UDAP, fraud, or fiduciary duty claim.[155]

NAIC has produced model laws regarding title insurers and title insurance agents, which, among other things, prohibit fee splitting for referrals.[156] Only a limited number of states, however, have adopted all, or even some, of these provisions.[157]

---

146 Iowa Code § 16.91 (establishing the title guaranty program) as part of the Iowa Finance Authority. Although state law expressly permits collection of title protection fees only for a title guaranty issued by the Iowa Finance Authority, a recent Iowa Supreme Court opinion appears to permit lenders to collect fees for conventional title insurance issued by out-of-state underwriters. Gardin v. Long Beach Mortgage Co., 661 N.W.2d 193 (Iowa 2003).

147 *In re* Radian Guaranty, File No. SF 15404-A, Before the Insurance Commissioner of the State of California (June 18, 2003) (Center for Public Interest Law, Brief of Amici Curiae), *available at* www.cpil.org/download/Amici_Curiae_Brief.pdf (describing concentration and reverse competition in the title insurance market); Birny Birnbaum, Testimony to Texas Title Insurance Biennial Rate Hearing, Clearinghouse No. 55624, (Oct. 14, 1997); Title Insurance Advisory Committee, Final Report to the State Board of Insurance, Austin, Texas, Clearinghouse No. 55625 (Sept. 1986).

148 Reg. X, 24 C.F.R. pt. 3500 App. A. *See* § 12.2.1, *infra*.

149 Charles Szypszak, *Public Registries and Private Solutions: An Evolving American Real Estate Conveyance Regime*, 24 Whittier L. Rev. 663 (Spring 2003).

150 Birny Birnbaum, Testimony to Texas Title Insurance Biennial Rate Hearing, Clearinghouse No. 55624, (Oct. 14, 1997).

151 Some of these kickback arrangements are structured as captive-reinsurance deals, where, for example, the insurer agrees to reinsure all business it receives from a producer, such as a

homebuilder or realtor, with a reinsurance entity controlled by or affiliated with the producer. For an example of such an arrangement, see Stipulation for Entry of Final Agency Order, *In re* The Matter of the Certificate Authority of First Am. Title Ins. Co., Division of Insurance, State of Colorado, Clearinghouse No. 55621, Order No. O-05-143 (Feb. 18, 2005).

152 *See* National Consumer Law Center, Truth in Lending, § 3.9.6.3 (5th ed. 2003 and Supp.).

153 12 U.S.C. § 2607; Reg. X, 24 C.F.R. § 3500.14; Moll v. U.S. Life Title Ins. Co. of New York, 700 F. Supp. 1284 (S.D.N.Y. 1988) (Moll II) (discussing the equitable tolling doctrine and its application to the claim challenging "referral fees" under RESPA, RICO and the state insurance law; the court assumes the underlying viability of a RESPA claim for title insurance kickbacks). For further discussion of this issue, see § 12.2.1, *infra;* National Consumer Law Center, Foreclosures and Repossessions, § 16.7.8.8 (5th ed. 2002 and Supp.).

154 Office of the Comptroller of the Currency v. Chicago Title Ins. Co., No. AA-EC-2004-84 (stipulation and consent order Feb. 24, 2005), *available at* www.occ.treas.gov/ftp/eas/ea2005-12.pdf (settling claims against the title insurer by the OCC, OTS, HUD and the Texas Dep't of Ins.). The federal regulators determined that Chicago Title had engaged in a pattern or practice of violations of section 4 of RESPA by providing inaccurate HUD-1 Settlement Statements to lenders and borrowers that did not accurately reflect all of the actual settlement charges and adjustments. The settlement requires Chicago Title to restructure its settlements nationwide, change the training of employees and officers, audit its practices, and better oversee its Board of Directors.

155 *See* § 8.7, *infra*, for a discussion of remedy issues. Note that a fiduciary duty claim also may be available to a consumer where the title agent did not properly disburse funds or execute documents upon settlement.

156 NAIC Title Insurers Model Act, Clearinghouse No. 55623. NAIC Title Insurance Agent Model Act, Clearinghouse No. 55622. The text for both of these model acts is available on Westlaw in the insurance directory under NAIC model laws, regulations and guidelines.

157 Conn. Gen. Stat. §§ 38a-400 to 38a-425; Haw. Rev. Stat. §§ 431:20-101 to 431:20-125; Kan. Stat. Ann. §§ 40-1134 to 40-1141; La. Rev. Stat. Ann. §§ 22:2091.12 to 22:2095; Mont.

8.3.2.3 Debt Cancellation and Debt Suspension Agreements

Credit insurance may soon be replaced by debt cancellation or debt suspension agreements in the consumer loan context.[158] One reason for this anticipated shift is that many states do not regulate these products, having decided that they are "banking products" and thus do not constitute "insurance."[159] In the public arena, single-premium credit insurance has fallen out of favor in the mortgage-lending context.[160] In addition, federal banking agencies, which are increasingly scrutinizing credit insurance transactions, have given banks a green light to sell debt cancellation and suspension products with minimal regulation.[161]

From where the consumer stands, however, a debt cancellation or suspension agreement functions much like traditional credit insurance. For a fee (akin to a premium), the lender agrees to cancel payment on the consumer's loan in the event of death, serious illness or injury, unemployment, or loss of collateral securing the loan or suspend payments for some of these same events as well as when divorce, family leave from work, military relocation, and even incarceration of a spouse occur. The fee for such an agreement may be paid as a monthly charge or may be payable at the outset of the loan and financed over the loan term. Both credit insurance and debt cancellation agreements eliminate some or all of the consumer's indebtedness. Credit insurance, however, usually involves a third-party insurer, whereas debt cancellation or suspension agreements are between the consumer and the lender.

From the creditor's perspective, the primary purpose of a debt cancellation or suspension agreement is to protect the creditor from a risk of income loss (the monthly or periodic payments the consumer owes on the loan) caused by a particular covered event. The fees collected are used to create reserves to cover the creditor's interest in the loan should the indebtedness be reduced, deferred, or canceled by an enumerated contingency.

Although similar in structure, debt cancellation and suspension agreements generally offer far fewer benefits than credit insurance due to differences in covered or triggering events and the types of benefits provided. For example, unlike credit insurance, death benefits under most debt protection products generally apply only in case of accidental death. As a result, only about ten percent of the eligible claims under a credit life insurance policy would result in a payment of benefits under a debt cancellation agreement. Moreover, a debt suspension agreement provides even more limited benefits than those provided by a debt cancellation agreement; instead of canceling payment of interest and principal, it simply waives the monthly finance charge for the covered months. Most credit card credit insurance programs have been replaced by these limited debt suspension agreement programs.[162]

Code §§ 33-25-104 to 33-25-403; Neb. Rev. Stat. §§ 44-1978 to 44-19,123; S.C. Code Ann. §§ 38-75-905 to 38-75-1000; Wyo. Stat. Ann. §§ 26-23-301 to 26-23-336.

158 Debt cancellation coverage is treated similarly to credit insurance under the Truth in Lending Act. *See* 12 C.F.R. §§ 226.4(b)(7), (10), 226.4(d)(1), (3). Regulations regarding debt cancellation protection apply whether or not it is treated as insurance under applicable law. See Appx. J.2 for the OCC debt cancellation regulations. For a comprehensive review of debt cancellation and suspension products, see Center for Economic Justice, The Impact of Debt Cancellation Contracts on State Insurance Regulation (July 2003), *available at* www.cej-online.org/cej%20first%20dcc%20report%20no%20app.pdf. *See also* Caroline E. Mayer, *Lenders Peddle Protection, at a Hefty Profit*, Washington Post (Mar. 13, 2004).

159 *See, e.g.*, First Nat'l Bank of Eastern Arkansas v. Eubanks, 740 F. Supp. 1427 (E.D. Ark. 1989) (sale of debt cancellation products does not constitute business of insurance and thus is not subject to regulation by state insurance department; department had sought to regulate such products); Auto. Funding Group Inc. v. Garamendi, 7 Cal. Rptr. 3d 912 (Cal. Ct. App. 2003); 1994 Md. AG. LEXIS 50 (Oct. 17, 1994) (debt cancellation agreements do not constitute contracts of insurance). In Texas, the state Finance Commission adopted a new rule expressly authorizing the sale by state-charted banks of debt cancellation and suspension products on consumer loans and allowing the financing of such premiums. 7 Tex. Admin. Code § 12.33. Similarly, the South Dakota Legislature adopted a provision allowing state-charted banks to sell debt cancellation and suspension products. S.D. Codified Laws § 51A-4 through 46.

160 Neither Fannie Mae nor Freddie Mac invests in mortgages that contain single-premium credit insurance. *See* www.freddiemac.com/singlefamily/anti-predatory.html; www.fanniemae.com/newsreleases/2000/0710.jhtml.

161 12 C.F.R. § 37 (OCC) (OCC's new rule is discussed later in this section.); OTS Chief Counsel Letter (Dec. 18, 1995), *available at* www.ots.treas.gov/docs/5/56521.pdf; 12 C.F.R. § 721.3(g) (National Credit Union Administration); Opinion Letter from Sheila A. Albin, Assoc. Gen. Counsel, National Credit Union Admin. to Barbara Means, AVP, Aon Integramark (Jan. 28, 2004), *available at* www.ncua.gov/RegulationsOpinionsLaws/opinion_letters/2003_letters/03-1039.htm (a federal credit union may offer debt cancellation agreements to its members as an exercise of incidental powers without having to comply with state law; this does not constitute the business of insurance); Opinion Letter from Sheila A. Albin, Assoc. Gen. Counsel, National Credit Union Admin. to Robert K. Rusch, VP, CUNA

Mut. Group (Jan. 28, 2004), *available at* www.ncua.gov/RegulationsOpinionsLaws/opinion_letters/2003_letters/03-1120.htm (state laws attempting to limit or prohibit charges related to debt cancellation or suspension agreements are preempted). *See also* First Nat'l Bank v. Taylor, 907 F.2d 775 (8th Cir. 1990) (court held that a state insurance commissioner could not prohibit a national bank from entering into debt cancellation agreements because the National Bank Act gave national banks "incidental" powers to conduct business; furthermore, although debt cancellation contracts may transfer some risk from the borrower to the bank, the court found that the contracts do not require the bank to take an investment risk or to make payment to the borrower's estate and thus are not "insurance").

162 *See* Center for Economic Justice, The Impact of Debt Cancellation Contracts on State Insurance Regulation (July 2003), *available at* www.cej-online.org/cej%20first%20dcc%20report%20no%20app.pdf.

A look at some statistics shows the drastic loss suffered by consumers when credit insurance is replaced with a debt cancellation or suspension product.[163]

What the Shift from Credit Insurance to DCC/DSA Means for Credit Card Consumers

	Credit Insurance	DCC/DSA	Difference
Premiums/Fees Annually	$2,000,000,000	$2,500,000,000	25.0%*
Benefit Ratios	40%	5%	−84.4%**
Benefit Dollars	$800,000,000	$125,000,000	$650,000,000***

*Accordingly DCC/DSA costs are 25% more expensive than credit insurance.

**Accordingly DCC/DSA benefits are over 84% less than credit Insurance benefits, keeping fees constant.

***Accordingly DCC/DSA provide $675,00,000 less in benefits than does credit insurance, keeping fees constant.

Guaranteed Auto Protection (GAP) agreements are among the most common forms of debt cancellation agreements currently on the market. Under a GAP plan, when a consumer finances the purchase of a car, the creditor agrees to hold the consumer harmless for the difference between the balance on the debt and the amount paid under an automobile physical damage insurance policy in the event that the vehicle is totaled or stolen.[164] A creditor can provide GAP protection to a consumer through a simple waiver provision in a loan contract, or through a separate agreement. That separate contract may be executed simply between the creditor and the consumer, where the creditor serves as the obligor, or may involve a third-party administrator or property insurer. The two-party agreement between the creditor and the consumer, whether part of the loan contract or provided for in a separate document, is not considered to be insurance. Where a third-party obligor is involved, the question of whether it is considered to be insurance (and thus whether it is regulated by state insurance rules) varies by state. While the bona fide insurance arrangement is subject to state insurance regulation, these arrangements are quite rare. Because the arrangements generally are not subject to state insurance regulation, loss ratios—which indicate the ratio of premiums or GAP charges paid *in* to claims paid *out* (essentially the profit ratio)—are not publicly available. When they are available, for example through litigation, such ratios may not provide the full story because, at least in some cases, the numbers are based upon the amount the finance company charged the dealer not the amount the dealer charged the consumer.

Importantly, a GAP waiver or agreement between the creditor and the consumer provides fewer benefits than actual GAP insurance. For example, many GAP insurance policies will cover the primary insurance company's deductible up to $1,000, while a GAP waiver or agreement often does not. Even where a consumer obtains the broader GAP insurance, the terms of the policy may not be provided to the consumer. Rather, the consumer's loan documents may simply summarize the terms of the GAP insurance coverage and identify the cost, while providing that any conflict between the summary and the actual policy will be resolved by the language in the policy.

Regulations issued by the OCC[165] have opened the floodgates for the sale of debt cancellation and suspension agreements (collectively "DCAs") as banking products rather than insurance. The OCC has codified its long-held view that DCAs are not insurance[166] and it has provided only minimal substantive consumer protections. While the regulations prohibit the use of single-premium financing for DCAs sold in connection with residential mortgage loans, prohibit a lender from conditioning the availability of credit upon a customer's purchase of a DCA, and require lenders offering lump-sum payment DCAs to also offer a bona fide periodic payment option, they do not set limits on fees or require any refund of a lump-sum premium (on loans other than residential mortgages) in the event of prepayment or refinancing.[167] The OCC primarily relies on disclosure of the terms of the agreement to protect consumers.[168] Because of preemption under the Gramm-Leach Bliley Act,[169] state provisions that limit fees, require refunds of lump-sum premiums in the event of prepayment, and otherwise treat DCAs as insurance appear to no longer apply to national banks.[170]

---

163 This information is based on a chart which available from the Center for Economic Justice report on Debt Cancellation Contracts. *See* Center for Economic Justice, The Impact of Debt Cancellation Contracts on State Insurance Regulation (July 2003), *available at* www.cej-online.org/cej%20first%20dcc%20report%20no%20app.pdf.

164 For a discussion of GAP plans and hidden finance charges, see § 7.4.2, *supra*. GAP in connection with negative equity in the car-financing context is discussed in § 11.6.3, *infra*.

165 *See* 67 Fed. Reg. 58962 (Sept. 19, 2002) (reprinted in Appx. C.2, *infra*).

166 Perhaps ironically, the OCC has modeled its DCA regulations on those requirements that apply to banks' insurance sales. *See* 67 Fed. Reg. 58963 (Sept. 19, 2002).

167 *See id.*

168 *See id.*

169 For a discussion of the Gramm-Leach-Bliley Act, see § 8.4.1.5.2, *infra*.

170 *See, e.g.,* Opinion Letter Regarding Banks Sales of Debt Suspension Agreements and Debt Cancellation Contracts, Clearinghouse No. 54,591 (New York State Ins. Dep't Apr. 4, 2003) (national banks selling DCAs in New York are not subject to regulation by the state insurance department, although it is generally the department's position that "debt cancellation contracts are considered insurance under New York Insurance Law"). A few states are explicitly retaining the power to regulate DCAs as insurance for some classes of financial institutions. *See, e.g.,* Utah Ins. Admin. Code § 31A-1-301(79); Utah Code Ann. § 7-1-324 (debt cancellation and suspension products fall within definition of insurance in insurance code, but depository institutions are exempt from such regulation); Opinion Letter Regarding Regulation of National Banks Offer-

While most of the OCC regulations concerning DCAs became effective on June 16, 2003, implementation of certain key provisions has been indefinitely delayed due to industry concerns. The OCC announced that it is delaying the date for mandatory compliance with regulations requiring creditors to offer a periodic payment option in cases of broker sales ("unaffiliated, non-exclusive agents of a national bank that offer that bank's DCC or DSA in connection with closed-end consumer credit").[171] Related disclosure requirements have also been suspended. These regulations primarily affect auto dealers who originate car loans, who have expressed concerns that their software systems are not capable of adding a monthly pay product. As some commentators have noted, the notion that such dealers should simply suspend sales of lump-sum DCAs until a system is available to accommodate both types of payment systems apparently was not considered.[172]

The Federal Reserve Board may take action regarding DCAs in the future. In connection with proposed revisions to several consumer credit regulations and staff commentaries, Board staff requested information about debt protection products, including how they are sold, how they compare with credit insurance, what types of disclosures are made, and how they might be addressed under Regulation Z.[173]

8.3.3 Non-Credit Insurance Distinguished

Creditors, particularly finance companies, may offer to sell ancillary insurance, unrelated to the debt itself. This insurance does not protect the creditor against any risk relating to the account, unlike credit insurance where the beneficiary is the creditor or the debtor's account. However, the creditor will finance the premium for this "separately" purchased product. The creditor may sell cancer insurance, accidental death and dismemberment insurance,[174] or level term non-credit life insurance (in addition to the credit life). Insurance packing schemes frequently involve abusive sales techniques in the offering of these forms of non-credit insurance.[175]

The Minnesota Supreme Court took note of the distinction between credit life and non-credit life insurance sold by lenders in that state. It ruled that the state Regulated Loan Act[176] authorized only the sale of credit insurance, so the sale of a non-credit life insurance policy was prohibited.[177] The policy in question could not be categorized as credit insurance because it did not provide for the indemnity of the creditor and the policy term is unrelated to the loan.[178]

Like Minnesota, the North Carolina Consumer Finance Act prohibits covered lenders from soliciting or transacting any business other than making loans and selling credit insurance. The banking commissioner denied a lender's request for permission to sell a non-credit form of insurance known as (euphemistically) "Liberator Income Protector Plan" (LIPP) based, in part, upon the testimony of a legal service attorney.[179] LIPP is income replacement disability insurance. In the event of disability, LIPP would not pay off the balance of the loan but, rather, would make a payment directly to the borrower. Thus, the indebtedness of the loan would not be reduced. Since the insurance premium was to be financed as part of the loan, interest would be earned on the premium. Practitioners should be mindful of the administrative advocacy opportunities that may exist to prevent lenders from introducing new non-credit products into their repertoire especially where they drive up the cost of credit.

ing Debt Cancellation Contracts and Debt Suspension Agreements, Clearinghouse No. 54,593 (Nevada Div. of Ins. Apr. 2, 2003) (state regulation of national banks is preempted under Gramm-Leach-Bliley, but other types of financial institutions are subject to insurance regulation for sales of debt protection products). It is still an open question whether states that historically have treated DCAs as insurance will be influenced by the OCC's regulations to allow lenders other than national banks to sell them without substantial state regulation. Approximately forty states have "parity statutes" that give state-chartered financial institutions the same rights as federally-chartered counterparts. These laws potentially could serve as a basis for state-chartered banks to argue that they have the right to sell DCAs free of any state regulation. Center for Economic Justice, The Impact of Debt Cancellation Contracts on State Insurance Regulation 21 (July 2003).

171 68 Fed. Reg. 35283 (June 13, 2003).

172 Letter from Consumer Federation of America and Center for Economic Justice to Office of the Comptroller of the Currency (July 14, 2003), *available at* www.cej-online.org/cfa_cej_dcc_delay_030714.pdf.

173 68 Fed. Reg. 68793 (Dec. 10, 2003). The FRB then published an update, noting that "the products are being made available by an increasing number of creditors in connection with many types of credit, on a wide and growing variety of terms." 69 Fed. Reg. 16770 (Mar. 31, 2004). While stakeholders are urging the FRB to take action, so far the Board only collected information.

174 These types of specialized insurance policies have often been criticized by insurance professionals. They are expensive for the protection they buy and because they cover only specialized risks, are less likely to be of benefit than comprehensive health coverage or regular life insurance. See, e.g., Cancer Insurance: Exploiting Fear for Profit (An Examination of Dread Disease Insurance), Select Comm. on Aging, 97th Cong. 1st Sess. 2d Ed. (Comm. Print Oct. 1981).

175 *See* § 8.5.4.3, *infra*.

176 Minn. Stat. ch. 56.

177 Hawkins v. Thorp Credit & Thrift Co., 441 N.W.2d 470 (Minn. 1989). *See generally* § 8.5.4.3, *infra*.

178 *Cf.* Official Staff Commentary to Truth in Lending Regulation Z, § 226.4(d)-6 ("Insurance is not credit life, accident, health or loss of income insurance if the creditor or the credit account of the consumer is not the beneficiary of the insurance coverage").

179 Beneficial North Carolina, Inc. v. State, 484 S.E.2d 808 (N.C. App. 1997).

8.4 Types of Regulation

8.4.1 Sources of Regulation

8.4.1.1 Overview

It goes without saying that one must consider all applicable laws, regulations and administrative orders in examining a credit transaction for potential claims involving credit insurance. But it is not always an easy task to find all that information. Sources of law governing the sale of credit insurance include:

- Insurance statutes and regulations;[180]
- Insurance department bulletins that are not officially published;
- Credit laws governing the specific type of transaction; and
- Licensing laws governing the type of creditor involved.

From all these sources, the consumer's attorney further must determine what, if any, provision provides the statutory remedy for a particular impropriety. For example, ordinarily, rates will be set by insurance laws, but credit or licensing laws are likely to define the legal effect of improper insurance charges and provide the borrower's remedy.

In reviewing the regulatory structure, it must be kept in mind that there are at least two theoretically distinct parties involved, in addition to the consumer—the creditor and the insurer. Some of the provisions may regulate the conduct of the insurer only, some the creditor only. Similarly, the administrative agency responsible for enforcing and administering the rules will differ. The state insurance department has authority over the insurers; the creditors are subject to oversight by the relevant state licensing authority, such as the state banking department.

8.4.1.2 Insurance Statutes and Regulations

Most states specifically designate in their insurance codes chapters devoted to credit insurance. The majority of these are based on the Model Credit Life, Accident and Health Insurance Act, developed by the National Association of Insurance Commissioners in 1960.[181] Even where that Act is

not specifically adopted in a state, the Act often influences the substance of the state's credit insurance regulation.[182] In 2001, the NAIC finally adopted a credit personal property insurance model act.[183] Where similar provisions are enacted by the states,[184] this act can help curb some of the abuses in this market, most especially excessive cost of this type of insurance. Its key provisions are described in §§ 8.3.5.1, *supra*, and 8.4.2.2.1, *infra*.

Another source of insurance legislation dealing with credit insurance, in addition to the state's special chapter on credit insurance, is the state's general group insurance laws.[185] Additionally, the state insurance department may promulgate administrative rules pursuant to either the credit insurance or group insurance statutes to further interpret and implement those statutes. The NAIC has developed model

---

180 Note that in limited instances insurance companies selling credit insurance have been exempted from state regulation under a special charter. *See, e.g.*, Indiana Dep't of Ins. v. Vernon Gen. Ins. Co., 784 N.E.2d 556 (Ind. Ct. App. 2003).

181 Model Bill to Provide for the Regulation of Credit Life Ins. and Credit Accident and Health Ins., National Association of Ins. Commissioners, Model Regulatory Service, 360-1, 370-1, and 375-1 (NIARS Corp., 1984); Alaska Stat. §§ 21.57.010 to 21.57.160; Ariz. Rev. Stat. Ann. §§ 20-1602 to 20-1616.01; Ark. Stat. Ann. §§ 23-87-101 to 23-87-119; Cal. Ins. Code

§§ 779.1 to 779.36; Colo. Rev. Stat. §§ 10-10-101 to 10-10-119; Conn. Gen. Stat. §§ 38a-645 to 38a-658; Del. Code Ann. tit 18, §§ 3701 to 3713; Ga. Code §§ 33-31-1 to 33-31-12; Haw. Rev. Stat. §§ 431:10B-101 to 431:10B-114; Idaho Code §§ 41-2301 to 41-2316; 215 Ill. Comp. Stat. Ann. §§ 5/155.51 to 155.65; Ind. Code §§ 27-8-4-1 to 27-8-4-14; Ky. Rev. Stat. §§ 304.19-010 to 304.19-140; Me. Rev. Stat. Ann. tit. 24-A, §§ 2851 to 2865; Md. Ins. Code Ann. §§ 13-101 to 13-117; Mich. Comp. Laws §§ 550.601 to 550.624; Minn. Stat. §§ 62B.01 to 62B.14; Mo. Rev. Stat. §§ 385.010 to 385.080; Mont. Code Ann. § 33-21-101 to 33-21-207; Neb. Rev. Stat. §§ 44-1701 to 44-1713; Nev. Rev. Stat. §§ 690A.010 to 690A.280; N.H. Rev. Stat. Ann. §§ 408-A:1 to 408-A:15; N.J. Stat. Ann. §§ 17B:29-1 to 17B:29-13; N.M. Stat. Ann. §§ 59A-25-1 to 59A-25-14; N.C. Gen. Stat. § 58-57-1 to 58-57-80; N.D. Cent. Code §§ 26.1-37-01 to 26.1-37-16; Ohio Rev. Code Ann. §§ 3918.01 to 3918.99; Or. Rev. Stat. §§ 743.371 to 743.380; Pa. Stat. Ann. tit. 40, §§ 1007.1 to 1007.15; Tex. Ins. Code Ann. §§ 1153.001 to 1153.703; Utah Code Ann. §§ 31A-22-801 to 31A-22-809; Vt. Stat. Ann. tit. 8, §§ 4101 to 4115; Va. Code Ann. §§ 38.2-3717 to 38.2-3738; Wash. Rev. Code §§ 48.34.010 to 48.34.910; Wyo. Stat. §§ 26-21-101 to 26-21-114. *See also* N.Y. Ins. Law § 3201.

182 *E.g.*, Tenn. Code Ann. § 56-7-901 *et. seq.*

183 *See* NAIC Credit Personal Property Insurance Model Act, Clearinghouse No. 53,564.

184 Two states have adopted similar provisions. Ariz. Rev. Stat. Ann. §§ 20-1621 to 20-1621.11; W. Va. Regs. §§ 114-61-1 to 114-61-9. Several other states have some protections, but they fall short of adopting all of the major provisions of the NAIC model act. Ala. Admin. Code r. 482-1-093-.01 to -.14; 4 Colo. Code Regs. § 902-1; Fla. Stat. Ann. § 624.605(j); Fla. Admin. Code § 69O-184.006; Kan. Stat. Ann. §§ 16a-4-301, -302, -304; Kan. Stat. Ann. § 16a-2-501; Kan. Admin. Regs. 75-6-9; Kan. Op. Att'y Gen. No. 86-42 (1986), 1986 WL 238275 (Kan. A.G.); Mo. Ann. Stat. §§ 385.010 to .080; Mo. Code Regs. Ann. tit. 140-3.041; N.Y. Ins. § 2340; N.Y. Banking § 357; N.Y. Comp. Codes R. & Regs. tit. 11, §§ 186.1-.13; N.C. Gen. Stat. § 58-57-90; N.D. Cent. Code §§ 26.1-37-01 to -16; Okla. Stat. Ann. tit. 14A, §§ 4-301, -302, -304; 31 Pa. Code §§ 112.1-.12; Va. Code. Ann. § 38.2-233.

185 *E.g.*, Iowa Code ch. 509, 515; Vt. Stat. Ann. tit. 8, §§ 3805, 3806.

regulations to flesh out the Model Credit Insurance Act, but they have not been widely adopted.[186]

For purposes of examining a debt for insurance-related overcharges, the most important state insurance law provisions regulating credit insurance are those dealing with rate structure and any restrictions on coverage, such as insured amount or term of the insurance. Premium rates are set by statute or regulation, or approved in accordance with formulae set by insurance regulations.[187] The nature of this rate and other substantive regulation will be discussed more fully in § 8.4.2, *infra*.

8.4.1.3 Consumer Credit Laws Regulating Credit Insurance

Special usury laws, such as small loan acts, consumer loan acts, industrial loan acts, second mortgage laws or general credit statutes, including retail installment sales acts, may contain important limitations on the sale of credit insurance. It is critical to be aware of these statutes' insurance provisions because it generally is these statutes that place limits on the *creditor* in relation to credit insurance charges. Furthermore, unlike most credit insurance codes, credit and licensing statutes often will provide a viable consumer remedy for violations of their provisions.

Most importantly for usury purposes, special usury statutes usually establish limitations on the premium cost, often by providing that insurance must be written in compliance with the credit insurance code,[188] or by otherwise referring to the insurance department rate limitations.[189] These statutes often specify, implicitly or explicitly, the conditions which must be met in order for the insurance premiums to be excluded from the finance charge, such as that the insurance must be voluntary,[190] or that the charges must be imposed in compliance with specified statutory provisions.[191]

Special usury statutes also may impose disclosure requirements in addition to those of the Truth in Lending Act.[192] They may also specify what type of insurance may be sold in conjunction with a covered transaction,[193] thus rendering premiums for any type of unlisted insurance an unauthorized additional charge.[194]

Any applicable restrictions on credit property insurance typically will be found in special usury statutes, because the NAIC's 1960 model credit insurance code does not cover credit property insurance. This should change over time if states begin enacting NAIC's Model Act covering personal property credit insurance adopted in 2001.[195] Restrictions on credit property insurance may include standards for the premium cost,[196] and limitations on the kinds of loans on which property insurance may be written.[197]

States adopting comprehensive consumer credit codes generally have detailed provisions regarding credit insurance in transactions subject to the credit code.[198] Article 4 of the Uniform Consumer Credit Code (UCCC) is the primary example of such a statute, and it in turn is derived in part from the NAIC Model Act.[199] However, the 1960 NAIC

---

186 Fonseca, Handling Consumer Credit Cases 484–485 (3d ed. 1986).

187 Where a premium is financed, or where a service charge is applied for making installment payments, the state premium financing statute may apply. *See* Smith v. Foremost Ins. Co., 884 So. 2d 341 (Fla. Ct. App. Sept. 10, 2004) (finding, in an auto insurance case, that the state premium financing statute, applied to the insurer's service fees for making installment payments).

188 *E.g.*, Fla. Stat. Ann. (West) § 516.35; N.H. Rev. Stat. Ann. § 399-A:11 (Lender Licensing).

189 *E.g.*, Del. Code Ann. tit. 6, § 4307 (RISA); Ga. Code Ann. § 7-3-14(3) (Ind. Loan); Vt. Stat. Ann. tit. 9, § 2355(g).

190 *E.g.*, Ala. Code § 5-19-20; Iowa Code § 537.2501(2); La. Rev. Stat. tit. 9, § 3542(A).

191 *E.g.*, Ala. Code § 5-19-1(1); Ga. Code Ann. § 7-3-14(3). *See also* Singleton v. Protective Life Ins. Co., 857 So. 2d 803 (Ala. 2003) (applying *McCullar* and finding that borrowers failed to establish sale of excess insurance where net coverage was sold and finding that state rate requirements were followed); McCullar v. Universal Underwriters Life Ins. Co., 687 So. 2d 156 (Ala. 1996) (plurality) (regulatory language requiring that when

repayment is in substantially equal installments, the credit insurance can "never exceed approximate unpaid balance of the loan" prohibits gross coverage notwithstanding contrary agency interpretations; question of fact whether creditor's telling consumers that gross amount of insurance was needed to pay off debt in event of death constituted fraud; *see also* Gartman v. The Independent Life and Accident Ins. Co., 1998 U.S. Dist. LEXIS 22069 (S.D. Ala. Oct. 9, 1998) (class certified, by consent, in case challenging insurance charges based on total of payments, relying on *McCullar* decision); *but see* Gall v. American Heritage Life Ins. Co., 3 F. Supp. 2d 1344 (S.D. Ala. 1998) (court states it is not bound by plurality in *McCullar* and, agreeing with the dissent, finds that insurance can be calculated on the total of payments); Liberty Bank & Trust Co. v. Splane, 959 P.2d 600 (Okla. Ct. App. 1998) (court construed provision in U.C.C.C. restricting the amount of the permissible credit insurance to that which does not "exceed the debt" and another provision in Oklahoma insurance law restricting the amount of such insurance to "the approximate unpaid balance of the loan" to allow insurance premiums to be calculated on the total of payments; court specifically rejects the plurality in *McCullar*.).

192 *E.g.*, Conn. Gen. Stat. Ann. § 36a-566; N.D. Cent. Code § 51-13-02; Vt. Stat. Ann. tit. 9, § 2355(f)(4).

193 *E.g.*, N.D. Cent. Code § 13-03.1-17.

194 *Cf.* Ex Parte New Fin. Ltd, 284 Ala. 374, 225 So. 2d 782, 784 (1969) (Small Loan Acts strictly inclusive as to permissible charges); Hawkins v. Thorp Credit & Thrift Co., 441 N.W.2d 470 (Minn. 1989) (non-credit insurance not an authorized charge; its sale violated licensing act). *See also* §§ 8.5.3.2, 9.2.1.6, *infra*.

195 *See* discussion in §§ 8.3.1.5.1, *supra*, and 8.4.2.2.1, *infra*.

196 *E.g.*, Ala. Code § 5-19-20(b); Ariz. Rev. Stat. Ann. § 6-636; Cal. Fin. Code § 18294 (Industrial Loan); U.C.C.C. § 4-301.

197 Some states require that the amount financed and the value of the insured collateral meet a minimum floor in order for property insurance to be written, *e.g.*, Ala. Code § 5-19-20(g); Colo. Rev. Stat. § 5-4-301.

198 *E.g.*, La. Rev. Stat. tit. 9, § 3542–3550; U.C.C.C. § 4-101, *et seq*.

199 Comment #1, U.C.C.C. § 4-102 (1974).

Model Act governs only credit life and A&H, while the UCCC model also regulates credit property insurance.[200] The UCCC model governs creditor conduct, rather than insurer conduct.

Because many special consumer credit regulatory statutes regulate all types of charges which may be imposed, violations of applicable credit insurance provisions generally implicate the remedies available for violations of special licensing statutes as would any type of overcharge. If, for example, the small loan act provides that loans will be void if any consideration or charges in excess of that permitted by the statute is assessed, insurance charges not in compliance with applicable insurance law provisions can void the loan.[201]

8.4.1.4 Unfair Trade Practices Laws

Unfair and Deceptive Acts and Practices (UDAP) laws should not be overlooked as a source for establishing the consumer's rights and remedies. However, care must be taken to assure that the state UDAP statute does not exclude credit or insurance transactions from coverage.[202]

In addition to general UDAP statutes, every state has adopted some version of an "unfair insurance trade practices act" (UNIP),[203] again based on an NAIC Model UNIP Act. Though UDAP and UNIP statutes will generally be of little value in dealing with usury issues raised by credit insurance, it is important to be aware of them, as they may squarely address some of the marketing abuses often involved in credit insurance sales. Among these abuses are coercive sales tactics,[204] and the sale of insurance which may be worthless to borrowers who are clearly ineligible for benefits.[205] The UNIP statutes generally prohibit debtor coercion through tie-in arrangements, whereby creditors require that insurance be purchased from particular insurers or agents.[206] Additionally, UNIP statutes generally prohibit misrepresentation concerning the "terms, conditions and extent of insurance policy coverage."[207] Usually there is no explicit private right of action under UNIP statutes, although a private right of action may be implied, or a UNIP violation

may constitute a violation of a state UDAP statute.[208] Similarly, if a special licensing statute provides generally that an insurance charge "made in violation of the law," implicates the remedies authorized by that law, a UNIP violation may make that statute's penalty provisions applicable.[209]

8.4.1.5 Federal Laws

8.4.1.5.1 Truth in Lending

The Truth in Lending Act is a disclosure statute which does not substantively regulate the cost or terms of credit insurance. The most important TIL provisions relating to credit insurance set forth the conditions under which the lender may exclude the premium cost from the calculation of the finance charge for TIL disclosure purposes.[210] The premium cost may be excluded only if the insurance is not a factor in approving the credit, and the consumer is so informed.[211] Further, the cost of any such insurance must be disclosed, and the borrower must give specific affirmative written indication of a desire to purchase it.[212] Otherwise, credit insurance charges are treated as part of the finance charge.

Credit property insurance may be excluded from the TIL calculation of the finance charge if two conditions are met: the borrower must be informed that he or she may choose the insurance provider, and the cost of the insurance, if purchased through the creditor, must be disclosed.[213] In order to be excluded from the finance charge, vendor's single interest property insurance must comply with regular property insurance disclosures, and the insurer must also waive all subrogation rights against the consumer.[214]

Additionally, for loans entered into on or after October 1, 2002, single premium credit insurance and debt cancellation coverage are included in the "points and fees" calculation when determining whether the Homeownership and Equity Protection Act (HOEPA) applies.[215] As a result, high-cost loans with substantial single premium credit insurance or debt cancellation coverage are more likely to be covered by HOEPA and therefore subject to additional restrictions, prohibitions and disclosure requirements.

---

200 U.C.C.C. §§ 4.301–4.304.

201 *See* § 8.5.3.2, *infra*.

202 *See* National Consumer Law Center, Unfair and Deceptive Acts and Practices §§ 2.2.1, 2.3.1 (6th ed. 2004 and Supp.).

203 *See id.* § 5.3.2.

204 *See* § 8.5.2, *infra*.

205 *See* § 8.5.5, *infra*.

206 National Consumer Law Center, Unfair and Deceptive Acts and Practices § 5.3.6 (6th ed. 2004 and Supp.).

207 *Id.* Misrepresentations in the sales of credit insurance also can be challenged using state fraud statutes. *See* Byrd v. Metropolitan Corp., Clearinghouse Nos. 54596A, 54596B, & 54596C (Minn. Dist. Ct. Apr. 29, 2002) (jury finding in a class action that a car dealer used false statements in the retail installment contract when the dealer kept as profit almost half of a credit insurance premium it had agreed to pay to the insurer on behalf of the consumer).

208 *Id.* § 5.3.6.

209 *E.g.*, Iowa Code § 537.4101(2).

210 Calculating the finance charge for TIL purposes is different than calculating interest for purposes of the state usury law. *See* § 8.5.2.2, *infra*.

211 15 U.S.C. § 1605(b)(1); 12 C.F.R. § 226.4(d)(1).

212 15 U.S.C. § 1605(b)(2); 12 C.F.R. § 226.4(d)(1).

213 15 U.S.C. § 1605(c); 12 C.F.R. § 226.4(d)(2).

214 12 C.F.R. § 226.4(d)(2) n.5. For further details of TIL requirements relating to credit insurance disclosures, see National Consumer Law Center, Truth in Lending § 3.9.4 (5th ed. 2003 and Supp.).

215 Reg. Z § 226.32(b)(1)(iv).

8.4.1.5.2 Bank Holding Company Act and the Gramm-Leach-Bliley Act

The insurance-related activities of banks and bank holding companies are subject to the requirements of the Bank Holding Company Act and Regulation Y.[216] The Act prohibits tying credit to the purchase of credit insurance from the bank, holding company, or an affiliate.[217] It also limits the right of regulated banks and bank holding companies to underwrite insurance to those circumstances where the underwriter's performance could "reasonably be expected to produce benefits to the public."[218]

In 1999, Congress passed financial services reform legislation, the Gramm-Leach-Bliley Act, which largely eliminates the barriers separating the banking, insurance, and securities industries.[219] Though the Act was expected to set off a wave of mergers and acquisitions in the financial services industry, this has not yet occurred between banks and insurance companies.[220] Banks have focused their efforts to date "on rationalizing and expanding their existing structures for distributing insurance products under the Act's liberal provisions."[221]

Of relevance to credit insurance, the Act does not change the longstanding prohibition against banks or their subsidiaries underwriting insurance.[222] Nor does the Act affect the provisions of the Bank Holding Act described above.[223] On the other hand, the Act prohibits the states, by way of statute, regulation, or other action, from preventing or significantly interfering with the ability of an insured depository institution (or a subsidiary or affiliate thereof) from engaging in any insurance sales, solicitations, or cross-marketing activity.[224] This preemption is subject to thirteen exceptions that preserve the states' rights to regulate a bank's insurance sales so long as the restrictions are no more burdensome or restrictive than the provisions outlined in the Act and do not discriminate against or impose a disparate burden on banks and their affiliates.[225] These thirteen areas that the states may regulate include referral fees, licensing, regulatory inspection of books, release of information and privacy issues, conditioning extension of credit upon purchase of insurance, disclosures regarding choice of providers if the insurance is required, disclosures regarding the fact that the insurance is not insured by the FDIC, and financing of the premium.[226]

The Gramm-Leach-Bliley Act also requires the various federal banking agencies to publish customer protection regulations within one year from the date of enactment that apply to the retail sales practices, solicitations, advertising, or offers of any insurance products by a depository institution or affiliate.[227] This provision lists the types of customer protections contemplated which include: antitying and anticoercion rules; disclosure requirements that are meaningful; consumer acknowledgment mandate; prohibition regarding certain misrepresentations; physical separation requirement between the taking deposits and the sale of insurance; prohibition against discrimination if the applicant is a victim of domestic violence or a service provider to such persons; and the creation of a consumer grievance process. These regulations have not yet been published.

In 2000, the Office of the Comptroller of the Currency, the Federal Reserve Board, the Federal Deposit Insurance Corporation, and the Office of Thrift Supervision issued joint regulations under this provision of the Act.[228] The effective date was October 1, 2001.[229] The regulations cover prohibited practices, disclosures, restrictions on where insurance activities may take place, and insurance sales personnel licensing requirements and qualifications. Following publication of the regulations, these agencies issued responses to questions from the American Bankers Insurance Association and the American Bankers Association. The topics covered include: under what circumstance private

---

216 12 U.S.C. § 1843(c)(8); 12 C.F.R. § 225.28(b)(11) (1999). *See* Hinkle, *Insurance Activities of National Banks and Bank Holding Companies*, 105 Banking L.J. 137 (1988).

217 12 U.S.C. § 1972.

218 12 U.S.C. § 1843(c)(8).

219 Pub. L. No. 106-102 (1999), codified as 15 U.S.C. §§ 6701 *et seq.*, 6801 *et seq.*, 6901 *et seq.*

220 Board of Governors of the Federal Reserve System, Report to the Congress on Financial Holding Companies Under the Gramm-Leach-Bliley Act (Nov. 2003), *available at* www.federalreserve.gov/boarddocs/rptcongress/glbarptcongress.pdf. Nevertheless, consolidation in the banking industry, which was well underway before Gramm-Leach-Bliley, is continuing, and cross-fertilization by securities, banking and insurance firms certainly is developing. Arthur E. Wilmarth, Jr., *The Transformation of the U.S. Financial Services Industry, 1975–2000: Competition, Consolidation, and Increased Risks*, 2002 U. Ill. L. Rev. 215 (2002); Edward D. Herlihy, et al., *Financial Institutions Mergers and Acquisitions 2001: Adapting to the Challenges of a Changing Landscape* (Practicing Law Institute, 1299 PLI/Corp 11, Feb.–Mar. 2002).

221 James M. Cain, *Financial Institution Insurance Activities—Gramm-Leach-Bliley—One Year Later*, 56 Bus. Lawyer 1191, 1191 (May 2001).

222 15 U.S.C. § 6712.

223 15 U.S.C. § 1601(d)(2)(viii)(I). The OCC published a notice in 2004 providing contact information for questions concerning tying and reiterating the prohibition on conditioning credit availability on the purchase of credit insurance. This prohibition—at least in the Bank Holding Act—applies to banks but not to nonbank affiliates of a bank or other nonbank entities. Press Release, Office of the Comptroller of the Currency (Mar. 23,

2004), *available at* www.occ.treas.gov/scripts/newsrelease.aspx ?Doc=5585SPNY.xml.

224 15 U.S.C. § 6701(d). *See* Association of Banks in Ins., Inc. v. Duryee, 270 F.3d 397 (6th Cir. 2001) (Ohio's licensing laws and restrictions on solicitations of customers were preempted by Gramm-Leach-Bliley).

225 15 U.S.C. § 6701(d)(2)(B) and (e).

226 15 U.S.C. § 6701(d)(2)(B)(i)–(xiii).

227 § 305 of Gramm-Leach-Bliley which amends the Federal Insurance Deposit Act at 12 U.S.C. § 1831x.

228 65 Fed. Reg. 75822 (Dec. 4, 2000).

229 66 Fed. Reg. 15345 (Mar. 19, 2001).

mortgage insurance and renewals of insurance are covered by the regulations and timing of disclosures when solicitation of the customer to purchase insurance does not occur until after the loan application has been approved. This document is available at www.occ.treas.gov/abaqa8-13.doc.

Regarding prohibited acts, any covered person[230] may not lead a consumer to believe that an extension of credit is conditional upon either: (1) the purchase of an insurance product or an annuity from the bank or any of its affiliates or (2) an agreement by the consumer not to obtain, or a prohibition on the consumer from obtaining, any insurance product or annuity from an unaffiliated entity. Further, covered persons may not mislead any person into believing that the insurance product or annuity is backed by the federal government or insured by the FDIC, or that any product which involves investment risk does not have such risk or cannot lose its value. Finally, covered persons may not consider the fact that a consumer is a victim of domestic violence in the underwriting, pricing, renewal, or scope of coverage or with regard to the payment of claims except as required or expressly permitted under state law.[231]

Banks and covered persons must disclose to consumers several pieces of information related to the above-described prohibited practices. Such disclosures must state that: the insurance product or annuity is not a deposit, or other obligation of or guaranteed by the bank or an affiliate; such product is not insured by the FDIC or any other agency; and if the product involves investment risk, that the risk exists, including the possibility of loss.[232] These disclosures must be provided both orally and in writing before the completion of the initial sale of an insurance product or annuity.[233] Further, the bank must disclose that it cannot condition the purchase of an insurance product on the extension of credit or that the consumer agree not to obtain an insurance product or annuity from an unaffiliated entity. This information must be provided orally and in writing at the time the consumer applies for an extension of credit.[234] The disclosures must be "readily understandable," clear and conspicuous, and designed to call attention to the nature and significance of the information provided.[235] In addition, the

disclosures must be given in a "meaningful" form.[236]

If disclosures are provided electronically, the consent requirements set forth in the Electronic Signatures in Global and National Commerce Act apply.[237] The bank may provide the mandated written disclosures electronically "if the consumer affirmatively consents to receiving the disclosures electronically and if the disclosures are provided in a format that the consumer may retain or obtain later, for example, by printing or storing electronically (such as by downloading)."[238] If the information is provided electronically, oral disclosures need not be given. Electronic disclosures are not meaningfully provided if the consumer can bypass the visual text before purchasing the insurance product or annuity.[239]

Significantly, the regulations require that the consumer acknowledge receipt of the mandated disclosures in writing or electronically.[240] The consumer is not specifically entitled to a copy of this acknowledgment, however.

Two additional substantive restrictions apply to these types of transactions. First, where practicable, the bank must physically separate its insurance business from where it conducts its retail deposit business. The insurance product or annuity sales section of the bank must be "clearly delineated" and "distinguished" from the other bank functions. However, bank personnel employed in the deposit section of the bank may refer consumers to the insurance or annuity portion of the bank only if that person received no more than a "nominal" fee of a fixed dollar amount for each referral.[241] Second, a bank may not allow any person who sells or offers for sale any such products to do so in its offices or to act on its behalf unless that person is qualified and licensed under applicable state insurance licensing rules regarding the specific products being recommended or sold.[242]

The Office of the Comptroller of the Currency published for comment three requests that the OCC determine that certain state insurance laws are preempted by Gramm-Leach-Bliley.[243] The OCC acted upon only two of these

---

230 A covered person is defined as a bank or "any other person only when the person sells, solicits, advertises, or offers an insurance product or annuity to a consumer at an office of the bank or on behalf of a bank." 12 C.F.R. § 208.82(j) (the regulation also discusses what are activities performed on behalf of a bank) (FRB regulations).
231 12 C.F.R. § 208.83 (FRB regulations).
232 12 C.F.R. §§ 208.84(a) and (b) (FRB regulations).
233 12 C.F.R. § 208.84(c)(1) (FRB regulations) (if a sale is conducted by mail, oral disclosures need not be provided; if a sale is conducted or application is taken by telephone, the timing rules for the provision of the written disclosure change, see §§ 208.84(2) and (3)).
234 *Id.*
235 12 C.F.R. § 208.84(c)(5) (FRB regulations) (the regulation provides some examples of statements that could be used in advertisements which are simple, direct, readily understandable,

and formatted in a way to call attention to the nature and significance of the information as well as a list of the types of methods that could be used to satisfy this requirement, see § 208.84(c)(5), (c)(6)).
236 12 C.F.R. § 208.84(c)(6) (FRB regulations).
237 12 C.F.R. § 208.84(c)(4) (FRB regulations). The Electronic Signatures in Global and National Commerce Act, 12 U.S.C. § 7001 *et seq.*, is discussed in § 9.2.10, *infra.*
238 12 C.F.R. § 208.84(c)(4) (FRB regulations).
239 12 C.F.R. § 208.84(c)(6)(iii) (FRB regulations).
240 12 C.F.R. § 208.84(c)(7) (FRB regulations) (special rules apply if the transaction is conducted by telephone).
241 12 C.F.R. § 208.85 (FRB regulations) (and the payment of the fee cannot depend on whether the referral results in a sale).
242 12 C.F.R. § 208.86 (FRB regulations).
243 65 Fed. Reg. 35420 (June 2, 2000) (West Virginia Insurance Sales Commission Protection Act); 65 Fed. Reg. 57427 (Sept. 22, 2000) (Rhode Island Financial Institutions Insurance Sales Act); 65 Fed. Reg. 43827 (July 14, 2000) (certain provisions of

requests, the ones addressing West Virginia and Massachusetts law. The agency opined that some provisions of West Virginia insurance law are preempted and some are not.[244] On the other hand, the OCC found that all of the sections of Massachusetts law at issue are preempted.[245] Both West Virginia and Massachusetts challenged the legality of these letters in federal appellate courts. The Fourth Circuit upheld the OCC's preemption of the West Virginia provisions.[246] The court ruled that the OCC has the authority to interpret Gramm-Leach-Bliley and that the OCC's reasoning in finding the West Virginia provisions to be preempted was valid.[247] This was the first time a federal court had ruled on the OCC's preemption of state law under Gramm-Leach-Bliley. Unlike the Fourth Circuit, the First Circuit held that it had no jurisdiction under Article III of the Constitution because the OCC's opinion letter had no legal effect and was not coercive, and thus did not give rise to a "case or controversy."[248] Subsequently, a group of lenders challenged in district court the Massachusetts laws relating to sales, solicitations, and marketing of insurance products (thus providing an actual case). The court held that all four

challenged provisions were preempted by Gramm-Leach-Bliley.[249] Applying a *Barnett*[250] analysis, the court found that the state law substantially burdened a lender's ability to cross-market and sell insurance products by significantly decreasing marketing opportunities, impeding lenders from offering insurance until after a consumer is likely to have purchased it elsewhere, and imposing "more costs" in its requirement for separate insurance-related space. The state has declined to appeal the case.

Response to the OCC's letters also has reached beyond the judicial forum. In August 2002, the National Conference of State Legislatures approved a resolution opposing the OCC's practice of issuing interpretations of federal law.[251]

It is way too early to understand and predict the effect of this new federal law upon the sale of credit insurance by depository institutions. One thing is certain at this point: the sale of credit insurance by banks and their affiliates will be governed by a mish-mash of state and federal statutes and regulations which will make understanding the whole picture more complicated.

8.4.1.6 Insurance Premium Financing Laws

Insurance premium financing laws do not regulate the sale of credit insurance, even though that sale is financed as part of the loan it insures. Instead, these laws regulate the financing of ordinary insurance premiums, often allowing high interest rates on these transactions, which are actually credit sales. Insurance premium financing statutes commonly apply to automobile insurance premiums, where the insured cannot afford to pay the entire amount in a single installment. However, these statutes may also apply, in some instances, to a lender's sale of extraneous insurance, such as cancer policies, level term non-credit-life, or accidental death and dismemberment policies, as are often sold in insurance-packing schemes. Some of these statutes do not apply to traditional lenders, however. Consequently, it is important to be aware of the scope and requirements of insurance premium financing statutes in those states which currently have them.[252] Other claims may arise in this

---

the Massachusetts bank insurance sales statute and regulations).

244 66 Fed. Reg. 51502 (Oct. 9, 2001). *Preempted* were provisions: (1) requiring financial institutions to use separate employees' for insurance solicitations; (2) restricting the timing of bank employees' referral or solicitation of insurance business from customers who have loan applications pending with the bank; (3) restricting the sharing of information with bank affiliates acquired by a financial institution in the course of a loan transaction to solicit or offer insurance; (4) requiring that financial institutions segregate the place of solicitation or sale of insurance so that it is readily distinguishable from deposit-taking and lending areas. *Not* preempted were provisions: (1) prohibiting a requirement or implication that the purchase of an insurance product is required as a condition of a loan; (2) prohibiting a financial institution from offering an insurance product in combination with other products unless all of the products are available separately; (3) requiring that, where insurance is required as a condition of credit, the insurance and credit transactions be completed independently and through separate documents.

245 67 Fed. Reg. 13405 (Mar. 22, 2002). The affected provisions prohibited non-licensed bank personnel from referring prospective customers to a licensed insurance agent except upon an inquiry initiated by the customer; prohibited non-licensed bank personnel from receiving any additional compensation for making a referral; prohibited banks from telling loan applicants that insurance products are available through the bank until the application is approved and, in the case of a loan secured by a mortgage on real property, until after the customer has accepted the bank's written commitment to extend credit.

246 Cline v. Hawke, 51 Fed. Appx. 392, 2002 WL 31557392 (4th Cir. Nov. 19, 2002).

247 *Id.*

248 Bowler v. Hawke, 320 F.3d 59 (1st Cir. 2003). One judge on the Fourth Circuit panel dissented from the majority on the same basis, arguing that the matter did not meet the "case or controversy" requirement of Article III of the Constitution. Cline v. Hawke, 51 Fed. Appx. 392, 2002 WL 31557392 (4th Cir. 2002) (King, J., dissenting).

249 Massachusetts Bankers Ass'n v. Bowler, 2005 WL 61458 (D. Mass. Jan. 10, 2005). The provisions at issue: prohibit bank employees who are not licensed insurance agents from referring a bank customer to a licensed insurance agent unless the customer inquires about insurance; forbids banks from paying insurance referral fees; allows banks to solicit loan applicants for insurance sales only after written approval and disclosures have been provided; and requires insurance solicitation to be physically separate from other bank functions.

250 Barnett Bank of Marion County v. Nelson, 517 U.S. 25 (1996) (where state law forbids or significantly impairs a congressional grant of authority, state law is preempted).

251 *State Legislators Oppose OCC's Role In Ruling on Preemption of State Laws*, Banking Rep. (BNA) Vol. 79, No. 7, at 276 (Monday Aug. 12, 2002).

252 *E.g.*, Ala. Code § 27-40-1, *et seq.*; Alaska Stat. § 06.40.010 *et*

context. Truth in Lending disclosures must be given in certain circumstances.[253] Breach of fiduciary duty and UDAP claims have survived motions to dismiss where the insurance premium finance company and the insurance company were connected and failed to disclose this information to the consumer.[254]

8.4.2 Substance of Credit Insurance Regulations

8.4.2.1 Rates

8.4.2.1.1 General

Most states have a prescribed mechanism for establishing authorized rates for credit life and disability insurance. Few states have any rate regulation for credit property or involuntary unemployment insurance. Consequently, this discussion relates primarily to credit life and disability rates.

With respect to credit life, a few states have established maximum rates by statute or regulation.[255] These are generally cast as x cents per $100 of the initial indebtedness per year, e.g., 60¢/$100/yr.[256] The more common approach for both credit life and disability, however, is not an inflexible statutory maximum ceiling, but the more fluid concept of *prima facie* rates. Because the majority of the states have adopted some variant of the 1960 NAIC Model Act,[257] the NAIC rate-setting system will be used to illustrate this problem. (The new NAIC model act governing credit property insurance establishes the same 60% loss-ratio benchmark as the 1960 act. Thus, the following discussion applies to the new model act as well.[258])

Under the NAIC Model Act, insurers are required to file "all policies, certificates of insurance, notices of proposed insurance, applications for insurance, endorsements and riders and the schedules of premium rates pertaining thereto" with the state insurance commission, which has the authority to disapprove any forms or premium schedule. The Act *requires* the Commissioner to disapprove the form if "the benefits provided therein are not reasonable in relation to the premium charge."[259] Similar language has been interpreted to give the insurance department the authority, in effect, to set rate standards.[260]

The generally used method of determining what premium rate would be "reasonable in relation to the benefits" is to adopt a "benchmark loss-ratio," and then to attempt to establish rates expected to produce that benchmark loss-ratio. (Recall that a loss-ratio is that portion of each premium dollar paid out in claims to insureds. The higher the loss-ratio, the less of the premium dollar is retained by the insurer and creditor for expenses and profits.) The rates are purportedly chosen on the basis of actual experience, derived from determining the ratio of "incurred claims" to "earned premiums" for a given period.[261] Of course, authorized rates cannot be established retroactively, as using actual loss-ratios would suggest, so insurance commissions are authorized to establish prima facie rates, which they anticipate will meet the loss-ratio benchmark. The prima facie "reasonable" rate, derived by this system, becomes the "authorized" premium rate.

The NAIC recommends a benchmark standard for a "reasonable charge" to be a 60% loss-ratio for both credit life and credit A & H.[262] However, most states utilize a 50% benchmark loss-ratio. The applicable benchmark may be established by statute, by administrative regulation, or by letters or bulletins issued by the insurance department. Some states set different benchmark loss-ratios for life than for disability insurance.

---

seq.; Ariz. Rev. Stat. Ann. § 6-1401 *et seq.*; Idaho Code §§ 28-43-205; Ky. Rev. Stat. § 304.30-010 et. seq. ; Minn. Stat. Ann. § 59A.01 *et seq.*

253 Official Staff Commentary § 226.2(a)(14)-1. *See* Harris v. Illinois Vehicle Premium Fin. Co., 2000 U.S. Dist. LEXIS 13763 (N.D. Ill. Sept. 7, 2000). *See also* National Consumer Law Center, Truth in Lending § 2.2.4.1 (5th ed. 2003 and Supp.). *But see* Hobson v. Lincoln Ins. Agency, Inc., 2001 U.S. Dist. LEXIS 476 (N.D. Ill. Jan. 22, 2001) (breach of fiduciary duty dismissed pursuant to an Illinois statute that expressly negates the existence of a fiduciary duty; RICO claims dismissed).

254 *See* Harris v. Illinois Vehicle Premium Fin. Co., 2000 U.S. Dist. LEXIS 13763 (N.D. Ill. Sept. 7, 2000); Hobson v. Lincoln Ins. Agency, Inc., 2000 U.S. Dist. LEXIS 13314 (N.D. Ill. Sept. 7, 2000) (note that RICO claims were dismissed but with leave to amend in these cases).

255 In Texas, the maximum fee is 30% above the "presumptive" rate. *See* Service Life & Cas. Ins. Co. v. Montemayor, 150 S.W.3d 649 (Tex. App. 2004).

256 *E.g.*, Ky. Rev. Stat. § 304.19-080; Mo. Ann. Stat. § 385.070 (Vernon); Tenn. Code Ann. § 56-7-908(a).

257 *See* note 181, *supra*.

258 No state has passed the new model act. For a description of

many of its significant provisions, see §§ 8.3.1.5.1, *supra*, 8.4.2.2.1, *infra*.

259 Model Bill to Provide for the Regulation of Credit Life Ins. and Credit Accident and Health Ins., National Ass'n of Ins. Comm'rs, Model Regulatory Service § 7B (NIARS Corp., 1984).

260 Old Republic Life Ins. Co. v. Wikler, 9 N.Y.2d 524, 175 N.E.2d 147 (1961).

261 A practitioner can derive this information from filings insurance companies must provide annually to insurance departments in states where they do business. For a guide which assists in this information gathering process, *see* David Birnbaum, *A Consumer Advocate's Guide to Getting, Understanding, and Using Insurance Data*, Center for Economic Justice (Aug. 1999), *available at* www.cej-online.org/intro.php.

262 Fagg, Credit Life and Disability Insurance 382–383 (1986).

8.4.2.1.2 Problems with prima facie rates

One problem with prima facie rates is that they result from a guess as to what will achieve the benchmark loss-ratio, though past experience is supposed to guide the process. The guessing historically has been on the high side. The original prima facie rate for credit life insurance in many states was $1 or more per hundred per year.[263] By 1994, forty-five states had established a prima facie rate for single decreasing credit life rates of 65¢ or less per hundred per year.[264] In addition, the *actual* experience of many insurers shows that even the authorized prima facie rates often result in loss ratios far lower than the targeted loss ratio. The 1979 Senate hearings indicated that sixteen states had rates which resulted in loss ratios of less than 37%.[265] By 1990, twenty-four states had loss ratios that low.[266] By 1997, the picture improved a bit as fourteen states claimed loss ratios under 37%, though four others were between 37–38%.[267] Unfortunately, by 2000, this number had increased to seventeen states with loss-ratios below 37%, a worse record than in 1979.[268]

8.4.2.1.3 Deviations

As the term indicates, the prima facie rate is a presumptive standard of reasonable benefits. An insurer may request that the insurance department grant an "upward deviation," which then allows it to charge a higher premium. Theoretically, the insurer must present actuarial evidence to the department to establish that the prima facie rate is insufficient. Only a few states have mandatory downward deviations if the rates charged do not meet the benchmark loss-ratio.[269]

One problem with the upward deviation process is that some insurers may look upon the loss-ratio benchmark as a guaranteed return, and may seek a deviation even if the loss-ratio exceeds the benchmark by only a little. Since many consumer experts in the field argue that a loss-ratio of 70–80% provides ample return to insurers and creditors,[270] granting a deviation in such circumstances excessively burdens consumers. For this reason, some states authorize upward deviations only if the insurer's loss-ratio exceeds a specified "loss-ratio corridor." For example, if a state has a 50% benchmark, an upward deviation may not be granted unless the insurer's loss-ratio is over 60%.[271] Or there may be a "no-action corridor," where no change is implemented if the new rate would be within a specified "corridor" from the current rate.[272]

8.4.2.1.4 Challenging prima facie rates

The NAIC Model Act specifies in mandatory terms that the insurance commissioner has authority to require rates that are reasonable in relation to benefits. Therefore, a commissioner who has authorized prima facie rates which result in loss-ratios lower than the state's target benchmark loss-ratio may be vulnerable to a mandamus challenge from consumers. This rarely has been done, though consumers were ultimately successful in Ohio and Illinois when this

---

263 National Ass'n of Ins. Comm'rs, A Background Study of the Regulation of Credit Life and Disability Insurance 70 (1970).

264 The Cost of Personal Borrowing published by Financial Publishing Company, contains state by state charts of credit insurance rates. Increased public attention has led to more attention by insurance commissions. *See* discussion in § 8.2, *supra*.

265 *Credit Life Insurance Hearing Before the Subcomm. on Antitrust, Monopoly and Business Rights of the Senate Comm. on the Judiciary*, 96th Cong, 1st Sess. 2–3, 41, 49 (1979).

266 *Credit Life Insurance Revisited: A Continuing Consumer Ripoff*, Statement of Consumer Federation of America and National Insurance Consumer Organization, Clearinghouse No. 47,773A (May 20, 1992), updating *Credit Life Insurance: The Nation's Worst Insurance Ripoff*, Clearinghouse No. 47,773 (June 4, 1990). The 1994 survey showed 19 states with loss ratios under 37%. Credit Life Insurance Revisited II (second update of Consumer Federation of America/National Insurance Consumer Organization July 25, 1995, Clearinghouse No. 45,773B). The numbers in 1995 were even worse: 22 states with loss ratios under 37%. Most Credit Life Insurance Still a Rip-Off, Clearinghouse No. 45,773C (update to Consumer Federation of America/National Insurance Consumer Organization July 25, 1995, Clearinghouse No. 45,773B). The Wall Street Journal reported that, of the ten largest credit life insurers in the country, only the credit union's underwriter met a 60% loss ratio in 1989. ITT Lyndon Life, with $50 million in premiums, had a 26.5% loss ratio. American Bankers Life Assurance Co. of Florida, with $117 million in premiums, had a 40% loss ratio. Christi Harlan, *As Credit Insurers Aim High, Beware*, Wall St. J., June 12, 1991 at C1. *See also* Union Security Life Ins. Co. v. Crocker, 667 So. 2d 688 (Ala. 1995) (case noting one company's credit life loss ratios ranging only from 16.3% to 21.1% during a four year period), *vacated on other grounds*, 116 S. Ct. 1872 (1996) ($2 million punitive damage award was sent back to Alabama Supreme Court for further consideration in light of BMW of N. Am., Inc. v. Gore, 517 U.S. 559, 116 S. Ct. 1589 (1996)), *upon remand from Supreme Court*, 709 So. 2d 1118 (Ala. 1997) (court reduced punitive damages award to $1 million by weighing reprehensible conduct of insurance company's agent (though an apparently isolated instance) coupled with the "catastrophic" economic injury to Ms. Crocker facing foreclosure of her mobile home in the wake of her husband's death against percentage of award to insurance companies' net worth).

267 Mary Griffin & Birny Birnbaum, *Credit Insurance: The $2 Billion a Year Rip-Off*, Consumers Union and the Center for Economic Justice 7 (Mar. 1999).

268 Jack Gillis, James Hunt, D.J. Powers, Birny Birnbaum, *Credit Insurance Overcharges Hit $2.5 Annually*, Consumer Federation of America and Center for Economic Justice 6 (Nov. 2001).

269 *E.g.*, Ohio Admin. Code § 3901-1-14(C)(8).

270 *E.g.*, *Credit Life Insurance Hearing Before the Subcomm. on Antitrust, Monopoly and Business Rights of the Senate Comm. on the Judiciary*, 96th Cong, 1st Sess. 12, 52–53 (1979).

271 Fagg, Credit Life and Disability Insurance 181 (1986).

272 The NAIC Model Regulation uses 5% as the "no-action corridor." Thus if the indicated new rate is within 5% of the old rate, no deviation will be authorized. Fagg, Credit Life and Disability Insurance 181 (1986).

approach was tried.[273] Probably these mandamus actions are unusual because attorneys evaluating a client's credit transaction for excess charges generally limit their scrutiny to the issue of whether the premium exceeds the maximum ceiling approved by the state. Consumer attorneys rarely consider the validity of the authorized rate itself. That is a different lawsuit, but one which others may pursue more vigorously in light of the successes by consumers in Ohio and Illinois.

In Georgia, a different litigation approach was taken to challenge rates which exceed target loss-ratios. Rather than filing a mandamus against the insurance commissioner for approving such rates, the insurers themselves were sued in a series of related cases.[274] The plaintiffs contended that the prima facie reasonable rate set an *outside* limit, and that a state administrative regulation required insurers to further reduce rates annually to an amount which would result in at least a 50% loss-ratio. The regulation also created a presumption that a commission in excess of 40% operates to prevent the insurer from reaching that 50% target loss-ratio.

The defending insurers lost important preliminary rounds in the litigation. In denying one insurer's motion to dismiss,[275] the court held that the regulations have the force of law and form a part of the contract. It further found that Georgia law would recognize a private cause of action to provide a remedy: acting contrary to a legal duty constitutes actionable fraud;[276] a state statute provides that "for every

right there shall be a remedy;"[277] and, of course, breach of contract, since lawful regulations are an implied term of every contract.

In a companion case, *Shellman v. Investors National Life Insurance Co.*,[278] the insurer argued that the target loss-ratio was simply a mechanism to assure the financial solvency of the insurers, and placed no burden on it to lower rates to meet that. It further argued that there was an implied approval of its rates by virtue of its filings with the Insurance Department, and that an insurer indeed is not *permitted* to charge less than the maximum rates set by regulation. The court rejected all those arguments in denying the defendants' motion to dismiss.[279] Though this litigation was only one of several factors, the result of bringing attention to bear in Georgia was to improve dramatically the situation for consumers, who will save an estimated $32.8 million annually as a result of the 40% rate reduction.[280]

8.4.2.1.5 Filed-Rate Doctrine

The filed-rate doctrine has developed as a result of a regulatory system in which, in many states, insurance companies, and other entities, file and seek approval for their rates from state regulatory bodies.[281] The doctrine requires courts to accord state administrative and regulatory bodies deference regarding approved rates.[282]

---

273 Madrigal v. O'Connor, No. 81 L 27570, Clearinghouse No. 41,268 (Cook Cty. Cir. Ct. Mar. 4, 1987); State Ex. Rel. Consumers League v. Ratchford, 457 N.E.2d 878 (Ohio App. 1982). In 1988, the Illinois Department of Insurance completed the review process begun as a result of the mandamus in *Madrigal, supra*. Many policies were disapproved, and rates lowered by 23%. The plaintiffs' attorneys estimated a savings of $22 million a year to consumers.

Though the Ohio case was dismissed on standing grounds, the court did conclude that the insurance department was under a duty to seek a rate reduction. The department subsequently did so.

It has been suggested that the loss-ratio experience is not strictly enforced because states wish to encourage lending and insurance business, and there is no countervailing consumer pressure regarding this rather arcane topic. *Credit Insurance: Abuse and Reform*, 10 B.C. Ind. & Com. L. Rev. 439, 454 n.87 (1969). *See also* § 8.2.3.1, *supra*.

274 *See, e.g.*, Griffin v. American Life Ins. Co., Clearinghouse No. 44,823 (Super. Ct., Richmond Cty., filed Aug. 23, 1989), in which the plaintiffs sued the insurer for paying commissions to its creditor/agents in excess of the commission caps authorized under state regulations and exceeding lawful premiums. Causes of action alleged were: fraud (seeking a constructive trust on the excess fund); breach of contract, in that each contract incorporates existing law and regulations into its terms; unconscionability; and the state RICO Act. The matter was ultimately resolved when the state insurance commission lowered the rates.

275 Colvin v. Citizens & Southern Life Ins. Co., Clearinghouse No. 45,775 (Super. Ct., Richmond Cty., motion to dismiss denied Jan. 8, 1990). *Accord* Shellman v. Investors Nat'l Life Ins. Co., Clearinghouse No. 45,774 (Super. Ct., Richmond Cty., defendant's motion for summary judgment denied Aug. 16, 1990).

276 Ga. Code Ann. § 23-2-51(b).

277 Ga. Code Ann. § 9-2-3.

278 Clearinghouse No. 45,774 (Super. Ct., Richmond Cty., defendant's motion for summary judgment denied Aug. 16, 1990).

279 These and a number of related cases were subsequently settled after parallel hearings before the state Insurance Commissioner resulted in the credit life rate being lowered to .45¢/$100. *See* Aldrich v. Georgia Int'l Life Ins. Co., Clearinghouse No. 50,417 (Super. Ct. Richmond Cty. Va., stipulation of settlement filed Apr. 14, 1994).

280 *See* Credit Life Insurance Revisited II (second update of Consumer Federation of America/National Insurance Consumer Organization July 25, 1995, Clearinghouse No. 45,773B).

281 Many jurisdictions apply the filed rate doctrine to insurance rates. *See, e.g.*, Kirksey v. Am. Bankers Ins. Co. of Fla., 114 F. Supp. 2d 526 (S.D. Miss. 2000); Allen v. State Farm Fire & Cas. Co., 59 F. Supp. 2d 1217 (S.D. Ala. 1999); Morales v. Attorneys' Title Ins. Funds, Inc., 983 F. Supp. 1418 (S.D. Fla. 1997); Horwitz v. Bankers Life & Cas. Co., 745 N.E.2d 591 (Ill. Ct. App. 2001); Amundson & Assoc. Art Studio, Ltd. v. National Council on Compensation Ins., Inc., 988 P.2 1208 (Kan. Ct. App. 1999).

282 In Richardson v. Standard Guaranty Ins. Co., 853 A.2d 955 (N.J. Super. Ct. 2004), a consumer class action alleging that a credit card bank fraudulently induced consumers to purchase credit insurance policies, the court acknowledged the controversial nature of the filed-rate doctrine, yet it still found that it is bound by it. Even the U.S. Supreme Court has noted that it "may seem harsh in some circumstances." *Central Office*, 524 U.S. 214, 222 (1998). The Court however explained that, at least in the communications context, the strict application of the filed-rate doctrine is important to prevent carriers from offering shippers rebates or discounts and to ensure that all consumers pay the same price. In the credit insurance context, however, the prob-

As a result, the doctrine bars claims for monetary relief where the plaintiff seeks to enforce a rate other than that filed with the state (the "nondiscrimination" strand).[283] A component of this strand is that a consumer is presumed to have suffered no monetary loss if she paid a filed rate, even if she claims that the amount was obtained through a misrepresentation.[284] Additionally, other types of claims against regulated entities may be limited or dismissed because consumers are presumed to have constructive knowledge of the filed rate (the "nonjusticiability" strand) and thus could not have relied upon misrepresentations or other fraud perpetrated by the regulated entity.[285]

The doctrine is limited, however, to where the court decision would have an impact upon state regulatory procedures and rate determinations. Thus, a rescission claim or a claim that insurance was sold without the consumer's knowledge does not implicate the filed-rate doctrine.[286]

The artificial nature of this doctrine presuming consumer knowledge is apparent in light of the doctrine's failure to bar similar claims against an unregulated entity, such as a bank, selling the regulated product.[287] Moreover, where the industry in question is not closely regulated by a particular state, the court, where it chooses to apply this doctrine, is providing deference to a hollow process that can gravely harm consumers.[288]

8.4.2.2 Non-Rate Regulation

8.4.2.2.1 NAIC model acts

In addition to rates, there are a number of other aspects of the credit insurance transaction that may be governed by insurance, credit, or UNIP statutes. This section will first review the NAIC Model Act governing credit life and

disability and then discuss the Model Act covering personal property insurance, the latter having just been adopted in 2001.

For credit life and disability, the term of coverage may be limited;[289] the NAIC Model Code excludes long-term credit transactions from its coverage. Relying upon a similar provision in Georgia law, the Georgia Insurance Commissioner brought an enforcement proceeding against a lender who sold credit insurance in connection with loans whose terms exceeded ten years.[290] Following a hearing, the Commissioner ordered the lender to cease selling such insurance on loans with a duration of more than ten years.

In addition, the Model Act limits initial coverage to the initial indebtedness,[291] interpreted to mean the total of payments.[292] Many states require that credit life be written on a

---

lem is that consumers are all held to non-competitive, high prices and fraud can be used to hold a consumer to a higher price than she reasonably could have expected to pay.

283 *See, e.g.,* Smith v. Tower Loan of Mississippi, Inc., 216 F.R.D. 338 (S.D. Miss. 2003) (filed-rate doctrine bars allegation of excessive rates; court approved a class action settlement alleging other credit insurance abuses).

284 Richardson v. Standard Guar. Ins. Co., 853 A.2d 955 (N.J. Super. Ct. 2004).

285 In addition to barring consumer claims, the nondiscrimination strand also has been found to bar antitrust claims. Square D Co. v. Niagara Frontier Tariff Bureau, Inc., 476 U.S. 409 (1986).

286 *See* Richardson, 853 A.2d 955 (N.J. Super. Ct. 2004); Gulf States Util. Co. v. Alabama Power Co., 824 F.2d 1465 (5th Cir.), *op. amended,* 831 F.2d 557 (5th Cir. 1987); Nordlicht v. New York Tel. Co., 617 F. Supp. 220 (S.D.N.Y. 1985).

287 Smith v. SBC Comm. Inc., 839 A.2d 850 (N.J. 2004). An agent, but not a retailer, can avail itself of the filed-rate doctrine in this context. This rule creates an incentive for purveyors of insurance to fashion themselves as agents in order to shield themselves from a broad array of legal claims.

288 *See* Allan Kanner, *The Filed Rate Doctrine and Insurance Fraud Litigation,* 76 N.D. L. Rev. 1 (2000).

289 The NAIC Model Act applies only to credit life and disability policies of less than 10 years duration. Longer term insurance is subject to general insurance laws. State versions may vary.

290 In the matter of Associates Fin. Life Ins. Co., Case No. 99C-014B (Ga. Office of Insurance and Safety Fire Commissioner, Jan. 31, 2000), Clearinghouse No. 52,508A. The decision was based upon Ga. Code Ann. § 33-31-2(c). *See also* Darden v. Ford Consumer Fin. Co., Clearinghouse No. 53,570 (Ga. Super. Ct. Aug. 20, 2001) (settlement agreement) (class action filed claiming that the lender and its insurance company sold credit life and health and accident insurance policies in connection with loans of more than 10 years in duration certified for settlement purposes; class members to receive a refund of entire insurance premium plus a $300 or $500 cash payment plus a 0.5% reduction in the loan interest rate depending upon whether the class members cancel the insurance, the loan is still held by the lender, and other factors).

291 Model Bill to Provide for the Regulation of Credit Life Ins. and Credit Accident and Health Ins., National Ass'n of Ins. Comm'rs, Model Regulatory Service § 4 (NIARS Corp., 1984). Under the revised NAIC model act, net coverage would be mandated. NAIC Consumer Credit Insurance Model Act § 4(A) (1994).

292 Winkle v. Grand Nat'l Bank, 601 S.W.2d 559, 571 (Ark. 1980). *But cf.* McCullar v. Universal Underwriters Life Ins. Co., 687 So. 2d 156 (Ala. 1996) (plurality) (interpreting Alabama regulation limiting coverage to "approximate unpaid balance of the loan" to require net coverage, despite agency interpretation that gross coverage was permissible); *see also* Gartman v. The Independent Life and Accident Ins. Co., 1998 U.S. Dist. LEXIS 22069 (S.D. Ala. Oct. 9, 1998) (class certified, by consent, in case challenging insurance charges based on total of payments, relying on *McCullar* decision); Singleton v. Protective Life Ins. Co., 857 So. 2d 803 (Ala. 2003) (applying *McCullar* in finding that borrowers failed to establish sale of excess insurance where net coverage was sold; also finding that state rate requirements were followed); *see* Gall v. American Heritage Life Ins. Co., 3 F. Supp. 2d 1344 (S.D. Ala. 1998) (court states it is not bound by plurality in *McCullar* and, agreeing with the dissent, finds that insurance can be calculated on the total of payments); Liberty Bank & Trust Co. v. Splane, 959 P.2d 600 (Okla. Ct. App. 1998) (court construed provision in U.C.C.C. restricting the amount of the permissible credit insurance to that which does not "exceed the debt" and another provision in Oklahoma insurance law restricting the amount of such insurance to "the approximate unpaid balance of the loan" to allow insurance premiums to be calculated on the total of payments; court specifically rejects the plurality in *McCullar*).

declining-term basis to reflect the fact that the balance declines as payments are made.[293]

The Model Act prohibits charging for a policy the term of which extends more than fifteen days beyond the scheduled maturity date of the transaction.[294] If a credit transaction is refinanced, the old insurance must be canceled and required rebates made before writing new insurance, thus prohibiting the practice of "pyramiding" insurance.[295] The Model Act specifies the information which must be disclosed to the borrower in the policy or certificate of insurance, such as the identity and address of the insurer, the premium cost, a description of the coverage, any applicable restrictions, and the distribution of any surplus.[296] This information is to be given to the debtor at the time of the consummation, either in the policy or certificate or, somewhat abbreviated, in a copy of the application or notice of proposed insurance.[297] In any event, a copy of the policy or certificate must be delivered within thirty days from the date of consummation.[298]

The Model Act requires that all policies and other forms be submitted to the insurance commissioners for approval. In addition to the authority to disapprove a policy if the benefits "are not reasonable in relation to the premium charge," the commissioner may disapprove a policy if it contains provisions which are "unjust, unfair, inequitable, misleading, deceptive, or encourage misrepresentation of the coverage, or are contrary to any provision of the Insurance Code...."[299] It is illegal for an insurer to use a disapproved form.[300]

It is also unlawful under the Model Act for an insurer to charge premium rates which exceed that on file with, and

approved by, the commissioner,[301] and the premium amount charged to a debtor cannot exceed the premiums charged by the insurer.[302] If the policy is terminated before its scheduled maturity, rebates are required.[303] Finally, the Model Act has an anti-tie-in or anti-coercion provision which requires that borrowers be given a choice of insurers.[304]

In 2001, the NAIC adopted a credit personal property insurance model act.[305] Two states have adopted this model act.[306] The Act does not cover insurance on motor vehicles designed for highway use and mobile homes, insurance written in connection with a credit transaction that is secured by a real estate mortgage or deed of trust, force-placed insurance, non-filing insurance, or insurance for which no identifiable charge is made or collected from the consumer.[307]

The Act's key non-rate provisions include a prohibition against using gross debt in calculating the premium.[308] This is a significant improvement over the model credit life and disability act. Insurance premium rebates must be made by the pro rata method.[309] For closed-end loans, the credit insurance cannot exceed the amount of the underlying debt, unless otherwise required by state law, nor can the insurer sell insurance with a term that exceeds the scheduled term of the underlying credit transaction.[310]

The credit insurance cannot be sold unless the loan amount exceeds a minimum amount to be set by each adoptive state.[311] The insurance cannot be bundled with other types of insurance and it must be optional and not a condition of obtaining credit approval.[312] Consumers must receive a pre-purchase clear and conspicuous disclosure describing certain rights contemporaneously with the extension of credit (or, if the insurance is sold after the initial extension of credit, within ten days after the election or the date any written material is provided to the consumer).[313] The insurer must provide consumers with certificates of insurance that shall contain certain information.[314]

Like the life and disability model act, all policies, certificates of insurance, application forms, endorsements and

293 Model Bill to Provide for the Regulation of Credit Life Ins. and Credit Accident and Health Ins., National Ass'n of Ins. Comm'rs, Model Regulatory Service § 4(A)(1) (NIARS Corp., 1984). *Cf.* NAIC Consumer Credit Insurance Model Act § 4(A)(1) (1994), which would mandate net debt coverage.

294 *Id.* § 5.

295 *Id. See also* In the matter of Associates Fin. Life Ins. Co., Case No. 99C-014A (Ga. Office of Insurance and Safety Fire Commissioner, Jan. 31, 2000), Clearinghouse No. 52,508 (when lender sold multiple policies, it incorrectly calculated unearned premium for each insurance product separately and failed to rebate when each rebate was lower than the $10 floor per Ga. Comp. R. & Regs. R. 120-2-27-.18, e.g., if each rebate was less than $10 but, combined, exceeded $10, both must be refunded); MIC Life Ins. Co. v. Hicks, 825 So. 2d 616 (Miss. 2002) (affirming the lower court's ruling that state law requires a refund of unearned insurance premiums within 30 days of termination of the policy).

296 Model Bill to Provide for the Regulation of Credit Life Ins. and Credit Accident and Health Ins., National Ass'n of Ins. Comm'rs, Model Regulatory Service § 6B (NIARS Corp., 1984). For further discussion of the distribution of surpluses, see § 8.5.6, *infra.*

297 Model Bill to Provide for the Regulation of Credit Life Ins. and Credit Accident and Health Ins., National Ass'n of Ins. Comm'rs, Model Regulatory Service § 6D (NIARS Corp., 1984).

298 *Id.*

299 *Id.* § 7B.

300 *Id.* § 7C.

301 *Id.* § 8A.

302 *Id.* § 8D.

303 *Id.* § 8B. *See also* § 8.6, *infra.*

304 Model Bill to Provide for the Regulation of Credit Life Ins. and Credit Accident and Health Ins., National Ass'n of Ins. Comm'rs, Model Regulatory Service § 11 (NIARS Corp., 1984).

305 NAIC Credit Personal Property Insurance Model Act, Clearinghouse No. 53,564.

306 *See* § 8.4.1.2, *supra.*

307 *Id.* § 2.

308 *Id.* § 4(G).

309 *Id.* § 10.

310 *Id.* §§ 4(B), (C).

311 *Id.* § 4(A).

312 *Id.* §§ 4(F), 5(a)(2).

313 *Id.* §§ 5(A), (B).

314 *Id.* §§ 5(D), (E).

riders must be filed with the state insurance commissioner before being used. Only approved rates and forms may be used.[315]

Interestingly, no claim may be denied because the consumer was ineligible for coverage later than ninety days after the initiation of coverage unless the consumer misrepresented a material fact. If a claim is denied because the consumer misrepresented a material fact or was ineligible for coverage within ninety days of the initiation of coverage, the insurer must refund all of the premium paid *and* the creditor must refund any finance charge paid on the premium.[316]

8.4.2.2.2 Substantive credit regulation and unfair trade practices statutes

Statutes governing consumer credit and unfair trade practices statutes both may further regulate credit insurance coverage, marketing, and disclosure practices. Such statutes may require that credit property insurance be written only on collateral,[317] and that coverage be limited to either the loan amount or the value of the property.[318] Further, there may be a limitation on writing property insurance in connection with loans below a specified amount.[319]

State insurance laws often require that the insurer obtain a certificate of authority or license before soliciting insurance applications or transacting insurance in the state or from offering insurance in other states from an office in that state.[320] If the insurer does not obtain the necessary permission from the state insurance agency to operate, the insurance contract may be void.[321]

Many credit statutes require that credit insurance must be sold by a licensed agent.[322] The statutes often reiterate the requirement that borrowers be given a choice of insurers,

thus making this requirement applicable to *creditors*,[323] or do so implicitly by requiring that all insurance written comply with the credit insurance code. These statutes may also impose additional disclosure requirements, such as information regarding whether insurance is compulsory.[324] Trade practices rules regarding insurance sales are discussed in § 8.4.1.4, *supra*.

8.5 Common Abuses and Possible Remedies

8.5.1 Introduction

As a general rule, credit insurance is considered to benefit borrowers as well as creditors, and therefore premium charges are not considered interest for usury purposes.[325] However, for nearly two centuries, it has been recognized that insurance schemes can be a pretext for usury.[326] This is particularly true with credit insurance, and thus transactions involving its sale should be carefully scrutinized.[327] If its sale is not in accordance with applicable law, the premiums, or any excess portion of them, may be considered interest.[328] If, when added to other interest charged, the yield exceeds the ceiling, the borrower has a usury claim. (Remember that in a deregulated state, where the maximum allowable charge is set by the contract itself, excess insurance charges, like any hidden interest, can be argued to exceed the maximum.[329]) Further, some statutory language suggests that the imposition of an improper charge in and of itself gives rise to a claim for excess charges or statutory penalties, irrespective of whether the total interest exceeds the maximum usury limit.[330] Other remedies also may be available to attack overpricing or a variety of abusive marketing prac-

315 *Id.* § 6.
316 *Id.* § 11(D).
317 *E.g.,* Ariz. Rev. Stat. Ann. § 6-636 (consumer loans); Iowa Code Ann. §§ 536.27, 536A.23(3), 537.2501(2); Miss. Code Ann. § 75-67-121 (small loans); U.C.C.C. § 4-301(1).
318 *E.g.,* 12 C.F.R. § 225.25(b)(8)(B)(ii)(A); Ariz. Rev. Stat. Ann. § 6-636(E); S.C. Code Regs. 69-11.1C(1)(d).
319 *E.g.,* Ala. Code § 5-19-20(g) (no property insurance unless loan amount exclusive of charges is $300 or over and value of property is $300 or more); Colo. Rev. Stat. § 5-4-301 (same provisions, but with amounts of $1,000 in each case).
320 *See, e.g.,* Fla. Stat. § 624.401.
321 *See* Fabricant v. Sears Roebuck, 202 F.R.D. 310 (S.D. Fla. 2001) (class certified on this type of claim).
322 *E.g.,* Ariz. Rev. Stat. Ann. § 6-636(D); Iowa Code Ann. § 536.26. *See also* Bailey v. Defenbaugh & Co. of Cleveland, Inc., 513 F. Supp. 232, 243 (N.D. Miss. 1981); In the matter of Associates Fin. Life Ins. Co., Case No. 99C-014A (Ga. Office of Insurance and Safety Fire Commissioner, Jan. 31, 2000), Clearinghouse No. 52,508 (also check state insurance law for a similar requirement as the Insurance Commissioner in this case brought an enforcement proceeding for, among other reasons, the lender could not show that only licensed agents in the lender's shop were selling the credit insurance).
323 *E.g.,* Miss. Code Ann. § 63-19-33 (MVRISA).
324 *Compare* U.C.C.C. §§ 2-2501(2), 3-2501(2) (1968); U.C.C.C. § 2-2501(2) (1974) (notice of voluntary nature of life and A&H must be given in order to exclude premiums from finance charge) *with* Tex. Fin. Code Ann. § 348.204 (clear and conspicuous notice mandated if insurance is required).
325 *See* § 8.5.2.3, *infra*.
326 *See* Vernon, *Regulated Credit Life and Disability Insurance and the Small Loan*, 29 N.Y.U.L. Rev. 1098, 1100–01 (1954).
327 *See, e.g.,* Robinson v. Rebsamen Ford, Inc., 530 S.W.2d 660, 662 (Ark. 1975); Tribble v. State, 80 S.E.2d 711 (Ga. Ct. App. 1954).
328 *But see* Lemelledo v. Beneficial Mgmt., 674 A.2d 582 (N.J. Super. Ct. App. Div. 1996) (New Jersey law excludes credit life insurance premiums from its definition of interest; no discussion, however, of whether the coercive sale of credit insurance transforms the premiums into a usury claim), *aff'd on other grounds*, 696 A.2d 546 (N.J. 1997).
329 *See* § 9.2.8, *infra*.
330 *E.g.,* U.C.C.C. § 4-104(2); Attorney General of Md. v. Equitable Trust Co., 450 A.2d 1273, 1292 (Md. Ct. App. 1982).

tices that are all-too common in connection with credit and ancillary non-credit insurance sales.[331]

8.5.2 Voluntariness

8.5.2.1 General: The Law and the Practice

One of the first steps in examining a transaction involving credit insurance is to determine whether the insurance purchase was voluntary. Few lenders explicitly require borrowers to purchase insurance from the lender. State law rarely authorizes such a requirement. Even if it does, Truth in Lending only allows exclusion of insurance premiums from the TIL finance charge if their purchase is voluntary.[332] The question of whether the purchase of insurance was voluntary is a question of fact.[333]

However, the existence of a signed "voluntary" insurance authorization as required by the TILA does not end the inquiry.[334] Clients must be questioned to ascertain whether they knew they purchased credit insurance, whether they were orally informed that the insurance was required, or whether the creditor implied that the insurance was necessary.[335] The allegations in a recent case are instructive.[336]

There the borrowers were alleged to be lacking in established credit, could not obtain credit elsewhere, and were desperate for money. They were given an illusory "option" to buy insurance since all loans were packaged with credit insurance even if not requested by borrowers. The complaint further alleged that the loan documents were prepared before the borrowers arrived to sign and already included credit insurance. Further, if the borrowers questioned or

---

331 In fact, an Australian subsidiary of Household Finance lost its lending license after a finding by authorities that "dishonesty, unfairness and sharp practice were accepted standards of behavior." Among those "sharp practices" were indicating (or telling) consumers credit insurance was required, automatically pre-including insurance premiums in quoting loan amounts to customers, and failing to rebate insurance premiums after the loan terminated. In the Matter of an Application by H.F.C. Fin. Servs., Ltd., Clearinghouse No. 44,821 (Credit Licensing Authority, Sept. 12, 1989). These are not at all uncommon practices in this country.

332 The limited exception is property insurance. *See* § 8.5.2.2, *infra*.

333 *See* § 8.5.2.5, *infra*.

334 A consumer may be able to make a claim under state law that the contract is illegal. In London v. Wal-Mart Stores, Inc., 340 F.3d 1246 (11th Cir. 2003), the court, which retained supplemental jurisdiction after TILA claims were settled, held that a credit card applicant who obtained related credit insurance had suffered "injury in fact," even though he knew the insurance was not required and the enrollment form stated it was optional. The creditor, however, did not comply with a state law requirement to disclose to an applicant that purchasing the insurance is not a prerequisite to obtaining the loan. The court ruled that the applicant suffered injury *per se* by paying consideration for an illegal contract.

335 It is also worthwhile to check whether the initials on the credit insurance authorization are forged. *See* Vickers v. Interstate Dodge, 882 So. 2d 1236 (La. Ct. App. 2004) (because buyer's initials were forged by dealership, premium amount should have been disclosed as a finance charge).

336 Lemelledo v. Beneficial Mgmt., 674 A.2d 582 (N.J. Super. Ct. App. Div. 1996), *aff'd on other grounds*, 696 A.2d 546 (N.J. 1997). *See also* Fabricant v. Sears Roebuck & Co., 202 F.R.D. 310 (S.D. Fla. 2001) (certifying class in case of retailer selling credit card plan with package of credit life, disability, property, and unemployment insurance without properly advising con-

sumer that the package was optional), *subsequent history*, Order on Motions for Summary Judgment, Clearinghouse No. 54,563 (S.D. Fla. Mar. 5, 2002) (granting summary judgment on two of plaintiffs' counts and voiding the contracts as unenforceable on public policy grounds); Baron v. Best Buy Co., 75 F. Supp. 2d 1368 (S.D. Fla. 1999) (similar allegations as in *Fabricant*; motion to compel arbitration clause denied as defendant failed to show that the arbitration forum is a neutral, inexpensive forum to litigate the issues raised); Fed. Trade Comm'n v. Stewart Fin. Co., Civ. No. 103CV-2648 (N.D. Ga. filed Sept. 4, 2003), *available at* www.ftc.gov/os/caselist/103cv2648.htm (in a recently filed enforcement action, the FTC, which had already obtained a temporary restraining order and asset freeze, alleged that a subprime lender and nine related companies sold credit insurance and other add-on products, such as car club memberships, to consumers by telling them that it was required—even where the consumer was not eligible for the insurance or did not own a car—and by representing that the products were free; the lender also allegedly collected illegal fees by deceptively promoting a "direct deposit program" and violated the Credit Practices Rule by taking security for small personal loans); FTC v. Citigroup, Inc., Civil No. 010CV-0606 (N.D. Ga. filed Mar. 6, 2001), *available at* www.ftc.gov/os/2001/03/citigroupcmp.pdf (in a recently settled enforcement action, in which Citigroup agreed to pay $240 million, the FTC alleged that the Associates trained its employees to add the cost of a "total payment protection" package of credit insurance products to the monthly payment which they quoted to borrowers without explaining that this payment included the premium charges; employees instructed to discuss only the "benefits" of the insurance and not the costs or limitations on coverage); Easterling v. Gulf Guaranty Ins. Co., 60 F. Supp. 2d 586 (S.D. Miss. Aug. 24, 1999) (case remanded to state court; claims included a challenge to the condition of purchasing credit insurance in order to get the loan); Roberson v. Money Tree of Alabama, Inc., 954 F. Supp. 1519 (M.D. Ala. 1997) (borrowers allege that the lender misrepresented that they would not qualify for credit unless they purchased credit insurance and financed the cost through the loan; merits not reached as court upheld an arbitration clause and stayed case pending arbitration); Compton v. Altavista Motors, Inc., 121 F. Supp. 2d 932 (W.D. Va. 2000) (credit insurance "protection plan" form not given to car buyer until after the credit contract was signed; summary judgment to creditor on usury claim due to alleged lack of choice in purchasing the protection plan denied). *But see* Williams v. Norwest Fin. Alabama, Inc., 723 So. 2d 97 (Ala. Civ. App. 1998) (a claim that the lender fraudulently misrepresented that the purchase of credit insurance was required to obtain the loan failed because credit insurance was not sold by the vendor in all of the several loan transactions with the borrower, no employee told the borrower that the insurance was required, (though the "voluntary" disclosure was given as one of the several documents which she was instructed to sign without explanation), and the borrower was relatively sophisticated.).

objected to the unrequested insurance, the salesperson implied that the borrowers would not be given the loan proceeds at that time but would have to return (presumably because the documents would have to be re-done). The named plaintiff in this class action sought a loan of $2000 to pay her daughter's college tuition, but was given a loan for $2538.17 of which $335.28 was for credit insurance. This insurance charge added 15.2% to the cost of her loan.[337] Beyond the conventional notions of coercion and voluntariness, there is also an argument that credit insurance is not voluntary when the insurance is valueless. This argument might apply when the consumer cannot recover any benefits because of ineligibility.[338]

In addition to the facts of individual cases, the pervasiveness of the coercion issue is also indicated by the portion of credit transactions which include credit insurance sales (called the penetration rate). A Federal Reserve Board survey found a 62% penetration rate, with finance companies having a 75% penetration rate.[339] Though only 1.2% of the survey borrowers had asked for insurance, and over 25% thought it was required or "strongly recommended," the FRB concluded that coercion was not a problem.[340] However, that conclusion is questionable. A survey done in conjunction with a class-certification motion in one insurance packing case found 88% of respondents complained of coercion (explicit or implicit), sliding, and other problems with the insurance and other ancillary products.[341] Other data contemporaneous with the FRB survey indicated that the penetration rate was even higher than the FRB estimates, as high as 90 to 100% in some markets.[342] Further, a

significant number of borrowers purchase insurance without realizing it,[343] perhaps as a result of what loan officers call "sliding,"—where the insurance charges are pre-included in the loan documents and the authorization is silently "slid" in among all the other lines marked for the customer to sign. And while many experts claim more than 25% of credit customers receive implicit pressure to purchase credit insurance,[344] even a 25% figure is, as the FTC has put it, "unacceptable."[345] This kind of data suggests that a client who claims to have thought the insurance was necessary may well have been given reason to think so.

8.5.2.2 Truth in Lending and Usury Distinguished

Any discussion of coerced credit insurance must begin with a reminder of the distinction between Truth in Lending analysis and usury analysis. The Truth in Lending Act requires that credit life, A&H, or loss of income premiums be included in the TIL-defined finance charge unless there is

---

337 *Lemelledo, supra,* at 674 A.2d 584.

338 *See* § 8.5.5.1, *infra* (discussion of post-claim underwriting).

339 *Tie-in of Sale of Insurance by Banks and Bank Holding Companies, Hearings Before the Senate Committee on Banking, Housing and Urban Affairs,* 96th Cong., 1st Sess. 20 (1979).

340 *Id.* at 20, 48. With touching naiveté, the FRB concluded that if there had been coercion, there should be borrower resentment. Because their survey indicated that most borrowers thought credit insurance was "a good thing" and inexpensive to boot, *Id.* at 20–21, they concluded the high penetration rate was because it was a valued product, a conclusion readily acceded to by the industry, see Fagg, Credit Life and Disability Insurance 433–441 (1986). However, because a full understanding of both the cost and value of credit insurance requires an unusual degree of sophistication, such simplistic survey questions yield no credible data. *See* § 8.2.3.1, *supra.*

341 James v. ITT Fin. Servs., Report of Prof. Robert Hartley, submitted in support of Plaintiff's Motion to Certify Class, Oct. 10, 1989, Clearinghouse No. 44,801X. *See also* Miller v. Dobbs Mobile Bay, Inc., 661 So. 2d 203 (Ala. 1995) (allegation that customer tried twice to decline credit insurance, explaining he was in ill health, but auto dealer informed him he could not buy car without it and health would not be a problem [case challenging insurer's refusal to pay death benefits]).

342 *Tie-in of Sale of Insurance by Banks and Bank Holding Companies, Hearings Before the Senate Committee on Banking, Housing and Urban Affairs,* 96th Cong., 1st Sess. 334–335 (1979) (testimony of Dr. Emmett Vaughn, Professor of Insurance, University of Iowa), 122–23 (Federal Trade Commission

study). *See also Equity Predators: Stripping, Flipping and Packing Their Way to Profits: Hearing before the Special Committee on Aging United States Senate,* 105th Cong. 2d Sess. 33-34, Serial No. 105-18 (Mar. 16, 1998) (statement of Jim Dough, former employee of predatory lender); Lopez v. Associates Fin. Servs. of Hawaii, Inc., Civil No. 97-01384 (D. Haw., Motion for Summary Judgment filed Oct. 29, 1998), Clearinghouse No. 52,509 (Associates answers to interrogatories show that in 1995, it made 689 mortgage loans, 408 of which included credit life [penetration rate of 59%]; in 1996, it made 628 mortgage loans, 341 of which included credit life [penetration rate of 54%]; and in 1997, it made 530 mortgage loans, 197 of which included credit life [penetration rate of 37%]).

343 *Tie-in of Sale of Insurance by Banks and Bank Holding Companies, Hearings Before the Senate Committee on Banking, Housing and Urban Affairs,* 96th Cong., 1st Sess. 334–335 (1979) (Vaughn testimony: 9%), 124 (FTC Survey: 40% of retail customers unaware of purchase).

344 College of Bus. Adm., Ohio Univ., Consumer Credit Life and Disability Insurance 75 (C. Hubbard, ed. 1973) (26% of finance company borrowers thought credit life was required); *Tie-in of Sale of Insurance by Banks and Bank Holding Companies, Hearings Before the Senate Committee on Banking, Housing and Urban Affairs,* 96th Cong., 1st Sess. 312, 313 (1979) (over 50% of purchases subject to some pressure); *Id.* at 278 (testimony of Robert Sable, coercion present in 36%–59%); *Credit Life Insurance Hearing Before the Subcomm. on Antitrust, Monopoly and Business Rights of the Senate Comm. on the Judiciary,* 96th Cong, 1st Sess. 22 (1979) (45% of finance company purchasers, 37% of retail purchasers, and 36% of bank purchasers thought it was required or strongly recommended). *Cf.* James v. ITT Fin. Servs., Report of Prof. Robert Hartley, submitted in support of Plaintiff's Motion to Certify Class, Oct. 10, 1989, Clearinghouse No. 44,801X. In this survey of ITT customers taken as part of a class certification motion in one Ohio county, 88% of respondents complained of coercion (explicit or implicit), sliding, and other insurance-related problems.

345 *Tie-in of Sale of Insurance by Banks and Bank Holding Companies, Hearings Before the Senate Committee on Banking, Housing and Urban Affairs,* 96th Cong., 1st Sess. 126 (1979).

a disclosure of the cost of the credit and of the fact that the insurance is not a factor in the approval of the credit. Additionally, the consumer must give a "specific, affirmative written indication of [the] desire to purchase the insurance after receiving the disclosure."[346] Property insurance on collateral may be excluded from the TIL finance charge even though required, so long as there is a written disclosure of the cost if the creditor's proffered insurance is purchased, and disclosure of the borrower's choice of providers.[347] Even if insurance premiums may be considered interest for purposes of state usury law, they may not be a finance charge for TIL purposes if they meet the criteria for exclusion set forth in the Act.[348] Of course, the converse is true as well. A proper exclusion of premiums from the finance charge under TIL does not necessarily insulate the insurance component of the transaction from usury claims. State law, not TILA, must be the controlling reference as to when insurance premiums are interest for purposes of state usury claims.

8.5.2.3 Compulsory Insurance and Usury

8.5.2.3.1 General

The passage of time and changes in the regulatory environment have marked shifts in how the courts have treated compulsory insurance. Prior to the development of credit insurance, insurance companies, when acting as lenders, sometimes required borrowers to purchase life insurance from them as a condition of receiving the loan. Courts generally considered such mandatory insurance premiums to be interest, constituting usury if this interest payment combined with the loan's other interest charges exceeded state limits.[349] Compulsory premiums were either *per se* interest, or the requirement created a presumption that the intention was to circumvent the usury laws.[350]

A minority view, however, considered this insurance to be a collateral transaction to provide the lender with additional security. Under this view, compulsory insurance premiums were not interest unless the premium charge or amount of

coverage was excessive.[351] As credit insurance in its modern incarnation became more prevalent, this became the majority view.[352]

By mid-century, at least in the absence of specific statutory provisions, creditors generally were permitted to require insurance as a condition of obtaining credit, unless there were factors indicating that the insurance requirement was a pretext for circumventing usury laws instead of as loan security.[353] Among the factors which courts considered in determining whether the premiums should be considered interest were:[354]

- Whether the lender retained commission or profit from the premiums; and if so, how much;
- Whether the premiums exceeded the fair rate;
- Whether the loan was amply secure without it;
- Whether the amount of insurance was excessive;
- Whether there was a choice of insurers; and
- Whether an insurance policy was actually purchased.

Where the relevant special usury statutes do not specifically address the voluntariness issue, these cases still provide sound precedent for making a usury claim in such circumstances.

However, today the regulation of credit insurance is much more pervasive, and relevant statutes and rules in many states specifically address the voluntariness issue. The UCCC, for example, specifically prohibits compulsory credit life or disability insurance. It incorporates the TIL requirement that the borrower be informed that such purchase is not a factor in obtaining the credit, as well as TIL's cost disclosure and signature requirements.[355] Premiums must be included as interest for the purposes of the state usury ceiling if *all* these conditions are not met.[356] Many

---

346 15 U.S.C. § 1605(b); 12 C.F.R. §§ 226.4(b)(7), (10), 226.4(d)(1), (3). Note that regulations regarding debt cancellation fees apply whether or not it is treated as insurance under applicable law.

347 15 U.S.C. § 1605(c); 12 C.F.R. §§ 226.4(b)(8), 226.4(d)(2).

348 Hickman v. Cliff Peck Chevrolet, 566 F.2d 44 (8th Cir. 1977). *See generally* National Consumer Law Center, Truth in Lending § 3.9.4 (5th ed. 2003 and Supp.).

349 Vernon, *Regulated Credit Life and Disability Insurance and the Small Loan*, 29 N.Y.U.L. Rev. 1098, 1105 (1954). *Cf.* Pacific Eastern Corp. v. Gulf Life Holding Co., 902 S.W.2d 946 (Tenn. Ct. App. 1995) (question of fact whether life insurance policy required as collateral on life of a principal in a commercial loan was pretext for usury; insurer was one of lenders).

350 *Id.* at 1106.

351 *Id.* at 1106–07.

352 *Id.*; *Credit Insurance: Abuse and Reform*, 10 B.C. Ind. & Com. L. Rev. 439, 454 n.87 (1969).

353 Vernon, *Regulated Credit Life and Disability Insurance and the Small Loan*, 29 N.Y.U.L. Rev. 1098, 1106–07 (1954); Annot., 91 A.L.R. 2d 1344 (1963). *Cf.* Farber v. Republic Pension Serv., 553 N.Y.S.2d 179 (App. 1990) (court invoked principle that mandatory life insurance not interest so long as policy issued at same rate and on same terms as policies issued to non-borrowers).

354 Annot., 91 A.L.R.2d at 1348. *See also* Standard Sav. Ass'n v. Greater New Canaan Missionary Baptist Church, 786 S.W.2d 774 (Tex. App. 1990) (noting Texas law holds insurance to be interest when it is required as a condition of accepting the loan and the borrower shows he or she had no role in selecting the insurance).

355 U.C.C.C. §§ 2-202(2), 3-202(2) (1968); U.C.C.C. § 2-501(2) (1974).

356 U.C.C.C. § 2-202(2), comment ¶ 2; 3-202(2) (1968). *See also* Compton v. Altavista Motors, Inc., 121 F. Supp. 2d 932 (W.D. Va. 2000) (summary judgment to creditor on usury claim due to alleged lack of choice in purchasing the protection plan denied where credit insurance "protection plan" form not given to car buyer until after the credit contract was signed).

other consumer credit statutes also prohibit compulsory credit life and disability insurance.[357]

8.5.2.3.2 Choice of insurers

Some credit statutes do not specifically address compulsory insurance, but do prohibit the creditor from tying the extension of credit to purchase of insurance from a particular insurer. Most states permit creditors to require property insurance on collateral as long as the borrower has a choice of providers.[358] (Some states may prohibit property insurance on loans under a specified dollar amount,[359] or limit the amount of required coverage.)[360]

The Model NAIC Credit Life and Disability Act provides that borrowers must have the option of supplying required insurance through an insurer of their choice.[361] The NAIC's Model Unfair Insurance Practices Act also prohibits the tie-in of credit to the purchase of insurance from particular providers.[362] Even in the absence of a statutory provision, the failure to give the borrower a choice of providers "converts the premiums into interest."[363]

As a practical matter, though, with the exception of property insurance, it is very difficult for a borrower to purchase credit insurance from someone other than the creditor. Credit insurance is not sold independently of the credit transaction it insures. A finance company borrower, for example, could not insure her loan with the cheaper credit insurer used by credit unions. A borrower would have to purchase a regular life or disability policy.

8.5.2.4 Proving Coercion

It rarely happens today that creditors openly admit that they require insurance. Most credit documents include a boiler-plate insurance authorization containing the TIL disclosure that life and disability is not required, and that there is a choice of providers if property insurance is required. However, a signature on such an authorization is not the end of the analysis for usury purposes, and may not be for TIL purposes, either.[364]

The mere fact that a borrower did not read the insurance authorization form indicating the purchase is voluntary, before signing it is unlikely to warrant a finding that the insurance was compulsory.[365] However, parol evidence may be admissible to show usury,[366] at least where there are allegations of fraud, illiteracy or duress.[367] Since compulsory tied-insurance is prohibited in most states, fraud or duress may be present if the borrower does not freely choose to purchase the insurance. (It is important to recall that the parol evidence rule is simply a doctrine of contract construction.[368] Claims and defenses which arise independently of the contract, such as the state UDAP statute, misrepresentation, unconscionability, or the duty to disclose should not be subject to the parol evidence rule in any event.[369])

Since it is unlikely that a creditor will admit to the court that it required an insurance purchase, the consumer's attorney must take some care to present a credible case of

---

357 *E.g.*, Ala. Code § 5-19-20(a); Cal. Civ. Code § 1802.10 (RISA); Cal. Fin. Code § 18291(b) (Industrial Loans); Cal. Fin. Code § 22314 (Consumer Loans); Conn. Gen. Stat. Ann. § 36a-566 (Small Loans).

358 *E.g.*, Ala. Code § 5-19-20(a) & (e); U.C.C.C. §§ 2-202(2)(a), 3-202(2)(a) (1968); U.C.C.C. § 2-501(2)(a) (1974); U.C.C.C. § 4-109 (1968 and 1974).

359 *E.g.*, Ala. Code § 5-19-20(g); U.C.C.C. § 4-301(3).

360 *See* § 8.4.1.3, *supra*; § 8.5.3.4, *infra*.

361 Model Bill to Provide for the Regulation of Credit Life Ins. and Credit Accident and Health Ins., National Ass'n of Ins. Comm'rs, Model Regulatory Service § 11 (NIARS Corp., 1984).

362 NAIC Model Unfair Insurance Practices Act § 5.

363 North Am. Acceptance Corp. v. Warren, 451 S.W.2d 921, 925 (Tex. Civ. App. 1970).

364 *See* § 8.5.2.5, *infra*.

365 Universal C.I.T. Credit Corp. v. Lackey, 228 Ark. 101, 305 S.W.2d 858 (1957); Swyters v. Motorola Employees Credit Union, 535 S.E.2d 508 (Ga. App. 2000) (consumer is bound to read the contract in absence of illiteracy; summary judgment granted to creditor on whether insurance was required); Andrus v. Ellis, 887 So. 2d 175 (Miss. 2004) (consumer generally is assumed to have read documents; failure to read loan documents does not support claim for fraudulent concealment and therefore statute of limitations was not tolled at loan closing). *See also* Anthony v. Community Loans & Inv. Corp., 559 F.2d 1363 (5th Cir. 1977).

366 Aclin Ford v. Cordell, 625 S.W.2d 459 (Ark. 1982). *See also* Fisher v. Beneficial Fin. Co. of Hoxsie, 383 F. Supp. 895 (D.R.I. 1974) (borrower could introduce evidence that defendant actually required insurance by its conduct). *But see* Dixon v. S&S Loan Serv. of Waycross, 754 F. Supp. 1567 (S.D. Ga. 1990) (parol evidence rule invoked to bar borrower's claim of coerced non-credit accidental death and dismemberment insurance where contract form stated purchase is voluntary; court invoked rule despite damning memorandum obtained in discovery instructing that "all new and former borrower's [sic] are to have AD&D on this loan.").

367 Anthony v. Community Loans & Inv. Corp., 559 F.2d 1363, 1369 (5th Cir. 1977); Knapp v. American Gen. Fin Inc., 111 F. Supp. 2d 758 (S.D. W. Va. 2000); Wiegand v. Walser Automotive Groups, 683 N.W.2d 807 (Minn. 2004). A class action case based on such a claim, however, will face the additional hurdle of demonstrating to the court that the oral representations were not so individualized so as to defeat class certification. *See* Frelin v. Oakwood Homes Corp., 2002 WL 31863487 (Ark. Cir. Ct. Nov. 25, 2002) (declining to certify "false insurance class" primarily because the case requires "individualized transaction-by-transaction showing" of the oral presentations made to consumers; the court did note that plaintiff's counsel had failed to provide sample jury forms or other documents to demonstrate how this issue could be overcome).

368 Even so, there are a number of exceptions, some of which might be applicable in a given case. *See generally* National Consumer Law Center, Consumer Warranty Law § 3.7 (2d ed. 2001 and Supp.).

369 *See* §§ 8.5.2.5, 8.5.4, 8.7.2–8.7.5, *infra* and National Consumer Law Center, Consumer Warranty Law § 3.6.8 (2d ed. 2001 and Supp.) for discussions of other potential claims which should be unaffected by the parol evidence rule.

coercion in what is likely to be a swearing contest.[370] At the outset, an understanding of the economic pressures on the creditor to sell the insurance is important,[371] as this can provide direction for discovery strategies. For example, it is often helpful to depose individual loan officers to find out what their sales practices are, what training or instruction they receive, and what their employer's performance expectations are.[372]

The subtle coercion of a customer can begin at the initial inquiry stage. At least in the consumer finance segment of the market, most lenders automatically assume the transaction will include insurance. When a prospective borrower calls to ask the terms on a loan, the quotes given by the lender automatically (and often without explanation) include the price of insurance premiums in the quotation on monthly payments.[373] Typically, the documents are generally typed up beforehand, ready for the borrower's signature, with all the figures reflecting an insured loan.[374] It is pos-

sible that nothing will be said concerning the insurance; the borrower may simply be told what lines to sign, including the insurance authorization. (In the industry, this is called "sliding.")

The creditor may even contradict the written voluntariness disclosure, and orally inform the borrower that the insurance is required.[375] In such a case the insurance is compulsory, and the premium is considered interest.[376] In addition, if the evidence indicates the borrower is unable to read the authorization he or she signed, and its provisions were not explained, it should be considered compulsory, and may therefore constitute interest.[377]

Because credibility likely will be an issue in such cases, it is important to have buttressing evidence. A good source for suggestions as to the type of corroborative evidence which may be probative is found in *In re USLIFE* and other Federal Trade Commission enforcement cases.[378]

In *USLIFE*, the FTC argued that Truth in Lending required that the credit insurance premiums be included in the finance charge because, despite proper written disclosures on the printed form, USLIFE in reality coerced the insurance sales. Ultimately, the Fifth Circuit disagreed, holding that TIL required written disclosures only, that parol evidence concerning the undermining of properly made written disclosures was irrelevant to a TIL claim, and that literal,

---

370 *Cf.* Miller v. Dobbs Mobile Bay, Inc., 661 So. 2d 203 (Ala. 1995) (court denied creditor and insurer's motions for summary judgment where deceased borrower's representative alleged auto dealer said purchase of insurance was required and ill health did not matter; case challenging insurer's failure to pay, not the coercion). *But cf.* Standard Sav. Ass'n v. Greater New Canaan Missionary Baptist Church, 786 S.W.2d 774 (Tex. App. 1990) (borrower's affidavit that insurance purchase was required was insufficient evidence to warrant finding of usury on motion for summary judgment; "stricter standard of proof" required because of "harshness and finality of summary judgments").

371 *See* § 8.2, *supra.* One court has suggested in dicta that a consumer alleging coerced insurance purchases made a strategic error in failing to plead causes of action predicated upon the creditor's profit from the insurance. *In re* Milbourne, 108 B.R. 522, 540, 543 n.8 (Bankr. E.D. Pa. 1989).

372 At least two wrongful discharge cases have been brought by former finance company employees alleging they were fined for failure to push insurance hard enough. Laws v. Aetna Fin., 667 F. Supp. 342 (N.D. Miss. 1987) (Aetna's motion for summary judgment denied, court holding that plaintiff stated a cognizable cause of action for wrongful discharge where the alleged ground for discharge was a refusal to engage in illegal acts for the employer); Zimmer v. Thorp Credit, Civ. No. 33,073 (Iowa Dist. Ct., Marion County, filed Dec. 1984) (case dismissed upon negotiated settlement). (Apart from that stick, carrots of free trips to Aruba may also lead to excessive sales pressure on consumers.) *But cf. In re* Milbourne, 108 B.R. 522 (Bankr. E.D. Pa. 1989) (court refused to interpret creditor's internal memorandum to its loan closers telling them to explain insurance as evidence that it was sent in response to a previous problem with employees requiring insurance).

373 *See Equity Predators: Stripping, Flipping and Packing Their Way to Profits: Hearing before the Special Committee on Aging United States Senate,* 105th Cong. 2d Sess. 33-34, Serial No. 105-18 (Mar. 16, 1998) (statement of Jim Dough, former employee of predatory lender).

374 This is usually treated as a positive practice by management. *See Credit Life Insurance Hearing Before the Subcomm. on Antitrust, Monopoly and Business Rights of the Senate Comm. on the Judiciary,* 96th Cong, 1st Sess. 47 (1979). Lemelledo v. Beneficial Mgmt., 674 A.2d 582 (N.J. Super. Ct. App. Div. 1996) (the allegations in a recent case are instructive. There the

borrowers were alleged to be lacking in established credit, could not obtain credit elsewhere, and were desperate for money. They were given a "negative" option to buy insurance since all loans are packaged with credit insurance even if not requested by borrowers. The complaint further alleged that the loan documents were prepared before the borrowers arrived to sign and already included credit insurance. Further, if the borrowers questioned or objected to the unrequested insurance, the salesperson implied that the borrowers would not be given the loan proceeds at that time but would have to return (presumably because the documents would have to be re-done). The named plaintiff in this class action sought a loan of $2,000 to pay her daughter's college tuition, but was given a loan for $2,538.17 of which $335.28 was for credit insurance. This insurance charge added 15.2% to the cost of her loan.), *aff'd on other grounds,* 696 A.2d 546 (N.J. 1997). *See also Equity Predators: Stripping, Flipping and Packing Their Way to Profits: Hearing before the Special Committee on Aging United States Senate,* 105th Cong. 2d Sess. 33-34, Serial No. 105-18 (Mar. 16, 1998) (statement of Jim Dough, former employee of predatory lender).

375 Knapp v. American Gen. Fin Inc., 111 F. Supp. 2d 758 (S.D. W. Va. 2000). *See* allegations in Hager v. American Gen. Fin., Inc., 37 F. Supp. 2d 778 (S.D. W. Va. 1999) (lender's motion for summary judgment denied on the TIL credit insurance claim based upon disputes of fact regarding the voluntary nature of the insurance).

376 Aclin Ford v. Cordell, 625 S.W.2d 459, 461 (Ark. 1982); § 8.5.2.3, *supra.*

377 *In re* Bogan, 281 F. Supp. 242, 251 (W.D. Tenn. 1968).

378 *In re* USLIFE Credit Corp. & USLIFE Corp., 91 FTC 984, Consumer Cred. Guide CCH ¶ 97,938 (1978), *modified on other grounds,* 92 FTC 353 (1978), *rev'd on other grounds* 599 F.2d 1387 (5th Cir. 1979).

technical compliance is all that TIL requires.[379] It is questionable whether *USLIFE* is still good law for TIL purposes.[380]

Irrespective of whether the case is still good TIL law, the FTC's evidence used to prove the *factual* allegation of a coerced insurance purchase is relevant to a usury analysis. Among the factors considered by the FTC, as well as other courts and regulators looking at coerced insurance sales are:

- The creditor's penetration rate (i.e., that portion of loans which include insurance).[381] In the case of USLIFE, the penetration rate on credit life was 80–90%.[382] The penetration rate has been a factor in usury cases, as well.[383]
- The creditor's pecuniary interest in making the sale.[384]

- A practice of including insurance in quoting monthly repayment figures to prospective borrowers.[385]
- The automatic pre-inclusion of premiums in loan documents.[386]
- Placing a "x" by the authorization signature line or otherwise indicating the borrower should sign it.[387]
- Presenting pre-typed loan agreements for signature without disclosing the purpose of the signature.[388]

---

379 *In re* USLIFE Corp., 599 F.2d 1387 (5th Cir. 1979). *See also* Dixon v. S&S Loan Serv. of Waycross, 754 F. Supp. 1567 (S.D. Ga. 1990) (following *US Life*). *But see* Hager v. American Gen. Fin., Inc., 37 F. Supp. 2d 778 (S.D. W. Va. 1999) (court disagreed with USLIFE finding that if a lender misrepresents to its customers that insurance is required, even though the loan contracts unequivocally state that the purchase of insurance is optional, a violation of the TILA may be established).

380 *See* § 8.5.2.5, *infra. But see* Dixon v. S&S Loan Serv. of Waycross, 754 F. Supp. 1567 (S.D. Ga. 1990) (court followed *U.S. Life*, but there is no indication from the decision that the arguments made in § 8.5.2.5, *infra* were advanced).

381 The penetration rate for credit insurance in the prime market is less than 6%; whereas self-reporting major subprime lenders indicate penetration rates ranging up to 57%. Eric Stein, Quantifying the Economic Cost of Predatory Lending, Coalition for Responsible Lending, at 2-6 (July 25, 2001), *available at* www.responsiblelending.org.

382 *In re* USLIFE Credit Corp. & USLIFE Corp., 91 FTC 984, 996, Consumer Cred. Guide CCH ¶ 97,938 (1978), *modified on other grounds*, 92 FTC 353 (1978), *rev'd on other grounds* 599 F.2d 1387 (5th Cir. 1979).

383 Aclin Ford v. Cordell, 625 S.W.2d 459 (Ark. 1982) (salesman denied telling consumer insurance was required, but had a 100% penetration rate on his credit sales). *But cf. In re* Milbourne, 108 B.R. 522 (Bankr. E.D. Pa. 1989) (in case alleging coerced life and disability insurance purchase as TIL and UDAP violation, court declined to find a 99.55% penetration rate of credit life as *per se* proof of required purchase without knowing why it was not sold on the other .45% of loans; court also troubled by a complete lack of data on penetration rate concerning credit disability insurance). [*Note:* Such a small segment of uninsured loans suggests that those might have been made by borrowers ineligible for benefits, e.g., older than an age cut-off. *Cf.* Kaminski v. Shawmut Credit Union, 494 F. Supp. 723 (D. Mass. 1980) (100% penetration rate for customers under 70 years old). For many lenders, the statistical probability is that a larger portion of borrowers would be ineligible for benefits under a disability policy, many of which require that the insured actively be at work at least 30 hours a week, and some further exclude self-employed workers. Thus part-time workers, retired borrowers, Social Security recipients, borrowers with disability or welfare benefits as income, and Donald Trump all may be ineligible for the typical credit disability coverage.]

384 *In re* USLIFE Credit Corp. & USLIFE Corp., 91 FTC 984, 1027, Consumer Cred. Guide CCH ¶ 97,938 (1978), *modified on other grounds*, 92 FTC 353 (1978), *rev'd on other grounds* 599

F.2d 1387 (5th Cir. 1979); Aclin Ford v. Cordell, 625 S.W.2d 459, 461 (Ark. 1982). One court has suggested in dicta that a consumer alleging coerced insurance purchases made a strategic error in failing to plead causes of action predicated upon the creditor's profit from the insurance. *In re* Milbourne, 108 B.R. 522, 540, 543 n.8 (Bankr. E.D. Pa. 1989).

Note: when doing discovery on this element, it is important to learn *all* of the profit sources, not just front-end commissions, and to ask about both corporate profit and profit to individual loan officers. *See* § 8.2, *supra.* Counsel for borrowers in Hawkins v. Thorp Credit & Thrift Co., 441 N.W.2d 470 (Minn. 1989) (*see* § 8.5.4.3, *infra*) calculated that the creditor made almost 100% profit on $48 million worth of sales on one insurance product when increased interest return, commissions, and profits received through reinsurance agreements were considered.

385 *In re* USLIFE Credit Corp. & USLIFE Corp., 91 FTC 984, 1024–1025, Consumer Cred. Guide CCH ¶ 97,938 (1978), *modified on other grounds*, 92 FTC 353 (1978), *rev'd on other grounds* 599 F.2d 1387 (5th Cir. 1979). *See also Equity Predators: Stripping, Flipping and Packing Their Way to Profits: Hearing before the Special Committee on Aging United States Senate*, 105th Cong. 2d Sess. 33-34, Serial No. 105-18 (Mar. 16, 1998) (statement of Jim Dough, former employee of predatory lender).

386 *Id.*; FRB Letter No. 1286, excerpts published in Truth in Lending, Special Releases—Correspondence, April 1969 to October 1978, ¶ 31,777 (CCH) (1979). *See also* Lemelledo v. Beneficial Mgmt., 674 A.2d 582 (N.J. Super. Ct. App. Div. 1996), *aff'd on other grounds*, 696 A.2d 546 (N.J. 1997); *Equity Predators: Stripping, Flipping and Packing Their Way to Profits: Hearing before the Special Committee on Aging United States Senate*, 105th Cong. 2d Sess. 33-34, Serial No. 105-18 (Mar. 16, 1998) (statement of Jim Dough, former employee of predatory lender).

387 *In re* USLIFE Credit Corp. & USLIFE Corp., 91 FTC 984, 1029–1030, Consumer Cred. Guide CCH ¶ 97,938 (1978), *modified on other grounds*, 92 FTC 353 (1978), *rev'd on other grounds* 599 F.2d 1387 (5th Cir. 1979); W.T. Grant Co., 83 FTC 1328, 1337 (1974) (consent order). *But cf.* Credithrift of America, Inc. v. Whitley, 380 S.E.2d 489 (Ga. Ct. App. 1989) (court held that creditors' statement that "although they were not required by law to purchase certain insurance . . . as a practical matter they would probably not be approved for the loan unless the insurance was purchased" did not constitute fraudulent misrepresentation or a violation of the state fair business practices act. *Note:* the court's reasoning is viable only where creditors are legally free to deny credit if consumers refuse insurance, as Georgia law may have done. But in many, if not most jurisdictions, consumer credit regulation laws do not permit creditors to require credit life or disability insurance as a condition of receiving the loan, in which case this decision would be inapposite).

388 *In re* USLIFE Credit Corp. & USLIFE Corp., 91 FTC 984, 1024, Consumer Cred. Guide CCH ¶ 97,938 (1978), *modified on*

- Suggesting the loan may be delayed if the borrower does not purchase the insurance.[389]

A creditor's "going over" loan documents with the borrower, that is, explaining the insurance charges pre-included in the documents, does not negate the inherent coercion, but may reinforce the notion that the insurance is required.[390]

One court held that a TILA[391] or UDAP[392] claim predicated upon an allegation that the credit insurance purchase was compulsory required proof of two elements: 1) the lender affirmatively represented, by words or conduct, that insurance was required in fact, and 2) the borrower purchased insurance as a result of the lender's action which he or she otherwise would not have done. The borrower further should be permitted to introduce evidence to prove those elements, despite the existence of a signed voluntariness disclosure executed pursuant to TIL or a similar state law.[393]

Beginning in the mid-1980s, allegations of insurance packing received widespread attention. The subsequent investigations of insurance packing cases[394] suggested another factual element which may prove valuable in establishing implicit or explicit coercion. The training given by the company to loan officers as to how to make insurance sales may stress just such factors as the FTC considered coercive in *USLIFE*.[395] Employees may feel pressured to achieve high penetration rates. In *USLIFE*, loan officers testified that they were under standing orders not to write uninsured loans.[396] Former employees of companies involved in some insurance packing investigations have reported pressure on the job to achieve high penetration rates.[397] Some said they were fired because they did not meet insurance sales performance standards.[398] In fact, at least two wrongful discharge lawsuits have been brought by former employees of ITT Financial affiliates alleging they were fired because they did not pack their customers' loans[399] or meet required insurance sales quotas.[400] A 1986 credit insurance text makes clear that penetration rates are closely monitored by creditors:

> Successful promotion of the product at the producer level [lending institution] depends on management commitment. If the producer's top management does not take an active role in stressing the importance of the product's sale, the attitude filters down through the organization. One tool for management review is a penetration report . . . *Statistics are maintained by individual lending officer* and summarized by branch or location. The mere compilation and publication of a penetration report improves the awareness of the importance of the product. (emphasis added)[401]

---

other grounds, 92 FTC 353 (1978), *rev'd on other grounds* 599 F.2d 1387 (5th Cir. 1979).

389 FRB Letter No. 1286, excerpts published in Truth in Lending, Special Releases—Correspondence, April 1969 to October 1978, ¶ 31,777 (CCH) (1979); *see also* Lemelledo v. Beneficial Mgmt., 674 A.2d 582 (N.J. Super. Ct. App. Div. 1996), *aff'd on other grounds*, 696 A.2d 546 (N.J. 1997). *See also Equity Predators: Stripping, Flipping and Packing Their Way to Profits: Hearing Before the Special Committee on Aging United States Senate*, 105th Cong. 2d Sess. 33-34, Serial No. 105-18 (Mar. 16, 1998) (statement of Jim Dough, former employee of predatory lender).

390 *In re* USLIFE Credit Corp. & USLIFE Corp., 91 FTC 984, 1028, Consumer Cred. Guide CCH ¶ 97,938 (1978), *modified on other grounds*, 92 FTC 353 (1978), *rev'd on other grounds*, 599 F.2d 1387 (5th Cir. 1979).

391 *See* § 8.5.2.5, *infra*.

392 *See* § 8.5.2.6, *infra*.

393 *In re* Milbourne, 108 B.R. 522 (Bankr. E.D. Pa. 1989).
     Note: It is arguable that, at least as to the UDAP claim, that second element imposes a reliance requirement, though most UDAP statutes use a tendency to deceive standard. *See* National Consumer Law Center, Unfair and Deceptive Acts and Practices § 4.2.2 (6th ed. 2004 and Supp.). *See also* Hager v. American Gen. Fin., Inc., 37 F. Supp. 2d 778 (S.D. W. Va. 1999) (court disagreed with USLIFE finding that if a lender misrepresents to its customers that insurance is required, even though the loan contracts unequivocally state that the purchase of insurance is optional, a violation of the TILA may be established; unconscionability claim raised on other grounds).

394 *See* § 8.5.4, *infra*.

395 Aggressive marketing may be held up as an example by proud executives, as in the case of the executive who praised as his two best managers men who automatically pre-included both life and disability on loans and only retracted if forced to by the

customer. "They do not . . . give the customer a chance to turn it down before it is even written into the loan." Letter to Gov. Bucher, Board of Governors, Federal Reserve System, Nov. 29, 1974 from C.M. Tobin, Sec., FTC, reprinted in *Hearings on Consumer Information Before the Subcommittee on Consumer Affairs with House Committee on Banking, Currency, and Housing*, 94th Cong., 1st Sess. at 51–53.

396 *In re* USLIFE Credit Corp. & USLIFE Corp., 91 FTC 984, 1026, Consumer Cred. Guide CCH ¶ 97,938 (1978), *modified on other grounds*, 92 FTC 353 (1978), *rev'd on other grounds*, 599 F.2d 1387 (5th Cir. 1979). *But see* Dixon v. S&S Loan Serv. of Waycross, 754 F. Supp. 1567 (S.D. Ga. 1990) (parol evidence rule invoked to prevent claim of coerced non-credit insurance where preprinted contract form stated purchase is voluntary, despite discovery of internal memorandum stating all new loans must have it).

397 *See Equity Predators: Stripping, Flipping and Packing Their Way to Profits: Hearing before the Special Committee on Aging United States Senate*, 105th Cong. 2d Sess. 33-34, Serial No. 105-18 (Mar. 16, 1998) (statement of Jim Dough, former employee of predatory lender).

398 Bogdanich, *Unwanted Extras: Irate Borrowers Accuse ITT's Loan Companies of Deceptive Practices*, Wall St. J., Feb. 26, 1985 at 1, Col. 1, 22.

399 For a discussion of insurance packing including ITT Financial's practices, see § 8.5.4, *infra*.

400 Laws v. Aetna Fin., 667 F. Supp. 342 (N.D. Miss. 1987) (Aetna's motion for summary judgment denied, court holding that plaintiff stated a cognizable cause of action for wrongful discharge where the alleged ground for discharge was a refusal to engage in illegal acts for the employer); Zimmer v. Thorp Credit, Civ. No. 33,073 (Iowa Dist. Ct., Marion County, filed Dec., 1984) (case dismissed upon negotiated settlement).

401 Fagg, Credit Life and Disability Insurance 89 (1986).

Seeking discovery of any job evaluations of the loan officer who closed the loan may be helpful, as it may indicate whether he or she was under pressure which could lead to coercive selling tactics.

Before seeking production of documents or doing a deposition, the consumer's attorney should perform some informal investigation. Annual reports filed by the companies can be informative about the corporate relationship between the creditor and insurer, if any, and, in gross terms, about the relative profitability of the various corporate entities. These reports may be filed with the state insurance agency or may be available at university or public libraries.

Corroborative evidence of coercive sales practices also may be found in the testimony of borrowers other than the client. The client may know of other borrowers who may have had a similar experience with the same creditor. Attorneys who specialize in consumer matters may hear the same complaints from several clients regarding a particular lender. In conjunction with a motion for class certification in one insurance packing case, a court-approved survey was sent to the defendant's borrowers from one county. The responses included complaints from 88% of the customers, which led the expert analyzing the results to conclude that there were pervasive problems.[402]

8.5.2.5 Truth in Lending

The Fifth Circuit is the only circuit to address the issue of *actual* coercion in the sale of credit insurance as a TIL claim. The Fifth Circuit has held that TIL is only a disclosure law. Technical compliance with the requirements on the forms was all that was necessary. Parol evidence was inadmissible to contradict the written disclosures, absent allegations of illiteracy, fraud or duress.[403] (Though even under this approach, a TIL claim apparently would still be allowed if it can be proven that the lender specifically and unequivocally required the insurance despite the proper disclosures.)[404] Thus, the Fifth Circuit does not recognize as a TIL violation creditor conduct which undermines or negates the import of the voluntariness disclosure, as the FTC sought to do in *USLIFE.*

The Fifth Circuit approach has been roundly criticized as ignoring the statutory purpose of the TIL insurance requirement, which is to assure that the credit insurance purchase is the result of a genuinely free and informed choice. The analysis also ignores the remedial purposes of the TIL Act,

the sounder reasoning of contrary judicial authority, and the expressed opinion of the Federal Reserve Board to the contrary.[405]

The precedential effect of the Fifth Circuit approach is open to question because of the Supreme Court's subsequent decision in *Ford Motor Credit Co. v. Milhollin.*[406] The Court there held that the opinions of the Federal Reserve Board as to the interpretation of Truth in Lending are to be given great deference unless "demonstrably irrational."[407] The FRB position as expressed in staff letters, even prior to the Fifth Circuit cases, was that voluntariness was a factual issue, ascertainable only "by reference to all of the circumstances of a particular transaction. Inquiry into those circumstances is, of course, not foreclosed by the presence of a customer's signature in an insurance authorization."[408] The FRB subsequently restated this position in its Official Staff Commentary promulgated as the official FRB interpretation to TIL Regulation Z. The commentary states that "whether the insurance is in fact required or optional is a factual question."[409]

The FRB's reaffirmation of its earlier position, in light of *Milhollin,* suggests that evidence that a creditor engaged in conduct undermining or contradicting the voluntariness disclosure should give rise to a TIL claim. The Fifth Circuit's superficial analysis should not be viewed as controlling post-*Milhollin.* This is true as to both credit and non-credit insurance.[410]

Since *Milhollin,* a bankruptcy court specifically rejected the Fifth Circuit cases, holding that "a borrower should be permitted, by the borrower's own testimony or otherwise, to rebut the contents of a declaration, in a written contract, that the insurance purchase is not required," and that a lender who, by conduct or words, affirmatively represented that insurance was required would not be insulated by a properly executed TIL voluntariness disclosure form.[411] In that case,

---

402 *See* James v. ITT Fin. Servs., Report of Prof. Robert Hartley, submitted in support of Plaintiff's Motion to Certify Class, Oct. 10, 1989, Clearinghouse No. 44,801X. (The report also includes the questionnaire and a description of the survey.)

403 USLIFE Credit Corp. v. FTC, 599 F.2d 1387 (5th Cir. 1979); Anthony v. Community Loan & Inv. Corp., 559 F.2d 1363 (5th Cir. 1977).

404 Mims v. Dixie Fin. Co., 426 F. Supp. 627, 631 (N.D. Ga. 1976).

405 Sheffey, *Credit Life and Disability Insurance Disclosures Under Truth in Lending: The Triumph of Form Over Substance,* 8 Fla. St. U.L. Rev. 463, 477–490 (1980).

406 444 U.S. 555 (1980).

407 *Id.*

408 FRB Letter No. 1270, excerpts published in Truth-In-Lending, Special Releases—Correspondence, April 1969 to October 1978 ¶ 31,756 (CCH) (1979). *See also* FRB Letter No. 1286, excerpts published in Truth in Lending, Special Release—Correspondence, April 1969 to October 1978 ¶ 31,777 (CCH) (1979) letter elaborates on factors which may suggest that ostensibly optional non-credit insurance is in reality required, and thus should be included in the finance charge). The Official Staff Commentary to revised Reg. Z, § 226.4(b)(7) and (8) ¶ 4 reiterates the position that required non-credit insurance *also* is a finance charge; Sheffey, *Credit Life and Disability Insurance Disclosures Under Truth in Lending: The Triumph of Form Over Substance,* 8 Fla. St. U.L. Rev. 463, 481–483 (1980).

409 Official Staff Commentary to Reg. Z § 226.4(d) ¶ 5.

410 *See* notes 270–271, *supra.*

411 *In re* Milbourne, 108 B.R. 522, 541 (Bankr. E.D. Pa. 1989). *See also* Kaminski v. Shawmut Credit Union, 494 F. Supp. 723, 729 (D. Mass. 1980) (100% penetration rate among borrowers under

however, the borrower did not prove the elements the court held necessary to establish a coercion claim.[412] The court indicated in dicta, however, that a claim that the creditor's retention of substantial commissions constituted impermissible finance charges or an unfair trade practice might have been easier to prove than coercion.[413]

Ten years after the *USLIFE* decision, the Federal Trade Commission recently initiated an enforcement complaint which further underscores its position that the voluntariness of the insurance is a factual issue not determinable solely by reference to the written disclosure. The complaint in *Matter of Tower Loan of Mississippi*[414] alleged that the creditor violated TIL by requiring credit insurance and failing to include premiums in the finance charge. It further alleged that the creditor violated the FTC unfair and deceptive practices act[415] by obtaining false statements from the consumers stating that the purchase was voluntary.

8.5.2.6 UDAP

Virtually all states have some version of an Unfair and Deceptive Trade Practices law (UDAP), based generally upon the Federal Trade Commission Act prohibiting unfair or deceptive acts or practices in or affecting trade or commerce.[416] Though the federal act does not give aggrieved individuals a private right of action, all state UDAP statutes so provide.[417] Many state UDAP Acts, by statute or judicial interpretation, give some precedential effect to FTC positions as to what constitutes an unfair or deceptive practice.[418]

Overtly misrepresenting or intimating that the credit will not be granted without insurance is certainly deceptive.[419] Other types of conduct undermining the borrower's sense of a free choice is at least unfair, and probably deceptive as well.[420] The FTC administrative law judge in the *USLIFE* case noted that the same facts alleged to create a TIL violation as to the genuine voluntariness of the insurance purchase may establish a violation of the FTC Act, though the FTC had not pled such a violation.[421] The FTC has used its UDAP authority to issue a cease and desist order prohibiting a creditor from misrepresenting that credit would be unavailable without credit insurance and from pre-including insurance charges on the contracts.[422] In another case, the FTC alleged that a finance company violated UDAP law by obtaining false statements from consumers that the insurance was voluntary.[423]

---

70 established required insurance purchase, notwithstanding the signed voluntariness disclosures, therefore, was a finance charge as to all class members; however named plaintiff lost out because he testified he knew he bought it and would have done so even if not required). *Cf.* Wojcik v. Courtesy Auto Sales, Inc., 2002 WL 31663298 (D. Neb. Nov. 25, 2002) (credit insurance was properly included as part of amount financed rather than finance charge because consumer signed documents stating the insurance was optional, even though consumer had not read the loan documents and was told by the lender that the insurance was required). *But see* Dixon v. S&S Loan Serv. of Waycross, 754 F. Supp. 1567 (S.D. Ga. 1990) (court held *U.S. Life* binding on it; no indication from published opinion as to whether these arguments were advanced).

412   *See* § 8.5.2.4, *supra*.

413   *In re* Milbourne, 108 B.R. 522, 540, 543 n.8 (Bankr. E.D. Pa. 1989). *See also* Hager v. American Gen. Fin., Inc., 37 F. Supp. 2d 778 (S.D. W. Va. 1999) (court disagreed with *USLIFE* finding that if a lender misrepresents to its customers that insurance is required, even though the loan contracts unequivocally state that the purchase of insurance is optional, a violation of the TILA may be established; lender's motion for summary judgment denied); Kaminski v. Shawmut Credit Union, 494 F. Supp. 723, 729 (D. Mass. 1980) (100% penetration rate among borrowers under 70 established required insurance purchase, notwithstanding the signed voluntariness disclosures, therefore, was a finance charge as to all class members; however named plaintiff lost out because he testified he knew he bought it and would have done so even if not required).

414   Consumer Cred. Guide Rpt. No. 579; FTC Docket No. 9241 (filed July 5, 1990).

415   15 U.S.C. § 45(a)(1).

416   *See generally* National Consumer Law Center, Unfair and Deceptive Acts and Practices (6th ed. 2004 and Supp.).

417   *Id.* at Ch. 8.

418   *Id.* § 3.4.4.

419   *See, e.g.*, Matter of Tower Loan of Mississippi, Consumer Cred. Guide Rpt. No. 579, FTC Docket No. 9241 (filed July 5, 1990) in which the FTC alleges that the creditor violated the FTC unfair and deceptive practices act by obtaining false statements from consumers stating that the purchase of credit insurance was voluntary, when the creditor was in fact requiring the purchase and failing to include the premiums in the finance charge in violation of TIL. *But see* Credithrift of America, Inc. v. Whitley, 380 S.E.2d 489 (Ga. Ct. App. 1989) (court held that creditors' statement that "although they were not required by law to purchase certain insurance . . . as a practical matter they would probably not be approved for the loan unless the insurance was purchased" did not constitute fraudulent misrepresentation or a violation of the state fair business practices act. *Note*: the court's reasoning is viable only if creditors are free under state law to deny credit if consumers refuse to buy insurance. But in many, if not most states, consumer credit regulation laws do not permit creditors to require credit life or disability insurance as a condition of receiving the loan, in which case decision is inapposite).

420   *See e.g.,* Fox v. Industrial Casualty Ins. Co., 424 N.E.2d 839 (Ill. App. 1981) (state Consumer Fraud Act designed to protect plaintiffs sold credit auto insurance without having been advised of additional cost, term of policy, and that less expensive policies available).

421   *In re* USLIFE Credit Corp. & USLIFE Corp., 91 FTC 984, 1015–16, Consumer Cred. Guide CCH ¶ 97,938 (1978), *modified on other grounds*, 92 FTC 353 (1978), *rev'd on other grounds*, 599 F.2d 1387 (5th Cir. 1979). The case was brought solely pursuant to the FTC's enforcement authority over Truth in Lending. (*Note*: the ALJ's recommended decision, to the effect that *USLIFE* did not violate TIL, was not adopted by the full commission. 91 FTC at 1017–46.)

422   *See In re* The Money Tree, Inc., 62 Fed. Reg. 7232 (Feb. 18, 1997) (notice of proposed order), 62 Fed. Reg. 35819 (July 2, 1997) (notice of final order); *In re* Peacock Buick, Inc., 86 FTC 1532, 1558, 1567 (1975), *appeal denied* 553 F.2d 97 (4th Cir. 1977).

423   Matter of Tower Loan of Mississippi, Consumer Cred. Guide Rpt. No. 579; FTC Docket No. 9241 (filed July 5, 1990).

One court articulated its test for establishing allegations of coerced credit insurance purchases as a UDAP claim: 1) the lender affirmatively represented, by words or conduct, that insurance was required in fact, and 2) the borrower purchased insurance as a result of the lender's action which he or she otherwise would not have done. The borrower further should be permitted to introduce evidence to prove those elements, despite the existence of a signed voluntariness disclosure executed pursuant to TIL or a similar state law.[424]

For purposes of a state UDAP claim, whether the challenged acts are unfair or deceptive may not be as difficult an issue as whether credit transactions or insurance transactions are included in the scope of the state UDAP act.[425] Though credit insurance often has been held to fall under the scope of UDAP,[426] either insurance or credit transactions may be specifically excluded, because either product is not a sale of a "good" or "service," which is the most common definition of those transactions covered by UDAP acts, or because the lender or insurer is exempt.

If the transaction is covered by the statute, there are a number of advantages to a UDAP claim. Direct use can be made of FTC precedent that implicit coercive conduct is unfair or deceptive.[427] In addition, evidence of oral misrepresentations in the sales pitch is admissible despite any subsequent written disclosures in the loan documents themselves.[428]

In some states a violation of another statute designed to protect the public is a *per se* UDAP violation.[429] Because both the NAIC's Model UNIP statute[430] and the NAIC Model Credit Insurance Act,[431] both adopted in some form in most states, prohibit at least the tie-in of credit to particular providers, a coerced sale to the lender's insurer is arguably a *per se* UDAP violation.

8.5.2.7 Antitrust; McCarran-Ferguson Act

8.5.2.7.1 Unlawful tie-in arrangements

Perhaps because of its complexity, especially where insurance is involved, antitrust law has not been frequently invoked as a private remedy for credit insurance abuses. While a sophisticated analysis of the issues involved is beyond the scope of this work,[432] a general overview is appropriate.

The possibility of an antitrust claim arises when there is explicit or implied[433] coercion in the sale of credit insurance. Tie-in arrangements, in which the sale of one product is tied to the sale of a second product, are generally condemned under the antitrust laws.[434] As was discussed earlier, despite the TIL voluntariness notice on the documents, all too frequently borrowers feel that their chances of obtaining the credit are jeopardized without the insurance purchase.[435] The high penetration rates of credit insurance, an expensive insurance product for the coverage purchased, suggest that the insurance purchase may in fact be tied to the sale of the credit. In addition, some creditors sell credit insurance as a package deal, i.e., to get any one type of insurance, the consumer must purchase two or more.[436]

---

424 *In re* Milbourne, 108 B.R. 522 (Bankr. E.D. Pa. 1989). *See* § 8.5.2.4, *supra. But see* Strong v. First Family Fin. Servs., Inc., 202 F. Supp. 2d 536 (S.D. Miss. 2002) (clear and conspicuous TILA disclosures regarding credit insurance preclude plaintiffs' argument that lender failed to disclose material terms of the insurance); Hayes v. Osterman Jewelers, 2002 WL 1608445 (Ohio Ct. App. Apr. 19, 2002) (although plaintiff did not discuss the credit insurance with the creditor and did not read the document that she signed accepting credit insurance, the court presumed she had read and understood the terms of the agreement and held that the creditor had not committed a deceptive act by selling the insurance); *cf.* Harrison v. Commercial Credit Corp., 2003 WL 1844464 (S.D. Miss. Mar. 20, 2003) (one of a series of cases holding that a lender's omission or misrepresentation regarding the terms and conditions of credit insurance does not constitute fraudulent concealment—and thus does not toll the statute of limitations—where the loan documents disclose the insurance information, whether or not the consumer has read the papers); Agnew v. Washington Mutual Fin. Group, 244 F. Supp. 2d 672 (N.D. Miss. 2003) (same); Singleton v. Protective Life Ins. Co., 857 So. 2d 803 (Ala. 2003) (same).

425 National Consumer Law Center, Unfair and Deceptive Acts and Practices §§ 2.2.1 (credit), 2.3.1 (insurance) (6th ed. 2004 and Supp.).

426 *E.g.,* Ortego v. Merit Ins. Co., 433 F. Supp. 135 (N.D. Ill. 1977); Browder v. Hanley-Dawson Cadillac, 62 Ill. App. 3d 623, 379 N.E.2d 1206 (1978); State v. Ralph Williams North West Chrysler-Plymouth, Inc., 87 Wash. 2d 298, 553 P.2d 423 (1976). *See also* Fox v. Industrial Casualty Ins. Co., 424 N.E.2d 839 (Ill. App. 1981) (state Consumer Fraud Act designed to protect plaintiffs sold credit auto insurance without having been advised of additional cost, term of policy, and that less expensive policies available).

427 *See* notes 420, 421, *supra.*

428 *See* National Consumer Law Center, Unfair and Deceptive Acts and Practices § 4.2.15 (6th ed. 2004 and Supp.). *See also In re* Milbourne, 108 B.R. 522, 541 (Bankr. E.D. Pa. 1989).

429 *See* National Consumer Law Center, Unfair and Deceptive Acts and Practices § 3.2.7 (6th ed. 2004 and Supp.).

430 *See* § 8.4.1.4, *supra.*

431 *See* note 181, *supra.*

432 And this author.

433 Though the legal issues are generally the same, the factual issues establishing the claim are more difficult in cases of implicit coercion.

434 As a practical matter, Section 1 of the Sherman Act, 15 U.S.C. § 1 *et. seq.,* would be the applicable statute, as the Clayton Act, though forbidding tying arrangements, does not apply to intangibles such as credit or insurance. Polden, *The Antitrust Implications of Credit Insurance Tying Arrangements,* 32 Drake Law Rev. 862, 882 n.78 (1982–1983) (much of this discussion is derived from this article).

435 *See* § 8.5.2.1, *supra.*

436 For an example of this phenomenon, see Fabricant v. Sears Roebuck & Co., 202 F.R.D. 310 (S.D. Fla. 2001) (certifying class in case of retailer selling credit card plan that automatically

It seems well-established now that credit can be the tying (the desired) product under the Sherman Act.[437] A tie-in requires evidence of at least three case elements:

- A tie of two products, (here arguably, the credit and the credit insurance);
- The challenged conduct has "affected a not insubstantial amount of commerce in the market for the tied product" (the tied product being credit insurance);
- "The defendant has substantial economic power in the market for the tying product" (the tying product here being credit).

A showing of coercion may also be required.[438]

The elements regarding economic power may be the most difficult ones to prove. One commentator suggests that the penetration rate itself is evidence of economic power, especially when coupled with the high price of credit insurance in relation to comparable ordinary insurance.[439] Further, though a defendant is likely to argue that the credit marketplace is competitive, and that market dominance is lacking, a number of factors can limit consumers' choices. One of the most fundamental is the extent of borrower sophistication required if he or she is to perceive the full implications of the tie-in arrangement. As was noted earlier, most borrowers focus on the credit, not the ancillary insurance product.[440] Only a very small portion of the borrowing public is likely to understand the cost of credit insurance in relation to its benefits.[441] The fact that the relevant credit market may be segmented as a result of geographic or income factors may suggest that a defendant has sufficient economic power despite the presence of other types of creditors serving other geographic or income markets.[442] Because of the complexity of this issue, the practitioner may wish to seek expert assistance.

This discussion has focused on the tying of credit insurance to the extension of credit. However, there are other tie-ins in credit insurance. Though credit life insurance may be sold alone, rarely is credit disability made available separately. Rather, it must be purchased with credit life coverage. For example, a borrower with standard life insurance adequate to cover all expenses and debts in the event of death may view credit life as superfluous, and wish to insure only against disability. Many lenders would provide such a borrower only with a choice between both credit life and credit disability or neither. Policies cast as loss-of-income policies covering both disability and involuntary-unemployment also in effect, present a tie-in.[443]

The issues involved in the tying of one type of credit insurance to another type of credit insurance apparently have been little explored in cases or commentary.[444] Arguably most of the analysis of that type of tie-in would be similar to that in situations where the insurance is tied to the purchase of credit. However, it is conceivable that the "business of in-

---

includes package of credit life, disability, property, and unemployment insurance without properly advising consumer that the package was optional) (no antitrust claim raised), *subsequent history, Order on Motions for Summary Judgment*, Clearinghouse No. 54,563 (S.D. Fla. Mar. 5, 2002) (granting summary judgment on two of plaintiffs' counts and voiding the contracts as unenforceable on public policy grounds); Baron v. Best Buy Co., 75 F. Supp. 2d 1368 (S.D. Fla. 1999) (same but Best Buy calls the package the "Payment Maker Protection Plan"; court found arbitration clause unenforceable), *rev'd and vacated*, 260 F.3d 625 (11th Cir. 2001) (court reversed denial of motions to compel arbitration).

437 Fortner Enterprises, Inc. v. United States Steel Corp., 394 U.S. 495 (1969); Homestead M. Homes, Inc. v. Foremost Corp. of America, 603 F. Supp. 767 (N.D. Tex. 1985) (where mobile home financing arrangements tied to insurance, conduct not exempt from antitrust as business of insurance. Further, because insurer acted in concert with a non-exempt entity, exemption would have been forfeited in any case).

438 Polden, *The Antitrust Implications of Credit Insurance Tying Arrangements*, 32 Drake Law Rev. 862, 880 (1982–1983). This manual does not address the distinction between pleading and proving a *per se* tying case and a tying case analyzed under the rule of reason, as that is beyond the scope of this manual. The concepts, however, are important in litigating an antitrust tie-in case. *See generally id.* at 881; Jefferson Parish Hosp. Dist. No. 2 v. Hyde, 466 U.S. 2 (1984).

439 Polden, *The Antitrust Implications of Credit Insurance Tying Arrangements*, 32 Drake Law Rev. 862, 895–96 (1982–1983).

440 *See* § 8.2.3.1, *supra.*

441 *Id.*

442 Polden, *The Antitrust Implications of Credit Insurance Tying Arrangements*, 32 Drake Law Rev. 862, 984–92 (1982–1983). In a rural area, there are likely to be fewer choices as to credit providers. During a farm recession, which may cause rural banks with a high volume of troubled agricultural credit to restrict their lending to lower-income consumers, for example, the finance company segment of the lending market may assume greater economic control, at least in relation to that class of borrowers. *See also* § 11.1, *infra.*

443 California requires that loss of income (LOI) insurance and disability insurance must be offered separately, even if a combination plan is offered. Cal. Fin. Code § 18292.5(e) (Industrial Loan).

444 *Compare* Kenty v. Bank One, Columbus, N.A., 1992 WL 170605, 1992 U.S. Dist LEXIS 16645 (S.D. Ohio Apr. 23, 1992), *aff'd in relevant part* 92 F.3d 384 (6th Cir. 1996) (claim under anti-tying provision of Bank Holding Co. Act, 12 U.S.C. § 1972, dismissed where allegation that credit loss endorsements were tied to force-placed property insurance purchase) *with* Boyd v. Society Bank & Trust, Clearinghouse No. 47,939A (Ct. Com. Pleas, Ohio, *order on motion to dismiss* Oct. 29, 1991) (same claim survived motion to dismiss). For an example of this phenomenon but where antitrust claims have not been raised, see Fabricant v. Sears Roebuck & Co., 1999 U.S. Dist. LEXIS 16574 (S.D. Fla. Sept. 30, 1999) (Sears card "credit plan" is sold as a package which automatically includes credit life, disability, property, and unemployment insurance) (antitrust claim not raised); Baron v. Best Buy Co., 75 F. Supp. 2d 1368 (S.D. Fla. 1999) (same but Best Buy calls the package the "Payment Maker Protection Plan"), *rev'd*, 260 F.3d 625 (11th Cir. 2001) (court reversed denial of motions to compel arbitration).

surance" factor may be weighed differently where insurance is both the tying and tied product, or where the *insurer*, rather than a creditor, creates the tied package.[445]

8.5.2.7.2 *Effect of the McCarran-Ferguson Act on antitrust challenges to credit insurance practices*

The McCarran-Ferguson Act[446] may impede the use of federal antitrust laws to challenge credit insurance sales practices. The Act does not exclude *all* state laws regulating insurance from antitrust laws. Rather, Congress intended the Act to free state insurance laws and regulations from "inadvertent"—as opposed to intentional—federal preemption.[447] Accordingly, the Act merely reverses the standard rules for preemption by creating a "clear-statement rule . . . that state laws enacted 'for the purpose of regulating the

business of insurance' do not yield to conflicting federal statutes unless a federal statute specifically requires otherwise."[448]

Generally speaking, the Act leaves the "business of insurance" to state regulation and mandates that state law overrides conflicting federal law *unless* the federal law specifically relates to the business of insurance.[449] For federal laws in general, such a conflict arises when it would "invalidate, impair, or supersede" any state law "regulating the business of insurance."[450] Further, the antitrust laws *do*

---

445 *See* Kintner, Bauer & Allen, *Application of the Antitrust Laws to the Activities of Insurance Companies*, 63 N.C.L. Rev. 431, 465 (1985).

446 15 U.S.C. §§ 1012, 1013. The McCarran-Ferguson exclusion provision reads in its entirety as follows:

> (b) Federal regulation. No Act of Congress shall be construed to invalidate, impair, or supersede any law enacted by any State for the purpose of regulating the business of insurance, or which imposes a fee or tax upon such business, unless such Act specifically relates to the business of insurance: *Provided, That after June 30, 1948, the Act of July 2, 1890, as amended, known as the Sherman Act [15 U.S.C. §§ 1* et seq.], and the Act of October 15, 1914, as amended, known as the Clayton Act, and the Act of September 26, 1914, known as the Federal Trade Commission Act, as amended [*15 U.S.C. §§ 41* et seq.], shall be applicable to the business of insurance to the extent that such business is not regulated by State law.

15 U.S.C. § 1012(b) (emphasis added).

Congress expressed the intent behind the exclusion as follows:

> Congress hereby declares that the continued regulation and taxation by the several States of the business of insurance is in the public interest, and that silence on the part of the Congress shall not be construed to impose any barrier to the regulation or taxation of such business by the several States.

15 U.S.C. § 1011.

447 Merchants Home Delivery Servs. v. Frank B. Hall & Co., 50 F.3d 1486, 1488–89 (9th Cir.), *cert. denied sub nom.* Prometheus Funding Corp. v. Merchants Home Delivery Servs., 516 U.S. 964 (1995). If Congress specifically intends a particular statute to regulate the business of insurance, that statute controls and no McCarran-Ferguson exclusion inquiry is needed. *See, e.g.,* Patton v. Triad Guar. Ins., 277 F.3d 1294, 1298 (11th Cir. 2002) (holding that the federal Real Estate Settlement Procedures Act was not subject to McCarran-Ferguson's exclusion provision because by explicitly referring to mortgage insurance, Congress displayed an intent to regulate it).

448 U.S. Dept. of the Treasury v. Fabe, 508 U.S. 491, 507 (1993). Furthermore, the McCarran-Ferguson Act's protections are triggered only when an entity is engaged in the "business of insurance." Sec. & Exch. Comm'n v. National Sec., Inc., 393 U.S. 453, 460 (1969).

449 15 U.S.C. § 1012(b); Barnett Bank of Marion County v. Nelson, 517 U.S. 25, 38–39 (1996) (holding that federal statute granting national banks in small towns the authority to sell insurance preempted state law prohibiting such banks from selling insurance). Courts have described the test for state law supremacy in two different ways. The Fifth Circuit has a four part test as follows: The Act allows a state law to override federal law if: (1) the federal statute does not "specifically relate[] to the business of insurance"; (2) if the acts challenged are part of the "business of insurance"; (3) if the state has enacted a law "for the purpose of regulating insurance"; and (4) if application of the federal statute would "invalidate, impair, or supersede" the state law. Edwards v. Your Credit, 148 F.3d 427, 433 (5th Cir. 1998) (quoting 15 U.S.C. § 1012). *See also* DeHoyos v. Allstate, 345 F.3d 290 (5th Cir. 2003) (holding, in a case alleging pricing discrimination due to use of credit scores, that federal civil rights statutes are not "reverse preempted" because they do not interfere with any identified state insurance statute or regulatory goal), *cert. denied,* 124 S. Ct. 2074 (2004); Highmark, Inc. v. UPMC Health Plan, Inc., 276 F.3d 160, 169–170 (3d Cir. 2001) (following analysis similar to that of *Edwards*). The Seventh Circuit uses a broader test expressed in three parts as follows: a state law preempts a federal statute under the Act if: (1) the federal statute at issue does not "specifically relate to the business of insurance"; (2) the state statute was "enacted . . . for the purpose of regulating the business of insurance"; and (3) application of the federal statute would "invalidate, impair or supersede" the state law. Autry v. Northwest Premium Servs., 144 F.3d 1037, 1043 (7th Cir. 1998). *See also* Standard Sec. Life Ins. Co. v. West, 267 F.3d 821, 823–24 (8th Cir. 2001) (three step analysis); Moore v. Liberty Nat'l Life Ins. Co., 267 F.3d 1209, 1220–21 (11th Cir. 2001) (same); Mayard-Paul v. Mega Life & Health Ins. Co., 2001 U.S. Dist. LEXIS 22256, at *6 (S.D. Fla. Dec. 21, 2001) (same). The three part test does not address the activity being challenged, but rather allows state law to preempt federal law even if the specific activity at issue does not relate to the business of insurance, so long as a state law governs it. The Supreme Court recently ruled that the analysis under this provision does not carry over to control the interpretation of ERISA's savings clause, 29 U.S.C. § 1144(b)(2)(A). Ky. Ass'n of Health Plans, Inc. v. Miller, 538 U.S. 329, 123 S. Ct. 1471, 1479, 155 L. Ed. 2d 468 (2003) (holding that Kentucky statutory provisions that prohibited health benefit plans from discriminating against certain providers were laws regulating insurance which ERISA saved from preemption).

450 15 U.S.C. § 1012(b). *See* Humana Inc. v. Forsyth, 525 U.S. 299, 307 (1999) ("invalidate" means "to render ineffective, generally without providing a replacement rule or law"; "supersede"

apply "to the business of insurance to the extent that such business is not regulated by State law."[451] Third, the Sherman Act in particular always applies to any "act of boycott, coercion or intimidation."[452]

As construed by the Supreme Court, the second clause of the exemption, which addresses the relationship of the antitrust laws to insurance practices, exempts only a limited set of such practices from antitrust laws.[453] That exemption is to be read narrowly,[454] and exempts from the antitrust laws *only* such practices that meet all three of the following criteria: (1) the practices constitute the "business of insurance"; (2) the practices are "regulated by state law"; and (3) the practices do not constitute a boycott, coercion, or intimidation.[455]

Applying these criteria to coercive credit insurance sales strongly supports the argument that a state law should not override federal antitrust challenges to such practices. An antitrust challenge to a credit insurance practice should be viable based upon one of the following arguments: (1) the specific practice is not the "business of insurance" because it arises from a creditor-borrower relationship, not an insurer-insured relationship; (2) even if the practice falls within the "business of insurance," the state's laws do not specifically regulate the practice; or (3) even if the practice is part of the "business of insurance," and is specifically regulated by the state, the antitrust claim would not invalidate, impair or supersede the state's regulating law.

The mere fact that a practice involves an insurance policy does not place the practice within the "business of insurance."[456] For example, the Fifth Circuit has held that the

---

ordinarily means "to displace (and thus render ineffective) while providing a substitute rule"; "impair" means a direct conflict with state regulation and the frustration of state policy or interference with a state's administrative regime) (using these definitions, the Court held that RICO did not invalidate, supersede, or impair Nevada's Unfair Insurance Practices Act).

451 15 U.S.C. § 1012(b). The first clause and the second clause of 15 U.S.C. § 1012(b) address two different functions of the McCarran-Ferguson Act. The first clause of § 1012(b) acts to allow states to freely regulate insurance companies without fear of Commerce Clause attack, while the second serves an entirely different purpose, to give insurance companies only a limited exemption from antitrust laws. Group Life & Health Ins. Co. v. Royal Drug Co., 440 U.S. 205, 219 (1979). As construed by the Court, Congress intended to establish that the insurance industry would no longer have a general immunity from the antitrust laws. U.S. Dept. of Treasury v. Fabe, 508 U.S. 491, 505 (1993). *Royal Drug*, 440 U.S. at 220. Thus, the Supreme Court has treated the second clause of 15 U.S.C. § 1012(b), which describes the relationship of the Sherman Act, Clayton Act, and Federal Trade Commission Acts, as specifically defining the relationship between those Acts and the protection offered by the McCarran-Ferguson Act. That is, the McCarran-Ferguson Act will exempt a particular practice from those Acts *only* if it is the business of insurance, *and* it is regulated by state law. *Royal Drug*, 440 U.S. at 219. Furthermore, even if a practice falls within the immunity clause because it is the business of insurance and regulated by state law, the Sherman Act will nonetheless apply to any practice that is a boycott or other conduct described by 15 U.S.C. § 1013(b). *Id.* at 210.

452 15 U.S.C. § 1013(b). The Supreme Court interpreted the boycott element of § 1012(b)'s antitrust clause in Hartford Fire Ins. Co. v. Calif., 509 U.S. 764, 802–806 (1993), holding that the plaintiffs had sufficiently alleged that the defendants, a group of reinsurers, had engaged in a boycott to avoid having their Sherman Act claim dismissed on the grounds that the defendant's activities were exempt by way of the McCarran-Ferguson Act from the antitrust laws.

453 Group Life & Health Ins. Co. v. Royal Drug Co., 440 U.S. 205, 220 (1979). See also Humana, Inc. v. Forsyth, 525 U.S. 299, 309 (1999) (discussing the differences between the two clauses of 15 U.S.C. § 1012(b)); U.S. Dept. of Treasury v. Fabe, 508 U.S. 491, 504 (1993) (describing the immunity given insurance practices from the antitrust laws by the second clause as "narrower" than the immunity given from other laws by the first.).

454 Union Labor Life Ins. Co. v. Pireno, 458 U.S. 119, 126 (1982).

455 *Id.* at 124.

456 To determine whether particular conduct falls within "the business of insurance," courts have used a three part test derived from three Supreme Court decisions: Union Labor Life Ins. Co. v. Pireno, 458 U.S. 119 (1982); Group Life & Health Ins. Co. v. Royal Drug Co., 440 U.S. 205 (1979); S.E.C. v. National Sec., Inc., 393 U.S. 453 (1969). This test asks: whether the practice has the effect of transferring or spreading a policyholder's risk; whether the practice is an integral part of the policy relationship between the insurer and the insured; and whether the practice is limited to entities within the insurance industry. See, e.g., U.S. Dept. of Treasury v. Fabe, 508 U.S. 491, 501–02 (1993) (to the extent a state law furthers the interests of policyholders, it regulates the business of insurance, to the extent it furthers the interests of others, it does not, therefore portion of state bankruptcy priority statute that gave priority to policyholders regulated business of insurance, but portion that gave priority to other creditors did not and therefore that portion was not protected by the McCarran-Ferguson Act from preemption by federal statute that granted priority to the government); O'Connor v. Unum Life Ins. Co., 146 F.3d 959, 962 (D.C. Cir. 1998); Autry v. Northwest Premium Servs., 144 F.3d 1037, 1044 (7th Cir. 1998) (a statute is enacted for the purpose of regulating the "business of insurance" if "it possesses the end, intention or aim of adjusting, managing, or controlling the relationship between the insurance company and the policyholder, directly or indirectly") (holding that an Illinois statute requiring insurance premium finance agreements to disclose certain information did not regulate the business of insurance, and therefore McCarran-Ferguson did not bar TILA claim, because the law addressed the relationship between a creditor and debtor, not the relationship between an insurance company and a policyholder, that the money borrowed ultimately paid insurance premiums was "incidental"); Perry v. Fidelity Union Life Ins. Co., 606 F.2d 468, 471 (5th Cir. 1979) (where defendant insurance company acted as a creditor, not as an insurer, its premium financing was not the "business of insurance" and therefore Act did not bar TILA; focus is on the nature of the activity itself, not the type of business that is conducting it); *In re* EVIC Class Action Litig., 2002 WL 1766554, at *5 (S.D.N.Y. July 31, 2002) (state unfair competition and consumer protection laws were not enacted for the purpose of regulating the business of insurance for purposes of McCarran-Ferguson Act analysis, and therefore were not protected from preemption); FTC v. Manufacturer's Hanover Consumer Serv., 567 F. Supp. 992, 995–96 (E.D. Pa. 1983) (upholding power of

---

McCarran-Ferguson Act did not bar the FTC from investigating whether finance companies were violating the Federal Trade Commission Act[457] by misrepresenting to borrowers that they must purchase credit insurance to obtain credit.[458] The court reasoned that the appropriate focus is not on the sale of the insurance, but on the extension of credit, which is not "the business of insurance," and accordingly falls outside of the McCarran-Ferguson Act.[459] Similar reasoning should preserve federal antitrust law challenges to such credit practices as well.[460]

Even if a particular practice involves the business of insurance, it must be "regulated by State Law" to be exempt from federal antitrust laws. While lines of authority differ as to the degree of state regulation necessary to invoke the exemption,[461] the more thoroughly-reasoned view requires that the state both specifically authorize the conduct at issue *and* actively regulate it.[462] Since many states prohibit creditors from requiring insurance in credit transactions,[463] and all states require creditors to give the consumer a choice of provider in any case,[464] no state has expressed a policy of allowing credit insurance tie-ins, and thus the exemption should not apply.[465]

Furthermore, regardless of whether state law regulates the practice, to the extent the tie-in is achieved by coercion or intimidation, the McCarran-Ferguson Act explicitly subjects the practice to the Sherman Act.[466]

Finally, the McCarran-Ferguson Act defense can be escaped by asserting a state claim, where appropriate. For example, some state antitrust laws may prohibit credit insurance tie-ins. McCarran-Ferguson, of course, would not be a threshold issue if a state antitrust law formed the basis of the claim.

Note that pursuant to its first clause McCarran-Ferguson may also be raised to defend against a consumer's use of other federal statutes, such as the Truth in Lending Act and RICO, to challenge credit-related insurance practices. The Act generally does not bar such claims at least as to a creditor's conduct because they do not meet the first clause of the anti-preemption provision, allowing the state law to override federal law only where the federal law would "invalidate, impair, or supersede" the state law.[467] The U.S.

FTC to investigate credit insurance tie-ins to automobile financing); Allen v. Pacheco, 71 P.3d 375, 383, 384 (Colo. 2003) (holding that statute need not relate solely to insurance to fall within McCarran-Ferguson's savings clause and avoid preemption; accordingly, state statute regulating HMO contracts was not preempted by the Federal Arbitration Act). *See also* Ruthardt v. United States, 303 F.3d 375, 380 (1st Cir. 2002) (even when antitrust is not involved, "business of insurance" should be read restrictively, focusing on the insurance contract and protection of policyholders). *But see* Standard Sec. Life Ins. Co. v. West, 267 F.3d 821, 823 (8th Cir. 2001) (McCarran-Ferguson barred application of Federal Arbitration Act because state statute prohibiting arbitration clauses in insurance contracts involved the business of insurance); Balaban Zilke v. CIGNA Healthcare of Cal., Inc., 2003 WL 21228038, at *3, *4 (Cal. Ct. App. May 28, 2003) (state statute requiring certain disclosures in health care service plans that required binding arbitration " 'regulat[ed] the business of insurance' " and accordingly the McCarran-Ferguson Act protected them from preemption by the Federal Arbitration Act); Imbler v. PacifiCare of Cal., Inc., 103 Cal. App. 4th 567, 577 (2002) (same); Pagarigan v. Super. Ct., 102 Cal. App. 4th 1121, 1133, 1134 (2002) (same); Smith v. PacifiCare Behavioral Health of Cal., Inc., 113 Cal. Rptr. 2d 140, 155 (Cal. Ct. App. 2001) (state law requiring specific disclosures in health care service plans' binding arbitration clauses were enacted for the purpose of regulating the business of insurance and therefore McCarran-Ferguson prevented application of Federal Arbitration Act to contract clause); Cox v. Woodmen of the World Ins. Co., 556 S.E.2d 397, 401–02 (S.C. Ct. App. 2001) (where state law specifically excepted arbitration clauses in insurance contracts from enforcement under state arbitration act, McCarran-Ferguson barred enforcement of Federal Arbitration Act).

457 15 U.S.C. § 45(a)(2).

458 FTC v. Dixie Fin. Co., 695 F.2d 926, 930 (5th Cir. 1983), *cert. denied*, 461 U.S. 928 (1983).

459 *Id.*

460 *See, e.g.,* Homestead M. Homes, Inc. v. Foremost Corp. of America, 603 F. Supp. 767, 771–72 (N.D. Tex. 1985) (where mobile home financing arrangements tied to insurance, conduct not exempt from antitrust as business of insurance; further, because insurer acted in concert with a non-exempt entity, exemption would have been forfeited in any case). *But see* Gilchrist v. State Farm Mut. Auto. Ins. Co., 390 F.3d 1327, 1333 (11th Cir. 2004) (holding that automobile policy holder's antitrust claim based on allegations that insurers had lowered the quality and cost of repairs by specifying inferior parts and had further failed to pass the savings onto policy holders was barred; court reasoned that the heart of Gilchrist's complaint is that claim went "to the heart of 'the relationship between insurer and insured' and attack[ed] the 'reliability, interpretation, and enforcement' of the insurance policy itself") (quoting S.E.C. v. National Sec., Inc., 393 U.S. 453, 460 (1969)). *See generally*

Polden, *The Antitrust Implications of Credit Insurance Tying Arrangements*, 32 Drake Law Rev. 862, 903–05 (1982–1983); Kintner, Bauer & Allen, *Application of the Antitrust Laws to the Activities of Insurance Companies*, 63 N.C.L. Rev. 431, 461–65 (1985).

461 *See* Polden, *The Antitrust Implications of Credit Insurance Tying Arrangements*, 32 Drake Law Rev. 862, 906, nn.183–84 (1982–1983), *discussing* Klamath-Lake Pharmaceutical Ass'n v. Klamath Medical Serv. Bureau, 701 F.2d 1276 (9th Cir.), *cert. denied*, 464 U.S. 822 (1983) *and* Dexter v. Equitable Life Assurance Society, 527 F.2d 233 (2d Cir. 1975).

462 *See* Polden, *The Antitrust Implications of Credit Insurance Tying Arrangements*, 32 Drake Law Rev. 862, 906–08 (1982–1983), *discussing, inter alia*, United States v. Crocker Nat'l Corp., 656 F.2d 428 (9th Cir. 1981), *rev'd on other grounds*, BankAmerica Corp. v. United States, 462 U.S. 122, (1983).

463 *See* § 8.5.2.3, *supra*.

464 *Id.*

465 Polden, *The Antitrust Implications of Credit Insurance Tying Arrangements*, 32 Drake Law Rev. 862, 907, 910–11 (1982–1983).

466 15 U.S.C. § 1013(b).

467 *E.g.,* American Chiropractic Ass'n v. Trigon Healthcare, Inc., 367 F.3d 212, 231 (4th Cir. 2004) (McCarran-Ferguson Act did not bar application of federal RICO statute because RICO furthered state policy in policing insurance fraud, did not frustrate any declared state policy, and did not interfere with state's

Supreme Court has defined "impair" in *Humana v. Forsyth* to mean " '[t]o weaken, to make worse, to lessen in power,

administrative scheme even though RICO's damages provisions were more severe than many of the state's laws); Dehoyos v. Allstate Corp., 345 F.3d 290, 298 (5th Cir. 2003) (McCarran-Ferguson Act did not bar civil rights action arising from insurers' use of credit scoring system to price insurance policies, rejecting argument that such actions would frustrate states' ability to regulate insurance pricing policies); Ruthardt v. United States, 303 F.3d 375, 382–83 (1st Cir. 2002) (while state's bankruptcy priority statute's provision granting priority to guaranty funds was not preempted by federal priority statute, its one-year claims deadline was because it was not sufficiently directed to policyholder protection to fall within McCarran-Ferguson's protection); Highmark, Inc. v. UPMC Health Plan, Inc., 276 F.3d 160, 168 (3d Cir. 2001) (Lanham Act not overridden by state insurance law because it did not invalidate, impair or supersede the state law, notwithstanding that state law imposed a different standard of liability and provided for administrative enforcement without private remedies); Moore v. Liberty Nat'l Life Ins. Co., 267 F.3d 1209, 1221–22 (11th Cir. 2001) (McCarran-Ferguson did not bar application of civil rights laws to insurer because they neither frustrated any state regulation nor conflicted with any statute enacted to regulate insurance); Lander v. Hartford Life & Annuity Ins. Co., 251 F.3d 101, 115–16 (2d Cir. 2001) (McCarran-Ferguson did not prevent application of Securities Litigation Uniform Standards Act to insurance companies); BancOklahoma Mortg. Corp. v. Capital Title Co., 194 F.3d 1089, 1099–1100 (10th Cir. 1999) (upholding RICO claim against McCarran-Ferguson preemption argument); LaBarre v. Credit Acceptance Corp., 175 F.3d 640, 643–44 (8th Cir. 1999) (RICO claim against RISC assignee arising from assignee's purchase of vendor-single-interest insurance not barred by McCarran-Ferguson, though plaintiff's claims against insurers were so barred because they fell within a state insurance provision); Edwards v. Your Credit, Inc., 148 F.3d 427, 434 (5th Cir. 1998) (McCarran-Ferguson did not protect finance company from alleged TILA violation arising from failure to include "nonfiling insurance premium" in disclosed amount financed); Autry v. Northwest Premium Servs., 144 F.3d 1037, 1044–45 (7th Cir. 1998) (McCarran-Ferguson did not bar TILA claim based on alleged misstatements in premium financing agreement for automobile insurance policy); Sabo v. Metropolitan Life Ins. Co., 137 F.3d 185, 192–93 (3d Cir. 1998) (RICO not overridden by state unfair insurance practices statute because it did not invalidate, supersede, or impair the statute), *cert. denied*, 525 U.S. 1129 (1999); Kenty v. Bank One, Columbus, N.A., 92 F.3d 384, 392–93 (6th Cir. 1996) (McCarran-Ferguson did not protect bank from RICO claim with respect to forced-place insurance, but did protect insurer); Garcia v. Island Program Designer, Inc., 4 F.3d 57, 62 (1st Cir. 1993) (state's bankruptcy filing deadline not protected from preemption by McCarran-Ferguson because it was not reasonably necessary to further the goal of protecting policyholders); Mayard-Paul v. Mega Life & Health Ins. Co., 2001 U.S. Dist. LEXIS 22256, at *5–9 (S.D. Fla. Dec. 21, 2001) (since no conflict between state law and Federal Arbitration Act with respect to the arbitrability of rescission of an insurance policy, McCarran-Ferguson did not bar application of Federal Arbitration Act); *In re* MetLife Demutualization Litig., 156 F. Supp. 2d 254, 263 (E.D.N.Y. 2001) (state law regarding demutualization did not override federal Securities Act under McCarran-Ferguson because it did not displace any provision of the state law); Sandwich Chef of Texas, Inc. v. Reliance Nat'l Indemnity Ins. Co., 111 F. Supp. 2d 867, 877 (S.D. Tex. 2000) (state's filed-rate doctrine did not cause Act to bar plaintiff's

RICO claim based on defendant's overbilling for worker's compensation insurance); Harris v. Illinois Vehicle Premium Fin. Co., 2000 U.S. Dist. LEXIS 13763, at *8 (N.D. Ill. Sept. 12, 2000) (unpublished) (TILA not preempted by state premium financing law); Fabricant v. Sears Roebuck & Co., 1999 U.S. Dist. LEXIS 16574, at *7 n.2 (S.D. Fla. Sept. 30, 1999) (unpublished) (Act did not bar application of TILA to defendant's sale of credit insurance made in connection with credit card, no direct conflict with state regulation or frustration of declared state policy or administrative regime); Cunningham v. PFL Life Ins. Co., 42 F. Supp. 2d 872, 882 (N.D. Iowa 1999) (non-credit life insurance case; RICO held not preempted by McCarran-Ferguson), *vacated in part on other grounds*, 1999 U.S. Dist. LEXIS 16574 (S.D. Fla. Sept. 30, 1999); Celtic Life Ins. Co. v. McLendon, 814 So. 2d 222, 226 (Ala. 2001) (Alabama's anti-arbitration statute did not override application of Federal Arbitration Act under principles of McCarran-Ferguson). *See also* Barber v. Unum Life Ins. Co. of Am., 383 F.3d 134, 141 (3d Cir. 2004) (holding that ERISA preempted a state bad faith statute because while it may have been "specifically directed toward entities engaged in insurance," it did not "substantially affect the risk pooling arrangement between the insurer and the insured.") (quoting Ky. Ass'n of Health Plans, Inc. v. Miller, 538 U.S. 329, 341–42 (2003)); Perrin v. First Money, L.L.C., 1999 U.S. Dist. LEXIS 6039 (E.D. La. 1999) (dismissing RICO claim in connection with the sale of credit life insurance based on plaintiff's failure to appropriately plead injury); Bermudez v. First of America Bank Champion, N.A., 860 F. Supp. 580, 589–90 (N.D. Ill. 1994), *case subsequently withdrawn pursuant to settlement*, 886 F. Supp. 643 (N.D. Ill. 1995) (McCarran-Ferguson no bar to RICO and TILA challenge to force-placed insurance practices); Moore v. Fidelity Fin. Servs., Inc., 884 F. Supp. 288, 291–92 (N.D. Ill. 1995) (same) (later the court dismissed the RICO count in *Moore*, 897 F. Supp. 378 (N.D. Ill. 1995), on the grounds that the plaintiff failed to adequately plead an "enterprise"); National Consumer Law Center, Truth in Lending § 3.9.4.2 (5th ed. 2003 and Supp.). Nonetheless, several federal statutes have been ruled to be overridden by a state insurance law by virtue of the federal law's anticipated effect on state policy. *See, e.g.*, Standard Sec. Life Ins. Co. v. West, 267 F.3d 821, 823 (8th Cir. 2001) (in case against insurer, McCarran-Ferguson barred application of Federal Arbitration Act because it would invalidate, impair or supersede state arbitration act with conflicting provisions); Grider v. Keystone Health Plan Cent., Inc., 2003 WL 22182905, at *9 (E.D. Pa. Sept. 13, 2003) (McCarran-Ferguson Act barred RICO suit by car buyer against insurers that allegedly schemed to provide costlier vendor single interest insurance in place of limited physical damage insurance because RICO would frustrate state's policy of addressing such conduct through administrative process); American Chiropractic Ass'n v. Trigon Healthcare, Inc., 151 F. Supp. 2d 723, 733–35 (W.D. Va. 2001) (under McCarran-Ferguson, state insurance law overrode application of federal RICO statute, because allowing claim would impair state policy of not allowing private causes of action under insurance laws); Gerlach v. Allstate Ins. Co., 338 F. Supp. 642, 649 (S.D. Fla. 1972) (state laws and regulations governing premium financing caused Act to preclude application of TILA); Gordon v. Ford Motor Credit Co., 868 F. Supp. 1191, 1196–97 (N.D. Cal. 1992) (RICO); Smith v. PacifiCare Behavioral Health of Cal., Inc., 93 Cal. App. 4th 139, 113 Cal. Rptr. 2d 140, 150–52 (2001) (under McCarran-Ferguson, state law requiring certain specific disclosures for arbitration clauses in health insurance contracts overrode Federal Arbitration Act).

diminish, or relax, or otherwise affect in an injurious man-

Furthermore, though RICO actions against the creditor may not be barred, actions against the insurance company itself may be. A line of cases holds that where a state's comprehensive insurance scheme does not provide for a private cause of action, the McCarran-Ferguson Act will bar a RICO claim against an insurer because such a claim, by allowing a private cause of action to replace the state's administrative enforcement, would hurt the state's regulation of insurers. *See, e.g.,* Doe v. Norwest Bank Minn., N.A., 107 F.3d 1297, 1306–07 (8th Cir. 1997) (McCarran-Ferguson Act barred RICO claim based on alleged insurance fraud because claim could impair state's own scheme for regulating the insurance market, a scheme that did not allow private claims); *In re* Managed Care Litig., 185 F. Supp. 2d 1310, 1321–22 (S.D. Fla. 2002) (McCarran-Ferguson Act barred RICO claims based on alleged insurance fraud, because state laws did not allow a private cause of action for such fraud and therefore allowing RICO claim would frustrate state's declared policy), *amended by* 2002 WL 1359736 (S.D. Fla. Mar. 25, 2002); Ambrose v. Blue Cross & Blue Shield of Va., Inc., 891 F. Supp. 1153, 1158 (E.D. Va. 1995) (state insurance laws were enacted for the purpose of regulating insurance, and since they allowed only the state insurance commissioner to enforce them, RICO claim would impair state law by allowing private cause of action that could result in treble damages to supplant state's enforcement mechanisms), *aff'd,* 95 F.3d 41 (table), 1996 WL 482689 (4th Cir. 1996); Everson v. Blue Cross & Blue Shield of Ohio, 898 F. Supp. 532, 543–44 (N.D. Ohio 1994) (Act barred RICO claim based on withheld discounts because state insurance laws did not allow for a private cause of action); Wexco Inc. v. IMC, Inc., 820 F. Supp. 194, 199–200 (M.D. Pa. 1993) (Act barred claim based on fictitious policy issued by defendant's employee because it would "reward" plaintiff and thereby "upset the balance" of relationship between insured and insurer as set forth by state scheme, which did not offer a private remedy for such behavior); LeDuc v. Kentucky Cent. Life Ins. Co., 814 F. Supp. 820, 829 (N.D. Cal. 1992) (RICO action by agents based on allegedly fraudulent nondisclosure of insurance company's financial condition barred by McCarran-Ferguson Act, availability of treble damages and attorney fees would undermine and disrupt state's regulatory supervision of insurers' financial conditions); Senich v. Transamerica Premier Ins. Co., 766 F. Supp. 339, 340 (W.D. Pa. 1990) (Act barred RICO claim based on force-placed collateral protection insurance because claim would impair state regulatory scheme and its administrative remedies); American Int'l Group, Inc. v. Superior Ct., 285 Cal. Rptr. 765, 777 (Cal. Ct. App. 1991) (RICO claim, which alleged mail and wire fraud in connection with allegedly fraudulent scheme by workers' compensation insurers to avoid paying premium refunds, was barred by McCarran-Ferguson Act because the conduct involved—the marketing, sale, and performance of insurance contracts and representations made in connection with such—were within the business of insurance, and allowing RICO claim to recover treble damages would interfere with state scheme, which provided only administrative remedies) (granting writ of mandamus), *cert. denied,* 504 U.S. 911 (1992).

However, in contrast to these decisions, where the courts focused on the difference between the RICO remedy and state-provided remedies, courts that have instead focused on the alleged acts underlying the claim have ruled that a RICO claim based on behavior that would violate state law does not interfere with the state's regulation of insurance companies, even if the state scheme provides a different, administrative, remedy for the misconduct. They reason that if the conduct would not be

ner.' "[468] In that case, a health care insurer sought to use McCarran-Ferguson to evade a federal RICO claim that alleged that the insurer failed to pass cost discounts it received from service providers on to its consumers. The Court upheld the RICO claim, reasoning that it did not impair Nevada's Unfair Insurance Practices Act because the state's many remedies to victims of insurance fraud showed that the federal statute would complement and advance state policy, rather than impair it.[469]

8.5.3 Excessive Cost of Credit Insurance

8.5.3.1 Calculating Credit Insurance Charges

8.5.3.1.1 Introduction

There are at least three ways in which a creditor can overcharge for credit insurance. One is to charge a premium rate higher than that permitted by law or regulation.[470] Another is to purchase insurance coverage in excess of that allowable under the law or necessary to protect the loan. Finally, a level life policy may be sold where a decreasing life policy is required. To check for an overcharge of these types, it is necessary to understand how the premium amount on any given credit insurance policy is calculated. Before proceeding, however, it is critical to note that the formulas discussed in subsequent sections apply where the insurance rates are

---

permitted by state law, no harm comes from allowing a plaintiff to use a federal law to recover for it, even a law that authorizes treble damages and attorney fees. Merchants Home Delivery Serv., Inc. v. Frank B. Hall & Co., 50 F.3d 1486, 1492 (9th Cir.) (California law) (since state insurance law prohibited the acts alleged to support plaintiff's RICO claim, there was no conflict between federal and state laws and McCarran-Ferguson did not bar claim), *cert. denied,* 516 U.S. 964 (1995); Thacker v. N.Y. Life Ins. Co., 796 F. Supp. 1338, 1343 (E.D. Cal. 1992) (gravamen of RICO complaint lay in fraud, not business of insurance, and therefore McCarran-Ferguson Act did not apply; even if considered business of insurance, RICO claim would not interfere with state statutory scheme, although such scheme did not allow a private cause of action, because RICO claim was based on mail fraud, and state law allowed common law fraud actions, declining to follow *American Int'l Group, Inc.*). The split in decisions may be based in part on the sensitivity of any particular court to RICO's treble damages remedy, and the fear that such an attractive remedy would upset a state's determination that only the regulatory head of insurance, and not private parties, should be able to enforce the state's laws, even in the case of egregious fraud.

468 525 U.S. 299, 309–310 (1999) (quoting Black's Law Dictionary 752 (6th ed. 1990)).

469 *Id.* at 311–312.

470 *See, e.g.,* Smith v. Tower Loan of Miss., Inc., 216 F.R.D. 338 (S.D. Miss. 2003) (discussing the filed rate doctrine in approving a class action settlement for various credit insurance abuses and holding that the doctrine bars allegations of excessive rates), *aff'd,* 2004 WL 507572 (5th Cir. Mar. 16, 2004) (unpublished, citation limited).

expressed as x¢ per $100 per annum (life) or x¢ per $100 (A&H) in the regulation or statute, and the borrower pays a single premium charge. They will not work in certain states where the rates are determined by more complicated formulas.[471] Nor will they work with an outstanding balance rate, usually expressed as a " 'per thousand dollars per month' rate,"[472] or where the coverage provided by the insurance provides only net payoff coverage.[473]

8.5.3.1.2 Credit life

The statute, regulation, or other administrative ruling establishing the approved rates for credit life insurance will usually couch the rate in terms of the cost per $100 of the obligation per year, e.g., 65¢/$100/year. The insurance is usually written to insure the total of payments on a closed-end loan, which includes both the anticipated interest and the insurance premiums themselves.

This in itself is an overcharge in an economic sense, though legal in most states. It is excessive because more insurance is sold than is needed. At any time before the last payment is made, the outstanding balance includes unearned interest, which must be rebated if the account is paid before maturity.[474] If the borrower dies before the loan matures, the loan is prepaid. The coverage thus includes the unearned interest, coverage the borrower does not need. The policies, and many state laws, require that the difference be paid to the estate of the borrower. Often the family does not realize that there is extra money due and creditors or insurance companies do not voluntarily pay back this difference. The practice of writing insurance on the total of payments (called "gross coverage") is, however, valid in most states, though some now require net coverage.[475] The Vermont Supreme

Court upheld the validity of such a regulation under Vermont's revision of the NAIC Model Credit Insurance Act.[476]

The Model NAIC Act provides that the initial amount of credit life insurance cannot exceed the total amount repayable under the contract of indebtedness,[477] and indebtedness is further defined to mean the total amount repayable.[478] Thus the formula below uses the term "total of payments," as TIL defines it, because that generally is equal to the initial insured indebtedness. However, in some cases, the initial insured indebtedness will differ from the total of payments. In that situation the initial insured indebtedness should be substituted for the total of payments in the formula. This may occur, for example, if the loan is for a term longer than a legally permissible term for credit insurance, or if the loan amount exceeds the amount of permissible coverage under group insurance laws. Another example is if the full term of the loan takes the borrower past his or her 66th birthday, an age beyond which many credit insurers will not insure debtors. The certificate of insurance will state the amount of initial insured indebtedness.

Where credit life rates are expressed in dollars or cents per $100 per year, the rate may be calculated for a particular transaction by dividing the premium (that is, the amount charged for credit life insurance in that transaction) by the number of years in the transaction. That number (or pre-

---

471 Such as the decremental rate. *See* Financial Publishing Co., The Cost of Personal Borrowing, pp. 44–45 (1998).

472 *Id.* at 43–44. This method of calculation is commonly used in connection with open-end credit. Fagg, Credit Life and Disability Insurance 487 (1986).

473 Net payoff coverage covers net indebtedness plus accrued interest. Fagg, Credit Life and Disability Insurance 14 (1986). *See also* Financial Publishing Co., The Cost of Personal Borrowing, pp. 46–49 (1998).

474 *See generally* Ch. 5, *supra*.

475 *See* note 473, *supra*, for an explanation and sources on net pay-off coverage. *See, e.g.*, Code Me. Rules, § 02-031, ch. 220, sec. 5(B); N.Y. Admin. Code tit. 11, § 185.6(2)(1); Vt. Ins. Reg. I-84-1 (revised) § 3(10); Wash. Rev. Code § 48.34.060 (for group coverage). *See also* Gartman v. The Independent Life and Accident Ins. Co., 1998 U.S. Dist. LEXIS 22069 (S.D. Ala. Oct. 9, 1998) (class certified, by consent, in case challenging insurance charges based on total of payments, relying on McCullar decision); Dixon v. Ford Motor Credit, 2000 U.S. Dist. LEXIS 7934 (E.D. La. May 31, 2000) (allegations that Louisiana law mandates net coverage, that the terms of the insurance were not properly disclosed, and that excessive commissions were paid to sell the insurance product warrants denial of motion for summary judgment on RICO claim), *subsequent proceedings*, 137 F. Supp. 2d 702 (E.D. La. 2000) (RICO claim dismissed; supple-

mental state law claims dismissed); Singleton v. Protective Life Ins. Co., 857 So. 2d 803 (Ala. 2003) (applying *McCullar* and finding that borrowers failed to establish sale of excess insurance where net coverage was sold and finding that state rate requirements were followed); McCullar v. Universal Underwriters Life Ins. Co., 687 So. 2d 156 (Ala. 1996) (plurality) (Alabama law requires net coverage, though regulatory agencies had been interpreting it to permit gross coverage). *But see* Gall v. American Heritage Life Ins. Co., 3 F. Supp. 2d 1344 (S.D. Ala. 1998) (court states it is not bound by plurality in *McCullar* and, agreeing with the dissent, finds that insurance can be calculated on the total of payments); Robertson v. PHF Life Ins. Co., 702 So. 2d 555 (Fla. Dist. Ct. App. 1997) (Florida law permitted calculation based on the total of payments); Liberty Bank & Trust Co. v. Splane, 959 P.2d 600 (Okla. Ct. App. 1998) (court construed provision in U.C.C.C. restricting the amount of the permissible credit insurance to that which does not "exceed the debt" and another provision in Oklahoma insurance law restricting the amount of such insurance to "the approximate unpaid balance of the loan" to allow insurance premiums to be calculated on the total of payments; court specifically rejects the plurality in *McCullar*).

476 Consumer Credit Insurance Administration v. Vermont, 149 Vt. 305, 544 A.2d 1159 (Vt. 1988).

477 Model Bill to Provide for the Regulation of Credit Life Ins. and Credit Accident and Health Ins., National Ass'n of Ins. Comm'rs, Model Regulatory Service § 4A(1) (NIARS Corp., 1984). *But cf.* NAIC Consumer Credit Insurance Model Act § 4(A) (1994) (NAIC model act now would mandate net coverage).

478 Model Bill to Provide for the Regulation of Credit Life Ins. and Credit Accident and Health Ins., National Association of Ins. Commissioners, Model Regulatory Service, § 2B(5) (NIARS Corp., 1984). *See* Winkle v. Grand Nat'l Bank, 601 S.W.2d 559 (Ark. 1980).

mium per year) is then divided by the total amount repayable. Finally, that figure (or the premium per dollar per year) is multiplied times 100, resulting in the rate per hundred per year. This computation may be expressed by the following formula:[479]

$$\text{Rate per \$1,000 per year} = \frac{\text{Premium}}{\text{Years in a Transaction}} \times \frac{100}{\text{Total of Payments}}.$$

It is important to check the certificate of insurance to confirm the term of the insurance. For instance, a 45-day first payment period on a two year loan under some state laws may be charged as a 25-month transaction. Where, as in such a case, the transaction involves parts of years, substitute for years the number of months divided by 12. Therefore, the formula may be written:[480]

$$\text{Rate per \$1,000 per year} = \frac{\text{Premium} \times 12}{\text{Months in Transaction}} \times \frac{100}{\text{Total of Payments}}.$$

An example may be helpful. The state authorizes a credit life rate of 65¢/$100/year for single, declining term coverage. A $210.60 credit life premium was charged on a six year loan with a Total of Payments of $5400. To determine the propriety of that premium, the calculation would be:

$$\frac{\$210.60 \text{ (Premium)}}{6 \text{ (Years of Transaction)}} \times \frac{100}{\$5400 \text{ (Total of Payments)}}$$

$$= 65¢/\$100/\text{year}.$$

The rate charged is at the maximum rate allowed.

One might also wish to use an alternative formula to calculate what the maximum allowable premium would be for a given transaction. That formula is:[481]

$$\text{Maximum Premium} =$$
$$\frac{\text{Legal Max. Rate} \times \text{Yrs. of Transaction} \times \text{Total of Payments}}{100}$$

The answer is then compared to the premium actually charged to derive the amount of an overcharge, if any. In the example above, the maximum legal premium could be derived as follows:

$$\frac{65¢ \times 6 \times \$5,400}{100} = \$210.60.$$

As that was the amount actually charged, there was no overcharge.

In comparing the premium rate actually charged to the legally allowable rate, it is, of course necessary to be sure one is comparing the appropriate rate. Thus one must check the certificate of insurance to see if the insurance is single or joint, declining or level.[482] The legal rate for joint life may be separately established at a specific amount, e.g., $1.07/$100/year, or it may be listed as an adjustment factor to be derived from the single life coverage. If the latter, one must do yet another calculation. To check the authorized rate for joint life, where an adjustment factor is given, multiply the factor times the legal single coverage rate. For example, if the legal rate for single life is 60¢/$100/yr., and the adjustment factor for joint life is 1.50%, the allowable joint life rate is:

$$60¢ \times 1.50 = 90¢/\$100/\text{year}.$$

If the insurance sold is level life, there may be an overcharge even if the rate *per se* is authorized, as many states do not permit level credit life in consumer transactions.[483]

8.5.3.1.3 Credit accident & health

Approved rates for credit accident and health, also called credit disability insurance, are generally derived from estimates as to what rate will result in a specified target loss-ratio.[484] As was noted earlier, there are different kinds of disability coverage: retroactive and non-retroactive; seven-, fourteen-, or thirty-day waiting periods or elimination periods.[485] Because insurance company losses will be different, depending on the type of coverage, there are generally different approved rates for each of the different types of coverage. If these rates are not published in the state administrative code, they are likely to be the subject of an insurance department bulletin or directive. All consumer law practitioners should have a copy of this approved rate schedule, which can be obtained from the insurance department. *The Cost of Personal Borrowing*, published by the Financial Publishing Company, is a valuable resource containing a summary of credit insurance rates for all states.[486]

As with credit life insurance, it is important to know for credit disability insurance what type of coverage was written in order to compare the rate charged with the applicable legal rate. That information usually can be obtained from the certificate of insurance. If the client does not have the certificate, it is usually safe to guess that the coverage is fourteen-day retroactive, as that is the most commonly sold type of policy. (While one, of course, must confirm through discovery or a check with the insurance commission as to what type of coverage the company sells, this estimate will give the practitioner an idea of the highest allowable pre-

---

479 Substitute "initial insured indebtedness" if that amount is different from the loan "total of payments." That figure may be obtained by checking the certificate of insurance, which should have been given to the borrower.
480 *Id.*
481 *Id.*

482 *See* § 8.3.1.2, *supra.*
483 *See* § 8.5.3.3.1, *infra.*
484 *See* § 8.4.2.1, *supra.*
485 § 8.3.1.3, *supra.*
486 *See* § 1.5, *supra.*

mium in most states, as the rest of the common types of coverage usually are cheaper.)[487]

Disability policies, and the approved rates, are based on the full term of the transaction, not on a yearly basis. The rates are set on a sliding scale which establishes a maximum rate per hundred dollars for loans of various lengths; the longer the loan, the higher the rate, though the increase generally is not proportional.[488] In most states the rates are expressed in dollars per $100 of loan. The formula below will not work in states with more complex rate structures.

As with credit life, the amount of coverage usually is based on the total of payments as TIL defines the term. To find the rate charged, the disability premium is divided by the total of payments, and that figure is multiplied by 100.

$$\frac{A \& H\ Premium}{Total\ of\ Payments} \times = Rate\ Charged$$

An example may be helpful. Consider a disability premium of $53.28 on a three-year loan with a total of payments of $1296.00. To determine the rate that was charged, the calculation is:

$$\frac{\$53.28}{\$1,296.00} \times 100 = \$4.11.$$

Assume the state has in effect a rate schedule as described in note 488, *supra*. The appropriate rate for a fourteen-day retroactive policy on a three-year loan would then be $3.80. Therefore, there appears to be an overcharge.

To determine the amount of the apparent excess charge, one can use this formula to determine the maximum legal premium:

$$Max.\ Premium = \frac{Legal\ Max.\ Rate \times Total\ of\ Payments}{100}$$

In this example, the calculation would be:

$$\frac{\$3.80\ (legal\ Max.\ Rate) \times \$1,296\ (Total\ of\ Payments)}{100} = \$49.25.$$

Therefore, there may have been an overcharge of $4.03 ($53.28 − $49.25).

However, there is one more step to take before determining if there is an excess charge. If the calculations reveal an overcharge, the next step is to contact the insurance department to see if that insurer has been granted an upward deviation. If so, the rate as authorized by the deviation is the maximum allowable rate, not the rate on the regular schedules. To see if it is within the authorized deviated rate, the authorized deviation rate is substituted for the "legal maximum rate" in the above formula.

The insurance department, upon inquiry about an upward deviation, simply may supply the authorized rate for that type of coverage, saying, for example, that Calm Yourself Insurance Co. may charge $4.02/$100 for fourteen-day retroactive coverage on a three-year loan. Or, the insurance department may force the practitioner back to the calculator by authorizing a uniform percentage increase to all the authorized rates on the standard chart. For example, a 125% upward deviation, applied to fourteen-day retro coverage on a three-year loan in the state described in note 291 would be calculated as follows:

$$3.80 \times 1.25 = \$4.75.$$

So Calm Yourself Insurance could charge $4.75/$100 for this coverage on this three year loan.

As was discussed earlier, it may turn out that the approval of that deviation is subject to challenge, if it results in a return that exceeds the target loss ratio.[489] That is a separate legal challenge and probably would not support a usury claim on a transaction written while it was authorized by the insurance department.[490]

8.5.3.1.4 Credit property insurance

In 2001, the NAIC adopted a model act that sets a 60% loss-ratio as the standard and requires the insurer to calculate coverage based upon the amount financed, not the total of payments.[491] States are beginning to adopt some or all of this model act.

Credit property insurance generally is not subject to rate regulation. However, the borrower may have purchased excess coverage,[492] which could give rise to an overcharge claim. It may be a simple matter to determine the amount of coverage by referring to the certificate of property insurance. However, if the certificate of insurance is unavailable, or if it does not contain the amount of coverage, the practitioner may have to try to calculate the amount of coverage sold.

Unlike credit life or disability, there may be two unknowns in the mathematical equation for credit property insurance, so some preliminary inquires must be made. First, since there usually is no rate regulation, it is necessary to supply a rate to use in the formula. A call to the insurance

---

Seven-day retroactive is more expensive, but it is rarely sold because many states do not allow it. Even more rare are the yet more expensive three-day retroactive policies.

488 For example, a state may have approved a rate scale of 14-day retroactive coverage similar to the following:

Length of Loan	Max. Rate Per $100 of Total of Payments
1–12 months	$2.20/$100
13–24 months	$3.00/$100
25–36 months	$3.80/$100
37–48 months	$4.30/$100
49–60 months	$4.70/$100

For longer terms, the insurance department rule usually will specify the adjustment factor.

489 *See* § 8.4.2.1, *supra*.

490 Keniston v. American Nat'l Ins. Co., 31 Cal. App. 3d 810, 811, 107 Cal. Rptr. 583, 588 (1973).

491 *See* discussion in §§ 8.3.1.5.1 and 8.4.2.2.1, *supra*.

492 *See* § 8.5.3.4, *infra*.

department staffer who works with credit insurance can yield information about the most common rates used in the state for credit property. If the practitioner knows the name of the insurer, the insurance department probably can supply the rate used by that company.[493] As noted above the certificate of insurance or the master policy may also state the rate on its face, and this rate should then be used.

The second unknown is the amount of coverage. Unlike credit life and A&H, one should not assume that the coverage is equivalent to the total of payments, though it may be. Because some insurers have a minimum amount of coverage available, e.g., $1,000, a borrower may pay for $1,000 of insurance coverage even though the total of payments on the loan may be only $750.

After having obtained from the client's insurance documents or from the insurance department the rate/$100/year charged by the company, the formula to determine the amount of coverage is:

$$\text{Amount of coverage} = \frac{\text{Premium} \times 100}{\text{Rate} \times \text{Number of years}}.$$

Consider an example: a charge for household contents insurance of $60 was made on a two-year loan with a total of payments of $576. The insurance policy stated that the rate was $2 per $100 per year. To determine the amount of coverage the consumer purchased, the formula is:

$$\frac{\$60 \text{ (premium)} \times 100}{\$2 \text{ (rate)} \times 2 \text{ (term of loan)}} = \$1,500 \text{ Amount of Coverage.}$$

This consumer purchased $1,500 of property insurance coverage on a total of payments of $576. Though the insurance department does not regulate the property insurance rate, state credit laws may in some fashion require property insurance to relate to the loan amount. If that is the case, this property insurance may be an excessive charge.[494]

8.5.3.2 Excess Premium Charges As Usury

8.5.3.2.1 General

Generally, charging the borrower a premium in excess of that allowed by law is usury. In most circumstances, the statutory foundation for such a claim is found in the usury law applicable to the credit transaction in question rather than in the credit insurance code. The NAIC Model Act provides that insurers shall not issue a policy "for which the premium rate exceeds that determined by the schedules of such insurer as then on file with the Commissioner,"[495] and

that the amount then charged to a debtor "shall not exceed the premiums charged by the insurer."[496] However, in most states the credit insurance code regulates the insurers, not the creditors, and there is usually no direct private remedy granted to insured debtors under the credit insurance codes.[497]

When read together with the law governing the credit transaction, however, most state statutory schemes should support a usury claim against the creditor. Many of the comprehensive consumer credit codes which govern creditors, for example, include some variation on language that limits the charge to the debtor to the authorized premium permitted for such coverage,[498] or exclude from the definition of finance charge only premiums for "permissible" or "authorized" insurance.[499] Some statutes specifically provide that an excess premium charge is subject to the penalties prescribed for excess charges generally.[500]

Small loan, industrial loan or consumer loan acts may specifically authorize the imposition of credit insurance premiums only under specified conditions.[501] Since many such special usury statutes prohibit any charges except "as authorized,"[502] if all the prescribed conditions are not met, including any incorporated rate or coverage limitations or voluntariness requirements, the premiums should be an unauthorized charge.[503] Most RISA[504] and industrial loan[505]

Comm'rs, Model Regulatory Service § 8(A) (NIARS Corp., 1984).

496 *Id.* § 8(D).

497 Cope v. Aetna Fin. Co. of Maine, 412 F.2d 635, 640 (1st Cir. 1969); Jennings v. Globe Life & Accident Insurance Co., 922 P.2d 622 (Okla. 1996) (court also rejected the creative argument that the Oklahoma version of the U.C.C.C. provided a private right of action to enforce violations of regulations promulgated by the Insurance Commissioner; the U.C.C.C. is specifically limited to "creditor" not "insurer" violations).

498 *E.g.*, Ala. Code § 5-19-20; Colo. Rev. Stat. § 5-4-107(1); Kan. Stat. Ann. § 16a-4-107(1); La. Rev. Stat. tit. 9, § 3545; U.C.C.C. § 4-107(1) (1968).

499 *E.g.*, Ala. Code § 5-19-1(1). *Cf.* Kenty v. Bank One, Columbus, N.A., 1992 WL 170605 (S.D. Ohio Apr. 23, 1992), *aff'd in part, rev'd in part on other grounds*, 92 F.3d 384 (6th Cir. 1996) (cost in force-placed insurance premium for unauthorized coverage and coverage unnecessary to protect the collateral is interest under the National Bank Act [*NB*: This type of insurance is not subject to credit insurance statute. Court relied on common law principles.]).

500 U.C.C.C. § 4-104(2) (1968, 1974); Colo. Rev. Stat. § 5-4-104(2); Kan. Stat. Ann. § 16a-4-104; La. Rev. Stat. tit. 9, § 3552 (penalties for violating the provisions of Consumer Credit Law). Under the U.C.C.C., there are additional requirements which must be met as well to insulate insurance premiums from a usury claim §§ 2-202 (1968), 3-202 (1968), 2-501 (1974).

501 *E.g.*, Ariz. Rev. Stat. Ann. § 6-636; Conn. Gen. Stat. Ann. § 362-566.

502 *E.g.*, Conn. Gen. Stat. Ann. § 36a-563(h).

503 Dickinson v. Buck, 220 So. 2d 48, 51 (Fla. Dist. Ct. App. 1969) (insurance commissions authorized only under circumstances authorized by law).

504 *E.g.*, Alaska Stat. § 45.10.130; Del. Code Ann. tit. 6, § 4307.

505 *E.g.*, Iowa Code Ann. § 536A.23.

---

493 The insurance department may even know which insurance is with a particular transaction simply from the identity of the creditor.

494 *See* §§ 8.4.1.3, *supra*, 8.5.3.3, *infra*.

495 Model Bill to Provide for the Regulation of Credit Life Ins. and Credit Accident and Health Ins., National Ass'n of Ins.

statutes are similarly structured to prohibit creditors from charging debtors for insurance premiums in excess of the rates authorized by the insurance department.

If a special usury statute is silent as to whether insurance premiums are authorized, an argument can be made that the debtor cannot be charged at all for insurance premiums,[506] though the majority of courts have allowed them, in the absence of lender profit, as a third-party expense.[507] Since most special usury statutes now specifically refer to credit life, disability, and property, this issue may arise only with respect to non-traditional insurances, such as involuntary unemployment insurance, or non-credit insurance policies, such as term life or accidental death and dismemberment policies not insuring the debt.[508]

It is necessary that practitioners making this usury claim develop the case properly through discovery, and present evidence as to the lender's profit and role in selecting the insurer. In some instances, courts have refused to hold creditors liable for improper or unauthorized credit insurance charges on the grounds that the creditor merely passes through the premiums to a third party—the insurer. Thus, in this view, the premiums do not represent compensation retained by the creditor.[509] Similarly, at least one court has

implied that creditors might not be liable for excess premiums if the insurer set the premiums.[510]

There are several flaws in such analyses. First, many special usury statutes focus on those charges which the borrower must pay, rather than on what charges the lender receives.[511] For example, if the statute prohibits a licensed lender from "charging, collecting or receiving" any charges except those specifically authorized, then merely "charging" the borrower the unauthorized amount is a violation of the statute. This interpretation is recognized in a number of cases under small loan acts which find usury even where the illegal amounts were never paid, because the act prohibits "charging" or "contracting for" any charges not specifically authorized.[512]

Secondly, to look at credit insurance premiums simply as a charge passed through to a third party, while ignoring compensation retained by the lender, is to ignore the realities of the substantial profit accruing to lenders in the sale of insurance.[513] *In re Galea'i* is one example of this incomplete (and naive) analysis. In that case, the industrial loan law had prohibited the sale of credit insurance.[514] The court merely analogized the charge to a pass-through of an appraisal charge, with no discussion whatsoever of the amount of compensation the lender received from the sale. Undoubtedly, the lender did receive compensation from that sale in a number of ways,[515] though there is no indication in the opinion that such evidence was presented. Since the legislature did not authorize licensees to sell the insurance at all, obviously there was no legislative authority for them to retain any compensation from the sale of such insurance.[516]

---

506 *Ex parte* New Fin., Ltd., 284 Ala. 374, 225 So. 2d 784 (1969) (small loan act); Sunderland v. Day, 12 Ill. 2d 50, 145 N.E.2d 39 (1957); Home Fin. Co. v. Padgett, 54 So. 2d 813, 817 (La. Ct. App. 1951); Hawkins v. Thorp Credit & Thrift Co., 441 N.W.2d 470 (Minn. 1989) (non-credit life insurance not authorized under state regulated loan act, see § 8.5.4.3 for further discussion of this case). *See also* Moran v. American Funding, Ltd., 238 N.J. Super. 263, 569 A.2d 841, 842 (1989) (at issue a prior version of New Jersey's second mortgage act under which title insurance was not a specifically authorized charge and therefore was prohibited by the catch-all provision preventing the creditor from receiving anything other than "charges authorized by this Act"); Garrison v. First Fed. Saving & Loan Ass'n of S.C., 402 S.E.2d 24 (Va. 1991) (risk management fee was not specifically authorized, and thus constituted excess interest); Opinion of the Michigan Att'y Gen., No. 6594, 5 Consumer Cred. Guide (CCH) ¶ 95,775 (July 17, 1989) (MVRISA statute did not authorize any charges other than those specifically itemized, therefore documentary fees, service fees or inspection fees imposed on installment buyers of cars as part of cash price of car were prohibited charges). *See generally* § 9.3.1.2, *infra.*

507 *See* cases cited in *In re* Richards, 272 F. Supp. 480, 485 n.12 (D. Me. 1967), *rev'd on other grounds and remanded*, 412 F.2d 635 (1st Cir. 1969), *on remand* 304 F. Supp. 817 (1969); § 8.5.2.7, *supra. Cf.* Jones v. Jones, 301 S.W.2d 737 (Ark. 1957) (credit insurance premium charge in excess of actual cost of insurance purchased was interest).

508 *See* § 8.5.4.3, *infra.* After initially running into trouble with at least two states for selling involuntary unemployment credit insurance in the absence of authorizations, the industry has been successful in getting it statutorily authorized in a number of states.

509 *E.g., In re* Galea'i, 31 B.R. 629 (Bankr. D. Haw. 1981); Universal C.I.T. Credit Corp. v. Lackey, 305 S.W.2d 858, 862 (Ark. 1957). *See also* General Motors Acceptance Corp. v. Baymon, 732 So. 2d 262 (Miss. 1999) (jury verdict for consumer for $35,000 in compensatory damages and $5 million in punitive

damages reversed and remanded for new trial; grounds for mistrial to allow evidence of excessive profits, that rates amounted to "gouging" and that GMAC had manipulated the rate approval process).

510 Cope v. Aetna Fin. Co. of Maine, 412 F.2d 635, 642 (1st Cir. 1969) (dicta).

511 Sunderland v. Day, 12 Ill. 2d 50, 145 N.E.2d 39 (1957). *See also* Vernon, *Regulated Credit Life and Disability Insurance and the Small Loan*, 29 N.Y.U.L. Rev. 1098, 1109 (1954).

512 *E.g.,* Clyde v. Liberty Loan Corp., 287 S.E.2d 551 (Ga. 1982); Danziger v. San Jacinto Sav. Ass'n, 732 S.W.2d 300, 303–04 (Tex. 1987) (pay-off quotation containing excessive interest constituted "charging" usurious interest); Nationwide Fin. Corp. v. English, 604 S.W.2d 458 (Tex. Ct. App. 1980). *See also* Kaiser Agr. Chemicals, Inc. v. Peters, 417 N.W.2d 437 (Iowa 1987) (general usury statute providing that no one shall "receive" excess interest does not require that the borrower actually pay it to establish a violation of the statute; "it is the agreement to exact and pay usurious interest," not the performance which renders it usurious). *See generally* § 10.5.4.2, *infra.*

513 *See* § 8.2, *supra.*

514 31 B.R. 629 (Bankr. D. Haw. 1981). The contrary arguments and precedent discussed in § 8.5.3.2.1, *supra,* were apparently not raised. The precise language of the statute at issue there is unknown.

515 *See* § 8.2, *supra.*

516 *Cf.* Bailey v. Defenbaugh & Co. of Cleveland, Inc., 513 F. Supp. 232, 242–43 (N.D. Miss. 1981); Hatridge v. Home Life & Acc't

Thus the *Galea'i* court's analysis fails even on its own terms. Further, as a matter of logic, it fails because it is the creditor-licensee who makes the sale of the insurance—a sale prohibited under the licensing statute—not the insurer. Cases such as *Galea'i* make it clear that the consumer's attorney, to be safe, should always present evidence concerning the full extent of creditor compensation.

Thirdly, cases which suggest that the creditor should have no liability where an excess rate is set by the insurer also ignore the business realities of the creditor-insurer relationship. The First Circuit, recognizing the ease with which such a dichotomous view could facilitate an evasion of the law, held that the creditor was liable where there was essentially a joint decision because of a captive insurer relationship.[517] The evidence showed that "in essence, the [parent company] commanded its wholly-owned insurance subsidiary to set a rate and its own wholly-owned loan company to pass it on."[518]

As a practical matter, even outside the captive insurer (or captive lender) situation, the creditor is not isolated from the decision making. It is, after all, the creditor which chooses the insurance it sells to its customers. The reverse competition phenomenon is a large part of the reason a creditor selects among the independent insurers competing for its business: the higher the premium, the higher the creditors' commission.[519] Since corporate lenders are well aware of the prevailing legal limits on credit insurance charges, they should not escape liability for choosing non-compliant insurers, especially since the lender retains the consequent excessive commissions. Normal usury analysis supports this view. "Reasonable" third-party expenses may not be considered interest.[520] However, it is not a "reasonable" expense if it is in excess of that authorized by law. In such a situation, the practitioner would do well to find out through discovery why the creditor chose or retained a particular insurer, and what efforts the creditor routinely makes to be sure the insurer is operating within the law. Further, many times an excess premium amount is charged on a transaction not because the insurer has set an unauthorized rate, but because the creditor's calculations include an excess amount. In such cases, it is the creditor's liability, not the insurers, though the practitioner may still have to deflect a pass-through defense.

8.5.3.2.2 Creditor compensation as interest

A number of early cases considered whether credit insurance premiums constituted usury under state small loan acts. As phrased in the Uniform Small Loan Law:

> In addition to the interest herein provided for, no further or other charge or amount for any examination, service, brokerage, expense, fee, or bonus or otherwise shall be directly or indirectly charged, contracted for, or received.[521]

The Small Loan Act was generally construed strictly, and thus such language precluded the imposition of any charge not specifically authorized, including credit insurance premiums.[522] This strict language, moreover, raised the related question of whether small loan licensees could retain commissions, even assuming the insurance sale was authorized. One early court allowed the creditor to require insurance as security, but held that it must be purchased from an outside insurer.[523] Some states permitted tie-in sales, but prohibited commissions;[524] others authorized them as compensation for services rendered.[525]

Perhaps in reaction to adverse legal developments, small loan acts were amended specifically to authorize credit life, disability and property insurance charges, to provide that the premiums were not considered interest, and that profit to the creditor from the insurance sale should not be considered interest.[526] However, this was also the era when regulation of credit insurance was strengthening, as with the adoption of the NAIC Model Credit Insurance Act, which required approval of premium rates. Such statutes must be read in *pari materia*, so that the rate regulation is not rendered meaningless. Thus the language of statutes which exclude insurance profits from the definition of interest can only be

---

Ins. Co., 246 S.W.2d 666, 671 (Tex. Civ. App. 1951) (commissions from writing an unauthorized type of insurance constitute interest).

517 Cope v. Aetna Fin. Co. of Maine, 412 F.2d 635 (1st Cir. 1969), *on remand* 304 F. Supp. 817 (D. Me. 1969).

518 *Id.* 412 F.2d at 641.

519 *See* § 8.2.3.1, *supra.*

520 *See* § 7.3, *supra.*

521 Sixth Draft of Uniform Small Loan Law, § 13, *reprinted in* Hubacheck, Annotations on Small Loan Laws 70–80 (1938).

522 *Ex parte* New Fin., Ltd., 284 Ala. 374, 225 So. 2d 782, 784 (1969); Sunderland v. Day, 12 Ill. 2d 50, 145 N.E.2d 39 (1957); Home Fin. v. Padgett, 54 So. 2d 813, 817 (La. Ct. App. 1951). *See also* Hawkins v. Thorp Credit & Thrift Co., 441 N.W.2d 470 (Minn. 1989) (interpreting Minnesota Regulated Loan Act, which evolved from the state's small loan act; court interpreted language restricting insurance sales to prohibit the sale of non-credit insurance); *see* § 9.3.1.2, *infra.* A minority of states, however, allowed credit insurance premiums under the rationale that credit insurance was a collateral transaction for security.

523 Martorano v. Capitol Fin. Co., 289 N.Y. 21, 43 N.E.2d 705 (1942). *See generally* Vernon, *Regulated Credit Life and Disability Insurance and the Small Loan*, 29 N.Y.U.L. Rev. 1098, 1109–10 (1954); *Credit Insurance: Abuse and Reform*, 10 B.C. Ind. & Com. L. Rev. 439, 441–42 (1969).

524 *See* Mors, *Small Loan Laws and Credit Insurance*, 1954 Ins. L.J. 778, 792; Vernon, *Regulated Credit Life and Disability Insurance and the Small Loan*, 29 N.Y.U.L. Rev. 1098, 1117 n.80 (1954).

525 *Credit Insurance: Abuse and Reform*, 10 B.C. Ind. & Com. L. Rev. 439, 442 (1969).

526 *E.g.*, Ariz. Rev. Stat. § 6-636(H).

rationally interpreted to mean that authorized commissions from authorized insurance premiums are excluded from interest.[527]

Some states provided that the authorized premium was limited to the "actual cost of any premium paid."[528] Such language has been interpreted to mean the cost of insurance to the small loan licensee, exclusive of the licensee's profit.[529] One court noted that the authorized interest rate for small loan licensees is quite high as it is, and the legislature would have authorized additional commissions if it so desired.[530] (Two state supreme courts have rejected that view, however, holding that premiums commonly encompass commissions, and creditors may charge the maximum premium rate irrespective of the commissions.[531]) Other states in fact did specifically regulate creditor profit; some clearly designate retained commissions as interest.[532] Nearly one half the states now have set limits on creditor compensation.[533] In a California case, the state's authority to impose

such caps was upheld.[534] The court held that the reverse compensation and captive market factors create influences "detrimental to insureds if left uncontrolled," and that limiting compensation is an appropriate means to assure that the insurance cost is reasonable in relation to the benefits.[535] Apparently only a few states strictly enforce compensation caps,[536] so it is not improbable that these ceilings are being violated. If so, the excess commission would be unauthorized, and thus should be considered interest,[537] subject to whatever penalties are provided for excess charges.[538] Examining charges for force-placed property insurance (not a rate-regulated insurance), one court has held that the commissions, kickbacks or rebates given to the creditor from the premium are interest under the National Bank Act, as is interest on the excess premium.[539]

Another possible source of limitation on creditors commissions may be found in insurance laws. The Mississippi

---

527 Cope v. Aetna Fin. Co. of Maine, 412 F.2d 635, 642 (1st Cir. 1969); Bank of Winnfield & Trust v. United States, 540 F. Supp. 219 (W.D. La. 1982) (fact that creditor is authorized to sell insurance does not implicitly authorize it to retain commissions from sales where such is prohibited); Hatridge v. Home Life & Accident Ins. Co., 246 S.W.2d 666 (Tex. Civ. App. 1951); *see also* Bailey v. Defenbaugh & Co. of Cleveland, Inc., 513 F. Supp. 232 (N.D. Miss. 1981); Browder v. Hanley-Dawson Cadillac, 379 N.E.2d 1206, 1212 (Ill. Ct. App. 1978) (claim survived motion to dismiss). *Cf.* Hawkins v. Thorp Credit & Thrift Co., 441 N.W.2d 470 (Minn. 1989) (sale of non-credit life insurance, not specifically authorized by the Regulated Loan Act, is prohibited).

528 *E.g.*, Miss. Code Ann. § 75-67-121.

529 Bailey v. Defenbaugh & Co. of Cleveland, Inc., 513 F. Supp. 232 (N.D. Miss. 1981). A similar claim survived a Motion to Dismiss in Browder v. Hanley-Dawson Cadillac, 62 Ill. App. 3d 623, 379 N.E.2d 1206, 1212 (1978).

530 Bailey v. Defenbaugh & Co. of Cleveland, Inc., 513 F. Supp. 232, 242, 243 (N.D. Miss. 1981).

531 Spears v. Colonial Bank of Alabama, 514 So. 2d 814 (Ala. 1987) (Ala. Code § 5-10-20 provides "[t]he charge to the debtor for any such insurance shall not exceed the authorized premium permitted for such coverages." Where premiums charged were within lawful maximum established by state banking department, fact that creditors received 50% commission from the premium did not violate § 5-19-20); Tew v. Dixieland Fin. Co., 527 So. 2d 665 (Miss. 1988) (creditor may charge maximum authorized premium rate under Small Loan Regulatory Law regardless of commission paid to creditor; premiums allowable are those "usually and customarily paid for life insurance" and it is customary for sellers in state to charge the maximum premium; also definition of premium may include commission to seller; *But cf. In re* Milbourne, 108 B.R. 522, 540, 543 n.8 (Bankr. E.D. Pa. 1989) (indicating in dicta that it was a strategic error on the borrower's part to fail to allege lender's receipt of substantial commissions as improper finance charges).

532 *See* Equitable Life Assurance Soc. of U.S. v. Ins. Comm., 251 Md. 143, 246 A.2d 604 (1968).

533 California, Colorado, Georgia, Illinois, Indiana, Maine, Maryland, Massachusetts (only state-chartered banks), Michigan, Mississippi, Missouri, Montana, Nebraska, Nevada, New York, Ohio, Oklahoma, Pennsylvania, South Dakota, Tennessee, Utah,

Washington, Wyoming; Arkansas; *see* Fagg, Credit Life and Disability Insurance 534–536 (1986).

534 Credit Ins. Gen. Agents Assoc. v. Payne, 83 Cal. App. 3d 870, 148 Cal. Rptr. 141 (1978).

535 *Id.* at 148 Cal. Rptr. 143–44. The captive market factor results because the borrower cannot shop for credit insurance. It is not sold separately from its related credit transaction, and the creditor generally offers only a single insurer. Furthermore, the borrower may be a poor credit risk with limited options. *Id.* at 143–44, n.2.

536 Fagg, Credit Life and Disability Insurance 377 (1986). *Cf.* Shellman v. Investors Nat'l Life Ins. Co., Clearinghouse No. 45,774 (Super. Ct., Richmond Cty., Ga., defendants' motion for summary judgment denied Aug. 16, 1990) (though Georgia has a 40% commission cap, evidence in connection with this summary judgment showed the defendant insurer paid 55% to 90% commissions to one of its creditors. The case and companion cases are discussed in more detail at § 8.4.2.1.4, *supra*).

537 *See* Bank of Winnfield & Trust v. United States, 540 F. Supp. 219 (W.D. La. 1982) (fact that creditor is authorized to sell insurance does not implicitly authorize it to retain commissions from sales where such is prohibited); Hatridge v. Home Life & Accident Ins. Co., 246 S.W.2d 666 (Tex. Civ. App. 1951); *see also* Bailey v. Defenbaugh & Co. of Cleveland, Inc., 513 F. Supp. 232 (N.D. Miss. 1981); Browder v. Hanley-Dawson Cadillac, 379 N.E.2d 1206, 1212 (Ill. Ct. App. 1978) (claim survived motion to dismiss). If excessive compensation is retained by a small loan licensee, even a provision holding that profit from insurance sales is not deemed a violation of any other law would not immunize the lender. That provision must be read *in pari materia* with statutes regulating the cost of the insurance to mean that only authorized benefits from an authorized premium is excluded from interest. *Cf.* Cope v. Aetna Fin., 412 F.2d 635, 641–43 (1st Cir. 1969).

538 In some jurisdictions, however, a violation of a regulation may not offer the same remedies as a statutory violation. *See, e.g.*, Robinson v. Central Loan & Fin. Corp., 609 F.2d 170 (5th Cir. 1980). For another approach to challenging insurance charges with excessive commissions, see § 8.4.2.1.4, *supra*.

539 Kenty v. Bank One, Columbus, N.A., 1992 WL 170605 (S.D. Ohio Apr. 23, 1992), *aff'd in part, rev'd in part on other grounds*, 92 F.3d 384 (6th Cir. 1996). (The latter point recognizes that, since the capitalized premium contains hidden interest, the effect is to compound interest. See § 7.4.2, *supra*.)

insurance code, for example, prohibited acceptance of a commission by one not licensed as an insurance agent. Since a corporate-creditor could not be licensed as an insurance agent, the creditor could not retain the commissions. (The creditors generally had one or more employees licensed as agents, but it was the corporate creditor that retained the commissions, not the licensed individual agents, thereby violating the law). However, the court recognized that the legislature created a conflict in other legislation (and administrative regulations) recognizing that corporate creditors do receive commissions from the sale of credit insurance. The court resolved the conundrum by holding that it was illegal for the unlicensed corporate creditor to receive the commissions, but making its ruling prospective, thus giving the legislature and administrative agencies time to adjust to the ruling.[540]

8.5.3.3 Excess Coverage As Illegal Overcharge

8.5.3.3.1 Level term credit life insurance

Even if premium rates are properly calculated, a usury claim may lie if the insurance coverage exceeds that permitted by law. As § 8.3.1.2, *supra* explained, writing level life on an installment loan provides excessive coverage, because it always insures the full amount of the original loan, and does not reflect the fact that the loan balance declines. Since it does provide this excessive coverage, it is much more expensive than declining term life.[541] Consequently, most states prohibit the writing of level term credit life insurance. The NAIC Model Act, for example, provides that where the debt "is repayable in substantially equal installments, the amount of insurance shall at no time exceed the scheduled or actual amount of unpaid indebtedness, whichever is greater."[542] Where a state prohibits level life, a creditor charging the borrower the higher level life premium would be charging in excess of that permitted by law, and thus would be vulnerable to a usury claim under the same analysis as if it were engaged in a rate overcharge.[543] If, however, the statute does not specifically prohibit level term, the courts are unlikely to infer such a prohibition.[544]

8.5.3.3.2 Amount of coverage

Courts have long recognized that usury may exist when lenders charge borrowers for coverage in an amount "greater than the amount of the loan with a purpose of increasing the proportion of charges to the amount of money lent."[545] Some regulations similarly restrict credit life and disability coverage to the amount and term of the indebtedness. This limitation is found in both the credit insurance codes,[546] and often in the special credit regulatory laws.[547] Charges for any greater coverage would be in excess of that authorized by law, and therefore subject to penalties for

---

540 Tew v. Dixieland Fin., Inc., 527 So. 2d 665 (Miss. 1988).

541 In the event a claim is made, there would be a surplus which should be paid to the borrower's estate.

542 Model Bill to Provide for the Regulation of Credit Life Ins. and Credit Accident and Health Ins., National Ass'n of Ins. Comm'rs, Model Regulatory Service § 4A(1) (NIARS Corp., 1984).

543 *See* § 8.5.3.2, *supra*.

544 Mason v. Service Loan & Fin. Co., 128 Ga. App. 828, 198 S.E.2d 391 (1973).

545 Western Guaranty Loan Co. v. Dean, 309 S.W.2d 857, 862 (Tex. Civ. App. 1957); Industrial Fin. Serv. Co. v. Riley, 295 S.W.2d 498, 506 (Tex. Civ. App. 1956), *rev'd in part on other grounds*, 302 S.W.2d 652 (Tex. 1957).

546 *E.g.*, Model Bill to Provide for the Regulation of Credit Life Ins. and Credit Accident and Health Ins., National Ass'n of Ins. Comm'rs, Model Regulatory Service §§ 4(A) (Life), 4(B) (A&H), 5 (Term) (NIARS Corp., 1984).

547 *E.g.*, Ala. Code §§ 5-18-17 (small loan), 5-19-20 (Credit Code). *See also* Gartman v. The Independent Life and Accident Ins. Co., 1998 U.S. Dist. LEXIS 22069 (S.D. Ala. Oct. 9, 1998) (class certified, by consent, in case challenging insurance charges based on total of payments, relying on *McCullar* decision); McCullar v. Universal Underwriters Life Ins. Co., 687 So. 2d 156 (Ala. 1996) (plurality) (interpreting Ala. law to mandate net coverage, not gross coverage, as agencies had interpreted it) (the original opinion found at 1995 WL 577025 (Ala. 1995) was withdrawn upon rehearing; the substituted opinion affirms the earlier decision and, in addition, rejects the defendants' argument that the decision should not have retroactive effect; the lengthy dissent claims the retroactive application will damage the Alabama economy "beyond estimate" and "only allows for predatory attacks on legitimate businesses. . . . The termites are swarming" (meaning that the consumer bar will feed on such creditors: what a rare reversal!); the dissent includes an appendix listing every other state's definition of total indebtedness for purposes of calculating credit insurance premiums). *But see* Gall v. American Heritage Life Ins. Co., 3 F. Supp. 2d 1344 (S.D. Ala. 1998) (court states it is not bound by plurality in *McCullar* and, agreeing with the dissent, finds that insurance can be calculated in total of payments); Dixon v. Ford Motor Credit, 2000 U.S. Dist. LEXIS 7934 (E.D. La. May 31, 2000) (allegations that Louisiana law mandates net coverage, that the terms of the insurance were not properly disclosed, and that excessive commissions were paid to sell the insurance product warrants denial of motion for summary judgment on RICO claim), *subsequent proceedings*, 137 F. Supp. 2d 702 (E.D. La. 2000) (RICO claim dismissed; supplemental state law claims dismissed); Liberty Bank & Trust Co. v. Splane, 959 P.2d 600 (Okla. Ct. App. 1998) (court construed provision in U.C.C.C. restricting the amount of the permissible credit insurance to that which does not "exceed the debt" and another provision in Oklahoma insurance law restricting the amount of such insurance to "the approximate unpaid balance of the loan" to allow insurance premiums to be calculated on the total of payments; court specifically rejects the plurality in *Mccullar*); Robertson v. PHF Life Ins. Co., 702 So. 2d 555 (Fla. Dist. Ct. App. 1997) (with no discussion, court holds that Florida law allows credit life insurance to be calculated based upon the total of payments rather than the principal amount of the loan).

excess charges applicable under the statute governing the transaction,[548] or common law claims.[549] It is clear that the creditor, not the insurer is responsible for excessive coverage, unlike the situation with respect to excessive rates, where there is an argument that the insurer is responsible.[550] This is because the creditor is the one who determines the amount of coverage.

Defining the appropriate limits of coverage for an open-end credit account, in which the amount of debt varies, is more difficult. The UCCC provides that coverage on an open-end account should be "reasonably commensurate with the amount of debt as it exists from time to time."[551] An opinion of the Kansas Attorney General defines open-end credit to include lines of credit.[552] Thus, if a borrower has opened a $10,000 line of credit to have available in case of emergencies, but generally carries a balance of less than $2,000, any credit insurance should relate to the $2,000 balance.

8.5.3.4 Special credit property issues

8.5.3.4.1 Scope of insurable interest

Credit property insurance has been the source of particular abuse because it is rarely regulated. In 2001, the NAIC finally adopted a credit personal property insurance model act.[553] If enacted by the states, this act will curb some of the abuses in this market, most especially excessive cost of this type of insurance. Its key provisions are described in §§ 8.3.5.1 and 8.4.2.2.1, *supra*. Currently, most credit insurance codes do not address this type of insurance at all. Furthermore, unlike credit life and disability insurance, creditors typically are permitted to require borrowers to purchase property insurance to protect collateral, although creditors generally must give the borrower a choice of insurance provider.[554] Excess property insurance may be

manifested in a number of different ways. The creditor may sell it in transactions where it is not permitted by law; it may sell coverage for an amount greater than the collateral (or the debt) is worth; it may insure property which is not collateral; it may add additional types of coverage beyond that which is authorized or necessary; or it may insure a phantom risk.

A number of states' *credit* statutes, however, place some limitations on the sale of credit property insurance. Some states prohibit creditors from requiring credit property insurance in conjunction with very small loans.[555] Other states prohibit writing credit property insurance at all unless the amount financed (exclusive of insurance charges) and the value of the collateral each exceed a specified minimum.[556] Other credit statutes more generally require that credit property insurance charges be "reasonable" in relation to both the value of the insured property and the amount of the loan[557] or, depending on the statute, to the greater[558] or lesser[559] of these two amounts. Some states require that coverage be reasonable in relation to the risk, not to exceed the loan amount.[560] The UCCC prohibits property insurance charges unless the insurance covers: a) a substantial risk of loss or damage to property related to the transaction; b) the amount, terms and conditions of the insurance are reasonable in relation to the character and value of the property, and the term is reasonable in relation to the terms of credit, i.e. if it is customary and closely coincides with the term of the credit transaction.[561] Read together with the UCCC's general credit insurance provisions limiting credit insurance coverage generally to the value of the debt, the statute requires that the amount of property insurance coverage is limited to *the lesser of* the amount of the debt or the value of the property.[562]

A number of statutes specify that property insurance can only be written on collateral. The UCCC provides that property insurance can be written on property "related to the credit transaction."[563] Thus, property insurance written on

---

548 An insurance charge may purchase some hidden *types* of additional coverage, which may not be authorized, and would, therefore constitute interest. *See, e.g.*, the discussion of force-placed insurance in § 8.5.3.4, *infra*.

549 *See, e.g.*, McCullar v. Universal Underwriters Life Ins. Co., 687 So. 2d 156 (Ala. 1996), discussed in § 8.7.3, *infra*.

550 *See* § 8.5.3.2.1, *supra*.

551 U.C.C.C. § 4.202.

552 Opinion of Kansas Att'y Gen., No. 88-13, Consumer Cred. Guide (CCH) ¶ 95,910 (Feb. 2, 1988). The opinion includes lines of credit within the scope of the definition of "open-end credit," or revolving credit, and distinguishes them from "credit commitments," in which the appropriate insurance coverage may combine both the current debt and the limits of the commitment.

553 *See* NAIC Credit Personal Property Insurance Model Act, Clearinghouse No. 53,564.

554 *E.g.*, Ala. Code § 5-19-20(a), (e); U.C.C.C. §§ 2-201, 3-201 (1968); U.C.C.C. § 2-501(2)(a) (1974).
    Cf. Sunwest Bank of El Paso v. Gutierrez, 819 S.W.2d 673 (Tex. App. 1991) (fact that consumer had not authorized creditor's purchase of VSI insurance did not, by itself, turn premium into interest).

555 Ga. Comp. R. & Regs. §§ 120-1-11.04(3) and 120-1-14-17(3); Robinson v. Central Loan & Fin. Corp., 609 F.2d 170, 175 (5th Cir. 1980).

556 *E.g.*, Ala. Code § 5-19-20(g); U.C.C.C. § 4-301.

557 *E.g.*, Ga. Code Ann. § 7-3-14(3) (industrial loan); U.C.C.C. § 4-301.

558 *E.g.*, Ariz. Rev. Stat. § 6-636(E) (consumer loan act).
    But see § 8.5.3.4.3 on "phantom coverage," *infra*.

559 *E.g.*, Bailey v. Defenbaugh & Co. of Cleveland, Inc., 513 F. Supp. 232, 241 (D. Miss. 1981) (interpreting Miss. Code Ann § 75-67-121 (Regs. VI(A)(2))).

560 *E.g.*, Tenn. Code Ann. § 45-5-305(3)(C). *See also* § 8.5.3.4.3 on "phantom coverage," *infra*.

561 U.C.C.C. § 4-301.

562 Opinion of Kansas Att'y Gen., No. 87-3, Consumer Cred. Guide (CCH) ¶ 95,980 (Jan. 9, 1987); *modified by* opinion of Kansas Att'y Gen., No. 87-47, Consumer Cred. Guide (CCH) ¶ 95,981 (Mar. 12, 1987).

563 U.C.C.C. § 4-301(1)(a). *See* Department of Fin. Inst. v. Beneficial Fin. Co. of Madison, 426 N.E.2d 711, 713 (Ind. Ct. App. 1981).

non-collateral property should be an excessive charge where a statute limits the specified authorized charges to an inclusive list.[564] Interpreting UCCC language permitting property insurance to cover a risk of loss on "property related to the credit transaction," and requiring that insurance be of benefit to the borrower, the Kansas Attorney General has ruled that a creditor cannot sell property insurance on household goods unless there is a purchase-money security interest in the household goods which would be valid under the FTC Credit Practices Rule;[565] if there is no valid security interest, it cannot be property "related to the credit transaction." Further, a creditor cannot shortcut this requirement by taking a valid purchase money-security interest in *some* household goods, and then naming itself as loss payee on a policy insuring *all* household goods.[566] Property insurance cannot be "required"—either explicitly or implicitly—where the lender has no interest in the insured property, as in an unsecured loan,[567] or where the coverage extends beyond the collateral.[568] Other statutes authorize credit property on security if it is sold at "standard" rates, reasonably insuring against loss considering the circumstances, and if sold through licensed agents.[569] Generally, charging premiums for excess coverage should constitute usury,[570] though only if it is established that the excess coverage added cost to the premium charged the borrower.[571]

8.5.3.4.2 Force-placed insurance

The possibility of insurance premiums paying for extra unauthorized types of coverage has arisen in the context of "force-placed" insurance. In automobile-secured loans, borrowers are typically required to furnish proof of insurance (in favor of the creditor) and to maintain it throughout the loan. If the borrower does not, the creditor usually is authorized by the contract to purchase insurance and add the charge to the borrower's balance. This type of insurance has recently crept into the mortgage lending context as well.[572]

A number of cases have been filed in which borrowers allege that the creditor has force-placed insurance with extraneous endorsements. In addition to the ordinary coverage against damage to the collateral, conversion, embezzlement, mechanics liens, premium deficiency, repossession expense, repossession storage expense and repossessed vehicle coverages were also purchased. Such extra types of coverage may not be authorized by either statute or contract, are unnecessary to protect the collateral, and the premiums attributable to them would be considered interest.[573]

8.5.3.4.3 Phantom coverage

Excess coverage may also be argued in situations where the coverage buys illusory benefits. This may occur, for example, in connection with open-end accounts, where the account balance reflects non-durable purchases, such as lunches at the department store restaurant, tune-ups at the auto-center, or cosmetics. Phantom coverage may also occur where the property insured is worth less than the total of payments. Coverage in the amount of the total of payments may be illusory in part, if the policy limits liability to the value of the property. In such a case, coverage in the full loan amount would not meet a statutory requirement that the insurance be reasonable in relation to the risk, even if the statute would otherwise permit coverage to equal the total

564 *See* § 8.5.3.2, *supra*; *see also* § 8.5.4.4, *infra*.
565 Opinion of Kansas Attorney General, No. 87-3, Consumer Cred. Guide (CCH) ¶ 95,980 (Jan. 9, 1987), *modified by* Opinion of Kansas Att'y Gen., No. 87-47, Consumer Cred. Guide (CCH) ¶ 95,981 (Mar. 12, 1987). *See* § 8.5.4.4, *infra* for a brief discussion of what may constitute a valid security interest under the FTC rule.
566 Opinion of Kansas Attorney General, No. 87-3, Consumer Cred. Guide (CCH) ¶ 95,980 (Jan. 9, 1987), *modified by* Opinion of Kansas Att'y Gen., No. 87-47, Consumer Cred. Guide (CCH) ¶ 95,981 (Mar. 12, 1987).
567 *In re* Bogan, 281 F. Supp. 242, 251 (W.D. Tenn. 1968).
568 Opinion of Kansas Att'y Gen., No. 87-3, Consumer Cred. Guide (CCH) ¶ 95,980 (Jan. 9, 1987), *modified by* Opinion of Kansas Att'y Gen., No. 87-47, Consumer Cred. Guide (CCH) ¶ 95,981 (Mar. 12, 1987). (Selling property insurance to cover non-collateral property is one of the insurance packing tricks. *See* § 8.5.4.4, *infra*.)
569 Cal. Fin. Code § 22313 (consumer loans).
570 Bailey v. Defenbaugh & Co. of Cleveland, 513 F. Supp. 232, 241–242 (N.D. Miss. 1981). *See also* Western Guaranty Loan Co. v. Dean, 309 S.W.2d 857 (Tex. Civ. App. 1957).
571 *See* Coner v. Morris S. Berman, Unltd., 65 Md. App. 514, 501 A.2d 458, 462 (1985).
572 *See, e.g.*, Kirkland v. Midland Mortgage Co., CV198-083 (S.D. Ga. Jan. 4, 2000) (defendant's motion for reconsideration of denial of summary judgment and grant of class certification denied; motion for certification of interlocutory appeal granted), Clearinghouse No. 52,504 and 52,504A.
573 *See, e.g.*, Kenty v. Bank One, Columbus, N.A., 1992 WL 170605 (S.D. Ohio Apr. 23, 1992) (interest under the National Bank Act), *aff'd in part, rev'd in part on other grounds*, 92 F.3d 384 (6th Cir. 1996) (without disturbing the ruling that the excess premium cost would constitute interest, court held that there was no usury because the national bank defendant was entitled to most favored lender status, and thus was entitled to assert the unlimited interest privilege granted Ohio thrifts under Ohio law. *NB*: *See* §§ 3.4.3, *supra* for discussion of most favored lender, 8.3.5.4.2, *supra* for a longer discussion of force-placed insurance, and 9.2.8, *infra* for an argument as to why, even without an applicable interest rate ceiling, the excess fees as interest might nonetheless be actionable); *contra* Doe v. Norwest Bank Minnesota, N.A., 107 F.3d 1297 (8th Cir. 1997); Boyd v. Society Bank & Trust, Clearinghouse No. 47,939A (Ct. Com. Pleas, Ohio, *order on motion to dismiss*, Oct. 29, 1991) (state usury law). *See generally* National Consumer Law Center, Unfair and Deceptive Acts and Practices § 5.3.11 (6th ed. 2004 and Supp.) for an overview of other issues and causes of action relating to force-placed insurance. A variety of challenges are taken in, *e.g.*, *Kenty*, *supra*; Kenty v. Transamerica Premium Ins. Co., 650 N.E.2d 863 (Ohio 1995); and National Consumer Law Center, Consumer Law Pleadings No. 1, Ch. 2 (Cumulative CD-Rom and Index Guide) (selected documents in a force-placed insurance case).

amount of the obligation.[574] Even in states where the statute specifically authorizes property insurance coverage related to either the value of the property or the amount of the loan whichever is greater,[575] excess coverage should be argued in this situation. Such a provision can only rationally be interpreted to allow full coverage of the property's value even if it exceeds the total of payments, as, for example, where a $5,000 car is offered as security on a $1,000 loan. To hold otherwise would require the assumption that the legislature intended to authorize the sale of phantom insurance, an irrational result not lightly to be reached under principles of statutory construction. Some of these excess coverage issues arise in the context of insurance packing situations, and will be dealt with more fully in the following subsection.

8.5.4 Insurance Packing

8.5.4.1 Overview

Insurance packing refers to increasing a consumer's debt by padding or "packing" the amount financed through the sale of expensive, unnecessary and often unwanted products, such as insurance. This is not a new phenomenon, nor is its judicial condemnation new.[576] The systematic practice of packing by multi-state lenders, however, attracted the attention of the public and some regulators in the mid-1980s, and significant litigation ensued.[577]

There are a number of ways insurance packing can take place. However it is done, as the examples below show, insurance packing has a dramatic effect on borrowers. Their debt is dramatically increased for largely (or wholly) illusory benefits, and they may risk the loss of their homes. In larger home equity loans, credit insurance premiums of as much as $10,000 may be packed into a loan, adding considerably to the risk of default.

A number of claims can be raised to challenge packing practices: usury, UDAP, breach of fiduciary duty, RICO. Some of these theories are discussed below and some will be discussed in later sections.[578] It should be noted, as well, that the types of coercive sales practices described in § 8.5.2, *supra* often are utilized in connection with insurance packing, so the theories and evidentiary suggestions discussed in that section should also be considered in challenging packing schemes. The excessive charge challenges discussed in § 8.5.3, *supra* are also often warranted.

It should also be noted that insurance packing often goes hand-in-hand with flipping abuses (frequent refinancing), as insurance is one of the elements of the refinancing price escalator, described further in §§ 6.1, 6.3, *supra*.[579]

8.5.4.2 Packing As an Equity-Skimming Tool to Exceed Critical Statutory Thresholds

The primary motivation for insurance packing is increased profits through the sale of additional profitable products. But in some cases there may be additional forces driving the effort. It is a remarkably effective tool to use in equity-skimming,[580] and there may be statutory thresholds that a creditor may wish to cross to get to greener pastures.

---

574 *See* Opinion of Kansas Att'y Gen., No. 87-3, Consumer Cred. Guide (CCH) ¶ 95,980 (Jan. 9, 1987) *modified by* Opinion of Kansas Att'y Gen., No. 87-47, Consumer Cred. Guide (CCH) ¶ 95,981 (Mar. 12, 1987) (where value of property is less than the debt, coverage should be limited to property value, even if policy would pay in excess of value of property, resulting in surplus; public policy forbids this result, as creditor could benefit in excess of its rights under security interest; even if borrower received surplus, public policy should forbid this, as borrower may have unknowingly contracted for insurance neither needed or desired).

575 *E.g.*, Ariz. Rev. Stat. § 6-636(E).

576 *See, e.g.*, Tribble v. State, 80 S.E.2d 711 (Ga. Ct. App. 1954) (credit insurance was 34% and 42% of the face amount of two notes, respectively, the creditor required both life and disability insurance be purchased through him, and he retained 85% of the premium as commission, *inter alia*).

577 *See* Bogdanich, *Unwanted Extras: Irate Borrowers Accuse ITT's Loan Companies of Deceptive Practices*, Wall St. J. Feb. 26, 1985, pg. 1; California v. ITT Fin. Servs., Clearinghouse No. 44,801S and T, No. 656038-0 (Calif. Super. Ct., Alameda Cty., complaint and settlement filed Sept. 21, 1989); State v. Aetna Fin. Co., Case No. 84 CV0103, Clearinghouse No. 36,151 (Wis. Cir. Ct., Dane Cty., Feb. 20, 1984); Memorandum of Agreement between Colo. Att'y Gen. and Aetna Fin. Co., Clearinghouse No. 38,916 (Apr. 16, 1985); Settlement Agreement between Iowa Att'y Gen. and Thorp Credit, announced June 6, 1984. *See* § 8.7.4, *infra* for a more complete listing of insurance packing case documents available through National Clearinghouse for Legal Services.

578 *See* § 8.7, *infra. See also* Ch. 11, *infra*.

579 Some of the current litigation challenges the overreaching from the combined impact of insurance packing and frequent flipping. *See, e.g.*, Emery v. American General Fin., Inc., 71 F.3d 1343 (7th Cir. 1995) (flipping can state a cause of action under RICO) (see full discussion of this case and its subsequent history in § 12.7, *supra*). *See also* Hager v. American Gen. Fin., Inc., 37 F. Supp. 2d 778 (S.D. W. Va. 1999) (flipping case where multiple insurances were sold at each refinancing; court denied lender's motion for summary judgment on the unconscionability claim based upon borrowers' allegation that defendants induced them to enter into high interest rate loans and to mortgage their residence without realizing the magnitude of the debt they were incurring or the ramifications of these transactions); McCrae v. Commercial Credit Corp., 892 F. Supp. 1385 (M.D. Ala. 1995) (defendant unsuccessfully tried to remove plaintiff's state court action challenging refinancing and credit insurance practices to federal court); Dean v. American General Fin., Inc., 191 B.R. 463 (M.D. Ala. 1996) (same). For a description of the ways in which the costs of a loan blossom when it is constantly refinanced, see affidavit filed in Hager v. American Gen. Fin., Inc. in Appx. L, *infra*.

580 *See* § 11.5.1, *infra*. In defining the triggering charges for the Home Ownership and Equity Protection Act of 1994, Pub. L. No. 103-325, 108 Stat. 2160 (Sept. 23, 1994), Congress gave the FRB authority to add additional charges to the list of trigger

One of the more subtle mechanisms by which insurance packing can be maximized is to stretch a loan's term, since the cost of the premiums increases with the term of the loan. Consider the following actual fact situation:[581] a customer wished to borrow approximately $1,400, and informed the lender she could afford a $75 per month payment. The creditor could have written the loan for a three-year term, a common term for such a small amount. In a three-year loan at the lender's already ample 28.09% rate, the borrower's loan would have looked like this:

Net Proceeds to Borrower	$1,440.22
Credit Life Insurance	49.42
Credit Disability	96.31
Property Insurance	114.05
AMOUNT FINANCED	$1,700.00
36 Mo. Payments @	70.40
Finance Charge	834.43
TOTAL OF PAYMENTS	$2,543.43

Such a loan would have served the customer's needs: $1,400 to her with less than a $75 monthly payment. The lender would have had a fully insured loan, and a very high return of 28.09%.

But the lender was not satisfied with that. Rather, the lender (not the borrower) decided to write the loan for a six-year term. As the loan was finally written, it looked like this:

Net Proceeds to Borrower	$1,442.23
Credit Life Insurance	210.60
Credit Disability Insurance	275.40
Property Insurance	486.00
Real Estate Security Fees	184.00
AMOUNT FINANCED	$2,598.23
72 Mo. Payments @	75.00
Finance Charge	2,801.77
TOTAL OF PAYMENTS	$5,400.00

For two dollars more in loan proceeds than she would have in a three-year transaction, the customer received slightly higher monthly payments, was obligated to make those monthly payments twice as long, and more than doubled her debt. Further, as one can guess from the real estate security fees, the loan was secured by the customer's home.

This example shows the need to look behind the mere numbers on a document. If one did just the rate calculations, one would find that this lender did not charge a higher rate per $100 than allowed under applicable law. But that should not be the end of the analysis. It is important to ask why a lender does something unusual like this. The unusually long

term and high fees in relation to the borrower's proceeds should raise suspicions. The extra interest and extra commissions on higher premiums may be ample motivation alone, but in this case, there was a further reason for padding the amount financed with huge insurance premiums. The state in which this loan took place prohibited security interests in consumers' residences unless the amount financed exceeded $2,000.[582] The padding of the amount financed took the borrower's loan over the magic threshold, from $1,700 to $2,598, and placed the borrower's home at risk for $1,440 in loan proceeds. The insurance padding took place to provide the creditor with excessive collateral— excessive as defined by the legislature in enacting such a threshold. Though that loan, which in effect embezzled $3,000 from the borrower, was ruled unconscionable,[583] it was small potatoes compared to a Mississippi lender who, by the same trick, skimmed an extra $23,000 out of a home equity loan.[584]

There may be other statutory thresholds which a lender may try to cross by packing a loan with insurance premiums. For example, the UCCC permits a seller to take a purchase-money security interest in goods sold, but in no other

---

[582] Several states have limitations on real estate as security in connection with small loan amounts. *See, e.g.,* Fla. Stat. Ann. § 516.031(1); U.C.C.C. §§ 2-307(a), 3-301 (1974).

[583] Besta v. Beneficial Loan Co., 855 F.2d 532 (8th Cir. 1988). *See* § 8.7.5, *infra.*

[584] Compare a $9250 loan, written as a 10-year loan and packed with nearly *$12,000* worth of insurance premiums, to a fully insured 5-year loan of the same amount.

	AS WRITTEN (10 Year)	WITHOUT STRETCHING THE LOAN TERM (5 years)
PROCEEDS TO BORROWER	$ 9,241.22	$ 9,261.66
Life Insurance Premium	$ 7,277.92	$ 1,655.40
Disability Insurance Premium	$ 3,719.52	$ 1,282.94
Note Principal	$20,288.66	$12,250.00
AMOUNT OF MONTHLY PAYMENTS	$ 378.00	$ 344.89
Loan Term	120 months	60 months
Interest at Maximum Rate Permitted	$25,071.34	$ 8,442.52
TOTAL OF PAYMENTS	$43,360	$20,692.52
APR	18.94%	22.94%

The combination of term-stretching and insurance packing thus netted this creditor nearly $23,000 extra for nothing. (Mississippi is one of the few states which allows the unnecessary and expensive level life, *see* § 8.3.1.2, *supra,* and which authorizes among the highest rates in the country. [*Note:* that the 5-year term has a higher APR. Mississippi usury statute had a 4-tier split rate ceiling. On the 10-year loan, a larger portion of the principal was earning interest at the lowest 14% tier, thus lowering the APR, which is a blended rate. *See* § 4.3.4, *supra* for an explanation of split-rate interest ceilings.]) (NCLC case files).

---

charges if they are used to facilitate evasion of the statute. Credit insurance was specifically identified as one to watch. H.R. Conf. Rep. No. 652, 103d Cong. 2d Sess. 147, 159 (1994) (accompanying H.R. 3474).

[581] *See* Besta v. Beneficial Loan Co., 855 F.2d 532 (8th Cir. 1988).

personalty unless the debt meets a minimum amount.[585] Such padding may also be desirable to creditors in states which have deregulated all lending except for small loans. The lender might wish to pad the amount financed in order to increase the loan beyond the maximum small loan size, thus allowing the creditor freedom to charge whatever interest rate it chooses.

While a number of theories are appropriate for this kind of overreaching,[586] courts should look behind a facially proper transaction to see if otherwise legitimate charges are imposed in bad faith, to serve as a pretext for usury. In the six-year loan described above, it is hard to think of a "good faith" rationale for the lender's actions. In the past, courts have found charges, including insurance premiums, to be unreasonable and evasive in intent when viewed in relation to the *real* consideration to the borrower.[587] Courts, in finding usury in insurance coverage which exceeded the loan, have noted that the purpose and effect of such is to increase the proportion of the charges to the amount of money lent,[588] an impact and purpose similarly found in this kind of loan padding.

8.5.4.3 Packing with Sales of Non-Credit Insurance and Other Ancillary Products

The insurance packing practices of ITT Financial, challenged by consumers and the attorneys general in several states,[589] took a different form. A number of suits alleged that ITT Financial or its subsidiaries, usually unbeknownst to its customers, "packed" or loaded various types of expensive optional insurance onto consumer loans along with traditional credit insurance. Typically the debtor would request a loan in a specified amount. The lender would telephone back that the loan plus optional insurance had been approved with a stated monthly payment, never mentioning the total loan amount. When the debtor arrived at the lender's offices for the closing, all loan and insurance documents had been typed and intermingled, making them look like one transaction.

Actually, what many ITT Financial customers had purchased in addition to the loan was some combination of the following:

- Credit life insurance and credit accident and health insurance.
- "Unipay," a single premium policy covering certain types of accidental death and dismemberment until age 65. This policy is not credit insurance, and is unrelated to the credit life and A&H policies purchased. Because one premium payment keeps the policy in force until age 65, premiums cost as much as $475. Sometimes ITT Financial sold separate policies to the husband and the wife.
- "SPT-5," a 5-year term, single premium life insurance policy, again totally unrelated to the credit life policy. The single premium payment could cost as much as $523.
- "ITT Thrift Club" costing $24.50 that gives the debtor discounts on hotels, rental cars, and other purchases.
- Credit property insurance on household goods taken as collateral for the personal loan, even if the debtor already had property insurance on those goods, and often when the consumer had no idea that household goods would be required as collateral on the loan.
- Credit property insurance on household goods that were *not* collateral on the loan (in effect, "non-credit property insurance"); or excessive property insurance on collateral, the value of which had been artificially inflated.

Suits alleged that many debtors never realized that they were purchasing any insurance from ITT Financial lenders. Other debtors believed that they were buying just credit insurance, or thought the insurance was required because the papers were already made out. Loan officers faced with heavy insurance sales quotas used various techniques to persuade hesitant customers to sign up for insurance. For example, where debtors needed cash right away, loan officers might claim that retyping the papers would take three or four days, or that the loan would have to be resubmitted for approval.[590]

Because the prices for most of the insurance sold by ITT Financial and its subsidiaries was unregulated, one issue in the Wisconsin Attorney General's case[591] was whether such insurance premiums were unconscionably high. Not only were Aetna's customers purchasing large amounts of "optional insurance," but they were also financing these insurance payments at high small loan interest rates—23% APR

---

585 U.C.C.C. § 2-3301(1). Note also that the FTC Credit Practices Rule restricts the right of most lenders to take non-purchase money security interests in household goods, irrespective of amounts.

586 *See* § 8.7, Ch. 11, *infra.*

587 Home Fin. Co. v. Padgett, 54 So. 2d 813, 814–15 (La. Ct. App. 1951).

588 Western Guaranty Loan Co. v. Dean, 309 S.W.2d 857 (Tex. Civ. App. 1957); Industrial Fin. Serv. Co. v. Riley, 295 S.W.2d 498 (Tex. Civ. App. 1956), *rev'd in part on other grounds,* 302 S.W.2d 652 (Tex. 1957). *See also* Strickler v. State Auto Fin. Co., 220 Ark. 565, 249 S.W.2d 307 (1952) (premiums were 10% of principal); Wilson v. Whitworth, 197 Ark. 675, 125 S.W.2d 112 (1939) ($150 real proceeds, $3500 insurance required); Tribble v. State, 80 S.E.2d 711 (Ga. Ct. App. 1954).

589 *See* § 8.7.4, *infra,* for a complete listing of insurance packing case documents available through Clearinghouse.

590 For an example of some complaints, see James v. ITT Fin. Servs., Report of Prof. Robert Hartley, submitted in support of Plaintiff's Motion to Certify Class, Oct. 10, 1989, Clearinghouse No. 44,801X.

591 Case No. CV0103, Clearinghouse No. 36,151 (Wis. Cir. Ct., Dane Cty., Feb. 20, 1984).

in Wisconsin. (Insurance premium financing should be of-fered at lower interest rates than personal loans because of the risk-free nature of the premium loan. The lender can cancel the insurance upon debtor's default.)

The unconscionability of insurance packing schemes is revealed by their dramatic financial impact on borrowers. One ITT Financial customer asked to borrow $500. Her pre-prepared loan documents gave her $600 in proceeds, $120 in property insurance (for $2,000 coverage!), $49.25 disability premium, $25.27 life premiums, and, unbe-knownst to her a second loan of $396 to buy the UNIPAY death and dismemberment policy. Her $500 request obli-gated her to repay $1,700.[592] The impact on larger loans is even more dramatic: one couple had $5,000 of insurance charges in a loan with $10,000 proceeds.[593]

Practices challenged in *California v. ITT Consumer Fi-nancial Corp.*,[594] involved the sale of the whole gamut of ITT's collateral products: credit life and disability insurance; property insurance, (household contents and auto collision and comprehensive insurance); the SPT-5 non-credit 5-year term life insurance policies; and membership in ITT's Thrift Club. The company was alleged to have made misrepresen-tations concerning the optional nature of insurance when it was routinely added and padded the loans with charges for insurance and the Thrift Club, which customers either did not know they were purchasing, thought were required, or were led to believe were free. Additionally, it was alleged ITT failed to cancel and rebate the household contents insurance on refinancing; would refinance, or "flip"[595] low-rate side loans financing insurance premiums into high-rate loans; and required an excessive amount of household con-tents insurance, which it would sell for a term exceeding the loan term. Other property insurance abuses alleged included selling household contents insurance in excess of the rea-sonable value of the insured property; selling duplicative property insurance; and taking security interests in personal property as a device to sell household contents insurance. As had been true in some other ITT cases, it was also alleged that credit disability insurance was sold to borrowers who would not be eligible for benefits. These actions were all alleged to violate the California UDAP statutes.[596] Though

ITT Financial took the brunt of the litigation, other finance companies maybe vulnerable to similar claims.[597]

Collateral contracts, such as those involved in the sale of non-credit insurance items in packing cases, can be viewed as "a device to extract an exorbitant rate of interest," even if the theoretically independent contract is not "illegal, improper, or illusory, nor totally lacking in substance."[598] The questionable value of the types of ancillary products sold in packing cases, combined with the implicitly coercive or deceptive sales tactics which often accompany such sales should make these kinds of packing cases fall within the definition of a device to extract an exorbitant rate of inter-est[599] thus subject to challenge.

Furthermore, it is worth looking carefully at the scope of the authority granted a licensee under a special usury statute to make such sales. Such statutes, like small loan acts, may specifically authorize the licensee to sell credit insurance and impose premium charges, but make no mention of non-credit insurance charges. As has been discussed, such statutes are to be interpreted strictly, and charges not spe-cifically authorized should not be permitted.[600] Moreover, the relevant licensing statute may contain a provision similar to that from the Uniform Small Loan Act, which prohibits conducting other business at the same location as its lending business, unless authorized by the regulatory authority upon a finding that "the granting of such authority would not facilitate evasions" of the statute.[601] The sale of products, including insurance products not specifically listed as au-thorized, should constitute "conducting other business" that is not permitted. Certainly, the profits to the lender or its affiliates from insurance packing, accompanied by the fre-quently coercive or deceptive sales practices, suggest this "other business" tends to circumvent or evade the special usury statutes.[602]

The strict interpretation of Minnesota's version of the small loan statute led the state supreme court to rule that the sale of non-credit life insurance by a finance company

592 Funk & Thorp Credit, Inc., No. 82-310-A (S.D. Iowa, filed June 7, 1982).

593 Urbina v. Aetna Fin. Co., Civ. 83-452 TUC-ACM, (D. Ariz. filed June 30, 1983).

594 Clearinghouse Nos. 44,801S and T, No. 656038-0 (Cal. Super. Ct., Alameda Cty., settlement filed Sept. 21, 1989). *See ITT Loan Fraud Settlement to Cost $50 Million or More*, 53 Banking Rep. 641 (BNA) (Oct. 30, 1989); McCoy, *ITT Unit Settles Fraud Charges in California*, Wall St. J., Sept. 22, 1989 at A3, col. 4. *See also* Golann, *Consumer Litigation in the Age of Combat Banking*, 45 Bus. L. 1761 (June 1990).

595 *See* § 6.4.3, *supra* for a discussion of schemes to flip lower rate sales-financing agreements into higher-rate loan agreements.

596 Cal. Bus. & Prof. Code §§ 17200, 17500.

597 *See, e.g.*, Hager v. American Gen. Fin., Inc., 37 F. Supp. 2d 778 (S.D. W. Va. 1999) (flipping case in which borrowers were sold non-credit life insurance and credit life insurance; claims in-cluded TIL, unconscionability, and fraud); Baron v. Best Buy Co., 75 F. Supp. 2d 1368 (S.D. Fla. 1999) (in credit card context, allegations include claims of insurance packing via a "payment maker protection plan" in which the consumer is sold a package of credit life, disability, property, and unemployment insurance in connection with purchases of merchandise; court denied defendant's motion to compel arbitration); Fabricant v. Sears Roebuck & Co., 1999 U.S. Dist. LEXIS 16574 (S.D. Fla. 1999) (same; defendant's motion for summary judgment denied as to TIL claim).

598 *In re* Rosner, 48 B.R. 538, 550 (Bankr. E.D.N.Y. 1985).

599 *See also* § 8.5.2, *supra* on voluntariness, which will often be a factual issue in packing cases.

600 *See* § 7.4.2.2.1, *supra*; § 8.5.4.3, *infra*.

601 Uniform Small Loan Act § 12.

602 *Cf.* Beneficial Fin. Co. v. State Corp. Comm., 339 S.E.2d 192 (Va. 1986).

licensed under the Minnesota Regulated Loan Act[603] was prohibited in *Hawkins v. Thorp Credit and Thrift Co.*[604] Minn. Stat. § 56.155 subd. 1 was the provision under discussion. It provides in part:

> No licensee shall, directly or indirectly, sell or offer for sale any insurance in connection with any loan made under this chapter except as and to the extent authorized by this section. The sale of credit life and credit accident and health insurance is subject to the provisions of chapter 62B,.... Life, accident, and health insurance, or any of them, may be written upon or in connection with any loan but must not be required as additional security for the indebtedness.

The court reviewed the history of the provision, which is the current incarnation of Minnesota's small loan act, noting that it prohibited licensees from engaging in any other business than lending.[605] The provision at issue was an exception to allow for the sale of *credit* insurance.[606] The first sentence of section 56.155 subd. 1 made it clear, however, that licensees still could not engage in the insurance business beyond that limited exception.[607] (Note that the distinction between credit insurance and non-credit insurance is central to this ruling.[608])

Plaintiffs had also challenged ITT Financial's sale of buying club memberships as part of the loans. While not ruling directly on the issue, the state supreme court reversed the trial court's finding that those sales were not in violation of the law, and remanded the issue to make specific findings of practices used in their sale and to determine the legality of those practices.

This claim of illegality, which is separate from any issues of unfair and deceptive practice in marketing this insurance, may be available in other states, given the prevalence of similar restrictively worded statutes.[609]

Following the court's decision in *Hawkins*, a class was certified, and the case was consolidated for settlement purposes with several other insurance packing cases pending in Minnesota against ITT Financial entities.[610] In addition to a $17 million cash fund for members of the *Hawkins* class—one injunctive provision which should be particularly useful is that no optional insurance or non-loan product (such as Buyer's Club memberships) can be sold without a written comparison of the basic loan terms with and without the product: principal loan amount; monthly payment amount; the cost of each product or policy; the amount of coverage of any insurance; the amount the monthly payment increases (including the finance charge) for each policy or product; and a statement that the loan is approved either with or without these other products. Property insurance cannot exceed the *lesser* of the value of the collateral or the note amount, and borrowers must be told that a loss-payable endorsement on their current insurance will suffice, and how to obtain it.[611]

One recent challenge to an ancillary accidental death and dismemberment (AD&D) insurance product, predicated on the assertion that it was coerced, and thus a finance charge under state and TIL law, failed.[612] However, the facts described as to one of the named plaintiffs raise some intriguing "what if" questions: what if the economic impact of these policies had been demonstrated in the context of an insurance packing and/or loan flipping challenge?[613]

---

603 Minn. Stat. Ch. 56 (Regulated Loans).

604 441 N.W.2d 470 (Minn. 1989).

605 Minn. Stat. § 56.12. This provision was in the Uniform Small Loan Act, and is common in small loan and regulated loan acts derived from the Act. *See* Seventh Draft of the Uniform Small Loan Act § 12 (1942), *reprinted* in Curran, Trends in Consumer Credit Regulation (1965).

606 Hawkins v. Thorp Credit & Thrift Co., 441 N.W.2d 470, 474 (Minn. 1989). The Minnesota amendment was part of a similar movement in other states to allow small loan licensees to sell credit insurance. Curran, Trends in Consumer Credit Regulation 27–29 (1965).

607 *Cf.* Herndon v. ITT Consumer Fin. Corp., 789 F. Supp. 720 (W.D.N.C. 1992) (North Carolina statute had similar provision, but also had provision allowing other business if "not contrary to best interest of the borrowing public" and if it was authorized in writing by the State Banking Commissioner; court held sale of non-credit life and disability was not *per se* illegal during period when Commissioner had given written authorization to sell it. *Note*: The Commission withdrew that authority in 1990). A federal court, interpreting the Georgia Industrial Loan Act, accepted an argument rejected in *Hawkins* with regard to non-credit accidental death and dismemberment insurance: that the credit insurance provisions did not apply to non-credit insurance and therefore its sale did not violate these provisions. Unlike the Minnesota Supreme Court, however, the Georgia court failed to look at the non-credit insurance sale in the context of the licensing act as a whole, including the section immediately following the one it interpreted, which, like the Minnesota statute, excludes any insurance charges not specifically authorized. Dixon v. S&S Loan Serv. of Waycross, 754 F. Supp. 1567 (S.D. Ga. 1990) interpreting G.I.L.A. § 7-3-14(c) and ignoring G.I.L.A. § 7-3-15.

608 *See* § 8.3.2.1, *supra*.

609 *See also* § 9.3.1, *infra*.

610 In addition to *Hawkins*, the consolidated case for settlement includes Hohn v. Thorp, Clearinghouse No. 44,801F, No. 4-87-808 (D. Minn., filed Sept. 11, 1987). *See* § 8.7.4 note 799, *infra* for a summary of the allegations in that case.

    The consolidated amended complaint is available as *Hawkins v. Thorp*, Clearinghouse No. 44,801V (second amended complaint), and the settlement documents are available as Clearinghouse No. 44,801W.

611 ITT Financial has cut back on its small loan business (to what extent is unclear), but these settlement terms may be useful guidance in litigation involving other companies engaging in similar practices.

612 Mitchell v. Industrial Credit Corp., 898 F. Supp. 1518 (N.D. Ala. 1995).

613 Statements of fact in reported opinions, are, of course, always truncated. It is possible such evidence was presented, but the judge found it not important enough to mention.

The pattern of loans for one named plaintiff was as follows:

Loan # 1 May 6, 1992: $1,257 amount financed, included $70 for $10,000, 2-year, AD&D policy;
Loan # 2 Aug. 3, 1992: $3,315 amount financed, included $70 for $10,000, 2-year, AD&D policy;
Loan # 3 Nov. 17, 1992: $1,651 amount financed, included $72 for a $3,000, 2-year, AD&D policy;[614]
Loan # 4 Feb. 17, 1993: $3,317 amount financed, including $72, $3,000, 2-year, AD&D policy.

It is unclear from the opinion whether these were parallel loans, refinanced loans or a combination. Industry practice is such, though, the financing is more likely. As the flipping discussions elsewhere note,[615] loading up frequently refinanced loans with non-rebated charges plays an significant role in artificially inflating the debt. Unlike credit insurance policies, which are required to be cancelled and to have the unearned premiums rebated upon refinancing, premiums for these non-credit ancillary policies generally are not rebated. (Since they are not credit insurance, they are still effective for their scheduled term, at least in theory.) Insurance packing and flipping have met with judicial disapproval, and this arguably is simply part of such schemes.[616] These ancillary insurance products are usually of minimal value to the borrowers in the ordinary course of events, and the economic value to the lenders is considerable.[617] But beyond those problems, there is in these facts a further question of whether there might be phantom coverage in a lending pattern like this. During a good portion of the period between May, 1992 and January, 1995 (the end of the 24-month period on the last policy), there were multiple AD&D policies in effect on this borrower. Would the company actually pay multiple benefits in the (unlikely) event of a covered loss, or would it limit its pay-out to one policy? If the latter, it would be quite difficult to view the sale as

anything other than a devious mechanism to extract excess returns.[618]

8.5.4.4 Unnecessary Collateral, Duplicative Insurance

Another feature of packed loans may be unnecessary collateral taken as security in order to write profitable property insurance. A creditor may, for example, take a superfluous non-purchase money security interest in the borrower's old car which has little or no market value, and write property insurance for it into the loan. The most common example of unnecessary collateral is household goods, despite the legal restrictions on a creditor's right to take household goods as security. Consequently, a practitioner should examine a loan secured by insured household goods not only for claims relating to the insurance, but should examine as well the validity of the collateral itself.

The FTC restricts the right of creditors to take non-purchase money security interest in household goods.[619] The policy behind the prohibition is that ordinary household goods have little genuine value as security—they are generally taken for their *in terrorem* usefulness in debt collection and, perhaps more importantly, to justify writing property insurance on them. Because of the profitability of the insurance, some creditors aggressively attempt to take this security despite the legal restrictions.

One exception to the Rule is for purchase-money security interests, which are permitted. A creditor may attempt to improperly extend the purchase-money status of a security interest through cross-collateral clauses and refinancing.[620] A second exception arises in the definition of household goods provided in the FTC and related rules. Some items which either tend to have greater value, or are less necessary for daily living are excluded from the Rule's scope.[621] Some creditors have developed form contracts which purport to comply by taking a security interest in the excluded items. In some instances, a creditor may flatly overshoot its mark, and list a protected item. In other cases, it may use fuzzy contract language to try to comply. Depending upon the way

---

614 There is no stated explanation for the rate hike/benefit dive between the first two and the last two.

615 *See* §§ 6.1, 6.3, 6.4.1.3, *supra. See also* § 12.7, *infra.*

616 *Id.* and § 8.5.4 generally.

617 Given the limited risks insured by AD&D, the lack of adequate regulation on the ancillary products, and the high probability that many consumers are unaware of the nature of these policies (and therefore are unlikely to submit claims in any event), the loss-ratios are probably low, and the full package of resulting benefits to the creditors is undoubtedly quite generous. That explains the appeal of these products to lenders. *See, e.g.,* Balderos v. Illinois Vehicle Premium Fin. Co., 1997 WL 627650 (N.D. Ill. Oct. 2, 1997) (court certified class action where lender added a purported hospitalization policy premium into the financing of the consumer's purchase of auto insurance without informing the customer; value of additional "insurance" speculative in light of allegation that $85 of the $100 premium was kept as a commission; lack of disclosure about the supposed policy would likely result in a low loss ratio; claims raised include TILA, UDAP, breach of fiduciary duty, and RICO). *See generally* § 8.1, *supra.*

618 *Cf.* Arizona v. Associates Fin. Servs. Co., CV 92-21853 Clearinghouse No. 44,801Z (stipulated judgment filed Dec. 16, 1992), Clearinghouse No. 44,801Y (complaint) (UDAP and Cons. Loan Act challenges to insurance packing; among challenged practices: selling overlapping and duplicative memberships in a motor club as part of loan refinancings while the original membership is still effective; similar practice with non-filing insurance).

619 16 C.F.R. § 444. *See generally* National Consumer Law Center, Unfair and Deceptive Acts and Practices §§ 5.1.1.2–5.1.1.3 (6th ed. 2004 and Supp.).

620 For a discussion of the duration of purchase money security interests, see National Consumer Law Center, Repossessions and Foreclosures § 3.8 (5th ed. 2002 and Supp.).

621 *E.g.,* VCRs, a second television, artwork, jewelry other than wedding rings. 16 C.F.R. § 444.1(i).

the contract is written, it may be subject to challenge as well. An FTC Informal Staff Letter took the position that a contract which took a non-purchase money security interest in household goods, but included an exclusion for consumer transactions as to items covered by the FTC Rule, violates the Rule.[622] The FTC letter said the language was not clear enough to protect the consumer from the injury the Rule was designed to prevent—notably the *in terrorem* threats of repossession. Significantly, the letter goes on to add:

> We are also concerned about creditor efforts to evade the Rule. In our experience, a security interest in household goods is rarely taken in connection with business credit. Hence, we fail to see the necessity for including a household goods security interest provision in a contract and then creating an exclusion for the transactions as to which the security interest would be most likely to apply. The use of such a device might be regarded as an effort to evade the Rule and, as such, be an unfair or deceptive practice under the FTC Act.

One example of a finance company loan shows how some creditors are trying to comply technically with the FTC Credit Practices Rule while still keeping up their property insurance profits. The borrower wanted $500. He got $520 from ITT Financial: he also got *$992.43 of insurance premiums* packed into it. At the 32.7% interest rate charged, the premiums cost an extra $577.57 in interest. The packing thus added a total of $1,570 to the cost of his $500 loan.[623]

And the benefit of his bargain? He bought $20,000 worth of coverage on his household goods, though the collateral on the loan was only worth $500. (He also got credit life, and credit disability, and a general disability policy. The general disability policy was written by American Bankers Life Assurance Company, which cooperated with ITT Financial in the UNIPAY accidental death and dismemberment insurance, one of the packed insurances at issue in several of the packing cases.[624])

As an example like this makes clear, the property insurance arising from the security interest must be scrutinized as carefully as the security interest itself.[625] In insurance packing cases, property insurance can arguably be viewed as a pretext for usury: the collateral may be unnecessary because the loan is otherwise amply secured;[626] the collateral itself may be impermissible; the collateral may be of so little intrinsic value that as a practical matter it adds no security; or security may be listed with inflated values so as to increase the insurance sold.[627] The statutory provisions setting standards for the sale of credit property may dictate that property insurance is improper if it does not bear the required relationship to the risk, as the statute defines that relationship.[628] Where the statute requires that property insurance be written only on collateral, or that it bear a relationship to the creditor's risk, a creditor cannot sell property insurance on household goods unless there is a purchase-money security interest in the household goods which would be valid under the FTC Credit Practices

---

622   FTC Informal Staff Letter, Wilmore, Sept. 27, 1988, Clearinghouse No. 44,824. The letter was in response to the following inquiry:

> Is it permissible to include in a listing of items in which a security interest is taken in a non-purchase money contract, household goods prohibited by 16 C.F.R. § 444.2(a)(4) if the listing is followed by the following disclaimer:
>
> EXCLUSIONS: Secured Party specifically excludes from this security agreement the following items on a loan for a personal, family or household purpose, unless Secured Party has a purchase money security interest in the items:
>
> Clothing, furniture (except antiques), appliances, one radio, one television, linens, crockery, china, kitchenware, impersonal effects (including wedding rings but excluding other jewelry).
>
> If any items listed under "c" fall within the excluded items listed here and the Secured Party does not have a purchase money security interest in the item(s), then this preprinted language will supersede the items typed or written under "c" and Secured Party does not take a security interest in the excluded item.

623   *See* Besta v. Beneficial Loan Co., 855 F.2d 532 (8th Cir. 1988) discussed at § 8.5.4.2, *supra*, and § 8.7.5, *infra*.

624   In at least one state, ITT Financial was prohibited by the terms of its consent agreement from selling the American Bankers' UNIPAY policy. Settlement Agreement between Iowa Att'y Gen. and Thorp Credit, announced June 6, 1984. *See also* Hawkins v. Thorp Credit & Thrift Co., 441 N.W.2d 470 (Minn. 1989) (ITT's sale of non-credit SPT-5 life insurance illegal under Related Loan Act). *See generally* § 8.5.4.3, *supra*.

625   Many of the abuses discussed in this section concerning the sale of property insurance on unnecessary collateral and excessive or duplicative property insurance were alleged in the California insurance-packing case, California v. ITT Fin. Corp., Clearinghouse Nos. 44,801S and T, No. 656038-0 (Cal. Super. Ct. Alameda Cty., complaint and settlement filed Sept. 21, 1989). *See also* Hawkins v. Thorp; Hohn v. Thorp, Clearinghouse No. 44,801V (consolidated complaint), 44,801W (settlement) (D. Minn. 1991); Arizona v. Associates Fin. Servs. Co., CV 92-21853 Clearinghouse No. 44,801Z (stipulated judgment filed Dec. 16, 1992) (Clearinghouse No. 44,801Y, complaint). *See* § 8.5.2.4.3, *supra* for further discussion of these cases and 8.7.4, *infra* for a listing of some of the other insurance packing cases available from Clearinghouse.

626   *Cf.* Wilson v. Whitworth, 197 Ark. 675, 125 S.W.2d 112 (1939) ($3500 insurance required on $150 proceeds).

627   In its 1989 action involving insurance packing, the California attorney general alleged that security interests were taken in personal property as a pretext to sell household contents insurance, and that was unfair competition in violation of Cal. Bus. & Prof. Code § 17200. California v. ITT Consumer Fin. Corp., Clearinghouse No. 44801S ¶ 11-M, No. 656038-0 (Super. Ct. Alameda Cty., complaint filed Sept. 31, 1989). *See* § 8.5.4.3, *supra* for further discussion of this case.

628   *See* § 8.5.3.4, *supra*.

Rule.[629] Further, a creditor cannot shortcut this requirement by taking a valid purchase money-security interest in some household goods, and then be named loss payee on a policy insuring all household goods.[630]

As was the case in the above example where $20,000 coverage was purchased though the collateral was worth only $500, the loan documents may include a notice which clearly spells out that this property insurance covers all the household property, not just the collateral. This is clearly an effort to circumvent the earlier charges by consumers and regulators that selling property insurance on household goods which were not collateral, and which may have been duplicative of existing insurance coverage, was an unfair and deceptive practice. However, where state law prohibits selling property insurance on property which is not collateral, that notice cannot serve to legalize the practice.[631] Being up front about the action may, depending on the circumstances, save a practice from being deceptive; but if it is illegal anyway, it certainly cannot override the law.

Another factor in a number of insurance packing cases is that the property insurance on the collateral is duplicative of existing homeowner's or renter's policies. One case which addressed the issue of duplicative property insurance prior to the widespread activity concerning insurance packing illustrates the need to present a complete evidentiary picture, and also suggests the wisdom of pleading all relevant theories.

In *Department of Financial Institutions v. Beneficial Finance Co. of Madison*,[632] a state regulatory agency challenged the sale of duplicative property insurance, on the grounds that there was no risk of loss to the creditor, and the insurance thus was improper under the statute.[633] But the court noted that the relevant statute specifically referred to risk of loss to the property, not the creditor. The court also pointed out a few respects in which the creditor's insurance did not duplicate the consumer's own policy. The court therefore failed to find a violation of the statute.

This case should not be dispositive of the issue of duplicative insurance, however. The court decision does not indicate that this insurance was sold in an insurance-packing context which might suggest unfair and deceptive acts and practices or unconscionable practices, a breach of fiduciary duty,[634] or conduct designed to circumvent interest ceilings. Indeed, there were a number of other statutory provisions relevant to that case itself which were not addressed at all by the court, such as the creditor's need for the insurance

protection (which, in effect, does require insurance to relate to the creditor's risk of loss), the relation between the amount and terms of the credit and the insurance benefits, the potential benefits to the consumer[635] and the cost of the insurance in relation to its benefits.[636] Because a packing case involving duplicative insurance may utilize a large number of different statutory provisions and doctrine, the narrow scope of the *Beneficial Finance* holding and its incomplete analysis should not present an insurmountable barrier.

Interpreting its similar version of the UCCC, the Kansas Attorney General did look at the other provisions of the statute ignored by the Indiana court in the *Beneficial* case. The AG opinion noted that if the credit insurance policy had a *pro rata* clause, that would deny the consumer any benefit from the insurance sale, and would be unconscionable if the creditor did it knowingly.[637]

8.5.4.5 Non-Filing Insurance

Discovery in insurance packing cases brought to light yet another abusive charge.[638] These cases suggest that practitioners should examine carefully one small credit-related insurance charge which sometimes appears on secured loans—non-filing insurance. Ordinarily, a creditor taking a security interest in personal property files a record of its security interest in a county recorder's office as a means of protecting its interest in the collateral against other creditors.[639] However, sometimes creditors find it easier to purchase non-filing insurance than to perfect the security interest.

Non-filing insurance is simply a way for the creditor to avoid the cost and effort of filing the security interest with the county recorder's office as a means of establishing its priority over later creditors on the collateral. In theory, it pays the lender if the lender cannot repossess its collateral upon default, if the loss is occasioned by the fact that the

---

629 Opinion of Kansas Att'y Gen., No. 87-3, Consumer Cred. Guide (CCH) ¶ 95,980 (Jan. 9, 1987), *modified by* Opinion of Kansas Att'y Gen., No. 87-47, Consumer Cred. Guide (CCH) ¶ 95,981 (Mar. 12, 1987).

630 *Id.*

631 *Id. See generally* § 8.5.3.4, *supra.*

632 462 N.E.2d 711 (Ind. Ct. App. 1981).

633 Ind. Code § 24-4.5-4.301 (1)(a) (U.C.C.C. 4.301(1)(a)(1968)).

634 *See* § 8.7, *infra.*

635 Ind. Code § 24-4.5-4-106 (U.C.C.C. § 4-106).

636 Ind. Code § 24-4.5-5.108 (U.C.C.C. § 5-108).

637 Opinion of Kansas Att'y Gen., No. 87-3, Consumer Cred. Guide (CCH) ¶ 95,980 (Jan. 9, 1987); *modified by* Opinion of Kansas Att'y Gen., No. 87-47, Consumer Cred. Guide (CCH) ¶ 95,981 (Mar. 12, 1987).

638 Dixon v. S&S Loan Serv. of Waycross, 754 F. Supp. 1567, 1572–1574 (S.D. Ga. 1990) (creditor's motion for summary judgment denied where deposition suggested the purported non-recording insurance was not related to non-recording risks); Walmsley v. Mercury Fin. Co., Clearinghouse No. 49,164 (S.D. Fla., order on motions to dismiss Sept. 10, 1993) (court denied motion to dismiss, holding if economic reality was that creditor and insurer agreed to insure risks beyond non-filing, the premium should be a finance charge; nomenclature of policy is not controlling); Bagwell v. M. Kovens Co., Clearinghouse No. 44,801I, No. 88293033/CL 85964 (Cir. Ct. for Baltimore City filed Aug. 26, 1988) [*Note*: The complaint does not plead this issue, which came to light during discovery].

639 *See* U.C.C. Art. 9, Parts 3 and 4.

lender did not file its security interest.[640] As a practical matter, that is only going to happen when another secured party gets priority as a result of the creditor's failure to record its lien.[641]

The cost of non-filing premiums is generally fairly small, since Truth in Lending regulations require that the cost not exceed the actual cost of filing with the public officials in order for the insurance to be excluded from the TIL finance charge.[642] However, abuses are surfacing with non-filing insurance which could lead to usury claims. Certainly it is impermissible to both file and charge for the non-filing insurance.[643] The most egregious thus far is one in which the insurance purchased, while called non-filing insurance, seems actually nothing more than a default reserve. The lender sends the "premiums" to an insurer, who establishes a reserve fund, and then pays the fund (less an administrative fee)[644] back to the creditor for its uncollectible loans.[645] Discovery in a recent Alabama challenge to non-filing insurance confirms that at least some of these policies do not insure against the risks caused by non-filing: the policy clearly returns claims up to the reserve's cap "whenever [the creditor is] unable to secure the merchandise such as skips, bankruptcy, and merchandise destroyed."[646] Technically,

that is not even insurance, but at best, it is "default" insurance. That is always considered a finance charge under Truth in Lending,[647] and, as an unauthorized charge under most consumer credit licensing statutes, would be an illegal overcharge.[648] It is significant that one court, interpreting language providing that "each person who in any manner participates" in a usurious loan is subject to the statute, refused to dismiss the insurer from a usury challenge to a non-filing policy.[649]

640　*See* Fagg, Credit Life and Disability Insurance 522–523 (1986).

641　*See, e.g.,* White & Summers, Uniform Commercial Code § 33-4 (5th ed. 2002).

642　15 U.S.C. § 1605(d)(2); Reg. Z, 12 C.F.R. § 226.4(e)(2). *See generally* National Consumer Law Center, Truth in Lending § 3.9.7.3 (5th ed. 2003 and Supp.).

643　*See* Mitchell v. Industrial Credit Corp., 898 F. Supp. 1518 (N.D. Ala. 1995).

644　Dixon v. S&S Loan Serv. of Waycross, 754 F. Supp. 1567, 1572–1574 (S.D. Ga. 1990); Bagwell v. M. Kovens Co., No. 88293033/CL 85964 (Cir. Ct. for Baltimore City filed Aug. 26, 1988), Clearinghouse No. 44, 801I. In *Dixon*, the administrative fee was apparently 11%—the maximum "claim" by the creditor could not exceed 89% of the premiums paid. In *Bagwell*, the administrative fee was 20%. In Warehouse Home Furnishing Distributors, Inc. v. Whitson, 709 So. 2d 1144 (Ala. 1997), 93% of the premiums were returned to the creditor, with 7% to Voyager Insurance Co.

645　In *Bagwell*, the discovery suggested claims submitted by the creditor included losses from bankruptcy and "skips." In *Dixon*, the creditor's deposition suggested he would submit a claim where the collateral was not available for reasons totally unrelated to the consequences of non-filing. Further, the insurer had never either evaluated or rejected a claim submitted by the creditor. *See also* Christ v. Beneficial Corp. (*In re* Consolidated Non-Filing Ins. Fee Litig.), 195 F.R.D. 684 (M.D. Ala. 2000) (WESCO, Beneficial's insurance subsidiary, collected $20,380,766 in premiums between 1990 and 1997 and returned all but 10.82% to Beneficial finance company subsidiaries; national class certification granted on TILA and RICO claims); W.S. Badcock Corp. v. Myers, 696 So. 2d 766 (Fla. Dist. Ct. App. 1996). *But see* Edwards v. Your Credit, Inc., 971 F. Supp. 1045 (M.D. La. 1997) (no reserve account created and no monies paid back to lender; expected loss ratio of 89.25% did not transform non-filing insurance into a default reserve), *aff'd in part and rev'd in part*, 148 F.3d 427 (5th Cir. 1998).

646　That discovery document in Warehouse Home Furnishing Dis-

tributors, Inc. v. Whitson, 709 So. 1d 1144 (Ala. 1997) was in the instruction letter from the retailer's home office to store and credit managers. The fund's usage by both the insurer and retailer made it clear that the creditor's simply not repossessing was the trigger, not a loss of collateral to a competing secured credit with U.C.C. priority. *Cf.* Mitchell v. Industrial Credit Corp., 898 F. Supp. 1518, n.15 (N.D. Ala. 1995) (noting in passing that the insurer admitted all claims up to the cap were paid "with no questions asked," and finding nothing amiss in the procedure. *NB*: The *Whitson* court specifically rejected *Mitchell* as unpersuasive).

647　Edwards v. Your Credit Inc., 148 F.3d 427 (5th Cir. 1998); W.S. Badcock Corp. v. Myers, 696 So. 2d 766 (Fla. Dist. Ct. App. 1996). *See also* Adams v. Plaza Fin. Co., 168 F.3d 932 (7th Cir. 1999). TIL challenges to non-filing insurance are by no means uniformly successful, though the analysis in some is weak, e.g., Mitchell v. Industrial Credit Corp., 898 F. Supp. 1518 (N.D. Ala. 1995) (distinguished in Warehouse Home Furnishing Distributors, Inc. v. Whitson, 709 So. 2d 1144 (Ala. 1997). *See generally* National Consumer Law Center, Truth in Lending § 3.9.7.3 (5th ed. 2003 and Supp.); 15 U.S.C. § 1605(a)(5); Reg. Z § 226.4(b)(5). *See also* Walmsley v. Mercury Fin. Co., Clearinghouse No. 49,164 (S.D. Fla., order on motions to dismiss Sept. 10, 1993) (court denied motion to dismiss, holding if economic reality was that creditor and insurer agreed to insure risks beyond non-filing, the premium should be a finance charge; nomenclature of policy is not controlling).

648　*See* Warehouse Home Furnishing Distributors, Inc. v. Whitson, 709 So. 2d 1144 (Ala. 1997). *See also* Walmsley v. Mercury Fin. Co., Clearinghouse No. 49,164 (S.D. Fla., order on motions to dismiss Sept. 10, 1993) (court denied motion to dismiss, holding if economic reality was that creditor and insurer agreed to insure risks beyond non-filing, the premium should be a finance charge; nomenclature of policy is not controlling); Kenty v. Bank One, Columbus, N.A., 1992 WL 170605 (S.D. Ohio Apr. 23, 1992) (charge for unauthorized insurance coverage is interest under National Bank Act), *aff'd in part, rev'd in part on other grounds* 92 F.3d 384 (6th Cir. 1996) (without disturbing ruling that excess fees would constitute interest, court held no usury because national bank defendant entitled to most favored lender status which, under Ohio law, would leave it without any legal limit on the amount of interest it could charge. [*Cf.* § 9.2.8, *infra*]); Hawkins v. Thorp Credit & Thrift Co., 441 N.W.2d 470 (Minn. 1989) (non-credit life insurance not an authorized charge, and its sale violated licensing act); Garrison v. First Fed. Saving & Loan Ass'n of S.C., 402 S.E.2d 24 (Va. 1991) ("risk management fee" was not an authorized charge, and thus constituted excess interest. *Cf.* §§ 8.5.3.2.1, 8.5.4.3, *supra* (discussing types of authorized credit insurance); Mitchell v. Industrial Credit Corp., 898 F. Supp. 1518 (N.D. Ala. 1995), both discussed below. It may also constitute a UDAP violation.

649　Walmsley v. Mercury Fin. Co., Clearinghouse No. 49,164 (S.D. Fla., order on motions to dismiss Sept. 10, 1993), interpreting Fla. Stat. § 516.02(c).

Even if the charge is for real non-filing coverage, a non-filing premium may still be subject to challenge. Frequently, this insurance is sold where household goods are the security. However, it is precisely in the case of household goods that non-filing insurance is not necessary to protect the creditor against the risk covered by non-filing insurance. If the creditor's security interest is a purchase money security interest, it has priority over other secured creditors even without filing (therefore, except in very rare instances, it should never have a loss occasioned by non-filing).[650] Even if a statute allows a non-filing fee, the charge in this case may nonetheless be challenged as an excess charge. In another context, the Tennessee Supreme Court has said that a statutory authorization does not constitute permission to automatically impose a charge in all cases. Rather, the charge is prima facie valid, and the burden shifts to the borrower to show it does not bear a reasonable relation to the creditor's expense and service.[651] It is not reasonable to charge for protection against a virtually non-existent risk.[652] If not a pretext for usury, it may at least be an unfair and deceptive practice. And if the creditor's security interest in household goods is not purchase money, it quite possibly is an illegal security interest under the Credit Practices Rule, and therefore any insurance relating to it may be an illegal charge.[653]

A pair of recent cases from Alabama with conflicting results suggests that the manner in which facts are developed and presented is key. In June of 1995, a federal court reviewed Voyager's non-filing policy, found it to be worthy of the name, and thus not in violation of either the Alabama Mini-Code or TIL.[654] In contrast, a thoughtful and detailed opinion by the Alabama Supreme Court distinguished that decision, finding that *Mitchell* did not involve purchase money security interests in consumer goods.[655] The *Whitson* plaintiffs advanced three arguments as to why the charge did not qualify for exclusion from the finance charge as "a premium for insurance in lieu of perfecting a security interest,"[656] all of which the court found persuasive. First, there is no insurance involved at all. Two necessary characteristics of insurance are risk-shifting, and distribution of risk among similarly situated persons. In the arrangement at issue, the creditor's "claims" are paid simply by returning the premiums it pays in, less an administrative fee, so there is no risk shifted at all, nor is there any distribution of risk.[657] Second, even if it were insurance, it was not "in lieu of perfecting a security interest": it was, instead, default insurance. The insurer paid on losses due to bankruptcy, skips, and destroyed goods—none of which relate to risks created by non-filing. Finally, since the contracts in question were all purchase-money security interests in non-automotive consumer goods, the creditor's security interest was automatically perfected under the UCC, as noted above. The premium was not, therefore, "in lieu of perfecting."

This "non-filing insurance" premium therefore failed to qualify for the finance charge exemption in Alabama's mini-code, meaning the charge was considered interest. Since the admitted interest charged was at or very near the statutory maximum, this hidden interest took the contracts over the usury ceiling, with the prescribed result being forfeiture of the entire finance charge.[658]

The Alabama Supreme Court, however, reversed the trial court's grant of summary judgment on the issue of whether the imposition of the charges was deliberate which, if so, triggered the remedy of voiding the usurious loans. Instead, the court held that whether the charging of the non-filing fee was done with deliberateness was a question of fact to be decided by the jury.

An earlier decision from Florida outlined a similar variation of non-filing "insurance."[659] There the seller/creditor charged $7 for non-filing insurance every time a customer purchased goods in excess of $20. In lieu of filing a security interest statement, the entire charge was sent to American

---

650 U.C.C. §§ 9-302(1)(d), 9-307(2); White and Summers, Uniform Commercial Code §§ 31-9, 33-14 (4th ed. 1995). Bona fide purchasers who buy from the consumer have priority over holders of unfiled purchase money security interests in consumer goods.

651 Cumberland Capitol Corp. v. Patty, 556 S.W.2d 516 (Tenn. 1977). In a broad-scale challenge to Associates' insurance-packing practices, Arizona officials noted that a financing statement is effective for six years, though its non-filing insurance premium was effective for only five. Moreover, Associates would routinely assess a new non-filing premium with each refinancing, even when the original remained in effect. (*NB*: non-filing premiums, unlike credit life, disability, are typically not cancelled and rebated when a loan is paid off by renewal or otherwise.) The state's consent order provides that no new filing fee or non-filing premium can be charged unless the original financing statement or non-filing insurance will lapse during the renewal loan's term. Arizona v. Associates Fin. Servs. Co., CV 92-21853 Clearinghouse No. 44,801Z (stipulated judgment filed Dec. 16, 1992) (Clearinghouse No. 44,801Y, complaint).

652 *See* Warehouse Home Furnishing Distributors, Inc. v. Whitson, 709 So. 2d 1144 (Ala. 1997), discussed below.

653 *See* §§ 8.5.3.4, 8.5.4.4, *supra.*

654 Mitchell v. Industrial Credit Corp., 898 F. Supp. 1518 (N.D. Ala. 1995).

655 Warehouse Home Furnishing Distributors, Inc. v. Whitson, 709 So. 2d 1144 (Ala. 1997). The court noted that the *Mitchell* court held that the insurance premium did constitute a finance charge for the one plaintiff against whose property a security interest had been perfected.

656 Ala. Code § 5-19-1(1).

657 The "insurer" took no risk, because its maximum exposure was 93% of the premiums paid and it kept a guaranteed 7% administrative fee. Further since the pay-outs came entirely from premiums the creditor paid in, there was no distribution of risk. For example, if the premiums paid to insurance company totaled $100,000, the maximum payout would be $93,000 even if the *total value* of the property that could not be repossessed as a result of failing to file U.C.C.-1 financing statements was $750,000.

658 Ala. Code § 5-19-19.

659 W.S. Badcock Corp. v. Myers, 696 So. 2d 766 (Fla. Dist. Ct. App. 1996).

Bankers Ins. Co. pursuant to an agreement. American Bankers issued a non-filing insurance policy which limited the insurer's liability for losses to 90% of the premiums. American Bankers retained 10% of the premiums paid and returned the remaining 90% to the creditor to cover any losses that could occur. Since a purchase money security interest in consumer goods is perfected automatically without filing, the "losses" to the creditor would be few or none. The court held that this scheme was not insurance because there was no insurable interest since perfection occurred automatically. Further there was no risk of loss. Since this arrangement was not insurance, the court found that the creditor's behavior was subject to Florida's UDAP statute and upheld summary judgment in favor of the consumers on the merits.

Even if the evidence does not support a finding that the purported non-filing insurance is really a reserve fund, the insurance policy may, in fact, be a general default policy and not non-filing insurance. If so, the charge may be illegal under the state usury and/or credit insurance laws. For example, discovery in a case that reached the Fifth Circuit revealed that as many as 84.5% of the claims paid by the insurance company were based on losses not covered by the non-filing policy.[660] While this case only raised claims under the Truth-in-Lending Act, the type of evidence presented to defeat the creditor's motion for summary judgment can be used in pursuing usury or UDAP causes of action.

8.5.5 Post-Claim Underwriting, Ineligibility

8.5.5.1 Challenging the Sale of Insurance to Borrowers Unlikely to Benefit

So far in this section, two common credit insurance abuses have been discussed: involuntary or pressured sales and overcharges in sales to eligible borrowers. A third abuse is the sale of credit insurance to borrowers who are ineligible for the insurance coverage under the terms of the policies that they buy. Unlike ordinary insurance sales, creditors rarely ask borrowers for information relating to their eligibility for benefits under credit insurance policies, such as medical histories.[661] Instead, only after a claim is filed are

eligibility factors such as health, age, and employment checked to see if grounds exist for denying coverage. Other policies provide that there is a waiting period before coverage kicks in.[662] Many policies simply provide that the policy will be canceled and the premium refunded if ineligibility is determined. The result of this arrangement is that creditors and insurance companies keep the premiums paid by ineligible debtors who never file an insurance claim, while refusing to pay on the same policies if claims are ever filed.[663]

Most credit life policies have age restrictions, and many have pre-existing condition exclusions as well. Many disability policies have exclusionary periods whereby they will not pay for disabilities traceable to pre-existing conditions which occur within the first six months of coverage. Refinancing may begin a new exclusionary period. Given the prevalence of flipping in the consumer finance industry, borrowers may be subjected to rolling periods of ineligibility,[664] and the odds of becoming disabled during a period of eligibility are reduced. Such a practice may lead to a finding that an insurance sale is just a pretext for usury.[665] Currently, a number of states restrict the use of pre-existing condition exclusions on refinanced loans, at least where the same group policy is used to insure the refinanced loan.[666]

---

660 Edwards v. Your Credit Inc., 148 F.3d 427 (5th Cir. 1998); *accord* Adams v. Plaza Fin. Co., 168 F.3d 932 (7th Cir. 1999).

661 *See, e.g.,* Justus v. Mountain Life Ins. Co., 1999 Tenn. App. LEXIS 702 (Tenn. App. Oct. 15, 1999) (bank employee took no application but represented that a credit life insurance policy was in full force and effect). In insurance packing cases, where a creditor sells *non* credit life-related policies such as the UNIPAY policy sold by ITT Financial, the creditor may ask a few routine questions about treatment for medical conditions. Or some insurers now may ask a few questions on larger loans, though they still might not check the matter until after a claim has been filed. *See* Smith v. Globe Life Ins. Co., 597 N.W.2d 28 (Mich. 1999) (checks in boxes on credit insurance application regarding medial conditions may not have been filled in when

deceased signed the form; nevertheless, court held no dispute of material fact on insurer's defense that deceased misrepresented his pre-existing conditions, *reversing,* 565 N.W.2d 877 (Mich. App. 1997)) (see strong dissent on issue of whether insurer has to prove reliance on alleged misrepresentation).

662 Grimm v. USLIFE Credit Life Ins. Co., 1999 Ohio App. LEXIS 2445 (May 19, 1999) (credit life insurance application stated on the back side that the insurance was not effective until the first day of the month following approval of the application if approved by the 20th of the month, or was not effective until the first day of the second month following approval if approved after the 20th of the month; conflict between TILA disclosure regarding coverage [which appeared to make coverage co-extensive with the loan term] and the credit insurance application form prevents summary judgment to credit on negligent misrepresentation claim).

663 *See* Taylor v. American Bankers Ins. Group, Inc., 700 N.Y.S.2d 458 (N.Y. App. Div. 1999) (class certification granted in case where consumers allege practice of rejecting insurance claims on grounds that customers had not been paying for the appropriate type of insurance after disclosing the nature of the insurance in small, inconspicuous type). *See* Osborne v. Mountain Life Ins. Co., 130 S.W.3d 769 (Tenn. 2004) (insurer not estopped from asserting policy exclusion by failure to inquire about insured's health, where insured's medical situation, if known when insurance was purchased as part of credit contract, would have made insured ineligible for the insurance). *Cf.* Matter of Sprouse, 577 F.2d 989 (5th Cir. 1978) (discussing effect of overreaching contract language on consumers in transactions which are not litigated).

664 Dobson, *Credit Insurance: The Hidden Insurance,* 65 Mich. Bar Journal 168, 169 (Feb. 1986). *See generally* Ch. 6, *supra* on the incidence of refinancing.

665 *Cf.* Peebles v. State, 87 Ga. App. 649, 75 S.E.2d 35 (1953).

666 Fagg, Credit Life and Disability Insurance 117 (1986). *See also* Founders Life Assurance Co. v. Poe, 251 S.E.2d 247 (Ga. 1978)

One other abuse surprisingly common with low-income borrowers is the sale of insurance to protect against unforeseen loss of income (accident and health or involuntary unemployment) to people whose ability to repay will not be jeopardized by such loss because they are on a fixed income, such as Social Security or AFDC.[667] The benefit to such a borrower is utterly illusory, as most disability policies have some form of "actively at work" clause which effectively excludes people with a non-wage income from benefits.[668] The same problem may also arise with the sale of involuntary unemployment insurance to unemployed borrowers. Such insurance also has an actively at work clause, and usually excludes self-employed workers. Involuntary unemployment insurance policies also may be sold to those who are highly unlikely to be laid off, such as those in the military.

Such sales may be viewed as a pretext for usury, because the insurance provides no benefit to borrowers. The sole benefit is to the creditor and insurer, and thus should be argued to be a pretext for usury.[669]

Other appropriate claims involving the sale of insurance with no benefit to the insured includes the straight contract defense of failure of consideration, UDAP and unconscionability, or even fraud.[670] In its laundry list of factors which are relevant to determining unconscionability, the UCCC lists a sale of services where the seller knows the consumer

could not receive substantial benefits from the services sold.[671] Such a sale also should be a breach of fiduciary duty[672] or a breach of the common law duty of disclosure.[673] Section 8.5.5.3, *infra* discusses these and other theories which can be used to try to collect on the benefit of the bargain if the debtor should die or become disabled.

The creditor, not the insurer, is squarely responsible for the insurance sale; the creditor knows the borrower's employment situation from the credit application. Further, while most insurance contracts limit the insurer's liability to a return of the premium if it is determined the borrower was ineligible for coverage, it is unclear that the creditor would return the interest earned on the premium.

8.5.5.2 Incomplete Coverage

A somewhat related situation arises where the borrowers purchase insurance to "take care of the debt," only to find later that they were sold only partial coverage. As consumer loan balances grow larger, and terms longer, it is becoming more common for creditors to sell credit insurance which does not completely insure the loan. For example, a ten-year, $10,000 policy may be sold in connection with a fifteen-year, $15,000 loan.[674] If the benefits of such a policy are misrepresented as being full coverage, the consumer should have a UDAP claim, or a common law fraud claim.[675] Such policies may substantively create potential liability for their sellers, as well.

In *Marshall v. Citicorp Mortgage*[676] a $25,000, ten-year decreasing term policy was sold on a fifteen-year loan with a $30,000 principal ($85,500 total obligation). The insurance decreased from its original face value at a rate of $208.33 month. Concurrently, the lender was using the Rule of 78 as an accounting accrual method on the loan, which can result in negative amortization in the early years on a

---

(relating exclusionary period back to original transaction, though loan refinanced four times; court ordered recovery under the policy).

667 National Ass'n of Ins. Comm'rs, A Background Study of the Regulation of Credit Life and Disability Insurance 51 (1970).

668 One policy reads: "The disability insurance under this policy shall be conditional upon the Debtor being actively employed and working 30-hours or more each week at the time the insurance is applied for. If the Debtor is not so employed at the time the insurance is applied for, the company's liability shall be limited to the return of any premiums paid for the disability coverage." Also, in some disability or involuntary unemployment policies, self-employed borrowers are excluded from coverage.

669 *See* § 8.7.1, *infra*; *see also* § 7.2.3, *supra*.

670 *See* Union Sec. Life Ins. Co. v. Crocker, 709 So. 2d 1118 (Ala. 1997) (punitive damages award for fraud in sale of credit life insurance coverage to plaintiff and her husband when he was known to have disqualifying health problems; award was reduced after U.S. Supreme Court concluded that a higher amount would violate due process, see 517 U.S. 1230 (1996)); Lucas v. Cont'l Cas. Co., 170 S.E.2d 856 (Ga. Ct. App. 1969) (jury question existed regarding waiver of exclusion for prior illness where insured questioned auto dealer about whether prior heart condition would limit credit insurance availability). *But see* Southards v. Cent. Plains Ins. Co., 441 P.2d 808 (Kan. 1968) (plaintiff denied coverage under credit disability policy where he did not know at the time of purchase that he had a certain degenerative disease, although a medical expert could have detected it if the plaintiff would have been examined); S. Branch Valley Nat'l Bank v. Williams, 155 S.E.2d 845 (W. Va. 1967) (credit insurer was not liable under policy where cashier for bank processed insurance application for insured who was ineligible based on age).

671 U.C.C.C. § 5-108(4)(b).

672 § 8.7.2, *infra*.

673 *See* Suburban State Bank v. Squires, 145 Wis. 2d 445, 427 N.W.2d 393 (Ct. App. 1988) (where borrower had heart attack and collected on disability insurance and loan was refinanced, court upheld finding that creditor was negligent in not advising borrower that new disability policy would bar recovery if borrower had another heart attack). *See also* § 8.7.3, *infra*.

674 In some states, the statute governing credit insurance may authorize policies only up to 10-year terms. Additionally, the high cost of coverage for high-balance, long-term loans may generate buyer resistance. Fagg, Credit Life and Disability Insurance 19 (1986). As a consequence, policies which provide incomplete coverage have been devised.

675 *Cf.* Ginocchio v. American Bankers Life Assur. Co., 889 F. Supp. 1078 (N.D. Ill. 1995) (credit disability insurance sold with 15-year mortgage ambiguous as to meaning of 36-month truncated term; insurer's motion for summary judgment on breach of contract, UDAP, and improper claims practices denied).

676 601 So. 2d 669 (La. Ct. App. 1992).

long-term loan.[677] Hence the value of the policy declined while the loan balance was growing. Moreover, the insurance authorization did not disclose the decreasing value, nor that its value would drop to $0 five years before the end of the loan term. (An insurance certificate sent subsequently was held inadequate to inform the consumers.) The court held the combination of the two otherwise legal practices (sale of the decreasing insurance and use of the Rule of 78) was unconscionable and a violation of the state unfair and deceptive acts and practices statute, since no reasonable person who knew the results would buy the insurance.[678] The borrower was relieved of her obligation to pay the premium or interest on it (over $7500 combined) and to retain the value of the policy proceeds.

8.5.5.3 Collecting the Benefits of the Insurance Bargain

8.5.5.3.1 General

Selling insurance to someone likely to be ineligible for benefits as a loan padding tool causes harm enough to a debtor, but when the feared casualty actually befalls the consumer, the damage is greatly compounded. There are some theories, however, which can be used by a disabled debtor or a deceased debtor's family to challenge a post-claim denial of insurance benefits.

At the outset, it is necessary for the practitioner to determine whether the creditor/seller or insurance company is the appropriate defendant. Either or both may be liable, though the claims leading to liability may differ. It may be advisable to name both parties in many cases.

There are common patterns involved in this category of credit insurance cases. Sometimes the creditor knows of the condition which would render the debtor ineligible (or should have known), but does not inform the insurer.[679] The creditor may simply not inquire about relevant facts, such as health.[680] In some cases, there is no instruction from the

insurer to do so. On occasion, the creditor deliberately misstates information on the insurance application. Another wrinkle is when the creditor does not properly process the borrower's insurance application.[681] Which theories of recovery are most likely to succeed, of course, will depend on the fact pattern presented.

8.5.5.3.2 Theories of recovery against the insurer

Since credit insurance is sold only through creditors, never directly by the insurer, the insurer's liability may depend upon whether the creditor/seller is viewed as the insurer's agent, or the borrower's agent, about which there is a divergence of judicial opinion. If the creditor acts as the insurer's agent, its knowledge of disqualifying factors, or misrepresentations may be attributed to its principal, the insurer. Though the division appears to be too close for these labels to be accurate, they have been denominated as a majority rule and minority rule. The "majority" rule holds that a creditor acts as the agent of the insured borrower, so the insurer cannot be bound by the creditor's knowledge.[682] (That, though, has implications for the creditor's liabil-

---

677 *See* § 5.5.1, *supra*.

678 Louisiana Consumer Credit Law, La. Rev. Stat. Ann. § 9:3551 (unconscionability) and La. Rev. Stat. § 51:1401 *et seq.* (UDAP).

679 *See, e.g.,* Union Security Life Ins. Co. v. Crocker, 667 So. 2d 688 (Ala. 1995), *vacated on other grounds*, 116 S. Ct. 1872 (1996) ($2 million punitive damage award was sent back to Alabama Supreme Court for further consideration in light of BMW of N. Am., Inc. v. Gore, 517 U.S. 559, 116 S. Ct. 1589 (1996)), *upon remand from Supreme Court*, 709 So. 2d 1118 (Ala. 1997) (creditor knew of consumer's bad health but filled out the credit insurance application listing no prior illnesses); Miller v. Dobbs Mobile Bay, Inc., 661 So. 2d 203 (Ala. 1995).

680 In addition to the specific eligibility factors mentioned in § 8.5.5.1, *supra*, some life and disability policies have blanket "sound" health or "good" health conditions. Where an eligibility requirement is not specified or express, it will not be implied in law. *See, e.g.,* First Federated Life Ins. Co. v.

Citizen's Bank & Trust, 593 S.W.2d 97 (Ky. App. 1979). *See also* Justus v. Mountain Life Ins. Co., 1999 Tenn. App. LEXIS 702 (Tenn. App. Oct. 15, 1999) (bank employee took no credit insurance application information and represented that credit life insurance policy was in full force and effect).

681 In one extreme case, the creditor advertised credit insurance to credit card holders and collected premium payments, but never obtained any insurance or forwarded the premiums to an insurer. Card v. Chase Manhattan Bank, 669 N.Y.S.2d 117 (Civ. Ct. 1996) (holding bank liable for false advertising).

682 *See, e.g.,* Sadtler v. John Hancock Mutual Life Ins. Co., 291 A.2d 500 (D.C. App. Ct. 1972) (decision based on Michigan statute, M.C.L.A. § 500.4416, and on master policy clause denying agency; seller/car dealer knew of debtor's poor health, but issued sales contract stating debtor was in good health; court held neither dealer nor financier was insurer's agent and their knowledge not attributable to insurer); National Life Ins. Co. v. Harriott, 268 So. 2d 397 (Fla. App. 1972) (no creditor/insurer agency where debtor informed the creditor that his wife was ill; creditor had no duty to inquire further about the nature of the illness, but the debtor had obligation to fully disclose the health problems); Merchants Bank v. Gill, 1999 Tex. App. LEXIS 3252 (Tex. App. Apr. 29, 1999) (bank acted as agent for insured in procuring insurance; as such, however, bank held liable for failing to inform insured of insurer's insolvency); South Branch Valley Nat'l Bank v. Williams, 151 W. Va. 775, 155 S.E.2d 845 (1967) (insurer not liable for benefits where debtor was ineligible because of age requirement, despite fact that creditor knew debtor was too old). *See also* Palmer v. Newport Trust Co., 245 A.2d 438 (Me. 1968) and Martinson v. North Central Life Ins. Co., 222 N.W.2d 611 (1974), *rehearing denied*, 225 N.W.2d 604 (Wis. 1975). A review of the citations in this section (§ 8.5.5.3) suggests the possibility that the more recent trend may be tipping toward finding the necessary relationship between the creditor and insurer. Perhaps more widespread awareness of the economic (and often corporate) ties between creditors and credit insurers have tilted (or can tilt) the balance. *See* §§ 8.2, 8.5.4, *supra*.

ity.[683]) But about half the cases follow the "minority" rule, and conclude that the creditor is the insurer's agent.[684] Note that a creditor's knowledge of a condition which would make the borrower ineligible has been present in both lines of cases. For example, the Alabama Supreme Court upheld a jury verdict for $2 million punitive damages (later reducing the award to $1 million after remand from the United States Supreme Court) for fraud against both the creditor and insurer in a recent case involving sale of credit life insurance to a borrower in ill health. In *Union Security Life Insurance Co. v. Crocker*,[685] a creditor, knowing of the borrower's ill-health (and consequent ineligibility for insurance) nonetheless filled out an application for credit insurance indicating no history of prior illnesses. When the borrower died, the claim for credit life benefits was denied. The widow brought a successful action for fraud, concealment, and a scheme to defraud against both the creditor and insurer. The lender, acting as a knowledgeable agent for the insurer has a duty to disclose that benefits might not be payable. The widow alleged that the insurer's failure to pay benefits was part of a scheme to defraud.[686]

Other factors which courts have considered in holding a creditor to be the insurer's agent are its role in issuing and accepting applications, collecting and paying the premiums, and its receipt of a percentage of the premium.[687]

Practitioners should consider the problem that can arise by arguing an agency theory or joint collusion to defraud on the part of the lender and insurer. Arbitration clauses are in vogue and may exist in either the loan documents or the insurance contract (or both). There is an argument that even a non-signatory to the document containing the arbitration clause may successfully invoke arbitration on the theory that the borrower's claims against the lender and creditor involve agency or are intimately founded upon and intertwined with the underlying contract obligations.[688]

---

683 *See* § 8.5.5.3.3, *infra*.
684 *See, e.g.*, Ginocchio v. American Bankers Life Assur. Co., 889 F. Supp. 1078 (N.D. Ill. 1995) (creditor's representation regarding ambiguous term in credit disability policy at issue); Union Security Life Ins. Co. v. Crocker, 667 So. 2d 688 (Ala. 1995) (creditor and insurer shared joint and several liability for fraud where creditor intentionally filled out false medical information on credit insurance application and borrower's claim was subsequently denied), *vacated on other grounds*, 116 S. Ct. 1872 (1996), *upon remand*, 709 So. 2d 1118 (Ala. 1997) (court reduced punitive damages award to $1 million by weighing reprehensible conduct of insurance company's agent (though an apparently isolated instance) coupled with the "catastrophic" economic injury to Ms. Crocker facing foreclosure of her mobile home in the wake of her husband's death against percentage of $2 million award to insurance companies' net worth); Miller v. Dobbs Mobile Bay, Inc., 661 So. 2d 203 (Ala. 1995) (deceased borrower allegedly twice tried to decline insurance due to his ill health, auto dealer told him it was required to get the car and ill health did not matter, so he signed the paperwork stating he was in good health; court held summary judgment for insurer inappropriate, as jury could find that "misrepresentation" was the fault of auto-dealer as agent, and agent did have authority to bind insurer); Hardy v. American Southern Life Ins. Co., 211 So. 2d 559 (Fla. 1968) (policy had sound health clause; creditor had actual knowledge of debtor's poor health); Grimm v. USLIFE Credit Life Ins. Co., 1999 Ohio App. LEXIS 2445 (Ohio App. May 19, 1999) (Ohio statute makes the person who solicits and procures insurance the agent of the company issuing the insurance); Simonson v. Michigan Life Ins. Co., 194 N.W.2d 446 (Mich. App. 1971) (sound health clause at issue; that insured was obviously paralyzed in one arm and one leg at least created a duty to inquire further); Key v. Cherokee Credit Life Ins. Co., 298 So. 2d 892 (La. Ct. App. 1974); McDaniel v. Ins. Co. of Oregon, 410 P.2d 814 (Or. 1966); Justus v. Mountain Life Ins. Co., 1999 Tenn. App. LEXIS 702 (Tenn. App. Oct. 15, 1999) (bank employee's representation that insurance policy in full force and effect is binding on insurance company). *See also* Hayes Truck Lines, Inc. v. Investors Ins. Corp., 525 P.2d 1289 (Or. 1974), which does not concern itself with agency roles, but does hold that where no inquiry is made about health and the insured relies on the representation of insurance, sound health and pre-existing illness clauses will not constitute an ironclad defense against insurance liability. *See also* Barnes v. First Franklin Fin. Corp., 313 F. Supp. 2d 634 (S.D. Miss. 2004) (court assumes lender is agent of insurer but finds no liability for misrepresentation about whether credit insurance was required because of disclosures in loan documents). *Cf.* Vining v. Enterprise Fin. Group, Inc., 148 F.3d 1206 (10th Cir. 1998) (insurer, through its appointed agent at the car dealership, sold a credit life insurance policy to the deceased husband of the plaintiff; jury award of $800,000 upheld where plaintiff proved the insurers' deliberate, willful pattern of rescinding life insurance policies as soon as claims were made without determining whether it had good cause to do so).

685 667 So. 2d 688 (Ala. 1995) *vacated on other grounds*, 116 S. Ct. 1872 (1996), *upon remand from Supreme Court*, 709 So. 2d 1118 (Ala. 1997) (court reduced punitive damages award to $1 million by weighing reprehensible conduct of insurance company's agent (though an apparently isolated instance) coupled with the "catastrophic" economic injury to Mrs. Crocker facing foreclosure of her mobile home in the wake of her husband's death against percentage of $2 million award to insurance companies' net worth). *Cf.* Miller v. Dobbs Mobile Bay, Inc., 661 So. 2d 203 (Ala. 1995) (similar facts, but fraud claim dismissed because deceased borrower was sole obligor and credit insurance did not list widow or children as secondary beneficiary; fraud claim did not survive his death).

686 *Cf.* § 8.5.5.1, *supra* on the renumerability of post-claim underwriting. This lender had generated nearly $40 million in premiums in four years, during which the insurance product's loss ratios ranged from only 16.3 to 21.1%.

687 *See* Ford Life Ins. Co. v. Jones, 563 S.W.2d 399 (Ark. 1978); Vulcan Life & Accident Ins. Co. v. United Banking Co., 118 Ga. App. 36, 162 S.E.2d 798 (1968); Justus v. Mountain Life Ins. Co., 1999 Tenn. App. LEXIS 702 (Tenn. App. Oct. 15, 1999). *Cf.* Union Security Life Ins. Co. v. Crocker, 667 So. 2d 688 (Ala. 1995), *vacated on other grounds*, 116 S. Ct. 1872 (1996), *upon remand from Supreme Court*, 709 So. 2d 1118 (Ala. 1997); Miller v. Dobbs Mobile Bay, Inc., 661 So. 2d 203 (Ala. 1995) (court notes auto dealer/agent also allegedly told borrower he could not buy the car without purchasing the credit life insurance).

688 *See, e.g.*, Roberson v. Money Tree of Alabama, Inc., 954 F. Supp. 1519 (M.D. Ala. 1997); Staples v. Money Tree, Inc., 936 F. Supp. 856 (M.D. Ala. 1996). *Contra* First Family Fin. Servs., Inc. v. Rogers, 736 So. 2d 553 (Ala. 1999) (arbitration clause not

Without expressly discussing agency theory, other courts have invoked waiver or estoppel theory to decide the issue, though this implicitly accepts the "minority" view of agency.[689] For example, in *Larr v. Minnesota Mutual Life Ins. Co.*[690] the debtor had reached the cutoff age of seventy within nine months of purchasing the insurance with the loan, though the insurer accepted payment of three monthly premiums after that date.[691] The court held the acceptance of the premiums after the cutoff age waived the contract provision establishing an age limitation.[692]

Some cases however, hold that waiver and estoppel may avoid forfeiture of a policy, but cannot change, rewrite, or enlarge the contract's insured risks.[693] Moreover, the insured

borrower's certain knowledge of a disqualifying condition will preclude application of waiver and estoppel.[694] One should be careful not to concede that knowledge too readily, though, for a vague awareness of some health problems which may or may not cause disability or death may not constitute adequate knowledge on the debtor's part.[695] Moreover, an innocent misrepresentation may not be a basis to infer "intent to deceive" nor to preclude application of waiver and estoppel doctrines.[696]

In some circumstances, UDAP statutes[697] or even RICO may be used. For example, the Third Circuit recently reversed summary judgment in favor of the insurer and remanded a case where borrowers had alleged that the insurer failed to pay excess disability benefits as provided for in their policies.[698] Some states also have incontestability clauses, limiting the rights of the insurer to contest the validity of the policy in some specified circumstances.[699]

8.5.5.3.3 Theories of recovery against the creditor

Since the benefit of a credit insurance bargain is having a debt taken care of if the insured risk comes to pass, it probably does not matter to the debtor whether the insurer

---

enforceable against by insurer even though plaintiff alleged agency because arbitration provision limited its own applicability to the signatories to the loan documents); Med Center Cars, Inc. v. Smith, 727 So. 2d 9 (Ala. 1998) (buyer's order containing the arbitration clause was the "complete and exclusive" agreement and clause could not be invoked by nonsignatory); Jones v. Money Tree, 686 So. 2d 1166 (Ala. 1996) (court strictly applied contract law by holding that since the insurer was a non-signatory on the loan documents which contained the arbitration clause, it had no right to invoke arbitration).

689 *See* Spears v. Colonial Bank of Alabama, 514 So. 2d 814, 817 (Ala. 1987), *specially concurring opinion* by J. Jones, for an analysis of the "agency relationship" issue. The Alabama Supreme Court has now been explicit in viewing the creditor as the agent of the life insurer. *See* Union Security Life Ins. Co. v. Crocker, 667 So. 2d 688 (Ala. 1995) *vacated on other grounds*, 116 S. Ct. 1872 (1996), *upon remand*, 709 So. 2d 1118 (Ala. 1997); Miller v. Dobbs Mobile Bay, Inc., 661 So. 2d 203 (Ala. 1995).

690 567 So. 2d 239 (Miss. 1990), and 924 F.2d 65 (5th Cir. 1991). *See also* Commonwealth of Puerto Rico v. Pan Am. Life Ins. Co., 307 F. Supp. 1065 (D. P.R. 1969) (master policy between creditor and insurer contained a clause stating that all borrowers "whom the creditor believes to be in good health" were eligible for insurance; court held this clause implied no affirmative duty on the creditor to investigate the health of borrowers, and since the company had accepted the premiums, it was estopped from denying coverage; Keller v. First Nat'l Bank, 403 S.E.2d 424, 427 (W. Va. 1991) ("[m]ost people expect insurance once they pay the premium," therefore, acceptance of premium payments by the seller, or an agent, after ineligibility becomes ascertainable was found to be a waiver of any ineligibility clause in the policy by virtue of creating a reasonable expectation of insurance).

691 While a credit insurance premium appears as a single-payment, upfront charge on a closed-end loan, the creditor's payments to the insurer on the customers' loans may be in monthly installments. *See* § 8.2, *supra*.

692 The creditor's knowledge was attributed to the insurer, thus implicitly accepting the creditor's agency.

Where age is the ineligibility factor, actual or constructive knowledge should be easy to establish, as most credit applications and credit insurance applications ask for age or a date of birth.

693 *See, e.g.*, Great Am. Reserve Ins. Co. v. Mitchell, 335 S.W.2d 707 (Tex. Civ. App. 1960) (where insurer accepted premiums beyond age termination date, insured only entitled to refund of premium); *Great American* was not a credit insurance case, but

two subsequent Texas cases explicitly followed *Great American*. Minnesota Mutual Life Ins. Co. v. Morse, 487 S.W.2d 317 (Tex. 1972), and Hocutt v. Prudential Ins. Co., 501 S.W.2d 347 (Tex. Civ. App. 1973). *See also* Currie v. Occidental Life Ins. Co. of North Carolina, 17 N.C. 458, 194 S.E.2d 642 (1973) (age-limitation clause), and Sharp v. Richmond Life Ins. Co., 212 Va. 229, 183 S.E.2d 132 (1971) (pre-existing illness clause). *But cf.* Ginocchio v. American Bankers Life Assur. Co., 889 F. Supp. 1078 (N.D. Ill. 1995) (where credit disability insurance contract's term was ambiguous, creditor-agent's representation may fill the void).

694 *See* National Life Ins. Co. v. Harriott, 268 So. 2d 397 (Fla. 1972) (husband's purchase of credit life insurance on car loan clearly motivated by his wife's impending death, which he failed to disclose).

695 *See, e.g.*, Security Southwest Life Ins. Co. v. Gomez, 768 S.W.2d 505 (Tex. App. 1989), in which the court upheld a jury verdict finding that the debtor's representation on a credit insurance application that he was "in good health," despite treatment for ischemic heart disease, was not made with an intent to deceive. Here, the court observed that Mr. Gomez was a farmer who had an elementary education. He had been seen by his doctor over the years for various ailments, but never hospitalized or unable to work. Moreover, it was clear that his purpose in going to the bank was to obtain a loan for his farming operations, not for insurance to provide for his family upon his death. *See also* Gatlin v. World Serv. Life Ins. Co., 616 S.W.2d 606 (Tenn. 1981).

696 *See* Carter v. Service Life & Casualty Ins. Co., 703 S.W.2d 349 (Tex. App. 1985) (insurer had burden not only to plead and prove debtor's answers in application for credit insurance are false, but that debtor gave answers knowing them to be false).

697 *See generally* § 8.7.4, *infra*; National Consumer Law Center, Unfair and Deceptive Acts and Practices § 5.3 (6th ed. 2004 and Supp.).

698 Schroeder v. Acceleration Life, 972 F.2d 41 (3d Cir. 1992).

699 *E.g.*, Ala. Code § 27-18-4 (group life).

has to pay the creditor, or whether the creditor itself must absorb the loss. Consequently, the creditor's potential liability should always be assessed, too, particularly as it can be independent of the insurer's liability.

Contract, tort and some statutory claims may be appropriate. The end result for the borrower may be the same as if the insurer were liable on the policy, as actual damages may be measured as the benefit of the reasonably anticipated bargain.[700] The contract approach argues that the creditor committed a breach of an implied or express contract to obtain insurance coverage for the debtor. By charging for and collecting insurance premiums, the creditor assumes a contractual obligation to purchase the insurance,[701] and to do so properly.[702] (At least one court has held that an affirmative insurance authorization on the loan,[703] may create a contractual duty to purchase the insurance.[704]) Courts have denied a creditor's claim for a post-repossession deficiency where the creditor had failed to provide the consumer with claim forms necessary to apply for the disability insurance[705] and where the contract allowed repossession "to extent permitted by law" but state law regarding pending credit insurance claims was violated.[706]

Various tort theories may also be used. Some courts have held that, with respect to the sale of credit insurance, the creditor stands in a fiduciary or quasi-fiduciary relationship to the borrower.[707] At least one court has found a duty to disclose factors which may indicate that the insurance may not provide the protection anticipated.[708] In some circumstances a creditor's failure to disclose to the borrower that his bad health may preclude receiving benefits constitutes fraud.[709] Negligence or misrepresentation has also been used successfully.[710]

As is discussed in other sections, unconscionability may be appropriate in some circumstances,[711] as may state unfair and deceptive acts and practices statutes.[712] Remember, too,

---

700 *E.g.*, Barnett v. First Nat'l Bank, 253 So. 2d 480 (Fla. App. 1971) (creditor liable for damages equal to the benefits under the policy when it had insured the wrong person).

701 Pernell v. First Savings & Loan Ass'n, 336 So. 2d 764 (Miss. 1976); Watkins v. Valley Fidelity & Trust Co., 474 S.W.2d 915 (Tenn. 1971).

702 *E.g.*, Barnett v. First Nat'l Bank, 253 So. 2d 480 (Fla. App. 1971) (creditor liable for damages equal to the benefits under the policy when it had insured the wrong person); *In re* Estate of Carter, 116 N.W.2d 419 (Iowa 1962) (creditor held liable when it did not insure all of the loans involved).

703 *See* § 8.4.1.5.1, *supra*; National Consumer Law Center, Truth in Lending § 3.9.4.5.5 (5th ed. 2003 and Supp.).

704 Allied Elevator, Inc. v. East Texas State Bank of Buna, 965 F.2d 34 (5th Cir. 1992) (decedent initialed request on face of note for credit life insurance and premium charge included in loan; court remands for consideration of whether that was a material term, the breach of which would excuse the debtor's estate from paying the balance). In the absence of a contract, though, the creditor may have no obligation to procure the insurance. *E.g.*, Burgess v. Charlottesville Savings & Loan Ass'n, 349 F. Supp. 133 (W.D. Va. 1972), *rev'd on jurisdictional grounds*, 477 F.2d 40 (4th Cir. 1973); Peer v. First Federal Savings & Loan Ass'n of Cumberland, 273 Md. 610, 331 A.2d 299 (1975). However, in neither case did the creditor collect premiums, and in both cases it was not clear that an application for insurance had been made.

705 Cincinnati Central Credit Union v. Harper, 70 Ohio Misc. 2d 80, 652 N.E.2d 10 (Ohio Mun. Ct. 1995) ("had the employee assisted in the application for disability, there may have been no delinquency."). *See also* Chandler v. General Motors Acceptance Corp., 426 N.E.2d 521 (Ohio App. 1980) (court denied summary judgment to creditor in a deficiency suit where the facts revealed that the creditor refused to complete its portion of a credit disability insurance claim which the consumer needed to file for payment but later repossessed the car!) Oregon courts have interpreted U.C.C. Article 9 to mandate that creditors check to determine whether a consumer is eligible for purchased credit insurance benefits before repossessing collateral. *See* National Consumer Law Center, Repossessions and Foreclosures § 4.4 (5th ed. 2002 and Supp.).

706 McManis v. San Diego Postal Credit Union, 71 Cal. Rptr. 2d 617 (Cal. Ct. App. 1998).

707 *See* § 8.7.2, *infra*. In jurisdictions where the creditor is considered the agent of the borrower, instead of the insurer, a fiduciary duty should naturally flow from that.

708 *Compare* Merchants Bank v. Gill, 1999 Tex. App. LEXIS 3252 (Tex. App. Apr. 29, 1999) (bank had duty to tell insured that insurance company was insolvent); Suburban State Bank v. Squires, 145 Wis. 2d 445, 427 N.W.2d 393 (Ct. App. 1988) (where borrower had heart attack and collected on disability insurance prior to refinancing loan, court upheld finding that creditor was negligent in not advising borrower that new disability policy would bar recovery if borrower had another heart attack) *with* First United Bank of Poplarville v. Reid, 612 So. 2d 1131 (Miss. 1992) (bank was borrower's agent for purposes of processing credit insurance, owing duty of good faith and reasonable care. Court found no breach of that duty in bank's failure to inform borrowers that loan could not be renegotiated upon expiration if one were in poor health; no substantial credible evidence they would have sought other life insurance had they known it was not renewable). *See generally* § 8.7.3, *infra*.

709 *See* Union Security Life Ins. Co. v. Crocker, 667 So. 2d 688 (Ala. 1995) *vacated on other grounds*, 116 S. Ct. 1872 (1996), *upon remand from Supreme Court*, 709 So. 2d 1118 (Ala. 1997).

710 *See, e.g.*, Beiter v. Decatur Federal Savings & Loan Ass'n, 150 S.E.2d 687 (Ga. 1966) (where a creditor undertakes to procure insurance and fails to do so due to its own fraud or misrepresentation, it is liable for the debtor's loss to the limit of the agreed-upon policy); Robichaud v. Athol Credit Union, 352 Mass. 351, 225 N.E.2d 347 (1967); Musgrave v. Mutual Savings & Loan Ass'n, 174 S.E.2d 820 (N.C. App. 1970) (where there was a question as to whether a loan had been insured, bank's "custom and usage" of insuring loans indicated to the borrower that this loan was insured; court further stated that this custom and usage, viewed alongside the bank's disorganized system of handling insurance applications, supported the finding of negligence by the bank); Park Federal Savings & Loan Ass'n v. Lillie, 24 Ohio Misc. 271, 265 N.E.2d 339 (1970), *and* American Bank and Trust Co. of Houma v. Deroche, 357 So. 2d 1176 (La. App. 1978), also used the reasoning in *Beiter* to find the creditor liable. *See also* Strickler v. Neff Trailer Sales, Inc., 542 F.2d 890 (4th Cir. 1976) (recovery of punitive damages allowed from a creditor who "maliciously" disregarded debtor's application for credit insurance and retained premium payments).

711 *See* §§ 8.5.5.2, *supra*, 8.7.5, *infra*.

712 *See* § 8.7.4, *infra*.

that the creditor also may be vulnerable to claims based on the notion that the sale of insurance in these circumstances is a pretext to collect extra, and perhaps illegal charges on the debt.[713]

8.5.6 Surpluses, Secondary Beneficiaries

Because the purpose of credit life insurance is to protect the account from default in the event the borrower dies, the named primary beneficiary will be the creditor. However, any surplus should be distributed to a secondary beneficiary. While there is no reliable data, many people question whether insurance companies actually distribute any surplus to a secondary beneficiary.

There are several reasons why these funds are not likely to be distributed, the most important of which is that a borrower's beneficiaries will not realize there is excess insurance. As discussed above, the borrower's purpose is to insure the outstanding balance, but the creditor as a general practice overinsures the loan by insuring the total of payments to give the creditor better protection and provide a larger premium base for collection. When the survivors are notified that the loan is paid off by insurance, they are satisfied. Most people would not expect to receive extra cash benefits. Secondly, who would file the claim? In many transactions there is no secondary beneficiary designated. This is in part because the borrower does not expect excess benefits over the balance due. Only an informed secondary beneficiary would request such payment.

The issue of surplus virtually always will come up if level life is written on a transaction, as it by definition overinsures the loan.[714] A surplus will usually result even in the case of declining term life, unless the borrower was in default at the time of death. If the policy provides, for example, that the insurance "shall at no time exceed the scheduled or actual amount of unpaid indebtedness whichever is *greater*," there should be a surplus if the borrower was ahead in his or her scheduled payments at the time of death.[715] A similar issue may arise with respect to disability insurance.[716]

A surplus may also result from the combined effect of different forms of credit insurance. The classic example is

where there is property insurance on an automobile loan, and the borrower dies in an accident involving the insured auto. The property insurance should pay off the debt, and all of the benefits under the credit life policy would be a surplus.

The NAIC Model Act requires that each individual policy or certificate of insurance must state that benefits "shall be paid to the creditor to reduce or extinguish the unpaid indebtedness and, whenever the amount of insurance may exceed the unpaid indebtedness, that any such excess shall be payable to a beneficiary, other than the creditor, named by the debtor or to his estate."[717] Thus, failure to distribute the surplus would be a breach of the insurance contract. The NAIC Model Act language has been interpreted to impose a duty on the creditor to apply the benefits to the borrower's account and distribute the surplus. That may create a fiduciary duty on the creditor's part toward the borrowers, at least upon the insurer's payment of benefits.[718] Should the creditor retain the surplus, it should constitute compensation which the creditor is not authorized by law to receive, thus an illegal overcharge.

8.6 Rebates

The issue of refunding unearned insurance premium charges must be explored in any insured credit transaction. The premium usually pays for coverage for a term concurrent with the scheduled term of the loan.[719] The refund issue may arise when the credit transaction is prepaid, either by prepayment, refinancing or otherwise, or when the insurance policy is terminated.[720] Termination of the policy may occur

---

713 *See* § 8.5.5.1, *supra.*

714 *See* § 8.3.1.2, *supra.*

715 *See* Dublinske v. Pacific Fidelity Life Ins. Co., 230 N.W.2d 924 (Iowa 1975).

716 *See* Schroeder v. Acceleration Life, 972 F.2d 41 (3d Cir. 1992) (credit disability insurance contract which provided that insurance would terminate upon discharge of indebtedness, but also that termination would be without prejudice to any claim originating prior to termination, was interpreted to mean that monthly benefits would be paid from date of disability to scheduled maturity date, even if loan actually satisfied earlier. According to a prior state court decision, company's failure to do so constituted breach of contract. Those facts formed basis for RICO and state UDAP claims in federal court, and appellate court denied insurer's motion for summary judgment).

717 Model Bill to Provide for the Regulation of Credit Life Ins. and Credit Accident and Health Ins., National Ass'n of Ins. Comm'rs, Model Regulatory Service § 6(B) (NIARS Corp., 1984).

718 Wilson v. Household Fin. Corp., 131 Cal. App. 3d 649, 182 Cal. Rptr. 590, 593 (1982). A UDAP claim should also be warranted.

719 Occasionally, the insurance may be for a shorter term if, for example, the borrower will reach the age of ineligibility prior to the loan maturation date, or if the scheduled loan term is longer than the insurance term allowed under the state credit insurance code. Because of the expense of insurance coverage for long-term loans (and state law restrictions on long-term insurance), an alternative called "truncated life" has been developed recently, which may cover the first 5 years on a 10 year loan, or 1 to 3 years on shorter loans. Fagg, Credit Life and Disability Insurance 19 (1986). Similarly disability insurance may provide "critical period coverage," which would cover disability occurring any time during the loan term, but would limit monthly payments to a shorter period. For example, two year critical period coverage may be written on a 10-year loan. Truncated disability may also be written, with the coverage period coinciding with the term covered under a truncated life policy. *Id.* at 27–28.

720 For example, in the Federal Trade Commission's case against Stewart Finance, the company allegedly failed to rebate unearned insurance premiums upon refinancing of a consumer's loan. Complaint, Fed. Trade Comm'n v. Stewart Fin. Co., Civ.

on occasions which may or may not coincide with paying off the credit transaction by one of these means.

The NAIC Model Act requires that each credit life or A&H insurance policy provide for a prompt refund or credit "to the person entitled thereto" in the event of termination of *insurance* prior to the scheduled maturity date of indebtedness.[721] The Model Act also requires that the insurance be terminated when the account is prepaid by renewal or otherwise.[722] The two provisions together thus mandate a refund any time the debt is prepaid by refinancing or otherwise.[723] This Credit Insurance Code provision is often reiterated in the applicable credit statutes.[724]

State Insurance Departments generally will prescribe the method by which a rebate must be calculated, usually authorizing the generous Rule of 78 formula.[725] There may be a minimum amount below which rebates need not be made.[726] Should proper rebates not be credited, the lender has retained greater compensation than that to which it is entitled, and the amount retained would be interest.[727] For information on how to check the mathematical accuracy of a rebate, see Chapter 5, *supra* on Rebates.

Where the policy is terminated without paying off the debt, one common ploy minimizes the creditor's refund obligation. A contract term may provide that insurance premium refunds will be applied to the last maturing installments, and not to the principal remaining unpaid or to currently maturing installments. Such a provision contains "the seeds of usury" and, if utilized may render the transaction usurious.[728] The reason such a provision unfairly and illegally benefits the creditor is that the scheduled installments are calculated to retire the principal at a predicted rate. Since the premium cost is ordinarily a part of the principal, if initially imposed in accord with all applicable laws, the refund should reduce the principal immediately, thus reducing the base upon which earned interest is to be calculated for the remainder of the term. By applying it to the last due installments, the creditor deprives the borrower of the earlier, (and consequently cheaper) retirement of principal.

An important issue which may arise is whether a credit insurance rebate is required when a debt is in default, accelerated, or reduced to judgment. Some state statutes require that all unearned charges, including insurance, be rebated on prepayment, and further require that acceleration be treated as prepayment.[729] The lender, however, may not credit the account with a refund upon acceleration, arguing the policy will remain in force until the originally scheduled maturity, and that the insurance premium is therefore an "earned" charge not subject to the rebate requirement. Theoretically, leaving insurance policies in effect after default may not seem to be unfair to borrowers, but for the fact that borrowers, many of whom may not even know the account is insured in the first place, are unlikely to think about submitting insurance claims once the debt has been reduced to judgment. More importantly, the insurance in fact may not remain in force, depending on the terms of the policy. That, of course, would deprive the creditor's argument of any semblance of validity.

To determine whether the failure to rebate an insurance premium upon acceleration is actionable, it is necessary to review carefully both the statute and the terms of the master policy between the lender and the insurer, if group insurance, or the borrower's policy if individually insured. *Either* the statute or the insurance contract may give rise to a claim.

One Georgia case states that there is no general requirement that a lender cancel insurance upon acceleration. The court held that there is thus no violation of a statute requiring insurance refunds upon cancellation of the insurance when the creditor accelerates the debt in accordance with a properly drafted acceleration clause, without giving an insurance refund because the insurance is still in effect.[730] However, such a requirement may be implied by the general rebate statute, or a rebate may be required because the insurance was in fact canceled.

No. 103CV-2648 (N.D. Ga. filed Sept. 4, 2003), *available at* www.ftc.gov/os/caselist/103cv2648.htm.

721 Model Bill to Provide for the Regulation of Credit Life Ins. and Credit Accident and Health Ins., National Ass'n of Ins. Comm'rs, Model Regulatory Service § 8B (NIARS Corp. 1984).

722 *Id.* § 5.

723 The Supreme Court of Mississippi has ruled that an undue delay of a premium refund supports an award for punitive damages. Mic Life Ins. Co. v. Hicks, 825 So. 2d 616 (Miss. 2002) (finding that a punitive damages award is appropriate for a two-year delay, but holding that a $1 million award for failure to refund $637.99 is unconstitutionally excessive and that trial and evidentiary errors in this particular case preclude a punitive damage award against the insurer).

724 *E.g.,* Iowa Code § 537.2510. It may also be incorporated by a general reference in the credit statute to the applicability of the credit insurance code.

725 Even in states where interest rebates must be calculated by the actuarial method, the Rule of 78 may be authorized for credit insurance rebates. Other authorized methods are the pro rata method, an average of the 78 and pro rata methods, or the Rule of Anticipation. *See* Fagg, Credit Life and Disability Insurance 182–184 (1986).

726 Model Bill to Provide for the Regulation of Credit Life Ins. and Credit Accident and Health Ins., National Ass'n of Ins. Comm'rs, Model Regulatory Service § 8B (NIARS Corp., 1984).

727 For reasons which are unclear, a recent case appears to have challenged the insurer, rather than the creditor for routinely failing to rebate unearned credit insurance premiums unless asked by the borrowers. Though a district court judge condemned the practice as "reprehensible," he held it did not constitute mail fraud sufficient to state a RICO claim. Richards v. Combined Ins. Co., 55 F.3d 247 (7th Cir. 1995). A UDAP claim, consequently dismissed on jurisdictional grounds, may be more successful if it is refiled.

728 Ford Motor Credit v. Yarbrough, 567 S.W.2d 96 (Ark. 1978).

729 *E.g.,* Iowa Code §§ 537.2510(1) and (6).

730 Williams v. Charter Credit Co., 179 Ga. App. 721, 347 S.E.2d 635 (1986).

If a state statute specifically provides that all required rebates must be made upon acceleration as if there was prepayment, the argument that the policy can remain in force and therefore is not an "unearned" charge has little force. First, the clear legislative intent is to treat acceleration as if it were prepayment by any other means, and the creditor cannot leave the insurance in force in those circumstances. Further, the argument that credit insurance could remain in force until the end of the originally scheduled term proves too much: it would suggest that creditors do not need to rebate interest until a debt is actually paid, irrespective of when acceleration occurred, an interpretation that would render the rebate statute a nullity, and thus an interpretation which the courts should not adopt.[731]

Irrespective of state law regarding how rebates upon acceleration are to be handled, whether the insurance policy remains "in force" is a question of fact which the consumer practitioner must explore. Even if state law does not mandate termination of the policy, it may terminate upon default by its own terms, which then triggers the rebate requirement. First, the actual policy must be reviewed to see how it defines termination events. If the insurance is group insurance, the borrower's certificate will probably not include the relevant terms. (The master policy issued to the creditor must be reviewed. The master policy may be obtained from the creditor or the insurer. It also will be on file at the state insurance department.) Some policies include default-related events as events triggering the automatic termination of the loan. Such events may relate to the repossession of the loan's collateral, to a specified kind of default in payment on the loan (e.g., six month's nonpayment), or to entry of judgment on the debt.[732]

If the policy calls for automatic termination of the policy at a specific default-related time, the refund must be made as of the date of that termination,[733] even if the creditor took no action at that time to cause the cancellation. In fact, even if the creditor thinks the policy is still in force and continues to forward monthly premium installments on that account to the insurer, the policy still may have been automatically terminated,[734] thus triggering the refund requirement.

In addition to automatic termination situations under the insurance policy, the creditor may overtly take some action resulting in the cancellation of the insurance. The creditor will sometimes cancel the insurance when the borrower is in default even if the policy itself does not list default as a ground for termination.[735] As one method of checking this, the practitioner can determine through formal or informal discovery how the creditor forwards to the insurer the premiums on insurance in force. On open-end accounts, the borrower usually pays the insurance periodically, so that it is most likely to be forwarded from the creditor to insurer on a periodic basis as well. In closed-end credit, while the premium usually is assessed to the borrower as a single up-front charge, the creditor may nonetheless forward to the insurer the premium payments on policies in force on a monthly outstanding-balance basis.[736] If the creditor uses the monthly outstanding balance premium payment method, and the consumer's policy premium is not forwarded after default, acceleration, or judgment, the policy has been terminated and the refund should be credited as of the date of termination.[737]

In addition to the issue of whether the insurance policy as a matter of *fact* remained in force after default or acceleration, the credit contract language should be examined. Some usury statutes prohibit not only receiving excess charges, but also merely "contracting for" charges greater than that allowed by law.[738] If the contract on its face provides that the lender will accelerate insurance premiums, this contractual provision may violate such a statute, thus automatically implicating the penalties for usury, including forfeiture of interest.[739] This is true even if the policy form has been approved by the insurance department.[740] Furthermore, filing suit for an amount which includes unrebated insurance, if rebates are required, may constitute "charging" an illegal charge.[741]

---

731 Singer, 2A Sutherland on Statutory Construction § 46.06 (5th ed. 2000). *But see* Central Budget Corp. v. Blackett, 349 N.Y.S.2d 577 (Civ. Ct. NY 1973) (acceleration accelerates maturity date, therefore no credit due if paid or accelerated "before maturity").

732 *See, e.g., In re* Williams, 92 B.R. 761 (Bankr. S.D. Ohio 1988) (terms of credit insurance agreement between insurer and creditor provided that repossession of the collateral terminated the insurance coverage and gave rise to right to refund for unearned premiums, and borrower was to be given refund or credit on his account if insurance terminated before term expired); Carl v. G.M.A.C., 199 N.E.2d 452 (Ill. Ct. App. 1964). The insurance policy at issue provided for automatic termination " . . . (b) 90th day after continued default in payment of any installment of obligation when due, unless collateral is repossessed during 90-day period, (c) If repossessed on or before 90th day after default, then on the 15th day after repossession unless the debtor redeems and the creditor reinstates contract."

733 This is because the refund language in use in most states requires a "prompt" refund upon termination of the *insurance*. Model Bill to Provide for the Regulation of Credit Life Ins. and Credit Accident and Health Ins., National Ass'n of Ins.

Comm'rs, Model Regulatory Service § 8B (NIARS Corp., 1984).

734 *See* Palmer v. Newport Trust Co., 245 A.2d 438 (Me. 1968).

735 *See, e.g.,* F.D.I.C. v. Gulf Life Ins. Co., 737 F.2d 1513, 1518 n.4 (11th Cir. 1984).

736 This permits the creditor, who in the interim may retain the unearned portion of the premium, to obtain additional investment income. *See* § 8.2, *supra.*

737 Be aware, though, that forwarding the premiums will not keep the policy in force contrary to automatic termination provisions in the policy.

738 *See generally* § 10.5.4.2, *infra.*

739 Brown v. Associates Fin. Servs. Corp., 346 S.E.2d 873 (Ga. App. 1986). *See also* Varner v. Century Fin. Co., 738 F.2d 1143, 1149–50 n.10 (11th Cir. 1984).

740 Brown v. Associates Fin. Servs. Corp., 346 S.E.2d 873, 874 (Ga. App. 1986).

741 *See* § 10.5.4.2, *supra.*

Another way in which creditors may try to evade the requirement to rebate unearned insurance premiums is to use boilerplate language taking a security interest in insurance. Any purported security interest in insurance should be carefully examined: contract language giving a security interest in specified property "and insurance or other proceeds thereon" was held in one case to give rise to a security interest only in property insurance on the collateral. Neither it, nor any other provision in the contract, gave the creditor any right to retain refunds on the credit life and disability insuring the loan.[742]

8.7 Remedies

8.7.1 Usury

As has been noted throughout this chapter, excess insurance charges may be imposed in a number of ways—through excessive rates,[743] various types of excessive coverage,[744] or failure to comply with other conditions which applicable insurance and credit statutes impose as a necessary precondition to excluding insurance premiums from the finance charge, failure to rebate unearned premiums—and they should be considered interest.

Especially in insurance packing cases, the full impact of the insurance and method of its sale should be explored. When compulsory insurance was common, it was legal so long as it was sold in good faith and not as a pretext for usury.[745] Now, even if the insurance technically complies with the law, those cases should still provide sound precedent for an argument that the insurance charges are interest if the circumstances strongly suggest they were not imposed in good faith, but rather as a pretext for usury. It can be said of a wide array of the types of credit insurance practices discussed in this chapter that "[i]t is impossible to wink so hard as not to see what [is] expected by the contract—that its end [is] more interest on the money advanced than the law authorize[s]."[746] As discussed earlier in this chapter, certain situations do strongly suggest a lack of good faith

where there is little objective benefit to the borrower, but much benefit accrues to the creditor.

Careful attention must be paid to presenting evidence regarding the circumstances: the full extent of the creditor's profit; evidence regarding the borrower's level of sophistication or education; the borrower's impression of implicit or explicit coercion;[747] or the borrower's special relationship of confidence with the lender.[748] Lacking such specific evidence of overreaching, the court may view the premiums as a legitimate charge passed on to a third party, and may also view commissions as compensation for services in connection with the insurance just as any other agent commission is treated.[749] Where the credit insurance is hidden interest, any specific statutory remedy for excessive charge, or the more general array of traditional usury remedies should be available.[750] (If the statute provides only for administrative enforcement, it may be necessary to argue there is an implied private right of action.[751])

---

742 *In re* Williams, 92 B.R. 761 (Bankr. S.D. Ohio 1988). [*N.B.*: the right to a rebate of credit life and disability rebates arose because the insurance contract automatically terminated coverage upon repossession of collateral securing the loan.]

743 *See* §§ 8.5.3.1–8.5.3.2, *supra*.

744 *See* §§ 8.5.3.3, 8.5.4, 8.5.5.1, *supra*.

745 *See* § 8.5.2.3, *supra*.

746 Wilson v. Whitworth, 125 S.W.2d 112, 113–114 (Ark. 1939), *quoting* Heytle v. Archibald Logan, 1 A.K. Marsh, Ky, 529 (lender had required a $3,500 life insurance policy for a $150 loan from a borrower who earned 22 cents an hour working 5 to 8 hours a day). *Contra* Lemelledo v. Beneficial Mgmt., 674 A.2d 582 (N.J. Super. Ct. App. Div. 1996) (court found that insurance charges are not interest, citing state statutes excluding certain charges from the definition of interest), *aff'd on other grounds*, 696 A.2d 546 (N.J. 1997).

747 A number of cases declined to find usury where there was no indication the insurance was more expensive than if purchased elsewhere, or no circumstances of compulsion, duress, or fraud. *Compare* the Arkansas Supreme Court's analysis in Poole v. Bates, 520 S.W.2d 273 (Ark. 1975) *with* its analyses in Robinson v. Rebsamen Ford, Inc., 530 S.W.2d 660 (Ark. 1975) *and* Aclin Ford v. Cordell, 625 S.W.2d 459 (Ark. 1982). *See also* Coner v. Morris S. Berman Unlt'd, 65 Md. App. 514, 501 A.2d 458 (1985) ($25,000 coverage on a small loan not improper where there was no evidence that the excess coverage added cost to the premium).

748 *See* § 8.7.2, *infra*.

749 *See, e.g.,* Anthony v. Community Loans & Inv. Corp., 559 F.2d 1363 (5th Cir. 1977); Poole v. Bates, 520 S.W.2d 273 (Ark. 1975). *See also* § 8.5.3.2, *supra*. *But see* Kenty v. Bank One, Columbus, N.A., 1992 WL 170605 (S.D. Ohio Apr. 23, 1992) (commissions, kickbacks or rebates paid by insurer to creditor from premium charged to borrower's account are interest), *aff'd in part rev'd in part* 92 F.3d 384 (6th Cir. 1996) (without disturbing holding that those costs constitute interest, court held national bank defendant authorized under most favored lender status to charge unlimited interest under Ohio law, therefore no usury found [*cf.* § 9.2.8, *infra*]).

750 *See, e.g.,* Car Now Acceptance Co. v. Block, 2002 WL 32001272 (Ohio C.P. Nov. 25, 2002) (certifying class action in part based on usury claim where consumer asserted that the $35 he paid for VSI insurance should have been included in the finance charge rather than the amount financed, thus bringing the interest rate above the state usury ceiling), *aff'd*, 2003 WL 21714583 (Ohio App. July 24, 2003) (unpublished, citation limited). For a fuller discussion of usury claims, see § 10.8, *infra*.

751 *E.g.,* Bailey v. Defenbaugh & Co. of Cleveland, Inc., 513 F. Supp. 232, 240–41 (N.D. Miss. 1981); Transamerica Fin. Corp. v. Superior Court, 158 Ariz. 115, 761 P.2d 1019 (1988), *rev'g* Transamerica Fin. Corp. v. Superior Court, 155 Ariz. 327, 746 P.2d 497 (Ct. App. 1987); Tew v. Dixieland Fin., Inc., 527 So. 2d 665 (Miss. 1988). *See also* § 10.8, *infra*. *But see* Dixon v. S&S Loan Serv. of Waycross, 754 F. Supp. 1567 (S.D. Ga. 1990) (federal court holds no implied private right of action under Ga. Comp. R. & Regs. § 120, implementing the Georgia Industrial Loan Act).

8.7.2 *Breach of Fiduciary Duty*

Creditors may have a fiduciary duty to borrowers, which they may breach if they impose disadvantageous credit insurance charges. Ordinarily, debtors do not have a fiduciary relationship with creditors,[752] but one may be extrapolated with respect to credit insurance from a number of sources. It is a question of fact whether the creditor owes a fiduciary duty to any given borrower.[753]

Creditors which are part of a bank holding company have a fiduciary obligation when they sell credit insurance to borrowers.[754] In *In re Dickson*,[755] that duty was violated by selling insurance at inflated premiums, receiving a 25% commission and failing to disclose such facts.[756]

A source of a creditor's fiduciary duty where the creditor is not a bank holding company is that credit insurance sales are generally required to be made by licensed agents;[757] and state insurance laws may give rise to a fiduciary obligation on the creditor's part. At a minimum, a fiduciary relationship creates a duty to disclose the availability of cheaper insurance.[758]

Other cases have found the source of a fiduciary relationship in the "trust and confidence" which the borrower has reposed in the creditor, at least with respect to terms raised as part of "loan processing," after the central terms are agreed upon through arms' length negotiation. In *Stone v. Davis*,[759] an Ohio court found a fiduciary relationship to have arisen, after a mortgage had been arranged, when the lender purportedly broached the subject of mortgage insurance.[760] Another court found a quasi-fiduciary relationship in *Hutson v. Wenatchee Federal Savings and Loan Ass'n*[761] where the lender had advised the borrower on a number of things, giving rise at a minimum to a duty of disclosure.

Both of these factors were present in another case finding a fiduciary duty on the part of an auto dealer with respect to the sale of credit insurance, though the decision is unclear as to whether it might have reached the same result in their absence. In *Tomaszewski v. McKeon Ford, Inc.*[762] the dealer

---

752 *See* Ross v. Citifinancial, 344 F.3d 458 (5th Cir. 2003); Hutson v. Wenatchee Fed. Sav. & Loan Ass'n, 588 P.2d 1192, 1198 (Wash. Ct. App. 1979). *Cf.* Younker v. Citizens Commercial Bank & Trust Co., 2004 WL 1770439 (Ohio Ct. App. Aug. 9, 2004) (unreported) (creditor does not have fiduciary duty to offer credit insurance).

753 Browder v. Hanley-Dawson Cadillac, 62 Ill. App. 3d 623, 379 N.E.2d 1206, 1210–11 (Ill. App. 1978).

754 *In re* Dickson, 432 F. Supp. 752 (W.D.N.C. 1977), *interpreting* 12 C.F.R. § 225.4(a)(1), now appearing at 12 C.F.R. § 225.28(b)(11) (1999).

755 432 F. Supp. 752 (W.D.N.C. 1977).

756 *Id.* at 760. In order to avoid confusion when *Dickson* is used as precedent regarding the Bank Holding Company Act, it unfortunately is necessary to discuss the history of the Act as it relates to credit insurance. In 1971, the Federal Reserve Board granted bank holding companies the authority to act as insurance agents and brokers, selling credit life insurance, and stated that it expected lenders utilizing that authority to exercise a fiduciary responsibility to the insured borrower. The Board specifically suggested that lenders utilizing this authority must make their best effort to obtain insurance at the "lowest practicable cost to the consumer." *Id.* citing 36 Fed. Reg. 15526 (Aug. 17, 1971). In 1972, bank holding companies were also authorized to engage in some insurance underwriting activities. Those seeking to engage in underwriting activities were required to "show a public benefit in the form of a reduction in the premium cost of such insurance below the maximum or prima-facie rate established by the state and/or charged by credit insurance underwriters in the state." 51 Fed. Reg. 36201, 36204 (Oct. 9, 1986).
In 1986 the Federal Reserve Board amended rules on the authority of bank holding companies and their subsidiaries to sell and underwrite credit insurance, and deleted its ruling that the Bank Holding Company Act's public benefits requirement necessitated a reduction in insurance rates in order to allow a bank holding company to underwrite credit insurance. This change focused exclusively on the role of the bank holding company as an underwriter, and the relationship of a bank holding company's authorized rates to those authorized generally by state insurance commissions. The FRB's earlier position that when acting as insurance agents or brokers in *selling* insurance, the bank holding company lender should exercise a fiduciary responsibility. The Board recognized that coercion is "more likely to be exerted by an agent at the point of sale," rather than by the underwriter and thus such concerns are not properly addressed in underwriting rules. 51 Fed. Reg. at 36204 (Oct. 9, 1986). Though these regulations were overhauled in

1997 and renumbered, the Board specifically stated that the current regulation had not been changed. "Several commenters urged the Board to take a variety of steps to authorize broader insurance activities. The Board will continue to consider these suggestions in light of the specific terms of the BHC [Bank Holding Company] Act." 62 Fed. Reg. 9290 (Feb. 28, 1997).

757 Model Bill to Provide for the Regulation of Credit Life Ins. and Credit Accident and Health Ins., National Ass'n of Ins. Comm'rs, Model Regulatory Service § 9 (NIARS Corp., 1984).

758 *See, e.g.*, Robinson v. Rebsamen Ford, Inc., 530 S.W.2d 660 (Ark. 1975); Browder v. Hanley-Dawson Cadillac, 379 N.E.2d 1206, 1211–12 (Ill. App. 1978). Note that in Robinson v. Rebsamen Ford, *supra*, the Court stated that it was "influenced," but not "controlled" by state insurance laws requiring good faith. 530 S.W.2d at 662. Thus *Rebsamen Ford* may be used as precedent even in the absence of a similar statutorily imposed duty of good faith.

759 419 N.E.2d 1094 (Ohio 1981), *cert. denied*, 454 U.S. 1081 (1981). *Cf.* Blon v. Bank One, Akron, N.A., 519 N.E.2d 363 (Ohio 1988) (cites factors which led court to conclude no fiduciary relationship existed, hence no duty to disclose that finance charge included a finder's fee, and that finder's fee was on sliding scale which increased with higher interest rates. [*Ed. note*: It should be noted that the finder's fee was included in the disclosed APR, so there was no question of a "hidden" finance charge included in the loan principal as sometimes happens with broker's fees or finders' fee. *See* § 7.3.2, *supra*]).

760 *See also* Crow v. Fred Martin Motor Co., 2003 WL 1240119 (Ohio Ct. App. Mar. 19, 2003) (finding a fiduciary duty where the consumer applied for credit insurance in connection with her car purchase and "entrusted Appellee to process and forward the signed paperwork and insurance premium payment" to the insurer; the consumer subsequently was rejected for coverage but was not informed until she sought to file a claim).

761 588 P.2d 1192 (Wash. Ct. App. 1978).

762 573 A.2d 501 (N.J. Super. Ct. App. Div. 1990).

was a cousin of the borrower, a woman who wished to purchase the car in her own name. He advised her that her credit probably would not be approved on her income alone by Ford Motor Credit and that her husband (whose monthly earnings were almost three times as much as hers) would need to be joined as co-buyer. He also interceded with the creditor to approve the credit when it was questioned. Insurance was sold, without discussion or explanation, naming only the wife as the insured. (She did not specifically ask for coverage on her husband.) When her husband died, her income was not sufficient to make the payments, and the car was repossessed. The court held the dealer had a duty to inform Ms. McKeon of the significance of failing to insure her husband, the principal income earner.

One commentator has suggested that a creditor, when selling credit insurance, acts as the borrower's agent, thus giving rise to a fiduciary relationship.[763] This source of fiduciary responsibility, of course, is broader than the two previously discussed, as it would apply to all creditors who sell credit insurance to their customers.

In a special concurrence in *Spears v. Colonial Bank of Alabama*,[764] Justice Jones carefully considers the distinction between an insurance agent and an insurance broker. The opinion notes that creditors are in a unique position:

> [c]learly, the bargaining power of potentially thousands of customers each year puts [the creditor] in a situation where it can obtain the "most favorable terms from competing [insurance] companies." While brokers generally seek to obtain the most favorable terms for their *clients*, the *creditor*/broker uses the competition between in-

surance companies to obtain the highest compensation for *itself*.[765]

Such freedom to "shop around" for an insurer precludes the creditor from being defined as an "agent" of the insurance company, even though it chooses to deal with only one insurer. A creditor should not, "by such self-serving acts," be allowed to "avoid its fiduciary duty to the insured."[766]

While the above analysis would suggest that a creditor, when selling credit insurance, should be viewed to be a broker, and hence an agent of the insured, as a matter of law, Justice Jones suggests that, it should be a question of fact. In either case, if the creditor is a broker as a matter of law or fact, it is an agent of the insured borrower, with all the duties an agent owes to its principal. At a minimum, that would include advice as to price and the availability of cheaper insurance.[767]

Once a fiduciary relationship is established, whatever its source, there are a number of duties implicated: a duty of loyalty, the duty to use care and skill, to provide the borrower with information he or she "would desire to have," and to disclose any adverse interests the agent might have.[768] A breach of fiduciary duty claim would be particularly appropriate in insurance packing cases, as they often involve a breach of most duties a fiduciary has. The claim would also be appropriate in most other situations involving abuses discussed in this chapter.[769]

8.7.3 Breach of the Duty to Disclose; Fraud and Related Claims

8.7.3.1 Duty to Disclose

Even if the facts do not establish a duty which rises to the level of a fiduciary duty, there may nonetheless be a common law "duty to disclose." The *Restatement of Torts* describes a duty to disclose facts basic to a transaction if one party knows the other is about to enter into the agreement under a mistake as to the facts and if the other party, because

---

763 Budnitz, *The Sale of Credit Life Insurance: The Bank as Fiduciary*, 62 N.C.L. Rev. 295 (1984). *See also* Harris v. Illinois Vehicle Premium Fin. Co., 2000 U.S. Dist. LEXIS 13763 (N.D. Ill. Sept. 7, 2000); Hobson v. Lincoln Ins. Agency, Inc., 2000 U.S. Dist. LEXIS 13314 (N.D. Ill. Sept. 7, 2000) (breach of fiduciary duty and UDAP claims survived motions to dismiss where the insurance premium finance company and the insurance company were connected and failed to disclose this fact to the consumer; note that RICO claims were dismissed but with leave to amend in these cases); Robinson v. Rebsamen Ford, Inc., 530 S.W.2d 660 (Ark. 1975). *But see* Frye v. American Gen. Fin., 307 F. Supp. 2d 836 (S.D. Miss. 2004) (no fiduciary duty between creditor and borrower because insufficient course of dealing); Knapp v. American Gen. Fin. Inc., 111 F. Supp. 2d 758 (S.D. W. Va. 2000); Mans v. Peoples Bank of Imboden, 10 S.W.3d 885 (Ark. 2000) (no fiduciary relationship between bank and customer regarding credit insurance; bank acted as agent for insurance company); The Huntington Mortgage Co. v. DeBrota, 703 N.E.2d 160 (Ind. App. 1998) (no fiduciary duty between creditor and borrower absent special circumstances); Rossbach v. FBS Mortgage Corp., 1998 Minn. App. LEXIS 374 (Apr. 7, 1998); Green v. Paradise Pontiac, 483 N.E.2d 1213 (Ohio App. 1984) (where debtor admitted creditor was not his agent, and credit insurance was not required, but debtor requested it, there was no fiduciary relationship and no duty to disclose the creditor's commission).

764 514 So. 2d 814, 818 (Ala. 1987).

765 *Id.* at 819. *See generally* § 8.2.3.1, *supra* on reverse competition.

766 *Id.* at 820 (the opinion notes that while there are cases where the creditor was held to be the agent of the insurer, those holdings were generally in contexts in which such a result was for the protection of the insured-borrower in a dispute with the insurer. *Id.* at 818). *See generally* § 8.5.5.3.2, *supra*.

767 *Id.* at 820.

768 Budnitz, *The Sale of Credit Life Insurance: The Bank as Fiduciary*, 62 N.C.L. Rev. 322–23 (1984).

769 Note that such claims, and other credit-insurance claims, will be subject to the applicable statute of limitations and that the discovery rule likely will not be available to extend that period. *See* Bolden v. Kentucky Fin. Co., 316 F. Supp. 2d 406 (S.D. Miss. 2004) (statute of limitations not tolled by the discovery rule because plaintiffs could have found the alleged law violations at loan closing); Dixon v. First Family Fin. Servs. Inc., 2003 WL 21788959 (S.D. Miss. July 15, 2003) (same).

of the relationship involved, the customs of the trade or other objective circumstances, would reasonably expect disclosure of those facts.[770] The Colorado Court of Appeals has applied that doctrine in a situation in which the borrower testified he would not have purchased a credit disability policy had he known the monthly benefit did not fully cover his monthly obligation. The court stated that:

> [I]f a sale of insurance is included as part of a loan agreement, the lender has a duty to disclose to the borrower before the transaction is consummated, a brief written description of such insurance, including the type and amount of the coverages and, if a separate charge is made for the insurance, the amount of that charge. This duty may be fulfilled by making the disclosures clearly and conspicuously in any of the loan documents.[771] Certainly a lender has a duty to disclose to a borrower that he or she may be ineligible for benefits under the credit insurance policy being sold, particularly where the insurance agent, i.e., the creditor, is the agent of the insured.[772]

Most states require that information as to credit life and disability insurance be disclosed on the individual policy or certificate of insurance,[773] or that notice of proposed insurance containing the information be provided to the borrower at the time the indebtedness is incurred.[774] Whether the required disclosures were in fact given prior to consummation is a question of fact.[775]

Most consumer surveys suggest that little information is given orally regarding insurance, and the information is certainly not detailed.[776] As to whether written disclosure is routinely given prior to consummation, the practitioner could depose a loan officer as to whether the insurance certificates are included in loan sets. If they are, the order of the documents can be important; if not, a practitioner should ask whether the certificates are given to the borrower when the completed documents (note, security agreement, TIL disclosure) are signed. The certificate of insurance, unlike the other loan documents, does not generally include the borrower's signature. The certificate may therefore be at the bottom of the pile of papers, or not given to the borrower prior to obtaining the signature—which would ordinarily be the "consummation of the loan." Again, this duty to disclose may be relevant to a number of abusive credit insurance practices, including excessive coverage, duplicative insurance, insurance packing, or selling insurance to ineligible borrowers.

8.7.3.2 Fraud; Misrepresentation and Concealment

Fraud or related claims may be appropriate in some circumstances.[777] As is discussed in § 8.5.5.3.2, *supra* knowingly selling credit insurance to a borrower unlikely to be eligible for benefits has been found to be fraudulent under Alabama law.[778] One intriguing case raises the question of whether selling excessive insurance coverage may be fraudulent. The Alabama Supreme Court has held it is a factual question whether an automobile dealer fraudulently misrepresented the amount of insurance needed to pay off

---

770 Restatement (Second) of Torts § 551(2) (1977).

771 Bair v. Public Serv. Emp. Credit Union, 709 P.2d 961, 962 (Colo. Ct. App. 1985). *But see* Blon v. Bank One, Akron, N.A., 519 N.E.2d 363 (Ohio 1988) (bank had no duty to disclose details of its financing fee arrangement with auto dealer whereby dealer's finder's fee was on sliding scale which increased with higher rates. [*Note:* the finder's fee was included in the interest rate calculation, so there was no allegation of "hidden" interest padding the principal.]).

772 Union Security Life Ins. Co. v. Crocker, 667 So. 2d 688 (Ala. 1995), *vacated*, 116 S. Ct. 1872 (1996), *upon remand*, 709 So. 2d 1118 (Ala. 1997); Suburban State Bank v. Squires, 145 Wis. 2d 445, 427 N.W.2d 393 (Ct. App. 1988) (where borrower had heart attack and collected on disability insurance under a prior loan, court upheld finding that creditor was negligent in not advising borrower that new disability policy sold at refinancing would bar recovery if borrower had another heart attack). *See also* Smoot v. Physicians Life Ins. Co., 87 P.3d 545 (N.M. Ct. App. 2003) (allegation of failure to disclose that monthly life insurance premiums are more costly than an annual premium states a claim for statutory and common law duty to disclose a material fact); Merchants Bank v. Gill, 199 Tex. App. 3252 (Tex. App. Apr. 29, 1999) (bank had duty to notify insured of insurer's insolvency).

773 Model Bill to Provide for the Regulation of Credit Life Ins. and Credit Accident and Health Ins., National Ass'n of Ins. Comm'rs, Model Regulatory Service § 5(B) (NIARS Corp., 1984).

774 *Id.* § 6(C) & (D).

775 Bair v. Public Serv. Emp. Credit Union, 709 P.2d 961, 962 (Colo. Ct. App. 1985).

776 *See, e.g.*, College of Bus. Adm., Ohio Univ., Consumer Credit Life and Disability Insurance, 75 (C. Hubbard, ed. 1973).

777 Note that general claims of fraud regarding the terms of the insurance often will face the argument that a plaintiff has a duty to read the contract and cannot rely on oral misrepresentations regarding a written contract. *See, e.g.*, Ross v. Citifinancial, 344 F.3d 458 (5th Cir. 2003).

778 *See* Union Security Life Ins. Co. v. Crocker, 667 So. 2d 688 (Ala. 1995) *vacated on other grounds*, 116 S. Ct. 1872 (1996), *upon remand from Supreme Court*, 709 So. 2d 1118 (Ala. 1997). *See also* Cordell v. Greene Fin. of Georgetown, Ga., 953 F. Supp. 1391 (M.D. Ala. 1996) (misrepresentation claim which involved the selling of disability insurance including a provision which excluded from coverage anyone not working at least 30 hours per week on the effective date to a borrower whose only source of income was Social Security (and, therefore, not working) survived creditor's and insurer's motion for summary judgment) (interpreting Georgia law). *But see* Amerson v. Gardner, 681 So. 2d 570 (Ala. App. 1996) (claim for fraud not stated where borrower was simply asked if he wanted credit disability insurance, where creditor had no knowledge of any preexisting conditions, and where borrower failed to read the insurance application prior to signing which informed him of the conditions of eligibility).

the debt in the event of death.[779] The decision should have ramifications outside of Alabama, because the excessive coverage under scrutiny came in the form of the sale of gross, rather than net credit life insurance coverage.[780] The high court held that gross coverage in fact was illegal under Alabama law, holding that the plain meaning of "amount of credit" is the amount financed, not the total of payments. Further, upon rehearing, the court rejected the industry's argument that the decision should have no retroactive effect. As to fraud, the court held that the case could go to the jury only on a claim of innocent/mistaken misrepresentation because the creditor had calculated the premium relying upon an interpretation of the phrase "amount of credit" which the court found to be erroneous.[781] (In swift response to this decision, the Alabama legislature amended the applicable statute to favor net coverage for installment loans, stating that the amount of credit insurance on installment loans entered into after June 20, 1996 "shall not exceed the greater of the approximate unpaid balance of the debt, excluding unearned finance charges, if any, or the approximate unpaid scheduled balance of the debt, excluding unearned finance charges, if any, plus the amount of one scheduled payment"; for single payment consumer credit transactions, premiums may be based on the total of payments.)[782]

Another misrepresentation-based challenge to a common credit insurance practice survived a lender's motion for summary judgment on a RICO claim.[783] In a force-placed insurance case, borrowers alleged that the rebates given by the insurer to the lender ("kickbacks," according to borrowers, "commissions" according to the defendants) violated RICO.[784] The court held that the borrowers believed

they were being charged what it cost to purchase the insurance, and the bank's failure to pass along the rebates might be viewed as creating either fraudulent omissions or affirmative misrepresentations. Unfortunately, the court, upon rehearing, reversed itself and held that a false statement was not made by the bank when it told the borrower that it "may add such insurance premiums, and finance charges thereon, to any loan balance."[785] The court said that "premiums" could include commissions from the insurance company to the bank!

8.7.4 Unfair and Deceptive Acts and Practices

Unfair and Deceptive Acts and Practices (UDAP) statutes are well suited to challenge credit insurance abuses. A number of cases have held UDAP statutes applicable to credit insurance sales.[786] It is necessary to review the UDAP statute and case law in a particular jurisdiction carefully, because some UDAP statutes exclude credit or insurance transactions from their coverage.[787]

Many of the abuses described above would fall under the general unfairness standard. A practice is unfair when:

- The challenged practice causes the consumer to suffer substantial injury;

779 McCullar v. Universal Underwriters Life Ins. Co., 687 So. 2d 156 (Ala. 1996). Subsequently, the Alabama Supreme Court held that in evaluating the factual question of whether the premium calculation method was fraudulently suppressed, a claim will fail where the method for calculating the premiums is contained in the loan documents signed by the borrowers. *See* Singleton v. Protective Life Ins. Co., 857 So. 2d 803 (Ala. 2003). Moreover, where plaintiffs brought a purported class action alleging a common course of conduct in the sale of gross, rather than net, coverage of credit insurance, the Alabama Supreme Court found that a class can not be certified for claims of negligent supervision/hiring that led to fraudulent suppression because the allegations of oral misrepresentations do not allow for common questions of law and fact to predominate. Voyager v. Whitson, 867 So. 2d 1065 (Ala. 2003).

780 *See* §§ 8.3.1.2, 8.5.3.1.2, *supra* for an explanation of gross versus net coverage and for court decisions on this issue.

781 687 So. 2d 156 (Ala. 1996).

782 Ala. Code § 5-19-20(b)(2).

783 In pleading a RICO violation, keep in mind the $5,000 damage requirement under the statute. *See* Brown v. Protective Life. Ins. Co., 353 F.3d 405 (5th Cir. 2003) (holding that the named plaintiff's damages individually must meet the threshold).

784 Kenty v. Bank One, Columbus, N.A., 67 F.3d 1257 (6th Cir. 1995), *aff'd in part and rev'd in part*, 92 F.3d 384 (6th Cir. 1996) (insurer held exempt from RICO claim under McCarran-Fergu-

son; bank was not). *Cf.* Kenty v. Transamerica Premium Ins. Co., 650 N.E.2d 863 (Ohio 1995) (state claims related to same practice). The same practice may occur with respect to other types of credit insurance and credit-related ancillary insurance, as well. Lenders' compensation arrangements for credit-related insurance sometimes consists of both upfront commissions, and back-end compensation in a variety of forms, such as experience rebates.

785 *Kenty* at 92 F.3d 391. *See also* Weinberger v. Mellon Mortgage Co., 1998 WL 599192 (E.D. Pa. 1998) (RICO claim against insurance company in this mortgage loan case dismissed because mortgage servicer had warned homeowner in writing that forced-placed hazard insurance would cost substantially more and provide less coverage; therefore, no scheme to defraud even though the homeowner was not informed about the commissions paid by and between the insurer and servicer).

786 *E.g.*, Schroeder v. Acceleration Life, 972 F.2d 41 (3d Cir. 1992); *In re* Dickson, 432 F. Supp. 752 (W.D.N.C. 1977); Washington Mutual Bank v. Superior Court, 82 Cal. Rptr. 2d 564 (Cal. Ct. App. 1999), *rev'd and remanded*, 15 P.3d 1071 (Cal. 2001) (reversing class certification in class action involving allegations of kickback between lender and insurance companies and requiring the lower court to address the effect of the choice of law provision in the contract); Fox v. Industrial Casualty Ins. Co., 424 N.E.2d 839 (Ill. App. 1981); Browder v. Hanley-Dawson Cadillac, 379 N.E.2d 1206 (Ill. App. 1978); Marshall v. Citicorp Mtg., Inc., 601 So. 2d 669 (La. Ct. App. 1992); State v. Ralph Williams North West Chrysler Plymouth, Inc., 553 P.2d 423 (Wash. 1976).

787 *See generally* National Consumer Law Center, Unfair and Deceptive Acts and Practices, §§ 2.2.1, 2.3.1 (6th ed. 2004 and Supp.).

- Which he or she could not have reasonably avoided; and
- Which is not outweighed by countervailing benefits to the consumer or to competition.

Most credit insurance abuses cause the consumer economic injury, which is cognizable under UDAP. While credit insurance, sold properly and at reasonable cost has benefit to consumers, excessive, useless, or unwanted insurance has no benefit or only marginal benefit to consumers.[788] Practitioners also should consider a UDAP claim where insurance coverage was wrongfully denied.[789] The fact that the insurance is theoretically optional does not defeat the requirement that the consumer be unable to reasonably avoid the injury. The consumer is unable to reasonably avoid the injury when the creditor takes advantage of or creates an obstacle to the free exercise of decision-making. This may be done by withholding important information, use of coercive sales tactics, or exercising undue influence over highly susceptible classes of consumers,[790] any or all of which may be present in a given case involving credit insurance abuses.

It is currently unclear exactly what the FTC deception standard is,[791] but the one generally used by the courts is whether a practice has a tendency or capacity to deceive the least sophisticated consumer.[792] Deceptive practices include the use of misleading statements, partial truths, or the omission of material facts[793]—again all practices which are likely to be involved in insurance abuse cases. For example, allegations that a credit disability insurer defrauded its insureds by promising benefits it did not intend to pay, calculating benefits on a daily (instead of monthly basis), and prematurely terminating coverage stated a claim under the state UDAP and federal RICO statutes.[794] Additionally,

allegations in an FTC case that a creditor violated the FTC Act by failing to disclose cost and terms of credit insurance provided a basis in part for a temporary restraining order and two preliminary injunctions, as well as a freezing of the company owner's assets.[795]

An earlier section[796] discussed a UDAP challenge to creditor practices which undermine the written voluntariness disclosures. Courts have specifically held that failure to disclose the availability of cheaper credit insurance is a UDAP violation.[797] Most insurance packing cases have raised UDAP claims and one court found sufficient probability of success on the merits to issue a preliminary injunction.[798] Most of the insurance packing cases to date have settled so there are few decisions. However pleadings, briefs, and settlements from many of the cases are available from the National Clearinghouse for Legal Services.[799]

---

788 In a case which bears watching, a New York court affirmed an order granting class certification where the UDAP claim raised related to the defendant's practice of offering "easily available" credit insurance coverage in prominent print, relegating to small, inconspicuous print the precise terms of the insurance, and then rejecting claims on the ground that the customers had not been paying for the appropriate type of insurance. Taylor v. American Bankers Ins. Group, Inc., 700 N.Y.S.2d 458 (N.Y. App. Div. 1999). *But see* Vickers v. Interstate Dodge, 882 So. 2d 1236 (La. Ct. App. 2004) (plaintiff alleging forgery of election of purchase credit life insurance did not present evidence of actual damages under state's UDAP law).

789 For example, a consumer may have been denied credit life insurance coverage for health reasons where state law requires coverage to be provided notwithstanding health condition for coverage under a certain dollar amount.

790 National Consumer Law Center, Unfair and Deceptive Acts and Practices § 4.3 (6th ed. 2004 and Supp.). *See also* § 8.2.3.1, *supra.*

791 National Consumer Law Center, Unfair and Deceptive Acts and Practices § 4.2.11 (6th ed. 2004 and Supp.).

792 *Id.* §§ 4.2.9 and 4.2.11.

793 *Id.* §§ 4.2.13, 4.2.14.

794 Schroeder v. Acceleration Life, 972 F.2d 41 (3d Cir. 1992)

(credit disability contract provided that insurance would terminate upon discharge of debt, but also provided that termination would be without prejudice to previously originating claims; provision interpreted by state court in a breach of contract action to require benefits paid from onset of disability to loan's scheduled maturity. This case alleged fraudulent promise to pay excess benefits upon early termination and schemes to reduce benefits as UDAP and RICO violations). *Cf.* Fort Worth Mortgage Corp. v. Abercrombie, 835 S.W.2d 262 (Tex. App. 1992) (mortgagee's cancellation of policy and substituting one with less benefits without borrower's notice or consent was UDAP violation and unconscionable).

795 Order, Fed. Trade Comm'n v. Stewart Fin. Co., Civ. No. 103CV-2648 (N.D. Ga. filed Sept. 4, 2003), *available at* www.ftc.gov/os/caselist/103cv2648.htm.

796 *See* § 8.5.2.5.2, *supra.*

797 Browder v. Hanley-Dawson Cadillac, 379 N.E.2d 1206 (Ill. App. 1978); State v. Ralph Williams North West Chrysler Plymouth Inc., 553 P.2d 423 (Wash. 1976).

798 Balderos v. Illinois Vehicle Premium Fin. Co., 1997 WL 627650 (N.D. Ill. 1997) (court certified class action where lender added a purported hospitalization policy premium into the financing of the consumer's purchase of auto insurance without informing the customer; value of additional "insurance" speculative in light of allegation that $85 of the $100 "premium" was kept as a commission; lack of disclosure about this supposed policy would likely result in a low loss ratio; claims raised include TILA, UDAP, breach of fiduciary duty, and RICO); State v. Aetna Fin. Co., Case No. 84 CV0103, Clearinghouse No. 36,151 (Wis. Cir. Ct. Dane Cty., Feb. 20, 1984). *See also* Urbina v. Aetna Fin. Co., Civ. 83-452 TUC-ACM (D. Ariz., filed June 30, 1983); Samorano v. Aetna Fin. Co., No. 213316 (Ariz. Super. Ct. Pima Cty. filed Dec. 8, 1983); Fox v. Industrial Cas. Ins. Co., 98 Ill. App. 3d 543, 424 N.E.2d 839 (1981) (complaint regarding packing credit insurance sale with non-credit insurance stated a UDAP claim). For a discussion of these cases, see § 8.5.4, *supra.*

799 Clearinghouse No. 44,801. Following is an index to those documents.
ARIZONA: State of Ariz. v. Aetna Fin. Co., Clearinghouse No. 44,801J, No. CV87-30594 (Super. Ct. Ariz., Consent Judgment filed Nov. 9, 1987). Consent judgment between Arizona attorney general and ITT companies regarding proper insurance sales licensure, credit insurance sales practices, limitations on sale of certain non-credit insurance products. Samorano v.

One court suggested in dicta that a viable UDAP claim

might be stated if the borrower alleges the insurance is overpriced or that substantial undisclosed commissions unfairly increase insurance costs.[800]

Importantly, some states also have passed statutes that go beyond general UDAP laws by addressing specific abusive practices in high-cost mortgage lending. Some of these include prohibitions and restrictions regarding credit insurance. For example, the New York high-cost home loan law prohibits the financing of single premium insurance on high-cost home loans.[801] This prohibition applies to credit insurance, any other life or health insurance premiums, and any debt cancellation or suspension agreements.[802] Insur-

---

Aetna Fin. Co., Clearinghouse No. 44,801K, No. 84-1293-TUC-WBD (D. Ariz. 1984). The settlement agreement in a class action filed in federal district court in Arizona relating to the sale of non-credit life insurance (UNIPAY, SPT-5 and Extraguard); credit life and disability, and property insurance. Urbina v. Aetna Fin. Co., Clearinghouse No. 44,801L, No. CIV 83452 TUC ACM (D. Ariz. 1983). A complaint filed in federal district court in Arizona involving alleged packing of credit insurance and non-credit accidental death and dismemberment insurance, and disadvantageous refinancings in violation of the Arizona Consumer Fraud Act, and the state consumer loan act, breach of fiduciary duty, and unconscionability. Arizona v. Associates Fin. Servs. Co., CV 92-21853 Clearinghouse No. 44,801Z (stipulated judgment filed Dec. 16, 1992) (Clearinghouse No. 44,801Y, complaint) (various practices relating to credit property, non-filing insurance, and ancillary products such as auto club memberships).

CALIFORNIA: California v. ITT Consumer Fin. Corp. The complaint and stipulated judgment discussed § 8.5.2.4.2, *supra* are included as 44,801S and 44,801T, respectively. California v. ITT Fin. Servs., No. 656038-0 (Calif. Super. Ct., Alameda Cty., settlement filed Sept. 21, 1989).

FLORIDA: Jones v. Credithrift of America, Clearinghouse No. 44,801U, No. 89-441-Civ-Orl-19 (M.D. Fla. filed July 11, 1989). Amended complaint regarding, *inter alia*, deceptive practices in sale of non-credit life insurance, alleging violations of Truth in Lending, Florida Unfair Trade Practices Act, and unconscionability.

IOWA: Stansberry v. Thorp Loan, Clearinghouse No. 44,801M, Civ. No. CL 142-0289 (Dist. Ct. for Appanoose Cty.). State class action complaint alleging sale of excess credit property insurance in violation of state law and voluntary assurance previously entered into with state attorney general. Newton v. Thorp, Clearinghouse No. 44,801N (S.D. Iowa). Complaint alleging violations of Truth in Lending and state laws regarding, *inter alia*, excess property insurance and non-credit death and dismemberment insurance. Voluntary Cessation Agreement with the Attorney General, Clearinghouse No. 44,801O. The voluntary consent agreement entered into between the Iowa Attorney General and ITT Financial in 1984 regarding UNIPAY (AD&D), Thrift Club memberships, property insurance.

MARYLAND: Bagwell v. M. Kovens Co, Clearinghouse No. 44,801I, No. 88293033/CL85964 (Cir. Ct. for Baltimore City filed Aug. 26, 1988). A class action complaint filed in Maryland state court alleging violations of the Maryland Consumer Protection Act, Retail Installment Sales Act, Door-to-Door Sales Act, breach of fiduciary duty. U.C.C. and Truth in Lending for alleged insurance packing and excessive premium charges.

MINNESOTA: Hawkins v. Thorp Credit & Thrift Co., 441 N.W.2d 470 (Minn. 1989). Intervenor-amicus consumers' briefs in lower court and on appeal (draft) on issue of whether Minnesota Consumer Loan Act precludes sale of non-credit insurance (SPT-5) and buyer's club. Clearinghouse No. 44,801A-C. The Minnesota Supreme Court interlocutory decision (reported 441 N.W.2d 470 (Minn. 1989)) and subsequent class certification by the trial court (Dec. 5, 1989) are available as Clearinghouse No. 44,801D. Thomas v. Thorp, Clearinghouse No. 44,801E. A complaint in Minnesota state court alleging violations of Truth in Lending, the Regulated Loan Act, the state exemption law, arising out of a wide array of alleged insurance packing practices. Hohn v. Thorp, Clearinghouse No. 44,801F, No. 4-87-808 (D. Minn. filed Sept. 11, 1987). A complaint in Minnesota federal court alleging violations of

RICO, Truth in Lending, various state laws, and breach of fiduciary duty arising out of the full panoply of alleged packing practices.

The *Hawkins* and *Hohn* cases were consolidated for settlement purposes. A copy of the amended complaint in the consolidated case is available as Clearinghouse No. 44,801V. The preliminary order certifying settlement classes and approving the class settlement, and the class settlement agreement are available as Clearinghouse No. 44,801W. The settlement included a $17 million cash settlement for purchasers of SPT-5 non-credit insurance and $30 million in non-cash compensation for class members purchasing credit life, credit disability, property insurance and ITT Thrift Club memberships, as well as injunctive relief designed to prevent further marketing abuses.

OHIO: James v. ITT Fin. Servs., Clearinghouse No. 44,801G, No. 155436 (C.D. Cayahoga Cty.). A class action complaint filed in Ohio state court challenging practices related to sale of the non-credit life insurance (SPT-5) and Thrift Club membership under the state small loan act, RISA, Truth in Lending, and violation of fiduciary duty. The defendant's brief in support of its motion to dismiss is also included Clearinghouse No. 44,801H. In support of the motion for class certification, the plaintiff sent a survey to a sampling of the defendant's customers. The Report of the expert who analyzed the survey results (which are included) is available. James v. ITT Fin. Servs., Report of Prof. Robert Hartley, submitted in support of Plaintiff's Motion to Certify Class, Oct. 10, 1989, Clearinghouse No. 44,801X.

WISCONSIN: State of Wisconsin v. Aetna, Clearinghouse No. 44,801P, 84 CV0103 (Cir. Ct. Dane Cty.). Complaint alleges violations of Wisconsin Consumer Act in sale of UNIPAY (AD&D), SPT-5 (non-credit term life), household contents insurance, and Thrift Club memberships. Also includes plaintiff's proposed findings of fact, conclusions of law and order for temporary injunction, Clearinghouse No 44,801Q, and a stipulation and consent order, Clearinghouse No 44,801R.

800 *In re* Milbourne, 108 B.R. 522, 540, 543 n.8 (Bankr. E.D. Pa. 1989). *See also* Balderos v. Illinois Vehicle Premium Fin. Co., 1997 WL 627650 (N.D. Ill. 1997) (court certified class action where lender added a purported hospitalization policy premium into the financing of the consumer's purchase of auto insurance without informing the customer; value of additional "insurance" speculative in light of allegation that $85 of the $100 "premium" was kept as a commission; lack of disclosure about this supposed policy would likely result in a low loss ratio; claims raised include TILA, UDAP, breach of fiduciary duty, and RICO).

801 N.Y. Bank Law § 6-1(2)(h). For a discussion of similar laws, see § 2.3.3.7, *supra*.

802 *Id.*

ance premiums or other fees calculated and paid on a monthly basis are not considered "financed."[803]

8.7.5 Unconscionability

Unconscionability claims may also be raised to challenge credit insurance abuses. A number of states have incorporated unconscionability into their credit statutes.[804] Even absent a statutory reference, unconscionability is a common law concept which should be available in most states.[805] The UCCC defines unconscionability in the consumer credit context to be

> whether, in light of the background and setting of the market, the needs of the particular trade or case, and the condition of the particular parties to the conduct or contract, the conduct involved is, or the clauses involved are so one-sided as to be unconscionable. . . .[806]

Further, an agreement may be unconscionable, even if its terms are not, if the agreement was induced by unconscionable conduct.[807] With respect to credit insurance, the UCCC offers further guidance, requiring consideration of these factors:

- Potential benefits to the consumer, including satisfaction of his or her obligation;
- The creditor's need for the protection provided by the insurance; and
- The relation between the amount and terms of credit granted and the insurance benefits provided.[808]

Insurance which complies with all applicable laws is not "in itself" unconscionable.[809] The obvious implication is that insurance practices complying with applicable laws may still become unconscionable in some contexts. The sorts of facts which have historically led courts to consider otherwise legally required insurance to be a mere pretext for usury may be sound precedent for arguing that otherwise "legitimate" insurance is unconscionable in a context that suggests overreaching.

The Eighth Circuit, in reviewing the transaction described in § 8.5.4.2, *supra*, found it to be unconscionable. Juxtaposing the loan as it was written with the loan as it *could* have been written for a shorter term, the court said that the loan was "substantively unfair because there was no reasonable basis for writing the loan for a six-year period," but did not base its decision on that fact. Rather it held that the creditor's failure to tell the borrower "that she could have repaid the same loan with lower monthly payments in one-half the time deprived her of fair notice and amounted to unfair surprise—clearly no person in her senses would have accepted the more expensive term. This constituted, at least, procedural unconscionability."[810]

The court specifically said that the holding of unfair surprise was not based on a quasi-fiduciary duty to disclose disadvantageous terms. But, as the court noted, even a careful review of the contract by an average borrower could not have revealed the advantages of other options. The court seemed to find particularly offensive the fact that the creditor had initiated the offer to refinance the borrower's loan and advance extra funds it knew she wanted, then wrote up an "exorbitantly expensive" loan, without telling her "she could get everything she wants for less money and at a lower monthly payment."[811] (Practitioners should note that creditor-initiated invitations to refinance are quite frequent, especially among finance company lenders.)[812]

The fact that the credit insurance charges were lawful for a six-year loan, as the district court had found, did not

---

803   *Id.*

804   *E.g.*, U.C.C.C. §§ 4-106, 5-108.

805   *E.g.*, Besta v. Beneficial Loan Co., 855 F.2d 532, 535 (8th Cir. 1988) (a bargain is unconscionable "if it is such as no man in his senses and not under delusion would make on the one hand, and as no honest and fair man would accept on the other"); Williams v. Walker-Thomas Furn. Co., 350 F.2d 445 (D.C. Cir. 1965); Henningsen v. Bloommfield Motors, Inc., 161 A.2d 69 (N.J. 1960).

806   Comment to U.C.C.C. § 5-108 ¶ 3.

807   *Id.* ¶ 1.

808   U.C.C.C. § 4-106(1).

809   U.C.C.C. § 4-106.

810   Besta v. Beneficial Loan Co., 855 F.2d 532 (8th Cir. 1988).

811   *Id.* at 536. *See also* Hager v. American Gen. Fin., Inc., 37 F. Supp. 2d 778 (S.D. W. Va. 1999) (flipping case where multiple insurances were sold at each refinancing; court denied lender's motion for summary judgment on the unconscionability claim based upon borrowers' allegation that defendants induced them to enter into high interest rate loans and to mortgage their residence without realizing the magnitude of the debt they were incurring or the ramifications of these transactions); *In re* Milbourne, 108 B.R. 522 (Bankr. E.D. Pa. 1989) (series of flippings cost borrower extra $3000 over separate loans; failure to disclose that advantage to lender and disadvantage to borrower was UDAP violation). For a description of the ways in which the costs of a loan blossom when it is constantly refinanced, see affidavit filed in Hager v. American Gen. Fin., Inc. in Appx. L, *infra*.

812   *Cf.* Hager v. American Gen. Fin., Inc., 37 F. Supp. 2d 778 (S.D. W. Va. 1999) (flipping case where multiple insurances were sold at each refinancing; court denied lender's motion for summary judgment on the unconscionability claim based upon borrowers' allegation that defendants induced them to enter into high interest rate loans and to mortgage their residence without realizing the magnitude of the debt they were incurring or the ramifications of these transactions); *In re* Milbourne, 108 B.R. 522 (Bankr. E.D. Pa. 1989) (series of flippings cost borrower extra $3000 over separate loans; failure to disclose that advantage to lender and disadvantage to borrower was UDAP violation); *In re* Tucker, 74 B.R. 923 (Bankr. E.D. Pa. 1987) (dicta suggesting that, in some circumstances, frequent flipping may constitute violation of state unfair and deceptive acts and practices statute).

legitimate the transaction because this was not a "fairly negotiated" loan.

This action had been brought affirmatively by the borrower, advancing a number of federal and state claims, and the creditor counterclaimed. Following the lower court's ruling in favor of the creditor all around, only the state claim of unconscionability was at issue on appeal. The Eighth Circuit's remedy was to permit the creditor to collect on its judgment as if it had been written as a three-year loan, and essentially to invalidate the creditor's security interest on the borrower's home.[813] (Under state law, it could not have taken a valid security interest in the home if the amount financed were under $2,000, which would have been the case without the padding.)

It should be noted that the court based its finding of unconscionability on common law, as well as the state consumer credit code's statutory prohibition of unconscionability. Thus, even in states without statutory unconscionability provisions, the case should be useful precedent for claims under common law unconscionability or state unfair and deceptive acts and practices statutes.[814] The combination of selling partial coverage and using Rule of 78 accrual accounting on a mortgage, which meant that the value of the policy declined while the loan balance increased, was another example of an unconscionable credit insurance transaction.[815]

Even if the terms of the credit insurance agreement are not problematic, the lender's behavior in declaring a note in default where the credit disability insurer was obligated to make payments may be unconscionable. In *Bank One Milwaukee, N.A. v. Harris*, the Wisconsin Court of Appeals dismissed the creditor's replevin action and reinstituted the consumer's counterclaim for wrongful repossession where the creditor declared the loan in default even though the consumer had made a timely claim for payments under a credit disability policy.[816]

The facts revealed that the borrower was current on her loan (except for late charges that the lender carried over from month to month), became disabled, applied for the benefits of the credit disability insurance policy which the lender had sold her, and informed the lender of these developments during the month in which the payment was due (which she did not make). The insurance company honored her claim but did not make the first payment until almost a month later. Neither the installment loan contract nor the disability insurance contract informed the borrower that she could be in default for failing to pay the monthly payment that the insurer ultimately would pay. *After* the lender received the insurance payment, the lender filed a replevin action. The court had no trouble finding that, not only was the borrower not in default, the lender's behavior was unconscionable.[817]

8.7.6 Arbitration in the Insurance Context

As noted elsewhere in this treatise,[818] clauses in consumer credit and other contracts mandating arbitration are cropping up on an ever-increasing basis. Credit insurance agreements are no exception. The first issue to confront is whether the Federal Arbitration Act (FAA) applies to the agreement.[819] The FAA applies to any contract "evidencing a transaction involving interstate commerce."[820] Even when interstate commerce is implicated, state law and not the FAA, may apply to the arbitrability of a dispute relating to insurance.

As noted in § 8.5.2.7, *supra*, the federal McCarran-Ferguson Act prohibits *federal* regulation of insurance practices to the extent that they would invalidate, impair, or supersede *state* law enacted for the purpose of regulating the business of insurance, unless the federal law explicitly relates to the business of insurance.[821] The FAA does not explicitly relate to the business of insurance.[822] Thus, the general rule is that if a state statute regulating insurance limits the enforceability of an arbitration provision, this is in conflict with the FAA. State law, according to the McCarran-Ferguson Act,

813 Iowa Code § 537.5108 provides that a court can refuse to enforce those provisions of an agreement that it finds unconscionable.

814 *E.g., In re* Milbourne, 108 B.R. 522 (Bankr. E.D. Pa. 1989). *See generally* National Consumer Law Center, Unfair and Deceptive Acts and Practices (6th ed. 2004 and Supp.).

815 Marshall v. Citicorp Mtg., Inc., 601 So. 2d 669 (La. Ct. App. 1992) discussed in § 8.5.5.2, *supra*.

816 563 N.W.2d 543 (Wis. App. 1997). Chandler v. General Motors Acceptance Corp., 426 N.E.2d 521 (Ohio App. 1980) (though an unconscionability claim was not raised, court denied summary judgment to GMAC on its deficiency suit where the facts revealed that GMAC refused to complete its portion of a credit disability insurance form thwarting the consumer's efforts to see that GMAC got paid during his period of disability; breach of contract and wrongful repossession claim raised). *See also* National Consumer Law Center, Repossessions and Foreclosures § 4.4 (5th ed. 2002 and Supp.).

817 While the court could not precisely define "unconscionability," it quoted Justice Stewart from an obscenity case in this way: "[We] know [unconscionability] when [we] see it." *Harris*, 563 N.W.2d at 546, n.5. *See also* McManis v. San Diego Postal Credit Union, 71 Cal. Rptr. 2d 617 (Cal. Ct. App. 1998) (similar facts showing the consumer did everything she could and more to timely and adequately file her credit disability claim; causes of action included breach of contract, breach of covenant of good faith and fair dealing, and intentional infliction of emotional distress but not unconscionability).

818 *See* § 10.3, *infra*.

819 9 U.S.C. § 1. For a full discussion of the FAA, see National Consumer Law Center, Consumer Arbitration Agreements (4th ed. 2004); National Consumer Law Center, Unfair and Deceptive Acts and Practices § 7.6.7 (6th ed. 2004 and Supp.).

820 9 U.S.C. § 2.

821 15 U.S.C. § 1012(b). *See also* United States Department of the Treasury v. Fabe, 508 U.S. 491, 113 S. Ct. 2202, 124 L. Ed. 2d 449 (1993).

822 *See* American Bankers Ins. Co. of Florida v. Crawford, 757 So. 2d 1125 (Ala. 1999); Little v. Allstate Ins. Co., 705 A.2d 538 (Vt. 1997).

not the FAA, will then determine whether the arbitration provision is enforceable.[823] Unfortunately, many state stat-

utes limit the enforceability of arbitration, but are silent regarding insurance. Whether the FAA applies to trump these state arbitration statutes is discussed in the National Consumer Law Center, Consumer Arbitration Agreements (4th ed. 2004); National Consumer Law Center, Unfair and Deceptive Acts and Practices § 7.6.7 (6th ed. 2004 and Supp.).

---

823 Mutual Reinsurance Bureau v. Great Plains Mutual Ins. Co., 969 F.2d 931 (10th Cir. 1992), *cert. denied*, 506 U.S. 1001 (1992); Friday v. Trinity Universal of Kansas, 939 P.2d 869 (Kan. 1997); Little v. Allstate Ins. Co., 705 A.2d 538 (Vt. 1997). *See also* Davister Corp. v. United Republic Life Ins. Co., 152 F.3d 1277 (10th Cir. 1998), *cert. denied*, 525 U.S. 1177 (1999); Munich Am. Reinsurance Co. v. Crawford, 141 F.3d 585 (5th Cir. 1998); Murff v. Professional Med. Ins. Co., 97 F.3d 289 (8th Cir. 1996); Towe, Hester & Erwin, Inc. v. Kansas City Fire & Marine Ins. Co., 947 P.2d 594 (Okla. Ct. App. 1997) (while

recognizing that Oklahoma law that limits arbitration in insurance would oust the FAA, the dispute in that case between an insurance company and its employees did not relate to insurance).

The Statute: Determining the Applicable Statute and Principles of Statutory Construction

9.1 Introduction

This and the next chapter of this book consider usury issues from a litigation standpoint. Their purpose is to address usury questions that an attorney trying a usury case is likely to confront. Chapter Nine first considers the threshold question of what particular statute may control a disputed credit transaction, and then discusses general issues of statutory construction in the usury context. Chapter Ten addresses the actual elements of proving a borrower's usury claim, potential creditor defenses, and other litigation issues such as jurisdiction and the right to a jury trial. It concludes by reaching the issue of remedies: having proven the existence of usury, what remedies are available to the consumer?

9.2 Which Usury Statute Applies?

9.2.1 Nature of Distinctions Among Statutes; General Principles of Coverage

9.2.1.1 Overview

The first step in analyzing whether a consumer has a claim for violation of a statute regulating credit charges is to determine which statute is applicable. As was discussed in the overview in Chapter Two, most states have several different usury statutes, so an understanding of the state's regulatory scheme is critical to assure that the transaction is being assessed by the correct standards.

This subsection first examines five different characteristics that may determine whether an extension of credit is covered by a particular usury statute. The subsection then analyzes other potential sources of substantive limits on credit charges. First, if no other state usury law applies, a state criminal usury statute may still place a ceiling on charges. Second, even in a state that has "deregulated" credit charges, a creditor may violate an agreed-rate statute by, for example, charging more than the agreement with the borrower allows. The subsection then analyzes choice-of-

law rules by which a lender may seek to apply another state's law to a transaction. It concludes with an examination of the state and federal laws that control the formal requirements for electronic credit transactions.

9.2.1.2 Methods of Distinguishing the Transaction

The scope of a special usury statute[1] may be determined by one or more of the following characteristics,[2] which will be examined in more detail in this chapter:[3]

- *Purpose of loan*: frequently loans for business or commercial purposes are not covered by usury statutes; they are specifically excluded, or the statute applies by its terms only to consumer loans. Agricultural loans may also be excluded.
- *Type of credit*: requirements applying to loans may differ from those applicable to credit sales. Similarly, open-end or revolving credit may be subject to different provisions than closed-end credit. Loans and the financing of sales are further subdivided in some states. For example, the financing of home improvements and motor vehicle sales may each be governed by separate statutes.
- *Type of creditor*: depository lenders, such as banks, savings associations, or credit unions, are often subject to different statutes than non-depository creditors. There may be further distinctions as to applicable law within each of those categories: e.g., banks, savings associations (thrifts) or credit unions, state-chartered or federally-chartered, finance companies, retail sellers and pawnbrokers. Additionally some statutes may govern only creditors who "regularly" extend credit or are

---

1 *See* §§ 2.2 and 2.3, *supra* for a discussion of the distinction between general and special usury laws, and an overview of the distinctions between types of credit and types of creditors mentioned here.

2 Some statutes may include more than one characteristic in defining its scope. The Uniform Consumer Credit Code, for example, considers purpose (consumer purposes only); the identity of the creditor (only those who "regularly" extend credit); and only credit for which a finance charge is imposed or that is payable in installments. U.C.C.C. § 1.301 (1974).

3 *See* §§ 9.2.2–9.2.8, *infra*.

"in the business" of extending credit, while others may encompass one who makes even an isolated loan.

- *Loan size*: some usury statutes are determined by the size of the loan, e.g., small loan acts may apply to loans under a certain dollar amount, or other statutes may exclude large loans.
- *Type of security*: some statutes apply only where certain security is taken, as is the case with home equity or second mortgage regulation.

Because the stringency of requirements may vary widely among the differing usury statutes, the practitioner must not only determine which statute the creditor presumably wrote the transaction under, but also whether the creditor tried to fudge the facts in some way to evade the strictures of the statute which *should* be applicable. Courts will look at the substance, not the form of a transaction, and apply the correct law to the transaction.[4]

9.2.1.3 "Opting In" or Contracting for Coverage

It is also possible that a creditor will "opt in," or provide by contract that a specific regulatory statute will apply to the transaction, even though it would, in absence of that contractual provision, fall outside the scope of that statute. For example, a business-purpose loan may become subject to a consumer credit code, though otherwise excluded, because the contract so provides.[5] A creditor who inserts a choice of law clause into a contract may subject itself to that state's laws even if it could have relied on the laws of its home state.[6] If the creditor opts in, it then must comply with the requirements of that statute.

In contrast, an unlicensed lender cannot acquire the right to charge a higher interest rate allowed to licensed creditors under a special usury statute by including a clause in the contract which says that the parties agree the transaction will be governed by that statute.[7]

9.2.1.4 Deregulation; Criminal Usury

Some states have deregulated some or all credit transactions, taking specific rate caps out of their usury statutes. However, that does not necessarily mean the law permits

absolutely anything. Many legislatures simply substituted language allowing the creditor to charge any rate agreed to by the parties instead of a specific statutory rate cap, which means that a creditor may still violate the statute, if, for example, there is hidden interest in the transaction. This is discussed in § 9.2.8, *infra*.[8]

Moreover, some deregulated states retained criminal usury ceilings, which are still in force and may be applicable to "deregulated" transactions or credit otherwise exempt from usury laws.[9] Unconscionability also remains as a common law or statutory standard against which to measure credit costs.[10] Overreaching may also be challenged under UDAP or common law theories.[11]

9.2.1.5 Preemption

There is one final caveat. There is a possibility that an otherwise applicable state statute has been preempted by federal law. Chapter Three discusses the preemption issues most commonly arising in consumer credit transactions, and should be reviewed to determine if that is an issue in any given case. It may arise with some credit secured by first liens on homes,[12] "creative financing" mortgages,[13] the activities of a national bank, federal savings association, or federal credit union,[14] or the activities of an "exporting" national or state-chartered depository institution (which most commonly have involved credit card issues in recent years but also include tax refund anticipation loans and payday loans).[15]

9.2.1.6 Substance Not Form Dictates Nature of Transaction

In analyzing a transaction, the practitioner should take care not to accept without question the creditor's characterization as to its nature. Any number of tactics might be used to make the transaction itself or some of its terms appear to be something they are not in order to evade applicable strictures. For example, credit sales may be disguised as loans to take advantage of higher rates;[16] loans may be disguised as sale/repurchase or sale/leasebacks;[17] closed-

---

4 *See* § 9.2.1.6, *infra*.

5 *See, e.g.*, Mack Fin. Corp. v. Crossley, 550 A.2d 303 (Conn. 1988) (Retail Installment Sales Financing); First Northwestern National Bank v. Crouch, 287 N.W.2d 151 (Iowa 1980) (Iowa Consumer Credit Code); Farmers State Bank v. Haflich, 699 P.2d 553 (Kan. 1985) (Kansas Consumer Credit Code); Bank of Barron v. Gieske, 485 N.W.2d 426 (Wis. Ct. App. 1992) (Wisconsin Consumer Act).

6 *In re* Beck, 248 B.R. 229 (Bankr. W.D.N.Y. 2000) (dictum).

7 *See* Floyd v. Baton Rouge Sash & Door Co., 502 So. 2d 1073 (La. 1987). *See generally* §§ 9.2.4.5–9.2.4.6, *infra*, on the consequences of lending without required licenses.

8 *See also* Part 4, *supra*, for various commonplace methods of hiding interest.

9 *E.g.*, Norris v. Sigler Daisy Corp., 392 S.E.2d 242 (Ga. 1990). *See generally* §§ 9.2.7, 10.8.2.1 (on remedies), *infra*. To check whether a state has a criminal usury cap, see Appx. A, *infra*.

10 *See* § 9.2.7, *infra*.

11 *See* Ch. 11, *infra*.

12 *See* § 3.9.3, *supra*.

13 *See* § 3.10, *supra*.

14 *See* § 3.4, *supra*.

15 *See* §§ 3.4.5, 3.9.2.2, *supra*.

16 *See* § 9.2.3.3, *infra*.

17 Ch. 7, *supra*.

end credit as open-end;[18] and a vast array of techniques may be used to hide extra interest.[19] It is black letter law that courts will look behind the face of documents to ascertain the actual nature of the transaction; substance, not form dictates what law will govern.[20]

---

18 § 9.2.3.1, *infra*.

19 Chs. 7, 8, *supra*.

20 *See, e.g.,* Easter v. Am. West Fin., 381 F.3d 948 (9th Cir. 2004); ECE Technologies, Inc. v. Cherrington Corp., 168 F.3d 201 (5th Cir. 1999) (commercial case applying substance over form doctrine); Aaron v. Mattikow, 146 F. Supp. 2d 263 (E.D.N.Y. 2001), *aff'd*, 2003 WL 1973353 (2d Cir. Apr. 22, 2003) (table); Cashback Catalog Sales v. Price, 102 F. Supp. 2d 1375 (S.D. Ga. 2000) (declining to accept payday lender's attempt to disguise finance charges as the consumer's payment for catalog gift certificates); Hamilton v. York, 987 F. Supp. 953 (E.D. Ky. 1997) (alleged "deferred" presentment of a check really a loan); Khalif v. Khalif, 308 B.R. 614 (Bankr. N.D. Ga. 2004) (use of terms like "guarantor" and "investors" was contrivance); Brown v. Courtesy Consumer Discount Co., 134 B.R. 134 (Bankr. E.D. Pa. 1991) ("[b]ecause of the fertility of the minds of those who would devise schemes to circumvent remedial consumer protection laws, these laws must be interpreted with a flexibility necessary to preserve their spirit.") (RISA disguised as direct loan in order to charge a higher rate in a "body-dragging" case); Carter v. Four Seasons Funding Corp., 97 S.W.3d 387, 395 (Ark. 2003); Luebbers v. Money Store, Inc., 40 S.W.3d 745 (Ark. 2001); McElroy v. Grisham, 810 S.W.2d 933 (Ark. 1991) (sale-repurchase); Ghirardo v. Antonioli, 883 P.2d 960 (Cal. 1994) (trier of fact must look to substance, not form; "sensitive to the ingenuity and creativity of those entrepreneurs willing to engage in legal brinkmanship to maximize profits, courts have scrutinized the form of seemingly innocuous commercial transactions to determine whether the substance amounts to a usurious arrangement"; but settlement notes executed by sophisticated real estate purchasers at issue were exempt credit sale, not loan or forbearance); Sheehy v. Franchise Tax Bd., 100 Cal. Rptr. 2d 760 (App. 2000) (substance prevails over form, but delay in recovering taxes is neither a loan nor a forbearance); Hernandez v. Atlantic Fin., 164 Cal. Rptr. 279 (App. 1980) (in determining the applicability of consumer protection laws to particular transactions, substance, not form, dictates the results); Browner v. District of Columbia, 549 A.2d 1107, 1114 (D.C. App. 1988) (sale-leaseback was "transparent sham which masked an unlawful loan"); Oregrund Ltd. P'ship v. Sheive, 873 So. 2d 451, 457 (Fla. App. 2004); Low Cost Auto Pawn, Inc. v. Greco, 851 So. 2d 768 (Fla. App. 2003) (affirming judgment that vehicle marketing agreement was disguised title pawn loan); Party Yards, Inc. v. Templeton, 751 So. 2d 121 (Fla. Dist. Ct. App. 2000) (commissions in addition to interest may make loan usurious); Antonelli v. Neumann, 537 So. 2d 1027 (Fla. Dist. Ct. App. 1988); Bankwest, Inc. v. Oxendine, 598 S.E.2d 343 (Ga. Ct. App. 2004) (substance, not form, controls question whether payday lender or its rent-a-bank partner is the real lender); Williams v. Powell, 447 S.E.2d 45 (Ga. Ct. App. 1994); Jackson v. Commercial Credit Corp., 83 S.E.2d 76 (Ga. Ct. App. 1954); Wilcox v. Moore, 93 N.W.2d 288 (Mich. 1958) ("court must look squarely at the real nature of the transaction, thus avoiding . . . the betrayal of justice by the cloak of words, the contrivances of form, or the paper tigers of the crafty."); Aple Auto Cash Express of Okla., Inc. v. State *ex rel.* Oklahoma Dept. of Consumer Credit, 78 P.3d 1231 (Okla. 2003) (sale-leaseback was loan); Income Tax Buyers, Inc. v. Hamm, 1992 WL

9.2.2 Is the Loan for Consumer or Business Purposes?

9.2.2.1 Introduction

To determine what usury provision applies to a credit transaction, or whether the transaction is covered by a usury statute at all, it is often necessary to examine the purpose of the credit. Usury laws frequently distinguish business loans from consumer credit, allowing higher interest rates or completely eliminating usury ceilings for business transactions. The distinction may be accomplished by limiting the scope of any special usury laws to "consumer" credit. For example, the Uniform Consumer Credit Code applies only to credit extended "primarily for a personal, family, household, or agricultural purpose,"[21] so the statute does not reach business transactions. More frequently business loans are treated as a specific exception to a general usury law which would cover business transactions but for the exclusion. Under such a statutory scheme, the precise language of the usury exception is obviously critical. In some states, the exception may be limited to corporate loans, while in other states the exception may have been extended to entities such as partnerships, joint ventures, or individuals seeking credit for business purposes.[22]

12092431 (S.C. Com. Pleas Jan. 14, 1992) (sale of right to receive tax refund was loan); Pacific E. Corp. v. Gulf Life Holding Co., 902 S.W.2d 946 (Tenn. Ct. App. 1995); Swank v. Sverdlin, 121 S.W.3d 785 (Tex. App. 2003); Bantuelle v. Williams, 667 S.W.2d 810 (Tex. App. 1983); Zachman v. Whirlpool Acceptance Corp., 841 P.2d 27 (Wash. 1992). *See also* Adams v. Plaza Fin. Co., 168 F.3d 932 (7th Cir. 1999) (holding that court must look to substance of purported "non-filing" insurance, not form, to determine whether the premium is a hidden finance charge under TILA); Edwards v. Your Credit, Inc., 148 F.3d 427 (5th Cir. 1998) (same); Kjar v. Brimley, 497 P.2d 23, 25 (Utah 1972) (whether lease-purchase is in fact a sale, or is "a loan disguised as a sale to cover up a scheme to collect usurious interest" is a question of fact). *Cf.* First USA Mgmt., Inc. v. Esmond, 960 S.W.2d 625 (Tex. 1997) (substance rather than form controls, but arrangement here did not create usurious interest). *See generally* Creola Johnson, *Payday Loans: Shrewd Business or Predatory Lending?*, 87 Minn. L. Rev. 1, 18–26 (Nov. 2002) (documenting ways in which payday lenders disguise their loans); Singer, Sutherland Statutory Construction § 70.7 (6th ed. 2003); 47 C.J.S. *Interest and Usury* § 100(c) (1982); 45 Am. Jur. 2d *Interest and Usury* § 88 (1999). *But cf.* Jones v. Wells Fargo Bank, 5 Cal. Rptr. 3d 835 (Ct. App. 2003) (no sham when defendant intended to and did fit loan into exception to general usury law).

21 U.C.C.C. §§ 2.104, 2.106, 3.104 (1968 Model Code); U.C.C.C. §§ 1.301(12), 1.301(14), 1.301(15) (1974 Model Code). *See also* Edwards v. Alabama Farm Bureau Mut. Casualty Ins. Co., 453 So. 2d 746 (Ala. Ct. App. 1983) (definition of consumer credit transaction under Alabama "Mini-Code"). *See generally* Hall v. Owen Cty. State Bank, 370 N.E.2d 918 (Ind. App. 1978); Bill Brown Mfg. Inc. v. Crane, 589 P.2d 708 (Okla. Ct. App. 1978).

22 *See, e.g.,* GWC Restaurants, Inc. v. Hawaiian Floor Mills, Inc., 691 F. Supp. 274 (D. Haw. 1988) (restaurant is "merchant" and

It is also important to examine the statute carefully to determine whether the business purpose exemption displaces all of the otherwise applicable usury statute, or merely certain specific portions of it. For example, a Pennsylvania court has held that the business purpose exception in the statute governing residential mortgage transactions displaced only the maximum rate ceiling provision, not other provisions such as the prohibition against prepayment penalties.[23]

Finally, even if the general usury statute contains an exception for business loans, there may still be an applicable criminal usury ceiling, typically in the state criminal code.[24]

9.2.2.2 Justification for Business Loan Exemption

To the extent that business usury exemptions apply only to corporations, they are supported by several policy justifications.[25] First, corporations exist as a means for making profit, while it is generally the purpose of usury laws to protect necessitous borrowers from their own desperation[26] rather than to protect investors who are willing to risk their money for a profit.[27] Second, corporations often have greater leverage with lenders, and because of this bargaining power, have less need of usury protection.[28] Third, corporations have greater access to legal and economic advice than individuals, and can thus theoretically make better informed decisions. Finally, the risk assumed by any corporate shareholder when the corporation receives a loan is limited to the amount of that shareholder's investment. If a corporation defaults on a loan, its shareholders will generally not lose their homes.

While these justifications for a corporate usury exemption make sense when large corporations are involved, and may also apply to well-capitalized partnerships or joint ventures, they gradually lose their persuasive force as the size of the business entity diminishes and the effects of individual debt guarantees are considered. Although small businesses operate for profit just as large corporations, they may have little more access to expert advice than do individuals, and the livelihood of their proprietors or owners is often more closely tied to the business than is that of the shareholders of large businesses. Thus, small business owners who have fallen on hard times can fall prey to high rate lenders just as easily as individuals.[29] Moreover, since in most states the business usury exception is extended to guarantors of bona fide business debt,[30] and because creditors frequently require individual guarantees on small business debt, the consequences of a loan default may be just as severe for a small business owner as for an individual. In recognition of these differences between loans to small and large businesses, business exceptions in usury statutes may be written

---

therefore exempt from Hawaiian usury ceiling); Havens v. Woodfill, 266 N.E.2d 221 (Ind. App. 1971) (discussing extension of corporate usury exemption to trusts, partnerships, joint ventures etc.); Walker, Tooke & Lyons v. Sapp, 862 So. 2d 414 (La. Ct. App. 2003) (obligation to pay legal fees for employment discrimination claim is not for "commercial or business purposes" so 12% interest rate cap applies); Krause v. Griffis, 443 N.W.2d 444 (Mich. App. 1989) (statute provided business entity exception for credit extended to natural person who signed affidavit of business purpose; exception applied even without affidavit where all parties knew of business purpose and notarized land contract referred to property's "income potential"); Borowski v. Falleder, 296 A.D.2d 301, 744 N.Y.S.2d 177 (2002) (loan to individual in personal capacity is not business loan even if borrower owned a business and put the loan to corporate use); Ludlum Corp. Pension Plan Trust v. Matty's Superservice, Inc., 548 N.Y.S.2d 292 (App. Div. 1989) (usury exemption applied even though borrower had lost its official corporate status for nonpayment of franchise taxes and was only a de facto corporation).

23 *In re* Jungkurth, 74 B.R. 323 (Bankr. E.D. Pa. 1987) (failure to rebate unearned finance charges according to the actuarial method on a business loan violated the prepayment penalty prohibition of the residential mortgage act).

24 Hufnagel v. George, 135 F. Supp. 2d 406 (S.D.N.Y. 2001) (New York's 25% criminal usury ceiling applied to large business loan that was otherwise exempt from civil usury statute); RTC v. Minassian, 777 F. Supp. 385 (D.N.J. 1991) (New Jersey's 30% criminal usury law applied to commercial real estate loan); Committee of Unsecured Creditors v. RG Fin., Ltd. (*In re* Powerburst), 154 B.R. 307 (Bankr. E.D. Cal. 1993) (applying N.Y.'s criminal usury law to business loan); Norris v. Sigler Daisy Corp., 392 S.E.2d 242 (Ga. 1990) (Georgia's 60% criminal usury law applied to otherwise deregulated home-secured loan); Tower Funding, Ltd. v. David Berry Realty, Inc., 755 N.Y.S.2d 413 (App. Div. 2003) (defense of criminal usury may be asserted even by a corporation); Nikezic v. Balaz, 585 N.Y.S.2d 86 (App. Div. 1992) (business loans to corporate defendants with rates of 168%–192% were "unquestionably criminally usurious" under controlling statutes); Transmedia Restaurant Co. v. 33 E. 61st St. Restaurant Corp., 710 N.Y.S.2d 756 (Sup. Ct. 2000).

25 *See generally* Comment, *Usury Laws and the Corporate Exception*, 23 Md. L. Rev. 51 (1963).

26 *See* cases cited in § 9.3.1.1, *infra*.

27 *See* Paulman v. Filtercorp, 899 P.2d 1259 (Wash. 1995) (interpreting Washington's business purpose exception to apply to a corporate debtor even if loan guaranteed by a natural person).

28 *See, e.g.,* Trapp v. Hancuh, 530 N.W.2d 879 (Minn. Ct. App. 1995) (purpose of usury laws is "to protect the weak and necessitous from being taken advantage of by lender who can unilaterally establish the terms of the loan transaction"; distinguishing position of corporations, presumed to be in an equal bargaining position).

29 *See, e.g.,* Jersey Palm-Gross, Inc. v. Paper, 658 So. 2d 531 (Fla. 1995) (at issue usurious loan to business borrowers "in desperate financial straits" and "urgent" need of money). Cf. Paulman v. Filtercorp, 899 P.2d 1259 (Wash. 1995), in which separate opinions note that the loan at issue, "which would have made a loan shark proud," demonstrates the falseness of the assumption that small businesses and farmers are not driven by economic imperatives into oppressive situations, and call on the legislature to revisit whether complete exclusion from usury laws for business loans is "just."

30 *See, e.g.,* Snyder v. Woxo, Inc., 177 N.W.2d 281 (Neb. 1970); Republicbank Dallas N.A. v. Shook, 653 S.W.2d 278 (Tex. 1983); Wayne Cty. Bank v. Hodges, 338 S.E.2d 202 (W. Va. 1985); Annot., 63 A.L.R.2d 924 (1959). *See also* § 10.6.3, *infra* (standing to assert usury).

to apply only to loans over a set principal amount, on the assumption that businesses obtaining larger loans have the wherewithal to protect themselves from bad bargains.[31] Other ways to limit the business or corporate exception are to make it inapplicable if the borrower is a close corporation with a small number of shareholders,[32] or where the incorporation looks to be an evasive device.[33]

9.2.2.3 Requiring Incorporation or an Affidavit of Business Purpose

Regardless of the merits of a policy of excluding various business transactions from usury restrictions, merely the existence of such an exclusion raises usury issues because creditors sometimes attempt to structure transactions in order to take advantage of usury exclusions. In the case of business exemptions, creditors have frequently required borrowers to incorporate or to sign affidavits of business purpose before credit is issued so that business interest rates may be charged. To some extent this practice may be valid.

A majority of courts have held that it is permissible for a lender to require a borrower to incorporate to receive a loan under a corporate usury exception, provided that the loan is being made for a bona fide business purpose.[34] The basic idea is that incorporation of a true business operation is merely a matter of legal form, and that requiring a business to incorporate to obtain a loan is an attempt to comply with usury statutes rather than an attempt to evade them. It follows directly from this approach, sometimes called the New York rule, that the incorporation of individuals who have no bona fide business goals is a sham transaction which will not be recognized for usury purposes.[35]

The New York rule has some appeal because it follows the legislative goals behind corporate usury exemptions while foiling the more blatant attempts to evade usury ceilings. Yet this approach opens a significant loophole in usury laws because once some true business purpose exists, all usury protection vanishes. Lenders can and do require major stockholders in close corporations to transfer non-business assets to the corporation or, more frequently, to give personal guarantees of corporate debt before credit will be extended to the corporation. Such requirements are generally upheld by the courts either on the ground that guarantors fall within statutory corporate usury exceptions or on the broader ground that guarantors as a group lack standing to assert usury.[36]

The breadth of the usury loophole created by the combination of the New York rule and the ability of creditors to obtain personal guarantees of business debt has lead a minority of courts, most notably the courts of New Jersey, to take a different approach to corporate usury exemptions. Under the New Jersey rule, the question of whether a corporate loan is bona fide or merely a concealed individual loan is a question of fact which will not be determined merely by the existence of a business purpose.[37] Thus, the New Jersey rule gives more effect to the basic policy behind

---

31 *See, e.g., In re* Moorhous, 180 B.R. 138 (Bankr. E.D. Va. 1995) (Pa. law) (business loan over $10,000); Matter of Schlag, 60 B.R. 749 (Bankr. W.D. Pa. 1986) (business loan over $10,000); Tides Edge Corp. v. Central Fed. Sav., F.S.B., 542 N.Y.S.2d 763 (App. Div. 1989) (amount that triggers exemption from usury laws is amount agreed to be advanced rather than amount actually advanced); Smith v. Mitchell, 616 A.2d 17 (Pa. Super. Ct. 1992) (business loan over $10,000 exempt). *See also* § 9.2.5, *infra.*

32 *See* FDIC v. Caledonia Inv. Corp., 725 F. Supp. 90, 92–93 (D. P.R. 1989).

33 *E.g.,* N.Y. Gen. Oblig. Law. § 5-521(2) (exception to business exception where corporation formed within 6 months of loan and is secured by mortgage on a 1 or 2 family home which is the corporation's principal asset), *discussed in In re* L.G.H. Enterprises, Inc., 146 B.R. 612 (Bankr. E.D.N.Y. 1992); Millerton Properties v. Brescia Ent., 584 N.Y.S.2d 660 (App. Div. 1992).

34 *See, e.g.,* Matter of LeBlanc, 622 F.2d 872 (5th Cir. 1980); Briggs v. Capital Sav. & Loan Ass'n, 597 S.W.2d 600 (Ark. 1980); Jones v. Nelson, 432 N.W.2d 792 (Minn. Ct. App. 1988); Galloway v. Travelers Ins. Co., 515 So. 2d 678 (Miss. 1987); Schneider v. Phelps, 359 N.E.2d 1361 (N.Y. 1977); Jenkins v. Moyse, 172 N.E. 521 (N.Y. 1930); Republicbank Dallas NA v. Shook, 653 S.W.2d 278 (Tex. 1983); Skeen v. Glenn Justice Mortgage Co., 526 S.W.2d 252 (Tex. Civ. App. 1975).

35 *See, e.g., In re* Seisay, 49 B.R. 354 (S.D.N.Y. 1985), *aff'd*, 1986

WL 2826 (S.D.N.Y. Feb. 28, 1986); *In re* King, 68 B.R. 569 (Bankr. D. Minn. 1986); Rutter v. Troy Mortgage Servicing Co., 377 N.W.2d 846 (Mich. Ct. App. 1985) (cause of action stated); Allan v. M&S Mortgage Co., 359 N.W.2d 238 (Mich. Ct. App. 1984) (summary judgment reversed); Essex v. Newman, 655 N.Y.S.2d 595 (App. Div. 1997); Schneider v. Phelps, 359 N.E.2d 1361 (N.Y. 1977). *See also* Metcoff v. Mutual Trust Life Ins. Co., 339 N.E.2d 440 (Ill. App. 1975) (no business purpose); Havens v. Woodfill, 266 N.E.2d 221 (Ind. App. 1971) (no business enterprise).

36 *See* § 10.6.3, *infra* (standing to assert usury). *But cf.* Trapp v. Hancuh, 530 N.W.2d 879 (Minn. Ct. App. 1995) (New York rule and rule regarding standing of guarantors not applicable where individual has direct and primary liability, interpreting state's usury exception for loans to corporation).

37 *See, e.g.,* Sun Bank of Tampa Bay v. Spigrin Properties, 469 So. 2d 240 (Fla. Dist. Ct. App. 1985) (sham incorporation of partnership; loan held usurious); *In re* Greenberg, 121 A.2d 520 (N.J. 1956); Gelber v. Kugel's Tavern Inc., 89 A.2d 654 (N.J. 1952); Gottesfeld v. Kaminski, 524 A.2d 872 (N.J. Super. App. Div. 1987) (corporation set up by broker for borrower was shell and did not fall within corporate exception to usury doctrine); Walnut Discount Co. v. Weiss, 208 A.2d 26 (Pa. Super. 1965). *Cf.* Selengut v. Ferrara, 496 A.2d 725 (N.J. Super. 1985) (loan to bona fide corporation secured by mortgages on homes of shareholders fell within business exception to state second mortgage law); Whirlpool Fin. Corp. v. Sevaux, 96 F.3d 216 (7th Cir. 1996) (loan made to individual was a business loan where the individual was president and sole owner of a corporation, warranted that the note was a commercial transaction, deposited the proceeds into a corporate account, and used the money for business purposes); *see also* Damron v. Associates Fin. Servs. Co., 701 So. 2d 1146 (Ala. Civ. App. 1997) (since two-thirds of loan proceeds refinanced a commercial loan and one-third consolidated personal debts, court held loan was not "primarily" for personal, family, or household purposes).

usury limitations and greater protection to small businesses at the price of some uncertainty about how any particular personally guaranteed business loan will be treated.

Normally the question of whether a loan was for a business purpose is determined by an objective standard based on the borrower's representations, but if the lender manipulated the structure or rigged the documentation of the loan, then the borrower's subjective intent may be examined.[38] Borrowers' affidavits of business purpose have been given effect in cases where the lender had no reason to doubt that the loan was really a business loan.[39] Such affidavits have also been dispositive when the borrowers' oral representations were inconclusive.[40] However, statements or affidavits of business purposes which the lender knew or should have known to be false have been given no effect.[41]

---

38 *Compare* Brown v. Giger, 757 P.2d 523 (Wash. 1988) (en banc) (loan deemed for business purposes even though borrower was obtaining funds for friend and had no business purpose of her own; borrower signed documents stating specific business purpose) *with* Marashi v. Lannen, 780 P.2d 1341 (Wash. Ct. App. 1989) (borrowers' certificate stating business purpose in general, conclusory language was not dispositive; lender told borrowers that certificate was "just a formality" and did not explain its significance).

39 *See, e.g.,* Anglin v. J&G Assocs., Consumer Cred. Guide (CCH) ¶ 96,677 (D.D.C. 1983); *In re* Stipetich, 294 B.R. 635 (Bankr. W.D. Pa. 2003) (Md. law); Briggs v. Capital Sav. & Loan Ass'n, 597 S.W.2d 600 (Ark. 1980); Revocable Living Trust v. Wel-Co Group, Inc., 86 P.3d 818 (Wash. Ct. App. 2004); Castronuevo v. General Acceptance Corp., 905 P.2d 387 (Wash. Ct. App. 1995) (note and affidavits stated business purpose, and borrowers made no representations otherwise); Stevens v. Security Pac. Mortgage Co., 768 P.2d 1007 (Wash. Ct. App. 1989) (business exception applied despite the use of proceeds for personal purposes, where broker, but not lender, knew of real purpose and where sophisticated borrower, whose profession involved real estate financing, intended that representation to lender would be that it was for business purposes, and was represented by counsel at closing); Conrad v. Smith, 712 P.2d 866 (Wash. Ct. App. 1986).

40 Falk v. Riedel, 2000 Wash. App. LEXIS 1889 (Sept. 29, 2000) (unpublished, citation limited) (loan documents stated business purpose, and borrower's contrary evidence was unpersuasive); Marashi v. Lannen, 780 P.2d 1341, 1343 (Wash. Ct. App. 1989).

41 *See, e.g.,* Sheffield Commercial Corp. v. Clemente, 792 F.2d 282 (2d Cir. 1986) (question of fact whether creditor reasonably perceived the intended use of sports car to be commercial); *In re* Seisay, 49 B.R. 354 (S.D.N.Y. 1985), *aff'd,* 1986 WL 2826 (S.D.N.Y. Feb. 28, 1986), *later opinion at* 61 B.R. 940 (Bankr. S.D.N.Y. 1986); Family Fed. Sav. & Loan v. Davis, 172 B.R. 437 (Bankr. D.D.C. 1994) (lender told borrower business purpose statement was needed to obtain the loan); *In re* King, 68 B.R. 569 (Bankr. D. Minn. 1986) (court gives no effect to borrower's false statements where lender did not rely on them); Barco Auto Leasing Corp. v. House, 520 A.2d 162 (Conn. 1987) (seller bears the ultimate responsibility for the characterization of a transaction as business or consumer despite alleged buyer misrepresentations); Commercial Mtg. & Fin. Co. v. Life Savs. of America, 541 N.E.2d 661 (Ill. 1989) (when lender initiated idea of having borrower sign false business purpose statement, and borrower cooperated, borrower could assert usury and establish loans were for personal purpose); *In re* Estate of

9.2.2.4 Criteria for Business vs. Personal Purpose

Given the number of cases involving corporate or business usury exemptions, surprisingly few opinions discuss in any detail the difference between a business purpose and a personal or individual purpose.[42] The issue is generally

---

Backofen, 404 N.W.2d 675 (Mich. App. 1987) (borrower's written statement of business purpose not conclusive, evidence regarding knowledge which lender may have had concerning actual purpose of loan should have been admitted); Thelma Sanders & Assoc. v. Friedman, 524 N.Y.S.2d 768 (App. Div. 1988); Halco Fin. Servs., Inc. v. Foster, 770 S.W.2d 554 (Tenn. Ct. App. 1989) (lender constructed loan as sale/leaseback for business purposes; court found it to be a personal loan in reality, thus subject to usury statute); Brown v. Giger, 757 P.2d 523 (Wash. 1988) (en banc) (if objective evidence of loan's business purpose was rigged by creditor to evade usury restrictions, courts will not deny borrower protections against usury; *dicta*); Jansen v. Nu-West, Inc., 6 P.3d 98 (Wash. Ct. App. 2000) (if borrower's oral representations are different from the written representations, jury must decide the facts); McGovern v. Smith, 801 P.2d 250 (Wash. Ct. App. 1990) (written declaration does not necessarily control; where lender knew borrower burdened by personal liability on a pre-existing business debt, needed money in part for personal purposes, and knew debtor was not currently involved in business, loan was not for business purpose as a matter of law; case remanded); Marashi v. Lannen, 780 P.2d 1341 (Wash. Ct. App. 1989) (lender not entitled as a matter of law to rely on borrower's certificate of business purpose if lender's agent knew that funds were for personal use). *See also* Faison v. Nationwide Mortgage Corp., 839 F.2d 680 (D.C. Cir. 1987) (one of several alleged fraudulent and unfair acts for which jury awarded over $100,000 damages was extracting a business purpose statement for loan without explaining that had the effect of depriving borrower of protections under Truth in Lending Act), *cert. denied,* 488 U.S. 823 (1988); Ross v. Lake City Equity Fin. Co., 425 F.2d 1 (7th Cir. 1970) (usury claim rejected where borrowers fail to assert that affidavit stating business purpose was false); Metcoff v. Mutual Trust Life Ins. Co., 339 N.E.2d 440 (Ill. App. 1975) (letter from borrower to land trustee contains statement of business purpose, but statement given no effect because not made to lender, no reliance by lender, and no detail of purported business enterprise). *See generally* § 9.3.5.3, *infra* (estoppel against the assertion of usury).

42 In addition to the usury cases cited *infra* in this section, cases decided under the Truth in Lending Act, 15 U.S.C. § 1601 *et seq.,* may provide persuasive authority for the definition of "consumer" credit. (Note, however, that the current TILA excludes credit extended for agricultural purposes from its definition, unlike many state usury laws.) *See, e.g.,* Semar v. Platte Valley Fed. Sav. & Loan Ass'n, 791 F.2d 699 (9th Cir. 1986) (loan "primarily for personal purpose if primary purpose is to pay off second trust deed loan on consumer's home and only 10% of proceeds used for business purposes); Thorns v. Sundance Properties, 726 F.2d 1417 (9th Cir. 1984) (purchase of a limited partnership interest for investment purposes can be for personal, as opposed to business, purpose); Tower v. Moss, 625 F.2d 1161 (5th Cir. 1980) (home improvement transaction primarily for consumer purpose although home had been leased for nominal rent); Gallegos v. Stokes, 593 F.2d 372 (10th Cir. 1979) (purchase of truck primarily for personal use where borrower also intended to use truck for business but did not have an

viewed as a question of fact which will vary from case to case. Typically, loans used for direct investment or to finance a profit-making enterprise have been treated as business loans.[43] On the other hand, the absence of any profit-making enterprise suggests personal purposes.[44]

The borrower's intended purpose at the inception of the loan controls: a loan originally intended for business purposes does not lose that character if the borrower subsequently changes his mind and uses the proceeds for personal purposes.[45] (But note that this issue is distinct from whether the character of a loan may change upon refinancing.[46]) A contract to purchase land to live on is not a business transaction merely because the land had been classified as agricultural until the sale.[47] Courts have suggested that smaller loans will more likely be treated as personal,[48] as will loans which are expected to be repaid through income unrelated to the loan.[49]

9.2.2.5 Intermediaries; Refinancing

There are a few special circumstances which can create some uncertainty about how a loan should be treated. For example, it is unclear whether borrowers who act as intermediaries for other borrowers (typically for relatives who could not obtain a loan) have business purposes just because the third party borrowers do.[50] However, a debtor who signs

---

ongoing business nor the prospect of establishing one); Baskin v. G. Fox & Co., 550 F. Supp. 64 (D. Conn. 1982) (open-end consumer account); Dougherty v. Hoolihan, Neils, & Boland, Ltd., 531 F. Supp. 717 (D. Minn. 1982), *aff'd on other grounds*, 614 F.2d 968 (5th Cir. 1980); Weingarten v. First Mortgage Co., 466 F. Supp. 349 (E.D. Pa. 1979); Smith v. Chapman, 436 F. Supp. 58 (W.D. Tex. 1977) (car purchased primarily for personal use), *aff'd on other grounds*, 614 F.2d 968 (5th Cir. 1980); Allen v. City Dodge, Inc., Consumer Cred. Guide (CCH) ¶ 98,428, Clearinghouse No. 18,317 (N.D. Ga. 1977); Levites v. Chipman, 300 Mass. App. Ct. 356, 568 N.E.2d 639 (1991) (loan co-signed by parents with son to pay off son's business debt for which parents were guarantors was commercial even though parents did not participate in business); Stephens v. Chrysler First Fin. Servs. Corp., 1992 WL 108131 (Minn. Ct. App. May 26, 1992); Beck Enterprises, Inc. v. Hester, 512 So. 2d 672, 678 (Miss. 1987) (sale of truck not primarily for business purposes, where used to transport consumer and his tools to job, but not for transport of goods in the truck for payment, and both consumer and wife used it for family and personal purposes). *Cf.* Pollice v. National Tax Funding, 225 F.3d 379 (3d Cir. 2000) (credit for water and sewer service in non-owner occupied housing is business purpose); Quinn v. A.I. Credit Corp., 615 F. Supp. 151 (E.D. Pa. 1985) (loan to purchase commercial fire insurance policy on store and rental apartments was business purpose); Weber v. Langholz, 39 Cal. App. 4th 1578, 46 Cal. Rptr. 2d 677 (1995) (coin investment and speculation not consumer purposes); Broaddus v. National bank, 709 S.W.2d 461 (Ky. Ct. App. 1986) (loan to construct six-unit apartment building where borrower did not plan to live was for commercial or business purpose). *See generally* National Consumer Law Center, Truth in Lending §§ 2.2.3, 2.4.2 (5th ed. 2003 and Supp.). Cases interpreting similar definitions under the Fair Debt Collection Practices Act and state unfair and deceptive acts and practices (UDAP) statutes are discussed in National Consumer Law Center, Fair Debt Collection § 4.14.2 (5th ed. 2004 and Supp.) and Unfair and Deceptive Acts and Practices § 2.1.8 (6th ed. 2004 and Supp.).

43 *See, e.g.*, Matter of LeBlanc, 622 F.2d 872 (5th Cir. 1980); Ross v. Lake Equity Fin. Co., 425 F.2d 1 (7th Cir. 1970) (loan to acquire land for development was business loan even though development never occurred); Allen v. Mainway Fin. Corp., 446 F. Supp. 26 (N.D. Ill. 1977) (loan to purchase debenture); *In re* Stipetich, 294 B.R. 635 (Bankr. W.D. Pa. 2003) (Md. law) (loan to acquire ownership interest of any size in a business is a business loan); Briggs v. Capital Sav. & Loan Ass'n, 597 S.W.2d 600 (Ark. 1980); United Central Bank v. Kruse, 439 N.W.2d 849 (Iowa 1989) (property purchased both for residence and for business; evidence relating to method of handling interest and depreciation for tax purposes supported finding of business purpose loan); Krause v. Griffis, 443 N.W.2d 444 (Mich. App. 1989) (land contract for foster care facility); Galloway v. Travelers Ins. Co., 515 So. 2d 678 (Miss. 1987) (usury not available to one who forms corporation at lender's request to obtain loan which furthers profit-oriented business venture; usury defense is available if proceeds used to meet borrower's personal, non-business needs and obligations; court also suggests in dicta that if the principals of the corporation had been personally liable on the debt as endorsers or guarantors, the holding that the usury claim was not available in this case

"would likely be different" (*Id.* at 679 n.1)); Bollag v. Dresdner, 495 N.Y.S.2d 560 (N.Y.C. Civ. Ct. 1985); Pacesetter Real Estate, Inc. v. Fasules, 767 P.2d 961 (Wash. Ct. App. 1989) (loan for purchase of land to be used as combined residence, real estate office and farm, executed in borrower's corporate capacity and represented in documents as a commercial loan, was held to be such); Conrad v. Smith, 712 P.2d 866 (Wash. Ct. App. 1986); Wayne Cty. Bank v. Hodges, 338 S.E.2d 202 (W. Va. 1985). *See also* Schneider v. Phelps, 359 N.E.2d 1361 (N.Y. 1977) (remand for factual determination).

44 *See* Havens v. Woodfill, 266 N.E.2d 221 (Ind. App. 1971). *But see* Brown v. Giger, 757 P.2d 523 (Wash. 1988) (en banc) (loan obtained to re-lend to a friend at no interest for friend's business purpose was a business loan where the well-educated borrower did not make it clear to lender she had no interest in the venture, and the friend actively participated in loan negotiations and signed loan documents in three places describing the loan as business purpose).

45 Revocable Living Trust v. Wel-Co Group, Inc., 86 P.3d 818 (Wash. Ct. App. 2004); Jansen v. Nu-West, Inc., 6 P.3d 98 (Wash. Ct. App. 2000); Falk v. Riedel, 2000 Wash. App. LEXIS 1889 (Sept. 29, 2000) (unpublished, citation limited); Hommel v. Thweatt, 834 P.2d 1058 (Wash. Ct. App. 1992). *See also In re* Stipetich, 294 B.R. 635 (Bankr. W.D. Pa. 2003) (Md. law) (borrower had business purpose when she intended to invest funds in an enterprise, even though the enterprise defrauded her out of the money).

46 *See* § 9.2.2.3.3, *infra*.

47 Beltz v. Dings, 6 P.3d 424 (Kan. App. 2000).

48 *Compare* Allen v. Mainway Fin. Corp., 446 F. Supp. 26 (N.D. Ill. 1977) ($100,000 loan size suggests business purpose) *with* Havens v. Woodfill, 266 N.E.2d 221 (Ind. App. 1971) (three separate $100 loans; White, J., concurring suggests loan size indicates non-business purpose).

49 *See* Schneider v. Phelps, 359 N.E.2d 1361 (N.Y. 1977) (remand for factual determination).

50 *Compare* Metcoff v. Mutual Trust Life Ins. Co., 339 N.E.2d 440 (Ill. App. 1975) (bank lends money to parents who in turn

a genuine business purpose loan as surety is bound by the business characterization of the transaction just as the principal is.[51]

A second example is the question of whether loans refinancing pre-existing business debts continue to be treated as business debts the second time around. This may depend upon a combination of the borrower's motivation in seeking the refinancing and what the lender knows of the borrower's purpose. For example, if a delinquent business debt was secured by the borrower's residence, and refinancing was obtained to prevent foreclosure on the home which the lender was aware of, the second loan may be viewed as a personal loan.[52]

9.2.2.6 Burden of Proof

As a matter of evidence, if a loan is usurious on its face, the lender has the burden of proving the business purpose, rather than the debtor having to prove a nonbusiness purpose.[53] The absence of an exemption to the usury statute is not an element of usury.[54]

9.2.3 Distinctions Based on the Type of Credit

9.2.3.1 Introduction

In addition to the common distinction between consumer purpose and business purpose, a number of other distinctions among types of credit may be relevant to determining which usury statute is applicable. The most common distinctions are between open-end (revolving) and closed-end credit,[55] and between loans and installment credit sales.[56] To further complicate matters, some states will further subdivide their regulation of certain types of credit by reference to which creditor extends it. Thus there may be some regulatory provisions applicable to open-end credit extended by the seller (e.g., a department store credit card), and different provisions applicable to open-end credit extended by a third-party, such as a MasterCard or VISA issued by a bank, or an open-end line of credit from a bank or finance company. Moreover, where a third-party credit card is issued by an out-of-state bank, the possibility of federal preemption of the consumer's home state law must also be explored.[57]

9.2.3.2 Open-End or Closed-End Credit

As with any regulatory statute, some creditors may try to evade the more strict ones. As open-end credit regulation is often substantially looser, and requires less meaningful disclosures,[58] a creditor may seek to treat what is in reality a

---

re-lend funds to sons for business purposes; loan from bank to parents was not a business loan) *with* Simpson v. Aetna Fin. Co., 523 N.E.2d 762 (Ind. Ct. App. 1988) (where parents gave loan proceeds to son for "investment," loan was for business purpose); Brown v. Giger, 757 P.2d 523 (Wash. 1988) (en banc) (loan obtained to re-lend to a friend at no interest for friend's business purpose was a business loan where the well-educated borrower did not make it clear to lender she had no interest in the venture, and the friend actively participated in loan negotiations and signed loan documents in three places describing the loan as business purpose); Castronuevo v. General Acceptance Corp., 905 P.2d 387 (Wash. Ct. App. 1995) (business loans where parents borrowed money to finance son's business ventures); Conrad v. Smith, 712 P.2d 866 (Wash. Ct. App. 1986) (parents borrow money to start son in siding business; refinancing is a business loan).

51 *In re* Jungkurth, 74 B.R. 323 (Bankr. E.D. Pa. 1987); Simoni v. Time-Line, Ltd., 272 A.D.2d 537, 708 N.Y.S.2d 142 (2000). *See also* Holland v. Michigan Nat'l Bank-West, 420 N.W.2d 173 (Mich. App. 1988) (in reference to claim that cosigning wife was not engaged in the business being financed, if loan actually made for business purposes, and all borrowers aware of that purpose, business purpose exception applies irrespective of whether any single borrower has involvement in business beyond signing on the loan); McGovern v. Smith, 801 P.2d 250 (Wash. Ct. App. 1990) (the purpose of the transaction, not of the borrower is relevant; different parties cannot have conflicting purposes in context of the business exemptions).

52 *See* National Consumer Law Center, Truth in Lending § 2.4.2.2.2 (5th ed. 2003 and Supp.). *Compare* McGovern v. Smith, 801 P.2d 250 (Wash. Ct. App. 1990) (business purpose for one loan does not control as to purpose of subsequent loan refinancing the former; a loan refinancing a failed business loan that is a personal obligation may not be for a business purpose; in this case, a loan to pay off pre-existing business debt and provide living expenses to man who had lost his business, suffered a divorce and bankruptcy, all of which creditor knew, did not establish a business purpose as a matter of law; case remanded) *and In re* Jackson, 42 B.R. 76 (Bankr. D.D.C. 1984) (consolidation loan of previous business debts by new creditor to prevent foreclosure on homes was not exempt under D.C. usury law's business exemption) *with* Jansen v. Nu-West, Inc., 6 P.3d 98 (Wash. Ct. App. 2000) (original purpose clings to transaction through all refinancings) *and* Conrad v. Smith, 712 P.2d 866 (1986) (though purpose of refinancing was to prevent foreclosure, business characterization retained where borrower did not so inform the new lender, and in fact had emphasized the business purpose and obfuscated matters to the lender). *But see In re* Stipetich, 294 B.R. 635 (Bankr. W.D. Pa. 2003) (Md. law)

(if purpose of original loan was business, refinance is also business loan). The same issue arises in conjunction with the Truth in Lending Act's business exemption.

53 Hommel v. Thweatt, 834 P.2d 1058 (Wash. Ct. App. 1992); Marashi v. Lannen, 780 P.2d 1341 (Wash. Ct. App. 1989); Aetna Fin. Co. v. Darwin, 691 P.2d 581 (Wash. Ct. App. 1985). *See* § 9.3.3, *infra.*

54 Aetna Fin. Co. v. Darwin, 691 P.2d 581 (Wash. Ct. App. 1985).

55 The two different types of credit are discussed in § 2.3.2.3, *supra.*

56 *See* §§ 2.2.3.1, 2.2.3.2, 2.3.2.2, *supra.*

57 *See* §§ 3.4.5, 3.9.2.2, *supra.*

58 *E.g.,* open-end Truth in Lending regulations do not require disclosure of the total finance charge or total of payments, Reg. Z § 226, subpart B, for the reason that these *cannot* be determined in advance in the case of genuine open-end credit. However, with "spurious open-end credit," this information

closed-end transaction as revolving credit. The statute usually defines the characteristics of open-end credit, and a particular transaction may not meet all the necessary elements. Some states incorporate as one element of the definition of open-end transactions that repeated transactions be reasonably contemplated, similar to the Truth in Lending Act.[59]

The Washington Supreme Court, for example, scrutinized a purported revolving charge agreement and found it to be in reality a retail installment contract, to which greater disclosure requirements and a lower interest rate cap were applicable.[60] Similarly, a seller of funeral goods and services cannot "reasonably contemplate repeated transactions."[61] The purchase of big ticket items, such as cars,[62] satellite dishes,[63] or furniture[64] financed by a supposed revolving line of credit may not pass the likelihood of repeated transactions test. According to the North Dakota Supreme

Court, if there is a fixed due date to repay the extension of credit, it is closed-end, not open-end.[65]

On the other hand, the Seventh Circuit held in the Truth In Lending context that repeated transactions could reasonably be contemplated even though the $4,500 credit limit on the card the buyers received was only a few hundred dollars above the price of their purchases, a satellite dish and a year's worth of programming totalling about $4300.[66] The card could be used at hundreds of authorized retail dealers for goods and services related to the satellite dish, such as television sets or additional programming. The evidence showed that twenty percent of cardholders who used the card at least once made one or more additional purchases after the initial purchase, and the bank aggressively advertised repeat purchases. The court, however, ignored the "replenishing line of credit" factor, which may help to distinguish this decision from cases where evidence of this second criterion could be determinative. Another key distinction is that the plaintiffs did not seek a trial at which to prove that the bank's claim that it expected repeat transactions was not reasonable.[67] Since the determination of reasonableness is uniquely within the competence of juries, plaintiffs who do seek a trial on this issue should be granted one unless no rational jury could conclude that the lender acted unreasonably.[68]

One lending practice which raises serious questions about the distinction between open-end and closed-end credit is the writing of "open-end lines of credit" secured by the borrowers' home, in which the initial extension is at the line's maximum, and the "minimum" monthly payments are quite substantial but nonetheless reduce the principal only minimally.[69] Two contracts which NCLC reviewed are good examples of the problem.

The first had an initial advance which was greater than the credit limit. At 18%, the monthly payments were 1.5% of the balance, which put them at approximately $858.37 at the

---

could be determined at the outset. Since it might actually deter some cost-conscious consumers, an unethical creditor may choose to structure the loan to avoid providing meaningful cost information. The Home Ownership and Equity Protection Act, which substantively limits some loan terms on high cost mortgages, excludes open-end mortgages from its scope. 15 U.S.C. § 1602(aa)(1). *See* 12.2.2, *infra*.

59 15 U.S.C. § 1602(i), Reg. Z § 226.2(a)(20). *See, e.g., In re* Nair, Clearinghouse No. 24,757, Pov. L. Rep. ¶ 26,303 (S.D. Ohio 1978) (restrictions imposed on "open-end" plan lead court to find it other-than-open-end credit); Premier Federal Credit Union v. Douglas, 465 S.E.2d 338 (N.C. App. 1996). *See generally* National Consumer Law Center, Truth in Lending § 5.2 (5th ed. 2003 and Supp.).

60 Zachman v. Whirlpool Acceptance Corp., 841 P.2d 27 (Wash. 1992) (contract did not involve a retail seller, repeated transactions under a single agreement not possible, and creditor not obligated to approve subsequent purchases, so transaction did not meet statutory criteria to constitute a revolving charge agreement; statute subsequently amended). *But cf.* Sears, Roebuck & Co. v. Oszajca (*In re* Oszajca), 207 B.R. 41 (B.A.P. 2d Cir. 1997) (taking a security interest in goods purchased does not transform an open-end transaction into a closed-end transaction under Vermont statutory scheme).

61 *See, e.g.,* American Accounts Advisors, Inc. v. Hendrickson, 460 N.W.2d 83 (Minn. Ct. App. 1990) (state special usury statute governing open-end credit sales incorporated TIL definition, in which one element is that the creditor reasonably contemplate repeated transactions).

62 Premier Federal Credit Union v. Douglas, 465 S.E.2d 338 (N.C. App. 1996) (lender's motion for summary judgment denied).

63 Perry v. Household Retail Servs., Inc., 953 F. Supp. 1370 (M.D. Ala. 1996) (lender's motion for summary judgment denied), 180 F.R.D. 423 (M.D. Ala. 1998) (motion for class certification for statutory damages under TILA granted but denied as to actual damages under TILA, UDAP, RICO and fraud because the consumer passed away and the personal representative could not prove the consumer's reliance, a necessary element in each of these claims, according to the court), *on reconsideration*, 119 F. Supp. 2d 1258 (M.D. Ala. 2000) (granting assignee's motion for summary judgment on ground that it was not a creditor as defined by TILA), *aff'd without op.*, 268 F.3d 1067 (11th Cir. 2001).

64 Wise Furniture v. Dehning, 343 N.W.2d 26 (Minn. 1984).

65 Ag Acceptance Corp. v. Glinz, 684 N.W.2d 632 (N.D. 2004).

66 Benion v. Bank One, Dayton, 144 F.3d 1056 (7th Cir. 1998).

67 *Id.,* 144 F.3d at 1060.

68 Long v. Fidelity Water Sys., Inc., 2000 U.S. Dist. LEXIS 3982 (N.D. Cal. Mar. 16, 2000) (denying creditor's motion for summary judgment; whether creditor reasonably contemplated repeat transactions is jury question); Maes v. Motivation for Tomorrow, Inc., 356 F. Supp. 47 (N.D. Cal. 1973) (denying summary judgment to lender where plan allowed additional purchases only if creditor was satisfied with consumer's credit standing and on terms credit might later agree to and where consumer denied being told of possibility of future purchases); Premier Fed. Credit Union v. Douglas, 465 S.E.2d 338 (N.C. App. 1996) (denying summary judgment to lender who claimed car loan was under open-end credit plan; whether it was open-end and whether repeat transactions were contemplated are fact questions).

69 The loan may be non-amortizing or "barely-amortizing" at the minimum payment level, but the minimum payment levels are high enough that few borrowers could or would routinely make higher payments.

outset. When the cost of credit insurance was added, the principal balance declined at a snail's pace, thus freeing up very little room in the line for new advances. (This is significant, as a replenishing line of credit is implicit in the definition of open-end credit, and may be an explicit requirement, as well.[70]) Buried unobtrusively in the contract was a fifteen-year call provision. Without any subsequent draws on that $57,000 of credit, a conservative projection of the pay-off balance[71] at the end of fifteen years was still nearly $42,000, after over $137,000 in payments.

Under terms of a similar contract with a seventy-four-year-old consumer, the regular minimum payments on her initial draw of $4,000 would fail to open up even $500 after five years.[72] In such circumstances, arguably it is no more reasonable for these creditors to contemplate repeated transactions than it is for a funeral home to do so.[73] The Supreme Court of Alabama, interpreting the state's Mini-Code,[74] nonetheless found similar loans to be legitimate open-end credit,[75] presumably feeling that at least in the absence of licensing problems,[76] creditors are free to structure credit so as to receive the highest return.

Practitioners in other jurisdictions, however, may wish to consider making the argument that these are spurious open-end transactions[77] by raising additional claims not raised in the Alabama cases. In both Alabama cases, there actually was at least one additional extension of credit (though new agreements were in fact executed). There was apparently no evidence regarding the minimal degree to which the loan line would replenish itself through amortization. More importantly, to the extent any deception was alleged, it apparently was common law fraud or misrepresentation. If one advances, instead, a UDAP claim, the usual standard is the least sophisticated consumer,[78] rather than a "reasonably prudent person," and parol evidence rule problems are avoided.[79] Finally, some courts have held that creditors do not have unfettered freedom to structure credit in the most

profitable way, at least without so informing the consumer.[80] In the context of those types of claims, a court may be more willing than the Alabama court to find these spurious open-end credit transactions to be devices designed to evade more strict regulation, or, at a minimum, such courts may provide relief under the UDAP or unconscionability claim.

That fraud and UDAP claims are viable avenues to attack the essence of the sham is demonstrated by *Carlisle v. Whirlpool Fin. Nat'l Bank*,[81] in which the court upheld a significant jury award ($580 million punitive damages, reduced to $300 million) grounded squarely upon fraud and deception. Here, the elderly borrowers and their daughter bought a satellite dish, believing what they were told, that they would pay $34 per month for three years. Instead, it would take eight years to pay off the open-end account at the 22% interest rate in the agreement. The opinion highlights many of the facts which made the defendants' behavior "reprehensible," thus justifying the jury's outrage.

Other practices or contract terms that may be indicia of a spurious open-end home equity loan include: refinancing of closed-end loans into open-end or open-end into open-end especially by the same creditor;[82] prepayment penalties;[83] a

---

70 *Cf.* TIL Reg. Z, Official Staff Commentary § 226.2(a)(20)-5. *See* National Consumer Law Center, Truth in Lending § 5.2.2 (5th ed. 2003 and Supp.).

71 The note was a variable rate note starting at 18%; 15% after the first 1 1/2 years was the rate used in making the projection.

72 Moreover, after 15 years (at age 89), she would have paid over $12,000 to reduce this $4000 principal by less than $1300.

73 *See* American Accounts Advisors, Inc. v. Hendrickson, 460 N.W.2d 83 (Minn. Ct. App. 1990).

74 Ala. Code § 5-19-1(5) (1975). If closed-end the loans in question would have been subject to an 8% cap, rather than an 18% cap.

75 *See* Roper v. Associates Fin. Servs., 533 So. 2d 206 (Ala. 1988); Smith v. Citicorp Person-to-Person Fin. Centers, Inc., 477 So. 2d 308 (Ala. 1985).

76 *See* §§ 9.2.4.5–9.2.4.6, *infra*.

77 Courts look behind the face of the documents to determine the true nature of the transaction. *See* § 9.2.1.6, *supra*.

78 *See* National Consumer Law Center, Unfair and Deceptive Acts and Practices §§ 4.2.11.2, 4.3.8 (6th ed. 2004 and Supp.).

79 *Id.* § 4.2.15.

80 *See* Besta v. Beneficial Loan Co., 855 F.2d 532 (8th Cir. 1988); *In re* Milbourne, 108 B.R. 522 (Bankr. E.D. Pa. 1989). *See generally* Ch. 11, *infra*.

81 Civ. Action No. CV-97-068 (Circuit Court, Hale County, Ala., Post-Trial Order, Aug. 25, 1999), Clearinghouse No. 52,516.

82 The concept of refinancing an open-end account is essentially an oxymoron. If a customer needs additional cash for whatever reason, the customer will simply obtain a cash advance under the current account up to the credit line limit. There is no need to close one credit line and open another with a higher limit. If a borrower defaults, open-end creditors can simply terminate the account, eliminate the available credit, and sue for the balance. The creditor could also raise the credit line limit to allow a borrower to finance any arrears. The concept of refinancing an open-end account has no meaning in this context. What this practice reveals is that the loan is, in substance, a closed-end transaction. By structuring its portfolio in this fashion, the creditor retains the opportunity to collect points and fees to "refinance" which are not limited in amount by the terms of the contract as are the amounts of other fees, avoids potential coverage under the Home Ownership and Equity Protection Act (HOEPA), and effectively eliminates the extended right to rescind.

  If creditors claim that refinancing credit line accounts shows that they reasonably contemplated repeated transactions, this argument should fail. Under the Truth In Lending Act, § 1602(i), Congress clearly intended that there be one plan under which repeated transactions occur. The repeated transactions include the financing of *new* purchases or *new* cash advances under the *same* account.

  A refinancing, in contrast, is a new loan, generally between an existing creditor and borrower, the loan proceeds of which are used to pay off the pre-existing debt. The old debt is extinguished and an entirely new loan is created. To equate the concept of "repeated transactions" under one pre-existing plan with refinancing is to obliterate all distinctions between open-end and closed-end loans.

83 The imposition of prepayment penalties is completely inconsis-

call provision with or without a balloon payment;[84] or a term-limited draw provision coupled with a non-amortizing payment period.[85]

Lenders may also structure transactions as open-end rather than closed-end to avoid the strictures of the 1994 Home Ownership and Equity Protection Act (HOEPA).[86] Even while building in an exception for open-end mortgages, Congress was concerned enough about the possibility of evasion that it took the unusual step of directing the Federal Reserve Board to conduct a study of whether open-end mortgage borrowers were adequately protected.[87] In 2001, the Board amended Regulation Z to prohibit creditors from structuring home-secured loans as open-end credit plans to evade HOEPA's requirements.[88]

In a twist on the open-end versus closed-end issue, some mail order companies are in the business of selling merchandise through catalog sales to "members." At least one major company promoted itself to potential members by advising them that they had been pre-approved for a "gold card" with a $10,000 line of credit and for an annual fee had the right to make purchases from its catalog. Each time a member made a purchase by providing the account number, however, the company required the member to sign a new closed-end credit agreement. The Texas attorney general challenged the collection of an annual fee on the grounds that the issuance of a card with a line of credit constituted a retail credit card arrangement under state law which prohibited the charging of an annual fee. The court agreed.[89]

There may be circumstances in which borrowers will want to argue that payday loans fall under the state's revolving loan account law, which may impose stricter regulation than other alternatives. Payday lenders and borrowers often contemplate repeat transactions, and roll the amount due on one transaction over into the next, which satisfies one criterion of the typical revolving loan statute. One court has rejected such an argument,[90] but it might be successful in other jurisdictions, depending on the particular language of the statute.

9.2.3.3 Loans v. Credit Sales; Body-Dragging

Where a seller directly offers financing, it will be governed by a retail installment sales act (RISA) in most states.[91] However, if a sales transaction for some reason falls outside the scope of a RISA, the time-price usury exception may then come into play.[92] The scope of state RISAs is thus important for consumers. Many RISAs explicitly apply to sales of services as well as goods.[93] Even a RISA that only applies to "goods" may be construed to cover at least some service contracts.[94]

---

tent with the concept of open-end credit. The hallmark of revolving credit is that the borrowers pay as much or as little as they like subject to a minimum monthly payment. Such credit is openended in both directions: borrowers can pay for as short or as long a period of time as they choose. *See, e.g.,* Sears, Roebuck & Co. v. Oszajca (*In re* Oszajca), 207 B.R. 41, 47 (B.A.P. 2d Cir. 1997). The concept of "prepaying" has no meaning since there is no fixed term. Further, outside of the first lien mortgage lending context, the laws of many states forbid prepayment penalties in consumer credit transactions. *See* § 5.8, *supra*.

84 A call provision gives the creditor the right to close the account and require payment of the balance for any or no reason even when the account is current. Like the prepayment penalty provision, the call provision turns the concept of open-end lending on its head. Borrowers no longer have the right to repay over whatever period of time they choose.

85 Some equity line accounts contain a provision which limits the period during which a consumer can draw additional monies on the account to, e.g., the first ten years of the account. If the initial draw was equal or close to the account limit, it is very unlikely that account would replenish itself through monthly payments so that a consumer could actually draw additional sums during the draw period. The replenishing aspect inherent in a true open-end transaction is absolutely eliminated where a limited draw provision is coupled with a required payment amount that does not result in the loan amortizing during the same time-frame.

86 15 U.S.C. §§ 1602(ee), 1639. *See* § 12.2.2, *infra*.

87 *Id.* § 157(1).

88 12 C.F.R. § 226.34(b), effective Jan. 1, 2002.

89 State v. Allied Marketing Group, 949 S.W.2d 816 (Tex. App. 1997).

90 Porter v. Ace Cash Express, Inc., 2000 U.S. Dist. LEXIS 15996 (E.D. La. Oct. 25, 2000), *aff'd without op.*, 277 F.3d 1372 (5th Cir. 2001).

91 De La Rosa v. Western Funding, Inc., 24 P.3d 637 (Colo. App. 2001) (interpreting U.C.C.C.; considerations are whether the transaction involves a sale, whether the consumer has direct contact with the "lender," and whether the debt is originally payable to the seller). *Cf.* GMAC v. Kettelson, 580 N.E.2d 187 (Ill. App. Ct. 1991) (installment purchase of car financed by sales finance company governed by RISA, not the general usury statute applicable to loans). *But see* Prudential Dev. Co. Pension Plan Trust v. Rebector (*In re* Rebector), 208 B.R. 867 (W.D. Tex. 1997) (court reversed grant of summary judgment to borrower finding that there was a dispute of material fact as to borrower's understanding about whether home improvement company was financing the work on her home as opposed to a third party lender and as to whether she was offered a cash price and a credit price by the seller).

92 *See, e.g.,* Southwest Concrete Co. v. Gosh Constr., 798 P.2d 1247 (Cal. 1990); Saul v. Midlantic Nat'l Bank/South, 572 A.2d 650 (N.J. Super. App. Div. 1990) (car sale falling outside scope of RISA subject to time-price exception). *Cf.* Ghirardo v. Antonioli, 883 P.2d 960 (Cal. 1994) (real estate credit sale exempt from usury law; notes executed to settle dispute were modifications of exempt transactions and did not constitute separate non-exempt loan). *See generally* § 10.5.2.2, *infra*.

93 *See, e.g.,* Marshall v. JRS Farms (*In re* Marshall), 1998 Bankr. LEXIS 515 (Bankr. M.D.N.C. Mar. 2, 1998) (construction of a well is a service as defined in state RISA).

94 Westside Health and Racquet Club, Inc. v. Jefferson Fin. Servs., Inc., 19 S.W.3d 796 (Tenn. App. 1999) (health club memberships are "personalty" because they convey a right or interest in things movable, i.e., the right to use the club's facilities and equipment, so are covered by RISA; club's transfer of membership contracts to finance company at discount was excluded from state usury laws by RISA).

Just as there is an incentive for lenders to disguise closed-end credit as open-end,[95] there may be an incentive for a lender (particularly a finance company) to treat what is in reality a sale as a loan. The incentive arises when the ceiling applicable to small loan credit or second mortgage loans is higher than that applicable to retail installment sales,[96] as it often is.[97] Depending upon the circumstances surrounding the transaction, the effort may or may not pass muster.

In a classic scenario called "body-dragging," sellers—particularly used car dealers and home improvement contractors—take their buyer over to a finance company (or a second mortgage company) with whom they routinely do business. Instead of financing the purchase with a usually lower-rate Retail Installment Sales Act contract, the lender writes a "direct, third-party loan" at the higher small loan or second mortgage loan rate, the proceeds of which are used to pay off the seller. Courts may find body-dragging to be an impermissible effort to evade the rate ceiling and other RISA or MVRISA requirements, and find the finance company's loan therefore usurious.[98] That is not always the case, however.[99] Another theory is that efforts to evade a lower-rate ceiling constitute a violation of a state unfair and deceptive acts and practices (UDAP) statute.[100] Where the consumer independently arranges for a bank or finance company loan for the express purpose of purchasing goods or services, it is more clear that it is a loan, not a sale,[101] at least in the absence of specific statutory language to the contrary.[102]

9.2.3.4 Land Installment Contracts

A land installment contract, known in some parts of the country as a "contract for deed" or "bond for deed," is often presented to low-income people as a way to acquire ownership of a home without having to deal with a bank or get credit approval. With a land contract, unlike a mortgage, the seller does not convey title to the buyer and retain a security interest; instead, title remains in the seller's name until the buyer has completed all the payments. Land installment contracts are subject to very little regulation in some jurisdictions, making it easy for fraudulent sellers to take advantage of buyers. Some inner-city slumlords and promoters of home ownership schemes use land installment contracts and the prospect of home ownership to lure people in, expecting to be able to declare a forfeiture and retake the home in most cases. Land installment contracts are also often used by non-professional sellers on a one-time basis.

A number of states have statutes that regulate some aspects of land installment contracts, for example, by re-

---

95 *See* § 9.2.3.2, *supra.*

96 Many states have not only a general Retail Installment Sales Act, but also one or more specialized statutes applying to particular types of retail sales such as motor vehicle or home improvement sales, each of which may carry its own interest rate ceiling and restrictions on credit terms. See § 9.2.4.5, *infra*, for a discussion of licensing requirements under such statutes, and Appx. A, *infra*, for a list of each state's statutes.

97 In some circumstances, there may be a higher ceiling for credit sales than for certain loans, which creates an incentive to disguise the transaction as a credit sale. *See* De La Rosa v. Western Funding, Inc., 24 P.3d 637 (Colo. App. 2001).

98 Gonzalez v. Old Kent Mortg. Co., 2000 U.S. Dist. LEXIS 14530 (E.D. Pa. Sept. 19, 2000) (home improvement contractor arranged for loan); Barber v. Fairbanks Capital Corp., (*In re Barber*), 266 B.R. 309 (Bankr. E.D. Pa. 2001) (home improvement finance law applied both to a loan for home improvements arranged by a broker to whom the contractor referred the consumer, and to a second loan for more work arranged later by the same broker at the consumer's request); Brown v. Courtesy Consumer Discount Co., 134 B.R. 134 (Bankr. E.D. Pa. 1991) (the court also found the usury violation to result in a misstatement of the Truth in Lending finance charge, because the disclosed charge, calculated under the Small Loan Act, did not reflect the legal obligation); Hernandez v. Atlantic Fin., 164 Cal. Rptr. 279 (App. 1980) (seller-assisted "direct" finance company loan for purchase of car is subject to the automobile sales finance act). *See also* Johnson v. Household Mortg. Servs., 2004 WL 2188111 (E.D. Pa. Sept. 9, 2004) (home improvement contractor that arranged loan may have engaged in body dragging).

  A related scenario, whereby a seller assigns RISA paper to a finance company which then quickly flips (refinances) the contract into a higher-rate loan, is discussed in § 6.4.3, *supra.*

99 Kinzel v. Southview Chevrolet, 892 F. Supp. 1211 (D. Minn. 1995) (unsecured lender who financed a side loan for consumer's down payment on a car was not a retail seller subject to state MVRISA, though seller had arranged financing); Mullen v.

Fifth Third Bank, 539 N.E.2d 683 (Ohio App. 1988) (RISA inapplicable because car buyer signed loan agreement establishing direct contractual relationship with bank, though car dealer arranged financing and buyer had no face-to-face contact with any bank representative); Collins v. Horizon Housing, Inc., 519 S.E.2d 534 (N.C. App. 1999) (RISA did not apply to mobile home loan where borrowers approached the bank directly; bank was not engaged, directly or indirectly, in sale of goods or furnishing of services); Briercroft Serv. Corp. v. de Los Santos, 776 S.W.2d 198 (Tex. Ct. App. 1988) (home improvement loan financed directly by third-party lender did not involve a time-price differential, and therefore could not be a retail installment transaction as defined by code, though home improvement contractor arranged financing).

100 *See generally* Ch. 11, *infra*; National Consumer Law Center, Unfair and Deceptive Acts and Practices § 5.5.6 (6th ed. 2004 and Supp.).

101 De La Rosa v. Western Funding, Inc., 24 P.3d 637 (Colo. App. 2001) (interpreting U.C.C.C.); Micro-Switch Employee's Credit Union v. Collier, 530 N.E.2d 595 (Ill. App. Ct. 1988) (where borrower obtained loan directly from credit union to purchase car which secured the loan, the state MVRISA, which covered seller-financed retail installment transactions, holders of retail installment transactions, and sales finance agencies, did not apply to the transaction).

102 For example, the provisions of the Uniform Consumer Credit Code governing credit sales apply across the board to any type of creditor subject to the Act extending purchase-money credit. *Cf.* Acker v. Provident Nat'l Bank, 512 F.2d 729 (3d Cir. 1975) (bank credit card account governed by state installment sales act ceiling under "most favored lender" doctrine).

quiring advance notice and an opportunity to cure a default before the contract can be forfeited[103] or by specifying that the seller must follow state foreclosure procedures if the buyer defaults.[104] Only a few states specifically regulate the credit terms for land installment contracts, however. The Uniform Consumer Credit Code, which includes limitations on finance charges and other terms,[105] defines "consumer credit sale" to include the sale of an interest in land that is payable in installments or is subject to a finance charge.[106] Most of the states that have adopted one form or another of the UCCC include this provision.[107] It only applies if the seller regularly engages as a seller in transactions of that type,[108] however, and therefore would not cover the nonprofessional seller. It also has an exception for land installment contracts where the APR does not exceed a certain figure, ranging from 10% to 18% in states that have adopted this provision.[109] Kansas limits interest rates to 15% unless the parties agree to subject the transaction to the Uniform Consumer Credit Code.[110] Maryland has a comprehensive statute that limits the interest rate and prohibits points.[111] Minnesota limits the interest rate to 4% above a specified Fannie Mae rate when the contract amount is less than $100,000.[112] Michigan treats land contracts the same as mortgage loans, allowing any rate of interest that is less than the criminal usury rate but restricting other terms such as prepayment penalties.[113] Some other states have statutes that require disclosure of the financial terms of these transactions.[114]

If the state does not have a specific statute regulating land installment contracts, it may be possible to argue that some other statute applies. Particularly when dealing with protections against forfeiture, some courts have found state mortgage loan laws applicable to land installment contracts.[115] State statutes regulating mortgage loan interest rates may specify that they apply to land contracts.[116] Land installment contracts are subject to general usury laws in Texas.[117] An Oregon court has held, however, that a statute that limited prepayment penalties for "loans" did not apply to a land installment contract, which it characterized as a credit sale rather than a loan of money.[118] The typical Retail Installment Sales Act only applies to goods and services, so is unlikely to be applied to a land installment contract.

There are fewer federal preemption issues with respect to land installment contracts than with other types of transactions. Most land installment sellers are not federally related, so the Depository Institutions Deregulation and Monetary Control Act of 1980 (DIDA)[119] does not prevent state limitations on interest and charges from applying. The Alternative Mortgage Transactions Parity Act (AMTPA),[120] which overrides state law restrictions on adjustable rate clauses and other non-traditional terms, applies to both loans and credit sales that are secured by an interest in residential real estate or a mobile home,[121] so it will cover land installment sellers if the transaction is considered secured by the real estate. AMTPA covers state depository institutions, HUD-approved mortgage lenders, and "housing creditors," defined as those who regularly make loans or credit sales secured by real estate or mobile homes.[122] Therefore, it will not apply to sellers who are not federally-related and who

---

103 *See, e.g.,* Me. Rev. Stat. tit. 14, § 6111, tit. 33 § 482; Minn. Stat. § 559.21; Tex. Prop. Code §§ 5.061–5.080.

104 *See, e.g.,* 735 Ill. Comp. Stat. Ann. § 5/15-1106.

105 *See, e.g.,* U.C.C.C. §§ 2-201 (maximum finance charges), 2-501 to 2-503 (restrictions on late charges and other fees), 3-308 (prohibition against balloon payments).

106 U.C.C.C. § 1-301.

107 *See* Colo. Rev. Stat. § 5-1-301(11); Idaho Code § 28-41-301(35) (definition of "regulated credit sale"); Iowa Code § 537.1301(12) (excludes transactions in which interest rate is no more than 12%); Me. Rev. Stat. tit. 9-A, § 1-301 (broader coverage than most); Okla. Stat. tit. 14A, § 2-104; S.C. Code § 37-2-104 (includes broad exemption for land contracts from most of the Act's restrictions); Wis. Stat. § 421.301(9); Wyo. Stat. § 40-14-204 (land contracts in which APR is less than 18% excluded). *See also* Ind. Code § 24-4.5-1-301 (including land contracts in definition of "mortgage transaction"); Iowa Code § 558.70 (disclosures); Kan. Stat. § 16-207(b); W. Va. Code § 46A-1-1-2(13) (not a U.C.C.C. state, but provision is very similar; Beltz v. Dings, 6 P.3d 424 (Kan. Ct. App. 2000) (applying U.C.C.C. rate ceiling to contract for deed). Utah does not appear to include this provision.

108 U.C.C.C. § 1-301 (1974).

109 *Id.*

110 Kan. Stat. § 16-207(b).

111 Md. Code Real Prop. §§ 10-101 to 10-110.

112 Wolf v. Kian, 2000 WL 1281109 (Minn. Ct. App. Sept. 12, 2000) (unpublished).

113 Mich. Comp. Laws Ann. § 438.31c.

114 Me. Rev. Stat. tit. 33, § 482; Ohio Rev. Code § 5313.02; Tex. Prop. Code Ann. §§ 5.069 to 5.071.

115 *In re* Faiman, 70 B.R. 74 (Bankr. D.N.D. 1987); H & L Land Co. v. Warner, 258 So. 2d 293 (Fla. Dist. Ct. App. 1972); Anderson Contracting Co. v. Daugherty, 417 A.2d 1227 (Pa. Super. 1979). *See* National Consumer Law Center, Repossessions and Foreclosures § 16.11 (5th ed. 2002 and Supp.).

116 *See, e.g.,* 815 Ill. Comp. Stat. Ann. § 105/4(2)(b) (restricting prepayment penalties and adjustable rates on bonds for deed). *See also* Tex. Prop. Code § 5.073 (restricting late payment charges and prepayment penalties in land contracts).

117 Stringer v. Perales, 2003 WL 1848594 (Tex. App. Apr. 10, 2003) (unpublished); Dixon v. Brooks, 604 S.W.2d 330 (Tex. Civ. App. 1980). *See also* Bastani v. Serrato, 2002 WL 31236411 (Tex. App. Oct. 3, 2002) (affirming usury judgment against land contract seller).

118 Carey v. Lincoln Loan Co., 165 Or. App. 657, 998 P.2d 724 (2000). *Cf.* Stonebraker v. Zinn, 286 S.E.2d 911 (W. Va. 1982) (discussing whether land installment contracts fall within time-price exception to usury; concluding that an interest rate on a land installment contract in excess of usury ceiling will not be usurious unless the total monthly payment, including interest, is grossly disproportionate to the property's rental value).

119 12 U.S.C. § 1735f-7a, *reproduced at* Appx. L.5.1 *infra*. *See generally* § 3.9, *supra*.

120 12 U.S.C. §§ 3801–3806, *reproduced at* Appx. L.6, *infra*. *See generally* § 3.10, *supra*.

121 12 U.S.C. § 3802(1).

122 12 U.S.C. § 3802(2)(C).

engage only occasionally in land installment contracts. If AMTPA applies to a land installment contract by a state depository institution or a HUD-approved lender, then the contract can include terms such as variable rates without regard to their legality under state law.[123] For transactions entered into on or after July 1, 2003, the AMPTA regulations allow "housing creditors" to preempt only state limits on variable rates.[124]

9.2.3.5 The "Finance Charge" Requirement

Where a statutory definition of credit (or creditor) includes within its scope transactions upon which a "finance charge" is imposed, it can sometimes be difficult to determine precisely what constitutes a finance charge.[125] "Finance charge" usually does not include default or delinquency charges imposed for unanticipated late payments,[126] but in certain transactions, it may be difficult to distinguish a "finance charge" from a "late charge." For example, some vendors call for payment within thirty days of billing, then impose a charge on the unpaid balance after that time. Whether that charge is a "late charge" or a "finance charge" may depend on the facts.

In *Landon v. Mapco Inc.*,[127] a propane gas vendor's course of dealing involved carrying balances on the account, and imposing charges on those balances more than thirty days old. The Iowa Supreme Court held that such a practice meant that these were not charges for unanticipated late payments, but rather monthly finance charges which were waived if the payment was made within 30 days.[128] The

transaction, therefore, fell within the scope of Iowa's version of the Uniform Consumer Credit Code.[129]

In other cases, there may be issues of whether a transaction involves hidden finance charges, such as when the sales price of goods payable in installments has been inflated, or in the case of sale/leasebacks. These and other examples of hidden finance charges are discussed in detail in Chapter 7, *supra*.

9.2.4 Distinctions Based on the Type of Creditor

9.2.4.1 Introduction

This subsection generally addresses statutes which regulate or apply to specific types of creditors. For the sake of simplicity, creditors are divided into three broad categories, state depository lenders, federal depository lenders, and non-depository creditors, as this is a common method of differentiating among lenders.[130] A given special usury statute, however, may also depend upon the frequency of the creditor's lending activity, or whether the creditor is in the lending business.[131] It should be noted, however, that it is even possible for an entity which is not a party to a credit transaction to be bound by the laws governing that transaction, and subject to liability for violating them. Thus where a collection agency tried to collect excessive interest on a consumer debt, a Texas court held that it could be held liable for usury penalties, since under the statute the penalties were available against "any person" who contracted for or charged usurious interest.[132]

123 *See* § 3.10.2, *supra*.
124 12 C.F.R. § 560.220.
125 The Uniform Consumer Credit Code defines a consumer credit transaction as one in which the debt is either payable in installments or a finance charge is imposed. *See, e.g.*, Iowa Code §§ 537.1301(12)(a)(4), 537.1301(14)(a)(4). *See also* Ala. Code § 5-19-1(3) ("creditor" refers only to creditors extending credit for which payment of a finance charge is required).
126 *See, e.g.*, Iowa Code § 537.1301(19)(b)(1); Ala. Code § 5-19-1(1); Alaskan Fireplace, Inc. v. Everett, 677 N.W.2d 378 (Wis. Ct. App. 2003). *See also* Seaton v. City of Lexington, 97 S.W.3d 72 (Mo. Ct. App. 2002); Harrell v. Chrysler Fin. Co., 811 A.2d 597 (Pa. Super. 2002) (finance charges are separate from late charges and statute allows both); Anchor, Inc. v. Laguna Enters., Inc., 2002 WL 287706 (Tex. App. Feb. 7, 2002) (discount given by seller for prompt payment is not interest). *But see* Ala. Code § 8-8-5 as interpreted in Cantrell v. Walker Builders, Inc., 678 So. 2d 169 (Ala. Civ. App. 1996); Tex. Rev. Civ. Stat. Ann. art. 5068-1.01(a) (now Tex. Fin. Code Ann. § 301.002) *discussed in* Pentico v. Mad-Wayler, Inc., 964 S.W.2d 708 (Tex. App. 1998).
127 405 N.W.2d 825 (Iowa 1987).
128 *Id.* at 828. *See also* Metric Constr., Inc. v. Great Plains Properties, 344 N.W.2d 679 (N.D. 1984) (including a contract provision adding compensation for delayed payment means late payment not unanticipated within meaning of state's provisions on payment of late payment collection charges). *But cf.* Anderson v. Houston Cty. Hosp. Bd., 381 So. 2d 68 (Ala. Civ. App. 1980), *cert. denied*, 381 So. 2d 71 (1980) (hospital securing

30-day, no-interest promissory note is not a creditor where interest charged after maturity and default); Alaskan Fireplace, Inc. v. Everett, 677 N.W.2d 378 (Wis. Ct. App. 2003) (1.5% per month late charge not a finance charge when it was imposed for actual unanticipated late payment and seller viewed buyers as in default).
129 This finance charge/late charge dichotomy is similar to that which must be resolved to establish coverage under Truth in Lending. 12 C.F.R. § 226.2(a)(17) ("creditor" is one, *inter alia*, who extends credit subject to a finance charge); 12 C.F.R. § 226.4(c)(2) (charges for actual unanticipated late payment are not finance charges). Therefore, cases interpreting this TIL language may be useful in interpreting similar language in usury statutes. *See, e.g.*, Bright v. Ball Memorial Hosp. Ass'n, 616 F.2d 328 (7th Cir. 1980); National Consumer Law Center, Truth in Lending § 3.9.3 (5th ed. 2003 and Supp.).
     This distinction between a late charge and a finance charge in defining the scope of coverage of some statutes probably arises from the traditional distinction between a forbearance or detention of money. *See* § 10.5.2, *infra*.
130 *See also* § 2.3.1, *supra*.
131 Again, this may be just one of several tests necessary to invoke a specific statute, such as those statutes based on the Uniform Consumer Credit Code. *See* § 9.2.1.2, *supra*.
132 Lupo v. Equity Collection Serv., 808 S.W.2d 122 (Tex. Ct. App.

9.2.4.2 Frequency Standard, or "In the Business" of Extending Credit

Some statutes use a standard relating to either the frequency with which one engages in lending (e.g., applying to one who "regularly extends credit,"[133]) or whether one is in the business of making loans. Of course lending is an integral part of the business of most depository lenders, such as banks and credit unions, so this requirement will typically only present an issue with some non-depository lenders, usually individuals. For example, someone who makes a single loan as an investment, or makes a loan to a friend, may not be considered to "regularly" extend credit, and therefore may fall outside the scope of a special usury statute so defined.[134] On the other hand, a court may consider a lender to be "in the business" if he makes only a single loan, at least if done as a business proposition as opposed to a personal accommodation for the borrower.[135]

9.2.4.3 State Depository Lenders

Though state depository lenders are the subject of specific statutory schemes providing for chartering and regulation, those statutes concentrate primarily on commercial soundness and depositor protection rather than on consumer protections in the lenders' business practices. The reason is historical. During the period special usury statutes were evolving, depository institutions usually did not engage in the high rate lending or the abusive practices which led to stricter licensing statutes for non-depository lenders.[136]

Consequently, when the creditor is a state bank, credit union, or other depository lender, the special usury statute setting forth the legal standards against which an individual contract is to be measured may be the one applicable to the type of credit involved, such as installment sales or revolving credit, rather than the statute regulating that type of creditor.[137] Absent preemption, for example, a comprehensive consumer credit code such as Iowa's[138] may apply irrespective of whether the creditor is a bank, a finance company, or a retail seller, provided it meets the other definitional elements of a consumer credit transaction. However, a RISA statute may by its terms apply only to seller-financed credit, or seller-arranged credit. In that case, a bank loan obtained directly by the consumer to finance the purchase of a car will be subject to the statute governing the bank's consumer lending, unless that law is preempted.[139] Of course, the statute governing the institution should be carefully reviewed for any provisions which are pertinent to the consumer credit transaction being examined in any case.[140]

An additional complexity is that many states have "parity" statutes that allow certain depository lenders to extend consumer credit under state statutes that on their face apply only to other types of creditors.[141] In addition, the possibility of federal preemption must always be evaluated. The extent to which state laws governing state depository lenders are exempted by federal law is discussed in detail in § 3.6, *supra*.

1991) (amount demanded by collection agency included nearly 200% interest).

133 *E.g.*, Ala. Code § 5-19-1(3), interpreted in *In re* Crotzer, 147 B.R. 252 (Bankr. N.D. Ala. 1992) (creditor who extended real estate secured credit 26 times during the year prior to transaction and 24 times during the year of transaction, as shown by county records, fell within that definition); Iowa Code § 537.1301 (14)(a)(1) ("regularly engaged in the business of making loans").

134 The legal or contractual usury statute, however, may apply.

135 *See, e.g.*, Gorman v. Marcon Capital Corp., 274 B.R. 351 (D. Vt. 2002) (out-of-state lender that proposed business loan to state resident was in business of making loans; court cites no evidence of other loans in state); Gottesfeld v. Kaminski, 524 A.2d 872, 875 (N.J. Super. App. Div. 1987) (that is apparently the test used). *See also In re* Rose, 266 B.R. 192 (Bankr. N.D. Cal. 2001) (lender who made 5 loans over 10 years and 2 commercial loans within 1-year period was engaged in the business). *But cf.* White v. Coors Distrib. Co. (*In re* White), 260 B.R. 870 (B.A.P. 8th Cir. 2001) (company not in the business of purchasing installment contracts where its primary business was unrelated to financing but it had accepted assignment of three installment contracts from a related company).

136 *See generally* Ch. 2, *supra*.

137 Even if the statute applicable to the type of creditor governs the transaction, advocates should carefully scrutinize it to determine if exceptions are made for state or federal depository lenders particularly in revolving credit card cases. *See, e.g.*, Va. Code § 6.1-330.63; Amaro v. Capital One Bank, 1998 U.S. Dist. LEXIS 8373 (N.D. Ill. May 19, 1998). *See also* Avila v. Cmty. Bank, 143 S.W.3d 1 (Mo. Ct. App. 2003) (bank that charged interest allowed by its home state and federal laws was in compliance with statute limiting it to "lawful" interest rates).

138 Iowa Code Ch. 537.

139 *E.g.*, Micro-Switch Employees' Credit Union v. Collier, 530 N.E.2d 595 (Ill. App. Ct. 1988) (where borrower obtained loan directly from a credit union to purchase a car, the state MVRISA, which covered seller-financed retail installment transactions, holders of retail installment sales transactions, and sales finance agencies, did not apply to the transaction). *Cf.* Mullen v. Fifth Third Bank, 539 N.E.2d 683 (Ohio App. 1988) (RISA inapplicable because car buyer signed loan agreement establishing direct contractual relationship with bank, even though car dealer arranged financing and buyer had no face-to-face contact with any bank representative); Briercroft Serv. Corp. v. de Los Santos, 776 S.W.2d 198 (Tex. Ct. App. 1988) (home improvement loan financed directly by third-party lender did not involve a time-price differential, and therefore could not be a retail installment transaction as defined by code, though home improvement contractor arranged financing). *But cf.* Brown v. Courtesy Consumer Discount Co., 134 B.R. 134 (Bankr. E.D. Pa. 1991) (where "body-dragging" involved in a direct third-party loan to finance home improvement, the transaction was subject to RISA and the loan was usurious); Hernandez v. Atlantic Fin., 164 Cal. Rptr. 279 (App. 1980) (seller-assisted "direct" finance company loan for purchase of car is subject to the automobile sales finance act); § 9.2.3.3, *supra*.

140 12 U.S.C. § 3803; 12 C.F.R. §§ 34.20 to 34.24. *See* §§ 3.7.3, 3.11, *supra*.

141 *See* § 3.14.1, *supra*.

9.2.4.4 Regulations Applicable to Federal Depository Lenders

National banks, federal savings associations, and federal credit unions are federally regulated. However, these institutions are also subject to some state law, including usury statutes, unless the state law directly conflicts with the federal regulation in which case the state law is preempted, or, as in the case of federal savings associations, the applicable federal regulatory agency claims field preemption.[142] Federal preemption and regulation are discussed in Chapter 3, *supra*.

Federal lenders are treated as most favored lenders under state law.[143] This means that a national bank, for example, can charge the highest rate on any given loan which any state lender, licensed or unlicensed, depository or non-depository, could charge on the same loan. Consequently, to determine what state statute might apply to a loan issued by a federal lender, a consumer's attorney should forget about any classification of lenders under state law and should consider only how state law classifies the credit itself. For example, is the credit a small loan, a second mortgage loan, revolving credit, etc., under the relevant state's usury laws? If the national bank issues a loan which falls within the parameters of the state's small loan law, the bank can charge the highest rate on that loan that any state lender could charge on a small loan.[144] Of course, to determine the type of lending activities in which a national bank or other federally regulated lender can engage, one must look to the applicable federal regulations.[145]

9.2.4.5 Non-Depository Creditors

Non-depository creditors are subject to a state's general usury law unless the creditor has situated itself to take advantage of a specific usury statute which allows the charging of higher interest rates or otherwise provides the creditor with special advantages. A non-depository creditor may be subject to one of these specific usury statutes in several ways. Merchants and other institutions engaged in non-credit business may incidentally or secondarily offer customers credit arrangements. For example, a retailer may offer charge accounts or revolving credit. These credit activities are likely to be governed by statutes regulating the type of credit, not the type of creditor. The merchant's credit card, for example, will be governed by the state statute regulating revolving accounts.[146]

State laws also sanction specific non-depository institutions established for the purpose of making consumer credit available. The primary examples of this type of lender are finance companies, operating under small loan acts, industrial loan acts, or consumer finance acts. The advantage of the often more lucrative rate ceilings available under these laws may be enjoyed only if the company has obtained a license and subjected itself to regulation and supervision.[147] Further, unlicensed lenders cannot take advantage of higher-rate special usury statutes by use of a contractual clause providing that the parties agree that the transaction will be subject to such a statute.[148] The state licensing statutes which regulate such non-depository creditors are critical in evaluating an individual transaction with such a creditor.[149] Special usury statutes governing licensed creditors usually specify the permissible terms of individual credit transactions and include significant penalties if they fail to obtain a required license or violate their licenses by ignoring statutory consumer protections. Licensees generally must comply with the statute's requirements in order to retain their licenses.[150] Since obtaining the requisite license may be a precondition to lending under some special usury statutes, failure to do so may give rise to a usury claim under the

---

142 *See* § 3.9, *supra*.
143 *See* §§ 3.4.3, 3.8, 3.9, *supra*.
144 As an alternative, the federal lender may charge the federal discount rate plus one percent. *See* §§ 3.4.2, 3.6, 3.9.2.1, *supra*. Federal credit unions, as an additional alternative, may charge the rate set under the National Credit Union Act.
145 *See, e.g.*, Holland v. Michigan Nat'l Bank-West, 420 N.W.2d 173 (Mich. Ct. App. 1988) (whether state banking law prohibited state banks from writing second mortgages was immaterial; creditor was a national bank, and applicable federal law authorized national banks to write second mortgages).
146 *See* § 9.2.3, *supra*.
147 *See, e.g.*, Ala. Code § 5-19-22; Farmer v. Hypo Holdings, Inc., 675 So. 2d 387 (Ala. 1996) (a mere assignee of an loan which makes no direct loans in Alabama or any other state is exempt from licensing requirements because it did not meet the definition of a creditor; the original creditor need not be licensed because the transaction was a "consumer credit sale" and not a "consumer loan") (It is evident that advocates must review the pigeonholes in the relevant state statute to determine if licensing is required given the nature of the transaction.); Ohio Rev. Code Ann. § 1321.02; Vt. Stat. Ann. tit 8 § 2201; U.C.C.C. § 3.502 (1968); U.C.C.C. § 2.301 (1974). *See also* Galatti v. Alliance Funding Co., 644 N.Y.S.2d 330 (App. 1996) (original mortgage lender exempt from usury limits because it was a licensed mortgage banker; assignee, though not licensed, can also claim exemption). *See generally* § 2.3.3, *supra*.
148 Floyd v. Baton Rouge Sash & Door Co., 502 So. 2d 1073 (La. 1987).
149 Some states have schemes which will require reference to both the licensing statute governing the creditor and the special usury statute governing the type of credit. In Iowa, for example, when making a consumer loan, a finance company must comply with both the Iowa Regulated Loan Act, Ch. 536, and the Iowa Consumer Credit Code, Ch. 537. *See* Iowa Code § 536.13(7). *See also* Schmidt v. Beneficial Fin. Co., 400 A.2d 1124 (Md. Ct. App. 1979).
    The special licensing statutes also supplant general usury statutes where there is a conflict. Benoit v. United Companies Mortg., 504 So. 2d 196 (Miss. 1987).
150 *See, e.g.*, Iowa Code § 536.9; Ohio Rev. Code Ann. § 1321.08; Vt. Stat. Ann. tit 8 § 2210; U.C.C.C. § 3.504 (1968); U.C.C.C. § 2.303 (1974).

statute.[151] A licensed lender who engages in transactions outside the scope of the license may not be able to claim the exemption from the general usury law that the licensing statute creates.[152] Moreover, the failure to obtain a license may itself void the transaction.[153] The consumer's remedies when the lender has failed to obtain a license are discussed in § 10.8.4, *infra*.

Other examples of licensed, non-depository creditors, in addition to finance companies, are pawnbrokers, second mortgage lenders, insurance premium finance companies, home improvement sellers, and finance or motor vehicle sales finance companies. In many states, these creditors may not engage in their particular business without complying with state licensing or registration requirements,[154] unless a statutory exemption applies.[155] There may also be a local ordinance that requires a license or permit.[156] Note that finance companies which purchase retail installment contracts (but do not originate them) more often than not need not obtain a license.[157]

In California, loans that are made or arranged by licensed real estate brokers and secured in whole or part by real estate are exempt from the constitutional usury ceiling.[158] A broker who acts for another and receives or expects to receive compensation for it is considered to have arranged a loan.[159]

The compensation can be in the form of a share of the profits from the venture.[160] One court has held that loan is exempt regardless of whether the role the broker played in the loan required a license.[161]

In Arizona, the legislature repealed the ceiling on interest rates in the general usury statute at the same time as it reenacted the Small Loan Act with its own rate ceilings. For a period of four years, until the legislature resolved the ambiguity,[162] this left the question whether lenders licensed under the Small Loan Act were bound by its interest rate ceilings or could take advantage of the unlimited interest rates permitted by the general usury statute. The Arizona Supreme Court concluded that the legislature would not have intended to do a futile act by reenacting a Small Loan Act that did not apply to any lenders, and held that licensees had to comply with the Small Loan Act ceilings.[163]

Most of the time, the licensing statute which applies to a creditor will be obvious. Because a number of licensing statutes require that licenses be posted at the place of business,[164] a visit to the creditor's office will reveal the nature of the license. Another way to tell what licenses a creditor has is to call the office of the state regulatory agency which has supervisory authority under the applicable special usury act. Many agencies publish annual reports which list the names and addresses of licensees. Some post this information on their websites.

In states which have both small loan and industrial loan acts, most finance companies will be licensed under both acts. Where a lender is a dual licensee, a practitioner must decide which hat the lender was wearing when writing the loan in question in order to determine the relevant statute. Though it should be a standard question in interrogatories or requests for admission, it is usually safe to assume the finance company is writing a loan under whichever statute allows it the highest return. Thus, if the amount borrowed is under the small loan maximum, a lender typically writes the loan pursuant to its small loan license, as that license generally allows the highest yield to the creditor for that loan amount.

Under limited circumstances, some state non-depository lenders may be treated as federal lenders and may follow

---

151 *See* § 9.2.4.5, *infra*.

152 Agapitov v. Lerner, 108 Cal. App. 4th 830, 133 Cal. Rptr. 2d 837 (2003). *But cf.* Thrasher v. Homecomings Fin. Network, Inc., 838 A.2d 392 (Md. Spec. App. 2003) (interpreting statute to create private cause of action only against lender who is completely unlicensed, not one who makes loans at locations other than those allowed by the license).

153 *Id.*

154 *See* § 9.2.4.6, *infra*.

155 Special usury licensing statutes often exempt creditors subject to other regulatory statutes. Absent a specific statutory exception though, such entities are not exempt from the licensing requirements. *In re* Parkwood, Inc., 461 F.2d 158 (D.C. Cir. 1971) (insurance company lender). However, the statute should be carefully reviewed, as it may require compliance with both its own licensing statute and the one governing the type of transaction at issue. *See* Attorney Gen. of Md. v. Equitable Trust, 450 A.2d 1273, 1285 (Md. Ct. App. 1982); Schmidt v. Beneficial Fin. Co., 400 A.2d 1124 (Md. Ct. App. 1979).

156 Malish v. City of San Diego, 101 Cal. Rptr. 2d 18 (App. 2000) (upholding city's right to require pawnbroker to obtain local permit, but striking down parts of ordinance that were inconsistent with state pawnbroker licensing law); Circle D Pawn #2, Inc. v. Norman, 956 P.2d 931 (Okla. Ct. App. 1998).

157 *See, e.g.*, Ala. Code § 5-19-22; Farmer v. Hypo Holdings, Inc., 675 So. 2d 387 (Ala. 1996) (a mere assignee of an loan which makes no direct loans in Alabama or any other state is exempt from licensing requirements because it did not meet the definition of a creditor; the original creditor need not be licensed because the transaction was a "consumer credit sale" and not a "consumer loan"). *But see* Gaspard v. Vanguard Acceptance Corp., 689 So. 2d 1352 (La. 1997) (applying former La. Rev. Stat. § 6:951(9) (1985) which required the assignee of retail installment contracts to be licensed).

158 Cal. Const. art. XV § 1; Cal. Civil Code § 1916.1.

159 Park Terrace Ltd. v. Teasdale, 100 Cal. App. 4th 802, 122 Cal.

Rptr. 2d 797 (2002). *But cf.* Gibbo v. Berger, 123 Cal. App. 4th 396, 19 Cal. Rptr. 3d 829 (2004) (real estate broker who merely prepared documents using pre-printed forms, obtained title insurance, and disbursed funds did not arrange the loan so was not exempt from usury provision).

160 Park Terrace Ltd. v. Teasdale, 100 Cal. App. 4th 802, 122 Cal. Rptr. 2d 797 (2002).

161 *Id.*

162 In 1984, the legislature amended the Act to require all consumer lenders to be licensed and thus regulated by the Act. *See* Aros v. Beneficial Arizona, Inc., 977 P.2d 784, 785 n.1 (Ariz. 1999). The statute was rewritten again in 1997.

163 Aros v. Beneficial Arizona, Inc., 977 P.2d 784 (Ariz. 1999).

164 *See, e.g.*, Ohio Rev. Code Ann. § 1321.05; Or. Rev. Stat. § 725.160; Vt. Stat. Ann. tit 8 § 2206.

federal regulations to the exclusion of state law. Specifically, most housing creditors may invoke Office of Thrift Supervision[165] regulations when they are issuing variable rate or balloon mortgages.[166] But a payday lender lost its argument that its relationship with an out-of-state FDIC-insured bank precluded state regulators from finding that it was the true lender and was governed by the state Industrial Loan Act.[167]

9.2.4.6 Challenging a Creditor's Efforts to Evade Licensing Requirements

Though the failure to obtain a license when necessary has serious ramifications for creditors, obviously no license is required if the creditor is not engaging in regulated activity, or if the entity does not fall within the scope of coverage of the statute in question.[168] As lending practices changed in the 1970s and 1980s, complications arose as lenders tried to test the limits of their licensing requirements. In particular, licensing became an issue as the consumer finance industry moved aggressively into real estate secured lending. Many small loan statutes do not permit lenders to impose the types of charges often associated with real estate lending: appraisal fees, title insurance or title search fees, attorney fees, etc. Some statutes prohibit outright the taking of real estate

as security for small loans.[169] Lenders attempted several gambits to avoid these restrictions, though they ultimately resolved the matter by obtaining legislative changes in some states.[170]

One tactic for making prohibited loans is to fail to obtain any license. For example, one unlicensed lender, having made mortgage loans in an amount below the small loan ceiling, argued the act did not apply: since the act prohibited real estate lending, and these were real estate loans, they fell outside the scope of the act. The court rightly rejected this sophistry. It held that the small loan act applied to loans in amounts below the small loan ceiling, and that the creditor had engaged in precisely the sort of evasion that the act was designed to prevent.[171] Failure to obtain a license does not insulate the creditor from liability for such subterfuges, for the "inhibitory provisions" of special usury licensing statutes apply to both licensees and non-licensees.[172]

Similarly, other lenders may try to have the best of both the licensed and unlicensed business worlds by retaining a small loan license for use with normal small loans, while creating a theoretically distinct corporate identity, unlicensed under the act, to make real estate secured loans.[173] In such cases, practitioners should observe that small loan statutes often forbid licensees from conducting any unregulated business at their registered location unless authorized to do so by the regulatory agency. Such permission is not to be given if the nature of the other business would "conceal or facilitate violation or evasion" of the act.[174] Thus a

---

165 Prior to August 9, 1989, the regulations were those of the Federal Home Loan Bank Board. That agency was abolished and its functions transferred to the newly created OTS.

166 *See* § 3.10, *supra*. Some balloon mortgages may also be subject to the Home Ownership and Equity Protection Act, 15 U.S.C. §§ 1602(aa), 1639.

167 Bankwest, Inc. v. Oxendine, 598 S.E.2d 343 (Ga. Ct. App. 2004). *See also* BankWest, Inc. v. Baker, 324 F. Supp. 2d 1333 (N.D. Gal. 2004) (upholding statutory amendments that apply Industrial Loan Act limits to purported agents of out-of-state lenders where the agent holds the predominant economic interest in the loan).

168 *See, e.g.,* Casey v. Travelers, 531 So. 2d 846 (Ala. 1988) (life insurance companies are exempt from state credit code licensing requirements, even if they also write other kinds of insurance); Goldstein v. Betty Ginsburg Interior Design, Inc., 519 So. 2d 645 (Fla. Dist. Ct. App. 1987) (interior decorator provided "home improvement services" within meaning of Florida Home Improvement Sales and Finance Act, but since she acquired liens only by operation of law, rather than taking a consensual security interest in the property, she did not fall under Act and was not required to seek licensure); Terrebonne Bank & Trust Co. v. Lacombe, 464 So. 2d 753 (La. Ct. App. 1984) (car dealer did not meet definition of sales finance company, so no license required); Eriksen v. Fisher, 421 N.W.2d 193 (Mich. Ct. App. 1988) (statutory prohibition against escalator rates applies only to specified regulated lenders, not to contracts between natural persons); Dilleree v. Devoe, 724 P.2d 171 (Mont. 1986) (no loan of money, so Consumer Loan Act inapplicable); First Nat'l Bank v. Dickinson, 308 N.W.2d 910 (Wis. Ct. App. 1981) ("sellers" not required to be licensed under Precomputed Loan Act). *But cf.* Hernandez v. Atlantic Fin., 164 Cal. Rptr. 279 (App. 1980) (though Motor Vehicle Sales Finance Act does not apply to supervised lending, the exemption does not apply to seller-assisted loans).

169 *Cf.* Iowa Code § 537.2307 (security interest in debtor's residence prohibited for loans under $2000 where rate exceeds 15%).

170 *E.g.,* Ariz. Rev. Stat. § 6-628(A) prior to 1984 (reprinted in historical note) with the later version (repealed in 1997), which added real-estate related costs as authorized charges.

171 Valley Acceptance Corp. v. Glasby, 337 S.E.2d, 291, 295 (Va. l985). As a Connecticut court stated in a similar effort to avoid a pawnbroker licensing statute, one cannot "avoid a tax on shoes by calling shoes slippers." Rhodes v. City of Hartford, 513 A.2d 124, 126 (Conn. 1986).

172 Robertson v. Burnett, 109 N.W.2d 716 (Neb. 1961), *vacated on other grounds sub nom.* Michigan Nat'l Bank v. Robertson, 372 U.S. 591 (1963) (judgment vacated and case remanded for further consideration of whether venue in Nebraska was proper); State *ex rel.* Beck v. Associates Discount Corp., 77 N.W.2d 215 (1956), *further proceedings,* 96 N.W.2d 55 (Neb. 1959). *See also* Murphy v. Citizens Discount Corp., 90 N.E.2d 622, 626 (Ct. Com. Pleas Ohio 1950). Of course, if the loan would not be subject to the statute in any case, this principle does not act to bring non-licensees within its scope. Albers v. Overland Nat'l Bank, 324 N.W.2d 396 (Neb. 1982); Pattavina v. Pignotti, 128 N.W.2d 817 (Neb. 1964); note 168, *supra.*

173 *See, e.g.,* Rosner v. Household Fin. Corp., Civ. 85-68 TUC RMB (D. Ariz. filed Aug. 21, 1985). Many versions of the small loan act contain prohibitions against circumventing or evading the act, thus strengthening a challenge to such efforts. *See, e.g.,* Ariz. Rev. Stat. § 6-603(B); Ohio Rev. Code Ann. § 1321.02; Va. Code § 6.1-251.

174 *E.g.,* Ariz. Rev. Stat. § 6-606(F) (amended following litigation); Iowa Code § 536.12; Va. Code § 6.1-267. *See also* U.C.C.C.

federal court in Arizona held that it was a question of fact whether Household Realty Corporation (HRC), making real estate secured loans under the small loan limit, was so closely related to Household Finance Corporation (HFC) as to make HRC's loans in fact loans from the licensee HFC, and whether the use of the HRC subsidiary constituted a subterfuge to evade the small loan requirements.[175] Arguably, in such a case, the non-licensed lending should be prohibited even if that entity was not merely a shell corporation.[176]

A lender may argue that no license is required because it is not regularly engaged in the business of making loans. The statute should be reviewed carefully to determine who must be licensed. Under New Jersey's Secondary Mortgage Act, for example, making a single second mortgage loan "may constitute engaging in the secondary loan business."[177] The threshold number is larger in other states and the statutes cover first lien mortgage lenders as well.[178] A

Ninth Circuit decision, interpreting Washington law, holds that a mortgage broker need not be licensed if it is engaging only in "table-funded" transactions in which it lends another party's funds, but if it is lending its own funds it must be licensed.[179]

Another argument to evade licensing requirements is that the originating lender is only table-funded by the true lender and is not, therefore, the true lender for licensing purposes. Table-funding means that the lender listed on the loan documents was given all of the funds by the assignee and did not actually extend its own funds to the borrower. The loan is immediately assigned to the funding lender. This argument was unsuccessful in a recent case where the court correctly held that the loan was initially payable to the originating lender, not the funding lender.[180] In addition, the debt was only assigned to the funding lender after the loan was made. Thus, the originating lender must be licensed.

Persons who engage in sale/leaseback schemes may be found to be engaging in unlicensed lending,[181] and borrowers victimized could argue that the transactions, therefore, are void.[182] Car dealers that finance the consumer's negative equity in a trade-in vehicle may also be considered to be lending money without a license in some states.

Another way that a lender may seek to evade usury laws is by disguising a transaction so that it appears to be governed by a different law. For example, if a lender has a license allowing it to charge high rates under a small loan law, it arguably should not be allowed to evade other applicable usury laws with lower interest limits by mischaracterizing the nature of a particular credit transaction. This "body-dragging" scenario is described in § 9.2.3.3, *supra*.

---

§ 3-512 (1968) § 2-309 (1974) (other business permitted unless for purpose of evasion or violation of the act). Even where a licensee has sought and obtained permission to engage in real estate lending, the transaction should be closely scrutinized to see if the lender has complied with any applicable restrictions. One small loan licensee sought permission to engage in mortgage lending at its small loan location, and obtained permission on the conditions that such mortgage lending neither take additional personal property as collateral, nor include the sale of property insurance. Nonetheless, the licensee did both. Beneficial v. State Corp. Comm., 339 S.E.2d 192 (Va. 1986).

175 Rosner v. Household Fin. Corp. Civ. No. 85-68 TUC, (D. Ariz., order Aug. 21, 1985). *See also* Transamerica Fin. Corp. v. Superior Court, 761 P.2d 1019 (Ariz. 1988) (if evidence establishes that loans made by unlicensed lender should be attributable to its licensed alleged alter ego, loans would be void, *dicta*), *but see on remand sub nom.* Ranscon v. Transamerica Fin. Corp., 812 P.2d 1019 (Ariz. Ct. App. 1990) (court holds a loophole existed for four-year period during which licensed lenders were permitted to charge a deregulated rate in excess of rates applicable to licensees). *See also* Murphy v. Citizens Discount Corp., 90 N.E.2d 622 (Ct. Com. Pleas Ohio 1950) (licensee claimed loans made under its general corporate power to lend money, not as small loan licensee. Court held small loan prohibitions and remedy applied to lenders in business of loaning amounts under the ceiling whether done as licensee, private person, or corporation).

176 *See* notes 171–172, *supra*. The court in *Rosner* did not address that issue.

177 Gottesfeld v. Kaminski, 524 A.2d 872, 875 (N.J. Super. App. Div. 1987) (test is apparently whether the loan is made as a business proposition or a personal accommodation). *See* § 9.2.4.2, *supra*.

178 *See, e.g.*, Maine Consumer Credit Code, Me. Rev. Stat. Ann. tit. 9-A, § 1-301 (coverage is triggered if more than 5 mortgage loans in the preceding calendar year); Maryland Mortgage Lender Law, Md. Code Ann. Fin. Inst. § 11-502 (1992) (more than 3 mortgage loans per calendar year). *See also* Gorman v. Marcon Capital Corp., 274 B.R. 351 (D. Vt. 2002) (lender's negotiation and preliminary agreement amounted to engaging in business of making loans, so license was required). *But cf.* White v. Coors Distrib. Co. (*In re* White), 260 B.R. 870 (B.A.P. 8th Cir. 2001) (company not in the business of purchasing

installment contracts where its primary business was unrelated to financing, but it had accepted assignment of three installment contracts from a related company).

179 Easter v. American W. Fin., 381 F.3d 948 (9th Cir. 2004).

180 St. Jean v. Racal Mortgage, 952 F. Supp. 22 (D. Me. 1997), *vacated on other grounds sub nom.* Reagan v. Racal Mortg. Inc., 155 F.3d 6 (1st Cir. 1998).

181 Browner v. District of Columbia, 549 A.2d 1107 (D.C. 1988) ("foreclosure specialists" engaging in sale/leasebacks were successfully prosecuted for making unlicensed loans under Loan Sharking Act).

182 *See* Browner v. District of Columbia, 549 A.2d 1107 (D.C. 1988) has good language concerning usury and loan-sharking statutes being enacted for the protection of the public, which would support a claim for voiding loans of unlicensed lenders in absence of special statute providing that remedy.

9.2.5 Distinctions Based on Loan Size; Loan-Splitting and Loan-Packing To Evade Regulation

9.2.5.1 General

Small loan acts and certain other special usury laws apply only to transactions whose principal amount falls within a specified range. Small loan laws, for example, originally governed only loans of less than $300, although that figure has been greatly increased in most states. Similarly, a second mortgage statute might apply only to real estate secured loans of less than $25,000[183] or a business exemption might apply only to large loans.[184]

9.2.5.2 Loan Splitting

In some state, the special usury statute's interest rate ceiling may apply only to transactions below a specified dollar amount. If the principal exceeds this ceiling, the state's general usury ceiling comes into play, and the permissible interest rate for the transaction is significantly lower. Historically, it was in a creditor's interest to structure its transactions so that loans fell within the scope of the special usury law, and the obvious solution was to split a large loan into several small ones. For example, if the small loan limit was $300, a creditor might issue a borrower who wanted $500 a pair of $250 loans on which the high small loan rate could be charged, rather than a single $500 loan to which the general usury ceiling would apply. This practice of loan-splitting had to be specifically prohibited by the small loan law in order for general usury ceilings to retain any significance.[185]

Loan-splitting is also attractive to lenders who are operating under a statute that allows per-loan fees. For example, a payday loan law may allow a minimum finance charge of a certain dollar amount regardless of the size of the loan. Splitting a loan into two smaller loans allows the lender to double these fees without extending any additional credit.[186]

Lenders may also engage in loan splitting in order to avoid giving the borrower meaningful information about the cost and terms of the loan. Most borrowers will, for example, be unable to calculate a composite interest rate for two loans issued on the same day. This issue has arisen in the Truth in Lending context, but can also arise in the context of state credit statutes that require credit terms to be disclosed in a single document. In the Truth in Lending context, the test courts have applied is whether "the debtor wants, requests, and expects to get a single loan consummated in a single transaction, but the lender instead documents and makes disclosures for the loan as if it were two separate transactions."[187]

9.2.5.3 Loan Packing

With the deregulation of credit in many states, the historical incentives have been reversed. Today, special usury statutes such as small loan laws often contain a state's only usury restrictions. If a transaction falls outside of the scope of the special usury laws because its principal amount is too large, it may be free of all usury restrictions. Under such circumstances, creditors clearly want to escape the special usury ceilings, rather than seek shelter under them. Creditors' attempts to claim that loans are too large to be covered by special usury statutes have raised two major questions in litigation: first, what loan fees may be counted as principal for purposes of reaching the threshold loan size needed for the exemption; and second, when can several smaller loans be claimed as one large loan which qualifies for an exemption.

183 *E.g.*, N.C. Gen. Stat. § 24-12. *Cf.* Gibbs v. Green Tree Acceptance, Inc., 373 S.E.2d 637 (Ga. Ct. App. 1988) (Motor Vehicle Sales Financing Act applicable to sale of mobile home, but if cash sale price exceeds $3000, MVSFA provision on finance charge limitation is different).

184 *See* § 9.2.2.2, *supra*.

185 *See* Uniform Small Loan Law, Seventh Draft (as revised June 1, 1942) § 15 *reprinted in* Curran, Trends in Consumer Credit Legislation (1966) (restricting use of small loan rates where aggregate debt to one borrower or married couple, either as principal borrower(s) or as guarantor(s), exceeds $300). *See also* Securities Inv. Co. v. Pearson, 143 S.E.2d 36 (Ga. App. 1965) (loan splitting where borrower on one debt was cosigner on another with same lender). Loan-splitting also may be used improperly to increase the yield under split-rate usury statutes, § 4.3.4, *supra*. *But see* Kinzel v. Southview Chevrolet Co., 892 F. Supp. 1211 (D. Minn. 1995) (no loan splitting issue where consumer financed down payment on a car purchase with loan from a finance company and financed remaining balance through the dealer; no allegation that this constituted scheme to avoid usury limits).

186 *See* Bellizan v. Easy Money of La., 2002 WL 1611648 (E.D. La. July 19, 2002) (denying summary judgment to payday lender whose loan-splitting allegedly violated payday loan statute).

187 *See* Kane v. Equity One, Inc., 2003 WL 22939377 (E.D. Pa. Nov. 21, 2003) (denying lender's motion for summary judgment where consumer alleged she expected single loan); Rendler v. Corus Bank, 154 F. Supp. 2d 1365 (N.D. Ill. 2001), *aff'd*, 272 F.3d 992 (7th Cir. 2001); Stokes v. World Savings Bank, 2001 WL 1002461 (N.D. Ill. Aug. 31, 2001) (upholding separate disclosure where plaintiff did not allege she requested or expected single loan); MorEquity v. Naeem, 118 F. Supp. 2d 885, 894–95 (N.D. Ill. 2000); Harris v. Illinois Vehicle Premium Fin. Co., 2000 U.S. Dist. LEXIS 13763 (N.D. Ill. Sept. 7, 2000); Vance v. National Benefit Ass'n, 1999 WL 731764 (N.D. Ill. Aug. 30, 1999) (denying motion to dismiss; whether loan splitting occurred is question of fact); Hemauer v. ITT Fin. Servs., 751 F. Supp. 1241 (W.D. Ky. 1990); *In re* Buckles, 189 B.R. 752 (Bankr. D. Minn. 1995). *See also* Kinzel v. Southview Chevrolet Co., 892 F. Supp. 1211 (D. Minn. 1995) (applying FRB regulation that creditor may disclose financing of down payment in credit sale as separate transaction). *See generally* National Consumer Law Center, Truth in Lending § 4.9.2.2 (5th ed. 2003 and Supp.).

The practice of adding fees to the face amount of a loan note in order to reach the minimum loan size needed for a usury exemption is sometimes known as "packing" or "padding" the principal.[188] To some extent, packing the loan principal is legal because most states recognize reasonable third party fees, such as credit insurance premiums, and sometimes limited fees for lender services, as valid non-interest expenses which a lender may properly finance as part of the loan principal.[189] However, if a lender includes fees which qualify as interest payments in the face amount of the note, then that note no longer represents the size of the loan for purposes of determining whether the threshold loan size for the usury exemption has been reached.[190] Thus, determining loan size is essentially a matter of deciding whether the stated loan principal really contains hidden interest charges. Typical examples of hidden interest are discussed in detail in Chapters 7 and 8, *supra.*[191]

In addition to padding a loan with extra charges, a lender may also do so by requiring or encouraging the borrower to consolidate other debts,[192] or by the added incremental costs that come with placing a borrower on a "frequent flipper"

program—soliciting him or her for frequent refinancings.[193] To the extent such practices work to the disadvantage of borrowers, there may be grounds for challenging these types of loan padding practices under non-usury theories, such as unconscionability or state UDAP statutes. *See* Chapter 11, *infra.*

A second question created by statutes that raise or eliminate usury ceilings for loans which exceed a certain size is whether several small loans, which do not individually reach the statutory threshold, may be treated as one loan to which the higher ceiling applies. This question depends on the specific language of the relevant usury statute, but most such statutes seem to apply a transactional approach. In other words, if a borrower and lender signed a contract under which the lender agreed to advance, in several installments, an aggregate sum in excess of the statutory threshold, this series of advances will generally be treated as a single loan, based on a single transaction.[194] If, however, the individual advances are not interrelated, in the sense that the creditor, having advanced some money, was never obligated to make further advances, then the advances will be viewed as individual loans which will not qualify for the usury exemption unless individually they satisfy the statutory size requirement.[195]

Because the raising or elimination of usury ceilings for specific transactions, such as large business loans, is often structured as an exception to a general usury rule, the courts have construed these usury exceptions narrowly[196] and have been, as a group, reluctant to allow a series of loans to qualify for a large loan exemption. Yet, when a single transaction of the required size has been present, numerous

---

188 In a state with a small loan law but no general interest ceiling, the incentives for a less than scrupulous lender to pack loan principal can be powerful. First, by inflating the principal amount, the lender does not actually lend as much money as it would normally have to lend to escape the small loan limits, so its risk is reduced, and it can lend more elsewhere. Second, except under careful examination the loan appears to be free from the small loan law, so the lender can apparently charge whatever interest rate it wants. Third, if the inflated principal exceeds $25,000 and is not secured by the borrower's home, the loan appears to be free from Truth in Lending disclosures, except, again, under careful examination. Finally, inflating loan principal enables the lender to understate the rate it is actually charging.

189 *See* § 7.3.1, *supra.*

190 *See* Aetna Fin. Co. v. Darwin, 691 P.2d 581 (Wash. Ct. App. 1984) (textbook case of packing principal); Sparkman & McLean Income Fund v. Wald, 520 P.2d 173 (Wash. Ct. App. 1974). The Seventh Draft of the Uniform Small Loan Act § 2 (as revised June 1, 1942), *reprinted in* Curran Trends in Consumer Credit Legislation (1966) provides: "For the purpose of this section, a loan shall be deemed to be in the amount of $300 or less if the net amount or value advanced to or on behalf of the borrower, after deducting all payments for interest, principal, expenses, and charges of any nature taken substantially contemporaneously with the making of the loan, does not exceed $300."

191 *Cf.* Besta v. Beneficial Loan Co., 855 F.2d 532 (8th Cir. 1988) (creditor unnecessarily and disadvantageously stretched loan term and padded the principal with the consequently higher credit insurance premiums in order to meet the threshold principal amount permitting it to take a security interest in residential real estate under state law; court reformed contract under unconscionability doctrine). Loan padding is the reason that the Home Ownership and Equity Protection Act, 15 U.S.C. § 1602(aa), uses non-interest fees and charges imposed on a transaction as one of the triggers for coverage. *See* § 12.2.2, *infra.*

192 *See* Wolf v. Kian, 2000 Minn. App. LEXIS 963 (Aug. 16, 2000) (unpublished, citation limited) (consolidating two debts owed to

same creditor pushed amount over $100,000 and made loan exempt).

193 *See* Ch. 6, *supra,* for a explanation of how refinancings add to the cost of a loan.

194 *See* Citizens & Southern S. DeKalb Bank v. Watkins, 225 S.E.2d 266 (Ga. 1976) (stating rule). *See also* Mohr, Inc. v. Bank of California, 443 F. Supp. 370 (D. Or. 1978), *aff'd,* 622 F.2d 594 (9th Cir. 1980) (line of credit); Negaard v. Miller Constr. Co., 396 N.W.2d 833 (Minn. Ct. App. 1986) (debts aggregated in construction contract).

195 *See* Henson v. Columbus Bank & Trust, 770 F.2d 1566 (5th Cir. 1985) (series of demand notes would not be aggregated to create single forbearance exempt from usury law); Citizens & Southern South DeKalb Bank v. Watkins, 225 S.E.2d 266 (Ga. 1976); Western Auto Supply v. Vick, 277 S.E.2d 360, *reaff'd on rehearing,* 283 S.E.2d 101 (N.C. 1981); Magee v. Dyrdahl, 926 P.2d 319 (Or. App. 1996); Dean Vivian Homes v. Sebera's Plumbing & Appliances, Inc., 615 S.W.2d 921 (Tex. Civ. App. 1981). *But cf.* Irving Trust Co. v. Smith, 349 F. Supp. 146 (S.D.N.Y. 1972) (series of cross-collateralized demand notes treated as one loan; no discussion of single agreement to advance funds); American Bank & Trust Co. v. Lichtenstein, 369 N.Y.S.2d 155 (App. Div. 1975) (same), *aff'd mem.,* 352 N.E.2d 132 (N.Y. 1976).

196 *See* Citizens & Southern S. DeKalb Bank v. Watkins, 225 S.E.2d 266 (Ga. 1976); Sparkman & McLean Income Fund v. Wald, 520 P.2d 173 (Wash. Ct. App. 1974).

usury challenges have been rejected. For example, the existence of several payees on a single loan note has not been interpreted as indicating the presence of several smaller loans to which usury ceilings would apply.[197] Similarly, when a valid debt clearly in excess of a $100,000 statutory threshold was replaced, pursuant to a settlement of insurance litigation, by a note for less than $100,000, the court determined that the usury exemption still applied because the new rate was a "partial renewal and extension" of the original debt.[198] At least one court has specifically stated that the presence of several notes which individually fail to meet the statutory threshold does not automatically preclude the aggregation of the debts because the notes may be sufficiently related to a single transaction to justify their treatment as a single loan.[199]

9.2.6 Distinctions Based on Security Taken

The existence of any security in a credit transaction and the identity of that security is, in most states, a subject that is intertwined with the identification of the particular credit statute that regulates the transaction. In many situations, the existence of a particular security will dictate which special usury statute will apply. For example, the presence of a second mortgage lien may compel the application of a second mortgage statute to a transaction which would, but for that security, be governed by another credit statute.[200] Similarly, the identity of goods purchased in a credit sale may affect the regulation of the transaction. For example,

motor vehicle or mobile home credit sales are often distinguished from the credit sale of other goods.[201]

While the presence of a particular kind of security may dictate the applicability of a particular credit statute, it is also true that the statute which seems to apply to a transaction based on the type of lender, the size of the credit given, or the structure of the transaction, may determine what security the creditor may permissibly retain. For example, real estate security may be prohibited in transactions that fall within the scope of a small loan law[202] or a retail installment sales act.[203] Similarly, considerations aside from security may dictate whether limitations on security will come into play at all. In some states, for example, special mortgage regulations apply only if the contract interest rate exceeds a specified amount.[204]

This interrelationship—between statutes whose scope is defined by the existence of some security and statutes whose scope is otherwise defined but which restrict the retention of security interests—can cause significant problems of statutory construction. Essentially, the question is which of two or more overlapping statutes should take priority. Creditors, of course, invariably invoke the less restrictive statute, while borrowers assert that the more restrictive law should govern.

A good example of such a statutory overlap was considered by the Supreme Court of Virginia in *Valley Acceptance Corporation v. Glasby*.[205] A creditor who was not a small loan licensee issued a "mortgage" loan, secured by the borrowers' home, for a principal sum which fell within the scope of the small loan act. The issuance of mortgage loans by this lender was generally permitted by Virginia law, but the small loan act prohibited the retention of real estate security on transactions to which it applied. The creditor argued that the presence of the mortgage removed the transaction from the scope of the small loan law, because that law did not govern mortgage transactions, while the borrower claimed that the transaction was, in fact, just a

---

197 *See* Peterson v. Harville, 445 F. Supp. 16 (D. Or. 1977), *aff'd*, 623 F.2d 611 (9th Cir. 1980); Salzman v. Cole, 567, 254 S.E.2d 888 (Ga. App. 1979).

198 Sulton v. General Elec. Credit Corp., 268 S.E.2d 789 (Ga. App. 1980).

199 Sparkman & McLean Income Fund v. Wald, 520 P.2d 173 (Wash. Ct. App. 1974). *But cf.* Olson v. Froslee, 2000 Minn. App. LEXIS 795 (Aug. 1, 2000) (unpublished, citation limited) (loan was separate from contemporaneous lease with option to purchase even though both were part of sale of business).

200 *See, e.g.*, Schmidt v. Beneficial Fin. Co., 400 A.2d 1124 (Md. 1979). *See also* Chroniak v. Golden Inv. Corp., 577 A.2d 1209 (N.H. 1990) (statutory provision applicable by its terms to lenders making loans secured by a mortgage applied to *any* such lender; not necessary that lender be "in the business of making second mortgage loans" as was the case with the state's second mortgage licensing act), *further proceedings*, 983 F.2d 1140 (1st Cir. 1993). *Cf.* Goldstein v. Betty Ginsburg Interior Design, Inc., 519 So. 2d 645 (Fla. Dist. Ct. App. 1987) (interior decorator performed services which would have fallen within scope of home improvement statute, but statute's requirement that a security interest be taken in order to fall within its scope not met by existence of lien arising by operation of law, instead of consensual security agreement). *But see* Corrigan v. Insilco Corp., 439 N.W.2d 350 (Mich. Ct. App. 1989) (where goods sold were construction materials for a new home, RISA applied despite fact that seller also took a mortgage on the home).

201 *Cf.* Yates v. Mobile America Sales Corp., 591 S.W.2d 453 (Tex. 1979) (prior to 8/27/79, mobile homes treated as regular "good" rather than motor vehicle, but special regulations apply after that date).

202 *See* Valley Acceptance Corp. v. Glasby, 337 S.E.2d 291 (Va. 1985). *Cf.* Besta v. Beneficial Loan Co., 855 F.2d 532 (8th Cir. 1988) (in order to meet the threshold principal loan amount permitting lender to take a security interest in residential real estate under state law, lender unnecessarily and disadvantageously stretched loan term and padded the principal with the consequently higher credit insurance premiums; court reformed contract under unconscionability doctrine).

203 *See* Anderson v. Pamilco Chem. Co., 470 F. Supp. 12 (E.D.N.C. 1977) (distinguishing sale subject to RISA from subsequent forbearance of debt); Girard Acceptance Corp. v. Wallace, 388 A.2d 582 (N.J. 1978).

204 *See, e.g.*, Iowa Code § 537.1301(12); § 537.2307. *See also* Streets v. MGIC Mortgage Corp., 378 N.E.2d 915 (Ind. Ct. App. 1978) (U.C.C.C. since amended); Greenberg v. Royal Commerce Bank, 577 S.W.2d 576 (Tex. Ct. App. 1979).

205 337 S.E.2d 291 (Va. 1985).

small loan with an illegal security in land. The court sided with the borrower, citing the remedial purpose of the small loan act, and the ease with which the act could be evaded if simply the retention of real estate security could prevent its application.

Apparent conflicts between credit statutes, such as that in *Glasby*, are usually resolved by reference to the legislative intent behind the relevant statutes. As both particular statutory schemes and the intent behind them vary significantly from state to state, it is difficult to generalize the priorities among different types of statutes. Nevertheless, at least one trend seems clear; in consumer transactions, the courts have protected borrowers in transactions involving junior liens on real estate by applying the most restrictive statute which is relevant to the transaction.[206] Most noticeably, special second mortgage statutes have been broadly construed to protect homeowners,[207] but just as importantly, usury exemptions for first mortgage transactions have been narrowly read,[208] unclear small loan laws have been held to apply to small loans secured by real estate,[209] and ambiguous sales

statutes have been read to prohibit real estate security entirely.[210] This judicial tendency to limit the ability of creditors to obtain real estate security is, in consumer transactions, entirely justified both because the potential for foreclosure on the borrower's home in the case of default threatens the borrower's most basic interests, and because of a history of fraud and price-gouging associated with non-purchase-money mortgages.[211] Under such circumstances, protective regulations should not be limited unless this is the clear intent of the legislature.

9.2.7 Criminal Usury Statutes; Unconscionability Standards to Regulate the Cost of Credit

In the wake of deregulation, when many states removed statutory interest rate caps, the market often was less than effective in keeping the cost of credit to reasonable limits. Thus used car loans cropped up with disclosed rates of 60% and small loans of over 200%,[212] not to mention payday loans, refund anticipation loans, bounce loans, and auto title pawn loans with effective interest rates in the triple digits.

With particularly high rate credit, it may warrant checking whether the state has a criminal usury ceiling which may be applicable. Some states, when deregulating their civil usury statutes, nonetheless retained their criminal usury ceilings,[213] which may be invoked to challenge high cost credit.

---

206 *See, e.g.*, Chroniak v. Golden Inv. Corp., 577 A.2d 1209 (N.H. 1990) (statutory provision applicable by its terms to lenders making loans secured by a mortgage applied to any such lender; not necessary that lender be "in the business of making second mortgage loans" as was the case with the state's second mortgage licensing act. Statutory exemption applicable to those making mortgage loan incidental to another business such as real estate or construction was relevant to loans made by real estate investment corporation, but court expressed skepticism that mortgage-secured loans obtained to make bail and buy a boat trailer would qualify as incidental to real estate investment), *further proceedings*, 983 F.2d 1140 (1st Cir. 1993).

207 *See, e.g.*, Johnson v. Ronamy Consumer Credit Corp., 515 A.2d 682 (Del. 1986); First Nat'l Consumer Discount Co. v. Fuller, 419 A.2d 940 (Del. 1980) (statute applied to personal guarantee of small business loan); Mayo v. Bank of Carroll County, 276 S.E.2d 660 (Ga. App. 1981) (suit under secondary security deed act not precluded by argument that act was aimed at lenders primarily in the second mortgage business); Schmidt v. Beneficial Fin. Co., 400 A.2d 1124 (Md. 1979); HIMC Inv. Co. v. Siciliano, 246 A.2d 502 (N.J. Super. 1968). *See generally* Annot. 43 A.L.R.4th 675 (1986) (construction and application of second mortgage statutes). *But cf.* Rewis v. Browning, 265 S.E.2d 316 (Ga. App. 1980) (business loan not within scope of secondary security deed act).

208 *See, e.g.*, Varady v. White, 595 P.2d 272 (1979), *later op. at* 661 P.2d 284 (Colo. App. 1982) (no first mortgage); Beebee v. Grettenberger, 266 N.W.2d 829 (Mich. App. 1978) (lower ceiling when lender trades first mortgage for a second mortgage). *See also* Mitchell v. Trustees of United States Mutual Real Estate Inv. Trust, 375 N.W.2d 424 (Mich. Ct. App. 1985) (no first lien to qualify loan for federal preemption). *Cf.* McConnell v. Sutherland, 898 P.2d 254 (Or. Ct. App. 1995) (interpreting Oregon's exemption for loans made to "finance the acquisition of real property"; applies to loans for direct purchase, not to loans for indirect facilitation of sales).

209 *See* Liberty Fin. Co. v. Catterton, 161 Md. 650, 158 A. 16 (1932); Valley Acceptance Corp. v. Glasby, 337 S.E.2d 291 (Va. 1985). *Cf.* Besta v. Beneficial Loan Co., 855 F.2d 532 (8th Cir. 1988) (in order to meet the minimum $2000 threshold loan amount permitting lender to take a security interest in residential

real estate under state law, it unnecessarily and disadvantageously stretched loan term and padded the principal with the consequently higher credit insurance premiums; court reformed contract under unconscionability doctrine).

210 *Compare* Girard Acceptance Corp. v. Wallace, 388 A.2d 582 (N.J. 1978) (RISA prohibited real estate security) *with* Anderson v. Pamilco Chem. Co., 470 F. Supp. 12 (E.D.N.C. 1977) (RISA prohibited real estate security but court distinguishes later forbearance on debt which may be secured; equity heavily favored the creditor in this case).

211 This history led to federal restrictions on a limited category of home equity mortgages. Home Ownership and Equity Protection Act, 15 U.S.C. §§ 1602(aa), 1639. *See also Hearings on Problems in Community Development Banking, Mortgage Lending Discrimination, Reverse Redlining, and Home Equity Lending, Before the Senate Comm. on Banking, Housing and Urban Affairs*, 103d Cong., 1st Sess. (Feb. 3, 17, 24, 1993) (S. Hrg. 103-137). This legislation is discussed in § 12.2.2, *infra*.

212 These are examples from contracts sent by Legal Services attorneys to NCLC for review.

213 *See, e.g.*, Florida, 25% (Fla. Stat. § 687.071(2), [statute also prescribes a civil penalty for violating criminal usury statute]); Georgia, 5% per month (Ga. Code Ann. § 7-4-18); New York, 25% (Penal Law § 190.40; Gen. Oblig. Law § 5-521[3]); New Jersey, 30% (N.J. Stat. Ann. § 2C:21-19(a)). *See also* Lawyers Title Ins. Corp. v. Wells, 881 So. 2d 668 (Fla. App. 2004) (criminal usury statute made debt unenforceable so lender had no insurable interest in it and title insurer was not obliged to cover it); People v. Farrell, 630 N.Y.S.2d 791 (App. Div. 1995) (criminal usury conviction upheld; terms at issue 3% weekly). See Appx. A for a list of state criminal usury statutes.

The Cost of Credit: Regulation and Legal Challenges

New York courts hold loans taken in violation of a criminal usury ceiling to be void, and thus unenforceable.[214] The Georgia Supreme Court has also held loans made in violation of the criminal usury statute to be illegal, and subject to usury penalties in a civil action.[215]

When it deregulated, Idaho took a different approach to controlling market excesses. Caps were removed from Idaho's Consumer Credit Code in 1983;[216] the prohibition against unconscionable agreements, however, was retained.[217] The state Banking Department issued a guideline advising that 45% was prima facie unconscionable and therefore unenforceable, though the threshold may be higher or lower, depending on the circumstances.[218] A number of states have similar statutes,[219] and Massachusetts has a UDAP regulation that prohibits mortgage loans with rates or terms that deviate significantly from industry-wide standards or that are otherwise unconscionable.[220]

---

214 *See, e.g.*, Fareri v. Rain's Int'l Ltd., 589 N.Y.S.2d 579 (App. Div. 1992); Hammelburger v. Foursome Inn Corp., 431 N.E.2d 278 (N.Y. 1980) (criminal usury ceilings created to protect society as a whole "from loan-sharking, 'one of the most heinous, virtually blood-sucking criminal activities of all times.' "). *See also* Fla. Stat. § 687.071(7) (credit extension in violation of criminal usury ceiling is not an enforceable debt). *But cf.* Brodie v. Schmutz (*In re* Venture Mortgage Fund), 282 F.3d 185 (2d Cir. 2002) (questioning whether loan that violates N.Y. criminal usury statute is void); American Equities Group, Inc. v. Ahava Dairy Prods. Corp., 2004 WL 870260 (S.D.N.Y. Apr. 23, 2004) (questioning whether criminal usury makes loan void; instead, remedy may be cancellation of all interest or of usurious amount).

215 Norris v. Sigler Daisy Corp., 392 S.E.2d 242 (Ga. 1990) (penalty in Georgia is forfeiture of interest and other charges). *See* §§ 10.8.2.1, 10.8.3, *infra* on remedies. *See also* Moore v. Comfed Sav. Bank, 908 F.2d 834 (11th Cir. 1990), *rehearing denied*, 917 F.2d 570 (11th Cir. 1990) (violation of criminal usury statute gives rise to right to civil action for remedy; Georgia law); S&A Indus., Inc. v. Bank Atlanta, 543 S.E.2d 743 (Ga. App. 2000) (equally divided court disagrees as to whether criminal usury statute applies to loans over $250,000). *Cf.* Glinton v. And R, Inc., 524 S.E.2d 481 (Ga. 1999) (criminal usury not applicable to pawn transactions, which are governed by separate pawnshop statute).

216 Idaho Code § 28-42-201.

217 Idaho Code § 28-45-106.

218 Idaho Dep't of Finance, Policy Statement 84-5 (Dec. 6, 1994) (determined after taking into account market conditions and experience of credit grantors in the state, and the guidelines of "gross disparity between amounts charged and prevailing market charges and the taking advantage of the inabilities of a debtor to protect his interest").

219 *See, e.g.*, S.C. Code Ann. § 37-5-108; Utah Code § 70C-7-106. *See also* Carboni v. Arrospide, 2 Cal. Rptr. 2d 845 (App. Ct. 1991) (200% loan unconscionable). *See generally* Robin Morris, *Consumer Debt and Usury: A New Rationale for Usury*, 15 Pepperdine L. Rev. 151 (1988).

220 940 Code Mass. Reg. § 8.06(6). *See* United Companies Lending v. Sargeant, 20 F. Supp. 2d 192 (D. Mass. 1998) (upholding and applying regulation).

9.2.8 Usury in "Deregulated" States

9.2.8.1 Exceeding an "Agreed Rate" Cap

In the late 1970s and early 1980s, numerous state legislatures decided to remove interest ceilings on some or all types of credit transactions.[221] However, even in deregulated states, there usually remain benchmarks which provide a consumer with possible claims or defenses if a creditor violates them. Two such benchmarks, criminal usury statutes and unconscionability standards, were discussed in the preceding section, § 9.2.7. This section will discuss another possible benchmark which may be breached—the credit agreement itself.

In some deregulating states, the approach taken was a simple repeal which removed a usury statute from the books entirely. But a greater number of "deregulated" states found it expedient to leave most of an existing usury statute intact and to alter only that portion of the statute which set a numerical interest rate ceiling. For example, a statute which had previously authorized any rate of interest, not to exceed ten percent, might be modified to permit any "agreed rate."[222] Such an amendment raises interesting usury questions because many lenders in the state will assume that they no longer need worry about usury regulations, while in fact they may still face serious sanctions if they assess charges which exceed the "agreed rate."[223]

The most obvious way that a creditor could violate an "agreed rate" usury statute would be to assess charges to

---

221 *See* Ponca Fin. Co. v. Esser, 132 S.W.3d 930 (Mo. App. 2004) (where state allowed any interest rate agreed to, court did not have discretion to order that judgment bear interest at less than the agreed-to 125% interest rate). *See generally* § 2.4, *supra*.

222 Another formula would limit the contract rate to ten percent unless the parties agree to a higher rate. Under many such statutes the agreement must be in writing. Oral agreements for a higher rate (in this example, for more than 10% interest) would then be usurious or, at least, unenforceable. *See In re* Bradford Realty, Inc., 55 B.R. 218 (Bankr. D.N.H. 1985) (oral agreement unenforceable); Northwestern Equip., Inc. v. Badinger, 403 N.W.2d 8 (N.D. 1987) (written agreement met by merely mailing unsigned invoices to borrower; statute specifically provided that, as between merchants, that constituted a written agreement unless the borrower objected to it in writing). *See also* Gus T. Handge & Son Painting Co. v. First Bank & Trust Co., 756 S.W.2d 652 (Mo. Ct. App. 1988) (statute requiring written agreement as to rate of interest complied with by precomputed note calling for specified payments of principal and interest totalling the precomputed face amount of note); Preston Farm & Ranch Supply v. Bio-Zyme Enters., 625 S.W.2d 295 (Tex. 1981) (no writing requirement in Texas statute).

223 *Cf.* Marshall v. Mercury Fin. Co., 550 So. 2d 1026 (Ala. Civ. App. 1989) (Ala. Code § 8-8-5(b) makes usury defense unavailable to borrowers where loan complies with § 8-8-5(a), authorizing "as agreed rate." N.B. The borrower was challenging the 29 1/2% contract rate as usurious, rather than alleging that the rate actually charged was greater than the agreed upon 29 1/2%).

which the borrower had not agreed.[224] A threshold issue may be whether there was an *agreement* to pay any specified rate at all.[225] If the statute allows an agreed *rate*, but there is no *rate* agreed to in the note, then the lender's receipt of

interest charges may also violate the cap, even if the note specifies the finance charges in some other way.[226]

In other cases, the critical issue may be whether the lender in fact imposed charges at the agreed rate. For example, a lender might contract to charge twelve percent interest while in fact charging a somewhat higher rate due to its use of a 365/360 interest calculation.[227] Similarly, a creditor might contract to charge a borrower its "prime rate" while in fact charging a higher rate.[228] A lender may charge more interest

---

224 *But cf.* Luttenegger v. Conseco Fin. Serv. Corp., 671 N.W.2d 425 (Iowa 2003) (HUD-1 settlement statement was "written agreement" on which charge could be based, even though lender did not sign it).

225 A series of cases has interpreted a Texas statute which sets a low interest ceiling for transactions in which the parties do not agree to a specified interest rate. The issue of what constitutes an agreement therefore has been frequently litigated. These opinions have been fairly generous in finding agreements. *Compare* Ginsberg 1985 Real Estate P'ship v. Cadle Co., 39 F.3d 528 (5th Cir. 1994) (Texas law) (where benchmark bank specified in variable rate contract failed, court found an implicit agreement to substitute an analogous prime rate); Preston Farm & Ranch Supply v. Bio-Zyme Enters., 625 S.W.2d 295 (Tex. 1981) (continued use of open-end commercial account after imposition of finance charge constituted agreement to rate charged; court expressly distinguishes consumer accounts); Rent America, Inc. v. Amarillo Nat'l Bank, 785 S.W.2d 190 (Tex. Ct. App. 1990) (contract for interest tied to the prime rate of a third-party bank sufficiently stated a rate of interest); Broady v. Johnson, 763 S.W.2d 832 (Tex. Ct. App. 1988) (Texas law allows 6% where no contract rate specified); Augusta Dev. Co. v. Fish Oil Well Serv., 761 S.W.2d 538 (Tex. Ct. App. 1988) (work tickets authorizing maximum amount permitted by law sufficient to permit 18% interest); Campbell v. First Bank & Trust of Cleveland, 714 S.W.2d 363 (Tex. Ct. App. 1986) (APR listed on face of note sufficiently specifies rate when "interest" space on note left blank); Dodson v. Citizens State Bank of Dalhart, 701 S.W.2d 89 (Tex. Ct. App. 1986) (contract provided for interest at "highest legal rate" after maturity of debt; this specified a rate sufficiently to avoid the 6% ceiling in effect when no rate is specified); Holmes v. Dallas Int'l Bank, 718 S.W.2d 59 (Tex. Ct. App. 1986) (contract providing for interest at 2% over banks prime rate sufficiently stated a rate of interest); Morgan v. Amarillo Nat'l Bank, 699 S.W.2d 930 (Tex. Ct. App. 1985) (post-maturity interest at "highest lawful rate" specified a definite interest rate) *with In re* Charter Co., 913 F.2d 1575 (11th Cir. 1990) (Texas statutory rate of 6% read into agreement where agreement contained non-interest charging alternatives for late payment and was silent as to interest; buyer's failure to object to interest charged on invoices sent by seller did not establish agreement to pay interest); Tubelite v. Risica & Sons, Inc., 819 S.W.2d 801 (Tex. 1991) (unilateral addition of late charges on acknowledgments and invoices did not constitute agreement to modify the contract which had no provision regarding late charges; purchaser's failure to object did not constitute implied modification; 6% statutory rate applicable and the 18% rate imposed was twice the legal rate); Triton Oil & Gas Corp. v. Marine Contractors & Supply, Inc., 644 S.W.2d 443 (Tex. 1982) (unilateral charges imposed by one joint venture partner on another were not agreed upon where never paid despite deduction of amount equal to charged interest from proceeds owed to debtor partner); Strasburger Enterprises, Inc. v. TDGT Ltd. P'ship, 110 S.W.3d 566, 579 (Tex. App. 2003) (borrower entitled to usury penalty when creditor demanded interest in excess of legal rate on a contract that was silent as to interest); Baker v. Howard, 799 S.W.2d 450 (Tex. Ct. App. 1990) (amortization chart not signed by either party and used as evidence of completed oral contract did not constitute the necessary written agreement).

The issue has been litigated under other statutes, as well. *See also* Redmond v. McClelland, 2000 Minn. App. LEXIS 779 (July 25, 2000) (unpublished, citation limited) (court construes facts to have created equitable mortgage and loan; since no interest rate was ever agreed to, creditor's attempt to charge more than the cap was usurious); Northwestern Equip., Inc. v. Badinger, 403 N.W.2d 8 (N.D. 1987) (written agreement met by merely mailing unsigned invoices to borrower; statute specifically provided that, as between merchants, that constituted a written agreement unless the borrower objected to it in writing); Lawler v. Lomas & Nettleton Mortgage Invs., 691 S.W.2d 593 (Tex. 1985) (different Texas statute) (would be usurious to charge a corporation more than 10% interest unless corporation agrees to pay higher rate; court finds agreement in this case). *Cf.* Power Equip., Inc. v. Tschiggfrie, 460 N.W.2d 861 (Iowa 1990) (court discusses factual circumstances in trial record, both for and against finding a written agreement, and remands to trial court to sort it out: factors suggesting agreement were invoices reciting the existence of the charge, creditor's billing in accordance with invoice, debtor's employees signing the invoices, and debtor's continued dealings with creditor; factors suggesting no agreement were that creditor did not always require signed invoices, nor assess charges in accord with invoices, and debtor consistently denied liability for them and refused to pay them).

226 Chroniak v. Golden Inv. Corp., 983 F.2d 1140 (1st Cir. 1993) (second mortgage statute required disclosure of rate of interest and set cap at agreed-upon rate of interest; note which specified the interest in a dollar amount, but no rate, violated the statute, thus invoking statutory penalty of forfeiture of interest. In determining that the failure to specify the rate is also a UDAP violation, court also notes that full disclosure of interest rates takes on added significance with the elimination of usury ceilings, *id.*, 1147). *But see* Dunnam v. Burns, 901 S.W.2d 628 (Tex. Ct. App. 1995) (agreed interest rate does not have to be specified as a numeric rate; adequate if it can be determined from terms of note. *NB*: This case may be distinguished by the fact that it was a business loan and the borrower drafted the terms).

227 *See* § 4.6.3, *supra.*

228 *Cf.* Briggs Transportation Co. v. Second Northwestern Nat'l Bank, 406 N.W.2d 7 (Minn. Ct. App. 1987) (breach of contract claim where borrower allegedly was charged higher rate than the lender's actual prime lending rate to most creditworthy commercial borrowers). *But cf.* NCNB Nat'l Bank v. Tiller, 814 F.2d 931 (4th Cir. 1987) (court scorned debtor's efforts to establish that bank should have calculated its own prime rate by a different method, especially since no institution in the country used the method put forth by debtor).

Contracts which call for interest payments at a bank's prime rate appear to be sufficiently specific to satisfy an agreed rate requirement, so long as the rate charged is indeed the bank's prime rate. *See* Pappas v. NCNB Nat'l Bank, 653 F. Supp. 699 (M.D.N.C. 1987) (agreed rate existed despite borrowers' claim that they did not understand the meaning of the term prime rate;

than allowed by the contract by calculating the interest due on late payments using the daily interest accruing on the note balance times the number of days since the last payment as opposed to calculating the interest on the amount of the monthly payment in arrears.[229] Or a lender may delay posting the borrowers' payments, thus extracting a few more days of interest each month than the contract allows,[230] or manipulate a variable rate contrary to the contract.[231] In these instances, an "agreed rate" statute may automatically convert a contract overcharge to a usury violation.

9.2.8.2 Hidden Interest in Agreed Rate Transactions

Because these statutes are pegged to an agreed rate, issues of hidden interest, as discussed in Chapters 7 and 8 *supra*, are just as relevant as with statutorily defined numerical rate caps. In fact, they may be more relevant, as the prospect of lending in a deregulated environment may make some lenders feel more comfortable taking chances at the margins of acceptable practices. The theory behind deregulation was that market forces would drive the interest rates. Thus these "as agreed" statutes do not limit the amount of interest a lender can charge; a 100% annual rate, if agreed upon, would theoretically be permissible under an agreed rate usury statute, although it might be unconscionable.[232] But the rate has to be the one agreed upon,[233] and creditors that charge rates in excess of the market may not wish to be very forthcoming about those rates. For example, few knowledgeable borrowers would agree to a finance company mortgage at 18% interest if the market rate was 10%, or a 60% car loan if the market rates were 16%.

So what is the response of high rate lenders in the face of such market pressures?[234] One answer is to lower rates and become more competitive. Another commonly employed

strategy is to actually charge an above-market interest rate, while stating a lower rate, and thus only *appear* to be competitive. One way to accomplish this is to inflate the loan principal through the inclusion of various "fees," such as points, service charges, commitment or other fees, or sham closing costs. These artifices have long been used by lenders to circumvent fixed usury ceilings, but they are equally useful in understating effective interest rates in an unrestricted market. Some of these devices, such as phony closing costs or unauthorized charges, have never been legitimately excluded from calculation of the interest rate, but others—particularly points—have been in certain circumstances, and so are commonly counted as part of the note's principal.[235] This fact goes a long way towards explaining why points and other such fees are so prevalent in "deregulated" credit markets where lenders can charge whatever rate the market will bear.[236]

The understatement of interest rates in a deregulated state is basically a disclosure problem.[237] At least in consumer transactions, it is theoretically addressed by the Truth in Lending Act (TILA) because points and some other fees are generally "finance charges" which must be included in the computation of the TILA's annual percentage rate (APR) disclosure.[238] However, the TILA does not apply to all credit

---

misunderstanding was the unilateral mistake of the borrowers); 1600 Capital v. Bankers First Fed. Savs. & Loan, 370 S.E.2d 668 (Ga. App. 1988) (setting rate in reference to bank's "base" rate, which was rate set by committee of bank officers, was sufficient to satisfy statutory requirement of agreement in writing expressed in "simple interest terms"); Holmes v. Dallas Int'l Bank, 718 S.W.2d 59 (Tex. Ct. App. 1986). (Note that lenders can no longer use internal rates which they control as the index on a variable-rate home equity line of credit. 15 U.S.C. § 1647(a); Reg. Z § 226.5(f)(1)(i).)

229 Karg v. Strickland, 919 S.W.2d 722 (Tex. App. 1996).

230 *See* § 4.6.3.5, *supra*.

231 *See* Siradis v. Chase Lincoln First Bank, 1999 U.S. Dist. LEXIS 15593 (Sept. 30, 1999) (denying lender's motion for judgment on pleadings on UDAP claim that it miscalculated variable rates). *See also 8 Billion in Mortgage Overcharges Seen*, Los Angeles Times, June 30, 1990 at D-5.

232 *See* § 9.2.7, *supra*; Ch. 11, *infra*.

233 *See* § 9.2.8.1, *supra*.

234 Actually the application of free market theory to low-income credit is questionable, for a number of reasons which are discussed in § 11.1, *infra*.

235 *See* Chs. 7, 8, *supra*.

236 This problem is recognized in Fidelity Fin. Servs. v. Hicks, 574 N.E.2d 15 (Ill. App. Ct. 1991), which ruled that a statute deregulating interest rates did not implicitly repeal a statutory limitation on points. Court notes possibility of misuse of points to gouge consumers, undercut legitimate competition and discriminate against disfavored borrowers. *See also* Chroniak v. Golden Inv. Corp., 983 F.2d 1140 (1st Cir. 1993) (specifying only dollar amount of interest where statute required disclosure of rate of interest and set cap at agreed upon rate of interest violates both that statute and also is a UDAP violation; court notes that full disclosure of interest rates takes on added significance with the elimination of usury ceilings, *id.*, 1147); Moore v. Comfed Sav. Bank, 908 F.2d 834 (11th Cir. 1990) (loans involved included "outrageous" charges of 20 to 38 points in contrast to average of 2 1/2 points during same period). *See generally* § 7.2.2, *supra*.

   Understating the effective interest rate is not the only incentive for the use of points, though: lenders can claim these fees are "earned" at the contract's consummation, and thus are not subject to rebate upon prepayment or other early termination. This increases their yield on loans which do not go to scheduled maturity. *See* § 5.2.2.1, Ch. 6, § 7.2.2, *supra*.

237 *See* Chroniak v. Golden Inv. Corp., 983 F.2d 1140 (1st Cir. 1993) (specifying only dollar amount of interest where statute required disclosure of rate of interest and set cap at agreed upon rate of interest violates that statute and also is a UDAP violation; court notes that full disclosure of interest rates takes on added significance with the elimination of usury ceilings, *id.* at 1147). *Cf.* Fidelity Fin. Servs. v. Hicks, 574 N.E.2d 15 (Ill. App. Ct. 1991) (in ruling that statute deregulating interest rates did not implicitly repeal a statutory limitation on points, court notes possibility of misuse of points to gouge consumers, undercut legitimate competition and discriminate against disfavored borrowers).

238 Some other types of hidden interest, such as broker fees, closing attorney fees, or inflated closing costs, however, are often

transactions, and even when it does apply, its disclosures can still be minimized by an unscrupulous lender. It is all too easy for a creditor, during the sales process, to refer exclusively to the understated rate on the loan note and to breeze the APR disclosures (even if properly calculated and filled out) past an unsuspecting consumer in the shuffle of papers that accompanies any loan closing.[239]

Depending on the precise wording of a deregulated state's agreed rate statute, an answer to an understated interest rate accomplished through the use of one-time fees may lie in the apparently emasculated usury statute. The usury statute sets the usury ceiling at a *rate* agreed upon by the parties, and under both normal usage and statutory definition, a rate is a percentage figure, not a total charge.[240] The rate stated on the face of the loan note will be lower than the effective interest rate if the lender has charged hidden interest fees, such as points or other charges. Since the rate stated on the face of the note is arguably the only *rate* to which the parties have agreed, then this rate is the usury ceiling for the transaction. By charging a higher effective rate, the lender has exceeded the usury ceiling, and the frequently serious sanctions that the legislature left on the books when it "deregulated" the usury statute can be invoked.[241]

The Virginia Supreme Court adopted this approach in *Garrison v. First Federal Savings and Loan Association*,[242] holding that a second mortgage was null, void and unenforceable, the penalty authorized for a violation of the usury statute,[243] though the rate ceiling on such loans had been removed. Virginia's deregulation provision permitted junior mortgage loans to be "lawfully enforced at the interest rate stated therein on the principal amount of the loan. . . ."[244] At the time Ms. Garrison's loan was made, the statute authorized a 2% service charge, but there was no limitation on points. As is most frequently the case in mortgage loans, the points—26 of them—were included in the $9,200 note principal and the agreed-upon interest rate was 18%.[245]

Conventional practice notwithstanding, the "economic reality" is that points are interest,[246] and the lender in *Garrison* conceded as much. Yet Ms. Garrison's 26 points were not included within the stated 18% interest rate. The court refused to "allow a second tier of interest to be collected" by way of points that were not reflected in the rate disclosed on the note.[247] In other words, points are interest, not principal, and an agreed-upon interest rate must be calculated accordingly. Otherwise, the rate, which, theoretically, is to be set by market forces, will be understated, which is inherently deceptive and anticompetitive.[248] As the court stated, "[n]othing could be more confusing or deceptive to the borrower than reciting an 'agreed' interest rate on one line and then adding additional interest on another."[249] The court reached this conclusion even though, as a result of a peculiarity in Virginia law,[250] the promissory note also listed the higher Truth in Lending APR, which included the points.

In addition to the points, there were other challenged charges which had been included in the note principal: a

---

excluded from the calculation of the TIL APR as well, as they are not categorically considered a finance charge, as are points. (In some factual circumstances, though, they are.) For a discussion of how finance charges may be hidden in TILA disclosures, see generally National Consumer Law Center, Truth in Lending Ch. 3 (5th ed. 2003 and Supp.).

239 Allegations of such a practice could support the argument that the APR was not the "agreed rate" for usury purposes because the borrower could not have agreed to an APR which he never saw. Of course, the failure to disclose the APR prior to the signing of the note may also constitute a TILA violation. The Home Ownership and Equity Protection Act of 1994, 15 U.S.C. § 1639(a), requires a three-day advance look at the APR for mortgages within its scope, in an effort to minimize this practice.

240 Chroniak v. Golden Inv. Corp., 983 F.2d 1140 (1st Cir. 1993).

241 Other possible challenges are discussed in Ch. 11, *infra*.

242 402 S.E.2d 25 (Va. 1991). The borrower's brief is available through National Clearinghouse for Legal Services, Clearinghouse No. 46,421. *See also* Anderson v. FNMA, Clearinghouse No. 42,568 (E.D. Va. 1988) (Civ. No. 87-0236) (Plaintiffs' Brief in Opposition to Defendants' Motion to Dismiss).

243 Va. Code § 6.1-330.47(A). (Following the state's notoriously bad experience with deregulated second mortgages, it re-regulated them. Va. Code § 6.1-330.71) The statute was amended to weaken the penalty in 1987, but the legislature specifically provided that the former law applied to subordinate mortgages closed prior to July 1, 1986, which the loan in question was. Acts 1987, c. 622, cl. 3.

244 Va. Code § 6.1-330.16E (1983).

245 This loan was originated by Landbank Equity, which went on to achieve some notoriety before collapsing into bankruptcy and criminal prosecutions. *See, e.g., High Rate Mortgage Lending Can Violate Georgia's Criminal Usury Law*, 9 NCLC REPORTS Consumer Credit & Usury Ed. 1 (July/Aug. 1990) (discussing Moore v. Comfed Savings Bank, 908 F.2d 834 (11th Cir. 1990).

246 Smith v. Anderson, 801 F.2d 661 (4th Cir. 1986); Garrison v. First Federal Savings & Loan Ass'n of South Carolina, 402 S.E.2d 25 (Va. 1991). The legal characterization of points may vary, depending upon statutory or factual circumstances. *See* § 7.2.2, *supra*.

247 *Garrison*, 402 S.E.2d at 30.

248 For example, a creditor who charged 25 points and a creditor who charged 2 points could both provide for an agreed rate of 15% on their notes, though the former is significantly more costly.

249 *Garrison*, 402 S.E.2d at 30. The court held the quoted statutory language simply meant that *allowable* charges not appearing in the note could be enforced so long as they are included in the Truth in Lending disclosure statement. *See also* Fidelity Fin. Servs., Inc. v. Hicks, 574 N.E.2d 15, 19 (Ill. App. 1991) (statutorily limiting points in agreed-rate transactions "helps prevent an unscrupulous lender from luring an unsophisticated borrower with low interest rates that may undercut legitimate competition, only to impose additional, onerous, or undisclosed fees to compensate for the artificially low interest rate").

250 Va. Code § 6.1-330.16E included a sentence which provided that "[d]isclosure of charges, not otherwise specified in the note, deed of trust, or mortgage, in an interest disclosure pursuant to the federal interest disclosures law, shall constitute compliance with this statute."

"risk management fee," which was not a type of charge authorized to be imposed in these loans; and an appraisal fee greater than was actually incurred.[251] These hidden finance charges in excess of those authorized by statute were also interest, thus further distorting the agreed rate of interest.[252]

Following its common sense approach in *Garrison*, the Virginia court torpedoed another subterfuge when it refused to recognize the accounting fiction behind a wraparound note,[253] and held that the transaction was really a usurious $4,300, 31.2% loan, rather than a 13 1/4%, $50,000 loan.[254] In the absence of an accurately stated rate in the note, the general usury ceiling of 8% applied.

The Montana Supreme Court has also held that points are not interest for purposes of a statute that exempts certain lenders from all limitations on the "rate of interest" they may charge.[255] Thus, while a lender could charge any interest rate it chose, it cannot charge points. The court held:

> the points charged on the loans in question are not interest; that is, they are not charged for the use, forbearance, or detention of money. Under the circumstances of this case and the provisions of the [Consumer Loan Act], the imposition of a flat fee, computed as a percentage of the loan, bearing no direct relation to actual costs of specific services performed, front-loaded into the loan, which did not constitute a charge for the use of the lender's money over time, is not interest.[256]

The court declined to interpret the state Consumer Loan Act "in such a way that it contains a loophole whereby predatory lenders may add points onto the beginning of an interest-bearing loan and thereby escape the requirement that such points be at least partially refunded if the loan is prepaid or refinanced."[257]

Two earlier decisions also discuss this approach to interpreting deregulated statutes. These illustrated both its po-

tential and its pitfalls. In *Howes v. Curtis*,[258] the Idaho Supreme Court interpreted a usury statute which exempted commercial loans from a 10% usury ceiling by allowing parties, who "agree in writing which clearly sets forth the rate of interest charged, to pay any rate of interest. . . ." The lender in *Howes* obtained a note for $44,600 at a stated 10% interest rate but, because of sham broker's fees and funds never advanced, the actual loan principal was only $37,500 with an effective interest rate in excess of 17%. The court ruled that:

> In such a posture, the note lost efficacy as a valid disclosure of the rate of interest which would bar the issue of usury. Only by reference to extrinsic evidence could the total amount of interest charged or the rate of interest be determined. Therefore, the disclosure did not comport with the statutory condition requiring a writing which clearly sets forth the rate of interest charged, . . . and a claim of usury could be properly raised.[259]

The *Howes* court held that an agreed rate usury statute can be violated by the inclusion of hidden interest fees in the face amount of a loan note, and by the corresponding understatement of the actual interest rate, at least when the statute requires the rate to be stated "clearly."[260]

Applying a different agreed rate statute to an otherwise similar transaction, however, a middle-level Arizona appeals court in *Layne v. Transamerica Financial Services, Inc.*,[261] refused to rule that the charging of points constituted a *per se* violation of an Arizona statute setting a ten percent annual interest ceiling "unless a different rate is contracted for in writing, in which event any rate of interest may be agreed to." The note in *Layne* stated that the "Agreed Rate of Charge is 19.9% per annum interest on the Total Amount of the Loan, plus a Prepaid Finance Charge of 10% of Total Amount of Loan." The borrower contended that since the points were not included in the 19.9% interest rate they constituted a charge in excess of the agreed-upon rate, and were therefore usurious. However, the court construed the statute to allow the parties to agree to any *effective* rate of interest, so it validated the parties' agreement to pay interest plus points.[262]

---

251 The statute listed permissible charges for subordinate mortgages: the risk management fee was not listed (and therefore was not a legal charge), and only the actual appraisal cost could be imposed. Va. Code § 6.1-330.24.

252 In those states which, by statute, specifically authorize a specified number of points, charging those points may be permissible in agreed rate transactions, just as here, the 2% statutorily authorized service charge was not considered part of the note interest. *See, e.g.*, Fidelity Fin. Servs., Inc. v. Hicks, 574 N.E.2d 15, 19 (Ill. App. 1991) (construing statutory limit on points to apply to agreed rate transactions). *Cf.* Norris v. Sigler Daisy Corp., 392 S.E.2d 242 (Ga. 1990) (question of statutory interpretation: points excluded from interest in civil usury statute; included as interest in criminal usury statute). *See generally* § 7.2.2, *supra*.

253 *See* § 7.4.3, *supra*.

254 Skinner v. Cen-Pen Corp., 414 S.E.2d 824 (Va. 1992).

255 Wombold v. Associates Fin. Servs. Co., 104 P.3d 1080 (Mont. 2004).

256 *Id.* at 1089.

257 *Id.*

258 104 Idaho 563, 661 P.2d 729 (1983).

259 *Id.* at 661 P.2d 732.

260 A creditor in another state might find it a bit awkward to try to distinguish *Howes* on the basis that the Idaho statute required the rate to be stated "clearly." The absence of the word "clearly" or its equivalent certainly would not suggest legislative approval of unclear disclosure.

261 707 P.2d 963 (Ariz. Ct. App. 1986). *See also* Scavenger Sale Investors L.P. v. Bryant, 2000 U.S. Dist. LEXIS 4426 (N.D. Ill. Mar. 22, 2000) (assuming that loan fees in a commercial case would be part of agreed rate).

262 The court followed this interpretation for four reasons, two of which related to specific Arizona case precedent and state legislative action relating to points passed subsequently. A third

While the *Howes* and *Layne* decisions illustrate how subtle distinctions in statutory analysis and legislative history can affect a court's analysis, the Virginia Supreme Court's decision in *Garrison* persuasively states the case for putting substance over form, and giving teeth to the agreed rate language. There are also additional policy arguments which support such a reading. First, if legislatures had intended to abolish usury statutes through deregulation they could easily have done so. Their decision to leave most of the text of deregulated statutes intact suggests that it is still meaningful, and a narrow construction of agreed rate language should be avoided because it would render much of the statute meaningless.

Second, the deregulation of interest rates in those states which have removed usury ceilings has generally been explained as a decision to allow the free market to govern a lender's return. Yet, the use of points and other hidden interest fees is inherently deceptive and anti-competitive. The anti-competitive effect of points is particularly pronounced if the lender takes the position, as many do, that points are not subject to rebate if the borrower refinances.[263] This makes it uneconomical for the borrower to refinance, and immunizes the lender from the market forces that at least theoretically might drive rates down, as other lenders compete for the borrower's business by offering to refinance at lower rates. Thus, interpreting agreed rate statutes as forbidding points that are not included in the stated rate is consistent with the fundamental theories on which they are based. Agreed rate statutes should be construed as allowing the lender any effective rate of return that the market will bear, so long as that *rate* is knowingly agreed upon.[264] Any

other approach merely encourages inefficient lenders and deceptive lending practices.

If agreed rate statutes are given effect as a form of disclosure statute, these statutes could have a dramatic impact in several situations beyond home equity lending, where much of the type of abuse described above has occurred. A particularly interesting example is the effect of an agreed rate ceiling on a credit sale[265] in which the seller has inflated the cash price of goods, perhaps through the use of seller's points.[266] For example, assume that an automobile dealer offers a car for $10,000 with either 0.0% financing, or a $1,000 rebate if the purchaser pays cash. This transaction contains $1,000 in hidden interest because it really involves a $9,000 car which a purchaser can buy on credit for an extra $1,000. If the term of the credit is two years with equal monthly installments, the effective simple interest rate in this example is a little over ten percent per annum. This interest rate might be permissible under a traditional usury ceiling. But if both the contract and the TIL disclosure statement show a 0.0% interest rate,[267] and the controlling installment sales act allows the charging of any rate (or amount)[268] agreed upon by the parties, there is a strong argument that usury is present. By any standards, the seller

---

court notes that full disclosure of interest rates takes on added significance with the elimination of usury ceilings, *id.* at 1147); Fidelity Fin. Servs. v. Hicks, 574 N.E.2d 15 (Ill. App. Ct. 1991) (in ruling that statute deregulating interest rates did not implicitly repeal a statutory limitation on points, court notes possibility of misuse of points to gouge consumers, undercut legitimate competition and discriminate against disfavored borrowers).

265 The ceiling would have to be in the RISA or MVRISA which controlled the transaction. A number of states have installment sales acts which allow the parties to agree upon the rate or finance charge in the credit sale of automobiles, though in a few there are still outside limits. *See, e.g.,* Ariz. Rev. Stat. Ann. § 44-291; Del. Code Ann. tit. 5, § 2908; N.H. Rev. Stat. Ann. § 361-A:8; Nev. Rev. Stat. § 97.195; N.D. Cent. Code § 51-13-03; Ohio Rev. Code Ann. § 1317.061 (but not to exceed 25%); Or. Rev. Stat. § 83.560. The precise wording of agreed rate statutes varies from state to state and the effect of each statute's particular language must be closely considered.

266 *See* § 7.4.6, *supra.*

267 The TIL amount financed would probably include the $1000 in hidden charges because the current version of Regulation Z excludes seller's points from the finance charge (12 C.F.R. § 226.4(c)(5)) and most automobile rebate programs have been constructed to resemble seller's points. The key usury issue, however, is the treatment of seller's points under state law, not under Regulation Z. The usury statute could be violated even if the TILA was not. Furthermore, the FRB position on seller's points should not be very persuasive authority because, prior to the TILA simplification, the FRB took the position that seller's points were finance charge if they were passed on to the buyer. *See* FRB Interpretation 226.406 (Oct. 23, 1970). The change seems to have had more to do with the simplification of disclosures than with any logical reason for distinguishing seller's points and the finance charge. Seller's points are discussed in § 7.4.6.2, *supra.*

268 Either statutes addressing agreed "rates" or those addressing agreed "amounts" could prohibit the inflation of a cash sale

---

reason invoked the traditional rationale for points—that they merely compensate the lender for the greater expenses it incurs at the loan's outset. As discussed in § 7.2.2, *supra,* this is more rationalization than rationale. First, in most states almost all separately identifiable lender expenses are already passed on to borrowers in the form of non-interest fees; to justify points as payment of these expenses is to seek double compensation. Second, to the extent that lender expenses are not already compensated by non-interest fees, they generally constitute overhead expense, and the decision to attribute it to the consummation of the loan rather than spreading it evenly throughout the loan is simply an arbitrary accounting practice, which has now been disapproved by the FASB. *See* § 5.5.2.2.2, *supra.* Third, to the extent most of these lenders finance the points, they do not provide an influx of cash at the outset to cover originating costs even if those expenses are higher. Finally, there were 10 points imposed in *Layne:* the idea that 5 times the average number of points charged is justified by otherwise uncompensated lender expense strains credulity. *Cf.* Moore v. Comfed Sav. Bank, 908 F.2d 834 (11th Cir. 1990), *rehearing denied,* 917 F.2d 570 (11th Cir. 1990) (20–38 points "outrageous" compared to average 2 1/2 points).

263 *See* § 5.5.2, *supra.*

264 *See also* Chroniak v. Golden Inv. Corp., 983 F.2d 1140 (1st Cir. 1993) (specifying only dollar amount of interest where statute required disclosure of rate of interest and set cap at agreed upon rate of interest violates that statute and also is a UDAP violation;

is charging more than the agreed rate.[269] The only question is whether the inflated cash price is recognized as an interest charge under the installment sales act, and there are compelling arguments that it should be.[270]

9.2.9 Choice of Laws

9.2.9.1 Overview

In deciding what usury law may control any given credit transaction, the first issue that a practitioner should consider is which state's laws should be applied.[271] In many cases, the answer will be obvious. But if the residence or place of business of both parties, the real estate given as security in the transaction, and the place where the contract was negotiated or executed are not all located in the same state, then conflicts between state laws may be an issue. Such conflicts are fairly common because interest ceilings or other substantive limitations differ between states, and creditors can potentially avoid lower interest or other caps by maintaining an office in a high rate state while issuing loans to borrowers who live in a neighboring low-rate state. The growth of credit card banks, operating nationwide from states with minimal regulation, has further complicated the issue of which state's law is applicable to those transactions due to federal preemption and the right of "exportation" by national banks and state-chartered banks.[272]

When conflicts of law arise in consumer credit cases, consumer attorneys must emphasize to courts the public policy reasons for applying a particular state's usury statute. This approach is needed to counteract a general tendency among courts and other legal authorities to avoid the application of usury restrictions, either through choice of laws or otherwise.[273] Many of the long-standing justifications for this proclivity do not apply to consumer transactions, especially given the modern deregulation of credit laws in many states. Consequently, consumer attorneys should argue that

precedent based on commercial cases is largely inapplicable to consumer usury issues. There are special public policy arguments that support application of a particular state's consumer usury law even when that argument may not apply to application of a commercial usury law.[274]

Conflict between the usury laws of different states is a topic which, unfortunately for the consumer, historically has been dominated by commercial cases and the judicial aversion to usury statutes which prevails in commercial contexts. In general, courts in interstate transactions bend over backwards to uphold credit contracts, provided that the contracts in question bear some reasonable relationship to a state under whose laws they are legal. The rule is succinctly stated in § 203 of the *Restatement of Conflict of Laws*:

> The validity of a contract will be sustained against the charge of usury if it provides for a rate of interest that is permissible in a state to which the contract has a substantial relationship and is not greatly in excess of the rate permitted by the general usury law of the state of the otherwise applicable law. . . .[275]

Many states follow this rule or a variant of it.[276]

The *Restatement*'s rule for usury questions is in contrast to its usual rule for contract cases that the law of the state with the most significant relationship to the parties and the transaction should apply.[277] In cases involving loans, this will normally be the state where the contract requires repayment to be made, unless some other state has a more

---

price because the borrower will have agreed to neither the rate nor the amount charged.

269 Furthermore, the seller in such a transaction may be charging more than twice the enforceable rate. *See* § 10.8.5.3.1, *infra. Cf.* Houston Sash & Door Co. v. Heaner, 577 S.W.2d 217 (Tex. 1979) (if no charge is permissible, then any charge imposed more than exceeds twice the permissible rate). Therefore, treble damages should be available under RICO.

270 *See* § 7.4.6, *supra.*

271 For a detailed and insightful analysis of choice of law issues in usury cases, see generally Comment, *Usury in the Conflict of Laws: The Doctrine of Lex Debitoris*, 55 Cal. L. Rev. 123 (1967).

272 The issue arises under the most favored lender doctrine of the National Bank Act and DIDA and the judicially created right of exportation. *See In re* Beck, 248 B.R. 229 (Bankr. W.D.N.Y. 2000) (discussing financing of credit card purchases by retailer's captive national bank). *See generally* Ch. 3, *supra.*

273 *See* § 9.3.1, *infra.*

274 *See* Continental Mortgage Investors v. Sailboat Key, Inc., 395 So. 2d 507 (Fla. 1981) (noting that most cases invalidating choice of law clauses involve individual consumers); State *ex rel.* Meierhenry v. Spiegel, Inc., 277 N.W.2d 298 (S.D. 1979), *appeal dismissed*, 444 U.S. 804 (1979) (stronger public policy concerns in consumer transactions).

275 Restatement of Conflict of Laws 2d § 203 (ALI 1971) (adopted May 23, 1969).

276 *See* Superior Funding Corp. v. Big Apple Capital Corp., 738 F. Supp. 1468 (S.D.N.Y. 1990) (citing New York as following "rule of validation" that favors state whose usury law would uphold the contract). *Cf.* Consolidated Jewelers, Inc. v. Standard Fin. Corp., 325 F.2d 31 (6th Cir. 1963) (Kentucky law upholds choice of law clause in usury case as long as "some vital element of the contract" is associated with the state whose laws are designated to control, and the transaction is entered into in good faith). *But see* Am. Equities Group, Inc. v. Ahava Dairy Prods. Corp., 2004 WL 870260 (S.D.N.Y. Apr. 23, 2004) (declining to adopt "rule of validation"; applying law of state with most significant contacts, even though loan may be usurious under that state's laws); U.S. Trust Co. v. LTV Steel Co. (*In re* Chateaugay Corp.), 150 B.R. 529 (Bankr. S.D.N.Y. 1993) (N.Y. courts have not uniformly adopted "rule of validation"; applying general choice of law rule for contracts to choose N.Y. law, which invalidated contract's compounding of interest), *aff'd*, 170 B.R. 551 (S.D.N.Y. 1994); Marder v. Levin, 244 A.D.2d 467, 664 N.Y.S.2d 344 (1997) (law of jurisdiction with most significant contacts should be applied to usury dispute).

277 Restatement of Conflict of Laws 2d § 188. *See In re* Wright, 256 B.R. 626 (Bankr. D. Mont. 2000) (comparing § 188 to § 203).

significant relationship to the transaction and the parties.[278] By contrast, on usury issues, courts that follow the *Restatement* may apply the law of any state that has some substantial relationship to the transaction, even if it does not have the most significant relationship.[279]

Under the *Restatement* approach to usury cases there are two major limitations on the principle that a court should apply the laws of the state with the higher interest ceiling. These are the "substantial relationship" test[280] and the "not greatly in excess of the rate permitted by the general usury law" limitation.[281] Such factors are not matters of law, but rather issues of fact requiring evidentiary hearings.[282] Another limitation on the *Restatement*'s formula is that the forum state may have a law that overrides these principles and dictates the choice of law.[283] Further, at least one court has held that § 203 does not apply at all where the question is the validity of a contract under a creditor licensing statute rather than a rate ceiling.[284] In addition, more traditional conflict of law analysis may be applied to challenges to credit charges that are based on grounds other than usury, such as UDAP violations, breach of contract, or breach of the duty of good faith.[285]

Article 1 of the UCC also has a choice of law rule. Section 1-105 validates a choice of law clause as long as the transaction bears a "reasonable relation" to the state whose law is chosen. If there is no choice of law clause, the court is to apply the forum state's UCC to transactions bearing "an appropriate relation" to the forum state.[286] A revised version of Article 1, approved by NCCUSL in 2001 for consideration by state legislatures, loosens these standards except in consumer transactions.[287] No state that has enacted Revised Article 1 has adopted more than a phrase or two from the new choice of law provision, however.

Most usury cases apply the *Restatement*'s choice of law rules rather than the UCC's. An Official Comment to Revised Article 1 states that its choice of law rules apply only to the UCC aspects of a transaction, not to the non-UCC aspects.[288] One treatise asserts that the choice of law rules of the pre-2001 version of Article 1 (still in effect in almost all jurisdictions) also apply only to the UCC aspects of transactions.[289] Nonetheless, some cases apply the pre-2001 UCC choice of law rules to usury questions when the transaction involves a negotiable instrument or a contract governed by the UCC.[290]

The first step in deciding a choice of law issue is to decide which state's choice of law rules to apply. Courts generally follow the choice of law rules of the state where they sit.[291]

9.2.9.2 Substantial Relationship Test

Of the two limitations expressed by the *Restatement*, the most important is the requirement of a "substantial relationship" between the contract and the state whose laws are adopted. The comments to Restatement § 203 suggest that a "substantial" relationship requires a "normal and natural" relationship to the contract and parties, which "is unlikely to

---

278 *Id.* § 195. *See* Shannon-Vail Five Inc. v. Bunch, 270 F.3d 1207 (9th Cir. 2001) (law of place of performance applies unless location of repayment was selected to circumvent usury laws or has a very tangential relation to the contract); C.I.O.S. Foundation v. Berkston Ins. A.V.V., 2000 U.S. Dist. LEXIS 2337 (N.D. Miss. Feb. 1, 2000).

279 Restatement of Conflict of Laws 2d § 203 at comment c.

280 *See* § 9.2.9.2, *infra*.

281 *See* § 9.2.9.3, *infra*.

282 *In re* Rexplore, Inc. Securities Litigation, 685 F. Supp. 1132 (N.D. Cal. 1988) (California law); Mencor Enterprises, Inc. v. Hets Equities Corp., 235 Cal. Rptr. 464 (App. 1987).

283 *See* § 9.2.9.4, *infra*.

284 American Security & Trust Co. v. Equitable Life Ins. Co. (*In re* Parkwood, Inc.), 461 F.2d 158, 194 n.78 (D.C. Cir. 1971). In such a case the rules favoring the state with the most significant relationship to the parties and the transaction would apply.

285 *See* Washington Mut. Bank v. Superior Court, 15 P.3d 1071 (Cal. 2001) (challenge to forced placement of insurance at excessive rates). *See generally* Ch. 11, *infra*, for a discussion of non-usury claims.

286 U.C.C. § 1-105.

287 Rev. U.C.C. § 1-301.

288 Official Comment 9 to Rev. U.C.C. § 1-301.

289 Fred H. Miller and Alvin C. Harrell, The Law of Modern Payment Sys. ¶ 1.03[3][a] n.108 (2003). *See In re* Cayer, 6 U.C.C. Rep. Serv. 869 (D. Me. 1969) (U.C.C. choice of law rules control only validity and construction of promissory note, not enforceability where interest exceeded that allowed by state small loan act).

290 *See, e.g.*, Admiral Ins. Co. v. Brinkcraft Development, Ltd., 921 F.2d 591 (5th Cir. 1991) (applying Texas U.C.C. to uphold choice of law provision in negotiable instrument); Woods-Tucker Leasing Corp. of Ga. v. Hutcheson-Ingram Dev. Co., 642 F.2d 744 (5th Cir. 1981) (applying Texas U.C.C. rules to uphold choice of law clause in lease-purchase agreement); Jett Racing & Sales, Inc. v. Transamerica Commercial Fin. Corp., 892 F. Supp. 161 (S.D. Tex. 1995) (applying Texas U.C.C. to uphold choice of law clause in floor plan financing agreement); Evans v. Harry Robinson Pontiac Buick, 983 S.W.2d 946 (Ark. 1999) (applying U.C.C. § 1-105 to uphold clause in retail installment contract that chose Texas law, under which contract would not be usurious); Nevins v. Tinker, 429 N.E.2d 332 (Mass. 1981) (applying U.C.C. choice of law rules to usury questions regarding negotiable instrument). *See also* § 9.2.9.5, *infra*.

291 *See, e.g.*, Klaxon Co. v. Stentor Elec. Mfg. Co., 313 U.S. 487, 61 S. Ct. 1020, 85 L. Ed. 1477 (1941) (in diversity cases, federal courts must apply forum state's conflict of laws rules); *In re* Presque Isle Apts., L.P., 118 B.R. 332 (Bankr. W.D. Pa. 1990) (concluding that bankruptcy courts should apply forum state's choice of law rules); Fu v. Fu, 733 A.2d 1133, 1152 (N.J. 1999); Vanderbilt Mortg. & Fin., Inc. v. Posey, 146 S.W.3d 302 (Tex. App. 2004); Waddoups v. Amalgamated Sugar Co., 54 P.3d 1054 (Utah 2002). *But see* Olympic Coast Investment, Inc. v. Wright (*In re* Wright), 256 B.R. 626, 631–632 (Bankr. D. Mont. 2000) (bankruptcy court must apply federal choice of law rules, not those of forum state, in core matters); Committee of Unsecured Creditors v. RG Fin., Ltd. (*In re* Powerburst), 154 B.R. 307 (Bankr. E.D. Cal. 1993) (federal common law choice of law rules, not those of forum state, apply in federal question cases, including bankruptcy core proceedings).

be based solely upon contacts purposely located in . . . [a] . . . state . . . in an attempt to gain the benefit of that state's usury statute."[292] Thus, the state of residence of the borrower will almost invariably have a substantial relationship to the contract, as will the state where the loan is to be repaid, so long as the "normal and natural" test is met.[293] The *Restatement* suggests that other "significant" contacts, such as the place where the loan was made, the lender's principal place of business, and the place where the contract was principally negotiated, as well as "lesser" contacts such as the place where the note was drawn and dated, the place where the money is to be used, and the situs of land given as security, may not individually constitute a substantial relationship, but may do so in conjunction with other contacts.[294]

As this analysis suggests, it is not difficult to create a substantial relationship to a high rate state, and a majority of courts considering conflict issues in usury cases have managed to discover such a relationship, and have upheld the disputed contracts,[295] or have at least applied the laws of the

state with lesser penalties.[296] However, courts have sometimes found the contacts between a credit transaction and a low-rate state to be sufficiently strong to compel the enforcement of that state's usury law.[297] This latter result seems particularly likely when real estate given as security is located in the low-rate state,[298] despite the *Restatement*'s view of real estate as a less significant contact.

9.2.9.3 Public Policy Concerns and the "Not Greatly In Excess" Requirement

The second limitation on the rule of adopting the laws of the state that would uphold a contract is the concern that

---

292 Restatement of Conflict of Laws 2d § 203 at Comment c. *See also* A. Conner General Contracting, Inc. v. Rols Capital Co., 535 N.Y.S.2d 420 (App. Div. 1988) (if party is really a NY partnership only nominally operating in NJ in order to avoid NY usury laws, NJ has no significant contacts; question of fact); Cook v. Frazier, 765 S.W.2d 546 (Tex. Ct. App. 1989) (choice of law provision in contract cannot be used to evade usury law; it will be held a sham if the contracts are not reasonably related or if they are contrived in order to substantiate the choice of law; Texas borrowers' formation of a Utah partnership was device to avoid Texas law and was not a valid contact with Utah).

293 *See, e.g.,* Direct Mail Specialist, Inc. v. Brown, 673 F. Supp. 1540 (D. Mont. 1987) (law of place where note is payable applies); Acorn Partners II v. Kiley, 193 A.D.2d 397, 597 N.Y.S.2d 63 (1993) (loan has substantial relationship to Connecticut where borrowers were Connecticut organizations, Connecticut attorney drafted the documents, and proceeds were released there to develop property there).

294 Restatement of Conflict of Laws 2d § 203 at Comment c.

295 *See, e.g.,* Bice Constr. v. CIT Corp., 700 F.2d 465 (8th Cir. 1983); McHenry Cty. Credit Co. v. Feuerhelm, 720 F.2d 525 (8th Cir. 1983) (follows § 203 to seek state with "substantial contacts" to uphold contract); Tiffany Indus. v. Commercial Grain Bin Co., 714 F.2d 799 (8th Cir. 1983); International City Bank v. Morgan Walton Properties, Inc., 675 F.2d 666 (5th Cir. 1982); Lockwood Corp. v. Black, 669 F.2d 324 (5th Cir. 1982); Roofing & Sheet Metal Serv. v. La Quinta Motor Inns, 689 F.2d 982 (11th Cir. 1982); FDIC v. Lattimore Land Corp., 656 F.2d 139 (5th Cir. 1981) (Georgia usury law chosen even though note assigned to Tennessee lender); Weiss v. FDIC, 654 F.2d 453 (6th Cir. 1981); *In re* Crabtree, 48 B.R. 528 (Bankr. E.D. Tenn. 1985) (no evidence of bad faith); Easton State Bank v. Winn, 19 B.R. 218 (Bankr. E.D. Ark. 1982) (though contract signed in Arkansas, Kansas law applies); GiantValley v. Meneley Motors, 14 B.R. 457 (Bankr. D. Nev. 1981) (sustains Nevada contract using a California "nexus" to avoid usury); Stacey v. St. Charles Custom Kitchens, 683 S.W.2d 225 (Ark. 1985) (both Arkansas and Tennessee have substantial connections with contract; Tennessee law chosen to avoid usury); Grogg v. Colley Home Center, Inc., 671 S.W.2d 733 (Ark. 1984); McMillen v. Winona Nat'l & Sav. Bank, 648 S.W.2d 460 (Ark. 1983) (accepted seller

financing in Minnesota, where note not usurious); Snow v. CIT Corp., 647 S.W.2d 465 (Ark. 1983) (Georgia law chosen where contract accepted, not Tennessee where sale consummated or Kansas where goods delivered); Peragallo v. Sklat, 466 A.2d 1200 (Conn. Super. Ct. 1983); Finance America Corp. v. Moyler, 494 A.2d 926 (D.C. Ct. App. 1985); Morgan Walton Properties, Inc. v. International City Bank & Trust, 404 So. 2d 1059 (Fla. 1981) (usury policy balances in favor of upholding contract); OFS Equities v. Conde, 421 So. 2d 651 (Fla. Dist. Ct. App. 1982) (uses "normal relationship" to import Colorado law; rejects "old policy" that usury overrides contract); Nevins v. Tinker, 429 N.E.2d 332 (Mass. 1981) (no usury on 8% Massachusetts notes signed in New York); Burrill v. First Nat'l Bank of Shawnee Mission, 668 S.W.2d 116 (Mo. Ct. App. 1984) (applying Kansas, not Missouri usury rules); Mostek Corp v. Chemetron Corp., 642 S.W.2d 20 (Tex. Ct. App. 1982); Hammel v. Ziegler Fin. Corp., 334 N.W.2d 913 (Wis. Ct. App. 1983) (applying Missouri law so that note not usurious). *See also* Becker v. Marketing & Research Consultants, 526 F. Supp. 166 (D. Colo. 1981) (substantial relationship analysis; insufficient facts to decide choice of law issue on summary judgment).

296 *See, e.g.,* W. Heller & Co. v. Chopp-Wincraft Printing Specialties, 587 F. Supp. 557 (S.D.N.Y. 1982) (choice of law favors lightest penalty for credit sale disguised as lease); Wood v. Sadler, 468 P.2d 42 (Idaho 1970). *But see* Speare v. Consolidated Assets Corp., 367 F.2d 208 (2d Cir. 1966) (criticizing approach of seeking out lower penalties).

297 *See, e.g.,* HIMC Inv. Co. v. Siciliano, 246 A.2d 502 (N.J. Super. 1968); North Am. Bank, Ltd. v. Schulman, 123 Misc. 2d 516, 474 N.Y.S.2d 383 (Co. Ct. 1984); Commercial Credit Corp. v. West, 677 S.W.2d 669 (Tex. Ct. App. 1984). *See also* People v. Fairfax Family Fund, Inc., 47 Cal. Rptr. 812 (Cal. App. 1964) (interstate commerce analysis), *appeal dismissed,* 382 U.S. 1 (1965).

298 *See, e.g.,* Johnson v. Ronamy Consumer Credit Corp., 515 A.2d 682 (Del. 1986) (second mortgage statute enforced); Ehlers v. Frey, 441 N.E.2d 651 (Ill. App. 1982) (usury law of *situs* controls); Oxford Consumer Discount Co. v. Stefanelli, 246 A.2d 460 (N.J. Ct. App. 1968), *supplemental op. at* 250 A.2d 593, *modified and aff'd,* 262 A.2d 874 (N.J. 1970), *appeal dismissed,* 400 U.S. 808, 923 (1970); Equilease Corp. v. Belk Hotel Corp., 256 S.E.2d 836 (N.C. App. 1979); Whitaker v. Spiegel, Inc., 623 P.2d 1147, *amended,* 637 P.2d 235 (Wash. 1980) (since usury law is a fundamental state policy, court declines to engage in conflict of law analysis), *appeal dismissed,* 454 U.S. 958 (1981). *But see* Clark v. Transouth Fin. Corp., 236 S.E.2d 135 (Ga. App. 1977) (site of real estate is only one contact among many).

such a rule may undermine the public policy of the state whose laws are not followed. This concern is not explicitly mentioned in the *Restatement*, but is an implicit underpinning of its rule that the law of a higher rate state is to be used only if the resulting contract rate is not greatly in excess of the ceiling in the state whose laws would normally apply.[299] This concern is also not entirely separate from the substantial relationship test because a state's public policy would be most seriously threatened if the laws of a state which had little or no contact with a transaction could be invoked. Nevertheless, public policy concerns are sufficiently separate from the substantial relationship analysis to have justified the enforcement of usury statutes in cases where the contacts test alone might allow the avoidance of usury.[300]

A rule which rejects the normally applicable law of a forum state in favor of a sister state's law solely because of the substance of the regulation clearly undermines to some extent the public policy behind the forum state's law. Generally, state courts have not found the application of a sister state's usury law to violate public policy.[301] Nevertheless, at times the infringement on public policy is seen as too severe to be permitted. For example, when a state legislature adopts usury legislation with the specific intent of controlling foreign lenders who do business in the state, courts have enforced the legislation even though the regulated transactions may have a substantial relation to another state.[302]

Public policy concerns may also dominate if the otherwise permissible interest rate shocks the conscience of the court,[303] or if the laws of the foreign jurisdiction impose no usury ceiling whatsoever.[304]

At the time the *Restatement* was drafted, this limitation on the scope of section 203 was apparently viewed as minor. Indeed, the expressly stated rationale behind the basic rule of section 203 is that "[o]rdinarily, the permissible rate of interest will vary only slightly from state to state," and that, therefore, applying the law of the high rate state "can hardly affect adversely the interests of another state when the stipulated interest is only a few percentage points higher than would be permitted by the local law . . ."[305] A number of decisions that uphold contracts explicitly rely on the fact that the interest rate was only slightly higher than that allowed by the state whose law would normally apply.[306] However, in the current partially deregulated market, in which some states maintain usury ceilings and others have none, the assumptions which lie behind the basic rule of section 203 are very frequently false, and the "not greatly in excess" language becomes a significant limitation on the scope of the basic rule.[307] Indeed, under the terms of the *Restatement* itself, the basic rule of section 203 should not apply to a choice of law between a state which maintains a usury ceiling and one which does not, so long as the amount by which the contract rate exceeds the former state's ceiling is not *de minimis*.[308]

---

299 Restatement of Conflict of Laws 2d § 203. *See* comment b to § 203, which discusses the interests of states in enacting usury laws to protect debtors against extortion.

300 *See* Oxford Consumer Discount Co. v. Stefanelli, 246 A.2d 460 (N.J. Ct. App. 1968), *supplemental op. at* 250 A.2d 593, *modified and aff'd*, 262 A.2d 874 (N.J. 1970), *appeal dismissed*, 400 U.S. 808, 923 (1970); State *ex rel.* Meierhenry v. Spiegel, Inc., 277 N.W.2d 298 (S.D. 1979), *appeal dismissed*, 444 U.S. 804 (1979). *Cf.* Southwest Livestock & Trucking Co. v. Ramon, 169 F.3d 317 (5th Cir. 1999) (prohibition of usury is important public policy in Texas, but no so inviolable as to require disregard of Mexican judgment). *But see* Jett Racing & Sales, Inc. v. Transamerica Commercial Fin. Corp., 892 F. Supp. 161 (S.D. Tex. 1995) (commercial case).

301 *See, e.g.*, Gamer v. duPont Walston, Inc., 135 Cal. Rptr. 230 (App. 1976); Ury v. Jewelers Acceptance Corp., 38 Cal. Rptr. 376 (App. 1964); Santoro v. Osman, 174 A.2d 800 (Conn. 1961); Continental Mortgage Investors v. Sailboat Key, Inc., 395 So. 2d 507 (Fla. 1981); Big Four Mills, Ltd. v. Commercial Credit Co., 211 S.W.2d 831 (Ky. 1948); Kronovet v. Lipchin, 415 A.2d 1096 (Md. 1980); Exchange Bank & Trust Co. v. Tamerius, 265 N.W.2d 847 (Neb. 1978); Grady v. Denbech, 251 N.W.2d 864 (Neb. 1977); Ferdie Sievers & Lake Tahoe Land Co. v. Diversified Mortgage Investors, 603 P.2d 270 (Nev. 1979).

302 *See* Oxford Consumer Discount Co. v. Stefanelli, 246 A.2d 460 (N.J. Ct. App. 1968), *supplemental op. at* 250 A.2d 593, *modified and aff'd*, 262 A.2d 874 (N.J. 1970), *appeal dismissed*, 400 U.S. 808, 923 (1970); Whitaker v. Spiegel, Inc., 623 P.2d 1147, *amended*, 637 P.2d 235 (Wash. 1981), *appeal dismissed*, 454 U.S. 958 (1981). *See also* Johnson v. Ronamy Consumer Credit Corp., 515 A.2d 682 (Del. 1986) (Delaware's law applies because it has interest in preventing predatory second mortgage

lending). *See generally* R. Leflar, *Choice-Influencing Considerations in Conflicts Law*, 41 N.Y.U.L. Rev. 267 (1966).

303 Trinidad Industrial Bank v. Romero, 466 P.2d 568 (N.M. 1970) (contract rate shocks court's conscience so court declines to consider whether it could be upheld under another state's law); Industrial Dev. Bank v. Bier, 565 N.Y.S.2d 980 (Sup. Ct. 1991) (not shocking to conscience to apply law of Israel, which had most substantial relation to the transaction, to uphold contract that would be usurious in New York), *aff'd*, 582 N.Y.S.2d 429 (App. Div. 1992); Ferdie Sievers & Lake Tahoe Land Co. v. Diversified Mortgage Investors, 603 P.2d 270 (Nev. 1979) (contract rate not sufficient to shock conscience of court).

304 *See* North Am. Bank, Ltd. v. Schulman, 123 Misc. 2d 516, 474 N.Y.S.2d 383 (Co. Ct. 1984).

305 Restatement of Conflict of Laws 2d § 203, Comment b.

306 Peragallo v. Sklat, 466 A.2d 1200 (Conn. Super. Ct. 1983); Shull v. Dain, Kalman & Quail, Inc., 267 N.W.2d 517 (Neb. 1978) (maximum permissible interest rates of the two states varied "only slightly"); North Am. Bank, Ltd. v. Schulman, 474 N.Y.S.2d 383 (Co. Ct. 1984) (court might allow "somewhat higher ceiling," but will not apply law of jurisdiction that has rejected usury laws altogether).

307 *See, e.g.*, SEC v. Elmas Trading Corp., 683 F. Supp. 743 (D. Nev. 1987) (applying Restatement §§ 188 and 203, court holds Arkansas law applicable despite possible "substantial relationship" with Nevada, since 500% return provided for in contract is wildly in excess of the 13% return allowed under Arkansas law), *aff'd*, 865 F.2d 265 (9th Cir. 1988) (table).

308 If the contract rate exceeded that permitted by local law by only a small amount, the absence of any ceiling in another state would not seem to invoke the "not greatly in excess" exception. *See* Restatement of Conflict of Laws 2d § 203 at Comment a.

Since Restatement § 203 requires a comparison between the rate charged and the rate permitted by the law of the state that would be "otherwise applicable," the court must determine which state's law would normally apply to the transaction.[309] This requires an analysis of which state has the "most significant relationship" to the transaction.[310] After this analysis, the court will be in a position to compare the law of the high-rate state with the law that would normally apply.

The role of special usury laws deserves particular attention. Under the *Restatement* a contract will be upheld only if the interest rate is not greatly in excess of the rate permitted by the general usury law, not the special usury law, of the state whose law would normally apply. Thus, if a state has an 8% general usury law but allows 24% for certain small loans by licensed lenders, the *Restatement* would allow the court to apply another state's law that allowed interest slightly above the 8% ceiling, but it does not endorse application of law that would allow interest above the 24% ceiling.[311] Special usury laws also often incorporate their own choice of law provisions,[312] and are supported by strong and explicit public policies.[313]

A review of case law suggests that decisions which enforce the usury law of a low-rate state, despite the existence of some contacts between the transaction and a state under whose laws the contract would be legal, often involve the special usury laws, such as the small loan laws, installment sales acts, and second mortgage statutes, of the former state.[314] This result is reasonable because states have a strong interest in protecting particularly vulnerable classes of borrowers, and because special usury statutes, which as a whole are comparatively modern enactments, reflect legislative concern about abuses in modern credit markets which harmed such borrowers.

9.2.9.4 State Statutes Governing Choice of Laws

Even if a state normally follows the conflict of laws rules set forth in the *Restatement*, it may have statutes that dictate the choice of law for certain types of transactions. For example, a Washington statute provides:

> Whenever a loan or forbearance is made outside Washington state to a person then residing in this state the usury laws found in chapter 19.52 RCW, as now or hereafter amended, shall be applicable in all courts of this state to the same extent such usury laws would be applicable if the loan or forbearance was made in this state.[315]

In other states, a rule about what state's law applies may be incorporated into a special usury statute. For example, a state law may require all companies doing business in the state to comply with the state's licensing requirements.[316] Or

---

However, if the contract provides for a variable rate which has the potential to exceed the local rate by a substantial amount, the local law may be enforced even though the actual rate charged under the contract only slightly exceeds the local usury ceiling. *See* O'Brien v. Shearson, Hayden, Stone, Inc., 586 P.2d 830 (1978), *on reconsideration* 605 P.2d 779 (Wash. 1980).

309 Shannon-Vail Five Inc. v. Bunch, 270 F.3d 1207 (9th Cir. 2001) (finding the high-rate state to be the state with the most substantial relationship to the transaction, thereby making analysis under § 203 unnecessary).

310 Restatement of Conflict of Laws 2d §§ 188, 195.

311 Restatement of Conflict of Laws 2d § 203. *See* comment f, which says "It is uncertain whether a contract will be upheld if it provides for a rate of interest which is permissible under a special usury statute of a state having a substantial relationship to the contract, and which is not greatly in excess of the rate permitted by a special usury statute of the state of the otherwise applicable law." There is nothing in the text of the Restatement that would allow the court to salvage such a contract.

312 *See* § 9.2.9.4, *infra*.

313 *See* § 9.3.1.1, *infra*.

314 *See* Lyles v. Union Planters Nat'l Bank, 393 S.W.2d 867 (Ark. 1965); People v. Fairfax Family Fund, Inc., 47 Cal. Rptr. 812 (App. 1964) (interstate commerce analysis), *appeal dismissed*, 382 U.S. 1 (1965) ; Johnson v. Ronamy Consumer Credit Corp., 515 A.2d 682 (Del. 1986) (second mortgage statute); HIMC Inv. Co. v. Siciliano, 246 A.2d 502 (N.J. Super. 1968); Oxford Consumer Discount Co. v. Stefanelli, 246 A.2d 460 (N.J. Ct. App. 1968), *supplemental op. at* 250 A.2d 593, *modified and aff'd*, 262 A.2d 874 (N.J. 1970), *appeal dismissed*, 400 U.S.

808, 923 (1970); State *ex rel.* Meierhenry v. Spiegel, Inc., 277 N.W.2d 298 (S.D. 1979) (commercial and consumer cases involve different public policy considerations), *appeal dismissed*, 444 U.S. 804 (1979); Whitaker v. Spiegel, Inc., 623 P.2d 1147 (1981), *amended*, 637 P.2d 235 (Wash. 1981), *appeal dismissed*, 454 U.S. 958 (1981). *See also* Continental Mortgage Investors v. Sailboat Key, Inc., 395 So. 2d 507 (Fla. 1981) (recognizing minority rule in consumer cases); North Am. Bank, Ltd. v. Schulman, 123 Misc. 2d 516, 474 N.Y.S.2d 383 (Co. Ct. 1984) (individual borrower).

315 Wash. Rev. Code § 19.52.034. *See* Whitaker v. Spiegel, Inc., 623 P.2d 1147 (1981), *amended*, 637 P.2d 235 (Wash. 1981) (Washington courts cannot engage in conflict of law analysis because state statute says Washington law controls), *appeal dismissed*, 454 U.S. 958 (1981); Falk v. Riedel, 2000 Wash. App. LEXIS 1889 (Sept. 29, 2000) (unpublished, citation limited) (applying Washington law to contract); Golden Horse Farms, Inc. v. Parcher, 629 P.2d 1353 (Wash. Ct. App. 1981) (Washington courts are not free to engage in conflict of law analysis to determine whether the parties' own choice of law provision should apply). Note that an earlier decision, O'Brien v. Shearson Hayden Stone, Inc., 586 P.2d 830 (1978), *later op. at* 605 P.2d 779 (Wash. 1980), applied *Restatement* § 203 to a conflict of laws question, without mentioning Wash. Rev. Code § 19.52.034. The *O'Brien* court reached the same conclusion that § 19.52.034 would have required: that the transaction was governed by Washington law and was usurious. The later decision in Whitaker v. Spiegel, Inc., 623 P.2d 1147, 1151 (Wash. 1981), appears to overrule this aspect of *O'Brien*, stating "[i]n an interstate loan transaction the Washington courts are not free to engage in conflict of law analysis" because of § 19.52.034.

316 *See* Gorman v. Marcon Capital Corp., 274 B.R. 351 (D. Vt. 2002) (out-of-state lender must comply with Vermont licensing law if it makes loans to be used in Vermont); People v. Fairfax

a state may specify that its laws apply to contracts made by out-of-state companies with state residents.[317] A state may also have a statute that sets a general choice of law standard for contracts.[318]

If a state has a choice of law statute, it will be binding on courts of that state,[319] and those courts will not need to analyze the factors set forth in the *Restatement*.[320] Courts have upheld the authority of states to enforce choice of law statutes against challenges based on due process, the Full Faith and Credit Clause, and the Commerce Clause of the Constitution.[321]

9.2.9.5 Contractual Choice of Law Clauses

Often a creditor inserts a clause in a contract stating that it will be governed by a particular state's laws. Under the *Restatement*, such a clause will not be upheld if the chosen state does not have a substantial relation to the transaction.[322] Nor will the clause be given effect if the result would be contrary to a fundamental policy of the state with the most significant relation to the transaction, as long as that state also has a materially greater interest in the issue.[323] But where there is a substantial relationship with the state specified in the clause, courts have generally enforced such clauses.[324] A number of these decisions, however, stress that

Family Fund, Inc., 47 Cal. Rptr. 812 (App. 1964), *appeal dismissed*, 382 U.S. 1 (1965). *See also* HIMC Inv. Co. v. Siciliano, 246 A.2d 502 (N.J. Super. 1968); Oxford Consumer Discount Co. v. Stefanelli, 246 A.2d 460 (N.J. Super. App. Div. 1968), *supplemental op. at* 250 A.2d 593 (N.J. Super. App. Div. 1969) (New Jersey second mortgage statute indicates legislative intent that New Jersey law apply to all contracts involving second mortgage on New Jersey real estate), *modified and aff'd*, 262 A.2d 874 (N.J. 1970), *appeal dismissed*, 400 U.S. 808, 923 (1970). *Cf.* Pilcher v. Direct Equity Lending, 189 F. Supp. 2d 1198 (D. Kan. 2002) (denying summary judgment on question whether Kan. U.C.C.C. licensure requirement applies to out-of-state lender; lender's out-of-state assignees, which had no contact with Kan., are exempt from licensure).

317 *See, e.g.,* Kan. Stat. Ann. § 16a-1-201 (specifying when consumer credit transaction is considered made in Kansas; Consumer Credit Code applies to all such loans); N.C. Gen. Stat. § 24-2.1 (any extension of credit is deemed to have been made in North Carolina and subject to its laws if borrower accepts or makes loan offer in North Carolina). *See also* Consumer Federation of America, Consumers at Risk from Online Payday Lending: CFA Survey of 100 Payday Loan Sites (Nov. 30, 2004), *available at* www.consumerfederation.org/backpage/payday/cfm.

318 *See* Cal. Civ. Code § 1646 (applying law of place of performance); Shannon-Vail Five Inc. v. Bunch, 270 F.3d 1207 (9th Cir. 2001).

319 *See* Restatement of Conflict of Laws 2d § 6; Resolution Trust Co. v. Northpark Joint Venture, 958 F.2d 1313 (5th Cir. 1992); McCorhill Publishing, Inc. v. Greater New York Sav. Bank (*In re* McCorhill Publishing, Inc.), 86 B.R. 783 (Bankr. S.D.N.Y. 1988).

320 Whitaker v. Spiegel, Inc., 623 P.2d 1147 (1981), *amended*, 637 P.2d 235 (Wash. 1981) (Washington courts will not engage in conflict of law analysis because state statute says Washington law controls), *appeal dismissed*, 454 U.S. 958 (1981).

321 Aldens, Inc. v. Miller, 610 F.2d 538 (8th Cir. 1979) (upholding application of state credit laws to out-of-state mail order seller); Aldens, Inc. v. LaFollette, 552 F.2d 745 (7th Cir. 1977) (same); Aldens, Inc. v. Packel, 524 F.2d 38 (3d Cir. 1975) (same). *See also* Valley Bank v. Plus Sys., Inc., 914 F.2d 1186 (9th Cir. 1990) (upholding state law that regulated agreements regarding ATM charges); Underhill Assocs., Inc. v. Bradshaw, 674 F.2d 293 (4th Cir. 1982) (requiring out-of-state securities broker-dealers to register with state before transacting business there does not violate Commerce Clause or due process). *Cf.* Arab African Int'l Bank v. Epstein, 10 F.3d 168 (3d Cir. 1993) (remanding for determination whether state law prohibiting foreign banks from doing business there is excessive burden on interstate commerce). *But cf.* Pioneer Military Lending, Inc. v. Manning, 2 F.3d 280 (8th Cir. 1993) (Commerce Clause pre-

vents Missouri from regulating out-of-state lender that had branch office in Missouri but made loans only to non-Missouri residents).

322 Restatement of Conflict of Laws 2d § 187. *See* Am. Honda Fin. Corp. v. GloMc, Inc., 820 F. Supp. 1157 (E.D. Ark. 1993) (finding substantial connection to Cal. law and upholding clause choosing Cal. law where borrower was sophisticated businessman, one of lender's officers signed the agreement in Cal., invoices were sent from Cal., and lender "swept" payments into a Cal. account); Brock v. First Fidelity Acceptance Corp. (*In re* Brock), 214 B.R. 877 (Bankr. E.D. Ark. 1997) (giving effect to clause choosing Texas law; Texas had substantial relationship to the transaction in that notification of authorization came from Texas, decision to fund the loan was made there, and funds were authorized there); Washington Mut. Bank v. Superior Court, 15 P.3d 1071 (Cal. 2001) (adopting *Restatement* analysis; consumer may defeat choice of law clause by showing it is unreasonable or contrary to fundamental state policy, or would cause substantial injustice); Culbert v. Rols Capital Co., 585 N.Y.S.2d 67 (App. Div. 1992) (reversing summary judgment for lender holding that New Jersey law applied; connection to New Jersey may be a sham to avoid New York usury laws). *See also* Gulfcoast Hospitality, Inc. v. Amstat Corp. (*In re* Gulfcoast Hospitality, Inc.), 305 B.R. 341 (Bankr. M.D. Fla. 2003) (question of fact whether transaction had "normal relation" to California so that clause choosing California law would be valid). Note that in usury cases, the requirement that the state whose law is applied have a substantial relationship to the transaction is already part of § 203. *See* § 203 at comment e.

323 Restatement of Conflict of Laws 2d § 187(2). *See* Orix Credit Alliance, Inc. v. CIT Group/Equipment Fin., Inc. (*In re* Hughes), 230 B.R. 213 (Bankr. M.D. Ga. 1998) (upholding choice of law clause in absence of "overwhelming public policy"). *See also* Mazzoni Farms, Inc. v. E.I. DuPont De Nemours & Co., 761 So. 2d 306 (Fla. 2000) (non-usury case; choice of law clause will generally be enforced unless it contravenes strong public policy). Note that the more a usury statute is riddled with exceptions and the more frequently the legislature has changed it, the less likely a court will consider it to express a fundamental policy of the state. *See* Continental Mortgage Investors v. Sailboat Key, Inc., 395 So. 2d 507 (Fla. 1981) (stressing commercial setting and upholding choice of law clause).

324 *See, e.g.,* Aetna Life Ins. Co. v. Great Nat'l Corp., 818 F.2d 19 (8th Cir. 1987) (commercial transaction); Jones v. First Fidelity Acceptance Corp. (*In re* Jones), 231 B.R. 66 (E.D. Ark. 1999) (same outcome though the originating lender was the out-of-state lender); Jett Racing & Sales, Inc. v. Transamerica Commercial Fin. Corp., 892 F. Supp. 161 (S.D. Tex. 1995) (contractual choice of law binding so long as it bears "some relation"

the parties were sophisticated business negotiators, and suggest that boilerplate choice of law clauses in consumer contracts will be subjected to closer scrutiny.[325]

A provision of Article 1 of the UCC provides that a contractual choice of laws clause will be upheld as long as the state selected bears a reasonable relation to the transac-

tion.[326] The National Conference of Commissioners on Uniform State Laws (NCCUSL) has adopted a revised version of Article 1 of the UCC that sets even looser rules for choice of law clauses in non-consumer transactions, but restricts waiver of consumer protections through choice of law clauses in transactions with consumers.[327] As of early 2005, Alabama, Delaware, Hawaii, Idaho, Minnesota, Texas, Virginia, and the Virgin Islands had adopted revised Article 1, but only the Virgin Islands and, in part, Virginia, adopted the new choice-of-law rules.

A choice of law clause in the contract between a payday lender and an out of state "rent-a-bank" has no effect on the authority of state regulators to apply their state law to the payday lender.[328] While choice of law clauses usually protect lenders from usury claims, a clause that subjects a contract to laws of a state under which it is usurious may also be upheld.[329]

9.2.10 Formal Requirements for Electronic Credit Transactions and the Interplay Between State and Federal Law

9.2.10.1 Introduction

Paperless lending is a developing issue in consumer credit. While electronic credit transactions offer new convenience for borrowers, they also create new opportunities for fraud. Either federal or state law, or both, may apply to these transactions. Electronic transactions of all sorts are examined in detail in Chapter 9 of NCLC's *Consumer Banking and Payments Law* (2d ed. 2002).

When confronting an electronic credit transaction, the key questions for the consumer's attorney are:

---

to the transaction; commercial case); Superior Funding Corp. v. Big Apple Capital Corp., 738 F. Supp. 1468 (S.D.N.Y. 1990) (choice of law clause will be upheld if transaction has reasonable relation with that state and the law chosen would not violate public policy); *In re* Wright, 256 B.R. 626 (Bankr. D. Mont. 2000) (upholding clause choosing Washington law where that state had most significant relationship to the transaction); Committee of Unsecured Creditors v. RG Fin., Ltd. (*In re* Powerburst), 154 B.R. 307 (Bankr. E.D. Cal. 1993) (upholding clause even though loans were usurious under law of chosen state); Matter of Mickler, 20 B.R. 346 (Bankr. M.D. Fla. 1982) (contractual choice of law provision upheld even though choice rendered contract usurious; commercial loan); Washington Mut. Bank v. Superior Court, 15 P.3d 1071 (Cal. 2001) (choice of law clause in consumer contract is not *per se* unenforceable, but may be invalidated if superior power was unfairly used in imposing it or if enforcing it would cause substantial injustice); Continental Mortgage Inv. v. Sailboat Key, Inc., 395 So. 2d 507 (Fla. 1981) (contractual choice of law clause upheld in commercial case; court recognizes that in consumer cases courts give them less deference); Kronovet v. Lipchin, 415 A.2d 1096 (Md. 1980) (upholding contractual choice of Maryland law where Maryland had substantial relationship to the transaction; commercial case); Goodwin Brothers Leasing, Inc. v. H&B Inc., 597 S.W.2d 303 (Tenn. 1980) (choice of law clause upheld where selected state had reasonable relation to the transaction; court stresses that parties were sophisticated, knowledgeable businessmen); Cook v. Frazier, 765 S.W.2d 546 (Tex. Ct. App. 1989) (where contract is to finance purchase of property in Utah, the site of the property is a reasonable relation to Utah sufficient to warrant choice of law; though if property had been merely collateral, rule would not apply); Hi Fashion Wigs Profit Sharing Trust v. Hamilton Inv. Trust, 579 S.W.2d 300 (Tex. Civ. App. 1979) (commercial case). *See also* Moyer v. Citicorp Homeowners, Inc., 799 F.2d 1445 (11th Cir. 1986) (applying Georgia law, under which contract was usurious, over lender's objection, where contract clause selected Georgia law and Georgia had substantial relation to the transaction); Evans v. Harry Robinson Pontiac Buick, 983 S.W.2d 946 (Ark. 1999) (applying U.C.C. rules to uphold choice of Texas law [no usury cap] as Texas had a reasonable relationship to the contract; loan approval, loan notification, and funding authorization came from Texas though the car was purchased, registered and housed in Arkansas; irrelevant to court that the originating lender was an Arkansas car dealer which then assigned loan to out-of-state lender). *But see* Whitaker v. Spiegel, Inc., 623 P.2d 1147, *amended*, 637 P.2d 235 (Wash. 1980) (contractual choice of law not followed where state law specified that Washington law applied to all loans to Washington residents).

325 Continental Mortgage Inv. v. Sailboat Key, Inc., 395 So. 2d 507 (Fla. 1981) (contractual choice of law clause upheld in commercial case; court recognizes that in consumer cases courts give them less deference); Goodwin Brothers Leasing, Inc. v. H&B Inc., 597 S.W.2d 303 (Tenn. 1980) ("This is not a case of the victimizing of an uninformed consumer by an avaricious finance company").

326 U.C.C. § 1-105(1). *See* Admiral Ins. Co. v. Brinkcraft Dev., Ltd., 921 F.2d 591 (5th Cir. 1991) (upholding note against usury claim where clause chose N.Y. law, lender's principal offices were in N.Y., and payments were made there); Davidson Oil Country Supply Co. v. Klockner, Inc., 908 F.2d 1238 (5th Cir. 1990) (applying U.C.C. rule to uphold choice of law clause in sales contract; under the law chosen, usury claim fails); Anderson v. Chainani (*In re* Kemper), 263 B.R. 773, 781 n.15 (E.D. Tex. 2001) (upholding clause selecting state where debtor lived, signed the notes, and generated payments); Evans v. Harry Robinson Pontiac Buick, 983 S.W.2d 946 (Ark. 1999) (upholding Texas choice-of-law clause in retail installment contract that was signed in Arkansas but approved by and assigned to company in Texas). *See generally* § 9.2.9.1, *supra*.

327 Revised U.C.C. § 1-301.

328 Bankwest, Inc. v. Oxendine, 598 S.E.2d 343 (Ga. Ct. App. 2004).

329 Moyer v. Citicorp Homeowners, Inc., 799 F.2d 1445 (11th Cir. 1986) (applying Georgia law, under which contract was usurious, over lender's objection, where contract clause selected Georgia law and Georgia had substantial relation to the transaction); Committee of Unsecured Creditors v. RG Fin., Inc.(*In re* Powerburst Corp.), 154 B.R. 307 (Bankr. E.D. Cal. 1993).

- Did the consumer actually agree to the terms of the electronic contract?[330] Since there will not be a traditional paper document with signatures, proof that the parties actually agreed to specific terms raises special issues in electronic transactions.

- Does the electronic document that the creditor produces accurately reflect the terms of the transaction?[331] Since electronic documents are so easily altered, this issue is particularly likely to arise in electronic transactions. If the consumer contests the creditor's version of the terms of the transaction, can the creditor prove that it met E-Sign's or UETA's document integrity requirements?[332]

- If state or federal law requires the contract, credit disclosures or later documents to be provided in writing to the consumer, do the electronic documents satisfy this requirement?[333] If not, then the consumer has the right to whatever remedies the state or federal law provides.

- Can the creditor prove delivery of any documents that it claims were delivered electronically?[334]

Before resolving any of these issues, the practitioner must determine whether state or federal law governs these questions.

9.2.10.2 Overview of E-Sign and UETA

Congress gave an impetus to electronic transactions by passing the Electronic Signatures in Global and National Commerce Act (E-Sign), effective October 1, 2000.[335] It provides that neither a signature nor a contract can be denied legal effect, validity, or enforceability solely because it is in electronic form.[336] It also provides that "if a statute, regulation, or other rule of law requires that information relating to a transaction or transactions in or affecting interstate or foreign commerce be provided or made available to a consumer in writing," the information can be provided electronically, as long as certain conditions are met.[337]

The federal statute applies not only to transactions that the consumer initiates electronically, but also to traditional paper transactions. It authorizes creditors to provide information electronically in transactions that are otherwise conducted entirely on paper, as long as the new statute's requirements are satisfied. For consumer transactions, the key requirement is that the consumer must consent in a very specific way to receive electronic disclosures.[338]

Many state credit laws require that the credit contract be in writing. Because of E-Sign, a contract cannot be invalidated solely because it is electronic rather than written, or solely because it was electronically signed.[339] These same credit laws also typically require that the consumer be given a copy of the written contract. E-Sign will override the requirement that delivery of the information be in written rather than electronic format, but only if the consumer follows E-Sign's specific electronic consent procedures and the transaction meets the other requirements of E-Sign.[340] Even if the consumer consents, however, E-Sign does not authorize electronic provision of certain important notices such as foreclosure notices.[341] E-Sign also establishes important consumer protections regarding document integrity, so that consumers will be able to retain electronic documents and produce them accurately for later reference.[342]

The federal statute allows states to supersede some of its provisions, including its key consumer protection provisions, by passing the Uniform Electronic Transactions Act (UETA)[343] or other state laws that are technologically neutral and consistent with the federal statute.[344] By 2005, most states had adopted some form of UETA. The complex question of whether a state's adoption of UETA has superseded portions of E-Sign is summarized in § 9.2.10.3, *infra*, and discussed in detail in National Consumer Law Center, *Consumer Banking and Payments Law* § 9.2 (2d ed. 2002 and Supp.).

Like E-Sign, UETA provides that contracts, other records, and signatures cannot be denied legal effect because they are

---

330 *See* § 9.2.10.8, *infra*; National Consumer Law Center, Consumer Banking and Payments Law § 9.9.4 (2d ed. 2002 and Supp.).

331 *See* §§ 9.2.10.7, 9.2.10.8, *infra*.

332 *See* § 9.2.10.7, *infra*.

333 *See* § 9.2.10.4, *infra*.

334 *See* § 9.2.10.6, *infra*.

335 Pub. L. No. 106-229, 114 Stat. 464 (June 30, 2000), *codified at* 15 U.S.C. § 7001 *et seq.*

336 15 U.S.C. § 7001(a); *see* Roger Edwards, Ltd. Liab. Co. v. Fiddes & Son, Ltd., 245 F. Supp. 2d 251 (D. Me. 2003) (e-mails may be sufficient to meet statute of frauds), *aff'd on other grounds*, 387 F.3d 90 (1st Cir. 2004); Med. Self Care, Inc. v. National Broad. Co., 2003 WL 1622181 (S.D.N.Y. Mar. 28, 2003) (e-mail satisfies contractual requirement of a writing; court states this result is arguably mandated by E-Sign).

337 15 U.S.C. § 7001(c). *See In re* Cafeteria Operators, Ltd. P'ship, 299 B.R. 411 (Bankr. N.D. Tex. 2003) (e-mails satisfied federal regulation's requirement of a writing).

338 *See* § 9.2.10.5, *infra*; National Consumer Law Center, Consumer Banking and Payments Law §§ 9.2.10.3, 9.4 (2d ed. 2002 and Supp.).

339 15 U.S.C. § 7001(a).

340 *See* § 9.2.10.5, *infra*; National Consumer Law Center, Consumer Banking and Payments Law § 9.4 (2d ed. 2002 and Supp.).

341 *See* § 9.2.10.9, *infra*; National Consumer Law Center, Consumer Banking and Payments Law § 9.2.2 (2d ed. 2002 and Supp.).

342 *See* § 9.2.10.7, *infra*; National Consumer Law Center, Consumer Banking and Payments Law § 9.6 (2d ed. 2002 and Supp.).

343 UETA can be found in the pocket part to Part 1 of 7A Uniform Laws Annotated. The text of UETA is also posted on the website of the National Conference of Commissioners on Uniform State Laws, www.nccusl.org, along with a list of the states that have adopted it.

344 15 U.S.C. § 7002(a).

in electronic form.[345] It also echoes E-Sign in providing that electronic documents and electronic signatures satisfy state laws that require writings.[346] But UETA is different in many ways from the federal statute. First, it does not require E-Sign's specific consent procedures. It merely requires that the parties agree to conduct transactions by electronic means.[347] Second, UETA does not make exceptions for important documents like foreclosure notices. Third, UETA allows tape recordings and other electronic records of oral communications to serve as a writing,[348] while E-Sign limits the use of recordings of oral communications.[349] UETA's document integrity requirements are also significantly weaker than E-Sign's.[350] States that displace E-Sign by enacting UETA have the option of preserving E-Sign's consumer protections, however.[351]

Except for laws that require physical signatures or written documents, both E-Sign and UETA leave state consumer protection and credit statutes unchanged. E-Sign provides that it does not "limit, alter, or otherwise affect any requirement imposed by a statute, regulation, or rule of law relating to the rights and obligations of persons under such statute, regulation, or rule of law other than a requirement that contracts or other records be written, signed, or in nonelectronic form."[352] UETA does not have such a specific savings clause, but states "[a] transaction subject to this Act is also subject to other applicable substantive law."[353] The official comments to UETA clarify that "the substantive rules of contracts remain unaffected by UETA,"[354] and that the uniform act takes a "minimalist" approach, leaving to other law the question whether a contract or signature has any effect.[355]

Both E-Sign and UETA also clear the way for electronic promissory notes.[356] Neither the federal statute nor UETA applies to a contract or other record (electronic document) "to the extent that it is governed by" Article 9 of the Uniform Commercial Code,[357] but the 1999 revision to Article 9, which all states have adopted, has its own provisions allowing electronic documents in secured transactions.[358]

9.2.10.3 What Law Applies: E-Sign, UETA, or Other State Laws?

9.2.10.3.1 Introduction

The first question in analyzing the legality of an electronic credit contract is what law applies. E-Sign has an unusual provision that allows states to opt out of certain of its provisions by passing a uniform version of UETA or another state law that is consistent with E-Sign and does not favor any particular electronic technology.[359] A state could also take both routes, adopting both UETA and a companion provision.[360] What law or laws apply depends on whether and when the state implemented any of these options. This complex issue is only summarized here, and is analyzed in detail in National Consumer Law Center, *Consumer Banking and Payments Law* § 9.2 (2d ed. 2002 and Supp.).

In most states, the consumer protection provisions of E-Sign are *not* preempted by state law. But even if a state has preempted E-Sign, the preemption only applies to state law requirements, and E-Sign's consumer protections continue to apply when a creditor makes federally-mandated disclosures or delivers federally-mandated documents to the consumer.[361]

As discussed in more detail below, the only states that have clearly displaced E-Sign are Arkansas and Louisiana. In Mississippi, Missouri, and Rhode Island, E-Sign's protections probably continue to apply, because when those states adopted UETA they did not expressly indicate an intent to displace E-Sign. Likewise, E-Sign probably continues to apply in Kentucky, because it adopted UETA before E-Sign was enacted so could not have intended to displace it. E-Sign also probably continues to apply in the District of Columbia, Michigan, Montana, New Mexico, North Dakota, Texas, and Wyoming, because those states adopted versions of UETA that were not completely uniform. In the remaining states, there is little or no question that E-Sign applies.

---

345 UETA § 7.
346 *Id.*
347 UETA § 5(b).
348 UETA § 2 cmt. 6, 7.
349 15 U.S.C. § 7001(c)(6).
350 *See* § 9.2.10.7, *infra*; National Consumer Law Center, Consumer Banking and Payments Law § 9.6 (2d ed. 2002 and Supp.).
351 *See* 9.2.10.3.5, *infra* (discussion of states that have adopted UETA after E-Sign's passage); National Consumer Law Center, Consumer Banking and Payments Law § 9.5 (2d ed. 2002 and Supp.).
352 15 U.S.C. § 7001(b)(1). *See* Comments of Sen. Leahy, 106th Cong., 2d Session, 146 Cong. Rec. S. 5221 (June 15, 2000) ("the bill does not limit any legal requirement or prohibition other than those involving the writing, signature, or paper form of a contract").
353 UETA § 3(d).
354 UETA Prefatory note, Par. 3.
355 UETA Prefatory note, Sec. B.
356 15 U.S.C. § 7021; UETA § 16. *See* § 10.6.1.1, *infra*.
357 15 U.S.C. § 7003(a)(3); UETA § 3(b).

358 *See* National Consumer Law Center, Repossessions and Foreclosures §§ 3.2.3, 10.4.8 (5th ed. 2002 and Supp.).
359 15 U.S.C. § 7002(a). E-Sign also requires that such companion provisions make specific reference to E-Sign if they are passed after E-Sign was adopted. 15 U.S.C. § 7002(a)(2)(B).
360 *See* Statement of Congressman Bliley, the House sponsor of E-Sign, 106th Cong., 2d Sess., 146 Cong. Rec. H 4352–4355 (June 14, 2000); Statement of Sens. Hollings, Wyden and Sarbanes Regarding the Electronic Signatures in Global and National Commerce Act, 106th Cong., 2d Sess., 146 Cong. Rec. S 5229–5230 (June 15, 2000).
361 *See* National Consumer Law Center, Consumer Banking and Payments Law § 9.5.2.2 (2d ed. 2002 and Supp.).

9.2.10.3.2 States that have not passed a statute addressing electronic commerce

As of this writing, four states[362] have not passed a uniform version of UETA or any other technologically neutral statute that is consistent with E-Sign. In these states, E-Sign and only E-Sign applies.

9.2.10.3.3 States that passed non-uniform versions of UETA before E-Sign was adopted

Seventeen states[363] passed non-uniform versions of UETA prior to E-Sign. Since E-Sign can be displaced only by a uniform version of UETA or by another consistent, technologically neutral statute that specifically refers to E-Sign, E-Sign remains in effect in all of these states, and preempts at least certain portions of these statutes.[364] In particular, E-Sign's consumer consent provisions apply in these states.[365]

9.2.10.3.4 States that passed uniform versions of UETA before E-Sign was adopted

One state, Kentucky, passed a uniform version of UETA before E-Sign was adopted.[366] The passage of UETA in this state cannot be construed as opting out of a federal statute that had not been enacted at the time. This is particularly so since E-Sign does not confer on UETA any automatic displacement effect, but instead gives states the option of either displacing or preserving E-Sign when they adopt UETA.[367] Therefore, E-Sign probably applies in Kentucky.

9.2.10.3.5 States that passed UETA or other laws after E-Sign's adoption

The remaining states and the District of Columbia have all taken some legislative action since the adoption of E-Sign. In evaluating whether E-Sign's consumer protections apply in those states, the practitioner must determine:

- Did the state explicitly preserve E-Sign's consumer protections when it passed its new law? If it did, then those protections continue to apply.
- Did the state adopt a uniform version of UETA? If it did, then E-Sign allows that state to override E-Sign's consumer protection provisions. However, E-Sign can be interpreted to require that the state explicitly express its intention to supersede E-Sign, so the practitioner must also determine whether the state expressed such an intention.
- If the state adopted a non-uniform version of UETA, or another electronic commerce law, is the law technologically neutral and consistent with E-Sign, and does it make an express reference to E-Sign? Only if these questions are answered affirmatively can the new state law override E-Sign's consumer protections.

Sixteen of these states preserved E-Sign's consumer protections, either by declining to opt out of E-Sign or by passing their own version of those same protections.[368] It is clear that E-Sign's protections apply in these states.

Three states, Mississippi,[369] Missouri,[370] and Rhode Island,[371] adopted a uniform post E-Sign UETA without E-Sign's consumer protections, but did not indicate an express intent to displace the federal law. There is a strong argument that, without such an express statement of intent to displace E-Sign, it continues to apply in those states.[372]

One state, Delaware,[373] passed a version of UETA with significant non-uniformities after E-Sign's enactment. Since E-Sign provides that it is not displaced by such a law, it should be clear that E-Sign still applies in Delaware. Six

---

362 Georgia, Illinois, New York, and Washington.

363 Ariz. Rev. Stat. § 44-7001 *et seq.*; Cal. Civ. Code §§ 1633.1 to 1633.17; Fla. Stat. Ann. § 668.50 *et seq.*; Haw. Rev. Stat. § 489E-1 *et seq.*; Idaho Code § 28-50-101 *et seq.*; Ind. Code § 26-2-8-101 *et seq.*; Iowa Code § 554D.101 *et seq.*; Kan. Stat. Ann. § 16-1601 *et seq.*; Me. Rev. Stat. tit. 10, § 9401 *et seq.*; Minn. Stat. § 325L.01 *et seq.*; Neb. Rev. Stat. § 86-2101 *et seq.*; Ohio Rev. Code § 1306.01 *et seq.*; Okla. Stat. tit. 12A, § 15-101 *et seq.*; Pa. Stat. Ann. tit. 73, § 2260.101 *et seq.*; S.D. Codified Laws § 53-12-1 *et seq.*; Utah Code § 46-4-101 *et seq.*; Va. Code Ann. § 59.1-479 *et seq.*

364 *See* National Consumer Law Center, Consumer Banking and Payments Law §§ 9.2.8, 9.5.5.2.3 (2d ed. 2002 and Supp.).

365 *See* § 9.2.10.4, *infra.*

366 Ky. Rev. Stat. § 369.101 *et seq.* National Consumer Law Center, Consumer Banking and Payments Law § 9.5.5.2.2 (2d ed. 2002 and Supp.).

367 *See also* Statement of Sens. Hollings, Wyden and Sarbanes, 106th Cong., 2d Sess., 146 Cong. Rec. S 5229–30 (June 15, 2000) ("A state which passed UETA before the passage of this Act could not have intended to displace these federal law requirements. These states would have to pass another law to supersede or displace the requirements of section 101."); Statement of Rep. Bliley, 106th Cong., 2d Sess., 146 Cong. Rec. H 4353 (June 14, 2000) ("The preemptive effects of this Act apply to both existing and future statutes, regulations, or other rules of law enacted or adopted by a state. Thus, a state could not argue that section 101 does not preempt its statutes, regulations, or

other rules of law because they were enacted or adopted prior to the enactment of the Act.").

368 Ala. Code § 8-1A-2; Alaska Stat. § 09.80.010(c); Colo. Rev. Stat. § 24-71.3-102; Conn. Gen. Stat. § 1-266 *et seq.*; Md. Code Ann. Com. Law § 21-101; Mass. Gen. Laws ch. 110G, § 1 *et seq.*; Nev. Rev. Stat. § 719-010; N.H. Rev. Stat. Ann. § 294-E:1; N.J. Stat. Ann. § 12A:12-1; N.C. Gen. Stat. § 66-311; Or. Rev. Stat. § 84.001; S.C. Code Ann. § 26-6-10; Tenn. Code Ann. § 47-10-101; Vt. Stat. Ann. tit. 9, § 270 *et seq.*; W. Va. Code § 39A-1-1; Wis. Stat. § 137.12(2p), (2r). *See* National Consumer Law Center, Consumer Banking and Payments Law § 9.5.5.3.1 (2d ed. 2002 and Supp.).

369 Miss. Code Ann. §§ 75-21-1 *et seq.*

370 Mo. Rev. Stat. § 432.200.

371 R.I. Gen. Laws §§ 42-127.1-1 *et seq.* (adopted after E-Sign's enactment date, but before E-Sign's effective date).

372 *See* National Consumer Law Center, Consumer Banking and Payments Law § 9.5.5.4.5 (2d ed. 2002 and Supp.).

373 Del. Code Ann. tit. 6, §§ 101 *et seq.* (adds choice of forum provision).

states and the District of Columbia[374] adopted versions of UETA that are not completely uniform, but that have only minimal variations. Courts could conceivably hold that these state laws are, in fact, uniform. However, the legislative intent suggests that a state must pass an *exactly* uniform version of UETA in order to displace E-Sign, so the better view is that E-Sign is still in effect in these states.

Two states—Arkansas and Louisiana—adopted a uniform version of UETA and specifically indicated an intent to override E-Sign.[375] It is clear that E-Sign has been displaced in these two states.

9.2.10.4 E-Sign and UETA Consumer Consent Requirements

9.2.10.4.1 E-Sign

E-Sign overrides the requirement in many state credit statutes that the consumer be given a copy of the contract or other information in writing, but only if certain strict requirements are met.[376] First, the consumer must consent.[377] Prior to consenting, the consumer must be given a clear and conspicuous statement of:

- Any right or option to get the copy of the contract in non-electronic form;
- The right to withdraw consent and the procedures for and consequences of doing so;
- What transactions the consumer's consent applies to;
- The procedures for updating the information needed to contact the consumer electronically; and
- How, after consenting to electronic provision of the information, the consumer may get a paper copy, and whether any fee will be imposed.[378]

The consumer must also be given a statement of the hardware and software requirements for access to and retention of electronic records.[379]

Most importantly, the consumer must also either give consent electronically to receive the copy of the contract electronically, or must confirm consent electronically.[380] In either case, the consent or confirmation of consent must be done "in a manner that reasonably demonstrates that the consumer can access information in the electronic form that will be used to provide the information that is the subject of the consent."[381] This means that the consumer must demonstrate, not just affirm, that he or she has access to the equipment and programs necessary to receive, open, and read electronic documents from the creditor.[382] Unscrupulous creditors may to try to evade this requirement through use of creditor-owned Palm Pilots or in-house terminals, but this would hardly meet the requirement of "reasonably demonstrat[ing] that the consumer can access information in electronic form." Merely consenting on the creditor's computer should not be sufficient since the consumer cannot independently access the disclosure.

E-Sign also provides that the legal effect, validity, or enforceability of an electronic record may be denied if it is not in a form that is capable of being retained and accurately reproduced.[383] Thus, posting information on a website in a way that precludes downloading or printing will not satisfy a state law requirement that the information be provided to the consumer in writing.

9.2.10.4.2 UETA

UETA lacks E-Sign's specific consumer consent protections (although, as described in § 9.2.10.3.5, *supra*, many states preserved them when adopting UETA). However, it

---

374 D.C. Code Ann. § 28-4901 *et seq.* (omits severability clause); Mich. Comp. Laws § 450.831 *et seq.* (renames and reorganizes sections and deletes severability clause); Mont. Code Ann. § 30-18-101 *et seq.* (omits severability clause); N.M. Stat. Ann. § 14-16-1 *et seq.* (omits severability clause); N.D. Cent. Code § 9-16-01 *et seq.* (missing one definition); Tex. Bus. & Com. Code Ann. § 43.001 *et seq.* (missing one definition); Wyo. Stat. Ann. § 40-21-101 *et seq.* (adds a definition and omits severability clause). *See* National Consumer Law Center, Consumer Banking and Payments Law § 9.5.5.3.3 (2d ed. 2002 and Supp.).

375 Ark. Code Ann. § 25-32-101, *et. seq.*; La. Rev. Stat. Ann. § 9:2601, *et. seq.*

376 *See* National Consumer Law Center, Consumer Banking and Payments Law § 9.4 (2d ed. 2002 and Supp.) for a full discussion of these requirements.

377 15 U.S.C. § 7001(c)(1)(A).

378 15 U.S.C. § 7001(c)(1)(B).

379 15 U.S.C. § 7001(c)(1)(C)(i).

380 15 U.S.C. § 7001(c)(1)(C)(ii).

381 *Id. See* Statement of Sens. Hollings, Wyden and Sarbanes, 106th Cong., 2d Session, 146 Cong. Rec. S. 5224 (June 15, 2000) ("The Act requires that consumers consent electronically—or confirm their consent electronically—in either case, in a manner that allows the consumer to test his capacity to access and retain the electronic records that will be provided to him.").

382 *See* Comments of Sen. Wyden, 106th Cong., 2d Session, 146 Cong. Rec. S. 5216 (June 15, 2000) ("Reasonably demonstrates means just that. It means the consumer can prove his or her ability to access the electronic information that will be provided. It means the consumer, in response to an electronic vendor enquiry, actually opens an attached document sent electronically by the vendor and confirms that ability in an e-mail response. . . . It is not sufficient for the consumer merely to tell the vendor in an e-mail that he or she can access the information in the specified formats.") One exchange in the legislative history, between Senators McCain and Abraham, suggests that language in the consent form acknowledging that the consumer can access electronic information in the designated format would be sufficient, but this is clearly a misinterpretation, since the statute requires a "demonstration," not an acknowledgment, that the consumer can access the information. Colloquy between Sens. McCain and Abraham, 106th Cong., 2d Session, 146 Cong. Rec. S. 5282 (June 16, 2000). Even Senator Abraham's comments on the previous day indicated that the consumer must give an electronic demonstration of the ability to access the information. Statement of Sen. Abraham, 106th Cong., 2d Session, 146 Cong. Rec. S. 5224 (June 15, 2000).

383 15 U.S.C. § 7001(e).

does leave considerable room for evaluation of whether the consumer actually agreed to conduct the transaction electronically. UETA allows electronic transactions only if the parties to agree to conduct transactions by electronic means, which is determined "from the context and surrounding circumstances, including the parties' conduct."[384] Unlike E-Sign, UETA does not establish a separate standard for consumer transactions, but the fact that agreement is to be determined by the context means that different standards should be applied to consumer transactions and commercial ones. The comments to UETA section 5 are particularly explicit about the need to go behind the documents to determine whether there is actual consent.

9.2.10.5 Effect of E-Sign and UETA on Timing and Format Requirements

E-Sign states that it does not affect requirements regarding the content or timing of disclosures.[385] In addition, it states more generally that it has no effect on any state laws other than those requiring that contracts or other documents be written, signed, or in nonelectronic form.[386] The legislative history shows that Congress considered format requirements, such as a requirement that disclosures be clear and conspicuous, to be an example of a requirement that was unaffected by E-Sign.[387]

Some state credit statutes require that contracts, or portions of contracts, be printed in a certain size type. While it is not entirely clear how such a format requirement will be translated to electronic format, it is reasonable to interpret it as requiring that the words appear at least as large to a person sitting an average distance from a computer screen as words printed in the required type size would appear to the average reader.

Other state credit statutes require contract provisions to be "clear and conspicuous." To meet these standards, electronic disclosures should be easily readable from a monitor, organized logically, and free from distracting stimuli such as flashing advertisements or sounds. The FTC has issued detailed guidelines for evaluating whether an electronic

disclosure is clear and conspicuous that may be useful in evaluating this question.[388]

UETA provides that if a state law requires a document to contain information that is formatted in a certain manner, an electronic version must be formatted in that same manner.[389] This requirement cannot be waived.[390] UETA does not provide guidance about how format requirements are to be translated to electronic documents, but leaves this question to the courts or the legislature.[391]

9.2.10.6 Manner of Transmitting Electronic Credit Documents Under E-Sign and UETA

Only three provisions of E-Sign address the manner of transmission of electronic information. First, E-Sign provides that states that pass UETA cannot circumvent the federal statute by imposing nonelectronic delivery methods.[392] Second, E-Sign mandates that, where other law requires a document to be delivered in a way such as certified mail that produces an acknowledgment of receipt, then electronic documents must be delivered in a way that produces a similar acknowledgment.[393] Third, E-Sign directed the Department of Commerce to report to Congress regarding the effectiveness of electronic delivery methods as compared to delivery of written records via U.S. Mail and private express mail services.[394] E-Sign does not otherwise affect state law requirements about the manner of delivery of documents or information.[395]

UETA takes a similar approach. State laws that require information to be sent, communicated, or transmitted by a specified method apply to electronic documents.[396]

---

384 UETA § 5(b). *See* § 9.2.10.9, *infra.*
385 15 U.S.C. § 7001(c)(2)(A). *See also* 15 U.S.C. § 7001(b)(1) (E-Sign does not undermine any statutory or regulatory requirements other than those that require contracts or other records to be written, signed, or in nonelectronic form).
386 15 U.S.C. § 7001(b)(1).
387 *Accord* Statement of Rep. Dingell, 106th Cong., 2d Session, 146 Cong. Rec. H. 4358 (June 14, 2000). *See* Statement of Sens. Hollings, Wyden, and Sarbanes, 106th Cong., 2d Session, 146 Cong. Rec. S. 5230 (June 15, 2000) ("if a statute requires that a disclosure . . . include specific language set forth *clearly and conspicuously*, [t]hat requirement could be met by an electronic disclosure . . . which . . . included the specified language, set forth *clearly and conspicuously*").
388 FTC, Dot Com Disclosures (2000) at 5-14, available on the FTC's website at www.ftc.gov. *See* National Consumer Law Center, Consumer Banking and Payments Law § 9.7 (2d ed. 2002 and Supp.) for a more detailed discussion of standards of conspicuousness in electronic transactions.
389 UETA § 8(b)(3).
390 *Id.*
391 *See* UETA § 8 cmt. 4 ("If those legal requirements can be satisfied in an electronic medium, e.g., the information can be presented in the equivalent of 20 point bold type as required by other law, this Act will validate the use of the medium, leaving to the other applicable law the question of whether the particular electronic record meets the other legal requirements.").
392 15 U.S.C. § 7002(c).
393 15 U.S.C. § 7001(c)(2)(B).
394 15 U.S.C. § 7005(a). The Department of Commerce released a report in 2001 that cogently analyzes the lower reliability and higher cost to the consumer of electronic delivery methods. Department of Commerce, National Telecommunications and Information Administration, Report to Congress: Electronic Signatures in Global and National Commerce Act, Section 105(a) (June 2001), *available at* www.ntia.doc.gov/ntiahome/ntiageneral/esign/105a/esign105a.htm
395 *See* National Consumer Law Center, Consumer Banking and Payments Law § 9.8 (2d ed. 2002 and Supp.) for a fuller discussion of these issues and a discussion of the allocation of the burden of proving that an electronic document was delivered.
396 UETA § 8(b). The comments to this section state that if a law

State law requirements about delivery of documents will provide consumers some protections against creditors who, whether as a cost-cutting measure or to conceal onerous terms, merely post their credit terms on a website rather than actually giving them to the consumer. For example, a state law requirement that a copy of the contract be "delivered" to the consumer should be interpreted to mean that the consumer must actually receive it. Information posted to a website that the consumer has not actually accessed has not been "delivered." Likewise, information in an e-mail message that is sent to a consumer but is bounced back to the creditor, or is never opened, has not been delivered.

Even state law requirements that documents be mailed to the consumer are unaffected by E-Sign. While E-Sign prohibits states from imposing new nonelectronic delivery methods as a means of circumventing E-Sign,[397] it does not override or undercut existing requirements for the manner of delivering documents. If a state law requires a document to be delivered by first class or certified mail, for example, creditors would still have to deliver the document in that fashion regardless of E-Sign.

9.2.10.7 Document Integrity

Another important protection in E-Sign, and one that goes well beyond UETA, relates to the integrity, accessibility, and retainability of electronic documents. If a statute, regulation or other rule of law requires that a document be in writing, E-Sign provides that the legal effect, validity, or enforceability of the document may be denied if it is not in a form that is "capable of being retained and accurately reproduced for later reference by *all parties* or persons who are entitled to retain the contract or other record."[398] This requirement means that the document must be in "locked" form, so that neither party can alter it. Furthermore, it must be capable of accurate reproduction at a later date, which means that it must be in a form that is not inadvertently altered when, for example, the consumer opens the document. Finally, it must be in a form that enables the consumer to save the document.[399]

---

required a notice to be delivered by first class mail, a party who wanted to deliver an electronic document could mail a disk. If state law requires first class mail but allows the parties to vary this requirement by agreement, it may be varied by agreement for electronic documents also. UETA § 8(d)(2).

397 15 U.S.C. § 7002(c). *See* Statement of Sen. Leahy, 106th Cong., 2d Session, 146 Cong. Rec. S. 5222 (June 15, 2000) ("Section .102(c) prevents States that enact UETA from circumventing the federal legislation through the enactment of new nonelectronic delivery methods").

398 15 U.S.C. § 7001(e) (emphasis added). *See* National Consumer Law Center, Consumer Banking and Payments Law § 9.6 (2d ed. 2002 and Supp.).

399 A related provision of E-Sign provides that, if a law requires that documents be retained, they may be retained electronically as long as they are in a form that is capable of being accurately reproduced for later reference and is accessible to all persons

UETA's protections[400] are considerably weaker. First, UETA's document integrity rules apply only to documents that a law requires to be retained, not to those that are required to be in writing. This means that many documents that creditors are required to give to consumers may not be covered by UETA's document integrity rules. Second, UETA does not specify to whom electronic documents must remain accessible and accurately reproducible for later reference. Finally, in contrast to E-Sign,[401] UETA does not provide a sanction for failure to comply with the document integrity rules.

9.2.10.8 Validity and Enforceability of Electronic Contracts and Signatures Under E-Sign and UETA

E-Sign and UETA contain functionally identical language about the validity and enforceability of electronic contracts. E-Sign provides:

> Notwithstanding any statute regulation, or other rule of law . . . with respect to any transaction in or affecting interstate or foreign commerce (1) a signature, contract, or other record relating to such transaction may not be denied legal effect, validity, or enforceability *solely* because it is in electronic form; and (2) a contract relating to such transaction may not be denied legal effect, validity, or enforceability *solely* because an electronic signature or electronic record was used in its formation.[402]

UETA provides:

> (a) A record or signature may not be denied legal effect or enforceability *solely* because it is in electronic form.
> (b) A contract may not be denied legal effect or enforceability *solely* because an electronic record was used in its formation.
> (c) If a law requires a record to be in writing, an electronic signature satisfies the law.
> (d) If a law requires a signature, an electronic signature satisfies the law.[403]

The drafters of UETA envisioned it as taking a "minimalist and procedural" approach, deferring to existing substantive law.[404]

---

who are entitled to access by statute, regulation, or rule of law. 15 U.S.C. § 7001(d).

400 UETA § 12.

401 *See* 15 U.S.C. § 7001(e) (legal effect, validity, or enforceability of non-complying contract may be denied).

402 15 U.S.C. § 7001(a) (emphasis added). *See* National Consumer Law Center, Consumer Banking and Payments Law § 9.9 (2d ed. 2002 and Supp.).

403 UETA § 12 (emphasis added).

404 Prefatory Note to UETA, § B.

Neither E-Sign nor UETA limits the range of electronic signatures. An electronic signature could consist of a name typed at the end of a e-mail by a sender, a PIN number, a mouse click, pressing a number on a touch-tone telephone, or biometrics.

The term "solely" in both E-Sign and UETA is of great significance. Even if an electronic contract or signature meets all the requirements of E-Sign or UETA or both, the contract is not automatically valid and enforceable.[405] The practitioner should still evaluate all the usual questions about the contract. For example, do its substantive terms violate a state or federal law? Is it unconscionable? Does the creditor have any licenses the jurisdiction requires? Did the creditor commit fraud or violate the state deceptive practices statute in inducing the consumer to agree to the contract, or to agree to conduct the transaction electronically?

There are also particular issues regarding the validity of electronic contracts that the practitioner should evaluate. First, electronic documents are easily altered. Is the document that the creditor has produced the same as the document the consumer agreed to? When the consumer electronically signed the document, was the action creating the signature attached to or logically associated with the contract or other record? Can the seller prove that the document it has produced is the same as the one the consumer signed? E-Sign provides that an electronic contract or document may be denied legal effect, validity, or enforceability if it is not in a form that is capable of being retained and accurately reproduced for later reference by all parties or persons who are entitled to retain it.[406] In other words, the document must be change-proof and tamper-proof. UETA has similar, although weaker protections.[407]

Second, was there a true meeting of the minds as to the terms of the contract, including the agreement that it could be conducted electronically? As Senators Hollings, Wyden, and Sarbanes noted, "the validity of a consent obtained as the result of an unfair or deceptive practice can be challenged and found to be invalid, in which case any records which were provided electronically will be deemed to not have been provided to the consumer."[408] UETA makes it particularly clear that "[w]hether the parties agree to conduct a transaction by electronic means is determined from the context and surrounding circumstances, including the parties' conduct,"[409] not just by the contract. This implies much less reliance on the language of the contract than is usual. Indeed, the comments to UETA give an example of the absence of true agreement: a standard form contract in

which an agreement to receive all notices electronically is buried in fine print.[410] Electronic transactions raise additional questions about whether the consumer's mouse click was actually an expression of consent to the contract, or whether it was, for example, a misplaced attempt to link to a different page.

In addition, forgery or fraudulent assumption of the consumer's identity is particularly easy in an electronic environment. Thus it must also be determined whether the consumer in fact, rather than some unauthorized person, took whatever action was necessary to create the electronic signature.

9.2.10.9 Subsequent Notices

Many state and federal laws require creditors to provide information to consumers in writing after the initial consummation of the transaction. For example, in open-end credit the Truth in Lending Act requires the creditor to give written periodic statements to the consumer.[411] State open-end credit laws may contain similar requirements. Many state laws also require documents such as default notices, right to cure notices, receipts for payments, and statements of the balance still owing that are generated during the course of a closed-end credit transaction to be provided in writing.

Under E-Sign, documents subsequent to the consummation of the transaction that other law requires to be provided in writing can generally be provided electronically if that is part of the consumer's agreement. However, the consumer can withdraw consent at any time.[412] Further, if the creditor changes its hardware or software requirements for accessing or retaining its electronic records, it has to inform the consumer and go through E-Sign's consent procedures again.[413] If the consumer loses Internet access, so that the creditor's e-mails to the consumer bounce back, then new consent procedures are not required but the creditor will have a difficult time arguing that it has met state law delivery requirements.[414]

E-Sign's validation of electronic post-consummation notices has important additional exceptions. Of relevance to consumer credit transactions, it does not apply to notices of default, acceleration, repossession, foreclosure, eviction or the right to cure under a credit agreement secured by, or a

405 *In re* Piranha, Inc., 297 B.R. 78 (N.D. Tex. 2003), *aff'd*, 2003 WL 22922263 (5th Cir. Dec. 9, 2003).
406 15 U.S.C. § 7001(e). This requirement applies where state law would otherwise require the contract to be in writing.
407 UETA § 12.
408 Statement of Sens. Hollings, Wyden, and Sarbanes, 106th Cong., 2d Session, 146 Cong. Rec. S. 5229 (June 15, 2000).
409 UETA § 5.
410 UETA § 5 cmt. 5(A).
411 12 C.F.R. §§ 226.5(a)(1), 226.7, 226.9.
412 15 U.S.C. § 7001(c)(1)(A). *See* National Consumer Law Center, Consumer Banking and Payments Law § 9.2.2.3 (2d ed. 2002 and Supp.).
413 15 U.S.C. § 7001(c)(1)(D). *See* National Consumer Law Center, Consumer Banking and Payments Law § 9.4.6.4.1 (2d ed. 2002 and Supp.).
414 *See* National Consumer Law Center, Consumer Banking and Payments Law § 9.8.2 (2d ed. 2002 and Supp.).

441

rental agreement for, an individual's primary residence.[415] For these notices, E-Sign does not validate electronic delivery even if no state law explicitly requires that they be in writing. Further, for these notices, the consumer's consent or lack of consent is irrelevant: regardless of the consumer's consent, a creditor cannot rely upon E-Sign to validate electronic delivery.

Unlike E-Sign, UETA makes no special provision for important post-consummation notices of these types. If a state adopts UETA and displaces E-Sign, the question arises whether these notices can be delivered electronically. The legislative history specifically cautions states against using their opt-out authority to allow electronic provision of the listed documents,[416] and the National Conference of Commissioners on Uniform State Laws now recommends that states add the E-Sign exceptions when they adopt UETA.[417]

9.2.10.10 Practice Tips When Dealing with Electronic Credit Contracts

If a creditor is relying on a consumer's electronic consent to the credit terms, the consumer's attorney should investigate the following issues.

- Assuming that E-Sign has not been superseded by a state law, did the creditor follow the E-Sign's strict consent and confirmation-of-consent provisions? Did the consumer actually have the equipment necessary to receive the contract documents in electronic form? (These same questions should be asked in states that have displaced E-Sign but have incorporated E-Sign's consumer protections into their own laws.)
- Did the consumer actually receive and agree to the credit contract electronically? If the credit terms were merely posted on a website that the consumer never visited or were e-mailed to an incorrect e-mail address, then as a matter of contract law it is unlikely that the consumer will be bound by them. Neither E-Sign nor UETA has any effect on state contract law requirements.[418]
- Was the contract in a format that allowed retention and accurate reproduction for later reference by the consumer, and did the consumer actually have the equipment to keep it?[419]

- Did the electronic contract meet any state law requirements regarding type size, conspicuousness, proximity of particular terms to the consumer's signature, warnings and other content and format requirements?
- Did the consumer actually consent to the contract terms? If the transaction is governed by UETA, does an examination of all the circumstances of the transaction show true consent to electronic provision of the contract terms by the consumer? Consent to electronic provision of a contract that is buried in fine print in a transaction that is conducted on paper in other respects is unlikely to be effective under UETA.[420] In addition, the contract terms may be procedurally unconscionable.[421]

If it appears that the creditor violated any of these requirements, a computer expert should be consulted about preserving the evidence. While E-Sign requires that electronic records be in a form that is capable of being accurately reproduced for later reference,[422] an unscrupulous creditor can easily alter an electronic document, so the consumer needs to secure proof of the document in its unaltered state.

9.3 Statutory Construction

9.3.1 Applying General Rules of Interpretation

9.3.1.1 Broad vs. Narrow Construction of Usury Statutes: Invoking the History and Purpose of Usury Statutes

Usury is a statutory offense rather than an infraction of common law, and principles of statutory construction come into play in the many cases where the controlling usury statutes are vague or ambiguous.[423] Unfortunately, the mis-

---

415   15 U.S.C. § 7003(b)(2)(B).
416   *See* Statement of Sens. Hollings, Wyden, and Sarbanes, 106th Cong., 2d Session, 146 Cong. Rec. S. 5230 (June 15, 2000). *See* National Consumer Law Center, Consumer Banking and Payments Law § 9.2.2.3 (2d ed. 2002 and Supp.).
417   Memorandum to Standing Committee for UETA, Clearinghouse No. 53,549 (Aug. 2, 2001). *See* National Consumer Law Center, Consumer Banking and Payments Law § 9.1.3 (2d ed. 2002 and Supp.).
418   15 U.S.C. § 7001(b); Prefatory Note to UETA.
419   *See* 15 U.S.C. § 7001(e) (electronic documents may be denied

legal effect if they are not in a form that is capable of being retained and accurately reproduced by all parties); UETA § 8(a) (electronic documents must be capable of being retained by recipient). Even though UETA does not have a specific requirement regarding accurate reproduction of electronic documents, without such procedures a seller would have difficulty laying a foundation for introduction of the document into evidence.
420   *See* UETA § 5 cmt. 5(b).
421   *See* § 12.7, *infra*.
422   15 U.S.C. § 7001(e).
423   Note that statutory construction is only an issue when some ambiguity exists for a court to construe. If statutory language is clear it must be applied as written. *See* Rhodes v. Hartford, 513 A.2d 124 (Conn. 1986). *See also In re* Jordan, 91 B.R. 673 (Bankr. E.D. Pa. 1988) (statute governing late charge ambiguous as to whether allowed 1 1/2% calculated on full delinquent balance or 1 1/2% calculated on only delinquent installment; court looked to general principles of statutory and contract law to interpret).

understood history of usury has created confusion as to how one important principle of statutory construction applies—that statutes in derogation of common law are to be strictly construed. Moreover, two other basic tenets of statutory construction—the broad construction of remedial statutes, and the strict construction of penal statutes—conflict when applied to the typical usury statute.[424] This is particularly a conundrum with consumer credit, as statutes regulating the various cost components of consumer credit are typically part of a statute designed for the purpose of consumer protection.[425]

The fact that specific usury ceilings did not exist at common law can be misleading: to some it suggests that the interest restrictions contained in modern usury statutes are novel restrictions on previously unregulated lending and thus these restrictions should be narrowly construed because they would be in derogation of common law. In fact, at early common law it was forbidden to charge *any* interest at all, and common law recognized an action to recover usury (i.e., interest) paid.[426] The first usury statutes legalized the previously prohibited practice of charging interest on loans. Thus, usury statutes are actually in derogation of common law only to the extent that they *allow* the charging of interest, *not* to the extent that they restrict interest charges. Therefore, when applying the rule that statutes in derogation of common law should be strictly construed, one must conclude that it is the right to *charge* interest in modern usury statutes which should be strictly construed. Conversely restrictions on that right should be broadly interpreted.[427] However, many courts have never been presented with this line of reasoning, and thus are unaware that the English usury statutes *legalized* the charging of interest. They instead assume that these statutes created novel restrictions on lending, and they quote without much thought the dogma that usury statutes should be interpreted against borrowers because they are in derogation of common law.[428]

Once such conventional wisdom has become lodged in a state's case law, it can be difficult to dispel even though it is historically unfounded. However, it may be useful to try.

The conflict between the broad construction of remedial statutes and the narrow construction of penal statutes also may cloud statutory construction issues. Specifically, usury statutes are remedial to the extent that they seek to protect necessitous debtors from the exploitation of avaricious lenders[429] and to compensate debtors for the damages they have

---

424 See generally, Singer, Sutherland Statutory Construction § 70.07 (6th ed. 2003).

425 E.g., Iowa Code § 537.1102.

426 See § 10.8.2.2, infra.

427 See generally Dennis v. Bradbury, 236 F. Supp. 683 (D. Colo. 1964), aff'd, 368 F.2d 905 (10th Cir. 1966); Whitworth & Yancy v. Adams, 5 Rand. 333, 26 Va. 415 (1827) (no interest could be charged under common law); Federal-Mogul Corp. v. Dep't of Treasury, 411 N.W.2d 169 (Mich. App. 1987) (statutes allowing interest are in derogation of common law, thus court strictly construes statute to deny authority of Tax Tribunal to award interest on franchise fee refund in absence of specific statutory grant of such authority); Smith v. Mitchell, 616 A.2d 17 (Pa. Super. Ct. 1992) ("At common law the taking of any interest whatever was illegal, and the right to charge it, being a privilege granted by statute, is subject to legislative control."); Note, Interest Rates and the Law: A History of Usury, 1981 Ariz. St. L.J. 61; Horack, A Survey of the General Usury Laws, 8 Law and Contemp. Probs. 7 (1941).

428 E.g., Cullen v. Bragg, 350 S.E.2d 798 (Ga. Ct. App. 1986); Jacobson v. General Fin. Corp., 592 N.E.2d 1121 (Ill. App. Ct.

1992); Schuran, Inc. v. Walnut Hill Assocs., 606 A.2d 885 (N.J. Super. Ct. 1991).

429 See, e.g., Ghirardo v. Antonioli, 883 P.2d 960 (Cal. 1994) (purpose of usury law is " 'to protect the necessitous, impecunious borrower who is unable to acquire credit from the usual sources and is forced by his economic circumstances to resort to excessively costly funds to meet his financial needs.' "); Jersey Palm-Gross, Inc. v. Paper, 658 So. 2d 531, 534 (Fla. 1995) (purpose of usury laws is to "protect borrowers from paying unfair and excessive interest to overreaching creditors"; and "to bind the power of creditors over necessitous debtors and prevent them from extorting harsh and undue terms in the making of loans"); Nelson v. Associates Fin. Servs. Co., 659 N.W.2d 635 (Mich. Ct. App. 2002) (purpose of restrictions on prepayment penalties is to protect loan customers from being locked in to high interest rates); Watkins v. Mississippi Bar, 589 So. 2d 660 (Miss. 1991) (central purpose of usury law is to protect borrowers from overreaching creditors); Scarr v. Boyer, 818 P.2d 381, 383 (Mont. 1991) ("Usury statutes protect borrowers who lack real bargaining power against overreaching by creditors"); Schneider v. Phelps, 359 N.E.2d 1361, 1365 (N.Y. 1977) ("The purpose of usury laws, from time immemorial, has been to protect desperately poor people from the consequences of their own desperation. Law-making authorities in almost all civilizations have recognized that the crush of financial burdens causes people to agree to almost any conditions of the lender and to consent to even the most improvident loans. Lenders, with the money, have all the leverage; borrowers, in dire need of money have none."); Seidel v. 18 E. 17th St. Owners, 598 N.E.2d 7 (N.Y. 1992) (same); Car Now Acceptance Co. v. Block, 2003 WL 21714583 (Ohio Ct. App. July 14, 2003) (unpublished); Smith v. Mitchell, 616 A.2d 17 (Pa. Super. Ct. 1992) (purpose of usury law, which applied to business loans under $10,000, "to protect the citizenry ... from being exploited at the hands of unscrupulous individuals seeking to circumvent the law at the expense of *unsuspecting* borrowers who may have no other avenue to secure backing for a, for example, business venture"); Whitworth & Yancy v. Adams, 5 Rand 333, 335, 26 Va. 333 (1827) ("These statutes were made to protect needy and necessitous persons from the oppression of usurers and monied men, who are eager to take advantage of the distress of others; while they, on the other hand, from the pressure of their distress, are ready to come to any terms; and with their eyes open, not only break the law, but complete their ruin."). Demopolis v. Galvin, 786 P.2d 804, 807 (Wash. Ct. App. 1990) (purpose is to protect desperate borrowers "driven to borrow money at any cost"). *See also* Trapp v. Hancuh, 530 N.W.2d 879 (Minn. Ct. App. 1995) (purpose of usury laws is "to protect the weak and necessitous from being taken advantage of by lenders who can unilaterally establish the terms of the loan transaction"; distinguishing position of corporations, presumed to be in an equal bargaining position); Paulman v. Filtercorp, 899 P.2d 1259 (Wash. 1995) ("The evil at which the usury laws are aimed ... is the oppression of the borrower 'who

incurred through the payment of usurious interest. The remedial purposes indicate that ambiguous provisions should be broadly constructed to protect the consumer in usury statutes.[430] Moreover, consumer credit regulatory stat-

utes may specify that they are to be construed broadly to effectuate their ends, and such a specific statutory directive must supersede any contrary common law.[431]

On the other hand, many usury statutes go beyond compensating the victims of usury and impose penalties and forfeitures upon creditors who are guilty of usury. For example, many usury statutes prohibit a lender from collecting *any* interest on a usurious loan, and some forbid the recovery of principal. Such penalties or forfeitures are designed for their deterrent effect.[432] Without these penalties, a lender could charge usurious interest as a matter of course and simply refund the excess over the legal rate if challenged. Consequently, these remedies are penal, and their presence suggests that usury statutes should be strictly construed.[433] (Of course, some usury statutes carry greater penalties than others. As the degree of the penalty decreases, any need to construe usury statutes in favor of lenders also decreases.[434]) Similarly, a criminal usury statute, if susceptible of multiple interpretations, may be strictly construed in favor of the party facing liability.[435]

---

by adversity and necessity of economic life [is] driven to borrow money at any cost' ''; protecting vulnerable borrowers from oppression is the objective ([distinguishing business debtors]). *Cf.* Sunburst Bank v. Keith, 648 So. 2d 1147 (Miss. 1995) (purpose of usury statutes and its remedy of forfeiture "is to discourage exorbitance"; business loans at issue). *See generally* Steven W. Bender, *Rate Regulation at the Crossroads of Usury and Unconscionability: The Case for Regulating Abusive and Commercial Interest Rates Under the Unconscionability Standard*, 31 Houston L. Rev. 721 (1994).

430 *For cases adopting liberal construction of usury statutes because of their remedial purposes, see, e.g.,* GMAC v. Mid-West Chevrolet Co., 66 F.2d 1 (10th Cir. 1933); *In re* Feldman, 259 F. Supp. 218 (D. Conn. 1966); Agapitov v. Lerner, 133 Cal. Rptr. 2d 837, 838 (Ct. App. 2003); State v. Weiner, 28 A.2d 16 (Del. 1942); Liberty Fin. Co. v. Catterton, 161 Md. 650, 158 A.16 (1932) (small loan law); Williams v. Standard Fed. Sav. & Loan Ass'n, 545 A.2d 708 (Md. App. 1988) (Md. usury statute interpreted as remedial and not penal for purpose of applying statute of limitations); Nelson v. Associates Fin. Servs. Co., 659 N.W.2d 635 (Mich. Ct. App. 2002) (restrictions on prepayment penalties); Pease v. Taylor, 496 P.2d 757 (Nev. 1972); Tilley v. Pacesetter Corp., 585 S.E.2d 292, 298 (S.C. 2003) (applying pre-1997 version of statute); Income Tax Buyers, Inc. v. Hamm, 1992 WL 12092431 (S.C. Com. Pleas Jan. 14, 1992); Risica & Sons, Inc. v. Tubelite, 794 S.W.2d 468, 470 (Tex. Ct. App. 1990) (" . . . 'since the time of the code of Hammurabi . . . legislatures have imposed exceedingly harsh penalties for usury.' The statutes that the legislatures have enacted, which are penal in nature, are enacted for the protection of those who owe money. They were enacted for the prevention of unjust oppression by unscrupulous persons who are ready to take undue advantage of others"), *aff'd*, 819 S.W.2d 801 (Tex. 1991); Valley Acceptance Corp. v. Glasby, 337 S.E.2d 291 (Va. 1985) (small loan law); Radford v. Community Mortgage & Inv. Corp., 312 S.E.2d 282 (Va. 1984); Dunlap v. Friedman's, Inc., 582 S.E.2d 841 (W. Va. 2003) (West Virginia Consumer Credit and Protection Act); State v. J.C. Penny Co., 179 N.W.2d 641 (Wis. 1970). *See also* Brown v. Courtesy Consumer Discount Co., 134 B.R. 134 (Bankr. E.D. Pa. 1991) ("Because of the fertility of the minds of those who would devise schemes to circumvent remedial consumer protection laws, these laws must be interpreted with a flexibility necessary to preserve their spirit."); *In re* Jordan, 91 B.R. 673 (Bankr. E.D. Pa. 1988) (where statute and contract were ambiguous as to whether 1 1/2% late charge on full delinquent balance or only on each delinquent installment, policy against compounding interest, pyramiding late charges, excessive penalty clauses, suggests statute should be read to limit it to 1 1/2% of installment; state department of banking's informal opinion to the contrary in amicus brief not persuasive where agency considered none of the above principles and had not issued a formal interpretation; fact that industry practice was to interpret it to allow 1 1/2% of full balance also not persuasive: "[i]t is not surprising that interested, sophisticated lenders consistently interpret ambiguous laws to their own advantage and to the disadvantage of their obviously less-sophisticated customers. This data only highlights the need of the disinterested courts to be vigilant to prevent industry-wide overreaching." *Id.* at 688); Hammelburger v. Foursome Inn Corp., 431 N.E.2d 278 (N.Y. 1980) (criminal usury ceilings created to

protect society as a whole "from loan-sharking, 'one of the most heinous, virtually blood-sucking criminal activities of all times.' "). *Cf.* Sunburst Bank v. Keith, 648 So. 2d 1147 (Miss. 1995) (remedy of forfeiture imposed; purpose "is to discourage exorbitance"; business loans).

See generally Annot., 43 A.L.R.4th 675 at §§ 3–4 (1986) (construction and application of second mortgage statutes).

431 *E.g.,* Iowa Code § 537.1102. *See* text accompanying notes 438–446, *infra. See generally* 17 Am. Jur. 2d Consumer Protection § 282 (2004) (state credit construed to effectuate purpose and courts strict in requiring compliance).

432 *See, e.g.,* Seidel v. 18 E. 17th St. Owners, 598 N.E.2d 7 (N.Y. 1992) (New York's severe penalty of voiding the loan reflects legislative view that severe "consequences are necessary to deter the evils of usury.").

433 For cases adopting strict construction of usury laws because of their penal nature, *see, e.g.,* Thrift v. Hubbard, 44 F.3d 348 (5th Cir. 1995); Allied Chem. Corp. v. Jack MacKay, 695 F.2d 854 (5th Cir. 1983); Morosani v. First Nat'l Bank of Atlanta, 539 F. Supp. 1171 (N.D. Ga. 1982), *rev'd on other grounds*, 703 F.2d 1220 (11th Cir. 1983); Anderson v. Chainani (*In re* Kemper) 263 B.R. 773 (E.D. Tex. 2001); Indian Springs State Bank v. Kelley's Auto Supply, Inc., 675 P.2d 379 (Kan. App. 1984); Ranson v. C.A. Snyder, 75 So. 2d 738 (Miss. 1954); Crisman v. Corbin, 128 P.2d 959 (Or. 1942); Maners v. Lexington County Sav. & Loan Ass'n, 267 S.E.2d 422 (S.C. 1980); Standard Sav. Ass'n v. Greater New Canaan Missionary Baptist Church, 786 S.W.2d 774 (Tex. Ct. App. 1990); Swank v. Sverdlin, 121 S.W.3d 785 (Tex. App. 2003); Domizio v. Progressive County Mut. Ins. Co., 54 S.W.3d 867 (Tex. App. 2001).

434 *See In re* Russell, 72 B.R. 855 (Bankr. E.D. Pa. 1987) (distinguishing penalty of three times the excess charges actually paid from more severe penalties of automatic forfeiture of principal and/or interest).

This difference in the amount of damage for which the creditor is liable led one court to distinguish a statutory usury claim (penal) from a common law usury claim (remedial): the former made the debtor more than whole, while the latter simply entitled the borrower to recover illegally taken property. Demopolis v. Galvin, 786 P.2d 804 (Wash. Ct. App. 1990).

435 Glinton v. And R, Inc., 524 S.E.2d 481 (Ga. 1999); Fleet Fin., Inc.

The conflict between these two principles of statutory construction, when applied to usury statutes, promotes a standard litigation posture in usury cases in which the borrower emphasizes the remedial purposes of usury laws, the lender claims strict construction, and each side cites plentiful authority to support its position. The result is a legal deadlock which effectively leaves the court free to construe usury statutes as it wishes, and usury decisions which involve any degree of statutory construction frequently seem based as much on the equities of the case or the predisposition of the court as on any compelling logical reason for choosing one rule of construction over another.[436]

Nevertheless consumer attorneys should not be dissuaded from arguing issues of statutory construction. First, if a creditor's argument for strict construction goes unrebutted, it many be accepted automatically by the court. Second, even if marginal usury cases are actually resolved by equitable considerations, a court which is predisposed to find in favor of a consumer will want legal principles and precedent to hang its hat on, and it is the obligation of a debtor's attorney to provide them. Finally, and most importantly, the resolution of individual usury cases depends on the interpretation of individual usury statutes, not on observations of the nature of usury laws in general, and there are sound reasons to argue that the particular usury statutes most often involved in consumer cases—small loan laws, installment sales acts, second mortgage acts and consumer credit codes—are distinguishable from general usury statutes and should be more liberally construed.[437]

General usury statutes were, for the most part, adopted prior to the twentieth century at a time when consumer credit was limited, almost to the point of non-existence.[438] The consumer loans that did exist were made by loan sharks, and the limited number of consumer credit sales which existed were beyond the scope of usury laws because of the time-price doctrine. Instead, usury statutes were primarily concerned with commercial transactions which, both then and now, have many different characteristics from consumer credit. Most significantly, commercial transactions are far more likely than consumer transactions to occur after detached consideration and after arm's length bargaining over both interest rate and other credit terms.[439] Furthermore, the payment of usurious interest by a business, while serious, will not directly cause the same individual loss or hardship that may be suffered by a consumer who is the victim of usury. Consequently, it is not surprising that nineteenth and early twentieth century courts, interpreting general usury statutes in a commercial setting, construed those statutes narrowly, preferring to limit the government's role in private contracts, especially in light of the serious consequences of a usury violation for the lender.

So-called special usury laws, such as small loan laws, industrial bank acts, retail installment sales acts, and second mortgage acts, almost all of which have been enacted since the 1920s, are clearly distinguishable. Small loan laws, for example, many of which are still in effect in some form, were specifically aimed at protecting individual borrowers.[440] As originally structured, they attempted to displace the monopoly of the loan sharks by luring commercial investors to the small loan market. The general approach was to allow interest rates which, especially by the standards of the day, were extremely generous to lenders, in return for strict licensing and regulation to prevent the recurrence of loansharking.[441]

The structure and purposes of many special usury statutes such as small loan laws can enable practitioners to distinguish commercial usury cases decided under general usury statutes, and to argue that the more carefully targeted special

of Georgia v. Jones, 430 S.E.2d 352 (Ga. 1993). *Cf.* Hartsfield Co. v. Fulwiler, 200 S.E. 309 (Ga. 1938) (in which the court, interpreting identical language in the Small Loan Act, reached the opposite result in a civil collection case, though the remedy therein was the "penal" one of voiding the loan. See the dissent in *Fleet Finance* for a discussion of the seeming inconsistency). *But see* Hammelburger v. Foursome Inn Corp., 431 N.E.2d 278 (N.Y. 1980) (criminal usury ceilings created to protect society as a whole "from loan-sharking, 'one of the most heinous, virtually blood-sucking criminal activities of all times.' ").

436　*See, e.g.,* Amaro v. Capital One Bank, 1998 U.S. Dist. LEXIS 8373 (N.D. Ill. May 19, 1998) (in construing Virginia law in the exportation context, an Illinois court opted for the position argued by the bank, i.e., the provision in Virginia law relating to revolving accounts which permitted banks to charge any "charges and fees" as agreed to by the parties applied; in contrast, another provision specifically involving late fees (the issue in the lawsuit) which arguably applied to all credit transactions and limited the fee to 5% of the late installment, though providing greater consumer protection, was rejected). A later Virginia Supreme Court decision, Perez v. Capital One Bank, 522 S.E.2d 874 (Va. 1999), answering a question certified to it by the federal court, held that the statute allowing any late fee agreed upon also overrode common law restrictions on late fees.

437　An example of a type of special usury law where liberal construction in favor of consumers is clearly the rule is the second mortgage statute. *See* Annot., 43 A.L.R.4th 675 at §§ 3–4 (1986) (construction and application of second mortgage statutes). *See also* Chroniak v. Golden Investment Corp., 577 A.2d 1209, 1213 (N.H. 1990) (purpose of act is to protect

homeowners finding themselves "forced to go into a second mortgage").

438　For a discussion of the development of consumer credit legislation, see generally § 2.2, *supra. See also* Curran, Trends in Consumer Credit Legislation (1966). *See also* Curran, *Legislative Controls as a Response to Consumer-Credit Problems,* 8 B.C. Ind. & Comm. L. Rev. 409 (1966–67).

439　*See* Curran, *Legislative Controls as a Response to Consumer-Credit Problems,* 8 B.C. Ind. & Com. L. Rev. 409, 427 *et seq.* (1966–67).

440　*See, e.g.,* Aros v. Beneficial Arizona, Inc., 977 P.2d 784 (Ariz. 1999).

441　*Id.* at 410–412. Seeing small loans currently at rates exceeding 200% in states which deregulated in the 1980s, one can only assume that the small loan acts, while they were in effect, did achieve their purpose. Without them, things have come full circle in this century for the borrower of small sums. *See* § 2.4.3, *supra.*

usury laws should be broadly construed to give effect to their remedial purposes, despite their penal provisions. Typically, the best way to evaluate the purposes of any one special usury statute is to examine the language of the statute itself. Such statutes frequently contain statements of legislative purpose which reveal remedial goals. For example, the declaration of legislative intent in the Seventh Draft of the Uniform Small Loan Law, which regulated loans of $300 or less, discusses the inadequacy of previously existing usury laws in governing small loans, recognizes the exorbitant charges, fraud, and oppressive collection practices prevalent among such loans, and specifies that legislation to control this class of loans is necessary to protect the public welfare.[442] This statute remains at the core of many contemporary consumer loan acts and that statement of purpose likewise remains.[443] Similarly, the Uniform Consumer Credit Code contains a statement of purpose which, although vastly more qualified than that of the Uniform Small Loan Law, inherently recognizes the need for special consumer credit legislation, specifies that one purpose of the UCCC is "to protect consumers against unfair practices by some suppliers of consumer credit, having due regard for the interest of legitimate and scrupulous creditors," and instructs that the Act "be liberally construed and applied to promote its underlying purposes and policies."[444]

Express statements of legislative intent or, in their absence, records of legislative history, can be used in several ways to distinguish the treatment courts should give special usury statutes from the traditional strict construction of general usury statutes. First, if a statute says that it is remedial and should be broadly construed, it is a simple matter to argue that this legislative intent should be respected. Second, special usury laws inherently recognize the existence of special classes of transactions or borrowers, and these statutes should be interpreted as reaching all of the transactions or borrowers in the protected class unless an exception was clearly intended by the legislature.[445] Third,

the enactment of special usury laws when a general usury statute is already in force clearly indicates the inadequacy of the pre-existing law either as written or as applied. Thus, rules of construction applied to pre-existing usury statutes need not automatically control the construction of the new statute. Finally, in the case of credit sales, it may be possible to argue that installment sales acts are technically not "usury" statutes and should not be interpreted as such because usury laws did not historically apply to credit sales under the time-price doctrine.[446]

9.3.1.2 *Expressio Unius Est Exclusio Alterius*: Limiting the Creditor's Ability to Add Extra Charges Not Specifically Authorized

As is discussed elsewhere in this manual,[447] creditors may try to increase their return by adding non-interest fees to a loan, and one statutory construction principle may be especially useful in challenging them as hidden interest. *Expressio unius est exclusio alterius*[448] is an important one to remember in interpreting usury statutes, particularly special usury statutes such as those with roots in Small Loan Acts. Current versions of small loan acts, (also called regulated loan acts or consumer loan acts), second mortgage laws or some retail installment sales acts have provisions similar to one in the Uniform Small Loan Act:

> In addition to the interest [or charges] herein provided for, no further or other charge or amount for any examination, service, brokerage, expense, fee, or bonus or otherwise shall be directly or indirectly charged, contracted for, or received.[449]

---

442 Seventh Draft of the Uniform Small Loan Law § 1(a) (as Revised June 1, 1942) *reprinted in* Curran, Trends in Consumer Credit Legislation p.144 *et seq.* (1966). *See also In re* Rose, 266 B.R. 192 (Bankr. N.D. Cal. 2001) (applying liberal construction mandate of California's Finance Lenders Law).

443 Most states have raised the threshold loan size significantly, and many have modernized the statute somewhat, but frequently much of the model act's purpose and thrust remains.

444 U.C.C.C. § 1.02 (1974 Model Code); Idaho Code § 28-41-102; Iowa Code § 537.1102; S.C. Code Ann. § 37-1-102. *See* State *ex rel.* Salazar v. Cash Now Store, Inc., 31 P.3d 161 (Colo. 2001) (citing and applying rule of liberal construction).

445 *See* Rhodes v. Hartford, 513 A.2d 124 (Conn. 1986) (broad construction of pawnbroker statute to protect those who must have recourse to pawnbrokers). *Cf.* Browner v. District of Columbia, 549 A.2d 1107 (D.C. 1988) (in case involving criminal prosecution under Loan Sharking Statute of unlicensed lenders engaged in sale/leaseback transactions with persons facing mortgage foreclosures, defendants argued transactions should not be viewed as loans because some "borrowers" were

comparatively well-educated; court reminded defendant that purpose of usury and loan-sharking laws was to protect persons from the consequences of their financial desperation: "Lenders with the money, have all the leverage; borrowers, in dire need of money, have none").

446 *See, e.g.*, Barco Auto Leasing Corp. v. House, 520 A.2d 162 (Conn. 1987) (liberal construction of Installment Sales Financing Act to promote its remedial purpose). Although the distinction between credit extended in sales as opposed to loans may not make much sense, and although installment sales acts are treated as just a variety of usury statute throughout most of this manual, nevertheless the distinction between "loans," to which "usury" statutes apply, and sales, to which they may not, is firmly established in the case law of many states, and consumers might as well play the distinction for what it is worth in the few instances when it may operate in the consumer's favor.

447 Ch. 7 (hidden interest), Ch. 8 (credit insurance), and § 9.2.5, *supra*.

448 Expression of one thing is the exclusion of another. Black's Law Dictionary 620 (8th ed. 2004). *See generally* Singer, Sutherland Statutory Construction §§ 47.23–47.24 (6th ed. 2000).

449 Sixth Draft of Uniform Small Loan Law, § 13, *reprinted in* Hubacheck, Annotations on Small Loan Laws, 70–80 (1938). *See, e.g.*, Alaska Stat. § 06.20.260; Ohio Rev. Stat. § 1321.13(G); Va. Code § 6.1-278.

The statutes then specifically list certain types of charges which the creditor can impose on the transaction. The language certainly signals that the list of authorized charges is an exhaustive list, not an illustrative listing. Thus the principle that the express mention of one thing implies the exclusion of others would dictate that no other costs should be permitted.[450]

9.3.1.3 Deference to Administrative Interpretations

Another principle of statutory construction that arises in usury cases is that courts will defer to the interpretation of a statute by an agency that is charged with administering it.[451] This principle sometimes helps consumers but some-

times hurts them. If the state agency that regulates financial institutions is overly friendly to the industry, its interpretations may be unhelpful to consumers.

In dealing with unhelpful agency interpretations, it should be remembered that the court should defer to an agency's interpretation only if the statute is ambiguous.[452] There is also authority for the proposition that a court engaged in constitutional scrutiny will not defer to an agency's interpretation.[453] This limitation is particularly important in states that include a usury ceiling in their state constitutions. Finally, where an agency has been inconsistent in its interpretation of a statute, its opinion will be entitled to less deference.[454] Mere inaction by a regulatory agency, such as failure to prohibit a creditor's practice, is not entitled to any deference as an administrative interpretation.[455]

Some states have codified the deference to agency interpretations by giving lenders a safe harbor if they rely on an agency interpretation.[456] A lender can only rely on an agency interpretation that is in existence, so one issued after the transaction in question cannot protect the lender.[457]

9.3.2 Retroactive Amendment of Usury Statutes

9.3.2.1 General Standards

The 1970s and 1980s were a time of dramatic changes in usury law. During this period, all states modified their consumer credit statutes to some extent, and, because of rising market interest rates during the late 1970s and early

---

450 *See, e.g., Ex parte* New Fin., Ltd., 225 So. 2d 784 (Ala. 1969); Sunderland v. Day, 145 N.E.2d 39 (Ill. 1957); Home Fin. Co. v. Padgett, 54 So. 2d 813 (La. Ct. App. 1951); Hawkins v. Thorp Credit & Thrift Co., 441 N.W.2d 470 (Minn. 1989) (where statute specifically authorized only sale of credit insurance, creditor was not authorized to sell noncredit life insurance policies as part of credit transactions); Wombold v. Associates Fin. Servs. Co., 104 P.3d 1080 (Mont. 2004) (where statute allowed any interest rate but no other charges, creditor could not charge points); Garrison v. First Fed. Saving & Loan Ass'n of S.C., 402 S.E.2d 25 (Va. 1991) (risk management fees not listed as a permissible charge for junior mortgage loans, and therefore was an illegal charge); Opinion of the Kansas Att'y Gen. No. 87-3, Consumer Cred. Guide (CCH) ¶ 95,980, 1987 Kan. AG LEXIS 194 (Jan. 9, 1987); *modified by* Opinion of the Kansas Att'y Gen., No. 87-47, Consumer Cred. Guide (CCH) ¶ 95,981, 1987 Kan. AG LEXIS 149 (Mar. 12, 1987) (cannot sell property insurance except on property subject to valid security interest under statute); Opinion of the Michigan Att'y Gen., No. 6594, Consumer Cred. Guide (CCH) ¶ 95,775, 1989 Mich. AG LEXIS 38 (July 17, 1989) (documentary fees, service fees or inspection fees added to cash price on installment car purchase not specifically enumerated as authorized charge, and were therefore prohibited; note that the specific provisions regarding documentary charges have since been repealed); Byrd v. Crosstate Mortg. and Investments, Inc., 34 Va. Cir. 17, 1994 Va. Cir. LEXIS 38 (1994). *But cf.* Alston v. Crown Auto, Inc., 224 F.3d 332 (4th Cir. 2000) (only charges imposed up front, not late charges, are interest); Luttenegger v. Conseco Fin. Servicing Corp., 671 N.W.2d 425 (Iowa 2003) (where Iowa U.C.C.C. capped finance charges at 21% and finance charge was defined broadly rather than limited to certain types of charges, creditor could assess a charge that was not listed as long as total charge was within the cap); S.C. Dept. of Consumer Affairs v. Rent-A-Center, Inc., 547 S.E.2d 881 (S.C. App. 2001) (where RTO statute does not specify allowable charges, creditor may impose other charges).

451 *See, e.g.,* Babbitt v. Sweet Home Chapter, 515 U.S. 687, 115 S. Ct. 2407, 132 L. Ed. 2d 597 (1995); Chevron U.S.A., Inc. v. National Resources Defense Council, 467 U.S. 837, 104 S. Ct. 2778, 81 L. Ed. 2d 694 (1984); Betts v. Ace Cash Express, Inc., 827 So. 2d 294 (Fla. Dist. Ct. App. 2002) (giving weight to advisory opinion issued by state Department of Banking and Finance); Hathaway v. First Family Fin. Servs., 1 S.W.3d 634 (Tenn. 1999) (agency's interpretation of state usury law would be persuasive if statute were ambiguous). *But see* Luttenegger v. Conseco Fin. Servicing Corp., 671 N.W.2d 425 (Iowa 2003) (giving no deference to chart published by agency showing what

fees were allowed, where chart did not reveal agency's analysis and contained disclaimer that it was not the law).

452 Food and Drug Admin. v. Brown & Williamson Tobacco Co., 529 U.S. 120, 120 S. Ct. 1291, 146 L. Ed. 2d 121 (2000) ("[a]lthough agencies are generally entitled to deference in the interpretation of statutes that they administer, a reviewing court, as well as the agency, must give effect to the unambiguously expressed intent of Congress"); Hathaway v. First Family Fin. Servs., 1 S.W.3d 634 (Tenn. 1999).

453 Miller v. Johnson, 515 U.S. 900, 115 S. Ct. 2475, 132 L. Ed. 2d 762 (1995).

454 Good Samaritan Hosp. v. Shalala, 508 U.S. 402, 113 S. Ct. 2151, 124 L. Ed. 2d 368 (1993). *See also* Independent Fin. Inst. v. Clark, 990 P.2d 845 (Okla. 1999) (court agrees with agency's new interpretation of statute, based on AG opinion, which departed from interpretation it had accepted for 27 years; court makes its ruling effective only from date agency issued its new interpretation). *Cf.* Smiley v. Citibank (South Dakota), N.A., 517 U.S. 735, 116 S. Ct. 1730, 135 L. Ed. 2d 25 (1996) (according deference to newly-minted agency interpretation even though it was inconsistent with prior less formal expressions of agency's views).

455 Wombold v. Associates Fin. Servs. Co., 104 P.3d 1080 (Mont. 2004).

456 *See, e.g.,* Alexander v. PSB Lending Corp., 800 N.E.2d 984 (Ind. App. 2003) (interpreting Ind. U.C.C.C. § 24-4.5-6-104).

457 *Id.*

1980s, these modifications often included increases in, or even the abolition of contract interest ceilings. Statutes regulating non-interest fees, rebate requirements, and prepayment penalties also were altered in many jurisdictions.

Due to the frequency of statutory amendments affecting legally permissible interest rates, the effective dates of such amendments were a common subject of litigation. Creditors whose conduct violated existing usury statutes claimed that subsequent amendments to those statutes retroactively validated the theretofore illicit practices. Many courts accepted this argument.[458]

The retroactive application of laws in general runs contrary to principles of American jurisprudence. *Ex post facto* laws are expressly prohibited by the U.S. Constitution.[459] However, it is recognized that the *ex post facto* prohibition applies only to criminal statutes,[460] and that Congress or the states may adopt civil statutes with retrospective effect so long as other constitutional limitations are respected. Most notably for the purposes of usury amendments, retrospective statutes may not impair the obligation of existing contracts,[461] and may not deny due process.[462]

It is fairly clear, however, that the retroactive repeal of a usury statute or the retroactive increase of a usury ceiling does not unconstitutionally infringe on a borrower's rights. The leading decision on this point is *Ewell v. Daggs*[463] in which the U.S. Supreme Court gave retroactive effect to an amendment to the state constitution of Texas which abolished usury statutes regulating written contracts in that state. The court ruled that the retroactive application of such a repeal did not deprive the borrower of vested rights or impair the obligation of contract because the statute merely removed the borrower's right to avoid an otherwise valid contractual obligation. The court reasoned that, despite the declaration in the previously existing Texas usury statute that usurious obligations were "void" as to interest, such language indicated that the contract was merely voidable.[464]

Moreover, because the usury statute invoked by the borrower had been penal in nature, the court stated that the retroactivity of the repeal should be presumed in the absence of a savings clause. Thus, a borrower's statutory right to usury forfeitures and penalties remains very vulnerable to legislative action until that right is reduced to final judgment,[465] and thereby becomes "vested." (Precisely when a judgment becomes final for purposes of usury amendments is an issue of individual state law,[466] but it is fairly clear that a lower court ruling does not constitute final judgment while appeal is pending.[467])

The *Ewell* decision has been widely cited and applied in the past century. In cases considering the retrospective application of usury amendments, it is almost a matter of black letter law that usury statutes are penal,[468] that a borrower has no vested right in penalties or forfeitures, and that an otherwise usurious contract may be retroactively validated by legislative action until the borrower has obtained a final judgment. A majority of the state courts that

---

This distinction carries some plausibility because usury statutes which invalidate only interest implicitly recognize that the remainder of the usurious contract—the obligation to repay principal—is legally sound and enforceable. If, however, a statute declares a transaction completely void from its inception and never recognizes that any contractual obligation of the borrower ever existed, then the reasoning in *Ewell* (i.e., a contractual obligation remains in effect during the term of the usurious contract, but that this obligation is merely unenforceable due to the usury statute), would not apply.

Moreover, some state courts have specifically held that the complete voiding of a loan is not a "penalty," Szerdahelyi v. Harris, 490 N.E.2d 517 (N.Y. 1986), which knocks down another of the underpinnings of the *Ewell* decision. *But see* Moran v. Am. Funding, Ltd., 569 A.2d 841 (N.J. Super. 1989) (prior legislation which declared usurious loan void as unenforceable was amended to provide for lesser penalty; court held the amendment retroactive).

Despite the theoretical limitations in the reasoning of *Ewell*, it is unlikely at this late date that the *Ewell* decision will be limited in any significant way by modern courts. The decision has already been widely accepted and broadly applied. Furthermore, the void and voidable distinction between various usury statutes has been criticized by at least one court. *See* American Sav. Life Ins. Co. v. Financial Affairs Mgmt. Co., 513 P.2d 1362 (Ariz. App. 1973).

---

458   *But see* Merritt v. Knox, 380 S.E.2d 160, 162 (N.C. Ct. App. 1989) ("majority rule" is that "changes in the legal rate will not be applied retroactively"); Arguelles v. Kaplan, 736 S.W.2d 782 (Tex. Ct. App. 1987) (settled rule that question of usury is determined at inception of contract; subsequent change in permissible rate will not validate it).

459   U.S. Const. art. 1 § 10 clause 1.

460   *See generally* Annot., 53 L. Ed. 2d 1146 (1978) (Supreme Court's views on scope of ex post facto clause).

461   U.S. Const. art. 1 § 10 cl. 1.

462   U.S. Const. Amendments 5, 14.

463   108 U.S. 143 (1883).

464   The Texas statute merely declared a usurious loan void as to interest. It did not remove the lender's right to recover principal. In light of this fact and in light of the court's indication that acts which are *mala prohibita* (prohibited by statute) may be void or voidable, depending on the nature and effect of the act prohibited, it is possible to argue that *Ewell* should be limited to the repeal of those usury statutes which, like the Texas statute in *Ewell*, do not render the contract void as to both principal and interest.

465   *See, e.g.*, Jacobson v. General Fin. Corp., 592 N.E.2d 1121 (Ill. App. Ct. 1992) (amendment legalizing use of Rule of 78 applied retroactively); L.E. Marlowe & Sons, Ltd. v. Farner, 406 N.W.2d 273 (Mich. App. 1987) (amendment expanding business exemption enacted five years after transaction extinguished borrower's usury defense to obligation).

466   *In re* Lara, 731 F.2d 1455 (9th Cir. 1984).

467   *See* Chapman v. Farr, 183 Cal. Rptr. 606 (App. 1982). *See also* Clouse v. Heights Fin. Corp., 510 N.E.2d 1 (Ill. App. 1987) (amendment solely affecting remedies for violation of Consumer Installment Loan Act, with no savings clause, applied retroactively). For relevant discussion of final judgment under Georgia law, see Dorsey v. West, 311 S.E.2d 816 (1984) (judgment had become final).

468   *But see* § 9.3.1.1, *supra*.

have considered the issue of retroactivity have followed precisely this line of reasoning.[469]

Yet, despite the wide application of *Ewell*, modifications of usury laws are not universally given retroactive effect. The main reason for this fact is that, as *Ewell* itself recognized, the effective date of any statute is decided first and foremost by legislative intent. If a usury statute expressly states in a savings clause that its application should be prospective only, or that it should not affect pending litigation, then that statute clearly should not be given retroactive effect, although the precise scope of such savings clauses is often disputed.[470] Note that, *Ewell* notwithstanding, the presence of a savings clause is not a prerequisite to finding that a legislature intended to amend a usury statute prospectively.[471]

When the legislative intent regarding the effective date of a usury statute is not clear, a few courts have given the relevant statute only prospective effect,[472] despite the statement in *Ewell* that retrospective effect should be presumed under these circumstances.[473] The reason is that, as suggested previously in this subsection, retroactive legislation goes against the grain of American jurisprudence. In many states, a strong presumption exists under state law that statutes operate only prospectively unless the legislature expressly indicates otherwise. Such presumptions developed in non-usury cases have been sufficiently strong in some states to refute the opposite presumption stated in *Ewell* which is, after all, merely persuasive authority on the issue of legal presumptions under state law.

Practitioners should check their state constitutions and state laws to determine whether, as a matter of state law, there are any limitations to the state legislature's ability to apply a statutory change retroactively. Alabama's constitution, for example, contains a section that essentially prohibits retroactive application of a statutory change to any suits that have been filed before the passage of the change.[474] This provision effectively trumps the retroactive application of any state law that would defeat a pending cause of action.[475] Maryland's highest court held that retroactive authorization of late fees for cable television service violated the state constitution.[476] Similarly, Maine passed a general "savings statute" that preserves remedies in effect at the time of any amendment for behavior which occurred prior to the amendment.[477]

A final point which should be made regarding the possible retroactive application of usury statutes is that the analysis

---

469 *See, e.g., In re* Lara, 731 F.2d 1455 (9th Cir. 1984) (applying California law); Wight v. Agristor Leasing, 652 F. Supp. 1000 (D. Kan. 1987) (little discussion); American Sav. Life Ins. Co. v. Financial Affairs Mgmt. Co., 20 Ariz. App. 479, 513 P.2d 1362 (1973); Orden v. Crawshaw Mortgage & Inv. Co., 167 Cal. Rptr. 62 (App. 1980); Ward v. Hudco Loan Co., 328 S.E.2d 729 (Ga. 1985); Fountain v. Dixie Fin. Co., 314 S.E.2d 906 (1984); Ehrman v. Manning, 339 S.E.2d 652 (Ga. App. 1986); Wasser v. Citizens & So. Nat'l Bank, 318 S.E.2d 518 (Ga. App. 1984); Sweeney v. Citicorp Fin., 510 N.E.2d 93 (Ill. App. 1987); Duff v. Bank of Louisville & Trust Co., 705 S.W.2d 920 (Ky. 1986); Krause v. Griffis, 443 N.W.2d 444 (Mich. App. 1989); Paul v. U.S. Mut. Fin. Corp., 389 N.W.2d 487 (Mich. App. 1986); First Fed. Sav. & Loan Ass'n v. Guildner, 295 N.W.2d 501 (Minn. 1980); United Realty Trust v. Property Dev., 269 N.W.2d 737 (Minn. 1978); Farmland Enterprises v. Schuemann, 322 N.W.2d 665 (Neb. 1982); Davis v. G.M.A.C., 127 N.W.2d 907 (Neb. 1964); Bokum v. First Nat'l Bank, 740 P.2d 693 (N.M. 1987); Vaughan v. Kalyvas, 342 S.E.2d 617 (S.C. Ct. App. 1986); Cazzanigi v. General Electric Credit Corp., 938 P.2d 819 (Wash. 1997). *See also* Moran v. American Funding, Ltd., 569 A.2d 841 (N.J. Super. 1989). *But see* Dua v. Comcast Cable, 805 A.2d 1061 (Md. 2002) (retroactive authorization of late fees on cable TV bills abrogated a vested right so violates state constitution).

470 *See* Mickler v. Maranatha Realty Assoc., 20 B.R. 346 (Bankr. M.D. Fla. 1982); Credit Alliance Corp. v. Timmco Equip. Co., 507 So. 2d 657 (Fla. Dist. Ct. App. 1987) (statute amending usury penalty expressly operative prospectively); Hamm v. St. Petersburg Bank & Trust Co., 379 So. 2d 1300 (Fla. Dist. Ct. App. 1980), *rev'd on other grounds*, 414 So. 2d 1071 (Fla. 1982); Farmland Enterprises v. Schuemann, 322 N.W.2d 665 (Neb. 1982); Hazen v. Cook, 637 P.2d 195 (Or. App. 1981), *rev'd in part on other grounds*, 646 P.2d 33 (Or. 1982) (attorney fee issue).

471 *See* Southern Guaranty Corp. v. Doyle, 353 S.E.2d 510 (Ga. 1987) (amendment given prospective effect despite absence of savings clause); Norstar Bank v. Pickard & Anderson, 547 N.Y.S.2d 734 (1989) (no savings clause in amendment but general provision in statute prohibits interest rate exceeding that authorized at time loan was made and thus limits amendment to prospective effect unless amendment expressly states otherwise); Hardwick v. Austin Gallery of Oriental Rugs, Inc., 779 S.W.2d 438 (Tex. Ct. App. 1989) (intended prospectivity found present by implication in statutory exception providing that increased interest rate would apply to renewals and extensions: only if increase were prospective would this exception be necessary; court also refused to apply new rate even though "charge" in issue occurred after date of amendment).

472 *See* Mapes v. Palo Alto Town & Country Village, Inc., 584 F. Supp. 508 (D. Nev. 1984) (applying Nevada Law); U.S. Trust Co. v. LTV Steel Co. (*In re* Chateaugay Corp.), 150 B.R. 529 (Bankr. S.D.N.Y. 1993) (giving only prospective effect to repeal of prohibition of compound interest), *aff'd*, 170 B.R. 551 (S.D.N.Y. 1994); Walker v. Pliss, 34 B.R. 432 (Bankr. D. Or. 1983) (applying Oregon law); Broussard v. Crochet Broussard & Co., 477 So. 2d 166 (La. Ct. App. 1985); U.S. Life Title Ins. Co. v. Brents, 676 S.W.2d 839 (Mo. Ct. App. 1984); Hazen v. Cook, 637 P.2d 195 (Or. App. 1981) (statutory increase in interest ceiling was not retroactive, but forfeiture of loan principal to the state was penal and was repealed retroactively), *rev'd in part on other grounds*, 646 P.2d 33 (Or. 1982) (attorney fee issue).

473 Ewell v. Daggs, 108 U.S. 143 (1883).

474 Section 95 of the Alabama Constitution.

475 United Companies Lending Corp. v. Autrey, 723 So. 2d 617 (Ala. 1998) (at issue was a change in the damages available for a violation of Alabama's points cap on mortgage loans); Smith v. Alfa Fin. Corp., 762 So. 2d 850 (Ala. 1999) (at issue was the retroactive application of the legislative elimination of a cause of action for a lender's failure to obtain a lending license).

476 Dua v. Comcast Cable, 805 A.2d 1061 (Md. 2002).

477 1 Me. Rev. Stat. Ann. § 302 (1989); Reagan v. Racal Mortgage, Inc., 715 A.2d 925 (Me. 1998) (harsher penalty for failure to obtain a license to make supervised loans in effect prior to an amendment which provided for a lesser penalty applied due to Maine's savings statute).

previously presented in this section has presumed that statutory modifications have raised or eliminated usury limitations, thus legalizing previously usurious transactions. It is, of course, possible for an amended usury statute to prohibit transactions which had previously been legal.[478] For example, a usury ceiling could be lowered, or a previously permissible fee could be prohibited. Under such circumstances it is clear that usury statutes do not have retroactive effect because retroactive application would impair the existing contractual obligation.[479]

9.3.2.2 Variable or Floating Usury Ceilings Distinguished

Although newly enacted usury legislation is often given retroactive effect, it is important to distinguish the legislative amendment of a usury statute from a mere change in a floating interest ceiling, that is, one determined by a variable rate usury statute which has itself not been amended. In trying to reconcile the policy underlying usury laws, protecting borrowers from overreaching lenders,[480] with the legitimate needs of creditors when the cost of funds were at historic highs in the late 1970s, many legislatures adopted variable, or floating interest rate ceilings. To avoid recurrence of the anomalous mismatch between statutory ceilings and market rates which led to widespread changes in usury laws at that time, many states adopted a floating cap, which would go up or down in relation to a specified market rate, called the index. The index and the margin are set by statute, but the actual numerical ceiling will change without any change in statute. Thus, for example, under Iowa Code § 535.2(3) the rate applicable to a particular type of loan in Iowa may have been 8.55% in 1990, and 5.33% in 1993, without any legislative action. The rate cap "floats" at a 2% margin above the index, which is the monthly average for 10-year Treasury notes and bonds, as published monthly by the banking department.

Generally, under variable rate statutes, the interest ceiling which applies to any given transaction is fixed on the date of the transaction. If the statutory ceiling later increases or decreases, due to a change in a market interest rate to which the statute is pegged, subsequent transactions will fall under the new rate limitations, but each existing transaction must continue to respect the limit in effect when that transaction was consummated.[481]

Although statutes which set variable usury ceilings typically fix the ceiling for any one transaction on the date the loan or forbearance is made, these statutes should nevertheless be read carefully because exceptions may exist. For example, some statutes allow the interest rate charged under a variable rate contract to rise above the ceiling which existed on the date the contract was consummated, so long as the rate assessed at any point during the contract term does not exceed the usury ceiling which exists at that time.[482]

A rise in a variable interest ceiling may also allow an increase in the rate that a consumer is charged if a loan is not paid off on time. This increase is possible because, although the interest ceiling for the term of the contract may be set at the time the contract is consummated, any subsequent forbearance is treated as a new transaction,[483] and the usury ceiling in effect on the date of the forbearance will control what may be charged for the forbearance.[484] However, the rate permitted for the forbearance may not be applied retroactively to increase the rate charged on the original loan or on earlier forbearances.[485]

---

478 Also, previously unregulated transactions can be brought under regulation, but statutes accomplishing this normally do not have retroactive reach. *See, e.g.*, Givens v. Rent-A-Center, Inc., 720 F. Supp. 160 (S.D. Ala. 1988), *aff'd mem.*, 885 F.2d 879 (11th Cir. 1989) (Alabama Rental Purchase Agreements Act).

479 *See* Hoyne v. Prudential S&L Ass'n, 711 S.W.2d 899 (Mo. Ct. App. 1986); Garrett v. Citizens Sav. Ass'n, 636 S.W.2d 104 (Mo. Ct. App. 1982); Weinstein v. Investors S&L Ass'n, 381 A.2d 53 (N.J. Super. 1977).

480 *See* §§ 1.3, 9.3.1.1, *supra*.

481 *See* Eikenberry v. Adirondack Spring Water Co., 480 N.E.2d 70 (N.Y. 1985); Bookman v. First Bank of Marietta, 1983 Ohio App. LEXIS 13566 (Ohio Ct. App. Feb. 18, 1983); Reagan v. City Nat'l Bank, N.A., 714 S.W.2d 425 (Tex. Ct. App. 1986) (ceiling set at time of original agreement; subsequent addition of co-maker was not alteration or renewal which would change the applicable ceiling). *Cf.* Heuberger v. Rounsefell, 776 P.2d 596 (Or. App. 1989) (subsequent note for same principal was new "loan" under usury statute subject to new rate limitations).

482 *Cf.* Mickler v. Maranatha Realty Assoc., 20 B.R. 346 (Bank. M.D. Fla. 1982) (statutory amendment applies to preexisting loans only if lender has contractual right to modify interest rate or to accelerate debt).

483 The same principle may apply to a loan renewal. *See* Bank of Evening Shade v. Lindsey, 644 S.W.2d 920 (Ark. 1983) (no obligation to renew loan); Heuberger v. Rounsefell, 776 P.2d 596 (Or. App. 1989) (subsequent note for same principal was new "loan" under usury statute subject to new rate limitations).

484 *See* Central Flying Serv., Inc. v. Cain, 686 S.W.2d 432 (Ark. 1985); Eikenberry v. Adirondack Spring Water Co., 480 N.E.2d 70 (N.Y. 1985).

485 *Id.*

The Trial: Jurisdiction; The Right to a Jury Trial; Elements of a Prima Facie Case; Creditor Defenses and Borrowers' Remedies

10.1 Introduction

The preceding chapter addressed the preliminary questions involved in litigating a usury case—that of determining and interpreting the applicable statute. This chapter addresses litigation issues: courts' jurisdiction over out-of-state lenders and trusts; whether creditors can impose mandatory arbitration; whether there is a right to a jury trial; what elements are necessary to establish a prima facie case for the borrower; typical creditor defenses; and typical remedies available upon a finding of usury or other types of illegal overcharges. Another litigation issue, whether the doctrine of complete preemption allows a creditor to remove a state lawsuit against a federally-related lender to federal court, is discussed in § 3.15, *supra*.

10.2 Long-Arm Jurisdiction over Out-of-State Lenders

10.2.1 Constitutional and Statutory Standards

As interstate and e-commerce transactions proliferate, long-arm jurisdiction questions are likely to become more common. Whether a court can exercise jurisdiction over an out-of-state creditor is a separate question from the question of which state's law to apply, which is discussed in § 9.2.9, *supra*. Nonetheless, both questions turn at least to some extent on similar factual issues relating to the out-of-state party's contacts with the forum state. Long-arm jurisdiction also affects the choice of law issue because courts generally follow the choice of law rules of the state where they sit.[1]

Courts must consider both the state's long-arm statute and due process principles when determining whether they can exercise jurisdiction over out-of-state defendants. Due process requires that a defendant, if not present in the state, have certain minimum contacts with it such that maintaining

the suit does not offend traditional notions of fair play and substantial justice.[2] Since many long-arm statutes state that they are intended to allow jurisdiction to the maximum extent allowed by the Constitution, the analysis of statutory issues tends to merge with that of constitutional issues.

In analyzing constitutional issues, courts draw a conceptual distinction between "general jurisdiction" and "specific jurisdiction." Courts have general jurisdiction over a defendant who has substantial or continuous and systematic contacts with the forum state. If a court has general jurisdiction, the constitution allows it to hear any cause of action against that defendant, regardless of whether the claim arose from the defendant's activities in the state.[3] For example, a company has continuous and systematic contact with the state where its headquarters are located, so can be sued there on any claim. The standard for general jurisdiction is fairly high.[4]

Even if a defendant does not have continuous and systematic contact with a state, however, the constitution allows a court to exercise "specific jurisdiction" over a cause of action that arises directly from the defendant's contacts with the forum state.[5] Specific jurisdiction is permissible if the defendant has purposefully availed itself of the privilege of conducting activities in the forum state.[6] Many courts also

---

1 *See* § 9.2.9.1, *supra*.

2 International Shoe v. Washington, 326 U.S. 310, 66 S. Ct. 154, 90 L. Ed. 95 (1945). *See also* Burger King Corp. v. Rudzewicz, 471 U.S. 462, 476, 105 S. Ct. 2174, 85 L. Ed. 2d 528 (1985) (jurisdiction can be exercised over defendant who never physically entered the forum state).

3 Heliocopteros Nacionales de Colombia v. Hall, 466 U.S. 408, 414 nn.8–9, 104 S. Ct. 1868, 80 L. Ed. 2d 404 (1984); Burger King Corp. v. Rudzewicz, 471 U.S. 462, 473 n.15, 105 S. Ct. 2174, 85 L. Ed. 2d 528 (1985); Lakin v. Prudential Securities, Inc., 348 F.3d 704, 707 (8th Cir. 2003).

4 ALS Scan v. Digital Serv. Consultants, Inc., 293 F.3d 707 (4th Cir. 2002) (standard for general jurisdiction is more demanding than for specific jurisdiction).

5 Heliocopteros Nacionales de Colombia v. Hall, 466 U.S. 408, 414 nn.8–9, 104 S. Ct. 1868, 80 L. Ed. 2d 404 (1984); Burger King Corp. v. Rudzewicz, 471 U.S. 462, 473 n.15, 105 S. Ct. 2174, 85 L. Ed. 2d 528 (1985).

6 Burger King v. Rudzewicz, 471 U.S. 462, 473 n.15, 105 S. Ct. 2174, 85 L. Ed. 2d 528 (1985).

require a separate showing that the acts of the defendant or the consequences caused by the defendant must have a substantial enough connection with the forum state to make the exercise of jurisdiction reasonable.[7] Random, fortuitous, or attenuated contacts are insufficient, but specific jurisdiction is permissible if a defendant has deliberately engaged in significant activities within a state or created continuing obligations with members of the forum state.[8]

To obtain personal jurisdiction over an out-of-state parent corporation based on the in-state activities of a subsidiary corporation, the plaintiff must show that the parent so dominated and controlled the affairs of the subsidiary that the latter's corporate existence was disregarded and the subsidiary was the parent's alter ego.[9]

10.2.2 Jurisdiction over Internet-Based Lenders

In some situations, a lender's contacts with state residents through the Internet can meet the "minimum contacts" test, so that courts in the borrower's home state can assert jurisdiction over the lender.[10] In analyzing whether Internet-based contacts are sufficient for specific jurisdiction, many courts have followed the seminal case, *Zippo Mfg. Co. v. Zippo Dot Com*,[11] and divided websites into three categories.[12] On one end of the scale are passive websites that do no more than post advertisements that are accessible by people in the forum state. Courts uniformly find that this sort of website is insufficient to give the forum state jurisdiction.[13] On the other end of the scale are websites by which

a defendant conducts business with residents of the forum state, for example by entering into contracts and exchanging files. Courts generally find that this activity meets the minimum contacts test,[14] as this activity shows that the

(passive website does not create specific jurisdiction because defendant is not directing its activities toward forum state residents in particular); GTE New Media Servs. Inc. v. Bellsouth Corp., 199 F.3d 1343 (D.C. Cir. 2000) (maintaining a website that is accessible to residents of the jurisdiction is insufficient); Am. Wholesalers Underwriting, Ltd. v. Am. Wholesale Ins. Group, Inc., 2004 WL 719187 (D. Conn. Mar. 30, 2004) (passive website that infringes on forum state company's trademark does not give forum state specific jurisdiction); Comer v. Comer, 295 F. Supp. 2d 201 (D. Mass. 2003) (out-of-state law firm's passive website insufficient); SCC Communications Corp. v. Anderson, 195 F. Supp. 2d 1257 (D. Colo. 2002); Uncle Sam's Safari Outfitters, Inc. v. Uncle Sam's Army Navy Outfitters, 96 F. Supp. 2d 919 (E.D. Mo. 2000); Search Force, Inc. v. Data Force Int'l, Inc., 112 F. Supp. 2d 771 (S.D. Ind. 2000) (job postings on sites like Monster.com are analogous to passive ads); Millennium Enterprises, Inc. v. Millennium Music, 33 F. Supp. 2d 907 (D. Or. 1999); Bensusan Restaurant Corp. v. King, 937 F. Supp. 295 (S.D.N.Y. 1996) (website does not create long-arm jurisdiction for trademark infringement claim where infringing goods were not shipped into forum state and no infringing activity was directed at forum state), *aff'd on other grounds*, 126 F.3d 25 (2d Cir. 1997) (affirmance deals only with interpretation of New York long-arm statute, not with minimum contacts test).

14 *See, e.g.*, Bridgeport Music, Inc. v. Still N the Water Publishing, 327 F.3d 472, 483 (6th Cir. 2003) (operating an interactive website that reveals specifically intended interaction with forum state residents may create specific jurisdiction, but not shown here); Bird v. Parsons, 289 F.3d 865 (6th Cir. 2002) (doing business over Internet with residents of forum statute sufficient for specific jurisdiction although not for general jurisdiction); Arnold v. Goldstar Fin. Sys., Inc., 2002 WL 1941546 at *6 (N.D. Ill. Aug. 22, 2002) (credit repair company's acceptance of payment on web page is "roughly analogous to . . . setting up a twenty-four hour storefront" in the forum state; this plus other contacts sufficient for specific jurisdiction); Stuart v. Hennesey, 214 F. Supp. 2d 1198 (D. Utah 2002); Euromarket Designs, Inc. v. Crate & Barrel Ltd., 96 F. Supp. 2d 824 (N.D. Ill. 2000) (Illinois residents could browse defendant's on-line catalog and place orders via Internet); Zippo Mfg. Co. v. Zippo Dot Com, Inc., 952 F. Supp. 1119 (W.D. Pa. 1997) (sale of services to forum state residents by credit card through website gave forum state jurisdiction over trademark infringement case); Alitalia-Linee Aeree Italiane S.P.A. v. Casinoalitalia.com, 128 F. Supp. 2d 340 (E.D. Va. 2001) (allowing forum state residents to place bets through out-of-state website sufficient for specific jurisdiction over claim that website infringed on plaintiff's trademark); State v. Beer Nuts, Ltd., 29 S.W.3d 828 (Mo. App. 2000) (media advertising and interactive website through which Missouri residents ordered product was sufficient to give Missouri jurisdiction); Thompson v. Handa-Lopez, Inc., 998 F. Supp. 738 (W.D. Tex. 1998) (website through which Texas resident purchased game tokens and gambled gave Texas jurisdiction). *Cf.* Molnlycke Health Care v. Dumex Medical Surgical Products Ltd., 64 F. Supp. 2d 448 (E.D. Pa. 1999) (website through which products can be ordered is sufficient to give specific jurisdiction but not general jurisdiction). *But see* Butler v. Beer Across America, 83 F. Supp. 2d 1261 (N.D. Ala. 2000) (sale of beer to minor in forum state via Internet site not sufficient for specific

---

7 Bridgeport Music, Inc. v. Still N the Water Publishing, 327 F.3d 472, 478 (6th Cir. 2003); Bird v. Parsons, 289 F.3d 865 (6th Cir. 2002); Panavision Int'l v. Toeppen, 141 F.3d 1316 (9th Cir. 1998).

8 Burger King Corp. v. Rudzewicz, 471 U.S. 462, 105 S. Ct. 2174, 2183–84. 85 L. Ed. 2d 528 (1985).

9 Epps v. Stewart Information Servs. Corp., 327 F.3d 642 (8th Cir. 2003).

10 *See* § 10.2.1, *supra*.

11 952 F. Supp. 1119 (W.D. Pa. 1997).

12 ALS Scan v. Digital Serv. Consultants, Inc., 293 F.3d 707 (4th Cir. 2002) (specific jurisdiction allowed over person who directs electronic activity into forum state with manifest intention of engaging in business or other transactions there and that activity creates a cause of action for a person in that state; passively placing information on the Internet insufficient); Revell v. Lidov, 317 F.3d 467 (5th Cir. 2002) (applying *Zippo* but interactive website insufficient where it was not aimed at forum state); Bird v. Parsons, 289 F.3d 865 (6th Cir. 2002) (citing *Zippo* favorably). *See also* Mink v. AAAA Development L.L.C., 190 F.3d 333 (5th Cir. 1999) (applying *Zippo* analysis to general jurisdiction; website here insufficiently interactive to allow jurisdiction); Metcalf v. Lawson, 148 N.H. 35, 802 A.2d 1221 (2002) (where sale by defendant occurs through an on-line auction site, *Zippo* test "not particularly helpful . . . because the majority of cases using it are based upon a defendant's conduct over its own website").

13 *See* Jennings v. AC Hydraulic A/S, 383 F.3d 546 (7th Cir. 2004)

defendant is targeting forum state residents or deliberately engaging in transactions with them.[15] In the middle are websites that are interactive in that the user can exchange information with the host computer, for example by ordering product information or sending e-mail to sales representatives. Whether maintaining such a website meets the minimum contacts test usually depends on the level of interactivity and the commercial nature of the exchange of information.[16] E-mail sent to a forum resident may also be

sufficient contacts for a court to find specific jurisdiction over a defendant.[17] For specific jurisdiction, there must also be a nexus between the plaintiff's injury and the Internet transaction.[18]

For general jurisdiction, the question is whether the defendant has substantial or continuing and systematic con-

---

jurisdiction; court characterizes website as having only limited interactivity).

15 Neogen Corp. v. Neo Gen Screening, Inc., 282 F.3d 883 (6th Cir. 2002); Bird v. Parsons, 289 F.3d 865 (6th Cir. 2002) (Internet website can be purposeful availment if it is interactive to a degree that reveals specifically intended interaction with state residents); Sys. Designs, Inc. v. New Customware Co., 248 F. Supp. 2d 1093 (D. Utah 2003) (website was intentional solicitation of business in forum state so, when combined with other contacts, allowed specific jurisdiction over tort claim of trademark infringement); Becker v. Hooshmand, 841 So. 2d 561 (Fla. Dist. Ct. App. 2003) (posting defamatory comments on Internet, targeted at Florida residents, gives Florida jurisdiction over tort claim). *But cf.* Toys "R" Us, Inc. v. Step Two, S.A., 318 F.3d 446 (3d Cir. 2003) (defendant did not purposefully avail itself of forum state [New Jersey] by use of website posted entirely in Spanish with prices indicated only in Pesetas or Euros, and products shipped only to addresses in Spain, so no specific jurisdiction); ALS Scan v. Digital Serv. Consultants, Inc., 293 F.3d 707 (4th Cir. 2002) (merely posting information insufficient because it does not show intent to engage in business in the state); Metcalf v. Lawson, 148 N.H. 35, 802 A.2d 1221 (2002) (no specific jurisdiction where defendant was seller on Internet auction site and winning bidder could potentially reside in any state).

16 Carefirst of Md., Inc. v. Carefirst Pregnancy Centers, Inc., 334 F.3d 390 (4th Cir. 2003) (generally accessible, semi-interactive website did not target forum state so insufficient for specific jurisdiction); Panavision Int'l v. Toeppen, 141 F.3d 1316 (9th Cir. 1998) (maintaining non-interactive website that diverted potential customers, plus attempt to extort money from trade name holder, gave court specific jurisdiction over cybersquatter); Electronic Broking Servs., Ltd. v. E-Business Solutions & Servs., 285 F. Supp. 2d 686 (D. Md. 2003) (maintenance of website that infringed on plaintiff's trademark insufficient for specific jurisdiction when it was not targeted toward forum state); Venture Tape Corp. v. McGills Glass Warehouse, 292 F. Supp. 2d 230 (D. Mass. 2003) (mere interactive website insufficient, but here defendant's Internet-based trademark infringement targeted forum state company); Sys. Designs, Inc. v. New Customware Co., 248 F. Supp. 2d 1093 (D. Utah 2003) (website that solicited business and through which customers could register and make payment sufficiently targeted forum state to allow specific jurisdiction over trademark infringement claim); Graduate Mgmt. Admission Council v. Raju, 241 F. Supp. 2d 589 (E.D. Va. 2003) (soliciting and making sales to two Virginia residents via website, in violation of plaintiff's copyright, does not meet due process requirements for specific jurisdiction even though it meets Virginia's long-arm statute, but court finds jurisdiction on other grounds); Mothers Against Drunk Driving v. DAMMADD, Inc., 2003 WL 292162 (N.D. Tex. Feb. 7, 2003) (website that allowed anonymous tip reporting, on-line donations, and limited sale of merchandise not sufficiently interactive to support specific jurisdiction); Stuart v. Hennesey,

214 F. Supp. 2d 1198 (D. Utah 2002) (website containing advertisements, video clip, employment opportunities, and an on-line purchase option is sufficiently interactive to warrant specific jurisdiction); iAccess, Inc. v. WEBcard Techs., Inc., 182 F. Supp. 2d 1183 (D. Utah 2002) (website where users could send e-mail to WEBcard, subscribe to receive regular e-mails from them, and view the progress of their transaction on-line was insufficient); Donmar, Inc. v. Swanky Partners, Inc., 2002 WL 1917258 (N.D. Ill. Aug. 20, 2002) (website not interactive enough to support finding of jurisdiction where customers view information and join mailing list on website, but out-of-state names are immediately removed from mailing list and advertisements are not directed to out-of-state consumers); Bell v. Imperial Palace Hotel/Casino, Inc., 200 F. Supp. 2d 1082 (E.D. Mo. 2001) (hotel website allowing customers to make reservations on-line insufficient for specific jurisdiction, as no money or anything of intrinsic value was transmitted on-line, and travel to outside state was required to actually transact business); Ty, Inc. v. Clark, 2000 WL 51816, 2000 U.S. Dist. LEXIS 383 (N.D. Ill. Jan. 13, 2000) (website that allowed customers to e-mail questions and receive information but not to place orders or enter into contracts insufficient); Biometrics, L.L.C. v. New Womyn, Inc., 112 F. Supp. 2d 869 (E.D. Mo. 2000) (specific jurisdiction established where website contained a "sales rep. locator" feature with a box labeled "Missouri" for the user to check off); Purco Fleet Servs., Inc. v. Towers, 38 F. Supp. 2d 1320 (D. Utah 1999) (maintaining interactive website through which at least one forum state resident had made purchase, plus attempt to extort money from trade name holder gave court specific jurisdiction over cybersquatter in trademark infringement case); JB Oxford Holdings, Inc. v. Net Trade, Inc., 76 F. Supp. 2d 1363 (S.D. Fla. 1999) (maintaining website that allowed mutual communication did not give court jurisdiction where site expressly declined transactions with residents of forum state); Bedrejo v. Triple E Canada, Ltd., 984 P.2d 739 (Mont. 1999) (maintaining interactive website insufficient where no evidence of transactions with forum state residents through the website); Mar-Eco, Inc. v. T & R & Sons Towing & Recovery, Inc., 837 A.2d 512 (Pa. Super. Ct. 2003) (interactive website provided basis for general jurisdiction).

17 Verizon Online Servs., Inc. v. Ralsky, 203 F. Supp. 2d 601 (E.D. Va. 2002) (in trespass to chattel case, transmission of unsolicited bulk e-mail through plaintiff ISP by out-of-state defendant is sufficient minimum contacts for specific jurisdiction). *See also* Internet Doorway, Inc. v. Parks, 138 F. Supp. 2d 773 (S.D. Miss. 2001) (in suit by ISP for trespass to chattel, specific jurisdiction proper over defendant who sent e-mail to state resident; active nature of e-mail satisfies minimum contact with state; tort occurred when state resident opened e-mail). *But cf.* Hydro Engineering, Inc. v. Landa, Inc., 231 F. Supp. 2d 1130 (D. Utah 2002) (no specific jurisdiction where only three of 400 e-mail messages could have reasonably been perceived as addressed to Utah residents, and plaintiff provided no evidence that a single e-mail actually reached a Utah resident).

18 Bird v. Parsons, 289 F.3d 865 (6th Cir. 2002); Bell v. Imperial Palace Hotel/Casino, Inc., 200 F. Supp. 2d 1082 (E.D. Mo. 2001) (plaintiff showed no connection between hotel's website and slip and fall accident at hotel).

tacts with the forum state.[19] Some courts find the *Zippo* three-category analysis unsuited to the determination of general jurisdiction.[20] A passive website is probably insufficient for general jurisdiction.[21] Even a website that allows forum state residents to transact business may not be sufficient.[22] However, general jurisdiction may be established where a company maintains a sophisticated website that is clearly and deliberately structured to operate as a virtual store or office in the forum state.[23]

Making a loan to a consumer through the Internet is likely to create at least specific jurisdiction over causes of action arising directly from that loan.[24] On the other hand, if the consumer merely gets information about a potential consumer credit transaction from a website, but then travels to the creditor's home state to enter into the transaction, the fact that the website was accessible in the consumer's home state is unlikely to meet the minimum contacts test. A state statute may define the location of a consumer credit transaction as within the forum state if the defendant seller solicited the transaction by Internet.[25]

10.2.3 Personal Jurisdiction over Securitization Trusts

10.2.3.1 Overview

Whether courts can exercise personal jurisdiction over a securitization trust that is located in another state is a significant question as more and more obligations are securitized.[26] In analyzing the question, it is important to separate the question of general jurisdiction from specific jurisdiction.[27] If a defendant has continuous and systematic contacts with the forum state, the U.S. Constitution allows the courts of that state to exercise general jurisdiction. Then the courts in that state can hear any case against that defendant regardless of whether the case arose from the defendant's contacts with the state. Even when general jurisdiction is unavailable, a state can exercise specific jurisdiction over a defendant who has purposefully directed its activities at state residents if the litigation arises out of or relates to those activities. In many cases against securitization trusts, specific jurisdiction will be a more fruitful possibility to pursue than general jurisdiction.

Another important question is whether the trust has a security interest in real or personal property located in the forum state. If it does, it is more likely that the state will have jurisdiction. A final question is the litigation context in which the claim is presented: whether the debtor seeks to assert an affirmative suit or a counterclaim to a collection suit, and whether the matter arises in bankruptcy court.

In evaluating the defendant's contacts with the forum state, it is important to consider both the acts of the defendant itself and the acts of its agents. The latter can be sufficient to give the forum state jurisdiction.[28]

---

19 *See* § 10.2.1, *supra.*

20 Lakin v. Prudential Securities, Inc., 348 F.3d 704 (8th Cir. 2003) (*Zippo* interactivity criteria insufficient for general jurisdiction analysis; must also analyze quantity of contacts with forum state); Revell v. Lidov, 317 F.3d 467 (5th Cir. 2002) (finding three-category analysis not well adapted to general jurisdiction questions); Bird v. Parsons, 289 F.3d 865 (6th Cir. 2002). *But see* Gator.com Corp. v. L. L. Bean, Inc., 341 F.3d 1072 (9th Cir. 2003) (applying *Zippo* analysis to general jurisdiction question), *appeal dismissed upon rehearing en banc*, 398 F.3d 1125 (9th Cir. 2005) (no case or controversy after settlement); Mink v. AAAA Development L.L.C., 190 F.3d 333 (5th Cir. 1999) (applying *Zippo* analysis to general jurisdiction; website here insufficiently interactive to allow jurisdiction).

21 ALS Scan v. Digital Serv. Consultants, Inc., 293 F.3d 707 (4th Cir. 2002) (merely maintaining website that reaches people in forum state insufficient for general jurisdiction); Mink v. AAAA Development L.L.C., 190 F.3d 333 (5th Cir. 1999) (website with information about products, a printable mail-in order form, the company's telephone number, mailing address, and e-mail address, but no ability to take orders was a passive advertisement that was insufficient for general jurisdiction); Juelich v. Yamazaki Mazak Optonics Corp., 682 N.W.2d 565 (Minn. 2004) (Internet site that served as advertisement insufficient); Cerberus Partners, Ltd. P'ship v. Gadsby & Hannah, L.L.P., 836 A.2d 1113 (R.I. 2003) (website advertising firm's services insufficient for general jurisdiction); Hitachi Shin Din Cable, Ltd. v. Cain, 106 S.W.3d 776 (Tex. App. 2003).

22 Bird v. Parsons, 289 F.3d 865 (6th Cir. 2002); Arriaga v. Imperial Palace, Inc., 252 F. Supp. 2d 380 (S.D. Tex. 2003) (interactive website that allowed customers to make reservations and pay is insufficient to establish general jurisdiction); Stuart v. Hennesey, 214 F. Supp. 2d 1198 (D. Utah 2002); Bell v. Imperial Palace Hotel/Casino, Inc., 200 F. Supp. 2d 1082 (E.D. Mo. 2001) (hotel's maintenance of interactive website for reservations insufficient); Reiff v. Toy, 115 S.W.3d 700 (Tex. App. 2003) (website that allowed forum state residents to make hotel reservations insufficient for general jurisdiction).

23 Lakin v. Prudential Securities, Inc., 348 F.3d 704 (8th Cir. 2003) (substantial and continuous Internet contacts may support general jurisdiction if quantity is high enough); Gorman v. Ameritrade, 293 F.3d 506 (D.C. Cir. 2002) (general jurisdiction could be established by brokerage firm's 24-hour website that allowed residents to enter into contracts, pay commissions, exchange information, etc., but court lacks jurisdiction for other reasons). *See also* Mar-Eco, Inc. v. T & R & Sons Towing & Recovery, Inc., 837 A.2d 512 (Pa. Super. Ct. 2003) (interactive website provided basis for general jurisdiction).

24 *See* Burger King v. Rudzewicz, 471 U.S. 462, 105 S. Ct. 2174, 85 L. Ed. 2d 528 (1985).

25 *See* Colo. Rev. Stat. § 5-1-201 ("[f]or purposes of this code, a consumer credit transaction is made in this state if . . . (b) a consumer who is a resident of this state enters into the transaction with a creditor who has solicited or advertised in this state by any means, including [Internet or other electronic means]").

26 For a description of securitization, see § 11.3, *infra.*

27 The distinction between general and specific jurisdiction is described in Burger King Corp. v. Rudzewicz, 471 U.S. 462, 472, 105 S. Ct. 2174, 85 L. Ed. 2d 528 (1985) and Helicopteros Nacionalies de Columbia, S.A. v. Hall, 466 U.S. 408, 414, 415 n.9, 104 S. Ct. 1868, 80 L. Ed. 2d 404 (1984). *See also* Lakin v. Prudential Securities, Inc., 348 F.3d 704, 707 (8th Cir. 2003).

28 Daynard v. Ness, Motley, Loadholt, Richardson & Poole, 290

10.2.3.2 General Jurisdiction

General jurisdiction allows a court to can hear any case, even one that is unrelated to the defendant's activities in the forum state. The U.S. Constitution allows a court to exercise general jurisdiction over a defendant who has continuous and systematic contacts with the forum state.[29] For example, courts have general jurisdiction over a bank that has branch bank locations in the forum state and that forecloses upon and acquires ownership of property there.[30]

In cases against securitization trusts, or against any defendant that does business on a nationwide basis, the defendant is likely to point to the small percentage of its business that relates to the forum state. However, the Third and Eighth Circuits have held that the that fact that only a small percentage of a company's sales occurs in a given state is generally irrelevant.[31] The more relevant inquiry is whether the percentage of a company's contacts with the forum state is substantial for the forum.[32] The trust's lack of employees or offices in the forum state is also not dispositive.[33]

Several district court decisions have held that general jurisdiction is not established by a trust's purchase of loans originated in the forum state and its holding of mortgages secured by property in the forum state.[34] To justify this

conclusion, these cases cite Supreme Court decisions that say that jurisdiction cannot be based on the "unilateral activity of another party or a third person."[35] But those Supreme Court cases involve markedly different factual contexts. In one case, a third party sent the out-of-state defendant checks drawn on a forum state bank account.[36] Obviously, the defendant had no control over where the third party did its banking. The defendant's acceptance of these checks did not give the forum state jurisdiction. Another case dealt with a New York vehicle dealer who sold a car to a New York resident in New York. The buyer then drove the car to Oklahoma and had an accident.[37] The Supreme Court held that "the fortuitous circumstance that a single Audi automobile, sold in New York to New York residents, happened to suffer an accident while passing through Oklahoma," was insufficient to give Oklahoma jurisdiction over the buyer's suit.[38] Other cases in which the Supreme Court has applied this principle have similarly involved acts over which the defendant had no control.[39] By contrast, a trust has complete control over the states from which it will acquire obligations. It can purposefully avail itself of that state's business or choose not to. In fact, the pooling and servicing agreement will probably specify the states from which obligations will be acquired. If the trust does not want to take obligations from these states, it can choose not to enter into that agreement.[40]

The Third Circuit has approved general jurisdiction over an out-of-state bank that had purchased a number of loans on

F.3d 42 (1st Cir. 2002); *see also* ACORN v. Household Int'l, Inc., 211 F. Supp. 2d 1160 (N.D. Cal. 2002) (court may exercise jurisdiction over holding company based on actions in forum state of its subsidiary, which was its general agent).

29 Burger King Corp. v. Rudzewicz, 471 U.S. 462, 473 n.15, 105 S. Ct. 2174, 85 L. Ed. 2d 528 (1985); Helicopteros Nacionalies de Columbia, S.A. v. Hall, 466 U.S. 408, 414, 415 n.9, 104 S. Ct. 1868, 80 L. Ed. 2d 404 (1984).

30 Williams v. FirstPlus Home Loan Owner Trust 1998-4, 310 F. Supp. 2d 981, 996 (W.D. Tenn. 2004).

31 Lakin v. Prudential Securities, Inc., 348 F.3d 704, 709 (8th Cir. 2003); Provident Nat'l Bank v. Cal. Fed. Sav. & Loan Ass'n, 819 F.2d 434 (3d Cir. 1987).

32 Lakin v. Prudential Securities, Inc., 348 F.3d 704, 709 (8th Cir. 2003).

33 Burger King v. Rudzewicz, 471 U.S. 462, 476, 105 S. Ct. 2174, 85 L. Ed. 2d 528 (1985); Lakin v. Prudential Securities, Inc., 348 F.3d 704, 709 (8th Cir. 2003) (Arkansas had general jurisdiction even though defendant's only physical office was located in Georgia).

34 Brooks v. Terra Funding, 2002 WL 1797785 (W.D. Tenn. July 31, 2002); Street v. PSB Lending Corp., 2002 WL 1797773 (W.D. Tenn. July 31, 2002); Williams v. FirstPlus Home Loan Trust, 209 F.R.D. 404 (W.D. Tenn. 2002); Mull v. Alliance Mortgage Banking Corp., 219 F. Supp. 2d 895 (W.D. Tenn. 2002); *see also* Easter v. Am. West Fin., 381 F.3d 948 (9th Cir. 2004) (finding specific jurisdiction but not general jurisdiction where trust acquired forum state mortgage loans but had no offices, employees, bank accounts, or business operations in forum state); Williams v. FirstPlus Home Loan Owner Trust, 310 F. Supp. 2d 981 (W.D. Tenn. 2004) (following *Barry*; holding notes secured by mortgages in forum state insufficient for general jurisdiction); Pilcher v. Direct Equity Lending, 189 F. Supp. 2d 1198, 1209 (D. Kan. 2002) (not distinguishing

between general and specific jurisdiction); Lobatto v. Berney, 1999 WL 672994 (S.D.N.Y. Aug. 26, 1999) (court does not have jurisdiction over assignee of unsecured obligations simply because the assignor was subject to personal jurisdiction); Barry v. Mortgage Servicing Acquisition Corp., 909 F. Supp. 65, 74, 75 (D.R.I. 1995) ("where the property is completely unrelated to the plaintiff's cause of action, the presence of the defendant's property in the forum will not alone support the exercise of jurisdiction").

35 Helicopteros Nacionalies de Columbia, S.A. v. Hall, 466 U.S. 408, 417, 104 S. Ct. 1868, 80 L. Ed. 2d 404 (1984); *see also* Burger King Corp. v. Rudzewicz, 471 U.S. 462, 475, 105 S. Ct. 2174, 85 L. Ed. 2d 528 (1985).

36 Helicopteros Nacionalies de Columbia, S.A. v. Hall, 466 U.S. 408, 411, 416, 417, 104 S. Ct. 1868, 80 L. Ed. 2d 404 (1984).

37 World-Wide Volkswagen Corp. v. Woodson, 444 U.S. 286, 100 S. Ct. 559, 62 L. Ed. 2d 490 (1980).

38 *Id.* at 295.

39 Kuklo v. Super. Ct., 436 U.S. 84, 93, 94, 98 S. Ct. 1690, 56 L. Ed. 2d 132 (1978) (mother's choice of state in which to live with the children did not give that state jurisdiction over other parent); Hanson v. Denckla, 357 U.S. 235, 78 S. Ct. 1228, 2 L. Ed. 2d 1283 (1958) (fact that person who created trust later moved to Florida did not give Florida courts jurisdiction over Delaware trustee).

40 *But cf.* Williams v. FirstPlus Home Loan Owner Trust 1998-4, 310 F. Supp. 2d 981, 995 (W.D. Tenn. 2004) (fact that loan pools "happened" to include mortgage loans in forum state insufficient for specific jurisdiction over trust; court does not consider whether terms of pooling and servicing agreement specified that obligations from forum state would be acquired).

the secondary market that arose in the forum state.[41] The bank's ownership of loans secured by property in the forum state, plus its maintenance of a bank account there, amounted to continuous and systematic contacts with the forum state. The reasoning of this decision could subject a securitization trust to jurisdiction in any state in which property securing a substantial number of loans is located. In another case, the Eighth Circuit cited the defendant's liens on hundreds to thousands of real properties in the forum state as a factor favoring general jurisdiction.[42]

10.2.3.3 Specific Jurisdiction When Claim Relates to Property in Forum State

Often a debtor's suit relates to a security interest held by the trust in real or personal property that is located in the forum state. For example, a consumer may have entered into a loan transaction in his or her home state, and given the creditor a mortgage on real estate located in that same state. If a trust later acquires the mortgage and note, can the consumer bring a suit arising out of the loan in the state where the loan originated and the secured property is located? Because the suit in this situation arises out of the trust's contacts with the forum state, the forum state may have specific jurisdiction over the case.

Specific jurisdiction requires a showing only that the defendant has purposefully directed its activities at forum state residents, not that the defendant has maintained continuous and systematic contacts with the forum state. As the Supreme Court has stated, parties who "reach out beyond one state and create continuing relationships and obligations with citizens of another state" are subject to jurisdiction in the other state for the consequences of their activities.[43]

A United States Supreme Court decision strongly suggests that the consumer's home state will have jurisdiction over a securitization trust to which the note and mortgage are assigned, as long as the consumer's claim relates to the mortgaged property. In *Shaffer v. Heitner*, the Supreme Court stated: "[W]hen claims to the property itself are the source of the underlying controversy between the plaintiff and the defendant, it would be unusual for the State where the property is located not to have jurisdiction. . . . The State's strong interests in assuring the marketability of property within its borders and in providing a procedure for peaceful resolution of disputes about the possession of that property would also support jurisdiction, as would the likelihood that important records and witnesses will be found in

the State."[44] This decision supports jurisdiction in the state where property is located whenever the claim relates to the existence or amount of a mortgage debt.[45]

The leading case is *Easter v. American West Financial*.[46] There, the Ninth Circuit held that a federal court could assert specific jurisdiction over trusts that acquired mortgage loans in the forum state, even though they had no offices, employees, or bank accounts in the forum state, conducted no business there, and had not contracted with any forum state resident. The court held that the trusts "have availed themselves of the protections of Washington law because they are beneficiaries of deeds of trust, which hypothecate Washington realty to secure payments on notes" they own.[47] According to the court, simply holding a deed of trust represents a significant contact with the forum state. When combined with the income stream from those loans, it demonstrates that the trusts "have purposefully availed themselves of the privilege of doing business" in the forum state.[48] Because the trial court had specific jurisdiction, it could hear a suit by borrowers arising out of allegedly excessive interest they paid on their notes.

Likewise, a district court held that Illinois had jurisdiction over an out-of-state bank that acquired an Illinois mortgage loan and then assigned the servicing rights to another entity. The court pointed out that "a party who holds a mortgage agreement with an Illinois resident on Illinois property is on notice that it might be sued in Illinois."[49] Such a party "should reasonably anticipate being haled into court there."[50]

Several district court opinions are sometimes cited for the proposition that an out-of-state securitization trust that acquires loans secured by property in the forum state is not subject to that state's long-arm jurisdiction. However, most of these cases are entirely inapposite. *Barry v. Mortgage Servicing Acquisition Corp.*,[51] involves a highly unusual fact pattern because the plaintiff obtained a loan in Rhode Island that was secured by a home mortgage on property in a different state. When the plaintiff sought to assert Truth in Lending claims against a bank to which the mortgage and note had been transferred, the bank objected to jurisdiction. The court held that the bank's status as assignee of 138 mortgages secured by Rhode Island real property was insufficient to give Rhode Island general jurisdiction over the bank.[52] The opinion suggests, however, that as the plaintiff's

---

41 Provident Nat'l Bank v. Cal. Fed. Sav. & Loan Ass'n, 819 F.2d 434 (3d Cir. 1987).

42 Lakin v. Prudential Securities, Inc., 348 F.3d 704, 710 (8th Cir. 2003).

43 Burger King Corp. v. Rudzewicz, 471 U.S. 462, 473, 105 S. Ct. 2174, 85 L. Ed. 2d 528 (1985) (quoting Travelers Health Ass'n v. Virginia, 339 U.S. 643, 647, 70 S. Ct. 927, 94 L. Ed. 2d 1154 (1950)).

44 433 U.S. 186, 208, 97 S. Ct. 2569, 53 L. Ed. 2d 683 (1977).

45 *See also* Abernathy v. Abernathy, 482 S.E.2d 265 (Ga. 1997) (action to resolve ownership of Georgia property can be brought in Georgia against non-resident).

46 381 F.3d 948, 960–61 (9th Cir. 2004).

47 *Id.* at 961.

48 *Id.*

49 Newman v. 1st 1440 Investment, Inc., 1990 WL 125369, at *2 (N.D. Ill. Aug. 22, 1990).

50 *Id.* at *3.

51 909 F. Supp. 65 (D.R.I. 1995).

52 There is substantial authority to the contrary. *See* § 10.2.3, *supra*.

claims related to the mortgaged property, the state where the property was located would have had jurisdiction over the claim.[53] Thus this decision supports specific jurisdiction over a trust in the state where the mortgaged property is located, as long as the claim relates to the property.

Another frequently cited case, *Rogers v. 5-Star Management, Inc.*,[54] also arose in a very atypical context. The debtor there had signed a note secured by real estate in four states: New Mexico, Arizona, California, and New York. The note was assigned to a Texas corporation that brought suit in New York to foreclose on the New York real estate. The debtor then brought suit in New Mexico to enjoin the New York foreclosure. The court held that the fact that the debtor had signed the note in New Mexico with the original creditor was insufficient to give New Mexico jurisdiction over the assignee. The court stressed that the action did not concern whether the defendant "properly possesses or could properly foreclose the New Mexico lien,"[55] thus suggesting, as in *Barry*, that there would have been jurisdiction in New Mexico if the suit had related to the New Mexico property.

Four cases from Tennessee also involve unusual facts.[56] In each case the plaintiffs sued a host of securitization trusts, but did not allege that any one of them held their loans. Thus, there was no tenable claim that the forum state had specific jurisdiction over the plaintiffs' claims. The courts also held that the fact that the trusts owned other mortgage loans in the forum state was insufficient to give the forum state general jurisdiction. Only in rare cases will consumers have reason to sue trusts that do not hold their loans.[57]

Only two cases decline to find jurisdiction where debtors entered into credit transactions in the forum state and gave mortgages on homes in the same state. In the first case, *Pilcher v. Direct Equity Lending*,[58] a court in the debtors' home state held that it did not have long-arm jurisdiction over an out-of-state trust to which the mortgages and notes had been assigned. The court held that the trust's interests in the real estate in the forum state were insufficient to confer jurisdiction because the trusts were not attempting to foreclose and the "essence" of the plaintiffs' case was not the lien but the loan interest and fees. *Pilcher* did not discuss or even cite the United States Supreme Court's ruling in *Shaffer v. Heitner* discussed above, so cannot be regarded as sound precedent. Further, the court erred in characterizing the plaintiffs' claim as unconnected to the trust's interest in the real property. The plaintiffs' claims went to the dollar amount of the trust's liens, and in fact could have resulted in voiding of the entire debt.

In the second case, *Williams v. FirstPlus Home Loan Owner Trust 1998-4*,[59] a federal district court held that a trust that acquired a loan pool that "happened" to include loans secured by Tennessee real estate did not thereby give Tennessee courts specific jurisdiction over it. If the court had before it a pooling and servicing agreement that showed the trust's specific intent to acquire the Tennessee loans, it might have reached a different conclusion.

If consumers sue a securitization trust in the state where the collateral is located, they should frame the complaint to make it clear that the relief they are seeking relates to the collateral. For example, the complaint could seek a declaratory judgment reducing or voiding the security interest, and an order requiring the trust to file documents in the local recording office to reflect the reduction or release of the security interest.

10.2.3.4 Specific Jurisdiction When Unsecured Debts Have Been Assigned to a Trust

Even when the obligations at issue are not secured by property in the forum state, there are good arguments in favor of jurisdiction over the trust that holds the obligation, when the plaintiff's claim arises out of that obligation. In *McGee v. International Life Insurance Co.*,[60] a California resident bought life insurance from an Arizona insurance company. Then a Texas company assumed the Arizona insurance company's obligations. The United States Supreme Court held that California had jurisdiction over the Texas company in a suit for policy benefits, even though the Texas company had no office or agent in California and this insurance policy was the only one it held for a California resident. While this case dates from 1957, the Supreme Court has cited it with approval in more recent decisions.[61]

---

53 909 F. Supp. at 73, 74.

54 946 F. Supp. 907 (D.N.M. 1996).

55 *Id.* at 911.

56 Brooks v. Terra Funding, 2002 WL 1797785 (W.D. Tenn. July 31, 2002); Street v. PSB Lending Corp., 2002 WL 1797773 (W.D. Tenn. July 31, 2002); Williams v. FirstPlus Home Loan Trust, 209 F.R.D. 404 (W.D. Tenn. 2002); Mull v. Alliance Mortgage Banking Corp., 219 F. Supp. 2d 895 (W.D. Tenn. 2002). See § 10.2.3, *supra*, for an opposing view of general jurisdiction based on a trust's ownership of mortgages on property in the forum state.

57 *See, e.g.*, Easter v. American West Fin., 381 F.3d 948 (9th Cir. 2004) (named plaintiffs do not have standing to assert claims against trusts that do not hold their loans); Landmann v. Bann-Cor, 2003 WL 23742558 (S.D. Ill. Feb. 10, 2003), *later op. at* 2004 WL 1944789 (S.D. Ill. Feb. 26, 2004) (named plaintiffs have standing to sue only their loan originator and the trust that currently holds their loan, not other trusts that purchased other class members' loans from same originator); Alexander v. PSB Funding Corp., 800 N.E.2d 984 (Ind. App. 2004).

58 189 F. Supp. 2d 1198 (D. Kan. 2002).

59 310 F. Supp. 2d 981, 995 (W.D. Tenn. 2004).

60 355 U.S. 220, 78 S. Ct. 199, 2 L. Ed. 2d 223 (1957); *see also* Kelly Investment, Inc. v. Basic Capital Mgmt., Inc., 85 S.W.3d 371 (Tex. App. 2002) (Texas courts have jurisdiction over California corporation that bought notes signed in Texas, where debtors had already sued original payee; notes were secured by out-of-state realty).

61 *See, e.g.*, Burger King Corp. v. Rudzewicz, 471 U.S. 462, 105 S. Ct. 2174, 85 L. Ed. 2d 528 (1985) (citing *McGee* throughout).

An Iowa Supreme Court decision is consistent with *McGee* and suggests that the state where the obligations were created has jurisdiction over a securitization trust to which the obligations have been assigned, as long as the claims arise out of those obligations. In *Ross v. First Savings Bank of Arlington*,[62] the Iowa Supreme Court dealt with retail installment contracts that the original seller had assigned to a bank. That bank then pooled them and sold fractional interests in the pools to other banks. The court held that the banks that bought the fractional interests—who would be the equivalent of investors who buy shares in a securitization trust—did not have sufficient contacts with Iowa to be subject to the jurisdiction of the Iowa courts. But its language strongly suggests that the bank to which the contracts were actually assigned—which would be the equivalent of a securitization trust—would be subject to Iowa jurisdiction. That bank holds the contracts, has contractual relationships with the debtors, has the right to assert contractual claims against the debtors, has the right to control collection, and is subject to liability for the debtors' claims under the FTC Holder Rule.[63] On the other hand the Seventh Circuit has held, in a commercial case, that an assignee of a business contract does not automatically step into the shoes of the assignor for jurisdictional purposes.[64]

10.2.3.5 Jurisdiction in Bankruptcy Court and Over Counterclaims

If the debtor is litigating claims against a securitization trust in bankruptcy court, long-arm jurisdiction is not an issue. Nationwide service of process is allowed in bankruptcy court,[65] without regard to whether the defendant has minimum contacts with the state in which the bankruptcy court is located.[66]

Long-arm jurisdiction and due process issues are also not a concern if the trust voluntarily submits itself to the jurisdiction of the forum state's courts. For example, if the trust brings suit or joins in a suit in the forum state against the consumer, it subjects itself to the consumer's counterclaims or even the consumer's affirmative claims in a related suit, regardless of whether it has minimum contacts with the forum state.[67]

---

62 675 N.W.2d 812 (Iowa 2004).

63 16 C.F.R. § 433.2.

64 Purdue Research Found. v. Sanofi-Synthelabo, S.A., 338 F.3d 773 (7th Cir. 2003); *see also* Pilcher v. Direct Equity Lending, 189 F. Supp. 2d 1198, 1209 (D. Kan. 2002) (not distinguishing between general and specific jurisdiction); Lobatto v. Berney, 1999 WL 672994 (S.D.N.Y. Aug. 26, 1999) (court does not have jurisdiction over assignee of unsecured obligations simply because the assignor was subject to personal jurisdiction).

65 Fed. R. Bankr. P. 7004(b); *see* National Consumer Law Center, Consumer Bankruptcy Law and Practice § 13.3.2.1 (7th ed. 2004).

66 *In re* Fed. Fountain, Inc., 165 F.3d 600 (8th Cir. 1999).

67 Gen. Contracting & Trading Co. v. Interpole, Inc., 940 F.2d 20

10.3 The Enforceability of Arbitration Agreements

10.3.1 General

Loan agreements frequently include a binding arbitration clauses which the lender hopes will protect it from juries, class actions, claims for punitive damages, discovery requests, and publicity about any resulting award. Another NCLC manual, *Consumer Arbitration Agreements* (4th ed. 2004), examines the enforceability of such agreements in detail. This section focuses on five grounds to challenge an arbitration clause that have special relevance to the type of litigation that is the subject of this volume. This section then concludes with a brief enumeration of other possible theories to challenge an arbitration agreement. For a discussion of these other theories, see NCLC's *Consumer Arbitration Agreements*.

The Federal Arbitration Act (FAA) states that arbitration agreements are enforceable "save upon such grounds as exist at law or in equity for the revocation of any contract."[68] Nevertheless, arbitration is a matter of contract and a party cannot be required to submit to arbitration any dispute which he has not agreed so to submit."[69] If the parties did not agree to arbitrate certain claims, then the consumer cannot be forced to arbitrate those claims, even if it would be more efficient to do so.

In addition, an agreement is not enforceable if general state contract principles find no binding agreement—such as where the consumer never signed the agreement, there was fraud in the factum, or unconscionability. With the exception of insurance regulation described below,[70] federal law does not permit states to single out arbitration agreements and limit their enforceability.[71] It only allows state law to attack an arbitration agreement as it would any other contract. This section explores several of these, including that an arbitration agreement may not be binding if the agreement is void, was never finalized, was superseded by a different agreement, or where the parties to a dispute were not parties to the arbitration agreement.

Perhaps the most fertile area of the law today to challenge an arbitration agreement is that it is unconscionable. Because this is a complex, varied, and evolving area treated in great detail in NCLC's *Consumer Arbitration Agreements* (4th ed. 2004), it will not be covered in this section.

(1st Cir. 1991); Threlkeld v. Tucker, 496 F.2d 1101 (9th Cir. 1974); Nobel Floral, Inc. v. Pasero, 130 Cal. Rptr. 2d 881 (Ct. App. 2003).

68 9 U.S.C. § 2.

69 AT&T Technologies, Inc. v. Communications Workers of America, 475 U.S. 643, 648, 106 S. Ct. 1415, 1418, 89 L. Ed. 2d 648 (1986).

70 *See* § 10.3.6, *infra*.

71 *See* Doctor's Assocs., Inc. v. Cassarotto, 517 U.S. 681 (1996).

10.3.2 Where an Agreement Is Void: Usurious, Illegal and Unlicensed Loan Agreements

Courts have found that arbitration agreements are not binding if the whole contract of which they are a part is void.[72] "Clearly, if a party cannot be forced to arbitrate if the contract does not contain a valid arbitration clause, then a party cannot be forced to arbitrate if the contract containing the arbitration clause, which gives the arbitration clause viability, is found to be void."[73]

State usury statutes may specify that a usurious contract is void. If the contract is usurious, the agreement and the arbitration clause therein cannot be enforced.[74] Some courts have decided that the issue of whether a contract is usurious, and the arbitration agreement therefore void, is to be determined by the court, not the arbitrator.[75] But a number of recent decisions have held otherwise.[76]

For example, the Sixth Circuit appears to distinguish between void *ab initio* and contracts later declared void. While a consumer cannot be bound by a contract that never really existed, that is void *ab initio*, a consumer can be bound by a contract that he intended to enter, but later discovered that certain terms of the contact may violate state usury law, thus voiding the contract.[77] More is required to void an arbitration clause than an allegation of statutory violation. There must be a failure to assent to the documents or a failure of signatory power.[78]

Thus courts might distinguish between void and voidable. If a contract is void by operation of law, the arbitration agreement is void. But if the law allows the consumer to seek to rescind a contract on certain grounds, then the contract is voidable, but not void, and the arbitrator must make that determination.[79] Nevertheless, a number of recent decisions have even sent an arbitrator cases where the consumer argued that the usury violation made the contract void *ab initio*.[80]

States often require merchants or lenders to become licensed, and state law specifies that operation of that business without a license makes any resulting contracts void.[81] If a contract is void for this reason, the arbitration clause is also void.[82] The determination as to whether a lender or other merchant's contracts are void for want of a license is to be determined by the court, not an arbitrator.[83] One current example of such unlicensed activity is credit agreements entered into by title pawn or payday lending companies, when state law requires small loan lenders to be licensed but these type of lending companies mistakenly believe they are not covered by this state requirement.[84]

---

72 *See* Sphere Drake Ins. Ltd. v. Clarendon Nat'l Ins. Co., 256 F.3d 587 (7th Cir. 2001).

73 Ala. Catalog Sales v. Harris, 794 So. 2d 312 (Ala. 2000); Pittsfield Weaving Co. v. Grove Textiles, Inc., 430 A.2d 638 (N.H. 1981).

74 Ala. Catalog Sales v. Harris, 794 So. 2d 312 (Ala. 2000) (payday lending); Cardegna v. Buckeye Check Cashing, Inc., 894 So. 2d 860 (Fla. 2005) (payday lending case); FastFunding The Co. v. Betts, 758 So. 2d 1143 (Fla. Dist. Ct. App. 2000) (payday lending case).

75 Ala. Catalog Sales v. Harris, 794 So. 2d 312 (Ala. 2000) (payday lending); Williams v. Showmethemoney Check Cashers, Clearinghouse No. 52,500 (Ark. Cir. Ct. Aug. 26, 1999) (payday lending case), *aff'd on other grounds*, 342 Ark. 112, 27 S.W.3d 361 (Ark. 2000); Cardegna v. Buckeye Check Cashing, Inc., 894 So. 2d 860 (Fla. 2005) (payday lending case); Fast-Funding The Co. v. Betts, 758 So. 2d 1143 (Fla. Dist. Ct. App. 2000) (payday lending case); Party Yards, Inc. v. Templeton, 751 So. 2d 121 (Fla. Dist. Ct. App. 2000).

76 Bess v. Check Express, 294 F.3d 1298 (11th Cir. 2002); Burden v. Check Into Cash of Kentucky, L.L.C., 267 F.3d 483 (6th Cir. 2001); Conner v. Instant Cash Advance, 2003 WL 446197 (S.D. Ind. Feb. 20, 2003).

77 Burden v. Check Into Cash of Kentucky, L.L.C., 267 F.3d 483 (6th Cir. 2001).

78 *Id.*

79 *See* Sphere Drake Ins. Ltd. v. Clarendon Nat'l Ins. Co., 256 F.3d 587 (7th Cir. 2001) (holding that, if a contract is void and wholly unenforceable, an arbitration clause within that contract will not be enforced; if a contract is merely voidable, such as a contract induced by fraud, the arbitration clause will be enforced); Haga v. Martin Homes, Inc., 1999 Ohio App. LEXIS 1740 (Ohio Ct. App. Apr. 19, 1999). *Cf. In re* FirstMerit Bank, 52 S.W.3d 749 (Tex. 2001) (that the consumer has revoked acceptance of a purchase does not void the arbitration agreement; revocation of acceptance does not automatically void a sales agreement).

80 Bess v. Check Express, 294 F.3d 1298 (11th Cir. 2002); Burden v. Check Into Cash of Kentucky, L.L.C., 267 F.3d 483 (6th Cir. 2001); Conner v. Instant Cash Advance, 2003 WL 446197 (S.D. Ind. Feb. 20, 2003).

81 *See* S. Metal Treating Co. v. Goodner, 271 Ala. 510 (1960).

82 *See* Cmty. Care of Am. of Ala., Inc. v. Davis, 850 So. 2d 283 (Ala. 2002); Camaro Trading Co. v. Nissei Sangyo Am., Ltd., 577 So. 2d 1274 (Ala. 1991); Cheatham v. Air Sys. Eng'g Co., Clearinghouse No. 51,969 (Cal. Super. Ct. Apr. 30, 1997); Island House Developers v. AMAC Constr. Co., 686 So. 2d 1377 (Fla. Dist. Ct. App. 1997); Jensen v. Quik Int'l, 801 N.E.2d 1124, 1126 (Ill. App. Ct. 2003) (franchisor's possession of state license is a condition precedent to any contract, so court must resolve allegation that defendant operated without license); Michelson v. Voison, 658 N.W.2d 188 (Mich. Ct. App. 2003) (viatical settlement by unlicensed securities dealer); Nature's 10 Jewelers v. Gunderson, 648 N.W.2d 804 (S.D. 2002) (unlicensed jewelry store franchisor); *see also* Ackel v. Ackel, 696 So. 2d 140 (La. Ct. App. 1997) (whether contract is void as against public policy is not arbitrable). *But see* Burden v. Check Into Cash of Kentucky, L.L.C., 267 F.3d 483 (6th Cir. 2001).

83 Harris v. Montgomery Catalog Sales, Clearinghouse No. 52,505 (Ala. Cir. Ct. May 21, 1999) (payday lending), *aff'd sub nom.* Ala. Catalog Sales v. Harris, 794 So. 2d 312 (Ala. 2000); *see* Brown v. Pool Depot, Inc., 853 So. 2d 181 (Ala. 2002) (unlicensed pool installation company); Cmty. Care of Am. of Ala., Inc. v. Davis, 830 So. 2d 283 (Ala. 2002) (unlicensed nursing home); Michelson v. Voison, 658 N.W.2d 188 (Mich. Ct. App. 2003); Nature's 10 Jewelers v. Gunderson, 648 N.W.2d 804 (S.D. 2002). *But see* Snowden v. Checkpoint Check Cashing, 290 F.3d 631 (4th Cir. 2002).

84 Harris v. Montgomery Catalog Sales, Clearinghouse No. 52,505 (Ala. Cir. Ct. May 21, 1999), *aff'd sub nom.* Ala. Catalog Sales

Similarly, if a contract is criminal in nature, courts will not enforce an agreement to arbitrate disputes under that contract.[85] No court will lend its assistance in any way towards carrying out the terms of an illegal contract.[86] Illegal promises will not be enforced in cases controlled by federal law.[87]

10.3.3 Where a Contract Was Never Finalized: "Yo-Yo" and Other Condition Precedent Contracts

A condition precedent contract is one that is not effective until a condition occurs. A condition subsequent contract is one that is effective, subject to being undone if a condition later occurs. For example, a consumer can enter into a condition precedent contract with a dealer to purchase a car, that will not be effective until financing goes through. If financing does not go through, the consumer never owned the car and the contract was never effective. In a condition subsequent sale, the dealer will have turned over title to the consumer and there is an agreement that, if the financing falls through, the consumer must turn title back to the dealer.

In a condition precedent transaction, where the condition precedent does not occur, there is no contract that was consummated, and an arbitration clause that was part of that contract is not effective. Then, for example, if the consumer wants to bring a tort or UDAP claim against the dealer for misrepresenting that the deal would go through, that claim can be brought in court, because the arbitration clause was never in effect.[88]

The result may be different if the consumer brings a claim on the contract, simultaneously claiming the contract is in effect and that the arbitration provision in the contract is not. For example, where a company rescinds a contract pursuant to a condition subsequent, and the consumer brings an action on that contract, claiming it should still be in effect, a court has found that the consumer cannot simultaneously seek to

avoid arbitration by claiming the arbitration clause in the same agreement has been rescinded.[89]

10.3.4 Where Arbitration Agreement Is Superseded by Later Agreement

Because an arbitration agreement is like any other agreement, it is not effective if that agreement has been superseded by a later agreement. In automobile finance and other consumer credit transactions, there are often a series of documents the consumer signs. Issues are raised when the arbitration clause is found in some of those documents, but not in the final installment sales agreement or loan agreement. For example, motor vehicle sales finance statutes and retail installment sales acts often require that the installment sale be evidenced by a writing that contains all the agreements of the parties with reference to the subject matter of the sale.[90]

If a car dealer places the arbitration agreement in the sales order or other preliminary document, but not in the installment sales agreement, then the arbitration agreement is not part of the final transaction, and is not binding on the consumer.[91] The sales order is not the installment sales agreement, and the final agreement does not contain the arbitration clause. Consequently, the final terms of the parties does not include an arbitration requirement.[92]

This is even the case where the arbitration clause in the sales order explicitly states it applies to the installment sales agreement. State installment sales acts typically either explicitly or implicitly require that the parties execute a single, comprehensive installment agreement, without side agreements or riders.[93] This single document requirement may also be found in state UDAP regulations or other state legislation. The attempt to put the arbitration clause in a side agreement runs afoul of this single document rule.[94]

---

v. Harris, 794 So. 2d 312 (Ala. 2000); Williams v. Showmethemoney Check Cashers, Clearinghouse No. 52,500 (Ark. Cir. Ct. Aug. 26, 1999), *aff'd on other grounds*, 342 Ark. 112, 27 S.W.3d 361 (Ark. 2000).

85 Cardegna v. Buckeye Check Cashing, Inc., 894 So. 2d 860 (Fla. 2005) (payday lending case); FastFunding The Co. v. Betts, 758 So. 2d 1143 (Fla. Dist. Ct. App. 2000) (payday lending case); Party Yards, Inc. v. Templeton, 751 So. 2d 121 (Fla. Dist. Ct. App. 2000).

86 McMullen v. Hoffman, 174 U.S. 639, 19 S. Ct. 839, 43 L. Ed. 1117 (1899).

87 Kaiser Steel Corp. v. Mullins, 455 U.S. 72, 102 S. Ct. 851, 70 L. Ed. 2d 833 (1982).

88 Eady v. Bill Heard Chevrolet, Co., 274 F. Supp. 2d 1284 (M.D. Ala. 2003); *Ex parte* Payne, 741 So. 2d 398 (Ala. 1999); *see also Ex parte* Horton Family Housing, Inc., 2003 WL 22753458 (Ala. Nov. 21, 2003). *But see* Jacobson v. J.K. Pontiac GMAC Truck, Inc., 2001 U.S. Dist. LEXIS 20393 (N.D. Ill. Dec. 10, 2001).

89 Celtic Life Ins. Co. v. McLendon, 814 So. 2d 222 (Ala. 2001).
90 *See, e.g.*, Mich. Comp. Laws §§ 492.112(a), 566.302.
91 Rugumbwa v. Betten Motor Sales, 136 F. Supp. 2d 729 (W.D. Mich. 2001).
92 *Id.*
93 *See, e.g.*, Cal. Civ. Code § 2985.8 (leasing); Wash. Rev. Code §§ 63.14.020, 63.14.040; Kroupa v. Sunrise Ford, 77 Cal. App. 4th 835, 92 Cal. Rptr. 2d 42 (Cal. Ct. App. 1999); Commonwealth v. Metro Chrysler-Plymouth Jeep-Eagle, Inc., Clearinghouse No. 52,028 (Pa. Commw. Ct. 1997); Kenworthy v. Bolin, 17 Wash. App. 650, 564 P.2d 835 (1977). *See also* Ohio Rev. Code § 1317.02. *But see* Sharlow v. Wally McCarthy Pontiac-GMC Trucks-Hyundai, Inc., 2000 U.S. App. LEXIS 15627 (8th Cir. July 6, 2000) (unpublished, citation limited) (following *Scott*); Scott v. Forest Lake Chrysler-Plymouth-Dodge, 611 N.W.2d 346 (Minn. 2000) (contingency clause need not be included in retail installment contract despite single document rule).
94 Rugumbwa v. Betten Motor Sales, 136 F. Supp. 2d 729 (W.D. Mich. 2001); Lozada v. Dale Baker Oldsmobile, Inc., 197 F.R.D. 321 (W.D. Mich. 2000).

In addition, an integration clause in the final contract itself may be enough to void an arbitration agreement in a side document. Such integration clauses often state that the agreement is the full, final, and only agreement between the parties. Similarly, where the arbitration clause is found in a proposed agreement, but the final agreement does not contain the arbitration clause, then the clause is not enforceable.[95]

Consumers often enter into a series of loan transactions with the same creditor, such as when a loan is flipped a number of times into new loans. Another example is where there are a series of payday loans. Where an arbitration agreement is included in one loan, but not in later loans between the parties, the arbitration agreement does not apply to a dispute relating to the later loans.[96]

10.3.5 Where the Parties to a Dispute Are Not Parties to the Arbitration Agreement

10.3.5.1 Are Co-signers and Other Non-signatories Bound by Arbitration Agreement?

Consumers are not bound by arbitration agreements they did not sign, even if their spouse or other related party signed the agreement.[97] For example, where the principal obligor has signed an arbitration agreement, that should not be binding on a surety or co-signer who did not sign the agreement.[98] Similarly, a consumer may not be bound by an arbitration agreement where the consumer only signed the financing agreement, and another consumer signed the sales agreement that contained the arbitration clause.[99] Nothing in the FAA authorizes a court to compel arbitration of parties not covered by the agreement.[100] "It goes without saying that a contract cannot bind a nonparty."[101]

Nevertheless, courts may find an arbitration provision enforceable when the plaintiffs are third party beneficiaries of consumers who did in fact sign the arbitration agreement.[102] To find a third party beneficiary status, at a minimum, the consumer's claim must seek the benefit of the agreement that contains the arbitration clause.[103] Thus where a consumer that has not signed the agreement brings a tort claim that does not rely on the agreement, no third party beneficiary status is created, and the consumer is not bound by the arbitration agreement.[104]

---

95 *See* Aceros Prefabricados, S.A. v. Tradearbed, Inc., 2001 U.S. Dist. LEXIS 3445 (S.D.N.Y. Mar. 28, 2001), *reconsideration denied*, 2001 U.S. Dist. LEXIS 5143 (S.D.N.Y. Apr. 26, 2001), *vacated on other grounds*, 282 F.3d 92 (2d Cir. 2002).

96 Smith v. Steinkamp, 318 F.3d 775 (7th Cir. 2003); Florida Title Loans, Inc. v. Christie, 770 So. 2d 750 (Fla. Dist. Ct. App. 2000).

97 *See* Fleetwood Enterprises, Inc. v. Gaskamp, 2002 U.S. App. LEXIS 933 (5th Cir. Jan. 24, 2002); Oakwood Mobile Homes, Inc. v. Godsey, 824 So. 2d 713 (Ala. 2001); Equifirst Corp. v. Ware, 808 So. 2d 1 (Ala. 2001); Med Ctr. Cars, Inc. v. Smith, 727 So. 2d 9 (Ala. 1998); *Ex parte* Dickinson, 711 So. 2d 984 (Ala. 1998); Buckner v. Tamarin, 98 Cal. App. 4th 140, 119 Cal. Rptr. 2d 489 (2002) (fact that patient had signed medical arbitration agreement compelling arbitration of all claims arising out of doctor's treatment and care did not waive right of adult daughters to sue for medical malpractice); Pacheco v. Allen, 55 P.3d 141 (Colo. Ct. App. 2001), *aff'd on other grounds*, 71 P.3d 375 (Colo. 2003); Shea v. Global Travel Mktg., Inc., 870 So. 2d 20 (Fla. Dist. Ct. App. 2003) (minor son was not bound by arbitration clause signed by mother on his behalf in wrongful death case brought by father after minor son was killed by hyenas on an African safari), *review granted*, 873 So. 2d 1223 (Fla. 2004); *see also* Grundstad v. Ritt, 106 F.3d 201 (7th Cir. 1997) (guarantor not bound by arbitration agreement); Kaplan v. First Options of Chicago, Inc., 19 F.3d 1503 (3d Cir. 1994), *aff'd*, 514 U.S. 938, 115 S. Ct. 1920, 131 L. Ed. 2d 985 (1995); Clausen v. Watlow Elec. Mfg. Co., 242 F. Supp. 2d 877 (D. Or. 2002) (corporation that signed arbitration agreement with independent contractor could not enforce agreement

against individual employee of the contractor); Liberty Communications, Inc. v. MCI Telecommunications Corp., 733 So. 2d 571 (Fla. Dist. Ct. App. 1999) (individual signed in corporate capacity and thus clause not binding on individual). *But see* Fluehmann v. Associates Fin. Servs., 2002 WL 500564 (D. Mass. Mar. 29, 2002) (finding wife bound by husband's signature on mortgage documents because wife "exploited or benefited from" the contract).

98 Grundstad v. Ritt, 106 F.3d 201 (7th Cir. 1997) (guarantor not bound by arbitration agreement).

99 Sikes v. Ganley Pontiac Honda, 2001 Ohio App. LEXIS 4065 (Ohio Ct. App. Sept. 13, 2001).

100 Equal Employment Opportunity Comm'n v. Waffle House, Inc., 534 U.S. 279, 122 S. Ct. 754, 151 L. Ed. 2d 755 (2002).

101 *Id.*

102 Ballard Servs., Inc. v. Conner, 807 So. 2d 519 (Ala. 2001); Colonial Sales-Lease-Rental, Inc. v. Target Auction & Land Co., 735 So. 2d 1161 (Ala. 1999); Westendorf v. Gateway 2000, Inc., 2000 Del. Ch. LEXIS 54 (Del. Ch. Mar. 16, 2000), *aff'd*, 763 A.2d 92 (Del. 2000); Terminix Int'l Co. v. Ponzio, 693 So. 2d 104 (Fla. Dist. Ct. App. 1997); *In re* FirstMerit Bank, 52 S.W.3d 749 (Tex. 2001); Nationwide of Bryan v. Dyer, 969 S.W.2d 518 (Tex. App. 1998). *But see* Kaplan v. First Options of Chicago, Inc., 19 F.3d 1503 (3d Cir. 1994), *aff'd*, 514 U.S. 938 (1995).

103 *See, e.g.*, Crayton v. Conseco Fin. Corp., 237 F. Supp. 2d 1322 (M.D. Ala. 2002) (finding no third party beneficiary status when mobile home purchaser took over financing a mobile home which was in the process of being repossessed from another consumer; even though original contract had contained an arbitration clause, purchaser did not have to arbitrate her claims because her claims were brought under her separate financing agreement with Conseco to take over the first consumer's account); Fluehmann v. Associates Fin. Servs., 2002 U.S. Dist. LEXIS 5755 (D. Mass. Mar. 29, 2002); Ballard Servs., Inc. v. Conner, 807 So. 2d 519 (Ala. 2001); *In re* FirstMerit Bank, 52 S.W.3d 749 (Tex. 2001).

104 Oakwood Mobile Homes, Inc. v. Godsey, 824 So. 2d 713 (Ala. 2001); Equifirst Corp. v. Ware, 808 So. 2d 1 (Ala. 2001).

10.3.5.2 Can a Party Not Named in the Arbitration Agreement Force the Consumer to Arbitrate Claims?

Consumers should be able to avoid arbitrating a dispute with a lender, broker, insurer or other entity where that entity is not a party to the arbitration clause and is not listed in the arbitration clause as a party to the agreement.[105] Arbitration is a matter of contract and a consumer is entitled to know, by looking at the terms of the arbitration agreement, what potential parties are covered by the agreement. The clear intent of the arbitration agreement is that the agreement applies only to the parties enumerated in the agreement.[106]

Nevertheless, there are situations where a court will find that consumers are bound to arbitrate claims against certain individuals or entities who were not explicitly listed in the original arbitration agreement. Courts sometimes find that a party not mentioned in the arbitration agreement can still enforce the agreement based on equitable estoppel.[107] Equitable estoppel may be found to apply only where the consumer sues a party not enumerated in the arbitration clause, and the consumer is relying on the terms of the agreement containing the arbitration clause in asserting claims against that party.[108]

If the consumer's claim is not based on the contract containing the arbitration agreement, then equitable estoppel should not apply, even if the defendant is closely related and has engaged in concerted misconduct with a party listed in the arbitration agreement.[109] Similarly, if there are two agreements, and the arbitration clause is in one, for estoppel to operate, the consumer's claims must be based on the contract containing the arbitration clause, and not the other agreement.[110]

Even then, finding equitable estoppel is in the court's discretion.[111] Usually, courts will also see whether the consumer also alleges interdependent and concerted misconduct between the merchant or creditor signing the arbitration agreement and the defendant.[112] Courts will also look to see whether the consumer is bringing a claim against the merchant or creditor enumerated in the arbitration agreement, and whether that claim will go to arbitration. If the merchant signing the contract is not or will not be involved in an arbitration proceeding, then courts are less likely to find equitable estoppel to apply.[113]

---

105 Jim Burke Automotive, Inc. v. McGrue, 826 So. 2d 122 (Ala. 2002); Monsanto Co. v. Benton Farm, 813 So. 2d 867 (Ala. 2001); Parkway Dodge, Inc. v. Yarbrough, 779 So. 2d 1205 (Ala. 2000).

106 Universal Underwriters Life Ins. Co. v. Dutton, 736 So. 2d 564 (Ala. 1999); First Family Fin. Servs, Inc. v. Rogers, 736 So. 2d 553 (Ala. 1999).

107 *See* Choctaw Generation Ltd. P'ship v. American Home Assurance Co., 271 F.3d 403 (2d Cir. 2001); MS Dealer Serv. Corp. v. Franklin, 177 F.3d 942 (11th Cir. 1999), *remanded with instructions to grant motion to compel arbitration*, 1999 U.S. Dist. LEXIS 10662 (N.D. Ala. July 9, 1999); Goodwin v. Ford Motor Credit Co., 970 F. Supp. 1007 (M.D. Ala. 1997) (FMCC can enforce arbitration agreement found in dealership's installment sales agreements when FMCC is the intended and actual assignee); Boyd v. Homes of Legend, Inc., 981 F. Supp. 1423 (M.D. Ala. 1997), *remanded on jurisdictional grounds*, 188 F.3d 1294 (11th Cir. 1999); Roberson v. Money Tree, 954 F. Supp. 1519 (M.D. Ala. 1997) (forced-placed insurer can benefit from arbitration provision); Staples v. Money Tree, Inc., 936 F. Supp. 856 (M.D. Ala. 1996); Usina Costa Pinto S.A. Acucar E Alcool v. Louis Dreyfus Sugar Co., 933 F. Supp. 1170 (S.D.N.Y. 1996); *Ex parte* Napier, 723 So. 2d 49 (Ala. 1998); *Ex parte* Isbell, 708 So. 2d 571 (Ala. 1997); Nissan Motor Acceptance Corp. v. Ross, 703 So. 2d 324 (Ala. 1997) (assignee steps into shoes of assignor); *Ex parte* Gray, 686 So. 2d 250 (Ala. 1996) (salesman can enforce arbitration agreement entered into by dealership employing the salesperson); *Ex parte* Gates, 675 So. 2d 371 (Ala. 1996). *But see* Boyd v. Homes of Legend, Inc., 981 F. Supp. 1423 (M.D. Ala. 1997) (finding estoppel theory inapplicable to the facts of the case), *remanded on jurisdictional grounds*, 188 F.3d 1294 (11th Cir. 1999); *In re* Knepp, 229 B.R. 821 (Bankr. N.D. Ala. 1999).

108 *In re* Humana Inc. Managed Care Litigation, 285 F.3d 971 (11th Cir. 2002), *rev'd on other grounds*, 538 U.S. 401 (2003); Choctaw Generation Ltd. P'ship v. American Home Assurance

Co., 271 F.3d 403 (2d Cir. 2001); MS Dealer Serv. Corp. v. Franklin, 177 F.3d 942 (11th Cir. 1999), *remanded with instructions to grant motion to compel arbitration*, 1999 U.S. Dist. LEXIS 10662 (N.D. Ala. July 9, 1999); Sunkist Soft Drinks, Inc. v. Sunkist Growers, Inc., 10 F.3d 753 (11th Cir. 1993).

109 *In re* Humana Inc. Managed Care Litigation, 285 F.3d 971 (11th Cir. 2002), *rev'd on other grounds*, 538 U.S. 401 (2003); Hill v. GE Power Sys., Inc., 282 F.3d 343 (5th Cir. 2002) (trial court did not abuse discretion); Grigson v. Creative Artists Agency, 210 F.3d 524 (5th Cir. 2000); Brown v. Anderson, 102 S.W.3d 245 (Tex. App. 2003). *But see* North Am. Ins. Co. v. Moore, 2002 WL 31050995, at *3 (N.D. Miss. Aug. 26, 2003) (non-signatory insurer can compel arbitration of insured's claims because those claims are "intertwined" with insured's state court claims against the defendant who signed the arbitration clause), *aff'd without op.*, 2003 WL 21418113 (June 10, 2003).

110 Southern Energy Homes, Inc. v. Kennedy, 774 So. 2d 540 (Ala. 2000). *See also* Carriage Homes v. Channell, 825 So. 2d 90 (Ala. 2002).

111 Hill v. GE Power Sys., Inc., 282 F.3d 343 (5th Cir. 2002).

112 *In re* Humana Inc. Managed Care Litigation, 285 F.3d 971 (11th Cir. 2002), *rev'd on other grounds*, 538 U.S. 401 (2003); Grigson v. Creative Artists Agency, 210 F.3d 524 (5th Cir. 2000); MS Dealer Serv. Corp. v. Franklin, 177 F.3d 942 (11th Cir. 1999), *remanded with instructions to grant motion to compel arbitration*, 1999 U.S. Dist. LEXIS 10662 (N.D. Ala. July 9, 1999); Jureczki v. Banc One Texas, 252 F. Supp. 2d 368 (S.D. Tex. 2003), *aff'd*, 2003 WL 22121027(5th Cir. Sept. 15, 2003) (unpublished, citation limited); Bellizan v. Easy Money of La., Inc., 2002 WL 1066750, at *6 (E.D. La. May 29, 2002); *In re* Hartigan, 107 S.W.3d 684 (Tex. App. 2003).

113 *In re* Humana Inc. Managed Care Litigation, 285 F.3d 971 (11th Cir. 2002), *rev'd on other grounds*, 538 U.S. 401 (2003); MS Dealer Serv. Corp. v. Franklin, 177 F.3d 942 (11th Cir. 1999), *remanded with instructions to grant motion to compel arbitration*, 1999 U.S. Dist. LEXIS 10662 (N.D. Ala. July 9, 1999).

In general, assignees[114] and individual employees of the corporate signatory[115] may be able to enforce an arbitration agreement. On the other hand, a credit insurer,[116] forced-placed insurer[117] or service contract company[118] will have difficulty piggy-backing on the dealer's arbitration clause. A number of cases also find that a corporation's arbitration clause does not cover claims against its president or principal.[119]

10.3.6 Special Rules for Insurance Transactions

10.3.6.1 General

While the Federal Arbitration Act (FAA) preempts state law that limits the enforceability of arbitration agreements, there is an important exception for insurance transactions. The federal McCarran-Ferguson Act prohibits federal regulation of insurance practices to the extent that they would invalidate, impair or supersede state law enacted for the purpose of regulating the business of insurance, unless the federal law explicitly relates to the business of insurance.[120] The FAA does not explicitly relate to the business of insurance.[121] Consequently, if a state statute regulating insurance limits the enforceability of an arbitration provision, the FAA conflicts with the state statute, and therefore state law, not the FAA, determines whether the arbitration provision is enforceable.[122]

There are two issues concerning whether state law limits the enforceability of an arbitration agreement as to insurance claims. One is whether a state statute is one enacted for the purpose of regulating the business of insurance, and the other is whether a state statute enacted for that purpose restricts the enforceability of arbitration agreements.

---

114 Goodwin v. Ford Motor Credit Co., 970 F. Supp. 1007 (M.D. Ala. 1997); Universal Underwriters Life Ins. Co. v. Dutton, 736 So. 2d 564 (Ala. 1999); Nissan Motor Acceptance Corp. v. Ross, 703 So. 2d 324 (Ala. 1997). *Cf.* Green Tree Fin. Corp. v. Channell, 825 So. 2d 90 (Ala. 2002) (where assignee could not take advantage of arbitration clause in one document between consumer and dealer, it could still take advantage of arbitration clause found in the installment sales agreement). *But cf.* Cheatham v. Air Sys. Eng'g Co., Clearinghouse No. 51,969 (Cal. Super. Ct. Apr. 30, 1997); Mohamed v. Auto Nation USA Corp., 89 S.W.3d 830 (Tex. App. 2002).

115 Monsanto Co. v. Benton Farm, 813 So. 2d 867 (Ala. 2001); *Ex parte* Gray, 686 So. 2d 250 (Ala. 1996) (salesman can enforce arbitration agreement entered into by dealership employing the salesperson).

116 *In re* Knepp, 229 B.R. 821 (Bankr. N.D. Ala. 1999); Universal Underwriters Life Ins. Co. v. Dutton, 736 So. 2d 564 (Ala. 1999); First Family Fin. Servs., Inc. v. Rogers, 736 So. 2d 553 (Ala. 1999). *But see* Staples v. Money Tree, Inc., 936 F. Supp. 856 (M.D. Ala. 1996); *Ex parte* Napier, 723 So. 2d 49 (Ala. 1998) (seller of physical damage insurance on mobile home).

117 *Ex parte* Jones, 686 So. 2d 1166 (Ala. 1996). *But see* Roberson v. Money Tree, 954 F. Supp. 1519 (M.D. Ala. 1997).

118 *But see* MS Dealer Serv. Corp. v. Franklin, 177 F.3d 942 (11th Cir. 1999) (claims against service contract company are based on the contract containing arbitration clause and are based on interdependent misconduct between dealer signing contract and service contract company), *remanded with instructions to grant motion to compel arbitration*, 1999 U.S. Dist. LEXIS 10662 (N.D. Ala. July 9, 1999).

119 Dumais v. American Golf Corp., 150 F. Supp. 2d 1182 (D.N.M. 2001), *aff'd on other grounds*, 299 F.3d 1216 (10th Cir. 2002); Suttle v. Decesare, 2001 Ohio App. LEXIS 3030 (Ohio Ct. July 5, 2001) (arbitration agreement running to corporation does not benefit corporation president individually); ACRS, Inc. v. Blue Cross & Blue Shield, 722 N.E.2d 1040 (Ohio Ct. App. 1998); St. Vincent Charity Hosp. v. URS Consultants, Inc., 677 N.E.2d 381 (Ohio Ct. App. 1996); Kline v. Oak Ridge Builders, 656 N.E.2d 992 (Ohio Ct. App. 1995); Teramar v. Rodier Corp., 531 N.E.2d 721 (Ohio Ct. App. 1987). *But see* Levitan v. Fanfare Media Works, Inc., 2003 WL 21028339 (Cal. Ct. App. May 8, 2003).

120 15 U.S.C. § 1012(b); *see also* United States Dep't of the Treasury v. Fabe, 508 U.S. 491, 113 S. Ct. 2202, 124 L. Ed. 2d 449 (1993).

121 *See* Standard Sec. Life Ins. Co. of N.Y. v. West, 267 F.3d 821, 823 (8th Cir. 2001) (noting agreement of parties that FAA does not specifically relate to business of insurance); Am. Bankers Ins. Co. v. Crawford, 757 So. 2d 1125 (Ala. 1999); Smith v. Pacificare Behavioral Health of Cal., Inc., 93 Cal. App. 4th 139, 154, 113 Cal. Rptr. 2d 140, 151 (2001) (noting agreement of parties that FAA does not specifically relate to business of insurance); Cox v. Woodmen of the World Ins. Co., 556 S.E.2d 397, 400 (S.C. Ct. App. 2001) (same); Little v. Allstate Ins. Co., 167 Vt. 171, 705 A.2d 538 (1997).

122 Standard Sec. Life Ins. Co. of N.Y. v. West, 267 F.3d 821 (8th Cir. 2001); Quackenbush v. Allstate Ins. Co., 121 F.3d 1372 (9th Cir. 1997) (insurance statute prohibiting insurance liquidator from being compelled to arbitrate disputes prevails over FAA); Stephens v. Am. Int'l Ins. Co., 66 F.3d 41 (2d Cir. 1995); Mut. Reinsurance Bureau v. Great Plains Mut. Ins. Co., 969 F.2d 931 (10th Cir.), *cert. denied*, 506 U.S. 1001 (1992); Balaban-Zilke v. Cigna Healthcare of Cal., Inc., 2003 WL 21228038 (Cal. Ct. App. May 28, 2003); Ciccarelli v. Blue Cross of Cal., 2003 WL 150045 (Cal. Ct. App. Jan. 22, 2003); Imbler v. PacifiCare of Cal., Inc., 103 Cal. App. 4th 567, 126 Cal. Rptr. 2d 715 (2002); Pagarigan v. Super. Ct., 102 Cal. App. 4th 1121, 126 Cal. Rptr. 2d 124 (2001); Smith v. Pacificare Behavioral Health of Cal., Inc., 93 Cal. App. 4th 139, 158, 161–62, 113 Cal. Rptr. 2d 140, 154, 156–57 (2001); Allen v. Pacheco, 71 P.3d 375 (Colo. 2003); Cont'l Ins. Co. v. Equity Residential Properties Trust, 255 Ga. App. 445, 565 S.E.2d 603 (2002); Friday v. Trinity Universal, 262 Kan. 347, 939 P.2d 869 (1997); Little v. Allstate Ins. Co., 167 Vt. 171, 705 A.2d 538 (1997); *see also* Davister Corp. v. United Republic Life Ins. Co., 152 F.3d 1277 (10th Cir. 1998), *cert. denied*, 525 U.S. 1177 (1999); Munich Am. Reinsurance Co. v. Crawford, 141 F.3d 585 (5th Cir. 1998); Murff v. Prof'l Med. Ins. Co., 97 F.3d 289 (8th Cir. 1996); Towe, Hester & Erwin, Inc. v. Kan. City Fire & Marine Ins. Co., 947 P.2d 594 (Okla. Ct. App. 1997) (while recognizing that Oklahoma law which limits arbitration in insurance would oust the FAA, the dispute in that case between an insurance company and its employees did not relate to insurance); Cox v. Woodmen of the World Ins. Co., 556 S.E.2d 397 (S.C. Ct. App. 2001) (South Carolina's anti-arbitration insurance provision not preempted by FAA, but provision does not apply to fraternal benefits association).

10.3.6.2 Is a State Law One Enacted for the Purpose of Regulating Insurance?

A number of state statutes limit the enforceability of arbitration, but do not mention insurance specifically.[123] Instead, these are laws of general application that apply to insurance and most other forms of commerce. The question is whether they are state laws enacted for the purpose of regulating insurance sufficient to trigger the McCarran-Ferguson Act.[124]

For example, Alabama law states that agreements to submit controversies to arbitration cannot be enforced.[125] That statute does not mention insurance and the Alabama courts find that the statute is not one regulating the business of insurance, so as to supersede the FAA under McCarran-Ferguson.[126]

On the other hand, a statute need not be enacted solely for the purpose of regulating insurance. For example, a number of states have enacted the Uniform Arbitration Act, but have explicitly stated that the provision concerning the enforceability of arbitration agreements does not apply to insurance or certain lines of insurance.[127] Such an exemption is a state enactment for the purpose of regulating insurance.[128]

10.3.6.3 Does State Insurance Law Restrict the Enforceability of Arbitration Agreements?

It is not enough that a state enact statutes regulating the business of insurance. These statutes must also restrict the enforceability of arbitration agreements. If they do not, there is no conflict with the FAA, and the FAA continues to apply.[129] State insurance law does not preempt the field, but only supersedes federal law that is inconsistent with it.[130]

A number of states clearly restrict the enforceability of arbitration agreements concerning certain lines of insurance. For example, South Dakota voids arbitration agreements in insurance policies,[131] and Wisconsin requires that arbitration clauses must be approved by the insurance commissioner.[132]

One important example is that a number of states have amended their enactment of the Uniform Arbitration Act to specify that arbitration agreements are enforceable except as to insurance claims.[133] Although there is some ambiguity here, the clear legislative intent is to prohibit the enforceability of arbitration agreements as to insurance claims.[134] Similarly, an insurance commissioner under authority of insurance legislation could prohibit the use of arbitration clauses relating to a particular line of insurance, or could refuse to approve of an insurance policy that contained an arbitration clause.

10.3.7 Other Challenges to Agreement's Enforceability

Other challenges to the enforceability of a consumer arbitration agreement are examined in NCLC's *Consumer Arbitration Agreements* (4th ed. 2004). These include:

• That the transaction is not in interstate commerce and

---

123 *See* National Consumer Law Center, Consumer Arbitration Agreements § 2.3.2 (4th ed. 2004).

124 For the most recent Supreme Court discussion about whether a statute "regulates the business of insurance," see UNUM Life Ins. Co. v. Ward, 526 U.S. 358, 119 S. Ct. 1380, 143 L. Ed. 2d 462 (1999).

125 Ala. Code § 8-1-41.

126 Am. Bankers Ins. Co. v. Crawford, 757 So. 2d 1125 (Ala. 1999); *see also* Clayton v. Woodmen of the World Life Ins. Soc'y, 981 F. Supp. 1447 (M.D. Ala. 1997); Celtic Life Ins. Co. v. McLendon, 814 So. 2d 222 (Ala. 2001). *See also* Triton Lines, Inc. v. S.S. Mut. Underwriting Ass'n, 707 F. Supp. 277, 279 (S.D. Tex. 1989) (dealing with interrelationship of Texas insurance code and state UDAP statute); Hart v. Orion Ins. Co., 453 F.2d 1358 (10th Cir. 1971); Hamilton Life Ins. Co. v. Republic Nat'l Life Ins. Co., 408 F.2d 606 (2d Cir. 1969). *But see In re* Knepp, 229 B.R. 821 (Bankr. N.D. Ala. 1999).

127 Ark. Code Ann. § 16-108-201; Ga. Code Ann. § 9-9-2(c)(3) (arbitration statute significantly different than the Uniform Arbitration Act); Kan. Stat. Ann. § 5-401; Mo. Stat. § 435.350; Mont. Code Ann. § 27-5-114(2)(c); Neb. Rev. Stat. § 25-2602.01(f)(4); Okla. Stat. Rev. tit 15, § 802; S.C. Code Ann. § 15-48-10(b)(4).

128 McKnight v. Chicago Title Ins. Co., 358 F.3d 854, 858 (11th Cir. 2004); Standard Security Life Ins. Co. v. West, 267 F.3d 821 (8th Cir. 2001); Mutual Reinsurance Bureau v. Great Plains Mut. Ins. Co., 969 F.2d 931 (10th Cir. 1992); Am. Health & Life Ins. Co. v. Heyward, 272 F. Supp. 2d 578, 582 (D.S.C. 2003); Friday v. Trinity Universal of Kansas, 939 P.2d 869 (Kan. 1997). *See also* Cox v. Woodmen of the World Ins. Co., 556 S.E.2d 397, 401–02 (S.C. Ct. App. 2001) (holding that provision of South Carolina Arbitration Act exempting any insured or insurance policy beneficiary is an insurance regulation that McCarran-Ferguson saves from preemption by the FAA, but finding that provision does not apply to defendant as fraternal benefits association). *But see* Little v. Allstate Ins. Co., 167 Vt. 171, 705 A.2d 538 (1997).

129 *See* Miller v. National Fid. Ins. Co., 588 F.2d 185 (5th Cir. 1979) (no law in Georgia insurance code is impaired by the Federal Arbitration Act).

130 Humana v. Forsyth, 525 U.S. 299, 119 S. Ct. 710, 142 L. Ed. 2d 753 (1999).

131 S.D. Code § 21-25A-3.

132 Wis. Stat. §§ 631.85, 631.20.

133 Ark. Code Ann. § 16-108-201; Ga. Code Ann. § 9-9-2(c)(3) (arbitration statute significantly different than the Uniform Arbitration Act); Kan. Stat. Ann. § 5-401; Mo. Stat. § 435.350; Mont. Code Ann. § 27-5-114(2)(c); Neb. Rev. Stat. § 25-2602.01(f)(4); Okla. Stat. Rev. tit 15, § 802.

134 Standard Security Life Ins. Co. v. West, 267 F.3d 821 (8th Cir. 2001); Mutual Reinsurance Bureau v. Great Plains Mut. Ins. Co., 969 F.2d 931 (10th Cir. 1992); Friday v. Trinity Universal of Kansas, 939 P.2d 869 (Kan. 1997); *see also* Cox v. Woodmen of the World Ins. Co., 556 S.E.2d 397, 401–02 (S.C. Ct. App. 2001) (holding that provision of South Carolina Arbitration Act exempting any insured or insurance policy beneficiary is an insurance regulation that McCarran-Ferguson saves from preemption by the FAA, but finding that provision does not apply to defendant as fraternal benefits association).

state law restricts arbitration agreements;

- That the agreement specifies it will be governed by a state's laws, and that state's laws restrict arbitration agreements;
- That the agreement to arbitrate was not knowingly, willingly, and intelligently given, or the agreement to arbitrate is ambiguous or equivocal;
- That the agreement is not signed or the consumer's signature was forged;
- That the arbitration clause is procedurally unconscionable or that substantive terms are unconscionable, such as limitations on remedies, non-mutuality of the arbitration requirement, bias by the arbitrator or arbitration mechanism, excessive fees and costs, inconvenient arbitration venue, loser pay rules;
- Fraud in the factum in the creation of the whole contract or fraud in the inducement as to the arbitration clause;
- Under defenses under state contract law or state statutory law applying to any contract;
- Where the contract has been cancelled or rescinded by law;
- The dispute is outside the scope of matters to be arbitrated;
- Where the arbitration requirement is imposed unilaterally by a bill stuffer;
- Where the lender's collection action or response to the consumer's litigation indicates it has waived its rights to insist on arbitration; or
- Where the arbitration agreement conflicts with a federal statute or prevents the effective vindication of federal statutory rights.

10.4 Right to Jury Trial

The right to a trial by jury in a state court is not addressed by the Seventh Amendment to the United States Constitution and is therefore a matter of state law, at least in civil cases.[135] Rules regarding civil jury trials vary from state to state. Most states, however, follow the federal approach: in the absence of express statutory treatment, juries are available by right in civil actions which were recognized at common law and in their modern statutory counterparts, while no right to a jury exists in actions previously recognized only in courts of equity.[136]

---

135 *See* City of Monterey v. Del Monte Dunes at Monterey, Ltd., 526 U.S. 687 (1999); Gasperini v. Center for Humanities, Inc., 518 U.S. 415 (1996); Hawkins v. Czarnecki, 1998 U.S. App. LEXIS 1690 (6th Cir. 1998); Elliott v. City of Wheat Ridge, 49 F.3d 1458 (10th Cir. 1995).

136 *See generally* Burlington N. R.R. Co. v. Warren, 574 So. 2d 758 (Ala. 1990) (ordinarily an action in equity does not provide a right to a jury trial); State v. Dutch Harbor Seafoods, Ltd., 965 P.2d 738 (Alaska 1998) (state constitution preserves right to jury to same extent as at common law, i.e., civil cases when the amount in controversy exceeds $250); Riggin v. Dierdorff, 790

The right to a jury in usury cases is seldom litigated because in the average usury case the presence of the right is obvious. Usury is usually raised as a debtor defense or counterclaim in the creditor's action on a debt. Such a creditor action is a suit seeking the recovery of money damages for breach of contract, which is the epitome of an action recognized at common law.[137] The debtor can thus request a jury by right as the defendant in the creditor's suit.

Obtaining a jury is similarly seldom a problem in affirmative usury actions. In many states,[138] although apparently not all,[139] a common law action for the recovery of usurious interest paid was recognized, and modern statutory usury remedies are thus just a continuation of common law rights. Even in the absence of a specific common law predecessor, most usury statutes provide the debtor with an action to recover money which inherently resembles an action at law more than a suit in equity.[140] A state may also treat the existence of a bona fide credit sale as an issue of fact to be decided by a jury.[141]

The one circumstance in which a debtor may have trouble obtaining a jury to hear a usury claim exists when the creditor is attempting to foreclose on property given as security for the debt and the debtor is raising usury as a defense to the foreclosure. In most states foreclosure is recognized as an equitable remedy.[142] The existence of an

---

S.W.2d 897 (Ark. 1990) (right to jury trial does not extend to equity); Claudio v. State, 585 A.2d 1278 (Del. 1991) (state constitution preserves, inter alia, common law right to jury for civil claims); Dickeman v. Millwood Gold & Racquet Club, Inc., 67 S.W.3d 724 (Mo. App. 2002) (no right to jury trial on rescission claim).

137 *See generally* Dairy Queen v. Wood, 369 U.S. 469, 82 S. Ct. 894, 8 L. Ed. 2d 44 (1962) (action to collect debt for breach of contract); Raedeke v. Gibraltor Sav. & Loan Ass'n, 517 P.2d 1157 (Cal. 1974); Whitfield v. Cornelius, 554 S.W.2d 870 (Ky. Ct. App. 1977).

138 *See* Commercial Credit Equip. Corp. v. West, 677 S.W.2d 669 (Tex. App. 1984); Flannery v. Bishop, 504 P.2d 778 (Wash. 1972). *See generally* § 10.8, *infra*.

139 *See* Smith v. Barnett Bank of Murray Hill, 350 So. 2d 358 (Fla. Dist. Ct. App. 1977), *overruled on other grounds*, Cerrito v. Kovitch, 457 So. 2d 1021 (Fla. 1984); *see generally* § 10.8.2.3, *infra*.

140 *See* Rowell v. Kaplan, 235 A.2d 91 (R.I. 1967) (usury action for monetary damages was action at law, but allegations insufficient to state a claim). *Cf.* Bryer v. Green-Venable, 2001 Cal. App. LEXIS 3238 (Dec. 12, 2001) (unpublished, citation limited) (question whether a transaction is usurious is mixed question of law and fact).

141 *See* Dehart v. R/S Fin. Corp., 337 S.E.2d 94 (N.C. App. 1985); Carper v. Kanawha Banking & Trust Co., 207 S.E.2d 897 (W. Va. 1974).

142 State law can vary on this issue, however, especially when the creditor simultaneously seeks foreclosure on security and recovery on the accompanying note. *See* Pernell v. Southall Realty, 416 U.S. 363 (1974); *Ex parte* Moore, 880 So. 2d 1131 (Ala. 2003); General Elec. Credit Corp. v. Richman, 338 N.W.2d 814 (N.D. 1983). *Compare* Cheatham v. Bynum, 568 P.2d 649 (Okla. Ct. App. 1977) (jury right in suit to recover

equitable action will generally not preclude the jury trial of legal claims arising from the same transaction.[143] Nonetheless, the debtor may have to demonstrate more clearly the presence of a significant legal issue. Thus, an Oklahoma court denied a jury request in a creditor's suit for foreclosure and recovery on a promissory note when the usury defense

did not dispute the amount of the debt.[144] Similarly, a debtor's suit in Rhode Island for the cancellation and rescission of notes and mortgages did not merit a jury when the complaint contained insufficient allegations to raise a claim for a monetary recovery.[145] Finally, in states which never recognized a common law action for the recovery of usurious interest, courts may narrowly construe the debtor's legal rights in foreclosure actions and may thus deny the debtor a jury.[146]

Even when there is a right to a jury trial, some issues may be questions of law. For example, a Washington court has held that it is for the jury to decide what the borrower told the lender about the purpose of a loan, but whether these facts make it a business loan is a question of law for the court.[147]

10.5 Elements of a Prima Facie Case

10.5.1 General

10.5.1.1 Overview of Elements

Once the statute which appears to control a given credit transaction has been identified,[148] that statute must be closely read so that the elements of a violation under the statute can be determined precisely. Each of the statutory elements must be proved in court. If it is being raised defensively,[149] usury may be an affirmative defense which must be pled or lost.[150]

The proof of usury need not be complicated. Merely the introduction of the credit contract may suffice in some cases if the stated interest rate exceeds the limit in an undisputedly applicable statute. However, the sufficiency of the contract as proof of usury should never be assumed. Credit contracts are usually drafted by creditors, and frequently contain

---

judgment on note and to foreclose security) *with* Songer v. Civitas Bank, 771 N.E.2d 61 (Ind. 2002) (where essential point of case is lender's attempt to take possession of collateral, and legal claims are merely incidental, case is equitable and jury trial not required); First Nat'l Bank of Olathe v. Clark, 602 P.2d 1299 (Kan. 1979) (defense in foreclosure action that note was not yet due is essentially equitable); Oliver-Mercer Electric Co-op, Inc. v. Davis, 678 N.W.2d 757 (N.D. 2004) (action to foreclose on collateral is equitable even if it includes claim for deficiency, so no right to jury trial). Furthermore, actions to recover specific property were recognized at common law, so some actions to recover property can be construed as legal rather than equitable.

143 *See* Dairy Queen, Inc. v. Wood, 369 U.S. 469, 82 S. Ct. 894, 8 L. Ed. 2d 44 (1962); Marseilles Hydropower L.L.C. v. Marseilles Land & Water Co., 299 F.3d 643 (7th Cir. 2002) (right to jury trial arose when landowner counterclaimed for back rent in tenant's suit for injunction and declaratory judgment); Eldredge v. Gourley, 505 F.2d 769 (3d Cir. 1974); Prudential Ins. Co. v. Bonney, 299 F. Supp. 794 (W.D. Okla. 1969); Eason v. Bynon, 781 So. 2d 238 (Ala. Civ. App. 2000) (homeowner entitled to jury trial on claim of fraud asserted in foreclosure action); Poston v. Gaddis, 335 So. 2d 165 (Ala. Civ. App. 1976), *cert. denied*, 335 So. 2d 169 (Ala. 1976), *rev'd on other grounds*, 372 So. 2d 1099 (Ala. 1979); Barth v. Florida State Constructors Serv., 327 So. 2d 13 (Fla. 1976); David Steed & Assocs., Inc. v. Young, 766 P.2d 717 (1988), *appeal after remand*, 825 P.2d 79 (Idaho 1992); Songer v. Civitas Bank, 771 N.E.2d 61 (Ind. 2002); State *ex rel.* Leonardi v. Sherry, 137 S.W.3d 462 (Mo. 2004) (jury trial available on counterclaims asserted in response to suit seeking primarily equitable relief); Welsh v. Case, 43 P.3d 445 (Or. App. 2002) (if borrower raises legal defenses or counterclaims in foreclosure action, right to jury trial is available, but not here where borrower raised claims only by way of recoupment); Rowell v. Kaplan, 103 R.I. 60, 235 A.2d 91 (1967); North Carolina Fed. Sav. & Loan Ass'n v. Dav Corp., 381 S.E.2d 903 (S.C. 1989); Gardner v. Travis, 450 S.E.2d 54 (S.C. App. 1994); First Western Bank v. Livestock Yards Co., 466 N.W.2d 853 (S.D. 1991); Green Spring Farms v. Spring Green Farms Assocs., 492 N.W.2d 392 (Wis. App. 1992). *See also* Williams Electronic Games, Inc., v. 366 F.3d 569 (7th Cir. 2004) (if both legal and equitable remedies are sought, legal issues should be tried first, and jury's findings will bind judge who tries the equitable issues); Nwosu v. Uba, 19 Cal. Rptr. 3d 416 (App. 2004) (where case involved mixed legal and equitable claims, equitable claims should be tried first; note that jurisdictions split on this issue). *But see* Morris v. Bank One, 789 N.E.2d 68 (Ind. App. 2003) (where bank's foreclosure and replevin claims were essentially equitable, no right to jury trial on counterclaims); Vanier v. Ponsoldt, 833 P.2d 949 (Kan. 1992); Oliver-Mercer Electric Co-op, Inc. v. Davis, 678 N.W.2d 757 (N.D. 2004) (counterclaim seeking money damages does not give right to jury trial if damage claim is incidental to and dependent upon primary claim where jury trial is not allowed). *See generally* Annot. 17 A.L.R.3d 1321 (1968) (right in equity suit to jury trial of legal counterclaim).

144 *See* McCrary v. Stephens, 94 P.2d 532 (Okla. 1938). *But cf.* Cheatham v. Bynum, 568 P.2d 649 (Okla. Ct. App. 1977) (right to jury in suit to recover judgment on note and foreclose security).

145 *See* Rowell v. Kaplan, 235 A.2d 91 (R.I. 1967).

146 *See* Cerrito v. Kovitch, 457 So. 2d 1021 (Fla. 1984) (overruling Smith v. Barnett Bank of Murray Hill, 350 So. 2d 358 (Fla. Dist. Ct. App. 1977)); *see also* Furber v. Sidell, 164 N.Y.S.2d 616 (Cty. Ct. 1957) (grant of jury trial where usury pleaded as defense to mortgage foreclosure lies within discretion of court and is denied here because untimely).

147 Jansen v. Nu-West, Inc., 6 P.3d 98 (Wash. Ct. App. 2000).

148 *See* § 9.2, *supra.*

149 Some state usury laws may only be raised defensively. *See* George v. Capital South Mortgage Investments, Inc., 961 P.2d 32 (Kan. 1998) (construing Kan Stat. Ann. § 16-207(a)). Kansas recognizes an affirmative claim for usury, however, under its common law. *Id.*

150 *See* Arnold Machinery Co. v. CSL Building Corp., 733 P.2d 115 (Or. 1987).

recitations of business purposes or other factual admissions which, if unrebutted by other evidence, may preclude a finding of usury. Furthermore, the applicability of a particular usury statute is often disputed, and it may be necessary or appropriate to introduce evidence showing that a statute which the creditor claims to be controlling is really inapposite. Finally, many usury violations, such as the collection of unearned interest upon the acceleration of a debt[151] or the imposition of hidden interest charges, are not revealed by the terms of the credit contract and so must be separately proven.[152]

In the traditional usury case there are four elements which a borrower must establish:[153] 1) the existence of a loan or forbearance; 2) an absolute obligation to repay principal; 3)

an interest overcharge; and 4) the usurious intent of the lender. These elements exist expressly or by judicial inference in most usury statutes, and serious attention should be paid to their proof in most cases. Yet, they are neither universal nor exclusive. Usurious intent, for example, need not be demonstrated under some statutes.[154] On the other hand, many statutes contain elements beyond these four, such as the existence of "consumer" credit, the size of loan principal, or the type of security taken. The statute may also grant the borrower a private cause of action only if certain additional facts, such as payment of a portion of the usurious charge, are shown.[155] In general, a consumer's attorney should examine with specificity the reasons that a particular usury statute applies, and the reasons why it has been violated. Evidence to support each of these reasons should be introduced in court. With this basic approach in mind, the four most common elements of a prima facie usury case will be examined in more detail.

10.5.1.2 Burden of Proof

Courts generally presume the validity of contracts, and a party who claims that a contract is usurious therefore carries the burden of proving the usury, whether the claim is being asserted as an independent cause of action or as an affirmative defense.[156] The major exception to this rule is that once

---

151 For such an alleged violation, though, remember that one of the basic principles is that for an agreement to be usurious, it must have been so when made. *See, e.g.,* Smith v. MRCC P'ship, 792 S.W.2d 301 (Ark. 1990). The downside of this proposition for creditors, however, may be that a refund might not be considered to purge a contract of usury in some states. *See, e.g.,* Riley v. Red River Marine, Inc., 664 S.W.2d 200 (Ark. 1984). There are exceptions to this general rule in practice. For example, though late charges are generally excluded from interest because they are contingent, they may on some occasions be so considered, see § 7.2.4.2, *supra,* and failure to rebate unearned interest upon acceleration may constitute usury, though that was a subsequent occurrence. *See* Ch. 5, *supra.*

152 Introducing evidence outside of the credit contract generally does not cause parol evidence problems in usury cases because courts widely recognize the need to examine all the facts and circumstances of a transaction to determine whether usury may be concealed. *See* § 9.2.1.6, *supra,* § 10.5.1.3, *infra.*

153 For cases specifying these four elements, see, Rae v. Estate of Van Buren (*In re* Rae), 2002 WL 832203 (4th Cir. May 2, 2002) (unpublished, citation limited) (Fla. law); Henson v. Columbus Bank & Trust, 770 F.2d 1566 (11th Cir. 1985) (applying Georgia law); Cashback Catalog Sales, Inc. v. Price, 102 F. Supp. 2d 1375 (S.D. Ga. 2000); *In re* Bogan, 281 F. Supp. 242 (W.D. Tenn. 1968); *In re* Hoberg, 300 B.R. 752 (Bankr. C.D. Cal. 2003); Varr v. Olimpia, 2002 WL 1425373 (Cal. Ct. App. July 1, 2002) (unpublished, citation limited); Bryer v. Green-Venable, 2001 Cal. App. LEXIS 3238 (Dec. 12, 2001) (unpublished, citation limited); Oregrund Ltd. P'ship v. Sheive, 873 So. 2d 451 (Fla. App. 2004) (similar but slightly different list); Bermil Corp. v. Sawyer, 353 So. 2d 579 (Fla. App. 1977); Dang v. F&S Land Dev. Corp., 618 P.2d 276 (Haw. 1980); Tyrcha v. Wesolek, 543 N.E.2d 222, 224 (Ill. App. 1989) ("loan must be of money or something circulating as money"); Wolf v. Kian, 2000 WL 1281109 (Minn. Ct. App. Sept. 12, 2000) (unpublished); Olson v. Froslee, 2000 Minn. App. LEXIS 795 (Aug. 1, 2000) (unpublished, citation limited); St. Paul Bank for Cooperatives v. Ohman, 402 N.W.2d 235 (Minn. Ct. App. 1987); Western Auto Supply Co. v. Vick, 277 S.E.2d 360, *on reh'g* 283 S.E.2d 101 (N.C. 1981); Liebergesell v. Evans, 613 P.2d 1170 (Wash. 1980); King v. Western United Assurance Co., 997 P.2d 1007 (Wash. Ct. App. 2000) (adds "money or its equivalent constituting the subject matter of the loan or forbearance" as a fifth element); Marashi v. Lannen, 780 P.2d 1341, 1343 (Wash. Ct. App. 1989); Cuevas v. Montoya, 740 P.2d 858, 860 (Wash. Ct. App. 1987) (states "money or its equivalent as the subject of the loan or forbearance" as fifth element). *See also* Sheehy v. Franchise Tax Board, 100 Cal. Rptr. 2d 760

(App. 2000) (listing only three elements, omitting absolute obligation to repay).

154 *See In re* Swartz, 37 B.R. 766 (Bankr. D.R.I. 1984) (small loans); Beneficial Fin. Co. v. Administrator of Loan Laws, 272 A.2d 649 (Md. 1971) (small loans); Duckworth v. Bernstein, 466 A.2d 517 (Md. Ct. Spec. App. 1983) (second mortgage law). Generally, intent requirements are not expressly stated in usury statutes, but have been inferred by the courts. A few statutes, however, expressly provide a bona fide error defense to usury which, depending upon what constitutes a bona fide error, may imply the existence of an intent requirement.

155 Egge v. Healthspan Servs. Co., 115 F. Supp. 2d 1126 (D. Minn. 2000). *See also* Polk v. Crown Auto, Inc., 228 F.3d 541 (4th Cir. 2000) (no usury claim where seller refunded unused vehicle registration fee to debtor). *See generally* § 10.8.2.1, *infra.*

156 *See, e.g.,* OMP v. Security Pac. Bus. Fin. Inc., 716 F. Supp. 239 (N.D. Miss. 1989) ("no 'presumption of usury' under Mississippi law: one claiming usury must furnish clear, positive, and certain proof of usury"); *In re* Borum, 60 B.R. 516 (Bankr. E.D. Ark. 1986) (burden of proof on debtor when contract not usurious on its face); Costello v. F&M Enters., 34 B.R. 211 (Bankr. M.D. Fla. 1983) (burden of proving intent on debtor); Smith v. MRCC P'ship, 792 S.W.2d 301 (Ark. 1990) (where usury not apparent on face of document, burden of proving intent on debtor); Rhode v. Kremer, 655 S.W.2d 410 (Ark. 1983); Naples Cay Dev. Corp. v. Ferris, 555 So. 2d 1272 (Fla. Dist. Ct. App. 1989) (burden of proof on debtor to affirmatively plead and prove usury where contract not usurious on face); Transmedia Restaurant Co. v. 33 East 61st St. Restaurant Corp., 710 N.Y.S.2d 756 (Sup. Ct. 2000) ("strong presumption against the finding of usury"); Ervin v. Muller, 2003 WL 21744332, at *5 (Wash. Ct. App. July 29, 2003) (unpublished, citation limited) (borrower has burden of proof unless usury is apparent on

a facially usurious interest rate has been demonstrated by the debtor, the burden may shift to the creditor to rebut the allegation of usury. Thus, a creditor who has assessed charges apparently in excess of the usury ceiling, but who claims that some of the charges are excluded from "interest" as reasonable transaction fees, may be required to demonstrate the reasonableness of those fees.[157] Similarly, if a debtor has shown that a general usury ceiling has been exceeded, but the creditor claims to be within a statutory exception to that ceiling, some courts have indicated that the burden of proof shifts to the creditor to demonstrate that the transaction fell within the scope of the exception.[158] Finally, in many jurisdictions usurious intent will be presumed if the contract on its face violates the statutory ceiling, and it is therefore up to the creditor to show any absence of intent.[159]

The precise standard of proof by which usury must be demonstrated varies significantly from jurisdiction to jurisdiction, and splits of authority within individual states are common.[160] Nevertheless, the most frequently applied standards in civil usury cases are "clear and convincing" evidence and "preponderance of the evidence" or some variation of these tests.[161]

10.5.1.3 Contract Construction

Issues of contract construction typically arise in usury cases in connection with the proof of some of the elements of usury. Most notably, a court's interpretation of a contract may determine its finding of usurious intent, the absolute obligation of the debtor to repay principal, or the presence of an overcharge.

Construction of a credit contract only becomes an issue if the contract is ambiguous on some relevant point.[162] A contract which unambiguously calls for usurious payments cannot be cured by a forgiving "interpretation."[163] (Indeed,

---

face of contract); Durias v. Boswell, 791 P.2d 282 (Wash. Ct. App. 1990) (party alleging usury has burden of proof where usury is not apparent on face of transaction); Carper v. Kanawha Banking & Trust Co., 207 S.E.2d 897 (W. Va. 1974). *See also* Burge v. Pack, 785 S.W.2d 207 (Ark. 1990) (as an affirmative defense, usury must be pled and proved). *See generally* Annot. 51 A.L.R.2d 1087 (1957).

157 *See* Kissell Co. v. Gressley, 591 F.2d 47 (9th Cir. 1979); Bunn v. Weyerhauser Co., 598 S.W.2d 54 (Ark. 1980) (burden on lender to show that late charge was not interest); United-Bilt Homes, Inc. v. Teague, 432 S.W.2d 1 (Ark. 1968); Freeman v. Gonzales County Sav. & Loan Ass'n, 526 S.W.2d 774 (Tex. Civ. App. 1975), *aff'd*, 534 S.W.2d 903 (Tex. 1976).

158 *See In re* Russell, 72 B.R. 855 (Bankr. E.D. Pa. 1987) (lender carries burden of proving applicability of federal usury preemption); Colter v. Consolidated Credit Corp., 157 S.E.2d 812 (Ga. App. 1967) (burden shifted to lender to show it was operating under and had complied with Industrial Loan Act); Revocable Living Trust of Harold G. Strand v. Wel-Co Group, Inc., 86 P.3d 818, 821 (Wash. Ct. App. 2004); Hommel v. Thweatt, 834 P.2d 1058 (Wash. Ct. App. 1992); Marashi v. Lannen, 780 P.2d 1341 (Wash. Ct. App. 1989); Stevens v. Security Pac. Mortgage Corp., 768 P.2d 1007 (Wash. Ct. App. 1989); Brown v. Giger, 738 P.2d 312 (Wash. Ct. App. 1987) (elements of usury apparent on face of loan; burden shifted to lender to prove it fell within business exemption), *rev'd on other grounds*, 757 P.2d 523 (Wash. 1988); Aetna Fin. Co. v. Darwin, 691 P.2d 581 (Wash. Ct. App. 1984) (lender bore burden of showing that transaction fell within usury exception for business loans over $50,000). *But see* American Century Mortgage Investors v. Regional Center, Ltd., 529 S.W.2d 578 (Tex. Civ. App. 1975).

159 *See* Easton State Bank v. Winn, 19 B.R. 218 (Bankr. E.D. Ark. 1982); Grotjohn Precise Connexiones Int'l, S.A. v. JEM Fin., Inc., 12 S.W.3d 859 (Tex. App. 2000) (if loan is usurious on its face, lender has burden of proving bona fide error); Carper v. Kanawha Banking & Trust Co., 207 S.E.2d 897 (W. Va. 1974). *See generally* § 10.5.5, *supra* (usurious intent).

160 *See* Annot. 51 A.L.R.2d 1087, "Quantum, degree, or weight of evidence to sustain usury charge" (1957) (comprehensive annotation). The West Virginia Supreme Court has declared a "further qualification to the diverse holdings" surveyed in this annotation by distinguishing between usury on the face of the

document and in the conduct of the parties. The former category, which includes documents urged to be legal under the time-price doctrine (*see* § 10.5.2.2, *infra*), requires only a preponderance of the evidence. The latter category requires stronger proof: "a clear and satisfactory preponderance of the evidence." Carper v. Kanawha Banking & Trust Co., 207 S.E.2d 897, 917–18 (W. Va. 1974). *See also* Standard Sav. Ass'n v. Greater New Canaan Missionary Baptist Church, 786 S.W.2d 774 (Tex. App. 1990) (without articulating precisely what standard would be applied, the court held that borrower's affidavit that insurance purchase and third-party loan pay-off were required, thus constituting hidden interest, was insufficient evidence to warrant finding of usury on motion for summary judgment; holding borrowers to "a stricter standard of proof").

161 *See, e.g.*, Rae v. Estate of Van Buren (*In re* Rae), 2002 WL 832203 (4th Cir. May 2, 2002) (unpublished, citation limited) (Fla. law) ("clear and satisfactory" evidence necessary); Carter v. Four Seasons Funding Corp., 97 S.W.3d 387 (Ark. 2003) (clear and convincing evidence); Smith v. MRCC P'ship, 792 S.W.2d 301 (Ark. 1990) (clear and convincing standard); Naples Cay Dev. Corp. v. Ferris, 555 So. 2d 1272 (Fla. Dist. Ct. App. 1989) (borrower has burden to establish usury by clear and satisfactory evidence when contract is not usurious on its face); Goldstein v. CIBC World Markets Corp., 776 N.Y.S.2d 12 (App. Div. 2004) (clear and convincing evidence); Transmedia Restaurant Co. v. 33 East 61st St. Restaurant Corp., 710 N.Y.S.2d 756 (Sup. Ct. 2000) (clear and convincing standard); El Paso Refining, Inc. v. Spurlock Permian Corp., 77 S.W.3d 374 (Tex. App. 2002) (preponderance of evidence).

162 Zwayer v. Ford Motor Credit Co., 665 N.E.2d 843 (Ill. App. 1996) (court held the contract was ambiguous and should be construed against the maker where it contained a clause allowing the use of the Rule of 78 to rebate upon prepayment but was silent if acceleration occurred).

163 *See* C.I.O.S. Foundation v. Berkston Ins., 2000 U.S. Dist. LEXIS 2337 (N.D. Miss. Jan. 28, 2000) (where usurious contract was unambiguous, parol evidence was not admissible); Giventer v. Arnow, 372 N.Y.S.2d 63 (N.Y. 1975); Matter of Estate of Dane, 390 N.Y.S.2d (App. Div. 1976); Brookshire v. Longhorn Chevrolet, Inc., 788 S.W.2d 209 (Tex. App. 1990) (where contract called for payment upon acceleration of the "unpaid balance of the total of payments," which latter term had a contractual definition calculating it to include the finance charges, creditor could not save it from usury claim by arguing that it meant "Unpaid Balance-Amount Financed"); Gemperle

even if the contract was usurious due to mutual mistake, a creditor may not be able to salvage it by seeking reformation.[164] Conversely, unambiguous contracts should not dissuade borrowers from attempting to prove usury which is not evident on the face of a contract. It is black letter law that a court will consider all the facts and circumstances surrounding a transaction to determine whether usury is concealed.[165] Thus the parol evidence rule will not exclude evidence of usury.[166]

The main problem for borrowers when facing questions of contract interpretation is the widely-accepted principle that the terms of a contract should be construed as non-usurious if the language of the contract as a whole is fairly susceptible to that construction.[167] This rule is obviously not important if a creditor has already demanded or accepted usurious payments, but if a statute forbids "contracting" for usury and the "contracting" is the sole issue before the court, the construction of the contract itself becomes critical. For example, when an acceleration clause in a precomputed credit contract does not specify the treatment of unearned interest upon acceleration, courts construing the acceleration clause often assume that the parties intend a legal transaction to avoid finding usury.[168]

There are essentially two ways for debtors to combat the tendency of courts to construe contracts in favor of creditors, both of which depend on a recognition of the fact that creditors write consumer credit contracts. First, because of this fact, a consumer's attorney should not rely on the contract alone to prove a usury case if there is any conceivable ambiguity in the contract terms. The contract will probably be drafted to defeat debtor defenses, for example by including a usury savings clause.[169] Relying on the contract to establish the elements of usury is risky.[170] Instead, remembering that a court should consider all the facts and circumstances around a transaction when considering usury, a debtor's attorney should attempt to build a record showing the intent of the parties at the time the transaction was consummated and, if a form contract is at issue, the manner in which the creditor has applied the disputed contract provision in other transactions.

The second method of dealing with unfavorable rules of contract construction is to attack them head-on, at least insofar as they apply to consumer credit contracts. It is widely recognized that contracts should be construed against their drafter,[171] and consumer credit contracts are not only written by creditors, they are almost uniformly contracts of adhesion which are offered to the consumer on a take-it-or-leave-it basis.[172] Recognizing the one-sidedness of this situation, some courts have held that a presumption of legality does not apply to consumer credit contracts.[173] Other courts, observing that ambiguous contract language can mislead consumers about their rights and dissuade them from asserting their rights, have suggested that consumer credit contracts should be construed as the average consumer would interpret them.[174]

v. Crouch, 724 P.2d 375 (Wash. Ct. App. 1986) (traditional rule, that if contract can be construed lawfully as well as unlawfully the lawful construction should be used, does not apply in usury cases if it would validate a usurious transaction by trumpeting form over substance).

164 *See* § 10.8.5, *infra*.

165 *See, e.g.,* Beausejour Corp., N.V. v. Offshore Dev. Co., 802 F.2d 1319 (11th Cir. 1986) (applying Florida law); Blessing v. Zeffero, 149 Mich. App. 558, 386 N.W.2d 590 (1986); Lowell & Austin, Inc. v. Traux, 507 A.2d 949 (Vt. 1985); Gemperle v. Crouch, 724 P.2d 375 (Wash. Ct. App. 1986); 47 C.J.S. *Interest & Usury* § 100(c). *See also* § 9.2.1.6, *supra*.

166 *Cf.* Howard O. Hunter, Modern Law of Contracts: Revised Edition ¶ 7.16 (1999) (parol evidence is "almost always" admissible to prove illegality).

167 *See, e.g., In re* Casbeer, 793 F.2d 1436 (5th Cir. 1986) (applying Texas usury law); Wall v. East Texas Teachers Credit Union, 533 S.W.2d 918 (Tex. 1976). *See also* Hoxie Implement Co. v. Baker, 65 S.W.3d 140 (Tex. App. 2001) (if ambiguous, creditor's demand letter should be interpreted not to "charge" usurious interest). *Cf.* Myles v. Resolution Trust Corp., 787 S.W.2d 616 (Tex. App. 1990) (contract provision calling for acceleration of "note total, making all sums immediately due" was not explicitly usurious and was construed to be nonusurious in light of rebate provisions and savings clause; more critically to the analysis, the note appears to have been an interest-bearing contract, so that "all sums" only would be unpaid principal balance plus accrued interest). The rule will not apply if a contract is usurious on its face. Gemperle v. Crouch, 724 P.2d 375 (Wash. Ct. App. 1986); Aetna Fin. Co. v. Darwin, 691 P.2d 581 (Wash. Ct. App. 1984).

168 *See* § 5.7.2, *supra*. *See also* Coxson v. Commonwealth Mortgage Co. (*In re* Coxson), 43 F.3d 189 (5th Cir. 1995); Watson v. Avco Fin. Servs., Int'l, 401 N.W.2d 485 (Neb. 1987) (lender did not illegally contract for attorney fees where contractual clause for such fees prefaced by words, "to the extent permitted by law").

169 *See* § 10.6.10, *infra*.

170 *See, e.g.,* Voyager Life Ins. Co. v. Whitson, 703 So. 2d 944 (Ala. 1997) (court relied on various rules of contract construction, e.g., "with a choice between a valid construction and an invalid one, the court will accept the construction that will uphold, rather than destroy, the contract," to find that lender did not contract to charge usurious interest).

171 Zwayer v. Ford Motor Credit Co., 665 N.E.2d 843 (Ill. App. 1996) (court held the contract was ambiguous and should be construed against the maker where it contained a clause allowing the use of the Rule of 78 to rebate upon prepayment but was silent if acceleration occurred).

172 For a discussion of the interpretation of adhesive contracts, see Drennan v. Security Pac. Nat'l Bank, 621 P.2d 1318 (Cal.), *cert. denied*, 454 U.S. 833 (1981).

173 *Cf.* Gonzalez v. Gainan's Chevrolet City, Inc., 690 S.W.2d 885 (Tex. 1985) (no presumption of legality for contracts under consumer credit code *except* in cases alleging usury).

174 *See In re* Sprouse, 577 F.2d 989 (5th Cir. 1978).

10.5.2 Loan or Forbearance

10.5.2.1 Introduction

The first element of almost all usury violations is the existence of a "loan" or "forbearance" of money. Although the definition of these terms may vary from statute to statute, a loan may generally be thought of as a temporary transfer of money or its equivalent from a creditor to a debtor or to a third party on the debtor's behalf.[175] A forbearance, on the other hand, is an agreement between an existing debtor and creditor under which the debtor gives consideration (i.e., pays interest) in return for the creditor's agreement to refrain from demanding immediate payment of a pre-existing debt

---

175 *See generally* Eikenberry v. Adirondack Spring Water Co., 480 N.E.2d 70 (N.Y. 1985) (distinguishing loan and forbearance); Miro v. Allied Fin. Co., 650 S.W.2d 938 (Tex. App. 1983) (no loan when loan instrument cancelled shortly after signing and never funded). Statutes which regulate charges for the "use" of money are generally addressing loans. *See* Tygrett v. University Gardens Home Ass'n, 687 S.W.2d 481 (Tex. App. 1985).

Examples of cases in which there was an issue whether a loan or credit existed include:

Finding loans: Kenty v. Bank One, Columbus, N.A., 92 F.3d 384 (6th Cir. 1996) (issue whether financing force-placed insurance premium was a loan or forbearance); Najarro v. SASI Int'l Ltd., 904 F.2d 1002, 1007 (5th Cir. 1990) (money supplied by plaintiffs to defendant to purchase European gray market perfume for resale in the United States was a loan, not an investment; "the name that the parties give to [a] contract is irrelevant for purposes of determining whether there was a loan"); Cashback Catalog Sales v. Price, 102 F. Supp. 2d 1375 (S.D. Ga. 2000) (denial of lender's motion for summary judgment) (payday lender's agreement not to cash post-dated checks until borrower's payday was a forbearance; fact that lender gave borrower gift certificates equal to face value of checks did not fool the court); Turner v. E-Z Check Cashing, Inc., 35 F. Supp. 2d 1042 (M.D. Tenn. 1999) (deferred presentment of check constitutes a loan, *see* § 7.5.5, *supra*); Hamilton v. York, 987 F. Supp. 953 (E.D. Ky. 1997) (same); SAL Leasing, Inc. v. Arizona *ex rel.* Napolitano, 10 P.3d 1221 (Ariz. Ct. App. 2000) (vehicle sale-leaseback scheme is loan); State *ex rel.* Salazar v. The Cash Now Store, Inc., 31 P.3d 161 (Colo. 2001) (tax refund assignments are loans); Oregrund Ltd. P'ship v. Sheive, 873 So. 2d 451 (Fla. Dist. Ct. App. 2004) (reversing dismissal of complaint; land conveyance with repurchase option may be loan); Betts v. McKenzie Check Advance of Fla., L.L.C., 879 So. 2d 667 (Fla. Dist. Ct. App. 2004) (payday loan); Short On Cash.Net of New Castle, Inc. v. Dept. of Fin. Inst., 811 N.E.2d 819 (Ind. Ct. App. 2004) (sale of Internet service with cash back is loan); Aple Auto Cash Express, Inc. v. State *ex rel.* Oklahoma Dept. of Consumer Credit, 78 P.3d 1231 (Okla. 2003) (sale-leaseback); Baxter v. Stevens, 773 P.2d 890 (Wash. Ct. App. 1989) (usury statute includes discounting commercial paper to be a loan where borrower makes himself liable as guarantor or maker). *See also* §§ 7.5.5.4, 7.5.5.6, *supra* (disguised payday loans).

Finding no loan or credit: Buckman v. American Bankers Ins. Co., 115 F.3d 892 (11th Cir. 1997) (an indemnity agreement for a bail bond containing a contingency note and mortgage which secured advances only if the defendant fails to appear in the criminal case not a credit transaction under Truth-in-Lending analysis); Cazenovia College v. Renshaw (*In re* Renshaw), 229 B.R. 552 (B.A.P. 2d Cir. 1999) (unpaid balance of tuition, room and board not a loan even though the college charged a 19.2% per year "service charge"), *aff'd*, 222 F.3d 82 (2d Cir. 2000);

Betts v. Advance Am., 213 F.R.D. 466 (M.D. Fla. 2003) (payday loan); Rivera v. AT&T Corp., 141 F. Supp. 2d 719 (S.D. Tex. 2001) (late payment of cable TV bill not a loan even though equipment was "loaned" to subscribers); *In re* Hoberg, 300 B.R. 752 (Bankr. C.D. Cal. 2003) (husband's obligation to pay money to satisfy spousal support and division of property claims not loan or forbearance); Simpson v. C.J.V. Constr. & Consulting, Inc., 690 So. 2d 363 (Ala. 1997) (home improvement contractor did not extend credit by billing customers for payments periodically as various stages of the project were completed even though a late fee of 1.5% per month of the overdue balance would be imposed); Berger v. State Dep't of Revenue, 910 P.2d 581 (Alaska 1996) (guaranty of repayment by sellers of state-issued dividend certificates if the state refused to pay on the dividends to the buyer did not constitute a loan or a forbearance; but see the dissent—sellers did have an unconditional repayment expectation); Carter v. Four Seasons Funding Corp., 97 S.W.3d 387 (Ark. 2003) (sale of accounts receivable by sophisticated business entity not a loan even though buyer had recourse against seller if accounts proved uncollectible); Rhode v. Kremer, 655 S.W.2d 410 (Ark. 1983) (mobile home sale with contingent financing never completed so no "credit"); Mackey v. Bristol W. Ins. Servs., 130 Cal. Rptr. 2d 536 (Ct. App. 2003) (financing of auto insurance policy not a credit transaction when insured was under no obligation to pay for full term, but could cancel after paying for any number of months); Betts v. Ace Cash Express, Inc., 827 So. 2d 294 (Fla. Dist. Ct. App. 2002) (check cashers who charged statutory fee for cashing checks, but then deferred depositing the checks, did not make loans); Butler v. Target, Inc., 601 So. 2d 1276 (Fla. Dist. Ct. App. 1992) (attorney fee agreement not a loan, so there could be no usury); McComb v. McWilliams, 505 N.E.2d 1378 (Ill. App. 1987) (obligation on promissory note arose from exchange of property; more properly a purchase and sale of property than loan, usury statute therefore inapplicable); People v. Lee, 526 N.W.2d 882 (Mich. 1994) (sale with repurchase option not loan because no obligation to repay; criminal usury prosecution; note dissent; *NB: See generally* § 7.5.2.2, *supra*); Korrody v. Miller, 126 S.W.3d 224 (Tex. App. 2003) (upholding factual finding that sale of accounts receivable not a loan even though parties never signed factoring agreement and account debtor was never notified of assignment); Hoxie Implement Co. v. Baker, 65 S.W.3d 140 (Tex. App. 2001) (demand for money allegedly due as a result of nonpayment of debt was not usury where jury found that no debt was actually owed); Benchmark Land Development, Inc. v. Wooley, 2001 Tex. App. LEXIS 8390 (Dec. 20, 2001) (agreement to repay unauthorized transfers of funds would not be loan); Ravkind v. Mortgage Funding Corp., 881 S.W.2d 203 (Tex. App. 1994) (assignment of payments due on contract for deed not a loan even though assignee had recourse against assignor); Sunwest Bank of El Paso v. Gutierrez, 819 S.W.2d 673 (Tex. App. 1991) (unauthorized vendor's single insurance premium charged to borrower not a loan or forbearance of money; rather, a "separate and additional consideration"). *See also* Carey v. Lincoln Loan Co., 998 P.2d 724 (Or. App. 2000) (installment land contract is not a loan as defined by statute that limits restrictions on prepayment).

which has come due.[176] Most usury statutes treat loans and forbearances interchangeably.[177]

In Arkansas, where the usury ceiling is found in the state constitution, the courts have the role of determining whether a transaction is a loan; the legislature does not have the authority to define a type of transaction as a non-loan.[178]

10.5.2.2 Credit Sales and the Time-Price Doctrine

10.5.2.2.1 Time-price exception to usury laws

Absent specific statutory guidance, the chief uncertainty about the definition of a loan is whether this term includes credit extended in connection with the installment sale of goods or services. Some courts have held that it does not.[179] Other courts have deemed credit sales to be within the general coverage of the usury laws but subject to an exception. Historically, many states recognized an exception to their usury laws known as the "time-price" doctrine.[180] This exception is a legal fiction derived from English case law which distinguishes credit extended in connection with sales from loans subject to usury law, at least under certain conditions. Those jurisdictions which still recognize the time-price doctrine[181] only invoke it when a buyer and seller agree to separate "cash" and "time" prices, the former being the price which would be paid if the buyer used cash or its equivalent, and the latter being the (invariably higher) price which the buyer will pay in return for the ability to pay in installments.[182] The difference between the time price and the cash price is not legally recognized as interest, but is instead labeled "time-price differential" which is not regulated by traditional usury laws, though it may be by retail installment sale statutes.[183] See § 10.5.2.2.2, *infra*.

It is important for attorneys to recognize that the time-price doctrine is merely a legal fiction. A modern credit sale is not logically distinguishable from either a forbearance by the seller or a loan from the seller to the buyer, which the buyer must use to pay for the goods being purchased. Nevertheless, several states continue to follow the common

---

176 *See generally* Kenty v. Bank One, Columbus, N.A., 92 F.3d 384 (6th Cir. 1996) (force-placed insurance premium was not a forbearance); Henson v. Columbus Bank & Trust Co., 770 F.2d 1566 (11th Cir. 1985) (refraining from calling a demand note is not a forbearance); Smith Machinery Co. v. Jenkins, 654 F.2d 693 (10th Cir. 1981) (detention, not forbearance); Sunburst Bank v. Keith, 648 So. 2d 1147 (Miss. 1995) (oral agreements to extend loan term accompanied by payment of foreclosure fee were forbearance agreements); Clark v. Darby, 639 N.Y.S.2d 549 (App. Div. 1996) (acceptance of a bond and mortgage by an employer from an employee who embezzled funds and an agreement to defer the employer's right to pursue legal remedies as long as employee paid back the amount owed with interest of 13 1/2% constituted a forbearance that was subject to New York's usury statute limiting interest to 11%); Eikenberry v. Adirondack Spring Water Co., 480 N.E.2d 70 (N.Y. 1985) (agreement was a forbearance); Lowell & Austin, Inc. v. Traux, 507 A.2d 949 (Vt. 1985) (no forbearance); Carper v. Kanawha Banking & Trust Co., 207 S.E.2d 897 (W. Va. 1974) (no reversible error in usury verdict where debtor's attorney claimed usurious "loan" in opening argument but later proved usurious "forbearance").

177 Edwards v. Alabama Farm Bureau Mut. Casualty Ins. Co., 509 So. 2d 232 (Ala. Civ. App. 1986) (no distinction between treatment of loan and forbearance in Alabama Mini-Code).

178 Luebbers v. Money Store, Inc., 40 S.W.3d 745 (Ark. 2001).

179 *See, e.g.,* Computer Sales Corp. v. Rousonelos Farms, Inc., 546 N.E.2d 761 (Ill. App. 1989); Citipostal, Inc. v. Unistar Leasing, Inc., 283 A.D.2d 916, 724 N.Y.S.2d 555 (2001) (neither a credit sale nor a lease constitutes a loan or forbearance); Carey v. Lincoln Loan Co., 998 P.2d 724 (Or. App. 2000) (land sale contract not loan for purposes of statute requiring lender to allow prepayment).

180 *See generally* Note, *Interest Rates and the Law: A History of Usury*, 27 Ariz. St. L.J. 61 (1981).

181 At least with respect to consumer credit sales, most jurisdictions have abolished the doctrine. *See* §§ 2.3.2.2, *supra*, 10.5.2.2.2, *infra*.

182 *See, e.g.,* G.M.A.C. v. Mackrill, 175 Neb. 631, 122 N.W.2d 742 (1963); Carper v. Kanawha Banking & Trust Co., 207 S.E.2d 897 (W. Va. 1974). *But see* Leasing Serv. Corp. v. Simpkins Metal Buildings, Inc., 638 F. Supp. 896 (S.D.N.Y. 1986) (applying Texas law; even if purported lease was a credit sale, the charge was a time-price difference and was excludable from interest even if separate cash and time prices were not stated).

183 For cases applying the exclusion of time-price differential from "interest" for usury purposes, see, e.g., Bartholomew v. Northampton Nat'l Bank, 584 F.2d 1288 (3d Cir. 1978); Wilkins v. M&H Fin. Inc., 476 F. Supp. 212 (D. Ark. 1979), *aff'd*, 621 F.2d 311 (8th Cir. 1980); Agristor Credit Corp. v. Lewellen, 472 F. Supp. 46 (N.D. Miss. 1979); Credit Alliance Corp. v. David O. Crump Sand & Fill Co., 470 F. Supp. 489 (S.D.N.Y. 1979); Scientific Products v. Cyto Medical Laboratory, Inc., 457 F. Supp. 1373 (D. Conn. 1978); Cavazos v. Mid-State Trust II (*In re* Hillsborough Holdings Corp.), 267 B.R. 882 (Bankr. M.D. Fla. 2001) (sale of home); *In re* Craft, 120 B.R. 84 (Bankr. E.D. Mich. 1989) (2% per month service charge on unpaid balance was a time-price differential not governed by any specific Michigan statutes); Southwest Concrete Co. v. Gosh Constr., 798 P.2d 1247 (Cal. 1990) (court utilized time-price doctrine in evaluating late charge on credit sale); Boerner v. Colwell Co., 577 P.2d 200 (Cal. 1978); Varr v. Olimpia, 2002 WL 1425373 (Cal. Ct. App. July 1, 2002) (unpublished, citation limited) (even after it was restructured, debt for accounting services was still exempted from usury laws by time-price doctrine); Phillips v. Allis-Chalmers Credit Corp., 339 S.E.2d 302 (Ga. App. 1985); Walker v. Fingerhut Corp., 2000 Minn. App. LEXIS 142 (Jan. 28, 2000) (unpublished); Woods v. Evans Products Co., 574 S.W.2d 488 (Mo. App. 1978); Perez v. Rent-A-Center, Inc., 866 A.2d 1000, 1013–16 (N.J. Super. App. Div. 2005) (neither criminal nor civil usury laws apply to rent-to-own contract); Servpro Indus. Inc. v. Pizzillo, 2001 Tenn. App. LEXIS 87 (Feb. 14, 2001); Servpro Indus., Inc. v. Pizzillo, 2001 Tenn. App. LEXIS 87 (Feb. 14, 2001) (sale of franchise); Anchor, Inc. v. Laguna Enters., Inc., 2002 WL 287706 (Tex. App. Feb. 7, 2002) (discount given by seller for prompt payment is not interest); Mid State Homes v. Sullivan, 592 S.W.2d 29 (Tex. Civ. App. 1979). *But cf.* Thelen v. Ducharme, 390 N.W.2d 264 (Mich. App. 1986) (time-price differential was interest where usury statute definition of interest incorporated all amounts defined as "finance charge" under Truth in Lending Act).

law distinction between these two fundamentally identical transactions, and this adherence has given creditors a significant motivation to restructure credit in the form of credit sales. Instead of arranging a car loan from a lender subject to usury limitations, for example, an auto dealer who is not subject to usury ceilings may extend credit directly to the consumer. The dealer then sells the consumer's credit contract or note to the bank or finance company which might otherwise have given the consumer a direct loan. The outcome is identical to a direct loan transaction—the consumer purchases a car; the dealer receives cash; and the third party financier holds the consumer's debt—but under the time-price doctrine, usury law does not apply because the form of the transaction is legally a credit sale, not a loan.[184]

In jurisdictions where the time-price doctrine remains in force, a buyer's attorney should closely examine any credit sale transaction to be certain that the exception actually applies. The time-price exception does not apply to sham sales where the "buyer" obtains coupons or scrip that can be used as cash.[185] Moreover, usury ceilings will apply to credit sales when the seller fails to go through the formalities of stating a separate cash price for the purchased goods and disclosing the time-price differential.[186] Whether the seller computes sales tax on the cash price or the time price may

be another factor.[187] Further, an extension of credit to refinance or consolidate an earlier credit sale does not itself arise out of a credit sale, and therefore is not subject to the time-price exception.[188]

A final limitation on the time-price usury exception arises from the contradictions between the traditional application of the doctrine to seller-financed sales, and the widespread commercial practice of assigning consumer credit contracts or notes to third party creditors. As mentioned previously in this section, the distinction between a direct purchase money loan from a bank or finance company to a consumer and the financing of a sale directly by the seller is one of form over substance, particularly when, in the latter transaction, the seller discounts the consumer paper to the bank or finance company shortly after the sale. At times the distinctions between the two characterizations of the transaction become so transparent that courts in jurisdictions which generally recognize the time-price exception have decided that transactions are not "true" credit sales but are merely disguised loans or forbearances to which usury limitations apply.[189] Such rulings are most common with open-end sales accounts or when a seller, immediately after a sale, assigns the credit contract to a third party creditor with whom it regularly deals and whose forms it may use. Generally, evidence that the third party financing was pre-arranged is evidence that the transaction was not a "true" credit sale.[190]

---

184 *See generally* Hare v. General Contract Purchase Corp., 249 S.W.2d 973 (Ark. 1952) (examining use of credit sale format for loans).

185 *See* W.T. Grant Co. v. Walsh, 241 A.2d 46 (N.J. Super. 1968) (coupons/scrip); Tuition Plan, Inc. v. Zicari, 335 N.Y.S.2d 95 (Dist. Ct. 1972) (retail installment contract for tuition money was a loan).

186 *See, e.g.,* Daniel v. First Nat'l Bank of Birmingham, 227 F.2d 353 (5th Cir. 1955), *reh'g denied,* 228 F.2d 803 (5th Cir. 1956); Pollice v. National Tax Funding, 59 F. Supp. 2d 474 (W.D. Pa. 1999) (time-price doctrine does not apply where buyer did not make conscious decision to pay for goods on credit at a higher price than cash price), *aff'd in part, rev'd in part on other grounds,* 225 F.3d 379 (3d Cir. 2000); GMAC v. Mackrill, 122 N.W.2d 742 (Neb. 1963); Western Auto Supply Co. v. Vick, 268 S.E.2d 842 (N.C. App. 1980), *aff'd,* 277 S.E.2d 360 (1981) *reh'g* 283 S.E.2d 101 (N.C. 1981); Davenport v. Unicapital Corp., 230 S.E.2d 905 (S.C. 1976); Kinerd v. Colonial Leasing Co., 800 S.W.2d 187 (Tex. 1990); El Paso Dev. Co. v. Berryman, 769 S.W.2d 584 (Tex. App. 1989) (inflated sales price of real estate constituted interest instead of valid time-price differential); Commercial Credit Equip. Corp. v. West, 677 S.W.2d 669 (Tex. App. 1984); Whitaker v. Spiegel, Inc., 623 P.2d 1147 (Wash.), *amended on other grounds,* 637 P.2d 235 (Wash.), *appeal dismissed,* 454 U.S. 958 (1981); Carper v. Kanawha Banking & Trust Co., 207 S.E.2d 897, 911–12 (W. Va. 1974) (convenient general summary of the factors to be considered in determining whether the time-price doctrine applies to a particular sales transaction). *See also* Walker v. Fingerhut Corp., 2000 Minn. App. LEXIS 142 (Minn. App. Jan. 28, 2000) (unpublished) (seller established separate cash and time prices so fell within time-price doctrine except in cases where it rebated credit charges upon prepayment, which is inconsistent with existence of separate time-price; court remands case for determination of usurious intent issue; as to sales found nonusurious, court minimizes fact that lender charged sales tax on

cash price and suggested that it would give rebate of credit charges upon prepayment).

187 Walker v. Fingerhut Corp., 2000 Minn. App. LEXIS 142 (unpublished) (other factors outweighed fact that seller computed sales tax on cash price rather than time price; time-price doctrine applied).

188 Butler v. Holt Machinery Co., 741 S.W.2d 169 (Tex. App. 1987), *corrected on denial of reh'g,* 739 S.W.2d 958 (1987).

189 *See, e.g.,* Daniel v. First Nat'l Bank of Birmingham, 227 F.2d 353 (5th Cir. 1955), *reh'g denied,* 228 F.2d 803 (5th Cir. 1956); Hare v. General Contract Purchase Corp., 249 S.W.2d 973 (Ark. 1952); St. Paul Bank for Cooperatives v. Ohman, 402 N.W.2d 235 (Minn. Ct. App. 1987) (contract was a forbearance, not a time-price sale; use of "time-price" language and similarity of transaction to automobile installment sales or revolving credit plans was not controlling); Lloyd v. Gutgsell, 124 N.W.2d 198 (Neb. 1963); State Wholesale Supply, Inc. v. Allen, 227 S.E.2d 120 (N.C. App. 1976) (open-end account); Midland Guardian & Co. v. Thacker, 314 S.E.2d 26 (S.C. App. 1984); National Bank of Commerce of Seattle v. Thomsen, 495 P.2d 332 (Wash. 1972). *Cf.* Scientific Products v. Cyto Medical Laboratory, Inc., 457 F. Supp. 1373 (D. Conn. 1978); First Nat'l Bank of Ottawa v. Larkins, 444 N.E.2d 818 (Ill. App. 1983) (mobile home financing was bona fide sale); Woods v. Evans Products Co., 574 S.W.2d 488 (Mo. Ct. App. 1978); Kinerd v. Colonial Leasing Co., 800 S.W.2d 187 (Tex. 1990).

190 Daniel v. First Nat'l Bank of Birmingham, 227 F.2d 353 (5th Cir. 1955), *reh'g denied* 228 F.2d 803 (5th Cir. 1956); Hare v. General Contract Purchase Corp., 249 S.W.2d 973 (Ark. 1952); Miller v. Diversified Loan Serv. Co., 382 S.E.2d 514 (W. Va. 1989); Carper v. Kanawha Banking & Trust Co., 207 S.E.2d 897 (W. Va. 1974).

If the equities of a credit sale transaction favor the consumer and the seller has close connections to a finance company to which it assigns its contracts, it may be appropriate for a practitioner to argue that a true credit sale does not exist. However, a word of caution is in order. Cases deciding whether a true credit sale or a concealed loan exist often seem result oriented. Despite numerous opinions, the courts have been unable to develop any rigorous tests to distinguish valid assignments of consumer paper from concealed loans, simply because there is no real difference beyond the speed or frequency with which the seller discounts the contracts it obtains. Because standards such as the speed and frequency of discounting are inherently imprecise, a practitioner who chooses to argue that a credit sale is really a concealed loan should understand that the outcome is seldom predictable.

10.5.2.2.2 The erosion of the time-price doctrine: direct regulation of consumer credit sales and RISAs

The time-price usury exception no longer applies to consumer credit transactions in most jurisdictions. The chief method of eliminating the doctrine has been the enactment of installment sales acts or consumer credit codes, most of which impose ceilings on the charges that may be assessed in connection with consumer credit sales.[191] However, in a few jurisdictions the doctrine has been put to rest judicially by courts which have recognized its illogic or which have simply applied usury statutes at their face value.[192]

Many of the jurisdictions which now regulate credit sales still nominally distinguish credit sales and loans, and may still employ terminology such as the "time-price differen-

tial" which originated in the time-price doctrine.[193] For example, a credit sale might be regulated by an installment sales act, while a loan could fall under a corresponding small loan act, and a consumer claiming an installment sales act violation might well be required to establish the existence of a "credit sale" or "installment sale" rather than a "loan" as an element of the statutory violation.[194] Yet such distinctions are as much a matter of form as of substance,[195] and practitioners should not assume that a jurisdiction applies the time-price usury exception merely because the terminology associated with the doctrine remains in use.

10.5.2.3 Forbearance and Detention

Usury statutes generally apply not only to loans but also to forbearances. A forbearance is an agreement between a creditor and debtor under which the creditor defers the enforcement of a debt which has come due in return for the debtor's payment of interest on that debt.[196] For example, if a balloon payment came due on a mortgage and the debtor was unable to make the payment, the lender might agree to forbear collection of the balloon payment for a year in return for continued or increased interest payments.

191 *Cf.* Saul v. Midlantic Nat'l Bank/South, 572 A.2d 650 (N.J. Super. App. Div. 1990) (car sale falling outside scope of New Jersey's RISA was subject to time-price exception). A number of states amended their credit sales statutes to permit "as agreed" ceilings in the 1980s. A clear majority, however, retained specific caps on this type of credit.

192 *See* Foreign Commerce v. Tonn, 789 F.2d 221 (3d Cir. 1986); Sloan v. Sears, Roebuck & Co., 308 S.W.2d 802 (Ark. 1957); State *ex rel.* Turner v. Younker Bros., 210 N.W.2d 550 (Iowa 1973); Rollinger v. J.C. Penny Co., 192 N.W.2d 699 (S.D. 1971); Cloud v. Whitley, 1996 Tex. App. LEXIS 4777 (Oct. 30, 1996) (home improvement contract which provided that the homeowner need not pay for the work until 15 days following completion constituted a loan subject to state usury limits); Whitaker v. Spiegel, Inc., 623 P.2d 1147 (Wash. 1981); State v. J.C. Penny Co., 179 N.W.2d 641 (Wis. 1970).

Note, however, that if a usury statute by its terms applies only to a "loan of money," a court might as a matter of statutory interpretation, without dealing with the time-price doctrine, exclude all credit sales *per se* from usury coverage. *See* Tyrcha v. Wesolek, 543 N.E.2d 222 (Ill. App. 1989) (though preamble to usury statute referred to "sales on credit," penalty section applied only to a "loan of money").

193 *See, e.g.,* Tauber v. Johnson, 291 N.E.2d 180 (Ill. App. 1972) (excessive time-price differential charged under motor vehicle retail installment sales act).

194 *Cf.* Briercroft Serv. Corp. v. de Los Santos, 776 S.W.2d 198 (Tex. App. 1988) (borrower could not establish violation of statute governing retail installment transactions because contract was a loan with interest, rather than a retail installment sale with a time-price differential; statute therefore did not apply).

195 *See* Girard Acceptance Corp. v. Wallace, 388 A.2d 582 (N.J. 1978). Distinctions between statutes regulating credit sales and "usury" statutes regulating loans may, however, be important under some circumstances. For example, courts often strictly construe "usury" statutes, but may be inclined to distinguish installment sales acts as remedial legislation which must be broadly construed. *See* § 9.3, *supra.*

196 *See generally* Cashback Catalog Sales v. Price, 102 F. Supp. 2d 1375 (S.D. Ga. 2000) (denial of lender's motion for summary judgment) (payday lender's agreement not to cash post-dated check until borrower's payday is a forbearance); Pollice v. National Tax Funding, 225 F.3d 379 (3d Cir. 2000) (installment payment agreement for pre-existing debt was forbearance, but interest was not consideration for the forbearance because creditor charged debtors the same rate they had paid before entering into the agreements); Sunburst Bank v. Keith, 648 So. 2d 1147 (Miss. 1995); Clark v. Darby, 639 N.Y.S.2d 549 (App. Div. 1996) (acceptance of a bond and mortgage by an employer from an employee who embezzled funds and an agreement to defer the employer's right to pursue legal remedies as long as employee paid back the amount owed with interest of 13 1/2% constituted a forbearance that was subject to New York's usury statute limiting interest to 11%); Eikenberry v. Adirondack Spring Water Co., 480 N.E.2d 70 (N.Y. 1985); Western Auto Supply Co. v. Vick, 277 S.E.2d 360 (1981) *reh'g* 283 S.E.2d 101 (N.C. 1981); Tygrett v. University Gardens Home Ass'n, 687 S.W.2d 481 (Tex. App. 1985); Whitaker v. Spiegel, Inc., 623 P.2d 1147 (Wash.) *amended on other grounds*, 637 P.2d 235 (Wash.), *appeal dismissed* 454 U.S. 958 (1981).

The fact that most usury statutes cover forbearances means that many transactions which are not normally considered extensions of credit may become subject to usury limitations. All that is needed is a debt which has come due and an agreement between the parties allowing the debt to be paid off over time. The underlying debt often need not have been a loan. Thus, an agreement between an attorney and client for the payment of overdue bills for legal services may be a forbearance subject to usury law.[197] A payment plan for delinquent taxes and water and sewer charges is a forbearance.[198] Even a judicial settlement which provides for the payment of interest on an agreed liability may be a forbearance.[199] Moreover, debts which are created through credit sales that are exempt from usury limitations may provide the basis for forbearances to which usury ceilings do apply.[200] Similarly, the Mississippi Supreme Court has held that credit transactions which were not usurious at their inception may become tainted by a subsequent forbearance agreement allowing for unlawful interest.[201]

The chief limitation on the definition of a forbearance is that a forbearance usually requires an agreement between the parties under which the creditor agrees to forego the collection of the existing debt at least temporarily.[202] In most transactions, however, when a debt such as an oil bill comes due but is not paid, the creditor simply starts assessing interest on the outstanding debt, often in the name of late charges, but does not agree to forego collection. Consequently, no forbearance exists. Instead, this situation technically constitutes the "detention" of money, and in many jurisdictions charges for the detention of money are not within the scope of usury laws.[203]

Generally speaking, the detention of money is the failure to pay a debt when it comes due without obtaining the agreement of the creditor. Some usury statutes do address the "detention" of money as well as the forbearance of a debt, and under these statutes charges assessed on overdue accounts must respect usury ceilings.[204] This general ap-

---

197 Eikenberry v. Adirondack Spring Water Co., 480 N.E.2d 70 (N.Y. 1985).

198 Pollice v. National Tax Funding, 225 F.3d 379, 396–97 (3d Cir. 2000). *Cf.* Sheehy v. Franchise Tax Board, 100 Cal. Rptr. 2d 760 (App. 2000) (no agreement to forbear collection of unpaid taxes, so usury laws did not apply).

199 *Compare* Farley v. Fischer 137 Mich. App. 668, 358 N.W.2d 34 (1984) (usurious divorce settlement) *with* Ghirardo v. Antonioli, 883 P.2d 960 (Cal. 1994) (notes executed in settlement of litigated dispute regarding an exempt credit sale constituted a modification, not a non-exempt loan or forbearance); Clifford v. Clifford, 453 N.W.2d 675 (Mich. 1990) (usury statute applies to judgment interest rate entered by consent in divorce case, but remedy is correction of order rather than forfeiture of interest); Wiley-Reiter Corp. v. Groce, 693 S.W.2d 701 (Tex. App. 1985) (settlement contained no loan or charge for the use/detention of money).

200 *See In re* Pillon-Davey & Assocs., 52 B.R. 455 (Bankr. N.D. Cal. 1985). *But see* Ghirardo v. Antonioli, 883 P.2d 960 (Cal. 1994) (notes executed in settlement of litigated dispute regarding an exempt credit sale constituted a modification, not a non-exempt loan or forbearance). Some statutes, however, limit forbearances to the forbearance of debt arising from a loan. *See* U.C.C.C. § 3.106(4) (1968 Act), U.C.C.C. § 1.301(25) (1974 Act).

201 *See, e.g.*, Sunburst Bank v. Keith, 648 So. 2d 1147 (Miss. 1995) (in consequence, damages of forfeiture of all interest on the original notes were awarded).

202 *See* Smith Machinery Co. v. Jenkins, 654 F.2d 693 (10th Cir. 1981); Terrell Inc. v. DeShazo Builders, 661 P.2d 303 (Idaho 1983). *Cf.* Rollingbrook Investment Co. v. Texas Nat'l Bank of Baytown, 790 S.W.2d 375 (Tex. App. 1990) (bank's renewal of note was not forbearance where it did not grant additional time for performance, but extended a 90-day offer to renew, collected a higher rate of interest during commitment period, and executed new note with differing interest rate and payments as well as amount due and maturity date).

203 *See, e.g.*, Pollice v. National Tax Funding, 225 F.3d 379, 393–96 (3d Cir. 2000) (nonpayment of taxes and water and sewer charges was detention and was exempt from Pennsylvania usury laws, though payment plan could be forbearance); Resolution Trust Corp. v. Oaks Apt. Joint Venture, 753 F. Supp. 1332, 1338 (N.D. Tex. 1990) (demand for payment of five times amount of principal and interest due is not a demand for compensation for the use forbearance or detention of money), *aff'd in relevant part, vacated in part on other grounds*, 966 F.2d 995 (5th Cir. 1992); Sheehy v. Franchise Tax Board, 100 Cal. Rptr. 2d 760 (App. 2000) (no agreement to forbear collection of unpaid taxes); Widmark v. Northrup King Co., 530 N.W.2d 588 (Minn. Ct. App. 1995) (no agreement to forbear, and "unlike typical credit arrangements," did not encourage to pay late to receive additional charges; commercial transaction); Protection Industries Corp. v. Kaskel, 691 N.Y.S.2d 457 (App. Div. 1999); T.F. James Co. v. Vakoch, 604 N.W.2d 459 (N.D. 2000) (nonpayment of rent is detention, and charges are covered by legal interest rate statute rather than usury law); Lowell & Austin, Inc. v. Traux, 507 A.2d 949 (Vt. 1985) (no agreement to forbear); Alaskan Fireplace, Inc. v. Everett, 667 N.W.2d 378 (Wis. Ct. App. 2003) (not a credit transaction when seller did not grant buyers the right to defer payment, but imposed 1.5% monthly late charge as means of dissuading late payment); Opinion of the Kansas Att'y Gen., No. 88-30, Consumer Cred. Guide (CCH) ¶ 95,908, 1988 Kan. AG LEXIS 160 (Mar. 3, 1988) (reasonable late fees charged by cable television company are not interest, as they are not in consideration for forbearance as long as actual efforts to collect are undertaken and delinquent users are not given payment options). *See also* Griffin v. Georgia-Pacific Corp., 177 Ga. App. 852, 341 S.E.2d 499 (1986) (specific statutory rate authorized for unpaid commercial accounts). *But cf.* Forest Point Venture #703 v. Forest Point Owners Assn., 2001 Tex. App. LEXIS 6625 (Oct. 3, 2001) (detention of lender's money is within scope of Texas usury statute, but not shown here). *See generally* Annot. 28 A.L.R. 3d 449 (1969) (interest after maturity as usurious or otherwise illegal). Charges for the detention of money are frequently treated as late fees which are excluded from "interest" in many states. *See* § 7.2.4, *supra*.

204 *See* Iowa Supreme Court Board of Professional Ethics and Conduct v. McKittrick, 683 N.W.2d 554, 560 (Iowa 2004) (interpreting and applying Iowa limits on finance charges and compounding of interest on accounts receivable); Walker, Tooke & Lyons v. Sapp, 862 So. 2d 414 (La. Ct. App. 2003) (interpreting usury cap to apply to contract that set interest rate if client did not make timely payment of legal fees); Scarr v. Boyer, 818 P.2d 381 (Mont. 1991); Ulviden v. Sorken, 237 N.W.

proach makes sense. As one court has stated: "If a borrower is to be protected from the extortion of an excessive rate for the use of money, there is no apparent reason why . . . [the protection] . . . should be limited to the term of the loan."[205] Furthermore, creditors clearly expect and tolerate late payment on accounts, at least to a limited extent. Thus, the line between a formal forbearance, which is subject to most usury laws, and a detention in which the debtor is regularly billed for and pays interest on an overdue account, which may not be subject to usury limitations, is rather fine.[206]

Nevertheless, the distinction between forbearance and detention is made by most statutes, or at least by most courts.[207] The majority view is that charges on overdue debt,

without a specific agreement to forbear, are simply penalties designed to encourage tardy debtors to pay up. Courts frequently state that nonpayment is a "voluntary" act of the debtor,[208] and that usury will not result from the occurrence of a contingency within the control of the debtor, even if the debtor ends up paying charges which, if treated as interest, would exceed the legal rate.[209] In other words, charges for the detention of money, even if computed at a monthly rate instead of a one-time assessment,[210] are treated the same as late fees, and are not subject to usury limitations, unless it can be shown that the nonpayment which gave rise to the detention was anticipated by the parties at the time the transaction was consummated, and that the supposed "detention" is thus a ruse to escape the usury laws.[211]

---

565 (S.D. 1931); C.K. Oil Props., Inc. v. Hrubetz Operating Co., 2002 WL 32344609 (Tex. App. Apr. 25, 2002) (unpublished); Hardwick v. Austin Gallery of Oriental Rugs, Inc., 779 S.W.2d 438, 443 (Tex. App. 1989). *Cf.* Domizio v. Progressive County Mut. Ins. Co., 54 S.W.3d 867 (Tex. App. 2001) (Texas usury laws apply to charges for detention of money only if the debt arises from a loan transaction; not applicable to charges imposed for late payment of insurance premiums); Tygrett v. Univ. Gardens Homeowners' Ass'n, 687 S.W.2d 481 (Tex. App. 1985) (late charges may be interest, but no lending relationship here between condominium owner and condominium association with respect to condominium assessments). *But see* Garcia v. Tex. Cable TV Partners, 114 S.W.3d 561 (Tex. App. 2003) (late charge on cable television bill is not for forbearance or detention).

205 Ulviden v. Sorken, 58 S.D. 466, 237 N.W. 565 (1931).

Accord Scarr v. Boyer, 818 P.2d 381, 383 (Mont. 1991) (a debtor who cannot pay a debt with legal interest certainly "lacks the resources to pay usurious interest").

206 *Cf.* Crestwood Lumber Co. v. Citizens Sav. & Loan Ass'n, 148 Cal. Rptr. 129 (App. 1978) (agreement to pay finance charge after maturity implies forbearance). The same distinction may be made using other terminology, such as determining whether charges on an overdue account are "finance charges" or "late charges." *See* § 9.2.3.5, *supra*.

207 *See, e.g.,* Smith Machinery Co. v. Jenkins, 654 F.2d 693 (10th Cir. 1981); Scientific Products v. Cyto Medical Laboratory, 457 F. Supp. 1373 (D. Conn. 1978); Rangen, Inc. v. Valley Trout Farms, Inc., 658 P.2d 955 (Idaho 1983); Terrell Inc. v. DeShazo Builders, 661 P.2d 303 (Idaho 1983); Kelso Oil Co. v. East West Truck Stop, Inc., 102 S.W.3d 655 (Tenn. Ct. App. 2002); Bowman Plumbing, Heating & Electrical, Inc. v. Logan, 59 Va. Cir. 446 (2002); *see generally* Annot. 28 A.L.R. 3d 449 (1969) (interest after maturity as usurious).

A minority of states have treated monthly charges on overdue accounts as interest. *See* A.Y. McDonald Mfg. Co. v. Shackelford, 652 S.W.2d 9 (Ark. 1983); Bunn v. Weyerhauser Co., 598 S.W.2d 54 (Ark. 1980); Crestwood Lumber Co. v. Citizens Sav. & Loan Ass'n, 148 Cal. Rptr. 129 (Cal. Ct. App. 1978); Thrift Funds of Baton Rouge, Inc. v. Jones, 274 So. 2d 150 (La. 1973), *cert. denied*, 414 U.S. 820 (1973); Begelfer v. Najarian, 381 Mass. 177, 409 N.E.2d 167 (1980). *See also* T.F. James Co. v. Vakoch, 604 N.W.2d 459 (N.D. 2000) (monthly charges on overdue rent are governed by legal interest rate statute but do not constitute usury so usury penalties do not apply).

Within California there is a split of authority. *Compare* Southwest Concrete Products v. Gosh Constr. Co., 263 Cal. Rptr. 387 (Ct. App. 1989) (1 1/2% monthly charge on bill not paid in full when due was not charge for forbearance and thus

was not subject to usury laws, rather it was charge imposed to encourage prompt payment and compensate seller for delay; further seller did not agree not to enforce its claim so there was no forbearance) *with* Mark McDowell Corp. v. LSM 128, 263 Cal. Rptr. 310 (Ct. App. 1989) (charge similar to one in *Gosh* held usurious).

208 The whole idea that normally usurious charges may be excused because they are caused by the "voluntary" action or inaction of the debtor is somewhat bizarre. If a borrower "voluntarily" enters into a contract which is usurious at its inception, the usury is certainly not excused on that basis. The courts would view such a borrower as one compelled by economic necessity—precisely the type of person usury law was designed to protect. Yet, how does this differ from the economic necessity which prevents most defaulted debtors from paying their bills? The problem is that courts generally fail to distinguish truly voluntary nonpayment from nonpayment caused by a lack of money, though some courts do, e.g., Scarr v. Boyer, 818 P.2d 381 (Mont. 1991) (debtors have greater need of protection after default; one who cannot pay debt at legal interest cannot afford to pay debt at usurious interest). Furthermore, the courts generally do not recognize that the imposition of charges above the normally applicable usury ceiling is at least as much the result of a lender's actions as of the borrower's: clauses imposing high delinquency charges on overdue payments exist in contracts because creditors consciously put them there in anticipation of the possibility of late payment. For an example of a court which did recognize this, see Metro Hauling, Inc. v. Daffern, 723 P.2d 32 (Wash. Ct. App. 1986) (modification of contract after default to provide for late charges was usurious).

209 Corvetti v. Hudson, 676 N.Y.S.2d 263 (App. Div. 1998) (commercial case); Bowman Plumbing, Heating & Electrical, Inc. v. Logan, 59 Va. Cir. 446 (2002).

210 The expression of a late charge as a monthly rate has often not been considered relevant to its status as an interest or non-interest charge. *See, e.g.,* Scientific Products v. Cyto Medical Laboratory, Inc., 457 F. Supp. 1373 (D. Conn. 1978). However, at least in Arkansas, a late charge seems more likely to be held to be a non-interest "penalty" if it is a one-time assessment, rather than a monthly charge. *Compare* Bunn v. Weyerhauser Co., 598 S.W.2d 54 (Ark. 1980) (monthly "service charge") *with* Smith v. Figure World Plus, 705 S.W.2d 433 (Ark. 1986) (large one-time late charge).

211 *See* Union Mortgage Banking & Trust Co. v. Hagood, 97 F. 360 (4th Cir. 1899); Davis v. Rider, 53 Ill. 416 (1870); Osborn v. McCowen, 25 Ill. 218 (1860); Carroll County Sav. Bank v. Strother, 6 S.E. 313 (S.C. 1888); Metro Hauling, Inc. v. Daffern,

That being said, however, in this as in most usury-related matters, applicable statutes must be carefully scrutinized. Just as late charges may be separately regulated, and the subject of claims for relief in the cases of overcharges,[212] default charges also may be separately regulated,[213] and the subject of statutory remedies.[214]

10.5.3 Absolute Obligation to Repay Principal

The second element of a traditional usury case is the debtor's absolute obligation to repay the principal amount of the money transferred to him or her.[215] In a way this second element is closely intertwined with the first, i.e., the existence of a loan, because in the absence of an absolute obligation to repay, it is quite plausible to argue that a transfer of money is a gift or an investment rather than a loan. Nevertheless, most courts treat the obligation to repay as a distinct element in a usury case, and so it is separately discussed here.

The requirement that the repayment obligation be absolute means that it cannot be contingent, a concept that is discussed at § 7.5.6, *supra*. Where an investor advances money to a business with an agreement that the business will repay the principal plus a portion of profits, for example, the amount repaid is contingent on the success of the business, so the transaction does not fall within the usury laws.[216] Some courts have held that purchase of a stake in litigation does not involve usury where there is no repayment obligation if the suit is unsuccessful.[217] A loan will not be

considered contingent unless the lender, by the terms of the loan, is subjected to some greater hazard than that the borrower will fail to repay the loan or that the security will depreciate in value.[218]

Whether there is an absolute obligation to repay is occasionally an issue in complex business transactions.[219] In the average consumer credit case, however, proving the existence of an absolute obligation to repay principal is not a problem; the obligation is stated on the face of the note or credit contract and can be established by the introduction of these documents into evidence. The obligation to repay is something creditors care a great deal about, so credit contracts are rarely ambiguous on this point.

However, occasionally creditors attempt to evade laws regulating credit and credit charges by constructing a transaction in a way in which this element appears to be missing. Courts typically will look behind the facade to determine the true nature of the agreement.[220] Some courts hold that economic facts may make the agreement to pay binding even though it is expressed as conditional.[221] Some of the most common subterfuges, and applicable case law, are discussed in more detail in Chapter 7: investments; sale/repurchase or sale/leaseback agreements; leases, including rent-to-own (RTO); various post-dated check cashing schemes; refund anticipation loans; and pawn arrangements.

10.5.4 Interest Overcharge

10.5.4.1 General

The heart of every usury case is an overcharge of interest. Logically, this element of proof can be divided into three parts:

- The creditor exacted or attempted to exact payments from the debtor.

723 P.2d 32 (Wash. Ct. App. 1986) (modification of contract after default; no contingency).

212 See § 7.2.4.2, *supra*; § 10.8.2.1, *infra*.

213 See, e.g., 15 U.S.C. § 1639(d) (high-cost mortgage subject to act cannot provide for post-default interest rate higher than the contract rate); Ala. Code § 5-18-15(j) (small loan maximum rate reduced to 8% six months after maturity). See also T.F. James Co. v. Vakoch, 604 N.W.2d 459 (N.D. 2000) (charges for detention covered by legal rate of interest statute).

214 See, e.g., 15 U.S.C. § 1640(a), as amended 1994 (remedies for violating requirements of 15 U.S.C. § 1639); Ala. Code § 5-18-15(h) (loan void if "*any* amount in excess of the charges permitted" is "charged, contracted for, or received.").

215 See Lawsuit Fin., L.L.C. v. Curry, 683 N.W.2d 233 (Mich. App. 2004).

216 Dublin v. Veal, 341 S.W.2d 776 (Ky. 1960).

217 Dopp v. Yari, 927 F. Supp. 814 (D.N.J. 1996). See also Kraft v. Mason, 668 So. 2d 679 (Fla. App. 1996) (no usury where borrower had duty to repay principal, but the usurious interest was contingent on litigation success); § 7.5.8, *supra. But cf.* Lawsuit Fin., L.L.C. v. Curry, 683 N.W.2d 233 (Mich. App. 2004) (repayment obligation was not contingent where borrower signed agreement after tortfeasor had admitted liability and jury had returned $27 million verdict); Rancman v. Interim Settlement Funding Corp., 789 N.E.2d 217 (Ohio 2003) (declining to decide whether nonrecourse advance of funds secured solely by interest in a pending lawsuit and at 180% interest is a loan; contract is void as champerty and maintenance).

218 Britz v. Kinsvater, 351 P.2d 986 (Ariz. 1960).

219 See D-Beam Ltd. P'ship v. Roller Derby Skates, Inc., 366 F.3d 972 (9th Cir. 2004) (repayment obligation was contingent where it was to come from royalty payments); Oregrund Ltd. P'ship v. Sheive, 873 So. 2d 451 (Fla. App. 2004) (reversing dismissal of complaint; economic facts may make repurchase obligation binding even if contract expresses it as conditional); Transmedia Restaurant Co. v. 33 East 61st St. Restaurant Corp., 710 N.Y.S.2d 756 (Sup. Ct. 2000) (money that network gave to restaurant would be repaid only if and when cardholders bought meals at restaurant; since network bore risk of loss, transaction was not a loan); Olson v. Froslee, 2000 Minn. App. LEXIS 795 (Aug. 1, 2000) (unpublished, citation limited) (lease of equipment with option to buy was not loan because no absolute obligation to pay option price). See also § 7.5.7, *supra*.

220 § 9.2.1.6, *supra*.

221 See, e.g., Oregrund Ltd. P'ship v. Sheive, 873 So. 2d 451 (Fla. App. 2004) (option to repurchase can be considered an unconditional obligation where there is a great disparity between sale price and true value).

- The payments were "interest" under the relevant usury statute.
- The total of payments exceeded the statutory limit.[222]

10.5.4.2 Charging, Contracting For, or Receiving Excess Interest

The precise wording of usury statutes varies,[223] but generally creditors may not "contract for," "collect," "exact," "receive," or "charge" payments in excess of those specifically permitted by statute. Under statutes which forbid a creditor to "contract for" excessive payments, merely the signing of an offending contract may constitute a usury violation even if the lender never attempts to collect the excessive charges,[224] and under such circumstances, simply

the introduction of a credit contract into evidence can show the violation.[225] In fact, even a general usury statute providing that no one shall "receive" greater interest than permitted by law has been interpreted to render a credit transaction usurious in the absence of payment of the excess interest. The Iowa Supreme Court said it is "the agreement to exact and pay" excess interest which renders the transaction usurious.[226] Moreover, in some states, a creditor cannot cure a usurious contract by refunding the excess charge.[227]

However, usurious payments may not always be revealed by the contract itself. For example, the lender might require the borrower to pay fees not mentioned by the contract.[228] Similarly, the lender might not give the borrower the full amount of principal stated in the contract or may not give the borrower the use of all the principal for the full loan term.[229]

---

222 Some statutes, however, may impose liability for imposing any charge in excess of that authorized, irrespective of whether the overall yield to the creditor would breach an applicable ceiling. *See* § 10.5.4.4, *infra*.

223 For example, the Uniform Small Loan Law, 7th Draft § 13(c) (June 1, 1942) provides that amounts beyond those allowed may not be "directly or indirectly charged, contracted for, or received." The U.C.C.C. § 5.201(3) (1974 Act) provides consumer remedies when a creditor has "contracted for or received" excess charges or has refused to give the consumer a valid refund within a reasonable time after demand.

224 *See, e.g.,* First Nat'l Mortgage Co. v. Arkmo Lumber Supply Co., 641 S.W.2d 31 (Ark. 1982) (contract that called for usurious commitment fee was usurious though lender never charged it; cannot purge usury by dropping charge when suit is filed, and option to impose it remained with lender); Equity Mortgage, Inc. v. Niro, 690 A.2d 407 (Conn. App. 1997) (court took unusual step of addressing usury apparent on the face of the loan on appeal even though not raised below; held contract unenforceable based upon the note which listed 15% as the contract rate when Connecticut law only permitted 12%); Jim Walter Homes v. Schuenemann, 668 S.W.2d 324 (Tex. 1984); Brookshire v. Longhorn Chevrolet, Inc., 788 S.W.2d 209 (Tex. App. 1990) (acceleration clause in contract rendered it usurious on its face where it expressly entitled creditor, upon happening of the contingency of default and acceleration, to exact greater than lawful interest by providing that creditor could demand the unpaid balance of the "Total of Payments," which includes the finance charges); Myles v. Resolution Trust Corp., 787 S.W.2d 616 (Tex. App. 1990). *See also* Washburn v. Michailoff, 613 N.W.2d 405 (Mich. App. 2000) (usury law applies if lender seeks to enforce contract, even if it does not seek the usurious interest; lender would have avoided usury if it had filed action to reform the contract). *But see* Power Equip., Inc. v. Tschiggfrie, 460 N.W.2d 861 (Iowa 1990) (invoices with excessive interest were not "contracted for" sufficient to warrant penalty when borrower never agreed to the charge and refused to pay them. *NB*: The same circumstances may, however, constitute "charging" illegal interest. *See* Kaier Agr. Chemicals, Inc. v. Peters, 417 N.W.2d 437 (Iowa 1987) (holding that open-end account statement and court petition listing interest greater than allowed by statute constituted an exaction of greater profit than was allowed by law); Poulsen's Inc. v. Wood, 756 P.2d 1162 (Mont. 1988) (though contract on its face provided for excess interest, where contract also had savings clause, and where demand letter properly calculated interest at nonusurious rate,

no usury found); First USA Mgmt. v. Esmond, 960 S.W.2d 625 (Tex. 1997) (employer did not charge "interest" by terminating an employee for failing to repay a loan from the employer and refusing to pay the employee the base salary for remainder of contract term); Martinez v. Teachers Credit Union, 758 S.W.2d 946 (Tex. App. 1988) (contract called for usurious daily rate, but also nonusurious annual rate and nonusurious specific payment schedule; latter controlled irrespective of stated rate). *See generally* § 5.7.2, *supra*, as this issue relates rebate issues upon acceleration and prepayment.

225 Equity Mortgage, Inc. v. Niro, 690 A.2d 407 (Conn. App. 1997) (court took unusual step of addressing usury apparent on the face of the loan on appeal even though not raised below; held contract unenforceable based upon the note which listed 15% as the contract rate when Connecticut law only permitted 12%); Brookshire v. Longhorn Chevrolet, Inc., 788 S.W.2d 209 (Tex. App. 1990). This is a risky tactic, however. *See* § 10.5.1.3, *supra*. In a variable rate transaction, the borrower cannot rely on the contract to show usury unless the initial interest rate was unlawful. Instead, the borrower must prove by independent evidence what the creditor charged or received. Creditors may stipulate to the payments made and the effective periodic rates charged, but in the absence of proof on these issues, a usury case may fail. *See* Farmland Enterprises v. Schuemann, 322 N.W.2d 665 (Neb. 1982).

226 Kaiser Agr. Chemicals, Inc. v. Peters, 417 N.W.2d 437 (Iowa 1987) (open-end account statement and court petition listing interest greater than allowed by statute constituted an exaction of greater profit than was allowed by law). *But cf.* Spellman v. Meridian Bank, 1995 U.S. App. LEXIS 37149 (3d Cir. Dec. 29, 1995) (interpreting the National Bank Act, court holds that § 86 does not authorize an affirmative cause of action for charges which were contracted for but not paid, though § 86 would allow a defense to the banks' collection effort; similar finding with respect to the Home Owners' Loan Act, 12 U.S.C. § 1463(g), which uses "receiving or charging"; analyzed as a standing issue).

227 *See, e.g.,* Riley v. Red River Marine, Inc., 664 S.W.2d 200 (Ark. 1984); Danziger v. San Jacinto Sav. Ass'n, 732 S.W.2d 300 (Tex. 1987). *See also* § 10.6.9, *infra*.

228 *In re* McCorhill Pub., Inc., 86 B.R. 783, 793–94 (Bankr. S.D.N.Y. 1988) (contract provided for no pre-default interest, but creditor imposed a flat fee for the use of the money).

229 *See, e.g.,* Edwards v. Alabama Farm Bureau Mut. Casualty Ins. Co., 509 So. 2d 232 (Ala. Civ. App. 1986) (payment collected

It may manipulate the calculation of a variable rate in a way that increases the interest charged.[230] Or, in the case of prepayment, the lender might not credit the borrower with a rebate which it was contractually, as well as legally obligated to give.[231] Under such circumstances, evidence beyond the contract itself would be necessary to show the payments that the creditor actually charged or received. Such evidence might include the borrower's testimony of the sum actually received as loan proceeds, checks given by the borrower for fees, or the creditor's payment records. Account statements, the creditor's demand letters or similar communications,[232]

affidavits, and court pleadings[233] have all been held to evidence the "charging" of usurious payments. For pleadings to constitute a usurious interest charge, though, they may have to be based on the underlying transaction.

The Texas Supreme Court, in 1992, clarified a split in its appellate courts as to whether a demand for interest found solely in a pleading constituted "charging" usurious interest. Reasoning that the purpose of usury laws is "to correct abusive practices in consumer and commercial transactions,"[234] a demand for excess interest arising from the judicial process, "rather than directly from a commercial or consumer transaction" is not a charging within the meaning of usury laws.[235] Many if not most consumer cases should

---

on date of loan consumation, rather than 30 days later, should have been treated as down payment and principal amount upon which finance charge assessed reduced accordingly); Hoffman v. Key Fed. Sav. & Loan, 416 A.2d 1265 (Md. 1979); Danziger v. San Jacinto Sav. Ass'n, 732 S.W.2d 300, 302–03 (Tex. 1987) (lender contracted for usurious interest when it contracted for interest on entire principal though contract called for multiple disbursements; lender's practice of crediting back the overcharge upon disbursement of the principal in portions does not purge the usury). [Texas practitioners should note that other state statutes may affect the merits of a claim similar to *Danziger. See, e.g.*, Mayfield v. San Jacinto Savings Ass'n, 788 S.W.2d 119 (Tex. App. 1990) (same practice described in *Danziger* held not to be usurious when alleged by customers who had prepaid their contracts, because Texas' applicable spreading statute specifically allowed that creditor's crediting back the overcharge upon the borrower's prepayment would avoid usury penalties).] *But cf.* Shelton v. Mutual Sav. & Loan Ass'n, 738 F. Supp. 1050 (E.D. Mich. 1990) (court holds there is no common law prohibiting charging pre-disbursement interest; distinguishes the two cases cited by borrowers [Lyle v. Tri-County Fed. Sav. & Loan, 363 A.2d 642, *aff'd*, 371 A.2d 424 (Md. 1977); Ceco Corp. v. Steve's Sash & Door Co., 714 S.W.2d 322 (Tex. App. 1986), *aff'd as modified*, 751 S.W.2d 473 (Tex. 1988)] by finding they were interpreting state usury statutes).

See also Leibert v. Finance Factors, 788 P.2d 833 (Haw. 1990) (in case decided upon UDAP and contract claims, not usury grounds, court held that APR disclosure in prepaid education plans for private school tuition deceptively understated the finance charge where interest to buyer was charged on full amount from beginning of school year, though seller had agreement with school whereby it paid the school in two installments to increase the seller's yield. Though usury was not discussed, if the difference took the effective rate over a statutory usury ceiling, or the stated contract rate in an "as agreed" state, see § 9.2.8, *supra*, the practice should also give rise to a usury claim).

230 *See* Siradas v. Chase Lincoln First Bank, 1999 U.S. Dist. LEXIS 15593 (S.D.N.Y. Sept. 30, 1999) (denying lender's motion for judgment on the pleadings on claim that banker's use of improper method to adjust interest rates was UDAP violation).

231 *See* Ch. 5, *supra*.

232 Najarro v. SASI Int'l Ltd., 904 F.2d 1002, 1007–08 (5th Cir. 1990), *cert. denied*, 498 U.S. 1048 (1991) (cover letters, attached to promissory notes, promising to pay "commission" in addition to repayment of principal were evidence of a charge for the use of money, especially where commissions were paid directly to lender); Kaiser Agr. Chemicals, Inc. v. Peters, 417 N.W.2d 437 (Iowa 1987) (open-end account statement and court petition constituted exaction of excess interest); Danziger v. San

Jacinto Sav. Ass'n, 732 S.W.2d 300, 303–04 (Tex. 1987) (payment of loan not necessary; mere inclusion of excess interest in pay-off quote constituted "charging" illegal interest); Strasburger Enterprises, Inc. v. TDGT Ltd. P'ship, 110 S.W.3d 566, 579 (Tex. App. 2003) (letter demanding debt plus interest at usurious rate was "charge," but court construes letter as seeking less than double allowable rate, so lesser penalty applies); Hoxie Implement Co. v. Baker, 65 S.W.3d 140 (Tex. App. 2001) (demand letter that enclosed copy of petition creditor intended to file in court constituted "charging," but an intent to seek interest on another debt was not a charge when it was never communicated to debtor); Torres v. Overby, 2000 Tex. App. LEXIS 2493 (Apr. 17, 2000) (unpublished, citation limited) (letter demanding late fee charged that fee, but its threat to assess future late fees did not); Pentico v. Mad-Wayler, Inc., 964 S.W.2d 708 (Tex. App. 1998) (amortization schedule attached to a demand letter constituted a "charge" of interest); Karg v. Strickland, 919 S.W.2d 722 (Tex. App. 1996) (excess interest demanded in letter constitutes charging interest; lender given opportunity on remand to prove defense of accidental and bona fide error in the way it calculated interest in demand letter; implication is that lender's ignorance may meet the elements of this lender defense).

But see Thrift v. Hubbard, 44 F.3d 348 (5th Cir. 1995) (interpreting demand letter to avoid usurious claim); Lairsen v. Slutzky, 80 S.W.3d 121, 127 (Tex. App. 2002) (construing demand letter's reference to note as limiting demand to amount allowed by note); Varel Mfg. Co. v. Acetylene Oxygen Co., 990 S.W.2d 486 (Tex. App. 1999) (statement on invoice that interest will be charged if payments are late is not "charging"); Heine v. Schendel, 797 S.W.2d 278 (Tex. App. 1990) (demand letter did not constitute charging usurious interest when drafted by creditor's lawyer without creditor's knowledge; lawyer acting beyond scope of his employment); White v. Groco Corp., 783 S.W.2d 24 (Tex. App. 1990) (original invoice which had printed notation that 1 1/2% per month would be charged on amount not paid after 30 days did not constitute charging or demanding excess interest where demand letter and court petition did not include amount greater than permitted by law).

233 *See, e.g.*, Kaiser Agr. Chemicals, Inc. v. Peters, 417 N.W.2d 437 (Iowa 1987) (open-end account statement and court petition constituted exaction of excess interest).

234 George A. Fuller Co. v. Carpet Servs., Inc., 823 S.W.2d 603, 605 (Tex. 1992).

235 Briones v. Solomon, 842 S.W.2d 278 (Tex. 1992); George A. Fuller Co. v. Carpet Servs., Inc., 823 S.W.2d 603, 604 n.1, 605–606 (Tex. 1992). *See also In re* CPDC, Inc., 337 F.3d 436 (5th Cir. 2003) (amending pleading to delete usurious charge precludes usury liability); Cavazos v. Mid-State Trust II (*In re*

still pass this test. For example, a contract may not specify that the creditor will use the Rule of 78, but the amount of the demand in the pleading may show that it did use that accounting method in a transaction where it was prohibited.[236] In that case, though the overcharge appeared "solely" on the pleadings, it arose directly out of the consumer transaction, and should constitute a "charging" of excess interest.[237] Similarly a contract provision may be ambiguous, and the creditor may try to construe it in court so as to salvage the clause,[238] or to negate intent.[239] A demand in a pleading which shows the creditor actually construed the clause to allow the excess should also qualify as "charging" an illegal charge.

10.5.4.3 "Interest" or Regulated Charge

Once the payments charged or received by a creditor have been identified, the next question is which of those payments constitute "interest" or an excess charge under the relevant statute. Most obviously, the creditor may simply calculate the interest erroneously.[240] For example, an auto financing loan which calculates interest at a 15% add-on rate would violate a statute which caps such loans at a 15% actuarial rate.[241] Similarly, applying a 15% actuarial rate to a weekly repayment loan as if the payments were monthly would violate a statute calling for a 15% actuarial ceiling.[242] If a statute regulates the amount of points or origination fees which can be charged, then any overcharge in that category would violate that cap.[243] Imposing a service charge on a

quick-flip loan may violate a statute.[244] Or failing to rebate unearned charges may be considered excess interest in the loan being terminated,[245] or, if refinanced by the same creditor, in the new loan.[246] Chapters 4 to 6 of this volume discuss various calculation issues relevant to examining a transaction for excess charges.

But beyond the obvious charge for the use of money, the definition of "interest" sometimes is a complicated issue which varies from statute to statute, and to which Chapter 7 of this manual is devoted. Nevertheless, most statutes classify all payments made by a borrower as either principal, interest, or non-interest fees in the following manner. First, non-interest fees are charges, such as insurance premiums or late fees, which are most often expressly excluded from interest by statute.[247] However, such charges are often subject to separate regulation by consumer credit regulatory statutes,[248] and may be among the types of charges for which statutory liability attaches if limits are exceeded.[249] Next, "principal" generally includes loan proceeds given to the borrower or paid on the borrower's behalf and often may include any non-interest fees which the lender pays on the

---

Hillsborough Holdings Corp.), 267 B.R. 882 (Bankr. M.D. Fla. 2001) (form filed with IRS does not constitute a charge); Hoxie Implement Co. v. Baker, 65 S.W.3d 140 (Tex. App. 2001) (testimony in court about amount sought does not constitute charging).

236 *See* §§ 5.5.1, 5.6.3.3, *supra.*

237 The *Fuller* Court specifically stated it was not addressing the question of pleadings claiming interest based on underlying documents. 823 S.W.2d at 604 n.1. *Cf.* Cigna Ins. Co. v. TPG Store, Inc., 894 S.W.2d 431 (Tex. App. 1995) (statement sent which failed to reflect rebate of unearned interest constituted usurious "charging"; subsequent credit of the excess amount will not purge the usury).

238 *See* § 10.5.1.3, *supra.*

239 *See* § 10.5.5, *infra.*

240 *See generally* Ch. 4, *supra.*

241 *See* §§ 4.3.1, 4.3.2, *supra.*

242 *See* § 4.6.2.2, *supra.*

243 Mayo v. Key Fin. Servs., Inc., 1994 Mass. Super. LEXIS 549 (June 22, 1994) (implied private right of action for violation of statute limiting points; assertable by a suitable common law remedy; borrowers choose to assert common law restitution), *aff'd, as modified, on other issues,* 678 N.E.2d 1311 (Mass. 1997). *But cf.* Fleet Fin., Inc. of Georgia v. Jones, 430 S.E.2d 352 (Ga. 1993) (statute did not limit number of points, *per se,* but spreading doctrine applied to salvage loans with unusually high number of points from usury challenge under statute limiting return "per month." *See* § 4.6.5, *supra*); Tarver v. Sebring Capital Credit Corp., 69 S.W.3d 708 (Tex. App. 2002)

(points are interest, not fees, so are not included in 3% cap on fees).

244 Some statutes prohibit the imposition of new service charges on a loan refinanced within a certain period of time, or, even where not explicitly prohibited, courts may consider them to be impermissible. *See* § 6.4.2, *supra.*

245 Ch. 5, *supra.*

246 *See* Ch. 6, *supra.*

247 Third party fees may also be treated as non-interest expenses by judicial interpretation of general usury laws. *See* § 7.3, *supra.*

248 Non-interest charges may be the subject of separate regulation even if the interest rate itself is deregulated. *See, e.g.,* Mayo v. Key Fin. Servs., Inc., 1994 Mass. Super. LEXIS 549 (June 22, 1994) (interpreting Mass. Gen. Laws ch. 183, § 63 re points), *aff'd, as modified, on other issues,* 678 N.E.2d 1311 (Mass. 1997); Torres v. Overby, 2000 Tex. App. LEXIS 2493 (Apr. 17, 2000) (unpublished, citation limited) (late fees are contingent additional charges treated as interest under the usury laws, although not under the common law definition). Similarly, real estate closing fees may be limited to actual or reasonable and necessary fees, Va. Code Ann. § 6.1-330.70-72.

249 *See, e.g.,* Alston v. Crown Auto, Inc., 224 F.3d 332 (4th Cir. 2000) (excessive late fees do not make loan usurious, but penalties in late fee statute apply); Smith v. Khalif (*In re* Khalif), 308 B.R. 614 (Bankr. N.D. Ga. 2004) (treating late charges as violating criminal usury cap); S&A Indus., Inc. v. Bank Atlanta, 543 S.E.2d 743 (Ga. App. 2000) (concurring opinion for half of equally divided court) (late charge is considered a fee under criminal usury statutes but did not exceed limits); Garrison v. First Fed. Sav. & Loan Ass'n of S.C., 402 S.E.2d 25 (Va. 1991) (risk management fee not listed among permissible charges and therefore was an illegal charge; only "actual" appraisal cost authorized, excess constituted interest). *See also* § 7.3, *supra,* § 10.8.2.2.2 (late fees), *infra. Cf.* Mayo v. Key Fin. Servs., Inc., 1994 Mass. Super. 549 (June 22, 1994) (implied private right of action for violation of statute limiting points; assertable by a suitable common law remedy; borrowers choose to assert common law restitution), *aff'd, as modified, on other issues,* 678 N.E.2d 1311 (Mass. 1997).

borrower's behalf.[250] Finally, "interest" is any payment not attributable to the repayment of principal or to non-interest fees.[251]

Those payments which a contract defines as interest will generally require no proof, beyond the introduction of the contract, in order to be identified as interest.[252] However, whether various "fees" should be included in or excluded from interest frequently requires careful scrutiny, which sometimes requires examination of evidence beyond the contract.[253]

First, the applicable provision should be examined closely. Though third party fees may be excluded from interest under general usury principles,[254] the relevant statute may be drafted restrictively, so that any charge—irrespective of the recipient—may constitute interest if it is not among those specifically authorized.[255] Second, even if the

type of charge is authorized, it should be examined to assure that it meets standards necessary to exclude it. For example, such charges may be excluded from interest only to the extent they are "actually" charged or are "bona fide and reasonable," qualifications which must be verified.[256] Some third-party fees may be excluded if they are unreasonably high.[257] Credit and ancillary non-credit insurance premiums may be in amounts[258] or of a type[259] which will make them subject to challenge,[260] or they may never have been forwarded to the insurer, which may turn an otherwise authorized charge into interest.[261]

Even amounts which would appear to be clearly non-interest charges, such as payments made to the borrower, cannot always be taken for granted. For example, one creditor listed separate amounts as proceeds to the borrower, one of which was a check which it had her endorse back to the lender. The complaint alleged that, unbeknownst to her, it was to purchase an insurance policy she did not ask for.[262]

Chapters 7 and 8 of this manual discuss in detail the various types of fees and charges which often are challenged as illegal overcharges, and relevant case law.

As a practice note, it is generally true that the larger that portion of the note principal that ends up in the lender or third parties' pockets, or the more exorbitant the overall cost, the more closely the practitioner should examine each component of the loan. Loan padding or high rates are signs of a creditor who is trying to maximize profits and stretch the limits of the law, and who may cross the line in doing so. Practitioners should also be aware that even if specific statutes regulating charges are not breached, overreaching may nonetheless be attacked under other legal theories discussed in Chapter 11, *infra*. Moreover, closed-end, residential home equity loans in which the total points and fees

250 "Principal" or "amount financed" is often statutorily defined. Observe that the principal amount of a loan in this functional sense may not be the face amount of the note signed by the borrower because lenders often include charges such as "points"—which really are compensation to the creditor—in the face amount of the note. Applicable law often sanctions this. *See* §§ 4.4.1, 7.2.2, *supra*.

251 *See, e.g.*, Yazzie v. Ray Vicker's Special Cars, Inc., 12 F. Supp. 2d 1230 (D.N.M. 1998) (pawn service fee exceeded legal limit); Fryer v. Easy Money Title Pawn, Inc., 183 B.R. 322, *rehearing denied*, 183 B.R. 654 (Bankr. S.D. Ga. 1995) (pawnbroker's 23% per month "service charge" was not to reimburse it for any specific expenses, and was therefore interest); Dunnam v. Burns, 901 S.W.2d 628 (Tex. App. 1995) (additional sum to be repaid with principal was interest, even though not denominated as such); Byrd v. Crosstate Mortgage & Investments, Inc., 34 Va. Cir. 17 (1994). *But see* Nicolas v. Deposit Guarantee Nat'l Bank, 182 F.R.D. 226 (S.D. Miss. 1998) (NSF fee held not interest under Mississippi law because it was not charged in connection with a credit transaction).

252 *See, e.g.*, Dillon v. RTC, 811 S.W.2d 765 (Ark. 1991) (contract defined payments as interest; creditor's subsequent unilateral effort to reallocate excess interest to principal cannot purge contract of usury, nor can subsequent modification agreement, as usury is determined as of inception of contract).

253 *See* Swank v. Sverdlin, 121 S.W.3d 785 (Tex. App. 2003) (fact question is raised when there is dispute in the evidence as to whether a charge in addition to interest is actually for additional consideration).

254 *See* § 7.3, *supra*.

255 *See, e.g.*, Hawkins v. Thorp Credit & Thrift Co., 441 N.W.2d 470 (Minn. 1989) (non-credit insurance was not permitted by state regulated loan act); Moran v. American Funding, Ltd., 569 A.2d 841 (N.J. Super. 1989) (at issue prior version of New Jersey's second mortgage act under which title insurance was not a specifically authorized charge and was therefore prohibited by the Act); Garrison v. First Fed. Sav. & Loan Ass'n of S.C., 402 S.E.2d 25 (Va. 1991) (risk management fee not authorized by statute was interest). *See also* Kenty v. Bank One, Columbus, N.A., 1992 U.S. Dist. LEXIS 16445 (S.D. Ohio Apr. 29, 1992) (premium attributable to extraneous types of property insurance coverage unauthorized by contract and unnecessary to protect collateral is interest under § 85 of the National Bank Act), *summary judgment for lender aff'd*, 92 F.3d 384 (6th Cir. 1996) (insurance premiums were loans on which state law

permitted lender to charge any amount of interest; does not directly address definition of interest). *But see* Doe v. Norwest Bank Minnesota, 107 F.3d 1297 (8th Cir. 1997) (collateral protection insurance premiums do not constitute interest under National Bank Act). *See generally* §§ 7.3.1, 9.3.1.2, *supra*.

256 *See, e.g.*, Garrison v. First Fed. Sav. & Loan Ass'n of S.C., 402 S.E.2d 25 (Va. 1991) (only "actual" appraisal cost authorized; excess is interest). *See generally* Ch. 7, *supra*.

257 *See* Fikes v. First Fed. S&L of Anchorage, 533 P.2d 251 (Alaska 1975); Altherr v. Wilshire Mortgage Corp., 448 P.2d 859 (Ariz. 1969).

258 *See* §§ 8.5.3.1–8.5.3.2, *supra*.

259 *See, e.g.*, §§ 8.5.3.4, 8.5.4.3, *supra*.

260 Even where the insurance may not exceed specific limits, the circumstances of the transaction may make it subject to challenge under other theories, such as UDAP or unconscionability. *See* §§ 8.5.2.5–8.5.2.7, 8.7, *supra*.

261 *See* United-Bilt Homes v. Knapp, 396 S.W.2d 40 (Ark. 1965). Credit insurance is discussed in Ch. 8, *supra*.

262 Jones v. Credithrift of America, Clearinghouse No. 44,8100 (M.D. Fla. complaint filed July 11, 1989). *See also Principal Padding: The Prepaid Payment Pyramid*, 9 NCLC REPORTS Consumer Credit & Usury 23 (May/June 1991) (advance interest-only payments withheld from proceeds arguably discount interest).

exceed the greater of $400 (adjusted annually for inflation) or 8% of the total loan amount are now subject to the Home Ownership and Equity Protection Act.[263]

10.5.4.4 Proving the Charge Is Excessive

Once the amount of interest charged or collected in connection with a contract has been determined, the last step to proving an interest overcharge is to show that the interest assessed by the creditor is excessive. Since most usury ceilings are expressed as rates, the easiest way to demonstrate an overcharge is normally to calculate the highest permissible interest charge under the controlling statutory rate formula, given the principal amount properly determined,[264] and the length of time the loan or credit has been outstanding[265] or was scheduled to be outstanding.[266]

If the amount of interest assessed by the creditor exceeds this statutory maximum, then a usurious overcharge is present regardless of the precise manner in which the creditor calculated or exacted the interest.[267] As a matter of proof, using an expert to make these calculations is always helpful, if not essential to proving the existence of usury. At the very least, such an expert may be necessary to rebut the creditor's claim that the loan is not usurious.[268]

In some limited circumstances, courts will find that the collection of interest in excess of the lawful rate is not usurious if collection of the entire interest depends upon a contingent event and the contract was entered into in good faith and without the intent to evade the usury laws.[269]

Keep in mind that, as part of the borrower's proof, it is necessary to establish what maximum that particular creditor can charge for that particular kind of transaction.[270] It is also important to establish that no preemption questions are involved.[271] Which party bears the burden of proof on these issues is discussed in § 10.5.1.2, *supra*.

10.5.5 Intent

10.5.5.1 When Proof of Intent Is Required

Some statutes, particularly those regulating charges in consumer credit transactions, may have no intent requirement.[272] Apart from those statutes, typically the final element of a usury claim is the usurious intent of the lender.[273]

---

263 15 U.S.C. §§ 1602(aa), 1639. The statute has a specific definition of fees and charges. 15 U.S.C. § 1602(aa)(4). *See generally* § 12.2.2, *infra*.

264 *See* § 10.5.4.3, Chs. 7, 8 *supra*.

265 *But see* § 5.7.1, *supra* where early termination is at issue.

266 *See* § 4.10, *supra* on proof of mathematical issues.

  For common interest calculation formulae, such as simple interest, add-on interest, or discount interest, parties can frequently stipulate to the accuracy of a published rate chart which will show the permissible finance charge for any given principal amount (or amount financed) and rate. A common source is The Cost of Personal Borrowing in the United States, published by the Financial Publishing Company, Boston, MA. Requests for admission might also be used. *See* Appx. L.2.2, *infra*.

267 *See* Aikens v. Wagner, 498 S.E.2d 766 (Ga. App. 1998) (court simply compared the rate specified in the contract and payment history to the maximum rate allowed by law at the time the contract was consummated). *See also* Smith v. Khalif (*In re* Khalif), 308 B.R. 614 (Bankr. N.D. Ga. 2004) (loan was usurious where maximum allowable interest per month was $1,250 but note required $1,562.50); Corcoran v. TranSouth Fin. Corp. (*In re* Corcoran), 268 B.R. 882 (Bankr. M.D. Fla. 2001); Strasburger Enterprises, Inc. v. TDGT Ltd. P'ship, 110 S.W.3d 566, 579 (Tex. App. 2003); Pentico v. Mad-Wayler, Inc., 964 S.W.2d 708 (Tex. App. 1998) (court determined maximum allowable interest by multiplying the principal by the rate of interest and multiplying that amount by the term of repayment and then compared that amount to the sum of the actual interest charged plus late fees [considered "interest" under state law]). *But see* § 4.6.5.1, *supra* on spreading.

268 Britt v. Jones, 472 S.E.2d 199 (N.C. App. 1996) (court relied upon borrower's expert to find that all payments made should be attributed to each of four loans in chronological order, i.e., not until the first was paid off would subsequent payments be attributed to the later loans; thus, loans would never be paid in

full due to negative amortization).

269 Dopp v. Yari, 927 F. Supp. 814 (D.N.J. 1996). *See* § 10.5.3, *supra*.

270 *See generally* § 9.2, *supra*.

271 *See* Ch. 3, *supra*.

272 *See, e.g., In re* Swartz, 37 B.R. 766 (Bankr. D.R.I. 1984) (small loans); Beneficial Fin. Co. v. Administrator of Loan Laws, 272 A.2d 649 (Md. 1971) (no intent requirement under Small Loan Act); Duckworth v. Bernstein, 466 A.2d 517 (Md. Ct. Spec. App. 1983) (no intent requirement under second mortgage law unless treble damages sought); Thelen v. Ducharme, 390 N.W.2d 264 (Mich. App. 1986); Commercial Credit Equip. Corp. v. West, 677 S.W.2d 669 (Tex. App. 1984). *See also* § 5.7.2, *supra*.

273 *For cases finding usurious intent to be present in a transaction, see, e.g.,* Brodie v. Schmutz (*In re* Venture Mortgage Fund), 282 F.3d 185 (2d Cir. 2002) (loan is usurious if lender intends to take and receive interest in excess of that allowed by law even though lender has no specific intent to violate usury laws; loans made by victims to Ponzi scheme operator because of promised high returns are void); American Timber & Trading Co. v. First Nat'l Bank of Or. [II], 690 F.2d 781 (9th Cir. 1982) (intent derived from fact of charging to increase effective rate, ignorance of usury as such irrelevant); Fox v. Peck Iron & Metal, 25 B.R. 674 (Bankr. S.D. Cal. 1982) (real estate sale and leaseback; conscious receipt of excessive interest sufficient intent); Howes v. Curtis, 661 P.2d 729 (Idaho 1983) (despite uncontroverted assertions to the contrary usurious intent inferred from lender's background); Duckworth v. Bernstein, 466 A.2d 517 (Md. Ct. Spec. App. 1983) (arranger was lender's agent so statutory violation was knowing); Citizen's Nat'l Bank of Willmar v. Taylor, 368 N.W.2d 913 (Minn. 1985) (lender need only intend to charge rate which is, in fact, usurious; lender need not know that rate is usurious); Angelo v. Brenner, 457 N.Y.S.2d 630 (App. Div. 1982) (even without specific intent to do usury usurious note is void); Babcock v. Berlin, 475 N.Y.S.2d (Sup. Ct. 1984); Alamo Lumber Co. v. Gold, 661 S.W.2d 926 (Tex. 1983) (intent implied from knowing taking); Brookshire v. Longhorn Chevrolet, Inc., 788 S.W.2d 209 (Tex. App. 1990) (only intent required is to make the bargain made); Esparza v.

The difficulty of establishing this element frequently depends on whether the usury is created by a facially improper contract interest rate or is instead apparent only when hidden interest, disguised credit, or improper collection practices are exposed.

10.5.5.2 Usury Apparent on Face of Contract; Bona Fide Error

In almost all states,[274] if usury appears on the face of a credit contract, the requisite usurious intent is merely the intent of the lender to charge the interest rate which, in fact, was contracted for. This intent may be presumed from the contract.[275] Thus, the courts widely agree that if an overcharge is facially apparent, a lender need not have known that the interest rate was legally usurious and need not have had any intent to violate the law, provided that the interest which it intended to charge in fact exceeded the statutory limit.[276]

Nolan Wells Communications, 653 S.W.2d 532 (Tex. App. 1983) (intent immaterial if $93.60 interest charged); Jim Walter Homes v. Schuenemann, 655 S.W.2d 264 (Tex. App. 1983) (intent to reach the bargain made); Cuevas v. Montoya, 740 P.2d 858 (Wash. Ct. App. 1987) (intent need not be culpable, merely intent to enter a transaction which in fact carries unlawful rate of interest); Metro Hauling, Inc. v. Daffern, 723 P.2d 32 (Wash. Ct. App. 1986) (no intent to violate usury statute necessary).

For cases where usurious intent was absent, see, e.g., Kendrick v. Jim Walter Homes, 545 F. Supp. 541 (S.D. Ind. 1981) (intent is required to show U.C.C.C. violation); Smith v. MRCC P'ship, 792 S.W.2d 301 (Ark. 1990) (intent will not be inferred or imputed where opposite result can be fairly and reasonably reached); McDermott v. Strauss, 678 S.W.2d 334 (Ark. 1984) (value of debtor's services did not constitute additional interest absent a showing of usurious intent); Rhode v. Kremer, 655 S.W.2d 410 (Ark. 1983) (cannot infer usurious intent where uncontroverted evidence of typographical error); Argento v. Reynolds, 452 So. 2d 135 (Fla. Dist. Ct. App. 1984) (error to limit testimony regarding intent); Letiziano v. Lytal, 427 So. 2d 321 (Fla. Dist. Ct. App. 1983) (no summary judgment because intent must be shown); Lockhart Co. v. Naef, 693 P.2d 1090 (Idaho App. 1984) (evidence must show that lender charged usurious rate "knowingly and with corrupt intent" where lender's failure to sign note made otherwise permissible rate unlawful); *In re* Pearson, 352 N.W.2d 415 (Minn. 1984) (no intention given "unique circumstances"); Washington Fed. Sav. & Loan Ass'n of Stillwater v. Baker, 374 N.W.2d 786 (Minn. Ct. App. 1985) (no intent to evade usury law); Hanson v. Bonner, 661 P.2d 421 (Mont. 1983) (lawyer representing both parties who miscalculated interest and tried to correct error had no intent to commit usury); Freitas v. Geddes Sav. & Loan Ass'n, 471 N.E.2d 436 (N.Y. 1984) (mislabeling of otherwise valid fee); Libowsky v. Lakeshore Commercial Fin. Corp., 330 N.W.2d 248 (Wis. Ct. App. 1982) (unpublished, text available on Lexis) (lender charging 365/360 because of programmer error, lacked intent to commit usury).

274 An exception is Florida which generally requires a showing of "corrupt intent." *See, e.g.*, North Am. Mortgage Investors v. Cape San Blas Joint Venture, 378 So. 2d 287 (Fla. 1979) (corrupt intent demonstrated); Dixon v. Sharp, 276 So. 2d 817 (Fla. 1973) (discussion of corrupt intent); Oregrund Ltd. P'ship v. Sheive, 873 So. 2d 451 (Fla. App. 2004) (shown by intent to charge more than law allows); Gergora v. Goldstein Professional Ass'n Defined Benefits Plan Pension & Trust, 500 So. 2d 695 (Fla. Dist. Ct. App. 1987) (no corrupt intent); Rebman v. Flagship First Nat'l Bank of Highlands County, 472 So. 2d 1360 (Fla. Dist. Ct. App. 1985); Steward v. Nangle, 103 So. 2d 649 (Fla. Dist. Ct. App. 1958) (no corrupt intent). *See also* Jersey Palm-Gross, Inc. v. Paper, 658 So. 2d 531 (Fla. 1995) (ill will or malevolent intent unnecessary; intent to extract excessive rate

of interest shown where lender actively sought and received the usurious amounts and knew that borrowers were in urgent need).

"Corrupt intent" is also required in North Carolina but, as interpreted by the courts of that state, only the intent to charge a rate in excess of the statutory limit need be shown. *See* Swindell v. Federal Nat'l Mortg. Ass'n, 409 S.E.2d 892, 895–96 (N.C. 1991); Swindell v. Overton, 342 S.E.2d 391 (N.C. Ct. App. 1986).

New Mexico has also now adopted the "corrupt intent" rule. In Maulsby v. Magnuson, 755 P.2d 67 (N.M. 1988) the court overturned Hays v. Hudson, 514 P.2d 31 (N.M. 1973) and held there was no forfeiture because there was no corrupt intent where all parties were experienced in business, and the borrowers suggested the interest. The lender was, however, limited to the legal interest rate.

275 *See In re* Venture Mortgage Fund, 245 B.R. 460, 474 (Bankr. S.D.N.Y. 2000), *aff'd on other grounds*, 282 F.3d 185 (2d Cir. 2002); Henson v. Columbus Bank & Trust Co., 770 F.2d 1566 (11th Cir. 1985); Duderwicz v. Sweetwater Sav. Ass'n, 595 F.2d 1008 (5th Cir. 1979) (applying Georgia law); *In re* McCorhill Pub., Inc., 86 B.R. 783 (Bankr. S.D.N.Y. 1988) (N.Y. law); *In re* Rosner, 48 B.R. 538 (Bankr. E.D.N.Y. 1985) (applying New York law); Fikes v. First Fed. Sav. & Loan Ass'n, 533 P.2d 251 (Alaska 1975); Citizen's Nat'l Bank of Willmar v. Taylor, 368 N.W.2d 913 (Minn. 1985); Fareri v. Rain's Int'l Ltd., 589 N.Y.S.2d 579 (App. Div. 1992) (court also invoked parol evidence rule to deny admission of creditor's evidence that it did not retain all of offending charge where contract unambiguously stated it was payable to the lender); Matter of Estate of Dane, 390 N.Y.S.2d 249 (App. Div. 1976); Cook v. Frazier, 765 S.W.2d 546 (Tex. App. 1989); Kollman v. Hunnicutt, 385 S.W.2d 600 (Tex. Civ. App. 1964); Cuevas v. Montoya, 740 P.2d 858 (Wash. Ct. App. 1987). *See also* Fogie v. Thorn Americas, Inc., 95 F.3d 645 (8th Cir. 1996) (applying Minnesota law), *cert. denied*, 520 U.S. 1166 (1997).

276 *See, e.g.*, Najarro v. SASI Int'l Ltd., 904 F.2d 1002, 1009 (5th Cir. 1990), *cert. denied*, 498 U.S. 1048 (1991) (where evidence showed intent to enter into usurious bargain, a specific intent to charge usury is irrelevant); Henson v. Columbus Bank & Trust Co., 770 F.2d 1566 (11th Cir. 1985); American Timber & Trading v. First Nat'l Bank of Oregon, 690 F.2d 781 (9th Cir. 1982); Duderwicz v. Sweetwater Sav. Ass'n, 595 F.2d 1008 (5th Cir. 1979); Kissell Co. v. Gressley, 591 F.2d 47 (9th Cir. 1979); Gillivan v. Austin, 640 F. Supp. 1325 (D. V.I. 1986); *In re* Rosner, 48 B.R. 538 (Bankr. E.D.N.Y. 1985); Southland Mobile Home Corp. v. Webster, 563 S.W.2d 430 (Ark. 1978); Varr v. Olimpia, 2002 WL 1425373 (Cal. Ct. App. July 1, 2002) (unpublished, citation limited); Mark McDowell Corp. v. LSM 128, 263 Cal. Rptr. 310 (App. 1989) (intent is material to a determination of what terms the parties agreed to, but otherwise is "more or less immaterial"; creditor is presumed to intend what he actually does); McClung v. Saito, 83 Cal. Rptr. 44 (App. 1970); Dang v. F&S Land Dev. Co., 618 P.2d 276 (Haw. 1980); Kaiser Agric. Chem., Inc. v. Peters, 417 N.W.2d 437 (Iowa

A lender's only defense to usury on the face of the contract is to rebut the presumption of usurious intent by demonstrating that a bona fide error occurred in the preparation of the contract and that the lender therefore did not intend to charge the stated rate. The defense of mistake or bona fide error is a narrow one which must be proven by the lender.[277] It is generally limited to non-recurring errors such as numerical transpositions or a non-recurring mathematical error.[278] Repeated "errors" such as overcharges caused by

the use of an improper rate calculation method or an improperly programmed computer will not establish a bona fide error defense.[279] Moreover, a mistake in law does not

1987); Citizen's Nat'l Bank of Willmar v. Taylor, 368 N.W.2d 913 (Minn. 1985); Trapp v. Hancuh, 530 N.W.2d 879 (Minn. Ct. App. 1995); Scarr v. Boyer, 818 P.2d 381 (Mont. 1991) (intent required is to charge a rate that is usurious in fact; lack of knowledge that the rate is illegal or intent to violate the law is irrelevant); Freitas v. Geddes Sav. & Loan Ass'n, 471 N.E.2d 436 (N.Y. 1984) (plurality opinion stating rule for facially usurious contract); Norstar Bank v. Pickard & Anderson, 547 N.Y.S.2d 734 (App. Div. 1989); Vee Bee Serv. Co. v. Household Fin. Co., 51 N.Y.S.2d 590 (Special Term 1944), *aff'd without op.*, 269 A.D. 772 (1944); Western Auto Supply Co. v. Vick, 277 S.E.2d 360 (N.C. 1981), *aff'd on reh'g*, 283 S.E.2d 101 (1981); Swindell v. Overton, 342 S.E.2d 391 (N.C. Ct. App. 1986); Alamo Lumber Co. v. Gold, 661 S.W.2d 926 (Tex. 1983); Cochran v. American Sav. & Loan Ass'n of Houston, 586 S.W.2d 849 (Tex. 1979); Hoxie Implement Co. v. Baker, 65 S.W.3d 140 (Tex. App. 2001); Brookshire v. Longhorn Chevrolet, Inc., 788 S.W.2d 209 (Tex. App. 1990) (only intent required is to make the bargain made); Hardwick v. Austin Gallery of Oriental Rugs, Inc., 779 S.W.2d 438 (Tex. App. 1989) (usurious intent means intent to make the agreement that was made); Cuevas v. Montoya, 740 P.2d 858 (Wash. Ct. App. 1987). *See also* SAL Leasing, Inc. v. State *ex rel.* Napolitano, 10 P.3d 1221 (Ariz. App. 2000) (unlawful intent is shown by mere fact of intentionally doing what is forbidden by statute); Robinson v. Poferl, 2000 Minn. App. LEXIS 58 (Jan. 25, 2000); Olson v. Froslee, 2000 Minn. App. LEXIS 795 (Aug. 1, 2000) (unpublished, citation limited).

277 *See* Cashback Catalog Sales v. Price, 102 F. Supp. 2d 1375 (S.D. Ga. 2000) (intent to charge unlawful interest may be inferred from other facts, but lender can attempt to rebut it); Cochran v. American Sav. & Loan Ass'n of Houston, 586 S.W.2d 849 (Tex. 1979); Grotjohn Precise Connexiones Int'l, S.A. v. JEM Fin., Inc., 12 S.W.3d 859 (Tex. App. 2000); Commerce Crowdus & Canton, Ltd. v. DKS Constr., Inc., 776 S.W.2d 615, 618–19 (Tex. App. 1989) (" 'bona fide error' defense is only available when the evidence shows that the charge of usury results from the ignorance of a material fact or from other unintentional mishaps in office practice or routine which may be fairly characterized as 'clerical' errors"). *See also* Commercial Credit Equip. Corp. v. West, 677 S.W.2d 669 (Tex. App. 1984); Perez v. Hernardez, 658 S.W.2d 697 (Tex. App. 1983) (pleading of defense). *Cf.* Jones v. Jones, 301 S.W.2d 737 (Ark. 1957) (creditor failed to prove mistake in overcharging for insurance premium where he failed to offer testimony corroborating his claim that insurance agent misinformed him of cost, and he never informed borrower of the overcharge); Lupo v. Equity Collection Serv., 808 S.W.2d 122 (Tex. App. 1991) (defendant's pleading bona fide error did not constitute summary judgment proof; thus creditor presented no evidence sufficient to defeat debtor's motion for summary judgment).

278 *See, e.g.*, Walters v. First Tennessee Bank, 855 F.2d 267 (6th Cir. 1988) (mistake in computation is defense under National Bank Act, 12 U.S.C. § 86), *cert. denied*, 489 U.S. 1067 (1989); Rhode

v. Kremer, 655 S.W.2d 410 (Ark. 1983) (typographical error); Szeray v. Schaub, 496 So. 2d 883 (Fla. Dist. Ct. App. 1986) (error in calculations alleged); Sumner v. Adel Banking Co., 259 S.E.2d 32 (Ga. 1979) (mistake in calculation or by inadvertence which is not part of a usurious design or otherwise intentional); Harlow v. Walton Loan Corp., 329 S.E.2d 616 (Ga. App. 1985) (clerical error in complaint); Huddleston v. Bossier Bank & Trust Co., 475 So. 2d 1082 (La. 1985) (clerical error); Fidelity Funds, Inc. v. Price, 491 So. 2d 681 (La. Ct. App. 1986) (error in hand calculation—no bad faith); United Companies Mortgage & Inv. v. Lester, 394 So. 2d 1350 (Miss. 1981); Wycoff v. Commerce Bank, 561 S.W.2d 399 (Mo. Ct. App. 1977); Freitas v. Geddes Sav. & Loan Ass'n, 471 N.E.2d 436 (N.Y. 1984) (plurality opinion) (erroneous description of otherwise valid fee); Heelan v. Security Nat'l Bank, 343 N.Y.S.2d 417 (Dist. Ct. Suffolk Cty. 1973) (computer error caused by borrower's excessive overdrafts); Tyra v. Bob Carroll Constr. Co., 639 S.W.2d 690 (Tex. 1982) (usury in creditor pleadings excused as attorney error); Mayfield v. San Jacinto Savings Ass'n, 788 S.W.2d 119 (Tex. App. 1990) (bona fide error defense established where creditor presented evidence that transposition error created an overcharge); Martinez v. Teachers Credit Union, 758 S.W.2d 946 (Tex. App. 1988) (bona fide error where contract called for usurious daily rate, but nonusurious annual rate and total of payments); Ervin v. Muller, 2003 WL 21744332, at *6 (Wash. Ct. App. July 29, 2003) (unpublished, citation limited) (computation errors in lender's hand-kept ledgers did not establish usury). *See also* Marshall v. JRS Farms (*In re* Marshall), 1998 Bankr. LEXIS 515 (Bankr. M.D.N.C. Mar. 2, 1998) (court finds that interest rate that exceeded maximum RISA rate by 2% was bona fide error, so only remedy is refund; court does not explain factual basis for holding). *See generally* Annot. 11 A.L.R. 3d 1498 (1967), *Usury as Affected by Mistake in Amount or Calculation of Interest or Service Charges for Loan.*

But cf. Miller v. Soliz, 648 S.W.2d 734 (Tex. App. 1983) (failure to credit $465 down payment violates usury statute; not a bona fide error); Clark v. Aetna Fin. Corp., 340 N.W.2d 747 (Wis. Ct. App. 1983) (loan officer stole part of loan; given apparent authority, company answerable in usury for unrefunded interest overcharges even though principal returned; no bona fide error defense).

279 *See* Ford Motor Credit Co. v. Hutcherson, 640 S.W.2d 96 (Ark. 1982) (usury because of shorter initial installment interval is not excusable error); Southland Mobile Home Corp. v. Webster, 563 S.W.2d 430 (Ark. 1978) (incorrect interest formula used in computer program); Ford Motor Credit Co. v. Catalani, 238 Ark. 561, 383 S.W.2d 99 (1964) (mistaken use of wrong interest rate did not negate usurious intent); Lawler v. Lomas & Nettleton Mortgage Investors, 691 S.W.2d 593 (Tex. 1985) (charging per diem rate based on 360-day year not accidental or bona fide error); Mackie's Automotive, Inc. v. Parks, 2004 WL 213716 (Tex. App. Feb. 4, 2004) (unpublished, citation limited). *See also* Norstar Bank v. Pickard & Anderson, 529 N.Y.S.2d 667 (App. Div. 1988) (computer error could be defense to usury, but affidavit from bank officer insufficient evidence). *But see* Heelan v. Security Nat'l Bank, 343 N.Y.S.2d 417 (Dist. Ct. Suffolk Cty. 1973) (bank had no usurious intent when borrower's excessive overdrafts caused computer to assess improper late charges and bank refunded the overcharge); Jordan v. Tri County Ag, Inc., 546 S.E.2d 528 (Ga. App. 2001) (creditor not liable for usury where overcharges were caused by software and creditor cor-

negate a lender's intent to charge the contract rate and is not a valid usury defense.[280] (Nor will a mistake in law as to the maximum rate support a creditor's effort to reform a usurious contract.[281]) Finally, a bona fide error defense cannot be

maintained in some states unless the creditor proves that it had maintained procedures designed to prevent error.[282]

10.5.5.3 Usury Not Apparent on Face of Contract

In many cases, a credit contract is not usurious on its face because the usury is based either on the exposure of "hidden interest," the occurrence of some contingency such as acceleration, or the revelation of the extension of credit in a disguised credit contract.[283] In such situations, the courts

---

rected them upon discovery); Libowsky v. Lakeshore Commercial Fin. Corp., 330 N.W.2d 248 (Wis. Ct. App. 1982) (unpublished, text available on Lexis) (lender lacked intent when 365/360 interest charged because of programmer error). *See generally* Annot. 11 A.L.R.3d 1498 (1967), *Usury as Affected by Mistake in Amount or Calculation of Interest or Service Charges for Loan.*

280   *See, e.g.,* American Timber & Trading Co. v. First Nat'l Bank of Oregon, 690 F.2d 781 (9th Cir. 1982); LaPetina v. Metro Ford Truck Sales, 648 F.2d 283 (5th Cir. 1981) (wrong rate class chosen in motor vehicle usury law); Household Fin. Co. v. Swartz, 37 B.R. 776 (Bankr. D.R.I. 1984) ($4 recording fee usurious where not permitted separately under statute; no good-faith error defense allowed); Edwards v. Alabama Farm Bureau Mut. Casualty Ins. Co., 509 So. 2d 232 (Ala. Civ. App. 1986), *cert. quashed*, 509 So. 2d 241 (1987) (payment collected date loan was executed should have been treated as a down payment, rather than principal; this was error of law, and not a computational error, which is the only type of error subject to the statutory bona fide error defense); Ford Motor Credit Co. v. Catalani, 238 Ark. 561, 383 S.W.2d 99 (1964); Varr v. Olimpia, 2002 WL 1425373 (Cal. Ct. App. July 1, 2002) (unpublished, citation limited) (lender had usurious intent despite reliance on exemption to usury law that court later struck down); McClung v. Saito, 84 Cal. Rptr. 44 (App. 1970); Sunburst Bank v. Keith, 648 So. 2d 1147 (Miss. 1995) (usurious forbearance agreements; mistake as to legal effect of purposeful act binds creditor); Vee Bee Serv. Co. v. Household Fin. Co., 51 N.Y.S.2d 590 (Sup. Ct. Special Term 1944), *aff'd without op.*, 55 N.Y.S.2d 870 (App. Div. 1944); Commerce, Crowdus & Canton, Ltd. v. DKS Constr., Inc., 776 S.W.2d 615, 618–19 (Tex. App. 1989) (mistaken interpretation of contract provision was not bona fide error); Hardwick v. Austin Gallery of Oriental Rugs, Inc., 779 S.W.2d 438, 443 (Texas Ct. App. 1989) (trial court's finding that lender acted upon "mistaken and unfounded belief" regarding contract provision could not be interpreted as finding bona fide error). *See also* Danziger v. San Jacinto Sav. Ass'n, 732 S.W.2d 300, 302–03 (Tex. 1987) (creditor cannot purge a usurious charge by a subsequent credit). *Cf.* Aetna Fin. Co. v. Brown, 323 S.E.2d 720 (Ga. App. 1984) (regulatory agency's approval of loan contract form filed with it does not enable lender to claim statutory defense for contracts made in good faith conformity with rule, regulation or appellate judicial interpretation); Walker v. Fingerhut Corp., 2000 Minn. App. LEXIS 142 (Jan. 28, 2000) (unpublished) (remanding case for determination whether precautions creditor took to avoid violating state usury laws negated usurious intent; trial court had found usurious intent but that precautions established a good faith defense). *But see* Pilcher v. Direct Equity Lending, 189 F. Supp. 2d 1198 (D. Kan. 2002) (statute provides defense for bona fide error of law or fact). See National Consumer Law Center, Truth in Lending § 7.4.2 (5th ed. 2003 and Supp.) for a discussion of an analogous statutory defense in TILA.

281   *See* Olsen v. Porter, 539 N.W.2d 523 (Mich. Ct. App. 1995). *Cf.* Robinson v. Poferl, 2000 Minn. App. LEXIS 58 (Jan. 25, 2000) (unpublished, citation limited) (taking reasonable precautions to avoid usury, such as consulting qualified third party, can negate intent; not shown where lender did not retain own attorney and refused to reform loan after borrower discovered the usury).

282   *See* Trapp v. Hancuh, 530 N.W.2d 879 (Minn. Ct. App. 1995); Sumrall v. Navistar Fin. Corp., 818 S.W.2d 548 (Tex. App. 1991) (where there was no procedure to verify the calculation, nor if it existed, was the procedure used in the case where the collection supervisor "just skimmed" statement, the creditor did not establish maintenance of procedures designed to avoid bona fide errors); Moore v. White Motor Credit Corp., 708 S.W.2d 465 (Tex. App. 1985). *Cf.* Edwards v. Alabama Farm Bureau Mut. Casualty Ins. Co., 509 So. 2d 232 (Ala. Civ. App. 1986) (interpreting Truth in Lending provision on "bona fide error notwithstanding the maintenance of procedures reasonably adapted to avoid any such error," court held creditor did not meet burden where witnesses testified as to the company's training program and three-tiered checking system, but none of creditor's witnesses had first-hand knowledge of execution of loan in question and no evidence was presented that employee involved ever received the training, utilized the procedures, or had any other experience in making loans). See National Consumer Law Center, Truth in Lending § 7.4.3 (5th ed. 2003 and Supp.) and National Consumer Law Center, Fair Debt Collection § 7.5 (5th ed. 2004 and Supp.) for a discussion of the statutory bona fide error defense to TIL and FDCPA claims.

283   Unfortunately, there is room for disagreement about when a contract is usurious on its face. *See* Freitas v. Geddes Sav. & Loan Ass'n, 471 N.E.2d 436 (N.Y. 1984) (mislabeling of fee not facially usurious). The issue is infrequently discussed. While, logically, usury on the face of a contract should include any transaction in which excess interest or other statutory violations are the necessary consequence of the signing or enforcement of the contract, many courts may implicitly employ a narrower definition, especially when more "technical" violations are involved. *See also* Kissell Co. v. Gressley, 591 F.2d 47 (9th Cir. 1979) (usury due to commitment fee and acceleration does not appear on face of contract); *In re* Rosner, 48 B.R. 538 (Bankr. E.D.N.Y. 1985) (apparently regarding usury as appearing on face of note only when stated contract rate exceeds usury ceiling); Medford v. Wholesale Electric Supply Co., 691 S.W.2d 857 (Ark. 1985) (given variable rate ceiling, contract cannot be usurious on its face); Allied Supplier & Erection, Inc. v. A. Baldwin & Co., 688 S.W.2d 156 (Tex. App. 1985) (no usury on face of variable rate commercial contract). *Compare* Kish v. Van Note, 692 S.W.2d 463 (Tex. 1985) (insurance premium financing disclosure) *and* Jim Walter Homes v. Schuenemann, 668 S.W.2d 324 (Tex. 1984) (usurious acceleration clause) *with* Lockhart Co. v. Naef, 693 P.2d 1090 (Idaho App. 1984) (lender's failure to sign contract makes rate usurious under state law, but court requires proof of knowing and corrupt intent).

The question of intent in the rebate context also leads to some fine distinctions, e.g., Butler v. Holt Machinery Co., 741 S.W.2d 169 (Tex. App. 1987), *corrected on denial of rehearing*, 739 S.W.2d 958 (discussing distinction between acceleration clauses calling for maturity of "debt," which would not call for col-

apply a broad spectrum of approaches to determine the existence of usurious intent. Although decisions within most jurisdictions show some inconsistency, three over-all approaches seem to exist.

First, in at least one state, the courts draw no distinction between facially usurious contracts and other forms of usury, and look only at the lender's objective intent to make the loan.[284] Thus, the Supreme Court of Texas held that usurious intent was established, despite a jury finding that a bank had no subjective intent to charge excess interest, when a borrower showed that the bank had required her to assume a debt of her son's in order to obtain a refinancing of her loan.[285] The borrower's proof, that the bank had required the assumption of her son's debt as a condition for the extension of credit, established that the assumed debt was interest on the refinanced loan under Texas law, and the lender's intent to exact this interest was presumed. Because the true interest rate on the new loan exceeded the statutory limit, usury was demonstrated.

A second and more common approach to cases where usury is not facially apparent is to deny the borrower the presumption of intent otherwise granted, and to regard the existence of intent as a question of fact.[286] Given the same facts which existed in the Texas case described above, courts following this approach would require proof not only of the fact that the lender required the assumption of the son's debt, but also that it did so with the intent to exact more interest.[287] Note, however, that such a showing is not the same as the demonstration of a knowing violation of the usury law.[288] If the lender intended to exact more interest through the borrower's assumption of third party debt, it need not have known that the addition of this interest would cause the true rate to exceed the statutory limit and, thereby, to violate

state usury law. Thus, the real difference between this approach and the one taken in Texas is not the intent which must be proved, but rather the presumptions which aid the proof.

The third approach, taken by only a small minority of courts, to usury which is not apparent on the face of the contract is to require proof that the lender subjectively intended to evade the usury laws by structuring the contract as it did.[289] Thus, a lender who entered a contract in "good faith" or without "corrupt intent" may not have committed usury even if it intended to charge interest at a rate which, in fact, exceeds the statutory limit.[290] (However, at least as the Florida courts interpret their "corrupt intent" requirement, it is not always clear that the borrower need prove any more than that the creditor consciously intended to make the charges which result in usury and did so.[291]) The "good faith" approach is particularly favored in a line of California

---

lection of unearned interest, and one calling for maturity of "note," which would call for entire face amount of note including unearned interest. Where clause called for acceleration of "obligation," meaning is unclear and the parties' intention is a question of fact). *See generally* § 5.7.2, *supra*.

284 *See* Alamo Lumber Co. v. Gold, 661 S.W.2d 926 (Tex. 1983).

285 *Id. See also* Najarro v. SASI Int'l Ltd., 904 F.2d 1002, 1009 (5th Cir. 1990), *cert. denied*, 498 U.S. 1048 (1991) (specifically relies on *Alamo* in deciding usurious intent irrelevant).

286 *See, e.g.*, Greglon Industries, Inc. v. Bowman, 572 A.2d 369 (Conn. Ct. App. 1990); Dang v. F&S Land Dev. Co., 618 P.2d 276 (Haw. 1980); A&M Dev. v. Sherwood & Roberts, Inc., 457 P.2d 439 (Idaho 1969); Freitas v. Geddes Sav. & Loan Ass'n, 471 N.E.2d 436 (N.Y. 1984) (plurality opinion); Norstar Bank v. Pickard & Anderson, 547 N.Y.S.2d 734 (App. Div. 1989); Western Auto Supply v. Vick, 277 S.E.2d 360 (N.C. 1981), *reaff'd on reh'g*, 283 S.E.2d 101 (1981).

287 Interest in this context would be defined as any payment to the lender for a loan or forbearance, as opposed to a bona fide payment for third party services or a payment for other services exempted from "interest" by statute. *See, e.g.,* Durante Bros. & Sons, Inc. v. Flushing Nat'l Bank, 652 F. Supp. 101 (E.D.N.Y. 1986).

288 *See* Western Auto Supply v. Vick, 277 S.E.2d 360 (N.C. 1981), *reaff'd on reh'g*, 283 S.E.2d 101 (1981).

289 *See, e.g.*, Handi Inv. Co. v. Mobil Oil Corp., 550 F.2d 543 (9th Cir. 1977) (applying California law); Warehouse Home Furnishing Distributors, Inc. v. Whitson, 709 So. 2d 1144 (Ala. 1997) (court reversed trial court's grant of summary judgment on issue of whether lender's imposition of an illegal non-filing insurance fee was "deliberate" under Ala. Code § 5-19-19 to trigger the remedy of voiding the usurious loan; case goes to the jury on this issue; unclear if a subjective standard would be allowed upon remand); McDermott v. Strauss, 678 S.W.2d 334 (Ark. 1984); McConnell v. Merrill, Lynch, Pierce, Fenner, & Smith, 578 P.2d 1375 (Cal. 1978); Arneill Ranch v. Petit, 134 Cal. Rptr. 456 (App. 1976); Steward v. Nangle, 103 So. 2d 649 (Fla. Dist. Ct. App. 1958) (corrupt intent); Lockhart Co. v. Naef, 693 P.2d 1090 (Idaho App. 1984); Walker v. Fingerhut Corp., 2001 Minn. App. LEXIS 520 (May 15, 2001) (unpublished, citation limited) (defendant's good faith efforts to comply with states' laws demonstrated lack of intent). On occasion, a lender may make that strikingly easy, e.g., Antonelli v. Newmann, 537 So. 2d 1027 (Fla. Dist. Ct. App. 1988) (letter to borrowers said "Have you found a way around paying the 20% as agreed, or will you have to pay the [legal rate of] 18% and the additional 2% under a different pretext?" Borrowers then entered into a landscape consulting agreement on which they made regular payments in an amount equal to 2% of their loan when they made their loan payments). *See generally* § 7.2.3, *supra* on sham contracts as hidden interest.

290 *See* McConnell v. Merrill, Lynch, Pierce, Fenner, & Smith, 578 P.2d 1375 (Cal. 1978); Gergora v. Goldstein Professional Ass'n, 500 So. 2d 695 (Fla. Dist. Ct. App. 1987) (Florida law); *see also* Washington Fed. Sav. & Loan of Stillwater v. Baker, 374 N.W.2d 786 (Minn. Ct. App. 1985). *See generally* Comment, *Usury's Intent Requirement: Should There Be a Good Faith Defense?* 1985 B.Y.U.L. Rev. 789 (generally advocating good faith standard and suggesting that burden of proving good faith be placed on lender).

291 *See, e.g.,* Rollins v. Odom, 519 So. 2d 652 (Fla. Dist. Ct. App. 1988). *See also* Jersey Palm-Gross, Inc. v. Paper, 658 So. 2d 531 (Fla. 1995) (ill will or malevolent intent unnecessary; intent to extract excessive rate of interest shown where lender actively sought and received the usurious amounts and knew that borrowers were in urgent need). *But cf.* Polakoff v. State, 586 So. 2d 385 (Fla. Dist. Ct. App. 1991) (in criminal usury and RICO case, state's failure to allege in information that usurious acts were willful and knowing was fatal defect).

cases in which challenged overcharges were based on the occurrence of some contingency.[292] This approach clearly places a heavy burden of proof on borrowers.

10.5.5.4 Inference of Intent

In the majority of consumer transactions, a court's decision to view usurious intent as a question of fact should not preclude a finding of usury even if subjective intent is at issue. The court will examine all the circumstances surrounding the transaction in deciding whether to infer intent. Consequently, the inference is more likely to be drawn in standard consumer cases involving experienced lenders and distressed borrowers than in transactions exhibiting arm's length bargaining or inexperienced lenders.[293] Usurious intent has been found even when the only direct testimony on this point was the lender's denial of any intended usury.[294] Nevertheless, a requirement that a lender must show some degree of subjective intent provides an opening for courts which do not favor usury claims to find in favor of lenders.[295] Practitioners should challenge the good faith of professional lenders who repeatedly overcharge borrowers or who maintain a deliberate ignorance of usury law in order to deny corrupt intent.

10.6 Creditor Defenses

10.6.1 Defenses of Assignees and Holders in Due Course

10.6.1.1 Overview of General UCC Rules and Consumer Exceptions

Retail sellers and mortgage companies, in particular, and also finance companies, banks, and other creditors often do not individually have enough capital to finance as many sales or loans as they can originate. In order to obtain cash to continue their operations and to limit the risk associated with the extension of credit, these creditors sell obligations that they receive from borrowers to third party creditors who may or may not have had any connection with the original credit transaction. This pattern of financing retail credit through a secondary market prevails in both commercial and consumer transactions and has traditionally been encouraged by the law, including the Uniform Commercial Code (UCC) and its predecessor on this subject, the Uniform Negotiable Instruments Law (NIL). One of the primary mechanisms to encourage this flow is the holder-in-due-course doctrine, which permits those who purchase "negotiable instruments"[296] to protect themselves from claims of any other parties, and to free themselves from many, but not all, defenses to payment on the instrument.[297] The idea is that a bank or other investor can purchase negotiable instruments with limited risks. If an instrument appears valid on its face, the investor does not have to worry that the instrument might have been stolen, or that the maker of the instrument (e.g., a credit buyer) might have a contract dispute with the original payee (e.g., the credit seller) which would justify the maker's refusal to pay on the instrument. So long as the holder qualifies as a holder in due course, its risks are limited to the inherent risks of nonpayment because of the maker's bankruptcy, etc., and to the possibility that the instrument itself was originally invalid. Because the risks of investors are limited, they are more willing to invest, capital flows, and everyone benefits. Or so goes the reasoning behind UCC Article 3.

Holder doctrine, however, is not absolute, and not all assignees can successfully assert it in response to a consumer's claims and defenses. Most importantly for practitioners, the insulation of holders has been severely restricted for many common consumer transactions, as the uneven bargaining power and unequal sophistication in these transactions meant the operation of the rule unfairly inflicted great hardships. Thus many state consumer credit statutes limit its

---

292 *See* McConnell v. Merrill, Lynch, Pierce, Fenner, & Smith, 578 P.2d 1375 (Cal. 1978). *See also* Handi Inv. Co. v. Mobil Oil Corp., 550 F.2d 543 (9th Cir. 1977) (applying California law); Arneill Ranch v. Petit, 134 Cal. Rptr. 456 (App. 1976). *But cf. In re* Pillon-Davey & Assocs., 52 B.R. 455 (Bankr. N.D. Cal. 1985) (good faith not relevant if note usurious as matter of law and usury not dependent on a contingency); Fox v. Peck Iron & Metal, 25 B.R. 674 (Bankr. S.D. Cal. 1983) (real estate sale and leaseback with option to buy is usurious variable rate loan; no good faith error when minimum rate usurious); McClung v. Saito, 84 Cal. Rptr. 44 (App. 1970) (usury despite belief contract was legally proper).

293 Dixon v. Sharp, 276 So. 2d. 817 (Fla. 1973) (borrower distress is factor in "corrupt intent"). *Compare* Howes v. Curtis, 661 P.2d 729 (Idaho 1983) (experienced lender) *with* Meridian Bowling Lanes, Inc. v. Brown, 412 P.2d 586 (Idaho 1966) (arm's length bargaining and creditor not a professional lender).

294 *See* Howes v. Curtis, 661 P.2d 729 (Idaho 1983); Rollins v. Odom, 519 So. 2d 652 (Fla. Dist. Ct. App. 1988); *see also* Ford Motor Credit Co. v. Catalani, 383 S.W.2d 99 (Ark. 1964).

295 *See* Dixon v. Sharp, 276 So. 2d. 817 (Fla. 1973) (discussing corrupt intent).

---

296 Checks and promissory notes are classic examples of instruments which generally fall within the U.C.C. definition of a "negotiable instrument." U.C.C. § 3-104.

297 U.C.C. § 3-305. *See* § 10.6.1.3.5, *infra*.

impact,[298] as does the FTC Preservation of Claims and Defenses Rule in the context of consumer retail sales.[299] In 1994 Congress limited the circumstances in which assignees of certain high-cost home equity loans can assert holder-in-due-course status.[300] Moreover, even under traditional UCC doctrine, the underlying obligation and assignee must meet UCC definitions of a "negotiable instrument" and "holder in due course,"[301] and a failure to meet all the technical elements will deprive the assignee of that status. Finally, certain types of claims and defenses may be asserted even against holders in due course.[302]

The meaning of "holder" takes on a new dimension as electronic transactions increase. The Uniform Electronic Transactions Act (UETA),[303] which many states have adopted, envisions electronic promissory notes, termed "transferable records," the rights to which can be transferred just as paper notes are assigned. In addition, Congress included provisions for electronic promissory notes in the Electronic Signatures in Global and National Commerce Act "E-Sign"),[304] although only for promissory notes secured by real property. Revised Article 9 of the Uniform Commercial Code, which all states have adopted, also allows electronic "chattel paper," a term that includes the typical motor vehicle installment sales contract or lease.[305] The development of electronic retail installment contracts and transferable electronic promissory notes faces a number of technological hurdles,[306] however, which are only now being overcome.[307] There must be a way to identify the original, so that electronic copies cannot be passed as originals. Second, the technology must allow the holder of the electronic document to record an assignment of the document, but must prevent non-holders

from doing so. Third, there must be a way to transfer control over the electronic document to an assignee. The advent of electronic promissory notes may introduce new uncertainty for debtors and courts about who actually is the holder of a note,[308] but otherwise the holder-in-due-course analysis will be unaffected.[309]

The following sections discuss first the consumer exceptions, and then the UCC standards.

10.6.1.2 Consumer Exceptions to the Holder-in-Due-Course Doctrine: State Limitations, the FTC Holder Rule, and High-Cost Mortgages

10.6.1.2.1 Rationale for consumer exceptions

The UCC concepts of negotiability and limitation of defenses may be appropriate for commercial transactions. Commercial borrowers usually have sufficient resources to protect themselves even if they cannot enforce defenses against assignees of their obligations and must instead proceed against the original credit seller or lender. Commercial buyers, for example, frequently have enough financial clout to negotiate favorable credit terms. They are not normally forced to do business with sellers that they cannot rely on, or they are savvy enough not to do so. If a seller improperly performs in a commercial transaction, businesses usually have the resources to enforce their legal rights against the seller, even if they have to pay a holder in due course in the meantime.

While negotiability does not unduly prejudice commercial debts, application of the holder-in-due-course doctrine for consumer transactions is widely recognized to have been an unmitigated disaster for individual consumer debtors.[310]

---

298 *See* National Consumer Law Center, Unfair and Deceptive Acts and Practices § 6.6.5.3 (6th ed. 2004 and Supp.) (collection of state statutes).

299 16 C.F.R. 433. *See* § 10.6.1.2, *infra.*

300 *See* § 10.6.1.2.3, *infra.*

301 § 10.6.1.3, *infra.*

302 *Id.*

303 UETA § 16. UETA is published at 7A U.L.A. Pt. 1 (Supp.). The text of UETA can also be found on the website of the National Conference of Commissioners on Uniform State Laws, www.nccusl.org. By the end of 2000, UETA had been adopted in 24 states.

304 15 U.S.C. § 7021. *See* § 9.2.10, *supra*, and National Consumer Law Center, Consumer Banking and Payments Law Ch. 9 (2d ed. 2002 and Supp.).

305 U.C.C. § 9-102(a)(11), (31). *See* ANSI X9.103-2004, *Motor Vehicle Retail Sale and Lease—Electronic Contracting, available at* http://webstore.ansi.org.

306 UETA § 16; UETA § 3 cmt. 6, § 16 cmt. 1.

307 *See* Press Release, *First Electronic Note Registered on MERS eRegistry* (Aug. 10, 2004), and *MERS Launches MERS eRegistry*, (Apr. 26, 2004), *available at* www.mersinc.org/newsroom/press.aspx. In addition, the American National Standards Institute has promulgated standards for the creation, storage, and assignment of electronic chattel paper. *See* ANSI X9.103-2004, *Motor Vehicle Retail Sale and Lease—Electronic Contracting, available at* http://webstore.ansi.org (standards for creation, storage, and assignment of electronic chattel paper).

308 *See* 15 U.S.C. § 7021(f) and UETA § 16(f), which require the person in control of a transferable record to provide the obligor "reasonable proof" of control.

309 *See* 15 U.S.C. § 7021(d), (e), and UETA § 16(d), (e), both of which refer to the U.C.C. for rules governing the rights of holders and obligors.

310 For a history of the holder-in-due-course rule and its codification, see Kurt Eggert, *Held Up In Due Course: Codification and the Victory of Form Over Intent in Negotiable Instrument Law*, 35 Creighton Law Rev. 363 (Feb. 2002). For an analysis of the role the holder-in-due-course rule plays in encouraging fraud and predatory lending, see Kurt Eggert, *Held Up In Due Course: Predatory Lending, Securitization, and the Holder In Due Course Doctrine*, 35 Creighton Law Rev. 503 (Apr. 2002). For a discussion of the many problems that the holder-in-due-course rule posed for consumers, see 40 Fed. Reg. 53506 (Nov. 18, 1975) (Statement of Basis and Purpose for adoption of FTC assignee notice requirement). *See also Hearings on Problems in Community Development Banking, Mortgage Lending Discrimination, Reverse Redlining, and Home Equity Lending, Before the Senate Comm. on Banking, Housing and Urban Affairs*, 103d Cong., 1st Sess. (Feb. 3, 17, 24, 1993) (S. Hrg. 103-137; ISBN:0-16-041270-6, for sale by GPO).

Take, for example, the following all-too-common situation. A sales representative of Fly-By-Night Construction Co. visits the home of Joe and Jane Gullible and convinces them that they need aluminum siding on their home. The Gullibles sign a credit contract which is secured by their home. Unbeknownst to them, the contract contains a waiver of assignee liability. Fly-By-Night does a shoddy job or no job at all, and the telephone number that the salesman gave to the Gullibles is disconnected. Soon, however, the Gullibles are contacted by Friendly Finance Co., which has purchased the contract from Fly-By-Night. Friendly Finance claims to have no knowledge of the status of the construction. Instead, Friendly says it is an innocent third party assignee that merely wants to know where its monthly payments are. When the Gullibles refuse to pay, Friendly claims the rights of a holder in due course and begins foreclosure proceedings against the Gullibles' home. The UCC holder rules have, at least potentially,[311] taken away the Gullible's legal right to refuse to pay for defective goods or services.

Courts reviewing transactions such as the one with the Gullibles have frequently recognized the inequities of the situation and have interpreted UCC requirements in consumers' favor.[312] For example, numerous decisions under the UCC, and the NIL before it, have followed the "close-connectedness" doctrine, also referred to as the "party-to-the-transaction" doctrine, which contests a finance company's assertion of holder-in-due-course status by disputing the "good faith" and "without notice" requirements of UCC § 3-302, where the financer played some part in the original transaction.[313] It has also been used to allow a

consumer to assert defenses to the enforcement of a non-negotiable instrument, such as a RISC or a lease, against a third party who would not otherwise be subject to such defenses.[314] Facts that suggest an overly close connection include the seller's use of forms drafted by the finance company; the finance company's establishment or approval of the seller's sales terms; direct contact between the finance company and the debtor at the time of the sale, such as through a credit check; heavy financial reliance on the finance company by the seller; and common or connected ownership or management between the seller and the finance company.[315] To be considered without "good faith," the financer need not actually know of fraud in the underlying sale, if through the connection it had some reason to know of an infirmity.[316]

More recently, allegations that the lenders were principals, and the contractors their agents, have resulted in significant jury verdicts against lenders in these types of cases. Even if the agency theory fails, a lender may be liable in its own right for the acts of a third party under a civil

---

311 In fact, many courts reviewing such home improvement contracts determined that the finance company purchasing the consumer paper had not acted in good faith and without notice of defenses and was therefore not a holder in due course. *See, e.g.*, Fin. Credit Corp. v. Williams, 229 A.2d 712 (Md. 1967) (NIL); General Inv. Corp. v. Angelini, 278 A.2d 193 (N.J. 1971); Mutual Home Dealers Corp. v. Alves, 258 N.Y.S.2d 786 (App. Div. 1965); Walter E. Heller & Co. v. Da-Jar Constr. Co., 460 S.W.2d 266 (Tex. Civ. App. 1970). *See also* Ch. 11, *infra*. *See generally* Annot. 36 A.L.R. 4th 212 (1985) (good faith under U.C.C. § 3-302).

312 *See* Leasing Serv. Corp. v. River City Constr., 743 F.2d 871 (11th Cir. 1984) (distinguishing consumers and commercial debtors in enforcement of waiver-of-defense clauses).

313 *See, e.g.*, Greene v. Gibraltar Mortgage Inv. Corp., 488 F. Supp. 177 (D.D.C. 1980); Commercial Credit Corp. v. Childs, 137 S.W.2d 260 (Ark. 1940); Jones v. Approved Bancredit Corp., 256 A.2d 739 (Del. 1969) (finance company was sister corporation of seller and had exclusive decision-making power regarding transaction); Calvert Credit Corp. v. Williams, 244 A.2d 494 (D.C. Ct. App. 1968) (finance company was "so intimately involved" in sales process as to create agency relationship with seller); Ramadan v. Equico Lessors, Inc., 448 So. 2d 60 (Fla. Dist. Ct. App. 1984) (finance company's name on preprinted form used by seller in conjunction with borrower's testimony raised genuine issue of close connection for purpose of summary judgment); Rehurek v. Chrysler Credit Corp., 262 So. 2d 452 (Fla. Dist. Ct. App. 1972); Local Acceptance Co. v. Kincade, 361 S.W.2d 830 (Mo. 1962) (financer's knowledge that

seller also executed suspect "sew" contract with buyers purportedly to pay for machine supports verdict making holder subject to obligor's claims against seller); Unico v. Owen, 232 A.2d 405 (N.J. 1967) (finance company formed by seller which had thorough knowledge of and extensive control over seller's operations was not holder in due course); HIMC Inv. Co. v. Siciliano, 246 A.2d 502 (N.J. Super. 1968); Arcanum Nat'l Bank v. Hessler, 433 N.E.2d 204 (Ohio 1982) (finance company was not holder in due course where it provided seller of livestock with credit forms and set interest rate, ran an independent credit check on borrower and shared common directors with seller); Security Central Nat'l Bank v. Williams, 368 N.E.2d 1246 (Ohio App. 1976) (bank's taking of large number of notes, at substantial discount and on form provided by bank, from seller in "suspect" business, indicated close connection); American Plan Corp. v. Woods, 240 N.E.2d 886 (Ohio App. 1968); Norman v. WorldWide Distributors, Inc., 195 A.2d 115 (Pa. Super. 1963); Miller v. Diversified Loan Serv. Co., 382 S.E.2d 514, 518 (W. Va. 1989) ("It is generally held that if the financing institution exercises control over the creditor by supplying the financing forms or determining the amount of credit extended and its terms, such interconnectedness precludes the financing company from becoming a holder in due course"). *See generally* Annot. 36 A.L.R. 4th 212 (1985) (good faith under U.C.C. § 3-302).

314 *See, e.g.*, Mercedes-Benz Credit Corp. v. Lotito, 703 A.2d 288 (N.J. Super. 1997) (allowing consumer to assert breach of warranty claims against assignee of automobile lease).

315 Arcanum Nat'l Bank v. Hessler, 433 N.E.2d 204 (Ohio 1982) (citing White & Summers, Uniform Commercial Code 481 (1972)).

316 *See* United States Fin. Co. v. Jones, 229 So. 2d 495 (Ala. 1969) (denying holder-in-due-course status to financer of home improvement contract where both the mortgage and the certificate of completion were signed at the time of sale, though no work had yet been done); Local Acceptance Co. v. Kincade, 361 S.W.2d 830 (Mo. 1962) (financer's knowledge that seller of sewing machines also executed a "sew" contract with buyers whereby the buyers were to sew pre-cut garments to make the payments was sufficient to raise issue of bad faith for the jury).

conspiracy or aiding and abetting theory.[317] These are discussed in more detail in Chapter 11, *infra*. Common law theories of participation, ratification, and acceptance of benefits with knowledge of the fraud can also make a lender liable for the acts of the originator.[318] To the extent that these theories require proof of intent and knowledge, it may be sufficient to show willful blindness, i.e., that the defendant had limited information but failed to inquire further because of fear of what the inquiry would show.[319]

10.6.1.2.2 State laws and the FTC Rule

State legislatures also stepped in to protect consumers with special statutes which prohibit contractual waivers of assignee liability.[320] Case law also may hold such waivers to be void as a matter of public policy.[321] State law may distinguish consumer notes from commercial notes and remove the former from the class of negotiable instruments.[322] Similarly, the UCCC prohibits creditors from accepting negotiable instruments other than checks in conjunction with consumer credit sales.[323]

Nevertheless, the efforts of the courts and legislatures were somewhat haphazard, and for many years the assignment of consumer notes and contracts posed serious problems for the enforcement of many consumers' contractual rights.

The white knight[324] in this story turned out to be Federal Trade Commission (FTC) which in 1975, after several years of consideration, issued a Trade Regulation Rule, pursuant to the Federal Trade Commission Act. The FTC Holder Rule declares that it is an "unfair or deceptive act or practice" under the Act for a seller to enter a consumer credit contract which fails to contain the following language:

NOTICE

Any holder of this consumer credit contract is subject to all claims and defenses which the debtor could assert against the seller of goods or services obtained pursuant hereto or with the proceeds hereof. Recovery hereunder by the debtor shall not exceed amounts paid by the debtor hereunder.[325]

The rule requires sellers to include this language in all instruments created in consumer credit sales financed directly by a seller of goods or services. The FTC Holder Rule also requires sellers to arrange for the language to be included in instruments embodying a debt that arises from a "purchase money loan," with a third party creditor. The rule defines "purchase money loan" as any loan used to purchase goods or services if the seller either refers the consumer to the lender or is affiliated with the lender by "common control, contract, or business arrangement."[326] "Business arrangement" is defined broadly to include any understanding, procedure, course of dealing, or arrangement, formal or informal, between a creditor and a seller.[327] Thus, the FTC Holder Rule encompasses a large percentage of sales-related consumer credit, stopping only at loans obtained at a consumer's own initiative, without the referral or influence of a seller.[328]

The effect of the FTC Holder Rule is quite dramatic. The rule eliminates contractual waivers of a consumer's right to assert defenses against an assignee, which had previously been permitted by the UCC.[329] It also means that the holder

---

317 *See, e.g.*, Williams v. Aetna Fin. Co., 700 N.E.2d 859 (Ohio 1998). *See also* England v. MG Investments, Inc., 93 F. Supp. 2d 718, 723 n.8 (S.D. W. Va. 2000) (facts suggesting that broker was agent of lender, despite their agreement to the contrary, defeated summary judgment on holder-in-due-course issue and agency).

318 Maberry v. Said, 927 F. Supp. 1456, 1461–63 (D. Kan. 1996).

319 United States v. Cunningham, 83 F.3d 218 (8th Cir. 1996) (affirming criminal fraud conviction); United States v. Camuti, 78 F.3d 738 (1st Cir. 1996) (affirming mail fraud conviction); Louis Vuitton S.A. v. Lee, 875 F.2d 584, 590 (7th Cir. 1989) (trademark infringement by selling counterfeit goods); Bosco v. Serhant, 836 F.2d 271, 276 (7th Cir. 1987) (brokerage's liability in securities fraud case), *cert. denied*, 486 U.S. 1056 (1988).

320 *See, e.g.*, Tex. Fin. Code Ann. § 348.412. *Cf.* Me. Rev. Stat. Ann. tit. 11 § 3-1106(4), 3-1302(7). *See generally* National Consumer Law Center, Unfair and Deceptive Acts and Practices § 6.6.5.3 (6th ed. 2004 and Supp.); Annot. 39 A.L.R.3d 518 (1971) (waiver of assignee liability in consumer sales contracts).

321 Several courts have held that waiver of assignee liability for usury, in particular, is void as a matter of public policy. *See* Industrial Loan Co. v. Grisham, 115 S.W.2d 214 (Mo. Ct. App. 1934); Motor Contract Co. v. Van DerVolgen, 298 P. 705 (Wash. 1931). *See also* Westervelt v. Gateway Fin. Serv., 464 A.2d 1203 (N.J. Super. 1983) (second mortgage statute).

322 *See* S.D. Codified Laws § 57A-3A-101 *et seq.*; *cf.* Tollett v. Green Tree Acceptance, 379 S.E.2d 2 (Ga. Ct. App. 1989) (RISA provided that seller or holder liable for usury violations, but first assignee who then resold paper to Government National Mortgage Assoc. (GNMA), retaining only servicing duties for GNMA, was neither seller nor holder, and was therefore not liable); Roosevelt Fed. Sav. & Loan Ass'n v. Crider, 722 S.W.2d 325 (Mo. Ct. App. 1986) (holder of obligation evidencing purchase of consumer goods is subject to consumer defenses; aluminum siding was a "consumer good").

323 *See* U.C.C.C. § 3-307 (1974 Model Code); U.C.C.C. § 2-403 (1968 Model Code).

324 The armor is a bit tarnished by its unwillingness to extend the rule to direct, unrelated lenders. *See generally* National Consumer Law Center, Unfair and Deceptive Acts and Practices §§ 6.6, 6.7 (6th ed. 2004 and Supp.).

325 *See* 16 C.F.R. § 433.2 (1986). *See generally* National Consumer Law Center, Unfair and Deceptive Acts and Practices § 6.6 (6th ed. 2004 and Supp.).

326 *See* 16 C.F.R. § 433.1(d) (1986). *See, e.g.*, Associates Home Equity Servs., Inc. v. Troup, 778 A.2d 529 (N.J. App. Div. 2001) (jury question whether loan met definition of purchase money loan); Iowa Assistant Attorney General Letter, May 22, 2001, Clearinghouse No. 53,560.

327 16 C.F.R. § 433.1(g).

328 *See, e.g.*, Beck Enterprises, Inc. v. Hester, 512 So. 2d 672, 678 (Miss. 1987).

329 *See* § 10.6.1.3.10, *infra*.

of an instrument such as a promissory note that includes the FTC Holder Notice is not and cannot be a holder in due course under UCC Article 3.[330] The consumer has the right to raise claims both defensively and affirmatively against the holder or assignee,[331] but any affirmative recovery is limited to the amount the consumer has paid under the contract.[332] Refusal to acknowledge liability under the FTC Holder Rule may be a violation of the state's deceptive practices statute.[333]

The insertion of the FTC notice provision in an "instrument" such as a note may have a second, even more far-reaching effect in the one state, New York, that has retained the pre-1990 version of Article 3. It arguably removes the instrument from the definition of a "negotiable instrument" under the UCC, because negotiable instruments must contain an unconditional promise to pay, and the FTC notice imposes conditions on payment.[334] This issue does not exist for negotiable instruments governed by the 1990 version of Article 3, however, as it explicitly provides that a promise to pay is unconditional even if the instrument includes the FTC Holder Notice.[335]

Assignees and holders in due course may nonetheless continue to give consumers problems in some credit transactions. First, the FTC Holder Notice may have been wrongfully omitted from the credit contract. This is particularly likely in the case of a purchase money loan that purports to be an independent third-party loan. The holder of such an instrument may claim holder-in-due-course status even while the seller is liable for unfair or deceptive practices under the FTC Act or state UDAP statutes. The revised version of UCC Article 9, now in effect in all states, addresses this problem by reading the FTC Holder Notice into any consumer contract that should have included it.[336] This provision does not apply to negotiable instruments such as promissory notes, but the National Conference of Commissioners on Uniform State Laws has approved revisions to Article 3 that imply the FTC Holder Notice into any prom-

issory note whenever it should have been inserted.[337] This provision, if adopted by the states, will apply to direct loans where the seller refers the consumer to the lender and the consumer then signs a note with the lender. Even without these UCC amendments, a number of courts have found grounds to read the FTC Holder Notice into contracts and notes that should have included it.[338]

Another limitation on the FTC Holder Rule is that it only applies to sales-related consumer contracts, and not to traditional straight loans.[339] Thus, in the case of a loan of money that is not connected to the sale of goods or services, if the original lender defrauds the consumer, and then assigns the note to another financial institution, the FTC Holder Notice will not be present in the note and the borrower will not be able to rely on it to assert the original lender's fraud against the assignee.[340]

A final limitation on the FTC Holder Rule is that it has been misconstrued or misunderstood in a number of cases, resulting in the denial of its protections to consumers.[341] The UCC rules of assignment and negotiability therefore remain relevant in a significant number of consumer credit transactions.[342]

---

330 U.C.C. § 3-106(d). *See* Official Comment 3 to U.C.C. § 3-106.

331 *See, e.g.*, Jaramillo v. Gonzales, 50 P.3d 554 (N.M. App. 2002); Beemus v. Interstate Nat'l Dealer Servs., Inc., 823 A.2d 979 (Pa. Super. Ct. 2003). Note, however, that a line of decisions, starting with Ford Motor Credit Co. v. Morgan, 536 N.E.2d 587 (Mass. 1989), has misconstrued the rule and limited affirmative claims to cases in which the consumer is entitled to rescind the transaction or has received little or nothing of value. The FTC staff has repudiated this position. *See also* National Consumer Law Center, Unfair and Deceptive Acts and Practices § 6.6.3.4.3 (6th ed. 2004 and Supp.).

332 For an interpretation of this limitation, see Home Savings Ass'n v. Guerra, 720 S.W.2d 636 (Tex. App. 1986). *See generally* National Consumer Law Center, Unfair and Deceptive Acts and Practices § 6.6.3 (6th ed. 2004 and Supp.).

333 Jaramillo v. Gonzales, 50 P.3d 554 (N.M. App. 2002).

334 *See* N.Y. U.C.C. § 3-104(1)(b) (pre-1990 amendment); § 10.6.1.3, *infra*.

335 U.C.C. § 3-106(d).

336 U.C.C. §§ 9-403, 9-404.

337 Rev. U.C.C. § 3-305(e). As of early 2005, Revised Article 3 had been adopted only by Arkansas and Minnesota.

338 *See, e.g.*, Associates Home Equity Servs., Inc. v. Troup, 343 N.J. Super. 254, 778 A.2d 529 (App. Div. 2001). *But see* Crisomia v. Parkway Morg., Inc., 2001 Bankr. LEXIS 1469 (Bankr. E.D. Pa. Aug. 21, 2001); Capital Bank & Trust Co. v. Lacey, 393 So. 2d. 668 (La. 1980) (lender not subject to claims and defenses where FTC Holder Notice was omitted from the note; underlying transaction may have been commercial rather than consumer sale); Pratt v. North Dixie Manufactured Hous., Ltd., 2003 WL 21040658 (Ohio Ct. App. May 9, 2003) (unpublished). *See generally* National Consumer Law Center, Unfair and Deceptive Acts and Practices § 6.6.5 (6th ed. 2004 and Supp.).

339 *Cf.* Barnes v. Michigan Nat'l Bank Corp., 407 N.W.2d 23 (Mich. App. 1987) (state MVSFA did not apply to direct loan entered into between bank and borrower to finance vehicle purchase where no recourse by bank against dealer or other relationship between bank and dealer); Collins v. Horizon Housing, Inc., 519 S.E.2d 534 (N.C. App. 1999) (state RISA did not apply to direct loan to finance purchase of mobile home where borrower approached the bank directly; bank was not engaged, directly or indirectly, in sale of goods or furnishing of services). This loophole has been somewhat limited in the context of certain high-cost home equity loans. § 10.6.1.2.3, *infra*.

340 *See* § 10.6.1.2.3, *infra*.

341 *See, e.g.*, LaBarre v. Credit Acceptance Corp., 175 F.3d 640 (8th Cir. 1999) (construing FTC Holder Rule not to extend assignee liability beyond existing state law); Jarvis v. South Oak Dodge, Inc., 773 N.E.2d 641 (Ill. 2002) (FTC Holder Rule inapplicable to consumer leases; TILA restrictions on assignee liability also shield assignee from UDAP liability that is based on TIL violations); Ford Motor Credit Co. v. Morgan, 536 N.E.2d 587 (Mass. 1989) (consumer can sue affirmatively only when seller's breach is so substantial as to justify rescission). *See generally* National Consumer Law Center, Unfair and Deceptive Acts and Practices §§ 6.6.3.4.3, 6.6.3.8.1, 6.6.3.11 (6th ed. 2004 and Supp.).

342 *See* § 10.6.1.3, *infra*.

10.6.1.2.3 Assignee liability for high-cost mortgages

As the example of the Gullibles shows, the consequences of holder-in-due-course status for consumers who were victims of predatory contractors, brokers, or home equity lenders can be drastic: loss of the home to pay a debt for which they might have perfectly valid defenses and counterclaims. Unfortunately, since the FTC Holder Rule only applies to credit sales and to purchase money loans where the seller refers customers to or is affiliated with the lender, holder-in-due-course status can still apply to many direct loans. The growth of the secondary market to purchase residential-secured loans was one of the factors contributing to the growth of "equity-skimming" lenders in the 1980s.[343] The unethical contractor or mortgage lender could make an overreaching loan without fearing any consequences, because it got its money, then passed the risk on to the secondary market purchaser. Too many of those purchasers, in turn, did not assure that they were doing business with reputable, ethical originators, since they could use the holder doctrine as a shield to protect themselves from the borrowers' defenses.[344]

As a consequence, Congress enacted the Home Ownership and Equity Protection Act of 1994 (HOEPA)[345] as an amendment to the Truth in Lending Act.[346] HOEPA singles out a certain category of closed-end home equity loan for special protection.[347] Among those special protections is a limitation on the holder doctrine for assignees of this category of mortgage credit. As with the FTC Holder Rule, the hope is that this will encourage the industry to do more self-policing, so unscrupulous originators find the market for resale of their paper drying up.[348]

A loan which is subject to HOEPA is one which meets the following criteria:

- Is closed-end consumer credit;[349]

- Is not a "residential mortgage transaction," i.e., is not used for the acquisition or construction of the property;[350]
- Is secured by the borrower's principal dwelling;[351] and
- Meets one of two alternative cost-triggers;
  - Has an APR, properly calculated, which in the case of a first-lien loan is eight percentage points above the rate for Treasury securities of a comparable term, or, in the case of a junior-lien loan is ten percentage points higher. For example, if the yield on 15-year Treasury securities is 6%, an APR of 16% on a 15-year junior-lien loan will meet the trigger;[352] *or*
  - has upfront fees and charges (including broker fees and credit insurance premiums)[353] that exceed the greater of
    - 8% of the loan amount; or
    - $400 (an amount which changes annually with the consumer price index and which had reached $510 as of January 1, 2005).

Assignees of these loans are subject to *all* claims[354] (not just TILA claims) and defenses of the borrower which could

---

343 *See* Kurt Eggert, *Held Up In Due Course: Predatory Lending, Securitization, and the Holder In Due Course Doctrine*, 35 Creighton Law Rev. 503 (Apr. 2002).

344 *Hearings on Problems in Community Development Banking, Mortgage Lending Discrimination, Reverse Redlining, and Home Equity Lending, Before the Senate Comm. on Banking, Housing and Urban Affairs*, 103d Cong., 1st Sess. (Feb. 3, 17, 24, 1993) (S. Hrg. 103-137; ISBN:0-16-041270-6, for sale by GPO); *The Home Equity Protection Act of 1993, Hearings on H.R. 3153 Before the Subcommittee on Consumer Credit and Insurance of the House Committee on Banking, Finance and Urban Affairs*, 103d Cong., 2d Sess. (Mar. 22, 1994).

345 15 U.S.C. §§ 1602(aa), 1639.

346 15 U.S.C. § 1601 *et seq.*

347 The requirements of the Act are discussed in detail in National Consumer Law Center, Truth in Lending Ch. 9 (5th ed. 2003 and Supp.) and in overview in § 12.2.2, *infra*.

348 H.R. Conf. Rep. No. 652, 103d Cong. 2d Sess. 13, 163 (1994) (accompanying H.R. 3474).

349 Consumer credit is defined by TIL, 15 U.S.C. § 1602(e)–(h). *See* National Consumer Law Center, Truth in Lending § 2.2 (5th

ed. 2003 and Supp.). Closed-end credit is that repayable on specific repayment terms over a specified term, in contrast to open-end credit, which is defined at 15 U.S.C. § 1602(i). It is possible that some lenders will disguise closed-end credit as open-end in an effort to evade this legislation. *See The Home Equity Protection Act of 1993, Hearings on H.R. 3153 Before the Subcommittee on Consumer Credit and Insurance of the House Committee on Banking, Finance and Urban Affairs*, 103d Cong., 2d Sess. (Mar. 22, 1994). Effective October 1, 2002, the FRB added a prohibition to Regulation Z against structuring a home-secured loan as an open-end plan to evade HOEPA. 12 C.F.R. § 226.34(b).

350 15 U.S.C. § 1602(aa) as defined in TIL 15 U.S.C. § 1602(w). This tracks the exclusion from TIL's rescission right. 15 U.S.C. § 1635. *See* National Consumer Law Center, Truth in Lending § 6.2.6.1 (5th ed. 2003 and Supp.).

351 15 U.S.C. § 1602(aa). This, too, tracks TIL's definitions for rescission purposes. 15 U.S.C. §§ 1602(v), 1635; Reg. Z, § 226.23; National Consumer Law Center, Truth in Lending § 6.2.2 (5th ed. 2003 and Supp.).

352 12 C.F.R. § 226.32(a)(1).

353 Fees and charges are specifically defined by 15 U.S.C. § 1602(aa)(4) and Reg. Z § 226.32(b) to include: (a) all components of the TIL finance charge except interest and time-price differential (Reg. Z § 226.4); (b) broker fees; (c) certain listed real-estate related fees unless (i) they are reasonable, (ii) the creditor does not receive direct or indirect compensation. 15 U.S.C. § 1602(aa)(4), and (iii) they are paid to unaffiliated third parties; and (d) credit insurance premiums that are charged up front.

354 Faircloth v. National Home Loan Corp., 313 F. Supp. 2d 544 (M.D.N.C. 2003), *aff'd on other grounds*, 87 Fed. Appx. 314 (4th Cir. 2004); Pulphus v. Sullivan, 2003 WL 1964333, at *21 n.11 (N.D. Ill. Apr. 28, 2003) (§ 1641(d) subjects assignees to suit for mortgage creditor's violation of state law); Dash v. FirstPlus Home Loan Trust, 248 F. Supp. 2d 489, 506 n.20 (M.D.N.C. 2003) (by removing holder-in-due-course defense, § 1641(d) allows consumers to assert any claim against their

have been raised against the originator. Where the assignee's liability is based solely upon this section, however, damages for non-Truth in Lending claims are capped at the total paid by the borrower and an offset against the remaining indebtedness.[355]

To alert assignees, these mortgages must carry a "prominent notice of the potential liability" under the HOEPA.[356] However, to avoid the problem of lenders trying to circumvent the statute by simply omitting the notice, an assignee of a qualifying loan is still subject to all claims and defenses unless it proves that it could not, with due care, have determined that the transaction was one subject to this act. It must prove, by a preponderance of the evidence, that a reasonable lender, exercising ordinary due diligence after looking at all the relevant documents,[357] could not tell that this was a high-cost mortgage subject to HOEPA. In practice that should be a successful claim only infrequently. Though equity-skimming lenders often understate the APR by mis-

allocating charges which should be part of the finance charge to the amount financed, the "reasonable person" purchasing loans is ordinarily going to be a financial institution in the business of lending. A reasonable lender should certainly be charged with understanding how to calculate loan charges, what typical charges are, and how to calculate an APR.

10.6.1.3 UCC Principles

10.6.1.3.1 Basic prerequisites

As noted above, if an assignee can establish that it is a holder in due course, ordinarily it takes the obligation free of claims and most defenses.[358] But if a note or other writing evincing the obligation does not qualify as a negotiable instrument, or if its holder for some reason does not qualify as a holder in due course, the holder takes the obligation subject to all claims and defenses to which the original payee was subject.[359] Consequently, if the transaction is not subject to one of the consumer exceptions, practitioners facing a claim of holder-in-due-course status must examine the transaction carefully to determine whether all UCC prerequisites are met. In addition, even if a holder achieves holder-in-due-course status, it is still subject to certain defenses specified in the UCC.

10.6.1.3.2 Is the assignee a holder?

One of the preconditions of holder-in-due-course status is that the assignee be a "holder" of a "negotiable instrument." If the instrument is payable to bearer, the person in possession of it is the holder; if it is payable to an identified person who has possession of it, that person is the holder.[360] For one buying the paper from the person to whom it is originally payable, such as a lender buying it on the secondary mortgage market, the endorsement necessary for negotiation must be either written on the instrument itself or on a paper "affixed" to it.[361] Such a separate paper for an endorsement is called an allonge.[362] For instruments governed by the pre-1990 version of Article 3, the allonge must be "a paper so firmly affixed thereto as to become a part thereof."[363]

---

assignee that they could assert against the loan originator); Lewis v. Delta Funding Corp. (*In re* Lewis), 290 B.R. 541, 556 (E.D. Pa. 2003); Cooper v. First Gov't Mortg. & Investors Corp., 238 F. Supp. 2d 50 (D.D.C. 2002); Vandenbroeck v. Contimortgage Corp., 53 F. Supp. 2d 965, 968 (W.D. Mich. 1999); Mason v. Fieldstone Mortg. Co., 2000 U.S. Dist. LEXIS 16415 (N.D. Ill. Oct. 10, 2000); Murray v. First Nat'l Bank, 239 B.R. 728, 732 (Bankr. E.D. Pa. 1999). *See also* Harvey v. EMC Mortgage Corp. (*In re* Harvey), 2003 WL 21460063 (E.D. Pa. June 9, 2003) (HOEPA abrogates holder-in-due-course defense and makes assignee liable for all claims except under laws that have conflicting assignee liability provisions); Bryant v. Mortgage Capital Res. Corp., 197 F. Supp. 2d 1357 (N.D. Ga. 2002); Rodrigues v. U.S. Bank (*In re* Rodrigues), 278 B.R. 683 (Bankr. D.R.I. 2002). *But see* Dowdy v. Bankers Trust, 2002 U.S. Dist. LEXIS 3978 (N.D. Ill. Feb. 7, 2002) (erroneously confusing derivative liability created by HOEPA with the standard for liability for one's own acts under state UDAP statute).

355 15 U.S.C. § 1641(d)(2). (The damages for violating HOEPA itself include the usual TIL damages plus a special enhanced damage award consisting of all finance charges and fees paid by the consumer. 15 U.S.C. § 1640. Some violations also give rise to the extended rescission right under 15 U.S.C. § 1635.)

Practitioners should note that the assignee may be liable under other theories, as well, § 10.6.1.3, § 12.10, *infra*. If the assignee of a high-cost loan is directly liable under these theories, rather than derivatively liable because of the HOEPA assignee liability rules, then the HOEPA limitations on liability will not apply. *See* National Consumer Law Center, Truth in Lending § 9.6 (5th ed. 2003 and Supp.).

356 The language of the notice is prescribed by 12 C.F.R. § 226.32(e)(3).

357 This places a burden on the prospective purchaser to review all the documentation, instead of just the note alone. Any documents which would itemize all disbursements, including fees and costs, must be reviewed. This would include Truth in Lending disclosures, including itemization of the amount financed, or any disbursal statement or RESPA settlement statement. (In effect, this should have the effect of making the secondary market demand that itemizations of the amount financed be given, something TIL itself does not require. Reg. Z § 226.18.) *See generally* National Consumer Law Center, Truth in Lending § 9.7 (5th ed. 2003 and Supp.).

---

358 *See* § 10.6.1.1, *supra*.

359 U.C.C. §§ 3-305, 3-306.

360 U.C.C. § 1-201(20). *See* England v. MG Investments, Inc., 93 F. Supp. 2d 718, 723 n.8 (S.D. W. Va. 2000) (denying summary judgment that creditor was holder in due course where evidence showed instrument had been assigned to a different entity).

361 U.C.C. § 3-204(a).

362 U.C.C. § 3-204 cmt. 1. *See generally* National Consumer Law Center, Unfair and Deceptive Acts and Practices § 6.7.2.3.2 (6th ed. 2004 and Supp.) (requirements for allonges).

363 U.C.C. §§ 3-202(1) and (2) (pre-1990 version). Note that if it is bearer paper, only delivery of the instrument is necessary.

In the absence of a qualifying endorsement, an assignee may not be a "holder" at all, much less a holder in due course.[364] Some courts have construed this strictly, for example, disqualifying improperly placed endorsements,[365] or separate assignment agreements.[366] (This may be a particularly fruitful inquiry where the holder acquired the loan as part of a bulk purchase of a large portfolio of loans on the secondary mortgage market.) The 1990 amendments to Article 3 still require that the endorsement be "made on [the] instrument" but add that "a paper affixed to the instrument is a part of the instrument."[367] The Official Comments state that under this language an allonge is valid even though there is sufficient space on the instrument for an endorsement.[368] The 1990 amendments do not appear to eliminate the requirement that the paper containing the endorsement be attached to the instrument in a permanent way, although it no longer must be affixed so firmly "as to become a part thereof."

10.6.1.3.3 Is there a negotiable instrument?

The UCC's holder-in-due-course rules only apply to negotiable instruments.[369] The requirements for negotiability of the instrument are set out in UCC § 3-104(1). The instrument must be an unconditional promise or order to pay a fixed amount of money, with or without interest, and must (a) be payable to the bearer or to order at the time it is issued or first comes into possession of a holder;[370] (b) be payable on demand or at a definite time; and (c) with some exceptions, not include any other undertaking by the debtor. (As one early case characterized it, this last requirement means

that a negotiable instrument must be a "courier without baggage."[371]) Other formal requirements are found in the definition of "promise" and "order" at UCC § 3-103. For example, a promise must be in writing and signed by the obligor. Checks and promissory notes are typical examples of negotiable instruments. Negotiability must be determinable from the face of the documents.[372]

The industry found, to its consternation, that some common creative financing mechanisms devised in the 1980s failed to meet these requirements. Thus variable rate interest notes were successfully challenged as not meeting the "sum certain" criterion of the pre-1990 version of Article 3.[373] A number of state legislatures subsequently amended their laws to specifically declare variable rate notes to be negotiable,[374] and the 1990 revisions to Article 3 also do so.[375] Similarly, a Fifth Circuit decision raised the question of whether line-of-credit notes sufficiently define a "sum certain" to constitute a negotiable instrument.[376]

An instrument is payable at "a definite time" if it is due on a specified date or dates or on a date that is readily ascertainable at the time the instrument is issued.[377] In *In re*

---

364 Family Fin. Servs. v. Spencer, 677 A.2d 479 (Conn. App. 1996) (court held that plaintiff was not a holder because there was no valid assignment under state law). *But cf.* § 10.6.1.3.6, *infra* (discussion of shelter rule).

365 *See, e.g.,* Crossland Savings Bank F.S.B. v. Constant, 737 S.W.2d 19, 4 U.C.C. Rep. 2d 1479 (Tex. App. 1987) (endorsement by stapling separate piece of paper to back of loan documents, separated from note itself; court notes separate document should be used only when no room for endorsement on note itself; even so, this was not attached to note at all; discusses whether stapling adequate method of affixing even if endorsement is affixed to note). *See also* Adams v. Madison Realty & Dev., Inc., 853 F.2d 163 (3d Cir. 1988) (endorsement sheets not affixed at all did not constitute a valid allonge; decision contains a good discussion of the development and purpose of the requirement).

366 Becker v. National Bank & Trust Co., 284 S.E.2d 793 (Va. 1981). *See also* Adams v. Madison Realty & Dev., Inc., 853 F.2d 163 (3d Cir. 1988) (separate, unattached papers folded into promissory notes without any attachment are not valid allonges, therefore purchaser was not holder in due course).

367 U.C.C. § 3-204(a).

368 Official Comment 1 to U.C.C. § 3-204.

369 U.C.C. §§ 3-302(a), 3-104(b).

370 *See* Leavings v. Mills, 2004 WL 1902536 (Tex. App. Aug. 26, 2004) (retail installment contract not negotiable instrument where not payable to bearer or to order).

371 Overton v. Tyler, 3 Pa. 346, 347 (1846) (in reference to a precursor of the U.C.C.'s holder-in-due-course rule). *See* P & K Marble, Inc. v. La Paglia, 537 N.Y.S.2d 682 (App. Div. 1989) (mortgage note not a negotiable instrument under pre-1990 version of Article 3 when it included numerous promises such as to keep the property insured). *Cf.* Wilson v. Toussie, 260 F. Supp. 2d 530 (E.D.N.Y. 2003) (referring to a mortgage does not make a note non-negotiable).

372 Taylor v. Roeder, 360 S.E.2d 191, 4 U.C.C. Rep. 2d 652, 655 (Va. 1987).

373 Taylor v. Roeder, 360 S.E.2d 191 (Va. 1987) (note providing for variable-rate interest tied to Chase Manhattan prime did not call for payment of a "sum certain," as it required reference to an outside source). *See also* National Union Fire Ins. v. Alexander, 728 F. Supp. 192 (S.D.N.Y. 1989). *But see* Carnegie Bank v. Shalleck, 606 A.2d 389 (N.J. Super. Ct. App. Div. 1992) (applying 1990 Article 3 amendments retroactively to hold that note was negotiable despite variable rate); Amberboy v. Societe de Banque Privee, 831 S.W.2d 793 (Tex. 1992) (variable rate notes in which the rate may be determined by reference to a published rate, i.e., either known or readily ascertainable by anyone, are negotiable instruments).

374 *See, e.g.,* Schwegmann Bank & Trust Co. v. Falkenberg, 931 F.2d 1091 (5th Cir. 1991); First City Federal Sav. Bank v. Bhoganonker, 715 F. Supp. 1216 (S.D.N.Y. 1989) (addressing New York's 1988 amendment to U.C.C. § 3-106).

375 U.C.C. § 3-112(b). *See* England v. MG Investments, Inc., 93 F. Supp. 2d 718, 723 n.8 (S.D. W. Va. 2000) (assignee may be holder in due course of variable rate note under 1990 amendments).

376 RTC v. Oaks Apt. Joint Venture, 966 F.2d 995 (5th Cir. 1992) (note calling for repayment of "$2 million or so much thereof as may be advanced" was not sufficiently certain to constitute a negotiable instrument. *NB*: the court rules that where the *principal* was not a "sum certain," cases or statutes holding that variable *interest* rate notes are negotiable are irrelevant. 966 F.2d at 1002, n.9).

377 U.C.C. § 3-108(b).

Boardwalk Marketplace Securities Litigation,[378] the notes in question included an estimated payment schedule, but provided that the lender would notify the borrower of the first payment due date. Because the payment schedule required reference to a separate written notice, it was not payable "at a definite time."[379] Again, the result was to defeat negotiability, and thus preclude the use of a holder-in-due-course defense.

These cases point up the importance of routinely examining the technical prerequisites. In many cases, such technical deficiencies may be easier to prove than some of the other challenges to Holder status, such as "good faith," thus making discovery more economical and streamlining litigation on the issue. Such defects would make the holder of the obligation subject to all claims and defenses to which the original payee was subject.[380]

10.6.1.3.4 Did the holder acquire the instrument in good faith, for value, and without notice?

Assuming that these formal prerequisites for a negotiable instrument are met, the holder still must establish that it qualifies for holder-in-due-course status. It must have acquired the instrument (a) for value,[381] (b) in good faith, and (c) without notice that it is overdue, that it has been dishonored, that there is an uncured default with respect to payment of another instrument issued as part of the same series, that any signature is unauthorized or altered, that any defense exists to payment on the instrument, or that any other party has a claim to it.[382] (Article 9 of the UCC imposes similar requirements on an assignee of a credit contract who seeks the protections of a waiver-of-defense clause.[383]) In consumer litigation, the most common sources of contention are the good faith and notice requirements, which are discussed in § 10.6.1.3.8, *infra*.

10.6.1.3.5 What defenses can be asserted against a holder in due course?

Achieving holder-in-due-course status protects the holder against many, but not all, of the obligor's defenses. Defenses which can be asserted against a holder in due course include infancy, the lack of the maker's capacity to execute the instrument,[384] duress, the illegality of the transaction, misrepresentation of the essential character or terms of the contract,[385] "fraud that induced the obligor to sign the instrument with neither knowledge nor reasonable opportunity to learn of its character or its essential terms,"[386] and bankruptcy.[387] Usury can be a defense to a holder in due course in some cases.[388]

10.6.1.3.6 Rights of subsequent transferees of negotiable instruments

Often negotiable instruments are transferred more than once. For example, the original payee may negotiate the instrument to an entity that qualifies as a holder in due course, and then that holder may transfer the instrument to a second entity. Under the UCC, the second entity acquires the rights of a holder in due course even if it would not qualify as a holder in due course on its own.[389] For example, if the second entity knew of a defense to the instrument before it acquired it, it would still acquire the rights of a holder in due course.[390] This protection is known as the shelter rule.

There is an important exception to the shelter rule if the second entity engaged in fraud or illegality affecting the instrument.[391] "A person who is party to fraud or illegality affecting the instrument is not permitted to wash the instrument clean by passing it into the hands of a holder in due course and then repurchasing it."[392]

The shelter rule only gives the transferee the rights of the transferor.[393] If the transferor did not have the rights of a holder in due course, then the transferee will not acquire those rights.

10.6.1.3.7 Electronic negotiable instruments

The Electronic Signatures in Global and National Commerce Act (E-Sign) validates electronic negotiable instru-

---

378 668 F. Supp. 115, 4 U.C.C. Rep. 2d 1464 (D. Conn. 1987).

379 The banks tried to argue in the alternative that these were demand notes, which are sufficiently definite under § 3-104(1)(c). The court held they were not. *In re* Boardwalk Marketplace Securities, 668 F. Supp. 115, 4 U.C.C. Rep. 2d 1464, 1472–1474 (D. Conn. 1987).

380 U.C.C. §§ 3-305, 3-306.

381 *See* U.C.C. § 3-303 (definition of "value"). *See, e.g.,* Ocwen Fed. Bank v. Russell, 53 P.3d 312 (Haw. Ct. App. 2002) (when assignment stated only that assignee took note for $1.00 and other valuable consideration, question of fact whether assignee was holder in due course).

382 U.C.C. § 3-302.

383 U.C.C. § 9-403(b). *See* § 10.6.1.3.9, *infra*.

384 *See, e.g.,* Shepard v. First Am. Mortgage Co., 347 S.E.2d 118 (S.C. Ct. App. 1986).

385 American Plan Corp. v. Woods, 240 N.E.2d 886 (Ohio App. 1968).

386 For a discussion of fraud as a defense to a holder in due course, see generally Annot. 78 A.L.R.3d 1020(1977); § 12.10, *infra*.

387 U.C.C. § 3-305(a)(1), (b). *See generally* National Consumer Law Center, Unfair and Deceptive Acts and Practices § 6.7.2.5 (6th ed. 2004 and Supp.).

388 *See* § 10.6.1.3.9, *infra*.

389 U.C.C. § 3-203.

390 Official Comments 2, 4 to U.C.C. § 3-203.

391 U.C.C. § 3-203(b).

392 Official Comment 2 to U.C.C. § 3-203; *see* Triffin v. Somerset Valley Bank, 777 A.2d 993 (N.J. Super. Ct. App. Div. 2001) (buyer of forged check from holder in due course entitled to assert rights of holder).

393 U.C.C. § 3-203(a), (b).

ments that relate to loans secured by real property.[394] E-Sign refers to these as "transferable records." The issuer of the instrument must expressly agree that it is a transferable record.[395] If the transferable record meets various E-Sign requirements designed to ensure that multiple copies of the instrument are not created, then the holder can acquire holder-in-due-course status by meeting the UCC's requirements.[396] Delivery, possession, and endorsement are not required, however, to obtain the rights of a holder in due course of a transferable record.[397]

10.6.1.3.8 Showing that a holder did not take usurious note in good faith and without notice of defenses

If a debtor signs a note which qualifies as a negotiable instrument under the UCC, or a credit contract which contains a waiver of assignee liability that is not invalidated by state law or the FTC Holder Rule, all is not lost. Claims relating to credit overcharges may nevertheless be asserted against an assignee under UCC law if an assignee took the instrument in bad faith or with notice of defenses. In that case, the assignee cannot either qualify as a holder in due course under UCC § 3-302 or defeat the obligor's defenses by means of a waiver of defense clause under section 9-206, and is subject to any claim or defense.

In many situations, it may be possible to show that a holder did not take a note in good faith and without notice of defenses, as required by sections 3-302 and 9-206.[398] The current definition of "good faith," in effect in all states except New York, is "honesty in fact and the observance of reasonable commercial standards of fair dealing,"[399] so the holder must act in a way that is fair according to commercial standards that are reasonable.[400] Clearly, if a note is usurious on its face, any holder has notice of the usury and cannot be a holder in due course.[401] More frequently, however, a note will be facially valid, because, for example, the usury is created by hidden interest or fees not reflected in the note, and some inquiry into the holder's subjective knowledge of the underlying transaction will be necessary. For example, if usurious payments are apparent in a credit contract but do not appear on the associated note, the note holder may nevertheless be held to have notice of the usury if it obtained a copy of the contract along with the note.[402] Finance companies or other assignees which have close business ties to the original creditor, such as a credit seller, have often been held, solely under the provisions of the UCC, to be so "closely connected" to the original seller as to be on notice of the original creditor's business practices, including usury.[403] The holder may also have been put on notice of the

---

394 15 U.S.C. § 7021.

395 15 U.S.C. § 7021(a)(1)(B).

396 15 U.S.C. § 7021(b), (c), (d).

397 15 U.S.C. § 7021(d).

398 *See, e.g.,* United States Fin. Co. v. Jones, 229 So. 2d 495 (Ala. 1969); Salter v. Vanotti, 599 P.2d 962 (Colo. App. 1979); Cromwell v. All State Credit Corp., 10 U.C.C. Rep. 403 (D.C. Sup. Ct. 1971); Ocwen Fed. Bank v. Russell, 53 P.3d 312 (Haw. Ct. App. 2002) (question of fact whether assignee was holder in due course when assignment occurred after borrower sued assignor); HIMC Inv. Co. v. Siciliano, 246 A.2d 502 (N.J. Super. 1968); Mutual Home Dealers Corp. v. Alves, 258 N.Y.S.2d 786 (App. Div. 1965) (judgment reopened); Fairbanks Capital Corp. v. Summerall, 2003 WL 1700487 (Ohio Ct. App. Mar. 31, 2003) (unpublished) (question of fact whether holder took instrument without notice of defenses, when debtor had rescinded the transaction and filed suit prior to transfer of the obligation); Davenport v. Unicapital Corp., 230 S.E.2d 905 (S.C. 1976); Walter E. Heller & Co. v. Da-Jar Constr. Co., 460 S.W.2d 266 (Tex. Civ. App. 1970) (NIL); Sparkman & McLean Income Fund v. Wald, 520 P.2d 173 (Wash. Ct. App. 1974). *Cf.* Hatton v. Money Lenders & Assocs., 469 N.E.2d 360 (Ill. App. 1984) (no notice). *See generally* Annot. 36 A.L.R. 4th 212 (1985).

399 U.C.C. § 3-103(a)(4). Revised Article 1, which had been adopted by about ten states as of early 2005, incorporates this definition and applies it to all of the U.C.C. except Article 5.

Accordingly, Revised Article 3 deletes the definition of good faith, since it is no longer necessary for each article of the U.C.C. to define the term. *See* Legislative Note to Rev. U.C.C. § 3-103. A few of the states that adopted Revised Article 1 did not, however, adopt the revised definition of good faith. As of early 2005, only Minnesota and Arkansas had adopted Revised Article 3.

400 Any Kind Checks Cashed, Inc. v. Talcott, 830 So. 2d 160 (Fla. App. 2002).

401 *See* Davenport v. Unicapital Corp., 230 S.E.2d 905 (S.C. 1976).

402 *See, e.g.,* Davenport v. Unicapital Corp., 267 S.C. 691, 230 S.E.2d 905 (1976); Walter E. Heller & Co. v. Da-Jar Constr. Co., 460 S.W.2d 266 (Tex. Civ. App. 1970) (NIL); Carper v. Kanawha Banking & Trust Co., 207 S.E.2d 897 (W. Va. 1974) (notice of usury imputed even though the transaction was couched in language of a sale arguably brought under the time-price exception to the usury law). *See also* General Inv. Corp. v. Angelini, 58 N.J. 396, 278 A.2d 193 (1971) (defense of failure of consideration). *But cf.* Barbour v. Handlos Real Estate & Bldg. Corp., 393 N.W.2d 581 (Mich. Ct. App. 1986) (mere receipt of mortgage does not constitute actual notice of its payment terms where they are different from those on the note secured by the mortgage).

403 *See* HIMC Inv. Co. v. Siciliano, 103 N.J. Super. 27, 246 A.2d 502 (1968). *See also* Greene v. Gibraltar Mortgage Inv. Corp., 488 F. Supp. 177 (D.D.C. 1980) (fraud and misrepresentation); United States Fin. Co. v. Jones, 285 Ala. 105, 229 So. 2d 495 (1969) (fraud); Commercial Credit Corp. v. Childs, 199 Ark. 1073, 137 S.W.2d 260 (1940) (warranty claims); Ramadan v. Equico Lessors, Inc., 448 So. 2d 60 (Fla. Dist. Ct. App. 1984) (fraud, failure of consideration and warranty claims, summary judgment for finance company reversed); Rehurek v. Chrysler Credit Corp., 262 So. 2d. 452 (Fla. Dist. Ct. App. 1972) (warranty claims); Kennard v. Reliance, Inc., 257 Md. 654, 264 A.2d 832 (1970) (judgment for assignee of note reversed and remanded for determination of applicability of close connectedness doctrine); Arcanum Nat'l Bank v. Hessler, 69 Ohio St. 2d 549, 433 N.E.2d 204 (1982) (want of consideration defense); American Plan Corp. v. Woods, 16 Ohio App. 1, 240 N.E.2d 886 (1965) (fraud); Norman v. WorldWide Distributors, Inc., 202 Pa. Super. 53, 195 A.2d 115 (1963) (fraud). *But see* Mellon Bank, N.A. v. Ternisky, 999 F.2d 791 (4th Cir. 1993) (lender's protections and power under loan agreement with developer of

assignor's practices if the consumer filed a lawsuit against the assignor, or if correspondence about the consumer's claims appears in the assignor's file.[404] Further, if the consumer defaulted prior to the assignment, this should be documented in the consumer's file, putting the holder on notice of the default.[405] Actual knowledge of the defense or default is unnecessary. Under the UCC, a person has "notice" of a fact when, "from all the facts and circumstances known to him at the time in question he has reason to know it exists."[406] In general, the UCC notice and good faith requirements for holder-in-due-course status have been much more broadly interpreted and more strictly enforced in consumer transactions than in comparable commercial transactions.[407]

Practitioners litigating against lenders who have financed fraudulent contractors have argued either that the lender is in reality a primary lender, not an assignee,[408] or that the financier was in fact a principal, with the originating contractors or brokers actually mere agents. Even if the originator and the holder of a note have agreed among themselves that neither is the agent of the other, agency may be found based on their conduct.[409] Certainly, if a financier knows of the fraudulent manner of operation of its business

client, the contractor or second mortgage company, it should be directly liable.[410] Similarly, a bank which lent money to people to invest in what the bank knew to be a Ponzi scheme at least may be unable to enforce promissory notes signed as a result of the fraud.[411] This "ostrich game" also may be evidence of fraud if a bank, for example, was "selectively careless" in handling its credit arrangements with the primary perpetrator.[412] Evidence concerning the price paid by the purchasing institution may have some bearing at least on whether a financier is entitled to assert a holder-in-due-course defense to borrower's claims and defenses on a note. The purchase of a note at a steep discount may be evidence of bad faith.[413]

If the obligation has been securitized, the pooling and servicing agreement may demonstrate that both the original

---

resort condominiums did not give lender such control over developer as to negate lender's holder-in-due-course status as assignee of individual condominium purchaser's mortgage note); White v. Gilliam, 224 Va. 113, 419 S.E.2d 247 (1992) (assignee of mortgage notes who had ownership interest in and regular dealings with mortgage company, was owed substantial sum by mortgage company, and took notes with full recourse and without supporting deeds of trust was nonetheless holder in due course). *See generally* National Consumer Law Center, Unfair and Deceptive Acts and Practices §§ 6.6.4.6, 6.7.2 (6th ed. 2004 and Supp.).

404 Ocwen Fed. Bank v. Russell, 53 P.3d 312 (Haw. App. 2002) (summary judgment for holder vacated where it acquired note after consumer had raised her defenses in court); Fairbanks Capital Corp. v. Summerall, 2003 WL 1700487 (Ohio App. Mar. 31, 2003).

405 *Id.*

406 U.C.C. § 1-201(25). *See* Any Kind Checks Cashed, Inc. v. Talcott, 830 So. 2d 160 (Fla. App. 2002) (unusual circumstances surrounding the acquisition of the instrument are sufficient to defeat holder-in-due-course status).

407 *See* Leasing Serv. Corp. v. River City Constr., Inc., 743 F.2d 871 (11th Cir. 1984).

408 Alco Collections, Inc. v. Poirier, 680 So. 2d 735 (La. App. 1996) (holding in an arguably analogous context, that an attempt to assign a debt to an agency for collection failed because the plain wording of the agreement did not show an intent to transfer ownership of the debt). *Practice tip*: carefully check the language of the assignment/transfer documents. This language may appear on the documents given to consumers but, more often, is contained in a separate contract between the assignee and assignor.

409 England v. MG Investments, Inc., 93 F. Supp. 2d 718, 723 n.8 (S.D. W. Va. 2000) (concealment of identity of finance company and immediate assignment of note despite paperwork that gave appearance of later assignment tended to show agency relationship).

410 *See, e.g.,* Union Mortgage Co. v. Barlow, 595 So. 2d 1335 (Ala. 1992). *Cf.* Anderson v. FNMA, Clearinghouse No. 42,568, Civ. No. 87-0236 (E.D. Va. 1988) (motion to dismiss RICO claim against institutions which purchased portfolios of loans from fraudulent second mortgage company on secondary market denied where borrowers alleged purchasers knew of company's operations).

411 Sheradsky v. West One Bank, 817 F. Supp. 423, 425 (S.D.N.Y. 1993) ("If fraud is involved in a transaction, a financing entity which deliberately shuts its eyes to clues concerning the fraud may be unable to enforce promissory notes signed as a result of the fraud;" decision on denial of bank's motion for summary judgment; unclear what relief plaintiffs sought against bank).

412 *Cf.* Brazell v. First Nat'l Bank & Trust, 982 F.2d 206, 209 (7th Cir. 1992) (dicta). A financier's failure to check the creditworthiness and reputation of the contractor whose paper it purchased was apparently part of the evidence intended to show the contractor's agency in one of the unreported Alabama decisions. *See* Gene A. Marsh, *Lender Liability for Consumer Fraud Practices of Retail Dealers and Home Improvement Contractors*, 45 Univ. of Ala. L. Rev. 1 (1993).

413 *Compare* Beatty v. Franklin Inv. Co., 319 F.2d 712 (D.C. Cir. 1963) (NIL); Greene v. Gibraltar Mortgage Inv. Corp., 488 F. Supp. 177 (D.D.C. 1980) (substantial discount); Union Mortgage Co. v. Barlow, 595 So. 2d 1335 (Ala. 1992) (borrowers alleging that financier was a primary, not a secondary lender, presented evidence of the discount on the purchased paper); United States Fin. Co. v. Jones, 285 Ala. 105, 229 So. 2d 495 (1969) (50% discount off face value of note was evidence to be considered by jury as indicative of bad faith on part of assignee); Stewart v. Thorton, 568 P.2d 414 (Ariz. 1977) (1/3 discount; holder-in-due-course status at issue); Anderson v. Lee, 103 Cal. App. 2d 24, 228 P.2d 613 (1951) (NIL); Salter v. Vanotti, 42 Colo. App. 448, 599 P.2d 962 (1979) (40% discount); Security Central Nat'l Bank v. Williams, 52 Ohio App. 2d 175, 368 N.E.2d 1246 (1976) (substantial discount rate, with other factors, was evidence of bad faith); Norman v. WorldWide Distributors, Inc., 202 Pa. Super. 53, 195 A.2d 115 (1963) (more than 20% discount off face value of note) *and* Fin. Credit Corp. v. Williams, 246 Md. 575, 229 A.2d 712 (1967) (NIL) *with* Northwestern Nat'l Ins. Co. v. Maggio, 976 F.2d 320 (7th Cir. 1992) (50% discount purchase of note in commercial investment transaction was not a suspicious circumstance that triggered a duty to inquire as to possible defenses on the note; holder's status as holder-in-due-course at issue. Posner poopoos *Stewart* in this case); Hatton v. Money Lenders & Assocs., 469 N.E.2d 360 (Ill. App. 1984) (U.C.C.).

payee and the trust to which the obligation was transferred had notice of defenses and did not act in good faith. For example, the agreement may describe some of the originator's questionable practices, give some indication of the likelihood of default, indicate that the notes are subject to the FTC Holder Rule, or state that the assignee will not be a holder in due course.

Keep in mind that it is the holder of a note who bears the burden of establishing its status as a holder in due course, although the debtor must initially raise any issue, such as the holder's knowledge of usury, which could preclude holder-in-due-course status.[414]

10.6.1.3.9 Whether usury can be asserted against a holder in due course

Another way usury or fraud can be asserted against an assignee applies even if an assignee of a note has clearly taken a negotiable instrument for value, without notice of defenses, and in good faith, and has thus attained the esteemed status of a holder in due course. The important UCC provision under these circumstances is section 3-305, which defines the rights of a holder in due course and which specifies that even a holder in due course is subject to the defense of the "illegality of the transaction, which, under other law, nullifies the obligation of the obligor."[415] Although there is some questionable authority to the contrary,[416] and although a few states have special rules,[417] it seems clear that a usury violation or a fraud which renders an obligation void under state law is an "illegality" which renders the obligation a "nullity" under the UCC and may thus be asserted as a defense against a holder in due course of the obligation.[418] Further, if a note is void because it was

issued by an unlicensed lender in violation of a state credit statute,[419] it will remain void when transferred to an innocent assignee, even if that assignee holds a license which would have authorized it to originate the loan.[420]

A more difficult question is the status of a usury defense when the existence of usury under state law voids only part of the obligation by, for example, voiding the interest on the obligation while allowing the creditor to recover principal. Some support exists for the argument that usury is a defense under the UCC to a holder in due course to the extent that it voids the obligation even if the obligation is not rendered entirely void.[421] However, courts interpreting the Negotiable Instruments Law were split on the issue, with some courts concluding that usury was not a defense to a holder in due course if the usury statute merely forbids the collection of the illegal portion of the interest.[422]

10.6.1.3.10 The UCC and waiver of defense clauses

If for some reason the FTC Holder Rule does not apply to a contract, UCC or common law rules will determine the liability of the assignee. In the absence of a waiver of defense clause, the assignee of a contract subject to UCC Article 9 is subject to all claims or defenses that the obligor may have against the assignor, as long as the claim or defense accrued before the obligor was notified of the assignment.[423] These claims and defenses can be asserted only to reduce the obligor's liability to the assignee, however.[424] Common law also states that the rights of the

---

414 *See* Bank of North Carolina v. Rock Island Bank, 630 F.2d 1243 (7th Cir. 1980); Beatty v. Franklin Inv. Co., 319 F.2d 712 (D.C. Cir. 1963) (NIL); Jackson v. Mundaca Fin. Servs., Inc., 76 S.W.3d 819 (Ark. 2002) (holder has burden of pleading and proving holder-in-due-course status); HIMC Inv. Co. v. Siciliano, 103 N.J. Super. 27, 246 A.2d 502 (1968).

415 *See generally* National Consumer Law Center, Unfair and Deceptive Acts and Practices § 6.7.2 (6th ed. 2004 and Supp.).

416 *See* Pilcher v. Direct Equity Lending, 189 F. Supp. 2d 1198 (D. Kan. 2002) (treating usurious loans as voidable despite statutory language that they are void); Beatty v. Franklin Inv. Co., 319 F.2d 712 (D.C. Cir. 1963) (NIL decision); Katz v. Simcha Co., 251 Md. 227, 246 A.2d 555 (1968) (dictum, citing *Beatty, supra*); *see also* Hatton v. Money Lenders & Assocs., Ltd., 469 N.E.2d 360 (Ill. App. 1984) (summary judgment awarded to note holder once good faith and absence of notice of usury defense established; no discussion of possibility that usury is defense against a holder in due course).

417 *See* Michigan Nat'l Bank v. Mattingly, 212 S.E.2d 754 (W. Va. 1975); Carper v. Kanawha Banking & Trust Co., 207 S.E.2d 897 (W. Va. 1974) (West Virginia usury statute amended to preclude recovery from holder in due course).

418 *See, e.g.,* Bank of North Carolina v. Rock Island Bank, 630 F.2d 1243 (7th Cir. 1980); Andrews v. Martin, 245 Ark. 995, 436 S.W.2d 285 (1969); Fuller v. Universal Acceptance Corp., 264

A.2d 506 (D.C. 1970); Lucas v. Beco Homes, Inc., 494 S.W.2d 417 (Mo. App. 1973); Westervelt v. Gateway Fin. Serv., 190 N.J. Super. 615, 464 A.2d 1203 (1983); Robinson v. Rudy, 666 S.W.2d 507 (Tex. App. 1984); Michigan Nat'l Bank v. Mattingly, 212 S.E.2d 754 (W. Va. 1975) (transaction prior to statutory amendment). *See also* National Consumer Law Center, Unfair and Deceptive Acts and Practices § 6.7.2 (6th ed. 2004 and Supp.).

419 *See* § 9.2.4.6, *supra*.

420 *See In re* Harrington, 6 B.R. 655 (Bankr. D.R.I. 1980).

421 *See* Lucas v. Beco Homes, Inc., 494 S.W.2d 417 (Mo. App. 1973); *see also* Fuller v. Universal Acceptance Corp., 264 A.2d 506 (D.C. 1970) (usury precludes holder-in-due-course status; assignee forfeits interest). *But cf.* Cromwell v. All State Credit Corp., 10 U.C.C. Rep. 403 (D.C. Sup. Ct. 1971) (usury renders debt voidable, not void, and so is not defense to holder in due course).

422 *See* Hall v. Mortgage Security Corp. of America, 119 W. Va. 140, 192 S.E. 145 (1937) (good discussion); Annot. 95 A.L.R. 735 (1935) (NIL as affecting defense of usury). *See also* Lydick v. Stamps, 316 S.W.2d 107 (Tex. Civ. App. 1958) (contract void as to interest even in the hands of an innocent purchaser; debtor recovers twice the usurious interest).

423 U.C.C. § 9-404(a)(2) (formerly § 9-206).

424 U.C.C. § 9-404(b). *See also* Lawson State Community College v. First Continental Leasing Corp., 529 So. 2d 926 (Ala. 1988) (interpreting former version of Art. 9 to allow only defensive use of claims and defenses against assignee, but acknowledging cases to the contrary).

assignee of a contract are subject to all claims or defenses of the obligor that accrued before the obligor received notification of the assignment.[425] Although it is not universal, a number of courts have held that these claims can only be asserted defensively.[426] Whether the assignment delegates the assignor's duties under the contract to the assignee depends on the terms of the contract.[427]

Despite these general rules of assignee liability, the UCC allows the assignee of a credit sale contract or lease that does not qualify as a "negotiable instrument" to acquire the same rights as a holder in due course if the contract contains a provision waiving the right of the buyer or lessee to assert defenses against assignees, and if the assignee takes the contract for value, in good faith, and without notice of any claims or defenses.[428] However, this waiver provision applies only to defenses which could not be asserted against a holder in due course, and it is expressly subject to any special rules regarding waivers that may apply to consumer transactions under other provisions of state law.[429] Since the FTC Holder Notice requirement applies broadly to consumer credit sales, it should nullify the effect of a waiver of defense clause in most consumer sales contracts.[430]

10.6.2 Collection Agencies' Liability for Illegal Overcharges

In a Texas case of first impression, a collection agency which had attempted to collect interest far exceeding the maximum on a consumer debt unsuccessfully tried to defend against a claim for usury penalties on the ground it was not a party to the original transaction.[431] The court noted that the statute limited the parties who could recover penalties, but not those who were liable for them.[432] It also noted that to rule otherwise would permit a collection agency to collect and profit from usurious interest with impunity.[433] An Illinois decision, while finding the interest rate legal, also holds that an assignee of a debt is subject to the same interest rate restrictions as the assignor.[434]

10.6.3 Standing to Assert Usury

Noting that usury statutes are designed to protect needy borrowers rather than to penalize lenders, courts have widely viewed usury as a claim that is personal to the borrower.[435] This rule is frequently raised by creditors as a defense in usury actions where the party seeking to assert usury is not the same party who received the credit proceeds. The issue is often framed as one of standing to assert usury.[436] Standing is a question of law for the court.[437]

It is fairly clear that any maker or obligor on a note has standing to assert usury. Thus, a co-signer can plead usury.[438] Furthermore, a person whose interest in the litiga-

---

425 Restatement (Second) of Contracts § 336(2). *See* Am. Transportation Corp. v. Exchange Capital Corp., 129 S.W.3d 312, 316 (Ark. App. 2003); Bank of Hawaii v. Davis Radio Sales & Serv., Inc., 727 P.2d 419 (Haw. 1986); Hammelburger v. Foursome Inn Corp., 54 N.Y.2d 580, 446 N.Y.S.2d 917, 921, 431 N.E.2d 278 (1981) (assignee of nonnegotiable bond and mortgage takes subject to any defense that would have prevailed against assignor, but estoppel certificate here may be valid); Wynnewood Bank & Trust v. State, 767 S.W.2d 491, 494 (Tex. App. 1989). *See also* DaimlerChrysler Servs. v. Ouimette, 830 A.2d 38 (Vt. 2003) (assignee of contract stands in shoes of seller).

426 *See* Dege v. Milford, 574 A.2d 288 (D.C. 1990) (assignee takes claim subject to all defenses of the obligor against the assignor that existed before notice of assignment, but is not subject to affirmative liability without express agreement); Restatement (Second) of Contracts § 336(2), cmt. c. *But cf.* Buchanan v. Brentwood Fed. S. & L. Ass'n, 74 Pa. D. & C.2d 754 (C.P. 1975) (allowing affirmative suit against assignee; assignee takes mortgage subject to all rights and duties of assignor).

427 Restatement (Second) of Contracts § 328. *See* Black v. Sullivan, 122 Cal. Rptr. 119 (App. 1975) (where deed of trust was transferred to assignee as security for a debt owed by assignor, assignee was merely a pledge and was not obligated to perform under original contract).

428 U.C.C. § 9-403.

429 *Id.*

430 *See* § 10.6.1.2.2, *supra.*

431 Lupo v. Equity Collection Serv., 808 S.W.2d 122 (Tex. App. 1991). The collector tried to rely on cases holding that the usury defense is personal to the debtor.

432 Tex. Fin. Code Ann. § 349.002 provides that "a person" who violates the statute may be held liable for penalties.

433 Lupo v. Equity Collection Serv., 808 S.W.2d 122, 124 (Tex. App. 1991).

434 Dawson v. The Bureaus, Inc., 2004 WL 2921871 (N.D. Ill. Dec. 14, 2004).

435 *See, e.g.*, Manohara v. Medifax, Inc., 2002 WL 1376212 (Cal. Ct. App. June 26, 2002) (unpublished, citation limited) (debtor's limited partner does not have standing); Ideal Loan & Fin. Corp. v. Little, 457 S.E.2d 274 (Ga. App. Ct. 1995) (judge could not exclude award of interest on grounds of usury in default judgment, as usury defense is personal to the borrower); Midwest Fed. Sav. v. West Bend Mut. Ins., 407 N.W.2d 690 (Minn. Ct. App. 1987) (insurance company could not assert usury claim both because claim was personal to the borrower-insureds and because the usury defense is unavailable to corporations); LaBarre v. Gold, 520 So. 2d 1327 (Miss. 1988); General Elect. Credit Corp. v. Best Refrigerated Express, Inc., 385 N.W.2d 81 (Neb. 1986); Smart v. Crawford Bldg. Material Co., 638 S.W.2d 228 (Tex. App. 1982). *But cf.* Focus Investments Assoc., Inc. v. American Title Ins. Co., 992 F.2d 1231 (1st Cir. 1993) (title insurer had standing to assert that usury rendered lender's mortgage uninsurable; insurer did not assert usury as defense to repayment of loan).

436 Texas courts have distinguished between assertion of a statutory usury penalty and assertion of a "common law" usury claim that the principal indebtedness should be reduced by the payments of usurious interest. Standing to make the latter assertion has been granted to junior lienholders outside the transaction. Allee v. Benser, 779 S.W.2d 61 (Tex. 1988).

437 El Paso Refining, Inc. v. Scurlock Permian Corp., 77 S.W.3d 374 (Tex. App. 2002).

438 *See* Bizzoco v. Chintz, 193 Conn. 304, 476 A.2d 572 (1984); Fidelcor Mortgage Co. v. Tyroff, 302 S.E.2d 96 (Ga. 1983) (individual co-maker had standing to assert usury but lost claim

tion derives from the borrower may be able to assert usury on the borrower's behalf, but the extent to which such derivative rights exist can vary significantly with the plaintiff and the state.[439] Thus, while a trustee or receiver can generally maintain a usury action on behalf of a named bankrupt,[440] states are split on the standing of the estate of a deceased borrower to assert usury on the borrower's behalf.[441]

Most cases where creditors dispute a plaintiff's standing to assert usury involve guarantors or sureties to a debt, and while a few opinions to the contrary exist, the large majority of courts hold that guarantors and sureties do not have standing to assert usury.[442] The litigation regarding guaran-

tors typically involves loans to close corporations secured by the individual guaranty of a major stockholder. In such cases the corporate borrower may be unable to claim usury because of a high or non-existent corporate usury ceiling, and the addition of the rule denying standing to guarantors essentially exempts the entire transaction from usury limitations.

One danger with denying guarantors the right to assert usury is that creditors may force individuals who are seeking personal loans to receive their loans through a shell corporation and to add their personal guaranty to the corporation's note. It is somewhat reassuring, therefore, that courts examining individually guaranteed loans to close corporations have frequently recognized the potential for usury evasion and have specifically looked at the purposes of such loans before upholding them.[443] The result of this judicial approach is that individual loans through close corporations probably cannot be attacked as usurious if the loans have a business purpose, even if they are actually loans to individuals, but individual guarantors can challenge usurious personal or consumer loans that are structured in this man-

---

because of business purpose usury exception); Ciminelli v. Ford Motor Credit Co., 624 S.W.2d 903 (Tex. 1981); Miller v. First State Bank of Bedford, 551 S.W.2d 89 (Tex. Civ. App. 1977), *aff'd*, 563 S.W.2d 572 (Tex. 1978); Williams v. Security Sav. & Loan Ass'n, 355 N.W.2d 370 (Wis. App. 1984).

439 *See, e.g.*, Family Fed. Sav. & Loan v. Davis, 172 B.R. 437 (Bankr. D.D.C. 1994) ("purchaser of equity of redemption in real estate who is in privity of estate or contract with the mortgagor and grantor can plead usury," D.C. law); Eisenstein v. DiPrimio, 2000 Ga. App. LEXIS 1140 (Sept. 15, 2000) (law firm had standing to claim usury as defense when its client's creditor sought to impose constructive trust over money in client trust account); Seidel v. 18 East 17th St. Owners, 598 N.E.2d 7 (N.Y. 1992) (original borrower's corporate transferee was essentially same people, and transfer occurred as a result of building's conversion to a co-op, not a sale to an independent third party; transferee therefore could assert usury).

440 *See, e.g.*, McCollum v. Hamilton Nat'l Bank, 303 U.S. 245 (1938) (trustee in bankruptcy); *In re* Giorgio, 62 B.R. 853 (Bankr. D.R.I. 1986); *In re* Pair, 14 B.R. 732 (Bankr. N.D. Ga. 1981) (trustee could assert usury on behalf of named bankrupt but not on behalf of another debtor); North v. Cecil B. De Mille Productions, Inc., 39 P.2d 199 (Cal. 1934) (receiver); Scott v. Hollingsworth, 9 P.2d 836 (Cal. 1932) (receiver). *See also* Nogueras v. Maisel & Assocs. of Mich., 369 N.W.2d 492 (Mich. App. 1985) (individual partners can assert usury, if at all, only after partnership fails to pay debt and partner is called upon to repay the loans himself); Williams v. Macchio, 329 N.Y.S.2d 405 (Sup. Ct. 1972) (wife can assert usury in note signed by husband when she was compelled, under duress, to enter contract which cancelled the usurious note).

441 *See, e.g.*, Chandlee v. Tharp, 137 So. 540 (Miss. 1931); Crabb v. Cole, 84 S.W.2d 597 (Tenn. App. 1935). *Compare* Barnes v. Hartman, 54 Cal. Rptr. 514 (App. 1966) (death of plaintiff did not abate usury cause of action, although plaintiff lacked standing for other reasons); McNish v. Gen. Credit Corp., 83 N.W.2d 1 (Neb. 1957) (standing of estate not contested) *and* Tilley v. Pacesetter Corp., 585 S.E.2d 292, 310 (S.C. 2003) (usury claim based on statute survives borrower's death) *with* Orr v. International Bank of Commerce, 649 S.W.2d 769 (Tex. App. 1983) (usury does not survive death of either the liable party or the party entitled to a penalty) *and* Snodgrass v. Sisson's Mobile Home Sales, Inc., 244 S.E.2d 321 (W. Va. 1978) (no common law survivability). On the other hand, a borrower can usually prosecute a usury action against the estate of the lender. *But see* Orr v. International Bank of Commerce, 649 S.W.2d 769 (Tex. App. 1983).

442 *See, e.g.*, Superior Funding Corp. v. Big Apple Capital Corp., 738 F. Supp. 1468 (S.D.N.Y. 1990) (guarantor of corporate debt

cannot assert usury as defense); Bizzoco v. Chintz, 476 A.2d 572 (Conn. 1984); Snyder v. Woxo, Inc., 177 N.W.2d 281 (Neb. 1970); Bokum v. First Nat'l Bank, 740 P.2d 693 (N.M. 1987) (corporate exception applied where sophisticated and experienced businessman-borrower signed individually and as president of solely owned corporation); Colonial Acceptance Corp. v. Northeastern Printcrafters, 330 S.E.2d 76 (N.C. Ct. App. 1985); El Paso Refining, Inc. v. Scurlock Permian Corp., 77 S.W.3d 374 (Tex. App. 2002); Rent America, Inc. v. Amarillo Nat'l Bank, 785 S.W.2d 190 (Tex. App. 1990); Western Bank-Downtown v. Carline, 757 S.W.2d 111 (Tex. App. 1988) (guarantors cannot assert usury); Allied Supplier & Erection Inc. v. A. Baldwin & Co., 688 S.W.2d 156 (Tex. App. 1985); Greenway Bank & Trust of Houston v. Smith, 679 S.W.2d 592 (Tex. App. 1984); Williams v. Security Sav. & Loan Ass'n, 355 N.W.2d 370 (Wis. App. 1984). *See also* First South Savings Ass'n v. First South Partners, II, Ltd., 957 F.2d 174 (5th Cir. 1992) (apparently unaware of this principle, the court describes the trial court's ruling to that effect as "somewhat cryptic," but proceeds to deny guarantor's usury claim on the ground that there was no compensation demanded for the guarantor's use, forbearance or detention of money). *But see* Martin v. Ajax Constr. Co., 124 Cal. App. 2d 425, 269 P.2d 132 (1954) (usury in business loan may be asserted by guarantors as well as by principal obligor); Johnson v. Ronamy Consumer Credit Corp., 515 A.2d 682 (Del. 1986) (second mortgage statute covered guarantors); First Nat'l Consumer Discount Co. v. Fuller, 419 A.2d 940 (Del. 1980) (same); Skeen v. Slavik, 555 S.W.2d 516 (Tex. Civ. App. 1977) (corporation's guarantor, who later executes personal note to lender assuming the debt of the corporation, may assert usury). *See generally* Annot. 63 A.L.R.2d 924 (1959), *Statute Denying Defense of Usury to a Corporation*.

443 *See, e.g.*, Bizzoco v. Chintz, 476 A.2d 572 (Conn. 1984) (no proof that debt was not corporate); Brint v. Ellin Express Corp., 273 N.Y.S.2d 860 (1966), *aff'd*, 282 N.Y.S.2d 450 (App. Div. 1967); Micrea Inc. v. Eureka Life Ins. Co., 534 S.W.2d 348 (Tex. Ct. App. 1976); Allied Supplier & Erection Inc. v. A. Baldwin & Co., 688 S.W.2d 156 (Tex. App. 1985).

ner.[444] Thus, the rule against guarantor standing effectively creates a usury exception similar to the business purpose exception that already exists in many states.

A second potential problem created by the rule against the standing of guarantors to assert usury is that a guaranty or surety agreement can be structured so that there is really no difference between the duties of the guarantor and those of the maker or obligor. It seems a triumph of form over substance to give usury protection to a borrower and then to deny it to a surety whose liability is "primary, direct and unconditional," and who may be sued prior to any action against the primary borrower, but this is the law in many states.[445] This rule may encourage creditors to obtain guarantors rather than co-signers in order to limit the number of potential usury plaintiffs.

Fortunately, such a scenario has not developed with any frequency in consumer transactions. The main reason may be that there must always be at least one obligor on a note and in a consumer transaction, unlike a corporate loan,[446] that obligor will usually be available to assert any usury claim. Furthermore, a few usury statutes specifically extend to guarantors or sureties on consumer credit contracts.[447] Finally, there is some precedent for finding parties that are liable on consumer debt to be obligors rather than guarantors when doubt about their status exists.[448]

Another party whose standing to assert usury may be questioned is the assignee of a credit buyer—i.e., the person who purchases used goods and who, in so doing, assumes the original buyer's rights and obligations under the original credit contract. While borrowers who have paid usurious interest do not lose their right to recover the penalty by assigning their interest in the contract to a third party,[449] several courts have held that usury claims may not be assigned.[450] The reasoning is that the assignee should not be able to step into the assignor's shoes and reap a windfall through a usury claim.

Although denying usury claims to assignees might make sense if the assignment were viewed as a form of champerty, denying usury claims can lead to hardship for an innocent consumer who, instead of arranging his own financing, simply assumes the payments of the previous owner, only to discover later that the payments are usurious. Such arrangements invariably require the permission of the creditor, and the failure of a court to recognize a new extension of credit, from the original creditor to the new owner, that would give the new owner standing to assert usury, seems unnecessarily narrow-minded. Nevertheless, this is the position taken by some courts.[451]

Other courts, however, have developed somewhat more even-handed rules. A New York decision, for example, allowed an assignee to claim usury after tendering the principal and legal interest to the creditor.[452] Another New York decision held that parties who bought real estate that was subject to a usurious loan could assert the usury claim, where the original agreement contemplated that the real estate would be transferred to them.[453] Finally, some retail installment sales acts extend to a buyer's legal successors in

---

444 The subject of sham corporate loans is discussed in § 9.2.2.3, *supra*.

445 *See* Colonial Acceptance Corp. v. Northeastern Printcrafters, 330 S.E.2d 76 (N.C. Ct. App. 1985). *See also* Dahmes v. Industrial Credit Co., 110 N.W.2d 484 (Minn. 1961).

446 Statutes creating corporate usury exceptions, it is important to note, are frequently the basis for the rule denying guarantors the standing to assert usury. *See, e.g.,* Colonial Acceptance Corp. v. Northeastern Printcrafters, 330 S.E.2d 76 (N.C. Ct. App. 1985). Such statutes will probably not apply to guarantors of consumer debt, and decisions denying standing to corporate guarantors may therefore be distinguishable from consumer cases.

447 *See* 69 Pa. Cons. Stat. Ann § 603(3) (Purdon 1965) (motor vehicle sales).

448 *See* Ciminelli v. Ford Motor Credit Corp., 624 S.W.2d 903 (Tex. 1981).

449 Mangold v. Wilson, 695 F. Supp. 841 (D. V.I. 1988).

450 *See* Eposti v. Rivers Bros. Inc., 207 Cal. 570, 279 P. 423 (1929); General Elec. Credit Corp. v. Best Refrigerated Express, Inc. 385 N.W.2d 81 (Neb. 1986); Radner v. Burnett, 122 N.W.2d 747 (Neb. 1963); Smart v. Crawford Bldg. Material Co., 638 S.W.2d

228 (Tex. App. 1982). *See also* Lenart v. Ragsdale, 385 N.W.2d 282 (Mich. App. 1986) (an undisclosed principal may raise usury but not an assignee); Moore v. Plaza Commercial Corp., 192 N.Y.S.2d 770 (App. Div. 1959), *aff'd*, 168 N.E.2d 390 (N.Y. 1960) (restrictions on assignee standing); Demopolis v. Galvin, 786 P.2d 804 (Wash. Ct. App. 1990) (one who purchases encumbered property from original borrower but does not assume liability on underlying note is not in privity and cannot assert usury; one exception is where original debtor joins in the claim or gives purchaser permission to pursue it); Snodgrass v. Sisson's Mobile Home Sales, Inc., 244 S.E.2d 321 (W. Va. 1978) (action to collect a statutory penalty generally not assignable in absence of statute allowing assignment).

451 *See* General Elec. Credit Corp. v. Best Refrigerated Express, Inc., 385 N.W.2d 81 (Neb. 1986) *following* Radner v. Burnett, 122 N.W.2d 747 (Neb. 1963). *See also* Nesbitt v. Citicorp Savings of Florida, 514 So. 2d 371 (Fla. Dist. Ct. App. 1987) (standing denied to subsequent property owners who apparently assumed mortgage).

452 Moore v. Plaza Commercial Corp., 192 N.Y.S.2d 770 (App. Div. 1959), *aff'd*, 168 N.E.2d 390 (N.Y. 1960). *See also* Benser v. Independence Bank, 735 S.W.2d 566 (Tex. App. 1987) (dicta suggesting that one in privity with the borrower may have a right to challenge a usurious contract if claim is derived from the borrower's right); Demopolis v. Galvin, 786 P.2d 804 (Wash. Ct. App. 1990) (one who purchases encumbered property from original borrower but does not assume liability on underlying note is not in privity and cannot assert usury; one exception is where original debtor joins in the claim or gives purchaser permission to pursue it. In case where original borrower had assigned to subsequent purchaser "all causes of action arising from the loans," court held that assignment was ineffective as to statutory usury claims because damages were penal and therefore not assignable, but was effective as to common law usury claim, which is remedial and therefore assignable).

453 Seidel v. 18 East 17th St. Owners, Inc., 79 N.Y.2d 735, 586 N.Y.S.2d 240, 598 N.E.2d 7 (1992).

interest and therefore should protect a buyer who assumes another buyer's installment sale contract.[454]

One case holds that a borrower seeking an affirmative usury remedy under section 86 of the National Bank Act does not have standing unless she paid the challenged charges.[455] This issue is usually analyzed in terms of whether one of the necessary elements of a *prima facie* usury claim has been met, rather than as a standing question, however.[456]

Standing issues can affect those not obligated on the debt, as well. Junior lienholders seeking to void a senior lien may run afoul of the general rule that only immediate parties to the transaction may raise usury.[457] On the other hand, a title insurer was permitted to use usury to deny coverage on its policy to the overcharging lender on the theory that the lender does not have an insurable interest if the underlying transaction is usurious.[458]

Though not framed as a standing issue, one creditor unsuccessfully tried to argue that usury laws should not protect sophisticated borrowers for public policy reasons. The California Supreme Court found that there was no sophisticated borrower exemption to usury laws.[459] On rare occasions, the sophistication of the borrower may be relevant to an estoppel or waiver defense, though.[460]

10.6.4 Estoppel and Waiver

10.6.4.1 Overview

Estoppel is a loosely defined equitable doctrine under which a party may be barred from asserting legal or factual claims in court for any one of numerous reasons including fraud, misrepresentation, previous judicial rulings (i.e., "collateral estoppel"), or waiver. In what is probably the most common application of the doctrine in usury cases, a party may be estopped from denying the truth of facts that

it previously asserted, if the party seeking the estoppel reasonably relied, to its detriment, on the earlier assertion.[461] In several cases, lenders have sought to invoke estoppel to prevent borrowers from claiming usury because of various real or supposed misrepresentations made by the borrower in obtaining the disputed loan. However, a review of the relevant decisions demonstrates that the doctrine is inapplicable to most consumer usury cases.

10.6.4.2 Borrower's Knowledge

The most common reason for estoppel asserted by lenders is that the borrower knew that the terms of the loan were usurious at the time of the transaction and induced the lender to issue a loan that the borrower knew would not have to be repaid. In fact, there are cases involving inexperienced individuals lending money to street-wise small businessmen where usury claims have been estopped on precisely those grounds.[462] Thus, there is a line of cases holding that in some unusual circumstances a borrower who initiates the usurious aspects of the transaction is then estopped from raising usury as a defense.[463]

---

454 See 69 Pa. Cons. Stat. Ann. § 603(3) (1965) (motor vehicle sales).

455 Ament v. PNC Nat'l Bank, 849 F. Supp. 1015 (W.D. Pa. 1994), *aff'd without op. sub nom.* Deffner v. Corestates Bank, 92 F.3d 1170 (3d Cir. 1996).

456 *See* § 10.5.4.2, *supra*.

457 Allee v. Benser, 779 S.W.2d 61 (Tex. 1988) (court distinguishes between statutory penalty voiding entire transaction and "constitutional voidness" of usurious interest; although right to assert former is personal to the obligor, a junior lienholder may have standing to assert the latter). *See also* Henslee v. Madison Guaranty Sav. & Loan, 760 S.W.2d 842 (Ark. 1988) (discussing impact of change in usury penalties on statute permitting rival lienholder to gain priority when other lienholder's rights are tainted by usury).

458 Focus Investments Assoc., Inc. v. American Title Ins. Co., 992 F.2d 1231 (1st Cir. 1993).

459 Ghirardo v. Antonioli, 883 P.2d 960 (Cal. 1994) (creditor prevailed on other grounds).

460 *See* § 10.6.4, *infra*.

461 The precise statement of the rule varies from court to court. *Compare* Murphy v. Hagan, 271 S.E.2d 311 (S.C. 1980) *with* First State Bank of Bedford v. Miller, 551 S.W.2d 89 (Tex. Ct. App. 1977), *modified on other grounds and aff'd as modified*, 563 S.W.2d 572 (Tex. 1978). *See also* Perlman v. First Nat'l Bank of Chicago, 305 N.E.2d 236 (Ill. App. 1973), *appeal dismissed*, 331 N.E.2d 65 (Ill. 1975) (bank overcharges); Cook v. Frazier, 765 S.W.2d 546 (Tex. App. 1989) (borrowers relying on contract for six years and claiming interest as tax deduction until IRS disallowed did not estop usury claims; only if lender deceived by borrower can it claim estoppel).

462 *See* Holt v. Rickett, 238 S.E.2d 706 (Ga. App. 1974); Broaddus v. National Bank of Lancaster, 709 S.W.2d 461 (Ky. Ct. App. 1986) (professional banker with expertise in commercial transactions estopped from asserting usury); Olson v. Froslee, 2000 Minn. App. LEXIS 795 (Aug. 1, 2000) (unpublished, citation limited) (recognizing estoppel defense if borrower knows of usury, but finding it not shown here); LaBarre v. Gold, 520 So. 2d 1327 (Miss. 1988) (a Byzantine set of facts resulting in the court invoking estoppel); Angelo v. Brenner, 457 N.Y.S.2d 630 (App. Div. 1982) (estoppel is issue of fact precluding summary judgment); Schylander v. Tsaruchas, 409 N.Y.S.2d 932 (N.Y. City Civ. Ct. 1978); Gilbert v. Otterson, 550 A.2d 550 (Pa. Super. Ct. 1988) (where employer borrowed money from employee, the documents were prepared by borrower-employer's attorney, and borrower may have suggested the interest rate, court ruled that estoppel was a permissible defense to the treble damage claim for violation of usury statute); Liebergesell v. Evans, 613 P.2d 1170 (Wash. 1980). *Cf.* Gillivan v. Austin, 640 F. Supp. 1325 (D. V.I. 1986) (estoppel appeared appropriate but could not be raised as defense by court *sua sponte*).

463 *Borrower estopped*: Massie v. Rubin, 270 F.2d 60 (10th Cir. 1959) (attorney who obtained money by drafting transaction in form of trust but which may have been loan at usurious interest could be estopped from raising usury defense); Holden v. Nevergall, 526 N.E.2d 928 (Ill. App. 1988) (daughter who insisted on usurious rate of interest when borrowing money from parents was estopped from raising usury defense and note

Yet such circumstances are the exception. Most lenders are in the business of lending money. They know or can find out what the usury laws are, and they do not rely on any representation of the borrower that the contract is legal.[464] The courts have widely ruled that no estoppel against usury can exist when the lender knew or should have known what the usury law was, even though the borrower was also aware of the usury.[465] Indeed, this position is the only one that can uphold the fundamental purpose of usury statutes—that of protecting desperate "borrowers 'driven to borrow money at any cost.'"[466] If courts estopped usury claims merely

---

was enforceable according to its terms); Cohn v. Receivables Fin. Co., 260 N.E.2d 67 (Ill. App. 1970) (where attorney borrowed money from client, prepared the loan documents and made payments for 25 years, he was estopped from asserting usury); Russo v. Carey, 706 N.Y.S.2d 760 (App. Div. 2000) (lender could raise defense of estoppel where he and borrower were friends, borrower prepared note and set interest rate, and some evidence suggested that borrower deliberately inserted usurious interest rate to avoid repayment); Abramovitz v. Kew Realty Equities, Inc., 580 N.Y.S.2d 269 (App. Div. 1992) (experienced and sophisticated businessmen who induced a friend to loan them money as an investment and knowingly prepared loan documents with usurious rates were estopped from asserting usury as a defense); Berry v. Martens, 58 Va. Cir. 315 (2002) (borrower who proposed the interest rate is estopped from claiming usury). *See also* Keezing v. Rodriguez, 765 N.Y.S.2d 196 (Sup. Ct. 2003) (reducing interest to legal rate but refusing to void loan when debtor initiated and structured the transaction and prepared the documents).

Borrower not estopped: Hufnagel v. George, 135 F. Supp. 2d 406 (S.D.N.Y. 2001) (no estoppel without special relationship, which is limited to attorney-client, fiduciary, trustee, or long-standing relationship or its equivalent; borrower's suggestion of interest rate is not a defense); Hornblower & Weeks, Inc. v. Blue Marlin Breweries, Inc., 2000 U.S. Dist. LEXIS 13748 (S.D.N.Y. Sept. 21, 2000) (borrower not estopped from raising criminal usury as defense even if it knew loan was usurious and its agent prepared documents), *aff'd without op.*, 2003 WL 21369246 (2d Cir. June 10, 2003); Mangold v. Wilson, 695 F. Supp. 841 (D. V.I. 1988) (lender argued borrowers originated transaction, so should be estopped from pleading usury; whether estoppel generally available in Virgin Islands or not, inappropriate here where lender was represented by counsel who reviewed the agreement); *In re* Venture Mortgage Fund, 245 B.R. 460 (Bankr. S.D.N.Y. 2000) (lender must show special relationship with borrower, a representation by borrower that the transaction is legal, intent to induce reliance, actual reliance, and injury; not shown here), *aff'd on other grounds*, 282 F.3d 185 (2d Cir. 2002); McElroy v. Grisham, 810 S.W.2d 933 (Ark. 1991) (borrower in dire financial straights who proposed deed with option to purchase as means of obtaining temporary financial relief was not estopped from asserting usury; creditors were aware of his situation and received an unfair advantage from it); Lane v. Fabert, 533 N.E.2d 546 (Ill. App. 1989) (enterprising pawnbroker tried to argue customer estopped from asserting usury because she initiated the pawn transaction; rejecting the argument, court pointed out she did not suggest a usurious rate, but merely initiated the transaction and paid the pawnbroker's going rate); Commercial Mtg. & Fin. Co. v. Life Savs. of America, 541 N.E.2d 661 (Ill. 1989) (where creditor initiated idea of having borrower sign false business purpose affidavit and borrower cooperated, borrower was not estopped from asserting usury; court notes distinction between borrower initiating transaction, which is virtually always the case, and borrower initiating the usurious terms); Seidel v. 18 East 17th Street Owners, Inc., 598 N.E.2d 7 (N.Y. 1992) (no estoppel where lender did not detrimentally rely on borrower's representation); Marashi v. Lannen, 780 P.2d 1341 (Wash. Ct. App. 1989) (borrowers not estopped from asserting usury by their certificate stating business purpose in general, conclusory language; lender told borrowers that certificate was "just a formality" and did not explain its significance). *See also* Dunnam v. Burns, 901 S.W.2d

628 (Tex. App. 1995) (if there is an absolute obligation to pay, usury law is not concerned with which party might have originated the usurious terms; though borrower had drafted the document, creditor agreed to receive usurious interest). *See generally* 47 C.J.S. *Interest and Usury* § 207, at 351–52.

In an interesting twist to this principle, the Mississippi Bar reprimanded an attorney who, as a borrower, proposed to pay usurious interest on loan from an individual. The state supreme court reversed, noting that the borrower does not break the law by agreeing to pay usurious interest, and he had not "practiced deceit" by entering into an unenforceable contract, since he had never raised usury as a defense to his debt. "That a lawyer might do something unethical 'if he chose' is not grounds for discipline." Watkins v. Mississippi Bar, 589 So. 2d 660 (Miss. 1991).

464 *Cf.* Brodie v. Schmutz (*In re* Venture Mortgage Fund), 282 F.3d 185 (2d Cir. 2002) (estoppel not shown because no special relationship and no reliance); *In re* King, 68 B.R. 569 (Bankr. D. Minn. 1986) (lender fails to show reliance on borrower's mis-representations of loan purpose; loan held usurious); Lenart v. Ragsdale, 385 N.W.2d 282 (Mich. App. 1986) (failure to raise usury defense for 13 years does not estop borrower; no lender reliance); Lucas v. Beco Homes, Inc., 494 S.W.2d 417 (Mo. Ct. App. 1973) (no estoppel when debtor paid installments for two years; no reliance or prejudice); Seidel v. 18 East 17th St. Owners, 598 N.E.2d 7 (N.Y. 1992) (essential element of estoppel is that conduct or representation was intended to and did influence the other party to his or her injury; not established in this case); Media Tech., Inc. v. Pena, Consumer Cred. Guide (CCH) ¶ 96,041 (N.Y. Sup. Ct. 1986) (borrower's bounced check is not grounds for estoppel against usury).

465 *See, e.g., In re* General Am. Communications Corp., 63 B.R. 534 (Bankr. S.D.N.Y. 1986); *In re* Seisay, 61 B.R. 940 (Bankr. S.D.N.Y. 1986), *aff'd*, 1986 WL 2826 (S.D.N.Y. Feb. 28, 1986); LaBarr v. Tombstone Territorial Mint, 580 P.2d 744 (Ariz. App.), *adopted*, 582 P.2d 639 (Ariz. 1978) (en banc); McIlroy Bank & Trust v. Seven Day Builders, 613 S.W.2d 837 (Ark. App. 1981); Bjornstad v. Perry, 443 P.2d 999 (Idaho 1968); Gudgel v. Kaelin, 551 S.W.2d 803 (Ky. Ct. App. 1977); Murphy v. Hagan, 271 S.E.2d 311 (S.C. 1980); First State Bank of Bedford v. Miller, 563 S.W.2d 572 (Tex. 1978); Arguelles v. Kaplan, 736 S.W.2d 782 (Tex. App. 1987) (no estoppel where debtor's attorney prepared note: creditor was attorney who could have easily discovered what applicable rate ceiling was); Marashi v. Lannen, 780 P.2d 1341 (Wash. Ct. App. 1989) (court points out that party claiming estoppel must show justified reliance on business purpose certification and thus cannot have known or had means to know true purpose; knowledge of lender's agent is imputed to lender and will defeat estoppel claim). *See generally* Annot. 16 A.L.R.3d 510 (1967), *Borrower's Initiation of or Fraud Contributing to Usurious Transaction as Affecting Rights or Remedies of the Parties.*

466 Demopolis v. Galvin, 786 P.2d 804, 807 (Wash. Ct. App. 1990) *quoting* Baskes v. Russell, 407 P.2d 434 (Wash. 1965). *See also* Schneider v. Phelps, 359 N.E.2d 1361, 1365 (N.Y. App. 1977)

because the borrower knew of the usury, any lender could evade the usury statutes simply by informing the borrower of the usury at the time of the transaction.[467]

10.6.4.3 False Contractual Statements

A second situation in which creditors raise estoppel as a usury defense centers upon contract clauses through which the borrower purportedly attests to the existence of facts which may exclude the transaction from the scope of usury statutes. For example, a loan contract executed in a jurisdiction that does not regulate interest rates on business loans may state that the borrower intends to use the loan proceeds for business purposes. Lenders have claimed that such a clause estops the borrower from asserting that the transaction was actually a personal loan at a usurious interest rate.[468]

("The purpose of usury laws, from time immemorial, has been to protect desperately poor people from the consequences of their own desperation. Law-making authorities in almost all civilizations have recognized that the crush of financial burdens causes people to agree to almost any conditions of the lender and to consent to even the most improvident loans. Lenders, with the money, have all the leverage; borrowers, in dire need of money have none."); Whitworth & Yancy v. Adams, 5 Rand 333, 335, 26 Va. 333 (1827) ("These statutes were made to protect needy and necessitous persons from the oppression of usurers and monied men, who are eager to take advantage of the distress of others; while they, on the other hand, from the pressure of their distress, are ready to come to any terms; and with their eyes open, not only break the law, but complete their ruin."). *See generally* § 9.3.1.1, *supra*.

467 *See* Commercial Mtg. & Fin. Co. v. Life Savs. of America, 541 N.E.2d 661 (Ill. 1989) (where creditor initiated idea of having borrower sign false business purpose affidavit and borrower cooperated, borrower was not estopped from asserting usury; court notes distinction between borrower initiating transaction, which is virtually always the case, and borrower initiating the usurious terms); Gudgel v. Kaelin, 551 S.W.2d 803 (Ky. Ct. App. 1977) (invoking estoppel even when a lender knows of usury would enable lenders to circumvent usury laws); Matter of Estate of Dane, 390 N.Y.S.2d 249 (App. Div. 1976) (if usury law did not apply when the borrower set the interest rate, lenders would avoid usury by requiring the borrower to set the rate). *Cf.* Lane v. Fabert, 533 N.E.2d 546 (Ill. App. 1989) (enterprising pawnbroker tried to argue customer estopped from asserting usury because she initiated the pawn transaction; rejecting the argument, court pointed out she did not suggest a usurious rate, but merely initiated the transaction and paid the pawnbroker's going rate).

468 *Compare* Conrad v. Smith, 712 P.2d 866 (Wash. Ct. App. 1986) ("business purpose" clause recognized) *with* Sheffield Commercial Corp. v. Clemente, 792 F.2d 282 (2d Cir. 1986) ("business purpose" clause ineffective) *and* Marashi v. Lannen, 780 P.2d 1341 (Wash. Ct. App. 1989) (borrowers' certificate stating business purpose in general, conclusory language was not dispositive; lender told borrowers that certificate was "just a formality" and did not explain its significance). *See also* Kreditbank N.V. v. E.S.I.C. Capital Corp. (*In re* Rosner), 48 B.R. 538 (Bankr. E.D.N.Y. 1985) (no estoppel when lender requires letter from borrower's attorney stating that contract is legal); Metcoff

As with cases involving the borrower's knowledge of the usury, courts have occasionally estopped usury claims because of a borrower's contractual misrepresentations of fact, but they have done so only after examining the substance of the transaction. For example, one court sustained a "business loan" usury defense after observing that the borrower had apparently made repeated representations of his business purposes to the lender, and that nothing in the record suggested that the lender knew otherwise.[469] Similarly, another court found that a borrower was estopped from denying the business purpose of a loan because the borrower had signed an affidavit voluntarily and without duress or undue influence.[470]

It is, of course, possible to quarrel with a court's factual findings regarding the "voluntary" action of a debtor who signs a paper acknowledging a fictitious business purpose. The important point, however, is that even courts which invoke estoppel because of a borrower's misrepresentations do so only after looking at the facts of the case. This approach is entirely appropriate both because of the equitable nature of estoppel, and because of the widely recognized need to foil any legal artifice that is designed to evade usury statutes.[471] A court will not estop a borrower from asserting usury simply because a contract states some "agreed" fact which, if true, would preclude a usury claim.[472] Moreover, in examining the facts behind allegedly false contractual statements of business purpose, courts have often found the disputed loans to be personal in nature and have given no effect to the clearly adhesive statements of loan purpose.[473]

---

v. Mutual Trust Life Ins. Co., 339 N.E.2d 440 (Ill. App. 1975) (letter from borrower to land trustee contains statement of business purpose, but no estoppel because statement not made to lender, no reliance was present, and no detail was given about the purported business).

469 Conrad v. Smith, 712 P.2d 866 (Wash. Ct. App. 1986).

470 Anglin v. J&G Assocs., Consumer Cred. Guide (CCH) ¶ 96,677 (D.D.C. 1983).

471 § 9.2.1.6, *supra*.

472 *See* Sheffield Commercial Corp. v. Clemente, 792 F.2d 282 (2d Cir. 1986) (remand for factual determination); Allan v. M&S Mortgage Co., 359 N.W.2d 238 (Mich. Ct. App. 1984) (summary judgment reversed); Hammelburger v. Foursome Inn Corp., 431 N.E.2d 278 (N.Y. 1980) (estoppel certificate invalid if signed under duress; remand for factual determination). *See also* Commercial Mortgage & Fin. Co. v. Life Saving of America, 541 N.E.2d 661 (Ill. 1989) (creditor could not claim estoppel where it had suggested to borrower that loan be falsely characterized as business purpose and borrower did so). Of course, it is important to allege the falsity of the affidavit of business purpose. *See* Ross v. Lake City Equity Fin. Co., 425 F.2d 1 (7th Cir. 1970) (affirming summary judgment for lender where borrower's summary judgment materials did not dispute the facts in the business purpose affidavit).

473 *See, e.g., In re* Seisay, 49 B.R. 354 (S.D.N.Y. 1985), *aff'd*, 1986 WL 2826 (S.D.N.Y. Feb. 28, 1986), *later op. at* 61 B.R. 940 (Bankr. S.D.N.Y. 1986); Sun Bank v. Spigrin, 469 So. 2d 240 (Fla. Dist. Ct. App. 1985) (sham incorporation); Gelber v. Kugel's Tavern, Inc., 89 A.2d 654 (N.J. 1952) (no estoppel

10.6.4.4 Waiver

A final situation in which a usury plaintiff may encounter the defense of estoppel is when the borrower has purportedly waived the right to assert usury.[474] A waiver is a knowing surrender of legal rights. It is possible for a borrower to waive a usury claim, for example, through a settlement agreement, negotiated at arm's length.[475] A usury claim may also be waived by failing to raise it in litigation.[476] However, it is not possible for the borrower to waive a usury defense through a provision in the usurious contract or related documents.[477] The reason for this restriction is

obvious: if usury claims could be waived in this manner, all credit contracts would contain waiver provisions, and usury laws would be rendered meaningless.

A more difficult question regarding the waiver of usury defense occurs when usurious credit agreements are renewed or refinanced at non-usurious rates. Creditors have been known to argue that such renewals constitute waivers or settlements of any usury claims which arose from the original agreement. The merits of this argument are discussed in § 6.2, *supra*. Similarly, a creditor may argue that participating in workout arrangements and delaying in filing suit is a waiver. However, that is not evidence of a waiver of a known right.[478] On the other hand, if the obligation is voluntarily satisfied without renewal or refinancing, the borrower may be held to have waived a usury defense, thus defeating a claim for restitution.[479]

10.6.5 Voluntary Payment Defense

A borrower who has already made payments on a usurious loan may have to contend with an ancient, sporadically-recognized defense, the voluntary payment doctrine. The doctrine developed in tax cases, and was created to prevent those who had paid illegally imposed taxes from recouping their payments from the tax collector.[480] The basis for the

---

when no evidence that borrower knew purpose of incorporation). *See generally* § 9.2.2.2, *supra* (sham incorporation).

474 Waivers of the right to assert claims and defenses against assignees are discussed at § 10.6.1, *supra*.

475 *See, e.g.*, Gunn Plumbing, Inc. v. Dania Bank, 252 So. 2d 1 (Fla. 1971); Munilla v. Perez-Cobo, 335 So. 2d 584 (Fla. Dist. Ct. App. 1976); Thompson v. First Nat'l Bank, 300 S.E.2d 529 (Ga. App. 1983); Hammelburger v. Foursome Inn Corp., 54 N.Y.2d 580, 446 N.Y.S.2d 917, 431 N.E.2d 278 (1981) (assignee who took loan in reliance on estoppel certificate, without knowledge of usury, can defeat criminal usury claim, but duress would invalidate estoppel certificate); Vordenbaum v. Rubin, 611 S.W.2d 463 (Tex. App. 1980); Dunbabin v. Brandenfels, 566 P.2d 941 (Wash. Ct. App. 1977). *See also* Higgins v. Erickson (*In re* Higgins), 270 B.R. 147 (Bankr. S.D.N.Y. 2001) (borrowers waived usury defense by signing confession of judgment after default). *But cf. In re* Vehm Eng'g, 521 F.2d 186 (9th Cir. 1975) (narrow construction of release; usury claim not waived); *In re* Giorgio, 62 B.R. 853 (Bankr. D.R.I. 1986) (settlement binds debtor but does not later bind debtor's trustee in bankruptcy); Victoria Bank & Trust Co. v. Brady, 779 S.W.2d 893 (Tex. App. 1989) (jury's finding that release was invalid upheld on various grounds, including borrower's ignorance of usury claim and failure of consideration), *aff'd in part and rev'd in part on other grounds*, 811 S.W.2d 931 (Tex. 1991) (finding no usury, but holding release ineffective as to borrower's other claims).

476 REG, Inc. v. Rayho, 2000 Neb. App. LEXIS 273 (Aug. 29, 2000) (unpublished); Holdgate v. Acton, 764 A.2d 187 (R.I. 2000).

477 *See, e.g.*, Aaron v. Mattikow, 146 F. Supp. 2d 263 (E.D.N.Y. 2001) (giving effect to contractual waiver would run counter to court's duty to uncover true nature of transaction), *aff'd*, 2003 WL 1973357 (2d Cir. Apr. 22, 2003); Kredietbank N.V. v. E.S.I.C. Capital Corp. (*In re* Rosner), 48 B.R. 538 (Bankr. E.D.N.Y. 1985) (no estoppel when lender requires letter from borrower's attorney stating that contract is legal); Transworld Telecommunications, Inc. v. Pacific Mezzanine Fund, Inc. (*In re* Transworld Telecommunications, Inc.*), 260 B.R. 204 (Bankr. D. Utah 2000), *rev'd and remanded on other grounds*, 309 F.3d 744 (10th Cir. 2002) (indemnification and limitation of liability provisions in loan contract are ineffective); LaBarr v. Tombstone Territorial Mint, 580 P.2d 744 (Ariz. App. 1978), *adopted* 582 P.2d 639 (Ariz. 1978) (usury cannot be waived at inception of loan, and making payments on usurious loan does not constitute waiver); HIMC Inv. Co. v. Siciliano, 246 A.2d 502 (N.J. Super. 1968) (waiver provision is contrary to public policy as expressed in second mortgage statute and has no effect even if borrowers signed with full knowledge of contract provisions and with intent to be bound by them). *See also* Sheffield

Commercial Corp. v. Clemente, 792 F.2d 282 (2d Cir. 1986) (express statutory prohibition of waivers).

478 El Paso Dev. Co. v. Berryman, 769 S.W.2d 584 (Tex. App. 1989) (waiver is intentional relinquishment of known right or intentional conduct inconsistent with claiming it; borrower's delay in filing suit and executing reinstatement agreements and modifications not evidence of waiver where borrower appeared to simply be foregoing claim as long as creditor was working with him, and he pursued claim only when foreclosure imminent).

479 *See, e.g.*, Thelen v. Ducharme, 390 N.W.2d 264 (Mich. App. 1986) (holding, however, that payment after judgment was rendered on note is not a voluntary payment, therefore usury defense was not waived). *Cf. In re* Estate of Backofen, 404 N.W.2d 675 (Mich. App. 1987) (usury defense not waived here; waived only to extent usurious interest is voluntarily repaid); § 10.8.2.3, *infra*. *Contra* Hardwick v. Austin Gallery of Oriental Rugs, Inc., 779 S.W.2d 438 (Tex. App. 1989) (court states common law rule that voluntary payment of usury can be recovered and grants such recovery in addition to statutory usury penalty of three times the usurious interest charged; borrower here, however, made payments out of necessity to free property of lien so that it could be sold).

480 *See, e.g.*, City of Little Rock v. Cash, 644 S.W.2d 229 (Ark. 1982) (applying doctrine), *cert. denied*, 462 U.S. 1111 (1983); Sullivan v. Board of Comm'rs of Oak Lawn Park Dist., 743 N.E.2d 1057 (Ill. Ct. App. 2001) (applying doctrine); Louisville & N. Ry. Co. v. Hopkins County, 9 S.W. 497 (Ky. Ct. App. 1888) (applying doctrine); Quaker Oats Co. v. Stanton, 96 S.W.3d 133 (Mo. Ct. App. 2003) (applying doctrine); Shenango Furnace Co. v. Fairfield Township, 78 A. 937 (Pa. 1911) (applying doctrine); City of Laredo v. South Tex. Nat'l Bank, 775 S.W.2d 729 (Tex. App. 1989) (doctrine did not apply to taxes paid into court registry pursuant to an agreement between the

doctrine lies in the fiscal concerns of a government that may need to be certain of the amount of funds available for disbursement. The doctrine protects it from having to refund collected taxes that it may have already spent in a previous year.[481]

To justify the doctrine, courts have employed the fiction that every person is supposed to know and understand the law and the limits it places on taxing authorities, and therefore a person who voluntarily makes a demanded but unauthorized payment may not later use ignorance of the law to justify a refund.[482] The doctrine has limits, though: it will not apply when the payment was not "voluntary," that is, when it was made under some compulsion.[483] Formal notice of protest will also deflect the doctrine, so taxes paid after filing a complaint are not considered voluntary.[484] The degree of compulsion necessary for a taxpayer to avoid the doctrine has been relaxed over the years by some courts.[485]

Nonetheless, despite some courts' distaste for the rule—the Missouri Supreme Court observed that it "shocks the equitable conscience"[486]—the doctrine continues to be applied occasionally.

In some states, the voluntary payment doctrine has been extended to apply not just to payments to taxing authorities, but payments to private businesses as well. As with the taxing authority version, the voluntary payment defense is rationalized on the basis that it allows one who receives payment to rely upon those funds, and that it operates as a means to settle disputes without resort to courts by requiring the person asserting an overcharge to notify the payee before payment.[487] These are, essentially, arguments of economic and judicial efficiency, concerns that should not trump a legitimate claim that one was tricked, defrauded, or otherwise overcharged by a party that knew or should have known that it was not entitled to the sums demanded. Furthermore, it is not at all obvious that the justifications for the doctrine in the tax collecting context extend to charges made by private parties. Unlike a taxing entity, which may well have to collect and disburse all sums within one fiscal period, businesses have the flexibility to plan for contingent funds. If a business wants to be certain that it will be able to keep the sums it has collected, it can ensure that it is fully entitled to them before charging them. The voluntary payment doctrine puts the burden of understanding the applicable laws, regulations and contract terms on the consumer, which can only encourage unscrupulous businesses to attempt to overcharge their customers in the hope that consumers will pay the excess before realizing the error.

---

taxing authority and the taxed); G. Heileman Brewing Co. v. City of LaCrosse, 312 N.W.2d 875 (Wis. Ct. App. 1981) (applying doctrine). *See also* Time Warner Entertainment Co. v. Whiteman, 802 N.E.2d 886 (Ind. 2004) (distinguishing between voluntary payment to government agency and voluntary payment to private business).

481 Quaker Oats Co. v. Stanton, 96 S.W.3d 133, 143 (Mo. Ct. App. 2003) (taxing authority needs to have certainty so that collector can disburse collected taxes); Putnam v. Time Warner Cable of Southeastern Wis., Ltd., 649 N.W.2d 626, 637 (Wis. 2002) (government needs to have stability and certainty over funds that have been transferred without dispute); G. Heileman Brewing Co. v. City of LaCrosse, 312 N.W.2d 875, 880 (Wis. Ct. App. 1981) (stating that any inequity of paying illegally collected taxes is outweighed by the government's need to know what amount of income it has available).

482 *See, e.g.*, City of Little Rock v. Cash, 644 S.W.2d 229, 232 (Ark. 1982), *cert. denied*, 462 U.S. 1111 (1983); Yates v. Royal Ins. Co., 65 N.E. 726, 727 (Ill. 1902).

483 Getto v. City of Chicago, 426 N.E.2d 844, 849 (Ill. 1981) (doctrine will not apply where payments made under duress or compulsion or if plaintiff did not have knowledge of the facts on which to frame a protest). The doctrine also does not apply when the tax statute authorizes recovery. *See, e.g.*, Balmoral Racing Club, Inc. v. Gonzales, 788 N.E.2d 269 (Ill. Ct. App. 2003).

484 Worth v. City of Rogers, 14 S.W.3d 471 (Ark. 2000) (reversing and remanding judgment for taxing authority). *See also* Conrad v. Home & Auto Loan Co., 385 N.Y.S.2d 979 (App. Div. 1976) (construing statutory remedy for usury not to preclude recovery of payments made under a reservation of rights and without prejudice after suit filed).

485 The taxpayer need not show that a gun was figuratively pointed at his or her head; it may be sufficient to show that serious consequences would ensue from failing to pay. Thus, the Illinois Supreme Court held that the risk of losing phone service if the tax was not paid amounted to sufficient compulsion to preclude the doctrine. Getto v. City of Chicago, 426 N.E.2d 844 (Ill. 1981). The risk that a business would lose its license established sufficient duress to avoid the doctrine in a decision by the Texas Supreme Court. State v. Conn. Gen. Life Ins. Co., 382 S.W.2d 745 (Tex. 1964). However, the Arkansas Supreme Court applied the doctrine to bar a taxpayer's refund claim for a utility tax, holding that the discretionary power of the municipal water-

works to terminate service for failure to pay did not constitute sufficient distress to escape the voluntary payment doctrine where it had no such termination policy and none of the taxpayers testified that they had paid the tax out of coercion. City of Little Rock v. Cash, 644 S.W.2d 229 (Ark. 1982), *cert. denied*, 462 U.S. 1111 (1983). The court stated that coercion sufficient to preclude the doctrine must consist of some actual or threatened exercise of power by the taxing authority that the taxpayer cannot avoid except by making payment. *Id.* at 233. A 1911 Pennsylvania Supreme Court case held that where no evidence of threat of legal process beyond demand for payment of improper taxes had been offered, the doctrine precluded the taxpayer from a refund. Shenango Furnace Co. v. Fairfield Township, 78 A. 937 (Pa. 1911). *See also* Dreyfus v. Ameritech Mobile Communications, Inc., 700 N.E.2d 162 (Ill. Ct. App. 1988) (a payment is involuntary if either the payor lacked knowledge of the facts upon which to protect the payment at the time or the payor paid under duress; the duress sufficient to establish compulsion exists where the taxpayer pays to prevent injury to himself, his business, or property without adequate opportunity to effectively resist the demand); Getto v. City of Chicago, 426 N.E.2d 844, 849–50 (Ill. 1981) ("the implicit and real threat" that the taxing entity would shut off telephone service amounted to compulsion that precluded the application of the voluntary payment doctrine).

486 Ring v. Metropolitan St. Louis Sewer Dist., 969 S.W.2d 716, 718 (Mo. 1998) (en banc) (applying doctrine).

487 Putnam v. Time Warner Cable of Southeastern Wis., Ltd., 649 N.W.2d 626, 633 (Wis. 2002).

The rule can lead to inequitable results for consumers. For example, a consumer who brought suit against a cable company that had advertised a pay-per-view concert as being three hours long, when it was only two, had his breach of contract claim dismissed because the court ruled that he had "voluntarily" remitted the charge to the cable company.[488] In another case, home sellers sued a mortgage company that assessed recording and tax service fees against them even though the services had been provided to the buyers, not the sellers.[489] The mortgage company did not notify them of the fees until just before closing, and the sellers paid them in order for the closing to proceed, then sued for money wrongfully had and received *in assumpsit.* Their claim was dismissed on the grounds that regardless of whether the fees were appropriate—there was no contract between the mortgage company and the seller that authorized them—the plaintiffs relinquished their claim by paying them.[490] The court rejected their argument that they were compelled to pay the illegitimate charge because the mortgage company would have shut down the closing had they refused.[491] The case shows how the rule can catch overcharged consumers unaware, essentially imposing an instant statute of limitations on their claim, before they have had time to fully assess the charge and its legitimacy.

Though lenders have asserted the voluntary payment defense in usury cases, the majority of jurisdictions addressing the issue have refused to apply it in those circumstances.[492] Even where the voluntary payment doctrine is

accepted in other contexts, courts have recognized that strong policy reasons argue against applying it in usury cases. First of all, allowing the defendant to retain the usurious interest would thoroughly undermine the purpose of usury laws, which seek to protect borrowers from overreaching lenders.[493] By allowing borrowers to recover the illegal interest they have paid, the state encourages the enforcement of the usury laws and the development of the policies under girding them. Second, the voluntary payment rule fails to recognize the imbalance of power between most lenders and their borrowers. In rejecting the doctrine, one Georgia court noted that the usurer is an "oppressor" and the debtor a "victim," thus payment of the usury was by definition involuntary.[494] In a few states, statutes have abrogated the common law doctrine.[495]

Nonetheless, a number of jurisdictions have applied the voluntary payment doctrine to bar a consumer from recovering usurious interest paid to a lender.[496] In addition to the

---

488   Smith v. Prime Cable of Chicago, 658 N.E.2d 1325 (Ill. Ct. App. 1995).

489   Butitta v. First Mortgage Corp., 578 N.E.2d 116 (Ill. Ct. App. 1991).

490   *Id.* at 119.

491   *Id. See also* Putnam v. Time Warner Cable of Southeastern Wis., Ltd., 649 N.W.2d 626, 631 (Wis. 2002) (voluntary payment doctrine precluded cable TV customers' restitution claim arising from allegedly illegal late payment fees).

492   *See, e.g.,* LaBarr v. Tombstone Territorial Mint, 580 P.2d 744 (Ariz. Ct. App.) (rejecting *in pari delicto* argument), *op. adopted by* 582 P.2d 639 (Ariz. 1978); Stock v. Meek, 221 P.2d 15 (Cal. 1950); Baruch Inv. Co. v. Huntoon, 65 Cal. Rptr. 131 (Cal. Ct. App. 1967); Richlin v. Schleimer, 7 P.2d 711 (Cal. Ct. App. 1932); Babcock v. Olhasso, 293 P. 141 (Cal. Ct. App. 1930); Morgan v. Shepherd, 154 S.E. 780 (Ga. 1930); Young v. Barker, 342 P.2d 150, 159 (Kan. 1959) (arguing that it would be futile to declare usury to be criminal while allowing the lender to keep the "fruits of [its] crime"); Kline v. Robinson, 428 P.2d 190, 194 (Nev. 1967) (overruling earlier authority that precluded recovery of usurious interest voluntarily paid on grounds that "the wiser and more just result" was to allow such recovery); Damico v. Mayer, 158 A. 847 (N.J. Sup. Ct. 1932) (plaintiff could recover usurious interest on mortgage contract that had been paid in full; interprets the right as arising from an implied promise of the lender to repay the usurious interest); Hardwick v. Austin Gallery of Oriental Rugs, Inc., 779 S.W.2d 438 (Tex. App. 1989). *See also* Dougherty v. North Fork Bank, 753 N.Y.S.2d 130 (App. Div. 2003) (voluntary payment of illegal fees for payoff quotes is not a defense); Siefkes v. Clark Title Ins. Co., 215 N.W.2d 648 (S.D. 1974) (citing with approval

the majority rule allowing borrowers to recover usurious interest that they paid).

493   *See, e.g.,* Baruch Inv. Co. v. Huntoon, 65 Cal. Rptr. 131 (Cal. Ct. App. 1967) (noting that usury laws are designed to protect society); Stock v. Meek, 221 P.2d 15, 20 (Cal. 1950) (rejecting *in pari delicto* reasoning on grounds that applying voluntary payment doctrine would vitiate the usury law).

494   Morgan v. Shepherd, 154 S.E. 780, 783 (Ga. 1930); *see also* Chakford v. Sturm, 65 So. 2d 864, 865 (Fla. 1953) (describing statute as regarding lender as oppressor and borrower as oppressed).

495   *See, e.g.,* Chakford v. Sturm, 65 So. 2d 864 (Fla. 1953) (under Fla. Stat. Ann. § 687.03, immaterial that usurious interest was paid voluntarily); Ostiguy v. A.F. Franke Constr., Inc., 347 P.2d 1049 (Wash. 1959) (citing Wash. Rev. Code § 19.52.030).

496   *See, e.g.,* Matter of Goehring, 23 B.R. 323 (Bankr. W.D. Mich. 1982); Lincoln Nat'l Bank v. Kaufman, 406 F. Supp. 448 (E.D. Mich. 1976); Bell v. Barnes, 190 So. 273 (Ala. 1939); Bizzoco v. Chinitz, 476 A.2d 572 (Conn. 1984) (based on Conn. Gen. Stat. § 37-2); Jenkins v. Concorde Acceptance Co., 802 N.E.2d 1270 (Ill. App. 2003) (barring plaintiffs from recovering document preparation fees), *review granted*, 809 N.E.2d 1287 (Ill. 2004); Christian v. Filbert, 249 Ill. App. 230 (1928); Bebee v. Grettenberger, 266 N.W.2d 829 (Mich. Ct. App. 1978); Wright v. First Nat'l Bank of Monroe, 297 N.W. 505 (Mich. 1941); Farmers' Bank & Trust Co. v. Redwine, 167 S.E. 687 (N.C. 1933). *See also* Wakefield v. Goldstein, 644 F.2d 707 (8th Cir. 1981) (usurious contract was voidable, not void, and by releasing security to lender debtor voluntarily fulfilled the contract); Gross v. Coffey, 20 So. 428 (Ala. 1896) (dicta); Union Guardian Trust Co. v. Crawford, 258 N.W. 248 (Mich. 1935) (dicta); Luebke v. Moser, 598 N.E.2d 760 (Ohio Ct. App. 1991) (Ohio Rev. Code § 1343.04 authorized setoff of excess usurious interest against principle balance due, but not for recovery of any remaining excess usurious interest that was paid over the amount of the principal and interest due, therefore common law voluntary payment rule applied to bar such recovery). These cases should be distinguished from decisions that bar plaintiffs from asserting a cause of action to recover illegal interest on the grounds that it may only be used defensively. *See, e.g.,* Ala. Cash Credit Corp. v. Bartlett, 144 So. 808 (Ala. 1932) (statute only prohibits requirement to pay usury, does not allow plaintiff to sue to recover usurious interest already paid); Carey v. The

general reasons cited to support the doctrine, one theory argues that because a usurious contract is illegal from its inception, the borrower and the lender are *in pari delicto*, and therefore the guilty borrower should not be rewarded by being allowed to recover the interest paid pursuant to the illegal agreement.[497]

Even where accepted, the defense has nuances that may help an overcharged borrower defeat its use by a lender. For example, while a payment made under a mistake of law is considered voluntary in many states,[498] one made under a mistake of fact is considered involuntary.[499] Under this reasoning, a borrower may recover an overpayment of interest made due to a mistaken calculation, but may not recover a payment of usury.[500] Other courts have distinguished cases where the loan has been only partially paid from those where the loan has been completely paid, allowing a borrower to recover usurious interest in the former, but not the latter.[501] However, payments considered involuntary, such as those made only after judgment was rendered against a borrower, may be recovered.[502] As with the tax version, compulsion precludes application of the doctrine.[503] Money

obtained through fraud is not considered voluntarily paid either.[504]

These cases suggest a number of strategies that may be used to defeat a lender's argument that it should not have to repay usurious interest paid by the borrower. The jurisprudence of the state should be examined to determine whether it recognizes the voluntary payment defense in any context, and, if so, whether it runs to the benefit of a private entity as opposed to a taxing authority. It can be fairly argued that a taxing authority's need for the doctrine differs substantially from a private party's. Even if the jurisdiction recognizes the doctrine in private party cases, it should not apply it to usury cases, which are special. Usury laws reflect a specific public policy of the state to prevent lenders from overcharging interest. Allowing them to keep that interest because it was deemed "voluntarily" paid by the borrower would vitiate the effect of the usury laws by allowing transgressing lenders to keep illegal interest. The defense would turn the policy on its head as lenders would be encouraged to make usurious loans in the hope of ultimately being able to retain the illicit profit. Furthermore, the voluntary payment defense fails to recognize the fundamental difference in power between borrower and lender. The *in pari delicto* justification may have had some basis in the past, for those loans made between parties of relatively equal bargaining power, but can no longer be rationalized today in the typical loan between an individual consumer and a large, sophisticated, multi-state lender. Though mistake of law has been considered insufficient to avoid the doctrine, the lender generally has far greater ability to determine the applicable usury laws and their effects on loans; hence it, and not the borrower, should bear the consequences of failing to comply with them.

Even if a court allows a lender to argue the voluntary payment defense in a usury case, the borrower can argue that the payments that were made were not in fact voluntary. Rather, the borrower was compelled to make the payments under the duress of the knowledge that failure to pay the

---

Discount Corp., 36 Haw. 107 (Haw. 1942) (plaintiff who had paid usurious interest could not maintain action *in assumpsit* to recover it); *see also* Cooledge v. Collum, 100 So. 143 (Ala. 1924) (action to recover usurious interest allowed in Jefferson County, due to separate statute applicable there declaring all usurious contracts void); Luebke v. Moser, 598 N.E.2d 760 (Ohio Ct. App. 1991) (pursuant to usury statute; no independent cause of action to recover usurious interest exists, borrower limited to claim of set-off).

497 *See, e.g.,* Wright v. First Nat'l Bank of Monroe, 297 N.W. 505 (Mich. 1941).

498 *But see* Time Warner Entertainment Co. v. Whiteman, 802 N.E.2d 886, 891–92 (Ind. 2004); Criterion Ins. Co. v. Fulgham, 247 S.E.2d 404 (Va. 1978).

499 *See, e.g.,* Durant v. Servicemaster, 159 F. Supp. 2d 977, 981 (E.D. Mich. 2001) (rejecting voluntary payment defense when plaintiffs alleged defendant overcharged them for a fuel surcharge to which it was not entitled); Luebke v. Moser, 598 N.E.2d 760 (Ohio Ct. App. 1991) (allowing defense where plaintiff paid usurious interest due to a mistake of law).

500 Bell v. Barnes, 190 So. 273, 275 (Ala. 1939).

501 *See, e.g.,* Lincoln Nat'l Bank v. Kaufman, 406 F. Supp. 448 (E.D. Mich. 1976) (allowing plaintiff to recover prepaid interest where loan had not yet been fully repaid); Matter of Goehring, 23 B.R. 323, 325–26 (Bankr. D. Mich. 1982) (allowing debtor to recoup interest paid on unfulfilled note, but barring claim based on fully paid note, on grounds payment was "voluntary"); Waldorf v. Zinberg, 307 N.W.2d 749 (Mich. Ct. App. 1981) (defendant must apply collected usurious interest against principal due on matured loan); Bebee v. Grettenberger, 266 N.W.2d 829 (Mich. Ct. App. 1978); Sienkiewicz v. Leonard Mortg. Co., 229 N.W.2d 352 (Mich. Ct. App. 1975).

502 Thelen v. Ducharme, 390 N.W.2d 264 (Mich. Ct. App. 1986).

503 *See, e.g.,* Richter v. Burdock, 100 N.E. 1063 (Ill. 1913) (finding that compulsion existed when note was assigned to an innocent third party); Jenkins v. Concorde Acceptance Corp., 802 N.E.2d 1270, 1277 (Ill. App. Ct. 2003) (plaintiff must plead compulsion in response to defendant's defense of voluntary payment), *review granted*, 809 N.E.2d 1287 (Ill. 2004); Peterson v. O'Neill,

---

255 Ill. App. 400 (1930) (affirming judgment for plaintiff on claim of money had and received when plaintiff had paid sums to defendant to procure deed for property that defendant should have conveyed in previous transaction in which plaintiff had been compelled to pay the sums to avoid forfeiting a resale of the property). *Cf.* Jenkins v. Mercantile Mfg. Co., 231 F. Supp. 2d 737 (N.D. Ill. 2003) (refusing to dismiss claim of borrower who sought to recover fees assessed by title company at closing which title company misrepresented as necessary to pay governmental charges).

504 Lawson v. First Union Mortgage Co., 786 N.E.2d 279, 284 (Ind. Ct. App. 2003) (voluntary payment rule does not apply when the payee was induced by fraud or improper conduct, reversing dismissal in favor of mortgage company that had charged borrowers a documentation fee prohibited by state statute). *But cf.* Jenkins v. Concorde Acceptance Co., 802 N.E.2d 1270 (Ill. App. 2003) (fraud exception not satisfied by UDAP violations since UDAP statute eliminates many fraud elements), *review granted*, 809 N.E.2d 1287 (Ill. 2004).

illegal interest would not only have invited legal action by the lender against the borrower, but would have put the borrower at risk of losing the security for the loan, which is a grave matter in the case of a home or car or household goods. Finally, if the consumer made any form of protest before or simultaneously with making a payment on an illegal loan, the payment may be "involuntary" for purposes of the doctrine. The more facts that show the plaintiff was pressured to accede to the usurious interest payments, the less likely a court will allow the lender to use the voluntary payment defense to shield itself from its own illegal acts.

10.6.6 Res Judicata

Closely related to the defense of equitable estoppel is the doctrine of res judicata, which prohibits the relitigation of issues previously decided by the courts. Essentially, a judgment estops the parties to that judgment, outside of the normal appeals process, from continuing to contest any issues decided by the judgment.[505] Thus, res judicata applies to two situations: first, where a party attacks a judgment directly and attempts to have it reopened or set aside; second, where a party brings a separate "collateral" action which would have the effect of undermining the initial judgment.

Direct attack upon a judgment often occurs in the case of default judgments where the borrower never appeared and therefore asserted no defenses at all.[506] Borrowers who have acquiesced in the entry of default judgments on their debt, only to realize later that they might have asserted a usury defense, occasionally attempt to have the default judgments set aside. The success of such efforts varies significantly from state to state depending on the grounds recognized as sufficient for setting aside judgments.[507] For example, New York courts find usury to be a "meritorious defense" which may justify the reopening of a default judgment.[508] On the

other hand, Georgia courts invariably reject attempts to reopen judgments on the basis of usury because, under Georgia law, a judgment will not be set aside unless it is void on its face or unless the pleadings affirmatively show that the plaintiff had no claim.[509]

The second situation in which res judicata affects usury claims arises from the ability of a borrower in most states to assert usury either as a defense to the lender's action or as an independent cause of action for statutory penalties. (While the independent cause of action is typically brought as a counterclaim to the lender's action on the debt, it can also be brought separately, in the absence of any lender action.) Borrowers who fail to raise the defense of usury in a lender's foreclosure or other collection action may argue that, while they have forfeited their usury *defense*,[510] they retain the right to bring an *action* for statutory usury forfeitures or penalties.[511] Lenders, on the other hand, argue that the original judgment precludes any subsequent usury action because it inherently affirms the validity of the debt and therefore the absence of usury. The question is whether the usury counterclaim which the borrowers could have brought in response to the lender's action is a compulsory counterclaim, which is forfeited if not asserted, or a permissive counterclaim, which may be asserted subsequently.

As a general rule, a defendant who could raise a claim as a counterclaim, but who fails to do so, is precluded from raising that claim subsequently in two situations: (1) the counterclaim is required to be imposed by a compulsory counterclaim statute or rule of court; or (2) the relationship

---

505 Judicial settlements, if negotiated at arm's length, may constitute a similar bar although technically they may operate as a release or waiver rather than res judicata. Higgins v. Erickson (*In re* Higgins), 270 B.R. 147 (Bankr. S.D.N.Y. 2001) (borrowers waived usury defense by signing confession of judgment after default). *See, e.g.*, Munilla v. Perez-Cobo, 335 So. 2d 584 (Fla. Dist. Ct. App. 1976); Thompson v. First Nat'l Bank, 300 S.E.2d 529 (Ga. App. 1983); Vordenbaum v. Rubin, 611 S.W.2d 463 (Tex. App. 1980); Dunbabin v. Brandenfels, 566 P.2d 941 (Wash. Ct. App. 1977).

506 This discussion assumes that proper service was made upon the borrower. Obviously, in the absence of service, default judgments may be challenged on jurisdictional or due process grounds, but this topic is beyond the scope of this manual.

507 For general statements of these grounds outside of the context of usury, see, e.g., Citizens Nat'l Bank of University City v. Gehl, 567 S.W.2d 423 (Mo. Ct. App. 1978) (moving party must show reasonable diligence); Household Fin. Co. v. Avery, 476 S.W.2d 165 (Mo. Ct. App. 1972) (lender could not reopen judgment).

508 *See* Mutual Home Dealers Corp. v. Alves, 258 N.Y.S.2d 786

(App. Div. 1965); National Travis, Inc. v. Gialousakis, 466 N.Y.S.2d 624 (Sup. Ct. 1983), *aff'd mem.*, 471 N.Y.S.2d 1023 (App. Div. 1984). *Cf.* Matter of Farrell, 27 B.R. 241 (Bankr. E.D.N.Y. 1982) (judgment not reopened for corporation). *See also In re* Hamlett, 63 B.R. 492 (Bankr. M.D. Fla. 1986) (usury is type of defense which allows Bankruptcy Court to look behind state court default judgment notwithstanding principles of res judicata).

509 *See* Clark v. Kaiser Agricultural Chemicals, 274 S.E.2d 648 (Ga. App. 1980) (citing Georgia cases); Hyman v. Plant Imp. Co., 260 S.E.2d 531 (Ga. App. 1979).

510 Usury as shield instead of a sword is an affirmative defense which must be raised or generally will be deemed waived. *See, e.g.*, FDIC v. Ramirez-Rivera, 869 F.2d 624 (1st Cir. 1989).

511 Other scenarios also occur. For example, a borrower who filed and lost an affirmative action alleging usury was subsequently precluded from asserting usury as a defense in the creditor's later action on the same note. Gelb v. Mazzeo, 169 N.Y.S.2d 58, *reargument and appeal denied*, 170 N.Y.S.2d 1005 (App. Div. 1958) (res judicata applied even though earlier dismissal was clearly erroneous; borrower should have appealed but missed the deadline). As another example, a California court ruled that a borrower who, in a lender's action on note A, filed a permissive counterclaim to recover usurious interest paid on a separate note B, could not subsequently bring another action for statutory usury penalties on note B. *See* Alston v. Goodwin, 343 P.2d 993 (Cal. Ct. App. 1959) (procedural nightmare). *See also In re* Giorgio, 62 B.R. 853 (Bankr. D.R.I. 1986) (consent decree signed by debtors did not bar trustee in bankruptcy from later asserting usury).

between the counterclaim and the plaintiff's claim is such that the successful prosecution of the second action would nullify the initial judgment or would impair rights established in the initial action.[512] Compulsory counterclaim statutes, to the extent that they exist, vary significantly from state to state and are not thoroughly treated here. Nevertheless, it is worth noting that Federal Rule of Civil Procedure 13 makes counterclaims compulsory, with some exceptions, if they arise out of the transaction or occurrence that is the subject matter of the opposing party's claim, and if they do not require for their adjudication the presence of third parties over whom the court cannot obtain jurisdiction. This rule arguably makes usury a compulsory counterclaim to an action on a note.[513]

In the absence of a controlling compulsory counterclaim statute, most decisions hold that a judgment for a creditor in a foreclosure action or an action on a note necessarily affirms the validity of a debt and would be undermined if subsequent usury claims were permitted. Consequently, usury is generally viewed as a "common law compulsory counterclaim" which is barred by res judicata if not asserted when a creditor's action on a debt is litigated.[514] Some authority to the contrary does exist, but much of it seems questionable in light of its age, later case law, or special circumstances.[515]

Despite the prevailing view that a judgment on a debt, whether directly or through a foreclosure action, bars a subsequent usury action on the same debt, practitioners should be careful in defining exactly what that "same debt" is. A judgment operates as res judicata only on issues actually or necessarily decided by the court,[516] and when a debtor and creditor have executed a series of notes, several courts have held that a judgment on one note need not

preclude the assertion of usury against the remaining notes[517] even if they are only extensions of the note on which judgment had been given.[518]

A related question is whether a federal court has the authority to adjudicate usury issues when there is a state court judgment on the debt. Federal courts must not only give the same preclusive effect to a state court judgment as the judgment would be given in courts of the state that rendered it, but also lack jurisdiction to review state court judgments.[519] Nor can federal courts exercise jurisdiction over claims that are inextricably intertwined with claims adjudicated in state court.[520] Thus, a federal court lacked jurisdiction to order a creditor to petition to amend state court judgments to delete usurious post-judgment interest.[521]

10.6.7 Statutes of Limitations

Usury, like other causes of action, is subject to statutes of limitations, so that affirmative usury claims must be filed within a set period after the time that they mature. The length of time allotted varies from state to state, but typically ranges from one to three years after the usury action accrues.[522] If a state recognizes a common law action for the

---

512 Restatement, Judgments 2d § 22 (1982). *See also* Circle v. Jim Walter Homes, 654 F.2d 688 (10th Cir. 1981).

513 *Cf.* John R. Alley & Co. v. Federal Nat'l Bank of Shawnee, 124 F.2d 995 (10th Cir. 1942).

514 *See, e.g.,* Circle v. Jim Walter Homes, 654 F.2d 688 (10th Cir. 1981) (citing cases); Andrews v. Reidy, 60 P.2d 832 (Cal. 1936); Madden v. Harlandale Bank, 574 SW.2d 590 (Tex. Ct. App. 1978). *See also* Fielder v. Credit Acceptance Corp., 188 F.3d 1031 (8th Cir. 1999) (claim that state court judgments included impermissible post-judgment interest cannot be raised in federal court because it is inextricably intertwined with claims adjudicated in state court). *See generally,* Annot. 98 A.L.R. 1027 (1935), *Judgment as Res Judicata of Usury Notwithstanding Question as to Usury Not Raised.*

515 *See* Flint v. Kimbrough, 115 P.2d 84 (N.M. 1941) (court in the underlying foreclosure action had not obtained personal jurisdiction over the borrower); Murphy v. Fidelity Inv. Co., 17 P.2d 472 (Okla. 1932); Weaver v. White, 164 S.W.2d 48 (Tex. Civ. App. 1942) (questionable authority after Madden v. Harlandale Bank, 574 S.W.2d 590 (Tex. Ct. App. 1978)); McDonald v. Smith, 53 Vt. 33 (1880).

516 *See* Henson v. Columbus Bank & Trust Co., 770 F.2d 1566 (11th Cir. 1985) (state court usury decision based solely on statute of limitations does not subsequently bar federal court's consideration of merits of the same usury claim).

517 *See* Alston v. Goodwin, 343 P.2d 993 (Cal. Ct. App. 1959); Yager v. Rubymar Corp., 216 N.Y.S.2d 577 (Sup. Ct. Special Term 1961) (interpreting New Jersey Law). *See also* Heine v. Albin Gustafson Co., 461 N.Y.S.2d 934 (Sup. Ct. 1983). *Cf.* Sunbelt Savings, F.S.B. v. Barr, 824 S.W.2d 600 (Tex. App. 1991) (a note and a guaranty are separate transactions; prior suit against individual in his capacity as guarantor was not res judicata as to suit against him as a partner on the partnership's note).

518 *See* Yager v. Rubymar Corp., 216 N.Y.S.2d 577 (Sup. Ct. Special Term 1961) (interpreting New Jersey Law).

519 Rooker v. Fidelity Trust Co., 263 U.S. 413 (1923); District of Columbia Court of Appeals v. Feldman, 460 U.S. 462 (1983).

520 *Id.*; Fielder v. Credit Acceptance Corp., 188 F.3d 1031 (8th Cir. 1999).

521 Fielder v. Credit Acceptance Corp., 188 F.3d 1031 (8th Cir. 1999).

522 *See, e.g.,* M. Nahas & Co. v. First Nat'l Bank, 930 F.2d 608 (8th Cir. 1991) (2 years under National Bank Act; plaintiff's argument that DIDA permitted state opt-out of National Bank Act's statute of limitation was rejected, and Arkansas did not opt-out in any event); Durante Bros. v. Flushing Nat'l Bank, 755 F.2d 239 (2d Cir. 1985) (two years under National Bank Act; three years under borrowed New York law for civil RICO collection of unlawful debt), *cert. denied*, 473 U.S. 906 (1985); Van Cleef v. Aeroflex Corp., 657 F.2d 1094 (9th Cir. 1981) (three years under Arizona usury statute); Kendrick v. Jim Walter Homes, Inc., 545 F. Supp. 538 (S.D. Ind. 1980) (one year under Indiana U.C.C.C.); Henson v. Columbus Bank & Trust Co., 240 S.E.2d 284 (Ga. App. 1977) (one year); Scott v. Forest Lake Chrysler-Plymouth Dodge, 637 N.W.2d 587 (Minn. App. 2002) (2-year statute for penalty applies to MVRISA claim); Trapp v. Hancuh, 1997 Minn. App. LEXIS 779 (July 15, 1997) (unpublished, citation limited) (two year statute for actions upon a statute for a penalty applies); Arrowhead, Inc. v. Safeway Stores, Inc., 587

recovery of usurious interest paid, the statute of limitations which applies to such an action may differ from the time limit which applies to the state's statutory cause of action for usury.[523] In most states, statutes of limitations are tolled under special circumstances, such as incompetence.[524]

At least as important as determining the time period provided by a statute of limitations is determining when the relevant period begins to run. If a one year statute of limitations were to begin to run on the day the loan agreement is consummated, many causes of action would be time barred before the borrower discovered the usury. With a few exceptions,[525] courts rule that statutes of limitations do not

begin to run against usury actions until the date of final payment on the usurious note.[526] Normally this is the date on which the loan was originally scheduled to terminate, but an earlier termination, such as the satisfaction of a debt through a foreclosure on secured property, may trigger the statute earlier,[527] and a later termination, through some form of extension agreement, may start the clock later.[528]

P.2d 411 (Mont. 1978) (two years); Englishtown Sportswear Ltd. v. Marine Midland Bank, 467 N.Y.S.2d 693 (App. Div. 1983) (one year for usury, but six years for recovery of contract overcharge below usury ceiling); Henderson v. Security Mortgage & Fin. Co., 160 S.E.2d 39 (N.C. 1968) (two years); Car Now Acceptance Co. v. Block, 2003 WL 21714583 (Ohio Ct. App. July 14, 2003) (unpublished) (six-year period for action upon liability created by statute other than a forfeiture or penalty applies to retail installment sales act (RISA) claim, as RISA is a remedial statute); Dunlap v. Friedman's, Inc., 582 S.E.2d 841 (W. Va. 2003) (construing statute liberally to apply four-year statute of limitations to credit sales); Snodgrass v. Sisson's Mobile Home Sales, 244 S.E.2d 321 (W. Va. 1978) (one year). *See also* U.C.C.C. §§ 5.202(1),(2) (1968 Model Code) (one year and two years respectively); U.C.C.C. § 5.201 (1974 Model Code) (one or two years depending on transaction).

523 *See* Easter v. Am. West Fin., 381 F.3d 948 (9th Cir. 2004) (different limitation periods and periods run from different events); Dennis v. Bradbury, 236 F. Supp. 683 (D. Colo. 1964), *aff'd*, 368 F.2d 905 (1966); Westman v. Dye, 4 P.2d 134 (Cal. 1931); § 10.8, *infra*.

524 *See In re* Giorgio, 62 B.R. 853 (Bankr. D.R.I. 1986) (reaffirmation of usurious debt tolls usury statute of limitation), *rev'd*, 862 F.2d 933 (1st Cir. 1988) (debtors could not toll the statute on the debt in question because they had already paid the debt in full; at the latest, cause of action accrued with last payment, which was two years past the limitation period at the time of filing); Carter v. Zachary, 418 S.W.2d 787 (Ark. 1967) (insufficient evidence of fraudulent concealment to toll usury statute of limitation). *But cf.* Henson v. Columbus Bank & Trust Co., 240 S.E.2d 284 (Ga. App. 1977) ("renewal statute" did not toll statute of limitations when federal court declined pendant jurisdiction over usury claim). *See generally* 51 Am. Jur. 2d, Limitation of Actions §§ 169 *et seq.* (2000) (discussing exceptions to statutes of limitations).

525 *See* Easter v. Am. West Fin., 381 F.3d 948 (9th Cir. 2004) (statute of limitations for common law usury claim runs from date of each payment; for statutory usury claim, from date when loan is paid in full or when final payment is due); Miller v. Pacific Shore Funding, 224 F. Supp. 2d 977 (D. Md. 2002) (statute of limitations for inclusion of charges forbidden by Second Mortgage Loan Law begins on day of consummation), *aff'd*, 2004 WL 144138 (4th Cir. Jan. 28, 2004); Henderson v. Security Mortgage & Fin. Co., 273 N.C. 253, 160 S.E.2d 39 (1968) (each payment of usurious interest gives rise to separate cause of action, and statute of limitation runs from each payment date, but unallocated payments attributed first to principal, so most interest payments occur at end of loan term and can be recovered); Merritt v. Knox, 380 S.E.2d 160 (N.C. Ct. App. 1989) (statute of limitation runs from date of payment for

remedy providing double recovery of interest, from date of contract for interest forfeiture remedy); Mayfield v. San Jacinto Savings Ass'n, 788 S.W.2d 119 (Tex. App. 1990) (interpreting Tex. Rev. Stat. Ann. art 5069-8.04(a), statute of limitations runs from later of date notes were signed or occurrence of violation; court also held that though one transaction can have multiple violations of "contracting for," "charging" and "receiving" usurious interest, no new limitations period runs from each event); Skinner v. Cen-Pen Corp., 414 S.E.2d 824 (Va. 1992) (Virginia treats each payment of an installment of interest as a usurious payment; since pay-off included usurious interest, action brought within two years of pay-off was not barred). *See also* Garver v. Brace, 55 Cal. Rptr. 2d 220 (App. 1996) (cause of action does not accrue until borrower actually pays excess interest; since payments on usurious note are deemed to apply first to principal, the statute of limitations does not begin to run until debtor has paid the entire principal amount of the debt); Tinter v. Sack, 646 N.Y.S.2d 516 (App. Div. 1996) (one year statute of limitations had run where parties had entered into oral loan agreement with no fixed termination date over 7 years before suit to recover usurious interest was filed; unclear in opinion when the one year began to run); Cook v. Frazier, 765 S.W.2d 546 (Tex. App. 1989) (payment of interest under usurious contract triggers limitation, not just payment of excess interest).

526 *See* Easter v. Am. West Fin., 381 F.3d 948 (9th Cir. 2004) (statute of limitations for statutory usury claim runs from date when loan is paid in full or when final payment is due; for common law usury claim, from date of each payment); Westman v. Dye, 4 P.2d 134 (Cal. 1931); Wenck v. Ins. Agents Fin. Corp., 99 So. 2d 883 (Fla. Dist. Ct. App. 1958); Miller v. York, 548 P.2d 941 (Nev. 1976); Snodgrass v. Sisson's Mobile Home Sales, 244 S.E.2d 321 (W. Va. 1978). *See also* Kendrick v. Jim Walter Homes, Inc., 545 F. Supp. 538 (S.D. Ind. 1980) (citing Indiana U.C.C.C.; Ind. Code § 24-4.5-5-202(1)); Beltz v. Dings, 6 P.3d 424 (Kan. App. 2000) (cause of action for usury accrues with each payment made on a continuing contract). *Cf. In re* Giorgio, 862 F.2d 933 (1st Cir. 1988) (debtors could not toll the statute on the debt in question because they had already paid the debt in full; at the latest, cause of action accrued with last payment, which was two years past the limitation period at the time of filing); Shelton v. Chrysler First Fin. Servs. Corp., 676 So. 2d 591 (La. 1996) (if borrower prepays, "date of final payment" under statute of limitations means the date of prepayment, not date of maturity of loan). *But see* Miller v. Pac. Shore Funding, 2004 WL 144138 (4th Cir. Jan. 28, 2004) (table) (statute of limitations for challenge to closing costs runs from day of closing because they are legally enforceable then, even if they are financed); *cf.* McCarthy v. First Nat'l Bank, 223 U.S. 493, 32 S. Ct. 240, 56 L. Ed. 523 (1912) (runs from date usurious interest is paid, not from date of final payment).

527 *See* Van Cleef v. Aeroflex Corp., 657 F.2d 1094 (9th Cir. 1981); Fidelity Funds, Inc. v. Price, 491 So. 2d 681 (La. Ct. App. 1986) (interpreting date of acceleration as date of "final payment").

528 *See* Gemperle v. Crouch, 724 P.2d 375 (Wash. Ct. App. 1986). *See also* Pacific Eastern Corp. v. Gulf Life Holding Co., 902

It is important to recognize that the statutes of limitations discussed in this section apply only to a borrower's affirmative action under a usury statute. Statutes of limitations normally do not bar the debtor's assertion of usury as a defense to a creditor's action on the relevant debt.[529] Even if a borrower's affirmative cause of action to recover penalties for usury is time barred, the borrower can still offset by way of recoupment the amount the lender seeks on the usurious note. In states allowing extrajudicial foreclosures, a "defensive" use of a claim relating to overcharges beyond the statute of limitations arguably may be used despite the fact that the borrowers must file suit in order to stop a foreclosure.[530]

10.6.8 De Minimis Violations

The *de minimis* defense to usury is the argument that penalties should not be assessed for trivial usury violations. This defense is rejected in some states on the grounds that its recognition by the courts in the face of mandatory statutory penalties would constitute judicial legislation be-

yond the courts' authority.[531] Nevertheless, the *de minimis* defense is recognized in other states,[532] and in these jurisdictions it can cause problems for usury claimants.

Even where the *de minimis* defense is recognized, there are few standards as to which violations can confidently be described as trivial and not worthy of judicial attention. The dollar amount of an overcharge clearly influences the court, but it is unclear how large a *de minimis* overcharge may be. The nature of the violation—for example, a disclosure violation as opposed to an interest overcharge—may also influence some courts, but other courts have rejected such

S.W.2d 946 (Tenn. Ct. App. 1995) (paying off a note is not a final payment if note is one of a series of notes that are part of a continuing transaction; however, it is a final payment if it is a novation, which extinguishes the existing contract and substitutes a new one).

529 *See, e.g.,* In re Bishop, 79 B.R. 94 (Bankr. D.D.C. 1987); Simmons v. Patrick, 27 Cal. Rptr. 347 (App. 1962); Young v. Wilder, 77 So. 2d. 604 (Fla. 1955); Adamson v. Trust Co. Bank, 271 S.E.2d 899 (Ga. App. 1980); Thrift Funds of Baton Rouge, Inc. v. Jones, 274 So. 2d. 150 (La. 1973), *cert. denied,* 414 U.S. 820 (1973); Fidelity Funds, Inc. v. Price, 491 So. 2d. 681 (La. Ct. App. 1986) (consumer credit law); Miley v. Steedley, 269 So. 2d. 522 (La. Ct. App. 1972); Miller v. York, 548 P.2d 941 (Nev. 1976); Rebeil Consulting Corp. v. Levine, 617 N.Y.S.2d 830 (App. Div. 1994) (affirmative defenses such as usury not subject to statute of limitations). *Cf.* Merritt v. Knox, 380 S.E.2d 160 (N.C. Ct. App. 1989) (since limitation period for interest forfeiture had run, lender was awarded interest at statutory "legal" rate from date of contract; interest reduced from contract rate on theory that contract interest provisions were illegal and void). *But cf.* Valley View State Bank v. Caulfield, 731 P.2d 316 (Kan. Ct. App. 1987) (series of notes; borrower cannot assert defenses in earlier notes in action to enforce later note) (narrow reading of U.C.C.C.); Negaard v. Miller Constr. Co., 396 N.W.2d 833 (Minn. Ct. App. 1986) (usury defense must arise from same debt that creditor is attempting to enforce).

530 In re Bishop, 79 B.R. 94 (Bankr. D.D.C 1987) (a "defensive use" of a usury claim permitted beyond statute of limitations in extrajudicial foreclosure jurisdiction); Richlin v. Schleirer, 7 P.2d 711 (Cal. 1932) (usury case: immaterial that due to nature of foreclosure proceedings under a deed of trust, debtor must act as plaintiff to seek to enjoin threatened foreclosure rather that asserting a defense in an action initiated by the creditor); King v. Kitchen Magic, Inc., 391 A.2d 1184 (D.C. 1978) (suit to nullify the mortgage based on fraud was an equitable action filed as a defensive measure against the foreclosure allowed despite statute of limitations); Hill v. Hawes, 144 F.2d 511 (D.C. Cir. 1944) (usury claim raised affirmatively beyond statute of limitations).

531 Georgia courts seem to reject *de minimis* arguments on a regular basis. *See, e.g.,* Matter of Ferris, 42 B.R. 374 (S.D. Ga 1984), *rev'd on other grounds,* 764 F.2d 1475 (11th Cir. 1985) ($16.56 overcharge was not *de minimis*); Georgia Inv. Corp. v. Norman, 204 S.E.2d 740 (Ga. 1974) ($1.00 notary fee not *de minimis*); Kelly v. Sylvan Motors, 287 S.E.2d 359 (Ga. Ct. App. 1981) ($1.27 overcharge not *de minimis*); Gray v. Quality Fin. Co., 204 S.E.2d 483 (Ga. Ct. App. 1974) (loan term exceeded statutory maximum by one day; not *de minimis*). Courts in other jurisdictions have apparently agreed with this approach although they have considered the issue less frequently. *See In re* Swartz, 37 B.R. 776 (Bankr. D.R.I. 1984) (loan void for $4 overcharge; court states that amount of overcharge is irrelevant); Scott v. Forest Lake Chrysler-Plymouth Dodge, 637 N.W.2d 587 (Minn. App. 2002) (*de minimis* exception does not apply to cases involving statutory interpretation); Dickey v. Bank of Clarksdale, 184 So. 314 (Miss. 1938) (overcharges between $0.50 and $1).

532 The *de minimis* defense has regularly been recognized in Texas in cases of small overcharges. *Compare* Ceco Corp. v. Steve's Sash & Door Co., 714 S.W.2d 322 (Tex. App. 1986), *aff'd as modified,* 751 S.W.2d 473 (Tex. 1988) ($245.69 was not *de minimis* on total contract price of $71,702.95) *with* Yates Ford v. Ramirez, 692 S.W.2d 51 (Tex. 1985) (monthly overcharges of $0.074 and $0.002 from improper odd day calculations were *de minimis*); Buendia v. Advanta Mortgage Corp.-USA, 2003 WL 21982321 (Tex. App. Aug. 21, 2003) (unpublished) ($2.36 overcharge is *de minimus*); HSAM Inc. v. Gatter, 814 S.W.2d 887 (Tex. App. 1991) (premature "charging" of late charge in pay-off quote *de minimis* where payment subsequently was indeed made late; fact that pay-off quote was solicited for purpose of creating a cause of action supported application of the equitable doctrine); Gawlik v. Padre Staples Auto Mart, 666 S.W.2d 161 (Tex. App. 1983) ($1.62 overcharge in purchase and sale of two cars was *de minimis*); Wayne Strand Pontiac-GMC v. Molina, 653 S.W.2d 45 (Tex. App. 1983) ($5.53 "license plate fee" plus $2.50 "official fees" were *de minimis*); Thornhill v. Sharpstown Dodge Sales, 546 S.W.2d 151 (Tex. Civ. App. 1976) ($0.24 overcharge on $5300 credit was *de minimis*). However, one Texas court refused to find that the failure of a creditor to use the term "retail installment contract" was *de minimis,* Anguianao v. Jim Walters Homes, 561 S.W.2d 249 (Tex. Civ. App. 1978), and another ruled that the *de minimis* argument did not apply under a statute that imposed serious penalties for overcharges in excess of twice the permissible rate, when the creditor exceeded twice the permissible rate by only a small amount. Bendele v. Tri-County Farmers Coop., 635 S.W.2d 459 (Tex. App.), *aff'd,* 641 S.W.2d 208 (Tex. 1982). *Cf. In re* Cadillac Wildwood Dev. Corp., 138 B.R. 854 (Bankr. W.D. Mich. 1992) ($3 overcharge on closing costs was "mistake of fact" needing correction, but was not a usurious overcharge).

distinctions.[533] Similarly, some suggestion has been made that the collection of an excessive but otherwise legal charge may be *de minimis*, while the imposition of a completely unauthorized charge may not, but this approach too has been rejected by some courts.[534]

In fact it may be impossible for courts to develop coherent principles regarding the *de minimis* defense because to do so would effectively dismantle whatever usury requirement was labeled *de minimis*. For example, if courts predictably ruled that a $1 overcharge was *de minimis*, creditors could uniformly charge the maximum interest plus $1 with impunity,[535] and the state's usury ceiling would effectively have been raised. Courts refusing to recognize the *de minimis* defense find that its recognition would constitute judicial legislation.

Because of the absence of predictable standards, consumer attorneys in jurisdictions which recognize a *de minimis* defense should attempt to change the focus of the argument, rather than to debate precisely what size overcharge is *de minimis*. A court looking at a single $1 overcharge in one solitary case may be inclined to tell the usury claimant that it has more important matters to worry about. However, overcharges not involving bona fide error usually result from a systematic practice of the creditor. With a little effort, the borrower's attorney can show that the overcharge was not just $1, but was really $1 per customer. If a bank, for example, makes a few thousand loans per year, such an overcharge amounts to a few thousand dollars per year, and courts looking at the $1 overcharge from this perspective may well be willing to follow the reasoning of the Supreme Court of Mississippi which, in rejecting the contention that overcharges of $1 or $0.50 were *de minimis*, stated: "[i]f these charges are so trifling that the court should close its eyes to them, they are so trifling that banks should not insist upon them as conditions of making small loans. . . ."[536]

10.6.9 *Industry Custom and Usage*

A less commonly raised usury defense is the argument that long-standing and widely accepted financial industry practices should not be deemed usurious or otherwise illegal. For example, in an Illinois case borrowers claimed that a bank had overcharged them by calculating interest on the basis of a 360-day year, and the bank replied that the banking industry universally calculated interest in this manner, that the borrowers should have known this (unpublicized) fact, and that this should be a defense to the borrower's challenge.[537]

The primary justification for the industry practice defense arises from common law principles of contract interpretation which provide that ambiguous contracts should be construed in the light of general customs and usage.[538] Yet, whatever the merits of this doctrine as a matter of contract construction, it is black letter law that industry practice may not contravene a statute, and the courts have universally held that industry practice is no defense to usury.[539] Furthermore, evidence of industry practice is inadmissible if offered to validate an otherwise usurious transaction.[540]

Despite the rule that industry practice is no defense to usury violations, widespread financial customs may occa-

---

533 For example, the Georgia Supreme Court seems to view overcharges as more serious than at least some disclosure violations. *See* Georgia Inv. Corp. v. Norman, 204 S.E.2d 740 (Ga. 1974). *See also* Jenkins v. Commercial Credit Plan, Inc., 419 S.E.2d 484 (Ga. App. 1992). Yet in Texas, which clearly recognizes the *de minimis* defense in cases of small overcharges, at least one court refused to apply the *de minimis* approach to a disclosure violation. *See* Anguianao v. Jim Walters Homes, 561 S.W.2d 249 (Tex. Civ. App. 1978).

534 *See* Wayne Strand Pontiac-GMC v. Molina, 653 S.W.2d 45 (Tex. App. 1983) (compare majority and dissenting opinions).

535 Actually, courts which recognize the *de minimis* defense frequently emphasize the good faith of the creditor. *See, e.g.,* Yates Ford v. Ramirez, 692 S.W.2d 51 (Tex. 1985). If it could be shown that an overcharge was made in anticipation of an effective *de minimis* defense, the defense might well be rejected, but such a proof could be very difficult. Should the creditor routinely impose that marginal overcharge, that might suggest a business decision to take the risk.

536 Dickey v. Bank of Clarksdale, 183 Miss. 748, 184 So. 314 (1938) (stating that the aggregate gain to the creditor from its overcharges is the same as the aggregate loss to the borrowers, and that the legal wrong is no less wrong when its effect is

diffused among many borrowers). For other cases recognizing the impact of repeated, small overcharges, see Matter of Ferris, 42 B.R. 374 (S.D. Ga. 1984), *rev'd on other grounds*, 764 F.2d 1475 (11th Cir. 1985); Georgia Inv. Corp. v. Norman, 204 S.E.2d 740 (Ga. 1974). *Cf. In re* Sprouse, 577 F.2d 989 (5th Cir. 1978) (discussing effect of overreaching contract language on consumers in transactions which are not litigated); Sander v. Lincoln Serv. Corp., 1993 U.S. Dist. LEXIS 4454 (N.D. Ill. Apr. 5, 1993) (lender with many customers can realize substantial profit from small individual overcharges; RESPA case). *But see* HSAM Inc. v. Gatter, 814 S.W.2d 887 (Tex. App. 1991) (while court recognized that excess late charges on thousands of contracts would not be *de minimis*, it was not swayed by that argument in this particular case, where the creditor appeared to have been "set-up" for the usury claim and, by court's calculation, the borrower's loss was only a hypothetical 2 cents).

537 The court disagreed with the bank's defense. *See* Perlman v. First Nat'l Bank of Chicago, 305 N.E.2d 236 (Ill. App. 1973).

538 *Id. See also* Cohen v. District of Columbia Nat'l Bank, 382 F. Supp. 270 (D.D.C. 1974) (good analysis).

539 *See* Cohen v. District of Columbia Nat'l Bank, 382 F. Supp. 270 (D.D.C. 1974) (custom of ignoring declining balance in interest calculation); Harmon v. Lehmann, 85 Ala. 379, 5 So. 197 (1888) (sales commission); Perlman v. First Nat'l Bank of Chicago, 305 N.E.2d 236 (Ill. App. 1973) (360-day year); Beneficial Fin. Co. v. Administrator of Loan Laws, 272 A.2d 649 (Md. 1971) (alleged custom of correcting errors discovered in lender's books without imposing penalty); Dickey v. Bank of Clarksdale, 184 So. 314 (Miss. 1938) (custom of imposing service charge on small loans); Cowgill v. Jones, 73 S.W. 995 (Mo. App. 1903) (sales commissions); Kollman v. Hunnicutt, 385 S.W.2d 600 (Tex. Ct. App. 1964) (car dealer floor plan financing). *See also* Barclay Kitchen, Inc. v. Calif. Bank, 25 Cal. Rptr. 383 (App. 1962) (bank deposits).

540 *See* Kollman v. Hunnicutt, 385 S.W.2d 600 (Tex. Ct. App. 1964).

sionally affect the outcome of usury cases. If, after the application of the standard principles of statutory construction, a usury statute is ambiguous regarding the legality of some practice, a court may well be reluctant to find that practice usurious in the face of long-standing custom. This judicial tendency is hard to quantify, but it is often expressed in terms of the narrow construction of usury statutes.[541] Most courts will be quite hesitant to impose significant penalties, which almost invariably follow the labeling of any widespread practice as usurious, unless there are firm statutory grounds for striking down the practice.

On the other hand, if the statute is ambiguous, some courts have recognized the equally valid policy grounds to refuse to give much deference to industry usage, particularly in the consumer credit context:

> It is not surprising that interested, sophisticated lenders consistently interpret ambiguous laws to their own advantage and to the disadvantage of their obviously less-sophisticated customers. This data only highlights the need of the disinterested courts to be vigilant to prevent industry-wide overreaching.[542]

The related issue of deference to an administrative agency's interpretation is discussed in § 9.3.1.3, *supra*.

10.6.10 Usury Saving Clauses

Many credit contracts contain boilerplate "saving clauses" which, in one form or another, recite that the parties to the contract intend to comply with applicable usury laws, and that the contract should not be interpreted as providing for usurious interest rates. Saving clauses frequently specify that any charge above the usury ceiling should be deemed a mistake, and that the overcharge should either be refunded to the borrower or be credited against the outstanding principal balance.

The aim of usury saving clauses is to convert apparently usurious overcharges to mere contract violations and thereby to avoid the statutory penalties associated with usury. Saving clauses attempt to negate usurious intent by denying the presence of any such intent. In addition, savings clauses purport to reclassify any interest overcharge as a principal payment or as money in some manner held by the creditor on the debtor's behalf. If a charge above the usury ceiling occurs, but the savings clause is given effect, the interest overcharge element of a usury violation is negated.

If saving clauses were broadly construed, they would circumvent the enforcement of usury statutes.[543] Whenever a borrower challenged an apparently usurious contract, the creditor either would deny any intent to assess overcharges which the contract provided for but which had not yet occurred, or would simply rebate excessive charges without penalty. Creditors' incentives to comply with usury statutes would be greatly reduced because unscrupulous creditors could retain the excessive contract charges from the majority of their contracts which would never be challenged, while losing little in disputed contracts.[544]

Because of the potential which saving clauses hold for undermining usury laws, courts have given them only limited effect.[545] Creditors cannot rebut usurious intent or otherwise avoid usury statutes simply by rebating excessive charges that the debtor has already paid.[546] Also, savings

---

541 See § 9.3.1.1, *supra*.

542 *In re* Jordan, 91 B.R. 673, 688 (Bankr. E.D. Pa. 1988). *See also* § 9.3.1.1, *supra*.

543 Transworld Telecommunications, Inc. v. Pacific Mezzanine Fund, Inc. (*In re* Transworld Telecommunications, Inc.), 260 B.R. 204 (Bankr. D. Utah 2000), *rev'd and remanded on other grounds*, 309 F.3d 744 (10th Cir. 2002); Eisenstein v. DiPrimio, 2000 Ga. App. LEXIS 1140 (Sept. 15, 2000) (savings clause would be a "win/win proposition" for unscrupulous lenders); Swindell v. FNMA, 409 S.E.2d 892, 896 (N.C. 1991), *modifying and aff'g* 387 S.E.2d 220 (N.C. App. 1990) (if valid, savings clause would shift onus onto borrower, contravening policy and depriving borrower of statute's protections). *See also* Jersey Palm-Gross, Inc. v. Paper, 658 So. 2d 531 (Fla. 1995) (if savings clause were to be absolute bar to usury claim, lender could relieve himself of legal penalties for his conduct by writing into the contract a disclaimer of any intent to do what he plainly did).

544 *Cf. In re* Sprouse, 577 F.2d 989 (5th Cir. 1978); Swindell v. FNMA, 409 S.E.2d 892, 896 (N.C. 1991), *modifying and aff'g* 387 S.E.2d 220 (N.C. App. 1990) ("A lender cannot charge usurious rates with impunity by making that rate conditional upon its legality and relying upon the illegal rate's automatic rescission when discovered and challenged by the borrower").

545 *See, e.g.*, Jersey Palm-Gross, Inc. v. Paper, 658 So. 2d 531 (Fla. 1995) (court rejects use of savings clause as absolute bar to usury claim; rather it is one factor to be considered in overall determination of creditor's intent; other factors listed as illustrative: how narrow the usurious margin, whether it is complex transactions in which a mathematical error made; whether the usury was contingent; lender's knowledge of the urgency of borrower's need; finding of usury upheld); Lawrimore v. Sun Fin. Co., 205 S.E.2d 110 (Ga. App.), *aff'd*, 208 S.E.2d 454 (Ga. 1974) (boilerplate clause stating that contract provisions will be ineffective to extent of any illegality could not be given effect, because to do so would nullify the regulatory statute). *But see* Lairsen v. Slutzky, 80 S.W.3d 121, 127 (Tex. App. 2002) (relying on savings clause without discussion); S&J Investments v. Am. Star Energy & Minerals Corp., 2001 Tex. App. LEXIS 7730 (Nov. 7, 2001) (giving effect to savings clause in open-end credit agreement that contemplated a succession of debts).

546 *See* Duderwicz v. Sweetwater Savings Ass'n, 595 F.2d 1008 (5th Cir. 1979) (cancellation of usurious escrow account); Kissell Co. v. Gressley, 591 F.2d 47 (9th Cir. 1979) (acceleration due to lender's misconduct; savings clause given no effect); Szerdahelyi v. Harris, 490 N.E.2d 517 (N.Y. 1986) (loan void despite tender of excess payments); Okla. Preferred Fin. & Loan Corp. v. Morrow, 497 P.2d 221 (Okla. 1972) (failure to rebate unearned interest until borrower complains); Danziger v. San Jacinto Sav. Ass'n, 732 S.W.2d 300 (Tex. 1987); Coppedge v. Colonial Sav. & Loan Ass'n, 721 S.W.2d 933 (Tex. App. 1986) (refund of usurious overcharge did not preclude finding of usury despite language in Texas "spreading" statute). *See also* Swindell v. FNMA, 409 S.E.2d 892 (N.C. 1991), *modifying and aff'g*

clauses will normally be given no effect where any reasonable interpretation of the contract clearly calls for the payment of usurious charges or such charges have already been demanded.[547] Nor will a savings clause be given effect

where the lender has not attempted to implement it but has persisted in demanding unlawful interest.[548]

The one situation in which saving clauses may carry some weight is in ambiguous contracts which can plausibly be interpreted as either usurious or non-usurious. For example, two notes might be construed as a single loan at a legal rate or as two loans, one of which was usurious.[549] Similarly, a precomputed contract might be unclear about whether the creditor was required to rebate unearned interest charges upon prepayment or acceleration.[550] Under such circumstances, saving clauses are frequently cited by courts as support for their choice of the non-usurious construction of the transaction.[551] Consequently, saving clauses can make it more difficult for debtors to prove the element of usurious intent in ambiguous contracts which are not usurious on their face, especially when the overcharge has not yet been assessed.

---

387 S.E.2d 220 (N.C. App. 1990) (savings clause held not to protect creditor even though no excess charge collected and creditor offered to reduce charge to legal maximum); § 10.6.11, *infra* (statutory defenses where creditor refunds excess charge). *Cf.* Dillon v. RTC, 811 S.W.2d 765 (Ark. 1991) (contract defined payments as interest; creditor's subsequent unilateral effort to reallocate excess interest to principal cannot purge contract of usury, nor can subsequent modification agreement, as usury is determined as of inception of contract. [No savings clause at issue]). *But see* Greeley Nat'l Bank v. Sloan, 677 P.2d 409 (Colo. App. 1983) (statute permits refund within 30 days without penalty).

547 *See* ECE Technologies, Inc. v. Cherrington Corp., 168 F.3d 201 (5th Cir. 1999); Mack v. Newton, 737 F.2d 1343 (5th Cir. 1984) (mere presence of savings clause cannot rescue transaction that is necessarily usurious by its explicit terms); Kissell Co. v. Gressley, 591 F.2d 47 (9th Cir. 1979) (savings clause cannot salvage contract which is usurious on its face); Mims v. Fid. Funding, Inc., 307 B.R. 849 (N.D. Tex. 2002) (savings clause did not save contract that was usurious on its face; hypothetical possibility that conditions for charging usurious fees would not occur did not make savings clause effective); Turner v. E-Z Check Cashing, Inc., 35 F. Supp. 2d 1042 (M.D. Tenn. 1999) (commercial case: usury savings clause not effective if usurious interest is in fact paid); Nevels v. Harris, 102 S.W.2d 1046 (Tex. 1937); Armstrong v. Steppes Apts., Ltd., 57 S.W.3d 37 (Tex. App. 2001); Hardwick v. Austin Gallery of Oriental Rugs, Inc., 779 S.W.2d 438, 442–43 (Tex. Ct. App. 1989) (disclaimer of intent to contract for usury is immaterial if usury has actually been charged); Victoria Bank & Trust Co. v. Brady, 779 S.W.2d 893 (Tex. App. 1989) (savings clause insufficient in itself to avoid usury; if usurious interest is charged, then usury occurs), *aff'd in part, rev'd in part on other grounds*, 811 S.W.2d 931 (Tex. 1991) (charge was not usurious; court does not refer to saving clause). *But see* Federal Sav. & Loan Ins. v. Kralj, 968 F.2d 500 (5th Cir. 1992) (looking at savings clause in light of circumstances surrounding transaction: savings clause found to remedy any defect); First South Savings Ass'n v. First South Partners, II, Ltd., 957 F.2d 174 (5th Cir. 1992) (in commercial loan to sophisticated businessmen, savings clause held to remedy demand for excess amount in demand letters and original judicial complaint); Szenay v. Schaub, 496 So. 2d 883 (Fla. Dist. Ct. App. 1986) (saving clause along with allegation of actual mistake supports finding of no intent despite usurious rate of interest in note; observe that Florida follows a minority rule on usurious intent, see § 10.5.5, *supra*); Poulsen's, Inc. v. Wood, 756 P.2d 1162 (Mont. 1988) (in commercial case where contract on its face provided for excess interest, but contract also had savings clause and demand letter properly calculated interest at nonusurious rate, no usury found); Watson v. Avco Fin. Servs., Int'l, 401 N.W.2d 485 (Neb. 1987) (lender did not illegally contract for attorney fees where contractual clause for such fees prefaced by words "to the extent permitted by law"); Armstrong v. Steppes Apts., Ltd., 57 S.W.3d 37 (Tex. App. 2001); Woodcrest Assocs. Ltd. v. Commonwealth Mortgage Corp., 775 S.W.2d 434 (Tex. App. 1989) (lender's demand letter for specific, excessive amount was a "charge" under the usury statute but savings clause in loan rendered excess unenforceable and avoided usury; large commercial transaction). *But cf.* Robert Joseph Phillips Living Trust v. Scurry, 988 S.W.2d 418 (Tex.

App. 1999) (giving effect to savings clause where note was not usurious on its face and lender was unaware of pre-existing first mortgage, making new loan a junior mortgage loan subject to a lower rate cap).

548 Armstrong v. Steppes Apts., Ltd., 57 S.W.3d 37 (Tex. App. 2001). *See also* Gibbo v. Berger, 123 Cal. App. 4th 396, 19 Cal. Rptr. 3d 829 (2004) (savings clause has no effect where lender continued to accept borrower's monthly interest-only payments for ten years without declaring any default).

549 *See, e.g.*, Spanish Village Ltd. v. American Mortgage Co., 586 S.W.2d 195 (Tex. Ct. App. 1979).

550 *See, e.g.*, Mack v. Newton, 737 F.2d 1343 (5th Cir. 1984) (citing Texas cases). *See also* Myles v. Resolution Trust Corp., 787 S.W.2d 616 (Tex. App. 1990) (court superfluously invokes savings clause against borrower's challenge to acceleration provision in an interest-bearing contract, where acceleration would not have resulted in charging of unearned interest in any event). *See* § 5.7.2, *supra*.

551 *See, e.g.*, In re Casbeer, 793 F.2d 1436 (5th Cir. 1986); Mack v. Newton, 737 F.2d 1343 (5th Cir. 1984) (citing Texas cases); Rickman v. Modern Am. Mortgage Corp., 583 F.2d 155 (5th Cir. 1978); Imperial Corp. v. Frenchman's Creek Corp., 453 F.2d 1338 (5th Cir. 1972); Rebman v. Flagship First Nat'l Bank, 472 So. 2d 1360 (Fla. Dist. Ct. App. 1985); Nevels v. Harris, 129 Tex. 190, 102 S.W.2d 1046 (1937); Pentico v. Mad-Wayler, Inc., 964 S.W.2d 708 (Tex. App. 1998) (contract is not explicitly usurious, therefore, savings clause is effective; usury only apparent after the total interest charges over the loan term at the non-usurious contract rate are added to excessive late fees considered "interest" under state law); Parhms v. B&B Ventures, Inc., 938 S.W.2d 199 (Tex. App. 1997) (where the collection of usurious interest was contingent solely upon the borrower making late payments and the extent of the tardiness of those payments, contract was ambiguous as to whether interest was charged in excess of that allowed by law; usury savings clause given effect); Edmondson v. First State Bank, 819 S.W.2d 605 (Tex. App. 1991) (savings clause given effect where no evidence of usurious rate charged; debtor apparently had alleged that the mere existence of multiple prime rates at the bank resulted in usury); Spanish Village Ltd. v. American Mortgage Co., 586 S.W.2d 195 (Tex. Ct. App. 1979). *See also* R.V. Industries v. Urdiales, 851 S.W.2d 306 (Tex. App. 1992) (savings clause reflects an intent to comply with usury laws and indicates spreading should be used to avoid charge of usury).

10.6.11 Correction of Error as a Defense

Allowing a creditor a period of time after notice to avoid liability by correcting the error is a common feature of usury statutes.[552] The Minnesota MVRISA was amended in 1996 to allow dealers a 120-day period to cure violations of the requirement to provide the buyer with a signed copy of the contract. Sending the buyer a letter stating that the buyer can request a copy is insufficient.[553]

A court cited a Louisiana statute that provides a similar right to cure as a reason for rejecting the lender's claim that the violation was merely technical and did not warrant a refund.[554] Having failed to take advantage of the opportunity to correct the error, the lender could not complaint that the remedy was too severe.

Texas provides a lender a statutory defense if it corrects the violation, including paying interest on any overcharge at the contract rate, within 60 days after discovering it and gives written notice of the violation to the obligor before the obligor gives written notice of the violation or files an action alleging the violation.[555] Sending a demand letter asking only for the non-usurious portion of the obligation, without explicitly releasing the usurious portion, is probably insufficient.[556] In addition, the creditor's notice to the obligor must acknowledge the specific usury violation.[557] Another Texas provision allows a lender another 60 days to correct the error after receiving notice of the violation.[558] Responding to the obligor's notice by arguing that there was no usury violation is insufficient.[559] In addition, a Texas constitutional provision makes a lender liable for certain violations only if it fails to correct an error within a reasonable time after receiving notice from the borrower.[560]

10.7 Special Defenses of Federal Receivers: *D'Oench* and Related Doctrines

10.7.1 Introduction

As a result of the dramatic bank failures of the Great Depression of the 1930s, the federal government created the Federal Deposit Insurance Corporation (FDIC).[561] In creating the FDIC, Congress sought to promote stability and confidence in the banking system, to insure deposits, and to keep open the channels of trade and commerce.[562]

In order to effectuate these goals, the FDIC and other similar agencies have been granted uniquely powerful special defenses by Congress and the courts. As another wave of bank failures hit the country in the 1980s, the courts expanded these defenses to the point where it is now extremely difficult for borrowers to win any claims or defenses arising out of the conduct of a failed lender.

Three separate sources provide special defenses to the federal agencies responsible for insuring banks and thrifts.[563] First, there is the "*D'Oench* doctrine," first articulated by the Supreme Court in the 1942 case, *D'Oench, Duhme & Co. v. FDIC*.[564] Second, there is a special statute,

---

552 *See, e.g.,* Vickers v. Interstate Dodge, 882 So. 2d 1236, 1244 (La. App. 2004) (creditor cannot complain of penalty for technical violation when it failed to correct the error after receiving notice).

553 Scott v. Forest Lake Chrysler-Plymouth Dodge, 637 N.W.2d 587 (Minn. App. 2002).

554 Vickers v. Interstate Dodge, 882 So. 2d 1236 (La. App. 2004).

555 Tex. Fin. Code Ann. § 305.103(a) (Vernon). *See In re* CPDC, Inc., 337 F.3d 436 (5th Cir. 2003) (sixty days run from lender's subjective discovery that lender has violated usury prohibition); Strasburger Enterprises, Inc. v. TDGT Ltd. P'ship, 110 S.W.3d 566 (Tex. App. 2003) (no defense when complaint that did not seek usurious interest was delivered to debtor only after creditor received usury notice).

556 Anderson v. Chainani (*In re* Kemper) 263 B.R. 773 (Bankr. E.D. Tex. 2001).

557 *Id. See also* Pagel v. Whatley, 82 S.W.3d 571 (Tex. App. 2002) (attachment to complaint acknowledging possibility of usury violation was sufficient where debtor first raised usury issue after receiving complaint).

558 Tex. Fin. Code § 305.006(c). *See also* Ohio Rev. Code § 1317.08 (similar provision allowing refund within 10 days after receiving notice).

559 Anderson v. Chainani (*In re* Kemper) 263 B.R. 773 (Bankr. E.D. Tex. 2001).

560 *See* Vincent v. Bank of Am., 109 S.W.3d 856 (Tex. App. 2003)

(requirement of notice and opportunity to cure bars class action).

561 In 1933, Congress developed the FDIC as a part of the Federal Reserve Act, now codified at 12 U.S.C. §§ 1811–1832. (For an excellent summary of the different functions performed by the FDIC today, see Timberland Design, Inc. v. First Servs. Bank for Savings, 932 F.2d 46, 48 (1st Cir. 1991). *See also Norcross, The Bank Insolvency Game: FDIC Superpowers The D'Oench Doctrine, and Federal Common Law*, 103 Bank. L.J. 316 (1986).) When a bank has failed, or is about to fail, the FDIC has three options: 1) become a receiver and liquidate the bank; 2) arrange for another bank to purchase the failed bank's assets and assume liabilities to depositors (the "purchase and assumption" transaction); or 3) "bail-out" the failed institution. 12 U.S.C. §§ 1821–23.

562 Prior to the Great Depression of the 1930s, the states alone regulated financial institutions. The bank failures of the 1930s were so pervasive that President Roosevelt was forced to declare an unprecedented "bank holiday." Proclamation No. 2040, 48 Stat. 1691 (1933); Proclamation No. 2039, 48 Stat. 1689 (1933).

563 These special defenses may be asserted by the RTC and the FSLIC as well as the FDIC. The Resolution Trust Corporation (RTC) is appointed receiver by the Office of Thrift Supervision created by the Financial Institutions Reform, Recovery and Enforcement Act of 1989 (FIRREA), Pub. L. No. 101-73, 103 Stat. 183. Among other things, FIRREA clarified and amended certain sections of the Federal Deposit Insurance Act, which includes 12 U.S.C. § 1823(e). As a result of FIRREA, duties of the former Federal Savings and Loan Insurance Corporation (FSLIC) have been transferred either to the FDIC or Resolution Trust Corporation (RTC). Assignees of these agencies are also protected.

564 315 U.S. 447, 62 S. Ct. 676, 86 L. Ed. 956 (1942).

12 U.S.C. § 1823(e), sometimes imprecisely referred to as a statutory codification of *D'Oench*. Finally, there is a flexible "super holder in due course" or "federal holder in due course" doctrine.

This section will provide an overview of these three doctrines, concentrating on cases which may be useful to borrowers in responding to these special federal insurer defenses. However, many cases grant the FDIC sweeping immunity, and this focus on the positive signs in recent cases should not lead the reader to underestimate the force of the ample precedent which interprets these doctrines extremely broadly.

A critically important preliminary question is whether section 1823(e) preempts the other two doctrines. This issue is discussed in the next subsection, followed by analyses of each of the three doctrines. The text then discusses what creditors can claim these defenses, and the effect of certain federal limitations on the holder-in-due-course defense, and concludes with a survey of claims making inroads in *D'Oench* and related defenses.

10.7.2 Does § 1823(e) Preempt D'Oench and the Federal Holder-in-Due-Course Doctrine?

The question whether section 1823(e) preempts the somewhat similar judge-created defenses—the *D'Oench* doctrine and the federal holder-in-due-course doctrine—revolves around the implications of the Supreme Court's decision in *O'Melveny & Myers v. FDIC.*[565] The Court there held that the Financial Institutions Reform, Recovery, and Enforcement Act of 1989 (FIRREA), which includes section 1823(e), is a comprehensive statute that does not provide for extension through federal common law. Although the decision does not specifically mention *D'Oench*, there is a strong implication that FIRREA entirely displaces the judge-made *D'Oench* and federal holder-in-due-course doctrines.

A second Supreme Court decision, *Atherton v. Federal Deposit Ins. Corp.*,[566] bolsters this argument. *Atherton* involved a suit brought by the FDIC against several former officers and directors of the failed institution for gross negligence, simple negligence, and breaches of fiduciary duty, claiming they had acted or failed to act in ways that led the bank to make bad loans. The district court dismissed all the gross negligence counts, but on appeal, the Third Circuit concluded that the FDIC could pursue claims for negligence or breach of fiduciary duty available as a matter of federal common law, rejecting the argument that FIRREA's negligence provision preempted common law claims.[567] In reversing the Third Circuit's decision, the Supreme Court

refused to find that the federal interests asserted by the FDIC were sufficient to warrant application of federal common law. Citing to *O'Melveny*, it held that federal common law should be created only when there was a significant conflict between a federal policy and the use of state law.

At this point the Third,[568] Eighth,[569] and D.C.[570] Circuits and a number of district courts and state courts[571] have held that *O'Melveny* has overridden those federal common law defenses to borrowers' claims that are not included in FIRREA. The First[572] and Ninth[573] Circuits have suggested that they agree. But the Fourth[574] and Eleventh[575] Circuits and a number of other courts[576] disagree, and the Tenth

---

565 512 U.S. 79, 114 S. Ct. 2048, 129 L. Ed. 2d 67 (1994). *See* discussions at § 10.7.8, *infra.*

566 519 U.S. 213, 117 S. Ct. 666, 136 L. Ed. 2d 656 (1997).

567 57 F.3d 1231, 1241 (3d Cir. 1995).

568 FDIC v. Deglau, 207 F.3d 153 (3d Cir. 2000) (holding that *O'Melveny* overruled *D'Oench*). *See also* DiMuzio v. RTC, 68 F.3d 777, 780 n.2 (3d Cir. 1995) (suggesting that *D'Oench* may no longer exist as a separate bar to defenses).

569 Kessler v. National Enters., Inc., 165 F.3d 596 (8th Cir. 1999) (*D'Oench* no longer in force); DiVall Insured Income Fund v. Boatmen's First Nat'l Bank, 69 F.3d 1398 (8th Cir. 1995) (FIRREA excludes federal common law defenses not specifically mentioned). *See also* RTC v. Massachusetts Mut. Life Ins. Co., 93 F. Supp. 2d 300 (W.D.N.Y. 2000) (*O'Melveny* effectively ended use of common law in cases governed by FIRREA, therefore defendant could assert state law affirmative defenses based on the FDIC's discretionary activities that occurred post-receivership to professional malpractice action brought by RTC); Sun NLF L.P. v. Sasso, 713 A.2d 538 (N.J. Super. 1998) (federal holder-in-due-course doctrine did not survive *O'Melveny*).

570 Murphy v. FDIC, 61 F.3d 34 (D.C. Cir. 1995) (*D'Oench*).

571 *See, e.g.,* Shapo v. Underwriters Mgmt. Corp., 2002 WL 31155059, at *18–19 (N.D. Ill. Sept. 27, 2002) (unpublished) (questioning *D'Oench's* continued viability and refusing to extend it to bar enforcement of a side agreement entered into by insurance company in action by insurance company's liquidator); S.E.C. v. Capital Consultants, L.L.C., 2002 WL 31441215, at *4 (D. Or. Jan. 3, 2002) (unpublished) (declining to extend *D'Oench* to bar defenses of borrower who had borrowed from an entity that was not federally-regulated); Stewart Title Guaranty Co. v. FDIC, 936 S.W.2d 266 (Tenn. App. 1996).

572 Gens v. RTC, 112 F.3d 569 (1st Cir. 1997) (suggesting that the "FDIC's right to invoke [either *D'Oench* or federal holder-in-due-course] doctrine[s] . . . is open to serious question" without deciding the issue), *cert. denied*, 522 U.S. 931 (1997); FDIC v. Houde, 90 F.3d 600 (1st Cir. 1996).

573 Ledo Fin. Corp. v. Summers, 122 F.3d 825, 829 n.2 (9th Cir. 1997) (*D'Oench* doctrine not applicable in light of *O'Melveny* and *Atherton* but declines to reach whether *D'Oench* overruled). *See also* RTC v. Miller, 67 F.3d 308, 1995 U.S. App. LEXIS 32993 (9th Cir. 1995) (unpublished).

574 Young v. FDIC, 103 F.3d 1180 (4th Cir. 1997) (*D'Oench* remains separate and independent ground for decision), *cert. denied*, 522 U.S. 928 (1997). *Cf.* RTC v. Maplewood Invs., 31 F.3d 1276 (4th Cir. 1994) (*O'Melveny* creates a heavy presumption in favor of applying state law rules of negotiability).

575 FDIC v. Murphy, 208 F.3d 959 (11th Cir. 2000) (FIRREA does not preempt *D'Oench*, reasonable interpretation is that Congress intended *D'Oench* to co-exist with FIRREA).

576 State St. Capital Corp. v. Gibson Tile, Inc., 1998 U.S. Dist. LEXIS 20104 (N.D. Tex. Dec. 16, 1998) (unpublished) (assuming *D'Oench* still good law); Rankin v. Toberoff, 1998 U.S. Dist. LEXIS 9714 (S.D.N.Y. June 30, 1998) (unpublished) (conclud-

Circuit has applied *D'Oench* without questioning its continued viability.[577]

If FIRREA preempts federal common law rules such as *D'Oench* and the federal holder-in-due-course doctrine,[578] then a defense may only be barred based on a specific provision of FIRREA or by state law.[579] In the absence of special federal holder status, ordinary state holder-in-due-course law will control.[580]

Of course, many if not most claims will still be barred by section 1823(e). But section 1823(e) has certain exceptions, discussed in § 10.7.4, *infra*. A defense is more likely to be preserved if it need only avoid one rather than three separate doctrines that might bar it.

10.7.3 D'Oench

10.7.3.1 Overview of the Doctrine

Since the Supreme Court has not yet definitively ruled whether the judge-made *D'Oench* doctrine remains viable in light of the adoption of section 1823(e), it is important to understand its origins and contours. In 1942, in *D'Oench, Duhme & Co. v. FDIC*,[581] the United States Supreme Court

crafted a federal common-law doctrine of equitable estoppel to prevent borrowers from asserting "secret side agreements" with bank officers as a defense against obligations being administered by the FDIC. The borrower, a sophisticated businessperson, had executed in 1926 a demand note which a bank officer had orally agreed not to enforce. The borrower knew the transaction gave the appearance of an asset where none existed. When the bank failed, the FDIC acquired the note and demanded payment, and the borrower asserted the secret, oral side agreement as a defense. In disallowing this defense, the Court reasoned:

> Plainly one who gives such a note to a bank with a secret agreement that it will not be enforced must be presumed to know that it will conceal the truth from the vigilant eyes of the bank examiners.[582]

Thus, if a claim or defense can be construed in any way to arise out of a secret agreement between the borrower and the failed bank, and is likely to mislead bank examiners attempting to determine a bank's true assets profile, *D'Oench* will bar it.

D'Oench applies only to claims raised by borrowers, not depositors.[583] Nor does *D'Oench* apply to agreements between the receiver and a party other than a borrower.[584] It applies only to lending relationships,[585] and only to banking

---

ing that *D'Oench* survives *O'Melveny* in Second Circuit); Bank of San Diego v. Schuette, 2002 WL 2017089, at *2–4 (Cal. Ct. App. Sept. 4, 2002) (unpublished) (citing *D'Oench*); RTC Mortg. Trust 1994-S2 v. Shlens, 72 Cal. Rptr. 2d 581 (Cal. Ct. App. 1998); FDIC v. Kefalas, 822 N.E.2d 329 (table), 2005 WL 277693, at *3 (Mass. Ct. App. 2005) (holding that *D'Oench* and section 1823(e) precluded borrower's defense due to an unwritten policy; no analysis of effect of *O'Melveny*); Republic Credit Corp. I v. Gallo *ex rel.* Trustee of Spaulding Realty Trust, 2002 WL 31862709, at *7 (Mass. Super. Ct. Oct. 21, 2002) (unpublished) (holding *D'Oench* barred enforcement of any oral amendments to construction loan agreement; no analysis of effect of *O'Melveny*); Ray & Assocs., P.C. v. SMS Fin. II, L.L.C., 2002 WL 997663, at *2–3 (Tex. App. May 15, 2002) (unpublished) (*D'Oench* doctrine barred guarantor from asserting that guaranteed note was never funded and from claiming defense of failure of consideration); Pinkston v. Diversified Fin. Sys., 2000 Tex. App. LEXIS 6962 (Oct. 16, 2000) (unpublished) (reaffirming federal holder-in-due-course doctrine to hold that assignee of note acquired from FDIC could claim holder-in-due-course status notwithstanding that note was overdue at time acquired). *Cf.* Depositors Economic Protection Corp. v. Proacacianti, 2002 WL 977496, at *9 (R.I. Super. Ct. May 2, 2002) (unpublished) (neither letter to lender nor proof of claim met requirements of state version of § 1823(e)).

577 Harrison v. Wahatoyas, 253 F.3d 552, 559 (10th Cir. 2001).

578 DiVall Insured Income Fund Ltd. P'ship v. Boatmen's First Nat'l Bank, 69 F.3d 1398 (8th Cir. 1995).

579 *Id.* at 1403. *See also* Bisson v. Eck, 430 Mass. 406, 720 N.E.2d 784 (1999) (holder-in-due-course status to be decided under state law).

580 *See, e.g.,* Calaska Partners, Ltd. v. Corson, 672 A.2d 1099, 1102 (Me. 1996) (under U.C.C. § 3-302, FDIC's assignee could not claim holder-in-due-course status because the FDIC took the note as a bulk purchaser).

581 315 U.S. 447, 62 S. Ct. 676, 86 L. Ed. 956 (1942).

582 *Id.* at 460.

583 Fletcher Village Condo. Ass'n v. FDIC, 864 F. Supp. 259 (D. Mass. 1994) (since FDIC's mission is to protect interests of depositors, barring their claims would defeat purpose of *D'Oench* doctrine).

584 *See, e.g.,* Maryland Nat'l Bank v. RTC, 895 F. Supp. 762 (D. Md. 1995).

585 *See also* Alexandria Assocs., Ltd. v. Mitchell Co., 2 F.3d 598 (5th Cir. 1993) (*D'Oench* does not apply to nonbanking transactions involving sale of partnership interests in real estate development partnerships); Thigpen v. Sparks, 983 F.2d 644 (5th Cir. 1993) (*D'Oench* does not apply to bank's sale of subsidiary); Shapo v. Underwriters Mgmt. Corp., 2002 WL 31155059, at *18–19 (N.D. Ill. Sept. 27, 2002) (unpublished) (questioning *D'Oench*'s continued viability, and refusing to extend it to bar enforcement of a side agreement entered into by insurance company in action by insurance company's liquidator); S.E.C. v. Capital Consultants, L.L.C., 2002 WL 31441215, at *4 (D. Or. Jan. 3, 2002) (unpublished) (declining to extend *D'Oench* to bar defenses of borrower who had borrowed from an entity that was not federally-regulated); Color Leasing 3, L.P. v. Federal Deposit Ins. Corp., 975 F. Supp. 177 (D.R.I. 1997) (finding that Color Leasing was not the bank's borrower but rather a holder of a valid purchase money security interest in a printing press sold to a borrower and therefore the *D'Oench* doctrine did not bar a claim of conversion against the FDIC); Cote d'Azur Homeowners Ass'n v. Venture Corp., 846 F. Supp. 827 (N.D. Cal. 1994). *But see* Winterbrook Realty, Inc. v. FDIC, 820 F. Supp. 27 (D.N.H. 1993) (in order to determine whether *D'Oench* and § 1823(e) apply outside traditional lender-borrower context must look at whether the plaintiff is more like a creditor-depositor or borrower and whether the plaintiff could have taken reasonable steps to protect himself with a written agreement).

transactions and not to so-called non-banking functions.[586] If an agreement would not ordinarily be part of the bank's record, *D'Oench* does not preclude its assertion.[587]

10.7.3.2 Treatment of Innocent Borrowers and Free-Standing Torts

The party seeking to enforce the note need not show that the borrower intended to deceive anyone.[588] Nonetheless, in *FDIC v. Meo*,[589] the Ninth Circuit recognized an "innocent borrower" defense to *D'Oench*, rejecting the broad application of *D'Oench* after carefully analyzing the borrower's conduct to determine whether that conduct created an estoppel. The *Meo* court found there was no "secret agreement," but rather that the borrower was "wholly innocent," and "not negligent" in dealing with the bank.

Notwithstanding *Meo*, the "innocent borrower" defense has been nearly eradicated in the years since it was decided. At least one innocent borrower has been forced to pay back a loan from which he had been previously released,[590] and another had to pay "back" a loan that he claimed the bank had never funded.[591]

Despite the erosion of the principles articulated in *Meo*, the "innocent borrower" defense still exists, at least theoretically, for cases in which the borrower is truly innocent of wrongdoing or negligence.[592] In addition, equitable consid-

erations have recently found some ground in *D'Oench* analysis.[593] For example, one court held that although a continuing guaranty had been found in the records of the bank, *D'Oench* would not prevent the guarantor from asserting that it had been agreed at the time that the guaranty would cover only some, not all, debts owed by the borrower to the bank.[594] Even the FDIC has published policy guidelines for use by its attorneys which advocate a more limited invocation of the doctrine.[595]

Recently, another exception to the *D'Oench* doctrine has emerged, the so-called "free standing tort" exception.

---

586 McGarry v. RTC, 909 F. Supp. 241 (D.N.J. 1995) (lease); Ameribanc Savings Banks v. RTC, 858 F. Supp. 576 (E.D. Va. 1994) (*D'Oench* inapplicable to deed of trust originating among private parties and assigned to bank RTC took over and to lien priority disputes). *But see* Avirex, Ltd. v. RTC, 876 F. Supp. 1135 (C.D. Cal. 1995) (*D'Oench* does apply to lease).

587 Maryland Nat'l Bank v. RTC, 895 F. Supp. 762 (D. Md. 1995) (settlement agreement between RTC and plaintiff could be enforced); Fleischer v. RTC, 882 F. Supp. 999 (D. Kan. 1995) (claim for relocation expenses by employee allowed), *summary judgment granted on other grounds*, 882 F. Supp. 1010 (D. Kan. 1995), *aff'd*, 113 F.3d 168 (10th Cir. 1996); Waynesboro Village, L.L.C. v. BMC Properties, 255 Va. 75, 496 S.E.2d 64 (1998) (restrictive covenants contained in deed of trust were not invalidated by *D'Oench* where they were properly recorded in the land records of the county.).

588 D'Oench, Duhme & Co. v. FDIC, 315 U.S. 447, 458–59, 62 S. Ct. 676, 86 L. Ed. 956 (1942).

589 505 F.2d 790 (9th Cir. 1974).

590 Franklin Credit Mgt. Corp. v. Nicholas, 1999 Conn. Super. LEXIS 1123 (Apr. 26, 1999) (unpublished).

591 Carson Props., Inc. v. NAB Asset Venture, III, L.P., 1998 Tex. App. LEXIS 1619 (Mar. 17, 1998) (unpublished) (the court reasoned that the note said on its face that it was being funded simultaneously with execution, the fact that the bank went under before it actually funded the note did not excuse the borrower from repaying funds it had never received). *See also* Ray & Assocs., P.C. v. SMS Fin. II, L.L.C., 2002 WL 997663, at *2–3 (Tex. App. May 15, 2002) (unpublished) (*D'Oench* doctrine barred guarantor from asserting that guaranteed note was never funded and from claiming defense of failure of consideration).

592 Notrica v. FDIC, 2 F.3d 961 (9th Cir. 1993). *But see* Young v. Federal Deposit Ins. Corp., 103 F.3d 1180 (4th Cir. 1997), *cert.*

denied, 522 U.S. 928 (1997) (holding that *D'Oench* doctrine applied even when customer completely innocent of any bad faith, recklessness, or negligence); Dendinger v. First Nat'l Corp., 16 F.3d 99 (5th Cir. 1994) (rejecting innocent borrower defense); Baumann v. Savers Federal Sav. & Loan Ass'n, 934 F.2d 1506 (11th Cir. 1991) (although innocent borrower defense still possible exception to application of *D'Oench*, no longer tenable because of expansion of doctrine's application), *cert. denied*, 504 U.S. 908 (1992); Point Developers, Inc. v. FDIC, 961 F. Supp. 449 (E.D.N.Y. 1997) (court found case law demonstrated a trend moving away from application of this doctrine and Second Circuit declined to apply it in recent decisions); RTC Mortg. Trust 1994-S2 v. Shlens, 72 Cal. Rptr. 2d 581 (App. 1998).

593 *See, e.g.*, Bolduc v. Beal Bank, 167 F.3d 667, 673 (1st Cir. 1999) (holding that the defense of mutual mistake was not barred: "The doctrine and statute are only directed at protecting the FDIC from unrecorded or oral agreements not in the insured bank's records; they do not preclude every possible defense to a bank claim—e.g., that the loan was to an underage borrower who lacked capacity to contract—merely because it may depend on information that is not contained in bank files."); John v. RTC, 39 F.3d 773 (7th Cir. 1994) (*D'Oench* not "limitless, per se guarantee of victory"); E.I. DuPont de Nemours & Co. v. FDIC, 32 F.3d 592 (D.C. Cir. 1994), *rehearing denied*, 45 F.3d 458 (D.C. Cir. 1995) (only if disclosure could have made a difference does *D'Oench* logically bar recovery for failure to disclose; "*D'Oench* should not be converted into a meat-axe for avoiding debts incurred in the ordinary course of business."); SEC v. Capital Consultants, L.L.C., 2002 U.S. Dist. LEXIS 670, at *11 (D. Or. Jan. 3, 2002) (unpublished) (reasoning that it would be "fundamentally unfair" to apply *D'Oench* to agreement between borrower and financial institution that was not a federally regulated banking institution but was later placed in federal receivership). *See also* Leavitt v. National Loan Investors, Ltd. P'ship, 799 N.E.2d 605 (table), 2003 WL 22881034, at *4 (Mass. App. Ct. 2003) (unpublished) (borrowers could not invoke *D'Oench* doctrine or section 1823(e) to avoid unjust enrichment claim brought by homebuilder for full costs of construction notwithstanding that the FDIC had settled note and mortgage executed for such costs for less than the full amount).

594 Cinco Enters., Inc. v. Benso, 995 P.2d 1080 (Okla. 1999) (citing evidence that showed that the guarantor and bank both intended that the guaranty would cover only one note, and other evidence indicating that the guaranty was never relied on for antecedent debts).

595 An FDIC memorandum to regional offices states that it may not always be appropriate to raise *D'Oench* and § 1823(e) defenses. In some instances, approval from Washington must be obtained before these are asserted, and usury is one of those cases. The following example is given of an instance where use of these shields is not appropriate.

While the *D'Oench* doctrine bars tort claims arising out of "secret" agreements, some courts have held that a tort claim which is "free standing," i.e., not linked to any unwritten agreement, may survive.[596] However, the Eleventh Circuit has ruled that the doctrine covers all torts that arise out of "ordinary banking transactions" if not properly memorialized, and accordingly barred a borrower's tort claims based on alleged oral agreements that additional monies could be loaned, that extensions could be granted, and that the bank would permit assumption of the mortgage by a qualified buyer.[597]

10.7.4 12 U.S.C. § 1823(e)

10.7.4.1 Outline of § 1823(e)

Eight years after the *D'Oench* decision, Congress enacted the Federal Deposit Insurance Act of 1950 (FDIA). The new law included a section, 15 U.S.C. § 1823(e), which added a new dimension to the limited immunity afforded by the equitable estoppel doctrine created in *D'Oench*. Section 1823(e) was reenacted in substantially similar language as part of the Financial Institutions Reform, Recovery and Enforcement Act of 1989 (FIRREA)[598] in response to the dramatic series of bank and thrift failures in the 1980s.

In its current version, section 1823(e) provides:

> (e) Agreements against interests of Corporation
> (1) In general
> No agreement which tends to diminish or defeat the interest of the Corporation in any asset acquired by it under this section or section 1821 of this title, either as security for a loan or by purchase or as receiver of any insured depository institution, shall be valid against the Corporation unless such agreement—
> (A) is in writing,
> (B) was executed by the depository institution and any person claiming an adverse interest thereunder, including the obligor, contemporaneously with the acquisition of the asset by the depository institution,
> (C) was approved by the board of directors of the depository institution or its loan committee, which approval shall be reflected in the minutes of said board or committee, and
> (D) has been, continuously, from the time of its execution, an official record of the depository institution.[599]

In addition, section 1821(d)(a) of FIRREA provides that "[a]ny agreement which does not meet the requirements set forth in [section 1823(e)] shall not form the basis of, or substantially comprise, a claim against the receiver or the corporation."

A rationale for section 1823(e) is that bank examiners often have to evaluate assets on an urgent "overnight" basis in a crisis situation and must be able to rely on what obligations are shown in the records.[600] Section 1823(e)'s requirements are particular pitfalls given that banks that fail are often correlatively poor at the sort of i-dotting and t-crossing requirements the statute requires. Yet it is the borrower—who has little if any control over the bank's recordkeeping practices—who suffers.[601]

---

3. The FDIC is attempting to collect on a note which the failed bank acquired from a mortgage broker. The note is at a 15% interest rate and the mortgage broker charged six and one half points. State law provides that interest shall be no more than 13% and that no more than one point may be charged. The FDIC may not defend the borrower's counterclaim of a usurious loan by asserting *D'Oench* or 1823(e). Here too, Washington approval must be obtained before asserting *D'Oench* or section 1823(e).

FDIC Guidelines for Use of *D'Oench* and Statutory Provisions, 52 Fed. Reg. 5984 (Feb. 10, 1997).

596 Hanson v. FDIC, 13 F.3d 1247 (8th Cir. 1994) (*D'Oench* does not bar constructive trust claim against FDIC based on tort wholly independent of any agreement); Vernon v. RTC, 907 F.2d 1101 (11th Cir. 1990), *as narrowed by* OPS Shopping Center, Inc. v. FDIC, 992 F.2d 306 (11th Cir. 1993) (*D'Oench* inapplicable to free standing tort claim unrelated to specific bank asset); Astrup v. Midwest Federal Savings Bank, 886 F.2d 1057 (8th Cir. 1989) (breach of fiduciary duty claim survives); Beckley Capital Ltd. P'ship v. DiGeronimo, 942 F. Supp. 728 (D.N.H. 1996) (no bar to alteration defense because no agreement when defense based on acts performed without consent), *aff'd*, 184 F.3d 52 (1st Cir. 1999); Fairfield Six/Hidden Valley P'ship v. RTC, 860 F. Supp. 1085 (D. Md. 1994) (tortious interference claims based on bank's conduct months after agreement entered into allowed to stand); *In re* NBW Commercial Paper Litig., 826 F. Supp. 1448 (D.D.C. 1992) (negligence claim not linked to unwritten agreement survives motion to dismiss). Note that the Federal Tort Claims Act may be the appropriate vehicle. *See* § 10.7.9, *infra*.

597 RTC v. Dunmar Corp., 43 F.3d 587 (11th Cir. 1995) (en banc), *rev'g* Jones v. RTC, 7 F.3d 1006 (11th Cir. 1993).

---

598 Pub. L. No. 101-73, 103 Stat. 183 (1989). *See* H.R. Conf. Rep. 101-222 (Aug. 4, 1989) (identifying purpose as to "strengthen the enforcement powers of federal regulators").

599 Federal Deposit Insurance Act of 1950 § 2(13)(e), *codified at* 12 U.S.C. § 1823(e), *as amended*. There is no debate of § 1823(e) in the Act's legislative history. 96 Cong. Rec. 10, 731–32 (1950).

600 Langley v. FDIC, 484 U.S. 86, 91–92, 108 S. Ct. 396, 98 L. Ed. 2d 340 (1987).

601 *See* Note, *Borrower Beware: D'Oench, Duhme and Section 1823 Overprotect the Insurer When Banks Fail*, 62 S. Cal. L. Rev. 253, 275 (1988) (arguing that courts have given overly broad protection to failed banks at borrowers' expense under § 1823 and *D'Oench*, in light of the language and history of the statute and the actual needs of the FDIC).

10.7.4.2 Requirements for Enforceability of Agreements

Courts have generally interpreted the requirements of enforceable agreements listed in section 1823(e) very rigidly, requiring an "explicit" writing in the bank's official records, or an "express written agreement" between the banking institution and the borrower.[602] The Tenth Circuit, in *FDIC v. Noel*,[603] pronounced that "[t]he FDIC has no duty to scour a failed institution's documents for inferences and hidden duties."[604] The bank must have properly papered and correctly filed the transaction. Thus, it has been held that a non-recourse agreement that was placed in the bank's files but was not signed by the bank does not meet the second requirement;[605] a letter in the bank's files claiming that the bank's board approved an agreement does not meet the third requirement;[606] and a letter agreement's presence in the files of the bank's attorney, who kept offices in the same building and on the same floor, does not meet the fourth.[607] Pleadings kept with the bank's records do not meet the requirement of an "agreement."[608] On the other hand, to meet the requirement of contemporaneous execution, the documents need not have been *created* contemporaneously, just executed,[609] and some courts have been willing to interpret "contemporaneously" quite broadly.[610]

10.7.4.3 What Is an "Agreement" Under § 1823(e)?

One limitation on section 1823(e) is that, by its terms, it applies only to "agreements." The Supreme Court has interpreted the term "agreement" broadly to mean the entire bargain between the parties, including the warranties the bank had made.[611] The term is not limited to agreements to perform acts in the future.[612] Thus, section 1823(e) barred a fraudulent inducement claim by borrowers that the bank, prior to the FDIC receivership, had misrepresented the size, quality and encumbrances of real estate they had purchased through a loan with the FDIC-insured bank. The Court held that these representations were part of the agreement, and since they were not recorded in the bank's records, they were barred by section 1823(e).[613] Indeed, section 1823(e) prevents the defense of fraud in the inducement even if the receiver had "actual knowledge" of the claim prior to taking over the lender bank.[614]

Despite this broad construction of "agreement," where the claim or defense does *not* arise from an agreement but from other conduct on the part of the bank, section 1823(e)'s requirements should not be relevant.[615] Furthermore, not

---

602 *See, e.g.*, Rhode Island Depositors Economic Protection Corp. v. Tasca, 729 A.2d 707 (R.I. 1999) (based on state version of § 1823(e)). *See also* YNN Holding Corp. v. FDIC, 354 F. Supp. 2d 1334, 1337 (S.D. Fla. 2005) (denying FDIC's motion for summary judgment in breach of contract suit alleging FDIC's predecessor had wrongfully paid a letter of credit where contract in the predecessor's files); Depositors Economic Protection Corp. v. Proacacianti, 2002 WL 977496, at *9 (R.I. Super. Ct. May 2, 2002) (unpublished) (neither letter to lender nor proof of claim met requirements of state version of § 1823(e)).

603 177 F.3d 911 (10th Cir. 1999), *cert. denied*, 528 U.S. 1116 (2000) (*D'Oench* prevents borrower from asserting claim that bank breached fiduciary duties, even though bank's subsidiary was itself the majority owner of borrower's general partner, and borrower put forth evidence that bank was the alter ego of the partner and well aware of the circumstances behind the note).

604 *Id.* at 918.

605 RTC Mortg. Trust 1994-S2 v. Shlens, 72 Cal. Rptr. 2d 581 (App. 1998).

606 Aurora Shores Homeowners Ass'n v. FDIC, 2 F. Supp. 2d 975 (N.D. Ohio 1998).

607 RTC v. McCrory, 951 F.2d 68 (5th Cir. 1992). *See also* First Valley Bank of Los Fresnos v. Martin, 144 S.W.3d 466, 471 n.20 (Tex. 2004) (secured creditor's director did not have apparent authority to release collateral on oral vote).

608 Randolph v. RTC, 995 F.2d 611 (5th Cir. 1993) (if pleadings qualified as bank records under *D'Oench*, regulators would have to speculate as to the outcome of pending lawsuits), *cert. denied sub. nom.* Beeson v. Phillips, King & Smith, 510 U.S. 1191 (1994).

609 Erbafina v. FDIC, 855 F. Supp. 9 (D. Mass. 1994).

610 *See, e.g.*, RTC v. Midwest Federal Savings Bank of Minot, 36 F.3d 785 (9th Cir. 1993) (contemporaneousness requirement satisfied by commitment letter executed more than two months

prior to final loan documents, considering general business practice with large loans); Remington Inv., Inc. v. Aidekman, 1996 U.S. Dist. LEXIS 10453 (S.D.N.Y. July 25, 1996) (unpublished) (written modification agreement signed two and a half months after note survives summary judgment); *In re* Miraj & Sons, Inc., 192 B.R. 297 (Bankr. D. Mass. 1996) (have to view contemporaneousness in terms of commercial realities so twelve day gap is not fatal), *amended by* 197 B.R. 737 (Bankr. D. Mass. 1996); Sun NLF L.P. v. Sasso, 713 A.2d 538 (N.J. Super. 1998) (three months satisfies requirement). *Cf.* OCI Mortg. Corp. v. Marchese, 774 A.2d 940 (Conn. 2001) (sixteen month time span fails to satisfy contemporaneous provision), *appeal dismissed*, 712 A.2d 449 (Conn. App. 1998).

611 Langley v. FDIC, 484 U.S. 86, 91, 108 S. Ct. 396, 98 L. Ed. 2d 340 (1987) (construing statute to be consistent with *D'Oench*).

612 *Id.*

613 *Id.*

614 Langley v. FDIC, 484 U.S. 86, 93–95, 108 S. Ct. 396, 98 L. Ed. 2d 340 (1987); NCUA Bd. v. Madar, 1998 U.S. Dist. LEXIS 10293, at *11 (E.D.N.Y. July 9, 1998) (unpublished) ("Even if Madar could establish that the Board knew of Amalgamated's alleged improper lending practices, under *Langley*, knowledge of the misrepresentation prior to acquiring the notes is irrelevant"). *See also* FDIC v. Deglau, 207 F.3d 153 (3d Cir. 2000) (section 1823(e) bars fraud in the inducement defense; note guarantors failed to produce sufficient evidence that their execution of a guaranty was procured by fraud in the factum).

615 *See* Bolduc v. Beal Bank, 167 F.3d 667 (1st Cir. 1999) (defense of mutual mistake); Beckley Capital Ltd. P'ship v. DiGeronimo, 942 F. Supp. 728 (D.N.H. 1996) (defense based on alleged alteration of documents survives because based in acts performed without consent thus no agreement), *aff'd*, 184 F.3d 52 (1st Cir. 1999); Communication Sys., Inc. v. Ironwood Corp., 930 F. Supp. 1162 (S.D. Tex. 1996) (acceleration clause in note not based on agreement so admissible to show when cause of action accrued); Wilsim Ltd. P'ship v. P&M Dev., 1996 Conn. Super. LEXIS 1676 (May 31, 1996) (unpublished) (equitable

every agreement with a bank need necessarily meet section 1823(e)'s exacting requirements. "The FDIC protection applies only to separate and collateral agreements;" thus if the agreement sought to be enforced is actually spelled out within the loan documents itself, then section 1823(e) will not prevent its enforcement.[616]

In a recent case, an assignee of the FDIC sought to invoke the provision against a borrower who claimed that the note the assignee sought to enforce had been paid. In fact, the note in the noteholder's records was marked "paid." But in an imaginative inversion of FIRREA's protections, the noteholder claimed that the borrower had a secret agreement with the bank to have the note marked "paid" without actually paying the note, thus attempting to void the written record with a secret agreement not recorded in the bank's records. The Texas court of appeals found no authority for "the proposition that a note marked paid constitutes a secret agreement," and affirmed the trial court's take nothing judgment.[617]

Some courts also recognize a "bilateral agreement exception" to *D'Oench*, finding that where the agreement in a bank file shows that duties were imposed upon both bank and borrower, the *D'Oench* doctrine does not immunize the FDIC from claims of breach of contract. For example, the Seventh Circuit found that *D'Oench* is inapplicable to bilateral agreements, and only applicable to notes or guarantees imposing a unilateral obligation to pay a sum certain, with the maker's defense dependent upon separate, undisclosed agreements.[618]

In addition, section 1823(e) only applies to conventional loan activities.[619]

10.7.4.4 Requirement That the Agreement Tend to Diminish or Defeat FDIC's Interest in an Asset

Another limitation on the applicability of section 1823(e) is that the agreement must be one that "tends to diminish or defeat" the FDIC's interest in an asset. Courts have begun to analyze this agreement more closely than in the past.[620]

---

defenses like laches not based in agreement are not barred by Section 1823(e)); Resiventure, Inc. v. National Loan Investors, 480 S.E.2d 212 (Ga. App. 1996) (payment defense allowed). *See also* FDIC v. Deglau, 207 F.3d 153 (3d Cir. 2000) (suggesting that a conflict of interest defense, arising from the representation of an attorney to the original transaction who allegedly induced them to sign the guaranty, would not be barred by § 1823(e) because it is not the sort of issue that would be the subject of bank records).

616 Interproperty Holdings, Inc. v. Craft-Barnett, Invs. 1999 U.S. Dist. LEXIS 220, at *6 (N.D. Tex. Jan. 7, 1999) (unpublished), *citing* FDIC v. McFarland, 33 F.3d 532 (5th Cir. 1994) (release given in return for deed-in-lieu-of-foreclosure, included with the loan documents themselves, released borrower from claims of FSLIC's assignee). *See also* Bank One Tex. v. Morrison, 26 F.3d 544, 551 (5th Cir. 1994) (policies of *D'Oench* and § 1823(e) not implicated when all the loan documents and memoranda consistently reflected that defendant did not guarantee loan sought to be enforced); Valley View Development v. Henrichs, 2004 WL 120090, at *11 (Cal. Ct. App. Jan. 27, 2004) (unpublished) (where FDIC's predecessor had actual knowledge that lot was to be released from leasehold mortgage, neither *D'Oench* nor § 1823(e) prevented reformation of settlement agreement with FDIC to reflect the parties' intent to release the lot).

617 Investment Co. of the Southwest v. Dugan, 2001 Tex. App. LEXIS 2769, at *4, *6 (Apr. 26, 2001) (unpublished).

618 John v. RTC, 39 F.3d 773 (7th Cir. 1994) (*D'Oench* doctrine does not apply to claim based on undisclosed subsistence problems in house sold by RTC where reliance not inconsistent with terms of sales contract); FDIC v. McFarland, 33 F.3d 532

(5th Cir. 1994) (*D'Oench* doctrine does not apply when agreement FDIC seeks to avoid is spelled out in loan documents); Howell v. Continental Credit Corp., 655 F.2d 743, 746 (7th Cir. 1981) ("[*D'Oench* is inapplicable] where the document the FDIC seeks to enforce is one, such as the leases here, which facially manifests *bilateral* obligations and *serves as the basis of the lessee's defense*."); *Howell* was later clarified in FDIC v. O'Neil, 809 F.2d 350 (7th Cir. 1987) (holding that rule applied when obligation appeared in the asset itself rather than in another agreement); *Howell* was not extended to unrecorded agreements in Bell & Murphy & Assocs. v. Interfirst Bank Gateway, 894 F.2d 750 (5th Cir.), *cert. denied*, 498 U.S. 895 (1990); National Credit Union Admin. v. Ticor Title Ins. Co., 873 F. Supp. 718 (D. Mass. 1995) (title insurance policy unenforceable on written terms); FDIC v. Glynn, 1995 U.S. Dist. LEXIS 13957 (N.D. Ill. Sept. 25, 1995) (unpublished) (*D'Oench* does not preclude argument re loan construction and capacity in which parties signed); In re Miraj & Sons, Inc., 192 B.R. 297 (Bankr. D. Mass. 1996) (*Howell* exception extended to apply when bilateral agreements contained in closely related or integral loan documents in bank's records), *amended by* 197 B.R. 737 (Bankr. D. Mass. 1996); Diversified Fin. Sys., Inc. v. Miner, 713 N.E.2d 293 (Ind. Ct. App. 1999) (follows *Howell*, where loan agreement on its face loan agreement referenced "floor plan agreement," a document which manifests bilateral obligations, *D'Oench* did not bar borrowers' counterclaim that FDIC and assignee/plaintiff caused borrowers' business to fail because it did not comply with the floor plan agreement, affirming denial of summary judgment for plaintiff); Sun NLF L.P. v. Sasso, 713 A.2d 538 (N.J. Super. 1998) (affirming denial of summary judgment for assignee, where letter agreement by bank containing "take out" commitment was in bank's files, though not referenced in subsequent notes). *See also* FDIC v. Marine Midland Realty Credit Corp., 17 F.3d 715 (4th Cir. 1994) (*D'Oench* does not bar claim based on loan participation agreement with failed bank); RTC v. Oaks Apt. Joint Venture, 966 F.2d 995 (5th Cir. 1992) (case remanded, *inter alia*, to determine whether a limited liability guaranty created a mutual obligation on the lender's part which was not performed and thus *D'Oench* would not be available to RTC); Howerton v. Designer Homes by Georges, Inc., 950 F.2d 281 (5th Cir. 1992); Twin Constr. Inc. v. Boca Raton, Inc., 925 F.2d 378 (11th Cir. 1991); FDIC v. White, 820 F. Supp. 1423 (N.D. Ga. 1993) (*D'Oench* does not bar defense based solely on interpretation of contract).

619 John v. RTC, 39 F.3d 773 (7th Cir. 1994) (statute does not apply to contract to sell house owned by RTC).

620 *See, e.g.*, FDIC v. Bracero & Rivera, Inc., 895 F.2d 824, 830 (1st Cir. 1990) (note discharged by another debtor's payment prior to FDIC's acquisition was not an asset protected by § 1823(e)); Commerce Fed. Sav. Bank v. FDIC, 872 F.2d 1240, 1245 (6th

For example, the Florida Supreme Court held that neither *D'Oench* nor section 1823(e) barred a plaintiff from asserting a secondary security interest in a note when the value of the note exceeded the judgment of the FDIC's assignee, because the assignee's interest was not put at risk by the plaintiff's claim.[621] The Eighth Circuit allowed condominium owners, who had purchased units from a developer that had failed to satisfy contractual conditions prior to foreclosure, to sue the successor bank to rescind the sales.[622] The court reasoned that the suit did not seek to diminish the bank's security interest in the unsold units, but rather went to the underlying value of the collateral, an interest that did not fall within section 1823.[623] Similarly, the Third Circuit has ruled that this "no asset" exception allowed a guarantor to offer documentation that did not comply with section 1823(e) that showed the original bank had discharged a debt before the FDIC's takeover, reasoning that if it had been discharged, the asset no longer existed.[624] It would be illogical, the court reasoned, to require such documentation to meet the requirements of section 1823(e) simply so that

it could prove that section 1823(e) did not apply and that therefore the documentation did not need to comply with the section.[625]

10.7.4.5 Equitable Considerations

In *Langley v. FDIC*,[626] the Supreme Court declined to "engraft an equitable exception" upon section 1823(e). Nonetheless, common sense and equity have begun to appear in decisions as well. A Delaware court suggested that it had "strong doubts" as to whether section 1823(e) could bar the effect of a settlement agreement that released an obligor where the settlement agreement was an integral part of a court judgment in a suit between the original bank and that obligor.[627] Equitable considerations influenced the court, which pointed out that the noteholder had relied heavily on beneficial provisions of the settlement agreement, notwithstanding that it did not comply with section 1823(e), on other issues in the litigation.[628] However, the Connecticut Supreme Court recently overturned a decision that allowed borrowers to set off their $220,000 mortgage against $900,000 owed them by a failed bank, stating that there is no catchall "equitable exception" to section 1823(e).[629] Furthermore, section 1823(e) is an affirmative defense that the FDIC waives if it fails to raise it appropriately.[630]

10.7.4.6 Differences Between § 1823(e) and *D'Oench*

The differences between section 1823(e) and the *D'Oench* doctrine become important in light of the Supreme Court's decision in *O'Melveny & Myers v. FDIC*,[631] which many lower courts have read as obliterating *D'Oench*.[632] If

---

Cir. 1989) (since evidence showed that note secured by mortgage that FDIC sought to enforce was paid in full, security was extinguished prior to FDIC's takeover and accordingly did not exist for FDIC to acquire); Grubb v. FDIC, 868 F.2d 1151, 1158–59 (10th Cir. 1989) (notes voided by court judgment before FDIC acquired them were not assets subject to § 1823(e)); Cote d'Azur Homeowners Ass'n v. Venture Corp., 846 F. Supp. 827 (N.D. Cal. 1994) (§ 1823(e) does not bar assertion of joint venture agreement as basis for plaintiff's claims, since the agreement does not diminish RTC's interest in a particular asset); FDIC v. Nemecek, 641 F. Supp. 740, 743 (D. Kan. 1986) (note that had been extinguished by accord and satisfaction could not be an asset acquired by the FDIC); Alaska Southern Partners v. Prosser, 972 P.2d 161 (Alaska 1999) (since evidence showed that failed bank had accepted an assignment of note's security in full satisfaction of the loan, loan extinguished and § 1823(e) did not apply as there was no asset for successor to acquire, notwithstanding that bank had not marked the credit in its files). *See also* Salgado v. FDIC, 2004 WL 2584689, at *3 (E.D. Pa. Nov. 15, 2004) (unpublished) (in FCRA suit against FDIC that alleged that FDIC's predecessor wrongfully reported a missed mortgage payment after orally agreeing to allow plaintiffs to skip it, oral agreement not subject to section 1823(e) because it did not relate to any interest in an asset given that the original mortgage had been fully paid and discharged); Breaux Bridge Bank & Trust Co. v. Simon, 570 So. 2d 156, 158 (La. Ct. App. 1990) (where debtor sued by FDIC had discharged obligation by assigning promissory note executed by third party that exceeded the amount of the original obligation, the agreement augmented, rather than diminished, the interest of the FDIC and therefore § 1823(e) did not apply).

621 Grayson v. National Enters., Inc., 706 So. 2d 99 (Fla. 1998).

622 Kessler v. National Enters., Inc., 165 F.3d 596 (8th Cir. 1999).

623 The court explained: "Thus, like the mechanic's lien at issue in Bateman v. FDIC, 970 F.2d 924, 928 (1st Cir. 1992) plaintiffs' ownership interests 'are not the *kinds* of interests that the FDIC examiner need (or would) necessarily rely upon the bank's documents to reflect. Such interests are not those *of* the bank; they are not contained in documents filed *with* the bank. Nor are they otherwise difficult to find.' " *Id.* at 600.

624 FDIC v. Deglau, 207 F.3d 153 (3d Cir. 2000).

625 *Id.* at 174–75 (vacating trial court's denial of borrowers' Rule 60(b) motion).

626 484 U.S. 86, 93, 108 S. Ct. 396, 98 L. Ed. 2d 340 (1987).

627 Beal Bank, SSB v. Lucks, 791 A.2d 752 (Del. Ch. 2000) (unpublished) (deferring issue to trial).

628 *Id.* at 31. *But see* OCI Mortg. Corp. v. Marchese, 774 A.2d 940 (Conn. 2001) (stating that there is no catchall "equitable exception" to section 1823(e) in holding that defendants, who had made a debenture loan to a savings and loan association that subsequently failed, could not assert the defense of setoff against a mortgage taken out from that association and subsequently assigned, through the FDIC, to the plaintiff noteholder).

629 OCI Mortg. Corp. v. Marchese, 774 A.2d 940 (Conn. 2001), *rev'g* 745 A.2d 819 (Conn. App. 2000). The debenture agreement that documented the loan from the borrowers to the bank was not contemporaneous with the acquisition of the asset, that is, the original mortgage, and therefore failed to meet section 1823(e)(2).

630 Schramm v. Cadle Co., 2004 WL 2618356, at *3 (Cal. Ct. App. Nov. 18, 2004) (unpublished) (ruling that FDIC could not raise issue of section 1823(e) on appeal).

631 512 U.S. 79, 114 S. Ct. 2048, 129 L. Ed. 2d 67 (1994).

632 *See* § 10.7.2, *supra*.

D'Oench is no longer viable, then any claim or defense raised against the receiver that fails to meet the section 1823(e) criteria would be allowed to stand, regardless of *D'Oench*.

The *D'Oench* doctrine and the requirements of section 1823(e) are closely intertwined, and courts often construe section 1823(e) to be consistent with *D'Oench*.[633] Nonetheless, the two doctrines are not identical. For example, section 1823(e) applies only to "agreements" that impair "assets," while *D'Oench* applies to any "agreement."[634] In 1990, a district court emphasized this distinction in response to the growing scholarly concern regarding the misreading and misapplication of the doctrine.[635] The court observed that though courts often applied section 1823(e) and the *D'Oench* doctrine as if they were coextensive, they are not.[636]

> Section 1823(e) specifically applies to "agreements" between the borrower and the bank, and thus, in application of section 1823(e), the borrower's conduct is irrelevant. The *D'Oench, Duhme* doctrine, however, is a rule of equitable estoppel and applies to any defense that a borrower may assert in which the borrower participated in a scheme which tends to deceive bank examiners. . . . In this respect, the statute is both broader and narrower than *D'Oench, Duhme.* It is broader in that it applies to *any* agreement, whether or not it was secret and regardless of the maker's participation in a scheme; it is narrower in that it applies *only* to agreements, and not to other defenses the borrower might raise.[637]

Murphy v. FDIC[638] is an example of how the differences between *D'Oench* and section 1823(e) can benefit the borrower. There, a real estate developer sued the FDIC for breach of fiduciary duty, fraud and other torts. The court found that because the plaintiff was an investor in a failed venture in which the bank was a participant, the "no asset" exception to section 1823(e) was invoked. Since the court

also concluded that *D'Oench* had been preempted by FIRREA, the defenses were allowed to stand because they were not barred by section 1823(e).

10.7.5 Federal Holder-in-Due-Course Doctrine

As the cost of the 1980s bank crisis mounted, and litigation ballooned, the protective policies of *D'Oench* and section 1823 were pushed even further, with the creation of "super holder in due course" or "federal holder in due course"[639] status for FDIC and RTC. While some courts at least required the federal entity to establish that it met the basic definitional elements of a standard holder in due course,[640] others were not so exacting.[641] Here, too, the expansive reading triggered concern. Some courts and com-

---

633 *See, e.g.,* Langley v. FDIC, 484 U.S. 86, 108 S. Ct. 396, 98 L. Ed. 2d 340 (1987).

634 *See, e.g.,* Winterbrook Realty, Inc. v. FDIC, 820 F. Supp. 27, 29 (D.N.H. 1993). *See also* Brookside Assocs. v. Rifkin, 49 F.3d 490 (9th Cir. 1995) (although court decides claim barred by *D'Oench* doctrine, good discussion of no asset exception to § 1823(e)); Joslin v. Shareholder Servs. Group, 948 F. Supp. 627 (S.D. Tex. 1996) (no asset transferred to FDIC because stock transferred to bank in violation of express restriction). *But see* Cadle Co. v. Johnson, 714 So. 2d 183 (La. Ct. App. 1998) (where loan made to borrower to purchase capital stock of bank violated securities laws, it was voidable, but not void *ab initio,* therefore borrower could not assert no asset exception).

635 Tuxedo Beach Club Corp. v. City Fed. Sav. Bank, 749 F. Supp. 635 (D.N.J. 1990).

636 *Id.* at 642.

637 *Id.* at 642 (emphasis in original).

638 61 F.3d 34 (D.C. Cir. 1995). Pages 38–40 include an excellent analysis of the *O'Melveny* decision.

639 Holder in due course is defined in U.C.C. § 3-302(a)(2) as

> the holder of an instrument if . . .
> (2) the holder took the instrument (i) for value, (ii) in good faith, (iii) *without notice that the instrument is overdue or has been dishonored* . . . (iv) without notice that the instrument contains an unauthorized signature or has been altered; . . . (vi) *without notice that any party has a defense or claim in recoupment* . . . [Emphasis added].

640 *See, e.g.,* FDIC v. Payne, 973 F.2d 403 (5th Cir. 1992) (declining to give federal holder-in-due-course protections where instrument not negotiable); FSLIC v. Mackie, 962 F.2d 1144, 1151 (5th Cir. 1992) (federal holder-in-due-course doctrine does not apply to non-negotiable instruments); Beckley Capital Ltd. P'ship v. DiGeronimo, 942 F. Supp. 728 (D.N.H. 1996) (similar holding), *aff'd,* 184 F.3d 52 (1st Cir. 1999); *In re* Miraj & Sons, Inc., 192 B.R. 297 (Bankr. D. Mass. 1996) (variable rate notes are not negotiable so no holder in due course for assignee of FDIC), *amended by* 197 B.R. 737 (Bankr. D. Mass. 1996); Haines Pipeline Constr. v. Exline Gas Sys., 921 P.2d 955 (Okla. App. 1996) (FDIC not holder in due course of guaranty which is not negotiable instrument); NAB Asset Venture III, L.P. v. John O'Brien & Assocs., 1999 Tex. App. LEXIS 1302 at 14 (Feb. 23, 1999) (unpublished) ("The federal holder-in-due-course doctrine applies when the FDIC acquires a negotiable instrument; it does not convert a non-negotiable instrument into a negotiable one;" holding that line of credit note that does not establish a sum certain was not a negotiable instrument); Mundaca Inv. Corp. v. Espinoza, 1996 Tex. App. LEXIS 5158 (Nov. 20, 1996) (unpublished) (*D'Oench* does not bar real as opposed to personal defenses, allowing illegality defense to stand).

641 RTC v. Davies, 824 F. Supp. 1002 (S.D. Miss. 1993) (RTC can be holder in due course under federal common law even if not under state law); Joslin v. Friends of Wayne Babovich, 699 So. 2d 1107 (La. Ct. App. 1997) (court agreed that once the FDIC or RTC acquired the instrument, it was accorded the status of holder in due course vis-à-vis the borrower, irrespective of state law requirements); Rhode Island Depositors Economic Protection Corp. v. Ryan, 697 A.2d 1087 (R.I. 1997); Hudspeth v. Investor Collection Servs., L.P., 985 S.W.2d 477 (Tex. App. 1998) (assignee of note could assert federal holder-in-due-course status though note was past due when acquired).

mentators[642] have questioned whether the protective policy considerations underlying the *D'Oench* doctrine, designed to provide "some immunity" to the FDIC, are outweighed by policies underlying the Uniform Commercial Code (UCC), designed to provide unity and predictability in the regulation of commercial relationships.[643]

One of the early articulations of the federal holder doctrine was in a usury case. In *FDIC v. Wood*,[644] though a bank had charged 15% interest in gross (and obvious) violation of a state usury statute which imposed a 7% interest limit, the FDIC was allowed to recover the full amount of the guarantor's note.[645] The *Wood* court held that the FDIC was a holder in due course, for in order for the FDIC to accomplish its statutory objectives, "when the FDIC in its corporate capacity, *as part of a purchase and assumption transaction*, acquires a note in good faith, for value, and without actual knowledge of any defense against the note, it [must] take[] the note free of all defenses that would not prevail against a holder in due course."[646] Consequently, the FDIC, as a holder in due course, was free of the "personal defense" of usury,[647] despite the fact that the blatantly usurious note

existed in the bank files and should have put the FDIC on notice of the defense. According to *Wood*, the FDIC has no duty to examine the assets of a failed bank before executing a purchase and assumption transaction.[648]

Wood fails to deal with the negative impact that allowing the FDIC "super holder" status has on commercial transactions, as a dissenting opinion in a subsequent usury case following *Wood* observed:

> [F]ederal common law [does not have] to reject state law in the interest of what seems to me an unnecessarily bureaucratic national uniformity. The majority's federal common law rule rudely displaces state law and disrupts the ordinary expectations of consumers and business[persons] based on that law, and it does not further the FDIC's administration of any statutory program or policy. . . .
>
> . . . To allow such immunity for the FDIC seriously undermines the expectations of borrowers and the symmetry of the law. If there were some indication that such an immunity is needed in order to preserve the banking system, that would be a different question. The FDIC has neither made, nor attempted to make, such a showing.[649]

There are ample cases reading the federal holder status broadly, but there also is moderating precedent. Some courts have held that the federal holder-in-due-course defense does not apply if some of the UCC prerequisites for standard holder-in-due-course status are missing. For example, one must hold a "negotiable instrument" to be a holder in due course.[650] Consequently, if the subject of the borrower's claim is a non-negotiable instrument, as variable-rate notes may be in some jurisdictions, or a retail installment sales contract, federal holder status may be denied as well.[651]

A Louisiana state court recently reasoned that federal holder-in-due-course status derives from *D'Oench*, and that accordingly, where *D'Oench* did not apply because the notemaker was not asserting defenses based on a secret agreement, the noteholder's holder-in-due-course status would be determined under state law.[652] A federal district court also held that the RTC was not entitled to summary

---

642   For example, *see* Gray, *Limitations on the FDIC's D'Oench Doctrine of Federal Common-Law Estoppel: Congressional Preemption and Authoritative Statutory Construction*, 31 S. Tex. L. Rev. 245 (1990).

643   The *D'Oench* doctrine should not take precedence over U.C.C. § 3-302(c)(ii), which states the holder-in-due-course rule is not available when an instrument is purchased as part of a bulk transaction not in the ordinary course of business of the transferor. *See also* Calaska Partners, Ltd. v. Corson, 672 A.2d 1099, 1102 (Me. 1996) (applying state's version of U.C.C. § 3-302 to find that assignee not a holder in due course where note acquired in bulk transaction).

644   758 F.2d 156 (6th Cir.), *cert. denied*, 474 U.S. 944 (1985).

645   The violation would otherwise have barred a lender or assignee from collecting. The scenario in *Wood* did not arise from a "scheme" under the *D'Oench* holding nor an "agreement" as defined by § 1823(e).

646   *Wood*, 758 F.2d at 161 (emphasis added). The holding in *Wood*, in effect, created a "superholder" status for the FDIC. The *Wood* court acknowledged: "Under state law, the FDIC cannot be a holder in due course, if it had notice that the note was overdue." *Id.* at 158. However, "[w]e believe that, if state law mandates that the corporate FDIC cannot be a holder in due course, then application of state law would frustrate important objectives of the federal program." *Id.* at 159. In short, the *Wood* court did not believe that treating the FDIC as a holder in due course would in any way "disrupt commercial relationships predicated on state law." *Id.* at 161. *Accord* Campbell Leasing Inc. v. FDIC, 901 F.2d 1244 (5th Cir. 1990). *See also* First South Savings Ass'n v. First Southern Partners, II, Ltd., 957 F.2d 174 (5th Cir. 1992) (usury claims not available against RTC; however, the alleged usury was not on face of documents, but in subsequent demands). This "superholder" status only applies when the FDIC is acting in its corporate capacity, not in its capacity as a receiver. First City, Texas-Beaumont v. Treece, 848 F. Supp. 727 (E.D. Tex. 1994).

647   While constitutional issues were not reached, the U.S. Supreme Court has acknowledged that usury and breach of fiduciary duty claims involve "private rights" at the "core" of Article III

courts. Coit Indep. Joint Venture v. FSLIC, 489 U.S. 561, 109 S. Ct. 1361, 103 L. Ed. 2d 602 (1989).

648   *Wood*, 758 F.2d at 162; FDIC v. Gilbert, 9 F.3d 393 (5th Cir. 1993) (filing of lawsuit does not constitute notice for purposes of FDIC holder-in-due-course defense). *See also* RTC v. Davies, 824 F. Supp. 1002 (S.D. Miss. 1993) (RTC can be a holder-in-due-course under federal common law even if not under state law).

649   FDIC v. Leach, 772 F.2d 1262, 1270 (6th Cir. 1985) (Judge Merritt, dissenting).

650   *See* §§ 10.6.1.3.1–10.6.1.3.4, *supra*.

651   *See* §§ 10.6.1.3.2–10.6.1.3.9, *supra*.

652   Johnson v. Drury, 763 So. 2d 103 (La. Ct. App. 2000) (affirming summary judgment in favor of noteholder on state law grounds).

judgment on a note which its predecessor bank had bought after maturity, reasoning that the government could not change "lead into gold."[653] To hold otherwise would only encourage the transferring of troubled loans to near insolvent banks for "new life."[654] Although the opinion is somewhat unclear, the defenses were allowed to stand, thereby suggesting that the RTC could not assert the *D'Oench* doctrine either. A Wyoming district court applied the same reasoning more persuasively.[655] Noting that the debtor's rights take precedence over the FDIC's, a refreshing point of view, the court held that *D'Oench* did not bar a defense attacking the existence of a debt for deficiency after foreclosure based on the bank's failure to properly notify the debtor under Wyoming's version of Article 9 of the UCC. Since the bank had no right to a deficiency judgment it could not transfer such a right to the FDIC.

Another retrenchment is reflected in *In re 604 Columbus Ave. Realty Trust*,[656] which limited the availability of defenses to the FDIC in its capacity as receiver seeking to enforce obligations against a bankrupt borrower, as opposed to its corporate capacity.[657] While a kickback agreement between the borrower and bank officials was found to be a "secret agreement" clearly subject to *D'Oench*, the borrower's tort claims of conversion and fraud stood on a factual basis independent of the kickback arrangement and were not barred by *D'Oench*. Though an expansive holder doctrine might promote "purchase and assumption transactions that preserve the going concern value of the bank," no such policy considerations so warrant when the FDIC is simply trying to collect in its capacity as receiver.[658] "The federal

holder-in-due-course doctrine was fashioned precisely for the purpose of expediting the purchase and assumption transaction . . . *It was never intended to relieve the FDIC of all the 'difficulties' arising from state law defenses and counterclaims during the liquidation of assets.*"[659]

Commentators have posited that providing "super holder" status to the FDIC unfairly distributes the cost of bank failures to note makers when the FDIC is completely immunized from otherwise valid state defenses: "By allowing makers of notes to assert valid state law defenses against the FDIC, the entire banking system would be forced to bear the risk of improper conduct by the failed bank."[660] Further, it has always been sound commercial philosophy that uniformity in market dealings is what promotes stability and confidence in the commercial world.[661]

One could also argue that enforcement of state law, and subjecting the FDIC to accountability for the misconduct of its predecessor, would promote the very market discipline needed to insure stability and integrity in the banking system as a whole, thus promoting FDIC and general federal objectives.[662] One might wonder how the public can be ex-

---

653 St. Bernard Sav. & Loan Ass'n v. Cella, 826 F. Supp. 985, 987 (E.D. La. 1993). *See also* Sunbelt Savings, F.S.B. Dallas, Texas v. Montross, 923 F.2d 353 (5th Cir. 1991); *reh'g granted*, 932 F.2d 363, *reinstated, in part, and remanded*, 944 F.2d 227 (5th Cir. 1991) (en banc); *In re* Miraj & Sons, Inc., 192 B.R. 297 (Bankr. D. Mass. 1996) (no holder in due course when assignee purchased notes from FDIC knowing they were overdue), *amended by* 197 B.R. 737 (Bankr. D. Mass. 1996); Rhode Island Depositors Economic Protection Corp. v. Ryan, 697 A.2d 1087 (R.I. 1997) (court noted that protection enjoyed by federal holder in due course was not absolute; most effective way to pierce protections would be for the party asserting the defense to establish that FDIC possessed actual knowledge of the defense before taking the note).

654 St. Bernard Sav. & Loan Ass'n v. Cella, 826 F. Supp. 985, 987 (E.D. La. 1993).

655 S&S Diversified Serves., L.L.C. v. Baldamar Arguello, 911 F. Supp. 498 (D. Wyo. 1995). *But see* Burns v. RTC, 880 S.W.2d 149 (Tex. 1994) (federal holder-in-due-course doctrine bars borrower's defenses to deficiency judgment based on breach of contract and lack of notice of acceleration).

656 968 F.2d 1332 (1st Cir. 1992). *See also* FDIC v. Craft, 157 F.3d 697 (9th Cir. 1998) (neither *D'Oench* nor § 1823(e) apply where FDIC acting solely as a receiver); *In re* Miraj & Sons, Inc., 192 B.R. 297 (Bankr. D. Mass. 1996) (FDIC not holder in due course when acting as receiver), *amended by* 197 B.R. 737 (Bankr. D. Mass. 1996).

657 *See* note 561, *supra*.

658 *In re* 604 Columbus Ave. Realty Trust, 968 F.2d 1332, 1352 (1st

Cir. 1992). Note that this holding applies only when the FDIC sues solely in its capacity as receiver on a loan which has never been transferred or been part of a purchase and assumption transaction. The court expressly states that the FDIC "enjoys holder-in-due-course status as a matter of federal common law whether it is acting in its corporate or receivership capacity (so long as a transfer or purchase of the asset has occurred)." *Id.*

659 *Id.* at 1353 (emphasis added). *Cf.* FDIC v. McFarland, 243 F.3d 876 (5th Cir. 2001) (FIRREA provision that prohibited state and local taxing authorities from foreclosing on property subject to an FDIC lien without its consent did not preempt Louisiana's mortgage reinscription requirement, therefore FDIC's lien lost ranking; state law did not significantly conflict with federal policy of speeding recovery of the assets of failed financial institutions).

660 Miller & Meacham, *The FDIC And Other Financial Institution Insurance Agencies As "SUPER" Holders in Due Course: A Lesson in Self-Pollinated Jurisprudence*, 40 Okla. L. Rev. 621, 636 (1987).

661 Miller v. Race, 1 Burr. 452, 97 Eng. Rep. 398 (K.B. 1758).

The Fifth Circuit reversed a lower court's decision to grant the FDIC's motion for summary judgment in a suit that involved eight claims against a failed bank including a deceptive trade practices claim. The court stated:

> *D'Oench, Duhme* does not of itself thwart the assertion of rights for relief from wrongful acceleration and unreasonable sale at foreclosure. (Citation omitted.) ("[N]either section 1823(e) nor the *D'Oench, Duhme* doctrine prevents plaintiffs from asserting claims or defenses that *do not depend on agreements.*" (emphasis supplied).) We repeat, *D'Oench, Duhme* only protects the FDIC and federally-created bridge banks from oral agreements that for some reason do not become part of the loan record (usually, oral agreements).

Texas Refrigeration Supply, Inc. v. FDIC, 953 F.2d 975, 981 (5th Cir. 1992).

662 *See also* United States v. Kimbell Foods, Inc., 440 U.S. 715, 99

pected to trust a national banking system which deprives them of legal rights and defenses, obligating them to pay for a transaction from which they have also been deprived of any benefit.

Policy arguments aside, the most compelling argument to strike federal holder-in-due-course status is that it is just the sort of federal common law that the Supreme Court intended to erase with *O'Melveny & Myers v. FDIC*,[663] discussed in detail in § 10.7.2, *supra*. Nearly every court to address the issue has held that federal holder-in-due-course status no longer exists and that federal agencies and their assignees must abide by the same state negotiable instrument laws that bind other noteholders.[664]

10.7.6 Who Can Claim Protection Under *D'Oench* and Related Doctrines

10.7.6.1 Subsidiaries, Institutions That Are Not Federally Insured

At least one court has held that *D'Oench* does not apply to subsidiaries of insured institutions.[665] But other courts have disagreed.[666] Recently a federal district court held that *D'Oench* did not apply to a borrower's breach of contract claim that alleged that a financial institution that was not a federally regulated banking institution failed to advance funds pursuant to an oral promise. Since the institution was not part of the federally regulated system, but was only in the equity receivership of the SEC, the court declared that

---

S. Ct. 1448, 59 L. Ed. 2d 711 (1979), regarding whether applying federal law would disrupt commercial relationships predicated on state laws.

663 512 U.S. 79, 114 S. Ct. 2048, 129 L. Ed. 2d 67 (1994).

664 FDIC v. Houde, 90 F.3d 600, 604 (1st Cir. 1996) (following *O'Melveny*, holder-in-due-course status of FDIC determined by state law); DiVall Insured Income v. Boatmen's First Nat'l Bank, 69 F.3d 1398, 1402–03 (8th Cir. 1995) (following *O'Melveny*, holder-in-due-course status of FDIC determined by state law); RTC v. Maplewood Invs., 31 F.3d 1276, 1293 (4th Cir. 1994) (RTC could not rely on federal holder-in-due-course doctrine to convert note that was not negotiable under state law into a negotiable instrument); RTC v. A.W. Assocs., 869 F. Supp. 1503, 1510 (D. Kan. 1994) (state law governs holder-in-due-course status); Calaska Partners, Ltd. v. Corson, 672 A.2d 1099, 1103 (Me. 1996); Bisson v. Eck, 720 N.E.2d 784, 789 (Mass. 1999); Sun NLF Ltd. P'ship v. Sasso, 313 N.J. Super. 546, 713 A.2d 538, 544 (1998) (rejecting federal holder-in-due-course doctrine); Cadle Co. v. Patoine, 772 A.2d 544, 547 (Vt. 2001). *But see* Rhode Island Depositors Econ. Protection v. Ryan, 697 A.2d 1087, 1093 (R.I. 1997) (applying federal holder-in-due-course doctrine). *See also* discussion at § 10.7.8, *infra*.

665 Lesal Interiors, Inc. v. Echotree Assocs., L.P., 47 F.3d 607 (3d Cir. 1995).

666 *See* Robinowitz v. Gibraltar Savings, 23 F.3d 951 (5th Cir. 1994), *cert. denied*, 513 U.S. 1078 (1995) and cases cited therein.

"it would be fundamentally unfair to apply the *D'Oench, Duhme* doctrine to [the borrower] given that it had no expectation or forewarning that it could be penalized for not adhering to the strictures of the doctrine."[667]

10.7.6.2 Assignees

In general, courts have allowed *D'Oench* and related defenses to be asserted by institutions who purchase the assets of failed banks or thrifts from the FDIC or like federal agency, then seek to enforce an obligation against a borrower.[668] The grounds for expanding *D'Oench*'s power to immunize the FDIC and similar agencies from borrowers' defenses have far less force, however, when applied to subsequent assignees of the debt, for once the obligation has transferred into private commerce it no longer burdens or benefits the federal government. After assignment, the interests in the balance are no longer between a reluctant FDIC seeking to stem losses from a failed bank and a borrower who had the misfortune to borrow from such a bank, but between that borrower and a private entity that voluntarily

---

667 SEC v. Capital Consultants, L.L.C., 2002 U.S. Dist. LEXIS 670, at *11 (D. Or. Jan. 3, 2002) (unpublished).

668 *See, e.g.*, UMLIC-Nine Corp. v. Lipan Springs Dev. Corp., 168 F.3d 1173 (10th Cir. 1999) (*D'Oench* applies to actions brought by FDIC's assignees as well as by FDIC itself), *cert. denied*, 528 U.S. 1005 (1999); FDIC v. Newhart, 892 F.2d 47 (8th Cir. 1989); Ranger Portfolio v. Greene, 1998 U.S. Dist. LEXIS 10347 (D. Mass. May 8, 1998) (unpublished) (*D'Oench* runs to successors of FDIC, otherwise FDIC's ability to market assets would be severely diminished); AAI Recoveries, Inc. v. Pijuan, 13 F. Supp. 2d 448 (S.D.N.Y. June 23, 1998) (successor in interest to FDIC could assert *D'Oench* to defeat defense of lack of consideration); RTC Mortg. Trust 1994-S2 v. Shlens, 72 Cal. Rptr. 2d 581 (Cal. Ct. App. 1998); Jackson v. Thewatt, 883 S.W.2d 171 (Tex. 1994) (FIRREA applies to assignees); Alma Group, L.L.C. v. Palmer, 143 S.W.3d 840, 845 (Tex. App. 2004) (assignees of the FDIC benefit from both *D'Oench* and federal holder-in-due-course doctrine, upholding assignment of note by FDIC's assignee); Bosque Asset Corp. v. Greenberg, 19 S.W.3d 514 (Tex. App. 2000) (FIRREA's protections extend not just to first assignee of FDIC but to subsequent assignees as well, therefore subsequent assignee could claim benefit of FIRREA's six year limitations period); Pierson v. SMS Fin., II, 959 S.W.2d 343, 349 (Tex. App. 1998) (*D'Oench*'s protections extend to assignee). *See also* 5636 Alpha Road v. NCNB Texas Nat'l Bank, 879 F. Supp. 655 (N.D. Tex. 1995) (discussing status of bridge bank under pre-FIRREA version of § 1823(e), *D'Oench*); United Mortg. Servicing, L.L.C. v. Long, 2004 WL 1926329, at *6 (Mass. Super. Ct. June 26, 2004) (unpublished) (holding that *D'Oench* did not create a defense for borrowers that would prevent the FDIC's assignee from action in equity to correct problems arising from inadvertent failure to record a deed). *But see* New Maine Nat'l Bank v. Gendron, 780 F. Supp. 52 (D. Me. 1991) (without explanation, rejecting argument of bridge bank carrying out receivership of FDIC that *D'Oench* precluded rescission liability under the Truth-in-Lending Act; note that 15 U.S.C. § 1641 specifically provides by statute for assignee liability for TIL rescission, which may have been the basis for the ruling.).

chose to purchase the obligation—often at a substantial discount. Arguably one who purchases commercial paper from a federal agency should not suffer any less risk than any other ordinary assignee of commercial paper. Nonetheless, many courts have expanded *D'Oench* to protect such assignees, not based on the holding of *D'Oench* itself, but rather to further the "marketability" of the failed bank's obligations. Such courts reason that if the FDIC can sell, along with the note, the shields of *D'Oench* and FIRREA, the obligations will be that much more attractive to potential purchasers and thereby ultimately recoup more of the losses suffered by the federal government in taking over the failed institution. Nonetheless, some judges might be mindful to the relative difference in positions between the FDIC and subsequent assignees; one court that recently declined to apply *D'Oench* to bar a defendant from asserting his previous release cited the lower court's remark that the plaintiff had "gambled when he bought discounted paper and lost his bet."[669]

10.7.6.3 Whether Assignees Benefit from FIRREA's Limitations Period

In addition to seeking the benefits of *D'Oench*, assignees seeking to enforce instruments they have acquired from the FDIC often assert the benefit of the six year limitations period that FIRREA grants to the FDIC (but not specifically to any other entity) to bring suit on debts.[670] Prior to *O'Melveny*, most courts simply extended FIRREA to the assignees by reasoning that under federal common law, assignees stepped into the shoes of their assignors.[671] Only one court ruled that the limitations period of FIRREA was personal to the RTC/FDIC, and could not be taken advan-

tage of by assignees.[672] Following *O'Melveny* and its language disapproving of federal common law, most courts have analyzed the issue not by applying the federal limitations period directly to the assignee, but by referring to the rights granted by the relevant state to an assignee: if state law generally allows assignees to step into the shoes of the assignor, then the courts will extend that right to allow them to adopt the federal limitations period,[673] which usually exceeds what would be available for a similar action under state law.

However, occasionally reference to state law can bring quite a different result than would rote application of FIRREA's period. For example, the First Circuit held in a suit against a dead guarantor that where the obligation was in default before the FDIC received it, the FDIC's assignee could not claim the benefit of the six year period, but was limited to the one year state limitations period that governed suits brought against estates.[674] Responding to the marketability argument that had persuaded other courts to extend *D'Oench* to protect note purchasers, the court said that

---

669 *Joslin v. Bengal Chef, Inc.*, 715 So. 2d 1266, 1268 (La. Ct. App. 1998). *See also See National Enters., Inc. v. First Western Fin. Corp.*, 1998 U.S. App. LEXIS 31075 (10th Cir. Dec. 10 1998) (unpublished) (assignee's suit barred by defendant's earlier settlement agreement with RTC which extinguished defendant's note along with any possible related *D'Oench* claims); *Eastern Savings Bank, F.S.B. v. Ruffolo*, 1996 Conn. Super. LEXIS 2269 (Aug. 28, 1996) (unpublished) (assignee who does not mention the RTC in its complaint not entitled to protection of *D'Oench*). *See also State St. Capital Corp. v. Rios*, 1996 Tex. App. LEXIS 2241 (Tex. App. June 6, 1996) (unpublished) (*D'Oench* and federal holder in due course are affirmative defense to rescission which are waived if not raised).

670 12 U.S.C. § 1821(d)(14) (the FDIC may take advantage of a longer state provision).

671 *See, e.g., FDIC v. Bledsoe*, 989 F.2d 805 (5th Cir. 1993); *Mountain States Fin. Resources Corp. v. Agrawal*, 777 F. Supp. 1550 (W.D. Okla. 1991); *White v. Moriarty*, 19 Cal. Rptr. 2d 200 (App. 1993); *Tivoli Ventures, Inc. v. Baumann*, 870 P.2d 1244 (Colo. 1994); *The Cadle Co. II, Inc. v. Lewis*, 864 P.2d 718 (Kan. 1993), *cert. denied*, 511 U.S. 1053 (1994); *Central States Resources v. First Nat'l Bank*, 501 N.W.2d 271 (Neb. 1993); *Thweatt v. Jackson*, 838 S.W.2d 725 (Tex. App. 1992), *aff'd* 883 S.W.2d 171 (Tex. 1994).

672 *WAMCO, III v. First Piedmont Mortg. Corp.*, 856 F. Supp. 1076 (E.D. Va. 1994).

673 *See, e.g., National Enters. v. Barnes*, 201 F.3d 331 (4th Cir. 2000) (assignee gets benefit of FIRREA's six year limitations period where under state law assignees of contracts step into the shoes of the assignor); *UMLIC-Nine Corp. v. Lipan Springs Dev. Corp.*, 168 F.3d 1173 (10th Cir. 1999) (holding that the limitations period "reset" when the RTC took over as receiver after the note had previously been held by the FDIC as receiver for a different bank); *Federal Fin. Co. v. Noe*, 983 S.W.2d 107 (Ark. 1998) (assignee could claim FIRREA's six year limitations period); *National Loan Investors Ltd. P'ship v. Heritage Square Assocs.*, 733 A.2d 876 (Conn. Ct. App. 1999) (assignee could assert FIRREA's six year limitations period because under Conn. U.C.C. law assignee steps into shoes of assignee; rejects assertion that S/L is personal); *Franklin Credit Mgt. Corp. v. Nicholas*, 1999 Conn. Super. LEXIS 1123 (Apr. 26, 1999) (unpublished) (same); *Global Fin. Servs. v. Duttenhefner*, 575 N.W.2d 667 (N.D. 1998) (following *O'Melveny*, one looks to state law to determine the limitations period, under North Dakota state law the assignee steps into the shoes of the assignee and thus the date of accrual along with the six year period of FIRREA applied to RTC's assignee's suit against the defendant on an automobile deficiency); *Twelfth RMA Partners v. National Safe Corp.*, 518 S.E.2d 44 (S.C. Ct. App. 1999). *See also Joslin v. Grossman*, 107 F. Supp. 2d 150 (D. Conn. 2000) (FDIC's assignee stepped into shoes of assignor for purposes of FIRREA's limitations period governing fraudulent transfers); *UMLIC 2 Funding Corp. v. Butcher*, 970 S.W.2d 211 (Ark. 1998), *cert. denied*, 528 U.S. 1005 (1999) (six-year limitations period applies, seems to rely in part on somewhat outdated federal holder-in-due-course status); *Brae Asset Fund v. Petkauskos*, 1997 Mass. Super. LEXIS 182 (Aug. 7, 1997) (unpublished) (applying FIRREA's limitations period without acknowledging state law rule for assignees). *But see Bosque Asset Corp. v. Greenberg*, 19 S.W.3d 514 (Tex. App. 2000) (holding that FIRREA's six year limitations period extended directly to the benefit of a subsequent assignee of the FDIC, without reference to state law).

674 *Beckley Capital L.P. v. DiGeronimo*, 184 F.3d 52 (1st Cir. 1999).

"[t]his will require private purchasers of FDIC notes to be as diligent as other local plaintiffs, but it is a reasonable enough requirement that should not have any significant impact on the marketability of FDIC assets."[675] In another sign that FIRREA's provisions will not be applied blindly for the benefit of assignees, two circuit courts have held that its statutory grant of jurisdiction to sue in federal court does not transfer to the assignee of an FDIC-owned note.[676]

10.7.7 Effect of the Consumer Limitations on the FTC Holder Rule

As is discussed in § 10.6.1.2, *supra*, there are two federal limitations on standard holder-in-due-course doctrine. In addition to arguments set out above, consumer lawyers also should argue that the *D'Oench* and related doctrines do not prevent these limitations from applying to federal receivers and their assignees.[677] Most, if not all, cases applying the *D'Oench* doctrines have involved sophisticated borrowers who are developers, investors, or higher level dealmakers. But Congress and the federal courts have traditionally created numerous rules to protect the ordinary, or less sophisticated, consumer of credit from the vagaries of marketplace (i.e., sellers' and creditors') misconduct.[678] Application of the *D'Oench* and related doctrines to ordinary consumer transactions would be an unjustified invasion into well-established consumer protection laws.

The *D'Oench* doctrine, as it has been extended by the federal courts of the 1980s, would conflict with the FTC

Holder Rule.[679] The FTC Holder Rule specifically ties a buyer's duty to pay to a seller's duty to perform, by compelling assignee-creditors (rather than consumer-buyers) to absorb the cost of seller misconduct. By contrast, the blanket immunity of *D'Oench* would permit situations where consumers were helplessly forced to continue to pay for goods and services from which they did not benefit, exactly the scenario Congress has repeatedly tried to prevent.

Beyond policy arguments, the present body of *D'Oench*-related law offers sound arguments as to why the FTC Holder Rule should preserve consumer claims and defenses against the FDIC. Because the rule works by requiring that it be included in the note, effectively making it a written contractual provision, it should be considered a "bilateral agreement," imposing duties on the bank. *D'Oench* does not protect the FDIC or RTC from breach of contract claims arising from written agreements.[680] One court apparently permitted recovery in a home improvement case against the RTC based on the FTC notice, and further ruled that the borrower was entitled to a recovery of payments made even

---

675 *Id.* at 58.

676 National Enters., Inc. v. Smith, 114 F.3d 561 (6th Cir. 1997) (ordering dismissal for lack of subject matter jurisdiction); New Rock Asset Partners, L.P. v. Preferred Entity Advancements, Inc., 101 F.3d 1492 (3d Cir. 1996). *See also* RTC Commercial Loan Trust 1995-NP1A v. Winthrop Mgt., 923 F. Supp. 83 (E.D. Va. 1996) (RTC cannot assign its status as federal party or right to sue in federal court); S1 IL304 L.L.C. v. ANB Cust. For LG, Cook Cty. *ex rel.* Hynes, 950 F. Supp. 242 (N.D. Ill. 1996) (same); Brae Asset Fund, L.P. v. Dion, 929 F. Supp. 29 (D. Mass. 1996) (assignee does not have FDIC's special right to remove).

677 See § 10.6.1.2.2, *supra* for a description of the FTC Holder Rule, and how it operates. *See also* National Consumer Law Center, Unfair and Deceptive Acts and Practices § 6.6 (6th ed. 2004 and Supp.). It should be noted here that the FTC Holder Rule does not create claims or defenses for consumers, but simply preserves consumers' contractual rights. See § 10.6.1.2.3, *supra* for a discussion of the limitation contained in the recent high-cost mortgage legislation.

678 *See, e.g.*, Federal Trade Commission Act, 15 U.S.C. § 45(a) (upon which state unfair and deceptive practices acts are based); National Consumer Law Center, Unfair and Deceptive Acts and Practices §§ 4.2.11, 4.3.7, 4.3.8 (6th ed. 2004 and Supp.); Truth in Lending, 15 U.S.C. § 1601 et seq.; *In re* Steinbrecher, 110 B.R. 155 (Bankr. E.D. Pa. 1990) (in enacting TIL, Congress intended to aid unsophisticated consumers and to protect borrowers who are not on an equal footing with creditors).

679 16 C.F.R. § 433. As described in § 10.6.1.2.2, *supra*, the FTC Holder Rule applies to sales-related consumer credit contracts, and declares that it is an "unfair or deceptive act or practice" under the Federal Trade Commission Act for a seller to enter a credit agreement without a contractual notice stating that the holder of the consumer credit contract is subject to all claims and defenses which the debtor could assert against the seller of goods or services obtained pursuant hereto or with the proceeds hereof.

680 *See* text accompanying note 618, *infra*. *See also* Allied Elevator v. East Texas State Bank, 965 F.2d 34 (5th Cir. 1992) (*D'Oench* inapplicable to breach of contract claim for bank's failure to procure credit life insurance requested in writing on the note); FDIC v. Parkway Exec. Office Ctr., 1997 U.S. Dist. LEXIS 12318 at 33–34 (E.D. Pa. Aug. 18, 1997) (unpublished) ("[t]he financial instruments in question imposed obligations on both parties. Atlantic was obligated under the Promissory Note to disburse funds to Defendants. Defendants had a concomitant obligation to make payments of interest and principal to repay those disbursements. Accordingly, § 1823(e)(1) does not apply"); Diversified Fin. Sys., Inc. v. Miner, 713 N.E.2d 293 (Ind. Ct. App. 1999) (where loan agreement referenced "floor plan agreement," a bilateral agreement, *D'Oench* did not bar borrowers' counterclaim that FDIC and assignee caused borrowers' business to fail by not complying with the agreement); Leavings v. Mills, 2004 WL 1902536, at *7, n.9 (Tex. App. Aug. 26, 2004) (unpublished) (FDIC and RTC take notes free only of terms or agreements that are not apparent from the face of the instrument, so Holder Notice preserved claims even if current holder acquired note from one of those agencies). *But see* OCI Mortg. Corp. v. Marchese, 774 A.2d 940 (Conn. 2001) (unwritten understanding that bank would apply payments due under debenture agreement representing loan from mortgagors to bank against payments due under the mortgage was not bilateral with mortgage agreement executed sixteen months previous); Carson Props., Inc. v. NAB Asset Venture, III, L.P., 1998 Tex. App. LEXIS 1619 (Mar. 17, 1998) (unpublished) (simple note did not represent bilateral agreement imposing duty on lender to fund note, where note recited simultaneous funding, even where borrowers alleged that lender never funded note).

though the RTC and its co-defendant did not receive the payments.[681]

The new high-cost mortgage limitation on the FTC Holder Rule should be similarly interpreted.[682] The policy arguments are precisely the same as with the FTC Holder Rule, as the purpose of the congressional limitation of the holder doctrine was to shift the risk to the institutional purchasers, and, in the process, encourage self-policing by the industry.[683] Also, to some extent, the arguments concerning the way the FTC Holder Rule operates may also be appropriate in these cases. The statute requires that mortgages carry a notice saying that assignees are liable.[684] Arguably that notice would suffice as a written agreement sufficient to withstand a *D'Oench* attack.

10.7.8 A Sampling of Claims and Defenses Making Inroads

As the bank crisis of the 1980s faded into the past, some courts expressed increasing concern about past misapplications of the *D'Oench* doctrine. Courts have likewise focused to a greater extent on the policy reasons against granting overly broad and extensive immunity to the FDIC, which occurs at the expense of innocent borrowers and unsophisticated consumers. Consequently, some common consumer claims have survived, or seem likely to survive, *D'Oench* and related defenses.

In *Tuxedo Beach Club Corp. v. City Federal Sav. Bank*,[685] a U.S. District Court decided an action brought by developers against a failed bank in the receivership of the Resolution Trust Corporation. The action rested on a number of theories, including breach of contract, tort and violation of the state Consumer Fraud Act.[686] The developers maintained that they began construction of a condominium project in reliance on the bank's written and oral promises to continue the funding. When the funding ceased, the half-built project was vulnerable to weather damage.

The RTC moved to dismiss, asserting that the claims were barred by both *D'Oench* and section 1823(e), as the oral understandings were not reduced to writing and "continuously available in the bank records for scrutiny," and hence

unenforceable.[687] The borrowers responded that *D'Oench* and section 1823(e) do not automatically bar every verbal contract with a failed bank; to so hold would defeat Congress's "expressed intention to continue to honor commitments made by the bank to creditworthy small businesses without interruption or termination."[688] The *Tuxedo Beach* court decided that the borrowers should be able to continue the discovery process to "integrate" all of the documents that were created throughout the relationship with the bank to connect to a fully enforceable agreement under section 1823(e).[689]

Further, the court held that the *D'Oench* doctrine was not an automatic bar to a state consumer fraud statutory violation:

> [I]t would in fact be *contrary* to Congressional intent to provide such banks with sweeping immunity from claims arising out of fraudulent practices. Notably, other states have applied their consumer fraud statutes against banks and savings institutions, and federal courts have considered similar state law claims in the face of the federal regulatory scheme.[690]

---

681 RTC v. Cook, 840 S.W.2d 42 (Tex. App. 1992).

682 15 U.S.C. § 1641(d).

683 *See* § 10.6.1.2.3, *supra*.

684 Home Ownership and Equity Protection Act, Subtitle B of Title I, Riegle Community Development and Regulatory Improvement Act of 1994, (H.R. 3474) Pub. L. No. 103-325, § 153(d)(4), 108 Stat. 2160 (Sept. 23, 1994) (codified at 15 U.S.C. § 1641(d)(4)).

685 749 F. Supp. 635 (D.N.J. 1990).

686 The complaint by the developers against the bank actually included ten theories: breach of fiduciary duty, constructive fraud, breach of duty to act fairly and in good faith, negligent misrepresentation, prima facie tort, tortious interference with prospective economic advantage, intentional misrepresentation, breach of contract, promissory estoppel, and consumer fraud.

687 *Tuxedo Beach*, 749 F. Supp. at 640.

688 *Id.* at 640 (citing to 12 U.S.C. § 1821 (n)(e)(B)).

689 The burden on a borrower piecing together the history of understandings in the course of a relationship with a bank is a great one. To enforce an agreement to fully fund a loan, numerous requirements under § 1823(e) must be satisfied. FDIC v. Texarkana Nat'l Bank, 874 F.2d 264 (5th Cir. 1989), *substituted op., in part,* 1989 U.S. App. LEXIS 11418 (July 19, 1989) (unpublished) (no setoff against claim by FDIC because written requirement not met), *cert. denied,* 493 U.S. 1043 (1990); FDIC v. La Rambla Shopping Ctr., Inc., 791 F.2d 215 (1st Cir. 1986) (lease executed prior to note not a defense because not contemporaneously executed); FDIC v. Amberson, 676 F. Supp. 777 (W.D. Tex. 1987) (requirement that agreement be continuously reflected in bank's records not met); FDIC v. Gardner, 606 F. Supp. 1484 (S.D. Miss. 1985) (board approval requirement not met). *See also* Varel v. BancOne Capital Partners, Inc., 55 F.3d 1016 (5th Cir. 1995) (*D'Oench* does not bar introduction of parol evidence to explain ambiguous contract term); *In re* Angel Fire Ski Corp., 176 B.R. 570 (Bankr. D.N.M. 1995) (court can look at all documents to construe the agreement and where documents clearly contradictory *D'Oench* does not apply because banking authorities will not be misled). *See also* the following cases construing the contemporaneous requirement broadly: RTC v. Midwest Federal Savings Bank of Minot, 36 F.3d 785 (9th Cir. 1993) (two month gap); Remington Invs., Inc. v. Aidekman, 1996 U.S. Dist. LEXIS 10453 (S.D.N.Y. July 25, 1996) (unpublished) (two and a half month gap); *In re* Miraj & Sons, Inc., 192 B.R. 297 (Bankr. D. Mass. 1996) (twelve day gap), *amended by* 197 B.R. 737 (Bankr. D. Mass. 1996); Sun NLF L.P. v. Sasso, 713 A.2d 538 (N.J. Super. 1998) (three month gap).

690 *Tuxedo Beach*, 749 F. Supp. at 649 (emphasis in original; footnote omitted). *See also* Flanagan v. Germania, 872 F.2d 231 (8th Cir. 1989) (state law will recognize tort claim by buyer against federal bank which is seller's creditor); Morse v. Mutual Fed. S&L Ass'n, 536 F. Supp. 1271 (D. Mass. 1982) (liability under UDAP statute can be imposed against bank which wrong-

In *In re 604 Columbus Ave. Realty Trust,*[691] the First Circuit also carved new limits on the reach of the FDIC's *D'Oench* protection when it declined to extend *D'Oench* to bar application of the bankruptcy law doctrine of equitable subordination.[692] The underlying question was whether it would be appropriate to impute the misconduct of bank officials of the defunct bank to the FDIC as federal receiver, or whether equitable subordination against a federal receiver should be prohibited as a matter of federal common law.[693] The court characterized the bank's conduct as "gross misconduct amounting to overreaching" and found it sufficiently egregious to justify equitable subordination.[694]

The *Columbus Realty* case upheld equitable subordination of the FDIC's secured claims only in an amount equal to the damages on the counts which were outside of the realm of *D'Oench*. In essence the court first did a *D'Oench* analysis and, only after determining that the doctrine did not apply to these claims, ruled that the FDIC could not invoke holder-in-due-course status to avoid equitable subordination. A more recent Massachusetts case extended *Columbus Realty*, holding that *D'Oench* simply does not apply to a claim seeking equitable subrogation based on alleged bad acts or inequitable conduct of bank officers.[695] The state court reasoned that since equitable subrogation is a doctrine which equitably adjusts the record title to property in the absence of any agreement between the parties, the *D'Oench* doctrine was inapplicable. In addition, the court implied that because the events justifying equitable subrogation all occurred prior to the FDIC's involvement, the FDIC never held an asset which had priority over the plaintiff's lien.

In *E.I. DuPont de Nemours & Co. v. FDIC,*[696] the D.C. Court of Appeals ruled that a borrower's argument that an escrow agreement had been extended through the conduct of the parties was not barred by *D'Oench* or section 1823(e). The plaintiff alleged that the FDIC had breached its fiduciary duty under the escrow agreement, which had expired by its terms but which the plaintiff alleged had been extended through conduct. First the court held that section 1823(e) did not govern the dispute because the bank never had an interest in the escrow funds, and therefore no asset of the bank was involved.[697] In rejecting the *D'Oench* argument, the court reasoned that the examination of an escrow agreement would not provide any information to a bank examiner deciding whether to liquidate or initiate a purchase and assumption. Analogizing the case to a free standing tort, the court concluded that "[t]hat the escrow agreement might have appeared to have expired could not possibly have caused the FDIC to act any differently in this case" and that the extension of the escrow agreement would not have been reflected in the ordinary banking records.[698] Thus, *D'Oench* also did not apply.

These and other cases suggest that, though the involvement of the FDIC or the RTC makes it much more difficult for a borrower, it is not necessarily an insurmountable hurdle. A summary list of claims which have survived challenge, or which might under some courts' analysis, would include:

---

fully froze account, refused to refinance and began foreclosure); Madsen v. Western Am. Mortg. Co., 694 P.2d 1228 (Ariz. Ct. App. 1985) (liability under UDAP can be imposed on lenders charging more money than provided in agreements deceiving borrowers into believing they were protected from market fluctuations of rates); Le Sage v. Norwest Bank Calhoun-Isles, N.A., 409 N.W.2d 536 (Minn. App. 1987) (error for lower court to dismiss consumer fraud statute claim by widow whose retirement income lost by bank). *But see* Sweeney v. RTC, 16 F.3d 1 (1st Cir.) (UDAP claim barred by *D'Oench* where based on closing documents), *cert. denied*, 513 U.S. 914 (1994).

691   968 F.2d 1332 (1st Cir. 1992).

692   *Id.* at 1353. "The doctrine permits a bankruptcy court to rearrange the priorities of creditors' interests, and to place all or part of the wrongdoer's claim in an inferior status." *Id.*

693   *Id. See In re* CTS Truss, Inc. v. FDIC, 868 F.2d 146 (5th Cir. 1989) (raising but not reaching this issue, as the court found that the debtor had failed to allege facts that demonstrated that the bank's conduct towards it could have invoked the equitable subordination doctrine of the assets later acquired by the FDIC).

694   *In re* 604 Columbus Ave. Realty Trust, 968 F.2d at 1362 (quoting *In re* Mayo, 112 B.R. 607, 650 (Bankr. D. Vt. 1990) (defining what is bank misconduct)).

695   Lawlor Corp. v. FDIC, 848 F. Supp. 1069 (D. Mass. 1994) (FDIC denied summary judgment on equitable subrogation claim brought by holder of mechanic's lien on property on which FDIC held mortgage). *See also* St. Bernard Sav. & Loan Ass'n v. Cella, 826 F. Supp. 985 (E.D. La. 1993) (suggesting that a holder-in-due-course analysis be undertaken first and only if the agency qualifies should *D'Oench* be considered). *See* discussion at § 10.7.3, *supra*.

696   32 F.3d 592 (D.C. Cir. 1994), *rehearing denied*, 45 F.3d 458 (D.C. Cir. 1995).

697   32 F.3d at 597. *See also* Joslin v. Bengal Chef, Inc., 715 So. 2d 1266 (La. Ct. App. 1998) (no-asset exception applied to prevent *D'Oench* from barring guarantors defense that they had been released, where even though the release was not in the bank's records or official minutes of meeting, testimony that bank's board approved release supported factual finding of release, and fact that guarantors were not listed on the relevant loan applications meant that "a reasonable bank examiner" would not have been misled into believing the guaranties were still in effect; given trial court's finding that the guarantors were released before the FDIC acquired the bank's assets, the FDIC's successor could not enforce the guaranties, which were "dead" assets). *But see* OCI Mortg. Corp. v. Marchese, 774 A.2d 940 (Conn. 2001) (borrowers were not entitled to set off funds owed them by failed bank pursuant to a debenture agreement against note asserted by bank's assignee, therefore note was not extinguished by setoff and remained a live asset for purposes of section 1823(e)); Cadle Co. v. Johnson, 714 So. 2d 183 (La. Ct. App. 1998) (where loan made to borrower to purchase capital stock of bank violated securities laws, it was voidable, but not void *ab initio*, therefore borrower could not assert no asset exception).

698   *Id.* at 597–600. *See also* Kessler v. National Enters., Inc., 165 F.3d 596, 599 (8th Cir. 1999) ("[I]t is not realistic to apply the bar of § 1823(e) to non-banking transactions or other types of agreements which would not customarily be 'scrutinized, approved, and recorded by the bank's executive committee or board' ").

- Claims that do not relate to a specific asset (these may not be barred by section 1823(e));[699]
- Breach of fiduciary duty and other so-called "free standing torts";[700]
- Claims based upon an asset of which the federal agency was not a holder in due course, using standard UCC holder analysis;[701]

- Claims based on an agreement that would not normally be found within the bank's records;[702]
- Equitable subordination claims;[703]
- Shareholder claims for securities, RICO and fraud violations;[704]
- Fraud in the factum;[705]
- Negligent misrepresentation;[706]
- Claims against former officers and directors of failed banks;[707]
- Claims based on the actions of the RTC or FDIC itself, and not on those of the failed bank;[708]

---

[699] Murphy v. FDIC, 61 F.3d 34 (D.C. Cir. 1995) (bank participant in real estate venture); E.I. DuPont de Nemours & Co. v. FDIC, 32 F.3d 592 (D.C. Cir. 1994), *rehearing denied*, 45 F.3d 458 (D.C. Cir. 1995) (escrow agreement); Murphy v. FDIC, 38 F.3d 1490 (9th Cir. 1994) (letter of credit); FDIC v. McFarland, 33 F.3d 532 (5th Cir. 1994) (good discussion of no asset exception). *See also* discussion at § 10.7.2.6, *supra*.

[700] Hanson v. FDIC, 13 F.3d 1247 (8th Cir. 1994) (constructive trust claim based on tort wholly independent of agreement not barred); Astrup v. Midwest Fed. Sav. Bank, 886 F.2d 1057 (8th Cir. 1989); Fairfield Six/Hidden Valley P'ship v. RTC, 860 F. Supp. 1085 (D. Md. 1994) (tortious interference claims based on bank conduct months after alleged agreement not barred); *In re* NBW Commercial Paper Litig., 826 F. Supp. 1448 (D.D.C. 1992) (if plaintiff can establish independent duty, breach of fiduciary duty claim not barred by *D'Oench*); New Bank of New England N.A. v. Callahan, 798 F. Supp. 73 (D.N.H. 1992) (claims based on bank's legal obligations, not agreements, are not barred by *D'Oench*; at issue breach of duty of good faith and fair dealing; failure to conduct a commercially reasonable foreclosure sale; breach of fiduciary duty with respect to foreclosure sale; and abuse of process); Central Nat'l Bank v. FDIC, 771 F. Supp. 161 (E.D. La. 1991) (*D'Oench* does not bar an action based on breach of fiduciary duty); Consolidated Asset Recovery Corp. v. Sweeney, 1995 Conn. Super. LEXIS 2862 (Oct. 13, 1995) (unpublished) (duty of good faith and fair dealing); First Commerce of America v. Mr. Travel Agent, Inc., 1995 Conn. Super. LEXIS 986 (Apr. 3, 1995) (unpublished) (summary judgment for FDIC denied on claim alleging breach of implied covenant of good faith and fair dealing); F.E. Appling Interests v. McCamish, Martin, Brown & Loeffler, 953 S.W.2d 405 (Tex. App. 1997), *aff'd*, 991 S.W.2d 787 (Tex. 1999) (attorney subject to negligent misconception claim for inaccurate representation that settlement agreement in lender liability suit met the requirements of § 1823(e)).

[701] Beckley Capital Ltd. P'ship v. DiGeronimo, 942 F. Supp. 728 (D.N.H. 1996), *aff'd*, 184 F.3d 52 (1st Cir. 1999) (non-negotiable); Joslin v. Shareholder Servs. Group, 948 F. Supp. 627 (S.D. Tex. 1996) (no asset transferred because violation of express restriction); St. Bernard Sav. & Loan Ass'n v. Cella, 826 F. Supp. 985 (E.D. La. 1993) (S&L bought loan after maturity and then transferred to RTC); Integon Life Ins. Corp. v. Southmark Heritage Retirement Corp., 813 F. Supp. 783 (N.D. Ala. 1992) (property sold before RTC took over is not asset of bank subject to *D'Oench*); *In re* Miraj & Sons, Inc., 192 B.R. 297 (Bankr. D. Mass. 1996) (purchased notes knowing overdue), *amended by* 197 B.R. 737 (Bankr. D. Mass. 1996); Cadle Co. v. Wallach Concrete, Inc., 897 P.2d 1104 (N.M. 1995) (no federal holder in due course when note specially endorsed); Haines Pipeline Constr. v. Exline Gas Sys., 921 P.2d 955 (Okla. App. 1996) (non-negotiable); Leavings v. Mills, 2004 WL 1902536, at *7, n.10 (Tex. App. Aug. 26, 2004) (unpublished) (FTC Holder Rule rendered consumer non-negotiable); Mundaca Inv. Corp. v. Espinoza, 1996 Tex. App. LEXIS 1069 (Nov. 20, 1996) (unpublished) (illegality defense). *See also* FDIC v. Aetna Cas. & Sur. Co., 947 F.2d 196 (6th Cir. 1991) (*D'Oench* is inappli-

cable to insurance contracts which are conditional agreements and not negotiable instruments).

[702] Waynesboro Village, L.L.C. v. BMC Properties, 496 S.E.2d 64 (Va. 1998).

[703] *In re* 604 Columbus Ave. Realty Trust, 968 F.2d 1332 (1st Cir. 1992); Lawlor Corp. v. FDIC, 848 F. Supp. 1069 (D. Mass. 1994).

[704] Adams v. Zimmerman, 73 F.3d 1164 (1st Cir. 1996) (*D'Oench* does not apply to claim of offering unregistered security interests in condominium; court notes statutory mandate not contracted duty); Vernon v. RTC, 907 F.2d 1101 (11th Cir. 1990); *In re* NBW Commercial Paper Litig., 826 F. Supp. 1448 (D.D.C. 1992) (*D'Oench* does not prevent tort claims in a securities fraud action which are independent of oral agreements otherwise barred). *See generally* Timberland Design, Inc. v. FDIC, 745 F. Supp. 784 (D. Mass. 1990), *aff'd*, 932 F.2d 46 (1st Cir. 1991).

[705] Langley v. FDIC, 484 U.S. 86, 108 S. Ct. 396, 98 L. Ed. 2d 340 (1987) (fraud in the inducement did not survive a § 1823(e) defense, though fraud in the factum would); FDIC v. Kagan, 871 F. Supp. 1522 (D. Mass. 1995); FDIC v. Turner, 869 F.2d 270 (6th Cir. 1989) (bank officer fraudulently altered guaranty); RTC v. Davies, 824 F. Supp. 1002 (D. Kan. 1993) (fraud in the factum requires "excusable ignorance" of the contents of the writing and no reasonable opportunity to obtain knowledge); FDIC v. Rusconi, 808 F. Supp. 30 (D. Me. 1992); Wilshire Credit Corp. v. Walsh, 1998 Conn. Super. LEXIS 2196 (July 30, 1998) (unpublished). *See also* Comment, *Langley v. FDIC: FDIC Superpowers—A License to Commit Fraud*, 8 Ann. Rev. Banking L. 559 (1989). *But see* FSLIC v. Murray, 853 F.2d 1251 (5th Cir. 1988); FDIC v. McClanahan, 795 F.2d 512 (5th Cir. 1986) (promissory note executed in blank and later "altered" held enforceable); FDIC v. Dureau, 261 Cal. Rptr. 19 (Ct. App. 1989) (*D'Oench* available to FDIC despite fact obligor told he was signing a corporate resolution, which bank knew was a guaranty).

Lawyers should be aware of breadth of conduct covered by this defense. It is not limited to forgeries. *See* Restatement (Second) of Contracts § 163 (1981): where misrepresentations occur so that party signing instrument is unaware of the character and essential terms of the instrument. For a good discussion of how fraud in the factum defense is supposed to be expansive, *see* Amsterdam v. DePaul, 175 A.2d 219 (N.J. Super. Ct. App. Div. 1961).

[706] Condus v. Howard Savings Bank, 1998 U.S. Dist. LEXIS 11300 (D.N.J. June 15, 1998) (unpublished).

[707] Brookside Assocs. v. Rifkin, 49 F.3d 490 (9th Cir. 1995); Crowe v. Smith, 848 F. Supp. 1248 (W.D. La. 1994).

[708] Franklin Credit Mgt. Corp. v. Nicholas, 1999 Conn. Super. LEXIS 1123 (Apr. 27, 1999) (unpublished).

The Cost of Credit: Regulation and Legal Challenges

- State consumer fraud (UDAP) claims;[709]
- Failure of consideration and fraud;[710]
- Economic duress;[711]
- Violation of corporate registration law which rendered contract void *ab initio*;[712]
- Wrongful acceleration and unreasonable sale at fore-closure;[713]
- Usury in a non-negotiable instrument,[714] or apparent on

face of document;[715]
- Breach of contract;[716]
- Truth in Lending rescission;[717]

---

709   Tuxedo Beach Club Corp. v. City Fed. Sav. Bank, 749 F. Supp. 635 (D.N.J. 1990) and cases cited therein. *See also* FSLIC v. Mackie, 962 F.2d 1144 (5th Cir. 1992) (UDAP and breach of duty of good faith claims not barred if based on obligations in written agreement; would be barred if based on oral promises and representations); FDIC v. Rusconi, 808 F. Supp. 30 (D. Me. 1992) (UDAP claim not barred if not based on oral represen-tations); Desmond v. FDIC, 798 F. Supp. 829 (D. Mass. 1992) (breach of duty of good faith and fair dealing also survived; court notes that breach of that duty violates Mass. UDAP, a claim which also survived); First Commerce of America v. Mr. Travel Agent, Inc., 1995 Conn. Super. LEXIS 986 (Mar. 28, 1995) (unpublished) (UDAP claim survives motion for sum-mary judgment when based on actions of bank in attempting to coerce refinancing and threatening interest rate higher than allowed by note). *But see* Sweeney v. RTC, 16 F.3d 1 (1st Cir.), *cert. denied,* 513 U.S. 914 (1994).

710   DiVall Insured Income Fund Ltd. P'ship v. Boatmen's First Nat'l Bank, 69 F.3d 1398 (8th Cir. 1995); RTC v. Davies, 824 F. Supp. 1002 (D. Kan. 1993); *In re* Boston Investors Group, L.P., 182 B.R. 637 (Bankr. D. Mass. 1995); FDIC v. Sather, 468 N.W.2d 347 (Minn. App. 1991), *aff'd,* 488 N.W.2d 260 (Minn. 1992). *But see* FDIC v. McCullough, 911 F.2d 593 (11th Cir. 1990) (defenses of fraud and failure of consideration barred because never memorialized and made part of bank records), *cert. denied,* 500 U.S. 941 (1991); FDIC v. McClanahan, 795 F.2d 512 (5th Cir. 1986); FSLIC v. Dillon Constr. Co., 681 F. Supp. 1359 (E.D. Ark. 1988).

711   RTC v. Davies, 824 F. Supp. 1002 (D. Kan. 1993) (suggests may be a defense although not properly raised). *But cf.* Vasapolli v. Rostoff, 39 F.3d 27 (1st Cir. 1994) (rejects defense as unproven, but includes history of its application and conflicting cases).

712   Brogdon v. Exterior Design, 781 F. Supp. 1396 (W.D. Ark. 1992) (*quantum meruit* recovery permitted; court relied on *Langley's* distinction between void and voidable instrument).

713   RTC v. Carr, 13 F.3d 425 (1st Cir. 1993); Texas Refrigeration Supply, Inc. v. FDIC, 953 F.2d 975 (5th Cir. 1992) (claims arising from the U.C.C. are not precluded by *D'Oench*, but notes that only claims or defenses *not based* on agreements are not barred; thus if basis for wrongful acceleration claim was an oral agreement, *D'Oench* would bar it); FDIC v. Blue Rock Shop-ping Center, Inc., 766 F.2d 744 (3d Cir. 1985) (court found that if FDIC acted improperly to impair collateral, *D'Oench* does not prevent borrower from discharge of debt under the Uniform Commercial Code); S&S Diversified Servs., L.L.C. v. Baldamar Arguello, 911 F. Supp. 498 (D. Wyo. 1995) (where debtor claims Article 9 notice provisions violated before FDIC stepped in, no right to deficiency acquired); New Bank of New England N.A. v. Callahan, 798 F. Supp. 73 (D.N.H. 1992); Wansley v. First Nat'l Bank of Vicksburg, 566 So. 2d 1218 (Miss. 1990). *But see* Burns v. RTC, 880 S.W.2d 149 (Tex. 1994).

714   FSLIC v. Mackie, 962 F.2d 1144, 1151 (5th Cir. 1992) (federal holder-in-due-course doctrine does not protect holders of non-negotiable notes); RTC v. Montross, 944 F.2d 227 (5th Cir. 1991); Beckley Capital Ltd. P'ship v. DiGeronimo, 942 F. Supp.

728 (D.N.H. 1996), *aff'd,* 184 F.3d 52 (1st Cir. 1999); *In re* Miraj & Sons, Inc., 192 B.R. 297 (Bankr. D. Mass. 1996), *amended by* 197 B.R. 737 (Bankr. D. Mass. 1996); Haines Pipeline Constr. v. Exline Gas Sys., 921 P.2d 955 (Okla. App. 1996). *Cf.* RTC v. Oaks Apt. Joint Venture, 966 F.2d 995 (5th Cir. 1992) (federal holder-in-due-course defense to guarantor's claim of contractual limited liability unavailable because note was not a negotiable instrument; as the note called for repay-ment of $2 million "or so much thereof as may be advanced," it did not call for repayment of a principal sum certain). *See also* Desmond v. FDIC, 798 F. Supp. 829 (D. Mass. 1992) (federal holder-in-due-course doctrine does not protect FDIC or RTC with respect to non-negotiable instruments, such as variable rate notes; § 1823(e), however, might apply to both negotiable and non-negotiable notes if a secret agreement is at issue). *Note*: in some jurisdictions, variable rate notes may not be negotiable instruments, §§ 9.3.5.1.3, 10.6.1.3.1–10.6.1.3.4, *supra,* nor may retail installment sales contracts, §§ 9.3.5.1.1, 9.3.5.1.2, 10.6.1.2.2, *supra.*

    Under these cases, the super-holder-in-due-course defense may not be available to the RTC/FDIC in such transactions against claims and defenses other than usury, if they fell outside the scope of *D'Oench* or § 1823(e).

715   RTC v. Minassian, 777 F. Supp. 385 (D.N.J. 1991) (holding FDIC v. Wood, 758 F.2d 156 (6th Cir. 1985) no longer good law to the extent it would bar usury claims apparent on the docu-ments; but held usury not apparent in the instant case). *See also* FDIC v. Bergan, 534 N.W.2d 250 (Mich. 1995) (FDIC protected from paying usury penalty after date of receivership but forfei-ture of interest prior to that date allowed).

716   Allied Elevator v. East Texas State Bank, 965 F.2d 34 (5th Cir. 1992) (borrower initialed request for credit life insurance on note and premium cost was included in note; court held that was written agreement, rendering *D'Oench* inapplicable to breach of contract claim for bank's failure to procure); Howell v. Conti-nental Credit Corp., 655 F.2d 743 (7th Cir. 1981) (*D'Oench* inapplicable to dispute arising from bilateral agreement in the bank files); FDIC v. White, 820 F. Supp. 1423 (N.D. Ga. 1993) (defense based solely on the language of the contract whose enforcement is being sought); FDIC v. Vernon Real Estate Invs., Ltd., 798 F. Supp. 1009 (S.D.N.Y. 1992) (claims based on bank's contractual obligations not barred); First Commerce of America, Inc. v. Haddad, 1995 Conn. Super. LEXIS 274 (Jan. 31, 1995) (unpublished) (defendant contesting validity of modi-fication agreements, same instrument bank seeking to enforce). *See also* text accompanying note 618, *supra.*

717   FDIC v. Monterrey, Inc., 847 F. Supp. 997 (D. P.R. 1994) (although FDIC not liable for civil or criminal penalties under TILA, rescission is available) (note that the logic of this case is inconsistent and confusing), *aff'd,* 45 F.3d 423 (1st Cir. 1995) (unpublished); New Maine Nat'l Bank v. Gendron, 780 F. Supp. 52 (D. Me. 1991) (*D'Oench* asserted by a bridge bank); Kasket v. Chase Manhattan Mortg. Corp., 695 So. 2d 431 (Fla. Dist. Ct. App. 1997) (court agreed FDIC and RTC not liable for civil or criminal penalties under TILA, but same exemption could not be raised by assignee in a voluntary assignment by a govern-ment agency; nor were *D'Oench* doctrine and § 1823(e) avail-able as defenses since any alleged TILA violations would come from the face of the documents of the institution itself). *See also* State St. Capital Corp. v. Rios, 1996 WL 307456 (Tex. App. 1996) (unpublished) (*D'Oench* and federal holder-in-due-course

- Negligent infliction of emotional distress;[718]
- Challenge to validity of lien under Texas homestead law;[719]
- UCC Article 9 defenses to a collection action for a deficiency, at least where liability not predicated on a negotiable instrument;[720]
- Intentional infliction of emotional harm;[721]
- Equal Credit Opportunity Act claims;[722]
- Abuse of process;[723]
- Claims brought by depositors;[724]
- Expiration of the statute of limitations;[725]

- Exception to bankruptcy discharge for making false financial statements;[726]
- Payment defense;[727]
- Release;[728]
- Equitable defenses such as laches;[729]
- Loan documents signed before section 1823(e) became effective;[730]
- Claim for check mishandling;[731]
- Defense based on alleged alteration of documents;[732]
- In general, claims arising out of bank's legal obligations, rather than purported agreements;[733]
- Defense that assignee is not legal owner and holder of the note;[734]
- Defense of mutual mistake.[735]
- Claims based on an agreement with a financial institution that was not part of the federally regulated banking system.[736]

---

defenses to rescission waived because not raised). *See generally* National Consumer Law Center, Truth in Lending § 6.9 (5th ed. 2003 and Supp.).

718 RTC v. Cook, 840 S.W.2d 42 (Tex. App. 1992) (purported tortious conduct that was subject of claim was independent of any agreement, and not action to which § 1823(e) or *D'Oench* defenses apply).

719 Patterson v. FDIC, 918 F.2d 540 (5th Cir. 1990) (homestead right exists independently of any agreement between the parties); *In re* Napier, 144 B.R. 719 (Bankr. W.D. Tex. 1992); Mundaca Inv. Corp. v. Espinoza, 1996 Tex. App. LEXIS 1069 (Tex. App. Nov. 20, 1996) (unpublished).

720 FDIC v. Payne, 973 F.2d 403 (5th Cir. 1992) (guarantor permitted to raise Article 9 defenses; guaranty is not a negotiable instrument, so FDIC is not protected by holder-in-due-course status); S&S Diversified Servs., L.L.C. v. Baldamar Arguello, 911 F. Supp. 498 (D. Wyo. 1995) (where debtor claims Article 9 notice provisions violated before FDIC stepped in, no right to deficiency judgment was acquired by FDIC); First City, Texas-Beaumont v. Treece, 848 F. Supp. 727 (E.D. Tex. 1994) (FDIC can only rely on federal holder-in-due-course doctrine when acting in corporate capacity; no holder-in-due-course protection for guaranty because not negotiable instrument, but defenses barred by *D'Oench*); St. Bernard Sav. & Loan Ass'n v. Cella, 826 F. Supp. 985 (E.D. La. 1993) (RTC has no holder-in-due-course status when failed bank bought note after maturity). *See* note 714, *supra* regarding what types of credit contracts may not be negotiable instruments. *Cf.* New Bank of New England N.A. v. Callahan, 798 F. Supp. 73 (D.N.H. 1992) (alleged failure to conduct commercially reasonable foreclosure sale not barred; claims based on legal obligations, rather than purported agreements not barred). *But see* Burns v. RTC, 880 S.W.2d 149 (Tex. 1994) (barring all of borrower's defenses).

721 FDIC v. Rusconi, 808 F. Supp. 30 (D. Me. 1992) (at least to the extent predicate facts are independent of oral agreements or representations).

722 Bolduc v. Beal Bank, 167 F.3d 667 (1st Cir. 1999) (under certain circumstances ECOA violation could be asserted preemptively in an action to enjoin foreclosure); CMF Virginia Land, L.P. v. Brinson, 806 F. Supp. 90 (E.D. Va. 1992) (ECOA claim not barred by *D'Oench*; also holding that it is a compulsory counterclaim, not a defense, though damages could equal claimant's liability on the debt); FDIC v. Notis, 602 A.2d 1164 (Me. 1992) (alleged ECOA violation did not fall under *D'Oench* or § 1823).

723 New Bank of New England N.A. v. Callahan, 798 F. Supp. 73 (D.N.H. 1992).

724 Fletcher Village Condominium Ass'n v. FDIC, 864 F. Supp. 259 (D. Mass. 1994).

725 Beckley Capital L.P. v. DiGeronimo, 184 F.3d 52 (1st Cir. 1999); Davidson v. FDIC, 44 F.3d 246 (5th Cir. 1995) (if bank's claim is time barred or otherwise void under state law when

FDIC appointed, claim cannot be revived); Beckley Capital Ltd. P'ship v. DiGeronimo, 942 F. Supp. 728 (D.N.H. 1996), *aff'd*, 184 F.3d 52 (1st Cir. 1999); Cadle Co. v. Henderson, 982 S.W.2d 543 (Tex. App. 1998) (amendment of assignee's rights to allow use of FDIC statute of limitations ineffective to revive the six year limitation period because state statute of limitations had run when amendment made).

726 RTC v. Hilton, 182 B.R. 483 (S.D. Miss. 1995); *In re* McKernan, 180 B.R. 350 (Bankr. D. Mass. 1995), *vacated on other grounds*, 207 B.R. 971 (D. Mass. 1997) (both cases hold *D'Oench* does not relieve RTC of burden of proving actual reliance).

727 Resiventure, Inc. v. National Loan Investors, 480 S.E.2d 212 (Ga. App. 1996).

728 Joslin v. Bengal Chef, Inc., 715 So. 2d 1266 (La. Ct. App. 1998).

729 SMS Fin. v. ABCO Homes Inc., 167 F.3d 235 (5th Cir. 1999) (estoppel claim that FDIC had falsely represented ownership of note presents genuine issue of material fact); Wilsim Ltd. P'ship v. P&M Dev., 1996 Conn. Super. LEXIS 1676 (May 31, 1996) (unpublished).

730 RTC Mortg. Trust 1994 S-3 v. Guadalupe Plaza, 918 F. Supp. 1441 (D.N.M. 1996). *See also* Harrison v. Wahatoyas, 253 F.3d 552, 559 (10th Cir. 2001) (FIRREA not retroactive).

731 Bufman Org. v. FDIC, 82 F.3d 1020 (11th Cir. 1996).

732 Beckley Capital Ltd. P'ship v. DiGeronimo, 942 F. Supp. 728 (D.N.H. 1996), *aff'd*, 184 F.3d 52 (1st Cir. 1999).

733 *Id.* (at issue; abuse of process, failure to conduct a commercially reasonable foreclosure sale; breach of fiduciary duty with respect to foreclosure sale; breach of duty of good faith and fair dealing); Alexandria Assocs. Ltd. v. Mitchell Co., 2 F.3d 598 (5th Cir. 1993) (*D'Oench* does not apply to non-banking transactions). Though not characterized in this way, a number of claims surviving *D'Oench* challenges in this list may represent this distinction.

734 Booker v. Sarasota, Inc., 707 So. 2d 886 (Fla. 1998) (before *D'Oench* can apply, assignee must properly prove its status as legal owner and holder of the note).

735 Bolduc v. Beal Bank, 167 F.3d 667 (1st Cir. 1999).

736 SEC v. Capital Consultants, L.L.C., 2002 U.S. Dist. LEXIS 670 (D. Or. Jan. 3, 2002) (unpublished).

10.7.9 FDIC/RTC Liability for Its Own Conduct

As a general rule, *D'Oench* and related doctrines will not protect the FDIC or RTC from claims or defenses arising out of its own conduct.[737] There is a broader developing question in the growing area of FDIC accountability: whether the Federal Tort Claims Act[738] (FTCA) affords a remedy for "negligent operation of the receivership" by the FDIC or RTC.[739] The key to whether the FTCA, generally, waives the sovereign immunity of the federal government is whether the tort committed would impose liability under state law if it had been committed by a non-governmental, or private, person.[740]

In *Federal Deposit Insurance Corp. v. Healey*,[741] the FDIC originally sued seven former directors and officers of a failed bank, alleging common law negligence, common law gross negligence, gross negligence under FIRREA, 12 U.S.C. § 1821(k), and breach of fiduciary duty. Two of the defendants raised affirmative defenses of failure to mitigate damages and contributory negligence for conduct of the FDIC post-receivership. In addition to an extensive discussion of the impact of the Supreme Court's decisions in *O'Melveny* and *Atherton*,[742] the *Healey* court reviewed the discretionary function exception to the Federal Tort Claims

Act,[743] and held that the FTCA would apply and the discretionary function exception would bar any claims based upon an act or omission in the execution of FIRREA, or based upon the exercise of a discretionary function.[744]

10.7.10 Claims Process

Pursuant to FIRREA, all parties asserting claims against failed institutions must participate in a mandatory administrative claims review process.[745] The requirements for this process are stringent and the failure to properly submit claims can result in a claim being barred altogether, so it is imperative that any consumer attorney confronting the possibility of a claim against a failed bank look closely at the statutory requirements.[746]

The following is a brief synopsis of the process. The receiver is required to mail a claim notice to all creditors.[747] Once this notice is mailed, the creditor has a specified period, usually ninety days, to file an administrative claim.[748] If it fails to do so, the creditor forfeits its right to pursue that claim against the bank's assets.[749] Once the

---

737 FDIC v. Blue Rock Shopping Center, Inc., 766 F.2d 744 (3d Cir. 1985) (*D'Oench* and § 1823(e) do not protect the FDIC from the consequences of its own conduct); Maryland Nat'l Bank v. RTC, 895 F. Supp. 762 (D. Md. 1995) (RTC cannot use *D'Oench* to contest enforceability of settlement agreement between the plaintiff and itself); Kuehl v. Numerica Fin. Corp., 1994 U.S. Dist. LEXIS 17259 (D.N.H. Nov. 23, 1994) (unpublished) (claim for misapplication of proceeds after FDIC stepped in is not barred); Franklin Credit Mgt. Corp. v. Nicholas, 1999 Conn. Super. LEXIS 1123 (Apr. 27, 1999) (unpublished) (neither *D'Oench* nor 1823 applied to borrower's claim that plaintiff's predecessor, the RTC, had released borrower from the debt); Cadle Co. v. Wallach Concrete, Inc., 897 P.2d 1104 (N.M. 1995) (claim based on FDIC's breach of duty of good faith and commercial reasonableness not barred). *See also* Coker v. Cramer Fin. Group, 992 S.W.2d 586 (Tex. App. 1999) (FDIC could not argue that *D'Oench* barred borrower's claim of tender made after FDIC took over failed bank).

738 28 U.S.C. § 2680, *et seq.*

739 The U.S. Supreme Court in Gaubert v. United States, 499 U.S. 315, 111 S. Ct. 1267, 113 L. Ed. 2d 335 (1991), *rev'g and remanding* 885 F.2d 1284 (5th Cir. 1989), found that a discretionary function exception shields FHLBB decisions upon takeover. (It should be noted, however, that as Justice Scalia observed in *Gaubert*, the lack of a factual record in this case made it quite difficult to find that the particular activities involved were properly shielded by DFE immunity. Since the Court could do little more than speculate about the nature of the FHLBB's alleged negligent decision-making, a properly developed factual record could produce a different result.)

740 *See* 28 U.S.C. § 1346(b). (It should be noted here that the FTCA is the exclusive remedy for tort claims against the FDIC.)

741 991 F. Supp. 53 (D. Conn. 1998).

742 *See* § 10.7.1, *supra.*

743 28 U.S.C. § 2680(a).

744 991 F. Supp. at 61–62 (citing with approval First Nat'l Insur. Co. of America v. FDIC, 977 F. Supp. 1060 (S.D. Cal. 1997) (if a claim of negligent misfeasance were brought against FDIC-receiver, FTCA would apply and acts of FDIC-receiver would be protected under discretionary function exception)), *aff'd in part, rev'd in part on other grounds*, 2001 U.S. App. LEXIS 1079 (9th Cir. Jan. 18, 2001) (unpublished); FDIC v. Meyer, 510 U.S. 471 (1994) (holding that the post-receivership conduct of FSLIC, to which FDIC is the successor agency, was protected by the FTCA); United States v. Gaubert, 499 U.S. 315, 111 S. Ct. 1267, 113 L. Ed. 2d 335 (1991); FDIC v. Oldenburg, 38 F.3d 1119 (10th Cir. 1994), *cert. denied*, 516 U.S. 861 (1995); FDIC v. Mijalis, 15 F.3d 1314 (5th Cir. 1994) (court following FDIC v. Bierman, 2 F.3d 1424 (7th Cir. 1993). *See also* FDIC v. Craft, 157 F.3d 697 (9th Cir. 1998).

745 12 U.S.C. § 1821(d). See RTC v. Kolea, 866 F. Supp. 197 (E.D. Pa. 1994) for a good discussion of the case law in this area.

746 *See, e.g.*, Hanson v. FDIC, 113 F.3d 866 (8th Cir. 1997) (failure to meet administrative review requirements raised jurisdictional bar to borrower's breach of contract and tort counterclaims).

747 12 U.S.C. § 1821(d)(3).

748 Filing an answer to a suit brought by the receiver does not constitute filing a claim. RTC v. Schonacher, 844 F. Supp. 689 (D. Kan. 1994).

749 12 U.S.C. § 1821(d)(5)(C)(i); RTC v. J.F. Assocs., 813 F. Supp. 951 (N.D.N.Y. 1993). At least one court has held that the claimant may file a suit seeking more than the amount in the claim so long as he has complied with the claims procedure. Interlease Corp. v. FDIC, 837 F. Supp. 1 (D.D.C. 1993).

The receiver's failure to mail notice to the claimant does not automatically toll the claims period. *See* Palumbo v. Roberti, 839 F. Supp. 80 (D. Mass. 1993); Espinosa v. DeVasto, 818 F. Supp. 438 (D. Mass. 1993) (claimant who was aware of FDIC's appointment as receiver but unaware of claims process not excused from time bars). Thus consumer attorneys must be careful to seek out information as to the status of failed banks and submit claims on a timely basis even if their clients have not received notice.

claim is filed, the agency has 180 days in which to make a decision as to the claim. Section 1821(d)(6)(A) then provides the claimant with sixty days from the agency's decision or the expiration of the 180 days, whichever is earlier, in which to file suit on the claim or continue an action commenced prior to the bank's failure.[750]

Certain defenses may not be subject to the claims procedure. Only defenses which could have been asserted independently against the bank or the receiver are covered.[751] Other defenses may be raised against the receiver without a claim having been filed.[752]

10.8 Remedies for Illegal Overcharges; Traditional Usury Remedies

10.8.1 Introduction

The remedies available to victims of illegal overcharges are primarily determined by individual state statutes.[753] Consequently, attorneys who are concerned about the remedies available in an individual overcharge case must first pay close attention to the statute under which the action is brought or the defense raised. Remedies for exceeding authorized cost ceilings vary widely from statute to stat-

ute,[754] so an earlier case decided under a different statute may have little precedential value.

Despite the preeminence of state statutes in determining what remedies are available for illegal overcharges in the consumer credit context, there is an ample body of law in other sources considering usury claims which should also be considered. For example, an action at common law for recovery of the usurious interest already paid to a lender is recognized in many states and, in the absence of statutory provisions addressing this topic, a common law action may be the sole means to obtain such a recovery. Similarly, a usury statute may apply only to actions on a debt, and a borrower may be forced to seek equitable intervention to prevent the foreclosure of a usurious mortgage. Finally, federal law provides statutory remedies both for usurious loans made by lenders operating under federal interest ceilings and for many other loans if the interest exceeds twice the enforceable rate. These topics are discussed in greater detail in the following subsections.

Apart from the remedies available specifically for usury or violations of other limitations on charges, practitioners should investigate related non-usury causes of action and remedies. Usury claims do not exist in a vacuum, and usurious transactions frequently involve other illegalities. For example, fraud and unfair or deceptive practices often go hand in hand with usury, and statutes prohibiting such practices should be considered.[755] Similarly, invalid security interests may be taken in usurious transactions which can lead to claims under the UCC.[756] Even if the failure to disclose information required under the state usury statute is not actionable under that law,[757] the failure to disclose may state a claim under the state's UDAP statute.[758] Last, but not least, basic contract theories and remedies should be kept in mind. The voiding of interest or principal for usury may lead

---

750 FIRREA's administrative claims process acts as a jurisdictional bar. Federal courts retain subject matter jurisdiction, however, over claims brought before the appointment of the receiver, but those cases are stayed while the plaintiff proceeds with the administrative claims process. RTC v. J.F. Assocs., 813 F. Supp. 951, 953 (N.D.N.Y. 1993).

751 Several courts have found that affirmative defenses are not subject to the claims process. Bolduc v. Beal Bank, 167 F.3d 667 (1st Cir. 1999) (borrower's challenge to foreclosure action not a FIRREA "claim" subject to exhaustion); RTC v. Love, 36 F.3d 972 (10th Cir. 1994) (defense to action for deficiency after foreclosure not "claim" or "action" as used in § 1821(d)(13)(D)); National Union Fire Ins. Co. v. City Savings, 28 F.3d 376 (3d Cir. 1994) (distinguishes between affirmative defense and counterclaim which would be barred); FDIC v. Parkway Exec. Office Ctr., 1997 U.S. Dist. LEXIS 12318 (E.D. Pa. Aug. 18, 1997) (unpublished); FDIC v. Wrapwell Corp., 922 F. Supp. 913 (S.D.N.Y. 1996) (debtor defenses based on U.C.C. not barred by administrative claims process); Calaska Partners Ltd. v. Corson, 672 A.2d 1099 (Me. 1996) (affirmative defense of violation of ECOA not subject to administrative exhaustion requirement); Bisson v. Eck, 720 N.E.2d 784 (Mass. 1999) (set-off claim not barred).

752 RTC v. Schonacher, 844 F. Supp. 689 (D. Kan. 1994). This case includes a thorough discussion of the administrative process and the treatment by the courts of counterclaims and affirmative defenses.

753 Overcharges resulting from contract terms which are illegal under the federal high-cost mortgage legislation will trigger those federal penalties. *See* Ch. 5, *supra*, Ch. 11, *infra* for discussions of that legislation. Also, overcharges which may not violate any specific statute, but may nonetheless constitute overreaching may be challenged under a variety of theories. *See* Ch. 11, *infra*.

754 *Compare* Alaska Stat. § 06.20.310 (usurious small loan unenforceable) *with* Alaska Stat. § 45.10.190 (recovery of cash price only on usurious RISA).

755 Cuevas v. Montoya, 740 P.2d 858 (Wash. Ct. App. 1987) (usury is a *per se* violation of state Consumer Fraud Act; attorney fees, costs, and damages based on usurious contract awarded). *But see* Hathaway v. First Family Fin. Servs., 1 S.W.3d 634 (Tenn. 1999) (if statute creates a new right and remedy, then the prescribed remedy is exclusive; state usury statute created exclusive remedy and, therefore, cannot use state UDAP act to create additional remedies as least for the usury violation; court suggests that other violations could trigger the UDAP act). *See generally* Ch. 11, *infra*; National Consumer Law Center, Unfair and Deceptive Acts and Practices (6th ed. 2004 and Supp.).

756 *See generally* National Consumer Law Center, Repossessions and Foreclosures (5th ed. 2002 and Supp.).

757 Cazzanigi v. General Electric Credit Corp., 938 P.2d 819 (Wash. 1997) (court held no cause of action to enforce any violation of the state RISA other than the charging of excess interest (called a "service fee") even though statute states: "any person . . . who does not comply with the provisions of this chapter . . . shall be barred from the recovery of any service charge. . . .").

758 *See* National Consumer Law Center, Unfair and Deceptive Acts and Practices §§ 2.2.1.2, 5.1.5, 5.1.7 (6th ed. 2004 and Supp.).

to contract claims such as failure of consideration in a renewal note,[759] and questionable lender practices, such as compounding of interest, may constitute breach of contract even if usury ceilings are not violated.[760] A lender's conduct may be unconscionable, or violate the duty of good faith and fair dealing that all parties to a contract owe the others.[761] Tort claims, such as fraud or failure of a duty to disclose, may also be warranted.[762]

10.8.2 State Statutory Remedies

10.8.2.1 Overview; Implying a Remedy When Statute Is Silent

At first glance, there seems to be little consistency among state laws that provide usury remedies. Ignoring for the moment cases decided in equity, usury remedies nonetheless vary from the mere forfeiture of the usurious portion of the contract interest to the requirement that the creditor return all of the payments on the contract and pay additional statutory penalties.[763] Some measure of order can be imposed on this chaos, however, if one recognizes that the outcome in any one case depends on the interaction of several variables that are common to almost all the statutes. Specifically, a debtor's obligation to repay principal on a usurious contract may be treated differently from her obligation to pay interest; payments already made on the contract may be treated differently from amounts still owed; and the portion of the interest in excess of the permissible amount may be treated differently from the remainder of the contract interest.

Some licensing statutes, such as small loan laws or consumer loan laws metamorphosing from small loan laws, may not include specific provisions for individual remedies, nor may other statutes limiting the right to impose certain charges. Some of the equitable remedies discussed in § 10.8.5, *infra*, particularly reformation of the contract, may be available to a debtor in this situation. In addition, the consumer may argue that such statutes create an implied private right of action.[764] There is also a common law

doctrine that contracts made by a party who lacks a required license are unenforceable.[765] Where a statute declares usurious loans void or bars the creditor from collecting usurious charges, a number of courts have implied a private cause of action to seek that remedy.[766] There may also be a common law action for recovery of usurious interest that the borrower has paid.[767]

Generally speaking, illegal contracts are unenforceable as a matter of common law, but whether a particular usurious contract fits into this category depends on the nature of the violation and public policy considerations.[768] Civil voidness penalties have been read into statutes for contracts violating their criminal provisions.[769] Usury cases have extended this principle even to the situation in which the criminal violation in question had no express civil penalty but other types

---

points; assertable by a suitable common law remedy; borrowers choose to assert common law restitution); Tew v. Dixieland Fin., Inc., 527 So. 2d 665 (Miss. 1988). *But see* Taylor v. Citizens Fed. Savs. & Loan, 846 F.2d 1320 (11th Cir. 1988) (no private right of action to enforce FHLBB regulations promulgated pursuant to Home Owner's Loan Act of 1933, 12 U.S.C. § 1461); Luckett v. Alpha Constr. & Dev., Inc., 2001 U.S. Dist. LEXIS 17623 (N.D. Ill. Oct. 22, 2001) (no private right of action under Ill. Residential Loan Act where there was no evidence of legislative intent to create private remedy and court found criminal penalty sufficient for enforcement); Doubet v. USA Fin. Servs., Inc., 714 F. Supp. 980 (C.D. Ill. 1987) (no implied private right of action for violations of disclosure provisions of installment loan act; improper disclosures omitted in list of violations that trigger interest forfeiture penalty); Miller v. Pacific Shore Funding, 224 F. Supp. 2d 977 (D. Md. May 17, 2002) (no private cause of action to enforce provision of licensing statute that limits lender's operations to certain locations), *aff'd on other grounds*, 2004 WL 144138 (4th Cir. Jan. 28, 2004); Staley v. Americorp Credit Corp., 164 F. Supp. 2d 578 (D. Md. 2001) (no private cause of action to enforce requirement that lender may operate only out of specific location); Lane v. Fabert, 533 N.E.2d 546 (Ill. App. 1989) (no implied private right of action under pawnbroker licensing statute; court, however, weighed fact that consumer had other remedies in so finding); Couture v. G.W.M., Inc., 2002 WL 31962752 (N.H. Super. Ct. Dec. 3, 2002). *See generally* § 10.8.3, *infra*.

765 *See* § 10.8.4.1, *infra*.

766 Transamerica Fin. Corp. v. Superior Court, 761 P.2d 1019 (Ariz. 1988); Wombold v. Assocs. Fin. Servs. Co., 104 P.3d 1080 (Mont. 2004) (implying private cause of action where statute said loan was void but was silent as to private cause of action); Couture v. G.W.M., Inc., 2002 WL 31962752 (N.H. Super. Ct. Dec. 3, 2002). *See* § 10.8.2.3, *infra*.

767 *See* § 10.8.2.3, *infra*.

768 *See* Siner v. Am. Gen. Fin., Inc., 2004 WL 2441185 (E.D. Pa. Oct. 28, 2004) (home improvement contract that included forbidden cash loan is illegal as an essential term violates public policy); Lloyd Capital Corp. v. Pat Henchar, Inc., 544 N.Y.S.2d 178 (App. Div. 1989), *aff'd*, 603 N.E.2d 246 (N.Y. 1992) (violation of SBA regulations insufficient to render contract unenforceable); Mincks Agri Center, Inc. v. Bell Farms, Inc., 611 N.W.2d 270 (Iowa 2000) (spelling out policy considerations, in non-usury case). *See generally* § 9.2.4.6, *supra*.

769 2B Singer, Sutherland Statutory Construction § 55.07 (6th ed. 2000).

---

759 *See In re* Feldman, 259 F. Supp. 218 (D. Conn. 1966).

760 *See* Giventer v. Arnow, 372 N.Y.S.2d 63 (N.Y. 1975).

761 *See* Ch. 11, *infra*.

762 *Id.*

763 For an excellent discussion of the distinctions between "forfeitures," "penalties," and the voiding of a loan, see Szerdahelyi v. Harris, 490 N.E.2d 517 (N.Y. 1986).

764 Bailey v. Defenbaugh & Co., 513 F. Supp. 232 (N.D. Miss. 1981); Transamerica Fin. Corp. v. Superior Court, 761 P.2d 1019 (Ariz. 1988), *rev'g*, 746 P.2d 497 (Ariz. Ct. App. 1987) (consumer loan act voiding usurious loans implied a right of action to seek that remedy). *See also* Mayo v. Key Fin. Servs., Inc., 1994 Mass. App. LEXIS 549 (Mass. Super. Ct. June 22, 1994), *aff'd on other grounds*, 678 N.E.2d 1311 (Mass. 1997) (implied private right of action for violation of statute limiting

of criminal violations did.[770] Or a court, finding a contract to be illegal due to a violation of a criminal usury statute, may order that interest and other charges be forfeited.[771]

10.8.2.2 Forfeiture of Creditor's Right to Recover Principal, Interest, Other Illegal Overcharges, or to Collect Attorney Fees

10.8.2.2.1 *Statutes that void the contract interest or other charges*

A most basic distinction made by many usury statutes is the difference between a debtor's obligation to repay the principal amount of a usurious loan and her obligation to pay the contract interest or other charges. Very often a statute will declare a usurious loan void as to all or part of the interest, while leaving the principal obligation intact.[772]

Under such statutes, the widely-accepted rule is that all payments already made on the contract, unless the parties have specifically agreed otherwise,[773] will be applied to the principal debt until that debt has been paid off.[774] Thus, the

770 Walker v. Peoples Fin. & Thrift Co., 49 P.2d 1005 (Ariz. 1935); G. Nicotera Loan Corp. v. Gallagher, 160 A. 426 (Conn. 1932); Hartsfield Co. v. Roberston, 173 S.E. 201 (Ga. App. 1934); Burque v. Brodeur, 158 A. 127 (N.H. 1932).

771 Moore v. Comfed Sav. Bank, 908 F.2d 834 (11th Cir. 1990); Norris v. Sigler Daisy Corp., 392 S.E.2d 242 (Ga. 1990). *See also* Schuran, Inc. v. Walnut Hill Assocs., 606 A.2d 885 (N.J. Super. Ct. 1991) (criminal usury statute silent as to penalty; court held it made only excessive interest illegal, not contract, thus severed illegal interest provision and permitted recovery of loan principal).

772 *See, e.g., In re* Vehm Eng'g Corp., 521 F.2d 186 (9th Cir. 1975); Speare v. Consolidated Assets Corp., 367 F.2d 208 (2d Cir. 1966); Daenzer v. Wayland Ford, Inc., 193 F. Supp. 2d 1030 (W.D. Mich. 2002) (finance charges void where seller does not give copy of contract to buyer at time buyer signs, but civil penalties under separate Motor Vehicle Sales Finance Act apply only if seller has sought prohibited charges); Smith v. Khalif (*In re* Khalif), 308 B.R. 614, 625 (Bankr. N.D. Ga. 2004); *In re* Rose, 266 B.R. 192 (Bankr. N.D. Cal. 2001) (voiding of entire loan is penalty only for consumer loans; for commercial loan, court merely disallows interest); Cantrell v. Walker Builders, Inc., 678 So. 2d 169 (Ala. Civ. App. 1996) (for discussion on changes to the Alabama Mini-Code); Patterson v. Green, 474 So. 2d 725 (Ala. Ct. App. 1985); Metcalf v. Bartrand, 491 P.2d 747 (Alaska 1971); Dillon v. RTC, 811 S.W.2d 765 (Ark. 1991) (state constitution makes usurious contract "void as to unpaid interest"; since void from inception, all interest paid is unlawful); Westman v. Dye, 214 Cal. 28, 4 P.2d 134 (1931); Brown v. Fenner, 757 P.2d 184 (Colo. Ct. App. 1988) (lender on note at usurious rate could recover principal and interest at maximum legal rate); Centrust Savings Bank v. Springs Community Ass'n, Inc., 580 So. 2d 654 (Fla. Dist. Ct. App. 1991) (where creditor contracts for excess interest, the penalty is forfeiture of all interest, and only principal can be enforced); Cornelius v. Auto Analyst, Inc., 476 S.E.2d 9 (Ga. App. 1996) (citing to *Pave Way*); Pave Way Constr. Co. v. Parrish, 370 S.E.2d 495 (Ga. App. 1988) (interest is forfeited in usurious loan but principal may be collected because usury does not make the loan void and unenforceable as illegal contract); Southern Discount Co. of Georgia v. Ector, 268 S.E.2d 621 (Ga. 1980); Bjornstad v. Perry, 443 P.2d 999 (Idaho 1968); Route 50 Auto Sales, Inc. v. Muncy, 771 N.E.2d 635 (Ill. App. 2002) (credit seller whose contract

did not include items required by MVRISA cannot recover interest, late charges, or repossession fees, but debt for principal is not void); Saskill v. 4-B Acceptance, 452 N.E.2d 771 (Ill. App. 1983); Bonfanti v. Davis, 487 So. 2d 165 (La. Ct. App. 1986); Waldorf v. Zinberg, 307 N.W.2d 749 (Mich. App. 1981); Trapp v. Hancuh, 530 N.W.2d 879 (Minn. Ct. App. 1995) (interpreting Minn. Stat. § 334.011, subd. 2, regarding usury on business and agricultural loans under $100,000); Thomas Lakes Owners Assoc. v. Riley, 612 N.W.2d 529 (Neb. App. 2000) (obligation to pay interest is void, and creditor cannot replace usurious interest with interest at legal rate); *In re* Castillian Apartments, Inc., 190 S.E.2d 161 (N.C. 1972); Britt v. Jones, 472 S.E.2d 199 (N.C. App. 1996) (North Carolina statute limits the recovery to the amount of usurious interest paid during the two years preceding the filing of the lawsuit, which amount can be doubled under certain circumstances); Tilley v. Pacesetter Corp., 585 S.E.2d 292 (S.C. 2003) (applying pre-1997 version of statute) (finance charge is forfeited and loan is non-interest-bearing when lender violated provision of usury statute unrelated to interest rate); First State Bank of Bedford v. Miller, 563 S.W.2d 572 (Tex. 1978). *See also* Walters v. PDI Mgmt. Serv., 2004 WL 2137513 (S.D. Ind. June 14, 2004) (under Ind. U.C.C.C., debtor is not required to pay usurious interest and may recover any amount already paid); Patzka v. Viterbo College, 917 F. Supp. 654 (W.D. Wis. 1996) (creditor not entitled to any interest where it failed to make cost of credit disclosures required by Wisconsin Consumer Protection Act).

773 *Compare* Cherry v. Berg, 508 S.W.2d 869 (Tex. Civ. App. 1974) (usurious bonus designated by parties as interest) *with In re* Vehm Eng'g Corp., 521 F.2d 186 (9th Cir. 1975) (payments under usurious agreement, although denominated as interest, will be deemed payment on principal); Barach Inv. Co. v. Huntoon, 65 Cal. Rptr. 131 (App. 1967) (no actual application to interest shown); Hubschnan v. Broda, 247 A.2d 698 (N.J. Super. 1968) (payments attributed to principal where lender's unilateral application to interest and principal was not made at time of payment); *and* Credit Alliance Corp. v. Timmco Equip. Co., 507 So. 2d 657 (Fla. Dist. Ct. App. 1987) (interest payments already made applied to principal).

774 *See, e.g., In re* Vehm Eng'g Corp., 521 F.2d 186 (9th Cir. 1975) (California law); Speare v. Consolidated Assets Corp., 367 F.2d 208 (2d Cir. 1966) (New Jersey law); *In re* Bogan, 281 F. Supp. 242 (W.D. Tenn. 1968) (Tennessee law); Westman v. Dye, 4 P.2d 134 (Cal. 1931); Gibbo v. Berger, 123 Cal. App. 4th 396, 19 Cal. Rptr. 3d 829 (2004); Marino v. Whitney, 2000 Conn. Super. LEXIS 2778 (Oct. 12, 2000); Route 50 Auto Sales, Inc. v. Muncy, 771 N.E.2d 635 (Ill. App. 2002); Tauber v. Johnson, 291 N.E.2d 180 (Ill. App. 1972) (decision under MVRISA); *In re* Castillian Apartments, Inc., 190 S.E.2d 161 (N.C. 1972); Magee v. Dyrdahl, 926 P.2d 319 (Or. App. 1996) (this principle is also applicable to a business loan which violated Oregon's usury statute); Packer v. Wardwell, 744 P.2d 1312 (Or. Ct. App. 1987) (where statute provides for forfeiture of interest in usurious contracts, payments made will be applied solely to principal); Stacks v. East Dallas Clinic, 409 S.W.2d 842 (Tex. 1966) (acknowledging general rule when parties have not designated payments as interest or principal). *See also* C&A Tractor Co. v. Branch, 520 So. 2d 909 (La. Ct. App. 1987) (illegally collected interest should be returned to debtor; debtor found entitled to return of illegally assessed 50 cent service charge plus legal

maximum amount that a debtor may owe upon judgment under a statute which voids only interest is the original principal amount minus the payments made on the contract.[775] The creditor should not be able to fall back on the legal rate of interest.[776]

Another question is what portion of the interest is forfeited when a loan is made usurious by acts subsequent to the initial extension of credit. The Mississippi Supreme Court has held that an unlawful forbearance agreement, executed well after the initial extension of credit, tainted the entire transaction, making all interest on the original note subject to the forfeiture remedy.[777]

Usury statutes allowing the creditor to collect only principal, less the usury penalty, may be interpreted to preclude an award of attorney fees and costs to a creditor suing on the usurious note, even if the contract provides for it.[778] Similarly, where non-interest charges such as late charges are limited by statute, a creditor which imposes excess charges may forfeit the right to collect any such fees,[779] for to merely

reduce fees to the statutorily allowed amount would give creditors an incentive to break the law.[780]

10.8.2.2.2 Statutes that void the entire obligation

Although many usury statutes limit usury remedies to a forfeiture of interest,[781] harsher sanctions are also found. Numerous statutes declare usurious obligations to be completely void and prohibit any creditor recovery whether or not the principal has been repaid.[782] This sanction is most common in small loan laws and consumer loan laws derived from them. They often deny the lender the right to "collect or receive" any principal or interest charges whatsoever.[783]

---

interest on that judgment). *But see* Bjornstad v. Perry, 443 P.2d 999 (Idaho 1968) (rule does not apply where statute provides for borrower's recovery of interest paid); Negaard v. Miller Constr. Co., 396 N.W.2d 833 (Minn. Ct. App. 1986) (payments are applied first to interest as a matter of law).

775 Observe that the principal debt does not include interest charges hidden in the face amount of a note. Metcalf v. Bartrand, 491 P.2d 747 (Alaska 1971).

776 Thomas Lakes Owners Assoc. v. Riley, 612 N.W.2d 529 (Neb. App. 2000).

777 Sunburst Bank v. Keith, 648 So. 2d 1147 (Miss. 1995) (business loans at issue).

778 *See, e.g.,* Dent v. Associates Fin. Servs. of America, Inc., 137 B.R. 78 (Bankr. S.D. Ga. 1992) (if contract is usurious, creditor may not add attorney fees to its secured claim in bankruptcy); Hansen v. Doerflein, 757 P.2d 997 (Wash. Ct. App. 1988); Cuevas v. Montoya, 740 P.2d 858 (Wash. Ct. App. 1987). *But see* Suncrete Corp. v. Glusman (*In re* Suncrete Corp.), 100 B.R. 102 (Bankr. M.D. Fla. 1989) (usury penalty limited to forfeiture of interest and does not prevent recovery of attorney fees); Hazen v. Cook, 646 P.2d 33 (Or. 1982) (where judgment granted creditor for principal only on usurious note, it was a prevailing party entitled to attorney fees).

779 *See, e.g., In re* Crotzer, 147 B.R. 252 (Bankr. N.D. Ala. 1992) (creditor which imposed excess late fees forfeited right to collect any; [interpreting "actual damages" for violating Ala. Mini-Code's late fee limitation]); LaBarr v. Tombstone Territorial Mint, 580 P.2d 744 (Ariz. Ct. App.), *adopted*, 582 P.2d 639 (Ariz. 1978) (en banc); Rea v. Breakers Ass'n, 674 So. 2d 496 (Miss. 1996) (finance charge in excess of amount allowed by 100% triggers forfeiture of principal and interest as well as repayment of any amounts paid; court applied this statute to late fees charged at the rate of 20% which were then added in to the next month's payment upon which interest was charged); Swindell v. FNMA, 409 S.E.2d 892 (N.C. 1991) (interpreting late fees as "interest" on detained money; statute calling for forfeiture of interest therefore called for forfeiture of all late charges); Bagri v. Desai, 349 S.E.2d 309 (N.C. Ct. App. 1986) (usurious loan for purchase of motel; lender could not recover share of profits from operation and resale of motel as provided in usurious agreement).

780 *See, e.g., In re* Crotzer, 147 B.R. 252 (Bankr. N.D. Ala. 1992) (creditor which imposed excess late fees forfeited right to collect any; [interpreting "actual damages" for violating Ala. Mini-Code's late fee limitation]). *Cf.* Matter of Sprouse, 577 F.2d 989 (5th Cir. 1978) (discussing effect of overreaching contract language in transactions which are not litigated).

781 *See, e.g.,* Williams v. Seeley (*In re* Williams), 227 B.R. 83 (Bankr. E.D. Va. 1998) (Virginia's secondary mortgage loan law provides for the recovery of the total amount of interest paid in excess of that permitted plus twice the total amount of interest paid during the two years immediately preceding the filing of the action plus court costs and attorney fees), *on remand*, 241 B.R. 387 (Bankr. E.D. Va. 1999), *rev'd on other grounds*, 2001 WL 652028 (4th Cir. June 13, 2001).

782 *See, e.g.,* Borowski v. Falleder, 296 A.D.2d 301, 744 N.Y.S.2d 177 (2002) (loan void where made to individual and interest rate exceeded 15%); Equity Mortgage, Inc. v. Niro, 690 A.2d 407 (Conn. App. 1997) (applying Conn. Gen. Stat. § 37-8; court took unusual step of addressing usury apparent on face of contract on appeal even though not raised below); Rea v. Breakers Ass'n, 674 So. 2d 496 (Miss. 1996) (finance charge in excess of amount allowed by 100% triggers forfeiture of principal and interest as well as repayment of any amounts paid); Seidel v. 18 East 17th St. Owners, 598 N.E.2d 7 (N.Y. 1992) (New York Gen. Obligations Law § 5-511[2] voids usurious loans; borrower relieved of further interest and principal payment and mortgages securing the loan are canceled); Hilal v. Lipton, 642 N.Y.S.2d 78 (App. Div. 1996) (usury of one of two individual investors who made the loan taints the entire loan and renders it unenforceable under New York Gen. Obligations Law § 5-511[2]); Ferrari v. Howard, 2002 WL 1500414 (Ohio App. July 11, 2002) (unpublished, citation limited) (contract that included illegal charge is unenforceable under former version of Ohio RISA); Commerce, Crowdus & Canton Ltd. v. DKS Constr., Inc., 776 S.W.2d 615 (Tex. App. 1989) (interest in excess of twice amount legally allowed results in forfeiture of principal as well as interest, in addition to penalty of three times amount of usurious interest). *But see* Southern Discount Co. v. Ector, 268 S.E.2d 621 (Ga. 1980) (interpreting Ga. law to require forfeiture of interest and charges but not voiding of obligation to pay principal). *But cf.* Brodie v. Schmutz (*In re* Venture Mortgage Fund), 282 F.3d 185 (2d Cir. 2002) (questioning whether loan that violates N.Y. criminal usury statute is void); Brest v. Kleidman, 751 N.Y.S.2d 473 (App. Div. 2002) (original non-usurious loan is not void even though post-default extension agreement is usurious and void).

783 *See* Bailey v. Defenbaugh & Co., 513 F. Supp. 232 (N.D. Miss. 1981); *In re* Perry, 272 F. Supp. 73 (D. Me. 1967); *In re* Tavares, 298 B.R. 195 (Bankr. D. Mass. 2003); *In re* Harrington, 6 B.R.

Second mortgage laws commonly provided for similar relief, at least prior to the general statutory loosening of standards in the deregulation wave of the 1980s.[784] It is also present under the UCCC when credit is extended by an unlicensed lender,[785] and in some states, where double or treble the amount of legal interest was charged.[786]

10.8.2.3 Borrower's Recovery of Payments Made

A critical question which often arises when a loan is declared usurious is: what happens to the money already paid to the creditor? The answer will depend partly on whether the statute voids the entire obligation or merely the interest. If only interest is forfeited, it is fairly clear, as mentioned in the previous section, that all payments made under the contract will be credited to the principal debt until that debt is satisfied, unless the parties have specifically attributed some of those payments to interest.[787] Less clear is what happens if the loan is completely void so that no principal debt technically ever existed, if payments exceed the amount of the principal originally extended to the borrower, or if the payments were expressly deemed to be interest payments by the parties.

Some statutes which declare usurious loans to be completely void spell out the debtor's right to recover payments made, in which case the problem is solved.[788] Small loan acts which declare usurious loans void and deny the creditor's right to "collect or receive" any charges on the contract have generally been interpreted as requiring a refund of all payments made, including principal.[789] A federal court in

655 (Bankr. D.R.I. 1980); McNish v. General Credit Corp., 83 N.W.2d 1 (Neb. 1957) (statute since amended); Conrad v. Home & Auto Loan Co. 385 N.Y.S.2d 979 (App. Div. 1976); Smashed Ice v. Lee, 200 N.W.2d 236 (S.D. 1972). *See also* Ferrigno v. Cromwell Dev. Ass'n, 708 A.2d 1371 (Conn. 1998) (Connecticut law states: "No action shall be brought to recover principal or interest, or any part thereof, in any loan prohibited by [the general usury law])." Court held that an exception to this prohibition for bona fide "mortgage" of real property in excess of $5000 includes actions not only to foreclose upon the property but also actions to sue on the debt or to obtain a deficiency judgment following foreclosure); Aikens v. Wagner, 498 S.E.2d 766 (Ga. App. 1998) (usury can be a defense to a foreclosure action but applicable statute forfeits interest only; transaction not void). *But cf.* Miller v. Pacific Shore Funding, 224 F. Supp. 2d 977 (D. Md. May 17, 2002) (loan made in violation of Second Mortgage Loan Law not void or voidable where statute did not explicitly provide that remedy), *aff'd on other grounds*, 2004 WL 144138 (4th Cir. Jan. 28, 2004). *See generally* Hubachek, Annotations on Small Loan Laws (Russell Sage Foundation 1938) (complete compilation of small loan act cases decided through 1938); Hubachek, *The Development of Regulatory Small Loan Laws*, 8 Law & Contemporary Problems 108 (1941) (including supplemental list of small loan cases through 1941).

784 *See, e.g.,* Garrison v. First Fed. Sav. & Loan Ass'n of S.C., 402 S.E.2d 25 (Va. 1991) (usurious second mortgage null and void and unenforceable under Virginia's second mortgage act, since revised in 1987); Moran v. American Funding, Ltd., 569 A.2d 841 (N.J. Super. 1989) (the words "void and unenforceable" mean just that in New Jersey's second mortgage act, since amended in 1987). *But see* Thoreson v. Shaffer, 683 A.2d 1153 (Md. App. 1996) (Maryland secondary mortgage loan law provides that any violation of the statute prevents the lender from collecting "any interest, costs, or other charges with respect to the loan;" court held that broker fee was not a charge with respect to the loan, and thus, collectible by the lender, unless the lender has a direct pecuniary interest or managerial influence or control over the broker).

785 *See* United Kansas Bank & Trust v. Rixner, 610 P.2d 116 (Kan. App.), *aff'd*, 619 P.2d 1156 (Kan. 1980) (1974 draft of U.C.C.C.); Kuykendall v. Malernee, 516 P.2d 558 (Okla. Ct. App. 1973) (1968 draft of U.C.C.C.). *See also* Edwards v. Alabama Farm Bureau Mut. Casualty Ins. Co., 509 So. 2d 232 (Ala. Civ. App. 1986), *cert. quashed*, 509 So. 2d 241 (1987) (loan by unlicensed lender voided under Alabama Mini-Code; borrower also entitled to refund of payments under statute). A credit contract with an unlicensed lender may be void in any case. *See generally* § 9.2.4.6, *supra*.

786 *See, e.g.,* Tex. Fin. Code § 305.002 (Vernon); Risica & Sons, Inc. v. Tubelite, 794 S.W.2d 468 (Tex. App. 1990), *aff'd*, 819 S.W.2d 801 (Tex. 1991) (where more than double the amount of legal interest charged, under Texas law principal ($42,920.25) was forfeited; the $10,000 paid by borrower was reimbursed; and three times the amount of excess interest charged ($19,536.33) was awarded as penalty).

787 *See* § 10.8.2.2.2, *supra*.
788 *See, e.g.,* U.C.C.C. § 5.202(2) (1968 Model Code); Edwards v. Alabama Farm Bureau Mut. Casualty Ins. Co., 509 So. 2d 232 (Ala. Civ. App. 1986), *cert. quashed*, 509 So. 2d 241 (1987) (loan by unlicensed lender voided under Alabama Mini-Code; borrower also entitled to refund of payments made); Ferrari v. Howard, 2002 WL 1500414 (Ohio Ct. App. July 11, 2002) (unpublished) (interpreting former version of retail installment sales act; when violation was willful, consumer has no further obligation on the contract, need not return the collateral, and is entitled to refund of all payments). Some versions of the uniform small loan act have denied the creditor the right to "retain" payments, so a refund is obviously required. *See* Young v. Barker, 342 P.2d 150 (Kan. 1959) (Kansas has since adopted a version of the U.C.C.C.). *See also* Ganus v. Jopes, 470 So. 2d. 237 (La. Ct. App. 1985) (statutory "forfeiture" required return of all interest payments); Chandlee v. Tharp, 137 So. 540 (Miss. 1931) (usury ceiling is 8%; payment to principal recoverable if contract rate exceeds 20%).

789 *See* Daenzer v. Wayland Ford, Inc., 210 F.R.D. 202 (W.D. Mich. 2002); Bailey v. Defenbaugh & Co. of Cleveland, 513 F. Supp. 232 (N.D. Miss. 1981); In re Harrington, 6 B.R. 655 (Bankr. D.R.I. 1980); McNish v. General Credit Corp., 83 N.W.2d 1 (Neb. 1957); Smashed Ice v. Lee, 200 N.W.2d 236 (S.D. 1972). *See also In re* Capobianco, 73 B.R. 101 (Bankr. D.R.I. 1987) (return of payments ordered where Secondary Mortgage Loan Act voided usurious loans and provided that lender has no right to receive "any principal, interest or charges whatsoever"); Kinerd v. Colonial Leasing Co., 800 S.W.2d 187 (Tex. 1990) (interest charged was more than twice that allowed by Texas' general usury statute; penalty was refund of amounts paid, collection of debt was barred, and a penalty of three times the usurious interest); Risica & Sons, Inc. v. Tubelite, 794 S.W.2d 468 (Tex. App. 1990), *aff'd*, 819 S.W.2d 801 (Tex. 1991) (where more than double the amount of legal interest charged, under Texas law principal ($42,920.25) was forfeited; the $10,000 payments made by borrower were reimbursed; and three times

Michigan allowed buyers to recover finance charges from a dealer under this type of statutory provision even though the dealer had sold and assigned the credit contracts to finance companies.[790] The court reasoned that the finance company's payment to the dealer was based at least in part on the present value of the interest payments the buyers were expected to make, so the dealer had received a benefit from those finance charges.

However, it can be difficult without such statutory or judicial authority to argue that payments to principal or interest may be recovered simply because the obligation is declared "void" by statute. The problem is multifaceted. First, strictly speaking, if a contract is "void," a court will generally refuse to recognize its existence and will leave the parties where it finds them.[791] This suggests that while a lender could not sue the debtor on the purported debt, neither could the debtor recover payments back without specific statutory authorization, although courts have sometimes rejected this reasoning because of the intent of usury statutes to protect borrowers.[792] Second, courts frequently reason that even though a statute declares a usurious debt to be "void," the debt is actually voidable at the option of the debtor.[793] This position has led some courts to hold that a borrower can waive the usury by "voluntary" payment,[794] and having so waived his rights, may not recover the

payments.[795] This issue is discussed in greater detail in § 10.6.4, *supra*.[796] Third, some usury statutes are structured so that usury remedies are exclusively defensive. For example, a statute might declare a usurious loan "void" but then proceed to provide merely that the creditor may not collect on the debt.[797]

One implication could be that no debtor recovery is available except by recoupment in a creditor's action. However, it is possible to argue that such statutes create an implied private right of action to enforce the borrower's rights under the usury statute, and, in the absence of clear statutory language making it solely defensive, the practitioner should explore that option. The Arizona Supreme Court, interpreting its Consumer Loan Act which, in common with other statutes based upon the Uniform Small Loan Act, voided usurious loans by licensees and prohibited the collection of principal, interest or other charges, held that the statute created a private right of action.[798] The court also

---

the amount of excess interest charged ($19,536.33) was awarded as penalty; statute provided for forfeiture of "all principal"). *But see* Conrad v. Home & Auto Loan, Inc., 385 N.Y.S.2d 979 (App. Div. 1976) (no refund of payments "voluntarily" made).

790 Daenzer v. Wayland Ford, Inc., 210 F.R.D. 202 (W.D. Mich. 2002).

791 *See* Szerdahelyi v. Harris, 490 N.E.2d 517 (N.Y. 1986) (voiding is neither penalty nor forfeiture). *But see* Kowalski v. Cedars of Portsmouth Condominium Assn., 769 A.2d 344 (N.H. 2001) (allowing recovery on unjust enrichment theory of payments made to unlicensed real estate broker).

792 *See In re* Harrington, 6 B.R. 655 (Bankr. D.R.I. 1980); Kuykendall v. Malernee, 516 P.2d 558 (Okla. Ct. App. 1973). *See also* Siner v. Am. Gen. Fin., Inc., 2004 WL 2441185 (E.D. Pa. Oct. 28, 2004) (home improvement contract that included forbidden cash loan is illegal as an essential term violates public policy; it is therefore unenforceable, but consumer cannot recover payments already made).

793 Elwell v. Daggs, 108 U.S. 143 (1883) (interpreting Texas statute); Wakefield v. Goldstein, 644 F.2d 707 (8th Cir. 1981) (Arkansas law); Pilcher v. Direct Equity Lending, 189 F. Supp. 2d 1198 (D. Kan. 2002); Chandlee v. Tharp, 137 So. 540 (Miss. 1931).

794 The precise distinction between the voluntary and involuntary payment of usury is far from obvious. It is apparently a question of fact. *See* Conrad v. Home & Auto Loan Co., 385 N.Y.S.2d 979 (App. Div. 1976) (remand for factual determination). *See also* Thelen v. Ducharme, 390 N.W.2d 264 (Mich. App. 1986) (payment by borrowers after judgment rendered against them is not voluntary payment which would waive usury); Sienkiewicz v. Leonard Mortgage Co., 229 N.W.2d 352 (Mich. App. 1975) (issue of voluntariness not properly raised); § 10.6.5, *supra*.

795 *See, e.g.,* Wakefield v. Goldstein, 644 F.2d 707 (8th Cir. 1981); Bizzoco v. Chintz, 476 A.2d 572 (Conn. 1984) (interpreting statute that expressly prohibited recovery of voluntary payments of interest); Waldorf v. Zinberg, 307 N.W.2d 749 (Mich. App. 1981); Sienkiewicz v. Leonard Mortgage Co., 229 N.W.2d 352 (Mich. App. 1975); Luebke v. Moser, 598 N.E.2d 760 (Ohio Ct. App. 1991) (Ohio common law is that usurious interest may not be recovered if voluntarily paid); Cherry v. Berg, 508 S.W.2d 869 (Tex. Civ. App. 1974) (borrower can have all payments applied to reduce principal of usurious loan, but voluntary payments made after principal has been fully repaid cannot be recovered). *See also* Chandlee v. Tharp, 137 So. 540 (Miss. 1931) (property sold pursuant to foreclosure at which no usury was alleged cannot be recovered because of waiver, although purchase price may be recovered); Conrad v. Home & Auto Loan Co., 385 N.Y.S.2d 979 (App. Div. 1976) (construing statutory usury remedy not to allow recovery of voluntary payments).

Other courts have held that usury voluntarily paid is nevertheless recoverable. *See* Kline v. Robinson, 428 P.2d 190 (Nev. 1967); Siefkes v. Clark Title Co., 215 N.W.2d 648 (S.D. 1974). *See also* Dougherty v. North Fork Bank, 753 N.Y.S.2d 130 (App. Div. 2003) (voluntary payment of illegal fees for pay-off quotes is not a defense). It is frequently unclear whether the opinions addressing the recovery of usurious interest paid are based on statutory interpretation or on the common law as it stands in the relevant jurisdiction.

796 *See also* National Consumer Law Center, Unfair and Deceptive Acts and Practices §§ 4.2.15.5, 9.7.5.4 (6th ed. 2004 and Supp.).

797 *See* Olsen v. Porter, 539 N.W.2d 523 (Mich. Ct. App. 1995) (Michigan law requiring prior interest paid be applied to principal applies only in defense to creditor's action to enforce usurious contract; creditor's action to reform the contract was not enforcement action, so remedy unavailable to borrowers); Michigan Mobile Homeowners Ass'n v. Bank of Commonwealth, 223 N.W.2d 725 (Mich. App. 1974) (discussing former Michigan law). *Cf.* Bank of Guam v. Demapan, 839 F.2d 1344 (9th Cir. 1988) (where statute merely limits the amount of interest a lender can recover when suing on the contract and does not otherwise provide for voiding the contract or punishing the lender, court will not enforce the contract for the excess; but borrower cannot recover interest paid).

798 Transamerica Fin. Corp. v. Superior Court, 761 P.2d 1019 (Ariz. 1988). *But see* Taylor v. Citizens Fed. Savs. & Loan, 846 F.2d

noted that the provisions of a licensing act are part of a loan contract by operation of law, and are thus enforceable in a contract action.[799] A New Hampshire trial court has also concluded that a borrower can sue affirmatively to recover finance charges and other charges that the usury statute bars the creditor from collecting.[800] The court reasoned that it would be illogical to require a buyer to stop making payments, and wait to be sued, in order to take advantage of this right.

A significant exception to the rule against the debtor's recovery of payments made, apart from statutes which specifically provide a recovery remedy, is that many states recognize a common law action for the recovery of the usurious portion of interest payments made on a contract.[801] Such a claim has particular potential in very high-rate credit such as payday loans, where the finance charges often exceed the principal after a few rollovers. Such an action can be invaluable to debtors if litigation occurs only after most of a loan is paid off because the creditor's forfeiture of future payments means little at this point. A common law recovery can also help debtors who have statute of limitations prob-

lems because the time limit for actions in assumpsit may exceed that in the usury statute.[802]

Attorneys who are interested in the availability of common law recovery in particular jurisdictions should check an *ALR* annotation and any updates on this point.[803] Not all states recognize the common law action, and in some states which formerly recognized the action, it has been abrogated by statute.[804] A few courts, though, have specifically held that the common law action has not been repealed by the enactment of specific statutory remedies, but that the common law action instead supplements the statutory remedies.[805] However, an effort to collect damages under a federal common law theory against a federally-chartered savings and loan for excess charges resulting from violations of FHLBB regulations failed.[806]

1320 (11th Cir. 1988) (no private right of action implied by the Home Owner's Loan Act of 1933 to seek damages for violations of FHLBB regulations promulgated pursuant thereto. State law claims for breach of contract, conversion and breach of fiduciary duty could be prosecuted in proper forum). See other cases cited in § 10.8.6, *infra. See also* § 10.8.3, *infra.*

799 Transamerica Fin. Corp. v. Superior Court, 761 P.2d 1019, 1022 (Ariz. 1988).

800 Couture v. G.W.M., Inc., 2002 WL 31962752 (N.H. Super. Ct. Dec. 3, 2002). *See also* Gibbo v. Berger, 123 Cal. App. 4th 396, 19 Cal. Rptr. 3d 829 (2004) (where state usury law barred lender from collecting any interest, borrower was entitled to refund on unjust enrichment theory of amount by which her payments exceeded the principal).

801 *See* Dennis v. Bradbury, 236 F. Supp. 683 (D. Colo. 1964), *aff'd*, 368 F.2d 905 (10th Cir. 1966); Westman v. Dye, 4 P.2d 134 (Cal. 1931); Beltz v. Dings, 6 P.3d 424 (Kan. Ct. App. 2000); Commercial Credit Equip. Corp. v. West, 677 S.W.2d 669 (Tex. App. 1984) (recovery extends to legal interest as well as usurious interest paid); Flannery v. Bishop, 504 P.2d 778 (Wash. Ct. App. 1972). *See also* Gibbo v. Berger, 123 Cal. App. 4th 396, 19 Cal. Rptr. 3d 829 (2004) (where state usury law barred lender from collecting any interest, borrower was entitled to refund on unjust enrichment theory of amount by which her payments exceeded the principal); Mayo v. Key Fin. Servs., Inc., 1994 Mass. App. LEXIS 549 (Mass. Super. Ct., June 22, 1994), *aff'd on other grounds*, 678 N.E.2d 1311 (Mass. 1997) (implied private right of action for violation of statute limiting points; assertable by a suitable common law remedy; borrowers choose to assert common law restitution). *But see* Marker v. Pacific Mezzanine Fund, 309 F.3d 744 (10th Cir. 2002) (provision for forfeiture of interest does not create right to recover interest already paid); Anderson v. Chainani (*In re* Kemper) 263 B.R. 773, 781 n.15 (Bankr. E.D. Tex. 2001) (noting Texas legislature's 1999 abolition of common law remedies for usury); Luebke v. Moser, 598 N.E.2d 760 (Ohio Ct. App. 1991) (Ohio common law is that borrower cannot recover usurious interest voluntarily paid, at least if payment involved mistake of law rather than mistake of fact).

802 *See* § 10.8.2.4, *infra* for a discussion of the attribution of contract payments to principal, interest, or usurious interest for purposes of a statute of limitation.

803 Annot. 59 A.L.R.2d 522 (1958) (right, in absence of statute expressly so providing, to recover back usurious payments). *See also* Bank of Guam v. Demapan, 839 F.2d 1344 (9th Cir. 1988) (where statute merely limits the amount of interest a lender can recover when suing on the contract and does not otherwise provide for voiding the contract or punishing the lender, court will not enforce the contract for the excess; but borrower cannot recover interest paid).

804 *See* Anderson v. Chainani (*In re* Kemper) 263 B.R. 773, 781 n.15 (Bankr. E.D. Tex. 2001) (noting Texas legislature's 1999 abolition of common law remedies for usury); Smith v. Barnett Bank of Murray Hill, 350 So. 2d. 358 (Fla. Dist. Ct. App. 1977), *overruled on other grounds*, 457 So. 2d. 1021 (Fla. 1984); Schlattman v. Stone, 511 P.2d 959 (Wyo. 1973).

805 Westman v. Dye, 4 P.2d 134 (Cal. 1931); Commercial Credit Equip. Corp. v. West, 677 S.W.2d 669 (Tex. App. 1984); Flannery v. Bishop, 504 P.2d 778 (Wash. 1972); Demopolis v. Galvin, 786 P.2d 804, 808 (Wash. Ct. App. 1990) ("statutory usury remedies do not abrogate the common law action to recover usurious interest"). *See also* Danziger v. San Jacinto Sav. Ass'n, 732 S.W.2d 300 (Tex. 1987) (allowing common law penalty of return of interest paid and cancellation of interest not yet paid, in addition to statutory penalties); El Paso Dev. Co. v. Berryman, 769 S.W.2d 584 (Tex. App. 1989) (allowing return of principal and cancellation of deed of trust where both common law and statutory causes of action pled), *further proceedings*, 838 S.W.2d 610 (Tex. App. 1992); Hardwick v. Austin Gallery of Oriental Rugs, Inc., 779 S.W.2d 438 (Tex. App. 1989) (statutory penalty awarded plus recovery of illegal interest paid as equitable restitution under theory of "money fraudulently 'had and received' "; court states that usury is recoverable even if paid voluntarily); Coppedge v. Colonial Sav. & Loan Ass'n, 721 S.W.2d 933 (Tex. App. 1986) (common law remedy is an alternative to statutory remedies; compare with *West, supra*). *But see* Anderson v. Chainani (*In re* Kemper) 263 B.R. 773, 781 n.15 (Bankr. E.D. Tex. 2001) (noting Texas legislature's 1999 abolition of common law remedies for usury).

806 Taylor v. Citizens Fed. Savs. & Loan Ass'n, 846 F.2d 1320 (11th Cir. 1988) (court also held federal statute created no private right of action; borrower's claims for breach of contract, conversion and breach of fiduciary duty could be prosecuted in proper forum. *Ed. Note*: The lack of a federal common law claim or private right of action under the Home Owner's Loan Act to *directly* enforce FHLBB/OTS regulations should not be

Consumer attorneys should be careful to plead a common law action, if available in their jurisdiction, separately in their complaint or counterclaim so that it will not be deemed waived.

10.8.2.4 Statutory Penalties

Beyond providing restitution to a borrower who has proved usury, usually in the form of a credit for or recovery of usurious interest paid, usury statutes often impose penalties on the creditor involved. The penalties frequently take the form of an award to the borrower of double or triple either the interest or the usurious portion of the interest paid on the contract.[807] (These penalties are often limited to that paid within a year or two of the filing of the suit.[808]) It is difficult to generalize about the interpretation or effect of penalty provisions because the terms of the statutes vary significantly. Nevertheless, a few issues arise with regularity.

The first issue is one of accounting. If the penalty only reaches *interest payments made* within a year or two of the date of filing suit, it is obviously important to figure out what portion of the payments made during that period should be attributed to interest. If the contract does not specifically address which payments will be credited to interest and which to principal, most courts will first credit payments to principal.[809] This rule can be either advantageous or disad-

vantageous to borrowers depending on the circumstances. If the total payments made on the contract do not exceed the principal debt and they are all credited against that debt, then no interest will have been paid for purposes of the penalty provision.[810] However, if the total payments made exceed the principal debt, then the rule attributing payments first to principal suggests that the last payments made on the contract—i.e., the payments on which the statute of limitations for the penalty has not yet expired—are exclusively interest payments.[811]

For example, if a statute provided a penalty of twice the interest paid within a year of the date suit was filed, all of the payments made within that year should be doubled to calculate the penalty, so long as previous payments on the contract had satisfied the principal debt. Similarly, if the recovery is calculated solely on the basis of the usurious portion of the interest paid, then unallocated contract payments will be attributed first to principal, next to any unforfeited legal interest, and only last to usurious interest, with consequences for the borrower that mirror those when the penalty is calculated on the basis of all interest payments within the period set by the statute of limitations.[812]

If the statute provides for a penalty of two or three times the amount of excess interest "*charged or contracted for,*" the question of allocating payments made is avoided. The amount of excess interest is determined by the charge imposed or contracted for, not the payments made.[813] However, if the loan has gone past maturity, there may be a question whether to use the interest up to the date of trial or just up to the maturity date.[814]

---

used to cloud the issue of a borrower's rights when OTS compliance is at issue because a creditor is claiming the protection of federal preemption. *See* Ch. 3, *supra*. A borrower may raise a state law usury claim where a creditor fails to comply with certain OTS regulations and thus cannot claim to be exempt from otherwise applicable state law by virtue of federal preemption legislation. *See* §§ 3.5.3.4 and 3.6, *supra*. In those cases, the borrower is not seeking to directly enforce OTS regulations, but to enforce the state usury law which is applicable to the transaction by virtue of the creditor's failure to comply with the relevant federal regulations).

807 *See, e.g.*, Trapp v. Hancuh, 530 N.W.2d 879 (Minn. Ct. App. 1995) (interpreting Minn. Stat. § 334.011 subd. 2 [small business/agricultural loans], providing for forfeiture of all interest plus recovery of twice interest actually paid). *Cf.* Tilley v. Pacesetter Corp., 585 S.E.2d 292 (S.C. 2003) (denying recovery of double the excess finance charge when violation of usury law related to loan closing procedures rather than interest, even though as a result of that violation lender forfeited the finance charge).

808 *See, e.g.*, Williams v. Seeley (*In re* Williams), 227 B.R. 83 (Bankr. E.D. Va. 1998) (Virginia's secondary mortgage loan law provides for the recovery of the total amount of interest paid in excess of that permitted plus twice the total amount of interest paid during the two years immediately preceding the filing of the action plus court costs and attorney fees), *on remand*, 241 B.R. 387 (Bankr. E.D. Va. 1999), *rev'd on other grounds*, 2001 WL 652028 (4th Cir. June 13, 2001); Skinner v. Cen-Pen Corp., 414 S.E.2d 824 (Va. 1992) (Va. Code § 6.1-330.46 interpreted to allow recovery of twice all interest paid within limitations period).

809 *See* § 10.8.2.2.1, *supra*. *Cf.* El Paso Dev. Co. v. Berryman, 769 S.W.2d 584 (Tex. App. 1989) (for purposes of calculating

excess interest for statutory penalties, maximum allowable interest should be calculated based on terms of contract at its inception), *further proceedings*, 838 S.W.2d 610 (Tex. App. 1992).

810 *See In re* Vehm Eng'g, 521 F.2d 186 (9th Cir. 1975). But note that many contracts specify that payments will be applied first to interest. *See, e.g., In re* Grigsby, 127 B.R. 759 (E.D. Pa. 1990) (where contract provided that payments would be applied first to interest, Pennsylvania law mandates award of three times amount of excess interest due on any given payment).

811 *See* Henderson v. Security Mortgage & Fin. Co., 160 S.E.2d 39 (N.C. 1968).

812 *See* Baruch. Inv. Co. v. Huntoon, 65 Cal. Rptr. 131 (App. 1967).

813 *See, e.g.*, Strasburger Enterprises, Inc. v. TDGT Ltd. P'ship, 110 S.W.3d 566, 579 (Tex. App. 2003) (penalty is based on difference between legal rate and interest creditor demanded, even though not paid); Risica & Sons, Inc. v. Tubelite, 794 S.W.2d 468 (Tex. App. 1990), *aff'd*, 819 S.W.2d 801 (Tex. 1991) (where more than double the amount of legal interest charged, under Texas law principal ($42,920.25) was forfeited; the $10,000 payments made by borrower was reimbursed; and three times the amount of excess interest charged ($19,536.33) was awarded as penalty; no payments to interest had been made, the amount of excess interest charged was determined from statements of account).

814 *See* Confederated Tribes v. Quantum Five, Inc., 91 P.3d 1255 (Mont. 2004) (discussing competing rationales, but using lesser amount here because of unique facts and equitable principles).

In cases involving accounts, where the statute calls for forfeiture of principal, determining what is the principal may be complicated. The Texas Supreme Court held in one case that the principal to be forfeited was that part of the account upon which the usurious interest was charged.[815]

A second issue that may arise in connection with statutory penalty provisions is the effect of such provisions in the absence of an express statutory forfeiture of the lender's right to receive future interest payments on the contract. Some creditors have argued that statutes which require the creditor to pay a penalty of, say, twice the interest contracted for, do not preclude the creditor from simultaneously recovering interest at the legal rate which would then be offset against the penalty. Courts have generally rejected this creditor argument on the grounds that it would undermine the effectiveness of the penalty provision.[816] Moreover, at least under some penalty provisions, a lender may not treat the penalty that it owes the borrower as an offset against any principal balance still outstanding, but instead must pay the full amount of the penalty to the borrower.[817]

A third issue may arise where a statute authorizes a penalty based on the "excess" over the "lawful rate": what statute applies to define the "lawful rate"? In a Pennsylvania case, the debtor argued that the lawful rate should be equated with the general usury statute's "legal" rate of 6%. The court rejected that argument, holding that the lawful rate was determined instead by reference to the special usury statute with which the court believed the creditor should have complied.[818]

However, the practitioner must be careful in deciding which statute to argue should have applied. For example, a Missouri statute authorized a flexible "market rate" ceiling where the parties so agreed in writing. The parties had a written agreement to pay 17%, when the maximum under that provision was 16.6%. The trial court had used 16.6% as the proper rate. On appeal, however, the appellate court held that the written agreement to pay the usurious rate invalidated the written agreement. Without the written agreement, the legal rate of 9% was the proper rate to apply where the borrower was seeking relief under the "defensive" usury penalty, allowing the usurious lender judgment for only principal and the "legal interest." On the other hand, as to the borrower's seeking affirmative recovery of twice the interest paid "greater than permitted by law," the court utilized the market rate which would have been authorized under that section of the law.[819]

Finally, it should be argued that the imposition of statutory penalties is mandatory,[820] at least in the absence of clear language to the contrary. If the law provides, for example, that the creditor "shall forfeit" a triple damage penalty to the borrower, that is mandatory on the court: such a penalty is "meant to punish and deter those who charge usuriously."[821] Moreover, statutory damages may be assessed against each separate entity guilty of usury.[822]

10.8.3 Equitable Remedies

Although most usury and other overcharge remedies exist under statutes or common law, there are circumstances when a debtor's appropriate remedy for usury is in equity. The most common occasion is when the creditor is attempting to foreclose upon security, often the borrower's home, given in conjunction with the usurious loan. Borrowers who want to enjoin foreclosures must typically invoke the court's equitable powers to do so. Equity may also control if a borrower wants to rescind an illegal credit sale contract, although rescission of consumer sales contracts is often controlled by statute.[823]

815 Steves Sash & Door Co. v. Ceco Corp., 751 S.W.2d 473 (Tex. 1988).

816 *See* Bjornstad v. Perry, 443 P.2d 999 (Idaho 1968) (no interest whatever on the principal can be charged or offset against the penalties); Commercial Credit Equip. Corp. v. West, 677 S.W.2d 669 (Tex. App. 1984). *See also* Bonfanti v. Davis, 487 So. 2d 165 (La. Ct. App. 1986) (forfeiture of interest means all interest, not just the difference between the contract rate and the legal rate); Thomas Lakes Owners Assoc. v. Riley, 612 N.W.2d 529 (Neb. App. 2000) (where usurious contract is not void, but recovery is limited to principal without interest, creditor cannot fall back on legal rate of interest). *Cf.* Merritt v. Knox, 380 S.E.2d 160 (N.C. Ct. App. 1989) (lender allowed to collect "legal" rate of interest, generally the lowest rate of various allowable ones, from contract date because limitation period for interest forfeiture had expired). *But cf.* Mark McDowell Corp. v. LSM 128, 263 Cal. Rptr. 310 (Ct. App. 1989) (usury resulted in note payable at maturity in principal amount only, but did not prevent creditor from earning postmaturity interest at legal rate).

817 *See* McCollum v. Hamilton Nat'l Bank, 303 U.S. 245 (1938) (National Bank Act penalties).

818 *In re* Russell, 72 B.R. 855 (Bankr. E.D. Pa. 1987). *Cf.* Dunnam v. Burns, 901 S.W.2d 628 (Tex. App. 1995) (Texas cap for agreed rates is 18%, 6% if no agreed rate; where loan specified a dollar amount of interest and terms from which the rate could be determined, the 18% ceiling applied. *NB*: compare § 9.2.8, *supra*). *See also In re* Marshall, 1998 Bankr. LEXIS 515 (Bankr. M.D.N.C. Mar. 2, 1998) (amount over rate cap of 16% in RISA is forfeited); Avila v. Cmty. Bank, 2003 WL 22002779 (Mo. Ct. App. Aug. 26, 2003) (bank that charged interest allowed by its

home state and federal laws was in compliance with statute limiting it to "lawful" interest rates); Stringer v. Perales, 2003 WL 1848594 (Tex. App. Apr. 10, 2003) (unpublished) (any interest charged in an interest-free period is in excess of twice the legal rate of zero).

819 Addison v. Jester, 758 S.W.2d 454 (Mo. Ct. App. 1988) (*NB*: The court also found that a usury defense was sufficient grounds to avoid payment of a late penalty except as to any late installments falling after judgment).

820 McElroy v. Grisham, 810 S.W.2d 933 (Ark. 1991) (provision that borrower "may recover" twice the amount of interest paid was mandatory; to read it otherwise would defeat purpose of discouraging usurious contracts).

821 Berryman v. El Paso Natural Gas, 838 S.W.2d 610 (Tex. App. 1992) (holding debtor entitled to recover full penalty even though he pled an incorrect amount).

822 *Id.*

823 *See* Barco Auto Leasing Corp. v. House, 520 A.2d 162 (Conn.

Seeking equitable remedies for usury can present serious problems for borrowers. The main obstacle is the rule that a party seeking equity must do equity which, in the case of a borrower facing foreclosure of a usurious mortgage, means tendering the principal balance owed on the debt,[824] sometimes with legal interest,[825] and sometimes with amounts expended by the lender to maintain the security.[826] Tender may be avoided if a statute declares the underlying debt to be void or if the payments already made on the contract exceed the principal originally lent, because in either case the principal balance owed is zero.[827] Yet, if principal is still owed, the debtor will have the difficult task of producing a large sum of money quickly. Courts are rarely swayed by the fact that the tender requirement imposes serious hardship upon consumer borrowers, or that such a requirement, in the face of demonstrated wrongdoing on the part of the creditor, hardly seems equitable.[828]

A second problem with equitable usury remedies is that the debtor may be unable to obtain in a foreclosure proceeding all the offsets or penalties which might be available in a creditor's action on the debt. While there are not always problems,[829] the precise language of the statutes varies greatly, and can sometimes create difficulties. In Connecticut, a statutory usury exception precluded the assertion of usury on bona fide mortgages over $5,000 even though usury may be raised as a defense in a deficiency action brought at law after foreclosure.[830] Similarly, prior to an amendment to Michigan law, that state's usury statute provided the borrower with a defense to the creditor's action on a note, but if the creditor instead attempted foreclosure, the borrower could be forced to tender principal plus legal interest.[831]

(Practitioners should note that home equity credit transactions which include illegal overcharges frequently also violate Truth in Lending's disclosure requirements, and TIL rescission may be a separate remedy available.[832] As TIL has both its own tender rules, which differ from those for

---

1987) (implied right of rescission under Retail Installment Sales Financing Act).

824 Speare v. Consolidated Assets Corp., 367 F.2d 208 (2d Cir. 1966) (applying New Jersey law); Metcalf v. Bartrand, 491 P.2d 747 (Alaska 1971); Winnett v. Roberts, 225 Cal. Rptr. 82 (App. 1986) (proper tender made; foreclosure sale set aside); Feemster v. Schurkman, 291 So. 2d. 622 (Fla. Dist. Ct. App. 1974); Citizens & Southern DeKalb Bank v. Watkins, 225 S.E.2d 266 (Ga. 1976); I.D.S. Homes Corp. v. Lucas, 186 S.E.2d 745 (Ga. 1972); Kawauchi v. Tabata, 413 P.2d 221 (Haw. 1966); Michigan Mobile Homeowners Ass'n v. Bank of Commonwealth, 223 N.W.2d 725 (Mich. App. 1974); Naumburg v. Pattison, 711 P.2d 1387 (N.M. 1985); Bohlinger v. Am. Credit Co., 594 S.W.2d 710 (Tenn. App. 1979). *But see* Williams v. Macchio, 329 N.Y.S.2d 405 (Sup. Ct. 1972) (no tender necessary when usurious contract signed under duress).

825 *See* Kawauchi v. Tabata, 413 P.2d 221 (Haw. 1966) (emphasizing the equities in this particular case); Bohlinger v. Am. Credit Co., 594 S.W.2d 710 (Tenn. Ct. App. 1979).

826 *Compare* Barco Auto Leasing Corp. v. House, 520 A.2d 162 (Conn. 1987) (creditor which violated Retail Installment Sales Financing Act was not entitled to offset for fair rental value of automobile when buyer rescinds contract) *and* Kuykendall v. Malernee, 516 P.2d 558 (Okla. App. 1973) (payment for excise taxes and expenses on automobile not recoverable) *with* Metcalf v. Bartrand, 491 P.2d 747 (Alaska 1971) (tender must include amount paid for real estate tax); Feemster v. Schurkman, 291 So. 2d. 622 (Fla. Dist. Ct. App. 1974) (lender can recover expenses related to prior lease and first mortgage); Pisaro v. Rand, 291 N.Y.S.2d 82 (App. Div. 1968) (under unjust enrichment theory, lender can recover sums spent for taxes and payments on outstanding senior mortgages).

827 *See* I.D.S. Homes Corp. v. Lucas, 186 S.E.2d 745 (Ga. 1972) (borrower must tender amount admittedly due; complete failure of consideration could obviate tender in proper case); Bjornstad v. Perry, 443 P.2d 999 (Idaho 1968) (recovery by borrowers exceeds remaining principal due); Pisaro v. Rand, 291 N.Y.S.2d 82 (App. Div. 1968) (mortgage was void).

828 The courts have some discretion to delay the time when tender must be made. *See* Speare v. Consolidated Assets Corp., 367 F.2d 208 (2d Cir. 1966) (bankruptcy case). Note also that the immediate payment of the full amount of principal might not be necessary if for some reason the payments were not yet due under the contract. For example, in a North Carolina case, a

senior mortgagee foreclosed on a parcel of land, leaving a surplus. The second mortgage note was held usurious, so the second mortgage lender was entitled to recover only its principal. The court held that because the borrower had never defaulted on the second mortgage note, no event had occurred to enable the second mortgage lender to accelerate its debt, and that the second mortgage lender was thus entitled only to periodic payments of principal from the surplus amount. *In re* Castillian Apartments, Inc., 190 S.E.2d 161 (N.C. 1972).

829 *See, e.g.*, Johnson v. Ronamy Consumer Credit Corp., 515 A.2d 682 (Del. 1986) (invalidation of second mortgage pursuant to second mortgage statute also reaches personal guarantees executed by debtors); Colter v. Consolidated Credit Corp., 154 S.E.2d 812 (Ga. App.), *later appeal,* 157 S.E.2d 812 (Ga. App. 1967) (affidavit of illegality allows borrower to set up any defense in a foreclosure action which could be brought in an action on the debt); El Paso Dev. Co. v. Berryman, 769 S.W.2d 584 (Tex. App. 1989), *further proceedings,* 838 S.W.2d 610 (Tex. App. 1992) (where borrower alleged both statutory and common law usury, court awarded statutory penalty of return of principal and forfeiture of interest plus cancellation of deed of trust under common law claim). *See also* Enell Corp. v. Longoria, 834 S.W.2d 132 (Tex. App. 1992) (first lien taken in retail installment sale contract in violation of Tex. Cons. Cred. Code was invalidated; to allow creditors to illegally take first liens with only payment of statutory penalty would allow creditors to avoid its duties and "profit from the very evil the legislature seeks to avoid." [Purpose of statute was to limit first liens to 10% or less; it requires creditors to choose between higher interest rates and less security or lower interest rates and greater security]).

830 *See* Maresca v. DeMatteo, 506 A.2d 1096 (Conn. App. 1986). *See also* Solomon v. Gilmore, 731 A.2d 280 (Conn. 1999) (failure to obtain a secondary mortgage loan license renders loan not enforceable in a foreclosure action).

831 *See* Michigan Mobile Homeowners Ass'n v. Bank of Commonwealth, 223 N.W.2d 725 (Mich. App. 1974).

832 15 U.S.C. § 1635. For a complete discussion of what transactions are subject to the rescission right, violations giving rise to the right, and the procedure, see generally National Consumer Law Center, Truth in Lending Ch. 6 (5th ed. 2003 and Supp.).

equitable rescission under common law, and its own rules regarding credits, offsets and penalties, a home foreclosure case should always be evaluated for TIL rescission rights, in addition to relief under state law.)

A final equitable issue that may arise in usury cases is the question of reformation. Creditors have sometimes sought to avoid usury penalties by requesting that usurious contracts be reformed to non-usurious rates. Such reformation has occasionally been granted on grounds of mutual mistake of the parties or on grounds of fraud by the borrower.[833] However, outside of these narrow circumstances, courts have viewed statutory usury remedies as mandatory and have refused to resort to equity.[834]

The one situation in which reformation may benefit borrowers arises when a transaction is declared usurious, perhaps by a criminal usury statute, but no civil statutory remedies are provided. In this circumstance, it is within the equitable power of a court at least to reform the contract to a legal rate, possibly to void the loan if the facts warrant such an action,[835] or invoke the clean hands doctrine to refuse an offending lender's claim for relief.[836] The court might imply a right of action from a criminal usury ceiling, and limit a creditor's right to recover solely to principal, forfeiting interest and charges.[837]

10.8.4 Consumer Remedies for Creditor's Failure to Obtain a License

10.8.4.1 Unlicensed Lending

The effects of failure to obtain a proper license vary.[838] Many licensing statutes clearly specify the impact of failure to obtain a required license. Sometimes the specified result is to void the transaction in which the unlicensed lender has participated.[839] This is the case with many small loan acts[840] as well as one version of the UCCC.[841] Other states may provide lesser penalties.[842] Operating without a required

---

833 *See* Turney v. Roberts, 501 S.W.2d 601 (Ark. 1973); Beach Assocs., Inc. v. Fauser, 401 N.E.2d 858 (Mass. App. 1980). *See generally* Annot. 74 A.L.R.3d 1239 (1976) (Reformation of Usurious Contracts). Reformation due to fraud or misrepresentation of the borrower is similar to a creditor's defense of estoppel. *See* § 10.6.4, *supra.*

834 *See* Varr v. Olimpia, 2002 WL 1425373 (Cal. Ct. App. July 1, 2002) (unpublished, citation limited) (confining reformation of contract to cases of scrivener's error); Bjornstad v. Perry, 443 P.2d 999 (Idaho 1968) (court cannot reform contract after action to enforce contract is brought and usury defense is raised); Olsen v. Porter, 539 N.W.2d 523 (Mich. Ct. App. 1995) (noting that reformation is generally not granted for errors of law, moreover, if it were permitted, unscrupulous lenders could collect "ill-gotten" interest when not discovered, and then simply seek reformation if it were, without any deterrent force in the law); Szerdahelyi v. Harris, 490 N.E.2d 517 (N.Y. 1986) (loan is void despite tender of excess interest to borrower); Matter of Dane's Estate, 390 N.Y.S.2d 249 (App. Div. 1976) (cannot invoke equity when statute mandates penalty). *Cf.* Missouri-Kansas-Texas Railroad Co. v. Fiberglass Insulators, 707 S.W.2d 943 (Tex. App. 1986) (in face of statute setting interest rate when contract states no specific rate, court cannot invoke equitable powers to grant lender a higher prejudgment rate on its recovery, and a demand for higher rate would be usurious; extensive discussion of Texas cases on point).

835 This approach has been taken in Massachusetts. *See* Begelfer v. Najarian, 409 N.E.2d 167 (Mass. 1980); Allegheny Int'l Credit Corp. v. Bio-Energy of Lincoln, Inc., 485 N.E.2d 965 (Mass. App. 1985); Beach Assocs., Inc. v. Fauser, 401 N.E.2d 858 (Mass. App. 1980).

836 *See, e.g.,* Brabson v. Valentine, 804 S.W.2d 451 (Tenn. Ct. App. 1990).

837 *See, e.g.,* Moore v. Comfed Sav. Bank, 908 F.2d 834 (11th Cir. 1990) (borrowers have a civil claim for violation of criminal usury statute; penalty as noted in text); Norris v. Sigler Daisy

Corp., 392 S.E.2d 242 (Ga. 1990) (same); Young v. Barker, 342 P.2d 150 (Kan. 1959) (criminal statute implies right of recovery). *See also* Schuran, Inc. v. Walnut Hill Assocs., 606 A.2d 885 (N.J. Super. Ct. 1991) (where criminal usury statute silent as to penalty, court held only illegal interest provision in contract was unenforceable; to permit forfeiture of principal would result in an inequitable windfall to a borrower who had been "fully advised by thorough and competent attorneys"). *Cf.* Conde v. O.F.S. Equities, Inc., 492 So. 2d 1153 (Fla. Dist. Ct. App. 1986) (applying Colorado law; maximum (civil?) effect of criminal usury violation would be reduction of interest to maximum permissible rate). *But cf.* Wilkerson v. Seder, 265 N.W.2d 807 (Mich. App. 1978) (criminal usury statute did not create private cause of action where civil remedies were available). *See generally* § 10.8.2.1, *supra.*

838 *See generally* Annot., 29 A.L.R.4th 884 (1984).

839 Beneficial Hawaii, Inc. v. Kida, 30 P.3d 895 (Haw. 2001) (loan arranged by unlicensed broker is void and unenforceable pursuant to Hawaii statute; holder may have equitable lien but only in amount of consideration it paid for the obligation); Gottesfeld v. Kaminski, 524 A.2d 872 (N.J. Super. App. Div. 1987) (second mortgage made by unlicensed lender voided the obligation under New Jersey Secondary Mortgage Act); Moran v. American Funding, Ltd., 569 A.2d 841 (N.J. Super. 1989) (same; Act since amended); Rancman v. Interim Settlement Funding Corp., 2001 Ohio App. LEXIS 4818 (Oct. 31, 2001) (loan made by unlicensed lender void under Small Loan Act).

840 *E.g.,* Ariz. Rev. Stat. § 6-603(B); Ohio Rev. Code Ann. § 1321.02. *See* Currier v. Tuck, 287 A.2d 625 (N.H. 1972); Smashed Ice v. Lee, 200 N.W.2d 236 (S.D. 1972). Whether "voiding" the transaction means completely voiding the debt, or merely voiding interest depends on state law. *See also* Community Nat'l Bank v. McClammy, 525 N.Y.S.2d 629 (App. Div. 1988) (City Adm. Code provides that home improvement contractors who fail to get license cannot recover against a homeowner on contract or in *quantum meruit;* effective against unlicensed contractor's assignee). *Compare* Hodges v. Community Loan & Inv. Corp., 216 S.E.2d 274 (Ga. 1975) *with* Southern Discount Co. v. Ector, 268 S.E.2d 621 (Ga. 1980); Moore v. Beneficial Fin., 281 S.E.2d 293 (Ga. App. 1981).

841 U.C.C.C. § 5.202(2)(1968). Furthermore, though a loan from an unlicensed lender under the U.C.C.C. may be void as to the lender's right to collect, it still gives the borrower the right to collect statutory penalties under the Act for other violations. Kuykendall v. Malernee, 516 P.2d 558 (Okla. Ct. App. 1973). *See also* United Kansas Bank & Trust Co. v. Rixner, 610 P.2d 116 (Kan. App.), *aff'd,* 619 P.2d 1156 (Kan. 1980).

842 *See, e.g.,* Smith v. Alfa Fin. Corp., 762 So. 2d 850 (Ala. 1999) (Alabama's mini-code was amended several times, first replac-

license is also a UDAP violation in many states.[843] A court may be willing to require an unlicensed entity to refund any money the consumer has already paid, on an unjust enrichment theory.[844]

Transactions with lenders who are not licensed, but should be, may be void even in the absence of a special statutory provision to that effect. The common law principle that "contracts made in violation of regulatory statutes enacted for the protection of the public [are] rendered null and unenforceable" has been applied where creditors failed to comply with appropriate licensing requirements.[845] This

general rule applies to licensing statutes enacted for the protection of the public, rather than those enacted merely to raise revenue. Special usury licensing statutes are clearly in the former category, as they are designed to protect borrowers "through the strict regulation and supervision of the creditors themselves."[846]

Some courts may not be willing to adopt an absolute rule that contracts made by unlicensed parties are void, but may apply a balancing test, weighing the interest in enforcing the contract against the public policy behind the licensing requirement.[847] This balancing approach is espoused by the *Restatement (Second) of Contracts* § 181. The factors that the *Restatement* lists as weighing in favor of enforcing the contract or contract term are:

- The parties' justified expectations;
- Any forfeiture that would result if enforcement were denied; and
- Any special public interest in the enforcement of the particular term.

The *Restatement* factors that weigh against enforcement are:

- The strength of the public policy, as manifested by legislation or judicial decisions;
- The likelihood that a refusal to enforce the term will further that policy;
- The seriousness of any misconduct involved and the extent to which it was deliberate; and
- The directness of the connection between that misconduct and the term.[848]

The fact that the unlicensed party will suffer a forfeiture should not be a decisive factor. As the *Restatement* notes, it is usually the case that the unlicensed party will have already performed, so will typically face a forfeiture.[849]

Applying these factors to the case of an unlicensed lender, the existence of any criminal penalty for unlicensed lending, and any legislative history showing the reasons behind the

ing the ultimate penalty of voiding the loan with recovery of actual damages, and then, in 1996, completely eliminated a cause of action for failure to obtain a license); Dixon v. Mercury Fin. Co., 694 N.E.2d 693 (Ill. App. 1998) (Illinois law allows recovery of actual damages only; court expressly distinguishes cases voiding contracts in absence of required license as limited to licensing requirements which could have a significant impact on public health or safety or where licensing statute does not contain a lesser penalty). The Maine Consumer Credit Code strips the finance charges from the loan. Me. Rev. Stat. Ann. tit. 9-A § 9-405. *See also* Gaspard v. Vanguard Acceptance Corp., 689 So. 2d 1352 (La. 1997) (Louisiana's Sales Finance Companies Licensing Law requires the payment of twice the interest and charges originally computed on the loan).

843 *See* National Consumer Law Center, Unfair and Deceptive Acts and Practices § 4.7.7.2 (6th ed. 2004 and Supp.).

844 Kowalski v. Cedars of Portsmouth Condominium Assn., 769 A.2d 344 (N.H. 2001) (unlicensed real estate broker).

845 Derico v. Duncan, 410 So. 2d 27, 29 (Ala. 1982) (loan of money was void as to principal and interest where defendant made loan at supervised lending rate without having obtained a license); Edwards v. Alabama Farm Bureau Mut. Casualty Ins., 509 So. 2d 232 (Ala. Civ. App. 1986) (casualty insurers were not expressly excluded from scope of Alabama's Mini-Code; note obtained from uninsured motorist on subrogation claim was consumer loan, requiring that insurer be licensed under Mini-Code; failure to obtain license voided the loan); Solomon v. Gilmore, 731 A.2d 280 (Conn. 1999) (mortgage taken by unlicensed lender is unenforceable); Family Constr. v. District of Columbia Dep't of Cons. & Regulatory Affairs, 484 A.2d 250 (D.C. 1984) (home improvement contractor who met definition of retail seller engaged in retail installment sales transactions was required to register; failure to register voided the transaction, and contractor was required to return the down payment). Other courts, however, have permitted recovery of principal, sometimes with interest at the general usury rate, where the statute is silent as to the effect of noncompliance. *See also* Gorman v. Marcon Capital Corp., 274 B.R. 351 (D. Vt. 2002) (even if statute's explicit voiding provision did not apply to pre-loan agreement with unlicensed lender, common law may make it unenforceable); RCDI Constr., Inc. v. Spaceplan/Architecture, Planning & Interiors, 148 F. Supp. 2d 607 (W.D.N.C. 2001) (contract with unlicensed construction firm is unenforceable), *aff'd on other grounds*, 2002 U.S. App. LEXIS 640 (4th Cir. Jan. 15, 2002). *See generally* cases collected in Annot. 29 A.L.R.4th 884, § 4[b]. *But see* Dixon v. Mercury Fin. Co., 694 N.E.2d 693 (Ill. App. 1998); Bennett v. Bourne, 5 S.W.3d 124 (Ky. 1999). *But cf.* Walters v. PDI Mgmt. Servs., 2004 WL 2137513 (S.D. Ind. June 14, 2004) (declining to void assignment of obligation since Indiana U.C.C. had other explicit remedies for violations).

846 Derico v. Duncan, 410 So. 2d 27, 31 (Ala. 1982). *Accord* Solomon v. Gilmore, 731 A.2d 280 (Conn. 1999) (secondary mortgage act imposes comprehensive set of rules, going far beyond lender's personal qualifications; mortgage by unlicensed lender is unenforceable). *See also* Vermont Dev. Credit Corp. v. Kitchel, 544 A.2d 1165 (Vt. 1988) (development credit corporations not specifically exempt under statute requiring license in order to make loans at greater than 12% interest; fact that purpose of corporation is to promote general welfare of state does not mean it can never charge excessive interest or engage in unfair practices); § 9.3.1.1, *infra*.

847 *See* Fabricant v. Sears Roebuck, Clearinghouse No. 54563B (S.D. Fla. Mar. 5, 2002) (citing *Restatement*; failure to obtain license to sell credit insurance makes contract void), *class certified*, 202 F.R.D. 310, 320 (S.D. Fla. 2001) (reiterating that unlicensed sale of credit insurance makes contracts void); Mincks Agri Center, Inc. v. Bell Farms, Inc., 611 N.W.2d 270 (Iowa 2000).

848 Restatement (Second) of Contracts § 178.

849 Restatement (Second) of Contracts § 181 cmt. c.

licensing requirement, will help demonstrate the strength of the public policy. The practitioner should stress that the licensing requirement is designed to protect the public rather than just raise revenue.[850] Common indications that the purpose goes beyond revenue are, according to the *Restatement*, provisions for examination to ensure minimum standards, a bond requirement, or procedures for license revocation to ensure that standards are maintained.[851] It also should not be difficult to show that refusing to enforce the loan contract would further the statute's public policies by providing a financial disincentive for unlicensed lending; to allow unlicensed lenders to reap the profits of illegal transactions would only encourage others to enter the business. As to the parties' justified expectations, a lender will have a difficult time arguing that it was justified in expecting repayment of an unlicensed loan at extortionate rates. A loan contract is unlikely to have any special impact on the public, so a court is unlikely to find any special public interest in enforcing it. How the other factors play out would depend on the facts of the particular case.

The failure to obtain a necessary license need not be willful to invoke a penalty.[852] However, statutory language providing for a bona fide error defense may be construed to insulate a creditor who reasonably and in good faith failed to obtain a license upon the advice of counsel.[853]

10.8.4.2 Remedies Where Licensed Creditor Violates Conditions of Licensure Statute

Even if a creditor has obtained a required license, it may not have complied with all the other requirements necessary to enable it to charge a particular rate. Thus, a South Carolina licensed creditor who neglected to file an annual rate schedule with the state as required was limited to an 18% APR and ordered to refund or credit any excess interest charged to borrowers while it was out of compliance.[854] Where the lender has not complied with the statute's requirements for licensed lenders, the loan may not qualify for the protections of the special usury law, making it subject to

a lower general usury ceiling.[855] The fact that a lender has a license does not mean that any loan it makes can take advantage of the higher usury ceiling in the licensing statute. If a licensee makes a loan that does not conform to the requirements of the licensing law, the loan will be subject to the general usury ceiling.[856] The borrower may also be able to make the violation the basis of a UDAP claim, assuming that causation and damages can be shown,[857] or assert an implied cause of action.[858]

On the other hand, some courts have viewed the question as whether a statutory cause of action is available for a lender's non-compliance with licensing requirements. A series of decisions from Maryland find no private cause of action to enforce a provision of a licensing statute that limits the lender's operations to certain locations.[859]

10.8.5 Federal Remedies

10.8.5.1 Remedies Under National Bank Act and DIDA

The National Bank Act establishes the remedy for a usurious loan issued by a national bank: the lender forfeits the entire contract interest, and the borrower may recover a penalty of twice the interest paid within two years of the action.[860] Similar, but not identical remedies apply to state banks, state and federal savings and loan institutions, and

---

850 *See* Restatement (Second) of Contracts § 181 cmt. b (contract not unenforceable if purpose of licensing requirement is merely to raise revenue).

851 *Id.*

852 Derico v. Duncan, 410 So. 2d 27, 31 (Ala. 1982); Edwards v. Alabama Farm Bureau Mut. Casualty Ins. Co., 509 So. 2d 232 (Ala. Civ. App. 1986) (failure to obtain license rendered loan void, whether willful or not; state banking department had advised insurer no license was necessary).

853 Rea v. Wichita Mortg. Corp. 747 F.2d 567 (10th Cir. 1984). *But see* Edwards v. Alabama Farm Bureau Mut. Casualty Ins. Co., 509 So. 2d 232 (Ala. Civ. App. 1986) (lender argued it acted upon advice of state banking department; court did not specifically address this issue, but held that failure to obtain required license whether willful or not voided loan).

854 Bell Fin. v. Dept. of Consumer Affairs, 374 S.E.2d 918 (S.C. Ct. App. 1988).

855 *See, e.g., Agapitov v. Lerner*, 133 Cal. Rptr. 2d 837 (Ct. App. 2003).

856 *Agapitov v. Lerner*, 133 Cal. Rptr. 2d 837 (Ct. App. 2003).

857 *See* § 12.5, *infra. But see* Rivera v. Grossinger Autoplex, Inc., 2000 U.S. Dist. LEXIS 11240 (N.D. Ill. June 14, 2000) (consumer does not have private cause of action against creditor for engaging in conduct which the licensing agency can consider as grounds to deny a license), *aff'd on other grounds*, 274 F.3d 1118 (7th Cir. 2001).

858 *See* § 10.8.2.1, *supra.*

859 Miller v. Pacific Shore Funding, 224 F. Supp. 2d 977 (D. Md. 2002) (no private cause of action to enforce provision of licensing statute that limits lender's operations to certain locations), *aff'd on other grounds*, 2004 WL 144138 (4th Cir. Jan. 28, 2004) (table); Staley v. Americorp Credit Corp., 164 F. Supp. 2d 578 (D. Md. 2001) (no private cause of action to enforce requirement that licensed lender operate only out of specific location); Rivera v. Grossinger Autoplex, Inc., 2000 WL 796158 (N.D. Ill. June 19, 2000) (no private cause of action for purchase of contract that violated RISA, where such a purchase was merely a factor in license revocation decision).

860 12 U.S.C. § 86. For cases interpreting these remedies, see, e.g., McCollum v. Hamilton Nat'l Bank, 303 U.S. 245 (1938); American Timber & Trading v. First Nat'l Bank of Ore., 690 F.2d 781 (9th Cir. 1982) (subclass recovers double interest paid on usurious loans, but prejudgment interest denied); First Nat'l Bank in Mena v. Nowlin, 509 F.2d 872 (8th Cir. 1975) (state remedies preempted); Bokum v. First Nat'l Bank, 740 P.2d 693 (N.M. 1987) (National Bank Act claim disallowed where not filed within two years). For a discussion of usury preemption under the National Bank Act, see Ch. 3, *supra.*

state and federal credit unions which are claiming federal preemption of state usury laws under the alternative ceiling provisions of the Depository Institutions Deregulation and Monetary Control Act of 1980 (DIDA).[861] If the alternative ceiling exceeds the interest rate allowed by the state, and the state ceiling is thereby preempted, but the lender charges a rate even higher than allowed by the DIDA alternative ceiling, then the lender forfeits the entire contract interest and the borrower may recover twice the amount of the interest paid within two years of the commencement of the action. If the state interest ceiling exceeds the DIDA alternative ceiling or if for some other reason, such as a state opt-out, the alternative ceiling preemption does not apply, the wording of DIDA suggests that state usury remedies control.

10.8.5.2 Remedies for HOEPA Violations

A separate set of federal remedies is available in the case of charges contracted for or imposed on certain high-cost mortgages in violation of the Home Ownership and Equity Protection Act of 1994.[862] While the Act specifically declares itself *not* to be a usury statute,[863] it does specifically limit or prohibit certain contract terms in high-cost mortgages which would result in excessive charges to consumers. Prepayment penalties (including the use of the Rule of 78), negatively amortizing terms, higher default rates, prepaid payment escrows are all prohibited or severely restricted. If they are contracted for or imposed in closed-end home equity loans subject to the Act, they trigger the Act's remedies: actual damages; statutory damages of twice the finance charge to a maximum of $2,000; in the case of "material" violations,[864] enhanced damages of all finance

charges and fees paid by the consumer.[865] Perhaps more critically, any covered mortgage loan containing a provision prohibited by the Act—whether invoked or not—is a violation which triggers Truth in Lending's extended rescission right, which gives consumers up to three years to rescind the transaction.[866]

10.8.5.3 RICO

10.8.5.3.1 Overview of RICO

The Racketeer Influenced and Corrupt Organizations Act (RICO)[867] provides powerful civil remedies,[868] including attorney fees and treble damages, to victims of a broadly defined range of "racketeering activity" and to those who have been subjected to the collection of an "unlawful debt." "Unlawful debt" includes any usurious debt bearing interest of at least twice the "enforceable rate."[869] RICO prohibits four activities, which are spelled out in section 1962, subsections (a) through (d).[870]

---

861 The remedy provisions are found at 12 U.S.C. §§ 1463(g)(2) (thrifts); 1785(g) (credit unions); 1831d(state banks). They are reprinted in Appx. G.1, *infra*. For a discussion of DIDA preemption, see § 3.9, *supra*.

862 15 U.S.C. §§ 1602(aa), 1639. *See generally* § 12.2.2, *infra*; National Consumer Law Center, Truth in Lending Ch. 9 (5th ed. 2003 and Supp.).

863 Subt. B of Title I, Riegle Community Development and Regulatory Improvement Act of 1994 (H.R. 3474), Pub. L. No. 103-325, § 152(a)(5), 108 Stat. 2160 (Sept. 23, 1994). "This subsection shall not be construed to limit the rate of interest or the finance charge that a person may charge a consumer for any extension of credit." Discussed at H.R. Conf. Rep. No. 652, 103d Cong. 2d Sess. 147, 158 (1994) (accompanying H.R. 3474) [hereinafter Conference Report]. This superfluous provision was put in at the behest of those who felt that regulating substantive terms on high-cost credit was a de facto rate cap, though it is difficult to see how it could have been so interpreted even without such a provision.

864 See National Consumer Law Center, Truth in Lending Ch. 9 (5th ed. 2003 and Supp.) for a discussion of this "materiality" standard, which is distinct from the materiality standard used in other provisions of TILA.

865 15 U.S.C. § 1640(a).

866 15 U.S.C. § 1639(j).

867 18 U.S.C. §§ 1961 *et seq*. For a detailed analysis of RICO, see National Consumer Law Center, Unfair and Deceptive Acts and Practices §§ 9.2, 9.3, Appx. C.2 (summaries of state RICO statutes) (6th ed. 2004 and Supp.); Mark E. Budnitz & Helen Davis Chaitman, The Law of Lender Liability, Ch. 6 (rev. ed. 1999 and 2004 Supp.). For further discussion of RICO as it may pertain to overreaching consumer credit transactions, see § 12.4, *infra*.

868 *See* 18 U.S.C. § 1964.

869 18 U.S.C. § 1961(6). The term also includes gambling debts that either arose from illegal gambling activity or are unenforceable due to state or federal usury laws. *Id.; see also* Kemp v. American Tel. & Tel. Co., 393 F.3d 1354, 1361–62 (5th Cir. 2004) (telecommunication carrier's billing on behalf of third party game operator could give rise to RICO claim where game illegal under Georgia gambling laws, affirming award of actual damages of $115.05, trebled under RICO, but reducing punitive damages award from $1,000,000 to $250,000).

870 (a) It shall be unlawful for any person who has received any income derived, directly or indirectly, from a pattern of racketeering activity or through collection of an unlawful debt in which such person has participated as a principal within the meaning of section 2, title 18, United States Code, to use or invest, directly or indirectly, any part of such income, or the proceeds of such income, in acquisition of any interest in, or the establishment or operation of, any enterprise which is engaged in, or the activities of which affect, interstate or foreign commerce. . . .

(b) It shall be unlawful for any person through a pattern of racketeering activity or through collection of an unlawful debt to acquire or maintain, directly or indirectly, any interest in or control of any enterprise which is engaged in, or the activities of which affect, interstate or foreign commerce.

(c) It shall be unlawful for any person employed by or associated with any enterprise engaged in, or the activities of which affect, interstate or foreign

At its core, RICO is aimed at organized crime and forbids the investment or use of money obtained through loansharking or a "pattern" of racketeering in any "enterprise" affecting interstate commerce. However, the statute is broadly written to encompass a myriad of fraudulent activities conducted by theoretically "legitimate" organizations such as banks and other creditors. Especially in light of the Supreme Court's decisions in *Sedima S.P.R.L. v. Imrex Company, Inc.*,[871] and *American National Bank and Trust Company of Chicago v. Haroco, Inc.*,[872] which overruled lower court attempts to limit the breadth of civil RICO, practitioners whose clients have been the victims of either fraudulent overcharging (indicating racketeering activity) or overcharging of at least twice the civil usury rate (indicating the collection of an unlawful debt) may wish to consider a RICO claim.

The essential elements of a civil RICO action depend upon which of the four subsections of section 1962 is alleged to have been violated. The following elements are common to any civil RICO cause of action:

- An enterprise must exist;
- The enterprise must be engaged in or affect interstate or foreign commerce;
- The defendant must have engaged in one or more of the four prohibited enumerated in section 1962; and
- The prohibited conduct must have caused injury to the plaintiff's business or property, a requirement discussed in more detail in § 10.8.5.3.4, *infra*.[873]

For the purposes of a RICO action, an "enterprise" includes almost any business organization, whether or not formally incorporated.[874] No criminal conviction is required before a RICO defendant may be pursued civilly, and the plaintiff need show no injury beyond that caused by the racketeering activity or the unlawful debt collection.[875]

In addition to these elements, every RICO violation must involve either "collection of an unlawful debt" or a "pattern of racketeering activity" that relates to the enterprise in the manner proscribed by the particular subsection of section 1962.[876] Of the four activities prohibited by section 1962, one, section 1962(c), generally requires that the plaintiff plead and prove an enterprise that is separate and distinct from the defendant person,[877] while subsections (a), (b), and (d) do not necessarily have that same requirement.[878]

10.8.5.3.2 Racketeering activity and the pattern requirement

A "racketeering activity" is conduct that violates any of a list of state and federal statutes. Most notably for consumer purposes, this list includes mail fraud, wire fraud, and extortion.[879] A "pattern" is a *minimum* of two incidents of racketeering activity.[880] The Supreme Court has stated that

commerce, to conduct or participate, directly or indirectly, in the conduct of such enterprise's affairs through a pattern of racketeering activity or collection of unlawful debt.

(d) It shall be unlawful for any person to conspire to violate any of the provisions of subsection (a), (b), or (c) of this section.

871 473 U.S. 479, 105 S. Ct. 3275, 87 L. Ed. 2d 346 (1985).

872 473 U.S. 479, 105 S. Ct. 3291, 87 L. Ed. 2d 437 (1985).

873 *See* Wilcox v. First Interstate Bank, 815 F.2d 522 (9th Cir. 1987); R.A.G.S. Couture, Inc. v. Hyatt, 774 F.2d 1350 (5th Cir. 1985); Haroco, Inc. v. American Nat'l Bank & Trust Co. of Chicago, 747 F.2d 384 (7th Cir. 1984), *aff'd per curiam*, 473 U.S. 606 (1985).

874 18 U.S.C. § 1961(4).

875 *See* Sedima, S.P.R.L. v. Imrex Co., 473 U.S. 479, 105 S. Ct. 3275, 87 L. Ed. 2d 346 (1985).

876 *See* 18 U.S.C. § 1961.

877 *See* Fogie v. THORN Americas, Inc., 190 F.3d 889 (8th Cir. 1999); Jaguar Cars, Inc. v. Royal Oaks Motor Car Co., 46 F.3d 258 (3d Cir. 1995) (officers or employees may properly be held liable under RICO as "persons" managing the affairs of their corporation as "enterprise" through pattern of racketeering activity); Guidry v. Bank of La Place, 954 F.2d 278 (5th Cir. 1992) (unincorporated sole proprietorship through which operator ran fraudulent scheme was not RICO "enterprise" distinct from RICO "person"); Miranda v. Ponce Federal Bank, 948 F.2d 41, 44–45 (1st Cir. 1991) (defendant bank could not be both the racketeer and the enterprise); Hastings v. Fidelity Mortgage Decisions Corp., 984 F. Supp. 600 (N.D. Ill. 1997) (in case alleging fraudulent yield spread premium payment, plaintiff adequately alleged distinct enterprise comprising mortgage broker and lender, though lender also pled as the RICO "person"); Purdie v. Ace Cash Express, Inc., 2002 WL 31730967 (N.D. Tex. Oct. 29, 2002) (plaintiff who sued payday lender failed to sufficiently show that the alleged association-in-fact had an existence separate and apart from the alleged unlawful debt collection activity, and therefore failed to meet RICO's enterprise element), *vacated upon plaintiff's motion in light of class action settlement*, 2003 WL 21447854 (N.D. Tex. June 13, 2003). Only the Eleventh Circuit held that a corporate defendant, in association with itself, can be both person and enterprise under section 1962(c), United States v. Hartley, 678 F.2d 961 (11th Cir. 1982), *cert. denied*, 459 U.S. 1183 (1983), but it abrogated this decision in U.S. v. Goldin Indus., Inc., 219 F.3d 1268 (11th Cir. 2000).

878 The issue that arises most often under § 1962(d), which prohibits conspiracy to violate one of the other subsections of § 1962, is whether a corporation can be deemed to conspire with its own parent, subsidiaries, officers or directors. *Compare* Fogie v. Thorn Americas, Inc., 190 F.3d 889 (8th Cir. 1999) (as a matter of law, a parent corporation and its wholly-owned subsidiaries are incapable of forming a conspiracy with one another) *with* Webster v. Omnitrition Int'l, Inc., 79 F.3d 776 (9th Cir.), *cert. denied*, 519 U.S. 865 (1996) (extends § 1962(d) liability to a wholly intracorporate conspiracy); Broussard v. Meineke Discount Muffler Shops, Inc., 945 F. Supp. 901 (W.D.N.C. 1996), *rev'd on other grounds*, 155 F.3d 331 (4th Cir. 1998).

879 18 U.S.C. § 1961(1).

880 18 U.S.C. § 1961(5). The Supreme Court has noted that the requirement of two incidents of racketeering activity is a minimum only, and has hinted that more elaborate proof of a true "pattern" may be required. *See* Sedima, S.P.R.L. v. Imrex Co.,

a pattern of racketeering activity need not involve organized crime, cannot be shown merely by proving two predicate acts, and does not require predicate acts that are part of separate illegal schemes.[881] When alleging predicate acts founded on fraud, practitioners should be alert to complying with Federal Rule of Civil Procedure 9(b)'s particularity requirements, which must be met as to each alleged act.[882]

In *H.J. Inc. v. Northwestern Bell Telephone Co.*,[883] the Supreme Court held that the concept of "pattern" has two separate properties that must be established: relationship and continuity.[884] The relationship property is met if the acts have "the same or similar purposes, results, participants, victims, or methods of commission, or are otherwise interrelated."[885] As for continuity, although the Court declined to express a specific test, it roughed out the requirement by providing that a plaintiff could meet it by showing either closed-ended or open-ended continuity.[886] A plaintiff could show closed-ended continuity "by proving a series of related predicates extending over a substantial period of time."[887] Alternatively, a plaintiff could show "open-ended" continuity by proving a threat of continued racketeering activity.[888] Practitioners should plead as many in-

cidents of racketeering activity as reasonably possible to demonstrate the existence of a pattern.

Lower court decisions reveal a good deal of doctrinal confusion with respect to the meaning of pattern, some of which may be particularly important to some consumer cases.[889] For instance, where identical fraudulent representations are made to a large number of potential purchasers, a restrictively minded court might hold that there is only one scheme and one criminal episode, and therefore, no pattern.[890] A flexible test that asks whether the acts alleged are sufficiently related and continuous to evidence a pattern[891] is more consistent with the Supreme Court's rejection of a multiple scheme requirement.[892] Identical fraudulent representations may establish open-ended continuity under the criteria established in *H.J. Inc.* A court found that allegations that a lender used identical fraudulent documents and letters could establish the continuity aspect of pattern by showing that they were part of the defendant's regular way

---

473 U.S. 479, 105 S. Ct. 3275, 3285, 87 L. Ed. 2d 346, 358–59 (1985). Alternatively, RICO claims based on the allegation of collection of unlawful debt apparently need not establish a "pattern" but must show that the defendant was in the "business of lending money or a thing of value" at a usurious rate. *See* 18 U.S.C. § 1961(6); Durante Bros. & Sons, Inc. v. Flushing Nat'l Bank, 755 F.2d 239 (2d Cir.) (overruled as to "racketeering injury" requirement by implication of *Sedima, supra*), *cert. denied*, 473 U.S. 906 (1985), *on remand* 652 F. Supp. 101 (E.D.N.Y. 1986).

881 H.J. Inc. v. Northwestern Bell Tel. Co., 492 U.S. 229 (1989).

882 *See* Vandenbroeck v. CommonPoint Mortgage Co., 210 F.3d 696 (6th Cir. 2000) (federal RICO); Goren v. New Vision Int'l Inc., 156 F.3d 721 (7th Cir. 1998) (federal RICO); McGee v. East Ohio Gas Co., 111 F. Supp. 2d 979 (S.D. Ohio 2000) (state RICO).

883 *Id.*

884 *Id.* at 239.

885 *Id.* at 240 (quoting 18 U.S.C. § 3575(e)).

886 *Id.* at 241.

887 *Id.* at 242. Predicate acts committed over just a few weeks or months would not satisfy closed-ended continuity; in such a case the plaintiff would have to show "open-ended" continuity to meet the continuity property of the pattern element.

888 *Id.* at 242. While declining to define open-ended continuity, the Court offered a couple of examples: open-ended continuity could be met if the racketeering acts themselves included a specific threat of repetition, extending indefinitely into the future, as with a "protection" racket, or if the predicate acts or offenses were part of an ongoing entity's regular way of doing business. *Id.* at 242–43. Given the facts alleged by the plaintiffs, that the defendants had paid five bribes to a utility commission over the course of six years, the Court reversed the lower court's dismissal of the claim and remanded. The court held that the bribes could be found to be related for a common purpose, meeting the relationship property, and the plaintiffs could meet the continuity property either under a closed-ended analysis, given the frequency of the acts, or under an open-ended analy-

sis, either by showing that the bribes were a regular way of conducting the defendant's ongoing business, or that bribery was a regular way of conducting or participating in the conduct of the alleged RICO enterprise, the utility company. *Id.* at 250.

889 *See, e.g.*, Hofstetter v. Fletcher, 905 F.2d 897 (6th Cir. 1988) (injuring numerous investors over the course of several years sufficient). *See also* Lawaetz v. Bank of Nova Scotia, 653 F. Supp. 1278 (D. V.I. 1987) (bank's fraudulent promise to extend credit through phone calls and letters to six plaintiffs constitutes pattern); National Consumer Law Center, Unfair and Deceptive Acts and Practices § 9.2.3.4 (6th ed. 2004 and Supp.) (detailed discussion of pattern).

890 *See, e.g*, Schlaifer Nance & Co. v. Estate of Andy Warhol, 119 F.3d 91 (2d Cir. 1997) (no pattern found, although scheme lasted three years and had some subparts); Leonard v. J.C. ProWear, Inc., 1995 U.S. App. LEXIS 24340 (4th Cir. Aug. 29, 1995) (unpublished) (single purpose, single set of victims, seven months insufficient; Fourth Circuit refused, however, to hold that a seven month scheme is *per se* insufficient); Tudor Assocs. Ltd., II v. AJ & AJ Servicing, Inc., 36 F.3d 1094 (4th Cir. 1994) (no pattern where scheme lasted more than ten years and involved many predicates, but single injury and single victim); Midwest Heritage Bank v. Northway, 576 N.W.2d 588 (Iowa 1998) (in suit by borrower alleging a scheme by bank to defraud in connection with a FmHA loan, the three alleged predicate acts were insufficiently related where they did not have a common purpose, only common participants and a common victim; claim also lacked continuity since borrower did not offer evidence that predicate acts were part of the bank's regular way of doing business).

891 Allwaste, Inc. v. Hecht, 65 F.3d 1523 (9th Cir. 1995) (flexible test; Ninth Circuit refused to adopt specific time period). *See also* Corley v. Rosewood Care Center, Inc., 142 F.3d 1041 (7th Cir. 1998) (plaintiff's allegations that nursing home's alleged bait and switch scheme involved not just the plaintiff but many other residents over a period of 12 to 14 months were sufficient evidence of pattern to withstand summary judgment); Schroeder v. Acceleration Life Ins. Co., 972 F.2d 41 (3d Cir. 1992) (reversing summary judgment for defendant on grounds that an alleged "benefits reduction scheme" based on a large number of credit disability insurance policies issued over a long period of time met definition of "pattern").

892 H.J. Inc. v. Northwestern Bell Tel. Co., 492 U.S. 229 (1989).

of conducting business.[893] In contrast, a case alleging a single transaction with a single victim, such as in the sale of a piece of real estate, may have more difficulty meeting the continuity requirement, even where the plaintiff alleges several predicate acts.[894]

For cases alleging a conspiracy under section 1962(d) to violate one of the other subsections of section 1692, the Supreme Court, relying on traditional conspiracy law, has ruled that RICO does not require that the defendant must commit or agree to commit two or more predicate acts. Instead, the defendant need only "intend to further an endeavor which, if completed, would satisfy all of the elements of a substantive criminal offense."[895] Lower court decisions have held that the plaintiff need only show that the defendant agreed that predicate acts would be committed on behalf of the conspiracy.[896]

10.8.5.3.3 Alleging a RICO claim based on the collection of an unlawful debt

An unlawful debt is either an illegal gambling debt or a debt incurred through the "business of lending money or a thing of value" at a usurious rate, provided that any part of the principal or interest is unenforceable under state or federal usury law and the rate charged is at least twice the enforceable rate.[897]

Civil RICO claims alleging the collection of an unlawful debt are much less common than those asserting injury from a pattern of racketeering activity.[898] Because the collection of an unlawful debt is a separate and distinct RICO violation from a "pattern of racketeering activity," a plaintiff does not have to demonstrate a "pattern" of collecting unlawful debts: collection of a single unlawful debt meets the statute's requirement.[899] However, the plaintiff must demonstrate that

---

893 Brown v. C.I.L., Inc., 1996 U.S. Dist. LEXIS 4917 (N.D. Ill. Jan. 28, 1996) (unpublished). *See also* Arenson v. Whitehall Convalescent & Nursing Home, 880 F. Supp. 1202 (N.D. Ill. 1995) (allegations that nursing home sent 75 bills fraudulently overcharging for drugs over five year period established closed-end continuity, and additionally established open-ended continuity by showing such fraud was part of defendant's regular way of conducting business); Robinson v. Empire of Am. Realty Credit Corp., 1991 U.S. Dist. LEXIS 2084 (N.D. Ill. Feb. 20, 1991) (unpublished) (allegations that mortgagor sent thousands of statements over a period of several years demanding excess escrow deposits met continuity requirement).

894 *See, e.g.,* Tucker v. Bank One, N.A., 265 F. Supp. 2d 923, 926 (N.D. Ill. 2003) (dismissing RICO claim based on foreclosure of plaintiff's property because single scheme involving single property could not satisfy pattern requirement); Pulphus v. Sullivan, 2003 WL 1964333, at *11 (N.D. Ill. Apr. 28, 2003) (dismissing RICO claims without prejudice; no closed-ended continuity where lender's involvement in home improvement loan scheme was limited to a single victim, a single transaction, and a few days, and no open-ended continuity where allegations that defendants had a practice of carelessly purchasing or originating fraudulent loans did not demonstrate intent to deliberately defraud customers as a matter of course); Mathon v. Marine Midland Bank, 875 F. Supp. 986 (E.D.N.Y. 1995) (no continuity). *See also* Hobson v. Lincoln Ins. Agency, Inc., 2000 U.S. Dist. LEXIS 13314 (N.D. Ill. Sept. 7, 2000) (plaintiff's allegations of ten payments made over a ten month period as part of a single, allegedly fraudulent, insurance transaction do not constitute a "pattern"); Travis v. Boulevard Bank, 1994 U.S. Dist. LEXIS 14615 (N.D. Ill. Oct. 7, 1994) (where alleged acts of mail fraud all related to the single alleged wrongful act of defendant's procurement of force-placed insurance on plaintiff's RISC, no continuity).

895 Salinas v. United States, 522 U.S. 52, 118 S. Ct. 469, 139 L. Ed. 2d 232 (1997).

896 Goren v. New Vision Int'l, Inc., 156 F.3d 721 (7th Cir. 1998) (defendant must agree that someone would commit two predicate acts on behalf of the enterprise); United States v. To, 144 F.3d 737 (11th Cir. 1998); American Automotive Accessories, Inc. v. Fishman, 991 F. Supp. 995 (N.D. Ill. 1998).

897 18 U.S.C. § 1961(6). See Merly v. D'Arcangelo, 1992 WL 11182 (Conn. Super. Ct. Jan. 16, 1992) (sufficient to allege "that the plaintiff was associated with the Gambino crime family, that each defendant was engaged in interstate commerce, and that the notes called for usurious interest (104%)"). *But see* Bellizan v. Easy Money of Louisiana, Inc., 2002 WL 1611648 (E.D. La. July 19, 2002) (rejecting argument that where loan was illegally split into two transactions to avoid interest rate limitations, allowable interest on second loan was zero for purposes of RICO's interest rate element); Porter v. Ace Cash Express, Inc., 2000 U.S. Dist. LEXIS 15996, at *20–21 (E.D. La. Oct. 26, 2000) (because term of loans made to plaintiff exceeded those defined by state payday loan act by 5 days, they fell outside its interest limitations; since loans were not usurious under state law they did not meet RICO's definition of an unlawful debt, action dismissed), *aff'd*, 277 F.3d 1372 (5th Cir. 2001).

898 For examples of unlawful debt collection cases, see United States v. Weiner, 3 F.3d 17 (1st Cir. 1993); Sundance Land v. Community First Fed. Sav. & Loan, 840 F.2d 653 (9th Cir. 1988) (where borrower claimed it was required to put up motels as security, no RICO claim for collection of unlawful debt stated because FHLBB regulations allegedly violated did not relate to amount of interest lender can charge); United States v. Biasacci, 786 F.2d 504 (2d Cir. 1986), *cert. denied*, 479 U.S. 827 (1986) (criminal RICO prosecution for unlawful debt collection); Durante Bros. & Sons, Inc. v. Flushing Nat'l Bank, 755 F.2d 239 (2d Cir.), *cert. denied*, 473 U.S. 906 (1985), *on remand* 652 F. Supp. 101 (E.D.N.Y. 1986); Furgason v. McKenzie Check Advance of Ind., Inc., 2001 U.S. Dist. LEXIS 2725 (S.D. Ind. Jan. 3, 2001) (granting payday lender's motion to compel arbitration of plaintiff's RICO and state usury claims); Blount Fin. Services v. Walter E. Heller & Co., 632 F. Supp. 240 (E.D. Tenn. 1986) (complaint must specify rate charged and controlling usury statute), *aff'd*, 819 F.2d 151 (6th Cir. 1987); Bandas v. Citizens State Bank of Silver Lake, 412 N.W.2d 818 (Minn. Ct. App. 1987), *rev'd and remanded on other grounds sub nom.* VanderWeyst v. First State Bank of Benson, 425 N.W.2d 803 (Minn. 1988), *cert. denied*, 488 U.S. 943 (1988). *See also* § 7.5.5.6, *supra*, regarding RICO claims in the payday loan context.

899 *See* United States v. Weiner, 3 F.3d 17 (1st Cir. 1993) and cases cited therein. *But cf.* Wright v. Sheppard, 919 F.2d 665 (11th Cir. 1990) (a single, isolated use of force by a law enforcement officer in trying to collect a debt owed a private creditor, which

the unlawful debt (if not from gambling) was "incurred in connection with ... the business of lending money or a thing of value, at a rate usurious under State or Federal law, where the usurious rate is at least twice the enforceable rate."[900] Two courts have interpreted this provision as requiring the plaintiff to show that the defendant was not just in the business of lending money, but in the business of lending money at a usurious rate.[901] Other courts have recited the requirement without focusing on this distinction.[902]

RICO usury cases are scarce, likely because most usurious overcharges on traditional loans are not so exorbitant as to reach twice the enforceable rate. However, in some transactions, where the essence of a consumer's problem is overcharging rather than fraud, or where the fraud presents proof problems, the defendant's collection of an unlawful debt may be the ideal basis for a RICO claim.

10.8.5.3.4 The "injury" element

Initially, fraudulent overcharge RICO cases met with little success, largely because the lower courts were requiring plaintiffs to establish a special "racketeering injury" apart from the injury directly caused by the individual predicate acts of racketeering activity. Under this approach, a borrower was faced with the difficult task of establishing, for example, not that he was directly harmed by a fraudulent interest overcharge, but rather that he was harmed by the pattern of the bank's fraudulent overcharging. This strained interpretation was expressly rejected by the Supreme Court in *Sedima*, which held that a RICO plaintiff need only demonstrate injury from the predicate acts of racketeering.[903] Moreover, in *Haroco* the Supreme Court affirmed a Seventh Circuit ruling that a borrower who had alleged a fraudulent interest overcharge had stated a claim under RICO.[904] Nevertheless, in *Holmes v. Securities Investor Protection Corp.*,[905] the Supreme Court somewhat narrowed RICO's injury element, holding that a RICO plaintiff must demonstrate that the injuries were directly and proximately caused by a defendant's racketeering activity. Several courts have construed *Holmes* as requiring that when alleging a section 1962(a) claim, the plaintiff must show more than simply injury from a predicate act; the plaintiff must show injury from the use or investment of the racketeering income.[906] However, when the claim arises from section 1962(c), which prohibits a person from conducting an enterprise's affairs through a pattern of racketeering activity or collection of an unlawful debt, simply showing injury from a predicate act may suffice.[907]

In its most recent decision on the injury element, *Beck v. Prupis*,[908] the Supreme Court continued to narrow the injury element, holding that when a claim arises from section 1962(d), which prohibits any person from conspiring to violate any of sections 1962(a)–(c), the plaintiff must show an injury that was caused by an overt act that is an act of racketeering or otherwise wrongful under RICO. The Court affirmed the dismissal of the case of a former employee who alleged that his firing was part of the defendant's conspiracy to violate RICO; the firing itself was not an overt act of racketeering or otherwise prohibited by the statute and therefore the claim failed to meet RICO's injury requirement.[909]

---

did not result in financial gain in the officer, did not constitute collection of an unlawful debt for RICO purposes).

900 18 U.S.C. § 1961(6)(B).

901 Weisel v. Pischel, 197 F.R.D. 231, 241 (E.D.N.Y. 2000) (reasoning that RICO's legislative history justified limiting the statute to loan sharkers, not ordinary businessmen who might make a usurious loan (quoting S. Rep. No. 91-617, 91st Cong., 1st Sess. 158 (1969)); VanderWeyst v. First State Bank of Benson, 425 N.W.2d 803 (Minn.) (must show defendant was in business of lending money at usurious rate), *cert. denied*, 488 U.S. 943 (1988).

902 Cashback Catalog Sales, Inc. v. Price, 102 F. Supp. 2d 1375 (S.D. Ga. 2000) (denying summary judgment on RICO claim); Arrington v. Colleen, Inc., 2000 U.S. Dist. LEXIS 20651, Clearinghouse No. 53,501 (D. Md. Aug. 7, 2000) (order and memorandum denying lender's motion for summary judgment); Burden v. York, Clearinghouse No. 52,502 (E.D. Ky. Sept. 29, 1999); Hamilton v. HLT Check Exchange, 987 F. Supp. 953 (E.D. Ky. 1997) (denying the motion of the defendant, a check cashing business, to dismiss RICO claim alleging the collection of an unlawful debt); Robidoux v. Conte, 741 F. Supp. 1019 (D.R.I. 1990) (car dealer was not in business of lending money). *See also* Henry v. Cash Today, Inc., 199 F.R.D. 566 (S.D. Tex. Sept. 19, 2000) (class certification granted in cash back ad sale case).

903 473 U.S. 479 (1985).

904 American Nat'l Bank & Trust Co. of Chicago v. Haroco, Inc., 473 U.S. 606, 105 S. Ct. 3291, 87 L. Ed. 2d 437 (1985).

905 503 U.S. 258 (1992).

906 *See* Fogie v. Thorn Americas, Inc., 190 F.3d 889 (8th Cir. 1999) (noting that seven of the eight circuits that have addressed the issue have required that a plaintiff suing for a violation of § 1962(a) must show that he or she suffered injury from the use or investment of racketeering income, and not just injury from unlawful debt collection).

907 *See* Bonilla v. Volvo Car Corp., 150 F.3d 62 (1st Cir. 1998) (defendant's excise fraud, which presumably lowered the cost of cars purchased by plaintiffs, could not support a RICO claim because plaintiffs were not injured by reason of the fraud), *cert. denied*, 526 U.S. 1098, 119 S. Ct. 1574, 143 L. Ed. 2d 670 (1999); First Nationwide Bank v. Gelt Funding Corp., 27 F.3d 763 (2d Cir. 1994); Ruiz v. Stewart Assocs., Inc., 171 F.R.D. 238 (N.D. Ill. 1997) (plaintiffs raised issue of fact as to injury suffered by reason of misrepresentation as to force-placed insurance; also certifying class); Red Ball Interior Demolition Corp. v. Palmadessa, 874 F. Supp. 576 (S.D.N.Y. 1995) (plaintiff must show direct relationship between plaintiff's injury and defendant's conduct). While a plaintiff must have suffered an injury, he need not have been injured by each predicate act he alleges—he need only have been injured by one of the predicate acts engaged in by the defendant. Terminate Control Corp. v. Horowitz, 28 F.3d 1335 (2d Cir. 1994).

908 529 U.S. 494 (2000).

909 *Id.* at 507. However, the Court expressly declined to decide whether "whether a plaintiff suing under § 1964(c) for a RICO

Similarly, a plaintiff advancing a claim based on the collection of an unlawful debt, rather than a pattern of racketeering activity, may have to show injury from the violation of the particular subsection. With respect to the injury element in an unlawful debt collection claim, the Eighth Circuit has ruled that plaintiffs injured by reason of usurious interest in a rent-to-own transaction, construed as the collection of an unlawful debt, must also demonstrate that they were injured by reason of the subsection of RICO they claimed.[910] Because they brought their claim under 18 U.S.C. § 1962(a), they had to show that they were injured by the use or investment of racketeering income, and not just from the unlawful debt collection.[911] Accordingly, practitioners should examine the law of their jurisdiction and carefully plead the injury element of RICO.

10.8.5.3.5 RICO and creditor overcharges

Several RICO cases involving allegedly fraudulent creditor overcharges have been litigated.[912] One common situation involves a bank that, after contracting to lend to a business at the "prime rate" that it charges its most creditworthy customers, in fact lends at a higher rate. Plaintiffs have alleged that the mailing of interest statements assessing excessive interest constitutes mail fraud and provides the underlying "predicate offense" to support the RICO action.[913] Following a somewhat similar theory, a depositor in a New York bank brought a RICO action against the bank for the advertisement of accounts paying interest at the highest rate allowed by law when its accounts in fact paid lower rates.[914]

---

conspiracy must allege an actionable violation under § 1962(a)–(c), or whether it is sufficient for the plaintiff to allege an agreement to complete a substantive violation and the commission of at least one act of racketeering that caused him injury." *Id.* at 506, n.10. Based on dicta, it does not appear that a plaintiff must necessarily have a claim under § 1962(c) in order to allege a violation of § 1962(d), which would functionally render § 1962(d) superfluous: "a plaintiff could, through a § 1964(c) suit for a violation of § 1962(d), sue co-conspirators who might not themselves have violated one of the substantive provisions of § 1962." The Third Circuit subsequently upheld such an interpretation, ruling that a defendant alleged to have conspired to violate § 1962(c) did not have to commit or agree to commit predicate acts to be liable for conspiracy under § 1962(d), so long as he knowingly agreed to facilitate a scheme that included operation or management of a RICO enterprise. Smith v. Berg, 247 F.3d 532 (3d Cir. Apr. 13, 2001).

910 Fogie v. Thorn Americas, Inc., 190 F.3d 889, 895 (8th Cir. 1999) (siding with majority of circuits that have addressed the issue, see cases cited therein).

911 *Id.*

912 *See* American Nat'l Bank & Trust Co. of Chicago v. Haroco, Inc., 473 U.S. 606, 105 S. Ct. 3291, 87 L. Ed. 2d 437 (1985), *aff'g*, 747 F.2d 384 (7th Cir. 1984) (fraudulent overcharging stated RICO claim); Emery v. American General Fin. Corp., 71 F.3d 1343 (7th Cir. 1995) (well-pled allegation of loan flipping may state a claim of RICO predicate act of mail fraud sufficient to withstand a motion to dismiss); Kerby v. Mortgage Funding Corp., 992 F. Supp. 787 (D. Md. 1998) (denying motion to dismiss RICO claim arising from allegedly fraudulent mortgage refinancing scheme); Hastings v. Fidelity Mortgage Decisions Corp., 984 F. Supp. 600 (N.D. Ill. 1997) (granting leave to plaintiffs to amend complaint alleging fraudulent yield spread premium payment so as to meet particularity requirements); Leff v. Olympic Federal Sav. & Loan Ass'n, 1987 WL 12921 (N.D. Ill. June 19, 1987) (granting class certification of RICO claim by mortgager for alleged overcharge for tax and insurance escrow), *vacated on reconsideration*, 1987 WL 15985 (N.D. Ill. Aug. 19, 1987) (vacating class certification because of named plaintiff's assignment of claim); Faircloth v. Certified Fin. Inc.,

2001 U.S. Dist. LEXIS 6793 (E.D. La. May 16, 2001) (court accepted settlement in class action that alleged that defendant had lent funds to plaintiffs with pending personal injury actions and then flipped the loans to create unlawful interest; judge approved attorney fee of more than $530,000); Matthews v. New Century Mortg. Corp., 185 F. Supp. 2d 874 (S.D. Ohio 2002) (plaintiffs adequately alleged pattern in state RICO claim brought against defendants who had allegedly been part of a fraudulent home improvement loan scheme targeting toward elderly women). *See also* Dixon v. Ford Motor Credit, 2000 U.S. Dist. LEXIS 7934 (E.D. La. May 31, 2000) (unpublished) (allegations that auto dealer failed to disclose commissions on credit life insurance sales could present predicate act of mail fraud sufficient to avoid dismissal of RICO claim). For earlier cases, see, e.g., Morosani v. First Nat'l Bank of Atlanta, 703 F.2d 1220 (11th Cir. 1983), *on remand* 581 F. Supp. 945 (N.D. Ga. 1984) (class action); Wilcox Dev. Co. v. First Interstate Bank of Oregon, 590 F. Supp. 445 (D. Or. 1984), *rev'd*, 815 F.2d 522 (9th Cir. 1987) (reversing summary judgment against RICO count); Charing Cross Inc. v. Riggs Nat'l Bank, 1983 WL 2193 (D.D.C. Oct. 7, 1983).

913 *See* American Nat'l Bank & Trust Co. of Chicago v. Haroco, Inc. 473 U.S. 606, 105 S. Ct. 3291, 87 L. Ed. 2d 437 (1985) (bank lied about its prime rate, on which rates to customers were based); Charing Cross Inc. v. Riggs Nat'l Bank, 1983 WL 2193 (D.D.C. Oct. 7, 1983) (denying motion to dismiss). Given the judicial hostility to RICO that exists in many jurisdictions, the practitioner may wish to challenge such "prime rate" overcharges on contract or, if applicable to the case at hand, usury theories. For example, some jurisdictions deregulated interest ceilings, leaving only an "as agreed" limitation. Such "prime rate" overcharges may thus violate the as-agreed "ceiling" and implicate whatever usury penalties remain in place. *See* § 9.2.3, *supra*. *Cf.* Briggs Transportation Co. v. Second Northwestern Nat'l Bank, 406 N.W.2d 7 (Minn. Ct. App. 1987) (breach of contract claim utilized).

914 Margolis v. Republic Nat'l Bank of New York, 585 F. Supp. 595, 596 (S.D.N.Y. 1984) (dismissing claims on grounds that the plaintiff had failed to allege an injury from a pattern of racketeering activity, an allegation that the Supreme Court ruled RICO did not require the next year, in *Sedima*). *See also* Lum Bank v. Bank of Am., 361 F.3d 217, 220 (3d Cir. 2004) (affirming dismissal of RICO claims of credit card holders who alleged that bank had promised them a rate based on bank's prime rate because plaintiffs failed to plead defendant's misrepresentations with sufficient specificity); *cf.* Walker v. Wash. Mut. Bank FA, 63 Fed. Appx. 316, 317 (9th Cir. 2003) (affirming summary judgment on RICO claim based on allegedly wrongful foreclosure of plaintiff's house on grounds that her mail fraud allegations, which were based on alleged TILA violations, failed because the defendant had not violated TILA).

Mail fraud is not the only predicate act that might appear in a creditor/borrower relationship. Where a creditor, as part of extending or collecting a debt, threatens to use overreaching means to collect on the debt, it may violate the federal loansharking statute,[915] which is a RICO predicate act.[916] That statute prohibits extortionate extensions of credit, those made with the understanding that failure to repay "could result in the use of violence or other criminal means to cause harm to the person, reputation, or property of any person,"[917] and further prohibits collecting a debt with the implicit or explicit threat to use violence or other criminal means to cause such harm.[918] One court liberally read collection letters sent to a plaintiff to find that they could suggest the threat of criminal means to collect the debt, and that the plaintiff thereby stated a class-action RICO claim based on loansharking against a consumer lender.[919] Another court sustained a RICO claim by a plaintiff who claimed that a bank threatened to jail his wife and call in the FBI unless he mortgaged his farm to secure an overdrawn account of his wife's employer.[920]

Many usurious consumer transactions are named not as the loans they are, but as sales or leases. An example of a common consumer transaction that may violate RICO through the collection of an unlawful debt in violation of RICO is the rent-to-own (RTO) appliance sale, discussed at length in Chapter 7, *supra*. These transactions resemble credit sales at exorbitant interest rates, but are disguised as leases with an option to purchase. Most states have legalized these high-rate transactions, but a few still place effective limits on their charges. In these states, if a practitioner can establish that the RTO contract in fact involves a credit sale under state usury law rather than a true lease,[921] the disguised interest will likely be more than double the enforce-able rate, and should serve to satisfy the "collection of an unlawful debt" element of RICO.[922] This approach should similarly provide RICO remedies for other hidden interest or mislabeled transactions such as the sham corporate loan or the sham real estate sale and repurchase.[923]

Post-dated check transactions may also be disguised loans for purposes of RICO.[924] Recently, a court denied summary judgment to a defendant that, though denying any lending activity, took post-dated checks in return for cash in an amount well under the face value of the check, along with an allegedly valueless gift certificate to an obscure catalog company in the amount of the difference.[925] Whether the gift certificate was actually "interest" under the usury statute, said the court, was for a trier of fact to decide.[926]

A transaction for which state law does not authorize *any* interest may also support an unlawful debt RICO claim. Some courts, interpreting state usury laws that trigger greater penalties when more than double the amount of legal interest is charged, have held that charging *any* interest where there is no interest authorized is double the legal rate of 0%,[927] which would qualify as an "unlawful debt" under RICO. It does not appear that this issue has been raised under RICO as yet, but the analysis should be the same.

One twist to making a RICO claim based on the collection of an unlawful debt (as opposed to a pattern of racketeering activity) is that by virtue of the definition of unlawful debt,[928] the individual state's small loan laws will usually

---

915 18 U.S.C. §§ 891–894.

916 18 U.S.C. § 1961(6).

917 18 U.S.C. §§ 891(6), 892.

918 18 U.S.C. §§ 891(7), 894.

919 Brown v. C.I.L., Inc., 1996 U.S. Dist. LEXIS 4917 (N.D. Ill. Jan. 28, 1996). The statements examined by the court included: "We can be reached at . . . any time should you wish to repay your debt in full without any damge [sic] to you or your credit"; "My 'ass' is being hung out to dry by you and I would like you to be man enough to tell me why? After you begged for us to loan you money, not once! but twice! My good Friends are interested to [sic]!"; and "Your attitude about this money you begged for is almost unbelievable. Our people in Mr. Carpenter's Office are watching with great interest. Stop being a coward, Big Man!" *Id.* at 40–41.

920 Ford v. Citizens & Southern Nat'l Bank, 700 F. Supp. 1121 (N.D. Ga. 1988) (allegations of blackmail sufficed to meet statute's requirement of "the use, or an express or implicit threat of use, of violence or other criminal means to cause harm to the person, reputation, or property of any person").

921 *See* Miller v. Colortyme, Inc., 518 N.W.2d 544 (Minn. 1994) (Minnesota's usury statute applies to rent-to-own contracts); Fogie v. Rent-A-Center, Inc., 518 N.W.2d 544 (Minn. 1994) (rent-to-own contracts are consumer credit sales under Minnesota law).

922 *See* Fogie v. Rent-A-Center, Inc., 1995 WL 649575 (D. Minn. 1995) (implicit interest in RTO contracts was usurious under state law and was more than twice the applicable rate; RICO predicate element of "unlawful debt" therefore established), *aff'd sub nom.*, Fogie v. Thorn Americas, Inc., 95 F.3d 645 (8th Cir. 1996) (declining to address RICO issue).

923 *See* §§ 7.5.2, 7.5.7, *supra*.

924 *Id.*

925 Cashback Catalog Sales, Inc. v. Price, 102 F. Supp. 2d 1375 (S.D. Ga. Mar. 20, 2000).

926 *Id.* at 1379–80.

927 *See In re* Giorgio, 62 B.R. 853 (Bankr. D.R.I. 1986); *In re* Marill Alarm Systems, 68 B.R. 399 (Bankr. S.D. Fla. 1986) (sham consulting fees are hidden interest; Florida RICO statute violated). *See* National Consumer Law Center, Unfair and Deceptive Acts and Practices § 9.2.7 (6th ed. 2004 and Supp.) for a listing of state RICO statutes.

928 18 U.S.C. § 1961(6) provides that an unlawful debt is:

> [A] debt (A) incurred or contracted in gambling activity which was in violation of the law of the United States, a State or political subdivision thereof, or which is unenforceable under State or Federal law in whole or in part as to principal or interest because of the laws relating to usury, and (B) which was incurred in connection with the business of gambling in violation of the law of the United States, a State or political subdivision thereof, *or the business of lending money or a thing of value at a rate usurious under State or Federal law, where the usurious rate is at least twice the enforceable rate.*

(Emphasis added.)

establish the enforceable rate for such a loan, the rate that the loan's rate must at least double to meet the definition. Unlike other state law offenses that are named as predicate acts—such as murder, kidnapping, robbery, or extortion—usury laws do not have a shared background in common law and accordingly vary widely from state to state.[929] Though fees for payday loans—usually assessed as a percentage of the face value of the check or in a flat amount—translate to an average annual percentage rate of close to 500%, such loans have drawn special treatment in many states, exempting them from the usury laws that govern other small loans.[930] Thus, one of the most pernicious abuses in consumer lending, the monstrous fees and interest charged on payday loans, may not lead to a RICO claim in a state that has chosen to exempt such loans from the more civilized limits that apply to other types of consumer credit arrangements. After ruling that the structure of payday loans allowed them to escape the usual limits, courts in Florida[931] and Louisiana[932] have dismissed RICO claims that were based on the exorbitant charges collected for cashing postdated checks.

State law may expressly permit fees that in substance are interest, precluding a RICO claim based on their collection. For example, the Fifth Circuit dismissed a RICO claim based on a loan broker's $1,500 fee assessed on a $2,000 loan on the grounds that the Texas Credit Services Organization Act permitted such fees and therefore they could not be characterized as disguised interest.[933] Meanwhile, the First Circuit allowed a lender to escape a RICO claim through a loophole in the Massachusetts criminal usury law that precludes criminal liability for loans bearing interest at a rate higher than the established ceiling of twenty percent per year if the lender simply sends a notice to the state attorney general that declares that the lender intends to charge such excess interest.[934]

In other states, however, check cashing operations and payday lenders have found themselves defending RICO actions that allege they were collecting unlawful debts, despite their arguments that they were not extending loans, but merely providing services for fees.[935] Accordingly, a usury-based RICO claim requires counsel to carefully review the appropriate state's small loan laws and the decisions interpreting those laws. Such claims are far more likely to have success in those states that require payday lenders to meet the same interest limits as other small loan laws.[936]

10.8.5.3.6 State RICO statutes

At least twenty-two states[937] have state RICO statutes that afford consumers a private cause of action in state court.[938] In addition, a state RICO statute may offer the alternative of equitable relief.[939] Where state court is a preferable forum to federal court, claims under state RICO statutes should be considered.

929 *See* § 7.5, *supra.*

930 *See* § 7.5.5, *supra.*

931 Betts v. Advance America, 213 F.R.D. 466 (M.D. Fla. 2003) (post-dated check transaction was not a loan for purposes of state usury laws, and therefore could not be the basis of a RICO claim), *citing* Betts v. Ace Cash Express, Inc., 827 So. 2d 294 (Fla. Ct. App. 2002) (holding that deferred deposit transactions are check-cashing transactions rather than loans subject to state usury laws).

932 Bellizan v. Easy Money of Louisiana, Inc., 2002 WL 31115249 (E.D. La. July 19, 2002) (because "overlapping" loans made by payday lender did not violate state laws prohibiting "rollover" or "renewal" loans, plaintiff failed to establish that defendant collected an unlawful debt; Porter v. ACE Cash Express, Inc., 2000 WL 1610632 (E.D. La. Oct. 26, 2000) (because term of loans made to plaintiff exceeded those defined by state payday loan act by 5 days, they fell outside its interest limitations; since loans were not usurious under state law they did not meet RICO's definition of an unlawful debt, action dismissed), *aff'd,* 277 F.3d 1372 (5th Cir. 2001) (table).

933 Lovic v. Ritemoney, Ltd., 378 F.3d 433, 44 (5th Cir. 2004).

934 Cannarozzi v. Fiumara, 371 F.3d 1, 5 (1st Cir. 2004).

935 *See* Cook v. Easy Money of Ky., Inc., 196 F. Supp. 2d 508 (W.D. Ky. 2001) (interpreting now-repealed version of state small loan law, refusing to dismiss §§ 1962(a) and (c) claims arising from interest and fees charged on deferred check presentment transactions); Arrington v. Colleen, Inc., 2000 U.S. Dist. LEXIS 20651, Clearinghouse No. 53,501 (D. Md. Aug. 7, 2000) (order and memorandum denying lender's motion for summary judgment); Burden v. York, Clearinghouse No. 52,502, Civil Action No. 98-268 (E.D. Ky. Sept. 29, 1999); Hamilton v. York, 987 F. Supp. 953 (E.D. Ky. 1997) (fees charged by check cashing firm were interest for purposes of usury laws, denying motion to dismiss RICO claim). *See also* Henry v. Cash Today, Inc., 199 F.R.D. 566 (S.D. Tex. 2000) (class certification granted in cash back ad sale case). *But see* Rivera v. AT&T Corp., 141 F. Supp. 2d 719, 723–25 (S.D. Tex. 2001) (late fee charged by cable companies was not interest under state law, therefore companies had not committed usury that would amount to collection of an unlawful debt; dismissing RICO class action with prejudice), *aff'd,* 2002 WL 663707 (5th Cir. Mar. 25, 2002) (table).

936 *See* § 7.5.5.5, *supra.*

937 Arizona, Colorado, Delaware, Florida, Georgia, Hawaii, Idaho, Indiana, Iowa, Louisiana, Mississippi, Nevada, New Jersey, New Mexico, North Carolina, North Dakota, Ohio, Oregon, Rhode Island, Utah, Washington, and Wisconsin.

938 *See also* Check 'N Go of Fla., Inc. v. State, 790 So. 2d 454 (Fla. Ct. App. 2001) (in action challenging a subpoena *duces tecum,* state attorney general had reason to believe that payday lender was violating state RICO statute with usurious "rollover" transactions). *But see* State v. Roderick, 704 So. 2d 49 (Miss. 1997) (finding state RICO statute unconstitutionally vague in case against payday lenders because it criminalized usury without providing fair warning), *cert. denied,* 524 U.S. 926 (1998). For a discussion of state RICO laws and a compilation of the statutes, see National Consumer Law Center, Unfair and Deceptive Acts and Practices § 9.3, Appx. C.2 (6th ed. 2004 and Supp.).

939 *See, e.g.,* Bowcutt v. Delta North Star Corp., 95 Wash. App. 311, 976 P.2d 643 (1999) (ruling homeowners could seek injunction against foreclosure pursuant to state RICO statute).

Many of these statutes explicitly list fraud and usury as predicate offenses, and some list violations of specific new consumer protection laws, such as those prohibiting equity skimming or telemarketing fraud. Some parallel the federal RICO statute by prohibiting collection of an unlawful debt.[940] These statutes demonstrate the legislative intent to treat consumer fraud as organized crime, and to afford victimized consumers the powerful remedies of the RICO laws. Several of these state RICO statutes allow for or mandate multiple damages.

10.8.6 Class Actions

Usury cases are well-suited to class action treatment.[941] Lenders who overcharge typically do so systematically, so there are common issues of law and fact. Often each borrower is entitled to a relatively small recovery, such as double the amount of the overcharge. A primary purpose of class actions is to provide a way to recover damage awards that are too small to make individual suits economically feasible.[942]

Usury class actions produce other benefits as well. As the California Supreme Court has noted, such actions often produce "several salutary by-products, including a therapeutic effect upon those sellers who indulge in fraudulent practices, aid to legitimate business enterprises by curtailing illegitimate competition, and avoidance to the judicial process of the burden of multiple litigation involving identical claims."[943] Even an unconscionability claim that requires examination of the comparative bargaining positions of the lender and consumers may be appropriate for class treatment where the consumers as a group share material characteristics.[944]

Individual issues are likely to be minimal in a usury class action.[945] Some usury statutes apply only to non-business loans, but, since in most cases the purpose of the loan is determined by the written representations the borrower made to the lender,[946] this can easily be determined from the lender's records. If there are individual factual questions about the purpose of the loan, they can be resolved through the claims process or by bifurcating the proceedings.[947] Damages can usually be determined from the lender's own records.[948] For nationwide class actions, however, the court will either have to find a basis for applying the law of a single state, or conclude that variations among the states' laws are not so significant as to make the class action unmanageable.[949]

---

940 *See In re* Giorgio, 62 B.R. 853 (Bankr. D.R.I. 1986) ("unlawful debt" under state RICO statute is any debt that is unenforceable in whole or in part due to usury), *rev'd*, 81 B.R. 766 (D.R.I. 1988) (debt could not be considered unenforceable where state court had entered non-collusive judgment on it two years earlier), *aff'd*, 862 F.2d 933 (1st Cir. 1988) (suggesting interpretation that would confine unlawful debt to gambling debts); *In re* Marill Alarm Systems, Inc., 68 B.R. 399 (Bankr. S.D. Fla. 1986) (usury in sham consulting fees triggers state RICO statute), *adopted by* 81 B.R. 119 (S.D. Fla. 1987), *aff'd*, 861 F.2d 725 (11th Cir. 1988) (table).

941 Violette v. P.A. Days, Inc., 214 F.R.D. 207 (S.D. Ohio 2003) (certifying class on claim that interest charge exceeded RISA limits); Car Now Acceptance Co. v. Block, 2002 WL 32001272 (Ohio C.P. Nov. 25, 2002), *aff'd*, 2003 WL 21714583 (Ohio Ct. App. July 14, 2003) (unpublished). Sample class action pleadings, including a complaint, class certification memos, and notices to the class, may be found on the CD-Rom accompanying this volume.

942 *See, e.g.*, Linder v. Thrifty Oil Co., 2 P.3d 27, 38 (Cal. 2000) (class action challenging surcharge imposed on customers who paid with credit card).

943 *Id.* (quoting from Vasquez v. Superior Court, 484 P.2d 964 (Cal. 1971)).

944 Dienese v. McKenzie Check Advance, 2000 U.S. Dist. LEXIS 20389 (E.D. Wis. Dec. 11, 2000).

945 *But see* Vincent v. Bank of Am., 109 S.W.3d 856 (Tex. App. 2003) (class certification would undermine statutory provision that usury remedy was available only if creditor filed to cure within reasonable time after receiving notice).

946 *See* § 9.2.2.3, *supra*.

947 *See* Fed. R. Civ. P. 23(c)(4)(A). *See also* Tay-Tay, Inc. v. Young, 80 S.W.3d 365 (Ark. 2002) (affirming certification of usury class action); Luttenegger v. Conseco Fin. Serv., 671 N.W.2d 425, 439–40 (Iowa 2003) (claims process can be used to determine nature of loans; individual damage issues to do preclude class certification when liability involves common questions). *See generally* 2 Newberg on Class Actions, §§ 9.53, 9.64 (4th ed. 2002).

948 *See* National Consumer Law Center, Consumer Class Actions § 9.3.5 (5th ed. 2002 and Supp.).

949 *See* Washington Mut. Bank v. Superior Court, 15 P.3d 1071 (Cal. 2001). *See generally* National Consumer Law Center, Unfair and Deceptive Acts and Practices § 8.5.5 (6th ed. 2004 and Supp.); National Consumer Law Center, Consumer Class Actions §§ 2.6.2, 2.6.3 (5th ed. 2002 and Supp.).

Chapter 11

The Credit Marketplace and a Sampling of Abuses *Du Jour*

11.1 Market Forces—Market Rationales—Market Failures

To effectively challenge overreaching credit,[1] it is important to understand both the articulated business rationales for the practices and the market failures which undermine the validity of those rationales.

Defenders of these practices frequently invoke "the sanctity of contract" and those policy considerations which attend that principle: a borrower signs the contract, gets the benefit of the bargain struck, and should be bound by it.[2] They argue that disclosure, rather than substantive regulation, not only suffices to meet consumers' interests, but is the preferred mechanism in a free market economy. Finally, they offer the conventional wisdom that high risk borrowers justify high rate credit, and that it is high risk borrowers who receive the high-cost credit. There are dangerous holes in that conventional wisdom due to market segmentation (the splitting of the market into prime, subprime, and predatory), steering, and information asymmetries.[3]

11.2 Barriers: Information, Understanding, Choice, and Steering

For basic contract principles, and to some extent, market theory, to work properly in practice requires equal knowledge and equal bargaining power on both sides. They both also assume the availability of other options for the borrower. Neither of these premises describe the reality for many people.[4] To some degree, the law now recognizes the inherently unequal bargaining power in the typical consumer contract,[5] though it is not always sufficient to convince a court to disturb the contract.[6] Moreover, those

---

1 Overreaching credit, as used in this book, refers both to substantive terms of a contract and to the process by which the contract is struck and enforced. It encompasses excessive cost in relation to the value of goods or services purchased on credit; excessive cost of the credit itself (however extracted); taking financial advantage of vulnerable or unsophisticated borrowers and buyers; and engaging in unfair or deceptive conduct at any stage of a credit transaction. "Overreaching" and "predatory" may not synonymous where "predatory" primarily is used to describe practices occurring in a segment of the subprime market. Over-reaching, on the other hand, can occur in any market, prime or subprime. For descriptions of the prime, subprime, and predatory mortgage markets, see Elizabeth Renuart, *An Overview of the Predatory Lending Process*, 15 Housing Pol'y Debate 467 (2004); Kathleen C. Engel & Patricia A. McCoy, *A Tale of Three Markets: The Law and Economics of Predatory Lending*, 80 Tex. L. Rev. 1255 (2002). For a description of the small loan market, see Lynn Drysdale & Kathleen E. Keest, *The Two-Tiered Consumer Financial Services Marketplace: The Fringe Banking System and its Challenge to Current Thinking About the Socio-Economic Role of Usury Law in Today's Society*, 51 S.C. L. Rev. 589 (2000). *See also* Joint Center for Housing Studies, Harvard University, *Credit, Capital and Communities: The Implications of the Changing Mortgage Banking Industry for Community Based Organizations* (Mar. 9, 2004), *available at* www.jchs.harvard.edu/publications/communitydevelopment/ccc04-1.pdf.

2 That perspective underlies basic common law contract principles, e.g., a party to a contract is presumed to know its terms absent duress, fraud, etc. *See, e.g.*, Roper v. Associates Fin. Servs., 533 So. 2d 206 (Ala. 1988) (a reasonably prudent person exercising ordinary care would have noticed the call option being challenged).

3 Kathleen C. Engel & Patricia A. McCoy, *A Tale of Three Markets: The Law and Economics of Predatory Lending*, 80 Tex. L. Rev. 1255, 1271–1283 (2002).

4 *See* Elizabeth Renuart, *An Overview of the Predatory Lending Process*, 15 Housing Pol'y Debate 467 (2004); Kathleen C. Engel & Patricia A. McCoy, *A Tale of Three Markets: The Law and Economics of Predatory Lending*, 80 Tex. L. Rev. 1255 (2002). *See also* Richard Lord, *American Nightmare: Predatory Lending and the Foreclosure of the American Dream* (Common Courage Press 2005). *See also* Till v. SCS Credit Corp., 541 U.S. 465, 124 S. Ct. 1951, 1962–1964, 158 L. Ed. 2d 787 (2004) (in the course of deciding the formula courts should apply to determine the rate of interest for a crammed-down car loan in the bankruptcy context, the Court recognized that the subprime auto finance market is not "perfectly" competitive and that creditors have much more information about the market than do consumers).

5 *E.g.*, American Fin. Serv. Ass'n v. FTC, 767 F.2d 957 (D.C. Cir. 1985), *cert. denied*, 475 U.S. 1011 (1986) (consumers' limited ability to shop for and bargain over terms cited as grounds for upholding FTC credit practice rule). *See also* Alan M. White & Cathy Lesser Mansfield, *Literacy and Contract*, 13.2 Stan. L. & Pol'y Rev. 233, 243–251 (2002).

6 *See, e.g.*, Alan M. White & Cathy Lesser Mansfield, *Literacy and Contract*, 13.2 Stan. L. & Pol'y Rev. 233, 251–256 (2002); Roper v. Associates Fin. Servs., 533 So. 2d 206 (Ala. 1988).

principles are meaningless with especially vulnerable consumers—the illiterate, the uneducated, the frail elderly, those for whom English is a second language, and those who have (or think they have) no other options. In addition, evidence has been presented in some cases that certain more vulnerable populations are targets of abusive sellers and expensive lenders.[7]

Disclosure is not an adequate counterweight. Foremost, in a country in which nearly 40% of the population is estimated to be functionally illiterate,[8] the concept of disclosure begins to lose meaning. The most recent literacy study used a typical advertisement for a home equity loan as one of its measures of "quantitative literacy," and only 4% of the adults sampled could calculate how much interest would be charged.[9] Similarly, a survey by the Consumer Federation of America showed that, while more than 70% of respondents knew what the letters APR stood for, only half that number understood its significance as the primary indicator of the cost of credit.[10] Add to that the tendency of too many creditors to understate or obscure the real cost of credit, (sometimes as permitted by law, other times not[11]), and the

inherently complex nature of credit,[12] and the concepts of "disclosure" and "consent to known terms of a freely negotiated bargain" are highly inadequate responses to creditor overreaching.

A return to the principle of *caveat emptor* seems an inappropriate solution, too, for at its core is a message to consumers: "assume that all business people are out to cheat you until proven otherwise." At least one court has rejected this "trust no one" approach,[13] and it is unlikely that ethical businesses, or our society as a whole, would consciously adopt that as a positive component of our economic system.

11.3 High Rate and High Risk: Myth or Fact?

The notion of risk is highly prized as a rationale for high-cost credit, but is insufficiently scrutinized to assess its validity. It presumes that the credit industry is sophisticated enough to properly identify who is "risky" and who is not,[14]

7　*See, e.g.,* Carlisle v. Whirlpool Fin. Nat'l Bank, Civil Action No. CV 97-068 (Circuit Court, Hale County, Ala., Post Trial Order, Aug. 25, 1999), Clearinghouse No. 52,516 (jury verdict in two satellite sale and financing cases for $580 million in punitive damages reduced $300 million though judge found defendants behavior "alarming" and "reprehensible," in part due to the evidence of sales practice designed to target and take advantage of the poor, under-educated elderly, and African-American citizens); § 11.3, *infra.*

8　*Adult Literacy in America*, National Center for Educ. Statistics, U.S. Dept. of Educ. (Sept. 1993) (available from the U.S. Gov't Printing Office, GPO stock number 065-000-00588-3), *discussed in, e.g.,* Alan M. White & Cathy Lesser Mansfield, *Literacy and Contract*, 13.2 Stan. L. & Pol'y Rev. 233, 235–242 (2002); Mary Jordan, *Literacy of 90 Million Is Deficient*, Washington Post, Sept. 9, 1993, at A1).

　　The figures are extrapolated from those in the survey performing in the lowest two of five levels of proficiency in prose, document, and quantitative skills. Document literacy tested comprehension of such documents as wage stubs or job applications. (Consider where a typical mortgage or promissory note would fall on that scale.) Proper use of a bank deposit slip was one of the tests of quantitative skills. (Consider that in relation to any consumer credit contract.)

9　*Adult Literacy in America*, National Center for Educ. Statistics, U.S. Dept. of Educ. (Sept. 1993) at 100. (The ad included all the information necessary to make the calculation: number and amount of monthly payments, and amount financed.)

10　Seventy-two percent of the respondents understood the acronym, but only 37% understood its significance as the best indicator of the cost of credit. *US Consumer Knowledge: The Results of a Nationwide Test*, (Survey conducted by the Educational Testing Service for the Consumer Federation of America and TRW 1990).

11　Even if the Truth in Lending disclosures are correct on their face, lenders sometimes use sales tactics and make representations which undermine or eliminate the effectiveness of otherwise accurate information. *See, e.g., In re* First Alliance Mortgage Co., 298 B.R. 652 (C.D. Cal. 2003); Diana B. Henriques

and Lowell Bergman, *Mortgaged Lives: A special report; Profiting from Fine Print with Wall Street's Help*, N.Y. Times, March 15, 2000, at A1 (reporting on allegations against First Alliance Mortgage about its sales tactics).

　　The APR itself, despite its original intent, is not always a true measure of the cost of credit even when calculated according to the Truth in Lending rules. By statute or FRB interpretation, a significant number of credit-related charges may be excluded from the APR, which means even a "proper" APR artificially understates the real cost of the transaction. *See generally* National Consumer Law Center, Truth in Lending Chs. 3, 9 (5th ed. 2003 and Supp.). Moreover, the disclosures are generally given after the consumer has made a decision based on whatever information the lender has given. Finally, the TIL disclosures fail miserably to alert consumers to the significant disadvantages built into many of these complex credit transactions, such as repeated refinancings.

12　Some credit has gotten so creative that even creditors' employees seem frequently not to understand it. The widespread occurrence of errors in calculating variable interest rates is one measure of this problem. *See, e.g., 8 Billion in Mortgage Overcharges Seen*, Los Angeles Times, June 30, 1990, at D-5, reporting on studies showing errors in over half of 7000 loans sampled. (For a real eye-opener look at an auto lease, and try to figure out the actual dollar penalty for turning the car in early.) *See generally* National Consumer Law Center, Truth in Lending Ch. 10 (5th ed. 2003 and Supp.).

13　Northwestern Bank v. Roseman, 344 S.E.2d 120 (N.C. Ct. App. 1986), *aff'd*, 354 S.E.2d 238 (N.C. 1987).

14　One study conducted by the Federal Reserve Bank of Boston found that 80% of all mortgage applicants had some blemish on their record which, if looked at in isolation, would have justified classifying them as not truly creditworthy. Munnell, Browne, McEneandy, Tootell, *Mortgage Lending in Boston: Interpreting HMDA Data*, Working Paper Series No. 92-7 (Federal Reserve Bank of Boston Oct., 1992). Thus, factors other than credit records came into play. The study found that the race of the applicant was a statistically significant factor. One startling piece of information shared by Fannie Mae lends a great deal of support for the proposition that some homeowners are not placed appropriately on the "risk-based" pricing scale.

how to price "risk,"[15] and that those setting the "risk" price are honest and wise enough not to conflate genuine risk with illegitimate factors.

Research suggests that the relationship between pricing and risk may be attenuated in the subprime mortgage market where significantly higher interest rates and points may create the risk, rather than compensate for it. For example, the interest rates charged by some subprime lenders in 1995 ranged from 5% to 17.99%.[16] In 1999, the range for the same lenders was 3% to 19.99%. The median interest rates for the same loans were 10% in 1996, 10.99% in 1997, and 11%—11.99% in 1998 and 1999. In contrast, during those same years, the annualized rate on conventional 30-year mortgages was 7.95% in 1995, 7.8% in 1996, 7.6% in 1997, 6.94% in 1998, and 7.43% in 1999.[17] Comparing the number of points or origination fees charged by subprime lenders is similarly disquieting. This industry appears to add from 5 to 25 points onto each deal,[18] while conventional lenders charge points averaging about .84 for purchase-money mortgages and 2 points for refinancings.[19]

A recent study found that legitimate risk-based pricing in the A- subprime market justified adding .90% to the interest rate for the potential increase in default rates and .25% due to higher servicing costs.[20] Thus, 1.15% above prime may be justifiable. The authors could account for a 1% additional

differential between prime and A- subprime interest rates. Further, at the end of 2000, considering the percentage distribution of all subprime loans among the categories of A-, B, and C credit, the weighted average interest rate of subprime loans over prime loans is only about 3%.[21] Arguably, price gouging occurs when rates exceed 3–5% above prime even on C credit loans. Another author reviewed a rate sheet from a major subprime lender and the existing research and observed that price and risk do not correlate closely and that credit losses are a small fraction of the high subprime mortgage rates and costs.[22]

Interestingly, a California study released in 2002 revealed that 60% of the borrowers surveyed believed they had good or excellent credit, yet they all received subprime loans.[23] Nearly half of the study participants received adjustable rate mortgages even though these consumers were often low-income consumers, seniors, and those who perceived themselves as having bad credit (all consumers who would be least able to handle an ever-changing monthly payment amount).[24] Further, almost 70% of all participants reported that key loan terms (interest rates, points and fees, fixed versus adjustable rates, prepayment penalty provisions) changed for the worse at closing compared to what the borrowers understood before closing.[25]

The common use of prepayment penalties in the subprime market is equally troubling. Borrowers do not incur the cost of a prepayment penalty at closing (unless they are refinancing a loan containing such a provision), like points and fees. Nor does the prepayment cost appear in the interest rate. Rather, prepayment penalties are triggered upon refinancing, payoff of the loan, or sometimes when the loan is accelerated and foreclosed. Approximately 80% of subprime mortgage loans contain prepayment penalties compared with only 2% of loans in the competitive prime market.[26] Consumer choice appears to be lacking. Lender choice may call

---

In 2000, Fannie Mae opined that almost half of all subprime borrowers could qualify for lower cost conventional financing. Fannie Mae, Press Release March 2, 2000, *available at* www.fanniemae.com/news/pressreleases/0667.html.

15 Indeed, one study concluded that its findings supported some suspicions within the industry that the price set for "good" customers may be set too low. C. Chmura, *A Loan Pricing Case Study*, 78 J. of Com. Lending 23, 32 (Dec. 1995). This suggests that the industry may be over-optimistic in its belief that it knows how to price risk. It also raises the question of whether those labeled "bad" risks are being priced to cross-subsidize those labeled "good" risks. Either way, "risk-based" pricing invites some objective scrutiny.

16 *See* Cathy Lesser Mansfield, *The Road to Subprime "HEL" Was Paved with Good Congressional Intentions: Usury Deregulation and the Subprime Home Equity Market*, 51 S.C.L. Rev. 473 (2000). As of December 1, 2000, the *average* interest rates on subprime loans by risk category were reported to be: A- loans—10%; B loans—11.8%; C loans—12.7%. *Inside B&C Lending*, Dec. 4, 2000.

17 *Id.* For a critique of the justification for the charging of high interest rates and points to cover risk, see Parts VI.A.1 and 2.

18 *See* Diana B. Henriques and Lowell Bergman, *Mortgaged Lives: A Special Report; Profiting from Fine Print with Wall Street's Help*, N.Y. Times, March 15, 2000, at A1.

19 *See* U.S. Census Bureau, Statistical Abstract of the United States: 1999, Table No. 819. An associate general counsel of Freddie Mac stated at a conference in June of 2000 that the total points and fees for conventional loans decreased from 1.6% in 1993 to 1.1% in 1999. Eric Stein, *Quantifying the Economic Cost of Predatory Lending*, Coalition for Responsible Lending at 7, n.17 (July 25, 2001), *available at* www.responsiblelending.org.

20 Howard Lax, Michael Manti, Paul Raca & Peter Zorn, *Subprime Lending: An Investigation of Economic Efficiency*, 15 Housing Pol'y Debate 533 (2004).

21 Eric Stein, *Quantifying the Economic Cost of Predatory Lending*, Coalition for Responsible Lending at 14 (July 25, 2001), *available at* www.responsiblelending.org.

22 Alan M. White, *Risk-Based Mortgage Pricing: Present and Future Research*, 15 Housing Pol'y Debate 503, 512–518 (2004).

23 Kevin Stein & Margaret Libby, *Stolen Wealth: Inequities in California's Subprime Mortgage Market*, California Reinvestment Committee at 21–22 (Dec. 2001).

24 *Id.* at 31.

25 *Id.* at 29.

26 Eric Stein, *Quantifying the Economic Cost of Predatory Lending*, Coalition for Responsible Lending at 7 (July 25, 2001). This author states: "Rational subprime borrowers with market power should prefer them no more often, and probably less often, than conventional borrowers so that they can refinance into a conventional loan as soon as credit improves." *See also* Roberto G. Quercia, Michael A. Stegman & Walter R. Davis, *The Impact of Predatory Loan Terms on Subprime Foreclosures: The Special Case of Prepayment Penalties and Balloon Payments* (Kenan Institute for Private Enterprise, University of North Carolina Jan. 25, 2005), *available at* www.kenan-flagler.unc.edu/assets/documents/foreclosurepaper.pdf (71.8% of loans in the study contained prepayment penalties).

the shots in the subprime market because prepayment penalties provide an extra source of income to such a degree that a whole class of securities are created based on this income stream, called class "P" securities.[27] One organization opines that prepayment penalty provisions cost 850,000 families about $2.3 billion per year.[28]

The proposition that higher costs result in higher foreclosure rates for subprime home equity loans has not been clearly established. What is irrefutable is that the delinquency and default rates for subprime loans are much higher than for conventional home equity loans. Between 1998 and 2003, one source reports foreclosure rates on subprime mortgage loans of approximately 4.5 to 11 times higher than the rates for prime loans.[29] Further, subprime loans with prepayment penalty and balloon provisions are much more likely to experience foreclosure than loans without these characteristics.[30] After controlling for certain neighborhood demographics and economic conditions, one study found that subprime loans in the Chicago area lead to foreclosure at 20 or more times the rate that prime loans do.[31]

Finally, a 1993 study of mortgage credit extended to low-income and minority borrowers under targeted CRA programs[32] suggested that loans to these borrowers performed as well as, or better, than equivalent loans to traditional, non-targeted borrowers.[33] Earlier research, too, failed to identify significant differences in the financial profile of low-rate and high-rate borrowers.[34] There are, on the contrary, suggestions that more insidious and unjustifiable factors may be at work.[35] A study showing race and gender discrimination in price negotiations on cars suggests that "sucker-pricing" may be involved, with the sellers' stereotypes operating as to which customers they might be able to get the highest mark-up from.[36] It stands to reason that those perceived to be "suckers" will be precisely those more vulnerable consumers. If the study is any indication, those stereotypes then turn into self-fulfilling prophecies.

---

27 Eric Stein, *Quantifying the Economic Cost of Predatory Lending*, Coalition for Responsible Lending at 8 (July 25, 2001).

28 *Id.* at 9.

29 Elizabeth Renuart, *An Overview of the Predatory Lending Process*, 15 Housing Pol'y Debate 467, 479 (2004). The source relied upon to create Figure 1 in this article was the National Delinquency Survey of the Mortgage Bankers Association of America. These numbers are understated because the foreclosure rate for prime loans was less than 1%.

30 Roberto G. Quercia, Michael A. Stegman & Walter R. Davis, *The Impact of Predatory Loan Terms on Subprime Foreclosures: The Special Case of Prepayment Penalties and Balloon Payments* (Kenan Institute for Private Enterprise, University of North Carolina Jan. 25, 2005), *available at* www.kenan-flagler.unc.edu/assets/documents/foreclosurepaper.pdf (the differential is about 20% higher for loans with prepayment penalties and 50% higher for loans with balloon payments).

31 Daniel Immergluck & Geoff Smith, *Risky Business—An Econometric Analysis of the Relationship Between Subprime Lending and Neighborhood Foreclosures* (Woodstock Institute 2004), *available at* http://woodstockinst.org/document/riskybusiness.pdf.

32 CRA is often criticized by the banking industry as forcing lenders to make "risky" loans.

33 *Sound Loans for Communities: An Analysis of the Performance of Community Reinvestment Loans* (Woodstock Institute, Oct. 1993).

34 *See, e.g.*, Boczar, "Competition Between Banks and Finance Companies," Credit Research Center Working Paper No. 9 (Purdue Univ. 1970) ("the evidence on borrower characteristics does not support the risk segmentation hypothesis."); Eisenbeis & Murphy, *Interest Rate Ceilings and Consumer Credit Rationing, a Multivariate Analysis of a Survey of Borrowers*, 41 S.

Econ. J. 115, 122 (1974) ("there is little evidence to support hypothesis of market risk segmentation."); Goudsward, *Consumer Credit Charges and Credit Availability*, S. Econ. J. 214, 217 (Jan. 1969) ("A systematic comparison of borrowers at low and high rate lenders shows little difference between them based on their risk characteristics."); A.C. Sullivan, *Competition in the Market for Consumer Loans*, 36 J. Econ. & Bus. 141, 148 (1984) ("The extent of risk segmentation of the consumer loan market appears to be dictated by the structure of rate ceilings."). *But see* Howard Lax, Michael Manti, Paul Raca & Peter Zorn, *Subprime Lending: An Investigation of Economic Efficiency*, 15 Housing Pol'y Debate 533 (2004) (subprime borrowers are accurately characterized as having higher credit risk but that 1% of the interest rate premium paid by these borrowers could not be explained by higher levels of risk).

35 It is likely that the primary operative factor is precisely that it is conventional wisdom: it is now assumed as fact, rather than an hypothesis still subject to empirical testing. However, a 1996 study by Freddie Mac found that 10 to 30% of homeowners in the subprime mortgage market would be eligible for prime-market mortgages. *Automated Underwriting: Making Mortgage Lending Simpler and Fairer for American Families*, Pub. No. 259 (Freddie Mac Sept. 1996). Attorneys representing high-cost, subprime-market borrowers might make it a matter of routine to check their client's "FICO" score—a standard credit-risk score. Whether a credit application was rejected or denied, a creditor to whom the application was submitted should have the FICO score or its equivalent.

36 The term is suggested by the explanation proffered for the discriminatory results in the study reported in Ian Ayres, *Fair Driving: Gender and Race Discrimination in Retail Car Negotiations*, 104 Harv. L. Rev. 817 (1991). Where profit is not evenly distributed over each item sold, the seller is looking for "sucker sales"—those willing to pay full markup, and stereotypes factor into their perception of who those consumers are. *Id.* at 854–57.

This study controlled for negotiating skills, the most commonly offered explanation of price differentials in car sales. Perhaps one of the most interesting results of the study is a comparison of the *initial* price quotes—before any negotiating began: the dealer profit in the first quote given white men was $818; in the initial quote given black women, $2169. *Id.* at 832. *See also* Ian Ayres, *Further Evidence of Discrimination in New Car Negotiations and Estimates of Its Cause*, 94 Mich. L. Rev. 109 (1995) (article suggests that the findings support more than one explanation for discriminatory pricing; discrimination against African-American women may stem from a belief that they are less informed about pricing and more adverse to bargaining than white males; discrimination against African-American males may be explained in part by "consequential animus"—a desire to disadvantage a certain group; note that this study looked not just at price differentials, but also at rates of concession and how long the bargaining process took).

There are also disquieting indications of discrimination, pure and simple, in pricing products and services.[37] Particularly disturbing are reports that examinations of the portfolios of a few lenders who purport to offer "tiered-pricing"—rates tied to the risk classification the lender assigns to the borrower—show discriminatory pricing even *within* risk categories,[38] which completely belies any legitimate business justification.

What is clear is that the subprime market is a "push" market where armies of telemarketers, brokers, and loan officers target borrowers and solicit business.[39] All credible research supports the observation that subprime mortgages are pushed disproportionately in minority neighborhoods.[40]

Further steering by prime lenders to subprime affiliates or the failure to refer up to a prime cousin may be prevalent. In a study of subprime lending in four cities in California, the authors reported that 25% of the surveyed borrowers took out loans from a subsidiary or affiliate of a regulated financial institution, yet none were referred to the prime lender for lower-cost loans. (It is worthy to note that 60% of all surveyed homeowners thought they had good or excellent credit.[41])

Though still hotly debated, there is now highly credible empirical evidence that race is a statistically significant factor in the credit decisions of even *mainstream* lenders. A

37 *Justice Settles First Suit on Overages; Also Settles with Bank on Illegal Rates*, 65 BNA Banking Rep. 667 (Oct. 23, 1995) (settlement involving allegation of higher "overages" to African Americans); *OCC Referred 20 Fair Lending Cases to DOJ or HUD During 2 1/2 Year Period*, 65 Banking Rep. (BNA) 918 (Dec. 4, 1995) (three referrals where institutions charged higher prices to African-American and Native-American borrowers than to similarly situated whites); *Hearings on Problems in Community Development Banking, Mortgage Lending Discrimination, Reverse Lending, and Home Equity Lending Before the Senate Comm. on Banking, Housing and Urban Affairs*, 103d Cong. 1st Sess. (Feb. 3, 17, & 24, 1993). *See also* National Consumer Law Center, Credit Discrimination § 8.4 (4th ed. 2005).

38 *See* Coleman v. General Motors Acceptance Corp., 196 F.R.D. 315 (M.D. Tenn. 2000) (allegations reveal that African Americans are about 200% more likely to be charged an interest rate mark-up than similarly situated whites when financing the purchase of a car, paying an average of $315 more than white customers), *vacated and remanded on other grounds*, 296 F.3d 443 (6th Cir. 2002) (reversed class certification); Fred Galves, *Housing and Hope Symposium: The Discriminatory Impact of Traditional Lending Criteria: An Economic and Moral Critique*, 29 Seton Hall L. Rev. 1467 (1999) (discussion regarding the role that the secondary market plays in perpetuating the discriminatory impact of lending criteria); *Pricing Credit: Tiered-Pricing and Yield-Spread Premiums*, 12 NCLC REPORTS Consumer Credit & Usury Ed. 46 (May/June 1994); National Consumer Law Center, Credit Discrimination § 8.4 (4th ed. 2005).

39 *See* Conseco Fin. Serv. Corp. v. North Am. Mortgage Co., 381 F.3d 811, 814–815 (8th Cir. 2004) (describes how Conseco conducted its outreach and that some of its employees worked on commission); *Testimony of Thomas J. Miller on Protecting Homeowners: Preventing Abusive Lending While Preserving Access to Credit*, U.S. House Subcommittee on Financial Institutions and Consumer Credit and the Subcommittee on Housing and Community Opportunity (Nov. 5, 2003), *available at* http://financialservices.house.gov/media/pdf/110503tm.pdf.

40 *See* Jim Campen, *Borrowing Trouble? V: Subprime Mortgage Lending in Greater Boston, 2000–2003* (Mass. Community & Banking Council Jan. 2005), *available at* www.masscommunityandbanking.org; Paul S. Calem, Jonathan E. Hershaff & Susan M. Wachter, *Neighborhood Patterns of Subprime Lending: Evidence from Disparate Cities*, 15 Housing Pol'y Debate 603 (2004) (minority status is significantly related to subprime borrowing in seven cities); Calvin Bradford, Center for Community Change, Risk or Race? Racial Disparities and the Subprime Refinance Market (May 2002) (significant racial disparities in subprime lending which increase as income increases; high concentrations of subprime lending and racial disparities exist in all

regions throughout the United States and in metropolitan areas of all sizes); Ken Zimmerman, Elvin Wyly & Hilary Btein, N.J. Inst. for Social Justice, Predatory Lending in New Jersey: The Rising Threat to Low-Income Homeowners 5, 6 (Feb. 2002), *available at* www.njisj.org/reports/predatory_lending.pdf (New Jersey African Americans are 2.5 times more likely than whites to be provided subprime loans); Ira Goldstein, *Predatory Lending: An Approach to Identify and Understand Predatory Lending*, The Reinvestment Fund (2002) (study shows that areas within the City of Philadelphia with a higher potential vulnerability to predatory lending tended to have greater concentrations of foreclosure sales; areas that are predominately African American and/or Latino also tended to have higher concentrations of foreclosure sales and were more vulnerable to predatory lending); Kevin Stein & Margaret Libby, *Stolen Wealth: Inequities in California's Subprime Mortgage Market*, California Reinvestment Committee at 41, 47, 50 (Dec. 2001) (25% of the surveyed borrowers took out loans from a subsidiary or affiliate of a regulated financial institution, yet none were referred to the prime lender for lower-cost loans; 60% of all surveyed homeowners thought they had good or excellent credit; about 62% of the participants were people of color; and about 45% of respondents were age 55 or older); HUD, *Unequal Burden: Income and Racial Disparities in Subprime Lending in America* (Apr. 2000) (report includes data from studies conducted in 5 cities, Atlanta, Baltimore, Chicago, Los Angeles, and New York; key findings show that: (1) from 1993–1998, the number of subprime refinancing loans increased ten-fold; (2) subprime loans are more than three times likely in low-income neighborhoods than in high-income neighborhoods; (3) subprime loans are five time more likely in black neighborhoods than in white neighborhoods; (4) homeowners in high-income black areas are twice as likely as homeowners in low-income white areas to have subprime loans; Debbie Gruenstein and Christopher E. Herbert, *Analyzing Trends in Subprime Originations and Foreclosures: A Case Study of the Boston Metro Area*, Abt Associates, Inc. (Sept. 2000); Daniel Immergluck and Marti Wiles, *Two Steps Back: The Dual Mortgage Market, Predatory Lending, and the Undoing of Community Development* (Woodstock Institute Nov. 1999) (data from Chicago shows that mortgage refinancing by subprime lenders occurred predominately in African-American neighborhoods; refinance lending by subprime lenders in African-American neighborhoods grew by almost 30 times during the period 1993–1998, much faster than in white neighborhoods (only 2.5 times)).

41 Kevin Stein & Margaret Libby, *Stolen Wealth: Inequities in California's Subprime Mortgage Market*, California Reinvestment Committee at 41, 47, 50 (Dec. 2001). About 62% of the participants were people of color and about 45% were age 55 or older.

milestone study of mortgage loan applications by the Federal Reserve Bank of Boston[42] showed that truly creditworthy borrowers received credit regardless of race, but that 80% of the applicants had problems that would constitute legitimate reasons for denial. Between the few highly creditworthy applicants and the clearly uncreditworthy, there is a lot of room for discretion, and the study showed that lenders gave the benefit of the doubt to white applicants more often than to similarly situated black applicants.[43]

The necessary implication of this finding is that some "risky" white borrowers get market-rate loans, while minority borrowers *of equal risk* either get no credit or are forced into other, more expensive sources. Add to that the broader marketing strategies of mainstream lenders which often bypass minority neighborhoods,[44] and the logical outcome is that there is no competitive downward pressure on the higher rate lenders who do move into the vacuum.[45]

Even if the discrimination is less than some suspect, a perception by some borrowers that their business is not wanted will result in self-selection out of the mainstream market. In either case, the possibility of choice, a necessary ingredient for a properly functioning market, is constricted.

Sucker-pricing can lead to a self-fulfilling prophecy in another critical way, as well: it helps create risk. Borrowers for whom fairly-priced products and market rate credit are within their ability to pay may become unable to pay the "sucker surcharge."[46] Why would a creditor create risk? For a start, the majority of loans are repaid, even to lenders with unusually high default rates. But the worst of this practice occurs in the context of fully secured loans. Consider an auto dealer operating near a reservation, who sells a used car with a book value of $1,800. By the time he marks up the cash price and finishes with add-ons, such as a $2,000 service contract and insurance, the loan amount is $5,000, and at 16% interest this results in a total obligation of about $6,810 for a four-year loan. If the borrower defaults halfway through the term, he will have paid nearly $3,405. Though that looks like a loss on the dealer's books, he will have made over $1,600 on that $1,800 car, which he can then repossess and resell.

The problem is most prevalent in home equity loans, which are fully secured by the homes.[47] Some predatory

---

42 Munnell, Browne, McEneaney, Tootell, *Mortgage Lending in Boston: Interpreting HMDA Data*, Working Paper Series No. 92-7 (Federal Reserve Bank of Boston Oct. 1992) (available from Federal Reserve Bank of Boston, Research Library-D, P.O. Box 2076, Boston, MA 02016-2076, (617) 973-3397, and also available as Clearinghouse No. 47,967).

43 The study found that merely being black or Hispanic increased the risk of denial by 56%. *Id.* at 2. A follow-up study confirms this. It notes that changing an African-American "bad" applicant to an African-American "good" applicant would not have improved the applicant's chances of approval as much as if he or she had magically changed to a white "bad" applicant. The authors speculate that this may result from the loan officers (usually white) identifying more with the white applicants. William C. Hunter & Mary Beth Walker, *The Cultural Affinity Hypothesis and Mortgage Lending Decisions*, Working Paper Series No. 95-8 (Federal Reserve Bank of Chicago July 1995) (available from Public Info. Center, Federal Reserve Bank of Chicago, 230 So. LaSalle St., P.O. Box 834, Chicago, IL 60690-0834; Phone (312) 322-5111, Fax (312) 322-5515).

44 *See, e.g.*, United States v. Chevy Chase Fed. Sav. Bank (Aug. 22, 1994) (consent decree), *reported in* 63 Banking Rpt. (BNA) 290 (Aug. 29, 1994).

45 *See* Coleman v. General Motors Acceptance Corp., 196 F.R.D. 315 (M.D. Tenn. 2000) (allegations reveal that African Americans are about 200% more likely to be charged an interest rate mark-up than similarly situated whites when financing the purchase of a car, paying an average of $315 more than white customers), *vacated and remanded on other grounds*, 296 F.3d 443 (6th Cir. 2002) (reversed class certification); Honorable v. Easy Life Real Estate Sys., 100 F. Supp. 2d 885 (N.D. Ill. 2000) (exploitation theory survived motion to dismiss in fair housing case; plaintiffs alleged that the real estate company targeted African Americans and lured them into buying homes that were not rehabbed and in good condition as claimed); Hargraves v. Capital City Mortgage Corp., 140 F. Supp. 2d 7 (D.D.C. 2000), *further proceedings*, 147 F. Supp. 2d 1 (D.D.C. 2001) (summary judgment dismissing ECOA and FHA claims raised by two plaintiffs who never applied for credit on their own behalf but did so on behalf of the church plaintiff); Daniel Immergluck and Marti Wiles, *Two Steps Back: The Dual Mortgage Market, Predatory Lending, and the Undoing of Community Development* (Woodstock Institute Nov. 1999) (data from Chicago shows that mortgage refinancing by subprime lenders occurred

predominately in African-American neighborhoods; refinance lending by subprime lenders in African-American neighborhoods grew by almost 30 times during the period 1993–1998, much faster than in white neighborhoods (only 2.5 times increase)).

46 For example a $23,000 sucker surcharge such as the one in the case cited in § 8.5.4.2, *supra*, can make the difference between an affordable loan and an unaffordable one.

47 The default rate on conventional mortgages has barely risen from 2.6% of outstanding loans in 1994 to 2.9% in 1998. The foreclosure rate on conventional loans has held constant at 0.7% during the same period. *See* U.S. Census Bureau, Statistical Abstract of the United States: 1999, Table No. 823. The national foreclosure rates for subprime loans for the period 1998–2003 were significantly higher than for conventional loans, ranging from over 3.5 to 10 times higher. *See* chart in Elizabeth Renuart, *An Overview of the Predatory Lending Process*, 15 Housing Pol'y Debate 467, 479 (2004). Despite these disparities, the ultimate risk of loss from a foreclosure may not be significantly greater than for conventional lenders for a variety of reasons. Alan M. White, *Risk-Based Mortgage Pricing: Present and Future Research*, 15 Housing Pol'y Debate 503 (2004); Kathleen C. Engel & Patricia A. McCoy, *Predatory Lending: What Does Wall Street Have to Do with It?*, 15 Housing Pol'y Debate 715, 728–739 (2004). "Credit enhancements" are often used to reduce the risk of loss to the investors in subprime mortgage securitizations. This means that other features of the loan or how it was structured make it more lucrative or safe. Some credit enhancements include an excess spread in the interest rate (which generates more income on a monthly basis) and over-collateralization, e.g., taking a security in more than one property. In addition, mortgage insurance can create more effective equity to cushion the pain of losses. About 45% of the subprime mortgage loans which Standard & Poors (S&P) rated in the last quarter of 2000 carried mortgage insurance, a significant jump from the third quarter

lenders engage in "asset-based lending," looking only to the value of the collateral, rather than the borrower's ability to pay from liquid assets.[48] (Asset-based lenders are part of the lending industry called "subprime" lenders, i.e., lenders who lend to those have blemishes on their credit record and do not qualify for "A" or prime rate loans.[49]) Most of their borrowers either repay, or refinance their obligations, the former often at the expense of other necessities, the latter usually only to get deeper in debt.[50] Even in the minority of loans which default, the creditor does not necessarily lose. While the foreclosure sale price may look like a loss, if one traces back to the actual investment these creditors put into

the loan, and forward to the price obtained upon resale after obtaining title at a foreclosure sale, the account may look very different.[51] Finally, the growth of the secondary mortgage market has made it possible for the unscrupulous originator to take its money upfront, and then sell the paper (and any risk) to a purchaser on the secondary market. Many of these purchasers, in turn, raise the holder in due course doctrine to protect themselves against the claims and defenses the borrower would have had against the originator.[52]

11.4 Fuel for the Subprime Market: Securitization

Another phenomenon, which gained momentum in the 1990s, is securitization. Securitization is the process of separating certain types of assets, in this instance, mortgage loans, from the risks associated with the original lender. These assets are sold to a third party who in turn issues securities to raise funds in the capital market at a lower cost to the original lender than obtaining a line of credit.[53] Consequently, the financial state of the original lender becomes much less relevant than the investment worthiness of the mortgage loans. The loans themselves become the commodity. This process brings together a variety of entities to accomplish these goals.

In its simplest form, securitization works like this: loans are pooled and transferred to a business entity whose purpose is to hold the pool of mortgages, oversee the servicing, and pay the investors at specified intervals.[54] These companies are separately incorporated from the original lender. Corporate separateness is strictly observed in order to avoid having the loan assets dragged into a bankruptcy that the original lender may subsequently file. They are often referred to generically as a "special purpose vehicle (SPV)" or "bankruptcy remote entity."[55] A trust is the most common form. Banks and trust companies often fulfill the role of the trustee.

---

when just 12% of S&P rated loans contained mortgage insurance. *Inside B&C Lending*, Feb. 2, 2001. In some cases, according to this industry newsletter, lenders are obtaining insurance coverage that cuts the effective loan-to-value ratio on the underlying mortgage to 50%. (*Editor's note*: Mortgage insurance generally pays 30% or so of foreclosure losses; if the loan-to-value ratio of the underlying mortgage is 75%, this means that the corrected loan-to-value ratio with mortgage insurance is only 45%, an incredibly risk-free loan.)

48 This practice lay behind that portion of the Home Ownership and Equity Protection Act of 1994 (HOEPA) which mandates that creditors look to the borrowers ability to pay. HOEPA, § 152(h), codified at 15 U.S.C. § 1639(h). For a more complete discussion, see *Hearings on Problems in Community Development Banking, Mortgage Lending Discrimination, Reverse Redlining, and Home Equity Lending Before the Senate Comm. on Banking, Housing and Urban Affairs*, 103d Cong., 1st Sess. (Feb. 3, 17, 24, 1993) (S. Hrg. 103-137); National Consumer Law Center, Truth in Lending Ch. 9 (5th ed. 2003 and Supp.).

49 *See* Elizabeth Renuart, *An Overview of the Predatory Lending Process*, 15 Housing Pol'y Debate 467, 474–479 (2004); Cathy Lesser Mansfield, *The Road to Subprime "HEL" Was Paved with Good Congressional Intentions: Usury Deregulation and the Subprime Home Equity Market*, 51 S.C.L. Rev. 473 (2000). Some subprime lenders conduct outreach to communities that the lenders *assume* contain riskier borrowers and make high rate loans regardless of these customer's good credit records. These lenders treat "A" borrowers the same way they treat "D" borrowers . . . to skyrocketing points (from 5–25 points, a point being 1% of the loan amount). Diana B. Henriques and Lowell Bergman, *Mortgaged Lives: A special report; Profiting from Fine Print with Wall Street's Help*, N.Y. Times, March 15, 2000, at A1. Note that conventional lenders charge points ranging from about .84 for purchase-money mortgages to 2 points for refinancings. *Id.*; U.S. Census Bureau, Statistical Abstract of the United States: 1999, Table No. 819. More insidious, some lenders convince borrowers through advertising, telemarketing, and direct representations that they cannot obtain less expensive credit elsewhere.

50 Among some of the principal players in Boston's second mortgage scandal of 1991, there appears to have been a hot potato game. One lender would refer a borrower with a high-rate balloon note coming due to another lender for refinancing, which, as was discussed in Ch. 6, *supra*, adds greatly to the debt, even if the borrower gets no new funds. If the borrower then defaults on monthly payments when the cost of refinancings has stripped the equity in the house, the cycle comes to a halt and foreclosure follows. Because the amount of the principal debt by then includes amounts that represent no real investment by the lenders, merely smoke and mirrors, what looks like a loss to the lender may not actually be one.

51 *See generally* Steven Wechsler, *Through the Looking Glass: Foreclosure By Sale As De Facto Strict Foreclosure—An Empirical Study of Mortgage Foreclosure and Subsequent Resale*, 70 Cornell L. Rev. 850 (1985).

52 *See* Kurt Eggert, *Held Up in Due Course: Predatory Lending, Securitization, and the Holder in Due Course Doctrine*, 35 Creighton L. Rev. 503 (2002); § 10.6.1, *supra*.

53 Steven Schwartz, *Structured Finance: A Guide to the Principles of Asset Securitization* § 1.1 (3d ed. 2002).

54 An example of this basic form of securitization is described in the Pooling and Servicing Agreement Related to First Alliance Mortgage Loan Trust 1999-4 (Dec. 1, 1999), *available at* www.sec.gov/Archives/edgar/data/1100333/0001024739-99-000157-index.html. Despite the relative simplicity of this securitization, this document is 114 single-spaced pages in length.

55 Kurt Eggert, *Held Up in Due Course: Predatory Lending, Securitization, and the Holder in Due Course Doctrine*, 35 Creighton L. Rev. 503, 538, 539 (2002). *See also* Kathleen C. Engel & Patricia A. McCoy, *Predatory Lending: What Does*

The trustee issues the certificates or securities that will ultimately be purchased by investors. Another company, called the underwriter or seller, often an investment bank, will purchase the certificates. This bank invites investors to buy certificates or mortgage-backed securities that pay an attractive interest rate over a specific term. The pools of loans represented by the certificates are rated by the various bond-rating agencies.[56] Securitizations can include additional players, resulting in the transfer of the mortgages and loans through one or two entities before reaching the trustee.[57] Insurance or bonding companies may provide credit enhancements to boost the rating of the pool of mortgages.[58]

The monthly payments made by the homeowners whose mortgage loans are in the pool of loans are used to pay the servicer, the trustee, and the investors.[59] The borrower's monthly interest payments on the loan must be high enough to cover the return to the investors, the costs of the securitization, and a profit to the lender. The risk of loss to the senior investors can be negligible, given mortgage and pool insurances, over-collateralization, senior-subordinate structures, and recourse agreements between the trust and the lender.[60] These "credit enhancements" provide so much protection to investors even for predatory loans that Fitch Ratings stated in a report: "Pending or existing predatory lending legislation is not expected to have any impact on performance, since sellers and issuers have provided protective measures to significantly reduce the risk of transactions and investors bearing the costs of assignee liability."[61]

Interestingly, the trail of players in the securitization process takes us from the originating lender to Wall Street. These entities are recognizing that they may be liable for the acts of the originating lender.[62] A jury in a federal court in Southern California awarded over $5 million to plaintiffs in a class action alleging that Lehman Brothers, Inc. aided and abetted a mortgage lender's fraud.[63] This decision is the first one in which consumers have successfully gone "upstream" from the originator to hold a Wall Street player directly responsible for its own actions. In this case, Lehman Brothers, Inc. provided a warehouse line of credit to First Alliance Mortgage Co. (FAMCO) and managed four of its securitizations, allowing FAMCO to perpetrate fraud.[64] Theories to attach liability to "upstream" parties are discussed in more detail in §§ 12.10 and 12.12, *infra*.

Securitization of conventional mortgage loans has been around for years. Indeed, the Government National Mortgage Association (Ginnie Mae), a quasi-governmental agency, guarantees pools of Federal Housing Administration (FHA) and Veteran Administration (VA) insured-loans for investment purposes. Creating capital flow in this way for subprime lenders, however, only took off following 1994. Creating capital flow in this manner for subprime lenders took off following 1994. The value of the mortgage-backed securities (MBS) issued by the subprime market grew from $11.05 billion in 1994 to $570 billion in 2004.[65]

Wall Street Have to Do with It?, 15 Housing Pol'y Debate 715, 717–720 (2004).

56 The rating companies include Standard and Poor's Rating Service, Moody's Investment Servs., Inc., Fitch Investors Service, C.P., or Duff & Phelps Credit Rating Co. Rating agencies are private companies whose business is assessing the risks associated with the payment of debt securities. The highest rating on long-term debt, such as mortgages, is typically AAA. The ratings then drop to AA, then to A, to BBB and so forth. The higher the rating, the lower the rating agency has assessed the risk associated with that particular security. A high rating more easily attracts investors and allows the special purpose vehicle (SPV) to charge a lower interest rate and still attract investors. The lower interest rate reduces the SPV's costs. This in turn lowers the financing cost of the original lender. Steven Schwartz, Structured Finance: A Guide to the Principles of Asset Securitization § 8.9 (3d ed. 2002).

57 For a description of how complicated these arrangements can be, see *Securitization of Financial Assets* § 4.02 (Jason H.P. Kravitz ed., 2d ed. 1997).

58 Kurt Eggert, *Held Up in Due Course: Predatory Lending, Securitization, and the Holder in Due Course Doctrine*, 35 Creighton L. Rev. 503, 540, 541 (2002).

59 *See* Clair Robinson, *Moody's Takes Tough Look at Role of Trustees*, Int'l Fin. L. Rev. 1 (Aug. 1, 2003), *available at* 2003 WL 18277316.

60 Kathleen C. Engel & Patricia A. McCoy, *Predatory Lending: What Does Wall Street Have to Do with It?*, 15 Housing Pol'y Debate 715, 728–739 (2004); Kurt Eggert, *Held Up in Due Course: Predatory Lending, Securitization, and the Holder in Due Course Doctrine*, 35 Creighton L. Rev. 503, 540, 541, 548, 549 (2002). For further information regarding securitization, see Cathy Lesser Mansfield, *The Road to Subprime "HEL" Was Paved with Good Congressional Intentions: Usury Deregulation and the Subprime Home Equity Market*, 51 S.C. L. Rev. 473 (2000) (specifically, Part IV, D and citations contained therein); Diana B. Henriques & Lowell Bergman, *Mortgaged Lives: A Special Report; Profiting from Fine Print with Wall Street's*

Help, N.Y. Times, Mar. 15, 2000, at A1. *See also* LaSalle Bank Nat'l Ass'n v. Lehman Bros. Holdings, Inc., 237 F. Supp. 2d 618 (D. Md. 2002) (involving a recourse agreement between two financial institutions, LaSalle Bank as trustee and Lehman Brothers as seller of a commercial loan; case shows an example of a recourse agreement upon which court granted summary judgment to LaSalle when Lehman failed to cure or repurchase the loan).

61 Fitch Ratings, *Global Structured Finance: 2004 Outlook and 2003 Review* (Dec. 10, 2003) at 5–6, *available at* www.fitchratings.com/corporate/reports/report_frame.cfm?rpt_id=191832.

62 *See* Robert Julavits, *Legal Risks Move the Financial World's Food Chain* (Apr. 12, 2000), *available at* www.AmericanBanker.com.

63 Copies of the jury verdict and jury instructions are *available at* Clearinghouse Nos. 55451A and 55451B, respectively.

64 For a description of FAMCO's sales tactics, the history of litigation against FAMCO, and Lehman's involvement with and knowledge of the fraud, see *In re* First Alliance Mortgage Co., 298 B.R. 652 (C.D. Cal. 2003). For another significant case in which the consumer held the lender responsible for the behavior of the home improvement contractor, see Williams v. Aetna Fin. Co., 700 N.E.2d 859 (Ohio 1998) (civil conspiracy theory).

65 Inside Mortgage Finance Publications, Inc., The 2005 Mortgage Market Statistical Annual, Vol. II, at 6–8.

This trend is disturbing. The easier the access to capital to fund predatory lenders of all stripes, the larger the problem becomes, and the more money is siphoned off from those least able to afford it. This tool to fund a revolving loan pool is not limited to mortgage loans. Subprime car, mobile home financing companies, and credit card lending can be fueled in the same way.[66]

11.5 Home-Secured Credit

11.5.1 Background: Equity-Skimming and Predatory Lending

One of the most important aspects of the phenomenal growth of consumer debt is that so much of it puts the family home at risk if a consumer becomes unable to repay.[67] While home-secured lending is touted as a boon to consumers because it is generally cheaper credit and may offer tax advantages, it has been an unmitigated nightmare for many consumers, particularly elderly, minority, and low-income homeowners. For these borrowers, the house as collateral may mean the credit is more expensive, not less expensive, as "predatory lenders" use exorbitantly priced credit simply as a mechanism to transfer the borrower's equity in the home (and the more of it, the better) to the lender.[68]

Some courts have recognized that allegations of equity-skimming can be the subject of a legal claim.[69] The totality of the circumstances often merit challenges under common law theories, such as fraud, as well.[70] Equity-skimming and the asset-based underwriting behind it were the bases for the improvident lending provision in the Home Ownership and Equity Protection Act.[71] It may be useful for practitioners to review NCLC's companion volumes, *Consumer Law Pleadings* and *Consumer Law in a Box*, where selected documents in cases involving overreaching on home-secured credit are included.

11.5.2 Home Improvement Credit

At the root of many credit disputes and threatened foreclosures is a home improvement transaction. Home improvement schemes often contain elements considered indicia of overreaching in other cases. Some are substantive, as in a gross disparity between the price of a product or service and its value; some are procedural, as in a misrepresentation about terms or benefits, or a failure to disclose material information. Of course, the two often go hand in hand, for a creditor offering a valuable product or service at reasonable terms has less need to dissemble. Thus, while it is important to be aware of the distinction between substance and process in judicial analysis of these cases, abuses of both types are usually present in overreaching cases and practitioners may be able to utilize both types of precedent in challenging particular conduct.

Home improvement transactions are subject to challenge under a wide variety of theories. If the contractor is around, and solvent, claims against the contractor certainly should be considered. But most often, the contractor is neither, and a separate entity is trying to collect the debt. That is less of a problem than it might seem. Most home improvement financing will be subject to the FTC Holder Rule, which makes the creditor liable for claims and defenses available against the seller.[72] Often, the nature of the relationship

---

66 *See Speeding Toward 2000: DCR Reviews 1999 Auto Issuance*, Duff & Phelps Credit Rating Co. (available at www.absnet.net/ include/showarticle.asp., with subscription).

67 Home equity debt (both open-end and closed-end) has risen dramatically since 1990. In 1990, the total home equity debt held by all lenders was $411 billion. By 1998, that figure rose to $787 billion. U.S. Census Bureau, Statistical Abstract of the United States: 1999, Table No. 821. A recent Harvard study noted that households cashed out an astonishing $333 billion from their homes between 2001 and 2003. Joint Center for Housing Studies of Harvard University, *The State of the Nation's Housing*, P 7 (2004), *available at* www.jchs.harvard.edu/ publications/markets/son2004.pdf. Between 1973 and 2004, homeowner's equity *fell*—from 68.3% to 55% through the second quarter in 2004. "In other words, Americans own less of their homes today than they did in the 1970s and early 1980s." Javier Silva, *A House of Cards: Refinancing the American Dream* at 4 (Jan. 2005), *available at* www.demos-usa.org/pubs/ AHouseofCards.pdf. *See also* §§ 2.3.3.7, 2.4.2, *supra*.

68 *See* § 11.3, *supra*; *Hearings on Problems in Community Development Banking, Mortgage Lending Discrimination, Reverse Redlining, and Home Equity Lending, Before the Senate Comm. on Banking, Housing and Urban Affairs*, 103d Cong., 1st Sess. (Feb. 3, 17, & 24, 1993) (S. Hrg. 103-137). For a description of the ways that lender and brokers skim equity, see Elizabeth Renuart, *An Overview of the Predatory Lending Process*, 15 Housing Pol'y Debate 467, 491–495 (2004).

69 *See, e.g.*, Young v. First Am. Fin. Servs., 977 F. Supp. 38 (D.D.C. 1997) (complaint states a cause of action for fraud and unconscionability in this equity-skimming case), *later proceedings*, 992 F. Supp. 440 (D.D.C. 1998) (motion for summary

judgment of lender granted on fraud claim as no evidence of agency; summary judgment on fraud claim against broker denied); Cheshire Mortgage v. Montes, 223 Conn. 80, 612 A.2d 1130 (1992) (recognizes equity-skimming may be unconscionable, though does not find it present in this case [Note dissent]); Fidelity Fin. Servs. v. Hicks, 574 N.E.2d 15 (Ill. App. Ct. 1991) (allegations of use of deceptive lending practices to make an unaffordable loan in order to acquire the equity stated a UDAP claim). *Cf.* Emery v. American Gen. Fin., Inc., 71 F.3d 1343 (7th Cir. 1995) (a well plead allegation of flipping [a device sometimes used in equity-skimming, *see* § 6.1, *supra*] may state a claim for mail fraud sufficient to withstand a motion to dismiss a RICO claim; *see* § 12.6, *infra*); U.C.C.C. § 5-108(4)(a) (1974) (especially Comment ¶ 4: selling goods to low-income consumers without expectation of payment, but with expectation of repossessing goods sold and reselling at a profit, is illustrative of unconscionable transaction).

70 *See* § 12.10, *infra*.

71 *See* 15 U.S.C. § 1639 (h). *See also* § 12.2.2, *infra*.

72 *See* § 10.6.1.2.2, *supra*; § 12.12, *infra* (this section contains a liability chart for quick reference). Those loans which fall

between the lender and the contractor is such that the lender could not successfully assert holder in due course status in any event.[73]

Some commonly available claims and defenses are not discussed in this manual, but should be explored. UCC claims such as rejection/revocation or breach of warranty are frequently available,[74] as is Truth in Lending rescission, an important remedy.[75] In addition, the lender may be responsible for the failure of the contractor to perform if the lender undertook to monitor the construction process.[76] State door-to-door solicitation acts and the FTC rule can also provide remedies where the required notice is not provided or where the three-day period is not properly calculated or undermined in some way.[77]

Excess price of the goods and home improvement work itself may be vulnerable to attack as hidden interest for usury purposes[78] or under an unconscionability theory.[79] Recently, situations which are relatively common for low-income homeowners have been the basis for large jury awards for fraud against the financer behind the contractor.[80]

Approximately thirty-one states have enacted home improvement statutes which require licensing or registration and regulate the behavior of contractors while wearing their

contractor hats.[81] About half of these states also mandate that the contractor be bonded or obtain insurance. Many of these states create criminal and civil liability for violations of these laws. Failure to obtain a required license may render the home improvement contract and accompanying credit contract void and unenforceable.[82] Several states created a fund from which homeowners can be compensated for the shoddy work of contractors.[83]

Some states also specifically regulate the contractor as lender.[84] Of these states, only three have set interest rate caps. In addition, these laws often require a highlighted disclosure that the lender is taking a security interest in the home and prohibit certain contract provisions or particular behavior. Under these statutes, it may be possible to assert a claim against a contractor who arranged for the financing directly with the lender or through an intermediary broker, even if the contractor did not originate the loan itself.[85] In the other states and the District of Columbia, more general lending laws may govern the contractor's behavior as lender. These typically include retail installment sales acts, small loan acts, industrial loan acts, second mortgage laws, and may include general usury statutes, constitutional provisions, or criminal laws.

Federal and state credit repair laws may also provide relief against home improvement contractors who "agree to help obtain financing," as is frequently the case.[86] The federal act applies to any person who performs or offers to perform any service, for a fee or other valuable consideration, for the purpose of improving a consumer's credit record, credit history, or credit rating.[87] The Act prohibits

---

between the cracks of the FTC Rule may be captured by HOEPA's broadened holder liability. *See* § 10.6.1.2.3, *supra*, § 12.2.2, *infra*.

73 *See* § 10.6.1, *supra*; §§ 12.10, 12.12, *infra* (this latter section contains a liability chart for quick reference); National Consumer Law Center, Unfair and Deceptive Acts and Practices § 6.6 (6th ed. 2004 and Supp.).

74 National Consumer Law Center, Consumer Warranty Law (2d ed. 2001 and Supp.). *Note especially* § 16.7, Special Issues Concerning Home Improvement Contracts.

75 *See* National Consumer Law Center, Truth in Lending Ch. 6 (5th ed. 2003 and Supp.). Note especially *id.*, § 6.5.3, on spiking. This is frequently an issue in home improvement lending.

The financier's liability for rescission is not a question. As an assignee, it is subject to rescission under 15 U.S.C. § 1641(c); National Consumer Law Center, Truth in Lending § 6.9 (5th ed. 2003 and Supp.). If it is the originating creditor, it is liable on its own hook. *See also* § 12.12, *infra* (this section contains a liability chart for quick reference).

76 Casey v. Hibernia Corp., 709 So. 2d 933 (La. Ct. App. 1998) (however, the claim against the bank in this new construction loan case failed due to a state statute requiring that such contracts be in writing).

77 *See* National Consumer Law Center, Unfair and Deceptive Acts and Practices § 5.8.2 (6th ed. 2004 and Supp.); Op. Ky. Att'y Gen. 92-41, 1992 WL 540962 (1992) (under Kentucky's home solicitation act, where sellers, e.g., home improvement contractors, finance or arrange financing for consumers, the contract is contingent until acceptable financing is found; effective date of contract is the date on which acceptable financing is found; three-day right to cancel flows from that date).

78 *See* § 7.4.6.1, *supra. See also* National Consumer Law Center, Truth in Lending § 3.10 (5th ed. 2003 and Supp.) (hidden finance charge).

79 *See* § 12.7, *infra*.

80 *See* § 12.10, *infra*.

81 1998 Survey of State Laws Regarding Home Improvement Contractors, AARP.

82 Antuna v. Nescor, Inc., 2002 Conn. Super. LEXIS 1003 (Conn. Super. Ct. Apr. 1, 2002) (court also held that the assignee cannot foreclose on the void mortgage).

83 *Id.*

84 *See, e.g.*, Cal. Bus. & Prof. Code §§ 7159.1–7159.2, 7163–7166; Fla. Stat. Ann. §§ 520.60–520.998; Md. Code Ann., Bus. Reg. §§ 8-501, 8-601; Mich. Comp. Laws §§ 445.1101–445.1431; Pa. Stat. Ann. tit. 14, §§ 500-101–500-602; N.J. Rev. Stat. §§ 17:16c-62–16c-94

85 *See, e.g.*, Bell v. Parkway Mortgage, Inc., 309 B.R. 139 (Bankr. E.D. Pa.), *reconsideration denied*, 314 B.R. 54 (Bankr. E.D. Pa. 2004); Armstrong v. Nationwide Mortgage Plan/Trust (*In re* Armstrong), 288 B.R. 404 (Bankr. E.D. Pa. 2003) (contractor arranged financing; state HIFA applies and assignee liable for violations); Barber v. Fairbanks Capital Corp. (*In re* Barber), 266 B.R. 309 (Bankr. E.D. Pa. 2001) (where contractor connected the homeowner to the broker and the broker obtains financing, state home improvement financing applies; even where the initial home improvement loan was refinanced through the same broker, the new loan is also subject to the HIFA); Cabbagestalk v. Wendover Fin. Servs., Inc., 270 B.R. 33 (W.D. Pa. 2001). *See also* Crisomia v. Parkway Mortgage, Inc. (*In re* Crisomia), 2002 WL 31202722 (Bankr. E.D. Pa. Sept. 13, 2002).

86 *See* the Federal Credit Repair Organizations Act. 15 U.S.C. §§ 1679–1679j.

87 15 U.S.C. § 1679a(3). The scope of this act and remedies available thereunder are discussed in Ch. 12, *infra* and in

such "organizations" from charging or receiving payment for their services until the service is fully performed. In addition, the consumer has a three-day right to cancel; the contract must provide certain information; and the credit repair organization cannot engage in any form of deception directed at the consumer. The remedies include actual and punitive damages, as well as costs and reasonable attorney fees.[88]

State credit repair acts may be even broader since they may cover the behavior of those who "obtain credit for a buyer." The Illinois Supreme Court held that a home improvement contractor was not subject to the state credit repair law, but only because it had not received a fee for the specific service of arranging credit.[89] In many cases, the home improvement contractor will have received a fee, either from the consumer (e.g., for document preparation) or from the financer.

State credit statutes may impose less obvious obligations on lenders when the credit is secured by the home. In one case, the Supreme Court of South Carolina held the contractor liable for failing to ascertain the preference of the homeowners regarding closing attorneys and certain insurers when it required a closing and required insurance.[90] As a result, the contractor owed the fees charged on the loan and could only collect on the principal without any interest.[91]

Credit repair statutes and their broad applicability to those soliciting to extend or broker credit are discussed more fully in § 12.4, *infra*.

11.5.3 Refinancing/Debt Consolidation

A close analysis of home-secured loans, including debt consolidation loans and refinancings, may well show evidence of overreaching, providing little or no benefit at considerable expense and risk for the consumers. Examples include:

- Consolidation loans with monthly payments about the same or higher than the combined monthly payments of the credit transactions consolidated or where the lender fails to pay off a particular debt as promised;[92]
- Consolidation loans paying off no-interest debts (e.g., medical bills, utility bills, or loans made by a governmental entity where the payments are deferred) or debts

with a significantly lower interest rate (e.g., a pre-1979 first mortgage);[93]
- Refinancing loans with prepayment or rebate penalties, excessive prepaid finance charges, or other costly add-ons;[94]
- Extending credit to a financially overburdened consumer or extending balloon payment transactions or demand transactions to consumers who do not have the resources to meet the terms;[95]

---

93 *See, e.g., In re* Stepanski, 20 B.R. 399 (Bankr. D.N.J. 1982) (although decided on a usury basis voiding the loan, Beneficial Finance's paying off a 9 1/4% mortgage with the proceeds of a 17% mortgage was criticized as "high handed conduct" and "sharp dealing").

94 *Cf.* Emery v. American Gen. Fin., Inc., 71 F.3d 1343 (7th Cir. 1995) (well-plead allegation of loan flipping may state a claim for mail fraud sufficient to withstand a motion to dismiss a RICO claim); Besta v. Beneficial Loan Co., 855 F.2d 532 (8th Cir. 1988) (see discussion at § 8.5.4.2, *supra*; § 12.7, *infra*); Hays v. Bankers Trust Co., 46 F. Supp. 2d 490 (S.D. W. Va. 1999) (lender's motion for summary judgment denied on civil conspiracy claim involving bait and switch resulting in a higher interest rate and a balloon payment); Hager v. American Gen. Fin., Inc., 37 F. Supp. 2d 778 (S.D. W. Va. 1999) (summary judgment for lender on borrowers' unconscionability claim denied where borrower's alleged that the defendants induced them to enter into high interest rate loans and to mortgage their residence without realizing the magnitude of the debt they were incurring or the ramifications of these transactions; United Companies Lending Corp. v. Sargeant, 20 F. Supp. 2d 192 (D. Mass. 1998) (charging 10 points on a loan substantially deviates from industry practice and can constitute an unfair and deceptive practice; conclusion was based upon a regulation promulgated under the Mass. UDAP act); *In re* Milbourne, 108 B.R. 522 (Bankr. E.D. Pa. 1989) (series of refinancings cost borrower over $3000 more than obtaining separate new loans, lender's failure to disclose refinancing option's advantage to lender and disadvantage to borrower violated state UDAP statute); Reynolds v. American Gen. Fin., Inc., 1999 Ala. Civ. App. LEXIS 858 (Ala. Civ. App. Dec. 3, 1999) (flipping case in which lender made five loans and represented that interest charged would be 20%, though the interest turned out to be higher; question involved whether statute of limitations was tolled given the alleged deceit), *on appeal*, 795 So. 2d 685 (Ala. 2000) (statute of limitations not tolled); Massachusetts v. First Alliance Mortgage Co., Civil Action No. 98-5534-A (Suffolk County Super. Ct., Mass. Nov. 27, 1998), Clearinghouse No. 52,511–52,513 (court preliminarily enjoined FAMCO from making mortgage loans in Massachusetts in which they charged more than 5 points). *See* Chapter 6, *supra* regarding the financial cost of flipping; Appendix L.2.6 which is an expert report on the spiraling costs to the borrower and profits to the lender due to multiple refinancings (the report was prepared for counsel in Hager v. American Gen. Fin., Inc., cited above). *See also* Gene Marsh, *Limitations on Flipping*, The Consumer Advoc., Sept./ Oct. 1998 at 4.

95 *See* 15 U.S.C. § 1639(h) (HOEPA specifically prohibits making a high-cost mortgage without regard to ability to repay from income); Young v. First Am. Fin. Serv., 977 F. Supp. 38 (D.D.C. 1997) (defendant lender's motion to dismiss fraud and unconscionability claims denied in case where homeowners allege that lender refinanced in an amount double the existing mortgage with the promise of another refinancing in a year to reduce

---

National Consumer Law Center, Fair Credit Reporting Ch. 15 (5th ed. 2002 and Supp.).

88 15 U.S.C. § 1679g(a).

89 Midstate Siding & Window Co. v. Rogers, 789 N.E.2d 1248 (Ill. 2003).

90 Tilley v. Pacesetter Corp., 508 S.E.2d 16 (S.C. 1998).

91 Tilley v. Pacesetter Corp., 585 S.E.2d 292 (S.C. 2003).

92 As to the latter practice, see Stewart v. Associates Consumer Discount Co., 183 F.R.D. 189 (E.D. Pa. 1998) (class action certified where practices appeared widespread and consistent).

- Providing a variable-rate/variable-payment loan to consumers with a fixed income or an income with little growth potential;[96]
- Baiting with promises of lower payments, lower interest rates, or other favorable terms that do not materialize;[97]
- Packing loans with unnecessary and expensive costs and fees that are of little or no benefit to the consumer, and are overpriced for their value.

An analysis of these loans, keeping in mind the mathematical manipulations described in Chapters 4, 5, 6 and the hidden interest issues in Chapters 7 and 8, may reveal violations of state regulatory statutes, RESPA or HOEPA. But equity-skimming and loan-bloating can also be challenged under UDAP, and the common law theories discussed in Chapter 12. As with home improvement loans, Truth in Lending rescission, too, should always be explored.

11.5.4 Loan Brokers/Mortgage Brokers

11.5.4.1 The Role of the Loan Broker

Loan brokers have contributed mightily to the problem of equity-skimming, and the involvement of a broker in a high-cost transaction warrants close examination.[98] Far from acting in accord with the commonly presumed role of a loan broker, in the predatory market, these brokers do not shop around on their borrowers' behalf for the credit best suited to their clients' financial needs and abilities. Brokers, on average, should charge up to 2% of the loan amount for

their time and effort.[99] However, brokers in the predatory mortgage market often charge much more.

At one extreme, the broker and lender may be, in effect, the same entity. The two may be comprised of the same principals, or the principals of each related by family ties or close business partnerships. Anyone who happens upon the broker, will, not surprisingly, have a loan arranged with this alter ego.

Similarly, some brokers simply act as "bird dogs" for a relatively small group of lenders, or even a single lender, with whom they have a referral relationship. Sometimes these brokers take the initiative, "flushing out" customers for these lenders by soliciting prospective borrowers. "Foreclosure specialists" monitor legal notices and contact the threatened homeowner, other brokers act in a "churning" operation, to solicit refinancing and consolidations.

Not all brokers take the initiative, and some may indeed be approached by consumers seeking a loan. The service performed may be to simply send the consumer down the street to a finance company (perhaps without any understanding as to a fee arrangement). Others may never quite make it clear that they are brokers, rather than lenders themselves, thus the added cost of a broker's fee is a surprise to the consumer at closing.[100] As may be the case with car salespeople (or home improvement contractors) who receive brokers' fees for placing loans with related lenders, the borrower may not know that an extra charge will be involved when a seller offers to arrange the financing. A broker may receive a fee from a solicitous lender even when the broker had nothing to do with the borrower or the transaction.[101]

A "correspondent lender" acts in the manner of a broker. It arranges "table-funded" loans in which, though the broker/correspondent lender is the nominal creditor on the documents, the assignee to which the loan is immediately assigned is the source of the loan funds.[102]

---

significantly the monthly payment), *later proceedings*, 992 F. Supp. 440 (D.D.C. 1998) (motion for summary judgment of lender granted on fraud claim as no evidence of agency; summary judgment on fraud claim against broker denied). *See also* Iowa Code § 537.5108(4)(a); S.C. Code Ann. § 37-5-108(4) (one factor in determining unconscionability is belief by a seller, lessor or lender at consummation that there is no reasonable probability of payment in full of the obligation by the consumer or debtor). *Cf.* Vern Countryman, *Improvident Credit Extension*, 27 Me. L. Rev. 1 (1975); Hersbergen, *The Improvident Extension of Credit As An Unconscionable Contract*, 23 Drake L. Rev. 225 (1974).

96 Dwight Golann, *Developments in Consumer Financial Services Litigation*, 43 Bus. Law. 1081, 1083–1085 (May 1988). (Recent legislation requires that creditors disclose a cap on rates, but it places no limit on what the cap is.) *See* National Consumer Law Center, Truth in Lending §§ 4.8.2, 4.8.3, 5.5.5.10 (5th ed. 2003 and Supp.).

97 *See, e.g.*, Hays v. Bankers Trust Co., 46 F. Supp. 2d 490 (S.D. W. Va. 1999) (a 9.7% conventional 30-year mortgage turned into a 10.65% balloon note).

98 For a more in-depth description of the roles brokers play and their contribution to ratcheting up the costs of mortgage loans, see Elizabeth Renuart, *An Overview of the Predatory Lending Process*, 15 Housing Pol'y Debate 467, 470, 480, 488–495 (2004).

99 U.S. Department of Housing and Urban Development, Office of Policy Development and Research, *Economic Analysis and Initial Regulatory Flexibility Analysis for RESPA Proposed Rule to Simplify and Improve the Process of Obtaining Mortgages to Reduce Settlement Costs to Consumers*, 67 Fed. Reg. 53958 (Aug. 20, 2002) at 5 (original).

100 The cooperative lender, though, automatically includes a sizeable fee to the broker as part of the loan principal.

101 *In re* Russell, 72 B.R. 855 (Bankr. E.D. Pa. 1987) (court found the fee to constitute a violation of state usury and UDAP statutes and Truth in Lending).

102 *See* Easter v. American West Fin., 381 F.3d 948 (9th Cir. 2004) (defines a table-funded transaction and holds that state usury laws do not apply to the correspondent lender if a three-part test is met); England v. MG Investments, Inc., 93 F. Supp. 2d 718 (S.D. W. Va. 2000) (court denied assignee's motion for summary judgment on regarding agency and on the holder-in-due course defense where the assignee and correspondent broker entered into a 16-page master agreement containing over 28 detailed requirements which the assignee imposed on the broker, suggesting that the broker was making the loan for the

That a broker dealing with high rate lenders may not be looking out for the most affordable deal for the borrower is understandable, in light of a reverse competition effect. At its most rudimentary, the more a lender pads a loan, the higher the broker's percentage-based commission will be. But there can be other highly remunerative arrangements by which a broker may get extra compensation from the creditor, paid for by the borrower, without the borrower's knowledge,[103] thus luring the broker into "a position in which to be honest must be a strain on him."[104]

11.5.4.2 Legal Status of Brokers

The triangular relationship among the loan broker, borrower and creditor creates as many complications as do the ones in romantic novels.[105] A loan broker is the borrower's agent, and thus owes a fiduciary duty to the borrower which is breached by many of the practices common to the brokers working with high rate lenders.[106]

The facts may show that the broker actually is not a separate and independent entity from the lender. In some cases the broker will be the same entity as the lender, operating under a trade name or other unregistered designation. Or two corporate entities may exist, but with identical or common principals.[107] As is discussed elsewhere, a close scrutiny may show the broker actually functions as the lender's agent.[108] In these cases, the close relationship can be a part of the cause of action,[109] and it can also make the lender liable for the broker's conduct under agency theory.

11.5.4.3 Range of Legal Claims Arising from Broker Involvement

Brokers may misrepresent or fail to explain their role or their fee.[110] They may misrepresent the nature or value of the credit they obtain for the borrower.[111] Such misrepresentations or omissions may constitute fraud, intentional misrepresentation, negligent representation, or support a UDAP claim.[112] As noted above, a broker usually owes

---

assignee). *See, e.g.*, Smith v. First Family Fin. Servs., Inc., 626 So. 2d 1266 (Ala. 1993). RESPA rules apply a common sense test, and do not consider assignment in this arrangement to be a secondary transaction for RESPA rules. *See generally* Ch. 12, *infra.*

103 One hidden compensation scheme is described in § 11.5.4.3, *infra.*

104 Frey v. Fraser Yachts, 29 F.3d 1153, 1159 (7th Cir. 1994) (quote relates to purpose of agency law to prevent broker from placing himself into such a position).

105 Not, you understand, that we know of any romantic novels involving a love triangle between a broker, borrower, and creditor. However, we see great possibilities for "The Banks of Madison County."

106 Barker v. Altegra Credit Co., 251 B.R. 250 (Bankr. E.D. Pa. 2000) (relationship between broker and borrower is primarily that of agent and principal); Arnold v. United Cos. Lending Corp., 511 S.E.2d 854 (W. Va. 1998) ("[W]here a loan broker acts as a true broker, not as a mere middleman, the broker is under a legal obligation (i.e., a duty) to disclose to the prospective borrowers all facts within his knowledge which are or may be material to the transaction for which he is employed or which might influence their action in relation to such transaction."); *In re* Dukes, 24 B.R. 40 (Bankr. E.D. Mich. 1982); Wyatt v. Union Mortgage Co., 24 Cal. 3d. 773, 157 Cal. Rptr. 392, 598 P.2d 45 (1979). *See also In re* Marill Alarm Sys., Inc., 81 B.R. 119 (S.D. Fla. 1987), *aff'd*, 861 F.2d 725 (11th Cir. 1988) (fee to broker who was acting as agent of borrower and lender held to be interest; loan transaction usurious); Modern Pioneers Ins. Co. v. Nandin, 437 P.2d 658 (Ariz. 1968) (agent of lender could not also be agent of borrower because of conflicting interests); National Amer. Life Ins. Co. v. Bayou Country Club, Inc., 403 P.2d 26 (Utah 1965) (broker's fee considered interest, contributing to usurious overcharge, where broker received commission from both borrower and lender). *But cf.* Marquess v. Spaner, 488 P.2d 698 (Ariz. Ct. App. 1971) (agency relationship between borrower and broker was for limited purpose of securing loan; after loan secured and commission paid, broker's acting as lender's agent to collect loan did not create conflict). *See generally* § 12.9, *infra.*

107 *See* Whitley v. Rhodes Fin. Serv. (*In re* Whitley), 177 B.R. 142 (Bankr. D. Mass. 1995) (TIL case; broker and lender shared business address and parent companies); Rollins v. Odom, 519 So. 2d 652 (Fla. Ct. App. 1988) (usury case; brokerage fee went to lender's wife who kept the books for herself and her husband); Coner v. Morris S. Berman, Unltd., 501 A.2d 458 (Md. Ct. Spec. App. 1985) (usury case; brokerage actually run by lender though nominally owned by lender's wife); § 7.3.2, *supra.* One can check corporate registration information with appropriate state or county agencies for necessary information.

108 *See* cases cited in § 7.3.2, *supra*, on brokers as the lender's agent; England v. MG Investments, Inc., 93 F. Supp. 2d 718 (S.D. W. Va. 2000) (court denied assignee's motion for summary judgment on regarding agency and on the holder-in-due course defense where the assignee and correspondent broker entered into a 16-page master agreement containing over 28 detailed requirements which the assignee imposed on the broker, suggesting that the broker was making the loan for the assignee). *See also* Jordon v. Washington Mut. Bank, 211 F. Supp. 2d 670 (D. Md. 2002) (a violation of the state mortgage broker law may be raised against the lender where agency is alleged).

109 *See, e.g.*, § 7.3.2, *supra*, broker's fee as interest; § 12.9, *infra* (breach of fiduciary duty); § 12.10, *infra* (fraud).

110 Young v. First Am. Fin. Servs., 992 F. Supp. 440 (D.D.C. 1998) (motion for summary judgment of lender granted on fraud claim where homeowner alleged that they were never informed that the broker was not the lender because no evidence of agency was presented; summary judgment on fraud claim against broker denied); Noel v. Fleet Fin., Inc., 971 F. Supp. 1102 (E.D. Mich. 1997) (similar allegations withstood a motion to dismiss).

111 Barker v. Altegra Credit Co., 251 B.R. 250 (Bankr. E.D. Pa. 2000) (broker assisted in the arranging of the refinancing of a special state-sponsored mortgage loan resulting in the doubling of the interest rate and a balloon payment; breach of fiduciary duty and fraud stated against the broker). *See, e.g.*, Hays v. Bankers Trust Co., 46 F. Supp. 2d 490 (S.D. W. Va. 1999) (a 9.7% conventional 30-year mortgage turned into a 10.65% balloon note).

112 *See* §§ 12.5; 12.10, *infra. See generally* National Consumer Law Center, Unfair and Deceptive Acts and Practices § 5.1.3.1 (6th ed. 2004 and Supp.).

a fiduciary duty to the borrower,[113] which is often violated in this type of transaction.

Some states have passed legislation specifically regulating mortgage brokers. A state may simply require licensing,[114] or it may impose more specific requirements.[115] A list of state broker laws appears in Appendix B, *infra*. If the statute itself provides no remedy, a violation may give rise to a UDAP claim.[116] State credit repair statutes may apply to mortgage brokers and provide significant remedies.[117] For a discussion of these laws, see § 12.4, *infra*.

One common form of lender kickback to the broker has been the subject of extensive litigation.[118] The "overage," or "yield spread premium" gives rise to a number of claims. It works like this. A creditor informs the broker that his client's application has been approved, and credit would be extended at, for example, 15%; that would be an adequate return for the creditor on this particular loan. However, if the broker can get the borrower to sign onto an 18% loan, the broker and creditor split this extra "yield spread premium."

It is undoubtedly rare for a broker to say to the client (whose best interests the broker is supposedly representing), "Would you like to pay an extra 3% on your loan so the creditor and I can have more money?" Absent that sort of honesty, the broker has breached his fiduciary duty to his client, engaged in unfair and deceptive practices and, perhaps, fraud.[119] If the transaction involved a mortgage loan, the anti-kickback provisions of the Real Estate Settlement Procedures Act may have been violated.[120]

Such price gouging also lends itself to "sucker-pricing."[121] Only those who do not know what the normal range of market rates is, or that they could get typical rates, or do not know that the rate is negotiable, will get the higher price. If this, in turn, means the creditor, acting through the broker, writes higher priced loans for the elderly, women, or minorities, then fair lending laws are violated, either because of the disparate impact on protected classes, or because it results quite clearly in disparate treatment.[122] If elderly borrowers are disproportionately harmed by differential pricing, special enhanced UDAP remedies may be available in some states, as well.[123]

Potential claims arising out of broker involvement are widely available against the lender, too. Should the facts establish a principal/agency relationship between the lender and broker,[124] the lender will be liable for the broker's acts under standard agency law.[125] In fact, an investigation may show that the lender was actively involved in its own right (and thus liable in its own right) in the activities giving rise to the claims.

The manner in which the broker's fee is treated for Truth in Lending purposes may create grounds for TIL rescission.[126] Brokers' fees in most of these home equity loans will now have to comply with RESPA's anti-kickback provisions.[127] Keep in mind, too, that the brokers' fee is part of

---

113 Barker v. Altegra Credit Co. (*In re* Barker), 251 B.R. 250 (Bankr. E.D. Pa. 2000). *See* § 12.9, *infra*.

114 *E.g.*, Ariz. Rev. Stat. § 6-903. *See, e.g.*, Beneficial Hawaii, Inc. v. Kida, 30 P.3d 895 (Haw. 2001) (mortgage and loan note void when arranged by an unlicensed mortgage broker; mortgage holder may be entitled to equitable lien on the property if it could prove that it paid consideration for the mortgage and note; lender failed to offer this proof in this case). Note that it may be possible to argue that a contract with a broker who fails to obtain a required license is void.

115 *See, e.g.*, State v. Western Capital Corp., 290 N.W.2d 467 (S.D. 1980) (South Dakota statute requires a 3-day cooling off period and certain disclosures; violation of these provisions constitutes a deceptive practice); Opportunity Mgmt. Co. v. Frost, 1999 Wash. App. LEXIS 336 (Wash. Ct. App. Feb. 16, 1999) (statute was violated where broker did not place loan on terms agreed upon with broker but, nevertheless, received a broker fee; lenders are covered as well); Idaho Admin. Code r. 04.02.01.200 (Idaho regulation prohibits brokers from receiving any fee either directly or indirectly until the loan is made or a written commitment is made to the consumer; broker must furnish a written contract to the consumer containing certain information); Mass. Regs. Code tit. 940, § 8.01–8.08 (promulgating regulations under state UDAP statute, e.g., failure to disclose facts which may have induced borrower not to enter into transaction; charging fees which significantly deviate from industry standard or are unconscionable).

116 *See* South Dakota v. Western Capital Corp., 290 N.W.2d 467 (S.D. 1980) (a violation of South Dakota broker law constitutes a UDAP violation and triggers restitution and civil penalties); National Consumer Law Center, Unfair and Deceptive Acts and Practices § 3.2.7 (6th ed. 2004 and Supp.).

117 *See, e.g.*, Lewis v. Delta Funding Corp. (*In re* Lewis), 290 B.R. 541 (Bankr. E.D. Pa. 2003) (lender and assignee may be liable for broker's violation of the state credit repair statute when the assignee funded the transaction knowing of the illegal payment of the broker fee); Barker v. Altegra Credit Co., 251 B.R. 250 (Bankr. E.D. Pa. 2000) (Pennsylvania's credit repair statute applies to the broker in this case; it enhances the principle that the broker's conduct constitutes a violation of the state UDAP, triggering treble damages).

118 *See* Ch. 12, *infra*.

119 *See* National Consumer Law Center, Unfair and Deceptive Acts and Practices §§ 5.1.2.1, 5.1.3 (6th ed. 2004 and Supp.). *Cf.* Smith v. First Family Fin. Servs., Inc., 626 So. 2d 1266 (Ala. 1993). This deception also strengthens an argument that the broker is acting as the lender's agent. *See* Adkinson v. Harpeth Ford Mercury, 1991 Tenn. App. LEXIS (Tenn. Ct. App. Feb. 15, 1991) (auto dealer who hiked financing rate by 2 1/2% and kept the excess for himself violated UDAP statute).

120 *See* Ch. 12, *infra*.

121 *See* § 11.1, *supra*.

122 *See* Letter From E. Philip A. Simpson, Jr., Vice Pres., Federal Reserve Bank of Boston, to First Federal Reserve District Member Banks (May 26, 1994), Clearinghouse No. 49,964; National Consumer Law Center, Credit Discrimination §§ 4.2, 4.3, 8.4 (4th ed. 2005).

123 *See* National Consumer Law Center, Unfair and Deceptive Acts and Practices § 8.4.1.1 (6th ed. 2004 and Supp.).

124 *See* § 7.3.2, *supra*.

125 *See* England v. MG Investments, Inc., 93 F. Supp. 2d 718 (S.D. W. Va. 2000). *See also* § 12.10, *infra* (fraud).

126 *See* National Consumer Law Center, Truth in Lending § 3.7.4 (5th ed. 2003 and Supp.).

127 *See* Ch. 12, *infra*.

the "fees and charges" trigger which determines when the HOEPA will apply.[128]

Even a breach of fiduciary duty on the broker's part, may, in some cases, create a corollary claim against the lender. Compensation arrangements such as the yield spread premium, in effect, seduce a broker into violating its fiduciary duty. Arguably that gives rise to a claim against the lender for interference with a contractual relationship.[129]

Where a broker acts as the originating creditor, and then assigns the loan to a lender, the lender may try to assert holder in due course status. If experience is any guide, the connection between the overreaching broker and lender is most often too close for that shield to succeed.[130] Even if the broker does not originate the credit, its role may trigger the applicability of a state home solicitation act[131] or a state home improvement financing act. In one case, the court held that the state HIFA applied where the contractor connected the homeowner to the broker and the broker connected the homeowner to the lender.[132]

One can use a national subscriber database to search for state regulatory actions against a particular broker. It is called Mortgage Asset Research Institute. The cost of the service is per search. For information, check out the website at www.mari-inc.com.

11.5.5 Post-consummation Profiteering

Most of the overreaching creditor behavior discussed in this chapter focuses on what occurs leading up to and at the consummation of the credit transaction. Recently, consumers and their attorneys have been paying increasing attention to junk fees, accounting fraud, charges imposed at payoff, and other creative methods to increase the profit of the lender and servicer *after* the consummation of the loan. To date, these practices have cropped up primarily in the mortgage lending context. Specific concerns include:

• Under-billing the monthly payments, advancing funds to cover the resulting escrow shortfall, and adding the advance into the principal on which interest accrues without notice to the homeowner.[133]

• Charging fax fees and payoff statement fees without notice or apparent authority to do so in the mortgage or note.[134]

• Placing monthly payments in "suspense" accounts which can result in the imposition of late fees and the collection of a larger amount of interest over the life of the loan.[135]

---

128 *See* § 12.2.2, *infra*; National Consumer Law Center, Truth in Lending Ch. 9 (5th ed. 2003 and Supp.).

129 § 12.9, *infra*.

130 *See* England v. MG Investments, Inc., 93 F. Supp. 2d 718 (S.D. W. Va. 2000); § 10.6.1, *supra*; National Consumer Law Center, Unfair and Deceptive Acts and Practices §§ 6.6.4, 6.7.4 (6th ed. 2004 and Supp.). Remember that the FTC Holder Rule, § 10.6.1.2.2, *supra*, is not implicated where no credit sale is involved. For other theories that may hold the lender liable for acts of the broker, *see* liability checklist in § 12.12, *infra*.

131 Bank of New York v. Kaiser, 2003 WL 23335972 (Ohio Com. Pl. Aug. 16, 2003).

132 Barber v. Fairbanks Capital Corp. (*In re* Barber), 266 B.R. 309 (Bankr. E.D. Pa. 2001) (significantly, where the initial home improvement loan was refinanced through the same broker, the new loan is also subject to the HIFA); Cabbagestalk v. Wendover Fin. Servs., Inc., 270 B.R. 33 (W.D. Pa. 2001) (sing along: "the knee bone's connected to the calf bone and the calf bone's connected to the ankle bone and the. . . .").

133 Or the converse, where the lender fails to reduce the escrow charge and treats the excess as profit. *See, e.g.*, Stewart v. Martin, 2001 Ark. App. LEXIS 602 (Ark. Ct. App. Sept. 12, 2001).

134 For an example of this practice, see Turner v. Ocwen Fed. Bank, F.S.B., Clearinghouse No. 53,571 (N.J. Super. Ct. Sept. 4, 2001) (national class certification granted). *See also* Sandlin v. Shapiro & Fishman, 919 F. Supp. 1564 (M.D. Fla. 1996) (pay-off fee charged when collection attorney sent a delinquency notice with the pay-off amount violated the mortgage provision prohibiting a prepayment penalty; the home owner had not requested a pay-off figure); *Ex parte* Ocwen Fed. Bank, Fed. Sav. Bank, 872 So. 2d 810 (Ala. 2003) (servicer attempted to collect prepayment penalty not contracted for; case is about pattern and practice discovery dispute and whether a writ of *mandamus* should issue). *But see* Cappellini v. Mellon Mortgage Co., 991 F. Supp. 31 (D. Mass. 1997) (pay-off fee not a prepayment penalty but summary judgment for lender denied on question of whether, by collecting such fees, it had breached clause in mortgage stating that upon payment of all sums secured by mortgage, lender would discharge its mortgage without additional charge); Krause v. GE Capital Mortgage Serv., Inc., 731 N.E.2d 302 (Ill. App. Ct. 2000) (distinguishing *Sandlin*, in which the pay-off amount was not requested by the borrower; also holding that mortgage does not prohibit the charging of pay-off and fax fees); Colangelo v. Norwest Mortgage Inc., 598 N.W.2d 14 (Minn. Ct. App. 1999) (lender's charge of a $10 fax fee to transmit a pay-off statement was not a prepayment penalty nor a fee listed as prohibited in the mortgage; therefore, it was permitted).

135 *See, e.g., In re* Hart, 246 B.R. 709 (Bankr. D. Mass. 2000) (for an example of the use of a suspense account and how this played out in creating liability for the servicer under a number of legal theories). Household Finance and Beneficial Finance, part of Household International Inc., allegedly engaged in this practice by using the "daily accrual accounting" method of collecting interest. *See* Iowa *ex rel.* Miller v. Household Int'l Inc. (Iowa Dist. Ct. Polk County Dec. 13, 2002) (complaint, ¶ 8I), *available at* www.state.ia.us/government/ag/latest_news/releases/dec_2002/hhold.htm (click on lawsuit). If the consumer paid more than 30 days after their last payment, Household charged interest for the days beyond the 30 days and placed the extra interest charge in a separate account. The next payment would be applied first to any new earned interest and then, if any remained, to pay down this amount. The result would be that the loan principal did not decline or declined more slowly than anticipated under normal amortization rules. Household agreed to change this practice in its consent judgment with the Attorney Generals. The Iowa version of this consent judgment is *available at* www.state.ia.us/government/ag/latest_news/releases/dec_2002/hhconsent.pdf. For several articles about Household's practices and the Attorney Generals' and private class action settlements, see 22 NCLC REPORTS *Consumer Credit &*

- Failing to timely pay the homeowner's hazard insurance from the escrow and then ordering force-placed insurance at rates higher than the original insurance.[136]
- Delaying credits and adjustments to the homeowner's escrow account which results in an unnecessary increase in the homeowner's monthly escrow payment.
- Failing to timely post monthly payments received from consumers resulting in the charging of late fees and collection of additional interest.[137]
- Conducting unnecessary "drive-by" property inspections when the homeowner is not in default and imposing a charge on the customer or conducting multiple inspections for one period of default and imposing multiple charges.[138]
- Improperly foreclosing or taking possession of the home illegally.[139]

- Improperly calculating interest on open-ended lines of credit or in variable rate loans.[140]
- Offering bi-weekly payment plans advertised as a way for homeowners to pay off their mortgages more quickly.[141]
- Attempting to collect a debt by demanding "the unpaid principal balance" in a certain amount and only generally stating that other charges may be added, e.g., unpaid interest, unpaid late fees, escrow advances and other charges.[142]
- Overcharging fees, late-fee abuses, and tacking on "monitoring" fees in the bankruptcy context.[143]
- Obtaining authorization from consumers to electroni-

Usury Ed. 15 (Jan./Feb. 2004); 22 NCLC REPORTS *Consumer Credit & Usury Ed.* 1 (July/Aug. 2003); 21 NCLC REPORTS *Consumer Credit & Usury Ed.* 13 (Jan./Feb. 2003); 21 NCLC REPORTS *Consumer Credit & Usury Ed.* 1 (July/Aug. 2002). A website about the Attorney Generals' settlement can be found at www.household-beneficial-settlement.com. The private class action settlement website is located at www.hblsettlement.com.

136   *See* Mary McCarty, *Predatory Lending Hits All Levels*, Dayton Daily News, Jan. 7, 2004, at B1 (article highlights one family's nightmare with this problem).

137   *See, e.g.,* Rawlings v. Dovenmuehle Mortgage, Inc., 64 F. Supp. 2d 1156 (M.D. Ala. 1999). Federal or state law may require prompt posting of payments. For example, the Truth in Lending Act requires prompt posting for credit card payments. 15 U.S.C. § 1666c; Official Staff Commentary § 226.10(a); National Consumer Law Center, Truth in Lending § 5.8.9.1 (5th ed. 2003 and Supp.). Iowa mandates the prompt crediting of payment in both the mortgage loan and credit card contexts. Iowa Code §§ 535.14, 537.3206(4).

138   *See* Ladd v. Equicredit Corp. of America, 2001 WL 1339007 (E.D. La. Sept. 7, 2001) (RICO claim stated for named plaintiff regarding the charging of a disputed "corporate advance" and for numerous drive-by inspections that allegedly were not performed; class action dismissed because reliance must be shown for each class member); *In re* Stark, 242 B.R. 866 (Bankr. W.D.N.C. 1999) (bankruptcy monitoring fees disallowed as ambiguous mortgage contract construed against lender). If the loan is an FHA-insured mortgage, the charges for inspections arguably cannot be passed onto the homeowner unless the mortgagee complies with 24 C.F.R. § 203.377: "[w]hen a mortgage is in default and a payment thereon is not received within 45 days of the due date, and efforts to reach the mortgagor by telephone within that period have been unsuccessful, the mortgagee shall be responsible for a visual inspection of the security property to determine whether the property is vacant." For the Fannie Mae Servicing Guides, see www.efanniemae.com (*Single Family Guides*). *But see* Walker v. Countrywide Home Loans, Inc., 121 Cal. Rptr. 2d 79 (Cal. Ct. App. 2002) (property inspections fees are not late fees; inspection fees are not illegal under California law; deed of trust allowed for these fees and for cost to be passed on to the homeowner).

139   Stark v. Sandberg, Phoenix & von Gontard, P.C., 381 F.3d 793 (8th Cir. 2004) (upholding arbitrator's award of $6 million in punitive damages due to the mortgage holder's forcible entry into the home in total disregard of the homeowner's rights).

140   *See, e.g.,* Cortez v. Keystone Bank, Inc., 2000 U.S. Dist. LEXIS 5705 (E.D. Pa. May 2, 2000) (alleged error arose when advances and payments were made on the same day); Siradas v. Chase Lincoln First Bank N.A., 1999 U.S. Dist. LEXIS 15593 (S.D.N.Y. Sept. 30, 1999) (miscalculation of interest due using the wrong index in variable rate transactions states a UDAP claim).

141   *See* Eva v. Midwest Nat'l Mortgage Banc, Inc., 143 F. Supp. 2d 862 (N.D. Ohio 2001) (court denied motion to dismiss claims against independent bi-weekly payment plan company who was not the loan holder). For a discussion of some of the issues raised by these payment plans, see § 4.6.7, *supra*. Household Finance and Beneficial Finance, part of Household International Inc., allegedly engaged in this practice in a misleading way. *See* Iowa *ex rel.* Miller v. Household Int'l Inc. (Iowa Dist. Ct. Polk County Dec. 13, 2002) (complaint, ¶¶ 8C, 8D), *available at* www.state.ia.us/government/ag/latest_news/releases/dec_2002/hhold.htm (click on lawsuit). Household agreed to change this practice in its consent judgment with the Attorney Generals. The Iowa version of this consent judgment is *available at* www.state.ia.us/government/ag/latest_news/releases/dec_2002/hhconsent.pdf. For several articles about Household's practices and the Attorney Generals' and private class action settlements, see 22 NCLC REPORTS *Consumer Credit & Usury Ed.* 15 (Jan./Feb. 2004); 22 NCLC REPORTS *Consumer Credit & Usury Ed.* 1 (July/Aug. 2003); 21 NCLC REPORTS *Consumer Credit & Usury Ed.* 13 (Jan./Feb. 2003); 21 NCLC REPORTS *Consumer Credit & Usury Ed.* 1 (July/Aug. 2002). A website about the Attorney Generals' settlement can be found at www.household-beneficial-settlement.com. The private class action settlement website is located at www.hblsettlement.com.

142   Miller v. McCalla, 214 F.3d 872 (7th Cir. 2000) (court holds that the unpaid principal balance listed is not the "debt" for purposes of the federal Fair Debt Collection Practices Act; court suggests appropriate language), *class cert. granted*, 198 F.R.D. 503 (N.D. Ill. 2001) (court awards maximum damages award allowed under the FDCPA; actual amount to be determined); Jackson v. Aman Collection Serv., 2001 U.S. Dist. LEXIS 22238 (S.D. Ind. Dec. 14, 2001) (collector's motion to dismiss denied on similar issue, court relying upon *Miller*). *See also* Schlosser v. Fairbanks Capital Corp., 323 F.3d 534 (7th Cir. 2003) (merits of FDCPA claim not reached; court held that holder of the loan that treated the loan as in default at the time it acquired the loan is a debt collector under the act).

143   For a discussion of these issues, see National Consumer Law Center, Consumer Bankruptcy Law and Practice § 13.4.3.4 (7th ed. 2004).

cally transfer funds from the consumers' accounts but withdrawing a larger amount than authorized, or withdrawing amounts early, causing overdrafts.[144]

These practices are being challenged under a number of legal theories including RESPA,[145] breach of contract,[146]

unjust enrichment, UDAP,[147] RICO,[148] and breach of duty of good faith and fair dealing,[149] and the FDCPA.[150] Many of

---

144 *See In re* Conseco Fin. Serv. Corp., Clearinghouse No. 55,600 (Kansas Office of the State Bank Comm'r 2002) (consent and settlement agreement).

145 The Real Estate Settlement Procedures Act applies to the escrowing of money to pay the taxes and hazard insurance and creates an affirmative obligation to make those payments in a timely way. *See* Ch. 12, *infra. See also* Miller v. Chevy Chase Bank, F.S.B., 1998 U.S. Dist. LEXIS 3651 (N.D. Ill. Mar. 24, 1998) (over-escrowing violates RESPA and the contract; lender's motion for summary judgment denied; RICO claim stated).

146 *See, e.g.,* Paslowski v. Standard Mortgage Corp., 1999 U.S. Dist. LEXIS 15787 (W.D. Pa. Mar. 10, 1999) (motion to dismiss denied where mortgage does not expressly permit the servicer's or holder's practice of under-billing the monthly payments, advancing the funds to cover the shortfall when the taxes and insurance came due, and adding the advance to the principal and in failing to capitalize monthly payments after doing so for several years), *later proceedings,* 129 F. Supp. 2d 793 (W.D. Pa. 2000) (Freddie Mac dismissed from case under the *Merrill* doctrine which states that a governmental entity cannot be bound by the unauthorized acts of its agents or employees [here, Freddie Mac either did not hold the note during the relevant period or did not authorize the conduct complained of]; alternative ground for dismissal involved argument that Freddie Mac did not affirmatively assume the errors in the accounts which occurred prior to its purchase of the loan); Miller v. Chevy Chase Bank, F.S.B., 1998 U.S. Dist. LEXIS 3651 (N.D. Ill. Mar. 24, 1998) (over-escrowing states a claim for breach of the contract; lender's motion for summary judgment denied; RESPA and RICO claims stated); Sandlin v. Shapiro & Fishman, 919 F. Supp. 1564, *class cert. denied,* 168 F.R.D. 662 (M.D. Fla. 1996) (payoff charge constituted a prepayment penalty; motion to dismiss complaint denied). *But see* Cappellini v. Mellon Mortgage Co., 991 F. Supp. 31 (D. Mass. 1997) (court granted motion to dismiss on breach of contract claim that the $15 fax fee and $25 duplicative statement fee charged for a payoff statement under the theory that while the mortgage and note did not expressly allow those charges, neither did it expressly prohibit them; the contract expressly allowed certain fees related to payments or defaults; fax and statement fees do not fall under this category but, rather, relate to special services outside of the scope of the basic services discussed in the mortgage and note; the homeowner could have gotten the statement for free by mail and there was no allegation that the lender required the use of fax, if so, the result may have been different; however, court *refused* to dismiss the breach of contract claim arising under a clause that said that upon payment of all sums secured by the instrument, the lender shall discharge the security instrument without charge to the borrower, except for recordation costs); Cain v. Source One Mortgage Serv. Corp., 1999 WL 674776 (Wash. Ct. App. Aug. 30, 1999) (court applies *Cappellini* reasoning to uphold dismissal of the complaint alleging that fax fee imposed for a payoff statement breached the contract; court, however, ignored the part of the *Cappellini* decision, directly applicable to the contract clause at issue in this case, where the court denied the creditor's motion). *See also* cases discussing charges construed as "prepayment

penalties" in § 5.8.1, *supra.* Note that one mortgage holder obtained a dismissal of a case against it for the imposition of a $25 mortgage recording fee and a $5 fax fee by raising the "voluntary payment" defense, arguing that both fees were clearly listed on the payoff statement and were paid voluntarily. Westfall v. Chase Lincoln First Bank, N.A., 685 N.Y.S.2d 181 (App. Div. 1999).

147 *See, e.g.,* Paslowski v. Standard Mortgage Corp., 1999 U.S. Dist. LEXIS 15787 (W.D. Pa. Mar. 10, 1999) (UDAP claim plead but it was dismissed due to the statute of limitations); *In re* Hart, 246 B.R. 709 (Bankr. D. Mass. 2000) (loan servicing agent violated state UDAP); Negrin v. Norwest Mortgage, Inc., 700 N.Y.S.2d 184 (N.Y. App. Div. 1999) (mortgage holder's motion to dismiss UDAP claim denied where homeowner alleged that holder charged a fax fee for a payoff statement and a recording fee), *further proceedings at* 741 N.Y.S.2d 287 (App. Div. 2000) (class certification reversed and remanded); Dwyer v. J.I. Kislak Mortgage Corp., 13 P.3d 240 (Wash. Ct. App. 2000) (charging fees not allowed by the mortgage and drafting the payoff statement to appear that such fees were required before the mortgage would be released is a UDAP violation). *See also* § 12.5, *infra. But see* Sewartz v. UST Corp., 2001 WL 1809798 (Mass. Super. Ct. Dec. 14, 2001) (no UDAP violation where holder corrected the monies debited from the homeowner's account before it sold the loan and before the subsequent holder started foreclosure).

148 *See, e.g.,* Ladd v. Equicredit Corp. of America, 2001 WL 1339007 (E.D. La. Sept. 7, 2001) (RICO claim stated for named plaintiff regarding the charging of a disputed "corporate advance" and for numerous drive-by inspections that allegedly were not performed; class action dismissed because reliance must be shown for each class member); Miller v. Chevy Chase Bank, F.S.B., 1998 U.S. Dist. LEXIS 3651 (N.D. Ill. Mar. 24, 1998) (over-escrowing states a claim for RICO; breach of the contract and RESPA claims also survived summary judgment). *See also* § 12.6, *infra.*

149 *See* § 12.8, *infra.*

150 An arbitrator awarded $1,000 in actual and $1,000 in statutory damages to two consumers plus attorney fees and $6,000,000 in punitive damages against the parent company of the collector. The news account is *available at* www.kansascity.com/mld/kansascity/business/4753684.htm?template=contentModules/printstory.jsp. The collector continued to contact the consumers directly even after receiving a clear letter from their attorney not to do so. The collector broke into the home and placed a sign in a window, embarrassing the family. It continued to contact the consumers at home and at work and sent notices of acceleration and the right to cure directly to the consumers. The arbitrator's award was ultimately upheld by the Eighth Circuit. Stark v. Sandberg, Phoenix & von Gontard, P.C., 381 F.3d 793 (8th Cir. 2004). *See also* Schlosser v. Fairbanks Capital Corp., 323 F.3d 534 (7th Cir. 2003) (merits of FDCPA claim not reached; court held that holder of the loan that treated the loan as in default at the time it acquired the loan is a debt collector under the act); Maxwell v. Fairbanks Capital Corp., 281 B.R. 101 (Bankr. D. Mass. 2002) (servicer demanded amounts of money from the homeowner that she did not owe and by demanding post-maturity interest on a 1991 loan; court stated that "Fairbanks, in a shocking display of corporate irresponsibility, repeatedly fabricated the amount of the homeowner's obligation to it out of thin air." *Id.* at 117). *Cf.* Hutchins v. Fairbanks Capital Corp., 2003 WL 1719997 (N.D. Ill. Mar. 31, 2003) (servicer did not

these cases are still in their early stages, as this is a developing area. For a more in-depth discussion of these issues, see National Consumer Law Center, Repossessions and Foreclosures (5th ed. 2002 and Supp.).

Fairbanks Capital Corp., one of the largest mortgage servicers, has recently undergone intense media scrutiny of its mortgage servicing practices. In 2003, a West Virginia court issued a restraining order preventing Fairbanks from foreclosing in that state based upon allegations that Fairbanks refused to credit payments in a timely fashion, assessed unauthorized fees, and illegally accelerated loan notes.[151] Faced with other individual and class lawsuits, as well as Federal Trade Commission (FTC) and HUD enforcement actions, Fairbanks has entered into a global settlement, with a private agreement and FTC order negotiated contemporaneously and cooperatively.[152] *Curry v. Fairbanks Capital Corp.*, filed in federal district court for the district of Massachusetts, consolidates and settles thirty-seven private lawsuits, and the FTC consent order was filed in a related action in the same court.

Fairbanks Capital's practices that were expressly covered by these settlements include: a) the assessment of excess or improper force-placed hazard insurance premiums; b) the payment or assessment of property tax penalties or excess interest on property taxes despite a valid and timely paid escrow account maintained by Fairbanks to cover property tax obligations; c) the assessment of broker's price opinion charges or inspection fees for work that was not completed due to reinstatement or payoff; d) the assessment of interest at the time of loan pay-offs that was not then due; or e) the assessment of interest due on corporate advances on the basis of improper rounding.

As part of the settlement, Fairbanks agreed to pay $35 million to refund home owners for certain fees it charged, upon the filing of claims by class members. It also set aside $5 million as redress for home owners who lost their homes due to wrongful foreclosures. Fairbanks will also spend at least $7 million to reimburse in full or reverse certain charges which remain outstanding on borrowers' accounts. Class members need not file a claim for the "reverse or reimburse" program. The reimbursement will be in cash regardless of whether the loan is still serviced by Fairbanks or whether the account is open, paid off, charged off, or in bankruptcy. Finally, the class settlement and FTC order require Fairbanks to adopt significant practice changes.[153] It will be interesting to see if industry practices as a whole are improved as a result of this settlement.

11.5.6 Property Flipping and Appraisal Fraud

Property flipping scams involve speculators who buy dilapidated residential properties at low prices and resell them to unsophisticated first-time home buyers at huge markups.[154] In ordinary real estate sales, bank officers, appraisers, building inspectors, building contractors, real estate agents, and the buyer's attorney safeguard against grossly over-priced sales. In property flipping scams, on the other hand, these parties may actively conspire with speculators to mislead buyers as to the property's market value and hide from buyers critical information.[155]

Generally, two types of flipping scams are targeted at unsophisticated low-income "first-time" home buyers, depending on the type of financing involved. Those home buyers with the worst credit ratings are steered to private subprime lenders. Home buyers with slightly higher incomes and cleaner credit reports get directed to lenders making FHA-insured loans.

An inflated appraisal is not only the linchpin of a property flipping scheme,[156] but is also a key part of many predatory

---

treat the homeowner as if he were in default at the time it acquired servicing rights because the letter it sent only said that if certain payments had not been paid, then the loan was in default, distinguishing *Schlosser*).

151 Lucas v. Fairbanks Capital Corp., Clearinghouse Nos. 55603A–55603C (W. Va. Cir. Ct. Lincoln County, Jan. 8, 2003) (complaint, motion for temporary restraining order, order). *See also* Lilly v. Bank One, Nat'l Ass'n, Clearinghouse Nos. 55604A–55604D (W. Va. Cir. Ct. Raleigh County, Apr. 5, 2004) (second amended complaint, motion for preliminary/temporary injunction, memorandum, stipulated order) (allegations against the servicer, HomeComings Financial Network, Inc. (HFN) include charging illegal fees, force placing home-owners insurance, and paying duplicate property taxes, and then pursuing foreclosure; parties agreed that all foreclosures on HFN serviced mortgages will stop for at least 120 days in West Virginia).

152 The FTC order was filed on November 12, 2003, and the private class settlement agreement was filed on November 14, 2003. Copies of the consolidated complaint, settlement agreement and release, FTC order, and related documents are available on the NCLC website at www.nclc.org. The class settlement provides: "This Settlement and the FTC Agreement are intended to jointly comprise a global settlement providing for consumer redress throughout the United States. The two settlements were negotiated simultaneously, and are inextricably intertwined." For an in-depth discussion of these settlements and a chart comparing and contrasting the injunctive relief, see 22 NCLC REPORTS *Bankruptcy & Foreclosures Ed.* 13 (Jan./Feb. 2004).

153 The injunctive relief is set out in the private settlement Appendix 1—"Default Resolution Program" (DRP) and Appendix 2—"Operational Practices Agreement" (OP). Both of these programs remain in effect for a minimum of five years. Significantly, Fairbanks's customers can raise as a defense to foreclosure Fairbanks's failure to comply with these obligations. The FTC order also provides for specific injunctive relief, with many of the provisions applying for periods of either five or ten years.

154 Thanks to Andre Weitzman and Cheryl Hystad, counsel in Hoffman v. Stamper, for contributing to this section.

155 See Hoffman v. Stamper, 867 A.2d 276 (Md. 2005) for a description of a property flipping scam in Baltimore.

156 Vaughn v. Consumer Home Mortg., Inc., 2003 WL 21241669 (E.D.N.Y. Mar. 23, 2003).

loan schemes in which loan brokers secure inflated appraisals to persuade lenders to extend loans larger than the borrower's income and assets justify.[157] In either case, the appraisal is essential to the scam artist's ultimate goal of bleeding away fees from a loan secured by the victim's property. More obviously, if property being sold for $100,000 is appraised for its true market value of $50,000, the deal will instantly crumble.

Appraisals in sub-prime transactions may be inflated by up to 300% above the actual fair market value in order to create a loan-to-value ratio of between 60% and 75% to satisfy the underwriting requirements of the lender and secondary market. Federal Housing Administration (FHA) appraisals typically are inflated by 30% to 50% because FHA-insured loans are made at close to 100% of the appraised value. Credit applications and downpayments also are routinely falsified in both "sub-prime" and FHA-financed transactions.

Both scams have a common result: an unqualified buyer is placed in a property in questionable condition and saddled with a debt load that exceeds the market value of the property. These homeowners will be unable to resell the home in an arms-length transaction because the mortgage indebtedness exceeds the fair market value of the property. Ultimately, the homeowners will lose their homes due to foreclosure sales because the home's condition is much worse than represented, promised repairs are not performed, and the consumer's mortgage payments may be higher than the consumer can afford. Then the scams can begin again against different homeowners if the wrongdoers or their confederates purchase the homes at the foreclosure sales.

Property flipping not only defrauds the buyer, but also whoever is on the hook if the consumer defaults on the mortgage. Despite this, the lender often actively participates in the flipping scheme, particularly where FHA-insured loans are utilized. The loan officer gets a commission and HUD is the one stuck with the bad loan. One recent case highlighted a loan officer who helped the speculator evade HUD requirements and defraud the consumer.[158]

Key then to property flipping litigation is the inclusion in the lawsuit of the various parties in the scam orbit. This not only adds deep pockets and provides more parties to contribute to a settlement, but also facilitates discovery from these parties and helps present the case to the judge in the correct light. This is not a case of buyers and sellers negotiating a price in a free market, but instead a scam where a number of parties who held themselves out as neutral or representing the consumer in fact conspired with the seller to defraud the consumer. For example, lawsuits have alleged various claims against the seller, the seller's officers, the corporate secretary for the seller, the realtor and the realtor's officers, the lender, the lender's officers, the seller's attorney, the buyer's attorney, the home inspector, and the appraiser.[159] Building contractors that were hired to renovate the buildings, but who either did not do the work or misrepresented the extent of the work required are also implicated.[160]

A variety of claims can be raised against these defendants, including fraud,[161] civil conspiracy, negligent misrepresentation, aiding and abetting, UDAP, breach of fiduciary duty,[162] and the federal False Claims Act (where submitting false insurance claims to the FHA).[163]

Appraiser fraud presents particular hurdles for the consumer. Consumers have limited contact with appraisers, so that appraisers' involvement in fraud may not be obvious. Nonetheless, the appraiser may be liable for fraud, civil conspiracy, UDAP violations, violation of state appraiser licensing laws, and even RICO violations. Investigating the facts surrounding the appraisal may also reveal how others—those who arranged for or used the appraisal—are tied into the fraud.

There can be little question that a falsified appraisal meets the standard of deception in a UDAP statute in most states, and is a misrepresentation that will support a negligent misrepresentation or even a fraud claim.[164] UDAP claims are particularly flexible since in most states the consumer does not have to show reliance,[165] privity of contract is

---

157 *See, e.g.,* Hill v. Meritech Mortg. Servs., Inc. (*In re* Hill), No. 01-30171SR, Adv. No. 01-848 (Bankr. E.D. Pa. Sept. 27, 2002); David Callahan, *Home Insecurity: How Widespread Appraisal Fraud Puts Homeowners at Risk* (Mar. 2005), *available at* www.DEMOS-USA.org/pubs/home_security_v3.pdf; Benjamin Wallace-Wells, *There Goes the Neighborhood: Why home prices are about to plummet—and take the recovery with them,* Washington Monthly (Apr. 2004) at 6, *available at* www.washingtonmonthly.com/features/2004/0404.Wallace-wells.html.

158 Hoffman v. Stamper, 867 A.2d 276 (Md. 2005).

159 Vaughn v. Consumer Home Mortgage, Inc., 2003 WL 21241669 (E.D.N.Y. Mar. 23, 2003); Banks v. Consumer Home Mortgage, Inc., 2003 WL 21251584 (E.D.N.Y. Mar. 28, 2003); Hoffman v. Stamper, 867 A.2d 276 (Md. 2005).

160 Polonetsky v. Better Homes Depot, Inc., 97 N.Y.2d 46, 735 N.Y.S.2d 479, 760 N.E.2d 1274 (2001) (UDAP claim against speculator for misrepresenting that contractors and attorneys to whom it steered the consumer were FHA-approved).

161 For ways to hold the lender liable for the acts of third parties, see §§ 12.10 and 12.12, *infra.*

162 Vaughn v. Consumer Home Mortgage, Inc., 2003 WL 21241669 (E.D.N.Y. Mar. 23, 2003); Banks v. Consumer Home Mortgage, Inc., 2003 WL 21251584 (E.D.N.Y. Mar. 28, 2003); Hoffman v. Stamper, 867 A.2d 276 (Md. 2005).

163 *See* National Consumer Law Center, Unfair and Deceptive Acts and Practices § 9.4.13 (6th ed. 2004 and Supp.). For the FHA's new anti-flipping regulations, see 24 C.F.R. § 203.37a. Making FHA-insured loans in violation of these guidelines should be evidence of conspiracy to defraud as should other attempts by the lender to evade these requirement, such as phony documentation.

164 Vaughn v. Consumer Home Mortg., Inc., 2003 WL 21241669, at *6 (E.D.N.Y. Mar. 23, 2003); Banks v. Consumer Home Mortg., Inc., 2003 WL 21252584, at *5 (E.D.N.Y. Mar. 28, 2003); Hoffman v. Stamper, 843 A.2d 153, 190 (Md. Ct. Spec. App. 2004), *appeal pending*; Moore v. Mortgagestar, Inc., Clearinghouse No. 55606, Civ. Action No. 2:01-0226 (S.D. W. Va. Dec. 18, 2002).

165 National Consumer Law Center, Unfair and Deceptive Acts and Practices § 4.2.12 (6th ed. 2004 and Supp.). *But cf.* Sampen v.

unnecessary,[166] and non-disclosure is just as actionable as affirmative deception.[167]

As to fraud or negligent misrepresentation, the general rule is that a party whose misrepresentation reaches third parties indirectly is liable as long as there was reason to expect that the third parties would learn of and rely on it.[168] Privity of contract is also unnecessary in most states.[169] Common law fraud or negligent misrepresentation requires proof that the consumers relied to their detriment on the misrepresentation, a showing that can be problematic if the consumer was not given the appraisal before consummation of the transaction. But an appraiser can be liable for aiding and abetting the other defendants' fraud even if the consumer never heard or relied on the appraiser's own misrepresentation.[170]

An appraiser can also be liable for the tort of civil conspiracy if its appraisal enabled others to defraud the consumer. The elements of a cause of action for civil conspiracy are generally an agreement by two or more persons to perform an overt act or acts in furtherance of the agreement to accomplish an unlawful purpose (or a lawful purpose by unlawful means), causing injury to another.[171] Every participant in the conspiracy is liable for the acts of all the other participants.[172] Thus, an appraiser whose falsified appraisal enabled the scam artist's fraud to succeed was liable for the entire fraud, and possibly for punitive damages, even though the consumers never read the appraisal.[173] A Maryland court held that an appraiser's representation about the value of a home was communicated to the buyer, indirectly, by the mere availability of financing to complete the transaction.[174] Another court held that, by giving the appraiser access to his home to perform the appraisal, the homeowner may have implicitly relied on him to perform the appraisal without deception.[175]

Submission of a falsified appraisal to a financial institution may also constitute bank fraud,[176] a predicate act under

---

Dabrowski, 584 N.E.2d 493 (Ill. App. 1991) (no UDAP claim where the appraiser was hired by the plaintiff directly but where the report, though inaccurate, did not contain inappropriate comparables or other false information to support the conclusion; no evidence of the appraiser's involvement in the sale or of other fraudulent behavior or inducements to the appraiser); Commonwealth v. Percudani, 844 A.2d 35, 48 (Pa. Commw. Ct. 2004) (reliance unnecessary in AG suit, but stating in *dictum* that for private UDAP action home buyer must show reliance on falsified appraisal).

166 *See* National Consumer Law Center, Unfair and Deceptive Acts and Practices § 4.2.15.3 (6th ed. 2004 and Supp.).

167 *See id.* § 4.2.14.

168 Restatement (2d) of Torts §§ 533, 552; National Consumer Law Center, Automobile Fraud § 7.5.2 (2d ed. 2003 and Supp.).

169 *See* Williams v. Polgar, 215 N.W.2d 149 (Mich. 1974) (court research shows that 35 states have abolished the privity requirement, at least in cases involving title searchers). *See also* Ensimger v. Terminix Int'l Co., 102 F.3d 1571 (10th Cir. 1996) (no need for privity between the pest inspector and the plaintiff); Petrillo v. Bachenberg, 655 A.2d 1354 (N.J. 1995) (attorney assumed duty to property purchaser to provide reliable information regarding percolation tests). In Ohio, the intermediate appellate courts are split on whether the privity rule applies between homeowners and appraisers. *Compare* Kenney v. Henry Fischer Builder, Inc., 716 N.E.2d 1189 (Ohio App. 1998) (privity defense reluctantly upheld) *with* Perpetual Fed. Sav. & Loan Ass'n, 609 N.E.2d 1324 (Ohio App. 1992) (adopted the Restatement of Torts 2d position abolishing privity but the case involved a specific representation related to compliance with zoning regulations; case did not involve an over-appraised property). The highest court has not directly addressed privity between homebuyers and appraisers but is split on the issue of privity in other contexts. *Compare* Haddon View Inv. Co. v. Coopers & Lybrand, 436 N.E.2d 212 (Ohio 1982) (privity rule abolished regarding accountants; court permits cases by third parties who are foreseen plaintiffs or members of a limited class whose reliance is specifically foreseen) *with* Thomas v. Guarantee Title & Trust Co., 91 N.E. 183 (Ohio 1910) (privity required to sue title abstractor).

170 *See, e.g.,* Banks v. Consumer Home Mortg., Inc., 2003 WL 21252584, at *5 (E.D.N.Y. Mar. 28, 2003) (describing aiding & abetting standards); Restatement (2d) of Torts § 876(b).

171 Adcock v. Brakegate, Ltd., 164 Ill. 2d 54, 645 N.E.2d 888 (1994). *See also* Banks v. Consumer Home Mortg., Inc., 2003 WL 21252584, at *5 (E.D.N.Y. Mar. 28, 2003) (home flipping case involving inflated appraisals); Moore v. Mortgagestar, Inc., Clearinghouse No. 55606, Civ. Action No. 2:01-0226 (S.D. W. Va. Dec. 18, 2002) (denying motion to dismiss conspiracy claim against appraiser in predatory lending scheme). *See generally* National Consumer Law Center, Unfair and Deceptive Acts and Practices § 6.5.2.3 (6th ed. 2004 and Supp.).

172 Matthews v. New Century Mortg. Corp., 185 F. Supp. 2d 874, 889 (S.D. Ohio 2002) (predatory loan with falsified income statement). *See also* Osburn v. Community Home Mortgage, L.L.C., Civil Action No. 02-C-1164 (Cir. Ct Kanawha County, W. Va. Jan. 13, 2005) (jury verdict awarding homeowners $50,000 in actual damages and $500,000 in punitive damages against the lender and broker for fraud and conspiracy based on the appraiser fraud), available on the CD-Rom accompanying this volume (complaint, jury instructions, interrogatories, and jury verdicts).

173 Hoffman v. Stamper, 867 A.2d 276, 290–293 (Md. 2005) (appraiser liable to home buyers on conspiracy count where the evidence showed a pattern of actual knowledge by the appraiser in some cases and the ability to know in others, that seller had purchased the properties only months earlier for a fraction of what the appraiser appraised them for; an attempt by the appraiser to justify the huge inflation through a variety of means; the appraiser derived 99% of his income from appraisals done for the lender; appraiser liable for aiding and abetting fraud even though the home buyer never read the appraisal).

174 Hoffman v. Stamper, 867 A.2d 276, 293 (Md. 2005) (home buyers proved that they were aware that if the appraisal was less than the contract price, they would have the right to cancel the contract and that, when that option was not afforded them because of the inflated appraisal, they relied and had a right to rely on the fact that the property was worth what they were paying for it).

175 Hill v. Meritech Mortg. Servs., Inc. (*In re* Hill), No. 01-30171SR, Adv. No. 01-848 (Bankr. E.D. Pa. Sept. 27, 2002).

176 18 U.S.C. § 1344. The bank may or may not be an innocent victim. Sometimes a bank officer whose compensation depends on bringing business into a bank is complicit in falsification, or the bank may be relying on passing the loan on to the secondary market or recovering from mortgage insurance.

the federal RICO statute, although the consumers may have to convince the court that they, in addition to the bank, are victims of this fraud.[177]

11.6 Used Car Financing

11.6.1 Introduction

For many Americans, cars are a necessity, not a luxury. In the absence of good mass transit systems, people need cars to go to work, to get to schools or training programs, to get to doctors. And, next to homes, cars are the biggest investment most households make. Buying the financing as well as the car at the lot is unfortunately an extraordinarily complex process, and, for some, dangerous to the pocketbook. "Subprime" auto financing, the very expensive credit available for "high-risk" (real and perceived) consumers, is often the source of credit for used cars.[178]

Diagnosing overreaching auto financing practices can be difficult. Probably most practitioners representing low-income consumers have seen car loans where the "cash price" of the vehicle was overpriced by any objective, fair-market standard. But untangling pricing problems relating to the sale of the vehicle and ancillary products from the credit-related problems can be daunting—particularly because the documents the consumer receives often bear little relationship to the real story.[179] The nature of the marketplace adds to the problem. Used vehicles are not mass-priced. Car lots are one of the few marketplaces in the American economy where it is common to haggle over price. These facts do not make it any more legal to bury credit-related costs in the underlying car sale than it is to bury them in magazine sales or any other retail sale.[180] They do, however, complicate the evidentiary questions and heighten the need for practitioners to take care in delineating the issues and presenting evidence in litigation. Is that exorbitant price just a bad deal? Or have indirect lender's financing costs been buried in it? If so, has

it been done illegally, and what evidence is necessary to establish that?[181] Or has negative equity been buried in that cash price?[182]

Buried financing costs are not the only credit-related headaches for consumers buying a car. In their eagerness to make sales, dealers often want to deliver the car to a prospective buyer on the spot—to get them locked psychologically and economically into a sale. But this "spot-delivery" or "yo-yo deal" often comes without the financing terms having been fully approved by the intended assignee. The consumer may then be told to return the car or make different financing arrangements—generally, of course, more disadvantageous.[183] And yield spread premiums, which result in interest rates higher than underwriting needs dictate in order to give the middleman compensation (here the dealer), are present in the car financing arena as well as in the mortgage lending field.[184] Loan-packing happens in car loans as well as other kinds of subprime loans.[185]

While the industry argues that subprime financing (sometimes called "specialty financing") makes credit available to people who could not otherwise obtain it, the economics sometimes perversely work against the consumer. As with subprime mortgage credit, the higher prices may create risk more than compensate for it, making less of a car cost more, and raising monthly payments.[186] Devoting more of a limited budget to service high financing costs (whether explicit or implicit) may mean that the car itself is of less value—less reliable and shorter-lived. That translates into higher repair expenses, or perhaps a debt that outlives the car. That, in turn, can lead to default. Who can afford to keep up payments on a car that does not run? The result can be a downward spiral for the consumers caught in this marketplace.

The nature of the subprime business has also exacerbated some insidious practices which undermine the integrity of this marketplace, making it difficult for market forces to work as well as theory would have it. One trend spawned by the nature of the subprime industry is the disappearance of price tags on used cars. Check out used car lots in lower income neighborhoods. The model year may be on the window, the down payment may be on the window, but not a price. Why? Because these deals commonly work backwards from the financing to the purchase terms. A TV news magazine captured a subprime lender at a dealer trade show explaining that "you never put the price on the car on the lot.

---

177 *Compare* Matthews v. New Century Mortg. Corp., 185 F. Supp. 2d 874 (S.D. Ohio 2002) (denying motion to dismiss RICO claim where broker submitted false information to lender) *with* Honorable v. Easy Life Real Estate Sys., Inc., 182 F.R.D. 553 (N.D. Ill. 1998) (granting motion to dismiss RICO claim on ground that banks, not consumers, were victims of realtors' falsification). State RICO statutes may explicitly state that a predicate act includes pursuing a pattern of skimming a homeowner's equity. *See, e.g.,* Wash. Rev. Code § 9A.82.010(1)(cc).

178 The need for close scrutiny of that rationalization is as applicable in the auto finance area as in any other. *See* § 11.1, *supra.*

179 For an overview of the kinds of documents typically kept in car dealer files and what information they can provide, see National Consumer Law Center, Unfair and Deceptive Acts and Practices § 5.4.2 (6th ed. 2004 and Supp.) and National Consumer Law Center, Automobile Fraud Ch. 2 (2d ed. 2003 and Supp.).

180 *See* § 7.4.6, *supra;* § 11.6.2, *infra. See also* National Consumer Law Center, Truth in Lending § 3.10 (5th ed. 2003 and Supp.).

181 *See* § 11.6.2, *infra. See generally* National Consumer Law Center, Truth in Lending §§ 3.7.8, 3.10 (5th ed. 2003 and Supp.).

182 *See* § 11.6.3, *infra.*

183 *See* § 11.6.5, *infra.*

184 *See* § 11.6.6, *infra.* For a discussion of yield spread premiums in mortgage lending, see § 11.5.4.3, *supra;* Ch. 12, *infra.*

185 *See* § 11.6.4, *infra.*

186 *See* § 11.1, *supra.*

Not in subprime."[187] It certainly hinders consumers' ability to negotiate if they do not even know the initial asking price of the car. And if they ask the seller for a price, the counter is likely to be "what kind of monthly payment were you thinking of?" Many of these deals start by the dealer figuring out a monthly payment, too often a maxed-out monthly payment, then working behind the scenes with the lender as to maximum finance terms and collateral requirements. Only after that is established are the terms of the sale fleshed out to fit the finance deal—the cash price of the car, any after-market add-ons, sometimes even which car! ("We can put you in this car right here.") The absence of the car's price tag is a distinct advantage to the seller in this kind of a scenario.[188] But there is a legal advantage as well: it is harder to prove that the price of the car was inflated to bury financing costs if there was no cash price for the consumer to see before the finance costs were factored in.

This section is not a full exploration of all the subprime credit practices,[189] nor all the legal issues and precedent involved in these practices, but it offers an introduction to the issues and a general overview of some of the legal theories which may be brought to bear on the problems.[190]

11.6.2 Lender-Imposed Financing Costs: Discounts and Acquisition Fees

11.6.2.1 Burying Credit Costs in Inflated Cash Prices

The financial arrangements by which a subprime lender pays the dealer for the retail installment contract vary. One method, which unfortunately leads to considerable price distortion for the consumer, is to purchase at a deep discount from the face value of the note. For example, a subprime lender may designate a buyer a "B" risk category under its criteria, and tell the dealer it will advance 75% of the amount financed to buy that consumer's paper. Or the lender

may impose a flat acquisition fee on the transaction, or some combination of the two.

It is not uncommon for the ultimate lender to pay a discounted price to a merchant for the consumer's obligation. For example, the price a credit card issuer pays a merchant may be a 2 to 3% discount. Merchants who let their customers use credit cards price their products accordingly. The customers at Store A may pay $40 for a widget because some of its customers will pay by credit card, though the widget might cost $39.20 at a store that does not take credit cards. Even though Store A took into account the credit card issuer's two percent discount in setting the widget's price, and hence is related to credit, the eighty cents differential is not a finance charge for purposes of Truth in Lending, and would not be under most state credit regulatory statutes. Cash and credit customers pay the same amount; the differential is not passed onto individual credit card users.

With subprime auto financing, in contrast, the discounts are much greater, and they are individualized. This combination of facts makes it more likely that the loan may contain hidden finance charges as the law defines them. The amount of the discount at which subprime lenders purchase paper may be too great for dealers to absorb within a normal negotiating range for the price of the vehicle, creating an economic incentive for the dealer to pass it on to the buyer. Subprime lenders, for example, may pay only 60 to 80% of the amount financed on the paper. (Some have paid as little as 50%.) Here's a basic example: The dealer acquires a used car at $3,700, puts $500 into fix-up, for a total acquisition cost of $4,200. If it wants to make $800 on the deal, it will price the car at $5,000. If customer A comes in, and has arranged the financing with her own bank, she walks out with the car for $5,000. But customer B is looking for financing as well as a car, so the dealer faxes a credit application off to Sublime Subprime Auto Finance. If the dealer gets approval from Sublime Subprime for a twenty-four month loan at 21% APR, a straightforward deal would give customer B monthly payments of $257 and a total cost of $6,168.

But if Sublime Subprime will pay the dealer only 75% of the amount financed to buy the contract, in this case, $3,750, the dealer will not make its profit and will lose $450.[191] Because the dealer listened carefully at that trade show, no price is posted on the car. So the dealer might be tempted to quote customer B a price that will mean the dealer still collects $5,000, in this case, a price of $6,700.[192] Here's how fudging the cash price changes the economics on this "21%" loan:

187 *Dateline* (NBC television broadcast Dec. 8, 1998). Dealers also know that if the advertised price and the sales price differ, they are in hot water under state UDAP acts. *See, e.g.,* Motzer Dodge Jeep-Eagle v. Ohio Atty. Gen., 642 N.E.2d 20 (Ohio Ct. App. 1994); Ciampi v. Ogden Chrysler Plymouth, Inc., 634 N.E.2d 448 (Ill. App. 1994); Sanders v. Francis, 561 P.2d 1003 (Or. 1977).

188 See the allegations in the complaint filed by the Iowa Attorney General against one used car seller and its subprime lending arm. State *ex rel.* Miller v. Dan Nelson Automotive Group, Inc., Equity No. CE 50210 (Dist. Ct. Polk County, Iowa filed Jan. 7, 2005) (complaint), *available at* www.state.ia.us/government/latest_news/releases/Jan_2005/dnelson.pdf.

189 For a text focusing on the unfair or deceptive aspects of car sales and auto financing, see National Consumer Law Center, Unfair and Deceptive Acts and Practices § 5.4 (6th ed. 2004 and Supp.).

190 Portions of this section are adapted from Kathleen Keest, *Recent Developments in Automobile Lending: Hot Spots*, 52 Cons. Fin. L. Qtrly. Rep. 287 (Summer 1998), with permission of the publisher.

191 Some lenders hold back a reserve, under which the dealer will get an additional portion back under specified conditions which indicate the contract will be performed. While some reserves actually pay out, others apparently are written with conditions which make it unlikely that the dealer will see any of the holdback.

192 $6700 × .75 = $5025. Hiking the price to cover a flat acquisi-

	Straight-forward deal	Fudged deal
Real cash price	$5,000	$5,000
Inflated cash price	NA	$6,700
Disclosed rate	21%	21%
Real credit cost as rate	21%	53.7%
Monthly payments (24)	$257	$344
Total of payments	$6,128	$8,256

See how well this subprime financing has worked for customer B? She gets the same car, nominally at the same APR, but her monthly payments are $87 higher and, at least economically, the real cost of credit is unquestionably nearly 54%, not 21%. The question is whether it is also legally considered a 54% rate.

There are a variety of legal issues triggered when the car's cash price is inflated to cover finance-related costs—the most obvious claims involve Truth in Lending and usury. That the price of a car or the valuation of a trade-in is "negotiable" is not a license to violate the cardinal rule that the price of credit and the price of the product being sold on credit are supposed to be two distinct—and accurately disclosed—things. Whether a TIL finance charge is buried in an inflated cash price on a car is exclusively a factual question. If the dealer absorbs the lender's discount as part of the cost of doing business and takes it into account in pricing all cars, the discount is not a finance charge. Rather, the dealer is absorbing the discount as part of a cost of doing business—just like the widget-selling merchant.[193]

However, the discount that the lender charges the dealer for purchasing the paper *is* a finance charge "if the consumer is required to pay the charges in cash, *as an addition to the obligation*, or as a deduction from the proceeds of the obligation."[194] According to the Commentary, the distinction between the two is whether the charge is imposed *separately* on the borrower.[195] Note that just because it is not identified explicitly as a separate charge does not mean that it was not imposed separately, however denominated.[196] To

think otherwise is to permit dishonesty in labeling to successfully circumvent Truth in Lending requirements.[197] The

---

tion fee works the same way. [*NB*: Acquisition fees are also charged in leases, but the legal issues are not the same, as leases do not have to disclose the equivalent of an APR.]

193   If applicable alike to cash and credit customers, then it is a charge "payable in a comparable cash transaction" and is not a finance charge. 15 U.S.C. § 1605(a); Reg. Z § 226.4(a); Official Staff Commentary § 226.4(a)-1.

194   Reg. Z § 226.4(b)(6).

195   Official Staff Commentary § 226.4(a)-2. *See generally* National Consumer Law Center, Truth in Lending § 3.7.8 (5th ed. 2003 and Supp.).

196   *See, e.g.*, Balderos v. City Chevrolet, 214 F.3d 849 (7th Cir. 2000) (even though car club membership fee was voluntary, part of it is a disguised finance charge if the consumer could prove that the excess part of the fee was imposed on buyers who did not purchase the membership and not imposed on those who did opt for it); Wallace v. Walker Auto Sales, Inc., 155 F.3d 927 (7th Cir. 1998); Knapp v. Americredit Fin. Serv., Inc., 245 F. Supp.

2d 841 (S.D. W. Va. 2003) (acquisition fee paid by dealer to lender based on the customer's creditworthiness may be a finance charge even though it was included in the cash price unbeknownst to the consumer and was charged only to "special" financing customers; dealer and lender motions for summary judgment denied on issue of whether the fee was "separately imposed"); Sampler v. City Chevrolet Buick Geo, Inc., 2000 U.S. Dist. LEXIS 2322 (N.D. Ill. Feb. 24, 2000), *rev'g* 10 F. Supp. 2d 934 (N.D. Ill. 1998) in light of Wallace v. Walker Auto Sales, Inc., 155 F.3d 927 (7th Cir. 1998) (in denying summary judgment, the court grappled with the issue of the type of proof necessary to show that the cost of the discount is separately imposed; court decided that the borrower may prevail on this TILA claim if she can prove: 1) the dealer set the negotiated price of cars it anticipates will be purchased on credit high enough to cover the cost of discount; 2) the dealer does not similarly raise the prices of cars sold for cash; 3) the dealer does not disclose the discount to credit customers; 4) the dealer anticipated a discount when negotiating the price of the borrower's car; 5) the dealer did not disclose the discount to this particular borrower; as these elements are akin to proving discrimination, the court further found that the borrower could prove by direct or indirect evidence that: 1) the dealer deducts the price of discounts from its profits on subprime cars but not on cash cars; 2) statistics demonstrate that the dealer's profits on cars bought with subprime credit are equal to or higher than the dealer's profits on cars bought with cash; 3) the dealer's sales managers knew that a particular customer is going to require subprime financing prior to setting a final price for the car. The proof presented by the consumer was sufficient to create a dispute of material fact, i.e., that discounts are listed on manager's sheets as a cost of subprime customers' cars and not on cash customers' cars shows that cost is imposed only on credit customers, profit margin is higher on subprime cars than on cash cars, the dealer knows the general rates of discount charged by subprime lenders and can reasonably approximate the amount to holdback in a particular transaction). *See also* Thomas B. Hudson, Michael A. Benoit, and Joseph D. Looney, *Indirect Auto Finance Dealer Compensation Litigation*, 54 Bus. Lawyer 1301 (May 1999) (industry representatives describe the difference between "dealer participation," discounted contracts, and upcharges and reviews some court decisions); Thomas B. Hudson, Michael A. Benoit & Joseph D. Looney, *Update on Indirect Auto Finance Dealer Compensation Litigation and Other Pertinent Litigation*, 55 Bus. Lawyer 1281 (May 2000); Thomas B. Hudson, Michael A. Benoit & Joseph D. Looney, *Update on Indirect Auto Finance Dealer Compensation Litigation and Other Pertinent Litigation*, 56 Bus. Lawyer 1113 (May 2001). *But see* Hoffman v. Grossinger Motor Corp., 218 F.3d 680 (7th Cir. 2000) (court found that consumer's general proof that a dealer, on average, charged subprime credit customers higher prices than it charged other customers was insufficient to survive a motion for summary judgment in light of dealer's proof that it used a unitary pricing system for its credit and cash customers which resulted in the salespeople trying to sucker everyone, even though a $400 holdback fee was imposed only in subprime financed transactions; while more general proof suffices at the motion to dismiss stage, not so for summary judgment). *See generally See generally* National Consumer Law Center, Truth in Lending §§ 3.6.5, 3.10 (5th ed. 2003 and Supp.).

197   *See* Wallace v. Walker Auto Sales, Inc., 155 F.3d 927, 934 n.9 (7th Cir. 1998); Sampler v. City Chevrolet Buick Geo, Inc.,

question then is the factual one of whether the dealer hikes the cash price on the cars purchased by customers like B, incident to their credit arrangements, or whether the dealer takes into account the fact that some will be financed at a discount when it prices all its cars.[198] In the TILA context, practitioners should be aware of the question of assignee liability in this context. For damage claims, assignees are liable for TIL violations that are apparent on the face of the document.[199] This standard has been strictly construed by the Seventh and Eleventh Circuits in hidden finance charge cases.[200]

The question of hidden interest in inflated finance charges can arise under state usury laws, as well.[201] For both TIL and usury, the evidentiary issue is crucial. Checking the price at which the vehicle was advertised in the newspaper may help establish the regular cash price. Or investigation may show that the lender actually helps the dealer figure out how to price the car to a borrower to cover the lender's discount. (One subprime lender made a chart to explain to its dealers how to set the "cash price" of the car to recoup the lender's discount.) And be sure to ask in discovery for all versions of the application and all correspondence between the dealer and the lender. Also review any facsimile time stamps. Sometimes the "cash price" listed for the car on the initial version of the application sent to the lender changes after the lender faxes back information on the financing terms.[202] One court denied summary judgment to the dealer after reviewing the discounts listed on the manager's sheets, the profit margin differential between subprime cars sold for cash and those sold on credit, and the dealer's knowledge of the general rates of discount charged by subprime lenders.[203]

Apart from the issue of hidden finance charges, there may also be UDAP issues. Irrespective of whether a car has a posted price tag, a dealer might have listed a cash price in an advertisement. While that should be good evidence that the dealer imposed a higher cash price for a credit buyer, in and of itself the higher price also may raise a separate issue of deceptive advertising.[204] It may also be deceptive for the dealer to fail to disclose its kickback from the assignee.[205]

In this situation, the argument is that the paperwork showing the dealer as lender is a sham. The dealer and lender were operating together and should be held accountable for their behavior. The lender cannot hide behind its "assignee" status. Alternatively, these facts can also be used to prove that the assignee is not a holder-in-due course if it participated in the fraud in the first instance.[206]

2000 U.S. Dist. LEXIS 2322 (N.D. Ill. Feb. 24, 2000), *rev'g*, 10 F. Supp. 2d 934 (N.D. Ill. 1998). In fact, many of the original cases challenging hidden finance charges in inflated cash prices were discount cases. *See generally* National Consumer Law Center, Truth in Lending § 3.10 (5th ed. 2003 and Supp.).

198 *See, e.g.*, Cornist v. B.J.T. Auto Sales, Inc., 272 F.3d 322 (6th Cir. 2001) (court reversed summary judgment to the dealer and finance company; consumer presented evidence that the dealer markups on the cash price for credit customers was 4 to 5 times that of cash customers; court distinguished cases holding that evidence under TILA must show *systematic* disparity in prices; systematic disparity is but one type of proof); Balderos v. City Chevrolet, 214 F.3d 849 (7th Cir. 2000) (even though car club membership fee was voluntary, part of it is a disguised finance charge if the consumer could prove that the excess part of the fee was imposed on buyers who did not purchase the membership and not imposed on those who did opt for it); Kilbourn v. Candy Ford-Mercury, Inc., 209 F.R.D. 121 (W.D. Mich. 2002) (summary judgment to dealer denied on issue of direct proof but granted as to indirect proof under *Cornist* standard). *Cf.* Hoffman v. Grossinger Motor Corp., 218 F.3d 680 (7th Cir. 2000) (court found that consumer's general proof that a dealer, on average, charged subprime credit customers higher prices than it charged other customers was insufficient to survive a motion for summary judgment in light of dealer's proof that it used a unitary pricing system for its credit and cash customers which resulted in the salespeople trying to sucker everyone, even though a $400 holdback fee was imposed only in subprime financed transactions). For a discussion of the standard necessary to overcome a motion to dismiss, where less proof is required, see Wallace v. Walker Auto Sales, Inc., 155 F.3d 927 (7th Cir. 1998); Sampler v. City Chevrolet Buick Geo, Inc., 2000 U.S. Dist. LEXIS 2322 (N.D. Ill. Feb. 24, 2000), *rev'g* 10 F. Supp. 2d 934 (N.D. Ill. 1998) (see lengthy discussion of this case in note 196, *supra*); Cemail v. Viking Dodge, 982 F. Supp. 1296 (N.D. Ill. 1997); Chancellor v. Gateway Lincoln-Mercury, Inc., 502 S.E.2d 799 (Ga. Ct. App. 1998) (buyer failed to prove cash price was increased to recoup the fee).

199 15 U.S.C. § 1641(a). *See, e.g.*, Irby-Greene v. M.O.R., Inc., 79 F. Supp. 2d 630 (E.D. Va. 2000) (discount not apparent on face of documents; no assignee liability under TILA); Jackson v. South Holland Dodge, Inc., 755 N.E.2d 462 (Ill. 2001), *appeal pending* (dealer practice of pocketing a portion of the service contract charge not apparent on the face; if no TILA liability, no Illinois UDAP liability against the assignee without specific knowledge).

200 For a discussion of this issue, see National Consumer Law Center, Truth in Lending § 7.3.2 (5th ed. 2003 and Supp.).

201 *See generally* § 7.4.6, *supra*.

202 *See also* Cemail v. Viking Dodge, 982 F. Supp. 1296 (N.D. Ill. 1997). For discussions of what other types of evidence might be relevant to establish the real cash price, see § 7.4.6.1, *supra*, and National Consumer Law Center, Truth in Lending § 3.10 (5th ed. 2003 and Supp.).

203 Sampler v. City Chevrolet Buick Geo, Inc., 2000 U.S. Dist. LEXIS 2322 (N.D. Ill. Feb. 24, 2000), *rev'g*, 10 F. Supp. 2d 934 (N.D. Ill. 1998) (see lengthy discussion of this case in note 196, *supra*).

204 *See, e.g.*, Motzer Dodge Jeep-Eagle v. Ohio Atty. Gen., 642 N.E.2d 20 (Ohio Ct. App. 1994); Ciampi v. Ogden Chrysler Plymouth, Inc., 634 N.E.2d 448 (Ill. App. Ct. 1994); Sanders v. Francis, 561 P.2d 1003 (Or. 1977); N.M. Admin. Code tit. 1, § 2.4.1–2.4.3.1. *See also* National Consumer Law Center, Unfair and Deceptive Acts and Practices § 4.6 (6th ed. 2004 and Supp.).

205 *See* National Consumer Law Center, Unfair and Deceptive Acts and Practices § 5.4.3.4 (6th ed. 2004 and Supp.).

206 *See* § 10.6.1, *supra*. Thanks to Tom Domonoske for fleshing out this theory.

11.6.2.2 Related Problems: Loan Packing or Shoddy Cars

Hiking the cash price is not the only option the dealer has to make up the shortfall. "Grossing up" the loan with add-ons will work, too. Adding a $1,000 service contract and $700 in credit insurance premiums to a $5,000 car will take the amount financed up to $6,700. (The dealer also gets the benefit of the mark-up on the service contract and commissions from the credit insurance.[207]) Whether there are hidden finance charges in these add-ons is a question of fact, as well, just as it is with the cash price of the car itself. If a service contract is offered to both cash and credit customers *for the same price*, then it is not a finance charge.[208] However, if service contracts are required only for credit customers, it is a finance charge.[209] Similarly, if credit customers are charged more for the service contract, then the price differential is a finance charge.[210]

Even if the price differential for service contracts is something other than the cash/credit distinction (thus, eliminating the claim that the price includes a hidden finance charge), there may be other problems. For example, differential pricing may violate applicable state regulations on discriminatory pricing.[211] Price differentials with a discriminatory impact on certain customers may raise UDAP and/or civil rights issues. That attorneys working with consumers in minority neighborhoods and on Native American reservations report some of the highest service contract prices in the country raise the question of whether these products may be vehicles for discriminatory pricing.[212] And irrespective of differential pricing issues in relation to add-ons, selling add-ons through "payment packing" raises UDAP issues and other issues, see § 11.6.4, *infra*.[213]

Dealers can accomplish "grossing up" the cash price in a variety of ways in addition to covering for any discount. These markups occur often with the blessing of the assignee funding the sale. These deals are usually spelled out in the dealer agreement. For example, the assignee may set a "funding cap" which allows a dealer to add to the manufacture's suggested retail price up to the cap. Allowable charges include "dealer prep," usually a percentage of the manufacture's suggested retail price, and "approved dealer value added products," such as GAP and other credit insurance products, service or extended warranty contracts (as just discussed), bird-dog fees (or referral fees), and auto theft registration protection (sometimes referred to as TT Theft Insurance). As long as the sales price minus any downpayment does not exceed the funding cap, the assignee is usually satisfied. Such fees, if separately itemized, could violate the state motor vehicle retail installment act or applicable lender licensing law. If the fees are separately paid by the consumer but do not show up as part of the downpayment or itemized as part of the amount financed, the dealer may be attempting to jack up the purchase price, a practice that could state a UDAP claim.[214] Improper disclosures could trigger TILA as well.[215] If the cash price is inflated to cover the downpayment in order to render its supposed reduction in the cost meaningless, TILA may provide the hook using the hidden finance charge theory discussed earlier in this section.[216]

Rather than messing with the numbers to cover finance-related costs on a subprime deal, a dealer may choose to

---

207 *See* Ch. 8, *supra*, for a discussion of credit insurance. Not only does the dealer profit from these products due to the markup and commission, the service or warranty contracts may also be bogus. Attorneys report that dealers sometimes deny the existence of the service or warranty contract. This occurs when the dealer pockets the entire charge rather than sending a portion to the service or warranting company. The dealer may engage in this unfair and deceptive practice hoping that the car would not need any covered work or, if it does, gambling that the customer will just drop the matter after being run around or that the customer could not produce the contract to prove its existence.

208 Reg. Z, Official Staff Commentary § 226.4(a)-1(i)(D).

209 Official Staff Commentary § 226.4(a)-1(ii)(C).

210 Official Staff Commentary § 226.4(a)-1(iii). In addition, TILA disclosure rules may be violated where the dealer lists the service contract fees as fully paid to a third party service provider, while actually pocketing a large percentage of the charge. *See* National Consumer Law Center, Truth in Lending §§ 3.10, 4.7.3.4 (5th ed. 2003 and Supp.).

211 *See, e.g.*, Iowa Admin. Code r. 191-23.22(6) (prohibiting "unfair discrimination" in rates charges for those service contracts to which the regulation applies. *NB*: The regulation does not apply to manufacturers' service contracts. *See* Iowa Admin. Code r.r. 191-23.4, 191-23.5).

212 *See generally* National Consumer Law Center, Credit Discrimination § 8.5.4 (4th ed. 2005).

213 *See* Taylor Auto Group, Inc. v. Jessie, 527 S.E.2d 256 (Ga. Ct. App. 1999) (upholding class certification order in case in which consumer alleged she was charged for services she did not receive and overcharged for services she did receive; claims include fraud, state RICO, motor vehicle finance act, and UDAP). Dealer "upcharges" or mark-ups on service contracts have also engendered litigation under Truth in Lending, see National Consumer Law Center, Truth in Lending § 4.7.3.4 (5th ed. 2003 and Supp.), and under state deceptive practices acts, see National Consumer Law Center, Unfair and Deceptive Acts and Practices § 5.4.3.6 (6th ed. 2004 and Supp.). *See also* T. Hudson, M. Benoit, J. Looney, *Indirect Auto Finance Dealer Compensation Litigation*, 54 Bus. Lawyer 1301, 1312–1315 (May 1999).

214 *See* Compton v. Altavista Motors, Inc., 121 F. Supp. 2d 932 (W.D. Va. 2000) (though this practice could state a UDAP claim, the plaintiff provided no actual proof that the price was inflated in this case). *See also* Taylor v. Bob O'Connor Ford, Inc., 2000 U.S. Dist. LEXIS 11486 (N.D. Ill. June 29, 2000).

215 Lifanda v. Elmhurst Dodge, Inc., 237 F.3d 803 (7th Cir. 2001) (disclosure of auto theft registration protection fee not clear and conspicuous under TILA for motion to dismiss purposes), *class cert. granted*, 2001 U.S. Dist. LEXIS 9210 (N.D. Ill. June 29, 2001). For disclosure of third party charges, see National Consumer Law Center, Truth in Lending § 4.7.3.4 (5th ed. 2003 and Supp.).

216 Ringenback v. Crabtree Cadillac-Oldsmobile, Inc., 99 F. Supp. 2d 199 (D. Conn. 2000).

switch cars. If the dealer switches to a car that it had acquired for less money, but keeps the $5,000 price tag, it can still make up the discount difference. The consumer gets less value in the car, and this kind of corner-cutting may be one way that subprime customers end up buying cars that break-down quickly.[217] If there appears to be a pattern of default and repossession, it might warrant examining the possibility of a churning scheme.[218]

11.6.3 Negative Equity: Driving "Upside Down"

When homeowners consider buying a different house, most are careful to protect themselves from selling their old house for less than the outstanding mortgage on it. Rather than becoming so burdened, many homeowners faced with that choice will delay buying the new house. Yet that same scenario is increasingly common in the case of auto financing. Given higher prices and the longer life of car loans,[219] the rapid depreciation of cars, and the increasing frequency with which consumers want (or, in the case of consumers who are driving cars that do not work, *need*) to change wheels, it is not at all unusual for the outstanding balance on a car loan to exceed the car's value. When that car is traded in on a new deal, the deficit—the "negative equity"—is likely to be refinanced as part of the loan on the new car. To illustrate: Harold wants a Honda, with a sticker price of $13,000. Harold has a Hyundai, with $8,000 left to pay. But his Hyundai has a fair market value of only $6,000, so Harold has $2,000 negative equity in the Hyundai he wants to trade-in for the Honda.

Dealer practices may vary as to how this $2,000 deficit is reflected on the new loan documents, but it appears to be common to hike the "cash price" of the newly purchased car to absorb—and disguise—the deficit on the trade-in. It works this way: on paper, the dealer gives a trade-in allowance value high enough to cover the payoff deficit (and perhaps a bit more.) In Harold's case, dealer might put down a paper allowance of $8,200, to cover the $2,000 deficit and make it look like Harold's still getting a net positive trade-in credit of $200. But if the dealer stopped with just an inflated trade-in allowance, it would have some real extra costs to absorb ($2,200 in this case). So the dealer then matches the inflated trade-in allowance with an upward ratchet on the

cash price of the car being purchased. The $13,000 purchase price becomes $15,200 on paper. After this numbers game is done, the deficit on the trade-in is totally buried in the inflated trade-in allowance and cash price. The paper figures wrongly make it appear to the consumer[220] as though there is a *positive* net trade-in value, though in fact the trade-in added to the new debt rather than reducing it.

Here's a comparison of Harold's Honda deal, with and without finagling to bury the negative equity:

	Unfinagled Numbers	Finagled Numbers
Cash Price on Honda being purchased	$ 13,000	$ 15,200
Trade-in Allowance	$ 6,000	$ 8,200
less payoff balance	−$8,000	−$8,000
Net trade-in (+/-)	($ 2,000)	$ 200
Unpaid Balance of Cash Price	$ 13,000	$ 15,000
Add other charges	+$2,000	none
		(payoff balance on trade-in)
Amount Financed	$ 15,000	$ 15,000

"So what's the problem?" you say, "the bottom line for the consumer is the same." In Harold's case, the bottom line was indeed the same. Dealers and the finance industry argue that these are just consolidation loans—a service which simply helps consumers get the new car they want. That may be true for some buyers. But it is not always a case of "no harm, no foul."

Deeper in debt: The first possible foul is that the numbers-shuffle can present an impediment to informed decision-making about the second most expensive purchase most people make. While some consumers undoubtedly understand that they are refinancing debt on the car they traded in, it is probable that many do not. Many people (probably most) think of trade-ins as *reducing* the cost of a new car purchase, not adding to it. To the extent that they think about it at all, some consumers may believe that they "sell" their trade-in to the dealer, with the agreed-upon trade-in allowance being the "selling price." The dealer then can recoup its investment (the sales price, any remaining debt assumed with it, and sprucing-up costs) when it sells it to the next customer.

If the numbers explaining the refinanced debt are clearly and comprehensibly laid out in front of them, some consumers may well decide not to stack new debt on top of this old debt—*especially* as it means continuing to pay on a car they no longer own. Those who can afford it may wish to avoid this by making a larger down payment, or pay off the

---

217 In the worst case, the dealer may sell cars it acquired cheaply because they were damaged, prior salvage, recycled lemons, or otherwise in bad condition.

218 *See* National Consumer Law Center, Repossessions and Foreclosures § 10.9.4 (5th ed. 2002 and Supp.).

219 In 1984, the average term for a new car loan was 48.3 months, and the average amount financed was $9,333. 73 Fed. Reserve Bull. A41, Table 1.56 (June 1987). By 1999, the average term for a new car loan was 52.7 months, and the average amount financed was $19,880. 83 Fed. Reserve Bull. A36, Table 1.56 (Feb. 2001).

220 While it would also appear in theory to conceal the negative equity from lenders, the apparent prevalence of the practice and resulting over-valuations which should be obvious to professionals invite questions as to whether they are in fact deceived.

deficit from savings. Others may decide they must buy a cheaper new car, in order to leave room in their budget for refinancing the deficit on the trade. And others, like the homeowners, would probably decide to delay buying a car until the old one was paid for.

Increased opportunity for pricing deception: It is easy for even educated consumers to lose track once the dealer employee called the "F&I" (finance and insurance) person starts shuffling numbers. The employee is playing a shell game with dollars, and in the process, it is not unheard of for a cash price to be inflated beyond the amount justified by the trade-in deficit. In Harold's case, for example, some dealers might have added an extra $500 or $1,000 to the cash price, and hence to his amount financed. In this case, it is clearly not a "no harm, no foul" situation.

Another way the shell game can be played is to "cover" the negative equity by reducing the value of the trade-in, which increases the amount of the negative equity. For example, if the trade-in is worth $8,800 but the balanced owed on it is $9,900, the trade-in is $1,100 "under water." The dealer may reduce the value of the trade-in, often unbeknownst to the consumer, to say $5,900 which jacks up the amount of the negative equity to $4,000 ($9,900 minus $5,900). The $4,000 (rather than the $1,100) is then added to the sales price to inflate the total cash price.

In addition, the dealer may also inflate the downpayment amount if the lender demands that the consumer put down a certain percentage of the cash price and refuses to fund a deal with negative equity. For example, a car loan may show a downpayment of $4,000 when the consumer will state that she only paid $2,500. The difference of $1,500 will be added to the cash price. The dealer file, including a recap sheet, an internal invoice, a finance disposition sheet and a trade-in valuation sheet help to show how the dealer inflated the numbers.

Understanding the numbers is a daunting task. The confusion is reasonable given how the dealer may finagle the math. In one case, the new lease transaction did not reflect the negative equity resulting from the trade-in of two cars in the lease document itself.[221] By disclosing this information in a variety of places, the consumers, not surprisingly, did not understand the effect of the negative equity. The angle of attack used was the California "single document rule." The appellate court found that this behavior violated the single document rule.[222]

Driving upside-down: Negative equity means the consumer is upside-down on the loan—the debt is greater than the value of the asset purchased from the git-go. That leaves the consumer with a bigger deficiency after repossession or an insurance pay-out after an accident. Consequently, a used car loan inflated by negative equity may leave the consumer with a loan that outlives the second car, making it that much harder for the consumer to find needed replacement transportation. Or a consumer struggling to meet the payments cannot sell the second car for an amount sufficient to cover the debt.[223]

There has been little litigation addressing problems arising from negative equity financing.[224] Whether that is because most consumers do not perceive it as a problem, or because most consumers do not perceive it at all (which itself could be a problem) is unknown. Depending on the facts and circumstances, it might raise questions under a number of laws.

Lemon law buy-backs: To date, more of the debate about negative equity has been in the context of lemon law buy-backs than in the context of front-end purchases. If the manufacturer is required to buy back a lemon car for the "cash price," is it the "cash price" that represents the real price of the lemon, or the listed "cash price" which included the negative equity on the trade-in? The applicable statutory definition of cash price may point to the contract figures,[225] in which case that should be determinative.[226] Proper disclosure of the negative equity deficit as a separate, identified component of the amount financed would avoid this issue.

Truth in Lending: The Official Staff Commentary to Regulation Z was amended in 1998 and 1999 to specifically address negative equity in credit sales. The primary purpose of the amendments was to provide instruction as to how to make disclosures relating to the down payment when there

---

221 Kroupa v. Sunrise Ford, 92 Cal. Rptr. 2d 42 (Cal. Ct. App. 1999).

222 *See* 11.6.8, *infra*.

223 One bankruptcy judge fretted about how difficult this problem makes it for debtors to get and keep necessary transportation: "In this manner, the initial bad judgment becomes self-perpetuating, and has a continuing adverse impact upon debtors." *In re* Brown, 170 B.R. 362, 365 (Bankr. S.D. Ohio 1994).

224 *See State ex rel.* Miller v. Dan Nelson Automotive Group, Inc., Equity No. CE 50210 (Dist. Ct. Polk County, Iowa filed Jan. 7, 2005) (complaint), *available at* www.state.ia.us/government/latest_news/releases/Jan_2005/dnelson.pdf. In the private litigation context, negative equity may create some headaches in the context of determining damages, without being an issue itself. *Compare* Dyer v. Quality Car & Truck Leasing, 1990 Ohio App. LEXIS 2481 (Ohio Ct. App. June 18, 1990) (court held the dealer to its paper valuations as to a positive net equity; lease) *with* Meade v. Nelson Auto Group, 1997 WL 208685 (Ohio Ct. App. Mar. 31, 1997) (consumers granted rescission of lease under Ohio Consumer Sales Practices Act, but return of negative equity pay-off was required without discussion).

225 *E.g.*, Iowa Code § 322G.4(2) pegs the buyback amount to the purchase price, defined in turn as "cash price paid for the motor vehicle appearing in the sales agreement of contract, including any net allowance given for a trade-in vehicle," Iowa Code § 322G.2(17).

226 *Cf.* Strachan v. Ford Motor Credit, 1997 WL 197301 (E.D. Pa. Apr. 17, 1997) (no documents in the lease transaction reflected negative equity, and they did show a trade-in allowance equal to the outstanding lien; defendant also unsuccessful in showing independent evidence of overvaluation on the trade-in).

is negative equity.[227] How the down payment should have been disclosed in a negative equity situation presented genuinely unchartered territory prior to the 1998 Commentary amendment. However, even prior to the 1998 amendment there was no defensible ground for burying the deficit in an inflated cash price, given Regulation Z's definition of cash price.[228] The Supplementary Information to the 1998 Commentary revision clarifies that the deficit "must appear in the itemization of the amount financed," and creditors are given leeway to add categories to the FRB model forms to explain that.[229] Improper disclosure of these items will not give rise to a claim for statutory damages under TIL.[230] Whether a claim might be made for actual damages would depend on the facts.[231] For example, what if Harold had bought his Hyundai under a special promotion, so the APR on the trade-in financing was 4.9%. If he did not understand that the $15,200 Honda price included a $2,000 refinance, and his new rate is 12%, he might have actual damages flowing from the failure to properly disclose the deficit in the itemization.

Where the car dealer charges the sales tax on both the negative equity from the trade-in and on the price of the new car, the dealer should disclose the portion of the sales tax generated by the negative equity as a finance charge because it is only imposed on credit customers.[232]

State credit and UDAP statutes: State credit and UDAP laws may raise questions similar to those under TIL, but definitions are likely to be important. For example, Ohio's retail installment sales act defines cash price as "the price, measured in dollars, agreed upon in good faith by the parties as the price at which the specific goods which are the subject matter of any retail installment sale would be sold if such sale were for cash. . . ."[233] The Ohio Supreme Court has said that, so long as the parties agree to it in good faith, negative equity can be included in "cash price" under that definition, which is a post-negotiation price.[234] But if the negative equity deficit is buried without good faith agreement, even under that definitional scheme there is arguably a RISA violation, as well as a potential UDAP violation.[235] Other states may have definitions of cash price more akin to Truth in Lending's definition, setting a more objective standard. For example, Iowa's definition of cash price is the price at which goods are sold by the seller to cash buyers in the ordinary course of business.[236] The Iowa Consumer Credit Code defines "amount financed," then, as the "cash price of the goods *plus the amount actually paid or to be paid by the seller pursuant to an agreement with the buyer to discharge a security interest in, a lien on, or a debt with respect to property traded in.* . . ."[237] This statutory scheme, like TIL's, seems to preclude burying the trade-in's deficit in the new car's cash price, as well as requiring the consumer's actual agreement that the negative equity be refinanced.

Negative equity might also raise other issues. For example, there may be a question as to whether dealers should

---

227 *See* Official Staff Commentary § 226.2(a)(18)-3, *as amended* 63 Fed. Reg. 16669, 16674 (Apr. 6, 1998), and 64 Fed. Reg. 16614 (Apr. 6, 1999). *See generally* National Consumer Law Center, Truth in Lending §§ 4.6.2.3, 4.6.2.4 (5th ed. 2003 and Supp.); K. Rojc & T. Juffernbruch, *The New Approach to Trade-In Vehicle Disclosures Under Regulation Z*, 54 Bus. Lawyer 1317 (May 1999). The 1999 amendment addresses the issue of how to make the down payment disclosure when there is both negative equity in the trade-in and a cash down payment, a situation which also affects the disclosure of the "total sale price," Reg. Z, § 226.18(j). The 1999 Commentary amendment gives guidance for that disclosure, as well, Official Staff Commentary § 226.18(j)-3, *as amended by* 64 Fed. Reg. 16614 (Apr. 6, 1999).

228 Reg. Z, § 226.2(a)(9). While the definition lists some permissible optional additions, they all relate to "the property that is the subject of the transaction," such as accessories, taxes, license fees, service contracts, etc. To analogize to the lease context, the "agreed upon value" of a leased vehicle does not encompass negative equity on a trade-in. Official Staff Commentary to Reg. M § 213.4(f)(1)-1.

229 *See* Supplemental Information, 63 Fed. Reg. at 16673, regarding Official Staff Commentary § 226.18(c)-2(iii), *as amended* 63 Fed. Reg. at 16677 (Apr. 6, 1998). *See also* K. Rojc & T. Juffernbruch, *The New Approach to Trade-In Vehicle Disclosures Under Regulation Z*, 54 Bus. Lawyer 1317, 1326–1328 (May 1999).

230 The itemization of the amount financed, the cash price, the down payment, and the total sale price are not among the enumerated violations which trigger statutory damages. *See generally* National Consumer Law Center, Truth in Lending §§ 4.7.3, 4.7.5, 8.6.5.2 (5th ed. 2003 and Supp.).

231 Actual damages are available for failure to comply with any disclosure requirement under Parts B (which includes the disclosure requirements), D and E of TIL, except as specifically limited. 15 U.S.C. § 1640(a)(1). The standard for actual damages, however, is difficult to meet. *See* National Consumer Law Center, Truth in Lending § 8.5 (5th ed. 2003 and Supp.).

232 Parra v. Borgman Ford Sales, 2001 U.S. Dist. LEXIS 16666 (W.D. Mich. Oct. 5, 2001).

233 Ohio Rev. Code Ann. § 1317.01(K).

234 Johns v. Ford Motor Credit, 551 N.E.2d 179 (Ohio 1990) (interpreting Ohio Rev. Code Ann. § 1317.01(K)). Since the Reg. Z Commentary clarification that the negative equity should be a line item in the amount financed, state definitions of "cash price" which would seem to permit buried negative equity deficits might be inconsistent with TIL. *See* K. Rojc & T. Juffernbruch, *The New Approach to Trade-In Vehicle Disclosures Under Regulation Z*, 54 Bus. Lawyer 1317, 1324–1325 (May 1999).

235 *See also* Castro v. Union Nissan, Inc., 2002 WL 1466810 (N.D. Ill. July 8, 2002) (dealer liable under UDAP act for selling a car for $1,000 over the advertised price; the inflated price likely occurred as a result of the negative equity, though this is not clear from the decision). *Cf.* Motzer Dodge Jeep Eagle v. Ohio Att'y Gen., 642 N.E.2d 20 (Ohio Ct. App. 1994) (dealer violated UDAP regulations by failing to make car available at advertised price; dealer's attempted use of negative equity as justification failed).

236 Iowa Code § 537.1301(8). It goes on to permit incidental additions similar to TIL's. *See also* K. Rojc & T. Juffernbruch, *The New Approach to Trade-In Vehicle Disclosures Under Regulation Z*, 54 Bus. Lawyer 1317 (May 1999).

237 Iowa Code § 537.1301(4)(a).

have lenders' licenses to make what is essentially a consolidation loan, financing more than just the purchase price of the new vehicle. However, in the wake of the greater attention focused on the issue of negative equity after the 1998 TIL Commentary amendments, there were efforts in several states to pass legislation to assure that dealers could finance the negative equity on a trade-in.[238]

Another possible issue relates to GAP insurance. GAP coverage is sold to cover the deficiency between an outstanding loan balance and the amount paid out by a property insurer after a loss on the collateral. However, GAP products may limit the payout to a percentage of the collateral's value, such as 110 to 120%. With coverage so limited, dealers must be careful how they tout the benefits of GAP products to consumers who are upside down from the outset due to negative equity (or any other reason), lest they make deceptive representations to sell it.[239]

Damage issues: If the cash price was inflated to cover the negative equity, the sales tax on the purchase was calculated on an inflated sales price on the new purchase. Depending on how sales taxes are calculated, an increase in the sale price of the car can result in the consumer paying more taxes. The difference in taxes is part of the damages incurred.

Where the consumer did not know about the negative equity and did not know that the sales price was raised to hide it, that consumer also did not know that she took out a direct loan from the dealer to pay down the negative equity. If the dealer charged an interest rate higher than the credit on the trade-in, the difference in the rates also constitute actual damages flowing from the non-disclosure.

11.6.4 Payment Packing

Loan packing, a major focus of litigation and enforcement activity against finance companies in the 1980s, is now attracting attention as it relates to auto financing.[240] Padding

a loan with add-ons—particularly the high margin add-ons such as service contracts and the various credit insurance products—gives the dealer considerably more income from a transaction. The lender also earns a higher yield from a higher principal balance. These benefits are evident to both the lender and the dealer. One subprime lender's sales representative excitedly explained at a dealer trade show that a service contract "can add six months to the [loan] term."[241] (It seems subprime logic to extend a debt horizon by six months by adding extra costs at subprime rates, when the rationale for those high rates is that the borrowers in this market are risky. One would think the rational thing to do would be to keep the debt horizon as short as possible, and the debt load as lean as possible to decrease the risk of default.[242])

One way of reducing customer resistance to costly add-ons is "payment packing." While the salesperson and prospective buyer are chatting about the car, the salesperson talks about a monthly payment amount. The natural assumption for the consumer is that the figure is the price of the car at the interest rate the dealer offers. But that payment amount has "room to pack" built in. The amount may be, for example, $20 or $30 higher than the amount that would buy that car. Then, when the salesperson sends the customer to the F&I (finance and insurance) employee, there is room in the payment to hike the cash price, to bump up the interest rate for a yield spread premium, or to pack in the add-ons like service contracts and insurance products. The Washington Attorney General has attacked payment packing as an unfair and deceptive practice.[243] However, two courts have held that state retail installment contract statutes do not prohibit dealer markups on service contracts.[244]

---

238 The Michigan Financial Institutions Bureau has opined that the total cash price can include the negative equity but only if it is separately itemized. Michigan Department of Consumer and Industry Services, Financial Institutions Bureau, *Disclosure of Negative Equity on an Installment Sale Contract*, Motor Vehicle Bulletin 1999-1 Clearinghouse No. 53,511 (July 6, 1999). An example of the manner in which negative equity must be listed is attached to the Bulletin. *See also* K. Rojc & T. Juffernbruch, *The New Approach to Trade-In Vehicle Disclosures Under Regulation Z*, 54 Bus. Lawyer 1317 (May 1999).

239 *See generally* National Consumer Law Center, Truth in Lending § 3.9.4.7 (5th ed. 2003 and Supp.) (discussing 1996 amendments to Reg. Z, §§ 226.4(b)(10), 226.4(d)(3) concerning GAP insurance).

240 *See* § 8.5.4, *supra*. That does not mean the problem has been solved with respect to finance companies, of course. It was among the problems mentioned in Senate hearings on predatory home equity lending practices conducted in 1998. *See Equity Predators: Stripping, Flipping and Packing Their Way to Prof-

its: Hearing before the Special Committee on Aging United States Senate*, 105th Cong. 2d Sess., 33–34, Serial No. 105-18 (Mar. 16, 1998).

241 The exchange was recorded by Dateline NBC for a segment on subprime lending which aired December 8, 1998. This particular exchange did not appear in the broadcast.

   In some instances, either the dealer or the lender (or both) may also have an ownership interest in the company producing the add-on products, or a reinsurance company, so that the financial rewards are greater than just commissions and mark-up.

242 One might speculate that perhaps another reason for high margin add-ons, high-rates, and artificially increased loan terms is that there simply is not enough margin on affordable rates for affordable cars to attract creditors in these heady days. The "risk" of the borrower, in that case, would be just a convenient excuse to avoid dealing with what is, instead, a structural problem in the economy.

243 Washington v. Resource Dealer Group, Inc., Clearinghouse No. 52,057 (Wash. Super. Ct. May 22, 1998). *See* National Consumer Law Center, Unfair and Deceptive Acts and Practices § 5.4.3.7 (6th ed. 2004 and Supp.). *See also* Ferrari v. Howard, 2002 WL 1500414 (Ohio App. July 11, 2002) (charging $19 extra for a filing fee is a UDAP violation).

244 King v. Ford Motor Credit Co., 668 N.W.2d 357 (Mich. Ct. App. 2003); Homziak v. Gen. Elec. Capital Warranty Corp., 839 A.2d 1076 (Pa. Super. Ct. 2003).

11.6.5 Yo-Yo Deals, a.k.a. Spot Delivery

"We'd like to think it over" is not a phrase that is music to a seller's ears. A dealer may try, instead, to get the buyer psychologically and economically invested, and preferably contractually bound. (And, of course, some buyers may be just as eager to drive that new car off the lot right away.) To clinch the deal immediately, dealers may ask the consumers to sign a purchase agreement and a fully completed retail installment contract, so they can buy that new beauty on the spot. But financing arrangements may not be complete, as the dealer has no intention of keeping the account in-house. Its intent is to transfer the paper to an indirect lender, so, at least in the dealer's mind, the deal is contingent on its ability to assign the paper. Whether that is so as a legal matter is often the issue the practitioner faces.[245]

Just how obvious this contingency is to the consumer varies considerably. And the degree of good faith involved in the dealer's representations to the consumer of the possibility of finalizing the contract at those terms also varies: perhaps the dealer has received final approval from the lender (who later backs out); perhaps the lender gave only preliminary approval, subject to verification. Perhaps the dealer has not gotten any bites at all, or has not even tried—and is using phony, low-balled finance terms as a deceptive inducement.

If the dealer does not place the loan, or does not place it on the terms reflected in the retail installment contract, it then contacts the consumers and offers them one or more options: bring the car back; find their own financing; or sign a new contract at different terms. In the latter case, it is usually at a higher rate, and perhaps asks for additional money down.[246] Particularly if the consumer's trade-in has been sold, the consumer is stuck. Or the consumer may already have incurred other costs, such as more expensive insurance on the new car.[247] If the consumer does not return

the car or sign the new, harsher terms, the dealer may repossess the car, even though the consumer has not defaulted.[248] Some contracts even purport to give the dealer the right to keep the trade-in if the financing falls through as "liquidated damages." That is clearly improper, and some state attorneys general have brought UDAP enforcement actions against this practice.[249]

Spot delivery can raise a range of legal concerns: basic contract principles;[250] retail installment sales acts issues;[251]

---

245 Attorneys should discover all of the dealer files on the transaction with particular attention paid to getting the outside part of the "dealer's jacket." This may list the consumer's credit score which helps to determine if the dealer knew from the outset that the consumer would or would not obtain favorable financing or any financing at all. The jacket may also contain notes of relevant conversations.

246 Industry slang suggests that this may not always be done in the best of faith. "Gimme back," "yo-yo deal" and "bushing" (short for "ambushing," perhaps?) are some of the terms used to describe this practice. For a fuller description of the yo-yo deal, see Christopher V. Langone and Joel D. Dabisch, *Have You Been "Spotted"? Recognizing and Attacking One of the Most Widespread Automobile Abuses*, 12 Loy. Consumer L. Rep. 108 (2000).

247 *See, e.g.,* Sapia v. Regency Motors of Metairie, Inc., 276 F.3d 747 (5th Cir. 2002) ("voluntary" return of the consumer's car by his father after the financing fell through when the consumer left the country on a trip and did not respond to requests to return the car held not a wrongful repossession); Johnson v. Grossinger Motorcorp, Inc., 753 N.E.2d 431 (Ill. App. 2001)

(conversion and wrongful repossession claim dismissed where a credit contingency clause existed in the contract).

248 *See, e.g.,* Ed Bozarth Chevrolet, Inc. v. Black, 96 P.3d 272 (Kan. App. 2003) (in the context of a replevin action, court finds that the consumer knew of the conditional financing arrangement because she took the car home after signing conditional agreements, even though she was not given a copy of the yo-yo contract until a few days later).

249 Illinois, Pennsylvania, and Washington, among them.

250 Harris v. Castle Motor Sales, Inc., 2001 U.S. Dist. LEXIS 5797 (N.D. Ill. May 7, 2001) (court denied dealer's motion to dismiss where the consumer alleged that the contract signed a blank buyer's order and installment contract; dealer did not inform the consumer of the credit terms until 10 days later, beyond a 5-day limit in the contract); Fox v. The Montell Corp., 2001 U.S. Dist. LEXIS 3403 (N.D. Ill. Mar. 19, 2001) (dealer's motion to dismiss denied based upon an ambiguous contract term related to cancellation; extrinsic evidence permissible to clarify); Walker Mobile Home Sales, Inc. v. Walker, 965 S.W.2d 271 (Mo. App. 1998) (consumer did not breach retail installment contract entered into with mobile home dealer before financing fell through because the RISC superseded the purchase agreement; the RISC unconditionally stated that the buyer pay the mobile home dealer monthly payments which the consumer had tendered each month; consumer's counterclaim against the lender failed because the consumer could not prove damages arising from the lender's conduct in pulling out of the financing after its commitment since the consumer could enforce the RISC against the dealer). *But see* Burns v. Elmhurst Auto Mall, Inc., 2001 U.S. Dist. LEXIS 6385 (N.D. Ill. May 16, 2001) (binding contract at the outset even though no time frame to cancel or notify the customer included).

251 Even when a dealer includes a contingency clause, the clause may be invalid. For example, a state's installment sale statute may not allow such conditional sales. *See* National Consumer Law Center, Unfair and Deceptive Acts and Practices § 5.4.5 (6th ed. 2004 and Supp.). Other possible TILA violations include failing to provide consumers with their copy of the TIL disclosures when they become obligated. *See* National Consumer Law Center, Truth in Lending § 4.3.6 (5th ed. 2003 and Supp.). Calculating the APR using the wrong consummation date is actionable. Rucker v. Sheehy Alexandria, Inc., 228 F. Supp. 2d 711 (E.D. Va. 2002). For a larger discussion of the TILA ramifications in the yo-yo context, see National Consumer Law Center, Truth in Lending § 4.4.2 (5th ed. 2003 and Supp.). *See also* Pennsylvania v. Metro Chrysler-Plymouth Jeep-Eagle, Inc., No. 1208 M.D. 1996 (Pa. Commonw. Court, Jan. 10, 1997), Clearinghouse No. 52,518A (enforcement action filed by the attorney general; consent petition for permanent injunction entered requiring compliance with the state motor vehicle retail installment sales act in spot delivery case); Michigan Department of Commerce, Financial Institutions Letter to Licensee (May 22, 1989), Clearinghouse No. 52,519 (agency determination that motor vehicle installment sales contract con-

UDAP claims;[252] Truth in Lending;[253] fraudulent suppres-

ditioned upon assignment violates the motor vehicle installment sales finance act); Michigan Automobile Dealers Association, Dealer Advisory (Oct. 10, 1997), Clearinghouse No. 52,519. However, some states have amended their laws to allow conditional retail installment contracts or buyer orders under certain conditions. These provisions may be found in the retail installment contract act or in motor vehicle titling or insurance laws. *See, e.g.,* La. Rev. Stat. § 32:1254(N)(3)(f) (prohibits spot delivery transaction except under certain conditions); N.H. Rev. Stat. Ann. § 361-A:10-b (requiring a disclosure of the conditional nature of the sale and of the obligations of the parties in the event the financing is approved or disapproved); N.C. Gen. Stat. § 20-75.1 (permits the "conditional" delivery of a car providing dealer's insurance covers the car until the financing is final); Va. Code § 46.2-1530(A)(12) (requires a bold type notice in the buyer's order stating that the sale is conditional upon approval of the "proposed" retail installment sales contract and buyer may cancel if the car is returned in the same condition, normal wear and tear excepted, within 24 hours of notification of the denial of credit); Wash. Rev. Code § 46.70.180(4) (spot delivery prohibited except in certain circumstances). *See also* King v. King Motor Co. of Ft. Lauderdale, 2005 WL 545098 (Fla. Dist. Ct. App. 2005) (indicating that Florida statutes recognize and, therefore permit, conditional sales agreements).

252 Castro v. Union Nissan, Inc., 2002 WL 1466810 (N.D. Ill. July 8, 2002) (summary judgment for the consumer granted where the dealer refused to return the downpayment and trade-in after the dealer was unable to obtain financing); Williams v. Thomas Pontiac-GMC-Nissan-Hyundai, 1999 U.S. Dist. LEXIS 15045 (N.D. Ill. Sept. 24, 1999) (motion to dismiss UDAP claim denied where consumer alleged that the dealer misrepresented that it was willing to sell her an automobile on the terms agreed to in the retail installment contract; contract signed on August 24, 1998 contained clause allowing dealer to cancel within 3 days; dealer tried to cancel about 10 days later and repossessed the car when buyer refused); Valley Nissan v. Davilla, 133 S.W.2d 702 (Tex. App. 2003) (consumer was told that financing for a used truck was approved when it was not; consumer's trade-in was sold; consumer was awarded economic damages for UDAP violation which were trebled, mental anguish, loss of use of her truck, and attorney fees). *But see* Geller v. Onyx Acceptance Corp., 2001 WL 1711313 (Cal. Super. Ct. Nov. 13, 2001) (court discusses spot delivery and agrees that dealers using a standard California form do create a condition subsequent and that dealers do immediately transfer ownership and title). For the most comprehensive discussion of UDAP claims in this context, see National Consumer Law Center, Unfair and Deceptive Acts and Practices § 5.4.5 (6th ed. 2004 and Supp.).

253 Bragg v. Bill Heard Chevrolet, Inc., 374 F.3d 1060 (11th Cir. 2004) (under Florida law, consumation occurred when the consumer signed the RISCs; any other holding would permit the dealer to give TIL disclosures after the consumer signed the contracts); Holley v. Gurnee Volkswagon and Oldsmobile, Inc., 2001 WL 243191 (N.D. Ill. Jan. 4, 2001) (dealer's motion for summary judgment denied on timing of TILA disclosures); Rayburn v. Car Credit Center Corp., 2000 U.S. Dist. LEXIS 14944 (N.D. Ill. Oct. 10, 2000) (lender's motion to dismiss denied where there was a question of fact as to the accuracy of the TILA disclosures and as to whether the contract for financing was firm at the outset); Fogle v. William Chevrolet/Geo, Inc., 2000 U.S. Dist. LEXIS 11556 (N.D. Ill. 2000) (summary judgment for dealer denied on one of two car transactions at issue in the case as the facts were disputed regarding whether

the documents were signed in blank); Heltzel v. Mecham Pontiac, 730 P.2d 235 (Ariz. 1986) (purchase order and retail installment contract was a binding agreement; jury award for dealer's breach of contract in repossessing car on claiming that the buyer was in default and for estoppel claim upheld). *See also* Nigh v. Koons Buick Pontiac GMC, Inc., 319 F.3d 119 (4th Cir. 2003), *cert. granted on other grounds*, 124 S. Ct. 1144 (2004) (consumer became obligated when he signed a buyer's order and retail installment contract even though the contract was superseded by a subsequent agreement; TILA applied and it was violated due to charge for a "Silencer" product), *aff'd on other grounds*, Koons Buick Pontiac GMC, Inc. v. Nigh, 125 S. Ct. 460 (2004); Rucker v. Sheehy Alexandria, Inc., 228 F. Supp. 2d 711 (E.D. Va. 2002) (in yo-yo sale, dealer miscalculated the APR by using the date of the first financing contract, not the date of the true consummation (the date of the second contract)); Losada v. Dale Baker Oldsmobile, Inc., 91 F. Supp. 2d 1087 (W.D. Mich. 2000) (copies of TIL disclosures not given until several days after consummation [i.e., consummation being the date on which contract was signed by consumer, not date financing approved] which violated TIL), *later proceedings*, 197 F.R.D. 321 (W.D. Mich. 2000) (class certification granted), 136 F. Supp. 2d 719 (W.D. Mich. 2001) (damages are available under the motor vehicle retail installment sales act for failure to provide disclosures in a timely way); Williams v. Thomas Pontiac-GMC-Nissan-Hyundai, 1999 U.S. Dist. LEXIS 15045 (N.D. Ill. Sept. 24, 1999) (motion to dismiss TILA claim denied where consumer alleged that the disclosures were inaccurate because she never received the credit as stated in the contract; retail installment contract signed on August 24, 1998 contained clause allowing dealer to cancel within 3 days; dealer tried to cancel about 10 days later and repossessed the car when buyer refused). *But see* Janikowski v. Lynch Ford Inc., 210 F.3d 765 (7th Cir. 2000) (court found no TIL violation where separate disclosures were provided before consumer signed each of two contracts; consumer was aware that financing was not firm and the consumer could have cancelled and returned the car in between financing deals as the contingency applied to both parties; bad facts drove this decision); Scroggins v. LTD, Inc., 251 F. Supp. 2d 1277 (E.D. Va. 2003) (no TILA violation as court held that disclosures were accurate at the time of consummation; court did not distinguish between conditions precedent and conditions subsequent); Najieb v. William Chrysler-Plymouth, 2002 WL 31906466 (N.D. Ill. Dec. 31, 2002) (summary judgment for dealer granted on TILA claim; dealer need not mark the APR as an estimate where contract contained a condition precedent); Harris v. Castle Motor Sales, Inc., 2001 U.S. Dist. LEXIS 5797 (N.D. Ill. May 7, 2001) (court denied dealer's motion to dismiss TILA claim where the consumer alleged that the contract signed a blank buyer's order and installment contract); Burns v. Elmhurst Auto Mall, Inc., 2001 U.S. Dist. LEXIS 6385 (N.D. Ill. May 16, 2001) (TILA claim dismissed; court found a binding contract at the outset even though no time frame to cancel or notify the customer included); Fogle v. William Chevrolet/Geo, Inc., 2000 U.S. Dist. LEXIS 11556 (N.D. Ill. 2000) (summary judgment for dealer granted regarding one of two car transactions at issue in this case on same grounds as in *Janikowski*); Fox v. The Montell Corp., 2001 U.S. Dist. LEXIS 3403 (N.D. Ill. Mar. 19, 2001) (dealer's motion to dismiss TILA claim denied based upon an ambiguous contract term related to cancellation; extrinsic evidence permissible to clarify); Jasper v. New Rogers Pontiac, Inc., 1999 U.S. Dist. LEXIS 17578 (N.D. Ill. Nov. 5, 1999) (no TIL violation based upon a scant record on the issue of when credit was

sion;[254] the Equal Credit Opportunity Act notice require-ments;[255] wrongful repossession;[256] usury;[257] and even conversion if the trade-in is not returned.[258] The dealer may also be estopped from denying validity of the original purchase order when the consumer relied upon it in good faith to her detriment.[259] Given outrageous facts, even a kidnapping-type of claim can prevail.[260]

11.6.6 Yield Spread Premiums

Yield spread premiums in the mortgage context are described in § 11.5.4.3, *supra*.[261] There are fewer tools to attack yield spread premiums in the auto loan context than in the mortgage context.[262] Case law challenging yield spread premiums in the car finance context is mixed. The facts are very important: if the borrower is not sophisticated, and perhaps the dealer made representations about getting the buyer a good financing deal and/or there is an agency relationship between the dealer and the consumer of which the lender was aware, a UDAP[263] or

---

actually extended); Johnson v. Grossinger Motorcorp, Inc., 753 N.E.2d 431 (Ill. App. 2001) (court accepted argument that there was never a contract in the first place as contract was conditional; therefore, no TILA claim possible as no credit contract). For a full discussion of TIL violations in spot delivery cases, see National Consumer Law Center, Truth in Lending §§ 4.3.2, 4.3.6, 4.4.5 (5th ed. 2003 and Supp.).

254 *See* Pescia v. Auburn Ford-Lincoln Mercury, Inc., 68 F. Supp. 2d 1269 (M.D. Ala. 1999) (summary judgment for dealer denied on claim that dealer failed to disclose that the sale was not final, was subject to financing approval, and that the terms and conditions of the final contract may differ from the contract that the consumer signed), *aff'd without op.*, 31 Fed. Appx. 202, 2001 U.S. App. LEXIS 29758 (11th Cir. 2001).

255 Treadway v. Gateway Chevrolet Oldsmobile Inc., 362 F.3d 971 (7th Cir. 2004) (car dealer solicited consumer and then decided not to send her credit information to any lender; dealer, nevertheless, brought the consumer in to tell her that a lender would only finance a new car, not a used one, and that she needed a co-signor; the co-signor actually ended up buying and financing the car in her own right, unbeknownst to her; court decided that a car dealer that regularly decides not to send credit applications to any lender is a "creditor" under the Equal Credit Opportunity Act and must send an adverse action notice; Fair Credit Reporting Act adverse action provisions implicated as well); Cannon v. Metro Ford, Inc., 242 F. Supp. 2d 1322 (S.D. Fla. 2002); Davis v. Regional Acceptance Corp., 2002 U.S. Dist. LEXIS 16775 (E.D. Va. Sept. 5, 2002); Fox v. The Montrell Corp., 2001 WL 293632 (N.D. Ill. Mar. 19, 2001; Williams v. Thomas Pontiac-GMC-Nissan-Hyundai, 1999 U.S. Dist. LEXIS 15045 (N.D. Ill. Sept. 24, 1999).

256 Holley v. Gurnee Volkswagon and Oldsmobile, Inc., 2001 WL 243191 (N.D. Ill. Jan. 4, 2001) (wrongful repossession can state a UDAP and fraud claim where dealer acted as though the consumer was in default when she alleges she was not); Rayburn v. Car Credit Center Corp., 2000 U.S. Dist. LEXIS 14944 (N.D. Ill. Oct. 10, 2000) (claim for wrongful repossession stated).

257 The argument is that the retail installment contract should not impose interest on the consumer until the consumer got the benefit of the credit. In the yo-yo situation, the "benefit" arguably occurs when the dealer signs title over to the consumer and delivers the car.

258 *See generally* National Consumer Law Center, Unfair and Deceptive Acts and Practices § 5.4.6.13 (6th ed. 2004 and Supp.) for a discussion of some of the applicable legal theories which can be brought when spot delivery occurs.

259 *See* Heltzel v. Mecham Pontiac, 730 P.2d 235 (Ariz. 1986).

260 *See* Ron Nissimov, *Kids Awarded $22,000 With Mom as Lawyer; Woman Says Car Dealer Tried to Use Children as "Ransom,"* The Houston Chronicle, Dec. 11, 1999 at A1.

261 That's where the interest rate is hiked over the rate underwriting guidelines dictate, and the middleman, in this case the dealer, takes a slice of the difference. *See also* Geller v. Onyx Acceptance Corp., 2001 WL 1711313 (Cal. Super. Ct. Nov. 13, 2001) (discussion of how dealer participation works, at least with this lender; court agreed with lender's rendition of why dealer participation payments are not kickbacks and, therefore, do not violate UDAP act; failure to disclose the payment also is not a UDAP violation). "Dealer participation" is a related concept. This is "one of the most prevalent methods by which finance companies compensate dealers who sell installment paper." Thomas B. Hudson, Michael A. Benoit & Joseph D. Looney, *Update on Indirect Auto Finance Dealer Compensation Litigation and Other Pertinent Litigation*, 56 Bus. Lawyer 1113, 114 n.5 (May 2001). It occurs when the finance company buys the contract from the dealer for the amount financed listed on the loan documents plus a portion of the finance charge disclosed on the contract. *Id.*

262 The Real Estate Settlement Procedures Act (RESPA) applies to mortgage loans only. *See* Ch. 12, *infra*. Some cases hold that mortgage brokers have a fiduciary responsibility, as well, §§ 11.5.4.2, *supra*, 12.9, *infra*. However, dealers are sellers, and at least nominally creditors, though they act as arrangers; the duty of a creditor to a debtor is not ordinarily that of a fiduciary. *See* § 12.9, *infra*.

263 *Compare* Gaddy v. Galarza Motor Sport L.T.D., 2000 U.S. Dist. LEXIS 13881 (N.D. Ill. Sept. 20, 2000) (the failure to disclose states a UDAP claim; Taylor v. Bob O'Connor Ford, Inc., 2000 U.S. Dist. LEXIS 11486 (June 29, 2000) (consumer's allegation regarding agency survived a motion to dismiss); Adkinson v. Harpeth Ford Mercury, 1991 Tenn. App. LEXIS 114 (Tenn. Ct. App. Feb. 15, 1991) (auto dealer who hiked financing rate by 2 1/2% and kept the excess violated state UDAP statute) *and* Fairman v. Schaumburg Toyota, Inc., 1996 WL 392224 (N.D. Ill., July 10, 1996) (dealer promised to find financing on the best terms available) *with* Baldwin v. Laurel Ford Lincoln Mercury, Inc., 32 F. Supp. 2d 894 (S.D. Miss. 1998) (no duty to disclose absent affirmative misrepresentation); *Ex parte* Ford Motor Credit, 717 So. 2d 781 (Ala. 1997) (dealer had no duty to disclose a "commission" which resulted in a 3% higher interest rate, even though buyer had asked the direct question of why the interest rate was so high; dealer had responded it was because buyer was a poor credit risk. Because there was no duty to disclose, there was no fraudulent suppression of a material fact within Alabama's fraud law; given the buyer's personal history, any reliance on the salesman's representation would not have been justifiable. Bramlett had been employed at a dealership, and bought and sold 200 vehicles in his own used car business. Consequently he was "more than adequately knowledgeable."); Kunert v. Mission Fin. Serv. Corp., 1 Cal. Rptr. 3d 589 (Ct. App.

RICO[264] might be stated.

Like yield spread premiums in the mortgage context, there is a possibility that these premiums might be a vehicle for discriminatory pricing. Two federal courts in Tennessee granted class certification and denied virtually all of the defendants' motions to dismiss the ECOA claims in cases against the financing arms of two major auto manufacturers.[265] Documents in the two cases suggest that both NMAC and GMAC have a standard, nationwide policy of agreeing to make loans at one rate, but providing kickbacks to dealer who arrange the loans at higher interest rates. Both companies place borrowers in one of several risk tiers. Each tier has a published "buy rate," the interest rate at which the lender is willing to extend a car loan to consumers in that tier. GMAC and NMAC pay an administrative fee to dealers when they write up a loan at the buy rate. In addition, if the

dealer makes loans at rates higher than the buy rate, up to a set maximum, the lender pays the dealer a commission on the upcharge.

This system gives the dealer virtually unfettered discretion. Dealers can charge very different interest rates for identical risks, based on whatever factors the dealer chooses to take into account. One of the direct consequences of this practice is that a study of several Tennessee dealers in the *Coleman* case revealed that African Americans are about 200% more likely to be charged an interest rate markup than similarly situated whites (i.e., whites with the same buy rate). African Americans paid an average of $315.35 more than white customers.

Documents that help to uncover the differential between the actual interest rate (on the loan note) and the buy rate include a credit approval sheet and the dealer and lender rate sheets. The dealer's recap sheet should reveal who made what off of the deal, including the yield spread premium.

The National Automobile Dealers Association has released its explanation of the reasons for differential interest rate pricing above the par rate.[266]

11.6.7 What's in a Name? Who's Who in a Vehicle Retail Installment Sale?

In assessing potential challenges to questionable automobile financing practices, and which parties may be potentially liable, it is important to keep in focus the dual roles that dealers and lenders play in the typical motor vehicle retail installment sales transaction. The dealers' and lenders' nominal roles may differ from their functional roles. Sometimes their legal rights and responsibilities are determined by their functional roles, and sometimes by their legal roles. Experience indicates that this sometimes creates some confusion for all concerned, including dealers.[267]

When the consumer buys the financing and the car together, most often, the retail installment sales contract will name the dealer as the "creditor/seller."[268] The contract

---

2003) (dealer reserve or participation payments do not violate California statute governing conditional sales contracts because the transaction was not a direct lender loan; UDAP claim based on the theory that the buy rate disclosed to the borrower was deceptive failed; no allegation that the lender made any specific representations to the consumers regarding the interest rate); Blon v. Bank One, Akron, N.A., 519 N.E.2d 363 (Ohio 1988) (no duty to disclose rate hike and resulting fee paid to the dealer where no affirmative misrepresentations were made about getting the best deal and no special relationship existed between dealer and consumer); Beaudreau v. Larry Hill Pontiac/Oldsmobile/GMC, Inc., 2004 WL 2168387 (Tenn. App. Mar. 28, 2005) (dealer had no duty to reveal to the consumer that it got a portion of the interest rate increase above the buy rate); Harvey v. Ford Motor Credit Co., 1999 Tenn. App. LEXIS 448 (July 13, 1999), *reconsideration*, 8 S.W.3d 273 (Tenn. App. 1999) (UDAP claim dismissed against finance company where consumer did not tie the finance company to the failure on the part of the dealer to explain the rate structure to the customer) *and* Flowers v. Ford Motor Credit Co., 959 F. Supp. 1467 (M.D. Ala. 1997) (no reliance established). *See also* Balderos v. City Chevrolet, 214 F.3d 840 (7th Cir. 2000) (dealer is not the consumer's agent); Smith v. Precision Chevrolet, No. ATL-L-3156-96 (class cert. Aug. 25, 1998), *discussed in* 5 The Consumer Advocate 25 (Jan./Feb. 1997); T. Hudson, M. Benoit, J. Looney, *Indirect Auto Finance Dealer Compensation Litigation*, 54 Bus. Lawyer 1301, 1302–1306 (May 1999); § 11.6.2.1, *supra*, for a discussion of how to look behind the facade to determine who is the real lender, which can defeat assignee shields to liability.

264 *See* Perino v. Mercury Fin. Co., 912 F. Supp. 313 (N.D. Ill. 1995) (mere failure to disclose insufficient to support a RICO claim); Fairman v. Schaumburg Toyota, Inc., 1996 WL 392224 (N.D. Ill. July 10, 1996). *See also* § 12.6, *infra*.

265 Coleman v. General Motors Acceptance Corp., 196 F.R.D. 315 (M.D. Tenn. 2000), *vacated and remanded on other grounds*, 296 F.3d 443 (6th Cir. 2002) (reversed class certification); Cason v. Nissan Motor Acceptance Corp., Civil Action No. 3-98-0223 (M.D. Tenn. oral decision issued on Aug. 23, 2000), 212 F.R.D. 518 (M.D. Tenn. 2002) (class certified for injunctive and declaratory relief only; applying the Sixth Circuit decision in *Coleman*). These cases have received a fair amount of media attention since the court decisions. *See, e.g.*, Diana B. Henriques, *Extra Costs on Car Loans Draw New Legal Attacks*, N.Y. Times Oct. 27, 2000 A1; Michelle Singletary, *The Color of Money: At High Risk for High Interest Rates*, Washington Post Oct. 29, 2000 H1; ABC News 20/20, Oct. 27, 2000.

266 National Auto. Dealers Ass'n, Statement on Automobile Financing (Oct. 23, 2000), *available at* www.nada.org/Content/NavigationMenu/Newsroom/News_Releases/2000/Misc_10_24_00.htm.

267 It has caused some confusion in the courts, as well. In Riviere v. Banner Chevrolet, Inc., 158 F.3d 335 (5th Cir. 1998), the court held the dealer was not really a creditor, relying on case law interpreting a prior version of TIL's definition of creditor, since amended in relevant part. Upon rehearing, the court reversed itself and held that the dealer was a creditor and remanded as to whether the underlying transaction was a personal or commercial transaction. 184 F.3d 457 (5th Cir. 1999). The opinion was withdrawn, judgment vacated, and rehearing granted, 166 F.3d 727 (5th Cir. 1999). For non-TIL claims, however, looking at the substance, not the form, to argue that the dealer was not truly the lender, can expand the liability net.

268 Truth in Lending requires that the "creditor" be identified, 15 U.S.C. § 1638(a)(1); Reg. Z § 226.18(a).

commonly has an assignment printed on it, by which the "creditor/seller/dealer" assigns the contract to the lender. (Most dealers do not keep the contracts in-house. An exception is the buy-here, pay-here used car lot.[269]) Technically, the assignment is a separate contractual arrangement between the dealer and the lender. In legal form, there are two two-party transactions: one between the consumer and the dealer (the retail installment contract), and a back-end commercial agreement between the dealer and the lender (the assignment). The consumer is a stranger to the second contract—the assignment.[270] In form, the lender and the consumer thus have a relationship only because the lender, as "assignee," has stepped into the shoes of the original creditor, the dealer.

However, the "assignee"/lender frequently takes a quite direct role behind the scenes from the outset, little different from that of an originating lender. Not only may it have furnished the forms to its dealer-partners, but it is likely to have called the shots on any given individual buyer's financing arrangement from the outset. The F&I employee at the dealership probably will have faxed the prospective credit application to a lender, which made the initial credit-granting decision and set the credit terms for that consumer. In these situations, the dealer functions more as a middleman, while the "assignee"/lender acts very much like an original creditor. Furthermore, the second contract, the assignment, may take place immediately. These two transactions almost seem to be one. This difference between form and function gives some dealers an identity crisis. They often view themselves as merely an "arranger" of a contract between the real creditor (the indirect lender) and the consumer, which may lead them to ignore some basic obligations their contract with the buyer imposes on them, most particularly in the spot delivery context, discussed in § 11.6.5, *supra*.

In thinking about potential claims and allocating potential liability, it is important to remember that sometimes the legal role is determinative. But for other claims, responsibility should follow function, not form. In a spot delivery case, the fact that the dealer is the creditor on a credit contract should certainly define its contractual obligation to the consumer. With respect to statutory claims, the statutory definitions will be critical. For Truth in Lending purposes, the dealer, and the dealer only, is a "creditor" if the dealer's name is the one on the contract.[271] But for purposes of the Equal Credit Opportunity Act, the statutory definition of "creditor" broadly encompasses arrangers and assignees, as well as those who extend credit.[272] With the likely exception of TIL claims, the assignee of a consumer car loan, at a minimum, will face derivative liability for the seller's conduct under the FTC holder rule.[273] But if the lender was actively involved in the conduct being challenged, the evidence might warrant holding it jointly accountable with the dealer, primarily liable for its own wrong-doing. Some claims, such as UDAP, usury, common law misrepresentation or fraud, or RICO should permit going behind the contractual designations to look as a factual matter at each party's actual conduct, and each party's consequent liability.[274] A good example of the need to match claims with both form and function can be found in the discount financing context discussed in § 11.2.2.2, *supra*. If the cash price of the car included buried finance charges, the lender/assignee may avoid TIL liability, but the facts may establish a level of knowledge or culpability sufficient to find liability under other theories, such as UDAP, RICO or state credit laws.[275]

Good facts to help prove this theory and motivate a court to look at the substance of the transaction and not the form

---

269   For special problems at buy-here, pay-here lots, see National Consumer Law Center, Unfair and Deceptive Acts and Practices § 5.4.6.13 (6th ed. 2004 and Supp.).

270   As to the parties to the retail sales contract, see Walker Mobile Homes Sales, Inc. v. Walker, 965 S.W.2d 271 (Mo. Ct. App. 1998) (retail installment sales contract was a contract between the buyer and seller; not between the assignee and buyer). As to the second contract, the assignment, see, e.g., Weatherman v. Gary-Wheaton Bank, 676 N.E.2d 206, 212 (Ill. Ct. App.) ("the assignment of a mortgage is a transaction as to which the borrower is completely passive, indeed a stranger"), *subsequent proceedings on procedural matters*, 683 N.E.2d 893, 689 N.E.2d 1147 (Ill. 1997); Broyles v. Iowa Dept. of Soc. Serv., 305 N.W.2d 718, 721 (Iowa 1981) ("An assignment is a contract between the assignor and assignee.").

271   The "creditor" is the person to whom the obligation is initially payable on its face, and there can be only one. Even if a bank has to approve the deal, and takes immediate assignment, the dealer is the sole creditor. Reg. Z § 226.2(a)(17)(i)(B); Official Staff Commentary § 226.2(a)(17)(i)-2. *See generally* National Consumer Law Center, Truth in Lending § 2.3.5 (5th ed. 2003 and Supp.). The lender, the "assignee" has limited TIL liability under 15 U.S.C. § 1641. *See generally* National Consumer Law Center, Truth in Lending § 7.3 (5th ed. 2003 and Supp.).

272   15 U.S.C. § 1691a(e); Reg. B § 202.2(l). *See generally* National Consumer Law Center, Credit Discrimination § 2.2.5 (4th ed. 2005).

273   The Seventh and Eleventh Circuits have recently held that the FTC holder provision on these contracts does not serve to expand TIL's limited assignee liability as to TIL claims. Ellis v. General Motors Acceptance Corp., 160 F.3d 703 (11th Cir. 1998); Taylor v. Quality Hyundai, Inc., 150 F.3d 689 (7th Cir. 1998), *cert. denied*, 525 U.S. 1141 (1999). But if the lender had actual responsibility for the TIL violations, it should be liable as a primary party under UDAP claims, or perhaps under a civil conspiracy or aiding and abetting theory. (Particularly if it is dealing with a small dealer, an indirect lender may actually do the calculations and prepare the TIL forms for the dealership.) *See* § 12.10, *infra*.

274   *See generally* §§ 10.6.1.3.8, 10.6.1.3.9, *supra* (usury); § 12.10, *infra* (fraud and misrepresentation); § 12.12, *infra* (liability checklist); National Consumer Law Center, Unfair and Deceptive Acts and Practices § 6.6 (6th ed. 2004 and Supp.).

275   *See, e.g.*, Wallace v. Walker Auto Sales, Inc., 155 F.3d 927 (7th Cir. 1998). For example, in an instance where the lender coached the dealers as to how much to mark up the cars' prices to recoup financing discounts, it would be hard, indeed, not to consider the lender liable as a primary party.

include a combination of the following: the "assignee" pays a large cut of the interest rate to the dealer; other potential assignees allow for less of a cut to the dealer but the dealer chooses the highest for itself (the reverse competition factor); the dealer makes representations to the consumer that it would find the best rate available; the dealer claims that the assignee is really the lender; direct bonus or other compensation sharing occurs with the employee (often the F&I [finance and insurance] person) who dealt directly with the consumer; the assignee represents that it is the lender; and a sympathetic client who thought that the assignee was the lender and that the dealer was trying to find the best rate. A harmful fact is a recourse agreement because the dealer will argue that it still bears the risk of loss and should be compensated for that risk. Joint advertising with a dealer to promote special deals can help to break through the usual roadblocks to holding the assignee primarily liable.

11.6.8 Single Document and Disclosure Requirements

Many states include a "single document rule" in certain consumer credit statutes, usually a retail installment sales act or a motor vehicle installment sales law. The single document rule is an important deterrent to shell games by dealers and financers. It prevents such ploys as side agreements making the deal contingent, requiring additional consideration, or containing additional promises on the part of the dealer. It prevents the dealer or creditor from taking a "mix and match" approach to the contract, having the consumer sign multiple documents containing contract clauses and later assembling selected clauses into a contract.

The single document rule statutes are of two general types. The first type states that the entire agreement must be contained in a single document.[276] The second type does not

use words like "single document" but achieves the same result[277] by requiring the contract to contain all agreements of the parties.[278] The single document rule is by no means universal, however, and some states have statutes that say that a single document is *not* required.[279]

Many statutes that establish a single document rule also require disclosure of a list of items, usually financial terms such as the amount of the down payment, the cash price, and

---

276 *See* Alaska Stat. § 45.10.010 (except for open-end credit, catalog sales, and consolidated contracts, retail installment contract must be single document); Cal. Civ. Code §§ 2981.9 (motor vehicle retail installment contracts must contain in a single document all of the agreements of the buyer and seller), 2985.8 (similar rule for vehicle leases); Nev. Rev. Stat. § 97; N.Y. Pers. Property Law § 337 (retail lease agreement must be a single document); N.D. Cent. Code § 51-13-02(1) (retail installment contract must be in writing and contain all the agreements of the parties); Or. Rev. Stat. § 83.020 (retail installment contract must be single document and must contain the entire agreement of the parties, except for open-end credit, mail order sales, and consolidated contracts; Pa. Stat. tit. 69, § 1302 (retail installment contract must be single document containing entire agreement of parties; note that this statute does not apply to motor vehicle installment sales); Wash. Rev. Code § 63.14.020 (retail installment contract must be single document containing parties' entire agreement; exceptions for open-end credit, catalog sales, and consolidated sales); Wis. Stat. § 422.303 (consumer credit sales other than open-end credit and in which finance charge is more than a discount for prompt payment). *See also* Mont. Code § 31-1-231(1) (by negative implication, retail installment con-

tract must be single document if seller retains security interest); Wis. Code § 422.303 (in consumer credit sales other than open-end credit and contracts where only finance charge is a discount for prompt payment, customer's obligation to pay the total of payments must be evidenced by a single document; statute specifies several other items that contract must include).

277 *See* Rugumbwa v. Betten Motor Sales, 136 F. Supp. 2d 729, 733 (W.D. Mich. 2001) ("the clear language of the MVISCA and the MFVSA envision the execution of a single, comprehensive installment contract containing all of the agreements made by the parties with regard to the subject matter of the retail installment sale"); Lozada v. Dale Baker Oldsmobile, Inc., 197 F.R.D. 321, 339 (W.D. Mich. 2000). *But see* Scott v. Forest Lake Chrysler-Plymouth-Dodge, 611 N.W.2d 346 (Minn. 2000) (interpreting Minnesota "all agreements" statute to require only that all credit terms be included).

278 *See, e.g.,* Conn. Gen. Stat. § 36a-771(a) [formerly § 42-84] (retail installment contracts must "contain all of the agreements of the parties" and must be completed as to all essential provisions before buyer signs); Fla. Stat. Ann. § 520.07(1)(a) (West); Ky. Rev. Stat. § 190.100 (motor vehicle installment sale contract); Mich. Comp. Laws §§ 492.112 (contract subject to Motor Vehicle Sales Finance Act must "contain all of the agreements between the buyer and the seller relating to the installment sale of the motor vehicle sold" and must be completed in all essential provisions before buyer signs), 566.302 (Motor Vehicle Installment Sales Contract Act); Minn. Stat. § 168.71 (motor vehicle retail installment contracts); Neb. Rev. Stat. §§ 37-1281 (motorboat sales), 60.1417 (vehicle sales); N.J. Rev. Stat. §§ 17:16C-21 (retail installment contracts), 17:16C-63 (home repair contracts); N.Y. Pers. Prop. Law § 302 (motor vehicle retail installment contracts); N.C. Gen. Stat. § 20-303 (motor vehicle installment sales); Ohio Rev. Code §§ 1317.02 (retail installment contracts), 4517.26 (motor vehicle sales); Or. Rev. Stat. § 83.520 (motor vehicle retail installment sales); Pa. Stat. tit. 69, § 613 (motor vehicle sales finance contracts); Va. Code § 29.1-826 (retail installment sales of boats); Wis. Stat. §§ 218.0142 (motor vehicle sales financing), 218.0144 (motor vehicle pre-lease agreements). *See* Martinez v. Rick Case Cars, Inc., 278 F. Supp. 2d 1371 (S.D. Fla. 2003) (dealer's motion to dismiss denied when consumer alleged that the dealer failed to fill in certain essential information on the contract and did not sign it). *See also* N.Y. Pers. Prop. Law § 402(7) (all terms of retail installment contract need not be included in single document, but if they are not then contract must be an open-end credit contract).

279 *See, e.g.,* Fla. Stat. § 520.34(f) (retail installment contract need not be contained in single document); Ga. Code § 10-1-3(c) (retail installment contracts); Mich. Comp. Laws § 445.854 (RISA); Mo. Stat. § 408.260 (retail installment contracts); N.M. Stat. § 56-1-2 (retail installment sales; contracts must be completed as to all essential provisions but need not be a single document); N.Y. Pers. Prop. Law § 402 (same); Tenn. Code Ann. § 47-11-103 (retail installment contracts); Vt. Stat. Ann. tit. 9, § 2405(a) (retail installment contracts).

the payment amount. Such a list is not an exclusive list because, otherwise, the single document rule would be mere surplusage.[280] Agreements of the parties that are not on the list of items that must be disclosed must still be included in the single document.[281]

Single document rules make ineffective:

- An arbitration clause that is found in a buyer's order form but not in the installment sales contract;[282]
- A side agreement making an installment sales contract conditional on financing;[283] and
- Contracts that leave certain terms blank, to be filled in later once financing is arranged.[284]

It is a violation of the single document rule to have the buyer sign a separate agreement to roll negative equity into a new vehicle lease.[285] The agreement regarding the treatment of the negative equity must be included in the new lease.

Some single document rule statutes specify the consequences of a violation. In California[286] and Connecticut, for example, the contract is unenforceable if it is not contained in a single document. In New York, the single document statute applicable to leases says that a violation is a UDAP violation.[287] In a number of states, the credit statute sets forth a penalty, typically denial of the right to collect finance charges, that applies not just to overcharges but also to violation of the single document rule and other procedural requirements.[288] Where the statute does not specify a pen-

alty, or provides only a criminal penalty, a violation will be considered a UDAP violation in most states.[289]

In states that do not have a single document rule, state law requirements regarding disclosure, contract completion, and delivery may fill the gap to some extent. Many state installment credit statutes require that the contract be "completed as to all essential provisions" before the buyer signs and that an exact signed copy of the contract, containing certain specified terms, be delivered to the buyer.[290] These statutes may give the consumer a remedy against an installment seller who withholds the contract, planning to discard it if financing falls through.[291] In Minnesota, the consumer can recover the entire contract amount, plus attorney fees, if the seller intentionally fails to provide a signed copy of the contract.[292]

Usually, the state credit statute requires disclosures for all transactions that meet its definitions, even if the transaction

---

280 Kroupa v. Sunrise Ford, 77 Cal. App. 4th 835, 92 Cal. Rptr. 2d 42 (1999).

281 *Id. But see* LaChappelle v. Toyota Motor Credit Corp., 126 Cal. Rptr. 2d 32 (Cal. Ct. App. 2002) (not a violation of the rule to fail to include terms of a trade-in agreement on the car lease unless the trade-in agreement is part of the lease agreement).

282 Rugumbwa v. Betten Motor Sales, 136 F. Supp. 2d 729, 733 (W.D. Mich. 2001).

283 Lozada v. Dale Baker Oldsmobile, Inc., 197 F.R.D. 321, 339 (W.D. Mich. 2000). *But see* Scott v. Forest Lake Chrysler-Plymouth-Dodge, 611 N.W.2d 346 (Minn. 2000). *See generally* National Consumer Law Center, Unfair and Deceptive Acts and Practices § 5.4.5 (6th ed. 2004 and Supp.) (discussion of contract requirements for yo-yo sales; note that some states have rules or statutes that allow and regulate yo-yo sales despite single document rules).

284 Keyes v. Brown, 232 A.2d 486 (Conn. 1967); Weltchek v. Ford Motor Credit Co., 1982 Ohio App. LEXIS 15749 (July 30, 1982) (seller's assignee had no right to repossess vehicle when buyer's copy of contract did not include payment due date).

285 Kroupa v. Sunrise Ford, 77 Cal. App. 4th 835, 92 Cal. Rptr. 2d 42 (1999).

286 Cal. Civ. Code §§ 2983 (with some exceptions, motor vehicle retail installment contract is unenforceable if not contained in single document), 2988.7 (with some exceptions, lease is rescindable if not contained in single document). *See also* Angel v. YFB Hemet, Inc., 2004 WL 1058180 (Cal. Ct. App. Apr. 30, 2004) (not published) (court upheld jury verdict that the single document rule was violated and the trial court's award of restitution).

287 N.Y. Pers. Prop. Law § 346.

288 *See, e.g.,* Cal. Civ. Code §§ 1812.7 (RISA); Conn. Gen. Stat. § 36a-786 (willful violations); N.Y. Pers. Prop. Law §§ 307

(uncorrected willful violations in motor vehicle retail installment contracts), 414 (uncorrected willful violations in retail installment contracts); N.D. Cent. Code 51-13-07; Or. Rev. Stat. § 83.170 (bars collection of service charges, official fees, delinquency, or collection charges for nonconforming contracts); Pa. Stat. tit. 69, § 2202 (installment sales of goods or services); Wash. Rev. Code § 63.14.180; Wis. Stat. §§ 425.304 (RISA), 218.0142(5) (MVRISA). *See also* Lozada v. Dale Baker Oldsmobile, Inc., 136 F. Supp. 2d 719 (W.D. Mich. 2001) (denial of finance charge is penalty for violation of MVISCA single document rule, but not for denial of MVSFA requirement of delivery of contract), *later op. at* 145 F. Supp. 2d 878 (W.D. Mich. 2001); Cal. Civ. Code § 2988.5(a) (statutory damages for vehicle leases); Kenworthy v. Bolen, 564 P.2d 835 (Wash. Ct. App. 1977).

289 *See* National Consumer Law Center, Unfair and Deceptive Acts and Practices § 3.2.7 (6th ed. 2004 and Supp.). *But see* Nigh v. Koons Buick Pontiac GMC, Inc., 143 F. Supp. 2d 535 (E.D. Va. 2001) (consumer cannot assert UDAP claim for violation of requirement of delivery of retail installment contract that was contained in statute that created comprehensive scheme of administrative enforcement).

290 *See, e.g.,* Ariz. Rev. Stat. § 44-286; 815 Ill. Comp. Stat. Ann. § 375/3 (motor vehicle installment sales); Mich. Comp. Laws §§ 492.112 (Motor Vehicle Sales Finance Act), 566.302 (Motor Vehicle Installment Sales Contract Act); Mont. Code § 31-1-231 (RISA); Ohio Rev. Code § 1317.2 (RISA); Wis. Stat. §§ 218.0142 (motor vehicle installment sales), 218.0144 (motor vehicle pre-lease agreements). *See* Lozada v. Dale Baker Oldsmobile, Inc., 136 F. Supp. 2d 719 (W.D. Mich. 2001) (finding statutory penalty of denial of finance charges to be available for violation of MVISCA but not MVSFA). *See also* Miranda v. AutoNation USA Corp., Clearinghouse No. 53,558 (Fla. Dist. Ct. Oct. 31, 2000) (certifying class action), *aff'd in relevant part, rev'd in part on other grounds*, 789 So. 2d 1188 (Fla. App. 2001). *Cf.* Cullen v. Art Goebel, Inc., 1997 U.S. Dist. LEXIS 23682 (D. Minn. July 23, 1997) (copy delivered to buyer upon execution need only have buyer's signature).

291 *See* Daenzer v. Wayland Ford, Inc., 193 F. Supp. 2d 1030 (W.D. Mich. 2002) (denying finance charges to seller who did not give copy of contract to buyer at time buyer signed it); Lozada v. Dale Baker Oldsmobile, Inc., 197 F.R.D. 321, 340, 341 (W.D. Mich. 2000).

292 Scott v. Forest Lake Chrysler-Plymouth-Dodge, 637 N.W.2d 587 (Minn. App. 2002).

is exempt from the disclosure requirements of the federal Truth in Lending Act.[293] But, for transactions that the Truth in Lending Act covers, the state law may allow the seller to give those disclosures in lieu of meeting the state law disclosure requirements.[294]

In some states, the contract is voidable at the buyer's election until an exact signed copy is delivered, although this right may not apply if the goods have been delivered.[295] Even where the statute did not explicitly make the contract voidable, the Connecticut Supreme Court found that the buyer had the right to rescind a contract that was not completely filled in and was not given to the buyer at the time of execution. The court stressed the mandatory language of the statute and that it was intended to protect buyers.[296] A federal court has construed a Michigan MVRISA to deny finance charges to a seller who did not give a copy of the contract to the buyer at the time of execution.[297] Other states specify another penalty, such as denial of finance charges.[298] An Illinois court has interpreted its MVRISA as denying any right to collect the finance charge to a seller who fails to fill in all the required information on the contract.[299] A UDAP claim may also be a possibility,[300]

or the court may imply a private cause of action under the statute.[301]

11.7 Credit Cards: Background, Abuses and State Law Claims

11.7.1 The Rise of the Credit Card

11.7.1.1 The Massive Credit Card Debt Burden

The use of open-end credit is pervasive in American society, and credit cards have become an increasingly integral part of American lives. Three-quarters of all households have at least one credit card, and over half of cardholders carry credit card debt from month to month.[302] There are now almost 1.5 billion cards in circulation—over a dozen credit cards for every household in the country.[303] The amount of credit card debt outstanding at the end of 2004 was almost $800 billion,[304] over three times as much as in 1993.[305]

The explosion of credit card debt may have fueled the U.S. economy, but it has placed an enormous burden on millions of American consumers. Consumers across all income levels have experienced dramatically increased credit card debt in the past ten years:

- The average credit card debt has increased from $630 in 1970 to over $4,000 in 2001, and $7,519 in 2003.[306]

293 *See, e.g.,* Cal. Civ. Code § 2982. *See also* Or. Rev. Stat. § 83.811 (making its disclosure requirements applicable only to transactions not covered by Truth in Lending Act); Uniform Consumer Credit Code § 3-201.

294 *See, e.g.,* Minn. Stat. § 168.71(b); Mont. Code § 31-1-231(8). *See also* Cullen v. Art Goebel, Inc., 1997 U.S. Dist. LEXIS 23682 (D. Minn. July 23, 1997).

295 Mich. Comp. Laws § 445.853(b) (voidable unless buyer has received the goods or services); N.Y. Pers. Prop. Law § 302(3) (motor vehicle installment buyer can cancel contract unless vehicle has been delivered). *See also* Rulle v. Ivari Int'l, Inc., 192 Misc. 2d 266, 746 N.Y.S.2d 338 (App. Term 2002) (contract unenforceable if buyer cancelled before signed copy was mailed to her).

296 Keyes v. Brown, 232 A.2d 486 (Conn. 1967). *Accord* Barnes v. Holliday, 1990 Conn. Super. LEXIS 392 (June 5, 1990) (contract voidable at election of consumer). *But see* Rulle v. Ivari Int'l, Inc., 192 Misc. 2d 266, 746 N.Y.S.2d 338 (App. Term 2002) (failure to include required warnings on contract does not entitle buyer to cancel and obtain refund).

297 Daenzer v. Wayland Ford, Inc., 193 F. Supp. 2d 1030 (W.D. Mich. 2002).

298 *See, e.g.,* Mont. Code § 31-1-203; Wis. Stat. § 218.0142(5) (motor vehicle installment sales). *See also* Route 50 Auto Sales, Inc. v. Muncy, 771 N.E.2d 635 (Ill. App. 2002) (credit seller cannot collect interest and charges where contract did not include statutorily-required terms).

299 Route 50 Auto Sales, Inc. v. Muncy, 771 N.E.2d 635 (Ill. App. 2002).

300 Lozada v. Dale Baker Oldsmobile, Inc., 197 F.R.D. 321, 340, 341 (W.D. Mich. 2000); Kleidon v. Rizza Chevrolet, Inc., 527 N.E.2d 374 (Ill. App. 1988) (omission of APR from contract, contrary to motor vehicle installment sales statute, was UDAP violation). *But see* Nigh v. Koons Buick Pontiac GMC, Inc., 143 F. Supp. 2d 535 (E.D. Va. 2001) (consumer cannot assert UDAP claim for violation of requirement of delivery of retail installment contract that was contained in statute that created comprehensive scheme of administrative enforcement). *See gener-*

ally National Consumer Law Center, Unfair and Deceptive Acts and Practices § 3.2.7 (6th ed. 2004 and Supp.).

301 *See, e.g.,* Couture v. G.W.M., Inc., 2002 WL 31962752 (N.H. Super. Ct. Dec. 3, 2002) (debtor has affirmative cause of action to recover finance charges paid). *But see* Forrest v. Simonds, 1997 WL 610761 (N.D.N.Y. Sept. 30, 1997) (no private cause of action for violating RISA disclosure requirements).

302 Ana M. Aizcorbe, Arthur B. Kennickell, and Kevin B. Moore, *Recent Changes in U.S. Family Finances: Evidence from the 1998 and 2001 Survey of Consumer Finances,* Federal Reserve Bulletin (Jan. 2003), at 25.

303 U.S. Census Bureau, Statistical Abstract of the United States: 2003 at 751 (Table 1190): Credit Cards—Holders, Numbers, Spending, and Debt, 1990 and 2000, and Projections, 2005, *available at* www.census.gov/prod/2004pubs/03statab/banking.pdf; U.S. Bureau of the Census, *Projections of the Number of Households and Families in the United States*: 1995 to 2010 at 9 (1996), *available at* www.census.gov/prod/1/pop/p25-1129.pdf (projecting 108.8 million households by 2005).

304 Federal Reserve Board, Statistical Release No. G.19—Consumer Credit, March 2005, *available at* www.federalreserve.gov/releases/g19/20050307.

305 OCC Advisory Letter 96-7, Sept. 26, 1996 (96-7.txt at www.occ.treas.gov); FDIC Quarterly Banking Profile Graph Book, Fourth Quarter 1997.

306 Figures vary somewhat, and self-reported balance data may result in understated debts. *See generally* David S. Evans, *The Growth and Diffusion of Credit Cards in Society,* 2 Payment Card Economics Review 59, 64–66 (2004); Tamara Draut & Javier Silva, *Borrowing to Make Ends Meet: The Growth of Credit Card Debt in the '90s,* at 9–11 (Demos Sept. 2003),

During that time, the savings rate steadily declined and the number of personal bankruptcies filed climbed 125%.[307]

- The average credit debt of older Americans rose by 89% between 1992 and 2001, from $2,143 to $4,041.[308]
- The average credit card debt among young adults increased by 55% between 1992 and 2001 to $4,088 dollars, and these households now spend nearly 24% of their income on debt payments.[309]

While in the past credit card practices may have affected primarily middle-class consumers, low-income consumers have become a lucrative target for credit card lenders, because those consumers typically carry and pay big balances at high interest rates. The largest increase in credit card debt is among households with a reported annual income of less than $10,000.[310]

The negative consequences of this escalating mountain of debt on individual consumers as well as the American economy cannot be minimized. Personal bankruptcy rates increase on an annual basis,[311] and families become destabilized due to the financial pressures.[312] Although less well documented, more foreclosures result as well. When a homeowner has big credit card balances, it is hard to resist the lure of mortgage refinancing as a way to manage the debt.

At the same time that consumers have been drowning in credit card debt, credit card companies have enjoyed growing profits.[313] Even with a weak economy, credit card companies experience increasing earnings.[314] The industry's average pre-tax, return-on-assets for their credit card portfolios rose from 3.1% in 1999 to 4.5% in 2004.[315]

11.7.1.2 Escalating Debt Loads Caused by Industry Practices

The credit card industry bears a significant portion of the responsibility for the explosion in credit card debt over the last few decades. For one thing, credit card lenders have engaged in aggressive solicitation. In 2001 alone, credit card lenders mailed more than five billion card solicitations.[316] This means more than 45 mailings went out each year to every American household—not counting telephone solicitations.[317]

However, the credit card lender culpability is not limited to aggressive solicitation. Recent cases show that a significant amount of debt load is sometimes caused, not by consumer borrowing, but by the punitive tactics of the credit card industry. Many overburdened consumers struggle to pay their obligations, but credit card lenders keep consumers on a treadmill of debt, paying fees and charges, for as long as possible.

Consider a case about a consumer from Cleveland, Ohio who did try to repay her debt, but was driven hopelessly into default by her credit card lender.[318] In May 1997, Ruth Owens stopped using her credit card, made no further purchases or cash advances, and tried to pay off her debt to her credit card lender. At that time, she owed $1,963. Over the next six years, Ms. Owens made $3,492 in payments to this lender. One might assume this was enough to pay off her debt. After all, if Ms. Owens had made the same payments on a $2,000 loan with interest at 21% annual percentage rate (the usury limit in many states), her debt would be paid off.

From May 1997 until her account was sent for collection in May 2003, not one penny of Ms. Owens' $3,492 in payments went to reduce her balance. During this time, the credit card lender charged Ms. Owens various fees that

available at www.demos-usa.org/pubs/borrowing_to_make_ends_meet.pdf; Thomas A. Durkin, *Credit Cards: Use and Consumer Attitudes, 1970–2000*, Fed. Res. Bull. 623, 626 (Sept. 2000); Patrick McGeehan, *Mountains of Interest Add to Pain of Credit Card Debt*, New York Times, Nov. 21, 2004, at 1.

307 Tamara Draut & Javier Silva, *Borrowing to Make Ends Meet: The Growth of Credit Card Debt in the '90s*, at 9 (Demos Sept. 2003), *available at* www.demos-usa.org/pubs/borrowing_to_make_ends_meet.pdf.

308 Heather G. McGee & Tamara Draut, *Retiring in the Red: The Growth of Debt Among Older Americans* at 1 (Demos Jan. 2004), *available at* www.demos-usa.org/pubs/Retiring_2ed.pdf.

309 Tamara Draut & Javier Silva, *Generation Broke: The Growth of Debt Among Young Americans* at 1 (Demos Oct. 2004), *available at* www.demos-usa.org/pubs/Generation_Broke.pdf.

310 *See* Robert D. Manning, *Role of FCRA in the Credit Granting Process*, Testimony Before the House Subcommittee on Financial Institutions and Consumer Credit, June 12, 2003, at 5–6 and 18, Table 2, *available at* www.creditcardnation.com/pdfs/061203rm.pdf.

311 The number of personal bankruptcy filings has increased steadily during the past few decades, reaching 1,624,272 in 2004. Administrative Office of the U.S. Courts News Release, *Number of Bankruptcy Cases Filed in Federal Courts Down Less Than One Percent* (Aug. 27, 2004), *available at* www.uscourts.gov/Press_Releases/june04bk.pdf. Personal bankruptcy filings declined by a small number, 13,111, between 2003 and 2004.

312 *See* Elizabeth Warren & Amelia Warren Tyagi, The Two-Income Trap: Why Middle-Class Mothers and Their Families Are Going Broke (Basic Books 2003).

313 Board of Governors of the Federal Reserve System, *The Prof-*

itability of Credit Card Operations of Depository Institutions (June 2004), *available at* www.federalreserve.gov/boarddocs/rptcongress/creditcard/2004/ccprofit.pdf. While the profitability of the credit card industry as a whole has fluctuated somewhat over these years, this is largely due to the changeability of the group of banks included in the sample. *Id.* at 2.

314 Lavonne Kuykendall, *Review 2004: Card Lenders Earned More Despite Weak Portfolio Growth*, American Banker (Jan. 3, 2005).

315 Cardweb.com, *Card Profits 04*, (Jan. 24, 2005), *available at* www.cardweb.com/cardtrak/news/2005/january/24a.html.

316 BAI Global Inc., *All Time High Credit Card Mail Volume Set in 2001 Despite 9-11 Disaster and Anthrax Fears*, Press Release, April 2002.

317 U.S. Bureau of the Census, *Projections of the Number of Households and Families in the United States: 1995 to 2010* at 9 (1996), *available at* www.census.gov/prod/1/pop/p25-1129.pdf (projecting 108.8 million households by 2005).

318 Discover Bank v. Owens, 822 N.E.2d 869 (Ohio Mun. 2004).

consumed all of her payments and caused her debt to grow even larger. The following fees and interest were charged to Ms. Owens' account:

Fees and Interest

Over-limit Fees	$1,518.00
Late Fees	$1,160.00
Credit Insurance (CreditSafe)[319]	$ 369.62
Interest and Other Fees	$6,008.66
Total	$9,056.28

Despite having received substantial payments for six years, the lender claimed that Ms. Owens still owed $5,564 when it filed a collection lawsuit against her. In other words, after having paid $3,492 on a $1,963 debt, Ms. Owens' balance grew to $5,564.

The court held that Ms. Owens was not liable for this debt on the basis that her credit card lender would be unjustly enriched by a judgment in its favor. The court also held that the accumulation of fees was "manifestly unconscionable." It noted that her "instincts were always that she wanted to plug away at meeting her financial obligations. While clearly placing her on the moral high road, that same highway unfortunately was her road to financial ruin. How is it that the person who wants to do right ends up so worse off? It is plain to the court that the creditor also bears some responsibility."[320] The court also stated "This court is all too aware of the widespread financial exploitation of the urban poor by overbearing credit-card companies. [Ms. Owens] has clearly been the victim of plaintiff's unreasonable, unconscionable and unjust business practices."[321]

Another example of how credit card practices drive consumers into overwhelming debt comes from the bankruptcy case of Josephine McCarthy.[322] Ms. McCarthy had two accounts with one credit card lender. On one account, she made $3,058 in payments over a two year period during which her balance on the account increased from $4,888 to $5,357. She had made only $218.16 (net of store credit) in purchases during this time. All of her payments went to pay finance charges (at a 29.99% interest rate), late charges, over-limit fees, bad check fees, and phone payment fees. On the other

card, she made $2,008 in payments over the same period and the account balance increased from $2,020.90 to $2,607.66. During this time, she added only $203.06 in purchases.

	Total Payments	Purchases	Balance Increase	Total Interest and Fees in 2 year period
Account 1	$3,058.00	$218.16	$469.00	$3,308.84
Account 2	$2,008.00	$203.06	$586.76	$2,391.79

Other bankruptcy decisions shed further light on how high finance charges and junk fees, not irresponsible spending, may be the root cause of overwhelming credit card debt. In one proceeding, a bankruptcy court forced a major credit card lender to break out principal versus interest and fees in its claims against 31 separate debtors. The bankruptcy court's order reveals that on average, 57% of the debts consisted of interest and fees.[323]

11.7.2 Credit Card Abuses

11.7.2.1 Historical Perspective

Credit card companies were not always so free to engage in reprehensible behavior. Credit card deregulation, and the concomitant spiraling credit card debt of Americans, began in 1978, with the Supreme Court's decision in *Marquette National Bank of Minneapolis v. First of Omaha Service Corp.*[324] This case gave national banks the ability to take the most favored lender status from their home state across state lines, and preempt the law of the borrower's home state.[325] As a result, national banks and other depositories established their headquarters in states that eliminated or raised their usury limits, giving them free rein to charge whatever interest rate they wanted.[326] As of 1978, credit card debt was $50 billion.[327] From 1978 to 1995, credit card debt increased six-fold to $378 billion.[328]

In 1996, the Supreme Court paved the way for credit card banks to increase their income stream even more dramati-

---

319 Like many card customers, Ms. Owens was being charged for one of the numerous insurance-like products sold by card companies. In this case, Ms. Owens was charged approximately $10 per month for a Discover card product called CreditSafe Plus, which apparently provided for a suspension of payments and finance charges if Ms. Owens became unemployed, hospitalized, or disabled. Since Ms. Owens was already on Social Security Disability and unemployed, the CreditSafe product presumably would apply only if she became hospitalized. Ms. Owens was no doubt paying for a product that would likely never benefit her. See Chapter 8, *supra* for a discussion of the many issues concerning credit insurance.

320 Discover Bank v. Owens, 822 N.E.2d 869, 873 (Ohio Mun. 2004).

321 *Id.* at 875.

322 *In re* Josephine McCarthy, No. 04-10493-SSM (Bankr. E.D. Va. filed 2004), available on the companion CD-Rom.

323 Amended Order Overruling Objection to Claims, *In re* Blair (W.D.N.C. Feb. 10, 2004) available on the companion CD-Rom.

324 439 U.S. 299, 99 S. Ct. 540, 58 L. Ed. 2d 534 (1978). See § 3.4, *supra*, for an in-depth discussion of National Bank Act preemption.

325 It is worth noting that there was no interstate banking when the National Bank Act was passed.

326 Other depository institutions obtained the same most favored lender status when Congress enacted § 521 of the Depository Institutions Deregulation and Monetary Control Act of 1980 (codified at 12 U.S.C. § 1831d). See § 3.8, *supra*.

327 Diane Ellis, *The Effect of Consumer Interest Rate Deregulation on Credit Card Volumes, Charge-Offs, and in the Personal Bankruptcy Rate*, FDIC—Division of Insurance, Bank Trends, 98-05 (Mar. 1998), *available at* www.fdic.gov/bank/analytical/bank/bt_9805.html.

328 *See* Federal Reserve Board, Statistical Release—Consumer Credit Historical Data (Revolving), *available at* www.federalreserve.gov/releases/g19/hist/cc_hist_mt.txt.

cally. In *Smiley v. Citibank (South Dakota), N.A.*,[329] the court approved of the Office of the Comptroller of the Currency's (OCC) definition of interest that included a number of credit card charges, such as late payment, over-limit, cash advance, returned check, annual fees, and membership fees.[330] As a result, national banks and other depositories can charge fees in any amount to their customers as long as their home-state laws permit the fees and so long as the fees are "interest" under the OCC definition.

The following is a description of some credit card abuses that have been noted. This list is by no means exhaustive and will probably grow as creditors develop new ways to increase fees and income.[331]

11.7.2.2 Junk Fees and Fee Income

11.7.2.2.1 Introduction

Uncapping the amount of fees that credit card banks can charge has resulted in the rapid growth of and reliance on fee income by credit card lenders. It has also contributed significantly to the snowballing credit card debt of American consumers.

Since *Smiley*, penalty fee revenue has increased nearly nine-fold from $1.7 billion in 1996 to $14.8 billion in 2004.[332] The income from just three fees—penalty fees, cash advance fees and annual fees—reached $24.4 billion in 2004,[333] Fee income topped $30 billion if balance transfer fees, foreign exchange, and other fees are added to this total.[334]

Credit card lenders have grown this fee income by making fees higher in amount, imposing them more quickly, and assessing them more often. After *Smiley*, banks rushed to increase fee amounts. The average late payment fee has soared from $14 in 1996 to over $32 in 2004.[335] Over-limit fees have similarly jumped from $14 in 1996 to over $30 in 2004.[336]

Not only has the size of fee income for credit card lenders grown enormously, the types of fees have mushroomed as well. The Federal Reserve Board provides a list of fees to consumers in a brochure titled "Choosing a Credit Card."[337] The most common fees incurred in credit card transactions include:

NAME OF FEE	DESCRIPTION OF FEE
Annual fee (sometimes billed monthly).	Charged for having the card. Fees range from zero to $130.
Cash advance fee.	Charged when the card is used to obtain a cash advance; the fee is usually 3% of the advance, with a minimum of $5 and no maximum.
Balance-transfer fee.	Charged when the consumer transfers a balance from another credit card. Fees range from 2% to 3% of the amount transferred, with a minimum.
Late-payment fee.	Charged if the consumer's payment is received after the due date. Fees range from $10 to $49.
Over-the-credit-limit fee.	Charged if the consumer goes over the credit limit. Fees range from $10 to $39.
Credit-limit-increase fee.	Charged if the consumer asks for an increase in her/his credit limit.
Set-up fee.	One-time fee, charged when a new credit card account is opened.
Return-item fee.	Charged if the consumer pays the bill by check and the check is returned for non-sufficient funds.
Expedited-payment fee.	Charged when the consumer makes a payment over the phone. Fees range from $10 to $14.95.
Expedited-delivery fee.	Charged when the consumer requests an additional credit card and requests that it be delivered in an expedited way.
Replacement card fee.	Charged when the consumer's credit card is lost, stolen, damaged, or otherwise needs to be replaced.
Additional card fee.	Charged when the consumer requests a card for a family member or otherwise wishes an additional card.
Other fees.	Some credit card companies charge a fee to cover the costs of reporting to credit bureaus, reviewing the consumer's account, or providing other customer services.

---

329 517 U.S. 735, 116 S. Ct. 1730, 135 L. Ed. 2d 25 (1996).

330 The OCC definition of interest is found in 12 C.F.R. § 7.4001(a). *See* § 3.4, *supra.*

331 Consumer Action publishes an annual credit card report that describes many of the abuses *du jour. See* Linda Sherry, *Annual Credit Card Survey 2004*, Consumer Action, (Spring 2004), *available at* www.consumer-action.org. *See also* USPIRG, *The Credit Card Trap: How to Spot It, How to Avoid It* (Apr. 2001), *available at* www.truthaboutcredit.org.

332 Cardweb.com, *Fee Party* (Jan. 13, 2005), *available at* www.cardweb.com/cardtrak/news/2005/january/13a.html.

333 *Id.*

334 *Id.*

335 Cardweb.com, *Late Fees* (Jan. 28, 2005), *available at* www.cardweb.com/cardtrak/news/2005/january/28a.html.

336 Cardweb.com, *Overlimit Fees* (Feb. 2, 2005), *available at* www.cardweb.com/cardtrak/news/2005/february/2a.html.

337 Federal Reserve Board, *Choosing a Credit Card, available at* www.federalreserve.gov/pubs/shop.

Commentators have documented even more fees than the above, including fees for wire transfers, lottery tickets, and casino chips.[338] Some credit card lenders even charge fees for inactivity on a credit card.[339]

Credit card lenders no longer impose these fees as a way to curb undesirable behavior from consumers, which used to be the primary justification for imposing high penalties. Instead, these fees constitute a significant source of revenue for the bank. The problem with these charges, especially in combination with the penalty interest rates, is that they exacerbate the problems of consumers who have hit hard times. Too often, these charges drive consumers into bankruptcy, resulting in cascading losses to individuals, families and neighborhoods—of lost savings, lost homes, and forced moves, with all of the consequential financial and emotional tolls.

11.7.2.2.2 Late fees

In addition to raising the dollar amount of late payment fees, credit card lenders have been aggressively imposing them more quickly. Previously, credit card lenders gave consumers a leniency period of a few days before imposing late fees.[340] Now, credit card lenders will impose late fees if the consumer is even one day over the due date. In fact, some lenders have imposed late fees for payments received on the payment due date but after a certain cut-off time, a practice discussed more fully in § 11.7.2.3.3, *infra*.

11.7.2.2.3 Over-limit fees

Over-limit fees are particularly unfair because the card issuer technologically has the ability to decline over-limit transactions, but chooses to permit them and then reap penalty fee income. A few decades ago, credit card lenders did not require specific authorization of transactions under a certain amount due to costs.[341] However, for about the last decade, electronic authorizations have been employed on

effectively *all* card-based transactions originated in the United States.[342]

In addition, credit card lenders typically now "pad" the nominal credit limit.[343] For example, a consumer enters into a credit card agreement that specifies a credit limit of $2,000. Usually, after a relatively brief period during which the customer manages the account in an acceptable manner, the *pad* is instituted. The card issuer may increase the *effective* credit limit up to $2,500. The *effective* credit limit has become $2,500, even though the consumer may still believe the credit limit is the *nominal* amount of $2,000.

The original ostensible purpose of this pad is to avoid customer relations problems stemming from denials for proposed charges that would have resulted in a balance exceeding the nominal credit limit only by a relatively modest amount.[344] However, with the proliferation of fees, an additional impetus to do so has arisen for credit card lenders, namely, to generate substantial over-limit fees.

Credit card lenders have also been known to lower customers' credit limits during the middle of the billing cycle, then charge over-limit fees when unsuspecting consumers exceed the new limit at the end of the cycle.[345]

11.7.2.2.4 Balance transfer fees

Balance transfer fees can be insidious because they often involve consumers who have been carrying a large balance from month to month. Credit card lenders lure these consumers into transferring large balances by heavily advertising low or 0% APRs, but not disclosing the balance transfer fee as prominently. For example, a credit card solicitation might trumpet a "low 2.9% Fixed APR" for balance transfers using large type, but only disclose the balance transfer fee of 3% on the reverse page in 8-point type. A consumer transferring a balance of $2,000 would be faced with a $60 fee. As a result of a balance transfer, this consumer would add more to her debt burden, yet card issuer's advertising would have led her to believe that a balance transfer would save her money.

11.7.2.2.5 Currency conversion fees

Currency conversion fees constitute a double whammy, in that they are imposed in many cases twice—once by the card issuer and once by the MasterCard or VISA network. These fees were previously hidden by deceptively "padding" the exchange rate, i.e., giving the consumer a worse exchange rate than that obtained by the card issuer.[346]

338 USPIRG, The Credit Card Trap: How to Spot It, How to Avoid It (Apr. 2001), at 8–9, *available at* www.truthaboutcredit.org.

339 *Id.* at 15.

340 The *Role of FCRA in the Credit Granting Process: Hearing Before the Subcommittee on Financial institutions and Consumer Credit*, at 7 (June 12, 2003) (statement of Dr. Robert D. Manning, Caroline Werner Gannett Professor of Humanities, Rochester Institute of Technology), *available at* www.creditcardnation.com/pdfs/061203rm.pdf

341 Thanks to Professor James Brown, Center for Consumer Affairs, University of Wisconsin at Milwaukee, for his contribution to this section. The facts in this section are based upon Professor Brown's reading and information provided to him by members of the credit card industry through his tenure as: (1) Member, Board of Directors, TYME Corporation (1st shared EFT network in the U.S.), 1982–2002; (2) Member, Board of Directors, Electronic Funds Transfer Association, 1992–present; (3) Expert witness in the *In re* Visa Check/Master-Money Antitrust Litigation, No. CV 96-5238 (E.D.N.Y.).

342 *Id.*

343 *Id.*

344 *Id.*

345 *See* Complaint, State of Minnesota v. Capital One Bank, (Minn. Dist. Ct.—2d Jud. Dist. Dec. 30, 2004) *available at* www.ag.state.mn.us/consumer/PDF/PR/CapitalOneComplaint.pdf.

346 *See In re* Currency Conversion Fee Antitrust Litigation, 265 F. Supp. 2d 385 (S.D.N.Y. 2003).

11.7.2.3 Other Abuses

11.7.2.3.1 Penalty rates and universal default

A penalty rate is an increase in the initial APR triggered by the occurrence of a specific event, such as the consumer's making a late payment or exceeding the credit limit. These penalty interest rates can be as high as 30% to 40%.[347] The new terms apply to the old balance—leaving consumers stuck with paying often high balances at interest rates far higher than was originally agreed, with devastating consequences.

The existence of penalty rates for minor transgressions alone would be enough to draw criticism. Raising an APR from the mid-teens to 30% or higher, simply on the basis of a single transgression, itself is probably unjustified. After all, the card issuer has already collected a one-time charge for that late payment or over-limit transaction, which probably more than covers its costs. Increasing the consumer's APR simply allows card issuer to reap additional profit by playing "gotcha" with unsuspecting consumers.[348]

This practice is particularly problematic when a penalty interest rate is applied retroactively to an existing balance. No other industry in the country is allowed to increase the price of a product once it is purchased. Credit card lenders have already assessed a consumer's risk of not repaying the loan and presumably offered an interest rate based on that risk.

Credit card lenders have recently added insult to injury with universal default. With universal default, credit card lenders impose penalty rates on consumers, not for late payments or any behavior with respect to the consumer's account with that particular issuer, but for late payments to any of the consumer's other creditors. In some cases, lenders will impose penalties simply if the credit score drops below a certain number, whether or not the drop was due to a late payment or another factor.[349] A survey of credit card banks found that 44% surveyed had a universal default policy.[350]

The disclosure of universal default policies is also questionable. Some credit card solicitations will disclose that a late payment to "any other" creditor will trigger a penalty rate; however, a review of credit card solicitations found that none of them disclosed that a mere drop in credit score may be the trigger.[351] This is problematic because a drop in credit score is not always caused by late payments—it could be caused by having a high balance-to-limit ratio on revolving accounts, an excessive number of inquiries, or a number of other factors that have little to do with the consumer's ability or willingness to repay the credit.[352]

Another concern with using credit reports to trigger a penalty rate is the enormous problem with inaccuracies in credit scoring and credit reporting. A review of over 500,000 consumer credit files by the Consumer Federation of America and the National Credit Reporting Association found that 29% of consumers have credit scores that differ by at least 50 points between credit bureaus, while 4% have scores that differ by at least 100 points.[353] Other studies have found that between 50% to 70% of credit reports contain inaccurate information.[354]

The Truth in Lending Act does include some disclosure requirements for penalty rates; however, there are no substantive limitations on these rates.[355]

11.7.2.3.2 Deceptive marketing

Some credit card lenders have engaged in questionable marketing practices when soliciting consumers. "Bait and switch" tactics are common. For example, some credit card lenders have marketed "no annual fee" credit cards, then imposed an annual fee six months later using a change-in-terms notice.[356] They heavily advertise low "fixed" rates,

---

347 *See* Kathleen Day & Caroline Mayer, *Credit Card Fees Bury Debtors*, Washington Post, Mar. 7, 2005, at A1.

348 The CEO of Cardweb has spun out the following scenario which shows how a combination of late fees and penalty rates can significantly increase a consumer's debt burden "Late and over-limit fees alone can easily rack up $900 in fees, and a 30% interest rate on a $3,000 balance can add another $1,000, so you could go from $2,000 to $5,000 in just one year if you fail to make payments." *See* Kathleen Day & Caroline Mayer, *Credit Card Fees Bury Debtors*, Washington Post, Mar. 7, 2005, at A1.

349 *See* Patrick McGeehan, *Plastic Trap—Debt That Binds: Soaring Interest Compounds Credit Card Pain for Millions*, N.Y. Times, Nov. 21, 2004; Complaint, State of Minnesota v. Capital One Bank, (Minn. Dist. Ct.—2d Jud. Dist. Dec. 30, 2004) *available at* www.ag.state.mn.us/consumer/PDF/PR/CapitalOneComplaint.pdf. The New York Times article was the companion piece to the PBS Frontline television episode *The Secret History of the Credit Card*, (PBS Frontline broadcast Nov. 23, 2004), which focused on among other issues, universal default and change-in-terms.

350 Linda Sherry, *Annual Credit Card Survey 2004*, Consumer

Action (Spring 2004), *available at* www.consumer-action.org/English/CANews/2004_May_CreditCard/.

351 *See* National Consumer Law Center, et al, *Comments to the Federal Reserve Board's Advance Notice of Proposed Rulemaking—Review of the Open-End (Revolving) Credit Rules of Regulation Z, Docket No. R-1217*, March 28, 2004, at 40–41, *available at* www.consumerlaw.org (review of credit card solicitation disclosures on universal default).

352 *See* Fair, Isaac & Co., *What's In Your Score?*, *available at* www.myfico.com/CreditEducation/WhatsInYourScore.aspx?fire=5.

353 Consumer Federation of America and National Credit Reporting Association, *Credit Score Accuracy and Implications for Consumers* at 24 (Dec. 17, 2002), *available at* www.consumerfed.org/121702CFA_NCRA_Credit_Score_Report_Final.pdf. *See also* National Consumer Law Center, Fair Credit Reporting, §§ 7.2.1, 14.8.1 (5th ed. 2002 and Supp.).

354 U.S. Public Interest Research Group, *Mistakes Do Happen: Credit Report Errors Mean Consumers Lose* (1998), *available at* http://uspirg.org/uspirg.asp?id2=5970&id3=USPIRG&; Consumer Reports, *Credit Reports: How Do Potential Lenders See You?*, at 52–53 (July 2000).

355 *See* National Consumer Law Center, Truth in Lending, § 5.4.3.2.4 (5th ed. 2003 and Supp.).

356 Rossman v. Fleet Bank (R.I.) Nat'l Assn., 280 F.3d 384 (3d Cir. 2002).

but subsequently raise rates through change-in-terms notices and use penalty fees with punitive late payment and over-limit policies to trip consumers up.[357]

One credit card lender allegedly used telemarketers to lure consumers to transfer balances by promising guaranteed savings but evading requests for specifics. It also marketed a credit protection program that would make the monthly payment if the debtor was hospitalized or out of work, but failed to disclose significant restrictions on coverage and benefits. Finally, it marketed "no annual fee" credit cards without disclosing that the consumer was required to purchase credit protection at $156 a year, and promised "rewards" of up to $200 if the consumer opened a credit card account, without disclosing significant limitations.[358]

Another deceptive practice is that of "downselling" consumers by prominently marketing one package of credit card terms, but then approving consumers only for accounts with less favorable terms, and touting the approved account in a fashion designed to mislead the customer about the fact he or she had has received a more expensive card with less favorable terms.[359]

11.7.2.3.3 Late payment practices and posting cut-off policies

Some lenders have deliberately instituted practices that result in imposition of late payment fees. For example, some creditors will use a very early hour of the morning, such as 9:00 or 10:00 a.m., as the cut-off time for crediting payments received that day.[360] Consequently, if a consumer's payment is received on the payment due date, it will be considered late because in all likelihood, the U.S. Postal Service will not have delivered the mail so early in the morning.[361] Furthermore, when due dates fall on a weekend or holiday, credit card lenders will consider the payment late if not received on the prior business day.[362]

Another troublesome practice occurs when the creditor provides only a post office box as an acceptable payment address, effectively prevented consumers from making timely payments late in the billing cycle by using overnight and other forms of high speed mail that will not deliver to post offices boxes.

11.7.2.3.4 Tiny minimum monthly payments

Many credit card lenders have decreased the minimum monthly payments from 4% to 2% or 3% of the consumer's balance.[363] A few lenders have begun reversing this trend, but minimum payment rates are still well under 3%.[364] With lowered monthly minimum payments, consumers who pay only the minimum will take much longer to pay off the credit card debt and will pay substantially more in finance charges.

Consumers may not realize how much more time and money paying only the minimum will cost.[365] In consumer education programs conducted by one attorney general's office, for example, even college-educated consumers consistently underestimated how long it would take to pay off credit card balances.[366] This information is even more criti-

---

357 Roberts v. Fleet Bank (R.I.), Nat'l Assn, 342 F.3d 260 (3d Cir. 2003); Gaynoe v. First Union Direct Bank, Nat'l Assn., 571 S.E.2d 24 (N.C. Ct. App. 2002); Chavers v. Fleet Bank (RI), N.A., 844 A.2d 666 (R.I. 2004). For an interesting analysis of the alleged deceptiveness of Capital One's heavy promotion including its prolific TV ad campaign, see Complaint, State of Minnesota v. Capital One Bank, (Minn. Dist. Ct.—2d Jud. Dist. Dec. 30, 2004) *available at* www.ag.state.mn.us/consumer/PDF/PR/CapitalOneComplaint.pdf.

358 Consent Order, *In re* Providian Nat'l Bank, No. 2000-53 (Dept. of the Treasury, Office of the Comptroller of the Currency June 28, 2000), *available at* www.occ.treas.gov/FTP/EAs/ea2000-53.pdf.

359 *See, e.g.,* Consent Order, *In re* Direct Merchants Credit Card Bank, No. 2001-24 (Dept of Treasury, Office of the Comptroller of the Currency, May 3, 2001), *available at* www.occ.treas.gov/ftp/eas/ea2001-24.pdf.

360 *See, e.g.,* Lawrence v. Household Bank, 343 F. Supp. 2d 1101 (M.D. Ala. 2004) (9 a.m. cut-off for payment posting); Landreneau v. Fleet Fin. Group, 197 F. Supp. 2d 551 (M.D. La. 2002) (9 AM cut-off for payment posting); Bond v. Fleet Bank, 2002 WL 31500393 (D.R.I. Oct. 10, 2002); Schwartz v. Citibank (S.D.), Nat'l Assn, Clearinghouse No. 53,023, Case No. 00-00078 (JWJX) (C.D. Cal. May 5, 2000) (class action settlement notice in case challenging 10 a.m. cut-off); Marsh v. First U.S.A. Bank, N.A., C.N. 3-99CV0783-T (N.D. Tex. Apr. 8, 1999). At one point, one of the nation's largest credit card banks (MBNA) supposedly set the cut-off time as early as 6:00 a.m. Kevin Hoffman, *Lerner's Legacy—MBNA's Customers Wouldn't Write Such Flattering Obituaries*, Cleveland Scene, Dec.

18, 2002, *available at* www.clevescene.com/issues/2002-12-18/news/feature.html.

361 The Fair Credit Billing Act provisions of the Truth in Lending Act do contain a requirement for prompt posting of payments to open-end accounts. *See* National Consumer Law Center, Truth in Lending, § 5.8.9.1 (5th ed. 2003 and Supp.).

362 *See* Landreneau v. Fleet Fin. Group, 197 F. Supp. 2d 551 (M.D. La. 2002); Bond v. Fleet Bank, 2002 WL 31500393 (D.R.I. Oct. 10, 2002).

363 Linda Sherry, *Annual Credit Card Survey 2004*, Consumer Action (Spring 2004), *available at* www.consumer-action.org/English/CANews/2004_May_CreditCard.

364 Jane J. Kim, *Minimums Due on Credit Cards Are on the Increase*, Wall St. J., March 24, 2005, at D2. Although federal regulators admit concern over this widespread practice, new rules addressing the problem have been delayed. *See* Kathleen Day & Caroline Mayer, *Credit Card Fees Bury Debtors*, Washington Post, Mar. 7, 2005, at A1.

365 To address this issue, California passed a statute requiring creditors to provide information to each consumer on how long it would take to pay off their credit card balance if they paid only the minimum payment. A federal district court held this law to be preempted by federal banking statutes in American Bankers Assoc. v. Lockyer, 239 F. Supp. 2d 1000 (E.D. Cal. 2002). *See* National Consumer Law Center, Truth in Lending § 5.10.3.4.3 (5th ed. 2003 and Supp.). According to a Federal Reserve Board study, 89% of consumers surveyed thought this type of information would be helpful. Thomas A. Durkin, *Credit Cards: Use and Consumer Attitudes, 1970–2000*, Fed. Res. Bull. 623, 626 (Sept. 2000).

366 Center for Responsible Lending, Comments to Advance Notice

cal, given that the portion of cardholders who do not pay off their credit card debt in full every month grew from 37% in 1970 to 55% in 1998.[367]

Worse, the combination of the minimum monthly payments and the penalty interest rates often results in negatively amortizing debt. Even when the consumer is making the payments as requested and not incurring any new charges, the debt keeps climbing.

Federal banking regulators have issued guidance that discourages minimum payments that are so low as to create negative amortization, i.e., when minimum payments do not fully pay off the interest that has accrued since the last payment, thereby increasing the principal balance.[368]

11.7.2.3.5 Aggressive solicitation

Many credit card lenders now make offers of credit based solely on the credit score.[369] Credit scores supposedly measure the propensity to repay and the ratio of revolving credit used, but they do not measure whether the consumer's income is adequate to repay a new debt, or include a debt-to-income ratio that would show if the consumer is already overextended. As a result, credit card lenders often grant new credit cards to consumers who are already overextended.[370] Federal regulators have issued guidance urging credit card lenders to consider repayment capacity when granting new credit,[371] but this guidance is not mandatory or enforceable by injured consumers.

11.7.2.3.6 Shrinking grace periods

Most creditors have decreased the amount of time for grace periods to 25 or even 20 days, down from the historic one month.[372] Some creditors have eliminated grace periods.[373] Note that the Truth in Lending Act requires creditors, if they have a grace period, to mail the periodic statement at least fourteen days prior to the expiration the grace period.[374] Thus TILA effectively requires some sort of minimum for a grace period, but only if the creditor chooses to provide a grace period at all.

11.7.2.3.7 Payment allocation order

Many credit card companies heavily advertise low APRs in their solicitations that are only applicable to one category of transactions. They then allocate payments first to the balances with lower APRs. Disclosure of payment allocation order has been very minimal,[375] or nonexistent.[376]

11.7.2.3.8 Debt collection abuses

Credit card lenders, like many creditors, have been known to engage in plain old debt collection abuse—harassment, deception and abuse.[377] However, there are a few practices that are unique to credit card companies and their collectors.

Most important is the fact that credit card companies, or the debt buyers to whom they sell the debt, often initiate collection cases against consumers without any documentation of a credit card agreement signed by the consumer or periodic statements to show transaction activity.[378] Instead,

---

of Proposed Rulemaking—Regulation Z, Subpart B: Open-End Credit, Docket No. R-1217, March 28, 2004, at 22–23, available on the companion CD-Rom.

367 *See* Thomas A. Durkin, *Credit Cards: Use and Consumer Attitudes, 1970–2000*, Fed. Res. Bull. 623, 626 (Sept. 2000).

368 Federal Financial Institutions Examination Council, *Credit Card Lending Account Management and Loss Allowance Guidance*, (Jan. 2003), *available at* www.federalreserve.gov/BoardDocs/press/bcreg/2003/20030108/attachment.pdf.

369 *See* National Consumer Law Center, Fair Credit Reporting § 14.3 (5th ed. 2002 and Supp.); Elizabeth Warren and Amelie Warren Tyagi, *The Two-Income Trap: Why Middle-Class Mothers and Their Families Are Going Broke* Ch. 6 (Basic Books 2003).

370 *See, e.g.,* AT&T Universal Card v. Ellingsworth (*In re* Ellingsworth), 212 B.R. 326 (Bankr. W. D. Mo. 1997) (consumer sent pre-approved credit card with credit limit of $4,000 based on her FICO score of 759 even though she had 16 other credit cards); Universal Card Servs. Corp. v. Akins (*In re* Akins), 235 B.R. 866 (W.D. Tex. 1999) (card issuer approved consumer to use convenience check up to her full $4,000 credit limit based on acceptable FICO score even though she had two other credit cards totaling approximately $30,000 in debt, or 150% of her gross income).

371 Federal Financial Institutions Examination Council, *Credit Card Lending Account Management and Loss Allowance Guidance* (Jan. 2003), *available at* www.federalreserve.gov/BoardDocs/press/bcreg/2003/20030108/attachment.pdf.

372 USPIRG, *The Credit Card Trap: How to Spot It, How to Avoid It* (Apr. 2001), at 12, *available at* www.truthaboutcredit.org.

373 *Id.*

374 15 U.S.C. § 1666b(a). National Consumer Law Center, Truth in Lending § 5.6.2 (5th ed. 2003 and Supp.).

375 Broder v. MBNA Corp., 722 N.Y.S.2d 524 (N.Y. Sup. Ct. 2001) (promotional material ambiguously disclosed in small print footnote that card issuer "may" allocate payments to promotional balances first).

376 *See* Johnson v. Chase Manhattan Bank USA, 784 N.Y.S.2d 921 (N.Y. Sup. Ct. 2004).

377 *See, e.g.,* State of Minnesota v. Cross County Bank, No. MC 03-5549 (Minn. Dist. Ct. 4th Jud. Dist. Nov. 10, 2004) (order granting motion for temporary injunction), available on the companion CD-Rom.

378 *See, e.g.,* Nelson v. First Nat. Bank Omaha, 2004 WL 2711032 (Minn. Ct. App. Nov. 30, 2004) (reversing summary judgment for credit card lender); Citibank (S.D.) Nat'l Assn. v. Whiteley, 149 S.W.3d 599 (Mo. Ct. App. 2004) (judgment for borrower due to lack of documentation); Atlantic Credit and Fin., Inc. v. Giuliana, 829 A.2d 340 (Pa. Super. 2003); First Selection Corp. v. Grimes, 2003 WL 151940 (Tex. App. Jan. 23, 2003) (summary judgment for borrower). For more on defending collection actions brought by credit card lenders and debt buyers, see generally *Overlooked Credit Card Defenses*, 22 NCLC REPORTS *Debt Collection & Repossessions Ed.* 5 (Sept./Oct. 2003); *Effective Challenges to Debt Buyers' Proof of Claims*, 22

they simply offer up an affidavit from an employee in their loss recovery department and/or sue on an account-stated theory.[379] This deprives the consumer of the ability to challenge erroneous transactions or demonstrate how much of their debt is due to purchases versus finance charges and junk fees.

Indeed, there is evidence that credit card lenders would be unable to offer up the original agreement or application signed by the cardholder. In one case, a major card issuer admitted in litigation that it does not retain the original account application of cardholder's beyond five years.[380] Yet these same lenders may sue the consumer, claiming that the terms of the now-destroyed documents justify charges, fees, and the liability of co-signers.

Related to the credit card lenders' failure to keep and provide adequate documentation on credit card accounts are their attempts to impose liability on parties who are not liable for credit card debt. Practitioners have reported that credit card lenders have attempted to impose liability on surviving spouses or other partners when the cardholder dies. In these cases, the surviving spouse or partner was not a joint account holder, and in some cases not even an authorized user. Some of these cases occurred in states without community property laws, or the partners were not married.

Another practice peculiar to credit card debt is "zombie debt collection,"[381] where credit card lenders buy old credit card debts, and then offer the debtors new credit cards to revive the old debt. Oftentimes, the debts are time-barred by the statute of limitations and would constitute stale information on the consumer's credit report under the Fair Credit Reporting Act.[382] Of course, the debt-buying credit card lenders deceptively omit this critical fact or bury it in fine print. In addition, the debt buyer/credit card lenders may fail to provide required disclosures as debt collectors under the Fair Debt Collection Practices Act.[383]

11.7.2.3.9 Use of mandatory arbitration clauses

Almost all credit card lenders have inserted mandatory arbitration provisions into their agreements. Many of these mandatory arbitration provisions have been added using the change-in-terms notices discussed in § 11.7.2.4, *infra*.[384]

Another volume in this series discusses mandatory arbitration in depth.[385] In short, mandatory arbitration in credit card disputes is consumer unfriendly because the consumer's only option for relief is an expensive arbitration proceeding (often conducted by arbitration providers that are biased against consumers).[386]

Most shockingly, credit card lenders are now using arbitration provisions offensively, as a lopsided method to obtain judgments against unsuspecting consumers. Some of these consumers include victims of unauthorized use and identity theft.[387]

NCLC REPORTS *Bankruptcy & Foreclosures Ed.* 1 (July/Aug. 2004); *Debt Buyers Putting Increased Long Term Pressure on Consumers*, 23 NCLC REPORTS *Debt Collection & Repossessions Ed.* 1 (Mar./Apr. 2005).

379 *See e.g.*, Citibank (S.D.) Nat'l Assn. v. Whiteley, 149 S.W.3d 599 (Mo. Ct. App. 2004). Challenging a credit card lender's or debt buyer's ability to satisfy the elements for an account-stated claim can be an effective defense. *See also* Asset Acceptance Corp. v. Proctor, 804 N.E.2d 975 (Ohio Ct. App. 2004). *But see* McManus v. Sears, Roebuck & Co., 2003 WL 22024238 (Tex. App. Aug. 28, 2003) (credit card lender not required to prove all elements of account-stated claim because of nature of the goods and services it sells.). Another option for defeating an account-stated claim is to raise disputes under TILA. *See, e.g.*, Discover Bank v. Walker, 2004 WL 1385477 (N.Y. Sup. App. June 4, 2004) (consumer defeated creditor's motion for summary judgment on account-stated claim by notifying card issuer of unauthorized use). *See generally* National Consumer Law Center, Truth in Lending, §§ 5.8.7.2, 5.9.4.3, 5.9.5.1 (5th ed. 2003 and Supp.). For a discussion of account-stated claims, see National Consumer Law Center, Fair Debt Collection, § 14.5.2 (5th ed. 2004 and Supp.).

380 Johnson v. MBNA, 357 F.3d 426 (4th Cir. 2004) (credit card lender attempted to impose liability for debt on ex-wife of the cardholder, who claimed she was merely an authorized user on the debt; lender admitted in litigation that because of its five-year documentation retention policy, the cardholder's original account application, which would have shown whether the ex-wife was a joint obligor or an authorized user, was no longer in its possession).

381 The term is taken from Liz Pulliam Weston, *Zombie Debt Collectors Dig Up Your Old Mistakes*, MSNMoney.com,

available at http://moneycentral.msn.com/content/Savinganddebt/Managedebt/P74812.asp.

382 Brink v. First Credit Resources, 185 F.R.D. 567 (D. Ariz. 1999).

383 Carbajal v. Capitol One, F.S.B., 2003 WL 22595265 (N.D. Ill. Nov. 10, 2003).

384 *See, e.g.*, Lawrence v. Household Bank, 343 F. Supp. 2d 1101 (M.D. Ala. 2004) (compelling arbitration of TILA and FCBA claims challenging a 9 a.m. cut-off for payment posting); Kurz v. Chase Manhattan Bank, 319 F. Supp. 2d 457 (S.D.N.Y. 2004) (compelling arbitration of FCBA claims as well as retaliation under the ECOA). *Cf.* Providian v. Screws, 2003 WL 22272861 (Ala. Oct. 3, 2003) (compelling arbitration of state law claims challenging bait and switch APRs, billing errors, and late fees.); Johnson v. Chase Manhattan Bank USA, 784 N.Y.S.2d 921, 2004 WL 413213 (N.Y. Sup. Ct. 2004) (compelling arbitration of state law claims challenging payment allocation abuse).

385 National Consumer Law Center, Consumer Arbitration Agreements (4th ed. 2004).

386 According to documents produced by the National Arbitration Forum itself, the consumer prevailed in just 87 out of 19,705 arbitrations conducted by NAF for First USA Bank. Thus, the credit card company prevailed a disturbing 99.56% of the time!

387 A report issued by NCLC documents how credit card debt buyers use arbitration proceedings to obtain judgments for thousands of dollars against identity theft victims. Steve Tripoli & Paul Bland, *New Trap Door for Consumers: Card Issuers Use Rubber-Stamp Arbitration to Rush Debts into Default Judgments*, National Consumer Law Center & Trial Lawyers for Public Justice (Feb. 27, 2005), *available at* www.consumerlaw.org/initiatives/model/content/ArbitrationNAF.pdf.

11.7.2.4 Unilateral Change in Terms Provisions

The expansive change-in-terms provisions in many credit card agreements are the mechanism that permits credit card lenders to impose excessive junk fees and engage in abusive practices. Many lenders place extremely expansive change-in-term provisions in their credit card agreements, which allow the lenders to change any of the terms in the agreement at any time.[388] Some states even permit changes in the terms of a credit agreement without a change-in-terms clause in the credit agreement.[389]

There are at least two problems with these changes in terms notices. First, these expansive change-in-terms provisions deprive consumers of any "benefit of bargain." They make a mockery of contract law because the terms of the "bargain" are illusory. They also undermine the Truth in Lending Act's purpose in ensuring effective disclosure. A savvy consumer can select a credit card after reviewing the TIL application and solicitation disclosures, comparing terms, reading articles about picking a credit card—in other words, be the smart shopper that the TILA envisioned—then be faced with a change-in-terms notice that entirely changes the APR and other terms of the credit card. One court has described change-in-terms provisions as "an Orwellian nightmare, trapped in agreements that can be amended unilaterally in ways they never envisioned."[390]

Second, the vast majority of consumers probably do not read or understand change-in-terms notices. While not involving credit cards, the case of *Ting v. AT&T*[391] is instructive. In that case, AT&T mailed a consumer services agreement to its customers that, among other provisions, added a mandatory arbitration clause. Before mailing this agreement, AT&T conducted extensive market research designed to predict how consumers would react to the mailing. AT&T then designed its mailing to ensure that consumers would be less likely to read and understand the details of the agreement.

For instance, AT&T's research found that only 25% of customers would actually open up the envelope for the mailing if it was sent separately from the monthly bill. For those customers who did open up the envelope, AT&T's research found that only 30% of them would read the entire agreement.[392]

Furthermore, even when consumers do open and read change-in-terms notices, the notices are full of dense, impenetrable legal jargon that even seasoned practitioners have difficulty understanding.[393] The vast majority of consumers do not have the literacy ability to read and comprehend these notices.[394]

Under Regulation Z, which implements the Truth in Lending Act, creditors are required to provide a 15-day notice period for some changes in terms.[395] The change-in-terms provisions of Regulation Z may contribute to the problem because they legitimize the practice of changing terms.

---

388 A typical change-in-terms agreement provides:

> We may amend or change any part of your Agreement, including the periodic rates and other charges, or add or remove requirements at any time. If we do so, we will give you notice if required by law of such amendment or change. Changes to the annual percentage rate(s) will apply to your account balance from the effective date of the change, whether or not the account balance included items billed to the account before the change date and whether or not you continue to use the account. Changes to fees and other charges will apply to your account from the effective date of the change.

Stone v. Golden Wexler & Sarnese, P.C., 341 F. Supp. 2d. 189, 191 (E.D.N.Y. 2004).

389 *See, e.g.,* Del. Code Ann. tit. 5, § 952 (a).

390 Perry v. FleetBoston Fin. Corp., 2004 WL 1508518 at *4 n.5 (E.D. Pa. July 6, 2004). This court went on to say that it was "reminded of George Orwell's 1946 work, Animal Farm, in which the pigs assume power and change the terms of the animals' social contract, reducing the original Seven Commandments, which included 'All animals are equal,' to one—'All animals are equal, but some animals are more equal than others.' "

391 319 F.3d 1126 (9th Cir. 2003).

392 Similar data has been reported by industry analysts. A survey by Auriemma Consulting Group finding that only one-third of consumers who received change-in-terms notices were aware of the changed terms. Bill Burt, *Ignoring Credit Changes Can Cost You,* (Jan. 30, 2004) *available at* www.bankrate.com/brm/news/cc/20040129a1.asp.

393 For example, a sample change-in-terms notice states:

> Your Daily Periodic Rate and corresponding APR may increase or decrease from time to time according to the movements up or down of the Index, which is the highest Prime Rate published in the "Money Rates" section of the Midwest Edition of The Wall Street Journal in the last 90 days, before the date on which the billing cycle closed (in other words, the "statement date"). Any variable rate adjustment based on an Index change will be effective as of the first day of the billing cycle, and will apply to the new and outstanding Account balances and transactions subject to that variable rate.

Using the Flesch Reading Ease score built into Microsoft Word, this text rates at a mere 29.7 out of 100 (the higher the better, standard documents score around 60 to 70), and requires a 12th grade reading level. In addition, this particular change-in-terms agreement was written in 4 ½-point type, in a bill stuffer consisting of 16 folded panels.

394 *See* Alan M. White & Cathy Lesser Mansfield, *Literacy and Contract,* 13 Stan. L. & Pol'y Rev. 233 (2002) (according to National Adult Literacy Survey, only 3–4% of the American adult population has the documentary literacy skills necessary to utilize a table comparing the features of two credit cards, so as to identify two differences between the cards).

395 For a discussion of TILA's notice requirements for a change in terms to an open-end account, see National Consumer Law Center, Truth in Lending, § 5.7.3 (5th ed. 2003 and Supp.).

11.7.3 *Challenging Credit Card Abuse*

11.7.3.1 Breach of Contract

A breach of contract claim is probably one of the first theories that comes to mind when analyzing an abusive credit card practice for legal violations.[396] Obtaining and understanding the underlying contract, however, may not be as easy as it sounds—and not just because the contractual language is obscure. Many consumers do not keep their credit card contracts, often because they are a small print document that arrives in a separate envelope from the card itself.

Even if a consumer retains the original credit card agreement, it may not be the contract governing the transaction, given the ability of credit card lenders to make unilateral "change in terms."[397] Thus, it may be possible that the consumer is legally being charged a 15% interest rate even though the original credit contract provided for a fixed rate of 12%. This possibility must be considered before pursuing any contract claim.

Without obtaining the initial credit card agreement and any changes in terms notices, it is thus difficult to evaluate the merits of any claim. If the client does not have everything needed and the creditor will not send the necessary documentation voluntarily, it is available in discovery.

The quandary with planning a case around a discovery strategy is, of course, that it is difficult to determine the initial violation justifying commencing the case at all. One potential way around this problem is to look for a legal claim of any type based on the available documentation. For example, state unfair and deceptive practices arguments may be easier to identify for open-end credit then a breach of contract violation. The UDAP claim then provides a platform to file a case and pursue discovery. Other appropriate claims can then be raised by amending the initial pleadings.

11.7.3.2 State UDAP Statutes

Consumers may have claims against credit card lenders under their state's unfair and deceptive acts and practices (UDAP) statute.[398] Private class actions have asserted UDAP claims against credit card lenders for deceptive and unfair practices when charging fees.[399] The Office of the Comptroller of the Currency has taken action in several instances under the Federal Trade Commission Act against credit card lenders that have committed allegedly unfair or deceptive acts against consumers.[400]

Note that some states may exempt lenders from the scope of their UDAP statutes.[401] Furthermore, the issue of preemption must be considered when using UDAP statutes against federally-chartered institutions. While general challenges to deception may not be preempted, it may be an issued when challenging the size of a fee or its existence.[402]

11.7.3.3 Other Claims

In addition to breach of contract and UDAP claims, there are potential claims available under a number of other statutes and common law theories, such as the Racketeer Influenced and Corrupt Organizations Act,[403] unconscionability,[404] breach of the duty of good faith and fair dealing,[405] breach of fiduciary duty,[406] and common law fraud.[407] The advantage of federal statutory and state common law claims is practitioners may be more able to avoid a preemption issue than for state statutory claims.

11.7.3.4 Intersection with Federal Truth in Lending Act

The primary regulation of credit card lending at the federal level is the Truth in Lending Act. Another volume in this series discusses TILA's regulation of credit cards and

---

[396] *See, e.g.*, Chavers v. Fleet Bank (RI), N.A., 2004 WL 249605 (R.I. Feb. 11, 2004) (dismissing UDAP claim but permitting breach of contract claim to go forward).

[397] For a further discussion of contract issues in credit card cases, see Robert S. Green, *Litigating Credit Card Cases*, 5 The Consumer Advocate 4 (July/Aug. 1999), a publication of the National Association of Consumer Advocates, 1730 Massachusetts Ave., NW, Suite 710, Washington DC 20036.

[398] *See* Robert S. Green, *Litigating Credit Card Cases*, 5 The Consumer Advocate 4 (July/Aug. 1999), a publication of the National Association of Consumer Advocates, 1717 Massachusetts Ave., NW, Suite 704, Washington DC 20036. *See generally*

National Consumer Law Center, Unfair and Deceptive Acts and Practices (6th ed. 2004).

[399] *See, e.g.*, Rubin v. MasterCard Int'l, L.L.C., 342 F. Supp. 2d 217 (S.D.N.Y. 2004); Landreneau v. Fleet Fin. Group, 197 F. Supp. 2d 551 (M.D. La. 2002); Bond v. Fleet Bank, 2002 WL 31500393 (D.R.I. Oct. 10, 2002); Sims v. First Consumers Nat'l Bank, 758 N.Y.S.2d 284 (N.Y. App. Div. 2003).

[400] Consent Order, *In re* Providian Nat'l Bank, No. 2000-53 (Dept. of the Treasury, Office of the Comptroller of the Currency June 28, 2000), *available at* www.occ.treas.gov/FTP/EAs/ea2000-53.pdf; Consent Order, *In re* Direct Merchants Credit Card Bank, No. 2001-24 (Dept of Treasury, Office of the Comptroller of the Currency, May 3, 2001), *available at* www.occ.treas.gov/ftp/eas/ea2001-24.pdf.

[401] *See* National Consumer Law Center, Truth in Lending, § 2.6.3 (5th ed. 2003 and Supp.); National Consumer Law Center Unfair and Deceptive Acts and Practices § 2.3.3 (6th ed. 2004).

[402] *See generally* Ch. 3, *supra* and National Consumer Law Center Unfair and Deceptive Acts and Practices (6th ed. 2004 and Supp.).

[403] *See* § 12.6, *infra*.

[404] *See* § 12.7, *infra*.

[405] *See* § 12.8, *infra*.

[406] *See* § 12.9, *infra*.

[407] *See* § 12.10, *infra*.

open-end credit in general.[408] TILA is primarily a disclosure statute, although there are a handful of dispute resolution and substantive protections in the statute specifically for credit cards. Even so, TILA's protections are nowhere near adequate to control the myriad credit card abuses existing today. TILA's credit card protections, enacted before the sweeping expansion of preemption during the last decade,[409] were simply not designed to be the primary, if not sole, source of protection for credit card consumers. Despite the dearth of protections, Congress has resisted efforts to enact meaningful substantive regulations to stem these abuses.

11.7.3.5 Preemption and Credit Cards

11.7.3.5.1 General

The problems involved in analyzing an abusive credit card practice for legal violations is always complicated by the complex scheme of federal preemption of state law governing credit, because most credit card lenders are financial institutions who can avail themselves of the benefits of preemption.[410] Thus, it is rarely the substantive law of the state where the consumer lives that is applicable.[411] Interest rates, late charges and other terms (such as laws restricting changes in terms) will be governed by the law of the state where the lender is incorporated. Practitioners cannot assume that a creditor has disclosed an illegal term simply by checking their own state's law.

11.7.3.5.2 TILA preemption

In contrast, the Truth in Lending Act has a narrow scope of preemption.[412] Other than state laws relating to disclo-

sures concerning credit and charge cards applications, solicitations, or in renewal notices, TIL does not preempt state laws governing credit cards (or open-end credit in general) as long as these laws are not inconsistent with TIL requirements. For example, a state law concerning periodic statements in general would not be preempted by TILA.[413]

Despite the fact that TILA itself has a narrow scope of preemption, the ability of states to require credit card disclosures is significantly constrained with respect to federally-chartered financial institutions, which constitute the vast majority of credit card lenders. A federal court has held that the preemption provisions in the various banking statutes, and not TILA's preemption standard, control when analyzing whether state laws regarding credit card disclosures are preempted.[414]

11.7.4 Assisting Consumers Overwhelmed by Credit Card Debt

In many cases, consumers who come forward with problems concerning their credit card accounts are financially overwhelmed. Identifying state law or Truth in Lending violations may only partially resolve the consumers' needs. Consumers may be able to obtain relief by use of strategies such as debt prioritization, bankruptcy, and aggressive foreclosure defense. At the same time, practitioners should also consider educating consumers about careful use of available credit to avoid new problems in the future. Materials to educate consumers with credit card problems are available in National Consumer Law Center, *Guide to Surviving Debt* (2005 ed.).[415]

---

408 National Consumer Law Center, Truth in Lending Ch. 5 (5th ed. 2003 and Supp.).
409 *See* Ch. 3, *supra.*
410 *See generally* Ch. 3, *supra.*
411 *See generally* Chs. 2 and 3, *supra.*
412 *See* National Consumer Law Center, Truth in Lending § 2.6.3 (general TILA preemption), § 5.4.6 (TILA preemption for credit

card application and solicitation disclosures), § 5.7.4.3.5 (change in insurance coverage disclosure), § 5.8.10 (Fair Credit Billing Act preemption) (5th ed. 2003 and Supp.).
413 Official Staff Commentary § 226.28(d)-3.
414 American Bankers Ass'n v. Lockyer, 239 F. Supp. 2d 1000 (E.D. Cal. 2002).
415 Information about ordering is available on the NCLC website, www.consumerlaw.org, or by contacting the Publications Department at 617-542-9595 or by faxing 617-542-8028.

Chapter 12

Beyond Usury: Statutory and Common Law Challenges to Overreaching Credit

12.1 Introduction

The first analysis of a credit transaction that does not pass the "smell test" should be whether the creditor violated any specific statutory or regulatory mandate. As this book attempts to make clear, even following the deregulatory fervor of the 1980s, there is still considerable regulation of the substantive terms of credit, though specific numerical rate and fee caps may no longer be statutorily proscribed. Given the purposes of this legislation[1] and the charge to the courts to look behind the face of things to determine the true nature of the transaction,[2] those statutes may still be viable avenues for relief, even in deregulated states.[3]

In addition to the specific statutes that historically have been the primary source of regulation for consumer credit,[4] there are some other statutes that may offer a remedy. Two federal statutes relating specifically to home-secured credit have some substantive provisions that relate to the ultimate cost of credit.[5] The Real Estate Settlement Procedures Act (RESPA), which applies much more broadly as a result of 1992 amendments, has some substantive limitations in it.[6] The Home Ownership and Equity Protection Act of 1994 (HOEPA) similarly contains limitations on cost-related terms in covered home equity loans.[7] A growing number of states have enacted "HOEPA-like" laws regulating the terms of certain mortgage loans.[8]

Federal and state credit repair statutes may apply to the third parties involved in many credit transactions—brokers, home improvement contractors, and car dealers.[9]

That minority borrowers are too often targeted for high-cost credit means that fair lending, fair housing and civil rights statutes are a source of potential challenge to overreaching credit.[10]

In the auto financing context, many states have incorporated a "single document rule" into state consumer financing statutes.[11] These statutes require that all terms or obligations of the parties related to the transaction be contained in one document. The practice of many auto dealers is to spread the terms of the financing throughout several documents. These statutes can be used to attack this phenomenon.[12]

Finally, one of the most vital statutory tools which is widely available in cases of lender overreaching is the body of state unfair and deceptive practices acts (UDAP) law, which generally prohibits unfair or deceptive business practices.[13]

---

1 See § 9.3.1.1, *supra*.

2 See § 9.2.1.6, *supra*. See also Chs. 7, 8, *supra*.

3 It is possible to exceed applicable caps even if a statute does not specify a numerical cap, see §§ 9.2.7, 9.2.8, *supra*. Further, regarding common consumer credit transactions, regulation of cost-related terms may remain even in the absence of a usury or fee cap, e.g., the Rule of 78 may be prohibited; add-on or discount interest may be prohibited; or limits on default or delinquency charges may remain.

4 *E.g.*, small loan and consumer loan acts; RISAs; consumer credit codes; and the body of traditional usury law. These have been the primary focus of the other chapters in this book.

5 The Federal Truth in Lending Act, while applicable to most consumer credit, is primarily a disclosure statute. 15 U.S.C. §§ 1601–1666j.

6 See § 12.2.1, *infra*.

7 See § 12.2.2, *infra. See also* § 5.8.2, *supra*.

8 See § 12.2.3, *infra*.

9 See § 12.4, *infra*.

10 § 12.3, *infra. See generally* National Consumer Law Center, Credit Discrimination §§ 8.2, 8.5.4 (4th ed. 2005).

11 *See, e.g.*, Cal. Civ. Code § 1803.2; Wash. Rev. Code § 63.14.020; Rugumbwa v. Betten Motor Sales, 136 F. Supp. 2d 729 (W.D. Mich. 2001) (single document rule in state MVRISA was used to defeat motion to compel arbitration because the arbitration clause was not in the retail installment contract). For a fuller discussion of the single document rule and its use in auto financing litigation, *see* § 11.6.8, *supra*.

12 *See, e.g.*, Kroupa v. Sunrise Ford, 92 Cal. Rptr. 2d 42 (Cal. Ct. App. 1999) (the trade-in of two cars and the negative equity resulting from those trade-in were part and parcel of the transaction to lease the new car; therefore, the failure to add them into the new lease document violated the single document rule). *But see* Sharlow v. Wally McCarthy Pontiac-GMC Trucks-Hyundai, Inc., 2000 U.S. App. LEXIS 15627 (8th Cir. July 6, 2000) (Michigan single document rule not violated where "conditional delivery agreement" did not directly change the cost of credit terms in the retail installment sales contract); Scott v. Forest Lake Chrysler-Plymouth-Dodge, 611 N.W.2d 346 (Minn. 2000) (same), *appeal after remand on other grounds*, 637 N.W.2d 587 (Minn. Ct. App. 2002).

13 See § 12.5, *infra. See generally* National Consumer Law Center, Unfair and Deceptive Acts and Practices (6th ed. 2004 and Supp.).

The Cost of Credit: Regulation and Legal Challenges

The successful use in the credit context of common law theories based on notions of fairness demonstrate that courts and juries may be willing to take a critical look at creditor overreaching even where the letter of the law is not broken. Unconscionability,[14] the duty of good faith and fair dealing,[15] and fraud or misrepresentation[16] have all been successfully used. Breach of fiduciary duty claims are available against brokers who steer borrowers to predatory lenders, and, in limited circumstances, may also be available against lenders. Similarly, lenders may be vulnerable to claims for interference with contractual relations where they seduce brokers to arrange loans based on the brokers' own interests rather than the interests of the brokers' client-borrowers. In a number of cases, borrowers have won large damage awards from juries based on unfair lender conduct.[17]

In recent years, a number of non-bank finance companies have filed chapter 11 bankruptcy cases which makes it more difficult for homeowners to raise their claims and defenses when they believe the loans contain overreaching or predatory terms and conditions. While representing a consumer as a creditor in the bankruptcy court can seem daunting, such an effort may be critical to rectifying the wrongs committed by such companies. For a discussion of the special issues raised when lenders file bankruptcy, *see* National Consumer Law Center, *Consumer Bankruptcy Law and Practice* § 17.9.1 (7th ed. 2004).

This chapter will briefly discuss these theories as they apply to the types of problems that commonly arise for low-income borrowers. The chapter will conclude with an outline of the theories to hold assignees and lenders liable for the behavior of other parties.

12.2 Federal and State Statutes Relating to Real Estate Secured Credit

12.2.1 The Real Estate Settlement Procedures Act (RESPA)

12.2.1.1 Scope

The express purpose of the Real Estate Settlement Procedures Act (RESPA)[18] is to protect consumers from unnecessarily high settlement charges and certain abusive practices that have developed in the residential real estate industry.[19] It attempts to achieve this goal primarily by controlling the manner by which settlement services for residential real estate loan transactions are provided and compensated. It also requires advance disclosure of settlement costs, designed to enable a borrower to make an informed decision as to whether the offered terms are reasonable and acceptable. HUD is the agency designated to promulgate regulations under and to enforce RESPA. This section is not a complete discussion of RESPA, but rather highlights several areas that are likely to be of most relevance for practitioners.[20]

While RESPA initially applied only to loans secured by a first lien on residential real property of one to four units,[21] in 1992 it was amended to include all such loans secured by subordinate liens as well.[22] In addition, RESPA's scope is limited to "federally related mortgage loans," which are defined as those made by federally-insured depository lend-

---

14 *See* § 12.7, *infra.*

15 *See* § 12.8, *infra.*

16 *See* § 12.10, *infra.*

17 "Lender liability" litigation came to the fore in the context of business lending, where the stakes were very large, and so were the jury awards. Six of the ten largest jury awards in the country in 1987 were lender liability cases. *"Lender Liability": The Next Big Area for Your Firm?*, 7 Law Alert 496 (Sept. 5, 1988); *see also* Johnson & Gaffney, *Lender Liability: Perspectives on Risk and Prevention*, 105 Banking L.J. 325 (1988).

The activity in the commercial arena has settled since then. In addition to the reversal on appeal of some multi-million dollar jury verdicts, the banking industry fought back on other avenues, such as "getting special legislation" to protect them, and by restricting "the ability of their customers to sue them at all by insisting on arbitration clauses and by demanding waivers of the right to jury trials." *See* A. Barry Cappello & Frances E. Komoroske, *Current Developments in Lender Liability Litigation*, Second Annual ABA Satellite Seminar on Suing and Defending Banks, at 178 (ABA Section of Litig. and Div. for Prof'l Educ. May 20, 1993). Some of these restraints apply solely to commercial lending relationships, and so will not affect consumer disputes.

This business lending litigation did not create new theories. Rather its major import seemed to be that the debtor's lawyers brought to "contract" litigation the approach of a personal injury case, which tends to maximize damages. *Lender Liability: Perspectives on Risk and Prevention*, 105 Banking L.J. 325 n.8 (1988). This approach has similarly been brought successfully to consumer litigation. *See, e.g.,* Carlisle v. Whirlpool Fin. Nat'l Bank, Clearinghouse No. 52,516 (Circuit Court, Hale County, Ala., Post Trial Order, Aug. 25, 1999) (jury verdict in two satellite sale and financing cases for $580 million in punitive damages reduced $300 million, though judge found defendants behavior "alarming" and "reprehensible," in part due to the evidence of sales practice designed to target and take advantage of the poor, under-educated elderly, and African-American citizens). Note that the recently, the Supreme Court set tough standards regarding the award of punitive damages. *See* § 12.10, *infra.*

18 12 U.S.C. §§ 2601–2617.

19 Wanger v. EMC Mortgage Corp., 127 Cal. Rptr. 2d 685 (Cal. Ct. App. 2002) (RESPA is a consumer protection statute and should be liberally construed).

20 HUD has proposed certain reforms of RESPA and TILA in a joint report with the Federal Reserve Board issued in 1998 to Congress. *U.S. Dep't of Housing & Urban Dev. & Fed. Reserve Bd., Joint Report to Cong. Concerning Reform to the Truth in Lending Act and the Real Estate Settlement Procedures Act* (1998), *available at* www.federalreserve.gov/boarddocs/rptcongress/tila.pdf.

21 12 U.S.C. § 2602(1)(A).

22 Pub. L. No. 102-550, § 908, 106 Stat. 3672 (1992); *see also* 59 Fed. Reg. 6506, 6511 (Feb. 10, 1994).

ers (other than for temporary financing, such as a construction loan), HUD-related loans, loans intended to be sold on the secondary market to Fannie Mae (Federal National Mortgage Association) or Freddie Mac (Federal Home Loan Mortgage Corporation), or to creditors who make or invest more than $1 million a year in residentially secured loans.[23] Thus, most home equity loans, as well as refinancings and the like are now subject to RESPA requirements.

Mobile home purchase loans and construction loans are usually covered by RESPA if the loan will be secured by the property.[24] However, any loan secured by vacant land is excluded unless a structure or manufactured home will be constructed or placed on the real property using the loan proceeds within two years from the date of settlement.[25]

An exception to RESPA coverage that may prove troublesome is the exception for secondary market transactions.[26] A bona fide secondary market transaction is one where a mortgage lender makes loans for its own portfolio and finances these loans from its own or borrowed funds. The lender will usually hold the loan for varying periods of time with the option of selling its loans on the open market.[27] In contrast, a table-funded transaction, which *is* subject to RESPA, is one where the nominal "lender" is actually originating the loan for another entity whose money is used to fund the loan. The loan will be transferred within a relatively short period of time to the ultimate lender. HUD admonishes, though, that the substance, not the form, of the transaction should be reviewed.[28] Interestingly, in this situation, HUD defines the "lender" as the person to whom the obligation is initially assigned at or after settlement.[29]

The Fifth and Eighth Circuits have ruled on what constitutes a secondary market transaction based on the facts of the cases confronting them. In *Moreno v. Summit Mortgage Corp.*, the lender funded the loans initially through a warehouse line of credit by a bank and then sold them under a prior agreement with a purchaser (who was not the warehouse lender) that did not require the purchaser to buy any loans until it issued a commitment but, once it did, the lender had to use its best efforts to close the loan and transfer it to the purchaser.[30] The warehouse lender only funded "committed" loans, that is, loans that a purchaser had promised to buy. The court held that this constituted a secondary mortgage transaction and RESPA did not apply to it. In the Eighth Circuit case, the majority primarily looked at the source of the nominal lender's funding in making the loan, characterizing the line of credit as the lender's own monies. The dissent, however, pointed to prior "Purchase and Sale" agreements to pool and securitize the loans and transfer them through an entity to the trustee, Norwest Bank Minnesota. The funds from the securitization purchase allowed the nominal lender to repay the line of credit that funded the loan. Given these facts, the dissent characterized the transaction as "a pure circumvention" of RESPA.[31]

12.2.1.2 Cost Disclosure Provisions

RESPA requirements begin to play a role early in the home mortgage process. No later than three business days after application, the consumer must be given a "good faith estimate" of settlement costs.[32] However, no estimate is required for home equity lines of credit, as Regulation Z

---

23 12 U.S.C. § 2602(1)(B). In the latter category, "creditors" are defined by reference to the Truth in Lending definition. *See* 15 U.S.C. § 1602(f); *see also* Gardner v. First Am. Title Ins. Co., 294 F.3d 991 (8th Cir. 2002) (the home owner must plead that the loan is a "federally related mortgage loan" and that the defendant violated RESPA; complaint stated a claim though these allegations were buried in paragraphs 20 and 85); Brazier v. Sec. Pac. Mortgage, Inc., 245 F. Supp. 2d 1136 (W.D. Wash. 2003) (summary judgment granted to the lender when it represented that it made less than $1 million in loans and the consumer put forth no evidence to refute the allegation); National Consumer Law Center, Truth in Lending § 2.3 (5th ed. 2003 and Supp.).

  RESPA does not apply to commercial loans. Scocca v. Cendant Mortgage Corp., 2004 WL 2536837 (E.D. Pa. Nov. 9, 2004); Quinn v. McCoy, 2002 WL 1303407 (Cal. Ct. App. June 14, 2002).

24 Reg. X, 24 C.F.R. § 3500.5(a)(4).

25 *Id.*

26 Reg. X, 24 C.F.R. § 3500.5(a)(7).

27 Such lenders often obtain what is called a "warehouse" line of credit from a bank or investment bank. The loan and all related documents are "warehoused" for a given period of time until the loan is sold to an investor or securitized. Another variation is a repurchase agreement which functions as a line of credit to the lender. This type of transaction involves a short-term sale of the loan to the investment bank and subsequent repurchase of the loan by the originator after a specified period of time. It is less clear whether this latter arrangement is a true "secondary market" transaction to qualify for the exemption from RESPA.

28 Reg. X, 24 C.F.R. § 3500.5(a)(7). Easter v. American West Fin.,

---

381 F.3d 948 (9th Cir. 2004) (court will look at substance over form in deciding under what circumstances a table-funded transaction occurred).

29 Reg. X, 24 C.F.R. § 3500.2(b). In one case, a court held that if the transaction was a table-funded one, the nominal assignee ("lender" under HUD's definition) can be liable for RESPA violations and can be liable under the state UDAP act for these violations. Jenkins v. Mercantile Mortgage Co., 231 F. Supp. 2d 737 (N.D. Ill. 2002). *See also* Easter v. American West Fin., 381 F.3d 948 (9th Cir. 2004) (court relies upon the RESPA definition of lender in a non-RESPA case to held that the broker was not the actual lender and consequently was not subject to the state usury law).

30 Moreno v. Summit Mortgage Corp., 364 F.3d 574 (5th Cir. 2004). *See also* Novakovic v. Samutin, 820 N.E.2d 967 (Ill. App. 2004) (bona fide secondary market transaction occurred where the lender had a warehouse line of credit from Indy Mac and then sold the loans to Option One; profit to lender from the sale of the not subject to RESPA; however, payment to the broker, if not an employee of the lender, could be subject to RESPA).

31 Chandler v. Norwest Bank Minn., 137 F.3d 1053, 1058 (8th Cir. 1998).

32 12 U.S.C. § 2604(d).

already provides for disclosures in such transactions.[33] The lender or, in some circumstances, the mortgage broker is required to use a Good Faith Estimate form, a sample of which is attached to TILA's Regulation X.[34] This form itemizes every charge associated with the transaction, such as points and all the usual closing costs, including real estate agents' and broker fees.[35] Estimates of the amount or range for each charge must bear a reasonable relationship to the borrower's ultimate cost for each charge and must be based upon experience in the area in which the property is located.[36] HUD instructions to lenders on how to properly itemize charges on the good faith estimate and HUD-1 follow Regulation X in the Code of Federal Regulations.[37] In addition to this settlement statement, a booklet explaining these costs must be given.[38]

When the good-faith estimate of settlement costs precedes the loan closing, it may alert consumers to loans with excessive points or large, surprising broker fees, and help them avoid the trap. Of course, where the time between application and closing is less than three days, the RESPA statement may be just one more of the many papers presented at consummation to the borrower who does not have the time to review and absorb the information. Even where disclosure is made in a timely fashion, it may not have meaning for some consumers. However, information in

these disclosures still may prove useful long after closing of a covered transaction. For instance, it could aid practitioners in determining whether protection under the Home Ownership and Equity Protection Act of 1994 is triggered.[39] Also, equity-skimming generally would be easier to detect.

In addition to the early good faith estimate, all settlement agents must use the HUD-1 settlement statement at the closing which shall clearly and conspicuously itemize all charges actually imposed on the borrower.[40] The statute specifically requires that the statement indicate whether any title insurance premium included in the charges covers or insures the lender's or borrower's interests or both.[41] Further, the borrower is entitled to inspect the settlement statement at closing and receive a copy.[42] Upon request, the borrower also has the right to see the itemization during the business day immediately preceding the day of settlement.[43] The consumer can waive receipt of a copy of the HUD-1 at settlement if the consumer executes a written waiver at or before the closing.[44] In that event, the HUD-1 must be mailed or delivered to the consumer as soon as practicable after the settlement.

A review of the HUD-1 provided at settlement will reveal whether the estimate of the costs was at all close to the actual charges. If not, the consumer may have been baited with better terms then switched into a disadvantageous loan, thus raising fraud and UDAP claims.[45] No remedies are

---

33   Reg. X, 24 C.F.R. § 3500.7(f); *see* 15 U.S.C. § 1637a; National Consumer Law Center, Truth in Lending § 5.11 (5th ed. 2003 and Supp.).

34   U.S.C. § 2604(c); Reg. X, 24 C.F.R. § 3500.7. The form is located in Appx. C to this regulation. A mortgage broker must provide this disclosure, not the lender, when the loan application is received by the broker and the broker is not an exclusive agent of the lender.

35   Reg. X, 12 C.F.R. § 3500.7(c).

36   Reg. X, 24 C.F.R. §§ 3500.7(a) and (c)(2); *see also* Briggs v. Countrywide Funding Corp., 931 F. Supp. 1545 (yield spread premium to broker at issue; court denied lender's motion to dismiss, holding RESPA requires disclosure of yield spread premium, and it preempts Alabama state law to the extent state law does not require disclosure of the premium; a variety of state law claims were plead, including fraudulent concealment; improper interference with brokerage contract, inducement to breach fiduciary duties, and RICO), *vacated on other grounds*, 949 F. Supp. 812 (M.D. Ala. 1996); Weatherman v. Gary-Wheaton Bank, 713 N.E.2d 543 (Ill. 1999) (recording fees may be aggregated on one line of good faith estimate, in contrast to the HUD-1 used at settlement; dissent argues that a gross estimate of all recording fees is not adequate where the recording fees relate to different transactions, that is, the recordation of the new mortgage versus the release of the old). *But cf.* Bloom v. Martin, 77 F.3d 318 (9th Cir. 1996) (RESPA's disclosure requirement do not apply to demand and reconveyance fees); Smith v. Litton Loan Serv., L.P., 2005 WL 289927 (E.D. Pa. Feb. 4, 2005) (the GFE need not include the disclosure of the yield spread premium, though it cites no authority for this statement).

37   Reg. X, 24 C.F.R. § 3500.7(c)(2), App. A (reprinted in Appx. K.2, *infra*; *see also* Federal Reserve System Compliance Handbook, Clearinghouse No. 52,526, at 1-319 (Oct. 1997).

38   12 U.S.C. § 2604; Reg. X, 24 C.F.R. § 3500.6 (not required for refinancings, subordinate lien or reverse mortgages).

39   *See* § 12.2.2, *infra*; National Consumer Law Center, Truth in Lending Ch. 9 (5th ed. 2003 and Supp.).

40   12 U.S.C. §§ 2603(a) and (b); Reg. X, 24 C.F.R. §§ 3500.8(a) and (b). Federal Reserve System Compliance Handbook, Clearinghouse No. 52,526, at 1-320 (Oct. 1997). Financial institutions must retain copies for five years from the date of settlement. *Id.* at 1-321. Note that HUD, by regulation, excludes home equity lines of credit from this requirement. Reg. X, 24 C.F.R. § 3500.8(f). The statute does not contain these exceptions. *Cf.* 12 U.S.C. § 2603. The statute and regulation place the burden on the settlement agent to provide the HUD-1 and to fill it out accurately. However, the settlement agent is the agent of the lender. The lender should be responsible if the agent fails to perform its duties under RESPA. One court held that the lender is not liable. Turner v. Provident Funding Assoc., 2004 WL 1113151 (Cal. Ct. App. May 19, 2004).

41   12 U.S.C. § 2603(a).

42   12 U.S.C. § 2603(b)Reg. X, 24 C.F.R. § 3500.10.

43   Reg. X, 24 C.F.R. § 3500.10(a).

44   12 U.S.C. § 2603(b); Reg. X, 24 C.F.R. § 3500.10(c).

45   *See, e.g.*, Brophy v. Chase Manhattan Mortgage Co., 947 F. Supp. 879 (E.D. Pa. 1996) (borrowers could pursue state law claims in state court on issue of whether disparities between good faith estimate and HUD-1 settlement statement violated Pennsylvania's UDAP statute); *see also* The Provident Bank v. Wright, 2001 U.S. Dist. LEXIS 9621 (N.D. Ill. July 11, 2001) (drastic difference between the GFE and the HUD-1 states a UDAP claim); National Consumer Law Center, Unfair and Deceptive Acts and Practices §§ 4.6.1, 5.1.5, 5.1.7 (6th ed. 2004 and Supp.). *But see* Turner v. Provident Funding Assoc., 2004 WL 1113151 (Cal. Dist. Ct. App. May 19, 2004) (not a RESPA violation against the lender when broker fees change from the time the GFE is issued and the closing; broker not sued in this case).

prescribed for violations of these sections,[46] but failure to comply should constitute a violation of state unfair and deceptive acts and practices statutes.[47]

Also required, when a so-called "affiliated business arrangement" is involved, is a statement disclosing the nature of the relationship between the provider of the settlement service and the person or entity making the referral, and a written estimate of the charge or range of charges generally made by such provider.[48] The disclosures must be provided on a separate piece of paper at the time of the referral or at the time of application, with certain exceptions.[49] This document also is useful in determining whether any of the closing costs count towards the points and fees trigger for Home Ownership and Equity Protection Act purposes.[50]

HUD has not issued any formal policy statements regarding the cost disclosures with the exception of the instructions accompanying Regulation X.[51] In 2000, one of HUD's assistant general counsels, responded to a list of questions and answers from the Massachusetts Bankers Association

relating to disclosures on the HUD-1 form. This letter did not receive public attention until the Office of the Comptroller of the Currency circulated it to the chief executive officers of all of the national banks in the country.[52]

One of HUD's most interesting revelations relates to whether the actual dollar amount of the commission earned by the settlement agent or closing attorney for issuing a title insurance policy must be disclosed on the HUD-1. HUD unequivocally states that the commission must be listed.[53] The agency goes further and opines that line 1107 (attorney fees) or, alternatively, line 1113 (blank) on the HUD-1 must show the amount of the commission and the services provided for that fee. (Note that if the services listed are compensated for elsewhere on the HUD-1, the commission may be an illegal kickback under RESPA.[54])

In addition, if the closing agent bundles the cost of services into a lump sum as "attorney's fees" on line 1107, the HUD-1 must show what services were included in the lump sum. This additional information must be listed under line 1107. This specificity will help consumers and practitioners determine more accurately whether any fees are duplicative or inflated before filing a lawsuit.

Query whether there is any reason to treat single premium credit insurance different from title insurance: it appears from a close reading of Regulation X and Appendix A that, while the premium for credit insurance products should be listed, the commission for the sale of it need not be separately itemized, IF the insurance was not required by the lender. (As many consumer practitioners know, the sale of credit insurance products is fraught with abuse, the most common of which that the lender slides it into the loan, unbeknownst to the consumer or simply tells the consumer that it is required, despite the written disclaimers to the contrary.[55])

First, the definition of "settlement services" in Regulation X should be reviewed.[56] The "provision of services" involving mortgage life, disability, or similar insurance designed to pay a mortgage loan upon death or disability IS

46 Several courts have held that there is no private right of action under 12 U.S.C. § 2604: Collins v. FMHA-USDA, 105 F.3d 1366 (11th Cir. 1997); Beard v. Worldwide Mortgage Corp., 354 F. Supp. 2d 789 (W.D. Tenn. 2005); Wingert v. Credit Based Asset Serv. & Securitization, L.L.C., 2004 WL 2915306 (W.D. Pa. Aug. 26, 2004); Chow v. Aegis Mortgage Corp., 286 F. Supp. 2d 965 (N.D. Ill. 2003); Reese v. 1st Metro. Mortgage Co., 2003 WL 22454658 (D. Kan. Oct. 28, 2003); Marbury v. Colonial Mortgage Co., 2001 U.S. Dist. LEXIS 1632 (M.D. Ala. Jan. 12, 2001); Mentecki v. Saxon Mortgage Inc., 1997 U.S. Dist. LEXIS 1374 (E.D. Va. Jan. 10, 1997); Brophy v. Chase Manhattan Mortgage Co., 947 F. Supp. 879 (E.D. Pa. 1996); Campbell v. Machias Sav. Bank, 865 F. Supp. 26 (D. Me. 1994); Koch v. First Union Corp., 2002 WL 372939 (Pa. C.P. 2002). *See* § 12.2.1.10, *infra*.

47 *See, e.g.*, Chow v. Aegis Mortgage Corp., 286 F. Supp. 2d 965 (N.D. Ill. 2003); Anderson v. Wells Fargo Home Mortgage, Inc., 259 F. Supp. 2d 1143 (W.D. Wash. 2003) (failure to disclose the yield spread premium proves one element of a UDAP claim); Gardner v. First Am. Title Ins. Co., 2003 WL 221844 (D. Minn. Jan. 27, 2003); Brophy v. Chase Manhattan Mortgage Co., 947 F. Supp. 879 (E.D. Pa. 1996) (borrowers could pursue state law claims in state court on issue of whether disparities between good faith estimate and HUD-1 settlement statement violated Pennsylvania's UDAP statute); Wash. Mut. Bank v. Super. Ct., 89 Cal. Rptr. 2d 560 (Ct. App. 1999) (court specifically held that RESPA and Reg. X do not expressly preempt private rights of action under state laws for violations of their provisions); Koch v. First Union Corp., 2002 WL 372939 (Pa. C.P. 2002); *see also* National Consumer Law Center, Unfair and Deceptive Acts and Practices § 3.2.7 (6th ed. 2005 and Supp.). For further discussion regarding preemption issues, see § 12.2.1.8, *infra*.

48 12 U.S.C. § 2607(c)(4); Reg. X, 24 C.F.R. § 3500.15(a); *see also* Gardner v. First Am. Title Ins. Co., 2003 WL 221844 (D. Minn. Jan. 27, 2003) (class certification denied in case alleging violation of § 2607 due to alleged payment of kickbacks between affiliated companies).

49 12 U.S.C. § 2607(c)(4); Reg. X, 24 C.F.R. § 3500.15(a).

50 *See* National Consumer Law Center, Truth in Lending § 9.2.6.3.5 (5th ed. 2003 and Supp.).

51 *See* Reg. X, 24 C.F.R. pt. 3500, App. A (reprinted in Appendix C.3.2, *infra*).

52 At the time of its circulation by the OCC on May 31, 2000, the letter was available on the Internet. Now, however, it is only referenced on the website of the OCC. *See* www.occ.treas.gov/ftp/advisory/2000-5.doc.

53 HUD points to the Instructions contained in Appendix A to Regulation X. Appendix A states that the HUD-1 must "itemize all charges imposed upon the borrower and the seller by the lender and all sales commissions, whether to be paid at settlement or outside of settlement, and any other charges which either the Borrower or the Seller will pay for at settlement."

54 12 U.S.C. § 2607(c) (this section exempts payments by a title company to its agent from the kickback prohibitions but only if the payment was for services actually performed in the making of the loan; so, if the other charges paid to the closing agent include all the services the agent actually preformed, the commission could violate RESPA). For a discussion of payments that are legal and illegal under RESPA, see § 12.2.1.5, *infra*.

55 *See* §§ 8.2, 8.5.2, *supra*.

56 Reg. X, 24 C.F.R. § 3500.2.

a settlement service UNLESS the insurance is voluntary. So, the pivotal question is whether the insurance was required, as a matter of fact. If so, then the commission paid to or kept by the lender who sells the insurance through an affiliated or unrelated insurance company must be separately listed on the HUD-1, like the commission paid in the title insurance context.

In addition to these heightened disclosure requirements, other potential RESPA consequences arise, if the insurance was required. Because the services rendered are "settlement services" under RESPA, an affiliated business arrangement disclosure must be given if the insurance company is related to the lender.[57] The analysis regarding whether the title insurance commission is a kickback is similar to that which applies in the yield spread premium context.[58]

Even though services related to such products may not be a settlement service if the consumer truly elects to purchase the insurance, Appendix A to Regulation X, nevertheless, requires that the premium be listed on the HUD-1 Statement.[59]

Other important observations in the Letter:

- Neither RESPA nor Regulation X provides tolerances for variations between the figures disclosed on the GFE and the final charges listed on the HUD-1. HUD believes that a pattern or practice of quoting GFE amounts that are lower than the corresponding amounts later shown on settlement statements may serve as evidence that the disclosures were not made in good faith.

- The appearance of fees on the HUD-1 that were not indicated on the GFE suggests that the GFE was not provided in good faith unless the fees were unanticipated and unforeseeable at the time the GFE was prepared.

- If a bank pays a mortgage broker a flat "per loan fee" that is not paid by the borrower or from the loan proceeds, that fee must be separately itemized and disclosed on any of the blank lines provided in the 800 series of the HUD-1.

- When a lender charges a fee for document preparation, a portion of which is kept by the lender and a portion of which goes to the closing attorney, this fee must be split and placed in two separate HUD-1 line numbers. The portion kept by the lender should appear on one of the blank 800 lines. The portion kept by the attorney should be disclosed on line 1105 (document preparation) or line 1107 (attorney fees).

- Lenders must list the name of the person or firm ultimately receiving all payments, even those paid outside of closing (P.O.C.). HUD specifically mentions

yield spread premium payments to brokers as an example.

12.2.1.3 Servicer Obligations

In 1990, Congress added a new section to RESPA which mandates that servicers tell consumers about the possibility that the mortgage loans which they sign may be transferred and when a transfer is imminent.[60] A 1989 GAO report to Representative LaFalce regarding the problems home owners experienced when servicing of their loan was transferred led to the enactment of section 2605.[61]

Under these amendments, notice is required when servicing is to be transferred.[62] Importantly, the note holder or servicer cannot assess a late fee or treat a payment as late during the sixty-day period after the servicing has been transferred if the consumer pays the old servicer before the due date.[63] It created a mechanism for consumers to obtain

---

57　12 U.S.C. § 2607(c)(4); *see also* § 12.2.1.5.1, *infra.*

58　*See* § 12.2.1.5, *infra.*

59　The settlement agent must itemize, among other things, any other charges which either the borrower or the seller will pay at settlement.

60　12 U.S.C. § 2605. HUD has also promulgated regulations under § 2605 and created form notices. Reg. X, 24 C.F.R. § 3500, and Appendices. Certain governmental agencies, for example, the RTC and FDIC, or governmentally sponsored entities, such as Fannie Mae, Ginnie Mae, and others, are exempt from coverage in certain circumstances. 12 U.S.C. § 2605(i)(2). Section 2605(a) was considerably shortened in 1996 by the Omnibus Consolidated Appropriations Act, 1997, Pub. L. No. 104-208, 110 Stat. 3009 (Sept. 30, 1996). 12 U.S.C. § 2605 and Reg. X, 24 C.F.R. § 3500, are reprinted in Appx. K, *infra.*

61　United States General Accounting Office, Mortgage Servicing Transfers are Increasing and Causing Borrower Concern, Clearinghouse No. 55,458 (Nov. 1998) (available on the CD-Rom accompanying National Consumer Law Center, Repossessions and Foreclosures (5th ed. 2002 and Supp.)).

62　12 U.S.C. § 2605(b); 24 C.F.R. § 3500.21(d); *see* Fraley v. Ocwen Fed. Bank, Fed. Sav. Bank, 8 Fed. Appx. 509 (6th Cir. 2001) (RESPA not violated when notice of transfer of servicing was provided even though the loan had been rescinded under TILA); Porter v. Fairbanks Capital Corp., 2002 WL 31163702 (N.D. Ill. Sept. 27, 2002) ("effective date of transfer" is the date the borrower is told to first pay the new servicer per § 2605(i)(1), not the actual date when the right to payment was transferred); Wanger v. EMC Mortgage Corp., 127 Cal. Rptr. 2d 685 (Cal. Ct. App. 2002) (delivery of the notice of servicing transfer means placing the letter in the U.S. mail, first-class postage paid, addressed to the last known address of the recipient or hand delivery; the servicer has the duty to exercise reasonable care and diligence in determining the correct address of the borrower when mailing a notice of transfer; servicer may have either actual or constructive knowledge of an address change; court denied the servicer's motion for summary judgment because there was a question of fact as to whether the new servicer knew or should have known upon further review that the borrower had sent an address change to the old servicer three days before the transfer was effective); Rochester Home Equity, Inc. v. Upton, 767 N.Y.S.2d 201 (N.Y. Sup. Ct. Oct. 29, 2003) (lock-in agreement is akin to consummation and transfer of servicing statement should be given before presenting the lock-in agreement); *see also* Chase Manhattan Mortgage Corp., 2002 WL 187496 (N.D. Ill. Feb. 6, 2002) (class certification denied based on lack of numerosity).

63　12 U.S.C. § 2605(d); Reg. X, 24 C.F.R. § 3500.21(d)(5).

answers from their servicers[64] to questions which they may have about their accounts and to obtain corrections to their accounts where appropriate.[65] Further, this section placed a substantive duty upon servicers to pay the taxes, insurance, and other escrowed monies to the appropriate recipients.

Finally, Congress created a private right of action to enforce its provisions and to provide for the recovery of actual damages, statutory damages in certain circumstances, costs and attorney fees.[66] This section of RESPA is dis-

cussed in more detail in NCLC's *Repossessions and Foreclosures*.[67] Claims against the servicer may also arise under the federal or state fair debt collection practices act. The federal act applies if the servicer acquired servicing rights after the loan was in default.[68] For a discussion of the types of behavior that triggers liability under the federal act, see NCLC's *Fair Debt Collection*.[69] Note that HUD, by regulation, limited the servicing provisions of RESPA to first lien mortgage loans, explicitly excluding subordinate lien mortgages and home equity lines of credit.[70]

12.2.1.4 Escrow Limitations

RESPA limits the amount of money a lender can require the borrower to deposit into an escrow account to pay "taxes, insurance premiums, or other charges with respect to the property."[71] This section of RESPA also requires that the borrower receive a written escrow account statement at the time the account is opened, and annually thereafter. In addition, Regulation X includes a formula for calculating how much of a cushion the servicer can legitimately maintain in the account.[72] Further, the regulation creates rules

---

64   Servicer is defined as the person responsible for servicing (receiving payments from the consumer and sending them on to the holder of the mortgage loan, as well as making escrow payments if called for by the loan), including the lender or holder of the loan if that person also services the loan. 12 U.S.C. § 2605(i)(2). The regulation further distinguishes between a "master" servicer (the owner of the right to service) and a "subservicer" (a servicer who services on behalf of the master servicer). Reg. X, 24 C.F.R. § 3500.21(a); *see* MorEquity, Inc. v. Naeem, 118 F. Supp. 2d 885 (N.D. Ill. 2000) (if qualified written request does not relate to the "servicing" of the loan, the protections in § 2605 are not triggered).

65   *See* Mazzei v. The Money Store, 349 F. Supp. 2d 651 (S.D.N.Y. 2004) (lender's summary judgment denied on the issue of whether the servicer properly responded to the qualified written request); Cardiello v. The Money Store, Inc., 2001 U.S. Dist. LEXIS 7107 (S.D.N.Y. June 1, 2001) (court discussed what constitutes an adequate response to a qualified written request), *aff'd*, 29 Fed. Appx. 780 (2d Cir. 2002) (table); Williamson v. Advanta Mortgage Corp., 1999 U.S. Dist. LEXIS 16374 (N.D. Ill. Oct. 8, 1999) (motion to dismiss denied where plaintiff adequately pled a claim under RESPA regarding its applicability, the servicer's failure to respond to a qualified written request, and the defendant's actions in reporting delinquencies after receipt of a qualified written request). *See also* Ploog v. Homeside Lending, Inc., 2001 U.S. Dist. LEXIS 15697 (N.D. Ill. Sept. 28, 2001) (class certification denied where consumer alleged that the servicer failed to respond to the written request within sixty days and reported her to the credit bureau during that period). *But see* Scocca v. Cendant Mortgage Corp., 2004 WL 2536837 (E.D. Pa. Nov. 9, 2004) (complaint dismissed where pro se plaintiff failed to allege he sent a qualified written request); Walker v. Michael W. Colton Trust, 47 F. Supp. 2d 858 (E.D. Mich. 1999) (complaint fails to state RESPA servicing violation because it contains no allegations regarding whether a qualified written request was sent or whether the servicer failed to respond).

66   12 U.S.C. § 2605(f); *see also* Maxwell v. Fairbanks Capital Corp. (*In re* Maxwell), 281 B.R. 101 (Bankr. D. Mass. 2002) (failing to respond to two qualified written requests does not create a "pattern and practice" to trigger statutory damages but agrees with *Ploog* that failing to respond five times is a pattern and practice). *Compare* Ploog v. Homeside Lending, Inc., 209 F. Supp. 2d 863 (N.D. Ill. 2002) (actual damages can include recovery for emotional distress; statutory damages are capped at $1000 for all violations but can get actual damages for each violation; failure to respond to five qualified written requests constitutes a pattern and practice to obtain statutory damages); Johnstone v. Bank of Am., 173 F. Supp. 2d 809 (N.D. Ill. 2001) (consumer can recover actual damages for emotional distress, time and inconvenience; can recover actual damages for illegally reporting a late payment to a credit bureau but only if the bureau disseminated the report to a third party; to survive a motion to dismiss, the consumer need only allege that the damages were caused by the servicer's violation); Rawlings v.

Dovenmuehle Mortgage, Inc., 64 F. Supp. 2d 1156 (M.D. Ala. 1999) (actual damages includes mental anguish); Wanger v. EMC Mortgage Corp., 127 Cal. Rptr. 2d 685 (Cal. Ct. App. 2002) (actual damages can include out-of-pocket expenses, lost time and inconvenience, late fees, and damages related to wrongful foreclosure if the foreclosure occurred as a result of the failure; emotional distress not raised) *with* Katz v. The Dime Savings Bank, 992 F. Supp. 250 (W.D.N.Y. 1997) (actual damages does not include damages for personal injury; actual damages are available for each violation; a showing of a pattern and practice is required to obtain statutory damages, though court does not define "pattern and practice"); *In re* Tomasevic, 273 B.R. 682 (Bankr. M.D. Fla. 2002) (actual damages are limited to economic pecuniary injury; punitive damages are not recoverable under § 2607; allegation of a single violation does not create a pattern and practice for statutory damages).

67   National Consumer Law Center, Repossessions and Foreclosures §§ 15.2.4.3, 15.3.3.7.5 (5th ed. 2002 and Supp.).

68   National Consumer Law Center, Fair Debt Collection § 4.3.9 (5th ed. 2004 and Supp.); *see also* Schlosser v. Fairbanks Capital Corp., 323 F.3d 534 (7th Cir. 2003).

69   National Consumer Law Center, Fair Debt Collection Ch. 5 (5th ed. 2004 and Supp.).

70   Reg. X, 24 C.F.R. § 3500.21(a). The statute does not contain these exceptions. *Cf.* 12 U.S.C. §§ 2605, 2602(1)(A). One court has held that § 3500.21(a) is not entitled to deference as it clearly conflicts with the statute. Cortez v. Keystone Bank, Inc., 2000 WL 536666 (E.D. Pa. May 2, 2000).

71   12 U.S.C. § 2609; *see also* 58 Fed. Reg. 5520 (Jan. 21, 1993). In addition, under the Home Ownership and Equity Protection Act of 1994, prepaid payments which a lender sometimes withholds from loan proceeds and keeps in an escrow account for future payments on the loan, are limited to two. *See* Tomaiolo v. Mallinoff, 281 F.3d 1 (1st Cir. 2002) (RESPA's escrow provisions do not apply to municipalities); § 12.2.2.3, *infra*.

72   Reg. X, 24 C.F.R. § 3500.17; Federal Reserve System Compliance Handbook, Clearinghouse No. 52,526, at 1-323 (Oct. 1997).

about how the servicer should handle surpluses, shortages, and deficiencies.[73]

Many subprime and second mortgages do not include such escrows, but where they appear, they may be worth checking. Lenders generally assume responsibility for calculating these complex escrow estimates, giving unscrupulous lenders an opportunity to extract an involuntary interest-free loan by requiring the borrower to pay more than is necessary to cover the borrower's obligations.[74] A 1990 report indicated that approximately two-thirds of all home mortgages may have excessive escrow requirements.[75] A New York federal court decision describes in helpful detail how to perform the calculations to determine whether a lender is excessively escrowing.[76] Though the authority is split as to whether there is a private remedy for a violation of this section of RESPA,[77] a consumer arguably may recoup the overcharges under a breach of contract theory, or such overcharges may be challenged as a violation of a state unfair and deceptive acts and practices statute.[78]

12.2.1.5 Prohibition Against Kickbacks and Referral Fees

12.2.1.5.1 Introduction

RESPA recognizes that disclosure alone is inadequate security against a sophisticated industry whose consumers tend to be inexperienced in complicated financial transactions, and can easily be overwhelmed by the mere volume of legalistic documents usually just plunked down before them at closing. An even more important provision, which gets at the heart of the problem of undisclosed arrangements involving hidden fees for referral of borrowers, is the prohibition against kickbacks and unearned fees.[79] The private remedy for a violation of this provision is treble damages and attorney fees.[80]

Under section 2607(a), no person shall give and no person shall accept any fee, kickback, or other thing of value[81] pursuant to any oral or written agreement or understanding for the referral of a settlement service in the scope of loans described above.[82] Regulation X explicitly provides that the referral of settlement services is not compensable, thus making it a violation for a company to pay any other company or the employees of any other company for the referral of settlement services.[83] Section 2607(b) forbids the splitting of any charges made or received for the rendering of a settlement service in connection with a covered loan other than for services actually performed.[84] This provision and the issue of marked-up fees is addressed more fully in § 12.2.1.6, *infra*.

Examples of specific situations which do and not violate these rules can be found in Appendix B to Regulation X.[85]

---

73 Reg. X, 24 C.F.R. § 3500.17.

74 *See* Sanders v. Lincoln Serv. Corp., 1993 WL 112543 (N.D. Ill. Apr. 5, 1993) (citing Aitken v. Fleet Mortgage Corp., 1992 U.S. Dist. LEXIS 1687 (N.D. Ill. Feb. 12, 1992)).

75 The Attorneys General of California, Florida, Iowa, Massachusetts, Minnesota, New York, Texas, Overcharging on Mortgages: Violations of Escrow Account Limits by the Mortgage Lending Industry (Apr. 24, 1990).

76 Heller v. First Town Mortgage Corp., 1998 U.S. Dist. LEXIS 14427 (S.D.N.Y. Sept. 14, 1998).

77 *Compare* Louisiana v. Litton Mortgage, Co., 50 F.3d 1298 (5th Cir. 1995) (no private right of action); Allison v. Liberty Sav., 695 F.2d 1086 (7th Cir. 1982) (same); McAnaney v. Astoria Fin. Corp., 357 F. Supp. 2d 578 (E.D.N.Y. 2005) (same); Clayton v. Raleigh Fed. Sav. Bank, 194 B.R. 793 (M.D.N.C. 1996), *aff'd without op.*, 107 F.3d 865 (4th Cir. 1997) (table) (same) *with* Vega v. First Fed. Sav. & Loan Ass'n, 622 F.2d 918 (6th Cir. 1980) (holding that private right of action exists is briefly mentioned in footnote 8); Heller v. First Town Mortgage Corp., 1998 U.S. Dist. LEXIS 14427 (S.D.N.Y. Sept. 14, 1998) (finding a private right of action). HUD, however, may assess a penalty for failure to comply with the requirements regarding escrow account statements. 12 U.S.C. § 2609(d).

78 *See* National Consumer Law Center, Unfair and Deceptive Acts and Practices § 3.2.7 (5th ed. 2001 and Supp.); § 12.2.1.10, *infra; see also* Heller v. First Town Mortgage Corp., 1998 U.S. Dist. LEXIS 14427 (S.D.N.Y. Sept. 14, 1998); Markowitz v. Ryland Mortgage Co., 1995 U.S. Dist. LEXIS 11323 (N.D. Ill. Aug. 9, 1995) (lender's motion for summary judgment on consumer fraud claim denied where borrowers alleged it retained escrow greater than permitted by the contract); Sanders v. Lincoln Serv. Corp., 1993 U.S. Dist. LEXIS 4454 (N.D. Ill. Apr. 5, 1993) (class plaintiffs stated a claim for breach of contract and state UDAP where creditor alleged to maintain unauthorized surpluses in customers' escrow accounts).

79 12 U.S.C. § 2607; Reg. X, 24 C.F.R. § 3500.14.

80 12 U.S.C. § 2607(d).

81 "Thing of value" is broadly defined. *See* Aiea Lani Corp. v. Hawaii Escrow & Title, Inc., 647 P.2d 257 (Haw. 1982) (discount to developer on construction loan title insurance for referring individual subdivision closings to defendant constituted a "thing of value" within meaning of RESPA).

82 Reg. X, 24 C.F.R. § 3500.14(b). In an odd context, a court held that it is an illegal kickback for a lender to charge a closing agent a higher fee for the use of its offices at settlement for loans it closed for that lender than for loans it closes for other lenders. Lawyers Title Ins. Corp. v. Dearborn Title Corp., 939 F. Supp. 611 (N.D. Ill. 1996), *aff'd in part*, 118 F.3d 1157 (7th Cir. 1997), *upon remand*, 22 F. Supp. 2d 823 (N.D. Ill. 1998). There was no showing that the consumer paid a higher settlement cost as a result. In this case, the title insurance company sued the closing agent for fraudulently mishandling money held in escrow. The kickback issue arose as a defense to the title insurance company's attempts to attach monies which the closing agent had paid to the lender.

83 Reg. X, 24 C.F.R. § 3500.14(b).

84 Reg. X, 24 C.F.R. § 3500.14(c). Herein lies a potential loophole which leaves room for a party to assert the performance of some bogus service to justify payment or receipt of a fee. *See* § 12.2.1.8, *infra*.

85 *See* Appx. K.2, *infra*.

One court held that a referral arrangement between a large-volume institutional seller of real property and a provider of escrow and title services did not violate RESPA based upon an "economies of scale" analysis.[86] These entities negotiated lower-than-normal rates that the title company would charge the seller for basic escrow services and for owner's title insurance. The court determined that there was little or no conclusive proof that the fees depended upon a certain volume of business, though it was clear that some volume of business was anticipated. More importantly for the court, however, was the lack of evidence that the discounts were "abnormally low," distinguishing an example described by HUD in Appendix B to Regulation X where HUD determined that RESPA was violated. The Ninth Circuit affirmed.[87]

A potential exemption from RESPA liability exists for referral fees or the splitting of charges. If the payment is for goods or services actually rendered, the fee is legal.[88] There is little guidance in the statute or Regulation X as to what that means, but it is clear that mere referrals are not compensable.[89] Regulation X does require that the payment bear a reasonable relationship to the market value of the goods furnished or services provided.[90] However, this leaves an opening for settlement service providers and others to make up services merely to justify receipt of fees.[91] By the same token, prohibited payments also may be obtained for non-compensable services by billing consumers a blanket fee for eclectic tasks grouped under an ambiguous title such as document preparation.[92]

In 1999, HUD issued a policy statement fleshing out the standard to apply in determining when lender-paid broker

fees are illegal.[93] HUD's general counsel then issued an opinion letter on this subject.[94] In response to a court decision, HUD issued a second policy statement on this topic in 2001.[95] This series of events and various twists and turns are discussed in §§ 12.2.1.5.3 through 12.2.1.5.5, *infra*.

Other exceptions to the kickback and referral prohibitions include payments: to attorneys for services actually rendered or by a title company to its duly appointed agent for services actually performed in the issuance of a title insurance policy;[96] by a lender to its duly appointed agent for services actually performed in the making of a loan; the payment to any person of a bona fide salary;[97] payments made pursuant to cooperative brokerage and referral arrangements or agreements between real estate agents and brokers.[98]

Finally, payments or fees split between "affiliated" businesses may be exempt from the section 2607 prohibitions if certain disclosures are made at specific times to the borrower, the entity making the referral has not required the use of the services from the affiliated business (there are some exceptions), and the only thing of value received from the arrangement, other than specified types of payments, is a return on the ownership or franchise interest.[99] Due to reports that affiliated business relationships were being created to circumvent RESPA and were sham arrangements, HUD issued a policy statement in 1996.[100] The agency listed ten factors that it would weigh to determine if the entity is a bona fide provider of services.[101]

---

86 Lane v. Residential Funding Corp., 2000 U.S. Dist. LEXIS 10717 (N.D. Cal. June 6, 2000).

87 Lane v. Residential Funding Corp., 323 F.3d 739 (9th Cir. 2003) (see discussion of this case at end of § 12.2.1.5.5, *infra*).

88 12 U.S.C. § 2607(c); Reg. X, 24 C.F.R. § 3500.14(c) and (g).

89 Reg. X, 24 C.F.R. § 3500.14(b). "Referral" is defined at § 3500.14(f). See the discussion regarding lender-paid broker fees in § 12.2.1.5.2, *infra*.

90 24 C.F.R. § 3500.14(g)(2).

91 *See* United States v. Grissom, 814 F.2d 577 (10th Cir. 1987) (president of savings and loan being prosecuted for embezzlement tried unsuccessfully to invoke a defense under RESPA that his appropriation of part of an origination fee paid by a borrower was really compensation for his actual service to the borrower in arranging the loan); *see also* United States v. Gannon, 684 F.2d 433 (1981) (counterman for county recorder received a salary for processing land registration and transfer documents, a service for which a statutory fee was imposed; no other services were provided in official or unofficial capacity justifying amounts accepted which exceeded statutory fee).

92 *Cf.* Texas State Bar Prof. Ethics Comm., Opinion 490 (Oct. 20, 1993), 61 Banking Rep. (BNA) 903 (Dec. 6, 1993) (state ethics committee held that bank's plan to charge loan applicants a separate fee for its salaried in-house counsel's preparation of loan documents violated professional ethics rules against lawyer's fee-splitting where bank retained the fee; however, a blanket document preparation fee covering all bank personnel and overhead would not).

93 64 Fed. Reg. 10079 (Mar. 1, 1999) (reprinted in Appx. K.3, *infra*).

94 This letter is reprinted in Appx. K.4, *infra*.

95 66 Fed. Reg. 53052 (Oct. 18, 2001) (reprinted in Appx. K.3, *infra*).

96 *See* Title Insurance Practices in Florida, RESPA Statement of Policy 1996-4, 61 Fed. Reg. 49398 (Sept. 19, 1996) (HUD issued this policy statement indicating that the payments in this context must be for core title services).

97 Novakovic v. Amutin, 820 N.E.2d 967 (Ill. App. 2004) (whether the broker was an employee of the lender was a question of fact; the court reversed summary judgment for the lender because there were questions of material fact on this issue).

98 12 U.S.C. § 2607(c)(1)–(3).

99 12 U.S.C. § 2607(c)(4); Reg. X, 24 C.F.R. § 3500.14(b).

100 61 Fed. Reg. 29258 (June 7, 1996).

101 *Id.* at 29262.

"The Department will consider the following factors and will weigh them in light of the specific facts in determining whether an entity is a bona fide provider:

(1) Does the new entity have sufficient initial capital and net worth, typical in the industry, to conduct the settlement service business for which it was created? Or is it undercapitalized to do the work it purports to provide?

(2) Is the new entity staffed with its own employees to perform the services it provides? Or does the new entity have "loaned" employees of one of the parent providers?

There is little case law interpreting the affiliated business arrangement provisions. In one case, the court granted the defendant summary judgment on the issue of the affiliated business disclosure finding that the statement adequately disclosed the relationship between the referor (the realtor) and the referee (title company).[102] The court held that the notice from the realtor need not disclose the fact that the title

company then referred out many of the closing services to companies affiliated to it.[103] On the issue of whether the homeowner was required to use a particular service provider, the court indicated that it would look beyond the disclaimer on the disclosure to see what actually took place.

12.2.1.5.2 Lender-paid broker fees and pre-HUD policy statement court decisions

HUD estimates that mortgage brokers handle about 60% of all home mortgage loans each year.[104] Given this huge volume and the potential profits to be made, it is not surprising that lender kickbacks and other abuses have occurred in brokered loans.

Lender kickbacks to brokers for bringing them business are often paid in one of two ways: by a "yield spread premium" or "volume-based compensation." A yield spread premium is a fee from a mortgage lender to a mortgage broker paid when the broker arranges a consumer mortgage loan where the interest rate on the loan is inflated to an amount higher than the "par" rate to cover the cost of the fee.[105] The par interest rate is the base rate at which the lender will make a loan to a borrower on a given day. Some lenders also compensate brokers based upon the volume of loans which brokers steer their way.[106]

These payments to brokers can drive up the cost of mortgage loans and create reverse competition where brokers have incentives to steer borrowers to lenders that pay brokers the most rather than to lenders who give borrowers the most favorable terms. This problem is exacerbated for low-income borrowers (over 46% of all families below the federal poverty level own their homes[107]) because unscrupulous elements of the mortgage industry perceive them as vulnerable targets. In addition, because low-income borrowers have or perceive themselves to have fewer credit

---

(3) Does the new entity manage its own business affairs? Or is an entity that helped create the new entity running the new entity for the parent provider making the referrals?

(4) Does the new entity have an office for business which is separate from one of the parent providers? If the new entity is located at the same business address as one of the parent providers, does the new entity pay a general market value rent for the facilities actually furnished?

(5) Is the new entity providing substantial services, i.e., the essential functions of the real estate settlement service, for which the entity receives a fee? Does it incur the risks and receive the rewards of any comparable enterprise operating in the market place?

(6) Does the new entity perform all of the substantial services itself? Or does it contract out part of the work? If so, how much of the work is contracted out?

(7) If the new entity contracts out some of its essential functions, does it contract services from an independent third party? Or are the services contracted from a parent, affiliated provider or an entity that helped create the controlled entity? If the new entity contracts out work to a parent, affiliated provider or an entity that helped create it, does the new entity provide any functions that are of value to the settlement process?

(8) If the new entity contracts out work to another party, is the party performing any contracted services receiving a payment for services or facilities provided that bears a reasonable relationship to the value of the services or goods received? Or is the contractor providing services or goods at a charge such that the new entity is receiving a "thing of value" for referring settlement service business to the party performing the service?

(9) Is the new entity actively competing in the market place for business? Does the new entity receive or attempt to obtain business from settlement service providers other than one of the settlement service providers that created the new entity?

(10) Is the new entity sending business exclusively to one of the settlement service providers that created it (such as the title application for a title policy to a title insurance underwriter or a loan package to a lender)? Or does the new entity send business to a number of entities, which may include one of the providers that created it?"

102 Gardner v. First Am. Title Ins. Co., 296 F. Supp. 2d 1011 (D. Minn. 2003); Nowacki v. Federated Realty Group, Inc., Clearinghouse No. 53,509 (E.D. Wis. Mar. 27, 2000) (decision and order) (a title insurance company and broker were allegedly affiliated and the borrower paid an inflated price for title insurance while the title insurance company paid a percentage of

gross income to joint principals of the broker and title company).

103 The court did not address the argument that the title company should have provided its own disclosure about its affiliations.

104 U.S. Dep't of Hous. & Urban Dev., *Real Estate Settlement Procedures (RESPA); Simplifying and Improving the Process of Obtaining Mortgages to Reduce Settlement Costs to Consumers*, 67 Fed. Reg. 49134, 49,140 (July 29, 2002). HUD does not break down this 60% figure into percentages of brokers in the prime, subprime, or predatory markets, or into purchase money mortgages versus refinances.

105 For an example, see § 11.5.4.3, *supra*.

106 One court approved an agreement between a large real estate seller and a title company in which they negotiated the per transaction fees assuming volume would be involved, although a particular baseline of volume was not discussed. Generally, the fees were discounted. The court held that the fees were reasonable, using an "economies of scale analysis," and that the discounts were not abnormally low. Lane v. Residential Funding Corp., 323 F.3d 739 (9th Cir. 2003).

107 American Housing Survey for Selected Metropolitan Areas, 2001, tables 2-1 & 7-1.

choices, brokers often engage in steering with legal impunity. One study, based upon 2000 mortgage loans made by one affiliated group of lending institutions, concluded that mortgage brokers received about $1,100 more in fees in loans where yield spread premiums were paid than those in those where the broker received no payment from the lender.[108] The findings also strongly suggest that yield spread premiums serve primarily to increase compensation for mortgage brokers and constitute a deceptive device that the broker industry employs to extract unnecessary and excessive payments from unsuspecting home owners.

Since the early 1990s, when these lender payments to brokers began to surface, there have been numerous challenges filed arguing that these payments are illegal kickbacks under RESPA. The resulting decisions will be discussed in chronological order to give the full flavor of the debate.

The first reported decision came from Alabama where a federal court held that a yield spread premium could well be classified as an illegal kickback where the borrower also paid the broker for services rendered.[109] Next, the court in *Martinez v. Weyerhaeuser Mortgage Co.*[110] denied the lender's motion for summary judgment finding a genuine issue of material fact as to whether the payment was duplicative of the other fees already charged to the consumers.

Fast forward to Virginia, where another federal court in *Mentecki v. Saxon Mortgage* squarely held, in the context of denying the lender's motion to dismiss, that the payment of a yield spread premium is a referral prohibited by 12 U.S.C. § 2607(a) because, by its very nature, yield spread premiums are not compensation given for services actually performed by the broker where the broker has already charged the borrower directly for all services provided.[111] In this case, one of the named plaintiffs paid $14,304.00[112] to the broker who also received a yield spread premium of $2,204.30.

In *Culpepper v. Inland Mortgage Corp.*, another Alabama court found that the yield spread premium was a legal referral fee under section 2607(a) because it met the "payment for goods" exception under section 2607(c)(2).[113] The broker being the table-funded lender seemed to be a critical factor for the court,[114] which concluded that the yield spread premium was the fair market value of the broker's services for bringing business to the lender.

The court, though, ignored the fact that, in a table-funded transaction, the broker is only the nominal lender. The entity funding the loan usually owns the loan from the outset due to an agreement between it and the broker. The yield spread premium cannot be paid for the "purchase" of the loan as it was not "purchased." Under section 2607(c)(2), the payment must also be made for particular goods, facilities, or services. The referral itself cannot count as a "service."[115] Otherwise, no lender payment to a broker for bringing it business would ever violate RESPA. Lenders pay brokers premiums because the loan's value to the lender is greater the higher the interest rate. Thus, the court would legitimize any kickback that would be profitable for a lender. In addition, no "goods" were actually furnished to the borrower under section 2607(c)(2). The mortgage loan itself is not a "good" under RESPA; the broker under the section 2607(c)(2) exception must provide the borrower with tangible property. If Congress had meant subsection (c) to include intangibles, it would have used different terms.

Next, in *Barbosa v. Target Mortgage Corp.*,[116] the borrowers alleged that the payment of the premium was both an illegal referral fee under section 2607(a) and an illegal splitting of fees under section 2607(b). Despite its recognition that the premium was paid for the procurement of loan at an above-par rate, the court found the lender's payment of

---

108 Howell E. Jackson, *Predatory Mortgage Lending Practices: Abusive Uses of Yield Spread Premiums*, Testimony before the U.S. Senate Committee on Banking, Housing, and Urban Affairs (Jan. 8, 2002), *available at* www.senate.gov/%7Ebanking/02_01hrg/010802/jackson.htm; Howell E. Jackson & Jeremy Berry, Kickbacks or Compensation: The Case of Yield Spread Premiums 94 (Jan. 8, 2002), *available at* www.law.harvard.edu/faculty/hjackson/pdfs/january_draft.pdf (typical broker compensation for a par interest rate loan is 1.388% of the loan amount); Howell E. Jackson & Jeremy Berry, Yield Spread Premiums and the Trilateral Dilemma in Financial Regulation, Clearinghouse No. 54,554; *see also* John Hechinger, *Mortgage Brokers Benefit from a Refinancing Boom, Huge Fees Draw Scrutiny of Regulators and Spawn Lucrative Small Companies*, The Wall St. J., Feb. 24, 2003 (reporting that broker earnings average about $120,000 but that at least 5% of brokers earn $1 million per year or more; broker fees average 1% to 1.5% of the loan amount).

109 Briggs v. Countrywide Funding Corp., 931 F. Supp. 1545, *vacated on other grounds*, 949 F. Supp. 812 (M.D. Ala. 1996) (denying lender's motion to dismiss a variety of claims and holding that RESPA also requires the disclosure of the yield spread premium).

110 959 F. Supp. 1511, 1522 (S.D. Fla. 1996).

111 Mentecki v. Saxon Mortgage, 1997 U.S. Dist. LEXIS 1197

(E.D. Va. Jan. 10, 1997), *related decision*, 1997 U.S. Dist. LEXIS 1374 (E.D. Va. Jan. 31, 1997) (denying another motion to dismiss).

112 This total consisted of: $12,925, origination fee; $550, appraisal fee; $51, credit report; $68, tax service fee; $355, underwriting fee; $60, express fee; $295, processing fee. This total does not include approximately $1,651 for other settlement costs paid to third parties or the cost of a mortgage insurance premium.

113 953 F. Supp. 367 (N.D. Ala. 1997), *rev'd*, 132 F.3d 692 (11th Cir. 1998) (the appellate decision is discussed later in this section).

114 A broker who funds the loan from monies received from a lender and who then immediately sells the loan to the lender after settlement is called a correspondent broker or table-funded lender by the industry. Such an entity or person is considered a mortgage broker under RESPA. 24 C.F.R. § 3500.2.

115 Reg. X, 24 C.F.R. § 3500.14(b).

116 968 F. Supp. 1548 (S.D. Fla. 1997) ($1,128 in broker fees included a $361 origination fee, a $702 loan discount fee, and a $65 processing fee; the lender paid an additional $2,457 as the yield spread premium).

a yield spread premium was not a "referral fee," but a fee for the broker's procurement of a loan that matched one of three loan options the lender made available to brokers.[117]

On the other hand, the court held that the splitting of interest payments between the broker and the lender can be an illegal fee under section 2607(b) if the charge was not paid for "services actually performed." Unfortunately, it then engaged in an analysis which could never result in a favorable outcome for borrowers.

The borrowers' argued that above-par loans do not require more service than par loans. Therefore, the yield spread premium was not paid for any additional services. Nor were the services provided worth their cost, according to expert testimony.[118] The court rejected these arguments, holding that "if arms' length bargaining in the mortgage marketplace set the payment for the broker's services, the payment is reasonable enough."[119] A service is reasonably related to its value if borrowers are willing to pay it (assuming they are even aware of the charge). Additionally, the court held that the offer of a premium payment does not influence the broker's initial selection of the lender.

This approach contradicts the plain language of Regulation X which states that payment must bear a reasonable relationship to the market value of the goods or services "actually performed."[120] Similarly, this rationale ignores the mandate that, first and foremost, the payment must be made for particular services provided by the broker which cannot include the referral itself.[121] The court wrongly assumed that the $1,128 paid by the borrower at settlement was not adequate compensation for the services provided by the broker.

It is inconsistent for a court to find, on one hand, that the loan would have been made without the payment of the yield spread premium, and to conclude, on the other hand, that the premium was not a referral fee. If the lender would have made the loan without paying the yield spread premium, *by definition*, the payment of the premium can only constitute a referral fee. Finally, the yield spread premium is a poor measure of the value of the services performed by the broker. The way in which the payment is calculated, that is, a portion of the increase in the interest rate, bears no relationship to the amount of time spent or work performed by the broker in a given transaction.

In *Dubose v. First Security Savings Bank*, the next court to tackle these issues rendered a thoughtful opinion and denied the lender's motion for summary judgment, holding that the origination and sale of loans in a table-funded transaction cannot alone justify the payment of the premium because the funding lender owned the loan from the outset.[122] The payment, therefore, could well be an illegal referral fee.

Unlike *Barbosa*, this court was unwilling to assume that the broker was paid the yield spread premium for otherwise uncompensated services to the borrower where the lender produced no evidence to show this. The lender's only evidence was that it paid the fee to release the broker's servicing rights to the loan. The borrowers submitted numerous articles from the lending industry and the written agreement between the lender and broker to contradict this allegation. The case will proceed to trial on the issues of whether the defendants split the fees for duplicative or non-existent settlement charges and whether the fee was, therefore, illegal.

Following the decision in *Dubose*, an Illinois court denied the lender's motion to dismiss due to the lack of factual development in the case, given its posture.[123] In doing so, however, it agreed with the *Barbosa* court that the payment of yield spread premiums does not have the effect of influencing the broker's selection of a lender if the offering of such payments is a widespread practice in the mortgage-lending industry and if the premiums offered by a particular lender will tend to be very similar to those offered by other lenders.

On the other hand, it disagreed with the district court holding in *Culpepper* that the payment of the premium could be viewed as the purchase price paid by the lender for a "good" actually furnished, especially in this case where the lender originated the loan (in other words, the broker was not the table-funded lender). Adopting the reasoning of the *Barbosa* court on the issue of whether "services" were provided (in other words, whether the premium payment resulted from "arms-length bargaining in the mortgage marketplace"), the court refused to dismiss in light of allegations in the complaint that the payment did not reflect services actually performed and that the lender conspired with the broker to obtain inflated interest payments for itself.[124]

One of these cases, *Culpepper v. Inland Mortgage Corp.*, reached the appellate level.[125] The appellate court ultimately

---

117 This holding ignores market reality, that lenders are paying brokers a kickback to bring in profitable business. The higher interest rate in this case would generate additional income to the holder of $18,363 over the life of the loan.

118 Plaintiff's counsel made these arguments in its briefs but the court does not specifically address them in its opinion.

119 *Barbosa*, 968 F. Supp. at 1562.

120 Reg. X, 24 C.F.R. § 3500.14(g)(2).

121 12 U.S.C. § 2607(c)(2); Reg. X, 24 C.F.R. § 3500.14(b).

122 Dubose v. First Sec. Sav. Bank, 974 F. Supp. 1426 (N.D. Ala. 1997).

123 Hastings v. Fid. Mortgage Decisions Corp., 984 F. Supp. 600 (N.D. Ill. 1997).

124 Note that the court also refused to dismiss a RICO claim grounded on the payment of the yield spread premium. *See* § 12.6, *infra*.

125 132 F.3d 692 (11th Cir. 1998) (court reiterated that, at the summary judgment stage, the evidence did not tie the premium paid to the broker to services actually provided. Without such a tie, the premium could only be a referral fee, though the broker and lender would get another shot at trial (the consumers did not file a cross-motion for summary judgment).

addressed yield spread premium issues on at least two occasions following this first decision. In *Culpepper I*, the Eleventh Circuit resoundingly reversed the lower court on all points.[126] Because the lender gave value to the broker in the form of a yield spread premium, the payment was a referral fee.

Utilizing the *Dubose* reasoning, the court held that the loan was not for a "good" under section 2607(c) because, in a table-funded transaction, the lender, not the broker, owns the loan from the outset. Thus, the lender could not pay the broker for the value of the loan because it never "purchased" it from the broker. Further, the premium was not paid for services rendered by the broker for two reasons. First, the borrowers had directly paid the broker for its services in the form of an origination fee and there was no evidence to suggest that this fee was not intended to compensate the broker fully for its services. Second, it was undisputed that the broker expended the same amount of effort and provided the same services whether it originated an above par, par, or below par loan. The sole determinant of whether a premium would be paid was the interest rate on the loan. Thus, the way in which the payment was calculated, that is, a portion of the increase in the interest rate, bore no relationship to amount of time spent or work performed by the broker.[127]

This decision made it much more difficult for lenders to succeed with the argument that the yield spread premium represented anything other than an illegal referral fee or an illegal splitting of the fee where the broker was also paid directly by the borrower for services rendered, in cash or at settlement.

Drawing upon the ruling in *Culpepper*, a court in Minnesota created a thoughtful road map to assess RESPA liability using the statute and Regulation X.[128] Step one involves an assessment of whether the fee represented payment for goods, facilities, or services performed. Only if the fee was paid *for* good, facilities, or services is step two necessary. If so, the court must look at the reasonableness of the fee. In *Brancheau*, the court held that the consumers properly alleged that the broker did not furnish any legitimate goods or services to earn the yield spread premium at issue for several reasons on a class-wide basis. First, the lender/broker loan correspondent agreement unequivocally stated that the broker would be compensated by the customer, not the lender. Second, while the level of service to the customer did not change, the yield spread premium increased as the interest rate increased. Third, the lender calculated the fee based on the net asset value of the loan and the value of the servicing rights, not on the value of services performed. (Note that the court later reversed itself and adopted the industry's interpretation of the HUD Policy Statement described in § 12.2.1.5.3, *infra*.[129])

Other courts have denied defendant motions to dismiss in referral cases rather easily.[130] Until HUD issued its 2001 Policy Statement, courts had been significantly split on whether class certification is appropriate.[131]

12.2.1.5.3 1999 HUD policy statement on lender-paid broker fees

On February 22, 1999, HUD published an anticipated policy statement dealing with the thorny issue of the legality of lender-paid broker fees.[132] This statement was drafted in response to a congressional directive seeking clarification

---

126 For a discussion of *Culpepper II*, see § 12.2.1.5.4, *infra*.

127 *See also* Jackson v. Ford Consumer Fin. Co., No. 1:96-CV-1009-RLV (N.D. Ga. Feb. 3, 1998), Clearinghouse No. 52,033 (decided after *Culpepper*; lender's motion for summary judgment denied; focused on "services" issue and sent the case to trial because the lender made conflicting claims about the purpose of the lender payment of the $3,752 "service release fee" made to the broker on top of the borrower-paid broker fee of $4,403.66 [both fees totaling over 8% of the loan amount], the fee would not be paid if the loan did not close [even though the broker would have performed the same services], and the fee was not based on the amount of actual work done but was based solely on the amount of the loan); Lawyers Title Ins. Corp. v. Dearborn Title Corp., 118 F.3d 1157, 1162 (7th Cir. 1997) ($200 payment that the lender received from closing agent for use of its office to conduct the settlement was an illegal kickback; because the cost of the space was no greater if used by one closing agent or lender than another, the "only plausible explanation for the $200 premium [was] that it was compensation to United for steering its borrowers to Dearborn to handle the closing.").

128 Brancheau v. Residential Mortgage, 182 F.R.D. 579 (D. Minn. 1998).

129 187 F.R.D. 591 (D. Minn. 1999) (class decertified and defendant's motion for summary judgment granted). This decision is discussed in § 12.2.1.5.3, *infra*.

130 De Leon v. Beneficial Constr. Co., 55 F. Supp. 2d 819 (N.D. Ill. 1999) (allegations that borrower paid a broker fee of 8% only to be steered into a more expensive loan states a claim under RESPA even though the lender paid no compensation); Taylor v. Flagstar Bank, 181 F.R.D. 509, 521, 522 n.5 (M.D. Ala. 1998) (in denying class certification, court observed that: "[T]he merits of the case appear to be fairly good. Yield spread premiums are fairly difficult to justify in light of . . . the decision in *Culpepper*."); Lowery v. Ameriquest Mortgage Co., 1998 U.S. Dist. LEXIS 22775 (D.S.C. Dec. 17, 1998) (lender's motion for summary judgment denied; class certification denied); Moses v. Citicorp Mortgage, Inc., 982 F. Supp. 897 (E.D.N.Y. 1997) (claim under RESPA § 2607(a) stated where borrowers paid application and origination fees to broker and lender paid broker an additional $1,913.40; allegations of duplicative fees also states a claim under § 2607(b)). *But see* Moreno v. Summit Mortgage Corp., 364 F.3d 574 (5th Cir. 2004) (court held that the transaction was not subject to RESPA as it was a secondary mortgage transfer); Chandler v. Norwest Bank Minn., 137 F.3d 1053 (8th Cir. 1998) (same, over a thoughtful dissent); Newton v. United Companies Fin. Corp., 24 F. Supp. 2d 444 (E.D. Pa. 1998) (no RESPA violation where borrower paid the entire fee ($700) to the broker, lender paid nothing, and no allegation of steering).

131 *See* § 12.2.1.5.6, *infra*.

132 64 Fed. Reg. 10079 (Mar. 1, 1999) (reprinted in Appx. K.3, *infra*). The Policy Statement was effective immediately.

from HUD regarding its position on lender payments to mortgage brokers.[133] Meanwhile, HUD never finalized regulations proposed in October 1997.[134]

The policy enunciates a two-part test. At the outset, HUD makes clear that it does not consider yield spread premiums to be *per se* illegal, nor are they *per se* legal. In determining whether a lender payment to a broker is permissible under RESPA, the first question is whether goods or services were actually performed or facilities were actually provided *for* the compensation paid.[135] The policy statement provides a list of compensable services normally performed in the origination of the loan.[136] Though not dispositive, HUD will generally be satisfied that sufficient origination work was performed to justify compensation if a broker took information from the borrower, filled out an application, and then performed at least five additional items on the list.[137]

Next, the analysis turns to whether the payments are reasonably related to the value of the goods, facilities, or services actually provided. In answering this question, HUD believes that the total compensation to the broker should be scrutinized. "Total compensation" includes direct fees paid by the borrower and indirect fees by the lender or other parties, including volume-based compensation. Further, the total of payments:

> [M]ust be commensurate with the amount nor-
> mally charged for similar services, goods or fa-

cilities. This analysis requires careful consideration of fees paid in relation to price structures and practices in similar transactions and in similar markets.[138]

If the fee bears no reasonable relationship to the market value of the goods, facilities, or services, the excess may be evidence of a referral or unearned fee.[139] HUD defines "goods" to include appraisals, credit reports, and other documents. For the first time, however, the agency makes clear that the mortgage loan itself cannot be regarded as a "good." "Facilities" may encompass a reasonable portion of the broker's retail or store-front operation.[140]

Separate from the issue of the legality of the fees, HUD urges, though does not require, clearer disclosures of lender-paid fees. The agency opines that, at a minimum, all fees to the mortgage broker (from whatever source) be clearly labeled and properly estimated on the good faith estimate.[141] Codes like "YSP POC" are inadequate. Instead, HUD suggests that lenders describe a yield spread payment in the following way: "Mortgage broker fee from lender to XYZ Corp. (P.O.C.)." Otherwise, one goal of RESPA, to make mortgage transactions understandable to the consumer, is undermined.

---

133 See the Conference Report on the Departments of Veterans Affairs and Housing and Urban Development, and Independent Agencies Appropriations Act, 1999, H.R. Conf. Rep. No. 105-769, at 260 (1998).

134 *See* 62 Fed. Reg. 53912 (Oct. 16, 1997). The proposed regulation would provide mortgage brokers with a safe harbor from RESPA liability if they enter into a binding broker contract with a prospective borrower and make certain disclosures in the contract about its role and the fees it will collect from the borrower and lender.

135 64 Fed. Reg. at 10084.

136 64 Fed. Reg. at 10085. HUD includes in this list the provision of disclosures as a compensable service. However, RESPA expressly prohibits a lender from charging a fee "for or on account of the preparation and submission" of TILA and RESPA good faith estimates. 12 U.S.C. § 2610. As the lender/broker cannot charge a fee, preparing and providing these disclosures cannot be a service that is "compensable" for purposes of justifying a yield spread premium. One consumer advocate has made the argument that the broker performed less than minimal services using HUD's list and, therefore, the fee is a referral fee. *See* Lewis v. Delta Funding Corp., Adv. No. 2000-935 (Bankr. E.D. Pa.) (motion for summary judgment), reprinted in Appx. H, *infra*.

137 If the services provided were only "counseling-type" activities, the agency will look to see that meaningful counseling—not steering—occurred. The report includes criteria HUD would use to make that determination. 64 Fed. Reg. at 10085. See Home Owner's Motion for Summary Judgment on this issue in Appx. L.6, *infra*. Significantly, HUD opines that the loan itself is *not* a good, thereby disposing of the industry's argument that the loan itself justifies the yield spread premium. 64 Fed. Reg. at 10085.

138 64 Fed. Reg. at 10086. Courts have generally denied summary judgment on the issue of whether the fees charged were reasonably related to the services provided. *See* Brazier v. Sec. Pac. Mortgage Inc., 245 F. Supp. 2d 1136 (W.D. Wash. 2003); Szczubelek v. Cendant Mortgage Corp., 215 F.R.D. 107 (D.N.J. 2003); Apgar v. Homeside Lending, Inc. (*In re* Apgar), 291 B.R. 665 (Bankr. E.D. Pa. 2003); Lewis v. Delta Funding Corp. (*In re* Lewis), 290 B.R. 541 (Bankr. E.D. Pa. 2003); *see also* Anderson v. Wells Fargo Home Mortgage, Inc., 259 F. Supp. 2d 1143, 1147 n.2 (W.D. Wash. 2003) (the borrower obtains no benefit from her agreement to pay a higher interest rate where the yield spread premium is not used to pay closing costs). *But see* Hirsch v. BankAmerica Corp., 328 F.3d 1306 (11th Cir. 2003) (broker fee of 1.4% on $150,000 loan is reasonable; home owner did not contest this issue); Tidwell v. Homestar Real Estate Serv., 290 F. Supp. 2d 729 (S.D. Miss. 2003) (summary judgment for lender granted where the home owner put forth no evidence regarding the value of the services provided to contradict the lender's claims; court also held that total compensation of 5.2% is presumptively reasonable because state law permits brokers to charge up to 7.95%. [*Editor's Note: There should be no relationship between the amount permitted under state law and the amount that is reasonably related to the actual value of the services under RESPA, a separate federal law.*]); Chow v. Aegis Mortgage Corp., 286 F. Supp. 2d 956 (N.D. Ill. 2003) (home owner did not refute affidavit that the fee was reasonable for services provided; must do so to avoid summary judgment).

139 64 Fed. Reg. at 10086.

140 *Id.* at 10085.

141 *Id.* at 10086, 10087; *see* Brazier v. Sec. Pac. Mortgage Inc., 245 F. Supp. 2d 1136 (W.D. Wash. 2003) (failure to disclose the yield spread premium at all is a violation but disclosure listing "mortgage broker fee of 1.5%—1.5% is being paid by lender for this transaction" is adequate).

12.2.1.5.4 *Conflicting interpretations of the 1999 HUD policy statement*

By affirming that, in the first instance, the compensation must be paid *for* goods, services, or facilities provided, the agency articulates a two-part test which has been utilized by the Eleventh Circuit Court of Appeals and by two district courts, as discussed in § 12.2.1.5.2, *supra*.

Although the HUD statement provides that percentage-based fees be included in the "total compensation," this prong of the analysis only arises if the compensation at issue, that is, the yield spread premium, was paid *for* the goods, facilities, or services provided.

The industry, however, sees the policy statement as affirming its position that one simply adds up the value of the services, goods, and facilities provided on one side of the equation and compares it to the total amount of compensation paid directly or indirectly to the broker from whatever source.[142] In this way, lenders and brokers can try to avoid the more careful scrutiny that the statute requires.

Even under this interpretation, lender-paid fees should be suspect for several reasons. First, practitioners should review the services performed by the broker which must be itemized and clearly labeled on the Good Faith Estimate and HUD-1 Settlement Statement.[143] It is less likely that a broker can claim that fees are paid for services, goods, or facilities that are not properly disclosed to its customer.

Second, on the "value of the services provided" side of the equation, "value" should be measured in specific dollar amounts for each good, service, or facility provided. The reasonable value arguably cannot include percentages of the loan amount because the value of a particular service would then be tied to the value of the loan, not the local market.[144]

Third, compare several loans involving the same broker and lender. If the same services were provided in each transaction but the total compensation for each loan was a different dollar amount, the compensation received by the broker could not be related to the reasonable value of the goods, services, or facilities actually provided. Instead, the differences must be related to the value of the referral itself.

Fourth, if the lender-paid portion of the total compensation is always calculated as a percentage of the loan amount, regardless of the amount of the borrower paid fees, it is possible that the total compensation was not reasonably related to the goods, services, or facilities actually provided.[145]

Fifth, fees and payments should be analyzed to see if the lender payment duplicates direct compensation paid by the borrower for the services actually rendered.[146] If so, then section 2607 has been violated.

Finally, volume-based compensation, by definition, is paid to a broker because of the number of loans that it refers to the lender. "Total compensation" must include any volume-based payment. One of two things should occur when the lender makes such a payment. If the volume-based payment results in a reduction of borrower-paid fees, the total may be reasonably related to the value of what the broker provided. However, if there is no corresponding reduction in the borrower paid fees, the total compensation, by definition, will never be reasonably related to the value of the goods, services, or facilities (because the volume-based payment will unreasonably inflate the total fees paid).

Though HUD hoped the Policy Statement would clarify the law, instead, it fueled a judicial debate over its meaning. Several courts have used it to deny consumer motions for class certification and a few have granted summary judgment against the consumers on the merits.[147] For example, the Minnesota district court in *Brancheau* and *Levine* (same judge) reluctantly held that the Statement eased the *Culpepper I* standard and turned the analysis into an intensely factual one. Unlike the *Culpepper* test that required that the payment be made in exchange *for* the services actually performed, the Minnesota court understood the Policy Statement to mean that the broker need only perform some services or furnish some goods. The inquiry then shifts to whether the total compensation to the broker is reasonably

---

142 *See* E. Robert Levy, *HUD Policy Statement Helps Resolve Lender Paid Mortgage Broker Fee Issues*, New Eng. Mortgage Report 8 (Mar. 1999).

143 64 Fed. Reg. at 10086, 10087.

144 *Id*. at 10085. But see HUD 2001 policy statement wherein HUD indicates that a rate sheet is merely a mechanism for displaying the yield spread premium. A rate sheet alone cannot determine whether the payment is legal or not. 66 Fed. Reg. 53052, 53055 (Oct. 18, 2001).

145 64 Fed. Reg. at 10084. ("[H]igher interest rates alone cannot justify higher total fees to mortgage brokers."); *see* Apgar v.

Homeside Lending, Inc. (*In re* Apgar), 291 B.R. 665 (Bankr. E.D. Pa. 2003) (court discusses how the rate sheets operate and how the yield spread premium is calculated as a percentage of the loan amount). But see HUD 2001 policy statement wherein HUD indicates that a rate sheet is merely a mechanism for displaying the yield spread premium. A rate sheet alone cannot determine whether the payment is legal or not. 66 Fed. Reg. 53052, 53055 (Oct. 18, 2001).

146 64 Fed. Reg. at 10086. But see HUD 2001 policy statement wherein HUD indicates that a rate sheet is merely a mechanism for displaying the yield spread premium. A rate sheet alone cannot determine whether the payment is legal or not. 66 Fed. Reg. 53052, 53055 (Oct. 18, 2001).

147 McCrillis v. WMC Mortgage Corp., 133 F. Supp. 2d 470 (S.D. Miss. 2000) (summary judgment for lender granted); *In re* Old Kent Mortgage Co. Yield Spread Premium Litigation, 191 F.R.D. 155 (D. Minn. 2000) (motion to strike class certification granted; Golon v. Ohio Sav. Bank, 1999 U.S. Dist. LEXIS 16452 (N.D. Ill. Oct. 15, 1999) (class certification denied); Brancheau v. Residential Mortgage, 187 F.R.D. 591 (D. Minn. 1999) (decertification of the class; defendant's motion for summary judgment granted); Levine v. North Am. Mortgage, 188 F.R.D. 320 (D. Minn. 1999) (class certification denied); Schmitz v. Aegis Mortgage Corp., 48 F. Supp. 2d 877 (D. Minn. 1999) (same); Paul v. National City Mortgage Co., 1999 U.S. Dist. LEXIS 20512 (N.D. Ga. Mar. 11, 1999) (same but no discussion of the Policy Statement); Yasgur v. Aegis Mortgage Corp., 1999 U.S. Dist. LEXIS 20989 (D. Minn. Mar. 10, 1999) (same but no discussion of the Policy Statement).

related to the goods or services furnished. While the court agreed with the *Culpepper I* decision, it felt bound by HUD's Statement.

On the other hand, two different federal courts in Alabama held that HUD's 1999 policy did not change the *Culpepper I* analysis.[148] Another court denied the lender's motion for summary judgment.[149] In addition, two district courts have granted class certification after the 1999 policy statement was issued, though they did not rely upon it.[150]

Following these court decisions, HUD's General Counsel released a letter dated December 17, 1999 responding to questions from Congressman Bruce Vento about the Policy Statement.[151] HUD clearly and unequivocally repeated that, in the first instance, the broker services must have been performed *for*, that is, *in exchange for*, the yield spread premium. To date, only one court has addressed the effect of the General Counsel's letter.[152] The district court in Hawaii dismissed the letter for two reasons. The letter did not carry the same weight as the 1999 policy statement, the court found. And, the letter did not explicitly adopt the *Culpepper I* standard, a standard that renders all yield spread premiums illegal, according to this court. Arguably, however, the *Culpepper I* analysis most closely comports with the plain language of RESPA, that no person shall give or receive any fee *for* the referral of any settlement service.[153] Despite the nay-saying of the *Isara* court, lender payments to brokers are legal when services are provided *for* the fee and the total amount paid to the broker from all sources is reasonably related to their value.

12.2.1.5.5 HUD's second policy statement and its domino effect upon the courts

On June 15, 2001, the Eleventh Circuit released a second decision in the *Culpepper* case. By doing so, it became the first appellate court to apply the 1999 HUD policy statement in determining whether a class should be certified in a case challenging the legality of the premium payments.[154] The three-judge panel agreed that, in the first instance, the goods, services, or facilities must be performed or furnished *for* (that is, in exchange for) the lender-paid fee. Any other interpretation would likely conflict with the statute, the court found. In *Culpepper II*, the agreement between the lender and broker did not make payment of the premium contingent upon the performance of any services. No evidence suggested that the broker rendered less service in originating a below-par loan than it did for an above-par loan, or that the lender ever inquired into how much work the broker actually performed. Rather, the payment was calculated in the same way on each loan. For these reasons, valuing the services provided was unnecessary because the lender's program did not meet the first prong of the test. Accordingly, the court affirmed the class certification.

This decision did not end the matter. The industry reacted strongly to *Culpepper II*[155] and pushed HUD to step in and "clarify" its policy statement.[156] HUD accepted the invitation and issued its second policy statement on the subject on October 18, 2001.[157] (Note: this policy statement also discussed whether excessive fees constitute a RESPA violation, an issue reviewed in § 12.2.1.6, *infra*.)

The agency explicitly repudiated the decision in *Culpepper II*.[158] HUD articulated the standard thusly: the total compensation paid to the broker *from any source* (not just the lender-paid fee) must be for goods, services, or facilities.[159] Arguably, if the broker provided *any* goods, services, or facilities for *any* payment made or to be made to it, the first prong of the test is met. Of course, the broker will have

---

148 Heimmermann v. First Union Mortgage, 188 F.R.D. 403 (N.D. Ala. 1999) (class certification granted), *vacated and remanded*, 305 F.3d 1257 (11th Cir. 2002) (see discussion of this case, *infra*); Briggs v. Countrywide Funding Corp., 188 F.R.D. 645 (M.D. Ala. 1999).

149 Marbury v. Colonial Mortgage Co., 2001 U.S. Dist. LEXIS 1632 (M.D. Ala. Jan. 12, 2001) (defendant's contention that the yield spread premium was paid for the release of servicing rights does not support its claim that the premium represents goods, services, or facilities; servicing rights do not equal "goods" because they do not arise until after the loan is closed; class certification stayed pending appeals in other cases before the Eleventh Circuit).

150 Culpepper v. Inland Mortgage Corp., 189 F.R.D. 668 (N.D. Ala. 1999), *aff'd*, 253 F.3d 1324 (11th Cir. 2001), *cert. denied*, 534 U.S. 1118 (2002); Dujanovic v. Mortgageamerica, Inc., 185 F.R.D. 660 (N.D. Ala. 1999).

151 The full text of the letter is contained in Appx. K.4, *infra*.

152 Isara v. Community Lending, Inc., Civ. No. 99-00310SPK (D. Haw. Jan. 20, 2000) (class certification denied).

153 12 U.S.C. § 2607(a); *see also* § 12.2.1.5.5, *infra*.

154 Culpepper v. Irwin Mortgage Corp., 253 F.3d 1324 (11th Cir. 2001), *cert. denied*, 534 U.S. 1118 (2002).

155 *See, e.g.*, Robert Julavits, *Broker Fee Ruling Roils Mortgage Bank Lawyers*, Am. Banker (June 22, 2001).

156 *See* Letter from the Consumer Mortgage Coalition to Secretary Martinez, Dep't of Hous. & Urban Dev. (Sept. 25, 2001), *no longer available at* www.houselaw.net/alerts/092801a.pdf.

157 66 Fed. Reg. 53052 (Oct. 10, 2001) (reprinted in Appx. K.3, *infra*). The consumer representatives responded with grave concerns to the new policy. *See, e.g.*, Margot Saunders, No Shades of Gray—HUD's New Statement of Policy Hurts Homeowners and Will Cost Millions, *available at* www.nclc.org/initiatives/predatory_mortgage/press_release.shtml.

158 66 Fed. Reg. at 53054, 53055.

159 *Id*. at 53055; *see also* Lane v. Residential Funding Corp., 323 F.3d 739, 744 (9th Cir. 2003) ("When the HUD test is met, any 'things of value' a defendant receives are treated as compensation for goods, facilities, or services, even if the compensation is not offered in direct exchange for goods, facilities or services"; not a yield spread premium case); O'Sullivan v. Countrywide Home Loans, Inc., 319 F.3d 732, 740 (5th Cir. 2003) ("Instead, as the 2001 Policy Statement clarifies, there is no requirement that the lender and broker tie the disputed fee to specific services provided. So long as the *total* compensation paid to the broker is reasonably related to the *total* value of the good or services actually provided, there is no § 8 liability"; not a yield spread premium case).

done something in brokering each loan, so meeting the first prong may become *pro forma*.[160] Then, the consumer must show that the total compensation is not reasonable for the services provided.[161]

As far as class actions were concerned, HUD unequivocally opined that it is necessary to look at each transaction individually. The industry, understandably, lauded HUD's action as "a significant victory for the mortgage lending industry."[162]

Several court decisions, including one by the Eighth Circuit in *Glover v. Standard Federal Bank*, quickly endorsed the new HUD standard.[163] In *Glover*, the court spent considerable energy analyzing whether the 2001 HUD statement deserved deference. It held that the HUD regulation enacted pursuant to section 2607 mirrored an ambiguous *statute*, although the court did not discuss the exact nature of this ambiguity. Instead, it quoted HUD's purpose in publishing the second policy statement as eliminating any ambiguity concerning the *Department's* position.[164] In light of this perceived ambiguity, the court held that the HUD policy statement interpreting its own ambiguous regulation is con-

trolling authority, unless plainly erroneous or inconsistent with the regulation or the purposes of RESPA. Not finding these latter exceptions to apply, the court reversed the trial court's decision to grant class certification.

Is the Eighth Circuit correct in its deference analysis? This court focused primarily on the substance of the policies, paying little or no attention to the procedural prerequisites necessary to trigger deference. A careful analysis of Supreme Court deference standards casts doubts on the both procedural and substantive viability of HUD's actions.

As to procedure, the Supreme Court distinguishes between interpretations such as those contained in policy statements and fully dressed regulations.[165] Policy statements or opinion letters that have not been subject to formal adjudication or notice-and-comment rulemaking are entitled to "respect," but only to the extent the policy has the power to persuade. On the other hand, a formally promulgated regulation deserves adherence by a court if it contains a reasonable interpretation of an ambiguous statute.[166]

In another case, the Court reviewed its previous deference opinions when deciding whether a tariff ruling was entitled to deference when it was issued without a comment period.[167] In *Mead*, the Court indicated that courts can consider a range of factors when determining whether an agency action is entitled to deference or whether the issuance can claim only "respect according to its persuasiveness."[168] Administrative implementation of a particular statutory provision qualifies for deference when Congress delegated authority to the agency generally to make rules carrying the force of law and the agency interpretation was promulgated in the exercise of that authority. The lack of formal promulgation alone is not determinative.[169] The factors the Court identified as relevant include: the thoroughness evident in the agency's consideration; the consistency of the agency's position; the procedures followed to issue the interpretation (whether public notice and a comment period were provided); the agency's level of expertise on the subject; and the persuasiveness of the agency's position.[170] Ultimately, in that case, the Court held that a tariff ruling did not deserve deference because forty-six different offices issued from 10,000 to 15,000 tariff rulings each year. These rulings applied only to the particular importer and the goods involved so, by definition, they have no precedential effect.

In 1998, Congress directed HUD to issue a statement of policy regarding yield spread premiums within 90 days and

---

160 *See* Wingert v. Credit Based Asset Serv. & Securitization, L.L.C., 2004 WL 2915306 (W.D. Pa. Aug. 26, 2004); Chow v. Aegis Mortgage Corp., 286 F. Supp. 2d 956 (N.D. Ill. 2003) (first prong met because the broker performed "some" services; court did not analyze the nature and extent of the services actually performed).

161 Wingert v. Credit Based Asset Serv. & Securitization, L.L.C., 2004 WL 2915306 (W.D. Pa. Aug. 26, 2004) (consumer did not refute the defendant's expert affidavit which claimed that the fee was reasonable); summary judgment granted to lender).

162 *See* Tom Noto, *HUD Issues Policy Statement on Yield Spread Premium Payments and Unearned Fees Under RESPA*, Mortgage Banking Commentary by the law firm of Kirkpatrick & Lockhart L.L.P. (Oct. 23, 2001).

163 Glover v. Standard Fed. Bank, 283 F.3d 953 (8th Cir.), *cert. denied*, 537 U.S. 943 (2002); Geraci v. Homestreet Bank, 203 F. Supp. 2d 1211 (W.D. Wash. 2002) (lender's motion for judgment on the pleadings granted where the home owner failed to allege that the yield spread premium did not bear a reasonable relationship to the value of the goods or services provided; the decision was issued after *Glover* was decided but did not rely upon *Glover*), *aff'd*, 347 F.3d 749 (9th Cir. 2003); LaCasse v. Wash. Mut., Inc., 198 F. Supp. 2d 1255 (W.D. Wash. 2002) (class certification denied); Empalmado v. First Franklin Fin. Corp., 2002 U.S. Dist. LEXIS 1929 (N.D. Ill. Feb. 7, 2002) (reconsideration of class certification denial denied); Michalowski v. Flagstar Bank, Fed. Sav. Bank, 2002 U.S. Dist. LEXIS 1245 (N.D. Ill. Jan. 25, 2002) (lender motion to dismiss case denied because the legality of a yield spread premium is highly dependent on the facts of each case; court cites to the 2002 policy statement); Vargas v. Universal Mortgage Corp., 2001 U.S. Dist. LEXIS 19635 (N.D. Ill. Nov. 29, 2001) (class certification denied under the 2001 policy statement); Bankers Trust v. McFarland, 743 N.Y.S.2d 804 (N.Y. Sup. Ct. 2002) (summary judgment for loan holder granted based on evidence presented to show that services were provided and the payment was reasonably related to the value of the services).

164 In *Culpepper II*, on the other hand, the Eleventh Circuit found ambiguity in the 1999 policy statement and interpreted it in a way it believed was consistent with the statute.

165 *See* Christensen v. Harris County, 529 U.S. 576, 587, 120 S. Ct. 1655, 146 L. Ed. 2d 621 (2000); *see also* Smiley v. Citibank (S.D.), N.A., 517 U.S. 735, 116 S. Ct. 1730, 135 L. Ed. 2d 25 (1996).

166 *Christensen*, 529 U.S. at 587.

167 United States v. Mead Corp., 533 U.S. 218, 121 S. Ct. 2164, 150 L. Ed. 2d 292 (2001).

168 *Mead Corp.*, 533 U.S. at 221.

169 *Mead Corp.*, 533 U.S. at 226, 227.

170 *Mead Corp.*, 533 U.S. at 228.

directed the agency to consult with consumer representatives.[171] The 1999 release was the result of that mandate. In contrast, the 2001 statement was not ordered by Congress. Nor did HUD follow the usual publication and comment procedure. While HUD published its 2001 policy statement in the *Federal Register*, it did not provide a notice and comment period. The public was deprived of its formal opportunity for input. However, the policy statements were more formal than the tariff rulings addressed in *Mead* and the Secretary of HUD issued the statements, unlike the individual tariff offices.

Regarding substance, RESPA itself limits the Secretary's authority to enact regulations or issue interpretations to those that "may be necessary to achieve the purposes of [the statute]."[172] The purposes of RESPA are outlined in section 2601: namely, to provide consumers with more timely information about the nature and costs of the settlement process and to protect consumers from unnecessarily high settlement charges caused by abusive practices. Neither of these goals seems to be furthered by the policy statement. The chief intent of HUD appears to be one of stopping class actions.

But more significantly, is there ambiguity in the statute? Considering the many conflicting court decisions written over the years, it would seem so. However, as to the first prong of the HUD test, the statute seems clear (or at least clearer than the HUD iterations of it). Section 2607(c) states that *the* payment to any person of bona fide salary or compensation or other payment *for* goods, services, or facilities actually provided is not prohibited. It seems that Congress intended that the payment at issue be in exchange for the services, a position adopted by the court in *Culpepper II*.

Despite these concerns, two other circuit courts, including the Eleventh (!), have followed in the footsteps of the Eighth Circuit in the yield spread premium context.[173] Generally, both courts held that the policy statement has the force of law because HUD has statutory authority to interpret RESPA, both the statute and HUD's regulation are either ambiguous or do not address yield spread premium payments explicitly, and HUD's interpretation is based upon a permissible construction of the statute. The dissent in *Schuetz*, however, picked apart the HUD standard. Judge Kleinfeld argued that the statutory language is clear, creating no need for agency interpretation. Further, he said that the problem with treating the yield spread premium as payment for services rendered to the borrower is that the relationship between the amount of the payment and the value of services is purely fortuitous. "[I]t is precisely the fortuitousness that makes the yield spread premium violate RESPA."[174]

Several aspects of the Eleventh Circuit's opinion are noteworthy. First, the same panel that issued the *Culpepper* decisions heard the *Heimmermann* appeal. In fact, both *Culpepper* and *Heimmermann* were argued the same day.[175] Second, the court did not seem troubled by the fact that the 2002 Policy Statement articulated a standard that clashed with the court's earlier interpretation of the 1999 Policy Statement. Ironically, the *Culpepper II* court observed: "Irwin's reading of the [1999] Statement is not only inconsistent with the Statement itself; it also would make the Statement clash with § 8(c)'s language."[176] However, in *Heimmermann*, the court backtracked by stating that HUD's most recent interpretation does not violate Congress' intent in enacting RESPA.[177] Third, the intervening event that may have changed the court's mind might be the Supreme Court's decision in *Mead*, discussed above. *Culpepper II* was released on June 15, 2001, the Supreme Court issued *Mead* on June 18, 2001, and *Heimmermann* was decided over a year later.[178] Finally, the court in *Heimmermann* addressed the issue of retroactivity. It held that both policy statements are clarifications of existing law, rather than changes in the law. Therefore, the policies may be applied retroactively.[179]

Given the rulings by three federal appellate courts, class actions in the yield spread premium context may be a non-starter.[180] On the other hand, the concerns expressed by

---

171 *See* H.R. Conf. Rep. No. 105-769, at 260 (1998).

172 12 U.S.C. § 2617(a).

173 Heimmermann v. First Union Mortgage Corp., 305 F.3d 1257 (11th Cir. 2002); Schuetz v. Banc One Mortgage Corp., 292 F.3d 1004 (9th Cir. 2002); *see also* Hirsch v. BankAmerica Corp., 328 F.3d 1306 (11th Cir. 2003) (applying *Heimmerman*); Bjustrom v. Trust One Mortgage Co., 322 F.3d 1201 (9th Cir. 2003) (applying *Schuetz*; but see the concurrence). For lower court cases decided since *Glover*, see Dominguez v. Alliance Mortgage Co., 226 F. Supp. 2d 907 (N.D. Ill. 2002) (among other things, the court placed the burden of proof upon the home owner to show that the fee is unreasonable in relation to the services provided; because no evidence was offered regarding the cost of relevant services in the local market, summary judgment against the home owner was granted); Costa v. SIB Mortgage Corp., 210 F.R.D. 84 (S.D.N.Y. 2002; Apgar v. Homeside Lending, Inc. (*In re* Apgar), 291 B.R. 665 (Bankr. E.D. Pa. 2003) (adopts HUD's policy statement but indicates that it is entitled to no more than *Skidmore* deference because it is only an interpretative guideline, not a fully dressed regulation).

174 *Schuetz*, 292 F.3d 1014, 1015.

175 *Heimmermann*, 305 F.3d at 1259.

176 Culpepper v. Irwin Mortgage Corp., 253 F.3d 1324, 1329, 1330 (11th Cir. 2001).

177 *Heimmermann*, 305 F.3d at 1262.

178 In *Heimmermann*, the court relied upon *Mead* to decide that the 2001 Policy Statement is entitled to full deference because Congress expressly delegated to HUD the power to issue "interpretations" in § 2617(a). The court distinguished the result in *Mead* by noting that the tariff ruling in that case did not involved an express delegation of authority.

179 *Heimmermann*, 305 F.3d at 1260.

180 *See also* Schneider v. Citicorp. Mortgage, Inc., 324 F. Supp. 2d 372 (E.D.N.Y. 2004) (in the context of confirming a settlement in this case, the court notes that class actions are dead under the

at least two judges may carry some weight in the other circuit courts. As noted above, Judge Kleinfeld on the Ninth Circuit disagreed with the majority in *Schuetz*. In addition, Judge Easterbrook on the Seventh Circuit slammed HUD for issuing the 2002 Policy Statement without notice and comment.[181] Even though the merits of *Krzalic* dealt with the excessive fee part of the policy statement, Judge Easterbrook took the opportunity to note: "But I am confident that *Heimmermann* and *Schuetz* erred in thinking that the [Policy Statement] is itself conclusive under *Chevron*, as opposed to informative (and potentially persuasive)."[182]

HUD's analysis of the legality of yield spread premiums has bled into other referral or splitting of fees contexts. In *Lane v. Residential Funding Corp.*, the Ninth Circuit applied the Policy Statement to affirm summary judgment granted to the seller and the title company who had negotiated lower escrow and title insurance fees for borrowers referred by the seller.[183] More specifically, the court held that discounts that are reasonably related to the value of compensable services performed by a settlement provider for a referring party are not discounts *for* referrals. Rather only abnormally low discounts violate RESPA. In this case, there was no evidence that the discounts were passed on to the consumer. In another case, the Fifth Circuit denied class certification where a law firm acting as the settlement agent split a document preparation fee with the lender, even though the entire fee appeared on the HUD-1 as paid to the law firm.[184] However, this court relied on HUD's regulations, refusing to address whether the Policy Statements are entitled to any deference. Instead, the court held class certification is inappropriate where there is a dispute as to whether the document preparation fee bears a reasonable relation to the value of the services when the lender did not render the identical services in each transaction.

12.2.1.5.6 Broker kickback practice issues

Figuring out whether a yield spread premium has been paid to a broker can be tricky. While the premium must be disclosed on the second page of the HUD-1 Settlement Statement, the description can be quite cryptic. For example, some settlement statements will list "(P.O.C. ysp— $1,500)." If nothing remotely like this appears on the settlement statement, the rate sheet that the broker used to price the loan would have this information, though this sheet often is not readily available without formal discovery. The settlement officer can be approached to provide copies of the checks distributed at the settlement which may produce this information. One practitioner provides a sample rate sheet in an article he wrote and dissects its meaning.[185] It is helpful to review this analysis before attempting to understand rate sheets obtained in real cases.

Practitioners should expect lenders to immediately file motions to dismiss and for summary judgment. Consequently, the consumer's attorney should serve discovery as soon as possible requesting a laundry list of information.[186]

2001 HUD Policy Statement). Note that the Federal Trade Commission filed an *amicus* brief criticizing a proposed class settlement in a yield spread premium case pending in New York on the grounds, among other things, that class certification in this type of case is "highly unlikely." Brief is available at www.ftc.gov/os/2004/03/040317citicorpmemorandum.pdf.

181 Krzalic v. Republic Title Co., 314 F.3d 875, 882–884 (7th Cir. 2002) (concurring). Note that Judge Posner, writing the majority opinion, distinguished the yield spread premium part of the 2001 Policy Statement from the excessive fee section on the issue of deference. He argued that the Secretary issued the broker portion "after meeting with government representatives and a broad range of consumer and industry groups. Further, the broker portion contained a full discussion of the issue; whereas the unearned fee portion was perfunctory and contained no 'interpretative methodology' or evidence of abuses." *Id.* at 881, 882.

182 *Id.* at 882, 883.

183 323 F.3d 739 (9th Cir. 2003).

184 O'Sullivan v. Countrywide Home Loans, Inc., 319 F.3d 732 (5th Cir. 2003).

185 Alan White, *Risk-Based Mortgage Pricing: Present and Future Research*, 15 Housing Pol'y Debate 503 (2004), *available at* www.fanniemaefoundation.org/programs/hpd/pdf/hpd_1503_White.pdf. Sometimes the markup is reflected explicitly on an underwriting worksheet. The rate sheet (or rate matrix) will show the markup but you need to know which credit category in which the consumer was placed. There may be adjustments to the rates and payment to the broker depending on several factors, including the loan-to-value ratio, whether there will be a prepayment penalty, or whether the loan is a no documentation loan.

186 Much of the relevant information consists of: the rate sheet used for the loan in question; the identity of other lenders, if any, that the broker approached to place the loan in question; the rate sheets of those other lenders for the time period in question; the discussions and written agreements, if any, between the broker and the home owners (and between the lender and the home owners) about payment for services rendered by the broker and whether the home owner wished to pay the higher interest rate; if the broker is the table-funded lender, the purchase agreement between it and the funding lender; any written or oral agreements/discussions between the broker and the lender; what specific services the broker performed for the borrower and the amount of time it took to perform each; the underwriting criteria of the lender and that of any other lender with whom the broker tried to place the loan; whether the loan would have been made by the lender at par rate; number of loans made by the lender at par, below par, and above par; the amount of fees paid to the broker by the borrower in each such loan (whether designated as "broker fees" or not on the HUD-1 Settlement statement); and the method by which the yield spread premium was calculated [note that this calculation may be memorialized in a document in the file]. Some of these documents, particularly rate sheets and desktop underwriting programs, may be available only in an electronic form. See sample discovery in Appx. H.3, *infra. See also* Schauf v. Mortgage Bankers Serv. Corp., 2001 U.S. Dist. LEXIS 21350 (N.D. Ill. Dec. 21, 2001) (court approved discovery seeking all documents relating to loans in which there was both the payment of a yield spread premium and an increased interest rate; plaintiff's requests were a bit too broad and defendant's offer to provide documents was too narrow).

However, the courts have seemed unwilling to dismiss cases where there has been no opportunity for discovery given the speed at which the request for dismissal was filed and where factual development could prove crucial.[187]

It is important to sue both the broker and the lender. While the lender may successfully eliminate itself from the case through a motion to dismiss or for summary judgment, the broker may not because the borrower may have independent claims against the broker under other legal theories. In addition to alleging violations of RESPA, practitioners can include breach of fiduciary duty, fraud, misrepresentation, RICO, TILA, state UDAP, and usury claims where appropriate.[188]

Courts have generally denied class status on the grounds that the factual determination as to whether the fee bore any reasonable relationship to the value of the goods or services provided was suitable for trial only on an individual basis.[189] The courts that have approved class certification usually based their analysis upon the *Culpepper I* standard.[190] How-

ever, all of these decisions were issued before HUD released the 2001 policy statement. It is unlikely that courts will grant class certification in the future in cases involving yield spread premiums.

In any event, individual affirmative cases or defenses to foreclosure continue to be viable avenues to attack this industry practice.[191] The likelihood that the premium is a prohibited kickback is strongest the more the borrower pays directly to the broker. For example, the borrowers in *Mentecki* paid the broker for several specified services in addition to an origination fee totaling almost $13,000 while the lender kicked in over $2,000.[192] In *Jackson* the borrower paid almost $4,500, while the lender added another $3,700.[193] Finally, in *Mulligan*, the broker collected $4,570 from the home owners and another $3,720 from the lender.[194]

The statute of limitations runs for one year from the date the violation occurred[195] and is subject to equitable tolling.[196] Equitable tolling may be difficult to plead and prove given the heightened pleading requirements when fraud is alleged.[197]

---

187   *See, e.g.*, Hastings v. Fidelity Mortgage Decisions Corp., 984 F. Supp. 600 (N.D. Ill. 1997).

188   *See* §§ 12.3–12.12, *infra*. *See* Johnson v. Matrix Fin. Serv. Corp., 820 N.E.2d 1094 (Ill. App. 2004)(a violation of RESPA can constitute a UDAP claim). *But see* Byars v. SCME Mortgage Bankers, Inc., 135 Cal. Rptr. 2d 796 (Ct. App. 2003) (UDAP claim against the lender failed on grounds that if a yield spread premium is legal under RESPA, the failure to disclose the rate sheet is not a deceptive practice under state UDAP statute; court dismissed claim against the lender but opined that a UDAP claim against the unnamed broker could be successful); Shafer v. GSF Mortgage Corp., 2003 WL 21005793 (Minn. Ct. App. May 6, 2003) (court refused to admit evidence of a RESPA violation based on payment of a yield spread premium because the RESPA statute of limitations had run; court ruled this evidence is not relevant to a fraud claim).

189   *See, e.g.*, Richter v. Banc One Mortgage Corp., 1999 U.S. Dist. LEXIS 16074 (D. Ariz. Mar. 19, 1999) (class certification denied); McBride v. Reliastar Mortgage Corp., 1999 U.S. Dist. LEXIS 21654 (N.D. Ga. Apr. 29, 1999) (same); Golan v. Ohio Sav. Bank, 1999 U.S. Dist. LEXIS 16452 (N.D. Ill. Oct. 15, 1999) (same); Brancheau v. Residential Mortgage, 187 F.R.D. 591 (D. Minn. 1999) (decertification of the class; defendant's motion for summary judgment granted); Levine v. North Am. Mortgage, 188 F.R.D. 320 (D. Minn. 1999) (class certification denied); Schmitz v. Aegis Mortgage Corp., 48 F. Supp. 2d 877 (D. Minn. 1999) (same); Paul v. National City Mortgage Co., 1999 U.S. Dist. LEXIS 20512 (N.D. Ga. Mar. 11, 1999) (same but no discussion of the Policy Statement); Yasgur v. Aegis Mortgage Corp., 1999 U.S. Dist. LEXIS 20989 (D. Minn. Mar. 10, 1999) (same but no discussion of the Policy Statement); Lowery v. Ameriquest Mortgage Co., 1998 U.S. Dist. LEXIS 22775 (D.S.C. Dec. 17, 1998); Taylor v. Flagstar Bank, 181 F.R.D. 509 (M.D. Ala. 1998); Hinton v. First Am. Mortgage, 1998 U.S. Dist. LEXIS 2712 (N.D. Ill. Mar. 4, 1998); Conomos v. Chase Manhattan Mortgage Corp., 1998 U.S. Dist. LEXIS 3135 (S.D.N.Y. Mar. 17, 1998); Marinaccio v. Barnett Banks, Inc., 176 F.R.D. 104 (S.D.N.Y. 1997); Moniz v. Crossland Mortgage Corp., 175 F.R.D. 1 (D. Mass. 1997).

190   Heimmermann v. First Union Mortgage, 188 F.R.D. 403 (N.D. Ala. 1999) (class certification granted), *vacated and remanded*, 305 F.3d 1257 (11th Cir. 2002); Briggs v. Countrywide Funding

Corp., 188 F.R.D. 645 (M.D. Ala. 1999); Culpepper v. Inland Mortgage Corp., 189 F.R.D. 668 (N.D. Ala. 1999), *aff'd*, 253 F.3d 1324 (11th Cir. 2001), *cert. denied*, 534 U.S. 1118 (2002); Dujanovic v. Mortgageamerica, Inc., 185 F.R.D. 660 (N.D. Ala. 1999); Mulligan v. Choice Mortgage Corp. USA, 1998 U.S. Dist. LEXIS 13248 (D.N.H. Aug. 11, 1998); *see also* Taylor v. Flagstar Bank, 181 F.R.D. 509 (M.D. Ala. 1998) (court properly recognized that the payment must be compensation for some good, facility, or service provided by the broker; it then suggested, however, that the lender could defend on the ground that the premiums were additional payment for services it rendered for which the borrower also paid a fee, thus forcing the court to make individualized determinations for each class member).

191   For a sample complaint filed as a defense to a judicial foreclosure proceeding, see Appx. H.2, *infra*. Note that one court held that RESPA requires that the complaint plead specifically the total compensation and why this total is unreasonable. Johnson v. Matrix Fin. Serv. Corp., 820 N.E.2d 1094 (Ill. App. 2004).

192   Mentecki v. Saxon Mortgage, 1997 U.S. Dist. LEXIS 1197 (E.D. Va. Jan. 10, 1997), *related decision*, 1997 U.S. Dist. LEXIS 1374 (E.D. Va. Jan. 31, 1997) (denying another motion to dismiss).

193   *See also* Jackson v. Ford Consumer Fin. Co., Clearinghouse No. 52,033 (N.D. Ga. Feb. 3, 1998).

194   Mulligan v. Choice Mortgage Corp. USA, 1998 U.S. Dist. LEXIS 13248 (D.N.H. Aug. 11, 1998).

195   12 U.S.C. § 2614; *see* Snow v. First Am. Title Ins. Co., 332 F.3d 356 (5th Cir. 2003) (date of violation is ordinarily the date of closing); Mullinax v. Radian Guaranty Inc., 311 F. Supp. 2d 474 (M.D.N.C. 2004) (violation occurs when the consumer pays the kickback, that is, the date of closing). RESPA violations, however, may be raised at any time by way of recoupment. *See* Roberson v. Cityscape Corp. (*In re* Roberson), 262 B.R. 312 (Bankr. E.D. Pa. 2001) (adversary proceeding must allege that it was filed in response to a proof of claim or to an independent action filed by the creditor in order to raise the RESPA claim at any time by way of recoupment).

196   *See* § 12.2.1.10, *infra*.

197   *See* Mullinax v. Radian Guaranty Inc., 311 F. Supp. 2d 474 (M.D.N.C. 2004).

The statute provides for damages of three times the amount of "any charge paid for such settlement service,"[198] attorney fees, and costs.[199] One court held that the statute does not allow for injunctive relief.[200] Note that the attorney fee provision is different from those in the federal consumer protection statutes, TILA, FDCPA, and so forth. Section 2607(d)(5) allows the court to award fees to the prevailing *party*, not to the prevailing *consumer*. Given this language, a court could award fees to the defendant in a RESPA case if it successfully defends itself. However, the Ninth Circuit interpreted this provision to mean that successful plaintiffs are generally entitled to attorney fees but successful defendants may be awarded fees only where the plaintiff's action is found to be frivolous, unreasonable, or without foundation.[201]

12.2.1.6 Excessive, Unearned, and Duplicative Fees

Virtually every mortgage transaction involves an array of "settlement services" which have the potential to generate costs for the borrower. Those services include, but are not limited to, title services, the preparation of closing documents, the rendering of credit reports or appraisals, property surveys and inspections, real estate agent, loan broker, and attorney services, as well as loan origination and processing.[202] Such an array of services leaves ample opportunity for financial abuse of unwary and vulnerable consumers. Brokers, agents, and lenders play an especially powerful role because of their presence during the process from beginning to end, and because of the potential influence they wield as many consumers rely on their experience, judgment, and advice upon which to base important decisions. Moreover, as mortgage brokers and, in some areas, closing attorneys, have been major players in many of the seedier second mortgage scams, the prohibition against kickbacks and unearned fees may be of considerable benefit to consumers.[203]

Many of the mortgage scams involve "loan padding," in which the loan includes excessive, duplicative, unearned, and, sometimes, illegal fees. The statute prohibits the giving or accepting of any portion, split, or percentage of any charge for services not actually performed.[204] Regulation X gives a bow in that direction by giving HUD the authority to investigate high prices to see if they are caused by kickbacks or referral fees. While "high prices standing alone are not proof of a RESPA violation," if there is no "reasonable relationship to the market value of the goods or services provided," it may be considered that the excess is "unearned" and therefore a RESPA violation.[205] Significantly, HUD added the following sentence to Regulation X in 1992: "A charge by a person for which no or nominal services are performed or for which duplicative fees are charged is an unearned fee and violates this section."[206]

Excessive charges should be a violation of RESPA's prohibition on kickbacks. However, section 2607(b) is titled: "Splitting charges." For this reason and others, the majority of courts have required that at least two parties share in the benefit of a service charge. This distinction was a pivotal concept behind the holding in *Mercado v. Calumet Federal Savings & Loan Ass'n*,[207] wherein the court dismissed the borrower's lawsuit for failure to state a cause of action under the anti-kickback and unearned fees provision. There, the bank decided to accelerate Ms. Mercado's mortgage after she transferred the property to her son, who lived in the house and had made the mortgage payments for years. The bank justified this decision based on the contention that the transfer occurred without its permission in violation of Ms. Mercado's contract with them.[208] When Calumet offered to refinance Ms. Mercado's loan at a higher interest rate than the loan she already had, Ms. Mercado refused and sued on the theory that the bank's actions amounted to an

---

198 Three courts have decided that the amount of the "charge" is the portion of the charge that violates RESPA, not the entire charge. *See* Mullinax v. Radian Guaranty Inc., 311 F. Supp. 2d 474 (M.D.N.C. 2004); Moore v. Radian Group, Inc., 233 F. Supp. 2d 819 (E.D. Tex. 2002), *aff'd*, 69 Fed. Appx. 659 (5th Cir. 2003) (table); Morales v. Attorneys' Title Ins. Fund, Inc., 983 F. Supp. 1418 (S.D. Fla. 1997); *see also* Durr v. Intercounty Title Co. of Ill., 14 F.3d 1183 (7th Cir. 1994) (discusses the overcharged portion in context of sanctioning the home owner's attorney). These decisions may be a stingy interpretation of § 2607(d)(2) which states: "Any person or persons who violate the prohibitions or limitations of this section shall be jointly and severally liable to the person or persons charged for the settlement service involved in the violation in an amount equal to three times the *amount of any charge paid for such settlement service*." (emphasis added.).

199 12 U.S.C. § 2607(d)(2).

200 Mullinax v. Radian Guaranty Inc., 311 F. Supp. 2d 474 (M.D.N.C. 2004).

201 Lane v. Residential Funding Corp., 323 F.3d 739 (9th Cir. 2003); *see also* Petroski v. First Horizon Home Loans Inc., 2004 WL 1551736 (E.D. Pa. July 9, 2004) (defendant's motion for attorney fees after plaintiff dismissed the RESPA claim denied; court noted that the plaintiff filed the claim in good faith).

202 Loan origination and processing is a "settlement service" as a result of both the 1992 amendments to Regulation X, 57 Fed. Reg. at 49601, and the 1992 statutory amendment. Pub. L. No. 102-550, § 908(a), 106 Stat. 3672 (1992).

203 It is important to recognize its limits, however. *See* § 12.2.1.8, *infra*.

204 12 U.S.C. § 2607(b).

205 Reg. X, 24 C.F.R. § 3500.14(g)(2). This standard, articulated for HUD enforcement purposes in determining when exorbitant fees are "unearned," should serve equally well in private litigation.

206 Reg. X, 24 C.F.R. § 3500.14(c).

207 763 F.2d 269 (7th Cir. 1985).

208 *Id.* at 270. Arguably, Ms. Mercado was only acting in response to the bank's prompting to transfer title after it learned that insurance on the house was in her son's name and not in her name, the mortgagor.

attempt to seek new compensation (by way of closing fees) without providing new services, in violation of RESPA.

The court rejected Ms. Mercado's characterization of the transaction as a violation of RESPA. The court said that the unearned fee prohibition applies to charges applied for *referral* of business without performance of any other services justifying the fee.[209] Therefore, where no referral of settlement service is made, the provision does not apply. Here, because there was no other party to whom any settlement service was being referred and with whom fees would be shared, there was no violation of section 2607(b).

The court in *Mercado* distinguished the facts before it from those in a prior case where the same RESPA provision was held to have been violated even though only one party was involved in the prohibited transaction. In *United States v. Gannon*, the defendant was a counterman in the county recorder's office, whose job was to process land registration and transfer documents for title certification, and accept statutory fees for such services.[210] In addition to the prescribed fees, however, it was customary for persons presenting the documents (usually bank employees) to pay Gannon a $2 or $3 "gratuity," which he kept for himself. This so-called tip was not required, nor was there evidence that Gannon conditioned his services upon its payment; but it was against the rules governing operation of the recorder's office. Despite there being no passing of payments to a third party, the court upheld Gannon's conviction, *inter alia*, under section 2607(b). While the court in *Mercado* described the reasoning in *Gannon* as creating a legal fiction that treats an individual as both a giver and acceptor of fees for purposes of RESPA, the latter decision rested more on the intent of the law to prohibit "abusive practices," rather than on syntax or semantics.[211] "The fact that [Gannon] kept the entirety of the extra payments instead of passing a portion of them along to an unrelated third party does not, in [the court's] opinion render his conduct less abusive or insulate him from liability under [RESPA]."[212]

On two more recent occasions, one in 2001, the Seventh Circuit has affirmed the *Mercado* reasoning.[213] In *Echevar-*

ria, the title company charged the home owners $25 to record their deed and $45 to record their mortgage while the county recorder's office charged $25 and $31 respectively. The title company pocketed $8 on each such transaction. The homeowners argued that the 1992 amendment to Regulation X expanded RESPA liability to all unearned fees and that alleging a split of fees with another party was no longer an essential element under section 2607(b). The court rejected this argument relying on language accompanying the regulation to show that HUD merely intended to clarify the existing law, not expand it. Similarly, the court rejected the homeowners use of HUD policy statements contained in two policy letters and a informational booklet, finding that these documents were not entitled to deference. Because the regulation was not ambiguous, the court said, policy statements and other expressions of opinion deserved no special deference.

This Seventh Circuit decision seemed to seal the fate of unearned and excessive fee claims under RESPA. However, a few months after the court released this decision, HUD issued a policy statement that should, effectively, overrule *Echevarria*.[214] This policy statement unequivocally disagreed with this case and earlier judicial interpretations which it regarded as inconsistent with HUD's regulations and HUD's long-standing interpretations of section 2607(b). HUD documented what it described as its long-standing and consistent interpretation of RESPA to prohibit unearned fees.[215] The agency went on to state:

> In HUD's view, Section 8(b) forbids the paying or accepting of any portion or percentage of a settlement service—including up to 100%—that is unearned, whether the entire charge is divided or split among more than one person or entity or is retained by a single person. Simply put, given that Section 8(b) proscribes unearned portions or percentages as well as splits, HUD does not regard

209 *Id.* A UDAP challenge, or a claim based on breach of duty and fair dealing may have been more appropriate theories in these circumstances. *See generally* §§ 12.5, 12.7, *infra.*

210 684 F.2d 433, 435 (7th Cir. 1981) (*en banc*).

211 "To the extent that the payment is in excess of the reasonable value of the . . . services performed, the excess may be considered a kickback or referral fee proscribed by section 7 [§ 2607]." *Id.* at 438 (quoting S. Rep. No. 93-866 (1974), *reprinted in* 1974 U.S.C.C.A.N. 6551).

212 *Id.*

213 Echevarria v. Chicago Title & Trust Co., 256 F.3d 623 (7th Cir. 2001); Durr v. Intercounty Title Co., 826 F. Supp. 259 (N.D. Ill. 1993), *aff'd*, 14 F.3d 1183 (7th Cir. 1994); *see also* Willis v. Quality Mortgage U.S.A., Inc. 5 F. Supp. 2d 1306 (M.D. Ala. 1998) (finding that the 1992 amendments to Regulation X did not scrap the third party fee-splitting element); Duggan v. Independent Mortgage Corp., 670 F. Supp. 652 (E.D. Va. 1987) (broker's failure to lock in agreed upon interest rate even after

receiving and accepting fee for that purpose was not an offense within the meaning of RESPA's unearned fee provision). *But see* Christakos v. Intercounty Title Co., 196 F.R.D. 496 (N.D. Ill. 2000) (distinguishes *Durr* on the facts; here a $52.50 settlement charge on the HUD-1 Settlement Statement represented $23.50 to the previous lender to record a release and $29 to the defendant title company for "doing nothing;" complaint states a § 2607 violation); Wash. Mut. Bank v. Super. Ct., 89 Cal. Rptr. 2d 560 (Cal. Ct. App. 1999) (RESPA and Regulation X do not preempt private rights of action under state laws for violations of their provisions; claims revolved around alleged overcharging of settlement costs).

214 66 Fed. Reg. 53052 (Oct. 18, 2001) (this policy statement also contains HUD pronouncements on lender-paid broker fees, discussed in § 12.2.1.5.5, *supra*), *reprinted in* Appx. K.3, *infra.*

215 Courts have not accorded deference to this portion of the policy statement to the same extent that several courts have regarding the lender-paid broker fee portion (see § 12.2.1.5.5, *supra*). The criticism that this policy statement was not first published for comment applies. However, HUD's longstanding policy of prohibiting unearned fees ought to trigger deference.

the provision as restricting only fee splitting among settlement service providers. Further, since Section 8(b) on its face prohibits the giving or accepting of an unearned fee by any person, and 24 CFR 3500.14(c) speaks of a charge by "a person," it is also incorrect to conclude that the Section 8(b) proscription covers only payments or charges among settlement service providers.[216]

HUD concluded that unearned fees occur in, but are not limited to, cases where: (1) two or more persons split a fee for settlement services, any portion of which is unearned; or (2) one settlement-service provider marks up the cost of the services performed or goods provided by another settlement-service provider without providing additional actual, necessary, and distinct services, goods, or facilities to justify the additional charge; or (3) one settlement-service provider charges the consumer a fee where no nominal, or duplicative work is done, or the fee is in excess of the reasonable value of goods or facilities provided or the services actually performed.[217] This policy statement appeared to provide home owners with a reinvigorated cause of action under RESPA for what are believed to be widespread abuses in overpricing for settlement charges.[218]

Despite the HUD policy statement and HUD's active role in the appeal via an *amicus* brief, the Fourth Circuit ruled that excessive fees, unless the excess is split between two or more settlement-service providers, do not violate RESPA.[219] Its major objection to HUD's interpretation of section 2607 seemed to be that consumers themselves could be liable for having paid the excessive fee.[220] The court refused to defer to HUD's policy statement and HUD's position reflected in its *amicus* brief,[221] finding that the statute is clear on its face.

This case involved a charge of $65 for a credit report when the actual cost to the lender was $15 or less. The lender itself kept the excess.

The Seventh and Eighth Circuits quickly followed with opinions that endorsed *Boulware*.[222] In the Seventh Circuit case, the closing agent charged the consumers $50 to record the mortgage, but paid the recorder only $36. The consumers argued that the closing agent had accepted a portion (the extra $14) of a charge made for a settlement service (the $50 recording fee) that was not for services actually performed. Rejecting this argument, the Seventh Circuit held that the statute *only* prohibits kickbacks or splitting of fees. But this interpretation ignores the statutory language, which does not mention kickbacks and prohibits acceptance of any portion, split, *or* percentage of a settlement charge. If Congress had intended only to prohibit splitting of charges, it would not have used this more inclusive language.[223]

Nor should the language "no person shall give and no person shall accept" a portion of a charge be interpreted to require a kickback by one party to another. The language can just as easily be read to create two separate prohibitions: one against giving and the other against accepting a portion of a fee that is not for services actually performed.

It is interesting to note how the Eighth Circuit justified giving deference to the part of the HUD Policy Statement

---

216 66 Fed. Reg. 53052, 53058, 53059 (Oct. 18, 2001).

217 *Id.* at 53058.

218 *See also* Weil v. Long Island Sav. Bank, 77 F. Supp. 2d 313 (E.D.N.Y. 1999) (defendants' motion to dismiss RESPA claims denied where mortgage loan customers alleged that they unwittingly paid inflated legal fees in connection with their mortgages which financed an arrangement between the bank's CEO and his former law firm whereby the law firm performed all of the bank's mortgage work, in return for which the CEO and his family took payments from the law firm totaling over $11 million), *further proceedings*, 200 F.R.D. 164 (2001) (class certification granted), *class settlement approved*, 188 F. Supp. 2d 258 (E.D.N.Y. 2002).

219 Boulware v. Crossland Mortgage Corp., 291 F.3d 261 (4th Cir. 2002).

220 This belief was based on the court's review of § 2607(b) which, at the outset, says: "No person shall give and no person shall receive. . . ."

221 Boulware v. Crossland Mortgage Corp., Clearinghouse No. 54,552 (4th Cir. Feb. 2002) (amicus brief). One commentator describes the filing of this brief as an "aggressive" effort by the government. Kenneth Harney, *Justice Department Weighs in on Settlement Fee Issue*, Washington Post, Mar. 16, 2002.

222 Haug v. Bank of Am., 317 F.3d 832 (8th Cir. 2003); Krzalic v. Republic Title Co., 314 F.3d 875 (7th Cir. 2002). For lower courts applying the same rationale, *see* Welch v. Centex Home Equity Co., 323 F. Supp. 2d 1087 (D. Kan. 2004); Haehl v. Wash. Mut. Bank, F.A., 277 F. Supp. 2d 933 (S.D. Ind. 2003) (reconveyance fee kept by the lender); Welch v. Centex Home Equity Co., 262 F. Supp. 2d 1263 (D. Kan. 2003); Monroe v. Citywide Title Corp., 2003 WL 1342988 (N.D. Ill. Mar. 13, 2003) (motion to dismiss granted; title company paid the recordation fee and kept the overcharge); Doxie v. Impac Funding Corp., 2002 WL 31045387 (N.D. Ill. Sept. 11, 2002) (same); Jenkins v. Mercantile Mortgage Co., 231 F. Supp. 2d 737 (N.D. Ill. 2002) (same against title company); Santiago v. GMAC Mortgage Group, Inc., 2002 WL 32173572 (E.D. Pa. Sept. 30, 2003) (markup on tax service and flood certification fees retained by broker; overcharging on underwriting fee). *See also* Beard v. Worldwide Mortgage Corp., 354 F. Supp. 2d 789 (W.D. Tenn. 2005) (court granted leave to amend in allegations regarding the split of the fee). *But see* Szczubelek v. Cendant Mortgage Corp., 215 F.R.D. 107 (D.N.J. 2003) (company offering "appraisal management services" charges $275, listed as paid to the lender, but only $150 is transferred to the appraisal company; motion for summary judgment on fee splitting claim denied due to dispute as to whether the services performed by the company were bona fide); Lengle v. Attorney's Title Guaranty Fund, Inc., 2002 WL 31163672 (N.D. Ill. Sept. 7, 2002) (class certification denied on numerosity grounds; commonality was met, however, where the settlement agent kept a fee to record a mortgage release even though the prior lender charged a release fee and actually recorded the release; court's observation on the commonality issue preceded the decision in *Schuetz*).

223 The court asserts that a "split" means an even split, so "portion" and "percentage" refer to kickbacks of other than 50%. 314 F.3d at 879. However, none of a series of dictionaries consulted supports this meaning of "split."

related to yield spread premiums in *Glover* but refused to give it deference regarding excessive charges. The court simply said: Well, HUD interpreted two different subsections of section 2607; the yield spread premium issue was not directly mentioned in the statute; and section 2607(b), applicable to excessive fees, is simply not ambiguous.[224] On the other hand, Judge Easterbrook wrote a concurring opinion in *Krzalic* in which he slams HUD for issuing the Policy Statement without notice and comment. (HUD had attempted to overrule *Echevarria*, a Seventh Circuit case, which triggered the ire of both Judges Posner and Easterbrook.) Of this behavior, Judge Easterbrook says: "[HUD] has the power to prescribe regulations . . . but elected instead to announce its interpretation of the statute. It issued a broadside and hoped that the courts would kowtow." He argues, in no uncertain terms, that in private litigation, Supreme Court precedent holds that no weight is given to a declaration unaccompanied by the formalities of rulemaking.[225]

Of course, as the *Krzalic* court points out, the closing agent could simply have raised its charge by $14 instead of keeping part of the recording fee, and the bottom line would not have changed for the consumers. This observation supports a broader interpretation of section 2607(b) than that offered by the court. Otherwise, the settlement service provider can always just raise prices to make more profit. The court also argued that the consumers' reading of the statute would mean that consumers themselves would be liable for paying padded fees. But when consumers pay padded fees to a closing agent, they pay the whole fee, not a "portion, split, or percentage" of the fee. In this case, it was the closing agent that split the fee, paying a portion of it to the recorder and keeping the rest.

Holding padded fees permissible allows parties to evade section 2607(b) simply by cutting fewer checks. According to these courts, if a closing agent charges the consumer $50 and pays the full amount to a settlement service provider, and if the provider pays $14 back, it is a kickback violating RESPA. But if the closing agent charges the consumer $50 and pays just $36 to the provider, keeping the same $14, there is no RESPA violation. This is exactly the same transaction economically, but with fewer checks passing between the parties. The HUD policy statement correctly views both of these practices as violations of the statute.[226]

Interestingly, the Eleventh Circuit rejected the Seventh Circuit's interpretation in a case that should breathe life back into padded fee challenges.[227] The alleged facts reveal that Chase charged $50 for messenger services, but kept a portion of the charge. The court held that section 2607(b) does not require a showing of a culpable giver and culpable receiver of the unearned fee. Rather, the "and" between the "no person shall give" and "no person shall accept" operates to create two separate prohibitions: one against giving and the other against accepting.[228] Under this statutory reading, a single party may violate RESPA by marking up the charge of another settlement service provider when it does not perform services for the markup.

Despite this holding, the court affirmed dismissal of the consumer's complaint because the consumer did not allege that Chase performed no services for its share of the fee.[229] The court went further, though, finding that Chase arranged for the courier, and that this action benefited the consumer. Therefore, "we find it impossible to say that Chase performed no services for which its retention of a portion of the fees at issue was justified."[230]

Even more surprisingly, the Seventh Circuit in *Weizeorick v. ABN Amro Mortgage Group, Inc.* did not dismiss a consumer's complaint under section 2607(b).[231] Instead, the court found that it is sufficient to plead that the settlement agent paid a fee ($10) to a mortgage holder to record a release for which no services were performed and paid a fee ($25.60) to itself for the same service which it did perform. The funds came from the loan proceeds which the settlement agent had received from the lender.

The court distinguished its earlier decision in *Echevarria*. It characterized *Echevarria* as a case where the title company both collected and retained fees from the consumer in the same capacity. Similarly, in *Krzalic*, the settlement agent kept a portion of a recordation fee that it paid to the county recorder's office. In *Weizeorick*, however, the funds flowed from the lender to the settlement agent who shared the fee to record the release with the current mortgage holder.

---

224 *Haug*, 317 F.3d at 839.

225 *Krzalic*, 314 F.3d at 882. His concerns encompass the validity of the yield spread premium part of the policy statement as well. *Id.* at 882–883.

226 The portion of the HUD policy statement that addresses padded fees should be entitled to more, not less, deference by courts. Both parts of the statement interpret HUD regulations, and neither was preceded by notice and comment. But unlike HUD's current view of yield spread premiums, its interpretation of padded fees is not a change of position.

227 Sosa v. Chase Manhattan Mortgage Corp., 348 F.3d 979 (11th Cir. 2003).

228 The interpretation of the other circuit courts leads to absurd results, said the Eleventh Circuit. For these examples, see 348 F.3d at 983.

229 This holding contradicts a statement the court made about the plaintiff's allegations earlier in the opinion.

230 *Sosa*, 348 F.3d at 983. This dismissal conflicts with a recent and helpful decision from the Seventh Circuit in which that court indicated that the issue of whether the fee truly was unearned is "best left to discovery." Weizeorick v. ABN Amro Mortgage Group, Inc., 337 F.3d 827, 832 (7th Cir. 2003), *cert. denied*, 124 S. Ct. 1418 (Feb. 23, 2004).

231 Weizeorick v. ABN Amro Mortgage Group, Inc., 337 F.3d 827, 832 (7th Cir. 2003), *cert. denied*, 124 S. Ct. 1418 (Feb. 23, 2004), *class certification denied*, 2004 WL 1880008 (N.D. Ill. Aug. 3, 2004) (certification denied due to potential conflict between named plaintiff and class, the recalcitrance of the named plaintiff in appearing at a deposition, and potential conflict of interest of the class counsel who had represented the title company that closed the loan and who was added as a third party defendant in this case).

In the most recent appellate decision, the Second Circuit sided with the Eleventh Circuit but departed company with the Fourth, Seventh, and Eighth Circuits in *Kruse v. Wells Fargo Home Mortgage, Inc.*[232] The case involved the legality of both "markups" and "overcharges" and the distinction between the two were critical to the outcome of each under RESPA analysis.

The court defined a mark-up to occur when the lender outsources the settlement service to a third party, pays the vendor its fee, inflates the cost without itself performing any additional service, and passes the padded fee on to the homeowner. An overcharge arises when the lender itself performs the settlement service and pads the cost. The Second Circuit found that mark-ups violate RESPA, while overcharges do not.

Regarding mark-ups, the court reasoned that the language in section 2607(b) supports two divergent but plausible readings. On the one hand, the section could mean that there must be a giver *and* acceptor to trigger liability. On the other hand, the "and" arguably operates to create two separate prohibitions, giving *or* receiving. Due to the ambiguity, the court looked to the 2001 HUD Policy Statement and deferred to it.

As to overcharges, the court held that the charging of an unreasonably high fee is not an activity that section 2607(b) prohibits on its face. The court also relied on Congress' rejection of an amendment to RESPA that would have set price-controls when interpreting the language in that section. Consequently, the court did not reach the issue of HUD's Policy Statement because it held that the statute does not cover overcharges on its face.

HUD has been serious in cracking down on such practices. Shortly after issuance of the policy statement, the agency announced settlement of enforcement actions it had taken against 38 lenders for violations related to illegal referral fees and unearned fees.[233] In the wake of HUD's policy statement, settlement service providers have warned their employees about the repercussions of charging fees beyond the actual cost.[234] In a significant move, the Office of the Comptroller of the Currency instructed its bank examiners to apply the HUD policy statement, not the

Echevarria decision, to banks located throughout the country, with the exception of the Seventh Circuit.[235] It is unclear to what extent the HUD Policy Statement will be followed now that three federal appellate courts refuse to embrace the part related to section 2607(b) violations.

A settlement service provider who imposes an *illegal* fee may violate RESPA as well, although the policy statement does not directly address this question. For example, the Veterans Administration prohibits the lender from charging more than 1% of the loan amount if that charge is in lieu of all other charges relating to the costs of origination not expressly allowed by the regulation for VA-insured mortgage loans.[236] The Federal Housing Administration enacted a similar regulation for FHA-insured mortgage loans.[237] If a lender charged a settlement fee in excess of this cap, the difference would be an illegal fee and arguably violates RESPA. However, courts have rejected this theory based upon an interpretation of the regulations.[238] These courts hold that only fees paid directly by the borrower are counted toward the 1% cap and not yield spread premiums that the borrowers repays indirectly through an increase in the interest rate.

RESPA itself prohibits a lender or servicer from charging for the preparation of a TILA disclosure document, the HUD-1 settlement statement, and the escrow accounting statements.[239] Arguably, if a fee is imposed at closing for the

---

232 383 F.3d 49 (2d Cir. 2004); *see also* Wyder v. Bank of America, N.A., 360 F. Supp. 2d 1302 (S.D. Fla. 2005) (mere overcharges are not actionable under § 2607(b), distinguishing *Sosa*); Thompson v. First Union National Bank of Delaware, 2004 WL 1171738 (W.D.N.Y. Mar. 23, 2004) (mere overcharge does not violate RESPA; decision precedes *Kruze*).

233 *See* U.S. Dep't of Hous. & Urban Dev., News Release No. 01-118, HUD Moves to Protect Families from Illegal Mortgage Fees—Pay $2 million, *available at* www.hud.gov (click on newsroom); *see also* United States v. Mercantile Mortgage Co., Civil Action No. 02-C-5078 (N.D. Ill. July 18, 2002) (complaint and stipulated final judgment and order), *available at* www.ftc.gov/os/caselist/0023321.htm.

234 Kenneth Harney, *Realtor Group Warns About Fees*, Washington Post, Jan. 12, 2002, at H01.

235 *See* Office of the Comptroller of the Currency, Bulletin No. 2002-3, Real Estate Settlement Procedures Act Description: Examiner Guidance—Mark-up of Settlement Service Fees, *available at* www.occ.treas.gov (click on "issuances" and then on "bulletins" and scroll down).

236 38 C.F.R. § 36.4312(d)(2). The VA Handbook outlines the costs and fees intended to be covered by the 1% cap. VA Handbook No. 26-7, §§ 8.01, 8.02; VA Pamphlet 26-7. The Handbook is available at www.homeloans.va.gov/handbook.htm.

237 24 C.F.R. § 203.27(a)(2)(i).

238 Geraci v. Homestreet Bank, 347 F.3d 749 (9th Cir. 2003) (same result as *Bjustrom* under VA regulations); Bjustrom v. Trust One Mortgage Corp., 322 F.3d 1201 (9th Cir. 2003) (FHA regulation does not limit all broker compensation to 1%; 24 C.F.R. § 203.27 is read to mean that the 1% cap applies to charges paid by the borrower directly; therefore, yield spread premiums and servicing release fees are excluded from the 1% limit); Dominguez v. Alliance Mortgage Co., 226 F. Supp. 2d 907 (N.D. Ill. 2002) (FHA); Watson v. CBSK Fin. Group, Inc., 197 F. Supp. 2d 1118 (N.D. Ill.) (FHA), *as amended upon reconsideration*, 2002 WL 598521 (N.D. Ill. Apr. 18, 2002); Kolle v. SGB Corp., 2002 WL 31133183 (N.D. Ill. Sept. 25, 2002) (VA); Vargas v. Universal Mortgage Corp., 2001 WL 1545874 (N.D. Ill. Nov. 29, 2001) (FHA); Byars v. SCMA Mortgage Bankers, Inc., 135 Cal. Rptr. 2d 796 (Ct. App. 2003) (applying *Bjustrom*). *But see* Andrews v. Temple Inland Mortgage Corp., 2001 WL 1136160 (D. Minn. Sept. 24, 2001) (court refused to dismiss breach of contract and UDAP claims where it found that the yield spread premium most likely should be counted towards the 1% cap; RESPA claim was not at issue in the motion to dismiss), *class certification denied*, 2002 WL 31844706 (D. Minn. Dec. 13, 2002).

239 12 U.S.C. § 2610.

preparation of one or more of these documents, the fee is illegal and violates section 2607, if the home owner lives outside the Fourth, Seventh, and Ninth Circuits. There appears to be no direct cause of action under section 2610.[240]

In addition to RESPA, practitioners can successfully attack excessive, unearned, and duplicative fees under the Truth in Lending Act if the fees are not included in the finance charge and are not authorized under Regulation Z.[241] In addition, if the fee is one that is listed in section 226.4(c)(7) of Regulation Z and the creditor receives any direct or indirect compensation from it or the charge is unreasonable, then it counts toward the points and fees trigger for determining whether a loan is covered by the HOEPA.[242] Consumers can also challenge the excessive fee itself or the failure to disclose who is receiving it through state UDAP statutes.[243]

Query whether the lender can be on the RESPA hook under section 2607(b) if it pays an excessive fee charged by another settlement service provider through the loan proceeds but retains no portion of the excess nor pays a yield spread premium? The answer is: it may depend upon whether the lender individually underwrote and funded each loan, approved the loan fee paid to the broker, used an extensive network of brokers, and aided its brokers in obtaining unearned fees. HUD itself filed a RESPA enforcement action against one lender claiming that the lender was liable for excessive broker fees even when it did not keep any portion of the unearned fee and did not pay a yield spread premium.[244] (The lender did pay yield spread premiums to brokers in a bit more than a third of the loans; however, HUD also alleged RESPA violations against the lender when the borrower paid the broker fees through the loan proceeds.) Specifically, HUD alleged that the lender was aware that little or no services were being performed in exchange for broker fees and the lender knew that the broker compensation did not bear a reasonable relation to the level of goods or services provided, especially as the lender performed many of these services itself. Further, the loan principals often were increased to pay broker fees and the increased principals provided the lender with additional profit and with a mechanism through which to pay its brokers. In doing so, the lender paid a portion of the loan proceeds to brokers even though nominal or no services were provided.[245] This matter was settled without providing more definitive authority for this RESPA theory.

In another case, HUD filed a complaint against a mortgage lender under section 2607 because it accepted all of the loans referred by a particular broker and routinely approved and paid up to a 10% broker fee in each case.[246] This matter settled but the importance of the case is that HUD alleged a violation of section 2607 by the lender for approving and paying inflated broker fees, even though the lender kept none of the fee. The lesson here is that if HUD believes there is a good faith basis to file such a suit under RESPA given these alleged facts, then consumer attorneys can feel comfortable raising similar claims, particularly in circuits outside the Fourth, Seventh, and Ninth Circuits.

A relatively new mortgage insurance product, called "pool" or "secondary" insurance is sold by mortgage insurance companies to lenders who sell their loans on the secondary market to Fannie Mae or Freddie Mac. These two entities charge an annual guaranty fee to protect themselves against losses not covered by the private mortgage insurance. One way to reduce this cost to the lender is to obtain a pool insurance policy that protects the loan pool purchaser from this risk.[247] Some state insurance regulators are reviewing whether some of the mortgage insurance companies have, in practice, underpriced pool insurance for lenders who, in exchange, channel a large volume of private mortgage insurance to the insurers, in violation of RESPA.[248] Consumer challenges to pool insurance and other arrange-

240 McAnaney v. Astoria Fin. Corp., 357 F. Supp. 2d 578 (E.D.N.Y. 2005).

241 *See* National Consumer Law Center, Truth in Lending Ch. 3 (5th ed. 2003 and Supp.). Certain fees related to real estate transactions must be bona fide and reasonable in order to qualify for exclusion from the finance charge. 12 C.F.R. § 226.4(c)(7). An "excessive" fee is not a "reasonable" fee for TIL purposes.

242 *See* National Consumer Law Center, Truth in Lending Ch. 9 (5th ed. 2003 and Supp.).

243 *See* National Consumer Law Center, Unfair and Deceptive Acts and Practices §§ 2.2.5, 3.3 (6th ed. 2004 and Supp.); *see also* Szczubelek v. Cendant Mortgage Corp., 215 F.R.D. 107 (D.N.J. 2003) (questions of fact warrant a denial of lender's motion for summary judgment on UDAP claim); Christakos v. Intercounty Title Co., 196 F.R.D. 496 (N.D. Ill. 2000) (even where RESPA provides its own remedy, UDAP statute can provide a parallel cause of action); Jenkins v. Mercantile Mortgage Co., 231 F. Supp. 2d 737 (N.D. Ill. 2002) (deliberately charging for a service that it had no intent to provide or knew was unnecessary could violate state UDAP act); Watson v. CBSK Fin. Group, Inc., 197 F. Supp. 2d 1118 (N.D. Ill. 2002) (omission or concealment of a material fact about the yield spread premium can state a claim).

244 United States v. Delta Funding Corp., Clearinghouse Nos. 54,553A, 54,553B (E.D.N.Y. filed Mar. 30, 2000) (complaint and settlement).

245 The lender may be liable alternatively under § 2607(a) for paying a referral fee.

246 United States v. Mercantile Mortgage Co., Civil Action No. 02-C-5078 (N.D. Ill. July 18, 2002) (complaint and stipulated final judgment and order), *available at* www.ftc.gov/os/caselist/0023321.htm.

247 See discussion of private mortgage insurance in § 8.3.2.1, *supra*. Pool insurance and other types of agreements that may involve kickbacks or referrals are described in Mullinax v. Radian Guaranty, Inc., 199 F. Supp. 2d 311 (M.D.N.C. 2002) (the other arrangements include: captive reinsurance agreements and rebates through performance notes), *subsequent proceedings*, 311 F. Supp. 2d 474 (M.D.N.C. 2004).

248 *See Pool Mortgage Insurance Probed in N.Y., Calif.*, Boston Globe, Dec. 28, 1999, at D3.

ments have begun to surface in reported decisions, though not on the merits of whether they violate RESPA.[249]

12.2.1.7 Steering by Seller to Title Insurance Company

As discussed previously, the payment of referral fees and the splitting of fees for the provision of settlement services are generally prohibited under RESPA.[250] Congress went further in the context of steering that occurs between sellers of real property, particularly large development corporations, and title insurance companies. It specifically prohibited a seller of property to be purchased with the assistance of a covered mortgage loan from directly or indirectly requiring that the buyer obtain title insurance from a particular title company regardless of whether any referral fees are paid.[251]

"Requiring the use" of a particular title company to purchase the insurance is defined by Regulation X.[252] The general definition includes the:

> [S]ituation in which a person must use a particular provider of a settlement service in order to have access to some distinct service or property, and the person will pay for the settlement service of the particular provider or will pay a charge attributable, in whole or in part, to the settlement service.

Excluded from this definition is the offering of a package of discounts or rebates to consumers for the purchase of multiple settlement services so long as the package or discounts are optional to the purchaser. Sham discounts will not meet this exemption, for example, a discount that is made up by higher costs elsewhere in the settlement process.[253]

Any seller who violates this prohibition is liable to the buyer in an amount equal to three times *all* charges made for such title insurance.[254] The measure of damages is three times the entire fee, not three times the amount by which the fee for the insurance issued by the required title company exceeds that available to the buyer from another source. Claims under section 2608 must be brought within one year from the date of the occurrence of the violation.[255] Though

section 2608 does not specifically provide for the payment of attorney fees and costs to the prevailing party, Regulation X makes a violation of section 2608 a *per se* violation of section 2607 (the anti-kickback section of RESPA).[256] As section 2607 contains a fee-shifting provision, consumers can argue that fees are recoverable under section 2607.[257]

Though there are no reported decisions regarding the merits of a section 2608 claim, a court granted class certification in a case where the seller development company inserted a clause in the agreement of sale authorizing the seller to place title insurance with a particular title insurance company whose name was or would be inserted into a blank in the clause.[258] The court had little trouble finding that the commonality requirement was met despite the defendants' claim that different oral representations were made to purchasers and that some purchasers may have had the "blank" filled in with the name of a title company and others may not.

12.2.1.8 Preemption

RESPA includes an express provision relating to the preemption of inconsistent state laws.[259] If the state law provides greater protections than RESPA, then the law is not preempted.[260] In one case, the denial of the lender's motion to dismiss a RESPA complaint raising issues of inflated settlement costs and fee-padding as violations of the state UDAP act and state common law torts, prompted the lender to request a writ of mandamus from an appellate court to vacate the trial court's decision.[261] The lender argued that

---

249 Mullinax v. Radian Guaranty, Inc., 311 F. Supp. 2d 474 (M.D.N.C. 2004) (motion to dismiss granted as borrowers did not have standing); Barnes v. Republic Mortgage Ins. Co., 2003 WL 1738454 (S.D. Ga. Feb. 5, 2003) (class certification denied; settlement mooted the motion); Moore v. Radian Group, Inc., 233 F. Supp. 2d 819 (E.D. Tex. 2002), *aff'd*, 69 Fed. Appx. (5th Cir. 2003) (table) (plaintiffs do not have standing as they do not allege that their PMI policy was overpriced as a result of the reinsurance agreements; motion to dismiss granted).

250 *See* § 12.2.1.5.1, *supra*.

251 12 U.S.C. § 2608(a).

252 Reg. X, 24 C.F.R. § 3500.2(b).

253 Reg. X, 24 C.F.R. § 3500.2(b); Reg. X, 24 C.F.R. § 3500.16.

254 12 U.S.C. § 2608(b).

255 12 U.S.C. § 2614.

256 Reg. X, 24 C.F.R. § 3500.19(c).

257 *See* 12 U.S.C. § 2607(d)(5); *see also* Weisberg v. Toll Bros., Inc., 617 F. Supp. 539 (E.D. Pa. 1985) (court awarded attorney fees upon settlement of a § 2608 class action but did not discuss any authority for the award because, by agreement, the motion for fees was unopposed).

258 Rendler v. Gambone Bros. Dev. Co., 182 F.R.D. 152 (E.D. Pa. 1998).

259 12 U.S.C. § 2616 states:

> This Act does not annul, alter, or affect, or exempt any person subject to the provisions of this Act from complying with the laws of any State with respect to settlement practices, except to the extent that those laws are inconsistent with any provision of this Act, and then only to the extent of the inconsistency. The Secretary is authorized to determine whether such inconsistencies exist. The Secretary may not determine that any State law is inconsistent with any provision of this Act if the Secretary determines that such law gives greater protection to the consumer. In making these determinations the Secretary shall consult with the appropriate federal agencies.

260 Regulation X fleshes out its sister statutory provision. *See* 24 C.F.R. § 3500.13.

261 Wash. Mut. Bank v. Super. Ct., 89 Cal. Rptr. 2d 560 (Cal. Ct. App. 1999) (court specifically held that RESPA and Reg. X do not expressly preempt private rights of action under state laws for violations of their provisions).

RESPA preempted these state law claims because RESPA provides no private right of action for violations of some of its provisions. The court disagreed, specifically upholding the right of consumers to sue under state statutory or common law theories for violations of RESPA.[262]

Since RESPA does not completely preempt state law, removal of cases alleging RESPA violations should be remanded.[263]

State RESPA-like escrow laws may fall in the face of federal depository preemption if those laws are not consistent with RESPA. In one case, the court held that the Office of Thrift Supervision may establish nationwide regulations consistent with RESPA that will trump state law.[264]

An issue raised in a recent case is whether a claim under RESPA of illegal kickbacks between a mortgage insurance company and the mortgage lender was barred by the Mc-Carran-Ferguson Act. This Act, discussed in § 8.5.2.7.2, *supra*, prohibits federal intrusion into the regulation of insurance unless the federal law relates to the business of insurance.[265] The Eleventh Circuit held that RESPA itself relates to the business of insurance because, among other things, insurance products are mentioned in the RESPA definition of settlement services.[266] Therefore, the consumer claims based upon alleged kickbacks were not barred by the McCarran-Ferguson Act.

12.2.1.9 Electronic Provision of Information Required by RESPA

The Electronic Signatures in Global and National Commerce Act (E-Sign),[267] effective October 1, 2000, allows lenders to replace written documents with electronic documents in certain circumstances. If a statute, regulation, or other rule of law requires that information relating to a transaction be provided to the consumer in writing, then the information may be provided electronically if:

- Certain disclosures are made to the consumer;[268]
- The consumer consents electronically, or confirms his or her consent electronically, in a manner that reasonably indicates that he or she can access information electronically in the format used by the provider of the information;[269] and
- The electronic document is in a form that is capable of being retained and accurately reproduced for later reference by all parties or persons who are entitled to retain it.[270]

These requirements apply whenever a lender wants to use an electronic document to replace a document that RESPA requires to be in writing.[271] RESPA explicitly requires that certain notices about servicing[272] and about affiliated business arrangements[273] be given to the borrower in writing. It also requires that borrowers be given a "booklet" about real estate settlement costs,[274] which clearly refers to a tangible

---

262 *Id.* at 571. The court stated:

> Our review of the law demonstrates, and we now hold, that RESPA and Regulation X do not expressly preempt private rights of action under state laws for violations of their provisions. We find that private state causes of action are not inconsistent with the federal disclosure requirements, but rather are complementary to the federal requirements and in fact will promote full compliance with the disclosure law enacted by Congress. We do not believe that allowing borrowers to sue for unlawful disclosures or omissions will interfere in any way with the operation of the federal law, and we find no conflict between RESPA and private state law causes of action. We thus uphold the decision of the trial court to overrule the demurrer to the extent it alleged that plaintiffs' state law claims were preempted by RESPA and Regulation X.

See also Fardella v. Downey Sav. & Loan Assoc., 2001 U.S. Dist. LEXIS 6037 (N.D. Cal. May 9, 2001) (removal to federal court remanded; UDAP claim and other state law claims arising from the payment of a yield spread premium are not preempted by RESPA).

263 *See* § 12.2.1.10, *infra*.

264 Flagg v. Yonkers Sav. & Loan Ass'n, FA, 396 F.3d 178 (2d Cir. 2005). For a discussion of federal depository preemption for federal savings associations, see § 3.5, *supra*.

265 15 U.S.C. § 1012.

266 Patton v. Triad Guaranty Ins., 277 F.3d 1294 (11th Cir. 2002); Mullinax v. Radian Guaranty Inc., 199 F. Supp. 2d 311 (M.D.N.C. 2002), *subsequent proceedings*, 311 F. Supp. 2d 474 (M.D.N.C. 2004).

267 Pub. L. No. 106-229, 114 Stat. 464 (2000) (codified at 15 U.S.C. § 7001 *et seq.*).

268 15 U.S.C. § 7001(c)(1)(B), (c)(1)(C)(1); *see* § 9.2.10.4, *supra* (a more detailed discussion of these requirements).

269 15 U.S.C. § 7001(c)(1)(C)(ii); *see* § 9.2.10.4, *supra* (further discussion of this requirement).

270 15 U.S.C. § 7001(e).

271 15 U.S.C. § 7002 allows states to supersede E-Sign's effect on state law by passing the Uniform Electronic Transactions Act or a similar statute that is consistent with E-Sign. A state's enactment of superseding legislation would not, however, affect the application of E-Sign to federal statutes such as RESPA. *See* § 9.2.10, *supra*.

272 12 U.S.C. §§ 2605(b)(2)(C) (notice of assignment, sale, or transfer of servicing must be "in writing"), 2605(c)(2)(C) ("written notice" at time of settlement satisfies requirement that transferee give notice to borrower), 2605(e) (requiring written response to borrower's request for information about servicing); Reg. X, 24 C.F.R. §§ 3500.21(b)(3)(v) (initial servicing disclosure "must contain" a "written acknowledgment," signed by the applicant), 3500.21(c) (initial servicing disclosure must be delivered and signed by borrower at settlement, or mailed to borrower), 3500.21(d)(1) (requiring "written Notice of Transfer"), 3500.21(e)(1) (requiring written response to request for information about servicing), 3500.21(3) (same). Appendix MS-1 to the HUD RESPA regulations, which contains instructions for filling out the initial servicing disclosure, directs the lender to "use business stationery or similar heading."

273 12 U.S.C. § 2607(c); Reg. X, 24 C.F.R. § 3500.15(b)(1).

274 12 U.S.C. § 2604; Reg. X, 24 C.F.R. § 3500.6(a). See also Reg. X, 24 C.F.R. § 3500.6(c), which provides that "any size and quantity of paper" may be used for the booklet.

object so is the equivalent of a requirement that the information be in writing. With regard to escrow statements, the HUD regulations evince a similar requirement by stating that both the initial and annual statements must be handed or mailed to the borrower,[275] and referring to the initial statement as a "document"[276] with pages.[277] Likewise, the settlement statement must be on a "standard form" prescribed by HUD;[278] it must be filled in "by typewriter, hand printing, computer printing, or any other method producing clear and legible results";[279] it must be either delivered at settlement or mailed;[280] and it can be reproduced on any size pages, on separate pages, on the front and back of a single page, on one continuous page, or on multicopy tear-out sets.[281] As to the good faith estimate of settlement costs, the regulations similarly require that it be mailed or delivered,[282] and refer to it as having pages.[283]

HUD is likely to issue an interpretation of the effect of E-Sign on these and other RESPA requirements, but in the meantime practitioners should give careful scrutiny to any RESPA disclosures that were provided electronically. In particular, the consumer should investigate:

- Did the lender follow E-Sign's strict consent and confirmation-of-consent provisions?[284]
- Did the consumer's manner of giving or confirming consent to electronic disclosures reasonably demonstrate that the consumer can access information in the electronic form that will be used?[285]
- Did the lender give the consumer the required statement about electronic documents and go through the consent procedures *before* the electronic disclosures were given?[286]
- Did the consumer actually receive the electronic RESPA disclosures? If the lender sent them by e-mail that was unopened or bounced back as undeliverable, the lender may not have met RESPA's requirement that it "deliver" the disclosures to the consumer.[287] Posting

disclosures to a website that the consumer does not visit raises similar problems.[288]
- Did the lender meet RESPA's timing requirements? E-Sign does not undercut other statutes' timing requirements.[289]
- Were the electronic documents provided in a format that allowed retention and accurate reproduction for later reference by the consumer, and did the consumer actually have the equipment to keep them?[290]

Requirements in RESPA that information be provided in writing are overridden only if the lender complies with E-Sign's requirements. If the lender did not comply, then the consumer should be entitled to whatever penalty RESPA would provide if the information had not been provided.[291]

12.2.1.10 Practice Issues

As the discussion indicates, of these highlighted provisions[292] only three have specific statutory remedies. The chart below lists the citations to each duty imposed by RESPA pre-settlement, settlement, and post-settlement. The chart then indicates whether the statute specifies a remedy, provides a description of the remedy, and states the applicable statute of limitations.[293]

Whether or not RESPA creates a specific remedy for any particular violation, the failure to comply with any RESPA provision may well fall within the scope of a state UDAP statute which applies to the credit transaction at issue.[294] For example, failure to give the required settlement statement which might have alerted the consumer to exorbitant closing costs or broker fees in time to seek credit elsewhere could be

---

275 Reg. X, 24 C.F.R. § 3500.17(b) (definitions of "delivery" and "submit"), (g), (i)(3).
276 Reg. X, 24 C.F.R. § 3500.17(g)(1)(ii).
277 Reg. X, 24 C.F.R. § 3500.17(h)(2).
278 12 U.S.C. § 2603(a); Reg. X, 24 C.F.R. §§ 3500.7, 3500.8.
279 Reg. X, 24 C.F.R. pt. 3500, app. A.
280 Reg. X, 24 C.F.R. § 3500.10(b), (c).
281 Reg. X, 24 C.F.R. § 3500.9(a)(5).
282 Reg. X, 24 C.F.R. § 3500.7(a).
283 Reg. X, 24 C.F.R. pt. 3500, App. C n.1.
284 See § 9.2.10.3, *supra*, for a more detailed discussion of the consent and confirmation-of-consent requirements.
285 15 U.S.C. § 7001(c)(1)(C)(ii).
286 15 U.S.C. § 7001(c)(1)(B), (c)(1)(C)(i) (requiring disclosures about the electronic provision of information to be given to the consumer prior to consenting).
287 See 12 U.S.C. § 2604(d) (lender must provide booklet by delivering it or placing it in the mail); Reg. X, 24 C.F.R. §§ 3500.7(a) (good faith estimate must be delivered or placed in the mail), 3500.10(b) (settlement agent "shall deliver" settlement statement at or before settlement).
288 *See* § 9.2.10.6, *supra*.
289 15 U.S.C. § 7001(c)(2).
290 *See* 15 U.S.C. § 7001(e) (electronic documents may be denied legal effect if they are not in a form that is capable of being retained and accurately reproduced by all parties).
291 *See* §§ 12.2.1.2, 12.2.1.3, 12.2.1.4, *supra*.
292 The Act contains other provisions which are less relevant to the most common mortgage scams, but become more important if the consumer runs into post-consummation problems. See discussion on servicer obligations in § 12.2.1, *supra*.
293 Thanks to John Rao for creating this chart.
294 *See* Christakos v. Intercounty Title Co., 196 F.R.D. 496 (N.D. Ill. 2000) (even where RESPA provides its own remedy, UDAP statute can provide a parallel cause of action); Wash. Mut. Bank v. Super. Ct., 89 Cal. Rptr. 2d 560 (Cal. Ct. App. 1999) (court specifically held that RESPA and Reg. X do not expressly preempt private rights of action under state laws for violations of their provisions). *But see* Koch v. First Union Corp., 2002 WL 372939 (Pa. C.P. Jan. 10, 2002) (court finds no relief under UDAP act because RESPA specifically contains no private cause of action for alleged violations of "good faith estimates" provisions); *see also* National Consumer Law Center, Unfair and Deceptive Acts and Practices §§ 2.2.1, 2.3.3 (6th ed. 2004 and Supp.); *cf.* Carver v. Discount Funding Assoc., 2004 WL 2827229 (Ohio Com. Pl. June 10, 2004) (failure of broker to disclose the yield spread premium states a claim under the state Mortgage Broker Act).

CLAIM	CITATIONS	RIGHT OF ACTION	REMEDY	STATUTE OF LIMITATIONS
Pre-Settlement				
Duty to Provide Good Faith Estimate, Information Booklet	12 U.S.C. § 2604 Reg. X § 3500.7; Reg. X § 3500.6			
Duty to Provide Servicing Statement	12 U.S.C. § 2605(a) Reg. X § 3500.21	Yes § 2605(f) § 2614	actual damages, costs and attorney fees; plus $1,000 per violation if pattern and practice of non-compliance	3 years § 2614
Duty to Provide "Controlled Business Arrangement" Notice	12 U.S.C. § 2607 Reg. X § 3500.15	Yes § 2607(d) § 2614	3 times amount paid for settlement service, attorney fees, and costs	1 year § 2614
Settlement				
Duty to Provide HUD-1	12 U.S.C. § 2603 Reg. X § 3500.8			
Duty to Provide Initial Escrow Account Statement	12 U.S.C. § 2609 Reg. X § 3500.17(g)			
Prohibition against Kickbacks, Fee Splitting and Unearned Fees	12 U.S.C. § 2607 Reg. X § 3500.14(b)	Yes § 2607(d) § 2614	3 times amount paid for settlement service, attorney fees, and costs	1 year § 2614
Prohibition against Requiring Purchase of Title Insurance from Certain Title Co.	12 U.S.C. § 2608 Reg. X § 3500.16	Yes § 2608 § 2614	3 times all charges for title insurance	1 year § 2614
Prohibition against Charging Fee for Preparation of TIL disclosure, HUD-1	12 U.S.C. § 2610 Reg. X § 3500.12			
Post-Settlement				
Duty to Provide Annual Escrow Statement	12 U.S.C. § 2609 Reg. X § 3500.17(i)			
Duty to Perform Escrow Analysis	12 U.S.C. § 2609 Reg. X § 3500.17			
Requirements for Surpluses, Deficiencies and Shortages	12 U.S.C. § 2609 Reg. X § 3500.17(f)			
Duty to Make Timely Payments Out of the Escrow	12 U.S.C. § 2605(g) Reg. X § 3500.17(k)	Yes § 2605(f) § 2614	actual damages, costs and attorney fees; plus $1,000 per violation if pattern and practice of non-compliance	3 years § 2614
Duty to Respond to Qualified Written Request	12 U.S.C. § 2605(e) Reg. X § 3500.21	Yes § 2605(f) § 2614	actual damages, costs and attorney fees; plus $1,000 per violation if pattern and practice of non-compliance	3 years § 2614
Duty to Provide Transfer of Servicing Statement	12 U.S.C. § 2605(b) Reg. X § 3500.21	Yes § 2605(f) § 2614	actual damages, costs and attorney fees; plus $1,000 per violation if pattern and practice of non-compliance	3 years § 2614

considered either a *per se* UDAP violation, as a violation of applicable law,[295] or more generally as a deceptive practice as an omission of critical information.[296]

As with Truth in Lending, RESPA provides consumers with important information. The settlement statement, in fact, helps close one of TIL's loopholes. Because TIL does not mandate that consumers be given an itemization of the amount financed,[297] some of the overreaching mortgage lenders were able to conceal exorbitant costs and other forms of loan padding simply by providing a total amount financed. By requiring a list of the fees charged at settlement, RESPA helps consumers to determine if padding and duplication occur.

Moreover, the limitation on unearned charges and kickbacks, which carries the possibility of a maximum $10,000

---

295 National Consumer Law Center, Unfair and Deceptive Acts and Practices § 3.2.7 (6th ed. 2004 and Supp.).
296 *Id.* § 4.2.14.

297 Reg. Z, 12 C.F.R. § 226.18(c)(2); National Consumer Law Center, Truth in Lending § 4.7.3 (5th ed. 2003 and Supp.).

fine as well as the treble-damages private remedy, gives practitioners a handle on at least some of the loan padding techniques used by these lenders, although the authorization for attorney fees to the "prevailing party"[298] may be a deterrent to private enforcement.[299] When challenging a RESPA kickback settlement, one court found that the bond to be posted should not include a component representing anticipated attorney fees.[300]

Several courts have held that the statute of limitations is not jurisdictional, which subjects it to an equitable tolling argument.[301] In addition, RESPA claims can be raised by way of recoupment by the homeowner.[302] If a violation of the statute is being challenged as a UDAP violation, however, that state statute of limitations should apply.

---

298 12 U.S.C. § 2607(d)(5).
299 *See* § 12.2.1.5.5, *supra.*
300 Pedraza v. United Guaranty Corp., 313 F.3d 1323 (11th Cir. 2002); Baynham v. PMI Mortgage Ins. Co., 313 F.3d 1337 (11th Cir. 2002) (follows *Pedraza*); Downey v. Mortgage Guaranty Ins. Corp., 313 F.3d 1341 (11th Cir. 2002) (follows *Pedraza*).
301 Lawyers Title Ins. Corp. v. Dearborn Title Corp., 118 F.3d 1157 (7th Cir. 1997), *upon remand*, 22 F. Supp. 2d 820 (N.D. Ill. 1998) (applying the equitable tolling doctrine, court found that Lawyers Title failed to act with due diligence to discover its cause of action; statute of limitations, therefore, not tolled); Becker v. Chicago Title Ins. Co., 2004 WL 228672 (E.D. Pa. Feb. 4, 2004) (doctrine recognized; statute not tolled because inflated notary fees were disclosed at the closing and legal amount of notary fees are listed in public law); Mills v. Equicredit Corp., 294 F. Supp. 2d 903 (E.D. Mich. 2003) (regardless of whether RESPA is subject to tolling doctrine, the home owners here did not show grounds for tolling because the HUD-1 disclosed the yield spread premium); Estate of Henderson v. Meritage Mortgage Corp., 293 F. Supp. 2d 830 (N.D. Ill. 2003) (equitable tolling recognized; statute of limitations tolled due to home owner's mental incapacity and the estate's inability to uncover the legal defenses until after the home owner's death); Mullinax v. Radian Guaranty Inc., 199 F. Supp. 2d 311 (M.D.N.C. 2002) (recognized equitable tolling doctrine but plaintiff did not plead facts to support it in this case; leave to amend granted), *case dismissed*, 311 F. Supp. 2d 474 (M.D.N.C. 2004); Thomas v. Ocwen Fed. Bank, Fed. Sav. Bank, 2002 WL 99737 (N.D. Ill. Jan. 25, 2002) (doctrine recognized but consumer does not allege facts to invoke it); Pedraza v. United Guaranty Corp., 114 F. Supp. 2d 1347 (S.D. Ga. 2000) (equitable tolling doctrine recognized but tolling can only occur for three years; plaintiff did not adequately plead facts to support equitable tolling claim; complaint dismissed without prejudice); Kerby v. Mortgage Funding Corp., 992 F. Supp. 787 (D. Md. 1998). *See also* Reiser v. Residential Funding Corp., 380 F.3d 1027 (7th Cir. 2004) (since statute of limitations is an affirmative defense, it is not proper to decide whether the statute was tolled at the motion to dismiss stage); Salois v. Dime Sav. Bank, 128 F.3d 20 (1st Cir. 1997) (court assumes equitable tolling doctrine applies but finds that loan documents contained all of the information necessary to determine bases of claims; inquiry notice satisfied). *But see* Carver v. Discount Funding Assoc., 2004 WL 2827229 (Ohio Com. Pl. June 10, 2004) (court states that the failure to file timely is jurisdictional, though equitable tolling argument was not at issue).
302 Harvey v. EMC Mortgage Corp., 2003 WL 21460063 (Bankr. E.D. Pa. June 9, 2003).

RESPA may not support removal of the case from state to federal court because it does not completely preempt state law.[303] One court held that raising RESPA defensively in a state foreclosure proceeding does not permit the homeowner to remove the whole matter to federal court.[304] RESPA also contains its own venue provision in section 2614. Venue is proper in the district in which the property involved is located or where the violation occurred.[305]

Standing issues have arisen recently in some cases. Where the complaint fails to plead that the consumer was overcharged or harmed by the alleged RESPA violation, the consumer does not have standing to sue.[306]

Motions to compel arbitration have reared their heads in the RESPA context.[307] One court ordered arbitration between not only the lender and borrower but also with the non-signatory broker where the borrower alleged that the misconduct by the lender and broker was "substantially interdependent and concerted."[308]

12.2.2 Home Ownership and Equity Protection Act of 1994

12.2.2.1 Overview and Remedies

In response to allegations that predatory lending was in part a natural consequence of the abandonment of minority and low-income neighborhoods by mainstream lending institutions, Congress conducted a series of hearings on the enforcement of fair lending laws and the Community Reinvestment Act, reverse redlining, predatory lending, and

---

303 Jamal v. WMC Mortgage Corp., 2005 WL 724204 (E.D. Pa. Mar. 28, 2005) (court remanded case to state court because RESPA did not completely preempt state law); Integra Bank, N.A. v. Greer, 2003 WL 21544260 (S.D. Ind. June 26, 2003) (the home owner also erred by not removing before a judgment in the foreclosure case was entered).
304 Firstar Bank, NA v. West-Anderson, 2003 WL 21313849 (D. Kan. Apr. 22, 2003) (home owner also could not meet her burden in proving diversity jurisdiction).
305 *See* Webb v. Chase Manhattan Mortgage Corp., 2005 WL 106896 (S.D.N.Y. Jan. 18, 2005) (venue not proper in New York since the properties at issue were located in Tennessee and Colorado and where the servicing occurred in Ohio).
306 *See, e.g.*, Mullinax v. Radian Guaranty Inc., 311 F. Supp. 2d 474 (M.D.N.C. 2004) (consumers did not allege they were overcharged for private mortgage insurance); Contawe v. Crescent Heights of America, Inc., 2004 WL 2244538 (E.D. Pa. Oct. 1, 2004) (charge for title insurance was set by state law, therefore, no overcharging), *class certification denied*, 2004 WL 2966931 (E.D. Pa. Dec. 21, 2004).
307 For a full discussion of arbitration clauses and enforceability issues, see National Consumer Law Center, Consumer Arbitration Agreements (4th ed. 2004); National Consumer Law Center, Unfair and Deceptive Acts and Practices § 7.6.7 (6th ed. 2004 and Supp.).
308 Blount v. National Lending Corp., 108 F. Supp. 2d 666 (S.D. Miss. 2000).

community development banking.[309] One outcome was the Home Ownership and Equity Protection Act of 1994, part of the larger Riegle Community Development and Regulatory Improvement Act of 1994.[310]

The legislation, effective October 1, 1995, defines a special category of closed-end, home-secured loans which will fall within the scope of the act if they meet one of two cost-triggers. Such high-cost mortgage loans[311] are subject to special disclosure requirements and, more critically, to restrictions on substantive terms which were commonly used by the predatory lenders to manipulate the cost of these transactions. Violations of the Act, which amends Truth in Lending, are subject to three remedies. They trigger the usual TIL monetary damages and, where "material" (under a common law standard, not the TIL standard), enhanced damages of the sum of all finance charges and fees paid by the consumer.[312] More critically, violations of HOEPA's disclosure provisions are deemed "material" for purposes of TIL rescission,[313] and the inclusion of a prohibited term (whether invoked or not) is also deemed a material violation for purposes of TIL rescission.[314] (Violations of TIL deemed "material" by that Act trigger the extended rescission right.[315]) Finally, the law limits the right of assignees of high-cost mortgages to assert holder-in-due-course status to cut off consumer claims and defenses.[316]

12.2.2.2 Covered Mortgages

A loan subject to this Act is one which meets the following criteria:[317]

- Is closed-end consumer credit;[318]
- Is not a "residential mortgage transaction," in other words, is not used for the acquisition or construction of the property;[319]
- Is secured by the borrower's principal dwelling;[320] and
- Meets one of two alternative cost-triggers:
    — has an APR, properly calculated, which is 10% above the rate for Treasury securities of a comparable term or after October 1, 2002 is 8% above the rate for Treasury securities of a comparable term for first lien loans and remains at 10% for subordinate loans;[321] *or*
    — has upfront fees and charges (including broker fees) which are the greater of:
        — 8% of the loan amount;[322] or
        — $400 (an amount which can change annually with the CPI).[323]

---

309 *Hearings on Problems in Community Development Banking, Mortgage Lending Discrimination, Reverse Redlining, and Home Equity Lending Before the Senate Comm. on Banking, Housing and Urban Affairs*, 103d Cong., 1st Sess. (Feb. 3, 17, 24, 1993) (S. Hrg. 103-137) [hereinafter 1993 Senate Hearings]; *Hearing on S.924 Home Ownership and Equity Protection Act Before the Senate Banking Committee*, 103d Cong., 1st Sess. (May 19, 1993); *The Home Equity Protection Act of 1993, Hearings on H.R. 3153 Before the Subcommittee on Consumer Credit and Insurance of the House Committee on Banking, Finance and Urban Affairs*, 103d Cong., 2d Sess. (Mar. 22, 1994); *Hearing on Community Development Institutions, 103-2, Before the House Subcommittee on Financial Institutions Supervision, Regulation and Deposit Insurance*, 103d Cong., 1st Sess. (Feb. 2–4, 1993).

310 Pub. L. No. 103-325, subtit. B of tit. I, §§ 151–158, 108 Stat. 2160 (1994).

311 Originally, covered loans were so denominated, but the term was deleted at the request of the industry. However, no easy-to-use alternative term was substituted—''a mortgage referred to in section 103(aa)''—seems a bit awkward. As the triggers are set at sums which make covered loans high cost in fact, this manual will use that term.

312 15 U.S.C. § 1640(a); *see* H.R. Conf. Rep. No. 103-652, at 147, 162 (1994). The creditor has the burden of demonstrating that the violation is not material. The congressional intent that "materiality" as used in this section be a common law standard, not the TIL standard as defined in 15 U.S.C. § 1602(u) and Reg. Z, 12 C.F.R. § 226.23 n.48, is a bit confusing as other sections of the Home Ownership and Equity Protection Act deem violations to be material for TIL rescission purposes.

313 15 U.S.C. § 1602(u).

314 15 U.S.C. § 1639(j).

315 15 U.S.C. § 1635; Reg. Z, 12 C.F.R. § 226.23(a)(3). *See generally* National Consumer Law Center, Truth in Lending § 6.4.2 (5th ed. 2003 and Supp.).

316 *See* § 10.6.1.2.3, *supra*.

317 15 U.S.C. § 1602(aa).

318 Consumer credit is defined by TIL, 15 U.S.C. § 1602(e),(f),(h). *See* National Consumer Law Center, Truth in Lending §§ 2.2, 2.3 (5th ed. 2003 and Supp.). Closed-end credit is credit repayable on specific repayment terms over a specified term, in contrast to open-end credit, which is defined at 15 U.S.C. § 1602(i).

319 As defined in TIL, 15 U.S.C. § 1602(w). This tracks the exclusion from TIL's rescission right. 15 U.S.C. § 1635; *see* National Consumer Law Center, Truth in Lending § 6.2.6.1 (5th ed. 2003 and Supp.).

320 Dwelling is defined at 15 U.S.C. § 1602(v). This provision tracks TIL's definitions for rescission purposes. 15 U.S.C. § 1635; Reg. Z, 12 C.F.R. § 226.23; National Consumer Law Center, Truth in Lending § 6.2.2 (5th ed. 2003 and Supp.).

321 For example, if the yield on 15-year Treasury securities is 6%, an APR of 16% on a 15-year loan will meet the trigger. The statute specifies the relevant date to use in determining the Treasury yield. HOEPA, Pub. L. No. 103-325, § 152(a), 108 Stat. 2160 (1994).

322 Fees and charges are specifically defined by 15 U.S.C. § 1602(aa)(4) to include:

> a) all components of the TIL finance charge except interest and time-price differential (Reg. Z, 12 C.F.R. § 226.4); b) broker fees; and c) real-estate related fees as itemized in 15 U.S.C. § 1605(e) (except escrow taxes), provided they i) are reasonable, ii) provide no direct or indirect compensation to the creditor, and iii) are paid to third parties unaffiliated with the creditor.

In 2001, the Federal Reserve Board added premiums and other charges for credit life, accident, health, or loss-of-income insurance, or debt-cancellation coverage written in connection with the loan into the points and fees trigger. 12 C.F.R. § 226.32(b)(iv). This change is mandatory on October 1, 2002.

It is the creditor's burden to establish that the criteria for excluding these closing costs are met, because the creditor, not the consumer, has the information readily available. H.R. Conf. Rep. No. 103-652, at 147, 159 (1994).

323 The annual adjustments will be codified in TIL's Official Staff

The major exclusion from the scope of the Act is open-end credit. Because lenders may create "spurious open-end credit"[324] transactions in an effort to avoid this legislation, the Act takes the unusual step of requiring the Federal Reserve Board to study the adequacy of protections for open-end credit borrowers, so practitioners will have a place to direct examples of any abuses of the exclusion.[325] Reverse mortgages are also excluded, although the Act amends TIL to provide a separate disclosure that is more relevant to the product.[326]

12.2.2.3 Substantive Prohibitions

The most critical portion of the Act prohibits or severely limits the right of high-cost mortgage lenders to impose certain terms which had been the subject of abuse.[327] Some of the substantive prohibitions relate to matters discussed elsewhere in this book: prepayment penalties,[328] the Rule of 78,[329] negative amortization,[330] and call provisions.[331] It also prohibits default rates higher than the contract rate, balloon payments in covered loans with terms of less than five years, and prepaid payment escrows of more than two periodic payments.[332] Payments to home improvement contractors from the proceeds of covered loans may not be made directly to the contractor alone, to avoid the contractor being paid before the work is satisfactorily completed.[333]

One of the more important provisions of the Act attempts to limit improvident lending. Extending credit without regard to ability to pay is circumscribed. (This is directed at "asset-based lending," where a cash-poor, house-rich borrower is placed in jeopardy of losing the family home because the lender looks to the value of the collateral in making the loan, rather than to the borrower's repayment capacity.[334]) A creditor cannot engage in "a pattern or practice of extending credit to consumers [in covered loans] based on the consumers' collateral without regard to the consumers' repayment ability, including the consumers' current and expected income, current obligations, and employment."[335]

The Federal Reserve Board is required to prohibit acts or practices in connection with these loans that are unfair, deceptive or designed to evade the Act's requirements.[336] In addition, the Board is to prohibit acts or practices related to refinancing which it finds to be abusive or otherwise not in the interest of the borrower.[337] The standards used in interpreting state unfair and deceptive trade practices acts and the federal unfair and deceptive trade practices act are the guide.[338] Pursuant to this authority, as of October 1, 2002, the Board forbids a creditor from refinancing its own HOEPA loan into another HOEPA loan at any time within one year from the origination date, unless the refinancing is within the borrower's best interest.[339] The prohibition extends to assignees of that loan. Attempts to evade this rule, including engaging in a pattern or practice of arranging for the refinancing of the loans by the creditor's affiliate or another creditor are also banned. In addition, a creditor cannot structure a home-secured loan as an open-end plan to evade HOEPA.[340]

Advance warnings must be given at least three business days prior to consummation, in order to give the consumer time to reflect on the step. In addition to warning the consumer that the loan need not be consummated simply because the application has been made or disclosures received, the lender must also warn that the home and any equity in it might be lost in the event of nonpayment. The cost information which studies suggest are most important to consumers must also be provided at that time: the APR and the amount of regular monthly payments for fixed rate loans and, for variable rate loans, both the regular and maximum possible monthly payment.[341]

Commentary. *See* National Consumer Law Center, Truth in Lending § 9.2.6 (5th ed. 2003 and Supp.).

324 *See* National Consumer Law Center, Truth in Lending § 5.2.2 (5th ed. 2003 and Supp.); *see also The Home Equity Protection Act of 1993, Hearings on H.R. 3153 Before the Subcommittee on Consumer Credit and Insurance of the House Committee on Banking, Finance and Urban Affairs,* 103d Cong., 2d Sess. (Mar. 22, 1994).

325 HOEPA, Pub. L. No. 103-325, § 157(1), 108 Stat. 2160 (1994). Practitioners may also share such information with NCLC, if they wish.

326 15 U.S.C. § 1648.

327 All substantive prohibitions are found at 15 U.S.C. § 1639(c)–(i).

328 *See* § 5.8.2, *supra.*

329 *See* §§ 5.5.1, 5.6.3.3, 5.8.2, *supra.*

330 *See* § 4.3.1.2, *supra.*

331 12 C.F.R. § 226.32(d)(8). Note that this prohibition is not mandatory until October 1, 2002.

332 For examples of the problems addressed by the latter provision, see, e.g., *Therrien v. Resource Fin. Group,* 704 F. Supp. 322 (D.N.H. 1989); *Principal Padding: The Prepaid Payment Pyramid,* 9 NCLC REPORTS *Consumer Credit and Usury Ed.* 23 (May/June 1991). *See generally* National Consumer Law Center, Truth in Lending § 3.9.6.2 (5th ed. 2003 and Supp.).

333 The consumer may set up an escrow.

---

334 *See also* Opportunity Mgmt. Co. v. Frost, 1999 Wash. App. LEXIS 336 (Wash. Ct. App. Feb. 16, 1999) (jury verdict in favor of home owner finding that making a loan where consumer could not repay could be as a UDAP violation upheld on appeal). *See generally* § 11.3, *supra.*

335 15 U.S.C. § 1639(h).

336 15 U.S.C. § 1639(*l*)(2)(A).

337 15 U.S.C. § 1639(*l*)(2)(B). *See generally* Ch. 6, *supra.*

338 *See* H.R. Conf. Rep. No. 103-652, at 147, 162 (1994).

339 12 C.F.R. § 226.34(a)(3).

340 Reg. Z, 12 C.F.R. § 226.34(b).

341 15 U.S.C. § 1639(a),(b). Variable rate loans must also disclose the APR, and a statement that the rate and monthly payment may increase. The statute also requires new disclosures if terms change, and authorizes the FRB to promulgate rules for modifying the three-day advance notice requirement, presumably under circumstances similar to the rescission waiver provisions. *See* National Consumer Law Center, Truth in Lending (5th ed. 2003 and Supp.).

Two new pieces of information must be added to the HOEPA notice as of October 1, 2002. First, the creditor must state the total amount the consumer will borrow, defined to be the face amount of the note (that is, the principal).[342] This information is intended to alert consumers to a common tactic of high-cost lenders: inflating the loan amount to refinance a first lien mortgage (so the new lender can be in first lien position), finance high fees and costs, and pad the principal, without the knowledge or consent of the borrower. In addition, if the amount borrowed includes premiums or charges for optional credit insurance or debt cancellation coverage, that fact must be stated and grouped together with the disclosure of the amount borrowed.[343]

12.2.3 State High-Cost Mortgage Statutes

State predatory lending laws also can be powerful tools for challenging overreaching credit.[344] North Carolina was the first state to pass a predatory lending statute.[345] Its statute fills in a number of the gaps that HOEPA left, both by covering more loans and by outlawing more abusive loan terms.

Like HOEPA, North Carolina's statute focuses primarily on loans that exceed certain thresholds, but it has a lower points and fees threshold for loans of $20,000 or more (five percent instead of eight percent), and it adds a third alternative threshold that covers loans that include harsh prepayment penalties. For covered loans, North Carolina repeats HOEPA's prohibitions of balloon payments, negative amortization, and clauses that increase the interest rate upon default, but also prohibits clauses giving the lender the right to accelerate in the absence of default or to charge fees for modification, renewal, extension, amendment, or deferral, or an increase in the interest rate upon default.

The North Carolina statute also adds several substantive limits on points. Points and fees cannot be financed directly or indirectly by the lender. If the high-cost loan is used to refinance an older high-cost loan held by the same lender, no points or fees can be charged at all. Charges payable to third parties cannot be financed directly or indirectly by the lender. Nor is the lender allowed to finance prepayment fees or penalties that the borrower has to pay to refinance a debt held by the lender or an affiliate of the lender.

Like HOEPA, the statute prohibits making high-cost home loans without regard to the home owner's repayment ability, but the North Carolina provision is much stronger than HOEPA's.[346] The North Carolina statute also prohibits making high-cost loans without a certification from a housing counselor that the borrower received counseling on the advisability and appropriateness of the loan. Unlike HOEPA, however, the North Carolina statute does not contain an explicit assignee liability provision.[347]

Texas has taken a different approach, suitable given the background of its unique state constitutional provisions. Until January 1, 1998, its constitution completely prohibited most non-purchase money home mortgages. When this prohibition was repealed, it was replaced with protections against abusive home equity loans. These protections apply to all home equity loans, regardless of interest rate, and include a prohibition against balloon payments, a three percent cap on points, a prohibition against open lines of credit, and a limit on the percentage of equity that can be encumbered.[348]

Effective April 1, 2003, the New York legislature adopted a predatory loan law that goes beyond HOEPA in a number of respects.[349] It has a 9% APR trigger instead of 10% for non-first lien loans, and the points and fees trigger will also cover more loans than HOEPA. It imposes many restrictions on these high-rate loans that are similar to HOEPA's, but imposes more sweeping restrictions on such practices as balloon payments, refinancing, and lending without regard to ability to repay. It also restricts arbitration clauses, financing of credit insurance, financing of points and fees, kickbacks to home improvement contractors, and broker fees, and prohibits lenders from encouraging borrowers to default on existing loans. Refinancings of covered loans are subject to a "tangible net benefit" test. The law also affords

---

342   12 C.F.R. § 336.32(c)(5).

343   Official Staff Commentary § 226.32(c)(5); Official Staff Commentary § 226.32(c)(5)-1.

344   The following is an overview of many of the state predatory lending laws and their key provisions. This section is not meant as an all-inclusive catalogue of state laws, nor does it list every provision of the laws discussed. While several local provisions are discussed, these types of laws are not generally addressed in this section. Practitioners are encouraged to fully explore state and local laws that may apply in their cases.

345   N.C. Gen. Stat. § 24-1.1E; *see* Cathy Lesser Mansfield, *The Road to Subprime "HEL" Was Paved with Good Congressional Intentions: Usury Deregulation and the Subprime Home Equity Market*, 51 S.C. L. Rev. 473 (2000) (includes an overview of the North Carolina statute); Roberto G. Quercia, Michael A. Stegman, & Walter R. Davis, *Assessing the Impact of North Carolina's Predatory Lending Law*, House Policy Debate, Vol. 15, Issue 3 (2004) (finding that the North Carolina predatory lending law is decreasing predatory lending without increasing interest rates; the decrease in subprime lending occurred primarily in predatory refinancings).

346   The statute sets out a substantial list of factors that a lender must consider in assessing repayment ability and establishes a presumption that a loan is affordable if total monthly debt, including the loan, does not exceed 50% of verified gross monthly income. N.C. Gen. Stat. § 24-1.1E(c)(2).

347   North Carolina common law automatically applies usury claims to assignees. *See* Swindell v. Federal Nat. Mortgage Ass'n, 409 S.E.2d 892 (N.C. 1991).

348   *See* § 3.9.3.2.2, *supra*, for more detail on the Texas constitutional provision.

349   N.Y. Banking Law § 6-l (McKinney); N.Y. Real Prop. Acts. Law § 1302 (McKinney); N.Y. Gen. Bus. Law § 771-a (McKinney).

specific remedies to consumers, including rescission, statutory damages, attorney fees, and injunctions, and provides that any claims can be raised as a defense against an assignee in a foreclosure case. The New York Banking Department has revised its high-cost loan regulation, effective May 5, 2003, to be consistent with the new law.[350]

The City Council of New York also has passed a broad law prohibiting the city from contracting with, providing financial assistance to, or depositing city funds in any financial institution or its affiliate that issues, purchases, or invests in a minimum number of "predatory" high-cost mortgage loans. The law includes a points and fees threshold more inclusive than HOEPA and defines predatory loans as transactions that meet the threshold and that also contain at least one practice from a list of practices including, among other things, refinancings where the borrower does not receive a reasonable and tangible benefit, balloon payments, mandatory arbitration clauses that are unfair or unconscionable, prepayment penalties, or payments where the lender does not reasonably believe that the borrower has the ability to pay.[351] The city's mayor and a trade organization sued the city council to stop enforcement of the law. The state trial court found that the local law was preempted by several federal statutes and by state law.[352]

A Connecticut statute places restrictions that go beyond HOEPA's on certain high-cost mortgage loans, including a cap on the amount of prepaid finance charges, restrictions on fees for modification, renewal, or extension, a requirement that monthly-pay credit insurance be offered as an alternative to any single-premium credit insurance, a prohibition against lending without regard to repayment ability that does not require proof of a pattern, and a prohibition against loans that do not benefit the borrower.[353] A federal court[354] issued a preliminary injunction against enforcement of the Connecticut statute's prohibition of mandatory arbitration clauses on the ground that it is preempted by the Federal Arbitration Act but, otherwise the statute remains in effect.

Illinois adopted banking regulations that apply to many loans that HOEPA does not cover, and which include restrictions that go beyond HOEPA's.[355] A challenge to the regulations, arguing that they are preempted by the Alternative Mortgage Transactions Parity Act (AMTPA) is pending in federal court.[356] Subsequently, Illinois passed a statute that codifies the state banking regulation. It includes a host of restrictions, including those limiting prepayment penalties, financing of single premium credit insurance, and loan flipping. It also prohibits loans that a borrower does not have the ability to repay and includes a presumptive threshold for assessing whether the loan is unaffordable.[357] The statute effectively supersedes the regulations.

A California statute[358] applies to a broader group of loans than HOEPA, covering loans with APRs that are 8 percentage points or more above comparable Treasury securities,[359] as well as loans in which the points and fees constitute 6% of the total loan amount.[360] It contains restrictions greater than HOEPA's on such terms as prepayment penalties, withholding of advance payments from the proceeds, lending without regard to ability to repay, financing of single premium credit insurance, and refinancings. Unfortunately, the statute, by its terms, does not apply to assignees. An ordinance adopted by the city of Oakland, California, goes beyond the statute by using lower triggers, mandating pre-loan counseling, extending liability to assignees, and imposing additional restrictions on prepayment penalties. While a California appellate court held that the state law does not preempt the Oakland ordinance,[361] the California Supreme Court recently ruled that the state law preempts the Oakland ordinance because the broad scope of the state law indicates the legislature's intent to fully occupy the field. The opinion also prevents enforcement of a similar ordinance in Los Angeles.[362]

---

350 N.Y. Comp. Codes R. & Regs. tit. 3, pt. 41. The Office of Thrift Supervision has issued an opinion that provisions of the law that regulate the terms of the credit, loan-related fees, disclosure and advertising, and mortgage origination, refinancing, and servicing are preempted by the Home Owners' Loan Act from applying to federal savings associations. Office of Thrift Supervision, Chief Counsel Letter P-2003-2 (Jan. 30, 2003). See discussion of OTS preemption in § 3.5.3, *supra*. This letter is summarized in Appx. D.3, *infra*, and reproduced in full on the CD-Rom accompanying this volume.

351 2002 New York Local Law 36, *available at* www.council.nyc.ny.us/pdf_files/bills/law02036.pdf.

352 Mayor of New York v. Council of New York, 780 N.Y.S.2d 266 (Sup. Ct. 2004).

353 Conn. Gen. Stat. §§ 36a-746 to 746g.

354 Am. Fin. Services Assn. v. Burke, 169 F. Supp. 2d 62 (D. Conn. 2001).

355 Ill. Admin. Code tit. 38, 160, 190, 345, 1000, 1050, 1075.

356 Ill. Ass'n of Mortgage Brokers v. Office of Banks & Real Estate, 308 F.3d 762 (7th Cir. 2002) (vacating trial court's decision that AMTPA did not affect Ill. regulation, and remanding for analysis of which, if any, sections of regulation are preempted). See discussion in § 3.10, *supra*.

357 815 Ill. Comp. Stat. § 137/1.

358 Cal. Fin. Code §§ 4970 to 4979.7, *as amended by* Cal. Assembly Bill 489 of the 2001-02 Regular Session (effective as to loans applied for after July 1, 2002).

359 While the FRB has amended its HOEPA regulation, effective October 1, 2002, to cover first-position mortgage loans with APRs of 8 percentage points or more above comparable Treasury securities, junior position loans are still covered only if the APR is ten percentage points or more above this benchmark. 66 Fed. Reg. 65604 (Dec. 20, 2001).

360 Cal. Fin. Code § 4972 (West), *as amended by* Cal. Assembly Bill 489 of the 2001-02 Regular Session (effective as to loans applied for after July 1, 2002). The California statute defines points and fees somewhat more restrictively than HOEPA, however.

361 Am. Fin. Services Ass'n v. City of Oakland, 4 Cal. Rptr. 3d 745 (Ct. App. 2003).

362 Am. Fin. Servs. Ass'n v. City of Oakland, 2005 WL 221891 (Cal. Jan. 31, 2005).

Massachusetts adopted a sweeping statute,[363] effective November 7, 2004, that covers more loans than HOEPA and provides for assignee liability.[364] For covered loans, the law prohibits prepayment penalties and limits the financing of fees. It also requires housing counseling and prohibits clauses that improperly restrict borrowers to a non-judicial forum. All refinancings—not just those involving high-cost loans—must be made in the borrower's interest if refinanced within five years of the previous loan. The law also prohibits the financing of single-premium credit insurance or the costs of debt cancellation and suspension products on all real-estate-secured loans. A regulation on the refinancing standard has been enacted.[365]

New Jersey enacted a predatory lending statute on May 1, 2003.[366] It defines a high-cost home loan as one exceeding a points and fees threshold or a rate threshold. The points and fees threshold will in many circumstances be lower than the comparable HOEPA trigger. These loans are subject to special restrictions similar to HOEPA's plus several restrictions that go beyond HOEPA's, including: restrictions clauses such as arbitration clauses that force a borrower into a less convenient, more costly, or more dilatory forum; a prohibition against financing of points and fees in excess of 2% of the total loan commitment; and a requirement of nonprofit credit counseling before a borrower accepts a high-cost home loan that finances points and fees. Some practices, such as flipping, financing of credit insurance premiums, encouraging default on an existing mortgage, certain servicing abuses, payoff fees, and acceleration in the sole discretion of the creditor, are prohibited for a wider class of home loans or for all home loans. Any violation can be asserted as a UDAP violation. UDAP and other claims are also specifically preserved for misconduct that is not covered under the new law. In addition, the statute creates a separate cause of action for statutory damages for material violations. The statute also applies to mortgage brokers, and allows borrowers to assert claims and defenses against assignees under certain circumstances and subject to certain caps on damages. Effective November 27, 2003, a new regulation also requires that borrowers of certain high-cost residential loans receive pre-loan counseling.[367]

A New Mexico statute,[368] effective January 1, 2004, uses lower triggers to define high-cost home loans, and imposes restrictions on them that go beyond HOEPA's, including restrictions on financing of points and fees, arbitration clauses or other clauses that force a borrower into a less convenient, more costly, or more dilatory forum, lending without regard to repayment ability, and fees to modify, renew, extend, or amend the loan agreement. It also requires credit counseling before a consumer enters into a high-cost home loan. In addition, for all home loans, it prohibits financing of credit insurance premiums and knowingly and intentionally refinancing a loan without a net tangible benefit to the borrower. It includes a private cause of action for actual, statutory, and punitive damages, attorney fees, rescission, and injunctive or declaratory relief. The new law shelters an assignee from uncapped damages and class action liability if it took measures to avoid purchasing or otherwise taking assignment of high-cost home loans, including the use of reasonable due diligence. Notably, even if an assignee meets this standard, borrowers may still defend their homes by pursuing individual claims against the assignee for amounts required to reduce or extinguish the borrower's liability under the loan plus costs and attorney fees. A violation is also a UDAP violation.

A predatory lending law adopted by Kentucky in 2003[369] uses the same triggers as HOEPA but appears to include purchase money mortgages. It goes beyond HOEPA's restrictions in, among other things, restricting prepayment penalties, balloon payments, fees for modification, renewal, extension, or amendment of a loan, lending without regard to repayment ability, refinancing of subsidized mortgages, oppressive arbitration clauses, late fees and servicing abuses, and encouraging default on existing loans. It gives the borrower a UDAP claim for violations but is silent about assignee liability.

An Arkansas statute[370] uses the same APR trigger as HOEPA, but a lower points and fees trigger, and also appears to include purchase money mortgages. A number of its restrictions go beyond HOEPA's, including those relating to balloon payments, arbitration clauses, financing of credit insurance, refinancing without a net tangible benefit to the borrower, refinancing of subsidized mortgages, and encouraging default. It creates a private cause of action, plus a violation is a UDAP violation. Assignees are liable unless they exercised reasonable due diligence to avoid buying high-cost home loans, but it appears that a borrower retains the right to raise violations as a recoupment or setoff in a foreclosure action regardless of the assignee's due diligence.

---

363 Mass. Gen. Laws ch. 183, §§ 28C, 56, 59 & 66, and ch. 183C §§ 1-12. Note that this law replaces the earlier state regulations on this subject; the statute is similar but not identical to the regulations. The earlier regulations were codified at Mass. Regs. Code tit. 209, §§ 40.00, 32.32.

364 The assignee liability formula is a compromise similar to that found in the New Jersey and New Mexico laws. If the assignee knows that it is buying a high-cost loan, it is subject to full liability. If the assignee is following policies to avoid purchasing any high-cost loans but nevertheless purchases one in a pool of securitized mortgages, it is liable for violations only up to the amount of the loan plus reasonable attorney fees.

365 Mass. Regs. Code tit. 209, § 32.34(1)(c).

366 N.J. Stat. Ann. § 46:10B-22. The law became effective "on the 210th day following enactment."

367 N.J. Admin. Code tit. 3, § 25-4.

368 N.M. Stat. Ann. §§ 58-21A-1 to 58-21A-14.

369 Ky. Rev. Stat. Ann. § 360.100.

370 Ark. Code Ann. § 23-53-101.

Georgia's predatory lending law uses the same APR threshold as HOEPA but a lower points and fees threshold to define high-cost home loans.[371] The definition appears to include purchase money loans, but many types of creditors are excluded from the definition. For all home loans it prohibits financing of credit insurance premiums, prohibits encouraging default, restricts the unfair imposition of late charges, and limits payoff fees. For high-cost home loans, the law goes beyond HOEPA in its limits on prepayment penalties; balloon payments; clauses such as arbitration clauses that force a borrower into a less convenient, more expensive, or more dilatory forum; lending without regard to repayment ability; and fees for loan modification, renewal, extension, amendment, or deferment. It also requires a notice of intent to foreclose and a right to cure, and mandates credit counseling before a borrower enters into a high-cost home loan. The statute creates a private cause of action, and allows rescission up to five years after consummation. Assignees are subject to affirmative claims and defenses unless they show due diligence intended to avoid purchasing high-cost home loans, but relief is limited to an individual action for the amount remaining on the debt plus attorney fees and the statute includes poorly worded and unclear language about the statute of limitations. Georgia had originally adopted a stronger law, but amended it after the Standard & Poors rating organization threatened to stop rating Georgia loans.[372]

The District of Columbia adopted a strong law in 2000,[373] but then replaced it in 2002 with a weaker version.[374] The 2002 law sets lower triggers than HOEPA, but does not apply to federally-regulated lenders or certain subsidiaries. Nor does it apply to loans that are guaranteed by the FHA, the VA, a state or local authority, or the D.C. Housing Finance Agency. For loans that it does cover, the 2002 law imposes restrictions greater than HOEPA's on such practices as lending without regard to repayment ability, selling of single premium credit insurance, refinancing, and charging of points and fees.

In Oklahoma, a new predatory lending law tightens controls on mortgage brokerage and regulates certain high-cost mortgage loans. The statute tracks HOEPA's coverage and enhances loan disclosures to include the total amount borrowed, with an indication of how much is being paid for credit insurance or debt cancellation benefits, and a message to consumers encouraging them to shop around (of course, a disclosure made at loan closing makes it hard to take this advice) and reminding them to budget for and pay home owners insurance and property taxes. The law restricts demand clauses, limits refinancings of low-interest loans,

prohibits single premium credit insurance and lending without regard to repayment ability, and includes an assignee liability provision.[375]

Maine's law tracks HOEPA's coverage and includes some less common provisions, including a requirement that creditors report positive and negative credit histories to one of the three major consumer reporting agencies, restrictions on the charging of points in refinancings of high-cost loans, a requirement that creditors offer monthly premiums for credit insurance, and limitations on advertising claims regarding a consumer's ability to decrease her monthly payment. Assignees are subject to some liability under the statute; they are jointly and severally liable with the "lender" to refund or credit the borrower for any default charges, prepayment penalties or prepaid finance charges collected in excess of the limits set out in the law.[376]

Virginia enacted a prohibition on refinancing mortgage loans within twelve months unless the refinancing is in the borrower's best interest.[377] This prohibition was passed in 2003 to replace a previous standard that allowed refinancings within twelve months only in cases of a net tangible benefit to the borrower.[378] This prohibition applies to all mortgage loans, not just a class of high-cost loans, but does not apply if the borrower initiates the contact with the lender.

Several other jurisdictions, including Ohio,[379] Pennsylvania,[380] South Carolina,[381] Nebraska,[382] Nevada,[383] Maryland,[384] Florida,[385] Colorado,[386] Michigan,[387] Wisconsin,[388] Utah[389] and Indiana[390] have adopted predatory mortgage lending acts that do not significantly increase, and may even reduce, existing protections, and which, in some cases,

---

371 Ga. Code Ann. §§ 7-6A-1 to 13.

372 *See* Newsbrief, Mortgage Bankers Association of Georgia (Mar. 7, 2003), *available at* www.mbag.org/media/pdf/GAFLABulletin.rtf.pdf.

373 Predatory Lending and Mortgage Foreclosure Improvements Act of 2000, 1999 D.C. Law 13-263 (2000).

374 D.C. Code Ann. §§ 26-1151.01 to 1155.01.

---

375 Okla. Stat. tit. 14A, §§ 1-301(10), 3-309.4, 3-410 411, & 4-113. The statute became effective on January 1, 2004.

376 Me. Rev. Stat. Ann. tit. 9-A, § 8-206-A (16-A, 16-B & 18).

377 Va. Code Ann. § 6.1-422.1.

378 2001 Va. Acts ch. 510.

379 Ohio Rev. Code Ann. §§ 1349.25 to 1349.36 (West).

380 63 Pa. Cons. Stat. §§ 456.501 to 456.524.

381 S.C. Code Ann. §§ 37-23-10 to 37-23-85.

382 2003 Neb. Laws 218.

383 Nev. Rev. Stat. 598D.010 to 598D.150.

384 Md. Code Ann., [Commercial Law] §§ 12.124.1, 12.127, 12.409.1 & 12.1029.

385 Fla. Stat. ch. 494.0078 to 494.00797.

386 Colo. Rev. Stat. §§ 5-3.5-101 to 303.

387 Mich. Comp. Laws § 445.1631-1645.

388 2005 Wisc. Stat. 428.

389 2004 Utah Code Ann. §§ 61-2d & 70D-1-21.

390 2005 Ind. Code § 24-9. This law, while providing certain strong provisions such as the rule that mandatory arbitration clauses are unconscionable and void in high-cost loans, exempts depository institutions—and arguably their operating subsidiaries and affiliates—from its purview. (Indiana is the first state to do so.) It also requires individuals planning to file actions for a deceptive act under the law to first file a complaint with a state agency and then wait 90 days before filing. The law also preempts any stronger laws by political subdivisions.

override any ordinances by political subdivisions that are more protective than state law.

While Ohio's statute has been found to preempt the stronger Dayton municipal ordinance,[391] a state appeals court has upheld a Cleveland anti-predatory lending law that is more restrictive than state law.[392] The Cleveland ordinance requires pre-loan counseling, limits the financing of points and fees, and prohibits mandatory arbitration clauses and the financing of single-premium credit insurance. Violations of the law's provisions constitute misdemeanors and lenders must submit a certification of compliance with a city office. As part of its analysis, the court held that home rule is an express local power that cannot be revoked by the state[393] and that a state law that completely preempts all local legislation related to the state statute violates the state constitution. Further, following a state supreme court precedent, the court held that a local ordinance that is more protective than state law does not conflict with state law.

A few states also have statutes directed toward related abuses by "home savers," who induce homeowners in foreclosure to enter into disadvantageous sale/leaseback or sale transactions.[394]

12.3 Fair Lending Statutes and Civil Rights

12.3.1 Scope and Substantive Prohibitions

As noted earlier, too often elderly and minority borrowers are targeted by overreaching creditors and sellers.[395] These same borrowers, though, are among the protected classes under one or more of the fair lending statutes. A separate volume in this series discusses these issues in depth,[396] but they will be mentioned here to alert the practitioner to this potential avenue for relief.

The Equal Credit Opportunity Act prohibits discrimination in *any* aspect of credit on the basis of race, color, national origin, religion, sex or gender, marital status, age or public assistance status.[397] The Federal Fair Housing Act and its state counterparts prohibit discrimination on the basis of race, color, religion, sex or gender, disability or handicap, familial status (i.e., having children),[398] or national origin in the sale, rental or advertising of housing and in housing-related financing.[399] Both of these acts also allow consumers to pursue relief against actors higher up in the food chain than the original lender.

The ECOA definition of creditor explicitly includes assignees as long as they regularly participate in credit decisions, including setting the terms of credit.[400] It also includes sellers such as car dealers and home improvement contractors who arrange credit.[401] Arrangers, however, may be subject to only limited provisions of the ECOA unless they participate in setting the terms of credit or in making credit decisions.[402]

Section 3605 of the FHA prohibits discrimination in the making or purchasing of residential real estate loans and in providing other financial assistance related to the making of the loan.[403] It explicitly applies to the selling, brokering, or appraising of residential real estate and to any other entity providing financial assistance related to a loan covered by the Act.[404] Significantly, the FHA also applies to the activities of secondary market players in the purchasing of loans, debts, or securities, the pooling or packaging of these instruments, and the marketing and sale of securities issues on the basis of the loans or debts.[405]

To prove discrimination under these acts, the consumer must show that the defendants either used a prohibited factor as the basis for their decision or that there was a disparate

---

391 City of Dayton v. Ohio, 813 N.E.2d 707 (Ohio Ct. App. 2004) (appellate court affirms lower court opinion upholding state law's preemption of Dayton's municipal predatory lending law and finds that the state statute was a general law, the ordinance is an example of a state police power, the matter is not a self-government issue, and the ordinance conflicts with the state statute).

392 American Fin. Servs. Assoc. v. Cleveland, 2004 WL 2755808 (Ohio Ct. App. Dec. 2, 2004) (slip op.) (discussing the destruction wrought by predatory lending practices and citing Anna B. Ferguson, *Predatory Lending: Practices, Remedies & Lack of Adequate Protection for Ohio Consumers*, 48 Clev. St. L. Rev. 607 (2000)). The American Financial Services Association says it plans to appeal to the Ohio Supreme Court.

393 State law sought to bar municipalities from regulating the business of credit.

394 *See, e.g., In re* Phelps, 113 Cal. Rptr. 2d 217 (Ct. App. 2001) (interpreting Cal. Civ. Code §§ 1695.6, 2945.4 (West)).

395 *See* § 11.1, *supra.*

396 *See generally* National Consumer Law Center, Credit Discrimination (4th ed. 2005).

397 15 U.S.C. § 1691. The ECOA also prohibits discrimination against consumers who exercise their rights under the Consumer Credit Protection Act. *See generally* National Consumer Law Center, Credit Discrimination Ch. 3 (4th ed. 2005).

398 *See* 42 U.S.C. § 3602(k) (definition of familial status).

399 42 U.S.C. §§ 3604; 3605. State fair lending laws are compiled in National Consumer Law Center, Credit Discrimination Appx. E (3d ed. 2002 and Supp.). Section 3605 of the FHA specifically applies to real-estate-related financing transactions. It is less clear whether courts will also apply § 3604 to home equity lending. *See* National Consumer Law Center, Credit Discrimination § 2.3.3.1.2 (4th ed. 2005).

400 Regulation B, 12 C.F.R. § 202.2(*l*). The Commentary further clarifies that the definition of creditor includes an assignee or a potential purchaser of the obligation who influences the credit decision by indicating whether or not it will purchase the loan if the transaction is consummated. Official Staff Commentary, 12 C.F.R. § 202.2(*l*)-(1).

401 15 U.S.C. § 1691a(e); Reg. B, 12 C.F.R. § 202.2(l).

402 *See* National Consumer Law Center, Credit Discrimination § 2.2.5.3 (4th ed. 2005).

403 42 U.S.C. § 3605(b); 24 C.F.R. § 100.115.

404 42 U.S.C. § 3605.

405 24 C.F.R. § 100.125.

impact on that basis.[406] A reverse redlining claim must contain slightly different elements. In addition to being a member of a protected class, the consumer must show that the loans were given on grossly unfavorable terms and that the lender continued to provide loans to other applicants with similar qualifications but on significantly more favorable terms.[407] However, the consumer should not have to show that she could afford to repay a particular loan in question. Instead, the *prima facie* case in a reverse redlining claim should require the plaintiff to show that she could have afforded to repay a loan offered to her on favorable terms.[408]

In addition, the Civil Rights Acts provide that the same right to contract, purchase, and hold property available to white citizens must be extended to all citizens.[409] These statutes may be invoked in the lending context when, e.g., a homeowner is targeted for less favorable terms on the basis of race.[410]

Discriminatory pricing may be subject to challenge under one or more of these statutes. For example, a number of cases have challenged the discriminatory aspects of mark-up policies in the auto lending industry.[411] Allegations of reverse redlining in the mortgage lending context have successfully survived preliminary motions in recent decisions.[412]

12.3.2 ECOA Notice Requirements

The ECOA also imposes procedural requirements on creditors. A creditor must notify the applicant if it takes adverse action after receiving a credit application.[413] This requirement can give a consumer a cause of action for bait-and-switch tactics. For example, where homeowners applied for credit in the amount of the cost of home repairs, never received a denial of those applications, but were granted credit in much larger amounts, the lender violated ECOA's requirement of notifying them of its action on their original applications.[414] The mere failure to provide a writ-ten rejection notice is actionable, without allegations of discrimination.[415]

The Fair Credit Reporting Act also imposes notice requirements on creditors who take adverse action on a credit application based on information in the consumer's credit report.[416] Violations of this requirement should also be investigated whenever a creditor appears to have violated the ECOA's adverse action notice requirement.[417] The ECOA and FCRA notices can be combined.[418]

12.4 Federal and State Credit Repair Statutes

12.4.1 Overview

Federal and state credit repair organization laws cover a surprising number of entities involved in abusive credit transactions. The federal law, discussed in § 12.4.2, *infra*, covers organizations and individuals that advertise, offer, or perform credit repair services for a fee. Many credit card finders, as well as some loan brokers and low-end car dealers, use the prospect of an improved credit rating as a way of luring customers, so are potentially covered by the federal law.

State credit repair laws, discussed in § 12.4.3, *infra*, are even broader. Not only do they typically cover the same entities as the federal statute, but most also cover entities that obtain credit for consumers, even if they do not advertise or offer credit repair. These statutes potentially cover loan brokers, credit card finders, tax return preparers who arrange refund anticipation loans, and even sellers who arrange credit for people to buy their products.

The federal law, and most state laws, give the consumer a right to cancel the contract, broadly prohibit deception, and offer strong private remedies. Both state and federal credit repair laws are discussed in detail in National Consumer Law Center, *Fair Credit Reporting* Ch. 15 (5th ed. 2002 and Supp.).

---

406 *See generally* National Consumer Law Center, Credit Discrimination Ch. 4 (4th ed. 2005).

407 *See, e.g.,* Matthews v. New Century Mortgage Corp., 185 F. Supp. 2d 874 (S.D. Ohio 2002).

408 *See generally* National Consumer Law Center, Credit Discrimination § 8.3 (4th ed. 2005).

409 42 U.S.C. §§ 1981, 1982.

410 *See generally* National Consumer Law Center, Credit Discrimination § 2.4 (5th ed. 2005).

411 See *id.* § 8.4.

412 *Id.* § 8.2.

413 15 U.S.C. § 1691(d)(2); 12 C.F.R. § 202.9(a). *See generally* National Consumer Law Center, Credit Discrimination Ch. 10 (4th ed. 2005).

414 Newton v. United Cos. Lending, 24 F. Supp. 2d 444 (E.D. Pa. 1998). Counter-offers that are accepted or used are not considered to be "adverse actions" under the ECOA. There is a split among the courts whether written notice is required if there is no adverse action. See National Consumer Law Center, Credit Discrimination § 10.4 (5th ed. 2005).

415 *See* National Consumer Law Center, Credit Discrimination § 10.1 (4th ed. 2005).

416 15 U.S.C. §§ 1681m, 1681a(k) (definition of "adverse action"). *See* National Consumer Law Center, Fair Credit Reporting § 6.4 (5th ed. 2002 and Supp.).

417 *See, e.g.,* Treadway v. Gateway Chevrolet Oldsmobile Inc., 362 F.3d 971 (7th Cir. 2004)(allowing car buyer to replead FCRA notice claim along with ECOA notice claim).

418 FRB Official Staff Commentary § 202.9(b)(1)-1.

12.4.2 Federal Credit Repair Organizations Act

12.4.2.1 Coverage

The federal Credit Repair Organizations Act has a broad definition of "credit repair organization."[419] A credit repair organization means any person who performs or offers to perform any service, for a fee or other valuable consideration, for the express or implied purpose of—

(i) improving any consumer's credit record, credit history, or credit rating; or

(ii) providing advice and assistance to any consumer with regard to any activity or service described in clause (i).[420]

The definition only applies if the organization uses an instrumentality of interstate commerce, such as mail or telephone, in these activities.[421] There are exceptions for section 501(c)(3) non-profit organizations;[422] any "creditor" as defined in the Truth in Lending Act to the extent it is restructuring a consumer's debt to it;[423] and depository institutions, credit unions, and their subsidiaries or affiliates.[424]

Simply advertising or claiming to provide credit repair services is sufficient for coverage, even if the organization does not actually provide such services but instead switches the consumer to other products.[425] The main question in these cases is whether the seller is offering or performing the credit repair service in return for a fee. One court found no coverage where a dealer did not charge a separate fee for arranging for financing, but charged the same purchase price for cash and credit customers.[426] If a document preparation fee to the dealer is included in the contract, or if the dealer receives a yield spread premium or other kickback from the financer, it may satisfy this requirement.[427] The fee need not be paid directly by the consumer.[428]

Many of the statutory prohibitions apply not just to credit repair organizations but to any "person." Thus, individuals and organizations that do not meet the definition of credit repair organization can still be subject to liability if they violate or assist in a violation of these prohibitions.[429] In one case a bank that entered into a credit card marketing arrangement with a credit repair organization was held to be covered.[430]

12.4.2.2 Substantive Prohibitions

Credit repair organizations must provide their customers a form disclosure, setting forth specific terms and containing specified language, prior to executing any agreement with the consumer.[431] The organization must also enter into a signed written and dated contract with the consumer that describes the services in detail, provides a three-day right to cancel, and contains other specified terms.[432] The Act prohibits the credit repair organization from receiving any

---

419 15 U.S.C. § 1679a(3).

420 15 U.S.C. § 1679a(3)(A).

421 15 U.S.C. § 1679a(3)(A). *See* Sannes v. Jeff Wyler Chevrolet, Inc., 1999 U.S. Dist. LEXIS 21748 (S.D. Ohio Mar. 31, 1999) (advertising in regionally distributed newspaper meets interstate commerce requirement).

422 15 U.S.C. § 1679a(3)(B)(i). *But see* FTC v. Gill, 265 F.3d 944 (9th Cir. 2001) (defendants' conversion of credit repair business to a purportedly non-profit corporation was a means of evading preliminary injunction and justifies harsher permanent injunction).

423 15 U.S.C. § 1679a(3)(B)(ii).

424 15 U.S.C. § 1679a(3)(B)(iii).

425 Parker v. 1-800 Bar None, 2002 U.S. Dist. LEXIS 2139 (N.D. Ill. Feb. 11, 2002); Sannes v. Jeff Wyler Chevrolet, Inc., 1999 U.S. Dist. LEXIS 21748 (S.D. Ohio Mar. 31, 1999) (car dealer advertised "Have you wrecked your credit? . . . Reestablish your credit through one of the largest banks in Ohio!"; *In re* Nat'l Credit Management Group, L.L.C., 21 F. Supp. 2d 424 (D.N.J. 1998). *See also* Limpert v. Cambridge Credit Counseling Corp., 328 F. Supp. 2d 360 (E.D.N.Y. 2004) (representing the ability to perform credit repair services may be sufficient for coverage); Browning v. Yahoo!, Inc., 2004 WL 2496183 (N.D. Cal. Nov. 4, 2004) (denial of motion to dismiss) (company that represented that it could provide" personalized tips" on how consumers could improve their credit scores can be credit repair organization even though another entity actually provided the services); Wojcik v. Courtesy Auto Sales, Inc., 2002 WL 31663298 (D. Neb. Nov. 25, 2002) (dealership "could obviously fit into the credit repair organization category," but not

426 shown here as consumers were not lured in by any credit repair advertising).

426 Sannes v. Jeff Wyler Chevrolet, Inc., 1999 U.S. Dist. LEXIS 21748 (S.D. Ohio Mar. 31, 1999). *See also* Wojcik v. Courtesy Auto Sales, Inc., 2002 WL 31663298 (D. Neb. Nov. 25, 2002) (no coverage where dealer did not charge for the brief advice it gave about building a good credit record); Oslan v. Collection Bureau, 2001 WL 34355648 (E.D. Pa. Dec. 13, 2001) (debt collector is covered only if it receives or solicits payment beyond repayment of debt).

427 *See, e.g.,* Parker v. 1-800 Bar None, 2002 U.S. Dist. LEXIS 2139 (N.D. Ill. Feb. 11, 2002) (seller's payment of referral fee to credit repair organization satisfied consideration requirement). *But cf.* Cannon v. William Chevrolet/Geo, Inc., 794 N.E.2d 843 (Ill. App. Ct. 2003) (car dealership did not meet state statute's definition of credit repair organization even though it charged consumer a $46.88 documentary fee and required consumer to pay 4.5% higher interest than bank charged).

428 Parker v. 1-800 Bar None, 2002 U.S. Dist. LEXIS 2139 (N.D. Ill. Feb. 11, 2002).

429 Rodriguez v. Lynch Ford, Inc., 2004 WL 2958772 (N.D. Ill. Nov. 18, 2004); Lacey v. William Chrysler Plymouth Inc., 2004 U.S. Dist. LEXIS 2479 (N.D. Ill. Feb. 20, 2004) (prohibition against counseling a consumer to make false statements about creditworthiness applies to car dealer even though it is not a credit repair organization); Parker v. 1-800 Bar None, 2002 U.S. Dist. LEXIS 2139 (N.D. Ill. Feb. 11, 2002).

430 Vance v. National Benefit Ass'n, 1999 U.S. Dist. LEXIS 13846 (N.D. Ill. Aug. 26, 1999).

431 15 U.S.C. § 1679c(a).

432 15 U.S.C. §§ 1679d(a), (b), 1679c.

payment for services until those services are fully performed and at least three days have passed since the signing of the contract.[433]

The Act contains four broad prohibitions against deceptive acts. It prohibits untrue or misleading statements to consumers or others about the organization's services.[434] It also prohibits any person from making untrue or misleading statements to credit reporting agencies or actual or potential creditors of the consumer about the consumer's credit worthiness, credit standing, or credit capacity.[435] A seller or broker who falsifies the consumer's credit information and submits it to a potential lender or financer is likely to run afoul of this prohibition. The Act also prohibits certain acts that conceal the consumer's true identity from credit reporting agencies or actual or potential creditors.[436] Sellers and loan brokers who structure transactions in the name of a straw purchaser or straw borrower may violate this prohibition.[437] More broadly still, no person may "engage, directly or indirectly, in any act, practice, or course of business" that constitutes the commission of, or an attempt to commit, fraud or deception in connection with the offer or sale of the services of a credit repair organization.[438]

Importantly, these four prohibitions of deception apply to any "person," whether or not that person meets the definition of credit repair organization.[439] Thus, for example, entities that are not credit repair organization themselves but participate more indirectly in the scheme can be held liable.[440]

12.4.2.3 Remedies

Consumers have a three-day right to cancel a contract with a credit repair organization.[441] In addition, any contract not in compliance with the Act is treated as void, and may not be enforced by any court or other person.[442] Thus, if the contract fails to include the right to cancel and notice thereof, fails to include any of the terms and conditions required by the Act, or requires any act or statement which is prohibited, the contract is effectively void. Any arbitration clause in the contract will be void and unenforceable along with the rest of the contract.

Any person who violates the Act is liable in the sum of:

- The greater of actual damages or the amount paid to the credit repair organization;
- Such additional punitive damages as the court may allow, using a set of factors listed in the statute;[443] and
- Costs and reasonable attorney fees.[444]

The Act makes specific provision for class actions.[445]

Liability is not confined to credit repair organizations, but applies to "any person" who fails to comply with the Act. Thus, other entities that are directly or indirectly involved in deception—such as assignees of the credit repair organization's contracts, the owner or employees of the credit repair organization, or creditors who agree to accept referrals from the credit repair organization—may be liable.[446] In addition, any person who violates one of the four prohibitions against deception is liable, regardless of the existence or non-existence of any connection to a credit repair organization.[447]

Any person may sue a credit repair organization, as long as the credit repair organization has violated a requirement relating to the person suing.[448] Significantly, there is no requirement that the party suing have suffered actual injury.[449]

The Credit Repair Organization Act does not contain a specific grant of jurisdiction in the federal district courts. Whether this omission will deny federal courts jurisdiction to hear private claims or whether jurisdiction is created under the general federal question statute[450] remains to be seen. The statute of limitations is five years from the occur-

---

433 15 U.S.C. §§ 1679b(b), 1679d(a).

434 15 U.S.C. § 1679b(a)(3).

435 15 U.S.C. § 1679b(a)(1).

436 15 U.S.C. § 1679b(a)(2).

437 Rodriguez v. Lynch Ford, Inc., 2004 WL 2958772 (N.D. Ill. Nov. 18, 2004).

438 15 U.S.C. § 1679b(a)(4); Wojcik v. Courtesy Auto Sales, Inc., 2002 WL 31663298 (D. Neb. Nov. 25, 2002) (car dealer's statement that making payments on time would build good credit record was true so was not a violation).

439 15 U.S.C. § 1679b(a).

440 *See* Vance v. National Benefit Ass'n, 1999 U.S. Dist. LEXIS 13846 (N.D. Ill. Aug. 26, 1999) (bank that agreed that credit repair organization could sponsor people for the bank's credit card was subject to suit under CROA; assignees and individual owner of credit repair organization also liable). *See also* FTC v. Gill, 265 F.3d 944 (9th Cir. 2001) (lawyer who allowed credit repair organization to operate out of his office liable for all fees paid by consumers, even though he did not receive them).

441 15 U.S.C. § 1679d(a).

442 15 U.S.C. § 1679f(c).

443 15 U.S.C. § 1679g(b).

444 15 U.S.C. § 1679g(a).

445 15 U.S.C. § 1679g(a)(2)(B), (b)(4).

446 Parker v. 1-800 Bar None, 2002 U.S. Dist. LEXIS 2139 (N.D. Ill. Feb. 11, 2002); Vance v. National Benefit Ass'n, 1999 U.S. Dist. LEXIS 13846 (N.D. Ill. Aug. 26, 1999). *See also* FTC v. Gill, 265 F.3d 944 (9th Cir. 2001) (affirming $1.3 million restitution award against attorney who allowed credit repair operator to work out of his office and under his supervision).

447 15 U.S.C. § 1679b(a). *See* § 12.4.2.2, *supra*.

448 15 U.S.C. § 1679g(a) (violation must be "with respect to" the plaintiff).

449 Parker v. 1-800 Bar None, 2002 U.S. Dist. LEXIS 2139 (N.D. Ill. Feb. 11, 2002) (punitive damages can be awarded even if plaintiff suffers no actual damages). *See* Bigalke v. Creditrust Corp., 2001 U.S. Dist. LEXIS 14591 (N.D. Ill. Sept. 11, 2001) (consumers who received a misleading letter from credit repair organization could recover without showing actual damages or that they were actually misled). *See also* FTC v. Gill, 265 F.3d 944 (9th Cir. 2001) (affirming restitution award even though no actual damages proven).

450 28 U.S.C. § 1331.

rence of the violation.[451] Where the violation relates to the organization's material and willful failure to disclose, the five years begins to run when the consumer discovers the misrepresentation.[452]

12.4.3 State Credit Repair Laws

12.4.3.1 Coverage

Most states have passed their own statutes, typically termed the state Credit Services Organization Act, to deal with abuses by credit repair organizations.[453] All or nearly all of the state statutes duplicate the federal law's coverage of organizations that offer to improve an individual's credit rating. But most of the state statutes also cover organizations that assist or offer to assist consumers in obtaining extensions of credit (usually limited to credit for personal, family, or household use) in return for the payment of money or other consideration.

Entities potentially covered by the "obtaining credit" branch of state credit repair laws include:

- Credit card "finders" that claim to be able to procure credit cards for consumers.[454]
- Loan brokers and mortgage brokers. Most state credit repair statutes exclude licensed real estate brokers and securities brokers, but few exclude loan brokers. The West Virginia Supreme Court, interpreting language that is found in many other states' statutes, has held that a loan broker meets the definition of "credit services organization."[455]

- Tax preparers who offer, for a fee, to arrange refund anticipation loans for their clients. While tax preparers may not disclose any special fee for arranging a refund anticipation loan, most receive a substantial fee in the form of a kickback of part of the borrower's payment to the lender.
- "Home finders" that promise to help people buy homes. These operations often appear in cities and are usually fraudulent.
- "Home savers" that approach homeowners who are in foreclosure and offer to secure financing to enable them to save their homes.

Even if an organization does not meet the definition of a credit repair organization, it may be liable if it assisted a credit repair organization in violating the law.[456]

Even sellers of goods and services who arrange credit for their customers may be covered by these statutes. The key questions are whether the seller is providing the services in return for the payment of money or other valuable consideration and whether the seller falls into a specific statutory exemption. The Illinois Supreme Court has ruled that there must be a payment for the specific credit repair services.[457] The consumer's payment for the underlying goods and services is not enough. An Ohio decision, interpreting a somewhat differently-phrased statute, held that the consumer must show either payment of a fee specifically for the service of arranging credit or that the cost of this service was included in the price of the product sold.[458] Showing that a document preparation fee to the dealer is included in the contract, or that the dealer received a yield spread premium or other kickback from the financer, may be sufficient.[459]

State statutes vary in the parties they exempt, but most

451 15 U.S.C. § 1679i.

452 *Id.*

453 *See* National Consumer Law Center, Fair Credit Reporting Appx. B (5th ed. 2002 and Supp.).

454 *See* State v. Schlosser, 681 N.E.2d 911 (Ohio 1997) (affirming conviction of credit card finder under state RICO statute based on predicate offense of operating unlicensed credit services organization).

455 Arnold v. United Companies Lending Corp., 511 S.E.2d 854 (W. Va. 1998). *See also* Lovick v. Ritemoney Ltd., 378 F.3d 433 (5th Cir. 2004) (state credit services law covers loan broker and authorizes it to charge fees); Lewis v. Delta Funding Corp. (*In re* Lewis), 290 B.R. 541, 556 (E.D. Pa. 2003) (loan broker meets Pa. definition of credit services organization); *In re* Bell, 309 B.R. 139 (Bankr. E.D. Pa. 2004) (mortgage loan broker meets Pennsylvania definition of credit services organization), *on reconsideration in part*, 314 B.R. 54 (Bankr. E.D. Pa. 2004) (dealing with damages issues); Barker v. Altegra Corp. (*In re* Barker), 251 B.R. 250 (Bankr. E.D. Pa. 2000) (finding that loan broker was covered under Pa. credit repair statute, but basing decision on language that does not appear in most states' statutes); Chandler v. Am. Gen. Fin., Inc., 768 N.E.2d 60 (Ill. Ct. App. 2002) (consumers sufficiently alleged violation of consumer fraud statute by alleging that lender used bait-and-switch advertising that failed to disclose that advertised "new" loan was in fact a refinancing of a previous loan).

456 Lewis v. Delta Funding Corp. (*In re* Lewis), 290 B.R. 541 (Bankr. E.D. Pa. 2003) (bank that prepared non-complying contract documents for loan broker is liable under state credit repair statute). *But see* Allen v. Advanta Fin. Corp., 2002 U.S. Dist. LEXIS 11650 (E.D. Pa. Jan. 3, 2002) (parties who participated in the scheme and benefited from the fraud not liable unless they meet credit repair statute's definitions).

457 Midstate Siding & Window Co. v. Rogers, 789 N.E.2d 1248 (Ill. 2003). *See also* Thele v. Sunrise Chevrolet, Inc., 2004 WL 1194751 (N.D. Ill. May 28, 2004) (car dealer was not credit services organization where it did not charge fee for forwarding credit application to potential lenders); Cannon v. William Chevrolet/Geo, Inc., 794 N.E.2d 843 (Ill. App. Ct. 2003) (state credit repair law does not apply to car dealerships primarily in the business of selling cars).

458 Snook v. Ford Motor Co., 755 N.E.2d 380 (Ohio App. 2001) (2-1 decision; dissent would have affirmed, based on buyer's affidavit that she paid dealer for an inseparable "bundle" consisting of the vehicle plus the assistance in obtaining credit). The many trial court decisions in Ohio dealing with this issue are discussed in National Consumer Law Center, Fair Credit Reporting Ch. 8 (5th ed. 2002 and Supp.).

459 *But see* Cannon v. William Chevrolet/Geo, Inc., 794 N.E.2d 843 (Ill. App. Ct. 2003) (car dealership not a credit repair organization even though it charged consumer a $46.88 documentary

exempt non-profit organizations; licensed real estate brokers and attorneys when acting within the scope of their licenses;[460] broker-dealers registered with the SEC or CFTC; consumer reporting agencies; credit unions; banks eligible for FDIC or FSLIC insurance; banks and other lenders authorized under federal or state law; and lenders approved by HUD for participation in federal mortgage insurance.[461] These exemptions will exclude most licensed institutional lenders but will not exclude fringe lenders who lack state or federal licenses. Most states do not have an exemption for sellers who arrange credit for their customers, but some sellers will have a license under the state installment sales act that will result in an exemption.

12.4.3.2 Substantive Prohibitions

Typical requirements of state credit repair statutes include:

- Registration and bonding requirements that go beyond the federal statute.
- Disclosures to the buyer about rights available under the FCRA.
- A requirement of a signed written contract with specified provisions, including a description of the services to be provided.
- A prohibition against charging the consumer for a referral to a retail seller who will or may extend credit to the consumer on the same terms as those available to the general public.
- A three- or five-day right to cancel.[462]

Most, like the federal statute, also prohibit certain misrepresentations and deceptive acts. A number of state statutes explicitly prohibit waivers of the statutory protections.

Some state credit repair statutes, like the federal statute, prohibit organizations from accepting payment from the buyer before performing services. Many allow advance payment once the organization has posted a bond, however.

12.4.3.3 Private Causes of Action

Almost all state credit repair statutes provide a private right of action to consumers. Some do so both by making a violation actionable under the state UDAP statute[463] and by creating a special cause of action.

The special causes of action offered by state credit repair laws are often broader than those authorized by the state UDAP statute. Usually the statutes that create special causes of action authorize punitive damages and attorney fees. Many, like the federal statute,[464] set as minimum damages the total amount paid by the consumer.[465] A few set a dollar amount, such as $1,000, as minimum damages.

A few state statutes, like the federal law, do not require the consumer to have suffered actual damages, but most afford a cause of action only to an "injured person." Presumably any payment to a credit repair organization will constitute injury.

A number of state laws, like the federal Act, make non-complying contracts void and unenforceable. As a result, not only can the consumer get out of the contract and get all his or her money back, but any arbitration clause in the contract is void and unenforceable.[466] A declaration that all contracts are void, with an ancillary order for restitution, could conceivably be won in a Rule 23(b)(2) class action, which is easier to certify than a 23(b)(3) action.

12.5 Unfair and Deceptive Acts and Practices (UDAP) Statutes

Overreaching consumer credit transactions can often be challenged under state unfair and deceptive acts and practices (UDAP) law, which are the subject of a separate volume in this series of practice manuals.[467] As long as the

---

fee and required consumer to pay 4.5% higher interest rate than bank charged).

460 *See* King v. Rubin, 35 Phila. 571, 1998 Phila. Cty. Rptr. LEXIS 73 (Pa. C.P. July 1, 1998) (licensed real estate brokers were exempt even when holding credit workshops, as this was related to their real estate business).

461 *See* Brown v. Mortgagestar, Inc., 194 F. Supp. 2d 473 (S.D. W. Va. 2002) (HUD-approved lender exempt even though it was acting as broker in transaction with plaintiff).

462 Lewis v. Delta Funding Corp. (*In re* Lewis), 290 B.R. 541 (Bankr. E.D. Pa. 2003) (broker's failure to include notice of right to cancel in broker agreement violated state credit repair law, and this claim can be asserted against lender who prepared the agreement and presented it to borrower).

463 *See* Illinois v. Nat'l Credit Management Group, 1996 U.S. Dist. LEXIS 8722 (N.D. Ill. June 20, 1996) (violation of state credit repair law is UDAP violation); Barker v. Altegra Corp. (*In re* Barker), 251 B.R. 250 (Bankr. E.D. Pa. 2000) (any violation of state credit repair law is UDAP violation).

464 15 U.S.C. § 1679g(a)(1)(B).

465 *See* Bell v. Parkway Mortgage, Inc. (*In re* Bell), 309 B.R. 139 (Bankr. E.D. Pa. 2004) (awarding as damages the amount consumer paid to mortgage loan broker, including yield spread premium), *reconsideration granted in part*, 314 B.R. 54, 60 (Bankr. E.D. Pa. 2004) (violation of credit repair law is UDAP violation, but consumer suffers no actual damages where loan is rescinded, so is not entitled to have any amount trebled under UDAP statute); Barker v. Altegra Corp. (*In re* Barker), 251 B.R. 250 (Bankr. E.D. Pa. 2000) (amount paid must be awarded regardless of amount of actual damages).

466 *See* Mitchell v. Am. Fair Credit Ass'n, Inc., 99 Cal. App. 4th 1345, 122 Cal. Rptr. 2d 193 (2002) (invalidating arbitration clause in unsigned modification of contract because of failure to comply with signature requirement).

467 National Consumer Law Center, Unfair and Deceptive Acts and Practices (6th ed. 2004 and Supp.). *See also* §§ 8.5.2.6, 8.7.4, *supra* (application of UDAP statutes to credit insurance problems).

statute does not exclude the type of transaction or creditor involved,[468] UDAP statutes are particularly well-suited for these kinds of situations.[469] In many states, violation of another consumer protection statute is a *per se* UDAP violation.[470]

Substantive unfairness and procedural unfairness and deception taken together may lead to actionable overreaching. This may be true even if the procedural defect is simply a failure to disclose the disadvantageous cost or nature of a loan.[471] Procedural unfairness can occur when the lender does not translate important written information into the same language as principally used in the transaction. Such unfairness can give rise to a UDAP claim, even in the absence of a statute mandating the translation.[472]

Broker conduct may well give rise to a UDAP claim.[473] For example, where at the time the consumer engaged a loan broker, the broker failed to disclose the approximate amount of his (high) broker fee or that he already had a prearranged lender, the loan broker violated the state UDAP statute.[474] In this case, the court emphasized the consumer's vulnerability and lack of sophistication, the size of the broker fee ($1,344) compared to the net loan amount ($3,656), and the broker's lack of an active search for a lender. Yield spread premiums,[475] at least without disclosure, may violate a UDAP statute.[476] Hiding a broker's commission in the loan documents so that the consumer must pay extra at the closing is deceptive.[477] A broker can be individually liable for assisting in creating an unconscionable loan.[478]

---

468 *See* National Consumer Law Center, Unfair and Deceptive Acts and Practices §§ 2.2, 2.3 (6th ed. 2004 and Supp.).

469 *See, e.g.,* Chroniak v. Golden Inv. Corp., 983 F.2d 1140 (1st Cir. 1993) (note which specified interest in dollar amount, but with no rate given violated an as-agreed statute, invoked statutory penalties; court also rules this is a UDAP violation, as full disclosure of interest rates takes on added significance with the elimination of usury ceilings); Therrien v. Resource Fin. Group, 704 F. Supp. 322 (D.N.H. 1989); Heastie v. Community Nat'l Bank, 690 F. Supp. 716 (N.D. Ill. 1988); *In re* Milbourne, 108 B.R. 522 (Bankr. E.D. Pa. 1989); *In re* Dukes, 24 B.R. 404 (Bankr. E.D. Mich. 1982); Fidelity Fin. Servs. v. Hicks, 574 N.E.2d 15 (Ill. App. Ct. 1991). *Cf.* Besta v. Beneficial Loan Co., 855 F.2d 532 (8th Cir. 1988) (unconscionability); Salois v. Dime Sav. Bank, 128 F.3d 20 (1st Cir. 1997) (describing scheme in which negative amortization, variable and teaser rates enticed unwitting borrowers into improvident mortgage loans, but deciding case on statute of limitations defense without reaching merits).

470 *See, e.g.,* Barnes v. Fleet Nat'l Bank, 370 F.3d 164 (1st Cir. 2004) (violation of Truth in Savings Act is Mass. UDAP violation). *See generally* National Consumer Law Center, Unfair and Deceptive Acts and Practices § 3.2.7 (6th ed. 2004).

471 Besta v. Beneficial Loan Co., 855 F.2d 532 (8th Cir. 1988) (unconscionability); *In re* Milbourne, 108 B.R. 522 (Bankr. E.D. Pa. 1989) (UDAP). *See also* Fed. Trade Comm'n v. Stewart Fin. Co. Holdings, Inc., Civ. No. 1:03-CV-2648-JTC (N.D. Ga. filed Sept. 2003) (complaint, temporary restraining order), (Oct. 28, 2003) (consent orders for preliminary injunction), *available at* www.ftc.gov/03/2003/09/stewart.htm (failure to inform borrowers that separate loan would be less expensive than refinancing); Smoot v. Physicians Life Ins. Co., 87 P.3d 545 (N.M. App. 2003) (affirming denial of motion to dismiss claim that UDAP statute imposes duty on insurer to disclose dollar amount and effective annual percentage rate of the extra costs imposed for paying premium monthly instead of annually; detrimental reliance need not be alleged); Azar v. Prudential Ins. Co., 68 P.3d 909 (N.M. App. 2003) (insurer may have duty to disclose APR representing extra costs imposed for paying premium in monthly installments instead of annually). *See generally* National Consumer Law Center, Unfair and Deceptive Acts and Practices §§ 2.2.1, 2.2.5, 5.1 (6th ed. 2004 and Supp.); Dwight Golann, *Beyond Truth in Lending: The Duty of Affirmative Disclosure,* 46 Business Lawyer 1307 (May 1991).

472 *See* National Consumer Law Center, Unfair and Deceptive Acts and Practices § 5.2.1 (6th ed. 2004 and Supp.). State statutes that do require translations in certain lending contexts are compiled in that section.

473 *See generally* National Consumer Law Center, Unfair and Deceptive Acts and Practices § 5.1.3 (6th ed. 2004 and Supp.).

474 *In re* Dukes, 24 B.R. 404 (Bankr. E.D. Mich. 1982). *See also* Heastie v. Community Nat'l Bank, 690 F. Supp. 716 (N.D. Ill. 1988) (motion to dismiss UDAP claim denied where broker misrepresented itself as lender, thereby concealing brokerage fees, until consummation); Tomlin v. Dylan Mortgage Inc., Clearinghouse No. 54597 (N.C. Super. Ct. June 12, 2000) (allegations that broker received premiums for placing borrowers in high interest rate loans, keeping the arrangement secret, and receiving usurious, duplicative, and excessive fees stated a UDAP claim); State v. Western Capital Corp., 290 N.W.2d 467 (S.D. 1980) (broker offered to arrange loans it knew it could not secure and failed to give disclosures required by state law; broker conduct constituted deceptive practices). *Cf.* State v. Gartenberg, 488 N.W.2d 496 (Minn. Ct. App. 1992) (UDAP action brought by attorney general against loan broker for failure to disclose it was not a lender, misrepresentation of interest rates and acceptance rates, and "failure to inform consumers about numerous nonrefundable charges;" at issue in reported decision was legality of certain preliminary injunctive relief).

475 *See* § 11.5.4.3, *supra.* These have the capacity to be imposed in a discriminatory fashion, as well.

476 Watson v. CBSK Fin. Group, Inc., 2002 WL 598521 (N.D. Ill. Apr. 18, 2002) (UDAP claim based upon payment of yield spread premium survives even though the amount of the ysp was disclosed and the broker agreement claimed the broker was an independent contractor); Andrews v. Temple Inland Mortgage Corp., Clearinghouse No. 54,551 (DWF/AJB) (D. Minn. Sept. 24, 2001) (UDAP claim stated where yield spread premium was not clearly disclosed); The Provident Bank v. Wright, 2001 U.S. Dist. LEXIS 9621 (N.D. Ill. July 11, 2001) (the yield spread premium was disclosed in the final HUD-1, but the total amount paid to the broker changed drastically from the good faith estimate; UDAP claim stated where the borrower went from paying nothing directly to the broker to paying $6,960); Smith v. First Family Fin. Servs., Inc., 626 So. 2d 1266 (Ala. 1993). *See also In re* Commonpoint Mortgage Co., 283 B.R. 469 (Bankr. W.D. Mich. 2002) (class certified in lender/broker bankruptcy case in which borrowers alleged violations of UDAP and fiduciary duty due to the charging of discount points when no discount was allegedly made, when the borrowers did not know they would get a par plus rate, and when the broker failed to disclose its back-end payments and that the document preparation fee was illegal under state law).

477 Russell v. Fidelity Consumer Discount Co. (*In re* Russell), 72 B.R. 855 (Bankr. E.D. Pa. 1987).

478 Cooper v. First Gov. Mortgage & Inv. Corp., 206 F. Supp. 2d 33

Equity-skimming states a claim under a UDAP statute.[479] A sale and repurchase arrangement was held to be unfair, unconscionable, and deceptive in violation of the UDAP statute where the uneducated, desperate, low-income borrower "sold" her house for $20,000 and received a repurchase agreement for $32,000 at a variable 9–11% rate, which sum included a 20% realty commission.[480] Both the inflated price for the loan-related services and the improvi-

dent lending entered into the court's reasoning.[481] The court noted that the total contract price would have been $135,366, and that the lenders knew she could not afford the payments. The contract also required her to maintain the property to code standards, a requirement the lenders also knew she could not afford to meet. Flipping loans or otherwise engaging in disadvantageous refinancing may state a UDAP claim.[482] In addition, where the advertising surrounding a refinancing scheme is deceptive or fails to state material facts, a UDAP claims arises.[483] Evidence showing that a mortgage loan was made without regard to ability to repay and loan application income was falsified to justify extending credit supported a jury verdict in favor of the borrower on her UDAP claim.[484]

(D.D.C.), *further proceedings at* 238 F. Supp. 2d 50 (D.D.C. 2002). In this case, the plaintiffs settled with the broker and assignees. However, the trial proceeded against the original lender on Truth In Lending and UDAP (unconscionable loan terms) claims. The actual damages of the six plaintiffs for violations of the CPA ranged from $10,000 to $57,000. Statutory damages under TILA were either $2,000 or $4,000 per plaintiff. In addition, the jury awarded over $4 million in punitive damages.

479 *See, e.g.*, Stewart v. Associates Consumer Discount Co., 183 F.R.D. 189 (E.D. Pa. 1998) (class certification granted where allegations involved a scheme targeting borrowers who had difficulty obtaining credit from banks, sending them "live" checks, charging exorbitant points, upselling the loans from consumer loans to home-secured loans, promising to consolidate other debt but failing to do so, and repeatedly refinancing existing loans; claims raised under fraud, conspiracy, RICO, UDAP, TILA, and unjust enrichment theories); Bryant v. Woodland, 111 B.R. 474 (Bankr. E.D. Pa. 1990) (equity-skimming real estate broker engaged in sale/lease-back scheme liable for treble damages under UDAP act for unconscionable conduct; damages included lost equity in home); Fidelity Fin. Servs. v. Hicks, 574 N.E.2d 15 (Ill. App. Ct. 1991) (allegations of deceptive practices used to make unaffordable loan in order to acquire equity in home stated a UDAP claim). *See also* U.S. Home & Realty Corp. v. Lehnartz, Clearinghouse No. 43,259, Case No. 87-930 (Mich. Dist. Ct. Sept. 30, 1987).

480 U.S. Home & Realty Corp. v. Lehnartz, Clearinghouse No. 43,259, Case No. 87-930 (Mich. Dist. Ct. Sept. 30, 1987). *Accord* Boquilon v. Beckwith, 49 Cal. App. 4th 1697, 57 Cal. Rptr. 2d 503 (1996) (sale and leaseback arrangement can also violate state laws specifically created to regulate such transactions as in this case interpreting California's Home Equity Sales Contract Act). *See also* Jackson v. Byrd, Civ. Action No. 01-ca-825, Clearinghouse No. 55,605 (D.C. Super. Ct. May 14, 2004) (UDAP violation for homesaver to fail to disclose the appraised value of the home and that he was the other contracting party and would profit personally from the transaction; presenting himself as helping save the home when his real intention was to acquire it for a pittance; and acquiring the home at a grossly disproportionate price from an aged and infirm homeowner), *later order* (June 30, 2004) (awarding UDAP damages of treble the lost equity minus settlement amounts received from other parties; also awarding $100,000 punitive damages); Bryant v. Woodland, 111 B.R. 474 (Bankr. E.D. Pa. 1990) (equity-skimming real estate broker engaged in sale/leaseback scheme liable for treble damages under UDAP act for unconscionable conduct; damages included lost equity in home); Fidelity Fin. Servs. v. Hicks, 574 N.E.2d 15 (Ill. App. Ct. 1991) (allegations of deceptive practices used to make unaffordable loan in order to acquire equity in home stated a UDAP claim); Billingham v. Dornemann, 771 N.E.2d 166 (Mass. App. 2002) (foreclosure specialist may violate state UDAP act by fraudulently inducing a distressed homeowner to enter into a sale/leaseback arrangement).

481 Note that improvident lending may also state an unconscionability claim. *See* § 12.7, *infra*.

482 Hager v. American Gen. Fin., Inc., 37 F. Supp. 2d 778 (S.D. W. Va. 1999)(flipping case where court denied summary judgment on UDAP claim based upon unconscionability); *In re* Milbourne, 108 B.R. 522 (Bankr. E.D. Pa. 1989) (series of refinancings cost borrower over $3000 more than obtaining new separate loans; lender's failure to disclose refinancing option's advantage to it and disadvantage to borrower is a UDAP violation); Villegas v. Transamerica Fin. Servs., 708 P.2d 781 (Ariz. Ct. App. 1985) (where borrower sought to refinance loan to lower payments and new loan was more expensive, borrower stated a UDAP claim, but not a violation of the duty of good faith). *See also In re* Tucker, 74 B.R. 923 (Bankr. E.D. Pa. 1987) (*dicta* suggests frequent flipping may state UDAP claim even in absence of usury). *But see* Gonzales v. Associates Fin. Serv., 967 P.2d 312 (Kan. 1998) (court held no violation of Kansas UDAP act because it found that Associates did not willfully withhold relevant information about the cost of refinancing; dissent found summary judgment on UDAP claim inappropriate where evidence showed that Associates had a practice of soliciting customers to refinance, where it did not disclose that the $100 origination fee charged for each refinancing was, in fact, $100 on about $500 of new money and where the promissory note failed to state that the origination fee was included in the principal); Trevino v. Sample, 565 S.W.2d 93 (Tex. Civ. App. 1978) (no fraud in refinancing a migrant worker's mortgage with higher installments and interest rate). *But cf.* Sheppard v. GMAC Mortgage Corp. (*In re* Sheppard), 299 B.R. 753 (Bankr. E.D. Pa. 2003) (misrepresentation that refinancing at a lower rate in a year following modification of mortgage loan was not UDAP violation because it did not cause loss to homeowners). *See generally* §§ 6.1.1, 6.3.2, *supra*.

483 Chandler v. American Gen. Fin., Inc., 768 N.E.2d 60 (Ill. App. 2002).

484 *In re* Jones, 298 B.R. 451 (Bankr. D. Kan. 2003) (allegations regarding the homeowner's inability to repay and regarding the falsification of the loan application which occurred after the homeowner was instructed to sign states a UDAP claim based on unconscionability); Opportunity Management Co. v. Frost, 1999 Wash. App. LEXIS 336 (Wash. Ct. App. Feb. 16, 1999). *See also* § 12.7, *infra*; Williams v. First Government Mortgage and Investors Corp., 225 F.3d 738 (D.C. Cir. 2000) (jury verdict against the lender on grounds that it made a loan that the borrower could not afford to repay upheld); *cf.* Roether v. Worldwide Fin. Serv. Inc., 2003 WL 22138032 (Mich. Ct. App. Sept. 16, 2003) (a pre-approval letter was a conditional offer to approve a loan application and not a contract to loan; as such,

A UDAP statute has been held applicable in an action seeking recovery of excess interest charged upon prepayment[485] or charging an illegal prepayment penalty.[486] Collecting fees in excess of those allowed by state usury laws or by the contract may state a UDAP claim.[487] (A UDAP challenge to the price of credit *per se* may be preempted by the National Bank Act or other federal laws, however, depending on the identity of the lender.[488]) "Overcollaterization" also may be vulnerable to a UDAP challenge, as where a home is taken as security for a relatively small loan.[489]

An allegation of "loan-padding"—structuring a loan to increase its size without advancing additional funds to borrowers, thereby increasing lender profit or giving a larger loan on which to foreclose—has been held to state a cause

of action under a state UDAP statute.[490] Similarly, packing a loan with worthless products states a UDAP claim.[491]

Trying to cut off a borrower's rights against assignees or related lenders under the FTC holder rule by omitting the required notice from its contracts also gives rise to a UDAP claim against the lender.[492] Where the assignee of a mobile home financing contract containing the FTC Holder Notice fails to acknowledge liability under the FTC rule, this behavior, in and of itself, can constitute a UDAP violation.[493]

Home sale scams involving dilapidated and overpriced homes, or home construction and financing schemes deceptively marketed to purchasers, can be challenged under state

---

it did not meet the state's statute of frauds and could not serve as the basis of the consumer's UDAP claim). *But cf.* Clark v. U.S. Bank Nat'l Ass'n, 2004 WL 1380166 (E.D. Pa. June 18, 2004) (denying preliminary injunction where increase of payment from $600 to $791.71 not enough to show that lender knew borrower could not afford loan, and where evidence showed that borrower knew what income he was attesting to).

485 McTeer v. Provident Life & Accident Ins., 712 F. Supp. 512 (D.S.C. 1989). *But see* Stutman v. Chemical Bank, 731 N.E.2d 608 (N.Y. App. 2000) (collecting a $275 attorney fee for the simultaneous transfer of funds to allow the consumers' collateral to be available to secure the new loan at the time of prepayment of the current loan when the loan note permitted the consumers to repay without any prepayment charge does not state a UDAP claim; not clear that the fee constituted a prepayment charge, so no deception).

486 Nelson v. Associates Fin. Serv. Co. of Ind., 659 N.W.2d 635 (Mich. Ct. App. 2002).

487 Siradas v. Chase Lincoln First Bank. N.A., 1999 U.S. Dist. LEXIS 15593 (S.D.N.Y. Sept. 30, 1999) (miscalculation of interest due using the wrong index in variable rate transactions states a UDAP claim); Fielder v. Credit Acceptance Corp., 19 F. Supp. 2d 966 (W.D. Mo.), *remanded to state court*, 188 F.3d 1031 (8th Cir. 1998); Tavares v. Sprunk (*In re* Tavares), 298 B.R. 195 (Bankr. D. Mass. 2003) (violation of criminal usury statute by exceeding 20% cap when making a mortgage loan is a *per se* UDAP violation). *See also* Tomlin v. Dylan Mortgage Inc., Clearinghouse No. 54597 (Super. Ct. N.C. June 12, 2000) (charging fees in excess of that allowed by other provisions of state law can state a UDAP claim). *But see* Miller v. Pacific Shore Funding, 224 F. Supp. 2d 977 (D. Md. 2002) (charging fees in excess of state law without more does not necessarily state a UDAP claim; since no explicit representation was made about the legality of the fee, UDAP claim under Maryland law dismissed), *aff'd on other grounds*, 2004 WL 144138 (4th Cir. Jan. 28, 2004).

488 *See* Ch. 3, *supra. See also* National Consumer Law Center, Unfair and Deceptive Acts and Practices § 2.5.3 (6th ed. 2004).

489 McRaild v. Shepard Lincoln Mercury, 141 Mich. App. 406, 367 N.W.2d 404 (1985) (exchange of home worth $43,000 for $17,000 car and $10,000 cash violated UDAP statute). *See also* Victoria Bank & Trust Co. v. Brady, 779 S.W.2d 893 (Tex. App. 1989) (after loan had been paid, bank retained security interest in order to force payment of another loan that bank had previously told borrower he would not be liable for; large UDAP award), *aff'd in part, rev'd in part on other grounds*, 811 S.W.2d 931 (Tex. 1991).

490 Therrien v. Resource Fin. Group, 704 F. Supp. 322 (D.N.H. 1989) (lender required a payment escrow which they advanced as part of the loan, adding nearly $12,000 to the principal at 20 1/4% interest, placed the payment escrow in an interest-bearing account on which it credited borrowers with 5% interest and retained any excess; also lender double-charged for closing costs). *See also* Knapp v. Americredit Fin. Serv., Inc., 245 F. Supp. 2d 841 (S.D. W. Va. 2003) (practice of adding hidden acquisition fees into the cash price with the intention of deceiving consumers states a UDAP violation; injury is at least the increased sales tax paid by the consumer on the higher cash price); Fed. Trade Comm'n v. Stewart Fin. Co. Holdings, Inc., Civ. No. 1:03-CV-2648-JTC (N.D. Ga. filed Sept. 2003) (complaint, temporary restraining order), (Oct. 28, 2003) (consent orders for preliminary injunction), *available at* www.ftc.gov/03/2003/09/stewart.htm (charging small loan lender with packing loans with expensive add-on products, such as insurance and car club membership, soliciting customers to engage in costly refinancings, and urging customers to participate in a direct deposit program that triggers fees for the lender, despite representations that it is a free service); Siemer v. Associates First Capital Corp., 2000 U.S. Dist. LEXIS 21244 (D. Ariz. Dec. 14, 2000) (class certification on claims of UDAP, breach of contract, negligent supervision, and unjust enrichment granted regarding credit insurance loan packing scheme), *adopted by*, 2001 U.S. Dist. LEXIS 12810 (D. Ariz. Mar. 30, 2001). *Cf.* Fidelity Fin. Servs. v. Hicks, 574 N.E.2d 15 (Ill. App. Ct. 1991) (home improvement RISA contract of $6000 at 18% and $106 payments refinanced by 26%, $22,000 contract with $525 payments; allegation that deceptive practices used to make an unaffordable loan in order to acquire the equity in home stated a UDAP claim).

491 Taylor v. Bob O'Connor Ford, Inc., 2000 U.S. Dist. LEXIS 11486 (N.D. Ill. June 29, 2000). *See also* Fed. Trade Comm'n v. Stewart Fin. Co. Holdings, Inc., Civ. No. 1:03-CV-2648-JTC (N.D. Ga. filed Sept. 2003) (complaint, temporary restraining order), (Oct. 28, 2003) (consent orders for preliminary injunction), *available at* www.ftc.gov/03/2003/09/stewart.htm (entering TRO against lender that packed small personal loans with expensive add-on products such as insurance and car club memberships). *But see* Butler v. Sterling, Inc., 2000 U.S. App. LEXIS 6419 (6th Cir. Mar. 31, 2000) (credit insurance packing claims dismissed based on consumer's inability to show causation under Ohio UDAP act).

492 *See* Brown v. LaSalle Northwest Nat'l Bank, 820 F. Supp. 1078 (N.D. Ill. 1993) (bank's scheme to avoid putting FTC holder notice on its car financing paper stated consumer fraud act and RICO claims).

493 Jaramillo v. Gonzales, 50 P.3d 554 (N.M. App. 2002).

UDAP statutes.[494] Charging ten points or more on a loan which substantially deviates from industry-wide practice can constitute an unfair or deceptive practice.[495] Deception in the sale of a mortgage loan or financing of a mobile home can be the basis of a UDAP claim.[496] The behavior of a home improvement contractor in the advertising and sale of improvements is actionable under UDAP acts.[497] A UDAP claim may also be stated where the contractor back-dates a notice of right to cancel.[498] A mortgagee who breaches its duty of good faith under a power of sale by refusing to postpone a foreclosure sale when the homeowners had a binding, unconditional contract to sell violated the UDAP act.[499]

Failure to specify the rate of interest on a loan, at least where required, can also violate a UDAP statute.[500] The

---

494 Banks v. Consumer Home Mortgage, Inc., 2003 WL 21251584 (E.D.N.Y. Mar. 28, 2003) (UDAP claim stated in property flipping case against broker for misrepresentation of fair market value and other features of home, steering the homeowners to use a particular home improvement company which never finished the work, and telling the homeowners that only cosmetic repairs were needed; UDAP claim stated against home inspector for concealing numerous defects, for leading the home buyers to believe he was inspecting for HUD, and for certifying falsely that the work was competed satisfactorily); Vaughn v. Consumer Home Mortgage, Inc., 2003 WL 21241669 (E.D.N.Y. Mar. 23, 2003) (UDAP claim against broker stated, based on alleged misrepresentations regarding the value of the property, the intention to complete repairs, the rental value of an apartment to be constructed, and steering the home buyers to the lender and attorney); Lester v. Percundani, 217 F.R.D. 345 (M.D. Pa. 2003) (class action not certified in case alleging RICO and UDAP claims against construction company, lender, and appraiser when scheme to deceive homebuyers was alleged; Note: This case and the families allegedly harmed received recent press. *See* Michael Moss & Andrew Jacobs, *Blue Skies and Green Yards, All Lost to Red Ink*, N.Y. Times, Apr. 11, 2004, at A1; Andrew Jacobs, *Trying to Hang on in the Poconos, From Before Dawn to Way Past Dusk*, N.Y. Times, Apr. 12, 2004, at A18; Hoffman v. Stamper, 843 A.2d 153 (Md. Ct. Spec. App. 2004) ((affirming jury award to nine consumers of $129,000 in economic damages and $1.3 million in emotional distress damages against lender, loan officer, and appraiser on fraud, civil conspiracy and other claims in property flipping scheme; reversing trial court's refusal to allow jury to decide punitive damages against them; jury also awarded same compensatory damages plus $1.8 million in punitive damages against seller, who did not appeal), *aff'd in part, rev'd in part*, 867 A.2d 276 (Md. 2005) (affirming in all respects except emotional distress damages); Consumer Protection Div. v. Morgan, 2005 WL 1123019 (Md. Spec. App. May 13, 2005) (affirming administrative ruling requiring principals and appraiser in property flipping scheme to pay restitution and civil penalties); Polonetsky v. Better Homes Depot, Inc., 760 N.E.2d 1274 (N.Y. 2001) (violation of municipal UDAP law sufficiently stated by allegations that defendant showed potential buyers substandard properties at inflated prices, promised to perform repairs before title closed but often performed them poorly, incompletely or without required permits, and threatened to keep downpayments of buyers who sought to back out because of home's poor condition; defendant also falsely led buyers to believe that their interests were being protected throughout the sale and that FHA involvement would protect them). *See also* § 11.5.6, *supra*.

495 Massachusetts v. First Alliance Mortgage Co., 1998 Mass. Super. LEXIS 712 (Mass. Super. Ct. Nov. 27, 1998), Clearinghouse Nos. 52,511–52,513 (preliminary injunction granted prohibiting FAMCO from making mortgage loans in Massachusetts in which the points charged exceeded five), *aff'd*, No. 98-J-0857 (Mass. App. Ct. Jan. 7, 1999), Clearinghouse No. 52,512; United Cos. Lending Corp. v. Sargeant, 20 F. Supp. 2d 192 (D. Mass. 1998) (this conclusion was based upon a regulation promulgated under the Massachusetts UDAP act).

496 Szczubelek v. Cendant Mortgage Corp., 215 F.R.D. 107 (D.N.J. 2003) (UDAP claim survives motion for summary judgment

where mortgage lender misrepresented or intentionally concealed the fact that the appraisal fee contained charges for ordering the appraisal and for processing, as well as for the appraisal itself); Christakos v. Intercounty Title Co., 196 F.R.D. 496 (N.D. Ill. 2000) (UDAP claim stated where the settlement company represented that it would record a release of a mortgage, but did not, and collected a fee to perform this activity), *further proceedings*, 2001 U.S. Dist. LEXIS 1933 (N.D. Ill. Feb. 15, 2001); Pagter v. First Alliance, Clearinghouse No. 52,524 (Cal. Ct. App. Feb. 5, 1999) (decision on appeal dealt with unenforceability of arbitration clause; court upheld finding that FAMCO trained its employees to use various methods, including deception, to sell its services); Hawaii Community Fed. Credit Union v. Keka, 11 P.3d 1 (Haw. 2000) (UDAP claim stated when loan officer promised a 7 1/4% interest rate on a mortgage loan which turned into 9% at settlement whereupon the homeowners were told not to worry as they could refinance later; when "later" came, loan company refused to refinance); Kidd v. Delta Funding Corp., 704 N.Y.S.2d 66 (N.Y. App. Div. 2001) (lender practice of charging and collecting illegal processing fees and impliedly representing that it was entitled to do so states UDAP claim). *See also* Rossman v. Fleet Bank (R.I.) Nat'l Ass'n, 280 F.3d 384 (3d Cir. 2002) (baiting a consumer with advertisements and a credit card agreement stating that there will be no annual fee and subsequently imposing an annual fee within the first year states a claim under TILA; UDAP claim also pled but not addressed); Fed. Trade Comm'n v. Chase Fin. Funding, Inc., Case No. SACV04-549 GLT (ANx) (C.D. Cal. May 12, 2004) (complaint), *stipulated preliminary injunction entered* (May 28, 2004), *available at* www.ftc.gov/opa/2004/06/chasefinancial.htm (broker misrepresented that it was offering fixed-rate 30-year mortgage loans). *Cf.* Conseco Fin. Serv. Corp. v. Hill, Conseco Fin. Serv. Corp. v. Hill, 556 S.E.2d 468 (Ga. App. 2001) (lender allowed to re-open a default judgment under the Georgia UDAP act for alleged misrepresentations in mobile home financing transaction where the allegations were merely conclusory).

497 Basnight v. Diamond Developers, Inc., 146 F. Supp. 2d 754 (M.D.N.C. 2001) (allegations that the contractor misrepresented that the rescission period had expired, that newspaper ads were misleading, and that harassing phone calls were made go to the jury; summary judgment for the contractor denied).

498 *Id.*

499 Snowden v. Chase Manhattan Mortgage Corp., 2003 WL 22519518 (Mass. Super. Ct. Nov. 5, 2003).

500 Chroniak v. Golden Inv. Corp., 983 F.2d 1140 (1st Cir. 1993) (the note therefore also failed to comply with New Hampshire's "as agreed" rate ceiling, thus implicating usury penalties as well. *See* § 9.2.8, *supra*. *Cf.* Nilsson v. NBD Bank, 731 N.E.2d 774 (Ill. App. 1999) (insertion of a demand feature into a commercial note with a verbal explanation that contradicted the language of the provision will not state a UDAP claim where the borrower is a sophisticated businessperson).

First Circuit, in upholding a jury verdict to that effect, noted that laws requiring full disclosure of the rate of interest take on added significance in the wake of the elimination of usury laws.[501] Similarly, in the payday loan context, disguising a small loan as check cashing, and failing to disclose the interest rate and charges, constitutes a UDAP violation.[502] Disclosing a charge but listing it as a "carrying charge" rather than as "interest" states a UDAP claim.[503] Misleading or false telemarketing or high-pressured sales tactics in the credit card context also state a UDAP claim.[504]

In the automobile purchasing context, charging the borrower for insurance not authorized in the loan documents may constitute a claim under the state's UDAP statute.[505] In addition, failure to disclose a dealer upcharge on an extended warranty or service contract may also state a claim against the dealer under a UDAP statute.[506] Allegations in a "spot delivery" sale[507] that the dealer misrepresented that it was willing to sell the car at the terms contained in the retail installment financing contract stated a UDAP claim.[508] In

the context of the sale of personal property, the lender's "same-as-cash" advertisements may state a UDAP claim where the lender does not actually treat purchases under the program in the same way that cash purchases are treated.[509] When the dealer told the consumer that financing was approved, although it was not, and sold the consumer's trade-in, the dealer violated the UDAP act.[510]

Mortgage lenders often require borrowers to obtain private mortgage insurance when financing the purchase of a home if they are unable to pay at least 20% of the sales price as a down payment.[511] The insurance covers a percentage of the lenders' loss in the event of a foreclosure. The insurance premium is usually collected monthly as part of the mortgage payment. By contract or by state law, lenders may be required to terminate the insurance once the consumers' monthly payments cause the principal balance to drop below a specified percentage of either the original sales price or the present appraised value. The failure of lenders to terminate the policy when required can state a UDAP claim.[512]

There is an argument that where the same course of conduct gives rise to a traditionally recognized action such as breach of contract as well as a cause of action for unfair trade practices, recovery under both may be barred.[513] But if the unfair trade practices claim is not based solely upon the defendant's usurious conduct, recovery can occur under both

---

501 Chroniak v. Golden Inv. Corp., 983 F.2d 1140, 1147 (1st Cir. 1993) (that the note specified the interest charge in a dollar amount did not salvage it; the second mortgage statute places the burden of disclosure on the lender, as the average consumer would find it difficult to compute the rate).

502 Burden v. York, Civ. Action No. 98-268 (E.D. Ky. Sept. 29, 1999), Clearinghouse No. 52,502 (summary judgment to consumer granted). *See* discussion of payday lending in § 7.5.5, *supra*.

503 Delaware *ex rel.* Brady v. 3-D Auto World, Inc., 2000 Del. Super. LEXIS 17 (Del. Super. Ct. Jan. 19, 2000) (granting partial summary judgment; reserving for trial question whether dealer intended that others rely on the omission).

504 Sims v. First Consumers Nat'l Bank, 758 N.Y.S.2d 284 (App. Div. 2003) (high-pressured sales tactics allegedly lured consumers into accepting credit cards with hidden fees); People *ex rel.* Spitzer v. Telehublink Corp., 756 N.Y.S.2d 285 (App. Div. 2003) (permanent injunction upheld against telemarketing company that misrepresented to consumers that they were pre-approved for a low interest rate credit card upon payment of $220).

505 Moore v. Fidelity Fin. Servs., Inc., 949 F. Supp. 673 (N.D. Ill. 1997). *See also* Schauer v. General Motors Acceptance Corp., 819 So. 2d 809 (Fla. Dist. Ct. App. 2002).

506 Cirone-Shadow v. Union Nissan of Waukegan, 955 F. Supp. 938 (N.D. Ill. 1997); Bernhauser v. Glen Ellyn Dodge, Inc., 683 N.E.2d 1194 (Ill. App. Ct. 1997); Sutton v. Viking Oldsmobile Nissan, Inc., 2001 Minn. App. LEXIS 866 (July 31, 2001). *See also* Knapp v. Americredit Fin. Serv., Inc., 245 F. Supp. 2d 841 (S.D. W. Va. 2003) (practice of adding hidden acquisition fees into the cash price with the intention of deceiving consumers states a UDAP violation; injury is at least the increased sales tax paid by the consumer on the higher cash price). *But see* Harvey v. Ford Motor Credit Co., 8 S.W.3d 273 (Tenn. App. 1999) (no UDAP claim against the financing company/assignee because consumer did not tie it to the failure on the part of the dealer to explain the rate structure). For a discussion of dealer upcharges, see § 7.4.2, *supra*, and National Consumer Law Center, Truth in Lending § 4.7.3.4 (5th ed. 2003 and Supp.).

507 See discussion of "yo yo" or "spot delivery" car sale and financing scams in § 11.6.5, *supra*.

508 Williams v. Thomas Pontiac-GMC-Nissan-Hyundai, 1999 U.S. Dist. LEXIS 15045 (N.D. Ill. Sept. 24, 1999).

509 Prata v. Superior Court, 111 Cal. Rptr. 2d 296 (Ct. App. 2001).

510 Valley Nissan, Inc., Davilla, 133 S.W.2d 702 (Tex. App. 2003) (upholding jury verdict awarding damages for economic loss, loss of use of the trade-in, and attorney fees).

511 *See also* § 8.3.2.1, *supra*.

512 Perez v. Citicorp Mortgage, Inc., 703 N.E.2d 518 (Ill. App. 1998); Huntington Mortgage Co. v. DeBrota, 703 N.E.2d 160 (Ind. App. 1998); Kochlin v. Norwest Mortgage, Inc., 2001 Minn. App. LEXIS 848 (July 31, 2001) (upholding jury verdict for consumer on claim that lender breached its contract by failing to automatically terminate private mortgage insurance once the loan-to-value ratio reached 80%; also affirming denial of class certification); Negrin v. Norwest Mortgage, Inc., 700 N.Y.S.2d 184 (N.Y. App. Div. 1999); Walts v. First Union Mortgage Corp., 686 N.Y.S.2d 428 (N.Y. App. Div. 1999). *But see* Hinton v. Federal Nat'l Mortgage Ass'n, 945 F. Supp. 1052 (S.D. Tex. 1996) (no UDAP violation where there was no contractual obligation to terminate the PMI); White v. Mellon Mortgage Co., 995 S.W.2d 795 (Tex. App. 1999) (no UDAP violation not to inform home buyers of right to cancel where contract did not provide such a right, even though lender had policy allowing cancellation once loan-to-value ratio reached 80%). Breach of contact claims have not been successful where the loan documents required the payment of the premium "over the full term of the loan" or otherwise did not provide for automatic termination. Deerman v. Federal Home Loan Mortgage Corp., 955 F. Supp. 1393 (N.D. Ala. 1997), *aff'd*, 140 F.3d 1043 (11th Cir. 1998) (Mem.). The argument that there is a duty to cancel and a duty to disclose has dramatically improved with the passage of the Homeowner's Protection Act of 1998, which applies to loans made after July 1, 1999. *See* § 8.3.2.1, *supra*.

513 Marshall v. Miller, 268 S.E.2d 97 (N.C. Ct. App. 1980), *modified and affirmed*, 276 S.E.2d 397 (N.C. 1981).

causes of action.[514] Further, if the acts complained of are specifically authorized by other state or federal law, the state UDAP act may not be violated.[515] For example, Illinois courts have held that a UDAP claim cannot be based on disclosures that comply with the Truth in Lending Act.[516] But where the practices complained of are not specifically governed or authorized by TILA, a UDAP claim should survive a motion to dismiss.[517] And when TILA is violated,

a UDAP claim may also flow from the violation.[518] In addition, if the act complained of concerned the interpretation of a statute that had yet to be construed, a court may refuse to find that a violation of the UDAP statute occurred.[519]

Some UDAP statutes also impose certain preconditions to suit. Most require some showing of injury or loss on the part of the plaintiff; a few require the plaintiff to send notice to the defendant prior to suit; and a few require the plaintiff to show that the defendant's acts impact the public.[520]

12.6 RICO As a Remedy for Overreaching and Fraud

Section 10.8.3.2, *supra*, gives an overview of the Racketeer Influenced and Corrupt Organization Act (RICO), focusing on its applicability where a lender attempts to collect a debt arising from a usurious transaction.[521] RICO's scope goes beyond attempts to collect unlawful debts, however. Since mail fraud and wire fraud are predicate acts on which RICO claims can be based,[522] fraudulent lending practices may be actionable even if they do not involve usury.[523]

Recent consumer credit cases show that courts take inconsistent views of consumer credit practices through the RICO prism. Though facts alleged or arguments advanced in civil RICO claims may be similar, the rulings on motions to dismiss may well diverge.

As an example that can serve to teach, *Emery v. American General Finance*,[524] presented a well-founded set of RICO allegations based on the defendant's loan flipping,[525] allegations that the Seventh Circuit held could state a claim for the RICO predicate act of mail fraud sufficient to withstand a motion to dismiss. The opinion, written by a noted eco-

---

514 Williams v. First Gov't Mortgage and Investors Corp., 176 F.3d 497 (D.C. Cir. 1999) (compliance with TILA does not shield defendant from a UDAP claim where statutes have different purposes and requirements). *But see* Hardwick v. Austin Gallery of Oriental Rugs, Inc., 779 S.W.2d 438 (Tex. App. 1989) (applying provision of Texas UDAP statute which precluded recovery thereunder for the same act for which a usury penalty is awarded).

515 *See* National Consumer Law Center, Unfair and Deceptive Acts and Practices §§ 2.3.3, 2.5.3 (6th ed. 2004).

516 Jackson v. South Holland Dodge, Inc., 755 N.E.2d 462 (Ill. 2001) (where assignee is not liable under TILA solely because the TILA violation was not apparent on the face of the documents, no liability under Illinois UDAP act); Lanier v. Associate Fin., Inc., 499 N.E.2d 440 (Ill. 1986); Price v. FCC Nat'l Bank, 673 N.E.2d 1068 (Ill. App. Ct. 1996); Franks v. Rockenbach Chevrolet Sales, Inc., 1998 U.S. Dist. LEXIS 20553 (N.D. Ill. Dec. 31, 1998), *reconsideration denied*, 1999 U.S. Dist. LEXIS 3367 (N.D. Ill. Mar. 17, 1999) (UDAP claim against assignee based upon misdisclosure of extended warranty dismissed where court finds that the assignee complied with TILA [a misunderstanding on the court's part as the assignee itself could not "comply" with TILA as it was not the originating lender and made none of the disclosures; no separate UDAP claim pled against assignee based upon its own behavior]). *See also* Graham v. RRR, L.L.C., 202 F. Supp. 2d 483 (E.D. Va. 2002), *aff'd*, 55 Fed. Appx. 135, 2003 WL 139432 (4th Cir. 2003) (applies this rule to the Virginia UDAP act); Shafer v. GSF Mortgage Corp., 2003 WL 21005793 (Minn. Ct. App. May 6, 2003) (the sending of a letter to the consumer asking him to sign a statement agreeing not to rescind does not, alone, state a UDAP claim). *But see* Fed. Trade Comm'n v. OSI Fin. Serv., Inc., 2003 WL 1904013 (N.D. Ill. Apr. 17, 2003) (UDAP claims based upon misrepresentations related to balloon payments and as to whether the payments would include an escrow for taxes and insurance were not destroyed by TILA disclosures, especially when the consumers alleged they did not receive complete or timely TILA disclosures). *See generally* National Consumer Law Center, Unfair and Deceptive Acts and Practices § 2.2.1.6.3 (6th ed. 2004).

517 *See* Williams v. First Gov't Mortgage and Investors Corp., 176 F.3d 497 (D.C. Cir. 1999) (compliance with TILA does not shield defendant from a UDAP claim where statutes have different purposes and requirements); *In re* First Alliance Mortgage Co., 280 B.R. 246 (C.D. Cal. 2002); Parish v. Beneficial Illinois, Inc., 1996 WL 172127 (N.D. Ill. Apr. 10, 1996) (where fraud claim reaches beyond the scope of the loan documents, UDAP claim survives); Chandler v. American Gen. Fin., Inc., 768 N.E.2d 60 (Ill. App. 2002) (bait-and-switch claim takes this case out of the *Lanier* rule). *See also* Horvath v. Adelson, Golden & Loria, Prof'l Corp., 773 N.E.2d 478 (Mass App. Ct. 2002) (table) (text available at 2002 WL 1931997) (when TILA and RESPA did not impose a specific duty, UDAP act was not violated). *But see* Najieb v. William Chrysler-Plymouth, 2002 WL 31906466 (N.D. Ill. Dec. 31, 2002); Bernhauser v. Glen

Ellyn Dodge, Inc., 683 N.E.2d 1194 (Ill. App. 1997); Grimaldi v. Webb, 668 N.E.2d 39 (Ill. App. Ct. 1996); *cf.* Greisz v. Household Bank, 8 F. Supp. 2d 1031 (N.D. Ill. 1998), *aff'd*, 176 F.3d 1012 (7th Cir. 1999) (to the extent that the UDAP claim is based on a meritless TILA claim, it may be dismissed).

518 *Cf.* Horvath v. Adelson, Golden & Loria, Prof'l Corp., 773 N.E.2d 478 (Mass App. Ct. 2002) (table) (text available at 2002 WL 1931997) (consumer, however, failed to show causal connection for damages).

519 *See* Stern v. Norwest Mortgage, Inc., 688 N.E.2d 99 (Ill. App. Ct. 1996).

520 *See* National Consumer Law Center, Unfair and Deceptive Acts and Practices § 7.5 (6th ed. 2004).

521 See § 10.8.5.3, *supra* and also the discussion of the use of state RICO statutes in consumer credit cases in § 10.8.5.3, *supra. See generally* National Consumer Law Center, Unfair and Deceptive Acts and Practices § 9.2 (6th ed. 2004); Mark E. Budnitz & Helen Davis Chaitman, The Law of Lender Liability Ch. 6 (rev. ed. 1999 & 2004 Supp.).

522 18 U.S.C. § 1961(1)(B).

523 See also § 12.10, *infra* for a discussion of common law fraud.

524 71 F.3d 1343 (7th Cir. 1995).

525 *See* § 6.1, *supra. See also* §§ 6.3–6.4, *supra.*

nomic analyst of the law, Chief Judge Richard Posner,[526] is notable for the evident disdain it shows for the practice, irrespective of whether the practice is ultimately determined to constitute actionable fraud.

Ms. Emery's experience was typical of this quite common practice among finance companies. The amount financed in her initial loan, which bore an interest rate of 36%, was $1,983.81. Of that amount, nearly $172 was set aside for credit life and disability insurance premiums. American General took a security interest in five items of personal property[527] and charged $64.42 to insure those items, along with a $6 premium for the "non-filing" insurance. The total obligation was $3,310.89. Six months later, American General solicited her to borrow additional money. The $200 additional funds she borrowed could have cost her $440, had she borrowed it through a new transaction; however, by refinancing the original loan the additional funds cost her $1,267.[528] Not surprisingly, Ms. Emery was not told about the cheaper avenue.

The plaintiff filed a RICO action, alleging that the lender committed mail fraud, a RICO predicate act, by inducing unsophisticated consumers to obtain inordinately and unconscionably expensive new funds. Likening the practice to that of "twisting" insurance policies,[529] the plaintiff alleged that the lender routinely concealed from consumers the fact that refinancing costs were significantly higher than obtaining a separate, new loan, and that the lender targeted its solicitations to an audience of unsophisticated consumers who generally did not understand the complex calculations the loans entailed.

Though the Seventh Circuit held that the plaintiff had failed to plead the complaint with sufficient particularity, that failure could be cured. The substantive allegations, however, could establish mail fraud sufficient to overcome a motion to dismiss.[530]

In getting to that bottom line, Judge Posner had some rather pointed remarks about the practice. For her additional $200, Ms. Emery's monthly payments jumped from $89 to $108, and the incremental additional cost was $1,200, an implicit rate of over 110% by his calculations: "So much for

the Truth in Lending Act as a protection for borrowers."[531] The court noted that, while mere failure to disclose is not necessarily mail fraud, nonetheless omissions, concealments, and half-truths may be: the crime depends upon the context, including the defendant's state of mind.

The complaint adequately suggests such a possible context, as described by the court in unvarnished terms:

> [A]ssume . . . that these employees, desiring to exploit the financial naiveté of working-class borrowers, realizing that these borrowers do not read Truth in Lending Act disclosure forms intelligently, and hoping to trick them into overpaying disastrously for credit, drafted a letter that they believed would be effective in concealing the costs of refinancing. Read against this background of nefarious purpose, the letter is seen to be replete with falsehoods and half truths. . . .[532] She is no "Dear Verna" to them; she has not been selected to receive the letter because she is a good customer, but because she belongs to a class of probably gullible customers for credit; the purpose of offering her more money is not to thank her for her business but to rip her off; nothing has been "set aside" for her. "[W]e could write your check on the spot. Or, call ahead and I'll have the check waiting for you." Yes—along with a few forms to sign whereby for only $1,200 payable over three years at an even higher monthly rate than your present loan (and your present loan plus a separate loan for $200, which we could have made you), you can have a meager $200 now.[533]

The appellate court rejected the lower court's reasoning that the want of a TIL claim or an allegation of a fiduciary duty on the creditor's part salvaged the scheme. Rather, the court should take into account the sophistication of the borrower, for not all people

> are capable of being careful readers. . . . The allegation is that she belongs to a class of borrowers who are not competent interpreters of such forms and that the defendant knows this and sought to take advantage of it. Taking advantage of the vulnerable is a leitmotif of fraud . . . Competent people can protect themselves well enough against most forms of fraud. The incompetent are for that reason a frequent target of con men and other defrauders, and such targeting is, of course,

---

526   *See, e.g.,* Richard A. Posner, Economic Analysis of Law (4th ed. 1992).

527   The security consisted of a typewriter, an amplifier and speakers, a tape player, and a TV. Thanks to Cathleen Combs of Chicago, IL., one of Ms. Emery's attorneys, for supplying details not apparent in the court's decision.

528   *See* § 6.1.1, *supra.* Regarding the insurance packing, see § 8.5.4, *supra.*

529   *See* National Consumer Law Center, Unfair and Deceptive Acts and Practices § 5.3.2.2 (6th ed. 2004 and Supp.). An account of the New York Insurance Department's action against a major insurer shows remarkable similarities. *See* Jerry Ackerman, *Hancock Pays $1m Fine to Insurance Regulators in N.Y.: Charged with Misleading Customers to Sell Policies, Generate More Fees,* Boston Globe, Jan. 4, 1996, at 50. The practice is also similar to "churning" in the securities field.

530   71 F.3d at 1348.

531   71 F.3d at 1346. His 110% rate included the various add-on charges such as insurance. He noted that it was not necessary to determine at that stage whether those charges inured to Ms. Emery's benefit. *See generally* Ch. 8, *supra,* for a discussion of that issue.

532   In part, the letter read: "Dear Verna . . . I have extra spending money for you. . . . You're a good customer. To thank you for your business, I've set aside $750 in your name."

533   71 F.3d at 1347.

unlawful, and indeed earns the criminal a longer sentence.[534]

Having said that, Judge Posner specified that he was not prejudging American General to be guilty of fraud. Nor was the court holding that loan flipping constitutes fraud, or that the mail fraud statute "criminalizes sleazy sales tactics, which abound in a free commercial society,"[535] for American General's state of mind was crucial. But the allegations in the complaint were adequate to save the suit from dismissal, though the complaint wanted amending.

Upon remand, the plaintiffs filed an amended complaint to address the issues raised by the Seventh Circuit.[536] This time, the district court found that plaintiffs failed to state a claim under RICO because none of the "enterprise" corporations (American General Finance and its subsidiary's subsidiary, American General Finance, Inc.) involved was sufficiently distinct from the alleged RICO "person" (the defendant, American General Finance Corp.) to satisfy the distinctness requirement of section 1962(c).[537] The amended complaint alleged that AGFI took its marching orders from AGFC, and that the business was operated centrally, without regard to their nominal existence.[538] The court also held that the amended complaint failed to fully allege more than one violation of the mail fraud statute, necessary to establish a pattern, because the allegations that the lender had defrauded other consumers failed to assert that any of them had ever received a misleading solicitation through the mail or had even made their loan payments through the mail, missing that element of the crime.[539]

The final chapter in the *Emery* story occurred when the Seventh Circuit affirmed the dismissal of the third amended complaint without leave to amend for two reasons which are instructive.[540] First, the plaintiff was unable to specifically plead that additional named plaintiffs received the same letter that American General's subsidary sent to her. RICO requires that a plaintiff prove at least two separate criminal acts to establish a "pattern of racketeering activity;"[541] pleading that other plaintiffs received correspondence "substantially similar" to that scrutinized by the court in *Emery* was not adequate.[542] This ruling underscores the necessity of obtaining actual copies of the offending letters from clients prior to filing a case to avoid a dismissal. The court suggested that to avoid dismissal plaintiffs should attempt to obtain such letters from the lenders.[543] While this may not realistically result in the production of such letters, the effort may lay the groundwork for a court's decision to permit discovery before deciding a creditor's motion to dismiss.

The second lesson of *Emery*'s ultimate dismissal is that mere allegations that the predicate acts of mail fraud were committed by a corporation that has agents or affiliates is not sufficient to meet section 1962(c)'s requirement that the defendant have "conduct[ed] . . . the enterprise's affairs through a pattern of racketeering activity."[544] Instead, a plaintiff must identify corporate officers or some other controlling group within the company as responsible parties in order to meet that element of liability.

Subsequent to *Emery*, *Cannon v. Nationwide Acceptance Corp.*[545] upheld allegations of RICO claims against a different finance company (this time Nationwide Acceptance Corporation, its CEO, and certain insurance companies owned by the CEO), denying the defendant's motion for

---

534　*Id. See also* § 11.2, *supra*.

535　71 F.3d at 1348.

536　Emery v. American Gen. Fin. Co., 938 F. Supp. 495 (N.D. Ill. 1996). A third attempt to successfully plead a RICO claim failed to allege that the RICO enterprise was separate and distinct from the RICO person; failed to plead a pattern of racketeering; failed to plead fraud with particularly; and failed to allege causation. Emery v. American Gen. Fin. Co., 952 F. Supp. 602 (N.D. Ill. 1997).

537　*Id.* at 499.

538　938 F. Supp. at 496–97. *See also* Brannon v. Boatmen's First Nat'l Bank, 153 F.3d 1144, 1149 (10th Cir. 1998) (parent/subsidiary relationship, standing alone, did not establish the distinct "person" and "enterprise" necessary to state a claim in this forced-placed insurance case).

539　Many consumers' RICO claims that are based on predicate acts of mail fraud and wire fraud are vulnerable to being dismissed for failing to meet Rule 9(b)'s particularity requirements. For example, a case alleging that an insurance agent fraudulently sold automobile insurance without disclosing its financial relationship with the insurance company and the financer of the insurance premiums was dismissed because the plaintiff failed to identify the details of his claim, including when the defendant committed the fraud, when he pulled the plaintiff's credit report, when he mailed the underlying documents and when he received the plaintiff's premium payments. Harris v. Illinois Vehicle Premium Finance Co., 2000 U.S. Dist. LEXIS 13763, at *18 (N.D. Ill. Sept. 12, 2000). A similar case held that broad allegations that a defendant defrauded other auto insurance purchasers in the same way as the plaintiff will not suffice without names, dates, and other details involving the transactions with the other customers. Hobson v. Lincoln Ins. Agency, Inc., 2000 U.S. Dist. LEXIS 13314, at *12–13 (N.D. Ill. Sept. 7, 2000), *further proceedings*, 2001 U.S. Dist. LEXIS 476 (N.D. Ill. Jan. 18, 2001) (RICO claim dismissed again after opportunity to amend). *See also* Wagh v. Metris Direct, Inc., 363 F.3d 821 (9th Cir. 2003) (affirming dismissal of RICO claim based on allegations that defendant had caused the plaintiff's credit card issuer to bill plaintiff's card for membership in a program to which plaintiff had not subscribed on grounds, in part, that plaintiff had failed to comply with Rule 9(b)); Pulphus v. Sullivan, 2003 WL 1964333, at *9 (N.D. Ill. Apr. 28, 2003) (victims of home improvement loan scheme failed to allege mail and wire fraud with sufficient peculiarity, dismissing RICO claims without prejudice); Singleton v. Montgomery Ward Credit Corp., 2000 WL 796163, at *3 (N.D. Ill. June 19, 2000) (dismissing RICO claim based on defendant's allegedly deceptive credit insurance sales tactics).

540　Emery v. American Gen. Fin. Co., 134 F.3d 1321 (7th Cir. 1997), *cert. denied*, 525 U.S. 818 (1998).

541　18 U.S.C. § 1961(5).

542　134 F.3d at 1323.

543　*Id.* at 1323.

544　18 U.S.C. § 1962(c); 134 F.3d at 1325.

545　1997 U.S. Dist. LEXIS 20019 (N.D. Ill. Dec. 12, 1997).

summary judgment.[546] The court held that the borrower had adequately pleaded the commission of predicate acts of mail fraud by alleging that the lender solicited consumers to refinance existing loans at costs higher than the consumer would incur were the consumer to take out new loans instead.[547] As in *Emery*, the failure to tell the borrower that repeated refinancings would be significantly more expensive could constitute the requisite fraud. In addition, the solicitations themselves were misleading. The defendants failed in their attempt to distinguish the facts from *Emery* on the grounds that this borrower was not scammed as badly.

The increasing problem of consumers paying higher interest rates due to the divided loyalties of loan arrangers has also been challenged under RICO's mail fraud provisions, with differing results. One federal district court dismissed a RICO challenge to the practice of "upselling" the interest rate on an auto loan. (Upselling the rate works like the yield spread premium described in § 11.5.4.3, *supra*: A 30% return on a contract is an adequate return, but if the auto dealer can sucker a 41% deal, the dealer and the assignee which purchases the installment credit contract split the difference.) Looking solely to Truth in Lending as the standard for whether the failure to disclose this "kickback" might constitute mail fraud, the court held that it did not.[548]

Note, though, that in some circumstances the practice may be a UDAP violation.[549] Practitioners should review state retail installment sales acts to determine whether the car dealer may have illegally received any compensation from an assignee for closing the loan with a higher than par rate. Some acts allow the seller to receive a portion of the resulting higher finance charge only if that fact is disclosed to the consumer.[550]

In the mortgage lending context, the common lending practice of paying yield spread premiums to brokers to steer business may support a RICO claim.[551] The Real Estate Settlement Procedures Act requires the disclosure of such payments and prohibits the payment of illegal referral fees. A borrower can successfully plead a RICO claim when the payment of the premium is not disclosed, the cost of the premium is passed on to the borrower in the form of a higher interest rate, the broker represented that it would provide the lowest available mortgage rate, money flowed between the assignee, the funding lender, the broker, and its related title company, and the mails were used in furtherance of the scheme.[552] The beauty of this approach is that the RICO

---

546 *See also* Faircloth v. Certified Fin. Inc., 2001 U.S. Dist. LEXIS 6793, at *18, 36–37 (E.D. La. May 16, 2001) (accepting settlement in class action that alleged that defendant lent funds to plaintiffs with pending personal injury actions and then flipped the loans to create unlawful interest; approving attorney fee of more than $530,000); Stewart v. Associates Consumer Discount Co., 183 F.R.D. 189, 198 (E.D. Pa. 1998) (granting class certification where allegations involved a scheme targeting borrowers who had difficulty obtaining credit from banks, sending them "live" checks, charging exorbitant points, upselling the loans from consumer loans to home-secured loans, promising to consolidate other debt but failing to do so, and repeatedly refinancing existing loans; claims raised under fraud, conspiracy, RICO, UDAP, TILA, and unjust enrichment theories); Parish v. Beneficial Illinois, Inc., 1996 WL 172127, at *5 (N.D. Ill. Apr. 10, 1996) (applying *Emery* to decide that pleading a loan flipping scheme can constitute "racketeering activity;" case dismissed without prejudice on the issue of pleading a "pattern;" plaintiffs permitted to conduct limited discovery on this issue).

547 1997 U.S. Dist. LEXIS 20019 at *2, 20.

548 Taylor v. Bob O'Connor Ford, Inc., 1998 U.S. Dist. LEXIS 5095, at *41–56 (N.D. Ill. Apr. 13, 1998)(while agency allegations between consumer and dealer create a duty to disclose and, thus, failure to tell the consumer about the kickback is a material omission, complaint failed to adequately allege the scheme to defraud, a pattern of racketeering, and separate enterprises; leave granted to amend); Perino v. Mercury Fin. Co., 912 F. Supp. 313, 318–19 (N.D. Ill. 1995) (state claims also dismissed for lack of federal jurisdiction); *see also* Balderos v. City Chevrolet, Buick, Geo, Inc., 1998 U.S. Dist. LEXIS 4398, at *18–21 (N.D. Ill. Mar. 31, 1998)(agency allegations alone without also claiming that dealer promised to find best terms available not fraud), *aff'd in part, rev'd in part on other grounds*, 214 F.3d 849 (7th Cir. 2000) (auto dealer's Truth in Lending Act violations accomplished through wire and mail communications

did not, on their own, raise wire and mail fraud allegations sufficient to avoid dismissal of RICO claim). *But see* Ewing v. Midland Fin. Co., 1997 U.S. Dist. LEXIS 15694 (N.D. Ill. Sept. 26, 1997) (refusing to dismiss allegations relating to scheme to defraud; applying *Emery* in holding that "[t]he circumstances surrounding the challenged representations may demonstrate half-truths even absent any fiduciary or similar legal duty," but dismissing the RICO claim alleged against Mercury Finance Co. which had taken over ownership of the lender, because the complaint failed to allege Mercury had any role in the scheme that was distinct from the original lender); Fairman v. Schaumburg Toyota, Inc., 1996 U.S. Dist. LEXIS 9669, at *12–16 (N.D. Ill. July 10, 1996)(dealer allegedly promised to find the best terms available, which distinguishes this case from *Perino*, *Taylor*, and *Balderos*); Johnson v. Mercury Fin. Co., Clearinghouse No. 50,407, Case No. CV 93-952 (Ala. Cir. Ct. jury verdict Aug. 1994) *discussed in* § 11.10.2, *infra* (hiding additional financing cost in inflated sale price found to be fraud).

549 *See, e.g.*, Adkinson v. Harpeth Ford-Mercury, Inc., 1991 Tenn. App. LEXIS 114, at *17–19 (Tenn. Ct. App. Feb. 15, 1991). *See generally* National Consumer Law Center, Unfair and Deceptive Acts and Practices §§ 5.1.3.3, 5.4.3.4 (6th ed. 2004).

550 Md. Code Ann., Com. Law § 12-609(g); *see* McGraw v. Loyola Ford, Inc., 723 A.2d 502, 515–23 (Md. Ct. Spec. App. 1999) (penalty under the Maryland RISA appears to be that the holder cannot collect or receive any finance, delinquency, or collection charge; court did not reach the issue of the penalty).

551 *See* § 11.3.1.5, *supra*.

552 Kerby v. Mortgage Funding Corp., 992 F. Supp. 787 (D. Md. 1998); Briggs v. Countrywide Funding Corp., 931 F. Supp. 1545 (M.D. Ala. 1996) (the alleged scheme to defraud as the predicate act for RICO was that the arrangement induced brokers to steer borrowers to higher priced loans in exchange for hidden commission payments from the lender), *vacated on other grounds*, 949 F. Supp. 812 (M.D. Ala. 1996). *See also* Smith v. Berg, 247 F.3d 532, 538 (3d Cir. 2001) (refusing to dismiss a RICO class action by plaintiff home buyers against several realty service corporations that alleged that they had conspired with a developer to use fraudulent financial incentives to induce

claim does not stand or fall on the legality of the yield spread premium under RESPA because the RICO claim is predicated upon mail fraud, and not upon a RESPA violation. Similarly, in the mortgage lending context, RICO can provide a remedy when a lender says it will consolidate debt at a better rate than other lenders when, in reality, the loan failed to pay off the existing debt, included an interest rate of over 15%, and was packed with various insurances.[553]

As an example of secret premium liability, in *Hastings v. Fidelity Mortgage Decisions Corp.*,[554] the defrauded borrower successfully pleaded two predicate acts:[555] a scheme to defraud[556] and an enterprise.[557] However, the court dis-

missed the allegations of a pattern (with leave to amend after discovery) which included the claim that it was the "policy and practice" of the lender to make payments to mortgage brokers similar to the fee paid in this case. Merely alleging that the defendants had done the same thing to other parties was insufficient under Rule 9(b).[558]

The widespread practice of requiring borrowers to make higher escrow payments than warranted may be attacked under RICO. Where the servicer collects mortgage payments, transfers a portion of the payment to the lender and escrows the remainder, determines the escrow amount, and pays the disbursements, it is participating in the affairs of the enterprise itself, i.e., the investors or lenders who pool their mortgages, sufficient to meet section 1962(c)'s "conduct" requirement.[559]

Increasingly, mortgage lenders and servicers impose fees upon their customers for services which previously were considered part of the overhead, e.g., payoff statements, fax fees, copies of documents from the customer's file. These fees may be subject to attack under breach of contract and unjust enrichment theories where the loan documents and mortgage do not specifically provide that such fees may be charged.[560] More insidious and expensive for consumers was one servicer's practice of imposing a one time bankruptcy "monitoring processing fee" of $150 upon the filing of a bankruptcy. An Illinois federal court allowed the plaintiffs to amend their complaint and refused to dismiss RICO claims on the grounds that the letter demanding the fee contained a misrepresentation about the mandatory nature of the fee, even though the letter was also sent to the consumers' attorney who could have advised the borrowers of their obligations.[561]

---

plaintiffs to purchase homes they could not afford). *But see* Vandenbroeck v. CommonPoint Mortgage Co., 22 F. Supp. 2d 677 (W.D. Mich. 1998) (insufficient facts were pled to show the existence of the alleged association-in-fact between the defendant/lender and the investors without specifics as to the decision-making mechanism for conducting the group's affairs; distinguishing *Kirby*, where the enterprise members were identified by name and specific role in the alleged fraud; court also found no allegation that demonstrated the existence of an enterprise separate and apart from the alleged pattern of racketeering (which was alleged to be the charging of a loan discount fee without providing a discounted interest rate and failing to disclose that the loans were at an inflated interest rate)), *aff'd*, 210 F.3d 696 (6th Cir. 2000) (holding that the district court should have allowed the homeowners to amend their complaint to allege that the corporation itself was the enterprise (rather than alleging that the secondary mortgage market was part of it), but affirming dismissal on ground that the representation regarding the loan discount fees included in a written statement given to the consumers included two different definitions, one accurate and one not, so no intent to defraud could be shown).

553 Stewart v. Associates Consumer Discount Co., 1 F. Supp. 2d 469 (E.D. Pa. 1998) (RICO claim survived motion to dismiss), *later proceedings*, 183 F.R.D. 189 (E.D. Pa. 1998) (class certification granted on RICO claim and a variety of others).

554 984 F. Supp. 600 (N.D. Ill. 1997).

555 Commercial bribery in violation of the Travel Act, 18 U.S.C. § 1952; and mail fraud in violation of 18 U.S.C. § 1341.

556 The complaint alleged that the broker misrepresented its intention to obtain the best possible interest rate for the borrowers while secretly hoping to be rewarded by the lender for persuading the borrowers to agree to a loan at an above-market rate of interest. The court inferred that the defendants knew of this false representation made by the broker because the lender knew that the broker was persuading clients to accept loans at above-market rates and because the lender structured its broker premium fees so as to encourage brokers to negotiate above-market rates.

557 The association between the lender and the broker constituted an "enterprise" because the broker originated loans for the lender on a continuous basis and the lender provided the necessary capital to fund the loans. Further, the broker and lender agreed upon the appropriate broker fee. *But see* Vandenbroeck v. CommonPoint Mortgage Co., 22 F. Supp. 2d 677, 682 (W.D. Mich. 1998) (insufficient facts were plead to show the existence of the alleged association-in-fact between the defendant/lender and the investors without specifics as to the decision-making mechanism for conducting the group's affairs; court also found no allegation that demonstrated the existence of

an enterprise separate and apart from the alleged pattern of racketeering (which was alleged to be the charging of a loan discount fee without providing a discounted interest rate and failing to disclose that the loans were at an inflated interest rate)), *aff'd*, 210 F.3d 696 (6th Cir. 2000) (holding that the district court should have allowed the homeowners to amend their complaint to allege that the corporation itself was the enterprise (rather than alleging that the secondary mortgage market was part of it), but affirming dismissal on other grounds).

558 984 F. Supp. at 609–10.

559 Heller v. First Town Mortgage Corp., 1998 U.S. Dist. LEXIS 14427, at *23–25 (S.D.N.Y. Sept. 14, 1998); Miller v. Chevy Chase Bank, 1998 U.S. Dist. LEXIS 3651, at *4–11 (N.D. Ill. Mar. 24, 1998) (RICO claim stated where parent company and subsidiaries can constitute an enterprise and where the defendant bank participated in the enterprise).

560 *Cf.* Henry v. Homeside Lending, Inc., 1996 WL 943909 (N.D. Ala. Dec. 13, 1996) (remanding case to state court because amount in controversy did not meet diversity threshold; merits not reached).

561 Ventura v. Home Servicing of America, 1996 U.S. Dist. LEXIS 4583, at *14–16 (N.D. Ill. Apr. 11, 1996) (claims under California's UDAP act were also raised); *see also* Ladd v. Equicredit Corp. of America, 2001 WL 1339007, at *1–3 (E.D. La. Sept. 7, 2001) (RICO claim stated for named plaintiff regarding the charging of a disputed "corporate advance" and for numerous

Similarly, in the mortgage refinancing arena, another court held that allegations describing a scheme to charge homeowners dramatically higher interest rates and fees than the defendants promised, using certain disclosures to misrepresent certain loan terms which generated additional fees to an affiliate, making loans that the homeowners could not repay, and using inflated appraisals to jack up the loan amounts which obtained a higher yield on percentage-based fees stated a RICO claim.[562] Where the consumer can allege a civil conspiracy between the mortgage broker and lender and fraud in the selling of mortgage loans on terms different from those represented, a RICO claim may be stated, at least under the Ohio RICO statute.[563]

In the sale and financing of real estate, sellers, developers, and others may offer misleading and fraudulent incentives, such as tax abatements and mortgage "credit certificates" to induce consumers into buying homes they cannot not afford. One court has held that a RICO claim can be stated to address the resulting consumer injury.[564] When property sellers steer home buyers to purchase defective homes that are intentionally overpriced and over-appraised, that have mortgage or property tax payments dramatically higher than represented, that lack amenities promised by the sellers, and that are located in different towns and in worse neighborhoods than promised, RICO may provide a remedy.[565]

Similarly, RICO can provide a remedy when a lender says it will consolidate debt at a better rate than other lenders when, in reality, the loan failed to pay off the existing debt, included an interest rate of over 15%, and was packed with various insurances.[566]

Credit-related insurance, too, has received some RICO attention. The Sixth Circuit found that a lender did not engage in a deceitful practice sufficient to state a RICO claim in the representations it made concerning the type of coverage obtained on force-placed auto insurance.[567] On the other hand, a federal court in Illinois refused to grant summary judgment to the insurer under RICO, holding that the borrowers adequately pleaded misrepresentation and causation.[568] A few courts have been receptive to allegations

---

drive-by inspections that allegedly were not performed; class action dismissed because reliance must be shown for each class member).

562   Eva v. Midwest Nat'l Mortgage, 143 F. Supp. 2d 862 (N.D. Ohio 2001) (existence of association-in-fact, predicate acts, and fraudulent conduct were properly alleged to cover all but two individual defendants); *see also* Bryant v. Bigelow, 311 F. Supp. 2d 666 (S.D. Ohio 2004) (denying defendants' motion to dismiss RICO claim brought by homeowners based on equity-stripping scheme targeting homeowners who were facing foreclosure for failure to pay taxes); Pulphus v. Sullivan, 2003 WL 1964333 (N.D. Ill. Apr. 28, 2003) (in RICO claim arising from home improvement loan scheme, plaintiff sufficiently alleged conduct by assignees of loans by pleading that they had reviewed loan documents of originating lenders, underwrote the loans, and approved loan applications, and sufficiently alleged conduct by loan originator by pleading that employee of title company closed the fraudulent loan on the originator's behalf).

563   Matthews v. New Century Mortgage Corp., 185 F. Supp. 2d 874 (S.D. Ohio 2002).

564   Smith v. Berg, 2000 U.S. Dist. LEXIS 9929, at *10–11 (E.D. Pa. July 18, 2000) (this case involved the application of the recent Supreme Court's decision in Beck v. Prupis, 529 U.S. 494, 120 S. Ct. 1608, 146 L. Ed. 2d 561 (2000)), *aff'd*, 247 F.3d 532 (3d Cir. 2001) (liability under § 1962(d) is met by knowledge of the corrupt enterprise's activities and agreement to facilitate them). *But see* DeGeorge Fin. Corp. v. Novak (*In re* DeGeorge Fin. Corp.), 2002 WL 31096716, at *9 (Bankr. D. Conn. July 15, 2002) (allegations do not amount to a pattern of racketeering activity in a case where the homebuyers were sold a home in bad repair for a high price and ultimately could not obtain a certificate of occupancy).

565   Wilson v. Toussie, 260 F. Supp. 2d 530, 536–39 (E.D.N.Y. 2003) (fraud needed to be pleaded with more specificity; "enterprise" allegations were sufficient in this case).

566   Stewart v. Associates Consumer Discount Co., 1 F. Supp. 2d 469 (E.D. Pa. 1998) (RICO claim survived motion to dismiss), *later proceedings*, 183 F.R.D. 189 (E.D. Pa. 1998) (class certification granted on RICO claim and a variety of others).

567   Kenty v. Bank One, Columbus, N.A., 92 F.3d 384 (6th Cir. 1996); *see also* Hobson v. Lincoln Ins. Agency, Inc., 2000 U.S. Dist. LEXIS 13314 (Sept. 7, 2000) (plaintiff's allegations of ten payments made over a ten month period as part of a single, allegedly fraudulent, insurance transaction do not constitute a "pattern"), *further proceedings*, 2001 U.S. Dist. LEXIS 476 (N.D. Ill. Jan. 18, 2001) (RICO claim dismissed again after opportunity to amend); Weathersby v. The Associates Fin. Servs. Co., 1999 U.S. Dist. LEXIS 6392 (E.D. La. Apr. 28, 1999) (RICO claim dismissed due to failure to allege injury related to defendants' investment of racketeering proceeds or to the RICO person gaining an interest in or control of the enterprise through a pattern of racketeering); Weinberger v. Mellon Mortgage Co., 1998 U.S. Dist. LEXIS 14084 (E.D. Pa. Sept. 11, 1998) (RICO claim against insurance company in this mortgage loan case dismissed because mortgage servicer had warned homeowner in writing that the forced-placed hazard insurance would cost substantially more and provide less coverage; therefore, no scheme to defraud even though the homeowner was not informed about the commissions paid by and between the insurer and servicer); Moore v. Fidelity Fin. Servs., Inc., 949 F. Supp. 673 (N.D. Ill. 1997) (though borrower may state a claim under the state UDAP act), *later proceedings*, 1998 U.S. Dist. LEXIS 3282 (N.D. Ill. Mar. 11, 1998); Balderos v. Illinois Vehicle Premium Fin. Co., 1997 U.S. Dist. LEXIS 15683 (N.D. Ill. Oct. 2, 1997) (court certified class action where lender added a purported hospitalization policy premium into the financing of the consumer's purchase of auto insurance without informing the customer; value of additional "insurance" speculative in light of allegation that $85 of the $100 premium was kept as a commission; lack of disclosure about the supposed policy would likely result in a low loss ratio; claims raised include TILA, UDAP, breach of fiduciary duty, and RICO), *aff'd in part, rev'd in part on other grounds*, 214 F.3d 849 (7th Cir. 2000) (auto dealer's Truth in Lending Act violations accomplished through wire and mail communications did not on their own raise wire and mail fraud allegations sufficient to avoid dismissal of RICO claim); Travis v. Boulevard Bank, 1994 U.S. Dist. LEXIS 14615 (N.D. Ill. Oct. 14, 1994) (where alleged acts of mail fraud all related to the single alleged wrongful act of defendant's procurement of force-placed insurance on plaintiff's RISC, no continuity), *adopted in part*, 880 F. Supp. 1226 (N.D. Ill. 1995).

568   Ruiz v. Stewart Assocs., Inc., 171 F.R.D. 238 (N.D. Ill. 1997) (class also certified); *see also* Hammett v. American Bankers

---

of fraud arising from an insurance agent's failure to disclose its full financial interest in the transaction, whether via commission,[569] or ownership of the premium financing company.[570] Where credit insurance premiums should be calculated on the loan amount and not the total of payments, the violation of state law may state a RICO claim.[571]

Abusive debt collection tactics may give rise to a RICO claim if they violate federal laws prohibiting extortionate credit transactions, which are also predicate acts under RICO.[572] In this context, an Illinois federal court held that the borrowers adequately alleged the extortionate collection of credit and mail fraud to survive a motion to dismiss.[573]

The creditor made small loans to poor, unsophisticated borrowers at interest rates ranging from 179.66% to 557.15%. Of relevance to the RICO claim, the creditor engaged in "aggressive" collection efforts. These collection efforts included giving the borrowers a "things to remember" list which advised that if the borrower dropped out of sight, the creditor would find her/him; there was no place to hide; for at least seven years, the creditor would be a "daily concern" until the borrower paid; that the creditor employed off-duty police officers to track down borrowers; and that bankruptcy will not save the borrower. Collection letters were also regularly sent and marked to the borrowers' homes and places of employment, sometimes containing pejorative language and making veiled threats.

In the context of automobile extended service contracts, RICO may provide a vehicle to combat the practice of demanding a hefty inspection fee of, say, $612.95, before a dealer would decide to honor the contract.[574] In this case, the consumer bought a used car from a dealer for $4,800 and paid an additional $1,195 (25% of the sales price!) for the extended service contract. The contract capped per repair coverage to the N.A.D.A. wholesale value of the car and stipulated that the consumer would pay a $50 deductible per repair, but made no mention at all of any inspection fee. Nonetheless, as there was no evidence that anyone other than the dealer was involved in charging the fee, the court dismissed the claim against the dealer because it was not involved in an "enterprise."

12.7 Unconscionability

12.7.1 Overview

Following its application in 1965 in one of the most frequently cited consumer cases, *Williams v. Walker-Thomas Furniture Co.*,[575] the theory of unconscionability was used for the next decade or so, then seemingly fell into quiescence, perhaps because of the subsequent rise of consumer protection legislation such as UDAP statutes. However, some recent decisions suggest that it once again may be a viable option for consumers, particularly where the remedies under a state statute are not adequate, or where the transaction is not covered by the UDAP statute.

Ins. Co., 203 F.R.D. 690 (S.D. Fla. 2001) (nationwide class action not certified on RICO theory given reliance issues in this challenge to unemployment insurer's alleged failure to pay the minimum monthly payment on the credit card as represented). *Compare* Harris v. Illinois Vehicle Premium Fin. Co., 2000 U.S. Dist. LEXIS 13763 (N.D. Ill. Sept. 7, 2000); Hobson v. Lincoln Ins. Agency, Inc., 2000 U.S. Dist. LEXIS 13314 (N.D. Ill. Sept. 7, 2000) (dismissing RICO claims with leave to amend where insurance premium finance company and insurance company were connected and failed to disclose this fact to the consumer), *further proceedings*, 2001 U.S. Dist. LEXIS 476 (N.D. Ill. Jan. 18, 2001) (RICO claim dismissed again after opportunity to amend).

569 Dixon v. Ford Motor Credit, 2000 U.S. Dist. LEXIS 7934 (E.D. La. May 31, 2000) (allegations that auto dealer failed to disclose commissions on credit life insurance sales could present predicate act of mail fraud sufficient to avoid dismissal of RICO claim), *further proceedings*, 137 F. Supp. 2d 702 (E.D. La. 2000) (RICO claims ultimately dismissed because consumers did not rely upon the misrepresentations).

570 Harris v. Illinois Vehicle Premium Finance Co., 2000 U.S. Dist. LEXIS 13763 (N.D. Ill. Sept. 12, 2000) (auto insurance agent, who allegedly failed to disclose his role as sole director of both the insurance agency and financer of policy, could be found to have committed mail fraud if he had a fiduciary relationship with the plaintiff, or made a misleading half-truth; however, court dismissed RICO claim on plaintiff's failure to plead the fraud with particularity sufficient to meet Rule 9(b)). *But see* Anderson v. Lincoln Ins. Agency, Inc., 2003 WL 291928 (N.D. Ill. Feb. 10, 2003) (insurance agent had no duty to disclose affiliation with entity that financed plaintiffs' premiums, therefore no mail fraud, dismissing RICO claim).

571 Dixon v. Ford Motor Credit, 2000 U.S. Dist. LEXIS 7934 (E.D. La. May 31, 2000), *aff'd mem.*, 252 F.3d 1356 (5th Cir. 2001) (allegations that Louisiana law mandates net coverage, that the terms of the insurance were not properly disclosed, and that excessive commissions were paid to sell the insurance product warrants denial of motion for summary judgment on RICO claim), *further proceedings*, 137 F. Supp. 2d 702 (E.D. La. 2000) (RICO claims ultimately dismissed because consumers did not rely upon the misrepresentations).

572 18 U.S.C. §§ 891–894, 1961(1).

573 Brown v. CIL, Inc., 1996 WL 164294 (N.D. Ill. Apr. 1, 1996) (also holding that judgments against the borrowers in collection actions pertained to amounts due under loan documents (the extension of credit), so *res judicata* did not bar a subsequent RICO claim, which was based on later acts (collection of credit)); *see also* Schulenberg v. Rawlings Co., Ltd. Liab. Co., 2003 WL 22129230, at *6, *7 (D. Nev. Aug. 20, 2003) (dismissing claim of hospital patient against hospital that had

---

asserted a lien against patient's tort recovery; given that the state statute governing liens was subject to disputes over interpretation, plaintiff failed to establish that debt that hospital sought to collect was "unlawful"); Chisolm v. TranSouth Fin. Corp., 194 F.R.D. 538, 560 (E.D. Va. 2000) (allowing plaintiff to use presumed reliance doctrine in RICO action based on used car churning scheme that employed allegedly fraudulent repossession notices).

574 Williams v. Ford Motor Co., 980 F. Supp. 938 (N.D. Ill. 1997).

575 350 F.2d 445 (D.C. Cir. 1965).

Unconscionability case law has developed through several different vehicles: common law,[576] UCC § 2-302, non-UCC statutory unconscionability provisions,[577] and some UDAP statutes that either explicitly prohibit unconscionability or that meld unfairness or deception standards into unconscionability standards.[578] However, because there is considerable overlap,[579] case law as to what type of conduct or contract terms may be unconscionable should be helpful irrespective of which of the above vehicles was used. Attorneys should not be deterred from relying on case law

decided under an unconscionability statute in another state simply because their state has not codified the doctrine.

There are two forms of unconscionability: procedural and substantive. Procedural unconscionability involves the bargaining process when the contract was made. Substantive unconscionability focuses on the content of the contract.[580]

The most typical type of procedural unconscionability involves oppression or surprise in the bargaining process.[581] Oppression occurs when there is a disparity in bargaining power between the parties.[582] Oppressive contracts involve

---

576 The equitable concept of an unconscionable contract as one no person in her senses would make and no fair and honest person would accept was used as early as 1751 (Earl of Chesterfield v. Jansen, 28 Eng. Rep. 82 (Ch. 1751)) and continues as the 21st century begins. *See* Besta v. Beneficial Loan Co., 855 F.2d 532 (8th Cir. 1988); Williams v. E.F. Hutton Mortgage Corp., 555 So. 2d 158 (Ala. 1989). *See also* Hume v. United States, 132 U.S. 406, 410 (1889). For brief discussions of the common law origins of unconscionability, see National Consumer Law Center, Consumer Warranty Law § 11.2 (2d ed. 2001 and Supp.) (UCC unconscionability) and Spanogle, *Analyzing Unconscionability Problems*, 117 U. Pa. Rev. 931, 936–941 (1968–1969).

577 *See, e.g.*, Ala. Code § 5-19-16 (consumer credit transactions); Alaska Stat. § 45.12.108 (leases); Cal. Civ. Code § 1670.5; Cal. Fin. Code § 22302 (consumer loans by finance lenders); Colo. Rev. Stat. § 5-5-109 (UCCC); D.C. Code Ann. § 28-3812 (consumer credit transactions or direct installment loans); Idaho Code § 28-45-106 (UCCC); Ind. Code Ann. § 24-4.5-5-108 (UCCC); Iowa Code § 537.5108; Kan. Stat. Ann. §§ 16a-4-106, 16a-5-108, 16a-6-111 (UCCC); La. Rev. Stat. Ann. § 9:3551 (consumer credit transactions); Me. Rev. Stat. Ann. tit. 9-A, §§ 5-108, 9-402 (UCCC); N.C. Gen. Stat. § 25A-43 (consumer credit sales); Okla. Stat. tit. 14A, §§ 4-106, 5-108, 6-111 (UCCC); S.C. Code Ann. §§ 37-4-106, 37-5-108, 37-10-105 (UCCC); Tenn. Code Ann. § 47-14-117(c); Utah Code Ann. § 70C-7-106 (UCCC); W. Va. Code §§ 46A-2-121 (UCCC hybrid), 46B-2-2 (rent-to-own); Wis. Stat. § 425.107 (UCCC); Wyo. Stat. Ann. §§ 40-14-106, 40-14-508. California has enacted several statutes that must be reviewed, depending upon the context, in determining whether a contract provision is unconscionable. For example, Cal. Civ. Code § 1668 provides that it is against public policy for a contract to exempt anyone from responsibility for her own fraud or willful injury to the person or property of another or violation of law, whether willful or negligent. Further, the unconscionability of an arbitration clause may be measured against Cal. Civ. Proc. Code § 1281.2 (California's arbitration statute). *See also* Soltani v. Western & Southern Life Ins. Co., 258 F.3d 1038 (9th Cir. 2001) (Cal. Civ. Code § 1670.5 applied in a suit by insurance agents against their employer after they were terminated to strike down an employment contract provision requiring notice to the company 10 days before filing suit; however, a contract shortening the applicable statute of limitations upheld); Stirlen v. Supercuts, Inc., 60 Cal. Rptr. 2d 138 (Cal. Ct. App. 1997).

578 *See* National Consumer Law Center, Unfair and Deceptive Acts and Practice § 4.4 (6th ed. 2004 and Supp.).

579 *See, e.g.*, U.C.C.C. § 5.108 Comments ¶ 1, 3; Perdue v. Crocker Nat'l Bank, 702 P.2d 503, 511 n.10, *appeal dismissed*, 475 U.S. 1001 (1986). For a more complete discussion of unconscionability, see National Consumer Law Center, Consumer Warranty Law § 11.2 (2d ed. 2001 and Supp.).

580 *See generally* Soltani v. Western & Southern Life Ins. Co., 258 F.3d 1038 (9th Cir. 2001); A&M Produce v. FMC Corp., 135 Cal. App. 3d 473 (1982); National Consumer Law Center, Consumer Warranty Law § 11.2 (2d ed. 2001 and Supp.); Steven W. Bender, *Rate Regulation at the Crossroads of Usury and Unconscionability: The Case for Regulating Abusive and Commercial Interest Rates Under the Unconscionability Standard*, 31 Hous. L. Rev. 721 (1994); Leff, *Unconscionability and the Code—The Emperor's New Clause*, 115 U. Pa. L. Rev. 485, 509, 539 (1967); Note, *Reviving the Law of Substantive Unconscionability, Applying the Covenant of Good Faith and Fair Dealing to Excessively Priced Consumer Credit Contracts*, 33 UCLA L. Rev. 940, 944, 946 (1986).

581 Note, *Reviving the Law of Substantive Unconscionability, Applying the Covenant of Good Faith and Fair Dealing to Excessively Priced Consumer Credit Contracts*, 33 UCLA L. Rev. 940, 944 n. 456 (1986). For an explanation of "oppression" and "surprise," see A&M Produce v. FMC Corp., 135 Cal. App. 3d 473, 486 (1982) (" 'Oppression' arises from an inequality of bargaining power which results in no real negotiation and absence of meaningful choice. . . . 'Surprise' involves the extent to which the supposedly agreed-upon terms of the bargain are hidden in a prolix printed form drafted by the party seeking to enforce the disputed terms."); Sosa v. Paulos, 924 P.2d 357 (Utah 1996) (listing six factors it will weigh: (1) whether each party had a reasonable opportunity to understand the terms and conditions of the agreement; (2) whether there was a lack of opportunity for meaningful negotiation; (3) whether the agreement was printed on a duplicate or boilerplate form drafted solely by the party in the strongest bargaining position; (4) whether the terms of the agreement were explained to the weaker party; (5) whether the aggrieved party had a meaningful choice; (6) whether the stronger party employed deceptive practices to obscure key contractual provisions). *See also* Knapp v. American Gen. Fin. Inc., 111 F. Supp. 2d 758 (S.D. W. Va. 2000); Mallory v. Mortgage America, Inc., 67 F. Supp. 2d 601 (S.D. W. Va. 1999) (summary judgment cannot be based on documents alone; factual issues ordinarily abound).

582 Speidel, *Unconscionability, Assent and Consumer Protection*, 31 U. Pitt. L. Rev. 359 (1970). *See also* Luna v. Household Fin. Corp., 236 F. Supp. 2d 1166 (W.D. Wash. 2002) (contract of adhesion meets this standard); Knapp v. American Gen. Fin. Inc., 111 F. Supp. 2d 758 (S.D. W. Va. 2000); Mallory v. Mortgage America, Inc., 67 F. Supp. 2d 601 (S.D. W. Va. 1999) (summary judgment cannot be based on documents alone; factual issues ordinarily abound); Williams v. E.F. Hutton Mortgage Corp., 555 So. 2d 158 (Ala. 1989) (gross inequality of bargaining power); Howard v. Diolosa, 574 A.2d 995 (N.J. Super. Ct. App. Div. 1990). *Cf.* Taylor v. Bob O'Connor Ford, Inc., 2000 U.S. Dist. LEXIS 11486 (N.D. Ill. June 29, 2000) (allegations of lack of education and sophistication alone are not enough to state an unconscionability claim in this auto packing case); Marshall v. Mercury Fin. Co., 550 So. 2d 1026 (Ala. Civ.

no negotiation over the terms of the agreement.[583] For example, a form contract in which one party has no choice in the matter and cannot obtain better terms elsewhere might be oppressive.[584] Surprise occurs when creditors hide contract terms from the consumer in fine print or unusually complex clauses.[585] When a loan transaction is negotiated in a language other than English and the borrower was pressured to sign the documents quickly, procedural unconscionability may apply.[586]

Procedural unconscionability alone usually is not sufficient to invalidate a term of a contract.[587] The consumer must normally also show substantive unconscionability. A court will find substantive unconscionability if the contract unfairly and unjustifiably "reallocates the risks of the bargain in an objectively unreasonable or unexpected manner."[588]

App. 1989) (unconscionability is an extraordinary remedy reserved for parties who are uneducated and unsophisticated; plaintiff who had college education and understood transaction did not establish claim of unconscionability).

583 California has liberalized this standard somewhat. Even if the party raising unconscionability is well-educated and highly paid, procedural unconscionability will be found where there was no realistic opportunity to modify the terms of the contract which was a generic contract and presented after employment began. Stirlen v. Supercuts, Inc., 60 Cal. Rptr. 2d 138 (Cal. Ct. App. 1997). *See also* Luna v. Household Fin. Corp., 236 F. Supp. 2d 1166 (W.D. Wash. 2002) (arbitration rider was offered on a take it or leave it basis and the disparity in bargaining power between the homeowner and a major financial institution was vast); Graham v. Scissor-Tail, Inc., 623 P.2d 165 (Cal. 1981).

584 *See* Luna v. Household Fin. Corp., 236 F. Supp. 2d 1166 (W.D. Wash. 2002) (arbitration rider was offered on a take it or leave it basis and the disparity in bargaining power between the homeowner and a major financial institution was vast); Landreneau v. Fleet Fin. Group, 197 F. Supp. 2d 551 (M.D. La. 2002) (summary judgment for credit card company denied where credit card agreement may be a contract of adhesion); Carboni v. Arrospide, 2 Cal. Rptr. 2d 845 (Cal. Ct. App. 1991); Beneficial Mortgage Co. of Ohio v. Leach, 2002 WL 926759 (Ohio App. May 9, 2002); Kripke, *Gesture and Reality in Consumer Credit Reform*, 44 N.Y.U. L. Rev. 1, 7 (1969) ("The ghetto shopper is not a comparison shopper and does not have access to the lowest prices"). *Cf.* Williams v. First Gov't Mortgage & Investors Corp., 974 F. Supp. 17 (D.D.C. 1997)(entire contract not void for common law unconscionability, even though loan terms were unreasonably favorable to the lender, where homeowner refinanced several weeks before tax sale and had substantial experience in finding and shopping for mortgage loans, but upholding jury's verdict that lender violated UDAP unconscionability prohibition where lender knew there was no reasonable probability of payment in full and knowingly took advantage of borrower's inability to protect his interest), *aff'd in part, rev'd in part*, 225 F.3d 738 (D.C. Cir. 2000) (affirming UDAP unconscionability verdict; remanding common law unconscionability ruling for further consideration); § 11.1, *supra*.

585 A&M Produce v. FMC Corp., 135 Cal. App. 3d 473, 486 (1982). *See also* M&T Mortg. Corp. v. Miller, 323 F. Supp. 2d 405 (E.D.N.Y. 2004) (finding procedural and substantive unconscionability sufficiently alleged in property flipping scheme where defendants baited consumers with one home, then switched them to another highly overpriced and unaffordable home at last minute, presented inflated appraisal, and steered them to lender and attorney chosen by defendants); Moore v. Mortgagestar, Inc., 2002 U.S. Dist. LEXIS 27457 (S.D. W. Va. Dec. 18, 2002) (denying lender's motion for summary judgment on unconscionability claim where one borrower was illiterate, the other could read but could not understand mortgage documents' complex, confusing, inconsistent, and substantively unconscionable terms, lender misrepresented loan terms, and closing was rushed); Knapp v. American Gen. Fin. Inc., 111 F. Supp. 2d 758 (S.D. W. Va. 2000) (though the contract terms may have

been clear, the lender misrepresented the contents of the documents to consumers who could not read); Williams v. E.F. Hutton Mortgage Corp., 555 So. 2d 158 (Ala. 1989) (quoting Williams v. Walker Thomas, says it is relevant whether, considering education or lack of it, there was a reasonable opportunity to understand terms of contract or whether important terms were "hidden in a maze of fine print and minimized by deceptive sales practices"); Steven W. Bender, *Rate Regulation at the Crossroads of Usury and Unconscionability: The Case for Regulating Abusive and Commercial Interest Rates Under the Unconscionability Standard*, 31 Hous. L. Rev. 721 (1994).

586 *See* Prevot v. Phillips Petroleum Co., 133 F. Supp. 2d 937 (S.D. Tex. 2003) (involving arbitration agreement); *see also In re* Turner Bros. Trucking, Inc., 8 S.W. 3d 370 (Tex. App. 1999) (arbitration agreement unconscionable because employee who signed it was illiterate and had no one to explain it to him).

587 M&T Mortg. Corp. v. Miller, 323 F. Supp. 2d 405 (E.D.N.Y. 2004) (both procedural and substantive unconscionability required; sufficiently alleged here where defendants baited consumers with one home, then switched them to another highly overpriced and unaffordable home at last minute, presented inflated appraisal, and steered them to lender and attorney chosen by defendants); Carboni v. Arrospide, 2 Cal. Rptr. 2d 845 (Cal. Ct. App. 1991) (both procedural and substantive unconscionability must be present; however, the greater the degree of substantive unconscionability, the less the degree of procedural unconscionability that is required); A&M Produce v. FMC Corp., 135 Cal. App. 3d 473 (1982). *See also In re* Allen, 174 B.R. 293 (Bankr. D. Or. 1994) (RTO transaction not unconscionable; noting Oregon courts typically balance both procedural and substantive unconscionability); National Consumer Law Center, Consumer Warranty Law § 11.2.4.5 (2d ed. 2001 and Supp.). *But see* Luna v. Household Fin. Corp., 236 F. Supp. 2d 1166 (W.D. Wash. 2002) (plaintiff need only show procedural or substantive unconscionability under Washington law); Maxwell v. Fidelity Fin. Servs., Inc., 907 P.2d 51, 59 (Ariz. 1995) (unconscionability can be established with a showing of substantive unconscionability alone, especially in cases involving either price-cost disparity or limitation of remedies. "If only procedural irregularities are present, it may be more appropriate to analyze the claims under the doctrines of fraud, misrepresentation, duress, and mistake, although such irregularities can make a case of procedural unconscionability."); Sosa v. Paulos, 924 P.2d 357 (Utah 1996) (unclear if court would have declined to sever arbitration clause if it found procedural unconscionability only).

588 Maxwell v. Fairbanks Capital Corp. (*In re* Maxwell), 281 B.R. 101 (D. Mass. 2002) (standard applied was whether the terms of the loan drive too hard of a bargain); Luna v. Household Fin. Corp., 236 F. Supp. 2d 1166 (W.D. Wash. 2002) (standard applied was whether the terms of the arbitration rider were one-sided or overly harsh); Williams v. First Gov't Mortgage & Investors Corp., 974 F. Supp. 17 (D.D.C. 1997), *aff'd in part,*

It is important for practitioners to remember that special vulnerabilities often present with low-income consumers—such as financial distress or limited education—should be relevant in evaluating unconscionability.[589] The fact that consumer contracts are not only non-negotiable but also unreadable by the majority of consumers argues in favor of a liberal application of the unconscionability doctrine.[590]

In its enumeration of examples of unconscionability, the 1974 version of the UCCC includes such substantive standards as gross price disparity, contracting for insurance charges with the effect of making the transaction unconscionable, entering into a transaction knowing the consumer could not receive a substantial benefit from it, or entering into a transaction knowing there was no reasonable probability of payment in full by the consumer, as well as examples of procedural unconscionability.[591]

12.7.2 Unconscionability as Outer Limit on Price of Credit

In the absence of legislatively prescribed usury ceilings, unconscionability can serve as an outer limit on the price of credit.[592] Idaho, for example, removed its statutorily-defined interest rate caps in 1983, but retained the prohibition on unconscionable consumer transactions. Idaho's Department of Finance, after reviewing the guidelines described in the statute, issued a policy statement warning that a rate of 45% would be considered unconscionable, and unenforceable.[593]

---

176 F.3d 497 (D.C. Cir. 1999), *remanded after jury verdict*, 225 F.3d 738 (D.C. Cir. 2000) (upholding jury verdict on UDAP unconscionability claim; remanding trial court's rejection of common law unconscionability claim for further consideration); Howard v. Diolosa, 574 A.2d 995 (N.J. Super. Ct. App. Div. 1990) (standard used: whether there was patent unfairness in the contract such that no reasonable person would accept its terms unless acting out of compulsion or necessity; case involved a sale and leaseback of the home); Beneficial Mortgage Co. of Ohio v. Leach, 2002 WL 926759 (Ohio App. May 9, 2002); Sosa v. Paulos, 924 P.2d 357 (Utah 1996) (clause in arbitration paragraph in a medical malpractice contract was found substantively unconscionable where it required the patient to pay all costs incurred by the physician to defend the arbitration and all costs of the arbitration itself if the arbitrator awarded the patient less than one half of the amount she sought); A&M Produce v. FMC Corp., 135 Cal. App. 3d 473, 487 (1982). *But cf.* Shadoan v. World Sav. & Loan Ass'n, 268 Cal. Rptr. 207 (Ct. App. 1990) (using unconscionability standard to evaluate a UDAP claim, court held that contract combining a unilateral call provision and a prepayment penalty did not impermissibly reallocate risk; court notes that "significantly" the prepayment penalty would not attach if the lender exercised its call option).

589 *See, e.g., In re* Fleet, 95 B.R. 319 (E.D. Pa. 1989); Sosa v. Paulos, 924 P.2d 357 (Utah 1996) (many borrowers face dire consequences, e.g., foreclosure, if the loan they are seeking falls through, are under stress, feel rushed through the loan transaction, are given loan documents preprinted by the lender, are given little or no explanation about the contents of the documents, are told to sign with little or no opportunity to read the documents (assuming they are even readable), and are given no opportunity to negotiate the terms; not unlike the patient in this case who was given an arbitration agreement regarding medical malpractice minutes before surgery); Kugler v. Romain, 279 A.2d 640 (N.J. 1970).

590 Cathy Lesser Mansfield and Alan White, *Literacy and Contract*, 13 Stan. Law & Policy Rev. 503 (2003).

591 Uniform Consumer Credit Code (UCCC) § 5.108 (1974), and comments thereto. *See also* Idaho Code §§ 28-44-106, 28-45-106, 28-46-111; Iowa Code § 537.5108; S.C. Code Ann. § 37-5-108.

592 *See* 1 Arthur L. Corbin, Corbin on Contracts § 129, at 556 (1963), noting that, absent a usury statute, a contractual interest rate will be enforced "up to the point at which 'unconscionability' becomes a factor"); Sharp v. Chartwell Fin. Servs. Ltd., 2000 U.S. Dist. LEXIS 3143 (N.D. Ill. Mar. 6, 2000); Davis v. Cash For Payday, Inc., 193 F.R.D. 518 (N.D. Ill. 2000) (class certified on price unconscionability claim in payday loan context where state law does not provide an outer limit on interest rates); Van Jackson v. Check 'N Go of Illinois, Inc., 193 F.R.D. 544 (N.D. Ill. 2000) (same), *further proceedings*, 123 F. Supp. 2d 1079 (N.D. Ill. 2000) (summary judgment for consumer on TILA claims granted); Donnelly v. Illini Cash Advance, Inc., 2000 U.S. Dist. LEXIS 11906 (N.D. Ill. Aug. 16, 2000) (same); Hartke v. Illinois Payday Loans, Inc., 1999 U.S. Dist. LEXIS 14937 (C.D. Ill. Sept. 15, 1999) (lender's motion for summary judgment denied; Illinois recognizes substantive unconscionability); Johnson v. Tele-Cash, Inc., 225 F.3d 366 (3d Cir. 2000), *cert. denied*, 531 U.S. 1145 (2001) (refusing to dismiss price unconscionability claim in this payday loan case [APR of 917%] even though Delaware does not have any applicable usury caps), *rev'd on other grounds sub nom.* Johnson v. West Suburban Bank., 225 F.3d 366 (3d Cir. 2000); Gonzales v. Associates Fin. Service, 967 P.2d 312 (Kan. 1998) (observing that a loan origination fee, though legal in amount under Kansas U.C.C.C., may be unconscionable given the totality of a particular creditor's conduct; holding in this case that unconscionability can only be raised defensively; dissent finds summary judgment on unconscionability claim inappropriate in this flipping case given the totality of the circumstances). *Cf.* Paulman v. Filtercorp, 899 P.2d 1259, 1263 (Wash. 1995) (though this business loan "which would have made a loan shark proud" was held subject to the commercial exemption to the state's usury laws, two dissenters explicitly suggested that an argument "that this transaction [was] so outrageous as to be unconscionable and against public policy" might have been well taken, had it been made). *See generally* Steven W. Bender, *Rate Regulation at the Crossroads of Usury and Unconscionability: The Case for Regulating Abusive and Commercial Interest Rates Under the Unconscionability Standard*, 31 Hous. L. Rev. 721, n.258 (1994) (arguing that an unconscionability standard is preferable to usury ceilings: "[u]sury regulation has lapsed before, and a few cases date to the nineteenth century when at times there was no usury protection;" extensively reviewing statutory and common law unconscionability). *But see* Porter v. Ace Cash Express, Inc., 2000 WL 1610632 (E.D. La. Oct. 26, 2000) (where the fees charged in a payday loan transaction were permitted by law, the transaction cannot be unconscionable on that basis), *aff'd without opinion*, 277 F.3d 1372 (5th Cir. 2001).

593 Idaho Dep't of Fin., Policy Statement 84-5 (Dec. 6, 1984). The guidelines considered were price disparity between prevailing market rates and what was charged, taking advantage of the

Similarly, Massachusetts, by regulation, sets the outer limit on rates or terms at that which "significantly deviate[s] from industry-wide standards or which are otherwise unconscionable."[594] North Carolina prohibits fees for refund anticipation loans in amounts that the state regulator has determined to be unconscionable.[595]

A California court, analogizing to retail sales price unconscionability cases, had no trouble finding a 200% loan unconscionable.[596] Recognizing that both substantive and procedural unconscionability must be present, it held there is a "sliding scale" relationship—the greater one is, the less of the other is needed. In ruling for the borrower, the court also turned around the usual excuse high-rate, "last-resort" lenders advance for their conduct. The borrower had been unable to obtain a loan elsewhere, which the court held established unequal bargaining power and an absence of meaningful choice—the procedural unconscionability in this transaction.

Borrowers of mortgage loans on which forty points were charged have alleged that such excessive, nonrefundable charges are unconscionable.[597] The Georgia Supreme Court, while ruling in favor of high-rate lenders on the usury issue, seemed to almost invite an unconscionability or UDAP challenge to high-rate mortgage loans (19–20%) with over twenty-two points added to them.[598] Unconscionability may also be appropriate to challenge some of the banking or credit alternatives offered by the "fringe banking" market,[599] where they fall through the regulatory cracks.[600]

Not all unconscionability challenges to interest rates succeed,[601]

---

594 Mass. Regs. Code tit. 940, § 8.06(6). The validity of this regulation survived attack by one lender on a variety of grounds. United Cos. Lending Corp. v. Sargeant, 20 F. Supp. 2d 192 (D. Mass. 1998). *See also* Massachusetts v. First Alliance Mortgage Co., 1998 Mass. Super. LEXIS 712 (Mass. Super. Ct. Nov. 27, 1998), Clearinghouse Nos. 52,511–52,513 (preliminarily enjoining FAMCO from making mortgage loans in Massachusetts in which the points charged exceeded five, citing this regulation), *aff'd*, Clearinghouse No. 52,512, No. 98-J-0857 (Mass. App. Ct. Jan. 7, 1999).

595 N.C. Gen. Stat. § 53-250(4).

596 Carboni v. Arrospide, 2 Cal. Rptr. 2d 845 (Ct. App. 1991). *See also* Johnson v. Tele-Cash, Inc., 82 F. Supp. 2d 264, 278–79 (D. Del. 1999) (refusing to dismiss price unconscionability claim in this payday loan case [APR of 917%] even though Delaware does not have any applicable usury caps), *rev'd on other grounds sub nom.*, Johnson v. West Suburban Bank., 225 F.3d 366 (3d Cir. 2000).

597 Williams v. E.F. Hutton Mortgage Corp., 555 So. 2d 158 (Ala. 1989) (case dismissed because action brought on behalf of plaintiff class which had prepaid loans, and unconscionability not available as basis for affirmative relief. Discussion indicates a companion case on behalf of current borrowers was settled). *See also* Massachusetts v. First Alliance Mortgage Co., 1998 Mass. Super. LEXIS 712 (Mass. Super. Ct. Nov. 27, 1998), Clearinghouse Nos. 52,511–52,513 (preliminarily enjoining FAMCO from making mortgage loans in Massachusetts in which the points charged exceeded five, citing this regulation), *aff'd*, Clearinghouse No. 52,512, No. 98-J-0857 (Mass. App. Ct. Jan. 7, 1999); § 12.7.5, *infra. Cf.* Moore v. Comfed Sav. Bank, 908 F.2d 834 (11th Cir. 1990) (in case involving usury claim, court takes judicial notice that 20–40 points were "outrageous" in light of industry average of 2 1/2 points, as are APRs of 25–30% in light of industry average of 11–12%).

inability of debtors to protect themselves, and the market conditions and creditor's experience. It also warned that unconscionability could exist at lower rates in some circumstances. Conversely the threshold might rise if market conditions "change drastically" or other factors come into play.

598 Fleet Fin., Inc. v. Jones, 430 S.E.2d 352 (Ga. 1993) ("Although we do not condone Fleet's interest charging practices, which are widely viewed as exorbitant, unethical, and perhaps even immoral, and suggest that further regulation of the lending industry is needed by our General Assembly to insure the economic survival of individuals like the [borrowers], we are constrained to hold that the loans in question are legal and not usurious").

599 Johnson v. Tele-Cash, Inc., 82 F. Supp. 2d 264, 278–79 (D. Del. 1999)(court refused to dismiss price unconscionability claim in this payday loan case [APR of 917%] even though Delaware does not have any applicable usury caps); *In re* Wernly, 91 B.R. 702 (Bankr. E.D. Pa. 1988) (check-cashing fee of over 10% of face value is unconscionable where normal fee in the industry is 2%). "Fringe banking" refers to the high-priced alternatives to normal banking services which spring up in areas without bank branches. These include both the alternatives to deposit services, such as check-cashers, and credit such as pawnbrokers, pay-day loans, RTO and similar high-priced alternatives. *But see In re* Allen, 174 B.R. 293 (Bankr. D. Or. 1994) (RTO transaction not unconscionable). *See generally* John P. Caskey, Russel Sage Foundation, Fringe Banking: Check-Cashing Outlets, Pawnshops, and the Poor (1994); Mike Hudson, *The Poverty Industry*, 21 Southern Exposure 16 (Fall 1993).

600 *See, e.g.*, Johnson v. Cash Store, 68 P.3d 1099 (Wash. Ct. App. 2003) (Washington prohibits rollovers in payday lending when the old loan is paid off from the proceeds of the new one; payday lending company encouraged rollovers in which the customer brought in her own cash to pay off the old loan and then received the same cash back minus the loan fee immediately upon signing a new loan; court refused to vacate a default judgment against the lender on unconscionability grounds who rolled over the customer fourteen times even though the lender complied with the letter of state law); *see also* § 7.5.5.6, *supra* (discussion of unconscionability in the payday loan context).

601 *See, e.g.*, Brown v. Investors Mortgage Co., 121 F.3d 972 (9th Cir. 1997) (interest rates of two loans in question were 15% and 10%); *In re* Glaser, 2002 WL 32375007 (Bankr. E.D. Va. Oct. 25, 2002) (pawn transaction by sophisticated businessman not unconscionable); Family Fed. Sav. & Loan v. Davis, 172 B.R. 437 (Bankr. D.D.C. 1994) (educated person who demonstrated basic understanding of the loan terms did not succeed in challenging second mortgage in which more than 50% was for a disclosed finders fee, in a very complicated factual context); Bramlett v. Adamson Ford, 717 So. 2d 772 (Ala. Civ. App. 1996), *rev'd on other grounds*, 717 So. 2d 781 (Ala. 1997) (interest rate of 15.49% on an auto loan was not unconscionable, relying on Harris v. Howell, 739 F. Supp. 565 (N.D. Ala. 1989), *aff'd*, 902 F.2d 959 (11th Cir. 1990), which held that a 20% rate was not unconscionable); Marshall v. Mercury Fin. Co., 550 So. 2d 1026 (Ala. Civ. App. 1989) (car loan at 30% under "as agreed" statute not so excessive as to be unconscionable where debtor had a college education and understood the documents); Capitol Furniture & Appliance Co. v. Morris, 8 U.C.C. Rep. 321 (D.C. Ct. Gen. Sess. 1970), *aff'd*, 280 A.2d 775 (D.C. 1971) (sale price on furniture marked up more than 100% over

and such cases are fact-intensive.[602] "Lack of borrower sophistication, financial necessity, lender sharp practices, and lack of choice are deemed relevant in most of the interest pricing cases."[603] Unfortunately, such factors are all too common in the consumer cases coming into Legal Services offices. It is critical to develop the facts extensively and to piece together all information which illustrates the "smell" factor of the transaction.

The more outrageous the facts, the more likely it is that the court will find causes of action under a variety of statutes and common law theories. In Illinois, a lender made installment small loans to poor, unsophisticated borrowers. The interest rates ranged from 179.66% to 557.15%, which resulted in finance charges which were about equal to or exceeded the principal borrowed.[604] The creditor then engaged in what was alleged to be "extortionate collection of credit" efforts.[605] The court refused to dismiss the unconscionability count when it looked at the borrowers' lack of access to credit, the creditor's alleged tortious and criminal conduct, and the high interest rates charged.[606] The sale and leaseback of a home likely worth over $100,000 for only $25,000 by the homeowners who were desperate can be

unconscionable. In this case, the court refused to enforce the agreement.[607]

Even if the original interest rate is not unconscionable, the lender may have contracted for an unconscionably high default rate. For example, the hearings that led to the Home Ownership and Equity Protection Act of 1994 (HOEPA) showed that one tactic used by equity-skimmers was to contract for default interest rates as high as 42% per annum.[608] These may be challenged as unconscionable.[609] (Higher default rates are now prohibited in high cost mortgages subject to HOEPA.[610])

---

wholesale with 17.9% interest rate on the credit not unconscionable); Mobile Am. Corp. v. Howard, 307 So. 2d 507, 16 U.C.C. Rep. 625 (Fla. Dist. Ct. App. 1975) (11.75% APR on mobile home sale not unconscionable).

602 Equity Mortgage v. Johnson, 149 B.R. 284, 288 (Bankr. D. Conn. 1993).

603 Steven W. Bender, *Rate Regulation at the Crossroads of Usury and Unconscionability: The Case for Regulating Abusive and Commercial Interest Rates Under the Unconscionability Standard*, 31 Hous. L. Rev. 721 (1994). *Cf. In re* Moorhous, 180 B.R. 138 (Bankr. E.D. Va. 1995) (business loan involving knowledgeable, sophisticated debtor, and private investor/creditor; 22% was not unconscionable "under the circumstances of this case").

    One other factor which enters into these cases, but is rarely mentioned, is the "eye of the beholder" factor. The facts as portrayed by the majority opinion in Cheshire Mortgage Serv. v. Montes, 612 A.2d 1130 (Conn. 1992) look very different from the facts as portrayed by the dissent. See also Judge Posner's decision in Emery v. American Gen. Fin., Inc., 71 F.3d 1343 (7th Cir. 1995), discussed in § 12.6, *supra*. It is worth considering taking the determination of unconscionability to a jury, if jury trial is allowed.

604 Brown v. CIL, Inc., 1996 WL 164294 (N.D. Ill. Apr. 1, 1996).

605 These collection efforts included giving the borrowers a "things to remember" list which advised that if the borrower dropped out of sight, the creditor would find her/him; there was no place to hide; for at least seven years, the creditor would be a "daily concern" until the borrower paid; that the creditor employed off-duty police officers to track down borrowers; that bankruptcy will not save the borrower. Collection letters were also regularly sent and marked to the borrowers' homes and places of employment, sometimes containing pejorative language and making veiled threats.

606 The court also found that the borrowers adequately pled claims under RICO, Truth in Lending (disclosures were not conspicuous) and UDAP.

607 Howard v. Diolosa, 574 A.2d 995 (N.J. Super. Ct. App. Div. 1990). *See also* Davis v. Suderov (*In re* Davis), 169 B.R. 285 (E.D.N.Y. 1994) (exceedingly one-sided sale-leaseback agreement was unconscionable where the consumers did not understand it and were under time pressure yet were locked into the agreement by having made advance payments to the other party, who was a sophisticated real estate operator).

608 *See Hearings on Problems in Community Development Banking, Mortgage Lending Discrimination, Reverse Redlining, and Home Equity Lending Before the Senate Comm. on Banking, Housing and Urban Affairs*, 103d Cong., 1st Sess. (Feb. 3, 17, 24, 1993) (S. Hrg. 103-137) [hereinafter 1993 Senate Hearings]; *Hearing on S.924 Home Ownership and Equity Protection Act Before the Senate Banking Committee*, 103d Cong., 1st Sess. (May 19, 1993); *The Home Equity Protection Act of 1993, Hearings on H.R. 3153 Before the Subcommittee on Consumer Credit and Insurance of the House Committee on Banking, Finance and Urban Affairs*, 103d Cong., 2d Sess. (Mar. 22, 1994); *Hearing on Community Development Institutions, 103-2, Before the House Subcommittee on Financial Institutions Supervision, Regulation and Deposit Insurance*, 103d Cong., 1st Sess. (Feb. 2–4, 1993).

609 *E.g., In re* Hollstrom, 133 B.R. 535, 541 (Bankr. D. Colo. 1991) (finding a 36% default rate to be an unconscionable penalty; court imposed 12%); *In re* White, 88 B.R. 498 (Bankr. D. Mass. 1988) (finding a 48% default rate to be an unenforceable penalty; court disallowed any lesser rate). *See also In re* Kalian, 178 B.R. 308 (Bankr. D.R.I. 1995) (refusing to enforce a 36% default rate). *But see* St. Onge v. Zuccola (*In re* St. Onge), 2004 WL 2518432 (Bankr. D.N.H. 2004) (default interest rate of 1.5% per month on second mortgage where state law allowed this rate, even though this lender was not covered by that law). There is a line of cases in New Jersey involving commercial loans in which the courts have held that if the default rate is unconscionably high, it is unenforceable because it amounts to a penalty. *See, e.g.*, Stuchin v. Kasirer, 568 A.2d 907 (N.J. Super. Ct. App. Div. 1990) (interest rate raised from 9.5% to 24%; case remanded to trial court on issue of unconscionability); Spiotta v. William H. Wilson, Inc., 179 A.2d 49 (N.J. Super. Ct. App. Div.), *cert. denied*, 181 A.2d 12 (1962) (contract rate raised from 30.18% to 38.76%); Feller v. Architects Display Bldgs., Inc., 148 A.2d 634 (N.J. Super. Ct. App. Div. 1959) (default rate was 32.89% while contract rate was 17%). Remedy is to credit the penalty against the balance properly due on the mortgage. Constellation Bank v. Binghamton Plaza, 655 N.Y.S.2d 664 (App. Div. 1997) (applying New Jersey law).

610 15 U.S.C. § 1639(d). *See generally* § 12.2.2, *supra*.

12.7.3 Improvident Lending as Unconscionable

Improvident lending may also be attacked using unconscionability theories. In Connecticut, a court found both substantive and procedural unconscionability in a second mortgage loan. The loan terms required a monthly payment of $733.33 for a borrower with monthly income of $1,126.67 and a first mortgage payment of $1,011.00. It also required the borrower to pay a year's interest in advance and contained a balloon payment which exceeded the principal.[611] The subprime mortgage industry's practice of "grossing up" certain types of fixed income, such as Social Security, to support higher loan payments (which the homeowner often cannot afford because she never had access to the theoretically higher income) may be unconscionable as well.[612] In Massachusetts, a court found that a refinancing of a mortgage loan was unconscionable where the homeowner received nothing of value but her principal increased from about $137,600 to $149,150, the monthly payment increased to about $2,000 which constituted 98.5% of her income, and the monthly payments did not amortize the loan because a balloon payment was due in five years.[613]

In another improvident lending case in Ohio, a widow, appearing *pro se*, convinced the appellate court to reverse summary judgment entered against her in a foreclosure.[614] The homeowner and her husband added a pool to their backyard, financing the work with a $6,000 loan from Beneficial. Subsequently, her husband died. She could not keep up the pool loan payments, though she remained current on a first mortgage. She alleged that Beneficial threatened to take action against her to collect on the debt if she did not refinance. Beneficial also allegedly assured her that she would get a lower rate and it would refinance the pool loan. What actually happened raised the court's eyebrows and caused it to reverse summary judgment. The lender did not simply refinance the pool loan. It refinanced her fixed-rate, 9% first mortgage into an adjustable rate

---

611 Family Fin. Servs. v. Spencer, 677 A.2d 479 (Conn. App. Ct. 1996). *See also* Matthews v. New Century Mortgage Corp., 185 F. Supp. 2d 874 (S.D. Ohio 2002) (motion to dismiss denied in case involving falsified application and income information, larger loans than anticipated, inability to repay); City Fin. Servs. v. Smith, 2000 WL 288469 (Cuyahoga County Mun. Ct. Ohio, Jan. 4, 2000), Clearinghouse No. 52,489 (lender made a $3,000 mortgage loan at 22.5% interest plus $618 in insurance and other charges resulting in monthly payments of $355 when consumer only had monthly income of $574, was already in default on a loan with the lender and owed over $6,700 on credit card debt; court found loan unconscionable and criticized lender's underwriting guidelines which grossed up her disability income based on the fact that it was tax-free). *Cf.* Williams v. First Gov't Mortgage & Investors Corp., 974 F. Supp. 17 (D.D.C. 1997), *aff'd in part*, 176 F.3d 497 (D.C. Cir. 1999) (court held no unconscionability to void the entire contract where homeowner refinanced several weeks before a tax sale and had substantial experience in finding and shopping for mortgage loans even though court found that the terms of loan were unreasonably favorable to the lender. Homeowner did prevail before a jury on claim of unconscionability raised under the UDAP act based upon the knowledge of the lender that there was no reasonable probability of payment in full and knowingly taking advantage of a borrower's inability to protect his interest), *remanded after jury verdict*, 225 F.3d 738 (D.C. Cir. 2000) (trial court overturned jury verdict on the unconscionability claim; appellate court remands for additional findings). In 1994, Congress attacked improvident lending head-on with the Homeownership and Equity Protection Act which prohibits "a pattern or practice of extending credit to consumers [in certain high-rate mortgage loans] based on the consumers' collateral without regard to the consumers' repayment ability." 15 U.S.C. § 1639(h). For more details, see National Consumer Law Center, Truth in Lending Ch. 9 (5th ed. 2003 and Supp.).

612 City Fin. Servs. v. Smith, 2000 WL 288469, Clearinghouse No. 52,489 (Cleveland Mun. Ct., Ohio Dec. 31, 1999) (judgment entry). Be aware, however, that the practice of "grossing up" in the prime mortgage lending context has some support by the secondary market players, at least Fannie Mae. Lenders are allowed to adjust non-taxable income by the greater of 25% or by the actual taxation (based on state and federal rates) that would be paid by a wage earner in a similar tax bracket. The lenders must verify and document that the source of income is

nontaxable and that the income and tax status are likely to continue. When a lender decides to use "grossing up," it needs to make sure it treats all borrowers the same, meaning, the lender should use the 25% method for all borrowers or the taxation rate method for all borrowers. The rationale appears to be that these borrowers are being credited with money they do not have to pay in taxes. In addition, the federal banking agencies, the Department of Housing and Urban Development, the Department of Justice, and the Federal Trade Commission issued a joint Policy Statement on Discrimination in Lending in 1994. In it, these agencies stated that the failure to gross up non-taxable income may have a disparate impact on individuals with disabilities, seniors, and others on fixed incomes. Such an impact could be proven discriminatory. 59 Fed. Reg. 18,266, 18269 (Apr. 15, 1994), *available at* www.fdic.gov/regulations/laws/rules/5000-3860.html.

In the subprime mortgage market, grossing up Social Security or other fixed, nontaxable income can be a recipe for disaster,. and can lead to unconscionability claims. Consumers in this market often are allowed higher debt-to-income ratios, even though some of these borrowers are higher credit risks. Debt ratios are not good ability-to-repay measures at very low incomes, below about $1,500 per month. The more important issue is residual income, that is, how much money does the borrower have left to buy food, transportation, medicine and other necessities after making the proposed mortgage payment.

613 Maxwell v. Fairbanks Capital Corp. (*In re* Maxwell), 281 B.R. 101 (D. Mass. 2002).

614 Beneficial Mortgage Co. of Ohio v. Leach, 2002 WL 926759 (Ohio App. May 9, 2002). *See also In re* Jones, 298 B.R. 451 (Bankr. D. Kan. 2003) (allegations regarding the homeowner's inability to repay and regarding the falsification of the application after the homeowner was told to sign states a UDAP claim based on unconscionability). *But see* Bank One, Nat'l Ass'n v. Borovitz, 2002 WL 31312671 (Ohio Ct. App. Oct. 16, 2002) (no evidence to show that the homeowner was not capable of agreeing to the mortgage terms; no discussion of the issue of the homeowner's ability to repay; summary judgment on complaint for foreclosure upheld).

mortgage with an initial interest rate of 14% (which could rise to 21%). The old mortgage lender escrowed for taxes and insurance, while Beneficial did not. Beneficial paid off only a portion of the pool loan and, for the remainder of the debt, offered her a small side-loan at an interest rate of almost 21% with a term of 3 years. Her total monthly payments rose from $1,394 to $1,718, a difference of $324. To make matters worse, the homeowner alleged that she was not given an opportunity to review the loan documents at the closing and the notice of right to cancel was backdated. The court found that the new loan significantly improved the financial position of the lender. Before the refinancing, it retained a security interest only in household goods. After-wards, it became the first lienholder on the homeowner's house. While an interest rate of 14% alone is not unreason-able, the court held that the rate plus the other terms of the transaction were so unreasonably favorable to Beneficial as to be unconscionable in the light of the circumstances existing when the loan was made.

Property flipping schemes typically involve extending credit to unsophisticated first-time home buyers for dilapi-dated, overpriced homes they cannot afford. A court refused to dismiss an unconscionability count against property flip-pers, finding both procedural and substantive unconsciona-bility sufficiently alleged.[615] The defendants baited consum-ers with one home, then switched them to another highly overpriced and unaffordable home at last minute, presented an inflated appraisal, and steered them to a lender and an attorney who would not protect their interests.

More general allegations of unconscionability can survive a motion to dismiss where the homeowners alleged that the substantive terms of the loan were one-sided, that they were charged ten points, that the lender and broker held them-selves out as experts, that the borrowers had no choice as to the terms offered, and that the defendants contrived to trap the borrowers into making a loan that would inevitably default.[616]

12.7.4 Challenging Terms Other Than Interest Rate as Unconscionable

Unconscionability may be well-suited to challenge the non-interest rate tools used to quietly extract an excessive price for credit. It is especially appropriate to apply the unconscionability doctrine to these transactions since so few consumers are able to detect, much less understand, these methods of increasing the cost of credit.[617]

Unconscionability was successfully invoked to challenge a creditor's subtle manipulation of the non-interest rate terms of a loan, with the result that the cost of the loan more than doubled, though there was no additional benefit to the consumer. In *Besta v. Beneficial Loan Co.*, the concepts of substantive and procedural unconscionability overlapped.[618]

Beneficial doubled the cost of a loan by stretching the repayment term for a mere $1,450 loan proceeds to six years, and then packed the loan with insurance premiums for a six-year loan. In addition to doubling the cost of the loan, the insurance packing also took the amount financed over the statutory threshold necessary to enable the creditor to take a security interest in the borrower's residence.[619] (Real estate closing fees were then added, as well.)

The Eighth Circuit found the loan "substantively unfair" because there was no reasonable basis for a six-year repay-ment period. However, it based its decision on a finding of procedural unconscionability, holding there was lack of fair notice and unfair surprise in the creditor's failure to tell the borrower that she could have repaid the same loan for less money with lower monthly payments in half the time. Thus, in essence, the procedural unconscionability lay in the credi-tor's failure to tell the consumer that a much cheaper alternative was available to her. The court specifically stated that this ruling was not based on a quasi-fiduciary duty of disclosure of disadvantageous terms, but it noted that the average borrower could not have ascertained the existence of more advantageous options even by careful reading of the contract. Though Iowa codified unconscionability standards in its consumer credit code, the court specifically predicated its ruling upon both common law and statutory unconscio-nability. *Besta* thus should be good precedent even in states without a statutory unconscionability provision.[620]

---

615 M&T Mortg. Corp. v. Miller, 323 F. Supp. 2d 405 (E.D.N.Y. 2004).

616 Young v. First Am. Fin. Servs., 977 F. Supp. 38 (D.D.C. 1997); *see also* Fidler v. Central Coop. Bank, (*In re* Fidler), 210 B.R. 411 (Bankr. D. Mass. 1997) (borrowers survived summary judgment by alleging only that there was a gross disparity between the cost of the loan to the borrowers and the benefit given).

617 Cathy Lesser Mansfield and Alan White, *Literacy and Contract*, 13 Stan. L. & Policy Rev. 503 (2003).

618 855 F.2d 532 (8th Cir. 1988). *See also* Knapp v. American Gen. Fin. Inc., 111 F. Supp. 2d 758 (S.D. W. Va. 2000) (packing loan with several credit insurance products may be unconscionable due to fraudulent representation by lender that insurance was required when it was not); Vance v. National Benefit Ass'n, 1999 U.S. Dist. LEXIS 13846 (N.D. Ill. Aug. 26, 1999)(uncon-scionability claim survived motion to dismiss in membership and credit card deal; consumer purchased membership [fee was $1,209] in an association and was entitled to certain "benefits;" among them, an unsecured credit card with a starting limit of $300; consumer signed a retail installment contract to pay the membership fee but had to put down $219 which is charged to the credit card leaving only a small amount in available credit; credit card had interest rate of 19.9%).

619 See § 8.5.4.2, *supra*, for further discussion of this case. The court considered evidence that the same amount could have been loaned at the same (high) interest rate, been fully insured for the creditor's benefit, had lower monthly payments for the borrower's benefit, and cost half as much.

620 Common law unconscionability may be limited to a defensive shield, though. *See* § 12.7.5, *infra*.

Loan flipping, the refinancing of an old loan into a new one generally by the existing creditor,[621] can be expensive for the consumer (and lucrative for the lender). Unconscionability can be one way to attack this problem. In one case, a door-to-door salesman sold a homeowner a solar water heater for $6,512 which never functioned properly and was subsequently declared a hazard. The solar heater company's sales were financed by a finance company that charged 19.5% interest over a ten-year period resulting in a total finance charge of almost $9,000. To make matters worse, a security interest was taken in the home as well as the water heater. During the course of the term of this loan, the homeowner approached the finance company to borrow $800 for unrelated purposes. Instead of adding this sum to the outstanding balance of the existing loan or making a separate small loan, the lender refinanced the existing loan, added the $800, and sold the homeowner a $313 term life insurance policy. The term of the new loan was six years at 19.5% interest per year. An Arizona court found that such a transaction presents a question of grossly excessive price since the homeowner could end up paying half of $40,000, the value of her home, for a non-functioning water heater.[622] The "apparent injustice and oppression" in placing a mortgage on her home as security may also constitute substantive unconscionability. (In a separate but related holding of significance, the court dismissed the lender's argument that the doctrine of novation, the substitution by mutual agreement of a new debt for an existing one which is thereby extinguished, prevented the court from applying the doctrine of unconscionability to scrutinize the original loan. The court held that a condition precedent to a novation is a previous valid debt. As the previous debt might be unenforceable because the contract was unconscionable, novation does not prevent the court from analyzing the prior transaction.)

Padding the non-interest charges tacked onto credit is a common tool for exacting extra profit from consumers,[623] and these, too, may be vulnerable. Price unconscionability cases in retail credit sales,[624] for example, may help in challenging the price of loan add-ons inflated to hide interest.[625] Some of the charges for credit-related services, such as broker fees, appraisal fees, and attorney fees, may be so far above market price as to subject them to challenge.[626]

---

barrier as procedural unconscionability, but did not make it clear whether procedural unconscionability was a necessary prerequisite to the finding that the purchase price was excessive. In Lefkowitz v. ITM, Inc., 275 N.Y.S.2d 303 (N.Y. Sup. Ct. 1966), a merchant sold exorbitantly priced items in a fraudulently deceptive manner. Despite the obvious procedural unconscionability in the scheme, the court held that retail installment contracts in which the prices charged ranged from two to six times the cost per unit were unconscionable as a matter of law. Toker v. Pearl, 247 A.2d 701 (N.J. Super. Ct. Law Div. 1966), *aff'd*, 260 A.2d 244 (N.J. Super. Ct. App. Div. 1970) found that the seller had charged an exorbitant price and held that the contract was unconscionable. On appeal, the appellate division affirmed on the grounds of fraud, specifically expressing no opinion on the trial court's finding that the excessive price alone made the contract unenforceable. In Jones v. Star Credit Corp., 298 N.Y.S.2d 264 (N.Y. Sup. Ct. 1969), a welfare recipient entered into an installment sales contract with a door-to-door salesman for a freezer. The contract price, $1,234.80, was more than four times the retail value of $300. The court found the price charged unconscionable as a matter of law. In Toker v. Westerman, 274 A.2d 78 (N.J. Super. Ct. 1970), a New Jersey court held that a purchase price of $1,229.76 for a freezer worth between $350 and $400 was unconscionable, even though no misconduct took place in the bargaining process. The buyer had already paid $655.87 toward the freezer. Given the market value of approximately $400, the court regarded the amount paid as fair compensation for the freezer, relieving the buyer of the duty to pay the remaining balance, but failing to return to the buyer any of the amount paid. In Kugler v. Romain, 279 A.2d 640 (N.J. 1971), the defendants sold books worth approximately $110 for $279.95. The court held that when a seller charged a price two and one half times the reasonable market value and when the goods were defective, the excessive price alone rendered the contract unconscionable. *See also In re* Fleet, 95 B.R. 319 (E.D. Pa. 1989) ($195–$260 to credit counselor for services amounting to nothing more than referral to a bankruptcy lawyer was unconscionable); *In re* Wernly, 91 B.R. 702 (Bankr. E.D. Pa. 1988) (check-cashing fee of over 10% of face value is unconscionable where normal fee in the industry is 2%); Associates Home Equity Servs., Inc. v. Troup, 778 A.2d 529 (N.J. Super. Ct. App. Div. 2001) (dismissal of unconscionability claim reversed where allegations revealed that the higher interest rates and points charged the borrowers may not have been warranted).

625 *See* §§ 7.2.1, 7.3, 7.4.6, *supra.*

626 *See, e.g., In re* Dukes, 24 B.R. 404 (Bankr. E.D. Mich. 1982); U.S. Home & Realty Corp. v. Lehnartz, Clearinghouse No. 43,259, Case No. 87-SP-930 (Mich. Dist. Ct. Sept. 30, 1987). *See also In re* Fleet, 95 B.R. 319 (E.D. Pa. 1989) (fees of $195–$260 to a purported credit counseling service for referring consumers to a bankruptcy lawyer, a service available for free elsewhere, was an unconscionable price; court noted particularly that consumers were financially troubled and distraught, many unemployed, disabled, and facing foreclosure. Query whether similar reasoning may be applied to a "loan broker" who simply refers the consumer to a readily accessible lender such as a finance company. *But see* Fanning v. Fritz's Pontiac-Cadillac-Buick, Inc., 472 S.E.2d 242 (S.C. 1996) ($87.00 "procurement fee" added to the sales price of cars by a dealer was

---

621 *See* § 6.1, *supra.*

622 Maxwell v. Fidelity Fin. Servs., Inc., 907 P.2d 51 (Ariz. 1995). *See also* Hager v. American Gen. Fin., Inc., 37 F. Supp. 2d 778 (D. W. Va. 1999)(summary judgment for lender on borrower's unconscionability claim denied where borrowers alleged that the defendants induced them to enter into and refinance high interest rate loans and to mortgage their residence without realizing the magnitude of the debt they were incurring or the ramifications of these transactions).

623 *See* Ch. 7, *supra.*

624 For example, in Forstifresh Corp. v. Reynoso, 274 N.Y.S.2d 757 (N.Y. Dist. Ct. 1966), *rev'd as to damages*, 281 N.Y.S.2d 964 (N.Y. App. Term 1967), the sellers used an installment sale contract written in English to sell a refrigerator to Spanish-speaking buyers. The refrigerator cost the seller $348, but the sale price, including the credit payments, was $1,145.80. The court declared the contract unconscionable because of the excessive price. The opinion in dicta also stressed the language

Applying a statutory definition, a Tennessee court held that a creditor which imposed substantial late charges with no contractual authority in order to pressure repayment engaged in unconscionable conduct.[627]

Bank fees, unrelated to credit, have been challenged under California's unconscionability provisions. In *Perdue v. Crocker National Bank*,[628] the California Supreme Court held that a bank's charge for its expenses—in this case its insufficient funds check charge—could be unconscionable. The ruling came in a motion to dismiss, so no determination on the merits was made. But the court looked at the law on price unconscionability, and found that such factors as the market price for the service or good, the cost of the goods or services to the seller, the inconvenience imposed on the seller, and the true value of the product or service should be considered.[629]

In *Perdue*, the check charge was six dollars, while plaintiff alleged the actual cost to the bank to be between thirty cents and one dollar—at least a 600% profit margin.[630] Combined with the procedural unconscionability factors— that the contracts were essentially adhesion contracts, and there was an absence of equal bargaining power, full disclosure, or open negotiations—the court held that an evidentiary hearing should be allowed to determine whether a fee so far in excess of its cost was unconscionable.[631] In

contrast, a mark-up from a $1.50 cost to a $3.00 charge did not shock an appellate court's conscience, particularly as that was at the low end of the scale charged by other banks for the same fee.[632] *Perdue* may be helpful in looking at some of the creditor expenses described in Chapter 7, *supra*, if they seem excessively high.

Other forms of creditor overreaching meet the general standards for unconscionability as summarized in the UCCC codification: selling credit insurance to persons who do not qualify for benefits under the policy's terms; equity-skimming;[633] or some types of hidden interest schemes as described in earlier chapters.[634] Variable rate contracts may be misused in such a way as to trigger a challenge. Though mortgage loans must now include a contractual cap,[635] it can be set as high as the lender chooses, subject to any applicable usury cap.[636] Further, outside of mortgage credit no contractual cap is required, if it is a deregulated transaction. One commentator has suggested that using a variable rate provision to raise payments to a point where a borrower cannot meet them may be vulnerable to an unconscionability or unfairness challenge, at least absent either a reasonable cap or a clear and meaningful disclosure at the outset of the worst-case scenario.[637] Other substantive provisions of the loan may be unconscionable. For example, a cross-collateralization clause which gives a security interest in the consumer's property to secure all past and future debts may not

---

not unconscionable; the definition of unconscionability in consumer credit sales is limited by South Carolina statute to "gross disparity" between price charged and price at which similar property or services are readily obtainable by like consumers; court also believed that the disclosure of the fee gave the consumer the ability to negotiate it; consumer claims attacking the fee on grounds of fraud, misrepresentation, unfair trade practices survived summary judgment, however).

627 Bank of Crockett v. Culliper, 752 S.W.2d 84 (Tenn. Ct. App. 1988) (late charge increased obligation by $933 every 10 days; applying Tenn. Code Ann. § 47-14-117 which defines knowing imposition of excess charges, among other things, as unconscionable conduct).

628 702 P.2d 503 (Cal. 1985), *appeal dismissed*, 475 U.S. 1001 (1986), interpreting Cal. Civ. Code § 1670.5. *But see* Gruber v. Fed. Nat'l Mortgage Ass'n, 2003 WL 1091046 (Cal. Ct. App. Mar. 13, 2003) (loan assumption fee not unconscionable due to full disclosure that such fee could be imposed and disclosure of the actual amount of the fee prior to the assumption, distinguishing *Perdue*). *See generally* Annotation, Bank's Liability to Customer for Imposing Allegedly Excessive Service Charges, 73 A.L.R.4th 1028.

629 *Perdue*, 702 P.2d at 512.

With respect to the market price, the defendant bank had contended that the charge was at market price, and therefore could not be held unconscionable. The court said that, "[w]hile it is unlikely that a court would find a price set by a freely competitive market to be unconscionable [*citation omitted*], the market price set by an oligopoly should not be immune from scrutiny," and that the other "price justification" factors should be reviewed as well.

630 *Id.* at 513.

631 *Id.* at 513–14. *But see* Best v. United States Nat'l Bank, 739 P.2d 554 (Or. 1987) (unconscionability doctrine did not apply because NSF check charge was not a term of the contract; duty of

good faith, which arises with respect to performance of an existing contract, did apply). *See generally* § 12.8, *infra*.

632 California Grocers Ass'n v. Bank of America, 27 Cal. Rptr. 2d 396 (Ct. App. 1994) (the "DIR" fee, charged to a depositor who had the misfortune to have someone else's check bounce, ranged from $4.00 to $10.00 at other institutions).

633 Cheshire Mortgage Serv. v. Montes, 612 A.2d 1130 (Conn. 1992); Family Fin. Servs. v. Spencer, 677 A.2d 479 (Conn. App. Ct. 1996) (loan unconscionable where it called for balloon payment exceeding the principal, payment of a year's interest in advance, and a monthly payment of $733.33 for borrower who had first mortgage payment of $1011.00 and monthly income of $1126.67).

634 See description of scheme in which negative amortization, variable and teaser rates enticed unwitting borrowers into improvident mortgage loans, though case dismissed before reaching the merits due to statute of limitations defense. Salois v. Dime Sav. Bank, 128 F.3d 20 (1st Cir. 1997).

635 12 U.S.C. § 3806.

636 *See generally* §§ 4.3.6, 9.3.2.2, *supra*.

637 Dwight Golann, *Developments in Consumer Financial Services Litigation*, 43 Bus. Law. 1081, 1083–1085 (May 1988).

Variable rate mortgages subject to the Homeownership and Equity Protection Act of 1994 must provide advance-look disclosures which include the worst-case scenario as to monthly payments. 15 U.S.C. § 1639(a)(2)(B). It further specifically prohibits a pattern or practice of improvident lending. 15 U.S.C. § 1639(h). Other variable rate loans are not required to have particularly helpful, transaction-specific payment disclosures. *See, e.g.*, Reg. Z, Appx. G-14A (maximum and historic payment example based on hypothetical home-equity lines of credit); Appx. H-4. *See generally* National Consumer Law Center, Truth in Lending §§ 4.8, 5.5.5.10, 5.11.4.5.13 (5th ed. 2003 and Supp.).

pass scrutiny where the clause is shuffled in among other boilerplate provisions and where the consumer had no prior knowledge or understanding of the provision's effect.[638] A concurrence in a case involving a non-credit contract matter suggests that contracts with one-sided attorney fees provisions (as loans almost always have) may be unconscionable.[639] Requiring bank customers to waive the protection against seizure of their Social Security deposits is unconscionable.[640] Failing to properly disclose a balloon payment as required by state law can be unconscionable.[641] Courts are increasingly turning to the unconscionability doctrine to strike down arbitration clauses.[642]

12.7.5 Remedy for Unconscionability

The remedy for unconscionability is usually limited to a defense against the enforcement of the unconscionable contract or terms, and may not support an affirmative claim for restitutionary damages.[643] Despite this general rule, one court held that the consumer may raise common law unconscionability affirmatively in a declaratory judgment action.[644] Another court determined that unconscionability can be the basis of another cause of action, such as unjust enrichment or a UDAP claim.[645] In addition, state codifications of unconscionability or state UDAP statutes that prohibit unconscionability may offer other relief.[646]

12.8 Duty of Good Faith and Fair Dealing

The duty of good faith and fair dealing between parties to a contract is based both in common law[647] and the UCC.[648] Recent years have seen a greatly increased use of the doctrine in disputes between lenders and their customers,[649] probably as a result of the combination of lenders' expansiveness in the competitive environment in the early days of

---

638 *Cf.* Williams v. Walker-Thomas Furniture Co., 350 F.2d 445 (D.C. Cir. 1965). *But see* Alcantar v. Windsor-Orange County Credit Union, 2000 Tex. App. LEXIS 1576 (Mar. 9, 2000) (where the new advance or cross-collateralization clause is allowed under Texas law, its mere presence in the contract does not render it unconscionable); Bastaich v. Kenworth Northwest, Inc., 1997 Wash. App. LEXIS 635 (Wash. Ct. App. Apr. 28, 1997) (cross-collateralization clause not unconscionable because buyer knew of its existence, negotiated to change it, and, having failed, signed the contract).

639 HILB, Rogal & Hamilton Agency of Dayton, Inc. v. Reynolds, 610 N.E.2d 1102 (Ohio Ct. App. 1992) (concurring op.) (the contract provided for reimbursement of employer's attorneys fees to enforce an anti-piracy provision, but none for employees who prevailed. Court notes that California and Washington have statutes which mandate that contractual attorney fee provisions be reciprocal).

640 Miller v. Bank of America, 2004 WL 3153009 (Cal. Super. Mar. 4, 2005) (unpublished, citation limited).

641 Mallory v. Mortgage America, Inc., 67 F. Supp. 2d 601 (S.D. W. Va. 1999).

642 *See* § 10.6.10, *supra.*

643 Cowin Equip. Co. v. General Motors Corp., 734 F.2d 1581 (11th Cir. 1984); Williams v. E.F. Hutton Mortgage Corp., 555 So. 2d 158 (Ala. 1989); Gonzales v. Associates Fin. Serv., 967 P.2d 312 (Kan. 1998) (unconscionability can only be raised defensively under Kansas law; court observed, however, that a loan origination fee, though legal in amount under the Kansas U.C.C.C., may be unconscionable given the totality of a particular creditor's conduct; dissent finds summary judgment on unconscionability claim inappropriate in this flipping case given the totality of the circumstances); Best v. United States Nat'l Bank, 714 P.2d 1049 (1986), *aff'd on other grounds,* 739 P.2d 554 (Or. 1987). *But see* Johnson v. Tele-Cash, Inc., 82 F. Supp. 2d 264, 278–79 (D. Del. 1999)(court should not require the consumer to breach the loan agreement in order to become subject to the lawsuit so that she can then raise the defense of unconscionability). *See generally*, Steven W. Bender, *Rate Regulation at the Crossroads of Usury and Unconscionability: The Case for Regulating Abusive and Commercial Interest Rates Under the Unconscionability Standard,* 31 Hous. L. Rev. 721 (1994).

644 Eva v. Midwest Nat'l Mortgage Banc., Inc., 143 F. Supp. 2d 862, 895 (N.D. Ohio 2001).

645 *In re* First Alliance Mortgage Co., 280 B.R. 246 (C.D. Cal. 2002).

646 *See, e.g.,* D.C. Code Ann. § 28-3904(r); Iowa Code § 537.5108 (court may refuse to enforce unconscionable agreement in whole or in part, consumer may be awarded actual damages and attorneys fees).

647 Restatement (Second) of Çontracts § 205 (1979). *See also* Carreau & Co. v. Security Pacific Business Credit, Inc., 272 Cal. Rptr. 387, 398 (Ct. App. 1990); Cadle Co. v. Vargas, 771 N.E.2d 179 (Mass. App. 2002); Am. Bankers' Ins. Co. v. Wells, 819 So. 2d 1196, 1206–07 (Miss. 2001) (lender's purchase of force-placed insurance on gross rather than net balance may be a violation); GMAC v. Baymon, 732 So. 2d 262, 269 (Miss. 1999) (duty exists in all contracts, but lender's purchase of force-placed insurance her was not a breach); Noonan v. First Bank Butte, 740 P.2d 631 (Mont. 1987) (tortious breach of covenant of good faith and fair dealing requires action which is arbitrary, capricious or unreasonable and exceeds plaintiff's justifiable expectations); Kirke La Shelle Co. v. Paul Armstrong Co., 188 N.E. 163, 167 (N.Y. 1933) ("in every contract there exists an implied covenant of good faith and fair dealing"); Southface Condo. Owners Ass'n, Inc. v. Southface Condo. Ass'n, 733 A.2d 55, 58 (Vt. 1999). *Cf.* Arnold v. National County Mut. Fire Ins. Co., 725 S.W.2d 165 (Tex. 1987) (duty of good faith and fair dealing arises as a result of special relationship between contracting parties or if agreed to in contract; such relationship exists between insurer and insured). *But see* Lovell v. Western Nat'l Life Ins. Co., 754 S.W.2d 298 (Tex. 1988) (no duty of good faith and fair dealing between mortgagor and mortgagee absent special circumstances or explicit agreement); Victoria Bank & Trust Co. v. Brady, 779 S.W.2d 893, 902 (Tex. App. 1989) (no duty of good faith in absence of special relationship; debtor-creditor relationship insufficient), *aff'd in relevant part, rev'd in part on other grounds,* 811 S.W.2d 931 (Tex. 1991).

648 U.C.C. § 1-203.

649 *See generally* Symons, *The Bank-Customer Relation: Part II—The Judicial Decisions,* 100 Banking L.J. 325, 346–353 (1983); Johnson & Gaffney, *Lender Liability: Perspectives on Risk and Prevention,* 105 Banking L.J. 325 (1988); Annotation, *Bank's Liability for Breach of Implied Contract of Good Faith and Fair Dealing,* 55 A.L.R.4th 1026 (1987).

deregulation, followed shortly by a recession which led to a tightening up by the lenders.[650] The borrower, of course, is equally subject to the duty of good faith.[651]

Unlike unconscionability, which is ordinarily determined by looking at contract terms at the time the contract was made, the duty of good faith is imposed on parties to an existing contract "to prohibit improper behavior in the performance and enforcement" of that contract.[652] Thus, while onerous contract terms might be subject to challenge under other theories, such as unconscionability, UDAP, or fraud, the duty of good faith and fair dealing may be useful to challenge creditor overreaching in later stages of the relationship.[653] There is disagreement about the degree to which the duty of good faith and fair dealing circumscribes conduct specifically authorized by the contract.[654]

Much of the litigation of the 1980s took place in the commercial lending context, where the factual situation often included the lender's unwarranted intrusion into the conduct of the debtor's business.[655] The extent to which this precedent transfers into the consumer arena still is unclear. However, the policy behind the doctrine—to exclude conduct which "violate[s] community standards of decency, fairness or reasonableness"[656]—is certainly equally applicable in the consumer context. In some respects, the policy is stronger in the consumer context, where there is generally not equal bargaining power, many of the terms are not subject to negotiation, and the borrower is usually less sophisticated than business borrowers.[657]

At least two kinds of contract enforcement issues, sometimes used to the disadvantage of consumers in some equity-skimming or churning schemes, are arguably subject to the duty. For example, the credit terms may include a balloon payment, which the creditor knew the borrower would be unlikely to meet.[658] At the loan's maturity, the borrower

---

650 Johnson & Gaffney, *Lender Liability: Perspectives on Risk and Prevention*, 105 Banking L.J. 325, 496 (1988).

651 Teachers Insurance & Annuity Ass'n of America v. Butler, 626 F. Supp. 1229 (S.D.N.Y. 1986); Liebergesell v. Evans, 613 P.2d 1170 (Wash. 1980).

652 Baldwin v. Laurel Ford Lincoln-Mercury, Inc., 32 F. Supp. 2d 894 (S.D. Miss. 1998) (recognizing the duty but finding it inapplicable to a claim that consumer did not get the best terms available; the duty concerns the performance of the contract, not the negotiation leading to the agreement); Best v. United States Nat'l Bank, 739 P.2d 554 (Or. 1987) (bank must use good faith in exercising its discretion to set NSF fees; reversing summary judgment for bank because there were genuine issues of material fact. *See also* Continental Bank v. Modansky, 997 F.2d 309 (7th Cir. 1988) (no duty of good faith and fair dealing in contract negotiations); Birt v. Wells Fargo Home Mortgage, Inc., 75 P.3d 640 (Wyo. 2003) (duty does not arise until the parties have reached an agreement and does not bind them during earlier negotiations). *Cf.* Teachers Ins. & Annuity Ass'n of America v. Butler, 626 F. Supp. 1229 (S.D.N.Y. 1986) (implied duty of good faith and fair dealing includes a duty of good-faith negotiation where parties are already subject to a binding commitment agreement); LLMD of Michigan v. Marine Midland Realty Credit, 789 F. Supp. 657 (E.D. Pa. 1992) (same, thus where binding loan commitment made, future negotiations of final terms subject to duty; Michigan law).

653 Fisher v. American Gen. Fin. Co., 52 Fed. Appx. 601, 2002 WL 31760189 (4th Cir. Dec. 11, 2002) (taking a security interest in a larger parcel of land than the parties agreed upon can subject the creditor to this duty; but not breached here where the evidence of other dishonest acts of the creditor was not admissible); Osburn v. Community Home Mortg., L.L.C., Civil Action No. 02-C-1164 (W. Va. Cir. Ct., Kanawha Cty. Jan. 13, 2005) ($75,000 jury verdict for breach of duty of good faith where consumer alleged that lender insisted that she make payments by Western Union and refused to allow her to make payments on 15th of month despite its agent's representation). *But see* Johnstone v. Bank of America, 173 F. Supp. 2d 809 (N.D. Ill. 2001) (no independent cause of action for the breach of the duty of good faith and fair dealing, relying on *Voyles*); Citibank, N.A. v. Gifesman, 773 A.2d 993 (Conn. App. 2001) (the implied duty cannot be applied to achieve a result contrary to the clear expressed contract terms, unless those terms are contrary to public policy); Voyles v. Sandia Mortgage Co., 751 N.E.2d 1126 (Ill. 2001) (Illinois does not recognize an independent cause of action for the breach of the duty of good faith and fair dealing. The line, though, may be quite fine at times. *Compare* Perdue v. Crocker Nat'l Bank, 702 P.2d 503 (Cal. 1985), *appeal dismissed*, 475 U.S. 1001 (1986) (both unconscionability and duty of good faith implicated in the

bank's imposing NSF charges) *with* Best v. United States Nat'l Bank, 739 P.2d 554 (Or. 1987) (unconscionability doctrine not applicable to bank's NSF charges, because the specific fee was not part of agreement; duty of good faith and fair dealing was applicable).

654 *Compare* Duffield v. First Interstate Bank, 13 F.3d 1403 (10th Cir. 1993) (duty of good faith and fair dealing limits right to act unreasonably even if express terms of contract appear to permit unreasonableness; upholding $6 million jury verdict for failure to act in good faith in workout arrangements upon default) *and* Brazell v. First Nat'l Bank & Trust, 982 F.2d 206 (7th Cir. 1992) (good faith is a "gap-filler," and does not apply to contingencies expressly provided for in the contract; Illinois law) *with* Alan's of Atlanta, Inc. v. Minolta Corp., 903 F.2d 1414 (11th Cir. 1990) (implied covenant of good faith and fair dealing is not an independent contract term, but a doctrine governing the performance of the explicit contract terms); Deerman v. Federal Home Loan Mortgage Corp., 955 F. Supp. 1393 (N.D. Ala. 1997) (interpreting New York and Alabama common law to hold that covenant of good faith cannot expand contract rights beyond the terms of the contract; no breach of duty where mortgage contracts did not require FHLMC to notify the borrowers of any right to cancel private mortgage insurance but required borrowers to maintain insurance until the entire indebtedness was repaid); *and* Azar v. Prudential Ins. Co., 68 P.3d 909 (N.M. App. 2003) (implied covenant cannot be used to challenge charges expressly authorized by insurance contract).

655 *See, e.g.*, KMC Co. v. Irving Trust Co., 757 F.2d 752 (6th Cir. 1985); State Nat'l Bank v. Farah Mfg. Co., 678 S.W.2d 661 (Tex. App. 1984) (dismissed by agreement Mar. 6, 1985) (lender's conduct did not comport with standards of fair play). *See generally* Johnson & Gaffney, *Lender Liability: Perspectives on Risk and Prevention*, 105 Banking L.J. 325 (1988).

656 Restatement (Second) of Contracts § 205 (1979), Comment a.

657 One factor in a laundry list of "bad faith" conduct is "abuse of power to specify terms." Restatement (Second) of Contracts § 205, Comment a (1979).

658 Note that this conduct may violate unconscionability standards as well. *See* § 12.7, *supra*.

must then refinance or face foreclosure. While ordinarily a creditor's decision as to whether to extend credit is not subject to the duty, the creditor may be subject to some mandatory obligation to refinance such a loan, in which case the refinancing decision would be subject to the duty of good faith and fair dealing.[659] In a some circumstances, the mandate may be by virtue of statute.[660] Or, if the creditor initially made oral assurances which rise to the level of an enforceable promise to the borrower that the balloon would be refinanced, the duty of good faith would arguably apply,[661] particularly where the borrower's financial position

had not changed significantly. Practitioners should be aware that the industry subsequently succeeded in getting special legislation in many states to protect them from claims based on such promises, though the new statutes may affect primarily commercial lending.[662]

A second area where the doctrine may be useful relates to the creditor's decision to accelerate and foreclose on collateral, which has also been held to be subject to the duty of good faith and fair dealing.[663] Charging fees at the time of

---

659 *See, e.g.,* Flagship Nat'l Bank v. Gray Distribution Sys., Inc., 485 So. 2d 1336 (Fla. Dist. Ct. App. 1986).

660 *See, e.g.,* U.C.C.C. §§ 2-405, 3-402 (1968); § 3-308 (1974); Ala. Code § 5-19-7; Ky. Rev. Stat. Ann. § 367.390; and some RISA statutes, e.g., Del. Code Ann. tit. 6, § 4326. (Note that even if such statutes apply to home equity lending in some circumstances they may be preempted by federal law. *See* § 3.3.1, *supra.*)

661 *Cf.* Reid v. Key Bank of S. Maine, Inc., 821 F.2d 9 (1st Cir. 1987) (arbitrary termination of line of credit arrangement); KMC Co. v. Irving Trust Co., 757 F.2d 752 (6th Cir. 1985) (financing agreement authorized line of credit, and borrower and creditor had course of dealing regarding advance; despite demand provision in contract, duty of good faith required notice to borrower to permit it time to find alternative financing where creditor refused further advances); Weinberg v. Farmers State Bank, 752 P.2d 719 (Mont. 1988) (bank encouraged agricultural borrowers to expand, and under facts as found by jury, breached implied covenant of good faith and fair dealing in raising interest rates arbitrarily, capriciously, and unreasonably, and against justifiable expectation of parties). *But see* Roberts v. Wells Fargo Agric. Credit Corp., 990 F.2d 1169 (10th Cir. 1993) (bank's failure to renew a line of credit *despite* a purported oral agreement to do so was not subject to duty of good faith, but court notes that under Oklahoma law, a false representation as to a future act may be fraudulent if it was "accompanied by an intent not to perform and the promise is made with the intent to deceive the promisee into acting where he otherwise would not have done so." *Id.* at 1172); Terry A. Lambert Plumbing, Inc. v. Western Sec. Bank, 934 F.2d 976 (8th Cir. 1991) (no duty to refinance troubled loan); Kham & Nates Shoes No. 2, Inc. v. First Bank, 908 F.2d 1351 (7th Cir. 1990) (same); Price v. Wells Fargo Bank, 261 Cal. Rptr. 735, 742 (Cal. Ct. App. 1989) (contractual duty of good faith does not impose affirmative duty of moderation in enforcing creditor's legal rights; borrower's claims that loan officer promised renewals not proven as fraud claim); Shiplet v. First Security, 762 P.2d 242 (Mont. 1988) (facts did not bear out allegations of breach of implied covenant of good faith and fair dealing; bank performed according to reasonable expectations); Bloomfield v. Nebraska State Bank, 465 N.W.2d 144 (Neb. 1991) (though U.C.C. duty of good faith can exist in debtor-creditor relationship, borrower did not prove breach of that duty in creditor's decision to accelerate loan and cancel line of credit; there was no evidence of a promise or implied contract by the bank to continue the line of credit; court distinguishes cases in which creditor accelerated in absence of default and attempted to run the business); Union Bank v. Woell, 434 N.W.2d 712 (N.D. 1989) (U.C.C. obligation of good faith does not exist absent an underlying contract; in the case, the alleged oral commitment to loan was too indefinite to form an enforceable contract to loan money in the future).

662 Because many of the high-award lender liability cases involved allegations of a creditor's failure to honor an oral commitment to lend or refinance, a number of states enacted legislation amending their statute of frauds to preclude enforcement of such agreements absent a signed writing. *See, e.g.,* Ariz. Rev. Stat. Ann. § 44-101(9) (applicable only to large non-consumer loans); Cal. Civ. Code § 1624; Minn. Stat. Ann. § 513.33; N.C. Gen. Stat. § 22-5 (inapplicable to consumer and agricultural loans).

However, some states have drafted the legislation so as to exempt much (or all) consumer borrowing from the statutes' scope. This exemption may be achieved by categorically excluding consumer transactions (*e.g.,* Cal. Civ. Code § 1624); or by placing dollar limitations on the statutes' reach (*e.g.,* Colo. Rev. Stat. § 38-10-124(2) (transactions over $25,000); Tex. Bus. & Com. Code Ann. § 26.02(b) ($50,000 floor)). Real estate mortgages are also excluded in some instances (Kan. Stat. Ann. § 16-117(a); Or. Rev. Stat. § 41.580(1)(h) [it also categorically excludes consumer transactions]).

Anyone considering a claim based on such conduct must check for legislative action in the relevant jurisdiction. For surveys of state legislative activity and related issues, see J. Culhane & D. Gramlich, *Lender Liability Limitation Amendments to State Statutes of Frauds,* 45 Bus. Law. 1779 (June 1990), and Mark E. Budnitz and Helen Davis Chaitman, The Law of Lender Liability ¶ 5.03[2][b] (rev. ed. 1999 & 2004 Supp.).

663 *See, e.g.,* Duffield v. First Interstate Bank, 13 F.3d 1403 (10th Cir. 1993), *cert. denied,* 512 U.S. 1205 (1994)(duty of good faith and fair dealing limits right to act unreasonably even if express terms of contract appear to permit unreasonableness; upholding $6 million jury verdict for failure to act in good faith in workout arrangements upon default); Bank One, Texas, N.A. v. Taylor, 970 F.2d 16 (5th Cir. 1992), *cert. denied,* 508 U.S. 906 (1993)(acceleration of ostensible demand note subject to U.C.C. duty of good faith when fair reading of all documents suggests intention that demand clause would only be invoked in event of default); Knapp v. American Gen. Fin. Inc., 111 F. Supp. 2d 758 (S.D. W. Va. 2000) (claim for breach of duty of good faith and fair dealing is stated where dealer tried to repossess personal property based upon an allegedly invalid security agreement and by employing a repo man whom the lender directed to harass the consumers); *In re* Martin Specialty Vehicles, Inc., 87 B.R. 752 (Bankr. D. Mass. 1988), *rev'd on jurisdictional grounds,* 97 B.R. 721 (D. Mass. 1989)($500,000 contract damages for bad faith foreclosures where default was minor and could have been cured by ordinary practice of bank set-off); *In re* Peterson, 93 B.R. 323 (Bankr. D. Vt. 1988) (refusing to dismiss claim for breach of covenant and good faith dealing arising out of purported unlawful declaration of acceleration and overreaching in obtaining modification of original agreement); Farmers & Merchants Bank v. Hancock, 506 So. 2d 305, *modified,* 510 So. 2d 201 (Ala. 1987) (U.C.C. duty of good faith); Am. Bankers' Ins. Co. v. Wells, 819 So. 2d 1196, 1206–07 (Miss. 2001) (jury

payoff or default that are not authorized by statute or the loan documents may also violate this duty, though consumers have more often alleged breach of contract and UDAP claims in this context.[664] Similarly, the duty may be breached where the lender consistently overstated the payoff amount and improperly capitalized certain costs that should have been assessed as separate fees, all of which prevented the consumer from paying off the mortgage which led to foreclosure.[665] One court held that a mortgagee breaches its duty of good faith by refusing to postpone a foreclosure sale when the homeowner had a binding unconditional contract

to sell.[666] A related line of cases holds that lenders participating in guaranteed mortgage programs such as FHA and VA should explore nonmandatory forbearance alternatives to foreclosure, and their failure to do so is an equitable defense to a foreclosure suit.[667]

Creditor behavior which thwarts a consumer's ability to file for and obtain payments to the creditor under a credit disability policy may also state a cause of action under this theory.[668] Similarly, an insurance company has a duty to deal fairly and act in good faith with its insureds. This duty is breached where, in the credit insurance context or otherwise, it deliberately and willfully engages in a pattern of canceling insurance policies as soon as claims are filed without determining whether it has good cause to do so.[669] A lender's practice of force-placing mortgage hazard insurance that is several times more expensive than the homeowner's policy and receiving kickbacks from the insurance companies may also state a claim for breach of the covenant of good faith and fair dealing.[670]

The duty is also breached when the assignee of a loan attempts to enforce a guaranty against the former wife when the loan was entered into by the ex-husband after the wife signed an open-ended guaranty while married, the purpose of which was to resolve marital debts.[671]

In the credit card context, the duty of good faith may not apply to the unilateral cancellation of the card by the creditor

---

question whether lender violated duty of good faith by force-placing insurance on gross rather than net balance for borrowers whose own insurance lapsed); Noonan v. First Bank Butte, 740 P.2d 631 (Mont. 1987) (U.C.C. duty and common law duty both may apply to a transaction; reversed and remanded on basis of improper jury instructions. The dissent describes facts involving bank overreaching in creating the debt, and acting in bad faith in foreclosing); First Nat'l Bank v. Twombly, 689 P.2d 1226 (Mont. 1984) (punitive damages for bad faith acceleration); State Nat'l Bank v. Farah Mfg. Co., 678 S.W.2d 661 (Tex. App. 1984) (dismissed by agreement Mar. 6, 1985) (acceleration clauses do not permit acceleration when the facts make its use unjust or oppressive). *See also* Aronson v. Creditrust Corp., 7 F. Supp. 2d 589 (W.D. Pa. 1998) (employees of credit card company who falsely indicated that the consumer entered into a repayment agreement and breached it, could be liable for the tort of defamation; breach of duty of good faith and fair dealing could be alleged as well); *Lender Liability*, *supra* note 57, at 498 (banks which set up borrowers by promising to work with them during periods of financial distress, getting additional collateral, then "mov[ing] in for the kill" is a classic example of "bad faith").

But see Deerman v. Federal Home Loan Mortgage Corp., 955 F. Supp. 1393 (N.D. Ala. 1997) (interpreting New York and Alabama common law to hold that the covenant of good faith cannot expand contract rights beyond the terms of the contract; no breach of duty where mortgage contracts did not require FHLMC to notify the borrowers of any right to cancel private mortgage insurance but required borrowers to maintain insurance until entire indebtedness was repaid); Price v. Wells Fargo Bank, 261 Cal. Rptr. 735, 742 (Cal. Ct. App. 1989) (contractual duty of good faith does not impose affirmative duty of moderation in enforcing creditor's legal rights); Affiliated Capital v. Commercial Fed. Bank, 834 S.W.2d 521 (Tex. App. 1992) (no breach of duty of good faith where creditor acted in accord with terms of contract in commercial loan). *See generally* National Consumer Law Center, Repossessions and Foreclosures § 4.7 (5th ed. 2002 and Supp.); Annotation, *Bank's Liability for Breach of Implied Contract of Good Faith and Fair Dealing*, 55 A.L.R.4th 1026 (1987); Note, *Mortgage Lender Liability to the Purchasers of New or Existing Homes*, 1988 U. Ill. L. Rev. 191, 211–14.

NOTE: Some of the amendments to state statutes of frauds designed to limit lender liability may affect claims based on oral promises not to accelerate. *See* note 562, *supra*.

664 *See* §§ 5.8.1, 11.5.5, 12.5, *supra*.

665 Chedick v. Nash, 151 F.3d 1077 (D.C. Cir. 1998) (recognizing tort of promissory fraud, i.e., misrepresentation of present intent to perform an act in the future; the act here was its duty to act in good faith).

666 Snowden v. Chase Manhattan Mortgage Corp., 2003 WL 22519518 (Mass. Super. Ct. Nov. 5, 2003).

667 FNMA v. Wingate, 273 N.W.2d 448 (Mich. 1979); Associated E. Mortgage Co. v. Young, 394 A.2d 899 (N.J. Super. Ct. App. Div. 1978); Federal Nat'l Mortgage Ass'n v. Ricks, 372 N.Y.S.2d 485 (Sup. Ct. 1975); Union Nat'l Bank v. Cobbs, 567 A.2d 719 (Pa. Super. Ct. 1989); Fleet Real Estate Funding Corp. v. Smith, 530 A.2d 919 (Pa. Super. Ct. 1987). *See also* Prudential Ins. Co. v. Jackson, 637 A.2d 573 (N.J. Super. Ct. App. Div. 1994). *See generally* National Consumer Law Center, Repossessions and Foreclosures Chs. 16, 17, 20–22 (5th ed. 2002 and Supp.).

668 *See, e.g.*, Chandler v. General Motors Acceptance Corp., 426 N.E.2d 521 (Ohio Ct. App. 1980) (denying summary judgment to GMAC in deficiency suit where GMAC refused to complete its portion of credit disability insurance claim form but later repossessed the car; while only breach of contract and wrongful repossession claims were raised, a breach of the duty of good faith and fair dealing could have been raised).

669 For a good example with a recitation of the type of proof obtained by the deceased consumer's spouse, see Vining v. Enterprise Fin. Group, Inc., 148 F.3d 1206 (10th Cir. 1998).

670 Washington Mutual Bank v. Superior Court, 82 Cal. Rptr. 2d 564 (Cal. Ct. App.), *modified*, 70 Cal. App. 4th 1287, *further proceedings*, 15 P.3d 1071 (Cal. 2001) (nationwide class certification in a mortgage loan case reversed and remanded due to trial court's failure to adjudicate effect of choice of law provision in the mortgages). *But see* General Motors Acceptance Corp. v. Baymon, 732 So. 2d 262 (Miss. 1999)(while all contracts contain the duty, record reflected that GMAC operated according to the loan agreement in force-placing insurance by repeatedly notifying the consumer to allow her to obtain other insurance).

671 Cadle Co. v. Vargas, 771 N.E.2d 179 (Mass. App. 2002).

where the credit card agreement permits the termination for any reason.[672] However, one court has held that prior notice of the cancellation is required regardless of whether the card agreement calls for it.[673]

In sorting through the conflicting cases on the duty of good faith in lender liability cases, it is important to note the distinction between those sounding in tort and those sounding in contract. While the contractual obligation is firmly established and applies to every contract, tort liability for breach of the covenant of good faith is less widely recognized. Tort liability may require a showing of some special relationship, beyond that of lender and customer, such as special circumstances giving rise to a fiduciary or quasi-fiduciary relationship or other indicia of a heightened duty.[674]

12.9 Fiduciary or Quasi-Fiduciary Duty

12.9.1 Duties of a Fiduciary; Remedies for Breach of Fiduciary Duty

A fiduciary owes its principal a duty of loyalty.[675] As the agent in a principal/agent relationship, the fiduciary has a duty to act in the best interests of the principal.[676] The existence of a fiduciary or quasi-fiduciary duty at the least gives rise to a duty of fair and honest disclosure of all facts which might be presumed to influence the consumer in regard to his or her actions,[677] including those favorable to the creditor or a third party and adverse to the borrower's interest.[678] Certainly this includes "the fullest disclosure . . . and fullest comprehension" by the principal of a dual agency, where the agent arranges a transaction for the principal but is to receive compensation from both parties.[679]

A fiduciary relationship may be express or implied. An express fiduciary relationship is created by contract or by legal proceedings. A fiduciary relationship is implied in law based upon the specific factual circumstances surrounding the transaction and the relationship of the parties.[680]

When there is a duty to disclose, failure to do so should give rise to a tort action for nondisclosure,[681] or the silence may qualify as misrepresentation.[682] A principal has the right to repudiate a contract made by one individual acting as agent of both parties in violation of the agent's fiduciary duty.[683] The principal also may have a claim for damages, including return of commission.[684]

---

672 Shwartz v. American Express Travel Co., 2002 WL 1684440 (E.D. La. July 22, 2002).

673 *Id.*

674 *See, e.g.*, Foley v. Interactive Data Corp., 765 P.2d 373 (Cal. 1988) (tort for breach of implied covenant of good faith and fair dealing not available in employment contract cases; suggesting tort will only be recognized in insurance cases); Mitsui Mfrs. Bank v. Superior Court, 260 Cal. Rptr. 793 (Ct. App. 1989) (no tort liability for breach of duty of good faith). *See also* § 12.9, *infra* (discussion of fiduciary duty).

675 *See, e.g.*, Frey v. Fraser Yachts, 29 F.3d 1153 (7th Cir. 1994).

676 *Id. See also* MIC Life Ins. Co. v. Hicks, 2001 Miss. LEXIS 296 (Oct. 31, 2001) (insurance company's failure to refund unearned insurance premium in a timely way can constitute a breach of this duty; jury award of actual damages plus $6 million in punitive damages against the insurance company upheld in light of evidence of a pattern of failing to refund unearned premiums), *op. withdrawn, reh'g granted*, 825 So. 2d 616 (Miss. 2002) (remanding for a new trial on the issue of the amount of punitive damages).

677 Stewart v. Phoenix Nat'l Bank, 64 P.2d 101, 106 (Ariz. 1937).

678 Barrett v. Bank of America, 229 Cal. Rptr. 16 (Ct. App. 1986).

679 Frey v. Fraser Yachts, 29 F.3d 1153, 1156 (7th Cir. 1994) (undisclosed dual agency of yacht broker, receiving commission from buyer as well as seller, breached fiduciary duty to seller).

680 First Nat'l Bank & Trust Co. of the Treasurer Coast v. Pack, 789 So. 2d 411 (Fla. Dist. Ct. App. 2001) (fiduciary relationship implied in law based upon lender's behavior); Basile v. H&R Block, Inc., 777 A.2d 95 (Pa. Super. Ct. 2001) (confidential relationship can arise between tax preparer and customer depending on the circumstances, even where no agency exists). *See also* Crow v. Fred Martin Motor Co., 2003 WL 1240119 (Ohio Ct. App. Mar. 19, 2003).

681 Restatement (Second) of Torts § 551.

682 First Nat'l Bank v. Brown, 181 N.W.2d 178, 182 (Iowa 1970) (if the misrepresentation amounts to fraud in the inducement "whether innocent or not," that may give the defrauded party the right to avoid the contract in an action in equity). See also cases from the tax refund anticipation loan context where the courts are split on the issue of a fiduciary duty on the part of the tax preparer. Green v. H&R Block, Inc., 735 A.2d 1039 (Md. 1999)(tax preparer found to be agent of consumer thus creating fiduciary duty to advise the consumer that it receives payments and other benefits from the lender for facilitating the making of the loan). *But see* Basile v. H&R Block, Inc., 761 A.2d 1115 (Pa. 2000) (tax preparer not an agent of customer in tax refund loan transaction but see the dissents), *further proceedings*, 777 A.2d 95 (Pa. Super. Ct. 2001) (reversing and remanding trial court decision; tax preparer can create a confidential relationship with its customers, where, as in this case, the tax preparer and customer are in different positions of knowledge and where the tax preparer cultivated customer trust through an extended and extensive media ad campaign, focusing on tax preparer's expertise in tax matters and the trustworthy character of its services); Peterson v. H&R Block Tax Servs., Inc., 971 F. Supp. 1204 (N.D. Ill. 1997) (motion to dismiss on breach of duty of good faith and fair dealing denied; granted as to breach of fiduciary duty [difference in outcome of *Basile* and *Green* relates to how the courts interpret state law on whether the tax preparer is an agent of the consumer]), 174 F.R.D. 78 (N.D. Ill. 1997) (class certification granted on RICO and UDAP claim), 22 F. Supp. 2d 795 (N.D. Ill. 1998) (RICO claim dismissed due to inability to show H&R Block's deliberate fraud in failing to advise customers that tax refunds where the earned income tax credit is sought may be delayed beyond three weeks; state law claim remanded to state court); Carnegie v. H&R Block, Inc., 703 N.Y.S.2d 27 (App. Div. 2000)(RAL transaction not alleged to occur in context of a larger relationship of trust and confidence; no fiduciary duty); Beckett v. H&R Block, Inc., 714 N.E.2d 1033 (Ill. Ct. App. 1999)(tax preparer not an agent; no duty to disclose secret profit to consumer).

683 Frey v. Fraser Yachts, 29 F.3d 1153, 1159 (7th Cir. 1994).

684 *Id.*

12.9.2 Mortgage/Loan Brokers

A mortgage or loan broker[685] has the fiduciary duty of an agent to a principal.[686] This would include the duty to advise the borrower of the disadvantageous terms of a high-rate mortgage with a large balloon payment.[687] Accepting a kickback from a lender[688] who provides additional (hidden) compensation to the agent at the expense of the borrower certainly should breach the fiduciary duty.[689] Furthermore, a lender could be liable to the borrower for inducing a broker to breach its fiduciary duty when the lender knowingly participates in paying a kickback to the broker.[690] Steering a borrower to more expensive, loan-padding lenders to increase the broker's percentage commission certainly smacks of a violation of the duty of loyalty to the borrower as well.

12.9.3 Creditors' Fiduciary or Quasi-Fiduciary Role

Traditionally, there has been no special duty read into the creditor-debtor relationship; the transaction is considered to be an arms' length one in which "the lender is entitled to its profits . . . and the borrower knows this."[691] While a minor-

---

685   Mortgage and loan brokers should be distinguished from real estate brokers. Real estate brokers, in the process of selling property, may aid a prospective buyer in lining up a purchase money mortgage. However, controversial though it is, a real estate broker is legally the agent of the property's seller, unless there is a specific agreement to the contrary. *See, e.g.*, Hagar v. Mobley, 638 P.2d 127 (Wyo. 1981). *Cf. Realtors, Consumers Group Announce Push for Greater Disclosure in Transactions*, 60 Banking Rpt. (BNA) at 64 (Jan. 18, 1993) (announcing a campaign to encourage states to require disclosures clarifying the party whom the agent represents. There is also a growing movement in the real estate market to have "buyers' brokers," who represent the buyer rather than the seller). A state statute may also place some duties, such as honesty toward all parties, on real estate brokers. *See, e.g.*, Tex. Occ. Code § 1101.558.

686   *See, e.g.*, Barker v. Altegra Credit Co. (*In re* Barker), 251 B.R. 250 (Bankr. E.D. Pa. 2000); *In re* Dukes, 24 B.R. 404 (Bankr. E.D. Mich. 1982); Tomlin v. Dylan Mortgage Inc., Clearinghouse No. 54597 (N.C. Super. Ct. June 12, 2000); State v. WWWJ Corp., 980 P.2d 1257 (Wash. 1999)(enforcement action to revoke a mortgage broker's license); Arnold v. United Cos. Lending Corp., 511 S.E.2d 854 (W. Va. 1998); Wyatt v. Union Mortgage Co., 598 P.2d 45 (Cal. 1979). *See also* Watson v. CBSK Fin. Group, Inc., 2002 WL 598521 (N.D. Ill. Apr. 18, 2002) (existence of duty rests on whether there was an agent/principal relationship, which is a question of fact that cannot be determined on a motion to dismiss; Michaelowski v. Flagstar, F.S.B., 2002 U.S. Dist. LEXIS 1245 (N.D. Ill. Jan. 25, 2002) (mortgage broker and borrower relationship is not always one of agency; factual issue in each case so defendant's motion to dismiss denied); High v. McLean Fin. Corp., 659 F. Supp. 1561 (D.D.C. 1987) (defendant who took mortgage application and passed it on to undisclosed lender may have acted as broker and may have had duty to act in good faith with borrower's interests in mind; denying defendant's motion to dismiss); Koch v. First Union Corp., 2002 WL 372939 (Pa. Com. Pl. Jan. 10, 2002) (the existence of the duty depends upon the facts; sufficient facts pled in this case against the contractor and the broker to survive a demurrer). *But cf.* Bell v. Parkway Mortg., Inc. (*In re* Bell), 309 B.R. 139 (Bankr. E.D. Pa. 2004) (broker that had no contact with borrower had no confidential relationship with her, so no fiduciary duty), *reconsideration granted in part on other grounds*, 314 B.R. 54 (Bankr. E.D. Pa. 2004) .

   The National Association of Mortgage Brokers at one point adopted a Code of Ethics which required, among other things, that the brokers duty to the client is paramount:

   ¶ 3. In accepting employment as an agent, the mortgage broker pledges himself to protect and promote the interests of the client. The obligation of absolute fidelity to the client's interest is primary.

687   Wyatt v. Union Mortgage Co., 598 P.2d 45 (Cal. 1979) ($1000 actual and $200,000 punitive damages awarded for broker's failure to counsel borrowers about their interest rate, late charges, and balloon payment and those provisions' consequences).

688   *See* § 11.5.4.3, *supra* for a discussion of the yield spread premium.

689   *Cf.* Frey v. Fraser Yachts, 29 F.3d 1153 (7th Cir. 1994) (undisclosed dual agency of yacht broker, receiving commission from buyer as well as seller, breached fiduciary duty to seller); Briggs v. Countrywide Funding Corp., 931 F. Supp. 1545 (M.D. Ala. 1996) (denying lender's motion to dismiss a variety of claims, including claim that its offer of a yield spread premium induced the mortgage broker to breach alleged fiduciary duties), *vacated on other grounds*, 949 F. Supp. 812 (M.D. Ala. 1996).

690   Cunningham v. Equicredit Corp. of Ill., 256 F. Supp. 2d 785 (N.D. Ill. 2003) (lender's motion to dismiss denied).

691   Sallee v. Fort Knox Nat'l Bank (*In re* Sallee), 286 F.3d 878 (6th Cir. 2002) (ordinarily no fiduciary duty on bank to act in the borrower's interest; fraud claim actionable, however, where the bank kept one appraisal secret while revealing another, as duty to disclose arises from a partial disclosure of information where a party to the contract has superior knowledge; case involved business loans); Landreneau v. Fleet Fin. Group, 197 F. Supp. 2d 551 (M.D. La. 2002) (no duty by lender, though this is not a *per se* rule); Baldwin v. Laurel Ford Lincoln-Mercury, Inc., 32 F. Supp. 2d 894 (S.D. Miss. 1998) (ordinarily, no fiduciary relationship between creditor and debtor; no special facts alleged by consumer to find such a relationship with the car dealer who obtained financing through the car manufacturer); Citibank, N.A. v. Gifesman, 773 A.2d 993 (Conn. App. 2001); Geiger v. Crestar Bank, 778 A.2d 1085 (D.C. App. 2001) (relationship between bank and depositor is governed by the written agreement; ordinarily no fiduciary duty owed by the bank); Huntington Mortgage Co. v. DeBrota, 703 N.E.2d 160 (Ind. App. 1998) (no fiduciary duty between creditor and borrower absent special circumstances); Morton v. Bank of the Bluegrass, 18 S.W.3d 353 (Ky. App. 1999); Holmes v. Peoples State Bank, 796 So. 2d 176 (La. App. 2001) (relationship between bank and depositor is governed by the written agreement; ordinarily no fiduciary duty owed by the bank); Rossbach v. FBS Mortgage Corp., 1998 Minn. App. LEXIS 374 (Apr. 7, 1998); GMAC v. Baymon, 732 So. 2d 262 (Miss. 1999); Koch v. First Union Corp., 2002 WL 372939 (Pa. Com. Pl. Jan. 10, 2002); Hutson v. Wenatchee Fed. Sav. & Loan Ass'n, 588 P.2d 1192, 1198 (Wash. Ct. App. 1979). *See also* Sutton v. Viking Oldsmobile Nissan, Inc., 2001 Minn.

ity of courts seem to view this as a *per se* rule,[692] the majority rule holds that the presence of certain factors in the relationship may give rise to special duties to the borrower, up to and including a fiduciary duty. Query whether a lender or car dealer creates a fiduciary relationship when the lender or dealer require the consumer to sign a power of attorney for any purpose in the transaction? A power of attorney may be signed, for example, when actual title to a car is not readily available and the dealer wishes to transfer title. A car dealer may have a fiduciary relationship to a consumer in regard to credit insurance sold by the dealer to the consumer when the dealer is responsible for handling a refund of the insurance premium in the event the insurance is denied or terminated.[693]

A fiduciary relationship can arise where a party—generally a "weaker" party in the sense of the ability to protect itself—places trust and confidence in another.[694] Such a "duty of confidence"[695] arguably can arise if a lender acts in the role of advisor and knows or should have known the borrower trusted him.[696] As lenders go beyond giving a borrower what he or she has asked for, by offering extra services, a "quasi-fiduciary relationship of trust and confidence" may be created,[697] which at least gives rise to a duty of disclosure.[698] Such a relationship has been found where a lender gave a borrower advice about such things as qualifying for a special lending program, whether to finance a remodeling or a new house, and whether she could afford a certain type of credit insurance.[699] A fiduciary duty may arise when the lender undertakes to pay property taxes from escrow and acts as the agent of the borrower.[700] The attorney or closing agent for the lender ordinarily has no duty to the borrower.[701] However, the lender's settlement agent may

---

App. LEXIS 866 (July 31, 2001) (no fiduciary duty between consumer and car dealer).

692　*See, e.g.,* Centerre Bank v. Distributors, Inc., 705 S.W.2d 42 (Mo. Ct. App. 1985).

　　Note: At least one of the recent legislative amendments to the statute of frauds, designed to limit certain lender liability suits , also states that an agreement to lend money cannot be implied from the relationship, fiduciary or otherwise, between a creditor and a debtor. Minn. Stat. Ann. § 513.33, subd. 3(b).

693　Crow v. Fred Martin Motor Co., 2003 WL 1240119 (Ohio Ct. App. Mar. 19, 2003).

694　Mark Budnitz, *The Sale of Credit Life Insurance: The Bank as Fiduciary,* 62 N.C.L. Rev. 295 (1984).

695　J. Shepherd, The Law of Fiduciaries 31 n.70 (1981).

696　Stewart v. Phoenix Nat'l Bank, 64 P.2d 101, 106 (Ariz. 1937); Boatmen's Nat'l Bank v. Ward, 595 N.E.2d 622, *cert. denied,* 606 N.E.2d 1224 (Ill. App. Ct. 1992); First Nat'l Bank v. Brown, 181 N.W.2d 178, 182 (Iowa 1970); First Am. Nat'l Bank v. Mitchell, 359 So. 2d 1376 (Miss. 1988), *overruled on other grounds* by C&C Trucking v. Smith, 612 So. 2d 1092 (Miss. 1992) (mortgagor and mortgagee are in relationship of trust, mortgagee had duty to disclose higher price was available when it forced sale of collateral); Deist v. Wachholz, 678 P.2d 188 (Mont. 1984). *See also* Capital Bank v. MVB, Inc., 644 So. 2d 515 (Fla. Dist. Ct. App. 1994) (commercial transaction); Birt v. Wells Fargo Home Mortg., Inc., 75 P.3d 640, 660–62 (Wyo. 2003) (fiduciary duty may arise between lender and borrower, but not shown here). *See also* Watson v. CBSK Fin. Group, Inc., 2002 WL 598521 (N.D. Ill. Apr. 18, 2002) (consumer pled that the contractor and broker acted as financial advisors and actively sought to inspire confidence that they would act in the consumer's interest). *Cf.* Victoria Bank & Trust Co. v. Brady, 779 S.W.2d 893, 902 (Tex. App. 1989) (mere subjective trust on part of borrower will not alone create fiduciary relationship), *aff'd in part, rev'd in part on other grounds,* 811 S.W.2d 931 (Tex. 1991). *Compare* Bloomfield v. Nebraska State Bank, 465 N.W.2d 144 (Neb. 1991) (no fiduciary relationship between bank and agricultural borrower where borrower failed to establish bank's opportunity to influence him or other evidence of a special relationship; court also notes borrower's failure to present evidence of disparity in bargaining power, though states

that superior bargaining power alone does not create a fiduciary duty).

697　Johnson v. Robinson (*In re* Johnson), 292 B.R. 821 (Bankr. E.D. Pa. 2003) (acknowledging that lender could have fiduciary responsibilities to borrower under certain circumstances not present here); Morton v. Bank of Bluegrass, 18 S.W.3d 353 (Ky. Ct. App. 1999) (where bank loan officer was also agent of credit insurance company, fiduciary duty to disclose material facts about eligibility arose; summary judgment for lender reversed); Hutson v. Wenatchee Fed. Sav. & Loan Ass'n, 588 P.2d 1192, 1199 (Wash. Ct. App. 1979); Birt v. Wells Fargo Home Mortgage, Inc., 75 P.3d 640 (Wyo. 2003) (recognizing that lender can create fiduciary relationship with borrower, but not on these facts).

698　Restatement (Second) of Torts § 551 (1977). *See also* Deist v. Wachholz, 678 P.2d 188 (Mont. 1984) (where confidential relationship existed between bank and customer, bank employee had duty of disclosure and duty to do nothing which would place customer at a disadvantage).

699　Hutson v. Wenatchee Fed. Sav. & Loan Ass'n, 588 P.2d 1192 (Wash. Ct. App. 1979) (lender therefore had duty to disclose that the mortgage insurance purchased was not the credit life insurance requested by borrowers). *See also* First Nat'l Bank & Trust Co. of the Treasurer Coast v. Pack, 789 So. 2d 411 (Fla. Dist. Ct. App. 2001) (fiduciary relationship created when consumer asked the bank to help with the builder and to make sure the construction moved forward; bank undertook this responsibility and assured the consumer that it would be present at the walk-through and stated that defects would be corrected); Tomaszewski v. McKeon Ford, Inc., 573 A.2d 501 (N.J. Super. Ct. App. Div. 1990) (auto dealer who advised purchaser about how to qualify for credit approval from financier also had duty to advise her concerning credit insurance purchase, and insuring herself instead of co-buyer, who was the principal income earner). *But see* Mans v. Peoples Bank of Imboden, 10 S.W.3d 885 (Ark. 2000) (no fiduciary relationship between bank and customer regarding credit insurance; court ignores fact that the bank acted as agent for the insurance company).

700　Ploog v. Homeside Lending, Inc., 209 F. Supp. 2d 863 (N.D. Ill. 2002).

701　*See, e.g.,* Johnson v. Robinson (*In re Johnson*), 292 B.R. 821 (Bankr. E.D. Pa. 2003); Garrett v. Fleet Fin., Inc., 556 S.E.2d 140 (Ga. App. 2001); Horvath v. Adelson, Golden & Loria, P.C., 773 N.E.2d 478 (Mass. App. 2002) (however, a duty could arise if attorney knew that the non-client would rely on the services rendered; no duty here where attorney stated in writing that he represented lender only). However, if the closing attorney later tries to claim attorney-client privilege to avoid producing closing documents, one can argue that the privilege does not apply where it is contemplated that the documents would be commu-

owe a fiduciary duty to the borrower where it created an escrow account and wrongfully permitted funds to be paid to a home improvement contractor.[702] A settlement agent also may be liable to a borrower under a state "good funds" statute for failing to use collected funds (that is, deposited funds) from the lender to close and fund the loan.[703]

In a case where the proceeds of a small loan were to be used to finance a fraudulent sale, one court held that a financier's knowledge of the fraud in and of itself may give rise to the duty to disclose.[704] Further, it suggested that by accepting the benefits of the fraudulent sale—financing it and profiting from it—it may be held to account for the fraud even if the lender played no role in the fraud at the outset.[705]

A duty to disclose facts which put a lender at an advantage to a borrower in a trust and confidence relationship has been found where banks, knowing it would improve their position vis-a-vis other financially troubled customers of theirs, encouraged prospective borrowers to invest or contract with the bank's troubled customer.[706] One court has held it a question of fact whether a construction lender had a duty to disclose to a borrower facts known to the lender which diminished the value of the house being purchased.[707] The duty of disclosure or a fiduciary duty also may arise with respect to the sale of insurance in the credit context, which is discussed in more detail in §§ 8.7.2 and 8.7.3, *supra*.

It might be arguable that aggressive marketing techniques used by lenders today may suggest a "trust and confidence" relationship. Some lenders' advertising campaigns invite consumers to view them as trustworthy financial advisors. One lender's letter to a new borrower read "[t]here are many ways we can help . . . not only by lending money—but by giving you sound money management when you need it."[708] If a borrower succumbs to such pitches—entering into an unaffordable home equity loan because the lender touted the tax advantages; engaging in very expensive and disadvantageous flipping or loan consolidations at the lender's suggestion; or getting an insurance-packed loan—the facts should be viewed carefully in the light of these cases. In a recent decision in a case with a long history, a Pennsylvania appellate court held that carefully orchestrated and pervasive advertising intended to create confidence and trust can establish the *prima facie* elements of a confidential relationship.[709]

12.9.4 Intentional Interference with a Contractual Relationship

It seems only fair that lenders who quietly reward brokers for bringing borrowers to them, passing on the cost of that reward to the borrower,[710] should share blame for the brokers' breach of duty which naturally follows. One common law claim which may be a possible avenue to challenge the lender for suborning this breach of fiduciary duty is the intentional interference with a contractual relationship.[711]

The elements of this tort are: the existence of a contractual relationship; the defendant's knowledge of the contract; the intent to interfere; and the plaintiff suffers damages.[712]

nicated to third parties. *See* United States v. Aronson, 610 F. Supp. 217 (S.D. Fla. 1985), *aff'd*, 781 F.2d 1580 (11th Cir. 1986) (this case involved subpoenas issued by the IRS and the attorney was not a closing attorney).

702 Luckett v. Alpha Construction & Development, Inc., 2001 WL 1286815 (N.D. Ill. Oct. 24, 2001); *see also* Reich v. Chicago Title Ins. Co., 853 F. Supp. 1325 (D. Kan. 1994) (decision on unrelated issue is interesting because it describes the operation of one major title insurance and closing company).

703 *In re* Apponline.com, Inc., 284 B.R. 181 (Bankr. E.D.N.Y. 2002).

704 Commercial Credit Plan v. Beebe, 187 A.2d 502 (Vt. 1963).

705 *Id. See also* Richfield Bank & Trust v. Sjogren, 244 N.W.2d 648 (Minn. 1976) (bank financed contract for purchase of goods from one of its other customers, knowing the seller could not deliver the goods; had duty of disclosure to borrowers).

706 *See, e.g.*, Security Pac. Nat'l Bank v. Williams, Nos. 457727/457728 (Cal. Super. Ct. San Diego County 1987) [case discussed in Johnson & Gaffney, *Lender Liability: Perspectives on Risk and Prevention*, 105 Banking L.J. 325 (1988)]; Barnett Bank v. Hooper, 498 So. 2d 923 (Fla. 1986); First Nat'l Bank v. Brown, 181 N.W.2d 178 (Iowa 1970); Richfield Bank & Trust v. Sjogren, 244 N.W.2d 648 (Minn. 1976). *Cf.* Powell v. H.E.F. Partnership, 835 F. Supp. 762 (D. Vt. 1993) (lender holding purchase money in escrow account is agent with duty to disclose information about a known fraud being committed on the principal. Query whether a lender escrowing loan proceeds in a home improvement contract violates such a duty if it knows of a contractor's fraudulent conduct). *But see* Tokarz v. Frontier Fed. Sav. & Loan, 656 P.2d 1089 (Wash. Ct. App. 1983) (no duty to disclose to borrowers that the home improvement contractor was having financial problems which impaired its ability to perform).

707 Camp v. First Fed. Sav. & Loan, 671 S.W.2d 213 (Ark. Ct. App. 1984).

708 Other examples of such advertisements are found in Mark Budnitz, *The Sale of Credit Life Insurance: The Bank as Fiduciary*, 62 N.C.L. Rev. 295, 318 n.126 (1984).

709 Basile v. H&R Block, Inc., 777 A.2d 95 (Pa. Super. Ct. 2001).

710 *See* § 11.5.4.3, *supra* (yield spread premiums, for example).

711 A lender may also be liable to return money or property it received in consequence of another's breach of fiduciary duty, particularly if there was bad faith on the lender's part. *See, e.g.*, Briggs v. Countrywide Funding Corp., 931 F. Supp. 1545 (M.D. Ala. 1996) (denying lender's motion to dismiss variety of claims challenging yield spread premiums, including improper interference with brokerage contract and that offer of the yield spread premium induced the broker to breach its fiduciary duty), *vacated on other grounds*, 949 F. Supp. 812 (M.D. Ala. 1996). *Cf.* Trenton Trust Co. v. Western Surety Co., 599 S.W.2d 481 (Va. 1980).

712 *See, e.g.*, Optivision, Inc. v. Syracuse Shopping Ctr. Assocs., 472 F. Supp. 665, 684 (N.D.N.Y. 1979). *See also* Thrift v. Hubbard, 44 F.3d 348 (5th Cir. 1995) (stating elements under Texas law); Kenty v. Transamerica Premium Ins. Co., 650 N.E.2d 863 (Ohio 1995) (recognizing the tort in Ohio).

A kickback arrangement like the yield spread premium would arguably supply the necessary elements. Certainly the lender is aware of the relationship between the borrower and the lender. It would be hard to argue with a straight face that an agreement to hike the cost of a loan to a borrower, a portion of which is then secretly returned to the broker, is not intended to deprive the borrower of the services of an objective broker.[713] Borrowers who asserted this tort in relation to force-placed insurance with alleged excess coverage and inflated premiums survived a motion to dismiss.[714]

Even in those circumstances where the broker and borrower do not have a binding contract, a variant of this tort may be applicable. Intentional interference with prospective contractual relations[715] may be found if the borrower had a reasonable expectation of an economic benefit from an anticipated arrangement.[716]

12.10 Fraud and Misrepresentation

12.10.1 Parties Liable

One of the more striking developments in recent years is the effort to reach behind shoddy contractors, brokers and predatory second mortgage companies to the financiers who enable them to operate by providing them their financial lifeline.[717] The effort to hold these lenders accountable for

their role is important first because they are most often the ones holding the notes, and so the ability to raise claims and defenses against them is critical to protecting a home against foreclosure or other collection efforts. They may also be the only realistic defendants left standing: the contractor may have fled or filed for bankruptcy; the second mortgage companies or used car dealers also may have gone bankrupt, or are so thinly capitalized as to present no source of recovery, either. But more importantly than the deep pocket (or only pocket) for an individual victim is the potential for decreasing the volume of contractor and second mortgage scams by drying up their funding.[718]

The vicarious liability of the lender for a seller's wrongs under the FTC holder rule is discussed elsewhere,[719] as is the expanded assignee liability under the Home Ownership and Equity Protection Act.[720] However, recovery against the financiers under both provisions is limited. Hence to impose liability for damages sufficient to act as a deterrent, such as punitive damages for fraud, a borrower would need to establish some basis for direct fraud liability on the part of the financier. Theories on which a financier can be held directly liability for the fraud of the party who originated the transaction include:

- The initial party was the financier's employee[721] or

---

713 Certainly a lender should be held to know of the broker's duty to the borrower, and one who knowingly aids and abets a fiduciary in a breach of its duty is also liable. Jackson v. Smith, 254 U.S. 586, 589 (1921).

714 Kenty v. Transamerica Premium Ins. Co., 650 N.E.2d 863 (Ohio 1995) (construing facts in favor of plaintiff, the overcharge could have been a breach of contract induced by the insurer; civil conspiracy claim also survived dismissal). *See generally* §§ 8.3.1.4, 8.5.3.4.2, *supra*.

715 In Massachusetts, it is the tort of interference with advantageous business relations. *See* Comey v. Hill, 438 N.E.2d 811 (Mass. 1982); Elm Med. Lab. Inc. v. RKO General, 532 N.E.2d 675 (Mass. 1989).

716 86 C.J.S. Torts §§ 59, 62 (1997). *See also* Thrift v. Hubbard, 44 F.3d 348 (5th Cir. 1995) (elements under Texas law: reasonable probability that parties would have entered into a contractual arrangement; intentional and malicious act, with purpose of harming the plaintiff, prevented the relationship; defendant lacked privilege or justification to do the act; actual harm or damage resulted from the interference: noting difference from tort of interference with a contractual relationship in requiring proof of reasonable probability of obtaining a contract and defendant's malice or intent to harm).

717 This can be either by providing them with up-front operating credit for their ventures, or by providing the back-end cash flow when these lenders finance the individual borrowers' loans. The latter may be by taking assignment of theoretically "seller-financed" paper or by making direct "third-party" loans arranged by the contractor through a pre-existing business relationship between it and the lender. Or, more typically with second mortgage companies than contractors, loans originated

by the company are packaged and sold in bulk to other financial institutions on the secondary market.

718 The theory behind the FTC Holder Rule, 16 C.F.R. § 433, and the assignee liability provisions of the Home Ownership and Equity Protection Act is that making assignees and related lenders liable for acts of the seller will result in the industry better policing itself. Crooks, like the poor, will always be among us. But business and legal climates can operate either to encourage or discourage their number. Making the financial "enablers" accountable would, one hopes, discourage such operations.

719 16 C.F.R. § 433. *See generally*, § 10.6.1.2.2, *supra*; National Consumer Law Center, Unfair and Deceptive Acts and Practices § 6.6 (6th ed. 2004 and Supp.).

720 § 10.6.1.2.3, *supra*; National Consumer Law Center, Truth in Lending Ch. 9 (5th ed. 2003 and Supp.).

721 Schunk v. United Fin. Mortgage Corp., 2001 U.S. Dist. LEXIS 5685 (D. Kan. Apr. 11, 2001) (denying lender's motion to dismiss where its employee allegedly forged customer's initials on a document at direction of lender's vice-president; lender can be liable for tortious conduct of its employees); Holley v. Gurnee Volkswagon and Oldsmobile, Inc., 2001 U.S. Dist. LEXIS 7274 (N.D. Ill. Jan. 8, 2001) (car salesperson acted as agent of car dealer; car dealer is liable for acts of fraud of salesperson, at least at motion to dismiss stage); Inter Mountain Mortgage, Inc. v. Sulimen, 93 Cal. Rptr. 2d 790 (Ct. App. 2000) (employer is vicariously liable for fraud of employee who is acting within scope of employment); Daigle v. Trinity United Mortg., L.L.C., 890 So. 2d 583 (La. App. 204) (mortgage company liable for acts of its employee, even for representations he made after leaving employ, where company told consumers he was unavailable when they called, instead of revealing that he was no longer employed there); Hoffman v. Stamper, 843 A.2d 153 (Md. Ct. Spec. App. 2004) (lender liable for complicity of its loan officer in financing property flipping scheme;

acted as its agent;[722]
- The lender participated directly in the fraud;[723]

- The lender aided and abetted or conspired with the tortfeasor;[724]
- The lender knowingly obtained at least some of the fruits of the fraud;[725]
- The lender induced the broker to breach its fiduciary duty to the borrower;[726] or
- There were some special circumstances which required the lender to disclose to the borrower information it knew about the seller and failed to reveal.[727]

---

this issue apparently was not contested), *aff'd in part, rev'd in part*, 867 A.2d 276 (Md. 2005) (affirming in all respects except emotional distress damages). *Cf.* Werdann v. Mel Hambelton Ford, Inc., 79 P. 3d 1081 (Kan. Ct. App. 2003) (car dealership liable for malicious behavior of its employee in blocking the consumer's van when she attempted to rescind the contract and leave, refusing to refund her down payment, and threatening to call the police if she refused to hand over the keys to the van; employer ratified the conduct by never disciplining the salesman and by selling the consumer's van but never crediting any of the proceeds against the debt until a governmental agency intervened). *See generally* Restatement (2d) of Agency § 219 (master's liability for torts of servant).

722 *See* People *ex rel.* Spitzer v. Telehublink Corp., 756 N.Y.S.2d 285 (App. Div. 2003) (telemarketers acted within apparent or actual authority as agents of supposed credit card lender when the company failed to produce documentation to show otherwise); Carlisle v. Whirlpool Fin. Nat. Bank, Civil Action No. CV-97-068 (Cir. Ct., Hale County, Ala. Aug. 25, 1999), Clearinghouse No. 52,516 (upholding jury's finding that agency relationship existed between lender and seller where their agreement gave lender the right to inspect merchant's premises, to approve or disapprove any marketing, advertising, promotional, and other sale materials, to approve or deny credit, to set the terms of financing, to make decisions about extending credit before sales occurred, and to require merchant to use lender's documents; lender was holding merchant out to the public as having authority to represent lender and to explain financing terms and lender documents). *See also* Jones v. Federated Fin. Reserve Corp., 144 F.3d 961 (6th Cir. 1998) (principal can be held liable for agent's torts on three theories: express or implicit authorization; *respondeat superior* where agent acts for benefit of principal and within scope of employment; and apparent authority regardless of whether agent acted for own purposes or principal's); Pulphus v. Sullivan, 2003 WL 1964333 (N.D. Ill. Apr. 28, 2003) (assignee can be liable for the actions of its agents and, under certain circumstances, for the actions of the agent's agents; title company is the agent of the lender for RICO purposes at the motion to dismiss stage); Jordan v. Washington Mutual Bank, 211 F. Supp. 2d 670 (D. Md. 2002) (quite apart from fraud claims, principals may be liable for statutory claims that can be raised against an agent; in this case, violations of the state mortgage broker law may be raised against the lender); Smith v. Elzey (*In re* Smith), 280 B.R. 436 (Bankr. N.D. Ill. 2002) (assignee may have been agent for original lender where its letters so stated and it filed eviction action on behalf of original lender, but court rules against consumer on other grounds). *But see* Bescos v. Bank of Am., 129 Cal. Rptr. 2d 423 (Ct. App. 2003); LaChapelle v. Toyota Motor Credit Corp., 126 Cal. Rptr. 2d 32 (Ct. App. 2002) (when car dealer used assignee's lease forms but was not required to offer leases through that particular financing program and consumer could obtain leasing through any other source, car dealer was not assignee's agent).

723 *See, e.g.*, Union Mortgage Co. v. Barlow, 595 So. 2d 1335 (Ala. 1992); Hays v. Bankers Trust Co., 46 F. Supp. 2d 490 (S.D. W. Va. 1999) (denying assignee's motion for summary judgment on claim of civil conspiracy with loan originator); George v. Capital S. Mortgage Invest., Inc., 961 P.2d 32 (Kan. 1998) (lender and broker held liable for fraud and usury under joint venture theory); Williams v. Aetna Fin. Co., 700 N.E.2d 859 (Ohio 1998) (civil conspiracy). For a discussion of a series of similar Alabama cases generally, see Gene A. Marsh, *Lender Liability*

for Consumer Fraud Practices of Retail Dealers and Home Improvement Contractors, 45 U. Ala. L. Rev. 1 (1993).

724 *See* Halberstam v. Welch, 705 F.2d 472 (D.C. Cir. 1983) (case involved civil liability of a live-in companion for murder committed during a burglary; good discussion of the differences and similarities between liability as a conspirator and as an aider and abettor); Knapp v. Americredit Fin. Serv., Inc., 245 F. Supp. 2d 841 (S.D. W. Va. 2003) (civil conspiracy/joint venture claim; motion for summary judgment denied when testimony supported allegations that the lender's area manager trained the car dealer employees to carry out the creation of false pay stubs, false down payments, and charge an acquisition fee that was hidden in the cash price); Aiello v. Chisick (*In re* First Alliance Mortgage Co.), Clearinghouse No. 53,572 (C.D. Cal. Jan. 10, 2002) (denying dismissal of aiding and abetting claim against investment house that provided underwriting services for lender's securitization and provided a $150 million credit for the lender to make its loans; though it did not have direct involvement in lender's allegedly fraudulent scheme, it allegedly knew of the scheme and its credit made the scheme possible); Hoffman v. Stamper, 843 A.2d 153 (Md. Ct. Spec. App. 2004) (affirming jury award to nine consumers of $129,000 in economic damages and $1.3 million in emotional distress damages against lender, loan officer, and appraiser on fraud, civil conspiracy and other claims in property flipping scheme; reversing trial court's refusal to allow jury to decide punitive damages against them; jury also awarded same compensatory damages plus $1.8 million in punitive damages against seller, who did not appeal), *aff'd in part, rev'd in part*, 867 A.2d 276 (Md. 2005) (affirming in all respects except emotional distress damages).

725 *See* Pulphus v. Sullivan, 2003 WL 1964333 (N.D. Ill. Apr. 28, 2003); Cumis Ins. Society, Inc. v. Peters, 983 F. Supp. 787 (N.D. Ill. 1997); Beaton & Assoc. v. Joslyn Mfg. & Supply Co., 512 N.E.2d 1286 (Ill. App. Ct. 1987); Moore v. Pinkert, 171 N.E.2d 73 (Ill. App. Ct. 1960); Commercial Credit Plan, Inc. v. Beebe, 187 A.2d 502 (Vt. 1963) (lender who accepts the benefit of another's fraudulent act, knowing the methods used, may be liable for the fraud). *But cf.* Zekman v. Direct Am. Marketers, Inc., 695 N.E.2d 853 (Ill. 1998) (knowingly receiving fruits of the fraud does not state a UDAP claim as the recipient is not the person who performed the act which violated the statute).

726 *See* International Underwriters, Inc. v. Boyle, 365 A.2d 779 (D.C. App. 1976) (commercial case involving one company allegedly inducing an employee to leave another company and bring private data from his employer).

727 Maberry v. S.A.S. Auto Sales, Inc., 911 F. Supp. 1393 (D. Kan. 1995) (denying lender's motion for summary judgment where evidence created a reasonable inference that assignee knew of the odometer discrepancy and failed to inform the consumer), *further proceedings*, 927 F. Supp. 1456 (D. Kan. 1996) (assignee's post-trial motions denied; consumer's post-trial motions denied in part and granted in part); Jim Short Ford Sales, Inc. v. Washington, 384 So. 2d 83 (Ala. 1980) (trial court erroneously

Some of the cases discussed in the next section find liability against the lender based on agency, conspiracy, and these other theories.[728] The success of this line of cases suggests an approach which may actually help rid low-income neighborhoods of predatory contractors and their financiers. Multi-million judgments are undoubtedly a more powerful deterrent to such practices than the occasional loss of an account receivable to a Truth in Lending rescission claim.

Certainly if a financier knows of the fraudulent manner of operation of its business client, the contractor or second mortgage company, it should be directly liable.[729] This is particularly clear where the lender knew that its financing was enabling a home improvement contractor to perpetrate a fraud on an unsophisticated customer,[730] where the lender knew the seller was irretrievably insolvent and failed to warn its customer,[731] or where the broker, lender, and middleman companies engaged in a joint venture to inflate the principal amount of the loan and pocket the difference.[732] Similarly, a bank which lent money to people to invest in what the bank knew to be a Ponzi-scheme at least may be unable to enforce promissory notes signed as a result of the fraud.[733] This "ostrich game" also may be evidence of fraud if a bank, for example, was "selectively careless" in handling its credit arrangements with the primary perpetrator.[734] Evidence concerning the price paid by the purchasing institution may have some bearing at least on whether a financier is entitled to assert a holder-in-due course defense

---

granted directed verdict for finance company for car dealer's fraud when selling car insurance required by the finance company, where finance company knew that dealer's insurance agent was under investigation for overcharging and failing to write insurance policies and where finance company's loan documents and its approval of the transaction made the insurance sale possible; duty to disclose can arise in special circumstances) (note that decision's implication that existence of duty to disclose is a jury question was overruled in State Farm Fire & Cas. Co. v. Owen, 729 So. 2d 834 (Ala. 1998)); Millard v. Lorain Invest, Corp., 184 A.2d 630 (D.C. Mun. App. 1962) (sufficient evidence to raise jury issue regarding finance company's knowledge of dealer's misrepresentations about loan terms where dealer was major stockholder in finance company and financed many sales through it); Brown v. Cahill, 157 So. 2d 871 (Fla. Dist. Ct. App. 1963) (sufficient evidence to charge the financing company with the car dealer's fraud of selling a previously wrecked car as new because the finance company had previously lent money for another consumer to purchase this same car, which was wrecked and subsequently repossessed by the finance company and sold back to the dealer); Richfield Bank & Trust Co. v. Sjogren, 244 N.W.2d 648 (Minn. 1976) (commercial case where lender knew the seller was insolvent and failed to warn its customer).

728 See also § 12.12, *infra*, for a liability checklist.

729 *See, e.g.*, Hays v. Bankers Trust Co., 46 F. Supp. 2d 490 (S.D. W. Va. 1999) (lender's motion for summary judgment denied based solely upon inconsistent disclosures on face of commitment letter and the actual terms of the loan provided at closing); George v. Capital S. Mortgage Invests., Inc., 961 P.2d 32 (Kan. 1998) (lender, broker, and middleman held liable for fraud and usury under joint venture theory); Hoffman v. Stamper, 843 A.2d 153 (Md. Ct. Spec. App. 2004) (affirming jury award to nine consumers of $129,000 in economic damages and $1.3 million in emotional distress damages against lender, loan officer, and appraiser on fraud, civil conspiracy and other claims in property flipping scheme; reversing trial court's refusal to allow jury to decide punitive damages against them; jury also awarded same compensatory damages plus $1.8 million in punitive damages against seller, who did not appeal), *aff'd in part, rev'd in part*, 867 A.2d 276 (Md. 2005) (affirming in all respects except emotional distress damages); Williams v. Aetna Fin. Co., 700 N.E.2d 859 (Ohio 1998) (holding lender liable for acts of home improvement contractor under civil conspiracy claim where lender allowed contractor to have access to loan money that was necessary to further his fraudulent actions, lender selected "authorized" contractor and readily made loans to his customers despite knowledge of complaints about and problems with the contractor); Union Mortgage Co. v. Barlow, 595 So. 2d 1335 (Ala. 1992); *see also* United Cos. Fin. Corp. v. Brown, 584 So. 2d 470 (Ala. 1991) (financer steered borrowers

to contractor who failed to perform work and released escrow funds knowing work was not done; compensatory and punitive damages awarded); Lockhart v. Lovett, Clearinghouse No. 50,406 (Cir. Ct., Miss., complaint filed Feb. 17, 1993; a jury verdict in excess of $1.5 million was rendered in Aug. 1994, against the finance company financing a contractor's home improvement sales contracts). *Cf.* Anderson v. FNMA, Clearinghouse No. 42,568, Civ. No. 87-0236 (E.D. Va. 1988) (denying motion to dismiss RICO claim against institutions which purchased portfolios of loans from fraudulent second mortgage company on secondary market where borrowers alleged purchasers knew of company's operations). *But see* Howard v. Riggs Nat'l Bank, 432 A.2d 701 (D.C. 1981) (bank not liable for fraud where its employee's recommendation of home improvement contractor was made in good faith; employee not obliged to reveal her friendship with wife of contractor's co-owner); Miller Planning Corp. v. Wells, 678 N.Y.S.2d 340 (App. Div. 1998) (no evidence that lender had a relationship with the contractor or that lender participated in or had knowledge of the home improvement contractor's scheme).

730 Williams v. Aetna Fin. Co., 700 N.E.2d 859 (Ohio 1998).

731 Richfield Bank & Trust Co. v. Sjogren, 244 N.W.2d 648 (Minn. 1976) (commercial case). *But compare* Howard v. Riggs Nat'l Bank, 432 A.2d 701 (D.C. 1981) (bank not liable for fraud where its employee's recommendation of home improvement contractor was made in good faith, even though contractor defrauded consumer).

732 Wilson v. Toussie, 260 F. Supp. 2d 530 (E.D.N.Y. 2003) (fraudulent conduct alleged in a subdivision development scheme by developers/sellers, appraisers, lenders, abstract companies, and lawyers; fraud allegations were not sufficiently specific regarding the lenders when the complaint alleged that the lenders knowingly participated in a conspiracy to generate income through points and fees and that loan applications were falsified but failed to indicate which loan applications were falsified and the extent to which each lender participated in the fraud; leave to amend granted); George v. Capital S. Mortgage Invests., Inc., 961 P.2d 32 (Kan. 1998).

733 Sheradsky v. West One Bank, 817 F. Supp. 423, 425 (S.D.N.Y. 1993) ("If fraud is involved in a transaction, a financing entity which deliberately shuts its eyes to clues concerning the fraud may be unable to enforce promissory notes signed as a result of the fraud;" decision on denial of bank's motion for summary judgment; unclear what relief plaintiffs sought against bank).

734 *Cf.* Brazell v. First Nat'l Bank & Trust, 982 F.2d 206, 209 (7th Cir. 1992) (dicta).

to a borrower's claims and defenses on a note.[735] A steep discount (25% on a used car loan[736]) apparently was part of what convinced a jury that the finance company was the primary lender, not merely an assignee.[737]

A close relationship between the lender and assignee may defeat the holder-in-due course shield and create an agency relationship. Many mortgage assignees are actively involved in the making of loans because they intend to purchase them from the lender as long as the lender originates the loans according to certain specifications. Assignees often sign "master loan purchase" agreements with table-funded brokers.[738] These agreements specify in detail the types of loans that the assignee will purchase and the circumstances under which they will be bought.[739] While many of these agreements include a disclaimer of agency, for all intents and purposes, the originating lender is merely a straw person or conduit for the assignee. Typically, these assignees are out-of-state companies who want to make mortgage loans on a broad geographical basis without maintaining local offices. In a case involving facts like these, a West Virginia federal court denied the assignee's motion for summary judgment on the holder-in-due-course defense and on the agency allegation.[740] The sixteen-page master agreement contained over twenty-eight detailed requirements imposed on the originating lender. The court found that "the more the holder knows about the underlying transaction, . . . or becomes involved in it, the less he fits the role of a good faith purchaser for value[.]"[741]

In situations where loans are securitized[742] and a trust holds the mortgages, the trust most likely is the real party in interest in a foreclosure action. In this situation, the trust should be added to any case in which defenses to the mortgage may be raised. If the originating lender continues to claim that it holds the note when it does not and this causes the consumer time and expense in proving who holds the loan, one should consider adding fraud (upon the court, never mind upon the consumer) and civil conspiracy claims against the lender and the trust for perpetuating this fraud.

A lender and the insurer which issued its credit insurance policies were held jointly and severally liable for punitive damages for fraud, concealment and a scheme to defraud where credit life insurance was sold to a borrower who the lender knew was in bad health and ineligible for coverage.[743] Similarly, in an action challenging the legality of a

---

735 *Compare* Union Mortgage Co. v. Barlow, 595 So. 2d 1335 (Ala. 1992) (borrowers alleging that financier was a primary, not a secondary lender, presented evidence of the discount on the purchased paper) *and* Stewart v. Thorton, 568 P.2d 414 (Ariz. 1977) (1/3 discount; holder-in-due course status at issue) *with* Northwestern Nat'l Ins. Co. v. Maggio, 976 F.2d 320 (7th Cir. 1992) (50% discount purchase was not a suspicious circumstance that triggered a duty to inquire as to possible defenses on the note; holder's status as holder-in-due-course at issue. Judge Posner poo-poos *Stewart* in this case).

736 This financier, which specialized in lending to low-income and/or credit-impaired consumers, used this discount or "dealer reserve" system as a loss reserve. *See* Andrew Bary, *Mercury Finance: Steep Incline*, 74 Barrons 17 (Aug. 15, 1994).

737 Johnson v. Mercury Fin., Clearinghouse No. 50,407, Case No. CV 93-952 (Ala. Cir. Ct. jury verdict Aug. 1994) ($53.5 million fraud award). This case is discussed in § 12.10.2, *infra*.

738 A table-funded broker (also called a "correspondent lender") acts in the manner of a broker. It arranges "table-funded" loans in which, though it is the nominal lender on the documents, the assignee to which the loan is immediately sold is the source of the loan funds. *See* § 12.2.1.1, *supra*. The table funded broker and/or the lender standing behind the broker will likely have a "funding worksheet" for each loan. This document shows when the lender approved the loan, an itemization of fees and disbursements per the HUD-1, and other loan specific information. It may also reveal that the depositor in the eventual securitization had already agreed to purchase the loan before it closed. If so, this document may make it difficult for the true lender and investors to pin all illegalities upon the broker or claim lack of knowledge.

739 The contract may: require what specific information must be obtained from the borrower; itemize the documents which the broker must use; require that third party services be purchased from a specific vendor; describe the method by which interest must be calculated; require the broker to follow detailed underwriting guidelines and appraisal policies; and grant a power of attorney to the assignee. The underlying facts in this case are disturbingly typical. The borrowers alleged that they were enticed to apply for a 30-year variable rate loan at an initial interest rate of 11.9% on the promise that the rate would drop after a year to 8%. The loan documents at closing did not match the promise. Not only was there no provision dropping the interest rate, but the loan was payable in 83 monthly payments with one final whopping balloon payment. Upon questioning by the borrowers, the lender faxed a letter to the settlement office confirming that once the borrowers made 12 monthly payments, they would qualify for a fixed rate of 8% (amending the term was not mentioned). After the borrower's fulfilled their obligation, the lender failed or refused to recast the loan. At that point, the loan had long ago been sold.

740 England v. MG Investments, Inc., 93 F. Supp. 2d 718 (S.D. W. Va. 2000). *See also* Pulphus v. Sullivan, 2003 WL 1964333 (N.D. Ill. Apr. 28, 2003) (denying motion to dismiss homeowner's complaint on agency theory based upon facts about written agreement between original lender and assignee in RICO context, but dismissing RICO complaint for other reasons); Moore v. Mortgagestar, Inc., 2002 U.S. Dist. LEXIS 27457 (S.D. W. Va. Dec. 18, 2002) (assignee may be liable for acts of loan originator on agency or joint venture theory where originator knew in advance it would assign the loan to the assignee in accord with guidelines in its agreement with assignee, notwithstanding clause denying agency or joint venture); Osburn v. Community Home Mortg., L.L.C., Civil Action No. 02-C-1164 (W. Va. Cir. Ct., Kanawha Cty. Jan. 13, 2005) (jury finding that lender and broker were engaged in joint venture and agency relationship; awarding $50,000 actual damages and $500,000 punitive damages on fraud count).

741 *Id.* at 724, *quoting* One Valley Bank of Oak Hill v. Bollen, 425 S.E.2d 829, 832 (W. Va. 1992).

742 See discussion about securitization in § 11.3, *supra*.

743 Union Security Life Ins. Co. v. Crocker, 667 So. 2d 688 (Ala. 1995) ($5 million jury award remitted to $2 million; court upheld the $2 million saying it "does not exceed the amount necessary to promote society's goals of punishment and deterrence, in order to exorcise fraud and inequity from the marketing of credit life policies"), *vacated on other grounds*, 116 S. Ct.

yield spread premium given by a mortgage lender to a broker, the lender's motion to dismiss fraud-based claims was denied. Facts might establish either primary liability on the lender's part ("too close to the fraud" to escape) or derivative liability under an agency theory.[744]

The owner of a company which, in turn, owned a mortgage lending company can be liable in his individual capacity for misrepresentations made to a homeowner by an agent for the lender, where the owner hired the agent to list the property, received information from the agent about the homeowner's financial status, and made the decision to make the loan in the form in which it was offered.[745] This decision is important because holding the principals responsible for the acts of the corporation and its agents can be critical to collecting on a judgment at the end of the day. Corporations and other entities that are wholly owned by one or a few individuals may be merely a shell to protect the individuals from liability when the heat is applied thought lawsuits.

Further, a bank affiliated with a broker may be responsible for the acts of the broker and the lender in certain situations. Where the broker advertised in a letter that it offered good rates and payments on mortgage loans because it was "one of the largest and most secure banks" in the country and stated that it was the exclusive agent for the bank, the bank could be liable for certain acts of the broker and the lender who ultimately made the loan under civil conspiracy theory.[746] The bank participated in activities and took overt acts in furtherance of the alleged conspiracy between the lender and broker to make loans in which the homeowners would not know that the broker was not the lender. Under other theories, the bank could also be liable for the acts of the broker alone since the solicitation indicates that the broker is the agent of the bank.

A theory of lender liability not often used in the credit context is aiding and abetting. This theory is separate and distinct from a civil conspiracy theory.[747] While civil conspiracy involves a tortious act in concert with another or pursuant to a common design, aiding and abetting involves knowledge that another's conduct constitutes a breach of duty and substantial assistance or encouragement to the other.[748] In other words, conspiracy involves an agreement (explicit or by conduct) to participate in a wrongful activity. Aiding and abetting, on the other hand, focuses on whether the lender gave "substantial assistance" to someone who engaged in wrongful conduct. Agreement to join the wrongful conduct is irrelevant.[749]

A federal court jury in Southern California awarded over $5 million to plaintiffs in a class action alleging that Lehman Brothers, Inc. aided and abetted a mortgage lender's fraud.[750] This decision is the first one in which consumers have successfully gone "upstream" from the originator to hold a Wall Street player directly responsible for its own actions. In this case, Lehman Brothers, Inc. provided a warehouse line of credit to First Alliance Mortgage Co. (FAMCO) and managed four of its securitizations, allowing FAMCO to perpetrate fraud.[751] FAMCO targeted home owners sitting on substantial equity in their homes, and FAMCO loan officers strictly followed twelve presentation steps when "selling" the benefits of a FAMCO mortgage loan to prospective borrowers. The loan presentation was designed to conceal the loan origination fee (points), other fees, and the true principal amount from the consumer.

1872 (1996) (sending $2 million punitive damage award back to Alabama Supreme Court for further consideration in light of BMW of N. America, Inc. v. Gore, 517 U.S. 559, 116 S. Ct. 1589 (1996), *upon remand from Supreme Court*, 709 So. 2d 1118 (Ala. 1997) (reducing punitive damages award to $1 million by weighing reprehensible conduct of insurance company's agent (though an apparently isolated instance) coupled with the "catastrophic" economic injury to Ms. Crocker facing foreclosure of her mobile home in the wake of her husband's death against the percentage of $2 million award compared to the insurance companies' net worth).

744 Briggs v. Countrywide Funding Corp., 931 F. Supp. 1545, *vacated on other grounds*, 949 F. Supp. 812 (M.D. Ala. 1996).

745 Hargraves v. Capital City Mortgage Co., 140 F. Supp. 2d 7 (D.D.C. 2000) (memorandum opinion and order). *See also* Jones v. Federated Fin. Reserve Corp., 144 F.3d 961 (6th Cir. 1998) (employer may be liable for employee's tortious conduct based upon apparent authority; court applied this holding in a Fair Credit Reporting Act case); Banks v. Consumer Home Mortgage, Inc., 2003 WL 21251584 (E.D.N.Y. Mar. 28, 2003) (allegations against the president of the company selling the properties in a property flipping scam that held him responsible for fraud committed by corporate employees were sufficient; knowledge and control were alleged); Vaughn v. Consumer Home Mortgage, Inc., 2003 WL 21241669 (E.D.N.Y. Mar. 23, 2003) (same); Aiello v. Chisick (*In re* First Alliance Mortgage Co.), 2002 U.S. Dist. LEXIS 5858 (C.D. Cal. Jan. 10, 2002) (CEO of mortgage lender may be liable for equitable subordination under the Bankruptcy Code when the creditor-borrowers claim that he controlled the company and designed and implemented an allegedly fraudulent lending scheme).

746 Miller v. Equifirst Corp., 2001 U.S. Dist. LEXIS 4795, at *2, Clearinghouse No. 53,515 (S.D. W. Va. Jan. 31, 2001) (memorandum order). *But see* Johnson v. Robinson (*In re* Johnson), 292 B.R. 821 (Bankr. E.D. Pa. 2003) (granting motion to dismiss title company and closing agent when specific allegations of their involvement in the fraud were lacking; actions of broker and lender were sufficiently pleaded in this home improvement loan broker case).

747 *See* Halberstam v. Welch, 705 F.2d 472 (D.C. Cir. 1983) (discusses the similarities and differences between these theories).

748 Restatement (Second) of Torts § 876 (1979); Vaughn v. Consumer Home Mortgage, Inc., 2003 WL 21241669 (E.D.N.Y. Mar. 23, 2003) (aiding and abetting cause of action adequately pled against the closing attorneys in this property flipping case).

749 Halberstam v. Welch, 705 F.2d 472 (D.C. Cir. 1983).

750 Copies of the jury verdict and jury instructions are available at Clearinghouse Nos. 55,451A and 55,451B, respectively.

751 For a description of the sales tactics of FAMCO, the history of litigation against it, and Lehman's involvement with and knowledge of the fraud, see *In re* First Alliance Mortgage Co., 298 B.R. 652 (C.D. Cal. 2003).

FAMCO charged exorbitant points on its loans, ranging from 8 to 26 points.

In 1995, Lehman Brothers first approved a $25 million back-up line of credit to FAMCO, which FAMCO used sporadically. At that time, a "corporate level" due diligence review of FAMCO's business practices revealed high pressure sales practices, a number of loans made to seniors, legal problems caused by aggressive collection tactics, and the practice of making loans based solely on the value of the home. In 1996 and 1997, Lehman co-managed four of the securitizations of FAMCO loans. By December of 1998, Lehman possessed copies of complaints filed by the attorneys general of Illinois, Minnesota, Massachusetts and in six private cases and had a list of twelve other cases. It also knew that the Department of Justice was investigating. Nevertheless, Lehman agreed to provide FAMCO with a $150 million line of credit secured by FAMCO mortgages. This enabled FAMCO to make mortgage loans in 1999 and 2000. In exchange for the line of credit, Lehman received $2.2 million as a commitment fee, interest on any amounts outstanding on the line of credit, and a fee on the remainder of the line that was not being used. Lehman anticipated its total compensation for the deal to be $4.5 million. Despite continued investigation of and internal discussions about FAMCO and its litigation, Lehman did not revoke the line of credit. Rather, it managed four securitizations of FAMCO loans involving over $400 million in mortgage loans in 1999.

FAMCO filed for bankruptcy on March 23, 2000.[752] In the class action filed in the bankruptcy court that eventually resulted in the jury verdict, the class charged that FAMCO systematically used the loan officer "tracks" to obscure the amount of points it charged. Between December 30, 1998 and March 23, 2000, Lehman allegedly knew of FAMCO's fraud and continued to fund its operation, thereby substantially assisting FAMCO in perpetrating fraud. The jury agreed and awarded a total of almost $51 million. However, the jury limited Lehman's responsibility to 10%, making Lehman liable for about $5 million.

Practitioners should consider the problem that can arise by arguing an agency theory or joint collusion to defraud on the part of two apparently separate entities. Arbitration clauses are in vogue and may exist in either the loan documents, broker agreement, home improvement contract, or credit insurance agreement. There is an argument that even a non-signatory to the document containing the arbitration clause may successfully invoke arbitration on the theory that the borrower's claims against the defendants involve agency or are intimately founded upon and intertwined with the underlying contract obligations.[753]

12.10.2 Substantive Conduct Subject to Fraud and Misrepresentation Claims

12.10.2.1 General

The traditional elements of fraud are frequently more difficult to establish than a deception claim under a UDAP statute.[754] However, consumers have successfully used fraud to reach brokers, auto dealers, home improvement contractors and the financiers behind them. It is important to note that the facts in these cases are all-too typical of low-income consumers. Entrusting the case to juries, rather than judges, and treating them as personal torts seems to be what differentiates them, not the facts. When reviewing the punitive damage awards in these decisions, however, the reader should note that many were decided before the Supreme Court's decisions that set limits on punitive damages and before state caps on punitive damages were enacted.[755]

12.10.2.2 Home Improvement Fraud

Baker v. Harper[756] resulted in a $9 million jury award against a second mortgage company and a contractor in a home improvement scam targeted against low-income, uneducated homeowners. The loans were purportedly for home improvement work, much of which was never done. The borrowers alleged the mortgage company utilized a stable of contractors to market the fraudulent mortgages. A companion case in which the borrowers were awarded compensatory damages of $150,000 and punitive damages of $6 million from the ultimate financier due to fraud was the subject of an appeal to the Alabama Supreme Court. In *Union Mortgage Co., Inc. v. Barlow*,[757] the court upheld the verdict. The decision, which discusses in some detail the relationship between the home improvement contractor and

---

752 This sequence of events is discussed in *In re* First Alliance Mortgage Co., 2003 WL 21530096 (C.D. Cal. June 16, 2003).

753 *See, e.g.*, Roberson v. Money Tree, Inc., 954 F. Supp. 1519 (M.D. Ala. 1997); Staples v. Money Tree, Inc., 936 F. Supp. 856 (M.D. Ala. 1996). *Contra* Jones v. Money Tree, Inc., 686 So. 2d

1166 (Ala. 1996) (court strictly applied contract law by holding that because the insurer was a non-signatory on the loan documents which contained the arbitration clause, it had no right to invoke arbitration). *See also* National Consumer Law Center, Consumer Arbitration Agreements (3d ed. 2003); National Consumer Law Center, Unfair and Deceptive Acts and Practices § 7.7 (5th ed. 2001 and Supp.).

754 *See* National Consumer Law Center, Unfair and Deceptive Acts and Practices § 3.2.4 (6th ed. 2004 and Supp.).

755 *See* § 12.10.3, *infra*.

756 Cir. Ct., Barbour County, Ala. No. 48 (judgment) (July 24, 1991) *reported in* 57 Banking Rpt. (BNA) at 270 (Aug. 12, 1991) (the second mortgage company was Union Mortgage, which also had a $6 million judgment rendered against it in another Alabama county). Selected documents from this case can be found in National Consumer Law Center, Consumer Law Pleadings No. 1, Ch. 5 (Cumulative CD-Rom and Index Guide).

757 595 So. 2d 1335 (Ala. 1992).

the mortgage company as well as the type of evidence presented to the jury, is instructive.

In *Williams v. Aetna Finance Co.*,[758] the Ohio Supreme Court upheld a $1.5 million punitive damage award against a finance company for providing the funds that allowed a home improvement contractor to further his fraudulent actions against his customers. The court affirmed liability against ITT even though the contractor was neither an agent of ITT nor received payment from ITT. Instead, liability was based on a civil conspiracy claim.[759] Although ITT engaged in no misrepresentation, its fraudulent participation in the conspiracy was based upon its act of making loans to Williams and others knowing what it did about the contractor. In this case, ITT was found to know that the home improvement contractor was converting loan proceeds from new customers to pay off old jobs, financing the ongoing repair jobs, and making payments on loans for jobs the contractor failed to finish. (ITT's loan documents contained the FTC Holder Notice, so that ITT was on the hook for all claims and defenses the consumer had against the contractor but only up to the amount of the loan. The civil conspiracy theory created liability for punitive damages for its own fraud that was part of the conspiracy.)

A Mississippi jury levied a $1.7 million verdict against a finance company that took the paper from a local contractor. The contractor, a door-to-door seller, misrepresented the cost[760] and quality of the work.[761] Some of the plaintiffs were unaware that deeds of trust were taken on their homes. As all had limited educations or were illiterate, the documents would have been of little help, even had they been accurate, proper and timely given. The lender's liability was alleged both through agency doctrine and conspiracy.[762]

Mahaffey v. Investors National Security Co.,[763] involved a common home improvement fraud. The borrowers were promised home insulation which would cut fuel consumption in half, the borrower's home would be used for promotional purposes (fully compensated for), and the total cost would be $5,300. Work was begun before the three-day cooling-off period, but never completed, and what was done was done improperly. The contractors induced borrowers to sign a completion certificate despite the incomplete work by threatening them with "sky-rocketing interest rates" and "troubles." The assignee tried to foreclose, but the Nevada Supreme Court found the contract to be null and void because of the fraudulent inducement and failure of consideration on the contractor's part.[764]

In another home improvement case, *Faison v. Nationwide Mortgage Corp.*,[765] the lender, brokers, and settlement attorney failed to disclose prior to settlement the principal

---

758   700 N.E.2d 859 (Ohio 1998).

759   More particularly, that ITT formed a "malicious combination" with the home improvement contractor for the purpose of committing the fraud that damaged the consumer. *See also* Hays v. Bankers Trust Co., 46 F. Supp. 2d 490 (S.D. W. Va. 1999) (lender's motion for summary judgment denied based solely upon inconsistent disclosures on face of commitment letter and the actual terms of the loan provided at closing).

760   For example, one couple was told it would cost them $9,000. No total appeared on the contract, though the number and amount of payments were scrawled on the paper. The borrowers, elderly and with a limited education, did not know it came out to $17,000. When their daughter, who can multiply very well, tried to cancel the contract the next day as permitted by both Mississippi's Home Solicitation Sales Act and TIL, the work had begun, and the request to cancel was not honored.

761   Though fair lending and civil rights claims were not raised, this case also involved overt racial discrimination. In addition to racial slurs, the evidence included pictures comparing the quality of work done by the contractor on the homes of white customers with the quality of the work done by the contractor on the homes of African-American customers, according to plaintiffs' counsel. *See also* Chandler v. MVM Constr., Inc., 501 S.E.2d 533 (Ga. Ct. App. 1998) (fraud claims go to the jury; summary judgment denied on claim of fraudulent misrepresentation of the value of home improvements [value alleged to be $4,000 whereas contract price was $27,402]).

762   Lockhart v. Lovett, Clearinghouse No. 50,406 (Cir. Ct., Miss., complaint filed Feb. 17, 1993). Often, the home improvement contractor is not a notary and fails to have a notary present during consummation of the loan. This is often part and parcel of a scam to prevent the homeowner from realizing that the creditor is taking a security interest in the home. [The contractor may also "stack" the papers and direct the homeowner where to sign, effectively preventing her from reading them.] A notary later falsely acknowledges the homeowner's signature. State notary and acknowledgment laws should be checked to determine, aside from a fraud claim, what is the effect of the false notarization upon the transaction. Under New Jersey law, for example, the defective acknowledgment may render the mortgage lien void. *In re* Buchholz, 224 B.R. 13 (Bankr. D.N.J. 1998) (claim was rendered unsecured in the bankruptcy proceeding).

763   747 P.2d 890 (Nev. 1987).

764   The assignee was liable because the required FTC Notice of Preservation of Claims and Defenses clause appeared on the contract. The trial court, in clear derogation of the public policy behind the FTC rule, had nonetheless tried to protect the assignee from its impact by a novel use of estoppel doctrine. The Nevada Supreme Court would have none of that, noting that the assignee was aware of the problems prior to buying the note, and had refused to protect its own position by proceeding against the contractor under a recourse provision instead of against the innocent borrowers. *See also* Lang v. Vickers (*In re* Vickers), 247 B.R. 530 (Bankr. M.D. Fla. 2000) (fraud allegations in state court proceeding upon which a default judgment was entered against the contractor who then filed bankruptcy are sufficient to prevent dischargeability of the debt).

765   839 F.2d 680 (D.C. Cir. 1987), *cert. denied*, 488 U.S. 823 (discussing allocation among joint tortfeasors of jury's $110,000 compensatory and $63,500 punitive damages award for fraud claim; UDAP claim also made). *Cf.* Horvath v. Adelson, Golden & Loria, P.C., 773 N.E.2d 478 (Mass. App. 2002) (no duty on the part of a settlement attorney representing the lender that could be breached where claim of negligent misrepresentation rested on fact that loan proceeds would be paid as indicated on settlement statement, even though they were not paid accordingly and attorney signed a certification on the settlement statement).

amount of the loan, the sizeable discount fee, the broker fee, the balloon-payment loan structure for which no refinancing was available, the significance of characterizing the loan as a business purpose loan (i.e., loss of rights under Truth in Lending), the true interest rate, and the automatic assignment relationship between lender and assignee. These fraudulent acts which gave rise to compensatory and punitive damages, which the appellate court upheld.

12.10.2.3 Fraud in Home Sales and Refinancing

In *Peoples Trust & Savings Bank v. Humphrey*,[766] the consumers went to their own bank for a home construction loan. The bank promised them a "good loan" at a 9 1/2% rate. However, that was merely the initial rate. The permanent financing (after two temporary construction loans) was actually a variable-rate loan and contained a demand clause allowing the bank to demand payment of the balance of the loan at its discretion. Quoting from on an old, respected legal treatise, the court held: "[w]hen parties to a contract have a prior understanding about the contract's terms, and the party responsible for drafting the contract includes contrary terms and then allows the other party to sign it without informing him of the changes, the drafter's conduct is fraudulent."[767] The court in *Humphrey* dismissed the lender's foreclosure, reformed the contract by deleting the demand and variable-rate clauses, and awarded $1,000 actual and $40,000 punitive damages.[768]

Fraud in property flipping and subdivision development construction, sales, and financing has been the subject of several lawsuits.[769] While only one of these cases went to trial, the allegations are common and the decisions are instructive on pleading issues. In *Hoffman v. Stamper*, an intermediate appellate court in Maryland upheld a jury award to nine consumers of $129,020 in economic damages and $1.3 million in economic damages against a lender, its loan officer, and an appraiser who were involved in a property flipping scheme. The court also held that the trial court had erred in refusing to allow the jury to decide statutory damages against those parties. The jury also awarded the same compensatory damages, plus $1.3 million in punitive damages, against the seller, who did not appeal. Upon further appeal, the highest court in Maryland affirmed the decision in all respects except the emotional distress damages award.[770] The causes of action included civil conspiracy, fraud, fraud by way of concealment, and UDAP violations. Other cases have also held that an appraiser whose falsified appraisal enables others to succeed in defrauding a homeowner or home purchaser may be liable for the others' fraud on a joint venture, agency, or civil conspiracy theory.[771]

---

766 451 N.E.2d 1104 (Ind. Ct. App. 1983).

767 *Id.* at 1112. *See also* Osburn v. Community Home Mortg., L.L.C., Civil Action No. 02-C-1164 (W. Va. Cir. Ct., Kanawha Cty. Jan. 13, 2005) (jury verdict for $50,000 actual damages and $500,000 punitive damages where consumer alleged that broker concealed existence of balloon payment). *But cf.* Bell v. Parkway Mortg. (*In re* Bell), 309 B.R. 139, 159–60 (Bankr. E.D. Pa. 2004) (no fraud liability for non-disclosure of higher monthly payment and balloon feature, where borrower chose to rely on broker rather than reading the documents), *reconsideration granted in part on other grounds*, 314 B.R. 54 (Bankr. E.D. Pa. 2004) ; Roper v. Associates Fin. Servs., 533 So. 2d 206 (Ala. 1988) (prudent person exercising ordinary care would have noticed the call option).

768 Note that variable-rate clauses in residential mortgages have become much more common in the period since this decision, so their inclusion should be less surprising. Furthermore, subsequent legislation required variable-rate caps, which must be disclosed, which should make variable-rate terms apparent to borrowers. National Consumer Law Center, Truth in Lending § 4.8.2.1 (5th ed. 2003 and Supp.). *See also* 15 U.S.C. § 1639(a), (b). Nonetheless, the principle articulated in *Humphrey* should still hold true when any contrary terms included by the lender are not obvious.

769 M&T Mortg. Corp. v. Miller, 323 F. Supp. 2d 405 (E.D.N.Y. 2004) (denying motion to dismiss fraud claim; merger clause does not defeat fraudulent inducement claim); Wilson v. Toussie,

260 F. Supp. 2d 530 (E.D.N.Y. 2003) (subdivision development sale and financing case); Banks v. Consumer Home Mortgage, Inc., 2003 WL 21251584 (E.D.N.Y. Mar. 28, 2003) (property flipping case); Vaughn v. Consumer Home Mortgage, Inc., 2003 WL 21241669 (E.D.N.Y. Mar. 23, 2003) (same); Lester v. Percundani, 217 F.R.D. 345 (M.D. Pa. 2003) (subdivision development and sales case; Note: This case and the families allegedly harmed received recent press coverage. *See* Michael Moss & Andrew Jacobs, *Blue Skies and Green Yards, All Lost to Red Ink*, N.Y. Times, Apr. 11, 2004, at A1; Andrew Jacobs, *Trying to Hang on in the Poconos, From Before Dawn to Way Past Dusk*, N.Y. Times, Apr. 12, 2004, at A18); Hoffman v. Stamper, 867 A.2d 276 (Md. 2005) (property flipping case); Polonetsky v. Better Homes Depot, Inc., 760 N.E.2d 1274 (N.Y. 2001) (same). *See also* Consumer Protection Div. v. Morgan, 2005 WL 1123019 (Md. Spec. App. May 13, 2005) (applying UDAP statute to property flipping; lengthy description of property flippers' methods of operation). For press and developments regarding property flipping in New Jersey, see *House of Cards*, Asbury Park Press, *available at* www.injersey.com/news/cards. For a detailed description of legal claims in property flipping cases, see § 11.5.6, *supra*.

770 843 A.2d 153 (Md. Ct. Spec. App. 2004), *aff'd in part, rev'd in part*, 867 A.2d 276 (Md. 2005). This case is very instructive on the kinds of facts that support holding the lender (through its loan officer) and the appraiser liable for their participation in the fraud that was principally committed by the seller. The decision is also helpful on identifying the types of economic damages upon which a recovery could be based. *See also* Consumer Protection Div. v. Morgan, 2005 WL 1123019 (Md. Spec. App. May 13, 2005) (affirming award of restitution and civil penalties under UDAP statute against appraiser who acted in concert with others in property flipping scheme).

771 Banks v. Consumer Home Mortgage, Inc., 2003 WL 21251584 (E.D.N.Y. Mar. 28, 2003); Moore v. Mortgagestar, Inc., 2002 U.S. Dist. LEXIS 27457 (S.D. W. Va. Dec. 18, 2002); Osburn v. Community Home Mortg., L.L.C., Civil Action No. 02-C-1164 (W. Va. Cir. Ct., Kanawha Cty. Jan. 13, 2005) (jury verdict awarding $50,000 in actual damages and $500,000 in punitive damages where consumer alleged that broker arranged for inflated appraisal).

A Kansas jury awarded a total of $100,000 in punitive damages against the ultimate funder of the loan and the intermediary assignee who engaged in a joint venture to inflate the principal amount of the loan and pocket the difference.[772] (The broker, who defaulted in the case, was hit with a punitive damages verdict of $250,000). The borrowers bought a home for $40,000 from a relative and sought financing. The broker convinced the borrowers to agree to list $60,000 as the loan amount while telling them that, in reality, they were only indebted in the amount of $40,000. Further, the assignee instructed the closing agent not to show certain documents to the borrowers that would have alerted them to the fraud. The borrowers did not receive any papers at the settlement. Of the $60,000 loan, only $32,000 was disbursed to the seller of the home. The funder and assignee kept the difference. Good facts clearly drove this successful outcome pled under common law theories. Refinancing home owners out of a lower cost mortgage into a higher cost loan that did not escrow for taxes and insurance led to a jury award in another case of over $500,000.[773]

12.10.2.4 Hidden Fees and Other Credit Practices

Hidden charges and other hard-to-detect methods of increasing the cost of credit have also been challenged successfully on fraud theories. In one case involving hidden finance charges in the inflated loan amount on a used car purchase, a jury awarded $53.5 million.[774] The car, purchased by the dealer for $1,900, was offered for $3,000 cash. On the financing contract, a dealer reserve added to the price in accord with the dealer's standing arrangement with Mercury Finance, plus other add-ons, took the loan amount over $4,000, written at 26.3% interest. Mercury paid the dealer $2,700 for the paper. The jury considered the costly add-ons to constitute a fraudulent practice, designed to disguise a true 50% rate on an already expensive car loan. The evidence showed that the company targeted low-income or credit-impaired car buyers who needed transportation for work, and charged high interest rates even absent padding, and that the padding of credit contracts gave the company an undisclosed additional return of $1.1 billion over recent years.

The yield spread premium given by lenders to brokers[775] may be subject to fraud-based claims. In denying a lender's motion to dismiss, a federal court held that RESPA created a duty to disclose such a compensation arrangement, and noted that it might prohibit it entirely. The borrowers had alleged, among other claims, that the defendants fraudulently concealed the fact that the yield spread premium induced the broker to hike the borrower's interest rate on the loan.[776] Similarly, when a car dealer allegedly misrepresents that payments to a third-party service contract provider and to an insurance company were accurate, a fraud claim may be stated[777] (although the consumer later lost at trial).[778]

The deceptive use of open-end credit to finance large ticket items, such as satellite dishes, can be costly to the lender and merchant. In *Carlisle v. Whirlpool Finance National Bank*, a jury awarded $580 million in two individual cases joined for trial. The factual basis of this award, though reduced by the trial court to $300 million, was fully supported by the evidence, the trial court found.[779] The facts presented revealed, as the court described it, a malicious sales practice designed to target the poor, under-educated elderly, and African-American citizens of Alabama. The daughter and elderly parents who purchased one satellite dish understood that they could pay for it in thirty-six

---

772 George v. Capital S. Mortgage Invests., Inc., 961 P.2d 32 (Kan. 1998).

773 Holley Gilbert, *Portland Couple Awarded $545,000 in Mortgage Case Tied to Language*, The Oregonian, Feb. 1, 2004, *available at* www.oregonlive.com/news/oregonian/index.ssf?/base/news/1075640117239800.xml.

774 Johnson v. Mercury Fin., Clearinghouse No. 50,407, Case No. CV 93-952 (Ala. Cir. Ct. Aug. 1994) (jury verdict). Car dealers also run into trouble if they have customers sign binding purchase orders before disclosing the financing terms. In one case, the consumer agreed to buy a car, was given possession, traded in her old car, but was never given any disclosures about the financing terms until three days later. On the first visit, the consumer told her dealer that she wanted an interest rate lower than the 11% she had paid for the purchase of her trade-in. When she arrived three days later, the dealer told the that she would have to accept an interest rate of 15%. In addition, she was informed that the cost of an extended warranty ($595) was a price fixed by Ford Motor Credit Company. It turned out the actual cost was only $150. The court held that those facts stated claims under the Illinois Consumer Fraud Act. Grimaldi v. Webb, 668 N.E.2d 39 (Ill. App. Ct. 1996). *Cf.* Adkinson v. Harpeth Ford Mercury, 1991 WL 17177 (Tenn. Ct. App. 1991) (auto dealer's hiking interest rate on financing contract to keep excess was a UDAP violation). *But cf.* Perino v. Mercury Fin. Co., 912 F. Supp. 313 (N.D. Ill. 1995) (looking solely to Truth in Lending's disclosure standard, court held auto dealer's failure to disclose kickback from the financer on a 10% "rate upsell," from 30% to 40% on a used car financing contract did not constitute mail fraud sufficient to establish it as a RICO predicate act. *NB:* See National Consumer Law Center, Truth in

Lending §§ 3.6.2, 3.7.8 (5th ed. 2003 and Supp.) on the current adequacy and accuracy of TIL rules regarding disclosing the "discount").

775 *See* § 11.5.4.3, *supra.*

776 *See* Briggs v. Countrywide Funding Corp., 931 F. Supp. 1545 (RICO claim alleging a scheme to defraud by inducing brokers to steer borrowers to lender with inflated interest rates in exchange for hidden commissions also survived motion to dismiss), *vacated on other grounds*, 949 F. Supp. 812 (M.D. Ala. 1996).

777 Sutton v. Viking Oldsmobile Nissan, Inc., 2001 WL 856250 (Minn. App. July 31, 2001) (denying dealer's motion for summary judgment).

778 Sutton v. Viking Oldsmobile Nissan, Inc., 2004 WL 26595 (Minn. App. Jan. 6, 2004) (affirming jury verdict against consumer).

779 Carlisle v. Whirlpool Fin. Nat'l Bank, Civil Action No. CV 97-068 (Circuit Court, Hale County, Ala., Post Trial Order, Aug. 25, 1999), Clearinghouse No. 52,516.

installments of $34 each. Because the lender structured the loan as open-ended credit, the payments actually would have lasted for eight years at the interest rate charged (22%). Significantly, the court upheld liability against the lender under an agency theory based upon evidence showing that the lender and merchant agreement gave the lender the right to inspect the merchant's premises; to approve or disapprove of any marketing, advertising, promotional, and other sale materials; to approve or deny credit; to set the terms of the financing; to make decisions about extending credit before the sale occurred; and to require that the merchant use the lender's documents. Further, the court specifically found the lender was holding the merchants out to the public as having the authority to represent the lender and to explain the financing terms and lender documents.

Loan flipping, the practice of frequently refinancing debt, particularly debt laden with insurance premiums and extra charges,[780] has been challenged as fraudulent.[781] As the manner in which this practice insidiously ratchets up the cost of credit works mostly outside the APR disclosure, it is an almost inherently deceptive practice. A reported Seventh Circuit decision has held that a well-plead claim of loan flipping can state a claim for mail fraud sufficient to withstand a motion to dismiss a RICO claim.[782] On the other hand, the Kansas Supreme Court upheld summary judgment in a flipping case where the borrower alleged that the lender failed to tell him material facts about the cost of repeated refinancings in the context of the lender's "campaign" to get customers flip loans.[783] Though conceding that loan flipping, under certain circumstances, could rise to the level of

fraud, the court found no theory to support a duty on the lender's part to disclose the effect of refinancing on the borrower's overall picture. The court seemed influenced by the relative sophistication of the borrower.[784] The dissent, in contrast, looked to *The Restatement of Torts* which creates a duty to exercise reasonable care in order to prevent partial or ambiguous statements of facts from being misleading.[785] Characterizing a loan origination fee as a prepaid finance charge was ambiguous as the borrower understood that the $100 fee (for only $500 of new money) was simply an interest payment. If he had known that he was required to pay $100 to receive a small sum of money, he would not have done so. In light of this, the dissent believed that the grant of summary judgment was inappropriate.

The Alabama Supreme Court upheld a jury verdict against a lender and insurer for knowingly selling credit insurance to ineligible borrowers.[786] The jury had awarded a general verdict of $5 million, covering both compensatory and punitive damages. After a remand from the U.S. Supreme Court, the Alabama Supreme Court upheld $1 million of this verdict.

Misrepresentation was successfully raised in a foreclosure case, *Greene v. Gilbrator Mortgage Investment Corp.*[787] in which the court found the failure to disclose an unconscionably high broker fee and the lender's charging of interest on that fee to be a misrepresentation. The lender also falsely represented the loan amount and the offering of a market interest rate. One case raises the interesting question of whether a creditor's representation that gross credit life insurance coverage is necessary to pay off the loan in the event of the borrower's death, when in fact only (cheaper) net coverage would be sufficient, might constitute misrep-

780 *See* § 6.1, *supra.* Emery v. American Gen. Fin., Inc., 71 F.3d 1343 (7th Cir. 1995), discussed in detail at § 12.6, *supra.*

781 Stewart v. Associates Consumer Discount Co., 183 F.R.D. 189 (E.D. Pa. 1998) (class certification granted where allegations involved a scheme targeting borrowers who had difficulty obtaining credit from banks, sending them "live" checks, charging exorbitant points, upselling the loans from consumer loans to home-secured loans, promising to consolidate other debt but failing to do so, and repeatedly refinancing existing loans; claims raised under fraud, conspiracy, RICO, UDAP, TILA, and unjust enrichment theories). *See also* Reynolds v. American Gen. Fin, Inc., 1999 Ala. Civ. App. LEXIS 858 (Ala. Civ. App. Dec. 3, 1999) (lender's motion for summary judgment reversed in this flipping case where lender stated that interest rate was 20% but it was actually higher; issue was whether statute of limitations was tolled due to alleged fraud), *addressed on appeal*, 795 So. 2d 685 (Ala. 2000) (statute of limitations not tolled).

782 Emery v. American Gen. Fin., Inc., 71 F.3d 1343 (7th Cir. 1995), discussed in detail at § 12.6, *supra.*

783 Gonzales v. Associates Fin. Serv., 967 P.2d 312 (Kan. 1998). *See also* Brown v. Norwest Fin. Ala., Inc., 723 So. 2d 97 (Ala. Civ. App. 1998) (though acknowledging that a fraudulent suppression cause of action could arise from the practice of flipping, in Alabama the borrower must show that the lender had a duty to communicate, arising either from a confidential relationship or a request for information, neither of which existed in this case; contention that lender fraudulently suppressed the existence of the mortgage placed on her home also failed).

784 He was in the Air Force, had completed 43 hours of college credit, was a 13-year customer of Associates, and had obtained credit from numerous other creditors. *See also Ex parte* Ford Motor Credit Co., 717 So. 2d 781 (Ala. 1997)(though the consumer specifically asked why he was getting a car loan at such a high rate after the dealer told him it would get the best rate [and one would think this would be enough to state at least a suppression of material fact claim, as did the intermediate appellate court] and the dealer told him a half-truth or a lie, court found no suppression claim stated, mainly, it appears, because the consumer had been involved in the used car business).

785 Restatement (Second) of Torts §§ 551(2)(b), (c), (e) (1997).

786 Union Sec. Life Ins. Co. v. Crocker, 667 So. 2d 688 (Ala. 1995), *vacated on other grounds*, 116 S. Ct. 1872 (1996) ($2 million punitive damage award was sent back to Alabama Supreme Court for further consideration in light of BMW of N. America, Inc. v. Gore, 517 U.S. 559, 116 S. Ct. 1589 (1996)), *upon remand from Supreme Court*, 709 So. 2d 1118 (Ala. 1997) (reducing punitive damages award to $1 million by weighing reprehensible conduct of insurance company's agent (though an apparently isolated instance) coupled with the "catastrophic" economic injury to Ms. Crocker who was facing foreclosure of her mobile home in the wake of her husband's death, against the percentage $2 million award represented of insurance companies' net worth), discussed further in § 8.5.5.1, *supra.*

787 488 F. Supp. 177, 529 F. Supp. 186 (D.D.C. 1981).

resentation.[788] However, a car dealer's statement that he would try to get a "better deal" was held not to be a misrepresentation but only an opinion based upon a statement about a future event.[789]

12.10.2.5 Falsification and Forgery

Complaints by consumers and homeowners about car dealers and mortgage brokers inflating their income and falsifying credit applications are common. Courts may be reluctant to believe the consumer that these parties perpetrated the fraud, instead blaming the consumer. One recent decision should add credibility to these complaints.[790] The decision outlines a "massive pattern of fraud" alleged by the assignee who bought retail installment contracts and leases from a car dealer in the context of denying a motion to dismiss the fraud claim. In the mortgage context, inflating appraisals allows some lenders and brokers to refinance loans that would otherwise hit the brick wall of insufficient equity. The homeowner becomes irretrievably tied to the new lender because, once the inflated valuation is uncovered, the loan to value ratio will be so high that other potential lenders will refuse to refinance.[791] In addition to fraud claims, the broker or lender may be covered by the federal or state credit repair statutes.[792] Making a statement that is false usually violates these acts. Furthermore, falsifying a loan application or inflating an appraisal is a federal criminal offense.[793]

In these cases, the lender or another defendant may raise an affirmative defense of fraud against the consumer based upon participation in the falsification of the loan application. One court rejected this defense when the borrowers were told that the practice of getting false "gift" letters when the cash really came from the property seller was standard in such loans.[794]

A deed that is forged or altered is void *ab initio* and a purchaser does not acquire title,[795] though the purchaser may be entitled to an equitable lien for the value of the improvements made by the purchaser in good faith.[796]

---

788 *See* McCullar v. Universal Underwriters Life Ins. Co., 687 So. 2d 156 (Ala. 1996) (opinion decides that statute mandates net, not gross coverage; factual question whether creditor fraudulently misled consumer about necessary coverage; a concurring opinion suggests that there is a duty not to misrepresent the amount of insurance *necessary* even if a higher amount is legally *permissible* under state law). *But see* Baldwin v. Laurel Ford Lincoln-Mercury, Inc., 32 F. Supp. 2d 894 (S.D. Miss. 1998) (no duty to disclose the fact that the assignee paid the car dealer part of the higher interest rate in a commission and that the dealer kept part of the extended service fee; no representation that the consumer was getting the best deal); §§ 8.3.1.2, 8.5.3.1.2, *supra*, for discussions of gross versus net coverage.

789 Graham v. RRR, L.L.C., 202 F. Supp. 2d 483 (E.D. Va. 2002), *aff'd mem.*, 55 Fed. Appx. 135, 2003 WL 139432 (4th Cir. Jan. 21, 2003).

790 Gelco Corp. v. Major Chevrolet, Inc., 2002 WL 31427027 (N.D. Ill. Oct. 30, 2002). *See also* United States v. Rivera, 2004 WL 3153171 (D. Conn. Aug. 5, 2004) (denying motion to dismiss indictment charging that auto salesman submitted falsified information to finance company).Knapp v. Americredit Fin. Serv., Inc., 245 F. Supp. 2d 841 (S.D. W. Va. Feb. 18, 2003) (testimony supported consumer's allegations that lender trained the dealer to create false pay stubs and false downpayments and to charge an acquisition fee in addition to interest of twenty-one percent which were included in the cash price of the vehicle; civil conspiracy count survives motion for summary judgment); Cannon v. William Chevrolet/GEO, Inc., 794 N.E.2d 843 (Ill. App. Ct. 2003); State of Iowa *ex rel.* Miller v. Dan Nelson Automotive Group, Inc., Equity No. CE50210 (Iowa Dist. Ct., Polk Cty.), *available at* www.state.ia.us/government/latest_news/releases/jan_2005/dnelson.pdf. (complaint filed Jan. 7, 2005, alleging that auto dealer routinely submitted false credit information about customers to lender). Note that for FHA insured loans, altering or falsifying any document for the purpose of getting HUD to accept or insure the loan is a federal crime. 18 U.S.C. § 1010.

791 Examples of mortgage loan cases in which the broker's or lender's falsification of information on the loan applications was an issue or at least mentioned as part of the facts include: United States v. Robinson, 2004 WL 370234 (4th Cir. Mar. 1, 2004) (affirming conviction of mobile home seller for falsifying buyers' employment and income information and inflating down payments; defendant recruited accomplices to set up phone lines in their homes and verify bogus information when lenders called); Wilson v. Toussie, 260 F. Supp. 2d 530 (E.D.N.Y. 2003); Cunningham v. Equicredit Corp. of Ill., 256 F. Supp. 2d 785 (N.D. Ill. 2003); Matthews v. New Century Mortgage Corp., 185 F. Supp. 2d 874 (S.D. Ohio 2002); In re Jones, 298 B.R. 451 (Bankr. D. Kan. 2003); Hoffman v. Stamper, 843 A.2d 153 (Md. Ct. Spec. App. 2004) (loan officer complicit in the property seller's practice of creating false gift letters in order to qualify home buyers for FHA-insured loans), *aff'd in part, rev'd in part*, 867 A.2d 276 (Md. 2005) (affirming in all respects except emotional distress damages); Haser v. Wright, 2002 WL 31379971 (Mass. Super. Ct. Sept. 4, 2002); Opportunity Mgmt. Co. v. Frost, 1999 WL 96001 (Wash. Ct. App. Feb. 16, 1999).

792 *See* § 12.4, *supra*.

793 18 U.S.C. § 1014. Some appraisers are up in arms over the pressure they feel from lenders, mortgage brokers, and real estate brokers to assess a predetermined value to property. Over 8,300 of them signed a petition to the Federal Financial Institutions Council, as of May, 2005. *See* Concerned Appraisers from Across America Petition, *available at* http://appraiserspetition.com.

794 Hoffman v. Stamper, 843 A.2d 153 (Md. Ct. Spec. App. 2004), *aff'd in part, rev'd in part*, 867 A.2d 276 (Md. 2005) (affirming in all respects except emotional distress damages).

795 M.M.&G., Inc. v. Jackson, 612 A.2d 186 (D.C. 1992); Harding v. Ja Laur Corp., 315 A.2d 132 (Md. Ct. Spec. App. 1974); *see also* Ward v. Gray, 374 A.2d 15 (Del. Super. Ct. 1977) (when there is no jurisdiction to conduct a sale due to fraud or failure to meet notice requirements, the sale is void and any resulting title is a nullity).

796 M.M.&G., Inc. v. Jackson, 612 A.2d 186 (D.C. 1992).

12.10.2.6 Negligent Misrepresentation

Negligent misrepresentation, which has a lesser standard of proof than fraud,[797] has also been held to apply in some instances to the debtor-creditor relationship.[798] Such actions as representing that a loan had been approved to stop a foreclosure, when the loan was subsequently denied or offered on more disadvantageous terms, may be subject to such a claim even if no fraudulent intent is present.[799] Similarly, representations by retail sellers (car dealers, home improvement contractors) and loan brokers about the nature of the financing they will arrange may lead to claims for negligent misrepresentation.

12.10.2.7 Effect of Credit Documents That Contradict Oral Misrepresentations

It often happens that oral misrepresentations made to a borrower are glaringly contradicted by documents in the loan package.[800] Written notice that the lender is not obliged to refinance a balloon payment (even though it stated it would refinance) is one example; a document stating that the lender would not escrow for taxes and insurance (though it assured the borrower it would) is another. Quite often, the low-income borrower has not read these documents. Indeed, research has shown that consumers are unlikely to understand contemporary consumer contracts even if they attempt to read them.[801] If the lender induces the borrower to sign without reading the documents through fraud and misrepresentation, and the borrower exercised due care under the circumstances, that may constitute part of the fraud.[802] Where a lack of education, inability to read the language, or a disability makes it impossible for a borrower to read or understand, that simply may bolster claims of the lender's fraud. The parol evidence rule does not bar evidence of fraud.[803]

12.10.3 Constitutional and Statutory Restrictions on Punitive Damages

One of the benefits of a fraud claim is that punitive damages are available in most jurisdictions. In a number of states, however, punitive damages for some or most torts are capped by statute either at a fixed multiple of compensatory damages or at a dollar amount.[804]

In addition, the U.S. Supreme Court has held that the Due Process Clause prohibits a state from imposing grossly excessive punitive damages on a tortfeasor. The Court has identified three guideposts for determining whether a punitive damage award is grossly excessive:

---

797 The elements are: 1) a representation made in the course of business or in a transaction in which he has a pecuniary interest; 2) furnishing false information for guidance of others in their business transactions; 3) no reasonable care or competence exercised in obtaining or communicating the information; and 4) the other party has pecuniary loss caused by justifiable reliance on the information. No intent to deceive is required. Richter, S.A. v. Bank of Am. Nat'l Trust & Sav. Ass'n, 939 F.2d 1176, 1185 (5th Cir. 1991); Federal Land Bank v. Sloane, 825 S.W.2d 439, 442 (Tex. 1991); Birt v. Wells Fargo Home Mortg., Inc., 75 P.3d 640, 651–57 (Wyo. 2003).

798 *E.g.*, Richter, S.A. v. Bank of Am. Nat'l Trust & Sav. Ass'n, 939 F.2d 1176 (5th Cir. 1991) (bank's negotiating with debtor over restructuring debt without informing him it had decided to "disengage" from credit relationship supported jury finding of negligent misrepresentation, though bank had legal right to refuse loan); Fidler v. Central Coop. Bank (*In re* Fidler), 210 B.R. 411 (Bankr. D. Mass. 1997) (allegations that the lender negligently misrepresented the nature and terms of the loan stated a claim); Frame v. Boatmen's Bank, 824 S.W.2d 491 (Mo. Ct. App. 1991) (bank's oral representation that it would fund a loan to purchase real estate without informing debtor of all contingencies which must be met prior to approval held subject to claim; bank knew debtor relying on its professional judgment on the matter, and loan officer had duty of due care in providing information and advice); Federal Land Bank v. Sloane, 825 S.W.2d 439 (Tex. 1991) (negligent misrepresentation that it had approved loan application).

799 *But cf.* Birt v. Wells Fargo Home Mortg., Inc., 75 P.3d 640, 657–58 (Wyo. 2003) (negligent misrepresentation of future intent or opinion insufficient for claim; incorrect statement that loan would be approved not actionable).

800 *See, e.g.*, Young v. First Am. Fin. Servs., 977 F. Supp. 38 (D.D.C. 1997) (denying defendant lender's motion to dismiss fraud claim where homeowners allege that lender refinanced in an amount double the existing mortgage with the promise of another refinancing in a year to reduce significantly the monthly payment. Needless to say, the reduction of the high monthly payment never occurred).

801 Cathy Lesser Mansfield and Alan White, Literacy and Contract, 13 Stan. Law & Policy Rev. 503 (2003).

802 Hanson v. American Nat'l Bank & Trust, 844 S.W.2d 408 (Ky. 1992), *vacated and remanded on other grounds*, 509 U.S. 918 (1993), *on remand*, 865 S.W.2d 302 (Ky. 1993). *See also* Holveck v. Ameriquest Mortgage Co., 2003 WL 21149085 (N.D. Ill. May 19, 2003) (motion to dismiss denied when borrowers alleged that they were induced to sign a note based upon representations that it did not contain a prepayment penalty). *But see* Davis v. G.N. Mortg. Corp., 396 F.3d 869 (7th Cir. 2005) (borrowers' failure to read and compare two stacks of documents presented to them at closing negates justifiable reliance on lender's misrepresentation that prepayment penalty only applied for two years); Clark v. U.S. Bank N.A., 2004 WL 1380166 (E.D. Pa. June 18, 2004) (no justifiable reliance where borrower signed multiple documents at closing that guided him not to rely on oral representations and that stated that only loan terms were those contained in the documents); Moore v. Mortgagestar, Inc., 2002 U.S. Dist. LEXIS 27457 (S.D. W. Va. Dec. 18, 2002) (granting summary judgment to lender on fraud claim; borrowers cannot show justifiable reliance on oral misrepresentations about loan terms where they did not review the documents they signed; court denies summary judgment on other fraud claims and unconscionability claim).

803 *See, e.g.*, O'Brien v. Cacciatore, 591 N.E.2d 1384, 1390 (Ill. App. 1992). *See generally* National Consumer Law Center, Automobile Fraud § 7.7.2 (2d ed. 2003 and Supp.).

804 *See* National Consumer Law Center, Automobile Fraud § 7.10.4 (2d ed. 2003 and Supp.).

- The degree of reprehensibility on the part of the defendant;
- The disparity between the harm or potential harm suffered and the punitive damages awarded;
- The difference between the punitive damages awarded and the civil penalties authorized or imposed in comparable cases.[805]

Factors that courts should consider when weighing the reprehensibility of a defendant's conduct include:

- Whether the harm is physical as opposed to economic;
- Whether the tortious conduct shows an indifference to or reckless disregard of the health or safety of others;
- Whether the target of the conduct had financial vulnerability;
- Whether the conduct involved repeated actions or was only an isolated incident;
- Whether the harm resulted from intentional malice, trickery, or deceit, or mere accident.[806]

Some of these factors are likely to be pronounced in consumer credit cases. The harm will usually be economic rather than physical, but the creditor's actions may involve some threat to the consumer's health or safety, particularly if loss of a home, loss of utility service, or faulty home repairs are involved. The targets of fraud in consumer credit cases typically are financially vulnerable, and fraudulent creditors often specifically seek out these vulnerable consumers. Showing repetition and malicious intent is also often possible.

As to the ratio of punitive to compensatory damages, "few awards exceeding a single-digit ratio between punitive and compensatory damages, to a significant degree, will satisfy due process."[807] Nonetheless, the Supreme Court held that a higher ratio may be consistent with due process if an egregious act causes only a small amount of economic harm.[808] Many courts have applied this principle, upholding punitive damages well in excess of a single-digit ratio to compensatory damages where the compensatory damage award was relatively small.[809]

The constitutional standards for punitive damages are discussed in detail in another volume in this series.[810]

12.11 Other Lender Liability Theories

12.11.1 Duty of Due Care

A bank, by virtue of agreeing to process a mortgage loan application and lock in a specified interest rate for ninety days in exchange for a $144 payment for an appraisal and credit report fee, entered into a relationship which gave rise to a tort duty of due care in processing the application.[811] In this case, the court suggested that the duty might be measured by looking at industry standards, such as credit underwriting standards established by the Federal Home Loan Mortgage Corporation, in the case of mortgage lending.[812] A mortgage holder which held a pay-off check from a third party too long, with the result that the check bounced when the issuer went out of business, breached a duty of care to the borrower.[813]

12.11.2 Estoppel

The elements of an estoppel claim include that the party estopped must have engaged in conduct which amounted to a false representation or concealment of material facts, must have had an intention that such conduct would be acted upon by the other party, and must have known the real facts. The party asserting estoppel must show that she lacked knowledge of the true facts, relied upon the conduct of the party estopped, and prejudicially changed her position in reliance thereon.[814] A court confirmed that a homeowner may raise an estoppel argument to defend against a foreclosure when he relied upon the lender's statement that his previous mortgage loan would be paid in full from the proceeds of the new loan and this pay-off did not occur.[815]

---

805 State Farm Mut. Auto. Ins. Co. v. Campbell, 538 U.S. 408, 123 S. Ct. 1513, 155 L. Ed. 2d 585 (2003); BMW of N. Am., Inc. v. Gore, 517 U.S. 559, 116 S. Ct. 1589, 134 L. Ed. 2d 809 (1996).

806 State Farm Mut. Auto. Ins. Co. v. Campbell, 538 U.S. 408, 123 S. Ct. 1513, 1521, 155 L. Ed. 2d 585 (2003).

807 *Id.*, 123 S. Ct. at 1524.

808 *Id.*

809 *See, e.g.,* Mathias v. Accor Econ. Lodging, Inc., 347 F.3d 672 (7th Cir. 2003) (upholding 37.2-to-1 ratio where compensatory damage award to motel guest bitten by bedbugs was $5000). *See* National Consumer Law Center, Automobile Fraud § 7.10.6.3.4 (2d ed. 2003 and Supp.).

810 National Consumer Law Center, Automobile Fraud § 7.10.6 (2d ed. 2003 and Supp.).

811 Jacques v. First Nat'l Bank, 515 A.2d 756 (Md. Ct. Spec. App. 1986). *See also* High v. McLean Fin. Corp., 659 F. Supp. 1561 (D.D.C. 1987). *Cf.* Ferleger v. First Am. Mtg. Co., 662 F. Supp. 584 (N.D. Ill. 1987) (broker allegedly offered locked-in terms without disclosing the time limit, and would delay processing past expiration date, borrowers alleged RICO and UDAP claims; defendant's motion to dismiss denied).

812 Jacques v. First Nat'l Bank, 515 A.2d 756, 764 (Md. Ct. Spec. App. 1986). Query whether a similar duty might be breached by lenders who make high cost loans to people they know will not be able to repay, contravening underwriting standards?

813 *See* Family Fed. Sav. & Loan v. Davis, 172 B.R. 437 (Bankr. D.D.C. 1994).

814 First Union Nat'l Bank v. Tecklendburg, 769 N.Y.S.2d 573 (App. Div. 2003).

815 *Id. But cf.* Davis v. U.S. Bankcorp, 383 F.3d 761 (8th Cir. 2004) (no promissory estoppel claim where lender issued pre-qualifi-

In a yo-yo car case,[816] the court held that the dealer was estopped from denying that the original purchase order was valid when the consumer had relied upon it in good faith to her detriment.[817] The facts of this case undoubtedly drove the outcome. The consumer traded in her old car and signed the contract to buy another and paid a downpayment. The purchase order purported to be contingent upon financing. After the consumer went home with her new car, the dealer called and assured her that the financing had gone through at the special rate in effect for a limited time. The dealer then sold her trade-in. That same day, the dealer was told that the financing had not been approved and communicated this to the consumer. The next day, the dealer repossessed her car. The court placed the burden on the dealer to show that the consumer did not rely upon the claims of the dealer, finding that consumer reliance on car dealers is "expected."

In *First State Bank v. Phillips*,[818] the court held that a bank was estopped from enforcing a balloon payment clause in a note and dismissed the foreclosure. The consumer in *Phillips* had assumed a mortgage extended by the bank to the person from whom the consumer brought the house. The mortgage indicated it would be fully paid with monthly payments, though the promissory note provided that after a period of regular monthly payments, the balance of the note would be due in a single lump sum balloon payment. The mortgage, which the consumer saw, did not contain the balloon payment; the consumer never saw the note which did. When the consumer talked to bank employees about assuming the mortgage, the balloon payment was not disclosed. The court found that the nondisclosure of that term forfeited the bank's right to enforce it.

12.12 Liability Chart: Lender and Assignee Liability

One of the most important practical decisions for a consumer advocate to make in attacking abusive credit transactions is to determine which actors to sue and what legal theories support the liability of each defendant included in the lawsuit. Lenders and other third parties often work together or perform in parallel universes that intersect in ways which create legal liability.

For example, door-to-door home improvement contractors almost always operate hand-in-hand with a lender who stands in the background, approves the credit extended, and either makes the loan directly or purchases an installment contract immediately from the contractor. The obligation may then be transferred on the secondary market. Mortgage brokers are involved in more than half of all mortgage transactions, according to HUD.[819] The presence of brokers in high-cost mortgage loans is especially common. At one extreme, the broker and lender may be, in effect, the same entity. Other mortgage brokers act as bird dogs for a relatively small group of lenders with whom they have a referral relationship. The payments of kickbacks by lenders to mortgage brokers who bring them business has generated considerable controversy.[820]

In most credit transactions, it is critical to hold the entity (usually an assignee) which holds the loan note or credit contract responsible for its behavior and/or that of third parties for several reasons. Usually, the consumer must make payments to the assignee during any litigation or risk repossession of collateral, foreclosure, and adverse information reported to the credit bureau. Raising claims and defenses to the obligation itself can provide the consumer with significant practical relief from an overbearing debt. In addition, the third parties who were directly responsible for the illegal behavior may be judgment-proof, may have filed bankruptcy, or may have disappeared. The assignee may be the only deep pocket around to provide some relief to a harmed consumer. Assignees will try to hide behind the shield of the holder-in-due-course rule, claiming legal, if not actual, innocence.

Checklists One and Two list statutes or common law claims that pin liability on the *assignee* for the behavior of bad actors "upstream." Under some of these theories, the assignee will be involved in the illegal behavior to a certain extent. Under others, the assignee may be liable despite its actual innocence, though damages will be limited as a result. Checklist Three provides a short analysis of the responsibility flowing to creditors due to their involvement with the most common (and most troublesome) third parties, i.e., home improvement contractors, brokers, car dealers, door-to-door sellers, and others.

"Close-connection" liability refers to the responsibility of the entity in its own right for its involvement with third parties who harm the consumer to the full extent of any damages available under tort, contract, or statutory theories. "Derivative" liability refers to the accountability of an entity for the acts of others, regardless of its involvement in the illegal conduct. In most cases, derivative liability is created by statutes or regulations that also limit the extent of the creditor's or assignee's exposure.

cation letter but did not approve loan); Birt v. Wells Fargo Home Mortg., Inc., 75 P.3d 640, 651–57 (Wyo. 2003) (no promissory estoppel or equitable estoppel claim against bank that led consumers to believe that financing would be approved but then denied their application).

816 See § 11.6.5, *supra*.
817 Heltzel v. Mecham Pontiac, 730 P.2d 235 (Ariz. 1986).
818 681 S.W.2d 408 (Ark. Ct. App. 1984).

819 See § 12.2.1.5.2, *supra*.
820 See §§ 11.5.4, 12.2.1.5, *supra*.

Close-Connection Assignee Liability: Checklist One

Assignees can be "primarily" liable for acts of the originating lenders or third parties under these theories:

- Fraud/UDAP (where the assignee is involved in some way);[821]
- Agency;[822]
- Corporate/familial relationships between the parties;[823]
- Civil conspiracy between or among parties;[824]
- Aiding and abetting;[825]
- Knowledge of fraud and acceptance of the "fruits";[826]
- Knowledge of insolvency of seller;[827]
- RESPA violation if referral fees were paid or fees were split for the provision of settlement services in the mortgage loan context;[828]
- RICO;[829]
- ECOA;[830]
- Fair Housing Act;[831]
- Consumer Leasing Act, all violations if assignee is substantially involved in the deal.[832]

Derivative Liability of Assignees: Checklist Two

Assignees can be derivatively liable for the acts of originating lenders or sellers or lessees because of the:

- FTC preservation of claims and defenses of sellers up to amount of the sales contract;[833]
- TILA:
  - *Damage claims* arising in all consumer loans and leases—for TILA violations apparent on the face of the documents;[834]
  - *Rescission* claims arising in certain mortgage loans—for all TILA violations that are material under rescission rules even if not apparent on the face of the documents;[835]
  - *HOEPA mortgage loans*—for *all* claims/defenses (TILA or otherwise) against original creditor up to amount of the contract;[836]
  - *Consumer leasing*: all violations if assignee is substantially involved in the deal; non-disclosure violations regardless of involvement; otherwise, only liable for disclosure violations apparent on the face of the documents;[837]
- Assignees are generally liable, unless holder-in-due-course status is achieved[838] or, if the transaction involves a retail installment sales contract, a similar defense applies;[839]
- State retail installment sales acts may have special rules about assignee liability.[840]
- Licensing violation or other illegality in contract which renders it void.[841]

---

821 *See* § 12.10, *supra*; National Consumer Law Center, Unfair and Deceptive Acts and Practices §§ 5.1, 6.3 (6th ed. 2004 and Supp.).

822 *See* §§ 11.5.4, 12.10.1, *supra*; National Consumer Law Center, Unfair and Deceptive Acts and Practices §§ 5.1, 6.3, 6.4 (6th ed. 2004 and Supp.); National Consumer Law Center, Truth in Lending § 3.7.4 (5th ed. 2003 and Supp.).

823 *See* §§ 11.5.4, 12.10.1, *supra*; National Consumer Law Center, Unfair and Deceptive Acts and Practices §§ 5.1, 6.3, 6.4 (6th ed. 2004 and Supp.); National Consumer Law Center, Truth in Lending § 3.7.4 (5th ed. 2003 and Supp.).

824 *See* § 12.10.1, *supra*; National Consumer Law Center, Unfair and Deceptive Acts and Practices §§ 5.1, 6.5 (6th ed. 2004 and Supp.).

825 *See* § 12.10.1, *supra*; National Consumer Law Center, Unfair and Deceptive Acts and Practices § 6.5 (6th ed. 2004 and Supp.).

826 *See* § 12.10.1, *supra*.

827 *See id.*; National Consumer Law Center, Unfair and Deceptive Acts and Practices § 6.5.2 (6th ed. 2004 and Supp.).

828 *See* § 12.2, *supra*.

829 *See* §§ 10.8.5.3.3, 12.6, *supra*; National Consumer Law Center, Unfair and Deceptive Acts and Practices § 9.2 (6th ed. 2004 and Supp.).

830 *See* § 12.3, *supra*; National Consumer Law Center, Credit Discrimination § 2.2.5 (4th ed. 2005).

831 *See* § 12.3, *supra*; National Consumer Law Center, Credit Discrimination § 2.3.2.3 (4th ed. 2005).

832 National Consumer Law Center, Truth in Lending § 10.7.6.2 (5th ed. 2003 and Supp.).

833 *See* National Consumer Law Center, Unfair and Deceptive Acts and Practices § 6.6 (6th ed. 2004 and Supp.); § 10.6.1.2, *supra*. This includes liability for acts of third-party sellers who have referral or other relationships with the lender. *See* new U.C.C. § 9-403 which states that an omitted holder notice is part of the credit-dales agreement as a matter of law; the assignee is subject to the consumer's claims and defenses just as if the holder notice had been included. *See also* Official Comment 5 to that provision. This change, now in effect in virtually every state, applies even to loans consummated before the U.C.C. revision's effective date. U.C.C. § 9-702.

834 National Consumer Law Center, Truth in Lending §§ 7.3.2, 10.7.6.2 (5th ed. 2003 and Supp.).

835 *Id.* §§ 6.9, 7.3.3, 7.3.5.

836 *Id.* § 9.7.2.

837 *Id.* § 10.7.6.2.

838 *See* § 10.6.1.3, *supra*; National Consumer Law Center, Unfair and Deceptive Acts and Practices § 6.7.1 (6th ed. 2004 and Supp.); National Consumer Law Center, Repossessions and Foreclosure §§ 16.7.6.2, 16.7.6.3 (5th ed. 2002 and Supp.).

839 *See* U.C.C. §§ 9-403, 9-404.

840 *See* general discussion of RISAs in § 2.3.3.4, *supra*. Citations to all state RISAs can be found in App. A, *infra*.

841 *See* §§ 10.6.1.3.8, 10.6.1.3.9, *supra*.

Lender Liability for Acts of Specific Third Parties: Checklist Three

Originating lenders can be held primarily or derivatively responsible for the acts of third parties with whom they have some involvement under a wide variety of theories. If a creditor is liable under these theories, the assignee may also face accountability under Checklist One or Two.

Home improvement contractors and brokers:

When a home improvement contractor and/or broker are involved in connecting the consumer to the lender, consult Checklist One for theories to hold the lender responsible for the actions of these third parties. If only a broker but no contractor arranged the loan, the FTC preservation of claims and defenses rule will not apply. Note that a few states have enacted home improvement financing acts that apply if the contractor originated the loan that financed the work and also may apply if the contractor only arranged the loan.[842] These acts may place some derivative liability on the creditor for acts of the contractor. In addition, state door-to-door sales acts often allow the consumer to cancel the entire transaction, including the financing, if the act was violated.[843]

Car dealers:

In the most common scenario, the car dealer originates the retail installment contract and immediately assigns it to the funding lender who is the technical assignee. In these cases, the assignee may be held liable under the "close-connection" liability theories in Checklist One depending on the nature of its involvement in the underlying car sale and financing tactics of the dealer. Otherwise, the assignee may be responsible under the theories identified in Checklist Two.

Door-to-door sellers:

If the lender originates the loan, consult Checklist One. In addition, if the FTC Holder Rule applies due to a referral arrangement with the seller, the lender may have derivative responsibility. If the seller writes the retail installment contract, consult Checklist Two.

Door-to-door sales acts—certain violations trigger cancellation of the sale and the loan.[844]

Merchants:

- Billing errors and merchant behavior in the credit card context;[845]
- Providing substantial assistance to a telemarketer who violates the law;[846]
- FTC preservation of claims and defenses of sellers up to the amount of the contract.[847]

Debt collectors and repossession companies:

- Fraud/UDAP if creditor or assignee involvement;[848]
- Agency;[849]
- Corporate/familial relationships;[850]
- Civil conspiracy;[851]
- Aiding and abetting;[852]
- Knowledge of fraud and acceptance of the "fruits";[853]
- Non-delegable duty to avoid breach of the peace.[854]

---

845 *Id.* § 6.5.3; National Consumer Law Center, Truth in Lending § 5.8 (5th ed. 2003 and Supp.). *See* 15 U.S.C. § 1666i.

846 National Consumer Law Center, Unfair and Deceptive Acts and Practices § 6.5.5 (6th ed. 2004 and Supp.).

847 *See* National Consumer Law Center, Unfair and Deceptive Acts and Practices § 6.6 (6th ed. 2004 and Supp.); § 10.6.1.2, *supra.* This includes liability for acts of third-party sellers who have referral or other relationships with the lender. *See* new U.C.C. § 9-403 which states that an omitted holder notice is part of the credit-dales agreement as a matter of law; the assignee is subject to the consumer's claims and defenses just as if the holder notice had been included. *See also* Official Comment 5 to that provision. This change, now in effect in virtually every state, applies even to loans consummated before the U.C.C. revision's effective date. U.C.C. § 9-702.

848 *See* § 12.10, *supra*; National Consumer Law Center, Unfair and Deceptive Acts and Practices §§ 5.1, 5.6.1, 6.3 (6th ed. 2004 and Supp.).

849 *See* §§ 11.5.4, 12.10.1, *supra*; National Consumer Law Center, Unfair and Deceptive Acts and Practices §§ 5.1, 6.3, 6.4 (6th ed. 2004 and Supp.); National Consumer Law Center, Truth in Lending § 3.7.4 (5th ed. 2003 and Supp.); for repossession companies, see National Consumer Law Center, Repossessions and Foreclosures §§ 7.3.1.5, 13.10.4 (5th ed. 2002 and Supp.).

850 *See* §§ 11.5.4, 12.10.1, *supra*; National Consumer Law Center, Unfair and Deceptive Acts and Practices §§ 5.1, 6.3, 6.4 (6th ed. 2004 and Supp.); National Consumer Law Center, Truth in Lending § 3.7.4 (5th ed. 2003 and Supp.); for repossession companies, see National Consumer Law Center, Repossessions and Foreclosures §§ 7.3.1.5, 13.10.4 (5th ed. 2002 and Supp.).

851 *See* § 12.10.1, *supra*; National Consumer Law Center, Unfair and Deceptive Acts and Practices §§ 5.1, 6.5 (6th ed. 2004 and Supp.).

852 *See* § 12.10.1, *supra*; National Consumer Law Center, Unfair and Deceptive Acts and Practices § 6.5 (6th ed. 2004 and Supp.).

853 *See* § 12.10.1, *supra.*

854 Williamson v. Fowler Toyota, Inc., 956 P.2d 858 (Okla. 1998). *See* National Consumer Law Center, Repossessions and Foreclosures § 13.10.4.3 (5th ed. 2002 and Supp.).

---

842 *See* discussion in § 11.2.1.2, *supra.*

843 National Consumer Law Center, Unfair and Deceptive Acts and Practices § 5.8.2 (6th ed. 2004 and Supp.).

844 *Id.* § 5.8.2.5.

Officers, managers, directors, owners, parent companies:

- Personal liability of officers, managers, etc. especially where corporation is involved;[855]

- Piercing the corporate veil and related theories;[856]
- Liability of a successor corporation for the predecessor's behavior.[857]

---

855 National Consumer Law Center, Unfair and Deceptive Acts and Practices § 6.4.2 (6th ed. 2004 and Supp.). *See* § 12.10.1, *supra*.

856 National Consumer Law Center, Unfair and Deceptive Acts and Practices § 6.4.3 (6th ed. 2004 and Supp.).

857 *See* National Consumer Law Center, Unfair and Deceptive Acts and Practices § 6.4.6 (6th ed. 2004 and Supp.).

Appendix A — State Lending Statutes

This compilation of cites to state usury laws was as complete as possible as of the printing of this new edition. Practitioners should re-check their state laws for changes and updates to assure accuracy. A citation appearing in parentheses represents the specific section of the law that caps interest or finance charges.

Of those states which still have small or consumer loan laws on the books, some have removed any interest or fees caps and allow the lenders to charge any rate of interest and/or fees that the parties agree upon in writing. These states include: Delaware, Idaho, Illinois, Montana, New Mexico, Oregon, Utah, and Wisconsin. Other protections of these lending statutes, however, may still apply. South Dakota repealed its small loan law entirely. Even though New Jersey and New York removed usury caps in their small loan laws, both states have criminal usury caps that function in the same way.

Added to this Appendix are the citations for newer laws permitting very high rate loans variously called "payday loans" (the term used here), "cash advance loans," or "delayed deposit check loans and auto title loans."[1]

Alabama

Legal Interest Rate: Ala. Code § 8-8-1
Contract: Ala. Code § 8-8-1 *or* Ala. Code § 8-8-14 *or* Ala. Code § 8-8-5
Judgment: Ala. Code § 8-8-10
Small Loans: Ala. Code §§ 5-18-1 to 5-18-23 (§ 5-18-15) Small Loan Act
Installment Loans & Credit: Ala. Code §§ 5-19-1 to 5-19-31 (§ 5-19-3), Consumer Finance
Insurance Premium Finance: Ala. Code §§ 27-40-1 to 27-40-18 (§ 27-40-9)
Revolving Charge: Ala. Code § 8-8-14; Ala. Code § 5-19-3, Consumer Finance
Life Insurance and Annuity Policy Loans: Ala. Code § 27-15-8.1
Auto Title Loans: Ala. Code §§ 5-19A-1 to 5-19A-20 (interpreted in *Floyd v. Title Exch. & Pawn of Anniston, Inc.*, 620 So. 2d 576 (Ala. 1993) to permit auto title lending)
Payday Loans: Ala. Code §§ 5-18A-1 to 5-18A-22 (Deferred Presentment Services Act)

---

1 *See* § 2.2.3.1, *supra,* for the tale of their turn of the century progenitors, the "salary-lenders," and how, in the days when this was considered loan-shark-level interest rates, they led to the first reform movement ultimately leading to the modern consumer credit marketplace. For a full discussion of expensive, disguised credit, see § 7.5, *supra.*

Alaska

Legal Interest Rate: Alaska Stat. § 45.45.010
Contract: Alaska Stat. § 45.45.010
Judgment: Alaska Stat. § 09.30.070
Small Loans: Alaska Stat. §§ 06.20.010 to 06.20.920
Installment Loan Law: Alaska Stat. § 45.45.080
Sales Finance Act: Alaska Stat. §§ 45.10.010 to 45.10.230 (§ 45.10.120), Retail Installment Sales Act
Insurance Premium Finance: Alaska Stat. §§ 06.40.010 to 06.40.190 (§ 06.40.120), Premium Financing Act
Revolving Credit: Alaska Stat. § 45.10.120, Retail Installment Sales Act
Bank Credit Cards: Alaska Stat. §§ 45.10.010 to 45.10.230 (§ 45.10.120), Retail Installment Sales Act; Alaska Stat. § 06.05.209
Open End Loans: Alaska Stat. § 06.20.285, Open End Loans; Alaska Stat. § 06.20.230, Small Loans Act
Life Insurance and Annuity Policy Loans: Alaska Stat. § 21.45.080
Payday Loans: Alaska Stat. §§ 06.50.010 to 06.50.900, Deferred Deposit Advances

Arizona

Legal Interest Rate: Ariz. Rev. Stat. Ann. § 44-1201
Contract: Ariz. Rev. Stat. Ann. § 44-1201
Judgment: Ariz. Rev. Stat. Ann. § 44-1201, except on a condemnation, then interest, including interest payable pursuant to § 12-1123 (sub. B) is payable at rate prescribed by § 9-409 (if instituted by city or town), § 11-269.04 (if instituted by a county), § 28-7101 (if instituted by the department of transportation) and § 48-3628 (if instituted by county flood control district, power district, or agricultural improvement district)
Criminal Usury Cap: Ariz. Rev. Stat. Ann. § 13-2208
Small Loans: Ariz. Rev. Stat. Ann. §§ 6-601 to 6-638 (§§ 6-632), Consumer Loans Act
Installment Loan Act: Ariz. Rev. Stat. Ann. § 44-1205
Insurance Premium Finance: Ariz. Rev. Stat. § 6-1412
Auto Finance: Ariz. Rev. Stat. Ann. §§ 44-281 to 295 (§ 44-291), Motor Vehicle Time Sales Disclosure Act
Other Goods Finance: Ariz. Rev. Stat. Ann. § 44-6001 to 44-6006, Retail Installment Sales Transactions
Revolving Loan Credit: Ariz. Rev. Stat. Ann. § 44-1205, Interest Usury for closed-end loans up to $5,000 and revolving loans up to $10,000 provided the loans are not subject to the Small Loans provisions; if both Revolving Loan and Retail Installment Sales statutes apply, then the parties may agree which statute governs
Payday Loans: Ariz. Rev. Stat. §§ 6-1251 to 6-1263 (effective Sept. 1, 2000)

Revolving Sales Credit: Ariz. Rev. Stat. Ann. §§ 44-6001 to 44-6006, Retail Installment Sales Transactions

Arkansas

Legal Interest Rate: Ark. Const. art. 19, § 13(d)(i)
Contract: Ark. Const. art. 19 § 13(a)(i), see also Ark. Code Ann. §§ 4-57-101 to 4-57-108
Judgment: Ark. Code Ann. § 16-65-114
Consumer Loans & Credit Sales: Ark. Const. art. 19, § 13(b); *see also* Ark. Code Ann. §§ 4-57-101 to 4-57-108
Life Insurance and Annuity Policy Loans: Ark. Code Ann. § 23-81-109
Industrial Loans: Ark Code Ann. §§ 23-36-101 to 23-36-117
Payday Loans: Ark. Code Ann. §§ 23-52-101 to 23-52-117
Attorney General Opinions: Op. No. 99-199 (1999 Ark. AG LEXIS 105, May 7, 1999)

California

Legal Interest Rate: Cal. Const. art. XV, § 1; Cal. Civ. Code § 1916-1
Contract: Cal. Const. art. XV, § 1; *Usury Law of 1919*: Cal. Uncodified Initiative Measures and Statutes 1919-1 Ann. § 2 (Deering); Cal. Civ. Code § 1916-1
Usury Law of 1919: Cal. Gen. Laws Ann. act 3757, § 2 (Deering) (uncodified); Cal. Civ. Code §§ 1916-1 to 1916-5
Criminal Usury Cap: Cal. Civ. Code § 1916-3; Uncodified Initiative Measures and Statutes 1919-1 Ann. § 3
Judgment: Cal. Civ. Proc. Code § 685.010; Cal. Const. art. XV, § 1
Consumer Loans: Cal. Fin. Code §§ 22000 to 22754 (§§ 22303 and 22304), California Finance Lenders Law
Personal Property Brokers: Cal. Fin. Code §§ 22000 to 22754 (§§ 22009, 22303 and 22304), California Finance Lenders Law
Industrial Loan Companies: Cal. Fin. Code §§ 18212 to 18212.1, Industrial Loan Law
Insurance Premium Finance: Cal. Fin. Code §§ 18560 to 18643 (§ 18626), Insurance Premium Financing
Auto Finance: Cal. Civil Code §§ 2981 to 2984.5 (§ 2982(j)), Automobile Sales Finance Act
Other Goods Finance: Cal. Civ. Code §§ 1801 to 1812.20 (§ 1805.1), "Unruh Act" (Retail Installment Sales)
Revolving Sales Credit: Cal. Civ. Code §§ 1801 to 1812.20 (§ 1810.2), "Unruh Act" (Retail Installment Sales)
Revolving Loan Credit: Cal. Fin. Code §§ 22450 to 22467, Open-end loans; Cal. Fin. Code §§ 22300 to 22341, Loan Regulations and Retail Installment Contracts
Payday Loans: Cal. Fin. Code §§ 23000 to 23106
Attorney General Opinions: 78 Op. Atty. Gen. Cal. 101 (May 9, 1995)

Colorado

Legal Interest Rate: Colo. Rev. Stat. § 5-12-101
Contract: Colo. Rev. Stat. § 5-12-103
Judgment: Colo. Rev. Stat. § 5-12-102
Personal Injury Judgments: Colo. Rev. Stat. § 13-21-101
Appealed Judgments: Colo. Rev. Stat. § 5-12-106
Consumer Supervised Loans—Licensed Lenders: Colo. Rev. Stat. § 5-2-201(2). Colo. UCCC also includes revolving loan provision
Consumer Loans in General: Colo. Rev. Stat. §§ 5-1-301(15)(a),

(b), 5-2-301 (includes revolving loan provision)
Non-Consumer Loans: Colo. Rev. Stat. §§ 5-1.301(15), 5-2-502, Colo. UCCC
Consumer Credit Sales: Colo. Rev. Stat. § 5-2-201, Colo. UCCC
Insurance Premium Finance: Colo. Rev. Stat. §§ 5-2-201(8), 5-3-502, Colo. UCCC
Revolving Charge Accounts: Colo. Rev. Stat. § 5-2-213, Colo. UCCC
Payday Loans: Colo. Rev. Stat. §§ 5-3.1-101 to 5-3.1.-121 (Deferred Deposit Loan Act)

Connecticut

Legal Interest Rate: Conn. Gen. Stat. § 37-1
Contract: Conn. Gen. Stat. § 37-4
Judgment: Conn. Gen. Stat. §§ 37-3a and 37-3b
Criminal Usury Cap: Conn. Gen. Stat. §§ 37-4, 37-7
Small Loans: Conn. Gen. Stat. §§ 36a-555 to 573, Small Loan Law
Auto Finance: Conn. Gen. Stat. §§ 36a-770 to 36a-788 (§ 36a-772), Retail Installment Sales Financing
Retail Installment Sales (Other Goods): Conn. Gen. Stat. §§ 36a-770 to 36a-788 (§ 36a-772), Retail Installment Sales Financing
Retail Credit Transaction Statement Errors: Conn. Gen. Stat. §§ 42-100b, 42-100c
Insurance Premium Finance: Conn. Gen. Stat. §§ 38a-160 to 38a-170 (§ 38a-168), Insurance Premium Finance Companies
Revolving Credit: Conn. Gen. Stat. § 42-133c, Open End Credit
Life Insurance and Annuity Policy Loans: Conn. Gen. Stat. § 38a-444
Refund Anticipation Loans: Conn. Gen. Stat. § 42-480

Delaware

Legal Interest Rate: Del. Code Ann. tit. 6, § 2301
Contract: Del. Code Ann. tit. 6, § 2301
Judgment: Del. Code Ann. tit. 6, § 2301
Auto Finance: Del. Code Ann. tit. 5, §§ 2901-2914 (§ 2908) Motor Vehicle Sales Finance Act
Other Goods: Del. Code Ann. tit. 6, §§ 4301–4351 (§ 4315), Retail Installment Sales Law
Insurance Premium Finance: Del. Code Ann. tit. 18, §§ 4801-4812 (§ 4807)
Revolving Sales Credit: Del. Code Ann. tit. 5, §§ 2214–2226 (licensed lenders)
Bank Revolving Credit: Del. Code Ann. tit. 5, §§ 941–956 (§§ 943 and 945)
Regulated Closed End Credit: Del. Code Ann. tit. 5, §§ 961 to 978 (banks), §§ 2227 to 2238 (§ 2229) (licensed lenders)
Life Insurance and Annuity Policy Loans: Del. Code Ann. tit. 18, § 2911
Payday Loans: Del. Code Ann. tit. 5, §§ 976, 2235A. Check cashers prohibited from making payday loans by Del. Code Ann. tit. 5, § 2744

District of Columbia

Legal Interest Rate: D.C. Code Ann. § 28-3302(a)
Contract: D.C. Code Ann. § 28-3301
Judgment: D.C. Code Ann. § 28-3302(b), (c); § 15-108 (liquidated debts); § 15-109 (other contracts); § 15-110 (foreign contracts)
Small Loans: §§ 26-901 to 26-912 (§ 26-905)

Auto Finance: §§ 50-601 to 50-610 (§ 50-602); D.C. Code Ann. §§ 28-3601 to 28-3603 (§ 28-3602), Direct Motor Vehicle Installment Loans

Installment Loans: D.C. Code Ann. § 28-3308, Direct Installment Loans

Revolving Charge: D.C. Code Ann. §§ 28-3701 and 28-3702 (§ 28-3702), Revolving Credit Accounts

Insurance Premium Finance: D.C. Code Ann. §§ 31-1101 to 31-1112 (§ 31-1109), Insurance Premium Finance Companies

Payday Loans: D.C. Code §§ 26-1101 to 26-323

Florida

Legal Interest Rate: Fla. Stat. § 687.01

Contract: Fla. Stat. § 687.01, 687.02

Judgment: Fla. Stat. § 55.03

Criminal Usury Cap: Fla. Stat. §§ 687.03, 687.146

Small Loans: Fla. Stat. §§ 516.001 to 516.36 (§§ 516.031 and 516.035), Consumer Finance Act

Bank Installment Loans: Fla. Stat. § 658.49

Insurance Premium Finance: Fla. Stat. §§ 627.826 to 627.849 (§ 627.840)

Auto Finance: Fla. Stat. §§ 520.01 to 520.13 (§ 520.08), Motor Vehicle Retail Sales Finance Act

Other Goods Finance: Fla. Stat. §§ 520.30 to 520.42 (§ 520.34), Retail Installment Sales Act

Home Improvements: Fla. Stat. §§ 520.60 to 520.98 (§ 520.78), Home Improvement Sales and Finance Act

Revolving Credit: Fla. Stat. §§ 520.30 to 520.42 (§ 520.35), Retail Installment Sales Act

Life Insurance and Annuity Policy Loans: Fla. Stat. §§ 627.458 and 627.4585

Auto Title Loans: Fla. Stat. Ann. §§ 537.001 to 537.018 (§ 537.011)

Payday Loans: Fla. Stat. Ann. §§ 560.401 to 560.408

Georgia

Legal Interest Rate: Ga. Code Ann. § 7-4-2

Contract: Ga. Code Ann. § 7-4-2

Judgment: Ga. Code Ann. § 7-4-12

Criminal Usury Cap: Ga. Code Ann. § 7-14-18

Small Loans: Ga. Code Ann. §§ 7-3-1 to 7-3-29 (§ 7-3-14), Industrial Loan Act

Auto Finance: Ga. Code Ann. §§ 10-1-30 to 10-1-42 (§ 10-1-33), Motor Vehicle Sales Finance Act; Ga. Code Ann. § 7-4-3, Retail Installment Contracts and Mobile Homes and Motor Vehicles

Other Goods Finance: Ga. Code Ann. §§ 10-1-1 to 10-1-16 (§§ 10-1-3 and 10-1-4), The Retail Installment & Home Solicitation Sales Act

Insurance Premium Finance: Ga. Code Ann. §§ 33-22-1 to 33-22-16 (§ 33-22-9), Insurance Premium Finance Company Act

Revolving Loans: Ga. Code Ann. §§ 7-5-1 to 7-5-6 (§ 7-5-4), Credit Card and Credit Card Bank Act

Revolving Sales Credit: Ga. Code Ann. § 10-1-4

Auto Title Loans: Ga. Code Ann. §§ 44-12-130 to 44-12-138 (§ 44-12-131)

Payday Lending: Ga. Code Ann. §§ 16-17-1 to 16-17-10

Hawaii

Legal Interest Rate: Haw. Rev. Stat. § 478-2

Contract: Haw. Rev. Stat. § 478-4

Judgment: Haw. Rev. Stat. § 478-3

Consumer Loans in General: Haw. Rev. Stat. §§ 412:9-100 to 412:9-500 (§ 412:9-302) Financial Services Loan Companies

Consumer Sales Credit: Haw. Rev. Stat. §§ 476-1 to 476-32 (§ 476-28) Credit Sales Act

Open-end Consumer Loans: Haw. Rev. Stat. § 412:9-305, Financial Services Loan Companies

Life Insurance and Annuity Policy Loans: Haw. Rev. Stat. § 431:10D-103

Payday Loans: Haw. Rev. Stat. §§ 480F-1 to 480F-7

Idaho

Legal Interest Rate: Idaho Code § 28-22-104(1)

Contract: Idaho Code § 28-42-201

Judgment: Idaho Code § 28-22-104(2)

Consumer Sales Credit: Idaho Code §§ 28-41-101 to 28-49-107 (§ 28-42-201), Idaho UCCC

Life Insurance and Annuity Policy Loans: Idaho Code §§ 41-1901 to 41-1939 (§ 41-1909)

Payday Loans: Idaho Code §§ 28-46-401 to 28-46-413

Illinois

Legal Interest Rate: Ill. Comp. Stat. Ann. ch. 815, § 205/1

Contract: Ill. Comp. Stat. Ann. ch. 815, § 205/4

Judgment: Ill. Comp. Stat. Ann. ch. 735, § 5/2-1303

Criminal Usury Cap: Ill. Comp. Stat. Ann. ch. 720, § 5/39-1

Small Loans: Ill. Comp. Stat. Ann. ch. 815, § 205/4a, Interest Act. Ill. Comp. Stat. Ann. ch. 205, §§ 670/1 to 670/27 (§ 670/15), Consumer Installment Loan Act

Revolving Loans: Ill. Comp. Stat. Ann. ch. 815, § 205/4.2

Revolving Sales Credit: Ill. Comp. Stat. Ann. ch. 815, §§ 405/1 to 405/33 (§§ 405/27 and 405/28), Retail Installment Sales Act

Auto Finance: Ill. Comp. Stat. Ann. ch. 815, §§ 375/1 to 375/26, Motor Vehicle Retail Installment Sales Act

Insurance Premium Finance: Ill. Comp. Stat. Ann. ch. 215, §§ 5/513a1 to 5/513a12 (§ 5/513a10), Premium Finance Regulation

Life Insurance and Annuity Policy Loans: Ill. Comp. Stat. Ann. ch. 215, 5/229.5

Payday Loans: Ill. Admin. Code tit. 38, § 110.300 *et seq.*

Auto Title Loans: Ill. Admin. Code tit. 38, §§ 110.300 to 110.410

Refund Anticipation Loans: Ill. Comp. Stat. Ann. ch. 815, §§ 177/1 to 177/99

Indiana

Legal Interest Rate: Ind. Code § 24-4.6-1-102

Contract: See rates specified in consumer sections of UCCC. *See* Ind. Code §§ 24-4.5-3-601 to 24-4.5-3-605.

Judgment: Ind. Code § 24-4.6-1-101

Consumer Supervised Loans—Licensed Lenders: Ind. Code § 24-4.5-3-508, Ind. UCCC

Consumer Loans In General: Ind. Code § 24-4.5-3-201, Ind. UCCC

Revolving Loan Accounts: Ind. Code § 24-4.5-3-201(4), Ind. UCCC

Small Loans Other than "Consumer Loans": Ind. Code §§ 24-4.5-3-601 to 24-4.5-3-606 (§ 24-4.5-3-605), Ind. UCCC

Consumer Sales Credit: Ind. Code § 24-4.5-2-201, Ind. UCCC

Life Insurance and Annuity Policy Loans: Ind. Code §§ 27-1-12.3-1 to 27-1-12.3-6 (§ 27-1-12.3-2), Interest Rates on Insurance Policy Loans

Payday Loans: Ind. Code §§ 24-4.5-7-101 to 24-4.5-7-414

Iowa

Legal Interest Rate: Iowa Code § 535.2

Contract: Iowa Code § 535.2

Judgment: Iowa Code § 535.3

Small Loans: Iowa Code §§ 536.1 to 536.29 (§ 536.13) Iowa Regulated Loan Act

Industrial Loans: Iowa Code §§ 536A.1 to 536A.31 (§ 536A.23), Iowa Industrial Loan Law, Iowa Code §§ 537.1101 to 537.8101, Iowa UCCC

Consumer Credit Sales: Iowa Code §§ 537.2101 to 537.2601 (§ 537.2201), Iowa UCCC

Revolving Sales Accounts: Iowa Code §§ 537.2101 to 537.2601 (§ 537.2202), Iowa UCCC

Consumer Loans In General: Iowa Code §§ 537.2101 to 537.2601 (§ 537.2401, finance charges), (§ 537.1301, definition); (§ 537.2301, consumer loan licensees); Iowa UCCC

Consumer Revolving Loans: Iowa Code §§ 537.2101 to 537.2601 (§ 537.2402), Iowa UCCC

Auto Finance: Iowa Code §§ 322.1 to 322.35 (§§ 322.3, 322.19, & 322.33), Motor Vehicle Dealer's Licensing Act (requires compliance with Iowa UCCC); § 537.2201 (Iowa UCCC)

Life Insurance and Annuity Policy Loans: Iowa Code § 511.36

Payday Loans: Iowa Code §§ 533D.1 to 533D.16

Kansas

Legal Interest Rate: Kan. Stat. Ann. § 16-201

Contract: Kan. Stat. Ann. § 16-207

Judgment: Kan. Stat. Ann. § 16-204

Consumer Loans: Kan. Stat. Ann. §§ 16a-2-101 to 16a-2-510 (§ 16a-2-401, finance charges), (§ 16a-2-301, consumer loan licensees), Kan. UCCC

Consumer Credit Sales: Kan. Stat. Ann. §§ 16a-2-101 to 16a-2-510 (§ 16a-2-201), Kan. UCCC

Revolving Sales Accounts: Kan. Stat. Ann. §§ 16a-2-101 to 16a-2-510 (§ 16a-2-202), Kan. UCCC

Mortgages: Kan. Stat. Ann. § 16-207(b)

Insurance Premium Finance: Kan. Stat Ann. §§ 40-2601 to 40-2613 (§ 40-2610) Insurance Premium Finance Company Act

Life Insurance Policy Loans: Kan. Stat. Ann. §§ 40-420a to 40-420d

Payday Loans: Kan. Stat. Ann. § 16a-2-404

Attorney General Opinions: A.G. Op. 97-99 § 1997 Kan. AG Lexis 99 (Dec. 19, 1997)

Kentucky

Legal Interest Rate: Ky. Rev. Stat. Ann. § 360.010

Contract: Ky. Rev. Stat. Ann. § 360.010

Judgment: Ky. Rev. Stat. Ann. § 360.040

Small Loans: Ky. Rev. Stat. Ann. §§ 288.410 to 288.991 (§ 288.530), Consumer Loan Act

Industrial Loans: Ky. Rev. Stat. Ann. §§ 291.410 to 291.990 (§ 291.460), Industrial Loan Corporations

Bank Installment Loans: Ky. Rev. Stat. Ann. § 287.215

Auto Finance: Ky. Rev. Stat. Ann. §§ 190.090 to 190.140 (§ 190.110), Motor Vehicle Retail Installment Sales Act

Insurance Premium Finance: Ky. Rev. Stat. Ann. §§ 304.30-010 to 304.30-120 (§ 304.30-090), Insurance Premium Finance Companies

Bank Revolving Credit: Ky. Rev. Stat. Ann. §§ 287.710 to 287.770

Life Insurance and Annuity Policy Loans: Ky. Rev. Stat. Ann. § 304.15-115

Auto Title Loans: Ky. Rev. Stat. Ann. §§ 368.200 to 368.285, § 368.991 (Title Pledge Act)

Payday Loans: Ky. Rev. Stat. Ann. §§ 368.010 to 368.120 and 368.991

Attorney General Opinions: OAG 92-41, 1992 Ky. AG LEXIS 50 (Mar. 17, 1992)

Louisiana

Legal Interest Rate: La. Rev. Stat. Ann. § 9:3500

Contract: La. Rev. Stat. Ann. § 9:3500

Judgment: La. Rev. Stat. Ann. §§ 9:3500, 13:4202

Consumer Loans: La. Rev. Stat. Ann. §§ 9:3510 to 9:3568 (§ 9:3519), Louisiana Consumer Credit Law (LCCA)

Consumer Credit Sales: La. Rev. Stat. Ann. §§ 9:3510 to 9:3568 (§ 9:3520), LCCA

Auto Finance: La. Rev. Stat. Ann. §§ 6:969.1 to 6:969.41 (§§ 6:969.9 to 969.14), Motor Vehicle Sales Finance Act

Revolving Charge Accounts: La. Rev. Stat. Ann. §§ 9:3510 to 9:3568 (§ 9:3523), LCCA

Revolving Loan Accounts: La. Rev. Stat. Ann. §§ 9:3510 to 9:3568 (§ 9:3519), LCCA

Mortgages: La. Rev. Stat. Ann. § 9:3503

Lender Credit Cards: La. Rev. Stat. Ann. §§ 9:3510 to 9:3568 (§ 9:3524), LCCA

Insurance Premium Finance: La. Rev. Stat. Ann. §§ 9.3510 to 9:3568 (§ 9:3550), LCCA

Life Insurance and Annuity Policy Loans: La. Rev. Stat. Ann. § 22:170.1

Payday Loans: La. Rev. Stat. Ann. §§ 9:3578.1 to 3578.8

Attorney General Opinions: Op. No. 98-88, 1998 La. AG LEXIS 106 (Mar. 12, 1998); Op. No. 94-297, 1994 La. AG LEXIS 385 (July 21, 1994)

Maine

Legal Interest Rate: Me. Rev. Stat. Ann. tit. 9-B, § 432

Contract: Me. Rev. Stat. Ann. tit. 9-B, § 432

Judgment: Me. Rev. Stat. Ann. tit. 14, §§ 1602-B, 1602-C.

Consumer Supervised Loans—Licensed Lenders: Me. Rev. Stat. Ann. tit. 9-A §§ 1-301, 2-101 to 2-601 (§ 2-301), Maine UCCC

Consumer Credit Sales: Me. Rev. Stat. Ann. tit. 9-A, §§ 2-101 to 2-601 (§ 2-201), Maine UCCC

Revolving Charge Accounts: Me. Rev. Stat. Ann. tit. 9-A, §§ 2-101 to 2-601 (§ 2-202), Maine UCCC

Consumer Loans: Me. Rev. Stat. Ann. tit. 9-A, §§ 2-101 to 2-601 (§ 2-401), Maine UCCC

Revolving Loans: Me. Rev. Stat. Ann. tit. 9-A, §§ 2-101 to 2-601 (§ 2-402), Maine UCCC

Auto Finance: Me. Rev. Stat. Ann. tit. 9-A, § 2-201(9-A), Maine UCCC

Industrial Banks: Me. Rev. Stat. Ann. tit. 9-B, § 917

Insurance Premium Finance: Me. Rev. Stat. Ann. tit. 9-A, § 2-401(9)

Life Insurance and Annuity Policy Loans: Me. Rev. Stat. Ann. tit. 24-A, § 2553

Refund Anticipation Loans: Me. Rev. Stat. Ann. tit. 9-A, § 8-103-(I-1), 8-106(6)

Maryland

Legal Interest Rate: Md. Code Ann., Com. Law II § 12-102; Md. Const. art. III, § 57

Contract: Md. Code Ann., Com. Law II § 12-103

Judgment: Md. Code Ann., Cts. & Jud. Proc. §§ 11-106, 11-107

Consumer Loans: Md. Code Ann., Com. Law II §§ 12-301 to 12-317 (§ 12-306), Maryland Consumer Loan Law—Credit Provisions

Auto Finance: Md. Code Ann., Com. Law II §§ 12-601 to 12-636 (§ 12-609), Retail Installment Sales Act

Other Goods: Md. Code Ann., Com. Law II §§ 12-601 to 12-636 (§ 12-610), Retail Installment Sales Act

Insurance Premium Finance: Md. Code Ann., Ins. §§ 23-303, 23-304, 23-305 (Oct. 1, 1997) (replaced Md. Ann. Code art. 48A, §§ 486D, 486E)

Revolving Charge Account: Md. Code Ann., Com. Law II §§ 12-501 to 12-515 (§ 12-506)

Revolving Loans: Md. Code Ann., Com. Law II § 12-903

Closed End Credit: Md. Code Ann., Com. Law II §§ 12-1001 to 12-1029

Second Mortgage Loans: Md. Code Ann., Com. Law II § 12-404

Life Insurance and Annuity Policy Loans: Md. Code Ann., Ins. §§ 16-207 to 16-208 (Oct. 1, 1997) (replaced Md. Ann. Code art. 48A, §§ 394 and 394A)

Massachusetts

Legal Interest Rate: Mass. Gen. Laws Ann. ch. 107, § 3

Contract: Mass. Gen. Laws Ann. ch. 107, § 3

Judgment: Mass. Gen. Laws Ann. ch. 231, §§ 6B and 6C

Criminal Usury Cap: Mass. Gen. Laws Ann. ch. 271, § 49

Small Loans: Mass. Gen. Laws Ann. ch. 140, §§ 90 and 96

Industrial Banks: Mass. Gen. Laws. Ann. ch. 172A, §§ 1 to 15 (§ 9), Banking Company Act (*repealed effective March 30, 2005*)

Insurance Premium Finance: Mass. Gen. Laws. Ann. ch. 255C, § 14

Second Mortgages: Mass. Gen. Laws. Ann. ch. 140, § 90A

Auto Finance: Mass. Gen. Laws. Ann. ch. 255B, §§ 1 to 25 (§ 14), Motor Vehicle Retail Installment Sales

Other Goods Finance: Mass. Gen. Laws. Ann. ch. 255D, §§ 1 to 32 (§ 11), Retail Installment Sales and Services

Revolving Sales Credit: Mass. Gen. Laws. Ann. ch. 255D, §§ 1 to 32 (§ 27), Retail Installment Sales and Services

Open-End Credit Loans: Mass. Gen. Laws. Ann. ch. 140, § 114B

Life Insurance and Annuity Policy Loans: Mass. Gen. Laws Ann. ch. 175, § 142

Michigan

Legal Interest Rate: Mich. Comp. Laws § 438.31

Contract: Mich. Comp. Laws § 438.31

Judgment: Mich. Comp. Laws § 600.6013

Small Loans: Mich. Comp. Laws §§ 493.1 to 493.24 (§ 493.13), Regulatory Loan Act

Regulated Loans: Mich. Comp. Laws §§ 445.1851 to 445.1864, Credit Reform Act

Criminal Usury Cap: Mich. Comp. Laws § 438.41

Bank Installment and Credit Card Loans: Mich. Comp. Laws §§ 445.1851 to 445.1864, Credit Reform Act

Autos: Mich. Comp. Laws §§ 492.101 to 492.151 (§ 492.118), Motor Vehicle Sales Finance Act

Other Goods: Mich. Comp. Laws §§ 445.851 to 445.873 (§ 445.857), Retail Installment Sales Act

Home Improvement Loans: Mich. Comp. Laws §§ 445.1101 to 445.1431 (§§ 445.1204b and 445.1301), Home Improvement Finance Act

Insurance Premium Finance: Mich. Comp. Laws §§ 500.1501 to 500.1514 (§ 500.1509), Insurance Premium Finance Companies

Revolving Credit: Mich. Comp. Laws §§ 445.851 to 445.873 (§ 445.862), Retail Installment Sales Act

Secondary Mortgage Loans: Mich. Comp. Laws § 493.51 to 493.81 (§ 493.71)

Life Insurance and Annuity Policy Loans: Mich. Comp. Laws §§ 500.4022 and 500.4023

Credit Cards: Mich. Comp. Laws § 493.101 to 493.114 (§ 493.110)

Minnesota

Legal Interest Rate: Minn. Stat. § 334.01

Contract: Minn. Stat. §§ 47.59 subds. 2, 3, 334.01

Judgment: Minn. Stat. § 549.09

Small Loans: Minn. Stat. §§ 56.0001 to 56.26 (§ 56.131), Minn. Regulated Loan Act

Industrial Loans: Minn. Stat. § 53.04, Industrial Loan & Thrift Company Law

Bank and Savings Bank Loans: Minn. Stat. § 48.195, § 47.59

Auto Finance: Minn. Stat. §§ 168.66 to 168.77 (§ 168.72), Motor Vehicle Retail Installment Sales Act

Insurance Premium Finance: Minn. Stat. §§ 59A.01 to 59A.15 (§ 59A.09); Insurance Premium Finance Company Act § 47.59, subds. 2, 3

Revolving Credit: Minn. Stat. § 334.16, Finance Charges for Open End Credit Sales

Revolving Loans: Minn. Stat. § 48.185, Open End Loan Account Arrangements; § 47.59, subds. 2, 3

Consumer Credit Sales: Minn. Stat. §§ 325G.15 and 325G.16

Consumer Loans: Minn. Stat. §§ 47.59, subds. 2, 3, 47.60

Mortgages: Minn. Stat. §§ 47.20, 47.59

Life Insurance and Annuity Policy Loans: Minn. Stat. § 61A.03

Auto Title Loans: Minn. Stat. §§ 325J.01 to 325J.13 (§ 325J.095), Pawnbroker Regulation. Pawn transactions involving holding only the title of property are also subject to chapter 168A (Uniform Motor Vehicle Certificate of title and Anti-Theft Act) or 336 (UCC). § 325J.06(c)

Payday loans: Minn. Stat. § 47.60

Refund Anticipation Loans: Minn. Stat. § 270.30.

Mississippi

Legal Interest Rate: Miss. Code Ann. § 75-17-1

Contract: Miss. Code Ann. § 75-17-1 (§ 75-17-25, finance charge defined)

Judgment: Miss. Code Ann. § 75-17-7

Small Loans: Miss. Code Ann. § 75-17-21 and Miss. Code Ann. §§ 75-67-101 to 75-67-135, Small Loan Regulatory Law

Bank & Trust Company Installment Loans: Miss. Code Ann. § 81-5-79

Insurance Premium Finance: Miss. Code Ann. §§ 81-21-1 to 81-21-27 (§ 81-21-15), Insurance Premium Finance Companies

Other Installment Loans: Miss. Code Ann. § 75-67-39

Mobile Home Loans: Miss. Code Ann. § 75-17-23

Auto Finance: Miss. Code Ann. § 63-19-43, Motor Vehicle Sales Finance Law

Other Goods: No special provisions

Revolving Credit: Miss. Code Ann. § 75-17-19

Revolving Loans: Miss. Code Ann. § 75-17-1

Life Insurance and Annuity Policy Loans: Miss. Code Ann. § 83-7-26

Auto Title Loans: Miss. Code Ann. §§ 75-67-401 to 75-67-449, Mississippi Title Pledge Act

Payday Loans: Miss. Code Ann. §§ 75-67-501 to 75-67-639

Missouri

Legal Interest Rate: Mo. Rev. Stat. § 408.020, *see* Mo. Const. art. III, § 44

Contract: Mo. Rev. Stat. §§ 408.030, 408.035, 408.080, 408.455

Judgment: Mo. Rev. Stat. § 408.040

Small Loans: Mo. Rev. Stat. §§ 408.100 to 408.190 (§§ 408.120, 408.140) Consumer Loan Act

Auto Finance: Mo. Rev. Stat. §§ 365.010 to 365.160 (§§ 365.120 and 365.125), Motor Vehicle Time Sales Law

Other Goods: Mo. Rev. Stat. §§ 408.250 to 408.375 (§ 408.300), Retail Credit Sales

Loan and Investment Companies: Mo. Rev. Stat. § 368.040

Revolving Loans (and Credit Cards): Mo. Rev. Stat. § 408.140, 408.145, 408.455

Second Mortgages: Mo. Rev. Stat. § 408.232

Life Insurance Policy Loans: Mo. Rev. Stat. § 376.672

Auto Title Loans: Mo. Rev. Stat. §§ 367.500 to 367.533, Pawnbrokers and Small Loans

Payday Loans: Mo. Rev. Stat. §§ 408.500, 408.505; Mo. Code Regs. Ann. tit. 4, §§ 140-11.030, 14-11.040

Montana

Legal Interest Rate: Mont. Code Ann. § 31-1-106

Contract: Mont. Code Ann. § 31-1-107

Judgment: Mont. Code Ann. § 25-9-205

Small Loans: Mont. Code Ann. §§ 32-5-101 to 32-5-506 (§ 32-5-301), Consumer Loan Act

Credit Sales: Mont. Code Ann. §§ 31-1-201 to 31-1-243 (§ 31-1-241), Retail Installment Sales Act

Revolving Credit: Mont. Code Ann. §§ 31-1-201 to 31-1-243 (§ 31-1-241), Retail Installment Sales Act

Installment Loans By Regulated Lenders: Mont. Code Ann. § 31-1-112

Open End Loans: Mont. Code Ann. §§ 32-5-501 to 32-5-506

Insurance Premium Finance: Mont. Code. Ann. §§ 33-14-101 to 33-14-307 (§ 33-14-302)

Life Insurance and Annuity Policy Loans: Mont. Code Ann. §§ 33-20-131 and 33-20-135

Auto Title Loans: Mont. Code Ann. §§ 31-1-801 to 31-1-827, Title Loan Act

Payday Loans: Mont. Code Ann. §§ 31-1-701 to 31-1-725

Nebraska

Legal Interest Rate: Neb. Rev. Stat. § 45-102

Contract: Neb. Rev. Stat. §§ 45-101.03 and 45-101.04

Judgment: Neb. Rev. Stat. § 45-103

Small Loans: Neb. Rev. Stat. §§ 45-1002 to 45-1042 (§§ 45-1024, 45-1025), Installment Loan Act

Bank Installment Loans: Neb. Rev. Stat. § 8-820

Installment Sales, All Goods: Neb. Rev. Stat. §§ 45-334 to 45-353 (§ 45-338), Installment Sales Act

Revolving Credit: Neb. Rev. Stat. §§ 45-204 to 45-209 (§ 45-207), Revolving Charge Agreements

Life Insurance and Annuity Policy Loans: Neb. Rev. Stat. § 44-502.03

Payday Loans: Neb. Rev. Stat. Ann. §§ 45-901 to 45-929

Nevada

Legal Interest Rate: Nev. Rev. Stat. § 99.040

Contract: Nev. Rev. Stat. § 99.050

Judgment: Nev. Rev. Stat. § 17.130

Small Loans: Nev. Rev. Stat. §§ 675.010 to 675.470 (§ 675.363), Installment Loan and Finance Act

Thrift Company Loans: Nev. Rev. Stat. § 677.730

Installment Sales, All Goods: Nev. Rev. Stat. §§ 97.015 to 97.335 (§ 97.195), Retail Installment Sales of Goods and Services

Revolving Credit: Nev. Rev. Stat. §§ 97.015 to 97.335 (§ 97.245), Retail Installment Sales of Goods and Services; Nev. Rev. Stat. §§ 97A.010 to 97A.180, Debt Evidenced by Credit Card

Payday Loans: Nev. Rev. Stat. §§ 604.010 to 604.190

Attorney General Opinions: Op. No. 99-04, 1994 Nev. AG LEXIS 2 (Feb. 1, 1999)

Insurance Premium Finance: Nev. Rev. Stat. § 686A.440

Life Insurance & Annuity Policy Loans: Nev. Rev. Stat. 688A.110

Auto Title Loans: Nev. Rev. Stat. §§ 646.000 to 646.060; 1995 Nev. Op. Atty. Gen. No. 20, 1995 WL 737002 (Nov. 17, 1995) (persons making title loans are pawnbrokers)

New Hampshire

Legal Interest Rate: N.H. Rev. Stat. Ann. § 336:1 (Consumer loans, N.H. Rev. Stat. Ann. §§ 358-K:1 to 358K:6, exempted).

Contract: N.H. Rev. Stat. Ann. § 336:1

Judgment: N.H. Rev. Stat. Ann. § 336:1

Small Loans: N.H. Rev. Stat. Ann. §§ 399-A:1 to 399-A:19 (§ 399-A:12), Small Loan Law

Second Mortgages: N.H. Rev. Stat. Ann. §§ 398-A:1 to 398-A:14 (§ 398-A:2), Second Mortgage Home Loans

Insurance Premium Finance: N.H. Rev. Stat. Ann. §§ 415-B:1 to 415-B:13 (§ 415-B:7), Premium Finance Companies

Auto Finance: N.H. Rev. Stat. Ann. §§ 361-A:1 to 361-A:13 (§ 361-A:8), Retail Installment Sales of Motor Vehicles

Other Consumer Credit: N.H. Rev. Stat. Ann. §§ 358-K:1 to 358K:6, Regulation of Consumer Credit Transactions

Auto Title Loans: N.H. Rev. Stat. Ann. §§ 398:1 to 398:14, Pawnbrokers; N.H. Rev. Stat. Ann. §§ 399-A:1 to 399-A:19 (§ 399-A:14)

Payday Loans: N.H. Rev. Stat. Ann. § 399-A:1 to 399-A:19 (§ 399-A:13)

New Jersey

Legal Interest Rate: N.J. Rev. Stat. § 31:1-1
Contract: N.J. Rev. Stat. §§ 31:1-1 and 31:1-1.1
Criminal Usury Cap: N.J. Rev. Stat. § 2C:21-19
Judgment: No statutory provision; N.J. Superior, Tax & Surrogate Courts Civ. Rule 4:42-11
Small Loans: N.J. Rev. Stat. §§ 17:11C-1 to 17:11C-50 (§ 17:11C-32), Licensed Lenders
Bank Installment Loans: N.J. Rev. Stat. § 17:9A-54
Installment Sales Including Auto Finance: N.J. Rev. Stat. §§ 17:16C-1 to 17:16C-61 (§ 17:16C-41), Retail Installment Sales Act
Home Repair: N.J. Rev. Stat. §§ 17:16C-62 to 17:16C-94 (§ 17:16C-69), Home Repair Financing Act
Second Mortgage Loans: N.J. Rev. Stat. §§ 17:11C-1 to 17:11C-50 (§ 17:11C-28), Licensed Lenders
Insurance Premium Finance: N.J. Rev. Stat. §§ 17:16D-1 to 17:16D-16 (§ 17:16D-10), Insurance Premium Financing Company Act
Bank Revolving Loan Credit: N.J. Rev. Stat. §§ 17:3B-4 to 17:3B-46 (§§ 17:3B-7, 17:3B-8), Market Rate Consumer Loan Act
Bank Closed-End Credit: N.J. Rev. Stat. §§ 17:3B-4 to 17:3B-46 (§§ 17:3B-17, 17:3B-18), Market Rate Consumer Loan Act
Market Rate Consumer Loan Act: N.J. Rev. Stat. §§ 17:3B-4 to 17:3B-46
Revolving Retail Charge: N.J. Rev. Stat. § 17:16C-44.1

New Mexico

Legal Interest Rate: N.M. Stat. Ann. § 56-8-3
Contract: N.M. Stat. Ann. § 56-8-9
Judgment: N.M. Stat. Ann. § 56-8-4
Criminal Usury Cap: N.M. Stat. Ann. §§ 56-8-9, 56-8-14
Small Loans: N.M. Stat. Ann. §§ 58-15-1 to 58-15-31 (§ 58-15-23), Small Loan Act
Bank Installment Loans: N.M. Stat. Ann. §§ 58-7-1 to 58-7-9, Bank Installment Loan Act
Auto Finance: N.M. Stat. Ann. §§ 58-19-1 to 58-19-14, Motor Vehicle Sales Finance Act
Insurance Premium Finance: N.M. Stat. Ann. §§ 59A-45-1 to 59A-45-16, Insurance Premium Financing Law
Life Insurance and Annuity Policy Loans: N.M. Stat. Ann. § 59A-20-10
New Mexico Attorney General's Opinions: 1985 Op. N.M. Att'y Gen. No. 85-01
Auto Title Loans: N.M. Admin. Code tit. 12, §§ 18.4 and 18.6
Payday Loans: N.M. Admin. Code tit. 12, §§ 18.4 to 18.6

New York

Legal Interest Rate: N.Y. Gen. Oblig. Law § 5-501; N.Y. Banking Law § 14-a; N.Y. Comp. Codes R. & Regs. tit. 3, §§ 4.1 to 4.7 (Banking Board Regulations—interest rates)
Criminal Usury Cap: N.Y. Penal Code §§ 190.40, 190.42
Contract: N.Y. Gen. Oblig. Law § 5-501; N.Y. Banking Law § 108
Judgment: N.Y. Civ. Prac. L. & R. § 5004
Small Loans: N.Y. Banking Law §§ 340 to 361 (§ 351), Licensed

Lender Law
Bank Installment Loans: N.Y. Banking Law § 108
Auto Finance: N.Y. Pers. Prop. Law §§ 301 to 316 (§ 303), Motor Vehicle Retail Installment Sales Act
Other Goods Finance: N.Y. Pers. Prop. Law §§ 401 to 422 (§ 404), Retail Installment Sales Act
Insurance Premium Finance: N.Y. Banking Law §§ 554 to 578 (§ 568), Insurance Premium Finance Agencies
Revolving Credit: N.Y. Pers. Prop. Law §§ 401 to 422 (§ 413), Retail Installment Sales Act
Life Insurance and Annuity Policy Loans: N.Y. Ins. Law § 3206

North Carolina

Legal Interest Rate: N.C. Gen. Stat. § 24-1
Contract: N.C. Gen. Stat. § 24-1.1
Judgment: N.C. Gen. Stat. § 24-5
Small Loans: N.C. Gen. Stat. §§ 53-164 to 53-191 (§§ 53-173 and 53-176), Consumer Finance Act
Industrial Bank Loans: N.C. Gen. Stat. § 53-141, Industrial Banks
Bank Installment Loans: N.C. Gen. Stat. § 53-43(1)
Installment Sales Including Auto Finance: N.C. Gen. Stat. §§ 25A-1 to 25A-45 (§ 25A-15), Retail Installment Sales Act
Mortgages: N.C. Gen. Stat. § 24-1.1A (eff. Oct. 1, 1999); N.C. Gen. Stat. § 24-1.1E (antipredatory mortgage loan law) (eff. July 1, 2000)
Second Mortgages: N.C. Gen. Stat. §§ 24-12 to 24-17 (§ 24-14)
Insurance Premium Finance: N.C. Gen. Stat. §§ 58-35-1 to 58-35-100 (§ 58-35-55), Insurance Premium Financing
Revolving Charge: N.C. Gen. Stat. § 25A-14 and § 24-11
Open-end Loans: N.C. Gen. Stat. § 24-11
Home Equity Loans: N.C. Gen. Stat. § 24-1.2A
Life Insurance and Annuity Policy Loans: N.C. Gen. Stat. §§ 58-61-1 to 58-61-15 (§ 58-61-10), Regulation of Interest Rates on Life Insurance Policy Loans
Refund Anticipation Loans: N.C. Gen. Stat. §§ 53-245 to 53-254

North Dakota

Legal Interest Rate: N.D. Cent. Code § 47-14-05
Contract: N.D. Cent. Code § 47-14-09
Judgment: N.D. Cent. Code § 28-20-34
Criminal Usury Cap: N.D. Cent. Code §§ 47-14-09, 47-14-11 (*cf.* 12.1-31-02)
Small Loans: N.D. Cent. Code §§ 13-03.1-01 to 13-03.1-19 (§ 13-03.1-15), Consumer Finance Act
Installment Sales, All Goods: N.D. Cent. Code §§ 51-13-01 to 51-13-08 (§ 51-13-03), Retail Installment Sales Act
Insurance Premium Finance: N.D. Cent. Code § 26.1-20.1-07
Revolving Credit: N.D. Cent. Code §§ 51-14-01 to 51-14-05 (§ 51-14-03), Revolving Charge Accounts
Attorney General Opinions: 1997 Op. Atty. Gen. N.D. L-56, 1997 N.D. AG LEXIS 35 (May 27, 1997)
Payday Loans: N.D. Cent. Code §§ 13-08-01 to 13-08-15

Ohio

Legal Interest Rate: Ohio Rev. Code Ann. §§ 1343.01, 1343.03
Contract: Ohio Rev. Code Ann. §§ 1343.01, 1343.03
Judgment: Ohio Rev. Code Ann. § 1343.03
Criminal Usury Cap: Ohio Rev. Code Ann. §§ 2905.21, 2905.22

Small Loans Including Open-End Loans: Ohio Rev. Code Ann. §§ 1321.01 to 1321.20 (§§ 1321.13, 1321.131 and 1321.16), Small Loan Law

Installment Sales, All Goods: Ohio Rev. Code Ann. §§ 1317.01 to 1317.99 (§§ 1317.06 and 1317.061), Retail Installment Sales

Second Mortgages and Home Equity Loans: Ohio Rev. Code Ann. §§ 1321.51 to 1321.60 (§§ 1321.57, 1321.571 and 1321.58), Second Mortgage Loans

Bank Installment Loans: Ohio Rev. Code Ann. § 1109.20

Insurance Premium Finance: Ohio Rev. Code Ann. §§ 1321.71 to 1321.99 (§§ 1321.79 and 1321.791), Insurance Premium Finance Companies

Revolving Credit: Ohio Rev. Code Ann. §§ 1317.01 to 1317.99 (§ 1317.11), Retail Installment Sales

Bank Revolving Credit: Ohio Rev. Code Ann. § 1109.20

Life Insurance and Annuity Policy Loans: Ohio Rev. Code Ann. § 3915.051

Payday Loans: Ohio Rev. Code Ann. §§ 1315.35 to 1315.55

Auto Title Loans: Ohio Rev. Code § 4505.102, Certificate of Motor Vehicle Title Law; Ohio Rev. Code §§ 4727.01 to 4727.99 (§ 4727.06), Pawnbrokers.

Oklahoma

Legal Interest Rate: Okla. Stat. tit. 15, § 266; Okla. Const. art. 14, § 2

Contract: Okla. Stat. tit. 15, § 266 (see rates specified in consumer sections of Okla. UCCC); Okla. Const. art. 14, § 2

Judgment: Okla. Stat. tit. 12, §§ 727, 727.1

Supervised Loans: Okla. Stat. tit. 14A, §§ 3-508A and 3-508B, Okla. UCCC

Unsupervised Consumer Loans: Okla. Stat. tit. 14A, § 3-201, Okla. UCCC

Non-Consumer Loans: Okla. Stat. tit. 14A, §§ 3-601, 3-605 and 5-107(2), Okla. UCCC

Consumer Sales Finance Including Auto Finance: Okla. Stat. tit. 14A, § 2-201, Oklahoma UCCC

Revolving Credit: Okla. Stat. tit. 14A, § 2-207, Okla. UCCC

Banks: Okla. Stat. tit. 15, § 272

Life Insurance and Annuity Policy Loans: Okla. Stat. tit. 36, § 4008

Payday Loans: Okla. Stat. tit. 57, §§ 3101 to 3119

Oklahoma's Attorney General's Opinions: 1997 Op. Okla. Att'y Gen. No. 96-84 (regarding Okla. Stat. tit. 14A, §§ 3-508A, 3-508B); Op. No. 96-84, 1997 Okla. AG LEXIS 10 (Feb. 20, 1997)

Oregon

Legal Interest Rate: Or. Rev. Stat. § 82.010

Contract: Or. Rev. Stat. §§ 82.010, 82.025

Judgment: Or. Rev. Stat. § 82.010

Small Loans: Or. Rev. Stat. §§ 725.010 to 725.910 (§ 725.340), Consumer Finance Act

Bank Installment Loans: Or. Rev. Stat. § 708A.255

Auto Finance: Or. Rev. Stat. §§ 83.510 to 83.680 (§§ 83.095, 83.560, 83.565), Motor Vehicle Retail Installment Sales Act

Other Goods Finance: Or. Rev. Stat. §§ 83.010 to 83.190 (§ 83.095), Retail Installment Sales

Insurance Premium Finance: Or. Rev. Stat. §§ 746.405 to 746.530 (§ 746.485), Premium Financing

Life Insurance Policy Loans: Or. Rev. Stat. § 743.187

Payday Loans: Or. Rev. Stat. §§ 725.600 to 725.625; Or. Admin. R. §§ 441-730-0005 to 441-730-0320

Auto Title Loans: Or. Rev. Stat. §§ 725.600 to 725.625; Or. Admin. R. §§ 441-730-0005 to 441-730-0320

Pennsylvania

Legal Interest Rate: Pa. Stat. Ann. tit. 41, §§ 201 and 202

Contract: Pa. Stat. Ann tit. 41 § 201

Judgment: Pa. Cons. Stat. Ann. tit. 42, § 8101

Criminal Usury Cap: Pa. Cons. Stat. Ann. tit. 41, §§ 501, 505

Small Loans: Pa. Stat. Ann. tit. 7, §§ 6201 to 6219 (§ 6213), Consumer Discount Company Act

Bank Installment Loans: Pa. Stat. Ann. tit. 7, §§ 309 and 318

Auto Finance: Pa. Stat. Ann. tit. 69, §§ 601 to 637 (§ 619), Motor Vehicle Sales Finance Act

Other Goods: Pa. Stat. Ann. tit. 69, §§ 1101 to 2303 (§ 1501), Goods and Services Installment Sales Act

Improvement Loans: Pa. Stat. Ann. tit. 73, §§ 500-101 to 500-602 (§ 500-301), Home Improvement Finance Act

Revolving Loan Credit: Pa. Stat. Ann. tit. 7, §§ 6201 to 6219 (§ 6217.1), Consumer Discount Company Act

Revolving Charge Credit: Pa. Stat. Ann. tit. 69, §§ 1101 to 2303 (§ 1904), Goods and Services Installment Sales Act

Bank Revolving Loans: Pa. Stat. Ann. tit. 7, § 309

Insurance Premium Finance: Pa. Stat. Ann. tit. 40, §§ 3301 to 3314 (§ 3308)

Second Mortgages: Pa. Cons. Stat. Ann. tit. 7, §§ 6601 to 6626 (§ 6609) (Purdon), Secondary Mortgage Loan Act

Life Insurance and Annuity Policy Loans: Pa. Cons. Stat. Ann. tit. 40, § 510e

Puerto Rico

Legal Interest Rate: P.R. Laws Ann. tit. 31, § 4591

Contract: P.R. Laws Ann. tit. 10, §§ 998, 998n, tit. 31, § 4591

Judgment: P.R. Laws Ann. tit. 32, app. III, R. Civ. P. 44.3

Small Loans: P.R. Laws Ann. tit. 10, §§ 941 to 959 (§ 954), Small Personal Loan Act

Auto Finance: Rules & Regs. of P.R., tit. 10, ch. 36 (Maximum Credit Service Charges in Installment Sales of Motor Vehicles, § 773-21 *et seq.*)

Retail Installment Sales: P.R. Laws Ann. tit. 10, §§ 731 to 793 (§ 750), Retail Installment Sales of Goods and Services; Rules & Regs. of P.R., tit. 10, ch. 36 (Household Furniture: § 773-81 *et seq.*; Industrial, Agric. & Construction Machinery: § 773-101 *et seq.*; Commercial Electric Fixtures § 773-41 *et seq.*)

Loans: 10 P.R. Laws. Ann. §§ 998, 998n

Life Insurance and Annuity Policy Loans: P.R. Laws Ann. tit. 26, § 1308

Revolving Credit: P.R. Laws Ann. tit. 10, §§ 731-793 (§ 750), Retail Installment Sales of Goods and Services, Rules & Regs of P.R., tit. 10, ch. 36, (Maximum Service Charges for Revolving Account Credit Plan, § 773-1 *et seq.*)

Rhode Island

Legal Interest Rate: R.I. Gen. Laws § 6-26-1

Contract: R.I. Gen. Laws § 6-26-2

Judgment: R.I. Gen. Laws § 6-26-1

Criminal Usury Cap: R.I. Gen. Laws §§ 6-26-2, 6-26-3

Small Loans: R.I. Gen. Laws §§ 19-14.2-1 to 19-14.2-16 (§§ 19-14.2-8 and 19-14.2-10), Small Loan Lenders Act

Loan and Investment Company Loans: R.I. Gen. Laws §§ 19-14.1-1 to 19-14.1-12 (§ 19-14.1-2), Lenders and Loan Brokers

Installment Sales Finance: R.I. Gen. Laws §§ 6-27-1 to 6-27-11 (§ 6-27-4), Truth-in-Lending and Retail Selling Act

Revolving Credit: R.I. Gen. Laws §§ 6-27-1 to 6-27-11 (§ 6-27-4), Truth-in-Lending and Retail Selling Act

Insurance Premium Financing: R.I. Gen. Laws §§ 19-14.6-1 to 19-14.6-6 (§ 19-14.6-2), Insurance Premium Finance Act

Life Insurance and Annuity Policy Loans: R.I. Gen. Laws § 27-4-13.1

Payday Lending: R.I. Gen. Laws §§ 19-14.4-1 to 19-14.4-10 (§ 19-14.4-4(4))

South Carolina

Legal Interest Rate: S.C. Code Ann. § 37-10-106(1)

Contract: S.C. Code Ann. §§ 37-10-106(1) and 34-31-20

Judgment: S.C. Code Ann. § 34-31-20

"Restricted" Loans: S.C. Code Ann. §§ 34-29-10 to 34-29-260 (§ 34-29-140), Consumer Finance Law

"Supervised" Loans: S.C. Code Ann. §§ 37-3-500 to 37-3-515 (§ 37-3-501), Consumer Protection Code

Consumer Credit Sales: S.C. Code Ann. §§ 37-1-101 to 37-15-100 (§ 37-2-201), Consumer Protection Code

Consumer Loans in General: S.C. Code Ann. §§ 37-1-101 to 37-15-100 (§ 37-3-201), Consumer Protection Code

Non-Consumer Loans: S.C. Code Ann. §§ 37-1-101 to 37-15-100 (§ 37-3-605), Consumer Protection Code

Insurance Premium Finance: S.C. Code Ann. §§ 38-39-10 to 38-39-110 (§ 38-39-80), Insurance Premium Service Companies

Revolving Charge: S.C. Code Ann. §§ 37-1-101 to 37-15-100 (§ 37-2-207), Consumer Protection Code

Revolving Loans: S.C. Code Ann. §§ 37-1-101 to 37-15-100 (§ 37-3-201), Consumer Protection Code

Life Insurance and Annuity Policy Loans: S.C. Code Ann. §§ 38-63-240 and 38-63-250

Payday Loans: S.C. Code Ann. §§ 34-39-110 to 34-39-260

Auto Title Loans: S.C. Code Ann. § 37-3-413

South Dakota

Legal Interest Rate: S.D. Codified Laws Ann. § 54-3-16

Contract: S.D. Codified Laws Ann. § 54-3-1.1

Judgment: S.D. Codified Laws Ann. § 54-3-5.1

Installment Sales: S.D. Codified Laws Ann. §§ 54-3A-1 to 54-3A-25 (§ 54-3A-3), Consumer Installment Sales Contracts

Bank Revolving Loan Credit: S.D. Codified Laws Ann. § 51A-12-12

Revolving Charge: S.D. Codified Laws Ann. §§ 54-11-1 to 54-11-10 (§ 54-11-6.1), Credit Cards and Revolving Charge Accounts

Life Insurance and Annuity Policy Loans: S.D. Codified Laws Ann. §§ 58-15-15.4 to 58-15-15.12

Payday Loans: S.D. Codified Laws Ann. §§ 54-4-65, 54.4-66

Tennessee

Legal Interest Rate: Tenn. Const. art XI, § 7; Tenn. Code Ann. § 47-14-103

Contract: Tenn. Code Ann. § 47-14-103 (formula rate defined in § 47-14-102(6) and § 47-14-106)

Judgment: Tenn. Code Ann. § 47-14-121

Industrial Loans: Tenn. Code Ann. §§ 45-5-101 to 45-5-612 (§ 45-5-301), Industrial Loan and Thrift Companies

Bank Installment Loans: Tenn. Code Ann. § 45-2-1106

Revolving Credit: Tenn. Code Ann. §§ 47-11-101 to 47-11-110 (§ 47-11-104), Retail Installment Sales Act

Home Loans: Tenn. Code Ann. §§ 47-15-101 to 47-15-104 (§§ 47-15-102 and 47-15-104), Interest on Home Loans

Goods Finance: Tenn. Code Ann. §§ 47-11-101 to 47-11-110 (§ 47-11-103), Retail Installment Sales Act

Insurance Premium Finance: Tenn. Code Ann. §§ 56-6-301, 56-37-108

Installment Loans: Tenn. Code Ann. § 47-14-107

Home Improvement Loans: Tenn. Code Ann. § 45-3-705

Life Insurance and Annuity Policy Loans: Tenn. Code Ann. § 56-7-2307

Auto Title Loans: Tenn. Code Ann. §§ 45-15-101 to 45-15-120 (§ 45-15-111)

Payday Loans: Tenn. Code Ann. §§ 45-17-101 to 45-17-119

Attorney General Opinions: Op. No. 90-79, 1990 Tenn. AG LEXIS 78 (Aug. 17, 1990)

Texas

Legal Interest Rate: Tex. Const. art. 16, § 11; Tex. Fin. Code Ann. § 302.001

Contract: Tex. Const. art. 16, § 11; Tex. Fin. Code Ann. §§ 302.001, 302.002, 303.001 to 303.704

Judgment: Tex. Fin. Code Ann. §§ 304.001 to 304.007

Consumer Loans: Tex. Fin. Code Ann. §§ 342.001 to 342.560, Consumer Loans

Installment Sales: Tex. Fin. Code Ann. §§ 345.001 to 345.357, Retail Installment Sales

Auto Finance: Tex. Fin. Code Ann. §§ 348.001 to 348.413, Motor Vehicle Installment Sales

Other Goods Finance: Tex. Fin. Code Ann. §§ 345.001 to 345.357, Retail Installment Sales

Manufactured Homes: Tex. Fin. Code Ann. §§ 347.001 to 347.403, Manufactured Home Credit Transactions

Insurance Premium Finance: Tex. Ins. Code. Ann. §§ 1110.001 to 1110.008 (§ 1110.004)

Second Mortgages: Tex. Fin. Code Ann. § 342.301, Consumer Loans

Revolving Loans & Credit Cards: Tex. Fin. Code Ann. §§ 346.001 to 346.206, Revolving Credit Accounts

Revolving Credit: Tex. Fin. Code Ann. §§ 345.001 to 345.357, Retail Installment Sales

Life Insurance and Annuity Policy Loans: Tex. Ins. Code. Ann. §§ 1110.001 to 1110.008 (§ 1110.004)

Payday Loans: 7 Tex. Admin. Code § 1.605

Utah

Legal Interest Rate: Utah Code Ann. § 15-1-1

Contract: Utah Code Ann. §§ 15-1-1 and 70C-2-101

Judgment: Utah Code Ann. § 15-1-4

Criminal Usury Cap: Utah Code Ann. § 76-6-520

Consumer Credit: Utah Code Ann. §§ 70C-1-101 to 70C-8-203 (§ 70C-2-101), Utah UCCC

Life Insurance and Annuity Policy Loans: Utah Code Ann. § 31A-22-420
Payday Loans: Utah Code Ann. §§ 7-23-101 to 7-23-110
Auto Title Loans: Utah Code Ann. §§ 7-24-101 to 7-24-305

Vermont

Legal Interest Rate: Vt. Stat. Ann. tit. 9, § 41a
Contract: Vt. Stat. Ann. tit. 9, § 41a
Judgment: Vt. R. App. P. 37; Vt. R. Civ. P. 69
Criminal Usury Cap: Vt. Stat. Ann. tit. 9, § 50
Small Loans: *See* Licensed Lender Act, below
Installment Loans: Vt. Stat. Ann. tit. 9, §§ 41a(b)(2), (5)
Auto Finance: Vt. Stat. Ann. tit. 9, §§ 2351 to 2362 (§ 2356a), Motor Vehicle Retail Installment Sales Financing; Vt. Stat. Ann. tit. 9, § 41a(b)(4)
Other Goods Finance: Vt. Stat. Ann. tit. 9, §§ 2401 to 2410 (§ 2405), Retail Installment Sales, Vt. Stat. Ann. tit. 9, § 41a(b)(2)
Revolving Credit: Vt. Stat. Ann. tit. 9, §§ 2401 to 2410 (§ 2406), Retail Installment Sales, Vt. Stat. Ann. tit. 9, § 41a(b)(3), (9)
Insurance Premium Finance: Vt. Stat. Ann. tit. 8, §§ 7001 to 7011 (§ 7007), Insurance Premium Finance Companies
Subordinate Mortgages: Vt. Stat. Ann. tit. 9, § 41a(b)(7)
Life Insurance and Annuity Policy Loans: Vt. Stat. Ann. tit. 8, § 3731
Licensed Lender Act: Effective Jan. 1, 1997. Consolidation of all lender licensing provisions in one location. Consumer Cred. Guide (CCH) ¶ 6340. Vt. Stat. Ann. tit. 8, §§ 2200 to 2239 (§ 2230), Licensed Lenders

Virginia

Legal Interest Rate: Va. Code Ann. § 6.1-330.53
Contract: Va. Code Ann. § 6.1-330.55
Judgment: Va. Code Ann. § 6.1-330.54; Va. Code Ann. § 8.01-382 (prejudgment and postjudgment interest).
Small Loans: Va. Code Ann. §§ 6.1-244 to 6.1-309 (§§ 6.1-272.1 to 6.1-278) Consumer Finance Act
Industrial Loans: Va. Code Ann. § 6.1-330.68
Bank Installment Loans: Va. Code Ann. § 6.1-330.60
Installment Sales: Va. Code Ann. § 6.1-330.77, Consumer Credit
Insurance Premium Financing: Va. Code Ann. §§ 38.2-4700 to 38.2-4712 (§ 38.2-4705), Insurance Premium Finance Companies
Second Mortgages: Va. Code Ann. §§ 6.1-330.71 to 6.1-330.73
Bank Revolving Credit: Va. Code Ann. § 6.1-330.63
Credit Union Loans: Va. Code Ann. § 6.1-330.64
Other Revolving Loan or Charge Credit: Va. Code Ann. § 6.1-330.78
Open Accounts: Va. Code Ann. § 6.1-330.77:1
Life Insurance and Annuity Policy Loans: Va. Code Ann. § 38.2-3308
Payday Loans: Va. Code Ann. §§ 6.1-444 to 6.1-471; 10 Va. Admin. Code §§ 5-200-10 to 5-200-100

Virgin Islands

Legal Interest Rate: V.I. Code Ann. tit. 11, § 951
Contract: V.I. Code Ann. tit. 11, § 951
Judgment: V.I. Code Ann. tit. 5, § 426
Small Loans: V.I. Code Ann. tit. 9, §§ 181 to 204 (§ 183), Small Loan Law

Credit Cards: V.I. Code Ann. tit. 11, § 957
Life Insurance Policy Loans: V.I. Code Ann. tit. 22, § 958
Insurance Premium Finance: V.I. Code Ann. tit. 22, § 1634

Washington

Legal Interest Rate: Wash. Rev. Code § 19.52.010
Contract: Wash. Rev. Code § 19.52.010, 19.52.020
Judgment: Wash. Rev. Code § 4.56.110
Industrial Loans: Wash. Rev. Code §§ 31.04.005 to 31.04.902 (§§ 31.04.105 and 31.04.115), Consumer Loan Act
Installment Finance—All Goods: Wash. Rev. Code §§ 63.14.010 to 63.14.926 (§ 63.14.130), Retail Installment Sales of Goods and Services
Insurance Premium Finance: Wash. Rev. Code §§ 48.56.010 to 48.56.900 (§ 48.56.090), Insurance Premium Finance Company Act
Revolving Credit: Wash. Rev. Code §§ 63.14.010 to 63.14.926 (§ 63.14.130), Retail Installment Sales of Goods and Services
Life Insurance and Annuity Policy Loans: Wash. Rev. Code §§ 48.23.080 and 48.23.085
Payday Loans: Wash. Rev. Code Ann. §§ 31.45.010 to 31.45.900 (§ 31.45.073)

West Virginia

Legal Interest Rate: W. Va. Code §§ 47-6-5 to 47-6-5c
Contract: W. Va. Code § 47-6-5. Alternative rates for loans and credit sales set by Lending and Credit Rate Board under W. Va. Code § 47A-1-1. Alternative bank rate set by Commissioner of Banking under W. Va. Code § 31A-4-30a.
Judgment: W. Va. Code §§ 56-6-31 and 46A-3-111(4)
Small Loans: W. Va. Code §§ 46A-1-101 to 46A-8-102 (§ 46A-4-107), Consumer Credit & Protection Act
Bank and Other Installment Loans: W. Va. Code § 47-6-5a
Second Mortgages: W. Va. Code §§ 31-17-1 to 31-17-20 (§ 31-17-8), Secondary Mortgage Loans
Auto Finance: W. Va. Code §§ 46A-1-101 to 46A-8-102 (§ 46A-3-101(6)), Consumer Credit and Protection Act
Installment Sales—Other Goods: W. Va. Code § 47-6-5a and §§ 46A-1-101 to 46A-8-102 (§§ 46A-3-101 and 46A-3-104), Consumer Credit & Protection Act
Revolving Charge Accounts: W. Va. Code §§ 46A-1-101 to 46A-8-102 (§ 46A-3-103), Consumer Credit & Protection Act
Revolving Loans: W. Va. Code §§ 46A-1-101 to 46A-8-102 (§ 46A-3-106), Consumer Credit & Protection Act
Life Insurance and Annuity Policy Loans: W. Va. Code §§ 33-13-8 and 33-13-8a

Wisconsin

Legal Interest Rate: Wis. Stat. §§ 138.04, 138.05
Contract: Wis. Stat. §§ 138.04, 138.05
Judgment: Wis. Stat. §§ 814.04 and 815.05
Criminal Usury Cap: Wis. Stat. § 943.27
Residential Mortgage Loans: Wis. Stat. §§ 138.051 to 138.056
State Bank Loans: Wis. Stat. § 138.041
Small Loans: Wis. Stat. § 138.09, Precomputed Loan Law; Wis. Stat. §§ 421.101 to 427.105 (§ 422.201), Wis. UCCC
Credit Sales: Wis. Stat. §§ 421.101 to 427.105 (§ 422.201), Wis. UCCC

Installment Loans: Wis. Stat. § 138.05

Insurance Premium Finance: Wis. Stat. § 138.12, Insurance Premium Finance Companies

Auto Finance: Wis. Stat. §§ 218.0142, 422.201(3)

Revolving Credit: Wis. Stat. §§ 421.101 to 427.105 (§ 422.201(10s)), Wis. UCCC

Life Insurance and Annuity Policy Loans: Wis. Stat. Ann. § 632.475

Refund Anticipation Loans: Wis. Stat. §§ 421.301-(37m), 422.201, 422.310

Wyoming

Legal Interest Rate: Wyo. Stat. § 40-14-106

Contract: See rates specified in consumer sections of Wyo. UCCC (Wyo. Stat. §§ 40-14-101 to 40-14-702)

Judgment: Wyo. Stat. § 1-16-102

Consumer Supervised Loans; Licensed Lenders: Wyo. Stat. §§ 40-14-101 to 40-14-702 (§ 40-14-348) (includes revolving loans), Wyoming UCCC

Consumer Loans in General: Wyo. Stat. §§ 40-14-101 to 40-14-702 (§ 40-14-310), Wyo. UCCC

Non-Consumer & Non-Consumer Related Loans: Wyo. Stat. §§ 40-14-101 to 40-14-702 (§ 40-14-358), Wyo. UCCC

Consumer Credit Sales: Wyo. Stat. §§ 40-14-101 to 40-14-702 (§ 40-14-212), Wyo. UCCC

Non-Consumer Related Credit Sales: Wyo. Stat. §§ 40-14-101 to 40-14-702 (§ 40-14-260), Wyo. UCCC

Revolving Charge Accounts: Wyo. Stat. §§ 40-14-101 to 40-14-702 (§ 40-14-218), Wyo. UCCC

Life Insurance and Annuity Policy Loans: Wyo. Stat. § 26-16-108

Payday Loans: Wyo. Stat. §§ 40-14-362 to 40-14-364

Appendix B   State Mortgage Broker Laws

This compilation of cites to state mortgage broker laws was as complete as possible as of the printing of this new edition. Practitioners should re-check their state laws for changes and updates to assure accuracy. These statutes include requirements, where applicable, regarding: applications and licensing; bonds; audits; fees; record keeping; continuing education; minimum net worth; standards for license revocation; and civil liability and government enforcement. Some statutes also set out standards of conduct, outlaw discrimination by brokers, and/or define deceptive advertising or other representations by mortgage brokers.

Alabama

Mortgage Brokers Licensing Act, Ala. Code §§ 5-25-1 to 5-23-18

Alaska

None

Arizona

Ariz. Rev. Stat. §§ 6-901 to 6-910

Arkansas

Fair Mortgage Lending Act, Ark. Code Ann. §§ 23-39-501 to 23-59-506 (Michie)

California

Finance Lenders Law, Cal. Fin. Code §§ 22000 to 22780 (West)

Residential Mortgage Lending Act, Cal. Fin. Code §§ 50000 to 50706 (West)

Cal. Bus. & Prof. Code §§ 10130 to 10149 (real estate brokers) (West)

Colorado

None

Connecticut

Conn. Gen. Stat. §§ 36a-485 to 36a-534a

Delaware

Del. Code Ann. tit. 25, §§ 2101 to 2115

District of Columbia

Mortgage Lender and Broker Act, D.C. Code Ann. §§ 26-1101 to 26-1121

Florida

Florida Fair Lending Act, Fla. Stat. Ann. §§ 494.001 to 494.00797 (West)

Georgia

Georgia Fair Lending Act, Ga. Code Ann. §§ 7-1-1000 to 7-1-1021; Ga. Code Ann. §§ 7-6A-1 to 7-6A-13

Hawaii

Haw. Rev. Stat. §§ 454-1 to 454-8

Idaho

Residential Mortgage Practices Act, Idaho Code §§ 26-3101 to 26-3117 (Michie)

Illinois

Residential Mortgage License Act, 205 Ill. Comp. Stat. §§ 635/1-1 to 635/7-1

Fairness in Lending Act, 815 Ill. Comp. Stat. §§ 120/1 to 120/6

Indiana

Ind. Code §§ 24-9-1-1 to 24-9-9-4 (effective Jan. 1, 2005)

Ind. Code §§ 23-2-5-1 to 23-2-5-21 (loan brokers)

Iowa

Iowa Code §§ 535B.1 to 535B.16

Kansas

Kansas Mortgage Business Act, Kan. Stat. Ann. §§ 9-2201 to 9-2220

Kentucky

Mortgage Loan Company and Mortgage Loan Broker Act, Ky. Rev. Stat. Ann. §§ 294.010 to 294.990 (Michie)

Louisiana

Residential Mortgage Lending Act, La. Rev. Stat. Ann. §§ 6:1081 to 6:1099 (West)

La. Rev. Stat. Ann. §§ 9:3572.1 to 9:3572.12 (West) (loan brokers)

Maine

Maine Consumer Credit Code, Me. Rev. Stat. Ann. tit. 9-A, §§ 10-101 to 10-401 (West)

Maryland

Maryland Mortgage Lender Law, Md. Code Ann., Fin. Inst. §§ 11-501 to 11-520

Md. Code Ann., Com. Law §§ 12-801 to 12-809

Massachusetts

Mass. Gen. Laws ch. 255E, §§ 1 to 12

Michigan

Consumer Mortgage Protection Act, Mich. Comp. Laws §§ 445.1631 to 445.1645

Mortgage Brokers, Lenders, and Servicers Licensing Act, Mich. Comp. Laws §§ 445.1651 to 445.1684

Secondary Mortgage Loan Act, Mich. Comp. Laws §§ 493.51 to 493.81

Minnesota

Minnesota Residential Mortgage Originator and Service Licensing Act, Minn. Stat. §§ 58.01 to 58.17

Mississippi

Mississippi Mortgage Consumer Protection Law (repealed effective July 1, 2007), Miss. Code Ann. §§ 81-18-1 to 81-18-51

Missouri

Residential Mortgage Brokers License Act, Mo. Rev. Stat. §§ 443.800 to 443.893

Montana

Mortgage Broker and Loan Originator Licensing Act, Mont. Code Ann. §§ 32-9-101 to 32-9-133

Nebraska

Mortgage Bankers Registration and Licensing Act, Neb. Rev. Stat. §§ 45-701 to 45-721

Nevada

Nev. Rev. Stat. §§ 645B.010 to 645B.960 (mortgage brokers and agents), §§ 397-B:1 to 397-B:12 (mortgage loan servicing)

New Hampshire

N.H. Rev. Stat. Ann. §§ 397-A:1 to 397A-21

New Jersey

New Jersey Licensed Lenders Act, N.J. Stat. Ann. §§ 17:11C-1 to 17:11C-48 (West)

New Mexico

Mortgage Loan Company and Loan Broker Act, N.M. Stat. Ann. §§ 58-21-1 to 58-21-29 (Michie)

New York

N.Y. Banking Law, §§ 589 to 599 (McKinney)

North Carolina

Mortgage Lending Act, N.C. Gen. Stat. §§ 53-243.01 to 53-243.16

North Dakota

N.D. Cent. Code §§ 13-04.1-01 to 13-04.1-13

Ohio

Ohio Rev. Code Ann. §§ 1322.01 to 1322.99 (West)

Oklahoma

Mortgage Broker Licensure Act, Okla. Stat. tit. 59, §§ 2081 to 2093

Oregon

Oregon Mortgage Lender Law, Or. Rev. Stat. §§ 59.840 to 59.980

Pennsylvania

63 Pa. Cons. Stat. §§ 301 to 318

Mortgage Bankers and Brokers and Consumer Equity Protection Act, 63 Pa. Cons. Stat. §§ 456.301 to 456.3101

Rhode Island

R.I. Gen. Laws §§ 19-14-1 to 19-14-32 (licensed activities), §§ 19-14.1.1 to 19-14.1-12 (lenders and loan brokers)

South Carolina

Licensing Requirements Act of Certain Loan Brokers of Mortgages on Residential Real Property, S.C. Code Ann. §§ 40-58-10 to 40-58-110 (Law. Co-op.)

South Dakota

S.D. Codified Laws §§ 54-14-1 to 54-14-11 (Michie)

Tennessee

Tennessee Residential Lending, Brokerage and Servicing Act, Tenn. Code Ann. §§ 45-13-101 to 45-13-128

Texas

Mortgage Broker License Act, Tex. Fin. Code Ann. §§ 156.001 to 156.508 (Vernon)

Mortgage Banker Registration Act, Tex. Fin. Code Ann. §§ 157.001 to 157.011 (Vernon)

Utah

Utah Residential Mortgage Practices Act, Utah Code Ann. §§ 61-2c-101 to 61-2c-510

Vermont

Vt. Stat. Ann. tit. 8, §§ 2200 to 2237

Virginia

Mortgage Lender and Broker Act, Va. Code Ann. §§ 6.1-408 to 6.1-431 (Michie)

Washington

Mortgage Broker Practices Act, Wash. Rev. Code §§ 19.146.005 to 19.146.903

West Virginia

W. Va. Code §§ 31-17-1 to 31-17-20

Wisconsin

Wis. Stat. §§ 224.71 to 224.82

Wyoming

None

National Bank Act

This appendix excerpts portions of the National Bank Act and the Interstate Branching and Banking Efficiency Act (which amended portions of the National Bank Act). These provisions appear in C.1. Section C.2, includes selected regulations promulgated by the Office of the Comptroller of the Currency (OCC). In addition, the OCC issues Interpretive and Advisory Letters from time to time. Relevant letters are summarized in C.3. Finally, all formal Preemption Opinions released by the OCC are summarized in C.4. The full text of the Interpretive and Advisory Letters and the Preemption Opinions are included on the CD-Rom accompanying this volume and is updated in the annual supplement. In addition, the statutes and regulations reprinted in Appxs. C.1 and C.2, are also found on the companion CD-Rom.

C.1 Selected Statutory Provisions

TITLE 12—BANKS AND BANKING

CHAPTER 2—NATIONAL BANKS

SUBCHAPTER I—ORGANIZATION AND GENERAL PROVISIONS

* * *

§ 24.   Corporate powers of associations
§ 24a.   Financial subsidiaries of national banks

* * *

§ 36.   Branch banks

* * *

§ 43.   Interpretations concerning preemption of certain State laws

* * *

SUBCHAPTER IV—REGULATION OF THE BANKING BUSINESS; POWERS AND DUTIES OF NATIONAL BANKS

* * *

§ 85.   Rate of interest on loans, discounts and purchases
§ 86.   Usurious interest; penalty for taking; limitations

* * *

CHAPTER 3—FEDERAL RESERVE SYSTEM

SUBCHAPTER X—POWERS AND DUTIES OF MEMBER BANKS

§ 371.   Real estate loans

* * *

SUBCHAPTER XV—BANK EXAMINATIONS

* * *

§ 484.   Limitation on visitorial powers

* * *

TITLE 12—BANKS AND BANKING

CHAPTER 2—NATIONAL BANKS

SUBCHAPTER I—ORGANIZATION AND GENERAL PROVISIONS

* * *

12 U.S.C. § 24. Corporate powers of associations

Upon duly making and filing articles of association and an organization certificate a national banking association shall become, as from the date of the execution of its organization certificate, a body corporate, and as such, and in the name designated in the organization certificate, it shall have power—

First. To adopt and use a corporate seal.

Second. To have succession from February 25, 1927, or from the date of its organization if organized after February 25, 1927, until such time as it be dissolved by the act of its shareholders owning two-thirds of its stock, or until its franchise becomes forfeited by reason of violation of law, or until terminated by either a general or a special Act of Congress or until its affairs be placed in the hands of a receiver and finally wound up by him.

Third. To make contracts.

Fourth. To sue and be sued, complain and defend, in any court of law and equity, as fully as natural persons.

Fifth. To elect or appoint directors, and by its board of directors to appoint a president, vice president, cashier, and other officers, define their duties, require bonds of them and fix the penalty thereof, dismiss such officers or any of them at pleasure, and appoint others to fill their places.

Sixth. To prescribe, by its board of directors, bylaws not inconsistent with law, regulating the manner in which its stock shall be transferred, its directors elected or appointed, its officers appointed, its property transferred, its general business conducted, and the privileges granted to it by law exercised and enjoyed.

Seventh. To exercise by its board of directors or duly authorized officers or agents, subject to law, all such incidental powers as shall be necessary to carry on the business of banking; by discounting and negotiating promissory notes, drafts, bills of exchange, and other evidences of debt; by receiving deposits; by buying and selling exchange, coin, and bullion; by loaning money on personal security; and by obtaining, issuing, and circulating notes according to the provisions of title 62 of the Revised Statutes. The business of dealing in securities and stock by the association shall be limited to purchasing and selling such securities and stock without recourse, solely upon the order, and for the account of, customers, and in no case for its own account, and the association shall not underwrite any issue of securities or stock; *Provided,* That the association may purchase for its own account investment securities under such limitations and restrictions as the Comptroller of the Currency may by regulation prescribe. In no event shall the total amount of the investment securities of any one obligor or maker, held by the association for its own account, exceed at any time 10 per centum of its capital stock actually paid in and unimpaired and 10 per centum of its unimpaired surplus fund, except that this limitation shall not require any association to dispose of any securities lawfully held by it on August 23, 1935. As used in this section the term "investment securities" shall mean marketable obligations, evidencing indebtedness of any person, copartnership, association, or corporation in the form of bonds, notes and/or debentures commonly known as investment securities under such further definition of the term "investment securities" as may by regulation be prescribed by the Comptroller of the Currency. Except as hereinafter provided or otherwise permitted by law, nothing herein contained shall authorize the purchase by the association for its own account of any shares of stock of any corporation. The limitations and restrictions herein contained as to dealing in, underwriting and purchasing for its own account, investment securities shall not apply to obligations of the United States, or general obligations of any State or of any political subdivision thereof, or obligations of the Washington Metropolitan Area Transit Authority which are guaranteed by the Secretary of Transportation under section 9 of the National Capital Transportation Act of 1969, or obligations issued under authority of the Federal Farm Loan Act, as amended, or issued by the thirteen banks for cooperatives or any of them or the Federal Home Loan Banks, or obligations which are insured by the Secretary of Housing and Urban Development under title XI of the National Housing Act [12 U.S.C. § 1749aaa *et seq.*] or obligations which are insured by the Secretary of Housing and Urban Development (hereinafter in this sentence referred to as the "Secretary") pursuant to section 207 of the National Housing Act [12 U.S.C. § 1713], if the debentures to be issued in payment of such insured obligations are guaranteed as to principal and interest by the United States, or obligations, participations, or other instruments of or issued by the Federal National Mortgage Association, or the Government National Mortgage Association, or mortgages, obligations or other securities which are or ever have been sold by the Federal Home Loan Mortgage Corporation pursuant to Section 305 or Section 306 of the Federal Home Loan Mortgage Corporation Act [12 U.S.C. §§ 1434 or 1455], or obligations of the Federal Financing Bank or obligations of the Environmental Financing Authority, or obligations or other instruments or securities of the Student Loan Marketing Association, or such obligations of any local public agency (as defined in section 110(h) of the Housing Act of 1949 [42 U.S.C. § 1460(h)]) as are secured by an agreement between the local public agency and the Secretary in which the local public agency agrees to borrow from said Secretary, and said Secretary agrees to lend to said local public agency, monies in an aggregate amount which (together with any other monies irrevocably committed to the payment of interest on such obligations) will suffice to pay, when due, the interest on and all installments (including the final installment) of the principal of such obligations, which monies under the terms of said agreement are required to be used for such payments, or such obligations of a public housing agency (as defined in the United States Housing Act of 1937, as amended [42 U.S.C. § 1437 *et seq.*]) as are secured

(1) by an agreement between the public housing agency and the Secretary in which the public housing agency agrees to borrow from the Secretary, and the Secretary agrees to lend to the public housing agency, prior to the maturity of such obligations, monies in an amount which (together with any other monies irrevocably committed to the payment of interest on such obligations) will suffice to pay the principal of such obligations with interest to maturity thereon, which monies under the terms of said agreement are required to be used for the purpose of paying the principal of and the interest on such obligations at their maturity,

(2) by a pledge of annual contributions under an annual contributions contract between such public housing agency and the Secretary if such contract shall contain the covenant by the Secretary which is authorized by subsection (g) of section 6 of the United States Housing Act of 1937, as amended [42 U.S.C. § 1437d(g)], and if the maximum sum and the maximum period specified in such contract pursuant to said subsection 6(g) [42 U.S.C. § 1437d(g)] shall not be less than the annual amount and the period for payment which are requisite to provide for the payment when due of all installments of principal and interest on such obligations, or

(3) by a pledge of both annual contributions under an annual contributions contract containing the covenant by the Secretary which is authorized by section 6(g) of the United States Housing Act of 1937 [42 U.S.C. § 1437d(g)], and a loan under an agreement between the local public housing agency and the Secretary in which the public housing agency agrees to borrow from the Secretary, and the Secretary agrees to lend to the public housing agency, prior to the maturity of the obligations involved, moneys in an amount which (together with any other moneys irrevocably committed under the annual contributions contract to the payment of principal and interest on such obligations) will suffice to provide for the payment when due of all installments of principal and interest on such obligations, which moneys under the terms of the agreement are required to be used for the purpose of paying the principal and interest on such obligations at their maturity: *Provided,* That in carrying on the business commonly known as the safe-deposit business the association shall not invest in the capital stock of a corporation organized under

the law of any State to conduct a safe-deposit business in an amount in excess of 15 per centum of the capital stock of the association actually paid in and unimpaired and 15 per centum of its unimpaired surplus. The limitations and restrictions herein contained as to dealing in and underwriting investment securities shall not apply to obligations issued by the International Bank for Reconstruction and Development, the European Bank for Reconstruction and Development, the Inter-American Development Bank[1] Bank for Economic Co-operation and Development in the Middle East and North Africa,,[2] the North American Development Bank, the Asian Development Bank, the African Development Bank, the Inter-American Investment Corporation, or the International Finance Corporation,,[3] or obligations issued by any State or political subdivision or any agency of a State or political subdivision for housing, university, or dormitory purposes, which are at the time eligible for purchase by a national bank for its own account, nor to bonds, notes and other obligations issued by the Tennessee Valley Authority or by the United States Postal Service: *Provided,* That no association shall hold obligations issued by any of said organizations as a result of underwriting, dealing, or purchasing for its own account (and for this purpose obligations as to which it is under commitment shall be deemed to be held by it) in a total amount exceeding at any one time 10 per centum of its capital stock actually paid in and unimpaired and 10 per centum of its unimpaired surplus fund. Notwithstanding any other provision in this paragraph, the association may purchase for its own account shares of stock issued by a corporation authorized to be created pursuant to Title IX of the Housing and Urban Development Act of 1968 [42 U.S.C. § 3931 *et seq.*], and may make investments in a partnership, limited partnership, or joint venture formed pursuant to section 907(a) or 907(c) of that Act [42 U.S.C. § 3937(a) or 3937(c)]. Notwithstanding any other provision of this paragraph, the association may purchase for its own account shares of stock issued by any State housing corporation incorporated in the State in which the association is located and may make investments in loans and commitments for loans to any such corporation: *Provided,* That in no event shall the total amount of such stock held for its own account and such investments in loans and commitments made by the association exceed at any time 5 per centum of its capital stock actually paid in and unimpaired plus 5 per centum of its unimpaired surplus fund. Notwithstanding any other provision in this paragraph, the association may purchase for its own account shares of stock issued by a corporation organized solely for the purpose of making loans to farmers and ranchers for agricultural purposes, including the breeding, raising, fattening, or marketing of livestock. However, unless the association owns at least 80 per centum of the stock of such agricultural credit corporation the amount invested by the association at any one time in the stock of such corporation shall not exceed 20 per centum of the unimpaired capital and surplus of the association: *Provided further,* That notwithstanding any other provision of this paragraph, the association may purchase for its own

account shares of stock of a bank insured by the Federal Deposit Insurance Corporation or a holding company which owns or controls such an insured bank if the stock of such bank or company is owned exclusively (except to the extent directors' qualifying shares are required by law) by depository institutions or depository institution holding companies (as defined in section 1813 of this title) and such bank or company and all subsidiaries thereof are engaged exclusively in providing services to or for other depository institutions, their holding companies, and the officers, directors, and employees of such institutions and companies, and in providing correspondent banking services at the request of other depository institutions or their holding companies (also referred to as a "banker's bank"), but in no event shall the total amount of such stock held by the association in any bank or holding company exceed at any time 10 per centum of the association's capital stock and paid in and unimpaired surplus and in no event shall the purchase of such stock result in an association's acquiring more than 5 per centum of any class of voting securities of such bank or company. The limitations and restrictions contained in this paragraph as to an association purchasing for its own account investment securities shall not apply to securities that

(A) are offered and sold pursuant to section 4(5) of the Securities Act of 1933 (15 U.S.C. 77d(5));

(B) are small business related securities (as defined in section 3(a)(53) of the Securities Exchange Act of 1934 [15 U.S.C. § 78c(a)(53)]); or

(C) are mortgage related securities (as that term is defined in section 3(a)(41) of the Securities Exchange Act of 1934 (15 U.S.C. 78c(a)(41)).[4] The exception provided for the securities described in subparagraphs (A), (B), and (C) shall be subject to such regulations as the Comptroller of the Currency may prescribe, including regulations prescribing minimum size of the issue (at the time of initial distribution) or minimum aggregate sales prices, or both.

A national banking association may deal in, underwrite, and purchase for such association's own account qualified Canadian government obligations to the same extent that such association may deal in, underwrite, and purchase for such association's own account obligations of the United States or general obligations of any State or of any political subdivision thereof. For purposes of this paragraph—

(1) the term "qualified Canadian government obligations" means any debt obligation which is backed by Canada, any Province of Canada, or any political subdivision of any such Province to a degree which is comparable to the liability of the United States, any State, or any political subdivision thereof for any obligation which is backed by the full faith and credit of the United States, such State, or such political subdivision, and such term includes any debt obligation of any agent of Canada or any such Province or any political subdivision of such Province if—

(A) the obligation of the agent is assumed in such agent's capacity as agent for Canada or such Province or such political subdivision; and

(B) Canada, such Province, or such political subdivision

---

1 So in original. A comma should probably appear.

2 So in original. Only one comma should appear.

3 So in original. Only one comma should appear.

---

4 So in original. The period probably should be preceded by an additional closing parenthesis.

on whose behalf such agent is acting with respect to such obligation is ultimately and unconditionally liable for such obligation; and

(2) the term "Province of Canada" means a Province of Canada and includes the Yukon Territory and the Northwest Territories and their successors.

In addition to the provisions in this paragraph for dealing in, underwriting, or purchasing securities, the limitations and restrictions contained in this paragraph as to dealing in, underwriting, and purchasing investment securities for the national bank's own account shall not apply to obligations (including limited obligation bonds, revenue bonds, and obligations that satisfy the requirements of section 142(b)(1) of Title 26) issued by or on behalf of any State or political subdivision of a State, including any municipal corporate instrumentality of 1 or more States, or any public agency or authority of any State or political subdivision of a State, if the national bank is well capitalized (as defined in section 1831o of this title).

Eighth. To contribute to community funds, or to charitable, philanthropic, or benevolent instrumentalities conducive to public welfare, such sums as its board of directors may deem expedient and in the interests of the association, if it is located in a State the laws of which do not expressly prohibit State banking institutions from contributing to such funds or instrumentalities.

Ninth. To issue and sell securities which are guaranteed pursuant to section 1721(g) of this title.

Tenth. To invest in tangible personal property, including, without limitation, vehicles, manufactured homes, machinery, equipment, or furniture, for lease financing transactions on a net lease basis, but such investment may not exceed 10 percent of the assets of the association.

Eleventh. To make investments designed primarily to promote the public welfare, including the welfare of low- and moderate-income communities or families (such as by providing housing, services, or jobs). A national banking association may make such investments directly or by purchasing interests in an entity primarily engaged in making such investments. An association shall not make any such investment if the investment would expose the association to unlimited liability. The Comptroller of the Currency shall limit an association's investments in any 1 project and an association's aggregate investments under this paragraph. An association's aggregate investments under this paragraph shall not exceed an amount equal to the sum of 5 percent of the association's capital stock actually paid in and unimpaired and 5 percent of the association's unimpaired surplus fund, unless the Comptroller determines by order that the higher amount will pose no significant risk to the affected deposit insurance fund, and the association is adequately capitalized. In no case shall an association's aggregate investments under this paragraph exceed an amount equal to the sum of 10 percent of the association's capital stock actually paid in and unimpaired and 10 percent of the association's unimpaired surplus fund.

[R.S. § 5136; July 1, 1922, ch. 257, § 1, 42 Stat. 767; Feb. 25, 1927, ch. 191, § 2, 44 Stat. 1226; June 16, 1933, ch. 89, § 16, 48 Stat. 184; Aug. 23, 1935, ch. 614, title III, § 308, 49 Stat. 709; Feb. 3, 1938, ch. 13, § 13, 52 Stat. 26; June 11, 1940, ch. 301, 54 Stat. 261; June 29, 1949, ch. 276, § 1, 63 Stat. 298; July 15, 1949, ch.

338, title VI, § 602(a), 63 Stat. 439; Apr. 9, 1952, ch. 169, 66 Stat. 49; Aug. 2, 1954, ch. 649, title II, § 203, 68 Stat. 622; Aug. 23, 1954, ch. 834, § 2, 68 Stat. 771; July 26, 1956, ch. 741, title II, § 201(c), 70 Stat. 667; Pub. L. No. 86–137, § 2, 73 Stat. 285 (Aug. 6, 1959); Pub. L. No. 86–147, § 10, 73 Stat. 301 (Aug. 7, 1959); Pub. L. No. 86–230, § 1(a), 73 Stat. 457 (Sept. 8, 1959); Pub. L. No. 86–278, 73 Stat. 563 (Sept. 16, 1959); Pub. L. No. 86–372, title IV, § 420, 73 Stat. 679 (Sept. 23, 1959); Pub. L. No. 88–560, title VII, § 701(c), 78 Stat. 800 (Sept. 2, 1964); Pub. L. No. 89–369, § 10, 80 Stat. 72 (Mar. 16, 1966); Pub. L. No. 89–754, title V, § 504(a)(1), 80 Stat. 1277 (Nov. 3, 1966); Pub. L. No. 90–19, § 27(a), 81 Stat. 28 (May 25, 1967); Pub. L. No. 90–448, title VIII, §§ 804(c), 807 (j), title IX, § 911, title XVII, § 1705(h), 82 Stat. 543, 545, 550, 605 (Aug. 1, 1968); Pub. L. No. 91–375, § 6(d), 84 Stat. 776 (Aug. 12, 1970); Pub. L. No. 92–318, title I, § 133(c)(1), 86 Stat. 269 (June 23, 1972); Pub. L. No. 91–143, § 12(b) (Dec. 9, 1969), *as added* Pub. L. No. 92–349, title I, § 101, 86 Stat. 466 (July 13, 1972); Pub. L. No. 92–500, § 12(n), 86 Stat. 902 (Oct. 18, 1972); Pub. L. No. 93–100, § 5(c), 87 Stat. 344 (Aug. 16, 1973); Pub. L. No. 93–224, § 14, 87 Stat. 941 (Dec. 29, 1973); Pub. L. No. 93–234, title II, § 207, 87 Stat. 984 (Dec. 31, 1973); Pub. L. No. 93–383, title II, § 206, title VIII, § 805(c)(1), 88 Stat. 668, 726 (Aug. 22, 1974); Pub. L. No. 96–221, title VII, § 711, 94 Stat. 189 (Mar. 31, 1980); Pub. L. No. 97–35, title XIII, § 1342(a), 95 Stat. 743 (Aug. 13, 1981); Pub. L. No. 97–320, title IV, § 404(b), 96 Stat. 1511 (Oct. 15, 1982); Pub. L. No. 97–457, § 18, 96 Stat. 2509 (Jan. 12, 1983); Pub. L. No. 98–440, title I, § 105(c), 98 Stat. 1691 (Oct. 3, 1984); Pub. L. No. 98–473, title I, § 101(1) [title I, § 101], 98 Stat. 1884, 1885 (Oct. 12, 1984); Pub. L. No. 100–86, title I, § 108, 101 Stat. 579 (Aug. 10, 1987); Pub. L. No. 100–449, title III, § 308, 102 Stat. 1877 (Sept. 28, 1988); Pub. L. No. 101–513, title V, § 562(c)(10)(B), (e)(1)(B), 104 Stat. 2036, 2037 (Nov. 5, 1990); Pub. L. No. 102–485, § 6(a), 106 Stat. 2774 (Oct. 23, 1992); Pub. L. No. 103–182, title V, § 541(h)(1), 107 Stat. 2167 (Dec. 8, 1993); Pub. L. No. 103–325, title II, § 206(c), title III, §§ 322(a)(1), 347 (b), 108 Stat. 2199, 2226, 2241 (Sept. 23, 1994); Pub. L. No. 104–208, div. A, title I, § 101(c) [title VII, § 710(b)], title II, § 2704(d)(7), 110 Stat. 3009–121, 3009–181, 3009–489 (Sept. 30, 1996); Pub. L. No. 106–102, title I, § 151, 113 Stat. 1384 (Nov. 12, 1999).]

12 U.S.C. § 24a. Financial subsidiaries of national banks

(a) Authorization to conduct in subsidiaries certain activities that are financial in nature

(1) In general

Subject to paragraph (2), a national bank may control a financial subsidiary, or hold an interest in a financial subsidiary.

(2) Conditions and requirements

A national bank may control a financial subsidiary, or hold an interest in a financial subsidiary, only if—

(A) the financial subsidiary engages only in—

(i) activities that are financial in nature or incidental to a financial activity pursuant to subsection (b) of this section; and

(ii) activities that are permitted for national banks to engage in directly (subject to the same terms and conditions that govern the conduct of the activities by a national bank);

(B) the activities engaged in by the financial subsidiary as a principal do not include—

(i) insuring, guaranteeing, or indemnifying against loss, harm, damage, illness, disability, or death (except to the extent permitted under section 302 or 303(c) of the Gramm-Leach-Bliley Act [15 U.S.C. § 6712 or 6713(c)]) or providing or issuing annuities the income of which is subject to tax treatment under section 72 of Title 26;

(ii) real estate development or real estate investment activities, unless otherwise expressly authorized by law; or

(iii) any activity permitted in subparagraph (H) or (I) of section 1843(k)(4) of this title, except activities described in section 1843(k)(4)(H) of this title that may be permitted in accordance with section 122 of the Gramm-Leach-Bliley Act;

(C) the national bank and each depository institution affiliate of the national bank are well capitalized and well managed;

(D) the aggregate consolidated total assets of all financial subsidiaries of the national bank do not exceed the lesser of—

(i) 45 percent of the consolidated total assets of the parent bank; or

(ii) $50,000,000,000;

(E) except as provided in paragraph (4), the national bank meets any applicable rating or other requirement set forth in paragraph (3); and

(F) the national bank has received the approval of the Comptroller of the Currency for the financial subsidiary to engage in such activities, which approval shall be based solely upon the factors set forth in this section.

(3) Rating or comparable requirement

(A) In general

A national bank meets the requirements of this paragraph if—

(i) the bank is 1 of the 50 largest insured banks and has not fewer than 1 issue of outstanding eligible debt that is currently rated within the 3 highest investment grade rating categories by a nationally recognized statistical rating organization; or

(ii) the bank is 1 of the second 50 largest insured banks and meets the criteria set forth in clause (i) or such other criteria as the Secretary of the Treasury and the Board of Governors of the Federal Reserve System may jointly establish by regulation and determine to be comparable to and consistent with the purposes of the rating required in clause (i).

(B) Consolidated total assets

For purposes of this paragraph, the size of an insured bank shall be determined on the basis of the consolidated total assets of the bank as of the end of each calendar year.

(4) Financial agency subsidiary

The requirement in paragraph (2)(E) shall not apply with respect to the ownership or control of a financial subsidiary that engages in activities described in subsection (b)(1) of this section solely as agent and not directly or indirectly as principal.

(5) Regulations required

Before the end of the 270-day period beginning on November 12, 1999, the Comptroller of the Currency shall, by regulation, prescribe procedures to implement this section.

(6) Indexed asset limit

The dollar amount contained in paragraph (2)(D) shall be adjusted according to an indexing mechanism jointly established by regulation by the Secretary of the Treasury and the Board of Governors of the Federal Reserve System.

(7) Coordination with section 1843(l)(2) of this title

Section 1843(l)(2) of this title applies to a national bank that controls a financial subsidiary in the manner provided in that section.

(b) Activities that are financial in nature

(1) Financial activities

(A) In general

An activity shall be financial in nature or incidental to such financial activity only if—

(i) such activity has been defined to be financial in nature or incidental to a financial activity for bank holding companies pursuant to section 1843(k)(4) of this title; or

(ii) the Secretary of the Treasury determines the activity is financial in nature or incidental to a financial activity in accordance with subparagraph (B).

(B) Coordination between the Board and the Secretary of the Treasury

(i) Proposals raised before the Secretary of the Treasury

(I) Consultation

The Secretary of the Treasury shall notify the Board of, and consult with the Board concerning, any request, proposal, or application under this section for a determination of whether an activity is financial in nature or incidental to a financial activity.

(II) Board view

The Secretary of the Treasury shall not determine that any activity is financial in nature or incidental to a financial activity under this section if the Board notifies the Secretary in writing, not later than 30 days after the date of receipt of the notice described in subclause (I) (or such longer period as the Secretary determines to be appropriate under the circumstances) that the Board believes that the activity is not financial in nature or incidental to a financial activity or is not otherwise permissible under this section.

(ii) Proposals raised by the Board

(I) Board recommendation

The Board may, at any time, recommend in writing that the Secretary of the Treasury find an activity to be financial in nature or incidental to a financial activity for purposes of this section.

(II) Time period for secretarial action

Not later than 30 days after the date of receipt of a written recommendation from the Board under subclause (I) (or such longer period as the Secretary of the Treasury and the Board determine to be appropriate under the circumstances), the Secretary shall determine whether to initiate a public rulemaking proposing that the subject recommended activity be found to be financial in nature or incidental to a financial activity under this section, and shall notify the Board in writing of the determination of the Secretary and, in the event that the Secretary determines not to seek public comment on the proposal, the reasons for that determination.

(2) Factors to be considered

In determining whether an activity is financial in nature or incidental to a financial activity, the Secretary shall take into account—

(A) the purposes of this Act[1] and the Gramm-Leach-Bliley Act;

(B) changes or reasonably expected changes in the marketplace in which banks compete;

(C) changes or reasonably expected changes in the technology for delivering financial services; and

(D) whether such activity is necessary or appropriate to allow a bank and the subsidiaries of a bank to—

(i) compete effectively with any company seeking to provide financial services in the United States;

(ii) efficiently deliver information and services that are financial in nature through the use of technological means, including any application necessary to protect the security or efficacy of systems for the transmission of data or financial transactions; and

(iii) offer customers any available or emerging technological means for using financial services or for the document imaging of data.

(3) Authorization of new financial activities

The Secretary of the Treasury shall, by regulation or order and in accordance with paragraph (1)(B), define, consistent with the purposes of this Act[2] and the Gramm-Leach-Bliley Act, the following activities as, and the extent to which such activities are, financial in nature or incidental to a financial activity:

(A) Lending, exchanging, transferring, investing for others, or safeguarding financial assets other than money or securities.

(B) Providing any device or other instrumentality for transferring money or other financial assets.

(C) Arranging, effecting, or facilitating financial transactions for the account of third parties.

(c) Capital deduction

(1) Capital deduction required

In determining compliance with applicable capital standards—

(A) the aggregate amount of the outstanding equity investment, including retained earnings, of a national bank in all financial subsidiaries shall be deducted from the assets and tangible equity of the national bank; and

(B) the assets and liabilities of the financial subsidiaries shall not be consolidated with those of the national bank.

(2) Financial statement disclosure of capital deduction

Any published financial statement of a national bank that controls a financial subsidiary shall, in addition to providing information prepared in accordance with generally accepted accounting principles, separately present financial information for the bank in the manner provided in paragraph (1).

(d) Safeguards for the bank

A national bank that establishes or maintains a financial subsidiary shall assure that—

(1) the procedures of the national bank for identifying and managing financial and operational risks within the national bank and the financial subsidiary adequately protect the national bank from such risks;

(2) the national bank has, for the protection of the bank, reasonable policies and procedures to preserve the separate corporate identity and limited liability of the national bank and the financial subsidiaries of the national bank; and

(3) the national bank is in compliance with this section.

(e) Provisions applicable to national banks that fail to continue to meet certain requirements

(1) In general

If a national bank or insured depository institution affiliate does not continue to meet the requirements of subsection (a)(2)(C) of this section or subsection (d) of this section, the Comptroller of the Currency shall promptly give notice to the national bank to that effect describing the conditions giving rise to the notice.

(2) Agreement to correct conditions

Not later than 45 days after the date of receipt by a national bank of a notice given under paragraph (1) (or such additional period as the Comptroller of the Currency may permit), the national bank shall execute an agreement with the Comptroller of the Currency and any relevant insured depository institution affiliate shall execute an agreement with its appropriate Federal banking agency to comply with the requirements of subsection (a)(2)(C) of this section and subsection (d) of this section.

(3) Imposition of conditions

Until the conditions described in a notice under paragraph (1) are corrected—

(A) the Comptroller of the Currency may impose such limitations on the conduct or activities of the national bank or any subsidiary of the national bank as the Comptroller of the Currency determines to be appropriate under the circumstances and consistent with the purposes of this section; and

(B) the appropriate Federal banking agency may impose such limitations on the conduct or activities of any relevant insured depository institution affiliate or any subsidiary of the institution as such agency determines to be appropriate under the circumstances and consistent with the purposes of this section.

(4) Failure to correct

If the conditions described in a notice to a national bank under paragraph (1) are not corrected within 180 days after the date of receipt by the national bank of the notice, the Comptroller of the Currency may require the national bank, under such terms and conditions as may be imposed by the Comptroller and subject to such extension of time as may be granted in the discretion of the Comptroller, to divest control of any financial subsidiary.

(5) Consultation

In taking any action under this subsection, the Comptroller shall consult with all relevant Federal and State regulatory agencies and authorities.

(f) Failure to maintain public rating or meet applicable criteria

(1) In general

A national bank that does not continue to meet any applicable rating or other requirement of subsection (a)(2)(E) of this section after acquiring or establishing a financial subsidiary shall not, directly or through a subsidiary, purchase or acquire any additional equity capital of any financial subsidiary until the bank meets such requirements.

(2) Equity capital

For purposes of this subsection, the term "equity capital" includes, in addition to any equity instrument, any debt instrument issued by a financial subsidiary, if the instrument qualifies as capital of the subsidiary under any Federal or State law, regulation, or interpretation applicable to the subsidiary.

---

1 So in original.

2 So in original.

(g) Definitions

For purposes of this section, the following definitions shall apply:

(1) Affiliate, company, control, and subsidiary

The terms "affiliate", "company", "control", and "subsidiary" have the meanings given those terms in section 1841 of this title.

(2) Appropriate Federal banking agency, depository institution, insured bank, and insured depository institution

The terms "appropriate Federal banking agency", "depository institution", "insured bank", and "insured depository institution" have the meanings given those terms in section 1813 of this title.

(3) Financial subsidiary

The term "financial subsidiary" means any company that is controlled by 1 or more insured depository institutions other than a subsidiary that—

(A) engages solely in activities that national banks are permitted to engage in directly and are conducted subject to the same terms and conditions that govern the conduct of such activities by national banks; or

(B) a national bank is specifically authorized by the express terms of a Federal statute (other than this section), and not by implication or interpretation, to control, such as by section 25 or 25A of the Federal Reserve Act [12 U.S.C. §§ 601 *et seq.*, 611 *et seq.*] or the Bank Service Company Act [12 U.S.C. § 1861 *et seq.*].

(4) Eligible debt

The term "eligible debt" means unsecured long-term debt that—

(A) is not supported by any form of credit enhancement, including a guarantee or standby letter of credit; and

(B) is not held in whole or in any significant part by any affiliate, officer, director, principal shareholder, or employee of the bank or any other person acting on behalf of or with funds from the bank or an affiliate of the bank.

(5) Well capitalized

The term "well capitalized" has the meaning given the term in section 1831o of this title.

(6) Well managed

The term "well managed" means—

(A) in the case of a depository institution that has been examined, unless otherwise determined in writing by the appropriate Federal banking agency—

(i) the achievement of a composite rating of 1 or 2 under the Uniform Financial Institutions Rating System (or an equivalent rating under an equivalent rating system) in connection with the most recent examination or subsequent review of the depository institution; and

(ii) at least a rating of 2 for management, if such rating is given; or

(B) in the case of any depository institution that has not been examined, the existence and use of managerial resources that the appropriate Federal banking agency determines are satisfactory.

[R.S. § 5136A, *as added by* Pub. L. No. 106-102, Title I, § 121(a)(2), 113 Stat. 1373 (Nov. 12, 1999).]

* * *

12 U.S.C. § 36. Branch banks

The conditions upon which a national banking association may retain or establish and operate a branch or branches are the following:

(a) Lawful and continuous operation

A national banking association may retain and operate such branch or branches as it may have had in lawful operation on February 25, 1927, and any national banking association which continuously maintained and operated not more than one branch for a period of more than twenty-five years immediately preceding February 25, 1927, may continue to maintain and operate such branch.

(b) Converted State banks

(1) A national bank resulting from the conversion of a State bank may retain and operate as a branch any office which was a branch of the State bank immediately prior to conversion if such office—

(A) might be established under subsection (c) of this section as a new branch of the resulting national bank, and is approved by the Comptroller of the Currency for continued operation as a branch of the resulting national bank;

(B) was a branch of any bank on February 25, 1927; or

(C) is approved by the Comptroller of the Currency for continued operation as a branch of the resulting national bank.

The Comptroller of the Currency may not grant approval under clause (C) of this paragraph if a State bank (in a situation identical to that of the national bank) resulting from the conversion of a national bank would be prohibited by the law of such State from retaining and operating as a branch an identically situated office which was a branch of the national bank immediately prior to conversion.

(2) A national bank (referred to in this paragraph as the "resulting bank"), resulting from the consolidation of a national bank (referred to in this paragraph as the "national bank") under whose charter the consolidation is effected with another bank or banks, may retain and operate as a branch any office which, immediately prior to such consolidation, was in operation as—

(A) a main office or branch office of any bank (other than the national bank) participating in the consolidation if, under subsection (c) of this section, it might be established as a new branch of the resulting bank, and if the Comptroller of the Currency approves of its continued operation after the consolidation;

(B) a branch of any bank participating in the consolidation, and which, on February 25, 1927, was in operation as a branch of any bank; or

(C) a branch of the national bank and which, on February 25, 1927, was not in operation as a branch of any bank, if the Comptroller of the Currency approves of its continued operation after the consolidation.

The Comptroller of the Currency may not grant approval under clause (C) of this paragraph if a State bank (in a situation identical to that of the resulting national bank) resulting from the consolidation into a State bank of another bank or banks would be prohibited by the law of such State from retaining and operating as a branch an identically situated office which was a branch of the State bank immediately prior to consolidation.

(3) As used in this subsection, the term "consolidation" includes a merger.

(c) New branches

A national banking association may, with the approval of the Comptroller of the Currency, establish and operate new branches:

(1) Within the limits of the city, town or village in which said association is situated, if such establishment and operation are at the time expressly authorized to State banks by the law of the State in question; and

(2) at any point within the State in which said association is situated, if such establishment and operation are at the time authorized to State banks by the statute law of the State in question by language specifically granting such authority affirmatively and not merely by implication or recognition, and subject to the restrictions as to location imposed by the law of the State on State banks. In any State in which State banks are permitted by statute law to maintain branches within county or greater limits, if no bank is located and doing business in the place where the proposed agency is to be located, any national banking association situated in such State may, with the approval of the Comptroller of the Currency, establish and operate, without regard to the capital requirements of this section, a seasonal agency in any resort community within the limits of the county in which the main office of such association is located, for the purpose of receiving and paying out deposits, issuing and cashing checks and drafts, and doing business incident thereto: *Provided*, That any permit issued under this sentence shall be revoked upon the opening of a State or national bank in such community. Except as provided in the immediately preceding sentence, no such association shall establish a branch outside of the city, town, or village in which it is situated unless it has a combined capital stock and surplus equal to the combined amount of capital stock and surplus, if any, required by the law of the State in which such association is situated for the establishment of such branches by State banks, or, if the law of such State requires only a minimum capital stock for the establishment of such branches by State banks, unless such association has not less than an equal amount of capital stock.

(d) Branches resulting from interstate merger transactions

A national bank resulting from an interstate merger transaction (as defined in section 1831u(f)(6) of this title may maintain and operate a branch in a State other than the home State (as defined in subsection (g)(3)(B) of this section) of such bank in accordance with [12 U.S.C. § 1831u].

(e) Exclusive authority for additional branches
    (1) In general

Effective June 1, 1997, a national bank may not acquire, establish, or operate a branch in any State other than the bank's home State (as defined in subsection (g)(3)(B) of this section) or a State in which the bank already has a branch unless the acquisition, establishment, or operation of such branch in such State by such national bank is authorized under this section or section 1823(f), 1823(k), or 1831u of this title.
    (2) Retention of branches

In the case of a national bank which relocates the main office of such bank from 1 State to another State after May 31, 1997, the bank may retain and operate branches within the State which was the bank's home State (as defined in subsection (g)(3)(B) of this section) before the relocation of such office only to the extent the bank would be authorized, under this section or any other provision of law referred to in paragraph (1), to acquire, establish, or commence to operate a branch in such State if—
    (A) the bank had no branches in such State; or
    (B) the branch resulted from—

(i) an interstate merger transaction approved pursuant to section [1831u of this title]; or
(ii) a transaction after May 31, 1997, pursuant to which the bank received assistance from the Federal Deposit Insurance Corporation under section 13(c) of such Act.

(f) Law applicable to interstate branching operations
    (1) Law applicable to national bank branches
    (A) In general
The laws of the host State regarding community reinvestment, consumer protection, fair lending, and establishment of intrastate branches shall apply to any branch in the host State of an out-of-State national bank to the same extent as such State laws apply to a branch of a bank chartered by that State, except—
    (i) when Federal law preempts the application of such State laws to a national bank; or
    (ii) when the Comptroller of the Currency determines that the application of such State laws would have a discriminatory effect on the branch in comparison with the effect the application of such State laws would have with respect to branches of a bank chartered by the host State.
    (B) Enforcement of applicable State laws
The provisions of any State law to which a branch of a national bank is subject under this paragraph shall be enforced, with respect to such branch, by the Comptroller of the Currency.
    (C) Review and report on actions by Comptroller
The Comptroller of the Currency shall conduct an annual review of the actions it has taken with regard to the applicability of State law to national banks (or their branches) during the preceding year, and shall include in its annual report required under section 333 of the Revised Statutes (12 U.S.C. 14) the results of the review and the reasons for each such action. The first such review and report after July 3, 1997, shall encompass all such actions taken on or after January 1, 1992.
    (2) Treatment of branch as bank
All laws of a host State, other than the laws regarding community reinvestment, consumer protection, fair lending, establishment of intrastate branches, and the application or administration of any tax or method of taxation, shall apply to a branch (in such State) of an out-of-State national bank to the same extent as such laws would apply if the branch were a national bank the main office of which is in such State.
    (3) Rule of construction
No provision of this subsection may be construed as affecting the legal standards for preemption of the application of State law to national banks.

(g) State "opt-in" election to permit interstate branching through de novo branches
    (1) In general
Subject to paragraph (2), the Comptroller of the Currency may approve an application by a national bank to establish and operate a de novo branch in a State (other than the bank's home State) in which the bank does not maintain a branch if—
    (A) there is in effect in the host State a law that—
      (i) applies equally to all banks; and
      (ii) expressly permits all out-of-State banks to establish de novo branches in such State; and
    (B) the conditions established in, or made applicable to this paragraph by, paragraph (2) are met.

(2) Conditions on establishment and operation of interstate branch

(A) Establishment

An application by a national bank to establish and operate a de novo branch in a host State shall be subject to the same requirements and conditions to which an application for an interstate merger transaction is subject under paragraphs (1), (3), and (4) of section 1831u(b) of this title.

(B) Operation

Subsections (c) and (d)(2) of section 1831u of this title shall apply with respect to each branch of a national bank which is established and operated pursuant to an application approved under this subsection in the same manner and to the same extent such provisions of such section 1831u of this title apply to a branch of a national bank which resulted from an interstate merger transaction approved pursuant to such section 1831u of this title.

(3) Definitions

The following definitions shall apply for purposes of this section:

(A) De novo branch

The term "de novo branch" means a branch of a national bank which—

(i) is originally established by the national bank as a branch; and

(ii) does not become a branch of such bank as a result of—

(I) the acquisition by the bank of an insured depository institution or a branch of an insured depository institution; or

(II) the conversion, merger, or consolidation of any such institution or branch.

(B) Home State

The term "home State" means the State in which the main office of a national bank is located.

(C) Host State

The term "host State" means, with respect to a bank, a State, other than the home State of the bank, in which the bank maintains, or seeks to establish and maintain, a branch.

(h) Repealed. Pub. L. No. 104-208, div. A, tit. II, § 2204, 110 Stat. 3009–405 (Sept. 30, 1996)

(i) Prior approval of branch locations

No branch of any national banking association shall be established or moved from one location to another without first obtaining the consent and approval of the Comptroller of the Currency.

(j) Branch defined

The term "branch" as used in this section shall be held to include any branch bank, branch office, branch agency, additional office, or any branch place of business located in any State or Territory of the United States or in the District of Columbia at which deposits are received, or checks paid, or money lent. The term "branch", as used in this section, does not include an automated teller machine or a remote service unit.

(k) Branches in foreign countries, dependencies, or insular possessions

This section shall not be construed to amend or repeal section 25 of the Federal Reserve Act, as amended (12 U.S.C. 601 et seq.),

authorizing the establishment by national banking associations of branches in foreign countries, or dependencies, or insular possessions of the United States.

(*l*) "State bank" and "bank" defined

The words "State bank," "State banks," "bank," or "banks," as used in this section, shall be held to include trust companies, savings banks, or other such corporations or institutions carrying on the banking business under the authority of State laws.

[R.S. § 5155; Feb. 25, 1927, ch. 191, § 7, 44 Stat. 1228; June 16, 1933, ch. 89, § 23, 48 Stat. 189; Aug. 23, 1935, ch. 614, title III, § 305, 49 Stat. 708; July 15, 1952, ch. 753, § 2(b), 66 Stat. 633; Pub. L. No. 87–721, 76 Stat. 667 (Sept. 28, 1962); Pub. L. No. 103–328, title I, §§ 102(b)(1), 103 (a), 108 Stat. 2349, 2352 (Sept. 29, 1994); Pub. L. No. 104–208, div. A, title II, §§ 2204, 2205 (a), 110 Stat. 3009–405 (Sept. 30, 1996); Pub. L. No. 105–24, § 2(b), 111 Stat. 239 (July 3, 1997).]

* * *

12 U.S.C. § 43. Interpretations concerning preemption of certain State laws

(a) Notice and opportunity for comment required

Before issuing any opinion letter or interpretive rule, in response to a request or upon the agency's own motion, that concludes that Federal law preempts the application to a national bank of any State law regarding community reinvestment, consumer protection, fair lending, or the establishment of intrastate branches, or before making a determination under section 36(f)(1)(A)(ii) of this title, the appropriate Federal banking agency (as defined in section 1813 of this title) shall—

(1) publish in the Federal Register notice of the preemption or discrimination issue that the agency is considering (including a description of each State law at issue);

(2) give interested parties not less than 30 days in which to submit written comments; and

(3) in developing the final opinion letter or interpretive rule issued by the agency, or making any determination under section 36(f)(1)(A)(ii) of this title, consider any comments received.

(b) Publication required

The appropriate Federal banking agency shall publish in the Federal Register—

(1) any final opinion letter or interpretive rule concluding that Federal law preempts the application of any State law regarding community reinvestment, consumer protection, fair lending, or establishment of intrastate branches to a national bank; and

(2) any determination under section 36(f)(1)(A)(ii) of this title.

(c) Exceptions

(1) No new issue or significant basis

This section shall not apply with respect to any opinion letter or interpretive rule that—

(A) raises issues of Federal preemption of State law that are essentially identical to those previously resolved by the courts or on which the agency has previously issued an opinion letter or interpretive rule; or

(B) responds to a request that contains no significant legal basis on which to make a preemption determination.

(2) Judicial, legislative, or intragovernmental materials

This section shall not apply with respect to materials prepared for use in judicial proceedings or submission to Congress or a Member of Congress, or for intragovernmental use.

(3) Emergency

The appropriate Federal banking agency may make exceptions to subsection (a) of this section if—

(A) the agency determines in writing that the exception is necessary to avoid a serious and imminent threat to the safety and soundness of any national bank; or

(B) the opinion letter or interpretive rule is issued in connection with—

(i) an acquisition of 1 or more banks in default or in danger of default (as such terms are defined in section 1813 of this title); or

(ii) an acquisition with respect to which the Federal Deposit Insurance Corporation provides assistance under section 1823(c) of this title.

[R.S. § 5244, *as added by* Pub. L. No. 103-328, Title I, § 114, 108 Stat. 2367 (Sept. 29, 1994).]

* * *

SUBCHAPTER IV—REGULATION OF THE BANKING BUSINESS; POWERS AND DUTIES OF NATIONAL BANKS

* * *

12 U.S.C. § 85. Rate of interest on loans, discounts and purchases

Any association may take, receive, reserve, and charge on any loan or discount made, or upon any notes, bills of exchange, or other evidence of debt, interest at the rate allowed by the laws of the State, Territory, or District where the bank is located, or at a rate of 1 per centum in excess of the discount rate on ninety-day commercial paper in effect at the Federal reserve bank in the Federal reserve district where the bank is located, whichever may be the greater, and no more, except that where by the laws of any State a different rate is limited for banks organized under state laws, the rate so limited shall be allowed for associations organized or existing in any such State under this chapter. When no rate is fixed by the laws of the State, Territory, or District, the bank may take, receive, reserve or charge a rate not exceeding 7 per centum, or 1 per centum in excess of the discount rate on ninety-day commercial paper in effect at the Federal reserve bank in the Federal reserve district where the bank is located, whichever may be the greater, and such interest may be taken in advance, reckoning the days for which the note, bill, or other evidence of debt has to run. The maximum amount of interest or discount to be charged at a branch of an association located outside of the States of the United States and the District of Columbia shall be at the rate allowed by the laws of the country, territory, dependency, province, dominion, insular possession, or other political subdivision where the branch is located. And the purchase, discount, or sale of a bona fide bill of exchange, payable at another place than the place of such purchase, discount, or sale, at not more than the current rate of exchange for sight drafts in addition to the interest, shall be not considered as taking or receiving a greater rate of interest.

[R.S. § 5197; June 16, 1933, ch. 89, § 25, 48 Stat. 191; Aug. 23, 1935, ch. 614, title III, § 314, 49 Stat. 711; Pub. L. No. 93–501, title II, § 201, 88 Stat. 1558 (Oct. 29, 1974); Pub. L. No. 96–104, title I, § 101, 93 Stat. 789 (Nov. 5, 1979); Pub. L. No. 96–161, title II, § 201, 93 Stat. 1235 (Dec. 28, 1979); Pub. L. No. 96–221, title V, § 529, 94 Stat. 168 (Mar. 31, 1980).]

12 U.S.C. § 86. Usurious interest; penalty for taking; limitations

The taking, receiving, reserving, or charging a rate of interest greater than is allowed by section 85 of this title, when knowingly done, shall be deemed a forfeiture of the entire interest which the note, bill, or other evidence of debt carries with it, or which has been agreed to be paid thereon. In case the greater rate of interest has been paid, the person by whom it has been paid, or his legal representatives, may recover back, in an action in the nature of an action of debt, twice the amount of the interest thus paid from the association taking or receiving the same: *Provided*, That such action is commenced within two years from the time the usurious transaction occurred.

[R.S. § 5198.]

* * *

CHAPTER 3—FEDERAL RESERVE SYSTEM

SUBCHAPTER X—POWERS AND DUTIES OF MEMBER BANKS

12 U.S.C. § 371. Real estate loans

(a) Authorization to make real estate loans; orders, rules, and regulations of Comptroller of the Currency

Any national banking association may make, arrange, purchase or sell loans or extensions of credit secured by liens on interests in real estate, subject to section 1828(o) of this title and such restrictions and requirements as the Comptroller of the Currency may prescribe by regulation or order.

(b) Eligibility for discount as commercial paper of notes representing loans financing construction of residential or farm buildings; prerequisites

Notes representing loans made under this section to finance the construction of residential or farm buildings and having maturities not to exceed nine months shall be eligible for discount as commercial paper within the terms of the first paragraph of section 343 of this title if accompanied by a valid and binding agreement to advance the full amount of the loan upon the completion of the building entered into by an individual, partnership, association, or corporation acceptable to the discounting bank.

[Dec. 23, 1913, ch. 6, § 24, 38 Stat. 273; Sept. 7, 1916, ch. 461, 39 Stat. 754; Feb. 25, 1927, ch. 191, § 16, 44 Stat. 1232; June 27, 1934, ch. 847, § 505, 48 Stat. 1263; Aug. 23, 1935, ch. 614, title II, § 208, title III, § 328, 49 Stat. 706, 717; Mar. 28, 1941, ch. 31, § 8, 55 Stat. 62; July 22, 1937, ch. 517, § 15(a), *as added* Aug. 14, 1946, ch. 964, § 5, 60 Stat. 1079; May 25, 1948, ch. 334, § 9, 62 Stat. 265; Oct. 25, 1949, ch. 729, § 6, 63 Stat. 906; Apr. 20, 1950, ch. 94, title V, § 502, 64 Stat. 80; Sept. 1, 1951, ch. 378, title II, § 207, title V, § 503, 65 Stat. 303, 312; Aug. 15, 1953, ch. 510, 67 Stat. 613; July 22, 1954, ch. 561, 68 Stat. 525; Aug. 28, 1937, ch. 870, § 10(f), *as added* Aug. 17, 1954, ch. 751, § 1(4), 68 Stat. 736; Aug. 11, 1955, ch. 781, §§ 1, 2, 69 Stat. 633, 634; Pub. L. No. 85–536, § 3, 72 Stat. 396 (July 18, 1958); Pub. L. No. 86–251, § 4, 73 Stat. 489 (Sept. 9, 1959); Pub. L. No. 87–70, title VIII, § 804(c), title IX, § 902, 75 Stat. 188, 191 (June 30, 1961); Pub. L. No. 87–717, 76 Stat. 662 (Sept. 28, 1962); Pub. L. No. 88–341, 78 Stat. 233 (June 30, 1964); Pub. L. No. 88–560, title X, § 1004, 78 Stat. 807 (Sept. 2, 1964); Pub. L. No. 89–117, title II, § 201(b)(2), title XI, § 1111, 79 Stat. 465, 509 (Aug. 10, 1965); Pub. L. No. 89–754, title V, § 504(a)(2), 80 Stat. 1277 (Nov. 3, 1966); Pub. L. No. 90–19, § 26, 81 Stat. 28 (May 25, 1967); Pub. L. No. 90–448, title IV, § 416(b), title XVII, § 1718, 82 Stat. 518, 609 (Aug. 1, 1968); Pub. L. No. 91–351, title VII, § 704, 84 Stat. 462 (July 24, 1970); Pub. L. No. 91–609, title VII, § 727(c), 84 Stat. 1803 (Dec. 31, 1970); Pub. L. No. 93–383, title VII, § 711, title VIII, § 802(i)(1), 88 Stat. 716, 725 (Aug. 22, 1974); Pub. L. No. 97–320, title IV, § 403(a), 96 Stat. 1510 (Oct. 15, 1982); Pub. L. No. 102–242, title III, § 304(b), 105 Stat. 2354 (Dec. 19, 1991).]

* * *

SUBCHAPTER XV—BANK EXAMINATIONS

* * *

12 U.S.C. § 484. Limitation on visitorial powers

(a) No national bank shall be subject to any visitorial powers except as authorized by Federal law, vested in the courts of justice or such as shall be, or have been exercised or directed by Congress or by either House thereof or by any committee of Congress or of either House duly authorized.

(b) Notwithstanding subsection (a) of this section, lawfully authorized State auditors and examiners may, at reasonable times and upon reasonable notice to a bank, review its records solely to ensure compliance with applicable State unclaimed property or escheat laws upon reasonable cause to believe that the bank has failed to comply with such laws.

[R.S. § 5240; Feb. 19, 1875, ch. 89, 18 Stat. 329; Dec. 23, 1913, ch. 6, § 21, 38 Stat. 271; Pub. L. No. 97–320, Title IV, § 412, 96 Stat. 1521 (Oct. 15, 1982); Pub. L. No. 97-457, § 23(a), 96 Stat. 2510 (Jan. 12, 1983).]

* * *

C.2 Selected Regulations

TITLE 12—BANKS AND BANKING

CHAPTER I—COMPTROLLER OF THE CURRENCY, DEPARTMENT OF THE TREASURY

PART 5—RULES, POLICIES, AND PROCEDURES FOR CORPORATE ACTIVITIES

Subpart C—Expansion of Activities

* * *

§ 5.34   Operating subsidiaries.
§ 5.39   Financial subsidiaries.

* * *

PART 7—BANK ACTIVITIES AND OPERATIONS

Subpart A—Bank Powers

* * *

§ 7.1003   Money lent at banking offices or at other than banking offices.

* * *

Subpart D—Preemption

* * *

§ 7.4000 Visitorial Powers.

§ 7.4001   Charging interest at rates permitted competing institutions; charging interest to corporate borrowers.
§ 7.4002   National bank charges.

* * *

§ 7.4006   Applicability of State law to national bank operating subsidiaries.
§ 7.4007   Deposit-taking.
§ 7.4008   Lending.
§ 7.4009   Applicability of state law to national bank operations.

* * *

Subpart E—Electronic Activities

* * *

§ 7.5001   Electronic activities that are part of, or incidental to, the business of banking.
§ 7.5002   Furnishing of products and services by electronic means and facilities.

* * *

§ 7.5008   Location of a national bank conducting electronic activities.
§ 7.5009   Location under 12 U.S.C. 85 of national banks operating exclusively through the Internet.

* * *

PART 34—REAL ESTATE LENDING AND APPRAISALS

Subpart A—General

34.1   Purpose and scope.
34.2   Definitions.
34.3   General rule.
34.4   Applicability of State law.
34.5   Due-on-sale clauses.

Subpart B—Adjustable-Rate Mortgages

34.20   Definitions.
34.21   General rule.
34.22   Index.
34.23   Prepayment fees.
34.24   Nonfederally chartered commercial banks.
34.25   Transition rule.

* * *

Subpart D—Real Estate Lending Standards

34.61   Purpose and scope.
34.62   Real estate lending standards.

* * *

PART 37—DEBT CANCELLATION CONTRACTS AND DEBT SUSPENSION AGREEMENTS

37.1   Authority, purpose, and scope.

37.2 Definitions.

37.3 Prohibited practices.

37.4 Refunds of fees in the event of termination or prepayment of the covered loan.

37.5 Method of payment of fees.

37.6 Disclosures.

37.7 Affirmative election to purchase and acknowledgment of receipt of disclosures required.

37.8 Safety and soundness requirements.

Appendix A to Part 37 Short Form Disclosures

Appendix B to Part 37 Long Form Disclosures

* * *

TITLE 12—BANKS AND BANKING

CHAPTER I—COMPTROLLER OF THE CURRENCY, DEPARTMENT OF THE TREASURY

PART 5—RULES, POLICIES, AND PROCEDURES FOR CORPORATE ACTIVITIES

Subpart C—Expansion of Activities

* * *

12 C.F.R. § 5.34 Operating subsidiaries.

(a) *Authority.* 12 U.S.C. 24 (Seventh), 24a, 93a, 3101 *et seq.*

(b) *Licensing requirements.* A national bank must file a notice or application as prescribed in this section to acquire or establish an operating subsidiary, or to commence a new activity in an existing operating subsidiary.

(c) *Scope.* This section sets forth authorized activities and application or notice procedures for national banks engaging in activities through an operating subsidiary. The procedures in this section do not apply to financial subsidiaries authorized under § 5.39. Unless provided otherwise, this section applies to a Federal branch or agency that acquires, establishes, or maintains any subsidiary that a national bank is authorized to acquire or establish under this section in the same manner and to the same extent as if the Federal branch or agency were a national bank, except that the ownership interest required in paragraphs (e)(2) and (e)(5)(i)(B) of this section shall apply to the parent foreign bank of the Federal branch or agency and not to the Federal branch or agency.

(d) *Definitions.* For purposes of this § 5.34:

(1) *Authorized product* means a product that would be defined as insurance under section 302(c) of the Gramm-Leach-Bliley Act (Public Law 106-102, 113 Stat. 1338, 1407) (GLBA) (15 U.S.C. 6712) that, as of January 1, 1999, the OCC had determined in writing that national banks may provide as principal or national banks were in fact lawfully providing the product as principal, and as of that date no court of relevant jurisdiction had, by final judgment, overturned a determination by the OCC that national banks may provide the product as principal. An authorized product does not include title insurance, or an annuity contract the income of which is subject to treatment under section 72 of the Internal Revenue Code of 1986 (26 U.S.C. 72).

(2) *Well capitalized* means the capital level described in 12 CFR 6.4(b)(1) or, in the case of a Federal branch or agency, the capital level described in 12 CFR 4.7(b)(1)(iii).

(3) *Well managed* means, unless otherwise determined in writing by the OCC:

(i) In the case of a national bank:

(A) The national bank has received a composite rating of 1 or 2 under the Uniform Financial Institutions Rating System in connection with its most recent examination; or

(B) In the case of any national bank that has not been examined, the existence and use of managerial resources that the OCC determines are satisfactory.

(ii) In the case of a Federal branch or agency:

(A) The Federal branch or agency has received a composite ROCA supervisory rating (which rates risk management, operational controls, compliance, and asset quality) of 1 or 2 at its most recent examination; or

(B) In the case of a Federal branch or agency that has not been examined, the existence and use of managerial resources that the OCC determines are satisfactory.

(e) *Standards and requirements*—(1) *Authorized activities.* A national bank may conduct in an operating subsidiary activities that are permissible for a national bank to engage in directly either as part of, or incidental to, the business of banking, as determined by the OCC, or otherwise under other statutory authority, including:

(i) Providing authorized products as principal; and

(ii) Providing title insurance as principal if the national bank or subsidiary thereof was actively and lawfully underwriting title insurance before November 12, 1999, and no affiliate of the national bank (other than a subsidiary) provides insurance as principal. A subsidiary may not provide title insurance as principal if the state had in effect before November 12, 1999, a law which prohibits any person from underwriting title insurance with respect to real property in that state.

(2) *Qualifying subsidiaries.* An operating subsidiary in which a national bank may invest includes a corporation, limited liability company, or similar entity if the parent bank owns more than 50 percent of the voting (or similar type of controlling) interest of the operating subsidiary; or the parent bank otherwise controls the operating subsidiary and no other party controls more than 50 percent of the voting (or similar type of controlling) interest of the operating subsidiary. However, the following subsidiaries are not operating subsidiaries subject to this section:

(i) A subsidiary in which the bank's investment is made pursuant to specific authorization in a statute or OCC regulation (*e.g.,* a bank service company under 12 U.S.C. 1861 *et seq.* or a financial subsidiary under section 5136A of the Revised Statutes (12 U.S.C. 24a)); and

(ii) A subsidiary in which the bank has acquired, in good faith, shares through foreclosure on collateral, by way of compromise of a doubtful claim, or to avoid a loss in connection with a debt previously contracted.

(3) *Examination and supervision.* An operating subsidiary conducts activities authorized under this section pursuant to the same authorization, terms and conditions that apply to the conduct of such activities by its parent national bank. If, upon examination, the OCC determines that the operating subsidiary is operating in violation of law, regulation, or written condition, or in an unsafe or unsound manner or otherwise threatens the safety or soundness of the bank, the OCC will direct the bank or operating subsidiary to take appropriate remedial action, which may include requiring the bank to divest or liquidate the operating subsidiary, or discontinue specified activities. OCC authority under this paragraph is subject to the limitations and requirements of section 45 of the Federal Deposit Insurance Act (12 U.S.C. 1831v) and section 115 of the Gramm-Leach-Bliley Act (12 U.S.C. 1820a).

(4) *Consolidation of figures*—(i) *National banks.* Pertinent book figures of the parent national bank and its operating subsidiary shall be combined for the purpose of applying statutory or regulatory limitations when combination is needed to effect the intent of the statute or regulation, e.g., for purposes of 12 U.S.C. 56, 60, 84, and 371d.

(ii) *Federal branch or agencies.* Transactions conducted by all of a foreign bank's Federal branches and agencies and State branches and agencies, and their operating subsidiaries, shall be combined for the purpose of applying any limitation or restriction as provided in 12 CFR 28.14.

(5) *Procedures*—(i) *Application required.* (A) Except as provided in paragraph (e)(5)(iv) or (e)(5)(vi) of this section, a national bank that intends to acquire or establish an operating subsidiary, or to perform a new activity in an existing operating subsidiary, must first submit an application to, and receive approval from, the OCC. The application must include a complete description of the bank's investment in the subsidiary, the proposed activities of the subsidiary, the organizational structure and management of the subsidiary, the relations between the bank and the subsidiary, and other information necessary to adequately describe the proposal. To the extent the application relates to the initial affiliation of the bank with a company engaged in

insurance activities, the bank should describe the type of insurance activity that the company is engaged in and has present plans to conduct. The bank must also list for each state the lines of business for which the company holds, or will hold, an insurance license, indicating the state where the company holds a resident license or charter, as applicable. The application must state whether the operating subsidiary will conduct any activity at a location other than the main office or a previously approved branch of the bank. The OCC may require the applicant to submit a legal analysis if the proposal is novel, unusually complex, or raises substantial unresolved legal issues. In these cases, the OCC encourages applicants to have a pre-filing meeting with the OCC.

(B) A national bank must file an application and obtain prior approval before acquiring or establishing an operating subsidiary, or performing a new activity in an existing operating subsidiary, if the bank controls the subsidiary but owns 50 percent or less of the voting (or similar type of controlling) interest of the subsidiary. These applications are not subject to the filing exemption in paragraph (e)(5)(vi) of this section and are not eligible for the notice procedures in paragraph (e)(5)(iv) of this section.

(ii) *Exceptions to rules of general applicability.* Sections 5.8, 5.10, and 5.11 do not apply to this section. However, if the OCC concludes that an application presents significant and novel policy, supervisory, or legal issues, the OCC may determine that some or all provisions in §§ 5.8, 5.10, and 5.11 apply.

(iii) *OCC review and approval.* The OCC reviews a national bank's application to determine whether the proposed activities are legally permissible and to ensure that the proposal is consistent with safe and sound banking practices and OCC policy and does not endanger the safety or soundness of the parent national bank. As part of this process, the OCC may request additional information and analysis from the applicant.

(iv) *Notice process for certain activities.* A national bank that is "well capitalized" and "well managed" may acquire or establish an operating subsidiary, or perform a new activity in an existing operating subsidiary, by providing the appropriate district office written notice within 10 days after acquiring or establishing the subsidiary, or commencing the activity, if the activity is listed in paragraph (e)(5)(v) of this section. The written notice must include a complete description of the bank's investment in the subsidiary and of the activity conducted and a representation and undertaking that the activity will be conducted in accordance with OCC policies contained in guidance issued by the OCC regarding the activity. To the extent the notice relates to the initial affiliation of the bank with a company engaged in insurance activities, the bank should describe the type of insurance activity that the company is engaged in and has present plans to conduct. The bank must also list for each state the lines of business for which the

company holds, or will hold, an insurance license, indicating the state where the company holds a resident license or charter, as applicable. Any bank receiving approval under this paragraph is deemed to have agreed that the subsidiary will conduct the activity in a manner consistent with published OCC guidance.

(v) *Activities eligible for notice.* The following activities qualify for the notice procedures, provided the activity is conducted pursuant to the same terms and conditions as would be applicable if the activity were conducted directly by a national bank:

(A) Holding and managing assets acquired by the parent bank, including investment assets and property acquired by the bank through foreclosure or otherwise in good faith to compromise a doubtful claim, or in the ordinary course of collecting a debt previously contracted;

(B) Providing services to or for the bank or its affiliates, including accounting, auditing, appraising, advertising and public relations, and financial advice and consulting;

(C) Making loans or other extensions of credit, and selling money orders, savings bonds, and travelers checks;

(D) Purchasing, selling, servicing, or warehousing loans or other extensions of credit, or interests therein;

(E) Providing courier services between financial institutions;

(F) Providing management consulting, operational advice, and services for other financial institutions;

(G) Providing check guaranty, verification and payment services;

(H) Providing data processing, data warehousing and data transmission products, services, and related activities and facilities, including associated equipment and technology, for the bank or its affiliates;

(I) Acting as investment adviser (including an adviser with investment discretion) or financial adviser or counselor to governmental entities or instrumentalities, businesses, or individuals, including advising registered investment companies and mortgage or real estate investment trusts, furnishing economic forecasts or other economic information, providing investment advice related to futures and options on futures, and providing consumer financial counseling;

(J) Providing tax planning and preparation services;

(K) Providing financial and transactional advice and assistance, including advice and assistance for customers in structuring, arranging, and executing mergers and acquisitions, divestitures, joint ventures, leveraged buyouts, swaps, foreign exchange, derivative transactions, coin and bullion, and capital restructurings;

(L) Underwriting and reinsuring credit related insurance to the extent permitted under section 302 of the GLBA (15 U.S.C. 6712);

(M) Leasing of personal property and acting as an agent or adviser in leases for others;

(N) Providing securities brokerage or acting as a futures commission merchant, and providing related credit and other related services;

(O) Underwriting and dealing, including making a market, in bank permissible securities and purchasing and selling as principal, asset backed obligations;

(P) Acting as an insurance agent or broker, including title insurance to the extent permitted under section 303 of the GLBA (15 U.S.C. 6713);

(Q) Reinsuring mortgage insurance on loans originated, purchased, or serviced by the bank, its subsidiaries, or its affiliates, provided that if the subsidiary enters into a quota share agreement, the subsidiary assumes less than 50 percent of the aggregate insured risk covered by the quota share agreement. A "quota share agreement" is an agreement under which the reinsurer is liable to the primary insurance underwriter for an agreed upon percentage of every claim arising out of the covered book of business ceded by the primary insurance underwriter to the reinsurer;

(R) Acting as a finder pursuant to 12 CFR 7.1002 to the extent permitted by published OCC precedent;[1]

(S) Offering correspondent services to the extent permitted by published OCC precedent;

(T) Acting as agent or broker in the sale of fixed or variable annuities;

(U) Offering debt cancellation or debt suspension agreements;

(V) Providing real estate settlement, closing, escrow, and related services; and real estate appraisal services for the subsidiary, parent bank, or other financial institutions;

(W) Acting as a transfer or fiscal agent;

(X) Acting as a digital certification authority to the extent permitted by published OCC precedent, subject to the terms and conditions contained in that precedent; and

(Y) Providing or selling public transportation tickets, event and attraction tickets, gift certificates, prepaid phone cards, promotional and advertising material, postage stamps, and Electronic Benefits Transfer (EBT) script, and similar media, to the extent permitted by published OCC precedent, subject to the terms and conditions contained in that precedent.

(vi) *No application or notice required.* A national bank may acquire or establish an operating subsidiary without filing an application or providing notice to the OCC, if the bank is adequately capitalized or well capitalized and the:

(A) Activities of the new subsidiary are limited to those activities previously reported by the bank in connection with the establishment or acquisition of a prior operating subsidiary;

---

1 *See, e.g.,* the OCC's monthly publication "Interpretations and Actions." Beginning with the May 1996 issue, the OCC's Web site provides access to electronic versions of "Interpretations and Actions" (www.occ.treas.gov).

(B) Activities in which the new subsidiary will engage continue to be legally permissible for the subsidiary; and

(C) Activities of the new subsidiary will be conducted in accordance with any conditions imposed by the OCC in approving the conduct of these activities for any prior operating subsidiary of the bank.

(vii) *Fiduciary powers.* If an operating subsidiary proposes to exercise investment discretion on behalf of customers or provide investment advice for a fee, the national bank must have prior OCC approval to exercise fiduciary powers pursuant to § 5.26.

(6) *Annual Report on Operating Subsidiaries*—(i) *Filing requirement.* Each national bank shall prepare and file with the OCC an Annual Report on Operating Subsidiaries containing the information set forth in paragraph (e)(6)(ii) of this section for each of its operating subsidiaries that:

(A) Is not functionally regulated within the meaning of section 5(c)(5) of the Bank Holding Company Act of 1956, as amended (12 U.S.C. 1844(c)(5)); and

(B) Does business directly with consumers in the United States. For purposes of paragraph (e)(6) of this section, an operating subsidiary, or any subsidiary thereof, does business directly with consumers if, in the ordinary course of its business, it provides products or services to individuals to be used primarily for personal, family, or household purposes.

(ii) *Information required.* The Annual Report on Operating Subsidiaries must contain the following information for each covered operating subsidiary listed:

(A) The name and charter number of the parent national bank;

(B) The name (include any "dba" (doing business as), abbreviated names, or trade names used to identify the operating subsidiary when it does business directly with consumers), mailing address (include the street address or post office box, city, state, and zip code), e-mail address (if any), and telephone number of the operating subsidiary;

(C) The principal place of business of the operating subsidiary, if different from the address provided pursuant to paragraph (e)(6)(ii)(B) of this section; and

(D) The lines of business in which the operating subsidiary is doing business directly with consumers by designating the appropriate code contained in appendix B (NAICS Activity Codes for Commonly Reported Activities) to the Instructions for Preparation of Report of Changes in Organizational Structure, Form FR Y-10, a copy of which is set forth on the OCC's Web site at *http://www.occ.gov.* If the operating subsidiary is engaged in an activity not set forth in this list, a national bank shall report the code 0000 and provide a brief description of the activity.

(iii) *Filing time frames and availability of information.* Each national bank's Annual Report on Operating Subsidiaries shall contain information current as of December 31st for the year prior to the year the report is filed. The national bank shall submit its first Annual Report on Operating Subsidiaries (for information as of December 31, 2004) to the OCC on or before January 31, 2005, and on or before January 31st each year thereafter. The national bank may submit the Annual Report on Operating Subsidiaries electronically or in another format prescribed by the OCC. The OCC will make available to the public the information contained in the Annual Report on Operating Subsidiaries on its Web site at *http://www.occ.gov.*

[65 Fed. Reg. 12911 (Mar. 10, 2000), *as amended at* 66 Fed. Reg. 49097 (Sept. 26, 2001); 66 Fed. Reg. 62914 (Dec. 4, 2001); 68 Fed. Reg. 70131 (Dec. 17, 2003); 69 Fed. Reg. 64481 (Nov. 5, 2004)]

* * *

12 C.F.R. § 5.39 Financial subsidiaries.

(a) *Authority.* 12 U.S.C. 93a and section 121 of Public Law 106-102, 113 Stat. 1338, 1373.

(b) *Approval requirements.* A national bank must file a notice as prescribed in this section prior to acquiring a financial subsidiary or engaging in activities authorized pursuant to section 5136A(a)(2)(A)(i) of the Revised Statutes (12 U.S.C. 24a) through a financial subsidiary. When a financial subsidiary proposes to conduct a new activity permitted under § 5.34, the bank shall follow the procedures in § 5.34(e)(5) instead of paragraph (i) of this section.

(c) *Scope.* This section sets forth authorized activities, approval procedures, and, where applicable, conditions for national banks engaging in activities through a financial subsidiary.

(d) *Definitions.* For purposes of this § 5.39:

(1) *Affiliate* has the meaning set forth in section 2 of the Bank Holding Company Act of 1956 (12 U.S.C. 1841), except that the term "affiliate" for purposes of paragraph (h)(5) of this section shall have the meaning set forth in sections 23A or 23B of the Federal Reserve Act (12 U.S.C. 371c and 371c-1), as applicable.

(2) *Appropriate Federal banking agency* has the meaning set forth in section 3 of the Federal Deposit Insurance Act (12 U.S.C. 1813).

(3) *Company* has the meaning set forth in section 2 of the Bank Holding Company Act of 1956 (12 U.S.C. 1841), and includes a limited liability company (LLC).

(4) *Control* has the meaning set forth in section 2 of the Bank Holding Company Act of 1956 (12 U.S.C. 1841).

(5) *Eligible debt* means unsecured long-term debt that is:

(i) Not supported by any form of credit enhancement, including a guaranty or standby letter of credit; and

(ii) Not held in whole or in any significant part by any affiliate, officer, director, principal shareholder, or employee of the bank or any other person acting on behalf of or with funds from the bank or an affiliate of the bank.

(6) *Financial subsidiary* means any company that is controlled by one or more insured depository institutions, other than a subsidiary that:

(i) Engages solely in activities that national banks may engage in directly and that are conducted subject to the same terms and conditions that govern the conduct of these activities by national banks; or

(ii) A national bank is specifically authorized to control by the express terms of a Federal statute (other than section 5136A of the Revised Statutes), and not by implication or interpretation, such as by section 25 of the Federal Reserve Act (12 U.S.C. 601-604a), section 25A of the Federal Reserve Act (12 U.S.C. 611-631), or the Bank Service Company Act (12 U.S.C. 1861 *et seq.*)

(7) *Insured depository institution* has the meaning set forth in section 3 of the Federal Deposit Insurance Act (12 U.S.C. 1813).

(8) *Long term debt* means any debt obligation with an initial maturity of 360 days or more.

(9) *Subsidiary* has the meaning set forth in section 2 of the Bank Holding Company Act of 1956 (12 U.S.C. 1841).

(10) *Tangible equity* has the meaning set forth in 12 CFR 6.2(g).

(11) *Well capitalized* with respect to a depository institution means the capital level designated as "well capitalized" by the institution's appropriate Federal banking agency pursuant to section 38 of the Federal Deposit Insurance Act (12 U.S.C. 1831o).

(12) *Well managed* means:

(i) Unless otherwise determined in writing by the appropriate Federal banking agency, the institution has received a composite rating of 1 or 2 under the Uniform Financial Institutions Rating System (or an equivalent rating under an equivalent rating system) in connection with the most recent examination or subsequent review of the depository institution and, at least a rating of 2 for management, if such a rating is given; or

(ii) In the case of any depository institution that has not been examined by its appropriate Federal banking agency, the existence and use of managerial resources that the appropriate Federal banking agency determines are satisfactory.

(e) *Authorized activities.* A financial subsidiary may engage only in the following activities:

(1) Activities that are financial in nature and activities incidental to a financial activity, authorized pursuant to 5136A(a)(2)(A)(i) of the Revised Statutes (12 U.S.C. 24a) (to the extent not otherwise permitted under paragraph (e)(2) of this section), including:

(i) Lending, exchanging, transferring, investing for others, or safeguarding money or securities;

(ii) Engaging as agent or broker in any state for purposes of insuring, guaranteeing, or indemnifying against loss, harm, damage, illness, disability, death, defects in title, or providing annuities as agent or broker;

(iii) Providing financial, investment, or economic advisory services, including advising an investment company as defined in section 3 of the Investment Company Act (15 U.S.C. 80a-3);

(iv) Issuing or selling instruments representing interests in pools of assets permissible for a bank to hold directly;

(v) Underwriting, dealing in, or making a market in securities;

(vi) Engaging in any activity that the Board of Governors of the Federal Reserve System has determined, by order or regulation in effect on November 12, 1999, to be so closely related to banking or managing or controlling banks as to be a proper incident thereto (subject to the same terms and conditions contained in the order or regulation, unless the order or regulation is modified by the Board of Governors of the Federal Reserve System);

(vii) Engaging, in the United States, in any activity that a bank holding company may engage in outside the United States and the Board of Governors of the Federal Reserve System has determined, under regulations prescribed or interpretations issued pursuant to section 4(c)(13) of the Bank Holding Company Act of 1956 (12 U.S.C. 1843(c)(13)) as in effect on November 11, 1999, to be usual in connection with the transaction of banking or other financial operations abroad; and

(viii) Activities that the Secretary of the Treasury in consultation with the Board of Governors of the Federal Reserve System, as provided in section 5136A of the Revised Statutes, determines to be financial in nature or incidental to a financial activity; and

(2) Activities that may be conducted by an operating subsidiary pursuant to § 5.34.

(f) *Impermissible activities.* A financial subsidiary may not engage as principal in the following activities:

(1) Insuring, guaranteeing, or indemnifying against loss, harm, damage, illness, disability or death, or defects in title (except to the extent permitted under sections 302 or 303(c) of the Gramm-Leach-Bliley Act (GLBA)), 113 Stat. 1407-1409, (15 U.S.C. 6712 or 15 U.S.C. 6713) or providing or issuing annuities the income of which is subject to tax treatment under section 72 of the Internal Revenue Code (26 U.S.C. 72);

(2) Real estate development or real estate investment, unless otherwise expressly authorized by law; and

(3) Activities authorized for bank holding companies by section 4(k)(4)(H) or (I) (12 U.S.C. 1843) of the Bank Holding Company Act, except activities authorized under section 4(k)(4)(H) that may be permitted in accordance with section 122 of the GLBA, 113 Stat. 1381.

(g) *Qualifications.* A national bank may, directly or indirectly, control a financial subsidiary or hold an interest in a financial subsidiary only if:

(1) The national bank and each depository institution affiliate of the national bank are well capitalized and well managed;

(2) The aggregate consolidated total assets of all financial subsidiaries of the national bank do not exceed the lesser of 45 percent of the consolidated total assets of the parent bank or $50 billion (or such greater amount as is determined according to an indexing mechanism jointly established by regulation by the Secretary of the Treasury and the Board of Governors of the Federal Reserve System); and

(3) If the national bank is one of the 100 largest insured banks, determined on the basis of the bank's consolidated total assets at the end of the calendar year, the bank has at least one issue of outstanding eligible debt that is currently rated in one of the three highest investment grade rating categories by a nationally recognized statistical rating organization. If the national bank is one of the second 50 largest insured banks, it may either satisfy this requirement or satisfy alternative criteria the Secretary of the Treasury and the Board of Governors of the Federal Reserve System establish jointly by regulation. This paragraph (g)(3) does not apply if the financial subsidiary is engaged solely in activities in an agency capacity.

(h) *Safeguards.* The following safeguards apply to a national bank that establishes or maintains a financial subsidiary:

(1) For purposes of determining regulatory capital:

(i) The national bank must deduct the aggregate amount of its outstanding equity investment, including retained earnings, in its financial subsidiaries from its total assets and tangible equity and deduct such investment from its total risk-based capital (this deduction shall be made equally from Tier 1 and Tier 2 capital); and

(ii) The national bank may not consolidate the assets and liabilities of a financial subsidiary with those of the bank;

(2) Any published financial statement of the national bank shall, in addition to providing information prepared in accordance with generally accepted accounting principles, separately present financial information for the bank in the manner provided in paragraph (h)(1) of this section;

(3) The national bank must have reasonable policies and procedures to preserve the separate corporate identity and limited liability of the bank and the financial subsidiaries of the bank;

(4) The national bank must have procedures for identifying and managing financial and operational risks within the bank and the financial subsidiary that adequately protect the national bank from such risks;

(5) Sections 23A and 23B of the Federal Reserve Act (12 U.S.C. 371c and 371c-1) apply to transactions involving a financial subsidiary in the following manner:

(i) A financial subsidiary shall be deemed to be an affiliate of the bank and shall not be deemed to be a subsidiary of the bank;

(ii) The restrictions contained in section 23A(a)(1)(A) of the Federal Reserve Act shall not apply with respect to covered transactions between a bank and any individual financial subsidiary of the bank;

(iii) The bank's investment in the financial subsidiary shall not include retained earnings of the financial subsidiary;

(iv) Any purchase of, or investment in, the securities of a financial subsidiary of a bank by an affiliate of the bank will be considered to be a purchase of or investment in such securities by the bank; and

(v) Any extension of credit by an affiliate of a bank to a financial subsidiary of the bank may be considered an extension of credit by the bank to the financial subsidiary if the Board of Governors of the Federal Reserve System determines that such treatment is necessary or appropriate to prevent evasions of the Federal Reserve Act and the GLBA.

(6) A financial subsidiary shall be deemed a subsidiary of a bank holding company and not a subsidiary of the bank for purposes of the anti-tying prohibitions set forth in 12 U.S.C. 1971 et seq.

(i) *Procedures to engage in activities through a financial subsidiary.* A national bank that intends, directly or indirectly, to acquire control of, or hold an interest in, a financial subsidiary, or to commence a new activity in an existing financial subsidiary, must obtain OCC approval through the procedures set forth in paragraph (i)(1) or (i)(2) of this section.

(1) *Certification with subsequent notice.* (i) At any time, a national bank may file a "Financial Subsidiary Certification" with the appropriate district office listing the bank's depository institution affiliates and certifying that the bank and each of those affiliates is well capitalized and well managed.

(ii) Thereafter, at such time as the bank seeks OCC approval to acquire control of, or hold an interest in, a new financial subsidiary, or commence a new activity authorized under section 5136A(a)(2)(A)(i) of the Revised Statutes (12 U.S.C. 24a) in an existing subsidiary, the bank may file a written notice with the appropriate district office at the time of acquiring control of, or holding an interest in, a financial subsidiary, or commencing such activity in an existing subsidiary. The written notice must be labeled "Financial Subsidiary Notice" and must:

(A) State that the bank's Certification remains valid;

(B) Describe the activity or activities conducted by the financial subsidiary. To the extent the notice relates to the initial affiliation of the bank with a company engaged in insurance activities, the bank should describe the type of insurance activity that the company is engaged in and has present plans to conduct. The bank must also list for each state the lines of business for which the company holds, or will hold, an insurance license, indicating the state where the company holds a resident license or charter, as applicable;

(C) Cite the specific authority permitting the activity to be conducted by the financial subsidiary. (Where the authority relied on is an agency order or interpretation under section 4(c)(8) or 4(c)(13), respectively, of the Bank Holding Company Act of 1956, a copy of the order or interpretation should be attached);

(D) Certify that the bank will be well capitalized after making adjustments required by paragraph (h)(1) of this section;

(E) Demonstrate the aggregate consolidated total assets of all financial subsidiaries of the national bank do not exceed the lesser of 45 percent of the bank's consolidated total assets or $50 billion (or the increased level established by the indexing mechanism); and

(F) If applicable, certify that the bank meets the eligible debt requirement in paragraph (g)(3) of this section.

(2) *Combined certification and notice.* A national bank may file a combined certification and notice with the appropriate district office at least five business days prior to acquiring control of, or holding an interest in, a financial subsidiary, or commencing a new activity authorized pursuant to section 5136A(a)(2)(A)(i) of the Revised Statutes in an existing subsidiary. The written notice must be labeled "Financial Subsidiary Certification and Notice" and must:

(i) List the bank's depository institution affiliates and certify that the bank and each depository institution affiliate of the bank is well capitalized and well managed;

(ii) Describe the activity or activities to be conducted in the financial subsidiary. To the extent the notice relates to the initial affiliation of the bank with a company engaged in insurance activities, the bank should describe the type of insurance activity that the company is engaged in and has present plans to conduct. The bank must also list for each state the lines of business for which the company holds, or will hold, an insurance license, indicating the state where the company holds a resident license or charter, as applicable;

(iii) Cite the specific authority permitting the activity to be conducted by the financial subsidiary. (Where the authority relied on is an agency order or interpretation under section 4(c)(8) or 4(c)(13), respectively, of the Bank Holding Company Act of 1956, a copy of the order or interpretation should be attached);

(iv) Certify that the bank will remain well capitalized after making the adjustments required by paragraph (h)(1) of this section;

(v) Demonstrate the aggregate consolidated total assets of all financial subsidiaries of the national bank do not exceed the lesser of 45% of the bank's consolidated total assets or $50 billion (or the increased level established by the indexing mechanism); and

(vi) If applicable, certify that the bank meets the eligible debt requirement in paragraph (g)(3) of this section.

(3) *Exceptions to rules of general applicability.* Sections 5.8, 5.10, 5.11, and 5.13 do not apply to activities authorized under this section.

(4) *Community Reinvestment Act (CRA).* A national bank may not apply under this paragraph (i) to commence a new activity authorized under section 5136A(a)(2)(A)(i) of the Revised Statutes (12 U.S.C. 24a), or directly or indirectly acquire control of a company engaged in any such activity, if the bank or any of its insured depository institution affiliates received a CRA rating of less than "satisfactory record of meeting community credit needs" on its most recent CRA examination prior to when the bank would file a notice under this section.

(j) *Failure to continue to meet certain qualification requirements—(1) Qualifications and safeguards.* A national bank, or, as applicable, its affiliated depository institutions, must continue to satisfy the qualification requirements set forth in paragraphs (g)(1) and (2) of this section and the safeguards in paragraphs (h)(1), (2), (3) and (4) of this section following its acquisition of control of, or an interest in, a financial subsidiary. A national bank that fails to continue to satisfy these requirements will be subject to the following procedures and requirements:

(i) The OCC shall give notice to the national bank and, in the case of an affiliated depository institution to that depository institution's appropriate Federal banking agency, promptly upon determining that the national bank, or, as applicable, its affiliated depository institution, does not continue to meet the requirements in paragraph (g)(1) or (2) of this section or the safeguards in paragraph (h)(1), (2), (3), or (4) of this section. The bank shall be deemed to have received such notice three business days after mailing of the letter by the OCC;

(ii) Not later than 45 days after receipt of the notice under paragraph (j)(1)(i) of this section, or any additional time as the OCC may permit, the national bank shall execute an agreement with the OCC to comply with the requirements in paragraphs (g)(1) and (2) and (h)(1), (2), (3), and (4) of this section;

(iii) The OCC may impose limitations on the conduct or activities of the national bank or any subsidiary of the national bank as the OCC determines appropriate under the circumstances and consistent with the purposes of section 5136A of the Revised Statutes; and

(iv) The OCC may require a national bank to divest control of a financial subsidiary if the national bank does not correct the conditions giving rise to the notice within 180 days after receipt of the notice provided under paragraph (j)(1)(i) of this section.

(2) *Eligible debt rating requirement.* A national bank that does not continue to meet the qualification requirement set forth in paragraph (g)(3) of this section, applicable where the bank's financial subsidiary is engaged in activities other than solely in an agency capacity, may not directly or through a subsidiary, purchase or acquire any additional equity capital of any such

financial subsidiary until the bank meets the requirement in paragraph (g)(3) of this section. For purposes of this paragraph (j)(2), the term "equity capital" includes, in addition to any equity investment, any debt instrument issued by the financial subsidiary if the instrument qualifies as capital of the subsidiary under federal or state law, regulation, or interpretation applicable to the subsidiary.

(k) *Examination and supervision.* A financial subsidiary is subject to examination and supervision by the OCC, subject to the limitations and requirements of section 45 of the Federal Deposit Insurance Act (12 U.S.C. 1831v) and section 115 of the GLBA (12 U.S.C. 1820a).

[65 Fed. Reg. 12914 (Mar. 10, 2000)]

* * *

PART 7—BANK ACTIVITIES AND OPERATIONS

Subpart A—Bank Powers

* * *

§ 7.1003   Money lent at banking offices or at other than banking offices.

* * *

Subpart D—Preemption

* * *

§ 7.4000   Visitorial Powers.

§ 7.4001   Charging interest at rates permitted competing institutions; charging interest to corporate borrowers.

§ 7.4002   National bank charges.

* * *

§ 7.4006   Applicability of State law to national bank operating subsidiaries.

§ 7.4007   Deposit-taking.

§ 7.4008   Lending.

§ 7.4009   Applicability of state law to national bank operations.

* * *

Subpart E—Electronic Activities

* * *

§ 7.5001   Electronic activities that are part of, or incidental to, the business of banking.

§ 7.5002   Furnishing of products and services by electronic means and facilities.

* * *

§ 7.5008   Location of a national bank conducting electronic activities.

§ 7.5009 Location under 12 U.S.C. 85 of national banks operating exclusively through the Internet.

* * *

Subpart A—Bank Powers

12 C.F.R. § 7.1003 Money lent at banking offices or at other than banking offices.

(a) *General.* For purposes of what constitutes a branch within the meaning of 12 U.S.C. 36(j) and 12 CFR 5.30, "money" is deemed to be "lent" only at the place, if any, where the borrower in-person receives loan proceeds directly from bank funds:

(1) From the lending bank or its operating subsidiary; or

(2) At a facility that is established by the lending bank or its operating subsidiary.

(b) *Receipt of bank funds representing loan proceeds.* Loan proceeds directly from bank funds may be received by a borrower in person at a place that is not the bank's main office and is not licensed as a branch without violating 12 U.S.C. 36, 12 U.S.C. 81 and 12 CFR 5.30, provided that a third party is used to deliver the funds and the place is not established by the lending bank or its operating subsidiary. A third party includes a person who satisfies the requirements of Sec. 7.1012(c)(2), or one who customarily delivers loan proceeds directly from bank funds under accepted industry practice, such as an attorney or escrow agent at a real estate closing.

* * *

Subpart D—Preemption

* * *

12 C.F.R. § 7.4000 Visitorial Powers.

(a) *General rule.*

(1) Only the OCC or an authorized representative of the OCC may exercise visitorial powers with respect to national banks, except as provided in paragraph (b) of this section. State officials may not exercise visitorial powers with respect to national banks, such as conducting examinations, inspecting or requiring the production of books or records of national banks, or prosecuting enforcement actions, except in limited circumstances authorized by federal law. However, production of a bank's records (other than non-public OCC information under 12 CFR part 4, subpart C) may be required under normal judicial procedures.

(2) For purposes of this section, visitorial powers include:

(i) Examination of a bank;

(ii) Inspection of a bank's books and records;

(iii) Regulation and supervision of activities authorized or permitted pursuant to federal banking law; and

(iv) Enforcing compliance with any applicable federal or state laws concerning those activities.

(3) Unless otherwise provided by Federal law, the OCC has exclusive visitorial authority with respect to the content and conduct of activities authorized for national banks under Federal law.

(b) *Exceptions to the general rule.* Under 12 U.S.C. 484, the OCC's exclusive visitorial powers are subject to the following exceptions:

(1) *Exceptions authorized by Federal law.* National banks are subject to such visitorial powers as are provided by Federal law. Examples of laws vesting visitorial power in other governmental entities include laws authorizing state or other Federal officials to:

(i) Inspect the list of shareholders, provided that the official is authorized to assess taxes under state authority (12 U.S.C. 62; this section also authorizes inspection of the shareholder list by shareholders and creditors of a national bank);

. (ii) Review, at reasonable times and upon reasonable notice to a bank, the bank's records solely to ensure compliance with applicable state unclaimed property or escheat laws upon reasonable cause to believe that the bank has failed to comply with those laws (12 U.S.C. 484(b));

(iii) Verify payroll records for unemployment compensation purposes (26 U.S.C. 3305(c));

(iv) Ascertain the correctness of Federal tax returns (26 U.S.C. 7602);

(v) Enforce the Fair Labor Standards Act (29 U.S.C. 211); and

(vi) Functionally regulate certain activities, as provided under the Gramm-Leach-Bliley Act, Pub. L. 106-102, 113 Stat. 1338 (Nov. 12, 1999).

(2) *Exception for courts of justice.* National banks are subject to such visitorial powers as are vested in the courts of justice. This exception pertains to the powers inherent in the judiciary and does not grant state or other governmental authorities any right to inspect, superintend, direct, regulate or compel compliance by a national bank with respect to any law, regarding the content or conduct of activities authorized for national banks under Federal law.

(3) *Exception for Congress.* National banks are subject to such visitorial powers as shall be, or have been, exercised or directed by Congress or by either House thereof or by any committee of Congress or of either House duly authorized.

[61 Fed. Reg. 4869 (Feb. 9, 1996); 64 Fed. Reg. 60100 (Nov. 4, 1999); 69 Fed. Reg. 1895 (Jan. 13, 2004)]

12 C.F.R. § 7.4001 Charging interest at rates permitted competing institutions; charging interest to corporate borrowers.

(a) *Definition.* The term "interest" as used in 12 U.S.C. 85 includes any payment compensating a creditor or prospective creditor for an extension of credit, making available of a line of credit, or any default or breach by a borrower of a condition upon which credit was extended. It includes, among other things, the following fees connected with credit extension or availability: numerical periodic rates, late fees, creditor-imposed not sufficient funds (NSF) fees charged when a borrower tenders payment on a debt with a check drawn on insufficient funds, overlimit fees, annual fees, cash advance fees, and membership fees. It does not ordinarily include appraisal fees, premiums and commissions attributable to insurance guaranteeing repayment of any extension of credit, finders' fees, fees for document preparation or notarization, or fees incurred to obtain credit reports.

(b) *Authority.* A national bank located in a state may charge interest at the maximum rate permitted to any state-chartered or licensed lending institution by the law of that state. If state law permits different interest charges on specified classes of loans, a national bank making such loans is subject only to the provisions of state law relating to that class of loans that are material to the determination of the permitted interest. For example, a national bank may lawfully charge the highest rate permitted to be charged by a state-licensed small loan company, without being so licensed, but subject to state law limitations on the size of loans made by small loan companies.

(c) *Effect on state definitions of interest.* The Federal definition of the term "interest" in paragraph (a) of this section does not change how interest is defined by the individual states (nor how the state definition of interest is used) solely for purposes of state law. For example, if late fees are not "interest" under state law where a national bank is located but state law permits its most favored lender to charge late fees, then a national bank located in that state may charge late fees to its intrastate customers. The national bank may also charge late fees to its interstate customers because the fees are interest under the Federal definition of interest and an allowable charge under state law where the national bank is located. However, the late fees would not be treated as interest for purposes of evaluating compliance with state usury limitations because state law excludes late fees when calculating the maximum interest that lending institutions may charge under those limitations.

(d) *Usury.* A national bank located in a state the law of which denies the defense of usury to a corporate borrower may charge a corporate borrower any rate of interest agreed upon by a corporate borrower.[69 Fed. Reg. 1904 (Jan. 13, 2004)]

[61 Fed. Reg. 4869 (Feb. 9, 1996); 66 Fed. Reg. 34791 (July 2, 2001)]

12 C.F.R. § 7.4002 National bank charges.

(a) *Authority to impose charges and fees.* A national bank may charge its customers non-interest charges and fees, including deposit account service charges.

(b) *Considerations.* (1) All charges and fees should be arrived at by each bank on a competitive basis and not on the basis of any agreement, arrangement, undertaking, understanding, or discussion with other banks or their officers.

(2) The establishment of non-interest charges and fees, their amounts, and the method of calculating them are business decisions to be made by each bank, in its discretion, according to sound banking judgment and safe and sound banking principles. A national bank establishes non-interest charges and fees in accordance with safe and sound banking principles if the bank employs a decision-making process through which it considers the following factors, among others:

(i) The cost incurred by the bank in providing the service;

(ii) The deterrence of misuse by customers of banking services;

(iii) The enhancement of the competitive position of the bank in accordance with the bank's business plan and marketing strategy; and

(iv) The maintenance of the safety and soundness of the institution.

(c) *Interest.* Charges and fees that are "interest" within the meaning of 12 U.S.C. 85 are governed by § 7.4001 and not by this section.

(d) *State law.* The OCC applies preemption principles derived from the United States Constitution, as interpreted through judicial precedent, when determining whether State laws apply that purport to limit or prohibit charges and fees described in this section.

(e) *National bank as fiduciary.* This section does not apply to charges imposed by a national bank in its capacity as a fiduciary, which are governed by 12 CFR part 9.

[61 Fed. Reg. 4869 (Feb. 9, 1996); 66 Fed. Reg. 34791 (July 2, 2001)]

* * *

12 C.F.R. § 7.4006 Applicability of State law to national bank operating subsidiaries.

Unless otherwise provided by Federal law or OCC regulation, State laws apply to national bank operating subsidiaries to the same extent that those laws apply to the parent national bank.

[61 Fed. Reg. 4869 (Feb. 9, 1996); 66 Fed. Reg. 34792 (July 2, 2001)]

12 C.F.R. § 7.4007 Deposit-taking.

(a) *Authority of national banks.* A national bank may receive deposits and engage in any activity incidental to receiving deposits, including issuing evidence of accounts, subject to such terms, conditions, and limitations prescribed by the Comptroller of the Currency and any other applicable Federal law.

(b) *Applicability of state law.* (1) Except where made applicable by Federal law, state laws

that obstruct, impair, or condition a national bank's ability to fully exercise its Federally authorized deposit-taking powers are not applicable to national banks.

(2) A national bank may exercise its deposit-taking powers without regard to state law limitations concerning:

(i) Abandoned and dormant accounts;[1]

(ii) Checking accounts;

(iii) Disclosure requirements;

(iv) Funds availability;

(v) Savings account orders of withdrawal;

(vi) State licensing or registration requirements (except for purposes of service of process); and

(vii) Special purpose savings services;[2]

(c) *State laws that are not preempted.* State laws on the following subjects are not inconsistent with the deposit-taking powers of national banks and apply to national banks to the extent that they only incidentally affect the exercise of national banks' deposit-taking powers:

(1) Contracts;

(2) Torts;

(3) Criminal law;[3]

(4) Rights to collect debts;

(5) Acquisition and transfer of property;

(6) Taxation;

(7) Zoning; and

(8) Any other law the effect of which the OCC determines to be incidental to the deposit-taking operations of national banks or otherwise con-

---

1 This does not apply to state laws of the type upheld by the United States Supreme Court in Anderson Nat'l Bank v. Luckett, 321 U.S. 233 (1944), which obligate a national bank to "pay [deposits] to the persons entitled to demand payment according to the law of the state where it does business." *Id.* at 248–249.

2 State laws purporting to regulate national bank fees and charges are addressed in 12 CFR 7.4002.

3 But see the distinction drawn by the Supreme Court in *Easton v. Iowa*, 188 U.S. 220, 238 (1903) between "crimes defined and punishable at common law or by the general statutes of a state and crimes and offences cognizable under the authority of the United States." The Court stated that "[u]ndoubtedly a state has the legitimate power to define and punish crimes by general laws applicable to all persons within its jurisdiction * * *. But it is without lawful power to make such special laws applicable to banks organized and operating under the laws of the United States." *Id.* at 239 (holding that Federal law governing the operations of national banks preempted a state criminal law prohibiting insolvent banks from accepting deposits).

sistent with the powers set out in paragraph (a) of this section.

[69 Fed. Reg. 1904 (Jan. 13, 2004)]

12 C.F.R. § 7.4008 Lending.

(a) *Authority of national banks.* A national bank may make, sell, purchase, participate in, or otherwise deal in loans and interests in loans that are not secured by liens on, or interests in, real estate, subject to such terms, conditions, and limitations prescribed by the Comptroller of the Currency and any other applicable Federal law.

(b) *Standards for loans.* A national bank shall not make a consumer loan subject to this § 7.4008 based predominantly on the bank's realization of the foreclosure or liquidation value of the borrower's collateral, without regard to the borrower's ability to repay the loan according to its terms. A bank may use any reasonable method to determine a borrower's ability to repay, including, for example, the borrower's current and expected income, current and expected cash flows, net worth, other relevant financial resources, current financial obligations, employment status, credit history, or other relevant factors.

(c) *Unfair and deceptive practices.* A national bank shall not engage in unfair or deceptive practices within the meaning of section 5 of the Federal Trade Commission Act, 15 U.S.C. 45(a)(1), and regulations promulgated thereunder in connection with loans made under this § 7.4008.

(d) *Applicability of state law.* (1) Except where made applicable by Federal law, state laws that obstruct, impair, or condition a national bank's ability to fully exercise its Federally authorized non-real estate lending powers are not applicable to national banks.

(2) A national bank may make non-real estate loans without regard to state law limitations concerning:

(i) Licensing, registration (except for purposes of service of process), filings, or reports by creditors;

(ii) The ability of a creditor to require or obtain insurance for collateral or other credit enhancements or risk mitigants, in furtherance of safe and sound banking practices;

(iii) Loan-to-value ratios;

(iv) The terms of credit, including the schedule for repayment of principal and interest, amortization of loans, balance, payments due, minimum payments, or term to maturity of the loan, including the circumstances under which a loan may be called due and payable upon the passage of time or a specified event external to the loan;

(v) Escrow accounts, impound accounts, and similar accounts;

(vi) Security property, including leaseholds;

(vii) Access to, and use of, credit reports;

(viii) Disclosure and advertising, including laws requiring specific statements, information, or other content to be included in credit application forms, credit solicitations, billing statements, credit contracts, or other credit-related documents;

    (ix) Disbursements and repayments; and

    (x) Rates of interest on loans.[1]

    (e) *State laws that are not preempted.* State laws on the following subjects are not inconsistent with the non-real estate lending powers of national banks and apply to national banks to the extent that they only incidentally affect the exercise of national banks' non-real estate lending powers:

    (1) Contracts;

    (2) Torts;

    (3) Criminal law;[2]

    (4) Rights to collect debts;

    (5) Acquisition and transfer of property;

    (6) Taxation;

    (7) Zoning; and

    (8) Any other law the effect of which the OCC determines to be incidental to the non-real estate lending operations of national banks or otherwise consistent with the powers set out in paragraph (a) of this section.

[69 Fed. Reg. 1895, 1904 (Jan. 13, 2004)]

12 C.F.R. § 7.4009 Applicability of state law to national bank operations.

    (a) *Authority of national banks.* A national bank may exercise all powers authorized to it under Federal law, including conducting any activity that is part of, or incidental to, the business of banking, subject to such terms, conditions, and limitations prescribed by the Comptroller of the Currency and any applicable Federal law.

    (b) *Applicability of state law.* Except where made applicable by Federal law, state laws that obstruct, impair, or condition a national bank's ability to fully exercise its powers to conduct activities authorized under Federal law do not apply to national banks.

    (c) *Applicability of state law to particular national bank activities.* (1) The provisions of this section govern with respect to any national bank power or aspect of a national bank's opera-

---

tions that is not covered by another OCC regulation specifically addressing the applicability of state law.

    (2) State laws on the following subjects are not inconsistent with the powers of national banks and apply to national banks to the extent that they only incidentally affect the exercise of national bank powers:

    (i) Contracts;

    (ii) Torts;

    (iii) Criminal law,[1]

    (iv) Rights to collect debts;

    (v) Acquisition and transfer of property;

    (vi) Taxation;

    (vii) Zoning; and

    (viii) Any other law the effect of which the OCC determines to be incidental to the exercise of national bank powers or otherwise consistent with the powers set out in paragraph (a) of this section.

[69 Fed. Reg. 1904 (Jan. 13, 2004)]

* * *

Subpart E—Electronic Activities

* * *

12 C.F.R. § 7.5001 Electronic activities that are part of, or incidental to, the business of banking.

    (a) *Purpose.* This section identifies the criteria that the OCC uses to determine whether an electronic activity is authorized as part of, or incidental to, the business of banking under 12 U.S.C. 24 (Seventh) or other statutory authority.

    (b) *Restrictions and conditions on electronic activities.* The OCC may determine that activities are permissible under 12 U.S.C. 24 (Seventh) or other statutory authority only if they are subject to standards or conditions designed to provide that the activities function as intended and are conducted safely and soundly, in accordance with other applicable statutes, regulations, or supervisory policies.

    (c) *Activities that are part of the business of banking.* (1) An activity is authorized for national banks as part of the business of banking if the activity is described in 12 U.S.C. 24 (Seventh) or other statutory authority. In determining whether an electronic activity is part of the business of banking, the OCC considers the following factors:

    (i) Whether the activity is the functional equivalent to, or a logical outgrowth of, a recognized banking activity;

    (ii) Whether the activity strengthens the bank by benefiting its customers or its business;

    (iii) Whether the activity involves risks similar in nature to those already assumed by banks; and

    (iv) Whether the activity is authorized for state-chartered banks.

---

    (2) The weight accorded each factor set out in paragraph (c)(1) of this section depends on the facts and circumstances of each case.

    (d) *Activities that are incidental to the business of banking.* (1) An electronic banking activity is authorized for a national bank as incidental to the business of banking if it is convenient or useful to an activity that is specifically authorized for national banks or to an activity that is otherwise part of the business of banking. In determining whether an activity is convenient or useful to such activities, the OCC considers the following factors:

    (i) Whether the activity facilitates the production or delivery of a bank's products or services, enhances the bank's ability to sell or market its products or services, or improves the effectiveness or efficiency of the bank's operations, in light of risks presented, innovations, strategies, techniques and new technologies for producing and delivering financial products and services; and

    (ii) Whether the activity enables the bank to use capacity acquired for its banking operations or otherwise avoid economic loss or waste.

    (2) The weight accorded each factor set out in paragraph (d)(1) of this section depends on the facts and circumstances of each case.

12 C.F.R. § 7.5002 Furnishing of products and services by electronic means and facilities.

    (a) *Use of electronic means and facilities.* A national bank may perform, provide, or deliver through electronic means and facilities any activity, function, product, or service that it is otherwise authorized to perform, provide, or deliver, subject to § 7.5001(b) and applicable OCC guidance. The following list provides examples of permissible activities under this authority. This list is illustrative and not exclusive; the OCC may determine that other activities are permissible pursuant to this authority.

    (1) Acting as an electronic finder by:

    (i) Establishing, registering, and hosting commercially enabled web sites in the name of sellers;

    (ii) Establishing hyperlinks between the bank's site and a third-party site, including acting as a "virtual mall" by providing a collection of links to web sites of third-party vendors, organized by-product type and made available to bank customers;

    (iii) Hosting an electronic marketplace on the bank's Internet web site by providing links to the web sites of third-party buyers or sellers through the use of hypertext or other similar means;

    (iv) Hosting on the bank's servers the Internet web site of:

    (A) A buyer or seller that provides information concerning the hosted party and the products or services offered or sought and allows the submission of interest, bids, offers, orders and confirmations relating to such products or services; or

---

1 The limitations on charges that comprise rates of interest on loans by national banks are determined under Federal law. See 12 U.S.C. 85; 12 CFR 7.4001. State laws purporting to regulate national bank fees and charges that do not constitute interest are addressed in 12 CFR 7.4002.

2 See *supra*, note 5 regarding the distinction drawn by the Supreme Court in Easton v. Iowa, 188 U.S. 220, 238 (1903) between "crimes defined and punishable at common law or by the general statutes of a state and crimes and offences cognizable under the authority of the United States."

(B) A governmental entity that provides information concerning the services or benefits made available by the governmental entity, assists persons in completing applications to receive such services or benefits and permits persons to transmit their applications for such services or benefits;

(v) Operating an Internet web site that permits numerous buyers and sellers to exchange information concerning the products and services that they are willing to purchase or sell, locate potential counter-parties for transactions, aggregate orders for goods or services with those made by other parties, and enter into transactions between themselves;

(vi) Operating a telephone call center that provides permissible finder services; and

(vii) Providing electronic communications services relating to all aspects of transactions between buyers and sellers;

(2) Providing electronic bill presentment services;

(3) Offering electronic stored value systems; and

(4) Safekeeping for personal information or valuable confidential trade or business information, such as encryption keys.

(b) *Applicability of guidance and requirements not affected.* When a national bank performs, provides, or delivers through electronic means and facilities an activity, function, product, or service that it is otherwise authorized to perform, provide, or deliver, the electronic activity is not exempt from the regulatory requirements and supervisory guidance that the OCC would apply if the activity were conducted by non- electronic means or facilities.

(c) *State laws.* As a general rule, and except as provided by Federal law, State law is not applicable to a national bank's conduct of an authorized activity through electronic means or facilities if the State law, as applied to the activity, would be preempted pursuant to traditional principles of Federal preemption derived from the Supremacy Clause of the U.S. Constitution and applicable judicial precedent. Accordingly, State laws that stand as an obstacle to the ability of national banks to exercise uniformly their Federally authorized powers through electronic means or facilities, are not applicable to national banks.

* * *

12 C.F.R. § 7.5008 Location of a national bank conducting electronic activities.

A national bank shall not be considered located in a State solely because it physically maintains technology, such as a server or automated loan center, in that state, or because the bank's products or services are accessed through electronic means by customers located in the state.

12 C.F.R. § 7.5009 Location under 12 U.S.C. 85 of national banks operating exclusively through the Internet.

For purposes of 12 U.S.C. 85, the main office of a national bank that operates exclusively through the Internet is the office identified by the bank under 12 U.S.C. 22 (Second) or as relocated under 12 U.S.C. 30 or other appropriate authority.

* * *

PART 34—REAL ESTATE LENDING AND APPRAISALS

Subpart A—General

34.1   Purpose and scope.
34.2   Definitions.
34.3   General rule.
34.4   Applicability of State law.
34.5   Due-on-sale clauses.

Subpart B—Adjustable-Rate Mortgages

34.20   Definitions.
34.21   General rule.
34.22   Index.
34.23   Prepayment fees.
34.24   Nonfederally chartered commercial banks.
34.25   Transition rule.

* * *

Subpart D—Real Estate Lending Standards

34.61   Purpose and scope.
34.62   Real estate lending standards.

* * *

Authority: 12 U.S.C. 1 *et seq.*, 29, 93a, 371, 1701j–3, 1828(o), and 3331 *et seq.*

Subpart A—General

Source: 61 FR 11300, Mar. 20, 1996, unless otherwise noted.

12 C.F.R. § 34.1 Purpose and scope.

(a) *Purpose.* The purpose of this part is to set forth standards for real estate-related lending and associated activities by national banks.

(b) *Scope.* This part applies to national banks and their operating subsidiaries as provided in 12 CFR 5.34. For the purposes of 12 U.S.C. 371 and subparts A and B of this part, loans secured by liens on interests in real estate include loans made upon the security of condominiums, leaseholds, cooperatives, forest tracts, land sales contracts, and construction project loans. Construc-

tion project loans are not subject to subparts A and B of this part, however, if they have a maturity not exceeding 60 months and are made to finance the construction of either:

(1) A building where there is a valid and binding agreement entered into by a financially responsible lender or other party to advance the full amount of the bank's loan upon completion of the building; or

(2) A residential or farm building.

[61 Fed. Reg. 11300 (Mar. 20, 1996)]

12 C.F.R. § 34.2 Definitions.

(a) *Due-on-sale clause* means any clause that gives the lender or any assignee or transferee of the lender the power to declare the entire debt payable if all or part of the legal or equitable title or an equivalent contractual interest in the property securing the loan is transferred to another person, whether by deed, contract, or otherwise.

(b) *State* means any State of the United States of America, the District of Columbia, Puerto Rico, the Virgin Islands, the Northern Mariana Islands, American Samoa, and Guam.

(c) *State law limitations* means any State statute, regulation, or order of any State agency, or judicial decision interpreting State law.

[61 Fed. Reg. 11301 (Mar. 20, 1996)]

12 C.F.R. § 34.3 General rule.

(a) A national bank may make, arrange, purchase, or sell loans or extensions of credit, or interests therein, that are secured by liens on, or interests in, real estate (real estate loans), subject to 12 U.S.C. 1828(o) and such restrictions and requirements as the Comptroller of the Currency may prescribe by regulation or order.

(b) A national bank shall not make a consumer loan subject to this subpart based predominantly on the bank's realization of the foreclosure or liquidation value of the borrower's collateral, without regard to the borrower's ability to repay the loan according to its terms. A bank may use any reasonable method to determine a borrower's ability to repay, including, for example, the borrower's current and expected income, current and expected cash flows, net worth, other relevant financial resources, current financial obligations, employment status, credit history, or other relevant factors.

(c) A national bank shall not engage in unfair or deceptive practices within the meaning of section 5 of the Federal Trade Commission Act, 15 U.S.C. 45(a)(1), and regulations promulgated thereunder in connection with loans made under this part.

[61 Fed. Reg. 11301 (Mar. 20, 1996); 68 Fed. Reg. 70131 (Dec. 17, 2003); 69 Fed. Reg. 1904 (Jan. 13, 2004)]

12 C.F.R. § 34.4 Applicability of state law.

(a) Except where made applicable by Federal law, state laws that obstruct, impair, or condition a national bank's ability to fully exercise its Federally authorized real estate lending powers do not apply to national banks. Specifically, a national bank may make real estate loans under 12 U.S.C. 371 and § 34.3, without regard to state law limitations concerning:

(1) Licensing, registration (except for purposes of service of process), filings, or reports by creditors;

(2) The ability of a creditor to require or obtain private mortgage insurance, insurance for other collateral, or other credit enhancements or risk mitigants, in furtherance of safe and sound banking practices;

(3) Loan-to-value ratios;

(4) The terms of credit, including schedule for repayment of principal and interest, amortization of loans, balance, payments due, minimum payments, or term to maturity of the loan, including the circumstances under which a loan may be called due and payable upon the passage of time or a specified event external to the loan;

(5) The aggregate amount of funds that may be loaned upon the security of real estate;

(6) Escrow accounts, impound accounts, and similar accounts;

(7) Security property, including leaseholds;

(8) Access to, and use of, credit reports;

(9) Disclosure and advertising, including laws requiring specific statements, information, or other content to be included in credit application forms, credit solicitations, billing statements, credit contracts, or other credit-related documents;

(10) Processing, origination, servicing, sale or purchase of, or investment or participation in, mortgages;

(11) Disbursements and repayments;

(12) Rates of interest on loans;[1]

(13) Due-on-sale clauses except to the extent provided in 12 U.S.C. 1701j-3 and 12 CFR part 591; and

(14) Covenants and restrictions that must be contained in a lease to qualify the leasehold as acceptable security for a real estate loan.

(b) State laws on the following subjects are not inconsistent with the real estate lending powers of national banks and apply to national banks to the extent that they only incidentally affect the exercise of national banks' real estate lending powers:

(1) Contracts;

---

[1] The limitations on charges that comprise rates of interest on loans by national banks are determined under Federal law. *See* 12 U.S.C. 85 and 1735f-7a; 12 CFR 7.4001. State laws purporting to regulate national bank fees and charges that do not constitute interest are addressed in 12 CFR 7.4002.

(2) Torts;

(3) Criminal law;[2]

(4) Homestead laws specified in 12 U.S.C. 1462a(f);

(5) Rights to collect debts;

(6) Acquisition and transfer of real property;

(7) Taxation;

(8) Zoning; and

(9) Any other law the effect of which the OCC determines to be incidental to the real estate lending operations of national banks or otherwise consistent with the powers and purposes set out in § 34.3(a).

[69 Fed. Reg. 1904 (Jan. 13, 2004)]

12 C.F.R. § 34.5 Due-on-sale clauses.

A national bank may make or acquire a loan or interest therein, secured by a lien on real property, that includes a due-on-sale clause. Except as set forth in 12 U.S.C. 1701j-3(d) (which contains a list of transactions in which due-on-sale clauses may not be enforced), due-on-sale clauses in loans, whenever originated, will be valid and enforceable, notwithstanding any State law limitations to the contrary. For the purposes of this section, the term real property includes residential dwellings such as condominium units, cooperative housing units, and residential manufactured homes.

[61 Fed. Reg. 11300 (Mar. 20, 1996)]

Subpart B—Adjustable-Rate Mortgages

Source: 61 Fed. Reg. 11301 (Mar. 20, 1996), unless otherwise noted.

12 C.F.R. § 34.20 Definitions.

Adjustable-rate mortgage (ARM) loan means an extension of credit made to finance or refinance the purchase of, and secured by a lien on,

---

[2] But see the distinction drawn by the Supreme Court in *Easton v. Iowa*, 188 U.S. 220, 238 (1903) between "crimes defined and punishable at common law or by the general statutes of a state and crimes and offences cognizable under the authority of the United States." The Court stated that "[u]ndoubtedly a state has the legitimate power to define and punish crimes by general laws applicable to all persons within its jurisdiction * * *. But it is without lawful power to make such special laws applicable to banks organized and operating under the laws of the United States." *Id.* at 239 (holding that Federal law governing the operations of national banks preempted a state criminal law prohibiting insolvent banks from accepting deposits).

a one-to-four family dwelling, including a condominium unit, cooperative housing unit, or residential manufactured home, where the lender, pursuant to an agreement with the borrower, may adjust the rate of interest from time to time. An ARM loan does not include fixed-rate extensions of credit that are payable at the end of a term that, when added to any terms for which the bank has promised to renew the loan, is shorter than the term of the amortization schedule.

[61 Fed. Reg. 11301 (Mar. 20, 1996)]

12 C.F.R. § 34.21 General rule.

(a) *Authorization.* A national bank and its subsidiaries may make, sell, purchase, participate in, or otherwise deal in ARM loans and interests therein without regard to any State law limitations on those activities.

(b) *Purchase of loans not in compliance.* A national bank may purchase or participate in ARM loans that were not made in accordance with this part, except that loans purchased, in whole or in part, from an affiliate or subsidiary must comply with this part. For purposes of this paragraph, the terms affiliate and subsidiary have the same meaning as in 12 U.S.C. 371c.

[61 Fed. Reg. 11301 (Mar. 20, 1996)]

12 C.F.R. § 34.22 Index.

If a national bank makes an ARM loan to which 12 CFR 226.19(b) applies (i.e., the annual percentage rate of a loan may increase after consummation, the term exceeds one year, and the consumer's principal dwelling secures the indebtedness), the loan documents must specify an index to which changes in the interest rate will be linked. This index must be readily available to, and verifiable by, the borrower and beyond the control of the bank. A national bank may use as an index any measure of rates of interest that meets these requirements. The index may be either single values of the chosen measure or a moving average of the chosen measure calculated over a specified period. A national bank also may increase the interest rate in accordance with applicable loan documents specifying the amount of the increase and the times at which, or circumstances under which, it may be made. A national bank may decrease the interest rate at any time.

[61 Fed. Reg. 11301 (Mar. 20, 1996)]

12 C.F.R. § 34.23 Prepayment fees.

A national bank offering or purchasing ARM loans may impose fees for prepayments notwithstanding any State law limitations to the contrary. For purposes of this section, prepayments do not include:

(a) Payments that exceed the required payment amount to avoid or reduce negative amortization; or

(b) Principal payments, in excess of those necessary to retire the outstanding debt over the remaining loan term at the then-current interest rate, that are made in accordance with rules governing the determination of monthly payments contained in the loan documents.

[61 Fed. Reg. 11301 (Mar. 20, 1996)]

12 C.F.R. § 34.24 Nonfederally chartered commercial banks.

Pursuant to 12 U.S.C. 3803(a), a State chartered commercial bank may make ARM loans in accordance with the provisions of this subpart. For purposes of this section, the term "State" shall have the same meaning as set forth in § 34.2(b).

[61 Fed. Reg. 11301 (Mar. 20, 1996)]

12 C.F.R. § 34.25 Transition rule.

If, on October 1, 1988, a national bank had made a loan or binding commitment to lend under an ARM loan program that complied with the requirements of 12 CFR part 29 in effect prior to October 1, 1988 (see 12 CFR Parts 1 to 199, revised as of January 1, 1988) but would have violated any of the provisions of this subpart, the national bank may continue to administer the loan or binding commitment to lend in accordance with that loan program. All ARM loans or binding commitments to make ARM loans that a national bank entered into after October 1, 1988, must comply with all provisions of this subpart.

[61 Fed. Reg. 11301 (Mar. 20, 1996)]

* * *

Subpart D—Real Estate Lending Standards

Source: 57 Fed. Reg. 62889 (Dec. 31, 1992), unless otherwise noted.

12 C.F.R. § 34.61 Purpose and scope.

This subpart, issued pursuant to section 304 of the Federal Deposit Insurance Corporation Improvement Act of 1991, 12 U.S.C. 1828(o), prescribes standards for real estate lending to be used by national banks in adopting internal real estate lending policies.

12 C.F.R. § 34.62 Real estate lending standards.

(a) Each national bank shall adopt and maintain written policies that establish appropriate limits and standards for extensions of credit that are secured by liens on or interests in real estate, or that are made for the purpose of financing permanent improvements to real estate.

(b)(1) Real estate lending policies adopted pursuant to this section must:

(i) Be consistent with safe and sound banking practices;

(ii) Be appropriate to the size of the institution and the nature and scope of its operations; and

(iii) Be reviewed and approved by the bank's board of directors at least annually.

(2) The lending policies must establish:

(i) Loan portfolio diversification standards;

(ii) Prudent underwriting standards, including loan-to-value limits, that are clear and measurable;

(iii) Loan administration procedures for the bank's real estate portfolio; and

(iv) Documentation, approval, and reporting requirements to monitor compliance with the bank's real estate lending policies.

(c) Each national bank must monitor conditions in the real estate market in its lending area to ensure that its real estate lending policies continue to be appropriate for current market conditions.

(d) The real estate lending policies adopted pursuant to this section should reflect consideration of the Interagency Guidelines for Real Estate Lending Policies established by the Federal bank and thrift supervisory agencies.

Editor's Note: Appendix A to Subpart D of Part 34 contains Interagency Guidelines for Real Estate Lending. The agencies' regulations require that each insured depository institution adopt and maintain a written policy that establishes appropriate limits and standards for all extensions of credit that are secured by liens on or interests in real estate or made for the purpose of financing the construction of a building or other improvements. These guidelines are intended to assist institutions in the formulation and maintenance of a real estate lending policy that is appropriate to the size of the institution and the nature and scope of its individual operations, as well as satisfies the requirements of the regulation. The guidelines are not reprinted here.

* * *

PART 37—DEBT CANCELLATION CONTRACTS AND DEBT SUSPENSION AGREEMENTS

Authority: 12 U.S.C. 1 *et seq.*, 24 (Seventh), 93a, 1818.
Source: 67 Fed. Reg. 58976 (Sept. 19, 2002), unless otherwise noted.

12 C.F.R. § 37.1 Authority, purpose, and scope.

(a) Authority. A national bank is authorized to enter into debt cancellation contracts and debt suspension agreements and charge a fee therefor, in connection with extensions of credit that it makes, pursuant to 12 U.S.C. 24 (Seventh).

(b) Purpose. This part sets forth the standards that apply to debt cancellation contracts and debt suspension agreements entered into by national banks. The purpose of these standards is to ensure that national banks offer and implement such contracts and agreements consistent with safe and sound banking practices, and subject to appropriate consumer protections.

(c) Scope. This part applies to debt cancellation contracts and debt suspension agreements entered into by national banks in connection with extensions of credit they make. National banks' debt cancellation contracts and debt suspension agreements are governed by this part and applicable Federal law and regulations, and not by part 14 of this chapter or by State law.

12 C.F.R. § 37.2 Definitions.

For purposes of this part:

(a) Actuarial method means the method of allocating payments made on a debt between the amount financed and the finance charge pursuant to which a payment is applied first to the accumulated finance charge and any remainder is subtracted from, or any deficiency is added to, the unpaid balance of the amount financed.

(b) Bank means a national bank and a Federal branch or Federal agency of a foreign bank as those terms are defined in part 28 of this chapter.

(c) Closed-end credit means consumer credit other than open-end credit as defined in this section.

(d) Contract means a debt][1] cancellation contract or a debt suspension agreement.

(e) Customer means an individual who obtains an extension of credit from a bank primarily for personal, family or household purposes.

(f) Debt cancellation contract means a loan term or contractual arrangement modifying loan terms under which a bank agrees to cancel all or part of a customer's obligation to repay an extension of credit from that bank upon the occurrence of a specified event. The agreement may be separate from or a part of other loan documents.

(g) Debt suspension agreement means a loan term or contractual arrangement modifying loan terms under which a bank agrees to suspend all or part of a customer's obligation to repay an extension of credit from that bank upon the occurrence of a specified event. The agreement may be separate from or a part of other loan documents. The term *debt suspension agreement* does not include loan payment deferral arrangements in which the triggering event is the borrower's unilateral election to defer repayment, or the bank's unilateral decision to allow a deferral of repayment.

(h) Open-end credit means consumer credit extended by a bank under a plan in which:

(1) The bank reasonably contemplates repeated transactions;

---

1 So in original.

(2) The bank may impose a finance charge from time to time on an outstanding unpaid balance; and

(3) The amount of credit that may be extended to the customer during the term of the plan (up to any limit set by the bank) is generally made available to the extent that any outstanding balance is repaid.

(*i*) *Residential mortgage loan* means a loan secured by 1-4 family, residential real property.

12 C.F.R. § 37.3 Prohibited practices.

(a) *Anti-tying.* A national bank may not extend credit nor alter the terms or conditions of an extension of credit conditioned upon the customer entering into a debt cancellation contract or debt suspension agreement with the bank.

(b) *Misrepresentations generally.* A national bank may not engage in any practice or use any advertisement that could mislead or otherwise cause a reasonable person to reach an erroneous belief with respect to information that must be disclosed under this part.

(c) *Prohibited contract terms.* A national bank may not offer debt cancellation contracts or debt suspension agreements that contain terms:

(1) Giving the bank the right unilaterally to modify the contract unless:

(i) The modification is favorable to the customer and is made without additional charge to the customer; or

(ii) The customer is notified of any proposed change and is provided a reasonable opportunity to cancel the contract without penalty before the change goes into effect; or

(2) Requiring a lump sum, single payment for the contract payable at the outset of the contract, where the debt subject to the contract is a residential mortgage loan.

12 C.F.R. § 37.4 Refunds of fees in the event of termination or prepayment of the covered loan.

(a) *Refunds.* If a debt cancellation contract or debt suspension agreement is terminated (including, for example, when the customer prepays the covered loan), the bank shall refund to the customer any unearned fees paid for the contract unless the contract provides otherwise. A bank may offer a customer a contract that does not provide for a refund only if the bank also offers that customer a bona fide option to purchase a comparable contract that provides for a refund.

(b) *Method of calculating refund.* The bank shall calculate the amount of a refund using a method at least as favorable to the customer as the actuarial method.

12 C.F.R. § 37.5 Method of payment of fees.

Except as provided in § 37.3(c)(2), a bank may offer a customer the option of paying the fee for a contract in a single payment, provided the bank also offers the customer a bona fide option of paying the fee for that contract in monthly or other periodic payments. If the bank offers the customer the option to finance the single payment by adding it to the amount the customer is borrowing, the bank must also disclose to the customer, in accordance with § 37.6, whether and, if so, the time period during which, the customer may cancel the agreement and receive a refund.

12 C.F.R. § 37.6 Disclosures.

(a) *Content of short form of disclosures.* The short form of disclosures required by this part must include the information described in appendix A to this part that is appropriate to the product offered. Short form disclosures made in a form that is substantially similar to the disclosures in appendix A to this part will satisfy the short form disclosure requirements of this section.

(b) *Content of long form of disclosures.* The long form of disclosures required by this part must include the information described in appendix B to this part that is appropriate to the product offered. Long form disclosures made in a form that is substantially similar to the disclosures in appendix B to this part will satisfy the long form disclosure requirements of this section.

(c) *Disclosure requirements; timing and method of disclosures*—(1) *Short form disclosures.* The bank shall make the short form disclosures orally at the time the bank first solicits the purchase of a contract.

(2) *Long form disclosures.* The bank shall make the long form disclosures in writing before the customer completes the purchase of the contract. If the initial solicitation occurs in person, then the bank shall provide the long form disclosures in writing at that time.

(3) *Special rule for transactions by telephone.* If the contract is solicited by telephone, the bank shall provide the short form disclosures orally and shall mail the long form disclosures, and, if appropriate, a copy of the contract to the customer within 3 business days, beginning on the first business day after the telephone solicitation.

(4) *Special rule for solicitations using written mail inserts or "take one" applications.* If the contract is solicited through written materials such as mail inserts or "take one" applications, the bank may provide only the short form disclosures in the written materials if the bank mails the long form disclosures to the customer within 3 business days, beginning on the first business day after the customer contacts the bank to respond to the solicitation, subject to the requirements of § 37.7(c).

(5) *Special rule for electronic transactions.* The disclosures described in this section may be provided through electronic media in a manner consistent with the requirements of the Electronic Signatures in Global and National Commerce Act, 15 U.S.C. 7001 *et seq.*

(d) *Form of disclosures*—(1) Disclosures must be readily understandable. The disclosures required by this section must be conspicuous, simple, direct, readily understandable, and designed to call attention to the nature and significance of the information provided.

(2) Disclosures must be meaningful. The disclosures required by this section must be in a meaningful form. Examples of methods that could call attention to the nature and significance of the information provided include:

(i) A plain-language heading to call attention to the disclosures;

(ii) A typeface and type size that are easy to read;

(iii) Wide margins and ample line spacing;

(iv) Boldface or italics for key words; and

(v) Distinctive type style, and graphic devices, such as shading or sidebars, when the disclosures are combined with other information.

(e) Advertisements and other promotional material for debt cancellation contracts and debt suspension agreements. The short form disclosures are required in advertisements and promotional material for contracts unless the advertisements and promotional materials are of a general nature describing or listing the services or products offered by the bank.

12 C.F.R. § 37.7 Affirmative election to purchase and acknowledgment of receipt of disclosures required.

(a) *Affirmative election and acknowledgment of receipt of disclosures.* Before entering into a contract the bank must obtain a customer's written affirmative election to purchase a contract and written acknowledgment of receipt of the disclosures required by Sec. 37.6(b). The election and acknowledgment information must be conspicuous, simple, direct, readily understandable, and designed to call attention to their significance. The election and acknowledgment satisfy these standards if they conform with the requirements in Sec. 37.6(b) of this part.

(b) *Special rule for telephone solicitations.* If the sale of a contract occurs by telephone, the customer's affirmative election to purchase may be made orally, provided the bank:

(1) Maintains sufficient documentation to show that the customer received the short form disclosures and then affirmatively elected to purchase the contract;

(2) Mails the affirmative written election and written acknowledgment, together with the long form disclosures required by § 37.6 of this part, to the customer within 3 business days after the telephone solicitation, and maintains sufficient documentation to show it made reasonable efforts to obtain the documents from the customer; and

(3) Permits the customer to cancel the purchase of the contract without penalty within 30 days after the bank has mailed the long form disclosures to the customer.

(c) Special rule for solicitations using written mail inserts or "take one" applications. If the contract is solicited through written materials such as mail inserts or "take one" applications and the bank provides only the short form disclosures in the written materials, then the bank shall mail the acknowledgment of receipt of disclosures, together with the long form disclosures required by § 37.6 of this part, to the customer within 3 business days, beginning on the first business day after the customer contacts the bank or otherwise responds to the solicitation. The bank may not obligate the customer to pay for the contract until after the bank has received the customer's written acknowledgment of receipt of disclosures unless the bank:

(1) Maintains sufficient documentation to show that the bank provided the acknowledgment of receipt of disclosures to the customer as required by this section;

(2) Maintains sufficient documentation to show that the bank made reasonable efforts to obtain from the customer a written acknowledgment of receipt of the long form disclosures; and

(3) Permits the customer to cancel the purchase of the contract without penalty within 30 days after the bank has mailed the long form disclosures to the customer.

(d) Special rule for electronic election. The affirmative election and acknowledgment may be made electronically in a manner consistent with the requirements of the Electronic Signatures in Global and National Commerce Act, 15 U.S.C. 7001 et seq.

12 C.F.R. § 37.8 Safety and soundness requirements.

A national bank must manage the risks associated with debt cancellation contracts and debt suspension agreements in accordance with safe and sound banking principles. Accordingly, a national bank must establish and maintain effective risk management and control processes over its debt cancellation contracts and debt suspension agreements. Such processes include appropriate recognition and financial reporting of income, expenses, assets and liabilities, and appropriate treatment of all expected and unexpected losses associated with the products. A bank also should assess the adequacy of its internal control and risk mitigation activities in view of the nature and scope of its debt cancellation contract and debt suspension agreement programs.

**12 C.F.R. Part 37 Appendix A—
Short Form Disclosures**

- This product is optional

Your purchase of [PRODUCT NAME] is optional. Whether or not you purchase [PRODUCT NAME] will not affect your application for credit or the terms of any existing credit agreement you have with the bank.

- Lump sum payment of fee

[Applicable if a bank offers the option to pay the fee in a single payment]

[Prohibited where the debt subject to the contract is a residential mortgage loan]

You may choose to pay the fee in a single lump sum or in [monthly/quarterly] payments. Adding the lump sum of the fee to the amount you borrow will increase the cost of [PRODUCT NAME].

- Lump sum payment of fee with no refund

[Applicable if a bank offers the option to pay the fee in a single payment for a no-refund DCC]

[Prohibited where the debt subject to the contract is a residential mortgage loan]

You may choose [PRODUCT NAME] with a refund provision or without a refund provision. Prices of refund and no-refund products are likely to differ.

- Refund of fee paid in lump sum

[Applicable where the customer pays the fee in a single payment and the fee is added to the amount borrowed]

[Prohibited where the debt subject to the contract is a residential mortgage loan]

[Either:] (1) You may cancel [PRODUCT NAME] at any time and receive a refund; or (2) You may cancel [PRODUCT NAME] within [rule; 5] days and receive a full refund; or (3) If you cancel [PRODUCT NAME] you will not receive a refund.

- Additional disclosures

We will give you additional information before you are required to pay for [PRODUCT NAME]. [If applicable]: This information will include a copy of the contract containing the terms of [PRODUCT NAME].

- Eligibility requirements, conditions, and exclusions

There are eligibility requirements, conditions, and exclusions that could prevent you from receiving benefits under [PRODUCT NAME].

[Either:] You should carefully read our additional information for a full explanation of the terms of [PRODUCT NAME] or You should carefully read the contract for a full explanation of the terms of [PRODUCT NAME].

**12 C.F.R. Part 37 Appendix B—
Long Form Disclosures**

- This product is optional

Your purchase of [PRODUCT NAME] is optional. Whether or not you purchase [PRODUCT NAME] will not affect your application for credit or the terms of any existing credit agreement you have with the bank.

- Explanation of debt suspension agreement

[Applicable if the contract has a debt suspension feature]

If [PRODUCT NAME] is activated, your duty to pay the loan principal and interest to the bank is only suspended. You must fully repay the loan after the period of suspension has expired. [If applicable]: This includes interest accumulated during the period of suspension.

- Amount of fee

[For closed-end credit]: The total fee for [PRODUCT NAME] is [rule; 5].

[For open-end credit, either:] (1) The monthly fee for [PRODUCT NAME] is based on your account balance each month multiplied by the unit-cost, which is [rule; 5]; or (2) The formula used to compute the fee is [rule; 5]].

- Lump sum payment of fee

[Applicable if a bank offers the option to pay the fee in a single payment]

[Prohibited where the debt subject to the contract is a residential mortgage loan]

You may choose to pay the fee in a single lump sum or in [monthly/quarterly] payments. Adding the lump sum of the fee to the amount you borrow will increase the cost of [PRODUCT NAME].

- Lump sum payment of fee with no refund

[Applicable if a bank offers the option to pay the fee in a single payment for a no-refund DCC]

[Prohibited where the debt subject to the contract is a residential mortgage loan]

You have the option to purchase [PRODUCT NAME] that includes a refund of the unearned portion of the fee if you terminate the contract or prepay the loan in full prior to the scheduled termination date. Prices of refund and no-refund products may differ.

- Refund of fee paid in lump sum

[Applicable where the customer pays the fee in a single payment and the fee is added to the amount borrowed]

[Prohibited where the debt subject to the contract is a residential mortgage loan]

[Either:] (1) You may cancel [PRODUCT NAME] at any time and receive a refund; or (2) You may cancel [PRODUCT NAME] within [rule; 5] days and receive a full refund; or (3) If you cancel [PRODUCT NAME] you will not receive a refund.

- Use of card or credit line restricted

[Applicable if the contract restricts use of card or credit line when customer activates protection]

If [PRODUCT NAME] is activated, you will be unable to incur additional charges on the credit card or use the credit line.

- Termination of [PRODUCT NAME]

[Either]: (1) You have no right to cancel [PRODUCT NAME]; or (2) You have the right to cancel [PRODUCT NAME] in the following circumstances: [rule; 5].

[And either]: (1) The bank has no right to cancel [PRODUCT NAME]; or (2)The bank has the right to cancel [PRODUCT NAME] in the following circumstances: [rule; 10].

• Eligibility requirements, conditions, and exclusions

There are eligibility requirements, conditions, and exclusions that could prevent you from receiving benefits under [PRODUCT NAME].

[Either]: (1) The following is a summary of the eligibility requirements, conditions, and ex-clusions. [The bank provides a summary of any eligibility requirements, conditions, and exclusions]; or (2) You may find a complete explanation of the eligibility requirements, conditions, and exclusions in paragraphs [rule; 5] of the [PRODUCT NAME] agreement.

C.3 OCC Interpretive and Advisory Letters

This section summarizes informal OCC "advisory" and "inter-pretative" letters relating to the preemption of state laws, to the authority of national banks, to relevant branching issues, to lending practices, and to the definition of "interest," from 1992 forward. Certain of these letters are also discussed in Chapter 3, *supra*. The full text of the OCC letters summarized in this section can be found on the CD-Rom accompanying this volume. The Interpretive Letters from 1996 to the present can also be found at the OCC website: www.occ.treas.gov/interp/monthly.htm. Advisory Letters appear at www.occ.treas.gov/issue.htm. Formal Preemption Deter-minations are summarized in Appx. C.4.

Letter to Private Attorneys regarding Wells Fargo Bank, Minne-sota, N.A. v. Alberta Harris (January 14, 2005). A national bank as trustee for a securitized pool of mortgage loans is subject to the state consumer fraud act (CFA) where the bank did not originate the loan, did not fund the loan at inception, nor "purchase" the loan as part of any real estate lending program comprehended by the regulation. Rather, bank acted as trustees for the benefit of investors in the trust. The substance of the transaction is that the investors, not the bank, are purchasing the loans that have been made by the original lender. The investors own the beneficial interest in the loans held by the bank as trustee. The effect of any liability for violation of the CFA ultimately falls on the investors. The bank does not allege that it, as opposed to the trust it represents, is exposed to liability for any violation of the CFA.

Letter to Massachusetts Attorney General regarding the Lack of Complete Preemption in a Suit Filed by the AG (January 5, 2005). Standard regarding complete preemption is whether a federal cause of action supplants the state causes of action alleged by Massa-chusetts in a suit regarding fees charged by a private retailer for the use of its gift cards; OCC agrees that *Beneficial Nat'l Bank v. Anderson* dealt with usury claims and does not condone complete preemption outside of that context.

Interpretive Letter No. 1006 (August 19, 2004). Recent OCC deposit-taking regulation adopts the Supreme Court standards as to which types of state unclaimed property and escheat laws are not preempted.

Interpretive Letter No. 1004 (August 4, 2004). Broad state parity act may be read to allow national banks to charge prepayment fees because it permits banks to charge "interest" on loans as permitted by federal law and federal law allows federal savings associations to collect prepayment fees.

Letter to Private Attorney regarding New OCC Preemption Regu-lations (July 20, 2004). Supplements and explains the new OCC preemption regulations; agrees that the new regulation is based in part on the OTS preemption regulations.

Interpretive Letter No. 995 (June 22, 2004). National bank may export the state fiduciary law of any state in which it conducts fiduciary activities to any other state; state law that restricts foreign national banks from providing fiduciary services in its state unless certain conditions are met is preempted.

Interpretive Letter No. 1005 (June 10, 2004). None of the uniform provisions of the UCC are preempted. OCC does not address the non-uniform provisions that individual states may include in the body of their state commercial codes.

Interpretive Letter No. 1002 (May 13, 2004). OCC addressed table-funding not mentioned in its Letter No. 1000. Loans table-funded by a national bank or its operating subsidiary are not subject to the Georgia Fair Lending Act (GFLA).

Advisory Letter AL: 2004-4 (April 28, 2004). The OCC addresses a number of issues presented by certain secured credit card pro-grams, including credit, compliance, and reputation risks and the potential for inappropriate treatment of customers and provides guidance to national banks on how to avoid these risks.

Interpretive Letter No. 1000 (April 2, 2004). The only part of the Georgia Fair Lending Act not preempted is a provision that requires a lender to terminate a foreclosure once a default is cured. If a loan is arranged by a broker but made by a national bank, the GFLA is not applicable. But where the loan is arranged by a broker and made by another type of entity, the GFLA is not preempted. Letter does not address the applicability of the GFLA to the national bank if it purchased the loan from a non-bank or operating subsidiary originator. Nor does the letter address table-funding by a national bank.

Interpretive Letter No. 999 (March 9, 2004). OCC describes its 2004 preemption rule and highlights the consumer protection provisions.

Interpretive Letter No. 998 (March 9, 2004). State anti-discrimi-nation laws are not preempted, generally speaking. The OCC will use conflict analysis to review a specific law. State fair lending and anti-redlining laws are only enforceable against national banks by the OCC, however.

Advisory Letter AL 2004-2 (February 26, 2004). State officials may refer complaints to national banks; national banks should expedi-tiously resolve complaints; national banks are to advise the OCC if the state attempts to exercise any control or to argue that state law applies.

Interpretive Letter No. 980 (December 24, 2003). UPS drop boxes at various non-branch offices of a national bank do not constitute branches given the particular circumstances.

Interpretive Letter No. 974 (July 21, 2003). Operating subsidiary may originate loans and charge interest as authorized under § 85 and applicable Indiana law to borrowers residing in all states without regard to the location of the property securing the loan.

Advisory Letter AL 2003-3 (February 21, 2003). The OCC issues guidance to national banks on avoiding predatory and abusive mortgage lending practices in brokered and purchased loans. Practices that raise concerns include: frequent, sequential refinancings; refinancings of special subsidized mortgages; single-premium credit life insurance or similar products; negative amortization; balloon payments in short-term transactions; prepayment penalties that are not limited to the early years of a loan; financing points, fees, penalties, and other charges; interest rate increases upon default; mandatory arbitration clauses; and the acquisition of HO-EPA loans.

Interpretive Letter No. 968 (February 12, 2003). A holding company affiliate of a national bank may become an operating subsidiary of the bank. After this occurs, the operating subsidiary may impose and export interest charges under the same terms and conditions as the bank.

Interpretive Letter No. 959 (February 13, 2003). OCC determines that the risk weight for refund anticipation loans (RALS) is 100%, contrary to the bank's request for a 20% risk weight. If a bank securitizes RALS and retains more than a pro rata share of the risk associated with the asset, the OCC rules provide for a dollar-for-dollar capital charge on unrated, first loss positions retained on securitized assets.

Interpretive Letter No. 958 (January 27, 2003). States may not exercise visitorial powers over national banks and their operating subsidiaries in the conduct of their mortgage banking and servicing activities. States cannot request documents or other information.

Interpretive Letter No. 957 (January 27, 2003). State licensing laws do not apply to operating subsidiaries. States cannot exercise visitorial powers over operating subsidiaries even if they had obtained state licenses.

Interpretive Letter No. 971 (January 16, 2003). In response to inquiry by counsel to a state banking department, the OCC repeats its assertion of jurisdiction over operating subsidiaries and refuses to answer if and when state UDAP acts apply to the activities of operating subsidiaries, in this case, a subprime mortgage lender.

Interpretive Letter No. 954 (December 16, 2002). The OCC opines that a subsidiary of a national bank is entitled to the same pre-emptive rights as its parent.

Advisory Letter No. AL 2002-9 (November 25, 2002). The OCC affirms that national banks are subject to supervision, examination, and enforcement of federal and state laws only by the OCC; national bank are federal instrumentalities; state laws that do apply to national banks include contract, debt collection, acquisition and transfer of property, taxation, zoning, criminal, and tort law.

Interpretive Letter No. 952 (October 23, 2002). For purposes of the applicability of substantive state and federal laws, the corporate location of a national bank is where the bank currently maintains its main office. For purposes of diversity jurisdiction, the bank is a citizen of the state in which its principal place of business is located and of the state that was originally designated in its organization certificate and articles of association, or, if applicable, to the state which that designation has changed under other authority (*i.e.*, the state in which its main office is currently located).

Interpretive Letter No. 997 (April 15, 2002). OCC concludes that national banks have the authority to set NSF fees based on a given posting of checks and approves of high-to-low postings.

Advisory Letter No. AL 2002-3 (March 22, 2002). The OCC describes the standards it uses to evaluate whether an act or practice violates applicable law prohibiting unfair or deceptive acts or practices; provides guidance on what constitutes unfair or deceptive acts or practices; provides guidance on how banks and their operating subsidiaries can prevent reputation, compliance, and legal risks posed by certain practices; confirms that state UDAP acts may apply, citing to California's as an example.

Interpretive Letter (March 18, 2002). Certain provisions of the Massachusetts Consumer Protection Act Relative to the Sale of Insurance by Banks and accompanying regulations are preempted under the Gramm-Leach-Bliley Act.

Interpretive Letter No. 939 (October 15, 2001). Letter concludes that federal law would preempt laws in Massachusetts and Florida that purport to limit or restrict a national bank from establishing deposit-taking ATMs.

OCC Interpretive Letter No. 916 (May 22, 2001). OCC opines that national banks may decide upon a policy of posting checks for payment in any order it chooses as long as the decision is based upon the criteria in 12 C.F.R. § 7.4002(b).

Interpretive Letter No. 906 (January 19, 2001). Letter provides a lengthy justification for the OCC's position that state laws or local ordinances that limit the national banks' ability to charge ATM fees are preempted. The letter discusses the interplay between the Electronic Funds Transfer Act and the general powers of national banks.

Interpretive Letter No. 903 (December 28, 2000). Letter agrees that national banks have the authority to sell debt suspension products in connection with credit cards issued by the banks.

Interpretive Letter No. 872 (October 28, 1999). Letter confirms that a national bank may solicit and conduct trust business and operate non-branch trust offices in California, notwithstanding that the bank's main office is in a different state. Letter also confirms that state laws purporting to prohibit a national bank from engaging in these activities are preempted by federal law.

Interpretive Letter No. 866 (October 9, 1999). Federal law preempts state laws that purport to preclude national banks from soliciting trust business from customers located in states other than where the bank's main office is located. A national bank also may have trust representative offices in its home state as well as other states to market its fiduciary services.

Interpretive Letter No. 846 (June 29, 1998). Letter concludes that disbursal of loan proceeds by escrow agent affiliate of lender at nonbranch office of the lender does not cause that office to be considered a branch.

Interpretive Letter No. 838 (April 15, 1998). Letter concludes that under described facts, ATM sharing space with a LPO and courier service is not a branch.

Interpretive Letter No. 822 (February 17, 1998). Letter addresses use of home state and host state interest rates by interstate national banks. National banks may be located in both its home and host (branch) states and may charge the interest allowed in its home state unless certain functions are performed in the host state.

Interpretive Letter No. 821 (February 17, 1998). Letter states that Connecticut law that generally prohibits out-of-state banks from establishing ATMs in the state can be read so as to permit out-of-state national bank ATMs.

Interpretive Letter No. 817 (January 7, 1998). Letter clarifies status of certain fees as "interest" following termination of credit card account where outstanding balance remains on the account.

Interpretive Letter No. 803 (October 7, 1997). Letter opines on whether certain fees, such as account opening fees, fixed rate option fees, prepayment of a fixed rate option fees, early account closure fees, are interest under 12 U.S.C. § 85 and 12 CFR § 7.4001(a).

Unpublished Letter (July 7, 1997). New York law permitting state inspection of books and records of a national bank's insurance agency to determine compliance with applicable state law is not preempted.

Interpretive Letter No. 789 (June 27, 1997). Portions of the Colorado Electronic Funds Transfer Act prohibiting national banks from placing their names on ATMs and giving the state regulatory authority over national bank ATMs is preempted.

Interpretive Letter No. 776 (March 18, 1997). Letter concerns the exportation of main office state credit card rates by interstate national bank when it intended to merge with an affiliated bank in the consumer's state.

Interpretive Letter No. 772 (March 6, 1997). Automated loan machines are not branches under 12 U.S.C. § 36(J). The recently amended definition in 36(J) excludes ATMs and remote service units, which are unstaffed electronic devices that accept deposits, dispense withdrawals or make loans. Deposit boxes are (still) branches, and are not remote service units.

Interpretive Letter No. 749 (September 13, 1996). Texas insurance licensing laws that prevent or significantly interfere with a national bank's authority to sell annuities as agent is preempted, but State laws that are not preempted and applicable federal securities laws would apply to the sale of these products.

Interpretive Letter No. 744 (August 21, 1996). Prepayment fees constitute interest for purposes of section 85; bank chartered and located solely in a state which permits prepayment penalties may charge prepayment penalties in loans made to out-of-state residents.

Interpretive Letter No. 739 (August 15, 1996). Applicable Rhode Island insurance laws and regulations would apply to a national bank's insurance agency subsidiary.

Unpublished Letter (August 9, 1996). Provisions of the Texas Insurance Code that prevent national banks from selling annuities are preempted.

Interpretive Letter No. 706 (January 18, 1996). An Alabama law prohibiting Sunday operations is preempted for national banks.

Interpretive Letter No. 674 (June 9, 1995). A Texas regulation concerning the "naming and advertising of branch facilities" is not preempted for national banks.

Unpublished Letter (May 15, 1995). A Texas regulation requiring licensing of loan production offices as a condition for operation, and regulating the types of activities that can be conducted at such offices, is preempted for national banks.

Unpublished Letter (May 3, 1995). A Rhode Island law prohibiting the use of the word "bank" on signs or documents unless the user is a state-chartered bank is preempted for national banks.

Unpublished Letter (February 9, 1995). Provisions of the Idaho Consumer Credit Code that impose licensing requirements as a condition to extending consumer credit, recordkeeping and reporting requirements, and assessments of fees to defray the costs of supervision and examination is preempted with respect to national banks.

Interpretive Letter No. 644 (March 24, 1994). Provisions of the Georgia Residential Mortgage Act that impose registration and fee requirements as a condition to transacting business directly or indirectly as mortgage brokers or mortgage lenders is preempted with respect to national banks.

Interpretive Letter No. 628 (July 19, 1993). Texas statute that requires a national bank to register with the state as an investment advisor before providing investment advisory services to its trust customers is preempted.

Unpublished Letter (July 13, 1993). The anti-association provisions of the Florida Insurance Code, and provisions requiring national banks to give notice and obtain authorization to engage in the sale of annuities, as well as implementing regulations, conflict with the authority of national banks to sell annuities as agent and is therefore preempted.

Unpublished Letter (June 3, 1993). A subpoena issued by the Texas Home of Representatives seeking national bank books and records would represent an attempted exercise of visitorial powers by state authorities that conflicts with federal law.

Interpretive Letter No. 623 (May 10, 1993). A Connecticut statute that requires all sellers of variable annuities to be licensed by the state is preempted with respect to national banks.

Unpublished Letter (May 6, 1993). Provisions of the Idaho Consumer Credit Code requiring annual reports and payment of fees as a condition to being permitted to extend consumer credit is preempted.

Interpretive Letter No. 616 (February 26, 1993). A Massachusetts law that requires the reporting of credit card finance charges and fees to the state is preempted.

Unpublished Letter (February 1, 1993). Portions of the Nebraska Securities Act requiring national banks performing securities brokerage activities to register, and providing for state examination, is preempted.

Interpretive Letter No. 614 (January 15, 1993). Portions of the Idaho Credit Code (requiring credit card issuers, including national banks, to obtain licenses in order to issue credit cards to Idaho residents, and to subject to visitation or enforcement by state officials), the Wisconsin Consumer Act (requiring national banks making certain consumer credit transactions to comply with notification requirements and to submit to visitation and enforcement by state officials), and the Wyoming Uniform Consumer Credit Code (containing similar visitation and enforcement provisions) is preempted.

Unpublished Letter (December 7, 1992). Provisions of the Iowa Uniform Securities Act requiring national banks performing discount brokerage activities to register with the state, and providing for state examination, is preempted.

Unpublished Letter (November 2, 1992). A Texas administrative interpretation that the Texas Credit Code prohibits national banks from offering debt cancellation contracts is preempted.

Unpublished Letter (September 30, 1992). Residential mortgage loan terms prescribed by the Pennsylvania Banking Code would not apply to national banks (applying former 12 C.F.R. § 34.2), and the Pennsylvania state-chartered banks could choose to follow OCC regulations instead of state law (applying 12 U.S.C. § 3803).

Interpretive Letter No. 590 (June 18, 1992). Illinois restrictions on the establishment of federal branches would not limit the authority of the Comptroller to license federal branches of foreign banks in Illinois.

Unpublished Letter (June 10, 1992). A usury provision in the Arkansas constitution would apply to national banks in the same manner as it applies to state banks, and therefore is not preempted.

Unpublished Letter (February 4, 1992). Provisions of the Iowa Lender Credit Card Act regarding state licensing, supervision, and permissible rates and fees for credit card lenders is preempted for national banks.

Interpretive Letter No. 572 (January 15, 1992). The New Jersey Consumer Checking Act is preempted for national banks.

C.4 OCC Preemption Determinations

This section summarizes the Preemption Determinations formally published by the OCC in the *Federal Register*, in contrast to the interpretive and advisory letters contained in Appx. C.3. Those latter opinions are not formally published and may carry less weight than these formal pronouncements. The full text of these determinations are contained on the CD-Rom accompanying this volume.

Preemption Determination August 5, 2003. Neither national banks nor their operating subsidiaries that are engaging in business in Georgia must abide by any of the provisions of the original or amended Georgia Fair Lending Act. 68 Fed. Reg. 46264 (Aug. 5, 2003).

Preemption Determination October 9, 2001. Certain provisions of the West Virginia Insurance Sales Commission Protection Act are preempted; other provisions not preempted. 66 Fed. Reg. 51502 (Oct. 9, 2001).

Preemption Determination May 23, 2001. Michigan's motor vehicle sales finance act (MVSFA) that would regulate how a national bank could conduct its lending business "through" automobile dealers located in Michigan is preempted. 66 Fed. Reg. 28593 (May 23, 2001).

Preemption Determination May 10, 2001. Ohio law that prohibits the public sale of reclaimed leased vehicles frustrates the banks' ability to operate their leasing businesses in an economically efficient manner consistent with safe and sound banking principles and is, therefore, preempted. 66 Fed. Reg. 23977 (May 10, 2001).

Preemption Determination March 20, 2000. Pennsylvania law regulating auctioneers in the selling of certificate of deposits online using an auction format is preempted. 65 Fed. Reg. 15037 (Mar. 20, 2000).

Home Owners' Loan Act

This appendix excerpts portions of the Home Owners' Loan Act. These provisions appear in D.1. Section D.2, includes selected regulations promulgated by the Office of Thrift Supervision (OTS). In addition, the OTS issues Interpretive Letters from time to time. Relevant letters are summarized in D.3. The full text of these letters is included on the CD-Rom accompanying this volume and is updated in the annual supplements. The CD-Rom also contains the statutes and regulations reprinted in D.1 and D.2.

D.1 Selected Statutory Portions

TITLE 12—BANKS AND BANKING

CHAPTER 12—SAVINGS ASSOCIATIONS

§ 1461. Short title

* * *

§ 1463. Supervision of savings associations
§ 1464. Federal savings associations

* * *

12 U.S.C. § 1461. Short title

This chapter may be cited as the "Home Owners' Loan Act."

[June 13, 1933, ch. 64, Sec. 1, 48 Stat. 128; Pub. L. No. 101-73, title III, Sec. 301, 103 Stat. 277 (Aug. 9, 1989).]

* * *

12 U.S.C. § 1463. Supervision of savings associations

(a) Federal savings associations

(1) In general
The Director shall provide for the examination, safe and sound operation, and regulation of savings associations.

(2) Regulations
The Director may issue such regulations as the Director determines to be appropriate to carry out the responsibilities of the Director or the Office.

(3) Safe and sound housing credit to be encouraged
The Director shall exercise all powers granted to the Director under this chapter so as to encourage savings associations to provide credit for housing safely and soundly.

(b) Accounting and disclosure

(1) In general
The Director shall, by regulation, prescribe uniform accounting and disclosure standards for savings associations, to be used in determining savings associations' compliance with all applicable regulations.

(2) Specific requirements for accounting standards
Subject to section 1464(t) of this title, the uniform accounting standards prescribed under paragraph (1) shall—

(A) incorporate generally accepted accounting principles to the same degree that such principles are used to determine compliance with regulations prescribed by the Federal banking agencies;

(B) allow for no deviation from full compliance with such standards as are in effect after December 31, 1993; and

(C) prior to January 1, 1994, require full compliance by savings associations with accounting standards in effect at any time before such date not later than provided under the schedule in section 563.23-3 of title 12, Code of Federal Regulations (as in effect on May 1, 1989).

(3) Authority to prescribe more stringent accounting standards
The Director may at any time prescribe accounting standards more stringent than required under paragraph (2) if the Director determines that the more stringent standards are necessary to ensure the safe and sound operation of savings associations.

(c) Stringency of standards

All regulations and policies of the Director governing the safe and sound operation of savings associations, including regulations and policies governing asset classification and appraisals, shall be no less stringent than those established by the Comptroller of the Currency for national banks.

(d) Investment of certain funds in accounts of savings associations

The savings accounts and share accounts of savings associations insured by the Corporation shall be lawful investments and may be accepted as security for all public funds of the United States, fiduciary and trust funds under the authority or control of the United States or any officer thereof, and for the funds of all corporations organized under the laws of the United States (subject to any regulatory authority otherwise applicable), regardless of any limitation of law upon the investment of any such funds or upon the acceptance of security for the investment or deposit of any of such funds.

(e) Participation by savings associations in lotteries and related activities

(1) Participation prohibited

No savings association may—

(A) deal in lottery tickets;

(B) deal in bets used as a means or substitute for participation in a lottery;

(C) announce, advertise, or publicize the existence of any lottery; or

(D) announce, advertise, or publicize the existence or identity of any participant or winner, as such, in a lottery.

(2) Use of facilities prohibited

No savings association may permit—

(A) the use of any part of any of its own offices by any person for any purpose forbidden to the institution under paragraph (1); or

(B) direct access by the public from any of its own offices to any premises used by any person for any purpose forbidden to the institution under paragraph (1).

(3) Definitions

For purposes of this subsection—

(A) Deal in

The term "deal in" includes making, taking, buying, selling, redeeming, or collecting.

(B) Lottery

The term "lottery" includes any arrangement under which—

  (i) 3 or more persons (hereafter in this subparagraph referred to as the "participants") advance money or credit to another in exchange for the possibility or expectation that 1 or more but not all of the participants (hereafter in this paragraph referred to as the "winners") will receive by reason of those participants' advances more than the amounts those participants have advanced; and

  (ii) the identity of the winners is determined by any means which includes—

    (I) a random selection;

    (II) a game, race, or contest; or

    (III) any record or tabulation of the result of 1 or more events in which any participant has no interest except for the bearing that event has on the possibility that the participant may become a winner.

(C) Lottery ticket

The term "lottery ticket" includes any right, privilege, or possibility (and any ticket, receipt, record, or other evidence of any such right, privilege, or possibility) of becoming a winner in a lottery.

(4) Exception for State lotteries

Paragraphs (1) and (2) shall not apply with respect to any savings association accepting funds from, or performing any lawful services for, any State operating a lottery, or any officer or employee of such a State who is charged with administering the lottery.

(5) Regulations

The Director shall prescribe such regulations as may be necessary to provide for enforcement of this subsection and to prevent any evasion of any provision of this subsection.

(f) Federally related mortgage loan disclosures

A savings association may not make a federally related mortgage loan to an agent, trustee, nominee, or other person acting in a fiduciary capacity without requiring that the identity of the person receiving the beneficial interest of such loan shall at all times be revealed to the savings association. At the request of the Director, the savings association shall report to the Director the identity of such person and the nature and amount of the loan.

(g) Preemption of State usury laws

(1) Notwithstanding any State law, a savings association may charge interest on any extension of credit at a rate of not more than 1 percent in excess of the discount rate on 90-day commercial paper in effect at the Federal Reserve bank in the Federal Reserve district in which such savings association is located or at the rate allowed by the laws of the State in which such savings association is located, whichever is greater.

(2) If the rate prescribed in paragraph (1) exceeds the rate such savings association would be permitted to charge in the absence of this subsection, the receiving or charging a greater rate of interest than that prescribed by paragraph (1), when knowingly done, shall be deemed a forfeiture of the entire interest which the extension of credit carries with it, or which has been agreed to be paid thereon. If such greater rate of interest has been paid, the person who paid it may recover, in a civil action commenced in a court of appropriate jurisdiction not later than 2 years after the date of such payment, an amount equal to twice the amount of the interest paid from the savings association taking or receiving such interest.

(h) Form and maturity of securities

No savings association shall—

(1) issue securities which guarantee a definite maturity except with the specific approval of the Director, or

(2) issue any securities the form of which has not been approved by the Director.

[June 13, 1933, ch. 64, Sec. 4, *as added by* Pub. L. No. 101-73, title III, Sec. 301, 103 Stat. 280 (Aug. 9, 1989).]

12 U.S.C. § 1464. Federal savings associations

(a) In general

In order to provide thrift institutions for the deposit of funds and for the extension of credit for homes and other goods and services, the Director is authorized, under such regulations as the Director may prescribe—

(1) to provide for the organization, incorporation, examination, operation, and regulation of associations to be known as Federal savings associations (including Federal savings banks), and

(2) to issue charters therefor,

giving primary consideration of the best practices of thrift institutions in the United States. The lending and investment powers conferred by this section are intended to encourage such institutions to provide credit for housing safely and soundly.

(b) Deposits and related powers

(1) Deposit accounts

(A) Subject to the terms of its charter and regulations of the Director, a Federal savings association may—

  (i) raise funds through such deposit, share, or other accounts, including demand deposit accounts (hereafter in this section referred to as "accounts"); and

(ii) issue passbooks, certificates, or other evidence of accounts.

(B) A Federal savings association may not—

(i) pay interest on a demand account; or

(ii) permit any overdraft (including an intraday overdraft) on behalf of an affiliate, or incur any such overdraft in such savings association's account at a Federal reserve bank or Federal home loan bank on behalf of an affiliate.

All savings accounts and demand accounts shall have the same priority upon liquidation. Holders of accounts and obligors of a Federal savings association shall, to such extent as may be provided by its charter or by regulations of the Director, be members of the savings association, and shall have such voting rights and such other rights as are thereby provided.

(C) A Federal savings association may require not less than 14 days notice prior to payment of savings accounts if the charter of the savings association or the regulations of the Director so provide.

(D) If a Federal savings association does not pay all withdrawals in full (subject to the right of the association, where applicable, to require notice), the payment of withdrawals from accounts shall be subject to such rules and procedures as may be prescribed by the savings association's charter or by regulation of the Director. Except as authorized in writing by the Director, any Federal savings association that fails to make full payment of any withdrawal when due shall be deemed to be in an unsafe or unsound condition.

(E) Accounts may be subject to check or to withdrawal or transfer on negotiable or transferable or other order or authorization to the Federal savings association, as the Director may by regulation provide.

(F) A Federal savings association may establish remote service units for the purpose of crediting savings or demand accounts, debiting such accounts, crediting payments on loans, and the disposition of related financial transactions, as provided in regulations prescribed by the Director.

(2) Other liabilities

To such extent as the Director may authorize in writing, a Federal savings association may borrow, may give security, may be surety as defined by the Director and may issue such notes, bonds, debentures, or other obligations, or other securities, including capital stock.

(3) Loans from State housing finance agencies

(A) In general

Subject to regulation by the Director but without regard to any other provision of this subsection, any Federal savings association that is in compliance with the capital standards in effect under subsection (t) of this section may borrow funds from a State mortgage finance agency of the State in which the head office of such savings association is situated to the same extent as State law authorizes a savings association organized under the laws of such State to borrow from the State mortgage finance agency.

(B) Interest rate

A Federal savings association may not make any loan of funds borrowed under subparagraph (A) at an interest rate which exceeds by more than 1 3/4 percent per annum the interest rate paid to the State mortgage finance agency on the obligations issued to obtain the funds so borrowed.

(4) Mutual capital certificates

In accordance with regulations issued by the Director, mutual capital certificates may be issued and sold directly to subscribers or through underwriters. Such certificates may be included in calculating capital for the purpose of subsection (t) of this section to the extent permitted by the Director. The issuance of certificates under this paragraph does not constitute a change of control or ownership under this chapter or any other law unless there is in fact a change in control or reorganization. Regulations relating to the issuance and sale of mutual capital certificates shall provide that such certificates—

(A) are subordinate to all savings accounts, savings certificates, and debt obligations;

(B) constitute a claim in liquidation on the general reserves, surplus, and undivided profits of the Federal savings association remaining after the payment in full of all savings accounts, savings certificates, and debt obligations;

(C) are entitled to the payment of dividends; and

(D) may have a fixed or variable dividend rate.

(c) Loans and investments

To the extent specified in regulations of the Director, a Federal savings association may invest in, sell, or otherwise deal in the following loans and other investments:

(1) Loans or investments without percentage of assets limitation

Without limitation as a percentage of assets, the following are permitted:

(A) Account loans

Loans on the security of its savings accounts and loans specifically related to transaction accounts.

(B) Residential real property loans

Loans on the security of liens upon residential real property.

(C) United States government securities

Investments in obligations of, or fully guaranteed as to principal and interest by, the United States.

(D) Federal home loan bank and Federal National Mortgage Association securities

Investments in the stock or bonds of a Federal home loan bank or in the stock of the Federal National Mortgage Association.

(E) Federal Home Loan Mortgage Corporation instruments

Investments in mortgages, obligations, or other securities which are or have been sold by the Federal Home Loan Mortgage Corporation pursuant to section 305 or 306 of the Federal Home Loan Mortgage Corporation Act [12 U.S.C. §§ 1454 or 1455].

(F) Other Government securities

Investments in obligations, participations, securities, or other instruments issued by, or fully guaranteed as to principal and interest by, the Federal National Mortgage Association, the Student Loan Marketing Association, the Government National Mortgage Association, or any agency of the United States. A savings association may issue and sell securities which are guaranteed pursuant to section 306(g) of the National Housing Act [12 U.S.C. § 1721(g)].

(G) Deposits

Investments in accounts of any insured depository institution, as defined in section 3 of the Federal Deposit Insurance Act [12 U.S.C. § 1813].

(H) State securities

Investments in obligations issued by any State or political

subdivision thereof (including any agency, corporation, or instrumentality of a State or political subdivision). A Federal savings association may not invest more than 10 percent of its capital in obligations of any one issuer, exclusive of investments in general obligations of any issuer.

(I) Purchase of insured loans

Purchase of loans secured by liens on improved real estate which are insured or guaranteed under the National Housing Act [12 U.S.C. § 1701 *et seq.*], the Servicemen's Readjustment Act of 1944, or chapter 37 of Title 38.

(J) Home improvement and manufactured home loans

Loans made to repair, equip, alter, or improve any residential real property, and loans made for manufactured home financing.

(K) Insured loans to finance the purchase of fee simple

Loans insured under section 240 of the National Housing Act [12 U.S.C. § 1715z-5].

(L) Loans to financial institutions, brokers, and dealers

Loans to—

(i) financial institutions with respect to which the United States or an agency or instrumentality thereof has any function of examination or supervision, or

(ii) any broker or dealer registered with the Securities and Exchange Commission,

which are secured by loans, obligations, or investments in which the Federal savings association has the statutory authority to invest directly.

(M) Liquidity investments

Investments (other than equity investments), identified by the Director, for liquidity purposes, including cash, funds on deposit at a Federal reserve bank or a Federal home loan bank, or bankers' acceptances.

(N) Investment in the National Housing Partnership Corporation, partnerships, and joint ventures

Investments in shares of stock issued by a corporation authorized to be created pursuant to title IX of the Housing and Urban Development Act of 1968 [42 U.S.C. § 3931 *et seq.*], and investments in any partnership, limited partnership, or joint venture formed pursuant to section 907(a) or 907(c) of such Act [42 U.S.C. § 3937(a) or (c)].

(O) Certain HUD insured or guaranteed investments

Loans that are secured by mortgages—

(i) insured under title X of the National Housing Act [12 U.S.C. § 1749aa *et seq.*], or

(ii) guaranteed under title IV of the Housing and Urban Development Act of 1968, under part B of the National Urban Policy and New Community Development Act of 1970 [42 U.S.C. § 4511 *et seq.*], or under section 802 of the Housing and Community Development Act of 1974 [42 U.S.C. § 1440].

(P) State housing corporation investments

Obligations of and loans to any State housing corporation, if—

(i) such obligations or loans are secured directly, or indirectly through an agent or fiduciary, by a first lien on improved real estate which is insured under the provisions of the National Housing Act [12 U.S.C. § 1701 *et seq.*], and

(ii) in the event of default, the holder of the obligations or loans has the right directly, or indirectly through an agent or fiduciary, to cause to be subject to the satisfaction of such obligations or loans the real estate described in the first lien or the insurance proceeds under the National Housing Act.

(Q) Investment companies

A Federal savings association may invest in, redeem, or hold shares or certificates issued by any open-end management investment company which—

(i) is registered with the Securities and Exchange Commission under the Investment Company Act of 1940 [15 U.S.C. § 80a-1 *et seq.*], and

(ii) the portfolio of which is restricted by such management company's investment policy (changeable only if authorized by shareholder vote) solely to investments that a Federal savings association by law or regulation may, without limitation as to percentage of assets, invest in, sell, redeem, hold, or otherwise deal in.

(R) Mortgage-backed securities

Investments in securities that—

(i) are offered and sold pursuant to section 4(5) of the Securities Act of 1933 [15 U.S.C. § 77d(5)]; or

(ii) are mortgage related securities (as defined in section 3(a)(41) of the Securities Exchange Act of 1934) [15 U.S.C. § 78c(a)(41)],

subject to such regulations as the Director may prescribe, including regulations prescribing minimum size of the issue (at the time of initial distribution) or minimum aggregate sales price, or both.

(S) Small business related securities

Investments in small business related securities (as defined in section 78c(a)(53) of Title 15), subject to such regulations as the Director may prescribe, including regulations concerning the minimum size of the issue (at the time of the initial distribution), the minimum aggregate sales price, or both.

(T) Credit card loans

Loans made through credit cards or credit card accounts.

(U) Educational loans

Loans made for the payment of educational expenses.

(2) Loans or investments limited to a percentage of assets or capital

The following loans or investments are permitted, but only to the extent specified:

(A) Commercial and other loans

Secured or unsecured loans for commercial, corporate, business, or agricultural purposes. The aggregate amount of loans made under this subparagraph may not exceed 20 percent of the total assets of the Federal savings association, and amounts in excess of 10 percent of such total assets may be used under this subparagraph only for small business loans, as that term is defined by the Director.

(B) Nonresidential real property loans

(i) In general

Loans on the security of liens upon nonresidential real property. Except as provided in clause (ii), the aggregate amount of such loans shall not exceed 400 percent of the Federal savings association's capital, as determined under subsection (t) of this section.

(ii) Exception

The Director may permit a savings association to exceed the limitation set forth in clause (i) if the Director determines that the increased authority—

(I) poses no significant risk to the safe and sound operation of the association, and

(II) is consistent with prudent operating practices.

(iii) Monitoring

If the Director permits any increased authority pursuant to clause (ii), the Director shall closely monitor the Federal savings association's condition and lending activities to ensure that the savings association carries out all authority under this paragraph in a safe and sound manner and complies with this subparagraph and all relevant laws and regulations.

(C) Investments in personal property

Investments in tangible personal property, including vehicles, manufactured homes, machinery, equipment, or furniture, for rental or sale. Investments under this subparagraph may not exceed 10 percent of the assets of the Federal savings association.

(D) Consumer loans and certain securities

A Federal savings association may make loans for personal, family, or household purposes, including loans reasonably incident to providing such credit, and may invest in, sell, or hold commercial paper and corporate debt securities, as defined and approved by the Director. Loans and other investments under this subparagraph may not exceed 35 percent of the assets of the Federal savings association, except that amounts in excess of 30 percent of the assets may be invested only in loans which are made by the association directly to the original obligor and with respect to which the association does not pay any finder, referral, or other fee, directly or indirectly, to any third party.

(3) Loans or investments limited to 5 percent of assets

The following loans or investments are permitted, but not to exceed 5 percent of assets of a Federal savings association for each subparagraph:

(A) Community development investments

Investments in real property and obligations secured by liens on real property located within a geographic area or neighborhood receiving concentrated development assistance by a local government under title I of the Housing and Community Development Act of 1974 [42 U.S.C. § 5301 *et seq.*]. No investment under this subparagraph in such real property may exceed an aggregate of 2 percent of the assets of the Federal savings association.

(B) Nonconforming loans

Loans upon the security of or respecting real property or interests therein used for primarily residential or farm purposes that do not comply with the limitations of this subsection.

(C) Construction loans without security

Loans—

(i) the principal purpose of which is to provide financing with respect to what is or is expected to become primarily residential real estate; and

(ii) with respect to which the association—

(I) relies substantially on the borrower's general credit standing and projected future income for repayment, without other security; or

(II) relies on other assurances for repayment, including a guarantee or similar obligation of a third party.

The aggregate amount of such investments shall not exceed the greater of the Federal savings association's capital or 5 percent of its assets.

(4) Other loans and investments

The following additional loans and other investments to the extent authorized below:

(A) Business development credit corporations

A Federal savings association that is in compliance with the capital standards prescribed under subsection (t) of this section may invest in, lend to, or to[1] commit itself to lend to, any business development credit corporation incorporated in the State in which the home office of the association is located in the same manner and to the same extent as savings associations chartered by such State are authorized. The aggregate amount of such investments, loans, and commitments of any such Federal savings association shall not exceed one-half of 1 percent of the association's total outstanding loans or $250,000, whichever is less.

(B) Service corporations

Investments in the capital stock, obligations, or other securities of any corporation organized under the laws of the State in which the Federal savings association's home office is located, if such corporation's entire capital stock is available for purchase only by savings associations of such State and by Federal associations having their home offices in such State. No Federal savings association may make any investment under this subparagraph if the association's aggregate outstanding investment under this subparagraph would exceed 3 percent of the association's assets. Not less than one-half of the investment permitted under this subparagraph which exceeds 1 percent of the association's assets shall be used primarily for community, inner-city, and community development purposes.

(C) Foreign assistance investments

Investments in housing project loans having the benefit of any guaranty under section 221 of the Foreign Assistance Act of 1961 [22 U.S.C. § 2181] or loans having the benefit of any guarantee under section 224 of such Act [22 U.S.C. § 2184], or any commitment or agreement with respect to such loans made pursuant to either of such sections and in the share capital and capital reserve of the Inter-American Savings and Loan Bank. This authority extends to the acquisition, holding, and disposition of loans guaranteed under section 221 or 222 of such Act [22 U.S.C. § 2181 or 2182]. Investments under this subparagraph shall not exceed 1 percent of the Federal savings association's assets.

(D) Small business investment companies

A Federal savings association may invest in stock, obligations, or other securities of any small business investment company formed pursuant to section 301(d) of the Small Business Investment Act of 1958 [15 U.S.C. § 681(d)] for the purpose of aiding members of a Federal home loan bank. A Federal savings association may not make any investment under this subparagraph if its aggregate outstanding investment under this subparagraph would exceed 1 percent of the assets of such savings association.

(E) Bankers' banks

A Federal savings association may purchase for its own account shares of stock of a bankers' bank, described in Paragraph Seventh of section 24 of this title or in section 27(b) of this title, on the same terms and conditions as a national bank may purchase such shares.

---

1 So in original.

(F) New markets venture capital companies

A Federal savings association may invest in stock, obligations, or other securities of any New Markets Venture Capital company as defined in section 689 of Title 15, except that a Federal savings association may not make any investment under this subparagraph if its aggregate outstanding investment under this subparagraph would exceed 5 percent of the capital and surplus of such savings association.

(5) Transition rule for savings associations acquiring banks

(A) In general

If, under section 5(d)(3) of the Federal Deposit Insurance Act [12 U.S.C. § 1815(d)(3)], a savings association acquires all or substantially all of the assets of a bank that is a member of the Bank Insurance Fund, the Director may permit the savings association to retain any such asset during the 2-year period beginning on the date of the acquisition.

(B) Extension

The Director may extend the 2-year period described in subparagraph (A) for not more than 1 year at a time and not more than 2 years in the aggregate, if the Director determines that the extension is consistent with the purposes of this chapter.

(6) Definitions

As used in this subsection—

(A) Residential property

The terms "residential real property" or "residential real estate" mean leaseholds, homes (including condominiums and cooperatives, except that in connection with loans on individual cooperative units, such loans shall be adequately secured as defined by the Director) and, combinations of homes or dwelling units and business property, involving only minor or incidental business use, or property to be improved by construction of such structures.

(B) Loans

The term "loans" includes obligations and extensions or advances of credit; and any reference to a loan or investment includes an interest in such a loan or investment.

(d) Regulatory authority

(1) In general

(A) Enforcement

The Director shall have power to enforce this section, section 8 of the Federal Deposit Insurance Act [12 U.S.C. § 1818], and regulations prescribed hereunder. In enforcing any provision of this section, regulations prescribed under this section, or any other law or regulation, or in any other action, suit, or proceeding to which the Director is a party or in which the Director is interested, and in the administration of conservatorships and receiverships, the Director may act in the Director's own name and through the Director's own attorneys. Except as otherwise provided, the Director shall be subject to suit (other than suits on claims for money damages) by any Federal savings association or director or officer thereof with respect to any matter under this section or any other applicable law, or regulation thereunder, in the United States district court for the judicial district in which the savings association's home office is located, or in the United States District Court for the District of Columbia, and the Director may be served with process in the manner prescribed by the Federal Rules of Civil Procedure.

(B) Ancillary provisions

(i) In making examinations of savings associations, examiners appointed by the Director shall have power to make such examinations of the affairs of all affiliates of such savings associations as shall be necessary to disclose fully the relations between such savings associations and their affiliates and the effect of such relations upon such savings associations. For purposes of this subsection, the term "affiliate" has the same meaning as in section 2(b) of the Banking Act of 1933 [12 U.S.C. § 221a(b)], except that the term "member bank" in section 2(b) shall be deemed to refer to a savings association.

(ii) In the course of any examination of any savings association, upon request by the Director, prompt and complete access shall be given to all savings association officers, directors, employees, and agents, and to all relevant books, records, or documents of any type.

(iii) Upon request made in the course of supervision or oversight of any savings association, for the purpose of acting on any application or determining the condition of any savings association, including whether operations are being conducted safely, soundly, or in compliance with charters, laws, regulations, directives, written agreements, or conditions imposed in writing in connection with the granting of an application or other request, the Director shall be given prompt and complete access to all savings association officers, directors, employees, and agents, and to all relevant books, records, or documents of any type.

(iv) If prompt and complete access upon request is not given as required in this subsection, the Director may apply to the United States district court for the judicial district (or the United States court in any territory) in which the principal office of the institution is located, or in which the person denying such access resides or carries on business, for an order requiring that such information be promptly provided.

(v) In connection with examinations of savings associations and affiliates thereof, the Director may—

(I) administer oaths and affirmations and examine and to[2] take and preserve testimony under oath as to any matter in respect of the affairs or ownership of any such savings association or affiliate, and

(II) issue subpenas and, for the enforcement thereof, apply to the United States district court for the judicial district (or the United States court in any territory) in which the principal office of the savings association or affiliate is located, or in which the witness resides or carries on business.

Such courts shall have jurisdiction and power to order and require compliance with any such subpena.

(vi) In any proceeding under this section, the Director may administer oaths and affirmations, take depositions, and issue subpenas. The Director may prescribe regulations with respect to any such proceedings. The attendance of witnesses and the production of documents provided for in this subsection may be required from any place in any State or in any territory at any designated place where such proceeding is being conducted.

(vii) Any party to a proceeding under this section may apply to the United States District Court for the District of Columbia, or the United States district court for the judicial district (or the United States court in any territory) in which such

---

2 So in original.

proceeding is being conducted, or where the witness resides or carries on business, for enforcement of any subpena issued pursuant to this subsection or section 10(c) of the Federal Deposit Insurance Act [12 U.S.C. § 1820(c)], and such courts shall have jurisdiction and power to order and require compliance therewith. Witnesses subpenaed under this section shall be paid the same fees and mileage that are paid witnesses in the district courts of the United States. All expenses of the Director in connection with this section shall be considered as nonadministrative expenses. Any court having jurisdiction of any proceeding instituted under this section by a savings association, or a director or officer thereof, may allow to any such party reasonable expenses and attorneys' fees. Such expenses and fees shall be paid by the savings association.

(2) Conservatorships and receiverships

(A) Grounds for appointing conservator or receiver for insured savings association

The Director of the Office of Thrift Supervision may appoint a conservator or receiver for any insured savings association if the Director determines, in the Director's discretion, that 1 or more of the grounds specified in section 11(c)(5) of the Federal Deposit Insurance Act [12 U.S.C. § 1821(c)(5)] exists.

(B) Power of appointment; judicial review

The Director shall have exclusive power and jurisdiction to appoint a conservator or receiver for a Federal savings association. If, in the opinion of the Director, a ground for the appointment of a conservator or receiver for a savings association exists, the Director is authorized to appoint ex parte and without notice a conservator or receiver for the savings association. In the event of such appointment, the association may, within 30 days thereafter, bring an action in the United States district court for the judicial district in which the home office of such association is located, or in the United States District Court for the District of Columbia, for an order requiring the Director to remove such conservator or receiver, and the court shall upon the merits dismiss such action or direct the Director to remove such conservator or receiver. Upon the commencement of such an action, the court having jurisdiction of any other action or proceeding authorized under this subsection to which the association is a party shall stay such action or proceeding during the pendency of the action for removal of the conservator or receiver.

(C) Replacement

The Director may, without any prior notice, hearing, or other action, replace a conservator with another conservator or with a receiver, but such replacement shall not affect any right which the association may have to obtain judicial review of the original appointment, except that any removal under this subparagraph shall be removal of the conservator or receiver in office at the time of such removal.

(D) Court action

Except as otherwise provided in this subsection, no court may take any action for or toward the removal of any conservator or receiver or, except at the request of the Director, to restrain or affect the exercise of powers or functions of a conservator or receiver.

(E) Powers

(i) In general

A conservator shall have all the powers of the members, the

stockholders, the directors, and the officers of the association and shall be authorized to operate the association in its own name or to conserve its assets in the manner and to the extent authorized by the Director.

(ii) FDIC or RTC as conservator or receiver

Except as provided in section 21A of the Federal Home Loan Bank Act [12 U.S.C. § 1441a], the Director, at the Director's discretion, may appoint the Federal Deposit Insurance Corporation or the Resolution Trust Corporation, as appropriate, as conservator for a savings association. The Director shall appoint only the Federal Deposit Insurance Corporation or the Resolution Trust Corporation, as appropriate, as receiver for a savings association for the purpose of liquidation or winding up the affairs of such savings association. The conservator or receiver so appointed shall, as such, have power to buy at its own sale. The Federal Deposit Insurance Corporation, as such conservator or receiver, shall have all the powers of a conservator or receiver, as appropriate, granted under the Federal Deposit Insurance Act [12 U.S.C. § 1811 *et seq.*], and (when not inconsistent therewith) any other rights, powers, and privileges possessed by conservators or receivers, as appropriate, of savings associations under this chapter and any other provisions of law.

(F) Disclosure requirement for those acting on behalf of conservator

A conservator shall require that any independent contractor, consultant, or counsel employed by the conservator in connection with the conservatorship of a savings association pursuant to this section shall fully disclose to all parties with which such contractor, consultant, or counsel is negotiating, any limitation on the authority of such contractor, consultant, or counsel to make legally binding representations on behalf of the conservator.

(3) Regulations

(A) In general

The Director may prescribe regulations for the reorganization, consolidation, liquidation, and dissolution of savings associations, for the merger of insured savings associations with insured savings associations, for savings associations in conservatorship and receivership, and for the conduct of conservatorships and receiverships. The Director may, by regulation or otherwise, provide for the exercise of functions by members, stockholders, directors, or officers of a savings association during conservatorship and receivership.

(B) FDIC or RTC as conservator or receiver

In any case where the Federal Deposit Insurance Corporation or the Resolution Trust Corporation is the conservator or receiver, any regulations prescribed by the Director shall be consistent with any regulations prescribed by the Federal Deposit Insurance Corporation pursuant to the Federal Deposit Insurance Act [12 U.S.C. § 1811 *et seq.*].

(4) Refusal to comply with demand

Whenever a conservator or receiver appointed by the Director demands possession of the property, business, and assets of any savings association, or of any part thereof, the refusal by any director, officer, employee, or agent of such association to comply with the demand shall be punishable by a fine of not more than $5,000 or imprisonment for not more than one year, or both.

(5) "Savings association" defined

As used in this subsection, the term "savings association" includes any savings association or former savings association that retains deposits insured by the Corporation, notwithstanding termination of its status as an institution insured by the Corporation.

(6) Compliance with monetary transaction recordkeeping and report requirements

(A) Compliance procedures required

The Director shall prescribe regulations requiring savings associations to establish and maintain procedures reasonably designed to assure and monitor the compliance of such associations with the requirements of subchapter II of chapter 53 of Title 31.

(B) Examinations of savings associations to include review of compliance procedures

(i) In general

Each examination of a savings association by the Director shall include a review of the procedures required to be established and maintained under subparagraph (A).

(ii) Exam report requirement

The report of examination shall describe any problem with the procedures maintained by the association.

(C) Order to comply with requirements

If the Director determines that a savings association—

(i) has failed to establish and maintain the procedures described in subparagraph (A); or

(ii) has failed to correct any problem with the procedures maintained by such association which was previously reported to the association by the Director,

the Director shall issue an order under section 8 of the Federal Deposit Insurance Act [12 U.S.C. § 1818] requiring such association to cease and desist from its violation of this paragraph or regulations prescribed under this paragraph.

(7) Regulation and examination of savings association service companies, subsidiaries, and service providers

(A) General examination and regulatory authority

A service company or subsidiary that is owned in whole or in part by a savings association shall be subject to examination and regulation by the Director to the same extent as that savings association.

(B) Examination by other banking agencies

The Director may authorize any other Federal banking agency that supervises any other owner of part of the service company or subsidiary to perform an examination described in subparagraph (A).

(C) Applicability of section 8 of the Federal Deposit Insurance Act

A service company or subsidiary that is owned in whole or in part by a saving association shall be subject to the provisions of section 8 of the Federal Deposit Insurance Act [12 U.S.C. § 1818] as if the service company or subsidiary were an insured depository institution. In any such case, the Director shall be deemed to be the appropriate Federal banking agency, pursuant to section 3(q) of the Federal Deposit Insurance Act [12 U.S.C. § 1813(q)].

(D) Service performed by contract or otherwise

Notwithstanding subparagraph (A), if a savings association, a subsidiary thereof, or any savings and loan affiliate or entity, as identified by section 8(b)(9) of the Federal Deposit Insurance Act [12 U.S.C. § 1818(b)(9)], that is regularly examined or subject to examination by the Director, causes to be performed for itself, by contract or otherwise, any service authorized under this chapter or, in the case of a State savings association, any applicable State law, whether on or off its premises—

(i) such performance shall be subject to regulation and ex-

amination by the Director to the same extent as if such services were being performed by the savings association on its own premises; and

(ii) the savings association shall notify the Director of the existence of the service relationship not later than 30 days after the earlier of—

(I) the date on which the contract is entered into; or

(II) the date on which the performance of the service is initiated.

(E) Administration by the director

The Director may issue such regulations and orders, including those issued pursuant to section 8 of the Federal Deposit Insurance Act [12 U.S.C. § 1818], as may be necessary to enable the Director to administer and carry out this paragraph and to prevent evasion of this paragraph.

(8) Definitions

For purposes of this section—

(A) the term "service company" means

(i) any corporation—

(I) that is organized to perform services authorized by this chapter or, in the case of a corporation owned in part by a State savings association, authorized by applicable State law; and

(II) all of the capital stock of which is owned by 1 or more insured savings associations; and

(ii) any limited liability company—

(I) that is organized to perform services authorized by this chapter or, in the case of a company, 1 of the members of which is a State savings association, authorized by applicable State law; and

(II) all of the members of which are 1 or more insured savings associations;

(B) the term "limited liability company" means any company, partnership, trust, or similar business entity organized under the law of a State (as defined in section 3 of the Federal Deposit Insurance Act [12 U.S.C. § 1813]) that provides that a member or manager of such company is not personally liable for a debt, obligation, or liability of the company solely by reason of being, or acting as, a member or manager of such company; and

(C) the terms "State savings association" and "subsidiary" have the same meanings as in section 3 of the Federal Deposit Insurance Act.

(e) Character and responsibility

A charter may be granted only—

(1) to persons of good character and responsibility,

(2) if in the judgment of the Director a necessity exists for such an institution in the community to be served,

(3) if there is a reasonable probability of its usefulness and success, and

(4) if the association can be established without undue injury to properly conducted existing local thrift and home financing institutions.

(f) Federal Home Loan Bank membership

After the end of the 6-month period beginning on November 12, 1999, a Federal savings association may become a member of the Federal Home Loan Bank System, and shall qualify for such membership in the manner provided by the Federal Home Loan Bank Act [12 U.S.C. § 1421 *et seq.*].

(g) Preferred shares

Repealed. Pub. L. No. 101-73, tit. III, § 301, 103 Stat. 282 (Aug. 9, 1989)

(h) Discriminatory State and local taxation prohibited

No State, county, municipal, or local taxing authority may impose any tax on Federal savings associations or their franchise, capital, reserves, surplus, loans, or income greater than that imposed by such authority on other similar local mutual or cooperative thrift and home financing institutions.

(*i*) Conversions

(1) In general

Any savings association which is, or is eligible to become, a member of a Federal home loan bank may convert into a Federal savings association (and in so doing may change directly from the mutual form to the stock form, or from the stock form to the mutual form). Such conversion shall be subject to such regulations as the Director shall prescribe. Thereafter such Federal savings association shall be entitled to all the benefits of this section and shall be subject to examination and regulation to the same extent as other associations incorporated pursuant to this chapter.

(2) Authority of Director

(A) No savings association may convert from the mutual to the stock form, or from the stock form to the mutual form, except in accordance with the regulations of the Director.

(B) Any aggrieved person may obtain review of a final action of the Director which approves or disapproves a plan of conversion pursuant to this subsection only by complying with the provisions of section 1467a(j) of this title within the time limit and in the manner therein prescribed, which provisions shall apply in all respects as if such final action were an order the review of which is therein provided for, except that such time limit shall commence upon publication of notice of such final action in the Federal Register or upon the giving of such general notice of such final action as is required by or approved under regulations of the Director, whichever is later.

(C) Any Federal savings association may change its designation from a Federal savings association to a Federal savings bank, or the reverse.

(3) Conversion to State association

(A) Any Federal savings association may convert itself into a savings association or savings bank organized pursuant to the laws of the State in which the principal office of such Federal savings association is located if—

(i) the State permits the conversion of any savings association or savings bank of such State into a Federal savings association;

(ii) such conversion of a Federal savings association into such a State savings association is determined—

(I) upon the vote in favor of such conversion cast in person or by proxy at a special meeting of members or stockholders called to consider such action, specified by the law of the State in which the home office of the Federal savings association is located, as required by such law for a State-chartered institution to convert itself into a Federal savings association, but in no event upon a vote of less than 51 percent of all the votes cast at such meeting, and

(II) upon compliance with other requirements reciprocally equivalent to the requirements of such State law for the conversion of a State-chartered institution into a Federal savings association;

(iii) notice of the meeting to vote on conversion shall be given as herein provided and no other notice thereof shall be necessary; the notice shall expressly state that such meeting is called to vote thereon, as well as the time and place thereof; and such notice shall be mailed, postage prepaid, at least 30 and not more than 60 days prior to the date of the meeting, to the Director and to each member or stockholder of record of the Federal savings association at the member's or stockholder's last address as shown on the books of the Federal savings association;

(iv) when a mutual savings association is dissolved after conversion, the members or shareholders of the savings association will share on a mutual basis in the assets of the association in exact proportion to their relative share or account credits;

(v) when a stock savings association is dissolved after conversion, the stockholders will share on an equitable basis in the assets of the association; and

(vi) such conversion shall be effective upon the date that all the provisions of this chapter shall have been fully complied with and upon the issuance of a new charter by the State wherein the savings association is located.

(B)

(i) The act of conversion constitutes consent by the institution to be bound by all the requirements that the Director may impose under this chapter.

(ii) The savings association shall upon conversion and thereafter be authorized to issue securities in any form currently approved at the time of issue by the Director for issuance by similar savings associations in such State.

(iii) If the insurance of accounts is terminated in connection with such conversion, the notice and other action shall be taken as provided by law and regulations for the termination of insurance of accounts.

(4) Savings bank activities

(A) To the extent authorized by the Director, but subject to section 18(m)(3) of the Federal Deposit Insurance Act [12 U.S.C. § 1828(m)(3)]—

(i) any Federal savings bank chartered as such prior to October 15, 1982, may continue to make any investment or engage in any activity not otherwise authorized under this section, to the degree it was permitted to do so as a Federal savings bank prior to October 15, 1982; and

(ii) any Federal savings bank in existence on August 9, 1989, and formerly organized as a mutual savings bank under State law may continue to make any investment or engage in any activity not otherwise authorized under this section, to the degree it was authorized to do so as a mutual savings bank under State law.

(B) The authority conferred by this paragraph may be utilized by any Federal savings association that acquires, by merger or consolidation, a Federal savings bank enjoying grandfather rights hereunder.

(5) Conversion to national or State bank

(A) In general

Any Federal savings association chartered and in operation before November 12, 1999, with branches in operation before November 12, 1999, in 1 or more States, may convert, at its option, with the approval of the Comptroller of the Currency or the appropriate State bank supervisor, into 1 or more national or State banks, each of which may encompass 1 or more of the branches of the Federal savings association in operation before November 12, 1999, in 1 or more States, but only if each resulting national or State bank will meet all financial, management, and capital requirements applicable to the resulting national or State bank.

(B) Definitions

For purposes of this paragraph, the terms "State bank" and "State bank supervisor" have the meanings given those terms in section 3 of the Federal Deposit Insurance Act [12 U.S.C. § 1813].

(j) Subscription for shares

Repealed. Pub. L. No. 101-73, tit. III, 1989, 103 Stat. 282 (Aug. 9, 1989)

(k) Depository of public money

When designated for that purpose by the Secretary of the Treasury, a savings association the deposits of which are insured by the Corporation shall be a depository of public money and may be employed as fiscal agent of the Government under such regulations as may be prescribed by the Secretary and shall perform all such reasonable duties as fiscal agent of the Government as may be required of it. A savings association the deposits of which are insured by the Corporation may act as agent for any other instrumentality of the United States when designated for that purpose by such instrumentality, including services in connection with the collection of taxes and other obligations owed the United States, and the Secretary of the Treasury may deposit public money in any such savings association, and shall prescribe such regulations as may be necessary to carry out the purposes of this subsection.

(*l*) Retirement accounts

A Federal savings association is authorized to act as trustee of any trust created or organized in the United States and forming part of a stock bonus, pension, or profit-sharing plan which qualifies or qualified for specific tax treatment under section 401(d) of the Internal Revenue Code of 1986 [26 U.S.C. § 401(d)] and to act as trustee or custodian of an individual retirement account within the meaning of section 408 of such Code [26 U.S.C. § 408] if the funds of such trust or account are invested only in savings accounts or deposits in such Federal savings association or in obligations or securities issued by such Federal savings association. All funds held in such fiduciary capacity by any Federal savings association may be commingled for appropriate purposes of investment, but individual records shall be kept by the fiduciary for each participant and shall show in proper detail all transactions engaged in under this paragraph.

(m) Branching

(1) In general

(A) No savings association incorporated under the laws of the District of Columbia or organized in the District or doing business in the District shall establish any branch or move its principal office or any branch without the Director's prior written approval.

(B) No savings association shall establish any branch in the District of Columbia or move its principal office or any branch in the District without the Director's prior written approval.

(2) "Branch" defined

For purposes of this subsection the term "branch" means any office, place of business, or facility, other than the principal office as defined by the Director, of a savings association at which accounts are opened or payments are received or withdrawals are made, or any other office, place of business, or facility of a savings association defined by the Director as a branch within the meaning of such sentence.

(n) Trusts

(1) Permits

The Director may grant by special permit to a Federal savings association applying therefor the right to act as trustee, executor, administrator, guardian, or in any other fiduciary capacity in which State banks, trust companies, or other corporations which compete with Federal savings associations are permitted to act under the laws of the State in which the Federal savings association is located. Subject to the regulations of the Director, service corporations may invest in State or federally chartered corporations which are located in the State in which the home office of the Federal savings association is located and which are engaged in trust activities.

(2) Segregation of assets

A Federal savings association exercising any or all of the powers enumerated in this section shall segregate all assets held in any fiduciary capacity from the general assets of the association and shall keep a separate set of books and records showing in proper detail all transactions engaged in under this subsection. The State banking authority involved may have access to reports of examination made by the Director insofar as such reports relate to the trust department of such association but nothing in this subsection shall be construed as authorizing such State banking authority to examine the books, records, and assets of such associations.

(3) Prohibitions

No Federal savings association shall receive in its trust department deposits of current funds subject to check or the deposit of checks, drafts, bills of exchange, or other items for collection or exchange purposes. Funds deposited or held in trust by the association awaiting investment shall be carried in a separate account and shall not be used by the association in the conduct of its business unless it shall first set aside in the trust department United States bonds or other securities approved by the Director.

(4) Separate lien

In the event of the failure of a Federal savings association, the owners of the funds held in trust for investment shall have a lien on the bonds or other securities so set apart in addition to their claim against the estate of the association.

(5) Deposits

Whenever the laws of a State require corporations acting in a fiduciary capacity to deposit securities with the State authorities for the protection of private or court trusts, Federal savings associations so acting shall be required to make similar deposits. Securities so deposited shall be held for the protection of private or court trusts, as provided by the State law. Federal savings associations in such cases shall not be required to execute the bond usually required of individuals if State corporations under similar circumstances are exempt from this requirement. Federal savings associations shall have power to execute such bond when so required by the laws of the State involved.

(6) Oaths and affidavits

In any case in which the laws of a State require that a corporation acting as trustee, executor, administrator, or in any capacity specified in this section, shall take an oath or make an affidavit, the president, vice president, cashier, or trust officer of such association may take the necessary oath or execute the necessary affidavit.

(7) Certain loans prohibited

It shall be unlawful for any Federal savings association to lend any officer, director, or employee any funds held in trust under the powers conferred by this section. Any officer, director, or employee making such loan, or to whom such loan is made, may be fined not more than $50,000 or twice the amount of that person's gain from the loan, whichever is greater, or may be imprisoned not more than 5 years, or may be both fined and imprisoned, in the discretion of the court.

(8) Factors to be considered

In reviewing applications for permission to exercise the powers enumerated in this section, the Director may consider—

(A) the amount of capital of the applying Federal savings association,

(B) whether or not such capital is sufficient under the circumstances of the case,

(C) the needs of the community to be served, and

(D) any other facts and circumstances that seem to it proper.

The Director may grant or refuse the application accordingly, except that no permit shall be issued to any association having capital less than the capital required by State law of State banks, trust companies, and corporations exercising such powers.

(9) Surrender of charter

(A) Any Federal savings association may surrender its right to exercise the powers granted under this subsection, and have returned to it any securities which it may have deposited with the State authorities, by filing with the Director a certified copy of a resolution of its board of directors indicating its intention to surrender its right.

(B) Upon receipt of such resolution, the Director, if satisfied that such Federal savings association has been relieved in accordance with State law of all duties as trustee, executor, administrator, guardian or other fiduciary, may in the Director's discretion, issue to such association a certificate that such association is no longer authorized to exercise the powers granted by this subsection.

(C) Upon the issuance of such a certificate by the Director, such Federal savings association

(i) shall no longer be subject to the provisions of this section or the regulations of the Director made pursuant thereto,

(ii) shall be entitled to have returned to it any securities which it may have deposited with State authorities, and

(iii) shall not exercise thereafter any of the powers granted by this section without first applying for and obtaining a new permit to exercise such powers pursuant to the provisions of this section.

(D) The Director may prescribe regulations necessary to enforce compliance with the provisions of this subsection.

(10) Revocation

(A) In addition to the authority conferred by other law, if, in the opinion of the Director, a Federal savings association is unlawfully or unsoundly exercising, or has unlawfully or unsoundly exercised, or has failed for a period of 5 consecutive years to exercise, the powers granted by this subsection or otherwise fails or has failed to comply with the requirements of this subsection, the Director may issue and serve upon the association a notice of intent to revoke the authority of the association to exercise the powers granted by this subsection. The notice shall contain a statement of the facts constituting the alleged unlawful or unsound exercise of powers, or failure to exercise powers, or failure to comply, and shall fix a time and place at which a hearing will be held to determine whether an order revoking authority to exercise such powers should issue against the association.

(B) Such hearing shall be conducted in accordance with the provisions of subsection (d)(1)(B) of this section, and subject to judicial review as therein provided, and shall be fixed for a date not earlier than 30 days and not later than 60 days after service of such notice unless the Director sets an earlier or later date at the request of any Federal savings association so served.

(C) Unless the Federal savings association so served shall appear at the hearing by a duly authorized representative, it shall be deemed to have consented to the issuance of the revocation order. In the event of such consent, or if upon the record made at any such hearing, the Director shall find that any allegation specified in the notice of charges has been established, the Director may issue and serve upon the association an order prohibiting it from accepting any new or additional trust accounts and revoking authority to exercise any and all powers granted by this subsection, except that such order shall permit the association to continue to service all previously accepted trust accounts pending their expeditious divestiture or termination.

(D) A revocation order shall become effective not earlier than the expiration of 30 days after service of such order upon the association so served (except in the case of a revocation order issued upon consent, which shall become effective at the time specified therein), and shall remain effective and enforceable, except to such extent as it is stayed, modified, terminated, or set aside by action of the Director or a reviewing court.

(o) Conversion of State savings banks

(1) Subject to the provisions of this subsection and under regulations of the Director, the Director may authorize the conversion of a State-chartered savings bank that is a Bank Insurance Fund member into a Federal savings bank, if such conversion is not in contravention of State law, and provide for the organization, incorporation, operation, examination, and regulation of such institution.

(2)

(A) Any Federal savings bank chartered pursuant to this subsection shall continue to be a Bank Insurance Fund member until such time as it changes its status to a Savings Association Insurance Fund member.

(B) The Director shall notify the Corporation of any application under this chapter for conversion to a Federal charter by an institution insured by the Corporation, shall consult with the Corporation before disposing of the application, and shall notify the Corporation of the Director's determination with respect to such application.

(C) Notwithstanding any other provision of law, if the Corporation determines that conversion into a Federal stock savings bank or the chartering of a Federal stock savings bank is necessary to prevent the default of a savings bank it insures or to reopen a savings bank in default that it insured, or if the Corporation determines, with the concurrence of the Director, that severe financial conditions exist that threaten the stability of a savings bank insured by the Corporation and that such a conversion or charter is likely to improve the financial condition of such savings bank, the Corporation shall provide the Director with a certificate of such determination, the reasons therefor in conformance with the requirements of this chapter, and the bank shall be converted or chartered by the Director, pursuant to the regulations thereof, from the time the Corporation issues the certificate.

(D) A bank may be converted under subparagraph (C) only if the board of trustees of the bank—

(i) has specified in writing that the bank is in danger of closing or is closed, or that severe financial conditions exist that threaten the stability of the bank and a conversion is likely to improve the financial condition of the bank; and

(ii) has requested in writing that the Corporation use the authority of subparagraph (C).

(E)

(i) Before making a determination under subparagraph (D), the Corporation shall consult the State bank supervisor of the State in which the bank in danger of closing is chartered. The State bank supervisor shall be given a reasonable opportunity, and in no event less than 48 hours, to object to the use of the provisions of subparagraph (D).

(ii) If the State supervisor objects during such period, the Corporation may use the authority of subparagraph (D) only by an affirmative vote of three- fourths of the Board of Directors. The Board of Directors shall provide the State supervisor, as soon as practicable, with a written certification of its determination.

(3) A Federal savings bank chartered under this subsection shall have the same authority with respect to investments, operations, and activities, and shall be subject to the same restrictions, including those applicable to branching and discrimination, as would apply to it if it were chartered as a Federal savings bank under any other provision of this chapter.

(p) Conversions

(1) Notwithstanding any other provision of law, and consistent with the purposes of this chapter, the Director may authorize (or in the case of a Federal savings association, require) the conversion of any mutual savings association or Federal mutual savings bank that is insured by the Corporation into a Federal stock savings association or Federal stock savings bank, or charter a Federal stock savings association or Federal stock savings bank to acquire the assets of, or merge with such a mutual institution under the regulations of the Director.

(2) Authorizations under this subsection may be made only—

(A) if the Director has determined that severe financial conditions exist which threaten the stability of an association and that such authorization is likely to improve the financial condition of the association,

(B) when the Corporation has contracted to provide assistance to such association under section 13 of the Federal Deposit Insurance Act [12 U.S.C. § 1823], or

(C) to assist an institution in receivership.

(3) A Federal savings bank chartered under this subsection shall have the same authority with respect to investments, operations and activities, and shall be subject to the same restrictions, including those applicable to branching and discrimination, as would apply to it if it were chartered as a Federal savings bank under any other provision of this chapter, and may engage in any investment, activity, or operation that the institution it acquired was engaged in if that institution was a Federal savings bank, or would have been authorized to engage in had that institution converted to a Federal charter.

(q) Tying arrangements

(1) A savings association may not in any manner extend credit, lease, or sell property of any kind, or furnish any service, or fix or vary the consideration for any of the foregoing, on the condition or requirement—

(A) that the customer shall obtain additional credit, property, or service from such savings association, or from any service corporation or affiliate of such association, other than a loan, discount, deposit, or trust service;

(B) that the customer provide additional credit, property, or service to such association, or to any service corporation or affiliate of such association, other than those related to and usually provided in connection with a similar loan, discount, deposit, or trust service; and

(C) that the customer shall not obtain some other credit, property, or service from a competitor of such association, or from a competitor of any service corporation or affiliate of such association, other than a condition or requirement that such association shall reasonably impose in connection with credit transactions to assure the soundness of credit.

(2)

(A) Any person may sue for and have injunctive relief, in any court of the United States having jurisdiction over the parties, against threatened loss or damage by reason of a violation of paragraph (1), under the same conditions and principles as injunctive relief against threatened conduct that will cause loss or damage is granted by courts of equity and under the rules governing such proceedings.

(B) Upon the execution of proper bond against damages for an injunction improvidently granted and a showing that the danger of irreparable loss or damage is immediate, a preliminary injunction may issue.

(3) Any person injured by a violation of paragraph (1) may bring an action in any district court of the United States in which the defendant resides or is found or has an agent, without regard to the amount in controversy, or in any other court of competent jurisdiction, and shall be entitled to recover three times the amount of the damages sustained, and the cost of suit, including a reasonable attorney's fee. Any such action shall be brought within 4 years from the date of the occurrence of the violation.

(4) Nothing contained in this subsection affects in any manner the right of the United States or any other party to bring an action under any other law of the United States or of any State, including any right which may exist in addition to specific statutory authority, challenging the legality of any act or practice which may be proscribed by this subsection. No regulation or order issued by the Director under this subsection shall in any manner constitute a defense to such action.

(5) For purposes of this subsection, the term "loan" includes obligations and extensions or advances of credit.

(6) Exceptions

The Director may, by regulation or order, permit such exceptions to the prohibitions of this subsection as the Director considers will not be contrary to the purposes of this subsection and which conform to exceptions granted by the Board of Governors of the Federal Reserve System pursuant to section 1972 of this title.

(r) Out-of-State branches

(1) No Federal savings association may establish, retain, or operate a branch outside the State in which the Federal savings association has its home office, unless the association qualifies as a domestic building and loan association under section 7701(a)(19) of the Internal Revenue Code of 1986 [26 U.S.C. § 7701(a)(19)] or meets the asset composition test imposed by subparagraph (C) of that section on institutions seeking so to qualify, or qualifies as a qualified thrift lender, as determined under section 1467a(m) of this title. No out-of-State branch so established shall be retained or operated unless the total assets of the Federal savings association attributable to all branches of the Federal savings association in that State would qualify the branches as a whole, were they otherwise eligible, for treatment as a domestic building and loan association under section 7701(a)(19) or as a qualified thrift lender, as determined under section 1467a(m) of this title, as applicable.

(2) The limitations of paragraph (1) shall not apply if—

(A) the branch results from a transaction authorized under section 13(k) of the Federal Deposit Insurance Act [12 U.S.C. § 1823(k)];

(B) the branch was authorized for the Federal savings association prior to October 15, 1982;

(C) the law of the State where the branch is located, or is to be located, would permit establishment of the branch if the association was a savings association or savings bank chartered by the State in which its home office is located; or

(D) the branch was operated lawfully as a branch under State law prior to the association's conversion to a Federal charter.

(3) The Director, for good cause shown, may allow Federal savings associations up to 2 years to comply with the requirements of this subsection.

(s) Minimum capital requirements

(1) In general

Consistent with the purposes of section 908 of the International Lending Supervision Act of 1983 [12 U.S.C. § 3907] and the capital requirements established pursuant to such section by the appropriate Federal banking agencies (as defined in section 903(1) of such Act [12 U.S.C. § 3902(1)]), the Director shall require all savings associations to achieve and maintain adequate capital by—

(A) establishing minimum levels of capital for savings associations; and

(B) using such other methods as the Director determines to be appropriate.

(2) Minimum capital levels may be determined by Director case-by-case

The Director may, consistent with subsection (t) of this section, establish the minimum level of capital for a savings association at such amount or at such ratio of capital-to-assets as the Director determines to be necessary or appropriate for such association in light of the particular circumstances of the association.

(3) Unsafe or unsound practice

In the Director's discretion, the Director may treat the failure of any savings association to maintain capital at or above the mini-mum level required by the Director under this subsection or subsection (t) of this section as an unsafe or unsound practice.

(4) Directive to increase capital

(A) Plan may be required

In addition to any other action authorized by law, including paragraph (3), the Director may issue a directive requiring any savings association which fails to maintain capital at or above the minimum level required by the Director to submit and adhere to a plan for increasing capital which is acceptable to the Director.

(B) Enforcement of plan

Any directive issued and plan approved under subparagraph (A) shall be enforceable under section 8 of the Federal Deposit Insurance Act [12 U.S.C. § 1818] to the same extent and in the same manner as an outstanding order which was issued under section 8 of the Federal Deposit Insurance Act and has become final.

(5) Plan taken into account in other proceedings

The Director may—

(A) consider a savings association's progress in adhering to any plan required under paragraph (4) whenever such association or any affiliate of such association (including any company which controls such association) seeks the Director's approval for any proposal which would have the effect of diverting earnings, diminishing capital, or otherwise impeding such association's progress in meeting the minimum level of capital required by the Director; and

(B) disapprove any proposal referred to in subparagraph (A) if the Director determines that the proposal would adversely affect the ability of the association to comply with such plan.

(t) Capital standards

(1) In general

(A) Requirement for standards to be prescribed

The Director shall, by regulation, prescribe and maintain uniformly applicable capital standards for savings associations. Those standards shall include—

(i) a leverage limit;

(ii) a tangible capital requirement; and

(iii) a risk-based capital requirement.

(B) Compliance

A savings association is not in compliance with capital standards for purposes of this subsection unless it complies with all capital standards prescribed under this paragraph.

(C) Stringency

The standards prescribed under this paragraph shall be no less stringent than the capital standards applicable to national banks.

(D) Deadline for regulations

The Director shall promulgate final regulations under this paragraph not later than 90 days after August 9, 1989, and those regulations shall become effective not later than 120 days after August 9, 1989.

(2) Content of standards

(A) Leverage limit

The leverage limit prescribed under paragraph (1) shall require a savings association to maintain core capital in an amount not less than 3 percent of the savings association's total assets.

(B) Tangible capital requirement

The tangible capital requirement prescribed under paragraph (1) shall require a savings association to maintain tangible capital in an amount not less than 1.5 percent of the savings association's total assets.

(C) Risk-based capital requirement

Notwithstanding paragraph (1)(C), the risk-based capital requirement prescribed under paragraph (1) may deviate from the risk-based capital standards applicable to national banks to reflect interest-rate risk or other risks, but such deviations shall not, in the aggregate, result in materially lower levels of capital being required of savings associations under the risk-based capital requirement than would be required under the risk-based capital standards applicable to national banks.

(3) Transition rule

(A) Certain qualifying supervisory goodwill included in calculating core capital

Notwithstanding paragraph (9)(A), an eligible savings association may include qualifying supervisory goodwill in calculating core capital. The amount of qualifying supervisory goodwill that may be included may not exceed the applicable percentage of total assets set forth in the following table:

For the following period:	The applicable percentage is:
Prior to January 1, 1992	1.500 percent
January 1, 1992–December 31, 1992	1.000 percent
January 1, 1993–December 31, 1993	0.750 percent
January 1, 1994–December 31, 1994	0.375 percent
Thereafter	0 percent

(B) Eligible savings associations

For purposes of subparagraph (A), a savings association is an eligible savings association so long as the Director determines that—

    (i) the savings association's management is competent;

    (ii) the savings association is in substantial compliance with all applicable statutes, regulations, orders, and supervisory agreements and directives; and

    (iii) the savings association's management has not engaged in insider dealing, speculative practices, or any other activities that have jeopardized the association's safety and soundness or contributed to impairing the association's capital.

(4) Special rules for purchased mortgage servicing rights

(A) In general

Notwithstanding paragraphs (1)(C) and (9), the standards prescribed under paragraph (1) may permit a savings association to include in calculating capital for the purpose of the leverage limit and risk-based capital requirement prescribed under paragraph (1), on terms no less stringent than under both the capital standards applicable to State nonmember banks and (except as to the amount that may be included in calculating capital) the capital standards applicable to national banks, 90 percent of the fair market value of readily marketable purchased mortgage servicing rights.

(B) Tangible capital requirement

Notwithstanding paragraphs (1)(C) and (9)(C), the standards prescribed under paragraph (1) may permit a savings association to include in calculating capital for the purpose of the tangible capital requirement prescribed under paragraph (1), on terms no

less stringent than under both the capital standards applicable to State nonmember banks and (except as to the amount that may be included in calculating capital) the capital standards applicable to national banks, 90 percent of the fair market value of readily marketable purchased mortgage servicing rights.

(C) Percentage limitation prescribed by FDIC

Notwithstanding paragraph (1)(C) and subparagraphs (A) and (B) of this paragraph—

    (i) for the purpose of subparagraph (A), the maximum amount of purchased mortgage servicing rights that may be included in calculating capital under the leverage limit and the risk-based capital requirement prescribed under paragraph (1) may not exceed the amount that could be included if the savings association were an insured State nonmember bank; and

    (ii) for the purpose of subparagraph (B), the Corporation shall prescribe a maximum percentage of the tangible capital requirement that savings associations may satisfy by including purchased mortgage servicing rights in calculating such capital.

(D) Quarterly valuation

The fair market value of purchased mortgage servicing rights shall be determined not less often than quarterly.

(5) Separate capitalization required for certain subsidiaries

(A) In general

In determining compliance with capital standards prescribed under paragraph (1), all of a savings association's investments in and extensions of credit to any subsidiary engaged in activities not permissible for a national bank shall be deducted from the savings association's capital.

(B) Exception for agency activities

Subparagraph (A) shall not apply with respect to a subsidiary engaged, solely as agent for its customers, in activities not permissible for a national bank unless the Corporation, in its sole discretion, determines that, in the interests of safety and soundness, this subparagraph should cease to apply to that subsidiary.

(C) Other exceptions

Subparagraph (A) shall not apply with respect to any of the following:

    (i) Mortgage banking subsidiaries

    A savings association's investments in and extensions of credit to a subsidiary engaged solely in mortgage-banking activities.

    (ii) Subsidiary insured depository institutions

    A savings association's investments in and extensions of credit to a subsidiary—

        (I) that is itself an insured depository institution or a company the sole investment of which is an insured depository institution, and

        (II) that was acquired by the parent insured depository institution prior to May 1, 1989.

    (iii) Certain Federal savings banks

    Any Federal savings association existing as a Federal savings association on August 9, 1989—

        (I) that was chartered prior to October 15, 1982, as a savings bank or a cooperative bank under State law; or

        (II) that acquired its principal assets from an association that was chartered prior to October 15, 1982, as a savings bank or a cooperative bank under State law.

(D) Transition rule

(i) Inclusion in capital

Notwithstanding subparagraph (A), if a savings association's subsidiary was, as of April 12, 1989, engaged in activities not permissible for a national bank, the savings association may include in calculating capital the applicable percentage (set forth in clause (ii)) of the lesser of—

(I) the savings association's investments in and extensions of credit to the subsidiary on April 12, 1989; or

(II) the savings association's investments in and extensions of credit to the subsidiary on the date as of which the savings association's capital is being determined.

(ii) Applicable percentage

For purposes of clause (i), the applicable percentage is as follows:

For the following period:	The applicable percentage is:
Prior to July 1, 1990	100 percent
July 1, 1990–June 30, 1991	90 percent
July 1, 1991–October 31, 1992	75 percent
November 1, 1992–June 30, 1993	60 percent
July 1, 1993–June 30, 1994	40 percent
Thereafter	0 percent

(iii) Agency discretion to prescribe greater percentage

Subject to clauses (iv), (v), and (vi), the Director may prescribe by order, with respect to a particular qualified savings association, an applicable percentage greater than that provided in clause (ii) if the Director determines, in the Director's sole discretion, that the use of the greater percentage, under the circumstances—

(I) would not constitute an unsafe or unsound practice;

(II) would not increase the risk to the affected deposit insurance fund; and

(III) would not be likely to result in the association's being in an unsafe or unsound condition.

(iv) Substantial compliance with approved capital plan

In the case of a savings association which is subject to a plan submitted under paragraph (7)(D) of this subsection or an order issued under this subsection, a directive issued or plan approved under subsection (s) of this section, or a capital restoration plan approved or order issued under section 38 or 39 of the Federal Deposit Insurance Act [12 U.S.C. § 1831o, 1831p-1], an order issued under clause (iii) with respect to the association shall be effective only so long as the association is in substantial compliance with such plan, directive, or order.

(v) Limitation on investments taken into account

In prescribing the amount by which an applicable percentage under clause (iii) may exceed the applicable percentage under clause (ii) with respect to a particular qualified savings association, the Director may take into account only the sum of—

(I) the association's investments in, and extensions of credit to, the subsidiary that were made on or before April 12, 1989; and

(II) the association's investments in, and extensions of credit to, the subsidiary that were made after April 12,

1989, and were necessary to complete projects initiated before April 12, 1989.

(vi) Limit

The applicable percentage limit allowed by the Director in an order under clause (iii) shall not exceed the following limits:

For the following period:	The limit is:
Prior to July 1, 1994	75 percent
July 1, 1994 through June 30, 1995	60 percent
July 1, 1995 through June 30, 1996	40 percent
After June 30, 1996	0 percent

(vii) Critically undercapitalized institution

In the case of a savings association that becomes critically undercapitalized (as defined in section 38 of the Federal Deposit Insurance Act [12 U.S.C. § 1831o]) as determined under this subparagraph without applying clause (iii), clauses (iii) through (v) shall be applied by substituting "Corporation" for "Director" each place such term appears.

(viii) "Qualified savings association" defined

For purposes of clause (iii), the term "qualified savings association" means an eligible savings association (as defined in paragraph (3)(B)) which is subject to this paragraph solely because of the real estate investments or other real estate activities of the association's subsidiary, and—

(I) is adequately capitalized (as defined in section 38 of the Federal Deposit Insurance Act [12 U.S.C. § 1831o]); or

(II) is in compliance with an approved capital restoration plan meeting the requirements of section 38 of the Federal Deposit Insurance Act [12 U.S.C. § 1831o], and is not critically undercapitalized (as defined in such section).

(ix) FDIC's discretion to prescribe lesser percentage

The Corporation may prescribe by order, with respect to a particular savings association, an applicable percentage less than that provided in clause (ii) or prescribed under clause (iii) if the Corporation determines, in its sole discretion, that the use of a greater percentage would, under the circumstances, constitute an unsafe or unsound practice or be likely to result in the association's being in an unsafe or unsound condition.

(E) Consolidation of subsidiaries not separately capitalized

In determining compliance with capital standards prescribed under paragraph (1), the assets and liabilities of each of a savings association's subsidiaries (other than any subsidiary described in subparagraph (C)(ii)) shall be consolidated with the savings association's assets and liabilities, unless all of the savings association's investments in and extensions of credit to the subsidiary are deducted from the savings association's capital pursuant to subparagraph (A).

(6) Consequences of failing to comply with capital standards

(A) Prior to January 1, 1991

Prior to January 1, 1991, the Director—

(i) may restrict the asset growth of any savings association not in compliance with capital standards; and

(ii) shall, beginning 60 days following the promulgation of final regulations under this subsection, require any savings association not in compliance with capital standards to submit a plan under subsection (s)(4)(A) of this section that—

(I) addresses the savings association's need for increased capital;

(II) describes the manner in which the savings association will increase its capital so as to achieve compliance with capital standards;

(III) specifies the types and levels of activities in which the savings association will engage;

(IV) requires any increase in assets to be accompanied by an increase in tangible capital not less in percentage amount than the leverage limit then applicable;

(V) requires any increase in assets to be accompanied by an increase in capital not less in percentage amount than required under the risk-based capital standard then applicable; and

(VI) is acceptable to the Director.

(B) On or after January 1, 1991

On or after January 1, 1991, the Director—

(i) shall prohibit any asset growth by any savings association not in compliance with capital standards, except as provided in subparagraph (C); and

(ii) shall require any savings association not in compliance with capital standards to comply with a capital directive issued by the Director (which may include such restrictions, including restrictions on the payment of dividends and on compensation, as the Director determines to be appropriate).

(C) Limited growth exception

The Director may permit any savings association that is subject to subparagraph (B) to increase its assets in an amount not exceeding the amount of net interest credited to the savings association's deposit liabilities if—

(i) the savings association obtains the Director's prior approval;

(ii) any increase in assets is accompanied by an increase in tangible capital in an amount not less than 6 percent of the increase in assets (or, in the Director's discretion if the leverage limit then applicable is less than 6 percent, in an amount equal to the increase in assets multiplied by the percentage amount of the leverage limit);

(iii) any increase in assets is accompanied by an increase in capital not less in percentage amount than required under the risk-based capital standard then applicable;

(iv) any increase in assets is invested in low-risk assets, such as first mortgage loans secured by 1- to 4-family residences and fully secured consumer loans; and

(v) the savings association's ratio of core capital to total assets is not less than the ratio existing on January 1, 1991.

(D) Additional restrictions in case of excessive risks or rates

The Director may restrict the asset growth of any savings association that the Director determines is taking excessive risks or paying excessive rates for deposits.

(E) Failure to comply with plan, regulation, or order

The Director shall treat as an unsafe and unsound practice any material failure by a savings association to comply with any plan, regulation, or order under this paragraph.

(F) Effect on other regulatory authority

This paragraph does not limit any authority of the Director under other provisions of law.

(7) Exemption from certain sanctions

(A) Application for exemption

Any savings association not in compliance with the capital standards prescribed under paragraph (1) may apply to the Director for an exemption from any applicable sanction or penalty for noncompliance which the Director may impose under this chapter.

(B) Effect of grant of exemption

If the Director approves any savings association's application under subparagraph (A), the only sanction or penalty to be imposed by the Director under this chapter for the savings association's failure to comply with the capital standards prescribed under paragraph (1) is the growth limitation contained in paragraph (6)(B) or paragraph (6)(C), whichever is applicable.

(C) Standards for approval or disapproval

(i) Approval

The Director may approve an application for an exemption if the Director determines that—

(I) such exemption would pose no significant risk to the affected deposit insurance fund;

(II) the savings association's management is competent;

(III) the savings association is in substantial compliance with all applicable statutes, regulations, orders, and supervisory agreements and directives; and

(IV) the savings association's management has not engaged in insider dealing, speculative practices, or any other activities that have jeopardized the association's safety and soundness or contributed to impairing the association's capital.

(ii) Denial or revocation of approval

The Director shall deny any application submitted under clause (i) and revoke any prior approval granted with respect to any such application if the Director determines that the association's failure to meet any capital standards prescribed under paragraph (1) is accompanied by—

(I) a pattern of consistent losses;

(II) substantial dissipation of assets;

(III) evidence of imprudent management or business behavior;

(IV) a material violation of any Federal law, any law of any State to which such association is subject, or any applicable regulation; or

(V) any other unsafe or unsound condition or activity, other than the failure to meet such capital standards.

(D) Submission of plan required

Any application submitted under subparagraph (A) shall be accompanied by a plan which—

(i) meets the requirements of paragraph (6)(A)(ii); and

(ii) is acceptable to the Director.

(E) Failure to comply with plan

The Director shall treat as an unsafe and unsound practice any material failure by any savings association which has been granted an exemption under this paragraph to comply with the provisions of any plan submitted by such association under subparagraph (D).

(F) Exemption not available with respect to unsafe or unsound practices

This paragraph does not limit any authority of the Director under any other provision of law, including section 8 of the Federal Deposit Insurance Act [12 U.S.C. § 1818], to take any appropriate action with respect to any unsafe or unsound practice or condition of any savings association, other than the failure of such savings association to comply with the capital standards prescribed under paragraph (1).

(8) Temporary authority to make exceptions for eligible savings associations

(A) In general

Notwithstanding paragraph (1)(C), the Director may, by order, make exceptions to the capital standards prescribed under paragraph (1) for eligible savings associations. No exception under this paragraph shall be effective after January 1, 1991.

(B) Standards for approval or disapproval

In determining whether to grant an exception under subparagraph (A), the Director shall apply the same standards as apply to determinations under paragraph (7)(C).

(9) Definitions

For purposes of this subsection—

(A) Core capital

Unless the Director prescribes a more stringent definition, the term "core capital" means core capital as defined by the Comptroller of the Currency for national banks, less any unidentifiable intangible assets, plus any purchased mortgage servicing rights excluded from the Comptroller's definition of capital but included in calculating the core capital of savings associations pursuant to paragraph (4).

(B) Qualifying supervisory goodwill

The term "qualifying supervisory goodwill" means supervisory goodwill existing on April 12, 1989, amortized on a straightline basis over the shorter of—

(i) 20 years, or

(ii) the remaining period for amortization in effect on April 12, 1989.

(C) Tangible capital

The term "tangible capital" means core capital minus any intangible assets (as intangible assets are defined by the Comptroller of the Currency for national banks).

(D) Total assets

The term "total assets" means total assets (as total assets are defined by the Comptroller of the Currency for national banks) adjusted in the same manner as total assets would be adjusted in determining compliance with the leverage limit applicable to national banks if the savings association were a national bank.

(10) Use of comptroller's definitions

(A) In general

The standards prescribed under paragraph (1) shall include all relevant substantive definitions established by the Comptroller of the Currency for national banks.

(B) Special rule

If the Comptroller of the Currency has not made effective regulations defining core capital or establishing a risk-based capital standard, the Director shall use the definition and standard contained in the Comptroller's most recently published final regulations.

(u) Limits on loans to one borrower

(1) In general

Section 5200 of the Revised Statutes [12 U.S.C. § 84] shall apply to savings associations in the same manner and to the same extent as it applies to national banks.

(2) Special rules

(A) Notwithstanding paragraph (1), a savings association may make loans to one borrower under one of the following clauses:

(i) for any purpose, not to exceed $500,000; or

(ii) to develop domestic residential housing units, not to exceed the lesser of $30,000,000 or 30 percent of the savings association's unimpaired capital and unimpaired surplus, if—

(I) the purchase price of each single family dwelling unit the development of which is financed under this clause does not exceed $500,000;

(II) the savings association is and continues to be in compliance with the fully phased-in capital standards prescribed under subsection (t) of this section;

(III) the Director, by order, permits the savings association to avail itself of the higher limit provided by this clause;

(IV) loans made under this clause to all borrowers do not, in aggregate, exceed 150 percent of the savings association's unimpaired capital and unimpaired surplus; and

(V) such loans comply with all applicable loan-to-value requirements.

(B) A savings association's loans to one borrower to finance the sale of real property acquired in satisfaction of debts previously contracted in good faith shall not exceed 50 percent of the savings association's unimpaired capital and unimpaired surplus.

(3) Authority to impose more stringent restrictions

The Director may impose more stringent restrictions on a savings association's loans to one borrower if the Director determines that such restrictions are necessary to protect the safety and soundness of the savings association.

(v) Reports of condition

(1) In general

Each association shall make reports of conditions to the Director which shall be in a form prescribed by the Director and shall contain—

(A) information sufficient to allow the identification of potential interest rate and credit risk;

(B) a description of any assistance being received by the association, including the type and monetary value of such assistance;

(C) the identity of all subsidiaries and affiliates of the association;

(D) the identity, value, type, and sector of investment of all equity investments of the associations and subsidiaries; and

(E) other information that the Director may prescribe.

(2) Public disclosure

(A) Reports required under paragraph (1) and all information contained therein shall be available to the public upon request, unless the Director determines—

(i) that a particular item or classification of information should not be made public in order to protect the safety or soundness of the institution concerned or institutions concerned, the Savings Association Insurance Fund; or

(ii) that public disclosure would not otherwise be in the public interest.

(B) Any determination made by the Director under subparagraph (A) not to permit the public disclosure of information shall be made in writing, and if the Director restricts any item of information for savings institutions generally, the Director shall disclose the reason in detail in the Federal Register.

(C) The Director's determinations under subparagraph (A) shall not be subject to judicial review.

(3) Access by certain parties

(A) Notwithstanding paragraph (2), the persons described in subparagraph (B) shall not be denied access to any information contained in a report of condition, subject to reasonable requirements of confidentiality. Those requirements shall not prevent such information from being transmitted to the Comptroller General of the United States for analysis.

(B) The following persons are described in this subparagraph for purposes of subparagraph (A):

(i) the Chairman and ranking minority member of the Committee on Banking, Housing, and Urban Affairs of the Senate and their designees; and

(ii) the Chairman and ranking minority member of the Committee on Banking, Finance and Urban Affairs of the House of Representatives and their designees.

(4) First tier penalties

Any savings association which—

(A) maintains procedures reasonably adapted to avoid any inadvertent and unintentional error and, as a result of such an error—

(i) fails to submit or publish any report or information required by the Director under paragraph (1) or (2), within the period of time specified by the Director; or

(ii) submits or publishes any false or misleading report or information; or

(B) inadvertently transmits or publishes any report which is minimally late,

shall be subject to a penalty of not more than $2,000 for each day during which such failure continues or such false or misleading information is not corrected. The savings association shall have the burden of proving by a preponderence[3] of the evidence that an error was inadvertent and unintentional and that a report was inadvertently transmitted or published late.

(5) Second tier penalties

Any savings association which—

(A) fails to submit or publish any report or information required by the Director under paragraph (1) or (2), within the period of time specified by the Director; or

(B) submits or publishes any false or misleading report or information,

in a manner not described in paragraph (4) shall be subject to a penalty of not more than $20,000 for each day during which such failure continues or such false or misleading information is not corrected.

(6) Third tier penalties

If any savings association knowingly or with reckless disregard for the accuracy of any information or report described in paragraph (5) submits or publishes any false or misleading report or information, the Director may assess a penalty of not more than $1,000,000 or 1 percent of total assets, whichever is less, per day for each day during which such failure continues or such false or misleading information is not corrected.

(7) Assessment

Any penalty imposed under paragraph (4), (5), or (6) shall be assessed and collected by the Director in the manner provided in subparagraphs (E), (F), (G), and (I) of section 8(i)(2) of the Federal Deposit Insurance Act [12 U.S.C. § 1818(i)(2)(E), (F), (G), (I)] (for penalties imposed under such section), and any such assessment (including the determination of the amount of the penalty) shall be subject to the provisions of such subsection.

(8) Hearing

Any savings association against which any penalty is assessed under this subsection shall be afforded a hearing if such savings association submits a request for such hearing within 20 days after the issuance of the notice of assessment. Section 8(h) of the Federal Deposit Insurance Act [12 U.S.C. § 1818(h)] shall apply to any proceeding under this subsection.

(w) Forfeiture of franchise for money laundering or cash transaction reporting offenses

(1) In general

(A) Conviction of Title 18 offense

(I) Duty to notify

If a Federal savings association has been convicted of any criminal offense under section 1956 or 1957 of Title 18, the Attorney General shall provide to the Director a written notification of the conviction and shall include a certified copy of the order of conviction from the court rendering the decision.

(II) Notice of termination; pretermination hearing

After receiving written notification from the Attorney General of such a conviction, the Director shall issue to the savings association a notice of the Director's intention to terminate all rights, privileges, and franchises of the savings association and schedule a pretermination hearing.

(B) Conviction of Title 31 offenses

If a Federal savings association is convicted of any criminal offense under section 5322 or 5324 of Title 31 after receiving written notification from the Attorney General, the Director may issue to the savings association a notice of the Director's intention to terminate all rights, privileges, and franchises of the savings association and schedule a pretermination hearing.

(C) Judicial review

Subsection (d)(1)(B)(vii) of this section shall apply to any proceeding under this subsection.

(2) Factors to be considered

In determining whether a franchise shall be forfeited under paragraph (1), the Director shall take into account the following factors:

(A) The extent to which directors or senior executive officers of the savings association knew of, were[4] involved in, the commission of the money laundering offense of which the association was found guilty.

(B) The extent to which the offense occurred despite the existence of policies and procedures within the savings association which were designed to prevent the occurrence of any such offense.

(C) The extent to which the savings association has fully cooperated with law enforcement authorities with respect to the investigation of the money laundering offense of which the association was found guilty.

(D) The extent to which the savings association has implemented additional internal controls (since the commission of the offense of which the savings association was found guilty) to prevent the occurrence of any other money laundering offense.

(E) The extent to which the interest of the local community in

---

3 So in original. Probably should be "preponderance."

4 So in original. Probably should be "or were."

(3) Successor liability

This subsection shall not apply to a successor to the interests of, or a person who acquires, a savings association that violated a provision of law described in paragraph (1), if the successor succeeds to the interests of the violator, or the acquisition is made, in good faith and not for purposes of evading this subsection or regulations prescribed under this subsection.

(4) "Senior executive officer" defined

The term "senior executive officer" has the same meaning as in regulations prescribed under section 32(f) of the Federal Deposit Insurance Act [12 U.S.C. § 1831i(f)].

[June 13, 1933, ch. 64, § 5, 48 Stat. 132; Apr. 27, 1934, ch. 168, §§ 5, 6, 48 Stat. 645, 646; May 28, 1935, ch. 150, § 18, 49 Stat. 297; Aug. 10, 1939, ch. 666, title IX, § 909, 53 Stat. 1402; Aug. 6, 1947, ch. 503, 61 Stat. 786; July 3, 1948, ch. 825, § 1, 62 Stat. 1239; Oct. 20, 1951, ch. 521, title III, § 313(d), 65 Stat. 490; July 14, 1952, ch. 723, § 12, 66 Stat. 604; Aug. 2, 1954, ch. 649, title II, § 204(b), title V, § 503, 68 Stat. 622, 634; Aug. 11, 1955, ch. 783, title I, § 110, 69 Stat. 641; Aug. 7, 1956, ch. 1029, title VI, § 604, 70 Stat. 1114; Pub. L. No. 85–857, § 13(f), 72 Stat. 1264 (Sept. 2, 1958); Pub. L. No. 86–372, title VIII, § 805, 73 Stat. 687 (Sept. 23, 1959); Pub. L. No. 86–507, § 1(11), 74 Stat. 200 (June 11, 1960); Pub. L. No. 87–70, title IX, § 901, 75 Stat. 189 (June 30, 1961); Pub. L. No. 87–779, § 1, 76 Stat. 778 (Oct. 9, 1962); Pub. L. No. 87–834, § 6(e)(1), 76 Stat. 984 (Oct. 16, 1962); Pub. L. No. 88–560, title IX, §§ 901(a), 902–905, 907, 908, 910, 78 Stat. 804–806 (Sept. 2, 1964); Pub. L. No. 89–117, title II, § 201(b)(3), title XI, § 1110(a)–(c), 79 Stat. 465, 507 (Aug. 10, 1965); Pub. L. No. 89–695, title I, § 101(a), 80 Stat. 1028 (Oct. 16, 1966); Pub. L. No. 90–448, title III, § 304(b), title IV, § 416(c), title VIII, §§ 804(e), 807 (m), title XVII, § 1716, 82 Stat. 508, 518, 543, 545, 608 (Aug. 1, 1968); Pub. L. No. 90–505, § 5, 82 Stat. 858 (Sept. 21, 1968); Pub. L. No. 90–575, title I, § 118(b), 82 Stat. 1026 (Oct. 16, 1968); Pub. L. No. 91–152, title IV, § 416(b), 83 Stat. 401 (Dec. 24, 1969); Pub. L. No. 91–351, title VII, §§ 706, 708, 709, 84 Stat. 462, 463 (July 24, 1970); Pub. L. No. 91–609, title VII, § 727(d), title IX, § 907(b), (c), 84 Stat. 1803, 1811 (Dec. 31, 1970); Pub. L. No. 92–318, title I, § 133(c)(3), 86 Stat. 270 (June 23, 1972); Pub. L. No. 93–100, § 5(b), 87 Stat. 343 (Aug. 16, 1973); Pub. L. No. 93–383, title VII, §§ 702–706, title VIII, §§ 802(i)(2), 805 (c)(4), 88 Stat. 715, 716, 725, 727 (Aug. 22, 1974); Pub. L. No. 93–449, § 4(d), 88 Stat. 1367 (Oct. 18, 1974); Pub. L. No. 93–495, title I, § 101(e), 88 Stat. 1502 (Oct. 28, 1974); Pub. L. No. 94–60, 89 Stat. 301 (July 25, 1975); Pub. L. No. 94–375, § 22, 90 Stat. 1078 (Aug. 3, 1976); Pub. L. No. 95–128, title IV, §§ 401–405, 91 Stat. 1136, 1137 (Oct. 12, 1977); Pub. L. No. 95–147, § 2(a), 91 Stat. 1227 (Oct. 28, 1977); Pub. L. No. 95–630, title I, §§ 107(a)(3), (c)(3), (d)(3), (e)(3), 111 (c), title II, § 208(b), title XII, §§ 1202, 1204, title XVII, § 1701, 92 Stat. 3651, 3655, 3659, 3662, 3668, 3675, 3710, 3711, 3714 (Nov. 10, 1978); Pub. L. No. 96–153, title III, §§ 325, 326, 93 Stat. 1121 (Dec. 21, 1979); Pub. L. No. 96–161, title I, § 102, 93 Stat. 1233 (Dec. 28, 1979); Pub. L. No. 96–221, title III, §§ 304, 307, title IV, §§ 401–404, 407 (a), 408, 94 Stat. 146, 147, 151, 155, 156, 158–160 (Mar. 31, 1980); Pub. L. No. 97–320, title I, §§ 112, 114 (b), (c), 121, 141 (a)(2), (5), title II, § 202(b), title III, §§ 311–313, 321–325, 328–331, 334, 351, title IV, §§ 424(a), (d)(8), (e), 427 (a), 96 Stat. 1471, 1475, 1479, 1489, 1492, 1496, 1497, 1499–1504, 1507, 1522–1524 (Oct. 15, 1982); Pub. L. No. 97–457, §§ 2, 12, 14 (a)(1), (b), 96 Stat. 2507, 2508 (Jan. 12, 1983); Pub. L. No. 98–440, title I, § 105(a), 98 Stat. 1691 (Oct. 3, 1984); Pub. L. No. 98–620, title IV, § 402(9), 98 Stat. 3357 (Nov. 8, 1984); Pub. L. No. 99–514, § 2, 100 Stat. 2095 (Oct. 22, 1986); Pub. L. No. 99–570, title I, § 1359(b), 100 Stat. 3207–27 (Oct. 27, 1986); Pub. L. No. 100–86, title IV, §§ 406(a), 413 (a), title V, § 509(a), 101 Stat. 614, 621, 635 (Aug. 10, 1987); Pub. L. No. 101–73, title III, § 301, 103 Stat. 282 (Aug. 9, 1989); Pub. L. No. 102–242, title I, §§ 131(d), 133 (d), title IV, § 441, title V, § 501(c), 105 Stat. 2267, 2271, 2381, 2391 (Dec. 19, 1991); Pub. L. No. 102–310, 106 Stat. 276 (July 1, 1992); Pub. L. No. 102–550, title IX, § 953, title XV, § 1502(b), title XVI, §§ 1603(d)(8), 1606 (f)(1)–(3), 106 Stat. 3893, 4046, 4080, 4088 (Oct. 28, 1992); Pub. L. No. 103–325, title II, § 206(a), title III, § 322(b), title IV, § 411(c)(2)(D), 108 Stat. 2199, 2227, 2253 (Sept. 23, 1994); Pub. L. No. 104–208, div. A, title II, §§ 2216(b), 2303 (a)–(d), (f), 2704(d)(12)(A), 110 Stat. 3009–413, 3009–424, 3009–490 (Sept. 30, 1996); Pub. L. No. 105–164, § 3(a)(1), 112 Stat. 33 (Mar. 20, 1998); Pub. L. No. 106–102, title VI, § 603, title VII, § 739, 113 Stat. 1450, 1480 (Nov. 12, 1999); Pub. L. No. 106–554, § 1(a)(8) [§ 1(f)], 114 Stat. 2763, 2763A–665 (Dec. 21, 2000); Pub. L. No. 106–569, title XII, § 1201(b)(1), 114 Stat. 3032 (Dec. 27, 2000)]

* * *

D.2 Selected Regulations

The Office of Thrift Supervision conducted a comprehensive review of its regulations beginning in 1995. As a result, all of Part 545 was deleted and certain sections were renumbered and others added to new Part 560. The portions relevant to consumer lending and to the preemption of state laws are reprinted below. For a discussion of the OTS rationale for these changes, see 61 Fed. Reg. 50951 (Sept. 30, 1996). These changes were effective on October 30, 1996.

TITLE 12—BANKS AND BANKING

CHAPTER V—OFFICE OF THRIFT SUPERVISION, DEPARTMENT OF THE TREASURY

PART 528 NONDISCRIMINATION REQUIREMENTS

§ 528.1 Definitions.
§ 528.1a Supplementary guidelines.
§ 528.2 Nondiscrimination in lending and other services.
§ 528.2a Nondiscriminatory appraisal and underwriting.
§ 528.3 Nondiscrimination in applications.
§ 528.4 Nondiscriminatory advertising.
§ 528.5 Equal Housing Lender Poster.
§ 528.6 Loan application register.
§ 528.7 Nondiscrimination in employment.
§ 528.8 Complaints.
§ 528.9 Guidelines relating to nondiscrimination in lending.

* * *

PART 559 SUBORDINATE ORGANIZATIONS

Subpart A—Regulations Applicable to Federal Savings Associations

* * *

§ 559.3 What are the characteristics of, and what requirements apply to, subordinate organizations of Federal savings associations?

* * *

PART 560—LENDING AND INVESTMENT

§ 560.1 General.
§ 560.2 Applicability of law.
§ 560.3 Definitions.

Subpart A—Lending and Investment Powers for Federal Savings Associations.

§ 560.30 General lending and investment powers.

* * *

§ 560.33 Late charges.
§ 560.34 Prepayments.
§ 560.35 Adjustments to home loans.

* * *

Subpart B—Lending and Investment Provisions Applicable to All Savings Associations.

* * *

§ 560.110 Most favored lender usury preemption.

* * *

PART 591—PREEMPTION OF STATE DUE-ON-SALE LAWS

§ 591.1 Authority, purpose, and scope.
§ 591.2 Definitions.
§ 591.3 Loans originated by Federal savings associations.
§ 591.4 Loans originated by lenders other than Federal savings associations.
§ 591.5 Limitation on exercise of due-on-sale clauses.
§ 591.6 Interpretations.

TITLE 12—BANKS AND BANKING

CHAPTER V—OFFICE OF THRIFT SUPERVISION, DEPARTMENT OF THE TREASURY

PART 528 NONDISCRIMINATION REQUIREMENTS

Authority: 12 U.S.C. 1464, 2810 *et seq.,* 2901 *et seq.*; 15 U.S.C. 1691; 42 U.S.C. 1981, 1982, 3601–3619.

Source: 55 Fed. Reg. 1388 (Jan. 16, 1990), unless otherwise noted.

12 C.F.R. § 528.1 Definitions.

As used in this part 528—

(a) *Application.* For purposes of this part, an application for a loan or other service is as defined in Regulation C, 12 CFR 203.2(b).

(b) *Savings association.* The term "savings association" means any savings association as defined in § 561.43 of this chapter other than a State-chartered savings bank whose deposits are insured by the Bank Insurance Fund.

(c) *Dwelling.* The term "dwelling" means a residential structure (whether or not it is attached to real property) located in a state of the United States of America, the District of Colombia, or the Commonwealth of Puerto Rico. The term includes an individual condominium unit, cooperative unit, or mobile or manufactured home.

[55 Fed. Reg. 1388 (Jan. 16, 1990), *as amended at* 58 Fed. Reg. 4312 (Jan. 14, 1993); 63 Fed. Reg. 71212 (Dec. 24, 1998)]

12 C.F.R. § 528.1a Supplementary guidelines.

The Office's policy statement found at 12 CFR 528.9 supplements this part and should be read together with this part. Refer also to the HUD Fair Housing regulations at 24 CFR parts 100 *et seq.*, Federal Reserve Regulation B at 12 CFR part 202, and Federal Reserve Regulation C at 12 CFR part 203.

[63 Fed. Reg. 71212 (Dec. 24, 1998)]

12 C.F.R. § 528.2 Nondiscrimination in lending and other services.

(a) No savings association may deny a loan or other service, or discriminate in the purchase of loans or securities or discriminate in fixing the amount, interest rate, duration, application procedures, collection or enforcement procedures, or other terms or conditions of such loan or other service on the basis of the age or location of the dwelling, or on the basis of the race, color, religion, sex, handicap, familial status (having one or more children under the age of 18), marital status, age (provided the person has the capacity to contract) or national origin of:

(1) An applicant or joint applicant;

(2) Any person associated with an applicant or joint applicant regarding such loan or other service, or with the purposes of such loan or other service;

(3) The present or prospective owners, lessees, tenants, or occupants of the dwelling(s) for which such loan or other service is to be made or given;

(4) The present or prospective owners, lessees, tenants, or occupants of other dwellings in the vicinity of the dwelling(s) for which such loan or other service is to be made or given.

(b) A savings association shall consider without prejudice the combined income of joint applicants for a loan or other service.

(c) No savings association may discriminate against an applicant for a loan or other service on any prohibited basis (as defined in 12 CFR 202.2(z) and 24 CFR part 100).

Note: See also, § 528.9 (b) and (c).

[55 Fed. Reg. 1388 (Jan. 16, 1990), *as amended at* 63 Fed. Reg. 71212 (Dec. 24, 1998)]

12 C.F.R. § 528.2a Nondiscriminatory appraisal and underwriting.

(a) *Appraisal.* No savings association may use or rely upon an appraisal of a dwelling which the savings association knows, or reasonably should know, is discriminatory on the basis of the age or location of the dwelling, or is discriminatory per se or in effect under the Fair Housing Act of 1968 or the Equal Credit Opportunity Act.

(b) *Underwriting.* Each savings association shall have clearly written, non-discriminatory loan underwriting standards, available to the public upon request, at each of its offices. Each association shall, at least annually, review its standards, and business practices implementing them, to ensure equal opportunity in lending

Note: See also, § 528.9(b), (c)(6), and (c)(7).

[55 Fed. Reg. 1388 (Jan. 16, 1990), *as amended at* 63 Fed. Reg. 71212 (Dec. 24, 1998)]

12 C.F.R. § 528.3 Nondiscrimination in applications.

(a) No savings association may discourage, or refuse to allow, receive, or consider, any application, request, or inquiry regarding a loan or other service, or discriminate in imposing conditions upon, or in processing, any such application, request, or inquiry on the basis of the age or location of the dwelling, or on the basis of the race, color, religion, sex, handicap, familial status (having one or more children under the age of 18), marital status, age (provided the person has the capacity to contract), national origin, or other characteristics prohibited from consideration in § 528.2(c) of this part, of the prospective borrower or other person, who:

(1) Makes application for any such loan or other service;

(2) Requests forms or papers to be used to make application for any such loan or other service; or

(3) Inquires about the availability of such loan or other service.

(b) A savings association shall inform each inquirer of his or her right to file a written loan application, and to receive a copy of the association's underwriting standards.

Note: See also, § 528.9(a) through (d).

[55 Fed. Reg. 1388 (Jan. 16, 1990), *as amended at* 63 Fed. Reg. 71212 (Dec. 24, 1998)]

12 C.F.R. § 528.4 Nondiscriminatory advertising.

No savings association may directly or indirectly engage in any form of advertising which implies or suggests a policy of discrimination or exclusion in violation of title VIII of the Civil Rights Acts of 1968, the Equal Credit Opportunity Act, or this part 528. Advertisements for any loan for the purpose of purchasing, constructing, improving, repairing, or maintaining a dwelling shall include a facsimile of the following logotype and legend:

[69 Fed. Reg. 68239 (Nov. 24, 2004)]

12 C.F.R. § 528.5 Equal Housing Lender Poster.

(a) Each savings association shall post and maintain one or more Equal Housing Lender Posters, the text of which is prescribed in paragraph (b) of this section, in the lobby of each of its offices in a prominent place or places readily apparent to all persons seeking loans. The poster shall be at least 11 by 14 inches in size, and the text shall be easily legible. It is recommended that savings associations post a Spanish language version of the poster in offices serving areas with a substantial Spanish-speaking population.

(b) The text of the Equal Housing Lender Poster shall be as follows:

We Do Business In Accordance With Federal Fair Lending Laws.

UNDER THE FEDERAL FAIR HOUSING ACT, IT IS ILLEGAL, ON THE BASIS OF RACE, COLOR, NATIONAL ORIGIN, RELIGION, SEX, HANDICAP, OR FAMILIAL STATUS (HAVING CHILDREN UNDER THE AGE OF 18) TO:

[ ]Deny a loan for the purpose of purchasing, constructing, improving, repairing or maintaining a dwelling or to deny any loan secured by a dwelling; or

[ ]Discriminate in fixing the amount, interest rate, duration, application procedures, or other terms or conditions of such a loan or in appraising property.

IF YOU BELIEVE YOU HAVE BEEN DISCRIMINATED AGAINST, YOU SHOULD:
SEND A COMPLAINT TO:
Assistant Secretary for Fair Housing and Equal Opportunity, Department of Housing and Urban Development, Washington, DC 20410.
For processing under the Federal Fair Housing Act
AND TO:
Director, Consumer Affairs, Office of Thrift Supervision, Washington, DC 20552.
For processing under Office of Thrift Supervision Regulations.
UNDER THE EQUAL CREDIT OPPORTUNITY ACT, IT IS ILLEGAL TO DISCRIMINATE IN ANY CREDIT TRANSACTION:
[ ]On the basis of race, color, national origin, religion, sex, marital status, or age;
[ ]Because income is from public assistance; or
[ ]Because a right has been exercised under the Consumer Credit Protection Act.
IF YOU BELIEVE YOU HAVE BEEN DISCRIMINATED AGAINST, YOU SHOULD SEND A COMPLAINT TO:
Director, Consumer Affairs, Office of Thrift Supervision, Washington, DC 20552.

12 C.F.R. § 528.6 Loan application register.

Savings associations and other lenders required to file Home Mortgage Disclosure Act Loan Application Registers with the Office of Thrift Supervision in accordance with 12 CFR part 203 must enter the reason for denial, using the codes provided in 12 CFR part 203, with respect to all loan denials.

[58 Fed. Reg. 4312 (Jan. 14, 1993)]

12 C.F.R. § 528.7 Nondiscrimination in employment.

(a) No savings association shall, because of an individual's race, color, religion, sex, or national origin:
(1) Fail or refuse to hire such individual;
(2) Discharge such individual;
(3) Otherwise discriminate against such individual with respect to such individual's compensation, promotion, or the terms, conditions, or privileges of such individual's employment; or
(4) Discriminate in admission to, or employment in, any program of apprenticeship, training, or retraining, including on-the-job training.
(b) No savings association shall limit, segregate, or classify its employees in any way which

would deprive or tend to deprive any individual of employment opportunities or otherwise adversely affect such individual's status as an employee because of such individual's race, color, religion, sex, or national origin.

(c) No savings association shall discriminate against any employee or applicant for employment because such employee or applicant has opposed any employment practice made unlawful by Federal, State, or local law or regulation or because he has in good faith made a charge of such practice or testified, assisted, or participated in any manner in an investigation, proceeding, or hearing of such practice by any lawfully constituted authority.

(d) No savings association shall print or publish or cause to be printed or published any notice or advertisement relating to employment by such savings association indicating any preference, limitation, specification, or discrimination based on race, color, religion, sex, or national origin.

(e) This regulation shall not apply in any case in which the Federal Equal Employment Opportunities law is made inapplicable by the provisions of section 2000e-1 or sections 2000e-2 (e) through (j) of title 42, United States Code.

(f) Any violation of the following laws or regulations by a savings association shall be deemed to be a violation of this part 528:
(1) The Equal Employment Opportunity Act, as amended, 42 U.S.C. 2000e-2000h-2, and Equal Employment Opportunity Commission (EEOC) regulations at 29 CFR part 1600;
(2) The Age Discrimination in Employment Act, 29 U.S.C. 621–633, and EEOC and Department of Labor regulations;
(3) Department of the Treasury regulations at 31 CFR part 12 and Office of Federal Contract Compliance Programs (OFCCP) regulations at 41 CFR part 60;
(4) The Veterans Employment and Readjustment Act of 1972, 38 U.S.C. 2011–2012, and the Vietnam Era Veterans Readjustment Adjustment Assistance Act of 1974, 38 U.S.C. 2021–2026;
(5) The Rehabilitation Act of 1973, 29 U.S.C. 701 *et al.*; and
(6) The Immigration and Nationality Act, 8 U.S.C. 1324b, and INS regulations at 8 CFR part 274a.

12 C.F.R. § 528.8 Complaints.

Complaints regarding discrimination in lending by a savings association shall be referred to the Assistant Secretary for Fair Housing and Equal Opportunity, U.S. Department of Housing and Urban Development, Washington, DC 20410 for processing under the Fair Housing Act, and to the Director, Consumer Affairs, Office of Thrift Supervision, Washington, DC 20552 for processing under Office regulations. Complaints regarding discrimination in employment by a savings association should be referred to the Equal Employment Opportunity Commission, Washington, DC 20506 and a copy, for information only, sent to the Director, Consumer Affairs, Office of Thrift Supervision, Washington, DC 20552.

12 C.F.R. § 528.9 Guidelines relating to nondiscrimination in lending.

(a) *General.* Fair housing and equal opportunity in home financing is a policy of the United States established by Federal statutes and Presidential orders and proclamations. In furtherance of the Federal civil rights laws and the economical home financing purposes of the statutes administered by the Office, the Office has adopted, in part 528 of this chapter, nondiscrimination regulations that, among other things, prohibit arbitrary refusals to consider loan applications on the basis of the age or location of a dwelling, and prohibit discrimination based on race, color, religion, sex, handicap, familial status (having one or more children under the age of 18), marital status, age (provided the person has the capacity to contract), or national origin in fixing the amount, interest rate, duration, application procedures, collection or enforcement procedures, or other terms or conditions of housing related loans. Such discrimination is also prohibited in the purchase of loans and securities. This section provides supplementary guidelines to aid savings associations in developing and implementing nondiscriminatory lending policies. Each savings association should reexamine its underwriting standards at least annually in order to ensure equal opportunity.

(b) *Loan underwriting standards.* The basic purpose of the Office's nondiscrimination regulations is to require that every applicant be given an equal opportunity to obtain a loan. Each loan applicant's creditworthiness should be evaluated on an individual basis without reference to presumed characteristics of a group. The use of lending standards which have no economic basis and which are discriminatory in effect is a violation of law even in the absence of an actual intent to discriminate. However, a standard which has a discriminatory effect is not necessarily improper if its use achieves a genuine business need which cannot be achieved by means which are not discriminatory in effect or less discriminatory in effect.

(c) *Discriminatory practices*—(1) *Discrimination on the basis of sex or marital status.* The Civil Rights Act of 1968 and the National Housing Act prohibit discrimination in lending on the basis of sex. The Equal Credit Opportunity Act, in addition to this prohibition, forbids discrimination on the basis of marital status. Refusing to lend to, requiring higher standards of creditworthiness of, or imposing different requirements on, members of one sex or individuals of one marital status, is discrimination based on sex or marital status. Loan underwriting decisions must be based on an applicant's credit history and present and reasonably foreseeable economic prospects, rather than on the basis of assumptions regarding comparative differences in creditworthiness between married and unmarried individuals, or between men and women.

(2) *Discrimination on the basis of language.* Requiring fluency in the English language as a prerequisite for obtaining a loan may be a discriminatory practice based on national origin.

(3) *Income of husbands and wives.* A practice of discounting all or part of either spouse's income where spouses apply jointly is a violation of section 527 of the National Housing Act. As with other income, when spouses apply jointly for a loan, the determination as to whether a spouse's income qualifies for credit purposes should depend upon a reasonable evaluation of his or her past, present, and reasonably foreseeable economic circumstances. Information relating to child-bearing intentions of a couple or an individual may not be requested.

(4) *Supplementary income.* Lending standards which consider as effective only the non-overtime income of the primary wage-earner may result in discrimination because they do not take account of variations in employment patterns among individuals and families. The Office favors loan underwriting which reasonably evaluates the credit worthiness of each applicant based on a realistic appraisal of his or her own past, present, and foreseeable economic circumstances. The determination as to whether primary income or additional income qualifies as effective for credit purposes should depend upon whether such income may reasonably be expected to continue through the early period of the mortgage risk. Automatically discounting other income from bonuses, overtime, or part-time employment, will cause some applicants to be denied financing without a realistic analysis of their credit worthiness. Since statistics show that minority group members and low- and moderate-income families rely more often on such supplemental income, the practice may be racially discriminatory in effect, as well as artificially restrictive of opportunities for home financing.

(5) *Applicant's prior history.* Loan decisions should be based upon a realistic evaluation of all pertinent factors respecting an individual's creditworthiness, without giving undue weight to any one factor. The savings association should, among other things, take into consideration that:

(i) In some instances, past credit difficulties may have resulted from discriminatory practices;

(ii) A policy favoring applicants who previously owned homes may perpetuate prior discrimination;

(iii) A current, stable earnings record may be the most reliable indicator of credit-worthiness, and entitled to more weight than factors such as educational level attained;

(iv) Job or residential changes may indicate upward mobility; and

(v) Preferring applicants who have done business with the lender can perpetuate previous discriminatory policies.

(6) *Income level or racial composition of area.* Refusing to lend or lending on less favorable terms in particular areas because of their racial composition is unlawful. Refusing to lend, or offering less favorable terms (such as interest rate, downpayment, or maturity) to applicants because of the income level in an area can discriminate against minority group persons.

(7) *Age and location factors.* Sections 528.2, 528.2a, and 528.3 of this chapter prohibit loan denials based upon the age or location of a dwelling. These restrictions are intended to prohibit use of unfounded or unsubstantiated assumptions regarding the effect upon loan risk of the age of a dwelling or the physical or economic characteristics of an area. Loan decisions should be based on the present market value of the property offered as security (including consideration of specific improvements to be made by the borrower) and the likelihood that the property will retain an adequate value over the term of the loan. Specific factors which may negatively affect its short-range future value (up to 3–5 years) should be clearly documented. Factors which in some cases may cause the market value of a property to decline are recent zoning changes or a significant number of abandoned homes in the immediate vicinity of the property. However, not all zoning changes will cause a decline in property values, and proximity to abandoned buildings may not affect the market value of a property because of rehabilitation programs or affirmative lending programs, or because the cause of abandonment is unrelated to high risk. Proper underwriting considerations include the condition and utility of the improvements, and various physical factors such as street conditions, amenities such as parks and recreation areas, availability of public utilities and municipal services, and exposure to flooding and land faults. However, arbitrary decisions based on age or location are prohibited, since many older, soundly constructed homes provide housing opportunities which may be precluded by an arbitrary lending policy.

(8) *Fair Housing Act (title VIII, Civil Rights Act of 1968, as amended).* Savings associations, must comply with all regulations promulgated by the Department of Housing and Urban Development to implement the Fair Housing Act, found at 24 CFR part 100 et seq., except that they shall use the Equal Housing Lender logo and poster prescribed by Office regulations at 12 CFR 528.4 and 528.5 rather than the Equal Housing Opportunity logo and poster required by 24 CFR parts 109 and 110.

(d) *Marketing practices.* Savings associations should review their advertising and marketing practices to ensure that their services are available without discrimination to the community they serve. Discrimination in lending is not limited to loan decisions and underwriting standards; a savings association does not meet its obligations to the community or implement its equal lending responsibility if its marketing practices and business relationships with developers and real estate brokers improperly restrict its clientele to segments of the community. A review of marketing practices could begin with an examination of an association's loan portfolio and applications to ascertain whether, in view of the demographic characteristics and credit demands of the community in which the institution is located, it is adequately serving the community on a nondiscriminatory basis. The Office will systematically review marketing practices where evidence of discrimination in lending is discovered.

[54 Fed. Reg. 49666 (Nov. 30, 1989), *as amended at* 60 Fed. Reg. 66870 (Dec. 27, 1995). Redesignated at 63 Fed. Reg. 71212 (Dec. 24, 1998)]

* * *

PART 559 SUBORDINATE ORGANIZATIONS

Subpart A—Regulations Applicable to Federal Savings Associations

* * *

12 C.F.R. § 559.3 What are the characteristics of, and what requirements apply to, subordinate organizations of Federal savings associations?

A federal savings association ("you") that meets the requirements of this section, as de-

tailed in the following chart, may establish, or obtain an interest in an operating subsidiary or a service corporation. For ease of reference, this section cross-references other regulations in this chapter affecting operating subsidiaries and service corporations. You should refer to those regulations for the details of how they apply. The chart also discusses the regulations that may apply to lower-tier entities in which you have an indirect ownership interest through your operating subsidiary or service corporation. The chart follows:

	Operating subsidiary	Service corporation
(a) How may a federal savings association ("you") establish an operating subsidiary or a service corporation?	(1) You must file a notice satisfying § 559.11. Any finance subsidiary that existed on January 1, 1997, is deemed an operating subsidiary without further action on your part.	(2) You must file a notice satisfying § 559.11. Depending upon your condition and the activities in which the service corporation will engage, § 559.3(e)(2) may require you to file an application.
(b) Who may be an owner?	(1) Anyone may have an ownership interest in an operating subsidiary.	(2) Only savings associations with home offices in the state where you have your home office may have an ownership interest in any service corporation in which you invest.
(c) What ownership requirements apply?	(1) You must own, directly or indirectly, more than 50% of the voting shares of the operating subsidiary. No one else may exercise effective operating control.	(2) You are not required to have any particular percentage ownership interest and need not have control of the service corporation.
(d) What geographic restrictions apply?	(1) An operating subsidiary may be organized in any geographic location.	(2) A service corporation must be organized in the state where your home office is located.
(e) What activities are permissible?	(1) After you have notified OTS in accordance with § 559.11, an operating subsidiary may engage in any activity that you may conduct directly. You may hold another insured depository institution as an operating subsidiary.	(2)(i) If you are eligible for expedited treatment under § 516.5 of this chapter, and notify OTS as required by § 559.11, your service corporation may engage in the preapproved activities listed in § 559.4. You may request OTS approval for your service corporation to engage in any other activity reasonably related to the activities of financial institutions by filing an application in accordance with standard treatment processing procedures at part 516, subparts A and E of this chapter.

(ii) If you are subject to standard treatment under § 516.5 of this chapter, and notify OTS as required by § 559.11, your service corporation may engage in any activity that you may conduct directly except taking deposits. You may request OTS approval for your service corporation to engage in any other activity reasonably related to the activities of financial institutions, including the activities set forth in § 559.4(b)–(j), by filing an application in accordance with standard treatment processing procedures at part 516, subparts A and E of this chapter. |

(f) May the operating subsidiary or service corporation invest in lower-tier entities?	(1)(i) An operating subsidiary may itself hold an operating subsidiary. Part 559 applies equally to a lower-tier operating subsidiary. In applying the regulations in this part, the investing operating subsidiary should substitute "investing operating subsidiary" wherever the part uses "you" or "savings association." (ii) An operating subsidiary may also invest in other types of lower-tier entities. These entities must comply with all of the requirements of this part 559 that apply to service corporations except for paragraphs (b)(2) and (d)(2) of this section.	(2) A service corporation may invest in all types of lower-tier entities as long as the lower-tier entity is engaged solely in activities that are permissible for a service corporation. All of the requirements of this part apply to such entities except for paragraphs (b)(2) and (d)(2) of this section.
(g) How much may a federal savings association invest?	(1) There are no limits on the amount you may invest in your operating subsidiaries, either separately or in the aggregate.	(2) Section 559.5 limits your aggregate investments in service corporations and indicates when your investments (both debt and equity) in lower-tier entities must be aggregated with your investments in service corporations.
(h) Do federal statutes and regulations that apply to the savings association apply?	(1) Unless otherwise specifically provided by statute, regulation, or OTS policy, all federal statutes and regulations apply to operating subsidiaries in the same manner as they apply to you. You and your operating subsidiary are generally consolidated and treated as a unit for statutory and regulatory purposes.	(2) (i) If the federal statute or regulation specifically refers to "service corporation," it applies to all service corporations, even if you do not control the service corporation or it is not a GAAP-consolidated subsidiary. (ii) If the federal statute or regulation refers to "subsidiary," it applies only to service corporations that you directly or indirectly control.
(i) Do the investment limits that apply to federal savings associations (HOLA section 5(c) and part 560 of this chapter) apply?	(1) Your assets and those of your operating subsidiary are aggregated when calculating investment limitations.	(2) Your service corporation's assets are not subject to the same investment limitations that apply to you. The investment activities of your service corporation are governed by paragraph (e)(2) of this section and § 559.4.
(j) How does the capital regulation (part 567 of this chapter) apply?	(1) Your assets and those of your operating subsidiary are consolidated for all capital purposes.	(2) The capital treatment of a service corporation depends upon whether it is an includable subsidiary. That determination is based upon factors set forth in part 567 of this chapter, including your percentage ownership of the service corporation and the activities in which the service corporation engages. Both debt and equity investments in service corporations that are GAAP-consolidated subsidiaries are considered investments in subsidiaries for purposes of the capital regulation, regardless of the authority under which they are made.
(k) How does the loans-to-one-borrower (LTOB) regulation (§ 560.93 of this chapter) apply?	(1) The LTOB regulation does not apply to loans from you to your operating subsidiary or loans from your operating subsidiary to you. Other loans made by your operating subsidiary are aggregated with your loans for LTOB purposes.	(2) The LTOB regulation does not apply to loans from you to your service corporation or from your service corporation to you. However, § 559.5 imposes restrictions on the amount of loans you may make to certain service corporations. Loans made by a service corporation that you control to entities other than you or your subordinate organizations are aggregated with your loans for LTOB purposes.

(l) How do the transactions with affiliates (TWA) regulations (§ 563.41 of this chapter) apply?	(1) Section 563.41 of this chapter explains how TWA applies. Generally, an operating subsidiary is not an affiliate, unless it is a depository institution; is directly controlled by another affiliate of the savings association or by shareholders that control the savings association; or is an employee stock option plan, trust, or similar organization that exists for the benefit of shareholders, partners, members, or employees of the savings association or an affiliate. A non-affiliate operating subsidiary is treated as a part of the savings association and its transactions with affiliates of the savings association are aggregated with those of the savings association	(2) Section 563.41 of this chapter explains how TWA applies. Generally, a service corporation is not an affiliate, unless it is a depository institution; is directly controlled by another affiliate of the savings association or by shareholders that control the savings association; or is an employee stock option plan, trust, or similar organization that exists for the benefit of shareholders, partners, members, or employees of the savings association or an affiliate. If a savings association directly or indirectly controls a service corporation and the service corporation is not otherwise an affiliate under § 563.41 of this chapter, the service corporation is treated as a part of the savings association and its transactions with affiliates of the savings association are aggregated with those of the savings association.
(m) How does the Qualified Thrift Lender (QTL) (12 U.S.C. 1467a(m)) test apply?	(1) Under 12 U.S.C. 1467a(m)(5), you may determine whether to consolidate the assets of a particular operating subsidiary for purposes of calculating your qualified thrift investments. If the operating subsidiary's assets are not consolidated with yours for that purpose, your investment in the operating subsidiary will be considered in calculating your qualified thrift investments.	(2) Under 12 U.S.C. 1467a(m)(5), you may determine whether to consolidate the assets of a particular service corporation for purposes of calculating your qualified thrift investments. If a service corporation's assets are not consolidated with yours for that purpose, your investment in the service corporation will be considered in calculating your qualified thrift investments.
(n) Does state law apply?	(1) State law applies to operating subsidiaries only to the extent it applies to you.	(2) State law applies to service corporations regardless of whether it applies to you, except where there is a conflict with federal law.
(o) May OTS conduct examinations?	(1) An operating subsidiary is subject to examination by OTS.	(2) A service corporation is subject to examination by OTS.
(p) What must be done to redesignate an operating subsidiary as a service corporation or a service corporation as an operating subsidiary?	(1) Before redesignating an operating subsidiary as a service corporation, you should consult with the OTS Regional Director for the Region in which your home office is located. You must maintain adequate internal records, available for examination by OTS, demonstrating that the redesignated service corporation meets all of the applicable requirements of this part and that your board of directors has approved the redesignation.	(2) Before redesignating a service corporation as an operating subsidiary, you should consult with the OTS Regional Director for the Region in which your home office is located. You must maintain adequate internal records, available for examination by OTS, demonstrating that the redesignated operating subsidiary meets all of the applicable requirements of this part and that your board of directors has approved the redesignation.
(q) What are the consequences of failing to comply with the requirements of this part?	(1) If an operating subsidiary, or any lower-tier entity in which the operating subsidiary invests pursuant to paragraph (f)(1) of this section fails to meet any of the requirements of this section, you must notify OTS. Unless otherwise advised by OTS, if the company cannot comply within 90 days with all of the requirements for either an operating subsidiary or a service corporation under this section, or any other investment authorized by 12 U.S.C. 1464(c) or part 560 of this chapter, you must promptly dispose of your investment.	(2) If a service corporation, or any lower-tier entity in which the service corporation invests pursuant to paragraph (f)(2) of this section, fails to meet any of the requirements of this section, you must notify OTS. Unless otherwise advised by OTS, if the company cannot comply within 90 days with all of the requirements for either an operating subsidiary or a service corporation under this section, or any other investment authorized by 12 U.S.C. 1464(c) or part 560 of this chapter, you must promptly dispose of your investment.

[61 Fed. Reg. 66571 (Dec. 18, 1996), *as amended at* 62 Fed. Reg. 66262 (Dec. 18, 1997); 63 Fed. Reg. 65683 (Nov. 30, 1998); 66 Fed. Reg. 13006 (Mar. 2, 2001); 67 Fed. Reg. 77916 (Dec. 20, 2002); 67 Fed. Reg. 78152 (Dec. 23, 2002); 68 Fed. Reg. 57796 (Oct. 7, 2003)]

* * *

PART 560—LENDING AND INVESTMENT

Authority: 12 U.S.C. 1462, 1462a, 1463, 1464, 1467a, 1701j-3, 1828, 3803, 3806; 42 U.S.C. 4106.

Source: 61 Fed. Reg. 50971 (Sept. 30 1996), unless otherwise noted.

12 C.F.R. § 560.1 General.

(a) *Authority and scope.* This part is being issued by OTS under its general rulemaking and supervisory authority under the Home Owners' Loan Act (HOLA), 12 U.S.C. 1462 et seq. Subpart A of this part sets forth the lending and investment powers of Federal savings associations. Subpart B of this part contains safety-and-soundness based lending and investment provisions applicable to all savings associations. Subpart C of this part addresses alternative mortgages and applies to all savings associations.

(b) *General lending standards.* Each savings association is expected to conduct its lending and investment activities prudently. Each association should use lending and investment standards that are consistent with safety and soundness, ensure adequate portfolio diversification and are appropriate for the size and condition of the institution, the nature and scope of its operations, and conditions in its lending market. Each association should adequately monitor the condition of its portfolio and the adequacy of any collateral securing its loans.

12 C.F.R. § 560.2 Applicability of law.

(a) *Occupation of field.* Pursuant to sections 4(a) and 5(a) of the HOLA, 12 U.S.C. 1463(a), 1464(a), OTS is authorized to promulgate regulations that preempt state laws affecting the operations of federal savings associations when deemed appropriate to facilitate the safe and sound operation of federal savings associations, to enable federal savings associations to conduct their operations in accordance with the best practices of thrift institutions in the United States, or to further other purposes of the HOLA. To enhance safety and soundness and to enable federal savings associations to conduct their operations in accordance with best practices (by efficiently delivering low-cost credit to the public free from undue regulatory duplication and burden), OTS hereby occupies the entire field of lending regulation for federal savings associations. OTS intends to give federal savings associations maximum flexibility to exercise their lending powers in accordance with a uniform federal scheme of regulation. Accordingly, federal savings associations may extend credit as authorized under federal law, including this part, without regard to state laws purporting to regulate or otherwise affect their credit activities, except to the extent provided in paragraph (c) of this section or § 560.110 of this part. For purposes of this section, "state law" includes any state statute, regulation, ruling, order or judicial decision.

(b) *Illustrative examples.* Except as provided in § 560.110 of this part, the types of state laws preempted by paragraph (a) of this section include, without limitation, state laws purporting to impose requirements regarding:

(1) Licensing, registration, filings, or reports by creditors;

(2) The ability of a creditor to require or obtain private mortgage insurance, insurance for other collateral, or other credit enhancements;

(3) Loan-to-value ratios;

(4) The terms of credit, including amortization of loans and the deferral and capitalization of interest and adjustments to the interest rate, balance, payments due, or term to maturity of the loan, including the circumstances under which a loan may be called due and payable upon the passage of time or a specified event external to the loan;

(5) Loan-related fees, including without limitation, initial charges, late charges, prepayment penalties, servicing fees, and overlimit fees;

(6) Escrow accounts, impound accounts, and similar accounts;

(7) Security property, including leaseholds;

(8) Access to and use of credit reports;

(9) Disclosure and advertising, including laws requiring specific statements, information, or other content to be included in credit application forms, credit solicitations, billing statements, credit contracts, or other credit-related documents and laws requiring creditors to supply copies of credit reports to borrowers or applicants;

(10) Processing, origination, servicing, sale or purchase of, or investment or participation in, mortgages;

(11) Disbursements and repayments;

(12) Usury and interest rate ceilings to the extent provided in 12 U.S.C. 1735f-7a and part 590 of this chapter and 12 U.S.C. 1463(g) and § 560.110 of this part; and

(13) Due-on-sale clauses to the extent provided in 12 U.S.C. 1701j-3 and part 591 of this chapter.

(c) *State laws that are not preempted.* State laws of the following types are not preempted to the extent that they only incidentally affect the lending operations of Federal savings associations or are otherwise consistent with the purposes of paragraph (a) of this section:

(1) Contract and commercial law;

(2) Real property law;

(3) Homestead laws specified in 12 U.S.C. 1462a(f);

(4) Tort law;

(5) Criminal law; and

(6) Any other law that OTS, upon review, finds:

(i) Furthers a vital state interest; and

(ii) Either has only an incidental effect on lending operations or is not otherwise contrary to the purposes expressed in paragraph (a) of this section.

12 C.F.R. § 560.3 Definitions.

For purposes of this part and any determination under 12 U.S.C. 1467a(m):

Consumer loans include loans for personal, family, or household purposes and loans reasonably incident thereto, and may be made as either open-end or closed-end consumer credit (as defined at 12 C.F.R. 226.2(a)(10) and (20)). Consumer loans do not include credit extended in connection with credit card loans, bona fide overdraft loans, and other loans that the savings association has designated as made under investment or lending authority other than section 5(c)(2)(D) of the HOLA.

Credit card is any card, plate, coupon book, or other single credit device that may be used from time to time to obtain credit.

Credit card account is a credit account established in conjunction with the issuance of, or the extension of credit through, a credit card. This term includes loans made to consolidate credit card debt, including credit card debt held by other lenders, and participation certificates, securities and similar instruments secured by credit card receivables.

Home loans include any loans made on the security of a home (including a dwelling unit in a multi-family residential property such as a condominium or a cooperative), combinations of homes and business property (*i.e.*, a home used in part for business), farm residences, and combinations of farm residences and commercial farm real estate.

Loan commitment includes a loan in process, a letter of credit, or any other commitment to extend credit.

Real estate loan, for purposes of this part, is a loan for which the savings association substantially relies upon a security interest in real estate given by the borrower as a condition of making the loan. A loan is made on the security of real estate if:

(1) The security property is real estate pursuant to the law of the state in which the property is located;

(2) The security interest of the Federal savings association may be enforced as a real estate mortgage or its equivalent pursuant to the law of the state in which the property is located;

(3) The security property is capable of separate appraisal; and

(4) With regard to a security property that is a leasehold or other interest for a period of years, the term of the interest extends, or is subject to extension or renewal at the option of the Federal savings association, for a term of at least five years following the maturity of the loan.

Small business includes a small business concern or entity as defined by section 3(a) of the Small Business Act, 15 U.S.C. 632(a), and implemented by the regulations of the Small Business Administration at 13 C.F.R. Part 121.

Small business loans and *loans to small businesses* include any loan to a small business as defined in this section; or a loan that does not exceed $2 million (including a group of loans to one borrower) and is for commercial, corporate, business, or agricultural purposes.

[61 Fed. Reg. 60184 (Nov. 27, 1996); 62 Fed. Reg. 15825 (Apr. 3, 1997); 64 Fed. Reg. 46565 (Aug. 26, 1999); 66 Fed. Reg. 65825 (Dec. 21, 2001)]

Subpart A—Lending and Investment Powers for Federal Savings Associations.

12 C.F.R. § 560.30 General lending and investment powers of Federal savings associations.

Pursuant to section 5(c) of the Home Owners' Loan Act ("HOLA"), 12 U.S.C. 1464(c), a Federal savings association may make, invest in, purchase, sell, participate in, or otherwise deal in (including brokerage or warehousing) all loans and investments allowed under section 5(c) of the HOLA including, without limitation, the following loans, extensions of credit, and investments, subject to the limitations indicated and any such terms, conditions, or limitations as may be prescribed from time to time by OTS by policy directive, order, or regulation:

Lending and Investment Powers Chart

Category	Statutory authorization[1]	Statutory investment limitations (Endnotes contain applicable regulatory limitations)
* * *	* * *	* * *
Consumer loans	5(c)(2)(D)	Up to 35% of total assets.[2, 5]
Credit card loans or loans made through credit card accounts	5(c)(1)(T)	None.[6]
* * *	* * *	* * *
Home improvement loans	5(c)(1)(J)	None.[6]
Home (residential) loans[9]	5(c)(1)(B)	None.[6, 10]
HUD-insured or guaranteed investments	5(c)(1)(O)	None.[6]
Insured loans	5(c)(1)(I), 5(c)(1)(K)	None.[6]
* * *	* * *	* * *
Manufactured home loans	5(c)(1)(J)	None.[6, 13]
* * *	* * *	* * *
Nonconforming loans	5(c)(3)(B)	5% of total assets.
* * *	* * *	* * *

Notes:

1. All references are to section 5 of the Home Owners' Loan Act (12 U.S.C. 1464) unless otherwise indicated.
2. For purposes of determining a Federal savings association's percentage of assets limitation, investment in commercial paper and corporate debt securities must be aggregated with the Federal savings association's investment in consumer loans.
5. Amounts in excess of 30% of assets, in the aggregate, may be invested only in loans made by the association directly to the original obligor and for which no finder's or referral fees have been paid. A Federal savings association may include loans to dealers in consumer goods to finance inventory and floor planning in the total investment made under this section.
6. While there is no statutory limit on certain categories of loans and investments, including credit card loans, home improvement loans, education loans, and deposit account loans, OTS may establish an individual limit on such loans or investments if the association's concentration in such loans or investments presents a safety and soundness concern.
9. A home (or residential) loan includes loans secured by one-to-four family dwellings, multi-family residential property, and loans secured by a unit or units of a condominium or housing cooperative.
10. A Federal savings association may make home loans subject to the provisions of §§ 560.33, 560.34, and 560.35 of this part.
13. If the wheels and axles of the manufactured home have been removed and it is permanently affixed to a foundation, a loan secured by a combination of a manufactured home and developed residential lot on which it sits may be treated as a home loan.

[61 Fed. Reg. 66577 (Dec. 18, 1996); 65 Fed. Reg. 78901 (Dec. 18, 2000); 66 Fed. Reg. 15017 (Mar. 15, 2001); 66 Fed. Reg. 37407 (July 18, 2001); 66 Fed. Reg. 65825 (Dec. 21, 2001); 68 Fed. Reg. 75108 (Dec. 30, 2003)]

* * *

12 C.F.R. § 560.33 Late charges.

A Federal savings association may include in a home loan contract a provision authorizing the imposition of a late charge with respect to the payment of any delinquent periodic payment. With respect to any loan made after July 31, 1976, on the security of a home occupied or to be occupied by the borrower, no late charge, regardless of form, shall be assessed or collected by a Federal savings association, unless any billing, coupon, or notice the Federal savings association may provide regarding installment payments due on the loan discloses the date after which the charge may be assessed. A Federal savings association may not impose a late charge more than one time for late payment of the same installment, and any installment payment made by the borrower shall be applied to the longest outstanding installment due. A Federal savings association shall not assess a late charge as to any payment received by it within fifteen days after the due date of such payment. No form of such late charge permitted by this paragraph shall be considered as interest to the Federal savings association and the Federal savings association shall not deduct late charges from the regular periodic installment payments on the loan, but must collect them as such from the borrower.

12 C.F.R. § 560.34 Prepayments.

Any prepayment on a real estate loan must be applied directly to reduce the principal balance on the loan unless the loan contract or the borrower specifies otherwise. Subject to the terms of the loan contract, a Federal savings association may impose a fee for any prepayment of a loan.

12 C.F.R. § 560.35 Adjustments to home loans.

(a) For any home loan secured by borrower-occupied property, or property to be occupied by the borrower, adjustments to the interest rate, payment, balance, or term to maturity must comply with the limitations of this section and the disclosure and notice requirements of § 560.210 of this part.

(b) Adjustments to the interest rate shall correspond directly to the movement of an index satisfying the requirements of paragraph (d) of this section. A Federal savings association also may increase the interest rate pursuant to a formula or schedule that specifies the amount of the increase, the time at which it may be made, and which is set forth in the loan contract. A Federal savings association may decrease the interest rate at any time.

(c) Adjustments to the payment and the loan balance that do not reflect an interest-rate adjustment may be made if:

(1) The adjustments reflect a change in an index that may be used pursuant to paragraph (d) of this section;

(2) In the case of a payment adjustment, the adjustment reflects a change in the loan balance or is made pursuant to a formula, or to a schedule specifying the percentage or dollar change in the payment as set forth in the loan contract; or

(3) In the case of an open-end line-of-credit loan, the adjustment reflects an advance taken by the borrower under the line-of-credit and is permitted by the loan contract.

(d)(1) Any index used must be readily available and independently verifiable. If set forth in the loan contract, an association may use any combination of indices, a moving average of index values, or more than one index during the term of a loan.

(2) Except as provided in paragraph (d)(3) of this section, any index used must be a national or regional index.

(3) A Federal savings association may use an index not satisfying the requirements of paragraph (d)(2) of this section 30 days after filing a notice unless, within that 30-day period, OTS has notified the association that the notice presents supervisory concerns or raises significant issues of law or policy. If OTS notifies the association of such concerns or issues, the Federal savings association may not use such an index unless it applies for and receives OTS's prior written approval under the standard treatment processing procedures at part 516, subparts A and E of this chapter.

[66 Fed. Reg. 12993 (Mar. 2, 2001)]

* * *

Subpart B—Lending and Investment Provisions Applicable to All Savings Associations.

* * *

12 C.F.R. § 560.110 Most favored lender usury preemption.

(a) *Definition.* The term "interest" as used in 12 U.S.C. 1463(g) includes any payment compensating a creditor or prospective creditor for an extension of credit, making available of a line of credit, or any default or breach by a borrower of a condition upon which credit was extended. It includes, among other things, the following fees connected with credit extension or availability: numerical periodic rates, late fees, not sufficient funds (NSF) fees, overlimit fees, annual fees, cash advance fees, and membership fees. It does not ordinarily include appraisal fees, premiums and commissions attributable to insurance guaranteeing repayment of any extension of credit, finders' fees, fees for document preparation or notarization, or fees incurred to obtain credit reports.

(b) *Authority.* A savings association located in a state may charge interest at the maximum rate permitted to any state-chartered or licensed lending institution by the law of that state. If state law permits different interest charges on specified classes of loans, a federal savings association making such loans is subject only to the provisions of state law relating to that class of loans that are material to the determination of the permitted interest. For example, a federal savings association may lawfully charge the highest rate permitted to be charged by a state-licensed small loan company, without being so licensed, but subject to state law limitations on the size of loans made by small loan companies. Except as provided in this paragraph, the applicability of state law to Federal savings associations shall be determined in accordance with § 560.2 of this part. State supervisors determine the degree to which state-chartered savings associations must comply with state laws other than those imposing restrictions on interest, as defined in paragraph (a) of this section.

(c) *Effect on state definitions of interest.* The Federal definition of the term "interest" in paragraph (a) of this section does not change how interest is defined by the individual states (nor how the state definition of interest is used) solely for purposes of state law. For example, if late fees are not "interest" under state law where a savings association is located but state law permits its most favored lender to charge late fees, then a savings association located in that state may charge late fees to its intrastate customers. The savings association may also charge late fees to its interstate customers because the fees are interest under the Federal definition of interest and an allowable charge under state law where the savings association is located. However, the late fees would not be treated as interest for purposes of evaluating compliance with state usury limitations because state law excludes late fees when calculating the maximum interest that lending institutions may charge under those limitations.

* * *

PART 591—PREEMPTION OF STATE DUE-ON-SALE LAWS

Authority: 12 U.S.C. 1464 and 1701j–3.
Source: 54 Fed. Reg. 49718 (Nov. 30, 1989), unless otherwise noted.

12 C.F.R. § 591.1 Authority, purpose, and scope.

(a) *Authority.* This part contains regulations issued under section 5 of the Home Owners' Loan Act of 1933, as amended, and under section 341 of the Garn-St Germain Depository Institutions Act of 1982, Pub. L. 97-320, 96 Stat. 1469, 1505-1507.

(b) *Purpose and scope.* The purpose of this permanent preemption of state prohibitions on the exercise of due-on-sale clauses by all lenders, whether federally- or state-chartered, is to reaffirm the authority of Federal savings associations to enforce due-on-sale clauses, and to confer on other lenders generally comparable authority with respect to the exercise of such clauses. This part applies to all real property loans, and all lenders making such loans, as those terms are defined in § 591.2 of this part.

12 C.F.R. § 591.2 Definitions.

For the purposes of this part, the following definitions apply:

(a) *Assumed* includes transfers of real property subject to a real property loan by assumptions, installment land sales contracts, wraparound loans, contracts for deed, transfers subject to the mortgage or similar lien, and other like transfers. "Completed credit application" has the same meaning as completed application for credit as provided in § 202.2(f) of this title.

(b) *Due-on-sale clause* means a contract provision which authorizes the lender, at its option, to declare immediately due and payable sums secured by the lender's security instrument upon a sale of transfer of all or any part of the real property securing the loan without the lender's prior written consent. For purposes of this definition, a *sale or transfer* means the conveyance of real property of any right, title or interest therein, whether legal or equitable, whether voluntary or involuntary, by outright sale, deed, installment sale contract, land contract, contract for deed, leasehold interest with a term greater than three years, lease-option contract or any other method of conveyance of real property interests.

(c) *Federal savings association* has the same meaning as provided in § 541.11 of this chapter.

(d) *Federal credit union* means a credit union chartered under the Federal Credit Union Act.

(e) *Home* has the same meaning as provided in § 541.14 of this chapter.

(f) *Savings association* has the same meaning as provided in § 561.43 of this chapter.

(g) *Lender* means a person or government agency making a real property loan, including without limitation, individuals, Federal savings associations, state-chartered savings associations, national banks, state-chartered banks and state-chartered mutual savings banks, Federal credit unions, state-chartered credit unions, mortgage banks, insurance companies and finance companies which make real property loans, manufactured-home retailers who extend credit, agencies of the Federal government, any lender approved by the Secretary of Housing and Urban Development for participation in any mortgage insurance program under the National Housing Act, and any assignee or transferee, in whole or part, of any such persons or agencies.

(h) *Loan secured by a lien on real property* means a loan on the security of any instrument (whether a mortgage, deed or trust, or land contract) which makes the interest in real property (whether in fee, or in a leasehold or subleasehold) specific security for the payment of the obligation secured by the instrument.

(i) *Loan secured by a lien on stock in a residential cooperative housing corporation* means a loan on the security of:

(1) A security interest in stock or a membership certificate issued to a tenant stockholder or resident member by a cooperative housing organization; and

(2) An assignment of the borrower's interest in the proprietary lease or occupancy agreement issued by such organization.

(j) *Loan secured by a lien on a residential manufactured home, whether real or personal property*, means a loan made pursuant to an agreement by which the party extending the credit acquires a security interest in the residential manufactured home.

(k) *Loan originated by* a Federal savings association or other lender means any loan for which the lender makes the first advance of

credit thereunder, *Provided*, That such lender then held a beneficial interest in the loan, whether as to the whole loan or a portion thereof, and whether or not the loan is later held by or transferred to another lender.

(l) *Real property loan* means any loan, mortgage, advance or credit sale secured by a lien on real property, the stock or membership certificate allocated to a dwelling unit in a cooperative housing corporation, or a residential manufactured home, whether real or personal property.

(m) *Residential manufactured home* has the same meaning as provided in § 590.2(g) of this chapter.

(n) *Reverse mortgage* means an instrument that provides for one or more payments to a homeowner based on accumulated equity. The lender may make payment directly, through the purchase of an annuity through an insurance company, or in any other manner. The loan may be due either on a specific date or when a specified event occurs, such as the sale of the property or the death of the borrower.

(o) *State* means the several states, Puerto Rico, the District of Columbia, Guam, the Trust Territory of the Pacific Islands, the Northern Mariana Islands, the Virgin Islands, and American Samoa.

(p)(1) A *window-period loan* means a real property loan, not originated by a Federal savings association, which was made or assumed during a window-period created by state law and subject to that law, which loan was recorded, at the time of origination or assumption, before October 15, 1982, or within 60 days thereafter (December 14, 1982).

(2) The window-period begins on: (i) The date a state adopted a law (by means of a constitutional provision or statute) prohibiting the unrestricted exercise of due-on-sale clauses upon outright transfers of property securing loans subject to the state law creating the window- period, or the effective date of a constitutional or statutory provision so adopted, whichever is later; or

(ii) The date on which the highest court of the state rendered a decision prohibiting such unrestricted exercise (or if the highest court has not so decided, the date on which the next highest appellate court rendered a decision resulting in a final judgment which applies statewide), and ends on the earlier of the date such state law prohibition terminated under state law or October 15, 1982.

(3) Categories of state law which create window-periods by prohibiting the unrestricted exercise of due-on-sale clauses upon outright transfers of property securing loans subject to such state law restrictions include laws or judicial decisions which permit the lender to exercise its option under a due-on-sale clause only where:

(i) The lender's security interest or the likelihood of repayment is impaired; or

(ii) The lender is required to accept an assumption of the existing loan without an interest-rate change or with an interest-rate change below the market interest rate currently being offered

by the lender on similar loans secured by similar property at the time of the transfer.

[54 Fed. Reg. 49718 (Nov. 30, 1989), *as amended at* 67 Fed. Reg. 60554 (Sept. 26, 2002)]

12 C.F.R. § 591.3 Loans originated by Federal savings associations.

(a) With regard to any real property loan originated or to be originated by a Federal savings association, as a matter of contract between it and the borrower, a Federal savings association continues to have the power to include a due-on-sale clause in its loan instrument.

(b) Except as otherwise provided in § 591.5 of this part with respect to any such loan made on the security of a home occupied or to be occupied by the borrower, exercise by any lender of a due-on-sale clause in a loan originated by a Federal savings association shall be exclusively governed by the terms of the loan contract, and all rights and remedies of the lender and borrower shall at all times be fixed and governed by that contract.

12 C.F.R. § 591.4 Loans originated by lenders other than Federal savings associations.

(a) With regard to any real property loan originated by a lender other than a Federal savings association, as a matter of contract between it and the borrower, the lender has the power to include a due on sale clause in its loan instrument.

(b) Except as otherwise provided in paragraph (c) of this section and § 591.5 of this part, the exercise of due-on-sale clauses in loans originated by lenders other than Federal savings associations shall be governed exclusively by the terms of the loan contract, and all rights and remedies of the lender and the borrower shall be fixed and governed by that contract.

(c)(1) In the case of a window-period loan, the provisions of paragraph (b) of this section shall apply only in the case of a sale or transfer of the property subject to the real property loan and only if such sale or transfer occurs on or after October 15, 1985: *Provided*, That:

(i) With respect to real property loans originated in a state by lenders other than national banks, Federal savings associations, and Federal credit unions, a state may otherwise regulate such contracts by state law enacted prior to October 16, 1985, in which case paragraph (b) of this section shall apply only if such state law so provides; and

(ii) With respect to real property loans originated by national banks and Federal credit unions, the Comptroller of the Currency or the National Credit Union Administration Board, respectively, may otherwise regulate such contracts by regulations promulgated prior to October 16, 1985, in which case paragraph (b) of this section shall apply only if such regulation so provides.

(2) A lender may not exercise its options pursuant to a due-on-sale clause contained in a window-period loan in the case of a sale or transfer of property securing such loan where the sale or transfer occurred prior to October 15, 1982.

(d)(1) Prior to the sale or transfer of property securing a window-period loan subject to the provisions of paragraph (c) of this section.

(i) Any lender in the business of making real property loans may require any successor or transferee of the borrower to supply credit information customarily required by the lender in connection with credit applications, to complete its customary credit application, and to meet customary credit standards applied by such lender, at the date of sale or transfer, to the lender's similar loans secured by similar property.

(ii) Any lender not in the business of making loans may require any successor or transferee of the borrower to meet credit standards customarily applied by other similarly situated lenders or sellers in the geographic market within which the transaction occurs, for similar loans secured by similar property, prior to the lender's consent to the transfer.

(2) The lender may exercise a due-on-sale clause in a window-period loan if:

(i) The successor or transferee of the borrower fails to meet the lender's credit standards as set forth in paragraphs (b)(1)(i) and (b)(1)(ii) of this section; or

(ii) Upon transfer of the security property and not later than fifteen days after written request by the lender, the successor or transferee of the borrower fails to provide information requested by the lender pursuant to paragraph (d)(1)(i) or (d)(1)(ii) of this section, to determine whether such successor or transferee of the borrower meets the lender's customary credit standards.

(3) The lender shall, within thirty days of receipt of a completed credit application and any other related information provided by the successor or transferee of the borrower, determine whether such successor or transferee meets the customary credit standards of the lender and provide written notice to the successor or transferee of its decision, and the reasons in the event of a disapproval. Failure of the lender to provide such notice shall preclude the lender from exercise of its due-on-sale clause upon the sale or transfer of the property securing the loan.

(4) The lender's right to exercise a due-on-sale clause pursuant to this paragraph (d)(4) is in addition to any rights afforded the lender by state law regulating window-period loans with regard to the exercise of due-on-sale clauses and loan assumptions.

12 C.F.R. § 591.5 Limitation on exercise of due-on-sale clauses.

(a) *General.* Except as provided in § 591.4 (c) and (d)(4) of this part, due-on-sale practices of Federal savings associations and other lenders shall be governed exclusively by the Office's regulations, in preemption of and without regard to any limitations imposed by state law on either their inclusion or exercise including, without limitation, state law prohibitions against restraints on alienation, prohibitions against penalties and forfeitures, equitable restrictions and state law dealing with equitable transfers.

(b) *Specific limitations.* With respect to any loan on the security of a home occupied or to be occupied by the borrower,

(1) A lender shall not (except with regard to a reverse mortgage) exercise its option pursuant to a due-on-sale clause upon:

(i) The creation of a lien or other encumbrance subordinate to the lender's security instrument which does not relate to a transfer of rights of occupancy in the property: *Provided,* That such lien or encumbrance is not created pursuant to a contract for deed;

(ii) The creation of a purchase-money security interest for household appliances;

(iii) A transfer by devise, descent, or operation of law on the death of a joint tenant or tenant by the entirety;

(iv) The granting of a leasehold interest which has a term of three years or less and which does not contain an option to purchase (that is, either a lease of more than three years or a lease with an option to purchase will allow the exercise of a due-on-sale clause);

(v) A transfer, in which the transferee is a person who occupies or will occupy the property, which is:

(A) A transfer to a relative resulting from the death of the borrower;

(B) A transfer where the spouse or child(ren) becomes an owner of the property; or

(C) A transfer resulting from a decree of dissolution of marriage, legal separation agreement, or from an incidental property settlement agreement by which the spouse becomes an owner of the property; or

(vi) A transfer into an inter vivos trust in which the borrower is and remains the beneficiary and occupant of the property, unless, as a condition precedent to such transfer, the borrower refuses to provide the lender with reasonable means acceptable to the lender by which the lender will be assured of timely notice of any subsequent transfer of the beneficial interest or change in occupancy.

(2) A lender shall not impose a prepayment penalty or equivalent fee when the lender or party acting on behalf of the lender

(i) Declares by written notice that the loan is due pursuant to a due-on-sale clause or

(ii) Commences a judicial or nonjudicial foreclosure proceeding to enforce a due-on-sale clause or to seek payment in full as a result of invoking such clause.

(3) A lender shall not impose a prepayment penalty or equivalent fee when the lender or party acting on behalf of the lender fails to approve within 30 days the completed credit application of a qualified transferee of the security property to assume the loan in accordance with the terms of the loan, and thereafter the borrower transfers the security property to such transferee and prepays the loan in full within 120 days after receipt by the lender of the completed credit application. For purposes of this paragraph (b)(3), a *qualified transferee* is a person who qualifies for the loan under the lender's applicable underwriting standards and who occupies or will occupy the security property.

(4) A lender waives its option to exercise a due-on-sale clause as to a specific transfer if, before the transfer, the lender and the existing borrower's prospective successor in interest agree in writing that the successor in interest will be obligated under the terms of the loan and that interest on sums secured by the lender's security interest will be payable at a rate the lender shall request. Upon such agreement and resultant waiver, a lender shall release the existing borrower from all obligations under the loan instruments, and the lender is deemed to have made a new loan to the existing borrower's successor in interest. The waiver and release apply to all loans secured by homes occupied by borrowers made by a Federal savings association after July 31, 1976, and to all loans secured by homes occupied by borrowers made by other lenders after the effective date of this regulation.

(5) Nothing in paragraph (b)(1) of this section shall be construed to restrict a lender's right to enforce a due-on-sale clause upon the subsequent occurrence of any event which disqualifies a transfer for a previously-applicable exception under that paragraph (b)(1).

(c) *Policy considerations.* Paragraph (b) of this section does not prohibit a lender from requiring, as a condition to an assumption, continued maintenance of mortgage insurance by the existing borrower's successor in interest, whether by endorsement of the existing policy or by entrance into a new contract of insurance.

12 C.F.R. § 591.6 Interpretations.

The Office periodically will publish Interpretations under section 341 of the Garn-St Germain Depository Institutions Act of 1982, Pub. L. 97-320, 96 Stat. 1469, 1505-1507, in the *Federal Register* in response to written requests sent to the Secretary, Office of Thrift Supervision, 1700 G Street, NW., Washington, DC 20552.

D.3 OTS Interpretive Letters

This section summarizes OTS interpretive letters and releases relating both to the preemption of state laws and to the scope of OTS authority and saving association powers. Letters interpreting the Alternative Mortgage Transactions Parity Act are summarized in Appx. H.3.

, Certain of these letters may be referenced in Chapter 3, *supra*. The full text of these letters, with one exception mentioned below, can be found on the CD-Rom accompanying this supplement. New letters will be posted on the CD-Rom accompanying future supplements. These letters can also be obtained from the OTS website: www.ots.treas.gov, click on "issuances" and then on "legal opinions."

The letter dated October 17, 1994, which is summarized here, does not appear in full text on the OTS's website. The summary of this letter appears in a GAO report entitled "Role of the Office of Thrift Supervision and Office of the Comptroller of the Currency in the Preemption of State Law," GAO/GGD/OGC-00-51R (Feb. 7, 2000).

Date of Opinion	State Affected	State Laws/Provisions
October 28, 2004	Illinois	State law that imposes qualification limitations or restrictions on foreign corporations to act as trustee, administrator, executive, or in another fiduciary capacity in the state and imposes application or registration requirements and subjects the association to examination or supervision of a state agency is preempted.
October 25, 2004	General	The OTS opined that an agent need not comply with state licensing or registration laws where the agent and the association enter into a written agreement specifying certain duties and responsibilities; where the agent must undergo training from the association on the products and applicable laws before commencing its activities on behalf of the association; and where the agent is subject to the association's and OTS's supervision and control. Although the company was the exclusive agent of the association, this factor does not appear to be a precondition to the agent's qualifications for preemption.
September 17, 2004	General	OTS confirms that savings associations may charge the interest rate allowed by its home state regardless of where the loan is "made" or "booked"; or the state in which a branch exists, if the loan is "booked" in the branch's state. OTS distinguishes the more restrictive standards set forth in OCC and FDIC letters on this issue.
September 14, 2004	General	An operating subsidiary of a savings association may own, sell, underwrite, and deal in asset-backed securities to the same extent as the saving association could itself. OTS applies four factors in arriving at this decision.
October 6, 2003	New York	State law requiring payment of interest on mortgage escrow accounts is preempted. Choice of law provision that applies both federal and state law does not effect the preemption decision. OTS also decides that even in the absence of a specific contract incorporation of federal law, a Supreme Court case states that "the law of the jurisdiction" includes federal law.
September 2, 2003	New Mexico	Home Loan Protection Act is completely preempted, even the provision dealing with judicial foreclosure for high-cost loans and the provision which makes violations of the act unfair and deceptive acts under the state UDAP law.

Date of Opinion	State Affected	State Laws/Provisions
July 22, 2003	New Jersey	Homeownership Security Act is preempted, including the provision requiring use of judicial foreclosure for high-cost loans. OTS notes that a provision similar to the FTC holder rule, if applied to non-savings association originators, could apply to saving association assignees. OTS affirms principle that the preemption applies to federal saving associations and their operating subsidiaries when originating the loan.
January 30, 2003	New York	New York's Predatory Lending Law, a HOEPA-like state law, is preempted as it relates to savings associations and operating subsidiaries. Requirement in foreclosure context that holder prove compliance with the law is preempted as well.
January 21, 2003	Georgia	Georgia Fair Lending Law, a HOEPA-like state law, that regulates the terms of credit, some loan-related fees, disclosures, and refinancings is preempted for savings associations and their operating subsidiaries for loans originated in their name. Excluded from coverage of the letter are provisions regarding foreclosure procedures and consumer remedies.
October 1, 2002	California	California law requiring credit card issuers to provide cardholders a combination of warnings and estimates of the length of time necessary to pay off their balances and the total cost of credit if minimum payments are made, requiring a referral to credit counseling under certain circumstances, and requiring the maintenance of a toll-free number to provide payoff estimates is preempted.
June 12, 2002	Oklahoma	Oklahoma law restricting the installation, operation, or utilization of ATM machines by an out-of-state savings association or operating subsidiary with no in-state offices is preempted.
May 14, 2002	Wisconsin	Wisconsin law that imposes specific disclosure and substantive requirements on automobile finance leases that are the functional equivalent of loans as defined under OTS regulations is preempted.
March 21, 2002	Arizona	Arizona law requiring credit card lenders to report current interest rates and related information for each type of credit card it offers to the state superintendent of banks is preempted.
March 1, 2002	General	Exhaustive listing of and citations to authority for all of the powers of savings associations and operating subsidiaries.
January 10, 2002	General	An operating subsidiary of a savings association may conduct fiduciary activities to the same extent and in the same manner as the parent association.
December 14, 2001	Iowa	Restrictions in Iowa law on the amount of origination charges and the type of other charges allowed in connection with a purchase money mortgage loan or the refinancing of an existing loan are preempted.
June 26, 2001	General	Federal savings banks are not subject to local ordinances that prohibit a bank from charging a non-account holder an ATM fee.
May 16, 2001	Iowa, Texas, Wisconsin	Certain credit card lending requirements regarding notice to consumers to change the terms of an open-end credit arrangement, notice requirements of late fee on each periodic statement, and a mandate that certain minimum default events exist before declaring the balance on an open-end credit plan to be due are preempted.
January 3, 2001	Virginia	State law prohibiting a federal savings bank from exercising fiduciary powers is preempted as long as the bank has received approval from the OTS to engage in this activity.

Date of Opinion	State Affected	State Laws/Provisions
June 2, 2000	General	The term "reverse mortgage" includes an instrument providing for a lump-sum payment to a homeowner based on accumulated equity in the security property for purposes of OTS due-on-sale regulation.
April 21, 2000	New York	New York law that prohibits the charging of a fee for a payoff statement is preempted. A saving association can charge a fax fee to rapidly transmit a payoff statement, regardless of New York law.
December 7, 1999	Local Ordinance San Francisco, California	A local ordinance prohibiting a financial institution from charging a fee to a customer for accessing an automated teller machine (ATM) of that financial institution with an access device—a card, code or other means of access—to a customer's account not issued by that financial institution.
November 22, 1999	Local Ordinance Santa Monica, California	A local ordinance prohibiting a financial institution from charging a fee to a customer for accessing an ATM of that financial institution with an access device not issued by that financial institution.
July 29, 1999	Maryland	Maryland's Mortgage Lender Law requiring an operating subsidiary of a financial institution to obtain a state license before conducting banking business.
July 26, 1999	Maryland	Maryland's Mortgage Lender Law requiring state licensing and approval for mortgage lenders.
	Connecticut	A law requiring a subsidiary of any financial institution to obtain state approval before engaging in banking business.
March 10, 1999	California	California Unfair Competition Act provisions on lending activities in the areas of advertising, the forced placement of hazard insurance and the imposition of certain specified loans.
January 4, 1999	Connecticut	A provision requiring application and approval from the State Banking Commissioner before opening a de novo branch.
December 22, 1998	Massachusetts	Provisions restricting the establishment and operations of electronic branches, including ATMs, applying to federal savings associations.
July 1, 1998	Iowa	A law prohibits or limits out-of-state financial institutions from establishing an ATM.
	Wyoming	A law requiring state approval before financial institutions can establish ATMs and fees to be properly disclosed to the consumer.
July 1, 1998	Georgia	A law prohibiting or restricting an out-of-state savings and loan association from engaging in interstate pre-need funeral trust services and fiduciary activities.
	Missouri	A law prohibiting or restricting an out-of-state savings and loan association from engaging in interstate pre-need funeral trust services and fiduciary activities.
	Illinois	A law prohibiting or restricting an out-of-state savings and loan association from engaging in interstate pre-need funeral trust services and fiduciary activities.
	Connecticut	A law prohibiting any corporation other than a bank or an out-of-state bank that maintains a branch in the state from acting in a fiduciary capacity.
	Michigan	A law barring out-of-state federal savings associations and federal savings bank from acting as a fiduciary in the state.
	Kansas	A law allowing an out-of-state federal savings bank to act as a fiduciary in the state only if the federal savings bank's home state permits an out-of-state federal savings bank to act in a similar fiduciary capacity.

Date of Opinion	State Affected	State Laws/Provisions
May 11, 1998	New York	A tax law barring mortgage lenders from passing on to consumers a special mortgage recording tax.
September 2, 1997	Virgin Islands	A Virgin Islands Banking Board Order that prohibits charging against insurance settlement proceeds fees for the inspection of reconstructed properties securing mortgage loans and requires the refund of all such fees collected since September 15, 1995. A statutory provision requiring financial institutions to obtain license to do business in the Virgin Islands.
August 25, 1997	Ohio	Specific provisions adopted by the Ohio legislature did not constitute an opt-out of the Depository Institutions Deregulation and Monetary Control Act of 1980 preemption provisions regarding discount points and federal-related residential mortgage loans secured by a first lien on residential real property made after March 31, 1980.
August 19, 1997	New Jersey	Operating subsidiaries of a federal savings and loan association would be preempted from the New Jersey Licensed Lenders Act when making first and second mortgage loans.
December 24, 1996	Indiana	A provision of the Indiana Uniform Consumer Credit Code requiring specific lending disclosures and certain loan-related charges by savings and loan associations.
August 8, 1996	Louisiana	A law requiring a trustee to be a financial institution organized under the laws of Louisiana or of the United States and domiciled in Louisiana.
	Oregon	A law prohibiting an out-of-state fiduciary from performing as a trustee of a trust holding real estate.
	Texas	A law prohibiting out-of-state fiduciaries from marketing and advertising of trust services and from acting as trustee in the state unless the trust company's state permits Texas-chartered fiduciaries to act in such capacity.
	Virginia	A law prohibiting an out-of-state fiduciary from performing as a trustee of a trust holding real estate.
	Wisconsin	A law prohibiting out-of-state trust companies from acting in any fiduciary capacity in Wisconsin unless the foreign trust corporation's home state permits Wisconsin-chartered fiduciaries to act in a similar manner.
June 21, 1996	California	A law prohibiting out-of-state corporations, other than national banks with branch offices in the state and out-of-state banks authorized by the state, to conduct trust business.
	New York	A provision prohibiting out-of-state trust companies from acting as a fiduciary in the state unless their home states permit same for New York chartered trusts.
	Ohio	A law imposing filing and licensing requirements on out-of-state fiduciaries wanting to do trust business in the state.
	Vermont	A law prohibiting savings associations from trust services marketing unless supervised by Vermont Banking Commissioner.
March 28, 1996		Any state law requiring a license or prohibiting the performance of trust powers by a federal savings association.
January 18, 1996	Colorado	A law requiring all financial institutions accepting deposits in Colorado to file detailed annual reports with the state.
May 10, 1995	Georgia	Provisions of the Georgia Residential Mortgage Act, involving licensing, registration, advertising, disclosure, escrow accounts, financial reports, maintenance of books and records, and fees for registration and filing.

Date of Opinion	State Affected	State Laws/Provisions
December 14, 1994	Virginia	Money Order Sales Act requiring a person to obtain a money order license from the State Corporation Commission.
October 18, 1994	Wisconsin	A law requiring a savings association to provide an individual who requests a copy of a credit report without extra charge.
October 17, 1994	Arizona	A law requiring any company that wishes to engage in the mortgage banking business in that state to file an application for a license, register to do business, post bond, and maintain a minimum net worth.
	Maine	A law requiring any company that wishes to originate consumer loans in that state to file an application for a license and to demonstrate that it is financially responsible and prohibiting lenders from taking a security interest in real property for consumer loans under a specified amount.

Appendix E   Federal Credit Union Act

This appendix excerpts portions of the Federal Credit Union Act. These provisions appear in E.1. Section E.2 includes selected regulations promulgated by the National Credit Union Administration (NCUA). In addition, the NCUA issues Interpretive Letters from time to time. Relevant letters are summarized in E.3. The full text of these letters is included on the CD-Rom accompanying this volume and is updated in the annual supplements. The CD-Rom also includes the statutes and regulations reprinted in Appxs. E.1 and E.2.

E.1 Selected Statutory Provisions

TITLE 12—BANKS AND BANKING
CHAPTER 14—FEDERAL CREDIT UNIONS
SUBCHAPTER I—GENERAL PROVISIONS

* * *

§ 1756.   Reports and examinations

* * *

§ 1757.   Powers

* * *

§ 1785.   Requirements governing insured credit unions [*This section is reprinted in Appx. G.1, infra, not herein, because it was added by the Depository Institutions Deregulation and Monetary Control Act of 1980.*]

* * *

12 U.S.C. § 1756. Reports and examinations

Federal credit unions shall be under the supervision of the Board, and shall make financial reports to it as and when it may require, but at least annually. Each Federal credit union shall be subject to examination by, and for this purpose shall make its books and records accessible to, any person designated by the Board.

[June 26, 1934, ch. 750, title I, § 106, formerly § 6, 48 Stat. 1218; Dec. 6, 1937, ch. 3, § 1, 51 Stat. 4; 1947 Reorg. Plan No. 1, § 401, eff. July 1, 1947, 12 F.R. 4534, 61 Stat. 952; June 29, 1948, ch. 711, §§ 1, 2, 62 Stat. 1091; renumbered § 7 and amended Pub. L. No. 86–354, § 1, 73 Stat. 629 Sept. 22, 1959); Pub. L. No. 91–206, § 2(1), 84 Stat. 49 (Mar. 10, 1970); renumbered title I, § 106, Pub. L. No. 91–468, § 1(2), 84 Stat. 994 (Oct. 19, 1970); amended Pub. L. No. 95–630, title V, § 508, 92 Stat. 3683 (Nov. 10, 1978)]

* * *

12 U.S.C. § 1757. Powers

A Federal credit union shall have succession in its corporate name during its existence and shall have power—

(1) to make contracts;

(2) to sue and be sued;

(3) to adopt and use a common seal and alter the same at pleasure;

(4) to purchase, hold, and dispose of property necessary or incidental to its operations;

(5) to make loans, the maturities of which shall not exceed twelve years except as otherwise provided herein, and extend lines of credit to its members, to other credit unions, and to credit union organizations and to participate with other credit unions, credit union organizations, or financial organizations in making loans to credit union members in accordance with the following:

(A) Loans to members shall be made in conformity with criteria established by the board of directors: Provided, That—

(i) a residential real estate loan on a one-to-four-family dwelling, including an individual cooperative unit, that is or will be the principal residence of a credit union member, and which is secured by a first lien upon such dwelling, may have a maturity not exceeding thirty years or such other limits as shall be set by the National Credit Union Administration Board (except that a loan on an individual cooperative unit shall be adequately secured as defined by the Board), subject to the rules and regulations of the Board;

(ii) a loan to finance the purchase of a mobile home, which shall be secured by a first lien on such mobile home, to be used by the credit union member as his residence, a loan for the repair, alteration, or improvement of a residential dwelling which is the residence of a credit union member, or a second mortgage loan secured by a residential dwelling which is the residence of a credit union member, shall have a maturity not to exceed 15 years or any longer term which the Board may allow;

(iii) a loan secured by the insurance or guarantee of, or with advance commitment to purchase the loan by, the Federal Government, a State government, or any agency of either may be made for the maturity and under the terms and conditions specified in the law under which such insurance, guarantee, or commitment is provided;

(iv) a loan or aggregate of loans to a director or member of the supervisory or credit committee of the credit union making the loan which exceeds $20,000 plus pledged shares, be approved by the board of directors;

(v) loans to other members for which directors or members of the supervisory or credit committee act as guarantor or endorser be approved by the board of directors when such loans standing alone or when added to any outstanding loan or loans of the guarantor or endorser exceeds $20,000;

(vi) the rate of interest may not exceed 15 per centum per annum on the unpaid balance inclusive of all finance charges, except that the Board may establish—

(I) after consultation with the appropriate committees of the Congress, the Department of Treasury, and the Federal financial institution regulatory agencies, an interest rate ceiling exceeding such 15 per centum per annum rate, for periods not to exceed 18 months, if it determines that money market interest rates have risen over the preceding six-month period and that prevailing interest rate levels threaten the safety and soundness of individual credit unions as evidenced by adverse trends in liquidity, capital, earnings, and growth; and

(II) a higher interest rate ceiling for Agent members for the Central Liquidity Facility in carrying out the provisions of subchapter III of this chapter for such periods as the Board may authorize;

(vii) the taking, receiving, reserving, or charging of a rate of interest greater than is allowed by this paragraph, when knowingly done, shall be deemed a forfeiture of the entire interest which the note, bill, or other evidence of debt carries with it, or which has been agreed to be paid thereon. If such greater rate of interest has been paid, the person by whom it has been paid, or his legal representatives, may recover back from the credit union taking or receiving the same, in an action in the nature of an action of debt, the entire amount of interest paid; but such action must be commenced within two years from the time the usurious collection was made;

(viii) a borrower may repay his loan, prior to maturity in whole or in part on any business day without penalty, except that on a first or second mortgage loan a Federal credit union may require that any partial prepayments

(I) be made on the date monthly installments are due, and

(II) be in the amount of that part of one or more monthly installments which would be applicable to principal;

(ix) loans shall be paid or amortized in accordance with rules and regulations prescribed by the Board after taking into account the needs or conditions of the borrowers, the amounts and duration of the loans, the interests of the members and the credit unions, and such other factors as the Board deems relevant;

(x) loans must be approved by the credit committee or a loan officer, but no loan may be made to any member if, upon the making of that loan, the member would be indebted to the Federal credit union upon loans made to him in an aggregate amount which would exceed 10 per centum of the credit union's unimpaired capital and surplus.

(B) A self-replenishing line of credit to a borrower may be established to a stated maximum amount on certain terms and conditions which may be different from the terms and conditions established for another borrower.

(C) Loans to other credit unions shall be approved by the board of directors.

(D) Loans to credit union organizations shall be approved by the board of directors and shall not exceed 1 per centum of the paid-in and unimpaired capital and surplus of the credit union. A credit union organization means any organization as determined by the Board, which is established primarily to serve the needs of its member credit unions, and whose business relates to the daily operations of the credit unions they serve.

(E) Participation loans with other credit unions, credit union organizations, or financial organizations shall be in accordance with written policies of the board of directors: Provided, That a credit union which originates a loan for which participation arrangements are made in accordance with this subsection shall retain an interest of at least 10 per centum of the face amount of the loan.

(6) to receive from its members, from other credit unions, from an officer, employee, or agent of those nonmember units of Federal, Indian tribal, State, or local governments and political subdivisions thereof enumerated in section 1787 of this title and in the manner so prescribed, from the Central Liquidity Facility, and from nonmembers in the case of credit unions serving predominately low-income members (as defined by the Board) payments, representing equity, on—

(A) shares which may be issued at varying dividend rates;

(B) share certificates which may be issued at varying dividend rates and maturities; and

(C) share draft accounts authorized under section 1785 (f) of this title;

subject to such terms, rates, and conditions as may be established by the board of directors, within limitations prescribed by the Board.

(7) to invest its funds

(A) in loans exclusively to members;

(B) in obligations of the United States of America, or securities fully guaranteed as to principal and interest thereby;

(C) in accordance with rules and regulations prescribed by the Board, in loans to other credit unions in the total amount not exceeding 25 per centum of its paid-in and unimpaired capital and surplus;

(D) in shares or accounts of savings and loan associations or mutual savings banks, the accounts of which are insured by the Federal Savings and Loan Insurance Corporation or the Federal Deposit Insurance Corporation;

(E) in obligations issued by banks for cooperatives, Federal land banks, Federal intermediate credit banks, Federal home loan banks, the Federal Home Loan Bank Board,[1] or any corporation designated in section 9101 (3) of title 31 as a wholly owned Government corporation; or in obligations, participations, or other instruments of or issued by, or fully guaranteed as to principal and interest by, the Federal National Mortgage Association or the Government National Mortgage Association, or in mortgages, obligations, or other securities which are or ever have been sold by the Federal Home Loan Mortgage Corporation pursuant to section 1454 or 1455 of this title; or in obligations or other instruments or securities of the Student

---

1   This statute makes reference to the Federal Home Loan Bank Board (FHLBB) and its authority. The Financial Institutions Reform, Recovery and Enforcement Act of 1989 (FIRREA), Pub. L. No. 101-73, 103 Stat. 183 (Aug. 9, 1989), abolished the FHLBB and replaced it with the Office of Thrift Supervision (OTS). The relevant authority was transferred from the FHLBB to the OTS.

Loan Marketing Association; or in obligations, participations, securities, or other instruments of, or issued by, or fully guaranteed as to principal and interest by any other agency of the United States and a Federal credit union may issue and sell securities which are guaranteed pursuant to section 1721 (g) of this title;

(F) in participation certificates evidencing beneficial interests in obligations, or in the right to receive interest and principal collections therefrom, which obligations have been subjected by one or more Government agencies to a trust or trusts for which any executive department, agency, or instrumentality of the United States (or the head thereof) has been named to act as trustee;

(G) in shares or deposits of any central credit union in which such investments are specifically authorized by the board of directors of the Federal credit union making the investment;

(H) in shares, share certificates, or share deposits of federally insured credit unions;

(I) in the shares, stocks, or obligations of any other organization, providing services which are associated with the routine operations of credit unions, up to 1 per centum of the total paid in and unimpaired capital and surplus of the credit union with the approval of the Board: Provided, however, That such authority does not include the power to acquire control directly or indirectly, of another financial institution, nor invest in shares, stocks or obligations of an insurance company, trade association, liquidity facility or any other similar organization, corporation, or association, except as otherwise expressly provided by this chapter;

(J) in the capital stock of the National Credit Union Central Liquidity Facility;

(K) investments in obligations of, or issued by, any State or political subdivision thereof (including any agency, corporation, or instrumentality of a State or political subdivision), except that no credit union may invest more than 10 per centum of its unimpaired capital and surplus in the obligations of any one issuer (exclusive of general obligations of the issuer).[2]

(8) to make deposits in national banks and in State banks, trust companies, and mutual savings banks operating in accordance with the laws of the State in which the Federal credit union does business, or in banks or institutions the accounts of which are insured by the Federal Deposit Insurance Corporation or the Federal Savings and Loan Insurance Corporation, and for Federal credit unions or credit unions authorized by the Department of Defense operating sub-offices on American military installations in foreign countries or trust territories of the United States to maintain demand deposit accounts in banks located in those countries or trust territories, subject to such regulations as may be issued by the Board and provided such banks are correspondents of banks described in this paragraph;

(9) to borrow, in accordance with such rules and regulations as may be prescribed by the Board, from any source, in an aggregate amount not exceeding, except as authorized by the Board in carrying out the provisions of subchapter III of this chapter, 50 per centum of its paid-in and unimpaired capital and surplus: Provided, That any Federal credit union may discount with or sell to any Federal intermediate credit bank any eligible obligations up to the amount of its paid-in and unimpaired capital;

---

2 So in original. Probably should be a semicolon.

(10) to levy late charges, in accordance with the bylaws, for failure of members to meet promptly their obligations to the Federal credit union;

(11) to impress and enforce a lien upon the shares and dividends of any member, to the extent of any loan made to him and any dues or charges payable by him;

(12) in accordance with rules and regulations prescribed by the Board, to sell to members negotiable checks (including travelers checks), money orders, and other similar money transfer instruments, and to cash checks and money orders for members, for a fee;

(13) in accordance with rules and regulations prescribed by the Board, to purchase, sell, pledge, or discount or otherwise receive or dispose of, in whole or in part, any eligible obligations (as defined by the Board) of its members and to purchase from any liquidating credit union notes made by individual members of the liquidating credit union at such prices as may be agreed upon by the board of directors of the liquidating credit union and the board of directors of the purchasing credit union, but no purchase may be made under authority of this paragraph if, upon the making of that purchase, the aggregate of the unpaid balances of notes purchased under authority of this paragraph would exceed 5 per centum of the unimpaired capital and surplus of the credit union;

(14) to sell all or a part of its assets to another credit union, to purchase all or part of the assets of another credit union and to assume the liabilities of the selling credit union and those of its members subject to regulations of the Board;

(15) to invest in securities that—

(A) are offered and sold pursuant to section 77d (5) of title 15;

(B) are mortgage related securities (as that term is defined in section 78c (a)(41) of title 15), subject to such regulations as the Board may prescribe, including regulations prescribing minimum size of the issue (at the time of initial distribution) or minimum aggregate sales prices, or both; or

(C) are small business related securities (as defined in section 78c (a)(53) of title 15), subject to such regulations as the Board may prescribe, including regulations prescribing the minimum size of the issue (at the time of the initial distribution), the minimum aggregate sales price, or both;

(16) subject to such regulations as the Board may prescribe, to provide technical assistance to credit unions in Poland and Hungary; and

(17) to exercise such incidental powers as shall be necessary or requisite to enable it to carry on effectively the business for which it is incorporated.

[(June 26, 1934, ch. 750, title I, § 107, formerly § 7, 48 Stat. 1218; Dec. 6, 1937, ch. 3, § 2, 51 Stat. 4; July 31, 1946, ch. 711, § 1, 60 Stat. 744; 1947 Reorg. Plan No. 1, § 401, eff. July 1, 1947, 12 F.R. 4534, 61 Stat. 952; June 29, 1948, ch. 711, §§ 1, 2, 62 Stat. 1091; Oct. 25, 1949, ch. 713, § 1, 63 Stat. 890; May 13, 1952, ch. 264, 66 Stat. 70; renumbered § 8 and amended Pub. L. No. 86–354, § 1, 73 Stat. 630 (Sept. 22, 1959); Pub. L. No. 88–353, § 1, 78 Stat. 269 (July 2, 1964); Pub. L. No. 89–429, § 7, 80 Stat. 167 (May 24, 1966); Pub. L. No. 90–44, §§ 2, 3, 81 Stat. 110, 111 (July 3, 1967); Pub. L. No. 90–375, § 1(1)–(3), 82 Stat. 284 (July 5, 1968); Pub. L. No. 90–448, title VIII, § 807(n), 82 Stat. 545 (Aug. 1, 1968); Pub. L. No. 91–206, § 2(1), 84 Stat. 49 (Mar. 10, 1970); renumbered title I, § 107, and amended Pub. L. No. 91–468, §§ 1(2), 10, 84 Stat. 994, 1017 (Oct. 19, 1970); Pub. L. No. 92–318, title I,

§ 133(c)(4), 86 Stat. 270 (June 23, 1972); Pub. L. No. 93–383, title VII, § 721, title VIII, § 805(c)(5), 88 Stat. 719, 727 (Aug. 22, 1974); Pub. L. No. 93–495, title I, § 101(d), 88 Stat. 1502 (Oct. 28, 1974); Pub. L. No. 93–569, § 6, 88 Stat. 1866 (Dec. 31, 1974); Pub. L. No. 95–22, title III, §§ 302, 303, 91 Stat. 49, 51 (Apr. 19, 1977); Pub. L. No. 95–630, title V, § 502(b), title XVIII, § 1803, 92 Stat. 3681, 3723 (Nov. 10, 1978); Pub. L. No. 96–153, title III, § 323(d), 93 Stat. 1120 (Dec. 21, 1979); Pub. L. No. 96–161, title I, § 103(b), 93 Stat. 1234 (Dec. 28, 1979); Pub. L. No. 96–221, title III, §§ 305(b), 307, 309 (a)(1), 310, 94 Stat. 146–149 (Mar. 31, 1980); Pub. L. No. 97–320, title V, §§ 506–514, 516–518, 96 Stat. 1528–1530 (Oct. 15, 1982); Pub. L. No. 97–457, §§ 25, 26, 96 Stat. 2510 (Jan. 12, 1983); Pub. L. No. 98–440, title I, § 105(b), 98 Stat. 1691 (Oct. 3, 1984); Pub. L. No. 98–479, title II, § 206, 98 Stat. 2234 (Oct. 17, 1984); Pub. L. No. 100–86, title VII, §§ 702, 703, 101 Stat. 652 (Aug. 10, 1987); Pub. L. No. 101–179, title II, § 206(b), 103 Stat. 1311 (Nov. 28, 1989); Pub. L. No. 103–325, title II, § 206(b), 108 Stat. 2199 (Sept. 23, 1994); Pub. L. No. 104–208, div. A, title II, § 2306, 110 Stat. 3009–426 (Sept. 30, 1996)]

E.2 Selected Regulations[3]

TITLE 12—BANKS AND BANKING

CHAPTER VII—NATIONAL CREDIT UNION ADMINISTRATION

SUBCHAPTER A—REGULATIONS AFFECTING CREDIT UNIONS

PART 701—ORGANIZATION AND OPERATION OF FEDERAL CREDIT UNIONS

* * *

§ 701.21 Loans to members and lines of credit to members.

* * *

§ 701.23 Purchase, sale, and pledge of eligible obligations.

* * *

§ 701.31 Nondiscrimination requirements.

* * *

PART 706—CREDIT PRACTICES

§ 706.1 Definitions.

§ 706.2 Unfair credit practices.

§ 706.3 Unfair or deceptive cosigner practices.

§ 706.4 Late charges.

§ 706.5 State exemptions.

* * *

PART 721—INCIDENTAL POWERS

§ 721.1 What does this part cover?

§ 721.2 What is an incidental powers activity?

§ 721.3 What categories of activities are preapproved as incidental powers necessary or requisite to carry on a credit union's business?

§ 721.4 How may a credit union apply to engage in an activity that is not preapproved as within a credit union's incidental powers?

§ 721.5 What limitations apply to a credit union engaging in activities approved under this part?

§ 721.6 May a credit union derive income from activities approved under this part?

§ 721.7 What are the potential conflicts of interest for officials and employees when credit unions engage in activities approved under this part?

* * *

TITLE 12—BANKS AND BANKING

CHAPTER VII—NATIONAL CREDIT UNION ADMINISTRATION

SUBCHAPTER A—REGULATIONS AFFECTING CREDIT UNIONS

PART 701—ORGANIZATION AND OPERATION OF FEDERAL CREDIT UNIONS

* * *

12 C.F.R. § 701.21 Loans to members and lines of credit to members.

(a) *Statement of scope and purpose.* Section 701.21 complements the provisions of section 107(5) of the Federal Credit Union Act (12 U.S.C. 1757(5)) authorizing Federal credit unions to make loans to members and issue lines of credit (including credit cards) to members. Section 107(5) of the Act contains limitations on matters such as loan maturity, rate of interest, security, and prepayment penalties. Section 701.21 interprets and implements those provisions. In addition, § 701.21 states the NCUA Board's intent concerning preemption of state laws, and expands the authority of Federal credit unions to enforce due-on-sale clauses in real property loans. Also, while § 701.21 generally applies to Federal credit unions only, its provisions may be used by state-chartered credit unions with respect to alternative mortgage transactions in accordance with 12 U.S.C. 3801 *et seq.*, and certain provisions apply to loans made by federally insured state-chartered credit unions as specified in § 741.203 of this chapter. Part 722 of this chapter sets forth requirements for appraisals for certain real estate secured loans made under § 701.21 and any other applicable lending authority. Finally, it is noted that § 701.21 does not apply to loans by Federal credit unions to other credit unions (although certain statutory limitations in section 107 of the Act apply), nor to loans to credit union organizations which are governed by section 107(5)(D) of the Act and Part 712.

(b) *Relation to other laws*—

(1) *Preemption of state laws.* Section 701.21 is promulgated pursuant to the NCUA's Board's exclusive authority as set forth in section 107(5) of the Federal Credit Union Act (12 U.S.C 1757(5)) to regulate the rates, terms of repayment and other conditions of Federal credit union loans and lines of credit (including credit cards) to members. This exercise of the Board's authority preempts any state law purporting to limit or affect:

(i)(A) Rates of interest and amounts of finance charges, including:

(1) The frequency or the increments by which a variable interest rate may be changed;

(2) The index to which a variable interest rate may be tied;

(3) The manner or timing of notifying the borrower of a change in interest rate;

(4) The authority to increase the interest rate on an existing balance;

(B) Late charges; and

(C) Closing costs, application, origination, or other fees;

(ii) Terms of repayment, including:

(A) The maturity of loans and lines of credit;

(B) The amount, uniformity, and frequency of payments, including the accrual of unpaid interest if payments are insufficient to pay all interest due;

(C) Balloon payments; and

(D) Prepayment limits;

(iii) Conditions related to:

---

3 These regulations make reference to the Federal Home Loan Bank Board (FHLBB) and its authority. The Financial Institutions Reform, Recovery and Enforcement Act of 1989 (FIRREA), Pub. L. No. 101-73, 103 Stat. 183 (Aug. 9, 1989), abolished the FHLBB and replaced it with the Office of Thrift Supervision (OTS). The relevant authority was transferred from the FHLBB to the OTS.

(A) The amount of the loan or line of credit;

(B) The purpose of the loan or line of credit;

(C) The type or amount of security and the relation of the value of the security to the amount of the loan or line of credit;

(D) Eligible borrowers; and

(E) The imposition and enforcement of liens on the shares of borrowers and accommodation parties.

(2) *Matters not preempted.* Except as provided by paragraph (b)(1) of this section, it is not the Board's intent to preempt state laws that do not affect rates, terms of repayment and other conditions described above concerning loans and lines of credit, for example:

(i) Insurance laws;

(ii) Laws related to transfer of and security interests in real and personal property (see, however, paragraph (g)(6) of this section concerning the use and exercise of due-on-sale clauses);

(iii) Conditions related to:

(A) Collection costs and attorneys' fees;

(B) Requirements that consumer lending documents be in "plain language;" and

(C) The circumstances in which a borrower may be declared in default and may cure default.

(3) *Other Federal law.* Except as provided by paragraph (b)(1) of this section, it is not the Board's intent to preempt state laws affecting aspects of credit transactions that are primarily regulated by Federal law other than the Federal Credit Union Act, for example, state laws concerning credit cost disclosure requirements, credit discrimination, credit reporting practices, unfair credit practices, and debt collection practices. Applicability of state law in these instances should be determined pursuant to the preemption standards of the relevant Federal law and regulations.

(4) *Examination and Enforcement.* Except as otherwise agreed by the NCUA Board, the Board retains exclusive examination and administrative enforcement jurisdiction over Federal credit unions. Violations of Federal or applicable state laws related to the lending activities of a Federal credit union should be referred to the appropriate NCUA regional office.

(5) *Definition of State Law.* For purposes of paragraph (b) of this section "state law" means the constitution, laws, regulations and judicial decisions of any state, the District of Columbia, the several territories and possessions of the United States, and the Commonwealth of Puerto Rico.

(c) *General Rules—*

(1) *Scope.* The following general rules apply to all loans to members and, where indicated, all lines of credit (including credit cards) to members, except as otherwise provided in the remaining provisions of § 701.21.

(2) *Written policies.* The board of directors of each Federal credit union shall establish written policies for loans and lines of credit consistent with the relevant provisions of the Act, NCUA's regulations, and other applicable laws and regulations.

(3) *Credit applications and overdrafts.* Consistent with policies established by the board of directors, the credit committee or loan officer shall ensure that a credit application is kept on file for each borrower supporting the decision to make a loan or establish a line of credit. A credit union may advance money to a member to cover an account deficit without having a credit application from the borrower on file if the credit union has a written overdraft policy. The policy must: set a cap on the total dollar amount of all overdrafts the credit union will honor consistent with the credit union's ability to absorb losses; establish a time limit not to exceed forty-five calendar days for a member either to deposit funds or obtain an approved loan from the credit union to cover each overdraft; limit the dollar amount of overdrafts the credit union will honor per member; and establish the fee and interest rate, if any, the credit union will charge members for honoring overdrafts.

(4) *Maturity.* The maturity of a loan to a member may not exceed 12 years. Lines of credit are not subject to a statutory or regulatory maturity limit. Amortization of line of credit balances and the type and amount of security on any line of credit shall be as determined by contract between the Federal credit union and the member/borrower.

(5) *Ten percent limit.* No loan or line of credit advance may be made to any member if such loan or advance would cause that member to be indebted to the Federal credit union upon loans and advances made to the member in an aggregate amount exceeding 10% of the credit union's total unimpaired capital and surplus. In the case of member business loans as defined in § 723.1 of this chapter, additional limitations apply as set forth in §§ 723.8 and 723.9 of this chapter.

(6) *Early payment.* A member may repay a loan, or outstanding balance on a line of credit, prior to maturity in whole or in part on any business day without penalty.

(7) *Loan interest rates—*

(i) *General.* Except when a higher maximum rate is provided for in paragraph (c)(7)(ii) of this section, a Federal credit union may extend credit to its members at rates not to exceed 15 percent per year on the unpaid balance inclusive of all finance charges. Variable rates are permitted on the condition that the effective rate over the term of the loan (or line of credit) does not exceed the maximum permissible rate.

(ii) *Temporary rates—*

(A) *21 percent maximum rate.* Effective from December 3, 1980 through May 14, 1987, a Federal credit union may extend credit to its members at rates not to exceed 21 percent per year on the unpaid balance inclusive of all finance charges. Loans and line of credit balances existing on or before May 14, 1987, may continue to bear rates of interest of up to 21 percent per year after May 14, 1987.

(B) *18 percent maximum rate.* Effective May 15, 1987, a Federal credit union may extend credit to its members at rates not to exceed 18 percent per year on the unpaid balance inclusive of all finance charges.

(C) *Expiration.* After September 8, 2006, or as otherwise ordered by the NCUA Board, the maximum rate on federal credit union extensions of credit to members shall revert to 15 percent per year. Higher rates may, however, be charged, in accordance with paragraph (c)(7)(ii)(A) and (B) of this section, on loans and line of credit balance existing on or before September 8, 2006.

(8)(i) Except as otherwise provided herein, no official or employee of a Federal credit union, or immediate family member of an official or employee of a Federal credit union, may receive, directly or indirectly, any commission, fee, or other compensation in connection with any loan made by the credit union.

(ii) For the purposes of this section:

Compensation includes non monetary items, except those of nominal value.

Immediate family member means a spouse or other family member living in the same household.

Loan includes line of credit.

Official means any member of the board of directors or a volunteer committee.

Person means an individual or an organization.

Senior management employee means the credit union's chief executive officer (typically, this individual holds the title of President or Treasurer/Manager), any assistant chief executive officers (e.g., Assistant President, Vice President, or Assistant Treasurer/Manager), and the chief financial officer (Comptroller).

Volunteer official means an official of a credit union who does not receive compensation from the credit union solely for his or her service as an official.

(iii) This section does not prohibit:

(A) Payment, by a Federal credit union, of salary to employees;

(B) Payment, by a Federal credit union, of an incentive or bonus to an employee based on the credit union's overall financial performance;

(C) Payment, by a Federal credit union, of an incentive or bonus to an employee, other than a senior management employee, in connection with a loan or loans made by the credit union, provided that the board of directors of the credit union establishes written policies and internal controls in connection with such incentive or bonus and monitors compliance with such policies and controls at least annually.

(D) Receipt of compensation from a person outside a Federal credit union by a volunteer official or non senior management employee of the credit union, or an immediate family member of a volunteer official or employee of the credit union, for a service or activity performed outside the credit union, provided that no referral has been made by the credit union or the official, employee, or family member.

(d) *Loans and lines of credit to officials*—

(1) *Purpose.* Sections 107(5)(A) (iv) and (v) of the Act require the approval of the board of directors of the Federal credit union in any case where the aggregate of loans to an official and loans on which the official serves as endorser or guarantor exceeds $20,000 plus pledged shares. This paragraph implements the requirement by establishing procedures for determining whether board of directors's approval is required. The section also prohibits preferential treatment of officials.

(2) *Official.* An "official" is any member of the board of directors, credit committee or supervisory committee.

(3) *Initial approval.* All applications for loans or lines of credit on which an official will be either a direct obligor or an endorser, cosigner or guarantor shall be initially acted upon by either the board of directors, the credit committee or a loan officer, as specified in the Federal credit union's bylaws.

(4) *Board of Directors' review.* The board of directors shall, in any case, review and approve or deny an application on which an official is a direct obligor, or endorser, cosigner or guarantor if the following computation produces a total in excess of $20,000:

(i) Add:

(A) The amount of the current application.

(B) The outstanding balances of loans, including the used portion of an approved line of credit, extended to or endorsed, cosigned or guaranteed by the official.

(C) The total unused portion of approved lines of credit extended to or endorsed, cosigned or guaranteed by the official.

(ii) From the above total subtract:

(A) The amount of shares pledged by the official on loans or lines of credit extended to or endorsed, cosigned or guaranteed by the official.

(B) The amount of shares to be pledged by the official on the loan or line of credit applied for.

(5) *Nonpreferential treatment.* The rates, terms and conditions on any loan or line of credit either made to, or endorsed or guaranteed by—

(i) An official,

(ii) An immediate family member of an official, or

(iii) Any individual having a common ownership, investment or other pecuniary interest in a business enterprise with an official or with an immediate family member of an official,

shall not be more favorable than the rates, terms and conditions for comparable loans or lines of credit to other credit union members. "Immediate family member" means a spouse or other family member living in the same household.

(e) *Insured, Guaranteed and Advance Commitment Loans.* A loan secured, in full or in part, by the insurance or guarantee of, or with an advance commitment to purchase the loan, in full or in part, by the Federal Government, a State government or any agency of either, may be made for the maturity and under the terms and conditions, including rate of interest, specified in the law, regulations or program under which the insurance, guarantee or commitment is provided.

(f) *20-Year Loans.*

(1) Notwithstanding the general 12-year maturity limit on loans to members, a federal credit union may make loans with maturities of up to 20 years in the case of:

(i) a loan to finance the purchase of a mobile home if the mobile home will be used as the member-borrower's residence and the loan is secured by a first lien on the mobile home, and the mobile home meets the requirements for the home mortgage interest deduction under the Internal Revenue Code,

(ii) a second mortgage loan (or a nonpurchase money first mortgage loan in the case of a residence on which there is no existing first mortgage) if the loan is secured by a residential dwelling which is the residence of the member-borrower, and

(iii) a loan to finance the repair, alteration, or improvement of a residential dwelling which is the residence of the member-borrower.

(2) For purposes of this paragraph (f), mobile home may include a recreational vehicle, house trailer or boat.

(g) *Long-Term Mortgage Loans.*

(1) *Authority.* A federal credit union may make residential real estate loans to members, including loans secured by manufactured homes permanently affixed to the land, with maturities of up to 40 years, or such longer period as may be permitted by the NCUA Board on a case-by-case basis, subject to the conditions of this paragraph (g).

(2) *Statutory Limits.* The loan shall be made on a one to four family dwelling that is or will be the principal residence of the member-borrower and the loan shall be secured by a perfected first lien in favor of the credit union on such dwelling (or a perfected first security interest in the case of either a residential cooperative or a leasehold or ground rent estate).

(3) *Loan Application.* The loan application shall be a completed standard Federal Housing Administration, Veterans Administration, Federal Home Loan Mortgage Corporation, Federal National Mortgage Association or Federal Home Loan Mortgage Corporation/Federal National Mortgage Association application form. In lieu of use of a standard application the Federal credit union may have a current attorney's opinion on file stating that the forms in use meet the requirements of applicable Federal, state and local laws.

(4) *Security Instrument and Note.* The security instrument and note shall be executed on the most current version of the FHA, VA, FHLMC, FNMA, or FHLMC/FNMA Uniform Instruments for the jurisdiction in which the property is located. No prepayment penalty shall be allowed, although a Federal credit union may require that any partial prepayments be made on the date monthly installments are due and be in the amount of that part of one or more monthly installments that would be applicable to principal. In lieu of use of a standard security instrument and note, the Federal credit union may have a current attorney's opinion on file stating that the security instrument and note in use meet the requirements of applicable Federal, state and local laws.

(5) *First Lien, Territorial Limits.* The loan shall be secured by a perfected first lien or first security interest in favor of the credit union supported by a properly executed and recorded security instrument. No loan shall be secured by a residence located outside the United States of America, its territories and possessions, or the Commonwealth of Puerto Rico.

(6) *Due-On-Sale Clauses.*

(i) Except as otherwise provided herein, the exercise of a due-on-sale clause by a Federal credit union is governed exclusively by section 341 of Pub. L. 97-320 and by any regulations issued by the Federal Home Loan Bank Board implementing section 341.

(ii) In the case of a contract involving a long-term (greater than twelve years), fixed rate first mortgage loan which was made or assumed, including a transfer of the liened property subject to the loan, during the period beginning on the date a State adopted a constitutional provision or statute prohibiting the exercise of due-on-sale clauses, or the date on which the highest court of such state has rendered a decision (or if the highest court has not so decided, the date on which the next highest court has rendered a decision resulting in a final judgment if such decision applies statewide) prohibiting such exercise, and ending on October 15, 1982, a Federal credit union may exercise a due-on-sale clause in the case of a transfer which occurs on or after November 18, 1982, unless exercise of the due-on-sale clause would be based on any of the following:

(A) The creation of a lien or other encumbrance subordinate to the lender's security instrument which does not relate to a transfer of rights of occupancy in the property;

(B) The creation of a purchase money security interest for household appliances;

(C) A transfer by devise, descent, or operation of law on the death of a joint tenant or tenant by the entirety;

(D) The granting of a leasehold interest of 3 years or less not containing an option to purchase;

(E) A transfer to a relative resulting from the death of a borrower;

(F) A transfer where the spouse or children of the borrower become an owner of the property;

(G) A transfer resulting from a decree of a dissolution of marriage, a legal separation agreement, or from an incidental property settlement agreement, by which the spouse of the borrower becomes an owner of the property;

(H) A transfer into an inter vivos trust in which the borrower is and remains a beneficiary and which does not relate to a transfer of rights of occupancy in the property; or

(I) Any other transfer or disposition described in regulations promulgated by the Federal Home Loan Bank Board.

(7) *Assumption of real estate loans by non-members.* A federal credit union may permit a nonmember to assume a member's mortgage loan in conjunction with the nonmember's purchase of the member's principal residence, provided that the nonmember assumes only the remaining unpaid balance of the loan, the terms of the loan remain unchanged, and there is no extension of the original maturity date specified in the loan agreement with the member. An assumption is impermissible if the original loan was made with the intent of having a nonmember assume the loan.

(h) [Reserved]

(i) *Put option purchases in managing increased interest-rate risk for real estate loans produced for sale on the secondary market—*

(1) *Definitions.* For purposes of this § 701.21(i):

(i) *Financial options contract* means an agreement to make or take delivery of a standardized financial instrument upon demand by the holder of the contract at any time prior to the expiration date specified in the agreement, under terms and conditions established either by:

(A) A contract market designated for trading such contracts by the Commodity Futures Trading Commission, or

(B) By a Federal credit union and a primary dealer in Government securities that are counterparties in an over-the-counter transaction.

(ii) *FHLMC security* means obligations or other securities which are or ever have been sold by the Federal Home Loan Mortgage Corporation pursuant to section 305 or 306 of the Federal Home Loan Mortgage Corporation Act (12 U.S.C. 1454 and 1455).

(iii) *FNMA security* means an obligation, participation, or any instrument of or issued by, or fully guaranteed as to principal and interest by, the Federal National Mortgage Association.

(iv) *GNMA security* means an obligation, participation, or any instrument of or issued by, or fully guaranteed as to principal and interest by, the Government National Mortgage Association.

(v) *Long position* means the holding of a financial options contract with the option to make or take delivery of a financial instrument.

(vi) *Primary dealer in Government securities* means:

(A) A member of the Association of Primary Dealers in United States Government Securities; or

(B) Any parent, subsidiary, or affiliated entity of such primary dealer where the member guarantees (to the satisfaction of the FCU's board of directors) over-the-counter sales of financial options contracts by the parent, subsidiary, or affiliated entity to a Federal credit union.

(vii) *Put* means a financial options contract which entitles the holder to sell, entirely at the holder's option, a specified quantity of a security at a specified price at any time until the stated expiration date of the contract.

(2) *Permitted options transactions.* A Federal credit union may, to manage risk of loss through a decrease in value of its commitments to origi-

nate real estate loans at specified interest rates, enter into long put positions on GNMA, FNMA, and FHLMC securities:

(i) If the real estate loans are to be sold on the secondary market within ninety (90) days of closing;

(ii) If the positions are entered into:

(A) Through a contract market designated by the Commodity Futures Trading Commission for trading such contracts, or

(B) With a primary dealer in Government securities;

(iii) If the positions are entered into pursuant to written policies and procedures which are approved by the Federal credit union's board of directors, and include, at a minimum:

(A) The Federal credit union's strategy in using financial options contracts and its analysis of how the strategy will reduce sensitivity to changes in price or interest rates in its commitments to originate real estate loans at specified interest rates;

(B) A list of brokers or other intermediaries through which positions may be entered into;

(C) Quantitative limits (e.g., position and stop loss limits) on the use of financial options contracts;

(D) Identification of the persons involved in financial options contract transactions, including a description of these persons' qualifications, duties, and limits of authority, and description of the procedures for segregating these persons' duties,

(E) A requirement for written reports for review by the Federal credit union's board of directors at its monthly meetings, or by a committee appointed by the board on a monthly basis, of:

(1) The type, amount, expiration date, correlation, cost of, and current or projected income or loss from each position closed since the last board review, each position currently open and current gains or losses from such positions, and each position planned to be entered into prior to the next board review;

(2) Compliance with limits established on the policies and procedures; and

(3) The extent to which the positions described contributed to reduction of sensitivity to changes in prices or interest rates in the Federal credit union's commitments to originate real estate loans at a specified interest rate; and

(iv) If the Federal credit union has received written permission from the appropriate NCUA Regional Director to engage in financial options contracts transactions in accordance with this § 701.21(i) and its policies and procedures as written.

(3) *Recordkeeping and reporting.*

(i) The reports described in § 701.21(i)(2) (iii)(E) for each month must be submitted to the appropriate NCUA Regional Office by the end of the following month. This monthly reporting requirement may be waived by the appropriate NCUA Regional Director on a case-by-case basis for those Federal credit unions with a proven record of responsible use of permitted financial options contracts.

(ii) The records described in § 701.21(i) (2)(iii)(E) must be retained for two years from the date the financial options contracts are closed.

(4) *Accounting.* A federal credit union must account for financial options contracts transactions in accordance with generally accepted accounting principles.

[49 Fed. Reg. 30685 (Aug. 1, 1984); 49 Fed. Reg. 46105 (Nov. 23, 1984); 49 Fed. Reg. 46541 (Nov. 27, 1984); 50 Fed. Reg. 48077 (Nov. 21, 1985); 52 Fed. Reg. 8061 (Mar. 16, 1987); 52 Fed. Reg. 12368 (Apr. 16, 1987); 53 Fed. Reg. 19751 (May 31, 1988); 53 Fed. Reg. 29645 (Aug. 8, 1988); 54 Fed. Reg. 18472 (May 1, 1989); 54 Fed. Reg. 43278 (Oct. 24, 1989); 55 Fed. Reg. 1797 (Jan. 19, 1990); 55 Fed. Reg. 30207 (July 25, 1990); 56 Fed. Reg. 37831 (Aug. 9, 1991); 56 Fed. Reg. 48425 (Sept. 25, 1991); 57 Fed. Reg. 42488 (Sept. 15, 1992); 58 Fed. Reg. 6077 (Jan. 26, 1993); 58 Fed. Reg. 40043 (July 27, 1993); 59 Fed. Reg. 39425 (Aug. 1, 1994); 60 Fed. Reg. 51889 (Oct. 4, 1995); 60 Fed. Reg. 58504 (Nov. 28, 1995); 61 Fed. Reg. 4214 (Feb. 5, 1996); 61 Fed. Reg. 68128 (Dec. 27, 1996); 62 Fed. Reg. 40930 (July 31, 1997); 63 Fed. Reg. 51799 (Sept. 29, 1998); 63 Fed. Reg. 71214 (Dec. 24, 1998); 64 Fed. Reg. 5929 (Feb. 8, 1999); 64 Fed. Reg. 28729 (May 27, 1999); 64 Fed. Reg. 57365 (Oct. 25, 1999); 65 Fed. Reg. 15226 (Mar. 22, 2000); 65 Fed. Reg. 44977 (July 20, 2000); 67 Fed. Reg. 7059 (Feb. 15, 2002); 68 Fed. Reg. 46441 (Aug. 6, 2003); 69 Fed. Reg. 27828 (May 17, 2004); 70 Fed. Reg. 3863 (Jan. 27, 2005); 70 Fed. Reg. 8921 (Feb. 24, 2005)]

* * *

12 C.F.R. § 701.23 Purchase, sale, and pledge of eligible obligations.

(a) For purposes of this section:

(1) *Eligible obligation* means a loan or group of loans.

(2) *Student loan* means a loan granted to finance the borrower's attendance at an institution of higher education or at a vocational school, which is secured by and on which payment of the outstanding principal and interest has been deferred in accordance with the insurance or guarantee of the Federal Government, of a State government, or any agency of either.

(b) *Purchase.* (1) A Federal credit union may purchase, in whole or in part, within the limitations of the board of directors' written purchase policies:

(i) Eligible obligations of its members, from any source, if either: (A) They are loans it is empowered to grant or (B) they are refinanced with the consent of the borrowers, within 60 days after they are purchased, so that they are loans it is empowered to grant;

(ii) Eligible obligations of a liquidating credit union's individual members, from the liquidating credit union;

(iii) Student loans, from any source, if the purchaser is granting student loans on an ongoing basis and if the purchase will facilitate the purchasing credit union's packaging of a pool of such loans to be sold or pledged on the secondary market; and

(iv) Real estate-secured loans, from any source, if the purchaser is granting real estate-secured loans pursuant to § 701.21 on an ongoing basis and if the purchase will facilitate the purchasing credit union's packaging of a pool of such loans to be sold or pledged on the secondary mortgage market. A pool must include a substantial portion of the credit union's members' loans and must be sold promptly.

(2) A Federal credit union may make purchases in accordance with this paragraph (b), provided:

(i) The board of directors or investment committee approves the purchase;

(ii) A written agreement and a schedule of the eligible obligations covered by the agreement are retained in the purchasers office; and

(iii) For purchases under paragraph (b)(1)(ii) of this section, any advance written approval required by § 741.8 of this chapter is obtained before consummation of such purchase.

(3) The aggregate of the unpaid balance of eligible obligations purchased under paragraph (b) of this section shall not exceed 5 percent of the unimpaired capital and surplus of the purchaser. The following can be excluded in calculating this 5 percent limitation:

(i) Student loans purchased in accordance with paragraph (b)(1)(iii) of this section;

(ii) Real estate loans purchased in accordance with paragraph (b)(1)(iv) of this section;

(iii) Eligible obligations purchased in accordance with paragraph (b)(1)(i) of this section that are refinanced by the purchaser so that it is a loan it is empowered to grant;

(iv) An indirect lending or indirect leasing arrangement that is classified as a loan and not the purchase of an eligible obligation because the Federal credit union makes the final underwriting decision and the sales or lease contract is assigned to the Federal credit union very soon after it is signed by the member and the dealer or leasing company.

(c) *Sale.* A Federal credit union may sell, in whole or in part, to any source, eligible obligations of its members, eligible obligations purchased in accordance with paragraph (b)(1)(ii) of this section, student loans purchased in accordance with paragraph (b)(1)(iii) of this section, and real estate loans purchased in accordance with paragraph (b)(1)(iv) of this section, within the limitations of the board of directors' written sale policies, *Provided:*

(1) The board of directors or investment committee approves the sale; and

(2) A written agreement and a schedule of the eligible obligations covered by the agreement are retained in the seller's office.

(d) *Pledge.* (1) A Federal credit union may pledge, in whole or in part, to any source, eligible obligations of its members, eligible obligations purchased in accordance with paragraph (b)(1)(ii) of this section, student loans purchased

in accordance with paragraph (b)(1)(iii) of this section, and real estate loans purchased in accordance with paragraph (b)(1)(iv) of this section, within the limitations of the board of directors' written pledge policies, *Provided:*

(i) The board of directors or investment committee approves the pledge;

(ii) Copies of the original loan documents are retained; and

(iii) A written agreement covering the pledging arrangement is retained in the office of the credit union that pledges the eligible obligations.

(2) The pledge agreement shall identify the eligible obligations covered by the agreement.

(e) *Servicing.* A Federal credit union may agree to service any eligible obligation it purchases or sells in whole or in part.

(f) *10 Percent limitation.* The total indebtedness owing to any Federal credit union by any person, inclusive of retained and reacquired interests, shall not exceed 10 percent of its unimpaired capital and surplus.

[44 Fed. Reg. 27071 (May 9, 1979), *as amended at* 46 Fed. Reg. 38680 (July 29, 1981). Redesignated at 49 Fed. Reg. 30688 (Aug. 1, 1984), and *amended at* 53 Fed. Reg. 4844 (Feb. 18, 1988); 56 Fed. Reg. 15036 (Apr. 15, 1991); 56 Fed. Reg. 35811 (July 29, 1991); 60 Fed. Reg. 58504 (Nov. 28, 1995); 63 Fed. Reg. 70998 (Dec. 23, 1998)]

* * *

12 C.F.R. § 701.31 Nondiscrimination requirements.

(a) *Definitions.* As used in this part, the term:

(1) *Application* carries the meaning of that term as defined in 12 CFR 202.2(f) (Regulation B), which is as follows:

> An oral or written request for an extension of credit that is made in accordance with procedures established by a creditor for the type of credit requested;

(2) *Dwelling* carries the meaning of that term as defined in 42 U.S.C. 3602(b) (Fair Housing Act), which is as follows: "Any building, structure, or portion thereof which is occupied as, or designed or intended for occupancy as, a residence by one or more families, and any vacant land which is offered for sale or lease for the construction or location thereon of any building, structure, or portion thereof"; and

(3) *Real estate-related loan* means any loan for which application is made to finance or refinance the purchase, construction, improvement, repair, or maintenance of a dwelling.

(b) *Nondiscrimination in Lending.* (1) A Federal credit union may not deny a real estate-related loan, nor may it discriminate in setting or exercising its rights pursuant to the terms or conditions of such a loan, nor may it discourage an application for such a loan, on the basis of the

race, color, national origin, religion, sex, handicap, or familial status (having children under the age of 18) of:

(i) Any applicant or joint applicant;

(ii) Any person associated, in connection with a real estate-related loan application, with an applicant or joint applicant;

(iii) The present or prospective owners, lessees, tenants, or occupants of the dwelling for which a real estate-related loan is requested;

(iv) The present or prospective owners, lessees, tenants, or occupants of other dwellings in the vicinity of the dwelling for which a real estate-related loan is requested.

(2) With regard to a real estate-related loan, a Federal credit union may not consider a lending criterion or exercise a lending policy which has the effect of discriminating on the basis of race, color, national origin, religion, sex, handicap, or familial status (having children under the age of 18). Guidelines concerning possible exceptions to this provision appear in paragraph (e)(1) of this section.

(3) Consideration of any of the following factors in connection with a real estate-related loan is not necessary to a Federal credit union's business, generally has a discriminatory effect, and is therefore prohibited:

(i) The age or location of the dwelling;

(ii) Zip code of the applicant's current residence;

(iii) Previous home ownership;

(iv) The age or location of dwellings in the neighborhood of the dwelling;

(v) The income level of residents in the neighborhood of the dwelling.

Guidelines concerning possible exceptions to this provision appear in paragraph (e)(2) of this section.

(c) *Nondiscrimination in appraisals.* (1) A Federal credit union may not rely upon an appraisal of a dwelling if it knows or should know that the appraisal is based upon consideration of the race, color, national origin, religion, sex, handicap, or familial status (having children under the age of 18) of:

(i) Any applicant or joint applicant;

(ii) Any person associated, in connection with a real estate-related loan application, with an applicant or joint applicant;

(iii) The present or prospective owners, lessees, tenants, or occupants of the dwelling for which a real estate-related loan is requested;

(iv) The present or prospective owners, lessees, tenants, or occupants of other dwellings in the vicinity of the dwelling for which a real estate-related loan is requested.

(2) With respect to a real-estate related loan, a Federal credit union may not rely upon an appraisal of a dwelling if it knows or should know that the appraisal is based upon consideration of a criterion which has the effect of discriminating on the basis of race, color, national origin, religion, sex, handicap, or familial status (having children under the age of 18). Guidelines

concerning possible exceptions to this provision appear in paragraph (e)(1) of this section.

(3) A Federal credit union may not rely upon an appraisal that it knows or should know is based upon consideration of any of the following criteria, for such criteria generally have a discriminatory effect, and are not necessary to a Federal credit union's business:

(i) The age or location of the dwelling;

(ii) The age or location of dwellings in the neighborhood of the dwelling;

(iii) The income level of the residents in the neighborhood of the dwelling.

(4) Notwithstanding paragraph (c)(3) of this section, it is recognized that there may be factors concerning location of the dwelling which can be properly considered in an appraisal. If any such factor(s) is relied upon, it must be specifically documented in the appraisal, accompanied by a brief statement demonstrating the necessity of using such factor(s). Guidelines concerning the consideration of location factors appear in paragraph (e)(3) of this section.

(5) Each Federal credit union shall make available, to any requesting member/applicant, a copy of the appraisal used in connection with that member's real estate-related loan application. The appraisal shall be available for a period of 25 months after the applicant has received notice from the Federal credit union of the action taken by the Federal credit union on the real estate-related loan application.

(d) *Nondiscrimination in advertising.* No federal credit union may engage in any form of advertising of real estate-related loans that indicates the credit union discriminates on the basis of race, color, religion, national origin, sex, handicap, or familial status in violation of the Fair Housing Act. Advertisements must not contain any words, symbols, models or other forms of communication that suggest a discriminatory preference or policy of exclusion in violation of the Fair Housing Act or the Equal Credit Opportunity Act.

(1) *Advertising notice of nondiscrimination compliance.* Any federal credit union that advertises real estate-related loans must prominently indicate in such advertisement, in a manner appropriate to the advertising medium and format used, that the credit union makes such loans without regard to race, color, religion, national origin, sex, handicap, or familial status.

(i) With respect to written and visual advertisements, a credit union may satisfy the notice requirement by including in the advertisement a copy of the logotype, with the legend "Equal Housing Lender," from the poster described in paragraph (d)(3) of this section or a copy of the logotype, with the legend "Equal Housing Opportunity," from the poster described in § 110.25(a) of the United States Department of Housing and Urban Development's (HUD) regulations (24 CFR 110.25(a)).

(ii) With respect to oral advertisements, a credit union may satisfy the notice requirement

by a spoken statement that the credit union is an "Equal Housing Lender" or an "Equal Opportunity Lender."

(iii) When an oral advertisement is used in conjunction with a written or visual advertisement, the use of either of the methods specified in paragraphs (d)(1)(i) or (ii) of this section will satisfy the notice requirement.

(iv) A credit union may use any other method reasonably calculated to satisfy the notice requirement.

(2) *Lobby notice of nondiscrimination.* Every federal credit union that engages in real estate-related lending must display a notice of nondiscrimination. The notice must be placed in the public lobby of the credit union and in the public area of each office where such loans are made and must be clearly visible to the general public. The notice must incorporate either a facsimile of the logotype and language appearing in paragraph (d)(3) of this section or the logotype and language appearing at 24 CFR 110.25(a). Posters containing the logotype and language appearing in paragraph (d)(3) of this section may be obtained from the regional offices of the National Credit Union Administration.

(3) *Logotype and notice of nondiscrimination compliance.* The logotype and text of the notice required in paragraph (d)(2) of this section shall be as follows:

We Do Business in Accordance With the Federal Fair Lending Laws

UNDER THE FEDERAL FAIR HOUSING ACT, IT IS ILLEGAL, ON THE BASIS OF RACE, COLOR, NATIONAL ORIGIN, RELIGION, SEX, HANDICAP, OR FAMILIAL STATUS (HAVING CHILDREN UNDER THE AGE OF 18), TO:

- Deny a loan for the purpose of purchasing, constructing, improving, repairing or maintaining a dwelling, or deny any loan secured by a dwelling; or
- Discriminate in fixing the amount, interest rate, duration, application procedures or other terms or conditions of such a loan, or in appraising property.

IF YOU BELIEVE YOU HAVE BEEN DISCRIMINATED AGAINST, YOU SHOULD SEND A COMPLAINT TO:

Assistant Secretary for Fair Housing and Equal Opportunity
Department of Housing & Urban Development
Washington, D.C. 20410
For processing under the Federal Fair Housing Act
and to:
National Credit Union Administration
Office of Examination and Insurance
1775 Duke Street
Alexandria, VA 22314–3428
For processing under NCUA Regulations

UNDER THE EQUAL CREDIT OPPORTUNITY ACT, IT IS ILLEGAL TO DISCRIMINATE IN ANY CREDIT TRANSACTION:

- On the basis of race, color, national origin, religion, sex, marital status, or age
- Because income is from public assistance, or
- Because a right was exercised under the Consumer Credit Protection Act.

IF YOU BELIEVE YOU HAVE BEEN DISCRIMINATED AGAINST, YOU SHOULD SEND A COMPLAINT TO:

National Credit Union Administration
Office of Examination and Insurance
1775 Duke Street
Alexandria, VA 22314–3428

(e) *Guidelines.* (1) Compliance with the Fair Housing Act is achieved when each loan applicant's creditworthiness is evaluated on an individual basis, without presuming that the applicant has certain characteristics of a group. If certain lending policies or procedures do presume group characteristics, they may violate the Fair Housing Act, even though the characteristics are not based upon race, color, sex, national origin, religion, handicap, or familial status. Such a violation occurs when otherwise facially nondiscriminatory lending procedures (either general lending policies or specific criteria used in reviewing loan applications) have the effect of making real estate-related loans unavailable or less available on the basis of race, color, sex, national origin, religion, handicap, or familial status. Note, however, that a policy or criterion which has a discriminatory effect is not a violation of the Fair Housing Act if its use achieves a legitimate business necessity which cannot be achieved by using less discriminatory standards. It is also important to note that the Equal Credit Opportunity Act and Regulation B prohibit discrimination, either per se or in effect, on the basis of the applicant's age, marital status, receipt of public assistance, or the exercise of any rights under the Consumer Credit Protection Act.

(2) Paragraph (b)(3) of this section prohibits consideration of certain factors because of their likely discriminatory effect and because they are not necessary to make sound real estate-related loans. For purposes of clarification, the prohibited use of location factors in this section is intended to prevent abandonment of areas in which a Federal credit union's members live or want to live. It is not intended to require loans in those areas that are geographically remote from the FCU's main or branch offices or that contravene the parameters of a Federal credit union's charter. Further, this prohibition does not preclude requiring a borrower to obtain flood insurance protection pursuant to the National Flood Insurance Act and part 760 of NCUA's Rules and Regulations, nor does it preclude involvement with Federal or state housing insurance programs which provide for lower interest rates for the purchase of homes in certain urban or rural areas. Also, the legitimate use of location factors in an appraisal does not constitute a violation of the provision of paragraph (b)(3) of this section, which prohibits consideration of location of the dwelling. Finally, the prohibited use of prior home ownership does not preclude a Federal credit union from considering an applicant's payment history on a loan which was made to obtain a home. Such action entails consideration of the payment record on a previous loan in determining creditworthiness; it does not entail consideration of prior home ownership.

(3)(i) Paragraph (c)(3) of this section prohibits consideration of the age or location of a dwelling in a real estate-related loan appraisal. These restrictions are intended to prohibit the use of unfounded or unsubstantiated assumptions regarding the effect upon loan risk of the age of a

dwelling or the physical or economic characteristics of an area. Appraisals should be based on the present market value of the property offered as security (including consideration of specific improvements to be made by the borrower) and the likelihood that the property will retain an adequate value over the term of the loan.

(ii) The term "age of the dwelling" does not encompass structural soundness. In addition, the age of the dwelling may be used by an appraiser as a basis for conducting further inspections of certain structural aspects of the dwelling. Paragraph (c)(3) of this section does, however, prohibit an unsubstantiated determination that a house over X years in age is not structurally sound.

(iii) With respect to location factors, paragraph (c)(4) of this section recognizes that there may be location factors which may be considered in an appraisal, and requires that the use of any such factors be specifically documented in the appraisal. These factors will most often be those location factors which may negatively affect the short range future value (up to 3–5 years) of a property. Factors which in some cases may cause the market value of a property to decline are recent zoning changes or a significant number of abandoned homes in the immediate vicinity of the property. However, not all zoning changes will cause a decline in property values, and proximity to abandoned buildings may not affect the market value of a property because the cause of abandonment is unrelated to high risk. Proper considerations include the condition and utility of the improvement and various physical factors such as street conditions, amenities such as parks and recreation areas, availability of public utilities and municipal services, and exposure to flooding and land faults.

[54 Fed. Reg. 46223 (Nov. 2, 1989), *as amended at* 59 Fed. Reg. 36041 (July 15, 1994); 66 Fed. Reg. 48206 (Sept. 19, 2001)]

* * *

PART 706—CREDIT PRACTICES

12 C.F.R. § 706.1 Definitions.

(a) *Person.* An individual, corporation, or other business organization.

(b) *Consumer.* A natural person member who seeks or acquires goods, services, or money for personal, family, or household use.

(c) *Obligation.* An agreement between a consumer and a Federal credit union.

(d) *Debt.* Money that is due or alleged to be due from one to another.

(e) *Earnings.* Compensation paid or payable to an individual or for his or her account for personal services rendered or to be rendered by him or her, whether denominated as wages, salary, commission, bonus, or otherwise, including periodic payments pursuant to a pension, retirement, or disability program.

(f) *Household goods.* Clothing, furniture, appliances, one radio and one television, linens, china, crockery, kitchenware, and personal effects (including wedding rings) of the consumer and his or her dependents, provided that the following are not included within the scope of the term "household goods":

(1) Works of art;

(2) Electronic entertainment equipment (except one television and one radio);

(3) Items acquired as antiques; and

(4) Jewelry (except wedding rings).

(g) *Antique.* Any item over one hundred years of age, including such items that have been repaired or renovated without changing their original form or character.

(h) *Cosigner.* A natural person who renders himself or herself liable for the obligation of another person without receiving goods, services, or money in return for the credit obligation, or, in the case of an open-end credit obligation, without receiving the contractual right to obtain extensions of credit under the obligation. The term includes any person whose signature is requested as a condition to granting credit to a consumer, or as a condition for forbearance on collection of a consumer's obligation that is in default. The term does not include a spouse whose signature is required on a credit obligation to perfect a security interest pursuant to state law. A person is a cosigner within the meaning of this definition whether or not he or she is designated as such on a credit obligation.

12 C.F.R. § 706.2 Unfair credit practices.

(a) In connection with the extension of credit to consumers, it is an unfair act or practice for a Federal credit union, directly or indirectly, to take or receive from a consumer an obligation that:

(1) Constitutes or contains a cognovit or confession of judgment (for purposes other than executory process in the State of Louisiana), warrant of attorney, or other waiver of the right to notice and the opportunity to be heard in the event of suit or process thereon.

(2) Constitutes or contains an executory waiver or a limitation of exemption from attachment, execution, or other process on real or personal property held, owned by, or due to the consumer, unless the waiver applies solely to property subject to a security interest executed in connection with the obligation.

(3) Constitutes or contains an assignment of wages or other earnings unless:

(i) The assignment by its terms is revocable at the will of the debtor, or

(ii) The assignment is a payroll deduction plan or preauthorized payment plan, commencing at the time of the transaction, in which the consumer authorizes a series of wage deductions as a method of making each payment, or

(iii) The assignment applies only to wages or other earnings already earned at the time of the assignment.

(4) Constitutes or contains a nonpossessory security interest in household goods other than a purchase money security interest.

12 C.F.R. § 706.3 Unfair or deceptive cosigner practices.

(a) *Prohibited practices.* In connection with the extension of credit to consumers, it is:

(1) A deceptive act or practice for a Federal credit union, directly or indirectly, to misprepsent the nature or extent of cosigner liability to any person.

(2) An unfair act or practice for a Federal credit union, directly or indirectly, to obligate a cosigner unless the cosigner is informed prior to becoming obligated, which in the case of open-end credit means prior to the time that the agreement creating the cosigner's liability for future charges is executed, of the nature of his or her liability as cosigner.

(b) *Disclosure requirement.* (1) To comply with the cosigner information requirement of paragraph (a)(2) of this section, a clear and conspicuous disclosure statement shall be given in writing to the cosigner prior to becoming obligated. The disclosure statement will contain only the following statement, or one which is substantially equivalent, and shall either be a separate document or included in the documents evidencing the consumer credit obligation.

Notice to Cosigner

You are being asked to guarantee this debt. Think carefully before you do. If the borrower doesn't pay the debt, you will have to. Be sure you can afford to pay if you have to, and that you want to accept this responsibility.

You may have to pay up to the full amount of the debt if the borrower does not pay. You may also have to pay late fees or collection costs, which increase this amount.

The creditor can collect this debt from you without first trying to collect from the borrower. The creditor can use the same collection methods against you that can be used against the borrower, such as suing you, garnishing your wages, etc. If this debt is ever in default, that fact may become a part of your credit record.

This notice is not the contract that makes you liable for the debt.

(2) If the notice to cosigner is a separate document, nothing other than the following items may appear with the notice. Items (i) through (v) may not be part of the narrative portion of the notice to cosigner.

(i) The name and address of the Federal credit union;

(ii) An identification of the debt to be con-signed (e.g., a loan identification number);

(iii) The amount of the loan;

(iv) The date of the loan;

(v) A signature line for a cosigner to acknowledge receipt of the notice; and

(vi) To the extent permitted by state law, a cosigner notice required by state law may be included in the paragraph (b)(1) notice.

(3) To the extent the notice to cosigner specified in paragraph (b)(1) of this section refers to an action against a cosigner that is not permitted by state law, the notice to cosigner may be modified.

12 C.F.R. § 706.4 Late charges.

(a) In connection with collecting a debt arising out of an extension of credit to a consumer, it is an unfair act or practice for a Federal credit union, directly or indirectly, to levy or collect any delinquency charge on a payment, which payment is otherwise a full payment for the applicable period and is paid on its due date or within an applicable grace period, when the only delinquency is attributable to late fee(s) or delinquency charge(s) assessed on earlier installment(s).

(b) For purposes of this section, "collecting a debt" means any activity other than the use of judicial process that is intended to bring about or does bring about repayment of all or part of a consumer debt.

12 C.F.R. § 706.5 State exemptions.

(a) If, upon application to the NCUA by an appropriate state agency, the NCUA determines that:

(1) There is a state requirement or prohibition in effect that applies to any transaction to which a provision of this rule applies; and

(2) The state requirement or prohibition affords a level of protection to consumers that is substantially equivalent to, or greater than, the protection afforded by this rule; then that provision of this rule will not be in effect in the state to the extent specified by the NCUA in its determination, for as long as the state administers and enforces the state requirement or prohibition effectively.

(b) States that received an exemption from the Federal Trade Commission's Credit Practices Rule prior to September 17, 1987, are not required to reapply to NCUA for an exemption under paragraph (a) of this section provided that the state forwards a copy of its exemption determination to the appropriate Regional Office. NCUA will honor the exemption for as long as the state administers and enforces the state requirement or prohibition effectively. Any state seeking a greater exemption than that granted to it by the Federal Trade Commission must apply to NCUA for the exemption.

* * *

PART 721—INCIDENTAL POWERS

12 C.F.R. § 721.1 What does this part cover?

This part authorizes a federal credit union (you) to engage in activities incidental to your business as set out in this part. This part also describes how interested parties may request a legal opinion on whether an activity is within a federal credit union's incidental powers or apply to add new activities or categories to the regulation. An activity approved in a legal opinion to an interested party or as a result of an application by an interested party to add new activities or categories is recognized as an incidental powers activity for all federal credit unions. This part does not apply to the activities of corporate credit unions.

12 C.F.R. § 721.2 What is an incidental powers activity?

An incidental powers activity is one that is necessary or requisite to enable you to carry on effectively the business for which you are incorporated. An activity meets the definition of an incidental power activity if the activity:

(a) Is convenient or useful in carrying out the mission or business of credit unions consistent with the Federal Credit Union Act;

(b) Is the functional equivalent or logical outgrowth of activities that are part of the mission or business of credit unions; and

(c) Involves risks similar in nature to those already assumed as part of the business of credit unions.

12 C.F.R. § 721.3 What categories of activities are preapproved as incidental powers necessary or requisite to carry on a credit union's business?

The categories of activities in this section are preapproved as incidental to carrying on your business under § 721.2. The examples of incidental powers activities within each category are provided in this section as illustrations of activities permissible under the particular category, not as an exclusive or exhaustive list.

(a) *Certification services.* Certification services are services whereby you attest or authenticate a fact for your members' use. Certification services may include such services as notary services, signature guarantees, certification of electronic signatures, and share draft certifications.

(b) *Correspondent services.* Correspondent services are services you provide to other credit unions that you are authorized to perform for your members or as part of your operation. These services may include loan processing, loan servicing, member check cashing services, disbursing share withdrawals and loan proceeds, cashing and selling money orders, performing internal audits, and automated teller machine deposit services.

(c) *Electronic financial services.* Electronic financial services are any services, products, functions, or activities that you are otherwise authorized to perform, provide, or deliver to your members but performed through electronic means. Electronic services may include automated teller machines, electronic fund transfers, online transaction processing through a web site, web site hosting services, account aggregation services, and Internet access services to perform or deliver products or services to members.

(d) *Excess capacity.* Excess capacity is the excess use or capacity remaining in facilities, equipment, or services that: You properly invested in or established, in good faith, with the intent of serving your members; and you reasonably anticipate will be taken up by the future expansion of services to your members. You may sell or lease the excess capacity in facilities, equipment or services such as office space, employees and data processing.

(e) *Financial counseling services.* Financial counseling services means advice, guidance or services that you offer to your members to promote thrift or to otherwise assist members on financial matters. Financial counseling services may include income tax preparation service, electronic tax filing for your members, counseling regarding estate and retirement planning, investment counseling, and debt and budget counseling.

(f) *Finder activities.* Finder activities are activities in which you introduce or otherwise bring together outside vendors with your members so that the two parties may negotiate and consummate transactions. Finder activities may include offering third party products and services to members through the sale of advertising space on your web site, account statements and receipts, or selling statistical or consumer financial information to outside vendors to facilitate the sale of their products to your members.

(g) *Loan-related products.* Loan-related products are the products, activities or services you provide to your members in a lending transaction that protect you against credit-related risks or are otherwise incidental to your lending authority. These products or activities may include debt cancellation agreements, debt suspension agreements, letters of credit and leases.

(h) *Marketing activities.* Marketing activities are the activities or means you use to promote membership in your credit union and the products and services you offer to your members. Marketing activities may include advertising and other promotional activities such as raffles, membership referral drives, and the purchase or use of advertising.

(i) *Monetary instrument services.* Monetary instrument services are services that enable your members to purchase, sell, or exchange various currencies. These services may include the sale and exchange of foreign currency and U.S. commemorative coins. You may also use accounts you have in foreign financial institutions to facilitate your members' transfer and negotiation of checks denominated in foreign currency or engage in monetary transfer services for your members.

(j) *Operational programs.* Operational programs are programs that you establish within your business to establish or deliver products and services that enhance member service and promote safe and sound operation. Operational programs may include electronic funds transfers, remote tellers, point of purchase terminals, debit cards, payroll deduction, pre-authorized member transactions, direct deposit, check clearing services, savings bond purchases and redemptions, tax payment services, wire transfers, safe deposit boxes, loan collection services, and service fees.

(k) *Stored value products.* Stored value products are alternate media to currency in which you transfer monetary value to the product and create a medium of exchange for your members' use. Examples of stored value products include stored value cards, public transportation tickets, event and attraction tickets, gift certificates, prepaid phone cards, postage stamps, electronic benefits transfer script, and similar media.

(1)[4] *Trustee or custodial services.* Trustee or custodial services are services in which you are authorized to act under any written trust instrument or custodial agreement created or organized in the United States and forming part of a tax-advantaged savings plan, as authorized under the Internal Revenue Code. These services may include acting as a trustee or custodian for member retirement, education and health savings accounts.

[69 Fed. Reg. 45237 (July 29, 2004)]

12 C.F.R. § 721.4 How may a credit union apply to engage in an activity that is not preapproved as within a credit union's incidental powers?

(a) *Application contents.* To engage in an activity that may be within an FCU's incidental powers but that does not fall within a preapproved category listed in § 721.3, you may submit an application by certified mail, return receipt requested, to the NCUA Board. Your application must describe the activity, your explanation, consistent with the test provided in paragraph (c) of this section, of why this activity is within your incidental powers, your plan for implementing the proposed activity, any state licenses you must obtain to conduct the activity, and any other information necessary to describe the proposed activity adequately. Before you engage in the petition process you should seek an advisory opinion from NCUA's Office of General Counsel, as to whether a proposed activity fits into one of the authorized categories or is otherwise within your incidental powers without filing a petition to amend the regulation.

(b) *Processing of application.* Your application must be filed with the Secretary of the NCUA Board. NCUA will review your application for completeness and will notify you whether additional information is required or whether the activity requested is permissible under one of the categories listed in § 721.3. If the activity falls within a category provided in § 721.3, NCUA will notify you that the activity is permissible and treat the application as withdrawn. If the activity does not fall within a category provided in § 721.3, NCUA staff will consider whether the proposed activity is legally permissible. Upon a recommendation by NCUA staff that the activity is within a credit union's incidental powers, the NCUA Board may amend § 721.3 and will request public comment on the establishment of a new category of activities within § 721.3. If the activity proposed in your application fails to meet the criteria established in paragraph (c) of this section, NCUA will notify you within a reasonable period of time.

(c) *Decision on application.* In determining whether an activity is authorized as an appropriate exercise of a federal credit union's incidental powers, the Board will consider:

(1) Whether the activity is convenient or useful in carrying out the mission or business of credit unions consistent with the Act;

(2) Whether the activity is the functional equivalent or logical outgrowth of activities that are part of the mission or business of credit unions; and

(3) Whether the activity involves risks similar in nature to those already assumed as part of the business of credit unions.

12 C.F.R. § 721.5 What limitations apply to a credit union engaging in activities approved under this part?

You must comply with any applicable NCUA regulations, policies, and legal opinions, as well as applicable state and federal law, if an activity authorized under this part is otherwise regulated or conditioned.

12 C.F.R. § 721.6 May a credit union derive income from activities approved under this part?

You may earn income for those activities determined to be incidental to your business.

12 C.F.R. § 721.7 What are the potential conflicts of interest for officials and employees when credit unions engage in activities approved under this part?

(a) *Conflicts.* No official, employee, or their immediate family member may receive any compensation or benefit, directly or indirectly, in connection with your engagement in an activity authorized under this part, except as otherwise provided in paragraph (b) of this section. This section does not apply if a conflicts of interest

---

4 This should probably be (*l*).

provision within another section of this chapter applies to a particular activity; in such case, the more specific conflicts of interest provision controls. For example: An official or employee that refers loan-related products offered by a third-party to a member, in connection with a loan made by you, is subject to the conflicts of interest provision in § 701.21(c)(8) of this chapter.

(b) *Permissible payments.* This section does not prohibit:

(1) Payment, by you, of salary to your employees;

(2) Payment, by you, of an incentive or bonus to an employee based on your overall financial performance;

(3) Payment, by you, of an incentive or bonus to an employee, other than a senior management employee or paid official, in connection with an activity authorized by this part, provided that

your board of directors establishes written policies and internal controls for the incentive program and monitors compliance with such policies and controls at least annually; and

(4) Payment, by a person other than you, of any compensation or benefit to an employee, other than a senior management employee or paid official, in connection with an activity authorized by this part, provided that your board of directors establishes written policies and internal controls regarding third-party compensation and determines that the employee's involvement does not present a conflict of interest.

(c) *Business associates and family members.* All transactions with business associates or family members not specifically prohibited by paragraph (a) of this section must be conducted at arm's length and in the interest of the credit union.

(d) *Definitions.* For purposes of this part, the following definitions apply.

(1) *Senior management employee* means your chief executive officer (typically, this individual holds the title of President or Treasurer/Manager), any assistant chief executive officers (e.g. Assistant President, Vice President, or Assistant Treasurer/Manager), and the chief financial officer (Comptroller).

(2) *Official* means any member of your board of directors, credit committee or supervisory committee.

(3) *Immediate family member* means a spouse or other family member living in the same household.

E.3 NCUA Interpretive Letters

This section summarizes NCUA interpretative letters and releases relating to the preemption of state laws by federal credit unions issued from 1992 forward. The full text of these letters can be found on the CD-Rom accompanying this volume. Archived and recently released letters and opinions can be obtained from NCUA's website: www.ncua.gov. Under "resources," click on "regulations," then on "legal opinions and law" and finally on "legal opinion letters." Then search by year.

Date of Opinion	State Affected	State Laws/Provisions
March 12, 2004	Georgia	Further explanation of NCUA's change in its position regarding how it evaluates state laws generally and anti-predatory lending laws in particular regarding preemption.
February 10, 2004	New Mexico	State anti-predatory lending law is preempted, relying on the analysis in the November 10, 2003 letter regarding Georgia's law.
January 29, 2004	General	State laws that limit or prohibit charges related to debt cancellation or suspension agreements are preempted.
January 28, 2004	General	Federal credit unions may offer debt cancellation agreements to its members as an exercise of incidental powers without having to comply with state insurance licensing laws. NCUA does not believe that a federal credit union that offers debt cancellation agreements is engaging in the business of insurance.
January 28, 2004	New Jersey	State Homeownership Security Act (anti-predatory lending law) is preempted.
December 14, 2003	Texas	State debt collection act that is amended and only applies to third party collectors and will, therefore, not apply to federal credit unions. See earlier letter of November 26, 2003.
November 26, 2003	Texas	State debt collection act is not preempted for federal credit union members in that state. Some federal laws permit states to regulate in the same area. State laws of this sort normally apply to federal credit unions. The relevant federal law's preemption standards determine whether a state law is preempted. Further, the state FDCPA does not regulate the terms of lending.

Date of Opinion	State Affected	State Laws/Provisions
November 10, 2003	Georgia	Amended Georgia Fair Lending Act is preempted. NCUA amends its position and states that any state law that affects the rates, terms, and conditions of the loan is preempted regardless of whether another federal law permits the state to enact it.
May 23, 2003	District of Columbia	D.C.'s Home Loan Protection Act is preempted even though it is a state law more protective than the federal Homeownership Equity Protection Act.
December 23, 2002	General	Credit unions need not obtain stop-loss insurance coverage if it institutes a debt cancellation or suspension program. NCUA argues that these products are not insurance.
October 4, 2002	North Carolina	North Carolina's Mortgage Lending Act that requires financial institutions to file for an exemption from licensing requirements and that imposes a penalty if they fail to file for an exemption is preempted. HOEPA-like provisions are preempted to the extent of loans not covered by HOEPA and then to the extent that it limits or affects rates of interest, finance charges, late fees, closing costs, terms or repayment, and loan conditions.
October 3, 2002	Connecticut	Connecticut law that bars financial institutions from permitting borrowers to use credit cards to access a home equity line of credit is preempted.
July 29, 2002	Georgia	Georgia's Fair Lending Act is preempted in part. For loans covered by the Act and covered under the HOEPA, the Act is generally not preempted. For covered loans below the HOEPA triggers, the Act is preempted to the extent it limits or affects rates of interest, finance charges, late fees, closing costs, terms or repayment, and loan conditions.
June 26, 2002	California	California's minimum payment credit card disclosure act is preempted as it affects the terms of repayment.
March 2, 2001	New York HOEPA-like regulations.	NCUA's lending regulation does not preempt state laws that affect aspects of credit transactions that are primarily regulated by other federal laws or regulations. In these cases, preemption is defined under the standards in those other federal laws. NCUA's regulations preempt some but not all of New York's HOEPA-like regulations.
February 1, 1999	Connecticut	State law limiting finance charges on retail installment contracts does not apply to federal credit unions that buy loans from dealers that the federal credit unions approved before the financing was granted to the consumer. These are so-called "indirect" loans. Opinion expressly declines to discuss legality of the car dealer's role under state law. Opinion conflicts with the letter of June 24, 1992.
December 9, 1998	Wyoming	State law prohibiting a federal credit union from establishing an ATM unless it has a place of business in that state is preempted.
April 21, 1998	Maryland	Federal Credit Union Act does not regulate in the area of electronic branching; therefore, state law prohibiting federal credit unions from charging a fee to non-members who use their ATMs is not preempted.
September 4, 1997	Indiana	State law permitting consumers to refinance a balloon payment loan on the same terms and conditions as the original loan at maturity is preempted.
July 31, 1997	North Carolina	State law regarding late charges is preempted. The fact that North Carolina opted out of the National Housing Act preemption of interest rates is not relevant to FCU Act preemption.
April 14, 1997	Maine	State law restricting the finance charge that can be collected on open-end credit is preempted.

Date of Opinion	State Affected	State Laws/Provisions
December 30, 1996	Arizona	Whether a federal credit union is exempt from state transaction privilege tax will be referred to the United States Attorney as NCUA does not have direct authority to enforce § 122 of the FCU Act.
January 29, 1996	Wisconsin	State law regarding the advertising of loans is not preempted, if not specifically addressed by NCUA regulations; state law one-year notice rule for any change in terms and conditions of an open-end credit plan is preempted; state law collection requirements are not preempted.
April 26, 1995	General	State usury laws are preempted. The federal 18% cap applies.
January 21, 1993	Pennsylvania	If the state law restricts fees for the recordation of the satisfaction of a mortgage or for the federal credit union's preparation of a satisfaction, it is preempted.
July 7, 1992	South Dakota	State law affecting the disposition of funds in a decedent's accounts is not preempted because it does not affect the opening, maintaining, or closing of an account.
June 24, 1992	Texas	State motor vehicle retail installment sales law applies to loan originated by car dealers and purchased or assigned to a federal credit union. FCU Act preemption only applies to loans originated by federal credit unions regardless of the fact that all parties contemplate that the loan will be assigned immediately to the federal credit union.
June 11, 1992	Iowa	State law requiring credit card issuers whose principal place of business is not in Iowa to register and provide certain information is not preempted as it does not conflict with the FCU Act or frustrate the federal credit union's ability to carry out its regulatory duties. Only the NCUA can enforce state law against a federal credit union, however. Letter affirms the April 25, 1992 letter regarding the preemption of restrictions on security and balloon payments.
June 1, 1992	New York	Assuming the state's motor vehicle retail installment loan law applied to a federal credit union, then a limit on a grace period is preempted.
May 18, 1992	Massachusetts	Massachusetts law prohibiting the charging of a late fee unless the mortgage payment is at least 15 days late is preempted; state law stating that payments due on a Saturday or holiday may be made on the next business day is not preempted since it is a matter of statutory contract law.
April 25, 1992	Iowa	State credit card law, for the most part, is not preempted. The sections that impose limitations on the use of security for loans and balloon payments are preempted.

Appendix F — Federal Deposit Insurance Act

This appendix excerpts portions of the Federal Deposit Insurance Act. These provisions appear in F.1. Section F.2, includes selected regulations promulgated by the Federal Deposit Insurance Corporation (FDIC). In addition, the FDIC issues Interpretive Letters from time to time. Relevant letters are summarized in F.3. The full text of these letters is included on the CD-Rom accompanying this volume and is updated in the annual supplements. In addition, the statutes and regulations reprinted in Appxs. F.1 and F.2, are also found on the companion CD-Rom.

F.1 Selected Statutory Provisions

TITLE 12—BANKS AND BANKING

CHAPTER 16—FEDERAL DEPOSIT INSURANCE CORPORATION

* * *

§ 1815.   Deposit insurance

§ 1816.   Factors to be considered

* * *

§ 1831a.   Activities of insured State banks

* * *

§ 1831d.   State-chartered insured depository institutions and insured branches of foreign banks [*This section is reprinted in Appx. G.1, infra, not herein, because it was added by the Depository Institutions Deregulation and Monetary Control Act of 1980.*]

* * *

§ 1831u.   Interstate bank mergers

* * *

§ 1831w.   Safety and soundness firewalls applicable to financial subsidiaries of banks

* * *

12 U.S.C. § 1815. Deposit insurance

(a) Application to Corporation required

(1) In general

Except as provided in paragraphs (2) and (3), any depository institution which is engaged in the business of receiving deposits other than trust funds (as defined in section 1813 (p) of this title), upon application to and examination by the Corporation and approval by the Board of Directors, may become an insured depository institution.

(2) Interim depository institutions

In the case of any interim Federal depository institution that is chartered by the appropriate Federal banking agency and will not open for business, the depository institution shall be an insured depository institution upon the issuance of the institution's charter by the agency.

(3) Application and approval not required in cases of continued insurance

Paragraph (1) shall not apply in the case of any depository institution whose insured status is continued pursuant to section 1814 of this title.

(4) Review requirements

In reviewing any application under this subsection, the Board of Directors shall consider the factors described in section 1816 of this title in determining whether to approve the application for insurance.

(5) Notice of denial of application for insurance

If the Board of Directors votes to deny any application for insurance by any depository institution, the Board of Directors shall promptly notify the appropriate Federal banking agency and, in the case of any State depository institution, the appropriate State banking supervisor of the denial of such application, giving specific reasons in writing for the Board of Directors' determination with reference to the factors described in section 1816 of this title.

(6) Nondelegation requirement

The authority of the Board of Directors to make any determination to deny any application under this subsection may not be delegated by the Board of Directors.

(b) Foreign branch nonmember banks; matters considered

Subject to the provisions of this chapter and to such terms and conditions as the Board of Directors may impose, any branch of a foreign bank, upon application by the bank to the Corporation, and examination by the Corporation of the branch, and approval by the Board of Directors, may become an insured branch. Before approving any such application, the Board of Directors shall give consideration to—

(1) the financial history and condition of the bank,

(2) the adequacy of its capital structure,

(3) its future earnings prospects,

(4) the general character and fitness of its management, including but not limited to the management of the branch proposed to be insured,

(5) the risk presented to the Bank Insurance Fund or the Savings Association Insurance Fund,

(6) the convenience and needs of the community to be served by the branch,

(7) whether or not its corporate powers, insofar as they will be exercised through the proposed insured branch, are consistent with the purposes of this chapter, and

(8) the probable adequacy and reliability of information supplied and to be supplied by the bank to the Corporation to enable it to carry out its functions under this chapter.

(c) Protection to deposit insurance fund; surety bond, pledge of assets, etc.; injunction

(1) Before any branch of a foreign bank becomes an insured branch, the bank shall deliver to the Corporation or as the Corporation may direct a surety bond, a pledge of assets, or both, in such amounts and of such types as the Corporation may require or approve, for the purpose set forth in paragraph (4) of this subsection.

(2) After any branch of a foreign bank becomes an insured branch, the bank shall maintain on deposit with the Corporation, or as the Corporation may direct, surety bonds or assets or both, in such amounts and of such types as shall be determined from time to time in accordance with such regulations as the Board of Directors may prescribe. Such regulations may impose differing requirements on the basis of any factors which in the judgment of the Board of Directors are reasonably related to the purpose set forth in paragraph (4).

(3) The Corporation may require of any given bank larger deposits of bonds and assets than required under paragraph (2) of this subsection if, in the judgment of the Corporation, the situation of that bank or any branch thereof is or becomes such that the deposits of bonds and assets otherwise required under this section would not adequately fulfill the purpose set forth in paragraph (4). The imposition of any such additional requirements may be without notice or opportunity for hearing, but the Corporation shall afford an opportunity to any such bank to apply for a reduction or removal of any such additional requirements so imposed.

(4) The purpose of the surety bonds and pledges of assets required under this subsection is to provide protection to the deposit insurance fund against the risks entailed in insuring the domestic deposits of a foreign bank whose activities, assets, and personnel are in large part outside the jurisdiction of the United States. In the implementation of its authority under this subsection, however, the Corporation shall endeavor to avoid imposing requirements on such banks which would unnecessarily place them at a competitive disadvantage in relation to domestically incorporated banks.

(5) In the case of any failure or threatened failure of a foreign bank to comply with any requirement imposed under this subsection (c), the Corporation, in addition to all other administrative and judicial remedies, may apply to any United States district court, or United States court of any territory, within the jurisdiction of which any branch of the bank is located, for an injunction to compel such bank and any officer, employee, or agent thereof, or any other person having custody or control of any of its assets, to deliver to the Corporation such assets as may be necessary to meet such requirement, and to take any other action necessary to vest the Corporation with control of assets so delivered. If the court shall determine that there has been any such failure or threatened failure to comply with any such requirement, it shall be the duty of the court to issue such injunction. The propriety of the requirement may be litigated only as provided in chapter 7 of title 5, and may not be made an issue in an action for an injunction under this paragraph.

(d) Insurance fees
(1) Uninsured institutions
(A) In general

Any institution that becomes insured by the Corporation, and any noninsured branch that becomes insured by the Corporation, shall pay the Corporation any fee which the Corporation may by regulation prescribe, after giving due consideration to the need to establish and maintain reserve ratios in the Bank Insurance Fund and the Savings Association Insurance Fund as required by section 1817 of this title.

(B) Fee credited to appropriate fund

The fee paid by the depository institution shall be credited to the Bank Insurance Fund if the depository institution becomes a Bank Insurance Fund member, and to the Savings Association Insurance Fund if the depository institution becomes a Savings Association Insurance Fund member.

(C) Exception for certain depository institutions

Any depository institution that becomes an insured depository institution by operation of section 1814 (a) of this title shall not pay any fee.

(2) Conversions
(A) In general

(i) Prior approval required No insured depository institution may participate in a conversion transaction without the prior approval of the Corporation.

(ii) 5-year moratorium on conversions Except as provided in subparagraph (C), the Corporation may not approve any conversion transaction before the later of the end of the 5-year period beginning on August 9, 1989, or the date on which the Savings Association Insurance Fund first meets or exceeds the designated reserve ratio for such fund.

(B) "Conversion transaction" defined

For purposes of this paragraph, the term "conversion transaction" means—

(i) the change of status of an insured depository institution from a Bank Insurance Fund member to a Savings Association Insurance Fund member or from a Savings Association Insurance Fund member to a Bank Insurance Fund member;

(ii) the merger or consolidation of a Bank Insurance Fund member with a Savings Association Insurance Fund member;

(iii) the assumption of any liability by—

(I) any Bank Insurance Fund member to pay any deposits of a Savings Association Insurance Fund member; or

(II) any Savings Association Insurance Fund member to pay any deposits of a Bank Insurance Fund member;

(iv) the transfer of assets of—

(I) any Bank Insurance Fund member to any Savings Association Insurance Fund member in consideration of the assumption of liabilities for any portion of the deposits of such Bank Insurance Fund member; or

(II) any Savings Association Insurance Fund member to any Bank Insurance Fund member in consideration of the assumption of liabilities for any portion of the deposits of such Savings Association Insurance Fund member; and

(v) the transfer of deposits—

(I) from a Bank Insurance Fund member to a Savings Association Insurance Fund member; or

(II) from a Savings Association Insurance Fund member to a Bank Insurance Fund member;

in a transaction in which the deposit is received from a depositor at an insured depository institution for which a receiver has been appointed and the receiving insured depository institution is acting as agent for the Corporation in connection with the payment of such deposit to the depositor at the institution for which a receiver has been appointed.

(C) Approval during moratorium

The Corporation may approve a conversion transaction at any time if—

(i) the conversion transaction affects an insubstantial portion, as determined by the Corporation, of the total deposits of each depository institution participating in the conversion transaction;

(ii) the conversion occurs in connection with the acquisition of a Savings Association Insurance Fund member in default or in danger of default, and the Corporation determines that the estimated financial benefits to the Savings Association Insurance Fund or Resolution Trust Corporation equal or exceed the Corporation's estimate of loss of assessment income to such insurance fund over the remaining balance of the moratorium period established by subparagraph (A), and the Resolution Trust Corporation concurs in the Corporation's determination; or

(iii) the conversion occurs in connection with the acquisition of a Bank Insurance Fund member in default or in danger of default and the Corporation determines that the estimated financial benefits to the Bank Insurance Fund equal or exceed the Corporation's estimate of the loss of assessment income to the insurance fund over the remaining balance of the moratorium period established by subparagraph (A).

(D) Certain transfers deemed to affect insubstantial portion of total deposits

For purposes of subparagraph (C)(i), any conversion transaction shall be deemed to affect an insubstantial portion of the total deposits of an insured depository institution, to the extent the aggregate amount of the total deposits transferred in such transaction and in all conversion transactions occurring after August 9, 1989, does not exceed 35 percent of the lesser of—

(i) the amount which is equal to the sum of—

(I) the total deposits of such insured depository institution on May 1, 1989; and

(II) the total amount of net interest credited to the depository institution's deposits during the period beginning on May 1, 1989, and ending on the date of the transfer of deposits in connection with such transaction; or

(ii) the amount which is equal to the total deposits of such insured depository institution on the date of the transfer of deposits in connection with such transaction.

(E) Exit and entrance fees

Each insured depository institution participating in a conversion transaction shall pay—

(i) in the case of a conversion transaction in which the resulting or acquiring depository institution is not a Savings Association Insurance Fund member, an exit fee (in an amount to be determined and assessed in accordance with subparagraph (F)) which—

(I) shall be deposited in the Savings Association Insurance Fund; or

(II) shall be paid to the Financing Corporation, if the Secretary of the Treasury determines that the Financing

Corporation has exhausted all other sources of funding for interest payments on the obligations of the Financing Corporation and orders that such fees be paid to the Financing Corporation;

(ii) in the case of a conversion transaction in which the resulting or acquiring depository institution is not a Bank Insurance Fund member, an exit fee in an amount to be determined by the Corporation (and assessed in accordance with subparagraph (F)(ii)) which shall be deposited in the Bank Insurance Fund; and

(iii) an entrance fee in an amount to be determined by the Corporation (and assessed in accordance with subparagraph (F)(ii)), except that—

(I) in the case of a conversion transaction in which the resulting or acquiring depository institution is a Bank Insurance Fund member, the fee shall be the approximate amount which the Corporation calculates as necessary to prevent dilution of the Bank Insurance Fund, and shall be paid to the Bank Insurance Fund; and

(II) in the case of a conversion transaction in which the resulting or acquiring depository institution is a Savings Association Insurance Fund member, the fee shall be the approximate amount which the Corporation calculates as necessary to prevent dilution of the Savings Association Insurance Fund, and shall be paid to the Savings Association Insurance Fund.

(F) Assessment of exit and entrance fees

  (i) Determination of amount of exit fees

(I) **Conversions before January 1, 1997** In the case of any exit fee assessed under subparagraph (E)(i) for any conversion transaction consummated before January 1, 1997, the amount of such fee shall be determined jointly by the Corporation and the Secretary of the Treasury.

(II) **Assessments after December 31, 1996** In the case of any exit fee assessed under subparagraph (E)(i) for any conversion transaction consummated after December 31, 1996, the amount of such fee shall be determined by the Corporation.

(ii) **Procedures** The Corporation shall prescribe, by regulation, procedures for assessing any exit or entrance fee under subparagraph (E).

(G) Charter conversion of SAIF members

This subsection shall not be construed as prohibiting any savings association which is a Savings Association Insurance Fund member from converting to a bank charter during the period described in subparagraph (A)(ii) if the resulting bank remains a Savings Association Insurance Fund member.

(3) Optional conversions subject to special rules on deposit insurance payments

(A) Conversions allowed

Notwithstanding paragraph (2)(A), and subject to the requirements of this paragraph, any insured depository institution may participate in a transaction described in clause (ii), (iii), or (iv) of paragraph (2)(B) if the transaction is approved by the responsible agency under section 1828 (c)(2) of this title.

(B) Assessments on deposits attributable to former depository institution

  (i) **Assessments by SAIF** In the case of any acquiring, assuming, or resulting depository institution which is a Bank Insurance Fund member, that portion of the deposits of such member for any semiannual period which is equal to the adjusted attributable deposit amount (determined under subparagraph (C) with respect to the transaction) shall be treated as deposits which are insured by the Savings Association Insurance Fund.

(ii) Assessments by BIF In the case of any acquiring, assuming, or resulting depository institution which is a Savings Association Insurance Fund member, that portion of the deposits of such member for any semiannual period which is equal to the adjusted attributable deposit amount (determined under subparagraph (C) with respect to the transaction) shall be treated as deposits which are insured by the Bank Insurance Fund.

(C) Determination of adjusted attributable deposit amount
Except as provided in subparagraph (K), the adjusted attributable deposit amount which shall be taken into account for purposes of determining the amount of the assessment under subparagraph (B) for any semiannual period by any acquiring, assuming, or resulting depository institution in connection with a transaction under subparagraph (A) is the amount which is equal to the sum of—
    (i) the amount of any deposits acquired by the institution in connection with the transaction (as determined at the time of such transaction);
    (ii) the total of the amounts determined under clause (iii) for semiannual periods preceding the semiannual period for which the determination is being made under this subparagraph; and
    (iii) the amount by which the sum of the amounts described in clauses (i) and (ii) would have increased during the preceding semiannual period (other than any semiannual period beginning before the date of such transaction) if such increase occurred at a rate equal to the annual rate of growth of deposits of the acquiring, assuming, or resulting depository institution minus the amount of any deposits acquired through the acquisition, in whole or in part, of another insured depository institution.

(D) Deposit of assessment
That portion of any assessment under section 1817 of this title which—
    (i) is determined in accordance with subparagraph (B)(i) shall be deposited in the Savings Association Insurance Fund; and
    (ii) is determined in accordance with subparagraph (B)(ii) shall be deposited in the Bank Insurance Fund.

(E) Conditions for approval, generally
    (i) Information required An application to engage in any transaction under this paragraph shall contain such information relating to the factors to be considered for approval as the responsible agency may require, by regulation or by specific request, in connection with any particular application.
    (ii) No transfer of deposit insurance permitted This paragraph shall not be construed as authorizing transactions which result in the transfer of any insured depository institution's Federal deposit insurance from 1 Federal deposit insurance fund to the other Federal deposit insurance fund.
    (iii) Capital requirements A transaction described in this paragraph shall not be approved under section 1828 (c)(2) of this title unless the acquiring, assuming, or resulting depository institution will meet all applicable capital requirements upon consummation of the transaction.

(F) Certain interstate transactions
A Bank Insurance Fund member which is a subsidiary of a bank holding company may not be the acquiring, assuming, or resulting depository institution in a transaction under subparagraph (A) unless the transaction would comply with the requirements of section 1842 (d) of this title if, at the time of such transaction, the Savings Association Insurance Fund member involved in such transaction was a State bank that the bank holding company was applying to acquire.

(G) Allocation of costs in event of default
If any acquiring, assuming, or resulting depository institution is in default or danger of default at any time before this paragraph ceases to apply, any loss incurred by the Corporation shall be allocated between the Bank Insurance Fund and the Savings Association Insurance Fund, in amounts reflecting the amount of insured deposits of such acquiring, assuming, or resulting depository institution assessed by the Bank Insurance Fund and the Savings Association Insurance Fund, respectively, under subparagraph (B).

(H) Subsequent approval of conversion transaction
This paragraph shall cease to apply if—
    (i) after the end of the moratorium period established by paragraph (2)(A), the Corporation approves an application by any acquiring, assuming, or resulting depository institution to treat the transaction described in subparagraph (A) as a conversion transaction; and
    (ii) the acquiring, assuming, or resulting depository institution pays the amount of any exit and entrance fee assessed by the Corporation under subparagraph (E) of paragraph (2) with respect to such transaction.

(I) "Acquiring, assuming, or resulting depository institution" defined
For purposes of this paragraph, the term "acquiring, assuming, or resulting depository institution" means any insured depository institution which—
    (i) results from any transaction described in paragraph (2)(B)(ii) and approved under this paragraph;
    (ii) in connection with a transaction described in paragraph (2)(B)(iii) and approved under this paragraph, assumes any liability to pay deposits of another insured depository institution; or
    (iii) in connection with a transaction described in paragraph (2)(B)(iv) and approved under this paragraph, acquires assets from any insured depository institution in consideration of the assumption of liability for any deposits of such institution.

(J) Redesignated (I)
(I) Redesignated (I)[1]
(K) Adjustment of adjusted attributable deposit amount
The amount determined under subparagraph (C)(i) for deposits acquired by March 31, 1995, shall be reduced by 20 percent for purposes of computing the adjusted attributable deposit amount for the payment of any assessment for any semiannual period that begins after September 30, 1996 (other than the special assessment imposed under section 2702(a) of such Act), for a Bank Insurance Fund member bank that, as of June 30, 1995—
    (i) had an adjusted attributable deposit amount that was less than 50 percent of the total deposits of that member bank; or

---

1 Probably should be deleted.

(ii)
    (I) had an adjusted attributable deposit amount equal to less than 75 percent of the total assessable deposits of that member bank;
    (II) had total assessable deposits greater than $5,000,000,000; and
    (III) was owned or controlled by a bank holding company that owned or controlled insured depository institutions having an aggregate amount of deposits insured or treated as insured by the Bank Insurance Fund greater than the aggregate amount of deposits insured or treated as insured by the Savings Association Insurance Fund.

(e) Liability of commonly controlled depository institutions
  (1) In general
  (A) Liability established
Any insured depository institution shall be liable for any loss incurred by the Corporation, or any loss which the Corporation reasonably anticipates incurring, after August 9, 1989, in connection with—
    (i) the default of a commonly controlled insured depository institution; or
    (ii) any assistance provided by the Corporation to any commonly controlled insured depository institution in danger of default.
  (B) Payment upon notice
An insured depository institution shall pay the amount of any liability to the Corporation under subparagraph (A) upon receipt of written notice by the Corporation in accordance with this subsection.
  (C) Notice required to be provided within 2 years of loss
No insured depository institution shall be liable to the Corporation under subparagraph (A) if written notice with respect to such liability is not received by such institution before the end of the 2-year period beginning on the date the Corporation incurred the loss.
  (2) Amount of compensation; procedures
  (A) Use of estimates
When an insured depository institution is in default or requires assistance to prevent default, the Corporation shall—
    (i) in good faith, estimate the amount of the loss the Corporation will incur from such default or assistance;
    (ii) if, with respect to such insured depository institution, there is more than 1 commonly controlled insured depository institution, estimate the amount of each such commonly controlled depository institution's share of such liability; and
    (iii) advise each commonly controlled depository institution of the Corporation's estimate of the amount of such institution's liability for such losses.
  (B) Procedures; immediate payment
The Corporation, after consultation with the appropriate Federal banking agency and the appropriate State chartering agency, shall—
    (i) on a case-by-case basis, establish the procedures and schedule under which any insured depository institution shall reimburse the Corporation for such institution's liability under paragraph (1) in connection with any commonly controlled insured depository institution; or
    (ii) require any insured depository institution to make immediate payment of the amount of such institution's liability

under paragraph (1) in connection with any commonly controlled insured depository institution.
  (C) Priority
The liability of any insured depository institution under this subsection shall have priority with respect to other obligations and liabilities as follows:
    (i) Superiority The liability shall be superior to the following obligations and liabilities of the depository institution:
      (I) Any obligation to shareholders arising as a result of their status as shareholders (including any depository institution holding company or any shareholder or creditor of such company).
      (II) Any obligation or liability owed to any affiliate of the depository institution (including any other insured depository institution), other than any secured obligation which was secured as of May 1, 1989.
    (ii) Subordination The liability shall be subordinate in right and payment to the following obligations and liabilities of the depository institution:
      (I) Any deposit liability (which is not a liability described in clause (i)(II)).
      (II) Any secured obligation, other than any obligation owed to any affiliate of the depository institution (including any other insured depository institution) which was secured after May 1, 1989.
      (III) Any other general or senior liability (which is not a liability described in clause (i)).
      (IV) Any obligation subordinated to depositors or other general creditors (which is not an obligation described in clause (i)).
  (D) Adjustment of estimated payment
    (i) Overpayment If the amount of compensation estimated by and paid to the Corporation by 1 or more such commonly controlled depository institutions is greater than the actual loss incurred by the Corporation, the Corporation shall reimburse each such commonly controlled depository institution its pro rata share of any overpayment.
    (ii) Underpayment If the amount of compensation estimated by and paid to the Corporation by 1 or more such commonly controlled depository institutions is less than the actual loss incurred by the Corporation, the Corporation shall redetermine in its discretion the liability of each such commonly controlled depository institution to the Corporation and shall require each such commonly controlled depository institution to make payment of any additional liability to the Corporation.
  (3) Review
  (A) Judicial
Actions of the Corporation shall be reviewable pursuant to chapter 7 of title 5.
  (B) Administrative
The Corporation shall prescribe regulations and establish administrative procedures which provide for a hearing on the record for the review of—
    (i) the amount of any loss incurred by the Corporation in connection with any insured depository institution;
    (ii) the liability of individual commonly controlled depository institutions for the amount of such loss; and
    (iii) the schedule of payments to be made by such commonly controlled depository institutions.

(4) Limitation on rights of private parties

To the extent the exercise of any right or power of any person would impair the ability of any insured depository institution to perform such institution's obligations under this subsection—

(A) the obligations of such insured depository institution shall supersede such right or power; and

(B) no court may give effect to such right or power with respect to such insured depository institution.

(5) Waiver authority

(A) In general

The Corporation, in its discretion, may exempt any insured depository institution from the provisions of this subsection if the Corporation determines that such exemption is in the best interests of the Bank Insurance Fund or the Savings Association Insurance Fund.

(B) Condition

During the period any exemption granted to any insured depository institution under subparagraph (A) or (C) is in effect, such insured depository institution and all other insured depository institution affiliates of such depository institution shall comply fully with the restrictions of sections 371c and 371c–1 of this title without regard to section 371c (d)(1) of this title.

(C) Limited partnerships

(i) In general The Corporation may, in its discretion, exempt any limited partnership and any affiliate of any limited partnership (other than any insured depository institution which is a majority owned subsidiary of such partnership) from the provisions of this subsection if such limited partnership or affiliate has filed a registration statement with the Securities and Exchange Commission on or before April 10, 1989, indicating that as of the date of such filing such partnership intended to acquire 1 or more insured depository institutions.

(ii) Review and notice Within 10 business days after the date of submission of any request for an exemption under this subparagraph together with such information as shall be reasonably requested by the Corporation, the Corporation shall make a determination on the request and shall so advise the applicant.

(6) 5-year transition rule

During the 5-year period beginning on August 9, 1989—

(A) no Savings Association Insurance Fund member shall have any liability to the Corporation under this subsection arising out of assistance provided by the Corporation or any loss incurred by the Corporation as a result of the default of a Bank Insurance Fund member which was acquired by such Savings Association Insurance Fund member or any affiliate of such member before August 9, 1989; and

(B) no Bank Insurance Fund member shall have such liability with respect to assistance provided by or loss incurred by the Corporation as a result of the default of a Savings Association Insurance Fund member which was acquired by such Bank Insurance Fund member or any affiliate of such member before August 9, 1989.

(7) Exclusion for institutions acquired in debt collections

Any depository institution shall not be treated as commonly controlled, for purposes of this subsection, during the 5-year period beginning on the date of an acquisition described in subparagraph (A) or such longer period as the Corporation may determine after written application by the acquirer, if—

(A) 1 depository institution controls another by virtue of own-ership of voting shares acquired in securing or collecting a debt previously contracted in good faith; and

(B) during the period beginning on August 9, 1989, and ending upon the expiration of the exclusion, the controlling bank and all other insured depository institution affiliates of such controlling bank comply fully with the restrictions of sections 371c and 371c–1 of this title, without regard to section 371c (d)(1) of this title, in transactions with the acquired insured depository institution.

(8) Exception for certain FSLIC assisted institutions

No depository institution shall have any liability to the Corporation under this subsection as the result of the default of, or assistance provided with respect to, an insured depository institution which is an affiliate of such depository institution if—

(A) such affiliate was receiving cash payments from the Federal Savings and Loan Insurance Corporation under an assistance agreement or note entered into before August 9, 1989;

(B) the Federal Savings and Loan Insurance Corporation, or such other entity which has succeeded to the payment obligations of such Corporation with respect to such assistance agreement or note, is unable to continue such payments; and

(C) such affiliate—

(i) is in default or in need of assistance solely as a result of the failure to meet the payment obligations referred to in subparagraph (B); and

(ii) is not otherwise in breach of the terms of any assistance agreement or note which would authorize the Federal Savings and Loan Insurance Corporation or such other successor entity, pursuant to the terms of such assistance agreement or note, to refuse to make such payments.

(9) Commonly controlled defined

For purposes of this subsection, depository institutions are commonly controlled if—

(A) such institutions are controlled by the same depository institution holding company (including any company required to file reports pursuant to section 1843 (f)(6) of this title); or

(B) 1 depository institution is controlled by another depository institution.

[Sept. 21, 1950, ch. 967, § 2[5], 64 Stat. 876; Pub. L. No. 95–369, § 6(c)(7), 92 Stat. 616 (Sept. 17, 1978); Pub. L. No. 97–320, title VII, § 703(c), 96 Stat. 1539 (Oct. 15, 1982); Pub. L. No. 101–73, title II, §§ 201(a), 206 (a), 103 Stat. 187, 195 (Aug. 9, 1989); Pub. L. No. 102–242, title I, § 115(a), title III, § 302(e)(1), (2), title V, § 501(a), 105 Stat. 2249, 2349, 2388 (Dec. 19, 1991); Pub. L. No. 102–550, title XVI, §§ 1605(a)(5)(B), 1607 (a), 106 Stat. 4085, 4089 (Oct. 28, 1992); Pub. L. No. 102–558, title III, §§ 303(b)(6)(B), 305, 106 Stat. 4225, 4226 (Oct..28, 1992); Pub. L. No. 103–204, § 9, 107 Stat. 2388 (Dec. 17, 1993); Pub. L. No. 103–325, title III, § 319(b), title VI, § 602(a)(2), (3), 108 Stat. 2225, 2288 (Sept. 23, 1994); Pub. L. No. 104–208, div. A, title II, §§ 2201(a), 2702 (i), 2704 (d)(14)(B)–(E), 110 Stat. 3009–403, 3009–483, 3009–491 Sept. 30, 1996]

12 U.S.C. § 1816. Factors to be considered

The factors that are required, under section 1814 of this title, to be considered in connection with, and enumerated in, any certificate issued pursuant to section 1814 of this title and that are required, under section 1815 of this title, to be considered by the Board of

Directors in connection with any determination by such Board pursuant to section 1815 of this title are the following:

(1) The financial history and condition of the depository institution.

(2) The adequacy of the depository institution's capital structure.

(3) The future earnings prospects of the depository institution.

(4) The general character and fitness of the management of the depository institution.

(5) The risk presented by such depository institution to the Bank Insurance Fund or the Savings Association Insurance Fund.

(6) The convenience and needs of the community to be served by such depository institution.

(7) Whether the depository institution's corporate powers are consistent with the purposes of this chapter.

[Sept. 21, 1950, ch. 967, § 2[6], 64 Stat. 876; Pub. L. No. 101–73, title II, § 207, 103 Stat. 206 (Aug. 9, 1989); Pub. L. No. 104–208, div. A, title II, § 2704(d)(14)(F), 110 Stat. 3009–491 (Sept. 30, 1996)]

* * *

12 U.S.C. § 1831a. Activities of insured State banks

(a) Permissible activities

(1) In general

After the end of the 1-year period beginning on December 19, 1991, an insured State bank may not engage as principal in any type of activity that is not permissible for a national bank unless—

(A) the Corporation has determined that the activity would pose no significant risk to the appropriate deposit insurance fund; and

(B) the State bank is, and continues to be, in compliance with applicable capital standards prescribed by the appropriate Federal banking agency.

(2) Processing period

(A) In general

The Corporation shall make a determination under paragraph (1)(A) not later than 60 days after receipt of a completed application that may be required under this subsection.

(B) Extension of time period

The Corporation may extend the 60-day period referred to in subparagraph (A) for not more than 30 additional days, and shall notify the applicant of any such extension.

(b) Insurance underwriting

(1) In general

Notwithstanding subsection (a) of this section, an insured State bank may not engage in insurance underwriting except to the extent that activity is permissible for national banks.

(2) Exception for certain federally reinsured crop insurance

Notwithstanding any other provision of law, an insured State bank or any of its subsidiaries that provided insurance on or before September 30, 1991, which was reinsured in whole or in part by the Federal Crop Insurance Corporation may continue to provide such insurance.

(c) Equity investments by insured State banks

(1) In general

An insured State bank may not, directly or indirectly, acquire or retain any equity investment of a type that is not permissible for a national bank.

(2) Exception for certain subsidiaries

Paragraph (1) shall not prohibit an insured State bank from acquiring or retaining an equity investment in a subsidiary of which the insured State bank is a majority owner.

(3) Exception for qualified housing projects

(A) Exception

Notwithstanding any other provision of this subsection, an insured State bank may invest as a limited partner in a partnership, the sole purpose of which is direct or indirect investment in the acquisition, rehabilitation, or new construction of a qualified housing project.

(B) Limitation

The aggregate of the investments of any insured State bank pursuant to this paragraph shall not exceed 2 percent of the total assets of the bank.

(C) Qualified housing project defined

As used in this paragraph—

(i) Qualified housing project The term "qualified housing project" means residential real estate that is intended to primarily benefit lower income people throughout the period of the investment.

(ii) Lower income The term "lower income" means income that is less than or equal to the median income based on statistics from State or Federal sources.

(4) Transition rule

(A) In general

The Corporation shall require any insured State bank to divest any equity investment the retention of which is not permissible under this subsection as quickly as can be prudently done, and in any event before the end of the 5-year period beginning on December 19, 1991.

(B) Treatment of noncompliance during divestment

With respect to any equity investment held by any insured State bank on December 19, 1991, which was lawfully acquired before December 19, 1991, the bank shall be deemed not to be in violation of the prohibition in this subsection on retaining such investment so long as the bank complies with the applicable requirements established by the Corporation for divesting such investments.

(d) Subsidiaries of insured State banks

(1) In general

After the end of the 1-year period beginning on December 19, 1991, a subsidiary of an insured State bank may not engage as principal in any type of activity that is not permissible for a subsidiary of a national bank unless—

(A) the Corporation has determined that the activity poses no significant risk to the appropriate deposit insurance fund; and

(B) the bank is, and continues to be, in compliance with applicable capital standards prescribed by the appropriate Federal banking agency.

(2) Insurance underwriting prohibited

(A) Prohibition

Notwithstanding paragraph (1), no subsidiary of an insured State bank may engage in insurance underwriting except to the extent such activities are permissible for national banks.

(B) Continuation of existing activities

Notwithstanding subparagraph (A), a well-capitalized insured State bank or any of its subsidiaries that was lawfully providing insurance as principal in a State on November 21, 1991, may continue to provide, as principal, insurance of the same type to residents of the State (including companies or partnerships incorporated in, organized under the laws of, licensed to do business in, or having an office in the State, but only on behalf of their employees resident in or property located in the State), individuals employed in the State, and any other person to whom the bank or subsidiary has provided insurance as principal, without interruption, since such person resided in or was employed in such State.

(C) Exception

Subparagraph (A) does not apply to a subsidiary of an insured State bank if—

(i) the insured State bank was required, before June 1, 1991, to provide title insurance as a condition of the bank's initial chartering under State law; and

(ii) control of the insured State bank has not changed since that date.

(3) Processing period

(A) In general

The Corporation shall make a determination under paragraph (1)(A) not later than 60 days after receipt of a completed application that may be required under this subsection.

(B) Extension of time period

The Corporation may extend the 60-day period referred to in subparagraph (A) for not more than 30 additional days, and shall notify the applicant of any such extension.

(e) Savings bank life insurance

(1) In general

No provision of this chapter shall be construed as prohibiting or impairing the sale or underwriting of savings bank life insurance, or the ownership of stock in a savings bank life insurance company, by any insured bank which—

(A) is located in the Commonwealth of Massachusetts or the State of New York or Connecticut; and

(B) meets applicable consumer disclosure requirements with respect to such insurance.

(2) FDIC finding and action regarding risk

(A) Finding

Before the end of the 1-year period beginning on December 19, 1991, the Corporation shall make a finding whether savings bank life insurance activities of insured banks pose or may pose any significant risk to the insurance fund of which such banks are members.

(B) Actions

(i) **In general**—The Corporation shall, pursuant to any finding made under subparagraph (A), take appropriate actions to address any risk that exists or may subsequently develop with respect to insured banks described in paragraph (1)(A).

(ii) **Authorized actions**—Actions the Corporation may take under this subparagraph include requiring the modification, suspension, or termination of insurance activities conducted by any insured bank if the Corporation finds that the activities pose a significant risk to any insured bank described in paragraph (1)(A) or to the insurance fund of which such bank is a member.

(f) Common and preferred stock investment

(1) In general

An insured State bank shall not acquire or retain, directly or indirectly, any equity investment of a type or in an amount that is

not permissible for a national bank or is not otherwise permitted under this section.

(2) Exception for banks in certain States

Notwithstanding paragraph (1), an insured State bank may, to the extent permitted by the Corporation, acquire and retain ownership of securities described in paragraph (1) to the extent the aggregate amount of such investment does not exceed an amount equal to 100 percent of the bank's capital if such bank—

(A) is located in a State that permitted, as of September 30, 1991, investment in common or preferred stock listed on a national securities exchange or shares of an investment company registered under the Investment Company Act of 1940 [15 U.S.C. 80a–1 et seq.]; and

(B) made or maintained an investment in such securities during the period beginning on September 30, 1990, and ending on November 26, 1991.

(3) Exception for certain types of institutions

Notwithstanding paragraph (1), an insured State bank may—

(A) acquire not more than 10 percent of a corporation that only—

(i) provides directors', trustees', and officers' liability insurance coverage or bankers' blanket bond group insurance coverage for insured depository institutions; or

(ii) reinsures such policies; and

(B) acquire or retain shares of a depository institution if—

(i) the institution engages only in activities permissible for national banks;

(ii) the institution is subject to examination and regulation by a State bank supervisor;

(iii) 20 or more depository institutions own shares of the institution and none of those institutions owns more than 15 percent of the institution's shares; and

(iv) the institution's shares (other than directors' qualifying shares or shares held under or initially acquired through a plan established for the benefit of the institution's officers and employees) are owned only by the institution.

(4) Transition period for common and preferred stock investments

(A) In general

During each year in the 3-year period beginning on December 19, 1991, each insured State bank shall reduce by not less than 1/3 of its shares (as of December 19, 1991) the bank's ownership of securities in excess of the amount equal to 100 percent of the capital of such bank.

(B) Compliance at end of period

By the end of the 3-year period referred to in subparagraph (A), each insured State bank and each subsidiary of a State bank shall be in compliance with the maximum amount limitations on investments referred to in paragraph (1).

(5) Loss of exception upon acquisition

Any exception applicable under paragraph (2) with respect to any insured State bank shall cease to apply with respect to such bank upon any change in control of such bank or any conversion of the charter of such bank.

(6) Notice and approval

An insured State bank may only engage in any investment pursuant to paragraph (2) if—

(A) the bank has filed a 1-time notice of the bank's intention to acquire and retain investments described in paragraph (1); and

(B) the Corporation has determined, within 60 days of receiving such notice, that acquiring or retaining such investments does not pose a significant risk to the insurance fund of which such bank is a member.

(7) Divestiture
(A) In general
The Corporation may require divestiture by an insured State bank of any investment permitted under this subsection if the Corporation determines that such investment will have an adverse effect on the safety and soundness of the bank.
(B) Reasonable standard
The Corporation shall not require divestiture by any bank pursuant to subparagraph (A) without reason to believe that such investment will have an adverse effect on the safety and soundness of the bank.

(g) Determinations

The Corporation shall make determinations under this section by regulation or order.

(h) "Activity" defined

For purposes of this section, the term "activity" includes acquiring or retaining any investment.

(i) Other authority not affected

This section shall not be construed as limiting the authority of any appropriate Federal banking agency or any State supervisory authority to impose more stringent restrictions.

(j) Activities of branches of out-of-State banks
(1) Application of host State law
The laws of a host State, including laws regarding community reinvestment, consumer protection, fair lending, and establishment of intrastate branches, shall apply to any branch in the host State of an out-of-State State bank to the same extent as such State laws apply to a branch in the host State of an out-of-State national bank. To the extent host State law is inapplicable to a branch of an out-of-State State bank in such host State pursuant to the preceding sentence, home State law shall apply to such branch.
(2) Activities of branches
An insured State bank that establishes a branch in a host State may conduct any activity at such branch that is permissible under the laws of the home State of such bank, to the extent such activity is permissible either for a bank chartered by the host State (subject to the restrictions in this section) or for a branch in the host State of an out-of-State national bank.
(3) Savings provision
No provision of this subsection shall be construed as affecting the applicability of—
(A) any State law of any home State under subsection (b), (c), or (d) of section 1831u of this title; or
(B) Federal law to State banks and State bank branches in the home State or the host State.
(4) Definitions
The terms "host State", "home State", and "out-of-State bank" have the same meanings as in section 1831u (f) of this title.

[Sept. 21, 1950, ch. 967, § 2[24], *as added* Pub. L. No. 102–242, title III, § 303(a), 105 Stat. 2349 (Dec. 19, 1991); amended Pub. L. No. 102–550, title XVI, § 1605(a)(8), 106 Stat. 4086 (Oct. 28, 1992); Pub. L. No. 103–328, title I, § 102(b)(3)(B), 108 Stat. 2351 (Sept. 29, 1994); Pub. L. No. 104–208, div. A, title II, §§ 2217,

2704 (d)(14)(W), 110 Stat. 3009–414, 3009–494 (Sept. 30, 1996); Pub. L. No. 105–24, § 2(a), 111 Stat. 238 (July 3, 1997)]

* * *

12 U.S.C. § 1831u. Interstate bank mergers

(a) Approval of interstate merger transactions authorized
(1) In general
Beginning on June 1, 1997, the responsible agency may approve a merger transaction under section 1828 (c) of this title between insured banks with different home States, without regard to whether such transaction is prohibited under the law of any State.
(2) State election to prohibit interstate merger transactions
(A) In general
Notwithstanding paragraph (1), a merger transaction may not be approved pursuant to paragraph (1) if the transaction involves a bank the home State of which has enacted a law after September 29, 1994, and before June 1, 1997, that—
(i) applies equally to all out-of-State banks; and
(ii) expressly prohibits merger transactions involving out-of-State banks.
(B) No effect on prior approvals of merger transactions
A law enacted by a State pursuant to subparagraph (A) shall have no effect on merger transactions that were approved before the effective date of such law.
(3) State election to permit early interstate merger transactions
(A) In general
A merger transaction may be approved pursuant to paragraph (1) before June 1, 1997, if the home State of each bank involved in the transaction has in effect, as of the date of the approval of such transaction, a law that—
(i) applies equally to all out-of-State banks; and
(ii) expressly permits interstate merger transactions with all out-of-State banks.
(B) Certain conditions allowed
A host State may impose conditions on a branch within such State of a bank resulting from an interstate merger transaction if—
(i) the conditions do not have the effect of discriminating against out-of-State banks, out-of-State bank holding companies, or any subsidiary of such bank or company (other than on the basis of a nationwide reciprocal treatment requirement);
(ii) the imposition of the conditions is not preempted by Federal law; and
(iii) the conditions do not apply or require performance after May 31, 1997.
(4) Interstate merger transactions involving acquisitions of branches
(A) In general
An interstate merger transaction may involve the acquisition of a branch of an insured bank without the acquisition of the bank only if the law of the State in which the branch is located permits out-of-State banks to acquire a branch of a bank in such State without acquiring the bank.
(B) Treatment of branch for purposes of this section
In the case of an interstate merger transaction which involves the acquisition of a branch of an insured bank without the acquisi-

tion of the bank, the branch shall be treated, for purposes of this section, as an insured bank the home State of which is the State in which the branch is located.

(5) Preservation of State age laws

(A) In general

The responsible agency may not approve an application pursuant to paragraph (1) that would have the effect of permitting an out-of-State bank or out-of-State bank holding company to acquire a bank in a host State that has not been in existence for the minimum period of time, if any, specified in the statutory law of the host State.

(B) Special rule for State age laws specifying a period of more than 5 years

Notwithstanding subparagraph (A), the responsible agency may approve a merger transaction pursuant to paragraph (1) involving the acquisition of a bank that has been in existence at least 5 years without regard to any longer minimum period of time specified in a statutory law of the host State.

(6) Shell banks

For purposes of this subsection, a bank that has been chartered solely for the purpose of, and does not open for business prior to, acquiring control of, or acquiring all or substantially all of the assets of, an existing bank or branch shall be deemed to have been in existence for the same period of time as the bank or branch to be acquired.

(b) Provisions relating to application and approval process

(1) Compliance with State filing requirements

(A) In general

Any bank which files an application for an interstate merger transaction shall—

(i) comply with the filing requirements of any host State of the bank which will result from such transaction to the extent that the requirement—

(I) does not have the effect of discriminating against out-of-State banks or out-of-State bank holding companies or subsidiaries of such banks or bank holding companies; and

(II) is similar in effect to any requirement imposed by the host State on a nonbanking corporation incorporated in another State that engages in business in the host State; and

(ii) submit a copy of the application to the State bank supervisor of the host State.

(B) Penalty for failure to comply

The responsible agency may not approve an application for an interstate merger transaction if the applicant materially fails to comply with subparagraph (A).

(2) Concentration limits

(A) Nationwide concentration limits

The responsible agency may not approve an application for an interstate merger transaction if the resulting bank (including all insured depository institutions which are affiliates of the resulting bank), upon consummation of the transaction, would control more than 10 percent of the total amount of deposits of insured depository institutions in the United States.

(B) Statewide concentration limits other than with respect to initial entries

The responsible agency may not approve an application for an interstate merger transaction if—

(i) any bank involved in the transaction (including all insured

depository institutions which are affiliates of any such bank) has a branch in any State in which any other bank involved in the transaction has a branch; and

(ii) the resulting bank (including all insured depository institutions which would be affiliates of the resulting bank), upon consummation of the transaction, would control 30 percent or more of the total amount of deposits of insured depository institutions in any such State.

(C) Effectiveness of State deposit caps

No provision of this subsection shall be construed as affecting the authority of any State to limit, by statute, regulation, or order, the percentage of the total amount of deposits of insured depository institutions in the State which may be held or controlled by any bank or bank holding company (including all insured depository institutions which are affiliates of the bank or bank holding company) to the extent the application of such limitation does not discriminate against out-of-State banks, out-of-State bank holding companies, or subsidiaries of such banks or holding companies.

(D) Exceptions to subparagraph (B)

The responsible agency may approve an application for an interstate merger transaction pursuant to subsection (a) of this section without regard to the applicability of subparagraph (B) with respect to any State if—

(i) there is a limitation described in subparagraph (C) in a State statute, regulation, or order which has the effect of permitting a bank or bank holding company (including all insured depository institutions which are affiliates of the bank or bank holding company) to control a greater percentage of total deposits of all insured depository institutions in the State than the percentage permitted under subparagraph (B); or

(ii) the transaction is approved by the appropriate State bank supervisor of such State and the standard on which such approval is based does not have the effect of discriminating against out-of-State banks, out-of-State bank holding companies, or subsidiaries of such banks or holding companies.

(E) Exception for certain banks

This paragraph shall not apply with respect to any interstate merger transaction involving only affiliated banks.

(3) Community reinvestment compliance

In determining whether to approve an application for an interstate merger transaction in which the resulting bank would have a branch or bank affiliate immediately following the transaction in any State in which the bank submitting the application (as the acquiring bank) had no branch or bank affiliate immediately before the transaction, the responsible agency shall—

(A) comply with the responsibilities of the agency regarding such application under section 2903 of this title;

(B) take into account the most recent written evaluation under section 2903 of this title of any bank which would be an affiliate of the resulting bank; and

(C) take into account the record of compliance of any applicant bank with applicable State community reinvestment laws.

(4) Adequacy of capital and management skills

The responsible agency may approve an application for an interstate merger transaction pursuant to subsection (a) of this section only if—

(A) each bank involved in the transaction is adequately capitalized as of the date the application is filed; and

(B) the responsible agency determines that the resulting bank will continue to be adequately capitalized and adequately managed upon the consummation of the transaction.

(5) Surrender of charter after merger transaction

The charters of all banks involved in an interstate merger transaction, other than the charter of the resulting bank, shall be surrendered, upon request, to the Federal banking agency or State bank supervisor which issued the charter.

(c) Applicability of certain laws to interstate banking operations

(1) State taxation authority not affected

(A) In general

No provision of this section shall be construed as affecting the authority of any State or political subdivision of any State to adopt, apply, or administer any tax or method of taxation to any bank, bank holding company, or foreign bank, or any affiliate of any bank, bank holding company, or foreign bank, to the extent such tax or tax method is otherwise permissible by or under the Constitution of the United States or other Federal law.

(B) Imposition of shares tax by host States

In the case of a branch of an out-of-State bank which results from an interstate merger transaction, a proportionate amount of the value of the shares of the out-of-State bank may be subject to any bank shares tax levied or imposed by the host State, or any political subdivision of such host State that imposes such tax based upon a method adopted by the host State, which may include allocation and apportionment.

(2) Applicability of antitrust laws

No provision of this section shall be construed as affecting—

(A) the applicability of the antitrust laws; or

(B) the applicability, if any, of any State law which is similar to the antitrust laws.

(3) Reservation of certain rights to States

No provision of this section shall be construed as limiting in any way the right of a State to—

(A) determine the authority of State banks chartered by that State to establish and maintain branches; or

(B) supervise, regulate, and examine State banks chartered by that State.

(4) State-imposed notice requirements

A host State may impose any notification or reporting requirement on a branch of an out-of-State bank if the requirement—

(A) does not discriminate against out-of-State banks or bank holding companies; and

(B) is not preempted by any Federal law regarding the same subject.

(d) Operations of the resulting bank

(1) Continued operations

A resulting bank may, subject to the approval of the appropriate Federal banking agency, retain and operate, as a main office or a branch, any office that any bank involved in an interstate merger transaction was operating as a main office or a branch immediately before the merger transaction.

(2) Additional branches

Following the consummation of any interstate merger transaction, the resulting bank may establish, acquire, or operate additional branches at any location where any bank involved in the transaction could have established, acquired, or operated a branch under applicable Federal or State law if such bank had not been a party to the merger transaction.

(3) Certain conditions and commitments continued

If, as a condition for the acquisition of a bank by an out-of-State bank holding company before September 29, 1994—

(A) the home State of the acquired bank imposed conditions on such acquisition by such out-of-State bank holding company; or

(B) the bank holding company made commitments to such State in connection with the acquisition,

the State may enforce such conditions and commitments with respect to such bank holding company or any affiliated successor company which controls a bank or branch in such State as a result of an interstate merger transaction to the same extent as the State could enforce such conditions or commitments against the bank holding company before the consummation of the merger transaction.

(e) Exception for banks in default or in danger of default

If an application under subsection (a)(1) of this section for approval of a merger transaction which involves 1 or more banks in default or in danger of default or with respect to which the Corporation provides assistance under section 1823 (c) of this title, the responsible agency may approve such application without regard to subsection (b) of this section, or paragraph (2), (4), or (5) of subsection (a) of this section.

(f) Applicable rate and other charge limitations

(1) In general

In the case of any State that has a constitutional provision that sets a maximum lawful annual percentage rate of interest on any contract at not more than 5 percent above the discount rate for 90-day commercial paper in effect at the Federal reserve bank for the Federal reserve district in which such State is located, except as provided in paragraph (2), upon the establishment in such State of a branch of any out-of-State insured depository institution in such State under this section, the maximum interest rate or amount of interest, discount points, finance charges, or other similar charges that may be charged, taken, received, or reserved from time to time in any loan or discount made or upon any note, bill of exchange, financing transaction, or other evidence of debt by any insured depository institution whose home State is such State shall be equal to not more than the greater of—

(A) the maximum interest rate or amount of interest, discount points, finance charges, or other similar charges that may be charged, taken, received, or reserved in a similar transaction under the constitution or any statute or other law of the home State of the out-of-State insured depository institution establishing any such branch, without reference to this section, as such maximum interest rate or amount of interest may change from time to time; or

(B) the maximum rate or amount of interest, discount points, finance charges, or other similar charges that may be charged, taken, received, or reserved in a similar transaction by a State insured depository institution chartered under the laws of such State or a national bank or Federal savings association whose main office is located in such State without reference to this section.

(2) Rule of construction

No provision of this subsection shall be construed as superseding or affecting—

(A) the authority of any insured depository institution to take, receive, reserve, and charge interest on any loan made in any

State other than the State referred to in paragraph (1); or

(B) the applicability of section 1735f–7a of this title, section 85 of this title, or section 1831d of this title.

(g) Definitions

For purposes of this section, the following definitions shall apply:

(1) Adequately capitalized

The term "adequately capitalized" has the same meaning as in section 1831o of this title.

(2) Antitrust laws

The term "antitrust laws"—

(A) has the same meaning as in subsection (a) of section 12 of title 15; and

(B) includes section 45 of title 15 to the extent such section 45 relates to unfair methods of competition.

(3) Branch

The term "branch" means any domestic branch.

(4) Home State

The term "home State"—

(A) means—

(i) with respect to a national bank, the State in which the main office of the bank is located; and

(ii) with respect to a State bank, the State by which the bank is chartered; and

(B) with respect to a bank holding company, has the same meaning as in section 1841 (o)(4) of this title.

(5) Host State

The term "host State" means, with respect to a bank, a State, other than the home State of the bank, in which the bank maintains, or seeks to establish and maintain, a branch.

(6) Interstate merger transaction

The term "interstate merger transaction" means any merger transaction approved pursuant to subsection (a)(1) of this section.

(7) Merger transaction

The term "merger transaction" has the meaning determined under section 1828 (c)(3) of this title.

(8) Out-of-State bank

The term "out-of-State bank" means, with respect to any State, a bank whose home State is another State.

(9) Out-of-State bank holding company

The term "out-of-State bank holding company" means, with respect to any State, a bank holding company whose home State is another State.

(10) Responsible agency

The term "responsible agency" means the agency determined in accordance with section 1828 (c)(2) of this title with respect to a merger transaction.

(11) Resulting bank

The term "resulting bank" means a bank that has resulted from an interstate merger transaction under this section.

[Sept. 21, 1950, ch. 967, § 2[44], *as added* Pub. L. No. 103–328, title I, § 102(a), 108 Stat. 2343 (Sept. 29, 1994); amended Pub. L. No. 106–102, title VII, § 731, 113 Stat. 1477 (Nov. 12, 1999)]

* * *

12 U.S.C. § 1831w. Safety and soundness firewalls applicable to financial subsidiaries of banks

(a) In general

An insured State bank may control or hold an interest in a subsidiary that engages in activities as principal that would only be permissible for a national bank to conduct through a financial subsidiary if—

(1) the State bank and each insured depository institution affiliate of the State bank are well capitalized (after the capital deduction required by paragraph (2));

(2) the State bank complies with the capital deduction and financial statement disclosure requirements in section 24a (c) of this title;

(3) the State bank complies with the financial and operational safeguards required by section 24a (d) of this title; and

(4) the State bank complies with the amendments to sections 23A and 23B of the Federal Reserve Act [12 U.S.C. 371c and 371c–1] made by section 121(b) of the Gramm-Leach-Bliley Act.

(b) Preservation of existing subsidiaries

Notwithstanding subsection (a) of this section, an insured State bank may retain control of a subsidiary, or retain an interest in a subsidiary, that the State bank lawfully controlled or acquired before November 12, 1999, and conduct through such subsidiary any activities lawfully conducted in such subsidiary as of such date.

(c) Definitions

For purposes of this section, the following definitions shall apply:

(1) Subsidiary

The term "subsidiary" means any company that is a subsidiary (as defined in section 1813 (w)(4) of this title) of 1 or more insured banks.

(2) Financial subsidiary

The term "financial subsidiary" has the meaning given the term in section 24a (g) of this title.

(d) Preservation of authority

(1) This chapter

No provision of this section shall be construed as superseding the authority of the Federal Deposit Insurance Corporation to review subsidiary activities under section 1831a of this title.

(2) Federal Reserve Act

No provision of this section shall be construed as affecting the applicability of the 20th undesignated paragraph of section 9 of the Federal Reserve Act [12 U.S.C. 335].

[Sept. 21, 1950, ch. 967, § 2[46], *as added* Pub. L. No. 106–102, title I, § 121(d)(1), 113 Stat. 1380 (Nov. 12, 1999)]

* * *

F.2 Selected Regulations

TITLE 12—BANKS AND BANKING

CHAPTER III—FEDERAL DEPOSIT INSURANCE CORPORATION

PART 303—FILING PROCEDURES

Subpart A—Rules of General Applicability

* * *

§ 303.14   Being "engaged in the business of receiving deposits other than trust funds."

* * *

Subpart G—Activities of Insured State Banks

§ 303.120   Scope.

§ 303.121   Filing procedures.

§ 303.122   Processing.

* * *

Subpart H—Activities of Insured Savings Associations

§ 303.140   Scope.

§ 303.141   Filing procedures.

§ 303.142   Processing.

* * *

TITLE 12—BANKS AND BANKING

CHAPTER III—FEDERAL DEPOSIT INSURANCE CORPORATION

PART 303—FILING PROCEDURES

Subpart A—Rules of General Applicability

* * *

12 C.F.R § 303.14 Being "engaged in the business of receiving deposits other than trust funds."

(a) Except as provided in paragraphs (b), (c), and (d) of this section, a depository institution shall be "engaged in the business of receiving deposits other than trust funds" only if it maintains one or more non-trust deposit accounts in the minimum aggregate amount of $500,000.

(b) An applicant for federal deposit insurance under section 5 of the FDI Act, 12 U.S.C. 1815(a), shall be deemed to be "engaged in the business of receiving deposits other than trust funds" from the date that the FDIC approves deposit insurance for the institution until one year after it opens for business.

(c) Any depository institution that fails to satisfy the minimum deposit standard specified in paragraph (a) of this section as of two consecutive call report dates (*i.e.*, March 31st, June 30th, September 30th, and December 31st) shall be subject to a determination by the FDIC that the institution is not "engaged in the business of receiving deposits other than trust funds" and to termination of its insured status under section 8(p) of the FDI Act, 12 U.S.C. 1818(p). For purposes of this paragraph, the first three call report dates after the institution opens for business are excluded.

(d) Notwithstanding any failure by an insured depository institution to satisfy the minimum deposit standard in paragraph (a) of this section, the institution shall continue to be "engaged in the business of receiving deposits other than trust funds" for purposes of section 3 of the FDI Act until the institution's insured status is terminated by the FDIC pursuant to a proceeding under section 8(a) or section 8(p) of the FDI Act. 12 U.S.C. 1818(a) or 1818(p).

* * *

Subpart G—Activities of Insured State Banks

12 C.F.R § 303.120 Scope.

This subpart sets forth procedures for complying with notice and application requirements contained in subpart A of part 362 of this chapter, governing insured state banks and their subsidiaries engaging in activities which are not permissible for national banks and their subsidiaries. This subpart sets forth procedures for complying with notice and application requirements contained in subpart B of part 362 of this chapter, governing certain activities of insured state nonmember banks, their subsidiaries, and certain affiliates. This subpart also sets forth procedures for complying with the notice requirements contained in subpart E of part 362 of this chapter, governing subsidiaries of insured state nonmember banks engaging in financial activities.

12 C.F.R § 303.121 Filing procedures.

(a) *Where to file.* A notice or application required by subpart A, subpart B, or subpart E of part 362 of this chapter shall be submitted in writing to the appropriate FDIC office.

(b) *Contents of filing.* A complete letter notice or letter application shall include the following information:

(1) *Filings generally.* (i) A brief description of the activity and the manner in which it will be conducted;

(ii) The amount of the bank's existing or proposed direct or indirect investment in the activity as well as calculations sufficient to indicate compliance with any specific capital ratio or investment percentage limitation detailed in subpart A, B, or E of part 362 of this chapter;

(iii) A copy of the bank's business plan regarding the conduct of the activity;

(iv) A citation to the state statutory or regulatory authority for the conduct of the activity;

(v) A copy of the order or other document from the appropriate regulatory authority granting approval for the bank to conduct the activity if such approval is necessary and has already been granted;

(vi) A brief description of the bank's policy and practice with regard to any anticipated involvement in the activity by a director, executive office or principal shareholder of the bank or any related interest of such a person; and

(vii) A description of the bank's expertise in the activity.

(2) [Reserved]

(3) *Copy of application or notice filed with another agency.* If an insured state bank has filed an application or notice with another federal or state regulatory authority which contains all of the information required by paragraph (b) (1) of this section, the insured state bank may submit a copy to the FDIC in lieu of a separate filing.

(4) *Additional information.* The FDIC may request additional information to complete processing.

12 C.F.R § 303.122 Processing.

(a) *Expedited processing.* A notice filed by an insured state bank seeking to commence or continue an activity under § 362.3(a)(2)(iii)(A)(2), § 362.4(b)(3)(i), or § 362.4(b)(5) of this chapter will be acknowledged in writing by the FDIC and will receive expedited processing, unless the applicant is notified in writing to the contrary and provided a basis for that decision. The FDIC may remove the notice from expedited processing for any of the reasons set forth in § 303.11(c)(2). Absent such removal, a notice processed under expedited processing is deemed approved 30 days after receipt of a complete notice by the FDIC (subject to extension for an additional 15 days upon written notice to the bank) or on such earlier date authorized by the FDIC in writing.

(b) *Standard processing for applications and notices that have been removed from expedited processing.* For an application filed by an insured state bank seeking to commence or continue an activity under § 362.3(a)(2)(iii)(A)(2), § 362.3 (b)(2)(i), § 362.3(b)(2)(ii)(A), § 362.3(b)(2)(ii) (C), § 362.4(b)(1), § 362.4(b)(4), § 362.5(b)(2), or § 362.8(b) or seeking a waiver or modification under § 362.18(e) or § 362.18(g)(3) of this chapter or for notices which are not processed pursuant to the expedited processing procedures, the FDIC will provide the insured State bank with written notification of the final action as soon as the decision is rendered. The FDIC will normally review and act in such cases within 60 days after receipt of a completed application or notice (subject to extension for an additional 30 days upon written notice to the bank), but failure of the FDIC to act prior to the expiration of these periods does not constitute approval.

* * *

Subpart H—Activities of Insured Savings Associations

12 C.F.R § 303.140 Scope.

This subpart sets forth procedures for complying with the notice and application requirements contained in subpart C of part 362 of this chapter, governing insured state savings associations and their service corporations engaging in activities which are not permissible for federal savings associations and their service corporations. This subpart also sets forth procedures for complying with the notice requirements contained in subpart D of part 362 of this chapter, governing insured savings associations which establish or engage in new activities through a subsidiary.

12 C.F.R § 303.141 Filing procedures.

(a) *Where to file.* All applications and notices required by subpart C or subpart D of part 362 of this chapter are to be in writing and filed with the appropriate FDIC office.

(b) *Contents of filing—*(1) *Filings generally.* A complete letter notice or letter application shall include the following information:

(i) A brief description of the activity and the manner in which it will be conducted;

(ii) The amount of the association's existing or proposed direct or indirect investment in the activity as well as calculations sufficient to indicate compliance with any specific capital ratio or investment percentage limitation detailed in subpart C or D of part 362 of this chapter;

(iii) A copy of the association's business plan regarding the conduct of the activity;

(iv) A citation to the state statutory or regulatory authority for the conduct of the activity;

(v) A copy of the order or other document from the appropriate regulatory authority granting approval for the association to conduct the activity if such approval is necessary and has already been granted;

(vi) A brief description of the association's policy and practice with regard to any anticipated involvement in the activity by a director, executive officer or principal shareholder of the association or any related interest of such a person; and

(vii) A description of the association's expertise in the activity.

(2) [Reserved]

(3) *Copy of application or notice filed with another agency.* If an insured savings association has filed an application or notice with another federal or state regulatory authority which contains all of the information required by paragraph (b)(1) of this section, the insured state bank may submit a copy to the FDIC in lieu of a separate filing.

(4) *Additional information.* The FDIC may request additional information to complete processing.

12 C.F.R § 303.142 Processing.

(a) *Expedited processing.* A notice filed by an insured state savings association seeking to commence or continue an activity under § 362.11(b)(2)(ii) of this chapter will be acknowledged in writing by the FDIC and will receive expedited processing, unless the applicant is notified in writing to the contrary and provided a basis for that decision. The FDIC may remove the notice from expedited processing for any of the reasons set forth in § 303.11(c)(2). Absent such removal, a notice processed under expedited processing is deemed approved 30 days after receipt of a complete notice by the FDIC (subject to extension for an additional 15 days upon written notice to the bank) or on such earlier date authorized by the FDIC in writing.

(b) *Standard processing for applications and notices that have been removed from expedited processing.* For an application filed by an insured state savings association seeking to commence or continue an activity under § 362.11(a)(2)(ii), § 362.11(b)(2)(i), § 362.12(b)(1) of this chapter or for notices which are not processed pursuant to the expedited processing procedures, the FDIC will provide the insured state savings association with written notification of the final action as soon as the decision is rendered. The FDIC will normally review and act in such cases within 60 days after receipt of a completed application or notice (subject to extension for an additional 30 days upon written notice to the bank), but failure of the FDIC to act prior to the expiration of these periods does not constitute approval.

(c) *Notices of activities in excess of an amount permissible for a federal savings association; subsidiary notices.* Receipt of a notice filed by an insured state savings association as required by § 362.11(b)(3) or § 362.15 of this chapter will be acknowledged in writing by the FDIC. The notice will be reviewed at the appropriate FDIC office, which will take such action as it deems necessary and appropriate.

F.3 FDIC Letters, Opinions, and Advisories

This section summarizes letters released by the Federal Deposit Insurance Corporation relating to the preemption of state laws by FDIC-insured state-chartered banks and to the "location" of the state-chartered bank for exportation purposes. The earliest letters by the FDIC dealing with these subjects date from 1981. The full text of these letters can be found on the CD-Rom accompanying this volume. Archived and recently released letters and opinions can be obtained from the FDIC's website: www.fdic.gov. Click on "Regulation and Examination," then on "Laws and Regulations" and select "FDIC legal staff advisory opinions" and scroll down to "staff advisory opinions" (listed by topic) or "General Counsel's Opinions." General Counsel Opinions are also published in the *Federal Register*. Where applicable, the *Federal Register* cite is provided below.

Date of Opinion	State Laws/Provisions
December 19, 2002	The Michigan motor vehicle retail installment sales act is pre-empted by § 521 for insured state-chartered banks only to the extent that the state law is interpreted to require an out-of-state bank to comply, directly or through its agent, with the law's interest rate and remedy provisions when making loans through car dealers acting as the bank's agents. Other parts of the act are not preempted, however. Section 85 of the National Bank Act and § 521 of DIDA should be construed the same. The state's ruling affects the lending of out-of-state banks by implication (even if not directly since the ruling was directed to policing the actions of bank agents, not the banks themselves) because it specifically provides that the lender's status as a bank does not mean that entities entering into agency arrangements with a bank may do so without complying with the licensing require-ments of the act and imposes compliance obligations.
May 18, 1998	General Counsel's Opinion No. 11, 63 Fed. Reg. 27282 (May 18, 1998). The lengthy opinion analyzes § 1831d of the FDI Act regarding the issue of which state's law applies for the most favored lender doctrine and exportation purposes, i.e., the "loca-tion" of the bank for exportation purposes. The FDIC adopts OCC Interpretive Letter No. 822. Therefore, an insured state-chartered bank can be located for purposes of § 1831d in the state in which it is chartered as well as where the branches are located, under certain circumstances. State banks should make an appropriate disclosure to the customer of the relevant state which will govern the transaction.
April 17, 1998	General Counsel Opinion No. 10, 63 Fed. Reg. 19258 (April 17, 1998). The definition of interest for § 521 purposes is the same for national banks and savings associations. Therefore, one looks to the OCC regulation on this point, 12 C.F.R. § 7.4001.
September 26, 1997	Certain courier/messenger services constitute branch banking where the bank hires the contract employee who works exclu-sively for the bank and where the employee picks up deposits from customers and delivers them to the bank. However, it is not branch banking where a truly independent company per-forms these services for the bank. The letter also discusses variations on these facts and the effect on the outcome of this issue.
July 8, 1997	An automated loan machine is not a branch even if it approves the loan and disburses the loan proceeds due to an amendment to the FDIA in 1996.
October 4, 1995	Soliciting borrowers, accepting loan applications, reviewing and processing loan applications, and forwarding the applications to an out-of-state bank does not turn a "loan production office" into a bank branch; however, the office becomes a branch if it approves loans and funds the loans.

July 12, 1993	The FDIC interprets § 521 to include the preemption of common law restrictions as well as statutory and constitutional restrictions on interest rates. In a lengthy letter, the FDIC reviewed court decisions and legislative history in interpreting the scope of § 521.
July 8, 1992	Section 521 of DIDA authorizes insured state-chartered banks to export the same fees and charges that are a component of interest or material to the determination of interest on interstate loans as national banks may export under the NBA. Purposes of § 501 and § 521 of DIDA are different and cases interpreting one section are not necessarily applicable to the other.
June 29, 1988	If the state where the loan is made opted out of § 521 of DIDA, then the usury law of that state applies. Where a loan is made is a factual determination. The letter does not list any determinative factors other than the contract terms and all facts. Rejects the proposition that the only a bank's home state has the right to countermand preemption regarding loans made by that bank.
October 20, 1983	The analysis under § 85 of the National Bank Act applies with equal force to § 521 of DIDA regarding a state bank making a loan to a borrower in another state that opted out of § 521. The bank may rely on the interest rate provisions of the state where the bank is located in extending credit to the residents of its state and of other states.
March 17, 1981	A state bank, making an interstate loan, would determine the permissible interest rates by referring only to the laws of the state in which it is located (i.e., chartered), and not to the state in which the borrower resides or any other state.

The FDIC also issues advisories to state-charted banks on a variety of topics. These can be found at the FDIC's website: www.fdic.gov. Click on "Regulation and Examination," then on "Laws and Regulations" and select "FDIC legal staff advisory opinions" and scroll down to "financial institutions letter." Many of these advisories are released jointly with the other federal banking agencies, i.e., the Office of the Comptroller of the Currency, the Office of Thrift Supervision, and the Board of Governors of the Federal Reserve System.

Of relevance to practitioners include: the letters addressing subprime lending (FIL-44-97); high loan-to-value residential real estate lending (FIL-94-99); subprime lending (FIL-9-2001); unfair or deceptive acts or practices (FIL-57-2002); Uniform Commercial Code (FIL-18-2001); credit card lending (FIL-2-2003); mortgage banking activities (FIL-15-2003); unfair or deceptive acts or practices by state-chartered banks (FIL-26-2004); overdraft protection programs (FIL-11-2005). The FDIC's Guidelines for Payday Lending (July 2003) are located at www.fdic.gov/regulations/examinations/index.html.

Depository Institutions Deregulation and Monetary Control Act of 1980

This appendix contains the Depository Institutions and Deregulation and Monetary Control Act of 1980 which are codified throughout Title 12 of the United States Code. These provisions appear in G.1. Section G.2 includes relevant regulations promulgated by the Office of Thrift Supervision (OTS). The statutes and regulations reprinted in Appxs. G.1 and G.2 are also found on the companion CD-Rom.

G.1 Statutory Provisions[1]

TITLE 12—BANKS AND BANKING

CHAPTER 13—NATIONAL HOUSING

SUBCHAPTER V—MISCELLANEOUS

* * *

§ 1735f-7a.   State constitution or laws limiting mortgage interest, discount points, and finance or other charges; exemption for obligations made after March 31, 1980

* * *

CHAPTER 14—FEDERAL CREDIT UNIONS

SUBCHAPTER II—SHARE INSURANCE

* * *

§ 1785.   Requirements governing insured credit unions

* * *

CHAPTER 16.—FEDERAL DEPOSIT INSURANCE CORPORATION

* * *

§ 1831d.   State-chartered insured depository institutions and insured branches of foreign banks

* * *

---

1 This Act makes reference to the Federal Home Loan Bank Board (FHLBB) and its authority. The Financial Institutions Reform, Recovery and Enforcement Act of 1989 (FIRREA), Pub. L. No. 101-73, 103 Stat. 183 (Aug. 9, 1989), abolished the FHLBB, and replaced it with the Office of Thrift Supervision (OTS). The relevant authority was transferred from the FHLBB to the OTS.

TITLE 12—BANKS AND BANKING

CHAPTER 13—NATIONAL HOUSING

SUBCHAPTER V—MISCELLANEOUS

* * *

12 U.S.C. § 1735f-7a. State constitution or laws limiting mortgage interest, discount points, and finance or other charges; exemption for obligations made after March 31, 1980

(a) Applicability to loan, mortgage, credit sale, or advance; applicability to deposit, account, or obligation

(1) The provisions of the constitution or the laws of any State expressly limiting the rate or amount of interest, discount points, finance charges, or other charges which may be charged, taken, received, or reserved shall not apply to any loan, mortgage, credit sale, or advance which is—

(A) secured by a first lien on residential real property, by a first lien on all stock allocated to a dwelling unit in a residential cooperative housing corporation, or by a first lien on a residential manufactured home;

(B) made after March 31, 1980; and

(C) described in section 527(b) of the National Housing Act (12 U.S.C. 1735f-5(b)), except that for the purpose of this section—

(i) the limitation described in section 527(b)(1) of such Act [12 U.S.C. § 1735f-5(b)(1)] that the property must be designed principally for the occupancy of from one to four families shall not apply;

(ii) the requirement contained in section 527(b)(1) of such Act [12 U.S.C. § 1735f-5(b)(1)] that the loan be secured by residential real property shall not apply to a loan secured by stock in a residential cooperative housing corporation or to a loan or credit sale secured by a first lien on a residential manufactured home;

(iii) the term "federally related mortgage loan" in section 527(b) of such Act [12 U.S.C. § 1735f-5(b)] shall include a credit sale which is secured by a first lien on a residential manufactured home and which otherwise meets the definitional requirements of section 527(b) of such Act [12 U.S.C. § 1735f-5(b)], as those requirements are modified by this section;

(iv) the term "residential loans" in section 527(b)(2)(D) of such Act [12 U.S.C. § 1735f-5(b)(2)(D)] shall also include loans or credit sales secured by a first lien on a residential manufactured home;

(v) the requirement contained in section 527(b)(2)(D) of such Act [12 U.S.C. § 1735f-5(b)(2)(D)] that a creditor make or invest in loans aggregating more than $1,000,000 per year shall not apply to a creditor selling residential manufactured homes financed by loans or credit sales secured by first liens on residential manufactured homes if the creditor has an arrangement to sell such loans or credit sales in whole or in part, or if such loans or credit sales are sold in whole or in part to a lender, institution, or creditor described in section 527(b) of such Act [12 U.S.C. § 1735f-5(b)] or in this section or a creditor, as defined in section 103(f) of the Truth in Lending Act [15 U.S.C. § 1602(f)], as such section was in effect on the day preceding March 31, 1980, if such creditor makes or invests in residential real estate loans or loans or credit sales secured by first liens on residential manufactured homes aggregating more than $1,000,000 per year; and

(vi) the term "lender" in section 527(b)(2)(A) of such Act [12 U.S.C. § 1735f-5(b)(2)(A)] shall also be deemed to include any lender approved by the Secretary of Housing and Urban Development for participation in any mortgage insurance program under the National Housing Act [12 U.S.C. § 1701 et seq.], and any individual who finances the sale or exchange of residential real property or a residential manufactured home which such individual owns and which such individual occupies or has occupied as his principal residence.

(2)(A) The provisions of the constitution or law of any State expressly limiting the rate or amount of interest which may be charged, taken, received, or reserved shall not apply to any deposit or account held by, or other obligation of a depository institution. For purposes of this paragraph, the term "depository institution" means—

(i) any insured bank as defined in section 3 of the Federal Deposit Insurance Act (12 U.S.C. 1813);

(ii) any mutual savings bank as defined in section 3 of the Federal Deposit Insurance Act (12 U.S.C. 1813);

(iii) any savings bank as defined in section 3 of the Federal Deposit Insurance Act (12 U.S.C. 1813);

(iv) any insured credit union as defined in section 101 of the Federal Credit Union Act (12 U.S.C. 1752);

(v) any member as defined in section 2 of the Federal Home Loan Bank Act (12 U.S.C. 1422); and

(vi) any insured institution as defined in section 408 of the National Housing Act (12 U.S.C. 1730a).

(b) Applicability to loan, mortgage, credit sale, or advance made in any State after April 1, 1980

(1) Except as provided in paragraphs (2) and (3), the provisions of subsection (a)(1) of this section shall apply to any loan, mortgage, credit sale, or advance made in any State on or after April 1, 1980.

(2) Except as provided in paragraph (3), the provisions of subsection (a)(1) of this section shall not apply to any loan, mortgage, credit sale, or advance made in any State after the date (on or after April 1, 1980, and before April 1, 1983) on which such State adopts a law or certifies that the voters of such State have voted in favor of any provision, constitutional or otherwise, which states explicitly and by its terms that such State does not want the

provisions of subsection (a)(1) of this section to apply with respect to loans, mortgages, credit sales, and advances made in such State.

(3) In any case in which a State takes an action described in paragraph (2), the provisions of subsection (a)(1) of this section shall continue to apply to—

(A) any loan, mortgage, credit sale, or advance which is made after the date such action was taken pursuant to a commitment therefor which was entered during the period beginning on April 1, 1980, and ending on the date on which such State takes such action; and

(B) any loan, mortgage, or advance which is a rollover of a loan, mortgage, or advance, as described in regulations of the Federal Home Loan Bank Board, which was made or committed to be made during the period beginning on April 1, 1980, and ending on the date on which such State takes any action described in paragraph (2).

(4) At any time after March 31, 1980, any State may adopt a provision of law placing limitations on discount points or such other charges on any loan, mortgage, credit sale, or advance described in subsection (a)(1) of this section.

(c) Applicability to loan, mortgage, credit sale, or advance secured by first lien on residential manufactured home

The provisions of subsection (a)(1) of this section shall not apply to a loan, mortgage, credit sale, or advance which is secured by a first lien on a residential manufactured home unless the terms and conditions relating to such loan, mortgage, credit sale, or advance comply with consumer protection provisions specified in regulations prescribed by the Federal Home Loan Bank Board. Such regulations shall—

(1) include consumer protection provisions with respect to balloon payments, prepayment penalties, late charges, and deferral fees;

(2) require a 30-day notice prior to instituting any action leading to repossession or foreclosure (except in the case of abandonment or other extreme circumstances);

(3) require that upon prepayment in full, the debtor shall be entitled to a refund of the unearned portion of the precomputed finance charge in an amount not less than the amount which would be calculated by the actuarial method, except that the debtor shall not be entitled to a refund which is less than $1; and

(4) include such other provisions as the Federal Home Loan Bank Board may prescribe after a finding that additional protections are required.

(d) Implementation of provisions applicable to residential manufactured home

The provisions of subsection (c) of this section shall not apply to a loan, mortgage, credit sale, or advance secured by a first lien on a residential manufactured home until regulations required to be issued pursuant to paragraphs (1), (2), and (3) of subsection (c) of this section take effect, except that the provisions of subsection (c) of this section shall apply in the case of such a loan, mortgage, credit sale, or advance made prior to the date on which such regulations take effect if the loan, mortgage, credit sale, or advance includes a precomputed finance charge and does not provide that, upon prepayment in full, the refund of the unearned portion of the precomputed finance charge is in an amount not less the amount which would be calculated by the actuarial method, except that the debtor shall not be entitled to a refund which is less than $1. The

Federal Home Loan Bank Board shall issue regulations pursuant to the provisions of paragraphs (1), (2), and (3) of subsection (c) of this section that shall take effect prospectively not less than 30 days after publication in the Federal Register and not later than 120 days from March 31, 1980.

(e) Definitions

For the purpose of this section—

(1) a "prepayment" occurs upon—

(A) the refinancing or consolidation of the indebtedness;

(B) the actual prepayment of the indebtedness by the consumer whether voluntarily or following acceleration of the payment obligation by the creditor; or

(C) the entry of a judgment for the indebtedness in favor of the creditor;

(2) the term "actuarial method" means the method of allocating payments made on a debt between the outstanding balance of the obligation and the precomputed finance charge pursuant to which a payment is applied first to the accrued precomputed finance charge and any remainder is subtracted from, or any deficiency is added to, the outstanding balance of the obligation;

(3) the term "precomputed finance charge" means interest or a time price differential within the meaning of sections 106(a)(1) and (2) of the Truth in Lending Act (15 U.S.C. 1605(a)(1) and (2)) as computed by an add-on or discount method; and

(4) the term "residential manufactured home" means a manufactured home as defined in section 603(6) of the National Mobile Home Construction and Safety Standards Act of 1974 [42 U.S.C. § 5402(6)] which is used as a residence.

(f) Rules, regulations, and interpretations

The Federal Home Loan Bank Board is authorized to issue rules and regulations and to publish interpretations governing the implementation of this section.

(g) Effective date

This section takes effect on April 1, 1980.

[Pub. L. No. 96-221, tit. V, § 501, 94 Stat. 161 (Mar. 31, 1980); Pub. L. No. 96-221, tit. II, § 207(b)(11), 94 Stat. 144 (Mar. 31, 1980); Pub. L. No. 96-399, tit. III, §§ 308(c)(6), 324(a), (e), 94 Stat. 1641, 1647, 1648 (Oct. 8, 1980); Pub. L. No. 97-35, tit. III, § 384, 95 Stat. 432 (Aug. 13, 1981)]

* * *

CHAPTER 14—FEDERAL CREDIT UNIONS

SUBCHAPTER II—SHARE INSURANCE

* * *

12 U.S.C. § 1785. Requirements governing insured credit unions

(a) Advertisement of insured status; exemptions; regulation of signs

Every insured credit union shall display at each place of business maintained by it a sign or signs indicating that its member accounts are insured by the Board and shall include in all of its advertisements a statement to the effect that its member accounts are insured by the Board. The Board may exempt from this requirement advertisements which do not relate to member accounts or advertisements in which it is impractical to include such a statement. The Board shall prescribe by regulation the forms of such signs, the manner of display, the substance of any such statement, and the manner of use.

(b) Restrictions

(1) Insured credit union activities with noninsured credit unions

Except as provided in paragraph (2), no insured credit union shall, without the prior approval of the Board—

(A) merge or consolidate with any noninsured credit union or institution;

(B) assume liability to pay any member accounts in, or similar liabilities of, any noninsured credit union or institution;

(C) transfer assets to any noninsured credit union or institution in consideration of the assumption of liabilities for any portion of the member accounts in such insured credit union; or

(D) convert into a noninsured credit union or institution.

(2) Conversion of insured credit unions to mutual savings banks

(A) In general

Notwithstanding paragraph (1), an insured credit union may convert to a mutual savings bank or savings association (if the savings association is in mutual form), as those terms are defined in section 1813 of this title, without the prior approval of the Board, subject to the requirements and procedures set forth in the laws and regulations governing mutual savings banks and savings associations.

(B) Conversion proposal

A proposal for a conversion described in subparagraph (A) shall first be approved, and a date set for a vote thereon by the members (either at a meeting to be held on that date or by written ballot to be filed on or before that date), by a majority of the directors of the insured credit union. Approval of the proposal for conversion shall be by the affirmative vote of a majority of the members of the insured credit union who vote on the proposal.

(C) Notice of proposal to members

An insured credit union that proposes to convert to a mutual savings bank or savings association under subparagraph (A) shall submit notice to each of its members who is eligible to vote on the matter of its intent to convert.—

(i) 90 days before the date of the member vote on the conversion;

(ii) 60 days before the date of the member vote on the conversion; and

(iii) 30 days before the date of the member vote on the conversion.

(D) Notice of proposal to Board

The Board may require an insured credit union that proposes to convert to a mutual savings bank or savings association under subparagraph (A) to submit a notice to the Board of its intent to convert during the 90-day period preceding the date of the completion of the conversion.

(E) Inapplicability of chapter upon conversion

Upon completion of a conversion described in subparagraph (A), the credit union shall no longer be subject to any of the provisions of this chapter.

(F) Limit on compensation of officials

(i) In general

No director or senior management official of an insured credit union may receive any economic benefit in connection with a conversion of the credit union as described in subparagraph (A), other than—

(I) director fees; and

(II) compensation and other benefits paid to directors or senior management officials of the converted institution in the ordinary course of business.

(ii) Senior management official

For purposes of this subparagraph, the term "senior management official" means a chief executive officer, an assistant chief executive officer, a chief financial officer, and any other senior executive officer (as defined by the appropriate Federal banking agency pursuant to section 1831i(f) of this title).

(G) Consistent rules

(i) In general

Not later than 6 months after August 7, 1998, the Administration shall promulgate final rules applicable to charter conversions described in this paragraph that are consistent with rules promulgated by other financial regulators, including the Office of Thrift Supervision and the Office of the Comptroller of the Currency. The rules required by this clause shall provide that charter conversion by an insured credit union shall be subject to regulation that is no more or less restrictive than that applicable to charter conversions by other financial institutions.

(ii) Oversight of member vote

The member vote concerning charter conversion under this paragraph shall be administered by the Administration, and shall be verified by the Federal or State regulatory agency that would have jurisdiction over the institution after the conversion. If either the Administration or that regulatory agency disapproves of the methods by which the member vote was taken or procedures applicable to the member vote, the member vote shall be taken again, as directed by the Administration or the agency.

(3) Insured credit union activities with other insured credit unions

Except with the prior written approval of the Board, no insured credit union shall merge or consolidate with any other insured credit union or, either directly or indirectly, acquire the assets of, or assume liability to pay any member accounts in, any other insured credit union.

(c) Considerations for waiver or enforcement of restrictions

In granting or withholding approval or consent under subsection (b) of this section, the Board shall consider—

(1) the history, financial condition, and management policies of the credit union;

(2) the adequacy of the credit union's reserves;

(3) the economic advisability of the transaction;

(4) the general character and fitness of the credit union's management;

(5) the convenience and needs of the members to be served by the credit union; and

(6) whether the credit union is a cooperative association organized for the purpose of promoting thrift among its members and creating a source of credit for provident or productive purposes.

(d) Prohibition

(1) In general

Except with prior written consent of the Board—

(A) any person who has been convicted of any criminal offense involving dishonesty or a breach of trust, or has agreed to enter into a pretrial diversion or similar program in connection with a prosecution for such offense, may not—

(i) become, or continue as, an institution-affiliated party with respect to any insured credit union; or

(ii) otherwise participate, directly or indirectly, in the conduct of the affairs of any insured credit union; and

(B) any insured credit union may not permit any person referred to in subparagraph (A) to engage in any conduct or continue any relationship prohibited under such subparagraph.

(2) Minimum 10-year prohibition period for certain offenses

(A) In general

If the offense referred to in paragraph (1)(A) in connection with any person referred to in such paragraph is—

(i) an offense under—

(I) section 215, 656, 657, 1005, 1006, 1007, 1008, 1014, 1032, 1344, 1517, 1956, or 1957 of Title 18; or

(II) section 1341 or 1343 of such title which affects any financial institution (as defined in section 20 of such title); or

(ii) the offense of conspiring to commit any such offense,

the Board may not consent to any exception to the application of paragraph (1) to such person during the 10-year period beginning on the date the conviction or the agreement of the person becomes final.

(B) Exception by order of sentencing court

(i) In general

On motion of the Board, the court in which the conviction or the agreement of a person referred to in subparagraph (A) has been entered may grant an exception to the application of paragraph (1) to such person if granting the exception is in the interest of justice.

(ii) Period for filing

A motion may be filed under clause (i) at any time during the 10-year period described in subparagraph (A) with regard to the person on whose behalf such motion is made.

(3) Penalty

Whoever knowingly violates paragraph (1) or (2) shall be fined not more than $1,000,000 for each day such prohibition is violated or imprisoned for not more than 5 years, or both.

(e) Security standards; reports; penalty

(1) The Board shall promulgate rules establishing minimum standards with which each insured credit union must comply with respect to the installation, maintenance, and operation of security devices and procedures, reasonable in cost, to discourage robberies, burglaries, and larcenies and to assist in the identification and apprehension of persons who commit such acts.

(2) The rules shall establish the time limits within which insured credit unions shall comply with the standards and shall require the submission of periodic reports with respect to the installation, maintenance, and operation of security devices and procedures.

(3) An insured credit union which violates a rule promulgated pursuant to this subsection shall be subject to a civil penalty which shall not exceed $100 for each day of the violation.

(f) Share draft accounts; maintenance, loans, etc.

(1) Every insured credit union is authorized to maintain, and make loans with respect to, share draft accounts in accordance with rules and regulations prescribed by the Board. Except as provided in paragraph (2), an insured credit union may pay dividends on share draft accounts and may permit the owners of such share draft accounts to make withdrawals by negotiable or transferable instruments or other orders for the purpose of making transfers to third parties.

(2) Paragraph (1) shall apply only with respect to share draft accounts in which the entire beneficial interest is held by one or more individuals or members or by an organization which is operated primarily for religious, philanthropic, charitable, educational, or other similar purposes and which is not operated for profit, and with respect to deposits of public funds by an officer, employee, or agent of the United States, any State, county, municipality, or political subdivision thereof, the District of Columbia, the Commonwealth of Puerto Rico, American Samoa, Guam, any territory or possession of the United States, or any political subdivision thereof.

(g) Interest rates

(1) If the applicable rate prescribed in this subsection exceeds the rate an insured credit union would be permitted to charge in the absence of this subsection, such credit union may, notwithstanding any State constitution or statute which is hereby preempted for the purposes of this subsection, take, receive, reserve, and charge on any loan, interest at a rate of not more than 1 per centum in excess of the discount rate on ninety-day commercial paper in effect at the Federal Reserve bank in the Federal Reserve district where such insured credit union is located or at the rate allowed by the laws of the State, territory, or district where such credit union is located, whichever may be greater.

(2) If the rate prescribed in paragraph (1) exceeds the rate such credit union would be permitted to charge in the absence of this subsection, and such State fixed rate is thereby preempted by the rate described in paragraph (1), the taking, receiving, reserving, or charging a greater rate than is allowed by paragraph (1), when knowingly done, shall be deemed a forfeiture of the entire interest which the loan carries with it, or which has been agreed to be paid thereon. If such greater rate of interest has been paid, the person who paid it may recover, in a civil action commenced in a court of appropriate jurisdiction not later than two years after the date of such payment, an amount equal to twice the amount of interest paid from the credit union taking or receiving such interest.

(h) Emergency merger

Notwithstanding any other provision of law, the Board may authorize a merger or consolidation of an insured credit union which is insolvent or is in danger of insolvency with any other insured credit union or may authorize an insured credit union to purchase any of the assets of, or assume any of the liabilities of, any other insured credit union which is insolvent or in danger of insolvency if the Board is satisfied that—

(1) an emergency requiring expeditious action exists with respect to such other insured credit union;

(2) other alternatives are not reasonably available; and

(3) the public interest would best be served by approval of such merger, consolidation, purchase, or assumption.

(i) Emergency purchase of assets; conversion to insured deposits

(1) Notwithstanding any other provision of this chapter or of State law, the Board may authorize an institution whose deposits or accounts are insured by the Federal Deposit Insurance Corporation or the Federal Savings and Loan Insurance Corporation to purchase any of the assets of or assume any of the liabilities of an insured credit union which is insolvent or in danger of insolvency, except that prior to exercising this authority the Board must attempt to effect the merger or consolidation of an insured credit union which is insolvent or in danger of insolvency with another insured credit union, as provided in subsection (h) of this section.

(2) For purposes of the authority contained in paragraph (1), insured accounts of the credit union may upon consummation of the purchase and assumption be converted to insured deposits or other comparable accounts in the acquiring institution, and the Board and the National Credit Union Share Insurance Fund shall be absolved of any liability to the credit union's members with respect to those accounts.

[June 26, 1934, ch. 750, tit. II, § 205, *as added* Oct. 19, 1970, Pub. L. No. 91-468, § 1(3), 84 Stat. 1002, and amended by Pub. L. No. 95-630, tit. V, § 502(b), 92 Stat. 3681 (Nov. 10, 1978); Pub. L. No. 96-221, tit. III, § 305(d), tit. V, § 523, 94 Stat. 147, 166 (Mar. 31, 1980); Pub. L. No. 97-320, tit. I, §§ 131, 141(a)(8), tit. VII, § 706(b), 96 Stat. 1486, 1489, 1540 (Oct. 15, 1982); Pub. L. No. 100-86, tit. V, § 509(a), 101 Stat. 635 (Aug. 10, 1987); Pub. L. No. 101-73, tit. IX, § 910(b), 103 Stat. 478 (Aug. 9, 1989); Pub. L. No. 103-322, tit. XXXII, § 320606, 108 Stat. 2119 (Sept. 13, 1994); Pub. L. No. 105-219, tit. II, § 202, 112 Stat. 919 (Aug. 7, 1998)]

* * *

CHAPTER 16.—FEDERAL DEPOSIT INSURANCE CORPORATION

* * *

12 U.S.C. § 1831d. State-chartered insured depository institutions and insured branches of foreign banks

(a) Interest rates

In order to prevent discrimination against State-chartered insured depository institutions, including insured savings banks, or insured branches of foreign banks with respect to interest rates, if the applicable rate prescribed in this subsection exceeds the rate such State bank or insured branch of a foreign bank would be permitted to charge in the absence of this subsection, such State bank or such insured branch of a foreign bank may, notwithstanding any State constitution or statute which is hereby preempted for the purposes of this section, take, receive, reserve, and charge on any loan or discount made, or upon any note, bill of exchange, or other evidence of debt, interest at a rate of not more than 1 per centum in excess of the discount rate on ninety-day commercial paper in effect at the Federal Reserve bank in the Federal Reserve district where such State bank or such insured branch of a foreign bank is located or at the rate allowed by the laws of the State, territory, or district where the bank is located, whichever may be greater.

(b) Interest overcharge; forfeiture; interest payment recovery

If the rate prescribed in subsection (a) of this section exceeds the rate such State bank or such insured branch of a foreign bank would be permitted to charge in the absence of this section, and such State fixed rate is thereby preempted by the rate described in subsection (a) of this section, the taking, receiving, reserving, or charging a greater rate of interest than is allowed by subsection (a) of this section, when knowingly done, shall be deemed a forfeiture of the entire interest which the note, bill, or other evidence of debt carries with it, or which has been agreed to be paid thereon. If such greater rate of interest has been paid, the person who paid it may recover in a civil action commenced in a court of appropriate jurisdiction not later than two years after the date of such payment, an amount equal to twice the amount of the interest paid from such State bank or such insured branch of a foreign bank taking, receiving, reserving, or charging such interest.

[Sept. 21, 1950, ch. 967, § 2[27], *as added* Mar. 31, 1980, Pub. L. No. 96-221, tit. V, § 521, 94 Stat. 164, and amended by Pub. L. No. 100-86, tit. I, § 101(g)(2), 101 Stat. 563 (Aug. 10, 1987); Pub. L. No. 101-73, tit. II, § 201(a)(1), 103 Stat. 187 (Aug. 9, 1989)]

* * *

Non-codified provisions relating to 12 U.S.C. §§ 1735f-7, 1785 and 1831d

* * *

Pub. L. No. 96-221, 94 Stat. 164 (March 31, 1980)

TITLE V—STATE USURY LAWS

Part C—Other Loans

* * *

EFFECTIVE DATE

Sec. 525.[2] The amendments made by sections 521 through 523 of this title shall only apply with respect to loans made in any State during the period beginning on April 1, 1980, and ending on the date, on or after April 1, 1980, on which such State adopts a law or certifies that the voters of such State have voted in favor of any provision, constitutional or otherwise, which states explicitly and by its terms that such State does not want the amendments made by such sections to apply with respect to loans made in such State, except that such amendments shall apply to a loan made on or after the date such law is adopted or such certification is made if such loan is made pursuant to a commitment to make such loan which was entered into on or after April 1, 1980, and prior to the date on which such law is adopted or such certification is made.

SEVERABILITY

Sec. 526. If any provision of this Act or the application of such provision to any person or circumstance shall be held invalid, the remainder of this Act and the application of such provision to any person or circumstance other than that as to which it is held invalid shall not to be affected thereby.

DEFINITION

Sec. 527. For purposes of these sections, the term "State" includes the several States, the Commonwealth of Puerto Rico, the District of Columbia, Guam, the Trust Territories of the Pacific Islands, the Northern Mariana Islands, and the Virgin Islands, except as provided in section 501(a)(2)(B).

EFFECT ON OTHER LAW

Sec. 528. In any case in which one or more provisions of, or amendments made by, this title, section 529 of the National Housing Act, or any other provisions of law, including section 5197 of the Revised Statutes (12 U.S.C. 85), apply with respect to the same loan, mortgage, credit sale, or advance, such loan, mortgage, credit sale, or advance may be made at the highest applicable rate.

[12 U.S.C. § 1735f-7 note]

REPEAL OF EXISTING LAW

Sec. 529. Effective at the close of March 31, 1980, Public Law 96-104, section 105(a)(2) of Public Law 96-161, and the amendments made by and the provisions of title II of Public Law 96-161 are hereby repealed, except that the provisions of such Public Law, the provisions of such section, the amendments made by such title, and the provisions of such title shall continue to apply to any loan made, any deposit made, or any obligation issued in any State during any period when those provisions were in effect in such State.

---

2   Sections 525, 527, and 528 now appear as a subsidiary note to 12 U.S.C. § 1785. Sections 526 and 529 only appear at 94 Stat. 167-168, *reprinted in* 1980 U.S.C.C.A.N.

G.2 Relevant Regulations

Title 12—Banks and Banking

CHAPTER V—OFFICE OF THRIFT SUPERVISION, DEPARTMENT OF THE TREASURY

PART 590—PREEMPTION OF STATE USURY LAWS

§ 590.1   Authority, purpose and scope.
§ 590.2   Definitions.
§ 590.3   Operation.
§ 590.4   Federally-related residential manufactured housing loans—consumer protection provisions.
§ 590.100   Status of Interpretations issued under Public Law 96-161.
§ 590.101   State criminal usury statutes.

Authority: Sec. 501, 94 Stat. 161, as amended (12 U.S.C. 1735f-7a).

Source: 54 Fed. Reg. 49715 (Nov. 30, 1989), unless otherwise noted.

12 C.F.R. § 590.1 Authority, purpose, and scope.

(a) *Authority.* This part contains regulations issued under section 501 of the Depository Institutions Deregulation and Monetary Control Act of 1980, Pub. L. 96-221, 94 Stat. 161.

(b) *Purpose and scope.* The purpose of this permanent preemption of state interest-rate ceilings applicable to Federally-related residential mortgage loans is to ensure that the availability of such loans is not impeded in states having restrictive interest limitations. This part applies to loans, mortgages, credit sales, and advances, secured by first liens on residential real property, stock in residential cooperative housing corporations, or residential manufactured homes as defined in § 590.2 of this part.

12 C.F.R. § 590.2 Definitions.

For the purposes of this part, the following definitions apply:

(a) *Loans* mean any loans, mortgages, credit sales, or advances.

(b) *Federally-related loans* include any loan:

(1) Made by any lender whose deposits or accounts are insured by any agency of the Federal government;

(2) Made by any lender regulated by any agency of the Federal government;

(3) Made by any lender approved by the Secretary of Housing and Urban Development for participation in any mortgage insurance program under the National Housing Act;

(4) Made in whole or in part by the Secretary of Housing and Urban Development; insured, guaranteed, supplemented, or assisted in any way by the Secretary or any officer or agency of the Federal government, or made under or in connection with a housing or urban development program administered by the Secretary, or a housing or related program administered by any other such officer or agency;

(5) Eligible for purchase by the Federal National Mortgage Association, the Government National Mortgage Association, or the Federal Home Loan Mortgage Corporation, or made by any financial institution from which the loan could be purchased by the Federal Home Loan Mortgage Corporation; or

(6) Made in whole or in part by any entity which:

(i) Regularly extends, or arranges for the extension of, credit payable by agreement in more than four installments or for which the payment of a finance charge is or may be required; and

(ii) Makes or invests in residential real property loans, including loans secured by first liens on residential manufactured homes that aggregate more than $1,000,000 per year; except that the latter requirement shall not apply to such an entity selling residential manufactured homes and providing financing for such sales through loans or credit sales secured by first liens on residential manufactured homes, if the entity has an arrangement to sell such loans or credit sales in whole or in part, or where such loans or credit sales are sold in whole or in part, to a lender or other institution otherwise included in this section.

(c) *Loans which are secured by first liens on real estate* means loans on the security of any instrument (whether a mortgage, deed of trust, or land contract) which makes the interest in real estate (whether in fee, or in a leasehold or subleasehold extending, or renewable, automatically or at the option of the holder or the lender, for a period of at least 5 years beyond the maturity of the loan) specific security for the payment of the obligation secured by the instrument: *Provided,* that the instrument is of such a nature that, in the event of default, the real estate described in the instrument could be subjected to the satisfaction of the obligation with the same priority as a first mortgage of a first deed of trust in the jurisdiction where the real estate is located.

(d) *Loans secured by first liens on stock in a residential cooperative housing corporation* means loans on the security of:

(1) A first security interest in stock or a membership certificate issued to a tenant stockholder or resident member by a cooperative housing organization; and

(2) An assignment of the borrower's interest in the proprietary lease or occupancy agreement issued by such organization.

(e) *Loans secured by first liens on residential manufactured homes* means a loan made pursuant to an agreement by which the party extending

the credit acquires a security interest in the residential manufactured home which will have priority over any conflicting security interest.

(f) *Residential real property* means real estate improved or to be improved by a structure or structures designed primarily for dwelling, as opposed to commercial use.

(g) *Residential manufactured home* shall mean a manufactured home as defined in the National Manufactured Home Construction and Safety Standards Act, 42 U.S.C. 5402(6), which is or will be used as a residence.

(h) *State* means the several states, Puerto Rico, the District of Columbia, Guam, the Trust Territories of the Pacific Islands, the Northern Mariana Islands, and the Virgin Islands, except as provided in section 501(a)(2)(B) of the Depository Institutions Deregulation and Monetary Control Act of 1980, Pub. L. 96-221, 94 Stat. 161.

12 C.F.R. § 590.3 Operation.

(a) The provisions of the constitution or law of any state expressly limiting the rate or amount of interest, discount points, finance charges, or other charges which may be charged, taken, received, or reserved shall not apply to any Federally-related loan:

(1) Made after March 31, 1980; and

(2) Secured by a first lien on:

(i) Residential real property;

(ii) Stock in a residential cooperative housing corporation when the loan is used to finance the acquisition of such stock; or

(iii) A residential manufactured home: *Provided,* that the loan so secured contains the consumer safeguards required by § 590.4 of this part;

(b) The provisions of paragraph (a) of this section shall apply to loans made in any state on or before the date (after April 1, 1980 and prior to April 1, 1983) on which the state adopts a law or certifies that the voters of such state have voted in favor of any law, constitutional or otherwise, which states explicitly and by its terms that such state does not want the provisions of paragraph (a) of this section to apply with respect to loans made in such state, except that—

(1) The provisions of paragraph (a) of this section shall apply to any loan which is made after such date pursuant to a commitment therefor which was entered into during the period beginning on April 1, 1980, and ending on the date the state takes such action;

(2) The provisions of paragraph (a) of this section shall apply to any rollover of a loan which loan was made, or committed to be made, during the period beginning on April 1, 1980, and ending on the date the state takes such action, if the mortgage document or loan note provided that the interest rate to the original borrower could be changed through the use of such a rollover; and

(3) At any time after the date of adoption of these regulations, any state may adopt a provi-

sion of law placing limitations on discount points or such other charges on any loan described in this part.

(c) Nothing in this section preempts limitations in state laws on prepayment charges, attorneys' fees, late charges or other provisions designed to protect borrowers.

[66 Fed. Reg. 65817 (Dec. 21, 2001)]

12 C.F.R. § 590.4 Federally-related residential manufactured housing loans—consumer protection provisions.

(a) *Definitions.* As used in this section:

(1) *Prepayment.* A "prepayment" occurs upon—

(i) Refinancing or consolidation of the indebtedness;

(ii) Actual prepayment of the indebtedness by the debtor, whether voluntarily or following acceleration of the payment obligation by the creditor; or

(iii) The entry of a judgment for the indebtedness in favor of the creditor.

(2) *Actuarial method.* The term *actuarial method* means the method of allocating payments made on a debt between the outstanding balance of the obligation and the finance charge pursuant to which a payment is applied first to the accumulated finance charge and any remainder is subtracted from, or any deficiency is added to, the outstanding balance of the obligation.

(3) *Precomputed finance charge.* The term *precomputed finance charge* means interest or a time/price differential as computed by the add-on or discount method. Precomputed finance charges do not include loan fees, points, finder's fees, or similar charges.

(4) *Creditor.* The term *creditor* means any entity covered by this part, including those which regularly extend or arrange for the extension of credit and assignees that are creditors under section 501(a)(1)(C)(v) of the Depository Institutions Deregulation and Monetary Control Act of 1980.

(b) *General.*

(1) The provisions of the constitution or the laws of any state expressly limiting the rate or amount of interest, discount points, finance charges, or other charges which may be charged, taken, received, or reserved shall not apply to any loan, mortgage, credit sale, or advance which is secured by a first lien on a residential mobile home if a creditor covered by this part complies with the consumer protection regulations of this section.

(2) *Relation to state law.*

(i) In making loans or credit sales subject to this section, creditors shall comply with state and Federal law in accordance with the following:

(A) *State law regulating matters not covered by this section.* When state law regulating matters not covered by this section is otherwise applicable to a loan or credit sale subject to this

section, creditors shall comply with such state law provisions.

(B) *State law regulating matters covered by this section.* Creditors need comply only with the provisions of this section, unless the Office determines that an otherwise applicable state law regulating matters covered by this section provides greater protection to consumers. Such determinations shall be published in the Federal Register and shall operate prospectively.

(ii) Any interested party may petition the Office for a determination that state law requirements are more protective of consumers than the provisions of this section. Petitions shall be sent to: Secretary to the Office of Thrift Supervision, 1700 G Street, NW., Washington, DC 20552, and shall include:

(A) A copy of the state law to be considered;

(B) Copies of any relevant judicial, regulatory, or administrative interpretations of the state law; and

(C) An opinion or memorandum from the state Attorney General or other appropriate state official having primary enforcement responsibilities for the subject state law provision, indicating how the state law to be considered offers greater protection to consumers than the Office's regulation.

(c) *Refund of precomputed finance charge.* In the event the entire indebtedness is prepaid, the unearned portion of the precomputed finance charge shall be refunded to the debtor. This refund shall be in an amount not less than the amount which would be refunded if the unearned precomputed finance charge were calculated in accordance with the actuarial method, except that the debtor shall not be entitled to a refund which is less than one dollar. The unearned portion of the precomputed finance charge is, at the option of the creditor, either:

(1) That portion of the precomputed finance charge which is allocable to all unexpired payment periods as originally scheduled, or if deferred, as deferred. A payment period shall be deemed unexpired if prepayment is made within 15 days after the payment period's scheduled due date. The unearned precomputed finance charge is the total of that which would have been earned for each such period had the loan not been precomputed, by applying to unpaid balances of principal, according to the actuarial method, an annual percentage rate based on those charges which are considered precomputed finance charges in this section, assuming that all payments were made as originally scheduled, or as deferred, if deferred. The creditor, at its option, may round this annual percentage rate to the nearest one-quarter of one percent; or

(2) The total precomputed finance charge less the earned precomputed finance charge. The earned precomputed finance charge shall be determined by applying an annual percentage rate based on the total precomputed finance charge (as that term is defined in this section), under the actuarial method, to the unpaid balances for the

actual time those balances were unpaid up to the date of prepayment. If a late charge or deferral fee has been collected, it shall be treated as a payment.

(d) *Prepayment penalties.* A debtor may prepay in full or in part the unpaid balance of the loan at any time without penalty. The right to prepay shall be disclosed in the loan contract in type larger than that used for the body of the document.

(e) *Balloon payments—*

(1) *Federal savings associations.* Federal savings association creditors may enter into agreements with debtors which provide for non-amortized and partially-amortized loans on residential manufactured homes, and such loans shall be governed by the provisions of this section and § 560.220 of this chapter.

(2) *Other creditors.* All other creditors may enter into agreements with debtors which provide for non-amortized and partially-amortized loans on residential manufactured homes to the extent authorized by applicable Federal or state law or regulation.

(f) *Late charges.*

(1) No late charge may be assessed, imposed, or collected unless provided for by written contract between the creditor and debtor.

(2) To the extent that applicable state law does not provide for a longer period of time, no late charge may be collected on an installment which is paid in full on or before the 15th day after its scheduled or deferred due date even though an earlier maturing installment or a late charge on an earlier installment may not have been paid in full. For purposes of assessing late charges, payments received are deemed to be applied first to current installments.

(3) A late charge may be imposed only once on an installment; however, no such charge may be collected for a late installment which has been deferred.

(4) To the extent that applicable state law does not provide for a lower charge or a longer grace period, a late charge on any installment not paid in full on or before the 15th day after its scheduled or deferred due date may not exceed five percent of the unpaid amount of the installment.

(5) If, at any time after imposition of a late charge, the lender provides the borrower with written notice regarding amounts claimed to be due but unpaid, the notice shall separately state the total of all late charges claimed.

(6) Interest after the final scheduled maturity date may not exceed the maximum rate otherwise allowable under State law for such contracts, and if such interest is charged, no separate late charge may be made on the final scheduled installment.

(g) *Deferral fees.*

(1) With respect to mobile home credit transactions containing precomputed finance charges, agreements providing for deferral of all or part of one or more installments shall be in writing, signed by the parties, and

(i) Provide, to the extent that applicable state law does not provide for a lower charge, for a charge not exceeding one percent of each installment or part thereof for each month from the date when such installment was due to the date when it is agreed to become payable and proportionately for a part of each month, counting each day as 1/30th of a month;

(ii) Incorporate by reference the transaction to which the deferral applied;

(iii) Disclose each installment or part thereof in the amount to be deferred, the date or dates originally payable, and the date or dates agreed to become payable: and

(iv) Set forth the fact of the deferral charge, the dollar amount of the charge for each installment to be deferred, and the total dollar amount to be paid by the debtor for the privilege of deferring payment.

(2) No term of a writing executed by the debtor shall constitute authority for a creditor unilaterally to grant a deferral with respect to which a charge is to be imposed or collected.

(3) The deferral period is that period of time in which no payment is required or made by reason of the deferral.

(4) Payments received with respect to deferred installments shall be deemed to be applied first to deferred installments.

(5) A charge may not be collected for the deferral of an installment or any part thereof if, with respect to that installment, a refinancing or consolidation agreement is concluded by the parties, or a late charge has been imposed or collected, unless such late charge is refunded to the borrower or credited to the deferral charge.

(h) *Notice before repossession, foreclosure, or acceleration.*

(1) Except in the case of abandonment or other extreme circumstances, no action to repossess or foreclose, or to accelerate payment of the entire outstanding balance of the obligation, may be taken against the debtor until 30 days after the creditor sends the debtor a notice of default in the form set forth in paragraph (h)(2) of this section. Such notice shall be sent by registered or certified mail with return receipt requested. In the case of default on payments, the sum stated in the notice may only include payments in default and applicable late or deferral charges. If the debtor cures the default within 30 days of the postmark of the notice and subsequently defaults a second time, the creditor shall again give notice as described in this paragraph (h)(1). The debtor is not entitled to notice of default more than twice in any one-year period.

(2) The notice in the following form shall state the nature of the default, the action the debtor must take to cure the default, the creditor's intended actions upon failure of the debtor to cure the default, and the debtor's right to redeem under state law.

To:
Date: ____, 19

Notice of Default and Right to Cure Default

Name, address, and telephone number of creditor
Account number, if any
Brief identification of credit transaction
You are now in default on this credit transaction. You have a right to correct this default within 30 days from the postmarked date of this notice. If you correct the default, you may continue with the contract as though you did not default. Your default consists of:

Describe default alleged

Cure of default: Within 30 days from the postmarked date of this notice, you may cure your default by (describe the acts necessary for cure, including, if applicable, the amount of payment required, including itemized delinquency or deferral charges).
Creditor's rights: If you do not correct your default in the time allowed, we may exercise our rights against you under the law by (describe action creditor intends to take).
If you have any questions, write (the creditor) at the above address or call (creditor's designated employee) at (telephone number) between the hours of and on (state days of week).
If this default was caused by your failure to make a payment or payments, and you want to pay by mail, please send a check or money order; do not send cash. [67 Fed. Reg. 60542, Sept. 26, 2002, effective July 1, 2003, *as amended by* 67 Fed. Reg. 76304, Dec. 12, 2002]

12 C.F.R. § 590.100 Status of Interpretations issued under Public Law 96-161.

The Office continues to adhere to the views expressed in the formal Interpretations issued under the authority of section 105(c) of Pub. L. 96-161, 93 Stat. 1233 (1979). These Interpretations, which relate to the temporary preemption of state interest ceilings contained in Pub. L. 96-161, may be found at 45 Fed. Reg. 2840 (Jan. 15, 1980); 45 Fed. Reg. 6165 (Jan. 25, 1980); 45 Fed. Reg. 8000 (Feb. 6, 1980); 45 Fed. Reg. 15921 (Mar. 12, 1980).

12 C.F.R. § 590.101 State criminal usury statutes.

(a) Section 501 provides that "the provisions of the constitution or laws of any state expressly limiting the rate or amount of interest, discount points, finance charges, or other charges shall not apply to any" federally-related loan secured by a first lien on residential real property, a residential manufactured home, or all the stock allocated to a dwelling unit in a residential housing cooperative. 12 U.S.C. 1735f-7a note (Supp. IV 1980). The question has arisen as to whether the federal statute preempts a state law which deems it a criminal offense to charge interest at a rate in excess of that specified in the state law.

(b) In the Office's view, section 501 preempts all state laws which expressly limit the rate or amount of interest chargeable on a federally-related residential first mortgage. It does not matter whether the statute in question imposes criminal or civil sanctions; section 501, by its terms, preempts "any" state law which imposes a ceiling on interest rates. The wording of the federal statute clearly expresses an intent to displace all direct state law restraints on interest. Any state law that conflicts with this Congressional purpose must yield.

Alternative Mortgage Transaction Parity Act of 1982

This appendix contains the Alternative Mortgage Transactions Parity Act (AMTPA). AMTPA is Title VIII of the Depository Institutions Act of 1982, also know as the Garn-St. Germain Act. These provisions appear in H.1. Section H.2 includes relevant regulations promulgated by the Office of Thrift Supervision (OTS). Finally, section H.3 summarizes OTS letters interpreting AMTPA. The statutes and regulations reprinted in Appxs. H.1 and H.2 are also found on the companion CD-Rom.

H.1 Statutory Provisions

TITLE 12—BANKS AND BANKING

CHAPTER 39—ALTERNATIVE MORTGAGE TRANSACTIONS

§ 3801. Findings and purpose
§ 3802. Definitions
§ 3803. Alternative mortgage authority
§ 3804. Applicability of preemption provisions
§ 3805. Applicability of consumer protection provisions
§ 3806. Adjustable rate mortgage caps

12 U.S.C. § 3801. Findings and purpose[1]

(a) The Congress hereby finds that—

(1) increasingly volatile and dynamic changes in interest rates have seriously impared[2] the ability of housing creditors to provide consumers with fixed-term, fixed-rate credit secured by interests in real property, cooperative housing, manufactured homes, and other dwellings;

(2) alternative mortgage transactions are essential to the provision of an adequate supply of credit secured by residential property necessary to meet the demand expected during the 1980's; and

(3) the Comptroller of the Currency, the National Credit Union Administration, and the Director of the Office of Thrift Supervision have recognized the importance of alternative mortgage transactions and have adopted regulations authorizing federally chartered depository institutions to engage in alternative mortgage financing.

(b) It is the purpose of this chapter to eliminate the discriminatory impact that those regulations have upon nonfederally chartered housing creditors and provide them with parity with federally chartered institutions by authorizing all housing creditors to make, purchase, and enforce alternative mortgage transactions so long as the transactions are in conformity with the regulations issued by the Federal agencies.

[Pub. L. No. 97-320, tit. VIII, § 802, 96 Stat. 1545 (Oct. 15, 1982); Pub. L. No. 101-73, tit. VII, § 744(c), 103 Stat. 438 (Aug. 9, 1989)]

12 U.S.C. § 3802. Definitions

As used in this chapter—

(1) the term "alternative mortgage transaction" means a loan or credit sale secured by an interest in residential real property, a dwelling, all stock allocated to a dwelling unit in a residential cooperative housing corporation, or a residential manufactured home (as that term is defined in section 5402(6) of Title 42)—

(A) in which the interest rate or finance charge may be adjusted or renegotiated;

(B) involving a fixed-rate, but which implicitly permits rate adjustments by having the debt mature at the end of an interval shorter than the term of the amortization schedule; or

(C) involving any similar type of rate, method of determining return, term, repayment, or other variation not common to traditional fixed-rate, fixed-term transactions, including without limitation, transactions that involve the sharing of equity or appreciation;

described and defined by applicable regulation; and

(2) the term "housing creditor" means—

(A) a depository institution, as defined in section 501(a)(2) of the Depository Institutions Deregulation and Monetary Control Act of 1980;

(B) a lender approved by the Secretary of Housing and Urban Development for participation in any mortgage insurance program under the National Housing Act [12 U.S.C.A. § 1701 et seq.];

(C) any person who regularly makes loans, credit sales, or advances secured by interests in properties referred to in paragraph (1); or

(D) any transferee of any of them.

A person is not a "housing creditor" with respect to a specific alternative mortgage transaction if, except for this chapter, in order to enter into that transaction, the person would be required to comply with licensing requirements imposed under State law,

---

1 12 U.S.C. § 3801 note, 12 U.S.C. §§ 3801–3806, Pub. L. No. 97-320, 96 Stat. 1469 (Oct. 15, 1982).

2 So in original. Should probably be "impaired."

unless such person is licensed under applicable State law and such person remains, or becomes, subject to the applicable regulatory requirements and enforcement mechanisms provided by State law.

[Pub. L. No. 97-320, tit. VIII, § 803, 96 Stat. 1545 (Oct. 15, 1982)]

12 U.S.C. § 3803. Alternative mortgage authority

(a) General authority; compliance by banks, credit unions and all other housing creditors with applicable regulations

In order to prevent discrimination against State-chartered depository institutions, and other nonfederally chartered housing creditors, with respect to making, purchasing, and enforcing alternative mortgage transactions, housing creditors may make, purchase, and enforce alternative mortgage transactions, except that this section shall apply—

(1) with respect to banks, only to transactions made in accordance with regulations governing alternative mortgage transactions as issued by the Comptroller of the Currency for national banks, to the extent that such regulations are authorized by rulemaking authority granted to the Comptroller of the Currency with regard to national banks under laws other than this section;

(2) with respect to credit unions, only to transactions made in accordance with regulations governing alternative mortgage transactions as issued by the National Credit Union Administration Board for Federal credit unions, to the extent that such regulations are authorized by rulemaking authority granted to the National Credit Union Administration with regard to Federal credit unions under laws other than this section; and

(3) with respect to all other housing creditors, including without limitation, savings and loan associations, mutual savings banks, and savings banks, only to transactions made in accordance with regulations governing alternative mortgage transactions as issued by the Director of the Office of Thrift Supervision for federally chartered savings and loan associations, to the extent that such regulations are authorized by rulemaking authority granted to the Director of the Office of Thrift Supervision with regard to federally chartered savings and loan associations under laws other than this section.

(b) Transactions deemed in compliance with applicable regulations

For the purpose of determining the applicability of this section, an alternative mortgage transaction shall be deemed to be made in accordance with the applicable regulation notwithstanding the housing creditor's failure to comply with the regulation, if—

(1) the transaction is in substantial compliance with the regulation; and

(2) within sixty days of discovering any error, the housing creditor corrects such error, including making appropriate adjustments, if any, to the account.

(c) Preemption of State constitutions, laws or regulations

An alternative mortgage transaction may be made by a housing creditor in accordance with this section, notwithstanding any State constitution, law, or regulation.

[Pub. L. No. 97-320, tit. VIII, § 804, 96 Stat. 1546 (Oct. 15, 1982); Pub. L. No. 101-73, tit. VII, § 744(c), 103 Stat. 438 (Aug. 9, 1989)]

12 U.S.C. § 3804. Applicability of preemption provisions

(a) The provisions of section 3803 of this title shall not apply to any alternative mortgage transaction in any State made on or after the effective date (if such effective date occurs on or after October 15, 1982, and prior to a date three years after October 15, 1982) of a State law or a certification that the voters of such State have voted in favor of any provision, constitutional or otherwise, which states explicitly and by its terms that such State does not want the preemption provided in section 3803 of this title to apply with respect to alternative mortgage transactions (or to any class or type of alternative mortgage transaction) subject to the laws of such State, except that section 3803 of this title shall continue to apply to—

(1) any alternative mortgage transaction undertaken on or after such date pursuant to an agreement to undertake such alternative mortgage transaction which was entered into on or after October 15, 1982, and prior to such later date (the "preemption period"); and

(2) any renewal, extension, refinancing, or other modification of an alternative mortgage transaction that was entered into during the preemption period.

(b) An alternative mortgage transaction shall be deemed to have been undertaken during the preemption period to which this section applies if it—

(1) is funded or extended in whole or in part during the preemption period, regardless of whether pursuant to a commitment or other agreement therefor made prior to that period; or

(2) is a renewal, extension, refinancing, or other modification of an alternative mortgage transaction entered into before the preemption period and such renewal, extension, or other modification is made during such period with the written consent of any person obligated to repay such credit.

[Pub. L. No. 97-320, tit. VIII, § 805, 96 Stat. 1547 (Oct. 15, 1982); Pub. L. No. 98-181, tit. IV, § 472, 97 Stat. 1237 (Nov. 30, 1983)]

12 U.S.C. § 3805. Applicability of consumer protection provisions

Section 501(c)(1) of the Depository Institutions Deregulation and Monetary Control Act of 1980 shall not apply to transactions which are subject to this chapter.

[Pub. L. No. 97-320, tit. VIII, § 806, 96 Stat. 1548 (Oct. 15, 1982)]

12 U.S.C. § 3806. Adjustable rate mortgage caps

(a) In general

Any adjustable rate mortgage loan originated by a creditor shall include a limitation on the maximum interest rate that may apply during the term of the mortgage loan.

(b) Regulations

The Board of Governors of the Federal Reserve System shall prescribe regulations to carry out the purposes of this section.

(c) Enforcement

Any violation of this section shall be treated as a violation of the Truth in Lending Act [15 U.S.C.A. § 1601 et seq.] and shall be subject to administrative enforcement under section 108 [15 U.S.C.A. § 1607] or civil damages under section 130 of such Act [15 U.S.C.A. § 1640], or both.

(d) Definitions

For the purpose of this section—

(1) the term "creditor" means a person who regularly extends credit for personal, family, or household purposes; and

(2) the term "adjustable rate mortgage loan" means any consumer loan secured by a lien on a one- to four-family dwelling unit, including a condominium unit, cooperative housing unit, or mobile home, where the loan is made pursuant to an agreement under which the creditor may, from time to time, adjust the rate of interest.

(e) Effective date

This section shall take effect upon the expiration of 120 days after August 10, 1987.

[Pub. L. No. 100-86, tit. XII, § 1204, 101 Stat. 662 (Aug. 10, 1987); Pub. L. No. 102-550, tit. IX, § 952, 106 Stat. 3893 (Oct. 28, 1992)]

H.2 Relevant Regulations

Title 12—Banks and Banking

CHAPTER V—OFFICE OF THRIFT SUPERVISION, DEPARTMENT OF THE TREASURY

PART 560—LENDING AND INVESTMENT

* * *

Subpart C—Alternative Mortgage Transactions.

§ 560.210 Disclosures for variable rate transactions.

§ 560.220 Alternative Mortgage Parity Act.

Authority: 12 U.S.C. 1462, 1462a, 1463, 1464, 1467a, 1701j-3, 1828, 3803, 3806; 42 U.S.C. 4106.

Source: 61 Fed. Reg. 50971 (Sept. 30 1996), unless otherwise noted.

12 C.F.R. § 560.210 Disclosures for variable rate transactions

A savings association must provide the initial disclosures described at 12 CFR 226.19(b) and the adjustment notices described at 12 CFR 226.20(c) for variable rate transactions, as described in those regulations. The OTS administers and enforces those provisions for savings associations.

[63 Fed. Reg. 38463 (July 17, 1998)]

12 C.F.R. § 560.220 Alternative Mortgage Transaction Parity Act.

(a) *Applicable housing creditors.* A housing creditor that is not a commercial bank, a credit union, or a federal savings association, may make an alternative mortgage transaction as defined at 12 U.S.C. 3802(1), by following the regulations identified in paragraph (b) of this section, notwithstanding any state constitution, law, or regulation. See 12 U.S.C. 3803.

(b) *Applicable regulations.* OTS identifies §§ 560.35 and 560.210 as appropriate and applicable for state housing creditors. All other OTS regulations are not identified, and are inappropriate and inapplicable for state housing creditors. State housing creditors engaged in credit sales should read the term "loan" as "credit sale" wherever applicable in applying these regulations.

[67 Fed. Reg. 60542 (Sept. 26, 2002), effective July 1, 2003, *as amended by* 67 Fed. Reg. 76304 (Dec. 12, 2002)]

TITLE VIII—ALTERNATIVE MORTGAGE TRANSACTIONS

SHORT TITLE

Sec. 801. This title may be cited as the "Alternative Mortgage Transaction Parity Act of 1982."

EFFECTIVE DATE

Sec. 807. (a) This title shall be effective upon enactment.

(b) Within sixty days of the enactment of this title, the Comptroller of the Currency, the National Credit Union Administration and the Federal Home Loan Bank Board shall identify, describe and publish those portions or provisions of their respective regulations that are inappropriate for (and thus inapplicable to), or that need to be conformed for the use of, the nonfederally chartered housing creditors to which their respective regulations apply, including without limitation, making necessary changes in terminology to conform the regulatory and disclosure provisions to those more typically associated with various types of transactions including credit sales.

H.3 OTS AMTPA Interpretive Letters

Date of Opinion	State Affected	Issue
December 2, 2003	General	"Interest only fixed rate" mortgages under which the borrower pays interest only for a fixed period and then the loan becomes fully amortizing is an alternative mortgage transaction subject to AMTPA. Similarly, a "one time rate reduction" mortgage loan under which the interest rate decreases if the borrower makes a specified number of timely payments is an alternative mortgage transaction. Neither, however, is a variable rate loan.
February 10, 1997	General	Variable rate home equity lines of credit and fixed term variable rate loans secured by first or subordinate liens on real property are alternative mortgage transactions.
November 27, 1996	General	Fixed-rate mortgage containing a default interest rate is an alternative mortgage transaction under AMPTA which permits the lender to include such a provision regardless of state law.
April 30, 1996	Wisconsin	A law restricting prepayment penalties on variable rate mortgage loans is preempted.

Appendix I   Gramm-Leach-Bliley Act

This appendix contains portions of the Gramm-Leach-Bliley Act related to insurance and the preemption of state insurance laws. These provisions appear in section I.1. Regulations jointly issued by three federal banking agencies addressing the sale of insurance products by depository institutions appear in I.2. The statutes and regulations reprinted in Appxs. I.1 and I.2, are also found on the companion CD-Rom.

I.1 Selected Statutory Provisions Related to Insurance

TITLE 12—BANKS AND BANKING

CHAPTER 16—FEDERAL DEPOSIT INSURANCE CORPORATION

* * *

§ 1831x.   Insurance customer protections

TITLE 15—COMMERCE AND TRADE

CHAPTER 93—INSURANCE

§ 6701.   Operation of State law

* * *

TITLE 12—BANKS AND BANKING

CHAPTER 16—FEDERAL DEPOSIT INSURANCE CORPORATION

* * *

12 U.S.C. § 1831x. Insurance customer protections

(a) Regulations required

(1) In general

The Federal banking agencies shall prescribe and publish in final form, before the end of the 1-year period beginning on November 12, 1999, customer protection regulations (which the agencies jointly determine to be appropriate) that—

(A) apply to retail sales practices, solicitations, advertising, or offers of any insurance product by any depository institution or any person that is engaged in such activities at an office of the institution or on behalf of the institution; and

(B) are consistent with the requirements of this chapter and provide such additional protections for customers to whom such sales, solicitations, advertising, or offers are directed.

(2) Applicability to subsidiaries

The regulations prescribed pursuant to paragraph (1) shall extend such protections to any subsidiary of a depository institution, as deemed appropriate by the regulators referred to in paragraph (3), where such extension is determined to be necessary to ensure the consumer protections provided by this section.

(3) Consultation and joint regulations

The Federal banking agencies shall consult with each other and prescribe joint regulations pursuant to paragraph (1), after consultation with the State insurance regulators, as appropriate.

(b) Sales practices

The regulations prescribed pursuant to subsection (a) of this section shall include antitying and anticoercion rules applicable to the sale of insurance products that prohibit a depository institution from engaging in any practice that would lead a customer to believe an extension of credit, in violation of section 1972 of this title, is conditional upon—

(1) the purchase of an insurance product from the institution or any of its affiliates; or

(2) an agreement by the consumer not to obtain, or a prohibition on the consumer from obtaining, an insurance product from an unaffiliated entity.

(c) Disclosures and advertising

The regulations prescribed pursuant to subsection (a) of this section shall include the following provisions relating to disclosures and advertising in connection with the initial purchase of an insurance product:

(1) Disclosures

(A) In general

Requirements that the following disclosures be made orally and in writing before the completion of the initial sale and, in the case of clause (iii), at the time of application for an extension of credit:

    (i) Uninsured status As appropriate, the product is not insured by the Federal Deposit Insurance Corporation, the United States Government, or the depository institution.

    (ii) Investment risk In the case of a variable annuity or other insurance product which involves an investment risk, that there is an investment risk associated with the product, including possible loss of value.

    (iii) Coercion The approval of an extension of credit may not be conditioned on—

        (I) the purchase of an insurance product from the institution in which the application for credit is pending or of any affiliate of the institution; or

        (II) an agreement by the consumer not to obtain, or a prohibition on the consumer from obtaining, an insurance product from an unaffiliated entity.

(B) Making disclosure readily understandable

Regulations prescribed under subparagraph (A) shall encourage the use of disclosure that is conspicuous, simple, direct, and readily understandable, such as the following:

    (i) "NOT FDIC—INSURED".

    (ii) "NOT GUARANTEED BY THE BANK".

    (iii) "MAY GO DOWN IN VALUE".

    (iv) "NOT INSURED BY ANY GOVERNMENT AGENCY".

(C) Limitation

Nothing in this paragraph requires the inclusion of the foregoing disclosures in advertisements of a general nature describing or listing the services or products offered by an institution.

(D) Meaningful disclosures

Disclosures shall not be considered to be meaningfully provided under this paragraph if the institution or its representative states that disclosures required by this subsection were available to the customer in printed material available for distribution, where such printed material is not provided and such information is not orally disclosed to the customer.

(E) Adjustments for alternative methods of purchase

In prescribing the requirements under subparagraphs (A) and (F), necessary adjustments shall be made for purchase in person, by telephone, or by electronic media to provide for the most appropriate and complete form of disclosure and acknowledgments.

(F) Consumer acknowledgment

A requirement that a depository institution shall require any person selling an insurance product at any office of, or on behalf of, the institution to obtain, at the time a consumer receives the disclosures required under this paragraph or at the time of the initial purchase by the consumer of such product, an acknowledgment by such consumer of the receipt of the disclosure required under this subsection with respect to such product.

(2) Prohibition on misrepresentations

A prohibition on any practice, or any advertising, at any office of, or on behalf of, the depository institution, or any subsidiary, as appropriate, that could mislead any person or otherwise cause a reasonable person to reach an erroneous belief with respect to—

(A) the uninsured nature of any insurance product sold, or offered for sale, by the institution or any subsidiary of the institution;

(B) in the case of a variable annuity or insurance product that involves an investment risk, the investment risk associated with any such product; or

(C) in the case of an institution or subsidiary at which insurance products are sold or offered for sale, the fact that—

    (i) the approval of an extension of credit to a customer by the institution or subsidiary may not be conditioned on the purchase of an insurance product by such customer from the institution or subsidiary; and

    (ii) the customer is free to purchase the insurance product from another source.

(d) Separation of banking and nonbanking activities

(1) Regulations required

The regulations prescribed pursuant to subsection (a) of this section shall include such provisions as the Federal banking agen-

cies consider appropriate to ensure that the routine acceptance of deposits is kept, to the extent practicable, physically segregated from insurance product activity.

(2) Requirements

Regulations prescribed pursuant to paragraph (1) shall include the following requirements:

(A) Separate setting

A clear delineation of the setting in which, and the circumstances under which, transactions involving insurance products should be conducted in a location physically segregated from an area where retail deposits are routinely accepted.

(B) Referrals

Standards that permit any person accepting deposits from the public in an area where such transactions are routinely conducted in a depository institution to refer a customer who seeks to purchase any insurance product to a qualified person who sells such product, only if the person making the referral receives no more than a one-time nominal fee of a fixed dollar amount for each referral that does not depend on whether the referral results in a transaction.

(C) Qualification and licensing requirements

Standards prohibiting any depository institution from permitting any person to sell or offer for sale any insurance product in any part of any office of the institution, or on behalf of the institution, unless such person is appropriately qualified and licensed.

(e) Domestic violence discrimination prohibition

(1) In general

In the case of an applicant for, or an insured under, any insurance product described in paragraph (2), the status of the applicant or insured as a victim of domestic violence, or as a provider of services to victims of domestic violence, shall not be considered as a criterion in any decision with regard to insurance underwriting, pricing, renewal, or scope of coverage of insurance policies, or payment of insurance claims, except as required or expressly permitted under State law.

(2) Scope of application

The prohibition contained in paragraph (1) shall apply to any life or health insurance product which is sold or offered for sale, as principal, agent, or broker, by any depository institution or any person who is engaged in such activities at an office of the institution or on behalf of the institution.

(3) Domestic violence defined

For purposes of this subsection, the term "domestic violence" means the occurrence of one or more of the following acts by a current or former family member, household member, intimate partner, or caretaker:

(A) Attempting to cause or causing or threatening another person physical harm, severe emotional distress, psychological trauma, rape, or sexual assault.

(B) Engaging in a course of conduct or repeatedly committing acts toward another person, including following the person without proper authority, under circumstances that place the person in reasonable fear of bodily injury or physical harm.

(C) Subjecting another person to false imprisonment.

(D) Attempting to cause or cause damage to property so as to intimidate or attempt to control the behavior of another person.

(f) Consumer grievance process

The Federal banking agencies shall jointly establish a consumer complaint mechanism, for receiving and expeditiously addressing consumer complaints alleging a violation of regulations issued under the section, which shall—

(1) establish a group within each regulatory agency to receive such complaints;

(2) develop procedures for investigating such complaints;

(3) develop procedures for informing consumers of rights they may have in connection with such complaints; and

(4) develop procedures for addressing concerns raised by such complaints, as appropriate, including procedures for the recovery of losses to the extent appropriate.

(g) Effect on other authority
(1) In general

No provision of this section shall be construed as granting, limiting, or otherwise affecting—

(A) any authority of the Securities and Exchange Commission, any self-regulatory organization, the Municipal Securities Rule-making Board, or the Secretary of the Treasury under any Federal securities law; or

(B) except as provided in paragraph (2), any authority of any State insurance commission (or any agency or office performing like functions), or of any State securities commission (or any agency or office performing like functions), or other State authority under any State law.

(2) Coordination with State law
(A) In general

Except as provided in subparagraph (B), insurance customer protection regulations prescribed by a Federal banking agency under this section shall not apply to retail sales, solicitations, advertising, or offers of any insurance product by any depository institution or to any person who is engaged in such activities at an office of such institution or on behalf of the institution, in a State where the State has in effect statutes, regulations, orders, or interpretations, that are inconsistent with or contrary to the regulations prescribed by the Federal banking agencies.

(B) Preemption

(i) In general If, with respect to any provision of the regulations prescribed under this section, the Board of Governors of the Federal Reserve System, the Comptroller of the Currency, and the Board of Directors of the Corporation determine jointly that the protection afforded by such provision for customers is greater than the protection provided by a comparable provision of the statutes, regulations, orders, or interpretations referred to in subparagraph (A) of any State, the appropriate State regulatory authority shall be notified of such determination in writing.

(ii) Considerations Before making a final determination under clause (i), the Federal agencies referred to in clause (i) shall give appropriate consideration to comments submitted by the appropriate State regulatory authorities relating to the level of protection afforded to consumers under State law.

(iii) Federal preemption and ability of States to override Federal preemption If the Federal agencies referred to in clause (i) jointly determine that any provision of the regulations prescribed under this section affords greater protections than a comparable State law, rule, regulation, order, or interpretation, those agencies shall send a written preemption notice to the appropriate State regulatory authority to notify the State that the Federal provision will preempt the State

provision and will become applicable unless, not later than 3 years after the date of such notice, the State adopts legislation to override such preemption.

(h) Non-discrimination against non-affiliated agents

The Federal banking agencies shall ensure that the regulations prescribed pursuant to subsection (a) of this section shall not have the effect of discriminating, either intentionally or unintentionally, against any person engaged in insurance sales or solicitations that is not affiliated with a depository institution.

Sept. 21, 1950, ch. 967, § 2[47], *as added* Pub. L. No. 106–102, title III, § 305 (Nov. 12, 1999), 113 Stat. 1410]

* * *

TITLE 15—COMMERCE AND TRADE
CHAPTER 93—INSURANCE

12 U.S.C. § 6701. Operation of State law

(a) State regulation of the business of insurance

The Act entitled "An Act to express the intent of Congress with reference to the regulation of the business of insurance" and approved March 9, 1945 (15 U.S.C. 1011 et seq.) (commonly referred to as the "McCarran-Ferguson Act") remains the law of the United States.

(b) Mandatory insurance licensing requirements

No person shall engage in the business of insurance in a State as principal or agent unless such person is licensed as required by the appropriate insurance regulator of such State in accordance with the relevant State insurance law, subject to subsections (c), (d), and (e) of this section.

(c) Affiliations
(1) In general

Except as provided in paragraph (2), no State may, by statute, regulation, order, interpretation, or other action, prevent or restrict a depository institution, or an affiliate thereof, from being affiliated directly or indirectly or associated with any person, as authorized or permitted by this Act or any other provision of Federal law.

(2) Insurance

With respect to affiliations between depository institutions, or any affiliate thereof, and any insurer, paragraph (1) does not prohibit—

(A) any State from—

(i) collecting, reviewing, and taking actions (including approval and disapproval) on applications and other documents or reports concerning any proposed acquisition of, or a change or continuation of control of, an insurer domiciled in that State; and

(ii) exercising authority granted under applicable State law to collect information concerning any proposed acquisition of, or a change or continuation of control of, an insurer engaged in the business of insurance in, and regulated as an insurer by, such State;

during the 60-day period preceding the effective date of the acquisition or change or continuation of control, so long as the collecting, reviewing, taking actions, or exercising authority by the State does not have the effect of discriminating, intentionally or unintentionally, against a depository institution or an affiliate thereof, or against any other person based upon an association of such person with a depository institution;

(B) any State from requiring any person that is acquiring control of an insurer domiciled in that State to maintain or restore the capital requirements of that insurer to the level required under the capital regulations of general applicability in that State to avoid the requirement of preparing and filing with the insurance regulatory authority of that State a plan to increase the capital of the insurer, except that any determination by the State insurance regulatory authority with respect to such requirement shall be made not later than 60 days after the date of notification under subparagraph (A); or

(C) any State from restricting a change in the ownership of stock in an insurer, or a company formed for the purpose of controlling such insurer, after the conversion of the insurer from mutual to stock form so long as such restriction does not have the effect of discriminating, intentionally or unintentionally, against a depository institution or an affiliate thereof, or against any other person based upon an association of such person with a depository institution.

(d) Activities

(1) In general

Except as provided in paragraph (3), and except with respect to insurance sales, solicitation, and cross marketing activities, which shall be governed by paragraph (2), no State may, by statute, regulation, order, interpretation, or other action, prevent or restrict a depository institution or an affiliate thereof from engaging directly or indirectly, either by itself or in conjunction with an affiliate, or any other person, in any activity authorized or permitted under this Act and the amendments made by this Act.

(2) Insurance sales

(A) In general

In accordance with the legal standards for preemption set forth in the decision of the Supreme Court of the United States in Barnett Bank of Marion County N.A. v. Nelson, 517 U.S. 25 (1996), no State may, by statute, regulation, order, interpretation, or other action, prevent or significantly interfere with the ability of a depository institution, or an affiliate thereof, to engage, directly or indirectly, either by itself or in conjunction with an affiliate or any other person, in any insurance sales, solicitation, or crossmarketing activity.

(B) Certain State laws preserved

Notwithstanding subparagraph (A), a State may impose any of the following restrictions, or restrictions that are substantially the same as but no more burdensome or restrictive than those in each of the following clauses:

(i) Restrictions prohibiting the rejection of an insurance policy by a depository institution or an affiliate of a depository institution, solely because the policy has been issued or underwritten by any person who is not associated with such depository institution or affiliate when the insurance is required in connection with a loan or extension of credit.

(ii) Restrictions prohibiting a requirement for any debtor, insurer, or insurance agent or broker to pay a separate charge in connection with the handling of insurance that is required in connection with a loan or other extension of credit or the provision of another traditional banking product by a deposi-

tory institution, or any affiliate of a depository institution, unless such charge would be required when the depository institution or affiliate is the licensed insurance agent or broker providing the insurance.

(iii) Restrictions prohibiting the use of any advertisement or other insurance promotional material by a depository institution or any affiliate of a depository institution that would cause a reasonable person to believe mistakenly that—

(I) the Federal Government or a State is responsible for the insurance sales activities of, or stands behind the credit of, the institution or affiliate; or

(II) a State, or the Federal Government guarantees any returns on insurance products, or is a source of payment on any insurance obligation of or sold by the institution or affiliate;

(iv) Restrictions prohibiting the payment or receipt of any commission or brokerage fee or other valuable consideration for services as an insurance agent or broker to or by any person, unless such person holds a valid State license regarding the applicable class of insurance at the time at which the services are performed, except that, in this clause, the term "services as an insurance agent or broker" does not include a referral by an unlicensed person of a customer or potential customer to a licensed insurance agent or broker that does not include a discussion of specific insurance policy terms and conditions.

(v) Restrictions prohibiting any compensation paid to or received by any individual who is not licensed to sell insurance, for the referral of a customer that seeks to purchase, or seeks an opinion or advice on, any insurance product to a person that sells or provides opinions or advice on such product, based on the purchase of insurance by the customer.

(vi) Restrictions prohibiting the release of the insurance information of a customer (defined as information concerning the premiums, terms, and conditions of insurance coverage, including expiration dates and rates, and insurance claims of a customer contained in the records of the depository institution or an affiliate thereof) to any person other than an officer, director, employee, agent, or affiliate of a depository institution, for the purpose of soliciting or selling insurance, without the express consent of the customer, other than a provision that prohibits—

(I) a transfer of insurance information to an unaffiliated insurer in connection with transferring insurance in force on existing insureds of the depository institution or an affiliate thereof, or in connection with a merger with or acquisition of an unaffiliated insurer; or

(II) the release of information as otherwise authorized by State or Federal law.

(vii) Restrictions prohibiting the use of health information obtained from the insurance records of a customer for any purpose, other than for its activities as a licensed agent or broker, without the express consent of the customer.

(viii) Restrictions prohibiting the extension of credit or any product or service that is equivalent to an extension of credit, lease or sale of property of any kind, or furnishing of any services or fixing or varying the consideration for any of the foregoing, on the condition or requirement that the customer obtain insurance from a depository institution or an affiliate of a depository institution, or a particular insurer, agent, or broker, other than a prohibition that would prevent any such depository institution or affiliate—

    (I) from engaging in any activity described in this clause that would not violate section 106 of the Bank Holding Company Act Amendments of 1970 [12 U.S.C. 1971 et seq.], as interpreted by the Board of Governors of the Federal Reserve System; or

    (II) from informing a customer or prospective customer that insurance is required in order to obtain a loan or credit, that loan or credit approval is contingent upon the procurement by the customer of acceptable insurance, or that insurance is available from the depository institution or an affiliate of the depository institution.

(ix) Restrictions requiring, when an application by a consumer for a loan or other extension of credit from a depository institution is pending, and insurance is offered or sold to the consumer or is required in connection with the loan or extension of credit by the depository institution or any affiliate thereof, that a written disclosure be provided to the consumer or prospective customer indicating that the customer's choice of an insurance provider will not affect the credit decision or credit terms in any way, except that the depository institution may impose reasonable requirements concerning the creditworthiness of the insurer and scope of coverage chosen.

(x) Restrictions requiring clear and conspicuous disclosure, in writing, where practicable, to the customer prior to the sale of any insurance policy that such policy—

    (I) is not a deposit;

    (II) is not insured by the Federal Deposit Insurance Corporation;

    (III) is not guaranteed by any depository institution or, if appropriate, an affiliate of any such institution or any person soliciting the purchase of or selling insurance on the premises thereof; and

    (IV) where appropriate, involves investment risk, including potential loss of principal.

(xi) Restrictions requiring that, when a customer obtains insurance (other than credit insurance or flood insurance) and credit from a depository institution, or any affiliate of such institution, or any person soliciting the purchase of or selling insurance on the premises thereof, the credit and insurance transactions be completed through separate documents.

(xii) Restrictions prohibiting, when a customer obtains insurance (other than credit insurance or flood insurance) and credit from a depository institution or an affiliate of such institution, or any person soliciting the purchase of or selling insurance on the premises thereof, inclusion of the expense of insurance premiums in the primary credit transaction without the express written consent of the customer.

(xiii) Restrictions requiring maintenance of separate and distinct books and records relating to insurance transactions, including all files relating to and reflecting consumer complaints, and requiring that such insurance books and records be made available to the appropriate State insurance regulator for inspection upon reasonable notice.

(C) Limitations

    (i) OCC deference Section 6714 (e) of this title does not apply with respect to any State statute, regulation, order, interpretation, or other action regarding insurance sales, solicitation,

or cross marketing activities described in subparagraph (A) that was issued, adopted, or enacted before September 3, 1998, and that is not described in subparagraph (B).

(ii) Nondiscrimination Subsection (e) of this section does not apply with respect to any State statute, regulation, order, interpretation, or other action regarding insurance sales, solicitation, or cross marketing activities described in subparagraph (A) that was issued, adopted, or enacted before September 3, 1998, and that is not described in subparagraph (B).

(iii) Construction Nothing in this paragraph shall be construed—

    (I) to limit the applicability of the decision of the Supreme Court in Barnett Bank of Marion County N.A. v. Nelson, 517 U.S. 25 (1996) with respect to any State statute, regulation, order, interpretation, or other action that is not referred to or described in subparagraph (B); or

    (II) to create any inference with respect to any State statute, regulation, order, interpretation, or other action that is not described in this paragraph.

(3) Insurance activities other than sales

State statutes, regulations, interpretations, orders, and other actions shall not be preempted under paragraph (1) to the extent that they—

(A) relate to, or are issued, adopted, or enacted for the purpose of regulating the business of insurance in accordance with the Act entitled "An Act to express the intent of Congress with reference to the regulation of the business of insurance" and approved March 9, 1945 (15 U.S.C. 1011 et seq.) (commonly referred to as the "McCarran-Ferguson Act");

(B) apply only to persons that are not depository institutions, but that are directly engaged in the business of insurance (except that they may apply to depository institutions engaged in providing savings bank life insurance as principal to the extent of regulating such insurance);

(C) do not relate to or directly or indirectly regulate insurance sales, solicitations, or cross marketing activities; and

(D) are not prohibited under subsection (e) of this section.

(4) Financial activities other than insurance

No State statute, regulation, order, interpretation, or other action shall be preempted under paragraph (1) to the extent that—

(A) it does not relate to, and is not issued and adopted, or enacted for the purpose of regulating, directly or indirectly, insurance sales, solicitations, or cross marketing activities covered under paragraph (2);

(B) it does not relate to, and is not issued and adopted, or enacted for the purpose of regulating, directly or indirectly, the business of insurance activities other than sales, solicitations, or cross marketing activities, covered under paragraph (3);

(C) it does not relate to securities investigations or enforcement actions referred to in subsection (f) of this section; and

(D) it—

    (i) does not distinguish by its terms between depository institutions, and affiliates thereof, engaged in the activity at issue and other persons engaged in the same activity in a manner that is in any way adverse with respect to the conduct of the activity by any such depository institution or affiliate engaged in the activity at issue;

    (ii) as interpreted or applied, does not have, and will not have, an impact on depository institutions, or affiliates thereof, engaged in the activity at issue, or any person who has an association with any such depository institution or affiliate, that is substantially more adverse than its impact on other persons engaged in the same activity that are not depository institutions or affiliates thereof, or persons who do not have an association with any such depository institution or affiliate;

(iii) does not effectively prevent a depository institution or affiliate thereof from engaging in activities authorized or permitted by this Act or any other provision of Federal law; and

(iv) does not conflict with the intent of this Act generally to permit affiliations that are authorized or permitted by Federal law.

(e) Nondiscrimination

Except as provided in any restrictions described in subsection (d)(2)(B) of this section, no State may, by statute, regulation, order, interpretation, or other action, regulate the insurance activities authorized or permitted under this Act or any other provision of Federal law of a depository institution, or affiliate thereof, to the extent that such statute, regulation, order, interpretation, or other action—

(1) distinguishes by its terms between depository institutions, or affiliates thereof, and other persons engaged in such activities, in a manner that is in any way adverse to any such depository institution, or affiliate thereof;

(2) as interpreted or applied, has or will have an impact on depository institutions, or affiliates thereof, that is substantially more adverse than its impact on other persons providing the same products or services or engaged in the same activities that are not depository institutions, or affiliates thereof, or persons or entities affiliated therewith;

(3) effectively prevents a depository institution, or affiliate thereof, from engaging in insurance activities authorized or permitted by this Act or any other provision of Federal law; or

(4) conflicts with the intent of this Act generally to permit affiliations that are authorized or permitted by Federal law between depository institutions, or affiliates thereof, and persons engaged in the business of insurance.

(f) Limitation

Subsections (c) and (d) of this section shall not be construed to affect—

(1) the jurisdiction of the securities commission (or any agency or office performing like functions) of any State, under the laws of such State—

(A) to investigate and bring enforcement actions, consistent with

section 77r (c) of this title, with respect to fraud or deceit or unlawful conduct by any person, in connection with securities or securities transactions; or

(B) to require the registration of securities or the licensure or registration of brokers, dealers, or investment advisers (consistent with section 80b−3a of this title), or the associated persons of a broker, dealer, or investment adviser (consistent with such section 80b−3a of this title); or

(2) State laws, regulations, orders, interpretations, or other actions of general applicability relating to the governance of corporations, partnerships, limited liability companies, or other business associations incorporated or formed under the laws of that State or domiciled in that State, or the applicability of the antitrust laws of any State or any State law that is similar to the antitrust laws if such laws, regulations, orders, interpretations, or other actions are not inconsistent with the purposes of this Act to authorize or permit certain affiliations and to remove barriers to such affiliations.

(g) Definitions

For purposes of this section, the following definitions shall apply:

(1) Affiliate

The term "affiliate" means any company that controls, is controlled by, or is under common control with another company.

(2) Antitrust laws

The term "antitrust laws" has the meaning given the term in subsection (a) of section 12 of this title, and includes section 45 of this title (to the extent that such section 45 relates to unfair methods of competition).

(3) Depository institution

The term "depository institution"—

(A) has the meaning given the term in section 1813 of title 12; and

(B) includes any foreign bank that maintains a branch, agency, or commercial lending company in the United States.

(4) Insurer

The term "insurer" means any person engaged in the business of insurance.

(5) State

The term "State" means any State of the United States, the District of Columbia, any territory of the United States, Puerto Rico, Guam, American Samoa, the Trust Territory of the Pacific Islands, the Virgin Islands, and the Northern Mariana Islands.

[Pub. L. No. 106−102, title I, § 104, 113 Stat. 1352 (Nov. 12, 1999)]

* * *

I.2 Selected Banking Regulations Related to Credit Insurance

I.2.1 12 C.F.R. Part 14—Office of the Comptroller of the Currency Regulations Regarding Consumer Protection in Sales of Insurance

§ 14.10   Purpose and scope.

§ 14.20   Definitions.

§ 14.30   Prohibited practices.

§ 14.40   What a covered person must disclose.

§ 14.50   Where insurance activities may take place.

§ 14.60   Qualification and licensing requirements for insurance sales personnel.

Appendix A to Part 14 Consumer Grievance Process

Authority: 12 U.S.C. 1 *et seq.*, 24 (Seventh), 92, 93a, 1818, and 1831x.

12 C.F.R. § 14.10 Purpose and scope.

(a) *General rule.* This part establishes consumer protections in connection with retail sales practices, solicitations, advertising, or offers of any insurance product or annuity to a consumer by:

(1) Any national bank; or

(2) Any other person that is engaged in such activities at an office of the bank or on behalf of the bank.

(b) *Application to operating subsidiaries.* For purposes of § 5.34(e)(3) of this chapter, an operating subsidiary is subject to this part only to the extent that it sells, solicits, advertises, or offers insurance products or annuities at an office of a bank or on behalf of a bank.

12 C.F.R. § 14.20 Definitions.

As used in this part:

(a) *Affiliate* means a company that controls, is controlled by, or is under common control with another company.

(b) *Bank* means a national bank or a Federal branch, or agency of a foreign bank as defined in section 1 of the International Banking Act of 1978 (12 U.S.C. 3101, *et seq.*).

(c) *Company* means any corporation, partnership, business trust, association or similar organization, or any other trust (unless by its terms the trust must terminate within twenty-five years or not later than twenty-one years and ten months after the death of individuals living on the effective date of the trust). It does not include any corporation the majority of the shares of which are owned by the United States or by any State, or a qualified family partnership, as defined in section 2(o)(10) of the Bank Holding Company Act of 1956, as amended (12 U.S.C. 1841(o)(10)).

(d) *Consumer* means an individual who purchases, applies to purchase, or is solicited to purchase from a covered person insurance products or annuities primarily for personal, family, or household purposes.

(e) *Control* of a company has the same meaning as in section 3(w)(5) of the Federal Deposit Insurance Act (12 U.S.C. 1813(w)(5)).

(f)(1) *Covered person* means:

(i) A bank; or

(ii) Any other person only when the person sells, solicits, advertises, or offers an insurance product or annuity to a consumer at an office of the bank or on behalf of a bank.

(2) For purposes of this definition, activities on behalf of a bank include activities where a person, whether at an office of the bank or at another location sells, solicits, advertises, or offers an insurance product or annuity and at least one of the following applies:

(i) The person represents to a consumer that the sale, solicitation, advertisement, or offer of any insurance product or annuity is by or on behalf of the bank;

(ii) The bank refers a consumer to a seller of insurance products or annuities and the bank has a contractual arrangement to receive commissions or fees derived from a sale of an insurance product or annuity resulting from that referral; or

(iii) Documents evidencing the sale, solicitation, advertising, or offer of an insurance product or annuity identify or refer to the bank.

(g) *Domestic violence* means the occurrence of one or more of the following acts by a current or former family member, household member, intimate partner, or caretaker:

(1) Attempting to cause or causing or threatening another person physical harm, severe emotional distress, psychological trauma, rape, or sexual assault;

(2) Engaging in a course of conduct or repeatedly committing acts toward another person, including following the person without proper authority, under circumstances that place the person in reasonable fear of bodily injury or physical harm;

(3) Subjecting another person to false imprisonment; or

(4) Attempting to cause or causing damage to property so as to intimidate or attempt to control the behavior of another person.

(h) *Electronic media* includes any means for transmitting messages electronically between a covered person and a consumer in a format that allows visual text to be displayed on equipment, for example, a personal computer monitor.

(i) *Office* means the premises of a bank where retail deposits are accepted from the public.

(j) *Subsidiary* has the same meaning as in section 3(w)(4) of the Federal Deposit Insurance Act (12 U.S.C. 1813(w)(4)).

12 C.F.R. § 14.30 Prohibited practices.

(a) *Anticoercion and antitying rules.* A covered person may not engage in any practice that would lead a consumer to believe that an extension of credit, in violation of section 106(b) of the Bank Holding Company Act Amendments of 1970 (12 U.S.C. 1972), is conditional upon either:

(1) The purchase of an insurance product or annuity from the bank or any of its affiliates; or

(2) An agreement by the consumer not to obtain, or a prohibition on the consumer from obtaining, an insurance product or annuity from an unaffiliated entity.

(b) *Prohibition on misrepresentations generally.* A covered person may not engage in any practice or use any advertisement at any office of, or on behalf of, the bank or a subsidiary of the bank that could mislead any person or otherwise cause a reasonable person to reach an erroneous belief with respect to:

(1) The fact that an insurance product or annuity sold or offered for sale by a covered person or any subsidiary of the bank is not backed by the Federal government or the bank, or the fact that the insurance product or annuity is not insured by the Federal Deposit Insurance Corporation;

(2) In the case of an insurance product or annuity that involves investment risk, the fact that there is an investment risk, including the potential that principal may be lost and that the product may decline in value; or

(3) In the case of a bank or subsidiary of the bank at which insurance products or annuities are sold or offered for sale, the fact that:

(i) The approval of an extension of credit to a consumer by the bank or subsidiary may not be conditioned on the purchase of an insurance product or annuity by the consumer from the bank or a subsidiary of the bank; and

(ii) The consumer is free to purchase the insurance product or annuity from another source.

(c) *Prohibition on domestic violence discrimination.* A covered person may not sell or offer for sale, as principal, agent, or broker, any life or health insurance product if the status of the applicant or insured as a victim of domestic violence or as a provider of services to victims of domestic violence is considered as a criterion in any decision with regard to insurance underwriting, pricing, renewal, or scope of coverage of such product, or with regard to the payment of insurance claims on such product, except as required or expressly permitted under State law.

12 C.F.R. § 14.40 What a covered person must disclose.

(a) *Insurance disclosures.* In connection with the initial purchase of an insurance product or annuity by a consumer from a covered person, a covered person must disclose to the consumer, except to the extent the disclosure would not be accurate, that:

(1) The insurance product or annuity is not a deposit or other obligation of, or guaranteed by, the bank or an affiliate of the bank;

(2) The insurance product or annuity is not insured by the Federal Deposit Insurance Corporation (FDIC) or any other agency of the United States, the bank, or (if applicable) an affiliate of the bank; and

(3) In the case of an insurance product or annuity that involves an investment risk, there is investment risk associated with the product, including the possible loss of value.

(b) *Credit disclosure.* In the case of an application for credit in connection with which an insurance product or annuity is solicited, offered, or sold, a covered person must disclose that the bank may not condition an extension of credit on either:

(1) The consumer's purchase of an insurance product or annuity from the bank or any of its affiliates; or

(2) The consumer's agreement not to obtain, or a prohibition on the consumer from obtaining, an insurance product or annuity from an unaffiliated entity.

(c) *Timing and method of disclosures.* (1) *In general.* The disclosures required by paragraph (a) of this section must be provided orally and in writing before the completion of the initial sale of an insurance product or annuity to a consumer. The disclosure required by paragraph (b) of this section must be made orally and in writing at the time the consumer applies for an extension of credit in connection with which an insurance product or annuity is solicited, offered, or sold.

(2) *Exception for transactions by mail.* If a sale of an insurance product or annuity is conducted by mail, a covered person is not required to make the oral disclosures required by paragraph (a) of this section. If a covered person takes an application for credit by mail, the covered person is not required to make the oral disclosure required by paragraph (b).

(3) *Exception for transactions by telephone.* If a sale of an insurance product or annuity is conducted by telephone, a covered person may provide the written disclosures required by paragraph (a) of this section by mail within 3 business days beginning on the first business day after the sale, excluding Sundays and the legal public holidays specified in 5 U.S.C. 6103(a). If a covered person takes an application for credit by telephone, the covered person may provide the written disclosure required by paragraph (b) of this section by mail, provided the covered person mails it to the consumer within three days beginning the first business day after the appli-

cation is taken, excluding Sundays and the legal public holidays specified in 5 U.S.C. 6103(a).

(4) *Electronic form of disclosures.* (i) Subject to the requirements of section 101(c) of the Electronic Signatures in Global and National Commerce Act (12 U.S.C. 7001(c)), a covered person may provide the written disclosures required by paragraph (a) and (b) of this section through electronic media instead of on paper, if the consumer affirmatively consents to receiving the disclosures electronically and if the disclosures are provided in a format that the consumer may retain or obtain later, for example, by printing or storing electronically (such as by downloading).

(ii) Any disclosures required by paragraphs (a) or (b) of this section that are provided by electronic media are not required to be provided orally.

(5) *Disclosures must be readily understandable.* The disclosures provided shall be conspicuous, simple, direct, readily understandable, and designed to call attention to the nature and significance of the information provided. For instance, a covered person may use the following disclosures in visual media, such as television broadcasting, ATM screens, billboards, signs, posters and written advertisements and promotional materials, as appropriate and consistent with paragraphs (a) and (b) of this section:

- NOT A DEPOSIT
- NOT FDIC-INSURED
- NOT INSURED BY ANY FEDERAL GOVERNMENT AGENCY
- NOT GUARANTEED BY THE BANK [OR SAVINGS ASSOCIATION]
- MAY GO DOWN IN VALUE

(6) *Disclosures must be meaningful.* (i) A covered person must provide the disclosures required by paragraphs (a) and (b) of this section in a meaningful form. Examples of the types of methods that could call attention to the nature and significance of the information provided include:

(A) A plain-language heading to call attention to the disclosures;

(B) A typeface and type size that are easy to read;

(C) Wide margins and ample line spacing;

(D) Boldface or italics for key words; and

(E) Distinctive type style, and graphic devices, such as shading or sidebars, when the disclosures are combined with other information.

(ii) A covered person has not provided the disclosures in a meaningful form if the covered person merely states to the consumer that the required disclosures are available in printed material, but does not provide the printed material when required and does not orally disclose the information to the consumer when required.

(iii) With respect to those disclosures made through electronic media for which paper or oral disclosures are not required, the disclosures are not meaningfully provided if the consumer may

bypass the visual text of the disclosures before purchasing an insurance product or annuity.

(7) *Consumer acknowledgment.* A covered person must obtain from the consumer, at the time a consumer receives the disclosures required under paragraphs (a) or (b) of this section, or at the time of the initial purchase by the consumer of an insurance product or annuity, a written acknowledgment by the consumer that the consumer received the disclosures. A covered person may permit a consumer to acknowledge receipt of the disclosures electronically or in paper form. If the disclosures required under paragraphs (a) or (b) of this section are provided in connection with a transaction that is conducted by telephone, a covered person must:

(i) Obtain an oral acknowledgment of receipt of the disclosures and maintain sufficient documentation to show that the acknowledgment was given; and

(ii) Make reasonable efforts to obtain a written acknowledgment from the consumer.

(d) *Advertisements and other promotional material for insurance products or annuities.* The disclosures described in paragraph (a) of this section are required in advertisements and promotional material for insurance products or annuities unless the advertisements and promotional materials are of a general nature describing or listing the services or products offered by the bank.

12 C.F.R. § 14.50 Where insurance activities may take place.

(a) *General rule.* A bank must, to the extent practicable, keep the area where the bank conducts transactions involving insurance products or annuities physically segregated from areas where retail deposits are routinely accepted from the general public, identify the areas where insurance product or annuity sales activities occur, and clearly delineate and distinguish those areas from the areas where the bank's retail deposit-taking activities occur.

(b) *Referrals.* Any person who accepts deposits from the public in an area where such transactions are routinely conducted in the bank may refer a consumer who seeks to purchase an insurance product or annuity to a qualified person who sells that product only if the person making the referral receives no more than a one-time, nominal fee of a fixed dollar amount for each referral that does not depend on whether the referral results in a transaction.

12 C.F.R. § 14.60 Qualification and licensing requirements for insurance sales personnel.

A bank may not permit any person to sell or offer for sale any insurance product or annuity in any part of its office or on its behalf, unless the person is at all times appropriately qualified and licensed under applicable State insurance licensing standards with regard to the specific products being sold or recommended.

Appendix A to Part 14—Consumer Grievance Process

Any consumer who believes that any bank or any other person selling, soliciting, advertising, or offering insurance products or annuities to the consumer at an office of the bank or on behalf of the bank has violated the requirements of this part should contact the Customer Assistance Group, Office of the Comptroller of the Currency, (800) 613-6743, 1301 McKinney Street, Suite 3710, Houston, Texas 77010-3031.

I.2.2 12 C.F.R. § 208—Membership of State Banking Institutions in the Federal Reserve System (Regulation H)

Subpart H—Consumer Protection in Sales of Insurance

§ 208.81   Purpose and scope.

§ 208.82   Definitions for purposes of this subpart.

§ 208.83   Prohibited practices.

§ 208.84   What you must disclose.

§ 208.85   Where insurance activities may take place.

§ 208.86   Qualification and licensing requirements for insurance sales personnel.

Appendix A to Subpart H Consumer Grievance Process

Authority: 12 U.S.C. 24, 36, 92a, 93a, 248(a), 248(c), 321–338a, 371d, 461, 481–486, 601, 611, 1814, 1816, 1818, 1820(d)(9), 1823(j), 1828(o), 1831, 1831o, 1831p-1, 1831r-1, 1831w, 1831x, 1835a, 1882, 2901–2907, 3105, 3310, 3331-3351, and 3906-3909; 15 U.S.C. 78b, 78l(b), 78l(g), 78l(i), 78o-4(c)(5), 78q, 78q-1, and 78w; 31 U.S.C. 5318, 42 U.S.C. 4012a, 4104a, 4104b, 4106, and 4128.

12 C.F.R. § 208.81 Purpose and scope.

This subpart establishes consumer protections in connection with retail sales practices, solicitations, advertising, or offers of any insurance product or annuity to a consumer by:

(a) Any state member bank; or

(b) Any other person that is engaged in such activities at an office of the bank or on behalf of the bank.

12 C.F.R. § 208.82 Definitions for purposes of this subpart.

As used in this subpart:

(a) *Affiliate* means a company that controls, is controlled by, or is under common control with another company.

(b) *Bank* means a state member bank.

(c) *Company* means any corporation, partnership, business trust, association or similar organization, or any other trust (unless by its terms the trust must terminate within twenty-five years or not later than twenty-one years and ten months after the death of individuals living on the effective date of the trust). It does not include any corporation the majority of the shares of which are owned by the United States or by any State, or a qualified family partnership, as defined in section 2(o)(10) of the Bank Holding Company Act of 1956, as amended (12 U.S.C. 1841(o)(10)).

(d) *Consumer* means an individual who purchases, applies to purchase, or is solicited to purchase from you insurance products or annuities primarily for personal, family, or household purposes.

(e) *Control* of a company has the same meaning as in section 3(w)(5) of the Federal Deposit Insurance Act (12 U.S.C. 1813(w)(5)).

(f) *Domestic violence* means the occurrence of one or more of the following acts by a current or former family member, household member, intimate partner, or caretaker:

(1) Attempting to cause or causing or threatening another person physical harm, severe emotional distress, psychological trauma, rape, or sexual assault;

(2) Engaging in a course of conduct or repeatedly committing acts toward another person, including following the person without proper authority, under circumstances that place the person in reasonable fear of bodily injury or physical harm;

(3) Subjecting another person to false imprisonment; or

(4) Attempting to cause or causing damage to property so as to intimidate or attempt to control the behavior of another person.

(g) *Electronic media* includes any means for transmitting messages electronically between you and a consumer in a format that allows visual text to be displayed on equipment, for example, a personal computer monitor.

(h) *Office* means the premises of a bank where retail deposits are accepted from the public.

(i) *Subsidiary* has the same meaning as in section 3(w)(4) of the Federal Deposit Insurance Act (12 U.S.C. 1813(w)(4)).

(j)(1) *You* means:

(i) A bank; or

(ii) Any other person only when the person sells, solicits, advertises, or offers an insurance product or annuity to a consumer at an office of the bank or on behalf of a bank.

(2) For purposes of this definition, activities on behalf of a bank include activities where a person, whether at an office of the bank or at another location sells, solicits, advertises, or offers an insurance product or annuity and at least one of the following applies:

(i) The person represents to a consumer that the sale, solicitation, advertisement, or offer of any insurance product or annuity is by or on behalf of the bank;

(ii) If the bank refers a consumer to a seller of insurance products or annuities and the bank has a contractual arrangement to receive commissions or fees derived from the sale of an insurance product or annuity resulting from that referral; or

(iii) Documents evidencing the sale, solicitation, advertising, or offer of an insurance product or annuity identify or refer to the bank.

12 C.F.R. § 208.83 Prohibited practices.

(a) *Anticoercion and antitying rules.* You may not engage in any practice that would lead a consumer to believe that an extension of credit, in violation of section 106(b) of the Bank Holding Company Act Amendments of 1970 (12 U.S.C. 1972), is conditional upon either:

(1) The purchase of an insurance product or annuity from the bank or any of its affiliates; or

(2) An agreement by the consumer not to obtain, or a prohibition on the consumer from obtaining, an insurance product or annuity from an unaffiliated entity.

(b) *Prohibition on misrepresentations generally.* You may not engage in any practice or use any advertisement at any office of, or on behalf of, the bank or a subsidiary of the bank that could mislead any person or otherwise cause a reasonable person to reach an erroneous belief with respect to:

(1) The fact that an insurance product or annuity sold or offered for sale by you or any subsidiary of the bank is not backed by the Federal government or the bank or the fact that the insurance product or annuity is not insured by the Federal Deposit Insurance Corporation;

(2) In the case of an insurance product or annuity that involves investment risk, the fact that there is an investment risk, including the potential that principal may be lost and that the product may decline in value; or

(3) In the case of a bank or subsidiary of the bank at which insurance products or annuities are sold or offered for sale, the fact that:

(i) The approval of an extension of credit to a consumer by the bank or subsidiary may not be conditioned on the purchase of an insurance product or annuity by the consumer from the bank or a subsidiary of the bank; and

(ii) The consumer is free to purchase the insurance product or annuity from another source.

(c) *Prohibition on domestic violence discrimination.* You may not sell or offer for sale, as principal, agent, or broker, any life or health insurance product if the status of the applicant or insured as a victim of domestic violence or as a provider of services to victims of domestic violence is considered as a criterion in any decision with regard to insurance underwriting, pricing, renewal, or scope of coverage of such product, or with regard to the payment of insurance claims on such product, except as required or expressly permitted under State law.

12 C.F.R. § 208.84 What you must disclose.

(a) *Insurance disclosures.* In connection with the initial purchase of an insurance product or annuity by a consumer from you, you must disclose to the consumer, except to the extent the disclosure would not be accurate, that:

(1) The insurance product or annuity is not a deposit or other obligation of, or guaranteed by, the bank or an affiliate of the bank;

(2) The insurance product or annuity is not insured by the Federal Deposit Insurance Corporation (FDIC) or any other agency of the United States, the bank, or (if applicable) an affiliate of the bank; and

(3) In the case of an insurance product or annuity that involves an investment risk, there is investment risk associated with the product, including the possible loss of value.

(b) *Credit disclosure.* In the case of an application for credit in connection with which an insurance product or annuity is solicited, offered, or sold, you must disclose that the bank may not condition an extension of credit on either:

(1) The consumer's purchase of an insurance product or annuity from the bank or any of its affiliates; or

(2) The consumer's agreement not to obtain, or a prohibition on the consumer from obtaining, an insurance product or annuity from an unaffiliated entity.

(c) *Timing and method of disclosures.* (1) *In general.* The disclosures required by paragraph (a) of this section must be provided orally and in writing before the completion of the initial sale of an insurance product or annuity to a consumer. The disclosure required by paragraph (b) of this section must be made orally and in writing at the time the consumer applies for an extension of credit in connection with which insurance is solicited, offered, or sold.

(2) *Exceptions for transactions by mail.* If a sale of an insurance product or annuity is conducted by mail, you are not required to make the oral disclosures required by paragraph (a) of this section. If you take an application for credit by mail, you are not required to make the oral disclosure required by paragraph (b) of this section.

(3) *Exception for transactions by telephone.* If a sale of an insurance product or annuity is conducted by telephone, you may provide the written disclosures required by paragraph (a) of this section by mail within 3 business days beginning on the first business day after the sale, excluding Sundays and the legal public holidays specified in 5 U.S.C 6103(a). If you take an application for such credit by telephone, you may provide the written disclosure required by paragraph (b) of this section by mail, provided you mail it to the consumer within three days beginning the first business day after the application is taken, excluding Sundays and the legal public holidays specified in 5 U.S.C. 6103(a).

(4) *Electronic form of disclosures.* (i) Subject to the requirements of section 101(c) of the Electronic Signatures in Global and National Commerce Act (12 U.S.C. 7001(c)), you may provide the written disclosures required by paragraphs (a) and (b) of this section through electronic media instead of on paper, if the consumer affirmatively consents to receiving the disclosures electronically and if the disclosures are provided in a format that the consumer may retain or obtain later, for example, by printing or storing electronically (such as by downloading).

(ii) Any disclosures required by paragraphs (a) or (b) of this section that are provided by electronic media are not required to be provided orally.

(5) *Disclosures must be readily understandable.* The disclosures provided shall be conspicuous, simple, direct, readily understandable, and designed to call attention to the nature and significance of the information provided. For instance, you may use the following disclosures, in visual media, such as television broadcasting, ATM screens, billboards, signs, posters and written advertisements and promotional materials, as appropriate and consistent with paragraphs (a) and (b) of this section:

- NOT A DEPOSIT
- NOT FDIC-INSURED
- NOT INSURED BY ANY FEDERAL GOVERNMENT AGENCY
- NOT GUARANTEED BY THE BANK
- MAY GO DOWN IN VALUE

(6) *Disclosures must be meaningful.* (i) You must provide the disclosures required by paragraphs (a) and (b) of this section in a meaningful form. Examples of the types of methods that could call attention to the nature and significance of the information provided include:

(A) A plain-language heading to call attention to the disclosures;

(B) A typeface and type size that are easy to read;

(C) Wide margins and ample line spacing;

(D) Boldface or italics for key words; and

(E) Distinctive type size, style, and graphic devices, such as shading or sidebars, when the disclosures are combined with other information.

(ii) You have not provided the disclosures in a meaningful form if you merely state to the consumer that the required disclosures are available in printed material, but you do not provide the printed material when required and do not orally disclose the information to the consumer when required.

(iii) With respect to those disclosures made through electronic media for which paper or oral disclosures are not required, the disclosures are not meaningfully provided if the consumer may bypass the visual text of the disclosures before purchasing an insurance product or annuity.

(7) *Consumer acknowledgment.* You must obtain from the consumer, at the time a consumer receives the disclosures required under paragraphs (a) or (b) of this section, or at the time of the initial purchase by the consumer of an insurance product or annuity, a written acknowledgment by the consumer that the consumer received the disclosures. You may permit a consumer to acknowledge receipt of the disclosures electronically or in paper form. If the disclosures required under paragraphs (a) or (b) of this section are provided in connection with a transaction that is conducted by telephone, you must:

(i) Obtain an oral acknowledgment of receipt of the disclosures and maintain sufficient documentation to show that the acknowledgment was given; and

(ii) Make reasonable efforts to obtain a written acknowledgment from the consumer.

(d) *Advertisements and other promotional material for insurance products or annuities.* The disclosures described in paragraph (a) of this section are required in advertisements and promotional material for insurance products or annuities unless the advertisements and promotional materials are of a general nature describing or listing the services or products offered by the bank.

12 C.F.R. § 208.85 Where insurance activities may take place.

(a) *General rule.* A bank must, to the extent practicable, keep the area where the bank conducts transactions involving insurance products or annuities physically segregated from areas where retail deposits are routinely accepted from the general public, identify the areas where insurance product or annuity sales activities occur, and clearly delineate and distinguish those areas from the areas where the bank's retail deposit-taking activities occur.

(b) *Referrals.* Any person who accepts deposits from the public in an area where such transactions are routinely conducted in the bank may refer a consumer who seeks to purchase an insurance product or annuity to a qualified person who sells that product only if the person making the referral receives no more than a one-time, nominal fee of a fixed dollar amount for each referral that does not depend on whether the referral results in a transaction.

12 C.F.R. § 208.86 Qualification and licensing requirements for insurance sales personnel.

A bank may not permit any person to sell or offer for sale any insurance product or annuity in any part of its office or on its behalf, unless the person is at all times appropriately qualified and licensed under applicable State insurance licensing standards with regard to the specific products being sold or recommended.

Appendix A to Subpart H—Consumer Grievance Process

Any consumer who believes that any bank or any other person selling, soliciting, advertising, or offering insurance products or annuities to the consumer at an office of the bank or on behalf of the bank has violated the requirements of this subpart should contact the Consumer Complaints Section, Division of Consumer and Community Affairs, Board of Governors of the Federal Reserve System at the following address: 20th & C Streets, NW, Washington, D.C. 20551.

I.2.3 12 C.F.R. Part 343—Federal Deposit Insurance Corporation Regulations Regarding Consumer Protection in Sales of Insurance

§ 343.10 Purpose and scope.
§ 343.20 Definitions.
§ 343.30 Prohibited practices.
§ 343.40 What you must disclose.
§ 343.50 Where insurance activities may take place.
§ 343.60 Qualification and licensing requirements for insurance sales personnel.

Appendix A to Part 343 Consumer Grievance Process

Authority: 12 U.S.C. 1819 (Seventh and Tenth); 12 U.S.C. 1831x.

12 C.F.R. § 343.10 Purpose and scope.

This part establishes consumer protections in connection with retail sales practices, solicitations, advertising, or offers of any insurance product or annuity to a consumer by:

(a) Any bank; or

(b) Any other person that is engaged in such activities at an office of the bank or on behalf of the bank.

12 C.F.R. § 343.20 Definitions.

As used in this part:

(a) *Affiliate* means a company that controls, is controlled by, or is under common control with another company.

(b) *Bank* means an FDIC-insured, state-chartered commercial or savings bank that is not a member of the Federal Reserve System and for which the FDIC is the appropriate federal banking agency pursuant to section 3(q) of the Federal Deposit Insurance Act (12 U.S.C. 1813(q)).

(c) *Company* means any corporation, partnership, business trust, association or similar organization, or any other trust (unless by its terms the trust must terminate within twenty-five years or not later than twenty-one years and ten months after the death of individuals living on the effective date of the trust). It does not include any corporation the majority of the shares of which are owned by the United States or by any State, or a qualified family partnership, as defined in section 2(o)(10) of the Bank Holding Company Act of 1956, as amended (12 U.S.C. 1841(o)(10)).

(d) *Consumer* means an individual who purchases, applies to purchase, or is solicited to purchase from you insurance products or annuities primarily for personal, family, or household purposes.

(e) *Control* of a company has the same meaning as in section 3(w)(5) of the Federal Deposit Insurance Act (12 U.S.C. 1813(w)(5)).

(f) *Domestic violence* means the occurrence of one or more of the following acts by a current or former family member, household member, intimate partner, or caretaker:

(1) Attempting to cause or causing or threatening another person physical harm, severe emotional distress, psychological trauma, rape, or sexual assault;

(2) Engaging in a course of conduct or repeatedly committing acts toward another person, including following the person without proper authority, under circumstances that place the person in reasonable fear of bodily injury or physical harm;

(3) Subjecting another person to false imprisonment; or

(4) Attempting to cause or causing damage to property so as to intimidate or attempt to control the behavior of another person.

(g) *Electronic media* includes any means for transmitting messages electronically between you and a consumer in a format that allows visual text to be displayed on equipment, for example, a personal computer monitor.

(h) *Office* means the premises of a bank where retail deposits are accepted from the public.

(i) *Subsidiary* has the same meaning as in section 3(w)(4) of the Federal Deposit Insurance Act (12 U.S.C. 1813(w)(4)).

(j) (1) *You* means:

(i) A bank; or

(ii) Any other person only when the person sells, solicits, advertises, or offers an insurance

product or annuity to a consumer at an office of the bank or on behalf of a bank.

(2) For purposes of this definition, activities on behalf of a bank include activities where a person, whether at an office of the bank or at another location sells, solicits, advertises, or offers an insurance product or annuity and at least one of the following applies:

(i) The person represents to a consumer that the sale, solicitation, advertisement, or offer of any insurance product or annuity is by or on behalf of the bank;

(ii) The bank refers a consumer to a seller of insurance products or annuities and the bank has a contractual arrangement to receive commissions or fees derived from a sale of an insurance product or annuity resulting from that referral; or

(iii) Documents evidencing the sale, solicitation, advertising, or offer of an insurance product or annuity identify or refer to the bank.

12 C.F.R. § 343.30 Prohibited practices.

(a) *Anticoercion and antitying rules.* You may not engage in any practice that would lead a consumer to believe that an extension of credit, in violation of section 106(b) of the Bank Holding Company Act Amendments of 1970 (12 U.S.C. 1972), is conditional upon either:

(1) The purchase of an insurance product or annuity from the bank or any of its affiliates; or

(2) An agreement by the consumer not to obtain, or a prohibition on the consumer from obtaining, an insurance product or annuity from an unaffiliated entity.

(b) *Prohibition on misrepresentations generally.* You may not engage in any practice or use any advertisement at any office of, or on behalf of, the bank or a subsidiary of the bank that could mislead any person or otherwise cause a reasonable person to reach an erroneous belief with respect to:

(1) The fact that an insurance product or annuity sold or offered for sale by you or any subsidiary of the bank is not backed by the Federal government or the bank, or the fact that the insurance product or annuity is not insured by the Federal Deposit Insurance Corporation;

(2) In the case of an insurance product or annuity that involves investment risk, the fact that there is an investment risk, including the potential that principal may be lost and that the product may decline in value; or

(3) In the case of a bank or subsidiary of the bank at which insurance products or annuities are sold or offered for sale, the fact that:

(i) The approval of an extension of credit to a consumer by the bank or subsidiary may not be conditioned on the purchase of an insurance product or annuity by the consumer from the bank or a subsidiary of the bank; and

(ii) The consumer is free to purchase the insurance product or annuity from another source.

(c) *Prohibition on domestic violence discrimination.* You may not sell or offer for sale, as principal, agent, or broker, any life or health insurance product if the status of the applicant or insured as a victim of domestic violence or as a provider of services to victims of domestic violence is considered as a criterion in any decision with regard to insurance underwriting, pricing, renewal, or scope of coverage of such product, or with regard to the payment of insurance claims on such product, except as required or expressly permitted under State law.

12 C.F.R. § 343.40 What you must disclose.

(a) *Insurance disclosures.* In connection with the initial purchase of an insurance product or annuity by a consumer from you, you must disclose to the consumer, except to the extent the disclosure would not be accurate, that:

(1) The insurance product or annuity is not a deposit or other obligation of, or guaranteed by, the bank or an affiliate of the bank;

(2) The insurance product or annuity is not insured by the Federal Deposit Insurance Corporation (FDIC) or any other agency of the United States, the bank, or (if applicable) an affiliate of the bank; and

(3) In the case of an insurance product or annuity that involves an investment risk, there is investment risk associated with the product, including the possible loss of value.

(b) *Credit disclosure.* In the case of an application for credit in connection with which an insurance product or annuity is solicited, offered, or sold, you must disclose that the bank may not condition an extension of credit on either:

(1) The consumer's purchase of an insurance product or annuity from the bank or any of its affiliates; or

(2) The consumer's agreement not to obtain, or a prohibition on the consumer from obtaining, an insurance product or annuity from an unaffiliated entity.

(c) *Timing and method of disclosures.* (1) *In general.* The disclosures required by paragraph (a) of this section must be provided orally and in writing before the completion of the initial sale of an insurance product or annuity to a consumer. The disclosure required by paragraph (b) of this section must be made orally and in writing at the time the consumer applies for an extension of credit in connection with which an insurance product or annuity is solicited, offered, or sold.

(2) *Exception for transactions by mail.* If a sale of an insurance product or annuity is conducted by mail, you are not required to make the oral disclosures required by paragraph (a) of this section. If you take an application for credit by mail, you are not required to make the oral disclosure required by paragraph (b).

(3) *Exception for transactions by telephone.* If a sale of an insurance product or annuity is conducted by telephone, you may provide the written disclosures required by paragraph (a) of this section by mail within 3 business days beginning on the first business day after the sale,

excluding Sundays and the legal public holidays specified in 5 U.S.C. 6103(a). If you take an application for credit by telephone, you may provide the written disclosure required by paragraph (b) of this section by mail, provided you mail it to the consumer within three days beginning the first business day after the application is taken, excluding Sundays and the legal public holidays specified in 5 U.S.C. 6103(a).

(4) *Electronic form of disclosures.* (i) Subject to the requirements of section 101(c) of the Electronic Signatures in Global and National Commerce Act (12 U.S.C. 7001(c)), you may provide the written disclosures required by paragraph (a) and (b) of this section through electronic media instead of on paper, if the consumer affirmatively consents to receiving the disclosures electronically and if the disclosures are provided in a format that the consumer may retain or obtain later, for example, by printing or storing electronically (such as by downloading).

(ii) Any disclosure required by paragraphs (a) or (b) of this section that is provided by electronic media is not required to be provided orally.

(5) *Disclosures must be readily understandable.* The disclosures provided shall be conspicuous, simple, direct, readily understandable, and designed to call attention to the nature and significance of the information provided. For instance, you may use the following disclosures in visual media, such as television broadcasting, ATM screens, billboards, signs, posters and written advertisements and promotional materials, as appropriate and consistent with paragraphs (a) and (b) of this section:

- NOT A DEPOSIT
- NOT FDIC-INSURED
- NOT INSURED BY ANY FEDERAL GOVERNMENT AGENCY
- NOT GUARANTEED BY THE BANK
- MAY GO DOWN IN VALUE

(6) *Disclosures must be meaningful.* (i) You must provide the disclosures required by paragraphs (a) and (b) of this section in a meaningful form. Examples of the types of methods that could call attention to the nature and significance of the information provided include:

(A) A plain-language heading to call attention to the disclosures;

(B) A typeface and type size that are easy to read;

(C) Wide margins and ample line spacing;

(D) Boldface or italics for key words; and

(E) Distinctive type size, style, and graphic devices, such as shading or sidebars, when the disclosures are combined with other information.

(ii) You have not provided the disclosures in a meaningful form if you merely state to the consumer that the required disclosures are available in printed material, but do not provide the printed material when required and do not orally disclose the information to the consumer when required.

(iii) With respect to those disclosures made through electronic media for which paper or oral

disclosures are not required, the disclosures are not meaningfully provided if the consumer may bypass the visual text of the disclosures before purchasing an insurance product or annuity.

(7) *Consumer acknowledgment.* You must obtain from the consumer, at the time a consumer receives the disclosures required under paragraphs (a) or (b) of this section, or at the time of the initial purchase by the consumer of an insurance product or annuity, a written acknowledgment by the consumer that the consumer received the disclosures. You may permit a consumer to acknowledge receipt of the disclosures electronically or in paper form. If the disclosures required under paragraphs (a) or (b) of this section are provided in connection with a transaction that is conducted by telephone, you must:

(i) Obtain an oral acknowledgment of receipt of the disclosures and maintain sufficient documentation to show that the acknowledgment was given; and

(ii) Make reasonable efforts to obtain a written acknowledgment from the consumer.

(d) *Advertisements and other promotional material for insurance products or annuities.* The disclosures described in paragraph (a) of this section are required in advertisements and promotional material for insurance products or annuities unless the advertisements and promotional materials are of a general nature describing or listing the services or products offered by the bank.

12 C.F.R. § 343.50 Where insurance activities may take place.

(a) *General rule.* A bank must, to the extent practicable, keep the area where the bank conducts transactions involving insurance products or annuities physically segregated from areas where retail deposits are routinely accepted from the general public, identify the areas where insurance product or annuity sales activities occur, and clearly delineate and distinguish those areas from the areas where the bank's retail deposit-taking activities occur.

(b) *Referrals.* Any person who accepts deposits from the public in an area where such transactions are routinely conducted in the bank may refer a consumer who seeks to purchase an insurance product or annuity to a qualified person who sells that product only if the person making the referral receives no more than a one-time, nominal fee of a fixed dollar amount for each referral that does not depend on whether the referral results in a transaction.

12 C.F.R. § 343.60 Qualification and licensing requirements for insurance sales personnel.

A bank may not permit any person to sell or offer for sale any insurance product or annuity in any part of its office or on its behalf, unless the person is at all times appropriately qualified and licensed under applicable State insurance licensing standards with regard to the specific products being sold or recommended.

Appendix A to Part 343—Consumer Grievance Process

Any consumer who believes that any bank or any other person selling, soliciting, advertising, or offering insurance products or annuities to the consumer at an office of the bank or on behalf of the bank has violated the requirements of this part should contact the Division of Compliance and Consumer Affairs, Federal Deposit Insurance Corporation, at the following address: 550 17th Street, NW., Washington, DC 20429, or telephone 202-942-3100 or 800-934-3342, or e-mail dcainternet@fdic.gov.

I.2.4 12 C.F.R. Part 536—Office of Thrift Supervision Regulations Regarding Consumer Protection in Sales of Insurance

§ 536.10   Purpose and scope.

§ 536.20   Definitions.

§ 536.30   Prohibited practices.

§ 536.40   What you must disclose.

§ 536.50   Where insurance activities may take place.

§ 536.60   Qualification and licensing requirements for insurance sales personnel.

Appendix A to Part 536 Consumer Grievance Process.

Authority: 12 U.S.C. 1462a, 1463, 1464, 1467a, and 1831x.

12 C.F.R. § 536.10 Purpose and scope.

(a) *General rule.* This part establishes consumer protections in connection with retail sales practices, solicitations, advertising, or offers of any insurance product or annuity to a consumer by:

(1) Any savings association; or

(2) Any other person that is engaged in such activities at an office of a savings association or on behalf of a savings association.

(b) *Application to operating subsidiaries.* For purposes of § 559.3(h) of this chapter, an operating subsidiary is subject to this part only to the extent that it sells, solicits, advertises, or offers insurance products or annuities at an office of a savings association or on behalf of a savings association.

12 C.F.R. § 536.20 Definitions.

As used in this part:

Affiliate means a company that controls, is controlled by, or is under common control with another company.

Company means any corporation, partnership, business trust, association or similar organization, or any other trust (unless by its terms the trust must terminate within twenty-five years or not later than twenty-one years and ten months after the death of individuals living on the effective date of the trust). It does not include any corporation the majority of the shares of which are owned by the United States or by any State, or a qualified family partnership, as defined in section 2(o)(10) of the Bank Holding Company Act of 1956, as amended (12 U.S.C. 1841(o)(10)).

Consumer means an individual who purchases, applies to purchase, or is solicited to purchase from a covered person insurance products or annuities primarily for personal, family, or household purposes.

Control of a company has the same meaning as in section 3(w)(5) of the Federal Deposit Insurance Act (12 U.S.C. 1813(w)(5)).

Domestic violence means the occurrence of one or more of the following acts by a current or former family member, household member, intimate partner, or caretaker:

(1) Attempting to cause or causing or threatening another person physical harm, severe emotional distress, psychological trauma, rape, or sexual assault;

(2) Engaging in a course of conduct or repeatedly committing acts toward another person, including following the person without proper authority, under circumstances that place the person in reasonable fear of bodily injury or physical harm;

(3) Subjecting another person to false imprisonment; or

(4) Attempting to cause or causing damage to property so as to intimidate or attempt to control the behavior of another person.

Electronic media includes any means for transmitting messages electronically between a covered person and a consumer in a format that allows visual text to be displayed on equipment, for example, a personal computer monitor.

Office means the premises of a savings association where retail deposits are accepted from the public.

Subsidiary has the same meaning as in section 3(w)(4) of the Federal Deposit Insurance Act (12 U.S.C. 1813(w)(4)).

You means:

(1) A savings association, as defined in § 561.43 of this chapter; or

(2) Any other person only when the person sells, solicits, advertises, or offers an insurance product or annuity to a consumer at an office of a savings association, or on behalf of a savings association. For purposes of this definition, activities on behalf of a savings association include

activities where a person, whether at an office of the savings association or at another location, sells, solicits, advertises, or offers an insurance product or annuity and at least one of the following applies:

(i) The person represents to a consumer that the sale, solicitation, advertisement, or offer of any insurance product or annuity is by or on behalf of the savings association;

(ii) The savings association refers a consumer to a seller of insurance products and annuities and the savings association has a contractual arrangement to receive commissions or fees derived from a sale of an insurance product or annuity resulting from that referral; or

(iii) Documents evidencing the sale, solicitation, advertising, or offer of an insurance product or annuity identify or refer to the savings association.

12 C.F.R. § 536.30 Prohibited practices.

(a) *Anticoercion and antitying rules.* You may not engage in any practice that would lead a consumer to believe that an extension of credit, in violation of section 5(q) of the Home Owners' Loan Act (12 U.S.C. 1464(q)), is conditional upon either:

(1) The purchase of an insurance product or annuity from a savings association or any of its affiliates; or

(2) An agreement by the consumer not to obtain, or a prohibition on the consumer from obtaining, an insurance product or annuity from an unaffiliated entity.

(b) *Prohibition on misrepresentations generally.* You may not engage in any practice or use any advertisement at any office of, or on behalf of, a savings association or a subsidiary of a savings association that could mislead any person or otherwise cause a reasonable person to reach an erroneous belief with respect to:

(1) The fact that an insurance product or annuity you or any subsidiary of a savings association sell or offer for sale is not backed by the Federal government or a savings association, or the fact that the insurance product or annuity is not insured by the Federal Deposit Insurance Corporation;

(2) In the case of an insurance product or annuity that involves investment risk, the fact that there is an investment risk, including the potential that principal may be lost and that the product may decline in value; or

(3) In the case of a savings association or subsidiary of a savings association at which insurance products or annuities are sold or offered for sale, the fact that:

(i) The approval of an extension of credit to a consumer by the savings association or subsidiary may not be conditioned on the purchase of an insurance product or annuity by the consumer from the savings association or a subsidiary of a savings association; and

(ii) The consumer is free to purchase the insurance product or annuity from another source.

(c) *Prohibition on domestic violence discrimination.* You may not sell or offer for sale, as principal, agent, or broker, any life or health insurance product if the status of the applicant or insured as a victim of domestic violence or as a provider of services to victims of domestic violence is considered as a criterion in any decision with regard to insurance underwriting, pricing, renewal, or scope of coverage of such product, or with regard to the payment of insurance claims on such product, except as required or expressly permitted under State law.

12 C.F.R. § 536.40 What you must disclose.

(a) *Insurance disclosures.* In connection with the initial purchase of an insurance product or annuity by a consumer from you, you must disclose to the consumer, except to the extent the disclosure would not be accurate, that:

(1) The insurance product or annuity is not a deposit or other obligation of, or guaranteed by, a savings association or an affiliate of a savings association;

(2) The insurance product or annuity is not insured by the Federal Deposit Insurance Corporation (FDIC) or any other agency of the United States, a savings association, or (if applicable) an affiliate of a savings association; and

(3) In the case of an insurance product or annuity that involves an investment risk, there is investment risk associated with the product, including the possible loss of value.

(b) *Credit disclosures.* In the case of an application for credit in connection with which an insurance product or annuity is solicited, offered, or sold, you must disclose that a savings association may not condition an extension of credit on either:

(1) The consumer's purchase of an insurance product or annuity from the savings association or any of its affiliates; or

(2) The consumer's agreement not to obtain, or a prohibition on the consumer from obtaining, an insurance product or annuity from an unaffiliated entity.

(c) *Timing and method of disclosures.* (1) *In general.* The disclosures required by paragraph (a) of this section must be provided orally and in writing before the completion of the initial sale of an insurance product or annuity to a consumer. The disclosure required by paragraph (b) of this section must be made orally and in writing at the time the consumer applies for an extension of credit in connection with which an insurance product or annuity is solicited, offered, or sold.

(2) *Exception for transactions by mail.* If you conduct an insurance product or annuity sale by mail, you are not required to make the oral disclosures required by paragraph (a) of this section. If you take an application for credit by

mail, you are not required to make the oral disclosure required by paragraph (b) of this section.

(3) *Exception for transactions by telephone.* If a sale of an insurance product or annuity is conducted by telephone, you may provide the written disclosures required by paragraph (a) of this section by mail within 3 business days beginning on the first business day after the sale, solicitation, or offer, excluding Sundays and the legal public holidays specified in 5 U.S.C. 6103(a). If you take an application for credit by telephone, you may provide the written disclosure required by paragraph (b) of this section by mail, provided you mail it to the consumer within three days beginning the first business day after the application is taken, excluding Sundays and the legal public holidays specified in 5 U.S.C. 6103(a).

(4) *Electronic form of disclosures.* (i) Subject to the requirements of section 101(c) of the Electronic Signatures in Global and National Commerce Act (12 U.S.C. 7001(c)), you may provide the written disclosures required by paragraph (a) and (b) of this section through electronic media instead of on paper, if the consumer affirmatively consents to receiving the disclosures electronically and if the disclosures are provided in a format that the consumer may retain or obtain later, for example, by printing or storing electronically (such as by downloading).

(ii) You are not required to provide orally any disclosures required by paragraphs (a) or (b) of this section that you provide by electronic media.

(5) *Disclosures must be readily understandable.* The disclosures provided shall be conspicuous, simple, direct, readily understandable, and designed to call attention to the nature and significance of the information provided. For instance, you may use the following disclosures in visual media, such as television broadcasting, ATM screens, billboards, signs, posters and written advertisements and promotional materials, as appropriate and consistent with paragraphs (a) and (b) of this section:

- NOT A DEPOSIT
- NOT FDIC-INSURED
- NOT INSURED BY ANY FEDERAL GOVERNMENT AGENCY
- NOT GUARANTEED BY THE SAVINGS ASSOCIATION
- MAY GO DOWN IN VALUE

(6) *Disclosures must be meaningful.* (i) You must provide the disclosures required by paragraphs (a) and (b) of this section in a meaningful form. Examples of the types of methods that could call attention to the nature and significance of the information provided include:

(A) A plain-language heading to call attention to the disclosures;

(B) A typeface and type size that are easy to read;

(C) Wide margins and ample line spacing;

(D) Boldface or italics for key words; and

(E) Distinctive type size, style, and graphic devices, such as shading or sidebars, when the disclosures are combined with other information.

(ii) You have not provided the disclosures in a meaningful form if you merely state to the consumer that the required disclosures are available in printed material, but do not provide the printed material when required and do not orally disclose the information to the consumer when required.

(iii) With respect to those disclosures made through electronic media for which paper or oral disclosures are not required, the disclosures are not meaningfully provided if the consumer may bypass the visual text of the disclosures before purchasing an insurance product or annuity.

(7) *Consumer acknowledgment.* You must obtain from the consumer, at the time a consumer receives the disclosures required under paragraphs (a) or (b) of this section, or at the time of the initial purchase by the consumer of an insurance product or annuity, a written acknowledgment by the consumer that the consumer received the disclosures. You may permit a consumer to acknowledge receipt of the disclosures electronically or in paper form. If the disclosures required under paragraphs (a) or (b) of this section are provided in connection with a transaction that is conducted by telephone, you must:

(i) Obtain an oral acknowledgment of receipt of the disclosures and maintain sufficient documentation to show that the acknowledgment was given; and

(ii) Make reasonable efforts to obtain a written acknowledgment from the consumer.

(d) *Advertisements and other promotional material for insurance products or annuities.* The disclosures described in paragraph (a) of this section are required in advertisements and promotional material for insurance products or annuities unless the advertisements and promotional material are of a general nature describing or listing the services or products offered by a savings association.

12 C.F.R. § 536.50 Where insurance activities may take place.

(a) *General rule.* A savings association must, to the extent practicable:

(1) Keep the area where the savings association conducts transactions involving insurance products or annuities physically segregated from areas where retail deposits are routinely accepted from the general public;

(2) Identify the areas where insurance product or annuity sales activities occur; and

(3) Clearly delineate and distinguish those areas from the areas where the savings association's retail deposit-taking activities occur.

(b) *Referrals.* Any person who accepts deposits from the public in an area where such transactions are routinely conducted in a savings association may refer a consumer who seeks to purchase an insurance product or annuity to a qualified person who sells that product only if the person making the referral receives no more than a one-time, nominal fee of a fixed dollar amount for each referral that does not depend on whether the referral results in a transaction.

12 C.F.R. § 536.60 Qualification and licensing requirements for insurance sales personnel.

A savings association may not permit any person to sell or offer for sale any insurance product or annuity in any part of the savings association's office or on its behalf, unless the person is at all times appropriately qualified and licensed under applicable State insurance licensing standards with regard to the specific products being sold or recommended.

Appendix A to Part 536—Consumer Grievance Process

Any consumer who believes that any savings association or any other person selling, soliciting, advertising, or offering insurance products or annuities to the consumer at an office of the savings association or on behalf of the savings association has violated the requirements of this part should contact the Director, Consumer Programs, Office of Thrift Supervision, at the following address: 1700 G Street, NW, Washington, DC 20552, or telephone 202-906-6237 or 800-842-6929, or e-mail consumer.complaint@ots.treas.gov.

Appendix J   Other Federal Statutory Limits on Credit Terms

This appendix collects provisions from a variety of federal laws that regulate the cost of credit in certain circumstances and which do not appear in other appendices. One imposes a lifetime interest rate cap in adjustable rate mortgages, another prohibits the use of the Rule of 78's in certain loans, and the last sets a usury cap for loans made to servicemembers before entering active duty. These provisions are also found on the companion CD-Rom.

J.1 Adjustable Rate Mortgages Caps

Competitive Equality Banking Act of 1987, 12 U.S.C. § 3806, Pub. L. No. 100-86, 101 Stat. 662, tit. XII, § 1204 (Aug. 10, 1987), *as amended by* Pub. L. No. 102-550, 106 Stat. 3893, tit. IX, § 952 (Oct. 28, 1992).

This legislation requires that each adjustable rate mortgage loan specify a maximum rate that can apply to the loan (a "lifetime cap"), though it does not place any limitation on the value of the cap.

TITLE 12. BANKS AND BANKING

CHAPTER 39—ALTERNATIVE MORTGAGE TRANSACTIONS

12 U.S.C. § 3806. Adjustable rate mortgage caps

(a) In general

Any adjustable rate mortgage loan originated by a creditor shall include a limitation on the maximum interest rate that may apply during the term of the mortgage loan.

(b) Regulations

The Board of Governors of the Federal Reserve System shall prescribe regulations to carry out the purposes of this section.

(c) Enforcement

Any violation of this section shall be treated as a violation of the Truth in Lending Act [15 U.S.C. § 1601 *et seq.*] and shall be subject to administrative enforcement under section 108 [15 U.S.C. § 1607] or civil damages under section 130 of such Act [15 U.S.C. § 1640], or both.

(d) Definitions

For the purpose of this section—

(1) the term "creditor" means a person who regularly extends credit for personal, family, or household purposes; and

(2) the term "adjustable rate mortgage loan" means any consumer loan secured by a lien on a one- to four-family dwelling unit, including a condominium unit, cooperative housing unit, or mobile home, where the loan is made pursuant to an agreement under which the creditor may, from time to time, adjust the rate of interest.

(e) Effective date

This section shall take effect upon the expiration of 120 days after August 10, 1987.

[Pub. L. No. 100-86, tit. XII, § 1204, 101 Stat. 662 (Aug. 10, 1987); Pub. L. No. 102-550, tit. IX, § 952, 106 Stat. 3893 (Oct. 28, 1992)]

J.2 Federal Rebate Statute

Housing and Community Development Act of 1992, 15 U.S.C. § 1615, Pub. L. No. 102-550, 106 Stat. 3891, tit. IX, § 933 (Oct. 28, 1992).

Though codified within the Truth in Lending Act, this statute was not enacted as part of that Act.

TITLE 15. COMMERCE AND TRADE

CHAPTER 41—CONSUMER CREDIT PROTECTION

SUBCHAPTER I—CONSUMER CREDIT COST DISCLOSURE

Part A—General Provisions

15 U.S.C. § 1615. Prohibition on use of "Rule of 78's" in connection with mortgage refinancings and other consumer loans

(a) Prompt refund of unearned interest required

(1) In general

If a consumer prepays in full the financed amount under any consumer credit transaction, the creditor shall promptly refund any unearned portion of the interest charge to the consumer.

(2) Exception for refund of de minimis amount

No refund shall be required under paragraph (1) with respect to the prepayment of any consumer credit transaction if the total amount of the refund would be less than $1.

(3) Applicability to refinanced transactions and acceleration by the creditor

This subsection shall apply with respect to any prepayment of a consumer credit transaction described in paragraph (1) without regard to the manner or the reason for the prepayment, including—

(A) any prepayment made in connection with the refinancing, consolidation, or restructuring of the transaction; and

(B) any prepayment made as a result of the acceleration of the obligation to repay the amount due with respect to the transaction.

(b) Use of "Rule of 78's" prohibited

For the purpose of calculating any refund of interest required under subsection (a) of this section for any precomputed consumer credit transaction of a term exceeding 61 months which is consummated after September 30, 1993, the creditor shall compute the refund based on a method which is at least as favorable to the consumer as the actuarial method.

(c) Statement of prepayment amount

(1) In general

Before the end of the 5-day period beginning on the date an oral or written request is received by a creditor from a consumer for the disclosure of the amount due on any precomputed consumer credit account, the creditor or assignee shall provide the consumer with a statement of—

(A) the amount necessary to prepay the account in full; and

(B) if the amount disclosed pursuant to subparagraph (A) includes an amount which is required to be refunded under this section with respect to such prepayment, the amount of such refund.

(2) Written statement required if request is in writing

If the customer's request is in writing, the statement under paragraph (1) shall be in writing.

(3) 1 free annual statement

A consumer shall be entitled to obtain 1 statement under paragraph (1) each year without charge.

(4) Additional statements subject to reasonable fees

Any creditor may impose a reasonable fee to cover the cost of providing any statement under paragraph (1) to any consumer in addition to the 1 free annual statement required under paragraph (3) if the amount of the charge for such additional statement is disclosed to the consumer before furnishing such statement.

(d) Definitions

For the purpose of this section—

(1) Actuarial method

The term "actuarial method" means the method of allocating payments made on a debt between the amount financed and the finance charge pursuant to which a payment is applied first to the accumulated finance charge and any remainder is subtracted from, or any deficiency is added to, the unpaid balance of the amount financed.

(2) Consumer, credit

The terms "consumer" and "creditor" have the meanings given to such terms in section 1602 of this title.

(3) Creditor

The term "creditor"—

(A) has the meaning given to such term in section 1602 of this title; and

(B) includes any assignee of any creditor with respect to credit extended in connection with any consumer credit transaction and any subsequent assignee with respect to such credit.

[Pub. L. No. 102-550, tit. IX, § 933, 106 Stat. 3891 (Oct. 28, 1992)]

J.3 Servicemembers Civil Relief Act

TITLE 50 APPENDIX. WAR AND NATIONAL DEFENSE SERVICEMEMBERS CIVIL RELIEF ACT

TITLE I.—GENERAL PROVISIONS

* * *

§ 511.   Definitions

* * *

TITLE II.—GENERAL RELIEF

* * *

§ 527.   Maximum rate of interest on debts incurred before military service

* * *

TITLE 50 APPENDIX. WAR AND NATIONAL DEFENSE

SERVICEMEMBERS CIVIL RELIEF ACT

TITLE I.—GENERAL PROVISIONS

* * *

50 U.S.C. app. § 511. Definitions

For the purposes of this Act [sections 501 to 596 of this Appendix]:

(1) Servicemember

The term "servicemember" means a member of the uniformed services, as that term is defined in section 101(a)(5) of title 10, United States Code.

(2) Military service

The term "military service" means—

(A) in the case of a servicemember who is a member of the Army, Navy, Air Force, Marine Corps, or Coast Guard—

(i) active duty, as defined in section 101(d)(1) of title 10, United States Code, and

(ii) in the case of a member of the National Guard, includes service under a call to active service authorized by the President or the Secretary of Defense for a period of more than 30 consecutive days under section 502(f) of title 32, United States Code, for purposes of responding to a national emergency declared by the President and supported by Federal funds;

(B) in the case of a servicemember who is a commissioned officer of the Public Health Service or the National Oceanic and Atmospheric Administration, active service; and

(C) any period during which a servicemember is absent from duty on account of sickness, wounds, leave, or other lawful cause.

(3) Period of military service

The term "period of military service" means the period beginning on the date on which a servicemember enters military service and ending on the date on which the servicemember is released from military service or dies while in military service.

(4) Dependent

The term "dependent", with respect to a servicemember, means—

(A) the servicemember's spouse;

(B) the servicemember's child (as defined in section 101(4) of title 38, United States Code); or

(C) an individual for whom the servicemember provided more than one-half of the individual's support for 180 days immediately preceding an application for relief under this Act [sections 501 to 596 of this Appendix].

(5) Court

The term "court" means a court or an administrative agency of the United States or of any State (including any political subdivision of a State), whether or not a court or administrative agency of record.

(6) State

The term "State" includes—

(A) a commonwealth, territory, or possession of the United States; and

(B) the District of Columbia.

(7) Secretary concerned

The term "Secretary concerned"—

(A) with respect to a member of the armed forces, has the meaning given that term in section 101(a)(9) of title 10, United States Code;

(B) with respect to a commissioned officer of the Public Health Service, means the Secretary of Health and Human Services; and

(C) with respect to a commissioned officer of the National Oceanic and Atmospheric Administration, means the Secretary of Commerce.

(8) Motor vehicle

The term "motor vehicle" has the meaning given that term in section 30102(a)(6) of title 49, United States Code.

(9) Judgment

The term "judgment" means any judgment, decree, order, or ruling, final or temporary.

[Oct. 17, 1940, ch. 888, § 101, *as added* Pub. L. No. 108-189, § 1, 117 Stat. 2836 (Dec. 19, 2003); Pub. L. No. 108-454, tit. VII, § 701, 118 Stat. 3624 (Dec. 10, 2004)]

* * *

TITLE II.—GENERAL RELIEF

* * *

50 U.S.C. app. § 527. Maximum rate of interest on debts incurred before military service

(a) Interest rate limitation

(1) Limitation to 6 percent

An obligation or liability bearing interest at a rate in excess of 6 percent per year that is incurred by a servicemember, or the servicemember and the servicemember's spouse jointly, before the servicemember enters military service shall not bear interest at a rate in excess of 6 percent per year during the period of military service.

(2) Forgiveness of interest in excess of 6 percent

Interest at a rate in excess of 6 percent per year that would otherwise be incurred but for the prohibition in paragraph (1) is forgiven.

(3) Prevention of acceleration of principal

The amount of any periodic payment due from a servicemember under the terms of the instrument that created an obligation or liability covered by this section shall be reduced by the amount of the interest forgiven under paragraph (2) that is allocable to the period for which such payment is made.

(b) Implementation of limitation

(1) Written notice to creditor

In order for an obligation or liability of a servicemember to be subject to the interest rate limitation in subsection (a), the servicemember shall provide to the creditor written notice and a copy of the military orders calling the servicemember to military service and any orders further extending military service, not later than 180 days after the date of the servicemember's termination or release from military service.

(2) Limitation effective as of date of order to active duty

Upon receipt of written notice and a copy of orders calling a servicemember to military service, the creditor shall treat the debt in accordance with subsection (a), effective as of the date on which the servicemember is called to military service.

(c) Creditor protection

A court may grant a creditor relief from the limitations of this section if, in the opinion of the court, the ability of the servicemember to pay interest upon the obligation or liability at a rate in excess of 6 percent per year is not materially affected by reason of the servicemember's military service.

(d) Interest

As used in this section, the term "interest" includes service charges, renewal charges, fees, or any other charges (except bona fide insurance) with respect to an obligation or liability.

[Oct. 17, 1940, ch. 888, § 207, *as added* Pub. L. No. 108-189, § 1, 117 Stat. 2844 (Dec. 19, 2003)]

Appendix K   Real Estate Settlement Procedures Act

This appendix excerpts portions of the Real Estate Settlement Procedures Act (RESPA). These provisions appear in K.1. Section K.2 includes selected regulations promulgated by the Department of Housing and Urban Development (HUD). In addition, HUD has issued two formal Policy Statements that appear in full in K.3. Finally, informal HUD letters are reproduced in full in K.4. All of these materials are also found on the companion CD-Rom.

K.1 Selected Statutory Provisions

TITLE 12—BANKS AND BANKING

CHAPTER 27—REAL ESTATE SETTLEMENT PROCEDURES

§ 2601.	Congressional findings and purpose
§ 2602.	Definitions
§ 2603.	Uniform settlement statement
§ 2604.	Special information booklets
§ 2605.	Servicing of mortgage loans and administration of escrow accounts.
§ 2606.	Exempted transactions
§ 2607.	Prohibition against kickbacks and unearned fees
§ 2608.	Title companies; liability of seller
§ 2609.	Limitation on requirement of advance deposits in escrow accounts
§ 2610.	Prohibition of fees for preparation of truth-in-lending, uniform settlement, and escrow account statements
§§ 2611–2613	[Repealed]
§ 2614.	Jurisdiction of courts; limitations
§ 2615.	Contracts and liens; validity
§ 2616.	State laws unaffected; inconsistent Federal and State provisions
§ 2617.	Authority of Secretary

12 U.S.C. § 2601. Congressional findings and purpose

(a) The Congress finds that significant reforms in the real estate settlement process are needed to insure that consumers throughout the Nation are provided with greater and more timely information on the nature and costs of the settlement process and are protected from unnecessarily high settlement charges caused by certain abusive practices that have developed in some areas of the country. The Congress also finds that it has been over two years since the Secretary of Housing and Urban Development and the Administrator of Veterans' Affairs submitted their joint report to the Congress on "Mortgage Settlement Costs" and that the time has come for the recommendations for Federal legislative action made in that report to be implemented.

(b) It is the purpose of this chapter to effect certain changes in the settlement process for residential real estate that will result—

    (1) in more effective advance disclosure to home buyers and sellers of settlement costs;

    (2) in the elimination of kickbacks or referral fees that tend to increase unnecessarily the costs of certain settlement services;

    (3) in a reduction in the amounts home buyers are required to place in escrow accounts established to insure the payment of real estate taxes and insurance; and

    (4) in significant reform and modernization of local recordkeeping of land title information.

[Pub. L. No. 93-533, § 2, 88 Stat. 1724 (Dec. 22, 1974).]

12 U.S.C. § 2602. Definitions

For purposes of this chapter—

    (1) the term "federally related mortgage loan" includes any loan (other than temporary financing such as a construction loan) which—

      (A) is secured by a first or subordinate lien on residential real property (including individual units of condominiums and cooperatives) designed principally for the occupancy of from one to four families, including any such secured loan, the proceeds of which are used to prepay or pay off an existing loan secured by the same property; and

      (B)

        (i) is made in whole or in part by any lender the deposits or accounts of which are insured by any agency of the Federal Government, or is made in whole or in part by any lender which is regulated by any agency of the Federal Government, or

        (ii) is made in whole or in part, or insured, guaranteed, supplemented, or assisted in any way, by the Secretary or any other officer or agency of the Federal Government or under or in connection with a housing or urban development program administered by the Secretary or a housing or related program administered by any other such officer or agency; or

        (iii) is intended to be sold by the originating lender to the Federal National Mortgage Association, the Government National Mortgage Association, the Federal Home Loan Mortgage Corporation, or a financial institution from which it is to be purchased by the Federal Home Loan Mortgage Corporation; or

(iv) is made in whole or in part by any "creditor", as defined in section 1602(f) of title 15, who makes or invests in residential real estate loans aggregating more than $1,000,000 per year, except that for the purpose of this chapter, the term "creditor" does not include any agency or instrumentality of any State;

(2) the term "thing of value" includes any payment, advance, funds, loan, service, or other consideration;

(3) the term "settlement services" includes any service provided in connection with a real estate settlement including, but not limited to, the following: title searches, title examinations, the provision of title certificates, title insurance, services rendered by an attorney, the preparation of documents, property surveys, the rendering of credit reports or appraisals, pest and fungus inspections, services rendered by a real estate agent or broker, the origination of a federally related mortgage loan (including, but not limited to, the taking of loan applications, loan processing, and the underwriting and funding of loans), and the handling of the processing, and closing or settlement;

(4) the term "title company" means any institution which is qualified to issue title insurance, directly or through its agents, and also refers to any duly authorized agent of a title company;

(5) the term "person" includes individuals, corporations, associations, partnerships, and trusts;

(6) the term "Secretary" means the Secretary of Housing and Urban Development;

(7) the term "affiliated business arrangement" means an arrangement in which

(A) a person who is in a position to refer business incident to or a part of a real estate settlement service involving a federally related mortgage loan, or an associate of such person, has either an affiliate relationship with or a direct or beneficial ownership interest of more than 1 percent in a provider of settlement services; and

(B) either of such persons directly or indirectly refers such business to that provider or affirmatively influences the selection of that provider; and

(8) the term "associate" means one who has one or more of the following relationships with a person in a position to refer settlement business:

(A) a spouse, parent, or child of such person;

(B) a corporation or business entity that controls, is controlled by, or is under common control with such person;

(C) an employer, officer, director, partner, franchisor, or franchisee of such person; or

(D) anyone who has an agreement, arrangement, or understanding, with such person, the purpose or substantial effect of which is to enable the person in a position to refer settlement business to benefit financially from the referrals of such business.

[(Pub. L. No. 93–533, § 3, 88 Stat. 1724 (Dec. 22, 1974); Pub. L. No. 94–205, § 2, 89 Stat. 1157 (Jan. 2, 1976); Pub. L. No. 98–181, tit. IV, § 461(a), 97 Stat. 1230 (Nov. 30, 1983); Pub. L. No. 102–550, tit. IX, § 908(a), (b), 106 Stat. 3873, 3874 (Oct. 28, 1992); Pub. L. No. 104–208, div. A, tit. II, § 2103(c)(1), 110 Stat. 3009–400(Sept. 30, 1996)]

12 U.S.C. § 2603. Uniform settlement statement

(a) The Secretary, in consultation with the Administrator of Veteran's Affairs, the Federal Deposit Insurance Corporation, and the Director of the Office of Thrift Supervision, shall develop and prescribe a standard form for the statement of settlement costs which shall be used (with such variations as may be necessary to reflect differences in legal and administrative requirements or practices in different areas of the country) as the standard real estate settlement form in all transactions in the United States which involve federally related mortgage loans. Such form shall conspicuously and clearly itemize all charges imposed upon the borrower and all charges imposed upon the seller in connection with the settlement and shall indicate whether any title insurance premium included in such charges covers or insures the lender's interest in the property, the borrower's interest, or both. The Secretary may, by regulation, permit the deletion from the form prescribed under this section of items which are not, under local laws or customs, applicable in any locality, except that such regulation shall require that the numerical code prescribed by the Secretary be retained in forms to be used in all localities. Nothing in this section may be construed to require that that part of the standard form which relates to the borrower's transaction be furnished to the seller, or to require that that part of the standard form which relates to the seller be furnished to the borrower.

(b) The form prescribed under this section shall be completed and for inspection by the borrower at or before settlement by the person conducting the settlement, except that

(1) the Secretary may exempt from the requirements of this section settlements occurring in localities where the final settlement statement is not customarily provided at or before the date of settlement, or settlements where such requirements are impractical and

(2) the borrower may, in accordance with regulations of the Secretary, waive his right to have the form made available at such time. Upon the request of the borrower to inspect the form prescribed under this section during the business day immediately preceding the day of settlement, the person who will conduct the settlement shall permit the borrower to inspect those items which are known to such person during such preceding day.

[Pub. L. No. 93–533, § 4, 88 Stat. 1725 (Dec. 22, 1974); Pub. L. No. 94–205, § 3, 89 Stat. 1157 (Jan. 2, 1976); Pub. L. No. 104–208, div. A, tit. II, § 2103(g)(1), 110 Stat. 3009–401 (Sept. 30, 1996)]

12 U.S.C. § 2604. Special information booklets

(a) Distribution by Secretary to lenders to help borrowers.
The Secretary shall prepare and distribute booklets to help persons borrowing money to finance the purchase of residential real estate better to understand the nature and costs of real estate settlement services. The Secretary shall distribute such booklets to all lenders which make federally related mortgage loans.

(b) Form and detail; cost elements, standard settlement form, escrow accounts, selection of persons for settlement services; consideration of differences in settlement procedures.

Each booklet shall be in such form and detail as the Secretary shall prescribe and, in addition to such other information as the Secretary may provide, shall include in clear and concise language—

(1) a description and explanation of the nature and purpose of each cost incident to a real estate settlement;

(2) an explanation and sample of the standard real estate settlement form developed and prescribed under section 2603 of this title;

(3) a description and explanation of the nature and purpose of escrow accounts when used in connection with loans secured by residential real estate;

(4) an explanation of the choices available to buyers of residential real estate in selecting persons to provide necessary services incident to a real estate settlement; and

(5) an explanation of the unfair practices and unreasonable or unnecessary charges to be avoided by the prospective buyer with respect to a real estate settlement.

Such booklets shall take into consideration differences in real estate settlement procedures which may exist among the several States and territories of the United States and among separate political subdivisions within the same State and territory.

(c) Estimate of charges.

Each lender shall include with the booklet a good faith estimate of the amount or range of charges for specific settlement services the borrower is likely to incur in connection with the settlement as prescribed by the Secretary.

(d) Distribution by lenders to loan applicants at time of receipt or preparation of applications.

Each lender referred to in subsection (a) of this section shall provide the booklet described in such subsection to each person from whom it receives or for whom it prepares a written application to borrow money to finance the purchases of residential real estate. Such booklet shall be provided by delivering it or placing it in the mail not later than 3 business days after the lender receives the application, but no booklet need be provided if the lender denies the application for credit before the end of the 3-day period.

(e) Printing and distribution by lenders of booklets approved by Secretary.

Booklets may be printed and distributed by lenders if their form and content are approved by the Secretary as meeting the requirements of subsection (b) of this section.

[Pub. L. No. 93–533, § 5, 88 Stat. 1725 (Dec. 22, 1974); Pub. L. No. 94–205, § 4, 89 Stat. 1158 (Jan. 2, 1976); Pub. L. No. 102–550, tit. IX, § 951, 106 Stat. 3892 (Oct. 28, 1992)]

12 U.S.C. § 2605. Servicing of mortgage loans and administration of escrow accounts.

(a) Disclosure to applicant relating to assignment, sale, or transfer of loan servicing.

Each person who makes a federally related mortgage loan shall disclose to each person who applies for any such loan, at the time of application for the loan whether the servicing of any such loan may be assigned, sold, or transferred to any other person at any time while such loan is outstanding.

(b) Notice by transferor of loan servicing at time of transfer.

(1) Notice requirement.

Each servicer of any federally related mortgage loan shall notify the borrower in writing of any assignment, sale, or transfer of the servicing of the loan to any other person.

(2) Time of notice.

(A) In general.

Except as provided under subparagraphs (B) and (C), the notice required under paragraph (1) shall be made to the borrower not less than 15 days before the effective date of transfer of the servicing of the mortgage loan (with respect to which such notice is made).

(B) Exception for certain proceedings.

The notice required under paragraph (1) shall be made to the borrower not more than 30 days after the effective date of assignment, sale, or transfer of the servicing of the mortgage loan (with respect to which such notice is made) in any case in which the assignment, sale, or transfer of the servicing of the mortgage loan is preceded by—

(i) termination of the contract for servicing the loan for cause;

(ii) commencement of proceedings for bankruptcy of the servicer; or

(iii) commencement of proceedings by the Federal Deposit Insurance Corporation or the Resolution Trust Corporation for conservatorship or receivership of the servicer (or an entity by which the servicer is owned or controlled).

(C) Exception for notice provided at closing.

The provisions of subparagraphs (A) and (B) shall not apply to any assignment, sale, or transfer of the servicing of any mortgage loan if the person who makes the loan provides to the borrower, at settlement (with respect to the property for which the mortgage loan is made), written notice under paragraph (3) of such transfer.

(3) Contents of notice.

The notice required under paragraph (1) shall include the following information:

(A) The effective date of transfer of the servicing described in such paragraph.

(B) The name, address, and toll-free or collect call telephone number of the transferee servicer.

(C) A toll-free or collect call telephone number for (i) an individual employed by the transferor servicer, or (ii) the department of the transferor servicer, that can be contacted by the borrower to answer inquiries relating to the transfer of servicing.

(D) The name and toll-free or collect call telephone number for (i) an individual employed by the transferee servicer, or (ii) the department of the transferee servicer, that can be contacted by the borrower to answer inquiries relating to the transfer of servicing.

(E) The date on which the transferor servicer who is servicing the mortgage loan before the assignment, sale, or transfer will cease to accept payments relating to the loan and the date on which the transferee servicer will begin to accept such payments.

(F) Any information concerning the effect the transfer may have, if any, on the terms of or the continued availability of mortgage life or disability insurance or any other type of optional insurance and what action, if any, the borrower must take to maintain coverage.

(G) A statement that the assignment, sale, or transfer of the servicing of the mortgage loan does not affect any term or condition of the security instruments directly related to the servicing of such loan.

(c) Notice by transferee of loan servicing at time of transfer.
(1) Notice requirement.

Each transferee servicer to whom the servicing of any federally related mortgage loan is assigned, sold, or transferred shall notify the borrower of any such assignment, sale, or transfer.

(2) Time of notice.
(A) In general.

Except as provided in subparagraphs (B) and (C), the notice required under paragraph (1) shall be made to the borrower not more than 15 days after the effective date of transfer of the servicing of the mortgage loan (with respect to which such notice is made).

(B) Exception for certain proceedings.

The notice required under paragraph (1) shall be made to the borrower not more than 30 days after the effective date of assignment, sale, or transfer of the servicing of the mortgage loan (with respect to which such notice is made) in any case in which the assignment, sale, or transfer of the servicing of the mortgage loan is preceded by—

(i) termination of the contract for servicing the loan for cause;
(ii) commencement of proceedings for bankruptcy of the servicer; or
(iii) commencement of proceedings by the Federal Deposit Insurance Corporation or the Resolution Trust Corporation for conservatorship or receivership of the servicer (or an entity by which the servicer is owned or controlled).

(C) Exception for notice provided at closing.

The provisions of subparagraphs (A) and (B) shall not apply to any assignment, sale, or transfer of the servicing of any mortgage loan if the person who makes the loan provides to the borrower, at settlement (with respect to the property for which the mortgage loan is made), written notice under paragraph (3) of such transfer.

(3) Contents of notice.

Any notice required under paragraph (1) shall include the information described in subsection (b)(3) of this section.

(d) Treatment of loan payments during transfer period.

During the 60-day period beginning on the effective of the servicing of any federally related mortgage loan, a late fee may not be imposed on the borrower with respect to any payment on such loan and no such payment may be treated as late for any other purposes, if the payment is received by the transferor servicer (rather than the transferee servicer who should properly receive payment) before the due date applicable to such payment.

(e) Duty of loan servicer to respond to borrower inquiries.
(1) Notice of receipt of inquiry.
(A) In general.

If any servicer of a federally related mortgage loan receives a qualified written request from the borrower (or an agent of the borrower) for information relating to the servicing of such loan, the servicer shall provide a written response acknowledging receipt of the correspondence within 20 days (excluding legal public holidays, Saturdays, and Sundays) unless the action requested is taken within such period.

(B) Qualified written request.

For purposes of this subsection, a qualified written request shall be a written correspondence, other than notice on a payment coupon or other payment medium supplied by the servicer, that—

(i) includes, or otherwise enables the servicer to identify, the name and account of the borrower; and
(ii) includes a statement of the reasons for the belief of the borrower, to the extent applicable, that the account is in error or provides sufficient detail to the servicer regarding other information sought by the borrower.

(2) Action with respect to inquiry.

Not later than 60 days (excluding legal public holidays, Saturdays, and Sundays) after the receipt from any borrower of any qualified written request under paragraph (1) and, if applicable, before taking any action with respect to the inquiry of the borrower, the servicer shall—

(A) make appropriate corrections in the account of the borrower, including the crediting of any late charges or penalties, and transmit to the borrower a written notification of such correction (which shall include the name and telephone number of a representative of the servicer who can provide assistance to the borrower);
(B) after conducting an investigation, provide the borrower with a written explanation or clarification that includes—

(i) to the extent applicable, a statement of the reasons for which the servicer believes the account of the borrower is correct as determined by the servicer; and
(ii) the name and telephone number of an individual employed by, or the office or department of, the servicer who can provide assistance to the borrower; or

(C) after conducting an investigation, provide the borrower with a written explanation or clarification that includes—

(i) information requested by the borrower or an explanation of why the information requested is unavailable or cannot be obtained by the servicer; and
(ii) the name and telephone number of an individual employed by, or the office or department of, the servicer who can provide assistance to the borrower.

(3) Protection of credit rating.

During the 60-day period beginning on the date of the servicer's receipt from any borrower of a qualified written request relating to a dispute regarding the borrower's payments, a servicer may not provide information regarding any overdue payment, owed by such borrower and relating to such period or qualified written request, to any consumer reporting agency (as such term is defined under section 1681a of Title 15).

(f) Damages and costs.

Whoever fails to comply with any provision of this section shall be liable to the borrower for each such failure in the following amounts:

(1) Individuals.

In the case of any action by an individual, an amount equal to the sum of—

(A) any actual damages to the borrower as a result of the failure; and
(B) any additional damages, as the court may allow, in the case of a pattern or practice of noncompliance with the requirements of this section, in an amount not to exceed $1,000.

(2) Class actions.

In the case of a class action, an amount equal to the sum of—
(A) any actual damages to each of the borrowers in the class as a result of the failure; and
(B) any additional damages, as the court may allow, in the case of a pattern or practice of noncompliance with the requirements of this section, in an amount not greater than $1,000 for each member of the class, except that the total amount of damages under this subparagraph in any class action may not exceed the lesser of—
    (i) $500,000; or
    (ii) 1 percent of the net worth of the servicer.

(3) Costs.

In addition to the amounts under paragraph (1) or (2), in the case of any successful action under this section, the costs of the action, together with any attorneys fees incurred in connection with such action as the court may determine to be reasonable under the circumstances.

(4) Nonliability.

A transferor or transferee servicer shall not be liable under this subsection for any failure to comply with any requirement under this section if, within 60 days after discovering an error (whether pursuant to a final written examination report or the servicer's own procedures) and before the commencement of an action under this subsection and the receipt of written notice of the error from the borrower, the servicer notifies the person concerned of the error and makes whatever adjustments are necessary in the appropriate account to ensure that the person will not be required to pay an amount in excess of any amount that the person otherwise would have paid.

(g) Administration of escrow accounts.

If the terms of any federally related mortgage loan require the borrower to make payments to the servicer of the loan for deposit into an escrow account for the purpose of assuring payment of taxes, insurance premiums, and other charges with respect to the property, the servicer shall make payments from the escrow account for such taxes, insurance premiums, and other charges in a timely manner as such payments become due.

(h) Preemption of conflicting State laws.

Notwithstanding any provision of any law or regulation of any State, a person who makes a federally related mortgage loan or a servicer shall be considered to have complied with the provisions of any such State law or regulation requiring notice to a borrower at the time of application for a loan or transfer of the servicing of a loan if such person or servicer complies with the requirements under this section regarding timing, content, and procedures for notification of the borrower.

(i) Definitions.

For purposes of this section:
(1) Effective date of transfer.
The term "effective date of transfer" means the date on which the mortgage payment of a borrower is first due to the transferee servicer of a mortgage loan pursuant to the assignment, sale, or transfer of the servicing of the mortgage loan.
(2) Servicer.
The term "servicer" means the person responsible for servicing of a loan (including the person who makes or holds a loan if such person also services the loan). The term does not include—
(A) the Federal Deposit Insurance Corporation or the Resolution Trust Corporation, in connection with assets acquired, assigned, sold, or transferred pursuant to section 1823(c) of this title or as receiver or conservator of an insured depository institution; and
(B) the Government National Mortgage Association, the Federal National Mortgage Association, the Federal Home Loan Mortgage Corporation, the Resolution Trust Corporation, or the Federal Deposit Insurance Corporation, in any case in which the assignment, sale, or transfer of the servicing of the mortgage loan is preceded by—
    (i) termination of the contract for servicing the loan for cause;
    (ii) commencement of proceedings for bankruptcy of the servicer; or
    (iii) commencement of proceedings by the Federal Deposit Insurance Corporation or the Resolution Trust Corporation for conservatorship or receivership of the servicer (or an entity by which the servicer is owned or controlled).
(3) Servicing.
The term "servicing" means receiving any scheduled periodic payments from a borrower pursuant to the terms of any loan, including amounts for escrow accounts described in section 10, and making the payments of principal and interest and such other payments with respect to the amounts received from the borrower as may be required pursuant to the terms of the loan.

(j) Transition.
(1) Originator liability.
A person who makes a federally related mortgage loan shall not be liable to a borrower because of a failure of such person to comply with subsection (a) of this section with respect to an application for a loan made by the borrower before the regulations referred to in paragraph (3) take effect.
(2) Servicer liability.
A servicer of a federally related mortgage loan shall not be liable to a borrower because of a failure of the servicer to perform any duty under subsection (b), (c), (d), or (e) of this section that arises before the regulations referred to in paragraph (3) take effect.
(3) Regulations and effective date.
The Secretary shall, by regulations that shall take effect not later than April 20, 1991, establish any requirements necessary to carry out this section. Such regulations shall include the model disclosure statement required under subsection (a)(2) of this section.

[Pub. L. No. 93–533, § 6, *as added* Pub. L. No. 101–625, tit. IX, § 941, 104 Stat. 4405 (Nov. 28, 1990); amended Pub. L. No. 102–27, tit. III, § 312(a), 105 Stat. 154 (Apr. 10, 1991); Pub. L. No. 103–325, tit. III, § 345, 108 Stat. 2239 (Sept. 23, 1994); Pub. L. No. 104–208, div. A, tit. II, § 2103(a), 110 Stat. 3009–399 (Sept. 30, 1996)]

12 U.S.C. § 2606. Exempted transactions

(a) In general.

This chapter does not apply to credit transactions involving extensions of credit—
(1) primarily for business, commercial, or agricultural purposes; or

(2) to government or governmental agencies or instrumentalities.

(b) Interpretation.

In prescribing regulations under section 2617(a) of this title, the Secretary shall ensure that, with respect to subsection (a) of this section, the exemption for credit transactions involving extensions of credit primarily for business, commercial or agricultural purposes, as provided in subsection (a)(1) of this section shall be the same as the exemption for such credit transactions under 1603(1) of Title 15.

[Pub. L. No. 93–533, § 7, *as added* Pub. L. 103–325, tit. III, § 312, 108 Stat. 2221 (Sept. 23, 1994); amended Pub. L. No. 104–208, div. A, tit. II, § 2103(b), 110 Stat. 3009–399 (Sept. 30, 1996)]

12 U.S.C. § 2607. Prohibition against kickbacks and unearned fees

(a) Business referrals.

No person shall give and no person shall accept any fee, kickback, or thing of value pursuant to any agreement or understanding, oral or otherwise, that business incident to or a part of a real estate settlement service involving a federally related mortgage loan shall be referred to any person.

(b) Splitting charges.

No person shall give and no person shall accept any portion, split, or percentage of any charge made or received for the rendering of a real estate settlement service in connection with a transaction involving a federally related mortgage loan other than for services actually performed.

(c) Fees, salaries, compensation, or other payments.

Nothing in this section shall be construed as prohibiting
(1) the payment of a fee
(A) to attorneys at law for services actually rendered or
(B) by a title company to its duly appointed agent for services actually performed in the issuance of a policy of title insurance or
(C) by a lender to its duly appointed agent for services actually performed in the making of a loan,
(2) the payment to any person of a bona fide salary or compensation or other payment for goods or facilities actually furnished or for services actually performed,
(3) payments pursuant to cooperative brokerage and referral arrangements or agreements between real estate agents and brokers,
(4) affiliated business arrangements so long as
(A) a disclosure is made of the existence of such an arrangement to the person referred and, in connection with such a referral, such person is provided a written estimate of the charge or range of charges generally made by the provider to which the person is referred
    (i) in case of a face-to-face referral or a referral made in writing or by electronic media, at or before the time of the referral (and compliance with this requirement in such case may be evidenced by a notation in a written, electronic, or similar system of records maintained in the regular course of business);

    (ii) in the case of a referral made by telephone, within 3 business days after the referral by telephone, (and in such case an abbreviated verbal disclosure of the existence of the arrangement and the fact that a written disclosure will be provided within 3 business days shall be made to the person being referred during the telephone referral); or
    (iii) in the case of a referral by a lender (including a referral by a lender to an affiliated lender), at the time the estimates required under section 2604(c) of this title are provided (notwithstanding clause (i) or (ii); and any required written receipt of such disclosure (without regard to the manner of the disclosure under clause (i), (ii), or (iii)) may be obtained at the closing or settlement (except that a person making a face-to-face referral who provides the written disclosure at or before the time of the referral shall attempt to obtain any required written receipt of such disclosure at such time and if the person being referred chooses not to acknowledge the receipt of the disclosure at that time, the fact shall be noted in the written, electronic, or similar system of records maintained in the regular course of business by the person making the referral),
(B) such person is not required to use any particular provider of settlement services, and
(C) the only thing of value that is received from the arrangement, other than the payments permitted under this subsection, is a return on the ownership interest or franchise relationship, or
(5) such other payments or classes of payments or other transfers as are specified in regulations prescribed by the Secretary, after consultation with the Attorney General, the Secretary of Veterans Affairs, the Federal Home Loan Bank Board,[1] the Federal Deposit Insurance Corporation, the Board of Governors of the Federal Reserve System, and the Secretary of Agriculture. For purposes of the preceding sentence, the following shall not be considered a violation of clause (4)(B):
    (i) any arrangement that requires a buyer, borrower, or seller to pay for the services of an attorney, credit reporting agency, or real estate appraiser chosen by the lender to represent the lender's interest in a real estate transaction, or
    (ii) any arrangement where an attorney or law firm represents a client in a real estate transaction and issues or arranges for the issuance of a policy of title insurance in the transaction directly as agent or through a separate corporate title insurance agency that may be established by that attorney or law firm and operated as an adjunct to his or its law practice.

(d) Penalties for violations; joint and several liability; treble damages; actions for injunction by Secretary and by State officials; costs and attorney fees; construction of State laws.

(1) Any person or persons who violate the provisions of this section shall be fined not more than $10,000 or imprisoned for not more than one year, or both.
(2) Any person or persons who violate the prohibitions or limitations of this section shall be jointly and severally liable to the

---

1 *Editor's Note*: This Act makes reference to the Federal Home Loan Bank Board (FHLBB) and its authority. The Financial Institutions Reform, Recovery and Enforcement Act of 1989 (FIRREA), Pub. L. No. 101-73, 103 Stat. 183 (Aug. 9, 1989), abolished the FHLBB, and replaced it with the Office of Thrift Supervision (OTS). The relevant authority was transferred from the FHLBB to the OTS.

person or persons charged for the settlement service involved in the violation in an amount equal to three times the amount of any charge paid for such settlement service.

(3) No person or persons shall be liable for a violation of the provisions of subsection (c)(4)(A) of this section if such person or persons proves by a preponderance of the evidence that such violation was not intentional and resulted from a bona fide error notwithstanding maintenance of procedures that are reasonably adapted to avoid such error.

(4) The Secretary, the Attorney General of any State, or the insurance commissioner of any State may bring an action to enjoin violations of this section.

(5) In any private action brought pursuant to this subsection, the court may award to the prevailing party the court costs of the action together with reasonable attorneys fees.

(6) No provision of State law or regulation that imposes more stringent limitations on affiliated business arrangements shall be construed as being inconsistent with this section.

[Pub. L. No. 93–533, § 8, 88 Stat. 1727 (Dec. 22, 1974); Pub. L. No. 94–205, § 7, 89 Stat. 1158 (Jan. 2, 1976); Pub. L. No. 98–181, tit. IV, § 461(b), (c), 97 Stat. 1231 (Nov. 30, 1983); Pub. L. No. 100–242, tit. V, § 570(g), 101 Stat. 1950 (Feb. 5, 1988); Pub. L. No. 102–54, § 13(d)(4), 105 Stat. 275 (June 13, 1991); Pub. L. No. 104–208, div. A, tit. II, § 2103(c)(2), (d), 110 Stat. 3009–400 (Sept. 30, 1996)]

12 U.S.C. § 2608. Title companies; liability of seller

(a) No seller of property that will be purchased with the assistance of a federally related mortgage loan shall require directly or indirectly, as a condition to selling the property, that title insurance covering the property be purchased by the buyer from any particular title company.

(b) Any seller who violates the provisions of subsection (a) of this section shall be liable to the buyer in an amount equal to three times all charges made for such title insurance.

[Pub. L. No. 93–533, § 9, 88 Stat. 1728 (Dec. 22, 1974)]

12 U.S.C. § 2609. Limitation on requirement of advance deposits in escrow accounts

(a) In general.

A lender, in connection with a federally related mortgage loan, may not require the borrower or prospective borrower—

(1) to deposit in any escrow account which may be established in connection with such loan for the purpose of assuring payment of taxes, insurance premiums, or other charges with respect to the property, in connection with the settlement, an aggregate sum (for such purpose) in excess of a sum that will be sufficient to pay such taxes, insurance premiums and other charges attributable to the period beginning on the last date on which each such charge would have been paid under the normal lending practice of the lender and local custom, provided that the selection of each such date constitutes prudent lending practice, and ending on the due date of its first full installment payment under the mortgage, plus one-sixth of the

estimated total amount of such taxes, insurance premiums and other charges to be paid on dates, as provided above, during the ensuing twelve-month period; or

(2) to deposit in any such escrow account in any month beginning with the first full installment payment under the mortgage a sum (for the purpose of assuring payment of taxes, insurance premiums and other charges with respect to the property) in excess of the sum of

(A) one-twelfth of the total amount of the estimated taxes, insurance premiums and other charges which are reasonably anticipated to be paid on dates during the ensuing twelve months which dates are in accordance with the normal lending practice of the lender and local custom, provided that the selection of each such date constitutes prudent lending practice, plus

(B) such amount as is necessary to maintain an additional balance in such escrow account not to exceed one-sixth of the estimated total amount of such taxes, insurance premiums and other charges to be paid on dates, as provided above, during the ensuing twelve-month period: Provided, however, That in the event the lender determines there will be or is a deficiency he shall not be prohibited from requiring additional monthly deposits in such escrow account to avoid or eliminate such deficiency.

(b) Notification of shortage in escrow account.

If the terms of any federally related mortgage loan require the borrower to make payments to the servicer (as the term is defined in section 2605(i) of this title) of the loan for deposit into an escrow account for the purpose of assuring payment of taxes, insurance premiums, and other charges with respect to the property, the servicer shall notify the borrower not less than annually of any shortage of funds in the escrow account.

(c) Escrow account statements.
(1) Initial statement
(A) In general

Any servicer that has established an escrow account in connection with a federally related mortgage loan shall submit to the borrower for which the escrow account has been established a statement clearly itemizing the estimated taxes, insurance premiums, and other charges that are reasonably anticipated to be paid from the escrow account during the first 12 months after the establishment of the account and the anticipated dates of such payments.

(B) Time of submission.

The statement required under subparagraph (A) shall be submitted to the borrower at closing with respect to the property for which the mortgage loan is made or not later than the expiration of the 45-day period beginning on the date of the establishment of the escrow account.

(C) Initial statement at closing.

Any servicer may submit the statement required under subparagraph (A) to the borrower at closing and may incorporate such statement in the uniform settlement statement required under section 2603 of this title. The Secretary shall issue regulations prescribing any changes necessary to the uniform settlement statement under section 2603 of this title that specify how the statement required under subparagraph (A) of this section shall be incorporated in the uniform settlement statement.

(2) Annual statement.

(A) In general.

Any servicer that has established or continued an escrow account in connection with a federally related mortgage loan shall submit to the borrower for which the escrow account has been established or continued a statement clearly itemizing, for each period described in subparagraph (B) (during which the servicer services the escrow account), the amount of the borrower's current monthly payment, the portion of the monthly payment being placed in the escrow account, the total amount paid into the escrow account during the period, the total amount paid out of the escrow account during the period for taxes, insurance premiums, and other charges (as separately identified), and the balance in the escrow account at the conclusion of the period.

(B) Time of submission.

The statement required under subparagraph (A) shall be submitted to the borrower not less than once for each 12-month period, the first such period beginning on the first January 1st that occurs after November 28, 1990, and shall be submitted not more than 30 days after the conclusion of each such 1-year period.

(d) Penalties.

(1) In general.

In the case of each failure to submit a statement to a borrower as required under subsection (c) of this section, the Secretary shall assess to the lender or escrow servicer failing to submit the statement a civil penalty of $50 for each such failure, but the total amount imposed on such lender or escrow servicer for all such failures during any 12-month period referred to in subsection (b)[2] of this section may not exceed $100,000.

(2) Intentional violations.

If any failure to which paragraph (1) applies is due to intentional disregard of the requirement to submit the statement, then, with respect to such failure—

(A) the penalty imposed under paragraph (1) shall be $100; and

(B) in the case of any penalty determined under subparagraph (A), the $100,000 limitation under paragraph (1) shall not apply.

[Pub. L. No. 93–533, § 10, 88 Stat. 1728 (Dec. 22, 1974); Pub. L. No. 94–205, § 8, 89 Stat. 1158 (Jan. 2, 1976); Pub. L. No. 101–625, tit. IX, § 942(a), 104 Stat. 4411 (Nov. 28, 1990); Pub. L. No. 104–208, div. A, tit. II, § 2103(g)(2), 110 Stat. 3009–401 (Sept. 30, 1996)]

12 U.S.C. § 2610. Prohibition of fees for preparation of truth-in-lending, uniform settlement, and escrow account statements

No fee shall be imposed or charge made upon any other person (as a part of settlement costs or otherwise) by a lender in connection with a federally related mortgage loan made by it (or a loan for the purchase of a mobile home), or by a servicer (as the term is defined under section 2605(i) of this title), for or on account of the preparation and submission by such lender or servicer of the statement or statements required (in connection with such loan) by sections 2603 and 2609(c) of this title or by the Truth in Lending Act [15 U.S.C. 1601 et seq.].

[Pub. L. No. 93–533, § 12, 88 Stat. 1729 (Dec. 22, 1974); Pub. L. No. 101–625, tit. IX, § 942(b), 104 Stat. 4412 (Nov. 28, 1990)]

12 U.S.C. § 2614. Jurisdiction of courts; limitations

Any action pursuant to the provisions of section 2605, 2607 or 2608 of this title may be brought in the United States district court or in any other court of competent jurisdiction, for the district in which the property involved is located, or where the violation is alleged to have occurred, within 3 years in the case of a violation of section 2605 of this title and 1 year in the case of a violation of section 2607 or 2608 of this title from the date of the occurrence of the violation, except that actions brought by the Secretary, the Attorney General of any State, or the insurance commissioner of any State may be brought within 3 years from the date of the occurrence of the violation.

[Pub. L. No. 93–533, § 16, 88 Stat. 1731 (Dec. 22, 1974); Pub. L. No. 98–181, tit. IV, § 461(d), 97 Stat. 1232 (Nov. 30, 1983); Pub. L. No. 104–208, div. A, tit. II, § 2103(e), 110 Stat. 3009–400 (Sept. 30, 1996)]

12 U.S.C. § 2615. Contracts and liens; validity

Nothing in this chapter shall affect the validity or enforceability of any sale or contract for the sale of real property or any loan, loan agreement, mortgage, or lien made or arising in connection with a federally related mortgage loan.

[Pub. L. No. 93-533, § 17, 88 Stat. 1731 (Dec. 22, 1974)]

12 U.S.C. § 2616. State laws unaffected; inconsistent Federal and State provisions

This chapter does not annul, alter, or affect, or exempt any person subject to the provisions of this chapter from complying with, the laws of any State with respect to settlement practices, except to the extent that those laws are inconsistent with any provision of this chapter, and then only to the extent of the inconsistency. The Secretary is authorized to determine whether such inconsistencies exist. The Secretary may not determine that any State law is inconsistent with any provision of this chapter if the Secretary determines that such law gives greater protection to the consumer. In making these determinations the Secretary shall consult with the appropriate Federal agencies.

[Pub. L. No. 93-533, § 18, 88 Stat. 1731 (Dec. 22, 1974); Pub. L. No. 94-205, § 9, 89 Stat. 1159 (Jan. 2, 1976)]

12 U.S.C. § 2617. Authority of Secretary

(a) Issuance of regulations; exemptions

The Secretary is authorized to prescribe such rules and regulations, to make such interpretations, and to grant such reasonable exemptions for classes of transactions, as may be necessary to achieve the purposes of this chapter.

---

2 So in original. Probably should be subsection "(c)".

(b) Liability for acts done in good faith in conformity with rule, regulation, or interpretation

No provision of this chapter or the laws of any State imposing any liability shall apply to any act done or omitted in good faith in conformity with any rule, regulation, or interpretation thereof by the Secretary or the Attorney General, notwithstanding that after such act or omission has occurred, such rule, regulation, or interpretation is amended, rescinded, or determined by judicial or other authority to be invalid for any reason.

(c) Investigations; hearings; failure to obey order; contempt

(1) The Secretary may investigate any facts, conditions, practices, or matters that may be deemed necessary or proper to aid in the enforcement of the provisions of this chapter, in prescribing of rules and regulations thereunder, or in securing information to serve as a basis for recommending further legislation concerning real estate settlement practices. To aid in the investigations, the Secretary is authorized to hold such hearings, administer such oaths, and require by subpena the attendance and testimony of such witnesses and production of such documents as the Secretary deems advisable.

(2) Any district court of the United States within the jurisdiction of which an inquiry is carried on may, in the case of contumacy or refusal to obey a subpena of the Secretary issued under this section, issue an order requiring compliance therewith; and any failure to obey such order of the court may be punished by such court as a contempt thereof.

(d) Delay of effectiveness of recent final regulation relating to payments to employees

(1) In general

The amendment to part 3500 of title 24 of the Code of Federal Regulations contained in the final regulation prescribed by the Secretary and published in the Federal Register on June 7, 1996, which will, as of the effective date of such amendment—

(A) eliminate the exemption for payments by an employer to employees of such employer for referral activities which is currently codified as section 3500.14(g)(1)(vii) of such title 24; and

(B) replace such exemption with a more limited exemption in new clauses (vii), (viii), and (ix) of section 3500.14 of such title 24,

shall not take effect before July 31, 1997.

(2) Continuation of prior rule

The regulation codified as section 3500.14(g)(1)(vii) of title 24 of the Code of Federal Regulations, relating to employer-employee payments, as in effect on May 1, 1996, shall remain in effect until the date the amendment referred to in paragraph (1) takes effect in accordance with such paragraph.

(3) Public notice of effective date

The Secretary shall provide public notice of the date on which the amendment referred to in paragraph (1) will take effect in accordance with such paragraph not less than 90 days and not more than 180 days before such effective date.

[Pub. L. No. 93-533, § 19, *as added* Pub. L. No. 94-205, § 10, 89 Stat. 1159 (Jan. 2, 1976); amended Pub. L. No. 98-181, tit. IV, § 461(e), 97 Stat. 1232 (Nov. 30, 1983); Pub. L. No. 104-208, div. A, tit. II, § 2103(f), 110 Stat. 3009–401 (Sept. 30, 1996)]

K.2 Selected Regulation X Provisions

Title 24—Housing and Urban Development

CHAPTER XX—OFFICE OF ASSISTANT SECRETARY FOR HOUSING—FEDERAL HOUSING COMMISSIONER, DEPARTMENT OF HOUSING AND URBAN DEVELOPMENT

PART 3500—REAL ESTATE SETTLEMENT PROCEDURES ACT

* * *

§ 3500.2   Definitions.

* * *

§ 3500.4   Reliance upon rule, regulation or interpretation by HUD.

§ 3500.5   Coverage of RESPA.

§ 3500.6   Special information booklet at time of loan application.

§ 3500.7   Good faith estimate.

§ 3500.8   Use of HUD-1 or HUD-1A settlement statements.

§ 3500.9   Reproduction of settlement statements.

§ 3500.10   One-day advance inspection of HUD-1 or HUD-1A settlement statement; delivery; recordkeeping.

* * *

§ 3500.12   No fee.

§ 3500.13   Relation to State laws.

§ 3500.14   Prohibition against kickbacks and unearned fees.

§ 3500.15   Affiliated business arrangements.

§ 3500.16   Title companies.

§ 3500.17   Escrow accounts.

§ 3500.19   Enforcement.

§ 3500.21   Mortgage servicing transfers.

Authority: 12 U.S.C. 2601 *et seq.*; 28 U.S.C. 2461 note; 42 U.S.C. 3535(d).

Source: 57 Fed. Reg. 49607 (Nov. 2, 1992), unless otherwise noted.

24 C.F.R. § 3500.2 Definitions.

(a) *Statutory terms.* All terms defined in RESPA (12 U.S.C. 2602) are used in accordance with their statutory meaning unless otherwise defined in paragraph (b) of this section or elsewhere in this part.

(b) *Other terms.* As used in this part:

Application means the submission of a borrower's financial information in anticipation of a credit decision, whether written or computer-generated, relating to a federally related mortgage loan. If the submission does not state or identify a specific property, the submission is an application for a pre-qualification and not an application for a federally related mortgage loan under this part. The subsequent addition of an identified property to the submission converts the submission to an application for a federally related mortgage loan.

Business day means a day on which the offices of the business entity are open to the public for carrying on substantially all of the entity's business functions.

Dealer means, in the case of property improvement loans, a seller, contractor, or supplier of goods or services. In the case of manufactured home loans, "dealer" means one who engages in the business of manufactured home retail sales.

Dealer loan or dealer consumer credit contract means, generally, any arrangement in which a dealer assists the borrower in obtaining a federally related mortgage loan from the funding lender and then assigns the dealer's legal interests to the funding lender and receives the net proceeds of the loan. The funding lender is the lender for the purposes of the disclosure requirements of this part. If a dealer is a "creditor" as defined under the definition of "federally related mortgage loan" in this part, the dealer is the lender for purposes of this part.

Effective date of transfer is defined in section 6(i)(1) of RESPA (12 U.S.C. 2605(i)(1)). In the case of a home equity conversion mortgage or reverse mortgage as referenced in this section, the effective date of transfer is the transfer date agreed upon by the transferee servicer and the transferor servicer.

Federally related mortgage loan or mortgage loan means as follows:

(1) Any loan (other than temporary financing, such as a construction loan):

(i) That is secured by a first or subordinate lien on residential real property, including a refinancing of any secured loan on residential real property upon which there is either:

(A) Located or, following settlement, will be constructed using proceeds of the loan, a structure or structures designed principally for occupancy of from one to four families (including individual units of condominiums and cooperatives and including any related interests, such as a share in the cooperative or right to occupancy of the unit); or

(B) Located or, following settlement, will be placed using proceeds of the loan, a manufactured home; and

(ii) For which one of the following paragraphs applies. The loan:

(A) Is made in whole or in part by any lender that is either regulated by or whose deposits or accounts are insured by any agency of the Federal Government;

(B) Is made in whole or in part, or is insured, guaranteed, supplemented, or assisted in any way:

(*1*) By the Secretary or any other officer or agency of the Federal Government; or

(*2*) Under or in connection with a housing or urban development program administered by the Secretary or a housing or related program administered by any other officer or agency of the Federal Government;

(C) Is intended to be sold by the originating lender to the Federal National Mortgage Association, the Government National Mortgage Association, the Federal Home Loan Mortgage Corporation (or its successors), or a financial institution from which the loan is to be purchased by the Federal Home Loan Mortgage Corporation (or its successors);

(D) Is made in whole or in part by a "creditor", as defined in section 103(f) of the Consumer Credit Protection Act (15 U.S.C. 1602(f)), that makes or invests in residential real estate loans aggregating more than $1,000,000 per year. For purposes of this definition, the term "creditor" does not include any agency or instrumentality of any State, and the term "residential real estate loan" means any loan secured by residential real property, including single-family and multifamily residential property;

(E) Is originated either by a dealer or, if the obligation is to be assigned to any maker of

mortgage loans specified in paragraphs (1)(ii)(A) through (D) of this definition, by a mortgage broker; or

(F) Is the subject of a home equity conversion mortgage, also frequently called a "reverse mortgage," issued by any maker of mortgage loans specified in paragraphs (1)(ii)(A) through (D) of this definition.

(2) Any installment sales contract, land contract, or contract for deed on otherwise qualifying residential property is a federally related mortgage loan if the contract is funded in whole or in part by proceeds of a loan made by any maker of mortgage loans specified in paragraphs (1)(ii)(A) through (D) of this definition.

(3) If the residential real property securing a mortgage loan is not located in a State, the loan is not a federally related mortgage loan.

Good faith estimate means an estimate, prepared in accordance with section 5 of RESPA (12 U.S.C. 2604), of charges that a borrower is likely to incur in connection with a settlement.

HUD-1 or HUD-1A settlement statement (also HUD-1 or HUD-1A) means the statement that is prescribed by the Secretary in this part for setting forth settlement charges in connection with either the purchase or the refinancing (or other subordinate lien transaction) of 1- to 4-family residential property.

Lender means, generally, the secured creditor or creditors named in the debt obligation and document creating the lien. For loans originated by a mortgage broker that closes a federally related mortgage loan in its own name in a table funding transaction, the lender is the person to whom the obligation is initially assigned at or after settlement. A lender, in connection with dealer loans, is the lender to whom the loan is assigned, unless the dealer meets the definition of creditor as defined under "federally related mortgage loan" in this section. See also § 3500.5(b)(7), secondary market transactions.

[Editor's Note: HUD promulgated the following change to this subsection but stayed its effective date. It is possible that the proposed change may be withdrawn. Check for developments in the Federal Register. Add to subsection (b):

Managerial employee means an employee of a settlement service provider who does not routinely deal directly with consumers, and who either hires, directs, assigns, promotes, or rewards other employees or independent contractors, or is in a position to formulate, determine, or influence the policies of the employer. Neither the term "managerial employee" nor the term "employee" includes independent contractors, but a managerial employee may hold a real estate brokerage or agency license.

[61 Fed. Reg. 29238, 29252 (June 7, 1996); 61 Fed. Reg. 51782 (Oct. 4, 1996)]]

Manufactured home is defined in § 3280.2 of this title.

Mortgage broker means a person (not an employee or exclusive agent of a lender) who brings a borrower and lender together to obtain a

federally related mortgage loan, and who renders services as described in the definition of "settlement services" in this section. A loan correspondent approved under § 202.8 of this title for Federal Housing Administration programs is a mortgage broker for purposes of this part.

Mortgaged property means the real property that is security for the federally related mortgage loan.

Person is defined in section 3(5) of RESPA (12 U.S.C. 2602(5)).

Public Guidance Documents means documents that HUD has published in the *Federal Register*, and that it may amend from time-to-time by publication in the *Federal Register*. These documents are also available from HUD at the address indicated in 24 CFR 3500.3.

Refinancing means a transaction in which an existing obligation that was subject to a secured lien on residential real property is satisfied and replaced by a new obligation undertaken by the same borrower and with the same or a new lender. The following shall not be treated as a refinancing, even when the existing obligation is satisfied and replaced by a new obligation with the same lender (this definition of "refinancing" as to transactions with the same lender is similar to Regulation Z, 12 CFR 226.20(a)):

(1) A renewal of a single payment obligation with no change in the original terms;

(2) A reduction in the annual percentage rate as computed under the Truth in Lending Act [15 U.S.C. § 1601 et seq.] with a corresponding change in the payment schedule;

(3) An agreement involving a court proceeding;

(4) A workout agreement, in which a change in the payment schedule or change in collateral requirements is agreed to as a result of the consumer's default or delinquency, unless the rate is increased or the new amount financed exceeds the unpaid balance plus earned finance charges and premiums for continuation of allowable insurance; and

(5) The renewal of optional insurance purchased by the consumer that is added to an existing transaction, if disclosures relating to the initial purchase were provided.

Regulation Z means the regulations issued by the Board of Governors of the Federal Reserve System (12 CFR part 226) to implement the Federal Truth in Lending Act (15 U.S.C. 1601 et seq.), and includes the Commentary on Regulation Z.

Required use means a situation in which a person must use a particular provider of a settlement service in order to have access to some distinct service or property, and the person will pay for the settlement service of the particular provider or will pay a charge attributable, in whole or in part, to the settlement service. However, the offering of a package (or combination of settlement services) or the offering of discounts or rebates to consumers for the purchase of multiple settlement services does not constitute a required use. Any package or discount must be optional to the purchaser. The discount must be a true discount below the prices that are otherwise generally available, and must not be made up by higher costs elsewhere in the settlement process.

RESPA means the Real Estate Settlement Procedures Act of 1974, 12 U.S.C. 2601 *et seq.*

Servicer means the person responsible for the servicing of a mortgage loan (including the person who makes or holds a mortgage loan if such person also services the mortgage loan). The term does not include:

(1) The Federal Deposit Insurance Corporation (FDIC) or the Resolution Trust Corporation (RTC), in connection with assets acquired, assigned, sold, or transferred pursuant to section 13(c) of the Federal Deposit Insurance Act [12 U.S.C. § 1823(c)] or as receiver or conservator of an insured depository institution; and

(2) The Federal National Mortgage Corporation (FNMA); the Federal Home Loan Mortgage Corporation (Freddie Mac); the RTC; the FDIC; HUD, including the Government National Mortgage Association (GNMA) and the Federal Housing Administration (FHA) (including cases in which a mortgage insured under the National Housing Act (12 U.S.C. 1701 et seq.) is assigned to HUD); the National Credit Union Administration (NCUA); the Farmers Home Administration or its successor agency under Public Law 103-354 [Oct. 13, 1994, 108 Stat. 3178; see Tables for classification]; and the Department of Veterans Affairs (VA), in any case in which the assignment, sale, or transfer of the servicing of the mortgage loan is preceded by termination of the contract for servicing the loan for cause, commencement of proceedings for bankruptcy of the servicer, or commencement of proceedings by the FDIC or RTC for conservatorship or receivership of the servicer (or an entity by which the servicer is owned or controlled).

Servicing means receiving any scheduled periodic payments from a borrower pursuant to the terms of any mortgage loan, including amounts for escrow accounts under section 10 of RESPA (12 U.S.C. 2609), and making the payments to the owner of the loan or other third parties of principal and interest and such other payments with respect to the amounts received from the borrower as may be required pursuant to the terms of the mortgage servicing loan documents or servicing contract. In the case of a home equity conversion mortgage or reverse mortgage as referenced in this section, servicing includes making payments to the borrower.

Settlement means the process of executing legally binding documents regarding a lien on property that is subject to a federally related mortgage loan. This process may also be called "closing" or "escrow" in different jurisdictions.

Settlement service means any service provided in connection with a prospective or actual settlement, including, but not limited to, any one or more of the following:

(1) Origination of a federally related mortgage loan (including, but not limited to, the taking of loan applications, loan processing, and the underwriting and funding of such loans);

(2) Rendering of services by a mortgage broker (including counseling, taking of applications, obtaining verifications and appraisals, and other loan processing and origination services, and communicating with the borrower and lender);

(3) Provision of any services related to the origination, processing or funding of a federally related mortgage loan;

(4) Provision of title services, including title searches, title examinations, abstract preparation, insurability determinations, and the issuance of title commitments and title insurance policies;

(5) Rendering of services by an attorney;

(6) Preparation of documents, including notarization, delivery, and recordation;

(7) Rendering of credit reports and appraisals;

(8) Rendering of inspections, including inspections required by applicable law or any inspections required by the sales contract or mortgage documents prior to transfer of title;

(9) Conducting of settlement by a settlement agent and any related services;

(10) Provision of services involving mortgage insurance;

(11) Provision of services involving hazard, flood, or other casualty insurance or homeowner's warranties;

(12) Provision of services involving mortgage life, disability, or similar insurance designed to pay a mortgage loan upon disability or death of a borrower, but only if such insurance is required by the lender as a condition of the loan;

(13) Provision of services involving real property taxes or any other assessments or charges on the real property;

(14) Rendering of services by a real estate agent or real estate broker; and

(15) Provision of any other services for which a settlement service provider requires a borrower or seller to pay.

Special information booklet means the booklet prepared by the Secretary pursuant to section 5 of RESPA (12 U.S.C. 2604) to help persons understand the nature and costs of settlement services. The Secretary publishes the form of the special information booklet in the *Federal Register*. The Secretary may issue or approve additional booklets or alternative booklets by publication of a Notice in the *Federal Register*.

State means any State of the United States, the District of Columbia, the Commonwealth of Puerto Rico, and any territory or possession of the United States.

Table funding means a settlement at which a loan is funded by a contemporaneous advance of loan funds and an assignment of the loan to the person advancing the funds. A table-funded transaction is not a secondary market transaction (see § 3500.5(b)(7)).

Title company means any institution, or its duly authorized agent, that is qualified to issue title insurance.

[61 Fed. Reg. 13233 (Mar. 26, 1996), *as amended at* 61 Fed. Reg. 29252 (June 7, 1996); 61 Fed. Reg. 58475 (Nov. 15, 1996); 62 Fed. Reg. 20080 (Apr. 24, 1997)]

* * *

24 C.F.R. § 3500.4 Reliance upon rule, regulation or interpretation by HUD.

(a) *Rule, regulation or interpretation.*—

(1) For purposes of sections 19 (a) and (b) of RESPA (12 U.S.C. 2617 (a) and (b)) only the following constitute a rule, regulation or interpretation of the Secretary:

(i) All provisions, including appendices, of this part. Any other document referred to in this part is not incorporated in this part unless it is specifically set out in this part;

(ii) Any other document that is published in the *Federal Register* by the Secretary and states that it is an "interpretation," "interpretive rule," "commentary," or a "statement of policy" for purposes of section 19(a) of RESPA [19 U.S.C. § 2617(a)]. Such documents will be prepared by HUD staff and counsel. Such documents may be revoked or amended by a subsequent document published in the *Federal Register* by the Secretary.

(2) A "rule, regulation, or interpretation thereof by the Secretary" for purposes of section 19(b) of RESPA (12 U.S.C. 2617(b)) shall not include the special information booklet prescribed by the Secretary or any other statement or issuance, whether oral or written, by an officer or representative of the Department of Housing and Urban Development (HUD), letter or memorandum by the Secretary, General Counsel, any Assistant Secretary or other officer or employee of HUD, preamble to a regulation or other issuance of HUD, Public Guidance Document, report to Congress, pleading, affidavit or other document in litigation, pamphlet, handbook, guide, telegraphic communication, explanation, instructions to forms, speech or other material of any nature which is not specifically included in paragraph (a)(1) of this section.

(b) *Unofficial interpretations; staff discretion.* In response to requests for interpretation of matters not adequately covered by this part or by an official interpretation issued under paragraph (a)(1)(ii) of this section, unofficial staff interpretations may be provided at the discretion of HUD staff or counsel. Written requests for such interpretations should be directed to the address indicated in § 3500.3. Such interpretations provide no protection under section 19(b) of RESPA (12 U.S.C. 2617(b)). Ordinarily, staff or counsel will not issue unofficial interpretations on matters adequately covered by this Part or by official interpretations or commentaries issued under paragraph (a)(1)(ii) of this section.

(c) All informal counsel's opinions and staff interpretations issued before November 2, 1992, were withdrawn as of that date. Courts and administrative agencies, however, may use previous opinions to determine the validity of conduct under the previous Regulation X.

[61 Fed. Reg. 13233 (Mar. 26, 1996)]

24 C.F.R. § 3500.5 Coverage of RESPA.

(a) *Applicability.* RESPA and this part apply to all federally related mortgage loans, except for the exemptions provided in paragraph (b) of this section.

(b) *Exemptions.*

(1) A loan on property of 25 acres or more.

(2) *Business purpose loans.* An extension of credit primarily for a business, commercial, or agricultural purpose, as defined by Regulation Z, 12 CFR 226.3(a)(1). Persons may rely on Regulation Z in determining whether the exemption applies.

(3) *Temporary financing.* Temporary financing, such as a construction loan. The exemption for temporary financing does not apply to a loan made to finance construction of 1- to 4-family residential property if the loan is used as, or may be converted to, permanent financing by the same lender or is used to finance transfer of title to the first user. If a lender issues a commitment for permanent financing, with or without conditions, the loan is covered by this part. Any construction loan for new or rehabilitated 1- to 4-family residential property, other than a loan to a *bona fide* builder (a person who regularly constructs 1- to 4-family residential structures for sale or lease), is subject to this part if its term is for two years or more. A "bridge loan" or "swing loan" in which a lender takes a security interest in otherwise covered 1- to 4-family residential property is not covered by RESPA and this part.

(4) *Vacant land.* Any loan secured by vacant or unimproved property, unless within two years from the date of the settlement of the loan, a structure or a manufactured home will be constructed or placed on the real property using the loan proceeds. If a loan for a structure or manufactured home to be placed on vacant or unimproved property will be secured by a lien on that property, the transaction is covered by this part.

(5) *Assumption without lender approval.* Any assumption in which the lender does not have the right expressly to approve a subsequent person as the borrower on an existing federally related mortgage loan. Any assumption in which the lender's permission is both required and obtained is covered by RESPA and this part, whether or not the lender charges a fee for the assumption.

(6) *Loan conversions.* Any conversion of a federally related mortgage loan to different terms that are consistent with provisions of the original mortgage instrument, as long as a new note is not required, even if the lender charges an additional fee for the conversion.

(7) *Secondary market transactions.* A *bona fide* transfer of a loan obligation in the secondary market is not covered by RESPA and this part, except as set forth in section 6 of RESPA (12 U.S.C. 2605) and § 3500.21. In determining what constitutes a *bona fide* transfer, HUD will consider the real source of funding and the real interest of the funding lender. Mortgage broker transactions that are table-funded are not secondary market transactions. Neither the creation of a dealer loan or dealer consumer credit contract, nor the first assignment of such loan or contract to a lender, is a secondary market transaction (see § 3500.2.)

[61 Fed. Reg. 13235 (Mar. 26, 1996), *as amended at* 61 Fed. Reg. 58475 (Nov. 15, 1996)]

24 C.F.R. § 3500.6 Special information booklet at time of loan application.

(a) *Lender to provide special information booklet.* Subject to the exceptions set forth in this paragraph, the lender shall provide a copy of the special information booklet to a person from whom the lender receives, or for whom the lender prepares, a written application for a federally related mortgage loan. When two or more persons apply together for a loan, the lender is in compliance if the lender provides a copy of the booklet to one of the persons applying.

(1) The lender shall provide the special information booklet by delivering it or placing it in the mail to the applicant not later than three business days (as that term is defined in § 3500.2) after the application is received or prepared. However, if the lender denies the borrower's application for credit before the end of the three-business-day period, then the lender need not provide the booklet to the borrower. If a borrower uses a mortgage broker, the mortgage broker shall distribute the special information booklet and the lender need not do so. The intent of this provision is that the applicant receive the special information booklet at the earliest possible date.

(2) In the case of a federally related mortgage loan involving an open-ended credit plan, as defined in § 226.2(a)(20) of Regulation Z (12 CFR), a lender or mortgage broker that provides the borrower with a copy of the brochure entitled "When Your Home is On the Line: What You Should Know About Home Equity Lines of Credit", or any successor brochure issued by the Board of Governors of the Federal Reserve System, is deemed to be in compliance with this section.

(3) In the categories of transactions set forth at the end of this paragraph, the lender or mortgage broker does not have to provide the booklet to the borrower. Under the authority of section 19(a) of RESPA (12 U.S.C. 2617(a)), the Secretary may issue a revised or separate special

information booklet that deals with these transactions, or the Secretary may choose to endorse the forms or booklets of other Federal agencies. In such an event, the requirements for delivery by lenders and the availability of the booklet or alternate materials for these transactions will be set forth in a Notice in the *Federal Register*. This paragraph shall apply to the following transactions:

(i) Refinancing transactions;

(ii) Closed-end loans, as defined in 12 CFR 226.2(a)(10) of Regulation Z, when the lender takes a subordinate lien;

(iii) Reverse mortgages; and

(iv) Any other federally related mortgage loan whose purpose is not the purchase of a 1- to 4-family residential property.

(b) *Revision.* The Secretary may from time to time revise the special information booklet by publishing a notice in the *Federal Register*.

(c) *Reproduction.* The special information booklet may be reproduced in any form, provided that no change is made other than as provided under paragraph (d) of this section. The special information booklet may not be made a part of a larger document for purposes of distribution under RESPA and this section. Any color, size and quality of paper, type of print, and method of reproduction may be used so long as the booklet is clearly legible.

(d) *Permissible changes.*

(1) No changes to, deletions from, or additions to the special information booklet currently prescribed by the Secretary shall be made other than those specified in this paragraph (d) or any others approved in writing by the Secretary. A request to the Secretary for approval of any changes shall be submitted in writing to the address indicated in § 3500.3, stating the reasons why the applicant believes such changes, deletions or additions are necessary.

(2) The cover of the booklet may be in any form and may contain any drawings, pictures or artwork, provided that the words "settlement costs" are used in the title. Names, addresses and telephone numbers of the lender or others and similar information may appear on the cover, but no discussion of the matters covered in the booklet shall appear on the cover.

(3) The special information booklet may be translated into languages other than English.

[59 Fed. Reg. 6513 (Feb. 10, 1994); 59 Fed. Reg. 37423 (July 22, 1994); 61 Fed. Reg. 13233 (Mar. 26, 1996)]

24 C.F.R. § 3500.7 Good faith estimate.

(a) *Lender to provide.* Except as provided in this paragraph (a) or paragraph (f) of this section, the lender shall provide all applicants for a federally related mortgage loan with a good faith estimate of the amount of or range of charges for the specific settlement services the borrower is likely to incur in connection with the settlement. The lender shall provide the good faith estimate required under this section (a suggested format is set forth in Appendix C of this part) either by delivering the good faith estimate or by placing it in the mail to the loan applicant, not later than three business days after the application is received or prepared.

(1) If the lender denies the application for a federally related mortgage loan before the end of the three-business-day period, the lender need not provide the denied borrower with a good faith estimate.

(2) For "no cost" or "no point" loans, the charges to be shown on the good faith estimate include any payments to be made to affiliated or independent settlement service providers. These payments should be shown as P.O.C. (Paid Outside of Closing) on the Good Faith Estimate and the HUD-1 or HUD-1A.

(3) In the case of dealer loans, the lender is responsible for provision of the good faith estimate, either directly or by the dealer.

(4) If a mortgage broker is the exclusive agent of the lender, either the lender or the mortgage broker shall provide the good faith estimate within three business days after the mortgage broker receives or prepares the application.

(b) *Mortgage broker to provide.* In the event an application is received by a mortgage broker who is not an exclusive agent of the lender, the mortgage broker must provide a good faith estimate within three days of receiving a loan application based on his or her knowledge of the range of costs (a suggested format is set forth in Appendix C of this part). As long as the mortgage broker has provided the good faith estimate, the funding lender is not required to provide an additional good faith estimate, but the funding lender is responsible for ascertaining that the good faith estimate has been delivered. If the application for mortgage credit is denied before the end of the three-business-day period, the mortgage broker need not provide the denied borrower with a good faith estimate.

(c) *Content of good faith estimate.* A good faith estimate consists of an estimate, as a dollar amount or range, of each charge which:

(1) Will be listed in section L of the HUD-1 or HUD-1A in accordance with the instructions set forth in Appendix A to this part; and

(2) That the borrower will normally pay or incur at or before settlement based upon common practice in the locality of the mortgaged property. Each such estimate must be made in good faith and bear a reasonable relationship to the charge a borrower is likely to be required to pay at settlement, and must be based upon experience in the locality of the mortgaged property. As to each charge with respect to which the lender requires a particular settlement service provider to be used, the lender shall make its estimate based upon the lender's knowledge of the amounts charged by such provider.

(d) *Form of good faith estimate.* A suggested good faith estimate form is set forth in Appendix

C to this part and is in compliance with the requirements of the Act [12 U.S.C. § 2601 et seq.] except for any additional requirements of paragraph (e) of this section. The good faith estimate may be provided together with disclosures required by the Truth in Lending Act, 15 U.S.C. 1601 *et seq.*, so long as all required material for the good faith estimate is grouped together. The lender may include additional relevant information, such as the name/signature of the applicant and loan officer, date, and information identifying the loan application and property, as long as the form remains clear and concise and the additional information is not more prominent than the required material.

(e) *Particular providers required by lender.*

(1) If the lender requires the use (see § 3500.2, "required use") of a particular provider of a settlement service, other than the lender's own employees, and also requires the borrower to pay any portion of the cost of such service, then the good faith estimate must:

(i) Clearly state that use of the particular provider is required and that the estimate is based on the charges of the designated provider;

(ii) Give the name, address, and telephone number of each provider; and

(iii) Describe the nature of any relationship between each such provider and the lender. Plain English references to the relationship should be utilized, e.g., "X is a depositor of the lender," "X is a borrower from the lender," "X has performed 60% of the lender's settlements in the past year." (The lender is not required to keep detailed records of the percentages of use. Similar language, such as "X was used [regularly] [frequently] in our settlements the past year" is also sufficient for the purposes of this paragraph.) In the event that more than one relationship exists, each should be disclosed.

(2) For purposes of paragraph (e)(1) of this section, a "relationship" exists if:

(i) The provider is an associate of the lender, as that term is defined in 12 U.S.C. 2602(8);

(ii) Within the last 12 months, the provider has maintained an account with the lender or had an outstanding loan or credit arrangement with the lender; or

(iii) The lender has repeatedly used or required borrowers to use the services of the provider within the last 12 months.

(3) Except for a provider that is the lender's chosen attorney, credit reporting agency, or appraiser, if the lender is in an affiliated business relationship (see § 3500.15) with a provider, the lender may not require the use of that provider.

(4) If the lender maintains a controlled list of required providers (five or more for each discrete service) or relies on a list maintained by others, and at the time of application the lender has not yet decided which provider will be selected from that list, then the lender may satisfy the requirements of this section if the lender:

(i) Provides the borrower with a written statement that the lender will require a particular

provider from a lender-controlled or -approved list; and

(ii) Provides the borrower in the Good Faith Estimate the range of costs for the required provider(s), and provides the name of the specific provider and the actual cost on the HUD-1 or HUD-1A.

(f) *Open-end lines of credit (home-equity plans) under Truth in Lending Act.* In the case of a federally related mortgage loan involving an open-end line of credit (home-equity plan) covered under the Truth in Lending Act [15 U.S.C. § 1601 *et seq.*] and Regulation Z, a lender or mortgage broker that provides the borrower with the disclosures required by 12 CFR 226.5b of Regulation Z at the time the borrower applies for such loan shall be deemed to satisfy the requirements of this section.

[59 Fed. Reg. 6513 (Feb. 10, 1994); 59 Fed. Reg. 14749 (Mar. 30, 1994); 59 Fed. Reg. 37423 (July 22, 1994); 61 Fed. Reg. 13236 (Mar. 26, 1996), *as amended at* 61 Fed. Reg. 58476 (Nov. 15, 1996)]

24 C.F.R. § 3500.8 Use of HUD-1 or HUD-1A settlement statements.

(a) *Use by settlement agent.* The settlement agent shall use the HUD-1 settlement statement in every settlement involving a federally related mortgage loan in which there is a borrower and a seller. For transactions in which there is a borrower and no seller, such as refinancing loans or subordinate lien loans, the HUD-1 may be utilized by using the borrower's side of the HUD-1 statement. Alternatively, the form HUD-1A may be used for these transactions. Either the HUD-1 or the HUD-1A, as appropriate, shall be used for every RESPA-covered transaction, unless its use is specifically exempted, but the HUD-1 or HUD-1A may be modified as permitted under this part. The use of the HUD-1 or HUD-1A is exempted for open-end lines of credit (home-equity plans) covered by the Truth in Lending Act [15 U.S.C. § 1601 *et seq.*] and Regulation Z.

(b) *Charges to be stated.* The settlement agent shall complete the HUD-1 or HUD-1A in accordance with the instructions set forth in Appendix A to this part.

(c) *Aggregate Accounting At Settlement.*

(1) After itemizing individual deposits in the 1000 series using single-item accounting, the servicer shall make an adjustment based on aggregate accounting. This adjustment equals the difference in the deposit required under aggregate accounting and the sum of the deposits required under single-item accounting. The computation steps for both accounting methods are set out in § 3500.17(d). The adjustment will always be a negative number or zero (-0-). The settlement agent shall enter the aggregate adjust-

ment amount on a final line in the 1000 series of the HUD-1 or HUD-1A statement.

(2) During the phase-in period, as defined in § 3500.17(b), an alternative procedure is available. The settlement agent may initially calculate the 1000 series deposits for the HUD-1 and HUD-1A settlement statement using single-item analysis with only a one-month cushion (unless the mortgage loan documents indicate a smaller amount). In the escrow account analysis conducted within 45 days of settlement, however, the servicer shall adjust the escrow account to reflect the aggregate accounting balance. Appendix E to this part sets out examples of aggregate analysis. Appendix A to this part contains instructions for completing the HUD-1 or HUD-1A settlement statements using an aggregate analysis adjustment and the alternative process during the phase-in period.

[59 Fed. Reg. 6514 (Feb. 10, 1994); 59 Fed. Reg. 14749 (Mar. 30, 1994); 59 Fed. Reg. 53901 (Oct. 26, 1994); 60 Fed. Reg. 8816 (Feb. 15, 1995); 60 Fed. Reg. 24734 (May 9, 1995); 61 Fed. Reg. 13237 (Mar. 26, 1996), *as amended at* 61 Fed. Reg. 29252 (June 7, 1996); 61 Fed. Reg. 51782 (Oct. 4, 1996); 61 Fed. Reg. 58476 (Nov. 15, 1996)]

24 C.F.R. § 3500.9 Reproduction of settlement statements.

(a) *Permissible changes—HUD-1.* The following changes and insertions are permitted when the HUD-1 settlement statement is reproduced:

(1) The person reproducing the HUD-1 may insert its business name and logotype in Section A and may rearrange, but not delete, the other information that appears in Section A.

(2) The name, address, and other information regarding the lender and settlement agent may be printed in Sections F and H, respectively.

(3) Reproduction of the HUD-1 must conform to the terminology, sequence, and numbering of line items as presented in lines 100-1400. However, blank lines or items listed in lines 100-1400 that are not used locally or in connection with mortgages by the lender may be deleted, except for the following: Lines 100. 120, 200, 220, 300, 301, 302, 303, 400, 420, 500, 520, 600, 601, 602, 603, 700, 800, 900, 1000, 1100, 1200, 1300, and 1400. The form may be shortened correspondingly. The number of a deleted item shall not be used for a substitute or new item, but the number of a blank space on the HUD-1 may be used for a substitute or new item.

(4) Charges not listed on the HUD-1, but that are customary locally or pursuant to the lender's practice, may be inserted in blank spaces. Where existing blank spaces on the HUD-1 are insufficient, additional lines and spaces may be added and numbered in sequence with spaces on the HUD-1.

(5) The following variations in layout and format are within the discretion of persons reproducing the HUD-1 and do not require prior HUD approval: size of pages; tint or color of pages; size and style of type or print; vertical spacing between lines or provision for additional horizontal space on lines (for example, to provide sufficient space for recording time periods used in prorations); printing of the HUD-1 contents on separate pages, on the front and back of a single page, or on one continuous page; use of multicopy tear-out sets; printing on rolls for computer purposes; reorganization of Sections B through I, when necessary to accommodate computer printing; and manner of placement of the HUD number, but not the OMB approval number, neither of which may be deleted. The designation of the expiration date of the OMB number may be deleted. Any changes in the HUD number or OMB approval number may be announced by notice in the *Federal Register*, rather than by amendment of this part.

(6) The borrower's information and the seller's information may be provided on separate pages.

(7) Signature lines may be added.

(8) The HUD-1 may be translated into languages other than English.

(9) An additional page may be attached to the HUD-1 for the purpose of including customary recitals and information used locally in real estate settlements; for example, breakdown of payoff figures, a breakdown of the borrower's total monthly mortgage payments, check disbursements, a statement indicating receipt of funds, applicable special stipulations between buyer and seller, and the date funds are transferred. If space permits, such information may be added at the end of the HUD-1.

(10) As required by HUD/FHA in FHA-insured loans.

(11) As allowed by § 3500.17, relating to an initial escrow account statement.

(b) *Permissible changes—HUD-1A.* The changes and insertions on the HUD-1 permitted under paragraph (a) of this section are also permitted when the HUD-1A settlement statement is reproduced, except the changes described in paragraphs (a)(3) and (6) of this section.

(c) *Written approval.* Any other deviation in the HUD-1 or HUD-1A forms is permissible only upon receipt of written approval of the Secretary. A request to the Secretary for approval shall be submitted in writing to the address indicated in § 3500.3 and shall state the reasons why the applicant believes such deviation is needed. The prescribed form(s) must be used until approval is received.

[59 Fed. Reg. 6514 (Feb. 10, 1994); 59 Fed. Reg. 14749 (Mar. 30, 1994); 61 Fed. Reg. 13238 (Mar. 26, 1996)]

24 C.F.R. § 3500.10 One-day advance inspection of HUD-1 or HUD-1A settlement statement; delivery; recordkeeping

(a) *Inspection one day prior to settlement upon request by the borrower.* The settlement agent shall permit the borrower to inspect the HUD-1 or HUD-1A settlement statement, completed to set forth those items that are known to the settlement agent at the time of inspection, during the business day immediately preceding settlement. Items related only to the seller's transaction may be omitted from the HUD-1.

(b) *Delivery.* The settlement agent shall provide a completed HUD-1 or HUD-1A to the borrower, the seller (if there is one), the lender (if the lender is not the settlement agent), and/or their agents. When the borrower's and seller's copies of the HUD-1 or HUD-1A differ as permitted by the instructions in Appendix A to this part, both copies shall be provided to the lender (if the lender is not the settlement agent). The settlement agent shall deliver the completed HUD-1 or HUD-1A at or before the settlement, except as provided in paragraphs (c) and (d) of this section.

(c) *Waiver.* The borrower may waive the right to delivery of the completed HUD-1 or HUD-1A no later than at settlement by executing a written waiver at or before settlement. In such case, the completed HUD-1 or HUD-1A shall be mailed or delivered to the borrower, seller, and lender (if the lender is not the settlement agent) as soon as practicable after settlement.

(d) *Exempt transactions.* When the borrower or the borrower's agent does not attend the settlement, or when the settlement agent does not conduct a meeting of the parties for that purpose, the transaction shall be exempt from the requirements of paragraphs (a) and (b) of this section, except that the HUD-1 or HUD-1A shall be mailed or delivered as soon as practicable after settlement.

(e) *Recordkeeping.* The lender shall retain each completed HUD-1 or HUD-1A and related documents for five years after settlement, unless the lender disposes of its interest in the mortgage and does not service the mortgage. In that case, the lender shall provide its copy of the HUD-1 or HUD-1A to the owner or servicer of the mortgage as a part of the transfer of the loan file. Such owner or servicer shall retain the HUD-1 or HUD-1A for the remainder of the five-year period. The Secretary shall have the right to inspect or require copies of records covered by this paragraph (e).

[59 Fed. Reg. 6515 (Feb. 10, 1994); 61 Fed. Reg. 13238 (Mar. 26, 1996)]

* * *

24 C.F.R. § 3500.12 No fee.

No fee shall be imposed or charge made upon any other person, as a part of settlement costs or otherwise, by a lender in connection with a federally related mortgage loan made by it (or a loan for the purchase of a manufactured home), or by a servicer (as that term is defined under 12 U.S.C. 2605(i)(2)) for or on account of the preparation and distribution of the HUD-1 or HUD-1A settlement statement, escrow account statements required pursuant to section 10 of RESPA (12 U.S.C. 2609), or statements required by the Truth in Lending Act, 15 U.S.C. 1601 *et seq.*

[61 Fed. Reg. 13239 (Mar. 26, 1996)]

24 C.F.R. § 3500.13 Relation to State laws.

(a) State laws that are inconsistent with RESPA or this part are preempted to the extent of the inconsistency. However, RESPA and these regulations do not annul, alter, affect, or exempt any person subject to their provisions from complying with the laws of any State with respect to settlement practices, except to the extent of the inconsistency.

(b) Upon request by any person, the Secretary is authorized to determine if inconsistencies with State law exist; in doing so, the Secretary shall consult with appropriate Federal agencies.

(1) The Secretary may not determine that a State law or regulation is inconsistent with any provision of RESPA or this part, if the Secretary determines that such law or regulation gives greater protection to the consumer.

(2) In determining whether provisions of State law or regulations concerning affiliated business arrangements are inconsistent with RESPA or this part, the Secretary may not construe those provisions that impose more stringent limitations on affiliated business arrangements as inconsistent with RESPA so long as they give more protection to consumers and/or competition.

(c) Any person may request the Secretary to determine whether an inconsistency exists by submitting to the address indicated in § 3500.3, a copy of the State law in question, any other law or judicial or administrative opinion that implements, interprets or applies the relevant provision, and an explanation of the possible inconsistency. A determination by the Secretary that an inconsistency with State law exists will be made by publication of a notice in the *Federal Register.* "Law" as used in this section includes regulations and any enactment which has the force and effect of law and is issued by a State or any political subdivision of a State.

(d) A specific preemption of conflicting State laws regarding notices and disclosures of mortgage servicing transfers is set forth in § 3500.21(h).

[57 Fed. Reg. 56857 (Dec. 1, 1992); 61 Fed. Reg. 13239 (Mar. 26, 1996), *as amended at* 61 Fed. Reg. 58476 (Nov. 15, 1996)]

24 C.F.R. § 3500.14 Prohibition against kickbacks and unearned fees.

(a) *Section 8 violation.* Any violation of this section is a violation of section 8 of RESPA (12 U.S.C. 2607) and is subject to enforcement as such under § 3500.19.

(b) *No referral fees.* No person shall give and no person shall accept any fee, kickback or other thing of value pursuant to any agreement or understanding, oral or otherwise, that business incident to or part of a settlement service involving a federally related mortgage loan shall be referred to any person. Any referral of a settlement service is not a compensable service, except as set forth in § 3500.14(g)(1). A company may not pay any other company or the employees of any other company for the referral of settlement service business.

[*Editor's Note: HUD promulgated the following change to this subsection but stayed its effective date. It is possible that the proposed change may be withdrawn. Check for developments in the Federal Register. Replace the last sentence in subsection (b) with:*

A business entity (whether or not in an affiliate relationship) may not pay any other business entity or the employees of any other business entity for the referral of settlement service business.

[*61 Fed. Reg. 22938, 29252 (June 7, 1996); 61 Fed. Reg. 51782 (Oct. 4, 1996)]*]

(c) *No split of charges except for actual services performed.* No person shall give and no person shall accept any portion, split, or percentage of any charge made or received for the rendering of a settlement service in connection with a transaction involving a federally related mortgage loan other than for services actually performed. A charge by a person for which no or nominal services are performed or for which duplicative fees are charged is an unearned fee and violates this section. The source of the payment does not determine whether or not a service is compensable. Nor may the prohibitions of this Part be avoided by creating an arrangement wherein the purchaser of services splits the fee.

(d) *Thing of value.* This term is broadly defined in section 3(2) of RESPA (12 U.S.C. 2602(2)). It includes, without limitation, monies, things, discounts, salaries, commissions, fees, duplicate payments of a charge, stock, dividends, distributions of partnership profits, franchise royalties, credits representing monies that may be paid at a future date, the opportunity to participate in a money-making program, retained or increased earnings, increased equity in a parent or subsidiary entity, special bank deposits or accounts, special or unusual banking terms, services of all types at special or free rates, sales or rentals at special prices or rates, lease or rental payments based in whole or in part on the amount of business referred, trips and payment of another person's expenses, or reduction in credit against an existing obligation. The term "payment" is used throughout §§ 3500.14 and 3500.15 as synonymous with the giving or receiving any "thing of value" and does not require transfer of money.

(e) *Agreement or understanding.* An agreement or understanding for the referral of business incident to or part of a settlement service need not be written or verbalized but may be established by a practice, pattern or course of conduct. When a thing of value is received repeatedly and is connected in any way with the volume or value of the business referred, the receipt of the thing of value is evidence that it is made pursuant to an agreement or understanding for the referral of business.

(f) *Referral*—

(1) A referral includes any oral or written action directed to a person which has the effect of affirmatively influencing the selection by any person of a provider of a settlement service or business incident to or part of a settlement service when such person will pay for such settlement service or business incident thereto or pay a charge attributable in whole or in part to such settlement service or business.

(2) A referral also occurs whenever a person paying for a settlement service or business incident thereto is required to use (see § 3500.2, "required use") a particular provider of a settlement service or business incident thereto.

(g) *Fees, salaries, compensation, or other payments.*

(1) Section 8 of RESPA [12 U.S.C. § 2607] permits:

(i) A payment to an attorney at law for services actually rendered;

(ii) A payment by a title company to its duly appointed agent for services actually performed in the issuance of a policy of title insurance;

(iii) A payment by a lender to its duly appointed agent or contractor for services actually performed in the origination, processing, or funding of a loan;

(iv) A payment to any person of a *bona fide* salary or compensation or other payment for goods or facilities actually furnished or for services actually performed;

(v) A payment pursuant to cooperative brokerage and referral arrangements or agreements between real estate agents and real estate brokers. (The statutory exemption restated in this paragraph refers only to fee divisions within real estate brokerage arrangements when all parties are acting in a real estate brokerage capacity, and has no applicability to any fee arrangements between real estate brokers and mortgage brokers or between mortgage brokers.)

(vi) Normal promotional and educational activities that are not conditioned on the referral of business and do not involve the defraying of expenses that otherwise would be incurred by persons in a position to refer settlement services or business incident thereto; or

(vii) An employer's payment to its own employees for any referral activities generating business for that employer.

(2) The Department may investigate high prices to see if they are the result of a referral fee or a split of a fee. If the payment of a thing of value bears no reasonable relationship to the market value of the goods or services provided, then the excess is not for services or goods actually performed or provided. These facts may be used as evidence of a violation of section 8 [12 U.S.C. § 2607] and may serve as a basis for a RESPA investigation. High prices standing alone are not proof of a RESPA violation. The value of a referral (i.e., the value of any additional business obtained thereby) is not to be taken into account in determining whether the payment exceeds the reasonable value of such goods, facilities or services. The fact that the transfer of the thing of value does not result in an increase in any charge made by the person giving the thing of value is irrelevant in determining whether the act is prohibited.

(3) *Multiple services.* When a person in a position to refer settlement service business, such as an attorney, mortgage lender, real estate broker or agent, or developer or builder, receives a payment for providing additional settlement services as part of a real estate transaction, such payment must be for services that are actual, necessary and distinct from the primary services provided by such person. For example, for an attorney of the buyer or seller to receive compensation as a title agent, the attorney must perform core title agent services (for which liability arises) separate from attorney services, including the evaluation of the title search to determine the insurability of the title, the clearance of underwriting objections, the actual issuance of the policy or policies on behalf of the title insurance company, and, where customary, issuance of the title commitment, and the conducting of the title search and closing.

(h) *Recordkeeping.* Any documents provided pursuant to this section shall be retained for five (5) years from the date of execution.

(i) *Appendix B of this part.* Illustrations in Appendix B of this part demonstrate some of the requirements of this section.

[61 Fed. Reg. 13239 (Mar. 26, 1996), *as amended at* 61 Fed. Reg. 29252 (June 7, 1996); 61 Fed. Reg. 58476 (Nov. 15, 1996)]

[*Editor's Note: HUD promulgated the following change to this subsection but stayed its effective date. It is possible that the proposed change may be withdrawn. Check for developments in the Federal Register. Replace subsection (g) with:*

(g) *Exemptions for fees, salaries, compensation, or other payments.*

(1) *The following are permissible:*

(i) *A payment to an attorney at law for services actually rendered;*

(ii) *A payment by a title company to its duly appointed agent for services actually performed in the issuance of a policy of title insurance;*

(iii) *A payment by a lender to its duly appointed agent or contractor for services actually performed in the origination, processing, or funding of a loan;*

(iv) *A payment to any person of a bona fide salary or compensation or other payment for goods or facilities actually furnished or for services actually performed;*

(v) *A payment pursuant to cooperative brokerage and referral arrangements or agreements between real estate agents and real estate brokers. (The statutory exemption restated in this paragraph refers only to fee divisions within real estate brokerage arrangements when all parties are acting in a real estate brokerage capacity, and has no applicability to any fee arrangements between real estate brokers and mortgage brokers or between mortgage brokers.)*

(vi) *Normal promotional and educational activities that are not conditioned on the referral of business and do not involve the defraying of expenses that otherwise would be incurred by persons in a position to refer settlement services or business incident thereto; or*

(vii) *A payment by an employer to its own bona fide employee for generating business for that employer.*

(viii) *In a controlled business arrangement, a payment by an employer of a bonus to a managerial employee based on criteria relating to performance (such as profitability, capture rate, or other thresholds) of a business entity in the controlled business arrangement. However, the amount of such bonus may not be calculated as a multiple of the number or value of referrals of settlement service business to a business entity in a controlled business arrangement; and*

(ix)(A) *A payment by an employer to its bona fide employee for the referral of settlement service business to a settlement service provider that has an affiliate relationship with the employer or in which the employer has a direct or beneficial ownership interest of more than 1 percent, if the following conditions are met:*

(1) *The employee does not perform settlement services in any transaction; and*

(2) *Before the referral, the employee provides to the person being referred a written disclosure in the format of the Controlled Business Arrangement Settlement Statement, set forth in Appendix D to this part.*

(B) *For purpose of this paragraph (g)(1)(ix), the marketing of a settlement service or product of an affiliated entity, including the collection and conveyance of information or the taking of an application or order for an affiliated entity, does not constitute the performance of a settlement service. Under this paragraph (g)(1)(ix), marketing of a settlement service or product may include incidental communications with the con-*

sumer after the application or order, such as providing the consumer with information about the status of an application or order; marketing shall not include serving as the ongoing point of contact for coordinating the delivery and provision of settlement services.

[*61 Fed. Reg. 29238, 29252 (June 7, 1996); 61 Fed. Reg. 51782 (Oct. 4, 1996)]*]

24 C.F.R. § 3500.15 Affiliated business arrangements.

(a) *General.* An affiliated business arrangement is defined in section 3(7) of RESPA (12 U.S.C. 2602(7)).

(b) *Violation and exemption.* An affiliated business arrangement is not a violation of section 8 of RESPA (12 U.S.C. 2607) and of § 3500.14 if the conditions set forth in this section are satisfied. Paragraph (b)(1) of this section shall not apply to the extent it is inconsistent with section 8(c)(4)(A) of RESPA (12 U.S.C. 2607(c)(4)(A)).

(1) The person making each referral has provided to each person whose business is referred a written disclosure, in the format of the Affiliated Business Arrangement Disclosure Statement set forth in Appendix D of this part, of the nature of the relationship (explaining the ownership and financial interest) between the provider of settlement services (or business incident thereto) and the person making the referral and of an estimated charge or range of charges generally made by such provider (which describes the charge using the same terminology, as far as practical, as Section L of the HUD-1 or HUD-1A settlement statement). The disclosures must be provided on a separate piece of paper no later than the time of each referral or, if the lender requires the use of a particular provider, the time of loan application, except that:

[*Editor's Note: HUD promulgated the following change to this subsection but stayed its effective date. It is possible that the proposed change may be withdrawn. Check for developments in the Federal Register. Replace subsection (1) with:*

(1) *Prior to the referral, the person making a referral has provided to each person whose business is referred a written disclosure, in the format of the Controlled Business Arrangement Disclosure Statement set forth in Appendix D of this part. This disclosure shall specify the nature of the relationship (explaining the ownership and financial interest) between the person performing settlement services (or business incident thereto) and the person making the referral, and shall describe the estimated charge or range of charges (using the same terminology, as far as practical, as Section L of the HUD-1 or HUD-1A settlement statement) generally made by the provider of settlement services. The disclosure must be provided on a separate piece of paper no later than the time of each referral or, if the lender*

requires the use of a particular provider, the time of loan application, except that:

[61 Fed. Reg. 29238, 29252 (June 7, 1996); 61 Fed. Reg. 51782 (Oct. 4, 1996)]]

(i) Where a lender makes the referral to a borrower, the condition contained in paragraph (b)(1) of this section may be satisfied at the time that the good faith estimate or a statement under § 3500.7(d) is provided; and

(ii) Whenever an attorney or law firm requires a client to use a particular title insurance agent, the attorney or law firm shall provide the disclosures no later than the time the attorney or law firm is engaged by the client. Failure to comply with the disclosure requirements of this section may be overcome if the person making a referral can prove by a preponderance of the evidence that procedures reasonably adopted to result in compliance with these conditions have been maintained and that any failure to comply with these conditions was unintentional and the result of a *bona fide* error. An error of legal judgment with respect to a person's obligations under RESPA is not a *bona fide* error. Administrative and judicial interpretations of section 130(c) of the Truth in Lending Act [15 U.S.C. § 1640(c)] shall not be binding interpretations of the preceding sentence or section 8(d)(3) of RESPA (12 U.S.C. 2607(d)(3)).

(2) No person making a referral has required (as defined in § 3500.2, "required use") any person to use any particular provider of settlement services or business incident thereto, except if such person is a lender, for requiring a buyer, borrower or seller to pay for the services of an attorney, credit reporting agency, or real estate appraiser chosen by the lender to represent the lender's interest in a real estate transaction, or except if such person is an attorney or law firm for arranging for issuance of a title insurance policy for a client, directly as agent or through a separate corporate title insurance agency that may be operated as an adjunct to the law practice of the attorney or law firm, as part of representation of that client in a real estate transaction.

(3) The only thing of value that is received from the arrangement other than payments listed in § 3500.14(g) is a return on an ownership interest or franchise relationship.

(i) In an affiliated business arrangement:

(A) *Bona fide* dividends, and capital or equity distributions, related to ownership interest or franchise relationship, between entities in an affiliate relationship, are permissible; and

(B) *Bona fide* business loans, advances, and capital or equity contributions between entities in an affiliate relationship (in any direction), are not prohibited—so long as they are for ordinary business purposes and are not fees for the referral of settlement service business or unearned fees.

(ii) A return on an ownership interest does not include:

(A) Any payment which has as a basis of calculation no apparent business motive other than distinguishing among recipients of pay-

ments on the basis of the amount of their actual, estimated or anticipated referrals;

(B) Any payment which varies according to the relative amount of referrals by the different recipients of similar payments; or

(C) A payment based on an ownership, partnership or joint venture share which has been adjusted on the basis of previous relative referrals by recipients of similar payments.

(iii) Neither the mere labelling of a thing of value, nor the fact that it may be calculated pursuant to a corporate or partnership organizational document or a franchise agreement, will determine whether it is a *bona fide* return on an ownership interest or franchise relationship. Whether a thing of value is such a return will be determined by analyzing facts and circumstances on a case by case basis.

(iv) A return on franchise relationship may be a payment to or from a franchisee but it does not include any payment which is not based on the franchise agreement, nor any payment which varies according to the number or amount of referrals by the franchisor or franchisee or which is based on a franchise agreement which has been adjusted on the basis of a previous number or amount of referrals by the franchisor or franchisees. A franchise agreement may not be constructed to insulate against kickbacks or referral fees.

(c) *Definitions.* As used in this section:

(1) *Associate* is defined in section 3(8) of RESPA (12 U.S.C. 2602(8)).

(2) *Affiliate relationship* means the relationship among business entities where one entity has effective control over the other by virtue of a partnership or other agreement or is under common control with the other by a third entity or where an entity is a corporation related to another corporation as parent to subsidiary by an identity of stock ownership.

(3) *Beneficial ownership* means the effective ownership of an interest in a provider of settlement services or the right to use and control the ownership interest involved even though legal ownership or title may be held in another person's name.

(4) *Control,* as used in the definitions of "associate" and "affiliate relationship," means that a person:

(i) Is a general partner, officer, director, or employer of another person;

(ii) Directly or indirectly or acting in concert with others, or through one or more subsidiaries, owns, holds with power to vote, or holds proxies representing, more than 20 percent of the voting interests of another person;

(iii) Affirmatively influences in any manner the election of a majority of the directors of another person; or

(iv) Has contributed more than 20 percent of the capital of the other person.

(5) *Direct ownership* means the holding of legal title to an interest in a provider of settlement service except where title is being held for the beneficial owner.

(6) *Franchise* is defined in 16 CFR 436.2(a).

(7) *Franchisor* is defined in 16 CFR 436.2(c).

(8) *Franchisee* is defined in 16 CFR 436.2(d).

(9) *Person who is in a position to refer settlement service business* means any real estate broker or agent, lender, mortgage broker, builder or developer, attorney, title company, title agent, or other person deriving a significant portion of his or her gross income from providing settlement services.

(d) *Recordkeeping.* Any documents provided pursuant to this section shall be retained for 5 years after the date of execution.

(e) *Appendix B of this part.* Illustrations in Appendix B of this part demonstrate some of the requirements of this section.

[57 Fed. Reg. 56857 (Dec. 1, 1992); 59 Fed. Reg. 6515 (Feb. 10, 1994); 61 Fed. Reg. 13240 (Mar. 26, 1996), *as amended at* 61 Fed. Reg. 29252 (June 7, 1996); 61 Fed. Reg. 51782 (Oct. 4, 1996); 61 Fed. Reg. 58476 (Nov. 15, 1996)]

24 C.F.R. § 3500.16 Title companies.

No seller of property that will be purchased with the assistance of a federally related mortgage loan shall violate section 9 of RESPA (12 U.S.C. 2608). Section 3500.2 defines "required use" of a provider of a settlement service. Section 3500.19(c) explains the liability of a seller for a violation of this section.

[59 Fed. Reg. 6515 (Feb. 10, 1994); 61 Fed. Reg. 13241 (Mar. 26, 1996)]

24 C.F.R. § 3500.17 Escrow accounts.

[*Editor's Note: The regulation concerning calculation and accounting procedures for escrow accounts established in conjunction with mortgage loans, such as those established for payment of property taxes and property insurance premiums, was published at 61 Fed. Reg. 13241 (Mar. 26, 1996) and amended by 63 Fed. Reg. 3214 (Jan. 21, 1998) and 68 Fed. Reg. 12789 (Mar. 17, 2003). It is not reprinted here.*]

* * *

24 C.F.R. § 3500.19 Enforcement.

(a) *Enforcement Policy.* It is the policy of the Secretary regarding RESPA enforcement matters to cooperate with Federal, State or local agencies having supervisory powers over lenders or other persons with responsibilities under RESPA. Federal agencies with supervisory powers over lenders may use their powers to require compliance with RESPA. In addition, failure to comply with

RESPA may be grounds for administrative action by the Secretary under part 24 of this title concerning debarment, suspension, ineligibility of contractors and grantees, or under part 25 of this title concerning the HUD Mortgagee Review Board. Nothing in this paragraph is a limitation on any other form of enforcement which may be legally available.

(b) *Violations of section 8 of RESPA (12 U.S.C. 2607), § 3500.14, or § 3500.15.* Any person who violates §§ 3500.14 or 3500.15 shall be deemed to violate Section 8 of RESPA and shall be sanctioned accordingly.

(c) *Violations of section 9 of RESPA (12 U.S.C. 2608) or § 3500.16.* Any person who violates Section 3500.16 of this part shall be deemed to violate Section 9 of RESPA and shall be sanctioned accordingly.

(d) *Investigations.* The procedures for investigations and investigational proceedings are set forth in 24 CFR part 3800.

[61 Fed. Reg. 13247 (Mar. 26, 1996)]

* * *

24 C.F.R. § 3500.21 Mortgage servicing transfers.

(a) *Definitions.* As used in this section:

Master servicer means the owner of the right to perform servicing, which may actually perform the servicing itself or may do so through a subservicer.

Mortgage servicing loan means a federally related mortgage loan, as that term is defined in § 3500.2, subject to the exemptions in § 3500.5, when the mortgage loan is secured by a first lien. The definition does not include subordinate lien loans or open-end lines of credit (home equity plans) covered by the Truth in Lending Act [15 U.S.C. § 1601 *et seq.*] and Regulation Z, including open-end lines of credit secured by a first lien.

Qualified written request means a written correspondence from the borrower to the servicer prepared in accordance with paragraph (e)(2) of this section.

Subservicer means a servicer who does not own the right to perform servicing, but who does so on behalf of the master servicer.

Transferee servicer means a servicer who obtains or who will obtain the right to perform servicing functions pursuant to an agreement or understanding.

Transferor servicer means a servicer, including a table funding mortgage broker or dealer on a first lien dealer loan, who transfers or will transfer the right to perform servicing functions pursuant to an agreement or understanding.

(b) *Servicing Disclosure Statement and Applicant Acknowledgement; requirements.*

(1) At the time an application for a mortgage servicing loan is submitted, or within 3 business days after submission of the application, the lender, mortgage broker who anticipates using table funding, or dealer who anticipates a first lien dealer loan shall provide to each person who applies for such a loan a Servicing Disclosure Statement. This requirement shall not apply when the application for credit is turned down within three business days after receipt of the application. A format for the Servicing Disclosure Statement appears as Appendix MS-1 to this part. Except as provided in paragraph (b)(2) of this section, the specific language of the Servicing Disclosure Statement is not required to be used, but the Servicing Disclosure Statement must include the information set out in paragraph (b)(3) of this section, including the statement of the borrower's rights in connection with complaint resolution. The information set forth in Instructions to Preparer on the Servicing Disclosure Statement need not be included on the form given to applicants, and material in square brackets is optional or alternative language.

(2) The Applicant's Acknowledgement portion of the Servicing Disclosure Statement in the format stated is mandatory. Additional lines may be added to accommodate more than two applicants.

(3) The Servicing Disclosure Statement must contain the following information, except as provided in paragraph (b)(3)(ii) of this section:

(i) Whether the servicing of the loan may be assigned, sold or transferred to any other person at any time while the loan is outstanding. If the lender, table funding mortgage broker, or dealer in a first lien dealer loan does not engage in the servicing of any mortgage servicing loans, the disclosure may consist of a statement to the effect that there is a current intention to assign, sell, or transfer servicing of the loan.

(ii) The percentages (rounded to the nearest quartile (25%)) of mortgage servicing loans originated by the lender in each calendar year for which servicing has been assigned, sold, or transferred for such calendar year. Compliance with this paragraph (b)(3)(ii) is not required if the lender, table funding mortgage broker, or dealer on a first lien dealer loan chooses option B in the model format in paragraph (b)(4) of this section, including in square brackets the language "[and have not serviced mortgage loans in the last three years.]". The percentages shall be provided as follows:

(A) This information shall be set out for the most recent three calendar years completed, with percentages as of the end of each year. This information shall be updated in the disclosure no later than March 31 of the next calendar year. Each percentage should be obtained by using as the numerator the number of mortgage servicing loans originated during the calendar year for which servicing is transferred within the calendar year and, as the denominator, the total number of mortgage servicing loans originated in the calendar year. If the volume of transfers is less than 12.5 percent, the word "nominal" or the actual percentage amount of servicing transfers may be used.

(B) This statistical information does not have to include the assignment, sale, or transfer of mortgage loan servicing by the lender to an affiliate or subsidiary of the lender. However, lenders may voluntarily include transfers to an affiliate or subsidiary. The lender should indicate whether the percentages provided include assignments, sales, or transfers to affiliates or subsidiaries.

(C) In the alternative, if applicable, the following statement may be substituted for the statistical information required to be provided in accordance with paragraph (b)(3)(ii) of this section: "We have previously assigned, sold, or transferred the servicing of federally related mortgage loans."

(iii) The best available estimate of the percentage (0 to 25 percent, 26 to 50 percent, 51 to 75 percent, or 76 to 100 percent) of all loans to be made during the 12-month period beginning on the date of origination for which the servicing may be assigned, sold, or transferred. Each percentage should be obtained by using as the numerator the estimated number of mortgage servicing loans that will be originated for which servicing may be transferred within the 12-month period and, as the denominator, the estimated total number of mortgage servicing loans that will be originated in the 12-month period.

(A) If the lender, mortgage broker, or dealer anticipates that no loan servicing will be sold during the calendar year, the word "none" may be substituted for "0 to 25 percent." If it is anticipated that all loan servicing will be sold during the calendar year, the word "all" may be substituted for "76 to 100 percent."

(B) This statistical information does not have to include the estimated assignment, sale, or transfer of mortgage loan servicing to an affiliate or subsidiary of that person. However, this information may be provided voluntarily. The Servicing Disclosure Statements should indicate whether the percentages provided include assignments, sales or transfers to affiliates or subsidiaries.

(iv) The information set out in paragraphs (d) and (e) of this section.

(v) A written acknowledgement that the applicant (and any co-applicant) has/have read and understood the disclosure, and understand that the disclosure is a required part of the mortgage application. This acknowledgement shall be evidenced by the signature of the applicant and any co-applicant.

(4) The following is a model format, which includes several options, for complying with the requirements of paragraph (b)(3) of this section. The model format may be annotated with additional information that clarifies or enhances the model language. The lender or table funding mortgage broker (or dealer) should use the language that best describes the particular circumstances.

(i) *Model Format*: The following is the best estimate of what will happen to the servicing of your mortgage loan:

(A) *Option A.* We may assign, sell, or transfer the servicing of your loan while the loan is outstanding. [We are able to service your loan[.][,] and we [will] [will not] [haven't decided whether to] service your loan.]; or

(B) *Option B.* We do not service mortgage loans[.][,] [and have not serviced mortgage loans in the past three years.] We presently intend to assign, sell, or transfer the servicing of your mortgage loan. You will be informed about your servicer.

(C) As appropriate, the following paragraph may be used:

We assign, sell, or transfer the servicing of some of our loans while the loans are outstanding, depending on the type of loan and other factors. For the program for which you have applied, we expect to [assign, sell, or transfer all of the mortgage servicing][retain all of the mortgage servicing] [assign, sell, or transfer [rule; 3]% of the mortgage servicing].

(ii) [Reserved]

(c) *Servicing Disclosure Statement and Applicant Acknowledgement; delivery.* The lender, table funding mortgage broker, or dealer that anticipates a first lien dealer loan shall deliver Servicing Disclosure Statements to each applicant for mortgage servicing loans. Each applicant or co-applicant must sign an Acknowledgement of receipt of the Servicing Disclosure Statement before settlement.

(1) In the case of a face-to-face interview with one or more applicants, the Servicing Disclosure Statement shall be delivered at the time of application. An applicant present at the interview may sign the Acknowledgment on his or her own behalf at that time. An applicant present at the interview also may accept delivery of the Servicing Disclosure Statement on behalf of the other applicants.

(2) If there is no face-to-face interview, the Servicing Disclosure Statement shall be delivered by placing it in the mail, with prepaid first-class postage, within 3 business days from receipt of the application. If co-applicants indicate the same address on their application, one copy delivered to that address is sufficient. If different addresses are shown by co-applicants on the application, a copy must be delivered to each of the co-applicants.

(3) The signed Applicant Acknowledgment(s) shall be retained for a period of 5 years after the date of settlement as part of the loan file for every settled loan. There is no requirement for retention of Applicant Acknowledgment(s) if the loan is not settled.

(d) *Notices of Transfer; loan servicing.*

(1) *Requirement for notice.*

(i) Except as provided in this paragraph (d)(1)(i) or paragraph (d)(1)(ii) of this section, each transferor servicer and transferee servicer of any mortgage servicing loan shall deliver to the borrower a written Notice of Transfer, containing the information described in paragraph (d)(3) of this section, of any assignment, sale, or transfer of the servicing of the loan. The following transfers

are not considered an assignment, sale, or transfer of mortgage loan servicing for purposes of this requirement if there is no change in the payee, address to which payment must be delivered, account number, or amount of payment due:

(A) Transfers between affiliates;

(B) Transfers resulting from mergers or acquisitions of servicers or subservicers; and

(C) Transfers between master servicers, where the subservicer remains the same.

(ii) The Federal Housing Administration (FHA) is not required under paragraph (d) of this section to submit to the borrower a Notice of Transfer in cases where a mortgage insured under the National Housing Act is assigned to FHA.

(2) *Time of notice.*

(i) Except as provided in paragraph (d)(2)(ii) of this section:

(A) The transferor servicer shall deliver the Notice of Transfer to the borrower not less than 15 days before the effective date of the transfer of the servicing of the mortgage servicing loan;

(B) The transferee servicer shall deliver the Notice of Transfer to the borrower not more than 15 days after the effective date of the transfer; and

(C) The transferor and transferee servicers may combine their notices into one notice, which shall be delivered to the borrower not less than 15 days before the effective date of the transfer of the servicing of the mortgage servicing loan.

(ii) The Notice of Transfer shall be delivered to the borrower by the transferor servicer or the transferee servicer not more than 30 days after the effective date of the transfer of the servicing of the mortgage servicing loan in any case in which the transfer of servicing is preceded by:

(A) Termination of the contract for servicing the loan for cause;

(B) Commencement of proceedings for bankruptcy of the servicer; or

(C) Commencement of proceedings by the Federal Deposit Insurance Corporation (FDIC) or the Resolution Trust Corporation (RTC) for conservatorship or receivership of the servicer or an entity that owns or controls the servicer.

(iii) Notices of Transfer delivered at settlement by the transferor servicer and transferee servicer, whether as separate notices or as a combined notice, will satisfy the timing requirements of paragraph (d)(2) of this section.

(3) *Notices of Transfer; contents.* The Notices of Transfer required under paragraph (d) of this section shall include the following information:

(i) The effective date of the transfer of servicing;

(ii) The name, consumer inquiry addresses (including, at the option of the servicer, a separate address where qualified written requests must be sent), and a toll-free or collect-call telephone number for an employee or department of the transferee servicer;

(iii) A toll-free or collect-call telephone number for an employee or department of the trans-

feror servicer that can be contacted by the borrower for answers to servicing transfer inquiries;

(iv) The date on which the transferor servicer will cease to accept payments relating to the loan and the date on which the transferee servicer will begin to accept such payments. These dates shall either be the same or consecutive days;

(v) Information concerning any effect the transfer may have on the terms or the continued availability of mortgage life or disability insurance, or any other type of optional insurance, and any action the borrower must take to maintain coverage;

(vi) A statement that the transfer of servicing does not affect any other term or condition of the mortgage documents, other than terms directly related to the servicing of the loan; and

(vii) A statement of the borrower's rights in connection with complaint resolution, including the information set forth in paragraph (e) of this section. Appendix MS-2 of this part illustrates a statement satisfactory to the Secretary.

(4) *Notices of Transfer; sample notice.* Sample language that may be used to comply with the requirements of paragraph (d) of this section is set out in Appendix MS-2 of this part. Minor modifications to the sample language may be made to meet the particular circumstances of the servicer, but the substance of the sample language shall not be omitted or substantially altered.

(5) *Consumer protection during transfer of servicing.* During the 60-day period beginning on the effective date of transfer of the servicing of any mortgage servicing loan, if the transferor servicer (rather than the transferee servicer that should properly receive payment on the loan) receives payment on or before the applicable due date (including any grace period allowed under the loan documents), a late fee may not be imposed on the borrower with respect to that payment and the payment may not be treated as late for any other purposes.

(e) *Duty of loan servicer to respond to borrower inquiries.*

(1) *Notice of receipt of inquiry.* Within 20 business days of a servicer of a mortgage servicing loan receiving a qualified written request from the borrower for information relating to the servicing of the loan, the servicer shall provide to the borrower a written response acknowledging receipt of the qualified written response. This requirement shall not apply if the action requested by the borrower is taken within that period and the borrower is notified of that action in accordance with the paragraph (f)(3) of this section. By notice either included in the Notice of Transfer or separately delivered by first-class mail, postage prepaid, a servicer may establish a separate and exclusive office and address for the receipt and handling of qualified written requests.

(2) *Qualified written request; defined.*

(i) For purposes of paragraph (e) of this section, a qualified written request means a written correspondence (other than notice on a payment coupon or other payment medium supplied by the servicer) that includes, or otherwise enables the servicer to identify, the name and account of the borrower, and includes a statement of the reasons that the borrower believes the account is in error, if applicable, or that provides sufficient detail to the servicer regarding information relating to the servicing of the loan sought by the borrower.

(ii) A written request does not constitute a qualified written request if it is delivered to a servicer more than 1 year after either the date of transfer of servicing or the date that the mortgage servicing loan amount was paid in full, whichever date is applicable.

(3) *Action with respect to the inquiry.* Not later than 60 business days after receiving a qualified written request from the borrower, and, if applicable, before taking any action with respect to the inquiry, the servicer shall:

(i) Make appropriate corrections in the account of the borrower, including the crediting of any late charges or penalties, and transmit to the borrower a written notification of the correction. This written notification shall include the name and telephone number of a representative of the servicer who can provide assistance to the borrower; or

(ii) After conducting an investigation, provide the borrower with a written explanation or clarification that includes:

(A) To the extent applicable, a statement of the servicer's reasons for concluding the account is correct and the name and telephone number of an employee, office, or department of the servicer that can provide assistance to the borrower; or

(B) Information requested by the borrower, or an explanation of why the information requested is unavailable or cannot be obtained by the servicer, and the name and telephone number of an employee, office, or department of the servicer that can provide assistance to the borrower.

(4) *Protection of credit rating.*

(i) During the 60-business day period beginning on the date of the servicer receiving from a borrower a qualified written request relating to a dispute on the borrower's payments, a servicer may not provide adverse information regarding any payment that is the subject of the qualified written request to any consumer reporting agency (as that term is defined in section 603 of the Fair Credit Reporting Act, 15 U.S.C. 1681a).

(ii) In accordance with section 17 of RESPA (12 U.S.C. 2615), the protection of credit rating provision of paragraph (e)(4)(i) of this section does not impede a lender or servicer from pursuing any of its remedies, including initiating foreclosure, allowed by the underlying mortgage loan instruments.

(f) *Damages and costs.*

(1) Whoever fails to comply with any provision of this section shall be liable to the borrower for each failure in the following amounts:

(i) *Individuals.* In the case of any action by an individual, an amount equal to the sum of any

actual damages sustained by the individual as the result of the failure and, when there is a pattern or practice of noncompliance with the requirements of this section, any additional damages in an amount not to exceed $1,000.

(ii) *Class Actions.* In the case of a class action, an amount equal to the sum of any actual damages to each borrower in the class that result from the failure and, when there is a pattern or practice of noncompliance with the requirements of this section, any additional damages in an amount not greater than $1,000 for each class member. However, the total amount of any additional damages in a class action may not exceed the lesser of $500,000 or 1 percent of the net worth of the servicer.

(iii) *Costs.* In addition, in the case of any successful action under paragraph (f) of this section, the costs of the action and any reasonable attorneys' fees incurred in connection with the action.

(2) *Nonliability.* A transferor or transferee servicer shall not be liable for any failure to comply with the requirements of this section, if within 60 days after discovering an error (whether pursuant to a final written examination report or the servicer's own procedures) and before commencement of an action under this section and the receipt of written notice of the error from the borrower, the servicer notifies the person concerned of the error and makes whatever adjustments are necessary in the appropriate account to ensure that the person will not be required to pay an amount in excess of any amount that the person otherwise would have paid.

(g) *Timely payments by servicer.* If the terms of any mortgage servicing loan require the borrower to make payments to the servicer of the loan for deposit into an escrow account for the purpose of assuring payment of taxes, insurance premiums, and other charges with respect to the mortgaged property, the servicer shall make payments from the escrow account in a timely manner for the taxes, insurance premiums, and other charges as the payments become due, as governed by the requirements in § 3500.17(k).

(h) *Preemption of State laws.* A lender who makes a mortgage servicing loan or a servicer shall be considered to have complied with the provisions of any State law or regulation requiring notice to a borrower at the time of application for a loan or transfer of servicing of a loan if the lender or servicer complies with the requirements of this section. Any State law requiring notice to the borrower at the time of application or at the time of transfer of servicing of the loan is preempted, and there shall be no additional borrower disclosure requirements. Provisions of State law, such as those requiring additional notices to insurance companies or taxing authorities, are not preempted by section 6 of RESPA or this section, and this additional information may be added to a notice prepared under this section, if the procedure is allowable under State law.

[59 Fed. Reg. 65448 (Dec. 19, 1994); 60 Fed. Reg. 2642 (Jan. 10, 1995); 60 Fed. Reg. 14636 (Mar. 20, 1995); 61 Fed. Reg. 13248 (Mar. 26, 1996)]

24 C.F.R. 3500 Appendix A—Instructions for Completing HUD-1 and HUD-1A Settlement Statements; Sample HUD-1 and HUD-1A Statements

The following are instructions for completing sections A through L of the HUD-1 settlement statement, required under section 4 of RESPA and Regulation X of the Department of Housing and Urban Development (24 CFR part 3500). This form is to be used as a statement of actual charges and adjustments to be given to the parties in connection with the settlement. The instructions for completion of the HUD-1 are primarily for the benefit of the settlement agents who prepare the statements and need not be transmitted to the parties as an integral part of the HUD-1. There is no objection to the use of the HUD-1 in transactions in which its use is not legally required. Refer to the definitions section of Regulation X for specific definitions of many of the terms which are used in these instructions.

General Instructions

Information and amounts may be filled in by typewriter, hand printing, computer printing, or any other method producing clear and legible results. Refer to Regulation X regarding rules applicable to reproduction of the HUD-1. An additional page(s) may be attached to the HUD-1 for the purpose of including customary recitals and information used locally in settlements, for example, a breakdown of payoff figures; a breakdown of the Borrower's total monthly mortgage payments; check disbursements; a statement indicating receipt of funds; applicable special stipulations between Borrower and Seller, and the date funds are transferred.

The settlement agent shall complete the HUD-1 to itemize all charges imposed upon the Borrower and the Seller by the Lender and all sales commissions, whether to be paid at settlement or outside of settlement, and any other charges which either the Borrower or the Seller will pay for at settlement. Charges to be paid outside of settlement, including cases where a non-settlement agent (*i.e.*, attorneys, title companies, escrow agents, real estate agents or brokers) holds the Borrower's deposit against the sales price (earnest money) and applies the entire deposit towards the charge for the settlement service it is rendering, shall be included on the HUD-1 but marked "P.O.C." for "Paid Outside of Closing" (settlement) and shall not be included in computing totals. P.O.C. items should not be placed in the Borrower or Seller columns, but rather on the appropriate line next to the columns.

Blank lines are provided in section L for any additional settlement charges. Blank lines are also provided for additional insertions in sections J and K. The names of the recipients of the settlement charges in section L and the names of the recipients of adjustments described in section J or K should be included on the blank lines.

Lines and columns in section J which relate to the Borrower's transaction may be left blank on the copy of the HUD-1 which will be furnished to the Seller. Lines and columns in section K which relate to the Seller's transaction may be left blank on the copy of the HUD-1 which will be furnished to the Borrower.

Line Item Instructions

Instructions for completing the individual items on the HUD-1 follow.

Section A. This section requires no entry of information.

Section B. Check appropriate loan type and complete the remaining items as applicable.

Section C. This section provides a notice regarding settlement costs and requires no additional entry of information.

Sections D and E. Fill in the names and current mailing addresses and zip codes of the Borrower and the Seller. Where there is more than one Borrower or Seller, the name and address of each one is required. Use a supplementary page if needed to list multiple Borrowers or Sellers.

Section F. Fill in the name, current mailing address and zip code of the Lender.

Section G. The street address of the property being sold should be given. If there is no street address, a brief legal description or other location of the property should be inserted. In all cases give the zip code of the property.

Section H. Fill in name, address, and zip code of settlement agent; address and zip code of "place of settlement."

Section I. Date of settlement.

Section J. Summary of Borrower's Transaction. Line 101 is for the gross sales price of the property being sold, excluding the price of any items of tangible personal property if Borrower and Seller have agreed to a separate price for such items.

Line 102 is for the gross sales price of any items of tangible personal property excluded from Line 101. Personal property could include such items as carpets, drapes, stoves, refrigerators, etc. What constitutes personal property varies from state to state. Manufactured homes are not considered personal property for this purpose.

Line 103 is used to record the total charges to Borrower detailed in Section L and totaled on Line 1400.

Lines 104 and 105 are for additional amounts owed by the Borrower or items paid by the Seller prior to settlement but reimbursed by the Borrower at settlement. For example, the balance in the Seller's reserve account held in connection with an existing loan, if assigned to the Borrower in a loan assumption case, will be entered here. These lines will also be used when a tenant in the property being sold has not yet paid the rent, which the Borrower will collect, for a period of time prior to the settlement. The lines will also be used to indicate the treatment for any tenant security deposit. The Seller will be credited on Lines 404–405.

Lines 106 through 112 are for items which the Seller had paid in advance, and for which the Borrower must therefore reimburse the Seller. Examples of items for which adjustments will be made may include taxes and assessments paid in advance for an entire year or other period, when settlement occurs prior to the expiration of the year or other period for which they were paid. Additional examples include flood and hazard insurance premiums, if the Borrower is being substituted as an insured under the same policy; mortgage insurance in loan assumption cases; planned unit development or condominium association assessments paid in advance; fuel or other supplies on hand, purchased by the Seller, which the Borrower will use when Borrower takes possession of the property; and ground rent paid in advance.

Line 120 is for the total of Lines 101 through 112.

Line 201 is for any amount paid against the sales price prior to settlement.

Line 202 is for the amount of the new loan made by the Lender or first user loan (a loan to finance construction of a new structure or purchase of manufactured home where the structure was constructed for sale or the manufactured home was purchased for purposes of resale and the loan is used as or converted to a loan to finance purchase by the first user). For other loans covered by Regulation X which finance construction of a new structure or purchase of a manufactured home, list the sales price of the land on Line 104, the construction cost or purchase price of manufactured home on Line 105 (Line 101 would be left blank in this instance) and amount of the loan on Line 202. The remainder of the form should be completed taking into account adjustments and charges related to the temporary financing and permanent financing and which are known at the date of settlement.

Line 203 is used for cases in which the Borrower is assuming or taking title subject to an existing loan or lien on the property.

Lines 204–209 are used for other items paid by or on behalf of the Borrower. Examples include cases in which the Seller has taken a trade-in or other property from the Borrower in part payment for the property being sold. They may also be used in cases in which a Seller (typically a builder) is making an "allowance" to the Borrower for carpets or drapes which the

Borrower is to purchase separately. Lines 204–209 can also be used to indicate any Seller financing arrangements or other new loan not listed in Line 202. For example, if the Seller takes a note from the Borrower for part of the sales price, insert the principal amount of the note with a brief explanation on Lines 204–209.

Lines 210 through 219 are for items which have not yet been paid, and which the Borrower is expected to pay, but which are attributable in part to a period of time prior to the settlement. In jurisdictions in which taxes are paid late in the tax year, most cases will show the proration of taxes in these lines. Other examples include utilities used but not paid for by the Seller, rent collected in advance by the Seller from a tenant for a period extending beyond the settlement date, and interest on loan assumptions.

Line 220 is for the total of Lines 201 through 219.

Lines 301 and 302 are summary lines for the Borrower. Enter total in Line 120 on Line 301. Enter total in Line 220 on Line 302.

Line 303 may indicate either the cash required from the Borrower at settlement (the usual case in a purchase transaction) or cash payable to the Borrower at settlement (if, for example, the Borrower's deposit against the sales price (earnest money) exceeded the Borrower's cash obligations in the transaction). Subtract Line 302 from Line 301 and enter the amount of cash due to or from the Borrower at settlement on Line 303. The appropriate box should be checked.

Section K. Summary of Seller's Transaction. Instructions for the use of Lines 101 and 102 and 104–112 above, apply also to Lines 401–412. Line 420 is for the total of Lines 401 through 412.

Line 501 is used if the Seller's real estate broker or other party who is not the settlement agent has received and holds the deposit against the sales price (earnest money) which exceeds the fee or commission owed to that party, and if that party will render the excess deposit directly to the Seller, rather than through the settlement agent, the amount of excess deposit should be entered on Line 501 and the amount of the total deposit (including commissions) should be entered on Line 201.

Line 502 is used to record the total charges to the Seller detailed in section L and totaled on Line 1400.

Line 503 is used if the Borrower is assuming or taking title subject to existing liens which are to be deducted from sales price.

Lines 504 and 505 are used for the amounts (including any accrued interest) of any first and/or second loans which will be paid as part of the settlement.

Line 506 is used for deposits paid by the Borrower to the Seller or other party who is not the settlement agent. Enter the amount of the deposit in Line 201 on Line 506 unless Line 501 is used or the party who is not the settlement agent transfers all or part of the deposit to the settlement agent in which case the settlement agent will note in parentheses on Line 507 the amount of the deposit which is being disbursed as proceeds and enter in column for Line 506 the amount retained by the above described party for settlement services. If the settlement agent holds the deposit insert a note in Line 507 which indicates that the deposit is being disbursed as proceeds.

Lines 506 through 509 may be used to list additional liens which must be paid off through the settlement to clear title to the property. Other payoffs of Seller obligations should be shown on Lines 506–509 (but not on Lines 1303–1305). They may also be used to indicate funds to be held by the settlement agent for the payment of water, fuel, or other utility bills which cannot be prorated between the parties at settlement because the amounts used by the Seller prior to settlement are not yet known. Subsequent disclosure of the actual amount of these post-settlement items to be paid from settlement funds is optional. Any amounts entered on Lines 204–209 including Seller financing arrangements should also be entered on Lines 506–509.

Instructions for the use of Lines 510 through 519 are the same as those for Lines 210 to 219 above.

Line 520 is for the total of Lines 501 through 519.

Lines 601 and 602 are summary lines for the Seller. Enter total in Line 420 on Line 610. Enter total in Line 520 on Line 602.

Line 603 may indicate either the cash required to be paid to the Seller at settlement (the usual case in a purchase transaction) or cash payable by the Seller at settlement. Subtract Line 602 from Line 601 and enter the amount of cash due to or from the Seller at settlement on Line 603. The appropriate box should be checked.

Section L. Settlement Charges.

For all items except for those paid to and retained by the Lender, the name of the person or firm ultimately receiving the payment should be shown. In the case of "no cost" or "no point" loans, the charge to be paid by the lender to an affiliated or independent service provider should be shown as P.O.C. (Paid Outside of Closing) and should not be used in computing totals. Such charges also include indirect payments or back-funded payments to mortgage brokers that arise from the settlement transaction. When used, "P.O.C." should be placed in the appropriate lines next to the identified item, not in the columns themselves.

Line 700 is used to enter the sales commission charged by the sales agent or broker. If the sales commission is based on a percentage of the price, enter the sales price, the percentage, and the dollar amount of the total commission paid by the Seller.

Lines 701–702 are to be used to state the split of the commission where the settlement agent disburses portions of the commission to two or more sales agents or brokers.

Line 703 is used to enter the amount of sales commission disbursed at settlement. If the sales agent or broker is retaining a part of the deposit against the sales price (earnest money) to apply towards the sales agent's or broker's commission, include in Line 703 only that part of the commission being disbursed at settlement and insert a note on Line 704 indicating the amount the sales agent or broker is retaining as a "P.O.C." item.

Line 704 may be used for additional charges made by the sales agent or broker, or for a sales commission charged to the Borrower, which will be disbursed by the settlement agent.

Line 801 is used to record the fee charged by the Lender for processing or originating the loan. If this fee is computed as a percentage of the loan amount, enter the percentage in the blank indicated.

Line 802 is used to record the loan discount or "points" charged by the Lender, and, if it is computed as a percentage of the loan amount, enter the percentage in the blank indicated.

Line 803 is used for appraisal fees if there is a separate charge for the appraisal. Appraisal fees for HUD and VA loans are also included on Line 803.

Line 804 is used for the cost of the credit report if there is a charge separate from the origination fee.

Line 805 is used only for inspections by the Lender or the Lender's agents. Charges for other pest or structural inspections required to be stated by these instructions should be entered in Lines 1301–1305.

Line 806 should be used for an application fee required by a private mortgage insurance company.

Line 807 is provided for convenience in using the form for loan assumption transactions.

Lines 808–811 are used to list additional items payable in connection with the loan including a CLO Access fee, a mortgage broker fee, fees for real estate property taxes or other real property charges.

Lines 901–905. This series is used to record the items which the Lender requires (but which are not necessarily paid to the lender, *i.e.*, FHA mortgage insurance premium) to be paid at the time of settlement, other than reserves collected by the Lender and recorded in 1000 series.

Line 901 is used if interest is collected at settlement for a part of a month or other period between settlement and the date from which interest will be collected with the first regular monthly payment. Enter that amount here and include the per diem charges. If such interest is not collected until the first regular monthly payment, no entry should be made on Line 901.

Line 902 is used for mortgage insurance premiums due and payable at settlement, except reserves collected by the Lender and recorded in the 1000 series. A lump sum mortgage insurance premium paid at settlement should be inserted on Line 902, with a note that indicates that the premium is for the life of the loan.

Line 903 is used for hazard insurance premiums which the Lender requires to be paid at the time of settlement except reserves collected by the Lender and recorded in the 1000 series.

Lines 904 and 905 are used to list additional items required by the Lender (except for reserves collected by the Lender and recorded in the 1000 series) including flood insurance, mortgage life insurance, credit life insurance and disability insurance premiums. These lines are also used to list amounts paid at settlement for insurance not required by the Lender.

Lines 1000–1008. This series is used for amounts collected by the Lender from the Borrower and held in an account for the future payment of the obligations listed as they fall due. Include the time period (number of months) and the monthly assessment. In many jurisdictions this is referred to as an "escrow", "impound", or "trust" account. In addition to the items listed, some Lenders may require reserves for flood insurance, condominium owners' association assessments, etc.

After itemizing individual deposits in the 1000 series using single-item accounting, the servicer shall make an adjustment based on aggregate accounting. This adjustment equals the difference between the deposit required under aggregate accounting and the sum of the deposits required under single-item accounting. The computation steps for both accounting methods are set out in § 3500.17(d). The adjustment will always be a negative number or zero (-0-). The settlement agent shall enter the aggregate adjustment amount on a final line in the 1000 series of the HUD-1 or HUD-1A statement.

During the phase-in period, as defined in § 3500.17(b), an alternative procedure is available. If a servicer has not yet conducted the escrow account analysis to determine the aggregate accounting starting balance, the settlement agent may initially calculate the 1000 series deposits for the HUD-1 and HUD-1A settlement statement using single-item analysis with a one-month cushion (unless the mortgage loan documents indicate a smaller amount). In the escrow account analysis conducted within 45 days of settlement, the servicer shall adjust the escrow account to reflect the aggregate accounting balance.

Lines 1100–1113. This series covers title charges and charges by attorneys. The title charges include a variety of services performed by title companies or others and includes fees directly related to the transfer of title (title examination, title search, document preparation) and fees for title insurance. The legal charges include fees for Lender's, Seller's or Buyer's attorney, or the attorney preparing title work. The series also includes any fees for settlement or closing agents and notaries. In many jurisdictions the same person (for example, an attorney or a title insurance company) performs several of the services listed in this series and makes a single overall charge for such services. In such cases, enter the overall fee on Line 1107 (for attorneys), or Line 1108 (for title companies), and enter on that line the item numbers of the services listed which are covered in the overall fee. If this is done, no individual amounts need be entered into the borrower's and seller's columns for the individual items which are covered by the overall fee. In transactions involving more than one attorney, one attorney's fees should appear on Line 1107 and the other attorney's fees should be on Line 1111, 1112 or 1113. If an attorney is representing a buyer, seller, or lender and is also acting as a title agent, indicate on line 1107 which services are covered by the attorney fee and on line 1113 which services are covered by the insurance commission.

Line 1101 is used for the settlement agent's fee.

Lines 1102 and 1103 are used for the fees for the abstract or title search and title examination. In some jurisdictions the same person both searches the title (that is, performs the necessary research in the records) and examines title (that is, makes a determination as to what matters affect title, and provides a title report or opinion). If such a person charges only one fee for both services, it should be entered on Line 1103 unless the person performing these tasks is an attorney or a title company in which case the fees should be entered as described in the general directions for Lines 1100–1113. If separate persons perform these tasks, or if separate charges are made for searching and examination, they should be listed separately.

Line 1104 is used for the title insurance binder which is also known as a commitment to insure.

Line 1105 is used for charges for preparation of deeds, mortgages, notes, etc. If more than one person receives a fee for such work in the same transaction, show the total paid in the appropriate column and the individual charges on the line following the word "to."

Line 1106 is used for the fee charged by a notary public for authenticating the execution of settlement documents.

Line 1107 is used to disclose the attorney's fees for the transaction. The instructions are discussed in the general directions for Lines 1100–1113. This line should include any charges by an attorney to represent a buyer, seller or lender in the real estate transaction.

Lines 1108–1110 are used for information regarding title insurance. Enter the total charge for title insurance (except for the cost of the title binder) on Line 1108. Enter on Lines 1109 and 1110 the individual charges for the Lender's and owner's policies. Note that these charges are not carried over into the Borrower's and Seller's columns, since to do so would result in a duplication of the amount in Line 1108. If a combination Lender's/owner's policy is purchased, show this amount as an additional entry on Lines 1109 and 1110.

Lines 1111–1113 are for the entry of other title charges not already itemized. Examples in some jurisdictions would include a fee to a private tax service, a fee to a county tax collector for a tax certificate, or a fee to a public title registrar for a certificate of title in a Torrens Act transaction. Line 1113 should be used to disclose services that are covered by the commission of an attorney acting as a title agent when Line 1107 is already being used to disclose the fees and services of the attorney in representing the buyer, seller, or lender in the real estate transaction.

Lines 1201–1205 are used for government recording and transfer charges. Recording and transfer charges should be itemized. Additional recording or transfer charges should be listed on Lines 1204 and 1205.

Lines 1301 and 1302, or any other available blank line in the 1300 series, are used for fees for survey, pest inspection, radon inspection, lead-based paint inspection, or other similar inspections.

Lines 1303–1305 are used for any other settlement charges not referable to the categories listed above on the HUD-1, which are required to be stated by these instructions. Examples may include structural inspections or pre-sale inspection of heating, plumbing, or electrical equipment. These inspection charges may include a fee for insurance or warranty coverage.

Line 1400 is for the total settlement charges paid from Borrower's funds and Seller's funds. These totals are also entered on Lines 103 and 502, respectively, in sections J and K.

Line Item Instructions for Completing HUD-1A

NOTE: HUD-1A is an optional form that may be used for refinancing and subordinate lien federally related mortgage loans, as well as for any other one-party transaction that does not involve the transfer of title to residential real property. The HUD-1 form may also be used for such transactions, by utilizing the borrower's side of the HUD-1 and following the relevant parts of the instructions as set forth above. The use of either the HUD-1 or HUD-1A is not mandatory for open-end lines of credit (home-equity plans), as long as the provisions of Regulation Z are followed.

Background

The HUD-1A settlement statement is to be used as a statement of actual charges and adjustments to be given to the borrower at settlement, as defined in this part. The instructions for completion of the HUD-1A are for the benefit of the settlement agent who prepares the statement; the instructions are not a part of the statement and need not be transmitted to the borrower. There is no objection to using the HUD-1A in transactions in which it is not required, and its use in open-end lines of credit transactions (home-equity plans) is encouraged. It may not be used as a substitute for a HUD-1 in any transaction in which there is a transfer of title and a first lien is taken as security.

Refer to the "definitions" section of Regulation X for specific definitions of terms used in these instructions.

General Instructions

Information and amounts may be filled in by typewriter, hand printing, computer printing, or any other method producing clear and legible results. Refer to § 3500.9 regarding rules for reproduction of the HUD-1A. Additional pages may be attached to the HUD-1A for the inclusion of customary recitals and information used locally for settlements or if there are insufficient lines on the HUD-1A.

The settlement agent shall complete the HUD-1A to itemize all charges imposed upon the borrower by the lender, whether to be paid at settlement or outside of settlement, and any other charges that the borrower will pay for at settlement. In the case of "no cost" or "no point" loans, these charges include any payments the lender will make to affiliated or independent settlement service providers relating to this settlement. These charges shall be included on the HUD-1A, but marked "P.O.C." for "paid outside of closing," and shall not be used in computing totals. Such charges also include indirect payments or back-funded payments to mortgage brokers that arise from the settlement transaction. When used, "P.O.C." should be placed in the appropriate lines next to the identified item, not in the columns themselves.

Blank lines are provided in section L for any additional settlement charges. Blank lines are also provided in section M for recipients of all or portions of the loan proceeds. The names of the recipients of the settlement charges in section L and the names of the recipients of the loan proceeds in section M should be set forth on the blank lines.

Line Item Instructions

The identification information at the top of the HUD-1A should be completed as follows:

The borrower's name and address is entered in the space provided. If the property securing the loan is different from the borrower's address, the address or other location information on the property should be entered in the space provided. The loan number is the lender's identification number for the loan. The settlement date is the date of settlement in accordance with § 3500.2, not the end of any applicable rescission period. The name and address of the lender should be entered in the space provided.

Section L. Settlement Charges. This section of the HUD-1A is similar to section L of the HUD-1, with minor changes or omissions, including deletion of lines 700 through 704, relating to real estate broker commissions. The instructions for section L in the HUD-1, should be followed insofar as possible. Inapplicable charges should be ignored, as should any instructions regarding seller items.

Line 1400 in the HUD-1A is for the total settlement charges charged to the borrower. Enter this total on line 1602 as well. This total should include section L amounts from additional pages, if any are attached to this HUD-1A.

Section M. Disbursement to Others. This section is used to list payees, other than the borrower, of all or portions of the loan proceeds (including the lender, if the loan is paying off a prior loan made by the same lender), when the payee will be paid directly out of the settlement proceeds. It is not used to list payees of settlement charges, nor to list funds disbursed directly to the borrower, even if the lender knows the borrower's intended use of the funds.

For example, in a refinancing transaction, the loan proceeds are used to pay off an existing loan. The name of the lender for the loan being paid off and the pay-off balance would be entered in section M. In a home improvement transaction when the proceeds are to be paid to the home improvement contractor, the name of the contractor and the amount paid to the contractor would be entered in section M. In a consolidation loan, or when part of the loan proceeds is used to pay off other creditors, the name of each creditor and the amount paid to that creditor would be entered in section M. If the proceeds are to be given directly to the borrower and the borrower will use the proceeds to pay off existing obligations, this would not be reflected in section M.

Section N. Net Settlement. Line 1600 normally sets forth the principal amount of the loan as it appears on the related note for this loan. In the event this form is used for an open-ended home equity line whose approved amount is greater than the initial amount advanced at settlement, the amount shown on Line 1600 will be the loan amount advanced at settlement. Line 1601 is used for all settlement charges that are both included in the totals for lines 1400 and 1602 and are not financed as part of the principal amount of the loan. This is the amount normally received by the lender from the borrower at settlement, which would occur when some or all of the settlement charges were paid in cash by the borrower at settlement, instead of being financed as part of the principal amount of the loan. Failure to include any such amount in line 1601 will result in an error in the amount calculated on line 1604. P.O.C. amounts should not be included in line 1601.

Line 1602 is the total amount from line 1400.

Line 1603 is the total amount from line 1520.

Line 1604 is the amount disbursed to the borrower. This is determined by adding together the amounts for lines 1600 and 1601, and then subtracting any amounts listed on lines 1602 and 1603.

A. Settlement Statement

U.S. Department of Housing
and Urban Development

OMB Approval No. 2502-0265
(expires 9/30/2006)

B. Type of Loan					
1. ☐ FHA 2. ☐ FmHA 3. ☐ Conv. Unins. 4. ☐ VA 5. ☐ Conv. Ins.	6. File Number:	7. Loan Number:	8. Mortgage Insurance Case Number:

C. Note: This form is furnished to give you a statement of actual settlement costs. Amounts paid to and by the settlement agent are shown. Items marked "(p.o.c.)" were paid outside the closing; they are shown here for informational purposes and are not included in the totals.

D. Name & Address of Borrower:	E. Name & Address of Seller:	F. Name & Address of Lender:

G. Property Location:	H. Settlement Agent:	
	Place of Settlement:	I. Settlement Date:

J. Summary of Borrower's Transaction		K. Summary of Seller's Transaction	
100. Gross Amount Due From Borrower		**400. Gross Amount Due To Seller**	
101. Contract sales price		401. Contract sales price	
102. Personal property		402. Personal property	
103. Settlement charges to borrower (line 1400)		403.	
104.		404.	
105.		405.	
Adjustments for items paid by seller in advance		**Adjustments for items paid by seller in advance**	
106. City/town taxes to		406. City/town taxes to	
107. County taxes to		407. County taxes to	
108. Assessments to		408. Assessments to	
109.		409.	
110.		410.	
111.		411.	
112.		412.	
120. Gross Amount Due From Borrower		**420. Gross Amount Due To Seller**	
200. Amounts Paid By Or In Behalf Of Borrower		**500. Reductions In Amount Due To Seller**	
201. Deposit or earnest money		501. Excess deposit (see instructions)	
202. Principal amount of new loan(s)		502. Settlement charges to seller (line 1400)	
203. Existing loan(s) taken subject to		503. Existing loan(s) taken subject to	
204.		504. Payoff of first mortgage loan	
205.		505. Payoff of second mortgage loan	
206.		506.	
207.		507.	
208.		508.	
209.		509.	
Adjustments for items unpaid by seller		**Adjustments for items unpaid by seller**	
210. City/town taxes to		510. City/town taxes to	
211. County taxes to		511. County taxes to	
212. Assessments to		512. Assessments to	
213.		513.	
214.		514.	
215.		515.	
216.		516.	
217.		517.	
218.		518.	
219.		519.	
220. Total Paid By/For Borrower		**520. Total Reduction Amount Due Seller**	
300. Cash At Settlement From/To Borrower		**600. Cash At Settlement To/From Seller**	
301. Gross Amount due from borrower (line 120)		601. Gross amount due to seller (line 420)	
302. Less amounts paid by/for borrower (line 220)	( )	602. Less reductions in amt. due seller (line 520)	( )
303. Cash ☐ From ☐ To Borrower		**603. Cash ☐ To ☐ From Seller**	

Section 5 of the Real Estate Settlement Procedures Act (RESPA) requires the following: • HUD must develop a Special Information Booklet to help persons borrowing money to finance the purchase of residential real estate to better understand the nature and costs of real estate settlement services; • Each lender must provide the booklet to all applicants from whom it receives or for whom it prepares a written application to borrow money to finance the purchase of residential real estate; • Lenders must prepare and distribute with the Booklet a Good Faith Estimate of the settlement costs that the borrower is likely to incur in connection with the settlement. These disclosures are manadatory.

Section 4(a) of RESPA mandates that HUD develop and prescribe this standard form to be used at the time of loan settlement to provide full disclosure of all charges imposed upon the borrower and seller. These are third party disclosures that are designed to provide the borrower with pertinent information during the settlement process in order to be a better shopper.

The Public Reporting Burden for this collection of information is estimated to average one hour per response, including the time for reviewing instructions, searching existing data sources, gathering and maintaining the data needed, and completing and reviewing the collection of information.

This agency may not collect this information, and you are not required to complete this form, unless it displays a currently valid OMB control number.

The information requested does not lend itself to confidentiality.

L. Settlement Charges

	Paid From Borrowers Funds at Settlement	Paid From Seller's Funds at Settlement
700. Total Sales/Broker's Commission based on price $ @ % =		
Division of Commission (line 700) as follows:		
701. $ to		
702. $ to		
703. Commission paid at Settlement		
704.		
800. Items Payable In Connection With Loan		
801. Loan Origination Fee %		
802. Loan Discount %		
803. Appraisal Fee to		
804. Credit Report to		
805. Lender's Inspection Fee		
806. Mortgage Insurance Application Fee to		
807. Assumption Fee		
808.		
809.		
810.		
811.		
900. Items Required By Lender To Be Paid In Advance		
901. Interest from to @$ /day		
902. Mortgage Insurance Premium for months to		
903. Hazard Insurance Premium for years to		
904. years to		
905.		
1000. Reserves Deposited With Lender		
1001. Hazard insurance months@$ per month		
1002. Mortgage insurance months@$ per month		
1003. City property taxes months@$ per month		
1004. County property taxes months@$ per month		
1005. Annual assessments months@$ per month		
1006. months@$ per month		
1007. months@$ per month		
1008. months@$ per month		
1100. Title Charges		
1101. Settlement or closing fee to		
1102. Abstract or title search to		
1103. Title examination to		
1104. Title insurance binder to		
1105. Document preparation to		
1106. Notary fees to		
1107. Attorney's fees to		
(includes above items numbers:)		
1108. Title insurance to		
(includes above items numbers:)		
1109. Lender's coverage $		
1110. Owner's coverage $		
1111.		
1112.		
1113.		
1200. Government Recording and Transfer Charges		
1201. Recording fees: Deed $; Mortgage $; Releases $		
1202. City/county tax/stamps: Deed $; Mortgage $		
1203. State tax/stamps: Deed $; Mortgage $		
1204.		
1205.		
1300. Additional Settlement Charges		
1301. Survey to		
1302. Pest inspection to		
1303.		
1304.		
1305.		
1400. Total Settlement Charges (enter on lines 103, Section J and 502, Section K)		

Settlement Statement
Optional Form for
Transactions without Sellers

**U.S. Department of Housing
and Urban Development**

OMB Approval No. 2502-0265
(expires 9/30/2006)

Name & Address of Borrower:	Name & Address of Lender:
Property Location: (if different from above)	Settlement Agent:
	Place of Settlement:
Loan Number:	Settlement Date:

L. Settlement Charges		**M. Disbursement to Others**	
800. Items Payable In Connection with Loan		1501.	
801. Loan origination fee % to			
802. Loan discount % to		1502.	
803. Appraisal fee to			
804. Credit report to		1503.	
805 Inspection fee to			
806. Mortgage insurance application fee to		1504.	
807. Mortgage broker fee to			
808.		1505.	
809.			
810.		1506.	
811.			
900. Items Required by Lender to be Paid in Advance		1507.	
901. Interest from to @ $ per day			
902. Mortgage insurance premium for months to		1508.	
903. Hazard insurance premium for year(s) to		1509.	
904.		1510.	
1000.Reserves Deposited with Lender			
1001.Hazard insurance months @ $ per month		1511.	
1002.Mortgage insurance months @ $ per month			
1003.City property taxes months @ $ per month		1512.	
1004.County property taxes months @ $ per month			
1005.Annual assessments months @ $ per month		1513.	
1006. months @ $ per month			
1007. months @ $ per month		1514.	
1008. months @ $ per month			
1100.Title Charges		1515.	
1101.Settlement or closing fee to			
1102.Abstract or title search to		**1520. TOTAL DISBURSED** (enter on line 1603)	
1103.Title examination to			
1104.Title Insurance binder to			
1105.Document preparation to			
1106.Notary fees to			
1107.Attorney's fees to			
(includes above item numbers)			
1108.Title insurance to			
(includes above item numbers)			
1109.Lender's coverage $			
1110.Owner's coverage $			
1111.			
1112.			
1113.			
1200.Government Recording and Transfer Charges		**N. NET SETTLEMENT**	
1201.Recording fees:			
1202.City/county tax/stamps:		1600.Loan Amount	$
1203.State tax/stamps:			
1204.		1601.**Plus** Cash/Check from Borrower	$
1205.			
1300.Additional Settlement Charges		1602.**Minus** Total Settlement Charges (line 1400)	$
1301.Survey to			
1302.Pest inspection to		1603.**Minus** Total Disbursements to Others (line 1520)	$
1303.Architectural/engineering services to			
1304.Building permit to		1604.**Equals** Disbursements to Borrower	$
1305.		(after expiration of any applicable	
1306.		rescission period required by law)	
1307.			
1400.Total Settlement Charges (enter on line 1602)			

Borrower(s) Signature(s):

X_____

form **HUD-1A** (2/94)
ref. RESPA

865

Public reporting burden for this collection of information is estimated to average 0.35 hours per response, including the time for reviewing instructions, searching existing data sources, gathering and maintaining the data needed, and completing and reviewing the collection of information. This agency may not collect this information, and you are not required to complete this form, unless it displays a currently valid OMB control number.

Instructions for completing form HUD-1A

Note: This form is issued under authority of the Real Estate Settlement Procedures Act (RESPA), 12 U.S.C. 2601 *et seq.* The regulation for RESPA is Regulation X, codified as 24 CFR 3500, and administered by the Department of Housing and Urban Development (HUD). Regulation Z referred to in the next paragraph is the regulation implementing the Truth in Lending Act (TILA), 15 U.S.C. 1601 *et seq.* and codified as 12 CFR part 226.

HUD-1A is an optional form that may be used for refinancing and subordinate lien federally related mortgage loans, as well as for any other one-party transaction that does not involve the transfer of title to residential real property. The HUD-1 form may also be used for such transactions, by utilizing the borrower's side of the HUD-1 and following the relevant parts of the instructions set forth in Appendix A of Regulation X. The use of either the HUD-1 or HUD-1A is not mandatory for open-end lines of credit (home-equity plans), as long as the provisions of Regulation Z are followed.

Background

The HUD-1A settlement statement is to be used as a statement of actual charges and adjustments to be given to the borrower at settlement. The instructions for completion of the HUD-1A are for the benefit of the settlement agent who prepares the statement; the instructions are not a part of the statement and need not be transmitted to the borrower. There is no objection to using the HUD-1A in transactions in which it is not required, and its use in open-end lines of credit transactions (home-equity plans) is encouraged. It may not be used as a substitute for a HUD-1 in any transaction in which there is a transfer of title and a first lien is taken as security.

Refer to the "definitions" section of Regulation X for specific definitions of terms used in these instructions.

General Instructions

Information and amounts may be filled in by typewriter, hand printing, computer printing, or any other method producing clear and legible results. Additional pages may be attached to the HUD-1A for the inclusion of customary recitals and information used locally for settlements or if there are insufficient lines on the HUD-1A.

The settlement agent shall complete the HUD-1A to itemize all charges imposed upon the borrower by the lender, whether to be paid at settlement or outside of settlement, and any other charges that the borrower will pay for at settlement. In the case of "no cost" or "no point" loans, these charges include any payments the lender will make to affiliated or independent settlement service providers relating to this settlement. These charges shall be included on the HUD-1A, but marked "P.O.C." for "paid outside of closing," and shall not be used in computing totals. Such charges also include indirect payments or back-funded payments to mortgage brokers that arise from the settlement transaction. When used, "P.O.C." should be placed in the appropriate lines next to the identified item, *not in the columns themselves.*

Blank lines are provided in Section L for any additional settlement charges. Blank lines are also provided in Section M for recipients of all or portions of the loan proceeds. The names of the recipients of the settlement charges in Section L and the names of the recipients of the loan proceeds in Section M should be set forth on the blank lines.

Line item instructions

The identification information at the top of the HUD-1A should be completed as follows:

The borrower's name and address is entered in the space provided. If the property securing the loan is different from the borrower's address, the address or other location information on the property should be entered in the space provided. The loan number is the lender's identification number for the loan. The settlement date is the date of settlement in accordance with § 3500.2 of Regulation X, not the end of any applicable rescission period. The name and address of the lender should be entered in the space provided.

Section L. Settlement Charges. This section of the HUD-1A is similar to section L of the HUD-1, with the deletion of lines 700 through 704, relating to real estate broker commissions. The Instructions for filling out the HUD-1 as set forth in Appendix A of Regulation X provide additional information regarding Section L, if needed.

Line 1400 in the HUD-1A is for the total settlement charges charged to the borrower. Enter this total on line 1602 as well. This total should include Section L amounts from additional pages, if any are attached to this HUD-1A.

Section M. Disbursement to Others. This section is used to list payees, other than the borrower, of all or portions of the loan proceeds (including the lender, if the loan is paying off a prior loan made by the same lender), when the payee will be paid directly out of the settlement proceeds. It is not used to list payees of settlement charges, nor to list funds disbursed directly to the borrower, even if the lender knows the borrower's intended use of the funds.

For example, in a refinancing transaction, the loan proceeds are used to pay off an existing loan. The name of the lender for the loan being paid off and the pay-off balance would be entered in Section M. In a home improvement transaction when the proceeds are to be paid to the home improvement contractor, the name of the contractor and the amount paid to the contractor would be entered in Section M. In a consolidation loan, or when part of the loan proceeds is used to pay off other creditors, the name of each creditor and the amount paid to that creditor would be entered in Section M. If the proceeds are to be given directly to the borrower and the borrower will use the proceeds to pay off existing obligations, this would not be reflected in Section M.

Section N. Net Settlement. Line 1600 normally sets forth the principal amount of the loan as it appears on the related note for this loan. In the event this form is used for an open-ended home equity line whose approved amount is greater than the initial amount advanced at settlement, the amount shown on Line 1600 will be the loan amount advanced at settlement. Line 1601 is used for all settlement charges that are both included in the totals for lines 1400 and 1602 and are not financed as part of the principal amount of the loan. This is the amount normally received by the lender from the borrower at settlement, which would occur when some or all of the settlement charges were paid in cash by the borrower at settlement, instead of being financed as part of the principal amount of the loan. Failure to include any such amount in line 1601 will result in an error in the amount calculated on line 1604. P.O.C. amounts should not be included in line 1601.

Line 1602 is the total amount from line 1400.

Line 1603 is the total amount from line 1520.

Line 1604 is the amount disbursed to the borrower. This is determined by adding together the amounts for lines 1600 and 1601, and then subtracting any amounts listed on lines 1602 and 1603.

[Approved by the Office of Management and Budget under control number 2502-0265]

[57 Fed. Reg. 49607 (Nov. 2, 1992); 57 Fed. Reg. 56857 (Dec. 1, 1992), *as amended at* 59 Fed. Reg. 6515 (Feb. 10, 1994); 59 Fed. Reg. 53908 (Oct. 26, 1994); 60 Fed. Reg. 8816 (Feb. 15, 1995); 60 Fed. Reg. 24735 (May 9, 1995); 61 Fed. Reg. 13251 (Mar. 26, 1996); 63 Fed. Reg. 3237 (Jan. 21, 1998)]

24 C.F.R. 3500 Appendix B— Illustrations of Requirements of RESPA

The following illustrations provide additional guidance on the meaning and coverage of the provisions of RESPA. Other provisions of Federal or State law may also be applicable to the practices and payments discussed in the following illustrations.

1. *Facts*: A, a provider of settlement services, provides settlement services at abnormally low rates or at no charge at all to B, a builder, in connection with a subdivision being developed by B. B agrees to refer purchasers of the completed homes in the subdivision to A for the purchase of settlement services in connection with the sale of individual lots by B.

Comments: The rendering of services by A to B at little or no charge constitutes a thing of value given by A to B in return for the referral of settlement services business and both A and B are in violation of section 8 of RESPA.

2. *Facts*: B, a lender, encourages persons who receive federally-related mortgage loans from it to employ A, an attorney, to perform title searches and related settlement services in connection with their transaction. B and A have an understanding that in return for the referral of this business A provides legal services to B or B's officers or employees at abnormally low rates or for no charge.

Comments: Both A and B are in violation of section 8 of RESPA. Similarly, if an attorney gives a portion of his or her fees to another attorney, a lender, a real estate broker or any other provider of settlement services, who had referred prospective clients to the attorney, section 8 would be violated by both persons.

3. *Facts*: A, a real estate broker, obtains all necessary licenses under state law to act as a title insurance agent. A refers individuals who are purchasing homes in transactions in which A participates as a broker to B, an unaffiliated title company, for the purchase of title insurance services. A performs minimal, if any, title services in connection with the issuance of the title insurance policy (such as placing an application with the title company). B pays A a commission (or A retains a portion of the title insurance premium) for the transactions or alternatively B receives a portion of the premium paid directly from the purchaser.

Comments: The payment of a commission or portion of the title insurance premium by B to A, or receipt of a portion of the payment for title insurance under circumstances where no substantial services are being performed by A is a violation of section 8 of RESPA. It makes no difference whether the payment comes from B or the purchaser. The amount of the payment must bear a reasonable relationship to the services rendered. Here A really is being compensated for a referral of business to B.

4. *Facts*: A is an attorney who, as a part of his legal representation of clients in residential real estate transactions, orders and reviews title insurance policies for his clients. A enters into a contract with B, a title company, to be an agent of B under a program set up by B. Under the agreement, A agrees to prepare and forward title insurance applications to B, to re-examine the preliminary title commitment for accuracy and if he chooses to attempt to clear exceptions to the title policy before closing. A agrees to assume liability for waiving certain exceptions to title, but never exercises this authority. B performs the necessary title search and examination work, determines insurability of title, prepares documents containing substantive information in title commitments, handles closings for A's clients and issues title policies. A receives a fee from his client for legal services and an additional fee for his title agent "services" from the client's title insurance premium to B.

Comments: A and B are violating section 8 of RESPA. Here, A's clients are being double billed because the work A performs as a "title agent" is that which he already performs for his client in his capacity as an attorney. For A to receive a separate payment as a title agent, A must perform necessary core title work and may not contract out the work. To receive additional compensation as a title agent for this transaction, A must provide his client with core title agent services for which he assumes liability, and which includes, at a minimum, the evaluation of the title search to determine insurability of the title, and the issuance of a title commitment where customary, the clearance of underwriting objections, and the actual issuance of the policy or policies on behalf of the title company. A may not be compensated for the mere re-examination of work performed by B. Here, A is not performing these services and may not be compensated as a title agent under section 8(c)(1)(B). Referral fees or splits of fees may not be disguised as title agent commissions when the core title agent work is not performed. Further, because B created the program and gave A the opportunity to collect fees (a thing of value) in exchange for the referral of settlement service business, it has violated section 8 of RESPA.

5. *Facts*: A, a "mortgage originator," receives loan applications, funds the loans with its own money or with a wholesale line of credit for which A is liable, and closes the loans in A's own name. Subsequently, B, a mortgage lender, pur-

chases the loans and compensates A for the value of the loans, as well as for any mortgage servicing rights.

Comments: Compensation for the sale of a mortgage loan and servicing rights constitutes a secondary market transaction, rather than a referral fee, and is beyond the scope of section 8 of RESPA. For purposes of section 8, in determining whether a *bona fide* transfer of the loan obligation has taken place, HUD examines the real source of funding, and the real interest of the named settlement lender.

6. *Facts*. A, a credit reporting company, places a facsimile transmission machine (FAX) in the office of B, a mortgage lender, so that B can easily transmit requests for credit reports and A can respond. A supplies the FAX machine at no cost or at a reduced rental rate based on the number of credit reports ordered.

Comments: Either situation violates section 8 of RESPA. The FAX machine is a thing of value that A provides in exchange for the referral of business from B. Copying machines, computer terminals, printers, or other like items which have general use to the recipient and which are given in exchange for referrals of business also violate RESPA.

7. *Facts*: A, a real estate broker, refers title business to B, a company that is a licensed title agent for C, a title insurance company. A owns more than 1% of B. B performs the title search and examination, makes determinations of insurability, issues the commitment, clears underwriting objections, and issues a policy of title insurance on behalf of C, for which C pays B a commission. B pays annual dividends to its owners, including A, based on the relative amount of business each of its owners refers to B.

Comments: The facts involve an affiliated business arrangement. The payments of a commission by C to B is not a violation of section 8 of RESPA if the amount of the commission constitutes reasonable compensation for the services performed by B for C. The payment of a dividend or the giving of any other thing of value by B to A that is based on the amount of business referred to B by A does not meet the affiliated business agreement exemption provisions and such actions violate section 8. Similarly, if the amount of stock held by A in B (or, if B were a partnership, the distribution of partnership profits by B to A) varies based on the amount of business referred or expected to be referred, or if B retained any funds for subsequent distribution to A where such funds were generally in proportion to the amount of business A referred to B relative to the amount referred by other owners such arrangements would violate section 8. The exemption for controlled business arrangements would not be available because the payments here would not be considered returns on ownership interests. Further, the required disclosure of the affiliated business arrangement and estimated charges have not been provided.

8. *Facts*: Same as illustration 7, but B pays annual dividends in proportion to the amount of

stock held by its owners, including A, and the distribution of annual dividends is not based on the amount of business referred or expected to be referred.

Comments: If A and B meet the requirements of the affiliated business arrangement exemption there is not a violation of RESPA. Since the payment is a return on ownership interests, A and B will be exempt from section 8 if (1) A also did not require anyone to use the services of B, and (2) A disclosed its ownership interest in B on a separate disclosure form and provided an estimate of B's charges to each person referred by A to B (see appendix D of this part), and (3) B makes no payment (nor is there any other thing of value exchanged) to A other than dividends.

9. *Facts*: A, a franchisor for franchised real estate brokers, owns B, a provider of settlement services. C, a franchisee of A, refers business to B.

Comments: This is an affiliated business arrangement. A, B and C will all be exempt from section 8 if C discloses its franchise relationship with the owner of B on a separate disclosure form and provides an estimate of B's charges to each person referred to B (see appendix D of this part) and C does not require anyone to use B's services and A gives no thing a value to C under the franchise agreement (such as an adjusted level of franchise payment based on the referrals), and B makes no payments to A other than dividends representing a return on ownership interest (rather than, *e.g.*, an adjusted level of payment being based on the referrals). Nor may B pay C anything of value for the referral.

10. *Facts*: A is a real estate broker who refers business to its affiliate title company B. A makes all required written disclosures to the homebuyer of the arrangement and estimated charges and the homebuyer is not required to use B. B refers or contracts out business to C who does all the title work and splits the fee with B. B passes its fee to A in the form of dividends, a return on ownership interest.

Comments: The relationship between A and B is an affiliated business arrangement. However, the affiliated business arrangement exemption does not provide exemption between an affiliated entity, B, and a third party, C. Here, B is a mere "shell" and provides no substantive services for its portion of the fee. The arrangement between B and C would be in violation of section 8(a) and (b). Even if B had an affiliate relationship with C, the required exemption criteria have not been met and the relationship would be subject to section 8.

11. *Facts*: A, a mortgage lender is affiliated with B, a title company, and C, an escrow company and offers consumers a package of mortgage title and escrow services at a discount from the prices at which such services would be sold if purchased separately. Neither A, B, nor C, requires consumers to purchase the services of their sister companies and each company sells such services separately and as part of the package. A also pays its employees (i.e., loan officers,

secretaries, etc.,) a bonus for each loan, title insurance or closing that A's employees generate for A, B, or C respectively. A pays such employee bonuses out of its own funds and receives no payments or reimbursements for such bonuses from B or C. At or before the time that customers are told by A or its employees about the services offered by B and C and/of the package of services that is available, the customers are provided with an affiliated business disclosure form.

Comments: A's selling of a package of settlement services at a discount to a settlement service purchaser does not violate section 8 of RESPA. A's employees are making appropriate affiliated business disclosures and since the services are available separately and as part of a package, there is not "required use" of the additional services. A's payments of bonuses to its employees for the referral of business to A or A's affiliates, B and C, are exempt from section 8 under section 3500.14(g)(1). However, if B or C reimbursed A for any bonuses that A paid to its employees for referring business to B or C, such reimbursements would violate section 8. Similarly, if B or C paid bonuses to A's employees directly for generating business for them, such payments would violate section 8.

12. *Facts*: A, a real estate broker, is affiliated with B, a mortgage lender, and C, a title agency. A employs F to advise and assist any customers of A who have executed sales contracts regarding mortgage loans and title insurance. F collects and transmits (by computer, fax, mail, or other means) loan applications or other information to B and C for processing. A pays F a small salary and a bonus for every loan closed with B or title insurance issued with C. F furnishes the controlled business disclosure to consumers at the time of each referral. F receives no other compensation from the real estate or mortgage transaction and performs no settlement services in any transaction. At the end of each of A's fiscal years, M, a managerial employee of A, receives a $1,000 bonus if 20% of the consumers who purchase a home through A close a loan on the home with B and have the title issued by C. During the year, M acted as a real estate agent for his neighbor and received a real estate sales commission for selling his neighbor's home.

Comments: Under § 3500.14(g)(1), employers may pay their own *bona fide* employees for generating business for their employer (§ 3500.14(g)(1)(vii)). Employers may also pay their own *bona fide* employees for generating business for their affiliate business entities (§ 3500.14(g)(1)(ix)), as long as the employees do not perform settlement services in any transaction and disclosure is made. This permits a company to employ a person whose primary function is to market the employer's or its affiliate's settlement services (frequently referred to as a Financial Services Representative, or "FSR"). An FSR may not perform any settlement services including, for example, those services of a real estate agent, loan processor, settle-

ment agent, attorney, or mortgage broker. In accordance with the terms of the exemption at § 3500.14(g)(1)(ix), the marketing of a settlement service or product of an affiliated entity, including the collection and conveyance of information or the taking of an application or order for the services of an affiliated entity, does not constitute the performance of a settlement service. Under the exemption, marketing of a settlement service or product also may include incidental communications with the consumer after the application or order, such as providing the consumer with information about the status of an application or order; marketing may not include serving as the ongoing point of contact for coordinating the delivery and provision of settlement services.

Thus, in the circumstances described, F and M may receive the additional compensation without violating RESPA.

Also, employers may pay managerial employees compensation in the form of bonuses based on a percentage of transactions completed by an affiliated company (frequently called a "capture rate"), as long as the payment is not directly calculated as a multiple of the number or value of the referrals. 24 CFR 3500.14(g)(1) (viii). A managerial employee who receives compensation for performing settlement services in three or fewer transactions in any calendar year "does not routinely" deal directly with the consumer and is not precluded from receiving managerial compensation.

13. *Facts*. A is a mortgage broker who provides origination services to submit a loan to a Lender for approval. The mortgage broker charges the borrower a uniform fee for the total origination services, as well as a direct up-front charge for reimbursement of credit reporting, appraisal services or similar charges.

Comment. The mortgage broker's fee must be itemized in the Good Faith Estimate and on the HUD-1 Settlement Statement. Other charges which are paid for by the borrower and paid in advance are listed as P.O.C. on the HUD-1 Settlement Statement, and reflect the actual provider charge for such services. Also, any other fee or payment received by the mortgage broker from either the lender or the borrower arising from the initial funding transaction, including a servicing release premium or yield spread premium, is to be noted on the Good Faith Estimate and listed in the 800 series of the HUD-1 Settlement Statement.

14. *Facts*. A is a dealer in home improvements who has established funding arrangements with several lenders. Customers for home improvements receive a proposed contract from A. The proposal requires that customers both execute forms authorizing a credit check and employment verification, and, frequently, execute a dealer consumer credit contract secured by a lien on the customer's (borrower's) 1- to 4-family residential property. Simultaneously with the completion and certification of the home im-

provement work, the note is assigned by the dealer to a funding lender.

Comments. The loan that is assigned to the funding lender is a loan covered by RESPA, when a lien is placed on the borrower's 1- to 4-family residential structure. The dealer loan or consumer credit contract originated by a dealer is also a RESPA-covered transaction, except when the dealer is not a "creditor" under the definition of "federally related mortgage loan" in § 3500.2. The lender to whom the loan will be assigned is responsible for assuring that the lender or the dealer delivers to the borrower a Good Faith Estimate of closing costs consistent with Regulation X, and that the HUD-1 or HUD-1A Settlement Statement is used in conjunction with the settlement of the loan to be assigned. A dealer who, under § 3500.2, is covered by RESPA as a creditor is responsible for the Good Faith Estimate of Closing Costs and the use of the appropriate settlement statement in connection with the loan.

[57 Fed. Reg. 49607 (Nov. 2, 1992); 57 Fed. Reg. 56857 (Dec. 1, 1992), *as amended at* 59 Fed. Reg. 6521 (Feb. 10, 1994); 61 Fed. Reg. 13251 (Mar. 26, 1996); 61 Fed. Reg. 29253 (June 7, 1996); 61 Fed. Reg. 58476 (Nov. 15, 1996)]

Effective Date Note: At 61 Fed. Reg. 29253, June 7, 1996, appendix B to part 3500 was amended by revising Illustration 11, redesignating Illustrations 12 and 13 as Illustrations 13 and 14, respectively, and adding a new Illustration 12, effective Oct. 7, 1996. At 61 FR 51782, Oct. 4, 1996, the effective date was delayed until further notice. For the convenience of the user, the revised text is set forth as follows:

24 C.F.R. 3500 Appendix B—Illustrations of Requirements of RESPA

* * *

11. *Facts*: A, a mortgage lender, is affiliated with B, a title company, and C, an escrow company, and offers consumers a package of mortgage, title, and escrow services at a discount from the prices at which such services would be sold if purchased separately. A, B, and C are subsidiaries of H, a holding company, which also controls a retail stock brokerage firm, D. None of A, B, or C requires consumers to purchase the services of its sister companies, and each company sells such services separately and as part of the package. A also pays an employee T, a full-time bank teller who does not perform settlement services, a bonus for each loan, title insurance binder, or closing that T generates for A, B, or C. A pays T these bonuses out of A's own funds and receives no reimbursements for these bonuses from B, C, or H. At the time that T refers customers to B and C, T provides the customers with a disclosure using the controlled business arrangement disclosure format. Also, Z, a stockbroker employee of D, occasionally refers her customers to A, B, or C; gives a statement in the

controlled business disclosure format; and receives a payment from D for each referral.

Comments: Selling a package of settlement services at a discount is not prohibited by RESPA, consistent with the definition of "required use" in 24 CFR 3500.2. Also, A is always allowed to compensate its own employees for business generated for A's company. Here, A may also compensate T, an employee who does not perform settlement services in this or any transaction, for referring business to a business entity in an affiliate relationship with A. Z, who does not perform settlement services in this or any transaction, can also be compensated by D, but not by anyone else. Employees who perform settlement services cannot be compensated for referrals to other settlement service providers. None of the entities in an affiliated relationship with each other may pay for referrals received from an affiliate's employees. Sections 3500.15(b)(3)(i)(A) and (B) set forth the permissible exchanges of funds between controlled business entities. In all circumstances described a statement in the controlled business disclosure format must be provided to a potential consumer at or before the time that the referral is made.

* * *

24 C.F.R. 3500 Appendix D —Affiliated Business Arrangement Disclosure Statement Format; Notice

Affiliated Business Arrangement Disclosure Statement Format; Notice

To: _____

From: _____

_____
(Entity Making Statement)

Property: _____

_____

Date: _____

_____

This is to give you notice that [referring party] has a business relationship with [settlement services provider(s)]. [Describe the nature of the relationship between the referring party and the provider(s), including percentage of ownership interest, if applicable.] Because of this relationship, this referral may provide [referring party] a financial or other benefit.

[A.] Set forth below is the estimated charge or range of charges for the settlement services listed. You are NOT required to use the listed provider(s) as a condition for [settlement of your loan on] [or] [purchase, sale, or refinance of] the subject property. THERE ARE FREQUENTLY

OTHER SETTLEMENT SERVICE PROVIDERS AVAILABLE WITH SIMILAR SERVICES. YOU ARE FREE TO SHOP AROUND TO DETERMINE THAT YOU ARE RECEIVING THE BEST SERVICES AND THE BEST RATE FOR THESE SERVICES.

Provider and settlement service	Charge or range of charges

[B.] Set forth below is the estimated charge or range of charges for the settlement services of an attorney, credit reporting agency, or real estate appraiser that we, as your lender, will require you to use, as a condition of your loan on this property, to represent our interests in the transaction.

Provider and settlement service	Charge or range of charges

Acknowledgment

I/we have read this disclosure form, and understand that [referring party] is referring me/us to purchase the above-described settlement service(s) and may receive a financial or other benefit as the result of this referral.

_____
Signature

[INSTRUCTIONS TO PREPARER:] [Use paragraph A for referrals other than those by a lender to an attorney, a credit reporting agency, or a real estate appraiser that a lender is requiring a borrower to use to represent the lender's interests in the transaction. Use paragraph B for those referrals to an attorney, credit reporting agency, or real estate appraiser that a lender is requiring a borrower to use to represent the lender's interests in the transaction. When applicable, use both paragraphs. Specific timing rules for delivery of the affiliated business disclosure statement are set forth in 24 CFR 3500.15(b)(1) of Regulation X. These INSTRUCTIONS TO PREPARER should not appear on the statement.]

[61 Fed. Reg. 41944, Aug. 12, 1996; 61 Fed. Reg. 51782, Oct. 4, 1996; 61 Fed. Reg. 58476, Nov. 15, 1996.]

* * *

K.3 HUD Policy Statements

K.3.1 HUD Statement of Policy 1999-1: Regarding Lender Payments to Mortgage Brokers

DEPARTMENT OF HOUSING AND URBAN DEVELOPMENT

24 CFR Part 3500

[Docket No. FR–4450–N–01]

RIN 2502–AH33

Real Estate Settlement Procedures Act (RESPA) Statement of Policy 1999–1 Regarding Lender Payments to Mortgage Brokers

AGENCY: Office of the Assistant Secretary for Housing-Federal Housing Commissioner, HUD.

ACTION: Statement of Policy 1999–1.

SUMMARY: This Statement of Policy sets forth the Department of Housing and Urban Development's position on the legality of lender payments to mortgage brokers in connection with federally related mortgage loans under the Real Estate Settlement Procedures Act ("RESPA") and HUD's implementing regulations. While this statement satisfies the Conferees' directive in the Conference Report on the 1999 HUD Appropriations Act that the Department clarify its position on this subject, HUD believes that broad legislative reform along the lines specified in the HUD/ Federal Reserve Board Report remains the most effective way to resolve the difficulties and legal uncertainties under RESPA and the Truth in Lending Act (TILA) for industry and consumers alike. Statutory changes like those recommended in the Report would, if adopted, provide the most balanced approach to resolving these contentious issues by providing consumers with better and firmer information about the costs associated with home-secured credit transactions and providing creditors and mortgage brokers with clearer rules. Such an approach is far preferable to piecemeal actions.

EFFECTIVE DATE: This Statement of Policy is effective March 1, 1999.

FOR FURTHER INFORMATION CONTACT: Rebecca J. Holtz, Director RESPA/ILS Division Room 9146, Department of Housing and Urban Development, Washington, DC 20410; telephone 202–708–4560, or (for legal questions) Kenneth A. Markison, Assistant General Counsel for GSE/RESPA or Rodrigo Alba, Attorney for RESPA, Room 9262, Department of Housing and Urban Development, Washington, DC 20410; telephone 202–708–3137 (these are not toll free numbers). Hearing or speech-impaired individuals may access these numbers via TTY by calling the toll-free Federal Information Relay Service at 1–800–877–8339.

SUPPLEMENTARY INFORMATION: This Preamble to the Statement of Policy includes descriptions of current practices in the industry. It is not intended to take positions with respect to the legality or illegality of any practices; such positions are set forth in the Statement of Policy itself.

I. Background

A. General Background

The Conference Report on the Departments of Veterans Affairs and Housing and Urban Development, and Independent Agencies Appropriations Act, 1999 (H.R. Conf. Rep. No. 105–769, 105th Cong., 2d Sess. 260 (1998)) (FY 1999 HUD Appropriations Act) directs HUD to clarify its position on lender payments to mortgage brokers within 90 days after the enactment of the FY 1999 HUD Appropriations Act on October 21, 1998. The Report states that "Congress never intended payments by lenders to mortgage brokers for goods or facilities actually furnished or for services actually performed to be violations of [Sections 8](a) or (b) of the Real Estate Settlement Procedures Act (12 U.S.C. 2601 *et seq.*) (RESPA)]" (Id.). The Report also states that the Conferees "are concerned about the legal uncertainty that continues absent such a policy statement" and "expect HUD to work with representatives of industry, Federal agencies, consumer groups, and other interested parties on this policy statement" (Id.).

This issue of lender payments, or indirect fees, to mortgage brokers has proven particularly troublesome for industry and consumers alike. It has been the subject of litigation in more than 150 cases nationwide (see additional discussion below). To understand the issue and HUD's position regarding the legality of these payments requires background information concerning the nature of the services provided by mortgage brokers and their compensation, as well as the applicable legal requirements under RESPA.

During the last seven years, HUD has conducted three rulemakings respecting mortgage broker fees. These rulemakings first addressed definitional issues and issues concerning disclosure of payments to mortgage brokers in transactions covered under RESPA. (See 57 FR 49600 (November 2, 1992); 60 FR 47650 (September 13, 1995).) Most recently in a regulatory negotiation (see 60 FR 54794 (October 25, 1995) and 60 FR 63008 (December 8, 1995)) and then a proposed rule (62 FR 53912 (October 16, 1997)), HUD addressed the issue of the legality of payments to brokers

under RESPA. In the latter, HUD proposed that payments from lenders to mortgage brokers be presumed legal if the mortgage broker met certain specified conditions, including disclosing its role in the transaction and its total compensation through a binding contract with the borrower. This rulemaking is pending.

In July 1998, HUD and the Board of Governors of the Federal Reserve delivered to Congress a joint report containing legislative proposals to reform RESPA and the Truth in Lending Act. If the proposals in this reform package were to be adopted, the disclosure and legality issues raised herein would be resolved for any mortgage broker following certain of the proposed requirements, and consumers would be offered significant new protections.

B. Mortgage Brokerage Industry

When RESPA was enacted in 1974, single family mortgages were largely originated and held by savings and loans, commercial banks, and mortgage bankers. During the 1980's and 1990's, the rise of secondary mortgage market financing resulted in new wholesale and retail entities to compete with the traditional funding entities to provide mortgage financing. This made possible the origination of loans by retail entities that worked with prospective borrowers, collected application information, and otherwise processed the data required to complete the mortgage transaction. These retail entities generally operated with the intent of developing the origination package, and then immediately transmitting it to a wholesale lender who funded the loan. The rise in technology permitted much more effective and faster exchange of information and funds between originators and lenders for the retail transaction.

Entities that provide mortgage origination or retail services and that bring a borrower and a lender together to obtain a loan (usually without providing the funds for loans) are generally referred to as "mortgage brokers." These entities serve as intermediaries between the consumer and the entity funding the loan, and currently initiate an estimated half of all home mortgages made each year in the United States. Mortgage brokers generally fit into two broad categories: those that hold themselves out as representing the borrower in shopping for a loan, and those that simply offer loans as do other retailers of loans. The first type may have an agency relationship with the borrower and, in some states, may be found to owe a

Appx. K.3.1　　*The Cost of Credit: Regulation and Legal Challenges*

Federal Register / Vol. 64, No. 39 / Monday, March 1, 1999 / Rules and Regulations　　**10081**

responsibility to the borrower in connection with the agency representation. The second type, while not representing the borrower, may make loans available to consumers from any number of funding sources with which the mortgage broker has a business relationship.

Mortgage brokers provide various services in processing mortgage loans, such as filling out the application, ordering required reports and documents, counseling the borrower and participating in the loan closing. They may also offer goods and facilities, such as reports, equipment, and office space to carry out their functions. The level of services mortgage brokers provide in particular transactions depends on the level of difficulty involved in qualifying applicants for particular loan programs. For example, applicants have differences in credit ratings, employment status, levels of debt, or experience that will translate into various degrees of effort required for processing a loan. Also, the mortgage broker may be required to perform various levels of services under different servicing or processing arrangements with wholesale lenders.

Mortgage brokers vary in their methods of collecting compensation for their work in arranging, processing, and closing mortgage loans. In a given transaction, a broker may receive compensation directly from the borrower, indirectly in fees paid by the wholesaler or lender providing the mortgage loan funds, or through a combination of both.

Where a broker receives direct compensation from a borrower, the broker's fee is likely charged to the borrower at or before closing, as a percentage of the loan amount (e.g., 1% of the loan amount) and through direct fees (such as an application fee, document preparation fee, processing fee, etc.).

Brokers also may receive indirect compensation from lenders or wholesalers. Such indirect fees may be referred to as "back funded payments," "servicing release premiums," or "yield spread premiums." These indirect fees paid to mortgage brokers may be based upon the interest rate of each loan entered into by the broker with the borrower. These fees have been the subject of much contention and litigation. Another method of indirect compensation, also the subject of significant controversy and uncertainty, is "volume-based" compensation. This generally involves compensation to a mortgage broker by a lender based on the volume of loans that the mortgage broker delivers to the lender in a fixed

period of time. The compensation may come in the form of: (1) a cash payment to the broker based on the amount of loans the broker delivers to the lender in excess of a "threshold" or "floor amount"; or (2) provision of a lower "start rate" (often called a discount) for such loans; the compensation to the broker results from the difference in yield between the "start rate" and the loan rate. Volume based compensation may be received at settlement or well after a particular loan has closed.

Payments to brokers by lenders, characterized as yield spread premiums, are based on the interest rate and points of the loan entered into as compared to the par rate offered by the lender to the mortgage broker for that particular loan (e.g., a loan of 8% and no points where the par rate is 7.50% will command a greater premium for the broker than a loan with a par rate of 7.75% and no points).[1] In determining the price of a loan, mortgage brokers rely on rate quotes issued by lenders, sometimes several times a day. When a lender agrees to purchase a loan from a broker, the broker receives the then applicable pricing for the loan based on the difference between the rate reflected in the rate quote and the rate of the loan entered into by the borrower. In some cases, the broker can increase its revenues by arranging a loan with the consumer at a particular rate and then, based on market changes or other factors which decrease the par rate, increase his or her fees. Some consumers allege that the compensation system for brokers results in higher loan rates for borrowers and/or that this compensation system is illegal under RESPA.

Lender payments to mortgage brokers may reduce the up-front costs to consumers. This allows consumers to obtain loans without paying direct fees themselves.[2] Where a broker is not compensated by the consumer through a direct fee, or is partially compensated through a direct fee, the interest rate of the loan is increased to compensate the broker or the fee is added to principal. In any of the compensation methods described, all costs are ultimately paid by the consumer, whether through direct fees or through the interest rate.

---

[1] The term "par rate" refers to the rate offered to the broker (through the lender's price sheets) at which the lender will fund 100% of the loan with no premiums or discounts to the broker.

[2] In many instances, these loans are called "no cost" or "no fee" loans. This terminology, however, may prove confusing because in such cases the costs are still paid by the borrower through a higher interest rate on the loan or by adding fees to principal. HUD's regulations implementing RESPA use the name "no cost" or "no point" loans consistent with industry practice.

C. Coverage of This Policy Statement

HUD's RESPA rules, found at 24 CFR part 3500 (Regulation X), define a mortgage broker to be "a person (not an employee or exclusive agent of a lender) who brings a borrower and lender together to obtain a federally-related mortgage loan, and who renders * * * 'settlement services'" (24 CFR 3500.2(b)). In table funding, mortgage brokers may process and close loans in their own names. However, at or about the time of settlement, they transfer these loans to the lender, and the lender simultaneously advances the monies to fund the loan. In transactions where mortgage brokers function as intermediaries, the broker also provides loan origination services, but the loan funds are provided by the lender and the loan is closed in the lender's name.

In other cases, mortgage brokers may originate and close loans in their own name using their own funds or warehouse lines of credit, and then sell the loans after settlement in the secondary market. In such transactions, mortgage brokers effectively act as lenders under HUD's RESPA rules. Accordingly, the transfer of the loan obligation by, and payment to, these brokers after the initial funding is outside of RESPA's coverage under the secondary market exemption, found at 24 CFR 3500.5(b)(7), which states that payments to and from other loan sources following settlement are exempt from disclosure requirements and Section 8 restrictions. HUD's rule provides that in determining what constitutes a *bona fide* transfer in the secondary market, HUD considers the real source of funding and the real interest of the funding lender. (24 CFR 3500.5(b)(7).)

Because this Statement of Policy focuses on the legality of lender payments to mortgage brokers in transactions subject to RESPA, the coverage of this statement is restricted to payments to mortgage brokers in table-funded and intermediary broker transactions. Lender payments to mortgage brokers where mortgage brokers initially fund the loan and then sell the loan after settlement are outside the coverage of this statement as exempt from RESPA under the secondary market exemption.

D. RESPA and Its Legislative History

In enacting RESPA, Congress sought to protect the American home-buying public from unreasonably and unnecessarily inflated prices in the home purchasing process (S. Rep. No. 93–866 (1974) *reprinted in* 1974

U.S.C.C.A.N. 6548). Section 2 of the Act provides:

"significant reforms in the real estate settlement process are needed to insure that consumers throughout the Nation are provided with greater and more timely information on the nature and costs of the settlement process and are protected from unnecessarily high settlement charges caused by certain abusive practices that have developed in some areas of the country. * * * It is the purpose of this act to effect certain changes in the settlement process for residential real estate that will result—

in more effective advance disclosure to home buyers and sellers of settlement costs; [and]

(2) In the elimination of kickbacks or referral fees that tend to increase unnecessarily the costs of certain settlement services. * * *" 12 U.S.C. 2601.

Section 4(a) of RESPA requires the Secretary to create a uniform settlement statement which "shall conspicuously and clearly itemize all charges imposed upon the borrower and all charges imposed upon the seller in connection with the settlement" (12 U.S.C. 2603(a)).

Section 5(c) of RESPA requires the provision of a "good faith estimate of the amount or range of charges for specific settlement services the borrower is likely to incur in connection with the settlement as prescribed by the Secretary" (12 U.S.C. 2604(c)).

Section 8(a) of RESPA, prohibits any person from giving and any person from accepting any fee, kickback, or other thing of value pursuant to any agreement or understanding that business shall be referred to any person. (See 12 U.S.C. 2607(a).) Section 8(b) also prohibits anyone from giving or accepting any portion, split, or percentage of any charge made or received for the rendering of a settlement service other than for services actually performed. (12 U.S.C. 2607(b).) Section 8(c) of RESPA provides, however, that nothing in Section 8 shall be construed as prohibiting the payment to any person of a *bona fide* salary or compensation or other payment for goods or facilities actually furnished or services actually performed. (12 U.S.C. 2607(c)(2).)

Under Section 19 of RESPA, HUD is authorized to issue rules, establish exemptions, and make such interpretations as is necessary to implement the law. (12 U.S.C. 2618(a).)

RESPA's legislative history refers to HUD–VA Reports and subsequent hearings by the Housing Subcommittee as defining "major problem areas that [had to] be dealt with if settlement costs are to be kept within reasonable bounds." (S. Rep. No. 93–866, at 6547.) One "major problem area" identified was the "[a]busive and unreasonable

practices within the real estate settlement process that increase settlement costs to home buyers without providing any real benefits to them." Another major concern was "[t]he lack of understanding on the part of most home buyers about the settlement process and its costs, which lack of understanding makes it difficult for a free market for settlement services to function at maximum efficiency."

The legislative history reveals that Congress intended RESPA to guard against these unreasonable and excessive settlement costs in two ways. Under Section 4, Congress sought to "mak[e] information on the settlement process available to home buyers in advance of settlement and requir[e] advance disclosures of settlement charges." (S. Rep. 93–866, at 6548.) The Senate Report explained that "home buyers who would otherwise shop around for settlement services, and thereby reduce their overall settlement costs, are prevented from doing so because frequently they are not apprised of the costs of these services until the settlement date or are not aware of the nature of the settlement services that will be provided."

Under Section 8, Congress sought to eliminate what it termed "abusive practices"—kickbacks, referral fees, and unearned fees. In enacting these prohibitions, Congress intended that "the costs to the American home buying public will not be unreasonably or unnecessarily inflated." (S. Rep. 93–866 at 6548.) In describing the Section 8 provisions, the Senate Report explained that RESPA "is intended to prohibit all * * * referral fee arrangements whereby any payment is made or a 'thing of value' is provided for the referral of real estate settlement business." (S. Rep. 93–866, at 6551.)

The legislative history adds that "[t]o the extent the payment is in excess of the reasonable value of the goods provided or services performed, the excess may be considered a kickback or referral fee proscribed by Section [8]." (S. Rep. 93–866, at 6551.) The Senate Report states that "reasonable payments in return for services actually performed or goods actually furnished" were not intended to be prohibited (Id.)[3] It also provided that "[t]hose persons and companies that provide settlement

[3] One of the examples of abusive activities listed in the legislative history that RESPA was intended to remedy is "a title insurance company [that] may give 10% or more of the title insurance premium to an attorney who may perform no services for the title insurance company other than placing a telephone call to the company or filling out a simple application." (S. Rep. 93–866, at 6551.) Accordingly, where insufficient services are provided, RESPA is intended to prohibit payment.

services should therefore take measures to ensure that any payments they make or commissions they give are not out of line with the reasonable value of the services received." (*Id.*)

The Department has consistently held that the prohibitions under Section 8 of RESPA cover the activities of mortgage brokers, because RESPA applies to the origination, processing, and funding of a federally related mortgage loan. This became an issue when, in 1984, the 6th Circuit Court of Appeals held that in applying Section 8 as a criminal statute, the definition of settlement services did not clearly extend to the making of a mortgage loan. (*U.S.* versus *Graham Mortgage Corp.*, 740 F.2d 414 (6th Cir. 1984).) In 1992, Congress responded by amending RESPA to remove any doubt that, for purposes of RESPA, a settlement service includes the origination and making of a mortgage loan. (Section 908 of the Housing and Community Development Act of 1992 (Pub. L. 102–550, approved October 28, 1992; 104 Stat. 4413). At the same time, Congress also specifically made RESPA applicable to second mortgages and refinancings. (*Id.*)

E. HUD's RESPA Rules

On November 2, 1992 (57 FR 49600), the Department issued a major revision of Regulation X, the rule interpreting RESPA. The rule defined the term "mortgage broker" for the first time. Under the rule, mortgage brokers are required to disclose direct and indirect payments on the Good Faith Estimate (GFE) no later than 3 days after loan application. (See 24 CFR 3500.7(a) and (c).) Such disclosure must also be provided to consumers, as a final figure, at closing on the settlement statement. (24 CFR 3500.8; 24 CFR part 3500, Appendix A (Instructions for Filling Out the HUD–1 and HUD–1A).) On the GFE and the settlement statement, lender-paid mortgage broker fees must be shown as "Paid Outside of Closing" (P.O.C.), and not computed in arriving at totals. (See 24 CFR 3500.7(a)(2) and 24 CFR part 3500, Appendix A.) The 1992 rule treats mortgage brokers as settlement service providers whose fees are disbursed at or before settlement, akin to title agents, attorneys, appraisers, etc., whose fees are subject to disclosure and otherwise subject to RESPA, including Section 8.

The 1992 rule did not explicitly take a position on whether yield spread premiums or any other named class of back-funded or indirect fees paid by lenders to brokers are *per se* legal or illegal. By illustration, codified as Illustrations of Requirements of RESPA, Fact Situations 5 and 12 in Appendix B

Appx. K.3.1   *The Cost of Credit: Regulation and Legal Challenges*

Federal Register / Vol. 64, No. 39 / Monday, March 1, 1999 / Rules and Regulations   **10083**

to 24 CFR part 3500, the 1992 rule specifically listed "servicing release premiums" and "yield spread premiums" as fees required to be itemized on the settlement statement. Although the 1992 rule specifically acknowledged the existence of such fees and provided illustrations of how they were to be denominated on HUD disclosure forms, this requirement was intended to ensure their disclosure, but not to create a presumption of *per se* legality or illegality.

The anti-kickback, anti-referral fee and unearned fee provisions of RESPA are implemented by 24 CFR 3500.14. Regulation X repeats the Section 8 prohibitions against compensation for the referral of settlement service business and for the giving or accepting of any portion, split or percentage of any charge other than for services actually rendered. (24 CFR 3500.14(c).) Regulation X provides that a charge by a person for which no or nominal services are performed or for which duplicative fees are charged is an unearned fee and violates the unearned fee prohibition. (See 24 CFR 3500.14(c).) Moreover, 24 CFR 3500.14(g)(1)(iv) clarifies that Section 8 of RESPA permits "[a] payment to any person of a *bona fide* salary or compensation or other payment for goods or facilities actually furnished or for services actually performed."

The Department's regulations provide, under 24 CFR 3500.14(g)(2), that:

The Department may investigate high prices to see if they are the result of a referral fee or a split of a fee. *If the payment of a thing of value bears no reasonable relationship to the market value of the goods or services provided, then the excess is not for services or goods actually performed or provided.* These facts may be used as evidence of a violation of section 8 and may serve as a basis for a RESPA investigation. High prices standing alone are not proof of a RESPA violation. The value of a referral (i.e., the value of any additional business obtained thereby) is not to be taken into account in determining whether the payment exceeds the reasonable value of such goods, facilities or services. * * * (emphasis supplied).

In addition, Regulation X clarifies that "[w]hen a person in a position to refer settlement service business * * * receives a payment for providing additional settlement services as part of a real estate transaction, such payment must be for services that are actual, necessary and distinct from the primary services provided by such person." (24 CFR 3500.14(g)(3).)

Since 1992, HUD has provided various interpretations and other issuances under these rules stating the Department's position that the legality

of a payment to a mortgage broker is not premised on the name of the particular fee. Rather, HUD has consistently advised that the issue under RESPA is whether the compensation to a mortgage broker in covered transactions is reasonably related to the value of the goods or facilities actually furnished or services actually performed. If the compensation, or a portion thereof, is not reasonably related to the goods or facilities actually furnished or the services actually performed, there is a compensated referral or an unearned fee in violation of Section 8(a) or 8(b) of RESPA, whether the compensation is a direct or indirect payment or a combination thereof.

F. Recent HUD Rulemaking Efforts

The Department received comments on the 1992 rule's requirement that mortgage brokers disclose indirect payments from lenders on the GFE and the settlement statement. In response, the Department reviewed whether the disclosure of indirect or back-funded fees is necessary or in the borrower's interest and whether additional rulemaking was needed to clarify the legality of fees to mortgage brokers. Brokers had alleged that these disclosures were confusing to consumers and disadvantaged brokers as compared to other originators who were within the secondary market exemption and were not required to disclose their compensation for the subsequent sale of the loan. Consumer representatives said that consumers needed to understand the existence of indirect fees and whether brokers represented consumers in shopping for loans. On September 13, 1995, the Department issued a proposed rule (60 FR 47650) and in December 1995 through May 1996, embarked on a negotiated rulemaking on these subjects.

Although the negotiated rulemaking did not result in consensus, on October 16, 1997, HUD published a proposed rule (62 FR 53912) that was shaped by views from both industry and consumer representatives provided during the negotiated rulemaking (as well as by comments received from the September 13, 1995, proposed rule (60 FR 47650)). The 1997 proposed rule proposed a qualified "safe harbor" for payments to mortgage brokers under Section 8. Under the proposal, if a broker enters into a contract with consumers explaining the broker's functions (whether or not it represented the consumer) and the total compensation the broker would receive in the transaction, before the consumer applied for a loan, HUD would presume the broker fees, both direct and indirect,

to be legal. The 1997 proposal also provided, however, that this qualified safe harbor would only be available to those payments that did not exceed a test, to be established in the rulemaking, to preclude unreasonable fees. This proposal was intended, among other things, to establish that yield spread premiums paid to brokers meeting the rule's requirements were presumed legal when brokers provided consumers with prescribed information concerning the functions and compensation of mortgage brokers. The Department has received over 9,000 comments in response to this proposed rule.

G. Litigation

During the last several years, more than 150 lawsuits have been brought seeking class action certification based in whole or in part on the theory that the making of indirect payments from lenders to mortgage brokers violates Section 8 of RESPA. In various cases, plaintiffs have argued that yield spread premiums or other denominated indirect payments to brokers, regardless of their amount, constitute prohibited referral fees under Section 8(a). These plaintiffs generally argue that yield spread premiums are payments based upon the broker's ability to deliver a loan that is above the par rate. Some lawsuits have alleged that such yield spread premiums or other indirect payments are a split of fees between the lender and the broker, or are simply unearned fees and, therefore, also violate Section 8(b) of RESPA. Other challenges rely, in part, on the alleged unreasonableness of brokers' fees. These complaints assert that under the RESPA regulations, payments must bear a reasonable relationship to the market value of the good or the service provided and that payments in excess of such amounts must be regarded as forbidden referral fees.

Many of the lawsuits involve allegations that consumers were not informed by mortgage brokers concerning the mortgage brokers' role and compensation. A common element in many allegations is that borrowers were not informed about the existence or the amount of the yield spread premiums paid to the mortgage broker, and the relationship of the yield spread premium to the direct fees that the borrower paid. The facts in these cases suggest generally that even where there were proper disclosures on the GFE and the settlement statement, borrowers allege that they were unaware of, or did not understand, that a yield spread premium was tied to the interest rate they agreed to pay, and that they could have reduced this charge or their direct payment to the broker either by further negotiation or by engaging in additional shopping among mortgage loan providers.

Courts have been split in their decisions on these cases. Some of the decisions have concluded that yield spread premiums may be prohibited referral fees or duplicative fees in contravention of Section 8 of RESPA under the specific facts of the case. Some have held that the permissibility of yield spread premiums must be based on an analysis of whether the premiums constitute a reasonable payment, either alone or in combination with any direct fee paid by the borrower, for either the goods, services or facilities actually furnished. Because some courts have found that this necessitates an individual analysis of the facts of each transaction, some courts have denied plaintiffs' requests for class action certification. Some courts have certified a class without reaching a conclusion on the RESPA issues. Others have held that yield spread premiums constitute valid consideration to the mortgage broker in exchange for the origination of the loan and the sale of the loan to the lender. These courts have found that the payment of yield spread premiums is one method among many of compensating the broker for the origination services rendered.

H. Reform

In July 1998, the Department and the Federal Reserve Board delivered a report to Congress recommending significant improvements to streamline and simplify current RESPA and Truth In Lending Act requirements. The Report proposed that along with a tighter and more enforceable scheme for providing consumers with estimated costs for settlements, an exemption from Section 8's prohibitions should be established for those entities that offer a package of settlement services and a mortgage loan at a guaranteed price, rate and points for the package early in the consumer's process of shopping for a loan. Such an approach, which also includes other additional consumer protection recommendations, would largely resolve these issues for any mortgage broker who chooses to abide by the requirements of this exemption. The Report's consumer protection recommendations included, among other items, that Congress consider establishment of an unfair and deceptive acts and practices remedy.

Under the "packaging" proposal set forth in the Report, settlement costs would be controlled more effectively by market forces. Consumers would be better able to comparison-shop, thereby encouraging creditors and others to operate efficiently and pass along discounts and lower prices. In addition, the Report's recommendations would greatly simplify compliance for the industry and clarify legal uncertainties that create liability risks.

I. This Policy Statement

This policy statement provides HUD's views of the legality of fees to mortgage brokers from lenders under existing law. In accordance with the Conference Report, in developing this policy statement, HUD met with representatives of government agencies, as well as a broad range of consumer and industry groups, including the Office of Thrift Supervision, the Comptroller of the Currency, the Federal Deposit Insurance Corporation, the Federal Reserve Board, the National Association of Mortgage Brokers, the Mortgage Bankers Association of America, the American Bankers Association, the Consumer Mortgage Coalition, America's Community Bankers, the Consumer Bankers Association, the Independent Bankers Association of America, AARP, the National Consumer Law Center, Consumers Union, and the National Association of Consumer Advocates.

II. RESPA Policy Statement 1999–1

A. Introduction

The Department hereby states its position on the legality of payments by lenders to mortgage brokers under the Real Estate Settlement Procedures Act (12 U.S.C. 2601 *et seq.*) (RESPA) and its implementing regulations at 24 CFR part 3500 (Regulation X). This Statement of Policy is issued pursuant to Section 19(a) of RESPA (12 U.S.C. 2617(a)) and 24 CFR 3500.4(a)(1)(ii). HUD is cognizant of the Conferees' statement in the Conference Report on the FY 1999 HUD Appropriations Act that "Congress never intended payments by lenders to mortgage brokers for goods or facilities actually furnished or for services actually performed to be violations of [Sections 8](a) or (b) (12 U.S.C. Sec. 2607) in its enactment of RESPA." (H. Rep. 105–769, at 260.) The Department is also cognizant of the congressional intent in enacting RESPA of protecting consumers from unnecessarily high settlement charges caused by abusive practices. (12 U.S.C. 2601.)

In transactions where lenders make payments to mortgage brokers, HUD does not consider such payments (i.e., yield spread premiums or any other class of named payments), to be illegal *per se*. HUD does not view the name of the payment as the appropriate issue

under RESPA. HUD's position that lender payments to mortgage brokers are not illegal *per se* does not imply, however, that yield spread premiums are legal in individual cases or classes of transactions. The fees in cases or classes of transactions are illegal if they violate the prohibitions of Section 8 of RESPA.

In determining whether a payment from a lender to a mortgage broker is permissible under Section 8 of RESPA, the first question is whether goods or facilities were actually furnished or services were actually performed for the compensation paid. The fact that goods or facilities have been actually furnished or that services have been actually performed by the mortgage broker does not by itself make the payment legal. The second question is whether the payments are reasonably related to the value of the goods or facilities that were actually furnished or services that were actually performed.

In applying this test, HUD believes that total compensation should be scrutinized to assure that it is reasonably related to goods, facilities, or services furnished or performed to determine whether it is legal under RESPA. Total compensation to a broker includes direct origination and other fees paid by the borrower, indirect fees, including those that are derived from the interest rate paid by the borrower, or a combination of some or all. The Department considers that higher interest rates alone cannot justify higher total fees to mortgage brokers. All fees will be scrutinized as part of total compensation to determine that total compensation is reasonably related to the goods or facilities actually furnished or services actually performed. HUD believes that total compensation should be carefully considered in relation to price structures and practices in similar transactions and in similar markets.

B. Scope

In light of 24 CFR § 3500.5(b)(7), which exempts from RESPA coverage *bona fide* transfers of loan obligations in the secondary market, this policy statement encompasses only transactions where mortgage brokers are not the real source of funds (i.e., table-funded transactions or transactions involving "intermediary" brokers). In table-funded transactions, the mortgage broker originates, processes and closes the loan in the broker's own name and, at or about the time of settlement, there is a simultaneous advance of the loan funds by the lender and an assignment of the loan to that lender. (See 24 CFR 3500.2 (Definition of "table funding").) Likewise, in transactions where

Appx. K.3.1   *The Cost of Credit: Regulation and Legal Challenges*

Federal Register / Vol. 64, No. 39 / Monday, March 1, 1999 / Rules and Regulations   **10085**

mortgage brokers are intermediaries, the broker provides loan origination services and the loan funds are provided by the lender; the loan, however, is closed in the lender's name.

C. Payments Must Be for Goods, Facilities or Services

In the determination of whether payments from lenders to mortgage brokers are permissible under Section 8 of RESPA, the threshold question is whether there were goods or facilities actually furnished or services actually performed for the total compensation paid to the mortgage broker. In making the determination of whether compensable services are performed, HUD's letter to the Independent Bankers Association of America, dated February 14, 1995 (IBAA letter) may be useful. In that letter, HUD identified the following services normally performed in the origination of a loan:

(a) Taking information from the borrower and filling out the application; [4]

(b) Analyzing the prospective borrower's income and debt and pre-qualifying the prospective borrower to determine the maximum mortgage that the prospective borrower can afford;

(c) Educating the prospective borrower in the home buying and financing process, advising the borrower about the different types of loan products available, and demonstrating how closing costs and monthly payments could vary under each product;

(d) Collecting financial information (tax returns, bank statements) and other related documents that are part of the application process;

(e) Initiating/ordering VOEs (verifications of employment) and VODs (verifications of deposit);

(f) Initiating/ordering requests for mortgage and other loan verifications;

(g) Initiating/ordering appraisals;

(h) Initiating/ordering inspections or engineering reports;

(i) Providing disclosures (truth in lending, good faith estimate, others) to the borrower;

(j) Assisting the borrower in understanding and clearing credit problems;

(k) Maintaining regular contact with the borrower, realtors, lender, between application and closing to appraise them of the status of the application and gather any additional information as needed;

(l) Ordering legal documents;

(m) Determining whether the property was located in a flood zone or ordering such service; and

(n) Participating in the loan closing. While this list does not exhaust all possible settlement services, and while the advent of computer technology has, in some cases, changed how a broker's settlement services are performed, HUD believes that the letter still represents a generally accurate description of the mortgage origination process. For other services to be acknowledged as compensable under RESPA, they should be identifiable and meaningful services akin to those identified in the IBAA letter including, for example, the operation of a computer loan origination system (CLO) or an automated underwriting system (AUS).

The IBAA letter provided guidance on whether HUD would take an enforcement action under RESPA. In the context of the letter's particular facts and subject to the reasonableness test which is discussed below, HUD articulated that it generally would be satisfied that sufficient origination work was performed to justify compensation if it found that:

• The lender's agent or contractor took the application information (under item (a)); and

• The lender's agent or contractor performed at least five additional items on the list above.

In the letter and in the context of its facts, HUD also pointed out that it is concerned that a fee for steering a customer to a particular lender could be disguised as compensation for "counseling-type" activities. Therefore, the letter states that if an agent or contractor is relying on taking the application and performing only "counseling type" services—(b), (c), (d), (j), and (k) on the list above—to justify its fee, HUD would also look to see that meaningful counseling—not steering—is provided. In analyzing transactions addressed in the IBAA letter, HUD said it would be satisfied that no steering occurred if it found that:

• Counseling gave the borrower the opportunity to consider products from at least three different lenders;

• The entity performing the counseling would receive the same compensation regardless of which lender's products were ultimately selected; *and*

• Any payment made for the "counseling-type" services is reasonably related to the services performed and not based on the amount of loan business referred to a particular lender.

In examining services provided by mortgage brokers and payments to

mortgage brokers, HUD will look at the types of origination services listed in the IBAA letter to help determine whether compensable services are performed.[5] However, the IBAA letter responded to a program where a relatively small fee was to be provided for limited services by lenders that were brokering loans.[6]

Accordingly, the formulation in the IBAA letter of the number of origination services which may be required to be performed for compensation is not dispositive in analyzing more costly mortgage broker transactions where more comprehensive services are provided. The determinative test under RESPA is the relationship of the services, goods or facilities furnished to the total compensation received by the broker (discussed below). In addition to services, mortgage brokers may furnish goods or facilities to the lender. For example, appraisals, credit reports, and other documents required for a complete loan file may be regarded as goods, and a reasonable portion of the broker's retail or "store-front" operation may generally be regarded as a facility for which a lender may compensate a broker. However, while a broker may be compensated for goods or facilities actually furnished or services actually performed, the loan itself, which is arranged by the mortgage broker, cannot be regarded as a "good" that the broker may sell to the lender and that the lender may pay for based upon the loan's yield's relation to market value, reasonable or otherwise. In other words, in the context of a non-secondary market mortgage broker transaction, under HUD's rules, it is not proper to argue that a loan is a "good," in the sense of an instrument bearing a particular yield, thus justifying any yield spread premium to the mortgage broker, however great, on the grounds that such yield spread premium is the "market value" of the good.

D. Compensation Must Be Reasonably Related to Value of Goods, Facilities or Services

The fact that goods or facilities have been actually furnished or that services have been actually performed by the mortgage broker, as described in the IBAA letter, does not by itself make a payment by a lender to a mortgage

---

[4] In a subsequent informal interpretation, dated June 20, 1995, HUD stated that the filling out of a mortgage loan application could be substituted by a comparable activity, such as the filling out of a borrower's worksheet.

[5] In the June 20, 1995 letter, the Department clarified that the counseling test in the IBAA letter would not apply if an entity performed only non-counseling services (a, e, f, g, h, i, l, m, n) or a mix of counseling and non-counseling services (but did not rely only on the five counseling services (b, c, d, j, and k)).

[6] In the particular program reviewed by HUD in the IBAA letter, the average total compensation for performing six of the origination services listed above was below $200.

Real Estate Settlement Procedures Act **Appx. K.3.1**

10086   Federal Register / Vol. 64, No. 39 / Monday, March 1, 1999 / Rules and Regulations

broker legal. The next inquiry is whether the payment is reasonably related to the value of the goods or facilities that were actually furnished or services that were actually performed. Although RESPA is not a rate-making statute, HUD is authorized to ensure that payments from lenders to mortgage brokers are reasonably related to the value of the goods or facilities actually furnished or services actually performed, and are not compensation for the referrals of business, splits of fees or unearned fees.

In analyzing whether a particular payment or fee bears a reasonable relationship to the value of the goods or facilities actually furnished or services actually performed, HUD believes that payments must be commensurate with that amount normally charged for similar services, goods or facilities. This analysis requires careful consideration of fees paid in relation to price structures and practices in similar transactions and in similar markets.[7] If the payment or a portion thereof bears no reasonable relationship to the market value of the goods, facilities or services provided, the excess over the market rate may be used as evidence of a compensated referral or an unearned fee in violation of Section 8(a) or (b) of RESPA. (See 24 CFR 3500.14(g)(2).) Moreover, HUD also believes that the market price used to determine whether a particular payment meets the reasonableness test may not include a referral fee or unearned fee, because such fees are prohibited by RESPA. Congress was clear that for payments to be legal under Section 8, they must bear a reasonable relationship to the value received by the person or company making the payment. (S. Rep. 93–866, at 6551.)

The Department recognizes that some of the goods or facilities actually furnished or services actually performed by the broker in originating a loan are "for" the lender and other goods or facilities actually furnished or services actually performed are "for" the borrower. HUD does not believe that it is necessary or even feasible to identify or allocate which facilities, goods or services are performed or provided for the lender, for the consumer, or as a function of State or Federal law. All services, goods and facilities inure to the benefit of both the borrower and the lender in the sense that they make the loan transaction possible (e.g., an appraisal is necessary to assure that the

lender has adequate security, as well as to advise the borrower of the value of the property and to complete the borrower's loan).

The consumer is ultimately purchasing the total loan and is ultimately paying for all the services needed to create the loan. All compensation to the broker either is paid by the borrower in the form of fees or points, directly or by addition to principal, or is derived from the interest rate of the loan paid by the borrower. Accordingly, in analyzing whether lender payments to mortgage brokers comport with the requirements of Section 8 of RESPA, HUD believes that the totality of the compensation to the mortgage broker for the loan must be examined. For example, if the lender pays the mortgage broker $600 and the borrower pays the mortgage broker $500, the total compensation of $1,100 would be examined to determine whether it is reasonably related to the goods or facilities actually furnished or services actually performed by the broker.

Therefore, in applying this test, HUD believes that total compensation should be scrutinized to assure that it is reasonably related to goods, facilities, or services furnished or performed to determine whether total compensation is legal under RESPA. Total compensation to a broker includes direct origination and other fees paid by the borrower, indirect fees, including those that are derived from the interest rate paid by the borrower, or a combination of some or all. All payments, including payments based upon a percentage of the loan amount, are subject to the reasonableness test defined above. In applying this test, the Department considers that higher interest rates alone cannot justify higher total fees to mortgage brokers. All fees will be scrutinized as part of total compensation to determine that total compensation is reasonably related to the goods or facilities actually furnished or services actually performed.

In so-called "no-cost" loans, borrowers accept a higher interest rate in order to reduce direct fees, and the absence of direct payments to the mortgage broker is made up by higher indirect fees (e.g., yield spread premiums). Higher indirect fees in such arrangements are legal if, and only if, the total compensation is reasonably related to the goods or facilities actually furnished or services actually performed.

In determining whether the compensation paid to a mortgage broker is reasonably related to the goods or facilities actually furnished or services

actually performed, HUD will consider all compensation, including any volume based compensation. In this analysis, there may be no payments merely for referrals of business under Section 8 of RESPA. (See 24 CFR 3500.14.)[8]

Under HUD's rules, when a person in a position to refer settlement service business receives a payment for providing additional settlement services as part of the transaction, such payment must be for services that are actual, necessary and distinct from the primary services provided by the person. (24 CFR 3500.14(g)(3).) While mortgage brokers may receive part of their compensation from a lender, where the lender payment duplicates direct compensation paid by the borrower for goods or facilities actually furnished or services actually performed, Section 8 is violated. In light of the fact that the borrower and the lender may both contribute to some items, HUD believes that it is best to evaluate seemingly duplicative fees by analyzing total compensation under the reasonableness test described above.

E. Information Provided to Borrower

Under current RESPA rules mortgage brokers are required to disclose estimated direct and indirect fees on the Good Faith Estimate (GFE) no later than 3 days after loan application. (See 24 CFR 3500.7(a) and (b).) Such disclosure must also be provided to consumers, as a final exact figure, at closing on the settlement statement. (24 CFR 3500.8; 24 CFR part 3500, Appendix A.) On the GFE and the settlement statement, lender payments to mortgage brokers must be shown as "Paid Outside of Closing" (P.O.C.), and are not computed in arriving at totals. (24 CFR 3500.7(a)(2).) The requirement that all fees be disclosed on the GFE is intended to assure that consumers are shown the full amount of compensation to brokers and others early in the transaction.

The Department has always indicated that any fees charged in settlement transactions should be clearly disclosed so that the consumer can understand the nature and recipient of the payment. Code-like abbreviations like "YSP to DBG, POC", for instance, have been noted.[9] Also, the Department has seen

---

[7] HUD recognizes that settlement costs may vary in different markets. The cost of a specific service in Omaha, Nebraska, for example, may bear little resemblance to the cost of a similar service in Los Angeles, California.

[8] The Department generally has held that when the payment is based on the volume or value of business transacted, it is evidence of an agreement for the referral of business (unless, for example, it is shown that payments are for legitimate business reasons unrelated to the value of the referrals). (See 24 CFR 3500.14(e).)

[9] This is an example only. HUD recognizes that current practices may leave borrowers confused. However, the use of any particular terms, including abbreviations, may not, by itself, violate RESPA. Nevertheless, going forward, HUD recommends that

Appx. K.3.1　　　*The Cost of Credit: Regulation and Legal Challenges*

Federal Register / Vol. 64, No. 39 / Monday, March 1, 1999 / Rules and Regulations　　**10087**

examples on the GFE and/or the settlement statement where the identity and/or purpose of the fees are not clearly disclosed.

The Department considers unclear and confusing disclosures to be contrary to the statute's and the regulation's purposes of making RESPA-covered transactions understandable to the consumer. At a minimum, all fees to the mortgage broker are to be clearly labeled and properly estimated on the GFE. On the settlement statement, the name of the recipient of the fee (in this case, the mortgage broker) is to be clearly labeled and listed, and the fee received from a lender is to be clearly labeled and listed in the interest of clarity. For example, a fee would be appropriately disclosed as "Mortgage broker fee from lender to XYZ Corporation (P.O.C.)." In the interest of clarity, other fees or payments from the borrower to the mortgage broker should identify that they are mortgage broker fees from the borrower.[10]

There is no requirement under existing law that consumers be fully informed of the broker's services and compensation prior to the GFE. Nevertheless, HUD believes that the broker should provide the consumer with information about the broker's services and compensation, and agreement by the consumer to the arrangement should occur as early as possible in the process. Mortgage brokers and lenders can improve their ability to demonstrate the reasonableness of their fees if the broker discloses the nature of the broker's services and the various methods of compensation at the time the consumer first discusses the possibility of a loan with the broker.

The legislative history makes clear that RESPA was not intended to be a rate-setting statute and that Congress instead favored a market-based approach. (S. Rep. No. 93–866 at 6546 (1974).) In making the determination of whether a payment is *bona fide* compensation for goods or facilities actually furnished or services actually performed, HUD has, in the past, indicated that it would examine whether the price paid for the goods,

---

the disclosures on the GFE and the settlement statement be as described in the text. HUD recognizes that system changes may require time for lenders and brokers to implement.

[10] HUD recognizes that current software may not currently accommodate these additional disclosures. Both industry and consumers would be better served if these additional disclosures were included in future forms.

facilities or services is truly a market price; that is, if in an arm's length transaction a purchaser would buy the services at or near the amount charged. If the fee the consumer pays is disclosed and agreed to, along with its relationship to the interest rate and points for the loan and any lender-paid fees to the broker, a market price for the services, goods or facilities could be attained. HUD believes that for the market to work effectively, borrowers should be afforded a meaningful opportunity to select the most appropriate product and determine what price they are willing to pay for the loan based on disclosures which provide clear and understandable information.

The Department reiterates its long-standing view that disclosure alone does not make illegal fees legal under RESPA. On the other hand, while under current law, pre-application disclosure to the consumer is not required, HUD believes that fuller information provided at the earliest possible moment in the shopping process would increase consumer satisfaction and reduce the possibility of misunderstanding.

HUD commends the National Association of Mortgage Brokers and the Mortgage Bankers Association of America for strongly suggesting that their members furnish consumers with a form describing the function of mortgage brokers and stating that a mortgage broker may receive a fee in the transaction from a lender.

Although this statement of policy does not mandate disclosures beyond those currently required by RESPA and Regulation X, the most effective approach to disclosure would allow a prospective borrower to properly evaluate the nature of the services and all costs for a broker transaction, and to agree to such services and costs before applying for a loan. Under such an approach, the broker would make the borrower aware of whether the broker is or is not serving as the consumer's agent to shop for a loan, and the total compensation to be paid to the mortgage broker, including the amounts of each of the fees making up that compensation. If indirect fees are paid, the consumer would be made aware of the amount of these fees and their relationship to direct fees and an increased interest rate. If the consumer may reduce the interest rate through increased fees or points, this option also would be explained. HUD recognizes that in many cases, the industry has not been using

this approach because it has not been required. Moreover, new methods may require time to implement. HUD encourages these efforts going forward and believes that if these desirable disclosure practices were adhered to by all industry participants, the need for more prescriptive regulatory or legislative actions concerning this specific problem could be tempered or even made unnecessary.

While the Department is issuing this statement of policy to comply with a Congressional directive that HUD clarify its position on the legality of lender payments to mortgage brokers, HUD agrees with segments of the mortgage lending and settlement service industries and consumer representatives that legislation to improve RESPA is needed. HUD believes that broad legislative reform along the lines specified in the HUD/Federal Reserve Board Report remains the most effective way to resolve the difficulties and legal uncertainties under RESPA and TILA for industry and consumers alike. Statutory changes like those recommended in the Report would, if adopted, provide the most balanced approach to resolving these contentious issues by providing consumers with better and firmer information about the costs associated with home-secured credit transactions and providing creditors and mortgage brokers with clearer rules.

III. Executive Order 12866, Regulatory Planning and Review

The Office of Management and Budget (OMB) reviewed this Statement of Policy under Executive Order 12866, *Regulatory Planning and Review*. OMB determined that this Statement of Policy is a "significant regulatory action," as defined in section 3(f) of the Order (although not economically significant, as provided in section 3(f)(1) of the Order). Any changes made to the Statement of Policy subsequent to its submission to OMB are identified in the docket file, which is available for public inspection in the office of the Department's Rules Docket Clerk, Room 10276, 451 Seventh Street, SW, Washington, DC 20410–0500.

Dated: February 22, 1999.

William C. Apgar,

Assistant Secretary for Housing-Federal Housing Commissioner.

[FR Doc. 99–4921 Filed 2–26–99; 8:45 am]

BILLING CODE 4210–27–P

K.3.2 HUD Statement of Policy 2001-1: Clarification of Statement of Policy 1999-1 Regarding Lender Payments to Mortgage Brokers, and Guidance Concerning Unearned Fees Under Section 8(b)

DEPARTMENT OF HOUSING AND URBAN DEVELOPMENT

24 CFR Part 3500

[Docket No. FR-4714-N-01]

RIN 2502-AH74

Real Estate Settlement Procedures Act Statement of Policy 2001–1: Clarification of Statement of Policy 1999–1 Regarding Lender Payments to Mortgage Brokers, and Guidance Concerning Unearned Fees Under Section 8(b)

AGENCY: Office of the Assistant Secretary for Housing-Federal Housing Commissioner, HUD.

ACTION: Statement of Policy 2001–1.

SUMMARY: This Statement of Policy is being issued to eliminate any ambiguity concerning the Department's position with respect to those lender payments to mortgage brokers characterized as yield spread premiums and to overcharges by settlement service providers as a result of questions raised by two recent court decisions, *Culpepper* v. *Irwin Mortgage Corp.* and *Echevarria* v. *Chicago Title and Trust Co.*, respectively. In issuing this Statement of Policy, the Department clarifies its interpretation of Section 8 of the Real Estate Settlement Procedures Act (RESPA) in Statement of Policy 1999–1 Regarding Lender Payments to Mortgage Brokers (the 1999 Statement of Policy), and reiterates its long-standing interpretation of Section 8(b)'s prohibitions. *Culpepper* v. *Irwin Mortgage Corp.* involved the payment of yield spread premiums from lenders to mortgage brokers. *Echevarria* v. *Chicago Title and Trust Co.* involved the applicability of Section 8(b) to a settlement service provider that overcharged a borrower for the service of another settlement service provider, and then retained the amount of the overcharge.

Today's Statement of Policy reiterates the Department's position that yield spread premiums are not per se legal or illegal, and clarifies the test for the legality of such payments set forth in HUD's 1999 Statement of Policy. As stated there, HUD's position that lender payments to mortgage brokers are not illegal per se does not imply, however, that yield spread premiums are legal in individual cases or classes of transactions. The legality of yield spread premiums turns on the application of HUD's test in the 1999 Statement of Policy as clarified today.

The Department also reiterates its long-standing position that it may violate Section 8(b) and HUD's

implementing regulations: (1) For two or more persons to split a fee for settlement services, any portion of which is unearned; or (2) for one settlement service provider to mark-up the cost of the services performed or goods provided by another settlement service provider without providing additional actual, necessary, and distinct services, goods, or facilities to justify the additional charge; or (3) for one settlement service provider to charge the consumer a fee where no, nominal, or duplicative work is done, or the fee is in excess of the reasonable value of goods or facilities provided or the services actually performed.

This Statement of Policy also reiterates the importance of disclosure so that borrowers can choose the best loan for themselves, and it describes disclosures HUD considers best practices. The Secretary is also announcing that he intends to make full use of his regulatory authority to establish clear requirements for disclosure of mortgage broker fees and to improve the settlement process for lenders, mortgage brokers, and consumers.

EFFECTIVE DATE: October 18, 2001.

FOR FURTHER INFORMATION CONTACT: Ivy M. Jackson, Acting Director, RESPA/ILS Division, Room 9156, U.S. Department of Housing and Urban Development, 451 Seventh Street, SW., Washington, DC 20410; telephone (202) 708–0502, or (for legal questions) Kenneth A. Markison, Assistant General Counsel for GSE/RESPA, Room 9262, Department of Housing and Urban Development, Washington, DC 20410; telephone (202) 708–3137 (these are not toll-free numbers). Persons who have difficulty hearing or speaking may access this number via TTY by calling the toll-free Federal Information Relay Service at (800) 877–8339.

SUPPLEMENTARY INFORMATION:

General Background

The Department is issuing this Statement of Policy in accordance with 5 U.S.C. 552 as a formal pronouncement of its interpretation of relevant statutory and regulatory provisions. Section 19(a) (12 U.S.C. 2617(a)) of the Real Estate Settlement Procedures Act of 1974 (12 U.S.C. 2601–2617) (RESPA) specifically authorizes the Secretary "to prescribe such rules and regulations [and] to make such interpretations * * * as may be necessary to achieve the purposes of [RESPA]."

Section 8(a) of RESPA prohibits any person from giving and any person from accepting "any fee, kickback, or thing of value pursuant to an agreement or

understanding, oral or otherwise" that real estate settlement service business shall be referred to any person. See 12 U.S.C. 2607(a). Section 8(b) prohibits anyone from giving or accepting "any portion, split, or percentage of any charge made or received for the rendering of a real estate settlement service * * * other than for services actually performed." 12 U.S.C. 2607(b). Section 8(c) of RESPA provides, "Nothing in [Section 8] shall be construed as prohibiting * * * (2) the payment to any person of a bona fide salary or compensation or other payment for goods or facilities actually furnished or for services actually performed * * *" 12 U.S.C. 2607(c)(2). RESPA also requires the disclosure of settlement costs to consumers at the time of or soon after a borrower applies for a loan and again at the time of real estate settlement. 12 U.S.C. 2603–4. RESPA's requirements apply to transactions involving a "federally related mortgage loan" as that term is defined at 12 U.S.C. 2602(1).

I. Lender Payments to Mortgage Brokers

The Conference Report on the Department's 1999 Appropriations Act directed HUD to address the issue of lender payments to mortgage brokers under RESPA. The Conference Report stated that "Congress never intended payments by lenders to mortgage brokers for goods or facilities actually furnished or for services actually performed to be violations of [Sections 8](a) or (b) (12 U.S.C. sec. 2607) in its enactment of RESPA." H. Rep. 105–769, at 260. As also directed by Congress, HUD worked with industry groups, federal agencies, consumer groups and other interested parties in collectively producing the 1999 Statement of Policy issued on March 1, 1999. 64 FR 10080. Interested members of the public are urged to consult the 1999 Statement of Policy for a more detailed discussion of the background on lender payments to brokers addressed in today's Statement.

HUD's 1999 Statement of Policy established a two-part test for determining the legality of lender payments to mortgage brokers for table funded transactions and intermediary transactions under RESPA: (1) Whether goods or facilities were actually furnished or services were actually performed for the compensation paid and; (2) whether the payments are reasonably related to the value of the goods or facilities that were actually furnished or services that were actually performed. In applying this test, HUD believes that total compensation should be scrutinized to assure that it is reasonably related to the goods,

Real Estate Settlement Procedures Act Appx. K.3.2

Federal Register / Vol. 66, No. 202 / Thursday, October 18, 2001 / Rules and Regulations **53053**

facilities, or services furnished or performed to determine whether it is legal under RESPA. In the determination of whether payments from lenders to mortgage brokers are permissible under Section 8 of RESPA, the threshold question is whether there were goods or facilities actually furnished or services actually performed for the total compensation paid to the mortgage broker. Where a lender payment to a mortgage broker comprises a portion of total broker compensation, the amount of the payment is not, under the HUD test, scrutinized separately and apart from total broker compensation.

Since HUD issued its 1999 Statement of Policy, most courts have held that yield spread premiums from lenders to mortgage brokers are legal provided that such payments meet the test for legality articulated in the 1999 Statement of Policy and otherwise comport with RESPA. However, in a recent decision, *Culpepper* v. *Irwin Mortgage Corp.*, 253 F.3d 1324 (11th Cir. 2001), the Court of Appeals for the Eleventh Circuit upheld certification of a class in a case alleging that yield spread premiums violated Section 8 of RESPA where the defendant lender, pursuant to a prior understanding with mortgage brokers, paid yield spread premiums to the brokers based solely on the brokers' delivery of above par interest rate loans. The court concluded that a jury could find that yield spread premiums were illegal kickbacks or referral fees under RESPA where the lender's payments were based exclusively on interest rate differentials reflected on rate sheets, and the lender had no knowledge of what services, if any, the broker performed. The court described HUD's 1999 Statement of Policy as "ambiguous." *Id.* at 1327. Accordingly, and because courts have now rendered conflicting decisions, HUD has an obligation to clarify its position and issues this Statement today to provide such clarification and certainty to lenders, brokers, and consumers.

Because this clarification focuses on the legality of lender payments to mortgage brokers in transactions subject to RESPA, the coverage of this statement is restricted to payments to mortgage brokers in table funded and intermediary broker transactions. Lender payments to mortgage brokers where mortgage brokers initially fund the loan and then sell the loan after settlement are outside the coverage of this statement as exempt from RESPA under the secondary market exception.

II. Disclosure

Besides establishing the two-part test for determining the legality of yield spread premiums, the 1999 Statement of Policy discussed the importance of disclosure in permitting borrowers to choose the best loan for themselves. The mortgage transaction is complicated, and most people engage in such transactions relatively infrequently, compared to the other purchases they make. In some instances, borrowers have paid very large origination costs, either up front fees, yield spread premiums, or both, which they might have been able to avoid with timely disclosure. Timely disclosure would permit them to shop for preferable origination costs and mortgage terms and to agree to those costs and terms that meet their needs. The Department therefore is issuing a clarification of the importance of disclosure, with a description of disclosures that it considers to be best practices.

In this Statement of Policy, the Secretary is announcing that he intends to make full use of his regulatory authority as expeditiously as possible to provide clear requirements and guidance prospectively regarding disclosure of mortgage broker fees and, more broadly, to improve the mortgage settlement process so that homebuyers and homeowners are better served. Pending the promulgation of such a rule, the Secretary asks the industry to adopt new disclosure requirements to promote competition and to better serve consumers.

III. Unearned Fees

The 1999 Statement of Policy also touched upon another area of recurring questions under Section 8 of RESPA: the legality of payments that are in excess of the reasonable value of the goods or facilities provided or services performed. See 64 FR 10082–3.

Since RESPA was enacted, HUD has consistently interpreted Section 8(b) and HUD's RESPA regulations to prohibit settlement service providers from charging unearned fees, as occurred in *Echevarria* v. *Chicago Title & Trust Co.*, 256 F.3d 623 (7th Cir. 2001). Such an interpretation is consistent with Congress's finding, when enacting RESPA, that consumers need protection from unnecessarily high settlement costs. Through this Statement of Policy, HUD makes clear that Section 8(b) prohibits any person from giving or accepting any fees other than payments for goods and facilities provided or services actually performed. Payments that are unearned fees occur in, but are not limited to, cases where: (1) Two or more persons split a fee for settlement services, any portion of which is unearned; or (2) one settlement service provider marks-up the cost of

the services performed or goods provided by another settlement service provider without providing additional actual, necessary, and distinct services, goods, or facilities to justify the additional charge; or (3) one settlement service provider charges the consumer a fee where no, nominal, or duplicative work is done, or the fee is in excess of the reasonable value of goods or facilities provided or the services actually performed.

In a July 5, 2001 decision, the Court of Appeals for the Seventh Circuit concluded that unearned fees must be passed from one settlement provider to another in order for such fees to violate Section 8(b). Accordingly, the court held that a settlement service provider did not violate Section 8(b) when, in billing a borrower, it added an overcharge to another provider's fees and retained the additional charge without providing any additional goods, facilities or services. *Echevarria* v. *Chicago Title & Trust Co.* Other courts have held that two or more parties must split or share a fee in order for a violation of Section 8(b) to occur. Still other courts have stated, however, that a single provider can violate Section 8(b). Because the courts are now divided, HUD is issuing this Statement of Policy to reiterate its interpretation of Section 8(b).

The Court of Appeals for the Seventh Circuit rendered its conclusion in *Echevarria* "absent a formal commitment by HUD to an opposing position. * * *" *Id.* at 630. In issuing this Statement of Policy pursuant to Section 19(a), HUD reiterates its position on unearned fees under Section 8(b) of RESPA, which HUD regards as long standing.

IV. Statement of Policy 2001–1

To give guidance to interested members of the real estate settlement industry and the general public on the application of RESPA and its implementing regulations, the Secretary hereby issues the following Statement of Policy. The interpretations embodied in this Statement of Policy are issued pursuant to Section 19(a) of RESPA. 12 U.S.C. 2617(a).

Part A. Mortgage Broker Fees

Yield Spread Premiums

One of the primary barriers to homeownership and homeowners' ability to refinance and lower their housing costs is the up front cash needed to obtain a mortgage. The closing costs and origination fees associated with a mortgage loan are a significant component of these up front

Appx. K.3.2   *The Cost of Credit: Regulation and Legal Challenges*

53054   Federal Register / Vol. 66, No. 202 / Thursday, October 18, 2001 / Rules and Regulations

cash requirements. Borrowers may choose to pay these fees out of pocket, or to pay the origination fees, and possibly all the closing fees, by financing them; *i.e.,* adding the amount of such fees to the principal balance of their mortgage loan. The latter approach, however, is not available to those whose loan-to-value ratio has already reached the maximum permitted by the lender. For those without the available cash, who are at the maximum loan-to-value ratio, or who simply choose to do so, there is a third option. This third option is a yield spread premium.

Yield spread premiums permit homebuyers to pay some or all of the up front settlement costs over the life of the mortgage through a higher interest rate. Because the mortgage carries a higher interest rate, the lender is able to sell it to an investor at a higher price. In turn, the lender pays the broker an amount reflective of this price difference. The payment allows the broker to recoup the up front costs incurred on the borrower's behalf in originating the loan. Payments from lenders to brokers based on the rates of borrowers' loans are characterized as "indirect" fees and are referred to as yield spread premiums.[1]

A yield spread premium is calculated based upon the difference between the interest rate at which the broker originates the loan and the par, or market, rate offered by a lender. The Department believes, and industry and consumers agree, that a yield spread premium can be a useful means to pay some or all of a borrower's settlement costs. In these cases, lender payments reduce the up front cash requirements to borrowers. In some cases, borrowers are able to obtain loans without paying any up front cash for the services required in connection with the origination of the loan. Instead, the fees for these services are financed through a higher interest rate on the loan. The yield spread premium thus can be a legitimate tool to assist the borrower. The availability of this option fosters homeownership.

HUD has recognized the utility of yield spread premiums in regulations issued prior to the 1999 Statement of Policy. In a final rule concerning "Deregulation of Mortgagor Income Requirements," HUD indicated that up front costs could be lowered by yield spread premiums. 54 FR 38646 (September 20, 1989).

In a 1992 rule concerning RESPA, HUD specifically listed yield spread

premiums as an example of fees that must be disclosed. The example was codified as Illustrations of Requirements of RESPA, Fact Situations 5 and 13 in Appendix B to 24 CFR part 3500. (See also Instructions at Appendix A to 24 CFR part 3500 for Completing HUD–1 and HUD–1A Settlement Statements.) HUD did not by these examples mean that yield spread premiums were *per se* legal, but HUD also did not mean that yield spread premiums were *per se* illegal.

HUD also recognizes, however, that in some cases less scrupulous brokers and lenders take advantage of the complexity of the settlement transaction and use yield spread premiums as a way to enhance the profitability of mortgage transactions without offering the borrower lower up front fees. In these cases, yield spread premiums serve to increase the borrower's interest rate and the broker's overall compensation, without lowering up front cash requirements for the borrower. As set forth in this Statement of Policy, such uses of yield spread premiums may result in total compensation in excess of what is reasonably related to the total value of the origination services provided by the broker, and fail to comply with the second part of HUD's two-part test as enunciated in the 1999 Statement of Policy, and with Section 8.

The 1999 Statement of Policy's Test for Legality

The Department restates its position that yield spread premiums are not per se illegal. HUD also reiterates that this statement "does not imply * * * that yield spread premiums are legal in individual cases or classes of transactions." 64 FR 10084. The legality of any yield spread premium can only be evaluated in the context of the test HUD established and the specific factual circumstances applicable to each transaction in which a yield spread premium is used.

The 1999 Statement of Policy established a two-part test for determining whether lender payments to mortgage brokers are legal under RESPA. In applying Section 8 and HUD's regulations, the 1999 Statement of Policy stated:

> In transactions where lenders make payments to mortgage brokers, HUD does not consider such payments (*i.e.,* yield spread premiums or any other class of named payments) to be illegal *per se*. HUD does not view the name of the payment as the appropriate issue under RESPA. HUD's position that lender payments to mortgage brokers are not illegal *per se* does not imply, however, that yield spread premiums are legal in individual cases or classes of

transactions. The fees in cases and classes of transactions are illegal if they violate the prohibitions of Section 8 of RESPA.

In determining whether a payment from a lender to a mortgage broker is permissible under Section 8 of RESPA, the first question is whether goods or facilities were actually furnished or services were actually performed for the compensation paid. The fact that goods or facilities have been actually furnished or that services have been actually performed by the mortgage broker does not by itself make the payment legal. The second question is whether the payments are reasonably related to the value of the goods or facilities that were actually furnished or services that were actually performed.

In applying this test, HUD believes that total compensation should be scrutinized to assure that it is reasonably related to goods, facilities, or services furnished or performed to determine whether it is legal under RESPA. Total compensation to a broker includes direct origination and other fees paid by the borrower, indirect fees, including those that are derived from the interest rate paid by the borrower, or a combination of some or all. The Department considers that higher interest rates alone cannot justify higher total fees to mortgage brokers. All fees will be scrutinized as part of total compensation to determine that total compensation is reasonably related to the goods or facilities actually furnished or services actually performed. HUD believes that total compensation should be carefully considered in relation to price structures and practices in similar transactions and in similar markets. 64 FR 10084.

Culpepper

The need for further clarification of HUD's position, as set forth in the 1999 Statement of Policy, on the treatment of lender payments to mortgage brokers under Section 8 of RESPA (12 U.S.C. 2607), is evident from the recent decision of the Court of Appeals for the Eleventh Circuit in *Culpepper.*

In upholding class certification in *Culpepper,* the court only applied the first part of the HUD test, and then further narrowed its examination of whether the lender's yield spread payments were "for services" by focusing exclusively on the presumed intent of the lender in making the payments. The crux of the court's decision is that Section 8 liability for the payment of unlawful referral fees could be established under the first part of the HUD test alone, based on the facts that the lender's payments to mortgage brokers were calculated solely on the difference between the par interest rate and the higher rate at which the mortgage brokers delivered loans, and that the lender had no knowledge of what services, if any, the brokers had performed.

HUD was not a party to the case and disagrees with the judicial interpretation regarding Section 8 of

---

[1] Indirect fees from lenders are also known as "back funded payments," "overages," or "servicing release premiums."

Real Estate Settlement Procedures Act **Appx. K.3.2**

Federal Register / Vol. 66, No. 202 / Thursday, October 18, 2001 / Rules and Regulations **53055**

RESPA and the 1999 Statement of Policy.

Clarification of the HUD Test

It is HUD's position that where compensable services are performed, the 1999 Statement of Policy requires application of both parts of the HUD test before a determination can be made regarding the legality of a lender payment to a mortgage broker.

1. *The First Part of the HUD Test:* Under the first part of HUD's test, the total compensation to a mortgage broker, of which a yield spread premium may be a component or the entire amount, must be for goods or facilities provided or services performed. HUD's position is that in order to discern whether a yield spread premium was for goods, facilities or services under the first part of the HUD test, it is necessary to look at each transaction individually, including examining all of the goods or facilities provided or services performed by the broker in the transaction, whether the goods, facilities or services are paid for by the borrower, the lender, or partly by both.

It is HUD's position that neither Section 8(a) of RESPA nor the 1999 Statement of Policy supports the conclusion that a yield spread premium can be presumed to be a referral fee based solely upon the fact that the lender pays the broker a yield spread premium that is based upon a rate sheet, or because the lender does not have specific knowledge of what services the broker has performed. HUD considers the latter situation to be rare. The common industry practice is that lenders follow underwriting standards that demand a review of originations and that therefore lenders typically know that brokers have performed the services required to meet those standards.

Yield spread premiums are by definition derived from the interest rate. HUD believes that a rate sheet is merely a mechanism for displaying the yield spread premium, and does not indicate whether a particular yield spread premium is a payment for goods and facilities actually furnished or services actually performed under the HUD test. Whether or not a yield spread premium is legal or illegal cannot be determined by the use of a rate sheet, but by how HUD's test applies to the transaction involved.

Section 8 prohibits the giving and accepting of fees, kickbacks, or things of value for the referral of settlement services and also unearned fees. It is therefore prudent for a lender to take action so as to ensure that brokers are performing compensable services and

receiving only compensation that, in total, is reasonable for those services provided. As stated, however, in the 1999 Statement of Policy:

The Department recognizes that some of the goods or facilities actually furnished or services actually performed by the broker in originating a loan are "for" the lender and other goods or facilities actually furnished or services actually performed are "for" the borrower. HUD does not believe that it is necessary or even feasible to identify or allocate which facilities, goods or services are performed or provided for the lender, for the borrower, or as a function of State or Federal law. All services, goods and facilities inure to the benefit of both the borrower and the lender in the sense that they make the loan transaction possible. * * * 64 FR 10086.

The 1999 Statement of Policy provided a list of compensable loan origination services originally developed by HUD in a response to an inquiry from the Independent Bankers Association of America (IBAA), which HUD considers relevant in evaluating mortgage broker services. In analyzing each transaction to determine if services are performed HUD believes the 1999 Statement of Policy should be used as a guide. As stated there, the IBAA list is not exhaustive, and while technology is changing the process of performing settlement services, HUD believes that the list is still a generally accurate description of settlement services. Compensation for these services may be paid either by the borrower or by the lender, or partly by both. Compensable services for the first part of the test do not include referrals or no, nominal, or duplicative work.

2. *Reasonableness of Broker Fees:* The second part of HUD's test requires that total compensation to the mortgage broker be reasonably related to the total set of goods or facilities actually furnished or services performed.

The 1999 Statement of Policy said in part:

The Department considers that higher interest rates alone cannot justify higher total fees to mortgage brokers. All fees will be scrutinized as part of total compensation to determine that total compensation is reasonably related to the goods or facilities actually furnished or services actually performed. 64 FR 10084.

Accordingly, the Department believes that the second part of the test is applied by determining whether a mortgage broker's total compensation is reasonable. Total compensation includes fees paid by a borrower and any yield spread premium paid by a lender, not simply the yield spread premium alone. Yield spread premiums serve to allow the borrower a lower up front cash payment in return for a

higher interest rate, while allowing the broker to recoup the total costs of originating the loan. Total compensation to the broker must be reasonably related to the total value of goods or facilities provided or services performed by the broker. Simply delivering a loan with a higher interest rate is not a compensable service. The Department affirms the 1999 Statement of Policy's position on this matter for purposes of RESPA enforcement.

The 1999 Statement also said:

In analyzing whether a particular payment or fee bears a reasonable relationship to the value of the goods or facilities actually furnished or services actually performed, HUD believes that payments must be commensurate with the amount normally charged for similar services, goods or facilities. This analysis requires careful consideration of fees paid in relation to price structures and practices in similar transactions and in similar markets. If the payment or a portion thereof bears no reasonable relationship to the market value of the goods, facilities or services provided, the excess over the market rate may be used as evidence of a compensated referral or an unearned fee in violation of Section 8(a) or (b) of RESPA. 64 FR 10086.

The 1999 Statement of Policy also stated:

The level of services mortgage brokers provide in particular transactions depends on the level of difficulty involved in qualifying applicants for particular loan programs. For example, applicants have differences in credit ratings, employment status, levels of debt, or experience that will translate into various degrees of effort required for processing a loan. Also, the mortgage broker may be required to perform various levels of services under different servicing or processing arrangements with wholesale lenders. 64 FR 10081.

In evaluating mortgage broker fees for enforcement purposes, HUD will consider these factors as relevant in assessing the reasonableness of mortgage broker compensation, as well as comparing total compensation for loans of similar size and similar characteristics within similar geographic markets.

Also, while the Department continues to believe that comparison to prices in similar markets is generally a key factor in determining whether a mortgage broker's total compensation is reasonable, it is also true that in less competitive markets comparisons to the prices charged by other similarly situated providers may not, standing alone, provide a useful measure. As a general principle, HUD believes that in evaluating the reasonableness of broker compensation in less competitive markets, consideration of price structures from a wider range of

Appx. K.3.2   *The Cost of Credit: Regulation and Legal Challenges*

53056   Federal Register / Vol. 66, No. 202 / Thursday, October 18, 2001 / Rules and Regulations

providers may be warranted to reach a meaningful conclusion.

Part B. Providing Meaningful Information to Borrowers

In addition to addressing the legality of yield spread premiums in the 1999 Statement of Policy, HUD emphasized the importance of disclosing broker fees, including yield spread premiums.

There is no requirement under existing law that consumers be fully informed of the broker's services and compensation prior to the GFE. Nevertheless, HUD believes that the broker should provide the consumer with information about the broker's services and compensation, and agreement by the consumer to the arrangement should occur as early as possible in the process. 64 FR 10087.

HUD continues to believe that disclosure is extremely important, and that many of the concerns expressed by borrowers over yield spread premiums can be addressed by disclosing yield spread premiums, borrower compensation to the broker, and the terms of the mortgage loan, so that the borrower may evaluate and choose among alternative loan options.

In the 1999 Statement of Policy, HUD stated:

* * * HUD believes that for the market to work effectively, borrowers should be afforded a meaningful opportunity to select the most appropriate product and determine what price they are willing to pay for the loan based on disclosures which provide clear and understandable information.

The Department reiterates its long-standing view that disclosure alone does not make illegal fees legal under RESPA. On the other hand, while under current law, pre-application disclosure to the consumer is not required, HUD believes that fuller information provided at the earliest possible moment in the shopping process would increase consumer satisfaction and reduce the possibility of misunderstanding. 64 FR 10087.

HUD currently requires the disclosure of yield spread premiums on the Good Faith Estimate and the HUD–1. The 1999 Statement of Policy said:

The Department has always indicated that any fees charged in settlement transactions should be clearly disclosed so that the consumer can understand the nature and recipient of the payment. Code-like abbreviations like 'YSP to DBG, POC', for instance, have been noted. [Footnote omitted.] Also the Department has seen examples on the GFE and/or the settlement statement where the identity and/or purposes of the fees are not clearly disclosed.

The Department considers unclear and confusing disclosures to be contrary to the statute's and the regulation's purposes of making RESPA-covered transactions understandable to the consumer. At a minimum, all fees to the mortgage broker are to be clearly labeled and properly estimated

on the GFE. On the settlement statement, the name of the recipient of the fee (in this case, the mortgage broker) is to be clearly labeled and listed, and the fee received from a lender is to be clearly labeled and listed in the interest of clarity. 64 FR 10086–10087.

While the disclosure on the GFE and HUD–1 is required, the Department is aware and has stated that the current GFE/HUD–1 disclosure framework is often insufficient to adequately inform consumers about yield spread premiums and other lender paid fees to brokers. Under the current rules, the GFE need not be provided until after the consumer has applied for a mortgage and may have paid a significant fee, and the HUD–1 is only given at closing. Because of this, HUD has in recent years sought to foster a more consumer beneficial approach to disclosure regarding yield spread premiums through successive rulemaking efforts. This history is discussed more fully in the 1999 Statement of Policy.[2]

Representatives of the mortgage industry have said that since the 1999 Statement of Policy, many brokers provide borrowers a disclosure describing the function of mortgage brokers and stating that a mortgage broker may receive a fee in the transaction from the lender. While the 1999 Statement of Policy commended the National Association of Mortgage Brokers and the Mortgage Bankers Association of America for strongly suggesting such a disclosure to their respective memberships, the Statement of Policy added:

Although this statement of policy does not mandate disclosures beyond those currently required by RESPA and Regulation X, the most effective approach to disclosure would allow a prospective borrower to properly evaluate the nature of the services and all costs for a broker transaction, and to agree to such services and costs before applying for a loan. Under such an approach, the broker would make the borrower aware of whether the broker is or is not serving as the consumer's agent to shop for a loan, and the total compensation to be paid to the mortgage broker, including the amounts of each of the fees making up the compensation. 64 FR 10087.

In HUD's view, meaningful disclosure includes many types of information: what services a mortgage broker will perform, the amount of the broker's total compensation for performing those services (including any yield spread premium paid by the lender), and whether or not the broker has an agency

or fiduciary relationship with the borrower. The disclosure should also make the borrower aware that he or she may pay higher up front costs for a mortgage with a lower interest rate, or conversely pay a higher interest rate in return for lower up front costs, and should identify the specific trade-off between the amount of the increase in the borrower's monthly payment (and also the increase in the interest rate) and the amount by which up front costs are reduced. HUD believes that disclosure of this information, and written acknowledgment by the borrower that he or she has received the information, should be provided early in the transaction. Such disclosure facilitates comparison shopping by the borrower, to choose the best combination of up front costs and mortgage terms from his or her individual standpoint. HUD regards full disclosure and written acknowledgment by the borrower, at the earliest possible time, as a best practice.

Yield spread premiums are currently required to be listed in the "800" series of the HUD–1 form, listing "Items Payable in Connection with Loan." This existing practice, however, does not disclose the purpose of the yield spread premium, which is to lower up front cost to borrowers. To achieve this end it has been suggested to the Department that the yield spread premium should be reported as a credit to the borrower in the "200" series, among the "Amounts Paid by or in Behalf of Borrowers." The homebuyer or homeowner could then see that the yield spread premium is reducing closing costs, and also see the extent of the reduction.

HUD believes that improved early disclosure regarding mortgage broker compensation and the entry of yield spread premiums as credits to borrowers on the GFE and the HUD–1 settlement statement are both useful and complementary forms of disclosure. The Department believes that used together these methods of disclosure offer greater assurance that lender payments to mortgage brokers serve borrowers' best interests.

While the 1999 Policy Statement and IV. Part A. of this Statement only cover certain lender payments to mortgage brokers, as described above, HUD also believes that similar information on the trade-off between lower up front costs and higher interest rates and monthly payments should be disclosed to borrowers on all mortgage loan originations, not merely those originated by brokers. HUD is aware that while yield spread premiums are not used in loans originated by lenders, lenders are able to offer loans with low or no up

---

[2] In both the HUD/Federal Reserve Board Report on RESPA/TILA Reform, 1998, and the HUD/Treasury Report on Curbing Predatory Home Mortgage Lending, 2000, the agencies recommended earlier disclosures to facilitate shopping and lower settlement costs.

Real Estate Settlement Procedures Act **Appx. K.3.2**

Federal Register / Vol. 66, No. 202 / Thursday, October 18, 2001 / Rules and Regulations   **53057**

front costs required at closing by charging higher interest rates and recouping the costs by selling the loans into the secondary market for a price representing the difference between the interest rate on the loan and the par, or market, interest rate. Sale of such a loan achieves the same purpose as the yield spread premium does on a loan originated by a broker. The Department strongly believes that all lenders and brokers should provide the level of consumer disclosure that the purposes of RESPA intend and that fair business practices demand. As indicated in the 1999 Statement of Policy, HUD emphasizes that fuller information provided as early as possible in the shopping process would increase consumer satisfaction and reduce the possibility of misunderstanding. In the future, full and early disclosures are factors that the Department would weigh favorably in exercising its enforcement discretion in cases involving mortgage broker fees. Nevertheless, the Department also again makes clear that disclosure alone does not make illegal fees legal under RESPA. The Department will scrutinize all relevant information in making enforcement decisions, including whether transactions evidence practices that may be illegal.

Part C. Section 8(b) Unearned Fees

A. Background

RESPA was enacted in 1974 to provide consumers "greater and more timely information on the nature of the costs of the [real estate] settlement process" and to protect consumers from "unnecessarily high settlement charges caused by certain abusive practices * * *" 12 U.S.C. 2601.

Since RESPA was enacted, HUD has interpreted Section 8(b) as prohibiting any person from giving or accepting any unearned fees, i.e., charges or payments for real estate settlement services other than for goods or facilities provided or services performed. Payments that are unearned fees for settlement services occur in, but are not limited to, cases where: (1) Two or more persons split a fee for settlement services, any portion of which is unearned; or (2) one settlement service provider marks-up the cost of the services performed or goods provided by another settlement service provider without providing additional actual, necessary, and distinct services, goods, or facilities to justify the additional charge; or (3) one settlement service provider charges the consumer a fee where no, nominal, or duplicative work is done, or the fee is in excess of the reasonable value of

goods or facilities provided or the services actually performed.

In the first situation, two settlement service providers split or share a fee charged to a consumer and at least part, if not all, of at least one provider's share of the fee is unearned. In the second situation, a settlement service provider charges a fee to a consumer for another provider's services that is higher than the actual price of such services, and keeps the difference without performing any actual, necessary, and distinct services to justify the additional charge. In the third situation, one settlement service provider charges a fee to a consumer where no work is done or the fee exceeds the reasonable value of the services performed by that provider, and for this reason the fee or any portion thereof for which services are not performed is unearned.

HUD regards all of these situations as legally indistinguishable, in that they involve payments for settlement services where all or a portion of the fees are unearned and, thus, are violative of the statute. HUD, therefore, specifically interprets Section 8(b) as not being limited to situations where at least two persons split or share an unearned fee for the provision to be violated.

As already indicated in this Statement of Policy, meaningful disclosure of all charges and fees is essential under RESPA. Such disclosures help protect consumers from paying unearned or duplicate fees. However, as noted above, in the 1999 Statement of Policy the Department reiterated "its long-standing view that disclosure alone does not make illegal fees legal under RESPA." 64 FR 10087.

B. HUD's Guidance and Regulations

HUD guidance and regulations have consistently interpreted Section 8 as prohibiting all unearned fees. In 1976, HUD issued a Settlement Costs Booklet that provided that "[i]t is also illegal to charge or accept a fee or part of a fee where no service has actually been performed." 41 FR 20289 (May 17, 1976). Between 1976 and 1992, HUD indicated in informal opinions that unearned fees occur where there are excessive fees charged, regardless of the number of settlement service providers involved.[3]

---

[3] *See* e.g., Old Informal Opinion (6), August 16, 1976 and Old Informal Opinion (65), April 4, 1980; Barron and Berenson, *Federal Regulation of Real Estate and Mortgage Lending*, (4th Ed.1998). On November 2, 1992 (57 F.R. 49600), when HUD issued revisions to its RESPA regulations, it withdrew all of its informal counsel opinions and staff interpretations issued before that date. The 1992 rule provided, however, that courts and

In the preamble to HUD's 1992 final rule revising Regulation X (57 FR 49600 (November 2, 1992)), HUD stated: "Section 8 of RESPA (12 U.S.C. 2607) prohibits kickbacks for referral of business incident to or part of a settlement service and also prohibits the splitting of a charge for a settlement service, other than for services actually performed (i.e., no payment of unearned fees)." 57 FR 49600 (November 2, 1992).

HUD's regulations, published on November 2, 1992, implement Section 8(b). Section 3500.14(c)[4] provides:

No person shall give and no person shall accept any portion, split, or percentage of any charge made or received for the rendering of a settlement service in connection with a transaction involving a federally-related mortgage loan other than for services actually performed. A charge by a person for which no or nominal services are performed or for which duplicative fees are charged is an unearned fee and violates this Section. The source of the payment does not determine whether or not a service is compensable. Nor may the prohibitions of this part be avoided by creating an arrangement wherein the purchaser of services splits the fee.

24 CFR 3500.14(g)(2) states in part:

The Department may investigate high prices to see if they are the result of a referral fee or a split of a fee. If the payment of a thing of value bears no reasonable relationship to the market value of the goods or services provided, then the excess is not for services or goods actually performed or provided. These facts may be used as evidence of a violation of Section 8 and may serve as a basis for a RESPA investigation. High prices standing alone are not proof of a RESPA violation.

24 CFR 3500.14(g)(3) provides in part:

When a person in a position to refer settlement service business * * * receives a payment for providing additional settlement services as part of a real estate transaction, such payment must be for services that are actual, necessary and distinct from the primary services provided by such person.

---

administrative agencies could use HUD's previous opinions to determine the validity of conduct occurring under the previous version of Regulation X. *See* 24 CFR 3500.4(c).

[4] The heading to 24 CFR 3500.14 is titled "Prohibition against kickbacks and unearned fees." However, the heading of subsection (c) is titled "split of charges," and the preamble to the November 1992 rule states "[s]ection 8 of RESPA (12 U.S.C. 2607) prohibits kickbacks for referral of business incident to or part of a settlement service and also prohibits the splitting of a charge for a settlement service, other than for services actually performed (i.e., no payment of unearned fees)." 57 FR 49600 (November 2, 1992). The rule headings and preamble text are a generalized description of Section 8 that is more developed in the actual regulation text. As discussed in Section D of this Statement of Policy, HUD believes that the actual text of the rules, as amended in 1992, makes clear that Section 8(b)'s prohibitions against unearned fees apply even when only one settlement service provider is involved.

Appx. K.3.2   *The Cost of Credit: Regulation and Legal Challenges*

53058   Federal Register / Vol. 66, No. 202 / Thursday, October 18, 2001 / Rules and Regulations

In Appendix B to the HUD RESPA regulations, HUD provides illustrations of the requirements of RESPA. Comment 3 states in part:

> The payment of a commission or portion of the * * * premium * * * or receipt of a portion of the payment * * * where no substantial services are being performed * * * is a violation of Section 8 of RESPA. It makes no difference whether the payment comes from [the settlement service provider] or the purchaser. The amount of the payment must bear a reasonable relationship to the services rendered. Here [the real estate broker in the example] is being compensated for a referral of business to [the title company].

In 1996, in the preamble to the final rule on the Withdrawal of Employer/ Employee and Computer Loan Origination Systems Exemptions [5] (61 FR 29238 (June 7, 1996)), HUD reiterated its interpretation of Section 8(b) of RESPA as follows:

> HUD believes that Section 8(b) of the statute and the legislative history make clear that no person is allowed to receive 'any portion' of charges for settlement services, except for services actually performed. The provisions of Section 8(b) could apply in a number of situations: (1) where one settlement service provider receives an unearned fee from another provider; (2) where one settlement service provider charges the consumer for third-party services and retains an unearned fee from the payment received; or (3) where one settlement service provider accepts a portion of a charge (including 100% of the charge) for other than services actually performed. The interpretation urged [by the commenters to the proposed rule published on July 21, 1994], that a single settlement service provider can charge unearned or excessive fees so long as the fees are not shared with another, is an unnecessarily restrictive interpretation of a statute designed to reduce unnecessary costs to consumers. The Secretary, charged by statute with interpreting RESPA, interprets Section 8(b) to mean that two persons are not required for the provision to be violated. 61 FR 29249.

The latest revision to the Settlement Costs Booklet for consumers, issued in 1997, also provides "[i]t is also illegal for anyone to accept a fee or part of a fee for services if that person has not actually performed settlement services for the fee." 62 FR 31998 (June 11, 1997).

Further, HUD has provided information to the public and the mortgage industry in the "Frequently Asked Questions" section of its RESPA Web site, located at <*http://www. hud.gov/fha/sfh/res/resindus.html*>. Question 25 states:

Can a lender collect from the borrower an appraisal fee of $200, listing the fee as such on the HUD–1, yet pay an independent appraiser $175 and collect the $25 difference?

The answer reads:

> No, the lender may only collect $175 as the actual charge. It is a violation of Section 8(b) for any person to accept a split of a fee where services are not performed.

In 1999, by letter submitted at the request of the Superior Court of California, Los Angeles County, in the case of *Brown* v. *Washington Mutual Bank* (Case No. BC192874), HUD provided the following response to a specific question posed by the court on lender "markups" of another settlement service provider's fees:

> A lender that purchases third party vendor services for purposes of closing a federally related mortgage loan may not, under RESPA, mark up the third party vendor fees for purposes of making a profit. HUD has consistently advised that where lenders or others charge consumers marked-up prices for services performed by the third party providers without performing additional services, such charges constitute "splits of fees" or "unearned fees" in violation of Section 8(b) of RESPA.

HUD noted in its letter to the court that the response reflected the Department's long-standing position.

C. Recent Cases

Notwithstanding HUD's regulations and other guidance, the Court of Appeals for the Seventh Circuit held, in *Echevarria* v. *Chicago Title and Trust Co.*, 256 F.3d 623 (7th Cir. 2001), that Section 8(b) was not violated where a title company, without performing any additional services, charged the plaintiffs more money than was required by the recorder's office to record a deed and the title company then retained the difference. The court reasoned that plaintiffs "failed to plead facts tending to show that Chicago Title illegally shared fees with the Cook County Recorder. The Cook County Recorder received no more than its regular recording fees and it did not give to or arrange for Chicago Title to receive an unearned portion of these fees. The County Recorder has not engaged in the third party involvement necessary to state a claim under [RESPA § 8(b)]." Id. at 626. The court in essence concluded that unearned fees must be passed from one settlement provider to another in order for such fees to violate Section 8(b).

Earlier, in *Willis* v. *Quality Mortgage USA, Inc.*, 5 F. Supp. 2d 1306 (M.D. Ala. 1998), cited by the Seventh Circuit in support of its conclusion, the district court concluded that 24 CFR 3500.14(c),

"[w]hen read as a whole," prohibits payments for which no services are performed "only if those payments are split with another party." Id. at 1309. The *Willis* court held that there must be a split of a charge between a settlement service provider and a third party to establish a violation Section 8(b). The court also concluded that 24 CFR 3500.14(g)(3) only applied when there was a payment from a lender to a broker, or vice versa. The payment from a borrower to a mortgage lender could not be the basis for a violation of 24 CFR 3500.14(g)(3) and Section 8(b).

HUD was not a party to the cases and disagrees with these judicial interpretations of Section 8(b) which it regards as inconsistent with HUD's regulations and HUD's long-standing interpretations of Section 8(b).

D. Unearned Fees Under Section 8(b)

This Statement of Policy reaffirms HUD's existing, long-standing interpretation of Section 8(b) of RESPA. Sections 8(a) and (b) of RESPA contain distinct prohibitions. Section 8(a) prohibits the giving or acceptance of any payment pursuant to an agreement or understanding for the referral of settlement service business involving a federally related mortgage loan; it is intended to eliminate kickbacks or compensated referral arrangements among settlement service providers. Section 8(b) prohibits the giving or accepting of any portion, split, or percentage of any charge other than for goods or facilities provided or services performed; it is intended to eliminate unearned fees. Such fees are contrary to the Congressional finding when enacting RESPA that consumers need protection from unnecessarily high settlement charges. 12 U.S.C. 2601(a).

It is HUD's position that Section 8(b) proscribes the acceptance of any portion or part of a charge other than for services actually performed. Inasmuch as Section 8(b)'s proscription against "any portion, split, or percentage" of an unearned charge for settlement services is written in the disjunctive, the prohibition is not limited to a split. In HUD's view, Section 8(b) forbids the paying or accepting of any portion or percentage of a settlement service— including up to 100%—that is unearned, whether the entire charge is divided or split among more than one person or entity or is retained by a single person. Simply put, given that Section 8(b) proscribes unearned portions or percentages as well as splits, HUD does not regard the provision as restricting only fee splitting among settlement service providers. Further, since Section 8(b) on its face prohibits

---

[5] This final rule was delayed by legislation, but the Department implemented portions of the final rule that were not affected by the legislative delay on November 15, 1996. 61 FR 58472 (November 15, 1996).

Real Estate Settlement Procedures Act   Appx. K.3.2

Federal Register / Vol. 66, No. 202 / Thursday, October 18, 2001 / Rules and Regulations   **53059**

the giving or accepting of an unearned fee by any person, and 24 CFR 3500.14(c) speaks of a charge by "a person," it is also incorrect to conclude that the Section 8(b) proscription covers only payments or charges among settlement service providers.[6]

A settlement service provider may not levy an additional charge upon a borrower for another settlement service provider's services without providing additional services that are bona fide and justify the increased charge. Accordingly, a settlement service provider may not mark-up the cost of another provider's services without providing additional settlement services; such payment must be for services that are actual, necessary and distinct services provided to justify the charge. 24 CFR 3500.14(g)(3).[7] The HUD regulation implementing Section 8(b) states: "[a] charge by a person for which no or nominal services are performed or for which duplicative fees are charged is an unearned fee and violates this Section." 24 CFR 3500.14 (c).

The regulations also make clear that a charge by a single service provider where little or no services are performed is an unearned fee that is prohibited by the statute. 24 CFR 3000.14(c). A single service provider is also prohibited from charging a duplicative fee. Further, a

single service provider cannot serve in two capacities, e.g., a title agent and closing attorney, and be paid twice for the same service. The fee the service provider would be receiving in this case is duplicative under 24 CFR 3000.14(c) and not necessary and distinct under 24 CFR 3000.14(g)(3). Clearly, in all of these instances, the source of the payment—whether from consumers, other settlement service providers, or other third parties—is not relevant in determining whether the fee is earned or unearned because ultimately, all settlement payments come directly or indirectly from the consumer. See 24 CFR 3500.14(c). Therefore, a single settlement service provider violates Section 8(b) whenever it receives an unearned fee.

A single service provider also may be liable under Section 8(b) when it charges a fee that exceeds the reasonable value of goods, facilities, or services provided. HUD's regulations as noted state: "If the payment of a thing of value bears no relationship to the goods or services provided, then the excess is not for services or goods actually performed or provided." 24 CFR 3500.14(g)(2). Section 8(c)(2) only allows "the payment to any person of a bona fide salary or compensation or other payment for goods or facilities actually furnished or services actually performed," i.e., permitting only that compensation which is reasonably related to the goods or facilities provided or services performed. Compensation that is unreasonable is unearned under Section 8(b) and is not bona fide under Section 8(c)(2).

The Secretary, therefore, interprets Section 8(b) of RESPA to prohibit all

unearned fees, including, but not limited to, cases where: (1) Two or more persons split a fee for settlement services, any portion of which is unearned; or (2) one settlement service provider marks-up the cost of the services performed or goods provided by another settlement service provider without providing additional actual, necessary, and distinct services, goods, or facilities to justify the additional charge; or (3) one service provider charges the consumer a fee where no, nominal, or duplicative work is done, or the fee is in excess of the reasonable value of goods or facilities provided or the services actually performed.

V. Executive Order 12866, Regulatory Planning and Review

The Office of Management and Budget (OMB) has reviewed this Statement of Policy in accordance with Executive Order 12866, (captioned "Regulatory Planning and Review"). OMB determined that this Statement of Policy is a "significant regulatory action" as defined in Section 3(f) of the Order (although not an economically significant regulatory action under the Order). Any changes to the Statement of Policy resulting from this review are available for public inspection between 7:30 a.m. and 5:30 p.m. weekdays in the Office of the Rules Docket Clerk.

Dated: October 15, 2001.

John C. Weicher,

Assistant Secretary for Housing-Federal Housing Commissioner.

[FR Doc. 01–26321 Filed 10–15–01; 4:51 pm]

BILLING CODE 4210–27–P

---

[6] HUD is, of course, unlikely to direct any enforcement actions against consumers for the payment of unearned fees, because a consumer's intent is to make payment for services, not an unearned fee.

[7] HUD notes that some lenders have charged an additional fee merely for "reviewing" another settlement service provider's services. HUD does not regard such "review" as constituting an actual, necessary, or distinct additional service permissible under HUD's regulations.

K.4 HUD Letters

K.4.1 HUD Letter Regarding Statement of Policy 1999-1

December 17, 1999

U.S. Department of Housing and Urban Development
Washington, D.C. 20410-0500
Office of the General Counsel

The Honorable Bruce F. Vento
U.S. House of Representatives
Washington, D.C. 20515-2304

Dear Representative Vento:

This is in response to your letter dated December 7, 1999, asking three questions on behalf of your constituents regarding lender payments to mortgage brokers under the Real Estate Settlement Procedures Act (RESPA). Specifically, you ask: (1) whether, in its Statement of Policy 1999-1 (64 Fed. Reg. 10084), HUD intended to change existing law and create a new less stringent legal standard; (2) what factors HUD examines in determining whether payments to mortgage brokers are legal under RESPA; and (3) whether HUD intended the Policy Statement to weaken the referral fee prohibitions contained in RESPA.

Regarding the first question, as requested in the Conference Report on the Departments of Veterans Affairs and Housing and Urban Development and Independent Agencies Appropriations Act, 1999 (H.R. Conf. Rep. No. 105-769), on March 1, 1999, HUD issued Statement of Policy 1999-1 regarding the legality of mortgage lender payments to mortgage brokers under RESPA. The preamble to the Statement of Policy expressly states that it "provides HUD's views of the legality of fees to mortgage brokers from lenders under existing law." 64 Fed. Reg. 10084. In accordance with its express language, HUD did not intend for the Policy Statement to create a new legal standard or to change existing law.

As to the second question, the Policy Statement makes clear that HUD does not consider lender payments to mortgage brokers illegal *per se*. The Policy Statement articulates a two-part test to determine the legality of yield spread or other payments to mortgage brokers from lenders. HUD's position is that for a payment from a lender to a mortgage broker to be permissible under RESPA: (1) goods or facilities must have been furnished or services must have been performed "for"—i.e., in exchange for—the compensation paid to the broker; and (2) the broker's compensation must be reasonably related to the value of the services performed, or the goods or facilities provided, by the broker. 64 Fed. Reg. 10084. Regarding the first test, the Policy Statement sets out the minimum types and extent of services that a mortgage broker must perform in order to justify compensation to the broker. The Policy Statement then provides that "[t]he fact that goods or facilities have been actually furnished or that services have been actually performed by the mortgage broker . . . does not by itself make a payment by a lender to a mortgage broker legal." 64 Fed. Reg. 10085–6. Accordingly, the mere performance of any service by a mortgage broker is not in itself sufficient to establish that the payment to the broker was made in exchange for those services. "The next inquiry is whether the payment is reasonably related to

the value of the goods or services that were actually performed." 64 Fed. Reg. 10086. In applying this second test, the total compensation from the lender and the borrower should be scrutinized to assure that the payment is reasonably related to goods, facilities, or services furnished or performed. 64 Fed. Reg. 10084 and 10086. Moreover, the Policy Statement also makes clear that in analyzing whether any transaction under RESPA and its regulations involves compensation for "goods," a mortgage loan is not a "good," and that the referral of a loan is not a compensable service. 64 Fed. Reg. 10085 and 10086. HUD stated that mortgage brokers and lenders could better demonstrate the reasonableness of mortgage broker compensation if, at the time a consumer first discusses the possibility of a loan with a broker, the broker discloses the nature of its services and the various methods of compensation. At a minimum, mortgage brokers are required to clearly label and properly estimate their fees on the Good Faith Estimates. 64 Fed. Reg. 10087.

Finally, the preamble to the Policy Statement affirms that "[t]he Department has consistently held that the prohibitions under Section 8 of RESPA cover the activities of mortgage brokers." 64 Fed. Reg. 10082. Moreover, it says that "[t]he fees in cases or classes of transactions are illegal if they violate the prohibitions of Section 8 of RESPA." 64 Fed. Reg. 10084. HUD, therefore, never intended for its Policy Statement to weaken the prohibitions contained in Section 8 of RESPA and indeed, in elucidating the tests for when fees could be legal, sought to establish a brighter line defining illegal conduct. HUD is committed to assuring that consumers receive all of the protections that Congress afforded under RESPA.

I appreciate your interest in the Department's programs. If I can be of further assistance, please contact me.

Sincerely,

Gail W. Laster
General Counsel

K.4.2 HUD Letter Regarding Disclosures on Good Faith Estimate and HUD-1 Settlement Statement

AL 2000-5
OCC ADVISORY LETTER

Comptroller of the Currency
Administrator of National Banks

Subject: Real Estate Settlement Procedures Act (RESPA)
        Qs & As on the HUD-1 Settlement Statement

TO: Chief Executive Officers of All National Banks, Department and Division Heads, and All Examining Personnel

Attached is a series of questions and answers (Qs & As) prepared by the Department of Housing and Urban Development Office of General Counsel. The Qs & As were prepared in response to questions received from the Massachusetts Bankers Association relating to the HUD-1 settlement statement. These Qs & As are attached to assist you in complying with the relevant provisions in Regulation X (24 CFR 3500) governing the completion of the HUD-1 settlement statement.

Questions concerning this advisory should be directed to your supervisory office, the Community and Consumer Policy Division at (202) 874-4428, or the Division of Community and Consumer Law at (202) 874-5750.

Ralph E. Sharp
Deputy Comptroller for Community
and Consumer Policy

Attachment—HUD's Response to Questions from the Massachusetts Bankers Association

Date: May 31, 2000

U.S. Department of Housing and Urban Development
Washington, D.C. 20416-0508

February 25, 2000

Ms. Tanya M. Duncan
Director of Federal Regulatory and
Legislative Policy
Massachusetts Bankers Association
73 Tremont Street, Suite 306
Boston, Massachusetts 02108-3906

Re: *HUD-1 Questions*

Dear Ms. Duncan:

This is in response to your letter sent to Mr. Rodrgrigo Alba, a staff attorney in my office, from October 29, 1999, attaching frequently asked questions by your members relating to the HUD-1 form. Enclosed are HUD's responses which address the questions in the same order identified in your letter.

I trust this is responsive to your request.

Sincerely,

Kenneth A. Markison
Assistant General Counsel
GSE/RESPA Division

Enclosure
cc: Gail W. Laster, General Counsel

*HUD's Response to Questions from the Massachusetts
Bankers Association*

HUD-1 Questions

(1) The bank offers several loan programs (rates, term, etc.). A GFE is given within three days to match the product chosen by the applicant. If the applicant subsequently changes products (example, midway through the approval process), is a new Good Faith Estimate required?

Answer: The RESPA rules do not expressly impose any disclosure requirements beyond the initial Good Faith Estimate of settlement costs that must be provided to mortgage applicants within three days of application. However, where the loan product sought by the borrower is subsequently changed and the change results in different estimates of settlement costs, HUD strongly recommends that a new Good Faith Estimate be provided to the borrower.

(2) Is the person who is cosigning or guaranteeing a note (not the borrower) required to be listed on the HUD-1?

Answer: As per the instructions for filling out the settlement statement (24 C.F.R. 3500, Appendix A, Instructions for Complet-

ing HUD-1 and HUD-1A Settlement Statements [hereinafter "Instructions"]), where there is more than one borrower, the name and address of each borrower is required to be listed. Where two or more individuals are joint obligors with primary responsibility on a obligation, they must all be listed as borrowers on the settlement statement Guarantors, on the other hand, are not primary obligors and are not required to be listed on the settlement statement.

(3) The bank has a list of closing attorneys that a borrower may choose from. If one of the attorneys is on the bank's Board of Investment (acts similar to a Board of Directors)(this is a mutual savings bank), does an Affiliated Business Arrangement Disclosure need to be provided if this attorney is chosen by the applicant? What if the attorney is a member of the mutual savings bank Board of Trustees (meets quarterly, primarily to ratify Board of Investment decisions) or the Board of Corporators (meets annually)?

Answer: The relationships listed in question between the bank and the closing attorney would fall within the broad definition of "an affiliated business arrangement" under Section 3 of RESPA (12 U.S.C. 2602). In accordance with the requirements under 24 C.F.R. 3500.15(b), the bank would have to provide an Affiliated Business Arrangement Disclosure (in the format set forth under Appendix D of Regulation X). The disclosure must be provided regardless of whether the affiliated attorney is ultimately selected by the applicant.

(4) Does the fee paid the borrower's own attorney need to be listed on the HUD-1? The bank does not require (this attorney).

Answer: An item should be listed on the HUD-1 if it is required by the lender or if it is to be paid for at closing or settlement. The instructions provide that the HUD-1 shall itemize all charges imposed upon the borrower and the seller by the lender and all sales commissions, whether to be paid at settlement or outside of settlement, and any other charges which either the borrower or the seller will pay for at settlement. Charges to be paid outside of settlement shall be included on the HUD-1 and HUD-1A but marked "P.O.C." (Paid Outside of Closing) and shall not be included in computing totals. "P.O.C" items should not be placed in the borrower or seller columns, but rather on the appropriate line next to the columns and should not be used in computing totals. For all items except for those paid to and retained by the lender, the name of the person or firm ultimately receiving payment should be shown. In the case of "no cost" or "no point" loans, the charge to be paid by the lender to an affiliated or independent service provider should be shown as "P.O.C" (See Instructions).

(5) Do items paid by the seller well in advance of loan closing, which are required by the bank, need to be listed on the HUD-1?

Answer: See answer to Question #4. RESPA and Regulation X require that the settlement statement itemize all charges imposed upon the buyer or seller by the lender, whether to be paid at settlement or outside settlement. Items paid outside of settlement that are required by the lender should be listed as "P.O.C" and should be placed on the appropriate line next to the columns and should not be used in computing totals. (See instructions).

(6) Is there an acceptable tolerance level for different amounts between the GFE and the HUD-1 if there is no "pattern of differences"?

Answer: Neither RESPA nor Regulation X provide tolerances for variations between the figures disclosed on the Good Faith Estimate and the final charges listed on the HUD-1 or HUD-1A. HUD believes that a pattern or practice of quoting Good Faith Estimate amounts that are lower than the corresponding amounts later shown on settlement statements may serve as evidence that the disclosures were not made in good faith.

(7) If the bank accepts a normally required item previously obtained by the borrower (for example an appraisal) using their own funds well in advance of an application being submitted to the bank, does the bank need to list the item on the GFE or HUD-1? If so, how should the bank show the item on the GFE or HUD-1?

Answer: The Good Faith Estimate must estimate, as a dollar amount or range, each charge which will be listed on section L of the HUD-1 or HUD-1A, including the appraisal. (See 24 C.F.R. 3500.7(c)). If an item was previously obtained by the borrower, the item would be listed as "P.O.C." In all instances, the settlement statement must itemize the actual charges for those items required by the lender to close the transaction. For instruction on the proper method of disclosing "P.O.C." items on the HUD-1 or HUD-1A, see answer to Question #4.

(8) If the bank accepts work performed by a friend of the borrower for a required item (for example a plot plan) and the friend does not want to charge the borrower for this work, should the item be indicated on the HUD-1? If so, how should the zero cost be shown?

Answer: See answer to Question #4. When the lender requires that an item or service be purchased as a condition for obtaining a loan, HUD takes the position that the charge for such item or service, even if gratuitous, must be disclosed on the settlement statement. This item should be disclosed as zero (0) in the appropriate line of the settlement statement. In order to assure clarity, HUD recommends that a asterisk be placed next to the item, along with an explanation, either at the bottom of the HUD-1 form or on a separate page, that the required service was rendered gratuitously on behalf of the consumer.

(9) Is it a violation of RESPA if there are unexpected fees that appear on the HUD-1 that were not indicated in the GFE?

Answer: Regulation X provides that the Good Faith Estimate should list those charges that the borrower is likely to incur at settlement, based upon the lender's experience in the locality of the mortgaged property. It is therefore not a violation of RESPA to add fees to the HUD-1 or HUD-1A that were not disclosed on the Good Faith Estimate if such fees were, in good faith, unanticipated and unforeseeable at the time that the Good Faith Estimate was prepared. (See 24 C.F.R. 3500.7(c)). Where there is a pattern or practice of not disclosing fees on the GFE that are collected at settlement, particularly fees imposed by lenders, it may serve as evidence that the exclusion of such fees from the Good Faith Estimate was not in good faith.

(10) If a loan is to be sold by the bank after the closing, are costs associated with this sale but paid by the borrower at closing listed as "P.O.C."? (Services will not be performed until after the closing).

Answer: See answer to Question #4. Items that are either required by the lender to close the loan or items that are payable at the closing must be disclosed on the Good Faith Estimate and HUD-1 or HUD-1A. (See Instructions). Under the situation described above, the item should not be disclosed as a "P.O.C." item since it is a charge that the consumer is paying for at closing. The name of the person or firm ultimately receiving the payment should be disclosed. (Example: "Payment to [lender] for [XYZ] Servicer.") (See Instructions).

(11) A bank pays a mortgage broker $150 per loan, [and the loan] is consummated by the bank. This flat fee is not paid by the borrower or from any of the loan proceeds. Does this transaction need to be shown on the HUD-1? If so where? Should it also be shown as "P.O.C."?

Answer: The Instructions specifically indicate that charges to be paid by the lender to an affiliated or independent settlement service provider should be disclosed on the settlement statement and shown as "P.O.C." (See Instructions). The Instructions explicitly state that "[s]uch charges also include indirect payments or back-funded payments to mortgage brokers that arise from the settlement transaction." (See Instructions). The $150 payment should, therefore, be broken out from any other origination fee and disclosed on any of the blank lines provided in the 800 series of the HUD-1. However, given the nature of the payment described in this question, the lender must carefully review this payment to assure that it does not violate RESPA's anti-kickback or unearned fee provisions (12 U.S.C. 2607) and that it is in full compliance with HUD's Statement of Policy 1999-1, dated March 1, 1999, regarding lender payments to mortgage brokers (64 Fed. Reg. 10,080).

(12) The bank offers the customer a coupon for money toward closing costs. May the amount of the coupon be shown as credit on the front of the HUD-1? Or must it be applied toward particular closing fees?

Answer: This amount must be shown on lines 204–209, which are used to list "items paid by or on behalf of the borrower." (See Instructions).

(13) A bank collects an application fee. These monies are used for the appraisal and credit reports. The GFE shows the fees paid on line #808. The designated providers are given at application. On line #808 of the HUD-1, is the bank also required to enter the names of the providers on line #808 of the Settlement Statement?

Answer: The amount of the "application fee" should be disclosed on the Good Faith Estimate and the settlement statement, on line 808 or any other blank line in the 800 series. Since this fee is payable at or near the time of application, it should be marked as "P.O.C." and the charge should not be used in computing totals. The specific charges relating to the appraisal and the credit report must then be broken out on lines 803 and 804. As per the Instructions, these lines must identify the name of the person or firm ultimately receiving the payment, and also be marked as "P.O.C." (See Instructions). To assure that there is no confusion about double charging, fees listed in line numbers 803 or 804 should indicate that those fees are included in the "application fee" amount, or alternatively, the line in the 800 series containing the "application fee" could include an annotation clarifying that the charge includes those fees listed in 803 and 804.

(14) Who is responsible for the GFE and HUD-1 when the bank purchases a loan (table funds) from a correspondent lender?

Answer: Regulation X defines two alternatives for the delivery of the Good Faith Estimate. In instances where the correspondent lender is the exclusive agent of the bank, the responsibility for submitting the Good Faith Estimate falls on the correspondent lender or bank. (24 C.F.R. 3500.7(a)(4)). If the correspondent lender is not the bank's exclusive agent, the correspondent lender must provide the Good Faith Estimate within three days of receiving the loan application, and if this is done, the funding lender is not required to provide an additional Good Faith Estimate. In such cases, the funding lender remains responsible for ascertaining that the form has been delivered. 24 C.F.R. 3500.7(b). RESPA imposes the duty to prepare and deliver the HUD-1 or HUD-1A upon the "person conducting the settlement," which under Regulation X is the settlement agent or the lender if the lender acts as the settlement agent in the transaction. (See 12 U.S.C. 2603(b), 24 C.F.R. 3500.10(a)(b)).

(15) What HUD-1 line number should be used for overnight delivery fees?

Answer: Such fees should be listed in any of the blank lines in the series pertaining to the specific settlement service provider that requires the use of the service in question. For example, if a lender requires the use of overnight services, the fees pertaining to this service should be disclosed on one of the blank lines in the 800 series of the HUD-1 or HUD-1A.

(16) What HUD-1 line number should be used for Tax Service and Flood Determination fees?

Answer: Since such services are generally required by the lender, tax service and flood determination fees should be listed on any of the blank lines in the 800 series of the HUD-1 or HUD-1A.

(17) A bank charges a fee for document preparation. A portion of the fee goes to the bank and a portion goes to the attorney. Should this fee be split and placed on two separate HUD-1 line numbers? If so, which line number should be used?

Answer: The regulations specify that "[f]or all items, except for those paid to and retained by the lender, the name of the person or firm ultimately receiving the payment should be shown." (See Instructions). The correct method of disclosing this item would therefore be to separate that part of the fee that the bank pays the attorney and list it on line 1105 or 1007. The remaining portion of that fee, which relates to the document preparation work actually performed by the lender, should be separately identified in one of the blank lines of the 800 series. It is important to note that Section 8 of RESPA prohibits anyone from collecting any fee or portion thereof, unless it is for goods delivered or services actually rendered. (12 U.S.C. 2607 (a)–(c)).

(18) Are fees that are collected after closing, such as inspection fees on a construction loan (where the fee is deducted from each advance) required to be on the GFE or HUD-1?

Answer: Generally, construction loans are only covered where the lender has issued a commitment for permanent financing. (24 C.F.R. 3500.5(b)(3)). In instances where RESPA does cover transactions involving construction loans, inspection fees required to be paid as a condition for settlement must be disclosed on the settlement statement. (See Instructions). The fact that these inspection fees are collected after closing through a deduction from periodic advances does not alter this result; these fees are essentially equivalent to fees collected at closing from loan proceeds.

(19) If an error is discovered on the HUD-1 at closing, may a written correction be made at that time? And, should any or all parties, including the closing agent initial the correction? Since the HUD-1 does not need to be signed, how should an institution correct an error discovered after the settlement has occurred? Would the institution be required to get an acknowledgment from the borrower that they have received a corrected copy?

Answer: The instructions make clear that the settlement must list "actual charges and adjustments" in connection with the settlement. Pursuant to this requirement, any mistake discovered at settlement should be corrected at the time of settlement. Corrections may be handwritten, provided that they are appropriately initialed by the affected party or parties and the settlement agent. Moreover, servicers should act with due diligence in correcting any errors or omissions on any completed settlement statement forms

as quickly as possible, and must use all reasonable means to inform borrowers of any such changes or corrections. Although HUD does not require that an institution obtain a borrower's acknowledgement on any post-closing corrections to the settlement statement, HUD believes that obtaining consumers' signatures to demonstrate acknowledgement of any changes would constitute a prudent business practice.

Aggregate Accounting Adjustment Questions

(1) Is an institution required to enter a zero ("0") in the borrower's column on the last line of the 1000 series if the aggregate accounting adjustment equals zero?

Answer: Yes. The aggregate accounting adjustment is the difference between the required balance using aggregate analysis and the required balance using single item analysis. Since every escrow account can be analyzed using single item and aggregate analysis, the aggregate accounting adjustment can always be calculated. Absent a rounding error, the aggregate accounting adjustment is either a negative number or a zero (0). Whatever the aggregate accounting adjustment is, even if zero (0), that number must be entered on the final line of the 1000 series of the settlement statement. (See 24 C.F.R. 3500.8(c)).

(2) Experience has shown that there is occasionally a positive number that results when calculating the aggregate accounting adjustment when there is only one escrow item. In these instances, should this positive number be omitted when completing the HUD-1, or should the institution enter this positive number on line 1008?

Answer: The computation steps set forth under 24 C.F.R. 3500.17(d) should always yield a zero when there is only one escrow item.

(3) Is the aggregate adjustment calculation required to be reported if there is only one escrow item?

Answer: Yes.

"P.O.C" and Third Party Settlement Service Providers

(1) Does the bank need to indicate on the HUD-1 the different entities making the "P.O.C." payments? (Bank pays for some, borrower pays for some).

Answer: For all items, except for those paid to and retained by the lender, the name of the person or firm ultimately receiving the payment should be shown. (See Instructions). Making additional notations on the HUD-1 to identify the payment source of a particular fee serves to clarify the transaction. In HUD's Statement of Policy 1999-1, dated March 1, 1999, regarding lender payments to mortgage brokers (64 Fed. Reg. 10,080), the Department clarified that in the interest of clarity, any payment from a lender to a mortgage broker is to be clearly identified and labeled as a fee paid by the lender (Example: "Mortgage Broker Fee from lender to XYZ Corp. (P.O.C.)."). (64 F.R. 10087).

(2) If the answer to question #1 is yes, may the bank use symbols to indicate the entity making the payment (placing the symbol next to the "P.O.C.") and explaining the symbol at the bottom of the page?

Answer: If the lender determines it appropriate to disclose the name of the payee, this approach is acceptable.

(3) How should the bank complete a line item on the HUD-1 correctly if there is not enough room on the line item to indicate the name of the entity receiving payment and/or listing "P.O.C." and the name of the entity?

Answer: Such problems may be resolved by filling out the necessary disclosures by hand or placing an asterisk or other clear symbol or indication on the appropriate line and clearly explaining the asterisk or symbol at the bottom of the HUD-1 or HUD-1A or on a separate page attached to the HUD-1 or HUD-1A.

(4) The bank requires a Title V (Massachusetts Septic Compliance Certificate) to be presented at the closing. This is a cost paid for by the seller in advance of the closing when the inspection is performed. Does this cost need to be reflected on the HUD-1? If so, what is the location and proper format for this fee?

Answer: This item should be listed on one of the blank lines provided in the 1300 series of the HUD-1 or HUD-1A, which are used to list additional settlement charges relating to inspections. This item should be listed as "P.O.C." and identified as paid by the seller.

(5) Is the bank required to list all items paid to other parties in connection with the HUD-1 for a "no closing costs" loan product? If so, should all of these items be listed as "P.O.C."?

Answer: Yes. HUD's regulation at 24 C.F.R. 3500.7(a)(2) and the Instructions are very clear that for so-called "no cost" or "no point" loans, "the charge to be paid by the lender to an affiliated or independent settlement service provider should be shown as "P.O.C." (Paid Outside of Closing) and should not be used in computing totals." (See Instructions).

(6) If an applicant pays any fees at the time of application, is the bank required to list these fees as "P.O.C" of the GFE? If so, should these items be included or excluded in the "Total Estimated Closing Costs" amount shown on the GFE?

Answer: Regulation X at 24 C.F.R. 3500.7(c) requires that the Good Faith Estimate list an estimate of each charge "that the borrower will normally pay or incur at or before settlement." Items paid for by the applicants in advance of closing, such as application fees, must therefore be listed on the Good Faith Estimate and identified as "P.O.C." The Good Faith Estimate does not, however, require that there be a total estimated closing cost disclosure; this is only required on the settlement statement. (See Appendix C).

Questions Relating to Title Charges

(1) Is it required to indicate anywhere on the HUD-1 the actual dollar amount of the commission earned by the settlement agent (closing attorney) for issuing a title insurance policy?

Answer: Yes. The Instructions specifically state that the HUD-1 must "itemize all charges imposed upon the borrower and the seller by the lender *and all sales commissions*, whether to be paid at settlement or outside of the settlement." (See Instructions)(Italics added).

(2) Is it a requirement that line 1113 be completed indicating what services the closing agent did to earn his/her commission for the title insurance policy?

Answer: The Instructions clarify that payments to settlement agents are to be detailed on lines 1101 through 1106 in accordance with the services performed by the agent in the transaction. If an attorney acts as the agent, the total amount of the payment should be listed on line 1107, along with entries on the blank line immediately below to identify item numbers of the services listed which are covered by that overall fee. If line 1107 is already being used to disclose the fees and services of the attorney in representing any of the parties to the transaction, then line 1113 should be used to disclose the commission (and those services covered by the commission) that the attorney is earning in his or her role as title agent in the transaction. (See Instructions).

(3) If a closing agent bundles services under line 1107, must they indicate under line 1107 the items 1101–1106 that were included in the fee shown in 1107?

Answer: Yes, the HUD-1 form is clear in this regard. (See Instructions).

(4) If the fee listed on 1108 is for the cost of the title insurance policy, does the closing agent need to list any other numbers (1101–1106) beneath line 1108?

Answer: Yes, the HUD-1 form is clear in this regard. As per the Instructions, line 1108 should list the overall fee for the policy and the blank line beneath it should disclose the item numbers of the services which are covered in the overall. (See Instructions).

(5) Is it a true statement that there may be no duplicate numbers or services listed when describing the fees earned in 1107, 1108 and 1113? (For example, 1103 may not be listed in more than one of the three of the line numbers described above?).

Answer: This statement is correct. Section 8 of RESPA forbids duplicative fees. (See 24 C.F.R. 3500.14(g)(3)).

Appendix L

Sample Pleadings, Discovery, and Expert Witness Evidence

L.1 RISA Violations in Car Sale

These pleadings are intended solely for purposes of demonstration. They must be adapted by a competent professional to meet actual needs in light of the facts and local statutory and case law and local practice requirements. All pleadings in this appendix can also be found on the companion CD-Rom and are available in Microsoft Word or can be copied onto a word processor. A number of additional pleadings can be found on the companion CD-Rom.

L.1.1 Answer and Counterclaim

The first sample pleading is an answer and counterclaim in response to a collection action based upon the hypothetical car sale described in § 4.11, *supra*, and the state motor vehicle retail installment sales act used in that hypothetical (with a few added facts to make it more interesting). The sample interrogatories that follow are also based on this hypothetical.

IN THE DISTRICT COURT OF TERRA INCOGNITA
In and For Sample County

C.R. PYLE CLEAN USED CARS,	)))
Plaintiff	))
v.	) ANSWER, AFFIRMA-) TIVE DEFENSE AND) COUNTERCLAIM)
CONNIE CONSUMER,	)
Defendant	))

ANSWER

Comes now the defendant, Connie Consumer, and for answer to Plaintiff C.R. Pyles Clean Used Cars' complaint, states as follows

1. She [*admits*] [*lacks sufficient information or knowledge to be able to answer*] [*denies*] the allegations of Paragraph l that Plaintiff is a corporation organized and duly licensed[1] under the laws of Terra Incognita, with its principal office in Sample County, Terra Incognita. Defendant admits that Plaintiff is regularly engaged in the business of selling and financing the sale of automobiles.

2. She denies the allegations of Paragraph 2 of Plaintiff's complaint, except that on January 1, 1994, she purchased from Plaintiff a 1990 Ford Escort for $3727.50, and entered into a retail installment sales agreement for the financing of said sale.

3. She denies the allegations of Paragraphs 3 through 6 of Plaintiff's complaint, and denies all other allegations contained in the complaint not specifically responded to in the preceding paragraphs.

AFFIRMATIVE DEFENSES AND COUNTERCLAIMS

Factual Allegations

4. Defendant, and plaintiff on the counterclaims, Connie Consumer (hereinafter "Consumer") entered into this installment sales transaction to purchase an automobile which was to be used for personal, family, and household purposes.

5. Plaintiff, and defendant on the counterclaims, C.R. Pyle Clean Used Cars (hereinafter "Pyle" is engaged in the business of selling and financing the sales of motor vehicles, in Terra Incognita, and is an installment seller within the meaning of the Motor Vehicle Retail Installment Sales Act, T.I. Code § 50.3(4), subject to the provisions of that Act. Further, in the ordinary course of business, it regularly extends credit for which the payment of a finance charge is required, and is a creditor within the meaning of the Truth in Lending Act, 15 U.S.C. § 1602(a)(17), subject to the provisions of that act.

6. On January 1, 1994, Consumer purchased a 1990 Ford Escort for $3727.50 from Pyle through its salesman, C.R. Pyle, Jr., who was at all relevant times an agent and employee of Pyle acting within the scope of his employment.

7. In conjunction with the purchase of the automobile, Pyle offered to arrange financing. Pyle's agent asked what monthly payments Consumer could afford, and then said he would see what kind of financing he could arrange for her. He asked if she could return at 5:45 that afternoon. No discussion as to any terms other than monthly payment level took place.

8. Upon her return on January 1, all of the documents had been prepared prior to her arrival. As Pyle was preparing to close for the day, Pyle explained only that Consumer would have 36 payments of about $160.00, and had her hurriedly sign the documents. A copy of the Purchase Agreement is attached hereto as Exhibit A, and hereby incorporated by reference.[2] In conjunction with the transaction, Pyle also prepared a Truth in Lending Disclosure

---

1 Failure to obtain required licenses may give rise to additional claims. Or, if a required license under a special usury ceiling has not been obtained, then the provisions of the general usury statute—often with a lower ceiling—may apply. For this reason, proper licensing should never be taken for granted.

2 The purchase agreement upon which this complaint is based can be found at § 4.11.4, Chart 17, *supra*.

statement, attached hereto as Exhibit B and hereby incorporated by reference.[3]

9. In addition to the unpaid balance of the cash price in the amount of $3073.62, Pyle included additional charges in the amount of $40.00 for license, title, and registration fees, $103.17 for credit life insurance premiums, $286.58 for credit disability insurance premiums, and $500.00 for an extended service plan in the amount financed. (Exhibit A) Consumer neither requested nor bargained for the extended service contract. The contract further provided that late charges in the amount of the lesser of $5 or 5% of the payment ($7.97) will be imposed in the event a payment is more than 10 days late. (Exhibit B)

10. Subsequent to the purchase, Consumer experienced numerous problems with the car, necessitating the return of the car to Pyle for repairs on eight occasions between January 1 and April 25, 1994. On each occasion, Consumer asked if the cost of the repair would be paid by the extended service plan, and was told it was "not covered" under the plan. Upon information and belief, the service contract purchased in fact provided no benefit to Consumer and was imposed solely to provide extra recompense to Pyle on this credit transaction.

11. Upon information and belief, Pyle included charges in the contract which were neither authorized by law, nor supported by any consideration or benefit to Consumer, and such excess charges were imposed by Pyle willfully and solely as a pretext to obtain recompense in excess of that authorized by law. Such unauthorized charges include, but are not limited to (a) $40.00 for license, title and registration fees, which amount is in excess of that actually paid and payable in connection with this transaction; (b) $500 for a purported service contract which represented a charge for nonexistent services from which Consumer derived no benefit; and (c) premium charges for credit insurance in excess of that authorized by T.I. Code § 50.4 and the regulations of the T.I. Department of Insurance, T.I.A.C. § 9801, *et seq.*

[*Facts relating to any warranty claims under Article 2 of the UCC or MagnusonMoss or related tort claims should be inserted.*][4]

12. Consumer made two monthly payments on February 1, 1994 and March 9, 1994, with the April payment being paid in two installments (April 11, 1994 and April 28, 1994). No further payments were made, and on June 12, 1994, Pyle repossessed the car.

[*Facts relating to improper repossession or resale which may state a claim under Article 9 of the UCC or related tort claims should be inserted.*][5]

13. On July 19, 1994, Pyle sent a demand letter, seeking immediate payment of $3800 from Consumer. A copy of the letter is attached hereto as Exhibit C, and is hereby incorporated by reference.[6]

FIRST DEFENSE

14. The Terra Incognita Motor Vehicle Retail Installment Sales Act, T.I. Code § 50.l, *et seq.*, governs the credit sale of motor vehicles entered into within the state of Terra Incognita. Section 50.10 provides that a seller who violates the provisions of the act may not recover any finance charge, delinquency charge, or collection costs from the borrower.[7]

15. Pyle has imposed charges on Consumer in excess of those permitted by law for this transaction, and has thereby forfeited its right to recover any finance charge, delinquency charge, or collection costs from Consumer. The imposition of such illegal charges was done willfully and knowingly.

16. Pyle has violated the T.I. MVRISA in the following and other respects

   a. It has imposed a rate of charge on this sale in excess of 12% add-on, the maximum authorized rate of charge authorized by T.I. Code § 50.5(a) for a four-year old automobile.[8]

   b. Section § 50.5(b) provides that the maximum finance charge may be determined by applying the authorized 12% rate of charge to an amount financed as defined in § 50.4. In calculating the amount financed, Pyle included unauthorized charges in violation of § 50.4. Among such unauthorized charges are credit insurance premiums which exceed the rates filed with the Department of Insurance;[9] fees for license, title and registration which exceed the actual amount payable;[10] and a charge for a $500 service contract which represented the purchase of a nonexistent service.[11]

   c. Upon information and belief,[12] the amount sought in Pyle's demand letter and complaint includes two late charges in the amount of $7.97 imposed in violation of § 50.6, which provides that late payments in an amount not to exceed the lesser of $5 or 5% of the payment amount may be imposed on any installment which is 10 days late.

   d. Upon information and belief,[13] the amount sought in Pyle's demand letter and complaint includes unearned interest, insurance charges, and service contract charges, in violation of § 50.7, which provides that rebates of unearned charges, calculated according to the Rule of 78 based on unpaid balances as of the next succeeding monthly due date must be made.[14]

---

3 The Truth in Lending Disclosure statement is found at § 4.11.4, Chart 16, *supra*.

4 Sample pleadings for warranty and related claims can be found in National Consumer Law Center, Consumer Warranty Law Appxs. K–M (2d ed. 2001 and Supp.).

5 Sample pleadings for wrongful repossession and related claims can be found in National Consumer Law Center, Repossessions and Foreclosures Appxs. D, E (5th ed. 2002 and Supp.).

6 The demand letter is found at § 4.11.4, Chart 19, *supra*.

---

7 *See* § 10.8.2.2.2, *supra*.

8 *See* § 4.11.4, *supra*.

9 *See* §§ 7.4.1, 7.4.2, 8.5.3.2, *supra*.

10 *See* §§ 7.3.1, 7.4.1, 7.4.2, *supra*.

11 Sham contracts for non-existent collateral services or fees not actually expended may be considered hidden interest. *See, e.g.*, §§ 7.2.1, 7.2.3, *supra*. For the possibility of service contracts as a TIL finance charge, see Official Staff Commentary to Reg. Z, § 226.4(a)-1.

12 Practitioners must always comply with good faith pleading requirements, e.g., Fed. R. Civ. P. 11. In this case, the practitioner can plead the late charges and lack of rebates in good faith as a result of a mathematical analysis based on the documentation available to him. *See* § 4.11.4, *supra*.

13 *Id.*

14 *See* § 5.6.3.3.1, *supra*. Note that some statutes do not permit creditors to "round up" to the next due date when using the Rule of 78 in all cases. *See* § 5.6.2, *supra*.

[SECOND AFFIRMATIVE DEFENSE]

[*Insert any defenses which may arise from other claims, such as improper acceleration which may defeat a claim of default, or other repossession claim which would defeat a deficiency action.*[15] *Other affirmative defenses may arise from common law claims or warranty claims relating to the condition of the car.*][16]

COUNTERCLAIM
Count I

[*Insert any claim for affirmative recovery which may arise from the usury claim, including any statutory penalty which may be authorized,*[17] *or, if applicable, a claim for a refund of payments made.*[18] *The following paragraphs are examples for use when the applicable law would permit such a claim:*]

17. Consumer realleges and incorporates by reference the allegations of Paragraphs 1 through 16 herein.

18. T.I. MVRISA § 50.11 provides for a penalty in an amount equal to the finance charge in the event of willful violations of the act. Pyle willfully violated the act as specified in Paragraphs 15 and 16 herein.

19. Said violations entitle Consumer to judgment against Pyle in the amount of $1535.51.

Count II: Truth in Lending

[*Insert counterclaim counts for affirmative recovery based on Truth in Lending.*][19]

Count III: Terra Incognita Consumer Protection Act

[*Insert counterclaim counts for affirmative recovery based on state UDAP statute if applicable.*][20]

Count IV: Uniform Commercial Code Article 2

[*Insert counterclaim counts for affirmative recovery based on UCC warranty claims.*]

Count V: Magnuson-Moss

[*Insert counterclaim counts for affirmative recovery based on the Magnuson-Moss Act.*]

Count VI: Universal Commercial Code Article 9

[*Insert claims for affirmative relief based on improper repossession under Article 9 of the UCC.*]

Count VII, etc.

[*Insert other applicable claims, such as tort claims for conversion based on wrongful repossession, common law fraud claims, negligent misrepresentation, debt collection.*]

[*JURY DEMAND*][21]

[*If desired, and appropriate, include a jury demand in the form prescribed for the jurisdiction.*]

PRAYER FOR RELIEF

WHEREFORE, Consumer prays the court as follows:

A. Plaintiff Pyle's complaint be dismissed in its entirety.

B. Declare that Pyle has forfeited any right to collect delinquency charges or finance charges, and that the amount of the finance charge forfeited includes excess insurance premiums, licensing and registration fees, and the cost of the service contract, all in accord with T.I. Code § 50.1, *et seq.*

C. Award judgment to Consumer in the amount of $1535.51 for Count I, in accord with T.I. Code § 50.1, *et seq.*

D. Award judgment to Consumer in the amount of $1000 for Count II, in accord with 15 U.S.C. § 1640.

E. [*State all appropriate relief under other applicable statutes or common law claims, including, where appropriate, actual and punitive damages.*]

F. Award reasonable attorney fees and costs as provided by T.I. § 50.12; 15 U.S.C. § 1640; [*and other applicable law*].

G. Award such other relief as the court deems just and equitable.

Attorney for Defendant Consumer
Address
Phone Number
Jarndyce and Jarndyce
79 High Street
Jefford, Terra Incognita
(555) 555-1234

L.1.2 First Set of Interrogatories

This is a sample form for demonstration purposes only, and must be adapted by a competent professional to meet the individual facts and local procedural rules. Note also that Rule 33(a) of the Federal Rules of Civil Procedure limits the number of interrogatories to 25 including subparts. This limitation may be avoided only by leave of the court with a written stipulation of the parties.

This set of interrogatories is based on the factual situation described in § 4.11, *supra*, and used as the basis for the answer and counterclaim in L.1, *supra*.

Where permitted, practitioners should also consider seeking a request for admissions as a supplement to interrogatories. In a usury case, Requests for Admissions may be a particularly useful way to spell out for the court the proper formula required by state law for calculating interest or rebates, and the arithmetic application of the formula in the case in question. *See* L.2.2.

---

15 *See* note 5, *supra.*

16 *See* note 4, *supra.*

17 *See* § 10.8.2.4, *supra.*

18 *See* § 10.8.2.3, *supra.*

19 Sample pleadings for Truth in Lending violations may be found in National Consumer Law Center, Truth in Lending Appxs. E–G (5th ed. 2003 and Supp.).

20 *See* National Consumer Law Center, Unfair and Deceptive Acts and Practices (6th ed. 2004 and Supp.).

21 *See* § 10.2, *supra.*

Discovery should begin as soon as possible. It is wise, where possible, to serve discovery requests along with an answer or counterclaim. Ordinarily, it is not only good practice to move the case along promptly, but it lets the creditor know that this will not be a default or routine workout arrangement.

IN THE DISTRICT COURT OF TERRA INCOGNITA
In and For Sample County

_____)		
C.R. PYLE CLEAN USED	)	
CARS,	)	
Plaintiff	)	
	)	DEFENDANT'S
v.	)	INTERROGATORIES
	)	(FIRST SET)
CONNIE CONSUMER,	)	
Defendant	)	
_____)		

TO: C.R. PYLE CLEAN USED CARS

You are hereby directed to answer under oath, in accordance with T.I.R. Civ. P. 33, the following interrogatories. In providing the responses, please note:

A. All answers are to be furnished in writing and under oath within 30 days of the date of these interrogatories.

B. Each interrogatory should be answered upon your entire knowledge from all sources and all information in Plaintiff's possession or otherwise available from Plaintiff including information from Plaintiff's office, employees, agents, representatives, attorneys, investigators, or consultants and information which is known by each of them. An incomplete or evasive answer is a failure to answer.

C. Where an individual interrogatory calls for an answer which involves more than one part, each part of the answer should be clearly explained so that it is understandable.

D. If you cannot answer any or all of the following interrogatories in full, after exercising due diligence to do so, state your inability and answer to the extent possible, state reasons for your inability to answer the remainder (including a list of the sources which were consulted for a response), and state whatever information or knowledge you have concerning the unanswered portions.

E. Each interrogatory is considered continuing, and if Plaintiff obtains information which renders its answer or one of them, incomplete or inaccurate, Plaintiff is obligated to serve amended answers on the undersigned.

F. "Identify," when used with reference to a document or documents, means to state as applicable: (a) the type of document (e.g., installment contract, credit application, recourse agreement, letter, memorandum, notes, etc.); (b) the date of the document; (c) the name and present address of the originator thereof; (d) the name and present or last known address of each signatory thereto; (e) the name and address of its present custodian; and (f) if the original document was destroyed, the date and reason for or circumstances under which it was destroyed.

G. "The transaction," when used without qualification, means the transaction consummated by Connie Consumer on or before January 1, 1994, involving Consumer's purchase of the 1990 Ford Escort on credit, including all sale, loan and other contracts and agreements entered into between Plaintiff and Defendant.

H. The terms "document" or "documents" in these interrogatories shall refer to all writings and recorded materials, of any kind, that are or have been in the possession, control or custody of Plaintiff of which Plaintiff has knowledge, whether originals or copies. Such writings or recordings include, but are not limited to, contracts, documents, notes, rough drafts, inter-office memoranda, memoranda for the files, letters, research materials, correspondence, logs, diaries, forms, bank statements, tax invoices, diagrams, drawings, computer print-outs or tapes, reports, statistical computations, studies, graphs, charts, minutes, manuals, pamphlets, or books of all nature and kind whether handwritten, typed, printed, mimeographed, photocopied or otherwise reproduced, all tape recordings (whether for computer, audio, or visual replay) or other written, printed, and recorded matter of tangible things on which words, phrases, symbols or information are recorded.

I. "Identify," when used with reference to a person, means to provide the person's full name, current or last known home and work addresses and current or last known home and work telephone numbers, occupation, and business relationship to Plaintiff currently and on January 1, 1994.

1. Identify the person(s) answering these interrogatories. Include the position held, the length of time the respondent has held this position, and the duties performed for Plaintiff.

2. Please state:

a. Plaintiff's correct present legal name, and any changes since January 1, 1989.

b. Any other names which Plaintiff uses to identify itself, whether such names are registered with any official, and the date and place of such registration.

3. Please state:

a. In what business Plaintiff was principally engaged from January 1, 1993 to the present.

b. Whether Plaintiff was licensed to conduct the business identified in subpart a.

c. If so, please state the date(s) such license was issued, and identify the issuing agencies.

d. Identify any other licenses issued to Plaintiff or its employees in relation to the conduct of Plaintiff's business, including, but not limited to, licenses issued by the Department of Insurance, and the person or entity to whom all such the licenses were issued.

4. Please identify each person who participated in the transaction with Connie Consumer which is the subject of this action, including but not limited to, the person(s) who negotiated the sale, reviewed the credit application, approved the credit application, determined the terms of the financing arrangement, performed the calculations in arriving at the terms of the financing arrangement, prepared the documents memorializing this transaction, and logged payments on this account. Explain the function which each person identified herein performed.

5. Please identify all documents prepared or received by Plaintiff in conjunction with this transaction, including but not limited to, contracts, instruments, disclosure forms, insurance documents, service contracts, file memos, records of telephone calls, correspondence and ledger cards. Attach all documentation relating to this transaction.

6. Please identify, by payee, payee's business address, check number, date of issuance, amount and signator, all disbursals made on Connie Consumer's account arising from this transaction. Attach copies of all cancelled checks identified herein. If any dis-

bursals were made by means of other than check, identify such disbursals by payee, amount, date and method of payment.[22] Attach copies of all documentation relating to such disbursals.

7. Please describe the benefits provided in the Extended Service Plan issued in conjunction with this transaction; include the type of services or parts covered, and the term for which coverage was provided. If such benefits are described in booklet, pamphlet, or other written form, you may respond by producing a copy of such written document.

8. Please identify Tow Motor Co. by correct legal name and address of its principal place of business.[23]

9. For the period between January 1, 1993 and January 1, 1995, state the number of completed transactions for the sale of motor vehicles by Plaintiff.

    a. Of that number, how many completed transactions included the sale of an Extended Service Plan from Tow Motor Co? From any other service plan provider?

    b. Of the total number of completed sales transactions, how many were financed by Plaintiff?

    c. Of the total number of completed sales transactions financed by Plaintiff, how many included the sale of an Extended Service Plan from Tow Motor Co? From any other service plan provider?

10. How many requests were made for repairs to be performed under service contracts sold in conjunction with those transactions identified in response to Interrogatory 9(a)? With respect to those requests, please state:

    a. The number in which the insured was told the repair was not covered by the service contract;

    b. The number in which the requested repairs were completed;

    c. The average dollar value of completed repairs identified in response to Interrogatory 10(b).

11. How many requests were made for repairs to be performed under service contracts sold in conjunction with those transactions identified in response to Interrogatory 9(c)? With respect to those requests, please state:

    a. The number in which the insured was told the repair was not covered by the service contract;

    b. The number in which the requested repairs were completed;

    c. The average dollar value of completed repairs identified in response to Interrogatory 11(b).

12. Please state:

    a. The premium charged for the credit disability insurance issued in conjunction with this transaction and the amount and type of coverage obtained.

    b. The premium charged for the credit life insurance issued in conjunction with this transaction and the type of coverage obtained.

13. Please identify the method by which Plaintiff determined the finance charge to be imposed on this credit transaction. If Plaintiff utilizes charts, please identify by name, publisher, and date of publication the chart(s) used in preparing this transaction. If Plain-

tiff utilizes a computer program, please identify the program used.

14. Please identify the method by which Plaintiff determined the amount of premium charges to be imposed for the use of credit life and disability insurance in conjunction with this transaction. If charts were used, please identify by title, publisher, date of publication and page number the chart(s) used. If Plaintiff utilizes a computer program, please identify the program used.

15. Please explain what rebates, if any, were made on Plaintiff's account prior to filing this action.

    a. Specify which charges were rebated, *e.g.*, finance charge, credit life premium, credit disability premium, service contract.

    b. Specify the amount rebated for each charge.

    c. Specify the date each such rebate was credited to this account.

    d. Specify the formula used to calculate each rebate.

    e. Specify the dates and amounts used in the formula to calculate such rebate.

Attorney for Defendant Consumer
Address
Phone Number
Jarndyce and Jarndyce
79 High Street
Jefford, Terra Incognita
(555)555-1234

L.2 Insurance Packing, Loan Padding and Flipping

L.2.1 Complaint

This is a sample pleading for demonstration purposes only, and must be adapted by a competent professional to meet the circumstances of a given case and the requirements of local law and practice.[24]

The facts include some of the facts at issue in the example discussed in § 8.5.4.2, *supra*, but the pleading itself is not based upon the pleadings in that case.

IN THE DISTRICT COURT OF TERRA INCOGNITA
In and For Sample County

————————————)	
L. L. Pomfret,)	
Plaintiff)	
)	
v.)	
)	
Beneficent Financial Serv., Inc.)	COMPLAINT
and Oliver Proudie, individually)	
and in his capacity as agent and)	
employee of Beneficent)	
Financial Services, Inc.,)	
Defendants)	
————————————)	

---

22 This will help establish whether some of the charges which had been imposed in order to reimburse third parties were actually paid to those third parties, or if paid, were paid in the amount claimed.

23 Questions 8 to 11 will help establish if the service contract is actually a pretext for usury with the proceeds going to the creditor for a non-existent service.

24 For other sample pleadings, see 14A Am. Jur. Pl. & Pr. Forms (Rev), Interest and Usury.

INTRODUCTION

1. Plaintiff L.L. Pomfret brings this action pursuant to the T.I. Consumer Loan Act, T.I. Code Chap. 101, for a declaration that an obligation he entered into with Defendant Beneficent Financial Services, Inc. is written in violation of the provisions of that Act, and is therefore null and void, and for return of moneys previously paid. He further alleges that the contract in question is unconscionable, and should be declared unenforceable.

PARTIES

2. Plaintiff is a natural person residing in Sample County, Terra Incognita.

3. Defendant Beneficent Financial Services, Inc. (hereinafter "Beneficent") is a domestic corporation, duly authorized to do business in Terra Incognita. In the ordinary course of business, it regularly extends consumer credit in the amount of $10,000 or less for which the payment of a finance charge is required.[25] It is licensed under the provisions of the Consumer Loan Act, T.I. § 101.1 *et seq.*, and subject to the provisions therein.

4. Defendant Oliver Proudie (hereinafter "Proudie") is a natural person, residing in Sample County, Terra Incognita. At all times relevant to the allegations herein, he acted as an agent within the scope of his authority and as an employee of defendant Beneficent Financial Services, Inc.

FACTUAL ALLEGATIONS

5. On December 10, 1992, Plaintiff sought to borrow $1000 from Defendants in order to purchase a refrigerator and to pay outstanding medical bills. The parties entered into a consumer loan transaction, the terms of which called for Plaintiff to repay $1478.35 at 24% in 36 monthly installments of $58.00. A copy of that transaction is attached hereto as Exhibit A and is incorporated herein by reference. This loan will be referred to hereafter as Loan I.

6. Plaintiff made all payments as scheduled on Loan I through April 10, 1994. On April 13, he received a telephone solicitation from Proudie, an employee of Beneficent, soliciting Plaintiff for additional credit. At all times relevant hereto, Proudie was acting as an employee and agent of Beneficent. As Plaintiff's plumbing was in need of repair, he inquired about the terms for obtaining an additional extension of credit in the amount of $500.00. He informed Proudie he could manage monthly payments in the amount of no more than $75.00.

7. Proudie said he would "work something up." On April 15, 1994, Proudie telephoned Plaintiff to inform him that the papers were ready for his signature.

8. Upon Plaintiff's arrival, Proudie explained that he had worked out the terms so that Plaintiff's monthly payments would be $75.00 over a period of 6 years (72 months), and he could get $517.23 for his plumbing repairs. No terms other than the amount of monthly payment were discussed at any time, and all documents had been prepared prior to Plaintiff's arrival.

9. The amount financed by Loan II also included a pay-off of Loan I in the amount of $925, credit life insurance premium in the amount of $210.60, credit disability insurance premium in the amount of $275.40, household contents insurance in the amount of $486, and $184 in recording fees. A security interest was taken in Plaintiff's household goods and in Plaintiff's residence. A copy of Loan II is attached hereto as Exhibit B and hereby incorporated by reference.

10. The property insurance written in conjunction with this loan is issued by Hollow National, a wholly owned subsidiary of Beneficent. Upon information and belief, Beneficent receives a commission in excess of 50% of each property insurance premium received in conjunction with a loan.

STATUTORY AND REGULATORY FRAMEWORK

11. The Terra Incognita Consumer Loan Act, Chapter 101, governs credit transactions by licensed lenders, entered into within the state, for amounts under $10,000.

   a. Section 101.12(c) provides that no licensed lender shall take a security interest upon real estate in conjunction with a loan wherein the amount financed is less than $2000.

   b. Section 101.13(a) sets forth the maximum rate of interest which may be charged on loans made subject to the Act to be 9% discount, or its actuarial equivalent.

   c. Section 101.13(c) provides that no charges other than those specifically authorized by Chapter 101 may be "directly or indirectly charged, contracted for, or received."

   d. Section 101.13(d)(l) authorizes the sale of credit life and credit disability insurance, the charge for which may not exceed the premium charged by the insurer in conformance with any rate filings required by law and made by the insurer with the T.I. Commissioner for Insurance.

   e. Section 101.13(d)(2) provides that a creditor may contract for a separate charge for insurance against loss of or damage to property taken as security in conjunction with the loan, so long as the insurance charge is reasonable in relation to the value of the insured property and the amount of the loan.

   f. Section 101.15 provides that upon prepayment, all unearned charges shall be rebated according to the Rule of 78,[26] calculated on unpaid balances due on the anniversary date nearest the date of prepayment.

   g. Section 101.13(c) provides that if any amount in excess of the charges permitted by loan are charged, contracted for, or received, the contract shall be void, and the creditor has no right to receive any principal, charges, or recompense whatsoever.

12. The T.I. Credit Insurance Code, § 105.1, *et seq.*, provides that all credit insurances issued in conjunction with a loan must be terminated upon refinancing, and refunds credited prior to the issuance of any new insurance in connection with the refinanced indebtedness. T.I. Code §§ 105.5, 105.8.

13. The F.T.C. Credit Practices Rule, 16 C.F.R. § 444, prohibits non-purchase money security interests in household goods.

---

25 All allegations necessary to bring the creditor and the transaction within the scope of the applicable statute must be made. *See, e.g.,* Herring v. Vadala, 670 F. Supp. 1086 (D. Mass. 1987) (motion to dismiss usury count granted because no allegation or evidence that creditors engaged in the business of making loans in excess of 12%).

26 As of Sept. 30, 1993, federal law prohibits the use of the Rule of 78 on all consumer loans with terms longer than 61 months. 15 U.S.C. § 1615 [reprinted in Appx J.2, *supra*]. Any state law which permits use of the Rule of 78 on such loans would be preempted.

CAUSE OF ACTION

Count I: Consumer Loan Act

14. Upon information and belief, Defendants failed to properly calculate rebates due on unearned charges made in conjunction with Loan I when calculating the pay-off balance to be refinanced with Loan II in violation of T.I. Code § 101.15, thereby imposing charges in excess of those authorized by law.[27]

15. Defendant Beneficent's purported security interest in Plaintiff's household contents is taken in contravention of 16 C.F.R. § 455, and hence is invalid.

16. The property insurance written in conjunction with this loan provides for coverage in excess of $4000 on all household contents, which are not the subject of a valid security interest, and therefore may not be the subject of property insurance issued in connection with a loan written pursuant to T.I. Code § 101, *et seq.* The premium for property insurance is not reasonable in price or coverage and does not bear a reasonable and bona fide relation to the risk of loss. It is therefore not an authorized charge under the terms of T.I. Code § 101.13(d)(2).[28]

17. The taking of such unauthorized charges results in a usurious return to Defendant Beneficent in excess of 10% discount, in violation of T.I. Code § 101.13(a), as a consequence of which this loan is null and void pursuant to § 101.13(c).

Count II: Unconscionability[29]

18. Plaintiff realleges and incorporates by reference the allegations of Paragraphs 1 to 17 herein.

19. Plaintiff alleges that Defendants imposed the excessive insurance charges and determined the repayment terms of Loan II for the express purpose of evading and circumventing the prohibition of T.I. Code § 101.12(c) against taking security interest in real estate for loans in which the amount financed is under $2000, and further to provide additional recompense to Defendants beyond that authorized by law on a loan of the amount sought by Plaintiff, and that Plaintiff obtained no benefit or consideration whatsoever from Defendants' conduct in imposing such terms upon this loan.

20. The circumvention of the provisions of the law was accomplished by imposing insurance charges greatly in excess of that necessary to protect Defendant Beneficent and its legitimate interests in insuring collateral or providing additional security for the debt. Further, said charges were greatly in excess of that necessary to secure repayment of the credit sought by Plaintiff in the event of death, disability, or loss of collateral, and greatly in excess of the amount of the actual credit granted.

21. Defendants willfully misrepresented and deceived Plaintiff as to the repayment terms necessary to provide the credit he requested at the monthly payment level he sought with due allowance for the fullest profit the defendants are permitted by law.

22. Defendants' actions were unconscionable in taking advantage of their superior bargaining power and knowledge to obtain contract terms that were oppressive and could not be understood by Plaintiff.

[*Insert other applicable claims, such as Truth in Lending, breach of fiduciary duty or UDAP claims.*][30]

PRAYER FOR RELIEF

WHEREFORE, Plaintiff requests judgment as follows:

1. An order declaring his obligation to defendant Beneficent to be void and uncollectible and judgment in the amount of all payments made by him on this loan in accordance with T.I. Code § 101.13(c).

2. An order declaring the security interests on Plaintiff's residence and household goods to be void and unenforceable as made in contravention of T.I. Code § 101.12(c) and 16 C.F.R. § 444, respectively.

3. An order declaring the note and security interest to be unconscionable and unenforceable.

4. [*Include a prayer for such other relief as may be appropriate under these or other causes of action.*]

5. Reasonable attorney fees for the prosecution of this action [*should any authority in the jurisdiction authorize fees for an action of this type*].

6. Such other relief as the court deems appropriate.

Dated this __ day of _____, 1994.

_____
Attorney for Plaintiff
Jarndyce & Jarndyce
79 High Street
Jefford, Terra Incognita
(555) 555-1244

L.2.2 Sample Request for Admissions

This sample request for admissions is for demonstration purposes only, and must be adapted by a competent professional to meet the needs of the case and to comply with local law and practice.

These requests seek to establish some of the mathematical issues raised by the preceding pleading. Ways of establishing mathematical issues are discussed in § 4.10, *supra.* Since courts can take judicial notice of mathematics, theoretically an advocate could simply spell some of these calculations out in a brief. But since many judges—and even some opposing counsel—are not familiar with the mechanics of credit math, it will probably make things easier if all the mathematical premises are spelled out.

---

27 When the attorney knows the payment record, either through the client's records or because the ledger card is already available, the proper rebate can be calculated, enabling the advocate to plead that the creditor did not make the rebates, if that is the case. *See* Chapters 4 and 5, *supra.* If the advocate does not have sufficient information, he or she should find out through discovery what the payment record is, and how the defendant calculated the pay-off, including rebates. For sample interrogatories on rebates, see Appx. L.2.2, *infra.*

28 *See* § 8.5.3.4, *supra.*

29 *See* § 11.7, *supra.*

30 *See* §§ 8.7, 10.8, *supra* for other remedies. Note also that a Truth in Lending claim is stated by the facts alleged in Paragraph 14. *See* Steele v. Ford Motor Credit, 783 F.2d 1016 (11th Cir. 1986) (creditor's rounding up to next due date when calculating Rule of 78 rebate resulted in retention of unearned interest, which should have been considered a finance charge in the refinancing; resultant $24 understatement of finance charge was a material violation giving rise to a rescission right).

A request for admissions may be a useful way to do this. It is unlikely that a creditor would admit that they committed usury, or that they misapplied the law. However, there should be little valid ground for denying some of the basic arithmetic groundwork. For example, using the factual situation in the preceding complaint, one of the questions of law is whether the rebate statute permits "rounding up" to the next due date in making the calculation, or requires "rounding back" to the preceding due date in this situation. The requests for admissions (# 5 to 8) will spell out for the court what the proper amount of the rebate should be in either event. The creditor should not have valid objections to an admission like that, since it is a simple question of verifying the math, and makes no judgment about the legal issue. However, if they deny the request without legitimate ground, and you must establish it by other means—through an expert, for example—some jurisdictions may allow the court, in some circumstances, to shift the expense of proving the matter to the party denying the admission. *See, e.g.*, Fed. R. Civ. P. 36.

IN THE DISTRICT COURT OF TERRA INCOGNITA
In and For Sample County

L. L. Pomfret,	)
Plaintiff	)
	)
v.	) REQUEST FOR
	) ADMISSIONS
Beneficent Financial Serv., Inc.,	)
Defendant	)
	)

TO: BENEFICENT FINANCIAL SERVICES INC.

Pursuant to T.I. R. Civ. P. 36, Plaintiff requests that within 30 days after service of this Request for Admissions, Defendant admit for the purpose of this action only, and subject to all pertinent objections to admissibility which may be interposed at the time of trial, the truth of the following matters.

For purposes of these admissions, the term "Loan I" shall refer to the credit transaction entered into between Plaintiff and Defendant on December 10, 1992; and "Loan II" shall refer to the credit transaction entered into between Plaintiff and Defendant on April 15, 1994.

1. Beneficent Finance Corp. is a licensee under the provisions of T.I. Code Chapter 101, and subject to its provisions.

2. Defendant regularly extends consumer credit in the amount of $10,000 or less for which the payment of a finance charge is required.

3. Loans I and II entered into between Plaintiff and Defendant are consumer credit transactions.

4. Plaintiff made all scheduled payments on Loan I as due under the terms of that contract.

5. If rebates to be credited to the balance on Loan I were to be calculated according to the provisions of T.I. Code § 101.15 as of April 10, 1994, the proper rebates to be credited would be as follows:

a.   Finance charge: $192.22
       ($609.65 × .3153[31] = $192.22)

b.   Credit life insurance $ 12.84
       ($40.72 × .3153 = $12.84)

c.   Credit disability insurance $ 25.01
       ($79.34 × .3153 = $25.01)

d.   Household contents insurance $ 29.63
       ($93.96 × .3153 = $29.63)

6. If all finance charge and credit insurance rebates were calculated as of April 10, 1994, the pay-off balance necessary to refinance Loan I would have been $900.30.

$2088.00	total of payments
−928.00	payments made on account
−259.70	finance charge and insurance rebate credits
$ 900.30	pay-off balance

7. If rebates to be credited to the balance on Loan I were to be calculated according to the provisions of T.I. Code § 101.15 as of May 10, 1994, the proper rebates to be credited would be as follows:

a.   Finance charge $173.93
       ($609.65 × .2853[32] = $173.93)

b.   Credit life insurance $11.62
       ($40.72 × .2853 = $11.62)

c.   Credit disability insurance $22.64
       ($79.34 × .2853 = $22.64)

d.   Household contents insurance $26.81
       ($93.96 × .2853 = $26.81)

8. If all finance charge and credit insurance rebates were calculated as of May 10, 1994, the pay-off balance necessary to refinance Loan I would have been $925.

$2088.00	total of payments
−928.00	payments made on account
−235.00	finance charge and insurance rebate credits
$ 925.00	pay-off balance

9. Defendant, in calculating the pay-off balance refinanced by Loan II utilized the Rule of 78, calculated on the unpaid balance of Loan I as of May 10, 1994.

10. Defendant credited the account of Loan I with a rebate of unearned finance charges in the amount of $173.93 in calculating the pay-off balance on Loan I.

---

31 *See* §§ 5.6.2, 5.6.3.3.1, *supra*. From April 10, 1994, the 16th installment due date, the number of periods remaining in the term would be 20 (36 − 16 = 20). The Rule of 78 rebate factor would be

$$\frac{(20)(21)}{(36)(37)} = \frac{420}{1332} = .3153.$$

32 *See* §§ 5.6.2, 5.6.3.3.1, *supra*. From May 10, 1994, the 17th installment due date, the number of periods remaining in the term would be 19 (36 − 17 = 19). The Rule of 78 rebate factor would be

$$\frac{(19)(20)}{(36)(37)} = \frac{380}{1332} = .2853.$$

11. Defendant credited the account of Loan I with a rebate of unearned insurance premiums in the amount of $61.07.

12. In order to repay a loan with an amount financed of $1705 at an actuarial rate of 28.09% over a 36 month period, the borrower's monthly payments would be $70.61, and the total of payments would be $2541.96.[33]

13. If Defendant were to sell the same credit life, disability, and household contents insurance which it sold to Plaintiff in conjunction with Loan II on a 36 month loan with a total of payments of $2541.96, the premium costs would be:

a.	Credit life	$ 49.57
b.	Credit disability	96.59
c.	Household contents	114.38

Attorney for Plaintiff
Jarndyce and Jarndyce
79 High Street
Jefford, Terra Incognita
(555)555-1234

L.2.3 Sample Expert Affidavit: Broker Fee as Hidden Finance Charge

This affidavit is for demonstration only, and must be adapted to meet the needs of the particular case and the rules of the local jurisdiction. The subject of this affidavit is a broker's fee as a hidden finance charge (§ 7.3.2, *supra*). For other ways of proving mathematical issues, see § 4.10, *supra*.

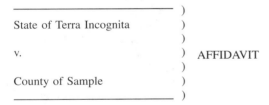

State of Terra Incognita   )
)
v.   )   AFFIDAVIT
)
County of Sample   )
)

Milo M. Bender, being first duly sworn, deposes and says:

SUMMARY

I am an [attorney/accountant] and a specialist in consumer credit transactions. I have analyzed the documents relating to the loan involving Beauregard Derrick and O.L. Derrick and House Lenders, Inc. The documents I have analyzed are attached and listed in Appendix A.[34] I calculated the interest rate of this loan assuming that

1. broker's fees, variously called in the documents "loan brokerage commissions," "brokerage commissions," "loan commissions" or "loan fees" were considered part of the interest on the loan and not part of the principal of the loan, and

2. the loan was to be paid off in accordance with the payment schedule called for in the documents. The results of my calculations are set out below with annual interest rate, rounded to the nearest 100th of a percent.

---

33 The consumer's attorney can easily derive these figures by the use of a financially programmed calculator.

34 The documents are not reprinted in this sample.

Face Amount of Note	Note Interest Rate	Broker's Fee	Loan Amount Excluding Broker's Fee	Interest Rate
$26,000	12%	$3,900	$22,100	18.34%

In the remainder of this affidavit I set out my qualifications and the details of the calculations.

I. Qualifications

I am a graduate of _____ College and _____ Law School. I have been a member of the bar since 1968. In 1974, I joined the staff of the_____ . One of the functions of the_____ is to advise attorneys throughout the country on the legality of consumer credit transactions entered into by their clients. I am a specialist on consumer credit transactions. Since 1974, I have personally analyzed hundreds of consumer credit transactions.

Part of that analysis is a determination of the interest rate charged. In the course of that work, I have studied the various types of interest calculations, and have taught courses to others on the calculation of interest rates.

II. Method of Determining Interest

A. *General Method*

For this loan I assumed

1. that the fees variously called in the documents "loan brokerage commissions," "brokerage commissions," "loan commissions" or "loan fees" were part of the interest on the loan and not part of the principal of the loan; and

2. that the loan was to be paid off according to the payment schedule in the documentation.

I then determined what annual interest rate would pay off the loan according to those assumptions.

To make those interest rate determinations, I used an IBM Personal Computer programmed by a member of our staff to solve the equation set out in Appendix J to "Regulation Z: Truth in Lending," 12 C.F.R. 226. The program uses the iteration process set out in section (b)(9) of Appendix J. To utilize the program, you must enter the following terms:

1. principal of loan

2. length of regular payment periods, e.g., monthly,

3. number of regular payment periods per year,

4. number of regular payments,

5. amount of regular payments,

6. which payments are regular,

7. which payment periods have irregular lengths and what the length is, e.g., first payment not due until one month and 15 days after loan starts,

8. which payments have irregular amounts and what the amounts are, e.g., final payments is balloon payment of $10,000.

The program then determines what the interest rate is for a loan with these terms.

While the equation is complex and the method, which uses iteration, or trial and error, is a lengthy one, the resulting table may be used to test the results with simple arithmetic.

For each loan, the program produces an "amortization table" which pays off the loan according to its terms by using the interest rate that the program has calculated is the correct one.

A sample table is set out as Chart 1. The first vertical column lists the payment number. The second column, labeled Old Balance, lists the loan balance, starting with the original principal of the loan. Column three shows the interest that would be charged on the Old Balance during the payment period. For a regular monthly payment, the interest rate is a twelfth of the annual interest rate determined by the program.

The fourth column shows the scheduled payment. The fifth column shows the New Balance. This is determined by deducting the interest from the amount of the payment and deducting that amount from the Old Balance. Finally, the sixth column records the cumulative sum of the interest payments.

On each horizontal line, you start with the Old Balance from column five of the line above and perform the same set of calculations.

If the interest rate chosen by the program is the correct one, then by making all the scheduled payments the loan should be paid off to a zero balance. The program adjusts the last payment to achieve the zero balance. If no adjustment is needed or the final adjustment is only a few pennies (necessitated by the need to round payments to the nearest cent), then the interest chosen is the correct one, in that it is the rate which will pay off the loan according to its scheduled terms.

If the interest rate chosen had been too high, the loan would not have been paid off fast enough (too much being allocated to interest) and the final payment would have to be increased over the scheduled amount.

If the interest rate chosen was too low, then the loan would have been paid off too fast (not enough being allocated to interest) and the final payment would have to be decreased compared to the scheduled amount.

Thus, the amortization table provides a simple check on the accuracy of the interest determination. Set out below is a simple amortization table illustrating the method and showing that 24.001% is the correct interest determination for a $1,000 loan payable in twelve installments of $94.56 each. Note that in every instance the interest in column three is 2% (1/12 of 24%) of the Old Balance column two.

Before turning to the specifics of the loan in question, two additional factors have to be taken into account.

First, the amortization chart shows that each payment is allocated first to interest, and the remainder to principal. It may be the case in some loans, and is the case in the loan under consideration, that the regular payment will not be sufficient to pay the interest due in any given period. There are two methods of dealing with this situation (called negative amortization), the "actuarial method" and the "U.S. Rule."

Under the actuarial method, the interest remaining unpaid after subtraction of the payment is added to unpaid principal to create the New Balance. Thus, the next month's interest calculation includes payment of interest on the unpaid interest from the previous month. This method results in the payment of "interest on interest" or "compounding," and is prohibited by some state laws.

The other method is referred to as the "U.S. Rule" after the U.S. Supreme Court's ruling in *Story v. Livingston*, 38 US 359 (1839), which held that under common law any unpaid interest is not added to the balance but kept, in effect, in a separate fund. New periodic interest charges are calculated only on the old principal balance. Interest is never charged on unpaid interest. The U.S. Rule is defined in Regulation Z, Appendix J.

In calculating this loan, as the tables indicate, I have used the actuarial method, charging interest on the interest. For example, in

Chart 3 the first month's interest is $664.43, while the payment is only $260.00. The balance on which the next month's interest is calculated increases by the difference ($404.33). As a result, a *lower* interest *rate* will amortize a loan with this initial principal, total interest amount and payment schedule than if the U.S. Rule were used. That is because that rate is applied against an increasingly larger balance. However, if the state of Terra Incognita prohibits compounding, then a higher interest rate would be needed to amortize the same loan under the U.S. Rule, because the same dollar amount of interest would be earned, but it would be calculated for each payment period on lower principal balances than under the actuarial rule. Thus, by using the actuarial rule, I have chosen the method which gives the lowest interest rate.

Another factor which must be taken into account is that the period between the time interest begins to run and the first payment is more than a month. The program and other calculations which I have made count the extra days beyond a month as one thirtieth of a month and multiply the original principal balance by the sum of the monthly interest rate plus the number of extra days divided by 30 times the monthly rate.

Thus, if the first period was one month and fifteen days, the regular monthly interest rate was 2% and the principal was $1,000.00, then the interest for the first month would be $30, calculated as follows: $1000 × [.02 + (15 ÷ 30 × .02)] or $1000 × .03 = $30.00.

B. *Derrick Loan*

The Note for this loan shows a $26,000.00 loan at 12% interest with 35 payments of $260.00 and a final balloon payment of interest and the remaining principal. All payments are monthly except the first payment which is due one month and twenty-nine days after interest begins to accrue.

The Borrowers' Final Closing Statement shows a loan commission of $3,900.00. If the loan commission is considered interest, there is a principal of $22,100.00. The program was therefore instructed to find an interest rate which would amortize a $22,100 loan to zero in accordance with the payment plan required by the Note. But to enter the payment plan of the Note it is necessary to know the dollar amount of the final balloon payment, which is expressed in the Note only as interest and remaining principal.

To determine the final payment, I first amortized a $26,000.00 loan under the terms of the Note. That table shows a final payment due of $26,615.80. That table is set forth in Chart 2.

Having determined the actual payment schedule provided by the Note, I could then calculate the interest rate on the loan considering the broker's fee as interest, using the actuarial method and the payment plan of the Note. Chart 3, is the amortization table for this loan. It shows an interest rate of 18.3447%, with an adjustment to the final payment of $.05.

Further affiant sayeth not.

_____

Milo M. Bender

Subscribed and sworn to before me this _____ day of _____ , 1994.

_____

Notary Public For the
State of Terra Incognita
My Commission Expires:

_____

CHART 1
Amortization Table
$1,000 Principal
12 Payments of $94.56

12 Periods/Year
Term is 12 Months
Finance Charge is $134.72
Amount Financed is $1000
Total of Payments is $1134.72

Actuarial Interest Rate is 24.001% yearly or 2.000083 % per period

Amortization Chart based on Rounding Nearest Follows:

Pay #	Old-Balance	+ Interest	− Payment	= New Balance	[IntEarn]
1	$1000.00	$20.00	$94.56	$925.44	$20.00
2	$925.44	$18.51	$94.56	$849.39	$38.51
3	$849.39	$16.99	$94.56	$771.82	$55.50
4	$771.82	$15.44	$94.56	$692.70	$70.94
5	$692.70	$13.85	$94.56	$611.99	$84.79
6	$611.99	$12.24	$94.56	$529.67	$97.03
7	$529.67	$10.59	$94.56	$445.70	$107.62
8	$445.70	$8.91	$94.56	$360.05	$116.53
9	$360.05	$7.20	$94.56	$272.69	$123.73
10	$272.69	$5.45	$94.56	$183.58	$129.18
11	$183.58	$3.67	$94.56	$92.69	$132.85
12	$92.69	$1.85	$94.54	$0.00	$134.70

Last Payment adjusted by $ − .02 to bring Amortization to zero.

CHART 2
Amortization of Note
$26,000 Principal
35 payments of $260
Final Payment of Interest and Principal
First Period—1 month, 29 days at 12%

Actuarial Interest Rate is 12% yearly or 1% per period

Amortization Chart based on Rounding Down Follows:

Pay #	Old-Balance	+ Interest	− Payment	= New Balance	[IntEarn]
1	$26000.00	$511.33	$260.00	$26251.33	$511.33
2	$26251.33	$262.51	$260.00	$26253.84	$773.84
3	$26253.84	$262.53	$260.00	$26256.37	$1036.37
4	$26256.37	$262.56	$260.00	$26258.93	$1298.93
5	$26258.93	$262.58	$260.00	$26261.51	$1561.51
6	$26261.51	$262.61	$260.00	$26264.12	$1824.12
7	$26264.12	$262.64	$260.00	$26266.76	$2086.76
8	$26266.76	$262.66	$260.00	$26269.42	$2349.42
9	$26269.42	$262.69	$260.00	$26272.11	$2612.11
10	$26272.11	$262.72	$260.00	$26274.83	$2874.83
11	$26274.83	$262.74	$260.00	$26277.57	$3137.57
12	$26277.57	$262.77	$260.00	$26280.34	$3400.34
13	$26280.34	$262.80	$260.00	$26283.14	$3663.14
14	$26283.14	$262.83	$260.00	$26285.97	$3925.97
15	$26285.97	$262.85	$260.00	$26288.82	$4188.82
16	$26288.82	$262.88	$260.00	$26291.70	$4451.70
17	$26291.70	$262.91	$260.00	$26294.61	$4714.61
18	$26294.61	$262.94	$260.00	$26297.55	$4977.55
19	$26297.55	$262.97	$260.00	$26300.52	$5240.52
20	$26300.52	$263.00	$260.00	$26303.52	$5503.52
21	$26303.52	$263.03	$260.00	$26306.55	$5766.55
22	$26306.55	$263.06	$260.00	$26309.61	$6029.61
23	$26309.61	$263.09	$260.00	$26312.70	$6292.70
24	$26312.70	$263.12	$260.00	$26315.82	$6555.82
25	$26315.82	$263.15	$260.00	$26318.97	$6818.97
26	$26318.97	$263.18	$260.00	$26322.15	$7082.15
27	$26322.15	$263.22	$260.00	$26325.37	$7345.37
28	$26325.37	$263.25	$260.00	$26328.62	$7608.62
29	$26328.62	$263.28	$260.00	$26331.90	$7871.90
30	$26331.90	$263.31	$260.00	$26335.21	$8135.21
31	$26335.21	$263.35	$260.00	$26338.56	$8398.56
32	$26338.56	$263.38	$260.00	$26341.94	$8661.94
33	$26341.94	$263.41	$260.00	$26345.35	$8925.35
34	$26345.35	$263.45	$260.00	$26348.80	$9188.80
35	$26348.80	$263.48	$260.00	$26352.28	$9452.28
36	$26352.28	$263.52	$26615.80	$0.00	$9715.80

CHART 3
Interest Determination and Amortization Table Note
Less Broker's Fee
(1st period 1 month and 29 days)

Actuarial Interest Rate is 18.3447% yearly or 1.528725% per period

Amortization Chart based on Rounding Nearest Follows:

Pay #	Old-Balance	+ Interest	− Payment	= New Balance	[IntEarn]
1	$22100.00	$664.43	$260.00	$22504.43	$664.43
2	$22504.43	$344.03	$260.00	$22588.46	$1008.46
3	$22568.46	$345.32	$260.00	$22673.78	$1353.78
4	$22673.78	$346.62	$260.00	$22760.40	$1700.40
5	$22760.40	$347.94	$260.00	$22848.34	$2048.34
6	$22848.34	$349.29	$260.00	$22937.63	$2397.63
7	$22937.63	$350.65	$260.00	$23028.28	$2748.28
8	$23028.28	$352.04	$260.00	$23120.32	$3100.32
9	$23120.32	$353.45	$260.00	$23213.77	$3453.77
10	$23213.77	$354.87	$260.00	$23308.64	$3808.64
11	$23308.64	$356.33	$260.00	$23404.97	$4164.97
12	$23404.97	$357.80	$260.00	$23502.77	$4522.77
13	$23502.77	$359.29	$260.00	$23602.06	$4882.06
14	$23602.06	$360.81	$260.00	$23702.87	$5242.87
15	$23702.87	$362.35	$260.00	$23805.22	$5605.22
16	$23805.22	$363.92	$260.00	$23909.14	$5969.14
17	$23909.14	$365.51	$260.00	$24014.65	$6334.65
18	$24014.65	$367.12	$260.00	$24121.77	$6701.77
19	$24121.77	$368.76	$260.00	$24230.53	$7070.53
20	$24230.53	$370.42	$260.00	$24340.95	$7440.95
21	$24340.95	$372.11	$260.00	$24453.06	$7813.06
22	$24453.06	$373.82	$260.00	$24566.88	$8186.88
23	$24566.88	$375.56	$260.00	$24682.44	$8562.44
24	$24682.44	$377.33	$260.00	$24799.77	$8939.77
25	$24799.77	$379.12	$260.00	$24918.89	$9318.89
26	$24918.89	$380.94	$260.00	$25039.83	$9699.83
27	$25039.83	$382.79	$260.00	$25162.62	$10082.62
28	$25162.62	$384.67	$260.00	$25287.29	$10467.29
29	$25287.29	$386.57	$260.00	$25413.86	$10853.86
30	$25413.86	$388.51	$260.00	$25542.37	$11242.37
31	$25542.37	$390.47	$260.00	$25672.84	$11632.84
32	$25672.84	$392.47	$260.00	$25805.31	$12025.31
33	$25805.31	$394.49	$260.00	$25939.80	$12419.80
34	$25939.80	$396.55	$260.00	$26076.35	$12816.35
35	$26076.35	$398.64	$260.00	$26214.99	$13214.99
36	$26214.99	$400.76	$26615.75	$0.00	$13615.75

Last payment adjusted by $ − .05 to bring Amortization to zero.

L.2.4 Expert Witness Testimony Regarding Loan Splitting (Besta v. Beneficial Financial)

This sample testimony relates to the type of factual situation presented by Besta v. Beneficial Finance, § 8.5.4.2, *supra,* an insurance packing case.

This sample is not a verbatim transcript.[35] It is merely a guide as to the kind of information which may prove useful. Readers should make sure they conform any relevant information to the facts of their particular case, and that all rules of evidence in their jurisdiction are followed, including qualifying witnesses, laying the foundation, relevance, etc.

DIRECT EXAMINATION

BY PLAINTIFF'S ATTORNEY

[Plaintiff's attorney elicits information on witness' educational and professional background to lay foundation.]

Q. Have you familiarized yourself with the plaintiff's documents?

A. I'm not sure I familiarized myself with everything that's been admitted as an exhibit. I know I have heard of the loan document that she has.

Q. Did you advise either Plaintiff or her [referring] attorney regarding this document?

DEFENDANT'S ATTORNEY: Your Honor, at this time we'd like to interpose an objection. We believe the purpose of the testimony of this witness is to testify as to the legal conclusions that she's drawn from the documents.

If she understands facts, short of what her legal conclusions might be, that might be an appropriate subject to testify about for an attorney; but for an attorney to testify about questions of law to the finder of fact I believe is not permitted under Rule 703, and I'd cite to you Mark and Company, Inc. versus Diners Club, 55 F.2d 505. It was in error to submit testimony to the Court concerning contract obligations.

And also I'd cite another case wherein their statement of expert testimony on the law by a lawyer is to be excluded, because the trial judge does not need—nor may he or she defer to the legal judgment of the witness and opinion from this witness for this purpose. It is entirely inappropriate, unusual and not permitted under the rules.

THE COURT: You may answer.

THE WITNESS: I made some suggestions to the attorney.

Defendant's Attorney enters continuing objection.

BY PLAINTIFF'S ATTORNEY:

Q. As a result of reviewing this document, did you make some calculations, financial calculations, analysis of this document?

A. Yes.

* * *

Q. And have you done this type of analysis as a part of your job as an attorney since graduation from law school?

A. Yes.

* * *

BY PLAINTIFF'S ATTORNEY:

Q. Could you describe or define what insurance packing consists of?

A. Insurance packing generically is the practice of loading a loan with insurance-related charges, particularly with respect to insurance charges that are of marginal or no usefulness to the borrower.

The reason that it is somewhat of a pejorative term is that the loan is packed because insurance is so profitable for the lender. It's profitable in a couple of ways which relate to both the way interest is calculated on the loan and the way the amount of credit insurance premiums themselves are calculated.

Credit insurance premiums, the rate for the premiums are established by state law or the state insurance commissioner, but they are ordinarily written on the total of payments of a loan.

The total of payments, of course, includes interest, and also includes the insurance premiums, so that you have this cyclical impact that the larger the loan, the larger the credit insurance premiums and the larger the interest, and it just keeps building on itself that way.

So what the concept of insurance packing is, is taking a loan where the actual proceeds to the borrower, the amount of money that the borrower actually gets the benefit of, is a relatively small amount, but the loan is packed with the insurance charges to make it a much more expensive loan for the borrower; and because of both the interest return on the loan and the commissions or other creditor compensation on the insurance, the lender gets sort of doubly blessed by it.

Q. How does that apply to the Plaintiff's Exhibit 16, the Betty Besta loan?

A. Well, if you look at the loan, the amount that Betty actually got the use of was the $1,150 to pay off an old loan, and $564 advance. The rest of the charges in this loan are charges that the lender put on the loan.

Q. Have you prepared an exhibit to describe or show that more clearly for the Court?

Exhibit 69	
Cash Advanced	$1440.22
Disability Insurance	96.31
Credit Life	49.42
Property Insurance	114.05
AMOUNT FINANCED	$1700.00
FINANCE CHARGE	$ 834.43
TOTAL OF PAYMENTS	$2534.43
PAYMENT SCHEDULE	36 monthly payments at $70.40/mo
ANNUAL PERCENTAGE RATE	28.09%
Cash Advanced	$1444.46
Disability Insurance	96.59
Credit Life Insurance	49.57
Property Insurance	114.38

---

35 The sample is, however, an edited excerpt of the testimony relied upon by the Eighth Circuit in the *Besta* case. The testimony was provided by a staff attorney at the National Consumer Law Center. Thanks to Plaintiff's attorney, Ken Dolezal, for providing the transcript.

AMOUNT FINANCED	$1705.00
FINANCE CHARGE	836.88
TOTAL OF PAYMENTS	$2541.88
PAYMENT SCHEDULE	36 monthly payments at $70.61/mo
ANNUAL PERCENTAGE RATE	28.09%

Q. I hand you what's been marked Plaintiff's Exhibit 69.

A. Yes.

Q. Are those calculations which you made recently in preparation of your testimony here today?

A. Yes.

Q. Regarding Exhibit 69, would you explain what you're attempting to demonstrate to the Court?

A. What that is showing is the impact of stretching the term of this loan to six years. What I did was look at the actual amount that the borrower needed there and calculated what it would have cost at the interest rate that they charged, had it been written for a three-year term.

Q. How did you determine the actual amount the borrower needed?

A. Well, in my mind, the critical factor here is that the amount financed at $2,000 becomes a critical threshold in Iowa, because under $2,000, lenders on these kinds of loans are not permitted to take a security interest in residential real estate.

So that to the extent that it would have been a normal thing for this loan to have been written for a three-year term, the amount financed would not have exceeded $2,000, and this could not have been a real estate secured loan.

Q. All right. How did you arrive at the amount financed for this loan?

A. In calculating the amount of the credit insurance premiums that can be charged, they are written on a total of payments, so you have to know the total of payments to get to the premiums; you have to know the premiums to get to the total of payment, so one way to do it is to take an educated guess as to one of the critical numbers and then do a series of iterations.

Q. Would you define iteration, please?

A. Start with a figure and calculate what the rates would be. In this case, I started with the amount financed, taking an educated guess as to what would work backwards to an actual net proceeds in the approximate amount of what she got when credit insurance was calculated.

Q. So the first item you did, you estimated the amount financed, and you estimated that amount to be in the top portion of the page, $1,700; is that correct?

A. Yes.

Q. Secondly, you assumed the A.P.R.?

A. Then I just figured out what a three-year loan at the contract rate—at the contract A.P.R. of 28.09% to see what the monthly payments, the finance charge and the total of payment would be.

Q. Okay.

A. And then that gave me the figures to work out the insurance premiums that would be written on the loan, and then that in turn showed me that what remained was in the neighborhood of what Betty's benefit was, and the amount financed was still under the $2,000 threshold.

Q. Let me go to the credit life insurance. How did you arrive at the $49.42 that you allocated for the charge for credit life insurance?

A. The maximum rate for single declining term coverage, which is what was written on this loan is 65 cents in Iowa. The formula for figuring that out is 65 cents per 100, per year, with $100 being based on total payments. And so in using that formula, I arrived at $49.42 on the total payments of $2,534.43.

Q. And how did you arrive at the next number, the credit A and H?

A. In Iowa, the maximum rate for 14-day retroactive coverage, which is what was written in this case, is set by the insurance commissioner. For a three-year term, it's $3.80 per $100 of loan, again, written on the total of payments. So using that formula, it comes out to $96.31.

Q. And lastly, then, the property insurance.

A. Property insurance is not rate regulated. I simply used the charge that I understand they used in connection with Miss Besta's loan cost, which was $1.50 per 100 per year.

Q. So by doing those calculations, you then were able to determine an actual net proceeds or what Betty Besta would be entitled to?

A. Yes. Without changing that, the amount financed was below the $2,000 threshold.

Q. And that amount, the actual net proceeds came out to $1,440.22?

A. Yes.

Q. And that was actually $2.01 less than what was the actual net proceeds in Plaintiff's Exhibit 16, the loan statement; is that correct?

A. Right.

Q. So then on the bottom half of the page you've done the same thing. By using an amount financed of $1,705, you came out with actual net proceeds greater than the amount of this Plaintiff's Exhibit 16?

A. Right. So that to come out with—I could have continued and obtained an amount of net proceeds exactly equal to her other loan, but it's clear that her monthly payments would have been in the neighborhood of $70 and some cents, and that in either case the amount financed would not have exceeded $2,000 had this been written for a three-year term, which is more common for loans of this size.

Q. Now, this does not take into consideration at all the fact that Betty Besta had a prior Beneficial loan which was refinanced; is that correct?

A. No. That's simply reflected in the actual net proceeds, the payoff on that.

Q. Could you define the term reverse competition?

A. Reverse competition is one of the things that explains why credit insurance is generally considered to be not a good deal for borrowers, in that it's insurance which creditors, in offering it, don't look for the lowest-cost insurance to offer their borrowers. They, rather, look for higher-cost insurance, because they get commissions and other forms of compensation, sometimes in the form of rebates.

So that the higher the cost of the insurance, the more profit they get. For the borrowers, generally it's a sideline which they aren't really focusing on, number 1; and number 2, even if they did look at the actual dollar amount, they have no way of knowing if it's a good buy or bad buy.

Q. Going back to Plaintiff's Exhibit 69, the monthly payments that you calculated would be actually less than the payments in the actual loan that the Plaintiff took out.

A. Yes.

Q. By what amount?

A. On an amount financed of $1,700, payments would been $70.40; and on $1,705 the approximate monthly payment would have been $70.61.

Q. And what term—how many months would that payment have been necessary?

A. This was calculated for a 36-month loan.

Q. Okay.

A. I might add that real estate costs were excluded from this, because they couldn't have been included, had it not been more than a $2,000 amount financed, so that's why those figures are excluded from these calculations.

Q. What was the effect of making this a 72-month loan?

A. The effect of making it a 72-month loan was to increase, obviously, the interest by doubling the term, which also increased the amount of the insurance premiums, which had the effect of throwing the amount financed over the $2,000 threshold, below which they could not have taken a security interest in her house.

PLAINTIFF'S ATTORNEY: I have no further questions.

CROSS-EXAMINATION

BY DEFENDANT'S ATTORNEY:

Q. Have you attempted to determine whether the charges for insurance on Exhibit 16 are within the permissible limits of the statutes that apply to those rates?

A. Yes, I have. And the rates that are charged do not exceed the 65 cents per 100 per year maximum for life. My recollection is that for a six-year loan disability, it's $5.10 per 100, and they do fall within those dollar limitations on the rate.

Q. So as far as what's permitted by the statute, it says insurance charges are permitted under this?

A. So far as what is permitted by the statute that sets the maximum rate per 100 for calculating the premium.

Q. So the rates charged here are permitted by law?

A. The premium rate is within that permitted by law.

Q. On all three of the insurance charges?

A. Property insurance is not rate regulated, so that would be a matter of contract.

Q. Do you know whether this rate that has been used here was approved by the insurance commissioner?

A. On property insurance?

Q. Yes.

A. I don't know. Since it's not rate regulated, I just don't know.

Q. So at least as far as you know, there's no violation of any statute that you're aware of with respect to the property insurance rate?

A. I didn't say that.

Q. Well, let me ask you then—

A. The rates, I said, are all right. Total premiums are a matter of different statutes.

Q. Well, do you know of any violation of any statute with respect to the rates of insurance charged here?

A. Not the rate, per se, to the extent that there's a mathematical calculation of 65 cents per 100 per year. No, I did not see any.

Q. And there are probably other lawyers in the country who may spend as much time, but you spend a lot of your time on that?

A. I spend all of my time.

Q. All of your time. Okay. Are you familiar with a case where the State of Indiana sued Beneficial with respect to the sale of household insurance?

A. Yes, I am, and actually have some opinions on the analysis in that case.

Q. Well, were you a counsel in that case?

A. No.

Q. Did you consult with them?

A. No.

Q. You don't agree with the result, apparently?

A. The Court did not discuss a couple of things that under the Indiana law they were supposed to discuss.

Q. You're aware, however, that the Court in Indiana found that there were distinctions between the household contents policy sold by Beneficial and the homeowner's policy that was sold by another insurance company to that customer?

A. Yes.

Q. And one of those was that the policy sold by Beneficial was a full replacement value of the policy. Were you aware of that distinction drawn by the Court?

A. Yes.

Q. Now, in this case, have you reviewed the household contents policy—

A. No, I haven't.

Q. —sold by Beneficial?

A. No, I haven't.

Q. Have you reviewed the homeowner's policy?

A. No, I haven't.

Q. Well, let me ask you to assume, as the evidence has previously demonstrated, that the household contents policy sold by Beneficial was a full replacement value, and that the homeowner's sold by IMT in this case to Miss Besta was not. Can you do that for me?

A. Yes.

Q. So at least with respect to that factor, if that was reviewed by the Indiana Court of Appeals and relied on, that would be the same factor we have here, isn't it?

A. I presume so.

Q. Are you aware that in this Indiana case, another factor that was considered by the Court in determining whether the sale of household insurance was proper under the statute was whether there was a deductible amount?

A. Yes.

Q. And you haven't reviewed the policies here with respect to a deductible either?

A. No.

Q. Let me ask you to assume that the evidence would show that in the policy sold by Beneficial there was no deductible except for $25 burglary deductible, and in the homeowner's policy there was a deductible of $100. Can you make that assumption for me?

A. Yes.

Q. Then in this case, the sale of the household contents policy to Mrs. Besta would again have one of the same distinctions drawn by the Indiana Court of Appeals in that case; correct?

A. Yes.

Q. Are you also aware that in that Indiana Court of Appeals case, that the Court found that there was a greater protection against certain natural hazards such as flooding and water damage in Beneficial's that were not present in the homeowner's policy? Are you aware of that?

A. I don't remember the whole list. I remember there were a number of coverage distinctions that the Court made in the case.

Q. Do you remember that one?

A. I don't have independent recollection, but I'll trust you.

Q. Let me ask you to assume that the policies in this case would make that same difference with respect to flood and water damage. Then we'd have present here another factor that was the same as the factors considered by the Indiana Court of Appeals; correct?

A. Yes.

Q. And also in that case it was established that the customer was not required to purchase the insurance in order to obtain the loan, do you recall that?

A. Yes.

Q. And that's the same situation we have here; correct?

A. I think that's a question of fact that I can't—I haven't heard the testimony.

Q. So with respect to the decision of the Indiana Court of Appeals about the propriety of the sale of the household contents policy, we have, from your own testimony at least some of the same distinctions and perhaps all of the distinctions?

A. Right. There were a number of things that the Court didn't discuss, or evidence wasn't put on that would affect it as well; but as to the distinctions you've mentioned, yes.

Q. You've apparently talked with the attorneys who represented Indiana to know that there are things in the record that weren't discussed?

A. Not things in the record. I'm sorry. Some things that could have been in the record or some issues of law that weren't discussed.

Q. But at least do you know of any other state court decision that says that the sale of the household contents policy by Beneficial is violative of the Code?

A. By Beneficial?

A. All of the cases that I'm aware of have been settled without reaching a decision, and I don't know who all the lenders have been.

Q. But do you know of any with respect to Beneficial about the sale of household contents insurance in Iowa?

A. Going to a decision, no. Whether there have been unreported cases that haven't been told to me in the last two years since I left, I don't know.

THE COURT: Do you know of any cases in any jurisdiction?

THE WITNESS: On the insurance packing, there is. Actually there are a number of cases that are pending.

THE COURT: Any decisions?

THE WITNESS: Any decision? There was a preliminary injunction decision issued in a Wisconsin insurance packing case. There are also cases—

THE COURT: But are there any final decisions that you know of?

THE WITNESS: Not on insurance packing, per se. There are cases that hold that insuring—writing property insurance for greater than the value of the collateral, for example, is a pretext to usury, and for that there are a number of cases. There are a number of cases that don't discuss insurance packing as a practice, but discuss over-insurance as a pretext for usury or as a violation of specific insurance regulations.

BY DEFENDANT'S ATTORNEY:

Q. This case you're talking about in Wisconsin involved Thorp; right?

A. Yes.

Q. And that's similar to the one that's reported in the Wall Street Journal article?[36]

A. Yes. I think the Wisconsin case was.

Q. One of the prime factors in that was that the amount of the insurance was larger than the amount of the loan; isn't that true?

A. The relationship of the premiums to the proceeds is one thing. Also, the voluminousness of it was an issue. The insurance packing issue is not that you pay more for insurance than for your loan; it's that you pay for more insurance than you need to be paying for insurance; and in that case, there are also allegations from a number of borrowers that they didn't know what they were doing.

Q. Well, isn't that what that article discusses, is borrowing more for insurance than borrowing money? Isn't that the problem that was connected with Thorp according to this article?

A. The pleadings on the insurance packing cases have not relied on the fact that the premiums were greater than the proceeds—none of the pleadings that I have seen.

Q. I'm trying to ask you about this article.

A. The examples that are chosen in here say—the first one they do. I don't remember what other ones they put in there.

Q. Well, please review the article then.

A. Okay.

THE COURT: Why don't you point out what you're getting at in the article.

DEFENDANT'S ATTORNEY: Well, I think the point is, Your Honor, the problem with Thorp—and my reason for wanting to keep this out of the entire proceeding is I believe what is discussed here is that Thorp was selling far more insurance premiums which they were selling for the amount of the loan, which is not the case we have in this situation, which, I think, that's what the Wisconsin Attorney General was after, and that's clearly not the case as we have here in the Indiana Court of Appeals case, but determines that the sale of household insurance is entirely within the UCC.

THE COURT: You're familiar with the article. Is that your understanding of its portent?

THE WITNESS: Actually, no, it's not my understanding of its portent. My understanding is that he chose these examples for the dramatic impact, not for their impact on the legal issues, and that's not what the pleadings filed by the Wisconsin attorney general—or any of the other insurance packing pleadings I've seen have said.

There is one case where it was $10,000, with $5,000 worth of insurance. On the last page of the article. The client had a $10,000 loan, and packed insurance premiums of $5,200 on a $10,000 loan.

BY DEFENDANT'S ATTORNEY:

Q. Well, let's take the sale of household insurance or the household contents insurance. Have you seen that before in other transactions?

A. Taking property insurance on collateral is common.

Q. And that's something that many borrowers agree to and many lenders offer and sell?

A. Many lenders offer and sell them. Most of the clients that I have had haven't known much of anything about the insurance in their loan, they just sign the papers, the clients I have talked with.

Q. Those are the clients that come to you for legal assistance?

A. Yes.

---

36 *See* § 8.5.2.4, *supra.* This article was discussed by an earlier witness.

Q. And have you talked with any other borrowers who aren't people who come to you for legal assistance?

A. You know, friends and people who share their experiences with the car dealer, that sort of thing.

Q. So you're aware, anyway, it's very common that this household insurance is sold throughout this loan industry?

A. Yes. And as I just explained, there are also cases that recognize the potential for danger with insurance loans written—or insurance premiums written in connection with loans.

Q. And it's the same with respect to the credit life and credit disability, isn't it, that there are a number of people in the industry who are accepting from their customers the decisions to purchase this insurance, and there are also many customers who were purchasing those kinds of insurance; correct?

A. Penetration rates are very high for credit insurance among the consumer finance industries.

Q. How high would you say?

A. There are some data that indicate as much as 85 to 95 percent for credit life, somewhat lower for A and H, and somewhat lower than that for property insurance. There are two ways to read that, and the FTC, in fact, has read that not to say it's popular, but that it's pushed and that it's often not voluntary.

Q. So are you of the opinion that all of these lenders who are selling credit life, credit disability and property insurance are not honest and fair minded people?

A. As to credit insurance, outside of the industry, virtually all of the literature that I've read is very critical of it as being overpriced for consumers and extremely profitable for lenders.

Q. Are you saying that no honest and fair person would accept such terms as a sale to a customer?

A. No customer.

Q. No. Are you saying that no person who would be an honest and fair lender would accept those terms to sell to a customer?

A. I think that there are strong economic pressure on lenders to move this insurance.

Q. I don't believe that's necessarily responsive to my question. My question is whether in your opinion that no honest and fair person would ever make such a deal from the perspective of the lender?

A. Personally, I don't believe that credit insurance is fair to borrowers, which would mean that lenders are not dealing fairly with borrowers by not telling them how expensive this is in relation to their benefits, or in this case, that charging—charging a six-year loan with all of the credit insurance charges that are going to take her loan over a critical threshold, it's going to put her house at issue.

There's a Colorado case, for example, that says there's a duty to disclose information that might affect a borrower's decision as to credit insurance, and that seems to me that that would have been a critical disclosure to make to this client; and that perhaps by not telling her the difference, not telling her the impact of spreading this loan over six years—that doesn't strike me as being—dealing fairly with her.

Q. Well, so you're saying that no honest or fair person would accept terms like this?

A. This particular case, this loan?

Q. Yes.

A. I don't think so.

Q. You've never seen any other loans like this one, is that what you're saying?

A. I have seen some that are being contested as being unconscionable in other courts and have been packed to the point where people are risking losing their homes for amounts that they should not have been, that are being challenged as being unconscionable or in violation of unfair deceptive acts and practices.

REDIRECT EXAMINATION

BY PLAINTIFF'S ATTORNEY:

Q. I'd like to refer back to your Exhibit 69, and does not 69 allow for Beneficial to provide all of the insurance they provided in the actual loan to Betty Besta only over a 36-month period instead of 72-month period?

A. Right. It's the same rate loan, same full coverage on the total of payments; same policies with same coverage.

Q. So all of these factors about the Indiana case really are irrelevant when you look at Plaintiff's Exhibit 69, because you're saying, hey, we can assume that we've given all of these benefits?

A. Yes.

L.2.5 Sample Expert Report on the Economic Cost of Debt Consolidation

This report analyzes the economic impact on a consumer when she was convinced to obtain a new mortgage loan through a broker that had connections with a home improvement company/mortgage loan company. She would have qualified for an unsecured loan through a local bank. Nevertheless, the broker obtained a new mortgage loan to fund $3060 worth of home improvements. As part of the deal, the mortgage company refinanced her first mortgage loan and other debts and stretched them out over a 240 month term. Note that the exhibits referred to are not attached to this sample report.

REPORT OF EXPERT WITNESS

1. I am an attorney on the staff of the National Consumer Law Center, 1629 K Street, N.W., Suite 600, Washington, D.C. 20006 and I focus on consumer credit transactions. My credentials are attached as Exhibit F.

2. To render the opinions described in this Report, I relied on the following documents:

A. Complaint;

B. Letter Advising Customer of Changed Amount of Cash to Borrower (R. 55);

C. Truth In Lending Disclosure Statement of June 15, 1995 (R. 56);

D. Revised HUD-1 Settlement Statement (R. 57–58);

E. Credit Report regarding consumer dated June 6, 1995 (R. 107–110);

F. Hand-written letter from consumer dated June 15, 1995 (R. 111);

G. _____ Bank billing statement of Apr. 9, 1995;

H. Uniform Residential Loan Application of June 2, 1995 (hand-written) (R. 152–154);

I. Credit Application (undated, typed) (R. 102–103);

J. _____, Inc. Home Improvement Agreement of May 22, 1995;

K. _____ Home Improvement Retail Installment Contract of Apr. 22, 1991;

L. _____ Contract and Disclosure Statement of June 12, 1993;

M. HUD-1 Settlement Statement of June 15, 1995 (R. 41–43);

N. Creditor Payoff letter of June 15, 1995;

O. Payoff letter from _____ of June 14, 1995 (R. 36);

P. Note of Feb. 9, 1977 between Consumer and _____ Mortgage Co.;

Q. Note of June 15, 1995 between Consumer and _____ Funding Co. (R. 10–11);

R. Deed of Trust of June 15, 1995 between Consumer and _____ Funding Co. (R. 12–19);

S. Consumer Credit Home Improvement Contract between Consumer and _____ Home Remodelers of June 16, 1996;

T. Affidavit of Ex-employee dated Jan. 27, 1999;

U. Affidavit of Ex-employee dated Feb. 12, 1999;

V. Affidavit of Defendant dated Feb. 17, 1999;

W. Computer printouts of loan amortizations attached as Exhibits A–E.

3. To render this report, I relied upon the following publications:

A. National Consumer Law Center, *Cost of Credit: Regulation and Legal Challenges* (2d ed. 2000 and Supp.); National Consumer Law Center, *Truth in Lending* (5th ed. 2003); National Consumer Law Center, *Unfair and Deceptive Acts and Practices* (5th ed. 2001 and Supp.);

B. Excerpts from Kirsch, Jungeblut, Jenkins, and Kolstad, *Adult Literacy on America: A First Look at the National Literacy Survey*, National Center for Education Statistics, U.S. Department of Education (Sept. 1993).

4. To render this report, I relied upon the following equipment and computer programs:

A. Hewlett Packard Business Calculator 10B;

B. An APR Program developed by the National Consumer Law Center. It is copyrighted and is sold in connection with NCLC's *Truth In Lending* (3d ed. 1999 & Supp.). The program prompts the user to enter the amount financed. It then asks for the monthly payments. The program will then calculate the APR based upon that information and print out an amortization chart of the loan.

5. In my opinion, the loan made to Consumer on June 15, 1995 by _____ Funding Company through the mortgage broker _____ Mortgage Services, Inc. which financed the cost of home improvements made or to be made by _____ Home Remodelers Inc. and which refinanced mortgage and consumer debts of Ms. Consumer:

A. Did not improve Ms. Consumer's financial circumstances and, in fact, put her in greater debt than she was in prior to the loan;

B. Cost her approximately twice what she would have paid if she had continued to pay her first mortgage and consumer debts to their completion;

C. Did not reduce Ms. Consumer's monthly payments in the long-term and, in fact, increased them over the 240 month term from what she would have been paying approximately 3 1/2 years after the 20 year loan was made.

6. Bases of opinions:

A. Loan of June 15, 1995 refinanced a much more favorable mortgage into a more expensive one. _____

Mortgage Co. loan of Feb. 9, 1977 was a 9% annual interest loan with monthly payments of $338.10 (PI). Approximately 222 payments had been made as of June 15, 1995, leaving only 138 to go. The new mortgage loan at 10.95% annual interest extended the remaining indebtedness of $28,989.56 (compare original principal of $56,000) back out to 240 months. This generated approximately $42,589.15 in interest that would be earned over the life of the new loan on this portion of the loan. In contrast, Ms. Consumer would have paid only about $17,651.23 in interest over 138 months if she had continued paying on the _____ Mortgage Co. loan.[37]

B. To finance the home improvements costing $3,060, Ms. Consumer paid a broker fee of 8% on $56,000 or $4,480 and closing costs of $1,231, totaling $5,711.00.

C. Ms. Consumer's monthly mortgage and consumer loan debt load just prior to June 15, 1995 was as follows:

_____ Mortgage Co:	$338.10 (PI)	Remaining term: 138 mos.
	$121.00 (TI)[38]	
Car loan:	$301.07[39]	Remaining term: 44 mos.
Credit card:	$45.00[40]	Remaining term: 58 mos.[41]
Finance Co. 1:	$124.33[42]	Remaining term: 10 mos.[43]

---

37 This figure is calculated by subtracting the approximate amount of interest paid as of June 15, 1995 ($62,050.75) from the total that would have been earned on the _____ Mortgage Co. loan had it been paid in full on schedule ($79,701.98). *See* Exhibit A.

38 *See* Uniform Residential Loan Application of June 2, 1995 (hand-written) (R. 152–154).

39 The monthly payment was figured based on information derived from the payoff letter of June 15, 1995 and the credit report. Since interest was rebated upon payoff, this car loan was a pre-computed loan. This means that each payment is subtracted from the total of payments (principal and interest over the term) leaving a resulting balance. Dividing the payment amount listed on the credit report ($301.07) into the original total of payments of $16,258 shows that the term was 54 months. Ms. Consumer made 10 payments prior to payoff ($3010.70) which accounts for the payoff of $13,247.96. Thus, Ms. Consumer had 44 payments remaining in June 1995.

40 This is the minimum payment listed in the billing statement of Apr. 9, 1995.

41 To determine the number of months it would take to payoff the balance due on June 15, 1995 of $1,738 at 17.9% per year @ $45 per month, I used the HP calculator to determine the term given these numbers. The interest earned over 58 months would have been about $870.62 plus the balance of $1,738 equals $2,608.62. I assumed that no additional charges were made on the account during the payoff period.

42 This is the monthly payment shown on the _____ Remodeling Home Improvement Retail Installment Contract of Apr. 22, 1991. *See also* the credit report.

43 Given the payoff balance, it appears that Ms. Consumer made 50 payments on this 60 month loan. *See* the contract, payoff figure on the HUD-1 Settlement Statement, and Exhibit C.

Finance Co 2:	$ 78.30[44]	Remaining term: none.[45]	
Hospital bill:	$ 25.00	Remaining term: 20 mos.[46]	
TOTAL MO. PMTS.	**$1,032.80**		

Given the remaining terms of the various loans, Ms. Consumer's monthly payment would decline in about 3 ½ years to approximately $504.10. Compare this to the monthly payment on the new mortgage loan of $576.12 (PI) plus $121 (TI) which total $697.12.

# mos. after 6/15/95	New total pmts.	Debt-to-income ratio
0	$1,032.80	43.7%[47]
1	$954.50	40.4%
10	$830.17	35.2%
20	$805.17	34.1%
44	$504.10	21.4%
58	$459.10	19.4%
138	0	0

Assuming Ms. Consumer did finance the home improvements costing $3060 through an alternative unsecured loan available through the broker at 15.99% over 48 months (terms identical to those made to her by an alternative lender the following year in the form of an unsecured loan), her monthly payment would have been about $86.71. If this monthly payment were included into her budget and she had not refinanced with the new mortgage loan, Ms. Consumer's total monthly payments on her mortgage and consumer loans nevertheless would have been affordable.

# mos. after 6/15/95	New total pmts.	Debt-to-income ratio
0	$1,119.51	47.4%
1	$1041.21	44.1%
10	$916.88	38.8%
20	$891.88	37.7%
44	$590.81	25%
48	$504.10	21.4%
58	$459.10	19.4%
138	0	0

D. If Ms. Consumer had paid all of the loans that were refinanced by the new mortgage loan in full according to the terms of the loans, her total of payments would have been approximately $64,335.98 (or $68,498.06 if an alternative unsecured loan for the home improvements is included). In contrast, she would have paid $138,268.80 under the terms of the new mortgage loan. The $64,335.98 was calculated as follows:

Lender	Total of pmts. due to end of term
_____ Mortgage Co.	$46,657.80[48]
Car Loan	$13,247.96[49]
Credit card	$2,608.62
Finance Co. 1	$1,243.30[50]
Finance Co. 2	$78.30
Hospital	$500.00
TOTAL	**$64,335.98**
Alternative, unsecured home imp. loan	$4,162.08[51]
TOTAL	**$68,498.06**

I reserve the right to alter or expand upon my opinions based upon additional information supplied to me.

[Expert's Signature]

L.2.6 Expert Report on the Spiraling Costs and Profits to Lenders Due to Multiple Refinancings

This report shows how a fairly small loan can grow dramatically over time due to increasing closing costs and insurance packing when the lender repeatedly refinances the customer.

REPORT OF ELIZABETH RENUART

A. OPINIONS AND BASIS

My opinions are based upon my education and legal experience set forth in Section C. below and my review of the documentation provided by Plaintiff's counsel in this case.

I. Analysis of six loans:[52]

Frequency of renewals: 5 loans in less than 1 ½ years.
Loan #1: May 24, 1994—renewed on June 3, 1994—10 days.
Loan #2: June 3, 1994—renewed on Nov. 7, 1994—157 days (5.23 months).
Loan #3: July 20, 1994—renewed on Nov. 7, 1994—110 days (3.67 months).
Loan #4: Nov. 7, 1994—renewed on Aug. 25, 1995—291 days (9.7 months).
Loan #5: Apr. 11, 1995—renewed on Aug. 25, 1995—136 days (4.53 months).
Loan #6: Aug. 25, 1995.

Upfront costs v. Consideration
Consideration:

---

44 This is the payoff amount shown on the HUD-1 Settlement Statement. Compare to the home improvement contract of June 12, 1993. See also the credit report.

45 Compare the loan contract, Exhibit D, and the HUD-1 Settlement Statement.

46 I assumed a payment of $25 each month to pay off the $500 bill listed on the HUD-1 Settlement Statement.

47 This percentage is calculated by dividing the total monthly payment amount in the adjacent column by the total monthly income of $2361 listed on the Uniform Residential Loan Application of June 2, 1995 (hand-written) (R. 152–154).

48 Payoff amount of $28,989.56 shows Ms. Consumer made about 222 payments. *See* payment line 221 on Exhibit A. Total of payments remaining equals $46,657.80 ($338.10 x 138).

49 *See* payoff letter of June 15, 1995.

50 Calculated by multiplying $124.33 by 10 months remaining.

51 *See* Exhibit E.

52 The numbers upon which this analysis is based can be found in the attached in Exhibit A, a chart based upon the loan documents produced by the Defendants, the Defendants' Answers and Supplemental Answers to Interrogatories, and the Deposition of the loan officer.

Total proceeds to consumers: **$7,574.96**
Upfront costs:
Total prepaid finance charges (no rebates): $443.97
Total credit life insurance charges (gross): $1,966.25
Total credit life insurance charges (after rebates): $1,272.41
Total non-credit life insurance charges (no rebates): $324.00
Title-related fees (no rebates): $293.00
Filing/non-filing fees (no rebates): $30.00
Recording fees (no rebates): $49.00
TOTAL Pyramided Fees and Charges (gross): $3,106.22
TOTAL Pyramided Fees and Charges (net): **$2,412.38**
PERCENTAGE of Fees and Charges (net) to Consideration: **32%**
PERCENTAGE of Fees and Charges (net) to Final Principal: **25.7%**

Growth of Debt Generally:
Amount financed: From $2,741.50 to $9,384.09 (242%).
Finance charge: From $806.43 to $8,706.59 (980%).
Loan term: From 24 months to 72 months (200%).
Monthly payment: From $147.00 to $251.17 (71%).

Growth of Debt from Loans 4&5 to Loan 6:[53]
Amount financed: From $8,633.49 to $9,384.09 (+ $750.60).
Finance charge: From $5,995.47 to $8,706.59 (+ $2,711.12).
Total of payments: From $14,628.96 to $18,090.68 (+ $3,461.72).
Amount of additional cash out: 0.

II. Repeated Refinancing:

1. Repeated refinancings of these transactions considering the amount of insurance charges and costs increased the cost to the consumer considerably in relation to the value obtained. This is accomplished in a way that ordinary consumers are unable to realize. Further, people that are unable to read are at an even greater disadvantage.

2. Insurance policies are a source of substantial additional profit to the lender and affiliates. In addition, the lender yields additional interest on the premiums since they are part of the principal for interest calculation purposes. As of the final loan, a considerable portion of the loan principal represents the cumulative pyramiding prepaid finance charges, insurance premiums, and other closing costs. The frequency and timing of the loans are suggestive of a pattern of flipping and packing.

3. The lender has an economic incentive to write loans which have expensive insurance premiums, particularly when they are to be refinanced in a short period of time. For the non-credit life insurance, none of the premiums are rebated upon refinancing. When charged a second time, they are stacked into the principal which increases the interest yield. Additionally, credit life insurance premiums are calculated on the total of payments due under the loan which includes the premiums themselves, unearned interest, and all other costs of the loan. Consequently, the insurance packing feeds on itself in terms of extra cost to the consumer.

4. In this case, the credit life insurance premiums were rebated upon refinancing in accordance with the Rule of 78's. This formula overstates the true amount earned during the short time the loan was in effect.

5. Finally, the commissions resulting from the sale of insurance products and other resulting revenue create the incentive to sell as much insurance as possible on as many loans as possible. Specifi-

cally, in the first loan of May 24, 1994, the Plaintiffs were sold *at the same time* a joint credit life insurance policy which would pay off the loan indebtedness to the Defendant in the event of the death of either or both of the Plaintiffs and two separate non-credit life insurance policies which would pay $5,000 in the event of the death of either of the Plaintiffs. The combined cost of these insurance products was $231.51. This additional cost added approximately $60.55 in interest charges to the cost of the loan. Even if the joint credit life insurance policy was arguably of some benefit to the Plaintiffs, the sale of the additional two products was unnecessary.

6. The Defendant compounded the cost by re-charging the Plaintiffs for the non-credit life *only ten days later* in the loan of June 3, 1994. The total life insurance costs added $394.47 to the cost of the loan. The total premiums when financed over 42 months added approximately $180.67 to the cost of the loan.

7. In addition, the credit life insurance company,_____ Life Insurance Co., is a wholly owned subsidiary of the Defendants' parent company.[54] _____ Life paid a commission to _____ Agency, Inc., a wholly owned subsidiary of the Defendants' parent company, for each credit life policy sold to the Plaintiffs of 36% of the amount of the premium. The commissions paid to _____ Agency, Inc. for the six credit life insurance policies totaled $688.18.[55] Further, the sale of insurance by a branch office contributes to whether the branch will receive a bonus. Employees are clearly motivated to add insurance products into the loans wherever possible.

8. Regarding the non-credit life insurance, _____ Life Insurance Co. paid commissions to the _____ Agency of 35% of the premiums. The total of these commissions equaled $113.40. On top of this, the agent received a 5% commission on each of the two occasions for each of the four policies. The District Manager also received a 1% commission for each of the four policies. These commissions totaled $19.44 for the four policies.

9. Chart regarding insurance premiums:

Loan	Credit life premium/ com. to Agency, Inc.	Non-credit premium/ com. to employees/to Agency Inc.
May 24, 1994	$69.50/$24.33	$162/$9.72/$56.70
June 3, 1994	$232.47/$81.36	$162/$9.72/$56.70
July 20, 1994	$3.00/$1.05	
Nov. 7, 1994	$644.55/$225.59	
Apr. 11, 1995	$9.44/$3.30	
Aug. 25, 1995	$1007.29/$352.55	
TOTALS	$1,966.25/$688.18	$324/$19.44/$113.40

The total commissions paid to _____ Agency Inc. and to Defendants' employees equals $821.02, which is 36% of total insurance premiums ($2,290.25) paid by the Plaintiffs.

9. Finally, the Defendant added mortgage impairment insurance into the loans of Nov. 7, 1994 and Aug. 25, 1995 for a total of

---

53 Loans 4 and 5 were refinanced by Loan 6.

54 All of the information provided in paragraphs 7–9 of this section is derived from Defendants Second Supplementary Answers to Plaintiffs' Interrogatories No. 2.

55 Defendants claims, however, that a proportionate share of the Interstate commissions were returned upon early payoff of the loan but failed to provide any dollar amounts.

$43.00. Of this premium, the _____ Agency received a 10% commission, or $2.30. The premium included in the Nov. 7, 1994 loan ($20) was not rebated upon refinancing.

III. Compulsory Insurance

1. A determination of whether the purchase of credit and non-credit life insurance was compulsory in this case is necessarily a factual determination. Assuming that the sale of these insurance products was required by the lender, it significantly understated the cost of credit to the consumer.

2. In none of the six loans did the lender include the cost of credit in the finance charge. This failure resulted in a material understatement of both the finance charge and annual percentage rate (APR).

Loan	Disclosed FC/Actual FC[56]	Disclosed APR/Actual APR
5/24/94	$806.43/1,037.94	25.5%/34.77%
6/3/94	$2,260.85/2,655.32	24%/29.965%
7/20/94	$63.68/66.68	35.59%/37.384%
11/7/94	$5,870.75/6,515.30	24.72%/28.807%
4/11/95	$124.72/134.16	27%/29.285%
8/25/95	$8,706.59/9,713.88	24.72%/29.65%

B. DATA OR INFORMATION CONSIDERED BY WITNESS IN FORMING OPINION

The data evaluated was derived from the Complaint and Answer, discovery requests and responses, Rule 26 disclosures by the Defendants, and the deposition transcripts of the Plaintiffs. In order to perform certain APR calculations, I relied upon an APR Program developed by the National Consumer Law Center and is one method of estimating APRs. It is copyrighted and is sold in connection with NCLC's *Truth in Lending* (5th ed. 2003 and Supp.). The program prompts the user to enter the amount financed. It then asks for the monthly payments. The program will then calculate the APR based upon that information.

C. QUALIFICATIONS

[*not reprinted herein*]

L.3 Disguised Credit

The first sample pleading is a complaint against a payday lender raising usury, small loan act, RICO, Truth In Lending, and UDAP claims. The next sample is a set of requests for production of documents and short set of interrogatories (combined in one set of written discovery which may not be permissible in all jurisdictions). These documents were filed by counsel in *Hamilton v. HLT Check Exchange, L.L.P.*, 987 F. Supp. 953 (E.D. Ky. 1997).[57] Thanks to Deborah Schmedemann, Stephen Sanders, and Addison Parker of Appalachian Research and Defense Fund in Prestonsburg, KY for sharing these materials. The response to is located on the companion CD-Rom.

---

56 FC means the finance charge.

57 These documents were written using Kentucky state law. Advocates should carefully compare the relevant Kentucky statutes and common law to their home state law before deciding what claims and defenses to raise against a payday loan.

A number of additional pleadings can be found on the companion CD-Rom, including a response to a motion to dismiss filed in this case and an amicus brief in the case of *State ex rel. Salazar v. The Cash Now Store, Inc.*, 31 P.3d 161 (Colo. 2001).[58]

L.3.1 Sample Complaint

COMMONWEALTH OF KENTUCKY
MODEL CIRCUIT COURT

_____)	
)	
GARY CONSUMER AND)	
JANET CONSUMER)	
PLAINTIFFS)	
)	
v.)	C.A. NO. 97-CI-__
)	DIVISION NO. __
JOHN SMITH D/B/A ZZZ)	
CHECK EXCHANGE, LLP,)	
DEFENDANT)	
_____)	

SERVE:

1. ZZZ Check Exchange, LLP   John Smith
_____ Street   _____ Street
Mytown, Kentucky 41702   Mytown, Kentucky 41702

2. Hon. Ben Chandler
Attorney General
State Capitol
Frankfort, Kentucky 40601

VERIFIED COMPLAINT

This Complaint is filed pursuant to the Consumer Protection Act and states causes of action pursuant to the Act and other applicable law. Counsel, therefore, requests that pursuant to K.R.S. 367.220(2), the clerk mail a copy of the Complaint to the Attorney General. Plaintiffs, Gary Consumer and Janet Consumer, by and through counsel, for their cause of action, state as follows:

Parties

1. The Plaintiffs, Gary Consumer and Janet Consumer, are natural persons; former residents of _____ County, Kentucky; and current residents of _____ County, Kentucky.

2. Defendant, ZZZ Check Exchange, LLP has a principal operating address of _____ Street, Mytown, Kentucky 41702. It transacts business at _____ Road in _____ ville, _____ County, Kentucky. John Smith is the owner and managing agent of ZZZ Check Exchange.

Jurisdiction and Venue

3. The amount sought in this complaint exceeds $4,000, and this Court has jurisdiction over this action. Venue is proper pursuant to

---

58 For other sample pleadings regarding high rate lenders, see National Consumer Law Center, Consumer Law Pleadings No. 3, Ch. 4 (Cumulative CD-Rom and Index Guide).

K.R.S. 452.450, 452.460, and 367.220, because the financial transactions occurred in _____ County.

Factual Allegations

4. Plaintiffs began doing business with Defendant ZZZ Check Exchange in _____ville, Kentucky on or about August 22, 1996 and engaged in financial transactions with Defendant on numerous occasions thereafter.

5. Plaintiffs engaged in two types of transactions with Defendant: check cashing transactions and deferral transactions.

6. In the "check cashing" transactions, Defendant advanced Plaintiffs credit as follows: Plaintiffs gave Defendant a document in the form of a check which was solicited by Defendant in exchange for cash. Defendant agreed to hold the "check" for two weeks before presenting it for payment or before requiring Plaintiffs to "pick up" the check by payment of the face amount.

7. As its charge for cashing and holding the check for two weeks, Defendant charged Plaintiffs 20% of the sum advanced. Defendant obtained its fee by requiring Plaintiffs to write a check 20% in excess of the sum advanced to Plaintiffs.

8. The charges described in paragraph 7 were wholly or in significant portion consideration for allowing Plaintiffs to delay payment on the check.

9. Defendant knew or reasonably should have known that at the time of each check cashing transaction, Plaintiffs were borrowing money to be repaid in two weeks and were paying a charge on the borrowed funds of 20% of the cash paid Plaintiffs by Defendant because Plaintiffs needed cash and did not have sufficient funds in the bank to cover the check on the date it was written.

10. In the deferral transactions, Defendant, from time to time, upon the expiration of two weeks, allowed Plaintiffs to defer presentment or pick-up of a check. For such deferrals, Defendant charged 10% of the sum originally advanced for each scheduled week of deferral. In all deferral transactions, upon Plaintiffs' payment of 20%, Defendant gave Plaintiffs an additional two weeks before presentment or before requiring Plaintiffs to pick up the check by payment of the face amount.

11. The deferral fees described in paragraph 10 were consideration for allowing Plaintiffs to defer payment on the original check.

12. Defendant knew or reasonably should have known that at the time of each deferral, Plaintiffs were borrowing money to be repaid in two weeks and were paying a charge of 20% on the borrowed funds because Plaintiffs did not have sufficient funds in the bank to cover the check on the date scheduled for pick-up.

13. The Plaintiffs deferred presentment or pick-up in this manner until approximately May 1, 1997.

14. At all times relevant, Defendant failed to furnish Plaintiffs the disclosures required by the Truth in Lending Act in the clear and conspicuous manner required by the Act. Among the disclosures the Defendant failed to furnish were the annual percentage rate, which was 520%; the finance charge, using that term; and the amount financed, using that term. Similarly, Defendant failed to disclose any finance charge or interest or other charges in connection with the furnishing of credit as required by applicable state law.

15. Had Plaintiffs known they were being charged finance charges at an annual percentage rate of 520% per year, Plaintiffs would have engaged in no check cashing or deferral transactions with Defendant.

16. At all times relevant, Plaintiffs incurred debt to Defendant for Plaintiffs' personal, family, and household use.

17. To enforce payment of the checks, Defendant tacitly and expressly threatened that in the event Plaintiffs' check did not clear on presentment for payment, or Plaintiffs failed to pick up their check or failed to pay the deferral fee for an additional deferral, Defendant would prosecute Plaintiffs for violation of Kentucky's bad check law, K.R.S. 514.040.

18. When Defendant made these threats, Defendant knew or reasonably should have known that the "checks" were not at the time of their writing payable on demand, were not backed by funds in the bank, and were not checks as defined by the Uniform Commercial Code, K.R.S. 355.3-104, and furthermore that Plaintiffs were not subject to criminal prosecution for writing bad checks under the provisions of K.R.S. 514.040 (theft by deception).

19. Defendant made these threats for the sole purpose of compelling Plaintiff to pay the charges described in paragraphs 7 and 10 for the extension of credit.

20. As a result of these threats, Plaintiffs paid the fees as described above to their damage.

21. Defendant contacted Plaintiff Janet Consumer at work, demanding payment and threatening criminal action against her and her husband, Plaintiff Gary Consumer.

22. Defendant ZZZ contacted the _____ County Attorney's office on or about June 4, 1997 in an attempt to scare the Plaintiffs into continuing to pay the charges described above.

23. During the preceding calendar year, for a fee, ZZZ cashed and held for delayed presentment or drawer pick-up more than twenty five checks.

Kentucky Usury Statute, K.R.S. 360.010 and 360.020

24. Plaintiffs incorporate by reference all previous allegations herein.

25. The check cashing charges described in paragraph 7 above were all, or in substantial portion, consideration for the right to defer payment on the check for a two week period.

26. The deferral charges described in paragraph 10 above were in their entirety consideration for deferred payment on the check.

27. Regardless of the terminology used to describe the charges, the check cashing and deferral charges were interest within the meaning of K.R.S. 360.010.

28. At all times relevant, Defendant charged interest at 520% per annum, in excess of that permitted by K.R.S. 360.010, and these charges were knowingly done within the meaning of K.R.S. 360.020.

29. Pursuant to K.R.S. 360.020(1), Defendant is liable to Plaintiffs in a sum of twice the interest charged, and Defendant must forfeit all unpaid interest.

Kentucky Consumer Loan Act, K.R.S. Ch. 288

30. Plaintiffs incorporate by reference all previous allegations.

31. At all times relevant, Defendant has been in the business of making consumer loans to Plaintiffs and others similarly situated without holding a license as required by K.R.S. 288.420.

32. The interest, charges, and fees charged by Defendant on the transactions were 520% per annum and exceed the limitations of K.R.S. ch. 288.

33. Pursuant to K.R.S. 288.991, the transactions described in this Complaint are void; Defendant has no right to collect any principal, charges, or recompense whatsoever; and Defendant is liable to Plaintiffs for all such sums as have been paid to Defendant.

Federal RICO: 18 U.S.C. § 1961 et seq.

34. Plaintiffs incorporate by reference all previous allegations.

35. At all times relevant, Defendant was an entity capable of holding a legal or beneficial interest in property.

36. Defendant engaged in collection of unlawful debt by lending money at a usurious rate under Kentucky law, which usurious rate was more than twice the enforceable rate.

37. Defendant received income from this unlawful debt collection (based on a usurious rate more than twice the enforceable rate under Kentucky law) and used the income to operate an enterprise engaged in or with activities affecting interstate commerce, including ZZZ Check Exchange, LLP, in violation of 18 U.S.C. § 1962(a).

38. Through its collection of unlawful debt (based on a usurious rate more than twice the enforceable rate under Kentucky law), Defendant maintained an interest in or control of enterprises engaged in activities affecting interstate commerce, including ZZZ Check Exchange, LLP, in violation of 18 U.S.C. § 1962(b).

39. Defendant was associated with, or an employee of, an enterprise that engaged in activities that affect interstate commerce, and Defendant conducted such enterprise's affairs, and obtained income for such enterprise, through a pattern of collection of unlawful debt (based on a usurious rate more than twice the enforceable rate under Kentucky law), in violation of 18 U.S.C. § 1962(c).

40. As a result of the foregoing actions, Defendant injured Plaintiffs in their property by forcing Plaintiffs to pay interest to Defendants at usurious rates.

41. Pursuant to 18 U.S.C. § 1964(c), Plaintiffs are entitled to triple damages from Defendant.

Federal Truth In Lending Act

42. Plaintiffs incorporate by reference all previous allegations.

43. Each check cashing transaction and each deferral transaction was a separate transaction within the meaning of the Truth In Lending Act, 15 U.S.C. § 1640 et seq.

44. The 10% per week charge (20% for a two week period) whether for check cashing or deferral of presentment or pick up, was a finance charge within the meaning of the Truth In Lending Act.

45. For each transaction in which Defendant failed to disclose the Annual Percentage Rate, Finance Charge, or Amount Financed in the manner required by the Truth In Lending Act, Defendant is liable to Plaintiffs for statutory damages pursuant to 15 U.S.C. § 1640 in the sum of twice the finance charge (the 10% per week charge), but not less than $100 per transaction and not more than $1,000 per transaction. In addition, Defendant is liable to Plaintiffs for any actual damages caused by Defendant's disclosure violations.

Disclosure Violations of K.R.S. § 360 et seq.

46. Plaintiffs incorporate by reference all previous allegations.

47. The transactions between Plaintiffs and Defendant were governed by the disclosure requirements of K.R.S. 360.210 et seq.

48. The check cashing fee and deferral fees that Defendant charged with respect to each transaction between Plaintiffs and Defendant were finance charges within the meaning of K.R.S. 360.215.

49. In each transaction with Plaintiffs, Defendant failed to furnish the disclosures required by K.R.S. 360.220, including without limitation the "percent per annum rate disclosure," and these failures were willful.

50. Plaintiffs are therefore entitled to recover all finance charges and other charges incurred in connection with the transactions and to an order barring recovery of any unpaid finance charges.

Fraud, Deceit, and Misrepresentation

51. Plaintiffs incorporate by reference all previous allegations.

52. Defendants engaged in a fraudulent scheme, artifice and device with the purpose of extracting usurious, illegal, and exorbitant charges from Plaintiffs. Defendant made the following false statements, knowing them to be false or acting recklessly with regard to the falsity, and with the intent that Plaintiffs act on the statements:

(a) that the documents that Plaintiffs executed were "checks" when, in fact, Defendant knew that the document was not payable on demand at the time of its writing, was not at the time of its writing backed by funds in the drawee bank, and thus did not constitute a check within the meaning of the Uniform Commercial Code or within the meaning of the "bad check law";

(b) that Defendant's charges on the financial transactions with Plaintiffs did not constitute interest; and

(c) that Defendant could utilize Kentucky's "bad check law" for the collection of monies for the Plaintiffs.

53. These statements were material to Plaintiffs in their decision to transact business with Defendant.

54. Plaintiffs relied upon the Defendant's misrepresentations and were injured as a result.

55. Defendant's actions were intended to cause Plaintiffs financial and other injury and constituted "fraud" and "malice" within the meaning of K.R.S. 411.186, thereby entitling Plaintiffs to punitive damages, in addition to actual damages.

Kentucky Consumer Protection Act, K.R.S. 367.170 et seq.

56. Plaintiffs incorporate by reference all previous allegations.

57. Defendant engaged in unfair, deceptive, false, misleading, and unconscionable acts and practices within the meaning of the Kentucky Consumer Protection Act, K.R.S. 361.110, by disguising their consumer loan business as a check cashing operation; failing to disclose their interest rates, finance charges, and annual percentage rates; and threatening criminal prosecution for writing bad checks in the event Plaintiffs failed to pay back the funds including the usurious interest charges of not less than 520% per annum.

58. Plaintiffs have suffered loss of money or property as a result of Defendant's actions and are entitled, pursuant to K.R.S. 367.220, to actual damages, equitable relief, and punitive damages.

WHEREFORE, Plaintiffs request the following relief:

1. That pursuant to Kentucky's Interest and Usury Statute, K.R.S. 360.010 and 360.020, Plaintiffs be awarded the sum of twice the interest paid and Defendant forfeit all unpaid interest.

2. That pursuant to the Kentucky Consumer Loan Act, K.R.S. 288.991, the transactions between Plaintiffs and Defendant be

declared void and Plaintiffs be awarded all sums paid to Defendant, including but not limited to principal, interest, and fees for each and every transaction.

3. That pursuant to RICO, 18 U.S.C. § 1964(c), Plaintiffs receive triple their damages and costs.

4. That pursuant to the federal Truth in Lending Act, 15 U.S.C. § 1640 et seq., and Regulation Z, Plaintiffs be awarded statutory damages of twice the finance charges, but not less than $100.00 per transaction and not more than $1,000.00 per transaction, and such actual damages as they may prove at trial.

5. That pursuant to the Kentucky Disclosure of Financing Charges Statute, K.R.S. 360.220, Plaintiffs be awarded a recovery of all finance charges and other charges paid in connection with the transactions and be granted an order barring recovery of finance charges.

6. That pursuant to their common law claims for fraud, deceit, and misrepresentation, Plaintiffs be awarded such actual damages as they may prove at trial, plus punitive damages.

7. That pursuant to the Kentucky Consumer Protection Act, K.R.S. 367.220, Plaintiffs be awarded such actual damages as they may prove at trial, appropriate equitable relief, and punitive damages.

8. That Plaintiffs be awarded pre-judgment and post-judgment interest.

9. That Defendant be ordered to cease its effort to collect monies from Plaintiffs through threats of criminal prosecution.

10. That Plaintiffs be granted trial by jury.

11. That Plaintiffs recover their costs, as well as attorney fees for services provided by attorneys other than those employed by or receiving compensation from Appalachian Research and Defense Fund, Inc.

12. That Plaintiffs be granted any other relief to which they may be entitled.

Respectfully submitted this __ day of _____ 1997.

_____

STEPHEN A. SANDERS
DEBORAH A. SCHMEDEMANN
Attorneys for Plaintiffs
Appalachian Research & Defense Fund
28 North Front Street
Prestonsburg KY 41653
Telephone Number
Fax Number

_____

Attorney for Plaintiffs
Law Firm
Address
Telephone Number

ADDISON PARKER
Attorney for Plaintiffs
Appalachian Research & Defense Fund
P.O. Box 567
Richmond KY 40476-0567
Telephone Number
Fax Number

L.3.2 Sample Discovery

UNITED STATES DISTRICT COURT
EASTERN DISTRICT OF KENTUCKY
_____VILLE DIVISION

Gary Consumer and	)
Janet Consumer	)
Plaintiffs	)
	)
v.	)
	)
John Smith d/b/a ZZZ Check	)
Exchange, LLP	)
Defendant	)
	)

PLAINTIFFS' REQUEST FOR PRODUCTION OF DOCUMENTS AND INTERROGATORIES

Request for Production of Documents

Pursuant to Rule 34 of the Federal Rules of Civil Procedure, Plaintiffs hereby request that the Defendant produce the documents below to Stephen A. Sanders, Appalachian Research and Defense Fund of Kentucky, 28 North Front Street, Prestonsburg, Kentucky 41653 within thirty (30) days after service.

If any document requested herein was but no longer is in the possession or control of Defendant or no longer exists, identify it and explain the reason it cannot be produced, stating whether it is missing or destroyed or transmitted to another person, describing the circumstances of such disposition, and identifying any person who may currently possess or control the document.

If Defendant refuses to produce any document in its possession or control, identify the document and state the reasons for such refusal.

The following definitions apply to this Request:

"Defendant" means John Smith d/b/a/ ZZZ Check Exchange, LLP; John Smith; ZZZ Check Exchange, LLP; John Smith d/b/a Mytown Check Exchange; or the staff of the preceding entities, as the case may be.

"Plaintiffs" means Gary Consumer, Janet Consumer, either, or both, as the case may be.

"Document" means any material in written form, whether handwritten, typed, printed, or computer-generated, as well as material in electronic or mechanical recordings or storage systems capable of translation into written form.

First Request: All documents showing the business organization of the Defendant, including but not limited to partnership agreements, Secretary of State filings, Certificates of Assumed Names.

Second Request: All documents submitted to or received from the Kentucky Department of Financial Institutions, or documenting contacts between Defendant and the Kentucky Department of Financial Institutions, in the latter's role as regulator of "check cashing" businesses, including but not limited to documents relating to initial licensure, renewal of licensure, inspections, and guidance as to permissible and impermissible business practices.

Third Request: All documents submitted to or received from county attorneys or other law enforcement officials, or documenting contacts between Defendant and county attorneys or other law enforcement officials, relating to the pursuit of bad check proceedings by Defendant against customers of Defendant, including but not limited to documents, if any, specifying that Defendant may pursue such proceedings and the procedures for doing so.

Fourth Request: All records of transactions between Defendant and the Plaintiffs, including but not limited to checks, receipts, acknowledgment forms, and correspondence regarding collection of amounts Defendant deemed to be owed by Plaintiffs.

Fifth Request: All documents showing the standard business practices of Defendant, including advertisements, training manuals for employees, policy statements or handbooks, postings, and notices and forms used with customers.

Sixth Request: All insurance policies which do or are reasonably believed by Defendant to cover this case.

Seventh Request: All other documents, not specifically requested above, which are pertinent to Plaintiffs' claims or Defendant's defenses.

Interrogatories

Pursuant to Rule 33 of the Federal Rules of Civil Procedure, Plaintiffs hereby ask the following Interrogatories of Defendant. Answers and objections, if any, are to be served on Stephen A. Sanders, Appalachian Research and Defense Fund of Kentucky, Inc., 28 North Front Street, Prestonsburg, Kentucky 41653 within thirty (30) days after service.

The following definitions apply to these Interrogatories:

"Defendant" is defined as set forth above.

"Plaintiffs" is defined as set forth above.

"Identify" means to state the person's full name, present or last known address, present or last known phone number, present or last known profession or employment, and present or last known job title.

Interrogatories:

1. Identify all past and present partners, investors, and owners of Defendant, indicating as to each the periods of such involvement with Defendant.

2. Identify all past and present employees of Defendant, indicating the beginning and, where applicable, ending employment dates of each individual as well as the primary location of that employment.

3. Identify all persons providing to Defendant the "Government interpretation of Kentucky state statutes" referred to in Defendant's Second Defense.

STEPHEN A. SANDERS
DEBORAH A. SCHMEDEMANN
Attorneys for Plaintiffs
Appalachian Research & Defense Fund
28 North Front Street
Prestonsburg KY 41653
phone (606) 886-3876
fax (606) 886-3704

ADDISON PARKER
Attorney for Plaintiffs
Appalachian Research & Defense Fund
P.O. Box 567
Richmond KY 40476-0567
phone (606) 624-1394

fax (606) 624-1396

Attorney for Plaintiffs
Law Firm
Address
Telephone Number

L.4 Rent-a-Bank

The sample complaints allege that agents of either a state-chartered FDIC-insured bank or a national bank were the true lenders despite the presence of the bank's name on the loan documents. In effect, the arrangements between these parties constitute renting the charter of the bank for purposes of circumventing state usury and lending laws. For a discussion of this phenomenon, see § 3.14, *supra*.

Note that an amicus brief filed in the case of *Goleta Nat'l Bank v. O'Donnell*, 239 F. Supp. 2d 745 (S.D. Ohio 2002) appears on the accompanying CD-Rom.

L.4.1 Complaint Challenging Rent-a-Bank Arrangements Involving a State-Chartered Bank

NORTH CAROLINA
IN THE GENERAL COURT OF JUSTICE
NEW HANOVER COUNTY
SUPERIOR COURT DIVISION

[CONSUMER 1], [CONSUMER 2], and [CONSUMER 3], on behalf of themselves and all other persons similarly situated, Plaintiffs,	))))))
v.	))
ADVANCE AMERICA, CASH ADVANCE CENTERS OF NORTH CAROLINA, INC.; ADVANCE AMERICA, CASH ADVANCE CENTERS, INC.; and WILLIAM M. WEBSTER, IV Defendants.	)))))))))

COMPLAINT

Plaintiffs, for their complaint against defendants, on behalf of themselves and all others similarly situated, allege and say as follows:

SUMMARY OF CLAIMS

1. Defendants have violated North Carolina law while engaged in the business of "payday lending" conducted at numerous North Carolina locations under the names "Advance America" and

"National Cash Advance." Payday lending involves a practice whereby the borrower writes a personal check drawn on his bank account for the amount borrowed, typically between $200–$500, plus a fee, and presents this check to the payday lender. The fee translates into a triple digit annual interest rate. The borrower is given funds in the amount borrowed. The lender agrees to defer presentment of the check until the customer's next payday (or date of next regular income payment), typically 14–30 days later. When the loan is due, the borrower may redeem the check for cash, allow the check to clear through the bank, or pay another fee to extend the loan until the next payday.

2. Advance America, Cash Advance Centers, Inc. ("Advance America"), Advance America, Cash Advance Centers of North Carolina, Inc. ("Advance America-NC") and William M. Webster, IV ("Webster") have violated North Carolina law in connection with their payday lending operations, including the following specific statutes:

(a) The North Carolina Consumer Finance Act, G.S. 53-166(a) and (b) which requires persons engaged "in the business of lending" to be licensed, prohibits loans of certain types, and applies to "any person who seeks to avoid [its requirements] by any device, subterfuge or pretense whatsoever."

(b) The North Carolina Check Cashing Statute, G.S. 53-276 through 283, which requires persons engaged in the business of "cashing" checks for a consideration to be licensed, prohibits check cashers from making loans, and limit fees that can be charged.

(c) The North Carolina Unfair Trade Practice Statute, G.S. 75-1.1, which prohibits unfair trade practices. Plaintiffs' G.S. 75-1.1 claims are based on multiple legal grounds:

• The use of a signed check in connection with lending operations;

• Engaging in payday lending operations after the North Carolina General Assembly allowed the law that authorized same to expire on August 31, 2001;

• Soliciting its payday loan customers to write checks when it has reason to believe that the payday loan customer does not have sufficient funds on deposit with the bank to cover the check; and

• The violation of other consumer protection statutes, identified in this complaint, which also constitute violations of the unfair practices prohibition of G.S. 75-1.1.

(d) G.S. 24-1.1, which prohibits loans of money at interest rates in excess of specified legal limits. Plaintiffs allege that defendants have attempted to circumvent North Carolina usury law, and, in the alternative, that Advance America and Advance America-NC are the actual *bona fide* lender in transactions that are designed to appear as loans made by non-North Carolina state-chartered banks.

(e) In the alternative, the North Carolina Loan Broker Statute, G.S. 66-106 *et seq.*, which requires persons engaged in business as "loan brokers" to provide certain disclosures, procure a bond, and file advertising with the Secretary of State.

Plaintiffs have further alleged multiple grounds of liability on the part of defendants Advance America and defendant Webster, including a claim for fraudulent transfers in violation of G.S. 39-23.4 and 39-23.5.

3. Plaintiffs assert claims with respect both to business transacted at North Carolina offices operating under the "Advance America" name, and also with respect to business transacted at North Carolina offices operating under the "National Cash Advance" name. National Cash Advance is an assumed name under which Advance America and Advance America-NC conduct some of their operations.

4. Plaintiffs seek a declaratory judgment that Advance America and Advance America-NC's business as conducted in North Carolina (both under the Advance America and National Cash Advance names) is unlawful under North Carolina law, an injunction barring continuing violations of North Carolina law, and an award of money damages.

5. Plaintiffs seek to maintain this case as a class action pursuant to Rule 23 of the North Carolina Rules of Civil Procedure on behalf of all persons who have obtained a "payday loan" at any North Carolina location doing business under the name "Advance America" or "National Cash Advance" at any time after August 31, 2001, in any transaction except for those that purported to involve a national bank as lender.

6. As stated in paragraphs 127-130 below, plaintiffs do not assert any claims under federal law; do not seek a recovery by any plaintiff (including any attorney fees, but exclusive of interest and costs as those terms are used in 28 U.S.C. § 1332) in excess of $75,000; do not assert claims against any bank; and do not assert claims in connection with transactions in which a national bank is identified as the purported lender on the payday loans made at Advance America or National Cash Advance locations.

PARTIES

Plaintiffs

7. Plaintiff [Consumer 1] is a resident of New Hanover County, North Carolina.

8. Plaintiff [Consumer 2] is a resident of Rowan County, North Carolina.

9. Plaintiff [Consumer 3] is a resident of Mecklenburg County, North Carolina.

The Advance America Companies

10. Defendant Advance America-NC is a Delaware corporation with its sole or principal business operations in North Carolina. Advance America-NC participates in operating retail payday lending establishments throughout North Carolina, including in New Hanover County, Rowan County, and Mecklenburg County, using the names "Advance America," "Advance America," "Cash Advance Centers" and "National Cash Advance."

11. Defendant Advance America is a Delaware corporation with its principal place of business in South Carolina. On information and belief, Advance America is a "management company" that oversees and directs the management and operations of Advance America-NC. On information and belief, Advance America was and is responsible for the decisions for Advance America-NC to engage in payday lending in North Carolina in the manner described in this complaint.

12. At some date prior to April 19, 2001, Advance America acquired control over all of the operations of another payday loan company, McKenzie Check Advance, LLC ("McKenzie Check Advance"). This acquisition included McKenzie Check Advance of North Carolina ("McKenzie Check Advance-NC). At that time, "National Cash Advance" was an assumed name for McKenzie

Check Advance. A founder of McKenzie Check Advance, Steve McKenzie, has at all relevant times been a substantial shareholder of Advance America. On August 13, 2003, McKenzie Check Advance-NC was merged into Advance America-NC. At all times relevant to this complaint, McKenzie Check Advance and/or McKenzie Check Advance-NC were wholly owned by or under common control with Advance America and/or Advance America-NC.

Defendant William M. Webster, IV

13. William M. Webster, IV is a resident of South Carolina. Defendant Webster is president and chief executive officer of Advance America, and is president of Advance America-NC. In addition, defendant Webster is a substantial shareholder, directly or indirectly, of both Advance America and Advance America-NC. On information and belief, defendant Webster has at all relevant times directed the affairs of Advance America and Advance America-NC, has been the chief executive officer and chairman of the board of directors of Advance America, and has been the individual controlling Advance America and Advance America-NC.

14. Defendant Webster participated personally in the decision to put Advance America and/or Advance America-NC's first payday office in North Carolina in November 1997, and since that date he has made or participated in all major decisions affecting Advance America and/or Advance America-NC's payday lending in North Carolina.

15. On information and belief, defendant Webster personally directed the unlawful actions of Advance America and/or Advance America-NC that are alleged herein. Moreover, defendant Webster caused McKenzie Check Advance-NC to be acquired by and later merged into Advance America-NC.

16. Defendant Webster decided or participated in the decision that Advance America and/or Advance America-NC would continue making payday loans in North Carolina after the law allowing the making of payday loans expired on August 31, 2001. Defendant Webster decided or participated in the decision that Advance America and/or Advance America-NC would enter into "rent-a-charter" arrangements with out-of-state banks (described below), and was substantively responsible for recommending the "rent-a-charter" device to other payday lenders doing business in North Carolina.

17. As a member of the South Carolina Bar (inactive) and a 1983 graduate of the University of Virginia's school of law, and as the immediate past president of the payday industry's trade association (the Community Financial Services Association or "CFSA"), defendant Webster has and had the legal ability to understand fully the meaning, scope and applicability of state laws affecting consumer lending.

18. By reason of his contacts with North Carolina and the effects of the North Carolina Advance America and/or Advance America-NC offices on North Carolina citizens, defendant Webster is subject to the *in personam* jurisdiction of the North Carolina courts.

FACTS COMMON TO ALL COUNTS

19. Unless the context clearly denotes otherwise, as used hereinafter, "Advance America" refers to Advance America and Advance America-NC, singularly and collectively, as well as to McKenzie Check Advance and/or McKenzie Check Advance-NC

prior to its 2003 merger with Advance America-NC. "Advance America" also refers to operations conducted under either or both of the "Advance America" or "National Cash Advance" names.

20. Advance America is the largest payday lender in North Carolina and nationally. There are over 100 stores in North Carolina operating under the name Advance America, as well as substantial additional locations doing business under the name "National Cash Advance." According to its website, Advance America is "America's leading payday advance provider with more than 2,000 locations in 35 states."

21. The Advance America offices located in North Carolina are, and at all times since August 31, 2001 have been, engaged in "payday lending."

22. Under Advance America's form of payday lending as practiced in North Carolina and elsewhere, a customer in need of a loan writes a personal check at one of defendants' outlets for a stated amount of $500 or less, and obtains a promise that the check will not be presented until a date a short time in the future, typically 14-30 days. The customer is given funds in the amount of the check, less a finance charge. In a typical transaction involving a loan in the amount of $425, for example, the customer writes a check in the amount of $500 and is given funds in the amount of $425. The fee for this loan is $75. The customer's check is held until the next payday. At the end of that short time period, the customer can pay $500 to get the check back, let the check clear the bank, or pay $75 to extend the loan until the next payday. Because the payday lender is agreeing to delay the deposit of the check (or "defer" the "presentment" of the check) such transactions are sometimes also referred to as "delayed deposit" or "deferred presentment" lending.

North Carolina's 1997 Authorization of Payday Lending

23. Prior to 1997, payday lending was illegal in North Carolina. A 1992 North Carolina Attorney General's opinion concluded that payday lending violated the North Carolina Consumer Finance Act (G.S. 53-164 *et seq.*) and North Carolina criminal law (G.S. 14-107(b)). This opinion, 60 N.C.A.G. 86 (1992), was reflected as an annotation to G.S. 53-166 in the published North Carolina General Statutes (West Publishing Company/Lexis).

24. On August 7, 1997, the North Carolina General Assembly adopted and enacted into law Chapter 391 of the 1997 Session Laws, authorizing and regulating the payday "Check-Cashing Businesses." Former G.S. 53-281 was one of the statutes enacted by Chapter 391, and it provided as follows:

> **"§ 53-281. *Postdated or delayed deposit checks.***
>
> *A licensee may defer the deposit of a personal check cashed for a customer for up to 31 days pursuant to the provisions of this section.*
>
> *The face amount of any postdated or delayed deposit check cashed pursuant to this section shall not exceed three hundred dollars ($300.00).*
>
> *Each postdated or delayed deposit check cashed by a licensee shall be documented by a written agreement that has been signed by the customer and the licensee. The written agreement shall contain a statement of the total amount of any fees charged, expressed both as a dollar amount and*

as an effective annual percentage rate (APR). The written agreement shall authorize the licensee to defer deposit of the personal check until a specific date not later than 31 days from the date the check is cashed.

A licensee shall not directly or indirectly charge any fee or other consideration for cashing a post-dated or delayed deposit check in excess of fifteen percent (15%) of the face amount of the check.

No check cashed under the provisions of this section shall be repaid by the proceeds of another check cashed by the same licensee or any affiliate of the licensee. A licensee shall not, for any consideration, renew or otherwise extend any postdated or delayed check or withhold such check from deposit for any period beyond the time set forth in the written agreement with the customer."

25. Former G.S. 53-281 became effective on October 1, 1997. The law was enacted on an experimental basis to determine how payday companies offered their services and how it affected consumers. Chapter 391 of the 2001 Session Laws provided that section 53-281 was subject to an expiration or "sunset" date of July 31, 2001.

Advance America and McKenzie Check Advance Begin North Carolina Operations

26. Following the enactment of Chapter 391 of the 1997 Session Laws, in or about November 1997, defendants Webster and Advance America caused Advance America-NC to be licensed by the North Carolina Commissioner of Banks as a check-cashing business, and caused Advance America offices using the "Advance America" name to engage in payday lending operations in North Carolina.

27. At approximately the same time, the managers of McKenzie Check Advance caused their entity to be chartered, to acquire a license from the North Carolina Commissioner of Banks, to file one or more assumed name certificates to do business under the name "National Cash Advance," and to begin engaging in payday lending in what it referred to as "deferred deposit services" or "delayed deposit services."

28. McKenzie Check Advance operated in the same manner as the offices doing business under the name "Advance America," but using the name "National Cash Advance."

29. During the years 1997-2000, Advance America and McKenzie Check Advance prospered in the North Carolina market. As of the year 2000, they were collectively North Carolina's largest payday lender, with a total of 126 offices and $31.7 million in annual revenue.

North Carolina Eliminates Authorization for Payday Lending

30. Under the 1997 Session Law enacting it, G.S. 53-281 was to expire on July 31, 2001. On July 31, 2001, the General Assembly enacted, and Governor Easley approved, a one month extension of the expiration date or "sunset" of G.S. 53-281.

31. On July 31, 2001, the North Carolina Commissioner of Banks released an "Urgent Memo" addressed to "[a]ll check-

cashing business licensees who are engaged in 'payday lending.' " On information and belief, this memorandum was sent to and received by Advance America. This memorandum advised the licensees that the sunset of G.S. 53-281 had been extended by one month. This memorandum also advised licensees that they should monitor developments in the General Assembly and should "prepare to cease all [new payday loans] after August 31, 2001, if the law is not re-enacted."

32. On August 30, 2001, the North Carolina Commissioner of Banks released a second "Urgent Memo" to "[a]ll check-cashing business licensees now engaged in 'payday lending.' " On information and belief, this memorandum was sent to and received by Advance America. This memorandum stated, in part:

*N.C.G.S. § 53-281 will expire on Friday, August 31, 2001, **and there is no lawful basis for 'payday lending' without such a law, including 'payday lending' transactions effected by 'agents' or 'facilitators' of out-of-state lending institutions.** . . .*

*Check-cashing businesses which engage in transactions involving postdated or delayed deposit checks should be prepared to cease all such new agreements after August 31, 2001. Any delayed deposit checks that a licensee is holding as of August 31, 2001 may, of course, be held and then deposited in accordance with the licensee's lawful contract with its consumers. **However, licensees should make no further payday loans after August 31, 2001, either directly or as agent for another**, since they are without legal authority to enter such transactions.*

(Emphasis added.)

33. The payday lending industry lobbied the North Carolina General Assembly extensively seeking action from it that would re-enact G.S. 53-281 or extend its expiration date to some date after August 31, 2001. Advance America participated in this lobbying effort. However, G.S. 53-281 was not re-enacted nor was its expiration date further extended. No other law authorizing payday lending or "delayed deposit" check cashing was enacted, or has since been enacted, in North Carolina.

Advance America's Reaction to Expiration of G.S. 53-281

34. With the expiration of the law authorizing delayed deposit checks and fees for such arrangements, payday lending came to be unlawful under the North Carolina statutes that had formerly prohibited payday lending.

35. At the time of the expiration of G.S. 53-281, Advance America had to make a decision whether to discontinue payday lending at its 126 stores in operation in North Carolina. All, or substantially all, of Advance America's North Carolina revenues were derived from payday lending, so discontinuing payday lending would be tantamount to closing the North Carolina operations and eliminating the $31.7 million in annual revenue.

36. Advance America decided to continue operations in North Carolina by creating an arrangement under which it purported to act as "agent" for a bank. These arrangements are often referred to, and are referred to in this complaint, as "rent-a-charter" arrangements.

37. Unlike the contract forms previously employed in North Carolina and most other states in which Advance America operated, Advance America's new loan contract forms for its North Carolina offices stated that it was acting as the "agent" of a bank. Advance America contended that because of this new contract form, North Carolina laws prohibiting payday lending operations were inapplicable, and that Advance America, as a bank's agent, could disregard such laws.

38. Defendant Webster decided or participated in the decision that Advance America would continue making payday loans in North Carolina after August 31, 2001. In addition, he recommended the "rent-a-charter" device to other payday lenders doing business in North Carolina.

39. In 2001, the national trade association of the payday loan industry, the Community Financial Services Association (CFSA), was under the leadership of the payday lenders who dominate the North Carolina market. Representatives of the top four payday lending companies, with 278 North Carolina offices in the year 2000 and $64 million in year 2000 North Carolina revenue, were all on CFSA's board of directors and constituted a majority of CFSA's officers, including its past presidents. CFSA encouraged payday lenders to adopt rent-a-charter arrangements in states that had prohibitions or restrictions that the payday lenders wished to avoid.

40. North Carolina's largest payday lenders, including Advance America, Check 'N Go, Check Into Cash and First Southern, all implemented rent-a-charter arrangements substantially similar to what was recommended by the CFSA.

41. Notwithstanding the payday industry's endorsement and implementation of rent-a-charter arrangements, it quickly became clear that both regulatory officials and courts regarded these arrangements as providing no shelter from payday lenders' duties to comply with state law.

42. Numerous regulatory bodies and courts have considered and rejected the payday industry's contentions that rent-a-charter arrangements insulate payday lenders from the obligation to comply with state law, such as North Carolina law referred to in this complaint. As stated by the Georgia Attorney General in a recently filed brief: "There is a clear consensus among courts, banking regulators and scholars that non-bank 'agents' who participate in [rent-a-charter] arrangements are subject to state usury and consumer protection laws."

43. In the fall of 2001, the North Carolina Attorney General commenced an investigation of ACE Cash Express's continued payday lending in North Carolina and its rent-a-charter arrangement with Goleta National Bank. The Attorney General filed suit against ACE in January 2002 contending that ACE's payday lending business conducted in North Carolina was unlawful notwithstanding the rent-a-charter relationship. During 2002, after suffering adverse decisions in the courts, ACE agreed to cease its payday lending in North Carolina.

44. Beginning in January 2002, the Office of the Comptroller of the Currency (OCC) brought four enforcement actions against payday lenders and national banks involved in rent-a-charter arrangements.

45. In January of 2003, the OCC brought Advance America's rent-a-charter arrangements with Peoples National Bank to a halt. In News Release NR 2003-06, issued January 31, 2003, the OCC commented on the Advance America situation and by clear impli-

cation described it as an arrangement for Advance America "to evade state and local consumer protection laws":

The Office of the Comptroller of the Currency announced today that Advance America, Cash Advance Centers, Inc. and Peoples National Bank, Paris, Texas, have agreed to end their payday lending arrangement and that the bank has agreed to pay $175,000 in civil money penalties.

The consent order marks the fourth such set of enforcement actions the OCC has taken since January 2002, involving national banks that have entered into arrangements with payday lenders. With these actions, no payday lenders are any longer carrying on business through a relationship with a national bank.

*"We have been greatly concerned with arrangements in which national banks **essentially rent out their charters to third parties who want to evade state and local consumer protection laws**," said Comptroller of the Currency John D. Hawke, Jr. "The preemption privileges of national banks derive from the Constitution and are not a commodity that can be transferred for a fee to nonbank lenders."*

* * * *

In signing the consent order, Advance America agreed to end its payday lending relationship with Peoples by February 28th [2003] for business conducted in North Carolina. . . .

(Emphasis added.)

46. Advance America was further ordered in the Consent Order not to enter into any rent-a-charter arrangements or other servicing relationships with any other national bank without advance permission from the OCC. On information and belief, no such permission has been granted by the OCC.

47. The consent order identified by the press release was entered pursuant to a Stipulation and Consent to the Issuance of Consent Order signed by defendant Webster, and dealt specially and separately with Advance America's payday lending in North Carolina. Defendant Webster personally made, or participated in making, the decision to request a special arrangement in the Consent Order. Defendant Webster had actual knowledge of, and was familiar with, the terms of the Consent Order issued by the Comptroller of the Currency on January 29, 2003.

48. Having been ordered to cease doing business with all national banks, Advance America thereupon entered into a new rent-a-charter arrangement with a non-North Carolina state-chartered bank, again contending that because of this rent-a-charter arrangement, Advance America was not subject to North Carolina law. At the same time, Advance America and payday industry lobbyists continued to endeavor to secure North Carolina legislative approval for payday lending, and, as these efforts failed, relied on contractual provisions with its customers purporting to limit borrower protections under North Carolina law.

Named Plaintiffs' Transactions at North Carolina Advance America Offices

49. Each of the named plaintiffs has obtained payday loans at Advance America retail offices in North Carolina in amounts less than $500.00. Each of the named plaintiffs has obtained payday loans at such offices in transactions in which the purported lender was identified on the loan paperwork as a non-North Carolina state-chartered bank.

50. Since August 31, 2001, named plaintiff [Consumer 1] has obtained several payday loans at an Advance America store located on Oleander Drive in Wilmington, North Carolina. He was charged a finance charge each time he obtained a loan.

51. To obtain a loan of $425 dollars, [Consumer 1] was instructed to write a personal check for $500. It was agreed that his check would be held for a short length of time (less than 30 days), at which time the check would be deposited or presented for payment.

52. On several occasions, [Consumer 1] was unable to pay the loan on the scheduled due date. He "rolled over" his loan by paying the finance charge and writing another check for the same amount he had borrowed previously, under the same terms. 53. Advance America treated each rollover as a new loan. [Consumer 1] was charged an additional $75 each time he extended his $500 loan.

54. On the occasions on which [Consumer 1] was instructed by Advance America to write a personal check in order to obtain a loan, his checking account did not or would not have sufficient funds with which to honor that check during the time period it was held by Advance America.

55. Since August 31, 2001, named plaintiff [Consumer 3] has obtained several payday loans at an Advance America store located on Albemarle Road in Charlotte, North Carolina.

56. To obtain a loan of $200 dollars, [Consumer 3] was instructed to write a personal check for $235. To obtain a loan of $300 dollars, [Consumer 3] was instructed to write a personal check for $352.50. It was agreed that these checks would be held for 14 days, at which time the check would be deposited or presented for payment.

57. On several occasions, [Consumer 3] was unable to pay the loan on the scheduled due date. He "rolled over" his loan by paying the finance charge and writing another check for the same or a higher amount than he had borrowed previously.

58. Advance America treated each rollover as a new loan. [Consumer 3] was charged an additional fee each time he extended his loan.

59. On the occasions on which [Consumer 3] was instructed by defendants Advance America to write a personal check in order to obtain a loan, his checking account did not or would not have sufficient funds with which to honor that check during the time period it was to be "held" by Advance America.

60. Since August 31, 2001, named plaintiff [Consumer 2] has obtained several payday loans at an Advance America store located on Jake Alexander Boulevard in Salisbury, North Carolina. [Consumer 2] does not recall the dates on which she entered into loans with Defendants or the terms of her loans, however, she has, upon information and belief, on repeated occasions during the past year, paid amounts similar to those paid by [Consumer 3] for similar short-term loans.

61. In connection with each of the transactions described herein, plaintiffs procured loans of $500 or less, for terms of 10 to 30 days, at a charge of 15% to 17.65% of the amount advanced to the borrower, resulting in an annual percentage rate finance charge of over 400% (and, typically, of 456% or 460%). Plaintiffs each paid not only the amount of the cash advance provided by Advance America, but also the fees described in this and preceding paragraphs.

CLASS ALLEGATIONS

62. Plaintiffs seek to bring this case as a class action pursuant to Rule 23 of the North Carolina Rules of Civil Procedure. The proposed plaintiff class consists of all persons who have entered into a "payday loan" transaction at North Carolina offices doing business under the names "Advance America" or "National Cash Advance" at any time after August 31, 2001, in transactions that did not purport to involve a national bank as lender.

63. On information and belief, the proposed plaintiff class is numerous: substantially in excess of 1,000 persons.

64. Common questions of law and fact predominate over any individual issues that may be presented, because defendants' operations in North Carolina are conducted pursuant to a uniform business method. Common questions include:

- Whether defendants' uniform business methods in the Advance America outlets in North Carolina violate the North Carolina Consumer Finance Act, either because they constitute loans made by defendants or because they violate G.S. 53-166(b)'s prohibition against persons seeking to avoid application of the North Carolina Consumer Finance Act "by any device, subterfuge or pretense whatsoever."
- Whether defendants' uniform business methods in the Advance America establishments in North Carolina constitute "engag[ing] in the business of cashing checks" (within the meaning of "cashing" as defined in the statute) in violation of the North Carolina Check Casher Act, G.S. 53-275 *et seq.*
- Whether defendants' uniform business methods in the Advance America establishments in North Carolina violate G.S. 75-1.1 by reason of:
  —The use of a signed check in connection with lending operations;
  —Engaging in payday lending operations after the North Carolina General Assembly allowed the law that authorized same to expire on August 31, 2001;
  —Soliciting its payday loan customers to write checks when it has reason to believe that the payday loan customer does not have sufficient funds on deposit with the bank to cover the check; and
  —The violations of other consumer protection statutes, identified in this complaint, which also constitute unfair trade practices.
- Whether defendants' uniform business methods in the Advance America operations in North Carolina constitute the business of acting as a "loan broker" in violation of the North Carolina Loan Broker Act, G.S. 66-106 *et seq.*
- Whether defendants' arrangements with non-North Carolina state-chartered lenders effectively exempt defendants from compliance with North Carolina law regulating checks written for insufficient funds, small loan practices and limits, check

cashing practices, loan broker requirements and unfair trade practice laws.

65. The named plaintiffs' claims are typical of the claims of the members of the proposed class. Defendants have engaged in standardized conduct toward the proposed class members in connection with defendants' "payday" lending in North Carolina.

66. The named plaintiffs are adequate representatives of the class in that the named plaintiffs do not have antagonistic or conflicting claims with other members of the class; the named plaintiffs have a sufficient interest in the outcome to ensure vigorous advocacy; and counsel for the named plaintiffs have the requisite qualifications and experience to conduct the proposed litigation competently and vigorously.

FIRST CLAIM FOR RELIEF
(Consumer Finance Act, G.S. 53-164 *et seq.*)

67. The allegations of paragraphs 1 through 66, and the other allegations of this complaint, are incorporated herein by reference.

68. G.S. 53-166(a) prohibits persons from being engaged in the "business of lending" loans of less than $10,000 except pursuant to a license issued by the North Carolina Commissioner of Banks, and except as permitted by G.S. 53-164 *et seq.*

69. Since August 31, 2001 (except for those transactions in which the payday loan was purportedly made by a national bank as lender), Defendants have been engaged in the "business of lending" within the meaning of G.S. 53-166(a). The transactions that have taken place at Advance America offices in North Carolina since August 31, 2001, and the transactions between the named plaintiffs and Advance America offices in North Carolina were loans of less than $10,000.

70. Defendants reaffirmed the accuracy of the description of Advance America's business in North Carolina as "making cash advances to individuals" in the annual reports filed with the North Carolina Secretary of State in 2002 and 2003.

71. Defendants reaffirmed the accuracy of the description of McKenzie Check Advance's business in North Carolina as "Deferred Presentment/Payday Advance" in the annual reports filed with the North Carolina Secretary of State in 2002 and 2003.

72. Since August 31, 2001, none of the defendants has been licensed by the North Carolina Commissioner of Banks.

73. In the course of making payday loans to plaintiffs and members of the class since August 31, 2001, Advance America repeatedly made loans at interest rates that exceed the rate of interest they would be permitted by law to charge if they were licensed by the North Carolina Commissioner of Banks.

74. In the course of making payday loans to plaintiffs and members of the class since August 31, 2001, Advance America repeatedly made loans in the same location where it was conducting other business, in violation of G.S. 53-172(a).

75. G.S. 53-166(b) is titled "Evasions" and provides: "The provisions of subsection (a) of this section shall apply to any person who seeks to avoid its application by any device, subterfuge or pretense whatsoever."

76. Defendants have sought to avoid the application of G.S. 53-166(a) and the North Carolina Consumer Finance Act by entering into arrangements with non-North Carolina state-chartered banks, whereby Advance America is identified as an "agent" for the state-chartered financial institutions. However, Advance

America has received most of the financial benefit from these lending operations in North Carolina, is itself "engage[d] in the business regulated by this Article" (G.S. 53-168(a)), and is itself "engaged in the business of lending" (G.S. 53-166(a)).

77. As hereinabove alleged, defendants have violated G.S. 53-164 *et seq.* even if defendants are not themselves the actual lenders or makers of the payday loans, because defendants are "engage[d] in the business of lending" and "engage[d] in the business regulated by this Article" and have sought to "avoid its application by [a] device, subterfuge or pretense." In the alternative, however, plaintiffs here allege that Advance America and/or Advance America-NC are the *bona fide* lender on the payday loans. In support of this alternative contention, plaintiffs incorporate by reference the allegations of paragraphs 115-116, below.

78. Plaintiffs do not, by this claim or in this complaint, challenge the right of non-North Carolina state-chartered banks to enter into loans with North Carolina residents at such rates as the bank's home state may permit. Rather, plaintiffs here complain of Advance America's actions in arranging such loans and receiving most of the financial benefit of such loans as participation in the "business of lending" and as an "evasion" prohibited by G.S. 53-166(b).

79. The named plaintiffs and the members of the plaintiff class have been damaged by Advance America's violations of G.S. 53-164 *et seq.* in that Advance America has charged fees not permitted because of its lack of licensure and other violations of the North Carolina Consumer Finance Act. Persons in violation of G.S. 53-164 *et seq.* may not retain "any principal or charges whatsoever with respect to such loan."

80. The named plaintiffs and the members of the plaintiff class are entitled to and request, pursuant to G.S. 1-253, a declaratory judgment that the payday transactions undertaken at Advance America outlets in North Carolina since August 31, 2001, with the exception of those transactions that involved a national bank as the purported lender, are in violation of G.S. 53-166(d).

81. The named plaintiffs and the members of the plaintiff class are further entitled to and request a preliminary and permanent injunction, barring Advance America from continuing to operate in violation of G.S. 53-164 *et seq.*

82. The named plaintiffs and the members of the plaintiff class are, pursuant to G.S. 53-166(d), entitled to recover back from defendants all amounts which defendants have received in connection with Advance America payday transactions in North Carolina since August 31, 2001 (except for those transactions in which the payday loan purports to be made by a national bank as lender), pursuant to G.S. 53-166(d)'s provision that any party in violation of the Act "shall have no right to collect, receive or retain any principal or charges whatsoever with respect to such loan."

SECOND CLAIM FOR RELIEF
(Check Cashing Statute, G.S. 53-276, 53-283)

83. The allegations of paragraphs 1 through 66, and all other allegations of this complaint, are incorporated herein by reference.

84. Notwithstanding the letter dated September 21, 2001, stating that Advance America "ceased [its] operations as [a] check-cashing business," defendants have continued to engage in the business of "cashing" checks in North Carolina.

85. G.S. 53-276 prohibits any person from engaging in the business of cashing checks for consideration in North Carolina

unless that person is licensed under Article 22 of Chapter 53 of the North Carolina General Statutes. G.S. 53-276 further provides that "[n]o person or other entity providing a check-cashing service may avoid the requirements of this Article by providing a check or other currency equivalent instead of currency when cashing payment instruments."

86. None of defendants holds a license as required by G.S. 53-276.

87. G.S. 53-283(1) prohibits a person required to be licensed under Article 22 of Chapter 53 of the General Statutes from charging fees in excess of those authorized in such Article 22 of Chapter 53.

88. Advance America's North Carolina operations charge fees in excess of those authorized in Article 22 of Chapter 53 of the North Carolina General Statutes.

89. G.S. 53-283(2) prohibits a person required to be licensed under Article 22 of Chapter 53 of the General Statutes from "engag[ing] in the business of making loans of money, or extensions of credit, or discounting notes, bills of exchange, items, or other evidences of debt. . . ."

90. Defendants have engaged in, and are currently engaging in, the business of making loans of money, of extending credit and of discounting items (customers' checks) in violation of G.S. 53-283.

91. Defendants' actions as hereinabove alleged constitute a violation of G.S. 53-276 and 53-283.

92. The named plaintiffs and the members of the plaintiff class have been damaged by defendants' business practices, in that the named plaintiffs and the members of the plaintiff class have paid fees in connection with Advance America's check cashing transactions and loans (except for those transactions in which the payday loan purports to be made by a national bank as lender) in North Carolina.

93. The named plaintiffs and the members of the plaintiff class are entitled, pursuant to G.S. 1-253, to a declaratory judgment that Advance America's actions as described herein have been and are in violation of G.S. 53-276, 53-283 and 75-1.1.

94. The named plaintiffs and the members of the plaintiff class are further entitled to a preliminary and permanent injunction, barring Advance America from continuing to operate in violation of G.S. 53-276, 53-283, and 75-1.1.

95. The named plaintiffs and the members of the plaintiff class are entitled to recover from defendants all fees or interest paid in connection with all Advance America transactions in North Carolina since August 31, 2001, except for those transactions which purported to involve a national bank as lender.

THIRD CLAIM FOR RELIEF
(Unfair Trade Practices—G.S. 75-1.1 *et seq.*)

96. The allegations of paragraphs 1 through 95 and 113-126, and all other allegations of this complaint, are incorporated herein by reference.

97. By this claim plaintiffs allege that the Advance America business operations in North Carolina, which were at all times conducted willfully, are contrary to the public policy of North Carolina, are substantially injurious to consumers of North Carolina, and constitute unfair trade practices under G.S. 75-1.1. Advance America's unfair practices include the following:

(a) Requiring that plaintiffs and members of the plaintiff class provide a personal check as security for, or as the basis for obtaining a payday loan.

(b) Engaging in payday lending after the law authorizing such transactions expired.

(c) Soliciting customers to write checks in order to obtain a payday loan, knowing that the customer lacks funds on deposit in the bank with which to honor the check.

(d) Engaging in violations of each of the specific consumer protection statutes alleged elsewhere in this complaint, the violations of which also constitute unfair trade practices.

98. In making payday loans to its customers, Advance America does not thoroughly evaluate a borrower's ability to repay the loan, but instead hold's the borrower's personal check as security for the loan.

99. Taking the borrower's personal check in connection with the payday loan deprives the customer of any opportunity to present defenses to the loan.

100. By securing a signed check from a borrower to assure repayment of a loan, Advance America places itself in a position to withdraw funds from the borrower's bank account or, if the account does not contain sufficient funds, to cause the borrower to incur "bounced check" or "NSF" fees from the bank and the payday lender, and to cause a deterioration of the borrower's relationship with his bank.

101. By securing a signed check from the borrower to assure repayment of the loan, Advance America also places the borrower in a position in which the borrower's other outstanding checks will be rejected by the borrower's bank for insufficient funds, thereby giving rise to bank "NSF" charges as well as returned check charges from other persons to whom the borrower has written checks, and to cause a deterioration of the borrower's financial relationship with the borrower's other creditors.

102. The loans are structured to make it difficult for consumers to pay in full at the end of the loan period without needing to borrow again before the next payday. Because of the consequences described in the preceding paragraph, payday loan borrowers are reluctant to default on payday loan obligations and, instead, frequently take out other payday loans to redeem the initial payday loan or "roll over" the loan for another 14 or 30 days by paying an additional loan fee.

103. Payday loans are structured in such a way so as to encourage extended borrowing through rollovers and replacement loans. Once a payday loan has been obtained, the cost to renew it or replace it is substantially smaller than the cost to pay it off. A substantial amount of payday loan revenues are derived from so-called "repeat customers."

104. With the sunset of G.S. 53-281, payday lending is no longer authorized under North Carolina law, and this form of business is contrary to North Carolina' public policy.

105. Defendant's practice of soliciting its customers to write personal checks when it is understood by the very nature of the transaction that the customer lacks the funds to cover the check being written also constitutes an unfair trade practice under G.S. 75-1.1. G.S. 14-107(b) makes it unlawful for any person to "solicit or to aid and abet any other person, firm or corporation to draw, make, utter or issue and deliver to any person, firm or corporation, any check or draft on any bank or depository for the payment of money or its equivalent, being informed, knowing or having reasonable grounds for believing at the time of the soliciting or the

aiding and abetting that the maker or the drawer of the check or draft has not sufficient funds on deposit in, or credit with, the bank or depository with which to pay the check or draft upon presentation."

106. Because Advance America engages in the payday loan business for the stated purpose of providing its customers with loans of funds the customers lack, all customers of Advance America are solicited to write checks at a time when defendants have "reasonable grounds for believing" that the maker of the check does not then have sufficient funds to pay the check.

107. Moreover, as alleged elsewhere in this complaint, defendants have violated other North Carolina statutes, specifically: G.S. 53-164 *et seq.* (the North Carolina Consumer Finance Act); G.S. 53-275 *et seq.* (the North Carolina Check Cashing Business Law); G.S. 24-1 *et seq.* (North Carolina usury law); and/or G.S. 66-106 *et seq.* (the North Carolina loan broker statutes), and such violations constitute also violations of G.S. 75-1.1.

108. Plaintiffs and members of the plaintiff class have been damaged by Advance America's violations of the Unfair Trade Practices statute. They were charged fees that were impermissible and are subject to refund.

109. Defendants have willfully caused the Advance America transactions hereinabove described to take place at Advance America outlets in North Carolina. Such transactions occur and have occurred in commerce in North Carolina.

110. The named plaintiffs and the members of the plaintiff class are entitled, pursuant to G.S. 1-253, to a declaratory judgment that the acts taken and being taken in North Carolina by Advance America are in violation of G.S. 75-1.1.

111. The named plaintiffs and the members of the plaintiff class are further entitled to a preliminary and permanent injunction, barring Advance America from continuing to operate in violation of G.S. 75-1.1.

112. The named plaintiffs and the members of the plaintiff class are entitled to recover from defendants all fees or interest paid in connection with Advance America transactions in North Carolina since August 31, 2001, except for those transactions which purported to involve a national bank as lender, and are further entitled to treble damages and attorney fees pursuant to G.S. 75-16.1.

FOURTH CLAIM FOR RELIEF
(Evading Usury, G.S. 24-1.1)

113. The allegations of paragraphs 1 through 66, and all other allegations of this complaint, are incorporated herein by reference.

114. By this alternative claim, it is contended that defendants have engaged in efforts to circumvent and evade the law of usury in North Carolina, and that the payday loan transactions constitute a loan of funds from defendants. Plaintiffs do not, by their complaint or this claim, challenge the right of out-of-state banks to enter into loans with North Carolina residents at such rates as the bank's home state may permit. Rather, plaintiffs complain here of Advance America's actions in arranging such loans and receiving most of the financial benefits of such loans as an evasion prohibited by Chapter 24 and cases decided under Chapter 24, and in the further alternative contend that Advance America was the true and *bona fide* lender in the loan transactions alleged herein.

115. On information and belief, defendants have controlled and conducted the business of making payday loans by Advance America in North Carolina as described herein. On information and

belief, the marketing of the payday loans made by Advance America in North Carolina has been and is conducted and controlled by defendants. The economic risk of such loans is (and has been) borne by defendants. The collection of such loans is (and has been) conducted by defendants. The corporate defendants have received most of the earnings generated by the deferred check presentment loans.

116. In North Carolina, Advance America has conducted business under the name "Advance America" and "National Cash Advance" rather than under the names of the non-North Carolina state-chartered financial institutions. The Advance America or National Cash Advance name has been continuously used rather than being changed to be consistent with the identity of the financial institutions with which defendants have entered into their various arrangements.

117. For loans structured under the "rent-a-charter" arrangements using state-chartered lending institutions, defendants are subject to Chapter 24 of the North Carolina General Statutes, and are not entitled to the usury protections of 12 U.S.C. § 1831d, as made applicable in North Carolina by G.S. 24-2.3(b).

118. Since September 1, 2001, for the payday loans it has made in North Carolina (with the exception of those loans made purportedly using a national bank as lender), Advance America has charged interest at rates in excess of the maximum rate permitted by Chapter 24 of the North Carolina General Statutes.

119. With the exception of those loans purportedly made using a national bank as lender, defendants have entered into, or caused others to enter into, loans of money, with an understanding that the money loaned shall be returned, with payment or an agreement to pay, a greater rate of interest than that allowed by law, and with a corrupt intent to take more than the legal rate for the use of the money loaned.

120. The named plaintiffs and the members of the plaintiff class are entitled to recover from defendants twice the amount of interest paid on all payday loans made by Advance America pursuant to a rent-a-charter agreement with a state-chartered bank, and to a release from any further obligation to make payments to Advance America on those loans.

FIFTH CLAIM FOR RELIEF
(Loan Broker Statute, G.S. 66-106 *et seq.*)

121. The allegations of paragraphs 1 through 66, and all other allegations of this complaint, are incorporated herein by reference.

122. In the alternative to the allegations made elsewhere in this complaint, plaintiffs here allege as an alternative claim that, with the exception of those transactions made purportedly using a national bank as lender, Advance America has operated and operates in North Carolina as a "loan broker" within the meaning of G.S. 66-106.

123. G.S. 66-106 *et seq.* require that all loan brokers doing business in North Carolina provide specified disclosure statements to prospective borrowers, obtain a bond or establish a trust account, and file certain materials with the Secretary of State.

124. Advance America has not complied with any of the requirements of Article 20 of Chapter 66 of the North Carolina General Statutes.

125. G.S. 66-111(d) provides that "[t]he violation of any provisions of this Article shall constitute an unfair practice under G.S. 75-1.1."

126. The allegations of paragraphs 109-112 are specifically incorporated here by reference, and plaintiffs are entitled to relief as there alleged.

LIMITATION OF CLAIMS

127. Plaintiffs do not assert in this action any claims under federal law, and specifically and without limitation do not assert any claims under 12 U.S.C. § 1831d.

128. Plaintiffs do not assert in this action any claim against any person not named herein, and specifically do not assert any claim against any bank.

129. Plaintiffs do not assert in this action any claim with respect to any loan in which the purported lender, as reflected in the writings signed by the borrower, is a national bank.

130. Plaintiffs do not assert in this action any claim for damages in the aggregate for any named plaintiff or member of the plaintiff class in excess of $75,000, exclusive of interest and costs within the meaning of those terms as used in 28 U.S.C. § 1332(b). The financial transactions at issue in this case involve payday loans of $500 or less.

LIABILITY OF ADVANCE AMERICA AND WEBSTER

131. Plaintiffs contend Advance America and Webster share all liability to which Advance America-NC is subject, and also contend that Advance America and Webster are liable for such funds as were originally obtained from North Carolina borrower payments and were ultimately transferred to Advance America or Webster or entities under their control (including, without limitation, to companies affiliated with Advance America).

Participation in Wrongdoing

132. The allegations of paragraph 1 to 131 and all other allegations of this complaint are incorporated herein by reference.

133. Plaintiffs contend that Advance America and Webster have joint and several liability with Advance America-NC by reason of their actual participation in the matters complained of herein.

134. As specific acts of actual participation by Advance America and Webster, plaintiffs allege:

(a) Advance America acted as the management company for the Advance America NC operations. Webster acted as Advance America's chief executive officer.

(b) Advance America determined the states in which Advance America would conduct operations.

(c) Advance America and Webster were aware of the North Carolina General Assembly's decision to eliminate the statute authorizing payday lending in North Carolina effective August 31, 2001.

(d) Advance America transmitted the September 20, 2001 letter to the North Carolina Commissioner of Banks falsely stating that Advance America-NC and McKenzie Check Advance "have ceased their operations as check-cashing businesses in the State of North Carolina."

(e) In or about September 2001, Advance America and Webster made the decision that Advance America-NC would continue in the payday lending business in North Carolina notwithstanding the expiration of the law that permitted such business and notwithstanding the North Carolina Commissioner of Banks' memoranda.

(f) In January of 2003, Advance America and Webster executed the January, 2003 Stipulation consenting to the issuance of the Consent Order by the Office of the Comptroller of the Currency against Advance America, and containing a specific provision addressing Advance America's rent-a-charter arrangements for North Carolina. In or about February 2003, Advance America and Webster nonetheless decided that Advance America would continue to operate its payday lending operations at its offices in North Carolina.

(g) Advance America and Webster participated in this decision with the other major North Carolina payday lenders, and elected to have the North Carolina Advance America operations follow the rent-a-charter model recommended by the CFSA, of which Webster was the president and a director, and of which Advance America was a founding member, and which was followed by the other major North Carolina payday lenders, including Check 'N Go, Check Into Cash and First Southern Cash Advance.

Liability to Return Funds
(G.S. 53-166(d); G.S. 39-23.4 and -23.5)

135. The allegations of paragraph 1 to 134 and all other allegations of this complaint are incorporated herein by reference.

136. Advance America and Webster, and entities under their control, have received funds from Advance America-NC and from the operations of the Advance America offices in North Carolina. Advance America and Webster are liable to return all such funds.

137. Such liability arises because Advance America and Webster are "other part[ies] in violation" under G.S. 53-166(d), which provides that "any other party in violation shall have no right to collect, receive or retain any principal or charges whatsoever with respect to such loan." The "violation" by Advance America and the individual defendants arises from their participation in and implementation of the acts and actions described in this Complaint.

138. Such liability also arises because funds transferred to or through Advance America and Webster, and entities under their control, constitute transfers made during a time at which Advance America-NC was "insolvent" within the meaning of that term as used in G.S. 39-23.2, after taking into consideration the amount of the liability represented by Advance America-NC's duty to make refunds to North Carolina customers. Plaintiffs allege that Advance America and Webster, and entities under their control, are receiving, and have received, transfers of funds that constitute "fraudulent transfers" under G.S. 39-23.5(a) in that Advance America-NC did not receive reasonably equivalent value in exchange for such transfers, and such transfers were made at a time when, after giving consideration to Advance America-NC's obligation to refund all fees paid by North Carolina customers, Advance America-NC was insolvent. Plaintiffs allege they are creditors of Advance America-NC whose claims arose prior to such transfers.

139. Plaintiffs further allege that such transfers were made with the intent to hinder creditors under G.S. 39-23.4(a). The fragmentation of Advance America operations into purportedly separate corporations and the transfers of funds from Advance America-NC done after the North Carolina payday authorization ended, but Advance America nonetheless continued to its North Carolina operations, were done with the intent to insulate Advance America and Webster, and others, against the risk of having to refund to North Carolina borrowers the funds that had been derived from

Advance America's unlawful deferred check presentment payday lending operations in North Carolina.

140. To the extent of transfers to Advance America or the individual defendants, or entities under their control, on account of antecedent debt, plaintiffs challenge such transfers as preferences under G.S. 39-23.5(b)

Conspiracy

141. The allegations of paragraph 1 to 140 and all other allegations of this complaint are incorporated herein by reference.

142. Advance America and the individual defendants share liability with Advance America-NC because they entered into a conspiracy to violate North Carolina law by agreeing with others (including defendant Advance America-NC) to perform acts in violation of North Carolina law as hereinabove alleged.

143. The actions hereinabove alleged were taken in furtherance of such conspiracy, and plaintiffs were injured as a proximate cause thereof, all as alleged herein.

Piercing Corporate Veil

144. The allegations of paragraph 1 to 143 are incorporated herein by reference.

145. Advance America-NC is a mere instrumentality of Advance America.

146. Advance America decided the states in which Advance America would do business, and caused approximately 29 purportedly separate organizations (such as Advance America-NC) to be set up for particular states. Those purportedly separate organizations such as Advance America-NC have no separate home office, no home office staff, no telephone, no telephone listing, no address, no board meetings, or other indicia of separate existence. The Stipulation agreeing to the Consent Order was signed by Webster and Advance America. The September 20, 2001 letter (falsely) stating that Advance America-NC and McKenzie Check Advance "have ceased their operations as check-cashing businesses in the State of North Carolina" was sent by Advance America. Advance America-NC is an alter ego of Advance America.

147. Advance America has used Advance America-NC to perpetrate violations of the statutory law of North Carolina. Plaintiffs have been proximately injured as a consequence thereof. Advance America shares liability with Advance America-NC for the matters alleged herein.

PRAYER FOR RELIEF

WHEREFORE, the plaintiffs, on behalf of themselves and all others similarly situated, pray that this Court grant relief as requested in this complaint, including that the Court:

A. Issue a declaratory judgment, declaring that the Advance America operations in North Carolina (both those conducted under the name "Advance America" and those conducted under the name "National Cash Advance") are in violation of North Carolina law;

B. Issue a preliminary and permanent injunction, barring defendants from offering, making, arranging, or collecting payday loans to North Carolina consumers;

C. Certify this case as a class action under Rule 23 of the North Carolina Rules of Civil Procedure;

D. Award the named plaintiffs and the members of the plaintiff class a refund of all amounts (principal, as well as fees and interest) paid by customers on payday loans described herein and obtained through Advance America offices in North Carolina;

E. Award the named plaintiffs and the other members of the plaintiff class treble damages pursuant to G.S. 75-1.1 and attorney fees pursuant to G.S. 75-16.1;

F. Award the named plaintiffs and the other members of the plaintiff class double the amount of fees paid pursuant to the Fourth Claim for Relief;

G. Award the plaintiffs and the other members of the class pre-judgment and post-judgment interest;

H. Order the disgorgement and refund of all monies, fees and interest unlawfully charged and that have been transferred to or through defendants or their affiliates; and

I. Award costs, and such other and further relief as the Court deems just and proper under the circumstances.

[Attorney for Plaintiff]

L.4.2 Complaint Challenging Rent-a-Bank Arrangements Involving a National Bank

CIRCUIT COURT FOR THE STATE OF MARYLAND
CITY OF BALTIMORE

```
––––––––––––––––––––––––––––  )
PLAINTIFF                      )
[Address]                      )
for herself and all others     )
similarly situated,            )
                    Plaintiffs  )
                               )
v.                             )
                               )
ACE CASH EXPRESS, INC.         )
[Address]                      )
UNKNOWN PERSONS                )
DOING BUSINESS AS              )
FRANCHISEES OF AND FOR         )
ACE CASH EXPRESS, INC.         )
                    Defendants  )
––––––––––––––––––––––––––––  )
```

COMPLAINT FOR DECLARATORY, INJUNCTIVE AND OTHER EQUITABLE RELIEF

I. PRELIMINARY STATEMENT

This lawsuit is brought on behalf of a statewide class of consumers in Maryland who are victimized by ACE Cash Express, Inc. (hereafter "ACE"), a predatory lending operation that charges interest rates of over 440 percent per year on the short-term "payday loans" that it makes to working-class and low-income borrowers. ACE and its franchisees market these "payday loans" to consumers who lack access to legitimate credit markets. The exorbitant interest rates that ACE and its franchisees extract from borrowers greatly exceed the interest rate ceilings set by Maryland anti-usury legislation, Md. Code Ann. §§ 12-101 *et seq.*, and also violate related restrictions that the State legislature has placed on interest rates that lenders charge for small consumer loans. Maryland Consumer Loan Law, Md. Code Ann. §§ 11-201 *et seq.* By brokering, lending and/or facilitating unsecured loans at unlawful interest rates, and by providing such financial services without a license, ACE and the other defendants are also in violation of Maryland's Unsecured Closed End Credit Regulation Act, 2001 Md. ALS 630. Defendants further violate this recently enacted legislation by knowingly requiring borrowers to unwittingly make dubious pledges of collateral that ACE uses in an attempt to evade the law, which applies only to unsecured loans. By knowingly collecting interest that they have no legal right to demand, ACE and its franchisees also violate the Maryland Consumer Debt Collection Act, Md. Code Ann. §§ 14-201 *et seq.* Finally, ACE and its franchisees violate the Maryland truth in lending provisions, Md. Code Ann. § 12-106, and the Unfair and Deceptive Trade Practices Act, Md. Code Ann. §§ 13-301 *et seq.*, by affirmatively misrepresenting and concealing their role and interests as lenders in the payday lending scheme.

ACE and its franchisees have developed a complex and evolving set of contrivances to make it appear to consumers and government officials that the payday loans they market are lawful and legitimate business practices. The defendants in this case have for years tried to evade regulation by government officials by changing the form and description of their payday loans—for some time claiming that ACE was simply charging "fees" for check cashing rather than charging interest on loans, more recently pretending that ACE merely acts as a conduit for loans made to consumers by Goleta National Bank (hereafter "Goleta"), and, in the most recent fiction designed to evade the State's new law governing unsecured loans, falsely purporting to require borrowers to post collateral when they apply for payday loans.

Through this lawsuit, plaintiff and the class of borrowers she represents seeks to end to defendants' illegal loan sharking operations in the State of Maryland. The violations of State law described above, taken together, render null and void the payday loan agreements that borrowers have entered into with ACE, and prohibit defendants from enforcing any contractual obligations that the agreements purport to impose on borrowers. The Plaintiff and Class members therefore ask the Court to issue a declaration of the parties' rights, status and legal relations under the purported contracts entered into in connection with the defendant's payday loan scheme, as authorized by the Maryland Declaratory Judgment Act, Md. Code Ann. §§ 3-401 *et seq.* The Plaintiff and Class members also request that the Court grant supplemental equitable relief, including an order rescinding any purported contractual relations arising from ACE's payday loan transactions, enjoining defendants from attempting to collect any interest or principal in connection with these transactions, requiring defendants to provide restitution to plaintiff and other borrowers, and ruling that defendants hold any funds obtained from plaintiffs through their payday loan scheme in a constructive trust for the benefit of the plaintiffs and other borrowers.

II. JURISDICTION AND VENUE

This Court has jurisdiction over this action under the Maryland Declaratory Judgment Act, Md. Code Ann. §§ 3-401 *et seq.* Venue is proper in this Court because ACE and its franchisees do business at over forty storefront outlets across the State, and the transactions that give rise to the named plaintiff's claims in this lawsuit occurred in the City of Baltimore, Maryland.

III. PARTIES

Plaintiff resides at [Address] She is employed as a data entry clerk by the City of Baltimore, Maryland.

ACE Cash Express, Inc. (hereafter "ACE"), is a corporation having its principal place of business in Texas at [Address]. ACE's registered agent in Maryland is Trust Inc., which accepts service of process for ACE at [Address].

IV. CLASS ACTION ALLEGATIONS

Plaintiff brings this lawsuit as a representative of members of a class of similarly situated persons pursuant to Rule 2-231 of the Maryland Rules of Civil Procedure. The "Class" consists of all those persons to whom ACE and its franchisees have lent money, or whom they have assisted or facilitated in the borrowing of money, or from whom defendants have collected or attempted to collect interest, or whom ACE has charged a fee for the delayed presentment of a check or other functionally equivalent bank draft, in transactions occurring in the State of Maryland since ACE began making payday loans in the State, on or about April 1, 2000.

The Class includes a subclass, referred to herein as the "Collateral Subclass" or the "Subclass," which consists of all those members of the Class to whom ACE and its franchisees have lent money, or assisted or facilitated the borrowing of money, since June 1, 2001, when defendants began purporting, albeit falsely, to require payday borrowers to post collateral when applying for payday loans.

The members of the Class and Subclass number in the thousand or tens of thousands, and are so numerous that joinder of all members of the Class and Subclass in a single action is impracticable.

Plaintiff's claims are typical of those of the Class. ACE and its franchisees have lent money to, or assisted or facilitated in borrowing by, and collected or attempted to collect interest and fees from, borrowers (including plaintiff) through standardized form transactions in which only the dates of the transactions and the amounts of the loans are different. Plaintiff's claims are also typical of those of the Subclass, as she and members of the Subclass obtained payday loans from ACE after June 1, 2001, when defendants began using a standardized form requiring borrowers to purport to pledge personal property as collateral for loans.

Plaintiffs are adequate representatives of the Class because their interests do not conflict with the interests of the Class and because they are represented by counsel who are competent and experienced in class action, consumer protection, and complex litigation.

Common questions of law and fact exist, and predominate over questions that affect only individual members of the Class. Among these questions of law and fact are the following:

a. Does the interest rate that ACE charges violate the Maryland anti-usury laws and/or the Maryland Consumer Loan Law?

b. Is ACE a lender or creditor subject to the State's anti-usury laws or other interest-limiting legislation and, if so, does ACE misrepresent its relationship with Goleta and its own true interest in payday loans when it represents to borrowers that "ACE is not involved in the decision to make any Bank

Loan" and that "Ace's involvement is only to transit or deliver information and other items" between the borrower and Goleta?

c. Do ACE's misrepresentations regarding its role as a lender violate the Maryland Unfair and Deceptive Trade Practices Act and the State's truth in lending provisions?

d. Were defendants' violations of the law knowing and intentional?

e. Does a payday borrower's advance authorization of debits to his or her checking account constitute a bank draft or check within the meaning of State laws that prohibit check cashers from charging excessive fees for delayed presentment of checks?

f. Do the statements that ACE now requires borrowers to make on standardized loan applications constitute valid pledges of collateral, so as to make payday loans "secured" and therefore immune regulation under the Maryland Unsecured Closed End Credit Regulation Act, 2001 Md. ALS 630?

g. If ACE does require a valid pledge of collateral from borrowers, does the requirement that borrowers pledge security for payday loans, all of which are under $500, violate the Maryland Consumer Loan Law, Md. Code Ann. § 12-311(b)(1)(ii), which prohibits lenders from requiring collateral for loans of under $700?

h. Does the marketing of payday loans at exorbitant interest rates to low-income people who have no alternative sources of credit constitute an unconscionable commercial practice, entitling plaintiffs to rescission of the payday loan contracts and restitution of the amounts defendants have wrongfully retained?

i. Are plaintiffs entitled to a declaration from this Court that any purported contracts arising from payday loans are void and unenforceable?

j. Are plaintiffs entitled to supplemental equitable relief, including but not limited to rescission, restitution, and an order that defendants cease their illegal activities in Maryland?

k. Do the Maryland Unsecured Closed End Credit Regulation Act and the Maryland Consumer Loan Law require defendants to obtain licenses as financial services concerns or consumer lenders, and, if so, does the fact that ACE is not so licensed render any accounts it acquires from Goleta unenforceable?

The class action is superior to other available methods for fair and efficient adjudication of this controversy. Many members of the Class and Subclass may be unaware that they have claims against defendants. In light of the small amount of each individual claim relative to the costs and burdens of bringing a lawsuit, moreover, it would be very difficult or impossible for members of the Class and Subclass to pursue their claims individually. Plaintiff and her counsel are aware of no factors that would make it especially difficult to manage this litigation as a class action. In fact, defendants have records of the names, addresses, and the borrowing and repayment histories of members of the Class and Subclass, so that any necessary communications with the Class and Subclass, and any assessment and distribution of restitution to the Class and Subclass can be accomplished without undue difficulty.

Defendants have acted or refused to act on grounds that are generally applicable to the Class and Subclass, so that declaratory relief and final injunctive relief to the Class and Subclass as a whole is appropriate and necessary.

The prosecution of separate lawsuits by individual members of the Class and Subclass would create the risk of adjudications and judgments which would, as a practical matter, be dispositive of the interests of other Class members or Subclass members not party to those adjudications, or might substantially impair their ability to protect their interests.

V. FACTUAL ALLEGATIONS

ACE is one of the nation's largest owners, operators, and franchisers of stores that sell basic financial services such as check cashing, bill payment and small short-term loans. ACE owns or controls a network of more than 1,221 stores in 34 states and in the District of Columbia. ACE is a publicly owned equity corporation whose shares are traded on the NASDAQ Stock Exchange.

Upon information and belief, until May 2000, ACE disguised its payday loan product as a check-cashing service. Under this "delayed presentment" rubric, the customer paid the principal and interest on a payday loan by delivering to ACE his or her postdated personal check for those combined amounts at the time that ACE provided the customer with principal loan amount in cash. ACE then presented the check to the customer's bank after a period of delay, obtaining repayment of the principal and collecting the interest as a "fee."

Beginning on or about May 1, 2000, defendants instituted a new device to conceal the true nature of its payday loan transactions, and effectively raised its interest rates significantly at the same time. Pursuant to an arrangement that ACE entered into with Goleta, ACE began admitting that its payday loans were in fact loans, but marketed the loans, and purported to process the loans, as if Goleta was the true lender and as if the customer's actual lender-borrower relationship was with Goleta rather than with ACE. ACE informs payday loan customers that Goleta is the lender, and affirmatively states on loan applications that "ACE is not involved in the decision to make any Bank Loan" and that "ACE's involvement is only to transit or deliver information and other items" between the borrower and Goleta. ACE intentionally conceals its actual interest and participation in the payday loans. Upon information and belief, ACE created and designed the loan product prior to any participation by Goleta, determines or heavily influences the lending criteria for its payday loan project, assumes substantial financial risk in the loans, handles all collections for the loans, guarantees to Goleta that ACE will repurchase loans from Goleta soon after the loans are made, and in fact does acquire the accounts soon after the loans are disbursed. ACE earns its profit based on the number and amount of the loans made and collected, ACE collects interest when it receives money for the loans and when it conducts its collection efforts. In sum, the presentation of Goleta as the lender is a mere formality and a sham. ACE is the lender in fact for its payday loan product.

Beginning on or about June 1, 2001, ACE began purporting to require that customers in Maryland pledge personal property as security for payday loans. The purported request for collateral was a subterfuge to evade the Maryland Unsecured Closed End Credit Regulation Act, which the Governor signed into law on May 18, 2001. ACE does not require consumers to post collateral for payday loans in Maryland: ACE merely requires borrowers to circle, on the loan application, either a watch, VCR player, camera/camcorder, home computer, secondary television, or secondary radio and to indicate the brand of the item. ACE requires no proof of ownership, does not investigate to determine if the property even exists, and makes, and has no intention of making, any attempt to move against collateral in the event of a default by the borrower. Based on the borrower's simply designating a type and brand of personal property as "security," ACE gives the customer a 14-day loan with an A.P.R. of 443 percent or higher.

ACE targets its loans to economically vulnerable individuals who have no access to legitimate credit markets. ACE actively markets the payday loan product with posters and brochures in each of its storefront financial services outlets. It advertises that money is available for borrowing without any credit check from any consumer credit reporting agency. It represents that it will lend money simply based on the customer providing a voided check from an active checking account, a recent checking account statement, a pay stub providing proof of income, and proof of residency. Although ACE advertises that these loans are intended as short-term solutions to immediate cash needs, ACE allows the customer to renew the loan up to three times or for a period of up to eight weeks.

Pursuant to the Payday Loan Scheme, defendants tried to conceal the true nature of the transactions, refusing to apply for and obtain appropriate licenses and permits in Maryland. Defendants together have executed a concerted and organized scheme of misrepresentations and material omissions to State officials and others to conceal the true nature of its business.

Throughout the Class Period, ACE solicited, encouraged, and permitted consumers to extend, renew, or continue their original transactions by the payment of additional fees or interest on or before the due date of the transactions.

The defendants' unfair and deceptive course of conduct can be seen from the experience just one member of the class, Plaintiff. On August 11, 2000, and on or about August 26, 2000, September 10, 2000, September 24, 2000, February 5, 2001, March 15, 2001, June 1, 2001, and July 6, 2001, Plaintiff visited an ACE check cashing store operated by the defendants in the City of Baltimore in the State of Maryland located at [Address]. On each occasion, the plaintiff obtained "short term" loan for $200 for a period of fourteen days by giving ACE a voided check and signing a promissory note for $230. As a condition of receiving the loans, Plaintiff was required to authorize that the loans be collected through an automatic debit from her checking account. The A.P.R. on the plaintiff's loans, according to ACE's computations, was in excess of 390 percent. The promissory notes indicated that ACE's only involvement was to transmit and deliver information and other items from the bank to the borrower and from the borrower to the bank.

On Plaintiff's first visit to ACE, on August 11, 2000, an ACE employee, upon processing her application, gave Plaintiff a plastic card with the words "Advance Cash Express ATM and Debit Card" and with the "ACE" insignia in the lower right corner. The ACE employee instructed Plaintiff to run the card through a machine at the counter and enter her "PIN." The employee then gave Plaintiff $200 in cash and a copy of her promissory note. The promissory note stated that she owed a payment of $230 on August 25, 2000.

On each subsequent visit to ACE, after Plaintiff had completed her loan application and the ACE employee had processed her application, she was instructed by the ACE employee to run her "Advance Cash Express ATM and Debit Card" (as described above in paragraph 24) through the machine located at the ACE counter. On each occasion, the employee would then give Plaintiff the principle amount of her "loan" in cash.

On or about September 24, 2000, Plaintiff learned of ACE's "refinancing" policy. Plaintiff was told by the ACE employee handling the transaction, in accordance with ACE policy, that she would be permitted to renew her loan at the end of the fourteen day period for another fourteen days and that she could renew her loan this way up to three times.

On or about September 24, 2000, February 5, 2001, March 15, 2001, June 1, 2001, and July 6, 2001, Plaintiff refinanced $200 loans from ACE by reducing the original loan amount by 5 percent, paying the interest that was due, and filling out the initial loan application papers again. Plaintiff was then told by an ACE employee that her loan was "refinanced" for an additional fourteen days. On each occasion, at the end of the second fourteen day period, Plaintiff refinanced her loans for a second time by paying an additional $41.80. At the end of the third fourteen day period, on each occasion, Plaintiff refinanced her loans for a third time by paying another $39.00. The A.P.R. listed on each of these "refinancing" transactions was in excess of 390 percent.

Beginning on or about June 1, 2001, in addition to filling out the loan application, Plaintiff was asked by the ACE employee handling the transaction to pledge personal property as collateral for her loan. Plaintiff listed a VCR on her application as her security interest. The ACE employee did not ask Plaintiff any questions to confirm the existence of or value of the VCR, nor did the employee request proof of ownership or possession. Additionally, the ACE employee did not tell Plaintiff that ACE would take her VCR if she failed to repay her loan.

Upon information and belief, the requirement that borrowers pledge collateral is a complete sham. ACE and its affiliates have no intent to gain any security interest in any property. ACE instructs its employees that the existence of or value of the collateral is of no concern to the company and that employees should ignore any indications that the property does not exist, is not owned by the borrower, or has little or no value.

ACE conducted and continues to conduct its payday loan program in an essentially identical manner to consumers across the State of Maryland.

Although all such transactions, including the specific transactions described, above, were handled entirely by ACE and it is ACE who holds the borrower's voided check and account information, each such transaction is memorialized by means of a preprinted promissory note purportedly payable by the customer to "Goleta National Bank."

On information and belief, ACE's representations that Goleta is the actual lender are pretextual. Goleta in turn authorizes and abets the subterfuge in exchange for a payment for each of the loans made and/or collected.

The loan that Plaintiff obtained on or about July 6, 2001, and renewed thereafter is still outstanding as of the commencement of this action.

VI. COUNT ONE: CLAIMS ARISING UNDER THE MARYLAND USURY STATUTE, MD. CODE ANN. §§ 12-101 *et seq.*

The allegations of each of the preceding paragraphs are incorporated by reference as if fully set forth herein.

The interest rates defendants have charged in connection with its payday loans are grossly in excess of the restrictions on interest that may be charged in the State of Maryland.

At all relevant times, defendants charged interest at amounts ranging from 390 percent to 443.21 percent per annum, in excess of that permitted by Md. Commercial Law Code Ann. § 12-103.

These charges were knowingly imposed in violation of law within the meaning of Md. Commercial Law Code Ann. § 12-103.

Plaintiffs and members of the Class and Subclass have been injured as a proximate result of defendants' illegal acts.

VII. COUNT TWO: CLAIMS ARISING UNDER THE MARYLAND CONSUMER LOAN LAW, MD. CODE ANN. §§ 12-301 *et seq.*

The allegations of each of the preceding paragraphs are incorporated by reference as if fully set forth herein.

At all relevant times, defendants have lent money and charged interest in amount ranging from 390 percent to 443.21 percent in connection with its payday loan product.

These charges were knowingly and willfully imposed in violation of law within the meaning of Md. Commercial Law Code Ann. § 12-313.

Defendants have collected and attempted to collect principal and interest in knowing and willful violation of law which prohibits the collection of principal or interest in connection with the payday loan practices under Md. Code Ann. § 12-314.

Defendants have lent or participated in the lending of money, and have acquired payday loan accounts for collection and collected or attempted to collect on the accounts despite the prohibition on such practices by non-licensed parties under Md. Code Ann. §§ 11-219.

Defendants' requirement that plaintiffs pledge personal property as security violates the prohibition on such practices in connection with loans under seven hundred dollars under Md. Code Ann. § 12-311(b)(1)(ii).

Plaintiffs and members of the Class and Subclass have been injured as a proximate result of defendants' illegal acts.

VIII. COUNT THREE: CLAIMS ARISING UNDER THE MARYLAND TRUTH IN LENDING ACT, MD. CODE ANN. § 12-106

The allegations of each of the preceding paragraphs are incorporated by reference as if fully set forth herein.

Defendants' misrepresentations of its actual interest in and role in the payday loan transactions violated the requirement that such information be truthfully provided to borrowers under § 12-106.

Plaintiffs and members of the Class and Subclass have been injured as a proximate result of defendants' illegal acts.

IX. COUNT FOUR: CLAIMS ARISING UNDER THE MARYLAND CONSUMER DEBT COLLECTION ACT, MD. CODE. ANN. §§ 14-201 *et seq.*

The allegations of each of the preceding paragraphs are incorporated by reference as if fully set forth herein.

Defendants' practice of demanding payment from plaintiffs of amounts that are not legally due, extracting authorization to debit debtors' bank accounts, and repeatedly attempting to access accounts with the consequence of incurring bank charges that the debtors must pay, contacting debtors at their place of employment and revealing private economic information, and verbally harassing and abusing debtors constitutes unfair debt collection practices and an abuse of debt collection.

Plaintiffs and members of the Class and Subclass have been directly and proximately injured by defendants' debt collection practices.

X. COUNT FIVE: CLAIMS ARISING UNDER THE MARYLAND UNSECURED CLOSED END CREDIT REGULATION ACT, 2001 MD. ALS 630

The allegations of each of the preceding paragraphs are incorporated by reference as if fully set forth herein.

Upon information and belief, ACE and its franchisees are credit service businesses that assist plaintiffs and members of the Class and Subclass in obtaining payday loans at rates that are in excess of those allowed under Maryland law.

ACE makes and uses false and misleading statements in selling its services in connection with payday lending and engages in the above-described fraud or deception in connection with the payday loan scheme.

Since June 1, 2001, ACE has marketed and assisted Maryland Sub-class plaintiffs in obtaining loans at interest rates that would be usurious under Maryland law. These loans were unsecured, closed end credit extensions. Defendants' pretensions to require a pledge of collateral in order to make it appear that they were not providing unsecured credit were pure shams. Defendants never confirmed or attempted to confirm in any way the ownership or existence of the purported collateral, never intended to seek to recover the collateral in the event of default, and, upon information and belief, have never attempted to move against any collateral. In fact, Defendants instructed ACE employees to ignore any indications the customer might give that the property did not exist or was not owned by the credit applicant.

Plaintiffs and members of the Class and Subclass have been injured as a proximate result of defendants' illegal act.

XI. COUNT SIX: CLAIMS ARISING UNDER THE MARYLAND CONSUMER PROTECTION ACT, MD. CODE. ANN. §§ 13-301 *et seq.*

The allegations of each of the preceding paragraphs are incorporated by reference as if fully set forth herein.

Defendants' marketing of payday loans incorporated the above-described misrepresentations and material omissions regarding the true nature of the transactions, the identity of the lender, the role of ACE in the transactions, the legality of the transactions, and the means that ACE would or legally could utilize to collect the debt, and the fact that payday loans constitute unconscionable transactions.

Defendants' misstatements have the capacity, tendency and effect of deceiving or misleading consumers, and its and material omissions deceives or tends to deceive consumers.

By knowingly and intentionally concealing, suppressing or omitting their true involvement in the loans and other material facts regarding the loans, ACE committed unlawful acts under the Maryland Consumer Protection Act, Md. Code Ann. Com, Law I § 13-301.

Plaintiffs and members of the Class and Subclass were injured by defendants' misleading, deceptive and unfair marketing and collection practices.

XII. COUNT SEVEN: CLAIMS FOR RESCISSION AND RESTITUTION UNDER THE COMMON LAW OF THE STATE OF MARYLAND

The allegations of each of the preceding paragraphs are incorporated by reference as if fully set forth herein.

Agreements entered into between Plaintiffs and members of the Class and Subclass and Defendants were and are unconscionable within the meaning of the common law of contracts, and Plaintiffs and members of the Class and Subclass are entitled to rescission of any agreements with defendants and a return of moneys that defendants are retaining as a consequence of their illegal course of conduct and benefits that Plaintiffs and members of the Class and Subclasses conferred on Defendants with no intent to make a gift to ACE, Goleta, or any of ACE's franchisees.

PRAYER FOR RELIEF

The plaintiffs respectfully request that this Court grant the following relief:

1. An Order declaring that the Defendants' payday loan practices are illegal and preliminarily and permanently enjoining defendants from their illegal conduct;

2. An Order declaring that plaintiffs' and all Classmembers' and Subclassmembers' obligations to the Defendants to be null and void;

3. An Order declaring that any moneys that Defendants have obtained from Plaintiffs, Classmembers and Subclassmembers be held in a constructive trust for the benefit of Plaintiffs, Classmembers and Subclassmembers and returned to them as restitution;

4. An Order dissolving ACE as an enterprise and prohibiting Defendants from operating any financial services business in the future;

5. An Order requiring that Defendants disgorge all wrongfully obtained profits from the payday loan business and pay such amounts to plaintiff Classmembers and Subclassmembers.

6. An award of costs and attorneys fees; and

7. Any other relief which this Court deems just.

Respectfully submitted,

[Attorney for Plaintiff]

L.5 Refund Anticipation Loan (RAL) Litigation

This appendix contains the complaint and discovery in a case challenging a refund anticipation (RAL) lender and tax preparation company for their practice of collecting debts for other RAL lenders, a common practice in the RAL industry. The complaint raises state fair debt, UDAP, and conversion claims against the lender, and aiding and abetting claims against the tax preparer. The complaint was filed in *Hood v. Santa Barbara Bank & Trust*, Case No. CGG03418466, Superior Court for the County of San Francisco. L.5.1 contains the first amended complaint. L.5.2 contains interrogatories served upon the bank. L.5.3 contains requests for production of documents directed to the bank. L.5.4 contains

interrogatories served upon the tax preparation company. L.5.5 contains requests for production of documents directed to the tax preparation firm.

Thanks to James C. Sturdevant and Monique Olivier of The Sturdevant Law Firm, who are co-counsel with NCLC on this case.

L.5.1 Sample Amended Complaint

SUPERIOR COURT OF THE STATE OF CALIFORNIA IN AND FOR THE COUNTY OF SAN FRANCISCO

[CONSUMER] and CONGRESS OF CALIFORNIA SENIORS, Plaintiffs, v. SANTA BARBARA BANK & TRUST and PACIFIC CAPITAL BANK NA, a California corporation, and JACKSONHEWITT TAX SERVICE a Virginia corporation, DOES 1 through 20, inclusive, Defendants.	*CLASS ACTION* *DEMAND FOR JURY TRIAL*

FIRST AMENDED COMPLAINT FOR VIOLATIONS OF CONSUMER LEGAL REMEDIES ACT, ROBBINS-ROSENTHAL FAIR DEBT COLLECTION PRACTICES ACT, BUSINESS & PROFESSIONS CODE §§ 17200 et seq., CONVERSION, AIDING & ABETTING, AND DECLARATORY RELIEF

INTRODUCTION

Plaintiffs [Consumer] and Congress of California Seniors, by their attorneys, bring this action to challenge the Defendants' unlawful and unfair practice of seizing consumers' tax refunds to repay debts owed to other third-party lenders without prior consent, permission or authorization. In the alternative, Plaintiffs challenge the Defendants' practice of misleading consumers into entering into loan agreements that permit the Defendants to seize tax refunds for debt collection purposes. Plaintiffs seek compensatory and punitive damages, injunctive relief, and attorney fees, costs and expenses.

JURISDICTION AND VENUE

This court has jurisdiction over the subject matter of this action pursuant to California Civil Code §§ 1780 and 1781, Civil Code § 1788.30 and Business and Professions Code §§ 17203 and 17204.

This court has personal jurisdiction over Defendant Pacific Capital Bank NA, also doing business as Santa Barbara Bank & Trust, as it is a California corporation.

This court has personal jurisdiction over Defendant Jackson Hewitt Tax Service as Jackson Hewitt does business throughout

California, including San Francisco County. Jackson Hewitt has offices and/or franchises in California.

Venue is proper in the County of San Francisco pursuant to California Civil Code § 1780(c) because Defendants are doing business in San Francisco.

THE PARTIES

1. Plaintiff [Consumer] is a natural person and a resident of Los Angeles, California. [Consumer] is employed as an administrative assistant. She supports two children and her mother. She has received the Earned Income Tax Credit from the Internal Revenue Service (IRS) during approximately the past nine (9) years.

2. The Congress of California Seniors (hereafter "CCS") is located in Sacramento, California. Established in 1977, CCS is a statewide nonprofit education and advocacy organization dedicated to improving the life of seniors and their families. CCS is an affiliate of the Alliance for Retired Americans, which was established eighteen (18) years ago for the purposes of representing the interests of the elderly throughout California.

3. Defendant Pacific Capital Bank NA is a California bank with its principal place of business in Santa Barbara, California. Pacific Capital Bank, NA is chartered by the Office of the Comptroller of Currency. Santa Barbara Bank & Trust is a division of Pacific Capital Bank NA. (Pacific Capital Bank, NA and Santa Barbara Bank & Trust hereinafter will be jointly referred to as "SBBT"). Among other functions, SBBT is engaged in the business of making refund anticipation loans (RALs) to consumers.

4. Defendant Jackson Hewitt Tax Service is a Virginia corporation with its principal office in Parsipanny, New Jersey. Jackson Hewitt is a subsidiary of Cendant Corporation, a Delaware corporation with its principal office in New York, NY. Jackson Hewitt is engaged in the business of tax preparation. It is, through its officers, agents, and employees, engaged in and sells tax preparation services, and is doing such business in California with offices and/or franchises located in San Francisco, California and many other California locations.

5. Plaintiffs are ignorant of the true names and capacities of Defendants sued herein as Does 1–20, and therefore sues these Defendants by such fictitious names. Plaintiffs are informed and believes that each of the fictitiously named Defendants, including any such Defendants that may be the agents, representatives, or parent or subsidiary corporations of the named Defendants, is responsible in some manner for the occurrences, events, transactions, and injuries alleged herein, and that the harm suffered by the persons Plaintiffs represent and by the general public as hereinafter set forth were proximately caused by said Defendants. Plaintiffs will amend this complaint to state the true names and capacities of said Doe Defendants when ascertained.

6. Plaintiffs are informed and believes and thereon alleges that each of the Defendants, including the Doe Defendants, acted in concert with each and every other Defendant, intended to and did participate in the events, acts, practices and courses of conduct alleged herein, and was a proximate cause of damage and injury thereby to Plaintiffs as alleged herein.

7. At all times herein mentioned, each Defendant was the agent or employee of each of the other Defendants and was acting within the course and scope of such agency or employment.

CLASS ALLEGATIONS

8. Pursuant to California Civil Code § 1781 and California Code of Civil Procedure § 382, Plaintiff [Consumer] brings this action on behalf of herself and all other persons similarly situated. The class that Plaintiff represents (hereinafter the "Plaintiff Class") is composed of all persons who have or have had at any time since March 18, 1999, had their refunds seized by SBBT as a result of the conduct challenged by this action.

9. The Plaintiff Class includes a subclass, referred to herein as the "No Contract Subclass" or the "Subclass," which consist of all those members of the Plaintiff Class who had their RAL Application/Agreements rejected by the Defendants, did not receive an "Accelerated Check Refund" from the Defendants, and had their refunds seized by the Defendants.

10. Plaintiff [Consumer] is informed and believes and on that basis alleges that the Plaintiff Class is so numerous that joinder of all members would be impracticable. The exact size of the Plaintiff Class, and the identity of the members of the class are ascertainable from the business records of Defendants.

11. Questions of law and fact common to the Plaintiff Class exist that predominate over questions affecting only individual members, including, *inter alia*, the following:

(a) whether Defendants have violated Civil Code § 1770(a)(5) by representing that RALs are a form of tax refund when they are, in fact, loans subject to seizure by the lender to pay off prior alleged RAL debts of individual taxpayers;

(b) whether Defendants have violated Civil Code § 1770(a)(14) by representing that they have rights and remedies that are prohibited by law, specifically that they have the right to collect the third party debt without providing notices required by law; and

(c) whether Defendants have violated Civil Code § 1770(a)(19) by including a provision authorizing cross-lender debt collection in their RAL Application/Agreements and whether without discussion or negotiation Defendants standardized the form contracts, drafted solely by them.

12. The claims asserted by Plaintiff [Consumer] in this action are typical of the claims of the members of the Plaintiff Class as described above, the claims arise from the same course of conduct by Defendants, and the relief sought is common.

13. Plaintiff [Consumer] will fairly and adequately represent and protect the interests of the members of the Plaintiff Class. Plaintiff [Consumer] has retained counsel who are competent and experienced in both consumer protection and class action litigation.

14. For class claims alleged under California Code of Civil Procedure § 382, a class action is superior to other methods for the fair and efficient adjudication of this controversy, since joinder of all members is impracticable. Furthermore, because the economic damages suffered by the individual class members may be relatively modest, albeit significant, compared to the expense and burden of individual litigation, it would be impracticable for members of the Plaintiff Class to seek redress individually for the wrongful conduct alleged herein. There will be no undue difficulty in the management of this litigation as a class action.

PRIVATE ATTORNEY GENERAL ALLEGATIONS

15. This action is brought by Plaintiffs acting as private attorneys general pursuant to the Unfair Competition Law, Business and Professions Code §§ 17200 *et seq.* Pursuant to Business and

Professions Code §§ 17203 and 17204, a private attorney general action is appropriate and necessary because SBBT has engaged in the acts described herein as a general business practice. Plaintiffs request that this Court decide that SBBT's practice of seizing tax refunds for debt collection purposes without the voluntary and knowing consent of consumers is unlawful, unfair, deceptive and unenforceable, and enjoin SBBT from engaging in this practice. Plaintiffs also request that this Court decide that SBBT's imposition of a contract provision permitting this debt collection practice is unlawful, unfair, deceptive and unenforceable, and enjoin SBBT from engaging in this practice.

FACTUAL ALLEGATIONS

16. On January 31, 2002, [Consumer] went to the Trotwood, Ohio office of Jackson Hewitt to have her taxes prepared. [Consumer] inquired into the option of getting her refund quickly.

17. A Jackson Hewitt employee informed [Consumer] about two options for getting her refund quickly, either the next day or in 48 hours. The Jackson Hewitt employee did not inform [Consumer] that both the next day and the 48 hour options actually were loans. Instead, the Jackson Hewitt employee characterized these options using the words "rapid refund." The employee also did not inform [Consumer] that the loan agreement contained a provision allowing SBBT to seize her refund if she had any prior RAL debts outstanding, including debts owed to other RAL lenders.

18. [Consumer] chose the RAL that would be received in 48 hours. [Consumer] did not realize that she was taking out a loan or that in seeking a "rapid refund," she might be agreeing to let SBBT take her refund to repay any outstanding RAL debts.

19. After preparing her tax returns, the Jackson Hewitt employee instructed [Consumer] to sign and initial a set of documents. [Consumer] did not have an opportunity to read the documents.

20. In the stack of documents signed by [Consumer], there was a loan application and agreement for a RAL. Paragraph 6.a. of the RAL Application/Agreement includes a Cross Lender Debt Provision which states

> COLLECTION OF DELINQUENT RAL You authorize JH and SBBT to exchange information about your current and prior RALs with other RAL lenders including Bank One, N.A., Beneficial National Bank/Household Bank, First Security Bank, River City Bank, County Bank of Rehobeth Beach, DE and Republic Bank & Trust Company/Refunds Now. If you have delinquent RALs from prior years with SBBT or any or one more of these lenders that have not been discharged in bankruptcy, you will not be eligible for a RAL but will instead receive an ACR. Upon receipt of your tax refund, you authorize SBBT to deduct from the Account, after deducting the applicable fees as set forth in Section 2 above, the total amount due on the prior year RALs and forward such amount to the appropriate RAL lender(s) prior to disbursing the balance of the Account to you.

A copy of the loan agreement is attached as Exhibit 1.

21. On Saturday, February 9, [Consumer] received a letter from Defendant SBBT stating that her RAL was denied because SBBT had been informed of an outstanding RAL debt with Household Bank. The letter also stated that if the IRS sent [Consumer's] refund to SBBT, those funds would be used to satisfy the outstanding RAL debt. A copy of this letter is attached as Exhibit 2.

22. [Consumer] never received her tax refund. Upon information and belief, [Consumer's] refund was seized by SBBT and paid to Household Bank to satisfy an outstanding RAL debt. [Consumer] also never received or was offered an "Accelerated Check Refund" (ACR). Upon information and belief, the ACR is a non-RAL product that represents a consumer's tax refund minus the tax preparation and ACR fees.

23. Subsequently, [Consumer] contacted a legal services program in Ohio seeking assistance. In June 2002, an attorney from the Equal Justice Foundation in Ohio sent letters on [Consumer's] behalf to Defendant SBBT and Household Bank requesting disclosure of the information upon which SBBT relied in denying [Consumer's] application. Copies of the responses from SBBT and Household Bank are attached as Exhibits 3 and 4.

24. Because of the loss of her tax refund, [Consumer] was unable to pay her rent and received an eviction notice. [Consumer] is still experiencing financial difficulties because of the loss of her tax refund.

SBBT's RAL program

25. A refund anticipation loan is a short term loan secured by a consumer's expected tax refund. RALs loan are usually *not* made by the tax preparer, but by a separate lender, usually a bank such as SBBT.

26. Pacific Capital Bank's filings with the Securities and Exchange Commission state that the company earned $26.4 million in gross income from RAL fees in 2001.

27. Upon information and belief, when SBBT makes a RAL, it prepares to collect on the loan by opening a temporary bank account to receive electronic deposit of the refund. The documents signed by the consumer instruct the IRS to direct deposit the refund into that account. SBBT is repaid when the consumer's refund appears in the temporary bank account.

28. Upon information and belief, if the consumer's refund is not deposited into the temporary bank account or is less than expected, the bank will hold the consumer liable for the full amount of the RAL.

29. Upon information and belief, there are only a handful of banks that make refund anticipation loans. The three banks that control most of the RAL market are Household Bank, Bank One and Defendant SBBT. Other banks that make RALs include Republic Bank & Trust (d.b.a. Refunds Now) and River City Bank.

30. Upon information and belief, banks that make RALs, including SBBT and Household Bank, have entered into a cooperative agreement with each other to collect back debts from RAL customers. RAL lenders include a provision their RAL Application/Agreements to implement this cooperative agreement.

FIRST CAUSE OF ACTION FOR INJUNCTIVE RELIEF
(Violation of Consumer Legal Remedies Act, California Civil Code §§ 1750 *et seq.*, asserted on behalf of Plaintiff [Consumer] and the Plaintiff Class against All Defendants)

31. [Consumer] realleges and incorporates herein as though set forth in full, the allegations of paragraphs 1 through 30 above.

32. [Consumer] brings this action on her behalf and on behalf of the Plaintiff Class seeking injunctive relief pursuant to the Consumer Legal Remedies Act (CLRA), California Civil Code §§ 1750 *et seq.* California Civil Code § 1770(a)(5) specifically prohibits representations that services have sponsorship, approval, characteristics, ingredients, uses, benefits, or quantities which they do not have. California Civil Code § 1770(a)(14) specifically prohibits representations that a transaction confers or involves rights, remedies, or obligations which it does not have or involve or which are prohibited by law. California Civil Code § 1770(a)(19) prohibits insertion of an unconscionable provision in a contract.

33. Defendants have violated California Civil Code § 1770(a)(5) because they have represented that the RALs are a form of tax refund when they are loans subject to seizure by the lender to pay off alleged prior RAL debts of individual taxpayers.

34. Defendants have violated § 1770(a)(14) of the Act by representing that they have rights and remedies that are prohibited by law, specifically that they have the right to collect a third party debt without providing notices required by law.

35. Defendants have violated § 1770(a)(19) of the Act by including the SBBT Cross-Lender Debt Collection Provision in their RAL Application/Agreements. Defendants possess bargaining strength and power far superior to that of [Consumer] and other customers. Without discussion or negotiation, Defendants offer standardized form contracts, drafted by Defendants, which are contracts of adhesion because they are offered on a take-it-or-leave-it basis.

36. The Cross-Lender Debt Collection Provision is substantially one-sided in favor of Defendants. There is no consideration for the SBBT Cross-Lender Debt Collection Provision. It is, therefore, unlawful, unfair, fraudulent and unconscionable.

37. The Cross-Lender Debt Collection Provision does not fall within the reasonable expectations of [Consumer] or of Defendants' other customers, and is unduly oppressive. It is, therefore, unlawful, unfair, fraudulent and unconscionable.

38. The Cross-Lender Debt Collection Provision unlawfully, unfairly and fraudulently deprives [Consumer] and the Defendants' other customers of their tax refunds without their voluntary, knowing and intelligent consent.

39. As a result of the unfair and deceptive acts and practices of Defendants hereinabove described, plaintiff [Consumer] and members of the Plaintiff Class have suffered substantial economic losses in an amount to be proven at trial.

40. Pursuant to California Civil Code §§ 1780 and 1781, plaintiff [Consumer] and the Plaintiff Class hereby request certification of the Plaintiff Class, injunctive relief, restitution, and attorneys' fees, costs and expenses pursuant to California Civil Code § 1780(d) and California Code of Civil Procedure § 1021.5.

SECOND CAUSE OF ACTION FOR DAMAGES AND PENALTIES
(Violation of the Robbins-Rosenthal Fair Debt Collection Practices Act; Asserted on behalf of [Consumer] Against All Defendants)

41. [Consumer] realleges and incorporates herein by reference each and every allegation set forth in paragraphs 1 through 30 above, except paragraphs 8 through 14.

42. The Robbins-Rosenthal Fair Debt Collection Practices Act (Robbins-Rosenthal Act), Civil Code §§ 1788 *et seq.*, prohibits unfair and deceptive acts and practices in the collection of consumer debts.

43. By their acts and practices as hereinabove described, Defendants have violated the Robbins-Rosenthal Act as follows, without limitation:

(a) In failing to inform consumers that SBBT would engage in debt collection practices during the loan application and approval process, Defendants have violated § 1788.13(i), which prohibits the false representation of the true nature of the business or services being rendered by the debt collector. Defendants have represented SBBT as a lender but have failed to disclose the material fact that it is acting as a debt collector with respect to the same transaction.

(b) By failing to include certain debt collection notices required by law.

44. Pursuant to § 1788.30 of the Robbins-Rosenthal Act, [Consumer] is entitled to recover her actual damages sustained as a result of Defendants' violations of the Robbins-Rosenthal Act. Such damages include, without limitation, the amount of her federal tax refund seized by SBBT, other resulting monetary losses and damages, and emotional distress suffered by [Consumer], which damages are in an amount to be proven at trial.

45. In addition, because Defendants' violations of the Robbins-Rosenthal Act were committed willingly and knowingly, [Consumer] is entitled to recover, in addition to her actual damages, penalties of at least $1,000 per violation as provided for in the Act.

46. Pursuant to § 1788.30(c) Robbins-Rosenthal Act, [Consumer] is entitled to recover all attorneys' fees, costs and expenses incurred in the bringing of this action.

THIRD CAUSE OF ACTION FOR INJUNCTIVE RELIEF AND RESTITUTION
(Violation of the Unfair Competition Law, California Business and Professions Code §§ 17200 *et seq.*, Brought by All Plaintiffs Against All Defendants)

47. Plaintiffs reallege and incorporate herein by this reference each and every allegation set forth in paragraphs 1 through 30 above.

48. Plaintiffs, as private attorneys general, challenge Defendants' practice of cross-lender debt collection and inclusion of the SBBT Cross-Lender Debt Collection Provision in the RAL Application/Agreement.

49. The Unfair Trade Practices Act defines unfair competition to include any "unlawful," "unfair" or "fraudulent" business act or practice. Bus. and Prof. Code § 17200.

50. Defendants' practices are unlawful, unfair and fraudulent business practices for the reasons set forth below, without limitation:

(a) The practice of cross-lender debt collection and the inclusion of the Cross-Lender Debt Collection Provision in RAL Agreements violate the Consumer Legal Remedies Act, §§ 1770 (a)(14) and (a)(19);

(b) The practice of cross-lender debt collection violates the Robbins-Rosenthal Act;

(c) The practice of cross-lender debt collection and the inclusion of the Cross-Lender Debt Collection Provision in RAL Agreements offends public policy, is oppressive and unscrupulous, and causes substantial injury to consumers; and

(d) Defendants' deceive and mislead consumers when they inducing consumers to sign RAL Agreements containing the Cross-Lender Debt Collection Provision, because consumers are not clearly and effectively informed about the existence and effect of the SBBT Cross-Lender Debt Collection Provision.

51. Pursuant to Business and Professions Code §§ 17200 *et seq.*, Plaintiffs are entitled to enjoin the practice of cross-lender debt collection and to obtain restitution of all funds obtained by Defendants by reason of and through the use of these unlawful, unfair and fraudulent acts and practices.

52. Pursuant to Business and Professions Code § 17203, Plaintiffs, individually, and on behalf of all members of the general public who are, have been or may be, subjected to the unlawful, unfair, and fraudulent practices of Defendants, hereby request injunctive relief prohibiting these practices in the future, and such other orders as may be necessary to restore to any person in interest, any money or property, real or personal, which may have been acquired by Defendants by means of this unlawful, unfair and fraudulent business practice, or to disgorge profits Defendants have earned thereby.

53. Pursuant to Code of Civil Procedure § 1021.5, Plaintiffs are entitled to recover their reasonable attorney's fees, costs and expenses incurred in bringing this action.

FOURTH CAUSE OF ACTION FOR DAMAGES
(Conversion, Asserted on Behalf of the No Contract Subclass Against All Defendants)

54. Plaintiffs reallege and incorporate herein by this reference each and every allegation set forth in paragraphs 1 through 30 above.

55. Defendants did not have a valid contract with Subclass members because they rejected the Subclass members' applications for RALs and did not give them ACRs. No contract was formed.

56. In the alternative, there was no consideration for the SBBT Cross-Lender Debt Collection Provision. It is, therefore, unlawful, unfair, fraudulent and unconscionable, and of no legal effect.

57. Because the contract and/or SBBT Cross-Lender Debt Collection Provision are null, void and of no legal effect, Defendants unlawfully, wrongfully and fraudulently exercised dominion and control over the property of the Subclass.

58. Defendants knowingly deprived the Subclass of the beneficial use of their property by these actions, and have committed the common law tort of conversion.

59. The Subclass is entitled to recover their actual damages sustained as a result of Defendants' conversion. Such damages include, without limitation, the amount of the Subclass' federal tax refunds seized by Defendants, interest from the time of the conversion, and other resulting monetary losses and damages, which damages are in an amount to be proven at trial.

FIFTH CAUSE OF ACTION
(Aiding and Abetting, Brought By All Plaintiffs Against Jackson Hewitt)

60. Plaintiffs reallege and incorporate herein by this reference each and every allegation set forth in paragraphs 1 through 30 above.

61. Jackson Hewitt knew or realized that the other Defendants were engaging in or planned to engage in the unlawful acts, as more particularly alleged above. Knowing or realizing that SBBT and other Defendants were engaged in the unlawful conduct, Jackson Hewitt nevertheless facilitated and continued to facilitate the commission of those unlawful acts as alleged above. Jackson Hewitt intended to encourage and facilitate the commission of the unlawful acts, and did encourage, facilitate, aid, promote and/or instigate the commission of unlawful acts, and thereby aided and abetted the other Defendants unlawful conduct. For these reasons, Jackson Hewitt is liable for the violations committed by SBBT.

SIXTH CAUSE OF ACTION
(Declaratory Relief, Brought by All Plaintiffs Against SBBT and Jackson Hewitt)

62. Plaintiffs reallege and incorporate herein as though set forth in full the allegations of paragraphs 1 through 30 above.

63. An actual controversy has arisen and now exists relating to the rights and duties of the parties herein. Plaintiffs contend that:

(a) Defendants' practice of cross-lender debt collection is unlawful, unfair and fraudulent;

(b) Defendants' practice of inducing consumers into entering into RAL Application/Agreements containing the SBBT Cross-Lender Debt Collection Provision is misleading, deceptive, fraudulent, unfair and unlawful; and

(c) The RAL Agreement/Application and/or SBBT Cross-Lender Debt Collection Provision are unconscionable, unlawful, unfair, unenforceable, oppressive, and are void and of no force or effect in all respects.

64. Plaintiffs contend that Defendants' practices have violated the Consumer Legal Remedies Act, the Robbins-Rosenthal Act, the Unfair Competition Law, Business and Professions Code §§ 17200 *et seq.* The Subclass also contends that Defendants have converted their property.

65. Defendants dispute Plaintiffs' contentions. They contend that its practice of cross-lender debt collection is lawful and that the SBBT Cross-Lender Debt Collection Provision is valid, creates binding contracts, and is enforceable in all respects.

66. Plaintiffs desire a declaration as to the lawfulness of Defendants' practice of cross-lender debt collection, the validity and enforceability of the SBBT Cross-Lender Debt Collection Provision, and whether Defendants' methods of inducing consumers to enter into the Provision is unlawful, unfair or fraudulent. A judicial declaration is necessary and appropriate at this time so that Plaintiffs may ascertain their rights and duties, and those of other affected persons.

PRAYER FOR RELIEF

WHEREFORE, Plaintiffs respectfully pray as follows:

1. That this Court certify this case as a class action and appoint Plaintiff [Consumer] as a class representative;

2. That this Court find and declare Defendants' acts and practices as described herein to be unlawful, unfair and fraudulent;

3. That Defendants be permanently enjoined from engaging in the unlawful, unfair and fraudulent acts and practices alleged herein;

4. That Defendants be ordered to disgorge all unjust enrichment obtained from the unlawful, unfair and fraudulent acts and practices alleged herein; and

5. That Plaintiffs and the Plaintiff Class be awarded compensatory damages according to proof at trial;

6. That Plaintiffs and the Plaintiff Class be awarded punitive damages according to proof at trial;

7. That Defendants be ordered to make restitution to all affected members of the general public;

8. That Plaintiffs be awarded attorneys' fees and expenses pursuant to California Civil Code § 1790(d), California Civil Code § 1788.30(c), and California Code of Civil Procedure § 1021.5.

9. For costs of suit herein incurred; and

10. For such other and further relief as the court may deem proper.

DEMAND FOR JURY TRIAL

Plaintiffs hereby demand a trial by jury as to all causes of action so triable.

DATED:

Respectfully submitted,

[Attorneys for Plaintiff]

L.5.2 Interrogatories to Bank

SUPERIOR COURT OF THE STATE OF CALIFORNIA
IN AND FOR THE COUNTY OF SAN FRANCISCO

————————————————)
[PLAINTIFF 1] and   )
[PLAINTIFF 2],   )
                    Plaintiffs,)
)
v.   )
)   CASE NO. CGG03418466
)
SANTA BARBARA BANK &   )
TRUST and PACIFIC   )   [PLAINTIFF 1'S] FIRST
CAPITAL BANK NA, a   )   SET OF INTERROGATO-
California corporation, and)   RIES TO DEFENDANT
JACKSONHEWITT TAX   )   SANTA BARBARA
SERVICE a Virginia   )   BANK & TRUST
corporation, DOES 1 through)
20, inclusive,   )
                    Defendants.)
————————————————)

PROPOUNDING PARTY: Plaintiff [Plaintiff 1]

RESPONDING PARTY: Defendant Santa Barbara Bank & Trust

SET NO.: One

INTERROGATORIES

INTERROGATORY NO. 1

IDENTIFY each PERSON consulted by SBBT in the preparation of responses to these Interrogatories and to [Plaintiff 1's] First Request for Production of Documents to SBBT.

The term "IDENTIFY" when referring to: i) an individual or a person, means to state, to the extent known, his or her full name, aliases, job title, last known business address, last known residential address, business telephone number, residential telephone number, and last-known employer or business affiliations; and ii) a company, corporation, business or other entity, means to state, to the extent known, its full name and its address. The term "PERSON" means, where applicable, natural persons, businesses, corporations, trusts, partnerships, incorporated or unincorporated associations, joint ventures, governmental units, and any other legal entity. The term "SBBT" refers to defendant Santa Barbara Bank & Trust, Santa Barbara Bank & Trust as a division of Pacific National Bank, Pacific Capital Bank doing business as Santa Barbara Bank & Trust, Pacific Capital Bank, and/or Pacific Capital Bancorp, and any of their principals, agents, employees, attorneys, representatives, predecessors, and any persons acting or purporting to act on their behalf, and any persons in active concert and participation with them, whether past or present, without regard to whether or not the relationship currently exists or has been terminated.

INTERROGATORY NO. 2

IDENTIFY each former or current SBBT employee or agent who was involved in any manner in SBBT's COLLECTION or attempts to COLLECT any debts purportedly owing by [Plaintiff 1], stating the nature and purpose of his/her involvement.

The term "IDENTIFY" when referring to: i) an individual or a person, means to state, to the extent known, his or her full name, aliases, job title, last known business address, last known residential address, business telephone number, residential telephone number, and last-known employer or business affiliations; and ii) a company, corporation, business or other entity, means to state, to the extent known, its full name and its address. The term "SBBT" refers to defendant Santa Barbara Bank & Trust, Santa Barbara Bank & Trust as a division of Pacific National Bank, Pacific Capital Bank doing business as Santa Barbara Bank & Trust, Pacific Capital Bank, and/or Pacific Capital Bancorp, and any of their principals, agents, employees, attorneys, representatives, predecessors, and any persons acting or purporting to act on their behalf, and any persons in active concert and participation with them, whether past or present, without regard to whether or not the relationship currently exists or has been terminated. The terms "COLLECTION" and "COLLECT," when referring to a debt, include the definition set forth at California Civil Code § 1788.2, and also refer to the taking, seizure, or offset of any monies held by SBBT or held in an SBBT deposit or other SBBT account for payment to satisfy any outstanding debt, obligation, bill, or amount owed by a consumer to any entity other than SBBT.

INTERROGATORY NO. 3

IDENTIFY each former or current SBBT employee or agent with a primary role or responsibility for developing, reviewing, approving, evaluating or implementing any SBBT policy, procedure or practice regarding offering RALs to consumers and COLLECTING RAL debts owed to entities other than SBBT, stating the nature and purpose of his/her responsibility.

The term "IDENTIFY" when referring to: i) an individual or a person, means to state, to the extent known, his or her full name, aliases, job title, last known business address, last known residential address, business telephone number, residential telephone number, and last-known employer or business affiliations; and ii) a company, corporation, business or other entity, means to state, to the extent known, its full name and its address. The term "RAL" refs to a loan that is secured by, or that the lender arranges to be repaid directly from, the proceeds of the borrower's income tax refund. The term "SBBT" refers to defendant Santa Barbara Bank & Trust, Santa Barbara Bank & Trust as a division of Pacific National Bank, Pacific Capital Bank doing business as Santa Barbara Bank & Trust, Pacific Capital Bank, and/or Pacific Capital Bancorp, and any of their principals, agents, employees, attorneys, representatives, predecessors, and any persons acting or purporting to act on their behalf, and any persons in active concert and participation with them, whether past or present, without regard to whether or not the relationship currently exists or has been terminated. The terms "COLLECTION" and "COLLECT," when referring to a debt, include the definition set forth at California Civil Code § 1788.2, and also refer to the taking, seizure, or offset of any monies held by SBBT or held in an SBBT deposit or other SBBT account for payment to satisfy any outstanding debt, obligation, bill, or amount owed by a consumer to any entity other than SBBT.

INTERROGATORY NO. 4

IDENTIFY each lender for whom SBBT has agreed to COLLECT RAL debts, stating the date(s) of such agreement(s) and the date(s) upon which SBBT began COLLECTING RAL debts for each lender.

The term "IDENTIFY" when referring to: i) an individual or a person, means to state, to the extent known, his or her full name, aliases, job title, last known business address, last known residential address, business telephone number, residential telephone number, and last-known employer or business affiliations; and ii) a company, corporation, business or other entity, means to state, to the extent known, its full name and its address. The term "RAL" refers to a loan that is secured by, or that the lender arranges to be repaid directly from, the proceeds of the borrower's income tax refund. The term "SBBT" refers to defendant Santa Barbara Bank & Trust, Santa Barbara Bank & Trust as a division of Pacific National Bank, Pacific Capital Bank doing business as Santa Barbara Bank & Trust, Pacific Capital Bank, and/or Pacific Capital Bancorp, and any of their principals, agents, employees, attorneys, representatives, predecessors, and any persons acting or purporting to act on their behalf, and any persons in active concert and participation with them, whether past or present, without regard to whether or not the relationship currently exists or has been terminated. The terms "COLLECTION" and "COLLECT," when referring to a debt, include the definition set forth at California Civil Code § 1788.2, and also refer to the taking, seizure, or offset of any monies held by SBBT or held in an SBBT deposit or other SBBT account for payment to satisfy any outstanding debt, obligation, bill, or amount owed by a consumer to any entity other than SBBT.

INTERROGATORY NO. 5

For each RAL lender for whom SBBT has agreed to COLLECT or does COLLECT RAL debts, IDENTIFY each PERSON from whom SBBT COLLECTED a tax refund to pay a RAL debt for each year from 1998 to the present, and state the amount COLLECTED, the date COLLECTED, and the amount of the RAL debt.

The term "IDENTIFY" when referring to: i) an individual or a person, means to state, to the extent known, his or her full name, aliases, job title, last known business address, last known residen-

tial address, business telephone number, residential telephone number, and last-known employer or business affiliations; and ii) a company, corporation, business or other entity, means to state, to the extent known, its full name and its address. The term "PERSON" means, where applicable, natural persons, businesses, corporations, trusts, partnerships, incorporated or unincorporated associations, joint ventures, governmental units, and any other legal entity. The term "RAL" refers to a loan that is secured by, or that the lender arranges to be repaid directly from, the proceeds of the borrower's income tax refund. The term "SBBT" refers to defendant Santa Barbara Bank & Trust, Santa Barbara Bank & Trust as a division of Pacific National Bank, Pacific Capital Bank doing business as Santa Barbara Bank & Trust, Pacific Capital Bank, and/or Pacific Capital Bancorp, and any of their principals, agents, employees, attorneys, representatives, predecessors, and any persons acting or purporting to act on their behalf, and any persons in active concert and participation with them, whether past or present, without regard to whether or not the relationship currently exists or has been terminated. The terms "COLLECTION" and "COLLECT," when referring to a debt, include the definition set forth at California Civil Code § 1788.2, and also refer to the taking, seizure, or offset of any monies held by SBBT or held in an SBBT deposit or other SBBT account for payment to satisfy any outstanding debt, obligation, bill, or amount owed by a consumer to any entity other than SBBT.

INTERROGATORY NO. 6

IDENTIFY all SBBT employees or agents who participated in any meetings or negotiations with other RAL lenders regarding COLLECTION of RAL debts.

The term "IDENTIFY" when referring to: i) an individual or a person, means to state, to the extent known, his or her full name, aliases, job title, last known business address, last known residential address, business telephone number, residential telephone number, and last-known employer or business affiliations; and ii) a company, corporation, business or other entity, means to state, to the extent known, its full name and its address. The term "RAL" refers to a loan that is secured by, or that the lender arranges to be repaid directly from, the proceeds of the borrower's income tax refund. The term "SBBT" refers to defendant Santa Barbara Bank & Trust, Santa Barbara Bank & Trust as a division of Pacific National Bank, Pacific Capital Bank doing business as Santa Barbara Bank & Trust, Pacific Capital Bank, and/or Pacific Capital Bancorp, and any of their principals, agents, employees, attorneys, representatives, predecessors, and any persons acting or purporting to act on their behalf, and any persons in active concert and participation with them, whether past or present, without regard to whether or not the relationship currently exists or has been terminated. The terms "COLLECTION" and "COLLECT," when referring to a debt, include the definition set forth at California Civil Code § 1788.2, and also refer to the taking, seizure, or offset of any monies held by SBBT or held in an SBBT deposit or other SBBT account for payment to satisfy any outstanding debt, obligation, bill, or amount owed by a consumer to any entity other than SBBT.

INTERROGATORY NO. 7

Describe in detail the financial and business relationship(s) between defendant SBBT and defendant JACKSON HEWITT, including a description and amount(s) of any compensation JACKSON HEWITT receives from SBBT and SBBT receives from JACKSON HEWITT.

The term "SBBT" refers to defendant Santa Barbara Bank & Trust, Santa Barbara Bank & Trust as a division of Pacific National Bank, Pacific Capital Bank doing business as Santa Barbara Bank & Trust, Pacific Capital Bank, and/or Pacific Capital Bancorp, and any of their principals, agents, employees, attorneys, representatives, predecessors, and any persons acting or purporting to act on their behalf, and any persons in active concert and participation with them, whether past or present, without regard to whether or not the relationship currently exists or has been terminated.

The term "JACKSON HEWITT" refers to defendant Tax Services of America, Inc. d/b/a Jackson Hewitt Tax Service, its parent Cendant Corporation, Jackson Hewitt Inc., any Jackson Hewitt franchise or subsidiary, and any of their principals, agents, employees, attorneys, representatives, predecessors, and any persons acting or purporting to act on their behalf, and any persons in active concert and participation with them, whether past or present, without regard to whether or not the relationship currently exists or has been terminated.

INTERROGATORY NO. 8

State the amount of any fee, commission or other monetary compensation that SBBT pays to JACKSON HEWITT for each RAL that JACKSON HEWITT facilitates, for each tax refund product that JACKSON HEWITT facilitates, and for each occasion when it COLLECTS or assists in COLLECTING RAL debts from consumers.

The term "RAL" refers to a loan that is secured by, or that the lender arranges to be repaid directly from, the proceeds of the borrower's income tax refund. The term "SBBT" refers to defendant Santa Barbara Bank & Trust, Santa Barbara Bank & Trust as a division of Pacific National Bank, Pacific Capital Bank doing business as Santa Barbara Bank & Trust, Pacific Capital Bank, and/or Pacific Capital Bancorp, and any of their principals, agents, employees, attorneys, representatives, predecessors, and any persons acting or purporting to act on their behalf, and any persons in active concert and participation with them, whether past or present, without regard to whether or not the relationship currently exists or has been terminated. The term "JACKSON HEWITT" refers to defendant Tax Services of America, Inc. d/b/a Jackson Hewitt Tax Service, its parent Cendant Corporation, Jackson Hewitt Inc., any Jackson Hewitt franchise or subsidiary, and any of their principals, agents, employees, attorneys, representatives, predecessors, and any persons acting or purporting to act on their behalf, and any persons in active concert and participation with them, whether past or present, without regard to whether or not the relationship currently exists or has been terminated. The terms "COLLECTION" and "COLLECT," when referring to a debt, include the definition set forth at California Civil Code § 1788.2, and also refer to the taking, seizure, or offset of any monies held by SBBT or held in an SBBT deposit or other SBBT account for payment to satisfy any outstanding debt, obligation, bill, or amount owed by a consumer to any entity other than SBBT.

INTERROGATORY NO. 9

IDENTIFY all SBBT employees or agents who participated in any meetings or negotiations with JACKSON HEWITT regarding COLLECTION of RAL debts.

The term "IDENTIFY" when referring to: i) an individual or a person, means to state, to the extent known, his or her full name, aliases, job title, last known business address, last known residential address, business telephone number, residential telephone number, and last-known employer or business affiliations; and ii) a company, corporation, business or other entity, means to state, to the extent known, its full name and its address. The term "RAL" refers to a loan that is secured by, or that the lender arranges to be repaid directly from, the proceeds of the borrower's income tax refund. The term "SBBT" refers to defendant Santa Barbara Bank & Trust, Santa Barbara Bank & Trust as a division of Pacific National Bank, Pacific Capital Bank doing business as Santa Barbara Bank & Trust, Pacific Capital Bank, and/or Pacific Capital Bancorp, and any of their principals, agents, employees, attorneys, representatives, predecessors, and any persons acting or purporting to act on their behalf, and any persons in active concert and participation with them, whether past or present, without regard to whether or not the relationship currently exists or has been terminated. The term "JACKSON HEWITT" refers to defendant Tax Services of America, Inc. d/b/a Jackson Hewitt Tax Service, its parent Cendant Corporation, Jackson Hewitt Inc., any Jackson Hewitt franchise or subsidiary, and any of their principals, agents, employees, attorneys, representatives, predecessors, and any persons acting or purporting to act on their behalf, and any persons in active concert and participation with them, whether past or present, without regard to whether or not the relationship currently exists or has been terminated. The terms "COLLECTION" and "COLLECT," when referring to a debt, include the definition set forth at California Civil Code § 1788.2, and also refer to the taking, seizure, or offset of any monies held by SBBT or held in an SBBT deposit or other SBBT account for payment to satisfy any outstanding debt, obligation, bill, or amount owed by a consumer to any entity other than SBBT.

INTERROGATORY NO. 10

IDENTIFY each provider of tax services which has an agreement, understanding or contract with SBBT to offer customers RALs provided by SBBT, stating the date(s) of such agreement(s) and the date(s) upon which SBBT began providing RALs for customers of each entity.

The term "IDENTIFY" when referring to: i) an individual or a person, means to state, to the extent known, his or her full name, aliases, job title, last known business address, last known residential address, business telephone number, residential telephone number, and last-known employer or business affiliations; and ii) a company, corporation, business or other entity, means to state, to the extent known, its full name and its address. The term "RAL" refers to a loan that is secured by, or that the lender arranges to be repaid directly from, the proceeds of the borrower's income tax refund. The term "SBBT" refers to defendant Santa Barbara Bank & Trust, Santa Barbara Bank & Trust as a division of Pacific National Bank, Pacific Capital Bank doing business as Santa Barbara Bank & Trust, Pacific Capital Bank, and/or Pacific Capital Bancorp, and any of their principals, agents, employees, attorneys, representatives, predecessors, and any persons acting or purporting to act on their behalf, and any persons in active concert and participation with them, whether past or present, without regard to whether or not the relationship currently exists or has been terminated.

INTERROGATORY NO. 11

Describe in detail the information and source of information from which SBBT learns or ascertains that a consumer seeking a RAL has an outstanding RAL debt.

The term "RAL" refers to a loan that is secured by, or that the lender arranges to be repaid directly from, the proceeds of the borrower's income tax refund. The term "SBBT" refers to defendant Santa Barbara Bank & Trust, Santa Barbara Bank & Trust as a division of Pacific National Bank, Pacific Capital Bank doing business as Santa Barbara Bank & Trust, Pacific Capital Bank, and/or Pacific Capital Bancorp, and any of their principals, agents, employees, attorneys, representatives, predecessors, and any persons acting or purporting to act on their behalf, and any persons in active concert and participation with them, whether past or present, without regard to whether or not the relationship currently exists or has been terminated.

INTERROGATORY NO. 12

State the amount of any fee, commission or other monetary compensation received by SBBT or any SBBT employees for each RAL debt COLLECTED, and state from whom such compensation is received. This interrogatory is limited to the time period from 1998 to the present.

The term "RAL" refers to a loan that is secured by, or that the lender arranges to be repaid directly from, the proceeds of the borrower's income tax refund. The term "SBBT" refers to defendant Santa Barbara Bank & Trust, Santa Barbara Bank & Trust as a division of Pacific National Bank, Pacific Capital Bank doing business as Santa Barbara Bank & Trust, Pacific Capital Bank, and/or Pacific Capital Bancorp, and any of their principals, agents, employees, attorneys, representatives, predecessors, and any persons acting or purporting to act on their behalf, and any persons in active concert and participation with them, whether past or present, without regard to whether or not the relationship currently exists or has been terminated. The terms "COLLECTION" and "COLLECT," when referring to a debt, include the definition set forth at California Civil Code § 1788.2, and also refer to the taking, seizure, or offset of any monies held by SBBT or held in an SBBT deposit or other SBBT account for payment to satisfy any outstanding debt, obligation, bill, or amount owed by a consumer to any entity other than SBBT.

INTERROGATORY NO. 13

Describe in detail the steps taken by SBBT or by JACKSON HEWITT as known to SBBT to process a customer's RAL application, approve or deny the application, and provide a RAL or COLLECT the customer's tax refund to pay a RAL debt. This interrogatory is limited to the time period from 1998 to the present.

The term "RAL" refers to a loan that is secured by, or that the lender arranges to be repaid directly from, the proceeds of the borrower's income tax refund. The term "SBBT" refers to defendant Santa Barbara Bank & Trust, Santa Barbara Bank & Trust as a division of Pacific National Bank, Pacific Capital Bank doing business as Santa Barbara Bank & Trust, Pacific Capital Bank, and/or Pacific Capital Bancorp, and any of their principals, agents,

employees, attorneys, representatives, predecessors, and any persons acting or purporting to act on their behalf, and any persons in active concert and participation with them, whether past or present, without regard to whether or not the relationship currently exists or has been terminated. The term "JACKSON HEWITT" refers to defendant Tax Services of America, Inc. d/b/a Jackson Hewitt Tax Service, its parent Cendant Corporation, Jackson Hewitt Inc., any Jackson Hewitt franchise or subsidiary, and any of their principals, agents, employees, attorneys, representatives, predecessors, and any persons acting or purporting to act on their behalf, and any persons in active concert and participation with them, whether past or present, without regard to whether or not the relationship currently exists or has been terminated. The terms "COLLECTION" and "COLLECT," when referring to a debt, include the definition set forth at California Civil Code § 1788.2, and also refer to the taking, seizure, or offset of any monies held by SBBT or held in an SBBT deposit or other SBBT account for payment to satisfy any outstanding debt, obligation, bill, or amount owed by a consumer to any entity other than SBBT.

INTERROGATORY NO. 14

Describe in detail the steps taken by SBBT or by JACKSON HEWITT as known to SBBT to process [Plaintiff 1's] RAL application at the JACKSON HEWITT office in Trotwood, Ohio and to COLLECT her tax refund and pay it to Household Bank.

The term "RAL" refers to a loan that is secured by, or that the lender arranges to be repaid directly from, the proceeds of the borrower's income tax refund. The term "SBBT" refers to defendant Santa Barbara Bank & Trust, Santa Barbara Bank & Trust as a division of Pacific National Bank, Pacific Capital Bank doing business as Santa Barbara Bank & Trust, Pacific Capital Bank, and/or Pacific Capital Bancorp, and any of their principals, agents, employees, attorneys, representatives, predecessors, and any persons acting or purporting to act on their behalf, and any persons in active concert and participation with them, whether past or present, without regard to whether or not the relationship currently exists or has been terminated. The term "JACKSON HEWITT" refers to defendant Tax Services of America, Inc. d/b/a Jackson Hewitt Tax Service, its parent Cendant Corporation, Jackson Hewitt Inc., any Jackson Hewitt franchise or subsidiary, and any of their principals, agents, employees, attorneys, representatives, predecessors, and any persons acting or purporting to act on their behalf, and any persons in active concert and participation with them, whether past or present, without regard to whether or not the relationship currently exists or has been terminated. The terms "COLLECTION" and "COLLECT," when referring to a debt, include the definition set forth at California Civil Code § 1788.2, and also refer to the taking, seizure, or offset of any monies held by SBBT or held in an SBBT deposit or other SBBT account for payment to satisfy any outstanding debt, obligation, bill, or amount owed by a consumer to any entity other than SBBT.

INTERROGATORY NO. 15

For each year from 1998 to the present, state the total dollar amount that SBBT COLLECTED from tax refunds to pay RAL debts and to whom those amounts were paid.

The term "RAL" refers to a loan that is secured by, or that the lender arranges to be repaid directly from, the proceeds of the borrower's income tax refund. The term "SBBT" refers to defendant Santa Barbara Bank & Trust, Santa Barbara Bank & Trust as a division of Pacific National Bank, Pacific Capital Bank doing business as Santa Barbara Bank & Trust, Pacific Capital Bank, and/or Pacific Capital Bancorp, and any of their principals, agents, employees, attorneys, representatives, predecessors, and any persons acting or purporting to act on their behalf, and any persons in active concert and participation with them, whether past or present, without regard to whether or not the relationship currently exists or has been terminated. The terms "COLLECTION" and "COLLECT," when referring to a debt, include the definition set forth at California Civil Code § 1788.2, and also refer to the taking, seizure, or offset of any monies held by SBBT or held in an SBBT deposit or other SBBT account for payment to satisfy any outstanding debt, obligation, bill, or amount owed by a consumer to any entity other than SBBT.

INTERROGATORY NO. 16

Describe in detail any training provided to former or current SBBT employees or agents that refers or relates to RALs or the COLLECTION of tax refunds to pay RAL debts. This interrogatory is limited to the time period from 1998 to the present.

The term "RAL" refers to a loan that is secured by, or that the lender arranges to be repaid directly from, the proceeds of the borrower's income tax refund. The term "SBBT" refers to defendant Santa Barbara Bank & Trust, Santa Barbara Bank & Trust as a division of Pacific National Bank, Pacific Capital Bank doing business as Santa Barbara Bank & Trust, Pacific Capital Bank, and/or Pacific Capital Bancorp, and any of their principals, agents, employees, attorneys, representatives, predecessors, and any persons acting or purporting to act on their behalf, and any persons in active concert and participation with them, whether past or present, without regard to whether or not the relationship currently exists or has been terminated. The terms "COLLECTION" and "COLLECT," when referring to a debt, include the definition set forth at California Civil Code § 1788.2, and also refer to the taking, seizure, or offset of any monies held by SBBT or held in an SBBT deposit or other SBBT account for payment to satisfy any outstanding debt, obligation, bill, or amount owed by a consumer to any entity other than SBBT.

INTERROGATORY NO. 17

State how many complaints, written or oral, that SBBT has received for each year from 1998 to the present regarding COLLECTION of RAL debts, and IDENTIFY the PERSONS who made each complaint, the date of the complaint, and the SBBT employee(s) who received each complaint.

The term "IDENTIFY" when referring to: i) an individual or a person, means to state, to the extent known, his or her full name, aliases, job title, last known business address, last known residential address, business telephone number, residential telephone number, and last-known employer or business affiliations; and ii) a company, corporation, business or other entity, means to state, to the extent known, its full name and its address. The term "PERSON" means, where applicable, natural persons, businesses, corporations, trusts, partnerships, incorporated or unincorporated associations, joint ventures, governmental units, and any other legal entity. The term "RAL" refers to a loan that is secured by, or that

the lender arranges to be repaid directly from, the proceeds of the borrower's income tax refund. The term "SBBT" refers to defendant Santa Barbara Bank & Trust, Santa Barbara Bank & Trust as a division of Pacific National Bank, Pacific Capital Bank doing business as Santa Barbara Bank & Trust, Pacific Capital Bank, and/or Pacific Capital Bancorp, and any of their principals, agents, employees, attorneys, representatives, predecessors, and any persons acting or purporting to act on their behalf, and any persons in active concert and participation with them, whether past or present, without regard to whether or not the relationship currently exists or has been terminated. The terms "COLLECTION" and "COLLECT," when referring to a debt, include the definition set forth at California Civil Code § 1788.2, and also refer to the taking, seizure, or offset of any monies held by SBBT or held in an SBBT deposit or other SBBT account for payment to satisfy any outstanding debt, obligation, bill, or amount owed by a consumer to any entity other than SBBT.

INTERROGATORY NO. 18

IDENTIFY and describe all reports and communications with governmental agencies relating to COLLECTION of RAL debts, identifying the PERSONS who prepared such reports or were involved in such communications.

The term "IDENTIFY" when referring to: i) an individual or a person, means to state, to the extent known, his or her full name, aliases, job title, last known business address, last known residential address, business telephone number, residential telephone number, and last-known employer or business affiliations; and ii) a company, corporation, business or other entity, means to state, to the extent known, its full name and its address. The term "PERSON" means, where applicable, natural persons, businesses, corporations, trusts, partnerships, incorporated or unincorporated associations, joint ventures, governmental units, and any other legal entity. The term "RAL" refers to a loan that is secured by, or that the lender arranges to be repaid directly from, the proceeds of the borrower's income tax refund. The terms "COLLECTION" and "COLLECT," when referring to a debt, include the definition set forth at California Civil Code § 1788.2, and also refer to the taking, seizure, or offset of any monies held by SBBT or held in an SBBT deposit or other SBBT account for payment to satisfy any outstanding debt, obligation, bill, or amount owed by a consumer to any entity other than SBBT.

INTERROGATORY NO. 19

Describe SBBT's procedures and policies with respect to the maintenance, preservation, and destruction of DOCUMENTS, noting any change in the procedures or policies and the nature of that change for the time period from 1998 to the present.

The term "SBBT" refers to defendant Santa Barbara Bank & Trust, Santa Barbara Bank & Trust as a division of Pacific National Bank, Pacific Capital Bank doing business as Santa Barbara Bank & Trust, Pacific Capital Bank, and/or Pacific Capital Bancorp, and any of their principals, agents, employees, attorneys, representatives, predecessors, and any persons acting or purporting to act on their behalf, and any persons in active concert and participation with them, whether past or present, without regard to whether or not the relationship currently exists or has been terminated. The term "DOCUMENT" mean any "writing," as defined in Evidence

Code section 250, *and any record regardless of the manner in which the record has been stored. This definition is specifically intended to include information and all data stored electronically, as well as information and data printed on paper.* This definition specifically includes any information and data, including databases and e-mails, recorded on or retrievable from any computer or electronic media, and further includes, without limitation, "originals" (as defined in Evidence Code § 255) and all non-conforming copies, no matter how prepared, and all drafts prepared in connection with such DOCUMENTS whether or not used, in the possession, custody, or control of defendants, their agents, attorneys, or any other persons acting on their behalf, regardless of where located.

INTERROGATORY NO. 20

IDENTIFY each DOCUMENT related in any way to the matters raised in this lawsuit that has been destroyed, including the date, reason, manner, and PERSON(S) responsible for such destruction. This interrogatory is limited to the time period from 1998 to the present.

The term "IDENTIFY" when referring to: i) an individual or a person, means to state, to the extent known, his or her full name, aliases, job title, last known business address, last known residential address, business telephone number, residential telephone number, and last-known employer or business affiliations; and ii) a company, corporation, business or other entity, means to state, to the extent known, its full name and its address. The term "PERSON" means, where applicable, natural persons, businesses, corporations, trusts, partnerships, incorporated or unincorporated associations, joint ventures, governmental units, and any other legal entity. The term "DOCUMENT" mean any "writing," as defined in Evidence Code section 250, *and any record regardless of the manner in which the record has been stored. This definition is specifically intended to include information and all data stored electronically, as well as information and data printed on paper.* This definition specifically includes any information and data, including databases and e-mails, recorded on or retrievable from any computer or electronic media, and further includes, without limitation, "originals" (as defined in Evidence Code § 255) and all non-conforming copies, no matter how prepared, and all drafts prepared in connection with such DOCUMENTS whether or not used, in the possession, custody, or control of defendants, their agents, attorneys, or any other persons acting on their behalf, regardless of where located.

DATED:
Respectfully submitted,

[Attorneys for Plaintiffs]

By:

_____
[Attorney]
Attorney for Plaintiffs

L.5.3 Requests for Production of Documents Directed to Bank

SUPERIOR COURT OF THE STATE OF CALIFORNIA
IN AND FOR THE COUNTY OF SAN FRANCISCO

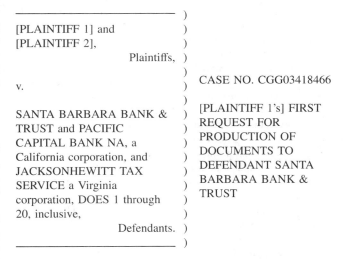

[PLAINTIFF 1] and [PLAINTIFF 2], Plaintiffs, v. SANTA BARBARA BANK & TRUST and PACIFIC CAPITAL BANK NA, a California corporation, and JACKSONHEWITT TAX SERVICE a Virginia corporation, DOES 1 through 20, inclusive, Defendants.	CASE NO. CGG03418466 [PLAINTIFF 1's] FIRST REQUEST FOR PRODUCTION OF DOCUMENTS TO DEFENDANT SANTA BARBARA BANK & TRUST

PROPOUNDING PARTY: Plaintiff [Plaintiff 1]

RESPONDING PARTY: Defendant Santa Barbara Bank & Trust

SET NO.: One

PLEASE TAKE NOTICE that pursuant to California Code of Civil Procedure § 2031, defendant Santa Barbara Bank & Trust (SBBT) is hereby required to produce for inspection and copying at the offices of The Sturdevant Law Firm, 475 Sansome Street, Suite 1750, San Francisco, California 94111 on or before July 25, 2003, the original and all non-conforming copies of each and every of the DOCUMENTS described below which are in the actual or constructive possession, custody or control of SBBT, including its attorneys, agents, officers and employees. SBBT is also required to serve upon the demanding party a written verified response to this set of document requests in conformity with the requirements of Code of Civil Procedure § 2031.

DEFINITIONS

1. As used in this request, the words "DOCUMENT" or "DOCUMENTS" mean any "writing," as defined in Evidence Code § 250, *and any record regardless of the manner in which the record has been stored. This definition is specifically intended to include information and all data stored electronically, as well as information and data printed on paper.* This definition specifically includes any information and data, including databases and e-mails, recorded on or retrievable from any computer or electronic media, and further includes, without limitation, "originals" (as defined in Evidence Code § 255) and all non-conforming copies, no matter how prepared, and all drafts prepared in connection with such DOCUMENTS whether or not used, in the possession, custody, or control of defendants, their agents, attorneys, or any other persons acting on their behalf, regardless of where located.

2. The term "SBBT" refers to defendant Santa Barbara Bank & Trust, Santa Barbara Bank & Trust as a division of Pacific National Bank, Pacific Capital Bank doing business as Santa Barbara Bank & Trust, Pacific Capital Bank, and/or Pacific Capital Bancorp, and any of their principals, agents, employees, attorneys, representatives, predecessors, and any persons acting or purporting to act on their behalf, and any persons in active concert and participation with them, whether past or present, without regard to whether or not the relationship currently exists or has been terminated.

3. The terms "YOU and "YOUR" refer jointly and severally to the corporate entity SBBT as defined in paragraph 2 above.

4. The term "JACKSON HEWITT" refers to defendant Tax Services of America, Inc. d/b/a Jackson Hewitt Tax Service, its parent Cendant Corporation, Jackson Hewitt Inc., any Jackson Hewitt franchise or subsidiary, and any of their principals, agents, employees, attorneys, representatives, predecessors, and any persons acting or purporting to act on their behalf, and any persons in active concert and participation with them, whether past or present, without regard to whether or not the relationship currently exists or has been terminated.

5. The term "RAL" refers to a loan that is secured by, or that the lender arranges to be repaid directly from, the proceeds of the borrower's income tax refund.

6. The term "COMPLAINT" refers to any complaint by a consumer, whether such complaints are formal or informal or written or oral, including but not limited to lawsuits and complaints made by or through the Federal Trade Commission, any state attorney general or district attorney, any Better Business Bureau, and by a consumer directly to SBBT.

7. The terms "COLLECTION" and "COLLECT," when referring to a debt, include the definition set forth at California Civil Code § 1788.2, and also refer to the taking, seizure, or offset of any monies held by SBBT or held in an SBBT deposit or other SBBT account for payment to satisfy any outstanding debt, obligation, bill, or amount owed by a consumer to any entity other than SBBT.

INSTRUCTIONS

Pursuant to Code of Civil Procedure § 2031(g), YOU are required to serve separate verified responses to each category of documents being demanded and state that YOU will (1) comply with the particular demand, (2) a representation that YOU lack the ability to comply with a particular demand or (3) an objection to a particular demand, and as further required by § 2031(g)(1)–(3).

If YOU object to producing any DOCUMENT, pursuant to § 2031(g)(3) YOU shall identify with particularity the DOCUMENT and clearly state the extent of, and the specific ground for, the objection. (*Wellpoint Health Networks v. Superior Court* (1997), 59 Cal. App. 4th 110, ["The information in the privilege log must be sufficiently specific to allow a determination of whether each withheld document is or is not in fact privileged"].) If YOU object to producing any DOCUMENT on the ground of attorney-client privilege, attorney work product, or other protection, YOU shall provide a log with YOUR written responses and state the following with respect to all such DOCUMENTS:

(1) The identity of the person(s) who prepared the DOCUMENTS, who signed it, and over whose name it was sent or issued;

(2) The identity of the person(s) to whom the DOCUMENT was directed;

(3) The nature and substance of the DOCUMENT with sufficient particularity to enable the Court and parties hereto to identify the DOCUMENT;

(4) The date of the DOCUMENT;

(5) The identify of the person(s) who has custody or, or control over the DOCUMENT and each copy thereof;

(6) The identity of each person to whom copies of the DOCUMENT were furnished;

(7) The number of pages;

(8) The basis on which any privilege or other protection is claimed; and

(9) Whether any non-privileged or non-protected matter is included in the DOCUMENT.

Pursuant to § 2031(g)(1), all DOCUMENTS produced shall either be produced as they are kept in the usual course of business, or be organized and labeled to correspond with the categories in the demand. If necessary, YOU shall translate any data compilations included in any demand into reasonably usable form.

DOCUMENTS REQUESTED

DOCUMENT REQUEST NO. 1
All DOCUMENTS which evidence, refer or relate to internal procedures, policies or practices of SBBT regarding RALs.

DOCUMENT REQUEST NO. 2
All DOCUMENTS which evidence, refer or relate to internal procedures, policies or practices of SBBT regarding COLLECTION of RAL debts held by entities other than SBBT.

DOCUMENT REQUEST NO. 3
All manuals, instructions, memoranda, or any other DOCUMENTS provided to SBBT employees regarding training or policies on offering RALs to consumers.

DOCUMENT REQUEST NO. 4
All manuals, instructions, memoranda, or any other DOCUMENTS provided to SBBT employees regarding training or policies on COLLECTION of RAL debts held by entities other than SBBT.

DOCUMENT REQUEST NO. 5
All agreements, contracts, memoranda of understanding or other DOCUMENTS that memorialize any agreement between SBBT and any other RAL lender concerning COLLECTION of RAL debts.

DOCUMENT REQUEST NO. 6
All agreements, contracts, memoranda of understanding or other DOCUMENTS that memorialize any agreement between SBBT and any provider of tax services concerning COLLECTION of RAL debts.

DOCUMENT REQUEST NO. 7
All DOCUMENTS which evidence, refer or relate to the process by which YOU determine that a consumer has an outstanding RAL debt.

DOCUMENT REQUEST NO. 8
Any computer system, software or other electronic program used by SBBT in its COLLECTION of outstanding RAL debts held by entities other than SBBT.

DOCUMENT REQUEST NO. 9

All DOCUMENTS, including computer records or electronic databases, containing the names of any consumer whose tax refund SBBT COLLECTED and paid over to another RAL lender to repay a RAL debt at any point from 1998 to the present.

DOCUMENT REQUEST NO. 10

All correspondence, memoranda, emails, and other DOCU-MENTS between SBBT and any RAL lender regarding that lender's COLLECTION of RAL debts for SBBT.

DOCUMENT REQUEST NO. 11

All correspondence, memoranda, emails, and other DOCU-MENTS between SBBT and any RAL lender regarding SBBT's COLLECTION of RAL debts for that lender.

DOCUMENT REQUEST NO. 12

All DOCUMENTS received by SBBT from any consumer whose tax refund SBBT used to pay a RAL debt owed to another RAL lender, including any RAL applications or RAL agreements signed by the consumer. This request is limited to documents created or used at any time between 1998 and the present.

DOCUMENT REQUEST NO. 13

All DOCUMENTS sent by SBBT to any consumer whose tax refund SBBT used to pay a RAL debt owed to another RAL lender. This request is limited to documents created or used at any time between 1998 and the present.

DOCUMENT REQUEST NO. 14

All written communications from SBBT to consumers which evidence, refer or relate to SBBT denials of applications for RALs because of existing RAL debts, including any notices sent pursuant to the Fair Credit Reporting Act or the Equal Credit Opportunity Act, and any responses by customers thereto. This request is limited to documents created or used at any time between 1998 and the present.

DOCUMENT REQUEST NO. 15

All written communications from SBBT to consumers which evidence, refer or relate to RAL debt COLLECTION on behalf of any entity other than SBBT, and any responses by customers thereto. This request is limited to documents created or used at any time between 1998 and the present.

DOCUMENT REQUEST NO. 16

All DOCUMENTS summarizing or memorializing any oral communications between SBBT and consumers regarding instances when SBBT denied RAL applications and when SBBT COLLECTED or attempted to COLLECT RAL debts held by entities other than SBBT. This request is limited to documents created or used at any time between 1998 and the present.

DOCUMENT REQUEST NO. 17

All DOCUMENTS which evidence, refer or relate to any COMPLAINTS against SBBT concerning SBBT's RALs or SBBT's COLLECTION or attempted COLLECTION of RAL debts held by entities other than SBBT. This request is limited to documents created at any time between 1997 and the present.

DOCUMENT REQUEST NO. 18

All DOCUMENTS containing summary or statistical information which evidence, refer or relate to the total number of times for each year from 1998 to the present that SBBT COLLECTED money from consumer tax refunds to pay RAL debts owed to other RAL lenders, including the total annual dollar amount thereof.

DOCUMENT REQUEST NO. 19

All DOCUMENTS containing summary or statistical information which evidence, refer or relate to the total number of consumers for each year from 1998 to the present whose tax refunds, or a portion of tax refunds, were COLLECTED by SBBT and paid over to other RAL lenders to satisfy RAL debts.

DOCUMENT REQUEST NO. 20

All DOCUMENTS containing summary or statistical information which evidence, refer or relate to any fees, commissions or other monies, received by SBBT for COLLECTING RAL debts on behalf of other RAL lenders, including the total dollar amount for each year from 1998 to the present.

DOCUMENT REQUEST NO. 21

All DOCUMENTS containing summary or statistical information which evidence, refer or relate to the number of consumers who applied to SBBT for RALs for each year from 1998 to the present.

DOCUMENT REQUEST NO. 22

All DOCUMENTS containing summary or statistical information which evidence, refer or relate to the number of consumers whose RAL application was denied by SBBT due to existing RAL debt for each year from 1998 to the present.

DOCUMENT REQUEST NO. 23

All DOCUMENTS containing summary or statistical information which evidence, refer or relate to the number of consumers whose tax refund or a portion thereof was taken by SBBT to pay an existing RAL debt for each year from 1998 to the present.

DOCUMENT REQUEST NO. 24

All DOCUMENTS which refer or relate to [Plaintiff 1].

DOCUMENT REQUEST NO. 25

All disclosure statements, notices, or other DOCUMENTS given to [Plaintiff 1] by SBBT in connection with any transaction between SBBT and [Plaintiff 1].

DOCUMENT REQUEST NO. 26

YOUR complete file(s) on each and every application made by [Plaintiff 1] for a RAL or other tax refund product.

DOCUMENT REQUEST NO. 27

All written communications between [Plaintiff 1] and SBBT or JACKSON HEWITT.

DOCUMENT REQUEST NO. 28

All written communications between SBBT and JACKSON HEWITT or Household Bank which refer or relate in any way to [Plaintiff 1].

DOCUMENT REQUEST NO. 29

All written communications between JACKSON HEWITT and Household Bank which refer or relate in any way to [Plaintiff 1].

DOCUMENT REQUEST NO. 30

All telephone log sheets, internal memoranda, notes, and other DOCUMENTS which evidence, refer or relate to [Plaintiff 1's] RAL application, the rejection of that application, and the payment of [Plaintiff 1's] tax refund(s) to Household Bank.

DOCUMENT REQUEST NO. 31

All DOCUMENTS summarizing or memorializing any oral communications between [Plaintiff 1] and SBBT.

DOCUMENT REQUEST NO. 32

All DOCUMENTS which evidence, refer or relate to any commissions, fees or bonuses paid to any individual, including but not limited to SBBT or JACKSON HEWITT employees or agents, in connection with the payment of [Plaintiff 1's] tax refund(s) to Household Bank.

DOCUMENT REQUEST NO. 33

All DOCUMENTS which evidence, refer or relate to SBBT's policies or procedures regarding compliance with federal and state consumer laws applicable to debt COLLECTION, including the federal Fair Debt Collection Practices Act, the Federal Trade Commission Act, the Robbins-Rosenthal Act, California Civil Legal Remedies Act, and California Business & Professions Code Section 172000.

DOCUMENT REQUEST NO. 34

All DOCUMENTS which evidence, refer or relate to SBBT's advertising and marketing of RALs to consumers.

DOCUMENT REQUEST NO. 35

All DOCUMENTS which evidence, refer or relate to any profiles or studies developed by YOU or at YOUR request of the personal characteristics of potential RAL customers, including but not limited to age, income, assets, education, ethnicity, and race.

DOCUMENT REQUEST NO. 36

All DOCUMENTS which evidence, refer or relate to any profiles or studies developed by YOU or at YOUR request of the personal characteristics of actual RAL customers, including but not limited to age, income, assets, education, ethnicity, and race.

DOCUMENT REQUEST NO. 37

All DOCUMENTS which evidence, refer or relate to YOUR record retention policies and procedures.

DOCUMENT REQUEST NO. 38

All notes, minutes and other DOCUMENTS which evidence, refer or relate to any meetings or negotiations between SBBT and other RAL lenders regarding COLLECTION of RAL debts.

DOCUMENT REQUEST NO. 39

All notes, minutes and other DOCUMENTS which evidence, refer or relate to any meetings or negotiations between SBBT and JACKSON HEWITT regarding COLLECTION of RAL debts.

DATED:
Respectfully submitted,

[Attorneys for Plaintiffs]

By:

_____
[Attorney for Plaintiffs]
Attorney for Plaintiffs

L.5.4 Interrogatories to Tax Preparer

SUPERIOR COURT OF THE STATE OF CALIFORNIA
IN AND FOR THE COUNTY OF SAN FRANCISCO

_____)	
[PLAINTIFF 1] and)	
[PLAINTIFF 2],)	
Plaintiffs,)	
)	
v.)	CASE NO. CGG03418466
)	
SANTA BARBARA BANK &)	[PLAINTIFF 1's] FIRST
TRUST and PACIFIC)	SET OF INTERROGATO-
CAPITAL BANK NA, a)	RIES TO DEFENDANT
California corporation, and)	JACKSON HEWITT
JACKSONHEWITT TAX)	
SERVICE a Virginia)	
corporation, DOES 1 through)	
20, inclusive,)	
Defendants.)	
_____)	

PROPOUNDING PARTY: Plaintiff [Plaintiff 1]

RESPONDING PARTY: Defendant Jackson Hewitt

SET NO.: One

INTERROGATORIES

INTERROGATORY NO. 1

IDENTIFY each PERSON consulted by JACKSON HEWITT in the preparation of responses to these Interrogatories and to Plaintiff [Plaintiff 1's] First Request for Production of Documents to JACKSON HEWITT.

The term "IDENTIFY" when referring to: i) an individual or a person, means to state, to the extent known, his or her full name, aliases, job title, last known business address, last known residential address, business telephone number, residential telephone number, and last-known employer or business affiliations; and ii) a company, corporation, business or other entity, means to state, to the extent known, its full name and its address. The term "PERSON" means, where applicable, natural persons, businesses, corporations, trusts, partnerships, incorporated or unincorporated associations, joint ventures, governmental units, and any other legal entity. The term "JACKSON HEWITT" refers to defendant Tax Services of America, Inc. d/b/a Jackson Hewitt Tax Service, its parent Cendant Corporation, Jackson Hewitt Inc., any Jackson Hewitt franchise or subsidiary, and any of their principals, agents, employees, attorneys, representatives, predecessors, and any persons acting or purporting to act on their behalf, and any persons in active concert and participation with them, whether past or present, without regard to whether or not the relationship currently exists or has been terminated.

INTERROGATORY NO. 2

IDENTIFY each former or present JACKSON HEWITT employee or agent who was involved in any manner in SBBT's COLLECTION or attempts to COLLECT any debts purportedly owing by [Plaintiff 1], stating the nature and purpose of his/her involvement.

The term "IDENTIFY" when referring to: i) an individual or a person, means to state, to the extent known, his or her full name, aliases, job title, last known business address, last known residential address, business telephone number, residential telephone number, and last-known employer or business affiliations; and ii) a company, corporation, business or other entity, means to state, to the extent known, its full name and its address. The term "JACKSON HEWITT" refers to defendant Tax Services of America, Inc. d/b/a Jackson Hewitt Tax Service, its parent Cendant Corporation, Jackson Hewitt Inc., any Jackson Hewitt franchise or subsidiary, and any of their principals, agents, employees, attorneys, representatives, predecessors, and any persons acting or purporting to act on their behalf, and any persons in active concert and participation with them, whether past or present, without regard to whether or not the relationship currently exists or has been terminated. The term "SBBT" refers to defendant Santa Barbara Bank & Trust, Santa Barbara Bank & Trust as a division of Pacific National Bank, Pacific Capital Bank doing business as Santa Barbara Bank & Trust, Pacific Capital Bank, and/or Pacific Capital Bancorp, and any of their principals, agents, employees, attorneys, representatives, predecessors, and any persons acting or purporting to act on their behalf, and any persons in active concert and participation with them, whether past or present, without regard to whether or not the relationship currently exists or has been terminated. The terms "COLLECTION" and "COLLECT," when referring to a debt, include the definition set forth at California Civil Code § 1788.2, and also refer to the taking, seizure, or offset of any monies held by SBBT or held in an SBBT deposit or other SBBT account for payment to satisfy any outstanding debt, obligation, bill, or amount owed by a consumer to any entity other than SBBT.

INTERROGATORY NO. 3

IDENTIFY each JACKSON HEWITT employee or agent with a primary role or responsibility for developing, reviewing, approving, evaluating or implementing any JACKSON HEWITT policy, procedure or practice regarding offering RALs to consumers and COLLECTING or assisting in the COLLECTION of RAL debts, stating the nature and purpose of his/her responsibility.

The term "IDENTIFY" when referring to: i) an individual or a person, means to state, to the extent known, his or her full name, aliases, job title, last known business address, last known residential address, business telephone number, residential telephone number, and last-known employer or business affiliations; and ii) a company, corporation, business or other entity, means to state, to the extent known, its full name and its address. The term "JACKSON HEWITT" refers to defendant Tax Services of America, Inc. d/b/a Jackson Hewitt Tax Service, its parent Cendant Corporation, Jackson Hewitt Inc., any Jackson Hewitt franchise or subsidiary, and any of their principals, agents, employees, attorneys, representatives, predecessors, and any persons acting or purporting to act on their behalf, and any persons in active concert and participation with them, whether past or present, without regard to whether or not the relationship currently exists or has been terminated. The term "RAL" refers to a loan that is secured by, or that the lender arranges to be repaid directly from, the proceeds of the borrower's income tax refund. The terms "COLLECTION" and "COLLECT," when referring to a debt, include the definition set forth at California Civil Code § 1788.2, and also refer to the taking,

seizure, or offset of any monies held by SBBT or held in an SBBT deposit or other SBBT account for payment to satisfy any outstanding debt, obligation, bill, or amount owed by a consumer to any entity other than SBBT.

INTERROGATORY NO. 4

IDENTIFY each entity which offers or provides RALs to customers of JACKSON HEWITT, stating the date(s) upon which JACKSON HEWITT began offering RALs from each entity to consumers.

The term "IDENTIFY" when referring to: i) an individual or a person, means to state, to the extent known, his or her full name, aliases, job title, last known business address, last known residential address, business telephone number, residential telephone number, and last-known employer or business affiliations; and ii) a company, corporation, business or other entity, means to state, to the extent known, its full name and its address. The term "RAL" refers to a loan that is secured by, or that the lender arranges to be repaid directly from, the proceeds of the borrower's income tax refund. The term "JACKSON HEWITT" refers to defendant Tax Services of America, Inc. d/b/a Jackson Hewitt Tax Service, its parent Cendant Corporation, Jackson Hewitt Inc., any Jackson Hewitt franchise or subsidiary, and any of their principals, agents, employees, attorneys, representatives, predecessors, and any persons acting or purporting to act on their behalf, and any persons in active concert and participation with them, whether past or present, without regard to whether or not the relationship currently exists or has been terminated.

INTERROGATORY NO. 5

IDENTIFY each PERSON from whom JACKSON HEWITT COLLECTED, or assisted in COLLECTING a RAL debt for each year from 1998 to the present, and state the amount COLLECTED, the date COLLECTED, and the amount of the RAL debt.

The term "IDENTIFY" when referring to: i) an individual or a person, means to state, to the extent known, his or her full name, aliases, job title, last known business address, last known residential address, business telephone number, residential telephone number, and last-known employer or business affiliations; and ii) a company, corporation, business or other entity, means to state, to the extent known, its full name and its address. The term "RAL" refers to a loan that is secured by, or that the lender arranges to be repaid directly from, the proceeds of the borrower's income tax refund. The term "PERSON" means, where applicable, natural persons, businesses, corporations, trusts, partnerships, incorporated or unincorporated associations, joint ventures, governmental units, and any other legal entity. The term "JACKSON HEWITT" refers to defendant Tax Services of America, Inc. d/b/a Jackson Hewitt Tax Service, its parent Cendant Corporation, Jackson Hewitt Inc., any Jackson Hewitt franchise or subsidiary, and any of their principals, agents, employees, attorneys, representatives, predecessors, and any persons acting or purporting to act on their behalf, and any persons in active concert and participation with them, whether past or present, without regard to whether or not the relationship currently exists or has been terminated. The terms "COLLECTION" and "COLLECT," when referring to a debt, include the definition set forth at California Civil Code § 1788.2, and also refer to the taking, seizure, or offset of any monies held by SBBT or held in an SBBT deposit or other SBBT account for payment to satisfy any outstanding debt, obligation, bill, or amount owed by a consumer to any entity other than SBBT. The terms

"COLLECTION" and "COLLECT," when referring to a debt, include the definition set forth at California Civil Code § 1788.2, and also refer to the taking, seizure, or offset of any monies held by SBBT or held in an SBBT deposit or other SBBT account for payment to satisfy any outstanding debt, obligation, bill, or amount owed by a consumer to any entity other than SBBT.

INTERROGATORY NO. 6

Describe in detail the financial and business relationship(s) between SBBT and JACKSON HEWITT, including a description and amount(s) of any compensation JACKSON HEWITT receives from SBBT and SBBT receives from JACKSON HEWITT.

The term "SBBT" refers to defendant Santa Barbara Bank & Trust, Santa Barbara Bank & Trust as a division of Pacific National Bank, Pacific Capital Bank doing business as Santa Barbara Bank & Trust, Pacific Capital Bank, and/or Pacific Capital Bancorp, and any of their principals, agents, employees, attorneys, representatives, predecessors, and any persons acting or purporting to act on their behalf, and any persons in active concert and participation with them, whether past or present, without regard to whether or not the relationship currently exists or has been terminated.

The term "JACKSON HEWITT" refers to defendant Tax Services of America, Inc. d/b/a Jackson Hewitt Tax Service, its parent Cendant Corporation, Jackson Hewitt Inc., any Jackson Hewitt franchise or subsidiary, and any of their principals, agents, employees, attorneys, representatives, predecessors, and any persons acting or purporting to act on their behalf, and any persons in active concert and participation with them, whether past or present, without regard to whether or not the relationship currently exists or has been terminated.

INTERROGATORY NO. 7

State the amount of any fee, commission or other monetary compensation that JACKSON HEWITT receives for each RAL that JACKSON HEWITT facilitates, for each tax refund product that JACKSON HEWITT facilitates, and for each occasion when it COLLECTS or assists in COLLECTING tax refunds from consumers to pay RAL debts, and by whom such compensation is paid.

The term "JACKSON HEWITT" refers to defendant Tax Services of America, Inc. d/b/a Jackson Hewitt Tax Service, its parent Cendant Corporation, Jackson Hewitt Inc., any Jackson Hewitt franchise or subsidiary, and any of their principals, agents, employees, attorneys, representatives, predecessors, and any persons acting or purporting to act on their behalf, and any persons in active concert and participation with them, whether past or present, without regard to whether or not the relationship currently exists or has been terminated. The term "RAL" refers to a loan that is secured by, or that the lender arranges to be repaid directly from, the proceeds of the borrower's income tax refund. The terms "COLLECTION" and "COLLECT," when referring to a debt, include the definition set forth at California Civil Code § 1788.2, and also refer to the taking, seizure, or offset of any monies held by SBBT or held in an SBBT deposit or other SBBT account for payment to satisfy any outstanding debt, obligation, bill, or amount owed by a consumer to any entity other than SBBT.

INTERROGATORY NO. 8

Describe in detail the steps taken by JACKSON HEWITT to process a customer's RAL application, approve or deny the application, and provide a RAL. This interrogatory is limited to the time period from 1998 to the present.

The term "JACKSON HEWITT" refers to defendant Tax Services of America, Inc. d/b/a Jackson Hewitt Tax Service, its parent Cendant Corporation, Jackson Hewitt Inc., any Jackson Hewitt franchise or subsidiary, and any of their principals, agents, employees, attorneys, representatives, predecessors, and any persons acting or purporting to act on their behalf, and any persons in active concert and participation with them, whether past or present, without regard to whether or not the relationship currently exists or has been terminated. The term "RAL" refers to a loan that is secured by, or that the lender arranges to be repaid directly from, the proceeds of the borrower's income tax refund.

INTERROGATORY NO. 9

Describe in detail the steps JACKSON HEWITT takes in COLLECTING or assisting in COLLECTING from consumers RAL debts owed to lenders. This interrogatory is limited to the time period from 1998 to the present.

The term "JACKSON HEWITT" refers to defendant Tax Services of America, Inc. d/b/a Jackson Hewitt Tax Service, its parent Cendant Corporation, Jackson Hewitt Inc., any Jackson Hewitt franchise or subsidiary, and any of their principals, agents, employees, attorneys, representatives, predecessors, and any persons acting or purporting to act on their behalf, and any persons in active concert and participation with them, whether past or present, without regard to whether or not the relationship currently exists or has been terminated. The term "RAL" refers to a loan that is secured by, or that the lender arranges to be repaid directly from, the proceeds of the borrower's income tax refund. The terms "COLLECTION" and "COLLECT," when referring to a debt, include the definition set forth at California Civil Code § 1788.2, and also refer to the taking, seizure, or offset of any monies held by SBBT or held in an SBBT deposit or other SBBT account for payment to satisfy any outstanding debt, obligation, bill, or amount owed by a consumer to any entity other than SBBT.

INTERROGATORY NO. 10

IDENTIFY all JACKSON HEWITT employees or agents who participated in any meetings or negotiations with SBBT regarding COLLECTION of RAL debts.

The term "IDENTIFY" when referring to: i) an individual or a person, means to state, to the extent known, his or her full name, aliases, job title, last known business address, last known residential address, business telephone number, residential telephone number, and last-known employer or business affiliations; and ii) a company, corporation, business or other entity, means to state, to the extent known, its full name and its address. The term "JACKSON HEWITT" refers to defendant Tax Services of America, Inc. d/b/a Jackson Hewitt Tax Service, its parent Cendant Corporation, Jackson Hewitt Inc., any Jackson Hewitt franchise or subsidiary, and any of their principals, agents, employees, attorneys, representatives, predecessors, and any persons acting or purporting to act on their behalf, and any persons in active concert and participation with them, whether past or present, without regard to whether or not the relationship currently exists or has been terminated. The term "SBBT" refers to defendant Santa Barbara Bank & Trust, Santa Barbara Bank & Trust as a division of Pacific National Bank, Pacific Capital Bank doing business as Santa Barbara Bank & Trust, Pacific Capital Bank, and/or Pacific Capital Bancorp, and any of their principals, agents, employees, attorneys, representatives, predecessors, and any persons acting or purporting to act on their behalf, and any persons in active concert and participation with them, whether past or present, without regard to whether or not the relationship currently exists or has been terminated. The term "RAL" refers to a loan that is secured by, or that the lender arranges to be repaid directly from, the proceeds of the borrower's income tax refund. The terms "COLLECTION" and "COLLECT," when referring to a debt, include the definition set forth at California Civil Code § 1788.2, and also refer to the taking, seizure, or offset of any monies held by SBBT or held in an SBBT deposit or other SBBT account for payment to satisfy any outstanding debt, obligation, bill, or amount owed by a consumer to any entity other than SBBT.

INTERROGATORY NO. 11

Describe in detail the information and source of information from which JACKSON HEWITT learns or ascertains that a consumer seeking a RAL has an outstanding RAL debt.

The term "JACKSON HEWITT" refers to defendant Tax Services of America, Inc. d/b/a Jackson Hewitt Tax Service, its parent Cendant Corporation, Jackson Hewitt Inc., any Jackson Hewitt franchise or subsidiary, and any of their principals, agents, employees, attorneys, representatives, predecessors, and any persons acting or purporting to act on their behalf, and any persons in active concert and participation with them, whether past or present, without regard to whether or not the relationship currently exists or has been terminated. The term "RAL" refers to a loan that is secured by, or that the lender arranges to be repaid directly from, the proceeds of the borrower's income tax refund.

INTERROGATORY NO. 12

Describe in detail the steps taken by JACKSON HEWITT to process [Plaintiff 1's] RAL application at the JACKSON HEWITT office in Trotwood, Ohio and to COLLECT her tax refund and pay it to Household Bank.

The term "JACKSON HEWITT" refers to defendant Tax Services of America, Inc. d/b/a Jackson Hewitt Tax Service, its parent Cendant Corporation, Jackson Hewitt Inc., any Jackson Hewitt franchise or subsidiary, and any of their principals, agents, employees, attorneys, representatives, predecessors, and any persons acting or purporting to act on their behalf, and any persons in active concert and participation with them, whether past or present, without regard to whether or not the relationship currently exists or has been terminated. The term "RAL" refers to a loan that is secured by, or that the lender arranges to be repaid directly from, the proceeds of the borrower's income tax refund. The terms "COLLECTION" and "COLLECT," when referring to a debt, include the definition set forth at California Civil Code § 1788.2, and also refer to the taking, seizure, or offset of any monies held by SBBT or held in an SBBT deposit or other SBBT account for payment to satisfy any outstanding debt, obligation, bill, or amount owed by a consumer to any entity other than SBBT.

INTERROGATORY NO. 13

For each year from 1998 to the present, state the total dollar amount that JACKSON HEWITT COLLECTED or assisted in COLLECTING from tax refunds to pay RAL debts and to whom those amounts were paid.

The term "JACKSON HEWITT" refers to defendant Tax Services of America, Inc. d/b/a Jackson Hewitt Tax Service, its parent Cendant Corporation, Jackson Hewitt Inc., any Jackson Hewitt franchise or subsidiary, and any of their principals, agents, employees, attorneys, representatives, predecessors, and any persons

acting or purporting to act on their behalf, and any persons in active concert and participation with them, whether past or present, without regard to whether or not the relationship currently exists or has been terminated. The term "RAL" refers to a loan that is secured by, or that the lender arranges to be repaid directly from, the proceeds of the borrower's income tax refund. The terms "COLLECTION" and "COLLECT," when referring to a debt, include the definition set forth at California Civil Code § 1788.2, and also refer to the taking, seizure, or offset of any monies held by SBBT or held in an SBBT deposit or other SBBT account for payment to satisfy any outstanding debt, obligation, bill, or amount owed by a consumer to any entity other than SBBT.

INTERROGATORY NO. 14

Describe in detail any training provided to former or current JACKSON HEWITT employees or agents that refers or relates to RALs or the COLLECTION of tax refunds to pay RAL debts. This interrogatory is limited to the time period from 1998 to the present.

The term "JACKSON HEWITT" refers to defendant Tax Services of America, Inc. d/b/a Jackson Hewitt Tax Service, its parent Cendant Corporation, Jackson Hewitt Inc., any Jackson Hewitt franchise or subsidiary, and any of their principals, agents, employees, attorneys, representatives, predecessors, and any persons acting or purporting to act on their behalf, and any persons in active concert and participation with them, whether past or present, without regard to whether or not the relationship currently exists or has been terminated. The term "RAL" refers to a loan that is secured by, or that the lender arranges to be repaid directly from, the proceeds of the borrower's income tax refund. The terms "COLLECTION" and "COLLECT," when referring to a debt, include the definition set forth at California Civil Code § 1788.2, and also refer to the taking, seizure, or offset of any monies held by SBBT or held in an SBBT deposit or other SBBT account for payment to satisfy any outstanding debt, obligation, bill, or amount owed by a consumer to any entity other than SBBT.

INTERROGATORY NO. 15

State whether JACKSON HEWITT employees or agents receive any compensation, bonus, incentives, or any other consideration for facilitating RALs, either on a per RAL basis or on an overall basis.

The term "JACKSON HEWITT" refers to defendant Tax Services of America, Inc. d/b/a Jackson Hewitt Tax Service, its parent Cendant Corporation, Jackson Hewitt Inc., any Jackson Hewitt franchise or subsidiary, and any of their principals, agents, employees, attorneys, representatives, predecessors, and any persons acting or purporting to act on their behalf, and any persons in active concert and participation with them, whether past or present, without regard to whether or not the relationship currently exists or has been terminated. The term "RAL" refers to a loan that is secured by, or that the lender arranges to be repaid directly from, the proceeds of the borrower's income tax refund.

INTERROGATORY NO. 16

State how many complaints, written or oral, that JACKSON HEWITT has received for each year from 1998 to the present regarding COLLECTION of RAL debts, and IDENTIFY the PERSONS who made each complaint, the date of the complaint, and the JACKSON HEWITT employee(s) who received each complaint.

The term "JACKSON HEWITT" refers to defendant Tax Services of America, Inc. d/b/a Jackson Hewitt Tax Service, its parent

Cendant Corporation, Jackson Hewitt Inc., any Jackson Hewitt franchise or subsidiary, and any of their principals, agents, employees, attorneys, representatives, predecessors, and any persons acting or purporting to act on their behalf, and any persons in active concert and participation with them, whether past or present, without regard to whether or not the relationship currently exists or has been terminated. The term "RAL" refers to a loan that is secured by, or that the lender arranges to be repaid directly from, the proceeds of the borrower's income tax refund. The term "IDENTIFY" when referring to: i) an individual or a person, means to state, to the extent known, his or her full name, aliases, job title, last known business address, last known residential address, business telephone number, residential telephone number, and last-known employer or business affiliations; and ii) a company, corporation, business or other entity, means to state, to the extent known, its full name and its address. The term "PERSON" means, where applicable, natural persons, businesses, corporations, trusts, partnerships, incorporated or unincorporated associations, joint ventures, governmental units, and any other legal entity. The terms "COLLECTION" and "COLLECT," when referring to a debt, include the definition set forth at California Civil Code § 1788.2, and also refer to the taking, seizure, or offset of any monies held by SBBT or held in an SBBT deposit or other SBBT account for payment to satisfy any outstanding debt, obligation, bill, or amount owed by a consumer to any entity other than SBBT.

INTERROGATORY NO 17

Describe JACKSON HEWITT's procedures and policies with respect to the maintenance, preservation, and destruction of DOCUMENTS, noting any change in the procedures or policies and the nature of that change for the time period from 1998 to the present.

The term "JACKSON HEWITT" refers to defendant Tax Services of America, Inc. d/b/a Jackson Hewitt Tax Service, its parent Cendant Corporation, Jackson Hewitt Inc., any Jackson Hewitt franchise or subsidiary, and any of their principals, agents, employees, attorneys, representatives, predecessors, and any persons acting or purporting to act on their behalf, and any persons in active concert and participation with them, whether past or present, without regard to whether or not the relationship currently exists or has been terminated. The term "DOCUMENT" mean any "writing," as defined in Evidence Code section 250, *and any record regardless of the manner in which the record has been stored. This definition is specifically intended to include information and all data stored electronically, as well as information and data printed on paper.* This definition specifically includes any information and data, including databases and e-mails, recorded on or retrievable from any computer or electronic media, and further includes, without limitation, "originals" (as defined in Evidence Code § 255) and all non-conforming copies, no matter how prepared, and all drafts prepared in connection with such DOCUMENTS whether or not used, in the possession, custody, or control of defendants, their agents, attorneys, or any other persons acting on their behalf, regardless of where located.

INTERROGATORY NO 18

IDENTIFY each DOCUMENT related in any way to the matters raised in this lawsuit that has been destroyed, including the date, reason, manner, and PERSON(S) responsible for such destruction. This interrogatory is limited to the time period from 1998 to the present.

The term "IDENTIFY" when referring to: i) an individual or a person, means to state, to the extent known, his or her full name, aliases, job title, last known business address, last known residential address, business telephone number, residential telephone number, and last-known employer or business affiliations; and ii) a company, corporation, business or other entity, means to state, to the extent known, its full name and its address. The term "PERSON" means, where applicable, natural persons, businesses, corporations, trusts, partnerships, incorporated or unincorporated associations, joint ventures, governmental units, and any other legal entity. The term "DOCUMENT" mean any "writing," as defined in Evidence Code section 250, *and any record regardless of the manner in which the record has been stored. This definition is specifically intended to include information and all data stored electronically, as well as information and data printed on paper.* This definition specifically includes any information and data, including databases and e-mails, recorded on or retrievable from any computer or electronic media, and further includes, without limitation, "originals" (as defined in Evidence Code § 255) and all non-conforming copies, no matter how prepared, and all drafts prepared in connection with such DOCUMENTS whether or not used, in the possession, custody, or control of defendants, their agents, attorneys, or any other persons acting on their behalf, regardless of where located.

DATED:

Respectfully submitted,

[Attorneys for Plaintiffs]

By: _____

[Attorney for Plaintiffs]

L.5.5 Requests for Production of Documents Directed to Tax Preparation Firm

SUPERIOR COURT OF THE STATE OF CALIFORNIA
IN AND FOR THE COUNTY OF SAN FRANCISCO

[PLAINTIFF 1] and [PLAINTIFF 2], 　　　　　　　Plaintiffs, v. SANTA BARBARA BANK & TRUST and PACIFIC CAPITAL BANK NA, a California corporation, and JACKSONHEWITT TAX SERVICE a Virginia corporation, DOES 1 through 20, inclusive, 　　　　　　　Defendants.	CASE NO. CGG03418466 [PLAINTIFF 1's] FIRST REQUEST FOR PRODUCTION OF DOCUMENTS TO DEFENDANT JACKSON HEWITT

PROPOUNDING PARTY: Plaintiff [Plaintiff 1]

RESPONDING PARTY: Defendant Jackson Hewitt

SET NO: One

PLEASE TAKE NOTICE that pursuant to California Code of Civil Procedure § 2031, defendant Santa Barbara Bank & Trust[59] (SBBT) is hereby required to produce for inspection and copying at the offices of The Sturdevant Law Firm, 475 Sansome Street, Suite 1750, San Francisco, California 94111 on or before July 25, 2003, the original and all non-conforming copies of each and every of the DOCUMENTS described below which are in the actual or constructive possession, custody or control of SBBT, including its attorneys, agents, officers and employees. SBBT is also required to serve upon the demanding party a written verified response to this set of document requests in conformity with the requirements of Code of Civil Procedure § 2031.

DEFINITIONS

1. As used in this request, the words "DOCUMENT" or "DOCUMENTS" mean any "writing," as defined in Evidence Code § 250, *and any record regardless of the manner in which the record has been stored. This definition is specifically intended to include information and all data stored electronically, as well as information and data printed on paper.* This definition specifically includes any information and data, including databases and e-mails, recorded on or retrievable from any computer or electronic media, and further includes, without limitation, "originals" (as defined in Evidence Code § 255) and all non-conforming copies, no matter how prepared, and all drafts prepared in connection with such DOCUMENTS whether or not used, in the possession, custody, or control of defendants, their agents, attorneys, or any other persons acting on their behalf, regardless of where located.

2. The term "JACKSON HEWITT" refers to defendant Tax Services of America, Inc. d/b/a Jackson Hewitt Tax Service, its parent Cendant Corporation, Jackson Hewitt, Inc. any Jackson Hewitt franchises or subsidiary and any of their principals, agents, employees, attorneys, representatives, predecessors, and any persons acting or purporting to act on their behalf, and any persons in active concert and participation with them, whether past or present, without regard to whether or not the relationship currently exists or has been terminated.

3. The terms "YOU and "YOUR" refer jointly and severally to the corporate entity SBBT as defined in paragraph 2 above.

4. The term "SBBT" refers to defendant Santa Barbara Bank & Trust, Santa Barbara Bank & Trust as a division of Pacific National Bank, Pacific Capital Bank doing business as Santa Barbara Bank & Trust, Pacific Capital Bank, and/or Pacific Capital Bancorp, and any of their principals, agents, employees, attorneys, representatives, predecessors, and any persons acting or purporting to act on their behalf, and any persons in active concert and participation with them, whether past or present, without regard to whether or not the relationship currently exists or has been terminated.

5. The term "RAL" refers to a loan that is secured by the lender, or that the lender arranges to be repaid directly from the proceeds of the borrower's income tax refund.

6. The term "COMPLAINT" refers to any complaint by a consumer, whether such complaints are formal or informal or written or oral, including but not limited to lawsuits and complaints made by or through the Federal Trade Commission, any state attorney general or district attorney, any Better Business Bureau, and by a consumer directly to SBBT.

7. The terms "COLLECTION" and "COLLECT," when referring to a debt, include the definition set forth at California Civil Code § 1788.2, and also refer to the taking, seizure, or offset of any monies held by SBBT or held in an SBBT deposit or other SBBT account for payment to satisfy any outstanding debt, obligation, bill, or amount owed by a consumer to any entity other than SBBT.

INSTRUCTIONS

Pursuant to Code of Civil Procedure § 2031(g), YOU are required to serve separate verified responses to each category of documents being demanded and state that YOU will (1) comply with the particular demand, (2) a representation that YOU lack the ability to comply with a particular demand or (3) an objection to a particular demand, and as further required by § 2031(g)(1)–(3).

If YOU object to producing any DOCUMENT, pursuant to section § (g)(3) YOU shall identify with particularity the DOCUMENT and clearly state the extent of, and the specific ground for, the objection. (*Wellpoint Health Networks v. Superior Court* (1997), 59 Cal. App. 4th 110, ["The information in the privilege log must be sufficiently specific to allow a determination of whether each withheld document is or is not in fact privileged"].) If YOU object to producing any DOCUMENT on the ground of attorney-client privilege, attorney work product, or other protection, YOU shall provide a log with YOUR written responses and state the following with respect to all such DOCUMENTS:

(1) The identity of the person(s) who prepared the DOCUMENTS, who signed it, and over whose name it was sent or issued;

(2) The identity of the person(s) to whom the DOCUMENT was directed;

(3) The nature and substance of the DOCUMENT with sufficient particularity to enable the Court and parties hereto to identify the DOCUMENT;

(4) The date of the DOCUMENT;

(5) The identify of the person(s) who has custody or, or control over the DOCUMENT and each copy thereof;

(6) The identity of each person to whom copies of the DOCUMENT were furnished;

(7) The number of pages;

(8) The basis on which any privilege or other protection is claimed; and

(9) Whether any non-privileged or non-protected matter is included in the DOCUMENT.

Pursuant to § 2031(g)(1), all DOCUMENTS produced shall either be produced as they are kept in the usual course of business, or be organized and labeled to correspond with the categories in the demand. If necessary, YOU shall translate any data compilations included in any demand into reasonably usable form.

DOCUMENTS REQUESTED

DOCUMENT REQUEST NO. 1

All DOCUMENTS which evidence, refer or relate to internal procedures, policies or practices of JACKSON HEWITT regarding RALs.

---

59 *Editor's Note*: So in the original.

DOCUMENT REQUEST NO. 2

All DOCUMENTS which evidence, refer or relate to internal procedures, policies or practices of JACKSON HEWITT regarding COLLECTION of RAL debts.

DOCUMENT REQUEST NO. 3

All manuals, instructions, memoranda, or any other DOCUMENTS provided to JACKSON HEWITT employees regarding training or policies on offering RALs to consumers.

DOCUMENT REQUEST NO. 4

All manuals, instructions, memoranda, or any other DOCUMENTS provided to JACKSON HEWITT employees regarding training or policies on COLLECTION of RAL debts.

DOCUMENT REQUEST NO. 5

All scripts provided to JACKSON HEWITT employees regarding RALs, including the COLLECTION of RAL debts.

DOCUMENT REQUEST NO. 6

All DOCUMENTS summarizing or memorializing any oral communications between JACKSON HEWITT and consumers regarding instances when consumer RAL applications were denied.

DOCUMENT REQUEST NO. 7

All DOCUMENTS summarizing or memorializing any oral communications between JACKSON HEWITT and consumers regarding instances when JACKSON HEWITT COLLECTED, attempted to COLLECT, or assisted in COLLECTING RAL debts. This request is limited to documents created or used at any time between 1998 and the present.

DOCUMENT REQUEST NO. 8

All agreements, contracts, memoranda of understanding, or other DOCUMENTS that memorialize any agreement between JACKSON HEWITT and SBBT or any other RAL lender concerning the COLLECTION of RAL debts.

DOCUMENT REQUEST NO. 9

All correspondence, memoranda, emails, or other DOCUMENTS between JACKSON HEWITT and SBBT concerning COLLECTION of RAL debts.

DOCUMENT REQUEST NO. 10

Any computer system, software or other electronic program used by JACKSON HEWITT in its COLLECTION or its assistance in COLLECTING RAL debts.

DOCUMENT REQUEST NO. 11

All DOCUMENTS, including computer records or electronic databases, containing the names of any JACKSON HEWITT consumer whose tax refund was used to pay a RAL debt. This request is limited to the time period from 1998 to the present.

DOCUMENT REQUEST NO. 12

All DOCUMENTS sent to JACKSON HEWITT from any consumer whose tax refund was used to pay an outstanding RAL debt. This request is limited to the time period from 1998 to the present.

DOCUMENT REQUEST NO. 13

All DOCUMENTS containing summary or statistical information which evidence, refer or relate to the total yearly amounts of tax refunds of JACKSON HEWITT customers COLLECTED and used to pay RAL debts.

DOCUMENT REQUEST NO. 14

All DOCUMENTS containing summary or statistical information which evidence, refer or relate to the total yearly number of JACKSON HEWITT consumers whose tax refunds were paid over to RAL lenders to pay outstanding RAL debts.

DOCUMENT REQUEST NO. 15

All written communications from JACKSON HEWITT to consumers which evidence, refer or relate to denials of RALs because of existing RAL debts, and any responses by consumers thereto. This request is limited to the time period from 1998 to the present.

DOCUMENT REQUEST NO. 16

All written communications from JACKSON HEWITT to consumers which evidence, refer or relate to RAL debt COLLECTION, and responses by consumers thereto. This request is limited to the time period from 1998 to the present.

DOCUMENT REQUEST NO. 17

All DOCUMENTS containing summary or statistical information which evidence, refer or relate to the number of JACKSON HEWITT consumers whose RAL application was denied due to existing RAL debt for each year from 1998 to the present.

DOCUMENT REQUEST NO. 18

All DOCUMENTS which refer or relate to [Plaintiff 1].

DOCUMENT REQUEST NO. 19

All disclosure statements, notices, or other DOCUMENTS given to [Plaintiff 1] by JACKSON HEWITT in connection with any transaction between JACKSON HEWITT or SBBT and [Plaintiff 1].

DOCUMENT REQUEST NO. 20

YOUR complete file(s) on each and every application made by [Plaintiff 1] for a RAL or other tax refund product.

DOCUMENT REQUEST NO. 21

All written communications between [Plaintiff 1] and SBBT or JACKSON HEWITT.

DOCUMENT REQUEST NO. 22

All written communications between JACKSON HEWITT and SBBT or Household Bank which refer or relate in any way to [Plaintiff 1].

DOCUMENT REQUEST NO. 23

All written communications between SBBT and Household Bank which refer or relate in any way to [Plaintiff 1].

DOCUMENT REQUEST NO. 24

All telephone log sheets, internal memoranda, notes, and other DOCUMENTS which evidence, refer or relate to [Plaintiff 1's] RAL application, the rejection of that application, and the payment of [Plaintiff 1's] tax refund(s) to Household Bank.

DOCUMENT REQUEST NO. 25

All DOCUMENTS summarizing or memorializing any oral communications between [Plaintiff 1] and JACKSON HEWITT.

DOCUMENT REQUEST NO. 26

All DOCUMENTS which evidence, refer or relate to any commissions, fees or bonuses paid to any individual, including but not limited to SBBT or JACKSON HEWITT employees or agents, in connection with the payment of [Plaintiff 1's] tax refund(s) to Household Bank.

DOCUMENT REQUEST NO. 27

All DOCUMENTS which evidence, refer or relate to JACKSON HEWITT's policies or procedures regarding compliance with federal and state consumer laws applicable to debt COLLECTION, including the federal Fair Debt Collection Practices Act, the Federal Trade Commission Act, the Robbins-Rosenthal Act, California Civil Legal Remedies Act, and California Business & Professions Code Section 172000.

DOCUMENT REQUEST NO. 28

All DOCUMENTS which evidence, refer or relate to any COMPLAINTS against JACKSON HEWITT concerning RALs or JACKSON HEWITT'S COLLECTION or attempted COLLECTION of RAL debts. This request is limited to documents created at any time between 1997 and the present.

DOCUMENT REQUEST NO. 29

All DOCUMENTS which evidence, refer or relate to JACKSON HEWITT's advertising and marketing of RALs to consumers.

DOCUMENT REQUEST NO. 30

All DOCUMENTS which evidence, refer or relate to any profiles or studies developed by YOU or at YOUR request of the personal characteristics of potential RAL customers, including but not limited to age, income, assets, education, ethnicity, and race.

DOCUMENT REQUEST NO. 31

All DOCUMENTS which evidence, refer or relate to any profiles or studies developed by YOU or at YOUR request of the personal characteristics of actual RAL customers, including but not limited to age, income, assets, education, ethnicity, and race.

DOCUMENT REQUEST NO. 32

All notes, minutes and other DOCUMENTS which evidence, refer or relate to any meetings or negotiations between SBBT and JACKSON HEWITT regarding COLLECTION of RAL debts.

DATED:

Respectfully submitted,

[Attorneys for Plaintiffs]

By:

_____

[Attorney for Plaintiff]

L.6 RESPA Pleadings

This appendix includes pleadings related to claims that can be raised under the Real Estate Settlement Procedures Act. This Act is discussed in § 11.3.1, *supra*. The servicer provisions are also addressed in National Consumer Law Center, *Repossessions and Foreclosures* (5th ed. 2002 and Supp.).

The first subsection, L.6.1, *infra*, contains an answer and affirmative defenses to a foreclosure proceeding. One of the defenses, raised by way of recoupment, is based upon RESPA. The creditor paid the broker a yield spread premium, allegedly not for goods, services, or facilities provided by the broker. Subsection L.6.2, *infra*, contains discovery from the same case. Thanks to Michelle Weinberg from Legal Assistance Foundation of Chicago for sharing her work.

The accompanying CD-Rom includes a motion for summary judgment in *Lewis v. Delta Funding Corp.* The homeowner pled a claim under RESPA based upon the payment of a broker fee of over $3000 that the lender approved and financed as part of the principal. In seeking summary judgment on the RESPA claim, the homeowner argued that the broker performed less than the minimal services identified by HUD in its 1999 Policy Statement (*see* discussion in § 11.3.1.5.4, *supra*) rendering the fee unearned and, therefore, a referral fee. Thanks to Alan White for supplying this motion.

L.6.1 Answer and Affirmative Defenses

IN THE CIRCUIT COURT OF COOK COUNTY, ILLINOIS
COUNTY DEPARTMENT, CHANCERY DIVISION

CHASE BANK OF TEXAS,	)
Plaintiff,	)
	)
v.	) No. 00 CH 3033
	)
[Defendant-Consumer],	)
Defendant.	)

SECOND AMENDED ANSWER AND AFFIRMATIVE DEFENSES TO COMPLAINT TO FORECLOSE MORTGAGE

Now comes Defendant, by and through her attorneys, the Legal Assistance Foundation of Chicago, and answers Plaintiff's Complaint, as follows:

1. Defendant admits paragraph 1 of Plaintiff's Complaint.

2. Defendant admits paragraph 2 of Plaintiff's Complaint.

3. Defendant has insufficient knowledge to admit or deny the facts alleged in paragraph 3 of Plaintiff's Complaint and demands strict proof thereof.

4. Defendant has insufficient knowledge to admit or deny the facts alleged in paragraph 4 of Plaintiff's Complaint and demands strict proof thereof.

5. Defendant denies paragraph 5 of Plaintiff's Complaint.

6. Defendant denies paragraph 6 of Plaintiff's Complaint.

WHEREFORE, Defendant prays that this Court enter an Order:

Dismissing the Complaint in this case with prejudice and entering judgment in favor of Defendant and against Plaintiff.

AFFIRMATIVE DEFENSES
STATEMENT OF FACTS

1. [Defendant-Consumer] is a 72-year-old woman who has owned the property at [Defendant Consumer's address] (hereinafter, "the home") for over thirty years.

2. The home was purchased for approximately $20,000 in 1970.

3. At all relevant times, [Defendant-Consumer] has resided in the home with her sons and grandchildren.

4. [Defendant-Consumer], as a senior citizen with limited education and income, but substantial equity in her home, was a prime target for predatory mortgage lenders and brokers.

5. [Defendant-Consumer] was an unsophisticated borrower who did not understand many of the basic terms and costs of a typical

mortgage loan transaction. For example, between 1995 and 1999, [Defendant-Consumer] entered into at least 4 costly home refinance loans as follows:

a. In July, 1995, [Defendant-Consumer] entered into a mortgage loan with Option One Mortgage Corporation, for a $48,750 loan amount at 12.85 percent Annual Percentage Rate, with closing costs of $4111.

b. In November, 1996, [Defendant-Consumer] refinanced the Option One loan with The Money Store, which paid off approximately $58,142 to Option One, paid off a few small credit card debts, and which purportedly gave her $16,327 cash to perform certain home improvements. She was charged approximately $7300 in closing costs for this loan, including almost $6000 in broker fees on a loan of approximately $80,000.

c. In April or May, 1997, [Defendant-Consumer] refinanced the Money Store loan with a mortgage lender/broker called Midwest America Financial Corp. Midwest paid The Money Store some $84,000 and charged [Defendant-Consumer] approximately $4000 in closing costs, a portion of which she was required to pay at the closing. The resulting loan was about $90,000, at 12.9 percent interest, with payments of $922 per month and a balloon after 15 years. In this transaction, [Defendant-Consumer] had received a preliminary Truth In Lending Disclosure which substantially differed from the final loan terms, but [she] did not realize the discrepancy due to her unsophistication.

d. In May, 1999, [Defendant-Consumer] took the loan presently at issue, described in more detail below, with a principal balance of $120,000 and monthly payments exceeding 80 percent of her total household monthly income.

e. In the space of four years, therefore, [Defendant-Consumer] increased the indebtedness secured by her home from $48,750 to $120,000, and paid over $20,000 in closing costs and mortgage fees (not counting regular interest on the loans), but received the benefit of only about $19,000 at most.

6. Each of the foregoing loans substantially reduced [Defendant-Consumer's] equity in her home and increased her monthly mortgage payments without providing her with a proportionate economic benefit.

7. In February 1999, [Defendant-Consumer] received a phone solicitation from Victoria Mortgage ("Victoria"), a mortgage broker. Victoria explained to [Defendant-Consumer] that it could offer her a new loan that would reduce her mortgage payments and provide her with some extra cash.

8. Because [Defendant-Consumer] was struggling to make her monthly mortgage payments of approximately $990 a month and because she needed about $1600 to repair her roof, she agreed to meet with Victoria.

9. Soon thereafter, a male Victoria agent visited [Defendant-Consumer] at her home. Victoria's agent repeated the assertions about the loan's benefits and urged [Defendant-Consumer] to complete loan application documents. In reliance on Victoria's promises that the loan would provide her with additional cash and lower her monthly mortgage payments, [Defendant-Consumer] signed these documents.

10. In or around March 1999, [Defendant-Consumer] went to the office of Victoria Mortgage near Central and Lawrence Avenue in Chicago and met with its agent, [Agent 1]. [Agent 1] again promised [Defendant-Consumer] that Victoria could provide a new mortgage loan that would reduce her mortgage payments and provide her with the cash to repair her leaking roof.

11. In reliance on [Agent 1's] assertions, [Defendant-Consumer] completed additional documents relating to the loan application.

12. Subsequently, a Victoria agent named [Agent 2] contacted [Defendant-Consumer] and informed her that her loan was ready to close. On or about May 27, 1999, [Defendant-Consumer] went to an office in downtown Chicago, where the closing was completed.

13. At the closing, [Defendant-Consumer] was presented with a myriad of loan documents to sign. A man showed [Defendant-Consumer] the documents and told her where to sign them. He stated that she did not need to read the documents because the signing was a mere formality. [Defendant-Consumer], with limited education and little ability to understand the complicated financial documents placed before her, signed all the documents. [Agent 2] was present at the closing.

14. Upon completing the closing, [Defendant-Consumer] asked [Agent 2] when she would receive the funds to repair her roof. [Agent 2] informed her that the loan they had arranged for her was insufficient to provide her with the $1600 in cash she had requested. Instead, [Agent 2] stated that Victoria would to pay [Defendant-Consumer's] first monthly mortgage payment.

15. A few days later, [Agent 2] called [Defendant-Consumer] and said that Victoria would not make the payment because they had just discovered some unpaid back taxes. [Defendant-Consumer] did not understand this because her previous mortgage company was supposed to pay the property taxes, and she was unaware of any tax arrearage.

16. The mortgage documents created a loan transaction between [Defendant-Consumer] and Saxon Mortgage, Inc. ("Saxon") for the principal amount of $120,000 with an Annual Percentage Rate of 12.042 percent. *See* Truth In Lending Statement and Itemization of Amount Financed, Exhibits A and B, attached.

17. On information and belief, Saxon reviewed [Defendant-Consumer's] application and prepared all the documents in connection with the loan. Moreover, Saxon had an arrangement or agreement with Victoria whereby Victoria referred borrowers to Saxon for mortgage loans. Therefore, Saxon authorized, approved, and/or ratified each document and procedure employed by Victoria in connection with the making of the loan.

18. The transaction created a 15-year loan which increased [Defendant-Consumer's] mortgage payments to $1142.79 (excluding taxes and insurance) with a balloon payment in the 180th month (when [Defendant-Consumer] is 84) of $101,686.62. *See* Exhibit A.

19. The loan also carried a prepayment penalty which would require [Defendant-Consumer] to pay an amount equal to six months interest if she paid off the loan within five years.

20. [Defendant-Consumer] had no idea that she would still owe $101,686.62 after making payments for fifteen years and would not have agreed to the loan had she known.

21. [Defendant-Consumer] relied on Victoria's representation that the loan would provide her with $1600 for the roof and would lower the monthly payment and interest rate. She would not have entered into the transaction had she been aware of the true nature of the loan.

22. [Defendant-Consumer's] reliance was reasonable under all of the circumstances, given her advanced age, limited education and lack of financial sophistication, and the fact that Victoria was a professional mortgage broker which undertook to assist and advise [Defendant-Consumer] in obtaining a loan.

23. According to the Itemization of Amount Financed attached to the Truth In Lending Statement, Victoria received $7800 from the loan proceeds for arranging the loan. Exhibit B, attached.

24. Victoria received at least $5597 from the loan proceeds.

25. Victoria received an additional payment of $3750 from Saxon, denominated "Broker's Compensation" in Exhibit C.

26. On information and belief, based on counsel's familiarity with mortgage industry practices, the $3750 was measured or calculated based on the rate of interest which Victoria was able to get [Defendant-Consumer] to sign for, *i.e.*, Victoria's compensation was increased by an amount corresponding to a higher rate of interest on the loan. The higher the rate, the more Victoria could receive. Such a payment is sometimes known in the mortgage industry as a "yield spread premium."

27. As part of the transaction, [Defendant-Consumer] paid thousands of dollars in fees to the mortgage broker for obtaining a balloon loan with an interest rate of 11 percent that increased her mortgage payments without providing her with any real economic benefit.

28. On information and belief, based on counsel's familiarity with the mortgage industry, the 11-percent interest rate exceeded Saxon's par rate on 15-year balloon loans for borrowers with similar credit histories to [Defendant-Consumer's].

29. Victoria was more than adequately compensated for its services by [Defendant-Consumer] from the loan proceeds. The mortgage broker provided no goods or services for the additional "yield spread premium" fee.

30. [Defendant-Consumer] received no real economic benefit from this transaction.

31. With respect to the loan transaction, Saxon was a "creditor" as that term is defined in the Truth-in-Lending Act, 15 U.S.C. § 1602(f) and Regulation Z, 12 C.F.R. § 226.2(a)(17).

32. The transaction between Saxon and [Defendant-Consumer] was a "consumer credit transaction" as that term is defined in the Truth-in-Lending Act, 15 U.S.C. § 1602(h) and Regulation Z, 12 C.F.R. § 226.2(a).

33. The transaction between Saxon and [Defendant-Consumer] was a "closed-end credit transaction" as the term is defined in 12 C.F.R. § 226.2(10) and is subject to the requirements for such transactions set forth in 15 U.S.C. § 1638 and 12 C.F.R. §§ 226.17–226.24.

34. The transaction between Saxon and [Defendant-Consumer] was one in which a security interest was taken in [Defendant-Consumer's] principal place of residence.

35. The transaction between Saxon and [Defendant-Consumer] was for the principal amount of $120,000.

36. The transaction between Saxon and [Defendant-Consumer] was for the Amount Financed of $111,705.66. *See* Exhibit A.

37. As such, the "total loan amount" for the transaction, as defined in 15 U.S.C. § 1602(aa)(1)(B) and 12 C.F.R. § 226.32(a)(1)(ii) was therefore a maximum of $111,705.66.

38. The total points and fees paid by [Defendant-Consumer] in connection with the loan exceeded 8 percent of the total loan amount.

39. When the total points and fees are greater than 8 percent of the total loan amount, the mortgage is defined as a high rate mortgage pursuant to 15 U.S.C. § 1602(aa).

40. The transaction between Saxon and [Defendant-Consumer] was therefore a high rate mortgage.

41. [Defendant-Consumer] has suffered economic and emotional damages as a result of the Third-Party Defendants' conduct described herein. She is faced with the possible loss of her home of over thirty years.

First Affirmative Defense:
Plaintiff's Assignor's Failure to Provide Required Truth in Lending Disclosures

42. As described above, the transaction between plaintiff's assignor and [Defendant-Consumer] was a high-rate mortgage. 15 U.S.C. § 1602(aa)(1)(B).

43. The transaction of May 27, 2000, between plaintiff's assignor and [Defendant-Consumer], was therefore one in which the provisions of 15 U.S.C. § 1639 and 12 C.F.R. § 226.32 were applicable.

44. Plaintiff's assignor violated the Truth-in-Lending [Act], *inter alia*,

a. by failing to provide the disclosures to the consumer required by 15 U.S.C. §§ 1639(a)(1) and (a)(2)(A) and 12 C.F.R. § 226.32(c)(1)–(3);

b. by failing to provide the above disclosures to the consumer required at least three business days prior to the consummation of the transaction, in violation of 15 U.S.C. §§ 1639(b)(1) and 12 C.F.R. § 226.31(c);

c. by failing to provide accurate disclosures as required by 15 U.S.C. § 1638(a) and Reg. Z §§ 226.17 and 226.18.

45. The failure to comply with any provision of 15 U.S.C. § 1639 is deemed a failure to deliver material disclosures for the purpose of 15 U.S.C. § 1635. *See* 15 U.S.C. § 1639(j).

46. Pursuant to the Truth-in-Lending Act, [Defendant-Consumer] had an absolute right to cancel the transaction for three business days after the transaction, or within three days of receiving proper disclosures from the plaintiff, after which she would not be responsible for any charge or penalty.

47. Plaintiff's assignor's violations of 15 U.S.C. §§ 1638, 1639 and 12 C.F.R. §§ 226.17, 226.18, 226.31 and 226.32, which are considered to be a failure to give all material disclosures, give rise to a continuing right of rescission on the part of [Defendant-Consumer].

48. [Defendant-Consumer] hereby elects to rescind the transaction between herself and plaintiff's assignor, pursuant to her continuing right of rescission.

49. When a consumer elects to rescind pursuant to the Truth-in-Lending Act, any security interest taken in connection with the transaction becomes void. 15 U.S.C. § 1635(b).

50. When a consumer elects to rescind pursuant to the Truth-in-Lending Act, the consumer is not liable for any finance or other charge. 15 U.S.C. § 1635(b).

51. The mortgage that is the subject of this foreclosure action was taken in connection with the transaction that [Defendant-Consumer] has elected to rescind.

52. Since the mortgage is now void, this foreclosure case is due to be dismissed.

WHEREFORE, [Defendant-Consumer] prays that this Court dismiss plaintiff's complaint, with prejudice.

Second Affirmative Defense:
Recoupment for Violation of the Real Estate Settlement and Procedures Act

53. The transaction between plaintiff's assignor and [Defendant-Consumer] was a "federally related mortgage loan" as that term is defined in the Real Estate Settlement and Procedures Act (RESPA), 12 U.S.C. § 2602(1).

54. Plaintiff's assignor's funding and origination of this transaction are "settlement services" as that term is defined in RESPA, 12 U.S.C. § 2601(3).

55. As part of the transaction, [Defendant-Consumer] paid fees to the mortgage broker of at least $11,550 for obtaining a balloon loan with an interest rate of 11 percent that increased her mortgage payments without providing her with any real economic benefit. *See* Exhibit D.

56. This interest rate exceeded plaintiff's assignor's par rate on 15-year balloon loans.

57. In exchange for submitting an above-par-rate loan, plaintiff's assignor paid the mortgage broker $3750. *See* Exhibit A. This payment was in addition to the money paid by [Defendant-Consumer], and was not for any services provided by the mortgage broker to plaintiff's assignor or [Defendant-Consumer].

58. The mortgage broker was more than adequately compensated for its services by [Defendant-Consumer].

59. The mortgage broker provided no goods or services for this fee.

60. Plaintiff's assignor's payment of this fee to the mortgage broker violates RESPA's prohibition against providers of settlement services from paying referral fees and kickbacks. 12 U.S.C. § 2607.

61. Plaintiff's violation of RESPA is a violation that subjects Plaintiff to a civil penalty of three times the amount of any charge paid for settlement services. 12 U.S.C. § 2607(d)(2).

Wherefore, [Defendant-Consumer] prays that this Court dismiss plaintiff's complaint, with prejudice, or, in the alternative, reduce the amount owed by [Defendant-Consumer] by the amount of damages available under RESPA.

Third Affirmative Defense:
Illinois Consumer Fraud and Deceptive Practices Act

62. [Defendant-Consumer] realleges paragraphs 1–50.

63. This defense is asserted pursuant to the Illinois Consumer Fraud and Deceptive Business Practices Act, 815 Ill. Comp. Stat. § 505 *et seq*.

64. Victoria Mortgage, [Agent 1], [Agent 2], and other unidentified employees and/or agents of Victoria Mortgage made misrepresentations to [Defendant-Consumer], as set forth above, including but not limited to statements that they would act in her best interest, obtain a loan which would be to her benefit, lower her monthly payment, and provide additional cash to repair her roof.

65. Victoria and its agents or employees also misrepresented the amount it was charging [Defendant-Consumer] for its purported services.

66. Saxon (plaintiff's assignor) misrepresented the terms and finance charges imposed on the loan.

67. Saxon's closing agent misrepresented the import and contents of the documents which he asked [Defendant-Consumer] to sign and concealed the terms of the loan while requiring [Defendant-Consumer] to sign the documents.

68. Saxon and Victoria entered into a conspiracy to defraud [Defendant-Consumer] by agreeing to the payment of a kickback (the "yield spread premium") from Saxon to Victoria for the purpose of getting [Defendant-Consumer] to accept the loan at a higher rate than Saxon was prepared to impose, without disclosing to [Defendant-Consumer] the purpose and nature of the kickback.

69. The misrepresentations were material in nature, as they concerned the basic terms and benefits of the loan.

70. Victoria and its employee agents knew that their representations were false at the time they were made.

71. Saxon knew that its Truth In Lending disclosures were inaccurate. Saxon's agent knew that representations to [Defendant-Consumer] at the closing were false.

72. The misrepresentations and omissions were made with the intent to induce [Defendant-Consumer's] reliance and thereby to enter into the transaction.

73. [Defendant-Consumer] reasonably relied on Saxon's and Victoria's misrepresentations to her detriment.

74. Plaintiff's assignor is a mortgage company with extensive experience and sophistication in transactions involving residential mortgages.

75. Conversely, [Defendant-Consumer] is a single family homeowner who is inexperienced and unsophisticated in matters involving consumer lending.

76. The fees charged to [Defendant-Consumer] far exceed the fees normally charged to consumers in home mortgage transactions.

77. In addition to the fees paid by [Defendant-Consumer] for the loan, plaintiff's assignor paid an illegal kickback to the mortgage broker of $3750 in violation of RESPA.

78. Furthermore, plaintiff's assignor failed to properly notify [Defendant-Consumer] about the high-cost nature of the loan and failed to provide accurate Truth In Lending disclosures.

79. Finally, the mortgage that plaintiff's assignor entered into with [Defendant-Consumer] increased her monthly mortgage payments by more than $150, left her with a balloon payment of $101,686.62 due when she is 84 years old and provided her with absolutely no real economic benefit.

80. Plaintiff's assignor's practices as described above are unfair, immoral, unethical, and unscrupulous.

81. Theses practices offend public policy.

82. As a result of plaintiff's assignor's unfair practices, in violation of the Consumer Fraud Act, 815 Ill. Comp. Stat. § 505, [Defendant-Consumer] suffered substantial injury in that she is now faced with the loss of her home.

83. Plaintiff, as holder of a high-cost loan, is liable for all claims and defenses that can be raised against its assignor. 15 U.S.C. § 1641(d)(1).

84. On information and belief, based on documents found in plaintiff's loan files, plaintiff knew that the terms of the loan had been misrepresented to [Defendant-Consumer].

85. Plaintiff knew that the Truth In Lending disclosures given to [Defendant-Consumer] were inaccurate. Such inaccuracy was apparent on the face of the documents assigned to plaintiff.

Wherefore, [Defendant-Consumer] prays that this Court dismiss Plaintiff's Complaint with prejudice, or, in the alternative, reduce the amount owed by [Defendant-Consumer] by the amount of damages available under the CFA.

Fourth Affirmative Defense:
Common Law Fraud

86. [Defendant-Consumer] incorporates paragraphs 1–74 above by reference herein.

87. Victoria Mortgage, [Agent 1], [Agent 2], and other unidentified employees and/or agents of Victoria Mortgage made misrepresentations to [Defendant-Consumer], as set forth above, including but not limited to statements that they would act in her best interest, obtain a loan which would be to her benefit, lower her monthly payment, and provide additional cash to repair her roof.

88. Victoria and its agents or employees also misrepresented the amount it was charging [Defendant-Consumer] for its purported services.

89. Saxon (plaintiff's assignor) misrepresented the terms and finance charges imposed on the loan.

90. Saxon's closing agent misrepresented the import and contents of the documents which he asked [Defendant-Consumer] to sign and concealed the terms of the loan while requiring [Defendant-Consumer] to sign the documents.

91. Saxon and Victoria entered into a conspiracy to defraud [Defendant-Consumer] by agreeing to the payment of a kickback (the "yield spread premium") from Saxon to Victoria for the purpose of getting [Defendant-Consumer] to accept the loan at a higher rate than Saxon was prepared to impose, without disclosing to [Defendant-Consumer] the purpose and nature of the kickback.

92. The misrepresentations were material in nature, as they concerned the basic terms and benefits of the loan.

93. Victoria and its employee agents knew that their representations were false at the time they were made.

94. Saxon knew that its Truth In Lending disclosures were inaccurate. Saxon's agent knew that representations to [Defendant-Consumer] at the closing were false.

95. The misrepresentations and omissions were made with the intent to induce [Defendant-Consumer's] reliance and thereby to enter into the transaction.

96. [Defendant-Consumer] reasonably relied on Saxon's and Victoria's misrepresentations to her detriment.

97. Plaintiff knew that the loan terms had been misrepresented to [Defendant-Consumer] and knew that the Truth In Lending disclosures given to [Defendant-Consumer] were inaccurate. Such inaccuracy was apparent on the face of the documents assigned to plaintiff.

98. Plaintiff accepted assignment of the note with notice that the documents contained therein were inaccurate and that the loan violated TILA and RESPA. Therefore plaintiff is subject to the defense of fraud raised herein.

99. Plaintiff, as holder of a high-cost loan, is liable for all claims and defenses that can be raised against its assignor. 15 U.S.C. § 1641(d)(1).

Wherefore, [Defendant-Consumer] prays that this Court dismiss Plaintiff's Complaint with prejudice, or, in the alternative, reduce the amount owed by [Defendant-Consumer] by the amount of her damages.

Fifth Affirmative Defense:
Violation of the Illinois Interest Act[60]

100. This defense is asserted pursuant to the Illinois Interest Act, 815 Ill. Comp. Stat. § 205.

101. The loan entered by plaintiff's assignor and [Defendant-Consumer] on May 27, 1999, was for the stated sum of $120,000.

102. The stated interest rate on the loan entered by plaintiff's assignor and [Defendant-Consumer] was 11.00 percent. *See* Exhibit D.

103. In addition to the stated interest, plaintiff's assignor charged [Defendant-Consumer] at least $12,044.34 in points and fees.

104. The points and fees paid by [Defendant-Consumer] are 10.04 percent of the principal amount of $120,000.

105. The points and fees charged to [Defendant-Consumer] are therefore in excess of 3 percent of the principal amount of the loan.

106. The loan made by plaintiff's assignor to [Defendant-Consumer] is secured by her home, which is residential real estate in the state of Illinois.

107. The loan requires the payment of interest at an interest rate in excess of 8 percent per annum. Section 4.1a of the Illinois Interest Act, 815 Ill. Comp. Stat. § 205/4.1a(f), limits the amount of certain charges, including "points," "service charge," "discounts," "commission," or otherwise, in the case of loans with an interest rate in excess of 8 percent per annum that are secured by residential real estate, to not more than 3 percent of the principal amount.

108. Plaintiff's actions as described in paragraphs 66–71 above were done "knowingly" as that term is used in Section 6 of the Interest Act. 815 Ill. Comp. Stat., § 205/6. A knowing violation of the Interest Act subjects the offender to a penalty of twice the total of all interest, discount and charges determined by the loan contract or paid by the obligor, whichever is greater. 815 Ill. Comp. Stat. § 205/6.

109. The total of all interest, discounts and charges determined by the loan contract in connection with the transaction far exceeds the payoff balance owed by [Defendant-Consumer].

110. Pursuant to Section 6 of the Interest Act, Plaintiff's statutory liability is not less than twice the total of all interest, discounts or charges determined by the loan contract. [Defendant-Consumer] is therefore entitled to a complete set-off against all amounts that Plaintiff claims are due, under the terms of the Mortgage. 815 Ill. Comp. Stat. § 205/6.

WHEREFORE, [Defendant-Consumer] prays that this Honorable Court dismiss plaintiff's complaint with prejudice.

One of Defendant's Attorneys

[Attorney's Name]
[Attorney's Law Firm and Address]

L.6.2 Discovery

INTERROGATORIES

1. State the name, job title, and business address of each person providing information in response to these discovery requests.

ANSWER:

2. Provide the following information for all employees and agents of Chase and/or its assignor and/or Victoria Mortgage who had any involvement in the transaction with plaintiff or in the

---

60 This Affirmative Defense (formerly denominated the "Fourth Affirmative Defense"), has been previously stricken by the Court. [Defendant-Consumer] includes it here solely in order to preserve her rights on appeal.

administration of her account, including but not limited [to] the origination, underwriting, disbursement and assignment of the subject account: full name, present or last known home and business addresses and telephone numbers; date first employed by you; whether presently employed by you; all job title(s) and dates during which each job was held; and, if not presently employed, Social Security number and exact date of birth. State, generally, each individual's involvement (*e.g.*, preparation of documents, notarizing signatures, approval of financing terms, communications with the borrower; sending of notices, disbursement of funds, etc.).

ANSWER:

3. State the date and subject matter of each communication (oral or written): (a) between or among any of the parties to this action, and (b) between you and any other person or entity (other than your counsel), relating to the subject account and/or transaction. Identify all documents reflecting or relating to such communications, including but not limited to letters, faxes, notes, internal memoranda, calendars, computer data, and credit applications, etc.

ANSWER:

4. State the date and amount of each payment (a) disbursed from the loan proceeds of the subject transaction and/or account; (b) received by you from anyone in connection with the subject account; and (c) paid to or received by anyone else in connection with the subject account (regardless of whether the payment came from the loan proceeds or another source). Identify the payor and payee of each such payment made or received, including but not limited to payments made to brokers, appraisers, title companies, credit reporting agencies, couriers and contractors, and identify all documents relating to same, including all canceled checks and receipts.

ANSWER:

5. Describe your policy and practice relating to the origination, approval or underwriting, preparation, disbursement and acceptance of assignment of a residential mortgage loan such as the subject transaction(s), including but not limited to all agreements with brokers, lenders, title companies, assignors, etc. Identify all documents relating to or reflecting such policy, practices and agreements, including all documentation required to be in assigned account files, and all forms given or sent to borrowers, information or forms which borrowers are requested to provide in order to obtain a loan, and all instructions, policy and procedure manuals, memoranda and guidelines given to brokers, title companies, lenders and/or closing agents, and any persons who review account files for approval and/or acceptance of assignment.

ANSWER:

6. If your response to any of the foregoing Requests To Admit is anything other than an unqualified admission, state in detail all facts upon which you rely on in denying the request, state whether any investigation was made to determine your response and describe any such investigation, and identify all documents reviewed or relied upon.

ANSWER:

7. If you are declining to produce any document or respond to any paragraph in whole or in part because of a claim of privilege, please: identify the subject matter, type (*e.g.*, letter, memorandum), date, and author of the privileged communication or information,

all persons that prepared or sent it, and all recipients or addressees; identify each person to whom the contents of each such communication or item of information have heretofore been disclosed, orally or in writing; state what privilege is claimed; and state the basis upon which the privilege is claimed.

ANSWER:

8. If any document requested was, but no longer is, in your possession or subject to your control, please state: the date of its disposition; the manner of its disposition (*e.g.*, lost, destroyed, or transferred to a third party); and an explanation of the circumstances surrounding the disposition of the document.

ANSWER:

9. With respect to each expert or opinion witness whom you will or may call upon to give evidence in connection with this case, please state: his or her name, address, telephone number, occupation, and current employment; the subject matter of his or her expertise; any matters which you contend qualify him or her as an expert; the substance of all facts and opinions to which he or she could testify if called as a witness; a summary of the grounds for each such opinion, and identify all documents, reports or statements made by any such expert.

ANSWER:

10. Describe and define all charges listed in Exhibits A, B and C to H's Affirmative Defenses, and explain any discrepancies in the listed figures, *i.e.*, explain why the Itemization of Amount Financed (Exhibit C to H's Affirmative Defenses) states that the Broker's Origination Fee was $7800, and that $500 was paid to Thomas Appraisals, while the HUD-1 Settlement Statement (Exhibit A to H's Affirmative Defenses) states that a $7032.63 "loan origination fee" plus $500 for an appraisal was paid to Victoria Mortgage.

ANSWER:

11. If you believe that other or different amounts were paid to Victoria Mortgage in connection with the subject transaction (other than what is disclosed in the Exhibits to H's Affirmative Defenses), please state what amounts were paid and explain the discrepancy. Identify each and every service or goods you believe were provided by Victoria Mortgage to Ms. H in connection with the transaction and the reasonable fair market value of those goods and services.

ANSWER:

12. State the amount that you believe is the "total loan amount" and the total "points and fees" involved in the subject transaction and explain how you arrived at those figures.

ANSWER:

13. Explain the basis and/or the manner in which the payments made to Victoria Mortgage were calculated (e.g., percentage of loan amount, interest rate of loan, specific services provided).

ANSWER:

14. State the name, residence and business addresses and phone numbers, and job position of all person(s) and/or entities not identified in response to any preceding Interrogatory who had any involvement in or has knowledge of any facts relating to matters alleged in H's Affirmative Defenses, and/or who may testify as witnesses at the trial or any hearing hereof. Identify each and every written or recorded statement made by such potential witnesses.

ANSWER:

15. Identify all agreements between Chase and Saxon Mortgage. State the number of residential mortgage loans assigned by Saxon to Chase in the last three years, and identify those in which Victoria Mortgage was the broker. Of these loans, state how many were in default of at least one month, within the first three years after they were made. State whether Chase has received any complaints (oral or written, whether or not filed with any judicial or administrative forum or consumer protection agency) from other borrowers in transactions in which either Saxon or Victoria Mortgage was involved, and identify all individuals who made such complaints.

ANSWER:

REQUESTS FOR PRODUCTION OF DOCUMENTS

1. Please produce all documents (including all computer or digital media-stored data) relating to Ms. H, the property located at [address], Chicago, Illinois, and the subject transaction and/or account, or which are indexed, filed or retrievable under her name or any number, symbol, designation or code (such as a transaction number or Social Security number) assigned to her or to the subject transaction(s), including but not limited to all documents relating to the origination, approval, disbursement, assignment and administration of the loan(s), all agreements between Chase and Saxon, and all correspondence related to the subject transaction.

2. All documents relating or referring to your policy and practice relating to the origination, approval or underwriting, preparation, disbursement and acceptance of assignment of a residential mortgage loan such as the subject transaction(s), including but not limited to all agreements with brokers, lenders, title companies, assignors, etc. Identify all documents relating to or reflecting such policy, practices and agreements, including all documentation required to be in assigned account files and all instructions, policy and procedure manuals, memoranda and guidelines given to brokers, title companies, lenders, closing agents, and/or any persons who review account files for approval and/or acceptance of assignment.

3. All documents relating to any judicial or administrative proceeding, public or private consumer protection agency or office, and all customer complaints in which Chase, Saxon or Victoria Mortgage were alleged to have made misrepresentations or violated any consumer protection statutes, rules or regulations relating to mortgages, mortgage brokers, or consumer credit.

4. Copies of all insurance policies which may afford coverage as to the matters complained of or under which a claim was made. Include any policy which refers to consumer protection coverage and any comprehensive general liability policy.

5. All documents identified in response to the above Interrogatories, and all documents referred to or reviewed in preparing the response to the above Interrogatories, not otherwise called for in these document production requests.

Respectfully submitted,
[Attorney for Plaintiff]

[Attorney for Plaintiff]
[Attorney's Law Firm and Address]

L.7 Bank Preemption Pleadings and Briefs

The first document (L.7.1) is an amicus brief that addresses the issue of whether the OCC has the authority to extend preemption rights to operating subsidiaries. This brief was filed in *Wachovia Bank, N.A. v. Burke* in the Second Circuit Court of Appeals. The lower court decision can be found at 319 F. Supp. 2d 275 (D. Conn. 2004). Thanks to Arthur E. Wilmarth, Jr., Professor of Law, George Washington University Law School, for this brief. The next subsection, L.7.2, *infra*, is the complaint filed by the New York Attorney General against an operating subsidiary of a depository alleging state law claims. Finally, the last document found in L.7.3, *infra*, is the amended complaint in a case filed against a national bank raising claims under state law. Thanks to James Sturdevant and Mark Johnson for sharing this pleading.

L.7.1 Amicus Brief in Wachovia Bank v. Burke

INTEREST OF *AMICI CURIAE*

This brief is submitted by the Attorneys General of 38 *amici* states, who are responsible for enforcing state laws regulating mortgage lenders and other providers of financial services. *Amicus* Conference of State Bank Supervisors is the professional association of state officials who regulate state-chartered banks and other state-licensed providers of financial services across the nation. *Amici* submit this brief in support of Appellant John P. Burke, Banking Commissioner of the State of Connecticut (the "Commissioner"). Connecticut's statutes authorize the Commissioner to license and regulate nonbank mortgage lenders in order to "protect consumers" from "unscrupulous lending practices." *Solomon v. Gilmore,* 731 A.2d 280, 284 (Conn. 1999). Connecticut's statutes are similar to the mortgage lending laws of many other states.

In the decision below, the District Court held that federal law preempted the Commissioner's authority to regulate a state-chartered nonbank mortgage lender that is an operating subsidiary of a national bank. The decision below is of great concern to *amici*, because it undermines core principles of federalism that are embodied in our systems of financial regulation and corporate governance.

INTRODUCTION AND SUMMARY OF ARGUMENT

Appellee Wachovia Mortgage Corporation ("Wachovia Mortgage") is a state-chartered nonbank corporation, organized under North Carolina law, that makes first and secondary mortgage loans to residents of Connecticut and other states. Prior to January 1, 2003, Wachovia Mortgage was a holding company affiliate of Appellee Wachovia Bank, N.A. ("Wachovia Bank"). During the same time period, Wachovia Mortgage obtained licenses from the Commissioner and acknowledged its duty to comply with Connecticut's laws governing nonbank mortgage lenders. On January 1, 2003, Wachovia Mortgage became a wholly-owned operating subsidiary of Wachovia Bank,[61] and Wachovia Mortgage thereafter

---

61 Under regulations adopted by the Office of the Comptroller of the Currency (OCC), a subsidiary of a national bank qualifies as

claimed that it was no longer required to follow Connecticut's mortgage lending regulations. Appellees pursued that claim by filing a lawsuit against the Commissioner.

The District Court held that federal law preempts six Connecticut statutes, which authorize the Commissioner to license and regulate Wachovia Mortgage. The District Court relied primarily on 12 C.F.R. § 7.4006, a regulation adopted in 2001 by the OCC. Section 7.4006 purports to extend 12 U.S.C. § 484(a) B a statute limiting the exercise of "visitorial powers" over "national banks" B to the operating subsidiaries of national banks. The District Court concluded that (i) "Congress . . . has not addressed the manner in which state law should apply to a national bank operating subsidiary," and (ii) § 7.4006 is a "reasonable interpretation of the National Bank Act." Joint Appendix ("J.A.") 106, 108.

The District Court should not have deferred to § 7.4006. The OCC's regulation conflicts with Congress' clearly-expressed intent and violates federalism principles underlying our systems of financial regulation and corporate governance. The unambiguous terms of § 484(a) and related federal statutes demonstrate that the limitation on "visitorial powers" under § 484(a) applies *only* to national banks and does *not* extend to operating subsidiaries and other "affiliates" of national banks. The decision below also contravenes the unmistakable purposes of Congress to separate national banks from their "affiliates" and to preserve the states' authority to regulate state-chartered providers of financial services.

ARGUMENT

A. The District Court's Decision Conflicts with Federalism Principles Inherent in Our Systems of Financial Regulation and Corporate Governance

1. National Banks Are Not Immune from State Regulation

The District Court concluded that 12 U.S.C. § 484(a) "evidences a broad intent to preempt state law as to national banks." J.A. 93. In support of that conclusion, the District Court cited *Beneficial National Bank v. Anderson,* 539 U.S. 1, 10 (2003), and *Marquette National Bank v. First of Omaha Serv. Corp.,* 439 U.S. 299, 314-15 (1978). J.A. 90. However, those decisions considered *only* the narrow question of whether state usury laws apply to national banks. In *Beneficial,* the Supreme Court determined that 12 U.S.C. §§ 85 & 86 provide "an exclusive federal cause of action for usury against national banks." 539 U.S. at 9. Previously, in *Marquette,* the Court held that the state usury laws do not govern national banks, because § 85 specifies the maximum interest rates allowed on loans by national banks. 439 U.S. at 308, 318-19. Thus, *Beneficial* and *Marquette* determined that usury is a *specific* area in which Congress has *expressly* preempted the application of state laws to national banks.

In contrast to the *special* case of usury laws, the courts have repeatedly upheld the states' *general* authority to regulate national banks.[62] In 1997, the Supreme Court declared, as a general prin-

ciple, that "federally chartered banks are subject to state law." *Atherton v. FDIC,* 519 U.S. 213, 222 (1997). As support for that principle, the Court cited decisions reaching back to an 1870 case, where the Court held that national banks

> . . . are subject to the laws of the State, and are governed in their daily course of business far more by the laws of the State than of the nation. All their contracts are governed and construed by State laws. Their acquisition and transfer of property, their right to collect their debts, and their liability to be sued for debts, are all based on State law. It is only when State law incapacitates the [national] banks from discharging their duties to the federal government that it becomes unconstitutional.

Id. at 222-23 (quoting *National Bank v. Commonwealth,* 76 U.S (9 Wall.) 353, 362 (1870)).

As the District Court noted (J.A. 93), the Supreme Court also held in 1996 that states have "the power to regulate national banks, where . . . doing so does not prevent or significantly interfere with the national bank's exercise of its powers." *Barnett Bank of Marion County, N.A. v. Nelson,* 517 U.S. 25, 33 (1996). In 1999, Congress determined that the "prevent or significantly interfere with" test is the controlling standard for evaluating preemption claims under *Barnett Bank. See* 15 U.S.C. § 6701(d)(2)(A); H.R. Rep. No. 106-434, at 156-57 (1999) (Conf. Rep.), reprinted in 1999 U.S.C.C.A.N. 245, 251. *Barnett Bank* is consistent with previous decisions holding that "national banks are subject to state laws unless those laws infringe the national banking laws or impose an undue burden on the performance of the banks' functions." *Anderson National Bank v. Luckett,* 321 U.S. 233, 248 (1944).[63]

Congress endorsed the general application of state laws to national banks when it passed the Riegle-Neal Interstate Banking and Branching Efficiency Act of 1994, 108 Stat. 2338 ("Riegle-Neal Act"). The Riegle-Neal Act provides that interstate branches of national banks must comply with state law in four broadly-defined areas B community reinvestment, consumer protection, fair lending and intrastate branching B *unless* federal law preempts the application of state law to national banks. 12 U.S.C. § 36(f)(1)(A).[64] In reviewing the terms of § 36(f), the conference report on the Riegle-Neal Act confirmed the states' longstanding

---

Review of Banking & Financial Law 225, 237–73 (2004).

63   *Accord* Lewis v. Fidelity & Deposit Co., 292 U.S. 559, 564–66 (1934) (explaining that Congress has followed a "policy of equalization" between national and state banks, based on the application of many aspects of state law to national banks); First Nat'l Bank in St. Louis v. Missouri, 263 U.S. 640, 656 (1924) (affirming that "the operation of general state laws upon the dealings and contracts of national banks" is the "rule," while preemption is an "exception" that applies only when state laws "expressly conflict with the laws of the United States or frustrate the purpose for which national banks were created, or impair their efficiency to discharge the duties imposed upon them by the law of the United States"); McClellan v. Chipman, 164 U.S. 347, 357 (1896) (same).

64   In adopting the Riegle-Neal Act, members of Congress explained that the application of state laws to interstate branches of national banks was necessary to preserve the vitality of the

---

an "operating subsidiary" if (i) the subsidiary engages in "activities that are permissible for a national bank to engage in directly," and (ii) the parent bank "controls" the subsidiary. 12 C.F.R. § 5.34(e)(1) & (2).

62   *See* Arthur E. Wilmarth, Jr., *The OCC's Preemption Rules Exceed the Agency's Authority and Present a Serious Threat to the Dual Banking System and Consumer Protection,* 23 Annual

authority to regulate national banks that conduct business within their borders:

> States have a strong interest in the activities and operations of depository institutions doing business within their jurisdictions, *regardless of the type of charter an institution holds.* In particular, States have a legitimate interest in protecting the rights of their consumers, businesses and communities. . . .
>
> Under well-established judicial principles, *national banks are subject to State law in many significant respects.* . . . Courts generally use a rule of construction that *avoids finding a conflict between the Federal and State law where possible.* The [Riegle-Neal Act] does not change these judicially established principles.

H.R. Rep. No. 103-651 (Conf. Rep.), at 53 (1994) (emphasis added), reprinted in 1994 U.S.C.C.A.N. 2068, 2074. By referring to "judicially established principles" under which "national banks are subject to State law in many significant respects," the Riegle-Neal conferees expressed their obvious agreement with the decisions in *Commonwealth, McClellan, Lewis, and Luckett,* cited above.

Until recently, most courts have applied a presumption in favor of applying state laws to the activities of national banks *unless* preemption is mandated in a particular area B such as usury B by "the clear and manifest purpose of Congress." *National State Bank v. Long,* 630 F.2d 981, 985 (3d Cir. 1980); *accord, Video Trax, Inc. v. NationsBank, N.A.,* 33 F. Supp. 2d 1041, 1048 (S.D. Fla. 1998), *aff'd,* 205 F.3d 1358 (11th Cir.) (per curiam), *cert. denied,* 531 U.S. 822 (2000); *Perdue v. Crocker National Bank,* 702 P.2d 503, 519-23 (Cal. 1985), *appeal dism'd,* 475 U.S. 1001 (1986). The foregoing presumption is consistent with the general presumption *against* preemption that the Supreme Court has applied in fields of traditional state regulation. *E.g., Medtronic, Inc. v. Lohr,* 518 U.S. 470, 475, 484-85 (1996); *N.Y. State Conference of Blue Cross & Blue Shield Plans v. Travelers Ins. Co.,* 514 U.S. 645, 654-56 (1995).

In *Bank of America v. City and County of San Francisco,* 309 F.3d 551, 559 (9th Cir. 2002), *cert. denied,* 538 U.S. 1069 (2003), the Ninth Circuit refused to apply a "presumption against preemption" when it struck down local ordinances that prohibited national banks from imposing surcharges on individuals who used the banks' automated teller machines. The Ninth Circuit's rejection of a presumption against preemption was clearly erroneous, because it conflicted with the Supreme Court precedents and congressional views discussed above.[65]

---

nation's dual banking system. *See* Wilmarth, *supra* note 62, at 269–70 & n.166.

65 In holding that a presumption against preemption was inapplicable, the Ninth Circuit relied primarily on *United States v. Locke,* 529 U.S. 89 (2000). *See Bank of America,* 309 F.3d at 558–59. *Locke,* however, did *not* deal with a state law regulating national banks. Instead, *Locke* invalidated state laws that imposed restrictions on oil tankers operating in navigable waterways. The Supreme Court refused to apply an " 'assumption' of non-preemption" in *Locke* because the challenged state laws interfered with "national and international maritime com-

In upholding the OCC's claim of preemption in § 7.4006, the District Court relied primarily on 12 U.S.C. § 484(a). J.A. 93, 100. Under § 484(a), "[n]o national bank shall be subject to any visitorial powers except as authorized by Federal law, vested in the courts of justice" or exercised under congressional authority. "Visitorial powers" include the right to examine a corporation's books and records and the power to enforce legal rules that bind the corporation. *E.g., Guthrie v. Harkness,* 199 U.S. 148, 159 (1905); *First Union National Bank v. Burke,* 48 F. Supp. 2d 132, 144 (D. Conn. 1999).

As shown by the plain language of § 484(a), the "courts of justice" are authorized to exercise "visitorial powers" over national banks. Based on that language in § 484(a) and its statutory antecedents, state officials and private parties have obtained *judicial remedies* in federal and state courts to enforce state laws against national banks.[66] In contrast, except as provided in § 484(b), § 484 does not allow state officials to examine national banks or to impose *administrative remedies* (e.g., cease-and-desist orders and civil money penalties) against national banks.[67]

The District Court noted that § 484(a) refers *only* to the exercise of visitorial powers over a "national bank," and that § 484(a) "does *not* speak expressly to subsidiaries of national banks." J.A. 101-02 (emphasis added). The District Court therefore recognized that 12 C.F.R. § 7.4006 is "the crux of the current controversy," because § 7.4006 is the "relevant conflicting [OCC] regulation" that purports to extend the preemptive effect of § 484(a) from national banks to their operating subsidiaries. J.A. 95, 99.

2. The District Court's Decision Conflicts with the States' Long-Established Authority to Regulate State-Chartered Corporations

Based on § 7.4006, the OCC claims that state-chartered operating subsidiaries of national banks are immune from state oversight. *See* J.A. 97, 108. In deferring to the OCC's claim, the District Court ignored the longstanding authority of each state (i) to

---

merce," an area in which Congress had shown a clear desire to establish a "uniformity of regulation." 529 U.S. at 108. By contrast, in *Atherton,* after reviewing the long tradition of state regulation of banks (including national banks), the Supreme Court concluded that federal policy did *not* require "uniformity" of regulatory treatment for federally-chartered banks. Accordingly, the Court refused in *Atherton* to adopt a federal common-law rule that would displace state law. 519 U.S. at 219–26. Similarly, the Supreme Court held in *St. Louis* and *McClellan* that the general application of state law to national banks is the "rule," while preemption is the "exception."

66 *E.g., St. Louis,* 263 U.S. at 259–61; *Burke,* 48 F. Supp. 2d at 145–46, 148–49, 150–51. *See also* Guthrie v. Harkness, 199 U.S. at 159 (holding that, under the predecessor of § 484, national banks were "liable to control in the courts of justice," and "the statute did not intend in withholding visitorial powers to take away the right to proceed in courts of justice to enforce . . . recognized rights"); Wilmarth, *supra* note 62, at 329–32 (discussing cases interpreting the "vested in the courts of justice" clause).

67 *See Long,* 630 F.2d at 987–89; *Burke,* 48 F. Supp. 2d at 143–50; 140 Cong. Rec. S 12786 (daily ed. Sept. 13, 1994) (colloquy between Sen. D'Amato and Sen. Riegle, explaining that 12 U.S.C. § 36(f)(1)(B) prevents state officials from examining or taking administrative enforcement measures against interstate branches of national banks).

exercise comprehensive supervision over the corporations it charters, and (ii) to license and regulate companies chartered by other
states that transact business within its borders. With regard to
locally-chartered companies, the Supreme Court has declared that:

> No principle of corporation law and practice is
> more firmly established than a State's authority to
> regulate domestic corporations. . . .
>
> It is thus an accepted part of the business
> landscape in this country for States to create
> corporations, to prescribe their powers, and to
> define the rights that are acquired by purchasing
> their shares.

CTS Corp. v. Dynamics Corp. of America, 481 U.S. 69, 89, 91
(1987).

With regard to foreign corporations, the Supreme Court has
affirmed that each state "is legitimately concerned with safeguarding the interests of its own people in business dealings with
corporations not of its own chartering but who do business within
its borders." *Union Brokerage Co. v. Jensen,* 322 U.S. 202, 208
(1944). Each state may therefore require foreign corporations to
comply with licensing requirements and other regulations enacted
"for the purpose of insuring the public safety and convenience."
Id. at 211 (internal quotation marks and citation omitted). The
courts have further noted that Congress has refrained from adopting a "federal corporate law" that would "overturn or at least
impinge severely on the tradition of state regulation of corporate
law." *Business Roundtable v. SEC,* 990 F.2d 406, 412 (D.C. Cir.
1990); *see also Santa Fe Industries, Inc. v. Green,* 430 U.S. 462,
478-79 (1977).

In the specific field of financial services, courts have frequently
upheld the states' authority to regulate banks and nonbanks for the
purpose of protecting their economy and their citizens from abusive practices. In 1980, the Supreme Court declared:

> We readily accept the submission that, both as a
> matter of history and as a matter of present com-
> mercial reality, banking and related financial ac-
> tivities are of profound local concern. . . . [S]ound
> financial institutions and honest financial practices
> are essential to the health of any State's economy
> and to the well-being of its people. Thus, it is not
> surprising that ever since the early days of our
> Republic, the States have chartered banks and
> have actively regulated their activities.

Lewis v. BT Investment Managers, Inc., 447 U.S. 27, 38 (1980).

In *BT Investment,* the Supreme Court also observed that 12
U.S.C. § 1846 reserves to the states a "general power to enact
regulations" applicable to bank holding companies and their banking and nonbanking subsidiaries, provided such "state legislation . . . operates within the boundaries marked by the Commerce
Clause." Id. at 48-49; *see also Old Stone Bank v. Michaelson,* 439
F. Supp. 252, 256 (D.R.I. 1977) ("It has long been recognized that
a state may regulate banking to protect the public welfare in the
exercise of its police powers"). In the field of mortgage lending,
courts have upheld state laws prohibiting lenders from engaging in
fraud, predatory lending, redlining and other unconscionable practices. *E.g., Long,* 630 F.2d at 985-87; *United Companies Lending*

Corp. v. Sargeant, 20 F. Supp. 2d 192, 200-04 (D. Mass. 1998);
Solomon v. Gilmore, 731 A.2d 280, 283-89 (Conn. 1999).

The District Court acknowledged that "there is no explicit
evidence of Congressional intent to preempt state regulation of
[operating subsidiaries]." J.A. 102. As demonstrated below in Part
B, that finding should have resulted in summary judgment for the
Commissioner. Given the lack of any evidence that Congress
contemplated preemption, the District Court should not have deferred to a federal agency regulation that abrogates the states'
longstanding authority to regulate state-chartered providers of
financial services.

B. The District Court Should Not Have Deferred to § 7.4006, Because That Rule Conflicts with Congressional Intent and Invades the States' Sovereign Authority to Regulate State-Chartered Corporations

1. Congress Has Not Preempted, or Authorized the OCC to Preempt, State Regulation of Operating Subsidiaries

a. Section 484(a) Does Not Apply to "Affiliates" of National Banks

The District Court concluded that it was "reasonable" for the
OCC to adopt a rule B § 7.4006 B that extends the limitation on
"visitorial powers" under 12 U.S.C. § 484(a) to operating subsidiaries of national banks. J.A. 108-12. That conclusion is clearly
erroneous, because § 484(a) applies *only* to "national banks" and
operating subsidiaries *cannot* qualify for treatment as "national
banks." The term "national bank," as used in § 484(a), is governed
by the definitions contained in 12 U.S.C. §§ 221 & 221a(a). As
those statutes and related federal laws make clear, a "national
bank" is a financial institution that (i) files articles of association
and an organization certificate with the OCC, pursuant to 12 U.S.C.
§§ 21-24 & 26; (ii) receives from the OCC a certificate of authority
to carry on the "business of banking," pursuant to §§ 24 & 27; and
(iii) is eligible to become a member of the Federal Reserve System
(FRS), pursuant to § 282. Operating subsidiaries do *not* qualify as
"national banks" under §§ 221 and 221a(a), because they are
chartered as *nonbank* corporations under *state* law, they do *not*
receive certificates of authority to conduct the "business of banking" from the OCC, and they *cannot* become members of the FRS.
Accordingly, operating subsidiaries are *not* entitled to any immunity from state supervision that "national banks" may enjoy under
§ 484(a).

The foregoing analysis is confirmed by § 221a(b), which defines
"affiliate" to include "any corporation" that controls or *is controlled by* a national bank. Under the OCC's regulations, an
operating subsidiary *must* be controlled by its parent national bank.
Therefore, an operating subsidiary is unquestionably an "affiliate"
of its parent bank under § 221a(b).

The separate legal status of "affiliates" is confirmed by 12
U.S.C. §§ 161(c) & 481. Under §§ 161(c) and 481, the OCC may
obtain reports from, and examine, "affiliates" of a national bank to
the extent "necessary to disclose fully the relations between such
bank and such affiliates" and "the effect of such relations upon the
affairs of such bank." In contrast to §§ 161(c) and 481, Congress
did *not* include the term "affiliates" in § 484. The only reasonable
conclusion is that § 484's limitation on visitorial powers applies
only to "national banks" and does *not* extend to their "affiliates,"

including their operating subsidiaries. *See Chicago v. Environmental Defense Fund,* 511 U.S. 328, 338 (1994) ("[I]t is generally presumed that Congress acts intentionally and purposely when it includes particular language in one section of a statue but omits it in another") (internal quotation marks and citation omitted).

In addition, §§ 161(c) and 481 do not impose any limitation on the authority of state officials to exercise visitorial powers over "affiliates" of national banks. The absence in those statutes of any restriction on state authority is highly significant, because the OCC's *nonexclusive* right to examine "affiliates" under § 481 is undoubtedly a "visitorial power." Taken together, §§ 161(c), 481 and 484 show that Congress has *not* preempted the authority of state officials to regulate state-chartered corporations that are "affiliates" of national banks.

Despite the unambiguous terms of § 221a(b), the District Court held that operating subsidiaries are not "affiliates." J.A. 102-05. In reaching that conclusion, the District Court relied heavily on 12 U.S.C. §§ 371c & 371c-1, which regulate certain transactions between national banks and their "affiliates." As the District Court noted, operating subsidiaries are exempted from "affiliate" status for purposes of both §§ 371c & 371c-1. Read in context, however, §§ 371c & 371c-1 demonstrate that operating subsidiaries *are* "affiliates" *for every other purpose.* Each section exempts operating subsidiaries from "affiliate" status *only* "[f]or the purpose of *this section,*" and each section authorizes the Federal Reserve Board to cancel that exemption in a particular case. 12 U.S.C. §§ 371c(b)(2)(A) & 371c-1(d)(1) (emphasis added). There would be no reason for Congress to exempt operating subsidiaries from "affiliate" status *specially* for purposes of §§ 371c and 371c-1, *unless* Congress understood that operating subsidiaries are *generally* treated as "affiliates" under § 221a(b).

In *Sec. Indus. Ass'n v. Bd. of Governors,* 468 U.S. 137 (1984), the Supreme Court held that commercial paper must be treated as "notes" and "securities" for purposes of the Banking Act of 1933 (popularly known as the "Glass-Steagall" Act). In reaching that conclusion, the Court observed that (i) commercial paper is a debt instrument that falls within the "ordinary meaning" of the statutory terms "notes" and "securities," and (ii) the Banking Act of 1933 did *not* contain any provision exempting commercial paper, in contrast to the special exemptions for commercial paper contained in *other* contemporaneous statutes. 468 U.S. at 149-52. Following the same reasoning, the District Court's approach must be rejected, because it ignores the literal definition of "affiliate" in § 221a(b) and fails to account for the *special* exemptions for operating subsidiaries contained in §§ 371c & 371c-1. Indeed, the District Court's view that operating subsidiaries are not "affiliates" for *any* purpose effectively reduces those special exemptions to "meaningless . . . surplusage." *Indep. Ins. Agents of Am. v. Hawke,* 211 F.3d 638, 643-44 (D.C. Cir. 2000); *see also Bd. of Governors v. Inv. Co. Inst.,* 450 U.S. 46, 58-59 n.24 (1981) (rejecting a proposed interpretation of the Banking Act of 1933 that would cause a provision dealing with "affiliates" to become "meaningless").

Section 221a(b) and other key statutes dealing with bank "affiliates" were enacted as part of the Banking Act of 1933. The District Court concluded that the 1933 Act was "directed at bank-related firms engaged in what Congress considered to be non-commercial bank functions . . ., not at operating subsidiaries conducting the 'business of banking.'" J.A. 104. That conclusion is plainly erroneous for two reasons. First, as shown above,

operating subsidiaries satisfy the literal definition of "affiliate" under § 221a(b). The alleged "purpose" of a statute cannot be used to alter "the plain language of the statute itself." *Bd. of Governors v. Dimension Fin. Corp.,* 474 U.S. 361, 369-70 (1986); *accord, SIA v. Bd. of Governors,* 468 U.S. at 153 ("[W]e cannot endorse the Board's departure from the literal meaning of the Act").

Second, as shown in the Commissioner's Brief, at 19-21, the legislative history of the Glass-Steagall Act shows that Congress intended to treat *all* companies controlled by national banks as "affiliates." Congress expected that the definition of "affiliate" in § 221a(b) would be applied strictly in accordance with its terms.[68] In addition, Congress wanted "[t]o separate as far as possible national . . . banks from *affiliates of all kinds,*" and "[t]o install a satisfactory examination of affiliates." S. Rep. No. 73-77, at 10 (1933) (emphasis added).

To accomplish these goals, Congress enacted three statutes B 12 U.S.C. §§ 52, 161(c) & 481. Section 52 requires national banks to separate their stock from the stock of any affiliates.[69] Sections 161(c) & 481 authorize the OCC to obtain reports from, and examine, all affiliates of national banks. While Congress imposed *additional* restrictions on securities affiliates of national banks in 1933 (and repealed those restrictions in 1999),[70] Congress clearly intended that the requirements of §§ 52, 161(c) and 481 would apply to *all* "affiliates" as defined in § 221a(b).

Section 133(a) of GLBA confirms that operating subsidiaries *cannot* be treated as "national banks." Under § 133(a), the Federal Trade Commission (FTC) may exercise its enforcement authority under the Federal Trade Commission Act against any "person" affiliated with a bank or savings association, as long as that "person . . . is not itself a bank or savings association."[71] In *Minnesota v. Fleet Mortgage Corp.,* 181 F. Supp. 2d 995 (D. Minn. 2001), the court determined that an operating subsidiary of a national bank is *not* "itself a bank" for purposes of § 133(a). The court concluded that § 133(a), which incorporates the definition of "bank" in 12 U.S.C. § 1813, is "unambiguous" and "simply does not include subsidiaries of banks." Id. at 1000. The court also found that an operating subsidiary "fits precisely into the category

---

68 The definition of "affiliate" in § 221a(b) was enacted as § 2(b) of the 1933 Act. 48 Stat. 162. The Senate committee report declared that § 2 "[d]efines the language used in the [Act] and *undertakes to make the meaning definite.*" S. Rep. No. 73-77, at 13 (1933) (emphasis added). Senator Bulkley confirmed that "the word 'affiliate,' as used in [the Act], is defined in section 2." 75 Cong. Rec. 9914 (1932).

69 The final paragraph of 12 U.S.C. § 52 was enacted by § 18 of the 1933 Act, 48 Stat. 192. The only affiliates exempted from § 52 are companies owning the premises of national banks as of June 16, 1934. *See* S. Rep. No. 73-77, at 16 (1933).

70 *See, e.g,* Sec. Indus. Ass'n v. Bd. of Governors, 839 F.2d 47, 54–62 (2d Cir.) (describing the restrictions imposed on securities affiliates under § 20 of the 1933 Act), *cert. denied,* 486 U.S. 1059 (1988). In 1999, Congress repealed § 20 of the 1933 Act. *See* Gramm-Leach-Bliley Act (GLBA), § 101, 113 Stat. 1341.

71 133 Stat. 1383, 15 U.S.C.A. § 41 note. Congress adopted § 133(a) to clarify the FTC's enforcement authority with regard to nondepository affiliates of banks and savings associations, because the FTC Act exempts "banks" and "savings and loan institutions" from the FTC's jurisdiction. *See* 15 U.S.C. § 45(a)(2); H.R. Rep. No. 106-74, at 137 (1999) (pt. 1); H.R. Rep. No. 106-434, at 161–62 (1999) (Conf. Rep.), reprinted in 1999 U.S.C.C.A.N. 245, 256–57.

of entities described in the language of § 133 as an entity controlled by a bank that is *not itself a bank* according to the prescribed definition." Id. (emphasis added). Accordingly, the court held that (i) the OCC did *not* have "exclusive jurisdiction" to enforce laws applicable to the mortgage lending subsidiary, and (ii) the subsidiary was subject to the shared enforcement authority of the FTC and state officials under an FTC regulation. Id. at 997-1002.

The definitions of "bank" and "affiliate" in 12 U.S.C. § 1813, the statute construed in *Fleet Mortgage,* are substantially similar to the definitions of the same terms in §§ 221 & 221a.[72] Therefore, *Fleet Mortgage* strongly supports the view that an operating subsidiary is an "affiliate" and cannot be treated as a "national bank" for purposes of §§ 221, 221a and 484(a).

b. Sections 24(Seventh) and 24a Do Not Preempt the State's Authority to Regulate Operating Subsidiaries

The District Court concluded that 12 U.S.C. §§ 24 (Seventh) and 24a provide "implicit" support for 12 C.F.R. § 7.4006. J.A. 93-95, 107-08. To the contrary, § 24(Seventh) and § 24a do *not* express any congressional purpose to bar the states from regulating operating subsidiaries. Under § 24(Seventh), a "national banking association" has authority "[t]o exercise . . . all such incidental powers as shall be necessary to carry on the business of banking." Like § 484(a), § 24(Seventh) refers *only* to national banks and does *not* grant any explicit authority or immunity to "affiliates." As the Supreme Court has observed, § 24(Seventh) "by its terms applies only to banks," while "[o]rganizations affiliated with banks . . . are dealt with by other sections of the [1933] Act." *Bd. of Governors v. ICI,* 450 U.S. at 58-59 n.24.

The District Court noted that three Supreme Court decisions have not questioned the authority of national banks to establish operating subsidiaries. J.A. 107. In two of those decisions, the Supreme Court upheld OCC interpretations of federal statutes that did *not* raise any preemption issues. *NationsBank of N.C., N.A. v. Variable Annuity Life Ins. Co.,* 513 U.S. 251, 254-55 (1995); *Clarke v. Sec. Indus. Ass'n,* 479 U.S. 388, 391-92 (1988). In the third decision, which concluded that 12 U.S.C. § 85 *did* preempt state law with regard to a national bank, the Court *declined* to decide whether the preemptive impact of § 85 extended to the bank's operating subsidiary. *Marquette,* 439 U.S. at 307-08. Thus, none of the three decisions supports the OCC's preemption claim set forth in § 7.4006.

While § 24(Seventh) may allow national banks to establish operating subsidiaries, it contains no language preempting the authority of states to regulate such entities. In fact, the first proviso cautions that "[e]xcept as hereinafter provided *or otherwise permitted by law,* nothing herein contained shall authorize the purchase by the [national bank] for its own account of any shares of stock of any corporation" (emphasis added). Thus, national banks do *not* have power under § 24(Seventh) to make investments in subsidiaries in violation of applicable "law" B a term whose plain meaning encompasses state law B *unless* the bank can point to a specific enabling grant of authority under a federal statute. *See Video Trax,* 33 F. Supp. 2d at 1047-49, 1058 (§ 24(Seventh) does *not* displace state laws through field preemption; preemption occurs *only if* state laws conflict with a specific power granted to

national banks); *Perdue,* 702 P.2d at 520-23 (same). Unlike other types of subsidiaries, operating subsidiaries do *not* derive their authority from any specific statutory grant.[73] Accordingly, the first proviso of § 24(Seventh) provides additional evidence that Congress has *not* preempted state regulation of operating subsidiaries.

Under established canons of statutory construction, the general grant of "incidental powers" to national banks under § 24(Seventh) must be construed in harmony with §§ 221a(b), 161(c) and 481, which specifically govern "affiliates." *See American Land Title Ass'n v. Clarke,* 968 F.2d 150, 157 (2d Cir. 1992) (the general grant of "incidental powers" under § 24(Seventh) must be interpreted in light of 12 U.S.C. § 92, which imposes specific limitations on the insurance activities of national banks), *cert. denied,* 508 U.S. 971 (1993); *IIAA v. Hawke,* 211 F.3d at 643-45 (same). As shown above, §§ 221a(b), 161(c) and 481 demonstrate that Congress has *not* preempted the states' authority to supervise state-chartered "affiliates" of national banks.

Section 24a, enacted in 1999 as part of GLBA, permits national banks to establish "financial subsidiaries" that may engage in certain activities (e.g., securities underwriting and dealing) that are not lawful for their parent banks. Under § 24a(g)(3), the term "financial subsidiary" does not include a subsidiary that "engages solely in activities that national banks are permitted to engage in directly and are conducted subject to the same terms and conditions that govern the conduct of such activities by national banks." Thus, § 24a(g)(3) exempts operating subsidiaries from *federal* statutory mandates (e.g., capital requirements, managerial ratings, and community reinvestment standards) that apply to financial subsidiaries under § 24a(a)-(f). Section 24a(g)(3) is not a power-granting provision, and it does not express any congressional purpose to bar the states from regulating operating subsidiaries. *See* S. Rep. No. 106-44, at 8 (1999) ("Nothing in this legislation is intended to affect any authority of national banks to engage in bank permissible activities through subsidiary corporations"); *Wilmarth, supra* note 62, at 342–43.

2. 12 C.F.R. § 7.4006 Is Not Entitled to Judicial Deference

a. Section 7.4006 Conflicts with Unambiguous Congressional Intent

Under the "first step" of the *Chevron* doctrine, a reviewing court must reject an agency interpretation that would "alter the clearly expressed intent of Congress." *Dimension,* 474 U.S. at 368. "In determining whether Congress has specifically addressed the question at issue, a reviewing court should not confine itself to examining a particular statutory provision in isolation. The meaning B or ambiguity B of certain words or phrases may only become evident when placed in context." *FDA v. Brown & Williamson Tobacco Corp.,* 529 U.S. 120, 132-33 (2000).

---

72 *Compare* 12 U.S.C. §§ 1813(a)(1)(A) (defining "bank") *and* 1813(w)(6) (incorporating the definition of "affiliate" from § 1841(k)) *with* id. §§ 221 & 221a(a) & (b).

73 The second, fourth and fifth provisos of § 24 (Seventh) authorize national banks to invest in subsidiaries that (i) conduct a "safe-deposit business," (ii) provide agricultural credit, and (iii) operate as "banker's banks." National banks may invest in "bank service companies" under 12 U.S.C. §§ 1861–67. In contrast, under the OCC's regulations, the term "operating subsidiary" does *not* include "a subsidiary in which the bank's investment is made pursuant to specific authorization in a statute." 12 C.F.R. § 5.34(e)(2)(i).

When § 484(a) is read in context with the statutes governing "affiliates" of national banks, it becomes clear that Congress has *not* preempted the authority of states to regulate operating subsidiaries of national banks. As previously shown, §§ 221a(b), 52, 161(c) and 481 demonstrate Congress' intent to separate national banks from their "affiliates" (including their operating subsidiaries) and to establish a distinct regulatory scheme for "affiliates." A comparison of §§ 161(c), 481 and 484(a) shows that (i) state officials must file lawsuits instead of administrative complaints to enforce state laws against national banks, but (ii) Congress has *not* restricted the authority of state officials to regulate state-chartered "affiliates" (including operating subsidiaries) of national banks.

Section 7.4006 is therefore invalid, because it contradicts the unambiguous statutory definitions of "national bank" and "affiliate" and also violates the clear intent of Congress. *ATLA v. Clarke*, 968 F.2d at 155-57; *IIAA v. Hawke*, 211 F.3d at 643-45. In *Dimension*, 474 U.S. at 368-75, the Supreme Court struck down a regulation that attempted to redefine "bank" in a way that conflicted with the governing statute's plain language. Section 7.4006 should be overruled for the same reason.

b. Section 7.4006 Violates Fundamental Tenets of Corporate Law and Invades the States' Sovereign Power to Regulate State-Chartered Corporations

The legal separation between a subsidiary and its parent corporation is a "general principle of corporate law deeply ingrained in our economic and legal systems." *United States v. Bestfoods*, 524 U.S. 51, 61 (1998) (citation and internal quotation marks omitted); *accord, Dole Food Co. v. Patrickson*, 538 U.S. 468, 474 (2003) ("[a] basic tenet of American corporate law is that the corporation and its shareholders are distinct entities"). Federal courts have consistently interpreted federal statutes in a manner that upholds corporate separation and other longstanding principles of state corporate law, absent clear evidence that Congress intended a different result.[74]

As shown above, Congress has *not* authorized the OCC to disregard the separate corporate existence of national banks and their operating subsidiaries. In fact, the National Bank Act requires a strict separation between national banks and their affiliates. Under 12 U.S.C. § 52, each national bank must separate its own stock from the stock of any affiliate. Sections 52, 161(c), 221a, 481 and other provisions of the 1933 Act were enacted "[t]o separate as far as possible national . . . banks from affiliates of all kinds." S.

Rep. No. 73-77, at 10 (1933). Sections 21-27, 221a & 282 establish that operating subsidiaries are "affiliates" and *cannot* be treated as "national banks." Accordingly, the OCC cannot claim any congressional mandate for its claim, embodied in § 7.4006, that operating subsidiaries are "in essence, incorporated departments or divisions of the [parent] bank." 66 F.R. 34784, 34788 (2001).

As indicated by 12 C.F.R. § 5.34(e), Wachovia Bank could have conducted all of Appellees' mortgage lending activities under its charter as a national bank. However, Appellees chose to establish Wachovia Mortgage as an operating subsidiary to take advantage of the legal protections provided by the subsidiary's state corporate charter.[75] Having made that choice, Appellees are in no position B even with the OCC's encouragement—to disregard the state-law duties that apply to Wachovia Mortgage by virtue of its charter. *See First Nat'l Bank of Logan v. Walker Bank & Trust Co.*, 385 U.S. 252, 261 (1966) (the Comptroller of the Currency may not "pick and choose what portion of the law binds him").

Based on § 7.4006, the OCC has claimed *exclusive* authority to regulate state-chartered operating subsidiaries of national banks. Section 7.4006 unlawfully invades sovereign state interests protected by the Tenth Amendment, because it attempts to transform state-chartered corporations into creatures of federal law without the chartering states' permission.[76] In an analogous case, the Supreme Court refused to defer to an agency's interpretation of federal law, because the agency's position created "significant constitutional and federalism questions" by "permitting federal encroachment upon a traditional state power" without any "clear indication that Congress intended that result." *Solid Waste Agency of Northern Cook County v. U.S. Army Corp. of Engineers*, 531 U.S. 159, 174, 172 (2001)*; see also Univ. of Great Falls v. NLRB*, 278 F.3d 1335, 1340-41 (D.C. Cir. 2002) (because "the constitutional avoidance canon of statutory interpretation trumps *Chevron* deference," the court declined to defer to an agency interpretation that raised serious constitutional questions and was not supported by any "affirmative intention of Congress clearly expressed").

---

74 *E.g., Dole Food Co.*, 538 U.S. at 475–76 (refusing to conclude that, "as a categorical matter, all subsidiaries are the same as the parent corporation," because "[t]he text of the [relevant statute] gives no indication that Congress intended us to depart from the general rules regarding corporate formalities"); *Bestfoods*, 524 U.S. at 62 (rejecting a proposed reading of a pollution control statute (CERCLA) that would impose automatic liability on a parent corporation for the acts of its subsidiary, because "nothing in CERCLA purports to reject this bedrock principle [of corporate separation], and against this venerable common law backdrop, the congressional silence is audible"); *CTS Corp.*, 481 U.S. at 85, 86 (refusing to construe a federal statute to "pre-empt a variety of state corporate laws of hitherto unquestioned validity," because the "longstanding prevalence of state regulation in this area suggests that, if Congress had intended to pre-empt all [such] state laws . . . it would have said so explicitly").

75 In an amicus brief filed in the District Court, four bank trade associations explained that national banks "establish[] operating subsidiaries as a vehicle to limit the portion of their capital exposed by their mortgage operations. . . . This protects the assets backing up the bank's entire deposit base . . . from being exposed to claims arising from the mortgage lending activities, as they would be if those activities were conducted directly in the bank." J.A. 74 (Amicus Brief of American Bankers Ass'n et al., at 14).

76 Hopkins Federal Savings & Loan Ass'n v. Cleary, 296 U.S. 315 (1935), held that a federal statute violated the Tenth Amendment by allowing state-chartered savings institutions to convert to federal charters without state permission. The Supreme Court declared that "[h]ow [state-chartered] corporations shall be formed, *how maintained and supervised,* and how and when dissolved, are matters of governmental policy, *which it would be an intrusion for another government to regulate by statute or decision,*" except as authorized by the federal Constitution. Id. at 337 (emphasis added). *See also* Chicago Title & Trust Co. v. 4136 Wilcox Bldg. Corp., 302 U.S. 120 (1937) (§ 77B of the federal Bankruptcy Act did not allow shareholders to file a bankruptcy petition on behalf of a corporation whose charter had expired under state law, because any such filing would be "an intrusion by the Federal Government on the powers of the [chartering] State" in contravention of the Tenth Amendment).

Under the same reasoning, the District Court should *not* have deferred to § 7.4006 in this case.

CONCLUSION

Amici respectfully urge this Court to reverse the decision below.

[Attorneys for Amici]

L.7.2 Complaint in New York v. First Horizon Home Mortgage

SUPREME COURT OF THE STATE OF NEW YORK
COUNTY OF ALBANY

————————————————)
)
PEOPLE OF THE STATE OF   )
NEW YORK, by ELIOT   )
SPITZER, attorney General of   )
the State of New York,   )
                     Plaintiffs,   )
)
v.   )
)
FIRST HORIZON LOAN CORP.)
                     Defendant.   )
————————————————)

COMPLAINT

The People of the State of New York, by their attorney, Eliot Spitzer, Attorney General of the State of New York, allege upon information and belief:

INTRODUCTION

1. The Attorney General brings this action, pursuant to General Business law (GBL) Article 29-H, § 602(2), to restrain and prevent defendant First Horizon Loan Corp. ("First Horizon") from violating and continuing to violate GBL § 601(8), and pursuant to GBL §§ 349(b) and 350-d, to permanently enjoin First Horizon from engaging in deceptive acts and practices and to recover restitution, statutory penalties and costs.

PARTIES AND JURISDICTION

2. Plaintiffs are the People of the State of New York, by their attorney, Eliot Spitzer, Attorney General of the State of New York.

3. Plaintiffs bring this action pursuant to GBL Article 29-H, § 602(2) under which the Attorney General is empowered to seek injunctive relief against any principal creditor who has engaged in unlawful debt collection practices, and pursuant to GBL §§ 349(b) and 350-d, which empower the Attorney General to seek injunctive relief, restitution and civil penalties when any person or entity has engaged in deceptive acts or practices in the conduct of business.

4. Defendant First Horizon is a foreign corporation with its principal place of business located at 4000 Horizon Way, Irving, Texas 75063.

5. First Horizon is a full-service mortgage banking company and a wholly-owned operating subsidiary of First Tennessee Bank, National Association. ("First Tennessee"). First Tennessee is a national bank headquartered in Memphis, Tennessee.

FACTS

6. In October 1974, Richard H. Consumer and Marsha P. Consumer purchased their residence at [Address], with a loan in the amount of $27,000 from Mechanics Savings Bank ("Mechanics Exchange").

7. The Consumers negotiated the terms of the loan and consummated the loan transaction on October 15, 1974. The terms of the loan are as follows: the loan would be repaid over twenty-five (25) years at an interest rate of eight and one half percent (8.5%) per annum, in three hundred (300) monthly payments of two hundred and one dollars and thirty one cents ($201.31), with the first payment due on November 15, 1974, and the final payment due on October 15, 1999.

8. As collateral for the loan, Mechanics Exchange received a first mortgage lien on the premises located at [Address].

9. the terms of the loan agreement were memorialized in a Disclosure Statement and Mortgage Bond, drafted by Mechanics Exchange and signed by the Consumers. The Mortgage and Mortgage Bond were filed with the Clerk of Rensselaer County on October 17, 1974, and were entered in Book 1112, Page 767.

10. In or around 1983, Mechanics Exchange merged with The Dime Savings Bank of New York, FSB ("Dime"), which acquired the Consumers Mortgage, as well as their checking accounts. Also around this time, the Consumers were divorced and Mr. Consumer assumed the obligations under the Mortgage Bond.

11. On or about June 16, 1993, Dime transferred the Mortgage Bond to Sunbelt National Mortgage Corp ("Sunbelt") through an Assignment. The Assignment was filed with the Clerk of Rensselaer County on July 15, 1993, and was entered in Book 2299, Page 203.

12. In or around 1995, First Horizon Home Loan Corporation merged with Sunbelt National Mortgage Corporation ("Sunbelt"), and acquired Mr. Consumer's mortgage in the process.

13. Around this time, Mr. Consumer authorized First Horizon to debit the amount of his monthly mortgage payment ($201.31) directly out of his checking account.

14. By November 15, 1999, Mr. Hall had fulfilled the obligations under the Mortgage Bond by making three hundred (300) timely payments of two hundred and one dollars and thirty one cents ($201.31), for a total of sixty thousand three hundred and ninety-three dollars ($60,393) to Mechanics Exchange and all subsequent holders of the Mortgage Bond.

15. Despite the fact that Mr. Consumer had completed his obligations under the loan agreement, First Horizon continued debiting two hundred and one dollars and thirty one cents ($201.31) from Consumer's checking account on or about the 15th of each month.

16. Mr. Consumer was unaware that he was making payments in excess of those owed under the Mortgage Bond, because he assumed he had taken out a thirty year mortgage, and had not recently looked at his mortgage paperwork.

17. In May 2003, Mr. Consumer received a letter from First Horizon. The letter included the following statements:

"[w]e strive to keep you informed of significant events involving your account, such as the upcoming maturity of your mortgage loan **on 10-99**" [emphasis added];

"Once we receive your 10/31/03 payment, your principal balance will reflect a paid-in-full status";

"Enclosed you will fin a payoff statement on your account if you decide to pay your loan in full **prior to 10-99**" [emphasis added];

"Should you decide to pay your account in full *after* this date, but still prior to 10-99, please contact our office for an updated payoff statement." [emphasis in original]

18. The "payoff statement" enclosed with Horizon's May 19, 2003 letter to Mr. Consumer alleged that Mr. Consumer owed $12,784.81 that was due on July 1, 2003. The "payoff statement" also included the following: "ONLY CERTIFIED FUNDS WILL BE ACCEPTED. NO PERSONAL CHECKS!"

19. Mr. Consumer was understandably confused by First Horizon's letter and contacted the bank at the number contained in the letter and spoke with a First Horizon representative. He was told that a representative would review his file and get back to him within one week. Mr. Consumer did not receive a response from First Horizon and called the bank several times over the next few weeks. Ultimately, Mr. Consumer was able to speak with a First Horizon representative named [Representative], who told him that she would look into the matter.

20. A few days later, Mr. Consumer received a letter from First Horizon (incorrectly dated July 9, 2002) stating, in relevant part:

"A review of the loan and the note executed October 15th, 1974 has revealed a discrepancy in the amortization. The note indicates a principal and interest (P&I) payment amount of $201.31. The loan, since inception, has carried a P&I amount of $201.31; however the payment amount of should [sic] have been $217.41, a difference of $16.10 per month. The current principal balance is $12,320.49. Had the loan been set up with the correct P&I amount the principal balance would have paid [sic] in full on October 15, 1999. Based on the current P&I the loan, as it stands will mature March 15, 2010."

21. This letter was the first time that Horizon communicated with Mr. Consumer about an alleged "discrepancy in the amortization" of his loan, and that Horizon was claiming that he should have paid $16.10 more each month. The letter acknowledged that Mr. Consumer would have "many questions regarding [the] issue" and advised him to call [Analyst], Executive Analyst.

22. After reviewing the letter, Mr. Consumer called Ms. Analyst at the number contained in the letter. Ms. Analyst told Mr. Consumer that it was a very complex issue and still under review. She also told him that he might want to request First Horizon to cease debiting his account.

23. By letter dated September 11, 2003, Mr. Consumer notified First Horizon to cease debiting his bank account. As of this date, First Horizon had debited an additional $9,461.57 over the amount due under the Mortgage Bond since it matured in October 1999.

24. Shortly thereafter, Mr. Consumer received a letter from First Horizon's Collections Department, dated October 2, 2003, notifying him that his loan "matured" in October 1999 and that the "unpaid principal balance" of $12,642.34 "is NOW due and payable." In addition, the letter informed Mr. Consumer that the "property securing [his] loan [would] be referred to an attorney for foreclosure" if he did not pay the amount due within thirty days. The letter did not disclosed the manner in which First Horizon arrived at the purported unpaid principal balance of $12,642.34.

25. After receiving this letter, Mr. Consumer met with his attorney [Attorney]. Ms. [Attorney] explained to First Horizon that any alleged miscalculation of the monthly payment was through no fault of Mr. Consumer, and that, in any event, Mr. Consumer had already paid more that $9,461.57 over the amount due under the Mortgage Bond.

26. In response, First Horizon offered to settle Mr. Consumer's account and discharge his mortgage if he paid an additional $7,500.00.

27. Although Mr. Consumer had already paid First Horizon $9,461.57 over the amount due under the Mortgage Bond, in an effort to avoid costly litigation, he authorized Ms. [Attorney] to offer to settle the matter with a payment to First Horizon in the amount of $5,000.

28. First Horizon rejected Mr. Consumer's offer to settle the account for $5,000 and reverted to its original demand for $12,642.34. In addition, First Horizon repeated its threat to foreclose on Mr. Consumer's home.

29. Horizon had no right to take any of the following actions which it has taken, or is threatening to take, with respect to Mr. Consumer's mortgage:

(a) unilaterally extending the maturity date on Mr. Consumer's mortgage from October 15, 1999 until March 15, 2010, thus threatening to hold a lien on Mr. Consumer's home for more than 11 years beyond the term of the mortgage;

(b) demanding that Mr. Consumer pay $201.31 per month for more that 11 years beyond the term of the mortgage, resulting in an additional payment of $25,163.75 beyond the amount required under the Mortgage Bond;

(c) continuing to debit funds from Mr. Consumer's account after October 15, 1999, without notice or authorization— and after receiving all payments to which it was entitled under the Mortgage Bond.

(d) threatening to foreclose on Mr. Consumer's home unless he paid an additional $12,320.49 within 30 days; and

(e) failing to discharge the mortgage on Mr. Consumer's home.

30. Horizon knew, or had reason to know, that if had no right to take the actions set forth above.

FIRST CAUSE OF ACTION PURSUANT TO GBL ARTICLE 29-H UNLAWFUL COLLECTION PRACTICES

31. New York GBL Article 29-H, § 601(8) provides that no principal creditor, as defined by GBL § 600(3), or his agent, shall "claim, or attempt or threaten to enforce a right with knowledge or reason to know that the right does not exist."

32. GBL § 600(3) defines "principal creditor" as "any person, firm, corporation or organization to whom a consumer claim is owed, due or asserted to be due or owed."

33. GBL § 600(1) defines "consumer claim" as "any obligation of a natural person for the payment of money or its equivalent which is or is alleged to be in default and which arises out of a transaction wherein credit has been offered or extended to a natural person, and the money, property or service which was the subject of the transaction was primarily for personal, family or household purposes."

34. Firs Horizon is a "principal creditor" as defined under GBL § 600(3) because it asserts that it is owed a debt arising out of a consumer's default on a loan wherein the money which was the subject of the loan was used for personal, family or household purposes.

35. By reason of the conduct described in paragraphs 15 through 29 above, First Horizon has violated and is continuing to violate GBL § 601(8).

SECOND CAUSE OF ACTION PURSUANT TO GENERAL BUSINESS LAW § 349 DECEPTIVE BUSINESS PRACTICES

36. Pursuant to GBL § 349, it is unlawful to engage in any deceptive acts or practices in the conduct of any business, trade, or commerce in this State.

37. By reason of the conduct described in paragraphs 15 through 29 above, First Horizon is engaging in deceptive acts and practices.

PRAYER FOR RELIEF

WHEREFORE, plaintiffs request that the Court grant relief pursuant to GBL §§ 349 and 602(2) by issuing an order and judgment as follows:

1. Permanently enjoining defendant from engaging in the unlawful collection practices and deceptive acts and practices described above;

2. Directing defendant to file a certificate with the Rensselaer County Clerk's office declaring that the mortgage currently held by defendant, which is filed in the Rensselaer County Clerk's office in Book 2299, Page 203, is satisfied;

3. Directing defendant to make restitution to Richard. H. Consumer.

4. Directing defendant to pay a civil penalty in the sum of $500.00 to the State of New York for each instance of violation of § 349, pursuant to GBL § 350-d;

5. Awarding plaintiffs the costs and disbursements of this action; and

6. Granting plaintiffs such other and further relief as the Court deems just and proper.

[Dated]

ELIOT SPITZER
Attorney General of the
State of New York
[Address]
[Telephone Number]

MARK FLEISCHER
MATTHEW BARBARO
Assistant Attorneys General

THOMAS CONWAY
Assistant Attorney General in Charge
Bureau of Consumer Frauds and Protection

L.7.3 Amended Complaint in Miller v. Bank of America

IN THE SUPERIOR COURT OF THE STATE OF CALIFORNIA
IN AND FOR THE COUNTY OF ALAMEDA

CASE NO. 801882-1

CLASS ACTION

PAUL CONSUMER, individually and on behalf of others similarly situated, Plaintiff, v. BANK OF AMERICA N.T. & S.A. a California corporation, and DOES 1//50, Defendants.	FIRST AMENDED COMPLAINT FOR FRAUD; VIOLATION OF CODE OF CIVIL PROCEDURE § 704.080; VIOLATION OF CODE OF CIVIL PROCEDURE § 1750 *et seq.*; INTENTIONAL INFLICTION OF EMOTIONAL DISTRESS; VIOLATION OF BUSINESS AND PROFESSIONS CODE § 17200 *et seq.*; VIOLATION OF BUSINESS AND PROFESSIONS CODE § 17500.

JURY TRIAL DEMANDED

Type of Case: Unfair Business Practices

INTRODUCTION

Plaintiff PAUL CONSUMER, by his attorneys, brings this action on behalf of himself and a class of similarly-situated persons to challenge defendant's unlawful and unfair practice of debiting Social Security direct deposit accounts for amounts protected from levy by law, and assessing unfair and unconscionable overdraft and return item fees from Social Security Direct Deposit accounts. Plaintiff seeks compensatory and punitive damages, restitution, declaratory and injunctive relief, and attorneys' fees, costs and expenses.

PARTIES

1. Plaintiff PAUL CONSUMER ("CONSUMER") is an individual, residing at all relevant times in the City and County of San Francisco, California. Plaintiff is a consumer who has a Social Security Direct Deposit Account with defendant BANK OF AMERICA. At all times material herein, Plaintiff CONSUMER's Social Security payments from the U.S. government were directly deposited into his account with defendant BANK OF AMERICA once each month. Defendant BANK OF AMERICA has repeatedly levied upon plaintiff CONSUMER's Social Security Direct Deposit account for debts allegedly owed to BANK OF AMERICA by CONSUMER, although BANK OF AMERICA erroneously

credited CONSUMER's account with funds that it later attempted to collect, and BANK OF AMERICA is prohibited by law from levying upon Social Security Direct Deposit funds. BANK OF AMERICA has imposed service charges on CONSUMER's account as a result of these improper levies and overdrafts resulting therefrom.

2. At all material times, defendant BANK OF AMERICA N.T.& S.A. ("BANK OF AMERICA") was, and is, a California corporation, with its principal place of business in San Francisco, California. BANK OF AMERICA is engaged in a nationwide business of marketing and providing banking and other financial services, including Social Security Direct Deposit Accounts. BANK OF AMERICA has offices throughout California, including in Alameda County. BANK OF AMERICA affirmatively solicits Social Security Direct Deposit customers residing in the State of California, and provides services to and collects payments from such customers.

3. Plaintiff is ignorant of the true names and capacities of defendants sued herein as DOES 1–50, and therefore sues these defendants by such fictitious names. Plaintiff will amend his complaint to state the true names and capacities when ascertained. Plaintiff is informed and believes that each of the fictitiously named defendants is responsible in some manner for the occurrences and damages alleged herein, and that plaintiff's damages as hereinafter set forth were proximately caused by said defendants.

4. Plaintiff is informed and believes and thereon alleges that each of the defendants acted in concert with each and every other defendant, intended to and did participate in the events, acts, practices and courses of conduct alleged herein, and was a proximate cause of damage and injury thereby to plaintiff as alleged herein.

5. At all times herein mentioned, each defendant was the agent or employee of each of the other defendants and was acting within the course and scope of such agency or employment.

ALLEGATIONS COMMON TO ALL CAUSES OF ACTION

6. On or about January 29, 1993, CONSUMER began receiving benefit payments from the Social Security Administration in the form of Social Security Disability Income and Supplemental Security Income (hereinafter collectively referred to as "SSI"). Individuals qualify for such benefit payments when they are permanently disabled and are unable to remain gainfully employed as a result of an ongoing physical or mental impairment. CONSUMER was physically assaulted in or around 1989 and suffered brain damage as a result of the assault. CONSUMER's sole source of income is his social security benefits, which he receives in the total amount of $670.40 per month. CONSUMER resides in a rent controlled apartment for which he pays approximately $530.60 per month in rent.

7. Plaintiff receives SSI benefits because of head injuries he received during a violent assault in 1989, resulting in brain damage. As a result, he suffers from recurrent depression, insomnia and other symptoms for which he takes medication on a regular basis and for which he is under the care of a physician, and sees a psychiatric counselor on a regular basis.

8. CONSUMER established a Social Security Direct Deposit account, in or around June 1994, with BANK OF AMERICA. Through May 14, 1998, CONSUMER paid a monthly service charge of approximately $2.50 to maintain this account. Plaintiff

elected to have his Social Security benefits directly deposited into his account because of the safety, security and convenience of that procedure. He believed that he would not have to wait to receive the check in the mail and then go to the bank to deposit it. He also believed that the check would never get lost or stolen as it could have been if delivered by regular mail.

9. BANK OF AMERICA knew at all times relevant herein that CONSUMER received Social Security benefit payments from the federal government.

10. On or about January 30, 1998, BANK OF AMERICA, through no fault of CONSUMER, erroneously credited CONSUMER's account with an amount of $1,799.83. This erroneous credit or deposit was made on the same date on which CONSUMER's regular monthly SSI payment was deposited. The erroneous deposit was assumed by CONSUMER to be a retroactive lump sum payment from the Social Security Administration for a possible underpayment during previous months.

11. Without prior notice, on or about April 16, 1998, BANK OF AMERICA reversed the $1,799.83 entry in CONSUMER's account. Plaintiff did not read or see any Debit Adjustment Notice concerning this transaction prior to May 3, 1998.

12. On or about May 1, 1998, Plaintiff's May Social Security benefits totaling $670.40 were deposited into the account. Unknown to Plaintiff, the account then still had a negative balance because of the April levy by BANK OF AMERICA. Also unknown to plaintiff, defendant BANK OF AMERICA appropriated these funds and applied them to the negative balance on plaintiff's account that had been created the Bank's reversal of its January mistake.

13. On or about May 3, 1998, Plaintiff learned through BANK OF AMERICA's automated telephone system that his account was overdrawn by an amount in excess of $1500.00. He immediately sought assistance from Bank of America representatives. BANK OF AMERICA personnel at his servicing branch told him that he needed to find a source of funds to repay BANK OF AMERICA, and suggested that he apply for a credit card.

14. On or about May 6, 1998, after an attorney had spoken with BANK OF AMERICA's legal department on his behalf, Plaintiff was advised that BANK OF AMERICA had agreed to release his Social Security benefits that had been received for the month of May . Plaintiff was told by personnel at his servicing BANK OF AMERICA branch that a new account could be opened and his Social Security benefits could be placed in the new account. A new VERSATEL checking account, [Number], was opened and the $670.40 Social Security benefits for May that had been levied by BANK OF AMERICA earlier were placed in the account. Plaintiff was told by BANK OF AMERICA personnel that money would not be taken from the new account to pay the debt on the old account.

15. Despite BANK OF AMERICA's promises, in June, 1998, BANK OF AMERICA levied upon Plaintiff's Social Security benefits deposited in the new account to satisfy its own claim against him. Once again, after an attorney intervened, the funds were returned to Plaintiff's account. Plaintiff was caused considerable inconvenience and hardship, as well as financial difficulties, because of defendant's actions.

16. For a third consecutive month, in July, 1998, BANK OF AMERICA levied upon the Social Security benefits deposited in Plaintiff's new account to pay the debt on the old account. After an attorney again intervened, the funds were returned to the new

account. As a result of this action by BANK OF AMERICA Plaintiff's rent check was returned unpaid for lack of funds. Had BANK OF AMERICA not continued its unlawful levies upon Plaintiff's Social Security Direct Deposit funds, there would have been sufficient funds in the account to cover the rent check. After the intervention of an attorney, the rent check was paid. Thereafter, Plaintiff was told by BANK OF AMERICA personnel that his Social Security funds would probably continue to be seized by the bank's collection system without notice in future months, so long as the debt remained unpaid.

17. Pursuant to Title 31, United States Code, section 3332, since 1995 Federal wage, salary, and retirement payments have been paid to authorized recipients by direct deposit electronic funds transfer, with certain exceptions. Effective January 1, 1999, all Federal payments shall be made by direct deposit electronic funds transfer, unless waiver is granted by the Secretary of the Treasury. Electronic funds transfer direct deposits thus have become, and will continue to be, a lucrative source of income for banks and other financial institutions, including without limitation BANK OF AMERICA, because of the large number of recipients of Federal wages, salaries, retirement benefits and other benefits and payments. Plaintiff is informed and believes and thereon alleges that this revenue stream is a significant incentive for BANK OF AMERICA to keep direct deposit accounts open despite overdraft and return activity that would otherwise warrant closing the accounts and to continue to levy charges upon the accounts for unpaid debts. BANK OF AMERICA has the power to close accounts without notice if, in the discretion of BANK OF AMERICA, overdraft and return activity or outstanding obligations warrant such action.

18. Plaintiff is informed and believes and thereon alleges that BANK OF AMERICA has established thousands of direct deposit accounts for recipients Government benefits, including but not limited to Social Security benefits. BANK OF AMERICA charges and collects substantial service fees for each of these accounts.

19. Plaintiff is informed and believes and thereon alleges that many of the recipients of Government benefits who have direct deposit accounts with BANK OF AMERICA for such benefits are Senior citizens, as defined by California Civil Code § 1761 (f) and California Business and Professions Code § 17206.1 (b) (1) and/or disabled persons, as defined by California Civil Code § 1761 (g) and California Business and Professions Code § 17206 (b) (2). Plaintiff is further informed and believes and thereon alleges that BANK OF AMERICA, through advertising, brochures and other promotional materials, has represented to its direct deposit customers and applicants for such accounts that its direct deposit accounts are safe and secure and that direct deposit is the safest and most reliable way to deposit pension or annuity checks, among others. Plaintiff is further informed and believes and thereon alleges that many of the BANK OF AMERICA customers who own, maintain and use Government benefit direct deposit accounts are unable, through age, infirmity and/or lack of understanding, fully to comprehend the nature and extent of charges, including but not limited to substantial recurring and escalating overdraft and return charges, and unauthorized levies, and other adverse consequences that could be and/or have been imposed upon direct deposit account holders by BANK OF AMERICA.

20. As a result of the practices described above, plaintiff PAUL CONSUMER and other BANK OF AMERICA customers have been damaged in that BANK OF AMERICA has knowingly and willfully debited their Government benefit direct deposit accounts for levies that are unconscionable and contrary to statute and therefore unlawful, and have further been damaged in that they have been deprived of access to the funds in their accounts and thus have been unable to purchase the goods and services for which Government benefits are provided.

CLASS ACTION ALLEGATIONS

21. Pursuant to California Code of Civil Procedure § 382 and California Civil Code § 1781, plaintiff brings this action on behalf of himself and all other persons similarly situated. The class that plaintiff represents (hereinafter the "Plaintiff Class") is composed of all California residents who have or have had a BANK OF AMERICA Government benefits direct deposit account at any time within four years preceding the filing of this lawsuit. A subclass of the Plaintiff Class (hereinafter the "Subclass") is composed of all members of the Plaintiff Class who are Senior citizens as defined by California Civil Code § 1761 (f) and California Business and Professions Code § 17206.1 (b) (1) and/or disabled persons as defined by California Civil Code § 1761 (g) and California Business and Professions Code § 17206 (b) (2). Plaintiff and the Plaintiff Class, including the subclass, are hereinafter referred to jointly as "plaintiffs."

22. Plaintiffs are unable to state the precise number of potential members of the Plaintiff Class because that information is in the possession of defendant BANK OF AMERICA. Plaintiffs are informed and believe and thereon allege that the Plaintiff Class numbers at least in the tens of thousands and is so numerous that joinder of all members would be impracticable. The exact size of the Plaintiff Class, and the subclass, and the identity of the members thereof, would be readily ascertainable from the business records of BANK OF AMERICA.

23. Questions of law and fact common to the Plaintiff Class exist that predominate over questions affecting only individual members, including, *inter alia,* the following:

   a. Whether BANK OF AMERICA has knowingly and willfully, and/or negligently, deducted from the Government benefit accounts of the Plaintiff Class charges that are unconscionable and therefore unlawful;

   b. Whether the actions of BANK OF AMERICA as hereinabove described violated California Code of Civil Procedure § 704.080;

   c. Whether the actions of BANK OF AMERICA as hereinabove described violated the Consumer Legal Remedies Act, California Civil Code § 1750 *et seq.*

   d. Whether the actions of BANK OF AMERICA as hereinabove described were fraudulent;

   e. Whether plaintiff and the other members of the Plaintiff Class were injured in their business or property by reason of the unlawful, unfair and/or fraudulent conduct of BANK OF AMERICA and the class-wide measure of damages;

   f. Whether plaintiff and the other members of the Plaintiff Class are entitled to injunctive relief and restitution.

24. The claims asserted by plaintiff CONSUMER in this action are typical of the claims of the members of the Plaintiff Class as described above, the claims arise from the same course of conduct by BANK OF AMERICA, and the relief sought is common.

25. Plaintiff CONSUMER will fairly and adequately represent and protect the interests of the members of the Plaintiff Class.

Plaintiffs have retained counsel competent and experienced in both consumer protection and class action litigation.

26. A class action is superior to other methods for the fair and efficient adjudication of this controversy, since joinder of all members is impracticable. Furthermore, because the economic damages suffered by the individual class members may be relatively modest, albeit significant, compared to the expense and burden of individual litigation, it would be impracticable for most Plaintiff Class members to seek redress individually for the wrongful conduct alleged herein. There will be no real difficulty in the management of this litigation as a class action.

FIRST CAUSE OF ACTION FOR DAMAGES AND PUNITIVE DAMAGES
(Violation of California Civil Code §§ 1709, 1710 (Fraud) Asserted on Behalf of Plaintiff and the Plaintiff Class)

27. Plaintiffs reallege and incorporate herein by reference the allegations set forth in paragraphs 1 through 26 above as if fully alleged herein.

28. At all times herein mentioned, defendant BANK OF AMERICA was in the business of providing banking services, including but not limited to bank deposit accounts, to the general public. Among the accounts provided were accounts into which direct deposits of Government benefits could be and were made.

29. At all times herein mentioned, BANK OF AMERICA represented to the public through brochures, advertisements, and other means that their direct deposit accounts were safe and secure. BANK OF AMERICA further represented to the public that direct deposit is the safest, most reliable way to deposit annuity, pension or retirement checks, including but not limited to Social Security benefits and Veterans' benefits.

30. BANK OF AMERICA's representations concerning safety and security were untrue in that at all times material herein BANK OF AMERICA imposed unexpected and unlawful levies, in violation of Californian Code of Civil Procedure § 704.080 upon its direct deposit account holders, rendering the direct deposit accounts unsafe and insecure.

31. BANK OF AMERICA made the representations herein alleged with the intention of inducing the public, including but not limited to plaintiffs, to purchase, maintain, and use BANK OF AMERICA's direct deposit accounts.

32. Plaintiffs were aware of BANK OF AMERICA's representations herein alleged and relied on them in purchasing and maintaining their direct deposit Government benefit accounts with BANK OF AMERICA.

33. At the time BANK OF AMERICA made the representations herein alleged, BANK OF AMERICA knew that the representations were false.

34. BANK OF AMERICA made the representations herein alleged with the intention of depriving plaintiffs of property or legal rights, to wit: the use of some or all of their direct deposit Government benefits, or otherwise causing injury, and was guilty of fraud.

35. As a proximate result of BANK OF AMERICA's intentional misrepresentations, plaintiffs were damaged by suffering the loss of some of their Government benefits and by being unable to acquire, possess, and use the goods and services ordinarily paid for by their Government benefits, in an amount to be proved at trial.

36. The wrongful conduct of BANK OF AMERICA, as herein alleged, was intentional and was done with malicious, oppressive or fraudulent intent. Plaintiffs are therefore entitled to recover punitive damages.

SECOND CAUSE OF ACTION FOR DAMAGES
(Violation of California Civil Code §§ 1709, 1710 (Negligent Misrepresentation) Asserted on Behalf of Plaintiff and the Plaintiff Class)

37. Plaintiffs reallege and incorporate herein by reference the allegations set forth in paragraphs 1 through 32 above as if fully alleged herein.

38. At the time BANK OF AMERICA made the misrepresentations herein alleged, BANK OF AMERICA had no reasonable grounds for believing the representations to be true.

39. As a proximate result of BANK OF AMERICA's negligent misrepresentations, plaintiffs were damaged by suffering the loss of some of their Government benefits and by being unable to acquire, possess, and use the goods and services ordinarily paid for by their Government benefits, in an amount to be proved at trial.

THIRD CAUSE OF ACTION FOR DAMAGES AND PUNITIVE DAMAGES
(Violation of Code of Civil Procedure § 704.080; Asserted on behalf of Plaintiff and the Plaintiff Class)

40. Plaintiffs reallege and incorporate herein by reference the allegations set forth in paragraphs 1 through 39 above as if fully alleged herein.

41. California Code of Civil Procedure § 704.080 provides that Social Security payments that are directly deposited by the U.S. government into a bank account are exempt from levy, regardless of the amount of the deposit. The statute further establishes that Social Security Direct Deposit accounts are exempt from levy, without the consumer having to make a claim of exemption, for amounts up to $2,000 for a single depositor account and for amounts up to $3,000 for an account with two or more depositors.

42. California Code of Civil Procedure § 704.080(d) also specifically requires a financial institution that holds a Social Security Direct Deposit account to follow certain procedures when processing a levy such that no exempt funds are seized.

43. Defendant BANK OF AMERICA has engaged and is continuing to engage in a business practice of unlawfully debiting accounts of Social Security Direct Deposit account holders for amounts sought through levy by alleged creditors including, without limitation, defendant BANK OF AMERICA and assessing service fees for the processing of such levies. Such practices violate California Code of Civil Procedure § 704.080 in that Social Security Direct Deposit funds are exempt from levy.

44. Defendants' violation of Code of Civil Procedure § 704.080 constitutes a tort in that it is a breach of a non-consensual duty owed to another. Code of Civil Procedure § 704.080 was enacted for the protection of plaintiffs and embodies a public policy that Social Security Direct Deposit accounts shall not be subject to levy. Accordingly, defendant's violation of said statute constitutes a tort and defendants are therefore liable for all damages suffered by plaintiffs.

45. As a result of defendants' unlawful practice, plaintiffs were denied funds to which they are statutorily entitled and were

charged improper service fees, and have suffered substantial damages, including without limitation, monetary losses.

46. Defendants have engaged in the aforementioned conduct willfully and for the specific purpose of denying plaintiffs rightful access to the funds in their accounts and collecting substantial bank service fees. Defendants have thus acted with oppression and malice in that they have deliberately engaged in conduct that has subjected plaintiffs and members of the plaintiff class to cruel and unjust hardship in conscious disregard of such individual's statutory rights; and have carried out such conduct with a willful and conscious disregard of the rights of plaintiffs. Accordingly, plaintiffs are entitled to an award of punitive damages according to proof at the time of trial.

FOURTH CAUSE OF ACTION FOR DAMAGES AND INJUNCTIVE RELIEF
(Violation of the Consumer Legal Remedies Act, California Civil Code § 1750, *et seq.*, Asserted on Behalf of Plaintiff and the Plaintiff Class)

47. Plaintiffs reallege and incorporate herein by reference the allegations set forth in paragraphs 1 through 46 above as if fully alleged herein.

48. The Consumer Legal Remedies Act, California Civil Code § 1750, *et seq.* (hereinafter "the CLRA"), was designed to protect consumers from unfair and deceptive business practices. To this end, the CLRA sets forth a list of unfair and deceptive acts and practices that are specifically prohibited in any transaction intended to result in the sale or lease of goods or services to a consumer. Cal. Civil Code § 1770. Defendant BANK OF AMERICA's acts and practices, as hereinabove described, violate the following provisions of the CLRA, without limitation:

    a. § 1770 (a) (5) in that BANK OF AMERICA represented that the services (direct deposit accounts) have characteristics, uses, benefits or quantities which they do not have, to wit: safety and security;

    b. § 1770 (a) (7) in that BANK OF AMERICA represented that the services (direct deposit accounts) are of a particular standard and quality of safety and security that the accounts did not possess;

    c. § 1770 (a) (13) in that BANK OF AMERICA made false and misleading statements concerning the safety and security of its direct deposit accounts;

    d. § 1770 (a) (14) in that BANK OF AMERICA represented that the banking transactions arising out of its direct deposit accounts conferred rights and remedies which they did not have or which are prohibited by law;

    e. § 1770 (a) (19) in that BANK OF AMERICA inserted unconscionable provisions in the contract for the provision of direct deposit accounts for Government benefits concerning assessment and collection of fees for overdrafts and return items.

49. On or about August 10, 1998, plaintiff CONSUMER, through counsel, sent a preliminary notice and demand to defendant BANK OF AMERICA, pursuant to § 1782 of the CLRA, notifying said defendant that it was alleged to have committed the acts and practices as hereinabove described, and violated the CLRA in the manner set forth above. Plaintiff demanded that BANK OF AMERICA take corrective action to discontinue the unlawful acts and practices and to remedy past violations. As of the date of the filing of this First Amended Complaint, defendant Bank of America has not responded by letter or otherwise to plaintiff's preliminary notice and demand. Plaintiff is informed and believes, and thereon alleges, that defendant BANK OF AMERICA has neither discontinued the unlawful acts alleged herein, nor remedied past violations.

50. As a result of the unfair and deceptive acts and practices of BANK OF AMERICA hereinabove described, plaintiff PAUL CONSUMER and members of the Plaintiff Class have suffered substantial economic losses in an amount to be proven at trial.

51. Pursuant to California Civil Code §§ 1780 and 1781, plaintiff and the Plaintiff Class hereby request certification of the Plaintiff Class, damages, injunctive relief, restitution and attorneys' fees, costs and expenses pursuant to California Civil Code § 1780 (d) and California Code of Civil Procedure § 1021.5.

FIFTH CAUSE OF ACTION FOR DAMAGE AND PUNITIVE DAMAGES
(Intentional Infliction of Emotional Distress; Asserted on Behalf of Plaintiff)

52. Plaintiff realleges and incorporates herein by reference the allegations set forth in paragraphs 1 through 20 and 27 through 50 as if fully alleged herein.

53. Defendants knew at all relevant times that debiting a Social Security Direct Deposit account pursuant to a levy and collecting substantial bank service fees for processing such levy, were contrary to the law and policy of the State of California, and in violation of the statutory rights of the plaintiff. Defendants further knew that plaintiff had limited income and that such acts would cause him considerable hardship and emotional distress. Nevertheless, defendants committed such acts deliberately and repeatedly, and with conscious disregard for the rights of the plaintiff.

54. As a result of defendants' acts as hereinabove described, plaintiff CONSUMER has suffered severe emotional distress, including without limitation, anger, stress, worry, anxiety, humiliation, fear, depression, fatigue and frustration.

55. Defendants committed the above-described wrongful and intentional acts because they felt confident in their position of wealth, sophistication and power, and in their ability to manipulate plaintiff and to coerce him into relinquishing rights guaranteed to them by law. Defendants deliberately, willfully and maliciously pursued this course of conduct because they had no fear that the plaintiff would understand the nature of the transactions and/or be able to assert his legal rights. Defendants have thus acted with oppression and malice in that they have engaged in despicable conduct, intended to cause cruel and unjust hardship to plaintiff, and have carried out such conduct with a willful and conscious disregard of the rights of plaintiff. Accordingly, plaintiff seeks and is entitled to awards of compensatory and punitive damages according to proof at the time of trial.

SIXTH CAUSE OF ACTION FOR RESTITUTION AND INJUNCTIVE RELIEF
(Violation of California Business and Professions Code § 17200, *et seq.*, Asserted on Behalf of Plaintiffs and All Affected Members of the General Public)

56. Plaintiffs reallege and incorporate herein by reference the allegations set forth in paragraphs 1 through 20 and 27 through 50 above as if fully alleged herein.

57. Plaintiffs bring this cause of action acting as a private attorney general on behalf of the public challenge defendant's business practices. California Business and Professions Code § 17200, The Unfair Competition Law (UCL), defines unfair competition to include any unlawful, unfair or fraudulent business act or practice. The UCL provides that a Court may order injunctive relief and restitution to affected members of the general public as remedies for any violation of the Act.

58. The business acts and practices of defendant BANK OF AMERICA, as hereinabove and hereinafter described, constitute an unlawful business practice in violation of the UCL for the reasons set forth below, without limitation:

a. The acts and practices violate California Civil Code §§ 1709 and 1710 for the reasons set forth in the First and Second Causes of Action, and are therefore unlawful;

b. The acts and practices violate California Civil Code § 1750, *et seq.*, for the reasons set forth in the Fourth Cause of Action and are therefore unlawful.

c. The acts and practices constitute violate California Business and Professions Code § 17500 for the reasons set forth in the Seventh Cause of Action and are therefore unlawful.

59. The business acts and practices of defendant BANK OF AMERICA as hereinabove described also constitute an unfair business practice in violation of the UCL in that such acts and practices are substantially injurious to consumers and offensive to established California public policy.

60. In addition, the business acts and practices of defendant BANK OF AMERICA as hereinabove described constitute a fraudulent business practice in violation of the UCL in that such acts and practices are likely to deceive California consumers as to their legal rights and obligations with respect to protection from levies on their Government benefit direct deposit accounts and protection from the consequences of excessive overdrafts.

61. Pursuant to California Business and Professions Code § 17203 plaintiffs seek to enjoin these acts and practices and to obtain restitution of all funds seized from plaintiffs by reason of and through the use of such unlawful, unfair and fraudulent acts and practices. Pursuant to California Business and Professions Code § 17203, plaintiff, individually, and on behalf of all members of the general public who are, have been or may be, subjected to these unlawful, unfair, and fraudulent business acts and practices of defendants, hereby requests preliminary and permanent injunctive relief prohibiting such practices in the future, and such other orders as may be necessary to restore to any person in interest, any money or property, real or personal, which may have been seized from plaintiffs by means of such unlawful, unfair and fraudulent business practices, and to disgorge all profits defendants have earned thereby. In addition, pursuant to California Code of Civil Procedure § 1021.5, plaintiffs are entitled to recover their reasonable attorney's fees, costs and expenses incurred in bringing this action.

SEVENTH CAUSE OF ACTION FOR RESTITUTION AND INJUNCTIVE RELIEF
(Violation of California Business and Professions Code § 17500, *et seq.*; Asserted on Behalf of Plaintiffs and All Affected Members of the General Public)

62. Plaintiffs reallege and incorporate herein by reference the allegations set forth in paragraphs 1 through 20, 27 through 50 and 56 through 60 above as if fully alleged herein.

63. Plaintiff brings this Cause of Action acting as a private attorney general on behalf of the public to challenge defendant's advertising practices. California Business and Professions Code § 17500, prohibits untrue or misleading advertising. A Court may order injunctive relief and restitution to affected members of the general public as remedies for any violations of Business and Professions Code § 17500 as part of the UCL.

64. At all times material herein defendant BANK OF AMERICA has engaged in advertising to the public, including plaintiffs, and offering to the public bank accounts that include a direct deposit feature ("direct deposit accounts.") The advertisements include, without limitation, brochures stating, A Bank of America's Direct Deposit is a safe and convenient means to deposit your money, no matter where you are. No more trips to the bank on payday to deposit regular monthly payments such as salary, pension, Social Security or Supplemental Security Income (SSI) checks. With direct deposit, your funds are electronically deposited into your designated bank and are instantly available," or words to that effect. The advertisements were disseminated to and received by the public in California.

65. Defendant BANK OF AMERICA engaged in the advertising herein alleged with the intent to induce the public to open, maintain and use BANK OF AMERICA direct deposit accounts for their Government benefits.

66. Defendant BANK OF AMERICA's advertising was untrue or misleading and likely to deceive the public in that while BANK OF AMERICA stated and implied that direct deposit accounts were safe and secure, the aforesaid accounts were subject to appropriation by defendant BANK OF AMERICA itself for alleged debts owed to the bank, as well as excessive, escalating, recurring and unconscionable levies, overdraft and return charges, rendering the direct deposit accounts unsafe and insecure. BANK OF AMERICA continued to keep open and collect fees from direct deposit accounts with excessive overdraft activity, thereby depriving the owners of those accounts of Government benefits of access to some or all of the funds in their accounts, thus impairing their ability to purchase the goods and services for which the Government benefits were provided.

67. In making and disseminating the statements herein alleged, BANK OF AMERICA knew, or by the exercise of reasonable care should have known, that the statements were and are untrue or misleading and so acted in violation of California Business and Professions Code § 17500.

68. The business acts and practices of defendant BANK OF AMERICA as hereinabove described also constitute an unfair business practice in violation of the UCL in that such acts and practices are substantially injurious to consumers and offensive to established California public policy.

69. In addition, the business acts and practices of defendant BANK OF AMERICA as hereinabove described constitute a fraudulent business practice in violation of the UCL in that such acts and practices are likely to deceive California consumers as to their legal rights and obligations with respect to the safety and security of their Government benefit direct deposit accounts and protection from levies by BANK OF AMERICA and from the consequences of excessive overdrafts.

70. Pursuant to California Business and Professions Code § 17535 plaintiffs seek to enjoin these acts and practices and to obtain restitution of all funds seized from plaintiffs by reason of and through the use of such false advertising. Pursuant to Califor-

nia Business and Professions Code § 17535, plaintiff, individually, and on behalf of all members of the general public who are, have been or may be, subjected to these unlawful, unfair, and fraudulent business acts and practices of defendants, hereby requests preliminary and permanent injunctive relief prohibiting such practices in the future, and such other orders as may be necessary to restore to any person in interest, any money or property, real or personal, which may have been seized from plaintiffs by means of such false advertising, and to disgorge all profits defendants have earned thereby. In addition, pursuant to California Code of Civil Procedure § 1021.5, plaintiffs are entitled to recover their reasonable attorney's fees, costs and expenses incurred in bringing this action.

PRAYER FOR RELIEF

WHEREFORE, plaintiffs respectfully pray as follows:

i. That this Court certify this case as a class action;

ii. That this Court find and declare the defendants' acts and practices as described herein to be unlawful, unfair and fraudulent;

iii. That plaintiffs and the Plaintiff Class be awarded compensatory damages according to proof at trial;

iv. That plaintiffs and the Plaintiff Class be awarded punitive damages according to proof at trial;

v. That the Subclass be awarded treble damages pursuant to California Civil Code § 3345;

vi. That defendants be preliminarily and permanently enjoined from engaging in the unlawful, unfair and fraudulent acts and practices alleged herein;

vii. That defendants be ordered to make restitution to all affected members of the general public;

viii. That plaintiffs be awarded attorneys' fees and expenses pursuant to California Code of Civil Procedure § 1021.5 and California Civil Code § 1780;

ix. That plaintiffs and the Plaintiff Class be awarded prejudgment interest on all sums collected;

x. For costs of suit herein incurred; and

xi. For such other and further relief as the Court may deem proper.

[Dated]

[Attorney for Plaintiffs]

Websites Relating to Consumer Credit Issues

Live web links can be found on the CD-Rom accompanying this volume.

Federal Regulators

Department of Housing and Urban Development: *www.hud.gov*
Federal Reserve Board: *www.federalreserve.gov*
Federal Trade Commission: *www.ftc.gov*
Federal Deposit Insurance Corp.: *www.fdic.gov*
National Credit Union Administration: *www.ncua.gov*
Office of the Comptroller of the Currency: *www.occ.treas.gov*
Office of Thrift Supervision: *www.ots.treas.gov*

Other Governmental and Quasi-Government Bodies

Fannie Mae: *www.fanniemae.com*
Freddie Mac: *www.freddiemac.com*
National Association of Attorneys General: *www.naag.org*
National Association of Consumer Credit Administrators: *www.naccaonline.org*
National Association of Insurance Commissioners: *www.naic.org*
National Conference of Commissioners on Uniform State Laws: *www.nccusl.org*
(drafts of uniform laws may be found on a University of Pennsylvania website,
www.law.upenn.edu/bll/ulc/ulc.htm)
Securities and Exchange Commission (EDGAR information): *www.sec.gov*
Thomas Database (Library of Congress federal legislation database): *www.thomas.loc.gov*
VA Home Loan Program: *www.homeloans.va.gov*

Advocacy Organizations

ACORN: *www.acorn.org*
Center for Community Change: *www.communitychange.org*
Center for Economic Justice: *www.cej-online.org*
Center for Responsible Lending: *www.responsiblelending.org*
Consumer Federation of America: *www.consumerfed.org*
Consumers Union: *www.consumer.org*
DEMOS: *www.demos-usa.org*
National Association of Consumer Advocates: *www.naca.net*
National Community Reinvestment Coalition: *www.ncrc.org*
National Consumer Law Center (website includes bibliographies of research and reports on predatory mortgage lending and high-cost non-mortgage lending): *www.consumerlaw.com*
National Training and Information Center: *www.ntic-us.org*
New Rules Project of the Institute for Local Self-Reliance: *www.newrules.org*
U.S. Public Interest Research Group: *www.uspirg.org*
Woodstock Institute: *www.woodstockinst.org*

Sources of Information

AARP Research Center: www.*research.aarp.org*
Annie E. Casey Foundation: *www.aecf.org*

Bankrate.com (compilation of information on personal finance): *www.bankrate.com*
British Bankers' Association (source of LIBOR rates):
www.bba.org.uk or *www.bankfacts.org.uk*
Brookings Institution: *www.brookings.org*
Center for Community Capitalism:
www.kenan-flagler.unc.edu/KI/commCapitalism/index.cfm
Fannie Mae Foundation: *www.fanniemaefoundation.org*
Ford Foundation: *www.fordfound.org*
Reinvestment Fund: *www.trfund.com*
Standard & Poors: *www.standardandpoors.com*

Industry Organizations

ABSNet (information about securitization): *www.absnet.net*
Association for Progressive Rental Organizations (RTO industry trade group):
www.apro-rto.com
Mortgage Asset Research Institute, Inc. (information service provider to the mortgage and
financial services industries): *www.mari-inc.com*
Mortgage Bankers Association: *www.mbaa.org*
National Home Equity Mortgage Association: *www.nhema.org*

Index

ACCELERATION
see also EARLY TERMINATION
due-on-sale clauses, 5.8.3
electronic notices, 9.2.10.9
prepayment distinguished, 5.8.1
rebates, calculation date, 5.6.2.1, 8.6
unconscionability, 8.7.5
unearned charges, collection, 5.7.2.1

ACCEPTANCE COMPANIES
see FINANCE COMPANIES

ACCIDENT AND HEALTH INSURANCE
see DISABILITY INSURANCE

ACCOMMODATION PARTIES
arbitration clauses, binding effect, 10.3.5.1
business loans, 9.2.2.5
side agreements as hidden interest, 7.2.3
standing to assert usury, 10.6.3

ACCRUED INTEREST
compounding, 4.6.1.1

ACTIONS
see REMEDIES

ACTUARIAL INTEREST TRANSACTIONS
see also SIMPLE INTEREST
Actuarial Rule, 4.3.1.2
amortization, 4.3.1.1
balloon payments, 4.3.1.2
calculation of interest, 4.3.1.1
capitalization of unpaid interest, 4.3.1.2
installment credit calculations, 4.3.1
interest-only loans, 4.3.1.2
negative amortization, 4.3.1.2
non-amortizing loans, 4.3.1.2
single payment transactions, 4.2
U.S. Rule, 4.3.1.2

ACTUARIAL METHOD
rebate calculations, 5.2.2, 5.6.3.4

ACTUARIAL RULE
see also ACTUARIAL INTEREST TRANSACTIONS
APR, calculation using, 4.4.2
compound interest, 4.6.1.1
negative amortization, 4.3.1.2
U.S. Rule, differences, 4.6.1.1

ADD-ON INTEREST
see also INTEREST
installment credit calculations, 4.3.2
precomputed interest calculation, 4.3.2

simple interest compared, 4.3.2
split rates, 4.3.2

ADJUSTABLE RATE MORTGAGES (ARMs)
see also MORTGAGES; VARIABLE RATE TRANSACTIONS
adjustment errors, 4.3.6.5
interest calculations, 4.3.6.2
interest caps and floors, 4.3.6.4, Appx. J.1
monthly payment caps, 4.3.6.4
negative amortization, 4.3.1.2
prepayment penalties, 5.8.3

ADJUSTED BALANCE
see also LOAN BALANCES
open-end credit calculations, 4.3.5

AFFIDAVITS
see also PLEADINGS
sample expert affidavit, Appx. L.2.3

AGENTS
arbitration clauses, application, 8.5.5.3.2, 12.10.1
creditors and insurers, relationship, 8.5.5.3.2
fiduciary duty, *see* FIDUCIARY DUTY
loan brokers as, 11.5.4.2
preemption rights, 3.4.6.4, 3.5.4

AIDING AND ABETTING
fraud, 12.10.1

ALLONGES
negotiable instruments, 10.6.1.3

ALTERNATIVE INTEREST CEILING
see also INTEREST CEILINGS
federally-insured lenders, 3.9.2.1
  DIDA opt-out, 3.9.4.3
national banks, 3.4.2
usury remedies under, 10.8.5.1

ALTERNATIVE MORTGAGE TRANSACTIONS PARITY ACT (AMTPA)
see also DEPOSITORY INSTITUTIONS ACT (DIA)
application, 3.2.4.2
HOEPA preemption, 3.10.1
land installment contracts, application, 9.2.3.4
mortgage deregulation, application, 2.4.2
OTS interpretive letters, Appx. H.3
overview, 3.1.1
preemption chart, 3.2.5
preemption scope, 3.10.1
regulatory scheme, 3.10.2
selected provisions, Appx. H.1
selected regulations, Appx. H.2

AMORTIZATION
see also AMORTIZED LOANS
actuarial interest transactions, 4.3.1.1
negative amortization, 4.3.1.2
rebate schedules, 5.6.3.4.2, CD-Rom
Rule of 78, use, 5.6.3.3.2
split rate loans, 4.3.4, 5.6.3.4.3
table, CD-Rom
variable rate loans, 4.3.6.3

AMORTIZED LOANS
see also AMORTIZATION
actuarial interest transactions, 4.3.1.1
level term insurance, restrictions, 8.3.1.2
split rate loans, 4.3.4, 5.6.3.4.3
variable rate loans, 4.3.6.3

AMOUNT FINANCED
see also PRINCIPAL AMOUNT
burying of finance charge, 7.4.6.1
defined, 4.4.1
TIL disclosures, 2.3.4, 4.4.1

ANNUAL INTEREST RATE
see ANNUAL PERCENTAGE RATE (APR)

ANNUAL PERCENTAGE RATE (APR)
see also INTEREST RATES
accuracy, 4.4.2
calculation, 4.4.2
  software program, CD-Rom
defined, 4.4.1
discount interest transactions, 4.3.3
odd payment periods, 4.6.2.1, 4.6.2.2
refinancing benefits, evaluating, 6.5
split rate loans, 4.3.4
TIL disclosures, 2.3.4, 4.4.1

ANTITRUST VIOLATIONS
credit insurance, 8.5.2.7

APPLIANCE LOANS
rent-to-own contracts, 7.5.3.2
repair contracts, rebate issues, 5.5.2.1

APPRAISAL FEES
interest status, 7.3.1
rebate issues, 5.5.2.1

APPRAISAL FRAUD
claims re, 12.10.2.5
described, 11.5.6

ARBITRATION CLAUSES
see also FEDERAL ARBITRATION ACT (FAA)
agency theory, effect, 8.5.5.3.2, 12.10.1
credit card accounts, 11.7.2.3.9
credit insurance, 8.7.6, 10.3.6
  insurers, invoking, 8.5.5.3.2
  state law preemption of FAA, 8.7.6, 10.3.6
enforceability, 10.3
  condition precedent contracts, 10.3.3
  insurance transactions, 8.7.6, 10.3.6
  non-signatories, against, 10.3.5.1
  non-signatories, by, 10.3.5.2
  other challenges, 10.3.7
  superseded agreements, 10.3.4
  void agreements, 10.3.2

payday loans, 7.5.5.8
RESPA violations, application, 12.2.1.10

ASSIGNEES
close-connection liability, 10.6.1.2.1, 12.12
D'Oench doctrine, asserting, 10.7.6.2
ECOA, application, 12.3.1
electronic documents, 10.6.1.1
FIRREA limitations, asserting, 10.7.6.3
high cost mortgages, liability, 10.6.1.2.3
holder rule
  asserting, 10.6.1.1
  exceptions, 10.6.1.2
  prerequisites, 10.6.1.3
liability chart, 12.12
national banks, status, 3.4.5.1.3
preemption protections, application, 3.2.2.7
retail installment sales, 11.6.7
table-funding, 9.2.4.6, 11.5.4.1, 12.2.1.5.2
true lender, as, 11.6.2.1, 11.6.7
usury claims, asserting, 10.6.3
usury liability, 10.6.2
VSI insurance, 8.3.1.5.2
waivers of liability, 10.6.1.2.2, 10.6.1.3.10

ASSIGNMENT TRANSACTIONS
government income to income buyers, 7.5.8.2
litigation finance, 7.5.8.3
loan status, 7.5.4.1
tax refunds, 7.5.4.1

ATMs
see AUTOMATED TELLER MACHINES (ATMs)

ATTORNEY FEES AND COSTS
hidden interest issues
  closing costs, 7.3.3.3
  default situations, 7.3.3.2
  generally, 7.3.3.1
unconscionability challenges, 12.7.4
usurious loans, creditor forfeiture, 10.8.2.2.1

AUTO LOANS
see also AUTO-SECURED LOANS
acquisition fees, 7.4.2, 11.6.2
balance protection plans, *see* GAP INSURANCE OR
  AGREEMENTS
dealer charges, interest status, 7.2.1, 7.4.2
differential interest rate pricing, 11.6.6
discounts, 7.4.2, 7.4.6.1, 11.6.2
disguised as RTO transactions, 7.5.3.6.7
force-placed insurance, 8.3.1.5.4, 8.5.3.4.2
fraud and misrepresentation claims, 12.10
inflated sale price, 7.4.6.1, 11.6.2.1, 11.6.2.2
lender liability for acts of dealer, 12.12
negative equity financing, 11.6.3
padding, 11.6.2.2, 11.6.4
repair contracts, rebate issues, 5.5.2.1
subprime, *see* SUBPRIME LENDERS
title pawns, *see* AUTO TITLE LOANS
UDAP violations, 12.5
upcharges, 7.4.2
upselling of interest rate, 12.6
used cars, *see* USED CAR PURCHASES
VSI insurance, 8.3.1.5.2
yield spread premiums, *see* YIELD SPREAD PREMIUMS

AUTO PAWN TRANSACTIONS
see AUTO TITLE LOANS

AUTO-SECURED LOANS
see also MOTOR VEHICLE RETAIL INSTALLMENT SALES
    ACTS (MVRISAs)
force-placed insurance, 8.3.1.5.4, 8.5.3.4.2
purchase loans, *see* AUTO LOANS
title pawns, *see* AUTO TITLE LOANS
VSI insurance, 8.3.1.5.2, 8.3.1.5.4

AUTO TITLE LOANS
see also FRINGE LENDERS
disguised as RTO transactions, 7.5.2.3.4, 7.5.3.6.7
form of auto-secured loan, 2.5, 7.5.2.3.3
hidden interest, 7.5.2.3
leasebacks, 7.5.2.3.2
overview, 7.5.2.3.1
pawn status, 7.5.2.3.2, 7.5.2.3.3
state law, 7.5.2.3.5
wrongful repossession claims, 7.5.2.3.5

AUTOMATED TELLER MACHINES (ATMs)
fees, regulation, 3.4.5.1.2

BAD CHECK LAWS
see also BOUNCED CHECKS
payday loans, application, 7.5.5.6

BALANCE PROTECTION PLANS
see DEBT CANCELLATION OR SUSPENSION AGREE-
    MENTS (DCAs); GAP INSURANCE OR AGREE-
    MENTS

BALANCES
see LOAN BALANCES

BALLOON PAYMENTS
see also NEGATIVE AMORTIZATION
actuarial interest transactions, 4.3.1.2
duty of good faith and fair dealing, 12.8
HOEPA prohibitions, 12.2.2.3
home equity loans, 4.3.1.2
odd payments resulting in, 4.6.2.1
payment holidays, after, 4.8.3
restrictions, 4.3.1.2
sum of the balances rebates, 5.6.3.3.4
variable rate transactions, 4.3.6.1, 4.3.6.4

BANK HOLDING COMPANY ACT
credit insurance, application, 8.4.1.5.2

BANKRUPTCY
prepayment penalties, disallowance, 5.8.1
rebate formula, 5.2.5
Rule of 78, use, 5.2.5, 5.6.3.3.1
securitization trusts, jurisdiction, 10.2.3.5
standing to assert usury, 10.6.3

BANKS
see also DEPOSITORY CREDITORS
ATM fees, out-of-state banks, 3.4.5.1.2
auto title lending, 7.5.2.3.5
Bank Holding Company Act, application, 8.4.1.5.2
bounce loans, 7.5.6
Community Reinvestment Act obligations, 6.5
credit card business, 2.3.1.2.1
credit insurance regulation, 8.4.1.5.2
daily interest calculation method, 4.6.3.4

deposit insurance, 2.3.1.2.1
DIDA, application, 3.9.2.2
    first lien preemption, 3.9.3.3
"dual" banking system, 3.7.1
failed banks
    claims process, 10.7.10
    D'Oench doctrine, 10.7.3
    FIRREA, application, 10.7.4
    receiver defenses, 10.7
FDIC, participation, 2.3.1.2.1, 10.7.1
FDIC definition, 3.7.2
federal banks, *see* NATIONAL BANKS
Federal Reserve System, establishment, 2.3.1.2.1
federally insured, *see* FEDERALLY INSURED LENDERS
fraud and misrepresentation claims, 12.10.1
Gramm-Leach-Bliley Act, application, 8.4.1.5.2
home loan banks, *see* BUILDING AND LOAN ASSOCIA-
    TIONS; SAVINGS AND LOAN ASSOCIATIONS
industrial banks, *see* INDUSTRIAL BANKS
installment loan laws, application, 2.3.3.4
insurance activities, regulation, 8.4.1.5.2
interstate banking, *see* INTERSTATE BANKING
location, determination, 3.4.5.1.2
national banks, *see* NATIONAL BANKS
payday lenders, partnerships, 3.13, 7.5.5.7
prepayment penalties, imposing, 5.8.3
rate exportation, *see* RATE EXPORTATION
regulatory history, 2.3.1.2.1
rent-a-charter arrangements, 3.13, 7.5.5.7
RICO actions against, 10.8.5.3.5
savings banks, *see* SAVINGS BANKS
state banks, *see* STATE BANKS
usurious loans, remedies, 10.8.5.1 ·
usury laws, application, 3.2–3.4

BODY-DRAGGING
credit sales, 9.2.3.3

BONUSES
non-cash as hidden interest, 7.2.3

BOUNCED CHECKS
see also BAD CHECK LAWS; CHECKS
NSF fees, interest status, 3.4.5.2
payday loans
    bad check laws, application, 7.5.5.6
    repeated presentment, 7.5.5.9.3
protection from, bounce loans, 7.5.6

BROKER FEES
see also COMMISSIONS; KICKBACKS; LOAN BROKERS
auto pawns disguised as, 7.5.2.3.4
circumstances, 11.5.4.1
hidden interest issues, 7.3.2
HUD policy statement
    conflicting interpretations, 12.2.1.5.4
    first statement (1999), 12.2.1.5.3, Appx. K.3.1
    letter regarding, Appx. K.4.1
    second statement (2001), 12.2.1.5.5, Appx. K.3.2
    unearned or excessive fees, 12.2.1.6
kickbacks and referral fees, 12.2.1.5
RESPA, application, 7.3.2, 11.5.4.3, 12.2.1.5.2
TIL rescission, 11.5.4.3
unconscionability, 12.7.4
yield spread premiums, *see* YIELD SPREAD PREMIUMS

BROKERS
see LOAN BROKERS; REAL ESTATE BROKERS

BUILDING AND LOAN ASSOCIATIONS
see also SAVINGS AND LOAN ASSOCIATIONS
historical development, 2.2.3.1, 2.3.1.2.2

BURDEN OF PROOF
see also EVIDENCE
bona fide error, 10.5.5.2
business purpose loan, 9.2.2.6
DIDA preemption, 3.9.3.1
elements of prima facie case, 10.5
high cost mortgages, assignee liability, 10.6.1.2.3
holder-in-due course status, 10.6.1.3.8
negligent misrepresentation, 12.10.2.6
usurious intent
    usury apparent on face of contract, 10.5.5.2
    usury not apparent on face of contract, 10.5.5.3
usury claims, 10.5.1.2

BUSINESS LOANS
see also SMALL BUSINESSES
affidavit of business purpose, 9.2.2.3
burden of proof, 9.2.2.6
consolidation with consumer loan, effect, 6.6
exemption justification, 9.2.2.2
incorporation prior to, 9.2.2.3
intermediaries, effect, 9.2.2.5
personal purpose distinguished, 9.2.2.4
refinancings, effect, 9.2.2.5
sham loans, 9.2.2.3, 10.6.4.3
stockholder guarantees, usury defense, 10.6.3
usury laws, application, 9.2.2

CALCULATIONS
see INTEREST CALCULATIONS; MATHEMATICAL
    FORMULAS

CAR DEALERS
see DEALERS

CAR LOANS
see AUTO LOANS

CASE LAW
see also COMMON LAW; RESEARCH AIDS
Clearinghouse citations, 1.5
D'Oench, see D'OENCH DOCTRINE
O'Melveny, see O'MELVENY DECISION

CASH-BACK ADS
disguised payday loans, 7.5.5

CHARGE ACCOUNTS
see CREDIT CARD ACCOUNTS; OPEN-END CREDIT

CHARGES
see FEES AND CHARGES

CHECK ADVANCEMENT LOANS
see PAYDAY LOANS

CHECKLISTS
analyzing the contract, 1.6.2
analyzing the legal issues
    fixed term credit, 1.6.3.2
    governing law, 1.6.3.1
assignee liability, 12.12
credit determination, 1.6.3.1.2

federal preemption of state law, 1.6.3.1.4, 3.2
    bureaucracy of preemption, 3.3.1
    first steps, 3.2.1
    mortgage loans, 3.2.4
    non-mortgage loans, 3.2.3
    preemption chart, 3.2.5
fixed term credit
    arithmetic, 1.6.3.2.1
    interest charges, 1.6.3.2.2
    maximum charges, 1.6.3.2.4
    non-rate violations, 1.6.3.2.5
    principal amount, 1.6.3.2.3
lender liability for third party actions, 12.12
regulatory chart, 3.3.1
state law, 1.6.3.1.3

CHECKS
see also NEGOTIABLE INSTRUMENTS
bounce loans, 7.5.6
face amount is maximum attainable, 7.5.5.9.4
payday loans and, 7.5.5.9
post-dated checks, 7.5.5.9.5
    disguised loan transactions, 10.8.5.3.5
repeated presentment of bounced checks, 7.5.5.9.3
stop payments, 7.5.5.9.6

CHOICE OF LAWS
contract provisions, 9.2.9.5
identifying applicable law, 3.2.2.5
    overview, 9.2.9.1
    public policy concerns, 9.2.9.3
rate exportation context, 3.9.2.2.2
Restatement approach, 9.2.9.1
    state statutes governing choice, 9.2.9.4
    substantial relationship test, 9.2.9.2
UCC rule, 9.2.9.1

CIVIL CONSPIRACY
appraisal fraud, 11.5.6
property flipping schemes, 11.5.6
RALs, 7.5.4.2

CIVIL RIGHTS ACTS
discrimination, prohibition, 12.3.1

CLASS ACTIONS
credit card abuses, 11.7.3.2
CROA, 12.4.2.3
usury, 10.8.6
yield spread premiums, 12.2.1.5.5, 12.2.1.5.6

CLEARINGHOUSE NUMBERS
see also SARGENT SHRIVER NATIONAL CENTER ON
    POVERTY LAW
unreported cases, 1.5

CLOSED-END CREDIT
see also CREDIT TRANSACTIONS; INSTALLMENT CREDIT
checklist
    arithmetic, 1.6.3.2.1
    interest ceilings, 1.6.3.2.4
    interest charges, 1.6.3.2.2
    non-rate violations, 1.6.3.2.5
    principal amount, 1.6.3.2.3
interest calculations
    generally, 4.3.1–4.3.4
    open-end differences, 4.3.5.1

CLOSED-END CREDIT (*cont.*)
interest rates, 2.3.2.3
open-end, distinction, 9.2.3.2
regulatory history, 2.3.2.3, 2.3.3.5
usury laws, application, 9.2.3.2

COERCION
credit insurance
    generally, 8.5.2.1
    non-usury claims, 8.5.2.5
    proving, 8.5.2.4

COLLATERAL
see also SECURITY INTERESTS
non-filing insurance, 7.3.1
pawnbrokers, regulation, 2.3.3.9
property insurance, 8.3.1.5, 8.5.4.4
secured credit transactions, regulation, 2.3.2.4
unnecessary, 8.5.4.4

COLLATERAL PROTECTION INSURANCE (CPI)
see CREDIT PROPERTY INSURANCE

COLLECTION ABUSES
credit card lenders, 11.7.2.3.8
RICO violations, 12.6

COLLECTION AGENCIES
RICO violations, 12.6
usury liability, 10.6.2

COLLECTION COSTS
attorney fees, creditor charges, 7.3.3.2

COMMERCIAL CREDIT
see BUSINESS LOANS

COMMISSIONS
see also BROKER FEES; KICKBACKS
credit insurance, creditor restrictions, 8.5.3.2.2
interest status, 7.3.1, 8.5.3.2.2

COMMITMENT FEES
see also POINTS
described, 7.2.2.3
hidden interest issues, 7.2.2.3
rate lock fees, 7.2.2.3

COMMON LAW
see also CASE LAW
contracts, *see* CONTRACT LAW
duty to disclose, 8.7.3.1
federal common law
    creation, 10.7.2
    equitable estoppel doctrine, 10.7.3.1
    super holder-in-due course status, 10.7.5
fiduciary duty, *see* FIDUCIARY DUTY
FIRREA preemption, 10.7.2
fraud claims, *see* FRAUD CLAIMS
holders-in-due course, *see* HOLDERS-IN-DUE COURSE
interest, restrictions, 9.3.1.1
late fees, treatment of, 7.2.4.2.1
tort claims, *see* TORT CLAIMS
unconscionability, *see* UNCONSCIONABILITY
usurious interest payments, recovery, 10.8.2.3
usury claims, 9.3.1.1, 10.8.1
usury remedies, 10.8.2.1
willful blindness, 10.6.1.2.1

COMMUNITY REINVESTMENT ACT
lending obligations, 6.5

COMPENSATING BALANCES
hidden interest, 7.4.4

COMPETITION
credit insurance, 8.2.3.1

COMPLAINT
see PLEADINGS

COMPOUND INTEREST
see also INTEREST
accrued unpaid interest, on, 6.4.1.2
discount interest, 4.6.1.1
hidden interest, 7.4.2
interest-bearing loans, 4.6.1.1
points as, 4.6.1.1, 6.4.1.3
refinancing rules, 6.4.1.2
restrictions, 4.6.1.1, 4.6.1.2
usury violations, 4.6.1.2

COMPTROLLER OF THE CURRENCY
see OFFICE OF THE COMPTROLLER OF THE CURRENCY
    (OCC)

CONFLICT OF LAWS
see CHOICE OF LAW

CONSOLIDATION OF LOANS
see also REFINANCING
business and consumer, 6.6
defined, 6.1.3
first and second mortgages, cost, 6.5
overreaching creditors, 11.5.3

CONSTRUCTION LOANS
see also HOME IMPROVEMENT LOANS
fraud and misrepresentation claims, 12.10.2.3

CONSUMER CREDIT CODES (STATE)
see also CONSUMER FINANCE LAWS (STATE); USURY
    LAWS (STATE)
comprehensive state codes, 2.3.3.10
UCCC, *see* UNIFORM CONSUMER CREDIT CODE (UCCC)

CONSUMER CREDIT TRANSACTIONS
see CREDIT TRANSACTIONS

CONSUMER FINANCE LAWS (STATE)
see also CONSUMER CREDIT CODES (STATE)
combined small and industrial loan laws, 2.3.3.2, 2.3.3.3

CONSUMER LOANS
see CREDIT TRANSACTIONS; LOANS

CONSUMER PROTECTION LAWS
ECOA, *see* EQUAL CREDIT OPPORTUNITY ACT (ECOA)
federal preemption of state laws, *see* FEDERAL PREEMPTION
federal statutes, preemptive effect, 3.12
HOEPA, *see* HOME OWNERSHIP AND EQUITY
    PROTECTION ACT (HOEPA)
small loan laws, *see* SMALL LOAN LAWS
state usury laws, *see* USURY LAWS (STATE)
TILA, *see* TRUTH IN LENDING ACT (TILA)

CONTINGENCIES
rule against usury through, 5.7.1, 5.8.1, 7.2.3

CONTRACT FOR DEED
see LAND INSTALLMENT CONTRACTS

CONTRACT LAW
credit card abuses, challenging, 11.7.3.1
duty of good faith and fair dealing, 12.8
federal rebate law violations as violations of, 5.7.3
prepayment penalties, challenging under, 5.8.1

CONTRACTS
see CREDIT AGREEMENTS

CONVENIENCE CREDITORS
see also NON-DEPOSITORY CREDITORS
state regulation, 2.3.1.3.3

COOPERATIVE SOCIETIES
credit unions, *see* CREDIT UNIONS
historical development, 2.2.3.1

CORPORATIONS
arbitration clauses, enforcement by principal or employees,
　10.3.5.2
jurisdiction over parent for activities of subsidiary, 10.2.1

CORRESPONDENT LENDERS
loan broker, acting as, 11.5.4.1

COSIGNERS
see ACCOMMODATION PARTIES

COST OF CREDIT
analyzing, 1.6
APR, *see* ANNUAL PERCENTAGE RATE (APR)
credit insurance, 8.2.3
disclosure, *see* DISCLOSURES (TIL)
discrimination, 11.3
early termination, *see* EARLY TERMINATION
federal preemption, *see* FEDERAL PREEMPTION
finance charge, *see* FINANCE CHARGE
interest, *see* INTEREST
NCLC manual
　organization, 1.4
　preemption chapter, 3.1.2
　purpose, 1.1
　scope, 1.2
refinancings, 6.3
research aids, 1.5
　relevant websites, Appx. M
standards for comparison, 4.4.1
state regulation, *see* USURY LAWS (STATE)
understating using points, 7.2.2.1
usury laws
　banks, *see* NATIONAL BANK ACT
　purpose, 1.3
　references, 1.5
　state, *see* USURY LAWS (STATE)

COUNTERCLAIMS
jurisdiction, voluntary submission, 10.2.3.5
usury, compulsory or permissive, 10.6.6

CREDIT
see CREDIT TRANSACTIONS

CREDIT AGREEMENTS
see also CREDIT TRANSACTIONS; LOANS
agreed rate caps, exceeding, 9.2.8.1, 9.2.8.2
analyzing, checklist, 1.6.2

arbitration clauses, *see* ARBITRATION CLAUSES
assignee defenses, 10.6.1
choice of law provisions, 9.2.1.3, 9.2.9.5
condition precedent contracts, 10.3.3
conflict of laws, 9.2.9
contract construction, issues, 10.5.1.3
duty of good faith and fair dealing, 12.8
electronic, *see* ELECTRONIC CREDIT TRANSACTIONS
holder clause, 10.6.1.2.2
illegal contracts, 10.3.2, 10.8.2.1
intentional interference, 12.9.4
integration clauses, 10.3.4
oral misrepresentations contradicted by, 12.10.2.7
reformation, 10.5.1.3, 10.8.3
rescission, *see* RESCISSION
"single document rule", 11.6.8
unconscionable, 12.7.1
usurious charges, evidence, 10.5.4.2
usurious intent, evidence, 10.5.5.2
usury saving clauses, 10.6.10
usury violations, *see* USURY VIOLATIONS
void agreements, 10.3.2, 10.8.2.2.2, 10.8.4.1

CREDIT CARD ACCOUNTS
see also OPEN-END CREDIT
abuses by lenders, 11.7.2
　challenging, 11.7.3
aggressive solicitation, 11.7.2.3.5
annual fees, 7.2.2.3
applicable usury law, 9.2.4.5
arbitration clauses, 11.7.2.3.9
balance transfer fees, 11.7.2.2.4
breach of contract, 11.7.3.1
collection practices, 11.7.2.3.8
currency conversion fees, 11.7.2.2.5
debt burden, 11.7.1.1
　assisting consumers, 11.7.4
　industry practices, 11.7.1.2
deceptive marketing, 11.7.2.3.2
federal regulation, 11.7.3.4
grace periods, 11.7.2.3.6
historical overview, 2.3.2.3
　bank involvement, 2.3.1.2.1
interest calculations, 4.3.5
interest rate exportation, 2.3.2.3
junk fees, 11.7.2.2
late fees, 11.7.2.2.2
late payment practices, 11.7.2.3.3
mail, account offers by, 2.3.3.8
minimum monthly payments, 11.7.2.3.4
over-limit fees, 11.7.2.2.3
payday loans marketed as, 7.5.5.6
payment allocation order, 11.7.2.3.7
penalty rates, 11.7.2.3.1
posting cut-off policies, 11.7.2.3.3
preemption issues, 11.7.3.5
　generally, 11.7.3.5.1
　TILA preemption, 11.7.3.5.2
retail sellers, 2.3.1.3.2
rise of the credit card, 11.7.1
small loan ceilings, application, 3.4.3.2
state regulation, 2.3.3.8
TILA, application, 11.7.3.4
UDAP violations, 11.7.3.2

References are to sections

CREDIT CARD ACCOUNTS (*cont.*)
unilateral change in terms, 11.7.2.4
universal default policies, 11.7.2.3.1

CREDIT CONTRACTS
see CREDIT AGREEMENTS

CREDIT COSTS
see COST OF CREDIT; FINANCE CHARGE; INTEREST

CREDIT INSURANCE
see also DEBT CANCELLATION OR SUSPENSION
      AGREEMENTS (DCAs)
acceleration of debt, effect, 8.6
accident and health, *see* DISABILITY INSURANCE
antitrust claims, 8.5.2.7
arbitration clauses, 8.7.6, 10.3.6
background, 8.2.1
banks, restrictions, 8.4.1.5.2
benefits to creditor, 8.2.2
choice of insurers, 8.5.2.3.2
common abuses, 8.5
consumer complaints, 8.3.1.1
creditor's obligation prior to repossession, 8.5.5.3.3
DCA alternative, 8.3.2.3
depository institutions, federal regulations, 8.4.1.5.2
disability insurance, *see* DISABILITY INSURANCE
disclosure, 8.7.3.1
excess coverage
    amount of coverage, 8.5.3.3.2
    credit property issues, 8.5.3.4
    fraud claims, 8.7.3.2
    level term life, 8.5.3.3.1
excessive cost
    calculating charges, 8.5.3.1
    excessive coverage, 8.5.3.3
    excessive premiums, 8.5.3.2
    loss-ratio, 8.2.3.2
    market failures, 8.2.3.1
    remedies, 8.7
    reverse competition, 8.2.3.1
    unemployment insurance, 8.3.1.4
federal regulation, 8.4.1.5, 8.5.2.7.2
force-placed, *see* FORCE-PLACED INSURANCE
fraud claims, 8.5.5.3.2, 8.7.3.2, 12.10.1, 12.10.2.4
good faith and fair dealing, 12.8
group policies, 8.2.1
hidden interest issues, 7.3.1
HOEPA calculations, inclusion, 8.4.1.5.1
incomplete coverage, 8.5.5.2
ineligible borrowers, sale to, 8.5.5.1, 8.5.5.3.2
life insurance, *see* CREDIT LIFE INSURANCE
loss insurance, *see* CREDIT LOSS INSURANCE
loss-of-income, *see* INVOLUNTARY UNEMPLOYMENT
    INSURANCE
misrepresentation, 12.10.2.4
mortgage insurance, *see* PRIVATE MORTGAGE INSURANCE
    (PMI)
NAIC model acts, *see* NAIC MODEL ACTS
no benefit insurance, 8.5.5.1
non-credit insurance distinguished, 8.3.3
non-rate regulation, 8.4.2.2
overview, 8.1
packing, *see* INSURANCE PACKING
post-claim denial, challenging, 8.5.5.3

premiums, *see* INSURANCE PREMIUMS
property insurance, *see* CREDIT PROPERTY INSURANCE
rate regulation, 8.4.2.1
    filed-rate doctrine, 8.4.2.1.5
rebates, *see* INSURANCE PREMIUM REBATES
refinancing, flipping penalty, 6.1.1.2
regulatory sources
    Bank Holding Company Act, 8.4.1.5.2
    consumer credit laws, 8.4.1.3
    Gramm-Leach-Bliley Act, 8.4.1.5.2, Appx. I.2
    insurance premium financing laws, 8.4.1.6
    NAIC model acts, 8.4.2.1.1, 8.4.2.2.1
    overview, 2.3.3.6, 8.4.1.1
    preemption issues, 8.5.2.7.2
    statutes and regulations, 8.4.1.2
    TIL, 8.4.1.5.1
    UDAP, 8.4.1.4, 8.4.2.2.2
re-insurance agreements, 8.2.2
remedies for abuses
    disclosure duty, 8.7.3.1
    fiduciary duty, 8.7.2
    UDAP, 8.7.4
    unconscionability, 8.7.5
    usury, 8.7.1
RICO claims, 12.6
secondary beneficiaries, 8.5.6
sliding, 8.5.2.1, 8.5.2.4
state regulation
    DCAs, 8.3.2.3
    preemption issues, 8.5.2.7.2
    sources, 8.4.1.2, 8.4.1.3, 8.4.1.4, 8.4.1.6
    substance, 8.4.2
surpluses, 8.5.6
tie-ins, 8.5.2.7.1
TIL claims, 8.5.2.5
title insurance, *see* TITLE INSURANCE
truncated policies, 8.3.1.2
types, 8.3.1
UDAP claims, 8.5.2.6
unemployment insurance, *see* INVOLUNTARY UNEMPLOY-
    MENT INSURANCE
usury claims, 8.5.1
voluntariness
    compulsory insurance, 8.5.2.3
    generally, 8.5.2.1
    non-usury coercion claims, 8.5.2.5
    proving coercion, 8.5.2.4
    TIL and usury distinguished, 8.5.2.2

CREDIT LIFE INSURANCE
see also CREDIT INSURANCE
background, 8.2.1
calculating charges, 8.5.3.1.2
compulsory, prohibition, 8.5.2.3.1
decreasing term, 8.3.1.2
excess coverage, 8.5.3.3.1
gross or net coverage, 8.5.3.1.2
joint life, 8.3.1.2
level term, 8.3.1.2, 8.5.3.3.1
NAIC model act, 8.4.2.2.1
overcharges, 8.5.3.1.2
overview, 8.3.1.2
prima facie rates, 8.4.2.1.1
rate regulation, 8.4.2.1.1

CREDIT LIFE INSURANCE (*cont.*)
rebates, 8.6
secondary beneficiaries, 8.5.6
surpluses, 8.5.6
tie-ins, 8.5.2.7.1

CREDIT LINES
see LINES OF CREDIT

CREDIT LOSS INSURANCE
see also CREDIT INSURANCE; CREDIT PROPERTY
        INSURANCE
auto loans, special issues, 8.3.1.5.4
charging consumer for, 8.3.1.5.2
deficiency insurance, *see* DEFICIENCY INSURANCE
force-placed insurance, 8.3.1.5.4

CREDIT MARKETPLACE
see also CREDITORS
barriers, 11.2
credit insurance, 8.2.3.1
custom and usage, creditor defense, 10.6.9
deregulation, effect, 1.1, 2.4
market forces, 11.1
modern consumer marketplace, described, 2.3
overreaching credit, challenging, 11.1, 12.1
post-deregulation, 2.5
risk factor, 11.3
subprime lenders, 11.3
TIL and state law relationship, 2.3.4
types of credit, 2.3.2
types of creditors, 2.3.1
types of usury statutes, 2.3.3
usury laws, purpose, 1.3

CREDIT MATH
see INTEREST CALCULATIONS; MATHEMATICAL
        FORMULAS

CREDIT PRACTICES RULE (FTC)
see also FEDERAL TRADE COMMISSION (FTC)
pyramiding late charges, 7.2.4.3

CREDIT PROPERTY INSURANCE
see also CREDIT INSURANCE
calculating charges, 8.5.3.1.4
compulsory, restrictions, 8.5.2.3.2
dual interest, 8.3.1.5
excess coverage
    calculating, 8.5.3.1.4
    duplicative insurance, 8.5.4.4
    force-placed insurance, 8.5.3.4.2
    packing, 8.5.4.3, 8.5.4.4
    phantom coverage, 8.5.3.4.3
    scope of insurable interest, 8.5.3.4.1
finance charge, exclusion, 8.4.1.5.1, 8.5.2.2
household goods, 8.5.3.4.1, 8.5.4.4
motor vehicles, *see* MOTOR VEHICLE CREDIT INSURANCE
NAIC model act, 8.3.1.5.1, 8.4.2.2.1, 8.5.3.1.4
overview, 8.3.1.5.1
scope of insurable interest, 8.5.3.4.1
state regulation, 8.4.1.3
vendor's single interest (VSI), 8.3.1.5.2

CREDIT REGULATION
see also DEREGULATION
banks, *see* NATIONAL BANK ACT

cost of credit, *see* USURY LAWS (STATE)
credit unions, *see* FEDERAL CREDIT UNION ACT
federal preemption, *see* FEDERAL PREEMPTION
government agencies, *see* REGULATORY AGENCIES
savings and loan associations, *see* HOME OWNERS' LOAN
        ACT
state law overview, 2.1

CREDIT REPAIR LAWS
federal, *see* CREDIT REPAIR ORGANIZATIONS ACT
home improvement contractors, application, 11.5.2
overview, 12.4.1
payday loans, application, 7.5.5.6
state laws, 12.4.3
    coverage, 12.4.3.1
    private causes of action, 12.4.3.3
    substantive provisions, 12.4.3.2

CREDIT REPAIR ORGANIZATIONS ACT
see also CREDIT REPAIR LAWS
coverage, 12.4.2.1
remedies, 12.4.2.3
substantive prohibitions, 12.4.2.2

CREDIT REPORTS
credit cards, penalty rates, 11.7.2.3.1
hidden interest status, 7.3.1

CREDIT SALES
see also INSTALLMENT CREDIT
applicable laws, checklist, 1.6.3.1.3
assignment of contract, 2.3.1.3.2
body-dragging, 9.2.3.3
concealed loans, 10.5.2.2.1
consumer credit sale, defined, 9.2.3.4
described, 2.3.2.2
DIDA, application, 3.9.3.4
disguised as leases
    generally, 7.5.3.1
    rent-to-own, 7.5.3.2
fixed-term, checklist, 1.6.3.2
fraud claims, 12.10
FTC Holder Rule, 10.6.1.2.2, 10.6.1.3
hidden interest
    disguised as leases, 7.5.3
    inflating sale price, 7.4.6.1
    seller's points, 7.4.6.2
insurance, regulation, 2.3.3.6
land installment contracts, 9.2.3.4
loan status, 2.2.2, 2.3.2.2
misrepresentation claims, 12.10
mobile homes, *see* MOBILE HOME LOANS
MVRISAs, *see* MOTOR VEHICLE RETAIL INSTALLMENT
        SALES ACTS (MVRISAs)
negative equity, 11.6.3
refinancings, 6.4.3
regulatory history, 2.3.2.2
rent-to-own, *see* RENT-TO-OWN (RTO) TRANSACTIONS
rescission of contract, 10.8.3
RISAs, *see* RETAIL INSTALLMENT SALES ACTS (RISAs)
spot delivery, 11.6.5
state regulation, 2.1, 2.2.2
time-price doctrine, 2.2.2, 2.3.2.2, 10.5.2.2
used cars, *see* USED CAR PURCHASES

References are to sections

CREDIT SALES (*cont.*)
usury law
   application, 9.2.1.2, 10.5.2.2.1
   historical development, 2.2.3.2
VSI insurance, 8.3.1.5.2
waiver of defenses against assignees, 10.6.1.3
yo-yo deals, 11.6.5

CREDIT TRANSACTIONS
adverse action, notice requirements, 12.3.2
analyzing, 1.6
closed-end credit, *see* CLOSED-END CREDIT
determining, checklist, 1.6.3.1.2
discrimination, 12.3
duty of good faith and fair dealing, 12.8
electronic, *see* ELECTRONIC CREDIT TRANSACTIONS
governing law, checklist, 1.6.3.1
holder rule, exceptions, 10.6.1.1
identifying, 3.2.2.2
interest bearing explained, 4.5.1
liability chart, 12.12
loans, *see* LOANS
open-end credit, *see* OPEN-END CREDIT
precomputed explained, 4.5.3
progress payments, 4.9
rebates, *see* REBATES
sale of goods, *see* CREDIT SALES
secured credit, *see* SECURED CREDIT
sophisticated borrowers, 10.6.3
state regulation, 2.1
substance not form, 9.2.1.6
time-price doctrine, application, 10.5.2.2.2
types of credit, 2.3.2
UDAP violations, 12.5
unconscionability, 12.7
usurious transactions, *see* USURY VIOLATIONS
variable rate, *see* VARIABLE RATE TRANSACTIONS

CREDIT UNIONS
see also DEPOSITORY CREDITORS
deposit insurance, 2.3.1.2.3
Federal Credit Union Act, application, 3.6
historical development, 2.2.3.1
interest ceilings, 3.1.1, 3.6.2
   mortgage loans, 3.2.4.1
mortgage loans, federal preemption, 3.2.4
most favored lender status, 3.6.2
NCUA regulation, 3.3.1, Appx. E.2
prepayment penalties, imposing, 5.8.3
regulatory history, 2.3.1.2.3
state-chartered federally-insured, *see* FEDERALLY INSURED
      LENDERS
state law, application, 3.6.2, 3.6.3
usurious loans, remedies, 10.8.5.1

CREDITOR DEFENSES
assignees, 10.6.1
bona fide error, 10.5.5.2
contract saving clauses, 10.6.10
correction of error, 10.6.11
de minimis violations, 10.6.8
estoppel, 10.6.4
FDIC, special defenses, 10.7
federal receivers, 10.7
high cost mortgages, 10.6.1.2.3

holders-in-due course, 10.6.1
   shelter rule, 10.6.1.3.6
industry custom and usage, 10.6.9
lack of standing, 10.6.3
lack of usurious intent, 10.5.5.2
removal to federal court, 3.15
res judicata, 10.6.6
voluntary payment doctrine, 10.6.5
waiver, 10.6.4.4

CREDITORS
see also CREDIT MARKETPLACE
abusive collection tactics, 12.6
bureaucracy of preemption, 3.3
credit insurance
   benefits, 8.2.2
   compensation as interest, 8.5.3.2.2
   excess charges, liability, 8.5.3.2.1
   fiduciary duty, 8.7.2
   liability for coverage, 8.5.5.3.3
defenses to usury claims, *see* CREDITOR DEFENSES
depository creditors, *see* DEPOSITORY CREDITORS (STATE);
      FEDERAL LENDERS
DIDA, application, 3.9.3.3
due care duty, 12.11.1
estoppel, 12.11.2
federal lenders, *see* FEDERAL LENDERS
federal regulation, 3.3.1
federally-insured lenders, *see* FEDERALLY INSURED
      LENDERS
fiduciary role, 12.9.3
fraud liability, 12.10.1
housing creditors, *see* HOUSING CREDITORS
insurers, agency relationship, 8.5.5.3.2
internet-based lenders, *see* ELECTRONIC CREDIT
      TRANSACTIONS
liability chart, 12.12
licensed, *see* LICENSED LENDERS
licensing requirements, 9.2.4.6, 10.8.4
most favored lender doctrine, *see* MOST FAVORED LENDER
      DOCTRINE
negotiable instruments, accepting, 10.6.1.2.2
non-depository creditors, *see* NON-DEPOSITORY CREDITORS
overreaching scenarios, 11.5
post-confirmation profiteering, 11.5.5
predatory lenders, *see* PREDATORY LENDERS
property-flipping schemes and, 11.5.6
retail installment sales, 11.6.7
state regulation, 2.1, 3.3.1
table-funding, *see* TABLE-FUNDED LOANS
types of creditors, 2.3.1
   identifying type, 3.2.2.4
usurious intent, 10.5.5
usury law application
   federal depository lenders, 3.4–3.6, 9.2.4.4
   FHA/VA-insured loans, 3.8
   frequency standard, 9.2.4.2
   generally, 9.2.1.2
   non-depository creditors, 3.2.4.2, 3.10, 9.2.4.5
   opting-in, 9.2.1.3
   preemption chart, 3.2.5
   preemption overview, 3.1.1
   state depository lenders, 3.7–3.11, 9.2.4.3

CRIMINAL USURY
business loans, application, 9.2.2
deregulated states, 9.2.1.3
violations, effect, 9.2.7

CUSTOM AND USAGE
creditor defense, 10.6.9

DAILY INTEREST RATES
see also INTEREST RATES
computation
    bankers' year, 4.6.3.4
    generally, 4.6.3.1
    360-day method, 4.6.3.3
    365-day method, 4.6.3.2
late charges in addition to, 4.8.1

DAMAGES
liquidated, *see* LIQUIDATED DAMAGES
punitive, *see* PUNITIVE DAMAGES
statutory, *see* STATUTORY PENALTIES

DE MINIMIS VIOLATIONS
see also USURY VIOLATIONS
creditor defense, 10.6.8

DEALERS
charges as hidden interest, 7.2.1, 7.4.2, 7.4.6.1
credit sales, 11.6
inflated sales prices, 7.4.6.1
lender liability for acts of, 12.12
retail installment sales, function, 11.6.7
upcharges, 7.4.2
yield spread premiums, *see* YIELD SPREAD PREMIUMS

DEBT CANCELLATION OR SUSPENSION AGREE-
    MENTS (DCAs)
see also CREDIT INSURANCE
auto loans, *see* GAP INSURANCE OR AGREEMENTS
generally, 8.3.2.3
hidden interest, 7.4.2
HOEPA calculations, inclusion, 8.4.1.5.1
insurance status, 8.3.2.3
negative equity issues, 11.6.3
regulations, 8.3.2.3
shift from credit insurance to, 8.3.2.3
state regulation, federal preemption, 8.3.2.3

DECEPTIVE PRACTICES
see also UDAP VIOLATIONS
credit repair organizations, 12.4.2.2

DEFAULT CHARGES
see also LATE CHARGES
attorney fees, 7.3.3.2
duty of good faith and fair dealing, 12.8
forbearance charges distinguished, 10.5.2.3
late charge distinguishing, 7.2.4.1
unconscionable default charges and rates, 12.7.2
usury laws, application, 10.5.2.3

DEFAULT JUDGMENTS
setting aside, res judicata, 10.6.6

DEFAULTED LOANS
see ACCELERATION

DEFENSES
arbitration clauses, 10.3.7

creditor defenses, *see* CREDITOR DEFENSES
holders-in-due course, against, 10.6.1.2.1, 10.6.1.3.5, 10.6.1.3.9
    waiver of defense clauses, 10.6.1.3.10
payday loans, 7.5.5.6
Servicemembers Civil Relief Act, 2.3.3.11
usury as defense, *see* USURY AS DEFENSE

DEFERRAL FEES
calculating, 4.8.2
payment holidays, 4.8.3
precomputed transactions, 4.5.3, 4.8.2
state law, 4.8.2

DEFERRED PRESENTMENT LOANS
see PAYDAY LOANS

DEFICIENCY INSURANCE
see also CREDIT LOSS INSURANCE
VSI misnomer, 8.3.1.5.2

DEFINITIONS
accurately disclosed APR, 4.4.2
"alternative mortgage transactions," 3.10.1
amount financed, 4.4.1, 10.5.4.3
APR, 4.4.1
business arrangement, 10.6.1.2.2
consolidation, 6.1.3
consumer credit sale, 9.2.3.4
credit repair organization, 12.4.2.1
enterprise, 10.8.5.3.1
finance charge, 4.4.1
"first lien," 3.9.3.2.1
flipping, 6.1.3
forbearance, 10.5.2.1
good faith, 7.5.5.9.3
hidden interest, 7.1.1
housing creditor, 3.10.1
impair, 8.5.2.7.2
interest, 5.5.2.2.3, 7.2.1, 10.5.4.3
loan, 10.5.2.1, 10.5.2.2.1
loan secured by first lien on real estate, 3.9.3.2.1
mark-up, 12.2.1.6
non-interest fees, 10.5.4.3
"obstruct, impair, or condition," 3.4.6.2
pattern, 10.8.5.3.2
preauthorized electronic fund transfer, 7.5.5.9.2
purchase money loan, 10.6.1.2.2
racketeering activity, 10.8.5.3.2
refinancing, 6.1.3
"requiring the use," 12.2.1.7
unconscionability, 8.7.5
unlawful debt, 10.8.5.3.3
wraparound mortgage, 7.4.3

DELINQUENCY CHARGES
see LATE CHARGES

DEPARTMENT OF HOUSING AND URBAN DEVELOP-
    MENT (HUD)
lender-paid mortgage broker fees, policy statement
    first statement (1999), 12.2.1.5.3, Appx. K.3.1
    conflicting interpretations, 12.2.1.5.4
    letter regarding, Appx. K.4.1
    second statement (2001), 12.2.1.5.5, Appx. K.3.2
    unearned or excessive fees, 12.2.1.6

Index   **DISCLOSURE**

References are to sections

DEPOSIT INSURANCE
see also FEDERAL DEPOSIT INSURANCE CORPORATION
 (FDIC); FEDERAL SAVINGS AND LOAN
 INSURANCE CORPORATION (FSLIC); NATIONAL
 CREDIT UNION SHARE INSURANCE FUND
banks, 2.3.1.2.1
credit unions, 2.3.1.2.3
federal receivers, special defenses, 10.7
savings and loan associations, 2.3.1.2.2

DEPOSITORY CREDITORS
federal, *see* FEDERAL LENDERS
state, *see* DEPOSITORY CREDITORS (STATE)

DEPOSITORY CREDITORS (STATE)
see also CREDITORS
AMTPA, application, 3.10.1
applicable law
 checklist, 1.6.3.1.4
 identifying, 3.2.2.5
banks, *see* BANKS
credit unions, *see* CREDIT UNIONS
D'Oench doctrine, application, 10.7.6.1
federal preemption, application
 federally-insured lenders, 3.9.2
 intrastate non-mortgage loans, 3.2.3.1
 mortgage loans, 3.9.3
 state-chartered banks, 3.7
federal receivers, special defenses, 10.7
federally-insured, *see* FEDERALLY INSURED LENDERS
identifying, 3.2.2.4
non-depository creditors, distinction, 2.3.1.1
savings and loan associations, *see* SAVINGS AND LOAN
 ASSOCIATIONS
usury laws, application, 9.2.4.3

DEPOSITORY INSTITUTIONS ACT (DIA)
overview, 3.10.1
 preemption, 3.1.1
preemption chart, 3.2.5
Title VIII, *see* ALTERNATIVE MORTGAGE TRANSAC-
 TIONS PARITY ACT (AMTPA)

**DEPOSITORY INSTITUTIONS DEREGULATION AND
 MONETARY CONTROL ACT (DIDA)**
choice of laws, 3.9.2.2.2
federally-insured lenders, 3.9.2
 alternative interest ceiling, 3.9.2.1
 exportation rights, 3.9.2.2
 most favored lender status, 3.7.2, 3.9.2.1
first mortgage preemption, 3.9.3
 first lien, defined, 3.9.3.2.1
 mobile home loans, 3.9.3.4, 5.2.3
 overview, 3.9.3.1
 qualifying lenders, 3.9.3.3
 special Texas issue, 3.9.3.2.2
legislative history, 3.9.1
mortgage deregulation, application, 2.4.2
overview, 3.1.1
preemption of state law, 3.9
 chart, 3.2.5
 federally related lenders, 3.9.2
 interstate banking, 3.9.2.2
 mortgage loans, 3.2.4.1, 3.9.3
 state banks, 3.7.2
purpose, 3.9.1

selected provisions, Appx. G.1
selected regulations, Appx. G.2
state opt out
 alternative ceiling, 3.9.4.3
 exportation rights, 3.9.2.2.1
 first liens, 3.9.4.2
 generally, 3.9.4.1
 most favored lender, 3.9.4.3
usury remedies, 10.8.5.1

DEREGULATION
credit marketplace, effect, 1.1
DIDA, *see* DEPOSITORY INSTITUTIONS DEREGULATION
 AND MONETARY CONTROL ACT (DIDA)
hidden interest issues, 9.2.8.2
interest ceilings, 2.4.1, 9.2.8.1
mortgages, 2.4.2
post-deregulation, 2.5
rate exportation, via, *see* RATE EXPORTATION
state parity laws, 3.1.1, 3.14

DETENTION OF MONEY
forbearance distinguished, 10.5.2.3
usury laws, application, 10.5.2.3

DIDA
see DEPOSITORY INSTITUTIONS DEREGULATION AND
 MONETARY CONTROL ACT (DIDA)

DISABILITY INSURANCE
see also CREDIT INSURANCE; INVOLUNTARY
 UNEMPLOYMENT INSURANCE
approved rate schedule, 8.5.3.1.3
calculating charges, 8.5.3.1.3
compulsory, prohibition, 8.5.2.3.1
elimination period, 8.3.1.3
"Liberator Income Protector Plan" (LIPP), 8.3.3
NAIC model act, 8.4.2.2.1
no benefit insurance, 8.5.5.1
non-credit insurance, 8.3.3
overview, 8.3.1.3
prima facie rates, 8.4.2.1.1
rate regulation, 8.4.2.1.1
rebates, 8.6
retroactive vs. non-retroactive, 8.3.1.3
tie-ins, 8.5.2.7.1
waiting period, 8.3.1.3

DISCLOSURE
credit insurance
 banks, federal regulations, 8.4.1.5.2
 common law duty, 8.7.3.1
 fiduciary duty, 8.7.2
 premium financing, 8.4.1.6
credit repair organizations, 12.4.2.2
electronic disclosures
 E-Sign provisions, 9.2.10.2, 9.2.10.4.1
 format requirements, 9.2.10.5
 RESPA disclosures, 12.2.1.9
fiduciary duty, 12.9.1, 12.9.3
 credit insurance, 8.4.1.6, 8.7.2
fraud and misrepresentation claims, 12.10.2.4
RESPA, *see* DISCLOSURES (RESPA)
TIL, *see* DISCLOSURES (TIL)
rent-to-own transactions, 7.5.3.5
"single document rule" and, 11.6.8

DISCLOSURES (RESPA)
affiliated business, 12.2.1.5.1
electronic provision, 12.2.1.9
settlement costs, 12.2.1.2
servicer obligations, 12.2.1.3

DISCLOSURES (TIL)
APR, *see* ANNUAL PERCENTAGE RATE (APR)
check advancement loans, 7.5.5
checklist, 1.6.3.2.1
credit insurance, 8.4.1.5.1, 8.5.2.2, 8.5.2.5
  premium financing, 8.4.1.6
discounts, 7.4.6.2
finance charge, *see* FINANCE CHARGE
generally, 2.3.4, 4.4.1
negative equity, 11.6.3
open-end credit calculations, 4.3.5.3
payday loans, 7.5.5.4, 7.5.5.6
private mortgage insurance, 8.3.2.1
variable rate calculations, 4.3.6.2

DISCOUNT INTEREST
see also INTEREST
compounding, 4.6.1.1
discount per annum, 4.3.3
hidden interest, 7.4.2
installment credit calculations, 4.3.3
precomputed interest calculation, 4.3.3
refinancing, effect, 6.1.1.2

DISCOUNT POINTS
see also POINTS
hidden interest, 7.2.2.1

DISCOUNTS
hidden interest issues, 7.4.2, 7.4.6.1, 11.6.2
subprime lenders, 11.6.2.1
TIL disclosures, 7.4.6.2
used car financing, 11.6.2

DISCOVERY
credit insurance
  excess charges, 8.5.3.2.1
  premiums after default, 8.6
  proving coercion, 8.5.2.4
refinanced loans, information sought, 6.3.2
sample discovery
  disguised credit, Appx. L.3.2
  RESPA, Appx. L.6.2
sample interrogatories
  RAL, Appx. L.5.2, Appx. L.5.4
  RISA violation, Appx. L.1.2
sample request for admissions, Appx. L.2.2
sample request for production of documents, Appx. L.3.2, Appx. L.5.3
true cash price, 7.4.6.1

DISCRIMINATION
civil rights remedies, 12.3.1
ECOA, *see* EQUAL CREDIT OPPORTUNITY ACT (ECOA)
fair lending statutes, remedies, 12.3.1
pricing of products and services, 11.3, 11.6.2.2
rent-to-own transactions, 7.5.3.6.6
yield spread premiums, 11.6.6

DOCTORS
see CONVENIENCE CREDITORS

DOCUMENT PREPARATION FEES
hidden interest, 7.2.1
unauthorized practice of law, 7.2.1

***D'OENCH* DOCTRINE**
assignees, asserting, 10.7.6.2
bilateral agreement exception, 10.7.4.3
"free standing tort" exception, 10.7.3.2
innocent borrowers and, 10.7.3.2
limitations on, 10.7.7
  FDIC/RTC conduct, 10.7.9
  sampling of claims, 10.7.8
overview, 10.7.3.1
section 1823(e)
  codification and preemption by, 10.7.2, 10.7.4.1
  differences, 10.7.4.6
scope, 10.7.6

DOOR-TO-DOOR SELLERS
see also HOME IMPROVEMENT CONTRACTORS
lender liability for acts of, 12.12

DUAL INTEREST INSURANCE
see also CREDIT PROPERTY INSURANCE
motor vehicles, 8.3.1.5.4
overview, 8.3.1.5.3

DUE CARE DUTY
lender liability, 12.11.1

DUE-ON-SALE CLAUSES
acceleration under, 5.8.3

DUE PROCESS
jurisdictional issues, 10.2.1
punitive damages, 12.10.3

DUTY
due care, *see* DUE CARE DUTY
fiduciary, *see* FIDUCIARY DUTY
good faith and fair dealing, *see* GOOD FAITH AND FAIR DEALING

EARLY TERMINATION
see also ACCELERATION; PREPAYMENT
federal law overview, 5.2.2
rebates, *see* REBATES
state law overview, 5.2.1

E-COMMERCE
see ELECTRONIC FUNDS TRANSFER ACT (EFTA);
      ELECTRONIC CREDIT TRANSACTIONS;
      ELECTRONIC SIGNATURES IN GLOBAL AND
      NATIONAL COMMERCE ACT (E-SIGN); INTERNET
      TRANSACTIONS; UNIFORM ELECTRONIC
      TRANSACTIONS ACT (UETA)

ELECTRONIC CREDIT TRANSACTIONS
applicable law, 9.2.10.3
  E-Sign overview, 9.2.10.2
  UETA overview, 9.2.10.2
consent requirements, 9.2.10.4
deregulation through exportation, 3.4.5.1.2
enforceability, 9.2.10.8
integrity of documents, 9.2.10.7
long-arm jurisdiction, 10.2.2
overview, 9.2.10.1
payday loans, 7.5.5.9
practice tips, 9.2.10.10

ELECTRONIC CREDIT TRANSACTIONS (*cont.*)
promissory note holder, 10.6.1.1
subsequent notices, 9.2.10.9
timing and format requirements, 9.2.10.5
transferable records, 10.6.1.1, 10.6.1.3.7
transmission of documents, 9.2.10.6

ELECTRONIC FUNDS TRANSFER ACT (EFTA)
National Banking Act, relationship, 3.4.5.1.2
payday loan repayments, application, 7.5.5.9.1, 7.5.5.9.2
    stop payments, 7.5.5.9.6
    unauthorized transfers, 7.5.5.9.4, 7.5.5.9.7
preauthorized transfers, *see* PREAUTHORIZED ELECTRONIC
        FUND TRANSFERS
preemptive effect, 3.4.5.1.2

**ELECTRONIC SIGNATURES IN GLOBAL AND
        NATIONAL COMMERCE ACT (E-SIGN)**
application, 9.2.10.3
consent requirements, 9.2.10.4.1
credit insurance disclosures, application, 8.4.1.5.2
document integrity, 9.2.10.7
electronic promissory notes, 10.6.1.1, 10.6.1.3.7
enforceability of contracts and signatures, 9.2.10.8
overview, 9.2.10.2, 12.2.1.9
post-consummation notices, 9.2.10.9
preemption by state law, 9.2.10.2, 9.2.10.3.1
RESPA disclosures, application, 12.2.1.9
timing and format requirements, 9.2.10.5
transmission requirements, 9.2.10.6
UETA override, 9.2.10.2

ENDING BALANCE
see also LOAN BALANCES
open-end credit calculations, 4.3.5

EQUAL CREDIT OPPORTUNITY ACT (ECOA)
discrimination, prohibition, 12.3.1
notice requirements, 12.3.2
rent-to-own transactions, application, 7.5.3.6.6
yield spread premiums, application, 11.6.6

EQUITABLE ESTOPPEL
see also ESTOPPEL
arbitration clauses, enforcement, 10.3.5.2
federal common-law defense, *see D'OENCH* DOCTRINE
FDIC defense, 10.7.3.1

EQUITABLE MORTGAGES
see also MORTGAGES
sale and repurchase agreements as, 7.5.2.1

EQUITABLE REMEDIES
see also USURY REMEDIES
usurious loans, 10.8.3

EQUITABLE SUBORDINATION
federal receivers, application, 10.7.8

EQUITY PARTICIPATION
hidden interest, 7.2.3

EQUITY-SKIMMING
HOEPA application, 12.2.2
insurance packing as, 8.5.4.2
loan brokers, participation, 11.5.4.1
predatory lenders, 11.5.1
refinancing, 6.1.1.3
RESPA disclosure, determination using, 12.2.1.2

RICO claims, 12.6
UDAP violations, 12.5
unconscionability challenges, 12.7.2

ERRORS
creditor defenses
    bona fide error, 10.5.5.2
    correction of error, 10.6.11

ESCROW
insurance premiums, 8.2.2
prepaid payments, HOEPA prohibitions, 12.2.2.3
RESPA provisions
    electronic compliance, 12.2.1.9
    escrow limitations, 12.2.1.4
    HUD regulations, 12.2.1.9
    servicer obligations, 12.2.1.3
RICO claims, 12.6

E-SIGN
see ELECTRONIC SIGNATURES IN GLOBAL AND
        NATIONAL COMMERCE ACT (E-SIGN)

ESTOPPEL
see also EQUITABLE ESTOPPEL
creditor defense, 10.6.4
creditor liability, 12.11.2
insurance disqualification, 8.5.5.3.2

EVIDENCE
see also BURDEN OF PROOF
business loan, 9.2.2.3, 9.2.2.4
credit insurance
    coercion, 8.5.2.4, 8.5.2.5
    tie-in, 8.5.2.7.1
expert evidence, *see* EXPERT WITNESSES
interest overcharge, 10.5.4
loan or forbearance, 10.5.2
mathematical issues, proving, 4.10
overcharge issues, uncovering, 4.11.2, 4.11.3
repayment obligation, 10.5.3
sample expert witness testimony and reports, Appx. L.2
true cash price, 7.4.6.1
usurious intent, 10.5.5
usury claim
    burden, 10.5.1.2
    contract construction, 10.5.1.3
    elements, 10.5
    excessive interest, 10.5.4.4
    intent, 10.5.5

EXPERT WITNESSES
proving usury, use, 10.5.4.4
sample affidavit, Appx. L.2.3
sample reports
    debt consolidation, Appx. L.2.5
    multiple refinancings, Appx. L.2.6
sample testimony, Appx. L.2.4

EXPORTATION OF INTEREST RATES
see RATE EXPORTATION

FAIR CREDIT REPORTING ACT (FCRA)
notice requirements, 12.3.2
private mortgage insurance (PMI), application, 8.3.2.1

FAIR HOUSING ACT
discrimination, prohibition, 12.3.1

FARM SUPPLY COMPANIES
see CONVENIENCE CREDITORS

FAVORED LENDERS
see MOST FAVORED LENDER DOCTRINE

FEDERAL ARBITRATION ACT (FAA)
see also ARBITRATION CLAUSES
credit insurance, application, 8.7.6, 10.3.6
preemption by state insurance law, 8.7.6, 10.3.6

FEDERAL BANKING SYSTEM
see also BANKS
"dual" banking system, 3.7.1
FDIC, *see* FEDERAL DEPOSIT INSURANCE CORPORA-
    TION (FDIC)
historical development, 2.3.1.2.1
reserve system, *see* FEDERAL RESERVE SYSTEM

FEDERAL BANKS
see NATIONAL BANKS

FEDERAL COURT
jurisdiction
    preemption issues, 3.15
    usury issues, 10.6.6
removal to, 3.15
state court judgments, relationship, 10.6.6

FEDERAL CREDIT UNION ACT
see also CREDIT UNIONS
most favored lender doctrine, 3.6.2
NCUA interpretive letters, Appx. E.3
overview, 3.6.1
preemption, 3.6
    beyond usury, 3.6.3
    interest rates, 3.6.2
    mortgage loans, 3.2.4.1
    preemption chart, 3.2.5
selected provisions, Appx. E.1
selected regulations, Appx. E.2

FEDERAL DEPOSIT INSURANCE ACT
see also FEDERAL DEPOSIT INSURANCE CORPORATION
    (FDIC)
FDIC opinion letters, Appx. F.3
selected provisions, Appx. F.1
selected regulations, Appx. F.2

FEDERAL DEPOSIT INSURANCE CORPORATION
    (FDIC)
see also FEDERAL BANKING SYSTEM; FEDERAL
    DEPOSIT INSURANCE ACT; FEDERAL RESERVE
    SYSTEM
advisory letters, Appx. F.3
creation, 2.3.1.2.1, 10.7.1
credit insurance, joint regulations, 8.4.1.5.2, Appx. I.2.3
equitable subordination, application, 10.7.8
FTCA, application, 10.7.9
liability for own conduct, 10.7.9
negligent operation of receivership, 10.7.9
opinion letters, Appx. F.3
payday lending, guidelines, 3.13.3
rent-a-charter arrangements, regulation, 3.13.3
special defenses, 10.7
    D'Oench doctrine, 10.7.3
    exception for own conduct, 10.7.9
    federal holder-in-due course doctrine, 10.7.5

section 1823(e), 10.7.4
state banks
    participation, 2.3.1.2.1
    regulation, 3.7.1
super holder-in-due-course status, 10.7.5

FEDERAL DISCOUNT RATE
alternative federal rate, relationship, 3.4.2

FEDERAL HOLDER-IN-DUE COURSE DOCTRINE
see also HOLDERS-IN-DUE COURSE
FIRREA preemption, 10.7.2
limitations on, 10.7.7, 10.7.8
overview, 10.7.5

FEDERAL HOME LOAN BANK BOARD
see also FEDERAL HOME LOAN BANK SYSTEM; OFFICE
    OF THRIFT SUPERVISION (OTS)
history, 2.3.1.2.2

FEDERAL HOME LOAN BANK SYSTEM
see also SAVINGS AND LOAN ASSOCIATIONS
Board, *see* FEDERAL HOME LOAN BANK BOARD
establishment, 2.3.1.2.2
FSLIC, *see* FEDERAL SAVINGS AND LOAN INSURANCE
    CORPORATION (FSLIC)
OTS, *see* OFFICE OF THRIFT SUPERVISION (OTS)
participation, 2.3.1.2.2

FEDERAL HOUSING ADMINISTRATION (FHA) LOANS
see also NATIONAL HOUSING ACT
foreclosure, duty of good faith and fair dealing, 12.8
mobile home loans, OTS regulations
    avoidance, 3.9.3.4
    compliance, 3.8.1
out-of-state lenders, authorization, 3.8.1
preemption of state interest ceilings, 3.1.1, 3.8
    preemption chart, 3.2.5
    state opt-out, 3.8.2
securitization, 11.4

FEDERAL LENDERS
see also FEDERALLY INSURED LENDERS
applicable law, checklist, 1.6.3.1.4
    regulatory chart, 3.3.1
depository institutions
    banks, *see* NATIONAL BANKS
    credit insurance regulation, 8.4.1.5.2
    credit unions, *see* CREDIT UNIONS
    D'Oench doctrine, application, 10.7.6.1
    savings and loan associations, *see* SAVINGS AND LOAN
        ASSOCIATIONS
    usury laws, application, 9.2.4.4
interest ceilings, 3.1.1
prepayment penalties, 5.8.3
regulation, overview, 3.3.1

FEDERAL PREEMPTION
see also PREEMPTION
agency regulations, deference, 3.3.2
AMTPA, 3.10
approaching, first steps, 3.2.1
bureaucracy of preemption, 3.3
checking for preemption, summary guide, 3.2
checklist, 1.6.3.1.4
    preemption chart, 3.2.5
conflict preemption, 3.4.6.1

FEDERAL PREEMPTION (*cont.*)
consumer protection statutes, 3.12, 5.9
credit card abuses and, 11.7.3.5
  generally, 11.7.3.5.1
  other claims, 11.7.3.3
  TILA, 11.7.3.5.2
  UDAP, 11.7.3.2
credit insurance, 8.4.1.5.2, 8.5.2.7.2
determining, 9.2.1.5
DCAs, 8.3.2.3
DIA, 3.10.1
DIDA, 3.7.2, 3.9
  first mortgage preemption, 3.9.3
  state opt-out, 3.9.4
EFTA, 3.4.5.1.2
FDIC, 3.7
federal court jurisdiction, 3.15
Federal Credit Union Act, 3.6
FHA loans, 3.8
  state opt-out, 3.8.2
field preemption, 3.5.3
FIRREA, 10.7.2
Gramm-Leach-Bliley Act, 8.3.2.3, 8.4.1.5.2
hidden interest and, 7.1.2
HOEPA, 5.9
HOLA, 3.5.3
interest ceilings, 2.4.1, 3.1.1
interpretative rulings and opinions
  deference, 3.3.2, 3.4.6.1
  FDIC, 3.7.2
  NCUA, 3.6.3
  OCC, 3.4.6.1
  OTS, 3.5.4
  publication for comment, 3.4.6.1
key statutes, 3.1.1
land installment contracts, 9.2.3.4
mortgage loans, 3.2.4
most favored lender doctrine
  credit unions, 3.6.2
  national banks, 3.4.3
  savings and loan associations, 3.5.2
  state banks, 3.7.2
National Bank Act, 3.4.6
NCLC manual organization, 3.1.2
NCUA regulations, 3.6.3
non-mortgage loans
  interstate, 3.2.3.2
  intrastate, 3.2.3.1
OCC regulations, 3.4.6.2
OTS regulations, 3.5.3
RALs, 7.5.4.2
rate exportation
  credit unions, 3.6.2
  federally-insured lenders, 3.9.2.2
  national banks, 3.4.5
  savings and loan associations, 3.5.2
  state banks, 3.7.2
rebates of unearned charges, 5.9
regulatory chart, 3.3.1
rent-a-charter arrangements, 3.13
RESPA, 12.2.1.8
sample pleadings, Appx. L.7
state parity laws, 3.14
step-by-step guide, 3.2.2

subsidiaries and agents, rights, 3.4.6.4, 3.5.4
TILA, 3.12
VA loans, 3.8
  state opt-out, 3.8.2
visitorial powers of OCC, 3.4.6.3

FEDERAL REBATE STATUTE
enactment, 5.2.2
points, status under, 5.5.2.2.3
preemptive effect, 3.1.1, 5.9
remedies for violation, 5.7.3
text, Appx. J.2

FEDERAL RECEIVERS
equitable subordination, application, 10.7.8
FDIC, *see* FEDERAL DEPOSIT INSURANCE CORPORATION (FDIC)
RTC, *see* RESOLUTION TRUST CORPORATION (RTC)
special defenses, 10.7
tort claims against, 10.7.9

FEDERAL RESERVE SYSTEM
see also FEDERAL BANKING SYSTEM; NATIONAL BANKS
establishment, 2.3.1.2.1
FDIC, *see* FEDERAL DEPOSIT INSURANCE CORPORATION (FDIC)
state banks, participation, 2.3.1.2.1

FEDERAL SAVINGS AND LOAN INSURANCE CORPORATION (FSLIC)
see also FEDERAL HOME LOAN BANK SYSTEM
creation, 2.3.1.2.2

FEDERAL TORTS CLAIMS ACT (FTCA)
discretionary function exemption, 10.7.9
federal receivers, application, 10.7.9

FEDERAL TRADE COMMISSION (FTC)
credit practices rule, *see* CREDIT PRACTICES RULE (FTC)
holder rule, *see* HOLDER RULE (FTC)

FEDERAL RESERVE BOARD (FRB)
credit insurance, joint regulations, 8.4.1.5.2
DCAs, future regulation, 8.3.2.3
state banks, regulatory function, 3.7.1

FEDERALLY INSURED LENDERS
credit unions, *see* CREDIT UNIONS
DIDA
  application, 3.1.1. 3.3.1, 3.9.2
  overview, 3.9.1
  qualifying lenders, 3.9.3.3
  state opt-out, 3.9.4
FDIC regulation, 3.3.1
first mortgage preemption, 3.9.3
interest rate ceilings, 3.1.1, 3.9.2
  alternative interest ceiling, 3.9.2.1
  non-mortgage loans, 3.2.3.1
most favored lender status, 3.4.3.1, 3.9.2.1
national banks, *see* BANKS; NATIONAL BANKS
rate exportation, 3.9.2.2
  choice of laws, 3.9.2.2.2
  credit cards, 3.2.3.2
  generally, 3.9.2.2.1
savings and loan associations, *see* SAVINGS AND LOAN ASSOCIATIONS
state banks, *see* BANKS; STATE BANKS

FEES AND CHARGES
see also POINTS
attorney fees, *see* ATTORNEY FEES AND COSTS
bounce loans, 7.5.6
broker fees, *see* BROKER FEES
commitment fees, 7.2.2.3
credit card fees, 11.7.2.2
   industry practices, 11.7.1.2
   penalty rates, 11.7.2.3.1
default charges, *see* DEFAULT CHARGES
delinquency fees, *see* LATE CHARGES
document preparation fees, 7.2.1
earned at consummation, 5.5.2.2.2
excessive charges as kickbacks, 12.2.1.6
expressio unius principle, 9.3.1.2
finance charge, *see* FINANCE CHARGE
hidden fees, *see* HIDDEN INTEREST
interest status, 3.4.5.2, 5.5.2.2.2, 5.5.2.2.3, 10.5.4.3
late charges, *see* LATE CHARGES
non-interest charges, 7.2.1, 10.5.4.3
NSF charges, 3.4.5.2
overcharge and mark-up distinguished, 12.2.1.6
post-confirmation profiteering, 11.5.5
principal, addition to, 7.4.2
rate lock fees, 7.2.2.3
referral fees, 12.2.1.5
refinancings, additional, 6.4.2
rent-to-own transactions, 7.5.3.6.4
RESPA restrictions, 12.2.1.5, 12.2.1.6
RICO claims, 12.6
settlement services, 12.2.1.6
state restrictions, 7.2.1, 7.3.1
third party services
   attorney fees, 7.3.3
   broker fees, 7.3.2
   general principles, 7.3.1
unconscionability challenges, 12.7.2
unearned
   intent to collect, 5.7.2
   rebates, *see* REBATES
   RESPA prohibition, 12.2.1.5, 12.2.1.6
usurious loans, forfeiture, 10.8.2.2.1

FIDUCIARY DUTY
credit card abuses as breach of, 11.7.3.3
credit insurance, 8.7.2
   premium financing, 8.4.1.6
creditors, 12.9.3
described, 12.9.1
loan brokers, 11.5.4.2, 12.9.2
remedies for breach, 12.9.1
tax preparers, RALs as breach of, 7.5.4.2

FILED-RATE DOCTRINE
described, 8.4.2.1.5

FINANCE CHARGE
see also FEES AND CHARGES; INTEREST RATES; LOAN
   FEES; POINTS
bounce loan fees, status, 7.5.6
burying in amount financed, 7.4.6.1
defined, 4.4.1
discounts for cash, 7.4.6.2
hidden, *see* HIDDEN INTEREST
inclusions, 9.2.3.5

insurance premiums, exclusion, 8.4.1.5.1, 8.5.2.1, 8.5.2.2
late charge, distinguishing, 9.2.3.5
lender discounts as, 11.6.2.1
minimum finance charge, 4.6.6
non-filing insurance, exclusion, 7.3.1
TIL disclosures, 2.3.4, 4.4.1

FINANCE COMPANIES
see also LICENSED LENDERS; NON-DEPOSITORY
   CREDITORS
applicable law, 9.2.4.5
captive insurer policies, marketing, 8.2.2
close-connectedness doctrine, 10.6.1.2.1
fraud and misrepresentation claims, 12.10.1, 12.10.2
holder-in-due-course defense, 10.6.1.2.1, 10.6.1.3.8
industrial banks, *see* INDUSTRIAL BANKS
insurance premiums, *see* INSURANCE PREMIUM FINANCE
   COMPANIES
licensing requirements, 9.2.4.5
party-to-the-transaction doctrine, 10.6.1.2.1
payday lenders, involvement, 7.5.5.7
rate exportation, 3.2.3.2
refinancing practices, 2.3.2.3
regulatory history, 2.3.1.3.1
retail installment contracts, purchasing, 2.3.1.3.2
small loans, movement away from, 7.5.5.1

FINANCIAL ACCOUNTING STANDARDS BOARD
   (FASB)
loans fees, accounting standards, 5.5.2.2.2

FINANCIAL INSTITUTIONS REFORM, RECOVERY
   AND ENFORCEMENT ACT (FIRREA)
claims process against failed institutions, 10.7.10
D'Oench doctrine, codification, 10.7.2, 10.7.4.1
federal common law, application, 10.7.2
judicial interpretations, 10.7.8
limitations period, asserting by assignees, 10.7.6.3
preemptive status, 10.7.2
savings and loan bail-out, 3.9.4.3
section 1823(e), 10.7.4
   D'Oench differences, 10.7.4.6
   equitable considerations, 10.7.4.5
   inroads against, 10.7.8
   overview, 10.7.4.1
   requirements, 10.7.4.2, 10.7.4.4
   scope, 10.7.4.3

FIRST MORTGAGES
see MORTGAGES

FIXED-TERM CREDIT
see CLOSED-END CREDIT

FLIPPING OF LOANS
see LOAN-FLIPPING

FLIPPING OF PROPERTY
see PROPERTY FLIPPING

FORBEARANCE
see also LOANS
definition, 10.5.2.1, 10.5.2.3
detention of money distinguished, 10.5.2.3
necessary element of usury violation, 10.5.2.1
usury law, application, 10.5.2.3

FORCE-PLACED INSURANCE
see also CREDIT INSURANCE
excess coverage, 8.5.3.4.2
motor vehicles, 8.3.1.5.4
NAIC Model Act, 8.3.1.5.4
premiums, interest status, 3.4.5.2
UCCC application, 8.3.1.5.4
VSI, *see* VENDOR'S SINGLE INTEREST (VSI) INSURANCE

FORECLOSURE
see also MORTGAGES
duty of good faith and fair dealing, 12.8
electronic notices, validity, 9.2.10.2, 9.2.10.9
enjoining, 10.8.3
FHA, 12.8
home defense, practice tips, 6.5
misrepresentation claims, 12.10.2.4
post-consummation profiteering, 11.5.5
prevention strategies, 11.5
recoupment extending statute of limitations, 10.6.7
refinancing alternative, 6.5
usury defense, right to jury trial, 10.4
Veteran's Administration, 12.8

FORFEITURE
unlicensed lenders, 10.8.4.1
usurious loans, 10.8.2.2

FORGERY
fraud claims, 12.10.2.5

FORMULAS
see MATHEMATICAL FORMULAS

FRAUD CLAIMS
aiding and abetting, 12.10.1
appraisal fraud, 11.5.6
credit card abuses, 11.7.3.3
credit insurance
    excess coverage, 8.7.3.2
    ineligible borrowers, 8.5.5.3.2
liable conduct, 12.10.2
liable parties, 12.10.1
open-end credit, 9.2.3.2
prepayment penalties, 5.8.1
RALs, 7.5.4.2
RICO, 10.8.5.3, 12.6
willful blindness, 10.6.1.2.1

FRINGE LENDERS
see also LOAN-SHARKING; PREDATORY LENDERS;
    SUBPRIME LENDERS
auto title pawns, *see* AUTO TITLE LOANS
interest ceilings and, 2.4.1
payday loans, *see* PAYDAY LOANS
rent-to-own transactions, *see* RENT-TO-OWN (RTO)
    TRANSACTIONS
small loan market, 2.3.1.1
tax refund advances, *see* REFUND ANTICIPATION LOANS
    (RALs)
unconscionability, 12.7.2

FTC
see FEDERAL TRADE COMMISSION (FTC)

FTC CREDIT PRACTICES RULE
see CREDIT PRACTICES RULE (FTC)

FTC HOLDER RULE
see HOLDER RULE (FTC)

FURNITURE AND APPLIANCE LOANS
see APPLIANCE LOANS

GAP INSURANCE OR AGREEMENTS
see also DEBT CANCELLATION OR SUSPENSION
    AGREEMENTS (DCAs)
described, 8.3.2.3
hidden interest, 7.4.2
negative equity issues, 11.6.3

GOOD FAITH AND FAIR DEALING
credit card abuses, 11.7.3.3
duty, overview, 12.8
RALs as breach of duty, 7.5.4.2
UCC good faith, defined, 7.5.5.9.3

GOVERNMENT AGENCIES
see REGULATORY AGENCIES

GOVERNMENT BENEFITS
assignment to income buyers, 7.5.8.2

GRADUATED INTEREST
see SPLIT RATE INTEREST

GRAMM-LEACH-BLILEY ACT
banks, insurance activities
    application, 8.4.1.5.2
    regulations, Appx. I.2
insurance protections, selected provisions, Appx. I.1
interstate loan pricing parity, 3.11
overview, 3.1.1, 8.4.1.5.2
preemption of state credit insurance laws, 8.3.2.3, 8.4.1.5.2

**GUARANTEED AUTO PROTECTION (GAP) INSUR-
    ANCE**
see GAP INSURANCE OR AGREEMENTS

GUARANTORS
see ACCOMMODATION PARTIES

HIDDEN INTEREST
see also INTEREST; INTEREST RATES
agreed-rate transactions, 9.2.8.2
auto financing, dealer charges, 7.2.1, 7.4.2
auto title loans, 7.5.2.3
bounce loans, 7.5.6
check advancement loans, 7.5.5
checklist, fixed-term credit, 1.6.3.2.2
commissions or kickbacks, 7.3.1
commitment fees, 7.2.2.3
compensating balances, 7.4.4
credit insurance, 8.2.3.1, 8.5.1
credit sales
    disguised as leases, 7.5.3
    inflating sale price, 7.4.6.1, 11.6.2.1
    seller's points, 7.4.6.2
deferred presentment loans, 7.4.1, 7.5.5
defined, 7.1.1
deregulated states, 9.2.8.2
discounts, 7.4.2
equitable mortgages, 7.5.2.1
equity participation, 7.2.3
expressio unius principle, 9.3.1.2
fees based on creditor expenses, 7.2.1

HIDDEN INTEREST (*cont.*)
fraud claims, 12.10.2.4
GAP insurance, 7.4.2
income buyers, 7.5.8
inflated sale price, 7.4.6.1, 11.6.2.1
joint venture investments, 7.5.7
late fees, 7.2.4.2
leaseback agreements, 7.5.2
non-cash bonuses, 7.2.3
non-credit transactions, 7.5
payday loans, 7.5.5
payments for third party services
    attorney fees, 7.3.3
    broker fees, 7.3.2
    dealer fees, 7.2.1
    general principles, 7.3.1
payments not posted when received, 7.2.1
points, 7.2.2
principal overstated
    added fees, 7.4.2
    compensating balances, 7.4.4
    credit sales, 7.4.6
    generally, 7.4.1
    indexing, 7.4.5
    wraparound mortgages, 7.4.3
rate exportation, 7.1.2
rent-to-own transactions, 7.5.3.2
RICO remedies, 10.8.5.3
sale and repurchase agreements, 7.5.2
sample expert affidavit, Appx. L.2.3
side agreements, 7.2.3
tax refund schemes
    assignments, 7.5.4.1
    RALs, 7.5.4.2
tip-offs, 7.1.1
unconscionability challenges, 12.7.2
upcharges, 7.4.2
wraparound mortgages, 7.4.3

HIGH-COST MORTGAGES
see also HOME EQUITY LOANS; HOME OWNERSHIP AND
    EQUITY PROTECTION ACT (HOEPA); MORTGAGES
assignee liability, 10.6.1.2.3
balloon payments, 4.3.1.2
credit insurance financing, 8.7.4
federal preemption, 5.9
HOEPA, application, 5.2.4, 10.6.1.2.3, 12.2.2
holders-in-due course, 10.7.7
prepayment penalties, restrictions, 5.2.4, 5.8.2, 5.9
rescission, 10.8.5.2
Rule of 78, restrictions, 5.2.4, 5.4.2, 5.6.3.3.1
state law, 12.2.3
unconscionability challenges, 12.7.2
usury remedies, 10.8.5.2

HISTORICAL DEVELOPMENT
see LEGISLATIVE HISTORY

HOLDER RULE (FTC)
see also FEDERAL TRADE COMMISSION (FTC);
    HOLDERS-IN-DUE COURSE
generally, 10.6.1.2.2
home improvement financing, application, 11.5.2
limitations on, 10.7.7

HOLDERS-IN-DUE COURSE
close-connectedness doctrine, 10.6.1.2.1
defenses against, 10.6.1.2.1, 10.6.1.3.5, 10.6.1.3.9
    waiver of defense clauses, 10.6.1.3.10
electronic promissory notes, 10.6.1.1
equitable subordination, application, 10.7.8
exceptions, 10.6.1.1, 10.6.1.2, 10.7.7
FDIC, 10.7.5
federal holder-in-due course, *see* FEDERAL HOLDER-IN-DUE
    COURSE DOCTRINE
for value, 10.6.1.3.4
FTC rule, *see* HOLDER RULE (FTC)
good faith, 10.6.1.3.4, 10.6.1.3.8
high cost mortgages, 10.6.1.2.3, 10.7.7
home improvement creditors, 11.5.2
party-to-the-transaction doctrine, 10.6.1.2.1
preemption protections, application, 3.2.2.7
RTC, 10.7.5
subsequent transfers, shelter rule, 10.6.1.3.6
super holder-in-due course, *see* FEDERAL HOLDER-IN-DUE
    COURSE DOCTRINE
UCC rule, 10.6.1.3
    basic prerequisites, 10.6.1.3.1
    overview, 10.6.1.1
    waiver of defense clauses, 10.6.1.3.10
without notice, 10.6.1.3.4, 10.6.1.3.8

HOME DEFENSE
practice tips, 6.5
refinancing option, 6.5

HOME EQUITY LOANS
see also MORTGAGES; REAL ESTATE SECURITY
AMTPA, application, 2.4.2
balloon payments, 4.3.1.2
consolidation loans, 11.5.3
deregulation, 2.4.2
DIDA
    application, 2.4.2
    first lien preemption, 3.9.3.1, 3.9.3.2.1
equity-skimming, 11.5.1, 11.5.3
federal regulation, 2.3.3.7, 2.4.2, 5.2.4, 5.6.3.1
first lien status, obtaining, 3.9.3.2.1
fraud and misrepresentation claims, 12.10
high-cost, *see* HIGH-COST MORTGAGES
HOEPA, application, 2.3.3.7, 5.2.4
home improvements, *see* HOME IMPROVEMENT LOANS
licensed lenders, 9.2.4.5
loan-padding, 12.2.1.6
open-end account fees, interest status, 3.4.5.2
overreaching creditors, 11.5
predatory lenders, 11.5.1
rebate rules, 5.6.3.1
refinancing versus consolidation, 6.5
refinancings, 6.1.1.3, 11.5.3
regulatory history, 2.3.3.7
RESPA, application, 12.2.1.1
state regulation, 2.3.3.7, 5.6.3.1
title insurance, 8.3.2.2
transferable records, 10.6.1.3.7

HOME IMPROVEMENT CONTRACTORS
body-dragging, 9.2.3.3
credit repair laws, application, 11.5.2
fraud and misrepresentation claims, 12.10.2.2

HOME IMPROVEMENT CONTRACTORS (*cont.*)
lender liability, 11.5.2, 12.12
payments from mortgage proceeds, prohibition, 12.2.2.3
state regulation, 11.5.2
UDAP violations, 12.5

HOME IMPROVEMENT LOANS
see also HOME EQUITY LOANS; MORTGAGES
AARP model law, 2.3.3.5
fraud and misrepresentation claims, 12.10.2.2
FTC Holder rule, application, 11.5.2
licensing of lenders, 9.2.4.5
overreaching, challenging, 11.5.2
progress payments, 4.9
regulatory history, 2.3.3.7
state regulation, 11.5.2
   RISA-type statutes, 2.3.3.5

HOME LOAN BANKS
see SAVINGS AND LOAN ASSOCIATIONS

HOME LOANS
see HOME EQUITY LOANS; MORTGAGES

HOME OWNERS' LOAN ACT
history and purpose, 3.5.1
most favored lender doctrine, 3.5.2
OTS interpretive letters, Appx. D.3
overview, 3.1.1
preemption
   chart, 3.2.5
   field preemption, 3.5.3
   generally, 3.1.1, 3.2.4.1
   subsidiaries and, 3.5.4
selected provisions, Appx. D.1
selected regulations, Appx. D.2

**HOME OWNERSHIP AND EQUITY PROTECTION ACT
   (HOEPA)**
AMTPA, preemption, 3.10.1
covered mortgages, 12.2.2.2
credit insurance and DCAs, inclusion in calculations, 8.4.1.5.1
high cost mortgages, application, 5.2.4, 10.6.1.2.3
motivation, 2.4.2
open-end mortgages, application, 9.2.3.2
overview, 12.2.2.1
preemptive effect, 3.1.1, 3.10.1, 5.9
prepayment penalties, restrictions, 5.8.2
remedies, 12.2.2.1
RESPA disclosure, using to determine application, 12.2.1.2
Rule of 78, prohibition, 5.2.4, 5.4.2, 5.6.3.3.1
scope, 2.3.3.7, 10.6.1.2.3
substantive prohibitions, 12.2.2.3
violations, remedies, 10.8.5.2

HOME PURCHASE LOANS
see MORTGAGES

HOME SALES
fraud and misrepresentation claims, 12.10.2.3

HOME-SECURED CREDIT
see HOME EQUITY LOANS; MORTGAGES; REAL ESTATE
   SECURITY

HOMEOWNER'S PROTECTION ACT OF 1998
private mortgage insurance, application, 8.3.2.1

HOSPITALS
see CONVENIENCE CREDITORS

HOUSEHOLD GOODS
credit property insurance
   non-filing insurance, 8.5.4.5
   packing, 8.5.4.4
   restrictions, 8.5.3.4.1
non-purchase money security interests, 8.5.4.4

HOUSING CREDITORS
see also MORTGAGES; NATIONAL HOUSING ACT; REAL
   ESTATE SECURITY
AMTPA, application, 3.2.4.2, 3.10.1
applicable law, 3.3.1, 9.2.4.5
defined, 9.2.3.4
land installment contracts, 9.2.3.4
OTS regulations, compliance, 3.10.2
   mobile homes, 3.9.3.4, 5.2.3

HUD
see DEPARTMENT OF HOUSING AND URBAN
   DEVELOPMENT (HUD)

IMPLIED PRIVATE RIGHT OF ACTION
remedy, 10.8.2.1

IMPROVIDENT LENDING
HOEPA application, 12.2.2.3
refinancing, 11.5.3
UDAP application, 12.5
unconscionability, 12.7.3

INCOME BUYERS
government income, assignment, 7.5.8.2
hidden interest, 7.5.8
litigation finance companies, 7.5.8.3
lottery winnings, assignment, 7.5.8.2

INDEXING LOAN PRINCIPAL
hidden interest, 7.4.5

INDUSTRIAL BANKS
see also BANKS; FINANCE COMPANIES
historical development, 2.2.3.1
regulatory history, 2.3.1.2.1, 2.3.3.3

INDUSTRIAL LOAN LAWS
combined consumer finance acts, 2.3.3.2, 2.3.3.3
historical development, 2.2.3.1, 2.3.3.3

INDUSTRY PRACTICES
creditor defense, 10.6.9

INSTALLMENT CREDIT
see also CLOSED-END CREDIT; CREDIT SALES
assignment of contract, 2.3.1.3.2
convenience creditors, 2.3.1.3.3
electronic transactions, *see* ELECTRONIC CREDIT
   TRANSACTIONS
interest calculations, *see under* INTEREST CALCULATIONS
land contracts, *see* LAND INSTALLMENT CONTRACTS
late charges, *see* LATE CHARGES
MVRISAs, *see* MOTOR VEHICLE RETAIL INSTALLMENT
   SALES ACTS (MVRISAs)
precomputed interest, 4.5.3
refinancing, 2.3.2.3, 6.4.3
regulation, 2.3.1.3.2, 2.3.1.3.3
rent-to-own transactions as, 7.5.3.2

INSTALLMENT CREDIT (*cont.*)
retail sellers, 2.3.1.3.2
RISAs, *see* RETAIL INSTALLMENT SALES ACTS (RISAs)
security interests, *see* COLLATERAL; PERSONAL PROPERTY
          SECURITY INTERESTS
time-price doctrine, 2.2.2, 2.3.2.2
unequal payments, 4.6.2.1

INSTALLMENT LOAN LAWS
application, 2.3.3.4
interpretation, 9.3.1.1
MVRISAs, *see* MOTOR VEHICLE RETAIL INSTALLMENT
          SALES ACTS (MVRISAs)
RISAs, *see* RETAIL INSTALLMENT SALES ACTS (RISAs)

INSTALLMENT SALES
see CREDIT SALES; INSTALLMENT CREDIT; LAND
          INSTALLMENT CONTRACTS

INSURANCE
characteristics of, 8.5.4.5
credit insurance, *see* CREDIT INSURANCE
deposit insurance, *see* DEPOSIT INSURANCE
mortgage insurance, *see* PRIVATE MORTGAGE INSURANCE
          (PMI)
non-filing, *see* NON-FILING INSURANCE
packing, *see* INSURANCE PACKING
premiums, *see* INSURANCE PREMIUMS
rebates, *see* INSURANCE PREMIUM REBATES
twisting, 6.1.1.1

INSURANCE PACKING
see also CREDIT INSURANCE
credit property, 8.3.1.5.1
duplicative insurance, 8.5.4.4
equity-skimming tool, 8.5.4.2
generally, 8.5.2.4
loan-flipping and, 8.5.4.1, 8.5.4.3
non-credit insurance, 8.3.3, 8.5.4.3
non-filing insurance, 8.5.4.5
overview, 8.5.4.1
unnecessary collateral, 8.5.4.4

INSURANCE PREMIUM FINANCE COMPANIES
regulation, 8.4.1.6, 9.2.4.5

INSURANCE PREMIUM REBATES
see also INSURANCE PREMIUMS; REBATES
early termination, 5.4.1
generally, 8.6
precomputed premiums, 5.1
refinancings, 6.3.1, 6.3.2, 6.4.1.1
Rule of 78, use, 5.6.3.3.2
state law overview, 5.2.1

INSURANCE PREMIUMS
see also CREDIT INSURANCE
calculating
    accident and health, 8.5.3.1.3
    life insurance, 8.5.3.1.2
    property insurance, 8.5.3.1.4
compulsory premiums, 8.5.2.3
credit sales, regulation, 2.3.3.6
earned, state law, 6.4.1.1
excess charges as usury
    creditor compensation as interest, 8.5.3.2.2
    generally, 8.5.3.2.1

finance charge, exclusion, 8.4.2.5.1, 8.5.2.1, 8.5.2.2
finance companies, *see* INSURANCE PREMIUM FINANCE
          COMPANIES
hidden interest issues, 7.3.1
interest charged on, 8.2.2
interest checklist, 1.6.3.2.2
interest status, 8.5.1, 8.5.2.2, 8.5.2.3.1
loss-ratio rate regulation, 8.2.3.2
property insurance, regulation, 8.3.1.5.1
rate regulation
    challenging rates, 8.4.2.1.4
    deviations, 8.4.2.1.3
    generally, 8.4.2.1.1
    problems with rates, 8.4.2.1.2
rebates, *see* INSURANCE PREMIUM REBATES
refinancings, 6.1.1.2
state law regulation, 8.4.1.2, 8.4.1.3, 8.4.2.1
TIL disclosures, 8.4.1.5.1, 8.5.2.2

INTENT
see USURIOUS INTENT

INTEREST
see also FINANCE CHARGE
accrued interest, *see* ACCRUED INTEREST
actuarial interest, 4.3.1
add-on interest, 4.3.2
attorney fees, status, 7.3.3
bounce loan fees, status, 7.5.6
broker fees, status, 7.3.2
calculations, *see* INTEREST CALCULATIONS
checklist, fixed-term credit, 1.6.3.2.2
commitment fees, exclusion from, 7.2.2.3
common law restrictions, 9.3.1.1
compound interest, *see* COMPOUND INTEREST
credit insurance
    credit compensation, status, 8.5.3.2.2
    premiums, status, 8.5.1, 8.5.2.2, 8.5.2.3.1
defined, 7.2.1, 10.5.4.3
    exportation purposes, 3.4.5.2
    federal common law definition, 5.5.2.2.3
discount interest, 4.3.3
early attitudes toward, 2.2.1
equity participation as, 7.2.3
finance charge, distinction, 4.4.1
forfeiture, 10.8.2.2
hidden interest, *see* HIDDEN INTEREST
interest bearing transactions, 4.5.1
late fees as, 7.2.4.2
late fees in addition to, 4.8.1
open-end transactions, 2.3.3.8, 4.3.5
overcharge, necessary element of usury claim, 10.5.4
penalties, distinguished, 2.2.2
points as, 5.5.2.2.2, 5.5.2.2.3, 7.2.2.2
precomputed interest, 4.3.2, 4.3.3, 4.5.3
rates, *see* INTEREST RATES
scope of term
    exportation context, 3.4.5.2
    hidden interest context, 7.2
simple interest, 4.2, 4.3.1.1
split rate interest, 4.3.4
spreading, *see* SPREADING
state law definition, 4.4.1
state regulation, *see* USURY LAWS (STATE)
third party payments, status, 7.3.1

INTEREST (*cont.*)
time price, status, 2.3.2.2
unearned
    intent to collect, 5.7.2
    rebates, *see* UNEARNED INTEREST REBATES
unpaid, capitalization, 4.3.1.2
usurious, remedies, *see* USURY REMEDIES
what is interest, 7.2
yield-spread premium, 7.3.2

INTEREST-BEARING LOANS
see also CREDIT TRANSACTIONS; INTEREST; LOANS
compound interest, 4.6.1.1
described, 4.5.1
payment holidays, 4.8.3
prepayment penalties, 5.8.1
rebate issues, 5.4.1, 5.5.1
Rule of 78, use, 5.5.1
unearned interest, 5.4.1, 5.5.1

INTEREST CALCULATIONS
actuarial interest, 4.3.1
add-on interest, 4.3.2
APR, 4.4.2
bi-weekly mortgage payments, 4.6.7
compound interest, 4.6.1
daily accrual accounting
    application of payments, 4.6.8.3
    with compounding, 4.6.8.2
    without compounding, 4.6.8.1
daily interest rates, 4.6.3
discount interest, 4.3.3
distinctions between open and closed-end, 4.3.5.1
formulas, *see* MATHEMATICAL FORMULAS
generally, 4.3
installment credit, 4.3
interest bearing transactions, 4.5.1
odd payment amounts, 4.6.2
odd payment periods, 4.6.2
open-end methods, 4.3.5.2
overcharge issues, uncovering, 4.11.4
precomputed transactions, 4.3.2, 4.3.3, 4.5.3
rounding, 4.6.4
scheduled loans, 4.6.8.1
single payment transactions, 4.2
special problems, 4.6
split rate interest, 4.3.4
spreading, 4.6.5
variable rate transactions, 4.3.6.2

INTEREST CEILINGS
see also CRIMINAL USURY; INTEREST; INTEREST RATES
abolishing, 2.4.1
agreed-rate caps, 9.2.8.1, 9.2.8.2
alternative federal ceiling
    federally related lenders, 3.9.2.1, 3.9.4.3
    national banks, 3.4.2
    usury remedies under, 10.8.5.1
business credit, 9.2.2
checklist, fixed-term credit, 1.6.3.2.4
conflicts of law, 9.2.9
deregulated states, 9.2.1.3, 9.2.7, 9.2.8
deregulation of usury law, 2.4.1, 9.2.8.1
DIDA, *see* DEPOSITORY INSTITUTIONS DEREGULATION
    AND MONETARY CONTROL ACT (DIDA)

exportation, *see* RATE EXPORTATION
federal credit unions, 3.1.1, 3.6.2
federal preemption, *see* FEDERAL PREEMPTION
federal savings associations, 3.1.1, 3.5.2
federally-insured lenders, 3.1.1, 3.9.2.1, 3.9.4.3
FHA loans, 3.1.1, 3.8
floating ceilings, 9.3.2.2
historical developments, 2.2, 2.4.1
loan size, application, 9.2.5
minimum finance charge, interrelationship, 4.6.6
mobile home loans, 3.8.1, 3.9.3.4
mortgage loans, 2.4.2, 3.2.4.1, 3.9.3
national banks
    alternative federal ceiling, 3.4.2
    calculating ceiling, 3.4.4
    most favored lender doctrine, 3.4.3
    National Bank Act, 3.1.1, 3.4.1
non-mortgage loans
    interstate, 3.2.3.2
    intrastate, 3.2.3.1
open-end credit, 2.3.3.8
purpose, 2.4.1
refinanced loans, 6.4.3
retroactive effect, 9.3.2.1
spreading, 4.6.5.1
state banks, 3.7.2
unconscionability standards, 12.7.2
VA loans, 3.1.1, 3.8
variable ceilings, 9.3.2.2
variable rate transactions, 4.6.5.1
violations, *see* USURY VIOLATIONS

INTEREST RATES
see also ANNUAL PERCENTAGE RATE (APR); INTEREST
add-on and simple compared, 4.3.2
agreed-rate transactions
    · exceeding agreed cap, 9.2.8.1
    hidden interest, 9.2.8.2
alternative federal rate, 3.4.2
APR, distinction, 4.4.1
calculations, *see* INTEREST CALCULATIONS
caps, *see* INTEREST CEILINGS
credit cards, 2.3.2.3
    penalty rates, 11.7.2.3.1
daily interest, 4.6.3
default rate, 5.4.2, 7.2.4.1, 12.7.2
deregulation, *see* DEREGULATION
discount and add-on compared, 4.3.3
discount and simple compared, 4.3.3
exportation, *see* RATE EXPORTATION
federal discount rate, 3.4.2
federal credit unions, 3.6
federal savings associations, 3.5.2
federally-insured lenders, 3.9.2.1, 3.9.4.3
fixed-term transactions, 2.3.2.3
graduated rates, *see* SPLIT RATE INTEREST
interstate loan pricing, 3.11
lawful rate, determination, 10.8.2.4
national banks, 3.4.2, 3.4.4, 3.4.5
open-end transactions, 2.3.2.3, 2.3.3.8
overage, 11.5.4.3
overreaching, challenging, 11.1
rate lock fees, 7.2.2.3
rent-to-own (RTO) transactions, 7.5.3.6.2

INTEREST RATES (*cont.*)
risk-based justifications, 2.4.1, 11.3
scope of term for exportation purposes, 3.4.5.2
Servicemembers Civil Relief Act, 2.3.3.11
split rates, *see* SPLIT RATE INTEREST
state banks, 3.7.2
state law definition, 4.4.1
subprime market, 11.3
sucker-pricing, 2.4.1, 11.3
unconscionable, 12.7.2
upselling, 12.6
usurious, *see* USURY VIOLATIONS
variable rates, *see* VARIABLE RATE TRANSACTIONS
yield-spread premium, 11.5.4.3

INTERNET TRANSACTIONS
credit transactions, *see* ELECTRONIC CREDIT TRANSAC-
    TIONS
electronic fund transfers, *see* ELECTRONIC FUNDS
    TRANSFER ACT (EFTA)
long-arm jurisdiction, 10.2.2
payday loans disguised as, 7.5.5.4

INTERSTATE BANKING
see also BANKS; INTERSTATE TRANSACTIONS;
    NATIONAL BANKS
Gramm-Leach-Bliley Act, 3.11
IBBEA, *see* INTERSTATE BANKING AND BRANCHING
    EFFICIENCY ACT (IBBEA)
National Bank Act, *see* NATIONAL BANK ACT
rate exportation, 3.4.5, 3.9.2.2
state parity laws, 3.14.1

**INTERSTATE BANKING AND BRANCHING EFFI-
    CIENCY ACT (IBBEA)**
see also INTERSTATE BANKING
overview, 3.1.1
preemption application, 3.3.2
    national banks, 3.4.5.1.2, 3.4.6.1
    state banks, 3.7.3

INTERSTATE TRANSACTIONS
applicable usury law, 9.2.9
banking, *see* INTERSTATE BANKING
DIDA, application, 3.9.2.2
federal preemption of state laws, 3.2
    non-mortgage loans, 3.2.3.2
jurisdiction, 10.2

INVESTMENTS
loans distinguished, 7.5.7, 10.5.3

INVOLUNTARY UNEMPLOYMENT INSURANCE
see also DISABILITY INSURANCE
excessive cost, 8.3.1.4
no benefit insurance, 8.5.5.1
overview, 8.3.1.4

JOINT VENTURES
hidden interest issues, 7.2.3, 7.5.7
loan status, 7.5.7

JURISDICTION
bankruptcy court, 10.2.3.5
counterclaims, 10.2.3.5
court referrals to OCC, 3.4.6.3
federal court to review state court, 10.6.6
general jurisdiction, 10.2.1, 10.2.3.2

internet-based lenders, 10.2.2
long-arm jurisdiction, 10.2
    constitutional and statutory standards, 10.2.1
parent corporations, 10.2.1
preemption issues, 3.15
primary jurisdiction doctrine, 3.4.6.3
removal to federal court, 3.15
securitization trusts, 10.2.3
specific jurisdiction, 10.2.1, 10.2.3.3, 10.2.3.4

JURY TRIALS
usury claims, right to, 10.4

KICKBACKS
see also COMMISSIONS
broker fees, 7.3.2, 11.5.4.3, 12.2.1.5
excessive charges as, 12.2.1.6
hidden interest issues, 7.3.1, 7.3.2
HUD policy statement
    conflicting interpretations, 12.2.1.5.4
    first statement (1999), 12.2.1.5.3, Appx. K.3.1
    letter regarding, Appx. K.4.1
    second statement (2001), 12.2.1.5.5, Appx. K.3.2
    unearned or excessive fees, 12.2.1.6
intentional interference with contractual relationship, 12.9.4
RESPA prohibition, 12.2.1.5
RICO claims, 12.6
settlement charges, 12.2.1.6
yield spread premiums, status, 12.2.1.5.2, 12.2.1.5.5

LAND INSTALLMENT CONTRACTS
mortgages distinguished, 9.2.3.4
regulation of, 9.2.3.4

LATE CHARGES
see also DEFAULT CHARGES; FEES AND CHARGES
calculation, 4.8.1
credit cards, 11.7.2.2.2
daily interest and, 4.8.1
finance charge, distinguishing, 9.2.3.5
generally, 7.2.4.1
hidden interest, 7.2.4.2
imposing, 7.2.4.1
interest status, 5.5.2.2.3, 7.2.4.2, 10.5.2.3
partial payments, 4.8.1
precomputed transactions, 4.5.3
pyramiding, 4.8.1, 7.2.4.3
refinancings, inclusion, 6.3.1, 6.3.2
usurious loans, forfeiture, 10.8.2.2.1

LAWYERS
see ATTORNEY FEES AND COSTS; CONVENIENCE
    CREDITORS

LEASEBACK AGREEMENTS
see also LEASES; SALE AND REPURCHASE AGREEMENTS
auto pawn transactions, 7.5.2.3.2
equitable mortgages, 7.5.2.1
hidden interest, 7.5.2
payday loans disguised as, 7.5.5.4
personal property, 7.5.2.2

LEASES
see also LEASEBACK AGREEMENTS
credit sales disguised as, 7.5.3.1
rent-to-own transactions, *see* RENT-TO-OWN (RTO)
    TRANSACTIONS

References are to sections

LEGAL FEES
see ATTORNEY FEES AND COSTS

LEGISLATIVE HISTORY
credit sales, 2.2.3.2
DIDA, 3.9.1
early attitudes toward interest, 2.2.1
exemptions, 2.2.3.1
federal home loan bank system, 2.3.1.2.2
general laws, 2.2.2
Home Owners' Loan Act, 3.5.1
industrial banks, 2.2.3.1
National Bank Act, 3.4.1
small loans, 2.2.3.1
special laws, 2.2.3
statutory interpretation, use, 9.3.1.1

LENDER PARTICIPATION MORTGAGES
see also MORTGAGES
hidden interest issues, 7.2.3

LENDERS
see CORRESPONDENT LENDERS; CREDITORS;
    DEPOSITORY CREDITORS (STATE); FEDERAL
    LENDERS; FEDERALLY INSURED LENDERS;
    LICENSED LENDERS; MOST FAVORED LENDER
    DOCTRINE; PREDATORY LENDERS

LIABILITY
assignees, 10.6.1, 12.12
checklists, 12.12
close-connection liability, 10.6.1.2.1, 12.12
collection agencies, 10.6.2
credit insurance benefits, 8.5.5.3
credit insurance overcharges, 8.5.3.2.1
derivative liability, 12.12
duty of due care, 12.11.1
estoppel, 12.11.2
fiduciaries, 12.9.1
fraud, 12.10.1
holders in due course, 10.6.1
lenders for third party actions, 12.12
misrepresentation, 12.10.1

LIABILITY DAMAGE WAIVERS (LDW)
rent-to-own transactions, 7.5.3.6.4

LICENSED LENDERS
see also CREDITORS; NON-DEPOSITORY CREDITORS
applicable law, 9.2.4.5
credit insurance sales, 8.4.2.2.2
examples, 9.2.4.5
failure to obtain license, 9.2.4.6, 10.8.4
   voiding of contract, 10.3.2, 10.8.2.1, 10.8.4.1
finance companies, *see* FINANCE COMPANIES
housing creditors, AMTPA, application, 3.2.4.2
non-depository lenders, 9.2.4.5
payday loans, 7.5.5.2
RALs, 7.5.4.2
regulatory history, 2.3.1.3.1
small loan laws, 2.3.3.2
usury laws, application, 9.2.4.5
violation of licensure statute, 10.8.4.2

LIENS
see HOME EQUITY LOANS; MORTGAGES; SECURITY
    INTERESTS

LIFE INSURANCE
see CREDIT LIFE INSURANCE

LIMITATIONS
see STATUTE OF LIMITATIONS

LINES OF CREDIT
see also OPEN-END CREDIT
masked closed-end credit, 9.2.3.2
notes, negotiable instrument status, 10.6.1.3
payday loans marketed as, 7.5.5.6

LIQUIDATED DAMAGES
late fees as, 7.2.4.2

LITIGATION FINANCE COMPANIES
disguised loans, 7.5.8.3

LOAN BALANCES
see also LOANS; PRINCIPAL AMOUNT
compensating balances, 7.4.4
declining balance, 4.3.1.1
increasing balance, 4.3.1.2
interest-only loans, 4.3.1.2
non-amortizing loans, 4.3.1.2
open-end credit
   adjusted balance, 4.3.5
   ending balance, 4.3.5
   modified average daily balance, 4.3.5
   previous balance, 4.3.5
   straight average daily balance, 4.3.5
   true actuarial average daily balance, 4.3.5

LOAN BROKERS
see also BROKER FEES
claims against, 11.5.4.3
fees as hidden interest, 7.3.2
fiduciary duty, 11.5.4.2, 12.9.2
intentional interference with contractual relationship, 12.9.4
kickbacks, 12.2.1.5
legal status, 11.5.4.2
lender liability for acts of, 12.12
referral fees, 12.2.1.5
RESPA disclosures, 12.2.1.2
RICO claims, 12.6
role, 11.5.4.1
state mortgage broker laws, Appx. B
state regulation, 11.5.4.3
UDAP violations, 12.5
yield-spread premiums, 7.3.2, 11.5.4.3, 11.6.6, 12.2.1.5.2

LOAN FEES
see also FEES AND CHARGES; POINTS
document preparation fees, 7.2.1
FASB accounting standards, 5.5.2.2.2
hidden interest, 7.2.1
refinancings, 6.4.2

LOAN-FLIPPING
see also REFINANCING
definition of flipping, 6.1.3
equity-skimmers, 6.1.1.3
fraud claims, 12.10.2.4
insurance packing and, 8.5.4.1, 8.5.4.3
refinancing, generally, 6.1.1.1
RICO claims, 12.6
small loan example, 6.1.1.2
unconscionability, 12.7.4

LOAN-PACKING
see LOAN-PADDING

LOAN-PADDING
credit insurance, *see* INSURANCE PACKING
fraud claims, 12.10.2.4
settlement services, 12.2.1.6
UDAP violations, 12.5
unconscionability challenges, 12.7.4
used car financing, 11.6.2.2, 11.6.4
usury restrictions, 9.2.5.3

LOAN-SHARKING
see also PREDATORY LENDERS
historical perspective, 2.2.3.1, 2.3.3.2, 2.3.3.3
RICO, application, 10.8.5.3.5
usury ceilings as means of preventing, 2.4.1

LOAN-SPLITTING
sample expert testimony, Appx. L.2.4
usury restrictions, 9.2.5.2

LOANS
see also CREDIT TRANSACTIONS
amortized, *see* AMORTIZED LOANS
assignee defenses, 10.6.1
auto-secured, *see* AUTO-SECURED LOANS
balance unpaid, *see* LOAN BALANCES
bounce loans, 7.5.6
business loans, *see* BUSINESS LOANS
check advancement, *see* PAYDAY LOANS
consolidation, *see* CONSOLIDATION OF LOANS
credit sales disguised as, 9.2.3.3
definition, 10.5.2.1, 10.5.2.2.1
discrimination, 11.3, 12.3
disguised as credit sales, 10.5.2.2.1
federal preemption of state laws, *see* FEDERAL PREEMPTION
fixed-term, *see* CLOSED-END CREDIT
flipping, *see* LOAN-FLIPPING; REFINANCING
forbearance, *see* FORBEARANCE
FTC Holder Rule, application, 10.6.1.2.2
home equity loans, *see* HOME EQUITY LOANS
home improvement loans, *see* HOME IMPROVEMENT LOANS
income buyers, 7.5.8
industrial banks, *see* INDUSTRIAL BANKS
installment loans, *see* INSTALLMENT LOAN LAWS
interest on, *see* INTEREST
interest-bearing loans, *see* INTEREST-BEARING LOANS
interest-only, 4.3.1.2
investments distinguished, 7.5.7, 10.5.3
joint ventures as, 7.5.7
level term insurance, restrictions, 8.3.1.2
litigation finance, 7.5.8.3
mortgage loans, *see* MORTGAGES
necessary element of usury violation, 10.5.2.1
non-amortizing loans, 4.3.1.2
novation, 6.2.3
payday loans, *see* PAYDAY LOANS
payment holidays, 4.8.3
penalties, *see* PENALTIES
post-confirmation profiteering, 11.5.5
post-dated check loans, *see* PAYDAY LOANS
precomputed loans, *see* PRECOMPUTED LOANS
principal amount, *see* PRINCIPAL
real property secured, *see* MORTGAGES; REAL ESTATE SECURITY

refinancing, *see* REFINANCING
Refund Anticipation Loans, *see* REFUND ANTICIPATION LOANS (RALs)
repayment obligation, absolute vs. contingent, 7.5.7, 10.5.3
sale of goods on credit, status, 2.2.2, 2.3.2.2
savings and loan associations, *see* SAVINGS AND LOAN ASSOCIATIONS
scheduled loans, 4.6.8.1
size determinations, 9.2.5
small loan lenders, *see* SMALL LOAN LENDERS
state regulation, 2.1, 2.2.2, 2.3.3
stretching the term, 6.1.1.2
table-funded loans, *see* TABLE-FUNDED LOANS
tax refund schemes as, 7.5.4.1
type of loan, identifying, 3.2.2.3
UDAP violations, 12.5
unconscionability, 12.7
unequal payments, 4.6.2.1
usurious
    renewal, 6.2
    voiding, 10.8.2.2, 10.8.2.3
usury laws
    application, 9.2.1.2, 10.5.2.2.1
    historical development, 2.2.3.1
variable rate, *see* VARIABLE RATE TRANSACTIONS

LOSS-OF-INCOME INSURANCE
see INVOLUNTARY UNEMPLOYMENT INSURANCE

LOTTERY WINNINGS
assignment to income buyers, 7.5.8.2

MARKETPLACE
see CREDIT MARKETPLACE

MATHEMATICAL FORMULAS
actuarial interest, 4.3.1.1, 5.6.3.4.2
add-on interest, 4.3.2
adjusted balance, 4.3.5
determining to prove mathematical issues, 4.10
disability insurance rates, 8.5.3.1.3
discount interest, 4.3.3
ending balance, 4.3.5
life insurance rates, 8.5.3.1.2
modified average daily balance, 4.3.5
one payment transactions, 4.2
previous balance, 4.3.5
pro rata formula, 5.6.3.2
property insurance, 8.5.3.1.4
rebates, 5.6.3
Rule of 78, 5.6.3.3.2
straight average daily balance, 4.3.5
sum of the balances, 5.6.3.3.4
true actuarial average daily balance, 4.3.5

MCCARRAN-FERGUSON ACT
credit insurance, application, 8.5.2.7.2
    arbitration clauses, 10.3.6.1
RESPA, relationship, 12.2.1.8

MERCHANTS
see RETAIL SELLERS

MISREPRESENTATION
appraisal fraud, 11.5.6, 12.10.2.5
credit insurance, excess coverage, 8.7.3.2
false contractual statements, 10.6.4.3

MISREPRESENTATION (*cont.*)
liable conduct, 12.10.2
liable parties, 12.10.1
loan brokers, 11.5.4.3
oral representations contradicted by loan documents, 12.10.2.7
negligent misrepresentation, 12.10.2.6
property flipping schemes, 11.5.6
RALs, 7.5.4.2

MOBILE HOME LOANS
AMTPA, application, 3.2.4.2
DIDA preemption, application, 3.9.3.4, 5.2.3
  qualifying lenders, 3.9.3.3
FHA loans, 3.8.1
OTS regulations, compliance, 3.9.3.4, 5.2.3
VA loans, 3.8.1

MODEL ACTS (NAIC)
see NAIC MODEL ACTS

MODIFIED AVERAGE DAILY BALANCE
see also LOAN BALANCES
open-end credit calculations, 4.3.5

MORRIS PLAN
industrial bank loans, 2.2.3.1, 2.3.3.3

MORTGAGE BROKERS
see LOAN BROKERS

MORTGAGES
see also HOME EQUITY LOANS; REAL ESTATE SECURITY
alternative mortgage transactions, 3.10.1
AMTPA, *see* ALTERNATIVE MORTGAGE TRANSACTIONS
      PARITY ACT (AMTPA)
applicable laws, checklist, 1.6.3.1.3, 1.6.3.1.4
ARMs, *see* ADJUSTABLE RATE MORTGAGES (ARMs)
balloon payments, 4.3.1.2
biweekly mortgage payments, 4.6.7
DCAs, regulations, 8.3.2.3
deregulation, 2.4.2
due-on-sale clauses, 5.8.3
equitable mortgages, 7.5.2.1
federal lenders, 5.8.3
federal preemption of state laws
    DIDA, 3.2.4.1, 3.9.3, 3.9.4.2
    first lien preemption, 3.9.3
    interest rates and charges, 3.2.4.1
    other contract terms, 3.2.4.2
high cost mortgages, *see* HIGH-COST MORTGAGES
HOEPA, application, 3.2.4.2, 5.2.4, 12.2.2.2
insurance, *see* PRIVATE MORTGAGE INSURANCE (PMI)
interest calculations, *see* INTEREST CALCULATIONS
interest ceilings, 2.4.2, 3.9.3
land installment contracts distinguished, 9.2.3.4
lender participation mortgages, 7.2.3
mobile homes, 3.9.3.4
payoff statement fees, 5.8.1
pools, 2.4.2
post-consummation profiteering, 11.5.5
prepayment penalties, 5.2.4, 5.8.2, 5.8.3
refinancing as foreclosure alternative, 6.5
RESPA, application, 12.2.1.1
reverse mortgages, *see* REVERSE MORTGAGES
Rule of 78, restrictions, 5.2.4, 5.4.2, 5.6.3.3.1
scheduled mortgages, 4.6.8.1
second mortgages, *see* HOME EQUITY LOANS

securitization, 2.4.2, 11.4
servicer obligations, 12.2.1.3
side agreements as hidden interest, 7.2.3
spurious open-end mortgages, 9.2.3.2
title insurance
    generally, 8.3.2.2
    steering by seller, 12.2.1.7
transferable records, 10.6.1.3.7
unconscionability, 12.7.2
variable rate, *see* ADJUSTABLE RATE MORTGAGES (ARMs)
wraparound mortgages, 7.4.3

MOST FAVORED LENDER DOCTRINE
see also FEDERAL PREEMPTION
federal credit unions, 3.6.2
federal savings associations, 3.5.2
federally-insured lenders
    application, 3.4.3.1
    DIDA extension, 3.9.2.1
    state opt-out, 3.9.4.3
national banks
    competing lender limitations, 3.4.3.2
    exportation, 3.4.5.1.1
    generally, 3.4.3.1
    material state restrictions, 3.4.3.4
    state lender limitations, 3.4.3.3
state banks, 3.7.2
state parity law interaction, 3.4.3.3, 3.14.3

MOTOR VEHICLE CREDIT INSURANCE
see also CREDIT INSURANCE; CREDIT PROPERTY
      INSURANCE
force-placed insurance, 8.3.1.5.4
special issues, 8.3.1.5.4

MOTOR VEHICLE RETAIL INSTALLMENT SALES
      ACTS (MVRISAs)
see also AUTO-SECURED LOANS; CREDIT SALES;
      INSTALLMENT CREDIT; INSTALLMENT LOAN
      LAWS; RETAIL INSTALLMENT SALES ACTS (RISAs)
body-dragging, application, 9.2.3.3
historical development, 2.2.3.2
installment contracts, regulation, 2.3.1.3.2
interpretation, 9.3.1.1
RTO transactions, application, 7.5.3.6.7
scope, 2.3.3.5
"single document rule," 11.6.8

NAIC MODEL ACTS
see also NATIONAL ASSOCIATION OF INSURANCE
      COMMISSIONERS (NAIC)
credit insurance
    choice of insurers, 8.5.2.3.2, 8.5.2.6
    creditor-placed insurance, 8.3.1.5.4
    excess premiums, 8.5.3.2.1
    life and disability, 8.4.2.2.1, 8.5.3.1.2, 8.5.3.3.1
    long-term transactions, application, 8.4.2.2.1
    non-rate regulation, 8.4.2.2.1
    personal property, 8.3.1.5.1, 8.4.2.2.1, 8.5.3.1.4
    rate regulation, 8.4.2.1.1
    rebates, 8.6
    surpluses, 8.5.6
    title insurance, 8.3.2.2
state adoption, 8.4.1.2
UNIP, *see* UNFAIR INSURANCE TRADE PRACTICES ACT
      (UNIP)

**NATIONAL ASSOCIATION OF INSURANCE COMMIS-
SIONERS (NAIC)**
consumer complaints, 8.3.1.1
loss ratios, compilation, 8.2.3.2
model acts, *see* NAIC MODEL ACTS

**NATIONAL AUTOMATED CLEARING HOUSE
ASSOCIATION (NACHA)**
payday loan repayment, application, 7.5.5.9.1
    preauthorized transfers, stop payments, 7.5.5.9.6
    re-presentment of checks, 7.5.5.9.2, 7.5.5.9.4
    unauthorized payments, 7.5.5.9.7

NATIONAL AUTOMOBILE DEALERS ASSOCIATION
differential interest rate pricing, explanation, 11.6.6

NATIONAL BANK ACT
alternative interest ceilings, calculating, 3.4.2
EFTA, relationship, 3.4.5.1.2
history and purpose, 3.4.1
most favored lender doctrine, 3.4.3
    state banks, application, 3.7.2
OCC interpretive and advisory letters, Appx. C.3
overview, 3.1.1
preemption
    agency regulations, 3.3.2
    chart, 3.2.5
    conflict preemption, 3.4.6.1
    generally, 3.1.1
    interest rates and charges, 3.2.4.1
    OCC determinations, Appx. C.4
    OCC regulations, 3.4.6, Appx. C.2
selected provisions, Appx. C.1
selected regulations, Appx. C.2
usury remedies, 10.8.5.1

NATIONAL BANKS
see also BANKS; FEDERAL BANKING SYSTEM; FEDERAL
    LENDERS; NATIONAL BANK ACT
ATM fees, 3.4.5.1.2
competing lender rule, 3.4.3.2, 3.4.3.3
interstate banking, 3.4.5
failed banks, *see under* BANKS
location, determination, 3.4.5.1.2
mortgage loans, federal preemption, 3.2.4
most favored lender status, 3.4.3
    competing lender limitations, 3.4.3.2
    exportation, 3.4.5.1.1
    generally, 3.4.3.1
    material state restrictions, 3.4.3.4
    state lender limitations, 3.4.3.3
OCC regulation, 3.3.1, Appx. C.2
    visitorial powers, 3.4.6.3
operating subsidiaries, 3.4.6.4
payday lenders, involvement, 3.13, 7.5.5.7
private actions against, 3.4.6.3
rate ceiling
    alternate ceiling, calculating, 3.4.2
    calculating, 3.4.4
    generally, 3.1.1
    mortgage loans, 3.2.4.1
rate exportation
    assignee status, effect, 3.4.5.1.3
    background, 3.4.5.1
    credit cards, 3.2.3.2
    location role, 3.4.5.1.2

scope of term "interest rate", 3.4.5.2
regulatory history, 2.3.1.2.1
reporting requirements, 3.5.6.4
state law, application, 3.4.6
    subsidiaries, 3.4.6.4
usurious loans, remedies, 10.8.5.1

NATIONAL CLEARINGHOUSE FOR LEGAL SERVICES
see SARGENT SHRIVER NATIONAL CENTER ON
    POVERTY LAW

NATIONAL CREDIT UNION ACT
see FEDERAL CREDIT UNION ACT

NATIONAL CREDIT UNION ADMINISTRATION (NCUA)
see also CREDIT UNIONS
interest rate ceiling, 3.1.1
interpretations
    deference, 3.3.2, 9.3.1.3
    publication for comment, 3.3.2, 3.4.6.1
interpretative letters, Appx. E.3
    preemption, 3.6.3
mortgage regulations, 3.10.2
regulations, selected text, Appx. E.2
regulatory function, 3.3.1, 3.6.1

NATIONAL CREDIT UNION SHARE INSURANCE FUND
see also CREDIT UNIONS
creation, 3.6.1
participation, 2.3.1.2.3

NATIONAL HOUSING ACT
see also HOUSING CREDITORS; FEDERAL HOUSING
    ADMINISTRATION (FHA) LOANS; VETERANS
    ADMINISTRATION (VA) LOANS
overview, 3.1.1

NEGATIVE AMORTIZATION
see also AMORTIZATION; BALLOON PAYMENTS
ARMs, 4.3.1.2
credit card minimum payments, 11.7.2.3.4
described, 4.3.1.2

NEGATIVE EQUITY
auto financing, 11.6.3

NEGLIGENCE
see also TORT CLAIMS
misrepresentations, 12.10.2.6

NEGOTIABLE INSTRUMENTS
allonges, 10.6.1.3.2
assignees, holder status, 10.6.1.3.2
checks, *see* CHECKS
creditors, accepting, 10.6.1.2.2
electronic instruments, 9.2.10.2, 10.6.1.1, 10.6.1.3.7
FTC holder notice, 10.6.1.2.2
holders-in-due course, *see* HOLDERS-IN-DUE COURSE
payable at "a definite time", 10.6.1.3.3
promissory notes, *see* PROMISSORY NOTES
qualifying endorsement, 10.6.1.3.2
requirements, 10.6.1.3.3
subsequent transferees, rights, 10.6.1.3.6
transferable records, 10.6.1.3.7

NON-DEPOSITORY CREDITORS
see also CREDITORS
convenience creditors, *see* CONVENIENCE CREDITORS
depository creditors, distinction, 2.3.1.1

NON-DEPOSITORY CREDITORS (*cont.*)
finance companies, *see* FINANCE COMPANIES
housing creditors, *see* HOUSING CREDITORS
licensed lenders, *see* LICENSED LENDERS
mortgage loans, AMTPA, application, 3.2.4.2
retail sellers, *see* RETAIL SELLERS
usury laws, application, 9.2.4.2, 9.2.4.5

NON-FILING INSURANCE
finance charge, exclusion, 7.3.1
hidden interest issues, 7.3.1
packing issues, 8.5.4.5

NOT SUFFICIENT FUNDS (NSF)
see also BOUNCED CHECKS
bank fees, interest status, 3.4.5.2

NOTICE
see also DISCLOSURE
adverse action, ECOA requirement, 12.3.2
electronic notices, 9.2.10.2, 9.2.10.9
FTC Holder Rule, 10.6.1.2.2
high cost mortgages, assignee liability, 10.6.1.2.3

NOVATION
concept discussed, 6.2.3
renewal distinguished, 6.2.3

OCC
see OFFICE OF THE COMPTROLLER OF THE CURRENCY
    (OCC)

ODD PAYMENTS
bi-weekly periods, 4.6.2.2, 4.6.7
generally, 4.6.2.1
weekly periods, 4.6.2.2

OFFICE OF THE COMPTROLLER OF THE CURRENCY
    (OCC)
see also NATIONAL BANKS
auto title loans, advisory letter, 7.5.2.3.5
credit insurance, joint regulations, 8.4.1.5.2, Appx. I.2.1
DCAs regulations, 8.3.2.3
interpretations
    deference, 3.3.2, 3.4.6.1, 9.3.1.3
    publication for comment, 3.3.2, 3.4.6.1
interpretive letters
    preemption doctrine, 3.4.6.1
    rate exportation, 3.4.5.1.2, 3.4.5.2
    text, Appx. C.3
interpretive rulings
    interest, 3.4.5.2
    preemption, Appx. C.4
mortgage regulations, 3.10.2
payday lenders, advisory letter, 3.13.3
preemption regulations
    broad 2004 regulations, 3.4.6.2
    payday lending, 3.13.3
    pre 2004, 3.4.6.1
    subsidiaries, 3.4.6.4
    text, Appx. C.2
RAL regulations, 7.5.4.2
regulatory function, 3.3.1
    visitorial powers, 3.4.6.3
regulations
    credit insurance, Appx. I.2.1
    preemption, 3.4.6

state banks, application, 3.7.3, 3.10.2
text, Appx. C.2
rent-a-charter arrangements, regulation, 3.13.3

OFFICE OF THRIFT SUPERVISION (OTS)
see also SAVINGS AND LOAN ASSOCIATIONS
credit insurance, joint regulations, 8.4.1.5.2, Appx. I.2.4
interest rate ceiling, 3.1.1
interpretations
    deference, 3.3.2, 9.3.1.3
    publication for comment, 3.3.2, 3.4.6.1
interpretive letters
    agents and preemption, 3.5.4
    HOLA, Appx. D.3
mobile home regulations, DIDA compliance requirement,
    3.9.3.4, 5.2.3
mortgage regulations, 3.10.2
payday lenders, advisory letter, 3.13.3
prepayment regulations, 5.8.3
regulations
    application to mortgage lenders, 3.3.1
    application to state lenders, 9.2.4.5
    credit insurance, Appx. I.2.4
    HOLA, Appx. D.2
    preemptive effect, 3.5.3
regulatory function, 2.3.1.2.2, 3.3.1
rent-a-charter arrangements, guidelines, 3.13.3
state housing creditors, regulation, 3.10.2
subsidiaries and preemption, regulations, 3.5.4

OIL COMPANIES
see CONVENIENCE CREDITORS

***O'MELVENY* DECISION**
FIRREA preemption, 10.7.2

OPEN-END CREDIT
see also CREDIT TRANSACTIONS
auto pawns disguised as, 7.5.2.3.4
closed-end, distinction, 2.3.2.3, 9.2.3.2
credit cards, *see* CREDIT CARD ACCOUNTS
fraud claims, 9.2.3.2, 12.10.2.4
HOEPA, application, 12.2.2.2
interest calculations
    closed-end differences, 4.3.5.1
    legal treatment of methods, 4.3.5.3
    methods of calculating, 4.3.5.2
    spreading, 4.6.5.2
lines of credit, *see* LINES OF CREDIT
regulatory history, 2.3.2.3, 2.3.3.8
retailers, 2.3.1.3.2
UDAP claims, 9.2.3.2
usury laws, application, 9.2.3.2

ORIGINATION FEES
see also POINTS
hidden interest, 7.2.2.1

OTS
see OFFICE OF THRIFT SUPERVISION (OTS)

OVERDRAFT PROTECTION
bounce loans, 7.5.6

OVERDUE CHARGES
see DEFAULT CHARGES; LATE CHARGES

PARITY LAWS (STATE)
constitutionality, 3.14.1
described, 3.14.1
impact, 3.1.1, 3.14.2
most favored lender interaction, 3.4.3.3, 3.14.3
state banks, application, 3.7.4

PAWNBROKING
auto-pawning, 2.5, 7.5.2.3
licensing requirements, 9.2.4.5
sale and repurchase agreements as, 7.5.2.2
state regulation, 2.3.3.9

PAYDAY LOANS
see also FRINGE LENDERS; LOAN-SHARKING
arbitration clauses, 7.5.5.8
bank partnerships, 3.13, 7.5.5.7
checks, repayment by, 7.5.5.9
    applicable law, 7.5.5.9.1
    postdated checks, early presentment, 7.5.5.9.5
    re-presentment, 7.5.5.9.3, 7.5.5.9.4
    right to stop payment, 7.5.5.9.6
    unauthorized payments, 7.5.5.9.7
described, 7.5.5.3
deregulation, effect, 2.4.1
electronic fund transfers, 7.5.5.9
    applicable law, 7.5.5.9.1
    conditioning loan on repayment by, 7.5.5.9.2
    preauthorized transfers, 7.5.5.9.2, 7.5.5.9.6
    right to stop payment, 7.5.5.9.6
    unauthorized transfers, 7.5.5.9.4, 7.5.5.9.7
hidden interest, 7.4.1, 7.5.5
historically, 2.2.3.1, 2.3.1.1, 7.5.5.1
overview of industry, 7.5.5.1, 7.5.5.2, 7.5.5.3
post-deregulation, 2.5
remedies, 7.5.5.6
rent-a-charter arrangements, 3.13, 7.5.5.7
revolving loan status, 9.2.3.2
RICO claims, 7.5.5.6, 10.8.5.3.5, 12.6
sample pleadings
    complaint, Appx. L.3.1
    discovery, Appx. L.3.2
state regulation, 7.5.5.5
types of abuses, 7.5.5.4
UDAP violations, 12.5

PAYMENT PACKING
see also LOAN-PADDING
auto financing, 11.6.4

PAYMENTS
see also PAYMENT PACKING
balloon payments, *see* BALLOON PAYMENTS
failure to post on date received, 7.2.1
holiday from, effect, 4.8.3
odd payments, *see* ODD PAYMENTS
prepayment, *see* PREPAYMENT
third party payments, *see under* THIRD PARTIES

PAYOFF STATEMENTS
fees as prepayment penalty, 5.8.1

PENALTIES
interest, distinguished, 2.2.2
late payments, *see* LATE CHARGES
prepayment, *see* PREPAYMENT PENALTIES

usury violations, *see* STATUTORY PENALTIES

PENALTY RATES
credit cards, 11.7.2.3.1

PERSONAL PROPERTY SECURITY INTERESTS
see also COLLATERAL; SECURITY INTERESTS
non-filing insurance, 7.3.1

PLEADINGS
sample amicus brief, Appx. L.7.1
sample answer and counterclaim, Appx. L.1.1
sample complaints
    disguised credit, Appx. L.3.1
    loan padding and flipping, Appx. L.2.1
    RALs, Appx. L.5.1
    rent-a-bank, Appx. L.4.1, Appx. L.4.2
    RESPA, Appx. L.7.2, Appx. L.7.3
sample expert affidavit, Appx. L.2.3
usurious charges in, 10.5.4.2

PMI
see PRIVATE MORTGAGE INSURANCE (PMI)

POINTS
see also FEES AND CHARGES; LOAN FEES; SERVICE
        CHARGES
abusive use, attacking, 5.5.2.3
agreed-rate transactions, 9.2.8.2
calculation
    described, 4.7.1
    legal issues arising, 4.7.2
compounding, 4.6.1.1
earned at consummation, 5.5.2.2.2, 7.2.2.1
exclusion from interest, 7.2.2.2
FASB accounting standards, 5.5.2.2.2
hidden interest, 7.2.2.1, 7.2.2.2, 9.2.8.2
interest status, 5.5.2.2.2, 5.5.2.2.3, 9.2.8.2
rebate issues, 5.4.1, 5.5.2.2
refinancings
    calculating, 4.7.2
    evaluating benefits, 6.5
    non-rebatable charges, 6.3.1, 6.4.1.3
seller's points as hidden interest, 7.4.6.2
table-funding arrangements as, 4.7.2
understating cost of credit, 7.2.2.1
yield-spread premiums as, 4.7.2, 7.3.2

POST-DATED CHECK LOANS
see PAYDAY LOANS

PRACTICE TIPS
see also CHECKLISTS; RESEARCH AIDS
analyzing consumer credit issues, 4.11
broker kickbacks, 12.2.1.5.6
calculating rebates, 5.6
credit card debt, assisting consumers overwhelmed by, 11.7.4
credit insurance, proving coercion, 8.5.2.4
credit math for practitioners, 4
electronic credit transactions, 9.2.10.10
expert witness testimony and reports, Appx. L.2
federal preemption, 3.2
foreclosure, enjoining, 10.8.3
formulas, *see* MATHEMATICAL FORMULAS
gathering information
    from client, 4.11.2
    from creditor and others, 4.11.3

References are to sections

PRACTICE TIPS (*cont.*)
getting started
    analyzing contract, 1.6.2
    analyzing legal issues, 1.6.3
    introduction, 1.6.1
hidden interest, 7.1.1, 10.5.4.3
home defense, refinancing alternative, 6.5
interest calculations, 4
interest rate ceiling for national banks, 3.4.4
liability chart, 12.12
mathematical issues, proving, 4.10
NCLC manual, organization, 1.4
    federal preemption, 3.1.2
overcharge issues, uncovering, 4.11, 10.5.4.3
potential claims, calculations and analysis, 4.11.4
refinancings
    analyzing, 6.1.2
    case study, 6.3.2
    evaluating as home defense, 6.5
regulatory chart, 3.3.1
RESPA implications, 12.2.1.10
sample pleadings and discovery, Appx. L
usurious charges, 4.11.4, 10.5.4.3
usury law, 1.5
yield spread premiums, 12.2.1.5.6

PREAUTHORIZED ELECTRONIC FUND TRANSFERS
see also ELECTRONIC FUNDS TRANSFER ACT (EFTA)
defined, 7.5.5.9.2
loan repayment by, 7.5.5.9.3
    credit conditional on, restrictions, 7.5.5.9.2
stop payments, 7.5.5.9.6

PRECOMPUTED LOANS
add-on interest, 4.3.2
described, 4.5.3
discount interest, 4.3.3
partial prepayments, 5.4.3
rebate requirements, 5.4.1, 5.4.3
refinancing case study, 6.3.2

PREDATORY LENDERS
see also CREDITORS; FRINGE LENDERS; SUBPRIME
       LENDERS
auto financing, 11.6.1
asset-based lending, 11.3
equity-skimming, 11.5.1
fraud liability, 12.10.1
interest ceilings, effect, 2.4.1
HOEPA, application, 12.2.2.1
RICO violations, 12.6
state law, *see* USURY LAWS (STATE)

PREEMPTION
D'Oench by FIRREA, 10.7.2
E-Sign by state law, 9.2.10.2, 9.2.10.3.1
FAA by state insurance law, 8.7.6, 10.3.6
federal holder-in-due course doctrine by FIRREA, 10.7.2
federal law by state insurance law, 8.5.2.7.2, 10.3.6.1
state law by federal law, *see* FEDERAL PREEMPTION

PREMIUM REBATES
see INSURANCE PREMIUM REBATES

PREMIUMS
see INSURANCE PREMIUMS

PREPAID PAYMENT PYRAMID
described, 7.4.2

PREPAYMENT
see also EARLY TERMINATION
acceleration distinguished, 5.8.1
fixing of date, 5.6.2.1
interest bearing transactions, 4.5.1
partial prepayments, 5.4.3
penalties, *see* PREPAYMENT PENALTIES
precomputed transactions, 4.5.3
rebates, *see* REBATES
restrictions on, 5.8.1
right to, 5.8.1
rounding intervals, 5.6.2.2, 5.6.3.4.2
spreading, effect, 4.6.5.3
unearned charges, collection, 5.7.2
unearned interest rebates, 4.5.3

PREPAYMENT PENALTIES
challenging, 5.8.1
credit unions, 2.3.1.2.3
generally, 5.8.1
high cost mortgages, 5.2.4, 5.8.2
HOEPA restrictions, 5.2.4, 5.8.2
junk fees as, 5.8.1
points as, 5.5.2.3, 5.8.1
rebate refusal, distinction, 5.8.1
refinancings, 6.3.1
refusal to accept payment as, 5.6.2.2, 5.8.1
Rule of 78, use as, 5.8.1
usury violations, 5.8.1

PREVIOUS BALANCE
see also LOAN BALANCES
open-end credit calculations, 4.3.5

PRICE
see SALE PRICE

PRINCIPAL AMOUNT
see also AMOUNT FINANCED; LOAN BALANCES
amortization, *see* AMORTIZATION
amount financed, distinction, 4.4.1
checklist, fixed-term credit, 1.6.3.2.3
compensating balances, 7.4.4
defined, 10.5.4.3
indexing, 7.4.5
inflating through fees, 7.4.2
inflating through refinancing, 6.3.1
installment credit
    balloon payments, 4.3.1.2
    declining balance, 4.3.1.1
    increasing balance, 4.3.1.2
insurance premiums, inclusion, 8.2.2
interest on, *see* INTEREST
loan-packing, 9.2.5.3
loan-splitting, 9.2.5.2
obligation to repay, necessary element of usury claim, 10.5.3
overstated, hidden interest issues, 7.4, 9.2.8.2
small loan laws, application, 9.2.5
statutory penalties, offsetting, 10.8.2.4
usurious loans, repayment, 10.8.2.2
wraparound mortgages, 7.4.3

PRIVATE MORTGAGE INSURANCE (PMI)
FCRA, application, 8.3.2.1

PRIVATE MORTGAGE INSURANCE (PMI) (*cont.*)
Homeowner's Protection Act, application, 8.3.2.1
overview, 8.3.2.1
premiums, collection, 8.2.2
state regulation, 8.3.2.1
TIL disclosures, 8.3.2.1
UDAP claims, 12.5
unregulated rates, 8.3.1.1, 8.3.2.1

PRO RATA FORMULA
rebate calculations, 5.6.3.2

PROGRESS PAYMENT TRANSACTIONS
usury violations, 4.9

PROMISSORY NOTES
see also NEGOTIABLE INSTRUMENTS
electronic, 9.2.10.2, 10.6.1.1
FTC Holder Notice, 10.6.1.2.2
variable rate notes, status, 10.6.1.3.3

PROOF
see BURDEN OF PROOF; EVIDENCE

PROPERTY FLIPPING
fraud and misrepresentation claims, 12.10.2.3
scams, 11.5.6
unconscionability, 12.7.3

PROPERTY INSURANCE
see CREDIT PROPERTY INSURANCE

PUNITIVE DAMAGES
fraud claims, 12.10.2.1
    constitutional and statutory restrictions, 12.10.3

PYRAMIDING
late charges, 4.8.1, 7.2.4.3

**RACKETEER INFLUENCED AND CORRUPT
    ORGANIZATIONS ACT (RICO)**
appraisal fraud, application, 11.5.6
auto pawns, application, 7.5.2.3.3
credit card abuses, 11.7.3.3
creditor overcharges, application, 10.8.5.3.5
injury, 10.8.5.3.4
mail and wire fraud, 12.6
overview, 10.8.5.3.1
pattern, 10.8.5.3.2
payday loans, application, 7.5.5.6, 10.8.5.3.5
racketeering activity, 10.8.5.3.2
RALs, application, 7.5.4.2
state RICO statutes, 10.8.5.3.6
unlawful debt, 10.8.5.3.3, 10.8.5.3.5
usury remedies, 10.8.5.3, 12.6
yield spread premiums, 11.6.6

RATE EXPORTATION
see also FEDERAL PREEMPTION
assignee status, effect, 3.4.5.1.3
background, 3.4.5.1
broad definition of interest, 7.1.2
choice of law considerations, 3.9.2.2.2
constitutional concerns, 3.4.5.1.1
credit cards, 2.3.2.3, 3.2.3.2
DIDA, application, 3.9.2.2
electronic lending, 3.4.5.1.2
federal credit unions, 3.6.2
federal savings associations, 3.5.2

federally-insured lenders, 3.9.2.2
finance companies, 3.2.3.2
interest rate, scope of term, 3.4.5.2
interstate banking, 3.4.5, 3.9.2.2
location of bank, role, 3.4.5.1.2
Marquette decision, 3.4.5.1
national banks, 3.4.5
non-mortgage loans, 3.2.3.2
overview, 3.4.5.1.1
payday loans, 7.5.5.7
state banks, 3.7.2

RATES
credit insurance, 8.4.2.1
exportation of rates, *see* RATE EXPORTATION
filed-rate doctrine, 8.4.2.1.5
interest rates, *see* INTEREST RATES

REAL ESTATE BROKERS
loans arranged by, 9.2.4.5

REAL ESTATE SECURITY
see also SECURITY INTERESTS
DIDA first lien preemption, 3.9.3
home equity loans, *see* HOME EQUITY LOANS
land installment contracts, 9.2.3.4
mortgages, *see* MORTGAGES
prepayment penalties, 5.8.3
small loan restrictions, 9.2.4.6, 9.2.6
title insurance, 8.3.2.2
transferable records, 10.6.1.3.7

**REAL ESTATE SETTLEMENT PROCEDURES ACT
    (RESPA)**
broker fees, application, 7.3.2, 11.5.4.3
disclosure provisions, 12.2.1.2
electronic disclosures, 12.2.1.9
escrow limitations, 12.2.1.4
exemptions, 12.2.1.1, 12.2.1.5.1
HUD letters, Appx. K.4
HUD policy statement on lender-paid broker fees
    conflicting interpretations, 12.2.1.5.4
    first statement (1999), 12.2.1.5.3, Appx. K.3.1
    letter regarding, Appx. K.4.1
    second statement (2001), 12.2.1.5.5, Appx. K.3.2
kickback prohibition, 12.2.1.5
limitations, 12.2.1.10
practice implications, 12.2.1.5.6, 12.2.1.10
scope, 12.2.1.1
secondary market exemption, 12.2.1.1
selected provisions, Appx. K.1
selected regulations, Appx. K.2
servicer obligations, 12.2.1.3
state law preemption, 12.2.1.8
title insurance, application
    generally, 8.3.2.2
    steering prohibition, 12.2.1.7
unearned fee prohibition, 12.2.1.5
violations, remedies, 12.2.1.10
    sample pleadings, Appx. L.6
    steering, 12.2.1.7
    unearned fees, 12.2.1.5.6
    venue and standing, 12.2.1.10

REAL PROPERTY
brokers, *see* REAL ESTATE BROKERS

REAL PROPERTY (*cont.*)
flipping scams, 11.5.6
security, *see* REAL ESTATE SECURITY

REBATES
actuarial rebates
   calculation, 5.6.3.4.2, CD-Rom
   legal status, 5.6.3.4.1
   split rates, 5.6.3.4.3
bankruptcy, calculating, 5.2.5
calculating
   fixing date, 5.6.2.1
   formulas, 5.6.3
   intervals, rounding, 5.6.2.3
charges and fees, 5.5.2
contractual provisions, 5.7.2.3
early termination, 5.4.2
federal law, 5.2.2, 5.5.2.2, 5.7.3
formulas
   actuarial rebates, 5.6.3.4
   determining which formula, 5.6.3.1
   pro rata rebates, 5.6.3.2
   Rule of 78, 5.6.3.3.2
   sum of the balances, 5.6.3.3.4
insurance premiums, *see* INSURANCE PREMIUM REBATES
intent to collect unearned charges, 5.7.2
mobile homes, credit secured by liens on, 5.2.3
partial prepayments, 5.4.3
points, 5.5.2.2
precomputed charges, 5.4.1
prepayment penalties, relationship, 5.8.1
pro rata rebates, 5.6.3.2
refinancings
   calculating, 6.4.1.1
   case study, 6.3.2
remedies for violations, 5.7
   federal rebate statute, 5.7.3
   intent, requirement, 5.7.2
   statutory remedies, generally, 5.7.1
requirements, 5.4
Rule of 78
   background and legal status, 5.6.3.3.1
   bankruptcy, using, 5.2.5, 5.6.3.3.1
   explanation, 5.6.3.3.2
   step by step calculation, 5.6.3.3.2
   sum of the balances variant, 5.6.3.3.4
   use in calculation, 5.5.1
service contracts, 5.5.2.1
state law overview, 5.2.1
sum of the balances rebates, 5.6.3.3.4
unearned interest, *see* UNEARNED INTEREST REBATES
violations as illegal charges, 5.7

RECAPTURE CLAUSES
variable rate transactions, 4.3.6.4

RECEIVERS
equitable subordination, application, 10.7.8
federal receiver defenses, 10.7

RECOUPMENT
statute of limitations, extension, 10.6.7

REDLINING
reverse redlining, remedies, 12.3

REFERRAL FEES
see BROKER FEES

REFINANCING
see also CONSOLIDATION OF LOANS
additional charges, 6.4.2
business and consumer loans together, 6.6
business loans, generally, 9.2.2.5
calculations, case study, 6.3.2
compounding interest, restrictions, 4.6.1.2
cost of refinancing
   case study, 6.3.2
   price, 6.3.1
credit insurance, 6.1.1.2
credit sales with new cash advance, 6.4.3
defined, 6.1.3
duty of good faith and fair dealing, 12.8
equity-skimmers, 6.1.1.3
finance company practices, 2.3.2.3
flipping penalty, *see* LOAN-FLIPPING
fraud claims, 12.10.2.3
frequent flipper programs, 9.2.5.3
interest ceilings, 6.4.3
legal issues, 6.1.2
mortgage foreclosure alternative, 6.5
novation and renewal distinguished, 6.2.3
overreaching creditors, 11.5.3
overview, 6.1.1.1, 6.1.2
points, calculation, 4.7.2
practice tips, 6.5
rebates
   calculation, 6.4.1.1
   compounding, 6.4.1.2
   non-rebatable charges, 6.4.1.3
release of usury claims, 6.2.3
RISAs, application, 6.4.3
Rule of 78, 6.1.1.2
service charges, 6.1.1.2
small loan example, 6.1.1.2
stretching the balance, 6.1.1.2
UDAP violations, 12.5
unconscionable points, 5.5.2.3
usurious taint, 6.2
   continuation of taint, 6.2.1
   purging of taint, 6.2.3
variables, evaluating, 6.5

REFORMATION
usurious contracts, 10.5.1.3, 10.8.3

REFUND ANTICIPATION LOANS (RALs)
see also FRINGE LENDERS; TAX REFUND SCHEMES
cross-lender debt collection, 7.5.4.2
federal preemption, 7.5.4.2
hidden interest, 7.5.4.2
OCC regulations, 7.5.4.2
rate exportation, 3.2.3.2
sample pleadings and discovery, Appx. L.5
state law claims, 7.5.4.2
unconscionability challenges, 12.7.2

REGULATORY AGENCIES
bureaucracy of preemption, 3.3
interpretations
   deference, 3.3.2, 3.4.6.1, 9.3.1.3
   preemption, publication, 3.4.6.1

REGULATORY AGENCIES (*cont.*)
NCUA, *see* NATIONAL CREDIT UNION ADMINISTRATION (NCUA)
OCC, *see* OFFICE OF THE COMPTROLLER OF THE CURRENCY (OCC)
OTS, *see* OFFICE OF THRIFT SUPERVISION (OTS)

RELEASES
usury claims through refinancing, 6.2.3

REMEDIES
appraisal fraud, 11.5.6
credit repair laws
    CROA, 12.4.2.3
    state laws, 12.4.3.3
home improvement contracts, 11.5.2
national banks, against, 3.4.6.3
negative equity financing, 11.6.3
property flipping schemes, 11.5.6
RESPA violations, 12.2.1.10
    broker kickbacks, 12.2.1.5.6
    title insurance steering, 12.2.1.7
RICO, 12.6
"single document rule" violations, 11.6.8
TILA, *see* TIL VIOLATIONS
UDAP, *see* UDAP VIOLATIONS
usury, *see* USURY REMEDIES

REMOVAL
see JURISDICTION

RENT SHARING
hidden interest, 7.2.3

RENT-A-CHARTER ARRANGEMENTS
banks and payday lenders
    challenging, 3.13.2
    generally, 3.13.1, 7.5.5.7
    OCC, OTS and FDIC regulation, 3.13.3
    sample pleadings, Appx. L.4

RENT-TO-OWN (RTO) TRANSACTIONS
see also FRINGE LENDERS
auto title loans disguised as, 7.5.2.3.4, 7.5.3.6.7
challenges, 7.5.3.6
    disguised high-cost loans, 7.5.3.6.7
    discrimination claims, 7.5.3.6.6
    history of, 7.5.3.4
    optional fees, 7.5.3.6.4
    repossession tactics, 7.5.3.6.5
    RICO remedies, 10.8.5.3.5
    UCC applicability, 7.5.3.6.5
    UDAP applicability, 7.5.3.6.3
    unconscionability, 7.5.3.6.2
described, 7.5.3.2
disclosure requirements, 7.5.3.5
disguised credit sales, 7.5.3.1
high-cost loans disguised as, 7.5.3.6.7
industry-friendly legislation, 7.5.3.5
industry overview, 7.5.3.3
liability damage waivers, 7.5.3.6.4
MVRISA, application, 7.5.3.6.7
post-deregulation, 2.5
RISA exemptions, 2.3.3.5, 7.5.3.5
state statutes, 7.5.3.5
trends, 7.5.3.3

REPAIR CONTRACTS
see SERVICE CONTRACTS

REPOSSESSION
auto pawns, 7.5.2.3.5
electronic notices, 9.2.10.9
rent-to-own transactions, 7.5.3.6.5

REPURCHASE AGREEMENTS
see LEASEBACK AGREEMENTS; SALE AND REPURCHASE AGREEMENTS

RES JUDICATA
creditor defense, 10.6.6

RESCISSION
high cost mortgages, 12.2.2.1
home improvement loans, 11.5.2
home secured loans, 11.5.3
usurious credit agreements, 10.8.3

RESEARCH AIDS
see also PRACTICE TIPS
brokers, state regulatory actions, 11.5.4.3
NCLC manual, organization, 1.4
usury issues, 1.5
websites relating to consumer credit, Appx. M

RESIDENTIAL MORTGAGES
see MORTGAGES

RESOLUTION TRUST CORPORATION (RTC)
defenses as federal receiver, 10.7
FTCA, application, 10.7.9
liability for own conduct, 10.7.9
negligent operation of receivership, 10.7.9
super holder-in-due-course status, 10.7.5

RETAIL INSTALLMENT SALES ACTS (RISAs)
see also CREDIT SALES; INSTALLMENT CREDIT; INSTALLMENT LOAN LAWS
body-dragging, application, 9.2.3.3
convenience creditors, application, 2.3.1.3.3
fees, restrictions, 7.2.1
historical development, 2.2.3.2
installment contracts, regulation, 2.3.1.3.2
interpretation, 9.3.1.1
motor vehicle sales, *see* MOTOR VEHICLE RETAIL INSTALLMENT SALES ACTS (MVRISA)
refinancings, application, 6.4.3
rent-to-own transactions, application, 2.3.3.5, 7.5.3.5
scope, 2.3.3.5
"single document rule", 11.6.8

RETAIL SELLERS
see also CREDIT SALES; NON-DEPOSITORY CREDITORS
automobiles, *see* AUTO LOANS
body-dragging, 9.2.3.3
credit card accounts, *see* CREDIT CARD ACCOUNTS
lender liability for acts of, 12.12
regulatory history, 2.3.1.3.2
RISAs, *see* RETAIL INSTALLMENT SALES ACTS (RISAs)
used cars, *see* USED CAR PURCHASES

RETAILERS
see RETAIL SELLERS

REVERSE COMPETITION
credit insurance, 8.2.3.1

REVERSE MORTGAGES
see also MORTGAGES
described, 6.5
HOEPA, application, 12.2.2.2

REVERSE REDLINING
remedies, 12.3

REVOLVING CREDIT PLANS
see CREDIT CARD ACCOUNTS; OPEN-END CREDIT

RICO
see RACKETEER INFLUENCED AND CORRUPT
    ORGANIZATIONS ACT (RICO)

ROUNDING
interest calculations, 4.6.4
intervals for rebates, 5.6.2.2, 5.6.3.4.2
refinancings, 6.4.1.1

RULE OF 78
background, 5.6.3.3.1
bankruptcy calculations, using, 5.2.5, 5.6.3.3.1
explanation of rule, 5.6.3.3.3
flipping penalty, small loan example, 6.1.1.2
formula, 5.6.3.3.2
high cost mortgages, restrictions, 5.2.4, 5.4.2, 5.6.3.3.1
interest-bearing transactions, use, 5.5.1
rebate calculations, 5.6.3.3.2, 8.6
restrictions on use, 5.2.2, 5.5.1, 5.5.2, 5.6.3.3.1
sum of the balances variant, 5.6.3.3.4
unearned interest charges, 5.4.1

RUSSELL SAGE FOUNDATION
small loan laws, 2.2.3.1, 2.3.3.2

SALARY LENDING
see PAYDAY LOANS

SALE AND REPURCHASE AGREEMENTS
see also LEASEBACK AGREEMENTS
equitable mortgage status, 7.5.2.1
hidden interest, 7.5.2
pawnbroking status, 7.5.2.2

SALE OF GOODS
credit transactions, *see* CREDIT SALES
price, *see* SALE PRICE
sellers, *see* RETAIL SELLERS

SALE PRICE
discrimination, 11.3, 12.3
hidden interest
    inflated price, 7.4.6.1
    seller's points, 7.4.6.2
inflating, 7.4.6.1, 11.6.2.1
rent-to-own (RTO) transactions, 7.5.3.6.2
sucker-pricing, *see* SUCKER-PRICING
unconscionability, 12.7.2

SALES CREDIT
see CREDIT SALES

**SARGENT SHRIVER NATIONAL CENTER ON
    POVERTY LAW**
see also CLEARINGHOUSE NUMBERS
document ordering information, 1.5

SAVINGS AND LOAN ASSOCIATIONS
see also DEPOSITORY CREDITORS

deposit insurance, 2.3.1.2.2
failed institutions
    claims process, 10.7.10
    federal receiver defenses, 10.7
Federal Home Loan Bank System, participation, 2.3.1.2.2
federally-insured, *see* FEDERALLY INSURED LENDERS
FIRREA bail-out, 3.9.4.3
FSLIC, participation, 2.3.1.2.2
historical development, 2.2.3.1
HOLA, history and purpose, 3.5.1
interest rate ceiling, 3.1.1, 3.5.2
    mortgage loans, 3.2.4.1
lending authority, 2.3.1.2.2
location, 3.5.2
mortgage loans, federal preemption, 3.2.4, 3.9.3
most favored lender status, 3.5.2
operating subsidiaries, 3.5.4
OTS regulation, 3.3.1, 3.5.3, Appx. D.2
payday lenders, involvement, 7.5.5.7, 3.13
prepayment penalties, 5.8.3
rate exportation, 3.5.2
regulatory history, 2.3.1.2.2
rent-a-charter arrangements, 7.5.5.7, 3.13
state-chartered associations, *see* FEDERALLY INSURED
    LENDERS
state law, application, 3.5.3
    subsidiaries, 3.5.4
supervision, *see* OFFICE OF THRIFT SUPERVISION (OTS)
usurious loans, remedies, 10.8.5.1

SAVINGS BANKS
see also BANKS; SAVINGS AND LOAN ASSOCIATIONS
Community Reinvestment Act obligations, 6.5
historical development, 2.2.3.1
regulatory history, 2.3.1.2.1

SECOND MORTGAGES
see HOME EQUITY LOANS

SECURED CREDIT
see also COLLATERAL; SECURITY INTERESTS
automobiles, *see* AUTO-SECURED LOANS
disguised as outright sale, 7.5.2
refinancing, equity-skimming, 6.1.1.3
regulatory history, 2.3.2.4

SECURITIES
churning, 6.1.1.1
mortgage-backed, 2.4.2, 11.4

SECURITIZATION OF DEBT
described, 11.4
jurisdiction over trust, 10.2.3
mortgage loans, 2.4.2, 11.4

SECURITY
see COLLATERAL

SECURITY INTERESTS
see also COLLATERAL; SECURED CREDIT
homes, *see* HOME EQUITY LOANS; MORTGAGES
household goods, 8.5.4.4
importance, 2.3.2.4
insurance, in, 8.6
non-filing insurance, *see* NON-FILING INSURANCE
personal property, *see* PERSONAL PROPERTY SECURITY
    INTERESTS

SECURITY INTERESTS (*cont.*)
real estate, *see* REAL ESTATE SECURITY
usury laws, applicable, 9.2.1.2, 9.2.6

SELLER'S POINTS
see also POINTS
hidden interest, 7.4.6.2

SERVICE CHARGES
see also FEES AND CHARGES; LOAN FEES; POINTS
finance charge, inclusion, 4.4.1
minimum finance charges, 4.6.6
refinancings
    additional charges, 6.4.2
    flipping penalty, 6.1.1.2
    non-rebatable charges, 6.3.1, 6.4.1.3

SERVICE CONTRACTS
hidden interest, 7.2.3
inflated pricing, 11.6.2.2, 11.6.4
rebate issues, 5.5.2.1
RICO claims, 12.6

SERVICEMEMBERS CIVIL RELIEF ACT
interest rate regulation, 2.3.3.11
selected text, Appx. J.3

SERVICER OBLIGATIONS
RESPA requirements, 12.2.1.3

SETTLEMENT ADVANCES
litigation finance companies, 7.5.8.3

SETTLEMENT CHARGES
disclosure requirements, 12.2.1.2
discount packages, 12.2.1.7
escrow limitations, 12.2.1.4
excessive charges, 12.2.1.6
HUD settlement statement, 12.2.1.9
kickback issues, 12.2.1.5, 12.2.1.6
overcharge and mark-up distinguished, 12.2.1.6
referral fees, prohibition, 12.2.1.5
RESPA regulation, 12.2.1.1, 12.2.1.5.1
splitting of charges, prohibition, 12.2.1.5.1, 12.2.1.6
title insurance, 12.1.1.7
unearned, prohibition, 12.1.1.5, 12.2.1.6

SHAMS
assignments, 11.6.2.1
business loans, 9.2.2.3
cash-back ads, 7.5.5
credit sales, 7.5.2, 9.2.3.3, 10.5.2.2.1
leases, 7.5.3, 7.5.5
loans, 9.2.3.3, 10.5.2.2.1
open-end credit, 9.2.3.2
outright sales, 7.5.2
tax refund schemes, 7.5.4.1

SIDE AGREEMENTS
hidden interest, 7.2.3

SIMPLE INTEREST
see also ACTUARIAL INTEREST TRANSACTIONS
actuarial calculation, 4.3.1.1
add-on interest compared, 4.3.2
described, 4.2

SINGLE DOCUMENT RULE
generally, 11.6.8

SLIDING
credit insurance, 8.5.2.1, 8.5.2.4

SMALL BUSINESSES
see also BUSINESS LOANS
usury laws, application, 9.2.2.2

SMALL LOAN LAWS
see also SMALL LOAN LENDERS
business loans, application, 9.2.2.2
combined consumer finance acts, 2.3.3.2, 2.3.3.3
credit card accounts, application, 3.4.3.2
credit insurance, application, 8.5.3.2.2
fringe lenders, avoidance, 2.3.1.1
historical development, 2.2.3.1, 2.3.3.2, 9.3.1.1
loan-packing to evade, 9.2.5.3
loan-splitting to fail within, 9.2.5.2
purpose, 9.3.1.1
real estate secured transactions, application, 9.2.4.6, 9.2.6
scope, 9.2.5

SMALL LOAN LENDERS
see also FINANCE COMPANIES
credit insurance restrictions, 8.5.3.2.2
flipping penalties, 6.1.1.2
fringe lenders, *see* FRINGE LENDERS
historical perspective, 2.2.3.1, 2.3.1.1, 2.3.1.2.1
post-deregulation, 2.5
real estate security, restrictions, 9.2.4.6
regulation, *see* SMALL LOAN LAWS
salary lenders, 2.5, 7.5.5

SOLDIERS' AND SAILORS' CIVIL RELIEF ACT
see SERVICEMEMBERS CIVIL RELIEF ACT

SPECIALTY FINANCING
see FRINGE LENDERS; SUBPRIME LENDERS

SPLIT RATE INTEREST
see also INTEREST
actuarial rebates, 5.6.3.4.3
add-on interest transactions, 4.3.2
amortization, 4.3.4
installment credit calculation, 4.3.4

SPOT DELIVERY
overview, 11.6.5
UDAP violations, 12.5

SPREADING
across notes, 4.6.5.3
contract restrictions, 4.6.5.4
fixed term loans, 4.6.5.1
open-end transactions, 4.6.5.2
term used, 4.6.5.3
usury ceilings, 4.6.5.1

STANDING
usury claims, 10.6.3

STATE BANKS
see also BANKS
FDIC
    participation, 2.3.1.2.1
    regulation, 3.7.1
most favored lender status, 3.7.2
parity acts, application, 3.7.4
powers, 3.7.1
preemption rights, 3.7.2, 3.7.3

STATE BANKS (*cont.*)
regulatory history, 2.3.1.2.1
regulatory overlay, 3.7.1
state law application, 3.7.3

STATE CLAIMS
fiduciary duty, *see* FIDUCIARY DUTY
fraud, *see* FRAUD CLAIMS
good faith and fair dealing, *see* GOOD FAITH AND FAIR
    DEALING
misrepresentation, *see* MISREPRESENTATION
UDAP, *see* UDAP VIOLATIONS
usury, *see* USURY CLAIMS

STATE LAW
see also USURY LAWS (STATE)
administrative interpretations, deference, 9.3.1.3
assignee liability, 10.6.1.2.2
auto title loans, 7.5.2.3.5
banking system, 2.3.1.2.1
bounced checks, re-presentment, 7.5.5.9.3
choice of law rules, 3.2.2.5, 9.2.9
claims, *see* STATE CLAIMS
credit deregulation, *see* PARITY LAWS (STATE)
credit insurance, 8.4.1.2, 10.3.6
credit regulation, overview, 2.1
credit repair laws, 12.4.3
deferral charges, 4.8.2
electronic transactions, 9.2.10.2, 9.2.10.3
    consent requirements, 9.2.10.4.2
    delivery of documents, 9.2.10.6
    format and timing requirements, 9.2.10.5
    subsequent notices, 9.2.10.9
federal credit unions, application, 3.6.2, 3.6.3
federal savings and loan associations, application, 3.5.3
high cost mortgage statutes, 12.2.3
home improvement contractors, 11.5.2
land installment contracts, 9.2.3.4
lending statutes, Appx. A
mortgage brokers, Appx. B
national banks, application, 3.4.6
parity laws, *see* PARITY LAWS (STATE)
preemption by federal law, *see* FEDERAL PREEMPTION
preemption of federal law, *see* PREEMPTION
private mortgage insurance (PMI), 8.3.2.1
punitive damages, restrictions, 12.10.3
RALs, 7.5.4.2
rebates of unearned charges, 5.2.1
rent-to-own (RTO) transactions, 7.5.3.5
RICO, 10.8.5.3.6
sale and leaseback of homes, 7.5.2.1
state banks, application, 3.7.3
UDAP, *see* UDAP VIOLATIONS
UNIP, *see* UNFAIR INSURANCE TRADE PRACTICES ACTS
    (UNIP)
usury laws, *see* USURY LAWS (STATE)

STATUTE OF LIMITATIONS
CROA, 12.4.2.3
FIRREA, asserting by assignees, 10.7.6.3
recoupment in nonjudicial foreclosure states, 10.6.7
RESPA claims, 12.2.1.10
    title insurance steering, 12.2.1.7
usury claims, 10.6.7

STATUTORY CONSTRUCTION
see also USURY STATUTES (STATE)
general rules of interpretation
    broad vs. narrow, 9.3.1.1
    expressio unius, 9.3.1.2
retroactive amendment
    general standards, 9.3.2.1
    variable or floating ceilings, 9.3.2.2

STATUTORY PENALTIES
offsetting, 10.8.2.4
usury violations, 10.8.2.4

STEERING
title insurance, RESPA prohibition, 12.2.1.7

STRAIGHT AVERAGE DAILY BALANCE
see also LOAN BALANCES
open-end credit calculations, 4.3.5

SUBPRIME LENDERS
see also FRINGE LENDERS; LOAN-SHARKING;
    PREDATORY LENDERS
acquisition fees, 11.6.2.1
auto financing, 11.6.1
deep discounts, 11.6.2.1
risk factor, 11.3
securitization of debt, 11.4
variable rate transactions, 4.3.6.1

SUBSIDIARIES
activities of, jurisdiction over parent, 10.2.1
D'Oench doctrine, application, 10.7.6.1
preemption rights, 3.4.6.4, 3.5.3

SUCKER-PRICING
see also SALE PRICE
interest ceilings and, 2.4.1
loan brokers, 11.5.4.3
overview, 11.3

SUM OF THE BALANCES
rebate calculations, 5.6.3.3.4

SUM OF THE DIGITS
see RULE OF 78

SURETIES
see ACCOMMODATION PARTIES

TABLE-FUNDED LOANS
correspondent lenders, 11.5.4.1
described, 4.7.2, 9.2.4.6
kickbacks, 12.2.1.5.2
licensing issues, 9.2.4.6
points, inclusion, 4.7.2
yield spread premiums, 12.2.1.5.2

TAX REFUND SCHEMES
disguised credit, 7.5.4.1
Refund Anticipation Loans, *see* REFUND ANTICIPATION
    LOANS (RALs)

TESTIMONY
see also EVIDENCE
sample expert witness, Appx. L.2.4

THIRD PARTIES
beneficiaries, status as, 10.3.5.1
lender liability for actions of, 12.12

THIRD PARTIES (*cont.*)
payments to
  attorney fees, 7.3.3
  broker fees, 7.3.2
  general principles, 7.3.1
  hidden interest issues, 7.3.1

THRIFT INSTITUTIONS
see OFFICE OF THRIFT SUPERVISION (OTS); SAVINGS
  AND LOAN ASSOCIATIONS

TIE-INS
credit insurance, 8.5.2.7.1

TIL CLAIMS
see TIL VIOLATIONS

TIL DISCLOSURES
see DISCLOSURES (TIL)

TIL VIOLATIONS
see also TRUTH IN LENDING ACT (TILA)
credit insurance coercion, 8.5.2.5
federal rebate law violations as, 5.7.3
inflated sale price, 7.4.6.1, 11.6.2.1
late charges, 4.8.1
odd payment periods, 4.6.2.2
payday loans, 7.5.5.4, 7.5.5.6
tax refund schemes, 7.5.4.1
uncovering, practical tips, 4.11

TIME-PRICE DOCTRINE
described, 2.2.2, 2.3.2.2, 10.5.2.2.1
erosion, 10.5.2.2.2
inflated sale price, application, 7.4.6.1
loans to finance purchases, application, 9.2.3.3
usury law exception, 10.5.2.2.1, 10.5.2.2.2

TITLE INSURANCE
kickbacks and fee-padding, 8.3.2.2
NAIC model laws, 8.3.2.2
real-estate-secured loans, generally, 8.3.2.2
steering by seller, RESPA prohibition, 12.2.1.7
TIL violations, 8.3.2.2

TITLE PAWNS
see AUTO TITLE LOANS

TORT CLAIMS
credit insurance, breach of duty, 8.7.2, 8.7.3.1
duty of due care, 12.11.1
duty of good faith, 12.8
federal receivers, against, 10.7.9
fraud, *see* FRAUD
free standing exception to *D'Oench*, 10.7.3.2
intentional interference with contractual relationship, 12.9.4
loan brokers, against, 11.5.4.3
misrepresentation, *see* MISREPRESENTATION

TRUE ACTUARIAL AVERAGE DAILY BALANCE
see also LOAN BALANCES
open-end credit calculations, 4.3.5

TRUTH IN LENDING ACT (TILA)
bounce loans, application, 7.5.6
credit cards, application
  change-in-terms notices, 11.7.2.4
  generally, 11.7.3.4
  grace periods, 11.7.2.3.6
preemption issues, 11.7.3.5.2
disclosure requirements, *see* DISCLOSURES (TIL)
federal rebate law, relationship, 5.2.2, 5.5.2.2.3
preemption overview, 3.1.1, 3.12
purpose, 2.3.4, 4.4.1
rebates of unearned charges, application, 5.5.2.2.3
scope, 2.3.4
state law, relationship, 2.3.4
violations, *see* TIL VIOLATIONS

UDAP VIOLATIONS
appraisal fraud, 11.5.6
credit card abuses, 11.7.3.2
credit insurance, 8.4.1.4, 8.5.2.6, 8.5.5.2, 8.7.4
  premium financing, 8.4.1.6
credit repair law violations as, 12.4.3.3
federal rebate law violations as, 5.7.3
federal savings associations, 3.4.6.1, 3.5.3
FTC Holder Rule, 10.6.1.2.2
inflated cash prices, 11.6.2.1
litigation finance companies, 7.5.8.3
loan brokers, 11.5.4.3, 12.5
national banks, 3.4.6.1
open-end credit, 9.2.3.2
overreaching credit, challenging as, 12.5
payday loans, 7.5.5.6
payment packing, 11.6.4
postdated checks, early presentment, 7.5.5.9.5
prepayment penalties, 5.8.1
property flipping schemes, 11.5.6
pyramiding late charges, 7.2.4.3
RALs, 7.5.4.2
rent-to-own transactions, 7.5.3.6.3
RESPA violations, 12.2.1.2, 12.2.1.4, 12.2.1.10
tax refund schemes, 7.5.4.1, 7.5.4.2
unconscionability, 12.7.5
yield spread premiums, 11.6.6

UNCONSCIONABILITY
arbitration clauses, 10.3.7
class actions alleging, 10.8.6
credit card abuses, 11.7.3.3
credit insurance, 8.7.5
credit transactions, 12.7
defined, 8.7.5
deregulated interest rates, 9.2.7
improvident lending, 12.7.3
loan flipping, 12.7.4
non-interest rate terms, 12.7.4
outer limit on credit price, 12.7.2
overview, 12.7.1
payday loans, 7.5.5.6
property flipping, 12.7.3
remedy, 12.7.5
rent-to-own pricing, 7.5.3.6.2

UNEARNED FEES AND CHARGES
HUD policy statement, 12.2.1.6
intent to collect, 5.7.2
rebates, *see* REBATES; UNEARNED INTEREST REBATES
RESPA prohibition, 12.2.1.5, 12.2.1.6

UNEARNED INTEREST REBATES
see also REBATES
calculation, 5.2.2
consumer credit transactions, 5.5.1

UNEARNED INTEREST REBATES (*cont.*)
early termination, 5.4.2
federal law overview, 5.2.2, 5.5.2.2.3
partial prepayments, 5.4.3
precomputed charges, 5.4.1
precomputed transactions, 4.5.3
refinancings, 6.3.1, 6.3.2, 6.4.1.1
spreading, application, 4.6.5.3, 4.6.5.4

UNEMPLOYMENT INSURANCE
see INVOLUNTARY UNEMPLOYMENT INSURANCE

UNFAIR AND DECEPTIVE ACTS AND PRACTICES
(UDAP)
see UDAP VIOLATIONS

UNFAIR INSURANCE TRADE PRACTICES ACTS (UNIP)
see also NAIC MODEL ACTS
credit insurance regulation, 8.4.1.4, 8.5.2.6

UNFAIR TRADE PRACTICES
see UDAP VIOLATIONS

UNIFORM COMMERCIAL CODE (UCC)
auto pawn transactions, application, 7.5.2.3.5
choice of law rule, 9.2.9.1
   contractual choice of law clauses, 9.2.9.5
electronic documents, 9.2.10.2, 10.6.1.1
holder-in-due-course rule
   basic prerequisites, 10.6.1.3
   overview, 10.6.1.1
home improvement loan remedies, 11.5.2
legal settlements, assignment of, application, 7.5.8.3
national banks, application, 3.4.6.1
payday loan checks, application, 7.5.5.9.1
   forged or altered checks, 7.5.5.9.7
   postdated checks, 7.5.5.9.5
   re-presentment of checks, 7.5.5.9.3, 7.5.5.9.4
rent-to-own transactions, application, 7.5.3.5, 7.5.3.6.5

UNIFORM CONSUMER CREDIT CODE (UCCC)
see also CONSUMER CREDIT CODES (STATE)
adoption, 2.3.3.1, 2.3.3.10
credit insurance, 8.4.1.3, 8.5.3.4.1
force-placed insurance, 8.3.1.5.4
historical development, 2.3.3.10
land installment contracts, application, 9.2.3.4
open-end interest calculations, 4.3.5.3
property insurance, 8.5.3.4.1
purpose, 9.3.1.1
unconscionability standards, 12.7.1

UNIFORM ELECTRONIC TRANSACTIONS ACT (UETA)
see also ELECTRONIC CREDIT TRANSACTIONS
consent requirements, 9.2.10.4.2
document integrity, 9.2.10.7
electronic promissory notes, 10.6.1.1
enforceability of contracts and signatures, 9.2.10.8
E-Sign, superseding of, 9.2.10.2, 9.2.10.3.1
overview, 9.2.10.2
post-consummation notices, 9.2.10.9
state adoption, 9.2.10.3
timing and format requirements, 9.2.10.5
transmission requirements, 9.2.10.6

UNITED STATES RULE
see also ACTUARIAL INTEREST TRANSACTIONS
accrued interest, 4.6.1.1

actuarial rule, differences, 4.6.1.1
APR, calculation using, 4.4.2
negative amortization, 4.3.1.2

UNPAID BALANCE
see LOAN BALANCES

USED CAR PURCHASES
see also AUTO LOANS
body-dragging, 9.2.3.3
cash price
   grossing up, 11.6.2.1, 11.6.2.2
   true cash price, 7.4.6.1
churning schemes, 11.6.2.2
financing
   discounts and acquisition fees, 11.6.2
   lender/dealer/assignee distinguished, 11.6.7
   lender-imposed financing costs, 11.6.2
   negative equity, 11.6.3
   overview, 11.6.1
   payment packing, 11.6.2.2, 11.6.4
   spot delivery, 11.6.5
   yield spread premiums, 11.6.6
RISA violations, sample pleadings and discovery, Appx. L.1.1

U.S. RULE
see UNITED STATES RULE

USURIOUS INTENT
necessary element, proof, 10.5.5
   apparent on face of contract, 10.5.5.2
   inference of intent, 10.5.5.4
   not apparent on face of contract, 10.5.5.3
   when required, 10.5.5.1
saving clauses, 10.6.10

USURY
see COST OF CREDIT; INTEREST CEILINGS; USURY AS
   DEFENSE; USURY CLAIMS; USURY REMEDIES;
   USURY LAWS (STATE); USURY VIOLATIONS

USURY AS DEFENSE
assignees, standing, 10.6.3
creditor defenses to usury claims, *see* CREDITOR DEFENSES
estoppel from asserting, 10.6.4
failed banks, claims process, 10.7.10
federal receivers, use against, 10.7
guarantors, 10.6.3
holders-in-due course, against, 10.6.1.3.9
innocent borrower defense, 10.7.3.2
jury trial right, 10.4
limitations, 10.6.7
pleading, 10.5.1
proof, 10.5.1
res judicata, 10.6.6
standing to assert, 10.6.3
sureties, 10.6.3
waiver, 10.6.4.4, 10.8.2.3

USURY CEILINGS
see INTEREST CEILINGS

USURY CLAIMS
see also USURY REMEDIES; USURY VIOLATIONS
applicable law, 9.2
assignment, 10.6.3
burden of proof, 10.5.1.2
calculations and analysis, 4.11.4

USURY CLAIMS (*cont.*)
class actions, 10.8.6
common law claims, 10.8.1
compulsory counterclaim, 10.6.6
defenses to, *see* CREDITOR DEFENSES
elements of claim
    generally, 10.5.1
    intent, 10.5.5
    interest overcharge, 10.5.4
    loan or forbearance, 10.5.2
    obligation to repay, 10.5.3
estoppel from asserting, 10.6.4
experts, using, 10.5.4.4
failed banks
    federal receiver defenses, 10.7
    process, 10.7.10
    sampling of claims, 10.7.8
jury trial, right to, 10.4
limitations, 10.6.7
prima facie case, 10.5
refinancing, effect, 6.2
release through novation, 6.2.3
pleadings, *see* PLEADINGS
standing, 10.6.3
uncovering, practice tips, 4.11
waiver, 10.8.2.3

USURY LAWS (STATE)
see also STATE LAW; STATUTORY CONSTRUCTION
administrative interpretations, deference, 9.3.1.3
applicable, determination, 9.2
    checklist, 1.6.3.1.3, 1.6.3.1.4
    distinctions among statutes, 9.2.1
    purpose of loan, 9.2.2
    size of loan, 9.2.5
    type of credit, 9.2.3
    type of creditor, 9.2.4
    type of security, 9.2.7
    which law, 3.2.2.6
    which state, overview, 3.2.2.5, 9.2.1.1
bounce loans, application, 7.5.6
business credit, application, 9.2.2
closed-end credit, application, 9.2.3.2
combined, *see* CONSUMER FINANCE LAWS (STATE)
conflict of laws, 9.2.9
consolidated, *see* CONSUMER CREDIT CODES (STATE)
contracting for coverage, 9.2.1.3
convenience creditors, application, 2.3.1.3.3
credit cards, 2.3.3.8
credit insurance, 8.4.1.3
depository lenders, 9.2.4.3
deregulation, 2.4, 9.2.1.4
detention of money, application, 10.5.2.3
federal depository lenders, application, 9.2.4.4
federal preemption, *see* FEDERAL PREEMPTION
forbearance, application, 10.5.2.3
frequency standard, 9.2.4.2
high-cost mortgage statutes, 12.2.3
historical development, *see* LEGISLATIVE HISTORY
home equity loans, 2.3.3.7
industrial loan laws, *see* INDUSTRIAL LOAN LAWS
installment loan laws, *see* INSTALLMENT LOAN LAWS
insurance premium credit, 2.3.3.6
insurance rebates, 5.2.1

interest ceilings, *see* INTEREST CEILINGS
interpretation, 9.3.1
interstate transactions, 9.2.9
land installment contracts, 9.2.3.4
late fees, 7.2.4.2.2
lender fees, 7.2.1
licensing statutes, 9.2.4.5, 9.2.4.6
modern statutes, interpretation, 2.2.2
MVRISAs, *see* MOTOR VEHICLE RETAIL INSTALLMENT
    SALES ACTS (MVRISAs)
national banks, application, 3.4.6.1
NCLC manual, scope, 2.1
non-depository creditors, 9.2.4.5
open-end credit, 2.3.3.8, 9.2.3.2
opting-in, 9.2.1.3
parity laws, 3.14
pawnbrokers, 2.3.3.9
payday loans, 7.5.5.5
points, 7.2.2.2
post-deregulation, 2.5
predatory lending statutes, 12.2.3
purpose, 1.3, 9.3.1.1
RALs, 7.5.4.2
rebates, 5.2.1
remedies, *see under* USURY REMEDIES
research aids, references, 1.5
retroactive amendment, 9.3.2
RISAs, *see* RETAIL INSTALLMENT SALES ACTS (RISAs)
scope, determination, 9.2.1.2
small loan laws, *see* SMALL LOAN LAWS
sophisticated borrowers, application, 10.6.3
special usury statutes, 2.3.3, 9.2.9.3
summary, Appx. A
tax refund schemes, application, 7.5.4.1
TILA, relationship, 2.3.4
time-price exception, *see* TIME-PRICE DOCTRINE
unearned interest rebates, 5.2.1
violation, *see* USURY VIOLATIONS
wraparound mortgages, application, 7.4.3

USURY REMEDIES
see also USURY CLAIMS; USURY VIOLATIONS
credit insurance abuses, 8.7.1
federal remedies
    DIDA, 10.8.5.1
    HOEPA, 10.8.5.2
    National Bank Act, 10.8.5.1
    RICO, 10.8.5.3, 12.6
forfeiture of creditor's recovery rights, 10.8.2.2
generally, 10.8.1
HOEPA, *see* HOME OWNERSHIP AND EQUITY
    PROTECTION ACT (HOEPA)
implied private right of action, 10.8.2.1
income buyers
    assignment of government income, 7.5.8.2
    litigation finance companies, 7.5.8.3
overreaching credit, challenging, 12
    overview, 12.1
payday loans, 7.5.5.6
RALs, 7.5.4.2
recovery of payments, 10.8.2.3
rent-to-own transactions, 7.5.3.6
rescission, *see* RESCISSION

USURY REMEDIES (*cont.*)
RESPA, *see* REAL ESTATE SETTLEMENT PROCEDURES
    ACT (RESPA)
RICO, 10.8.5.3, 12.6
state remedies
    equitable remedies, 10.8.3
    remedies at law, 10.8.2.1
statutory penalties, 10.8.2.4
UDAP, *see* UDAP VIOLATIONS
unconscionability, *see* UNCONSCIONABILITY
unlicensed lending, 10.8.4

USURY VIOLATIONS
see also USURY REMEDIES
bankers' year daily interest, 4.6.3.4
check advancement loans, 7.5.5
checklist, fixed-term credit
    interest charges, 1.6.3.2.4
    non-rate violations, 1.6.3.2.5
claims re, *see* USURY CLAIMS
collection agencies, liability, 10.6.2
common law, 9.3.1.1
compensating balances, 7.4.4
compound interest, 4.6.1.2
contingent events, 5.7.1
credit insurance
    compulsory premiums, 8.5.2.3.1
    excess charges, 8.5.3.2
    excess coverage, 8.5.3.3
    non-filing insurance, 8.5.4.5
creditor defenses, *see* CREDITOR DEFENSES
criminal usury, 9.2.7
de minimis violations, 10.6.8
deregulated states, 9.2.8
discounts as, 7.4.6.1
inflated sale price, 7.4.6.1, 7.4.6.2, 11.6.2.1
interest overcharge, 10.5.4.2
joint ventures, 7.5.7
license, failure to obtain, 10.8.4
mathematical issues, proving, 4.10
odd payment periods, 4.6.2.2
payday loans, 7.5.5
points as, 4.7.2, 6.4.1.3
prepayment penalties as, 5.8.1
prima facie case, elements, 10.5
progress payment transactions, 4.9
proof, 10.5.1
RALs, 7.5.4.2
rebate violations as, 5.7.1, 6.4.1.3
refinanced loans, 6.4
refinancing, effect, 6.2.1
reformation of contract, 10.5.1.3, 10.8.3
remedies, *see* USURY REMEDIES
rent-to-own transactions, 7.5.3.6
rounding, 4.6.4
sale and repurchase agreements, 7.5.2.1
saving clauses, 10.6.10
seller's points, 7.4.6.2
spreading defense, 4.6.5
statutory penalties, 10.8.2.4
uncovering, 4.11
unearned charges, intent to collect, 5.7.2
variable rate transactions, 4.6.5.1
wraparound mortgages, 7.4.3

UTILITIES
see CONVENIENCE CREDITORS

VARIABLE RATE TRANSACTIONS
amortization, 4.3.6.3
balloon payments, 4.3.6.1, 4.3.6.4
calculating current rate, 4.3.6.2
caps, 4.3.6.4
carry over clauses, 4.3.6.4
described, 4.3.6.1
escalator clauses, enforceability, 4.3.6.5
floors, 4.3.6.4
index substitution, 4.3.6.5
interest ceilings, 4.3.6.5
legal issues, 4.3.6.5
mortgages, *see* ADJUSTABLE RATE MORTGAGES (ARMs)
recapture clauses, 4.3.6.4
restrictions, 4.3.6.5
spreading
    fixed term loans, 4.6.5.1
    open-end transactions, 4.6.5.2
unconscionability challenges, 12.7.2

VENDOR'S SINGLE INTEREST (VSI) INSURANCE
see also FORCE-PLACED INSURANCE
credit property insurance, 8.3.1.5.2
    auto loans, 8.3.1.5.4

VETERANS ADMINISTRATION (VA) LOANS
see also NATIONAL HOUSING ACT
mobile home loans, OTS regulations
    avoidance, 3.9.3.4
    compliance, 3.8.1
preemption of state interest ceilings, 3.1.1, 3.8
    preemption chart, 3.2.5
    state opt-out, 3.8.2
securitization, 11.4

VOLUNTARY PAYMENT DOCTRINE
creditor defense to usury, 10.6.5

WAIVER
assignee liability, 10.6.1.2.2, 10.6.1.3.10
creditor defense, as, 10.6.4.4, 10.8.2.3
liability damage waivers, 7.5.3.6.4
usury claims through refinancing, 6.2.3

WEB RESOURCES
consumer credit issues, Appx. M

WITNESSES
see EVIDENCE; EXPERT WITNESSES

WRAPAROUND MORTGAGES
see also MORTGAGES
defined, 7.4.3
hidden interest, 7.4.3

YIELD-SPREAD PREMIUMS
class actions, 12.2.1.5.6
described, 4.7.2
fraud claims, 12.10.2.4
hidden interest, 7.3.2
kickback status, 12.2.1.5.2
    HUD policy statement, 12.2.1.5.3, 12.2.1.5.5
    practice issues, 12.2.1.5.6
mortgage financing, 11.5.4.3, 12.2.1.5
points, inclusion, 4.7.2, 7.3.2

YIELD-SPREAD PREMIUMS (*cont.*)
practice tips, 12.2.1.5.6
RICO claims, 12.6
used car financing, 11.6.6

YO-YO DEALS
arbitration clauses, 10.3.3
overview, 11.6.5

Quick Reference to the Consumer Credit and Sales Legal Practice Series

References are to sections in *all* manuals in NCLC's Consumer Credit and Sales Legal Practice Series. References followed by "S" appear only in a supplement.

Readers should also consider another search option available at ***www.consumerlaw.org/keyword***. There, users can search all sixteen NCLC manuals for a case name, party name, statutory or regulatory citation, or *any* other word, phrase, or combination of terms. The search engine provides the title, page number and context of every occurrence of that word or phrase within each of the NCLC manuals. Further search instructions and tips are provided on the web site.

The Quick Reference to the Consumer Credit and Sales Legal Practice Series pinpoints where to find specific topics analyzed in the NCLC manuals. References are to individual manual or supplement sections. For more information on these volumes, see *What Your Library Should Contain* at the beginning of this volume, or go to www.consumerlaw.org.

This Quick Reference is a speedy means to locate key terms in the appropriate NCLC manual. More detailed indexes are found at the end of the individual NCLC volumes. Both the detailed contents pages and the detailed indexes for each manual are also available on NCLC's web site, www.consumerlaw.org.

NCLC *strongly recommends,* when searching for PLEADINGS on a particular subject, that users refer to the *Index Guide* accompanying *Consumer Law Pleadings on CD-Rom*, and *not* to this *Quick Reference*. Another option is to search for pleadings directly on the *Consumer Law Pleadings* CD-Rom or on the *Consumer Law in a Box* CD-Rom, using the finding tools that are provided on the CD-Roms themselves.

The finding tools found on *Consumer Law in a Box* are also an effective means to find statutes, regulations, agency interpretations, legislative history, and other primary source material found on NCLC's CD-Roms. Other search options are detailed at page vii, *supra.*

Abbreviations

AUS	=	Access to Utility Service (3d ed. 2004)
Auto	=	Automobile Fraud (2d ed. 2003 and 2005 Supp.)
Arbit	=	Consumer Arbitration Agreements (4th ed. 2004)
CBPL	=	Consumer Banking and Payments Law (3d ed. 2005)
Bankr	=	Consumer Bankruptcy Law and Practice (7th ed. 2004)
CCA	=	Consumer Class Actions: A Practical Litigation Guide (5th ed. 2002 and 2005 Supp.)
CLP	=	Consumer Law Pleadings, Numbers One Through Ten (2004)
COC	=	The Cost of Credit (3d ed. 2005)
CD	=	Credit Discrimination (4th ed. 2005)
FCR	=	Fair Credit Reporting (5th ed. 2002 and 2005 Supp.)
FDC	=	Fair Debt Collection (5th ed. 2004 and 2005 Supp.)
Repo	=	Repossessions and Foreclosures (5th ed. 2002 and 2004 Supp.)
Stud	=	Student Loan Law (2d ed. 2002 and 2004 Supp.)
TIL	=	Truth in Lending (5th ed. 2003 and 2004 Supp.)
UDAP	=	Unfair and Deceptive Acts and Practices (6th ed. 2004)
Warr	=	Consumer Warranty Law (2d ed. 2001 and 2005 Supp.)

Abandonment of Apartment Building in Bankruptcy—Bankr § 17.8.2

Abbreviations Commonly Used by Debt Collectors—FDC App G.4

Abuse of Process—UDAP § 5.1.1.4; FDC § 10.6

Acceleration—COC §§ 5.6.2, 5.7.1; Repo § 4.1

Accessions—Repo § 3.5.3.2

Accord and Satisfaction—CBPL §§ 2.7, 9.3.1

Account Aggregation—CBPL § 3.12

Accountants—UDAP § 5.12.8

Accrediting Agencies, Student Loans—Stud § 9.4.1.2

Accurate Information in Consumer Reports—FCR § 7.8

ACH—*See* NACHA

Actual Damages—*See* Damages

Actuarial Rebates—COC § 5.6.3.4

Adhesion Contracts—UDAP § 5.2.3

Adjustable Rate Mortgages—TIL § 4.6.4; COC § 4.3.6

Administration of Lawsuit, Class Action—CCA Ch 13

Admissibility of Other Bad Acts—Auto § 9.8.1

Admissions, Requests for—CCA § 7.5; Repo App E.5, O.2.2S; CLP; COC App L; FDC App I.3; Auto App F.1.4

Advertisements as Warranties—Warr § 3.2.2.5

Advertising Credit Terms—TIL §§ 5.4, 10.4

Affordability Programs, Utilities—AUS Ch 9, App F

After-Acquired Property—Repo § 3.4.5.2

Age Discrimination re Credit—CD § 3.4.2

Airbags—AF §§ 2.8S, 6.3bS

Airline Fare Advertising—UDAP §§ 2.5, 5.4.13.1

Alteration of Checks—CBPL § 2.3.1.4

Alimony Discharged in Bankruptcy—Bankr § 14.4.3.5

Alimony, Protected Source under ECOA—CD §§ 3.4.1, 5.5.5.3

Alternative Dispute Mechanisms—Arbit; FDC § 15.4

American Arbitration Association—Arbit App B.1

Americans With Disabilities Act—CD § 1.6

Amortization Explained—COC § 4.3.1

Amortization Negative—COC § 4.3.1.2

Amount Financed—TIL § 4.6.2

Annual Percentage Rate—TIL §§ 4.6.4, 5.6.9; COC § 4.4

Answer and Counterclaims—Repo Apps D.1, D.2; O.2.1S; COC App L; CLP

Antecedent Debt Clauses—Repo § 3.9

Anti-Competitive Conduct as UDAP Violation—UDAP § 4.10

Anti-Deficiency Statutes—Repo § 12.6.3

Apartment Buildings Abandoned in Bankruptcy—Bankr § 17.8.2

Apartment Leases—Bankr § 12.9; UDAP §§ 2.2.6, 5.5.2

Appeal of Order Requiring Arbitration—Arbit § 9.5

Applications for Credit—CD § 5.4

Appraisal Fraud—COC § 11.5.6

Appraisals, Right to a Copy—CD § 10.11

APR—*See* Annual Percentage Rate

Arbitration—Arbit; Bankr § 13.3.2.5; COC § 10.6.11; FDC § 15.4; TIL § 7.7; Warr § 10.2

Arbitration and Class Actions—Arbit § 9.4; CCA Ch 2;

Arbitration & Collection Actions – Arbit Ch. 11

Arbitration Fees—Arbit § 5.4

As Is—Warr Ch 5; Auto § 7.8.2

Assignee Liability—UDAP § 6.6; TIL § 7.3

Assignment of Tax Refunds—COC § 7.5.4

Assistance for the Payment of Utility Service—AUS Ch 16

Assisted Living Facilities—UDAP § 5.11.4

Assistive Device Lemon Laws—Warr Ch 16aS

ATM Cards—CBPL Ch 3

ATM Machines, Bank Liability for Robberies at—CBPL § 3.5.4

ATM Machine Payments—CBPL Ch 3

ATM Machines, Access for Disabled—CBPL Ch 8

Attorney as Debt Collector—FDC §§ 4.2.7, 11.5.3

Attorney Fees—TIL § 8.9; Bankr Ch 15; Auto §§ 5.8.4, 9.12; CD § 11.7.6; FCR § 11.6; FDC §§ 6.8, 11.2.5, 11.3.5; UDAP § 8.8; Warr §§ 2.7.6, 10.8

Attorney Fees, Class Actions—CCA Ch 15, App C

Attorney Fees for Creditors—COC § 7.3.3; FDC § 15.2

Attorney Fees, Pleadings—Auto App L; FDC App K

Attorney General Enforcement—UDAP Ch 10

Attorneys Liable Under FDCPA—FDC §§ 4.2.7, 4.6.3

Attorneys Liable Under UDAP—UDAP §§ 2.3.9, 5.12.1

Auctions—Repo §§ 10.7.1, 10.9.3; Auto §§ 2.5.4, 2.6.4

Authorization to Represent—CCA App C

Authorization to Sue—CCA § 1.2.4

Automated Clearing House for Electronic Transfer—CBPL Ch3

Automatic Stay—Bankr Ch 9

Automobile Accessories—UDAP § 5.4.11

Automobile Auctions—*See* Auctions

Automobile Dealer Files—UDAP § 5.4.2

Automobile Dealer Licensing—Auto § 6.4, Appx. F

Automobile Dealers, Bonding Requirement—Auto § 9.13.4, App C

Automobile Dealers, Registration with Auction—Auto Appx. E.3

Automobile Fraud—Auto

Automobile Insurance, Force-Placed—*See* Force-Placed Auto Insurance

Automobile Leases, Article 9 Coverage—Repo § 14.2.1

Automobile Leases, Default and Early Termination—TIL Ch 10; UDAP § 5.4.8.3; Repo § 14.2

Automobile Leases, Misrepresentation—UDAP § 5.4.8

Automobile Leases, Odometer Rollbacks—Auto §§ 4.6.6.5, 5.2.6

Automobile Leases, Sublease Scams—UDAP § 5.4.10

Automobile Leases, Unconscionability—UDAP § 5.4.8.5

Automobile Manufacturers, List—Warr App N

Automobile Pawn Transactions—Bankr § 11.9; COC § 7.5.2.3; Repo § 3.5.5

Automobile Rentals—UDAP § 5.4.9

Automobile Repairs—Warr Ch 17; UDAP § 5.4.1

Automobile Repossession—*See* Repossessions

Automobile Safety Inspection Laws—Warr § 14.9

Automobile Sales—Warr Chs 13, 14; UDAP §§ 5.4.2, 5.4.6, 5.4.7

Automobile Service—Warr § 17.8; UDAP § 5.3.5

Automobile Spot Delivery Abuses—UDAP § 5.4.5; Repo § 4.5; TIL §§ 4.4.5, 4.4.6

Automobile Sublease Scams—UDAP § 5.4.10

Automobile Title—Auto §§ 2.3, 2.4, Apps. D, E; UDAP § 5.4.5; Warr § 14.5.5

Automobile Valuation—Bankr § 11.2.2.3.2

Automobiles, Theft Prevention, Federal Statutes & Regulations—Auto App B.2

Bad Checks—FDC §§ 5.6.4, 15.3

Bail (i.e. replevin)—Repo Ch 5

Bait and Switch—UDAP § 4.6.1

Balloon Payments—COC § 4.6.2, Ch 5; TIL § 2.2.4.2.2

Bank Accounts, Attachment—FDC Ch 12, CBPL § 4.2

Bank Accounts, Closing—CBPL § 2.6.3

Bank Account Garnishment—CBPL § 4.2, FDC Ch 12

Bank Accounts, Joint—FDC § 12.7

Bank Accounts, Set-Off—FDC § 12.6.7, CBPL § 4.3

Bank Fees—CBPL § 4.5

Bank Accounts, Unfair Practices—UDAP §§ 4.4.9, 5.1.10

Bankruptcy and Debt Collection—FDC §§ 2.2, 9.10; Bankr § 9.4.3

Bankruptcy and Security Interests—Repo Ch 8

Bankruptcy and Utility Service—AUS §§ 4.5, 12.1; Bankr § 9.8

Bankruptcy, Claims Against Landlords in—Bankr § 17.8

Bankruptcy, Claims Against Creditors, Merchants in—Bankr Ch 17; UDAP § 6.8

References are to sections in *all* manuals in NCLC's Consumer Credit and Sales Legal Practice Series

Bankruptcy Code, Text—Bankr App A
Bankruptcy, Consumer Reports of—FCR §§ 13.6.9, 7.8.4.10.2, 8.3.7
Bankruptcy Court as Litigation Forum—Bankr Ch 13
Bankruptcy Discharge of Student Loans—Stud Ch 7
Bankruptcy Forms—Bankr Apps D, E, F, G
Bankruptcy Petition Preparers—Bankr § 15.6
Benefit Overpayments and Bankruptcy—Bankr § 14.5.5.4
Bibliography—Bankr
Billing Errors—FDC § 5.7; Repo § 19.2.2
Billing Error Procedures, Credit Cards—CBPL § 6.5; TIL § 5.8
Bill Stuffers—Arbit § 3.8
Binding Arbitration—Arbit
Blanket Security Interests—Repo § 3.4.5.2.2
Bond, Claims Against Seller's—UDAP § 6.8; Auto § 9.13.4, App C
Bonding Statutes—Auto App C
Book-of-the-Month Clubs—UDAP § 5.8.5
Bounced Checks—CBPL § 2.5
Bounce Loans—TIL § 3.9.3.3, COC § 7.5.6
Breach of Contract—UDAP § 5.2.5
Breach of the Peace and Repossession—Repo § 6.4
Breach of Warranties—Warr; UDAP § 5.2.7.1
Briefs, Class Action—CCA Ch 9
Broker Fees—COC §§ 7.4.2, 11.5.4
Brokers, Auto—UDAP § 5.4.10
Brokers, Loan—*See* Loan Brokers
Brokers, Real Estate—*See* Real Estate Brokers
Budget Payment Plans—AUS § 6.4
Burglar Alarm Systems—UDAP § 5.6.2
Business Credit, Discrimination re—CD § 2.2.6.4
Business Opportunities—UDAP §§ 2.2.9.2, 5.13.1
Buy Here, Pay Here Car Sales—UDAP § 5.4.6.13
Buy Rate—UDAP § 5.4.7.6
Buying Clubs—UDAP § 5.10.6
Calculating Interest Rates—COC Ch 4
Campground Resort Memberships—UDAP §§ 2.2.8, 5.10.5
Cancellation Rights—TIL Ch 6; UDAP §§ 5.2.6, 5.8.2, 9.5
Cardholders' Defenses—TIL § 5.9.5
Carfax—Auto § 2.3.2, Appx. E.2
Cars—*See* Automobile
Case Selection—CCA § 1.2
Case Summaries, FDCPA—FDC App L
Cash Discounts—TIL § 5.9.6.4
Cashier's Checks—CBPL § Ch 5
Chapter 7 Bankruptcy—Bankr Ch 3
Chapter 11 Bankruptcy—Bankr §§ 6.3.4, 17.7
Chapter 12 Bankruptcy—Bankr Ch 16
Chapter 13 Bankruptcy—Bankr Ch 4
Charge Cards—TIL § 5.2.4.2
Charitable Contributions—Bankr § 1.1.2.5
Charitable Solicitations—UDAP § 5.13.5
Check 21—CBPL §§ 2.2, 2.4, App B
Check Advancement Loans—*See* Payday Loans
Check Approval Companies—FCR §§ 2.3.6.3, 2.6.1, 6.4.2.3.5, 13.2.2, 13.3.6
Check Cards—CBPL § 4.1.4.2
Check Cashing Services—UDAP §§ 5.1.10
Check Cashing Regulation—CBPL § 1.14
Check Guarantee Companies—FDC § 4.2.3
Checklist, Automobile Fraud Litigation—Auto § 1.4
Checklist, Debt Collection—FDC App G
Checklist, Truth in Lending—TIL §§ 1.6, 3.11
Checklist, Usury—COC § 1.6
Checks—CBPL Ch 2
Checks, Bad—FDC §§ 5.6.4, 15.3, CBPL § 2.5

Checks, Preauthorized Draft—UDAP §§ 5.1.10, CBPL § 2.3.5
Child Support, Credit Reports—FCR § 5.3.2
Child Support Discharged in Bankruptcy—Bankr § 14.4.3.5
Children in Household, Discrimination Based On—CD § 3.5.1
Choice of Laws—COC § 9.2.9; Repo § 2.18
Churning Repossession Schemes—Repo § 10.9.4
Civil Rights Act—CD § 1.5
Class Actions Fairness Act of 2005—CCA § 2.1aS, 11.5aS
Class Actions—CCA; Auto § 9.7, App H; FCR § 10.7.2; FDC §§ 6.2.1.3, 6.3.5, 6.6; TIL §§ 6.9.9, 8.8; UDAP § 8.5
Class Actions and Arbitration—Arbit § 9.4; CCA Ch 2
Class Actions of Diversity Jurisdiction—CCA § 2.1aS
Class Actions Guidelines for Settlement, NACA—CCA App B
Class Actions in Bankruptcy Court—Bankr §§ 13.7, 17.4.2
Class Actions, Removal to Federal Court—CCA § 2.1aS
Class Certification Motions, Sample—CCA App K; CLP
Class Definitions—CCA Ch 3
Class Notices—CCA Ch 10, App N
Client Authorization to Represent—CCA App C
Client Authorization to Sue—CCA § 1.2.4
Client Contacts with Other Parties—CCA §§ 1.2.6, 5.3
Client Handout on Bankruptcy—Bankr App I
Client Handout on Credit Discrimination—CD App I
Client Handout on Credit Reporting—FCR App J
Client Interview Checklist, Bankruptcy—Bankr App H
Client Interview Checklist, Debt Collection Harassment—FDC App G
Client Interview Sheet, Warranties—Warr App I
Client Retainer Forms, Sample—CLP
Closed-End Auto Leases—TIL Ch 10; Repo § 14.2
Closed-End Credit—TIL Ch 4
Closed School Discharge—Stud § 6.2
Closing Arguments, Sample—Auto App I; FCR App I.2
Coercive Sales Techniques—UDAP § 4.8
Collateral—Repo
Collection Fees—FDC § 15.2; Stud § 4.4
Collection of Student Loans—Stud Ch 4
College Transcripts and Bankruptcy—Bankr §§ 9.4.3, 14.5.5.2
Collision Damage Waiver (CDW)—UDAP § 5.4.9
Common Law Contract Defenses—UDAP § 9.5
Common Law Fraud, Misrepresentation—Warr § 11.4; UDAP § 9.6.3; Auto Ch 7
Common Law Right to Utility Service—AUS § 3.1
Common Law Violations and Credit Reporting—FCR § 10.2
Common Law Warranties—Warr § 17.4
Communications to Client from Other Attorney—CCA § 5.3; FDC § 5.3.3
Community Reinvestment Act—CD § 1.9
Compensating Balances—COC § 7.4.4
Complaint Drafting, Class Actions—CCA Ch 4
Complaints—Arbit App C; Auto App G; CD App G; CCA App D; COC App L; FCR App H; FDC App H; Repo Apps D.3, D.4, App OS; Warr App K; TIL Apps D, E; CLP
Compound Interest—COC § 4.6.1
Computers, Sale of—UDAP § 5.7.6
Condominiums—UDAP § 5.5.4.5
Condominium Warranties—Warr Ch 16
Consignment—Repo § 9.6.3.3
Consolidation Loan—Stud § 8.2
Conspiracy in Odometer Case—Auto § 4.7
Constitutionality of Arbitration Agreement—Arbit Ch 8
Contract Formation of Arbitration Agreement—Arbit Ch 3
Constructive Strict Foreclosure—Repo §§ 10.5.2, 12.5
Consumer Class Actions—CCA

References are to sections in *all* manuals in NCLC's Consumer Credit and Sales Legal Practice Series

Consumer Complaints to Government Agencies—UDAP § 9.8

Consumer Credit Reporting Reform Act of 1996—FCR § 1.4.6

Consumer Guide to Credit Reporting—FCR App J

Consumer Leasing Act—TIL Ch 10, App I.1

Consumer Recovery Funds—Auto § 9.13.5

Consumer Reporting Agencies—FCR

Consumer Reporting Agencies, Enforcement Agreements—FCR App H

Consumer Reporting Agency, Sample User Agreement—FCR App G.1

Consumer Reports, Disputing and Right to Use—FCR Ch 7

Consumer Reports, Keeping Credit Disputes Out of—FCR § 13.5.2

Consumer Reports for Business Transactions—FCR §§ 2.3.5.4, 2.3.6, 5.2.4.3, 5.2.9

Consumer Reports for Employment Purposes—FCR §§ 2.3.6.6, 5.2.5

Consumer Reports for Government Benefits—FCR §§ 2.3.6.8, 5.2.7

Consumer Reports for Insurance Purposes—FCR §§ 2.3.6.7, 5.2.6

Consumer Reports from Non-Reporting Agencies—FCR § 6.4.4

Consumer/Seller Liability under Odometer Act—Auto § 4.8.13

Contests—UDAP §§ 4.6.6, 5.13.4

Contract Defenses—UDAP § 9.5

Contractual Misrepresentations—UDAP § 5.2.4

Cooling Off Periods—*See* Cancellation

Correspondence Schools—Stud Ch 9

Cosigners—Bankr § 9.4.4; CD § 5.4; Repo § 12.9; TIL §§ 2.2.2.2, 8.2; UDAP § 5.1.1.2.9

Counseling the Debtor—Bankr Ch 6

Coupon Settlement, Class Actions—CCA §§ 11.5aS

Cramming—AUS § 2.7.5

Credit Abuses—COC; UDAP §§ 2.2.1, 5.1

Credit Accident and Health Insurance—COC § 8.3.1.3; TIL §§ 3.7.9, 3.9.4

Credit Balances—TIL § 5.6; UDAP § 5.1.9.4

Credit Card Finders—UDAP § 5.1.9.2

Credit Card Issuers, Raising Seller-Related Claims Against— UDAP § 6.6, TIL § 5.9.5; CBPL § 6.4

Credit Card Issuer's Security Interest in Goods Purchased—Repo § 3.6

Credit Card Surcharges—TIL § 5.9.6.4

Credit Card Unauthorized Use—TIL § 5.9.4

Credit Cards—TIL Ch 5; CBPL Ch 6; UDAP § 5.1; FDC § 4.2.3

Credit Cards, Reporting Services for Lost—UDAP § 5.1.5.5

Credit Charges—COC Ch 5; UDAP § 5.1.6

Credit Denial, Notice—CD § 10.5; FCR § 6.2

Credit Disability Insurance—COC §§ 8.3.1.3, 8.5.2.3; Repo § 16.7.5; TIL §§ 3.7.9, 3.9.4

Credit Evaluation—CD §§ 6.2, 6.3

Credit File, Disputing and Right to See—FCR Chs 4, 7

Credit Insurance—COC Ch 8; TIL §§ 3.7.9, 3.9.4; Repo § 4.4; UDAP § 5.3.10

Credit Life Insurance—COC §§ 8.3.1.2, 8.5.3.1.2; TIL §§ 3.7.9, 3.9.4

Credit Math—COC Ch 4

Credit Property Insurance—COC §§ 8.3.1.5, 8.5.3.1.4, 8.5.3.4, 8.5.4.4; TIL §§ 3.9.4.4, 3.9.4.6, 4.9.8

Credit Rating, Injury to—FCR § 13.4; FDC §§ 5.5.2.9, 8.3.8; UDAP § 8.3.3.6

Credit Regulation, History of—COC Ch 2

Credit Repair Organizations—FCR Ch 15; UDAP § 5.1.2.2

Credit Reporting Agencies, Contacting—FCR § 4.4.2

Credit Reporting Sample Forms—FCR App F

Credit Reports—FCR; TIL § 5.9.4.5

Credit Reports, Affiliate Sharing—FCR §§ 2.4.2, 4.4.1.5, 4.5.8, 6.4.4.4, 6.5.4

Credit Reports, Furnishers of Information Obligations—FCR Ch 3, § 13.5.1

Credit Reports, Keeping Credit Disputes Out of—FCR § 13.5.2

Credit Reports from Non-Reporting Agencies—FCR § 6.4.4

Credit Reports, Student Loans—Stud § 3.3

Credit Scams—UDAP §§ 5.1.2; 5.1.3; 5.1.8

Credit Scoring—CD § 6.4; FCR § 6.6.4, App JS

Credit Terms—COC; UDAP § 5.1.5; 5.1.7

Creditor Remedies—FDC Chs 12, 13, 15; UDAP § 5.1.1; 5.1.1

Creditors, Types of—COC Chs 2, 9

Creditors Filing Bankruptcy—Bankr Ch 17

Creditworthiness—Bankr § 6.2.2.3

Criminal Prosecution Threats—FDC § 15.3

Cross-Collateral—Repo § 3.7.2

Cross Metering, Utility Service—AUS § 5.2

Cruise Line Port Charges—UDAP § 5.4.13.2

Cure of Default—Repo §§ 4.8, 13.2.4.4

Cy Pres—CCA § 11.7

Daily Accrual Accounting—COC § 4.6.8

Damages—FDC §§ 2.5.2, 6.3, Ch 10; FCR Ch 11; Repo Ch 13; TIL Ch 8; UDAP § 8.3; Warr §§ 10.4–10.6

Damage to Credit Rating—UDAP § 8.3.3.6

Dance Studios—UDAP § 5.10.4

Daubert Doctrine—Warr § 10.1.7.5

Dealer's Only Auto Auctions—Repo § 10.9.3

Debit Cards—CBPL Ch 3

Debt Cancellation Agreements—TIL §§ 3.7.10, 3.9.4.7

Debt Collection—FDC; UDAP §§ 2.2.2, 5.1.1

Debt Collection and Bankruptcy—FDC § 2.2.5

Debt Collection by Arbitration—FDC § 15.4; Arbit Ch. 11

Debt Collection Case Preparation—FDC Ch 2

Debt Collection Procedures Act—FDC § 13.2.1.1

Debt Collectors—FDC § 1.2, Ch 4

Debt Collector's Common Abbreviations—FDC App G.4

Debt Harassment, How to Stop—FDC § 2.3

Debtor in Possession under Chapter 12—Bankr § 16.3

Debt Pooling—FDC § 1.5.5

Deceit—Warr § 11.4; UDAP § 9.6.3

Deception—UDAP § 4.2; FDC § 5.5

Deceptive Practices Statutes—*See* UDAP

Deceptive Pricing—UDAP § 4.6.3

Defamation—FDC § 10.5; FCR § 10.3.7

Defamatory Use of Mail—FDC § 9.1

Default—Repo Ch 4

Default Insurance—TIL § 3.7.7

Defective Automobile Title—Auto

Defenses as Grounds for Nonpayment—Repo § 4.6

Defenses to Credit Card Charges—CBPL § 6.4; TIL § 5.9.5; UDAP § 6.6

Deferment of Student Loan—Stud § 2.2

Deferral Charges—COC § 4.8.2

Deferred Payment Plans—AUS § 6.6

Deficiency Actions—Repo Ch 12, App C.1

Deficiency Judgments—Repo § 21.3

Delay—UDAP § 4.9.2

Delaying Tactics, Opposing—CCA Ch 6

Delinquency Charges—*See* Late Charges

Deliverable Fuels—AUS § 1.6

Demonstrator Vehicles—Auto §§ 1.4.8, 2.1.6

Denial of Credit, Notice—FCR § 6.2

Department of Housing and Urban Development (HUD)—CD

§ 12.3.1, App D; Repo Chs 16, 17, § 18.2

Department of Motor Vehicles—Auto Appx. D

Deposit, Consumer's Right to Return When Seller Files Bankruptcy—Bankr § 17.5

Depositions in Class Actions—CCA § 7.4.4, Ch 8

Deposition Notice, Sample—CLP

Deposition Questions, Sample—Auto § 9.5.5; FCR App I.4.2; CLP

Deposition Questions and Answers, Sample—CLP

Depository Creditors—COC Ch 2; FDC Ch 12

Deregulation of Utilities—AUS Ch 1

Detinue—Repo Ch 5

Digital Divide—CD § 3.8.2

Direct Deposits—CBPL Ch 10

Disabilities, Discrimination Based On—CD § 3.5.2

Disability Discharge—Stud § 6.6

Disabled Access to ATM machines—CBPL Ch 8

Discharge in Bankruptcy—Bankr Ch 14

Discharging Student Loan Obligations—Stud Ch 6, § 7.2.2S

Disclaimers, Warranties—Warr Ch 5

Disclosure and UDAP—UDAP § 4.2.14

Disclosure of Credit Terms—TIL

Disconnection of Utility Service—AUS Chs 11, 12

Discovery—Auto § 9.5, App H; *see also* Interrogatories; Document Requests

Discovery, Arbitration—Arbit § 9.1, App D

Discovery, Class Actions—CCA Ch 7, App E

Discovery, Motions to Compel—CCA Apps F, G, H

Discrimination in Collection Tactics—FDC § 9.8

Discrimination re Credit—CD

Disposition of Repo Collateral—Repo Chs 9, 10

Dispute Resolution Mechanisms—Warr §§ 2.8, 13.2.9

Disputing Information in Consumer Report—FCR § 13.5.2

Document Preparation Fees—TIL § 3.9.6; UDAP § 5.4.3.8

Document Production Requests, Sample—Arbit App D; Auto App F; CCA App E; CD App H; FDC App I.2; Repo Apps E.2, O.2.2S; TIL App F.3; Warr App L.3; CLP

Document Requests, Sample Objection to—CCA App J

D'Oench, Duhme Doctrine—COC § 10.7; Repo §§ 12.10, 16.7.7; UDAP § 6.7.5

Door-to-Door Sales—UDAP § 5.8.2; Warr § 17.6

Dragnet Clauses—Repo § 3.9

Driver Privacy Protection Act—Auto § 2.2.4, App A.2

Driver's Licenses and Bankruptcy—Bankr §§ 14.5.4, 14.5.5.1

Drunk Driving Debts in Bankruptcy—Bankr § 14.4.3.9

Dunning, How to Stop with Sample Letters—FDC § 2.3

Duress—UDAP § 9.5.12; AUS § 6.1.9

Duty of Good Faith and Fair Dealing—COC § 12.8

Early Termination Penalties in Auto Leases—TIL § 10.5

Earned Income Tax Credit—Bankr § 2.5.3

EBT—CBPL Ch 8

E-Commerce, Jurisdiction—COC § 9.2.9.4

Educational Loans—*See* Student Loans

EFT 99—CBPL Ch 10

Elderly, Special Foreclosure Problems—Repo § 16.10

Election of Remedy Statutes—Repo § 12.4

Electric Service—AUS § 1.2.2; UDAP § 5.6.9

Electric Industry Restructuring—AUS § 1.4

Electronic Banking—CBPL Ch 3; FDC § 12.6.6

Electronic Benefit Transfers—CBPL Ch 8

Electronic Check Conversion—CBPL Ch 3

Electronic Credit Transactions—COC § 9.2.10

Electronic Disclosure—TIL §§ 4.2.9, 5.3.6, 9.3.9; UDAP § 4.2.14.3.9

Electronic Fund Transfers—CBPL Chs 3, 10

Electronic Repossession—Repo § 6.6

Electronic Check Representment—CBPL Ch 2

Electronic Signatures and Records—CBPL Ch 11

Electronic Transaction Fraud—UDAP § 5.9.4; CBPL Ch 3

Electronic Transfer Account (ETA)—CBPL Ch 10

Employer Bankruptcy—Bankr § 17.7.11

Employment Agencies—UDAP § 5.13.2

Encyclopedia Sales—UDAP § 5.7.1

Endorsements—UDAP § 4.7.7

Energy Savings Claims—UDAP § 5.6.7

Enforceability of Arbitration Clause—Arbit

Equal Credit Opportunity Act—CD; AUS § 3.7.2; FCR §§ 6.4.5, 13.2.7

Equal Credit Opportunity Act Regulations—CD App B

E-Sign—CBPL Ch 11; COC § 9.2.10, 11.3.1.8a

ETAs (Electronic Transfer Accounts)—CBPL Ch 10

Ethnic Discrimination—CD § 3.3.3

Evictions—AUS § 12.4; UDAP § 5.5.2.10; FDC § 1.5.2

Evidence Spoilation—Warr § 10.1.2.5

Evidentiary Issues in Automobile Litigation—Auto § 9.8

Exempt Benefits and Bankruptcy—Bankr § 10.2.2.11

Exempting Interest Rates—COC Ch 3

Exemption Laws, Liberal Construction—FDC § 12.2

Exemption Planning—Bankr § 10.4.1

Exemptions, Benefits, Earnings, Due Process Protections—FDC Ch 12

Expert Inspection—Warr § 10.1.5.1

Experts, Attorney Fee Award for—UDAP § 8.8.7.3

Expert Witnesses—FDC § 2.4.14; Warr § 10.1

Expert Witnesses, Sample Questions—Auto App I

Exportation of Interest Rates—COC Ch 3

Express Warranties—Warr Ch 3

Expressio Unius Est Exclusio Alterius—COC § 9.3.1.2

Extended Warranties—*See* Service Contracts

Extortionate Collection—FDC § 9.5

FACT Act—FCR Supp

FACT Act Regulations—FCR Supp

Fair Credit Billing Act—CBPL § 6.5; TIL § 5.8; FCR § 13.5.2.2.1.1; AUS § 11.3.5

Fair Credit Reporting Act—FCR; FDC § 9.6

Fair Debt Collection Practices Act—FDC Chs 3–7, Apps A, B, L

Fair Housing Act—CD

Fair Housing Act Regulations—CD App D

False Certification Discharge—Stud § 6.3

False Pretenses, Obtaining Consumer Reports—FCR § 5.6

Family Expense Laws—FDC § 14.6; CD § 9.3

Farm Reorganizations, Bankruptcy—Bankr Ch 16

Farmworker Camps—UDAP §§ 2.2.7, 5.5.4

Faxes, Junk—UDAP § 5.9.2.2

Federal Agency Collection Actions—FDC Ch 13

Federal Arbitration Act—Arbit Ch 2, App A

Federal Benefit Payments, Electronic—CBPL Ch 10

Federal Civil Rights Acts—CD; AUS § 3.7.1

Federal Direct Deposit of Benefits—CBPL Ch 10

Federal Direct Student Loans—Stud

Federal Energy Regulatory Commission (FERC)—AUS § 1.2.2.2

Federal False Claims Act—UDAP § 9.4.13

Federal Family Education Loans—Stud

Federal Preemption—FDC §§ 2.2, 6.14; UDAP § 2.5

Federal Preemption of State Usury Laws—COC Ch 3

Federal Racketeering Statute—*See* RICO

Federal Reserve Board—*See* FRB

Federal Trade Commission—*See* FTC

Federally Insured Student Loans—Stud § 9.5

References are to sections in *all* manuals in NCLC's Consumer Credit and Sales Legal Practice Series

Fees—TIL § 3.7; COC § 7.2.1; FDC § 15.2
FHA Mortgage Foreclosure—Repo Ch 18
Fiduciary Duty—COC §§ 8.7.2, 12.9
Fifth Amendment Privilege—Auto § 9.8.6.7
Filed Rate Doctrine—UDAP § 5.6.10.1
Film Developing Packages—UDAP § 5.7.10
Finance Charge—TIL Ch 3; COC § 4.4
Finance Charges, Hidden—COC Ch 7; TIL § 3.10
Finance Companies—COC Ch 2; UDAP §§ 2.2.1, 5.1.5
Flipping—COC § 6.1; UDAP § 5.1.5
Flipping of Property—COC 11.5.6
Flood Damage to Vehicle—Auto § 2.1.3
Food Advertising—UDAP § 5.11.2
Food Stamps, Electronic Payment—CBPL Ch 8
Forbearance of Student Loans—Stud § 2.3
Force-Placed Auto Insurance—UDAP § 5.3.11; COC § 8.3.1.4; TIL § 3.9.4.4.2
Foreclosure—Repo
Foreclosure, False Threat—Repo Ch 6
Foreclosure, Government-Held Mortgages—Repo Ch 18
Foreclosure, Preventing Through Bankruptcy—Bankr Ch 9, §§ 10.4.2.6.4, 11.5, 11.6; Repo Ch 20
Foreclosure, Preventing Through Refinancing—COC § 6.5; Repo § 17.9.2
Foreclosure, Preventing Through Rescission—TIL Ch 6; Repo § 16.7.3.1
Foreclosure, Preventing Through Workouts—Repo Ch 17
Foreclosure, Setting Aside—Repo § 21.1
Foreclosure, Special Problems for Elderly—Repo § 16.10
Foreclosure, Summary of State Laws—Repo App I
Foreclosures and UDAP—UDAP § 5.1.1.5; Repo § 16.7.1.1
Forged Signatures, Indorsements—CBPL § 2.3.1.3
Franchises—UDAP §§ 2.2.9.2, 5.13.1
Fraud—UDAP; Warr § 11.4
Fraud and Arbitration—Arbit Ch 4
FRB Official Staff Commentary on Reg. B—CD App C
FRB Official Staff Commentary on Reg. M—TIL App I.3
FRB Official Staff Commentary on Reg. Z—TIL App C
Free Offers—UDAP § 4.6.4
Freezer Meats—UDAP § 5.7.2
FTC (Federal Trade Commission)—UDAP
FTC Act, No Private Action Under—UDAP § 9.1
FTC Cooling Off Period Rule—UDAP § 5.8.2, App B.3
FTC Credit Practices Rule—Repo § 3.4.2; UDAP § 5.1.1.2, App B.1; FDC § 8.4.2
FTC Debt Collection Law—FDC Ch 8
FTC FCR Enforcement Actions—FCR App H
FTC FCR Official Staff Commentary—FCR App C
FTC FDCPA Official Staff Commentary—FDC § 3.2.6, App C
FTC Funeral Rule—UDAP § 5.11.5, App B.5
FTC Holder Rule—UDAP § 6.6, App B.2
FTC Mail or Telephone Order Merchandise Rule—UDAP § 5.8.1.1, App B.4
FTC Staff Letters on FCR—FCR App D
FTC Staff Letters on FDCPA—FDC § 3.2.5, App B
FTC Telemarketing Sales Rule—UDAP App D.2.1
FTC Telephone and Dispute Resolution Rule—UDAP App D.2.2
FTC Used Car Rule—UDAP § 5.4.3.2, App B.6; Warr § 14.7, App D
Funds Availability—CBPL § 9.4
Funerals—UDAP § 5.11.5
Furniture Sales—UDAP § 5.7.3
Future Advance Clauses—Repo § 3.9
Future Service Contracts—UDAP § 5.10
GAP Insurance—TIL §§ 3.7.10, 3.9.4.7

Garnishment—FDC § 5.5.7, Ch 12, App D
Garnishment of Bank Account—CBPL § 4.2
Garnishment to Repay Student Loans—Stud § 5.3, App B.1.2A
Gas Service—AUS § 1.2.1; UDAP § 5.6.9
Gasoline, Price Gouging—UDAP § 5.6.8.5
Government Benefits—FCR §§ 2.3.6.8, 5.2.7
Government Checks—CBPL Ch 9
Government Collection Practices—FDC Ch 13; Stud Ch 4
Gramm-Leach-Bliley Act—COC §§ 3.9, 8.4.1.5.2; FCR § 1.5.3
Gray Market Sales—Auto § 1.4.11; Warr § 13.7
Guaranteed Student Loans—Stud
Guarantees—UDAP § 5.2.7.3
Guarantors—*See* Cosigners
Handguns—UDAP § 5.7.9
Handicapped, Discrimination Against—CD § 3.5.2
Handouts for Client—*See* Client Handouts
Health Care Bills—FDC Ch 14; Bankr § 6.2.2.4.1
Health Care Plans, Misrepresentations—UDAP § 5.11.6
Health Care Treatment, Discrimination In—CD § 2.2.2.6
Health Cures, Misrepresentations—UDAP § 5.11
Health Spas—UDAP § 5.10.3
Hearing Aids—UDAP § 5.11.1
Heating Fuel—AUS §§ 1.2, 1.6; UDAP § 5.6.8
HELC—TIL § 5.11
Hidden Interest—COC Ch 7; TIL § 3.10
High Cost Loans, State Laws—COC Ch 7
High Pressure Sales—UDAP § 4.8
Hill-Burton Act Compliance—UDAP § 5.11.5
Holder in Due Course—UDAP § 6.6; COC §§ 10.6.1
Home Builders—UDAP § 5.5.5.2
Home Equity Lines of Credit—TIL § 5.11
Home Equity Loans—TIL Ch 9
Home Foreclosure—*See* Foreclosure
Home Heating Fuel—AUS §§ 1.2, 1.6; UDAP § 5.6.8
Home Improvement Practices—TIL § 6.5.3; UDAP § 5.6.1; Warr § 17.7, Apps I.3, K.4
Home Mortgage Disclosure Act—CD § 4.4.5
Home Mortgage, Rescission of—TIL Ch 6, App E.3
Home Owners' Loan Act—COC § 3.5
Home Owners Warranty Program—UDAP § 5.5.5.2
Home Ownership & Equity Protection Act—TIL Ch 9, App E.4; Repo §§ 16.7.3.5, 14.11.3.2
Homes and UDAP—UDAP §§ 2.2.5, 5.5.5
Homes, Warranties—Warr § 1.4.3
Homestead Exemptions, Bankruptcy—Bankr § 10.2.2.2
Horizontal Privity—Warr § 6.3
Hospital Bills—FDC Ch 14
House Warranties—Warr Ch 16
Household Goods, Bankruptcy Exemption—Bankr §§ 10.2.2.4, 10.4.2.4
Household Goods Security Interest—Repo § 3.4; UDAP §§ 5.1.1.2; 5.1.1.5; TIL § 4.6.7
Household Goods Security Interest, Credit Property Insurance on—COC § 8.5.4.4
Houses and UDAP—UDAP §§ 2.2.5, 5.5
HOW Program—UDAP § 5.5.5.5.2
HUD—*See* Department of Housing and Urban Development
Identity Theft—FCR § 13.5.5
Illegal Conduct—UDAP §§ 4.3.9, 9.5.8
Illegality as Contract Defense—UDAP § 9.5.8
Immigrant Consultants, Deceptive Practices—UDAP § 5.12.2
Immigrant Status, Discrimination Based On—CD § 3.3.3.3
Implied Warranties—Warr Ch 4
Improvident Extension of Credit—UDAP § 5.1.4

References are to sections in *all* manuals in NCLC's Consumer Credit and Sales Legal Practice Series

Incomplete Information in Consumer Reports—FCR Ch 7

Inconvenient Venue—*See* Venue

Indian Tribal Law, Bankruptcy Exemptions—Bankr § 10.2.3.1

Industrial Loan Laws—COC Ch 2

Infancy—*See* Minority

Infliction of Emotional Distress—FDC § 10.2

In Forma Pauperis Bankruptcy Pilot Program—Bankr § 13.6.2

In Forma Pauperis Filings in Bankruptcy—Bankr §§ 13.6, 17.6

Informal Dispute Resolution—Warr § 2.8

Injunctions—UDAP § 8.6; FDC §§ 6.12, 12.6.2, 13.3

Insecurity Clauses—Repo § 4.1.6

Inspection by Experts—Warr § 10.1.5.1

Installment Sales Laws—COC §§ 2.3.3.4, 9.3.1.1

Insurance and Arbitration—Arbit § 2.3.3

Insurance and UDAP—UDAP §§ 2.3.1, 5.3

Insurance Consumer Reports—FCR §§ 2.3.6.7, 2.6.8, 5.2.6

Insurance, Credit—COC Ch 8; TIL §§ 3.7.9, 3.9.4; UDAP § 5.3.10

Insurance, Illusory Coverage—UDAP § 5.3.6

Insurance Packing—COC § 8.5.4; UDAP § 5.3.12

Insurance Redlining—CD § 7.3

Insurance, Refusal to Pay Claim—UDAP § 5.3.3

Intentional Infliction of Emotional Distress—FDC § 10.2

Intentional Interference with Employment Relationships—FDC § 10.4

Interest Calculations—COC §§ 4.2, 4.3

Interest, Hidden—COC Ch 7; TIL § 3.10

Interest Rates, Federal Preemption of—COC Ch 3

Interference with Employment Relationships—FDC § 10.4

International Money Orders and Wires—CBPL Ch 5

Internet Banking—CBPL Ch 3

Internet, Fraudulent Schemes—UDAP § 5.9

Internet, Invasion of Privacy—UDAP § 4.11

Internet Service Providers—UDAP § 5.6.10.7

Interrogatories—Arbit App D; Auto App F; CCA App E; CD App H; COC App L; FCR App I.2.1; FDC App I.1; Repo Apps E, O.2.2S, O.3.3S, O.3.4S; Warr App L; TIL App F.2; CLP

Interstate Banking and Rate Exportation—COC § 3.4.5

Intervenor Funding—AUS § 9.5

Interview Checklist for Debt Collection—FDC App G

Interview Form, Bankruptcy—Bankr App H

Interview Form for Clients, Warranties—Warr App I

Invasion of Privacy—FCR §§ 1.5, 10.3.8; FDC § 10.3

Investigative Reports—FCR Ch 9

Investments—UDAP §§ 2.2.9, 5.13

Involuntary Bankruptcy Cases—Bankr §§ 13.8, 16.1.2

Irrelevant Information in Consumer Reports—FCR § 7.8.4.10.3

JAMS—Arbit App B.3

Joint Bank Accounts, Seizure—FDC § 12.7

Joint Checking Accounts—CBPL §§ 2.6.3, 4.2, 4.3

Judicial Liens, Avoiding in Bankruptcy—Bankr § 10.4.2.3

Jury, Disclosure to, that Damages Will Be Trebled—UDAP § 8.4.2.8; Auto § 9.9.7

Jury Instructions, Sample—CCA Ch 14; Auto App G.6S; FDC App J.2; FCR App I.3; TIL App G

Jury Trial, Class Action—CCA Ch 14

Jury Trial, Preparing FDCPA Case—FDC § 2.5.7

Land Installment Sales—Repo § 16.11

Land Sales—UDAP §§ 2.2.5, 5.5.4.7

Land Trusts—TIL §§ 2.2.1.1, 2.4.3

Landlord Evictions—FDC § 1.5.2.2

Landlord's Removal of Evicted Tenant's Property—Repo § 15.7.4; FDC § 1.5.2.4

Landlord's Requested Disconnection of Utility Service—AUS § 12.4

Landlord's Termination of Utility Service—AUS Ch 4

Landlord-Tenant—Bankr §§ 12.9, 17.8; UDAP §§ 2.2.6, 5.5.2; FDC § 1.5.2

Landownership, Utility Service Conditioned on—AUS Ch 4

Late Charges—COC §§ 4.8, 7.2.4; TIL §§ 3.9.3, 4.7.7; UDAP §§ 5.1.1.2.8; 5.1.6

Late Charges, Utility Bills—AUS §§ 6.2, 6.3

Late Posting of Payments and Interest Calculation—COC § 4.6.3.5

Law, Unauthorized Practice of—FDC §§ 4.2.7.7.3, 11.5; Bankr § 15.6

Lawyer—*See* Attorney

Layaway Plans—UDAP § 4.9.1

Lease-Back of Home—COC § 7.5.2.1; TIL § 6.2.4.1

Leases—Repo Ch 14; TIL §§ 2.2.4.2, Ch 10; UDAP §§ 2.2.6, 5.4.8, 5.5.2; Warr Ch 19; Auto §§ 4.6.2.3, 4.6.6.5, 5.2.6; Bankr § 12.9; CD § 2.2.2.2; COC § 7.5.3; *see also* Rent to Own

Lease Terms for Residence—UDAP §§ 5.5.2.2, 5.5.2.3

Leased Vehicle Damages—Auto § 9.10.1.2

Legal Rights, Misrepresentation of—UDAP § 5.2.8

Lemon Cars Being Resold—Auto §§ 1.4.6, 2.1.5, 2.4.5.5, 6.3, App C; Warr § 14.5.3; UDAP § 5.4.6.7

Lemon Laws—Warr § 13.2, App F

Lender Liability—UDAP Ch 6

Letter to Debt Collector, Sample—FDC § 2.3

Liability of Agents, Principals, Owners—UDAP Ch 6; FDC § 2.8

Licenses to Drive and Bankruptcy—Bankr § 14.5.5.1

Liens—Repo Ch 15

Life Care Homes—UDAP § 5.11.3

Life Insurance, Excessive Premiums for—UDAP § 5.3.9

Lifeline Assistance Programs—AUS § 2.3.2

LIHEAP—AUS Ch 7, App D

Limitation of Remedies Clauses—Warr Ch 9

Living Trusts—UDAP § 5.12.3

Loan Brokers—UDAP §§ 2.2.1, 5.1.3; COC § 7.3.2

Loan Flipping—*See* Flipping

Loan Rehabilitation—Stud § 8.4

Loans, High Cost—COC Ch 7

Long Arm Jurisdiction—COC § 9.2.9.6; UDAP § 7.6.2

Lost Checks—CBPL §§ 2.8, 9.2

Lost Credit Card Reporting Services—UDAP § 5.1.5.5

Low Balling—UDAP § 4.6.5

Low Income Home Energy Assistance Program—AUS Ch 7, App D

Magazine Sales—UDAP § 5.7.1

Magnuson-Moss Warranty Act—Warr Ch 2, Apps A, B; Auto § 8.2.5

Magnuson-Moss Warranty Act Relation to Federal Arbitration Act—Arbit § 5.2.2, App G

Mail Fraud—UDAP § 9.2.4; FDC § 9.1

Mail Order Sales—UDAP § 5.8.1

Malicious Prosecution—FDC § 10.6.2

Managed Care, Misrepresentations—UDAP § 5.11.6

Manufacturer Rebates—UDAP § 4.6.3

Marital Status Discrimination—CD § 3.4.1

Mass Action—CCA § 2.1a.5.4S

Master Metering—AUS § 5.5

Math, Credit—COC Ch 4

McCarran-Ferguson Act—Arbit § 2.3.3; COC § 8.5.2.7; TIL § 2.4.9.5

Mechanical Breakdown Insurance—*See* Service Contracts

Mediation—Auto § 9.11.1.3

Medical—*See* Health Care

Mental Anguish Damages—FDC §§ 2.5, 6.3, 10.2

Mental Incompetence—UDAP § 9.5.7.3

Meter Tampering—AUS Ch 5

Migrant Farmworker Camps—UDAP §§ 2.2.7, 5.5.4

Mileage Disclosure—Auto §§ 2.4.5.8, 4.6.6

Military Personnel and Credit Protection—FDC § 9.12; FCR § 13.2.8.3; Repo §§ 6.3.5.1, 16.6

Mini-FTC Laws—*See* UDAP

Minority—UDAP § 9.5.7

Misrepresentation—UDAP § 4.2; Warr § 11.4; Auto § 8.4

Mistaken Undercharges, Utility Bills—AUS § 5.1.2

Mobile Home Defects—Warr § 15.1.3

Mobile Home Foreclosure—Repo § 16.12

Mobile Home Parks—UDAP §§ 2.2.6, 5.5.1

Mobile Homes, Federal Statutes—Warr App C

Mobile Homes and Interstate Rate Deregulation—COC Ch 3

Mobile Homes and Repossession—Repo §§ 2.2.2, 3.5, 4.8.3, 5.2, 6.3.3, 7.1

Mobile Homes, Sale by Consumer—Repo § 9.6.3

Mobile Homes and UDAP—UDAP §§ 2.2.5, 5.4.12

Mobile Homes, Utility Service—AUS § 5.6

Mobile Homes, Warranties—Warr Ch 15

Model Pleadings—*See* Complaints, Interrogatories, Document Requests, etc.

Money Orders—CBPL Ch 5

Mortgage Assistance Scams—UDAP § 5.1.2.1 Repo §§ 16.7.6, 15.10

Mortgage Assistance, State Programs—Repo § 17.9.4

Mortgage Fees—TIL § 3.9.6; COC Ch 7

Mortgage Loans—UDAP § 5.1.5

Mortgage Servicers—Repo § 17.2.4.3, Ch 19

Mortgage Servicing, Summary of State Laws—Repo App MS

Most Favored Lender—COC § 3.4.3

Motion in Limine, Sample—Auto App I; FDC App J.5

Motions for Class Certification—*See* Class Certification Motions

Motor Homes—CWL § 13.7b.45

Motor Vehicle Information and Cost Savings Act—Auto Chs 4, 5, App A.1

Motor Vehicle Installment Sales Act—COC § 2.3.3.5; Repo § 2.1

Multiple Damages—UDAP § 8.4.2; Auto § 5.8.1

Municipal Utilities (MUNIs)—AUS §§ 1.5, 12.2

NACA Class Actions Guidelines for Settlement—CCA App B

NACHA—CBPL Ch 3

National Arbitration Forum—Arbit App B.2, App H

National Origin Discrimination—CD § 3.3.3

"Nationwide" Reporting Agencies—FCR § 2.5.8

Native Americans and Repossession—Repo § 6.3.5.2

Necessities Laws—FDC § 14.6; CD § 9.3

Negative Equity—COC § 11.6.3

Negative Option Plans—UDAP § 5.8.5

Negligence—Warr Ch 12; FCR § 10.3.9; FDC §§ 10.2, 10.7

Negotiations, Class Actions—CCA Ch 11

New Car Lemon Laws—Warr § 13.2, App F

New Cars, Sales—Warr Ch 13; UDAP § 5.4.7

New Cars, Undisclosed Damage to—Auto §§ 1.4.5, 6.2.3

New House Warranties—Warr Ch 16

900 Numbers—UDAP §§ 5.9.3, 6.10, Apps D, E

Nonattorney Legal Service Providers, Deceptive Practices—UDAP § 5.12.2

Nondisclosure and UDAP—UDAP § 4.2.14

Non-English Speaking—UDAP § 5.2.1

Nonfiling Insurance—COC § 8.5.4.5

Nonpayment of Loans, When Excused—Repo § 4.6

Non-Signatories Rights and Obligations—Arbit §§ 6.3, 6.4

Notario Fraud—UDAP § 5.12.2

Notice Consumer Deducting Damages From Outstanding Balance—*See* Warr App J.2

Notice of Rescission—*See* Rescission Notice

Notice of Revocation—Warr App J.1

Notice to Class—CCA Ch 10

Notice to Quit, Deceptive—UDAP § 5.5.2.9

Not Sufficient Funds (NSF) Checks—CBPL § 2.5

Nursing Homes, Deceptive Practices—UDAP § 5.11.3

Obsolete Information in Consumer Reports—FCR Ch 8

Odometers—Auto; Warr § 14.5.2; UDAP § 5.4.6.5

Odometer Tampering—Auto §§ 4.3, 4.4

Offer of Judgment—FDC § 2.4.13; CCA § 6.3.1

Official Bankruptcy Forms—Bankr App D

Oil, Home Heating—AUS § 1.6; UDAP § 5.6.8

On-Line Fraud—UDAP § 5.9.4

On-Line Disclosures—UDAP § 4.2.14.3.9

On Us Checks—CBPL § 1.3.1.4

Open-End Credit—TIL Ch 5; COC § 2.3.2.3

Open-End Credit, Spurious—TIL § 5.2.3

Opening Statement, Sample—Auto App I

Outdated Information in Consumer Reports—FCR Ch 8

Overcharges by Creditor in Bankruptcy—Bankr § 13.4.3.3

Pain and Suffering Damages—FDC § 2.5; UDAP § 8.3.3.9

Paralegals, Attorney Fees for—UDAP §§ 8.6.11.6, 8.8.7.2

Parol Evidence—UDAP § 4.2.15.3; Warr § 3.7

Partial Prepayment—COC § 8.2

Pattern and Practice Evidence—Auto § 9.8

Payroll Cards—CBPL Ch 7

Pawnbrokers—COC §§ 2.3.3.9, 7.5.2.3; UDAP § 5.1.1.5.5

Payday Loans—COC § 7.5.5, App L

Payment Holidays for Interest-Bearing Loans—COC § 4.8.3

Payment Packing—COC § 11.6.4

Payment Plans, Utility Bills—AUS Ch 6

Pay Phones—AUS § 2.6

Pensions in Bankruptcy—Bankr §§ 2.5.2, 10.2.2.11

Percentage of Income Payment Plans—AUS § 9.2.3

Perkins Loans—Stud

Personal Injury Suits—UDAP § 2.2.11

Personal Property Seized with Repo—Repo Ch 7

Pest Control Services—UDAP § 5.6.3

Petroleum Products, Price Gouging—UDAP § 5.6.8.5

Photoprocessing Packages—UDAP § 5.7.10

Plain English—UDAP § 5.2.2

Pleadings—*See* Complaints, Interrogatories, Document Requests, etc.

Point of Sale (POS) Electronic Transfers—CBPL Ch 3

Points—COC §§ 4.7, 6.4.1.3, 7.2.1, 8.3.1.2; TIL § 3.7.5

Postal Money Order—CBPL Ch 5

Postdated Checks—CBPL § 2.6.1

Preauthorized Drafts—CBPL § 2.3.5

Precomputed Interest—COC § 4.5

Precut Housing—UDAP § 5.5.5.8

Preemption of State Usury Laws—COC Ch 3

Preemption and State Chartered Banks—COC Ch3

Preexisting Debt Clauses—Repo § 3.9

Prepayment—TIL § 4.7.6; COC Ch 5

Prepayment Penalties—COC § 5.8

Prescreening Lists—FCR § 5.3.8.4

Preservation of Documents, Class Actions—CCA § 5.2

Price Gouging in an Emergency—UDAP § 4.3.11

Pricing—UDAP § 4.6

Privacy, Invasion of—FCR § 10.3.8; FDC § 10.3

Privacy, Restrictions on Use of Consumer Reports—FCR § 1.5, Ch 5

Private Mortgage Insurance (PMI)—Repo § 16.7.8.7; COC § 8.3.2.1; UDAP § 5.3.13

Private Sale of Collateral—Repo § 10.5.7

Privity—Warr Ch 6; UDAP § 4.2.15.3
Prizes—UDAP § 5.13.4
Procedural Unconscionability—Warr § 11.2; COC § 12.7
Proceeds—Repo § 3.3.2
Progress Payments—COC § 4.9
Propane—AUS § 1.6; UDAP § 5.6.8
Property Flipping—COC § 11.5.6
Protective Orders—CCA § 5.2, App H
Public Assistance Status, Discrimination Based on—CD § 3.4.3
Public Housing, UDAP Coverage—UDAP §§ 2.3.3.3, 2.3.6
Public Housing, Utility Service—AUS Ch 8
Public Records—FCR § 7.2.3
Public Sale of Collateral—Repo § 10.7
Public Utilities—AUS
Public Utility Credit—TIL § 2.4.6
Punitive Damages—Auto § 7.10; CD § 11.7.4; FCR § 11.4; FDC § 2.6, Ch 10; UDAP § 8.4.3
Pyramid Sales—UDAP § 5.13.3
Pyramiding Late Charges—COC § 7.2.4.3; AUS § 6.2.6
Qualified Written Request—Repo App O.5S
Race Discrimination re Credit—CD § 3.3.1
Racketeering Statute—*See* RICO
Reachback Periods—Bankr § 6.5.3.4
Reaffirmations and Bankruptcy—Bankr § 14.5.2
Real Estate—UDAP §§ 2.2.5, 5.5.5
Real Estate Settlement Procedures Act—COC § 12.2.2; Repo Ch 19
Real Estate Tax Abatement Laws—Repo App J
Reassembled Cars from Parts—Auto §§ 1.4.3, 2.1.4; UDAP § 5.4.6.6
Rebates from Manufacturer—UDAP § 4.6.3.2; TIL § 3.7.5.2
Rebates of Interest—COC Ch 5, §§ 6.3, 6.4; TIL §§ 2.7, 3.7.2.2
Recoupment Claims—TIL §§ 6.3.3, 7.2.5; Bankr § 13.3.2.4
Redemption and Repo—Repo § 9.3
Redemption, Foreclosures—Repo §§ 16.2.6, 21.2
Redlining—CD §§ 7.1, 7.2
Referral Sales—UDAP § 5.8.3
Refinancings—COC Ch 6; Repo § 3.8; TIL § 4.9; UDAP § 5.1.5
Refund Anticipation Loans—COC § 7.5.4
Refunds—UDAP § 5.2.6
Regulation B, Text—CD App B
Regulation E—CBPL Ch 3, App D
Regulation M, Text—TIL App I.2
Regulation Z, Text—TIL App B
Regulation CC—CBPL § 9.4
Regulation DD—CBPL § 4.5
Rejection—Warr Ch 8
Reliance—TIL §§ 8.5.4.2, 8.5.5.7; UDAP § 4.2.12
Religious Discrimination re Credit—CD § 3.3.2
Rent and Bankruptcy—Bankr §§ 12.9, 14.5.5.3, 17.8
Rent to Own—UDAP § 5.7.4; Bankr § 11.8; COC § 7.5.3; Repo § 14.3
Rent, Utility Service—AUS Chs 4, 8
Rental Cars—UDAP § 5.4.9; Auto § 2.4.5.6
Rental Housing, Substandard—UDAP §§ 5.5.2.4, 5.5.2.5
Repairs—UDAP § 4.9.7
Repairs, Automobile—Warr § 17.8; UDAP § 5.4.1
Repayment Plan for Student Loans—Stud § 8.3
Replevin—Repo Ch 5
Reporting Agencies—FCR
Repossessions—Repo; UDAP § 5.1.1.5; FDC § 4.2.5
Repossessions, Stopping—Bankr Ch 9
Resale of Utility Service—AUS §§ 5.5, 5.6
Rescission—TIL Ch 6, App E.3; Auto § 7.11; Repo § 16.7.3.1; UDAP §§ 8.7, 9.5.2

Rescission by Recoupment—TIL § 6.3.3
Rescission Notice, Sample—TIL App D
Resisting Repossession, Liability for—Repo § 6.2.4.3
RESPA—COC § 12.2.2; Repo §§ 16.7.8.8, 17.2.4.3, 17.2.7.6, Ch 19; TIL §§ 4.1.1, 4.3.4
Retail Installment Sales Acts (RISA)—COC § 2.3.3.5; Repo § 2.5
Retail Sellers—COC §§ 2.3.1.3.2, 9.2.3.2
Retaliation for Exercise of TIL, CCPA Rights—CD § 3.4.4
Retroactive Statutes—UDAP § 7.4; COC § 9.3.2
Reverse Metering—AUS § 5.1
Reverse Redlining—CD §§ 8.2, 8.3
Review of Arbitration Decision—Arbit Ch 10
Revised Uniform Arbitration Act – Arbit Ch. 10
Revocation of Acceptance—Warr Ch 8
Revolving Repossessions—Repo § 10.9.4
RICO—UDAP §§ 9.2, 9.3, App C.1.1; COC § 12.6; FDC § 9.5; Auto § 8.5
Right to Cure Default—Repo § 4.8, App B; Bankr § 11.6.2
Right to See Consumer Reports—FCR § 4.3
Right to Utility Service—AUS Ch 3
RISA—COC § 2.3.3.5; Repo § 2.5
Rooker Feldman—FDC § 7.6.4
RTO Contracts—*See* Rent to Own
Rule of 78—COC § 5.6.3.3; TIL § 3.7.2.2.3; Repo § 11.3.2.2.2
Rural Electric Cooperatives (RECs)—AUS §§ 1.5, 12.2
Rustproofing—UDAP § 5.4.3.3
Safety—UDAP § 4.7.4
Sale and Lease-Back—COC § 7.5.2.1; TIL § 6.2.5
Sale of Collateral—Repo Ch 10
Salvage Auctions—Auto § 2.6.4.2
Salvage Vehicles, Sale of—Auto §§ 1.4.3, 2.1.4, 2.4.5.4, 6.2.1; Warr § 14.5.4
Salvaged Parts—UDAP § 5.4.6.6
Sample Answer and Counterclaims—*See* Answer and Counterclaims
Sample Attorney Fee Pleadings—*See* Attorney Fee Pleadings
Sample Client Retainer Forms— *See* Client Retainer Forms
Sample Closing Arguments—*See* Closing Arguments
Sample Complaints—*See* Complaints
Sample Deposition Questions—*See* Deposition Questions
Sample Discovery—*See* Interrogatories; Document Requests
Sample Document Production Requests—*See* Document Production Requests
Sample Forms, Bankruptcy—*See* Bankruptcy Forms
Sample Interrogatories—*See* Interrogatories
Sample Jury Instructions—*See* Jury Instructions
Sample Motion in Limine—*See* Motion in Limine Auto App I; FDC App J.5
Sample Motions for Class Certification—*See* Class Certification Motions
Sample Notice for Rescission—*See* Rescission Notice
Sample Notice of Deposition—*See* Deposition Notice
Sample Notice of Revocation—*See* Notice of Revocation
Sample Objection to Document Requests—*See* Document Requests, Sample Objection to
Sample Opening and Closing Statement—*See* Opening Statement; Closing Argument
Sample Pleadings—*See* Complaint, Interrogatories, Document Requests, etc.
Sample Requests for Admissions—*See* Admission Requests
Sample Trial Brief—*See* Trial Brief
Sample Trial Documents—*See* Trial Documents
Sample Voir Dire—*See* Voir Dire
School-Related Defenses to Student Loans—Stud § 9.5

Schools, Vocational—Stud Ch 9
Scope of Arbitration Agreement—Arbit Ch 6
Scrip Settlements, Class Actions—CCA § 11.6; CLP
Second Mortgage, Rescission of—TIL Ch 6
Secret Warranties—UDAP § 5.4.7.10.2; Warr § 13.5.3.2
Securities Law—UDAP § 9.4.10
Securitization of Consumer Paper—COC § 2.4.2
Security Deposits, Consumer's Rights to Reform Where Seller in Bankruptcy—Bankr § 17.8.4
Security Deposits, Tenant's—UDAP §§ 5.5.2.2, 5.5.2.3; FDC § 1.5.2.5
Security Deposits, Utility § 3.7
Security Interest Charges—TIL § 3.9
Security Interests—Repo Ch 3; TIL § 4.6.7
Security Interests, Avoiding in Bankruptcy—Bankr § 10.4.2.4, Ch 11
Security Systems—UDAP § 5.6.2
Seizure of Collateral—Repo
Self-Help Repossession—Repo Ch 6
Service Contracts—Warr Ch 18, App G; UDAP §§ 5.2.7.2, 5.4.3.5; Auto §§ 2.5.10, 2.6.2.11
Service Contracts, When Hidden Interest—COC §§ 7.2.3, 7.3.1; TIL § 3.6.5
Servicemembers Civil Relief Act—*See* Soldiers' and Sailors's Civil Relief Act
Servicer Abuses—Repo Ch 19
Services and Warranties—Warr Ch 17
Set Off, Banker's—CBPL Ch 4.3
Set-Offs—TIL §§ 5.9.3, 8.4; FDC § 12.6.7
Settlement, Auto Case—Auto § 9.11; Warr § 10.1.6
Settlement, Class Actions—CCA Chs 11, 12, Apps O, P
Settlement, Class Actions, Objections—CCA § 12.8, App Q
Settlement, Individual Prior to Class Action—CCA § 1.2
Settlements and Consumer Reports—FCR § 13.5.2
Sewer Service—AUS § 1.2.3
Sex Discrimination re Credit—CD § 3.3.4
Sexual Orientation, Discrimination Based On—CD § 3.7
Shell Homes—UDAP § 5.5.5.8
Single Document Rule—COC § 11.6.8
Slamming, Telephone Service—AUS § 2.7.5.1; UDAP § 5.6.11
Small Loan Laws—COC § 2.3.3.2
Smart Cards—CBPL § Ch 7
Social Security Benefit Offset to Repay Student Loan—Stud § 5.4
Social Security Payments, Electronic—CBPL Ch 10
Soldiers' and Sailors' Civil Relief Act—FDC § 9.12; FCR § 13.2.8.3; Repo § 6.3.5.1
Spendthrift Trusts in Bankruptcy—Bankr § 2.5.2
Spoilation of Evidence—Warr § 10.1.2.5
Spot Delivery of Automobiles—UDAP § 5.4.5; Repo § 4.5; TIL §§ 4.4.5, 4.4.6; COC § 11.6.5
Spouses, Consumer Reports on—FCR §§ 13.2.7, 13.3.7.2
Spreader Clauses—TIL § 4.6.7.6
Spurious Open-End Credit—TIL § 5.2.3
Stafford Loans—Stud
Standard Form Contracts, Unfair—UDAP § 5.2.3
State Arbitration Law—Arbit Ch 2
State Bonding Laws—Auto App C
State Chartered Banks and Preemption—COC Ch 3
State Cosigner Statutes—Repo § 12.9.6.2
State Credit Discrimination Laws—CD § 1.6, App E
State Credit Repair Laws—FCR App B
State Credit Reporting Laws—FCR § 10.4.1, App B
State Debt Collection Statutes—FDC § 11.2, App E
State Foreclosure Laws—Repo App I

State High Cost Loan Laws—COC Ch 7
State Home Improvement Statutes and Regs—Warr § 17.7.4
State Leasing Disclosure Statutes—TIL § 10.5.2.2
State Lemon Buyback Disclosure Laws—Auto App C
State Lemon Laws—Warr § 13.2, App F
State Lending Statutes—COC App A
State 900 Number Laws—UDAP App E
State Odometer Statutes—Auto App C
State Real Estate Tax Abatement Laws—Repo App J
State RICO Statutes—UDAP § 9.3, App C.2
State Right to Cure, Reinstate and Redeem Statutes—Repo App B
State Salvage Laws—Auto App C
State Service Contract Laws—Warr App G
State Telemarketing Laws—UDAP App E
State TIL Laws—TIL § 2.6
State Title Transfer Laws—Auto § 6.5, App C
State UDAP Statutes—UDAP App A
State Usury Statutes—COC App A
Statute of Limitations—Stud § 3.2; TIL § 7.2
Statute of Limitations as Consumer Defense to Collection Action—Repo § 12.7
Statutory Damages—TIL § 8.6; FDC §§ 6.4, 11.2; Repo § 13.2; UDAP § 8.4.1
Statutory Liens—Repo Ch 15
Statutory Liens, Avoiding in Bankruptcy—Bankr § 10.4.2.6.3
Staying Foreclosure—Bankr Ch 9
Stolen Checks—CBPL §§ 2.8, 9.2
Stolen Vehicles—Auto §§ 1.4.10, 2.1.7, 8.2.2
Stop Payment on Checks, Credit and Debit Cards—CBPL §§ 2.6.2, 6.4, Ch3
Storage of Evicted Tenant's Property—Repo § 15.7.4; UDAP § 5.5.2.5
Stored Value Cards—CBPL Ch 7, App F
Straight Bankruptcy—Bankr Ch 3
Strict Liability in Tort—Warr Ch 12
Student Loan Collection Abuse—Stud Ch 4
Student Loan Repayment Plans—Stud Ch 8
Student Loan Regulations—Stud App B
Student Loans—Bankr § 14.4.3.8; FCR §§ 8.6.9, 13.5.2.3, 13.6.11, 13.7.9; Stud; TIL § 2.4.5
Student Loans and Bankruptcy—Stud Ch 7
Student Loans, Private Loans—Stud § 1.9S
Student Loans, Reinstating Eligibility—Stud Ch 8
Summary Judgment Briefs, Sample—FDC App J.1; CLP
Surety for Consumer Debtor—Repo § 12.9
Surety Liability for Seller's Actions—Auto § 9.13.4
Survey Evidence—FDC § 2.9.3
Surveys, Use in Litigation—CCA § 7.6
Target Marketing Lists—FCR §§ 2.3.3, 5.2.9.1, 5.3.8.4.2
Tax Abatement Laws, State Property, Summaries—Repo App J
Tax Collections—FDC §§ 4.2.8S, 13.2
Tax Consequences, Bankruptcy Discharge—Bankr § 14.6
Tax Form 1099-C—CCA § 12.4a.5S
Tax Implications of Damage Award—CCA § 12.4a5
Tax Implications to Client of Attorney Fees—CCA § 15.6S
Tax Intercept—Bankr § 9.4.3
Tax Liens—Repo Ch 22
Tax Refund Intercepts—Stud § 5.2; FDC § 13.2
Tax Refunds—COC § 7.5.4
Tax Refunds in Bankruptcy—Bankr § 2.5.3
Tax Sales—Repo Ch 22
Taxis, Undisclosed Sale of—Auto § 2.4.5.6
Telechecks—UDAP §§ 5.1.10
Telecommunications Act of 1996—AUS Ch 2, App C

References are to sections in *all* manuals in NCLC's Consumer Credit and Sales Legal Practice Series

Telemarketing, Payment—CBPL §§ 2.3.5, 3.8

Telemarketing Fraud—UDAP § 5.9; FCR § 15.4

Telemarketing Fraud, Federal Statutes—UDAP App D

Telephone Cards, Prepaid—CBPL Ch 7

Telephone Companies as Credit Reporting Agencies—FCR § 2.6.9

Telephone Harassment—FDC § 9.3

Telephone Inside Wiring Maintenance Agreements—UDAP §§ 5.2.7.2, 5.6.10

Telephone Rates, Service—AUS Ch 2, App C

Telephone Service Contracts—UDAP §§ 5.2.7.2, 5.6.10

Telephone Slamming—AUS § 2.7.5.1; UDAP § 5.6.10

Teller's Checks—CBPL Ch 5

Tenant Approval Companies—FCR §§ 2.3.6.4, 2.6.1, 6.4.2.3.3, 13.3.2, 13.7.3

Tenant Ownership in Chapter 7 Liquidation—Bankr § 17.8.2

Tenant's Property Removed with Eviction—Repo § 15.7.4

Tenant's Rights When Landlord Files Bankruptcy—Bankr § 17.8; AUS § 4.5

Termination of Utility Service—AUS Chs 11, 12

Termite Control Services—UDAP § 5.6.3

Testers, Fair Housing—CD §§ 4.4.4, 11.2.2

Theft at ATM Machines, Bank Liability—CBPL § 3.5.4

Theft of Identity—FCR § 13.5.5

Third Party Liability Issues—AUS §§ 11.4, 11.5

Threats of Criminal Prosecution—FDC § 15.3

Tie-In Sale Between Mobile Home and Park Space—UDAP § 5.5.1.2

TIL—*See* Truth in Lending

Time Shares—UDAP § 5.5.5.10

Tire Identification—Auto § 2.2.3

Title, Automobile—Auto §§ 2.3, 2.4, Ch 3, Apps. D, E; UDAP § 5.4.5; Warr § 14.3.5

Tobacco—UDAP § 5.11.7

Tort Liability—FDC Ch 12

Tort Liability, Strict—Warr Ch 12

Tort Remedies, Unlawful Disconnections—AUS § 11.7.2

Tort Remedies, Wrongful Repossessions—Repo § 13.6

Towing—UDAP § 5.4.1.8; Repo Ch 15

Trade-in Cars—UDAP § 5.4.4.4

Trade Schools—Stud Ch 9; UDAP § 5.10.7

Trading Posts—UDAP § 5.1.1.5.5

Transcripts and Bankruptcy—Bankr § 14.5.5.2

Traveler's Checks—CBPL Ch 5, UDAP § 2.2.1.3

Travel Fraud—UDAP § 5.4.13

Treble Damages—UDAP § 8.4.2

Trebled, Disclosure to Jury that Damages Will Be—UDAP § 8.4.2.7.3

Trial Brief, Sample—FDC App J.4

Trial Documents, Sample—*See* Auto App I; FDC App J; Warr App M

Trustees in Bankruptcy—Bankr §§ 2.6, 2.7, 16.4.2, 17.7

Truth in Lending—TIL; COC §§ 2.3.4, 4.4.1; FDC § 9.4; Repo § 2.11

Truth in Mileage Act—Auto Chs 3, 4, 5

Truth in Savings—CBPL § 4.5

Tuition Recovery Funds—Stud § 9.6

Typing Services—Bankr § 15.6

UCC Article 2—Warr

UCC Article 2 and Comments Reprinted—Warr App E

UCC Article 2A—Repo §§ 2.3, 14.1.3.1; Warr Ch 19, App E.4; UDAP § 5.4.8.5

UCC Articles 3 and 4—CBPL Chs 1, 2, App A

UCC Article 9—Repo

UCC Article 9, Revised—Repo App A

UCC Article 9 and Comments Reprinted—Repo App A

UDAP—UDAP; AUS § 1.7.2; Auto § 8.4; COC §§ 8.5.2.6, 12.5; FDC § 11.3; FCR § 10.4.2; Repo §§ 2.7, 13.4.3; Warr § 11.1

Unauthorized Card Use—TIL § 5.9.4

Unauthorized Practice of Law—FDC §§ 4.2.7.7, 5.6.2, 11.5; Bankr § 15.6; UDAP § 5.12.2

Unauthorized Use of Checks, Credit and Debit Cards—CBPL §§ 2.3, 3.3, 6.3

Unauthorized Use of Utility Service—AUS § 5.3

Unavailability of Advertised Items—UDAP § 4.6.2

Unconscionability—Warr §§ 11.2, 19.2.6; COC §§ 8.7.5, 12.7; UDAP §§ 4.4, 5.4.6.5; Auto § 8.7

Unconscionability of Arbitration Clauses—Arbit §§ 4.2, 4.3, 4.4

Unearned Interest—COC Ch 5

Unemployment Insurance—COC § 8.3.1.4

Unfair Insurance Practices Statutes—UDAP § 5.3; COC § 8.4.1.4

Unfair Practices Statutes—*See* UDAP

Unfairness—UDAP § 4.3

Uniform Arbitration Act – Arbit. Ch. 10

Uniform Commercial Code—*See* UCC

United States Trustee—Bankr §§ 2.7, 17.7.2

Universal Telephone Service—AUS Ch 2

Unlicensed Activities—COC § 9.2.4.5

Unpaid Refund Discharge of Student Loan—Stud § 6.4

Unsolicited Credit Cards—TIL § 5.9.2

Unsolicited Goods—UDAP § 5.8.4; FDC § 9.2

Unsubstantiated Claims—UDAP § 4.5

Used as New—UDAP § 4.9.4

Used Car Lemon Laws—Warr § 14.8

Used Car Rule—Warr § 14.7, App D; UDAP § 5.4.6.2, App B.6

Used Cars—Auto; Warr Ch 14, App K.3, App L.6; UDAP § 5.4.6

Used Cars, Assembled from Salvaged Parts—Auto §§ 1.4.3, 2.1.4

Used Cars, Financing—COC § 11.6

Used Cars, Undisclosed Sale of Wrecked Cars—Auto §§ 1.4.4, 2.1.4

Users of Consumer and Credit Reports—FCR Ch 5

Usury, Trying a Case—COC Ch 10

Utilities—AUS; CD §§ 2.2.2.3, 2.2.6.2; TIL § 2.4.6; UDAP §§ 2.3.2, 5.6.9

Utilities and Bankruptcy—AUS §§ 4.5, 12.1; Bankr § 9.8

Utilities as Credit Reporting Agencies—FCR § 2.6.9

Utility Commission Regulation—AUS § 1.3, App A

Utility Service Terminated by a Landlord—AUS § 12.4

Utility Subsidies in Subsidized Housing—AUS Ch 8

Utility Termination, Remedies—AUS § 11.7; UDAP § 5.6.9.1; FDC § 1.5.6

Utility Terminations, Stopping—AUS Chs 11, 12; Bankr Ch 9

VA Mortgage Foreclosures and Workouts—Repo §§ 17.5.2, 18.3

Variable Rate Disclosures—TIL § 4.8

Variable Rates, Calculation—COC § 4.3.6

Vehicle Identification Number—Auto § 2.2.4

Venue, Inconvenient—FDC §§ 6.12.2, 8.3.7, 10.6.3, 11.7; UDAP § 5.1.1.4

Vertical Privity—Warr § 6.2

Vocational Schools—Stud Ch 9

Voir Dire, Sample Questions—FDC App J.2

Voluntary Payment Doctrine—UDAP § 4.2.15.5; COC § 10.6.5

Wage Earner Plans—Bankr Ch 4

Wage Garnishment—FDC Ch 12, App D

Waiver of Default—Repo § 4.3

Waiver of Right to Enforce Arbitration Clause—Arbit Ch 7

Wage Garnishment of Student Loans—Stud § 5.3, App B.1.2A

Warehouseman's Lien—Repo § 15.7.4

Warranties—Warr; Auto § 8.2; UDAP § 5.2.7

Warranties, Secret—Warr § 13.5.3.2; UDAP § 5.4.7.10.2
Warranty Disclaimers—Warr Ch 5
Warranty of Habitability, Utility Service—AUS § 4.4.1
Water Quality Improvement Systems—UDAP § 5.6.5
Water Service—AUS § 1.2.3, App I; UDAP § 5.6.11
Weatherization Assistance—AUS Ch 10
Web Sites, Consumer Advocacy—UDAP § 1.3
Welfare Benefits, Bankruptcy—Bankr §§ 10.2.2.11, 14.5.5
Welfare Benefits, Credit Discrimination—CD §§ 3.4.3, 5.5.2.5
Welfare Benefits, Credit Reporting—FCR §§ 2.3.6.8, 5.2.2, 13.3.5
Welfare Benefits, Exemptions—FDC § 12.5
"Wheelchair" Lemon Laws—Warr Ch 16aS
Wire Fraud—UDAP § 9.2.4.4

Wires—CBPL Ch 5
Withholding Credit Payments—Repo § 4.6.3; Warr § 8.5
Women's Business Ownership Act of 1988—CD § 1.3.2.4
Workers Compensation and Bankruptcy—Bankr § 10.2.2.1
Workout Agreements—TIL § 4.9.7
Workout Agreements, Foreclosures—Repo Ch 17
Wraparound Mortgages—COC § 7.4.3
Writ of Replevin—Repo Ch 5
Yield Spread Premiums—CD § 8.4; COC §§ 4.7.2, 7.3.2, 11.2.1.4.3, 11.2.2.6; UDAP §§ 5.1.3.3, 5.4.3.4
Yo-Yo Delivery of Automobiles—UDAP § 5.4.5; Repo § 4.5; TIL §§ 4.4.5, 4.4.6; COC § 11.2.2.5; CD § 10.4.2

About the Companion CD-Rom

CD-Rom Supersedes All Prior CD-Roms

This CD-Rom supersedes the CDs accompanying *The Cost of Credit* (2d ed. 2000) and its supplements. Discard all prior CD-Roms. This 2005 CD-Rom contains everything found on the earlier CDs and contains much additional material.

What Is on the CD-Rom

For a detailed listing of the CD's contents, see the CD-Rom Contents section on page xxxi of this book. Highlights and new additions include:

- A guide to analyzing a loan flipping case;
- 22 sample complaints;
- 23 sample discovery requests;
- Sample affidavits and expert witness testimony;
- 15 sample briefs;
- Class certification materials;
- Settlements, injunctive orders, jury instructions, and judgments;
- 12 key federal statutes;
- State lending statutes summarized and a model payday loan act;
- 11 sets of federal agency regulations;
- Web links;
- 55 new federal agency interpretation letters and the full text of numerous other hard-to-find statements of policy, interpretation letters, and opinion letters summarized in Appendices C and D; and
- Two different Windows-based credit math programs, "Consumer Law Math" and "NCLC APR Program," which compute APRs, generate amortization tables, and calculate Rule of 78 rebates:
  - In general, "Consumer Law Math" is the easier to use and is supported by Custom Legal Software. It can be used with irregular first payment amounts or periods and for irregular last payment amounts. It cannot be used where there are other irregularities in the payment schedule.
  - The NCLC APR program has the advantage of being able to perform more functions, including computing APRs for irregular payments or periods and evaluating split-rate transactions. The NCLC program is

created by Renaissance Software and we encourage users to report any bugs to APR@RenSoftware.com.

How to Use the CD-Rom

The CD's pop-up menu quickly allows you to use the CD—just place the CD into its drive and click on the "Start NCLC CD" button that will pop up in the middle of the screen. You can also access the CD by clicking on a desktop icon that you can create using the pop-up menu.[1] For detailed installation instructions, see *One-Time Installation* below.

All the CD-Rom's information is available in PDF (Acrobat) format, making the information:

- Highly readable (identical to the printed pages in the book);
- Easily navigated (with bookmarks, "buttons," and Internet-style forward and backward searches);
- Easy to locate with keyword searches and other quick-search techniques across the whole CD-Rom; and
- Easy to paste into a word processor.

While much of the material is also found on the CD-Rom in word processing format, we strongly recommend you use the material in PDF format—not only because it is easiest to use, contains the most features, and includes more material, but also because you can easily switch back to a word processing format when you prefer.

Acrobat Reader 5 and 7.0.1 come free of charge with the CD-Rom. **We strongly recommend that new Acrobat users read the Acrobat tutorial on the Home Page. It takes two minutes and will really pay off.**

How to Find Documents in Word Processing Format

Most pleadings and other practice aids are also available in Microsoft Word format to make them more easily adaptable for individual use. (Current versions of WordPerfect are

---

1 Alternatively, click on the D:\Start.pdf file on "My Computer" or open that file in Acrobat—always assuming "D:" is the CD-Rom drive on your computer.

able to convert the Word documents upon opening them.) The CD-Rom offers several ways to find those word processing documents. One option is simply to browse to the folder on the CD-Rom containing all the word processing files and open the desired document from your standard word processing program, such as Word or WordPerfect. All word processing documents are in the D:\WP_Files folder, if "D:" is the CD-Rom drive,[2] and are further organized by book title. Documents that appear in the book are named after the corresponding appendix; other documents have descriptive file names.

Another option is to navigate the CD in PDF format, and, when a particular document is on the screen, click on the corresponding bookmark for the "Word version of . . ." This will automatically run Word, WordPerfect for Windows, or *any other word processor* that is associated with the ".DOC" extension, and then open the word processing file that corresponds to the Acrobat document.[3]

Important Information Before Opening the CD-Rom Package

Before opening the CD-Rom package, please read this information. Opening the package constitutes acceptance of the following described terms. In addition, the *book* is not returnable once the seal to the *CD-Rom* has been broken.

The CD-Rom is copyrighted and all rights are reserved by the National Consumer Law Center, Inc. No copyright is claimed to the text of statutes, regulations, excerpts from court opinions, or any part of an original work prepared by a United States Government employee. Consumer Law Math is copyrighted 2002 by Custom Legal Software, all rights reserved. Consumer Law Math is the property of Custom Legal Software.

You may not commercially distribute the CD-Rom or otherwise reproduce, publish, distribute or use the disk in any manner that may infringe on any copyright or other proprietary right of the National Consumer Law Center or Custom Legal Software. Nor may you otherwise transfer the CD-Rom or this agreement to any other party unless that party agrees to accept the terms and conditions of this agreement. You may use the CD-Rom on only one computer and by one user at a time.

The CD-Rom is warranted to be free of defects in materials and faulty workmanship under normal use for a period of ninety days after purchase. If a defect is discovered in the CD-Rom during this warranty period, a replacement disk can be obtained at no charge by sending the defective disk,

---

2 The CD-Rom drive could be any letter following "D:" depending on your computer's configuration.

3 For instructions on how to associate WordPerfect to the ".DOC" extension, go to the CD-Rom's home page and click on "How to Use/Help," then "Word Files."

postage prepaid, with information identifying the purchaser, to National Consumer Law Center, Publications Department, 77 Summer Street, 10th Floor, Boston, MA 02110. After the ninety-day period, a replacement will be available on the same terms, but will also require a $20 prepayment.

The National Consumer Law Center and Custom Legal Software make no other warranty or representation, either express or implied, with respect to this disk, its quality, performance, merchantability, or fitness for a particular purpose. In no event will the National Consumer Law Center or Custom Legal Software be liable for direct, indirect, special, incidental, or consequential damages arising out of the use or inability to use the disk. The exclusion of implied warranties is not effective in some states, and thus this exclusion may not apply to you.

Users are subject to the license and warranty terms and limitations that they agree to when installing the Consumer Law Math program. These limitations and terms are in addition to those set out herein.

System Requirements

Use of this CD-Rom requires a Windows-based PC with a CD-Rom drive. (Macintosh users report success using NCLC CDs, but the CD has been tested only on Windows-based PCs.) The CD-Rom's features are optimized with Acrobat Reader 5 or later. Acrobat Reader versions 5 and 7.0.1 are included free on this CD-Rom, and either will work with this CD-Rom as long as it is compatible with your version of Windows. Acrobat Reader 5 is compatible with Windows 95/98/Me/NT/2000/XP, while Acrobat Reader 7.0.1 is compatible with Windows 98SE/Me/NT/2000/XP. If you already have Acrobat Reader 6.0, we *highly* recommend you install the 6.0.1 update from the Adobe web site at www.adobe.com because a bug in version 6.0 interferes with optimum use of this CD-Rom. The Microsoft Word versions of pleadings and practice aids can be used with any reasonably current word processor (1995 or later).

One-Time Installation

When the CD-Rom is inserted in its drive, a menu will pop up automatically. (Please be patient if you have a slow CD-Rom drive; this will only take a few moments.) If you do not already have Acrobat Reader 5 or 6.0.1, first click the "Install Acrobat Reader" button. Do not reboot, but then click on the "Make Shortcut Icon" button. (You need not make another shortcut icon if you already have done so for another NCLC CD.) Then reboot and follow the *How to Use the CD-Rom* instructions above.

[*Note*: If the pop-up menu fails to appear, go to "My Computer," right-click "D:" if that is the CD-Rom drive, and select "Open." Then double-click on "Read_Me.txt" for alternate installation and use instructions.]